CW00741153

BRITISH RAILWAYS ELECTRIC MULTIPLE UNITS TO 1975

Hugh Longworth

OPC
An imprint of
Ian Allan Publishing

Contents

Front cover: No 312103 takes part in a driver training run prior to introduction into passenger service on the Great Eastern outer suburban services out of Liverpool Street. *Malcolm Pudduck*

Previous page: The carriage sidings at Clapham Junction are full on 28 April 1976. Amongst the units on view are 4-VEP 7703, 4-CIG 7420 and some SR-designed 4-EPB units. *G. B. Wise*

Below: This view shows a typical line up of stock awaiting rush hour duties on the Fenchurch Street to Tilbury line. The flat-ended units are Class 302 and the units with raked back windows are Class 308/2.

To Doris and Heppy.
The two delights of my life.

I also want to specifically thank three couples who have supported and encouraged me and my family over the past ten difficult years.
Mark & Philippa Gee, Brian & Karen Duane,
Chris & Jane Gibbard. You've been a lifeline to us!

First published 2015

ISBN 978 0 86093 668 8

Published by Oxford Publishing Co

an imprint of Ian Allan Publishing Ltd, Addlestone, Surrey KT15 2SF.

Printed in Malta.

Visit the Ian Allan Publishing website at Ian Allan Publishing.com

Picture Credits
Every effort has been made to identify and correctly attribute photographic credits. Should any error have occurred this is entirely unintentional.

As always, I will be very glad to receive corrections or additional information. Please contact me via Ian Allan Publishing.

Introduction

This book completes my trilogy of books covering the coaching stock of British Railways.

My desire to prepare these books began when I first got hold of a BR diagram book describing and illustrating the whole of the British Railways coaching stock. These books were designed for the operating departments and showed the seating layouts, weights, dimensions and other details that would affect the use of the coaches. The diagram books are heavy tomes with pages that can be removed and replaced to keep them up to date. Straight away I decided to try and combine these diagrams with the lists of rolling stock that I had been trying to keep up-to-date over the years.

My first book covered all the first generation DMUs. An obvious choice as there is a great interest in that area, and Ian Allan Publishing felt that it would meet a need. And so it proved.

The second book covered hauled stock, specifically the Mark 1 & Mark 2 standard coaches and the BR built parcels coaches. This is something I had an interest in and wanted to put together, and I was pleasantly surprised to find that this book sold well too.

This led to this, the third book. Out of the three this was the one I had the most doubts about. If I was to follow the path of the other two I should only be including the BR units designed and built since 1948. This would have produced a slimmer book than the other two and I felt that such a book might be a bit boring, with less variety than the others. My memories of train spotting in the late 1960s and 1970s included many pre-nationalisation designs of EMU and for me that was where much of the interest lay. So with the encouragement of my publisher, I decided to broaden the chronological scope of this book. Laying aside my BR diagram books I headed off to the National Archives at Kew to locate older diagrams.

So what you see before you now is a book that covers all electric multiple unit trains that have run on the main lines of the railways of Britain, from the 1897 built Waterloo and City line units through to the PEP prototypes which appeared in the 1970s. I have excluded the London Underground, Liverpool Overhead, Glasgow Subway and similar lines, but I have included trains built by mainline companies which operated through-trains over some of these lines. I have included the PEP trains as they marked the start of something new, and the last of the standard types of EMU I have included are the class 312 units as they were similar to existing designs. As I have mentioned in a previous book, the aim is to cover classes that are substantially or completely extinct, leaving the rest for future historians to chronicle.

I feel that the decision to include the stock of pre-nationalisation and pre-grouping companies has been a good one and produces a well balanced book. It would be very hard to tell the story of the Southern EMUs in particular without giving the history of the stock of the LBSCR, LSWR and Southern Railways as well as the BR built units. The Southern's great tradition of making do and re-using, which continues until today, becomes clear as you trace through the different classes. I grew up in Liverpool and the railways south of the Thames always seemed mysterious and somewhat bland to me. At last I feel I have got a grasp of how that great system developed. I am typing this as I sit on a Southern Class 377 unit heading to Brighton (73843 in unit 377443, since you ask) and I really sense the history of the line I am travelling on.

This book divides itself easily into two main parts. The first section is the unit listing. Working through the regions I give a full listing of all units with a potted history for each. All the units are listed, with the formations and reformations of the units in those classes which usually maintained fixed formations. From about 1980 onwards TOPS unit numbers began to be applied, with the class number preceding the unit numbers. The ac TOPS numbered units are listed in numerical order as this gives more clarity, and in later years there was some transferring of these units between regions. The Southern region, individual as ever, resisted using TOPS numbers for its units. After a few Class 411 units were released with full six digit unit numbers, a change was soon made to 4-digit numbers which worked better for the Southern Operating department. Most units were renumbered but the first two digits were not carried on the units. These units are listed separately after the first list of Southern units.

The second part of the book is a listing of individual carriages. This is something I feel is often missing in published information on EMUs. Each different class of carriage in this section includes a diagram showing the coach and its layout. It also carries a full cross-reference to each unit the coach was allocated to in its lifetime.

You may be interested to know that my first attempt at producing a full listing of EMU stock in carriage number order took place in 1976. As new undergraduates at University College London we were introduced to computer programming on the College's IBM 360 mainframe computer. Yes, those were the days when the whole college used one computer (apart from four PDP-11 machines which we had access to in the computer science department). Before we were let loose on the IBM 360 we were warned not to use it for anything frivolous. My first personal project, coded in Fortran on punched cards, was to print out my EMU coach list in nicely tabulated columns. I think that nearly 40 years later it will be safe to own up to my frivolous use!

So enjoy this latest update to my 1976 book!

Hugh Longworth, November 2014

Electrification Schemes

The main electrification schemes in this country are listed below:

London Midland

In the London Midland area, the main electrification schemes were in the London, Liverpool and Manchester areas, with a small outpost in the Lancaster area. Later the West Coast main line was electrified on the high voltage overhead ac system.

- Wirral & Mersey lines 650v dc third rail.
- LYR Liverpool-Southport lines 630v dc third rail.
- LYR Manchester Bury line 1200v dc side-contact third rail.
- LYR Holcombe Brook 3600v dc overhead.
- LNWR London area 630v dc third and fourth rail. Later third rail only.
- MSJA Manchester Altrincham 1500v dc overhead.
- Lancaster Morecambe and Heysham 6.6kV 25Hz ac overhead. Later 6.6kV 50Hz ac overhead.
- Western Lines, Liverpool & Manchester to Birmingham and London. 25kV 50Hz ac overhead.

The LMS introduced a renumbering scheme in 1932 which was implemented from the beginning of 1933. EMUs were numbered in the series 28000-29899. This was divided into groups for Motors, Driving Trailers and Trailers. These groups were further sub-divided into groups for First, Third and Composite vehicles. These groups were then divided into groups for London area and Lancashire area units. Finally, within each block, numbers were allocated for LMS built stock, followed by a gap for new-build units, with the remaining stock taking up the higher end of the range.

The BR standard units built for the Western Lines, Bury and London were numbered in the BR standard number range. Earlier units were not renumbered on BR but carried an M suffix.

North Eastern

The North Eastern Railway introduced a service on North and South Tyneside using the 600v dc third rail system. The LNER renumbered all its coaching stock in 1943 into a series where North Eastern Railway stock began with the digit 2. These lines later used articulated stock and some BR standard built units.

Eastern

The Eastern Region of BR inherited two schemes started by the LNER before the war. They were both electrified at 1500v dc overhead and had almost identical stock.

- Liverpool Street - Shenfield. Stock numbered in the GE range beginning with the digit 6.
- Manchester - Glossop & Hadfield (Western end of the Manchester-Sheffield line). Stock numbered in the GC range beginning with the digit 5.

More dc stock was built for the GE line before the line was converted to 25kV/6.25kV ac overhead.

In the early sixties the ER ac units carried the prefix GE to denote the Great Eastern line, in common with hauled stock on the line. The units were numbered in ranges based on the lines they were designed for, as follows:

- 001-100 Liverpool Street - Chelmsford
- 101-200 Liverpool Street - Southend, Clacton & Walton
- 201-400 Fenchurch Street - Shoeburyness
- 401-500 Liverpool Street - Enfield & Chingford
- 501-600 Liverpool Street - Bishop's Stortford & Hertford East
- 601-700 Liverpool Street - Clacton & Walton Express Units

Scotland

The Scottish Region of British Railways electrified the North and South Clydeside lines on the 25kV/6.25kV ac overhead system, later converted to just 25kV. Class 303 and 311 units (formerly AM3 & AM11) worked on these lines.

Southern

The three main constituent parts of the Southern Railway had all developed plans for electrification schemes before 1923, but only the London Brighton & South Coast Railway (LBSCR) and London & South Western Railway (LSWR) had completed schemes before grouping. They used two completely different systems, the LBSCR using a 6700v ac overhead system, and the LSWR using 600c dc third rail. In August 1926 it was announced that the Southern Railway would use the third rail system and all the ac overhead lines were eventually converted to third rail dc operation.

The voltage on the Southern varied over time and according to the area.

- Original LSWR 600v
- Older SR 660v nominal, later upgraded
- Post War SR 750v
- Parts of Bournemouth line 850v
- W&C rebuilt 630v
- IOW 630v

EMUs on the Southern were generally kept in fixed formations. Early 3-SUB units were numbered from 1201 upwards with the corresponding trailer sets being numbered between 989 and 1199. In 1936 a numbering scheme for units was introduced. This remained in use until the 1980s when a TOPS based scheme was introduced. The 1936 scheme (with subsequent amendments) is shown below:

- 001-030 Departmental units
- 031-039 Isle of Wight three-car units
- 041-049 Isle of Wight four-car units
- 051-059 Departmental units
- 061-069 Two-car parcels units (withdrawn 1972)

- 301-399 Three-car trailer units
- 401-499 Four car trailer units
- 601 Six car trailer unit
- 701 Seven car trailer unit
- 1001-1999 Diesel-electric units
- 2001-2899 Two-car units
- 2901-2999 Four-car semi-fast units
- 3001-3999 Express units, four, five and six car units.
- 4001-4099 Double-deck four-car units (later 4901-4902). Later used for four-car high-density units.
- 4101-4899 SR design four-car suburban units with air brakes
- 5001-5599 Four-car suburban units with electro-pneumatic brakes
- 5601-5999 Two-car units with electro-pneumatic brakes
- 6001-6099 BR design semi-fast two-car units.
- 7001-7099 BR design express units with buffet car.
- 7101-7699 BR design express units without buffet car.
- 7701-7999 BR design semi-fast units
- 8001 Temporary eight-car unit

Units were classified on the Southern with a code which contained a number showing the number of coaches in the unit and up to three letters showing the type. These are listed below:

- 5-BEL Class 403 Brighton Belle Pullman
- 4-BEP Class 410 Buffet Electro-Pneumatic units
- 4-BIG Class 420 Buffet Intermediate Guard (Brighton) units
- 2-BIL Class 401 Bi-Lavatory (two toilets) units
- 4-BUF Class 404 Buffet units
- 4-CAP Class 413 Coastway HAP units
- 3-CEP Class 411 Corridor Electro-Pneumatic units
- 4-CEP Class 411 Corridor Electro-Pneumatic units
- 3-CIG Class 421 Corridor Intermediate Guard (Brighton) units
- 4-CIG Class 421 Corridor Intermediate Guard (Brighton) units
- 6-CIT City units (extra first class accommodation)
- 3-COP Class 421 Coastway units
- 4-COP Class 421 Coastway units
- 4-COR Class 404 Portsmouth Line Corridor units
- 4-COR(N) Class 404 Portsmouth Line Corridor units (reformed)
- 6-COR Class 404 Portsmouth Line Corridor units (reformed)
- 4-DD Double-deck units
- 8-DIG Double units. Permanently coupled BIG and CIG units
- 2-EPB Class 416 Electro-Pneumatic Braked SUB units
- 4-EPB Class 415 Electro-Pneumatic Braked SUB units
- 1-GLV Class 489 Gatwick Luggage Vans
- 4-GRI Class 404 Griddle units
- 2-HAL Class 402 Half-Lavatory (one toilet) units
- 2-HAP Class 414 Electro-Pneumatic HAL units
- 4-LAV Semi-fast Lavatory units
- 8-MIG Temporary CIG units with Miniature Buffet
- 1-MLV Class 419 Motor Luggage Vans
- 2-NOL Suburban units (No Lavatory)
- 2-PAN 2-HAL Parcels units
- 6-PAN Brighton Line Pantry units
- 2-PEP Class 446 Prototype EPB suburban unit
- 4-PEP Class 445 Prototype EPB suburban unit
- 4-PUL Brighton Line Pullman units
- 6-PUL Brighton Line Pullman units
- 3-REP Class 438 Restaurant Electro-Pneumatic units
- 4-REP Class 430 Restaurant Electro-Pneumatic units
- 6-REP Class 438 Restaurant Electro-Pneumatic units
- 4-RES Class 404 Portsmouth Line Restaurant units
- 2-SAP Class 418 Second Class downgraded HAP units
- 2-SL South London line units
- 3-SUB Suburban units
- 4-SUB Suburban units
- 4-SUB Class 405 Suburban units
- 2-T Trailer sets
- 3-TC Class 492 Control Trailer sets
- 4-TC Class 491 Control Trailer sets
- 5-TC Class 438 Control Trailer sets
- 6-TC Control Trailer sets
- 7-TC Control Trailer sets
- 4-TCT Class 438 Control Trailer sets
- 5-TCT Class 438 Control Trailer sets
- 4-TEP Class 411 Temporary Buffet CEP units
- 3-TIS Class 486 Isle of Wight (Vectis) units
- 1-TLV Class 499 Trailer Luggage Van
- 8-VAB Class 423 Eight car VEP unit
- 4-VEC Class 485 Isle of Wight (Vectis) units
- 4-VEP Class 423 Vestibule Electro-Pneumatic units
- 4-VEG Class 423 VEP Gatwick units
- 4-VIP Class 423 VEP reformed units
- 4-VOP Class 423 VEP South London Metro units
- 2-WIM Wimbledon line units

All the early SR suburban EMU coaches carried numbers between 8001-9999. The LBSCR ac coaches were renumbered on conversion and their numbers were reused. (These ac numbered coaches are listed at the end of the main section). The series 10401-10418 was also used for early stock. Main line stock and later suburban units were numbered in a range from 10001 upwards. Some number ranges in the 8001-9999 series were re-used for later suburban units.

The SR suburban and semi-fast units built before 1946 were on standard 62 foot length frames. The bodywork consisted of wooden frames covered with steel sheet. From 1946 all steel construction was used. The express units differed in length.

SR Suburban Units

The suburban stock of the Southern railway consisted for many years of three-car units (with their end bogies motored) augmented during the busy periods with two-car trailer units coupled between them.

In 1941 the first four-car suburban unit was built as part of a plan to use only such units. The existing units with sufficient life left in them were to be augmented with carriages from the trailer units, and a number of new augmentation trailers were built to complete the process. By 1950 some of these trailers became spare and new power cars were built to run with them

There were, therefore, two completely different types of 4-SUB units. The first type comprised those reformed from 3-SUB units with bodywork to the design of the three pre-grouping companies, and those of the early SR design. These sometimes could be found mixed within one unit, and to the mixture was added the new augmentation trailers built to the later Bulleid design and body profile.

The second type comprised new 4-SUB units, based on the design of the 1941 unit with changes to batches as they were delivered. Originally the units were fitted with the standard 275hp motors. Later units were fitted with lightweight 250hp motors. The earlier motored units became Class 405/1, the later were Class 405/2.

The new build 4-SUBs were '1936 stock', fitted with air-brakes and electro-pneumatic contactors. Subsequently '1951 stock' was introduced fitted with electro-pneumatic brakes. Suburban stock to this design was known as 4-EPB stock. Eighty-six SUB trailers were converted to EPB to run with newer units.

The EPB units were built to two different designs; the SR design and the BR design. Both of these appeared in two and four-car units.

British Railways

The British Railways classification scheme for all stock was developed at the end of the 1960s and came into general use in the 1970s. It is still in use today, and forms the basis of the TOPS scheme. (TOPS is the computerised Total Operations Processing System used to keep track of all BR stock.) EMUs in the period covered by this book are shown below:

AC units

- Class 301 Lancaster Morecambe & Heysham Class AM1
- Class 302 ER Class AM2 201-312
- Class 303 ScR Class AM3 001-091
- Class 304/1 LMR Class AM4/1 001-015
- Class 304/2 LMR Class AM4/2 016-035
- Class 304/3 LMR Class AM4/3 036-045
- Class 305/1 ER Class AM5/1 401-452
- Class 305/2 ER Class AM5/2 501-519
- Class 306 ER Class AM6 01-92/001-092
- Class 307 ER Class AM7 01s-32s/101-132
- Class 308/1 ER Class AM8/1 133-165
- Class 308/2 ER Class AM8/2 313-321
- Class 308/3 ER Class AM8/3 453-455
- Class 309/1 ER Class AM9/1 601-608
- Class 309/2 ER Class AM9/2 611-618
- Class 309/3 ER Class AM9/3 621-627
- Class 310 LMR Class AM10 046-095
- Class 311 ScR Class AM11 092-110
- Class 312/0 ER GN line
- Class 312/1 ER GE line
- Class 312/2 LMR line

SR DC units

- Class 401 2-BIL 2001-2152
- Class 402 2-HAL 2601-2700
- Class 403 5-BEL 3051-3053
- Class 404 4-COR, 4-COR(N), 6-COR, 4-BUF, 4-RES, 4-GRI 3101-3168 and between 3041 & 3088
- Class 405 4-SUB between 4101 & 4754
- Class 410 4-BEP 7001-7022
- Class 411/1 3-CEP 1199
- Class 411/3 4-CEP 7153
- Class 411/4 1951 4-CEP 7101-7104
- Class 411/4 3-CEP 1401-1406
- Class 411/5 1957 4-CEP 7105-7211
- Class 411/6 4-CEP 1697-1699
- Class 411/9 3-CEP 1101-1118
- Class 412 4-BEP 2301-2317 (ex-Class 410)
- Class 412/2 4-BEP 2321-2327 (ex-Class 410)
- Class 413/2 1951 4-CAP 3201-3213
- Class 413/3 1957 4-CAP 3301-3311
- Class 414/1 SR 2-HAP 5601-5636
- Class 414/2 1951 2-HAP 6001-6042
- Class 414/3 1957 2-HAP 6043-6173
- Class 415/1 SR 1951 4-EPB 5001-5260 & 5261-5281
- Class 415/2 BR 1957 4-EPB 5301-5370
- Class 415/4 Facelifted 1951 4-EPB 5401-5497
- Class 415/5 Reformed 4-EPB 5501-5532
- Class 415/6 Facelifted 1957 4-EPB
- Class 416/1 SR 2-EPB 5651-5684
- Class 416/2 BR 2-EPB 5701-5779 & 5781-5795
- Class 416/3 Facelifted SR 2-EPB 5601-5628
- Class 416/4 Refurbished SR 2-EPB 6401-6418
- Class 418/0 SR 2-HAP 5601-5636
- Class 418/1 1951 2-SAP 5901-5940
- Class 418/2 1957 2-SAP 5941-5951
- Class 419 Motor Luggage Van 68001-68010
- Class 420/1 1963 4-BIG 7039-7048
- Class 420/2 1970 4-BIG 7049-7058
- Class 421/1 1963 4-CIG 7301-7336
- Class 421/2 1970 4-CIG 7337-7438
- Class 421/3 4-CIG 1701-1753
- Class 421/4 4-BIG 1401-1411
- Class 421/4 4-CIG 1801-1891
- Class 421/5 4-CIG Greyhound units 1301-1322 & 1392-1399
- Class 421/6 4-CIG 1901-1908
- Class 421/7 3-COP 1401-1411
- Class 421/7 3-CIG 1497-1498
- Class 421/8 4-CIG 1392-1399
- Class 421/9 4-CIG 1901-1908
- Class 422 8-DIG 2001-2004
- Class 422/1 1963 4-BIG facelifted Class 420/1
- Class 422/2 1970 4-BIG facelifted Class 420/2
- Class 422/3 4-BIG
- Class 422/7 4-TEP 2701-2704
- Class 423 4-VEP 7701-7894
- Class 423/4 4-VEP 3401-3591 or 423/1
- Class 423/8 4-VEP 3801-3810 or 423/1
- Class 423/9 4-VOP 3901-3919 or 423/2
- Class 424 Networker Classic 76112
- Class 427 4-VEG 7901-7912
- Class 430 4-REP 3001-3015
- Class 432 4-REP ex class 430 2001-2015
- Class 438 4-TC ex Class 491 8001-8034
- Class 438/1 4-TCT 5-TCT 3-TC 5TC between 8101 & 8110
- Class 438/2 3-REP 4-REP 6-REP 2901-2906 2001-2007 1901-1905
- Class 445 4-PEP 4001-4002
- Class 446 2-PEP 2001
- Class 480 8-VAB 8001
- Class 482 8-MIG 2601-2602
- Class 482/7 4-TEP
- Class 485 4-VEC 041-046
- Class 486 4-TIS 031-036
- Class 487 Waterloo & City
- Class 488/2 2 coach Gatwick 8201-8210
- Class 488/3 3 coach Gatwick 8301-8319
- Class 489 Gatwick Luggage Van 9101-9110
- Class 491 4-TC 401-434
- Class 492 3-TC 301-303
- Class 492/0 5-TC 2804-2809
- Class 492/8 4-TC 2801-2807
- Class 499 Trailer Luggage Van 68201-68206

Original classification allocated to SR DC units

- Class 411 Original classification for 4-EPB Class 415/1
- Class 412 Original classification for 1951 2-HAP Class 414
- Class 413 Original classification for 2-EPB Class 416
- Class 414/1 Original classification for 1951 4-CEP Class 411
- Class 414/2 Original classification for 1951 4-BEP Class 410
- Class 421/1 Original classification for 1957 4-CEP Class 411
- Class 421/2 Original classification for 1957 4-BEP Class 410
- Class 422/1 Original classification for MLV Class 419
- Class 422/2 Original classification for TLV Class 499
- Class 423 Original classification for 4-EPB Class 415/2
- Class 424 Original classification for 1957 4-BEP Class 414/3
- Class 431/1 Original classification for 4-CIG Class 421
- Class 431/2 Original classification for 4-BIG Class 420
- Class 432 Original classification for 4-VEP Class 423 & 8-VAB Class 480
- Class 441 Original classification for 4-REP Class 430
- Class 442/1 Original classification for 3-TC Class 492
- Class 442/2 Original classification for 4-TC Class 491
- Class 453 Original classification for Waterloo & City Class 487
- Class 461 Original classification for PEP driving cars
- Class 462 Original classification for PEP intermediate cars

Other DC units

- Class 501 LMR London Area
- Class 502 LMR Liverpool-Southport Line
- Class 503 LMR Wirral & Mersey
- Class 504 LMR Manchester-Bury Line
- Class 505 Manchester-Altrincham Line
- Class 506 Manchester-Glossop & Hadfield Line

All BR built EMU coaches carried numbers in the 60999-78999 series as shown below:

- 61001-68199 EMU motor cars
- 68201-68206 Trailer luggage vans
- 69000-69999 Trailers with dining facilities
- 70001-74999 Non-dining intermediate Trailers
- 75001-78999 Driving Trailers

- 60001-60999 Diesel-Electric Multiple Units – see DMU book
- 79000-79999 This series was reserved for early DMUs but 79998 & 79999 were used in a battery-electric unit. As these were built to a DMU design, they are included in the DMU book.

In the early days the ranges for power cars and driving trailers were subdivided but these were abandoned in 1971:

- For the power cars, from 65300 upward was for cars intended for local work, a distinction that it was not easy to define. 68000 upwards was used for luggage vans.
- For trailer cars, DTCs for local work were numbered from 77100 upwards and DTSs for local work were numbered 77500 upwards .

A new division in the power car range was created in 1971 from 64300 upwards, used for power cars with driving controls.

In the period after the units described in this book the number ranges have been modified, stretched, re-used and generally ignored. Many recent EMUs have been numbered in the 3xxxx series, and in 2014 a new six digit carriage numbering series 4xxxxx is being introduced for new EMUs.

No 312115 is seen at Walton on the Naze working the 16.49 train to Liverpool Street on 20 May 1979. This unit carries the number 795 in the front cab window. The Eastern Region was seemingly not very happy with the numbers carried by these units, and they were soon renumbered in the 312/7 series, so that the unit numbers would follow on from the earlier three-digit numbers used for Eastern Region units. *Brian Morrison*

Layout of the book

This book is divided into two main parts.

Part 1 EMU Units

Part 1 of this book lists all the EMUs by the lines they ran on and lists their unit formations.

For many years (up until the experiments which led to the use of propelled trains on the Bournemouth line) there was in Britain a limit of two coaches being propelled in a passenger train. This had an impact on the formations of multiple unit trains. Three coach units usually had a driving motor car at one end with a trailer and driving trailer at the other. Four coach units would have two driving trailers with one non-driving motor and one trailer.

The Southern went about things differently. They always used driving motor cars at each end of the train, with one powered bogie at the outer end and one trailer bogie at the inner end. This allowed the formation of four, five and six car formations. This continued until the introduction of the CIG and BIG units on the Brighton line, which was the first time non-driving motor vehicles appeared on the Southern Region.

A typical listing from this section of the book is:

7189	61765	70538	70587	61764	02/61-11/71	
7189	61765	*70044*	70587	61764	11/71-08/81 ➲ *1587*	⤿
7190	61767	70539	70588	61766	03/61-09/82 ➲ **1568**	

The unit number is shown first followed by the formation of carriages within that unit. This is followed by the dates that the unit ran in this formation. Reformations of units are shown using the ⤿ symbol, with the unit number and the changes of formation shown in *italics*. In this case unit 7189 ran from February 1961 to November 1971 in the formation shown. Then 70538 was replaced by 70044 and it ran in this formation until August 1981. Only permanent reformations (or those thought to be permanent at the time) are shown.

The symbol ➲ is used to show when units were renumbered. If the new number is shown in **bold** (for example 1568 above) then the whole unit was renumbered. If the new number is in *italics* (1587 above), then the new unit formed was not in the same formation. The number shown is the unit that received most of the coaches from the old unit.

Part 2 EMU Coaches

Part 2 lists the individual carriages. The BR vehicles are shown first, followed by the relevant pre-Nationalisation companies and the pre-Grouping companies.

A typical listing from this section of the book is:

S70825	10/66-05/91	➲**977545**	**414**	10/66-09/86	**8014**	09/86-05/91			⊂**34996**
S70826	11/66-08/99	Ⓟ	**415**	11/66-10/86	**8015**	10/86-06/88	**8017**	09/88-09/91	
			417	09/91-01/98					⊂**34980**
S70827	10/66-10/91	⊗11/91	**416**	10/66-06/86	**8016**	06/86-10/88	**1903**	04/90-09/90	
			1902	12/90-10/91					⊂**34997**

The coach number is shown first followed by the dates that it ran in service with this number. This is followed by an indication of the fate of the vehicle. ⊗ is used to show scrapping dates, Ⓟ indicates the vehicle was preserved and ➲ shows that it was renumbered. This is followed by a list of the units that the coach belonged to, showing the period of time it was in that unit. The symbol ⊂ is used to show the previous number of the carriage (in this case it shows that these carriages were converted from Mark 1 hauled stock).

Two new symbols ↳ and are ↵ introduced in this book to cover the common practice on the Southern of building new carriages on the frames of old ones:

S9414S	③ 23-*06/54*	↳**15334**	**1201**	23-03/43	**4200**	03/43-*06/54*	⊂**7551**
S15334S	02/55-09/92	⊗10/92	**5156**	02/55-09/92			↵**9414**

The frame of 9414 was reused in February 1955 in the construction of 15334. Other symbols used are described in the class heading.

Note: The previous numbers of coaches converted from SECR and LBSCR hauled stock are given. The first number given is the pre-grouping number, and the second is the Southern Railway number. All SECR coaches converted to EMUs were of SER origin.

The BR coach classifications used for EMUs are shown below. The main codes are shown below, other more obscure codes are described in the relevant class headings. Third class was renamed second class in 1956. First class accommodation was removed from the Southern suburban area in October 1941.

- BDTBSO Battery Driving Trailer Brake Second Open
- BDTBSOL Battery Driving Trailer Brake Second Open Lavatory
- BDTC Battery Driving Trailer Composite
- BDTCOL Battery Driving Trailer Composite Open Lavatory
- BDTS Battery Driving Trailer Second
- BDTSO Battery Driving Trailer Second Open
- BDTSOL Battery Driving Trailer Second Open Lavatory
- DMBC Driving Motor Brake Composite
- DMBS Driving Motor Brake Second
- DMBSK Driving Motor Brake Second Corridor Lavatory
- DMBSO Driving Motor Brake Second Open
- DMBSOL Driving Motor Brake Second Open Lavatory
- DMBT Driving Motor Brake Third
- DMBTO Driving Motor Brake Third Open
- DMC Driving Motor Composite
- DMLV Driving Motor Luggage Van
- DMSO Driving Motor Second Open
- DMT Driving Motor Third
- DTBSO Driving Trailer Brake Second Open
- DTBS Driving Trailer Brake Second

- DTC Driving Trailer Composite
- DTCL Driving Trailer Composite Lavatory
- DTCOL Driving Trailer Composite Open Lavatory
- DTCso Driving Trailer Composite (semi-open)
- DTCsoL Driving Trailer Composite (semi-open) Lavatory
- DTLV Driving Trailer Luggage Van
- DTS Driving Trailer Second
- DTSO Driving Trailer Second Open
- DTSOL Driving Trailer Second Open Lavatory
- DTSso Driving Trailer Second (semi-open)
- DTSsoL Driving Trailer Second (semi-open) Lavatory
- DTT Driving Trailer Third
- DTTO Driving Trailer Third Open
- M Motor
- MBC Motor Brake Composite
- MBS Motor Brake Second
- MBSK Motor Brake Second Corridor Lavatory
- MBT Motor Brake Third
- MBSO Motor Brake Second Open
- MBSOL Motor Brake Second Open Lavatory
- MBTL Motor Brake Third Lavatory
- MBTO Motor Brake Third Open
- MBTP Motor Brake Third Pullman
- MF Motor First
- MLV Motor Luggage Van
- T Trailer
- TBSK Trailer Brake Second Corridor Lavatory
- TBSL Trailer Brake Second Lavatory
- TC Trailer Composite
- TCK Trailer Composite Corridor with Lavatory
- TCL Trailer Composite Lavatory
- TCP Trailer Composite Pullman
- TCsoL Trailer Composite Lavatory (semi-open)
- TF Trailer First
- TFK Trailer First Corridor with Lavatory
- TFK(P) Trailer First Corridor (Pantry)
- TFP Trailer First Pantry
- TFRBK Trailer First Buffet with Lavatory
- TRB Trailer Restaurant Buffet
- TRG Trailer Restaurant Griddle
- TRT Trailer Restaurant Third
- TS Trailer Second
- TSO Trailer Second Open
- TSOL Trailer Second Lavatory
- TSK Trailer Second Corridor with Lavatory
- TSP Trailer Second Pantry
- TT Trailer Third
- TTso Trailer Third (semi-open)
- TTK Trailer Third Corridor with Lavatory
- TTO Trailer Third Open

Accuracy of Dates

It should be noted that, while I have tried to be as accurate as I can with the dates shown in this book, there will always be inaccuracies in a work such as this. In general, older dates should not be expected to be as accurate as more recent ones. Research has shown that there was an amount of discrepancy in official dates, particularly in the mid to late 1940s when the 4-SUB units were being formed.

A variety of front ends are on display at Wimbledon carriage sheds on 18 February 1988. This was during the period when units were being renumbered and some units still carry their old numbers. Visible are 4-VEP 7774 (still carrying its old number even though it was officially renumbered 3074 in the previous October), 4-CIG 1248 (ex 7349), 2-HAPs 6062 and 4304 (ex 6064) and 4-CIG 1253 (ex 7353). *John H. Bird*

Bibliography

The following books have been helpful to me in the preparation of this book, and are worth studying if you want to delve deeper into the subject.

- **Southern Electric: Volume 1 Development of the London Suburban Network and Its Trains: A New History.** *David Brown.* Capital Transport Publishing. ISBN 978-1854143303
- **Southern Electric: Volume 2 Main Line Electrification, the War Years and British Railways: A New History.** *David Brown.* Capital Transport Publishing ISBN 978-1854143402
- **A Pictorial Record of Southern Electric Units: Drawings and Plans.** *Brian Golding.* Noodle Books ISBN 978-1906419349
- **Southern Electric Multiple-Units 1898-1948.** *Colin J. Marsden.* Ian Allan Publishing. ISBN 978-0711012530
- **Southern Electric Multiple Units 1948-83.** *Colin J. Marsden.* Ian Allan Publishing. ISBN 978-0711013148
- **DMU & EMU Recognition Guide.** *Colin J. Marsden.* Ian Allan Publishing. ISBN 978-0711037403
- **The DC Electrics.** *Colin J. Marsden.* Ian Allan Publishing. ISBN 978-0860936152
- **Pullman Profile Number 4. The Brighton Belle and Southern Electric Pullmans.** *Antony M Ford.* Noodle Books 2012. ISBN 978-1909328051
- **First Generation Southern EMUs (British Railway Pictorial).** *Kevin Robertson.* Ian Allan Publishing. 978-0711030879
- **Southern Electric.** *G.T. Moody & John Glover.* Ian Allan Publishing; 6th Revised edition edition ISBN 978-0711028074
- **Southern Electrics - A View from the Past.** *Graham Waterer.* Ian Allan Publishing 1998. ISBN 978-0711026216
- **The Electric Multiple Units of British Railways 1972.** *P Mallaband.* The Electric Railway Society.
- **London's North Western Electric - A Jubilee History.** *F.G.B. Atkinson & B.W.Adams.* The Electric Railway Society. 1962
- **Southern Region Multiple Unit Trains.** *G. D. Beecroft.* Southern Electric Group 1979 ISBN 978-0950237664
- **Southern Region Multiple Unit Trains.** *G. D. Beecroft & Bryan Rayner.* Southern Electric Group 1984 ISBN 978-0906988114
- **The '4-SUB' Story.** *Bryan Rayner.* Southern Electric Group 1983 ISBN 978-0906988091
- **DMU and EMU disposal.** *Ashley Butlin.* Coorlea Publishing 1988. ISBN 978-0948069086
- **British Multiple Units: Classes 410-499 & 508.** *Ashley Butlin.* Coorlea Publishing. ISBN 978-0948069208
- **British Multiple Units: EPBs, Haps, Saps and Caps v. 2.** *Ashley Butlin.* Coorlea Publishing. ISBN 978-0948069185
- **British Multiple Units: Classes 302-390 v. 3** *Ashley Butlin.* Coorlea Publishing; 2nd Revised edition edition. ISBN 978-0948069239
- **Midland Carriages – An Illustrated Review.** *David Jenkinson & Bob Essery.* Oxford Publishing Company 1984. ISBN 978-0860932918
- **The North Eastern Electrics. The History of the Tyneside Electric Passenger Services (1904-1967).** *K Hoole.* The Oakwood Press 1987. ISBN 978-0853613589
- **The Mersey Railway.** *G.W.Parkin.* The Oakwood Press
- **Lancashire & Yorkshire Passenger Stock.** *R. W. Rush.* The Oakwood Press 1984. ISBN 978-0853613060
- **Bogie Carriages of the South Eastern & Chatham Railway.** *David Gould.* The Oakwood Press 1993. ISBN 978-0853614555
- **Bogie Carriages of the London, Brighton and South Coast Railway.** *David Gould.* The Oakwood Press 1995. ISBN 978-0853614708
- **Service Stock of the Southern Railway.** *R. W. Kidner.* The Oakwood Press 1980. ISBN 978-0853612636
- **Pullman Trains of Great Britai**n *R. W. Kidner.* The Oakwood Press 1998. ISBN 978-0853615316
- **The Waterloo & City Railway.** *John C Gillham.* The Oakwood Press 2001. ISBN 978-0853615255
- **Tube Trains Under London.** *J Graeme Bruce.* London Transport 1968 ISBN 978-0853290230
- **Tube Trains on the Isle of Wight.** *Brian Hardy.* Capital Transport 2008. ISBN 978-1854142764
- **The Coaching Stock of British Railways.** *P Mallaband & L.J. Bowles.* The Railway Correspondence and Travel Society. 1972, 1974, 1976, 1978 & 1980
- **Ian Allan ABC Combined Volume** from 1948 to 1989.
- **Platform 5 Combined Volume** and pocket books 1980 onwards
- **Departmental Coaching Stock.** Platform 5. Produced every few years through the eighties and nineties.

I am also aware of a possible future work from Coorlea Publishing on the post-war SUB units, providing a definitive account of the entry of these units into service. So, if this is your particular area of interest, keep your eyes open for it.

My two previous books on coaching stock which complement this book are:

- **British Railways First Generation DMUs.** *Hugh Longworth.* OPC 2011. ISBN 978-0860936121
- **BR Mark 1 & Mark 2 Coaching Stock.** *Hugh Longworth.* OPC 2013. ISBN 978-0860936503

Part 1. EMUs listed by Units

London Midland Region

Western Lines

Class 304 AM4
London Midland Western Lines
25kV ac overhead
001-045

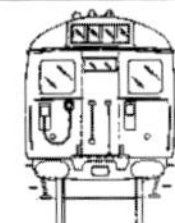

These units were built to work local services on the West Coast line. They were introduced in a number of batches as the electrification spread southwards from the initial Manchester & Liverpool to Crewe lines.

The Class 304/1 units were ordered for the Manchester-Crewe section and Class 304/2 followed for the Liverpool-Crewe section, but the units never were restricted to their own sections of line and common working was the rule. Class 304/3 were introduced as the electrification reached the Rugby and Birmingham area.

The units eventually settled down to work the Liverpool, Manchester and West Midlands services, rarely appearing at the southern end of the line. 016-023 worked on the GE line services out of Liverpool in the 1960-62 period to cover for a shortage of units on that line.

The MBS in the Class 304/1 units were originally fitted with eight compartments. They were converted to open coaches in 1984-86. The MBSO in the other units were built as open, but with seven bays of seats and an enlarged guard's compartment.

In 1979 the units were downgraded to second-class. In 1984-86 the TSsoL (formerly TCsoL) was removed from the units, reducing them to three-car units.

There was a plan to preserve one unit but this fell through and the class became extinct in 2000.

Class 304/1

	BDTSOL	*MBS*	*TCsoL*	*DTBSO*		
001	75045	61045	70045	75645	03/60-10/82	**➲304001**
002	75046	61046	70046	75646	04/60-04/82	**➲304002**
003	75047	61047	70047	75647	04/60-07/81	**➲304003**
004	75048	61048	70048	75648	05/60-09/83	**➲304004**
005	75049	61049	70049	75649	05/60-10/81	**➲304005**
006	75050	61050	70050	75650	05/60-12/82	**➲304006**
007	75051	61051	70051	75651	06/60-04/82	**➲304007**
008	75052	61052	70052	75652	06/60-08/81	**➲304008**
009	75053	61053	70053	75653	06/60-04/81	**➲304009**
010	75054	61054	70054	75654	06/60-12/81	**➲304010**
011	75055	61055	70055	75655	06/60-01/80	**➲304011**
012	75056	61056	70056	75656	07/60-04/82	**➲304012**
013	75057	61057	70057	75657	07/60-07/81	**➲304013**
014	75058	61058	70058	75658	07/60-06/81	**➲304014**
015	75059	61059	70059	75659	07/60-08/82	**➲304015**

Class 304/2

	BDTSOL	*MBSO*	*TCsoL*	*DTBSO*		
016	75680	61628	70483	75660	09/60-02/83	**➲304016**
017	75681	61629	70484	75661	09/60-08/82	**➲304017**
018	75682	61630	70485	75662	10/60-02/80	**➲304018**
019	75683	61631	70486	75663	10/60-12/81	**➲304019**
020	75684	61632	70487	75664	10/60-07/81	**➲304020**
021	75685	61633	70488	75665	10/60-12/81	**➲304021**
022	75686	61634	70489	75666	11/60-08/82	**➲304022**
023	75687	61635	70490	75667	11/60-05/82	**➲304023**
024	75688	61636	70491	75668	11/60-05/81	**➲304024**
025	75689	61637	70492	75669	12/60-02/80	**➲304025**
026	75690	61638	70493	75670	12/60-12/67	
027	75691	61639	70494	75671	12/60-07/83	**➲304027**
028	75692	61640	70495	75672	01/61-08/82	**➲304028**
029	75693	61641	70496	75673	01/61-06/81	**➲304029**
030	75694	61642	70497	75674	01/61-06/81	**➲304030**
031	75695	61643	70498	75675	02/61-06/81	**➲304031**
032	75696	61644	70499	75676	02/61-09/81	**➲304032**
033	75697	61645	70500	75677	02/61-10/84	**➲304033**
034	75698	61646	70501	75678	03/61-06/84	**➲304034**
035	75699	61647	70502	75679	06/61-04/82	**➲304035**

Class 304/3

	BDTSOL	*MBSO*	*TCsoL*	*DTBSO*		
036	75868	61873	70243	75858	07/61-04/82	**➲304036**
037	75869	61874	70244	75859	07/61-04/82	**➲304037**
038	75870	61875	70245	75860	07/61- *83*	**➲304038**
039	75871	61876	70246	75861	08/61- *83*	**➲304039**
040	75872	61877	70247	75862	08/61-02/82	**➲304040**
041	75873	61878	70248	75863	08/61-05/82	**➲304041**
042	75874	61879	70249	75864	09/61-04/81	**➲304042**
043	75875	61880	70250	75865	09/61-07/83	**➲304043**
044	75876	61881	70251	75866	09/61-10/82	**➲304044**
045	75877	61882	70252	75867	10/61-02/83	**➲304045**

Class 310 AM10
London Midland Western Lines
25kV ac overhead
046-095

As the West Coast electrification spread south from Crewe towards London there was a need for further units to work on the longer distance services at the southern end of the line. The Class 310 units were built to a modern integral design with no conventional underframes. The doors were concentrated near the centre of each coach, with another door over each bogie to even out the stresses in the integral body. They had distinctive cabs with wrap-around windscreens but these were later replaced with flat glass windscreens. The units were originally gangwayed in two sections, with no gangway between the two centre cars.

The units settled down to work the medium distance services out of Euston to Birmingham via Northampton. In 1988 they began to be replaced by Class 317 units and the units were transferred to East Ham to work on the Tilbury lines.

A number of units were refurbished to remain working in the Birmingham area. They were renumbered in the 3101xx series and were fitted with gangways throughout the whole set. They were later reduced to 3-car units

	BDTSOL	*MBSO*	*TSO*	*DTCOL*		
046	76130	62071	70731	76180	02/65- *83*	**➲310046**
047	76131	62072	70732	76181	03/65-03/82	**➲310047**
048	76132	62073	70733	76182	03/65-04/81	**➲310048**
049	76133	62074	70734	76183	03/65-08/81	**➲310049**
050	76134	62075	70735	76184	03/65-09/82	**➲310050**
051	76135	62076	70736	76185	09/65-06/81	**➲310051**
052	76136	62077	70737	76186	09/65-02/80	**➲310052**
053	76137	62078	70738	76187	09/65-11/82	**➲310053**
054	76138	62079	70739	76188	09/65-07/81	**➲310054**
055	76139	62080	70740	76189	08/65-12/81	**➲310055**
056	76140	62081	70741	76190	11/65-02/80	**➲310056**
057	76141	62082	70742	76191	10/65-03/82	**➲310057**
058	76142	62083	70743	76192	10/65-12/81	**➲310058**
059	76143	62084	70744	76193	10/65-09/71	
059	76143	62084	70744	*76205*	09/71-12/79	**➲310059**
060	76144	62085	70745	76194	10/65-04/81	**➲310060**
061	76145	62086	70746	76195	08/65-03/82	**➲310061**
062	76146	62087	70747	76196	11/65-02/83	**➲310062**
063	76147	62088	70748	76197	08/65-06/81	**➲310063**
064	76148	62089	70749	76198	08/65-04/81	**➲310064**
065	76149	62090	70750	76199	08/65-09/82	**➲310065**
066	76150	62091	70751	76200	09/65-04/69	
066	*76228*	62091	70751	76200	04/69-03/82	**➲310066**
067	76151	62092	70752	76201	09/65-03/82	**➲310067**
068	76152	62093	70753	76202	10/65-04/83	**➲310068**
069	76153	62094	70754	76203	10/65-01/80	**➲310069**
070	76154	62095	70755	76204	11/65-08/81	**➲310070**
071	76155	62096	70756	76205	12/65-01/70	
072	76156	62097	70757	76206	12/65-05/81	**➲310072**
073	76157	62098	70758	76207	02/66-12/81	**➲310073**
074	76158	62099	70759	76208	06/66-04/81	**➲310074**
075	76159	62100	70760	76209	07/66-04/83	**➲310075**
076	76160	62101	70761	76210	07/66-02/82	**➲310076**
077	76161	62102	70762	76211	07/66-12/81	**➲310077**
078	76162	62103	70763	76212	08/66-03/82	**➲310078**
079	76163	62104	70764	76213	08/66-08/81	**➲310079**
080	76164	62105	70765	76214	08/66-03/82	**➲310080**
081	76165	62106	70766	76215	09/66-03/82	**➲310081**
082	76166	62107	70767	76216	09/66-04/83	**➲310082**
083	76167	62108	70768	76217	09/66-10/81	**➲310083**
084	76168	62109	70769	76218	10/66-10/81	**➲310084**
085	76169	62110	70770	76219	11/66-04/83	**➲310085**
086	76170	62111	70771	76220	10/66-10/82	**➲310086**
087	76171	62112	70772	76221	02/67-12/81	**➲310087**
088	76172	62113	70773	76222	12/66-12/81	**➲310088**
089	76173	62114	70774	76223	01/67-06/81	**➲310089**

090	76174	62115	70775	76224	11/66-07/82	**➲310090**	
091	76175	62116	70776	76225	12/66-04/83	**➲310091**	
092	76176	62117	70777	76226	12/66-02/83	**➲310092**	
093	76177	62118	70778	76227	03/67-07/82	**➲310093**	
094	76178	62119	70779	76228	02/67-12/67		
094	*76998*	62119	*70780*	*76193*	04/75-01/83	**➲310094**	☜
095	76179	62120	70780	76229	05/67-12/67		
095	76179	62120	*70779*	76229	12/67-04/81	**➲310095**	☜

LNWR London Area

In 1907 the LNWR approved an electrification scheme for its London area suburban services. The heart of the plan was a new line to be built alongside the existing railway from London Euston to Watford Junction. The scheme eventually extended a lot further from Broad Street in the East to Richmond in the West, with branches to Croxley Green, Rickmansworth, Kew Bridge and Earls Court. It reached its greatest extent, and largest amount of stock, in 1933. It was electrified at 630V dc, using third and fourth rail, making it compatible with the other lines in the area that later became part of the Underground system.

LNWR London Area
Siemens 3-car sets
630V dc third & fourth rail

The first batch of units for the scheme comprised four 3-car multiple units built by the Metropolitan Carriage, Wagon & Finance Company. They were fitted with Siemens electrical equipment, and they ran in fixed formations for the whole of their life on the London services.

These units were not compatible with the later Oerlikon powered units and could not be used in multiple with any of the later units. These sets were used primarily (but not exclusively) on the Earls Court service.

The Earls Court service was withdrawn in October 1940 and the sets were placed in store, but nevertheless the first three sets were overhauled in 1945/46.

In 1953 the first three sets started work on the newly re-electrified Lancaster, Morecame & Heysham line. This had been converted to test the 50Hz ac overhead system and these units were fitted with new English Electric equipment, and new seating. The fourth unit joined them on this line in 1957. For this use they were reclassified AM1.

LNWR numbers.

DMBT	TC	DTT
1E	301E	601E
2E	302E	602E
3E	303E	603E
4E	304E	604E

LMS 1923 numbers.

DMBT	TC	DTT
5721	8801	9941
5722	8802	9942
5723	8803	9943
5724	8804	9944

LMS 1933 numbers. Rebuilt as overhead ac units for the Lancaster, Morecambe & Heysham line in 1952.

DMBT	TC	DTT	
28219	29721	29021	14-02/67
28220	29722	29022	14-02/67
28221	29723	29023	14-02/67
28222	29724	29024	14-02/67

LNWR London Area
Oerlikon 3-car sets
630V dc third & fourth rail

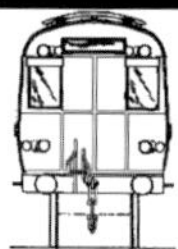

The next batch of stock built was similar to the Siemens stock, but it had electrical equipment built by Maschinenfabrik Oerlikon of Oerlikon, Switzerland.

Both the Siemens and Oerlikon sets were noted for their luxurious seating, and smooth riding qualities. They were comfortable and pleasant to travel in and were held in high regard by both passengers and staff.

The first batch of stock was built in 1915 and stored until the Kew Bridge and Richmond lines were electrified in October 1916. It comprised 38 3-car sets and five spare motor cars, but they worked for many years in 19 fixed 6-car sets.

A further order of stock was built in 1921 comprising 30 3-car sets and three spare motors, again these worked as 15 fixed 6-car trains.

From 1923 the unit formations started to become more flexible, but in general the trailer cars and driving trailers tended to stay together. In 1934 the vestibule connections between the vehicles in the Oerlikon & Siemens sets began to be removed.

Apart from accident damaged vehicles, the withdrawal of Oerlikon stock began in 1954, the last unit going in 1960 when the services were taken over completely by the new BR class 501 units.

Original fixed formations with 2 x 3-car units. Later formations more variable.

1915 stock.

DMBT	TC	DTT	DTT	TC	DMBT
5E	305E	605E	606E	306E	6E
7E	307E	607E	608E	308E	8E
9E	309E	609E	610E	310E	10E
11E	311E	611E	612E	312E	12E
13E	313E	613E	614E	314E	14E
15E	315E	615E	616E	316E	16E
17E	317E	617E	618E	318E	18E
19E	319E	619E	620E	320E	20E
21E	321E	621E	622E	322E	22E
23E	323E	623E	624E	324E	24E
25E	325E	625E	626E	326E	26E
27E	327E	627E	628E	328E	28E
29E	329E	629E	630E	330E	30E
31E	331E	631E	632E	332E	32E
33E	333E	633E	634E	334E	34E
35E	335E	635E	636E	336E	36E
37E	337E	637E	638E	338E	38E
39E	339E	639E	640E	340E	40E
41E	341E	641E	642E	342E	42E

spare DMBT	
43E	➲251E
44E	➲250E
45E	➲253E
46E	➲252E
47E	➲255E

1921 stock. *Not fixed formations.*

DMBT	TC	DTT
43E[2]	343E	643E
44E[2]	344E	644E
45E[2]	345E	645E
46E[2]	346E	646E
47E[2]	347E	647E
48E	348E	648E
49E	349E	649E
50E	350E	650E
51E	351E	651E
52E	352E	652E
53E	353E	653E
54E	354E	654E
55E	355E	655E
56E	356E	656E
57E	357E	657E
58E	358E	658E
59E	359E	659E
60E	360E	660E
61E	361E	661E
62E	362E	662E
63E	363E	663E
64E	364E	664E
65E	365E	665E
66E	366E	666E
67E	367E	667E
68E	368E	668E
69E	369E	669E
70E	370E	670E
71E	371E	671E
72E	372E	672E

spare DMBT
254E
256E
257E

1915 stock. *Not fixed formations.*

LMS 1923 numbers

DMBT	TC	DTT
5725	8805	9945
5726	8806	9946
5727	8807	9947
5728	8808	9948
5729	8809	9949
5730	8810	9950
5731	8811	9951
5732	8812	9952
5733	8813	9953
5734	8814	9954
5735	8815	9955
5736	8816	9956
5737	8817	9957
5738	8818	9958

5739	8819	9959
5740	8820	9960
5741	8821	9961
5742	8822	9962
5743	8823	9973
5744	8824	9974
5745	8825	9975
5746	8826	9976
5747	8827	9977
5748	8828	9978
5749	8829	9979
5750	8830	9980
5751	8831	9981
5752	8832	9963
5753	8833	9964
5754	8834	9965
5755	8835	9966
5756	8836	9967
5757	8837	9968
5758	8838	9969
5759	8839	9970
5760	8840	9971
5761	8841	9972
5762	8842	9982
5793		
5794		
5795		
5796		
5798		

1915 stock. *Not fixed formations.*
LMS 1923 numbers

DMBT	*TC*	*DTT*
5763	8843	9983
5764	8844	9984
5765	8845	9985
5766	8846	9986
5767	8847	9987
5768	8848	9988
5769	8849	9989
5770	8850	9990
5771	8851	9991
5772	8852	9992
5773	8853	9993
5774	8854	9994
5775	8855	9995
5776	8856	9996
5777	8857	9997
5778	8858	9998
5779	8859	9999
5780	8860	10000
5781	8861	10001
5782	8862	10002
5783	8863	10003
5784	8864	10004
5785	8865	10005
5786	8866	10006
5787	8867	10007
5788	8868	10008
5789	8869	10009
5790	8870	10010
5791	8871	10011
5792	8872	10012
5797		
5799		
5800		

1923 stock. *Not fixed formations.*
LMS 1923 numbers

DMBT	*TC*	*DTT*
5719	8873	10013
5720	8874	10014
	8875	10015
	8876	10016
	8877	10017
	8878	10018
	8879	10019

1915 stock. *Not fixed formations.*
LMS 1933 numbers

DMBT	*TC*	*DTT*
28223	29725	29025
28224	29726	29026
28225	29727	29027
28226		
28227	29729	29029
28228	29730	29030
28229	29731	29031
28230	29732	29032
28231	29733	29033
28232	29734	29034
28233	29735	29035
28234	29736	29036
28235	29737	29037
28236	29738	29038
28237	29739	29039
28238	29740	29040
28239	29741	29041
28240	29742	29042
28241	29743	29043
28242	29744	29044
28243	29745	29045
28244	29746	29046
28245	29747	29047
28246	29748	29048
28247	29749	29049
28248	29750	29050
28249	29751	29051
28250	29752	29052
28251	29753	29053
28252	29754	29054
28253	29755	29055
28254	29756	29056
28255	29757	29057
28256	29758	29058
28257	29759	29059
28258	29760	29060
28259	29761	29061
28260	29762	29062
28261		
28262		
28263		
28000		
28264		

1921 stock. *Not fixed formations.*
LMS 1933 numbers

DMBT	*TC*	*DTT*
28265	29763	29063
28266	29764	29064
28267	29765	29065
28268	29766	29066
28269	29767	29067
28270	29768	29068
28271	29769	29069
28272	29770	29070
28273	29771	29071
28274	29772	29072
28275	29773	29073
28276	29774	29074
28277	29775	29075
28278	29776	29076
28279	29777	29077
28280	29778	29078
28281	29779	29079
28282	29780	29080
28283	29781	29081
28284	29782	29082
28285	29783	29083
28286	29784	29084
28287	29785	29085
28288	29786	29086
28289	29787	29087
28290	29788	29088
28291	29789	29089
28292	29790	29090
28293	29791	29091
28294	29792	29092
28295		
28296		
28297		

1923 stock. *Not fixed formations.*
LMS 1933 numbers

DMBT	*TC*	*DTT*
28298	29793	29093
28299	29794	29094
	29795	29095
	29796	29096
	29797	29097
	29798	29098
	29799	29099

LNWR London Area
GEC 3-car sets
630V dc third & fourth rail

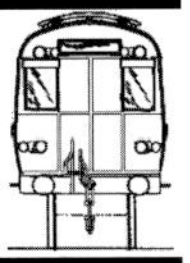

A new type of stock was introduced in 1927, known as the GEC or Compartment stock. It was part of a joint order for the London area and Liverpool area lines. Twelve 3-car units plus five trailers were built for the London area lines. Ten all-third compartment trailers were built in 1929 to allow seven-car trains to be run, the new trailers generally being inserted between the motor and motor composite vehicles of the GEC 3-car units.

A further batch of vehicles was built in 1933, and the stock was then generally reformed into 3-car sets, with the all-third trailers being converted to composites. In 1939, one trailer car, number 29401, was transferred to work on the Manchester South Junction & Altrincham line which used similar stock.

By 1957, the remaining vehicles were running as 25 3-car sets and the surplus trailers were withdrawn.

LMS 1923 numbers. Not fixed formations.

DMBT	TC	DTT
4605	4615	4611
4606	4616	4612
4607	4617	4613
4608	4618	4614
4609	5713	5236
4610	5714	5237
5801	5715	5238
8800	5716	5239
8880	5717	5240
8881	5718	5241
8882	10679	5242
8883	10680	5243
8884	1886	
8885		
8886		
8887		
8888		

LMS 1933 numbers.

DMBT	TC	DTT
28001	29600	28800
28002	29601	28801
28003	29602	28802
28004	29603	28803
28005	29604	28804
28006	29605	28805
28007	29606	28806
28008	29607	28807
28009	29608	28808
28010	29609	28809
28011	29610	28810
28012	29611	28811
28013	29612	
28014		
28015		
28016		
28017		

DMBT	TC	DTT
28018	29613	28812
28019	29614	28813
28020	29615	28814
28021	29616	28815
28022	29617	28816
28023	29618	28817
28024	29619	28818
28025	29620	28819
	29621	28820
		28821
	29622	28822
	29623	28823
	29624	28824

TT	
29400	➲29622
29401	➲MSJA 153 (29237)
29402	
29403	
29404	
29405	
29406	
29407	➲29623
29408	➲29624
29409	

LNWR London Area
Joint Tube Stock
630V dc third & fourth rail

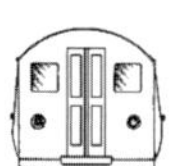

When the Bakerloo line was connected to the LNWR Watford line in 1917, new tube stock was needed to work over the through line. It was jointly ordered by the London Electric Railway and the LNWR, but technically two thirds of the cars were owned by the LNWR and one third by the LER. Ordered in 1914 from the Metropolitan Carriage Wagon and Finance Company, it was not delivered until 1920, meaning the new line had to open with borrowed stock.

The stock was formed as M-CT-M-T-T-M – the first time a motor car was formed in the centre of a London Underground train. The CT was a Control Trailer: a Driving Trailer in modern parlance. The units operated as 4-car units in the off-peak period, being augmented to 6-cars at the peak hours.

These units had the floors set 4½ inches higher than normal tube-stock as a compromise between the tube platform levels and the main line levels on the extension. They were fitted with hinged doors and a gateman was provided in each car to make sure they were locked. This led to slow loading and unloading at station stops, and the units were later replaced by cars with sliding doors in 1931-32.

Most of the stock was scrapped, but the LMS retained nine cars which it used on the Rickmansworth and Croxley Green services from 1931. They were fitted with modernised doors and were reformed into three third class only 3-car sets: 825-640-770, 2394-337-904 and 2415-593-2416.

With the outbreak of the Second World War the stock was placed in store and didn't work again. The vehicles were officially withdrawn in 1948, then scrapped in 1949.

Joint Tube Stock. Original J numbers. Not fixed formations, but the units were directional, with the formations as shown, North-South. Used as common joint stock but the actual vehicle owners are shown.

DMBT	DTT	DMBT	TT	TT	DMBT	
1J	402J	3J	201J	202J	2J	LNWR
5J	404J	6J	203J	207J	4J	LNWR
8J	405J	9J	208J	209J	7J	LNWR
10J	406J	12J	210J	211J	11J	LNWR
14J	407J	15J	212J	213J	13J	LNWR
17J	408J	18J	216J	218J	16J	LNWR
23J	409J	24J	219J	220J	22J	LNWR
30J	411J	27J	221J	224J	31J	LNWR
19J	401J	21J	204J	205J	20J	LER
26J	403J	32J	206J	214J	25J	LER
33J	410J	34J	215J	217J	28J	LER
35J	412J	36J	222J	223J	29J	LER

Retained Stock. LMS 1923 numbers. Fixed formations.

DMBT	TT	DMBT	DMBT	TT	DMBT
2394	337	904	825	640	770
2415	593	2416			

LMS 1933 numbers. Fixed formations.

DMBT	TT	DMBT	DMBT	TT	DMBT
28213	29497	28216	28218	29499	28217
28214	29498	28215			

Class 501
North London Watford Line
630V dc third & fourth rail, later third rail
133-189

These units were built at Eastleigh in 1957 as 3- car units on short frames, to replace the earlier units on the former LNWR London electrified system.

In common with other LMR dc units they did not carry unit numbers, but they remained in fixed formations, and were normally referred to by the last three digits of the carriage numbers, "133-182". They were later allocated the unit numbers 501135-501189, but these numbers were (in most cases) not carried.

The cars were fitted with bars on the windows due to the restricted clearance through Hampstead Heath tunnel. The intermediate Trailer Second vehicles were rebuilt as open at Croxley Green depot from 1975 onwards. Some sets were overhauled in the 1980s. The last units were withdrawn in 1985 and were replaced with Class 416 EPB stock.

	DMBSO	TS	DTBSO	
	61133	70133	75133	12/56-11/68
	61134	70134	75134	01/57-11/68
501135	61135	70135	75135	01/57-10/85
	61136	70136	75136	02/57-11/68
	61137	70137	75137	02/57-05/75
	61137	*70185*	*75185*	05/75-10/85
	61138	70138	75138	02/57-11/68
	61139	70139	75139	03/57-11/68
	61140	70140	75140	03/57-11/68
501141	61141	70141	75141	03/57-10/85
	61142	70142	75142	04/57-10/85
	61143	70143	75143	04/57-10/84
	61144	70144	75144	04/57-10/84
	61145	70145	75145	04/57-04/84
	61146	70146	75146	04/57-10/84
	61147	70147	75147	05/57-01/73
	61147	*70161*	*75161*	01/73-04/75
	61147	*70145*	*75145*	04/75-10/85
	61148	70148	75148	05/57-10/85

	61149	70149	75149	05/57-05/75		
	61149	*70166*	*75166*	05/75-10/84		↶
	61150	70150	75150	05/57-10/85		
	61151	70151	75151	05/57-*01/78*		
	61151	*70167*	75151	*01/78*-10/85		↶
	61152	70152	75152	06/57-10/85		
	61153	70153	75153	06/57-10/84		
	61154	70154	75154	06/57-10/84		
501155	61155	70155	75155	07/57-10/85		
	61156	70156	75156	07/57-10/85		
	61157	70157	75157	07/57-10/85		
501158	61158	70158	75158	07/57-10/85		
501159	61159	70159	75159	08/57-10/85		
	61160	70160	75160	08/57-10/85		
	61161	70161	75161	08/57-10/76		
	61162	70162	75162	08/57- 69	➲Dep	
	61163	70163	75163	09/57-10/84		
501164	61164	70164	75164	09/57-10/85		
	61165	70165	75165	09/57- 69	➲Dep	
	61166	70166	75166	09/57-05/75		
	61167	70167	75167	09/57-10/76		
	61167	*70151*	75167	10/76-10/76		↶
	61168	70168	75168	10/57-10/85		
	61169	70169	75169	10/57-10/85		
501170	61170	70170	75170	10/57-10/85		
501171	61171	70171	75171	10/57-10/85		
	61172	70172	75172	10/57-10/75		
	61173	70173	75173	11/57-07/75		
	61174	70174	75174	11/57-10/84		
	61175	70175	75175	11/57-10/75		
	61176	70176	75176	11/57-10/85		
	61177	70177	75177	11/57-10/84		
501178	61178	70178	75178	12/57-10/84	➲*Dep*	
	61179	70179	75179	12/57-10/84		
501180	61180	70180	75180	12/57-10/84	➲*Dep*	
	61181	70181	75181	12/57-10/84		
	61182	70182	75182	12/57-07/78		
	61183	70183	75183	01/58-10/84	➲*Dep*	
	61184	70184	75184	01/58-07/78		
	61185	70185	75185	01/58-02/75		
	61185	*70175*	*75175*	10/75-07/78		↶
501186	61186	70186	75186	01/58-10/85		
	61187	70187	75187	01/58-10/76		
501188	61188	70188	75188	02/58-10/85		
	61189	70189	75189	02/58-07/78	➲*Dep*	

Liverpool-Southport

Liverpool-Southport
Lancashire & Yorkshire 4-car sets
630V dc third rail

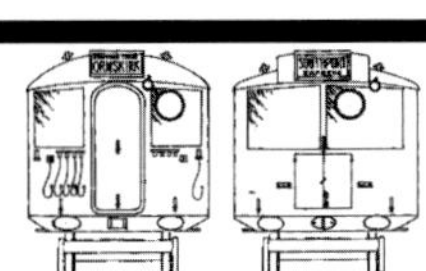

The Lancashire and Yorkshire Railway electrified the line from Liverpool to Southport on the 625V dc third rail system in 1904. The line was increasingly popular for commuters and pleasure trips, but it had been experiencing competition from the rival Cheshire Lines Committee route. The new vehicles were the widest ever seen on a British railway, being 10ft wide at the waist. They had clerestory roofs and straight sided vertical match-boarding on the sides. The motor vehicles were fitted with large luggage compartments behind the cabs and the door were recessed back and fitted at an angle of 25° in such a way that they did not project beyond the body-side when fully open. When first built the driving cabs were tapered towards the front, but they were later rebuilt to a box design. Later built trains were fitted with through gangways. Six trailer cars were fitted with half-width cabs in 1910 to allow trains to be shortened in off-peak periods. In 1913 the line to Ormskirk was electrified and additional trains were built. These later built cars had high elliptical roofs and domed ends and were longer than the previous cars.

Not fixed formations. Some units formed DMT TF TF DMT

LYR numbers

DMT	***TF***	***TT***	***DMT***	***Baggage***
3000	400	3100	3001	3028
3002	401	3101	3003	3029
3004	402	3102	3005	3066
3006	403	3103	3007	
3008	404	3104	3009	
3010	405	3105	3011	
3012	406	3106	3013	
3014	407	3107	3015	
3016	408	3108	3017	
3018	409	3109	3019	
3020	410	3110	3021	
3022	411	3111	3023	
3024	412	3112	3025	
3026	413	3113	3027	
3030	414	3114	3031	
3032	415	3115	3033	
3034	416	3116	3035	
3036	417	3117	3037	
3038	418	3118	3039	
3040	419	3119	3041	
3042	420	3120	3043	
3044	421	3121	3045	
3046	422	3122	3047	
3048	423	3123	3049	
3050	424	3124	3051	
3052	425	3125	3053	
3054	426	3126	3055	
3056	427	3127	3057	
3058	428	3128	3059	
3060	429	3129	3061	
3062	430	3130	3063	
3064	431	3131	3065	
	432	3132		
	433	3133		
	434	3134		
	435	3135		
	436	3136		
	437	3137		
	438	3138		
	439	3139		
	440	3140		
		3141		
		3142		
		3143		
		3144		
		3145		
		3146		
		3147		
		3148		
		3149		
		3150		

LMS 1923 numbers

DMT	***TF***	***TT***	***DMT***	***Baggage***
14501	10891	14616	14502	14529
14503	10892	14617	14504	14530
14505	10893	14618	14506	14567
14507	10894	14619	14508	
14509	10895	14620	14510	
14511	10896	14621	14512	
14513	10897	14622	14514	
14515	10898	14623	14516	
14517	10899	14624	14518	
14519	10900	14625	14520	
14521	10901	14626	14522	
14523	10902	14627	14524	
14525	10903	14628	14526	
14527	10904	14629	14528	
14531	10905	14630	14532	
14533	10906	14631	14534	
14535	10907	14632	14536	
14537	10908	14633	14538	
14539	10909	14634	14540	
14541	10910	14635	14542	
14543	10911	14636	14544	
14545	10912	14637	14546	
14547	10913	14638	14548	
14549	10914	14639	14550	
14551	10915	14640	14552	
14553	10916	14641	14554	
14555	10917	14642	14556	
14557	10918	14643	14558	
14559	10919	14644	14560	
14561	10920	14645	14562	
14563	10921	14646	14564	
14565	10922	14647	14566	
	10923	14648		
	10924	14649		
	10925	14650		
	10926	14651		
	10927	14652		
	10928	14653		
	10929	14654		
	10930	14655		
	10931	14656		
		14657		
		14658		
		14659		
		14660		
		14661		
		14662		
		14663		
		14664		
		14665		
		14666		

LMS 1933 numbers

DMT	*TF*	*TT*	*DMT*	*Baggage*
28433	29300	29500	28434	28497
28435	29301	29501	28436	28498
28437	29302	29502	28438	28499
28439	29303	29503	28440	
28441	29304	29504	28442	
28443	29305	29505	28444	
28445	29306	29506	28446	
28447	29307	29507	28448	
28449	29308	29508	28450	
28451	29309	29509	28452	
28453	29310	29510	28454	
28455	29311	29511	28456	
28457	29312	29512	28458	
28459	29313	29513	28460	
28461	29314	29514	28462	
28463	29315	29515	28464	
28465	29316	29516	28466	
28467	29317	29517	28468	
28469	29318	29518	28470	
28471	29319	29519	28472	
28473	29320	29520	28474	
28475	29321	29521	28476	
28477	29322	29522	28478	
28479	29323	29523	28480	
28481	29324	29524	28482	
28483	29325	29525	28484	
28485	29326	29526	28486	
28487	29327	29527	28488	
28489	29328	29528	28490	
28491	29329	29529	28492	
28493	29330	29530	28494	
28495	29331	29531	28496	
	29332	29532		
	29333	29533		
	29334	29534		
	29335	29535		
	29336	29536		
	29337	29537		
	29338	29538		
	29339	29539		
	29340	29540		
		29541		
		29542		
		29543		
		29544		
		29194		
		29195		
		29196		
		29197		
		29198		
		29199		

Liverpool-Southport
Liverpool Overhead Through Trains
630V dc third rail

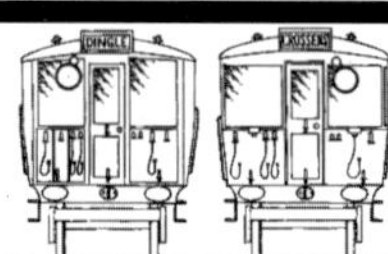

A connection to the Liverpool Overhead railway was opened in 1905, and agreement was made to run through services from Dingle to Southport. Specially built light-weight cars were constructed to operate through trains on this route, the prototype from Dick, Kerr and Co in Preston followed by eleven further cars from Newton Heath. The through trains were never a great success and the service was withdrawn in the War in 1915. The service was never re-instated apart from a limited amount of through running on Aintree race days.

LYR Numbers	*LMS 1923 numbers*	*LMS 1933 numbers*
DMC	*DMC*	*DMC*
1000	14610	28600
1001	14611	28601
1002	14612	28602
1003	11702	*28691*
1004	11703	*28692*
1005	11704	28693
1006	11705	28694
1007	11706	28695
1008	11707	28696
1009	11708	28697
1010	11709	28698
1011	11710	28699

Liverpool-Southport
LNWR 3-car sets
630V dc third rail

This was part of a joint order for the London area and Liverpool area lines. It was new type of stock introduced in 1927, known as the GEC or Compartment stock. Eleven 3-car units plus a spare trailer were built for the Liverpool area lines.

LMS 1923 numbers. Not fixed formations.

DMBT	*TC*	*DTT*
8889	10682	5244
8890	10683	5245
8891	10684	5246
8892	10685	5247
8893	10686	5248
8894	10687	5249
8895	10688	5250
8896	10689	5358
8897	10690	5359
8898	10691	5360
8899	10692	10020
	10693	

LMS 1933 numbers. Not fixed formations.

DMBT	*TC*	*DTT*
28300	29800	29100
28301	29801	29101
28302	29802	29102
28303	29803	29103
28304	29804	29104
28305	29805	29105
28306	29806	29106
28307	29807	29107
28308	29808	29108
28309	29809	29109
28310	29810	29110
	29811	

28496 and 28497 were motor luggage vans rebuilt from a compartment motor coach and driving trailer to replace similar L&Y vehicles 28498 and 28499. A driving cab was built into the opposite end to the existing cab and half the equipment transferred from the motor coach to the driving trailer as each operated singly.

Baggage
28496
28497

Class 502 Liverpool-Southport
LMS 2, 3 & 5-car sets
630V dc third rail

These units were built to replace life-expired LYR units on the Southport Line and later became Class 502. They were built at Derby in 1939-41 and bore a resemblance to the Class 503 units on the Wirral lines. They were of open arrangement and were fitted with air operated sliding doors.

They were originally formed into 3-car units (MBSO-TSO-DTCO) and 2-car part units (MBSO-TSO- or MBSO-TCO-), the part units designed to make up 5-car sets. Although no unit numbers were carried, the formations remained fairly constant.

The trailer composite coaches were later converted to TSO or DTCO and were renumbered accordingly. In the seventies many units were reformed into two and three car units with driving cabs at both ends.

The line was extended south through Liverpool city centre to join up with the newly electrified Garston line in 1977, and at the same time a new branch was electrified to Kirkby. The units were replaced by new Class 507 units in 1979.

Original Formations

DMBS	*TS*	*DTC*
28311	29545	29866
28312	29546	29867
28313	29547	29868
28314	29548	29869
28315	29549	29870
28316	29550	29871
28317	29551	29872
28318	29552	29873
28319	29553	29874
28320	29554	29875
28321	29555	29876
28323	29556	29877

28325	29557	29878
28327	29558	29879
28329	29559	29880
28331	29560	29881
28333	29561	29882
28335	29562	29883
28337	29564	29884
28339	29566	29885
28341	29568	29886
28343	29570	29887
28345	29572	*29888*
28347	29574	29889
28349	29576	29890
28351	29578	29891
28353	29580	29892
28355	29582	29893
28357	29584	29894
28359	29586	29895
28361	29588	29896
28363	29590	29897
28365	29592	29898
28367	29594	29899

DMBS	***TS***
28336	29563
28338	29565
28340	29567
28342	29569
28344	29571
28346	29573
28348	29575
28350	29577
28352	29579
28354	29581
28356	29583
28358	29585
28360	29587
28362	29589
28364	29591
28366	29593

DMBS	***TC***
28322	29812
28324	29813
28326	29814
28328	29815
28330	29816
28332	29817
28334	29818
28368	29819
28369	29820

Formation Changes

DMBS	***TS***	***DTC***	
28311	29545	29866	39-05/73
28311		29866	05/73-10/76
28311	*29599*	29866	10/76-12/77
28311	*29581*	*29863*	04/78-11/78
28311	*29599*		11/78-12/78
28312	29546	29867	39-11/80
28313	29547	29868	39-03/73
28313		29868	03/73-10/76
28313	*29586*	29868	10/76-12/77
28314	29548	29869	39-05/73
28314		29869	05/73-*02/74*
28314	*29547*	29869	01/77-12/78
28315	29549	29870	39- 68
28315	29549	*29874*	56-05/73
28315		29874	05/73-01/77
28315	*29577*	29874	01/77-12/77
28316	29550	29871	39-03/73
28317	29551	29872	39-10/68
28318	29552	29873	39-04/79
28318	29552	*29871*	04/79-11/79
28318	*29565*	*29886*	11/79-11/80
28319	29553	29874	39-*10/68*
28319	*29555*	*29890*	*10/68*-11/79
28319	*28334*		11/79-11/80
28320	29554	29875	39-02/50
28321	29555	29876	39-06/62
28322	29812		39- *50*
28322	*29595*		*50-10/68*
28322	29595	*29897*	*10/68*-02/74
28322	29595	*29866*	11/78-01/79
28323	29556	29877	39-11/80
28324	29813		39- *50*
28324	*29596*		*50*-10/68
28325	29557	29878	39-01/63
28326	29814		39- *50*
28326	*29597*		*50*-12/58
28326	*29573*		12/58- *63*
28326	29573	*29876*	*63*-01/79
28326	*29595*	*29866*	01/79-09/79
28327	29558	29879	39-09/70
28328	29815		39- *50*
28328	*29598*		*50*-11/59
28328	29598	*29864*	11/59-05/73
28328		29864	05/73-10/76
28328	*29554*	29864	10/76-09/79
28329	29559	29880	39-06/62
28330	29816		39- *50*
28330	*29599*		*50-06/71*
28330	29599	*29879*	*06/71*-03/73
28330		29879	03/73-10/76
28330	*29585*	29879	10/76-12/77
28330	29585	*29862*	12/77-05/79
28331	29560	29881	39-05/73
28331		29881	05/73-*02/76*
28331	*29568*	29881	*02/76*-09/79
28332	29817		39- *50*
28332	*29544*		*50*-01/63
28332	*29577*		01/63-*10/68*
28332	29577	*29872*	*10/68*-03/73
28332		29872	03/73-10/76
28332	*29566*	29872	10/76-06/80
28332	*29564*	29872	06/80-11/80
28333	29561	29882	39-05/73
28333		*29882*	05/73-12/77
28333	*29548*	29882	12/77-03/80
28334	29818		39-09/60
28334	*29559*	*29880*	06/62-11/79
28335	29562	29883	39-04/78
28335	*29561*		04/78-11/79
28335	29561	*29897*	11/79-01/80
28335	29561	*29894*	01/80-06/80
28336	29563		39-10/68
28337	29564	29884	39-06/80
28338	29565		39- *72*
28338		*29870*	*72*-10/76
28338	*29582*	29870	10/76-06/80
28338	*29561*	*29894*	06/80-11/80
28339	29566	29885	39-05/73
28339		29885	05/73-03/76
28339	*29598*	29885	01/77-05/79
28340	29567		39-03/73
28340		*29891*	03/73-01/77
28340	*29549*	29891	01/77-12/77
28341	29568	29886	39-*02/76*
28341	*29565*	29886	10/76-05/79
28342	29569		39- *59*
28342	29569	*29895*	*59*-10/68
28343	29570	29887	39-04/79
28343	*29573*	*29876*	04/79-08/79
28344	29571		39- 68
28344	29571	*29870*	56-12/71
28345	29572	*29888*	39-10/68
28346	29573		39-01/50
28347	29574	29889	39-11/80
28348	29575		39-10/68
28349	29576	29890	39-01/42
28349	*29554*	29875	50-06/71
28350	29577		39- 50
28350	29577	*29890*	50- *67*
28350	*29555*	29890	*67*-10/68
28351	29578	29891	39-12/58
28351	*29586*	*29862*	12/58-05/73
28351		29862	05/73-10/76
28351	*29561*	29862	10/76-12/77
28351	*29557*	*29878*	12/77-11/79
28351	29557	*29895*	11/79-11/80
28352	29579		39-*10/68*
28352	29579	*29888*	*10/68*-09/79
28353	29580	29892	39-05/79
28354	29581		39-09/60
28354	29581	*29863*	09/60-04/78
28354	*29562*	*29883*	04/78-11/80
28355	29582	29893	39-03/73
28355		29893	03/73-10/76
28355	*29545*	29893	10/76-09/79
28356	29583		39-*02/74*
28356		*29869*	*02/74*-03/76
28356	*29583*	*29879*	12/77-08/79
28357	29584	29894	39-01/80
28357	29584	*29587*	06/80-11/80
28358	29585		39-03/73
28358		*29871*	03/73-01/77
28358	*29599*	*29866*	12/77-11/78
28358	*29581*	*29863*	11/78-09/79
28359	29586	29895	39-12/58
28359	*29578*	*29891*	12/58-03/73
28359	*29578*		03/73-03/76
28359		*29885*	03/76-01/77
28359	*29578*	*29871*	01/77-04/79
28359	29578	*29873*	04/79-09/79

28360	29587			39-*04/59*	
28360	29587	*29865*		*04/59-02/74*	☜
28360		*29897*		*02/74*-11/79	☜
28361	29588	29896		39-08/80	
28362	29589			39-03/76	
28362		*29869*		03/76-01/77	☜
28362	*29589*	*29868*		12/77-12/78	☜
28363	29590	29897		39-10/68	
28364	29591			39-05/73	
28364		*29875*		05/73-01/77	☜
28364	*29567*	29875		01/77-11/80	☜
28365	29592	29898		39-10/68	
28366	29593			39-*10/68*	
28366	29593	*29895*		*10/68*-06/79	☜
28366	29593	*29874*		06/79-11/80	☜
28367	29594	29899		39-10/68	
28368	29819			39-*11/59*	
28368			Meols Cop Shunter	*11/59*-10/68	☜
28369	29820			39-*04/59*	
28369	*29557*	*29878*		07/62-12/77	☜

Liverpool-Southport
Ex-South Tyneside Line Motor Luggage Van
630V dc third rail

This Motor Luggage Van was transferred to the Southport Line in 1963 after its duties finished on the Tyneside system. It did not last very long, being withdrawn from service in 1964.

MLV	
68000	08/63- 64

Mersey Railway & Wirral Lines

Mersey Railway
1903 Stock
650V dc third rail

The Mersey Railway opened in 1886 forming an underground link from Liverpool to Birkenhead. It was steam-hauled from the start, but it was not a popular route because of the steam and smoke. When the weather was good, most people still preferred to use the ferry to get from one side of the Mersey to the other. The company was soon in serious financial difficulties and in 1899 a plan was prepared to electrify the line, to try and turn round the financial fortunes of the company.

In 1903 the new electrified line opened. The trains were British built by G.F. Milnes of Hadley, but were to a typical American design with straight match-boarded sides, clerestory roofs and open ends. The open ends were originally fitted with decorative lattice railings and a gate opened by a gate boy. These open ends were boxed in from 1912 to increase standing capacity. The trains were fitted with a control system which was new at the time, where the motors throughout the train could be controlled from the leading cab without the need to run a line-voltage power cable throughout the train. This was the first full-scale introduction of this method of multiple-working which became the standard for all future multiple unit trains.

Twenty-four motor cars and thirty-eight trailers were provided to work the services. They initially worked in trains of two or four cars except on Sundays when some single-car services were run. The electrification completely turned round the fortunes of the company and later, as traffic built up, five-car trains were introduced (two motor and three trailer cars).

Mersey Railway numbers. Not fixed formations.

MF	*TF*	*TT*	*TT*	*MT*
1	51	75	88	26
2	52	76	89	27
3	53	77	90	28
4	54	78	91	29
5	55	79	92	30
6	56	80	93	31
7	57	81	94	32
8	58	82	95	33
9	59	83	96	34
10	60	84	97	35
11	61	85	98	36
12	62	86	99	37
	63	87		

LMS 1933 type numbers; renumbered in 1948.

MF	*TF*	*TT*	*TT*	*MT*
28405	28787	29157	29169	28419
28406	28788	29158	29170	28420
28407	28789	29159	29171	28421
28408	28790	29160	29172	28422
28409	28791	29161	29173	28423
28410	28792	29162	29174	28424
28411	28793	29163	29175	28425
28412	28794	29164	29176	28426
28413	28795	29165	29177	28427
28414	28796	29166	29178	28428
28415	28797	29167	29179	28429
28416	28798	29168	29180	28430

Mersey Railway
1923 Stock
650V dc third rail

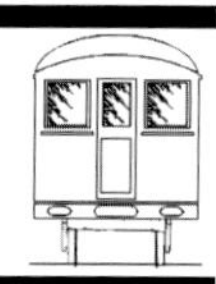

The Mersey Railway remained an independent company at the Railway Grouping in 1923. Some additional stock was delivered in 1923 and 1925. The new vehicles were similar to the earlier stock, but with a more modern appearance presented by larger windows, an elliptical roof and passenger entrances at each end of the car.

Mersey Railway numbers. Not fixed formations.

MF	*TF*	*TT*	*MT*
13	64	100	38
14		101	39

LMS 1933 type numbers; renumbered in 1948.

MF	*TF*	*TT*	*MT*
28417	28799	29181	28431
28418		29182	28432

Mersey Railway
1936 Stock
650V dc third rail

The last additions to the Mersey Railway fleet were ten new trailer cars introduced in 1936 to allow the existing trains to be lengthened to 6-cars. They were lighter in weight than the existing cars and were to a more modern design, with steel-skinned body sides. An eleventh car was built as a replacement for No. 84 which was damaged in the war.

Mersey Railway numbers. Not fixed formations.

TT	*TT*	*TT*
102	107	112
103	108	
104	109	
105	110	
106	111	

LMS 1933 type numbers; renumbered in 1948.

TT	*TT*	*TT*
29183	29188	29193
29184	29189	
29185	29190	
29186	29191	
29187	29192	

Class 503
Wirral & Mersey 1938 & 1956 Stock
650V dc third rail

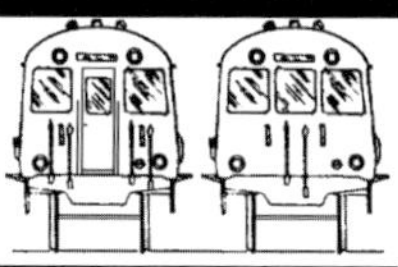

The Mersey Railway operated the line from Liverpool Central Low-Level to Birkenhead Park and Rock Ferry and it remained an independent company until it became part of BR in 1948. It was operated on the four-rail system until it was converted to third rail only in 1955.

In 1938 the New Brighton and West Kirby services of the former Wirral Railway were electrified and connected to the Mersey line to allow through trains to run to Liverpool. The LMS ordered nineteen three-car units for these new services. They were fitted with sliding doors and were of a modern appearance, with more curves than corners.

The earlier Mersey Railway stock was eventually displaced by the construction of more new BR units built to the LMS design in 1956. Twenty-four units were built plus four extra cars to replace war damaged stock. The units worked in fixed formations, but never carried unit numbers. All the stock was downgraded to second class only in 1971.

In 1977 a new single line loop was built at the Liverpool end of the line to connect with the main stations in Liverpool city centre. In preparation for this the Class 503 units were rebuilt from 1972 with end doors throughout to allow for emergency evacuation in the new tube section.

The units were later replaced by Class 508 units which were transferred from the Southern Region.

1938 stock

DMBS	TC	DTS	
28672	29702	29271	38-03/85
28673	29703	29272	38-10/84
28674	29704	29273	38-10/84
28675	29705	29274	38-10/84
28676	29706	29275	38-10/84
28677	29707	29276	38-10/84
28678	29708	29277	38-03/41
28678	*29155*	*29831*	56-10/84
28679	29709	29278	38-10/84
28680	29710	29279	38-05/85
28681	29711	29280	38-10/84
28682	29712	29281	38-10/84
28683	29713	29282	38-*06/82*
28684	29714	29283	38-10/84
28685	29715	29284	38-10/84
28686	29716	29285	38-02/83
28687	29717	29286	38-03/41
28687	*29156*	*29832*	56-10/84
28688	29718	29287	38-10/84
28689	29719	29288	38-10/84
28690	29720	29289	38-05/85

1956 stock

DMBS	TC	DTS	
28371	29838	29131	56- *57*
28371	*29843*	*29140*	*57*-05/85
28372	29841	29132	56-03/85
28373	29843	29140	56- *57*
28373	*29838*	*29131*	*57*-03/85
28374	29845	29137	56-10/84
28375	29821	29138	56-11/84
28376	29822	29146	56-12/84
28377	29823	29139	56-02/85
28378	29844	29134	56-12/84
28379	29824	29145	56-02/85
28380	29825	29135	56-10/84
28381	29837	29142	56-12/84
28382	29826	29147	56-10/84
28383	29840	29150	56-11/84
28384	29828	29151	56-11/84
28385	29839	29152	56-12/84
28386	29842	29149	56-10/84
28387	29829	29136	56- *57*
28387	*29846*	*29153*	*57*-02/85
28388	29846	29153	56- *57*
28388	*29829*	*29133*	*57*-11/84
28389	29833	29133	56- *57*
28389	29833	*29136*	*57*-10/84
28390	29830	29154	56-10/84
28391	29827	29148	56-02/85
28392	29834	29143	56-03/85
28393	29835	29144	56-02/85
28394	29836	29141	56-05/85

Manchester-Bury

Manchester-Bury
LYR 5-car sets
1200V dc side-contact third rail

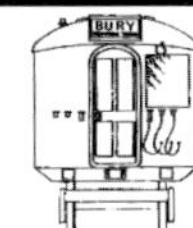

The Manchester-Bury line was electrified 1915, using a unique high voltage (1200V dc) side-contact third-rail system.

The Lancashire and Yorkshire electric stock for the Manchester-Bury line was different to that built for the Liverpool area. It was of all metal construction with straight sides and a high elliptical roof. But the general layout, with deeply recessed doors and a luggage compartment with roller shutters, was the same.

The stock was replaced with the BR Class 504 units in 1959.

Not fixed formations.
LYR numbers

DMBT	TT	DMBT	TF	DMBT
3502	3602	3503	500	3504
3505	3603	3506	501	3507
3508	3604	3509	502	3510
3511	3605	3512	503	3513
3514	3606	3515	504	3516
3517	3607	3518	505	3519
3520	3608	3521	506	3522
3523	3609	3524	507	3525
3526	3610	3527	508	3528
3529	3611	3530	509	3531
3532	3612	3533	510	3534
3535	3613	3536	511	3537
3538	3614	3539	512	
	3615		513	

LMS 1923 numbers

DMBT	TT	DMBT	TF	DMBT
14572	14669	14573	10933	14574
14575	14670	14576	10934	14577
14578	14671	14579	10935	14580
14581	14672	14582	10936	14583
14584	14673	14585	10937	14586
14587	14674	14588	10938	14589
14590	14675	14591	10939	14592
14593	14676	14594	10940	14595
14596	14677	14597	10941	14598
14599	14678	14600	10942	14601
14602	14679	14603	10943	14604
14605	14680	14606	10944	14607
14608	14681	14609	10945	
	14682		10946	

LMS 1933 numbers

DMBT	TT	DMBT	TF	DMBT
28500	29200	28501	28700	28502
28503	29201	28504	28701	28505
28506	29202	28507	28702	28508
28509	29203	28510	28703	28511
28512	29204	28513	28704	28514
28515	29205	28516	28705	28517
28518	29206	28519	28706	28520
28521	29207	28522	28707	28523
28524	29208	28525	28708	28526
28527	29209	28528	28709	28529
28530	29210	28531	28710	28532
28533	29211	28534	28711	28535
28536	29212	28537	28712	
	29213		28713	

Class 504
Manchester-Bury
1200V dc side-contact third rail
436-461

These units were built in 1959 to replace life-expired LYR units on the Manchester-Bury line. This line was electrified on the unique "third-rail side-contact" system. The third rail was at the relatively high voltage of 1200v dc and it was protected with a wooden box structure, contact being made on the side of the rail.

Substantially more units were built than were needed for the passenger service and by the late sixties the first eight units were stored. 77164 was transferred to the Eastern Region to replace a collision damaged Class 302 coach. Some of these stored units were later moved to Croxley Green where they supplied spare parts to Class 501 units. The remaining units were later given the numbers 50444-504461.

The remaining units were withdrawn when the line was taken over as part of the Manchester Metrolink system in 1991.

	DMBSO	DTCso		
	65436	77157		08/59- 70
	65437	77158		08/59- 70
	65438	77159	1970 stored	08/59-11/78
	65439	77160	1970 stored	08/59-05/82
	65440	77161		59-11/69
	65441	77162	1970 stored	59-05/82
	65442	77163	1970 stored	59-05/82
	65443	77164		59-09/70
504444	65444	77165		59-08/91
504445	65445	77166		59-08/91
504446	65446	77167		59-08/91
504447	65447	77168		59-07/91
	65448	77169		59-12/84
504449	65449	77170		59-07/91
504450	65450	77171		59-07/91
504451	65451	77172		59-08/91
504452	65452	77173		59-08/91
504453	65453	77174		59-08/91
504454	65454	77175		59-07/91
504455	65455	77176		59-07/91
504456	65456	77177		59-09/91
504457	65457	77178		59-09/91
504458	65458	77179		59-07/91

504459	65459	77180		59-07/91
504460	65460	77181		59-08/91
504461	65461	77182		59-08/91
	65436	65437	Used as depot shunter	70-05/82
	77157	77158	stored	70-05/82

Holcombe Brook

Holcombe Brook
LYR 2-car sets
3600V dc overhead

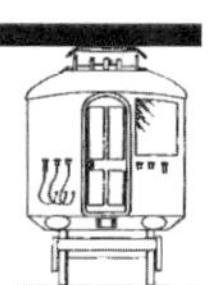

Prior to the electrification of the Manchester to Bury line, the line from Bury to Holcombe Brook was used experimentally by Dick, Kerr and company to try out a 3,600V overhead system. Two motor thirds and two trailer thirds were built at Newton Heath to work on the line and these operated successfully until 1919 when a major fault developed in the 3,600V supply.

The line was rebuilt to work at 1200V third rail, but until this could be completed the overhead line was fed at 1200V and the service was temporarily worked with a Holcombe Brook motor third (used to pick up the overhead line) connected to a Manchester-Bury motor third (which provided the driving power).

After this the Holcombe Brook stock was stored until 1928 when it was rebuilt by Beardmore & Sons to form an experimental four-coach diesel electric set. This unit spent the rest of its life working in the Blackpool area until it was withdrawn and broken up in 1933.

LYR numbers

DMBT	DTT
3500	3600
3501	3601

LMS 1923 numbers

DMBT	DTT
14570	14667
14571	14668

Manchester South Junction & Altrincham

Class 505 Manchester-Altrincham
MSJA 3-car sets
1500V dc overhead

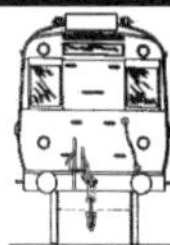

The Manchester South Junction and Altrincham line was jointly owned by the LMS and LNER. In 1931 it was agreed to electrify the route on the 1500V dc overhead system. Twenty-two three car sets plus two spare motor cars were built by Metropolitan-Cammell to a basically LNWR design. Some extra trailer cars were provided from converted LNWR Liverpool stock.

The cars were numbered in an individual system for the MSJ&A until 1948 when they were renumbered into the LMS series of numbers. They later became Class 505, but they never carried any unit numbers. They were all withdrawn in April 1971 when the system was converted to the 25kV ac system.

MSJA numbers. Not fixed formations.

DMBT	TC	DTT	
1	101	51	
2	102	52	
3	103	53	
4	104	54	
5	105	55	
6	106	56	
7	107	57	
8	108	58	
9	109	59	
10	110	60	
11	111	61	
12	112	62	
13	113	63	
14	114	64	
15	115	65	
16	116	66	
17	117	67	
18	118	68	
19	119	69	
20	120	70	
21	121	71	
22	122	72	
23			2 spare motors
24			
	151		
	152		
	153	74	
	154		
	155		
	156		
	157		
	158		

In 1948 BR numbered the coaches in the LMS 1933 series. Not fixed formations.

DMBT	TC	DTT
28571	29650	29231
28572	29651	29232
28573	29652	29233
28574	29653	29234
28575	29654	29235
28576	29655	29236
28577	29656	29237
28578	29657	29238
28579	29658	29239
28580	29659	29240
28581	29660	29241
28582	29661	29242
28583	29662	29243
28584	29663	29244
28585	29664	29245
28586	29665	29246
28587	29666	29247
28588	29667	29248
28589	29668	29249
28590	29669	29250
28591	29670	29251
28592	29671	29252
28593		
28594		
	29390	
	29391	
	29392	
	29393	
	29394	
	29395	
	29396	

Manchester, Glossop & Hadfield

Class 506
Manchester, Glossop & Hadfield
1500V dc overhead

These units were built to operate the local services at the Manchester end of the LNER's Manchester-Sheffield 1500V dc overhead electrified line. The units were almost identical to the Class 306 units on the GE line, but they carried coach numbers in the series reserved for Great Central line coaches (in the 5xxxx series). The driving trailer cars were built by Birmingham RC&W, the other cars by Metropolitan-Cammell. They were originally ordered in 1938 but the intervention of the war delayed the the completion of the electrification and the introduction of the units until 1954. They were downgraded to second class only in 1960.

The line was transferred to the London Midland Region in 1958. They received the correct M prefix, but also received an incorrect M suffix. Earlier they carried no suffix, and before that the correct E suffix.

In 1984, after the through line to Sheffield was closed, the line to Glossop & Hadfield was converted to 25kV ac overhead. The units were replaced by Class 303 and Class 304 units.

LNER 1943 numbers

DMBTO	TCO	DTTO	
59401	59501	59601	06/54-12/84
59402	59502	59602	06/54-12/84
59403	59503	59603	06/54-12/84
59404	59504	59604	06/54-12/84
59405	59505	59605	06/54-12/84
59406	59506	59606	06/54-11/83
59407	59507	59607	06/54-12/84
59408	59508	59608	06/54-07/84

Lancaster, Morecambe & Heysham

Lancaster, Morecambe & Heysham
Midland Railway
6.6kV 25Hz ac overhead

After unsuccessfully trying steam rail-motors on the Heysham line in 1904, the Midland Railway then successfully introduced an electrified scheme. The line was electrified at 6,600V 25Hz ac overhead in 1908. These were probably the world's first 'modern' electric trains. Three 60ft power cars were built with four 43ft trailers. The trains usually worked by a single motor flanked by two trailers.

In Midland railway days at least one other vehicle (01174) was converted as a driving trailer, and later in LMS days two 54ft vehicles were converted. They were withdrawn in 1952-1953 when they were life expired.

Midland Railway, LMS 1923 numbers.

DTT	DMT	DTT	or	DMT	DTT	DTT
2239	2236	2240		2236	2239	2240
2241	2237	2242		2237	2241	2242
	2238			2238		

LMS 1933 numbers.

DTT	DMT	DTT	or	DMT	DTT	DTT
29290	28610	29291		28610	29290	29291
29292	28611	29293		28611	29292	29293
29298	28612	29299		28612	29298	29299

AM1 Lancaster, Morecambe & Heysham
Ex-LNWR London Area Sets
6.6kV 50Hz ac overhead

In 1953 the line was converted to 50Hz ac to test out the new proposed BR standard electrification. Redundant LNWR London area Siemens units were converted to run on this line.

AM1-units, ex-LNWR London Area units.

DMBT	TC	DTT	
28219	29721	29021	08/53-02/67
28220	29722	29022	08/53-02/67
28221	29723	29023	08/53-02/67
28222	29724	29024	57-02/67

Eastern Region

Liverpool St. & Fenchurch St. Services

Class 306 AM6
Shenfield Line
1500V dc, later 25/6.25kV ac overhead 01-92, 001-092

Electrification of the lines from Liverpool Street to Shenfield on the 1500V dc overhead system was started before the Second World War. 92 three-car units were ordered in 1938 from Metropolitan-Cammell and Birmingham RC&W.

The war put the whole scheme on hold and many built and partially-built units were stored for the duration. The scheme was completed in 1949 although the last few units were not complete until the spring of 1950.

The units were numbered 01-92 and the coaches were numbered in the 1943 LNER scheme (the initial '6' indicating coaches for the GE section). They never carried the 'E' suffix that coaches in this number series should have carried. The diamond shaped pantograph was fitted at the driving end of the power car, where the roof was lowered to accommodate it. The units were fitted with siding doors. The units built later for the Manchester, Glossop and Hadfield service were to the same design.

In 1960-1962, the Shenfield line and Chelmsford lines were converted to the new standard 6.25/25kV ac overhead system. The units were rebuilt and renumbered as 001-092. During the rebuild, the pantograph was moved from the motor coach to the intermediate trailer, as space for the transformer and rectifier could not be found on the underframe of the power car. Most units were converted in 1959 and 1960, but had the new equipment switched out until the changeover.

Apart from 030 (which had been destroyed by fire in 1968) the units were withdrawn in 1981 being replaced by new Class 315 units. 017 was retained for working special services and has been preserved, and a number of coaches were retained in Internal User service at Ilford for a few years.

LNER 1943 numbers

DC units

	DMBTO	TTO	DTTO			
01	65201	65401	65601	11/49-	*60*	**➲001**
02	65202	65402	65602	11/49-	*60*	**➲002**
03	65203	65403	65603	11/49-	*60*	**➲003**
04	65204	65404	65604	11/49-	*60*	**➲004**
05	65205	65405	65605	11/49-	*60*	**➲005**
06	65206	65406	65606	11/49-	*60*	**➲006**
07	65207	65407	65607	11/49-	*60*	**➲007**
08	65208	65408	65608	11/49-	*60*	**➲008**
09	65209	65409	65609	11/49-	*60*	**➲009**
10	65210	65410	65610	11/49-	*60*	**➲010**
11	65211	65411	65611	11/49-	*60*	**➲011**
12	65212	65412	65612	11/49-	*60*	**➲012**
13	65213	65413	65613	11/49-	*60*	**➲013**
14	65214	65414	65614	11/49-	*60*	**➲014**
15	65215	65415	65615	11/49-	*60*	**➲015**
16	65216	65416	65616	11/49-	*60*	**➲016**
17	65217	65417	65617	11/49-	*60*	**➲017**
18	65218	65418	65618	11/49-	*60*	**➲018**
19	65219	65419	65619	11/49-	*60*	**➲019**
20	65220	65420	65620	11/49-	*60*	**➲020**
21	65221	65421	65621	11/49-	*60*	**➲021**
22	65222	65422	65622	11/49-	*60*	**➲022**
23	65223	65423	65623	11/49-	*60*	**➲023**
24	65224	65424	65624	11/49-	*60*	**➲024**
25	65225	65425	65625	11/49-	*60*	**➲025**
26	65226	65426	65626	11/49-	*60*	**➲026**
27	65227	65427	65627	11/49-	*60*	**➲027**
28	65228	65428	65628	11/49-	*60*	**➲028**
29	65229	65429	65629	11/49-	*60*	**➲029**
30	65230	65430	65630	11/49-	*60*	**➲030**
31	65231	65431	65631	11/49-	*60*	**➲031**
32	65232	65432	65632	11/49-	*60*	**➲032**
33	65233	65433	65633	11/49-	*60*	**➲033**
34	65234	65434	65634	11/49-	*60*	**➲034**
35	65235	65435	65635	11/49-	*60*	**➲035**
36	65236	65436	65636	11/49-	*60*	**➲036**
37	65237	65437	65637	11/49-	*60*	**➲037**
38	65238	65438	65638	11/49-	*60*	**➲038**
39	65239	65439	65639	11/49-	*60*	**➲039**
40	65240	65440	65640	11/49-	*60*	**➲040**
41	65241	65441	65641	11/49-	*60*	**➲041**
42	65242	65442	65642	11/49-	*60*	**➲042**
43	65243	65443	65643	11/49-	*60*	**➲043**
44	65244	65444	65644	11/49-	*60*	**➲044**
45	65245	65445	65645	11/49-	*60*	**➲045**
46	65246	65446	65646	11/49-	*60*	**➲046**
47	65247	65447	65647	11/49-	*60*	**➲047**
48	65248	65448	65648	11/49-	*60*	**➲048**
49	65249	65449	65649	11/49-	*60*	**➲049**
50	65250	65450	65650	11/49-	*60*	**➲050**
51	65251	65451	65651	11/49-	*60*	**➲051**
52	65252	65452	65652	11/49-	*60*	**➲052**
53	65253	65453	65653	11/49-	*60*	**➲053**
54	65254	65454	65654	11/49-	*60*	**➲054**
55	65255	65455	65655	11/49-	*60*	**➲055**
56	65256	65456	65656	11/49-	*60*	**➲056**
57	65257	65457	65657	11/49-	*60*	**➲057**
58	65258	65458	65658	11/49-	*60*	**➲058**
59	65259	65459	65659	11/49-	*60*	**➲059**
60	65260	65460	65660	11/49-	*60*	**➲060**
61	65261	65461	65661	11/49-	*60*	**➲061**
62	65262	65462	65662	11/49-	*60*	**➲062**
63	65263	65463	65663	11/49-	*60*	**➲063**
64	65264	65464	65664	11/49-	*60*	**➲064**
65	65265	65465	65665	11/49-	*60*	**➲065**
66	65266	65466	65666	11/49-	*60*	**➲066**
67	65267	65467	65667	11/49-	*60*	**➲067**
68	65268	65468	65668	11/49-	*60*	**➲068**
69	65269	65469	65669	11/49-	*60*	**➲069**
70	65270	65470	65670	11/49-	*60*	**➲070**
71	65271	65471	65671	11/49-	*60*	**➲071**
72	65272	65472	65672	11/49-	*60*	**➲072**
73	65273	65473	65673	11/49-	*60*	**➲073**
74	65274	65474	65674	11/49-	*60*	**➲074**
75	65275	65475	65675	11/49-	*60*	**➲075**
76	65276	65476	65676	11/49-	*60*	**➲076**
77	65277	65477	65677	11/49-	*60*	**➲077**
78	65278	65478	65678	11/49-	*60*	**➲078**
79	65279	65479	65679	11/49-	*60*	**➲079**
80	65280	65480	65680	11/49-	*60*	**➲080**
81	65281	65481	65681	11/49-	*60*	**➲081**

82	65282	65482	65682	11/49- *60*	⊃**082**
83	65283	65483	65683	11/49- *60*	⊃**083**
84	65284	65484	65684	11/49- *60*	⊃**084**
85	65285	65485	65685	11/49- *60*	⊃**085**
86	65286	65486	65686	11/49- *60*	⊃**086**
87	65287	65487	65687	11/49- *60*	⊃**087**
88	65288	65488	65688	11/49- *60*	⊃**088**
89	65289	65489	65689	11/49- *60*	⊃**089**
90	65290	65490	65690	11/49- *60*	⊃**090**
91	65291	65491	65691	11/49- *60*	⊃**091**
92	65292	65492	65692	11/49- *60*	⊃**092**

AC units

	DMBSO	*PTSB*	*DTSO*		
001	65201	65401	65601	*60*-04/81	
002	65202	65402	65602	*60*-03/81	
003	65203	65403	65603	*60*-08/80	⊃*072*
004	65204	65404	65604	*60*-05/80	
005	65205	65405	65605	*60*-11/81	
006	65206	65406	65606	*60*-03/81	
007	65207	65407	65607	*60*-09/81	
008	65208	65408	65608	*60*-03/81	
009	65209	65409	65609	*60*-04/81	
010	65210	65410	65610	*60*-11/81	
011	65211	65411	65611	*60*-04/80	
011	65211	*65472*	*65672*	04/80-05/80	
011	65211	*65444*	*65644*	05/80-03/81	
012	65212	65412	65612	*60*-03/81	
013	65213	65413	65613	*60*-03/81	
014	65214	65414	65614	*60*-11/81	
015	65215	65415	65615	*60*-11/81	
016	65216	65416	65616	*60*-03/81	
016	65216	*65435*	*65635*	03/81-06/81	
017	65217	65417	65617	*60*-11/81	
018	65218	65418	65618	*60*-03/81	
019	65219	65419	65619	*60*-08/81	
020	65220	65420	65620	*60*-03/81	
021	65221	65421	65621	*60*-08/81	
022	65222	65422	65622	*60*-06/81	
023	65223	65423	65623	*60*-05/81	
024	65224	65424	65624	*60*-03/81	
025	65225	65425	65625	*60*-03/81	
026	65226	65426	65626	*60*-03/81	
026	65226	65426	*65616*	03/81-06/81	
027	65227	65427	65627	*60*-11/80	
027	65227	*65446*	*65646*	11/80-03/81	
028	65228	65428	65628	*60*-08/81	
029	65229	65429	65629	*60*-08/81	
030	65230	65430	65630	*60*-04/68	
031	65231	65431	65631	*60*-09/81	
032	65232	65432	65632	*60*-06/81	
033	65233	65433	65633	*60*-08/81	
034	65234	65434	65634	*60*-11/81	
035	65235	65435	65635	*60*-03/81	⊃*016*
036	65236	65436	65636	*60*-03/81	
037	65237	65437	65637	*60*-11/81	
038	65238	65438	65638	*60*-06/81	⊃*083*
039	65239	65439	65639	*60*-03/81	
040	65240	65440	65640	*60*-08/81	
041	65241	65441	65641	*60*-09/81	
042	65242	65442	65642	*60*-03/81	
043	65243	65443	65643	*60*-08/81	
044	65244	65444	65644	*60*-05/80	⊃*011*
045	65245	65445	65645	*60*-03/81	
046	65246	65446	65646	*60*-10/80	⊃*027*
046	65246	*65474*	*65674*	10/80-03/81	
047	65247	65447	65647	*60*-09/81	
048	65248	65448	65648	*60*-03/81	
049	65249	65449	65649	*60*-01/81	
049	65249	*65454*	*65667*	04/81-09/81	
050	65250	65450	65650	*60*-06/81	
051	65251	65451	65651	*60*-03/81	
052	65252	65452	65652	*60*-09/81	
053	65253	65453	65653	*60*-03/81	
054	65254	65454	65654	*60*-04/81	
055	65255	65455	65655	*60*-08/81	
056	65256	65456	65656	*60*-03/81	
057	65257	65457	65657	*60*-03/81	
058	65258	65458	65658	*60*-11/81	
059	65259	65459	65659	*60*-03/81	
060	65260	65460	65660	*60*-03/81	
061	65261	65461	65661	*60*-11/81	
062	65262	65462	65662	*60*-11/81	
063	65263	65463	65663	*60*-11/81	
064	65264	65464	65664	*60*-03/81	
064	65264	65464	*65674*	03/81-08/81	
065	65265	65465	65665	*60*-03/81	
066	65266	65466	65666	*60*-03/81	⊃*090*
067	65267	65467	65667	*60*-01/81	
067	65267	65467	*65649*	01/81-06/81	
068	65268	65468	65668	*60*-11/81	
069	65269	65469	65669	*60*-09/81	
070	65270	65470	65670	*60*-05/81	⊃*082*
071	65271	65471	65671	*60*-06/81	
072	65272	65472	65672	*60*-04/80	⊃*011*
072	65272	*65403*	*65603*	08/80-03/81	⊃*084*
072	65272	*65480*	*65680*	03/81-11/81	
073	65273	65473	65673	*60*-09/81	
074	65274	65474	65674	*60*-10/80	⊃*046*
074	65274	*65427*	*65627*	11/80-06/81	
075	65275	65475	65675	*60*-06/81	
075	65275	65475	*65678*	06/81-09/81	
076	65276	65476	65676	*60*-09/81	
077	65277	65477	65677	*60*-09/81	
078	65278	65478	65678	*60*-03/81	
078	65278	*65484*	*65684*	03/81-08/81	
079	65279	65479	65679	*60*-08/81	
080	65280	65480	65680	*60*-03/81	⊃*072*
080	65280	*65492*	*65692*	03/81-09/81	
081	65281	65481	65681	*60*-03/81	
082	65282	65482	65682	*60*-06/81	
082	65282	*65470*	*65670*	06/81-11/81	
083	65283	65483	65683	*60*-06/81	
083	65283	*65438*	*65638*	06/81-09/81	
084	65284	65484	65684	*60*-03/81	⊃*078*
084	65284	*65403*	*65603*	04/81-11/81	
085	65285	65485	65685	*60*-09/81	
086	65286	65486	65686	*60*-08/81	
087	65287	65487	65687	*60*-03/81	
088	65288	65488	65688	*60*-09/81	
089	65289	65489	65689	*60*-03/81	
090	65290	65490	65690	*60*-03/81	
090	65290	*65466*	*65666*	03/81-09/81	
091	65291	65491	65691	*60*-06/81	
092	65292	65492	65692	*60*-03/81	⊃*080*

Class 307 AM7
Southend Line
1500V dc, later 25/6.25kV ac overhead
01s-32s, later 101-132

Class 307 comprised 32 four-car units that were built at Eastleigh for the Liverpool Street to Southend Victoria line. This was electrified on the 1500V dc overhead system, and the units were numbered 01s-32s (the 's' suffix standing for Southend to differentiate them from the earlier Shenfield line units).

These units where the first BR designed 4-car units for medium distance work and they set the layout for passenger accommodation for many subsequent designs.

When the line was converted to 6.25/25kV ac the units were rebuilt and renumbered as 101-132. As part of the rebuild the pantograph and guard's compartment was moved to one of the trailer vehicles. Many units were mis-formed during the changeover, but they soon settled down to their correct formations.

By 1990 the class was withdrawn from the original services on the Southend Line. After this some units were sent to Leeds to work the Doncaster services pending the arrival of the new Class 321/9 units. 307117 was sent to Edinburgh for trials on the Edinburgh to North Berwick service, but it was decided to use Class 305 units instead.

After withdrawal from service the units remained in storage. In 1993 75102 and 75114 were rebuilt to Propelling Control Vehicles (PCV) to work with parcels trains that needed propelling into the new Mail Centre at Wembley. This proved successful and a further 41 vehicles were converted.

	DTS	*MBS*	*TCsoL*	*DTSOL*		
01s	75001	61001	70001	75101	02/56- *61*	⊃**101**
02s	75002	61002	70002	75102	02/56- *61*	⊃**102**
03s	75003	61003	70003	75103	02/56-02/60	⊃**103**
04s	75004	61004	70004	75104	03/56- *61*	⊃**104**
05s	75005	61005	70005	75105	03/56- *61*	⊃**105**
06s	75006	61006	70006	75106	03/56- *61*	⊃**106**
07s	75007	61007	70007	75107	04/56- *61*	⊃**107**
08s	75008	61008	70008	75108	04/56- *61*	⊃**108**
09s	75009	61009	70009	75109	04/56- *61*	⊃**109**
10s	75010	61010	70010	75110	05/56- *61*	⊃**110**
11s	75011	61011	70011	75111	05/56- *61*	⊃**111**
12s	75012	61012	70012	75112	05/56- *61*	⊃**112**
13s	75013	61013	70013	75113	05/56- *61*	⊃**113**
14s	75014	61014	70014	75114	06/56- *61*	⊃**114**
15s	75015	61015	70015	75115	06/56- *61*	⊃**115**
16s	75016	61016	70016	75116	06/56- *61*	⊃**116**
17s	75017	61017	70017	75117	06/56- *61*	⊃**117**
18s	75018	61018	70018	75118	06/56- *61*	⊃**118**

19s	75019	61019	70019	75119	07/56- *61*	➲**119**
20s	75020	61020	70020	75120	07/56- *61*	➲**120**
21s	75021	61021	70021	75121	07/56- *61*	➲**121**
22s	75022	61022	70022	75122	07/56- *61*	➲**122**
23s	75023	61023	70023	75123	08/56- *61*	➲**123**
24s	75024	61024	70024	75124	08/56- *61*	➲**124**
25s	75025	61025	70025	75125	09/56- *61*	➲**125**
26s	75026	61026	70026	75126	09/56- *61*	➲**126**
27s	75027	61027	70027	75127	09/56- *61*	➲**127**
28s	75028	61028	70028	75128	09/56- *61*	➲**128**
29s	75029	61029	70029	75129	09/56- *61*	➲**129**
30s	75030	61030	70030	75130	10/56- *61*	➲**130**
31s	75031	61031	70031	75131	10/56- *61*	➲**131**
32s	75032	61032	70032	75132	10/56- *61*	➲**132**

	DTBS	*MS*	*TCsoL*	*DTSOL*		
101	75001	61001	70001	75101	*61*-11/82	➲**307101**
102	75002	61002	70002	75102	*61*-01/80	➲**307102**
103	75003	61003	70003	75103	02/60-10/82	➲**307103**
104	75004	61004	70004	75104	*61*-01/82	➲**307104**
105	75005	61005	70005	75105	*61*-09/82	➲**307105**
106	75006	61006	70006	75106	*61*-02/80	➲**307106**
107	75007	61007	70007	75107	*61*-12/81	➲**307107**
108	75008	61008	70008	75108	*61*-04/82	➲**307108**
109	75009	61009	70009	75109	*61*-02/82	➲**307109**
110	75010	61010	70010	75110	*61*-11/81	➲**307110**
111	75011	61011	70011	75111	*61*-01/83	➲**307111**
112	75012	61012	70012	75112	*61*-09/82	➲**307112**
113	75013	61013	70013	75113	*61*-12/82	➲**307113**
114	75014	61014	70014	75114	*61*-11/81	➲**307114**
115	75015	61015	70015	75115	*61*-12/81	➲**307115**
116	75016	61016	70016	75116	*61*-12/81	➲**307116**
117	75017	61017	70017	75117	*61*-07/82	➲**307117**
118	75018	61018	70018	75118	*61*-02/82	➲**307118**
119	75019	61019	70019	75119	*61*-06/82	➲**307119**
120	75020	61020	70020	75120	*61*-09/81	➲**307120**
121	75021	61021	70021	75121	*61*-04/82	➲**307121**
122	75022	61022	70022	75122	*61*-08/82	➲**307122**
123	75023	61023	70023	75123	*61*-10/81	➲**307123**
124	75024	61024	70024	75124	*61*-05/82	➲**307124**
125	75025	61025	70025	75125	*61*-10/82	➲**307125**
126	75026	61026	70026	75126	*61*-08/82	➲**307126**
127	75027	61027	70027	75127	*61*-01/82	➲**307127**
128	75028	61028	70028	75128	*61*-03/82	➲**307128**
129	75029	61029	70029	75129	*61*-06/82	➲**307129**
130	75030	61030	70030	75130	*61*-06/82	➲**307130**
131	75031	61031	70031	75131	*61*-05/82	➲**307131**
132	75032	61032	70032	75132	*61*-04/82	➲**307132**

Class 308/1 AM8

Clacton Line

25/6.25kV ac overhead

133-165

The Class 308/1 units were built at York in 1961. 133-141 were for use on the newly electrified Colchester to Clacton Line and 142-165 were added when the service was extended through Liverpool Street.

They were similar to the Class 307 units, but were fitted with new modern style cabs. The units were refurbished in 1981-1983; the vehicles were converted to open and through gangways were fitted within the unit. New seats and lighting were installed, and the first class section was moved to one of the driving trailers. At this time nearly all the units were working on the Tilbury Line, based at East Ham.

In 1993 the units were transferred to Birmingham to work on the Cross-City services. They were replaced on these services by new Class 323 units and they moved on again to Leeds to work the newly electrified Aire & Wharfe Valley services in 1995. They survived there until 2001 when they were replaced with Class 333 units.

	BDTSOL	*MBS*	*TCsoL*	*DTS*		
133	75878	61883	70611	75887	01/61-04/81	➲**308133**
134	75879	61884	70612	75888	01/61-08/81	➲**308134**
135	75880	61885	70613	75889	01/61-08/81	➲**308135**
136	75881	61886	70614	75890	01/61-01/82	➲**308136**
137	75882	61887	70615	75891	02/61-12/81	➲**308137**
138	75883	61888	70616	75892	02/61-12/81	➲*308138*
139	75884	61889	70617	75893	02/61-10/82	➲**308139**
140	75885	61890	70618	75894	02/61-05/81	➲**308140**
141	75886	61891	70619	75895	03/61-08/81	➲**308141**
142	75896	61892	70620	75929	03/61-01/82	➲**308142**
143	75897	61893	70621	75930	03/61-01/82	➲**308143**
144	75898	61894	70622	75931	03/61-12/81	➲**308144**
145	75899	61895	70623	75932	04/61-03/82	➲**308145**
146	75900	61896	70624	75933	04/61-02/80	➲**308146**
147	75901	61897	70625	75934	04/61-03/82	➲**308147**
148	75902	61898	70626	75935	04/61-12/82	➲**308148**
149	75903	61899	70627	75936	05/61-06/82	➲**308149**
150	75904	61900	70628	75937	05/61-03/82	➲**308150**
151	75905	61901	70629	75938	05/61-11/82	➲**308151**
152	75906	61902	70630	75939	07/61-05/83	➲**308152**
153	75907	61903	70631	75940	07/61-09/82	➲**308153**
154	75908	61904	70632	75941	07/61-10/82	➲**308154**
155	75909	61905	70633	75942	07/61-05/83	➲**308155**
156	75910	61906	70634	75943	07/61-05/83	➲**308156**
157	75911	61907	70635	75944	07/61-05/83	➲**308157**
158	75912	61908	70636	75945	07/61-02/80	➲**308158**
159	75913	61909	70637	75946	07/61-05/83	➲**308159**
160	75914	61910	70638	75947	08/61-05/83	➲**308160**
161	75915	61911	70639	75948	08/61-01/80	➲**308161**
162	75916	61912	70640	75949	09/61-07/83	➲**308162**
163	75917	61913	70641	75950	09/61-07/83	➲**308163**
164	75918	61914	70642	75951	09/61-02/80	➲**308164**
165	75919	61915	70643	75952	09/61-02/81	➲**308165**

Class 302 AM2

Tilbury Line

25/6.25kV ac overhead

201-312

The Class 302 units were built for the London, Tilbury and Southend services working out of Fenchurch Street. Electrification of the line was not completed until June 1962, but the units were built earlier so that they could cover the services out of Liverpool Street while the stock on that line was being rebuilt for ac working. Some units also worked in the Manchester area and a few appeared in Glasgow for trials. The units also worked on the north-east London area due to problems with the new stock for those lines; some of these units worked temporarily as three-car units. The first 25 units then remained on the GE lines, based at Ilford, while the rest transferred to their intended workings on the Tilbury line based at East Ham.

The units were based on the Mark 1 coach design, and were very similar to contemporary SR units.

In 1970 75292 in unit 244 was withdrawn after sustaining collision damage. It was replaced by 77164 from the Bury Line on the London Midland region. It later had its part-compartment interior converted to open.

Thirty units were refurbished at Eastleigh and Wolverton in the eighties. They were gangwayed within units and fitted with new bogies, fluorescent lighting and new seats and panels. These were the units numbered 302201-302230 in the 1990s.

Some units were renumbered in 1988. The Eastern region referred to their units by the last three digits of their six digit TOPS numbers. These units were renumbered to avoid clashes with new class 321 units were being built.

Four units were later converted to work parcels services and were renumbered 302990-302993. The TS was removed to form three-car units and they were fitted with roller shutter doors.

In 1987-88 some units ran temporarily as three-car units and they were renumbered in the 3024xx series.

	BDTSOL	*MBS*	*TCsoL*	*DTS*		
201	75085	61060	70060	75033	11/58-01/83	➲**302201**
202	75086	61061	70061	75034	12/58-06/83	➲**302202**
203	75087	61062	70062	75035	12/58-04/81	➲**302203**
204	75088	61063	70063	75036	12/58-04/81	➲**302204**
205	75089	61064	70064	75037	01/59-03/83	➲**302205**
206	75090	61065	70065	75038	01/59-03/81	➲**302206**
207	75091	61066	70066	75039	01/59-03/81	➲**302207**
208	75092	61067	70067	75040	01/59-04/81	➲**302208**
209	75093	61068	70068	75041	01/59-01/83	➲**302209**
210	75094	61069	70069	75042	01/59-05/85	➲**302210**
211	75095	61070	70070	75043	02/59-09/82	➲**302211**
212	75096	61071	70071	75044	02/59-05/81	➲**302212**
213	75097	61072	70072	75060	02/59-08/81	➲**302213**
214	75098	61073	70073	75061	02/59-04/81	➲**302214**
215	75099	61074	70074	75062	03/59-12/81	➲**302215**
216	75100	61075	70075	75063	02/59-06/83	➲**302216**
217	75190	61076	70076	75064	03/59-07/84	➲**302217**
218	75191	61077	70077	75065	04/59-06/81	➲**302218**
219	75192	61078	70078	75066	04/59-09/83	➲**302219**
220	75193	61079	70079	75067	04/59-09/83	➲**302220**
221	75194	61080	70080	75068	04/59-09/83	➲**302221**
222	75195	61081	70081	75069	04/59-06/82	➲**302222**
223	75196	61082	70082	75070	06/59-05/81	➲**302223**
224	75197	61083	70083	75071	06/59-07/81	➲**302224**
225	75198	61084	70084	75072	05/59-10/81	➲**302225**
226	75199	61085	70085	75073	06/59-10/81	➲**302226**
227	75200	61086	70086	75074	06/59- *83*	➲**302227**

228	75201	61087	70087	75075	05/59-11/81	➲**302228**
229	75202	61088	70088	75076	05/59-08/82	➲**302229**
230	75203	61089	70089	75077	05/59-12/83	➲**302230**
231	75204	61090	70090	75078	05/59-07/84	➲**302231**
232	75205	61091	70091	75079	05/59-03/85	➲**302232**
233	75206	61092	70092	75080	06/59-07/84	➲**302233**
234	75207	61093	70093	75081	06/59-12/83	➲**302234**
235	75208	61094	70094	75082	06/59-04/81	➲**302235**
236	75209	61095	70095	75083	06/59-01/80	➲**302236**
237	75210	61096	70096	75084	06/59-11/84	➲**302237**
238	75286	61097	70097	75211	06/59-05/81	➲**302238**
239	75287	61098	70098	75212	06/59-01/83	➲**302239**
240	75288	61099	70099	75213	06/59-11/82	➲**302240**
241	75289	61100	70100	75214	06/59-11/84	➲**302241**
242	75290	61101	70101	75215	07/59-01/82	➲**302242**
243	75291	61102	70102	75216	07/59-10/83	➲**302243**
244	75292	61103	70103	75217	07/59-10/70	
244	*77164*	61103	70103	75217	06/72-06/82	➲**302244** ✍
245	75293	61104	70104	75218	07/59-08/81	➲**302245**
246	75294	61105	70105	75219	07/59- *83*	➲**302246**
247	75295	61106	70106	75220	07/59-01/82	➲**302247**
248	75296	61107	70107	75221	07/59-03/83	➲**302248**
249	75297	61108	70108	75222	08/59-09/82	➲**302249**
250	75298	61109	70109	75223	08/59-04/82	➲**302250**
251	75299	61110	70110	75224	08/59-01/83	➲**302251**
252	75300	61111	70111	75225	08/59-08/82	➲**302252**
253	75301	61112	70112	75226	08/59-10/82	➲**302253**
254	75302	61113	70113	75227	08/59-03/83	➲**302254**
255	75303	61114	70114	75228	08/59-01/82	➲**302255**
256	75304	61115	70115	75229	09/59- *83*	➲**302256**
257	75305	61116	70116	75230	09/59-04/82	➲**302257**
258	75306	61117	70117	75231	09/59-05/81	➲**302258**
259	75307	61118	70118	75232	09/59-03/80	➲**302259**
260	75308	61119	70119	75233	09/59-05/81	➲**302260**
261	75309	61120	70120	75234	09/59-03/83	➲**302261**
262	75310	61121	70121	75235	09/59-10/82	➲**302262**
263	75311	61122	70122	75236	09/59-09/83	➲**302263**
264	75312	61123	70123	75237	09/59-05/82	➲**302264**
265	75313	61124	70124	75238	09/59-09/82	➲**302265**
266	75314	61125	70125	75239	09/59-07/84	➲**302266**
267	75315	61126	70126	75240	09/59-02/80	➲**302267**
268	75316	61127	70127	75241	11/59-09/82	➲**302268**
269	75317	61128	70128	75242	11/59-01/82	➲**302269**
270	75318	61129	70129	75243	11/59- *83*	➲**302270**
271	75319	61130	70130	75244	11/59-04/82	➲**302271**
272	75320	61131	70131	75245	11/59-06/83	➲**302272**
273	75321	61132	70132	75246	11/59-03/82	➲**302273**
274	75322	61190	70190	75247	11/59-05/82	➲**302274**
275	75323	61191	70191	75248	11/59-11/79	➲**302275**
276	75324	61192	70192	75249	11/59-01/80	➲**302276**
277	75325	61193	70193	75250	11/59-01/83	➲**302277**
278	75326	61194	70194	75251	01/60-11/84	➲**302278**
279	75327	61195	70195	75252	01/60-10/81	➲**302279**
280	75328	61196	70196	75253	01/60- *83*	➲**302280**
281	75329	61197	70197	75254	01/60-10/82	➲**302281**

Temporary three-car units working on the north-east London area lines

	BDTSOL	MBS	DTS	
282	75330	61198	75255	11/59-10/60
283	75331	61199	75256	12/59-11/60
284	75332	61200	75257	12/59-11/60
285	75333	61201	75258	12/59-11/60
286	75334	61202	75259	12/59-12/60
287	75335	61203	75260	11/59-12/60
288	75336	61204	75261	12/59-12/60
289	75337	61205	75262	01/60-12/60
290	75338	61206	75263	01/60-11/60
291	75339	61207	75264	01/60-11/60
292	75340	61208	75265	01/60-12/60
293	75341	61209	75266	01/60-12/60
294	75342	61210	75267	01/60-12/60
295	75343	61211	75268	01/60-12/60
296	75344	61212	75269	01/60-12/60
297	75345	61213	75270	02/60-12/60
298	75346	61214	75271	01/60-12/60
299	75347	61215	75272	01/60-12/60
300	75348	61216	75273	01/60-12/60
301	75349	61217	75274	01/60-12/60
302	75350	61218	75275	02/60-12/60
303	75351	61219	75276	06/60-12/60
304	75352	61220	75277	02/60-12/60
305	75353	61221	75278	01/60-12/60
306	75354	61222	75279	01/60-04/61
307	75355	61223	75280	01/60-04/61
308	75356	61224	75281	02/60-04/61
310	75358	61226	75283	04/60-04/61
311	75359	61227	75284	04/60-04/61
312	75360	61228	75285	05/60-04/61

	BDTSOL	MBS	TCsoL	DTS		
282	75330	61198	70198	75255	10/60-02/82	➲**302282**
283	75331	61199	70199	75256	11/60-02/83	➲**302283**
284	75332	61200	70200	75257	11/60-10/81	➲**302284**
285	75333	61201	70201	75258	11/60-06/83	➲**302285**
286	75334	61202	70202	75259	12/60-05/82	➲**302286**
287	75335	61203	70203	75260	12/60-01/80	➲**302287**
288	75336	61204	70204	75261	12/60-12/82	➲**302288**
289	75337	61205	70205	75262	12/60-01/80	➲**302289**
290	75338	61206	70206	75263	11/60-10/82	➲**302290**
291	75339	61207	70207	75264	11/60- *83*	➲**302291**
292	75340	61208	70208	75265	12/60-03/83	➲**302292**
293	75341	61209	70209	75266	12/60-08/81	➲**302293**
294	75342	61210	70210	75267	12/60-01/82	➲**302294**
295	75343	61211	70211	75268	12/60-02/82	➲**302295**
296	75344	61212	70212	75269	12/60-04/84	➲**302296**
297	75345	61213	70213	75270	12/60-10/81	➲**302297**
298	75346	61214	70214	75271	12/60-03/83	➲**302298**
299	75347	61215	70215	75272	12/60-03/83	➲**302299**
300	75348	61216	70216	75273	12/60-07/83	➲**302300**
301	75349	61217	70217	75274	12/60-01/83	➲**302301**
302	75350	61218	70218	75275	12/60-02/80	➲**302302**
303	75351	61219	70219	75276	12/60-07/83	➲**302303**
304	75352	61220	70220	75277	12/60-06/83	➲**302304**
305	75353	61221	70221	75278	12/60- *83*	➲**302305**
306	75354	61222	70222	75279	04/61-03/83	➲**302306**
307	75355	61223	70223	75280	04/61-10/83	➲**302307**
308	75356	61224	70224	75281	04/61-02/83	➲**302308**
309	75357	61225	70225	75282	01/60-02/80	➲**302309**
310	75358	61226	70226	75283	04/61-09/83	➲**302310**
311	75359	61227	70227	75284	04/61- *83*	➲**302311**
312	75360	61228	70228	75285	04/61- *83*	➲**302312**

Class 308/2 AM8

Tilbury Line
25/6.25kV ac overhead
313-321

Class 308/2 comprised nine units built for boat trains on the Tilbury Line. They were identical to the earlier Class 308 units, except for the power car which was built as a luggage van. (This appears to have been an afterthought as the original number series for these vehicles was left empty, and they were built to a later lot number than the rest of the unit.) It was intended to keep these on off-peak services, but this was difficult to achieve and in 1971 four of the MLVs were rebuilt as MBSs to increase the passenger accommodation. The remaining units (317-321) remained in off-peak use and in 1984 they were dedicated to parcels use, being renumbered 308991-308995.

	BDTSOL	MLV	TCsoL	DTS			
313	75920	68011	70644	75953	05/61-06/71		
313	75920	*62431*	70644	75953	06/71-01/82	➲**308313**	✍
314	75921	68012	70645	75954	09/61-03/72		
314	75921	*62434*	70645	75954	03/72-06/81	➲**308314**	✍
315	75922	68013	70646	75955	09/61-08/71		
315	75922	*62433*	70646	75955	08/71-02/82	➲**308315**	✍
316	75923	68014	70647	75956	10/61-07/71		
316	75923	*62432*	70647	75956	07/71-06/81	➲**308316**	✍
317	75924	68015	70648	75957	10/61- *82*	➲**308317**	
318	75925	68016	70649	75958	11/61-12/81	➲**308318**	
319	75926	68017	70650	75959	11/61-07/82	➲**308319**	
320	75927	68018	70651	75960	11/61-04/82	➲**308320**	
321	75928	68019	70652	75961	11/61-10/71		
321	75928	*62434*	70652	75961	10/71-03/72		✍
321	75928	*68012*	70652	75961	03/72- *82*	➲**308321**	✍

Class 305/1 AM5

North East London Lines
25/6.25kV ac overhead
401-452

Class 305/1 numbers 401-452 were three-car units, built at York to work the suburban services from Liverpool Street to Chingford and Enfield Town and they worked these services until they were replaced by new Class 315 units. After this a number of units were reformed with spare trailers as 4-car units 305521-305528.

	BDTSO	MBSO	DTSO		
401	75462	61429	75514	03/60-09/82	➲**305401**
402	75463	61430	75515	03/60-08/83	➲**305402**
403	75464	61431	75516	03/60-11/81	➲**305403**
404	75465	61432	75517	03/60-08/81	➲**305404**
405	75466	61433	75518	04/60-09/82	➲**305405**
406	75467	61434	75519	04/60-09/82	➲**305406**
407	75468	61435	75520	05/60-11/81	➲**305407**

408	75469	61436	75521	03/60-08/82	➲**305408**
409	75470	61437	75522	04/60-06/83	➲**305409**
410	75471	61438	75523	06/60-06/82	➲**305410**
411	75472	61439	75524	04/60- *83*	➲**305411**
412	75473	61440	75525	04/60-04/81	➲**305412**
413	75474	61441	75526	04/60-05/81	➲**305413**
414	75475	61442	75527	06/60-11/81	➲**305414**
415	75476	61443	75528	06/60-11/81	➲**305415**
416	75477	61444	75529	05/60-10/82	➲**305416**
417	75478	61445	75530	05/60- *83*	➲**305417**
418	75479	61446	75531	06/60-04/82	➲**305418**
419	75480	61447	75532	05/60-05/82	➲**305419**
420	75481	61448	75533	06/60-03/83	➲**305420**
421	75482	61449	75534	07/60-07/83	➲**305421**
422	75483	61450	75535	06/60-04/83	➲**305422**
423	75484	61451	75536	06/60-01/82	➲**305423**
424	75485	61452	75537	06/60-12/81	➲**305424**
425	75486	61453	75538	06/60-08/82	➲**305425**
426	75487	61454	75539	07/60- *83*	➲**305426**
427	75488	61455	75540	07/60-02/80	➲**305427**
428	75489	61456	75541	07/60-02/80	➲**305428**
429	75490	61457	75542	07/60-08/81	➲**305429**
430	75491	61458	75543	07/60-06/81	➲**305430**
431	75492	61459	75544	08/60-03/83	➲**305431**
432	75493	61460	75545	08/60- *83*	➲**305432**
433	75494	61461	75546	08/60-04/82	➲**305433**
434	75495	61462	75547	08/60-01/82	➲**305434**
435	75496	61463	75548	08/60-10/82	➲**305435**
436	75497	61464	75549	08/60-08/82	➲**305436**
437	75498	61465	75550	08/60-07/81	➲**305437**
438	75499	61466	75551	08/60-04/83	➲**305438**
439	75500	61467	75552	09/60-11/82	➲**305439**
440	75501	61468	75553	09/60-02/82	➲**305440**
441	75502	61469	75554	11/60-06/81	➲**305441**
442	75503	61470	75555	11/60-12/81	➲**305442**
443	75504	61471	75556	11/60-01/82	➲**305443**
444	75505	61472	75557	11/60-02/80	➲**305444**
445	75506	61473	75558	11/60-06/82	➲**305445**
446	75507	61474	75559	11/60-05/82	➲**305446**
447	75508	61475	75560	11/60-06/83	➲**305447**
448	75509	61476	75561	11/60-01/82	➲**305448**
449	75510	61477	75562	11/60-12/82	➲**305449**
450	75511	61478	75563	11/60-12/83	➲**305450**
451	75512	61479	75564	11/60-03/81	➲**305451**
452	75513	61480	75565	11/60-02/80	➲**305452**

Class 308/3 AM8

North East London Lines
25/6.25kV ac overhead
453-455

The final batch of Class 308 units comprised three Class 308/3 units numbered 453-455. Apart from being fitted with EE equipment instead of GEC, they were identical to Class 305 units 401-452 with which they ran in service.

	BDTSO	*MBSO*	*DTSO*		
453	75741	61689	75992	12/61-10/81	➲**308453**
454	75742	61690	75993	12/61-02/82	➲**308454**
455	75743	61691	75994	12/61-05/82	➲**308455**

Class 305/2 AM5

Bishops Stortford & Hertford East Lines
25/6.25kV ac overhead
501-519

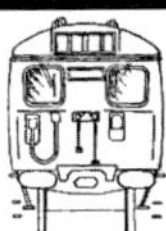

Class 305/2 numbers 501-519 were four-car units, built at Doncaster on frames built at York. The additional trailer composite provided first class accommodation and they worked on the Liverpool Street to Bishop's Stortford and Hertford East.

The units were refurbished in the 1980s. They were converted to open and fitted with gangways within the unit. The first class section was moved to the former BDTSOL coach.

From 1991 eleven units were transferred to the Manchester area to replace withdrawn Class 304 units, and they were reduced to three-car units. This was to cover for the late deliveries of new Class 323 units. Another five units were transferred to Scotland to work the Edinburgh to North Berwick services.

None of these units have been preserved.

	BDTSOL	*MBS*	*TCsoL*	*DTS*		
501	75424	61410	70356	75443	10/59-03/83	➲**305501**
502	75425	61411	70357	75444	03/60-04/83	➲**305502**
503	75426	61412	70358	75445	04/60-05/81	➲**305503**
504	75427	61413	70359	75446	04/60-11/81	➲**305504**
505	75428	61414	70360	75447	04/60-12/81	➲*305505*
506	75429	61415	70361	75448	05/60-07/81	➲**305506**
507	75430	61416	70362	75449	05/60-01/80	➲**305507**
508	75431	61417	70363	75450	06/60-03/83	➲**305508**
509	75432	61418	70364	75451	07/60- *83*	➲**305509**
510	75433	61419	70365	75452	07/60-03/83	➲**305510**
511	75434	61420	70366	75453	07/60-04/83	➲**305511**
512	75435	61421	70367	75454	08/60-09/81	
513	75436	61422	70368	75455	08/60-02/80	➲**305513**
514	75437	61423	70369	75456	09/60-02/81	➲**305514**
515	75438	61424	70370	75457	10/60-01/80	➲**305515**
516	75439	61425	70371	75458	10/60-02/83	➲**305516**
517	75440	61426	70372	75459	10/60-02/83	➲**305517**
518	75441	61427	70373	75460	11/60-08/81	➲**305518**
519	75442	61428	70374	75461	11/60-04/83	➲**305519**

Class 309 AM9

Clacton & Walton Express Stock
25/6.25kV ac overhead
601-627

The Class 309 express units were built for the Liverpool Street to Clacton & Walton services. They were fitted with Commonwealth bogies and designed for 100 mph running. They had distinctive front ends with wrap-around glass windscreens and a front gangway fitting to allow movement between units. The windscreens were later replaced with plain flat glass.

They were built originally in two and four car sets some with catering vehicles. This allowed 10-car trains to run from London to Thorpe-le-Soken, where the train split; the front four coaches running to Walton, leaving the rear six coaches (including Griddle car) to run to Clacton. The Griddle car E69105 in unit 616 was put into store in 1970 as it was suffering frame problems. It was withdrawn in 1972 and it was replaced by DMU buffet car W59831 which was converted and renumbered E69108, retaining its B4 bogies.

Over the years there were a number of reformations as the catering vehicles were withdrawn and the units were all augmented to 4-car sets using rebuilt Mark 1 coaches. This allowed 12-car trains to be operated.

The units were refurbished after 1985 with all the second class compartments removed. Hopper windows were fitted and they had a new PA system and new seats.

The units were replaced on the Clacton line in 1994, and a number of units were transferred to Manchester for use on the services to Crewe and Stafford, where they remained until 2000.

Two 3-car departmental units were formed in 2001 numbered 936101 & 936102. These were used on the West Coast Main Line as Alsthom Signalling Test Trains in connection with the introduction of the Class 390 Pendolinos.

Class 309/1

	DMBSK	*BDTSOL*	
601	61940	75984	09/62-08/81
602	61941	75985	12/62-10/81
603	61942	75986	01/63-09/81
604	61943	75987	02/63-10/81
605	61944	75988	02/63-05/74
606	61945	75989	03/63-03/74
607	61946	75990	03/63-04/74
608	61947	75991	03/63-04/74

Units strengthened to 3-car units with the addition of converted Mark 1 coaches.

	DMBSOL	*TCsoL*	*BDTSOL*		
601	61940	71573	75984	08/81-10/82	➲**309601**
602	61941	71574	75985	10/81-06/82	➲**309602**
603	61942	71575	75986	09/81-12/81	➲**309603**
604	61943	71576	75987	10/81-02/82	➲**309604**

Units strengthened to 4-car units with the addition of converted Mark 1 coaches

	DMBSK	*TSK*	*TCK*	*BDTSOL*	
605	61944	71108	71113	75988	05/74- 81
606	61945	71109	71112	75989	03/74- 81
607	61946	71107	71111	75990	04/74- 81
608	61947	71110	71114	75991	04/74-07/81

Units converted to 3-car units with the transfer of TSK to 309615-618 to allow withdrawal of Griddle cars.

	DMBSOL	*TCK*	*BDTSOL*		
605	61944	71113	75988	81-12/81	➲**309605**
606	61945	71112	75989	81-12/81	➲**309606**
607	61946	71111	75990	81-11/82	➲**309607**
608	61947	71114	75991	07/81-09/82	➲**309608**

Class 309/2

	BDTC	MBSK	TRB	DTCOL		
611	75637	61932	69100	75976	09/62-12/80	
612	75638	61933	69101	75977	10/62-05/81	
613	75639	61934	69102	75978	10/62-12/80	
614	75640	61935	69103	75979	12/62-02/81	
615	75641	61936	69104	75980	01/63- 81	
616	75642	61937	69105	75981	01/63-01/70	
616	75642	61937	*69108*	75981	06/72-01/80	➲**309616**
617	75643	61938	69106	75982	02/63- 81	
618	75644	61939	69107	75983	02/63-02/81	➲**309618**

Griddle cars removed and replaced with converted Mark 1 coaches (some transferred from 309605-309608).

	BDTC	MBSOL	TSOL	DTCOL		
611	75637	61932	71569	75976	12/80-03/81	➲**309611**
612	75638	61933	71570	75977	05/81-10/82	➲**309612**
613	75639	61934	71571	75978	12/80-06/82	➲**309613**
614	75640	61935	71572	75979	02/81-10/82	➲**309614**
615	75641	61936	71108	75980	81-09/82	➲**309615**
617	75643	61938	71107	75982	81-10/82	➲**309617**

Class 309/3

	BDTC	MBSK	TSOL	DTCsoL		
621	75962	61925	70253	75969	08/62-03/83	➲**309621**
622	75963	61926	70254	75970	11/62-02/82	➲**309622**
623	75964	61927	70255	75971	11/62-09/82	➲**309623**
624	75965	61928	70256	75972	12/62-05/82	➲**309624**
625	75966	61929	70257	75973	12/62-04/82	➲**309625**
626	75967	61930	70258	75974	12/62-03/82	➲**309626**
627	75968	61931	70259	75975	12/62-10/82	➲**309627**

Manchester South Junction & Altrincham

See under the London Midland Region section.

Manchester, Glossop & Hadfield

See under the London Midland Region section.

North Eastern Region

Tyneside Area

NER Tyneside Area
1904-1915 Stock
600V dc third rail

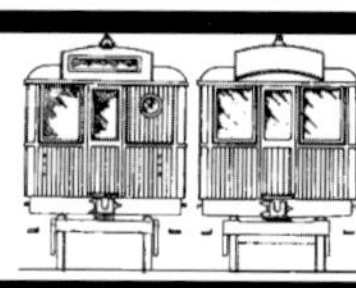

At the turn of the twentieth century the North Eastern Railway was experiencing a loss of traffic to the new tramways in the North and South Tyneside area. Its response was to plan an electrification scheme for this area which was approved at the end of 1902. The original plan specified 50 motor coaches and 50 trailers to be built at the Company's York carriage works, with British Thompson-Houston electrical equipment.

In the event only 90 vehicles were built to the 1904 design including two parcels cars, but some more were added later. The carriages were fitted with clerestory roofs and lower sides fitted with vertical matchboarding. The units worked in a variety of formations and some alterations were made to the stock in the light of service conditions. One feature of the Tyneside stock was the use of convertible areas of seating. Early morning trains had a larger proportion of third class users as workers set off to work. The proportion of first class users increased later in the morning. So some sections of the train were convertible; they had movable signs to designate them as first or third depending on the time of day. No change in the facilities offered, it was sufficient to keep the two groups separate!

On 11th August 1918 a disastrous fire took place in the Heaton car sheds, completely destroying thirty-four cars and resulting in the hasty re-introduction of steam services on some of the lines.

Variable 3-8 car formations
(2=cab each end)

DMBC	DMBC2	DMC	DMT	DMT2	DTT	DTT2	TT
3239	3237	3265	3212	3236	3185	3207	3180
3242	3238		3213	3268	3188	3208	3181
3243	3240		3214	3269	3189	3209	3182
3244	3241		3215	3519	3190	3210	3183
3245	3260		3216	3520	3191	3211	3184
3246	3261		3217	3521	3192		3186
3247	3263		3218	3522	3193		3187
3248	3264		3219	3523	3195		3194
3249	3770		3220	3524	3196		3201
3250	3771		3221		3197		3202
3251	3794		3222		3198		3203
3252			3223		3199		3204
3253			3224		3200		3205
3254			3225		3206		3781
3255			3226		3507		3782
3256			3227		3508		3783
3257			3228		3509		3784
3258			3229		3510		3785
3259			3230		3511		3786
3262			3231		3512		3787
			3232		3513		3788
			3233		3514		3789
			3234		3515		3790
			3235		3516		3791
MPV			3792		3517		
3266			3793		3518		
3267							
3525							

NER stock renumbered by the LNER in 1923 into the 23xxx series
1923 Numbers

DMBC	DMBC2	DMC	DMT	DMT2	DTT	DTT2	TT
23239	23237	23265	23213	23236	23185	23207	23181
23242	23240		23214	23269	23188	23208	23182
23244	23260		23215	23519	23189	23209	23183
23245	23261		23216	23522	23190	23210	23184
23247	23263		23218	23523	23191		23186
23248	23264		23220		23192		23187
23252	23770		23222		23193		23194
23253	23771		23223		23196		23201
23254	23794		23224		23199		23202
23255			23229		23200		23203
23256			23230		23206		23205
23257			23231		23509		23781
23258			23232		23510		23782
23259			23233		23511		23783
23262			23234		23514		23784
			23235		23515		23786
MPV			23792		23516		23787
23266			23793		23517		23789
23267							
23525							

NER Tyneside Area
Controlled Set
600V dc third rail

In 1929 a controlled-set was formed from six loco-hauled vehicles (replacing an earlier controlled set for which details are no longer available). These worked between two motor luggage vans. For many years it worked the same circuit including an early morning workman's train and one morning and one evening service.

1923 numbers

TC	TT	TT	TT	TT	TT
23694	23731	23733	23744	23745	23747

LNER 1943 numbers

TC	TT	TT	TT	TT	TT
29269	29270	29271	29272	29273	29274

NER Tyneside Area
1920-1922 Stock
600V dc third rail

As a result of the fire that destroyed thirty-four cars of the 1904 design, a similar number of new cars were built to replace them and they took the numbers of the vehicles they replaced. The 1920 stock was recognisable by the elliptical roof replacing the clerestory roof on the earlier stock.

DMBC	DMBC2	DMC	DMT	DMT2	DTT	DTT2	TT
23243	23238		23212	23268			23180
23246	23241		23217	23524			23195
23249			23219				23197
23250			23221				23198
23251			23225				23204
23253			23226				23211
24465			23227				23507
			23228				23508
			23520				23512
			23521				23513
MPV							23518
23795							23785
							23788
							23790
							23791

LNER 1943 numbers

DMT	TT
29175	29375

29176	29376
29177	29377
29178	29378
29179	29379
29180	29380
29181	29381
29182	29382
29183	29383
	29384

DMBC	***TT***
29184	29385
29185	29386
29186	29387
29187	29388
29189	29389
29190	29390
29191	29391
29192	29392

MPV
29493

Tyneside Area
1938 Stock
600V dc third rail

By 1937, the earlier Tyneside units were due for replacement and 64 articulated twin sets were ordered from Metropolitan-Cammell. They were fitted with bucket seats in both first and third class in the NER tradition.

The units came in four different varieties depending on the combination of vehicle types in the unit. In addition four single cars, two motor luggage third cars and two motor parcels vans were delivered from Metropolitan-Cammell at the same time.

Articulated type A units

DMT	***DTT***		
24145	24146	37-	43
24147	24148	37-	43
24149	24150	37-	43
24151	24152	37-	43
24153	24154	37-	43
24155	24156	37-	43
24157	24158	37-	43
24159	24160	37-	43
24161	24162	37-	43
24163	24164	37-	43
24165	24166	37-	43
24167	24168	37-	43

Articulated type B units

DMBT	***DTC***		
24169	24170	37-	43
24171	24172	37-	43
24173	24174	37-	43
24175	24176	37-	43
24177	24178	37-	43
24179	24180	37-	43
24181	24182	37-	43
24183	24184	37-	43
24185	24186	37-	43
24187	24188	37-	43
24189	24190	37-	43
24191	24192	37-	43
24193	24194	37-	43
24195	24196	37-	43
24197	24198	37-	43
24199	24200	37-	43

Articulated type C units

DMT	***TT***		
24201	24202	37-	43
24203	24204	37-	43
24205	24206	37-	43
24207	24208	37-	43
24209	24210	37-	43
24211	24212	37-	43
24213	24214	37-	43
24215	24216	37-	43
24217	24218	37-	43
24219	24220	37-	43
24221	24222	37-	43
24223	24224	37-	43
24225	24226	37-	43
24227	24228	37-	43
24229	24230	37-	*40*
24231	24232	37-	43
24233	24234	37-	43
24235	24236	37-	43

Articulated type D units

TC	***DMBT***		
24237	24238	38-	43
24239	24240	38-	43
24241	24242	38-	43
24243	24244	38-	43
24245	24246	38-	43
24247	24248	38-	43
24249	24250	38-	43
24251	24252	38-	43
24253	24254	38-	43
24255	24256	38-	43
24257	24258	38-	43
24259	24260	38-	43
24261	24262	38-	43
24263	24264	38-	43
24265	24266	38-	43
24267	24268	38-	43
24269	24270	38-	43
24271	24272	38-	43

DMBT		
24273	38-	43
24274	38-	43

Motor Parcels Van		
2424	38-	43
2425	38-	43

LNER 1943 Numbers

Articulated type A units

DMT	***DTT***	
29101	29301	43-04/67
29102	29302	43-06/67
29103	29303	43-04/67
29104	29304	43-04/67
29105	29305	43-06/67
29106	29306	43-06/67
29107	29307	43-06/67
29108	29308	43-04/67
29109	29309	43-04/67
29110	29310	43-04/67
29111	29311	43-06/67
29112	29312	43-08/51

Articulated type B units

DMBT	***DTC***	
29113	29313	43-06/67
29114	29314	43-06/67
29115	29315	43-06/67
29116	29316	43-06/67
29117	29317	43-06/67
29118	29318	43-06/67
29119	29319	43-06/67
29120	29320	43-06/67
29121	29321	43-06/67
29122	29322	43-06/67
29123	29323	43-06/67
29124	29324	43-06/67
29125	29325	43-06/67
29126	29326	43-04/67
29127	29327	43-06/67
29128	29328	43-06/67

Articulated type C units

DMT	***TT***		
29129	29229		43-06/64
29130	29230		43-04/67
29131	29231		43-08/51
29131	29231	new 29131 ex 29112	08/51-06/64
29132	29232		43-06/67
29133	29233		43-06/64
29134	29234		43-04/67
29135	29235		43-06/64
29136	29236		43-04/67
29137	29237		43-06/64
29138	29238		43-04/67
29139	29239		43-06/64
29140	29240		43-06/64
29141	29241		43-06/64
29142	29242		43-06/64
29144	29244		43-06/67
29145	29245		43-06/64
29146	29246		43-06/64

Articulated type D units

TC	***DMBT***	
29147	29247	43-06/67
29148	29248	43-04/67
29149	29249	43-06/67
29150	29250	43-06/64
29151	29251	43-04/67
29152	29252	43-06/67
29153	29253	43-04/67

29154	29254	43-06/64
29155	29255	43-06/64
29156	29256	43-06/67
29157	29257	43-04/67
29158	29258	43-04/67
29159	29259	43-06/67
29160	29260	43-06/67
29161	29261	43-06/67
29162	29262	43-06/64
29163	29263	43-06/67
29164	29264	43-06/67

DMBT	
29165	43-05/67
29166	43-05/67

Motor Parcels Van	
29467	43-06/67
29468	43-06/67

Tyneside
South Tyneside Line 2-car Standard Units
600V dc third rail

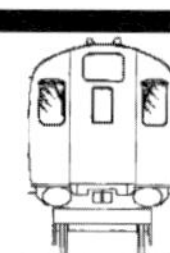

These units were built at Eastleigh for Tyneside to a very similar design to the Southern Region 2-EPB units. They differed from the Southern batch by having a larger guard's and luggage van, one less seating bay in the motor car and a first class compartment in the trailer vehicle. They carried a route destination blind and marker lights instead of a headcode box and carried no unit numbers.

The South Tyneside electric services ceased in 1963 and the units were sent south to work on the Southern Region as 2-EPBs 5781-5795. The composite vehicle was downgraded to second class and the Southern Region headcode box was fitted.

DMBS	***DTCoL***		
65311	77100	12/54-08/63	**➲5781**
65312	77101	12/54-10/63	**➲5782**
65313	77102	01/55-07/63	**➲5783**
65314	77103	01/55-08/63	**➲5784**
65315	77104	01/55-09/63	**➲5785**
65316	77105	02/55-09/63	**➲5786**
65317	77106	02/55-08/63	**➲5787**
65318	77107	02/55-08/63	**➲5788**
65319	77108	02/55-07/63	**➲5789**
65320	77109	02/55-08/63	**➲5790**
65321	77110	03/55-08/63	**➲5791**
65322	77111	03/55-09/63	**➲5792**
65323	77112	03/55-07/63	**➲5793**
65324	77113	03/55-08/63	**➲5794**
65325	77114	04/55-09/63	**➲5795**

Tyneside
South Tyneside Line Motor Luggage Van
600V dc third rail

At the same time as the new EPB build for Tyneside, a new Motor Luggage Van was built for use on the South Shields line. It was also fitted with batteries to allow operation away from the live rail supply for up to 20 minutes. It was trialled on the Southern region before being delivered to Tyneside.

After the Tyneside electrified system closed the unit transferred to the London Midland Region to work on the Liverpool-Southport line.

DMLV		
68000	08/63⇨**M**	55- *64*

Scottish Region

Class 303 AM3
Glasgow Suburban
25/6.25kV ac overhead
001-091

A total of 91 units were built for the Glasgow suburban electrification. When built they carried a light blue Caledonian Railway livery and they were known as the "Blue Trains". They were constructed by the Pressed Steel Company in Paisley and had very distinctive modern cabs with wrap-around windscreens. However, these were later replaced with plain glass windscreens (in common with other units that had similar wrap-around windscreens, classes 309, 310 & 311).

The North Side services were inaugurated in November 1960, but an explosion in the transformer of one of the units six weeks later led to the complete withdrawal of the services for 10 months while the problems were eradicated. The South Side services began in 1962. 001-056 originally worked on the North side and 057-091 on the South. Later 001-035 were swapped with 057-091, leaving 001-035 on the South and 036-091 on the North. Four or five units could usually be found working on the opposite side from usual due to operating requirements.

Class 303/1	Original units
Class 303/2	035 Thyristor control and Deans door gear (outside opening)
Class 303/3	071 converted 1964 with oil cooled silicon rectifiers.
Class 303/4	035 retaining thyristor control, but now with oil cooled silicon rectifiers. Deans door gear replaced with Peters door in 1971.
Class 303/5	072 Oil cooled silicon rectifiers (cooling common with transformer)
Class 303/6	040/4/6-70/81-91 Silicon rectifiers with separate oil cooling systems
Class 303/7	001-034/6-9/41-3/5 Air cooled silicon rectifiers

The later Class 311 units, built by Cravens, were to an identical design.

Many units were later refurbished with 2+2 seating and gangways within units. They had fewer seats and a lot more standing space, and they were not popular with the passengers.

In 1981-1983 thirteen unrefurbished units were transferred to the Crewe and Manchester areas to work local services and they stayed there until withdrawal.

In 1992 303049 was renumbered 303999 when it took part in the Intelligent Train Project.

	DTSO	***MBSO***	***BDTSO***			
001	75566	61481	75601	07/59-*11/79*	**➲303001**	
002	75567	61482	75602	09/59- 78		
003	75568	61483	75603	09/59-*11/79*	**➲303003**	
004	75569	61484	75604	11/59-*03/80*	**➲303004**	
005	75570	61485	75605	11/59-*03/80*	**➲303005**	
006	75571	61486	75606	11/59-*11/79*	**➲303006**	
007	75572	61487	75607	11/59- 78		
008	75573	61488	75608	12/59-*11/79*	**➲303008**	
009	75574	61489	75609	12/59-*03/80*	**➲303009**	
010	75575	61490	75610	12/59-*11/79*	**➲303010**	
011	75576	61491	75611	12/59-*05/79*	**➲303011**	
012	75577	61492	75612	01/60- *80*	**➲303012**	
013	75578	61493	75613	01/60- *80*	**➲303013**	
014	75579	61494	75614	01/60-*03/80*	**➲303014**	
015	75580	61495	75615	01/60-05/80	**➲303015**	
016	75581	61496	75616	02/60- *80*	**➲303016**	
017	75582	61497	75617	02/60-06/80	**➲303017**	
018	75583	61498	75618	02/60-07/80	**➲303018**	
019	75584	61499	75619	02/60-*03/80*	**➲303019**	
020	75585	61500	75620	02/60- *80*	**➲303020**	
021	75586	61501	75621	03/60-08/80	**➲303021**	
022	75587	61502	75622	03/60-06/80	**➲303022**	
023	75588	61503	75623	03/60-06/80	**➲303023**	
024	75589	61504	75624	03/60-*11/79*	**➲303024**	
025	75590	61505	75625	03/60-*08/79*	**➲303025**	
026	75591	61506	75626	04/60- *80*	**➲303026**	
027	75592	61507	75627	04/60-*03/80*	**➲303027**	
028	75593	61508	75628	04/60-*11/79*	**➲303028**	
029	75594	61509	75629	04/60-*03/80*	**➲303029**	
030	75595	61510	75630	04/60-*11/79*	**➲303030**	
031	75596	61511	75631	05/60- *80*	**➲303031**	
032	75597	61512	75632	05/60-*05/79*	**➲303032**	
033	75598	61513	75633	05/60-06/79		
033	75598	*61860*	75633	06/79-07/80	**➲303033**	☜
034	75599	61514	75634	05/60- *80*	**➲303034**	
035	75600	61515	75635	11/60-06/80	**➲303035**	
036	75746	61812	75802	05/60- *80*	**➲303036**	
037	75747	61813	75803	06/60-*03/80*	**➲303037**	
038	75748	61814	75804	06/60-*03/80*	**➲303038**	
039	75749	61815	75805	06/60-*08/79*	**➲303039**	
040	75750	61816	75806	06/60-*08/79*	**➲303040**	
041	75751	61817	75807	06/60-*11/79*	**➲303041**	
042	75752	61818	75808	06/60-*03/80*	**➲303042**	
043	75753	61819	75809	06/60-06/79		
043	*75572*	61819	75809	06/79-06/80	**➲303043**	☜
044	75754	61820	75810	06/60-06/80	**➲303044**	
045	75755	61821	75811	06/60-*03/80*	**➲303045**	
046	75756	61822	75812	06/60-06/80	**➲303046**	
047	75757	61823	75813	07/60-*11/79*	**➲303047**	
048	75758	61824	75814	07/60- *80*	**➲303048**	
049	75759	61825	75815	07/60- *80*	**➲303049**	
050	75760	61826	75816	07/60-*08/79*	**➲303050**	

051	75761	61827	75817	07/60-*03/80*	➲**303051**
052	75762	61828	75818	07/60-*03/80*	➲**303052**
053	75763	61829	75819	07/60-*03/80*	➲**303053**
054	75764	61830	75820	07/60-*03/80*	➲**303054**
055	75765	61831	75821	07/60-*08/79*	➲**303055**
056	75766	61832	75822	08/60-*03/80*	➲**303056**
057	75767	61833	75823	08/60- *80*	➲**303057**
058	75768	61834	75824	09/60-*03/80*	➲**303058**
059	75769	61835	75825	09/60- *80*	➲**303059**
060	75770	61836	75826	09/60- *80*	➲**303060**
061	75771	61837	75827	09/60-*05/79*	➲**303061**
062	75772	61838	75828	09/60- *80*	➲**303062**
063	75773	61839	75829	09/60-*03/80*	➲**303063**
064	75774	61840	75830	10/60-*08/79*	➲**303064**
065	75775	61841	75831	10/60- *80*	➲**303065**
066	75776	61842	75832	10/60- *80*	➲**303066**
067	75777	61843	75833	10/60-*03/80*	➲**303067**
068	75778	61844	75834	10/60-05/80	➲**303068**
069	75779	61845	75835	10/60- 78	
069	75779	61845	*75607*	*78*-*03/80*	➲**303069**
070	75780	61846	75836	10/60-05/80	➲**303070**
071	75781	61847	75837	11/60-*08/79*	➲**303071**
072	75782	61848	75838	11/60-*05/79*	➲**303072**
073	75783	61849	75839	12/60- *80*	➲**303073**
074	75784	61850	75840	12/60- 78	
075	75785	61851	75841	12/60-06/80	➲**303075**
076	75786	61852	75842	12/60-*03/80*	➲**303076**
077	75787	61853	75843	12/60-06/80	➲**303077**
078	75788	61854	75844	01/61-*03/80*	➲**303078**
079	75789	61855	75845	01/61- *80*	➲**303079**
080	75790	61856	75846	01/61-*08/79*	➲**303080**
081	75791	61857	75847	01/61-*08/79*	➲**303081**
082	75792	61858	75848	02/61-*03/80*	➲**303082**
083	75793	61859	75849	02/61-*03/80*	➲**303083**
084	75794	61860	75850	02/61- 78	
085	75795	61861	75851	02/61-*03/80*	➲**303085**
086	75796	61862	75852	02/61-07/80	➲**303086**
087	75797	61863	75853	02/61-*05/79*	➲**303087**
088	75798	61864	75854	02/61- *80*	➲**303088**
089	75799	61865	75855	03/61-*11/79*	➲**303089**
090	75800	61866	75856	04/61- *80*	➲**303090**
091	75801	61867	75857	07/61-08/79	➲**303091**

Class 311 AM11

Glasgow Suburban

25/6.25kV ac overhead

092-110

When the Glasgow Electric system was extended to the South bank of the Clyde further units were needed. The Class 311 units were built by Cravens to the same design as the Class 303 units and could be distinguished by their fluorescent interior lighting.

They were replaced in 1990 by the new Class 320 units. Two units were retained for departmental duties, and one unit was preserved.

	DTSO	*MBSO*	*BDTSO*		
092	76403	62163	76422	12/66-*05/79*	➲**311092**
093	76404	62164	76423	01/67-*03/80*	➲**311093**
094	76405	62165	76424	03/67-*03/80*	➲**311094**
095	76406	62166	76425	02/67-*11/79*	➲**311095**
096	76407	62167	76426	04/67-08/80	➲**311096**
097	76408	62168	76427	04/67-07/80	➲**311097**
098	76409	62169	76428	02/67-*08/79*	➲**311098**
099	76410	62170	76429	03/67-06/80	➲**311099**
100	76411	62171	76430	03/67-*05/79*	➲**311100**
101	76412	62172	76431	05/67-*05/79*	➲**311101**
102	76413	62173	76432	04/67-*03/80*	➲**311102**
103	76414	62174	76433	05/67-*05/79*	➲**311103**
104	76415	62175	76434	05/67-*11/79*	➲**311104**
105	76416	62176	76435	05/67-*08/79*	➲**311105**
106	76417	62177	76436	05/67-*03/80*	➲**311106**
107	76418	62178	76437	05/67-06/80	➲**311107**
108	76419	62179	76438	06/67-*03/80*	➲**311108**
109	76420	62180	76439	06/67-*08/79*	➲**311109**
110	76421	62181	76440	07/67- *80*	➲**311110**

Southern Region

Class 492 3-TC

Bournemouth Line Trailer Units

660-850V dc third rail (unpowered)

301-304

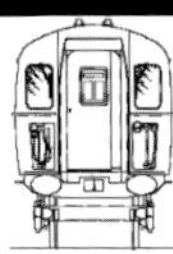

These 3-TC sets were built for the Bournemouth line in 1967. For details see the 4-TC units below.

	DTSO	*TBSK*	*DTSO*		
301	76325	70840	76326	05/67-06/74	➲*429*
302	76327	70841	76328	07/67-07/74	➲*430*
303	76329	70842	76330	08/67-06/74	➲*431*
304 spare	76270	70843		08/67-05/68	
304 spare	*76331*	70843		05/68-02/75	

Class 491 4-TC

Bournemouth Line Trailer Units

660-750V dc third rail (unpowered)

401-434

When the Bournemouth line was electrified in 1967, it was desired to find a way of running through trains to non-electrified Weymouth. A push-pull system was devised where a powerful tractor unit could propel non-powered trailer units to Bournemouth, where a Class 33/1 diesel locomotive would take the unit forward to Weymouth. The system was designed to be very flexible and the complete train could be driven in either push or pull mode from the front of the tractor unit (4-REP), trailer unit (4-TC), a Class 33/1 diesel locomotive or a Class 73 or 74 electro-diesel locomotive. A typical train would leave London Waterloo with two 4-TC sets leading and one 4-REP at the rear. At Bournemouth the REP unit was uncoupled from the rear and a Class 33 would attach to the front for the remainder of the journey to Weymouth. The return journey would repeat the procedure in reverse.

The three 3-TC and twenty-eight 4-TC units were converted from loco-hauled stock. The 3-TC units were built to allow 11-TC sets plus a locomotive to fit into the platform at Waterloo to work boat trains; the units were later augmented to four car units 429-431 in 1974 and additional units 432-434 were added in 1975, all converted from loco-hauled stock.

The TC units were Class 491/492 but they were reclassified to Class 438 when they were renumbered 8001-8034.

Temporary 3-car units

	DTSO	*TBSK*	*DTSO*		
421	76309	70832	76310	12/66-07/67	➲*421*
422	76311	70865	76312	12/66-07/67	➲*422*
423	76313	70834	76314	02/67-07/67	➲*423*
424	76315	70835	76316	03/67-07/67	➲*424*
425	76317	70836	76318	01/67-07/67	➲*425*
426	76319	70837	76320	02/67-10/67	➲*426*
427	76321	70838	76322	02/67-07/67	➲*427*
428	76323	70839	76324	03/67-07/67	➲*428*

	DTSO	*TBSK*	*TFK*	*DTSO*		
401	76332	70812	70844	76331	10/67-05/68	
401	76332	70812	70844	*76270*	05/68-07/86	➲**8001**
402	76271	70813	70845	76272	08/66-06/86	➲**8002**
403	76274	70814	70846	76273	08/66-11/86	➲**8003**
404	76276	70815	70847	76275	08/66-10/86	➲**8004**
405	76277	70816	70848	76278	08/66-05/85	
406	76279	70817	70849	76280	08/66-06/86	➲**8006**
407	76282	70818	70850	76281	09/66-12/86	➲**8007**
408	76283	70819	70851	76284	08/66-10/86	➲**8008**
409	76285	70820	70852	76286	09/66-12/86	
410	76287	70821	70853	76288	09/66-08/86	➲**8010**
410	76288	*70812*	*70859*	76287	09/91-08/96	
411	76289	70822	70854	76290	09/66-10/86	➲**8011**
412	76291	70823	70855	76292	09/66-06/86	➲**8012**
413	76294	70824	70856	76293	10/66-05/86	➲**8013**
414	76296	70825	70857	76295	10/66-09/86	➲**8014**
415	76298	70826	70858	76297	11/66-10/86	➲**8015**
416	76300	70827	70859	76299	10/66-06/86	➲**8016**
417	76301	70828	70860	76302	11/66-10/86	➲**8017**
417	76301	*70826*	70860	76302	09/91-01/98	
418	76304	70829	70861	76303	11/66-10/86	➲**8018**
419	76305	70830	70862	76306	11/66-08/86	➲**8019**
420	76308	70831	70863	76307	11/66-09/86	➲**8020**
421	76310	70832	70864	76309	07/67-10/86	➲**8021**
422	76311	70833	70865	76312	07/67-05/86	➲**8022**

423	76314	70834	70866	76313	07/67-06/86	➲**8023**
424	76315	70835	70867	76316	07/67-05/86	➲**8024**
425	76318	70836	70868	76317	07/67-05/86	➲**8025**
426	76320	70837	70869	76319	10/67-08/86	➲**8026**
427	76322	70838	70870	76321	07/67-06/86	➲**8027**
428	76323	70839	70871	76324	07/67-06/86	➲**8028**
429	76325	70840	71162	76326	06/74-10/86	➲**8029**
430	76327	70841	71163	76328	07/74-09/86	➲**8030**
431	76329	70842	71164	76330	06/74-10/86	➲**8031**
432	76944	70843	71165	76943	02/75-06/86	➲**8032**
433	76946	71160	71166	76945	02/75-09/86	➲**8033**
434	76948	71161	71167	76947	01/75-09/86	➲**8034**

6-TC

6-car Trailer Unit
660-750V dc third rail (unpowered)
601

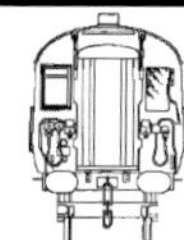

Following the success of the 7-TC unit, it was decided to create a series of 6-car units which would retain their cab controls and could be used in push-pull mode driven from the front cab. These were to be reformed from withdrawn PUL/PAN units.

In the event only one unit was formed, numbered 601. A Class 33 diesel locomotive number D6580 was converted and fitted with high-level jumper connections to work with this set. The set only operated on its intended duties (the Oxted line) for a short while, before being transferred to the Clapham Junction-Kensington Olympia service.

Although only one unit was formed, the principle had been successfully proved and it led to a fleet of Mark 1 3-TC and 4-TC units for the Bournemouth line and a fleet of 18 Class 33/1 locomotives converted to work with them.

	DTBS	*TSK*	*TSK*	*TSK*	*TSK*	*DTBS*	
601	11229	10041	11768	10009	10014	11154	06/65-10/71

7-TC

7-car Trailer Unit
660-750V dc third rail (unpowered)
900, later 701

In 1963 it was realised that there would be a shortage of electrically heated stock and this unit was created to meet that need. It was formed of the cars of 2-BIL unit number 2006 (to provide guard's accommodation) with four redundant augmentation trailers from 4-SUB units and a 4-SUB car 11485 used as a composite to provide first class accommodation. The unit was given the number 900 and was used as a locomotive hauled set on the Oxted line.

In 1966 it was overhauled and renumbered 701 to conform with the other TC units in which the first digit of the number indicated the number of carriages. Unlike the other TC units, 701 did not have any driving controls, these having been removed when it was converted.

After the unit was disbanded in 1969, the SUB cars returned to 4-SUB units. 11485 was converted for use in 4-EPB unit 5115 and was renumbered 15084.

	DTBS	*TS*	*TS*	*TS*	*TS*	*TC*	*DTBS*		
701	10573	10346	10349	10351	10353	11485	12107	06/66-05/69	

	DTBS	*TS*	*TS*	*TC*	*TS*	*TS*	*DTBS*		
900	10573	10346	10349	11485	10353	10351	12107	09/63-06/66	➲*701*

2-T

2-car Trailer Sets to run with 3-SUB units
660-750V dc third rail (unpowered)
989-1200

The LSWR first introduced 3-SUB units working with 2-T trailer sets on its lines out of Waterloon. These trailer units were numbered 1001-1024 in SR days.

In line with the introduction of further 3-SUB units on the Western and Eastern sections, more 2-car trailer sets were formed from loco-hauled stock to allow longer flexible trains to be formed on these lines.

1025-1037 were converted in 1925 from LBSCR 1921-built hauled stock to work with 3-SUB units 1285-1310 on the Western Section.

1038-1050 comprised three small batches of LSWR bodied vehicles.

1051-1120 were formed in 1925-26 from LBSCR nine-compartment bogie thirds to work on the Eastern Section.

The 1928-29 electrification programme produced more trailer units. 1121-1167 were formed with one SECR eight-compartment bogie and one eleven-compartment LSWR bogie coach. Another similar batch were formed in 1930, numbered 1188-1194.

The batch numbered 1168-1187 were converted in the late 1920s from ex-LBSCR stock. 1168-1180 of this batch were formed from pairs of ex-ac CP stock motor coaches. 1181-1187 comprised one ex-ac trailer coach and one converted steam hauled coach.

1195-1198 were ex-LSWR vehicles placed in stock in 1934. But they did not remain in that formation long, as there was a mass-reorganisation of trailers sets in 1934. The intention was to even out the accommodation in the trailer sets, many being reformed as one LBSCR 9-compartment coach and one LSWR 10-compartment vehicle. Some further units were numbered 989-1000 and 1199-1200 in 1937-38. At this point the sets were allocated 'Type' numbers as shown below.

During the war years, the majority of the trailers were used to strengthen the 3-SUB units which became 4-SUBs.

1938 Types

Type 1 Original LSWR sets with 9 compartment 51ft and 8 compartment 49ft vehicles.
Type 2 Original LSWR sets with 9 compartment 51ft and 8 compartment 51ft vehicles.
Type 3 LBSCR sets with two 9 compartment 54ft vehicles.
Type 4 LBSCR sets with 9 compartment 54ft and 8½ compartment 54ft vehicles.
Type 5 Sets with 8 compartment SECR vehicle and 11 compartment 62ft LSWR bodied vehicle.
Type 6 Sets with 10 compartment 62ft LSWR vehicle and 9 compartment 54ft LBSCR vehicle.
Type 7 Set with 9 compartment 54ft LBSCR vehicle and 11 compartment 62ft LSWR bodied vehicle.
Type 8 Sets with 9 compartment 54ft LBSCR vehicle and 10 compartment 62ft LSWR bodied vehicle.
Type 9 Sets with 9 compartment 54ft LBSCR vehicle and 10 compartment 61ft LSWR bodied vehicle.

SR/LBSCR Bodies.

Originally to have contained 2 x 104xx

	TT	*TT*		
989	10411	9100	Type 8	01/38-09/39
990	10417	9065	Type 8	01/38- 45
991	10410	9084	Type 8	02/38-01/42
992	10413	9039	Type 8	02/38-11/43
993	10403	9086	Type 8	03/38-10/44
994	10402	9106	Type 8	03/38- 44
995	10409	9101	Type 8	04/38-07/47
996	10415	9058	Type 8	04/38- 45
997	10406	9054	Type 8	05/38-08/46

LSWR/LBSCR Bodies

	TT	*TT*		
998	9299	9091	Type 8	09/37-09/48
999	9300	9035	Type 8	09/37-12/45
1000	9825	9024	Type 8	07/37-11/42

LSWR Bodies

	TT	*TT*		
1001	8925	8913	Type 2	23- 46
1002	8926	8901	Type 1	23- 48
1003	8927	8914	Type 2	23-06/38
1004	8928	8902	Type 1	23- 48
1005	8929	8915	Type 2	23-08/48
1006	8930	8903	Type 1	23- 48
1007	8931	8916	Type 2	23- 48
1008	8932	8904	Type 1	23- 48
1009	8933	8917	Type 2	23-11/40
1010	8934	8905	Type 1	23- 47
1011	8935	8918	Type 2	23-03/48
1012	8936	8906	Type 1	23- 47
1013	8937	8907	Type 1	23-11/37
1014	8938	8919	Type 2	23- 46
1015	8939	8920	Type 2	23-05/47
1016	8940	8908	Type 1	23-05/47
1017	8941	8909	Type 1	23-01/48
1018	8942	8921	Type 2	23-03/48
1019	8943	8922	Type 2	23- 48
1020	8944	8923	Type 2	23-12/47
1021	8945	8910	Type 1	23- 43
1022	8946	8911	Type 1	23-12/47
1023	8947	8924	Type 2	23-10/44
1024	8948	8912	Type 1	23-05/47

LBSCR Bodies

	TT	*TT*		
1025	8949	8950	Type 3	04/25-12/47
1026	8951	8952	Type 3	04/25-01/47
1027	8953	8954	Type 3	04/25- 47

1028	8955	8956	Type 3	04/25- 47	
1029	8957	8958	Type 3	04/25-11/46	➲Dep
1030	8959	8960	Type 3	04/25- 48	
1031	8961	8962	Type 3	04/25- 47	
1032	8963	8964	Type 3	04/25- 48	
1033	8965	8966	Type 3	04/25-07/47	
1034	8967	8968	Type 3	05/25- 48	
1035	8969	8970	Type 3	04/25-10/47	
1036	8971	8972	Type 3	04/25-06/47	
1037	8973	8974	Type 3	04/25- 48	

LSWR Bodies

1038-1050 reformed before entering service. Original formation not confirmed.

	TT	*TT*			
1038	9200	9201		06/36- 37	
1038	9200	*9020*	Type 8	37-09/40	↩

	TT	*TT*			
1039	9192	9196		*10/35-* 36	
1039	*9107*	*9000*	Type 8	37-10/40	↩
1040	9193	9197		*10/35-* 36	
1040	*9052*	*9195*	Type 8	36-10/45	↩
1041	9194	9198		*10/35-* 36	
1041	*9193*	*9034*	Type 8	36-08/47	↩
1042	9195	9199		*10/35-* 36	
1042	*9192*	*9047*	Type 8	36-08/48	↩

	TT	*TT*			
1043	9176	9184		07/35- 36	
1043	9176	*9045*	Type 8	36-05/47	↩
1044	9177	9185		07/35- 36	
1044	9177	*9028*	Type 8	36-08/47	↩
1045	9178	9186		07/35- 36	
1045	9178	*9097*	Type 8	36-08/47	↩
1046	9179	9187		07/35- 36	
1046	9179	*9093*	Type 8	36-09/42	↩
1047	9180	9188		07/35- 36	
1047	*9181*	*9067*	Type 8	36-09/42	↩
1048	9181	9189		07/35- 36	
1048	*9180*	*9036*	Type 8	36-11/42	↩
1049	9182	9190		07/35- 36	
1049	9182	*9123*	Type 6	36- 48	↩
1050	9183	9191		07/35- 36	
1050	9183	*9121*	Type 6	36-07/42	↩

LBSCR Bodies

	TT	*TT*			
1051	8999	9100		06/25- 38	
1051	8999	*10408*		38-08/48	↩
1052	9001	9002	Type 3	06/25-03/43	
1053	9013	9069	Type 3	05/25-11/45	➲Dep
1054	9048	9056	Type 3	05/25-10/40	
1054	*9291*	9056		10/40-10/41	↩
1055	9052	9115		05/25- 36	
1055	*9198*	9115	Type 8	36-12/40	↩
1056	9011	9014	Type 3	06/25- 48	
1057	9006	9008		06/25- *48*	
1058	9005	9103	Type 3	07/25- 48	
1059	9000	9012		07/25- 36	
1059	*9194*	9012	Type 8	36- 44	↩
1060	9003	9060	Type 3	07/25-11/45	➲Dep
1061	9063	9065		07/25- 38	
1061	9063	*10418*		38-02/44	↩
1062	9062	9064	Type 3	07/25-03/43	
1063	9015	9016	Type 3	07/25-09/40	
1064	9017	9071		07/25- 36	
1064	*9188*	9071	Type 8	36-05/48	↩
1065	9010	9061	Type 3	06/25-12/45	
1066	9004	9007		06/25-07/43	
1067	9019	9070		08/25- 37	
1067	*9030*	*9207*		37-08/46	↩
1068	9022	9077		08/25- 37	
1068	*9109*	*9206*	Type 8	37-08/48	↩
1069	9009	9068	Type 3	07/25-12/43	
1070	9021	9066		07/25- 36	
1070	9021	*9123*	Type 8	36-02/47	↩
1071	9036	9067		07/25- 36	
1071	*9066*	*9190*	Type 8	36- 46	↩
1072	9018	9020		07/25- 37	
1072	9018	*9201*	Type 8	37- 45	↩
1073	9034	9072		07/25- 36	
1073	*9199*	9072	Type 8	36-09/43	↩
1074	9073	9076	Type 3	07/25- 48	
1075	9081	9090	Type 3	09/25-07/43	
1076	9080	9108	Type 3	09/25- 48	
1077	9059	9082	Type 3	09/25-05/43	
1078	9078	9092	Type 9	09/25-08/48	
1079	9023	9053	Type 3	09/25-07/44	
1080	9043	9085	Type 3	10/25-04/42	
1081	9037	9094		10/25- 37	
1081	9037	*9827*		37-10/40	↩
1081	*9099*	9827		11/40-09/44	↩
1082	9074	9084		10/25- 38	
1082	9074	*10412*		38-06/45	↩
1083	9079	9089	Type 3	10/25-11/46	➲Dep
1084	9024	9095		10/25- 37	
1084	*9098*	*9828*		37-08/46	↩
1085	9035	9091		10/25-07/37	
1085	*9099*	*9830*		*09/37*-11/40	↩
1086	9038	9039		10/25-*02/38*	
1086	9038	*10414*		*02/38*-11/42	↩
1087	9027	9044		10/25- 35	
1087	*9175*	9044	Type 8	35-02/47	↩
1088	9083	9096	Type 3	10/25- 47	
1089	9040	9041	Type 3	12/25-11/42	
1090	9075	9086		10/25- 38	
1090	9075	*10404*		38-01/48	↩
1091	9042	9087	Type 3	10/25-12/47	
1092	9093	9097		10/25- 36	
1092	*9017*	*9189*	Type 8	36-07/47	↩
1093	9102	9106		11/25- 38	
1093	9102	*10401*		38-09/43	↩
1094	9088	9105	Type 3	11/25-09/43	
1095	9098	9099		11/25-*09/37*	
1095	*9094*	*9829*		37-01/46	↩
1096	9047	9104		11/25- 36	
1096	*9196*	9104	Type 8	36-02/47	↩
1097	9028	9045		12/25- 36	
1097	9122	*9187*	Type 6	36-09/42	↩
1098	9046	9107		11/25-03/37	
1098	*9022*	*9298*	Type 9	03/37-05/47	↩
1099	9049	9101		12/25-*02/38*	
1099	9049	*10407*		38-02/43	↩
1100	9029	9057	Type 3	12/25-03/43	
1101	9051	9110	Type 3	12/25-07/48	
1102	9031	9055	Type 3	12/25- *48*	
1103	9030	9109		12/25-*03/37*	
1103	*9046*	*9208*	Type 8	*03/37*-09/44	↩
1104	9033	9058		01/26- 38	
1104	9033	*10416*		38-06/44	↩
1105	9112	9113	Type 3	01/26- 48	
1106	9111	9114	Type 3	01/26-08/48	
1107	9025	9026	Type 3	01/26-03/42	
1108	9050	9054		12/25- 38	
1108	9050	*10405*		38-03/42	↩
1109	9032	9116		01/26-12/45	
1110	9119	9120	Type 3	02/26- 47	
1111	9121	9123		02/26- 36	
1111	*9184*	9126	Type 6	36-09/48	↩
1112	9124	*9126*		03/26- 36	
1112	9124	*9185*	Type 6	36-10/47	↩
1113	9125	9122		02/26- 36	
1113	9125	*9186*	Type 6	36-11/42	↩
1114	9117	9118	Type 3	02/26-03/43	
1115	9129	9132		*03/26-* 35	
1115	9129	*9170*	Type 6	35-01/43	↩
1116	9128	9131		*03/26-* 35	
1116	9128	*9173*	Type 6	35-09/42	↩

	TT	*TT*			
1117	9127	9130		04/26- 35	
1117	9127	*9168*	Type 6	35-05/45	↩

1118-1120 reformed before entering service. Original formation not documented

	TT	*TT*		
1118	9197	9202	Type 8	02/37-12/47
1119	9077	9203	Type 8	02/37-08/46
1120	9019	9204	Type 8	02/37-09/40

SECR Bodies

	TT	*TT*		
1121	8975	9209	Type 5	03/28-10/47
1122	8976	9210	Type 5	03/28-03/46
1123	8977	9211	Type 5	03/28-03/43
1124	8978	9212	Type 5	03/28-01/43
1125	8979	9213	Type 5	03/28-09/42
1126	8980	9214	Type 5	04/28-04/42
1127	8981	9215	Type 5	04/28-09/43
1128	8982	9216	Type 5	04/28-08/48
1129	8983	9217	Type 5	04/28-09/40
1130	8984	9218	Type 5	05/28-05/47
1131	8985	9219	Type 5	05/28-02/43
1132	8986	9220	Type 5	05/28-02/43
1133	8987	9221	Type 5	05/28-11/47
1134	8988	9222	Type 5	05/28-09/43
1135	8989	9223	Type 5	05/28-10/47
1136	8990	9224	Type 5	05/28-11/47
1137	8991	9225	Type 5	04/28-10/47

1138	8992	9226	Type 5	04/28-11/44	
1139	8993	9227	Type 5	04/28-10/40	
1139	8993	*9247*		12/40-02/44	☜
1140	8994	9228	Type 5	05/28-01/46	
1141	8995	9229	Type 5	05/28-02/44	
1142	8996	9230	Type 5	05/28-02/48	
1143	8997	9231	Type 5	05/28-08/43	
1144	8998	9232	Type 5	04/28-03/43	
1145	9133	9233	Type 5	04/28-07/47	
1146	9134	9234	Type 5	11/28-11/47	
1147	9135	9235	Type 5	11/28-11/42	
1148	9136	9236	Type 5	01/29-01/46	
1149	9137	9237	Type 5	10/28-08/47	
1150	9138	9238	Type 5	01/29-04/44	
1151	9139	9239	Type 5	01/29-08/46	
1152	9140	9240	Type 7	01/29-08/48	
1153	9141	9241	Type 5	12/28-08/46	
1154	9142	9242	Type 5	12/28-09/43	
1155	9143	9243	Type 5	12/28-07/48	
1156	9144	9244	Type 5	02/29-04/48	
1157	9145	9245	Type 5	02/29-08/43	
1158	9146	9246	Type 5	02/29-11/47	
1159	9147	9247	Type 5	02/29-11/40	
1160	9148	9248	Type 5	02/29-08/46	
1161	9149	9249	Type 5	01/29-01/44	
1162	9150	9250	Type 5	02/29-03/48	
1163	9151	9251	Type 5	02/29-09/43	
1164	9152	9252	Type 5	02/29-12/47	
1165	9153	9253	Type 5	02/29-12/47	
1166	9154	9254	Type 5	02/29-06/43	
1167	9155	9255	Type 5	02/29-08/47	

LBSCR Bodies (ex CP AC stock)

	TT	*TT*			
1168	9256	9257	Type 3	07/29-10/47	
1169	9258	9259	Type 3	07/29-05/48	
1170	9260	9261	Type 3	07/29-10/40	
1171	9262	9263	Type 3	07/29-12/47	
1172	9264	9265	Type 3	08/29- 45	
1173	9266	9267	Type 3	08/29- 46	
1174	9268	9269	Type 3	08/29-02/47	
1175	9270	9271	Type 3	08/29-08/48	
1176	9272	9273	Type 3	09/29-11/47	
1177	9274	9275	Type 3	09/29- 47	
1178	9276	9277	Type 3	09/29-08/48	
1179	9278	9279	Type 3	01/30-10/48	
1180	9280	9281	Type 3	01/30- 47	

LBSCR Bodies (ex CP/CW AC stock)

	TT	*TT*			
1181	9282	9283	Type 4	02/30-05/48	
1182	9284	9285	Type 4	02/30-04/47	
1183	9286	9287	Type 4	02/30- 45	
1184	9288	9289	Type 4	02/30-11/40	
1184	9288	*9260*	Type 4	11/40-11/47	☜
1185	9290	9291	Type 4	03/30-10/40	
1186	9292	9293	Type 4	03/30-06/47	

LBSCR Bodies (ex CP AC stock)

	TT	*TT*		
1187	9294	9295	Type 3	07/30-04/48
1188	9296	9297		07/30-07/47

LBSCR (ex CP AC stock)/SER stock

	TT	*TT*		
1189	9156	9157	Type 5	02/31-01/42
1190	9158	9159	Type 5	02/31-09/46
1191	9160	9161	Type 5	02/31-12/43
1192	9162	9163	Type 5	03/31-10/42
1193	9164	9165	Type 5	03/31-11/44
1194	9166	9167	Type 5	03/31-07/48

LSWR Bodies

	TT	*TT*			
1195	9168	9169		*09/34-* 35	
1195	*9130*	9169	Type 6	35-10/45	☜
1196	9170	9171		*10/34-* 35	
1196	*9132*	9171	Type 6	35-05/47	☜
1197	9173	9172		*11/34-* 35	
1197	*9131*	9172	Type 6	35-09/39	☜
1198	9175	9174		*11/34-* 35	
1198	*9027*	9174	Type 8	35-09/42	☜

LBSCR/LSWR Bodies

1199-1200 reformed before entering service. Original formation not documented

	TT	*TT*		
1199	9070	9205	Type 8	03/37- 46
	TT	*TT*		
1200	9095	9826	Type 8	07/37- 46

3-SUB units

As the Southern electrification quickly spread 3-SUB units working with 2-T trailer units were the standard suburban trains on the newly electrified suburban lines. The plan was to convert most of the new units from the steam-hauled suburban coaches they replaced, but 55 units were built new in 1925 to provide a pool of stock to allow the conversions to take place.

Most of the 3-SUB units were later converted to 4-SUB units with the addition of a trailer taken from the 2-T trailer units, or a new all-steel augmentation trailer built at Eastleigh.

The last 3-SUB units in service were working on the Hounslow loop until 1949, due to short platforms on that line.

3-SUB
LSWR Suburban Units
600V, later 660-750V dc third rail
1201-1284

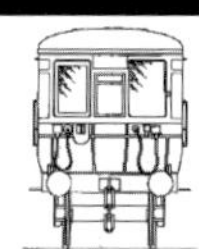

These units were the original LSWR sets which were renumbered 1201-1284 on the Southern Railway.

A *DMBT* *TC* *DMBT*
B *DMBT* *TC* *DMBT*
C *DMBT* *TC* *DMBC*

①②③ *Body style – see coach list*

					Rebuilt (Lengthening)				
1201	8001	9414	8002	A	37	③	23-03/43	➲**4200**	
1202	8003	9351	8004	B			23-12/39		
1203	8005	9372	8751	C	02/34	①	23-08/46	➲*4169*	
1204	8006	9373	8752	C	39	③	23-04/41	➲**4131**	
1205	8007	9415	8008	A	36	②	23-07/47	➲**4211**	
1206	8009	9352	8010	B	36	②	23- *38*		
1206	8009	*9366*	8010				*38*-08/43	➲**4218**	☜
1207	8011	9374	8753	C	02/34	①	23-10/45	➲**4160**	
1208	8012	9375	8754	C	34	①	23-06/44	➲**4152**	
1209	8013	9416	8014	A	37	③	23-08/43	➲**4202**	
1210	8015	9353	8016	B			23-12/39		
1211	8017	9376	8755	C	34	①	23-07/38		
1211	8017	*9344*	8755				07/38- *44*	➲**4154**	☜
1212	8018	9377	8756	C	39	③	23-*11/42*	➲**4146**	
1213	8019	9417	8020	A	39	③	23-09/42	➲**4199**	
1214	8021	9354	8022	B	39	③	23-02/44	➲**4226**	
1215	8023	9378	8757	C	35	①	23-09/44	➲**4153**	
1216	8024	9379	8758	C	39	③	23-06/45	➲**4158**	
1217	8025	9418	8026	A	37	③	23-09/43	➲**4203**	
1218	8027	9355	8028	B	39	③	23-11/47	➲**4232**	
1219	8029	9380	8759	C	36	①	23- 45	➲**4162**	
1220	8030	9381	8760	C	39	③	23- 44	➲**4156**	
1221	8031	9419	8032	A	39	③	23-01/46	➲**4207**	
1222	8033	9356	8034	B	36	①	23-08/46	➲**4229**	
1223	8035	9382	8761	C	37	②	23-08/46	➲**4170**	
1224	8036	9383	8762	C	37	②	23-12/45	➲**4164**	
1225	8037	9420	8038	A	37	③	23-08/46	➲**4208**	
1226	8039	9357	8040	B	38	③	23-02/43	➲**4223**	
1227	8041	9384	8763	C	34	①	23-01/43	➲**4141**	
1228	8042	9385	8764	C	34	①	23- 46	➲**4165**	
1229	8043	9421	8044	A	39	③	23-06/43	➲**4201**	
1230	8045	9358	8046	B	05/40	③	23-08/46	➲*4228*	
1231	8047	9386	8765	C	34	①	23-09/42	➲**4140**	
1232	8048	9387	8766	C	35	①	23-09/42	➲**4133**	
1233	8049	9422	8050	A	37	③	23-04/44	➲**4205**	
1234	8051	9359	8052	B	36	②	23-11/42	➲**4216**	
1235	8053	9388	8767	C	39	③	23-09/42	➲**4138**	
1236	8054	9389	8768	C	39	③	23-10/45	➲**4159**	
1237	8055	9423	8056	A	36	②	23-04/42	➲**4198**	
1238	8057	9360	8058	B	38	③	23-09/46	➲**4230**	
1239	8059	9390	8769	C	35	①	23-02/42	➲**4132**	
1240	8060	9391	8770	C	35	①	23- *42*	➲**4135**	
1241	8061	9424	8062	A	36	②	23-02/44	➲**4204**	
1242	8063	9361	8064	B	38	③	23-01/44	➲**4224**	
1243	8065	9392	8771	C	35	①	23-11/42	➲*4150*	
1244	8066	9393	8772	C	35	①	23- 46	➲**4167**	
1245	8067	9425	8068	A	37	③	23-01/46	➲**4209**	
1246	8069	9362	8070	B	36	①	23-09/43	➲**4220**	
1247	8071	9394	8773	C	39	③	23-03/42	➲**4134**	
1248	8072	9395	8774	C	35	①	23-10/42	➲*4147*	
1249	8073	9426	8074	A	37	③	23-08/47	➲**4213**	
1250	8075	9363	8076	B	38	③	23-10/47	➲**4231**	
1251	8077	9396	8775	C	34	①	23- 46	➲**4166**	

1252	8078	9397	8776	C	35	①	23- 44	⊃**4151**	
1253	8079	9427	8080	A	39	③	23-08/46	⊃**4210**	
1254	8081	9364	8082	B	38	③	23-09/43	⊃**4221**	
1255	8083	9398	8777	C	35	①	23-02/43	⊃**4143**	
1256	8084	9399	8778	C	34	①	23-05/45	⊃**4157**	
1257	8085	9428	8086	A	37	③	23-01/42	⊃**4195**	
1258	8087	9365	8088	B	36	②	23-08/43	⊃**4219**	
1259	8089	9400	8779	C	34	①	23-*12/40*		
1259	8089	9400	*8791*				*12/40*-11/42	⊃**4145**	☜
1260	8090	9401	8780	C	34	①	23-07/42	⊃**4137**	
1261	8091	9429	8092	A	36	①	23- 45	⊃**4206**	
1262	8093	9366	8094	B	36	②	23- *38*		
1262	8093	*9352*	8094				*38*-03/43	⊃**4217**	☜
1263	8095	9402	8781	C	34	①	23- 45	⊃**4163**	
1264	8096	9403	8782	C	35	①	23-01/42	⊃**4144**	
1265	8097	9430	8098	A	36	②	23-12/47	⊃**4214**	
1266	8099	9367	8100	B	38	②	23-11/47	⊃**4233**	
1267	8101	9404	8783	C	35	①	23-08/44	⊃*1692*	
1268	8102	9405	8784	C	34	①	23-08/46	⊃**4171**	
1269	8103	9431	8104	A	36	②	23-10/42	⊃**4196**	
1270	8105	9368	8106	B	38	③	23-12/43	⊃**4225**	
1271	8107	9406	8785	C	36	①	23-09/42	⊃**4139**	
1272	8108	9407	8786	C	37	②	23-11/42	⊃**4142**	
1273	8109	9432	8110	A	39	③	23-03/48	⊃**4215**	
1274	8111	9369	8112	B	39	③	23-11/47	⊃**4234**	
1275	8113	9408	8787	C	37	③	23-09/43	⊃**4149**	
1276	8114	9409	8788	C	37	②	23- 45	⊃**4161**	
1277	8115	9433	8116	A	37	③	23-07/47	⊃**4212**	
1278	8117	9370	8118	B	39	③	23-12/44	⊃**4227**	
1279	8119	9410	8789	C	34	①	23-09/43	⊃**4148**	
1280	8120	9411	8790	C	36	①	23-09/42	⊃**4136**	
1281	8121	9434	8122	A	39	③	23- 42	⊃**4197**	
1282	8123	9371	8124	B	38	②	23-02/43	⊃**4222**	
1283	8125	9412	8791	C	36	①	23-10/40		
1284	8126	9413	8792	C	34	①	23-01/46	⊃**4168**	

3-SUB

SR Steel-panelled Suburban Units

660-750V dc third rail

1285-1310

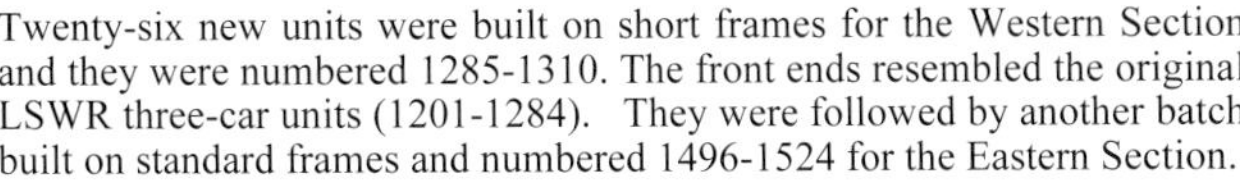

Twenty-six new units were built on short frames for the Western Section and they were numbered 1285-1310. The front ends resembled the original LSWR three-car units (1201-1284). They were followed by another batch built on standard frames and numbered 1496-1524 for the Eastern Section.

	DMBT	*TC*	*DMBT*			
1285	8127	9435	8128	*05/25-01/46*	⊃**4300**	
1286	8129	9436	8130	*05/25-01/46*	⊃**4301**	
1287	8131	9437	8132	*05/25-01/46*	⊃**4302**	
1288	8133	9438	8134	*05/25-11/45*	⊃**4303**	
1289	8135	9439	8136	*06/25-04/46*	⊃**4304**	
1290	8137	9440	8138	*06/25-01/46*	⊃**4305**	
1291	8139	9441	8140	*06/25-02/46*	⊃**4306**	
1292	8141	9442	8142	*06/25-*		
1292	8141	9442	*8155*	*-11/45*	⊃**4307**	☜
1293	8143	9443	8144	*06/25-12/45*	⊃**4308**	
1294	8145	9444	8146	*06/25-10/45*	⊃**4309**	
1295	8147	9445	8148	*06/25-11/45*	⊃**4310**	
1296	8149	9446	8150	*06/25-12/45*	⊃**4311**	
1297	8151	9447	8152	*07/25-12/45*	⊃**4312**	
1298	8153	9448	8154	*07/25-12/45*	⊃**4313**	
1299	8155	9449	8156	*07/25-*		
1299	*8142*	9449	8156	*-02/46*	⊃**4314**	☜
1300	8157	9450	8158	*07/25-08/45*	⊃**4315**	
1301	8159	9451	8160	*07/25-10/45*	⊃**4316**	
1302	8161	9452	8162	*07/25-02/46*	⊃**4317**	
1303	8163	9453	8164	*07/25-10/45*	⊃**4318**	
1304	8165	9454	8166	*07/25-07/45*	⊃**4319**	
1305	8167	9455	8168	*07/25*-04/41		
1305	8167	*9412*	8168	04/41-*02/46*	⊃**4320**	☜
1306	8169	9456	8170	*07/25-01/46*	⊃**4321**	
1307	8171	9457	8172	*08/25-11/45*	⊃**4322**	
1308	8173	9458	8174	*08/25-12/45*	⊃**4323**	
1309	8175	9459	8176	*08/25-02/46*	⊃**4324**	
1310	8177	9460	8178	*08/25-10/45*	⊃**4325**	

3-SUB

SER-bodied Suburban Units

660-750V dc third rail

1401-1495

1401-1495 and 1525-1534 were converted at Ashford in 1926 for the Eastern Section from SECR steam stock. Some of these worked temporarily as 4-car units when first built.

Temporary formations

	DMBT	*TC*	*TC*	*DMBT*	
1402	8229	9518	9521	8230	07/25-09/25
1403	8231	9499	9501	8232	07/25-09/25
1404	8233	9517	9519	8234	07/25-09/25
1405	8235	9502	9504	8236	07/25-09/25
1406	8237	9498	9500	8238	07/25-09/25
1407	8239	9524	9520	8240	07/25-09/25
1409	8243	9495	9513	8244	07/25-09/25
1410	8245	9549	9546	8246	07/25-09/25
1411	8247	9508	9512	8248	07/25-09/25
1412	8249	9507	9509	8250	07/25-09/25
1413	8251	9530	9534	8252	07/25-09/25
1414	8253	9510	9506	8254	07/25-09/25
1415	8255	9511	9505	8256	07/25-09/25
1416	8257	9532	9533	8258	07/25-09/25
1417	8259	9527	9528	8260	07/25-09/25
1418	8261	9491	9552	8262	07/25-09/25
1419	8263	9522	9523	8264	07/25-09/25
1420	8265	9526	9529	8266	07/25-09/25
1421	8267	9559	9564	8268	07/25-09/25
1422	8269	9486	9493	8270	07/25-09/25
1423	8271	9514	9515	8272	07/25-09/25
1424	8273	9485	9487	8274	07/25-09/25
1425	8275	9488	9494	8276	07/25-09/25
1426	8277	9574	9573	8278	07/25-09/25
1427	8279	9489	9490	8280	07/25-09/25
1429	8283	9548	9554	8284	
1430	8285	9545	9547	8286	
1432	8289	9492	9525	8290	
1433	8291	9512	9569	8292	
1434	8293	9567	9571	8294	
1435	8295	9561	9563	8296	
1436	8297	9560	9558	8298	
1437	8299	9550	9570	8300	
1438	8301	9516	9566	8302	
1440	8305	9540	9542	8306	
1444	8313	9556	9557	8314	
1445	8315	9555	9562	8316	

	DMBT	*TC*	*DMBT*			
1401	8227	9531	8228	*02/25*-11/49		
1402	8229	9518	8230	*02/25-04/47*	⊃**4432**	
1403	8231	9501	8232	*02/25-12/46*	⊃**4433**	
1404	8233	9517	8234	*02/25*-06/45		
1404	8233	9517	*8376*	06/45-*01/49*		☜
1405	8235	9502	8236	*02/25-03/47*	⊃**4434**	
1406	8237	9498	8238	*02/25-11/47*	⊃**4406**[2]	
1407	8239	9524	8240	*02/25-11/46*	⊃**4435**	
1408	8241	9496	8242	*02/25-11/49*		
1409	8243	9513	8244	*02/25*-08/47	⊃**4436**	
1410	8245	9546	8246	*03/25-11/46*	⊃**4437**	
1411	8247	9554	8248	*03/25-03/47*	⊃**4438**	
1412	8249	9509	8250	*03/25-12/46*	⊃**4439**[1]	
1413	8251	9534	8252	*03/25-03/47*	⊃**4440**	
1414	8253	9506	8254	*03/25*-10/40		
1414	*8372*	9506	8254	11/40-*01/47*	⊃**4441**	☜
1415	8255	9505	8256	*03/25-11/46*	⊃**4442**[1]	
1416	8257	9532	8258	*03/25-05/47*	⊃**4443**	
1417	8259	9528	8260	*03/25-*		
1417	*8299*	9528	8260	*-02/47*	⊃**4444**	☜
1418	8261	9552	8262	*04/25-12/46*	⊃**4445**	
1419	8263	9523	8264	*04/25-12/46*	⊃**4446**	
1420	8265	9526	8266	*04/25-06/47*	⊃**4447**	
1421	8267	9564	8268	*04/25*-11/49		
1422	8269	9493	8270	*04/25-10/46*	⊃**4448**	
1423	8271	9514	8272	*04/25-04/47*	⊃**4449**	
1424	8273	9487	8274	*04/25-03/47*	⊃**4450**	
1425	8275	9488	8276	*04/25*-11/49		
1426	8277	9573	8278	*04/25*-10/40		
1426	8277	9573	*8377*	11/40-*02/47*	⊃**4451**	☜
1427	8279	9490	8280	*05/25*-01/45		
1428	8281	9553	8282	*05/25*-04/41		
1428	8281	9553	*8290*	04/41-01/45		☜
1429	8283	9548	8284	*05/25*-01/47		
1429	*8366*	9548	8284	01/47-*02/47*	⊃**4452**	☜
1430	8285	9545	8286	*05/25*-11/49		
1431	8287	9565	8288	*05/25-01/47*	⊃**4453**	
1432	8289	9486	8290	*05/25*-11/40		
1433	8291	9512	8292	*05/25-01/47*	⊃**4454**	
1434	8293	9571	8294	*05/25*-11/40		
1434	8293	9571	*8485*	11/40-*11/46*	⊃**4455**	☜
1435	8295	9563	8296	*05/25-03/47*	⊃**4456**	
1436	8297	9560	8298	*06/25-06/47*	⊃**4457**	
1437	8299	9550	8300	*06/25-*		
1437	*8259*	9550	8300	*-04/47*	⊃**4458**	☜
1438	8301	9566	8302	*06/25*-11/49		
1439	8303	9538	8304	*06/25-10/46*	⊃**4459**	
1440	8305	9542	8306	*06/25*-11/49		
1441	8307	9570	8308	*06/25-02/47*	⊃**4460**	

	DMBT	TC	DMBT			
1442	8309	9522	8310	06/25-06/47	⊃**4461**	
1443	8311	9495	8312	06/25-02/47	⊃**4462**	
1444	8313	9555	8314	06/25-11/46	⊃**4463**	
1445	8315	9562	8316	07/25-11/49		
1446	8317	9544	8318	07/25-03/47	⊃**4464**	
1447	8319	9541	8320	07/25-10/46	⊃**4465**	
1448	8321	9543	8322	07/25-09/40		
1448	*8333*	9543	8322	09/40-11/49		☞
1449	8323	9536	8324	07/25-11/49		
1450	8325	9539	8326	07/25-03/47	⊃**4466**	
1451	8327	9535	8328	07/25-01/47	⊃**4467**	
1452	8329	9503	8330	07/25-11/47		
1452	8329	9503	*8374*	11/47- 47	⊃**4468**	☞
1453	8331	9574	8332	07/25-04/47	⊃**4469**	
1454	8333	9497	8334	08/25-09/40		
1455	8335	9499	8336	08/25-03/46		
1455	8335	9499	*8391*	03/46-06/47	⊃**4470**	☞
1456	8337	9547	8338	08/25-06/47	⊃**4471**	
1457	8339	9551	8340	08/25-12/41		
1457	8339	9551	*8349*	12/41-11/46	⊃**4472**	☞
1458	8341	9572	8342	08/25-11/49		
1459	8343	9559	8344	08/25-10/46	⊃**4473**	
1460	8345	9537	8346	08/25-04/47	⊃**4474**	
1461	8347	9511	8348	08/25-11/49		
1462	8349	9579	8350	09/25-12/41		
1463	8351	9577	8352	09/25-11/49		
1464	8353	9492	8354	09/25-05/47	⊃**4475**	
1465	8355	9519	8356	09/25-11/49		
1466	8357	9507	8358	09/25-10/46	⊃**4476**	
1467	8359	9485	8360	09/25-05/47	⊃**4477**	
1468	8361	9561	8362	09/25-12/46	⊃**4478**	
1469	8363	9504	8364	09/25-03/47	⊃**4479**	
1470	8365	9540	8366	09/25- 40		
1471	8367	9558	8368	10/25-06/47	⊃**4480**	
1472	8369	9557	8370	10/25-12/46	⊃*4481*	
1473	8371	9489	8372	10/25-10/40		
1474	8373	9527	8374	10/25-10/46	⊃*4254*	
1475	8375	9529	8376	10/25- 42		
1475	8375	9529	*8282*	42-05/47	⊃**4482**	☞
1476	8377	9568	8378	10/25-08/40		
1477	8379	9556	8380	10/25-04/47	⊃**4483**[1]	
1478	8381	9500	8382	10/25-05/47	⊃**4484**	
1479	8383	9549	8384	10/25-11/49		
1480	8385	9515	8386	11/25-03/47	⊃**4485**	
1481	8387	9533	8388	11/25-11/49		
1482	8389	9567	8390	11/25-11/49		
1483	8391	9508	8392	11/25-03/46		
1483	*8279*	9508	8392	03/46-05/47	⊃**4486**	☞
1484	8393	9520	8394	11/25-12/46	⊃**4487**	
1485	8395	9516	8396	11/25-01/47	⊃**4488**	
1486	8397	9569	8398	11/25-05/47	⊃**4489**	
1487	8399	9525	8400	11/25-11/49		
1488	8401	9491	8402	11/25-12/46	⊃**4490**	
1489	8403	9494	8404	12/25-10/46	⊃**4491**	
1490	8405	9521	8406	12/25-11/46	⊃**4492**	
1491	8407	9530	8408	12/25-06/47	⊃**4493**	
1492	8409	9510	8410	12/25-11/49		
1493	8411	9578	8412	12/25-05/47	⊃**4494**	
1494	8413	9576	8414	12/25-11/49		
1495	8415	9575	8416	12/25-11/49		

3-SUB
SR Steel-panelled Suburban Units
660-750V dc third rail
1496-1524

These units were part of the batch of 55 units built new in 1925 to provide a pool of stock to allow the conversions of steam-hauled stock to take place.

They were built on standard frames for the Eastern Section and were numbered 1496-1524. Some of these worked temporarily as 4-car units when first built.

Temporary Formations

	DMBT	TC	TC	DMBT	
1496	8417	9583	9582	8418	07/25-09/25
1497	8419	9592	9594	8420	07/25-09/25
1499	8423	9581	9584	8424	07/25-09/25
1500	8425	9601	9603	8426	07/25-09/25
1501	8427	9600	9604	8428	07/25-09/25
1502	8429	9602	9598	8430	07/25-09/25
1503	8431	9608	9606	8432	07/25-09/25
1504	8433	9605	9607	8434	07/25-09/25
1505	8435	9597	9595	8436	07/25-09/25
1506	8437	9586	9588	8438	07/25-09/25
1507	8439	9580	9587	8440	07/25-09/25

	DMBT	TC	DMBT			
1496	8417	9583	8418	09/25-09/45	⊃**4326**	
1497	8419	9595	8420	09/25-03/46	⊃**4327**	
1498	8421	9591	8422	09/25-07/45	⊃**4328**	
1499	8423	9584	8424	09/25-		
1499	*8428*	9584	8424	-06/45	⊃**4329**	☞
1500	8425	9603	8426	09/25-10/45	⊃**4330**	
1501	8427	9604	8428	09/25-		
1501	8427	9604	*8423*	-09/45	⊃**4331**	☞
1502	8429	9598	8430	09/25-06/45	⊃**4332**	
1503	8431	9606	8432	09/25-		
1503	*8460*	9606	8432	-04/46	⊃**4333**	☞
1504	8433	9607	8434	09/25-08/45	⊃**4334**	
1505	8435	9597	8436	09/25-03/46	⊃**4335**	
1506	8437	9588	8438	09/25-09/45	⊃**4336**	
1507	8439	9587	8440	09/25-09/45	⊃**4337**	
1508	8441	9596	8442	07/25-08/45	⊃**4338**	
1509	8443	9600	8444	07/25-07/45	⊃**4339**	
1510	8445	9589	8446	07/25-04/46	⊃**4340**	
1511	8447	9599	8448	07/25-07/45	⊃**4341**	
1512	8449	9582	8450	08/25-08/45	⊃**4342**	
1513	8451	9594	8452	08/25-06/45	⊃**4343**	
1514	8453	9592	8454	08/25-03/46	⊃**4344**	
1515	8455	9608	8456	08/25-03/46	⊃**4345**	
1516	8457	9586	8458	08/25-06/45	⊃**4346**	
1517	8459	9590	8460	09/25-		
1517	8459	9590	*8431*	-08/45	⊃**4347**	☞
1518	8461	9580	8462	09/25-	⊃**4348**	
1519	8463	9581	8464	09/25-04/46	⊃**4349**	
1520	8465	9593	8466	09/25-11/40		
1520	8465	9593	*8486*	11/40-11/45	⊃**4350**	☞
1521	8467	9601	8468	10/25-09/45	⊃**4351**	
1522	8469	9602	8470	10/25-07/45	⊃**4352**	
1523	8471	9585	8472	10/25-09/45	⊃**4353**	
1524	8473	9605	8474	10/25-06/45	⊃**4354**	

3-SUB
SER-bodied Suburban Units
660-750V dc third rail
1525-1534

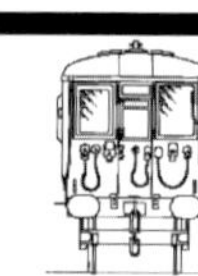

See 1401-1495 for details.

	DMBT	TC	DMBT		
1525	8475	9609	8476	06/26-02/48	⊃**4442**[2]
1526	8477	9612	8478	06/26-05/47	⊃**4495**
1527	8479	9611	8480	06/26-04/47	⊃**4496**
1528	8481	9610	8482	06/26-08/49	
1529	8483	9617	8484	06/26-05/47	⊃**4497**
1530	8485	9618	8486	06/26-11/40	
1531	8487	9613	8488	06/26-01/47	⊃**4498**
1532	8489	9614	8490	06/26-03/47	⊃**4499**
1533	8491	9616	8492	06/26-04/47	⊃**4500**
1534	8493	9615	8494	06/26-06/47	⊃**4501**

3-SUB
LSWR-bodied Suburban Units
660-750V dc third rail
1579-1599

1579-1599 were additional units converted from LSWR stock at Eastleigh in 1934-37 for services on the Western Section.

	DMBT	TC	DMBT		
1579	9789	9671	9790	08/37-12/46	⊃**4424**
1580	9791	9672	9792	09/37-11/46	⊃**4425**
1581	9793	9673	9794	10/37-02/47	⊃**4426**
1582	9795	9674	9796	10/37-01/47	⊃**4427**
1583	9797	9759	9798	11/37-03/47	⊃**4428**
1584	9799	9760	9800	12/37-02/47	⊃**4429**
1585	9831	9766	9832	11/35-11/46	⊃**4411**
1586	9833	9767	9834	11/35-02/47	⊃**4412**
1587	9835	9768	9836	11/35-10/46	⊃**4413**
1588	9837	9769	9838	10/35-05/47	⊃**4414**
1589	9839	9770	9840	10/35-04/47	⊃**4415**
1590	9841	9771	9842	10/35-04/47	⊃**4416**
1591	9843	9772	9844	10/35-06/47	⊃**4417**
1592	9845	9773	9846	09/35-12/46	⊃**4418**
1593	9847	9774	9848	09/35-06/47	⊃**4419**
1594	9849	9775	9850	09/35-03/47	⊃**4420**
1595	9851	9761	9852	08/34-02/47	⊃**4421**
1596	9853	9762	9854	08/34-11/46	⊃**4422**
1597	9855	9763	9856	08/34-04/47	⊃**4423**
1598	9857	9764	9858	07/34-06/44	
1599	9859	9765	9860	07/34-01/49	⊃**4518**

3-SUB
LBSCR-bodied Suburban Unit
660-750V dc third rail
1600

See 1801 for details.

	DMBT	TC	DMBT			
1600	8594	9670	8595	ex 1801	34-*08/47*	➲**4607**[1]

3-SUB
SER-bodied Suburban Units
660-750V dc third rail
1601-1630

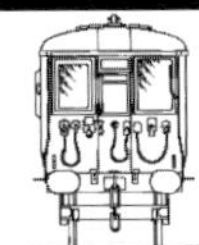

1601-1630 entered service in 1928 for use on the Central Section. Again these were converted from SECR stock.

	DMBT	TC	DMBT		
1601	8495	9619	8496	11/27-*02/49*	➲**4439**[2]
1602	8497	9620	8498	11/27-*12/46*	➲**4502**
1603	8499	9621	8500	11/27-*01/47*	➲**4503**
1604	8501	9622	8502	11/27-05/49	➲**4587**
1605	8503	9623	8504	11/27-*05/47*	➲**4504**
1606	8505	9624	8506	11/27-11/49	
1607	8507	9625	8508	*12/27*-11/49	
1608	8509	9626	8510	*12/27-04/47*	➲**4505**
1609	8511	9627	8512	*12/27-04/48*	➲**4588**
1610	8513	9628	8514	*12/27*-02/44	
1610	*8710*	9628	8514	02/44-*02/49*	➲**4483**[2]
1611	8515	9629	8516	*12/27-11/46*	➲**4506**
1612	8517	9630	8518	*12/27*-05/41	
1613	8519	9631	8520	*01/28-05/47*	➲**4507**
1614	8521	9632	8522	*01/28*-11/49	
1615	8523	9633	8524	*01/28-12/46*	➲**4508**
1616	8525	9634	8526	*01/28*-11/49	
1617	8527	9635	8528	*01/28-01/49*	➲**4589**
1618	8529	9636	8530	*02/28-04/47*	➲**4509**
1619	8531	9637	8532	*02/28*-11/49	
1620	8533	9638	8534	*02/28-03/48*	➲**4580**
1621	8535	9639	8536	*02/28*-06/44	
1621	8535	9639	*8513*	06/44-*01/47*	➲**4510**
1622	8537	9640	8538	*02/28*-11/49	
1623	8539	9641	8540	*02/28-11/46*	➲**4511**
1624	8541	9642	8542	*02/28-01/47*	➲**4512**
1625	8543	9643	8544	*03/28-04/47*	➲**4513**
1626	8545	9644	8546	*03/28-11/46*	➲**4514**
1627	8547	9645	8548	*03/28*-11/49	
1628	8549	9646	8550	*03/28-01/47*	➲**4515**
1629	8551	9647	8552	*03/28-06/47*	➲**4516**
1630	8553	9648	8554	*03/28-02/48*	➲**4586**

3-SUB
LBSCR-bodied Suburban Units
660-750V dc third rail
1631-1657

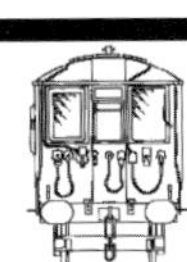

1631-1657 were converted at Ashford and Brighton from former LBSCR stock in 1929, followed by 1797-1801 to the same design in 1932.

	DMBT	TC	DMBT		
1631	8617	9675	8618	09/27-*04/48*	➲**4585**
1632	8619	9676	8620	10/27-11/48	
1633	8621	9677	8622	07/28-11/42	
1633	8621	9677	*8877*	11/42-11/48	
1634	8623	9678	8624	07/28-*08/47*	➲**4603**[1]
1635	8625	9679	8626	07/28-11/48	
1636	8627	9680	8628	07/28-*08/47*	➲**4605**[1]
1637	8629	9681	8630	07/28-*05/48*	➲**4522**
1638	8631	9682	8632	07/28-*02/48*	➲**4523**
1639	8633	9683	8634	08/28-*02/48*	➲**4524**
1640	8635	9684	8636	08/28-11/48	
1641	8637	9685	8638	08/28-10/48	
1642	8639	9686	8640	08/28-*04/48*	➲**4525**
1643	8641	9687	8642	09/28-*08/47*	➲**4601**[1]
1644	8643	9688	8644	09/28-*03/48*	➲**4562**
1645	8645	9689	8646	09/28-*08/47*	➲**4604**[1]
1646	8647	9690	8648	09/28-11/48	
1647	8649	9691	8650	10/28-*08/47*	➲**4610**
1648	8651	9692	8652	10/28-*08/47*	➲**4606**[1]
1649	8653	9693	8654	10/28-02/48	➲**4257**
1650	8655	9694	8656	10/28-*03/48*	➲**4575**
1651	8657	9695	8658	11/28-*02/48*	➲**4608**
1652	8659	9696	8660	11/28-*08/47*	➲**4613**
1653	8661	9697	8662	11/28-*08/47*	➲**4614**
1654	8663	9698	8664	12/28-11/48	
1655	8665	9699	8666	12/28-11/48	
1656	8667	9700	8668	05/28-11/48	
1657	8669	9701	8670	04/28-01/49	

3-SUB
LSWR-bodied Suburban Units
6660-750V dc third rail
1658-1701

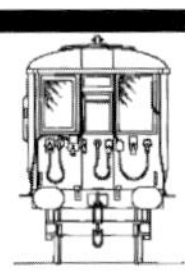

1658-1701 were converted from LSWR suburban stock in 1928 for working on the Western Section and 1773-1785 followed to the same design in 1930.

	DMBT	TC	DMBC		
1658	8179	9307	8793	09/27-08/46	➲**4172**
1659	8180	9308	8794	*01/28*-08/48	➲**4194**
1660	8181	9309	8795	*01/28-08/48*	➲**4193**
1661	8182	9310	8796	*01/28-05/47*	➲**4174**
1662	8183	9311	8797	*01/28-02/47*	➲**4177**
1663	8184	9312	8798	*01/28-12/47*	➲**4185**
1664	8185	9313	8799	*01/28-07/47*	➲**4180**
1665	8186	9314	8800	*01/28-08/47*	➲**4181**
1666	8187	9315	8801	*01/28-08/48*	➲**4192**
1667	8188	9316	8802	*01/28-06/45*	➲*4253*
1668	8189	9317	8803	*01/28-* 48	➲**4188**
1669	8190	9318	8804	*01/28-12/47*	➲**4249**
1670	8191	9319	8805	*02/28-10/47*	➲**4184**
1671	8192	9320	8806	*02/28-02/47*	➲**4173**
1672	8193	9321	8807	*02/28-* 48	➲**4187**
1673	8194	9322	8808	*02/28-10/47*	➲*4255*
1674	8195	9323	8809	*02/28-09/48*	➲**4189**
1675	8196	9324	8810	*02/28-08/47*	➲**4183**
1676	8197	9325	8811	*02/28-05/47*	➲**4178**
1677	8198	9326	8812	*02/28-07/47*	➲**4179**
1678	8199	9327	8813	*02/28-09/48*	➲**4250**[2]
1679	8200	9328	8814	*02/28*-12/41	
1679	8200	9328	*9903*	12/41-08/47	➲**4521**
1680	8201	9329	8815	*02/28-08/47*	➲**4182**
1681	8202	9330	8816	*03/28-09/48*	➲**4242**
1682	8203	9331	8817	*03/28-02/47*	➲**4175**
1683	8204	9332	8818	*03/28-05/48*	➲**4186**
1684	8205	9333	8819	*03/28-05/47*	➲**4176**
1685	8206	9334	8820	*03/28-07/48*	➲**4191**
1686	8207	9335	8821	*03/28-01/43*	➲**4236**
1687	8208	9336	8822	*03/28-11/42*	➲**4245**
1688	8209	9337	8823	*03/28*-11/42	
1688	8209	9337	*9809*	11/42-12/47	➲**4239**
1689	8210	9338	8824	*03/28-11/47*	➲**4237**
1690	8211	9339	8825	*03/28-08/48*	➲**4248**
1691	8212	9340	8826	*03/28-07/48*	➲**4243**
1692	8213	9341	8827	*04/28*-06/44	
1692	8213	*9404*	*8783*	08/44-09/44	➲**4155**
1693	8214	9342	8828	*04/28-04/48*	➲**4244**
1694	8215	9343	8829	*04/28-07/48*	➲**4247**
1695	8216	9344	8830	*04/28*-07/38	
1695	8216	*9376*	8830	07/38-05/47	➲**4235**
1696	8217	9345	8831	*04/28-08/47*	➲**4572**
1697	8218	9346	8832	*04/28*-10/40	
1697	8218	9346	*8779*	12/40-03/48	➲**4246**
1698	8219	9347	8833	*04/28-10/47*	➲**4240**
1699	8220	9348	8834	*04/28-10/47*	➲**4238**
1700	8221	9349	8835	*04/28-02/48*	➲**4241**
1701	8222	9350	8836	*04/28-03/47*	➲*4255*

3-SUB
LBSCR-bodied Suburban Units
660-750V dc third rail
1702-1716

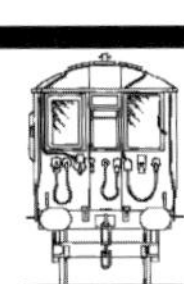

1702-1716 were LBSCR vehicles converted to provide units for the 1928-1930 electrification.

	DMBT	TC	DMBC		
1702	8671	9702	8837	10/27-09/48	
1703	8672	9703	8838	10/27-*02/48*	➲**4256**
1704	8673	9704	8839	10/27-*03/48*	➲**4576**
1705	8674	9705	8840	10/27-11/48	
1706	8675	9706	8841	07/28-*05/48*	➲**4577**
1707	8676	9707	8842	07/28-*08/47*	➲**4602**[1]
1708	8677	9708	8843	08/28-*01/49*	
1709	8678	9709	8844	08/28-*08/43*	➲**4250**[1]
1710	8679	9710	8845	09/28-07/48	

1711	8680	9711	8846	09/28-11/48		
1712	8681	9712	8847	10/28-08/48		
1713	8682	9713	8848	10/28-*04/48*	➲**4578**	
1714	8683	9714	8849	11/28-*03/48*	➲**4563**	
1715	8684	9715	8850	12/28-*03/48*	➲**4581**	
1716	8685	9716	8851	12/28-*03/48*	➲**4582**	

3-SUB

LBSCR-bodied Suburban Units (ex-AC Stock)
660-750V dc third rail
1717-1772

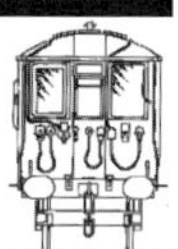

1717-1772 were LBSCR vehicles converted to provide more units for the 1928-1930 electrification. These were all converted from ex-ac stock of different types.

	DMBT	TC	DMBC			
1717	8686	9717	8852	01/29-*03/48*	➲**4566**	
1718	8687	9718	8853	01/29-*04/48*	➲**4567**	
1719	8688	9719	8854	02/29-*01/48*	➲**4568**	
1720	8689	9720	8855	02/29-08/47	➲**4569**	
1721	8690	9721	8856	02/29-*02/48*	➲**4570**	
1722	8691	9722	8857	02/29-04/41		
1723	8692	9723	8858	02/29-*01/48*	➲**4571**	
1724	8693	9724	8859	05/29-08/47	➲**4527**	
1725	8694	9725	8860	05/29-*02/48*	➲**4528**	
1726	8695	9726	8861	06/29-*02/48*	➲**4529**	
1727	8696	9727	8862	06/29-*04/48*	➲**4530**	
1728	8697	9728	8863	06/29-06/44		
1728	8697	*9490*	*8691*	45-08/47	➲**4520**	☞
1729	8698	9729	8864	06/29-08/47	➲**4531**	
1730	8699	9730	8865	09/29-*10/46*	➲*4254*	
1731	8700	9731	8866	09/29-08/47	➲*4532*	
1732	8701	9732	8867	07/29-03/49	➲**4533**	
1733	8702	9733	8868	07/29-*01/48*	➲**4534**	
1734	8703	9734	8869	08/29-*07/48*	➲**4535**	
1735	8704	9735	8870	08/29-*01/49*	➲**4536**	
1736	8705	9736	8871	08/29-03/44	➲**4251**	
1737	8706	9737	8872	06/29-08/47	➲**4537**	
1738	8707	9738	8873	06/29-*04/48*	➲**4538**	
1739	8708	9739	8874	06/29-*01/49*	➲**4539**	
1740	8709	9740	8875	06/29-*05/48*	➲**4540**	
1741	8710	9741	8876	06/29-02/44		
1742	8711	9742	8877	06/29-12/41		
1743	8712	9743	8878	07/29-*07/48*	➲**4541**	
1744	8713	9744	8879	07/29-*07/48*	➲**4542**	
1745	8714	9745	8880	08/29-10/40		
1746	8715	9746	8881	08/29-*02/48*	➲**4543**	
1747	8716	9747	8882	08/29-*03/48*	➲**4544**	
1748	8717	9748	8883	08/29-*03/48*	➲**4545**	
1749	8718	9749	8884	08/29-*07/48*	➲**4546**	
1750	8719	9461	8885	01/30-*05/48*	➲**4547**	
1751	8720	9462	8886	01/30-*03/48*	➲**4548**	
1752	8721	9463	8887	02/30-08/47	➲**4549**	
1753	8722	9464	8888	02/30-*01/48*	➲**4550**	
1754	8731	9465	8889	01/30-08/47	➲**4551**	
1755	8732	9466	8890	01/30-08/47	➲**4552**	
1756	8733	9467	8891	01/30-*02/48*	➲**4553**	
1757	8734	9468	8892	01/30-*07/48*	➲**4554**	
1758	8735	9469	8893	02/30-02/48		
1759	8736	9470	8894	02/30-08/47	➲**4556**	
1760	8737	9471	8895	02/30-11/40		
1761	8738	9472	8896	03/30-08/44	➲**4252**	
1762	8739	9473	8897	03/30-*03/48*	➲**4555**	
1763	8740	9474	8898	03/30-05/48		
1764	8741	9475	8899	03/30-05/48	➲**4557**	
1765	8742	9476	8900	03/30-*02/48*	➲**4558**	
1766	8743	9477	9801	03/30-08/47	➲**4561**	
1767	8744	9478	9802	04/30-*07/48*	➲**4559**	
1768	8745	9479	9803	04/30-*05/47*	➲**4560**	
1769	8746	9480	9804	06/30-08/47	➲**4564**	
1770	8747	9481	9805	06/30-10/47		
1771	8748	9482	9806	06/30-11/48		
1771	*8877*	9482	9806	11/48-02/49	➲**4590**	☞
1772	8749	9483	9807	06/30-*07/48*	➲**4565**	

3-SUB

LSWR-bodied Suburban Units
660-750V dc third rail
1773-1801

1773-1785 were converted from LSWR suburban stock in 1930 for working on the Western Section. They were built to the same design as 1658-1701.

1782 remained in departmental service for many years as a mobile class-room for CMEE staff, numbered S10 and later 053.

	DMBT	TC	DMBC			
1773	8555	9649	9808	*06/30-05/47*	➲**4401**	
1774	8556	9650	9809	*06/30*-11/42	➲*4253*	
1775	8557	9651	9810	*06/30-02/47*	➲**4402**	
1776	8558	9652	9811	*07/30-02/48*	➲**4519**	
1777	8559	9653	9812	*07/30-06/47*	➲**4403**	
1778	8560	9654	9813	*07/30-02/47*	➲**4404**	
1779	8561	9655	9814	*08/30-12/46*	➲**4405**	
1780	8562	9656	9815	*08/30-01/49*	➲**4573**	
1781	8563	9657	9816	*08/30-06/48*	➲**4574**	
1782	8564	9658	9817	*08/30*-08/47	➲**4579**	
1783	8223	9301	9822	*11/30-02/48*	➲**4594**	
1784	8224	9302	9823	*11/30-01/48*	➲**4517**	
1785	8225	9303	9824	*11/30*-11/40		
1785	8225	9303	*8895*	11/40-*07/48*	➲**4526**	☞

1786-1796 were converted from LSWR six-wheeled suburban vehicles originally built in 1901.

	DMBT	TC	DMBC			
1786	8226	9304	8565	*01/31-01/47*	➲**4406**[1]	
1787	8566	9305	8567	*01/31-10/46*	➲**4407**	
1788	8568	9306	8569	*01/31-02/47*	➲**4408**	
1789	8570	9484	8571	*01/31-10/46*	➲**4409**	
1790	8572	9659	8573	*01/31*-08/48	➲**4190**	
1791	8574	9660	8575	*02/31-02/49*	➲**4591**	
1792	8576	9661	8577	*02/31-02/49*	➲**4592**	
1793	8578	9662	8579	*02/31*-05/49	➲**4593**	
1794	8580	9663	8581	*02/31-03/47*	➲**4410**	
1795	8582	9664	8583	11/31-*01/47*	➲**4430**	
1796	8584	9665	8585	11/31-*01/47*	➲**4431**	

1797-1801 were converted at Ashford and Brighton from former LBSCR stock in 1932, to the same design as 1631-1657. 1801 was renumbered 1600 in 1934.

	DMBT	TC	DMBC			
1797	8586	9666	8587	01/32-*03/48*	➲**4583**	
1798	8588	9667	8589	01/32-*02/48*	➲**4584**	
1799	8590	9668	8591	01/32-05/41		
1799	*9876*	9668	8591	06/41-10/46		☞
1800	8592	9669	8593	01/32-05/48		
1801	8594	9670	8595	01/32- 34	➲**1600**	

2-SL

South London Units (ex-AC Stock)
660-750V dc third rail
1801-1808

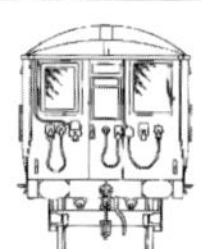

When the South London line was converted to third-rail from overhead working, the sixteen original driving vehicles were converted to form eight new two-car units. Originally built in 1908/9, they entered service in their new form in May 1929. They were distinctive units as they had a lowered roof section over the cab where the collector bow had previously been located.

They were numbered 1901-1908 but this was altered to 1801-1808 in 1934.

	DMBT	DTC	
1801	8723	9751	04/34-10/54
1802	8724	9752	04/34-06/51
1803	8725	9753	04/34-09/54
1804	8726	9754	04/34-09/54
1805	8727	9755	04/34-10/54
1806	8728	9756	04/34-09/54
1807	8729	9757	04/34-10/40
1808	8730	9758	04/34-09/54

2-WIM
Wimbledon-West Croydon Units (ex-AC Stock)
660-750V dc third rail
1809-1812

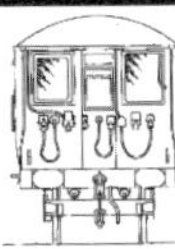

These four 2-car units were formed in 1929 for working the Wimbledon-West Croydon line, although it was not uncommon for them to also appear on the South London Line.

They were formed from the eight first-class trailers, originally built in 1909 for the South London Line. They were taken out of service on that line in 1910 and were used for the next 19 years as locomotive hauled firsts on the Brighton main line. They were converted back to electric stock in 1929 and fitted with full-width driving cabs, with one car-of each unit being a driving motor and one as a driving trailer.

They were numbered 1909-1912 but this was altered to 1809-1812 in 1934.

	DMBC	*DTT*	
1809	9818	9951	04/34-*01/54*
1810	9819	9952	04/34-10/54
1811	9820	9953	04/34-10/54
1812	9821	9954	04/34-08/54

2-NOL
Suburban Units (no toilets)
660-750V dc third rail
1813-1890

The 2-NOL (two-car non-lavatory suburban) units 1813-1890 were built in 1934-36 by putting existing LSWR hauled stock bodies onto new frames. The units originally worked on the Brighton-West Worthing routes and then began running on the Horsted Keynes to Seaford and Ore Line.

Later built units took over services on the Waterloo to Windsor & Weybridge lines. When the final eight were built they were fitted with electro-pneumatic control equipment for the first time on Southern EMUs. Some units had their power equipment removed during the war and were operated as trailer sets marshalled between two 4-SUB units. After 1943 the guard's van in these units was enlarged by removal of the adjacent third-class coupé.

All the units were returned to powered status after the war. 1813-1850 had the first class seating reinstated and worked mainly on the Central Section, while 1851-1890 became third-class only units, working mainly on the Waterloo-Windsor line services.

The last of these reliable units was withdrawn in 1959, and their underframes were re-used for new stock.

	DMBT	*DTC*	
1813	9861	9940	11/34-03/59
1814	9862	9941	11/34-02/59
1815	9863	9942	11/34-05/57
1815	*8605*	9942	07/57-07/59
1816	9864	9943	11/34-02/59
1817	9865	9944	11/34-07/59
1818	9866	9945	12/34-07/59
1819	9867	9946	12/34-01/51
1819	9867	*9975*	05/51-*05/58*
1820	9868	9947	12/34-07/59
1821	9869	9948	12/34-02/59
1822	9870	9949	12/34-07/59
1823	9871	9950	12/34-10/58
1824	9872	9964	01/35-02/59
1825	9873	9965	01/35-03/59
1826	9874	9963	01/35-08/59
1827	9875	9962	01/35-06/59
1828	9876	9961	01/35-05/41
1829	9877	9966	01/35-07/59
1830	9878	9967	01/35-08/59
1831	9879	9968	01/35-02/59
1832	9880	9969	02/35-07/59
1833	9881	9970	02/35-06/58
1834	9882	9971	02/35-06/59
1835	9883	9972	02/35-02/58
1836	9884	9973	02/35-06/59
1837	9885	9974	02/35-03/59
1838	9886	9975	02/35-*05/51*
1839	9887	9976	02/35-07/59
1840	9888	9977	03/35-07/59
1841	9889	9978	03/35-02/59
1842	9890	9979	03/35-07/59
1843	9891	9980	03/35-02/58
1844	9892	9981	03/35-06/59
1845	9893	9982	03/35-03/59
1846	9894	9983	03/35-03/59
1847	9895	9984	03/35-02/59
1848	9896	9985	04/35-06/59
1849	9897	9986	04/35-03/59
1850	9898	9987	04/35-03/59
1851	9899	9988	04/35-04/57
1852	9900	9989	04/35-12/57
1853	9901	9990	04/35-12/55
1854	9902	9991	04/35-11/57
1855	9903	9992	04/35-11/41
1856	9904	9993	04/35-07/57
1857	9905	9994	05/35-05/57
1858	9906	9995	05/35-04/57
1859	9907	9996	05/35-04/57
1860	9908	9997	05/35-09/57
1861	9909	9998	05/35-06/57
1862	9910	9999	05/35-06/57
1863	8596	9920	02/36-09/57
1864	8597	9921	02/36-09/57
1865	8598	9922	02/36-01/58
1866	8599	9923	02/36-09/57
1867	8600	9924	02/36-06/57
1868	8601	9925	02/36-12/57
1869	8602	9926	02/36-06/57
1870	8603	9927	02/36-07/56
1871	8604	9928	02/36-07/56
1872	8605	9929	02/36-07/57
1873	8606	9930	03/36-07/57
1874	8607	9931	03/36-04/57
1875	8608	9932	03/36-04/57
1876	8609	9933	03/36-07/57
1877	8610	9934	03/36-07/56
1878	8611	9935	03/36-07/56
1879	8612	9936	03/36-08/57
1880	8613	9937	03/36-10/57
1881	8614	9938	03/36-05/57
1882	8615	9939	03/36-09/57
1883	9781	9913	07/36-01/58
1884	9782	9914	07/36-06/57
1885	9783	9915	07/36-05/57
1886	9784	9916	07/36-12/57
1887	9785	9917	07/36-05/57
1888	9786	9918	07/36-09/57
1889	9787	9912	07/36-06/57
1890	9788	9919	07/36-02/58

2-SL
South London Units (ex-AC Stock)
660-750V dc third rail
1901-1908

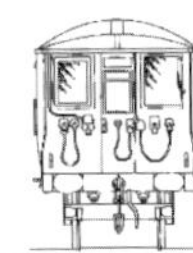

See 1801-1808 for details.

	DMBT	*DTC*		
1901	8723	9751	05/29-04/34	**➲1801**
1902	8724	9752	04/29-04/34	**➲1802**
1903	8725	9753	04/29-04/34	**➲1803**
1904	8726	9754	04/29-04/34	**➲1804**
1905	8727	9755	05/29-04/34	**➲1805**
1906	8728	9756	05/29-04/34	**➲1806**
1907	8729	9757	05/29-04/34	**➲1807**
1908	8730	9758	04/29-04/34	**➲1808**

2-WIM
Wimbledon-West Croydon Units (ex-AC Stock)
660-750V dc third rail
1909-1912

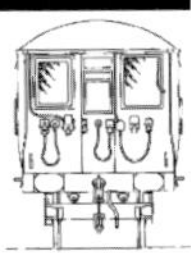

See 1809-1812 for details.

	DMBC	*DTT*		
1909	9818	9951	06/30-04/34	**➲1809**
1910	9819	9952	06/30-04/34	**➲1810**
1911	9820	9953	06/30-04/34	**➲1811**
1912	9821	9954	06/30-04/34	**➲1812**

Class 401 2-BIL
Outer-Suburban Units (two toilets)
660-750V dc third rail
1890-1920

See 2001-2030 for details.

	DMBTL	DTCL		
1890	10567	12101	02/35-01/36	➲**1900**
1891	10568	12102	*03/35*-01/37	➲**2001**
1892	10569	12103	*03/35*-01/37	➲**2002**
1893	10570	12104	*03/35*-01/37	➲**2003**
1894	10571	12105	*03/35*-01/37	➲**2004**
1895	10572	12106	*03/35*-01/37	➲**2005**
1896	10573	12107	*03/35*-01/37	➲**2006**
1897	10574	12108	*03/35*-01/37	➲**2007**
1898	10575	12109	*03/35*-01/37	➲**2008**
1899	10576	12110	*03/35*-01/37	➲**2009**
1900	10567	12101	01/36-01/37	➲**2010**

1901-1920 were renumbered in the 2011 series before entering service.

	DMBTL	DTCL		
1901	10577	12034	*08/36*-01/37	➲**2011**
1902	10578	12035	*08/36*-01/37	➲**2012**
1903	10579	12036	*08/36*-01/37	➲**2013**
1904	10580	12037	*08/36*-01/37	➲**2014**
1905	10581	12038	*08/36*-01/37	➲**2015**
1906	10582	12039	*08/36*-01/37	➲**2016**
1907	10583	12040	*08/36*-01/37	➲**2017**
1908	10584	12041	*08/36*-01/37	➲**2018**
1909	10585	12042	*09/36*-01/37	➲**2019**
1910	10586	12043	*09/36*-01/37	➲**2020**
1911	10587	12044	*09/36*-01/37	➲**2021**
1912	10588	12045	*09/36*-01/37	➲**2022**
1913	10589	12046	*09/36*-01/37	➲**2023**
1914	10590	12047	*09/36*-01/37	➲**2024**
1915	10591	12048	*09/36*-01/37	➲**2025**
1916	10592	12049	*10/36*-01/37	➲**2026**
1917	10593	12050	*10/36*-01/37	➲**2027**
1918	10594	12051	*10/36*-01/37	➲**2028**
1919	10595	12052	*10/36*-01/37	➲**2029**
1920	10596	12053	*10/36*-01/37	➲**2030**

4-LAV
Brighton Line Express Units
660-750V dc third rail
1921-1953

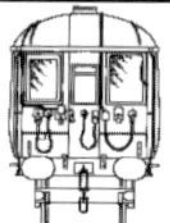

See 2921-2953 for details.

	DMBT	TCL	TC	DMBT		
1921	10501	12002	11501	10502	*07/31*-01/37	➲**2921**
1922	10503	12004	11502	10504	*07/31*-01/37	➲**2922**
1923	10505	12013	11517	10506	*07/31*-01/37	➲**2923**
1924	10507	12005	11506	10508	*07/31*-01/37	➲**2924**
1925	10509	12003	11510	10510	*07/31*-01/37	➲**2925**
1926	10511	12001	11509	10512	*08/31*-01/37	➲**2926**
1927	10513	12006	11504	10514	*08/31*-01/37	➲**2927**
1928	10515	12012	11508	10516	*08/31*-01/37	➲**2928**
1929	10517	12007	11503	10518	*08/31*-01/37	➲**2929**
1930	10519	12008	11518	10520	*08/31*-01/37	➲**2930**
1931	10521	12020	11520	10522	*09/31*-01/37	➲**2931**
1932	10523	12010	11507	10524	*09/31*-01/37	➲**2932**
1933	10525	12016	11516	10526	*09/31*-01/37	➲**2933**
1934	10527	12011	11514	10528	*09/31*-01/37	➲**2934**
1935	10529	12014	11513	10530	*09/31*-01/37	➲**2935**
1936	10531	12019	11515	10532	*10/31*-01/37	➲**2936**
1937	10533	12009	11519	10534	*10/31*-01/37	➲**2937**
1938	10535	12017	11511	10536	*10/31*-01/37	➲**2938**
1939	10537	12015	11505	10538	*10/31*-01/37	➲**2939**
1940	10539	12018	11512	10540	*10/31*-01/37	➲**2940**
1941	10541	12021	11521	10542	*10/31*-01/37	➲**2941**
1942	10543	12022	11522	10544	*11/31*-01/37	➲**2942**
1943	10545	12023	11523	10546	*12/31*-01/37	➲**2943**
1944	10547	12024	11524	10548	*01/32*-01/37	➲**2944**
1945	10549	12025	11525	10550	*01/32*-01/37	➲**2945**
1946	10551	12026	11526	10552	*02/32*-01/37	➲**2946**
1947	10553	12027	11527	10554	*03/32*-01/37	➲**2947**
1948	10555	12028	11528	10556	*04/32*-01/37	➲**2948**
1949	10557	12029	11529	10558	*05/32*-01/37	➲**2949**
1950	10559	12030	11530	10560	*06/32*-01/37	➲**2950**
1951	10561	12031	11531	10562	*07/32*-01/37	➲**2951**
1952	10563	12032	11532	10564	*08/32*-01/37	➲**2952**
1953	10565	12033	11533	10566	*09/32*-01/37	➲**2953**

Class 401 2-BIL
Outer-Suburban Units (two toilets)
660-750V dc third rail
1954-1971

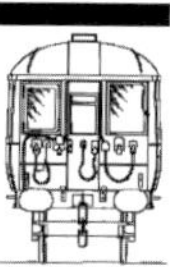

See 2031-2048 for details. These units were renumbered before entering service.

	DMBTL	DTCL		
1954	10597	12054	*10/36*-01/37	➲**2031**
1955	10598	12055	*10/36*-01/37	➲**2032**
1956	10599	12056	*11/36*-01/37	➲**2033**
1957	10600	12057	*11/36*-01/37	➲**2034**
1958	10601	12058	*11/36*-01/37	➲**2035**
1959	10602	12059	*11/36*-01/37	➲**2036**
1960	10603	12060	*11/36*-01/37	➲**2037**
1961	10604	12061	*11/36*-01/37	➲**2038**
1962	10605	12062	*11/36*-01/37	➲**2039**
1963	10606	12063	*12/36*-01/37	➲**2040**
1964	10607	12064	*12/36*-01/37	➲**2041**
1965	10608	12065	*12/36*-01/37	➲**2042**
1966	10609	12066	*12/36*-01/37	➲**2043**
1967	10610	12067	*12/36*-01/37	➲**2044**
1968	10611	12068	*12/36*-01/37	➲**2045**
1969	10612	12069	*12/36*-01/37	➲**2046**
1970	10613	12070	*12/36*-01/37	➲**2047**
1971	10614	12071	01/37-01/37	➲**2048**

Prototype main-line unit
Brighton Line Express Unit Prototype
660-750V dc third rail
2001

When the Brighton Line was electrified a number of six-car express units were built, most of them containing a Pullman car. Designed for a 75mph top speed they were gangwayed within the units. Power cars were all steel construction and were built by outside contractors and the intermediate trailers were built with wooden framing and roofs at Eastleigh.

A pair of prototype driving motor vehicles were built in 1931. They ran with some steam-stock intermediate trailers and a Pullman car and the unit was numbered 2001. The test unit was disbanded and 1932 and the driving cars later reappeared in 6-CIT units.

	DMBTO	DMBTO	
2001	11001	11002	11/31-11/32

6-PUL
Brighton Line Express Pullman Units
660-750V dc third rail
2001-2020

See 3001-3020 for details.

	DMBTO	TTK	TCK	TPCK	TCK	DMBTO		
2001	11043	10017	11783	Anne	11784	11044	*12/32*-01/37	➲**3001**
2002	11004	10002	11754	Rita	11753	11003	*09/32*-01/37	➲**3002**
2003	11006	10003	11755	Grace	11756	11005	*09/32*-01/37	➲**3003**
2004	11008	10006	11761	Elinor	11762	11007	*10/32*-01/37	➲**3004**
2005	11010	10008	11766	Ida	11765	11009	*10/32*-01/37	➲**3005**
2006	11012	10011	11772	Rose	11771	11011	*11/32*-01/37	➲**3006**
2007	11014	10013	11775	Violet	11776	11013	*11/32*-01/37	➲**3007**
2008	11045	10019	11788	Lorna	11787	11046	*12/32*-01/37	➲**3008**
2009	11018	10010	11769	Alice	11770	11017	*10/32*-01/37	➲**3009**
2010	11020	10016	11781	Daisy	11782	11019	*11/32*-01/37	➲**3010**
2011	11022	10018	11785	Naomi	11786	11021	*12/32*-01/37	➲**3011**
2012	11024	10020	11789	Bertha	11790	11023	*12/32*-01/37	➲**3012**
2013	11025	10001	11752	Brenda	11751	11026	*09/32*-01/37	➲**3013**
2014	11027	10004	11757	Enid	11758	11028	*09/32*-01/37	➲**3014**
2015	11029	10005	11759	Joyce	11760	11030	*10/32*-01/37	➲**3015**
2016	11031	10007	11764	Iris	11763	11032	*10/32*-01/37	➲**3016**
2017	11033	10009	11768	Ruth	11767	11034	*10/32*-01/37	➲**3017**
2018	11035	10012	11773	May	11774	11036	*11/32*-01/37	➲**3018**
2019	11037	10015	11780	Peggy	11779	11038	*11/32*-01/37	➲**3019**
2020	11039	10014	11777	Clara	11778	11040	*11/32*-01/37	➲**3020**

6-PAN

Eastbourne Line Express Pantry Units
660-750V dc third rail
2021-2037

See 3021-3037 for details.

	DMBTO	TTK	TFK	TFRBK	TTK	DMBTO		
2021	11047	10022	12260	12501	10021	11048	*03/35*-01/37	➲**3021**
2022	11049	10024	12261	12502	10023	11050	*03/35*-01/37	➲**3022**
2023	11051	10026	12262	12503	10025	11052	*03/35*-01/37	➲**3023**
2024	11064	10028	12263	12504	10027	11065	*03/35*-01/37	➲**3024**
2025	11066	10030	12264	12505	10029	11067	*04/35*-01/37	➲**3025**
2026	11054	10032	12265	12506	10031	11053	*04/35*-01/37	➲**3026**
2027	11068	10034	12266	12507	10033	11069	*04/35*-01/37	➲**3027**
2028	11070	10036	12267	12508	10035	11071	*04/35*-01/37	➲**3028**
2029	11055	10038	12268	12509	10037	11056	*04/35*-01/37	➲**3029**
2030	11072	10040	12269	12510	10039	11077	*05/35*-01/37	➲**3030**
2031	11057	10042	12270	12511	10041	11058	*05/35*-01/37	➲**3031**
2032	11074	10044	12271	12512	10043	11075	*05/35*-01/37	➲**3032**
2033	11059	10046	12272	12513	10045	11060	*05/35*-01/37	➲**3033**
2034	11076	10048	12273	12514	10047	11073	*06/35*-01/37	➲**3034**
2035	11061	10050	12274	12515	10049	11062	*06/35*-01/37	➲**3035**
2036	11078	10052	12275	12516	10051	11079	*06/35*-01/37	➲**3036**
2037	11080	10054	12276	12517	10053	11063	*06/35*-01/37	➲**3037**

6-CIT

Brighton Line Express City Units
660-750V dc third rail
2041-2043

See 3041-3043 for details.

	DMBTO	TFK	TFK	TPCK	TFK	DMBTO		
2041	11041	12254	12255	Gwladys	12256	11001	11/32-01/37	➲**3041**
2042	11002	12259	12258	Olive	12257	11042	*11/32*-01/37	➲**3042**
2043	11015	12253	12251	Ethel	12252	11016	12/32-01/37	➲**3043**

Class 403 5-BEL

Brighton Belle Pullman

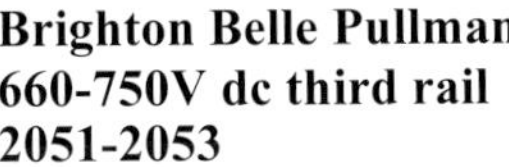

660-750V dc third rail
2051-2053

See 3051-3053 for details.

	DMPBS	TPS	TKRK	TKRK	DMPBS		
2051	89	86	Doris	Hazel	88	01/33-01/37	➲**3051**
2052	91	87	Audrey	Vera	90	01/33-01/37	➲**3052**
2053	93	85	Mona	Gwen	92	01/33-01/37	➲**3053**

Class 401 2-BIL

Outer-Suburban Units (two toilets)
660-750V dc third rail
2001-2152

Ten semi-fast main-line units entered traffic in 1935 for use on the Eastbourne Line. They were numbered 1890-1899; 1890 (the first built unit) being later renumbered to 1900.

The building of the power cars was split between Metropolitan-Cammell and Birmingham Railway Carriage & Wagon, and the trailer cars were built at Eastleigh.

The next units had a slightly larger guard's compartment and different power equipment. They were numbered from 1901 upwards, but all the 2-BILs were renumbered in a new series from 2001 upwards in 1936.

2011-2048 were built for use on the Waterloo-Portsmouth and Alton routes in 1936. 2049-2116 followed in 1937, being intended for the Central Section route to Portsmouth and Bognor Regis. The final batch was numbered 2117-2152 and these units were built in 1938 for the Waterloo-Reading route.

A number of accident damaged trailers were replaced by vehicles of the 2-HAL type.

The 2-BIL units were withdrawn in 1969-70 and many worked their last days as parcels units. 2037 was taken into departmental stock in 1970, spending much of its time in Derby.

	DMBTL	DTCL			
2001	10568	12102	01/37-04/69		
2002	10569	12103	01/37-05/69		
2003	10570	12104	01/37-04/69		
2004	10571	12105	01/37-03/69		
2005	10572	12106	01/37-04/69		
2006	10573	12107	01/37-09/63	➲*900*	
2007	10574	12108	01/37-07/68		
2008	10575	12109	01/37-08/51		
2008	10575	*12052*	08/51-04/69		☜
2009	10576	12110	01/37-04/69		
2010	10567	12101	01/37-07/68		
2011	10577	12034	01/37-11/70		
2012	10578	12035	01/37-09/69		
2013	10579	12036	01/37-09/69		
2014	10580	12037	01/37-05/43		
2015	10581	12038	01/37-05/69		
2016	10582	12039	01/37-07/71		
2017	10583	12040	01/37-10/70		
2018	10584	12041	01/37-04/69		
2019	10585	12042	01/37-01/70		
2020	10586	12043	01/37-05/69		
2021	10587	12044	01/37-06/70		
2022	10588	12045	01/37-11/70		
2023	10589	12046	01/37-09/69		
2024	10590	12047	01/37-04/71		
2025	10591	12048	01/37-11/70		
2026	10592	12049	01/37-02/70		
2027	10593	12050	01/37-11/70		
2028	10594	12051	01/37-10/66		
2028	10594	*12854*	03/69-04/71		☜
2029	10595	12052	01/37-08/51		
2029	10595	*12109*	08/51-10/70		☜
2030	10596	12053	01/37-09/69		
2031	10597	12054	01/37-01/70		
2032	10598	12055	01/37-04/71		
2033	10599	12056	01/37-04/71		
2034	10600	12057	01/37-07/71		
2035	10601	12058	01/37-01/70		
2036	10602	12059	01/37-06/71		
2037	10603	12060	01/37-02/70	➲Dep **024**	
2038	10604	12061	01/37-11/70		
2039	10605	12062	01/37-12/69		
2040	10606	12063	01/37-09/69		
2041	10607	12064	01/37-04/69		
2042	10608	12065	01/37-06/69		
2043	10609	12066	01/37-10/70		
2044	10610	12067	01/37-02/69		
2045	10611	12068	01/37-10/70		
2046	10612	12069	01/37-01/70		
2047	10613	12070	01/37-01/70		
2048	10614	12071	01/37-01/70		
2049	10615	12072	*06/37*-08/69		
2050	10616	12073	*06/37*-11/70		
2051	10617	12074	*06/37*-06/70		
2052	10618	12075	*06/37*-06/70		
2053	10619	12076	*06/37*-02/70		
2054	10620	12077	*06/37*-02/70		
2055	10621	12078	*06/37*-07/68		
2055	10621	*12108*	07/68-11/70		☜
2056	10622	12079	*06/37*-12/46		
2056	10622	*12231*	11/47-01/71		☜
2057	10623	12080	*06/37*-01/71		
2058	10624	12081	*07/37*-04/71		
2059	10625	12082	*07/37*-10/66		
2060	10626	12083	*07/37*-02/70		
2061	10627	12084	*07/37*-02/70		
2062	10628	12085	*07/37*-05/71		
2063	10629	12086	*07/37*-01/70		
2064	10630	12087	*07/37*-10/70		
2065	10631	12088	*07/37*-02/70		
2066	10632	12089	*07/37*-06/70		
2067	10633	12090	*07/37*-04/71		
2068	10634	12091	*08/37*-10/70		
2069	10635	12092	*08/37*-08/51		
2069	10635	*12858*	01/55-12/70		☜
2070	10636	12093	*08/37*-06/56		see **2601**
2070	10636	12093	08/57-02/70		☜
2071	10637	12094	*08/37*-06/69		
2072	10638	12095	*08/37*-04/71		
2073	10639	12096	*08/37*-09/69		
2074	10640	12097	*08/37*-04/71		
2075	10641	12098	*08/37*-10/70		
2076	10642	12099	*08/37*-09/69		
2077	10643	12100	*08/37*-09/69		
2078	10644	12111	*09/37*-01/71		
2079	10645	12112	*09/37*-07/69		
2080	10646	12113	*09/37*-05/69		
2081	10647	12114	*09/37*-01/71		
2082	10648	12115	*09/37*-06/70		

2083	10649	12116	09/37-01/71	
2084	10650	12117	09/37-01/71	
2085	10651	12118	09/37-12/69	
2086	10652	12119	09/37-05/71	
2087	10653	12120	09/37-09/70	
2088	10654	12121	10/37- 50	
2088	10654	*12807*	50-08/62	
2089	10655	12122	10/37-10/69	
2090	10656	12123	10/37-08/71	Ⓟ
2091	10657	12124	10/37-10/69	
2092	10658	12125	10/37-02/69	
2093	10659	12126	10/37-09/69	
2094	10660	12127	10/37-09/69	
2095	10661	12128	10/37-02/70	
2096	10662	12129	10/37-07/69	
2096	10662	*12101*	07/69-12/69	
2097	10663	12130	10/37-09/69	
2098	10664	12131	11/37-06/71	
2099	10665	12132	11/37-04/71	
2100	10666	12133	11/37-08/51	
2100	10666	*12857*	01/55-06/70	
2101	10667	12134	11/37-05/71	
2102	10668	12135	11/37-08/40	
2103	10669	12136	11/37-11/70	
2104	10670	12137	11/37-05/71	
2105	10671	12138	11/37-09/65	
2106	10672	12139	11/37-02/69	
2107	10673	12140	11/37-09/69	
2108	10674	12141	12/37-08/69	
2109	10675	12142	12/37-06/69	
2110	10676	12143	12/37-03/70	
2111	10677	12144	12/37-01/71	
2112	10678	12145	12/37-01/71	
2113	10679	12146	12/37-09/59	see **2611**
2113	10679	*12146*	03/62-02/71	
2114	10680	12147	12/37-11/70	
2115	10681	12148	12/37-10/69	
2116	10682	12149	12/37-09/70	
2117	10683	12150	08/38-09/70	
2118	10684	12151	08/38-12/69	
2119	10685	12152	08/38-12/44	
2120	10686	12153	08/38-04/69	
2121	10687	12154	08/38-08/69	
2122	10688	12155	08/38-02/69	
2123	10689	12156	08/38-01/68	
2123	10689	*12193*	02/68-12/70	
2124	10690	12157	08/38-09/70	
2125	10691	12158	08/38-08/69	
2126	10692	12159	08/38-09/69	
2127	10693	12160	09/38-09/69	
2128	10694	12161	09/38-10/69	
2129	10695	12162	09/38-07/69	
2130	10696	12163	09/38-01/71	
2131	10697	12164	09/38-08/40	
2132	10698	12165	09/38-04/71	
2133	10699	12166	09/38-11/52	
2133	10699	*12856*	02/55-01/71	
2134	10700	12167	09/38-06/70	
2135	10701	12168	09/38-06/71	
2136	10702	12169	10/38-06/70	
2137	10703	12170	10/38-03/71	
2138	10704	12171	10/38-10/69	
2139	10705	12172	10/38-01/71	
2140	10706	12173	10/38-08/71	
2141	10707	12174	10/38-01/71	
2142	10708	12175	10/38-05/69	
2143	10709	12176	10/38-07/69	
2144	10710	12177	10/38-10/69	
2145	10711	12178	11/38-01/70	
2146	10712	12179	11/38-01/71	
2147	10713	12180	11/38-03/71	
2148	10714	12181	11/38-05/69	
2149	10715	12182	11/38-10/69	
2150	10716	12183	11/38-09/70	
2151	10717	12184	11/38-02/70	
2152	10718	12185	11/38-02/70	

Class 446 2-PEP

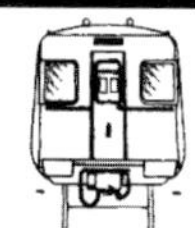

Experimental Suburban Prototype
660-750V dc third rail
2001

The PEP units arose from a plan to devise a new generation of high-density multiple unit trains. Two 4-car units and one 2-car unit were delivered from York to the Southern Region for evaluation. They appeared in passenger traffic from Waterloo in 1973.

Originally they were classified 461 and 462; uniquely among British EMUs the class numbers referred to the vehicle type rather than the unit type, Class 461 for the driving cars and Class 462 for intermediate cars. They were all motor vehicles with a motor on every axle to achieve a high acceleration rate. There was a mix of driving and non-driving vehicles. There was no guard's compartment, the guard was to travel in the rear driving cab. They were originally planned to be PER units but appeared with the PEP designation.

In 1974 the 2-car unit was converted to three cars with an additional trailer and transferred to departmental service for testing on the Eastern and Scottish Regions. The 4-car units were also later taken into departmental stock and used at Derby.

The new Classes 313, 314, 315, 455, 507 & 508 were developed directly from these prototypes.

	DMSO	DMSO		
2001	64300	64305	72-08/73	
2001	64300	*64301*	08/73-10/74	➲Dep

Class 402 2-HAL

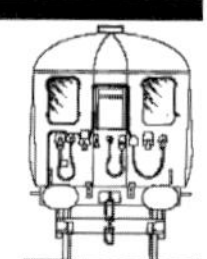

Outer-Suburban Units (one toilet)
660-750V dc third rail
2601-2692

A total of 99 semi-fast 2-HAL units were built from 1939-48 and another was added in 1955. All were built at Eastleigh on Lancing frames. They had one toilet per unit (HAL – half the number of lavatories compared to a BIL – bi(two)-lavatories)

2601-2676 were built for the Gillingham and Maidstone routes. They were transferred to the Central and South Western divisions in 1958 to work on services to Gatwick & Reading. This batch became Class 402/1.

2677-2692 followed for the Reading services. This batch became Class 402/2.

Most of the 2-HAL units were withdrawn in 1969-71. Many were used as parcels units for a short while, and six were officially transferred for these duties, becoming 2-PAN units 061-066. They were withdrawn in January 1972.

Other withdrawn units entered departmental stock as de-icing units.

	DMBT	DTCL		
2601	10719	12186	01/39-06/56	
2601	10719	*12093*	06/56-08/57	
2601	10719	*12186*	08/57-02/70	
2602	10720	12187	01/39-01/71	
2603	10721	12188	01/39-01/71	
2604	10722	12189	01/39-11/70	➲2-PAN **061**
2605	10723	12190	01/39-11/70	➲2-PAN **062**
2606	10724	12191	01/39-12/69	
2607	10725	12192	01/39-11/70	
2608	10726	12193	01/39-07/67	
2609	10727	12194	01/39-09/69	
2610	10728	12195	01/39-08/71	
2611	10729	12196	01/39-09/59	
2611	10729	*12146*	09/59-03/62	
2611	10729	*12196*	03/62-06/70	
2612	10730	12197	01/39-10/70	
2613	10731	12198	01/39-12/69	
2614	10732	12199	01/39-01/70	
2615	10733	12200	02/39-01/71	
2616	10734	12201	02/39-01/71	
2617	10735	12202	02/39-09/69	
2618	10736	12203	02/39-06/70	
2619	10737	12204	02/39-06/71	
2620	10738	12205	02/39-12/70	
2621	10739	12206	02/39-10/70	
2622	10740	12207	02/39-04/69	
2623	10741	12208	02/39-08/71	
2624	10742	12209	02/39-12/69	
2625	10743	12210	02/39-01/70	
2626	10744	12211	02/39-09/66	
2626	10744	*12051*	01/67-10/69	
2627	10745	12212	02/39-07/71	
2628	10746	12213	02/39-07/71	
2629	10747	12214	02/39-07/71	
2630	10748	12215	03/39-02/70	
2631	10749	12216	03/39-01/70	
2632	10750	12217	03/39-01/71	
2633	10751	12218	03/39-01/71	
2634	10752	12219	03/39-01/70	
2635	10753	12220	03/39-12/69	
2636	10754	12221	03/39-10/70	
2637	10755	12222	03/39-05/69	
2638	10756	12223	03/39-06/70	➲2-PAN **063**

Unit	DMBT	DTCL	Dates	Notes
2639	10757	12224	03/39-07/69	
2640	10758	12225	03/39-10/70	
2641	10759	12226	03/39-07/71	
2642	10760	12227	03/39-12/69	
2643	10761	12228	03/39-02/70	
2644	10762	12229	03/39-04/69	
2645	10763	12230	03/39-11/70	⊃2-PAN **064**
2646	10764	12231	04/39-11/47	
2647	10765	12801	04/39-02/70	
2648	10766	12802	04/39-01/71	
2649	10767	12803	04/39-01/71	
2650	10768	12804	04/39-02/70	
2651	10769	12805	04/39-10/69	
2652	10770	12806	04/39-12/69	
2653	10771	12807	04/39- 50	
2653	10771	*12854*	01/51-02/69	⇦
2654	10772	12808	04/39-12/70	
2655	10773	12809	04/39-06/70	
2656	10774	12810	04/39-05/71	
2657	10775	12811	04/39-01/70	
2658	10776	12812	04/39-05/69	
2659	10777	12813	04/39-04/69	
2660	10778	12814	04/39-11/70	
2661	10779	12815	04/39-08/71	
2662	10780	12816	05/39-09/69	
2663	10781	12817	05/39-01/70	
2664	10782	12818	05/39-01/70	
2665	10783	12819	05/39-04/71	
2666	10784	12820	05/39-10/70	
2667	10785	12821	05/39-01/71	
2668	10786	12822	05/39-01/71	
2669	10787	12823	05/39-12/69	
2670	10788	12824	05/39-09/69	
2671	10789	12825	05/39-01/70	
2672	10790	12826	05/39-03/71	
2673	10791	12827	05/39-12/69	
2674	10792	12828	05/39-08/71	
2675	10793	12829	05/39-11/70	
2676	10794	12830	05/39-04/71	
2677	10795	12831	11/39-05/71	
2678	10796	12832	11/39-08/69	
2679	10797	12833	11/39-07/71	
2680	10798	12834	11/39-04/56	
2681	10799	12835	11/39-06/70	
2682	10800	12836	11/39-06/69	
2683	10801	12837	12/39-12/70	
2684	10802	12838	12/39-04/71	
2685	10803	12839	12/39-05/71	
2686	10804	12840	12/39-06/70	
2687	10805	12841	12/39-12/70	
2688	10806	12842	12/39-03/68	
2688	10806	*12855*	03/68-06/69	⇦
2689	10807	12843	12/39-10/70	⊃2-PAN **065**
2690	10808	12844	12/39-10/70	
2691	10809	12845	12/39-01/70	
2692	10810	12846	12/39-12/70	⊃2-PAN **066**

Class 402 2-HAL

Outer-Suburban Units (one toilet)
660-750V dc third rail
2693-2700

2693-2699 were built with all steel bodies in 1948 to cover war losses. They had a different cab-design, looking more like suburban units. Five additional trailers were built in 1950-54 to replace losses in this class and the 2-BILs. The last unit (2700) came into stock in 1955 formed from one of these trailers and a 4-SUB power car.

Unit	DMBT	DTCL	Dates	Notes
2693	10811	12847	11/48-07/70	
2694	10812	12848	11/48-08/71	
2695	10813	12849	11/48-08/71	
2696	10814	12850	12/48-10/69	
2696	10814	*12855*	10/69-04/71	⇦
2697	10815	12851	12/48-04/71	
2698	10816	12852	12/48-07/71	
2699	10817	12853	12/48-07/71	
2700	12664	12855	02/55-03/68	

4-LAV

Brighton Line Semi-Fast Units
660-750V dc third rail
2921-2953

This was the first batch of main-line units built for the Southern Railway. Units 1921-1953 were built in 1931-32 as semi-fast units for the Brighton Line. Seven more units were included in the order, but the order for these was cancelled. They were renumbered 2921-2953 in 1937. Later three of the first class compartments in the TC were downgraded to second class.

The vehicles were built on steel underframes with the bodies being constructed of a hard-wood framing with steel panelling. The driver's cab and guard's compartment were slightly inset, giving a tapered appearance to the MBS vehicle. Periscopes were fitted to the guard's compartment giving a view of the line ahead.

These units spent their entire lives on the Victoria-Brighton/Worthing main line.

Unit	DMBT	TCL	TC	DMBT	Dates	Notes
2921	10501	12002	11501	10502	01/37-01/68	
2922	10503	12004	11502	10504	01/37-04/68	
2923	10505	12013	11517	10506	01/37-10/68	
2924	10507	12005	11506	10508	01/37-05/69	
2925	10509	12003	11510	10510	01/37-02/68	
2926	10511	12001	11509	10512	01/37-10/47	
2926	*10764*	12001	11509	10512	02/48-09/61	⇦
2926	10764	*10359*	11509	10512	01/62-10/67	⇦
2926	10764	10359	11509	*10542*	12/67-05/68	⇦
2927	10513	12006	11504	10514	01/37-02/68	
2928	10515	12012	11508	10516	01/37-02/69	
2929	10517	12007	11503	10518	01/37-01/68	
2930	10519	12008	11518	10520	01/37-03/68	
2931	10521	12020	11520	10522	01/37-03/68	
2932	10523	12010	11507	10524	01/37-05/67	
2932	*10939*	12010	11507	*10940*	06/67-02/68	⇦
2933	10525	12016	11516	10526	01/37-07/68	
2934	10527	12011	11514	10528	01/37-01/68	
2935	10529	12014	11513	10530	01/37-01/68	
2936	10531	12019	11515	10532	01/37-03/68	
2937	10533	12009	11519	10534	01/37-07/68	
2938	10535	12017	11511	10536	01/37-01/68	
2939	10537	12015	11505	10538	01/37-02/69	
2940	10539	12018	11512	10540	01/37-02/68	
2941	10541	12021	11521	10542	01/37-12/67	
2942	10543	12022	11522	10544	01/37-05/68	
2943	10545	12023	11523	10546	01/37-11/66	
2943	*10671*	12023	11523	10546	11/66-05/68	⇦
2944	10547	12024	11524	10548	01/37-02/68	
2945	10549	12025	11525	10550	01/37-01/68	
2946	10551	12026	11526	10552	01/37-03/68	
2947	10553	12027	11527	10554	01/37-05/68	
2948	10555	12028	11528	10556	01/37-05/68	
2949	10557	12029	11529	10558	01/37-02/69	
2950	10559	12030	11530	10560	01/37-02/69	
2951	10561	12031	11531	10562	01/37-05/68	
2952	10563	12032	11532	10564	01/37-03/68	
2953	10565	12033	11533	10566	01/37-01/68	

4-LAV

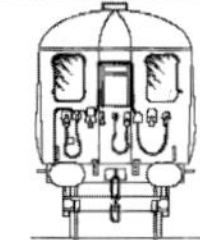

Brighton Line Semi-Fast Units
660-750V dc third rail
2954-2955

Two more units numbered 2954-2955 were built in 1940. They were to the same internal design, but externally they were similar to the 2-HAL units.

Unit	DMBT	TCL	TC	DMBT	Dates
2954	10497	11999	11534	10498	02/40-05/68
2955	10499	12000	11535	10500	05/40-07/68

6-PUL

Brighton Line Express Pullman Units
660-750V dc third rail
3001-3020

Twenty units were built in 1932, each of which was fitted with a Pullman car. The Pullman cars were built by Metropolitan-Cammell for the Pullman Car company and they were all given girl's names and were painted in the Pullman chocolate and cream livery, the rest of the units being in standard SR green. They were composite vehicles, and they were fitted with cooking and pantry facilities.

The units were numbered 2001-2020 and this was altered to 3021-3020 in 1937. The Pullman cars were stored from May 1942, leaving the units to work as 5-car sets until 1946.

	DMBTO	TTK	TCK	TPCK	TCK	DMBTO			
3001	11043	10017	11783	Anne	11784	11044	01/37- 48		
3001	11043	10017	11783	*Bertha*	11784	11044	48-04/66	➲*3043*[2]	↩
3002	11004	10002	11754	Rita	11753	11003	01/37-05/46		
3002	11004	10002	11754	*Olive*	11753	11003	05/46-12/65	➲*3046*	↩
3003	11006	10003	11755	Grace	11756	11005	01/37-01/48		
3003	*11056*	10003	11755	Grace	11756	11005	06/49-01/66		↩
3004	11008	10006	11761	Elinor	11762	11007	01/37-01/64		
3005	11010	10008	11766	Ida	11765	11009	01/37-02/66	➲*3050*	
3006	11012	10011	11772	Rose	11771	11011	01/37-04/65		
3006	11012	10011	11772	*Iris*	11771	11011	04/65-09/65	➲*3042*[2]	↩
3007	11014	10013	11775	Violet	11776	11013	01/37-09/65		
3008	11045	10019	11788	Lorna	11787	11046	01/37-02/66		
3009	11018	10010	11769	Alice	11770	11017	01/37-09/64	➲*3027*	
3010	11020	10016	11781	Daisy	11782	11019	01/37-11/65	➲*3044*	
3011	11022	10018	11785	Naomi	11786	11021	01/37-12/65		
3012	11024	10020	11789	Bertha	11790	11023	01/37- 48		
3012	11024	10020	11789	*Anne*	11790	11023	48-09/65		↩
3013	11025	10001	11752	Brenda	11751	11026	01/37-03/66		
3014	11027	10004	11757	Enid	11758	11028	01/37-08/58		
3014	*11074*	*10044*	11757	Enid	11758	11028	08/58-01/59		↩
3014	*11075*	10044	11757	Enid	11758	11028	01/59-01/64		↩
3015	11029	10005	11759	Joyce	11760	11030	01/37-12/65		
3016	11031	10007	11764	Iris	11763	11032	01/37-03/65		
3017	11033	10009	11768	Ruth	11767	11034	01/37-05/46		
3017	11033	10009	11768	*Gwladys*	11767	11034	05/46-01/64		↩
3018	11035	10012	11773	May	11774	11036	01/37-05/46		
3018	11035	10012	11773	*Ethel*	11774	11036	05/46-01/64		↩
3019	11037	10015	11780	Peggy	11779	11038	01/37-01/64		
3020	11039	10014	11777	Clara	11778	11040	01/37-01/64		

6-PAN

Eastbourne Line Express Pantry Units

660-750V dc third rail

3021-3037

The seventeen 6-PAN units were built for the electrification of the Eastbourne and Hastings lines in 1935. The units were numbered 2021-2037 and later became 3021-3037. They were similar to the 6-PUL units but had the Pullman car replaced with a Trailer First with a Pantry. These were used for serving light refreshments and were usually manned by Pullman personnel.

The motor-cars in these units were fitted with a new design of single air-stream ventilators above the windows, designed to give draught free ventilation. They worked on London-Eastbourne, Hastings, Brighton & West Worthing routes, often with 6-PUL and 6-CIT units.

Many of these units were reformed with redundant PUL vehicles in 1965 to form 6-COR units 3041-3050, being finally withdrawn in 1969.

	DMBTO	TTK	TFK	TFRBK	TTK	DMBTO			
3021	11047	10022	12260	12501	10021	11048	01/37-03/66		
3022	11049	10024	12261	12502	10023	11050	01/37-02/66		
3023	11051	10026	12262	12503	10025	11052	01/37-09/65		
3024	11064	10028	12263	12504	10027	11065	01/37-09/65		
3025	11066	10030	12264	12505	10029	11067	01/37-06/49		
3025	*11054*	10030	12264	12505	10029	11067	06/49-03/65		↩
3026	11054	10032	12265	12506	10031	11053	01/37-06/49		
3026	*11006*	10032	12265	12506	10031	11053	06/49-12/65		↩
3027	11068	10034	12266	12507	10033	11069	01/37-01/64		
3027	11068	*10014*	12266	*11768*	*10009*	11069	01/64-08/64		↩
3027[2]	*11018*	*10010*	*11769*	*11757*	*11758*	*11035*	10/64-*09/65*		↩
3028	11070	10036	12267	12508	10035	11071	01/37-09/64	➲*3048*	
3029	11055	10038	12268	12509	10037	11056	01/37-01/48		
3029	11055	*10037*	12268	12509	*10038*	*11066*	06/49-03/66		↩
3030	11072	10040	12269	12510	10039	11077	01/37-05/43		
3030	11072	10040	12269	12510	11077		05/43- *45*		↩
3030	11072	10040	12269	12510	*10039*	11077	*45*-12/65	➲*3045*	↩
3031	11057	10042	12270	12511	10041	11058	01/37-01/64		
3032	11074	10044	12271	12512	10043	11075	01/37-08/58		
	3032 often ran with a pullman car when the rest of a 6-PUL set was being serviced								
3033	11059	10046	12272	12513	10045	11060	01/37-01/64		
3034	11076	10048	12273	12514	10047	11073	01/37-12/65		
3035	11061	10050	12274	12515	10049	11062	01/37-12/65	➲*3047*	
3036	11078	10052	12275	12516	10051	11079	01/37-09/65		
3037	11080	10054	12276	12517	10053	11063	01/37-01/66		

6-CIT

Brighton Line Express City Units

660-750V dc third rail

3041-3043

Three other Pullman units were built concurrently with the 6-PUL units. These were for working on the London Bridge to Brighton service, which was used by City commuters, and they were known as the 6-CIT sets. The main difference from the 6-PUL units was that the three trailers were all first-class seating in seven compartments. These units were numbered 2041-2043 until 1937 when they were renumbered 3041-3043.

The Pullman cars were stored from May 1942, leaving the units to work as 5-car sets until 1946. From 1947 two of the trailer vehicles were converted to composites, due to reduced demand for first class on these services.

	DMBTO	TFK	TFK	TPCK	TFK	DMBTO			
3041	11041	12254	12255	Gwladys	12256	11001	01/37-07/46		
3041	11041	12254	12255	*10073*	12256	11001	07/46-02/47		↩
3041	11041	*10113*	11862	*May*	*11863*	11001	04/47-09/65		↩
	coaches renumbered (derated)								
3041	11041	10113	11862	*Alice*	11863	11001	09/65-03/66	➲*3041*[2]	↩
3042	11002	12259	12258	Olive	12257	11042	01/37-07/46		
3042	11002	12259	12258	*11859*	12257	11042	07/46-02/47		↩
3042	11002	*10114*	*11864*	*Ruth*	*11865*	11042	12/47-09/65		↩
	coaches renumbered (derated)								
3043	11015	12253	12251	Ethel	12252	11016	01/37-12/47		
3043	11015	*10115*	*11866*	*Rita*	*11867*	11016	12/47-03/66		↩
	coaches renumbered (derated)								

Class 404 6-COR

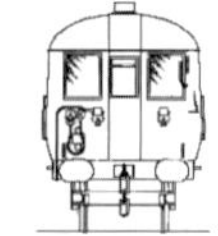

Portsmouth Line Express Units (reformed)

660-750V dc third rail

3041-3050

Late in 1965 a start was made to form ten 6-COR units numbered 3041-3050 utilising redundant 6-PUL/6-PAN vehicles. They differed from the other CORs by having a full-width cab with no corridor connection between units. They worked on South Eastern division services as a stop-gap while new stock was being built, and were also used on summer relief trains to the Kent Coast in 1967.

	DMBSO	TSK	TCK	TFK	TSK	DMBSO		
3041[2]	11041	10113	11862	12273	10048	11001	03/66-*06/68*	
3042[2]	11012	10011	11772	12268	10037	11011	03/66-01/69	
3043[2]	11043	10017	11783	12260	10021	11044	04/66-10/68	
3044	11020	10016	11781	12262	10026	11019	11/65-01/69	
3045	11077	10039	11782	12269	10040	11072	12/65-01/69	
3046	11004	10002	11754	12263	10025	11003	12/65-01/69	
3047	11062	10049	11753	12274	10050	11061	01/66-01/69	
3048	11022	10018	11785	12267	10036	11021	01/66- 66	
3048	11022	*10035*	*11756*	12267	10036	11021	66-01/69	↩
3049	11029	10005	11759	12265	10032	11030	02/66-01/69	
3050	11010	10008	11766	12261	10024	11009	02/66-01/69	

Class 403 5-BEL

Brighton Belle Pullman

660-750V dc third rail

3051-3053

These three five-car units were built for the Brighton line services in 1932 and they remained the property of the Pullman Company until taken over by BR in 1963. They were built by Metropolitan-Cammell to all-Pullman standards. The service was initially named "The Southern Belle", but this was changed to "The Brighton Belle" in 1934. They carried the chocolate and cream livery of the Pullman livery until 1968-69 when they were repainted in BR blue and grey and the names were removed.

In service two units generally worked together as a ten-coach train with one unit remaining spare. In 1941 the units were put into store for the war years. 3052 received war damage at Victoria and had to be returned to the builder before re-entering service in 1947.

Because they had spent the war years out of service they were still in good condition when the other Pullman stock was due for retirement in 1965. The service eventually finished in April 1972 and all the Pullman cars were sold. Many were used as restaurants and a number later found their way into the VSOE luxury Pullman train. In 2014 an exciting plan is underway to recreate a complete 5-car Brighton Belle unit.

Carriages later renumbered and names removed.

	DMPBS	TPS	TKRK	TKRK	DMPBS		
3051	89	86	Doris	Hazel	88	01/37-02/69	
3051	289	286	282	279	288	02/69-04/72	↩

3052	91	87	Audrey	Vera	90	01/37-12/68
3052	291	287	280	284	290	12/68-04/72
3053	93	85	Mona	Gwen	92	01/37-05/69
3053	293	285	283	281	292	05/69-04/72

Class 404 4-RES

Portsmouth Line Express Restaurant Units

660-750V dc third rail

3054-3072

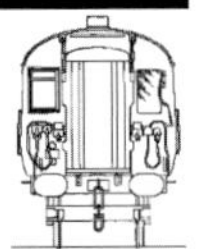

The nineteen 4-RES units were built in 1937 to provide restaurant facilities on the newly electrified Waterloo-Portsmouth line. The units operated with the 4-COR sets and were numbered 3054-3072. The power cars were constructed at Eastleigh, the first class restaurant car by Metropolitan Cammell and the third class trailer by Birmingham RC&W.

Unit 3072 was involved in a fire in 1952, which destroyed the restaurant car. When it was rebuilt this car was fitted out in cafeteria style and it was reclassified 4-BUF.

Units 3058, 3060 & 3063 were deleted during the war and they were replaced by 4-COR units 3156-3158.

In 1962 three units (3056, 3065 & 3068) were taken out of service and converted to Griddle sets. The restaurant cars were rebuilt internally to contain a buffet saloon, a kitchen and a bar section. In 1963 these three 4-GRI units were renumbered 3086-3088.

Five units were reformed with a Pullman car replacing the Restaurant car in 1964 and these became 4-PUL units.

The remaining units were reformed to become 4-COR(N) units 3065-3071 in 1964.

	DMBTO	TRKB	TFRK	DMBTO		
3054	11139	12619	12248	11140	*04/37- 45*	
3054	*11177*	12619	12248	11140	*45*-01/64	➲*3054*
3055	11142	12610	12246	11141	*04/37*-01/64	➲*3055*
3056	11143	12609	12245	11144	*04/37*-12/63	➲**3086**
3057	11145	12611	12247	11146	*04/37*-01/64	➲*3057*
3058	11147	12606	12234	11148	*04/37-12/40*	
3059	11149	12612	12250	11150	*04/37- 45*	
3059	11149	12612	*12242*	*11172*	*45*-01/64	➲*3059*
3060	11151	12615	12249	11152	*04/37-01/41*	
3061	11153	12607	12233	11154	*04/37*-01/64	➲*3056*
3062	11155	12616	12235	11156	*04/37*-01/64	➲*3065*
3063	11157	12617	12232	11158	*04/37-06/44*	
3064	11159	12601	12236	11160	*05/37*-01/64	➲*3068*
3065	11162	12605	12237	11161	*05/37- 45*	
3065	11162	12605	12237	*11202*	*45*-12/63	➲**3087**
3066	11163	12604	12238	11164	*05/37*-01/64	➲*3066*
3067	11165	12608	12239	11166	*05/37*-01/64	➲*3067*
3068	11167	12602	12240	11168	*05/37*-12/63	➲**3088**
3069	11169	12603	12241	11170	*05/37*-01/64	➲*3069*
3070	11171	12614	12242	11172	*05/37- 45*	
3070	11171	12614	*12250*	*11229*	*45*-01/64	➲*3070*
3071	11173	12618	12243	11174	*05/37*-01/64	➲*3071*
3072	11175	12613	12244	11176	*05/37*-05/71	

3072 was 3-car unit 07/54-07/55, while 12613 was converted to cafeteria car. Reclassified 4-BUF.

4-PUL

Portsmouth Line Express Pullman Units

660-750V dc third rail

3054-3059

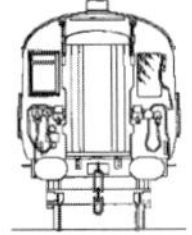

During 1964 five 4-RES units had their restaurant cars replaced with Pullman cars removed from withdrawn 6-PUL sets. They were reclassified 4-PULs and operated on the Central division for the next four years.

	DMBSO	TPCK	TRKB	DMBSO		
3054	11177	Clara	12248	11140	01/64-06/66	➲*3161*
3055	11142	Gwladys	12246	11141	01/64-06/66	➲*3162*
3056	11153	Ethel	12233	11154	01/64-09/64	
3056	11153	Ethel	12233	*11214*	09/64-07/65	
3057	11145	Elinor	12247	11146	01/64-02/66	
3057	11145	*Lorna*	12247	11146	02/66-03/66	➲*3163*
3059	11149	Enid	12242	11172	01/64-09/64	
3059	11149	*Alice*	12242	*11128*	09/64-07/65	

Class 404 4-COR(N)

Portsmouth Line Express Units (reformed)

660-750V dc third rail

3065-3071

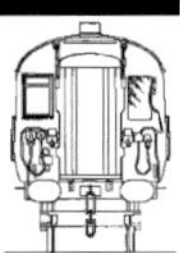

In 1964 the restaurant cars were removed from six 4-RES sets and one 6-PUL set. After some reformation these appeared as seven 4-COR(N) units numbered 3065-3071. In this form they could be seen working the Victoria-Worthing and Littlehampton routes.

	DMBSO	TSK	TFK	DMBSO		
3065	11155	12235	10034	11156	01/64-05/66	➲*3164*
3066	11164	12238	10033	11163	01/64-05/66	➲*3165*
3067	11166	12239	10046	11165	01/64-05/66	➲*3166*
3068	11160	12236	10045	11159	01/64-09/65	➲*3160*
3069	11170	12241	10042	11169	01/64-05/66	➲*3167*
3070	11229	12250	10041	11171	01/64- *64*	
3071	11174	12243	10044	11173	01/64-07/66	➲*3168*

Class 404/1 4-BUF

Portsmouth Line Express Buffet Units

660-750V dc third rail

3073-3085

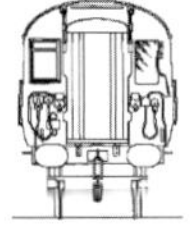

Thirteen buffet car sets were constructed to work on the Portsmouth Line in 1938. They were numbered 3073-3085 and were unusual in that the buffet cars had no windows in the buffet part of the coach. The Buffet cars were stored out of use during the Second World War.

3073-85 ran without buffet 05/42-01/46

	MBSO	TCK	TRB	MBSO		
3073	11229	11846	12518	11230	*05/38-09/40*	
3073	*11148*	11846	12519	11230	*12/40*-10/70	➲*3121*
3074	11231	11847	12519	11232	*05/38-09/40*	
3074	11231	11847	*12518*	*11213*	10/48-09/64	
3074	11231	11847	12518	*11172*	09/64-10/70	
3075	11233	11848	12520	11234	*05/38*-01/71	
3076	11235	11849	12521	11236	*05/38*-10/70	
3077	11237	11850	12522	11238	*06/38*-02/71	
3078	11239	11851	12523	11240	*06/38- 45*	
3078	*11249*	*11856*	12523	11240	*45*-10/70	
3079	11241	11852	12524	11242	*06/38*-09/62	➲*3134*
3080	11243	11853	12525	11244	*06/38- 45*	
3080	11243	11853	12525	*11250*	*45*-01/71	
3081	11245	11854	12526	11246	*06/38-12/68*	
3082	11247	11855	12527	11248	*07/38-06/44*	
3082	*11206*	11855	12527	11248	*06/44*-10/70	
3083	11249	11856	12528	11250	*07/38- 45*	
3083	*11191*	*11851*	12528	*11112*	*45*-10/70	
3084	11251	11857	12529	11252	*07/38*-10/70	
3085	11253	11858	12530	11254	*07/38*-02/71	

Class 404/1 4-GRI

Portsmouth Line Express Griddle Units

660-750V dc third rail

3086-3088

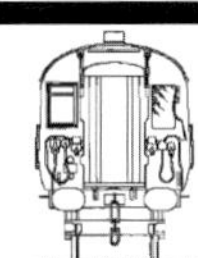

In 1962 three 4-RES units were taken out of service and converted to Griddle sets. The restaurant cars were rebuilt internally to contain a buffet saloon, a kitchen and a bar section. In 1963 these three 4-GRI units were renumbered 3086-3088.

	DMBSO	TFRK	TRKG	DMBSO		
3086	11144	12245	12605	11143	12/63-05/71	
3087	11162	12237	12602	11202	12/63-05/71	➲Dep 054
3088	11168	12240	12609	11167	12/63-05/71	

Class 430 4-REP

Bournemouth Line Tractor Units

660-850V dc third rail

3001-3015

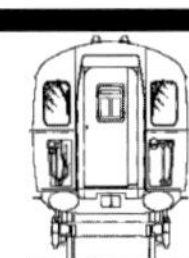

These were the tractor units built to work with the TC units on the Bournemouth line. See the 4-TC units 401-434 for more details of this scheme. The 4-REP units were constructed at York. The powerful DMS vehicles were built new, while the other coaches were converted from Mark 1 hauled stock. Eleven units (3001-3011) were built initially, and a further four units (3012-3015) were built in 1974. Each of the TBFK vehicles was named, the name being appearing in a glass panel behind the serving counter.

Although originally allocated Class 441, the 4-REPs started life as Class 430; they were later reclassified to 432 and renumbered 2001-2015.

For the extension of the electrification to Weymouth 24 new 5-WES units were ordered. To save on costs electrical components were reused from the REP units and this meant that from 1986 they were progressively taken out of stock for component recovery. This caused extensive reformation of units in order to keep the services moving.

In 1986 units 2801-2807 were formed with a buffet vehicle from a REP unit replacing the TFK in a TC unit. Later the asbestos-contaminated buffet cars were withdrawn and this series was reformed and renumbered as 8101-8106. In 1988 they were again reformed into 5-TC units 2804-2809, 5-TC sets 8101 & 8110 and 3-TCs 8102 & 8104.

Further reformations in 1987 formed six 3-REP units (2901-2906) with one DMSO removed and replaced with a Class 73 locomotive. After a short while these were reformed into three 4-REPs (2001, 2003 & 2007). Then the DMS vehicles were reformed with TC vehicles to make units 1901 & 1902. Finally, in 1990-91 the remaining serviceable vehicles were formed in 6-REP units 1901-1906.

	DMSO	TBFK	TRB	DMSO		
3001	62141	70801	69319	62142	03/67-06/86	➲**2001**
3002	62143	70802	69320	62144	03/67-05/86	➲**2002**
3003	62145	70803	69321	62146	03/67-09/86	➲**2003**
3004	62147	70804	69322	62148	05/67-06/86	➲**2004**
3005	62149	70805	69323	62150	06/67-08/86	➲**2005**
3006	62151	70806	69324	62152	05/67-06/86	➲**2006**
3007	62153	70807	69325	62154	06/67-06/86	➲**2007**
3008	62155	70808	69326	62156	05/67-09/86	
3009	62157	70809	69327	62158	06/67-06/86	➲**2009**
3010	62159	70810	69328	62160	07/67-09/86	➲**2010**
3011	62161	70811	69329	62162	07/67-09/86	➲**2011**
3012	62477	71156	69022	62476	09/74-05/86	➲**2012**
3013	62479	71157	69023	62478	10/74-05/86	➲**2013**
3014	62481	71158	69024	62480	11/74-04/86	➲**2014**
3015	62483	71159	69025	62482	12/74-04/86	➲**2015**

Class 404/2 4-COR
Portsmouth Line Express Units
660-750V dc third rail
3101-3168

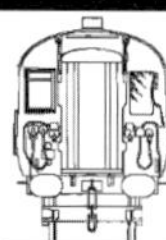

3101-3129 were built in 1937 for the services from Waterloo to Portsmouth and 3130-3155 followed a year later for the Victoria to Bognor & Portsmouth route. The units were known as the "Nelsons" or the "Pompey" stock. The Nelson name referred to their one-eyed look, with only one window at the front end. The units were gangwayed throughout to provide access to the Buffet units marshalled in the train.

The units suffered from a considerable amount of war damage and more coaches were built to the original design in 1946, many of them taking the numbers of the vehicles they replaced. Units 3156-3158 were formed after the war from various new and repaired war-damaged vehicles, taking the place of some war damaged 4-RES units. In 1965-66 ten more units numbered 3159-3168 were formed using trailers from the older PUL & PAN units and power cars from 4-RES units.

The 4-COR units were relegated to other services as they were replaced on their former duties by newer stock. They appeared on outer suburban services on the South Western and Central divisions, and minor duties such as the Waterloo-Reading and South Coast lines. The final survivors were withdrawn in 1972.

	DMBTO	TTK	TCK	DMBTO		
3101	11081	10055	11791	11082	02/37-06/44	
3101	11081	10055	11791	11244	45-01/72	↩
3102	11083	10056	11792	11084	02/37-10/72	
3103	11085	10057	11793	11086	02/37-05/72	
3104	11087	10058	11794	11088	02/37-05/72	
3105	11089	10059	11795	11090	02/37-05/72	
3106	11091	10060	11796	11092	02/37-05/72	
3107	11093	10061	11797	11094	02/37-01/72	
3108	11095	10062	11798	11096	02/37-09/72	
3109	11097	10063	11799	11098	02/37-09/72	
3110	11099	10064	11800	11100	03/37-10/71	
3111	11101	10065	11801	11102	03/37-05/72	
3112	11103	10066	11802	11104	03/37- 45	
3112	11103	10066	11839	11216	45-01/72	↩
3113	11105	10067	11803	11106	03/37-01/72	
3114	11107	10068	11804	11108	03/37-05/72	
3115	11109	10069	11805	11110	03/37-01/72	
3116	11111	10070	11806	11112	03/37- 45	
3116	11111	10070	11806	11150	45- 64	↩
3116	11211	10070	11806	11150	64-12/72	↩
3117	11113	10071	11807	11114	03/37-01/41	
3117	11118	10071	11809	11114	09/46-05/72	↩
3118	11115	10072	11808	11116	03/37-01/70	
3118	11133	10072	11765	11116	01/70-08/72	↩
3119	11117	10073	11809	11118	03/37-01/41	
3119	11117	10073	11859	11192	02/47-05/72	↩
3120	11119	10074	11810	11120	04/37-05/72	
3121	11121	10075	11811	11122	04/37-05/71	
3121	11230	10075	11811	11148	05/71-10/71	↩
3122	11123	10076	11812	11124	04/37-08/72	
3123	11125	10077	11813	11126	04/37-12/72	
3124	11127	10078	11814	11128	04/37-06/64	
3124	11127	11814	10078	11034	06/64-07/65	↩
3124	11127	10078	11814	11128	07/65-10/71	↩
3125	11129	10079	11815	11130	04/37-01/72	
3126	11131	10080	11816	11132	04/37-01/72	
3127	11133	10081	11817	11134	04/37-01/70	
3128	11135	10082	11818	11136	04/37-09/72	
3129	11137	10083	11819	11138	04/37-05/72	
3130	11178	10084	11820	11177	05/38- 45	
3130	11178	10084	11820	11139	45-05/72	↩
3131	11180	10085	11821	11179	05/38-09/72	
3132	11182	10086	11822	11181	05/38-09/72	
	3 coaches stranded at Portsmouth with war damage, 01/41 to 09/46. New 11181 built.					
3133	11184	10087	11823	11183	05/38-05/72	
3134	11185	10088	11824	11186	05/38- 45	
3134	11195	10088	11824	11186	45-02/63	↩
3134	11195	10088	11852	11241	04/64-01/72	↩
3135	11188	10089	11825	11187	05/38-09/72	
3136	11190	10090	11826	11189	05/38-09/72	
3137	11192	10091	11827	11191	05/38-08/40	
3137	11113	10091	11827	11082	02/47-08/72	↩
3138	11194	10092	11828	11193	06/38-11/68	
3138	11194	10092	11808	11193	11/68-01/70	↩
3138	11115	10092	11808	11193	01/70-01/72	↩
3139	11196	10093	11829	11195	06/38- 45	
3139	11196	10093	11829	11185	45-01/72	↩
3140	11198	10094	11830	11197	06/38-05/72	
3141	11200	10095	11831	11199	06/38-09/72	
3142	11202	10096	11832	11201	06/38- 45	
3142	11161	10096	11832	11201	45-12/72	↩
3143	11204	10097	11833	11203	06/38-10/72	
3144	11206	10098	11834	11205	06/38-08/40	
3144	11157	10111	11834	11205	10/46-10/71	↩
3145	11207	10099	11835	11208	06/38- 64	
3145	11207	10099	11835	11111	64- 72	↩
3146	11210	10100	11836	11209	06/38-01/72	
3147	11211	10101	11837	11212	07/38- 64	
3147	11171	10101	11837	11212	64-07/65	↩
3147	11171	10101	11837	11147	07/65-01/72	↩
3148	11214	10102	11838	11213	07/38- 45	
3148	11214	10102	11838	11147	45-06/64	↩
3148	11036	10102	11838	11208	06/64-07/65	↩
3148	11214	10102	11838	11208	07/65-12/71	↩
3149	11216	10103	11839	11215	07/38- 45	
3149	11215	10103	11802	11104	45-01/72	↩
3150	11218	10104	11840	11217	07/38- 45	
3150	11239	10104	11840	11217	45-12/71	↩
3151	11220	10105	11841	11219	07/38-08/72	
3152	11222	10106	11842	11221	07/38-01/72	
3153	11224	10107	11843	11223	07/38-01/72	
3154	11226	10108	11844	11225	07/38-09/72	
3155	11228	10109	11845	11227	07/38-01/72	
3156	11218	10098	11807	11232	10/46-01/72	
3157	11151	10112	11860	11152	10/46-01/72	
3158	11158	10110	11861	11247	10/46-02/64	
3158	11158	10110	11824	11247	02/64-05/72	↩
3159	11159	10045	11773	11160	10/65-09/72	
3160	11149	10007	11764	11153	10/65-01/72	
3161	11177	10010	11765	11140	07/66-11/68	
3161	11140	10003	11828	11246	11/68-10/71	↩
3162	11142	10053	11789	11141	06/66-10/71	
3163	11145	10054	11788	11146	06/66-07/70	
3163	11249	10054	11788	11146	10/70-05/72	↩
3164	11155	10034	11787	11156	05/66-05/72	
3165	11163	10033	11751	11164	05/66-05/72	
3166	11165	10046	11775	11166	05/66-10/71	
3167	11169	10042	11784	11170	05/66-01/72	
3168	11173	10044	11776	11174	07/66-01/72	

4-DD
Double-Deck Units
660-750V dc third rail
4001-4002

These unique units entered service in 1949 as an experiment to help reduce overcrowding on the South Eastern Division suburban services. They were not true double-deck units (impossible in the restricted British loading gauge) but the seating was on two levels, alternatively high and low with steps from the lower compartments leading to the higher compartments. In effect, the passengers in the upper deck were seated above the heads of those in the lower deck, giving restricted headroom all-round.

The units were built to the very extremes of the loading gauge, and were restricted to working on the Charing Cross and Cannon Street to Dartford lines (with special clearance to work to Eastleigh for overhaul) for the whole of their existence. As a result of their size opening windows could not be fitted and the units were fitted with pressure ventilation. There was no space for external footboards on the outside of the units. One advantage was that as the upper compartments had no external doors, small folding seats could be provided at each end for additional passengers to perch on.

The experiment was not a great success. Passenger loading was slow at the stations and the passengers felt cramped in the compartments, particularly on the upper-level. As a result of this experiment it was decided to solve the overcrowding problem with platform lengthening and 10-car trains on the busy routes.

In spite of the problems the units did survive in service for many years, until withdrawal in 1971. They were renumbered in 1970 from 4001 & 4002 to 4901 & 4902 to release space for the new PEP units which were then being planned.

Two of these unique vehicles have survived in preservation.

	DMBT	TT	TT	DMBT		
4001	13001	13501	13502	13002	10/49-10/70	➲**4901**
4002	13003	13504	13503	13004	10/49-10/70	➲**4902**

Class 445 4-PEP
Experimental Suburban Prototype
660-750V dc third rail
4001-4002

See 2-PEP 2001 for details.

	DMS	MS	MS	DMS		
4001	64301	62427	62428	64302	05/71-08/73	
4001	*64305*	62427	62428	64302	08/73-09/78	➲Dep
4002	64303	62426	62429	64304	07/71-08/78	➲Dep

4-SUB units

The first 4-SUB unit to enter service was the newly built Sheba unit 4101 in 1941. From this point on the 4-SUB unit story followed two parallel paths; new built units and augmented 3-SUB units. The augmented units received an extra carriage from either redundant trailer units, or a new built augmentation trailer.

The mass conversion of 3-SUB units into 4-SUB sets began in 1942, when units in the 1201 fleet were strengthened and became 4-car sets in the 4131 and 4195 fleets.

In 1947-48, the 3-SUBs in the 1658 fleet were strengthened with ex-LSWR compartment trailers and were renumbered in the 4172 and 4235 fleets.

4250-4257 were units reformed in 1948-49, using war-damaged three-car sets.

The majority of the remaining 3-SUBs were then augmented with new all-steel trailers. The first batch was 10230-10345. 10449-10471 and 11448-11470 were built for the 4355-4377 batch of 4-SUBs but delays to the construction of electrical equipment meant they were used for augmentation. Most of the final build of augmentation trailers numbered 10167-10229 then found their way into 4355-4377.

As the later standard 4-SUBs in the 46xx and 47xx series entered service, many of the augmented units were withdrawn from service, most having gone by the late 1950s. Eighty-six augmentation trailers were converted to work with EPB units.

Two units numbered 4131 & 4132 were formed in 1969 using 2-HAL motor coaches, with redundant all-steel trailers. They were withdrawn in 1971.

The standard 4-SUBs were taken out of service from 1976 onwards. There was growing concern at this time about the use of compartment TS vehicles. There had been a growing number of cases of vandalism, and worries about the safety of passenges in these vehicles. As a result, when units were taken out of service, the TSO vehicles were retained and swapped with the TS vehicles of units which were still in service.

Class 405 4-SUB
"Sheba" Suburban Units
660-750V dc third rail
4101-4110

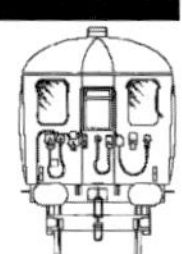

The first of the new units was 4101 built in 1941 as the first of an order for thirty units. The rest were put on hold due to the war, and eventually only nine more of this type appeared in 1944 & 45, the rest appearing to a revised design as 4111-4130.

4101 went into service on the South Eastern Division, where it gained the title "Sheba" (from 1Kings 10:2 in the Old Testament, *"The Queen of Sheba had a very great train"*).

The Shebas were designed to fit as many seats as possible into to the unit, including an 11-compartment trailer. They first unit also included a trailer composite with some first class compartments, but first class was abolished in the suburban area just before 4101 went into service. Regular travellers would soon learn which compartments to head for! The 11-compartment TT proved to be too tight a fit and all later builds had only 10 compartments in the trailers.

The other difference from later units was the cabs, which had roofs made of steel which sloped down to meet the front of the car which was made of three flat planes joined at a distinct angle. Two windows were fitted at the end with a two-digit route indicator in between. This used metal stencils over a lighted glass panel to display the route numbers.

	DMBT	TC/TT	TT	DMBT	
4101	10941	11471	10419	10942	09/41-05/72
4102	10943	11472	10420	10944	12/44-05/72
4103	10945	11473	10421	10946	01/45-12/68
4103	10945	11473	10421	*10762*	04/69-01/72
4104	10947	11474	10422	10948	01/45-01/72
4105	10949	11475	10423	10950	01/45-01/72
4106	10951	11476	10424	10952	02/45-04/72
4107	10953	11477	10425	10954	02/45-05/72
4108	10955	11478	10426	10956	03/45-01/61
4108	10955	*10356*	10426	10956	01/61-05/72
4109	10957	11479	10427	10958	03/45-01/72
4110	10959	11480	10428	10960	03/45-05/72

Class 405 4-SUB
Standard Suburban Units
660-750V dc third rail
4111-4120

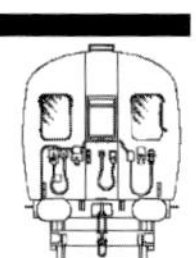

The next batch was 4111-4120. They were fitted with a 10-compartment TT and downgraded TC. They carried a new style cab-front which became the standard for all future batches.

	DMBT	TC/TT	TT	DMBT	
4111	10961	11481	10429	10962	04/46-05/72
4112	10963	11482	10430	10964	04/46-05/74
4113	10965	11483	10431	10966	05/46-10/73
4114	10967	11484	10432	10968	05/46-05/72
4115	10969	11485	10433	10970	06/46-09/63
4115	10969	*10396*	10433	10970	09/63-01/72
4116	10971	11486	10434	10972	06/46-05/72
4117	10973	11487	10435	10974	06/46-10/73
4118	10975	11488	10436	10976	07/46-01/72
4119	10977	11489	10437	10978	07/46-10/73
4120	10979	11490	10438	10980	07/46- *61*
4120	10979	11490	10438	*11363*	02/62-05/72

Class 405 4-SUB
Standard Suburban Units
660-750V dc third rail
4121-4132

4121-4130 was the last part of the original order. Internally they were different to the earlier units; all except the downgraded TC had saloon accommodation with 3+2 seats.

	DMBT	TC/TT	TTO	DMBT		
4121	10981	11491	10439	10982	08/46-04/76	➲Dep 005
4122	10983	11492	10440	10984	08/46-03/72	
4123	10985	11493	10441	10986	08/46-10/71	
4124	10987	11494	10442	10988	08/46-04/76	
4125	10989	11495	10443	10990	09/46-04/76	➲Dep 009
4126	10991	11496	10444	10992	09/46-01/75	
4126	10991	10448	10444	10992	01/75-04/76	➲Dep 011
4127	10993	11497	10445	10994	09/46-03/75	
4127	10993	10446	10445	10994	03/75-04/76	
4128	10995	11498	10446	10996	09/46-05/74	
4129	10997	11499	10447	10998	09/46-06/72	
4130	10999	11500	10448	11000	10/46-05/74	

Class 405 4-SUB
Suburban Units
660-750V dc third rail
4121-4132

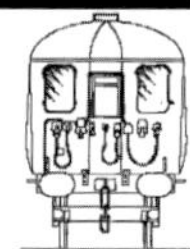

These units were formed in 1969 from 2-HAL power cars with 10 compartment trailers, including three from the disbanded 7-TC unit 701.

	DMBS	TS	TS	DMBS	
4131[2]	10740	10149	10346	10777	06/69-10/71
4132[2]	10755	10349	10351	10806	09/69-10/71

4-SUB
Augmented Suburban Units
660-750V dc third rail
4131-4171

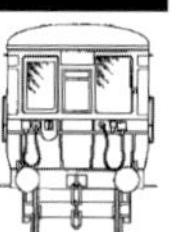

The conversion of 3-SUB units into 4-SUB sets began in 1942, when units in the LSWR 1201 fleet were strengthened and became 4-car sets in the 4131 and 4195 fleets.

	DMBT	TC	TT	DMBC	
4131	8006	9373	10411	8752	04/41-12/55
4132	8059	9390	9172	8769	02/42-02/55
4133	8048	9387	9174	8766	09/42-07/55
4133	8048	9717	9719	8766	07/55-05/56
4134	8071	9394	10405	8773	03/42-03/53
4134	8071	9472	9728	8773	03/53-05/56
4135	8060	9391	9204	8770	42-12/55
4136	8120	9411	9173	8790	09/42-05/54
4137	8090	9401	9183	8780	07/42-11/54
4138	8053	9388	9181	8767	09/42-04/55
4139	8107	9406	9179	8785	09/42-01/54
4140	8047	9386	9187	8765	09/42-06/54
4141	8041	9384	9170	8763	01/43-02/55
4142	8108	9407	9186	8786	11/42-06/56
4143	8083	9398	10407	8777	02/43-09/54
4144	8096	9403	10410	8782	01/42-09/54
4145	8089	9400	9825	8791	11/42-12/54
4146	8018	9377	10414	8756	11/42-05/54
4147	8072	9395	9180	8771	11/42-11/54
4148	8119	9410	9199	8789	09/43-03/55
4149	8113	9408	10401	8787	09/43-11/55
4150	8065	9392	10413	8774	43-10/55
4151	8078	9397	9194	8776	44-03/55
4152	8012	9375	10416	8754	06/44-08/55
4153	8023	9378	9827	8757	09/44-09/54
4154	8017	9344	10418	8755	09/44-08/53
4155	8213	9404	9208	8783	09/44-01/54
4156	8030	9381	10402	8760	44-06/55
4157	8084	9399	9168	8778	05/45-07/54
4158	8024	9379	10412	8758	06/45-09/55
4159	8054	9389	9169	8768	10/45-12/55
4160	8011	9374	9195	8753	10/45-08/55
4161	8114	9409	9201	8788	45-10/47
4161	8114	9409	9201	8808	10/47-11/53
4162	8029	9380	10417	8759	45-11/55
4163	8095	9402	10415	8781	45-09/54
4164	8036	9383	9300	8762	12/45-08/55
4165	8042	9385	9826	8764	46-12/54
4166	8077	9396	9190	8775	46-12/55
4167	8066	9393	9205	8772	46-08/54
4168	8126	9413	9829	8792	01/46-01/55
4169	8046	9372	9207	8751	08/46-08/55
4170	8035	9382	9828	8761	08/46-01/56
4171	8102	9405	10406	8784	08/46-06/55

4-SUB
Augmented Suburban Units
660-750V dc third rail
4172-4194

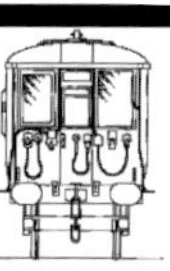

In 1947-48, the LSWR bodied 3-SUBs in the 1658 fleet were strengthened with ex-LSWR compartment trailers and were renumbered in the 4172 and 4235 fleets.

	DMBT	TC	TT	DMBC	
4172	8179	9307	9203	8793	08/46-10/53
4173	8192	9320	9191	8806	02/47-10/53
4174	8182	9310	9171	8796	05/47-10/53
4175	8203	9331	9196	8817	02/47-09/53
4176	8205	9333	9298	8819	05/47-01/56
4177	8183	9311	9175	8797	02/47-05/52
4177	8183	9311	9175	9845	05/52-07/53
4178	8197	9325	9176	8811	05/47-11/54
4179	8198	9326	10409	8812	07/47-08/53
4180	8185	9313	9189	8799	07/47-12/53
4181	8186	9314	9193	8800	08/47-04/55
4182	8201	9329	9178	8815	08/47-05/54
4183	8196	9324	9177	8810	08/47-07/53
4184	8191	9319	9185	8805	10/47-08/52
4185	8184	9312	9202	8798	12/47-09/53
4186	8204	9332	9188	8818	05/48-09/53
4187	8193	9321	9182	8807	48-12/54
4188	8189	9317	10404	8803	48-03/54
4189	8195	9323	9184	8809	09/48-07/53
4190	8572	9659	9078	8573	08/48-01/56
4191	8206	9334	10403	8820	07/48-04/53
4192	8187	9315	10408	8801	08/48-05/53
4193	8181	9309	9206	8795	08/48-06/49
4194	8180	9308	9192	8794	08/48-09/54

4-SUB
Augmented Suburban Units
660-750V dc third rail
4195-4234

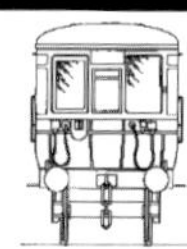

LSWR bodied. See the 4131 series for details.

	DMBT	TC	TT	DMBT	
4195	8085	9428	9157	8086	01/42-05/55
4196	8103	9431	9163	8104	10/42-06/55
4197	8121	9434	9217	8122	42-08/54
4198	8055	9423	9214	8056	04/42-04/55
4199	8019	9417	9213	8020	09/42-04/55
4200	8001	9414	9232	8002	03/43-06/54
4201	8043	9421	9254	8044	06/43-06/55
4202	8013	9416	9215	8014	09/43-03/54
4203	8025	9418	9251	8026	09/43-10/54
4204	8061	9424	9247	8062	02/44-11/55
4205	8049	9422	9238	8050	04/44-09/55
4206	8091	9429	9265	8092	45-01/56
4207	8031	9419	9236	8032	01/46-04/54
4208	8037	9420	9241	8038	08/46-09/55
4209	8067	9425	9228	8068	01/46-02/55
4210	8079	9427	9239	8080	08/46-10/55
4211	8007	9415	9297	8008	07/47-06/54
4212	8115	9433	9233	8116	07/47-03/55
4213	8073	9426	9237	8074	08/47-10/55
4214	8097	9430	9252	8098	12/47-03/55
4215	8109	9432	9255	8110	03/48-05/55
4215	8109	9432	10224	8110	05/55-05/56
4216	8051	9359	9235	8052	11/42-07/54
4217	8093	9352	9211	8094	03/43-07/55
4218	8009	9366	9231	8010	08/43-07/56
4219	8087	9365	9245	8088	08/43-11/55
4220	8069	9362	9242	8070	09/43-10/54
4221	8081	9364	9222	8082	09/43-12/55
4222	8123	9371	9220	8124	02/43-11/47
4223	8039	9357	9219	8040	02/43-12/54
4224	8063	9361	9249	8064	01/44-04/48
4224	8063	9361	9249	8123	06/48-04/54
4225	8105	9368	9161	8106	12/43-05/54
4226	8021	9354	9229	8022	02/44-05/55
4227	8117	9370	9226	8118	12/44-06/54
4228	8005	9358	9210	8045	08/46-04/55
4229	8033	9356	9248	8034	08/46-10/54
4230	8057	9360	9159	8058	09/46-10/54
4231	8075	9363	9225	8076	10/47-11/55
4232	8027	9355	9246	8028	11/47-10/55
4233	8099	9367	9221	8100	11/47-04/52
4234	8111	9369	9224	8112	11/47-05/55

4-SUB
Augmented Suburban Units
660-750V dc third rail
4235-4249

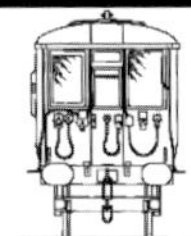

LSWR bodied. See the 4172 series for details.

	DMBT	TC	TT	DMBC		
4235	8216	9376	9218	8830	05/47-07/53	
4236	8207	9335	9212	8821	01/43-02/54	
4237	8210	9338	9234	8824	11/47-08/53	
4238	8220	9348	9223	8834	10/47-09/54	
4239	8209	9337	9253	9809	12/47-05/54	
4240	8219	9347	9209	8833	10/47-09/53	
4241	8221	9349	9230	8835	02/48-07/53	
4242	8202	9330	9220	8816	09/48-12/53	
4243	8212	9340	9167	8826	07/48-08/53	
4244	8214	9342	9244	8828	04/48-12/53	
4245	8208	9336	9216	8822	08/48-03/54	
4246	8218	9346	9250	8779	03/48-09/53	
4247	8215	9343	9243	8829	07/48-12/54	
4248	8211	9339	9240	8825	08/48-11/53	
4249	8190	9318	9197	8804	12/47-08/53	

4-SUB
Augmented Suburban Units
660-750V dc third rail
4250-4257

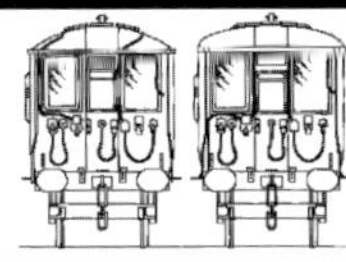

4250-4257 were units reformed in 1948-49, using miscellaneous war-damaged three-car sets.

	DMBT	TC	TC	DMBC		
4250[1]	8678	9709	9722	8844	08/43-11/47	
4250[2]	*8199*	*9327*	*9299*	*8813*	09/48-01/55	⇦
4251	8705	9736	9741	8871	03/44-11/56	⊃**4518**[2]
4252	8738	9728	9472	8896	08/44-03/53	⊃*4519*
4253	8556	9650	9316	8802	07/45-06/53	
4254	9876	9730	9527	8865	10/46-03/56	
4255	8194	9322	9350	8836	12/47-05/53	
4256	8672	9703	9505	8838	02/48-10/49	
	DMBT	**TC**	**TC**	**DMBT**		
4257	8653	9693	9670	8654	02/48-10/49	

Class 405/2 4-SUB
Standard Suburban Units
660-750V dc third rail
4277-4299

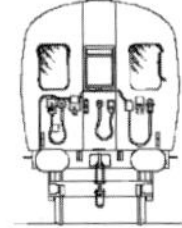

This batch (which followed the 4378 batch) had the new lighter 250hp motors and were classified Class 405/2.

	DMBTO	TTO	TT	DMBTO		
4277	10849	10121	10144	10850	12/48-06/76	
4277	10849	10121	*10463*	10850	06/76-09/83	⇦
4278	10851	10122	10145	10852	12/48-08/58	
4278	10851	10122	10145	10852	08/59-06/81	⇦
4278	10851	10122	*12372*	10852	06/81-09/83	⇦
4279	10853	10123	10146	10854	01/49-05/56	
4279	10853	10123	*10267*	10854	05/56-08/57	⇦
4279	10853	10123	*10146*	10854	08/57-05/76	⇦
4279	10853	10123	*10439*	10854	05/76-07/82	⇦
4279	10853	10123	*8947*	10854	07/82-09/83	⇦
4280	10855	10124	10147	10856	01/49-06/81	
4281	10857	10125	10148	10858	01/49-06/81	
4282	10859	10126	10149	10860	01/49-03/68	
4283	10861	10127	10150	10862	01/49-06/81	
4284	10863	10128	10151	10864	02/49-03/75	
4284	10863	10128	*12374*	10864	03/75-05/82	⇦
4285	10865	10129	10152	10866	02/49-05/76	
4285	10865	10129	*12353*	10866	05/76-10/82	⇦
4286	10867	10130	10153	10868	02/49-08/70	
4286	10867	10130	10153	*10880*	08/70-06/81	⇦
4287	10869	10131	10154	10870	02/49-03/81	
4287	10869	10131	*12359*	10870	03/81-05/82	⇦
4288	10871	10132	10155	10872	02/49-06/81	
4289	10873	10133	10156	10874	02/49-02/63	
4289	*11323*	10133	10156	10874	03/63-06/81	⇦
4290	10875	10134	10157	10876	03/49-12/76	
4290	*12660*	10134	10157	10876	12/76-04/81	⇦
4291	10877	10135	10158	10878	03/49-06/76	
4291	10877	10135	*9004*	10878	06/76-08/83	⇦
4292	10879	10136	10159	10880	03/49-07/70	
4293	10881	10137	10160	10882	03/49-05/76	
4293	10881	10137	*8979*	10882	05/76-10/82	⇦
4294	10883	10138	10161	10884	03/49-05/76	
4294	10883	10138	*9007*	10884	05/76-05/83	⇦
4295	10885	10139	10162	10886	03/49-06/81	
4296	10887	10140	10163	10888	04/49-06/81	
4297	10889	10141	10164	10890	04/49-07/76	
4297	10889	10141	*12358*	10890	07/76-09/82	⇦
4298	10891	10142	10165	10892	04/49-07/76	
4298	10891	10142	*10442*	10892	07/76-09/83	⇦
4299	10893	10143	10166	10894	04/49-11/73	
4299	10893	10143	*12380*	11339	06/74-06/81	⇦

4-SUB
Augmented Suburban Units
660-750V dc third rail
4300-4325

SR units augmented with new all-steel trailers.

	DMBT	TT	TC	DMBT		
4300	8127	10384	9435	8128	01/46-03/58	
4301	8129	10383	9436	8130	01/46-10/60	
4302	8131	10381	9437	8132	01/46-11/60	
4303	8133	10371	9438	8134	11/45-02/60	
4304	8135	10397	9439	8136	04/46-06/60	
4305	8137	10382	9440	8138	01/46-05/61	
4306	8139	10388	9441	8140	02/46-04/60	
4307	8141	10374	9442	8155	11/45-04/60	
4308	8143	10380	9443	8144	12/45-11/60	
4308	8143	*10357*	9443	8144	11/60-11/60	⇦
4309	8145	10369	9444	8146	10/45-04/58	
4309	8145	10369	*10372*	8146	04/58-09/60	⇦
4310	8147	10372	9445	8148	11/45-03/58	
4310	8147	*9444*	9445	8128	04/58-05/60	⇦
4311	8149	10379	9446	8150	12/45-04/61	
4312	8151	10378	9447	8152	12/45-06/60	
4313	8153	10376	9448	8154	12/45-12/49	
4313	8153	*11456*	9448	8154	12/49-05/60	⇦
4314	8156	10389	9449	8142	02/46-04/61	
4315	8157	10357	9450	8158	08/45-11/60	
4316	8159	10366	9451	8160	10/45-03/60	
4317	8161	10390	9452	8162	02/46-03/60	
4318	8163	10367	9453	8164	10/45-02/60	
4319	8165	10355	9454	8166	07/45-07/60	
4320	8167	10387	9412	8168	02/46-05/50	
4320	8167	10387	*9593*	8168	05/50-04/60	⇦
4321	8169	10385	9456	8170	01/46-12/59	
4322	8171	10375	9457	8172	11/45-12/60	
4322	8171	10375	*10383*	8172	12/60-10/61	⇦
4323	8173	10377	9458	8174	12/45-04/61	
4324	8175	10386	9459	8176	02/46-02/61	
4324	8175	10386	*10385*	8176	02/61-10/61	⇦
4325	8177	10370	9460	8178	10/45-05/60	

4-SUB
Augmented Suburban Units
660-750V dc third rail
4326-4354

SR units augmented with new all-steel trailers.

	DMBT	TT	TC	DMBT		
4326	8417	10362	9583	8418	09/45-04/61	
4327	8419	10394	9595	8420	03/46-01/60	
4328	8421	10351	9591	8422	07/45-08/60	⊃*Dep S99*
4329	8428	10346	9584	8424	06/45-01/62	
4330	8425	10368	9603	8426	10/45-01/62	
4331	8427	10361	9604	8423	09/45-10/51	
4331	8427	*10195*	9604	8423	10/51-07/60	⊃*Dep S101* ⇦
4332	8430	10348	9598	8429	06/45-11/48	
4332	8430	10348	9598	*8465*	05/50-09/60	⊃*Dep S101* ⇦
4333	8460	10398	9606	8432	04/46- 51	
4333	8460	*10449*	9606	8432	05/52-05/60	⇦
4333	8460	*10373*	9606	8432	05/60-11/61	⇦
4334	8433	10356	9607	8434	08/45-08/60	⊃*Dep S96*
4335	8435	10391	9597	8436	03/46-06/52	
4335	8435	*10376*	9597	8436	10/52-11/60	⇦
4335	8435	10376	*10381*	8436	11/60-01/62	⇦
4336	8437	10365	9588	8438	09/45-01/60	
4337	8439	10364	9587	8440	09/45-01/62	
4338	8441	10359	9596	8442	08/45-11/61	

4339	8443	10352	9600	8444	*07/45*-04/58	
4339	8443	10352	9600	*8148*	04/58-11/60	☜
4340	8445	10396	9589	8446	*04/46*-07/60	➲*Dep S93*
4341	8447	10354	9599	8448	*07/45*-05/60	
4342	8449	10358	9582	8450	*08/45*-06/60	➲*Dep*
4343	8451	10347	9594	8452	*06/45*-04/61	
4344	8453	10395	9592	8454	*03/46*-07/60	➲*Dep S95*
4345	8455	10392	9608	8456	*03/46*-04/59	➲*Dep S92*
4346	8457	10349	9586	8458	*06/45*-12/61	
4347	8459	10360	9590	8431	*08/45*-05/61	
4348	8461	10393	9580	8462	*03/46*-06/51	
4348	8461	*10361*	9580	8462	*10/51*-03/61	☜
4348	8461	10361	*10352*	8462	03/61-01/62	☜
4349	8463	10400	9581	8464	*04/46*-07/60	➲*Dep S94*
4350	8465	10373	9593	8486	*11/45*-05/50	
4351	8467	10399	9601	8468	*04/46*-04/59	
4351	8467	10399	*9608*	8468	04/59-08/60	➲*Dep S98* ☜
4352	8469	10353	9602	8470	*07/45*-11/61	
4353	8471	10363	9585	8472	*09/45*-08/60	➲*Dep S97*
4354	8473	10350	9605	8474	*06/45*-11/59	

Class 405 4-SUB

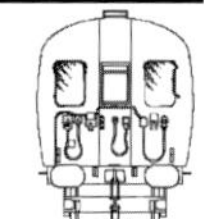

Standard Suburban Units
660-750V dc third rail
4355-4387

When the 4355-4377 batch was built the electrical equipment was delayed and as a result all the trailers were used as augmentation trailers and their places exchanged with others intended for that purpose. They were originally to have been allocated 10449-10471 and 11448-11470. Nine of these units did not receive a composite trailer but by that time it had been decided not to reinstate first class facilities in the suburban area, so it was of no consequence. 10463 was built as a saloon with no internal partitions and this was the prototype for later units.

	DMBT	TT	TT	DMBT		
4355	10895	10220	10221	10896	06/48-03/72	
4355	10895	10220	10221	*10952*	04/72-05/72	☜
4356	10897	10218	10219	10898	06/48-01/74	
4357	10899	10216	10217	10900	05/48-07/73	
4358	10901	10214	10215	10902	05/48-01/74	
4359	10903	10209	10210	10904	05/48-06/58	
4359	*10914*	10209	10210	10904	06/58-01/74	☜
4360	10905	10207	10208	10906	04/48-09/64	
4361	10907	10205	10206	10908	04/48-05/74	➲*Dep 004*
4362	10909	10199	10200	10910	04/48-10/73	
4363	10911	10197	10198	10912	04/48-02/74	
4364	10913	10196	11461	10914	03/48-06/58	
4364	10913	10196	11461	*10903*	06/58-04/70	☜
4364	10913	10196	*10353*	*10811*	*07/70*-02/74	☜
4365	10915	10173	11462	10916	03/48-02/68	
4366	10917	10172	11469	10918	03/48-01/74	
4367	10919	10171	11470	10920	02/48-10/73	➲Dep 055
4368	10921	10170	11468	10922	01/48-05/66	
4368	10921	10170	*8941*	10922	05/66-08/67	☜
4368	*10860*	10170	*11468*	10922	03/68-05/72	☜
4369	10923	10464	11466	10924	01/48-03/68	
4369	*10924*	*10359*	11466	*12664*	04/69-10/73	☜
4370	10925	10461	11467	10926	01/48-05/73	
4371	10927	10462	11463	10928	12/47-10/73	
4372	10929	10465	11464	10930	12/47-05/72	
4373	10931	10455	11465	10932	12/47-01/74 ⊠10/73-12/73	
4374	10933	10454	11460	10934	11/47-05/74	
4375	10935	10457	11459	10936	11/47-02/74	
4376	10937	10458	11458	10938	10/47-10/73	
4377	10939	10463	11457	10940	06/48-06/67	
4377	*10939*	10463	11457	10940	02/68-04/76	➲*Dep 012* ☜

This batch of units was built with all open coaches without partitions apart from the TT.

	DMBT	TT	TTO	DMBT		
4378	10830	10472	12351	10829	09/48-05/72	➲*Dep 024*
4379	10832	10473	12352	10831	10/48-08/67	
4379	10832	*10173*	*11462*	10831	04/69-05/74	☜
4380	10834	10474	12353	10833	10/48-04/76	➲*Dep 006*
4381	10836	10475	12354	10835	10/48-11/73	
4382	10838	10476	12355	10837	11/48-05/74	
4383	10840	10477	12356	10839	09/48-04/72	
4384	10842	10478	12357	10841	10/48-04/76	
4385	10844	10479	12358	10843	10/48-04/76	➲*Dep*
4386	10846	10480	12359	10845	10/48-05/74	
4387	10848	10481	12360	10847	11/48-04/76 ⊠05/74-10/74	

4-SUB

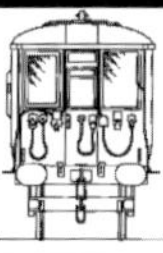

Augmented Suburban Units
660-750V dc third rail
4401-4405

LSWR bodied units augmented with new all-steel trailers.

	DMBT	TC	TT	DMBC	
4401	8555	9649	10332	9808	*05/47-03/53*
4402	8557	9651	10292	9810	*02/47-02/53*
4403	8559	9653	10338	9812	*06/47-07/51*
4404	8560	9654	10288	9813	*02/47-08/51*
4405	8561	9655	10254	9814	*12/46-03/53*

4-SUB

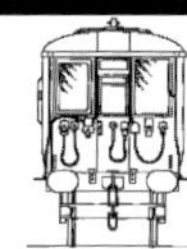

Augmented Suburban Units
660-750V dc third rail
4406-4410

LSWR bodied units augmented with new all-steel trailers.

	DMBT	TC	TT	DMBT		
4406[1]	8226	9304	10270	8565	01/47-11/47	
4406[2]	*8237*	*9498*	10270	*8238*	*11/47-07/50*	
4407	8566	9305	10234	8567	*10/46-07/51*	
4408	8568	9306	10281	8569	*02/47-02/53*	
4409	8570	9484	10238	8571	*10/46*-02/53	
4409	8570	9484	*9651*	8571	02/53-04/54	☜
4410	8580	9663	10302	8581	*03/47-07/51*	

4-SUB

Augmented Suburban Units
660-750V dc third rail
4411-4423

LSWR bodied units augmented with new all-steel trailers.

	DMBT	TC	TT	DMBT		
4411	9831	9766	10251	9832	*11/46*-03/53	
4411	9831	9766	*10405*	9832	03/53-04/54	☜
4412	9833	9767	10280	9834	*02/47-07/53*	
4412	9833	9767	*9306*	9834	*07/53*-12/53	☜
4413	9835	9768	10239	9836	*10/46-06/51*	
4414	9837	9769	10319	9838	*05/47-08/51*	
4415	9839	9770	10308	9840	*04/47-07/51*	
4416	9841	9771	10312	9842	*04/47*-05/50	
4416	9841	9771	*9412*	9842	05/50-07/53	☜
4417	9843	9772	10345	9844	*06/47-07/51*	
4417	9843	9772	*9619*	9844	*07/51-11/51*	☜
4418	9845	9773	10266	9846	*12/46*-05/52	
4418	*8562*	9773	10266	9846	06/52-03/53	☜
4418	8562	9773	*9655*	9846	03/53-03/54	☜
4419	9847	9774	10335	9848	*06/47-01/52*	
4420	9849	9775	10298	9850	*03/47*-05/53	
4420	9849	9775	*9345*	9850	05/53-06/54	☜
4421	9851	9761	10289	9852	*02/47-10/50*	
4422	9853	9762	10253	9854	*11/46-07/51*	
4422	9853	9762	*9305*	9854	*07/51-10/51*	☜
4423	9855	9763	10316	9856	*04/47-07/51*	
4423	9855	9763	*9770*	9856	*07/51-09/51*	☜

4-SUB

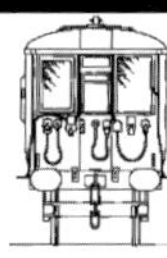

Augmented Suburban Units
660-750V dc third rail
4424-4429

LSWR bodied units augmented with new all-steel trailers.

	DMBT	TC	TT	DMBT	
4424	9789	9671	10260	9790	*12/46*-04/56
4425	9791	9672	10246	9792	*11/46*-04/56
4426	9793	9673	10285	9794	*02/47*-03/56
4427	9795	9674	10275	9796	*01/47*-04/56
4428	9797	9759	10299	9798	*03/47*-04/56
4429	9799	9760	10283	9800	*02/47*-04/56

4-SUB
Augmented Suburban Units
660-750V dc third rail
4430-4431

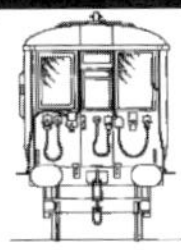

LSWR bodied units augmented with new all-steel trailers.

	DMBT	TC	TT	DMBT	
4430	8582	9664	10269	8583	01/47-08/51
4431	8584	9665	10268	8585	01/47-09/51

4-SUB
Augmented Suburban Units
660-750V dc third rail
4432-4494

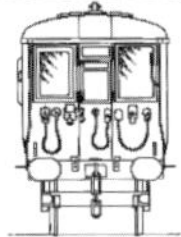

SER bodied units augmented with new all-steel trailers.

	DMBT	TC	TT	DMBT	
4432	8229	9518	10306	8230	04/47-02/51
4433	8231	9501	10258	8232	12/46-06/50
4434	8235	9502	10300	8236	03/47-02/51
4435	8239	9524	10249	8240	11/46-05/50
4436	8243	9513	10230	8244	08/47-06/50
4437	8245	9546	10243	8246	11/46-02/51
4438	8247	9554	10296	8248	03/47-06/50
4439[1]	8249	9509	10255	8250	12/46-02/49
4439[2]	*8495*	*9619*	10255	*8496*	02/49-07/51
4440	8251	9534	10290	8252	03/47-07/50
4441	8254	9506	10276	8372	01/47-04/50
4441	8254	9506	*9609*	8372	04/50-04/51
4442[1]	8255	9505	10242	8256	11/46-02/48
4442[2]	*8475*	*9609*	10242	*8476*	02/48-04/50
4443	8257	9532	10330	8258	05/47-12/50
4444	8299	9528	10282	8260	02/47-06/50
4444	8299	9528	*9501*	8260	06/50-09/50
4445	8261	9552	10265	8262	12/46-04/50
4445	8261	9552	*9500*	8262	04/50-05/51
4446	8263	9523	10263	8264	12/46-09/50
4447	8265	9526	10339	8266	06/47-03/51
4448	8269	9493	10240	8270	10/46-03/50
4449	8271	9514	10307	8272	04/47-01/51
4450	8273	9487	10294	8274	03/47-01/51
4451	8277	9573	10284	8377	02/47-04/51
4452	8284	9548	10233	8366	02/47-12/50
4453	8287	9565	10271	8288	01/47-11/50
4454	8291	9512	10279	8292	01/47-04/50
4455	8293	9571	10250	8485	11/46-10/50
4456	8295	9563	10297	8296	03/47-04/50
4456	8295	9563	*9495*	8296	04/50-05/51
4457	8297	9560	10344	8298	06/47-06/50
4458	8300	9550	10314	8259	04/47-08/50
4459	8303	9538	10236	8304	10/46-10/50
4460	8307	9570	10286	8308	02/47-10/50
4461	8309	9522	10343	8310	06/47-12/50
4462	8311	9495	10287	8312	02/47-03/50
4463	8313	9555	10248	8314	11/46-04/50
4463	8313	9555	*9541*	8314	04/50-05/51
4464	8317	9544	10293	8318	03/47-06/50
4465	8319	9541	10237	8320	10/46-04/50
4466	8325	9539	10305	8326	03/47-11/50
4467	8327	9535	10274	8328	01/47-07/50
4468	8329	9503	10334	8374	12/47-09/50
4469	8331	9574	10317	8332	04/47-12/50
4470	8335	9499	10340	8391	06/47-03/51
4471	8337	9547	10336	8338	06/47-03/51
4472	8339	9551	10247	8349	11/46-06/50
4473	8343	9559	10232	8344	10/46-09/50
4474	8345	9537	10318	8346	04/47- 49
4474	*8380*	9537	10318	8346	49-06/50
4475	8353	9492	10331	8354	05/47-11/50
4476	8357	9507	10235	8358	10/46-04/51
4477	8359	9485	10322	8360	05/47- 50
4477	8359	9485	*11450*	8360	50-09/50
4478	8361	9561	10259	8362	12/46-04/50
4478	8361	9561	*9558*	8362	04/50-05/51
4479	8363	9504	10295	8364	03/47-11/50
4480	8367	9558	10337	8368	06/47-03/50
4481	8369	9557	10256	8370	12/46- 50
4481	*8365*	9557	10256	8370	50-01/51
4482	8375	9529	10329	8282	05/47-10/50
4483[1]	8379	9556	10310	8380	04/47-02/49
4483[2]	*8514*	*9628*	10310	*8710*	02/49-06/51
4484	8381	9500	10325	8382	05/47-04/50
4485	8385	9515	10301	8386	03/47-09/50
4486	8392	9508	10327	8279	05/47-09/50
4487	8393	9520	10261	8394	12/46-04/50
4488	8395	9516	10230	8396	01/47-07/47
4488	8395	9516	*10291*	8396	07/47-04/50
4489	8397	9569	10324	8398	05/47-01/51
4490	8401	9491	10264	8402	12/46-04/50
4491	8403	9494	10231	8404	10/46-11/50
4492	8405	9521	10245	8406	11/46-04/50
4492	8405	9521	*9493*	8406	04/50-06/51
4493	8407	9530	10342	8408	06/47-12/50
4494	8411	9578	10323	8412	05/47-07/50

4-SUB
Augmented Suburban Units
660-750V dc third rail
4495-4501

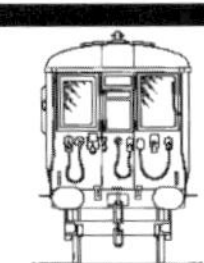

SER bodied units augmented with new all-steel trailers.

	DMBT	TC	TT	DMBT	
4495	8477	9612	10320	8478	05/47-04/50
4496	8479	9611	10303	8480	04/47-09/50
4497	8483	9617	10321	8484	05/47-07/50
4498	8487	9613	10267	8488	01/47-08/50
4499	8489	9614	10304	8490	03/47-07/50
4500	8491	9616	10311	8492	04/47-11/50
4501	8493	9615	10341	8494	06/47-03/51

4-SUB
Augmented Suburban Units
660-750V dc third rail
4502-4516

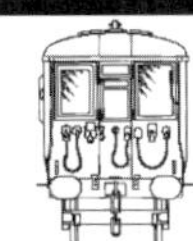

SER bodied units augmented with new all-steel trailers.

	DMBT	TC	TT	DMBT	
4502	8497	9620	10257	8498	12/46-09/51
4503	8499	9621	10277	8500	01/47-07/52
4503	8499	9621	*9185*	8500	08/52-10/54
4504	8503	9623	10326	8504	05/47-09/51
4505	8509	9626	10309	8510	04/47-04/53
4506	8515	9629	10244	8516	11/46-09/51
4507	8519	9631	10328	8520	05/47-12/51
4508	8523	9633	10262	8524	12/46-02/51
4509	8529	9636	10313	8530	04/47-08/51
4510	8513	9639	10278	8535	01/47-07/53
4511	8539	9641	10252	8540	11/46-01/51
4512	8541	9642	10273	8542	01/47-09/51
4513	8543	9643	10315	8544	04/47-02/51
4514	8545	9644	10241	8546	11/46-08/51
4514	8545	9644	*9660*	8546	08/51-09/51
4515	8549	9646	10272	8550	01/47-04/53
4515	8549	9646	*9626*	8550	04/53-01/55
4516	8551	9647	10333	8552	06/47-12/51

4-SUB
Augmented Suburban Units
660-750V dc third rail
4517-4519

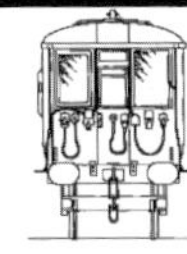

Miscellaneous LSWR bodied units augmented with new all-steel trailers.

	DMBT	TC	TT	DMBC	
4517	8224	9302	10175	9823	01/48-04/53

	DMBT	TC	TT	DMBT	
4518	9859	9765	10203	9860	01/49-01/52
4518	9859	9765	*9647*	9860	01/52-12/53

	DMBT	TC	TT	DMBC	
4519	8558	9652	10177	9811	02/48-05/53
4519	8558	9652	*9649*	9811	05/53-01/54

4-SUB
Augmented Suburban Units
660-750V dc third rail
4520

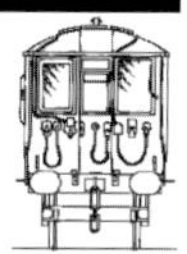

LBSCR bodied units augmented with new all-steel trailers.

	DMBT	TC	TT	DMBT		
4520	8691	9490	10470	8697	08/47-07/53	
4520	8106	10229	10470	8697	10/54-02/56	☞

4-SUB
Augmented Suburban Units
660-750V dc third rail
4521-4526

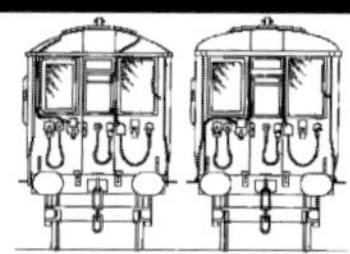

Miscellaneous LSWR bodied units augmented with new all-steel trailers.

	DMBT	TC	TT	DMBT		
4521	8200	9328	10456	9903	08/47-03/53	
4522	8629	9681	10203	8630	05/48-01/49	
4523	8631	9682	10180	8632	02/48-01/49	
4524	8633	9683	10182	8634	02/48-05/49	
4525	8639	9686	10202	8640	04/48-01/49	
4526	8225	9303	10228	8895	07/48-11/51	
4526	8225	9303	9762	8895	11/51-02/56	☞

4-SUB
Augmented Suburban Units
660-750V dc third rail
4527-4571

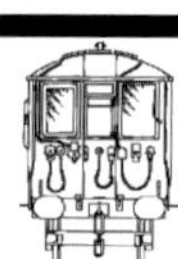

LBSCR bodied units augmented with new all-steel trailers.

	DMBT	TC	TT	DMBC			
4527	8693	9724	10471	8859	08/47-07/56	➲4504	
4528	8694	9725	10183	8860	02/48-06/55	➲4510	
4528	8739	9725	10183	8860	06/55-11/56		☞
4529	8695	9726	10182	8861	05/49-08/56		
4530	8696	9727	10193	8862	08/49-08/56		
4531	8698	9729	10180	8864	01/49-11/56	➲Dep	
4532	8866	9731	10469	8700	08/47-04/50		
4532	8866	9731	10188	8877	05/50-09/56	➲4507	☞
4533	8701	9732	10185	8867	03/49-12/56	➲4514	
4534	8702	9733	10167	8868	01/48-07/56	➲4503	
4535	8703	9734	10226	8869	07/48-09/56		
4536	8704	9735	10202	8870	01/49-05/53		
4537	8706	9737	10466	8872	08/47-08/55		
4537	8036	9737	10466	8762	08/55-05/56		☞
4538	8707	9738	10194	8873	04/48-10/56	➲4508	
4539	8708	9739	10191	8874	01/49-12/56	➲4512	
4540	8709	9740	10211	8875	05/48-06/56		
4541	8712	9743	10225	8878	07/48-11/56	➲4509	
4542	8713	9744	10222	8879	07/48-03/56		
4543	8715	9746	10178	8881	02/48-09/56	➲Dep	
4544	8716	9747	10186	8882	08/49-10/56		
4545	8717	9748	10190	8883	02/49-08/56	➲4506	
4546	8718	9749	10223	8884	07/48-09/53		
4546	8718	9749	10223	8798	09/53-06/56		☞
4547	8719	9461	10204	8885	01/49-08/56		
4548	8720	9462	10188	8886	05/49-04/50		
4548	8700	9462	10469	8886	04/50-10/56		☞
4549	8721	9463	10468	8887	08/47-05/56	➲4504	
4550	8722	9464	10168	8888	01/48-12/56	➲4513	
4551	8731	9465	10453	8889	08/47-10/51		
4551	8731	9657	10453	8889	11/51-10/56	➲4511	☞
4552	8732	9466	10450	8890	08/47-09/56		
4553	8733	9467	10176	8891	02/48-06/56	➲4502	
4554	8734	9468	10227	8892	07/48-01/57	➲4516	
4555	8739	9473	10187	8897	03/48-06/55		
4555	8694	9473	10187	8897	06/55-01/57	➲4515	☞
4556	8736	9470	10451	8894	08/47-08/56	➲4505	
4557	8741	9475	10212	8899	06/48-10/56	➲S90	
4558	8742	9476	10179	8900	02/48-12/56	➲4517	
4559	8744	9478	10229	9802	07/48-10/54		
4560	8745	9479	11450	9803	08/49- 50		
4560	8745	9479	10322	9803	50-03/56		☞
4561	8743	9477	10467	9801	08/47-07/56		
4562	8643	9688	10191	8644	03/48-01/49		
4563	8683	9714	10185	8849	03/48-03/49		
4564	8746	9480	10459	9804	08/47-02/56		
4565	8749	9483	10224	9807	07/48-04/55		
4566	8686	9717	10189	8852	02/49-06/52		
4566	8686	9717	9719	8852	06/52-07/55		☞
4567	8687	9718	10201	8853	01/49-02/52		
4567	8687	9718	9774	8853	02/52-02/56		☞
4568	8688	9719	10169	8854	01/48-06/52		
4569	8689	9720	10449	8855	08/47-05/52		
4570	8690	9721	10181	8856	05/49-04/51		
4571	8692	9723	10174	8858	01/48-06/52		
4571	8692	9723	9720	8858	06/52-03/56		☞

4-SUB
Augmented Suburban Units
660-750V dc third rail
4572-4614

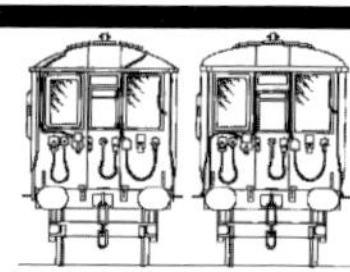

Miscellaneous units augmented with new all-steel trailers.

	DMBT	TC	TT	DMBC/DMBT			
4572	8217	9345	10452	8831	08/47-05/53		
4572	8217	9735	10452	8831	05/53-05/56		☞
4573	8562	9656	11454	9815	01/49-11/51		
4573	8562	9656	9772	9815	11/51-06/52		☞
4573	8689	9656	9772	9815	06/52-03/55		☞
4573	8689	9656	9478	9815	03/55-02/56		☞
4574	8563	9657	10213	9816	06/48-09/51		
4575	8655	9694	10190	8656	03/48-02/49		
4576	8673	9704	10193	8839	03/48-08/49		
4577	8675	9706	10204	8841	05/48-01/49		
4578	8682	9713	10195	8848	04/48-10/49		
4579	8564	9658	10460	9817	08/47-07/53	➲S10	
4580	8533	9638	10192	8534	03/48-08/53		
4580	8533	9638	9639	8534	08/53-03/54		☞
4581	8684	9715	10186	8850	03/48-08/49		
4582	8685	9716	10188	8851	03/48-05/49		
4583	8586	9666	10189	8587	03/48-02/49		
4584	8588	9667	10181	8589	02/48-05/49		
4585	8617	9675	10201	8618	04/48-01/49		
4586	8553	9648	10184	8554	02/48-06/52		
4586	8553	9648	9319	8554	08/52-01/55		☞
4587	8501	9622	11453	8502	05/49-05/51		
4588	8511	9627	10195	8512	10/49-10/51		
4589	8527	9635	11449	8528	01/49-01/51		
4590	9806	9482	11451	8877	02/49-05/50		
4590	9806	9482	11451	12664	05/50-07/54		☞
4590	9806	9482	11451	8023	09/54-03/56		☞
4591	8574	9660	11448	8575	02/49-10/50		
4591	9852	9660	10289	8575	10/50-08/51		☞
4592	8576	9661	11452	8577	02/49-06/51		
4593	8578	9662	11455	8579	05/49-03/51		
4594	8223	9301	11456	9822	03/49-12/49		
4594	8223	9301	10376	9822	12/49-10/52		☞
4594	8223	9301	9367	9822	10/52-12/53		☞
4601	8641	9687	11453	8642	08/47-05/49		
4602	8676	9707	11448	8842	08/47-06/48		
4603	8623	9678	11452	8624	08/47-02/49		
4604	8645	9689	11455	8646	08/47-05/49		
4605	8627	9680	11451	8628	08/47-02/49		
4606	8651	9692	11454	8652	08/47-01/49		
4607	8594	9670	11456	8595	08/47-02/48		
4608	8657	9695	11456	8658	02/48-02/49		
4610	8649	9691	11448	8650	06/48-02/49		
4613	8659	9696	11450	8660	08/47-08/49		
4614	8661	9697	11449	8662	08/47-01/49		

4-SUB
Augmented Suburban Units
660-750V dc third rail
4501-4518

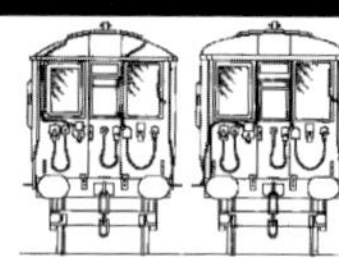

Second Series

	DMBS	TC	TS	DMBC		
4501²	8895	9730	9656	9815	06/56-01/60	
4502²	8733	9720	9467	8891	06/56-12/59	
4503²	8718	9478	9733	8868	07/56-12/59	
4504²	8721	9463	9724	8859	07/56-10/59	
4505²	8736	9461	9470	8894	08/56-05/58	
4506²	8717	9719	9748	8883	08/56-04/58	
4506²	8717	9719	9748	8719	04/58-01/60	☞
4507²	8703	9728	9731	8866	09/56-10/59	
4508²	8707	9472	9738	8873	10/56-01/60	
4509²	8712	9726	9743	8878	11/56-11/59	
4510²	8739	9746	9725	8860	11/56-12/59	
4511²	8731	9737	9657	8889	11/56-12/59	

Unit					Dates
4512[2]	8708	9729	9739	8874	12/56-12/59
4513[2]	8722	9475	9464	8888	12/56-11/59
4514[2]	8701	9747	9732	8867	12/56-10/59
4515[2]	8694	9462	9473	8897	01/57-11/59
4516[2]	8734	9734	9468	8892	01/57-10/59
4517[2]	8742	9727	9476	8900	01/57-11/59
4518[2]	8705	9741	9736	8871	01/57-11/58

Class 405 4-SUB
Standard Suburban Units
660-750V dc third rail
4601-4607, 4617-4620

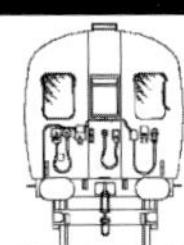

4601-4607 were formed from newly built motors with older trailers.

12650-12664 were built to work with redundant augmentation trailers from units in the 4401-4516 range that were then being withdrawn. 12664 went to 4590 to replace an old car, then it moved on to new 2-HAL unit 2700.

The remaining units were renumbered 4617-4620 in 1977.

Unit	DMBTO	TT	TT	DMBTO	Dates	Notes
4601[2]	12650	10245	10240	12651	04/50-10/58	
4601[2]	12650	10245	10240	12681	06/59-06/76	
4601[2]	12650	10444	10448	12681	06/76-05/77	⇒4617
4602[2]	12652	10276	10242	12653	04/50-06/72	⇒4620
4603[2]	12654	10297	10287	12657	04/50-06/76	
4603[2]	12654	10446	10445	12657	06/76-05/77	⇒4618
4604[2]	12658	10325	10265	12659	04/50-04/76	
4605[2]	12655	10259	10337	12656	04/50-07/75	
4605[2]	12655	10259	12359	12656	07/75-05/77	⇒4619
4606[2]	12660	10248	10237	12661	04/50-04/76	
4607[2]	12662	10373	10312	12663	05/50-05/60	
4607[2]	12662	10449	10312	12663	05/60-12/73	
4607[2]	12662	10449	8941	11382	03/74-04/76	

Unit	DMBSO	TS/TSO	TS/TSO	DMBSO	Dates
4617	12650	10444	10448	12681	05/77-06/82
4618	12654	10446	10445	12657	05/77-10/82
4619	12655	10259	12359	12656	05/77-02/81
4620	12652	12403	10242	12653	06/72-05/76
4620	12652	12403	8970	12653	05/76-05/83

Class 405/2 4-SUB
Standard Suburban Units
660-750V dc third rail
4621-4754

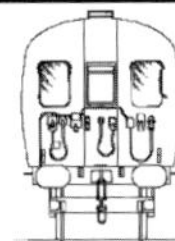

This batch was practically identical to the 4277 batch, but many were built on old frames. Although designed for use with new light-weight motors, many were at first fitted with the old style 275hp type.

The batch from 4667 onwards was the last batch of 4-SUBs. All the compartment trailers were taken from augmented 3-SUB units. All the other coaches except for three were built on reclaimed underframes.

Unit	DMBTO	TT	TTO	DMBTO	Dates	Notes
4621	11302	8901	12361	11301	05/49-09/72	
4621	12747	8901	12361	11301	09/72-06/76	
4621	12665	8980	12361	11301	06/76-12/80	
4622	11304	8902	12362	11303	05/49-05/74	
4623	11306	8903	12363	11305	05/49-07/72	
4623	11306	8903	8947	11305	10/72-07/81	
4623	11306	10124	8947	11305	07/81-05/82	
4624	11308	8904	12364	11307	05/49-07/72	
4624	11308	8904	12364	11305	07/72-10/72	
4624	11308	8904	12364	11307	10/72-04/76	
4625	11309	8905	12365	11310	06/49-03/71	
4625	10815	8905	12365	11310	04/71-05/74	
4626	11311	8906	12366	11312	06/49-05/76	
4626	11311	9026	12366	11312	05/76-02/79	
4626	11311	9026	12366	11383	02/79-10/82	
4627	11313	8907	12367	11314	06/49-02/68	
4627	11313	8907	12367	10915	02/68-01/72	
4627	11313	8907	12367	10840	04/72-05/76	
4627	11313	12386	12367	11351	05/76-06/81	
4628	11315	8908	12368	11316	06/49-06/81	
4629	11318	8909	12369	11317	07/49-06/81	
4629	11318	12368	12369	11317	06/81-09/83	
4630	11320	8910	12370	11319	07/49-06/81	
4630	11320	12357	12370	11319	06/81-05/83	
4631	11322	8911	12371	11321	07/49- 51	
4631	11322	10328	12371	11321	05/52-07/81	
4631	11322	12390	12371	11321	07/81-05/82	
4632	11324	8912	12372	11323	07/49-02/63	
4632	11324	8912	12372	10873	02/63-09/78	
4632	11324	8912	12372	10873	06/79-06/81	
4633	11326	8913	12373	11325	07/49-06/76	
4633	11326	12384	12373	11325	06/76-10/82	
4634	11327	8914	12374	11328	07/49-05/74	
4635	11329	8915	12375	11330	08/49-07/73	
4635	11329	8915	12375	11343	07/73-06/81	
4636	11332	8916	12376	11331	09/49-06/81	
4637	11334	8917	12377	11333	09/49-05/76	
4637	11334	8956	12377	11333	05/76-05/82	
4637	11334	8956	12371	11333	05/82-10/82	
4638	11336	8918	12378	11335	09/49-06/81	
4639	11338	8919	12379	11337	09/49-03/75	
4639	11338	12362	12379	11337	03/75-05/82	
4640	11340	8920	12380	11339	10/49-11/73	
4641	11342	8921	12381	11341	10/49-06/81	
4642	11343	8922	12382	11344	10/49-05/73	
4643	11345	8923	12383	11346	10/49-04/81	
4644	11347	8924	12384	11348	10/49-04/76	
4645	11349	8925	12385	11350	11/49-12/75	
4645	11349	8984	12385	11350	12/75-10/82	
4646	11351	8926	12386	11352	11/49-04/76	
4647	11354	8927	12387	11353	11/49-04/76	
4648	11355	8928	12388	11356	11/49-05/81	
4649	11357	8929	12389	11358	11/49-03/75	
4649	11357	12355	12389	11358	03/75-06/82	
4650	11360	8930	12390	11359	12/49-04/58	
4650	11360	10244	12390	11359	06/58-06/81	
4651	11362	8931	12391	11361	12/49-07/76	
4651	11362	9020	12391	11361	07/76-10/79	
4651	11362	12402	12391	11361	10/79-10/82	
4652	11364	8932	12392	11363	12/49-04/61	
4653	11366	8933	12393	11365	12/49-06/81	
4654	11368	8934	12394	11367	01/50-07/76	
4654	11368	12364	12394	11367	07/76-10/82	
4655	11370	8935	12395	11369	01/50-09/78	
4655	11370	8935	12395	10873	09/78-06/79	
4655	11370	8935	12395	11369	06/79-06/81	
4656	11372	8936	12396	11371	01/50-06/76	
4656	11372	9032	12396	11371	06/76-10/82	
4657	11374	8937	12397	11373	01/50-05/76	
4657	11374	8992	12397	11373	05/76-07/83	
4658	11375	8938	12398	11376	02/50-05/76	
4658	11375	9014	12398	11376	05/76-10/82	
4659	11377	8939	12399	11378	02/50-06/76	
4659	11377	8978	12399	11378	06/76-12/80	
4659	11377	8978	12399	11301	12/80-10/82	
4660	11380	8940	12400	11379	02/50-07/81	
4660	11380	10130	12400	11379	07/81-04/83	
4661	11382	8941	12401	11381	02/50-06/51	
4661	11382	8941	12401	12767	06/51-02/59	
4661	11382	8941	12401	11381	02/59-05/66	
4661	11382	11468	12401	11381	11/66-08/67	
4661	11382	8941	12401	11381	08/67-03/74	
4662	11384	8942	12402	11383	02/50-07/76	
4662	11384	8965	12402	11383	07/76-02/79	
4663	11385	8943	12403	11386	02/50-05/72	
4664	11387	8944	12404	11388	03/50-08/67	
4664	11387	8944	12404	12686	08/67-01/68	
4664	11387	8944	12404	11388	01/68-11/80	⇒Dep 013
4665	11389	8945	12405	11390	03/50-04/76	
4666	11391	8946	12406	11392	03/50-05/76	
4666	11391	8993	12406	11392	05/76-05/83	
4667	12665	10291	8947	12666	05/50-11/70	
4668	12667	10264	8948	12668	05/50-06/76	
4668	12667	8983	8948	12668	06/76-05/83	
4669	12670	10261	8949	12669	05/50-07/81	
4669	12670	10127	8949	12669	07/81-05/82	
4670	12671	10249	8950	12672	05/50-06/76	
4670	12671	12387	8950	12672	06/76-05/83	
4671	12674	10279	8951	12673	05/50-06/76	
4671	12674	8991	8951	12673	06/76-10/82	
4672	12676	10320	8952	12675	05/50-05/76	
4672	12676	9016	8952	12675	05/76-10/82	
4673	12678	10344	8953	12677	06/50-05/81	
4673	12678	8961	8953	12677	05/81-10/82	
4674	12679	10296	8954	12680	06/50-06/76	
4674	12679	8974	8954	11354	06/76-12/77	
4674	12679	8974	8954	12680	12/77-10/82	
4675	12681	10258	8955	12682	06/50-10/58	
4675	12651	10258	8955	12682	04/59-06/81	
4676	12683	10230	8956	12684	06/50-04/76	
4677	12686	10247	8957	12685	06/50-08/67	
4677	12686	10247	8957	12685	01/68-06/81	
4678	12687	10323	8958	12688	07/50-06/76	
4678	12687	8982	8958	12688	06/76-05/83	

4679	12689	10318	8959	12690	07/50-07/59	
4679	*12699*	10318	8959	*12700*	07/59-05/76	↩
4679	12699	*12405*	8959	12700	05/76-08/81	↩
4679	*10862*	12405	8959	12700	08/81-10/82	↩
4680	12691	10304	8960	12692	07/50-10/59	
4680	*8654*	10304	8960	*8655*	10/59-05/76	↩
4680	8654	*9003*	8960	8655	05/76-07/83	↩
4681	12693	10321	8961	12694	07/50-05/81	
4682	12695	10293	8962	12696	07/50-06/76	
4682	12695	*8968*	8962	12696	06/76-04/83	↩
4683	12697	10290	8963	12698	08/50-07/81	
4683	12697	*8957*	8963	12698	07/81-10/82	↩
4684	12700	10270	8964	12699	08/50-07/59	
4684	*12690*	10270	8964	*12689*	07/59-07/81 ⊠04/76-04/76	↩
4684	12690	*8975*	8964	12689	07/81-05/82	↩
4685	12702	10314	8965	12701	08/50-04/76	
4686	12703	10274	8966	12704	08/50-08/58	
4686	12703	10274	8966	*10852*	08/58-04/59	↩
4686	12703	10274	8966	*12704*	04/59-04/76	↩
4687	12706	10267	8967	12705	09/50-05/56	
4687	12706	10267	8967	12705	*08/57*-06/76	↩
4687	12706	*9000*	8967	12705	06/76-12/82	↩
4687	12706	9000	8967	*8646*	01/83-05/83	↩
4688	12708	11450	8968	12707	09/50-04/76	
4689	12709	10301	8969	12710	09/50-06/81	
4690	12712	10282	8970	12711	09/50-04/76	
4691	12713	10303	8971	12714	09/50-04/76	
4692	12715	10232	8972	12716	09/50-05/81	
4692	12715	*8989*	8972	12716	05/81-12/82	↩
4692	12715	8989	8972	*8644*	12/82-05/83	↩
4693	12717	10327	8973	12718	09/50-06/81	
4694	12719	10263	8974	12720	09/50-04/76	
4695	12722	10334	8975	12721	09/50-06/81	
4696	12723	11448	8976	12724	10/50-01/65	
4696	*12771*	11448	8976	12724	01/65-06/76	↩
4696	12771	*12357*	8976	12724	06/76-03/77	↩
4696	*10847*	12357	8976	12724	06/77-05/81	↩
4697	12726	10286	8977	12725	10/50-06/81	
4698	12727	10329	8978	12728	10/50-04/76	
4699	12730	10236	8979	12729	10/50-04/76	
4700	12731	10250	8980	12732	10/50-04/76	
4701	12733	10305	8981	12734	11/50-11/65	
4701	12733	10305	8981	*8649*	11/65-06/81	↩
4702	12735	10331	8982	12736	11/50-04/76	
4703	12738	10311	8983	12737	11/50-11/70	
4703	12738	10311	8983	*12665*	11/70-06/73	↩
4703	12738	10311	8983	*12747*	06/73-04/76	↩
4704	12740	10295	8984	12739	11/50-*07/58*	
4704	*12754*	10295	8984	12739	07/58-09/75	↩
4705	12742	10271	8985	12741	11/50-06/81	
4706	12743	10231	8986	12744	11/50-04/76	
4707	12746	10343	8987	12745	12/50-04/76	
4708	12747	10317	8988	12748	12/50-09/72	
4709	12749	10233	8989	12750	12/50-05/81	
4710	12751	10342	8990	12752	12/50-06/76	
4710	12751	*8986*	8990	12752	06/76-03/78	↩
4710	*12767*	8986	8990	12752	03/78-07/83	↩
4711	12754	10330	8991	12753	12/50-10/56	
4711	*12740*	10330	8991	12753	07/58-12/70	↩
4711	12740	10330	8991	12753	05/71-04/76	↩
4712	12755	10294	8992	12756	01/51-04/76	
4713	12758	10256	8993	12757	01/51-04/76	
4714	12760	10324	8994	12759	01/51-05/81	
4714	12760	*8976*	8994	12759	05/81-07/83	↩
4715	12761	10307	8995	12762	01/51-11/74	
4716	12763	10300	8996	12764	02/51-07/81	
4716	12763	*12378*	8996	12764	07/81-07/83	↩
4717	12765	10306	8997	12766	02/51-04/76	
4718	12767	10252	8998	12768	02/51-06/51	
4718	*11381*	*8911*	8998	12768	05/52-02/59	↩
4718	*12767*	8911	8998	12768	02/59-06/76	↩
4718	12767	*8987*	8998	12768	06/76-01/78	↩
4719	12769	10243	8999	12770	03/51-07/81	
4719	12769	*12376*	8999	12770	07/81-06/83	↩
4720	12771	10340	9000	12772	03/51-12/64	
4720	*10906*	10340	9000	*12723*	*01/65*-04/76	↩
4721	12773	10339	9001	12774	03/51-06/76	
4721	12773	*10443*	9001	12774	06/76-09/83	↩
4722	12776	10341	9002	12775	04/51-03/71	
4722	12776	10341	9002	*8620*	10/71-05/76	↩
4722	12776	*9021*	9002	8620	05/76-01/83	↩
4722	12776	9021	9002	*11349*	01/83-05/83	↩
4723	12777	11455	9003	12778	04/51-04/76	
4724	12779	10284	10181	12780	04/51-07/51	
4724	12779	10284	*9004*	12780	07/51-04/76	↩
4725	12782	10235	9005	12781	04/51-06/76	
4725	12782	*9028*	9005	12781	06/76-10/81	↩
4726	12784	10336	9006	12783	05/51-06/76	
4726	12784	*8971*	9006	12783	06/76-07/83	↩
4727	12785	10315	9007	12786	05/51-04/76	
4728	12788	11449	9008	12787	06/51-04/76	
4729	12789	10393	9009	12790	06/51-03/74	
4730	12791	10262	9010	12792	06/51-11/74	
4730	*12762*	*8995*	9010	12792	11/74-12/81	↩
4730	*12781*	8995	9010	12792	12/81-10/82	↩
4731	12794	10252	9011	12793	06/51-04/76	
4732	12796	10239	9012	12795	06/51-11/74	
4732	12796	10239	*12354*	12795	11/74-10/83	↩
4733	12798	11453	9013	12797	06/51-10/75	
4733	*12739*	*12365*	9013	12797	10/75-05/82	↩
4734	12799	10338	9014	12800	07/51-04/76	
4735	8617	10234	9015	8616	07/51-06/81	
4736	8618	10181	9016	8619	07/51-12/70	
4736	*12740*	10181	9016	8619	12/70-05/71	↩
4736	*8618*	10181	9016	8619	05/71-04/76	↩
4737	8620	10308	9017	8621	08/51-10/71	
4738	8622	10310	9018	8623	08/51-03/76	
4738	8622	*9011*	9018	*12793*	04/76-08/83	↩
4739	8624	11452	9019	8625	08/51-06/76	
4739	8624	*12360*	9019	8625	06/76-06/81	↩
4740	8626	10255	9020	8627	08/51-04/76	
4741	8629	10288	9021	8628	08/51-04/76	
4742	8630	10319	9022	8631	08/51-07/81	
4742	8630	*8977*	9022	8631	07/81-06/83	↩
4743	8633	10273	9023	8632	09/51-06/76	
4743	8633	*9008*	9023	8632	06/76-05/83	↩
4744	8634	10313	9024	8635	09/51-01/76	
4745	8636	10241	9025	8637	09/51-10/73	
4746	8639	10316	9026	8638	09/51-04/76	
4747	8640	10269	9027	8641	10/51-05/81	
4747	8640	*12388*	9027	8641	05/81-05/83	↩
4748	8643	10213	9028	8642	10/51-03/74	
4748	*12789*	10213	9028	8642	03/74-04/76	↩
4749	8645	10268	9029	8644	10/51-05/76	
4749	8645	*8997*	9029	8644	05/76-09/82	↩
4750	8647	10289	9030	8646	10/51-06/76	
4750	8647	*8966*	9030	8646	06/76-10/82	↩
4751	8648	10302	9031	8649	10/51-11/65	
4751	8648	10302	9031	*12734*	*01/66*-07/81	↩
4751	8648	*12375*	9031	12734	07/81-07/83	↩
4752	8650	10244	9032	8651	11/51-06/58	
4752	8650	*8930*	9032	8651	06/58-04/76	↩
4753	8653	10326	9033	8652	12/51-09/78	
4754	8654	10257	9034	8655	12/51-10/59	
4754	*12691*	10257	9034	*12692*	10/59-06/81	↩
4754	12691	*10140*	9034	12692	06/81-09/83	↩

4-DD
Double-Deck Units
660-750V dc third rail
4901-4902

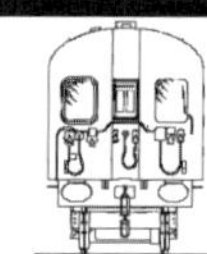

See 4001-4002 for details.

	DMBS	*TS*	*TS*	*DMBS*		
4901	13001	13501	13502	13002	10/70-10/71	⊂**4001**
4902	13003	13504	13503	13004	10/70-10/71	⊂**4002**

Class 415/1 4-EPB
EPB Suburban Units
660-750V dc third rail
5001-5260

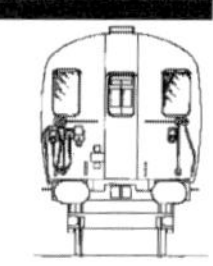

The EPBs were virtually identical with the final 4-SUBs. The main change was the incorporation of electro-pneumatic brake control. The cab end was redesigned with no external cab doors (entry being through the guard's van). The units were fitted with roller blind indicators as standard.

Most of the carriages in the units were built on reclaimed frames. The old frames were completely dismantled and then reassembled at Lancing, the inner and outer sole-bars being transposed as part of the process. Compartment trailers for the units came from augmented 4-SUB units; they were re-wired and renumbered for use in the EPB units.

The first nine units were built carrying carriage numbers following on from the final 4-SUB units, 8656-8673 and 9035-9043. The compartment trailer cars carried their 4-SUB numbers. Units 5001 & 5002 had the carriages renumbered in March 1952, the rest were renumbered before entering service.

Units from 5138 onwards had detail differences including the provision of a rainstrip above the level of the doors for the full length of the unit. (Previously the rainstrips had been mounted higher up on the roofs).

The units worked on suburban services on all divisions, and later also appeared on outer-suburban and main-line duties on the Central and Western sections.

Attention was turned to the facelifting of the units in the 1970s after it was realised that no replacement stock would be available for a number of years. Unit 5263 was formed using two 2-SAP motor coaches and two 4-SUB trailers. The unit featured a much improved interior; lower ceilings with fluorescent lighting, new seating and a public address system.

As a result of this conversion, many more units were facelifted (although without lowered ceilings to reduce the costs). They were converted at Eastleigh and at Horwich and all coaches were converted to open. The units were reclassified 415/4 and were renumbered in the 54xx series. The remaining 2-SAP motor coaches were also incorporated in the reformed units. A number of redundant 4-SUB trailers were upgraded and renumbered as part of this scheme.

During the 1980s there had been increasing cases of vandalism in compartment stock, but things came to a head after the murder of a young woman in a compartment. This led to the reforming of a large number of unrefurbished units to concentrate the remaining compartment stock into a small number of units which were to be used in rush hours only. They were renumbered 5501-5532 and were identified with a red line above the doors. They were taken out of traffic in 1991.

The remaining units in the 50xx series were renumbered from 5265 upwards in 1988.

Unit	*DMBSO*	*TS*	*TSO*	*DMBSO*	Dates		
5001	14001	15001	15101	14002	12/51-01/84		
5001	14001	*15429*	15101	14002	01/84-11/88	➲**5265**	☜
5001	14001	*15207*	15101	14002	11/90-03/95		☜
5002	14004	15002	15102	14003	02/52-04/85	➲*5466*	
5003	14006	15003	15103	14005	03/52-03/85	➲*5467*	
5004	14007	15004	15104	14008	03/52-06/85	➲*5469*	
5005	14010	15005	15105	14009	04/52-04/88	➲*5531*	
5006	14012	15006	15106	14011	04/52-08/85		
5006	*14100*	15006	15106	14011	08/85-07/87		☜
5007	14013	15007	15107	14014	04/52-11/81		
5007	14013	15007	15107	*14057*	01/82-07/85	➲*5477*	☜
5008	14016	15008	15108	14015	05/52-08/59		
5008	14016	*15080*	15108	14015	08/60-06/85	➲*5476*	☜
5009	14017	15009	15109	14018	05/52-08/85	➲*5482*	
5010	14019	15010	15110	14020	06/52-06/85	➲*5475*	
5011	14021	15011	15111	14022	06/52-02/85	➲**5462**	
5012	14024	15012	15112	14023	07/52-05/86	➲**5489**	
5013	14025	15013	15113	14026	08/52-05/88	➲*5532*	
5014	14028	15014	15114	14027	08/52-10/86	➲*5493*	
5015	14029	15015	15115	14030	08/52-01/86	➲*5491*	
5016	14031	15016	15116	14032	04/53-05/88	➲*5511*	
5017	14033	15017	15117	14034	05/53-07/87		
5018	14036	15018	15118	14035	05/53-04/88	➲*5508*	
5019	14037	15019	15119	14038	05/53-03/85	➲**5463**	
5020	14039	15020	15120	14040	05/53-06/58		
5020	14039	*15332*	*15382*	14040	11/58-03/85		☜
5020	14039	*15234*	15382	14040	03/85-11/88	➲**5266**	☜
5021	14041	15021	15121	14042	05/53-02/59		
5021	*14062*	*15023*	*15123*	14042	10/59-02/84		☜
5021	14062	15023	*15027*	*14054*	02/84-09/84	➲**5455**	☜
5022	14043	15022	15122	14044	06/53-05/88	➲*5517*	
5023	14045	15023	15123	14046	06/53-07/58		
5024	14048	15024	15124	14047	06/53-07/87	➲*Dep*	
5025	14050	15025	15125	14049	06/53-12/85		
5026	14052	15026	15126	14051	07/53-11/85	➲*5483*	
5027	14053	15027	15127	14054	07/53-02/84		
5027	14053	*15123*	15127	*14042*	02/84-11/88	➲**5267**	☜
5028	14056	15028	15128	14055	08/53-06/86		
5028	*65303*	15028	*15083*	14055	06/86-07/87		☜
5029	14057	15029	15129	14058	08/53-09/79		
5029	*14493*	15029	15129	14058	09/79-08/85	➲*5473*	☜
5030	14059	15030	15130	14060	08/53-09/85	➲*5478*	
5031	14061	15031	15131	14062	08/53-09/58		
5031	14061	15031	15131	*14046*	09/58-12/85	➲*5484*	☜
5032	14063	15032	15132	14064	08/53-05/88	➲*5516*	
5033	14065	15033	15133	14066	09/53-08/85	➲*5474*	
	DMBSO	***TSO***	***TSO***	***DMBSO***			
5034	14067	15159	15134	14068	09/53-04/85		
5034	14067	*15141*	15134	14068	04/85-12/85		☜
5035	14069	15160	15135	14070	09/53-05/88		
5035	14069	*15113*	15135	14070	05/88-11/88	➲**5268**	☜
5036	14071	15161	15136	14072	09/53-01/86	➲*5486*	
5037	14073	15162	15137	14074	10/53-11/86	➲*5494*	
5038	14076	15163	15138	14075	10/53-04/88	➲*5504*	
5039	14078	15164	15139	14077	10/53-06/77		
5039	14078	15164	15139	*14094*	08/77-04/88		☜
5039	14078	*15118*	15139	14094	04/88-11/88	➲**5269**	☜
5040	14080	15165	15140	14079	10/53-05/88		
5040	14080	*15122*	15140	14079	05/88-11/88	➲**5270**	☜
5041	14081	15166	15141	14082	10/53-04/85	➲*5464*	
5042	14083	15167	15142	14084	11/53-09/85		
5042	14083	*15130*	15142	14084	09/85-11/88	➲**5271**	☜
5043	14085	15168	15143	14086	11/53-04/88	➲*5529*	
5044	14087	15169	15144	14088	11/53-07/85		
5044	14087	*15345*	15144	14088	07/85-11/88	➲**5272**	☜
5045	14090	15170	15145	14089	11/53-08/85		
5045	14090	*15129*	15145	14089	08/85-11/88	➲**5273**	☜
5046	14091	15171	15146	14092	11/53-07/87		
5046	14091	*15364*	15146	14092	07/87-11/88	➲**5274**	☜
5047	14093	15172	15147	14094	11/53-06/77		
5048	14095	15173	15148	14096	11/53-12/86	➲*5495*	
5049	14098	15174	15149	14097	12/53-09/80		
5049	14098	*15271*	15149	14097	09/80-09/88	➲**5275**	☜
5050	14100	15175	15150	14099	01/54-01/85		
5050	14100	15175	15150	*14300*	01/85-01/85	➲*5150*	☜
5051	14101	15176	15151	14102	01/54-04/88		
5051	14101	*15143*	15151	14102	04/88-11/88	➲**5276**	☜
5052	14104	15177	15152	14103	01/54-06/72		
5052	14104	15177	15152	*14495*	06/72-03/85		☜
5052	14104	*15103*	15152	14495	03/85-11/88	➲**5277**	☜
5053	14105	15178	15153	14106	02/54-12/85	➲*5485*	
5101	14201	15179	15154	14202	11/53-04/88	➲*5530*	
5102	14204	15180	15155	14203	12/53-10/84		
5103	14205	15181	15156	14206	12/53-09/71		
5104	14207	15182	15157	14208	01/54-05/81		
5104	14207	*15409*	15157	14208	05/81-11/92		☜
5105	14210	15183	15158	14209	01/54-04/88	➲*5512*	
5106	14212	15184	15231	14211	02/54-03/85	➲*5468*	
5107	14213	15185	15235	14214	02/54-12/85		
5107	14213	*15153*	15235	14214	12/85-10/90		☜
5108	14215	15186	15236	14216	03/54-11/86		
5108	14215	15186	*15162*	14216	11/86-07/87		☜
5109	14218	15187	15237	14217	03/54-10/86		
5109	14218	15187	*15014*	14217	10/86-07/87		☜
5110	14220	15188	15238	14219	03/54-11/83		
5110	*14349*	*15353*	15238	14219	11/83-07/87	➲*5187*	☜
5111	14221	15189	15239	14222	03/54-05/88	➲*5520*	
5112	14223	15190	15240	14224	03/54-08/86	➲*5492*	
5113	14225	15191	15241	14226	04/54-04/81		
5113	14225	*15376*	15241	14226	04/81-05/91		☜
5114	14227	15192	15242	14228	04/54-05/81		
5114	14227	*15426*	15242	14228	05/81-02/92	➲Dep	☜
5115	14230	15193	15243	14229	04/54-01/69		
5115	14230	*15084*	15243	14229	08/69-07/88		☜
5115	14230	*15350*	15243	14229	07/88-10/92		☜
5116	14232	15194	15244	14231	04/54-04/88	➲*5523*	
5117	14234	15195	15245	14233	05/54-04/88	➲*5527*	
5118	14236	15196	15246	14235	05/54-11/83		
5118	14236	15196	15246	*14350*	11/83-04/85	➲*5465*	☜
5119	14238	15197	15247	14237	05/54-04/88	➲*5509*	
5120	14240	15198	15248	14239	05/54-09/81	➲*5420*	
5121	14242	15199	15249	14241	06/54-04/88		
5121	14242	*15247*	15249	14241	04/88-09/91		☜
5121	*14413*	15247	15249	14241	09/91-10/92		☜
5122	14243	15200	15250	14244	06/54-04/71		
5122	14243	*15215*	*15265*	14244	09/71-06/85		☜
5122	14243	*15336*	15265	14244	06/85-12/86		☜
5122	14243	*15328*	*15173*	14244	12/86-07/87		☜
5123	14246	15201	15251	14245	06/54-06/85		
5123	14246	*15104*	15251	14245	06/85-02/87	➲**5497**	☜
5124	14248	15202	15252	14247	06/54-09/81		
5124	14248	*15248*	15252	14247	09/81-01/93		☜
5125	14250	15203	15253	14249	06/54-01/86		
5125	14250	*15015*	15253	14249	01/86-05/88	➲*5501*	☜
5126	14252	15204	15254	14251	07/54-01/85		
5126	14252	15204	15254	*14376*	01/85-04/88		☜
5126	14252	*15244*	15254	14376	04/88-07/92		☜
5127	14253	15205	15255	14254	07/54-06/85		
5128	14255	15206	15256	14256	08/54-05/85	➲*5471*	
5129	14257	15207	15257	14258	08/54-05/88	➲*5528*	
5130	14260	15208	15258	14259	08/54-12/73		
5131	14261	15209	15259	14262	09/54-07/81		
5131	14261	*15412*	15259	14262	07/81-05/93		☜
5132	14264	15210	15260	14263	09/54-08/85	➲*5480*	
5133	14265	15211	15261	14266	09/54-05/88		
5133	14265	*15132*	15261	14266	05/88-12/91		☜
5134	14267	15212	15262	14268	09/54-12/81		
5134	14267	*15444*	15262	14268	12/81-03/82		☜
5134	*65383*	15444	15262	14268	03/82-09/92		☜
5135	14269	15213	15263	14270	09/54-12/85		
5135	*14050*	15213	15263	14270	12/85-05/88	➲*5521*	☜
5136	14272	15214	15264	14271	10/54-04/88	➲*5525*	
5137	14274	15215	15265	14273	10/54-03/70		
5137	14274	*15072*	*15442*	14273	03/70-01/76		☜
5137	14274	*15320*	15442	*14383*	01/76-05/88	➲*5519*	☜
5138	14275	15216	15266	14276	10/54-03/81		
5138	14275	*15423*	15266	14276	03/81-09/93		☜
5139	14277	15217	15267	14278	10/54-05/88		
5139	14277	*15442*	15267	14278	05/88-02/92		☜

5140	14280	15218	15268	14279	11/54-05/87		
5140	*14359*	15218	15268	14279	05/87-05/88	⊃*5503*	↺
5141	14281	15219	15269	14282	11/54-07/61	⊃*5245*	
5142	14284	15220	15270	14283	11/54-04/85		
5142	14284	*15102*	15270	14283	04/85-12/86		↺
5143	14285	15221	15271	14286	11/54-09/80	⊃*5403*	
5144	14287	15222	15272	14288	11/54-05/88	⊃*5524*	
5145	14290	15223	15273	14289	11/54-04/88		
5145	14290	*15158*	15273	14289	04/88-04/93		↺
5146	14291	15224	15274	14292	12/54-08/85		
5146	14291	*15133*	15274	14292	08/85-01/91		↺
5147	14294	15225	15275	14293	12/54-05/88	⊃*5518*	
5148	14296	15226	15276	14295	12/54-08/85		
5148	14296	*15343*	15276	14295	08/85-11/90		↺
5149	14297	15227	15277	14298	01/55-10/80	⊃*5408*	
5150	14300	15228	15278	14299	01/55-05/63		
5150	14300	*15228*[2]	*15278*[2]	14299	05/63-01/85		↺
5150	14099	*15175*	15278[2]	14299	01/85-11/85		↺
5150	14099	*15370*	15278[2]	14299	09/87-05/91		↺
5151	14302	15229	15279	14301	01/55-04/88	⊃*5506*	
5152	14303	15230	15280	14304	01/55-01/81	⊃*5406*	
5153	14305	15231	15281	14306	01/55-05/85		
5153	14305	*15256*	15281	14306	05/85-05/93		↺
5154	14308	15232	15282	14307	02/55-04/88		
5154	14308	*15279*	15282	14307	04/88-04/93		↺
5155	14309	15233	15283	14310	02/55-07/85		
5155	14309	*15107*	15283	14310	07/85-11/92		↺
5156	14311	15284	15334	14312	02/55-05/88		
5156	14311	*15272*	15334	14312	05/88-09/92		↺
5157	14313	15285	15335	14314	03/55-03/80		
5157	14313	*15381*	15335	14314	05/80-05/93		↺
5158	14315	15286	15336	14316	03/55-06/85	⊃*5470*	
5159	14317	15287	15337	14318	03/55-04/88		
5159	14317	*15105*	15337	14318	04/88-10/93		↺
5160	14319	15288	15338	14320	03/55-05/88		
5160	14319	*15268*	15338	14320	05/88-07/93		↺
5161	14322	15289	15339	14321	03/55-10/85	⊃*5479*	
5162	14323	15290	15340	14324	04/55-05/88	⊃*5505*	
5163	14325	15291	15341	14326	04/55-08/85		
5163	14325	*15260*	15341	14326	08/85-10/90		↺
5164	14328	15292	15342	14327	04/55-07/87		
5165	14330	15293	15343	14329	04/55-08/85	⊃*5481*	
5166	14331	15294	15344	14332	05/55-05/88		
5166	14331	*15253*	15344	14332	05/88-11/90		↺
5167	14333	15295	15345	14334	05/55-12/69		
5168	14335	15296	15346	14336	05/55-05/88		
5168	14335	*15340*	15346	14336	05/88-10/90		↺
5169	14337	15297	15347	14338	05/55-08/85		
5169	14337	*15109*	15347	14338	08/85-07/87		↺
5169	*65303*	15109	15347	14338	07/87-02/92		↺
5170	14339	15298	15348	14340	06/55-04/88		
5170	14339	*15245*	15348	14340	04/88-07/92		↺
5171	14341	15299	15349	14342	06/55-04/88	⊃*5507*	
5172	14344	15300	15350	14343	06/55-01/69		
5172	14344	*15193*	15350	14343	01/69-07/88	⊃*5510*	↺
5173	14345	15301	15351	14346	07/55-03/80		
5173	14345	15301	*15120*	14346	04/80-05/88		↺
5173	14345	*15116*	15120	14346	05/88-10/90		↺
5174	14348	15302	15352	14347	08/55-04/88		
5174	14348	*15138*	15352	14347	04/88-10/90	⊃*5278*	↺
5175	14349	15303	15353	14350	04/55-11/83		
5176	14352	15304	15354	14351	08/55-01/81		
5176	14352	*15396*	15354	14351	01/81- 95		↺
5177	14354	15305	15355	14353	08/55-05/88		
5177	14354	*15257*	15355	14353	05/88-05/93		↺
5178	14355	15306	15356	14356	08/55-10/80	⊃*5243*	
5179	14357	15307	15357	14358	09/55-05/88	⊃*5513*	
5180	14360	15308	15358	14359	09/55-12/85		
5180	14360	*15131*	15358	14359	12/85-05/87		↺
5181	14361	15309	15359	14362	09/55-03/86	⊃**5487**	
5182	14364	15310	15360	14363	09/55-05/88		
5182	14364	*15357*	15360	14363	05/88-10/91		↺
5183	14366	15311	15361	14365	10/55-05/88	⊃*5502*	
5184	14367	15312	15362	14368	10/55-05/88	⊃*5514*	
5185	14369	15313	15363	14370	10/55-10/80		
5185	14369	*15277*	15363	14370	10/80-01/93		↺
5186	14372	15314	15364	14371	10/55-07/87		
5187	14374	15315	15365	14373	10/55-07/87		
5187	14374	*15353*	15365	*14349*	07/87-04/88	⊃*5526*	↺
5188	14376	15316	15366	14375	11/55-01/85		
5189	14377	15317	15367	14378	11/55-10/85		
5189	14377	*15339*	15367	14378	10/85-11/90		↺
5190	14380	15318	15368	14379	11/55-05/88		
5190	14380	*15361*	15368	14379	05/88-04/93		↺
5191	14381	15319	15369	14382	11/55-08/85		
5191	14381	*15108*	15369	14382	08/85-10/90		↺
5192	14383	15370	15320	14384	11/55-01/76		
5192	*14273*	15370	*15208*	14384	01/76-04/85		↺
5192	14273	15370	*15246*	14384	04/85-08/86		↺
5192	14273	15370	*15190*	14384	08/86-07/87	⊃*Dep*	↺
5193	14386	15371	15321	14385	11/55-04/86	⊃**5488**	
5194	14388	15372	15322	14387	11/55-05/88		
5194	14388	15372	*15275*	14387	05/88-10/93		↺
5195	14389	15373	15323	14390	12/55-05/88		
5195	14389	15373	*15239*	14390	05/88-09/93		↺
5196	14392	15374	15324	14391	12/55-07/81		
5196	14392	15374	*15399*	14391	07/81-07/94		↺
5197	14394	15375	15325	14393	12/55-05/88	⊃*5522*	
5198	14396	15376	15326	14395	12/55-04/81	⊃*5413*	
5199	14397	15377	15327	14398	12/55-06/82	⊃**5441**	
5200	14400	15378	15328	14399	12/55-11/86	⊃*5496*	
5201	14402	15379	15329	14401	12/55-11/85		
5201	14402	15379	*15126*	14401	11/85-01/91		↺
5202	14404	15380	15330	14403	01/56-05/88		
5202	14404	15380	*15362*	14403	05/88-10/90		↺
5203	14406	15331	15381	14405	01/56-03/79		
5203	14406	*15072*	15381	14405	03/79-09/79		↺
5203	*14057*	15072	15381	14405	09/79-03/80		↺
5203	14057	*15285*	15381	14405	03/80-05/80		↺
5204	14407	15382	15332	14408	01/56-12/57	⊃*5020*	
5205	14410	15383	15333	14409	01/56-01/82	⊃**5429**	
5206	14411	15384	15394	14412	02/56-05/82	⊃**5437**	
5207	14413	15385	15395	14414	02/56-04/88	⊃*5515*	
5208	14416	15386	15396	14415	02/56-01/81		
5209	14418	15387	15397	14417	02/56-04/88		
5209	14418	*15395*	15397	14417	04/88-02/91		↺
5209	*14039*	15395	15397	14417	02/91-01/93		↺
5210	14420	15388	15398	14419	03/56-05/88		
5210	14420	*15263*	15398	14419	05/88-09/92		↺
5211	14421	15389	15399	14422	03/56-07/81	⊃*5416*	
5212	14423	15390	15400	14424	03/56-02/82	⊃**5431**	
5213	14425	15391	15401	14426	03/56-04/88		
5213	14425	*15353*	15401	14426	04/88-11/92		↺
5214	14428	15392	15402	14427	03/56-04/81	⊃*5407*	
5215	14430	15393	15403	14429	04/56-01/82	⊃*5428*	
5216	14431	15034	15404	14432	04/56-11/84	⊃**5458**	
5217	14434	15035	15405	14433	04/56-06/85		
5217	14434	*15366*	15405	14433	06/85-11/92		↺
5218	14435	15036	15406	14436	04/56-10/80	⊃**5404**	
5219	14438	15037	15407	14437	05/56-12/82	⊃**5449**	
5220	14440	15038	15408	14439	05/56-01/73		
5220	*14260*	15038	15408	14439	12/73-04/88		↺
5220	14260	*15349*	15408	14439	04/88-09/93		↺
5221	14441	15039	15409	14442	05/56-05/81	⊃*5414*	
5222	14443	15040	15410	14444	06/56-05/81		
5222	*14490*	15040	15410	14444	05/81-09/81		↺
5222	14490	*15421*	15410	14444	09/81-01/91	⊃*5280*	↺
5223	14446	15041	15411	14445	06/56-10/81		
5223	14446	*15427*	15411	14445	10/81-07/91	⊃*5281*	↺
5224	14447	15042	15412	14448	06/56-07/81	⊃*5424*	
5225	14449	15043	15413	14450	06/56-08/57		
5225	14449	*15020*	*15120*	*14407*	06/58-03/80		↺
5225	14449	15020	*15351*	14407	03/80-03/80	⊃**5402**	↺
5226	14451	15044	15414	14452	07/56-02/82		
5226	14451	*15280*	15414	14452	04/82-11/92		↺
5227	14453	15045	15415	14454	07/56-01/82	⊃*5427*	
5228	14455	15046	15416	14456	07/56-01/82		
5228	14455	*15415*	15416	14456	01/82-10/90		↺
5229	14458	15047	15417	14457	07/56-02/70		
5229	*14333*	15047	15417	14457	02/70-04/81		↺
5229	14333	*15435*	15417	14457	04/81-08/91		↺
5230	14460	15048	15418	14459	08/56-06/85		
5230	14460	*15110*	15418	14459	06/85-10/90		↺
5231	14461	15049	15419	14462	08/56-04/88		
5231	14461	*15264*	15419	14462	04/88-05/91		↺
5232	14464	15050	15420	14463	08/56-10/81		
5232	14464	*15422*	15420	14463	10/81-04/93		↺
5233	14466	15051	15421	14465	09/56-09/81	⊃*5415*	
5234	14467	15052	15422	14468	09/56-10/81	⊃*5422*	
5235	14470	15053	15423	14469	09/56-03/81	⊃*5405*	
5236	14472	15054	15424	14471	09/56-02/82	⊃**5433**	
5237	14473	15055	15425	14474	10/56-11/81	⊃*5419*	
5238	14475	15056	15426	14476	10/56-05/81	⊃*5411*	
5239	14478	15057	15427	14477	10/56-10/81	⊃*5417*	
5240	14479	15058	15428	14480	10/56-06/72		
5240	*14103*	15058	15428	14480	06/72-11/81		↺
5240	14103	*15425*	15428	14480	11/81-05/93		↺
5241	14482	15059	15429	14481	10/56-01/84		
5241	14482	15059	*15001*	14481	01/84-10/84	⊃**5456**	↺
5242	14483	15060	15430	14484	11/56-04/81		
5242	14483	*15402*	15430	14484	04/81-05/91		↺
5243	14486	15061	15431	14485	11/56-10/80		
5243	14486	*15306*	*15356*	14485	10/80-02/81		↺
5243	*14405*	15306	15356	14485	02/81-05/88		↺
5243	14405	*15375*	15356	14485	05/88-10/93		↺

5244	14487	15062	15432	14488	11/56-05/82	➲**5439**	
5245	14490	15063	15433	14489	11/56-07/61		
5245	14490	15063	*15219*	*14282*	09/61-05/81	➲*5418*	☞
5246	14492	15064	15434	14491	11/56-06/72		
5246	*65383*	15064	15434	14491	06/72-03/75		☞
5246	65383	*15181*	15434	14491	03/75-10/80		☞
5246	65383	*15061*	*15431*	14491	10/80-01/82	➲*5435*	☞
5247	14494	15065	15435	14493	12/56-11/67		
5247	14494	15065	15435	*65307*	11/67-10/71		☞
5247	14494	15065	15435	*14206*	10/71-04/81	➲*5409*	☞
5248	14495	15066	15436	14496	12/56-06/72		
5248	*14492*	15066	15436	14496	06/72-01/82		☞
5248	14492	*15443*	15436	*14510*	03/82-08/93		☞
5249	14498	15067	15437	14497	01/57-03/82	➲*5434*	
5250	14500	15068	15438	14499	01/57-09/81	➲*5421*	
5251	14502	15069	15439	14501	01/57-11/84	➲**5457**	
5252	14504	15070	15440	14503	01/57-11/82	➲**5443**	
5253	14505	15071	15441	14506	01/57-12/84	➲**5459**	
5254	14508	15072	15442	14507	02/57-02/70		
5254	14508	*15295*	*15345*	*14458*	05/70-07/85	➲*5472*	☞
5255	14510	15073	15443	14509	02/57-09/81		
5255	14510	*15438*	15443	14509	09/81-03/82	➲*5248/5430*	☞
5256	14511	15074	15444	14512	02/57-12/81	➲*5423*	
5257	14514	15075	15445	14513	02/57-08/82	➲**5440**	
5258	14515	15076	15446	14516	03/57-01/85	➲**5460**	
5259	14517	15077	15447	14518	03/57-01/82	➲*5426*	
5260	14519	15078	15448	14520	03/57-02/85	➲**5461**	

Class 415/1 4-EPB
Hybrid EPB Suburban Units
660-750V dc third rail
5261-5262

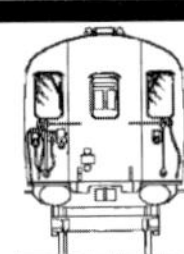

During 1965, two new units 5261 & 5262 were formed from existing spare BR standard power cars, one spare 4-EPB trailer and three spare 4-SUB trailers which were rewired.

	DMBS	TS	TSO	DMBS			
5261	65300	15081	15082	65310	08/65-08/87		
5261	65300	15081	*15413*	65310	08/87-04/88		☞
5261	65300	*15154*	15413	65310	04/88-07/93		☞
5262	65308	15083	15433	65303	12/65-01/72		
5262	*14205*	15083	15433	65303	01/72-06/86	➲*5028/5490*	☞

Class 415/1 4-EPB
EPB Suburban Units
660-750V dc third rail
5263-5281

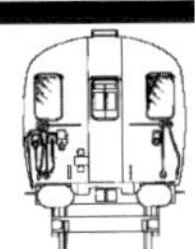

Prototype refurbished unit.

	DMBS	TS	TSO	DMBS		
5263	14556	15449	15450	14521	06/76-03/77	➲**5401**

Formed using 2-HAP motors.

	DMBS	TS	TSO	DMBS	
5264	14522	15258	15147	14523	09/77-11/92

Renumbered from units in the 50xx series.

	DMBS	TS	TSO	DMBS			
5265	14001	15429	15101	14002	11/88-11/90	➲*5001*	
5266	14039	15234	15382	14040	11/88-02/91		
5266	*14418*	15234	15382	14040	02/91-01/93		☞
5267	14053	15123	15127	14042	11/88-09/92		
5268	14069	15113	15135	14070	11/88-08/93		
5269	14094	15139	15118	14078	11/88-01/93		
5270	14079	15140	15122	14080	11/88-05/93		
5271	14083	15130	15142	14084	11/88-01/91		
5272	14087	15345	15144	14088	11/88-01/91		
5273	14089	15145	15129	14090	11/88-10/90		
5274	14091	15364	15146	14092	11/88-10/90		
5275	14097	15149	15271	14098	11/88-04/93		
5276	14101	15143	15151	14102	11/88-05/92		
5277	14495	15152	15103	14104	11/88-05/93		
5278	14085	15138	15352	14086	10/90-05/91		
5279	14257	15380	15429	14258	11/90-02/94		
5280	14231	15410	15421	14232	01/91-02/93		
5281	14349	15427	15411	14374	07/91-08/91		
5281	*14414*	15427	15411	14374	08/91-09/92		☞

Class 415/2 4-EPB
Hybrid EPB Suburban Units
660-750V dc third rail
5301-5302

Three years after the final SR EPB unit was built a series of BR EPB units were constructed at Eastleigh. The main external difference was the lack of quarter-lights above the windows in the doors. They were similar in design to the BR 2-EPBs in the 57xx series.

The first two units were hybrid units which were composed of three 4-EPB trailers, one 4-SUB trailer with new power cars (a combination of SR & BR vehicles).

	DMBS	TS	TSO	DMBS		
5301	61625	15413	15043	61626	01/60-08/87	
5302	61627	15079	15121	61872	01/61-01/72	
5302	61627	15079	15121	*65308*	01/72-12/83	☞

Class 415/2 4-EPB
BR Suburban Units
660-750V dc third rail
5303-5370

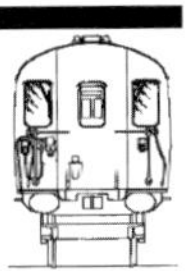

This was the main batch of BR 4-EPB units. 5301-5356 were built to work on the South Eastern section, and 5357-5370 for the South Western, but they were all soon pooled together working on the South Eastern and Central divisions.

From 1982-83 twenty-five units were facelifted. However the removal of asbestos insulation proved an expensive operation and the remaining 45 units were withdrawn and sent for scrap. The facelifted units became Class 415/6 and were renumbered 5601-5625. Three of these units were renumbered to 5626-5628 to designate units allocated to Ramsgate to supplement peak-hour mainline services.

	DMBS	TSso	TSso	DMBS			
5303	61516	70375	70376	61517	01/60-05/85		
5304	61518	70378	70377	61519	01/60-05/85		
5305	61520	70380	70379	61521	01/60-07/87	➲**5621**	
5306	61522	70382	70381	61523	01/60-05/85		
5307	61524	70384	70383	61525	01/60-05/84		
5308	61526	70385	70386	61527	01/60-05/84		
5309	61528	70387	70388	61529	02/60-05/84		
5310	61530	70389	70390	61531	02/60-05/85		
5311	61532	70391	70392	61533	02/60-07/87	➲**5613**	
5312	61534	70393	70394	61535	02/60-10/84		
5313	61536	70395	70396	61537	02/60-07/87	➲**5606**	
5314	61538	70397	70398	61539	02/60-06/87	➲**5603**	
5315	61540	70399	70400	61541	03/60-07/87	➲**5605**	
5316	61542	70401	70402	61543	03/60-06/87	➲**5612**	
5317	61544	70403	70404	61545	03/60-05/85		
5318	61546	70405	70406	61547	03/60-06/87	➲**5614**	
5319	61548	70407	70408	61549	03/60-05/84		
5320	61550	70409	70410	61551	03/60-07/87	➲**5601**	
5321	61552	70411	70412	61553	03/60-10/84		
5322	61554	70413	70414	61555	03/60-05/85		
5323	61556	70415	70416	61557	03/60-08/84		
5324	61558	70417	70418	61559	03/60-05/85		
5325	61560	70419	70420	61561	04/60-07/87	➲**5622**	
5326	61562	70421	70422	61563	04/60-07/87	➲**5619**	
5327	61564	70423	70424	61565	04/60-05/85		
5328	61566	70425	70426	61567	04/60-07/87	➲**5610**	
5329	61568	70427	70428	61569	04/60-12/83		
5330	61570	70429	70430	61571	04/60-07/87	➲**5611**	
5331	61572	70431	70432	61573	04/60-07/87	➲**5624**	
5332	61574	70433	70434	61575	04/60-05/85		
5333	61576	70435	70436	61577	05/60-07/87	➲**5616**	
5334	61578	70437	70438	61579	05/60-07/87	➲**5623**	
5335	61580	70439	70440	61581	05/60-05/85		
5336	61582	70441	70442	61583	05/60-07/87	➲**5602**	
5337	61584	70443	70444	61585	05/60-07/87	➲**5618**	
5338	61586	70445	70446	61587	05/60-05/84		
5339	61588	70447	70448	61589	06/60-06/87	➲**5604**	
5340	61590	70449	70450	61591	06/60-07/87	➲**5607**	
5341	61592	70451	70452	61593	06/60-07/87	➲**5617**	
5342	61594	70453	70454	61595	06/60-08/84		
5343	61596	70455	70456	61597	06/60-05/84		
5344	61598	70457	70458	61599	06/60-03/85		
5345	61600	70460	70459	61601	09/61-06/87	➲**5608**	
5346	61602	70461	70462	61603	10/61-07/87	➲**5620**	
5347	61604	70464	70463	61605	10/61-07/87	➲**5609**	
5348	61606	70466	70465	61607	10/61-05/85		
5349	61608	70467	70468	61609	10/61-05/84		
5349	61608	*70455*	70468	61609	05/84-07/87	➲**5625**	☞
5350	61610	70469	70470	61611	11/61-05/85		

5351	61612	70471	70472	61613	11/61-07/87	➲**5615**
5352	61614	70473	70474	61615	11/61-10/62	
5352	*61624*	70473	70474	61615	12/64-02/85	
5353	61616	70475	70476	61617	11/61-05/85	
5354	61618	70477	70478	61619	12/61-05/85	
5355	61620	70479	70480	61621	12/61-05/85	
5356	61622	70481	70482	61623	01/62-05/85	
5357	61989	70667	70668	61990	08/62-07/84	
5358	61991	70669	70670	61992	08/62-03/85	
5359	61993	70671	70672	61994	10/62-03/85	
5360	61995	70673	70674	61996	10/62-05/85	
5361	61997	70675	70676	61998	09/62-05/84	
5362	61999	70677	70678	62000	12/62-04/84	
5363	62001	70679	70680	62002	12/62-09/84	
5364	62003	70681	70682	62004	12/62-10/84	
5365	62005	70683	70684	62006	12/62-02/85	
5366	62007	70685	70686	62008	01/63-09/84	
5367	62009	70687	70688	62010	01/63-07/84	
5368	62011	70689	70690	62012	01/63-05/84	
5369	62013	70691	70692	62014	01/63-10/84	
5370	62015	70693	70694	62016	01/63-05/84	

Class 414/1 2-HAP (later 2-SAP)
EPB Outer-Suburban Units (one toilet)
660-750V dc third rail
5601-5636

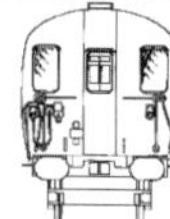

These SR design units were built on reclaimed 2-NOL underframes in 1958 for use on semi-fast trains on the Thanet routes. In 1969 some units were transferred to work on the Waterloo to Cobham line. These services were second class only and these units were reclassified 2-SAP. The official list shows these units as 5602-5/7-9/15-18/22/34/5, although 5602/5/9/15/6 were noted as not converted. In 1970 they reverted back to 2-HAP, but they became 2-SAP again in 1976.

Other units were transferred in 1969 to the Coastway route and the Central Division suburban services.

In the late seventies the MBS vehicles were refurbished (mainly at Horwich) to work in 4-EPB units, and the DTC vehicles were scrapped.

	DMBS	*DTCL*		
5601	14521	16001	02/58-04/76	
5602	14522	16002	02/58-09/77	
5603	14523	16003	02/58-09/77	
5604	14524	16004	02/58-05/83	
5605	14525	16005	02/58-05/83	
5606	14526	16006	06/58-02/83	
5607	14527	16007	06/58-01/81	
5608	14528	16008	07/58-01/81	
5609	14529	16009	07/58-03/82	
5610	14530	16010	07/58-06/82	
5611	14531	16011	06/58-07/82	
5612	14532	16012	08/58-08/82	
5613	14533	16013	08/58-10/82	
5614	14534	16014	08/58-02/82	
5615	14535	16015	08/58-05/82	
5616	14536	16016	08/58-04/83	
5617	14537	16017	08/58-04/82	
5618	14538	16018	08/58-10/80	
5619	14539	16019	09/58-09/82	
5620	14540	16020	09/58-03/82	
5621	14541	16021	09/58-07/82	
5622	14542	16022	09/58-10/80	
5623	14543	16023	09/58-02/82	
5624	14544	16024	09/58-11/67	
5624	*14493*	16024	11/67-09/79	
5624	*65409*	16024	09/79-05/83	
5625	14545	16025	09/58-05/83	
5626	14546	16026	09/58-04/83	
5627	14547	16027	09/58-03/82	
5628	14548	16028	09/58-09/82	
5629	14549	16029	10/58-09/82	➲Dep **019**
5630	14550	16030	10/58-08/82	
5631	14551	16031	10/58-02/83	
5632	14552	16032	10/58-10/82	
5633	14553	16033	10/58-05/82	
5634	14554	16034	10/58-04/82	
5635	14555	16035	10/58-05/83	
5636	14556	16036	10/58-04/76	

Class 416/1 2-EPB
EPB Suburban Units
660-750V dc third rail
5651-5684

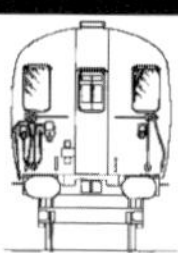

These 2-EPB units were built on the frames of 2-NOL units withdrawn in 1958-59. Interestingly, they were built *after* the BR designed 2-EPB units; they were the last units to be built on the re-used frames of SR stock.

These units were all second class and were designed for the Waterloo to Windsor and Weybridge services. The units underwent a major facelift programme in 1982-85 and were reclassified 416/3 and renumbered in the 63xx series. Some of these units were transferred to replace the Class 501 stock on the North London line, a line which included the restricted clearance through Hampstead Heath tunnel which led to the fitting of bars on the windows.

	DMBSO	*DTSO*		
5651	14557	16101	09/59-06/85	➲**6333**
5652	14558	16102	10/59-03/84	➲**6313**
5653	14559	16103	10/59-05/84	➲**6316**
5654	14560	16104	10/59-09/84	➲**6324**
5655	14561	16105	10/59-07/84	➲**6320**
5656	14562	16106	10/59-10/83	➲**6309**
5657	14563	16107	10/59-06/85	➲**6334**
5658	14564	16108	10/59-06/83	➲**6308**
5659	14565	16109	10/59-02/84	➲**6311**
5660	14566	16110	10/59-06/84	➲**6318**
5661	14567	16111	10/59-10/84	➲**6325**
5662	14568	16112	10/59-07/84	➲**6319**
5663	14569	16113	10/59-06/85	➲**6332**
5664	14570	16114	10/59-03/85	➲**6329**
5665	14571	16115	10/59-10/82	➲**6306**
5666	14572	16116	11/59-02/85	➲**6327**
5667	14573	16117	11/59-06/83	➲**6307**
5668	14574	16118	11/59-01/84	➲**6310**
5669	14575	16119	11/59-08/84	➲**6322**
5670	14576	16120	11/59-04/82	➲**6303**
5671	14577	16121	12/59-03/82	➲**6301**
5672	14578	16122	12/59-05/84	➲**6317**
5673	14579	16123	12/59-02/84	➲**6312**
5674	14580	16124	12/59-03/82	➲**6302**
5675	14581	16125	12/59-08/84	➲**6323**
5676	14582	16126	12/59-03/85	➲**6328**
5677	14583	16127	12/59-05/85	➲**6331**
5678	14584	16128	12/59-07/84	➲**6321**
5679	14585	16129	12/59-01/85	➲**6326**
5680	14586	16130	12/59-04/84	➲**6314**
5681	14587	16131	12/59-07/82	➲**6305**
5682	14588	16132	12/59-05/85	➲**6330**
5683	14589	16133	12/59-04/82	➲**6304**
5684	14590	16134	12/59-04/84	➲**6315**

Class 416/2 2-EPB
BR Suburban Units
660-750V dc third rail
5701-5779

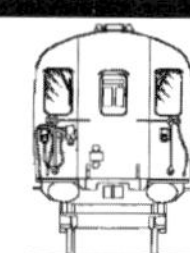

The first eleven of these BR designed 2-EPB units were built as replacements for the 2-SL and 2-WIM units on the South London and Wimbledon to West Croydon services.

The remainder were built for the South Eastern section as part of the 10-car train lengthening programme.

5779 and 5800 were built later as replacements for accident damaged vehicles (including 5766 which was lost in the wreck at St. Johns in 1957).

A number of the early units were disbanded in 1965. The DTS vehicles were used with DEMU vehicle units to form the Class 206 "Tadpole" units. The DMBS vehicles were formed into 4-EPB units 5261-5262.

In 1984 the units were renumbered in the 62xx series to match their class number. Eighteen units were refurbished in 1985-87 (the last EPB units to be so treated) and they were reclassified 416/4 and renumbered 6401-6418.

	DMBSO	*DTSso*		
5701	65300	77500	01/54-01/65	
5702	65301	77501	01/54-04/85	➲**6202**
5703	65302	77502	04/54-03/85	➲**6203**
5704	65303	77503	04/54-01/65	
5705	65304	77504	04/54-04/85	➲**6205**
5706	65305	77505	04/54-05/85	➲**6206**
5707	65306	77506	04/54-01/85	➲**6207**
5708	65307	77507	05/54-01/65	

5709	65308	77508	05/54-01/65		
5710	65309	77509	05/54-12/64		
5710	65309	*75636*	12/64-04/85	**➲6210**	☞
5711	65310	77510	05/54-01/65		
5712	65326	77511	08/54-03/85	**➲6212**	
5713	65327	77512	08/54-04/85	**➲6213**	
5714	65328	77513	08/54-09/84	**➲6214**	
5715	65329	77514	08/54-08/84	**➲6215**	
5716	65330	77515	09/54-03/85	**➲6216**	
5717	65331	77516	09/54-09/84	**➲6217**	
5718	65332	77517	09/54-09/84	**➲6218**	
5719	65333	77518	09/54-03/85	**➲6219**	
5720	65334	77519	10/54-05/85	**➲6220**	
5721	65335	77520	10/54-09/84	**➲6221**	
5722	65336	77521	10/54-03/85	**➲6222**	
5723	65337	77522	10/54-12/84	**➲6223**	
5724	65338	77523	10/54-01/85	**➲6224**	
5725	65339	77524	11/54-08/84	**➲6225**	
5726	65340	77525	11/54-02/85	**➲6226**	
5727	65341	77526	11/54-04/85	**➲6227**	
5728	65342	77527	04/55-08/84	**➲6228**	
5729	65343	77528	05/55-06/77		
5729	65343	77528	11/80-08/84	**➲6229**	☞
5730	65344	77529	05/55-12/84	**➲6230**	
5731	65345	77530	05/55-03/85	**➲6231**	
5732	65346	77531	05/55-07/85	**➲6232**	
5733	65347	77532	06/55-08/84	**➲6233**	
5734	65348	77533	06/55-09/84	**➲6234**	
5735	65349	77534	06/55-05/85	**➲6235**	
5736	65350	77535	06/55-09/84	**➲6236**	
5737	65351	77536	07/55-05/85	**➲6237**	
5738	65352	77537	07/55-05/85	**➲6238**	
5739	65353	77538	07/55-05/85	**➲6239**	
5740	65354	77539	07/55-09/84	**➲6240**	
5741	65355	77540	07/55-08/84	**➲6241**	
5742	65356	77541	08/55-03/85	**➲6242**	
5743	65357	77542	08/55-03/85	**➲6243**	
5744	65358	77543	08/55-08/84	**➲6244**	
5745	65359	77544	09/55-04/85	**➲6245**	
5746	65360	77545	09/55-01/85	**➲6246**	
5747	65361	77546	09/55-04/85	**➲6247**	
5748	65362	77547	09/55-04/85	**➲6248**	
5749	65363	77548	09/55-05/85	**➲6249**	
5750	65364	77549	10/55-03/85	**➲6250**	
5751	65365	77550	10/55-02/85	**➲6251**	
5752	65366	77551	10/55-08/84	**➲6252**	
5753	65367	77552	04/56-07/84	**➲6253**	
5754	65368	77553	05/56-07/84	**➲6254**	
5755	65369	77554	10/56-10/84	**➲6255**	
5756	65370	77555	05/56-08/84	**➲6256**	
5757	65371	77556	06/56-03/85	**➲6257**	
5758	65372	77557	10/56-04/85	**➲6258**	
5759	65373	77558	06/56-10/84	**➲6259**	
5760	65374	77559	05/56-12/84	**➲6260**	
5761	65375	77560	07/56-09/84	**➲6261**	
5762	65376	77561	06/56-07/84	**➲6262**	
5763	65377	77562	06/56-12/84	**➲6263**	
5764	65378	77563	07/56-03/85	**➲6264**	
5765	65379	77564	07/56-07/84	**➲6265**	
5766	65380	77565	07/56-12/57		
5767	65381	77566	08/56-09/84	**➲6267**	
5768	65382	77567	08/56-09/84	**➲6268**	
5769	65383	77568	09/56-09/71		
5769	*14206*	77568	09/71-10/71		☞
5769	*65307*	77568	10/71-04/85	**➲6269**	☞
5770	65384	77569	09/56-08/84	**➲6270**	
5771	65385	77570	09/56-09/84	**➲6271**	
5772	65386	77571	09/56-09/84	**➲6272**	
5773	65387	77572	09/56-08/84	**➲6273**	
5774	65388	77573	10/56-06/77		
5774	65388	77573	11/80-08/84	**➲6274**	☞
5775	65389	77574	10/56-08/84	**➲6275**	
5776	65390	77575	10/56-08/84	**➲6276**	
5777	65391	77576	11/56-08/84	**➲6277**	
5778	65392	77577	11/56-09/84	**➲6278**	
5779	65435	77578	06/58-08/84	**➲6279**	

Class 416/2 2-EPB (ex Tyneside)

BR Suburban Units
660-750V dc third rail
5781-5795

These units were the former Tyneside units which were transferred to the Southern Region in 1963.

They worked at first on the South Eastern Division before being transferred to the South Western Division working out of Waterloo. They could always be identified by their large guard's van. All were withdrawn in 1984 with many of the class later entering departmental service.

	DMBSO	*DTSso*		
5781	65311	77100	08/63-08/84	**➲6281**
5782	65312	77101	10/63-08/84	**➲6282**
5783	65313	77102	07/63-08/84	**➲6283**
5784	65314	77103	08/63-08/84	**➲6284**
5785	65315	77104	09/63-08/84	**➲6285**
5786	65316	77105	09/63-08/84	**➲6286**
5787	65317	77106	08/63-09/84	**➲6287**
5788	65318	77107	08/63-05/84	
5789	65319	77108	07/63-09/84	**➲6289**
5790	65320	77109	08/63-08/84	**➲6290**
5791	65321	77110	08/63-09/84	**➲6291**
5792	65322	77111	09/63-08/84	**➲6292**
5793	65323	77112	07/63-08/84	**➲6293**
5794	65324	77113	08/63-05/84	
5795	65325	77114	09/63-05/84	

Class 416/2 2-EPB

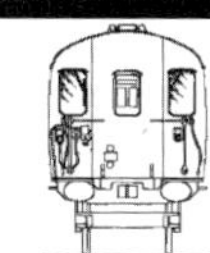

BR Suburban Units
660-750V dc third rail
5800

The first 5800 was formed in 1960 from power car 61624 and a newly built driving trailer 75636 which carried the unit battery. The unit was a replacement for accident damaged vehicles.

	DMBSO	*DTSso*	
5800	61624	75636	01/60-12/64

The second unit numbered 5800 was formed in 1977 with two power cars. It temporarily carried the number 5801 for a few months in 1977.

	DMBSO	*DMBSO*		
5800[2]	65343	65388	(temp **5801** 09/77-12/77)	06/77-11/80

Class 418 2-SAP

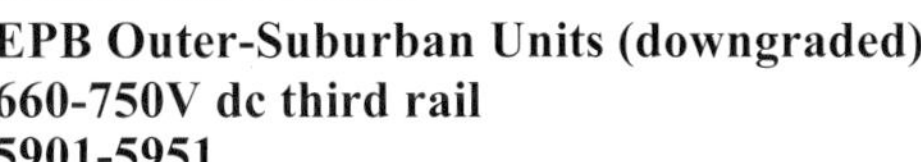

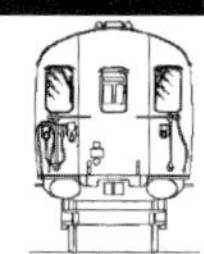

EPB Outer-Suburban Units (downgraded)
660-750V dc third rail
5901-5951

During the period from 1974 to 1977 some 2-HAP units were downgraded to second class only to work on South Western suburban routes. They were Class 418 and carried the numbers 5901-5951.

Class 418/1

	DMBSO	*DTSsoL*		
5901	65393	77115	05/74-02/80	**➲6001**
5902	65394	77116	05/74-05/80	**➲6002**
5903	65395	77117	05/74-04/80	**➲6003**
5904	65396	77118	04/74-07/80	**➲6004**
5905	65397	77119	04/74-04/80	**➲6005**
5906	65398	77120	04/74-09/80	**➲6006**
5907	65399	77121	04/74-04/80	**➲6007**
5908	65400	77122	04/74-05/80	**➲6008**
5909	65401	77123	04/74-09/80	**➲6009**
5910	65402	77124	05/74-04/80	**➲6010**
5911	65403	77125	04/74-04/80	**➲6011**
5912	65404	77126	04/74-03/80	**➲6012**
5913	65405	77127	05/74-05/80	**➲6013**
5914	65406	77128	04/74-04/80	**➲6014**
5915	65407	77129	05/74-05/80	**➲6015**
5916	65408	77130	05/74-02/80	**➲6016**
5917	65409	77131	05/74-03/79	
5918	65410	77132	04/74-04/80	**➲6018**
5919	65411	77133	04/74-03/80	**➲6019**
5920	65412	77134	05/74-05/80	**➲6020**
5921	65413	77135	04/74-03/80	**➲6021**
5922	65416	77138	04/74-02/80	**➲6024**
5923	65417	77139	04/74-03/80	**➲6025**
5924	65418	77140	04/74-02/80	**➲6026**
5925	65419	77141	04/74-02/80	**➲6027**
5926	65420	77142	04/74-03/80	**➲6028**
5927	65421	77143	04/74-04/80	**➲6029**
5928	65422	77144	05/74-03/80	**➲6030**
5929	65423	77145	03/74-04/80	**➲6031**
5930	65424	77146	04/74-02/80	**➲6032**
5931	65425	77147	05/74-02/80	**➲6033**
5932	65426	77148	04/74-02/80	**➲6034**
5933	65427	77149	04/74-04/80	**➲6035**
5934	65428	77150	04/74-06/80	**➲6036**
5935	65429	77151	04/74-06/80	**➲6037**
5936	65430	77152	04/74-02/80	**➲6038**
5937	65431	77153	04/74-02/80	**➲6039**

5938	65432	77154	04/74-02/80	➲**6040**	
5939	65433	77155	05/74-05/80	➲**6041**	
5940	65434	77156	04/74-02/80	➲**6042**	

Class 418/2

	DMBSO	*DTSsoL*			
5941	61241	75361	04/74-03/80	➲**6043**	
5942	61242	75362	04/74-02/80	➲**6044**	
5943	61243	75363	05/77-04/80	➲**6045**	
5944	61244	75364	05/77-03/80	➲**6046**	
5945	61245	75365	05/77-04/80	➲**6047**	
5946	61246	75366	05/77-03/80	➲**6048**	
5947	61247	75367	05/77-03/80	➲**6049**	
5948	61248	75368	05/77-02/80	➲**6050**	
5949	61249	75369	05/77-02/80	➲**6051**	
5950	61250	75370	05/77-05/80	➲**6052**	
5951	61251	75371	05/77-10/77	➲**6053**	

Class 414 2-HAP

EPB Outer-Suburban Units (one toilet)

660-750V dc third rail

6001-6173

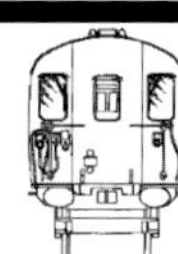

The 2-HAP units were the two-class equivalents of the BR 2-EPB units. 6001-6042 were built to replace the 2-HAL units on the Gillingham and Maidstone routes before the Ramsgate line was electrified. This batch was later classified 414/2 and had electro-pneumatic contactor control ('1951 stock'); all later builds had camshaft control and became 414/3 ('1957 stock'). 6043-6105 were built for the Thanet lines and 6106-6146 for the second phase of the Kent Coast Electrification Scheme. Finally 6147-6173 were built as additional units for the South Western and Central divisions and these were fitted with Commonwealth unpowered bogies.

During the period from 1974 to 1977 a number of units (6001-6053, missing out 6022 & 6023) were downgraded to second class only to work on South Western suburban routes. They were reclassified 418 and were renumbered 5901-5951, but resumed their earlier numbers when the first class section was later reinstated.

In 1982 forty-eight units were semi-permanently coupled to provide four-car units for working on the Coastway services. They were reclassified 4-CAP (Classes 413/2 & 413/3) and were renumbered in the 32xx and 33xx series.

The later surviving units were renumbered 4301-4322 in 1986 to match their class designations. Some of these were reformed to make additional 4-CAP units, numbered 3321-3325 and 3333 in 1991.

Ten MBSO vehicles were converted after withdrawal to make Gatwick Luggage Vans for use with converted Mark 2 hauled stock on the London Victoria to Gatwick services.

Class 414/2

	DMBSO	*DTCsoL*			
6001	65393	77115	06/57-05/74	➲**5901**	
6001	65393	77115	02/80-06/82	➲*3211*	⇦
6002	65394	77116	07/57-05/74	➲**5902**	
6002	65394	77116	05/80-05/84		⇦
6003	65395	77117	07/57-05/74	➲**5903**	
6003	65395	77117	04/80-05/82	➲*3203*	⇦
6004	65396	77118	08/57-04/74	➲**5904**	
6004	65396	77118	07/80-05/82	➲*3202*	⇦
6005	65397	77119	11/57-04/74	➲**5905**	
6005	65397	77119	04/80-05/82	➲*3213*	⇦
6006	65398	77120	11/57-04/74	➲**5906**	
6006	65398	77120	09/80-05/82	➲*3201*	⇦
6007	65399	77121	11/57-04/74	➲**5907**	
6007	65399	77121	04/80-05/85		⇦
6008	65400	77122	11/57-04/74	➲**5908**	
6008	65400	77122	05/80-05/85		⇦
6009	65401	77123	11/57-04/74	➲**5909**	
6009	65401	77123	09/80-05/82	➲*3201*	⇦
6010	65402	77124	11/57-05/74	➲**5910**	
6010	65402	77124	04/80-05/82	➲*3210*	⇦
6011	65403	77125	11/57-04/74	➲**5911**	
6011	65403	77125	04/80-10/84		⇦
6012	65404	77126	02/58-04/74	➲**5912**	
6012	65404	77126	03/80-05/82	➲*3207*	⇦
6013	65405	77127	02/58-05/74	➲**5913**	
6013	65405	77127	05/80-07/88	➲**4201**	⇦
6014	65406	77128	02/58-04/74	➲**5914**	
6014	65406	77128	04/80-04/82	➲*3212*	⇦
6015	65407	77129	02/58-05/74	➲**5915**	
6015	65407	77129	05/80-04/82	➲*3209*	⇦
6016	65408	77130	02/58-05/74	➲**5916**	
6016	65408	77130	02/80-05/84		⇦
6017	65409	77131	02/58-05/74	➲**5917**	
6018	65410	77132	03/58-04/74	➲**5918**	
6018	65410	77132	04/80-04/82	➲*3204*	⇦
6019	65411	77133	03/58-04/74	➲**5919**	
6019	65411	77133	03/80-05/84		⇦
6020	65412	77134	03/58-05/74	➲**5920**	
6020	65412	77134	05/80-05/82	➲*3202*	⇦
6021	65413	77135	03/58-04/74	➲**5921**	
6021	65413	77135	03/80-05/82	➲*3205*	⇦
6022	65414	77136	03/58-05/86		
6023	65415	77137	03/58-05/86		
6024	65416	77138	03/58-04/74	➲**5922**	
6024	65416	77138	02/80-05/84		⇦
6025	65417	77139	03/58-04/74	➲**5923**	
6025	65417	77139	03/80-05/84		⇦
6026	65418	77140	03/58-04/74	➲**5924**	
6026	65418	77140	02/80-05/84		⇦
6027	65419	77141	03/58-04/74	➲**5925**	
6027	65419	77141	02/80-04/82	➲*3206*	⇦
6028	65420	77142	03/58-04/74	➲**5926**	
6028	65420	77142	03/80-04/82	➲*3204*	⇦
6029	65421	77143	04/58-04/74	➲**5927**	
6029	65421	77143	04/80-05/84		⇦
6030	65422	77144	04/58-05/74	➲**5928**	
6030	65422	77144	03/80-05/82	➲*3205*	⇦
6031	65423	77145	04/58-03/74	➲**5929**	
6031	65423	77145	04/80-04/82	➲*3206*	⇦
6032	65424	77146	04/58-04/74	➲**5930**	
6032	65424	77146	02/80-05/82	➲*3203*	⇦
6033	65425	77147	04/58-05/74	➲**5931**	
6033	65425	77147	02/80-05/82	➲*3208*	⇦
6034	65426	77148	04/58-04/74	➲**5932**	
6034	65426	77148	02/80-05/84		⇦
6035	65427	77149	05/58-04/74	➲**5933**	
6035	65427	77149	04/80-06/82	➲*3211*	⇦
6036	65428	77150	05/58-04/74	➲**5934**	
6036	65428	77150	06/80-05/82	➲*3207*	⇦
6037	65429	77151	05/58-04/74	➲**5935**	
6037	65429	77151	06/80-05/82	➲*3208*	⇦
6038	65430	77152	05/58-04/74	➲**5936**	
6038	65430	77152	02/80-04/82	➲*3209*	⇦
6039	65431	77153	05/58-04/74	➲**5937**	
6039	65431	77153	02/80-06/84		⇦
6040	65432	77154	05/58-04/74	➲**5938**	
6040	65432	77154	02/80-05/82	➲*3213*	⇦
6041	65433	77155	05/58-05/74	➲**5939**	
6041	65433	77155	05/80-04/82	➲*3212*	⇦
6042	65434	77156	05/58-04/74	➲**5940**	
6042	65434	77156	02/80-05/82	➲*3210*	⇦

Class 414/3

	DMBSO	*DTCsoL*			
6043	61241	75361	11/58-04/74	➲**5941**	
6043	61241	75361	03/80-05/82	➲*3302*	⇦
6044	61242	75362	12/58-04/74	➲**5942**	
6044	61242	75362	02/80-10/83		⇦
6045	61243	75363	12/58-05/77	➲**5943**	
6045	61243	75363	04/80-05/82	➲*3310*	⇦
6046	61244	75364	12/58-05/77	➲**5944**	
6046	61244	75364	03/80-05/82	➲*3302*	⇦
6047	61245	75365	12/58-05/77	➲**5945**	
6047	61245	75365	04/80-05/84		⇦
6048	61246	75366	12/58-05/77	➲**5946**	
6048	61246	75366	03/80-05/82	➲*3308*	⇦
6049	61247	75367	01/59-05/77	➲**5947**	
6049	61247	75367	03/80-05/84		⇦
6050	61248	75368	01/59-05/77	➲**5948**	
6050	61248	75368	02/80-10/82		⇦
6051	61249	75369	01/59-05/77	➲**5949**	
6051	61249	75369	05/80-07/88	➲**4301**	⇦
6052	61250	75370	01/59-05/77	➲**5950**	
6052	61250	75370	05/80-04/82	➲*3303*	⇦
6053	61251	75371	01/59-05/77	➲**5951**	
6053	61251	75371	10/77-05/82	➲*3309*	⇦
6054	61252	75372	02/59-04/82	➲*3303*	
6055	61253	75373	02/59-05/82	➲*3301*	
6056	61254	75374	02/59-04/82	➲*3306*	
6057	61255	75375	02/59-05/82	➲*3301*	
6058	61256	75376	02/59-04/82	➲*3306*	
6059	61257	75377	03/59-05/82	➲*3309*	
6060	61258	75378	03/59-05/82	➲*3307*	
6061	61259	75379	03/59-10/84		
6062	61260	75380	03/59-06/88	➲**4302**	
6063	61261	75381	04/59-05/88	➲**4303**	
6064	61262	75382	04/59-12/87	➲**4304**	
6065	61263	75383	04/59-10/83		
6066	61264	75384	04/59-05/82	➲*3308*	
6067	61265	75385	05/59-10/82		
6068	61266	75386	05/59-05/82	➲*3310*	
6069	61267	75387	05/59-05/82		
6070	61268	75388	05/59-04/88	➲**4305**	

6071	61269	75389	05/59-05/82	
6072	61270	75390	06/59-08/87	➲**4306**
6073	61271	75391	06/59-05/82	➲*3307*
6074	61272	75392	06/59-05/82	
6075	61273	75393	06/59-10/87	➲**4307**
6076	61274	75394	06/59-09/82	
6077	61275	75395	06/59-07/87	➲**4308**
6078	61276	75396	07/59-07/87	➲**4309**
6079	61277	75397	07/59-09/82	
6080	61278	75398	07/59-05/88	➲**4310**
6081	61279	75399	07/59-05/82	➲*3305*
6082	61280	75400	07/59-05/82	
6083	61281	75401	07/59-05/82	
6084	61282	75402	07/59-04/82	➲*3304*
6085	61283	75403	07/59-04/82	➲*3304*
6086	61284	75404	07/59-05/82	
6087	61285	75405	08/59-10/84	
6088	61286	75406	08/59-05/82	
6089	61287	75407	08/59-07/87	➲**4311**
6090	61288	75408	08/59-07/88	➲**4312**
6091	61289	75409	08/59-10/83	
6092	61290	75410	08/59-07/87	➲**4313**
6093	61291	75411	08/59-05/82	➲*3311*
6094	61292	75412	08/59-05/82	
6095	61293	75413	08/59-10/82	
6096	61294	75414	08/59-07/87	➲**4314**
6097	61295	75415	09/59-11/87	➲**4315**
6098	61296	75416	09/59-12/87	➲**4316**
6099	61297	75417	09/59-05/82	➲*3311*
6100	61298	75418	09/59-04/87	➲**4317**
6101	61299	75419	09/59-05/82	
6102	61300	75420	09/59-05/87	➲**4318**
6103	61301	75421	09/59-10/84	
6104	61302	75422	09/59-05/82	➲*3305*
6105	61303	75423	09/59-06/87	➲**4319**
6106	61648	75700	03/61-05/82	
6107	61649	75701	04/61-05/82	
6108	61650	75702	04/61-10/83	
6109	61651	75703	04/61-10/83	
6110	61652	75704	04/61-05/82	
6111	61653	75705	04/61-10/83	
6112	61654	75706	05/61-11/87	➲**4320**
6113	61655	75707	05/61-10/83	
6114	61656	75708	05/61-05/83	
6115	61657	75709	05/61-05/82	
6116	61658	75710	05/61-10/83	➲**054**
6117	61659	75711	05/61-10/83	
6118	61660	75712	05/61-10/83	
6119	61661	75713	05/61-10/83	
6120	61662	75714	05/61-05/82	
6121	61663	75715	06/61-05/82	➲**052**
6122	61664	75716	06/61-05/82	
6123	61665	75717	06/61-05/82	
6124	61666	75718	06/61-05/83	
6125	61667	75719	06/61-10/83	
6126	61668	75720	07/61-05/88	➲**4321**
6127	61669	75721	07/61-01/82	
6128	61670	75722	08/61-05/83	
6129	61671	75723	08/61-05/82	
6130	61672	75724	08/61-05/82	
6131	61673	75725	09/61-05/83	
6132	61674	75726	09/61-05/82	
6133	61675	75727	09/61-10/83	
6134	61676	75728	09/61-01/82	
6135	61677	75729	09/61-05/82	
6136	61678	75730	09/61-09/82	
6137	61679	75731	10/61-09/82	
6138	61680	75732	10/61-05/82	
6139	61681	75733	11/61-10/83	
6140	61682	75734	11/61-05/83	
6141	61683	75735	11/61-06/88	➲**4322**
6142	61684	75736	11/61-05/82	➲**053**
6143	61685	75737	12/61-05/82	
6144	61686	75738	12/61-04/83	
6145	61687	75739	01/62-05/83	
6146	61688	75740	01/62-10/83	
6147	61962	75995	02/63-05/84	
6148	61963	75996	02/63-10/83	
6149	61964	75997	03/63-10/83	
6150	61965	75998	03/63-05/84	
6151	61966	75999	03/63-06/71	
6151	*61872*	75999	01/72-10/83	☜
6152	61967	76000	03/63-10/83	
6153	61968	76001	03/63-05/84	
6154	61969	76002	03/63-10/83	
6155	61970	76003	03/63-05/83	
6156	61971	76004	03/63-10/83	➲**051**
6157	61972	76005	04/63-10/83	
6158	61973	76006	04/63-10/83	
6159	61974	76007	04/63-05/84	
6160	61975	76008	04/63-10/83	
6161	61976	76009	04/63-05/84	
6162	61977	76010	04/63-05/84	
6163	61978	76011	04/63-05/84	
6164	61979	76012	04/63-06/82	
6165	61980	76013	05/63-10/83	
6166	61981	76014	05/63-05/84	
6167	61982	76015	05/63-05/84	
6168	61983	76016	05/63-10/83	
6169	61984	76017	05/63-05/84	
6170	61985	76018	05/63-10/84	
6171	61986	76019	05/63-05/84	
6172	61987	76020	05/63-05/84	
6173	61988	76021	05/63-10/84	

Class 410 4-BEP

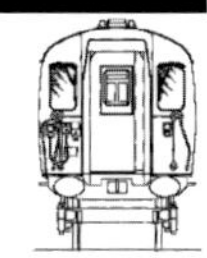

Kent Line Express Buffet Units
660-750V dc third rail
7001-7022

These 4-BEP buffet units were built to work with the 4-CEP units on the Kent Coast electrification. See the 4-CEP units for more details. They were later reclassified to 412 when they were renumbered in the later TOPS number series.

	DMBSO	*TCK*	*TRB*	*DMBSO*			
7001	61041	70041	69000	61042	07/56-05/80	➲*1501*	
7002	61043	70042	69001	61044	07/56-08/83	➲*1504*	
7003	61391	70346	69002	61390	03/59-09/81	➲*1532*	
7004	61393	70347	69003	61392	04/59-01/72		
7004	61393	70347	69003	*61385*	03/72-09/81	➲*1533*	☜
7005	61395	70348	69004	61394	04/59-03/82	➲*1542*	
7006	61397	70349	69005	61396	04/59-11/81	➲*1535*	
7007	61399	70350	69006	61398	04/59-11/81	➲*1536*	
7008	61401	70351	69007	61400	05/59-11/81	➲*1539*	
7009	61403	70352	69008	61402	05/59-11/80	➲*1519*	
7010	61405	70353	69009	61404	05/59-10/81	➲*1534*	
7011	61407	70354	69010	61406	05/59-08/83	➲*1562*	
7012	61409	70355	69011	61408	05/59-11/81	➲*1541*	
7013	61792	70601	69012	61793	01/61-05/82	➲*1574*	
7014	61794	70602	69013	61795	01/61-03/83	➲*1612*	
7015	61796	70603	69014	61797	03/61-07/70		
7015	*61748*	70603	69014	61797	07/70-11/81	➲*1582*	☜
7016	61798	70604	69015	61799	03/61-12/83	➲*2305*	
7017	61800	70605	69016	61801	04/61-07/83	➲*1617*	
7018	61802	70606	69017	61803	04/61-12/83	➲*2307*	
7019	61804	70607	69018	61805	05/61-02/82	➲*2301*	
7020	61806	70608	69019	61807	06/61-06/82	➲*1571*	
7021	61808	70609	69020	61809	06/61-12/83	➲*2306*	
7022	61810	70610	69021	61811	09/61-09/83	➲*1621*	

Class 420 4-BIG

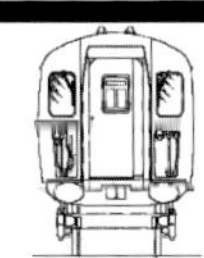

Brighton Line Express Buffet Units
660-750V dc third rail
7031-7058

These 4-BIG buffet units were built to work with the 4-CIG units on the Brighton line. Some ran as three car units without the buffet car when first built. See the 4-CIG units for more details. They were later reclassified to 422 when they were renumbered in the later TOPs number series.

Temporary 3-car units

	DTCsoL	*MBSO*	*DTCsoL*	
7031	76112	62053	76058	04/65-06/65
7032	76113	62054	76059	05/65-06/65
7033	76114	62055	76060	05/65-06/65
7034	76115	62056	76061	06/65-07/65
7035	76116	62057	76062	06/65-07/65
7036	76117	62058	76063	06/65-08/65
7038	76119	62060	76065	07/65-08/65
7039	76120	62061	76066	08/65-09/65

	DTCsoL	*MBSO*	*TSRB*	*DTCsoL*			
7031	76112	62053	69301	76058	06/65-09/85	➲**2111**	
7032	76113	62054	69302	76059	06/65-04/83		
7032	*76063*	62054	69302	76059	04/83-04/85	➲**2101**	☜
7033	76114	62055	69303	76060	07/65-03/86	➲**1711**	
7034	76115	62056	69304	76061	07/65-11/85	➲**2110**	
7035	76116	62057	69305	76062	08/65-10/86	➲*1719*	
7036	76117	62058	69306	76063	08/65-04/83		
7036	76117	62058	69306	*76113*	04/83-06/83		☜
7036	76117	62058	69306	*76051*	06/83-05/85	➲**2104**	☜
7037	76118	62059	69307	76064	08/65-04/85	➲**2106**	

7038	76119	62060	69308	76065	08/65-11/85	➲ *7323*
7038	*76098*	*62039*	69308	*76044*	11/85-07/86	➲ *7299*
7039	76120	62061	69309	76066	09/65-10/86	➲ *1724*
7040	76121	62062	69310	76067	11/65-08/79	➲ *7300*
7040	*76121*	62062	69310	76067	04/80-05/85	➲ **2105**
7041	76122	62063	69311	76068	11/65-04/85	➲ **2107**
7042	76123	62064	69312	76069	11/65-08/83	
7042	*76129*	62064	69312	76069	08/83-04/85	➲ **2102**
7043	76124	62065	69313	76070	12/65-04/85	➲ **2103**
7044	76125	62066	69314	76071	12/65-03/86	➲ *7300*
7045	76126	62067	69315	76072	12/65-04/86	➲ **2112**
7046	76127	62068	69316	76073	02/66-09/85	➲ **2108**
7047	76128	62069	69317	76074	02/66-05/86	➲ *1713*
7048	76129	62070	69318	76075	02/66-08/83	
7048	*76123*	62070	69318	76075	08/83-10/85	➲ **2109**
7049	76561	62277	69330	76571	05/70-06/85	➲ **2201**
7050	76562	62278	69331	76572	06/70-05/85	➲ **2202**
7051	76563	62279	69332	76573	06/70-04/85	➲ **2203**
7052	76564	62280	69336	76574	10/70-04/85	➲ **2204**
7053	76565	62281	69339	76575	11/70-04/85	➲ **2205**
7054	76566	62282	69338	76576		
			intended formation but not delivered as this (vehicles went to 7358)			
7054	*76602*	*62308*	69338	*76632*	11/70-04/85	➲ **2206**
7055	76567	62283	69333	76577	07/70-04/85	➲ **2207**
7056	76568	62284	69334	76578	08/70-04/85	➲ **2208**
7057	76569	62285	69335	76579	09/70-04/85	➲ **2209**
7058	76570	62286	69337	76580	10/70-04/85	➲ **2210**

Class 411 4-CEP

Kent Line Express Units

660-750V dc third rail

7101-7211

In 1956 six prototype mainline units were built for evaluation on the forthcoming Kent Coast electrification. 4-CEP units 7101-7104 and 4-BEP buffet units 7001-7002 were based on the Mark 1 design and were used on the Central Division. They were designed to work at 90mph, the highest speed for any Southern region units yet built. These prototype units had Electro-pneumatic contactor control ('1951 stock').

These proved successful and further units were built with camshaft control ('1957 stock'). 7105-7153 and 7003-7012 were ordered in 1958 for Phase 1 of the Kent Coast electrification and 7154-7204 and 7013-7022 in 1960 for Phase 2. The Phase 2 units were fitted with Commonwealth trailer bogies. A further small batch (7205-7211) was ordered in 1963 for the South Western Division, but these soon moved to join the others on the South East Division.

In 1975 unit 7153 was experimentally refurbished at Eastleigh Works. The second class compartment vehicle was converted to open and the Guard's compartment was transferred to the intermediate composite trailer. It was fitted with hopper windows.

This mid-life refurbishment was deemed to be a success and the whole class was similarly treated at Swindon between 1979 and 1984. They were initially renumbered in the 4115xx series, but as the Southern Region preferred to refer to their units by just 4 digits, they soon were renumbered in the 15xx series. Only seven of the Class 410 4-BEP units were refurbished; these units were reclassified as Class 412 and renumbered in the 23xx series. A number of Mark 1 coaches were converted to replace the rest of the buffet cars and form extra 4-CEP units.

Between 1983 and 1986 the 4-BIG units on the Brighton line were having asbestos removed, and to cover for the units in works four units were converted to 4-TEP 2701-2704. They were reformed with unrefurbished 4-BEP buffets; these were later withdrawn when the units were reformed back to CEPs.

In 1993 six 3-CEP 3-car units were formed to work on the Medway Valley, Tonbridge-Redhill and Sheerness services. They were numbered 1401-1406.

Three units were renumbered 1697-1699 in 1996 when they were fitted with B6 power bogies.

A further batch of 3-CEP units numbered 1101-1118 was formed for the South Eastern Division in 1998-99.

Two further 3-CEP units 1198 & 1198 were used on the Lymington Branch in 2003 & 2004, but they were soon replaced with 3-BIG units 1497-1499.

Further reformations took place in 2002 when South West Trains swapped the buffet cars in their 4-BEP and 4-CEP units to create more "Greyhound" units. (Greyhound units had an extra set of weak-field resistances to allow more rapid acceleration. See the 4-CIG units 1301-1322).

	DMBSO	*TSK*	*TCK*	*DMBSO*		
7101	61033	70033	70037	61034	02/56-10/82	➲ **1503**
7102	61035	70034	70038	61036	03/56-10/75	
7103	61037	70035	70039	61038	04/56-08/83	➲ *1505*
7104	61039	70036	70040	61040	05/56-12/80	➲ **1502**
7105	61230	70229	70235	61229	08/58-01/82	➲ **1537**
7106	61232	70230	70236	61231	08/58-12/83	➲ *1561*
7107	61234	70231	70237	61233	08/58-06/81	➲ **1531**
7108	61236	70232	70238	61235	09/58-03/81	➲ **1525**
7109	61238	70233	70239	61237	09/58-04/81	➲ **1527**
7110	61240	70234	70240	61239	09/58-03/81	➲ **1526**
7111	61304	70260	70303	61305	09/58-01/80	➲ **1508**
7112	61306	70261	70304	61307	09/58-02/82	➲ **1538**
7113	61308	70262	70305	61309	10/58-02/81	➲ **1524**
7114	61310	70263	70306	61311	10/58-10/82	
7114	61310	*70283*	*70326*	61311	10/82-04/83	➲ **1555**
7115	61312	70264	70307	61313	10/58-12/82	➲ **1550**
7116	61314	70265	70308	61315	10/58-06/82	➲ **1544**
7117	61316	70266	70309	61317	10/58-11/80	➲ **1517**
7118	61318	70267	70310	61319	11/58-10/80	➲ **1516**
7119	61320	70268	70311	61321	11/58-06/80	➲ **1512**
7120	61322	70269	70312	61323	11/58-04/82	➲ **1543**
7121	61324	70270	70313	61325	11/58-12/82	➲ **1551**
7122	61326	70271	70314	61327	11/58-08/80	➲ **1514**
7123	61328	70272	70315	61329	12/58-09/82	➲ **1547**
7124	61330	70273	70316	61331	12/58-06/81	➲ **1530**
7125	61332	70274	70317	61333	12/58-11/80	➲ **1518**
7126	61334	70275	70318	61335	12/58-02/80	➲ **1509**
7127	61336	70276	70319	61337	12/58-07/83	➲ *1558*
7128	61338	70277	70320	61339	12/58-11/82	➲ **1549**
7129	61340	70278	70321	61341	01/59-09/70	
7129	61340	70278	70321	*61796*	09/70-06/80	➲ **1513**
7130	61342	70279	70322	61343	01/59-03/79	
7131	61344	70280	70323	61345	01/59-09/80	➲ **1515**
7132	61346	70281	70324	61347	01/59-12/80	
7133	61348	70282	70325	61349	01/59-12/79	➲ **1506**
7134	61350	70283	70326	61351	01/59-10/82	
7135	61352	70284	70327	61353	01/59-12/80	
7136	61354	70285	70328	61355	02/59-05/81	➲ **1529**
7137	61356	70286	70329	61357	02/59-08/82	➲ **1546**
7138	61358	70287	70330	61359	02/59-07/82	➲ **1545**
7139	61360	70288	70331	61361	02/59-07/83	➲ *1557*
7140	61362	70289	70332	61363	02/59-01/80	➲ **1507**
7141	61364	70290	70333	61365	03/59-04/80	➲ **1510**
7142	61366	70291	70334	61367	03/59-05/80	➲ **1511**
7143	61368	70292	70335	61369	03/59-04/83	➲ **1554**
7144	61370	70293	70336	61371	03/59-06/83	➲ **1556**
7145	61372	70294	70337	61373	04/59-02/83	➲ **1552**
7146	61374	70295	70338	61375	04/59-10/82	➲ **1548**
7147	61376	70296	70339	61377	04/59-10/83	➲ **1559**
7148	61378	70297	70340	61379	05/59-04/81	➲ **1528**
7149	61380	70298	70341	61381	05/59-04/79	
7150	61382	70299	70342	61383	06/59-02/81	➲ **1523**
7151	61384	70300	70343	61385	06/59-04/71	
7151	61384	70300	70343	*61870*	04/71-03/82	➲ **1540**
7152	61386	70301	70344	61387	06/59-11/83	➲ **1560**
7153	61388	70302	70345	61389	06/59-11/85	➲ **1500**
7154	61695	70503	70552	61694	07/60-03/80	➲ **1606**
7155	61697	70504	70553	61696	08/60-06/81	➲ **1590**
7156	61699	70505	70554	61698	09/60-03/80	➲ **1607**
7157	61701	70506	70555	61700	09/60-02/82	➲ **1578**
7158	61703	70507	70556	61702	09/60-04/83	➲ **1614**
7159	61705	70508	70557	61704	09/60-02/81	➲ **1595**
7160	61707	70509	70558	61706	09/60-10/80	➲ **1599**
7161	61709	70510	70559	61708	09/60-01/81	➲ **1597**
7162	61711	70511	70560	61710	01/61-10/81	➲ **1585**
7163	61713	70512	70561	61712	10/60-04/80	➲ **1605**
7164	61715	70513	70562	61714	10/60-08/81	➲ **1586**
7165	61717	70514	70563	61716	10/60-01/81	➲ **1596**
7166	61719	70515	70564	61718	10/60-02/82	➲ **1577**
7167	61721	70516	70565	61720	10/60-08/80	
7168	61723	70517	70566	61722	10/60-11/82	➲ **1566**
7169	61725	70518	70567	61724	10/60-09/80	➲ **1600**
7170	61727	70519	70568	61726	11/60-05/82	➲ **1573**
7171	61729	70520	70569	61728	11/60-07/80	➲ *1603*
7172	61731	70521	70570	61730	11/60-04/81	➲ **1593**
7173	61733	70522	70571	61732	11/60-07/80	➲ **1604**
7174	61735	70523	70572	61734	11/60-06/82	➲ **1572**
7175	61737	70524	70573	61736	11/60-11/83	➲ *2304*
7176	61739	70525	70574	61738	11/60-08/82	➲ **1570**
7177	61741	70526	70575	61740	12/60-01/83	➲ **1563**
7178	61743	70527	70576	61742	12/60-07/81	➲ **1589**
7179	61745	70528	70577	61744	12/60-02/83	➲ **1609**
7180	61747	70529	70578	61746	12/60-10/81	➲ **1583**
7181	61749	70530	70579	61748	12/60-01/69	
7182	61751	70531	70580	61750	01/61-02/83	➲ **1610**
7183	61753	70532	70581	61752	01/61-03/82	➲ **1584**
7184	61755	70533	70582	61754	01/61-03/81	➲ **1594**
7185	61757	70534	70583	61756	01/61-12/81	➲ *1580*
7186	61759	70535	70584	61758	02/61-03/83	➲ *1611*

Unit					Dates	Renumbered	
7187	61761	70536	70585	61760	02/61-04/83	➲**1613**	
7188	61763	70537	70586	61762	02/61-01/83	➲*1565*	
7189	61765	70538	70587	61764	02/61-11/71		
7189	61765	*70044*	70587	61764	11/71-08/81	➲*1587*	✍
7190	61767	70539	70588	61766	03/61-09/82	➲**1568**	
7191	61769	70540	70589	61768	03/61-12/81	➲*1575*	
7192	61771	70541	70590	61770	03/61-04/82	➲**1576**	
7193	61773	70542	70591	61772	03/61-01/82	➲**1579**	
7194	61775	70543	70592	61774	04/61-06/83	➲*2302*	
7195	61777	70544	70593	61776	04/61-09/80	➲**1601**	
7196	61779	70545	70594	61778	06/61-05/81	➲**1592**	
7197	61781	70546	70595	61780	06/61-11/80	➲**1598**	
7198	61783	70547	70596	61782	06/61-08/82	➲**1569**	
7199	61785	70548	70597	61784	07/61-11/81	➲**1581**	
7200	61787	70549	70598	61786	07/61-10/82	➲**1567**	
7201	61789	70550	70599	61788	07/61-12/82	➲**1564**	
7202	61791	70551	70600	61790	08/61-06/81	➲**1591**	
7203	61869	70241	70043	61868	08/61-09/83	➲*1618*	
7204	61871	70242	70044	61870	09/61-04/71		
7205	61949	70660	70653	61948	12/62-11/83	➲**1620**	
7206	61951	70661	70654	61950	01/63-06/83	➲*1616*	
7207	61953	70662	70655	61952	01/63-10/83	➲**1619**	
7208	61955	70663	70656	61954	01/63-09/83	➲*2303*	
7209	61957	70664	70657	61956	02/63-05/83	➲**1615**	
7210	61959	70665	70658	61958	02/63-03/79		
7211	61961	70666	70659	61960	02/63-02/80	➲**1608**	

Class 421 4-CIG

Brighton Line Express Buffet Units
660-750V dc third rail
7301-7438 (plus 7299 & 7300)

These units were designed to replace the life-expired first generation express units on the London to Brighton, Worthing and Eastbourne lines. They were low-density units with fewer doors.

This stock made a real break from Southern tradition by having one brake motor car in the middle of the unit rather than two driving motor brakes at the end of the units. Two different theories have been forwarded to explain the IG designation: it either refers to "intermediate guard" reflecting the then unusual formation of the units, or it reflects the telegraphic code "IG" for Brighton.

These units differed from earlier CEP & BEP units by having rounded off edges to the cab tops (rather than an overhang) and jumper connections fitted in recesses on the ends.

The Central division units were numbered 7031-7048 for the BIG units (buffet), and 7301-7336 for the CIG units. These units were fitted with unique electric parking brakes and were Class 420/1 and 421/1.

A further order of units was to replace the COR, BUF and GRI stock on the Waterloo-Portsmouth line, and they were numbered 7049-7058 and 7337-7366. These and later units were Class 420/2 and 421/2 and they had conventional handbrakes. Next was another order of units for the Central and South Western divisions numbered 7367-7437 to replace the remaining 4-COR units on those lines. A final unit, 7438, was built to replace 7181 which had been written off in a collision.

From 1985 the units were renumbered to match their TOPS classifications. Class 420 became Class 422. Class 422/1 units were renumbered 2101-2112 and Class 422/2 became 2201-2210.

The earlier Class 421/1 units had been built with blue asbestos and this had to be removed from units from the mid 1980s onwards. Some units were facelifted as part of this process and they were renumbered from 1701 upwards. Others were not facelifted and these were renumbered 1100-1127 in 1987. As part of the asbestos removal program two 8-MIG 8-car units were formed including a buffet car. These were used on the Waterloo-Portsmouth line to release other 4-BIG units to the Brighton line while their units were in the works.

The later Class 421/2 units were renumbered 1201-1226 (7401-7426), 1237-1300 (7337-7400) and 1801-1813 (7427-7438). From 1988 onwards, these units were facelifted and they were renumbered 1814-1891 as Class 421/4.

In 1989 the Class 422/1 4-BIG units 2101-2112 were reformed to become Class 421/3 4CIG units 1751-1762.

In 1990-92 twenty-two 4-CIGs were modified to become 'Greyhound' units. They had an extra set of weak-field resistances to allow more rapid acceleration and were renumbered 1301-1322. They were used on the Waterloo-Portsmouth route.

Eight units were renumbered 1901-1908 in 1993-95 when they were fitted with B6 power bogies.

Between 1993 and 1997 four 8-DIG units were created to work on the London-Brighton "Capital Coast Express". They were formed from semi-permanently coupled BIG and CIG units and were numbered 2001-2004.

The BIG units 2203-2210 were considered surplus to requirements in 1997 and they were renumbered 1401-1411 as Class 421/4. Later that year, the buffet cars were removed and they were reclassified as Class 421/7 3-COP units for use on the Coastway services. Some of these later received a trailer coach from withdrawn CIG units to become 4-COP units.

Finally, in 1999, the remaining eight 4-BIG units based at Fratton had their Buffet cars replaced by CEP TSOs, to become Class 421/8 units 1392-1399.

Two units were retained under the Community Rail scheme after the rest had been withdrawn. 1497 & 1498 worked on the Lymington Pier branch and were painted in heritage liveries.

Unit	DTCsoL	MBSO	TSO	DTCsoL	Dates	Renumbered	
7299	76098	62039	71021	76044	07/86-08/86	➲*1720*	
7300	76121	62062	71106	76067	08/79-01/80		
7300	76121	62062	*70995*	76067	01/80-04/80		✍
7300²	76125	62066	71051	76071	03/86-06/87	➲**1100**	

Unit	DTCsoL	MBSO	TSO	DTCsoL	Dates	Renumbered	
7301	76076	62017	70695	76022	09/64-11/85	➲**1705**	
7302	76077	62018	70696	76023	10/64-06/86	➲**1714**	
7303	76078	62019	70697	76024	10/64-02/86	➲**1710**	
7304	76079	62020	70698	76025	10/64-04/86	➲**1712**	
7305	76080	62021	70699	76026	11/64-06/87	➲**1105**	
7306	76081	62022	70700	76027	11/64-10/86	➲**1718**	
7307	76082	62023	70701	76028	11/64-07/86	➲**1715**	
7308	76083	62024	70702	76029	12/64-09/86	➲**1717**	
7309	76084	62025	70703	76030	12/64-12/85	➲**1707**	
7310	76085	62026	70704	76031	12/64-06/87	➲**1110**	
7311	76086	62027	70705	76032	01/65-06/87	➲**1111**	
7312	76087	62028	70706	76033	01/65-07/85	➲**1701**	
7313	76088	62029	70707	76034	01/65-03/87	➲**1725**	
7314	76089	62030	70708	76035	02/65-06/87	➲**1114**	
7315	76090	62031	70709	76036	03/65-12/86	➲**1721**	
7316	76091	62032	70710	76037	03/65-06/87	➲**1116**	
7317	76092	62033	70711	76038	03/65-10/85	➲**1704**	
7318	76093	62034	70712	76039	04/65-06/87	➲**1118**	
7319	76094	62035	70713	76040	08/65-12/85	➲**1706**	
7320	76095	62036	70714	76041	08/65-11/87	➲**1731**	
7321	76096	62037	70715	76042	09/65-05/87	➲**1121**	
7322	76097	62038	70716	76043	09/65-09/85	➲**1703**	
7323	76098	62039	70717	76044	09/65-11/85	➲*7038*	
7323	*76119*	*62060*	70717	*76065*	11/85-07/86	➲**1123**	✍
7324	76099	62040	70718	76045	09/65-07/87	➲**1728**	
7325	76100	62041	70719	76046	10/65-08/86	➲*1716*	
7326	76101	62042	70720	76047	10/65-08/85	➲**1702**	
7327	76102	62043	70721	76048	10/65-06/87	➲**1127**	
7328	76103	62044	70722	76049	10/65-02/86	➲**1709**	
7329	76104	62045	70723	76050	11/65-07/87	➲**1729**	
7330	76105	62046	70724	76051	12/65-06/83		
7330	76105	62046	70724	*76113*	06/83-10/87	➲**1730**	✍
7331	76106	62047	70725	76052	12/65-01/87	➲**1722**	
7332	76107	62048	70726	76053	01/66-02/87	➲**1723**	
7333	76108	62049	70727	76054	01/66-12/78		
7334	76109	62050	70728	76055	01/66-05/87	➲**1726**	
7335	76110	62051	70729	76056	01/66-01/86	➲**1708**	
7336	76111	62052	70730	76057	02/66-06/87	➲**1727**	
7337	76581	62287	70967	76611	06/70-08/87	➲**1237**	
7338	76582	62288	70968	76612	05/70-06/87	➲**1238**	
7339	76583	62289	70969	76613	05/70-08/87	➲**1239**	
7340	76584	62290	70970	76614	06/70-09/87	➲**1240**	
7341	76585	62291	70971	76615	06/70-08/87	➲**1241**	
7342	76586	62292	70972	76616	08/70-09/87	➲**1242**	
7343	76587	62293	70973	76617	10/70-09/87	➲**1243**	
7344	76588	62294	70974	76618	10/70-06/87	➲**1244**	
7345	76589	62295	70975	76619	11/70-06/87	➲**1245**	
7346	76590	62296	70976	76620	01/71-06/87	➲**1246**	
7347	76591	62297	70977	76621	01/71-06/87	➲**1247**	
7348	76592	62298	70978	76622	06/70-06/87	➲**1248**	
7349	76593	62299	70979	76623	07/70-09/87	➲**1249**	
7350	76594	62300	70980	76624	07/70-08/87	➲**1250**	
7351	76595	62301	70981	76625	08/70-08/87	➲**1251**	
7352	76596	62302	70982	76626	08/70-09/87	➲**1252**	
7353	76597	62303	70983	76627	09/70-09/87	➲**1253**	
7354	76598	62304	70984	76628	09/70-11/87	➲**1254**	
7355	76599	62305	70985	76629	10/70-02/88	➲**1255**	
7356	76600	62306	70986	76630	11/70-06/87	➲**1256**	
7357	76601	62307	70987	76631	10/70-07/87	➲**1257**	
7358	76602	62308	70988	76632	intended formation but not delivered as this (vehicles went to 7054)		
7358	*76566*	*62282*	70988	*76576*	10/70-09/87	➲**1258**	
7359	76603	62309	70989	76633	10/70-06/87	➲**1259**	
7360	76604	62310	70990	76634	11/70-06/87	➲**1260**	
7361	76605	62311	70991	76635	11/70-08/87	➲**1261**	
7362	76606	62312	70992	76636	12/70-05/87	➲**1262**	

7363	76607	62313	70993	76637	12/70-07/87	➲**1263**	
7364	76608	62314	70994	76638	11/70-07/87	➲**1264**	
7365	76609	62315	70995	76639	12/70-12/78		
7366	76610	62316	70996	76640	01/71-05/87	➲**1266**	
7367	76717	62355	71035	76788	02/71-08/87	➲**1267**	
7368	76718	62356	71036	76789	02/71-06/87	➲**1268**	
7369	76719	62357	71037	76790	02/71-05/87	➲**1269**	
7370	76720	62358	71038	76791	03/71-08/87	➲**1270**	
7371	76721	62359	71039	76792	02/71-08/87	➲**1271**	
7372	76722	62360	71040	76793	02/71-06/87	➲**1272**	
7373	76723	62361	71041	76794	02/71-06/87	➲**1273**	
7374	76724	62362	71042	76795	03/71-06/87	➲**1274**	
7375	76725	62363	71043	76796	03/71-06/87	➲**1275**	
7376	76726	62364	71044	76797	04/71-08/87	➲**1276**	
7377	76727	62365	71045	76798	04/71-08/87	➲**1277**	
7378	76728	62366	71046	76799	04/71-06/87	➲**1278**	
7379	76729	62367	71047	76800	04/71-06/87	➲**1279**	
7380	76730	62368	71048	76801	04/71-06/87	➲**1280**	
7381	76731	62369	71049	76802	05/71-06/87	➲**1281**	
7382	76732	62370	71050	76803	05/71-06/87	➲**1282**	
7383	76733	62371	71051	76804	05/71-01/86		
7384	76734	62372	71052	76805	05/71-06/87	➲**1284**	
7385	76735	62373	71053	76806	05/71-06/87	➲**1285**	
7386	76736	62374	71054	76807	05/71-06/87	➲**1286**	
7387	76737	62375	71055	76808	05/71-06/87	➲**1287**	
7388	76738	62376	71056	76809	05/71-06/87	➲**1288**	
7389	76739	62377	71057	76810	06/71-07/87	➲**1289**	
7390	76740	62378	71058	76811	06/71-09/87	➲**1290**	
7391	76741	62379	71059	76812	06/71-06/87	➲**1291**	
7392	76742	62380	71060	76813	06/71-06/87	➲**1292**	
7393	76743	62381	71061	76814	06/71-06/87	➲**1293**	
7394	76744	62382	71062	76815	06/71-05/87	➲**1294**	
7395	76745	62383	71063	76816	07/71-08/87	➲**1295**	
7396	76746	62384	71064	76817	07/71-06/87	➲**1296**	
7397	76747	62385	71065	76818	08/71-06/87	➲**1297**	
7398	76748	62386	71066	76819	08/71-08/87	➲**1298**	
7399	76749	62387	71067	76820	08/71-05/87	➲**1299**	
7400	76750	62388	71068	76821	08/71-06/87	➲**1300**	
7401	76751	62389	71069	76822	09/71-05/83	➲*2601*	
7401	76751	62389	71069	76822	10/83-06/87	➲**1201**	✍
7402	76752	62390	71070	76823	09/71-05/83	➲*2601*	
7402	76752	62390	71070	76823	10/83-05/87	➲**1202**	✍
7403	76753	62391	71071	76824	09/71-05/83	➲*2602*	
7403	76753	62391	71071	76824	10/83-08/87	➲**1203**	✍
7404	76754	62392	71072	76825	09/71-05/83	➲*2602*	
7404	76754	62392	71072	76825	10/83-06/87	➲**1204**	✍
7405	76755	62393	71073	76826	09/71-07/87	➲**1205**	
7406	76756	62394	71074	76827	09/71-08/87	➲**1206**	
7407	76757	62395	71075	76828	09/71-12/86	➲**1812**	
7408	76758	62396	71076	76829	10/71-07/87	➲**1208**	
7409	76759	62397	71077	76830	10/71-07/87	➲**1209**	
7410	76760	62398	71078	76831	10/71-05/87	➲**1210**	
7411	76761	62399	71079	76832	10/71-08/87	➲**1211**	
7412	76762	62400	71080	76833	11/71-09/87	➲**1212**	
7413	76763	62401	71081	76834	11/71-09/87	➲**1213**	
7414	76764	62402	71082	76835	12/71-09/87	➲**1214**	
7415	76765	62403	71083	76836	12/71-08/87	➲**1215**	
7416	76766	62404	71084	76837	12/71-09/87	➲**1216**	
7417	76767	62405	71085	76838	12/71-09/87	➲**1217**	
7418	76768	62406	71086	76839	12/71-09/87	➲**1218**	
7419	76769	62407	71087	76840	12/71-09/87	➲**1219**	
7420	76770	62408	71088	76841	01/72-06/87	➲**1220**	
7421	76771	62409	71089	76842	01/72-08/87	➲**1221**	
7422	76772	62410	71090	76843	01/72-08/87	➲**1222**	
7423	76773	62411	71091	76844	01/72-08/87	➲**1223**	
7424	76774	62412	71092	76845	02/72-09/87	➲**1224**	
7425	76775	62413	71093	76846	02/72-08/87	➲**1225**	
7426	76776	62414	71094	76847	02/72-08/87	➲**1226**	
7427	76777	62415	71095	76848	02/72-03/86	➲**1801**	
7428	76778	62416	71096	76849	03/72-05/86	➲**1804**	
7429	76779	62417	71097	76850	03/72-03/86	➲**1802**	
7430	76780	62418	71098	76851	02/72-03/86	➲**1803**	
7431	76781	62419	71099	76852	02/72-11/86	➲**1811**	
7432	76782	62420	71100	76853	03/72-05/86	➲**1805**	
7433	76783	62421	71101	76854	03/72-06/86	➲**1806**	
7434	76784	62422	71102	76855	03/72-06/86	➲**1807**	
7435	76785	62423	71103	76856	03/72-07/86	➲**1808**	
7436	76786	62424	71104	76857	04/72-08/86	➲**1809**	
7437	76787	62425	71105	76858	05/72-09/86	➲**1810**	
7438	76859	62430	71106	76860	05/72-08/79		
7438	76859	62430	71106	76860	01/80-02/87	➲**1813**	✍

Class 423 4-VEP

Outer Suburban Units

660-850V dc third rail

7700-7894

The 4-VEP units were based on the successful 4-CIG units using a similar formation, but fitted out with high density 3+2 seating for use on outer-suburban services.

The first batch, 7701-7720, were designed for use on stopping services on the newly electrified Bournemouth line. The next batch ordered was for 95 units (7721-7815) to replace the 4-LAV units on the Brighton Line and the 2-BIL and 2-HAL units on the Central and South Western divisions. Another batch 7816-7853 followed, and the final batch (7854-7894) were delivered to the South Eastern division, displacing 2-HAP units.

The first fifty-five units had lifting lugs on the body sides at each bogie centre which projected from the otherwise smooth profile of the body.

After delivery, three units (7739, 7740 & 7741) were disbanded and some of the coaches were formed into an eight-car unit, 8-VAB 8001. This included a converted hauled buffet car and it was used on the Bournemouth line, standing in for non-available REPs. Four extra REPs were delivered in 1974; 8001 was disbanded and 7740 & 7741 were reformed.

In 1978 twelve units were converted to 4-VEG units 7901-7912 for working the services from London Victoria to Gatwick.

In 1987 the units were all renumbered in the 3xxx series to bring them in line with their 423 classification.

In 1988 a major facelifting programme began at Eastleigh. The motor coach had the most extensive refurbishment with the luggage space in the guard's van being reduced and replaced with extra seating bays. In order to speed the process up a float of MBS vehicles was formed, and all the MBSs ended up in different units from their original.

Twelve Porterbrook owned units were renumbered to 3801-3812 in 1995 to differentiate them from the Angel Trains units.

In 1999 nineteen units were downgraded to second class for working the South London Metro services. They were renumbered to 3901-3919 and reclassified to 4-VOP.

In 2003, the introduction of new Class 375 units had an impact on the stabling of stock and it was difficult to maintain the allocation of VEP and VOP units to the correct services. To ease the situation eight 4-VIP units were formed with one composite and one second only driving car, to reduce the impact when they were on the wrong line. They were numbered between 3813 and 3844.

	DTCsoL	*TSO*	*MBSO*	*DTCsoL*			
7700	76690	70798	62200	76639	10/84-05/86		
7700	*76804*	70798	62200	76639	05/86-08/87	➲**3000**	✍
7701	76230	70781	62121	76231	04/67-09/87	➲**3001**	
7702	76232	70782	62122	76233	04/67-06/87	➲**3002**	
7703	76234	70783	62123	76235	04/67-06/87	➲**3003**	
7704	76236	70784	62124	76237	04/67-06/87	➲**3004**	
7705	76238	70785	62125	76239	04/67-09/87	➲**3005**	
7706	76240	70786	62126	76241	04/67-07/72		
7706	76240	*70875*	62126	76241	07/72-04/75		✍
7706	76240	*70786*	62126	76241	04/75-06/87	➲**3006**	✍
7707	76242	70787	62127	76243	04/67-09/87	➲**3007**	
7708	76244	70788	62128	76245	04/67-09/87	➲**3008**	
7709	76246	70789	62129	76247	06/67-06/87	➲**3009**	
7710	76248	70790	62130	76249	06/67-11/68		
7710	*76369*	70790	62130	76249	11/68-10/87	➲**3010**	✍
7711	76250	70791	62131	76251	06/67-05/87	➲**3011**	
7712	76252	70792	62132	76253	06/67-08/87	➲**3012**	
7713	76254	70793	62133	76255	06/67-06/87	➲**3013**	
7714	76256	70794	62134	76257	06/67-04/71		
7714	*76248*	70794	62134	76257	01/72-08/87	➲**3014**	✍
7715	76258	70795	62135	76259	07/67-12/87	➲**3015**	
7716	76260	70796	62136	76261	07/67-06/87	➲**3016**	
7717	76262	70797	62137	76263	07/67-08/87	➲**3017**	
7718	76264	70798	62138	76265	07/67-12/80		
7718	76264	*70875*	62138	76265	12/80-06/87	➲**3018**	✍
7719	76266	70799	62139	76267	07/67-05/87	➲**3019**	
7720	76268	70800	62140	76269	07/67-07/87	➲**3020**	
7721	76333	70872	62182	76334	10/67-07/87	➲**3021**	
7722	76335	70873	62183	76336	10/67-07/87	➲**3022**	
7723	76337	70874	62184	76338	10/67-06/87	➲**3023**	
7724	76339	70875	62185	76340	11/67-06/68		
7724	76339	*70893*	62185	76340	06/68-06/84		✍
7724	*76639*	70893	62185	76340	06/84-10/84		✍
7724	76339	70893	62185	76340	10/84-08/86		✍
7724	76339	*71021*	62185	76340	08/86-12/87	➲**3024**	✍
7725	76341	70876	62186	76342	11/67-06/87	➲**3025**	
7726	76343	70877	62187	76344	11/67-05/87	➲**3026**	

Unit					Dates		
7727	76345	70878	62188	76346	12/67-06/87	⊃**3027**	
7728	76347	70879	62189	76348	12/67-06/87	⊃**3028**	
7729	76349	70880	62190	76350	12/67-06/87	⊃**3029**	
7730	76351	70881	62191	76352	12/67-05/87	⊃**3030**	
7731	76353	70882	62192	76354	12/67-05/87	⊃**3031**	
7732	76355	70883	62193	76356	12/67-05/87	⊃**3032**	
7733	76357	70884	62194	76358	12/67-06/87	⊃**3033**	
7734	76359	70885	62195	76360	01/68-06/87	⊃**3034**	
7735	76361	70886	62196	76362	01/68-04/68		
7735	76361	*70890*	62196	76362	04/68-06/87	⊃**3035**	☞
7736	76363	70887	62197	76364	01/68-04/80		
7737	76365	70888	62198	76366	02/68-06/87	⊃**3037**	
7738	76367	70889	62199	76368	02/68-08/87	⊃**3038**	
7739	76369	70890	62200	76370	02/68-04/68		
					Not taken into service in this formation		
7740	76371	70891	62201	76372	02/68-02/88	⊃**3040**	
7741	76373	70892	62202	76374	03/68-04/68		
					Not taken into service in this formation		
7741	76373	70892	62202	76374	02/75-06/87	⊃**3041**	☞
7742	76375	70893	62203	76376	03/68-04/68		
					Not taken into service in this formation		
7742	76375	*70886*	62203	76376	02/75-02/88	⊃**3042**	☞
7743	76377	70894	62204	76378	04/68-06/87	⊃**3043**	
7744	76379	70895	62205	76380	04/68-08/87	⊃**3044**	
7745	76381	70896	62206	76382	04/68-03/88	⊃**3045**	
7746	76383	70897	62207	76384	04/68-06/87	⊃**3046**	
7747	76385	70898	62208	76386	04/68-06/87	⊃**3047**	
7748	76387	70899	62209	76388	04/68-03/88	⊃**3048**	
7749	76389	70900	62210	76390	05/68-10/87	⊃**3049**	
7750	76391	70901	62211	76392	05/68-10/87	⊃**3050**	
7751	76393	70902	62212	76394	05/68-12/87	⊃**3051**	
7752	76395	70903	62213	76396	06/68-11/87	⊃**3052**	
7753	76397	70904	62214	76398	06/68-12/87	⊃**3053**	
7754	76399	70905	62215	76400	07/68-06/87	⊃**3054**	
7755	76401	70906	62216	76402	07/68-03/88	⊃**3055**	
7756	76441	70907	62217	76442	01/69-12/87	⊃**3056**	
7757	76443	70908	62218	76444	01/69-06/87	⊃**3057**	
7758	76445	70909	62219	76446	01/69-07/88	⊃**3058**	
7759	76447	70910	62220	76448	02/69-02/88	⊃**3059**	
7760	76449	70911	62221	76450	02/69-09/87	⊃**3060**	
7761	76451	70912	62222	76452	02/69-06/87	⊃**3061**	
7762	76453	70913	62223	76454	02/69-02/88	⊃**3062**	
7763	76455	70914	62224	76456	02/69-06/87	⊃**3063**	
7764	76457	70915	62225	76458	02/69-06/87	⊃**3064**	
7765	76459	70916	62226	76460	03/69-03/88	⊃**3065**	
7766	76461	70917	62227	76462	03/69-08/87	⊃**3066**	
7767	76463	70918	62228	76464	03/69-08/87	⊃**3067**	
7768	76465	70919	62229	76466	03/69-03/74		
7768	*76370*	70919	62229	76466	01/75-09/87	⊃**3068**	☞
7769	76467	70920	62230	76468	03/69-06/87	⊃**3069**	
7770	76469	70921	62231	76470	04/69-08/87	⊃**3070**	
7771	76471	70922	62232	76472	04/69-06/87	⊃**3071**	
7772	76473	70923	62233	76474	04/69-10/87	⊃**3072**	
7773	76475	70924	62234	76476	04/69-10/87	⊃**3073**	
7774	76477	70925	62235	76478	05/69-10/87	⊃**3074**	
7775	76479	70926	62236	76480	05/69-08/87	⊃**3075**	
7776	76481	70927	62237	76482	05/69-06/87	⊃**3076**	
7777	76483	70928	62238	76484	05/69-06/87	⊃**3077**	
7778	76485	70929	62239	76486	05/69-06/87	⊃**3078**	
7779	76487	70930	62240	76488	05/69-08/87	⊃**3079**	
7780	76489	70931	62241	76490	06/69-06/87	⊃**3080**	
7781	76491	70932	62242	76492	06/69-07/87	⊃**3081**	
7782	76493	70933	62243	76494	06/69-05/87	⊃**3082**	
7783	76495	70934	62244	76496	07/69-07/87	⊃**3083**	
7784	76497	70935	62245	76498	07/69-05/87	⊃**3084**	
7785	76499	70936	62246	76500	07/69-05/87	⊃**3085**	
7786	76501	70937	62247	76502	07/69-05/87	⊃**3086**	
7787	76503	70938	62248	76504	07/69-05/87	⊃**3087**	
7788	76505	70939	62249	76506	08/69-05/78	⊃**7901**	
7788	76505	70939	62249	76506	05/84-05/87	⊃**3088**	☞
7789	76507	70940	62250	76508	09/69-05/78	⊃**7902**	
7789	76507	70940	62250	76508	05/84-05/87	⊃**3089**	☞
7790	76509	70941	62251	76510	09/69-05/78	⊃**7903**	
7790	76509	70941	62251	76510	05/84-06/87	⊃**3090**	☞
7791	76511	70942	62252	76512	09/69-04/78	⊃**7904**	
7791	76511	70942	62252	76512	05/84-06/87	⊃**3091**	☞
7792	76513	70943	62253	76514	09/69-03/78	⊃**7905**	
7792	76513	70943	62253	76514	05/84-05/87	⊃**3092**	☞
7793	76515	70944	62254	76516	09/69-05/78	⊃**7906**	
7793	76515	70944	62254	76516	05/84-06/87	⊃**3093**	☞
7794	76517	70945	62255	76518	10/69-05/78	⊃**7907**	
7794	76517	70945	62255	76518	05/84-05/87	⊃**3094**	☞
7795	76519	70946	62256	76520	10/69-05/78	⊃**7908**	
7795	76519	70946	62256	76520	05/84-06/87	⊃**3095**	☞
7796	76521	70947	62257	76522	10/69-05/78	⊃**7909**	
7796	76521	70947	62257	76522	05/84-06/87	⊃**3096**	☞
7797	76523	70948	62258	76524	11/69-05/78	⊃**7910**	
7797	76523	70948	62258	76524	05/84-05/87	⊃**3097**	☞
7798	76525	70949	62259	76526	11/69-05/78	⊃**7911**	
7798	76525	70949	62259	*76364*	05/84-05/87	⊃**3098**	☞
7799	76527	70950	62260	76528	11/69-05/78	⊃**7912**	
7799	76527	70950	62260	76528	05/84-05/87	⊃**3099**	☞
7800	76529	70951	62261	76530	11/69-08/87	⊃**3100**	
7801	76531	70952	62262	76532	11/69-06/87	⊃**3101**	
7802	76533	70953	62263	76534	12/69-06/87	⊃**3102**	
7803	76535	70954	62264	76536	12/69-07/87	⊃**3103**	
7804	76537	70955	62265	76538	12/69-05/87	⊃**3104**	
7805	76539	70956	62266	76540	12/69-05/87	⊃**3105**	
7806	76542	70957	62267	76541	01/70-07/87	⊃**3106**	
7807	76544	70958	62268	76543	01/70-05/87	⊃**3107**	
7808	76546	70959	62269	76545	02/70-06/87	⊃**3108**	
7809	76548	70960	62270	76547	02/70-06/87	⊃**3109**	
7810	76550	70961	62271	76549	02/70-10/87	⊃**3110**	
7811	76552	70962	62272	76551	02/70-08/87	⊃**3111**	
7812	76554	70963	62273	76553	02/70-09/87	⊃**3112**	
7813	76556	70964	62274	76555	03/70-08/87	⊃**3113**	
7814	76558	70965	62275	76557	03/70-09/87	⊃**3114**	
7815	76560	70966	62276	76559	03/70-09/87	⊃**3115**	
7816	76642	70997	62317	76641	04/72-05/87	⊃**3116**	
7817	76644	70998	62318	76643	04/72-08/87	⊃**3117**	
7818	76646	70999	62319	76645	04/72-06/87	⊃**3118**	
7819	76648	71000	62320	76647	04/72-09/87	⊃**3119**	
7820	76650	71001	62321	76649	05/72-03/88	⊃**3120**	
7821	76652	71002	62322	76651	05/72-12/87	⊃**3121**	
7822	76654	71003	62323	76653	06/72-04/88	⊃**3122**	
7823	76656	71004	62324	76655	06/72-06/87	⊃**3123**	
7824	76658	71005	62325	76657	06/72-03/88	⊃**3124**	
7825	76660	71006	62326	76659	06/72-07/87	⊃**3125**	
7826	76662	71007	62327	76661	06/72-12/87	⊃**3126**	
7827	76664	71008	62328	76663	07/72-09/88	⊃**3127**	
7828	76666	71009	62329	76665	07/72-08/87	⊃**3128**	
7829	76668	71010	62330	76667	08/72-11/87	⊃**3129**	
7830	76670	71011	62331	76669	08/72-07/87	⊃**3130**	
7831	76672	71012	62332	76671	08/72-08/87	⊃**3131**	
7832	76674	71013	62333	76673	08/72-07/87	⊃**3132**	
7833	76676	71014	62334	76675	09/72-07/87	⊃**3133**	
7834	76678	71015	62335	76677	09/72-05/87	⊃**3134**	
7835	76680	71016	62336	76679	09/72-05/87	⊃**3135**	
7836	76682	71017	62337	76681	09/72-10/87	⊃**3136**	
7837	76684	71018	62338	76683	09/72-05/87	⊃**3137**	
7838	76686	71019	62339	76685	10/72-07/87	⊃**3138**	
7839	76688	71020	62340	76687	10/72-05/87	⊃**3139**	
7840	76690	71021	62341	76689	11/72-04/80		
7840	*76363*	*70887*	62341	76689	04/80-07/87	⊃**3140**	☞
7841	76692	71022	62342	76691	11/72-07/87	⊃**3141**	
7842	76694	71023	62343	76693	12/72-10/87	⊃**3142**	
7843	76696	71024	62344	76695	12/72-06/87	⊃**3143**	
7844	76698	71025	62345	76697	02/73-06/87	⊃**3144**	
7845	76700	71026	62346	76699	02/73-07/87	⊃**3145**	
7846	76702	71027	62347	76701	03/73-08/87	⊃**3146**	
7847	76704	71028	62348	76703	03/73-06/87	⊃**3147**	
7848	76706	71029	62349	76705	03/73-09/87	⊃**3148**	
7849	76708	71030	62350	76707	04/73-08/87	⊃**3149**	
7850	76710	71031	62351	76709	04/73-06/87	⊃**3150**	
7851	76712	71032	62352	76711	05/73-05/87	⊃**3151**	
7852	76714	71033	62353	76713	05/73-03/74		
7852	76714	71033	62353	*76465*	03/74-05/87	⊃**3152**	☞
7853	76716	71034	62354	76715	05/73-07/87	⊃**3153**	
7854	76862	71115	62435	76861	05/73-05/87	⊃**3154**	
7855	76864	71116	62436	76863	05/73-05/87	⊃**3155**	
7856	76866	71117	62437	76865	06/73-06/87	⊃**3156**	
7857	76868	71118	62438	76867	06/73-09/87	⊃**3157**	
7858	76870	71119	62439	76869	06/73-06/87	⊃**3158**	
7859	76872	71120	62440	76871	06/73-08/87	⊃**3159**	
7860	76874	71121	62441	76873	07/73-06/87	⊃**3160**	
7861	76876	71122	62442	76875	07/73-05/87	⊃**3161**	
7862	76878	71123	62443	76877	07/73-07/87	⊃**3162**	
7863	76880	71124	62444	76879	07/73-06/87	⊃**3163**	
7864	76882	71125	62445	76881	08/73-08/87	⊃**3164**	
7865	76884	71126	62446	76883	08/73-08/87	⊃**3165**	
7866	76886	71127	62447	76885	08/73-07/87	⊃**3166**	
7867	76888	71128	62448	76887	08/73-08/87	⊃**3167**	
7868	76890	71129	62449	76889	09/73-08/87	⊃**3168**	
7869	76892	71130	62450	76891	09/73-05/87	⊃**3169**	
7870	76894	71131	62451	76893	09/73-07/87	⊃**3170**	
7871	76896	71132	62452	76895	09/73-07/87	⊃**3171**	
7872	76898	71133	62453	76897	10/73-06/87	⊃**3172**	
7873	76900	71134	62454	76899	10/73-05/87	⊃**3173**	
7874	76902	71135	62455	76901	10/73-07/87	⊃**3174**	
7875	76904	71136	62456	76903	10/73-08/87	⊃**3175**	
7876	76906	71137	62457	76905	11/73-05/87	⊃**3176**	
7877	76908	71138	62458	76907	12/73-08/87	⊃*3177*	
7878	76910	71139	62459	76909	01/74-07/87	⊃**3178**	
7879	76912	71140	62460	76911	01/74-06/87	⊃**3179**	
7880	76914	71141	62461	76913	02/74-07/87	⊃**3180**	
7881	76916	71142	62462	76915	02/74-08/87	⊃**3181**	
7882	76918	71143	62463	76917	12/73-07/87	⊃*3182*	
7883	76920	71144	62464	76919	02/74-09/87	⊃**3183**	
7884	76922	71145	62465	76921	02/74-09/87	⊃**3184**	

7885	76924	71146	62466	76923	02/74-07/87	**➲3185**
7886	76926	71147	62467	76925	03/74-10/87	**➲3186**
7887	76928	71148	62468	76927	03/74-09/87	**➲3187**
7888	76930	71149	62469	76929	03/74-08/87	**➲3188**
7889	76932	71150	62470	76931	03/74-08/87	**➲3189**
7890	76934	71151	62471	76933	04/74-08/87	**➲3190**
7891	76936	71152	62472	76935	04/74-06/87	**➲3191**
7892	76938	71153	62473	76937	04/74-07/87	**➲3192**
7893	76940	71154	62474	76939	05/74-09/87	**➲3193**
7894	76942	71155	62475	76941	05/74-10/87	**➲3194**

Class 427 4-VEG

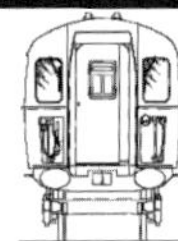

Outer Suburban Units (Gatwick) Units
660-850V dc third rail
7901-7912

In 1978 12 4-VEP units were converted to 4-VEG units 7901-7912 for working the services from London Victoria to Gatwick. Several rows of seats were removed and additional luggage racks were added. In 1984 the Gatwick Express units were introduced and the VEGs were converted back to their original seating arrangement and numbers 7788-7799.

	DTCsoL	*TSO*	*MBSO*	*DTCsoL*		
7901	76505	70939	62249	76506	05/78-05/84	**➲7788**
7902	76507	70940	62250	76508	05/78-05/84	**➲7789**
7903	76509	70941	62251	76510	05/78-05/84	**➲7790**
7904	76511	70942	62252	76512	04/78-05/84	**➲7791**
7905	76513	70943	62253	76514	03/78-05/84	**➲7792**
7906	76515	70944	62254	76516	05/78-05/84	**➲7793**
7907	76517	70945	62255	76518	05/78-05/84	**➲7794**
7908	76519	70946	62256	76520	05/78-05/84	**➲7795**
7909	76521	70947	62257	76522	05/78-05/84	**➲7796**
7910	76523	70948	62258	76524	05/78-05/84	**➲7797**
7911	76525	70949	62259	76526	05/78-06/80	
7911	76525	70949	62259	*76364*	10/80-05/84	**➲7798**
7912	76527	70950	62260	76528	05/78-05/84	**➲7799**

Class 480 8-VAB

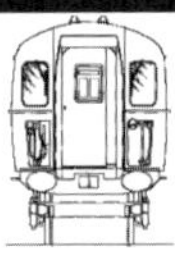

Outer Suburban Units
660-850V dc third rail
8001

This eight-car unit 8-VAB 8001 was formed from 4-VEP carriages. It included a converted hauled buffet car and it was used on the Bournemouth line, standing in for non-available REPs. After four extra REPs were delivered in 1974 8001 was disbanded.

	DTCsoL	*MBSO*	*TRB*	*MBSO*	*DTCsoL*	*DTCsoL*	*MBSO*	*DTCsoL*	
8001	76375	62203	1759	62200	76376	76373	62202	76374	04/68-01/75

Class 419 1-MLV

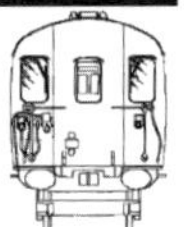

Kent Boat Trains Motor Luggage Vans
660-750V dc third rail
68001-68010

When the Kent Coast Lines were electrified it was decided that the Dover boat trains would also be worked by multiple units. In order to provide luggage accommodation some motor luggage vans were built to operate with 4-CEP units on the boat trains. They were fitted with batteries so that they could work over non-electrified lines in the port area, hauling up to two trailer vans if necessary. The first two were built in 1959 and eight more similar vans were built in 1960-61. They were not formed into any unit, but carried their car numbers on the end in the same location as a unit number.

	MLV	
68001	68001	04/59- 92
68002	68002	04/59- 92
68003	68003	12/60- 92
68004	68004	12/60- 92
68005	68005	01/61- 92
68006	68006	01/61-12/91
68007	68007	02/61- 92
68008	68008	03/61- 92
68009	68009	03/61- 92
68010	68010	03/61- 92

Class 499 1-TLV
Kent Boat Trains Trailer Luggage Vans
660-750V dc third rail (unpowered)
68201-68206

It was found that two luggage vans were needed on most boat trains and it became normal to see two MLVs heading their trains into Victoria. It therefore was decided to convert six standard locomotive hauled full-brakes (BGs) at Selhurst to work as trailer luggage vans on these services. In the mid seventies there was a downturn in traffic and these redundant coaches were transferred to departmental stock to work as Enparts vans (delivering diesel engine parts from works to depots).

TLV	
68201	*01/68-09/74*
68202	*01/68-09/74*
68203	*01/68-09/74*
68204	*01/68-09/74*
68205	*01/68-09/74*
68206	*01/68-09/74*

London, Brighton & South Coast Railway

In 1903 the London Brighton & South Coast Railway gained powers to electrify its suburban network. The South London line from London Bridge to Victoria via Denmark Hill was chosen as the first line to be electrified, as it was suffering greatly from completion from new tramways. After some deliberation a German system of electrification was chosen, 6,700V ac supplied from overhead cables.

The initial South London service opened in 1909 and was a great success and the network soon expanded. The electrified lines from London Bridge and Victoria to Crystal Palace opened in 1911 & 1912. Agreement for further electrification to Brighton/Eastbourne and Coulsdon North was reached, but the first World War intervened and the overhead electrification only reached as far as Coulsdon North & Sutton by 1925.

The Railway Grouping had taken place in 1923 and the newly formed Southern Railway had to make some decisions about the different electrification schemes it had inherited. At that time the third-rail electrification of the former LSWR lines formed a larger system and in August 1926 it was announced that all the overhead lines would be converted to third-rail dc operation.

All the overhead lines were converted by 1929 and the majority of redundant vehicles were converted for dc use at Peckham Rye.

SL

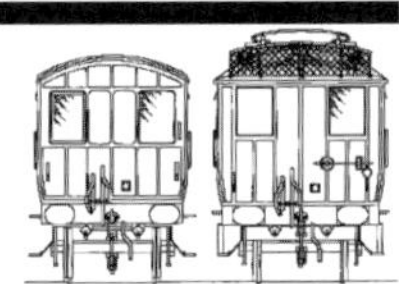

South London Stock
6.6kV 25Hz ac overhead
1E-8E

Eight three-car trains were built by the Metropolitan Amalgamated Carriage and Wagon Company to work the South London line when it was electrified in 1909.

The new service was a great success and the number of passengers increased. It soon became clear though that the provision of space on the trains needed some alteration. The peak hour trains were overcrowded, while the off-peak services were running half-empty. In addition there was an over-provision of first class accommodation throughout the day. So from 1910 onwards the first-class trailers were taken out of service, being converted to work as steam-hauled stock. Fourteen Driving Trailer Composite vehicles were built and these ran with the original Driving Motor Brake Thirds to form two-car units, which could run as up to three sets in multiple to cope with varying demand throughout the day.

Initial 3-car formations

	DMBT	*TF*	*DMBT*	
1E	3201	3202	3203	12/08- *10*
2E	3204	3205	3206	04/09- *10*
3E	3207	3208	3209	*05/09- 10*
4E	3210	3211	3212	*06/09- 10*
5E	3213	3214	3215	*06/09- 10*
6E	3216	3217	3218	*07/09- 10*
7E	3219	3220	3221	*07/09- 10*
8E	3222	3223	3224	*08/09- 10*

Later SL 2-car units. Not fixed formations		SR Numbers	
DMBT	*DTC*	*DMBT*	*DTC*
3201	3225	8601	9811
3203	3226	8602	9812
3204	3227	8603	9813
3206	3228	8604	9814
3207	3229	8605	9815

3209	3230	8606	9816
3210	4057	8607	9817
3212	4058	8608	9818
3213	4059	8609	9819
3215	4060	8610	9820
3216	4065	8611	9821
3218	4066	8612	9822
3219	4067	8613	9823
3221	4068	8614	9824
3222		8615	
3224		8616	

CP

Crystal Palace Stock
6.6kV 25Hz ac overhead

The stock ordered for the Crystal Palace electrification comprised 30 motor coaches and 30 driving trailers built by Metropolitan Amalgamated, and a further 30 driving trailers built at Lancing. The stock was only eight feet wide and fifty-seven and a half feet long, due to restricted clearances at Crystal Palace.

They normally ran in three or six coach formations.

3-car loose coupled
First DTC-DTC-DMBT
Later DTC-DMBT-DTC
Not fixed formations

DTC	DTC	DMTB	SR Numbers DTC	DMBT	DTC
4001	4002	3231	9825	8567	9826
4003	4004	3232	9827	8568	9828
4005	4006	3233	9829	8569	9830
4007	4008	3234	9831	8570	9832
4009	4010	3235	9833	8571	9834
4011	4012	3236	9835	8572	9836
4013	4014	3237	9837	8573	9838
4015	4016	3238	9839	8574	9840
4017	4018	3239	9841	8575	9842
4019	4020	3240	9843	8576	9844
4021	4022	3241	9845	8577	9846
4023	4024	3242	9847	8578	9848
4025	4026	3243	9849	8579	9850
4027	4028	3244	9851	8580	9852
4029	4030	3245	9853	8581	9854
4031	4032	3246	9855	8582	9856
4033	4034	3247	9857	8583	9858
4035	4036	3248	9859	8584	9860
4037	4038	3249	9861	8585	9862
4039	4040	3250	9863	8586	9864
4041	4042	3251	9865	8587	9866
4043	4044	3252	9867	8588	9868
4045	4046	3253	9869	8589	9870
4047	4048	3254	9871	8590	9872
4049	4050	3255	9873	8591	9874
4051	4052	3256	9875	8592	9876
4053	4054	3257	9877	8593	9878
4055	4056	3258	9879	8594	9880
4061	4062	3259	9881	8595	9882
4063	4064	3260	9883	8596	9884
4069	4070	3261	9885	8597	9886
4071	4072	3262	9887	8598	9888
4073	4074	3263	9889	8599	9890
4075	4076	3264	9891	8600	9892
4084	4085		9893		9894

CW

Coulsdon-Wallington Stock
6.6kV 25Hz ac overhead

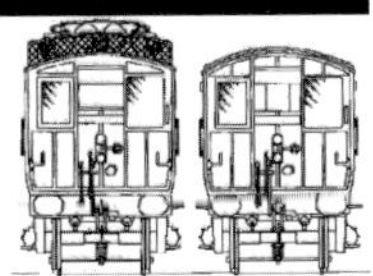

When the Coulsdon-Wallington electrification was being planned, a total of 60 Driving Trailer Composites were ordered from Lancing Works in 1913. These were to be numbered 4077-4136. The war disrupted the plans and eventually only 42 carriages were built, and all bar two went into service as steam hauled carriages (4084 & 4085 were the exceptions and they went to work on the Crystal Palace services for the whole of their lives).

Work resumed on the Coulsdon-Wallington electrification after the War and in 1921 more stock was ordered. By this time plans had changed and the new design used Motor Luggage Vans in the centre of units formed DTT-DTC-Motor-TC-DTT. The DTC vehicles were 20 of the previously built carriages reconverted back from steam stock. The rest were built new.

After the later conversion of the line to dc operation, the Motor Luggage Vans were stored for a while before being de-motored and converted into bogie goods brake vans, in which form they survived for many years.

5 coach sets. Not fixed formations. Some were built carying SR numbers.

DTT	DTC	Motor	TC	DTT
3265	4077	10101	4119	*3266*
3267	4078	10102	4120	*3288*
3289	4079	10103	4121	*3290*
3291	4080	10104	4122	*3292*
3293	4081	10105	4123	*3294*
3295	4082	10106	4124	*3296*
3297	4083	10107	4125	*3298*
3299	4086	10108	4126	*3300*
3301	4087	10109	4127	*3302*
3303	4088	10110	4128	*3304*
3268	4089	10111	*4129*	3269
3270	4090	10112	*4130*	3271
3272	4091	10113	*4131*	3273
3274	4092	10114	*4132*	3275
3276	4093	10115	*4133*	3277
3278	4094	10116	*4134*	3279
3280	4095	10117	*4135*	3281
3282	4096	10118	*4136*	3283
3284	4097	10119	*4137*	3285
3286	4098	10120	*4138*	3287
		10121		

SR Numbers

DTT	DTC	Motor	TC	DTT
9169	9895	10101	9664	9170
9171	9896	10102	9665	9172
9173	9897	10103	9666	9174
9175	9898	10104	9667	9176
9177	9899	10105	9668	9178
9179	9900	10106	9669	9180
9181	9901	10107	9670	9182
9183	9902	10108	9671	9184
9185	9903	10109	9659	9186
9187	9904	10110	9660	9188
9189	9905	10111	9655	9190
9191	9906	10112	9656	9192
9193	9907	10113	9657	9194
9195	9908	10114	9658	9196
9197	9909	10115	9661	9198
9199	9910	10116	9662	9200
9201	9911	10117	9663	9202
9203	9912	10118	9672	9204
9205	9913	10119	9673	9206
9207	9914	10120	9674	9208
		10121		

London & South Western Railway

3-SUB

LSWR Suburban Sets
600V dc third rail
E1-E84

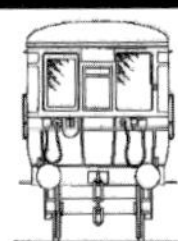

In 1913 the LSWR announced its intention to electrify its suburban services on the third rail dc system. The line from Waterloo to Wimbledon via East Putney opened in 1915. Other lines followed in 1916: the Kingston & Hounslow loops, the Shepperton and Hampton Court lines, and the Guildford line as far as Claygate. Further electrification was then postponed until after the First World War.

To work these lines 84 3-car sets were built, being converted from 1904 four-car steam hauled suburban sets. They were mounted on wooden underframes and carried distinctive 'torpedo' style cabs. They were numbered E1-E84 on the LSWR then became SR 1201-1284. In many ways they were forerunners of the 3-SUB units.

In 1934 a start was made in rebuilding these units on new 62ft steel underframes. The units were all later augmented to form 4-SUB units.

	DMBT	TC	DMBT/DMBC		
E1	6701	7551	6702	11/14-	23
E2	6703	7552	6704	11/14-	23
E3	6705	7553	7201	11/14-	23
E4	6706	7554	7202	06/14-	23
E5	6707	7555	6708	11/14-	23
E6	6709	7556	6710	11/14-	23
E7	6711	7557	7203	*12/14-*	23
E8	6712	7558	7204	*12/14-*	23
E9	6713	7559	6714	*12/14-*	23
E10	6715	7560	6716	*12/14-*	23
E11	6717	7561	7205	*01/15-*	23
E12	6718	7562	7206	*01/15-*	23
E13	6719	7563	6720	*01/15-*	23
E14	6721	7564	6722	*01/15-*	23

E15	6723	7565	7207	*01/15-*	23
E16	6724	7566	7208	*02/15-*	23
E17	6725	7567	6726	*02/15-*	23
E18	6727	7568	6728	*02/15-*	23
E19	6729	7569	7209	*02/15-*	23
E20	6730	7570	7210	*03/15-*	23
E21	6731	7571	6732	*03/15-*	23
E22	6733	7572	6734	*03/15-*	23
E23	6735	7573	7211	*03/15-*	23
E24	6736	7574	7212	*03/15-*	23
E25	6737	7575	6738	*04/15-*	23
E26	6739	7576	6740	*04/15-*	23
E27	6741	7577	7213	*04/15-*	23
E28	6742	7578	7214	*04/15-*	23
E29	6743	7579	6744	*05/15-*	23
E30	6745	7580	6746	*05/15-*	23
E31	6747	7581	7215	*05/15-*	23
E32	6748	7582	7216	*05/15-*	23
E33	6749	7583	6750	*06/15-*	23
E34	6751	7584	6752	*06/15-*	23
E35	6753	7585	7217	*06/15-*	23
E36	6754	7586	7218	*06/15-*	23
E37	6755	7587	6756	*07/15-*	23
E38	6757	7588	6758	*07/15-*	23
E39	6759	7589	7219	*07/15-*	23
E40	6760	7590	7220	*08/15-*	23
E41	6761	7591	6762	*08/15-*	23
E42	6763	7592	6764	*08/15-*	23
E43	6765	7593	7221	*09/15-*	23
E44	6766	7594	7222	*09/15-*	23
E45	6767	7595	6768	*09/15-*	23
E46	6769	7596	6770	12/15-	23
E47	6771	7597	7223	12/15-	23
E48	6772	7598	7224	12/15-	23
E49	6773	7599	6774	02/16-	23
E50	6775	7600	6776	02/16-	23
E51	6777	7601	7225	02/16-	23
E52	6778	7602	7226	03/16-	23
E53	6779	7603	6780	03/16-	23
E54	6781	7604	6782	03/16-	23
E55	6783	7605	7227	*06/16-*	23
E56	6784	7606	7228	*06/16-*	23
E57	6785	7607	6786	*07/16-*	23
E58	6787	7608	6788	*07/16-*	23
E59	6789	7609	7229	*08/16-*	23
E60	6790	7610	7230	*08/16-*	23
E61	6791	7611	6792	*09/16-*	23
E62	6793	7612	6794	*09/16-*	23
E63	6795	7613	7231	*10/16-*	23
E64	6796	7614	7232	*10/16-*	23
E65	6797	7615	6798	*10/16-*	23
E66	6799	7616	6800	*11/16-*	23
E67	6801	7617	7233	*11/16-*	23
E68	6802	7618	7234	*11/16-*	23
E69	6803	7619	6804	*12/16-*	23
E70	6805	7620	6806	*12/16-*	23
E71	6807	7621	7235	*12/16-*	23
E72	6808	7622	7236	*01/17-*	23
E73	6809	7623	6810	*01/17-*	23
E74	6811	7624	6812	*01/17-*	23
E75	6813	7625	7237	*02/17-*	23
E76	6814	7626	7238	*02/17-*	23
E77	6815	7627	6816	*02/17-*	23
E78	6817	7628	6818	*03/17-*	23
E79	6819	7629	7239	*03/17-*	23
E80	6820	7630	7240	*03/17-*	23
E81	6821	7631	6822	08/17-	23
E82	6823	7632	6824	08/17-	23
E83	6825	7633	7241	04/17-	23
E84	6826	7634	7242	08/17-	23

2-T

2-car LSWR Trailer Sets to run with 3-SUB sets
600V dc third rail (unpowered)
T1-T24

In 1920 the passenger numbers on the LSWR section had grown to the point were extra trains were needed. Rather than add additional services it was decided to lengthen the existing trains by creating some 2-car trailer units to work between the existing 3-car sets.

LSWR trailer units T1-T24 were converted from standard loco-hauled stock at Eastleigh work. They later were numbered 1001-1024.

LSWR Trailer sets

	TT	*TT*		
T1	7401	7402	01/20-	23
T2	7404	7403	01/20-	23
T3	7405	7406	04/20-	23
T4	7408	7407	04/20-	23
T5	7409	7410	04/20-	23
T6	7412	7411	01/20-	23
T7	7413	7414	04/20-	23
T8	7416	7415	05/20-	23
T9	7417	7418	05/20-	23
T10	7420	7419	05/20-	23
T11	7421	7424	10/20-	23
T12	7423	7422	10/20-	23
T13	7425	7426	12/21-	23
T14	7427	7428	12/21-	23
T15	7429	7430	12/21-	23
T16	7431	7432	12/21-	23
T17	7433	7434	12/21-	23
T18	7435	7436	12/21-	23
T19	7437	7438	11/22-	23
T20	7439	7440	12/22-	23
T21	7441	7442	12/22-	23
T22	7443	7444	12/22-	23
T23	7445	7446	12/22-	23
T24	7447	7448	12/22-	23

Isle of Wight

The Isle of Wight has long had a "hand-me-down" railway, often using ancient stock borrowed from the mainland. In the mid-sixties, with the end of steam looming, some big decisions had to be made. One option was to use some more modern steam tank engines now becoming redundant on the mainland. However, there was a problem with the restricted size of the tunnels at Ryde, where the tunnel base had had to be raised due to flooding problems. Closure was not an option as the line from Ryde to Shanklin down the eastern side of the island carried an enormous amount of summer tourist traffic from the end of the pier at Ryde to the tourist resorts.

The solution eventually arrived at was to purchase some redundant tube trains from London to work out their retirement on quieter trains in the countryside.

The line was electrified on the three-rail system and six 3-car trains and six 4-car trains were formed from ex-LT standard tube stock built between 1920 and 1931. They were rebuilt and converted from the LT four-rail electric system. The units were classified 4-VEC and 3-TIS – "Vectis" being the Roman name for the Isle of Wight.

They entered service in 1967, but car number 15 suffered a mishap at Ryde in 1968 and it was replaced by another car (which was given the same number) in 1971.

The stock served the line for many years, but a reduction in demand gradually saw the number of vehicles whittled down. The last units survived until 1989-90 when they were replaced by "modern" Class 483 units – 1938 built Underground stock which was then being phased out in London.

Class 486 3-TIS

Isle of Wight (ex-London Transport)
630V dc third rail
031-037, 486031-486036

	MBSO	*TSO*	*DTSO*						
031	1	47	26			03/67-	83		
031	*13*	47	26			83-	84		☜
032[1]	3	92	28			03/67-	68	⊃*042*	
032[2]	*42*	*29*	*22*			68-09/71		⊃*042*	☜
032[1]	*3*	*92*	*28*			09/71-	84		☜
033	5	93	30			03/67-	82		
034	7	94	32			03/67-	76		
034	*7*	94	32	*10*		76-	82		☜
034	*7*	94	32			82-	84		☜
035	9	95	34			03/67-09/73			
035[2]	*11*	*96*	*36*		ex 036	74-	83		☜
035	*9*	96	36			83-	84		☜
036	11	96	36			03/67-	74	⊃**035**	
036[2]	*46*	*49*	*8*		ex 046	10/80-	84		☜
037	Spare		10						

	MBSO	*TSO*	*DTSO*		
486031	13	47	26	84-	85
486032	3	92	28	84-	85
486034	7	94	32	84-	85
486035	9	96	36	84-	85
486036	46	49	8	84-	85

	MBSO	*MBSO*			
486031[2]	11	*20*	85-08/87		
486031[2]	11	*28*	08/87-	89	☜

486032[2]	15	22		85-08/87		
486032[2]	15	*20*		08/87- 88		↩

Class 485 4-VEC

Isle of Wight (ex-London Transport)
630V dc third rail
041-046, 485041-485045

	MBSO	*TSO*	*DTSO*	*MBSO*				
041	13	41	27	20		03/67- 83		
041	*1*	41	27	20		83- 84		↩
042[1]	15	42	29	22		03/67- 68	➲*032*	
042[2]	*3*	*92*	*28*	*10*		68-09/71	➲*032*	↩
042[1]	*15[2]*	*42*	*29*	*22*		09/71- 84		↩
043	19	43	31	2		03/67- 82		
043	*5*	43	31	2		82- 84		↩
044	21	44	33	4		03/67- 84		
045	23	45	48	6		03/67-09/73		
045[2]	*9*	*95*	*34*	*6*	ex 035	74- 83		↩
045[2]	*11*	95	34	6		83- 84		↩
046	25	46	49	8		03/67-09/75		
046	46	49	8			09/75-10/80	➲**036**	↩

	MBSO	*TSO*	*DTSO*	*MBSO*	
485041	1	41	27	20	84- 85
485042	15	42	29	22	84- 85
485043	19	43	31	2	84- 85
485044	21	44	33	4	84- 85
485045	11	95	34	6	84- 85

	MBSO	*DTSO*	*TSO*	*DTSO*	*MBSO*		
485041[2]	1	27	92	26	2	85- 89	
485042[2]	3	29	42	28	4	85- 87	
485042[2]	3	29	*95*	*47*	4	87- 89	↩
485043[2]	5	31	43	32	6	85- 89	
485044[2]	7	33	44	49	8	85- 89	
485045[2]	9	93	94	34	10	85- 89	

From 1989 the formations were very variable and the units were all withdrawn by 1990

Waterloo & City

The London & South Western Railway's terminus at Waterloo was a long way from the City of London and for many years this caused problems for people who wanted to commute into the City from the South Western suburbs of London. The problem was solved when the Railway built a 1 mile 46 chain electrified tube line from Waterloo to the City at Bank. Because it was built by the LSWR and it had only one sole purpose – that of transferring its own passengers further into London – it managed to avoid being taken into the Underground empire, becoming part of the Southern and later BR. The depot was at the end of the line at Waterloo and the only access to the rest of the world for the rolling stock was via a lift on the west side of Waterloo Station

1898 Stock

Waterloo & City
630V dc third rail

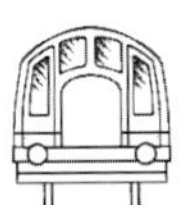

This is the earliest stock featured in this book. Built by the firm of Jackson & Sharp of Wilmington, USA, these coaches were shipped to the UK as kits of parts to be assembled at Eastleigh. They were formed into five four-car units with two trailers sandwiched between two single-ended motor cars. Wooden seating, was provided with no heating and very little lighting. A verandah was fitted at the inner end of the motor cars and both ends of the trailer cars, protected by trellis gates.

Two spare trailer cars were built by the Electric Tramway Company in Preston in 1904, and four further trailer cars were built at Eastleigh in 1922 to allow the original trains to be augmented to five cars.

1898 4-car units. Not fixed formations

DMT	*TT*	*TT*	*DMT*
1	21	22	2
3	23	24	4
5	25	26	6
7	27	28	8
9	29	30	10
11			12

Augmented to 5-car units. Not fixed formations

DMT	*TT*	*TT*	*TT*	*DMT*
1	21	22	33	2
3	23	24	34	4
5	25	26	35	6
7	27	28	36	8
9	29	30		10
11	31	32		12

Final formations just before withdrawal in 1940

	DMT	*TT*	*TT*	*TT*	*DMT*
A	10	21	22	23	9
B	8	24	25	26	5
C	6	27	28	29	12
D	4	31	32	33	2
E	3	34	35	36	11
spare	1	30			7

1899 Double Ended Stock

Waterloo & City
630V dc third rail

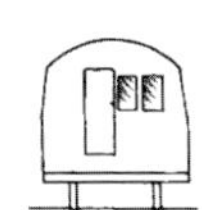

Five double-ended motor cars were built by Dick Kerr & Co in 1899-1900 to run as single cars in the off-peak periods.

DMT
13
14
15
16
17

Class 487 1940 Stock

Waterloo & City
630V dc third rail

When the 1898 stock needed replacing an order was placed with the English Electric Company for replacement tube stock. At the same time the line was modernised and the third rail was moved to the standard position. Normal operations were 5-car trains (two motors with three trailers between). The motor coaches were double ended and could be detached to work as one or two car units during quieter times of the day.

The units were delivered painted in SR green livery with unpainted aluminium cab ends and sliding doors.

Fixed formations were not kept but it was usual for trains to work with consecutively numbered power cars and trailer cars, with a few cars kept as spares. So it was common to have one unit in service as 51 71 72 73 52 and another as 61 84 85 86 62, with the other units carrying other numbers in between depending on which cars were currently out of service.

The line was again modernised in 1993 and new Class 482 units (based on LT Central Line stock) took over from the older units. Soon after this the line was finally absorbed into the London Underground system.

DMSO	*TSO*	*TSO*	*TSO*	*DMSO*
51	71	72	73	52
53	74	75	76	54
55	77	78	79	56
57	80	81	82	58
59	83			60
61	84	85	86	62

TOPS numbered AC units

Class 302 AM2

Tilbury Line
25kV ac overhead
302200-302993

	BDTCOL	*MBSO*	*TSOL*	*DTSO*			
302200	75091	61066	70066	75039	09/88-03/90		
302201	75085	61060	70060	75033	01/83-06/98		
302202	75086	61061	70061	75034	06/83-04/97		
302203	75087	61062	70062	75035	04/81-08/88	➲*Dep*	
302203[2]	*75311*	*61122*	*70122*	*75236*	09/88-06/96		↩
302204	75088	61063	70063	75036	04/81-02/98		
302205	75089	61064	70064	75037	03/83-06/97		
302206	75090	61065	70065	75038	03/81-02/92	➲*305599*	
302206	75090	61065	70065	75038	07/93-03/94		↩
302206	*75281*	61065	*70224*	*75356*	03/94-04/97		↩
302207	75091	61066	70066	75039	03/81-09/88	➲**302200**	
302207[2]	*75358*	*61226*	*70226*	*75283*	09/88-04/97		↩

302208	75092	61067	70067	75040	04/81-09/88	➲**302276**	
302208[2]	*75356*	*61224*	*70224*	*75281*	09/88-02/92	➲*305596*	♻
302208	75356	61224	70224	75281	07/93-01/94	➲*302206*	♻
302209	75093	61068	70068	75041	01/83-06/95		
302210	75094	61069	70069	75042	05/85-04/97		
302211	75095	61070	70070	75043	09/82-09/97		
302212	75096	61071	70071	75044	05/81-02/97		
302213	75097	61072	70072	75060	08/81-07/97		
302214	75098	61073	70073	75061	04/81-04/88	➲*Dep 937996*	
302214[2]	*75352*	*61220*	*70220*	*75277*	09/88-09/96		♻
302215	75099	61074	70074	75062	12/81-04/97		
302216	75100	61075	70075	75063	06/83-07/98		
302217	75190	61076	70076	75064	07/84-02/92	➲*305598*	
302217	75190	61076	70076	75064	07/93-04/97		♻
302218	75191	61077	70077	75065	06/81-07/97		
302219	75192	61078	70078	75066	09/83-04/97		
302220	75193	61079	70079	75067	09/83-02/92	➲*305595*	
302220	75193	61079	70079	75067	01/93-06/97		♻
302221	75194	61080	70080	75068	09/83-06/97		
302222	75195	61081	70081	75069	06/82-02/92	➲*305597*	
302222	75195	61081	70081	75069	12/92-06/96		♻
302223	75196	61082	70082	75070	05/81-08/88		
302223[2]	*75341*	*61209*	*70209*	*75266*	09/88-07/97		♻
302224	75197	61083	70083	75071	07/81-08/97		
302225	75198	61084	70084	75072	10/81-07/98		
302226	75199	61085	70085	75073	10/81-02/92	➲*305594*	
302226	75199	61085	70085	75073	01/93-01/98		♻
302227	75200	61086	70086	75074	83-10/85		
302227	*75335*	61086	70086	75074	10/85-02/88	➲*302427*	♻
302227[2]	75325	*61193*	*70193*	*75250*	09/88-01/98		♻
302228	75201	61087	70087	75075	11/81-07/98		
302229	75202	61088	70088	75076	08/82-09/97		
302230	75203	61089	70089	75077	12/83-08/88		
302230[2]	*75205*	*61091*	*70091*	*75079*	09/88-07/98		♻
302231	75204	61090	70090	75078	07/84-03/89		
302232	75205	61091	70091	75079	03/85-09/88	➲**302230**	
302233	75206	61092	70092	75080	07/84-02/88	➲*302433*	
302234	75207	61093	70093	75081	12/83-08/87	➲*302434*	
302234	75207	61093	*70120*	75081	01/88-01/91		♻
302235	75208	61094	70094	75082	04/81-12/88		
302235	75208	*61100*	70094	75082	12/88-03/89		♻
302236	75209	61095	70095	75083	01/80-02/86		
302237	75210	61096	70096	75084	11/84-12/88		
302237	*75333*	61096	70096	75084	12/88-03/89		♻
302238	75286	61097	70097	75211	05/81-08/88		
302238	*75360*	61097	*70112*	*75226*	08/88-09/89		♻
302239	75287	61098	70098	75212	01/83-08/87	➲*302439*	
302239	75287	61098	70098	*75278*	01/88-02/88		♻
302239	75287	61098	*70125*	75278	02/88-11/88		♻
302239	75287	61098	70125	*75272*	11/88-06/90		♻
302240	75288	61099	70099	75213	11/82-11/87		
302240	75288	61099	*70121*	75213	11/87-06/88		♻
302241	75289	61100	70100	75214	11/84-12/88		
302241	75289	*61094*	70100	75214	12/88-03/89		♻
302242	75290	61101	70101	75215	01/82-07/88		
302243	75291	61102	70102	75216	10/83-09/89		
302244	77164	61103	70103	75217	06/82-09/83		
302244	*75298*	61103	70103	75217	09/83-03/89		♻
302244	*75210*	61103	*70201*	75217	03/89-03/89		♻
302245	75293	61104	70104	75218	08/81-04/89		
302246	75294	61105	70105	75219	83-09/89		
302247	75295	61106	70106	75220	01/82-04/89		
302248	75296	61107	70107	75221	03/83-03/83	➲*302399*	
302248	75296	61107	70107	75221	05/83-03/89		♻
302249	75297	61108	70108	75222	09/82-09/89		
302250	75298	61109	70109	75223	04/82-02/83		
302250[2]	*75348*	*61216*	*70216*	*75273*	09/88-03/90		♻
302251	75299	61110	70110	75224	01/83-05/90		
302251	75299	61110	*70103*	75224	05/90-10/90		♻
302252	75300	61111	70111	75225	08/82-03/89		
302252	*75306*	61111	70111	75225	03/89-01/90		♻
302252	75306	61111	*70086*	75225	01/90-06/90		♻
302252	*75346*	61111	*70214*	*75271*	06/90-03/91		♻
302253	75301	61112	70112	75226	10/82-05/85		
302253[2]	*75349*	*61217*	*70217*	*75274*	09/88-06/90		♻
302254	75302	61113	70113	75227	03/83-03/89		
302254	75302	61113	*70123*	*75254*	03/89-09/89		♻
302255	75303	61114	70114	75228	01/82-07/83		
302255[2]	*75351*	*61219*	*70219*	*75276*	09/88-02/89		♻
302255[2]	*75092*	61219	70219	75276	02/89-01/90		♻
302256	75304	61115	70115	75229	83-03/89		
302256	*75326*	61115	70115	*75231*	03/89-09/89		♻
302257	75305	61116	70116	75230	04/82-03/89		
302257	75305	*61212*	*70212*	75230	03/89-09/89		♻
302258	75306	61117	70117	75231	05/81-11/88		
302258	*75326*	61117	70117	75231	11/88-03/89		♻
302258	*75304*	61117	70117	*75229*	03/89-09/89		♻

302259	75307	61118	70118	75232	03/80-11/87	➲*302459*	
302259	75307	61118	*70195*	75232	02/88-03/89		♻
302259	*75329*	61118	*70198*	75232	03/89-03/90		♻
302260	75308	61119	70119	75233	05/81-05/85		
302260[2]	*75321*	*61132*	*70132*	*75246*	09/88-09/89		♻
302261	75309	61120	70120	75234	03/83-01/88	➲*302461*	
302261	75309	61120	*70073*	75234	05/88-05/90		♻
302261	*75298*	61120	70073	75234	05/90-01/91		♻
302262	75310	61121	70121	75235	10/82-11/87	➲*302462*	
302262	75310	61121	*70131*	75235	02/88-07/90		♻
302263	75311	61122	70122	75236	09/83-09/88	➲**302203**	
302264	75312	61123	70123	75237	05/82-02/87		
302264	75312	61123	70123	*75254*	02/87-03/89		♻
302264	75312	61123	*70113*	*75227*	03/89-09/89		♻
302265	75313	61124	70124	75238	09/82-03/89		
302265	*75345*	*61213*	*70092*	75238	03/89-09/89		♻
302266	75314	61125	70125	75239	07/84-01/88		
302267	75315	61126	70126	75240	02/80-08/86		
302267[2]	*75355*	*61223*	*70223*	*75280*	09/88-10/90		♻
302268	75316	61127	70127	75241	09/82-08/86		
302268	*75315*	61127	70127	75241	08/86-09/89		♻
302269	75317	61128	70128	75242	01/82-06/88		
302269	*75342*	61128	70128	75242	06/88-09/89		♻
302270	75318	61129	70129	75243	83-09/89		
302271	75319	61130	70130	75244	04/82-06/88		
302271	75319	61130	70130	*75267*	06/88-07/88		♻
302271	75319	61130	*70121*	75267	07/88-08/88		♻
302271	*75290*	61130	70121	75267	08/88-11/88		♻
302272	75320	61131	70131	75245	06/83-02/88		
302272	75320	61131	*70086*	75245	02/88-04/89		♻
302272	*75359*	61131	70086	75245	04/89-01/90		♻
302272	75359	61131	*70111*	75245	01/90-06/90		♻
302273	75321	61132	70132	75246	03/82-08/85	➲*302302*	
302273[2]	*75354*	61222	*70202*	*75279*	09/88-03/90		♻
302274	75322	61190	70190	75247	05/82-04/89		
302274	*75334*	61190	*70222*	75247	04/89-01/91		♻
302275	75323	61191	70191	75248	11/79-07/83		
302275[2]	*75359*	*61227*	*70227*	*75284*	09/88-04/89		♻
302276	75324	61192	70192	75249	01/80-02/86		
302276[2]	*75092*	*61067*	*70067*	*75040*	09/88-02/89		♻
302277	75325	61193	70193	75250	01/83-09/88	➲**302227**	
302278	75326	61194	70194	75251	11/84-11/88		
302278	*75306*	61194	70194	75251	11/88-03/89		♻
302278	*75300*	61194	70194	75251	03/89-09/89		♻
302279	75327	61195	70195	75252	10/81-02/88		
302280	75328	61196	70196	75253	83-01/90		
302281	75329	61197	70197	75254	10/82-10/86		
302282	75330	61198	70198	75255	02/82-08/86		
302282	*75329*	61198	70198	75255	10/86-03/89		♻
302282	*75307*	61198	*70195*	75255	03/89-09/89		♻
302283	75331	61199	70199	75256	02/83-08/88		
302283	75331	61199	*70130*	75256	08/88-07/90		♻
302284	75332	61200	70200	75257	10/81-03/90		
302285	75333	61201	70201	75258	06/83-12/88		
302285	*75210*	61201	70201	75258	12/88-03/89		♻
302285	*75298*	61201	*70103*	75258	03/89-05/90		♻
302286	75334	61202	70202	75259	05/82-01/88		
302286	75334	61202	*70222*	75259	01/88-04/89		♻
302286	*75322*	61202	*70190*	75259	04/89-03/90		♻
302287	75335	61203	70203	75260	01/80-10/85		
302288	75336	61204	70204	75261	12/82-05/85		
302289	75337	61205	70205	75262	01/80-09/89		
302290	75338	61206	70206	75263	10/82-09/89		
302291	75339	61207	70207	75264	83-09/89		
302292	75340	61208	70208	75265	03/83-06/90		
302292	75340	61208	70208	*75272*	06/90-10/90		♻
302293	75341	61209	70209	75266	08/81-09/88	➲**302223**	
302294	75342	61210	70210	75267	01/82-11/87	➲*302494*	
302294	75342	61210	70210	75267	06/88-06/88		♻
302295	75343	61211	70211	75268	02/82-09/89		
302296	75344	61212	70212	75269	04/84-03/89		
302296	75344	*61116*	*70116*	75269	03/89-03/90		♻
302297	75345	61213	70213	75270	10/81-12/85		
302297	75345	61213	70213	*75282*	12/85-11/87	➲*302497*	♻
302297	75345	61213	*70092*	75282	02/88-07/88		♻
302297	75345	61213	70092	*75074*	07/88-03/89		♻
302297	*75313*	61213	*70124*	75074	03/89-03/89		♻
302298	75346	61214	70214	75271	03/83-06/90	➲*302252*	
302299	75347	61215	70215	75272	03/83-11/88		
302300	75348	61216	70216	75273	07/83-09/88	➲**302250**	
302301	75349	61217	70217	75274	01/83-09/88	➲**302253**	
302302	75350	61218	70218	75275	02/80-09/85		
302302	*75321*	61218	*70132*	*75246*	09/85-09/88	➲**302260**	♻
302303	75351	61219	70219	75276	07/83-09/88	➲**302255**	
302304	75352	61220	70220	75277	06/83-09/88	➲**302214**	
302305	75353	61221	70221	75278	83-04/87		
302305	75353	61221	*70197*	75278	04/87-08/87		♻
302305	75353	61221	70197	*75212*	09/87-01/90		♻

302306	75354	61222	70222	75279		03/83-01/88		
302306	75354	61222	*70202*	75279		01/88-09/88	➲ **302273**	☞
302307	75355	61223	70223	75280		10/83-09/88	➲ **302267**	
302308	75356	61224	70224	75281		02/83-09/88	➲ **302208**	
302309	75357	61225	70225	75282		02/80-12/85		
302310	75358	61226	70226	75283		09/83-09/88	➲ **302207**	
302311	75359	61227	70227	75284		*83*-09/88	➲ **302275**	
302312	75360	61228	70228	75285		*83*-07/85		
302312	75360	61228	*70112*	75226		07/85-08/88	➲ **302238**	☞
	BDTCOL	***MBSO***	***TSOL***	***DTSO***				
302399	75296	61107	70107	75223		03/83-05/83	➲ *302248*	

	BDTCOL	MBSO	DTSO			
302427	75335	61086	75074	02/88-06/88	➲ *302227*	
302433	75206	61092	75080	02/88-04/88	➲ *302233*	
302434	75207	61093	75081	08/87-01/88	➲ *302234*	
302439	75287	61098	75212	08/87-09/87		
302439	75287	61098	*75278*	09/87-01/88	➲ *302239*	☞
302459	75307	61118	75232	11/87-02/88	➲ *302259*	
302261	75309	61120	75234	01/88-05/88	➲ *302261*	
302462	75310	61121	75235	11/87-02/88	➲ *302262*	
302494	75342	61210	75267	11/87-06/88	➲ *302294*	
302497	75345	61213	75282	11/87-02/88	➲ *302297*	

	DTLV	MLV	DTLV	
302990	68100	68020	68207	03/89-10/95
302991	68101	68021	68208	03/89-10/95
302992	68102	68022	68209	[illegible]
302993	68103	68023	68210	03/90-03/96

Class 303 AM3

Glasgow Suburban
25kV ac overhead
303001-303091

	DTSO	MBSO	BDTSO	*® Refurbished units*			
303001	75566	61481	75601	®	*11/79*-12/02		
303003	75568	61483	75603	®	*11/79*-10/01		
303004	75569	61484	75604	®	*03/80*-12/02		
303005	75570	61485	75605		*03/80*-07/89		
303006	75571	61486	75606	®	*11/79*-06/02		
303008	75573	61488	75608	®	*11/79*-01/02		
303009	75574	61489	75609	®	*03/80*-08/00		
303009	75574	*61504*	75609		08/00-09/02		☞
303010	75575	61490	75610	®	*11/79*-01/01		
303011	75576	61491	75611	®	*05/79*-12/02		
303012	75577	61492	75612	®	*80*-02/02		
303013	75578	61493	75613	®	*80*-10/01		
303014	75579	61494	75614	®	*03/80*-07/01		
303015	75580	61495	75615		05/80-12/87		
303016	75581	61496	75616	®	*80*-10/90		
303016	*75750*	61496	75616		10/90-01/02		☞
303017	75582	61497	75617		06/80-12/82		
303018	75583	61498	75618		07/80-12/87		
303019	75584	61499	75619	®	*03/80*-03/02		
303020	75585	61500	75620	®	*80*-06/02		
303021	75586	61501	75621	®	08/80-06/02		
303022	75587	61502	75622		06/80-12/82		
303023	75588	61503	75623	®	06/80-07/02		
303024	75589	61504	75624	®	*11/79*-05/98		
303024	75589	*61489*	75624		08/00-08/00		☞
303025	75590	61505	75625	®	*08/79*-07/00		
303025	*75572*	61505	75625		09/00-09/00		☞
303026	75591	61506	75626		*80*-12/87		
303027	75592	61507	75627	®	*03/80*-09/02		
303028	75593	61508	75628	®	*11/79*-10/82		
303028	*75600*	61508	*75635*		10/82-07/99		☞
303028	75600	*61813*	*75845*		07/99-07/99		☞
303029	75594	61509	75629		*03/80*-08/90		
303029	*76420*	61509	75629		08/90-09/90		☞
303030	75595	61510	75630		*11/79*-12/87		
303031	75596	61511	75631		*80*-12/87	➲ *303044*	
303032	75597	61512	75632	®	*05/79*-06/02		
303033	75598	61860	75633	®	07/80-07/88		
303033	*75595*	61860	*75817*		07/88-06/02		☞
303034	75599	61514	75634	®	*80*-10/01		
303035	75600	61515	75635		06/80-12/80	➲ *303028*	
303036	75746	61812	75802	81⇨**M**	*80*-10/89		
303037	75747	61813	75803	®	*03/80*-07/91		
303037	*75781*	61813	75803		02/94-05/98		☞
303037	75781	*61508*	75803		07/99-04/02		☞
303038	75748	61814	75804	®	*03/80*-02/93		
303039	75749	61815	75805		*08/79*-09/90		
303040	75750	61816	75806		*08/79*-10/90		
303040	*75581*	61816	75806	®	10/90-02/01		☞
303041	75751	61817	75807	81⇨**M**	*11/79*-10/89		
303042	75752	61818	75808		*03/80*-09/89	➲ *303048*	
303043	75572	61819	75809		06/79-09/00		
303043	*75766*	61819	75809	®	09/00-08/01		☞
303044	75754	61820	75810		06/80-02/88		
303045	75755	61821	75811	®	*03/80*-09/02		
303046	75756	61822	75812	®	06/80-11/97		
303047	75757	61823	75813	®	*11/79*-10/01		
303048	75758	61824	75814	81⇨**M** 90⇨**SC**	*80*-03/90	➲ *303052*	
303048	*75758*	*61824*	*75814*	Renumbered carriages	10/90-03/96		☞
303049	75759	61825	75815	81⇨**M**	*80*-02/91	➲ **303999**	
303050	75760	61826	75816	81⇨**M**	*08/79*-10/89		
303051	75761	61827	75817	®	*03/80*-02/87		
303052	75762	61828	75818		*03/80*-03/90		
303052	*75758*	61828	*75814*		03/90-09/90	➲ *303048*	☞
303053	75763	61829	75819	81⇨**M**	*03/80*-10/89		
303054	75764	61830	75820	®	*03/80*-06/02		
303055	75765	61831	75821	®	*08/79*-03/01		
303056	75766	61832	75822	®	*03/80*-09/00		
303056	*75590*	61832	75822		09/00-03/01		☞
303057	75767	61833	75823	® 81⇨**M**	*80*-10/89		
303058	75768	61834	75824	®	*03/80*-03/01		
303059	75769	61835	75825	81⇨**M**	*80*-11/83		
303060	75770	61836	75826	81⇨**M**	*80*-12/92		
303061	75771	61837	75827	®	*05/79*-03/01		
303062	75772	61838	75828		*80*-09/90		
303063	75773	61839	75829		*03/80*-10/90		
303064	75774	61840	75830		*08/79*-07/88		
303065	[illegible]	[illegible]	[illegible]	®	*80*-06/01		
303066	75776	61842	75832	81⇨**M**	*80*-02/91		
303067	75777	61843	75833	81⇨**M**	*03/80*-10/89		
303068	75778	61844	75834		05/80-01/89		
303069	75779	61845	75607		*03/80*-07/90		
303070	75780	61846	75836	®	05/80-10/01		
303071	75781	61847	75837	®	*08/79*-07/89		
303072	75782	61848	75838		*05/79*-07/90		
303073	75783	61849	75839		*80*-07/96		
303075	75785	61851	75841		06/80-08/90		
303076	75786	61852	75842		*03/80*-09/90		
303077	75787	61853	75843	®	06/80-01/02		
303078	75788	61854	75844	81⇨**M**	*03/80*-10/89		
303079	75789	61855	75845	®	*80*-07/99		
303079	75789	61855	*75635*		07/99-06/02		☞
303080	75790	61856	75846	®	*08/79*-10/01		
303081	75791	61857	75847		*08/79*-01/89		
303082	75792	61858	75848	81⇨**M**	*03/80*-12/92		
303083	75793	61859	75849	®	*03/80*-09/02		
303085	75795	61861	75851	®	*03/80*-03/02		
303086	75796	61862	75852		07/80-05/98		
303087	75797	61863	75853	®	*05/79*-04/02		
303088	75798	61864	75854	®	*80*-12/02		
303089	75799	61865	75855	®	*11/79*-03/01		
303090	75800	61866	75856	®	*80*-04/02		
303091	75801	61867	75857	®	*08/79*-06/02		

Class 304 AM4

London Midland Western Lines
25kV ac overhead
304001-304045

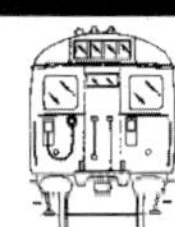

Class 304/1

	BDTSOL	MBSO	TSsoL	DTBSO		
304001	75045	61045	70045	75645	10/82-12/86	
304002	75046	61046	70046	75646	04/82-12/86	
304003	75047	61047	70047	75647	07/81-12/86	
304004	75048	61048	70048	75648	09/83-12/86	
304005	75049	61049	70049	75649	10/81-12/86	
304006	75050	61050	70050	75650	12/82-12/86	
304007	75051	61051	70051	75651	04/82-12/86	
304008	75052	61052	70052	75652	08/81-07/84	
304008	75052	61052	*70249*	75652	07/84-01/85	☞
304009	75053	61053	70053	75653	04/81-12/86	
304010	75054	61054	70054	75654	12/81-12/86	
304011	75055	61055	70055	75655	01/80-12/86	
304012	75056	61056	70056	75656	04/82-12/86	
304013	75057	61057	70057	75657	07/81-12/86	
304014	75058	61058	70058	75658	06/81-12/86	
304015	75059	61059	70059	75659	08/82-12/86	

Class 304/2

	BDTSOL	MBSO	TSsoL	DTBSO	
304016	75680	61628	70483	75660	02/83-05/86
304017	75681	61629	70484	75661	08/82-05/86
304018	75682	61630	70485	75662	02/80-12/84
304019	75683	61631	70486	75663	12/81-05/86
304020	75684	61632	70487	75664	07/81-05/86
304021	75685	61633	70488	75665	12/81-05/86
304022	75686	61634	70489	75666	08/82-12/84

Unit					Dates
304023	75687	61635	70490	75667	05/82-09/85
304023	75687	61635	*70494*	75667	09/85-05/86
304024	75688	61636	70491	75668	05/81-05/86
304025	75689	61637	70492	75669	02/80-12/84
304027	75691	61639	70494	75671	07/83-09/85
304028	75692	61640	70495	75672	08/82-09/85
304029	75693	61641	70496	75673	06/81-09/85
304030	75694	61642	70497	75674	06/81-05/85
304031	75695	61643	70498	75675	06/81-05/85
304032	75696	61644	70499	75676	09/81-10/84
304033	75697	61645	70500	75677	10/84-10/84
304034	75698	61646	70501	75678	06/84-10/84
304035	75699	61647	70502	75679	04/82-10/84

Class 304/3

	BDTSOL	*MBSO*	*TSsoL*	*DTBSO*	
304036	75868	61873	70243	75858	04/82-10/84
304037	75869	61874	70244	75859	04/82-10/84
304038	75870	61875	70245	75860	83-12/84
304039	75871	61876	70246	75861	83-10/84
304040	75872	61877	70247	75862	02/82-10/84
304041	75873	61878	70248	75863	05/82-10/84
304042	75874	61879	70249	75864	04/81-07/84
304043	75875	61880	70250	75865	07/83-10/84
304044	75876	61881	70251	75866	10/82-12/84
304045	75877	61882	70252	75867	02/83-10/84

Three car units

	BDTSOL	*MBS*	*DTBSO*	
304001	75045	61045	75645	12/86-07/92
304002	75046	61046	75646	12/86-04/96
304003	75047	61047	75647	12/86-05/94
304004	75048	61048	75648	12/86-03/96
304005	75049	61049	75649	12/86-12/94
304006	75050	61050	75650	12/86-12/93
304007	75051	61051	75651	12/86-05/92
304008	75052	61052	75652	01/85-05/94
304009	75053	61053	75653	12/86-03/96
304010	75054	61054	75654	12/86-09/94
304011	75055	61055	75655	12/86-01/91
304012	75056	61056	75656	12/86-05/92
304013	75057	61057	75657	12/86-05/94
304014	75058	61058	75658	12/86-09/94
304015	75059	61059	75659	12/86-06/94

	BDTSOL	*MBSO*	*DTBSO*	
304016	75680	61628	75660	05/86-07/92
304017	75681	61629	75661	05/86-03/96
304018	75682	61630	75662	12/84-12/84
304019	75683	61631	75663	05/86-04/95
304020	75684	61632	75664	05/86-04/92
304021	75685	61633	75665	05/86-05/94
304022	75686	61634	75666	12/84-12/84
304023	75687	61635	75667	05/86-10/91
304024	75688	61636	75668	05/86-06/94
304025	75689	61637	75669	12/84-12/84
304027	75691	61639	75671	09/85-05/94
304028	75692	61640	75672	09/85-05/92
304029	75693	61641	75673	09/85-05/94
304030	75694	61642	75674	05/85-11/93
304031	75695	61643	75675	05/85-06/87
304032	75696	61644	75676	10/84-05/96
304033	75697	61645	75677	10/84-04/96
304034	75698	61646	75678	10/84-01/94
304035	75699	61647	75679	10/84-11/91

	BDTSOL	*MBSO*	*DTBSO*	
304036	75868	61873	75858	10/84-12/95
304037	75869	61874	75859	10/84-06/95
304038	75870	61875	75860	12/84-12/84
304039	75871	61876	75861	10/84-04/92
304040	75872	61877	75862	10/84-04/95
304041	75873	61878	75863	10/84-07/92
304042	75874	61879	75864	07/84-06/96
304043	75875	61880	75865	10/84-05/94
304044	75876	61881	75866	12/84-12/84
304045	75877	61882	75867	10/84-07/92

Class 305/1 AM5

North East London Lines

25kV ac overhead

305401-305499

	BDTSO	*MBSO*	*DTSO*		
305401	75462	61429	75514	09/82-05/93	
305401	*75471*	61429	75514	05/93-06/96	
305402	75463	61430	75515	08/83-02/92	

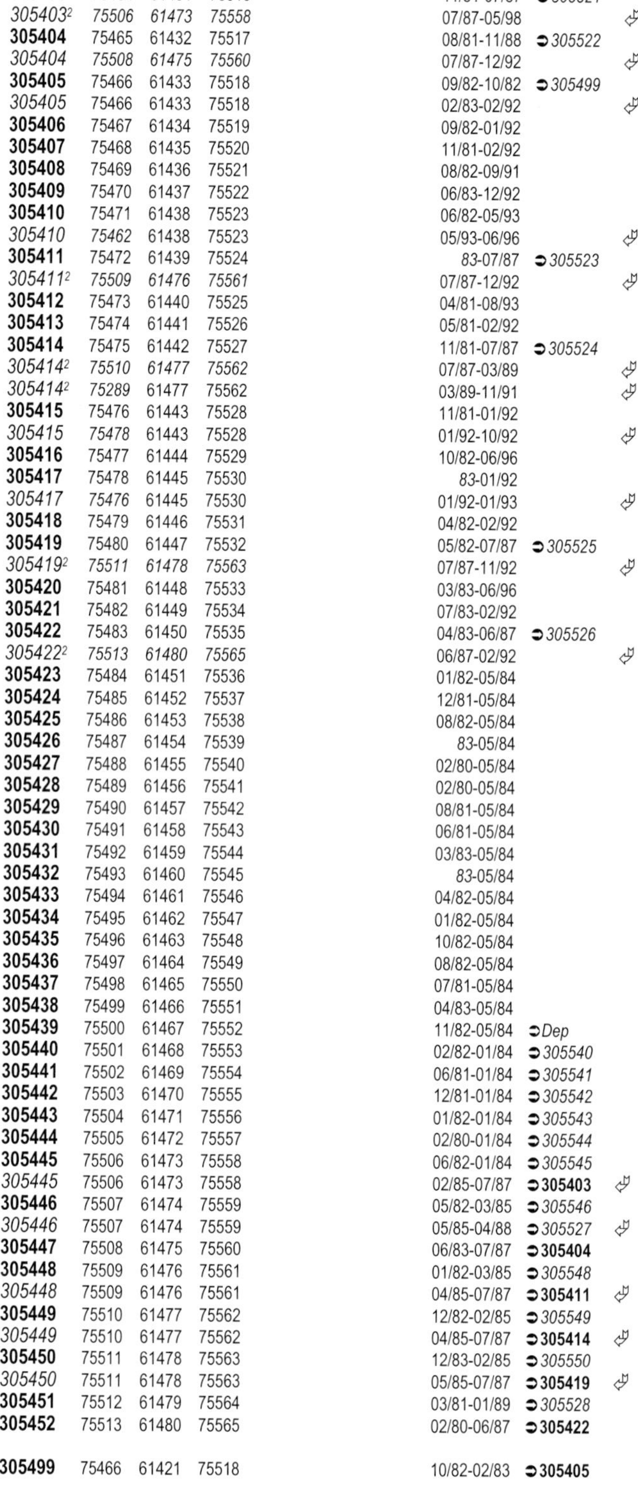

305403	75464	61431	75516	11/81-07/87	➲ *305521*
305403[2]	*75506*	*61473*	*75558*	07/87-05/98	
305404	75465	61432	75517	08/81-11/88	➲ *305522*
305404	*75508*	*61475*	*75560*	07/87-12/92	
305405	75466	61433	75518	09/82-10/82	➲ *305499*
305405	75466	61433	75518	02/83-02/92	
305406	75467	61434	75519	09/82-01/92	
305407	75468	61435	75520	11/81-02/92	
305408	75469	61436	75521	08/82-09/91	
305409	75470	61437	75522	06/83-12/92	
305410	75471	61438	75523	06/82-05/93	
305410	*75462*	61438	75523	05/93-06/96	
305411	75472	61439	75524	83-07/87	➲ *305523*
305411[2]	*75509*	*61476*	*75561*	07/87-12/92	
305412	75473	61440	75525	04/81-08/93	
305413	75474	61441	75526	05/81-02/92	
305414	75475	61442	75527	11/81-07/87	➲ *305524*
305414[2]	*75510*	*61477*	*75562*	07/87-03/89	
305414[2]	*75289*	61477	75562	03/89-11/91	
305415	75476	61443	75528	11/81-01/92	
305415	*75478*	61443	75528	01/92-10/92	
305416	75477	61444	75529	10/82-06/96	
305417	75478	61445	75530	83-01/92	
305417	*75476*	61445	75530	01/92-01/93	
305418	75479	61446	75531	04/82-02/92	
305419	75480	61447	75532	05/82-07/87	➲ *305525*
305419[2]	*75511*	*61478*	*75563*	07/87-11/92	
305420	75481	61448	75533	03/83-06/96	
305421	75482	61449	75534	07/83-02/92	
305422	75483	61450	75535	04/83-06/87	➲ *305526*
305422[2]	*75513*	*61480*	*75565*	06/87-02/92	
305423	75484	61451	75536	01/82-05/84	
305424	75485	61452	75537	12/81-05/84	
305425	75486	61453	75538	08/82-05/84	
305426	75487	61454	75539	83-05/84	
305427	75488	61455	75540	02/80-05/84	
305428	75489	61456	75541	02/80-05/84	
305429	75490	61457	75542	08/81-05/84	
305430	75491	61458	75543	06/81-05/84	
305431	75492	61459	75544	03/83-05/84	
305432	75493	61460	75545	83-05/84	
305433	75494	61461	75546	04/82-05/84	
305434	75495	61462	75547	01/82-05/84	
305435	75496	61463	75548	10/82-05/84	
305436	75497	61464	75549	08/82-05/84	
305437	75498	61465	75550	07/81-05/84	
305438	75499	61466	75551	04/83-05/84	
305439	75500	61467	75552	11/82-05/84	➲ *Dep*
305440	75501	61468	75553	02/82-01/84	➲ *305540*
305441	75502	61469	75554	06/81-01/84	➲ *305541*
305442	75503	61470	75555	12/81-01/84	➲ *305542*
305443	75504	61471	75556	01/82-01/84	➲ *305543*
305444	75505	61472	75557	02/80-01/84	➲ *305544*
305445	75506	61473	75558	06/82-01/84	➲ *305545*
305445	75506	61473	75558	02/85-07/87	➲ **305403**
305446	75507	61474	75559	05/82-03/85	➲ *305546*
305446	75507	61474	75559	05/85-04/88	➲ *305527*
305447	75508	61475	75560	06/83-07/87	➲ **305404**
305448	75509	61476	75561	01/82-03/85	➲ *305548*
305448	75509	61476	75561	04/85-07/87	➲ **305411**
305449	75510	61477	75562	12/82-02/85	➲ *305549*
305449	75510	61477	75562	04/85-07/87	➲ **305414**
305450	75511	61478	75563	12/83-02/85	➲ *305550*
305450	75511	61478	75563	05/85-07/87	➲ **305419**
305451	75512	61479	75564	03/81-01/89	➲ *305528*
305452	75513	61480	75565	02/80-06/87	➲ **305422**
305499	75466	61421	75518	10/82-02/83	➲ **305405**

Class 305/2 AM5

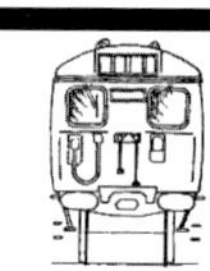

Bishops Stortford & Hertford East Lines

25kV ac overhead

305501-305599

	BDTCOL	*MBSO*	*TSOL*	*DTSO*		
305501	75424	61410	70356	75443	91⇨**SC**	03/83-12/01
305502	75425	61411	70357	75444		04/83-04/83
305502	75425	*61421*	70357	75444	91⇨**SC**	04/83-06/01
305503	75426	61412	70358	75445	91⇨**M**	05/81-03/93
305503	75426	61412	*70368*	75445		04/93-10/95
305504	75427	61413	70359	75446	91⇨**M**	11/81-03/93
305505	75435	61414	70360	75447		05/83-09/90
305506	75429	61415	70361	75448	91⇨**M**	07/81-03/93
305507	75430	61416	70362	75449	91⇨**M**	01/80-03/93
305508	75431	61417	70363	75450	91⇨**SC**	03/83-10/01
305509	75432	61418	70364	75451	91⇨**M**	83-03/93

Unit					Transfer	Dates		
305510	75433	61419	70365	75452	91⇨**M**	03/83-03/93		
305511	75434	61420	70366	75453	91⇨**M**	04/83-03/93		
305511	75434	61420	*70359*	75453		03/93-06/96		⇦
305513	75436	61422	70368	75455	91⇨**M**	02/80-03/93		
305514	75437	61423	70369	75456		02/81-03/93		
305515	75438	61424	70370	75457	91⇨**M**	01/80-03/93		
305515	75438	61424	*70362*	75457		03/93-07/96		⇦
305516	75439	61425	70371	75458	91⇨**M**	02/83-03/93		
305516	75439	61425	*70373*	75458		03/93-03/93		⇦
305517	75440	61426	70372	75459	91⇨**SC**	02/83-12/01		
305518	75441	61427	70373	75460	91⇨**M**	08/81-03/93		
305519	75442	61428	70374	75461	91⇨**SC**	04/83-12/01		

Three car units

	BDTCOL	*MBSO*	*DTSO*	
305503	75426	61412	75445	10/95-11/97
305504	75427	61413	75446	03/93-06/96
305506	75429	61415	75448	03/93-08/00
305507	75430	61416	75449	03/93-11/97
305509	75432	61418	75451	03/93-10/95
305510	75433	61419	75452	03/93-03/99
305511	75434	61420	75453	06/96-07/00
305513	75436	61422	75455	03/93-06/96
305515	75438	61424	75457	07/96-11/97
305516	75439	61425	75458	03/93-06/00
305518	75441	61427	75460	03/93-05/98

	BDTSO	*MBSO*	*TSOL*	*DTSO*	
305521	75464	61431	70098	75516	05/88-03/93
305522	75465	61432	70099	75517	11/88-12/92
305523	75472	61439	70221	75524	04/88-12/92
305524	75475	61442	70118	75527	11/88-12/92
305525	75480	61447	70213	75532	02/92-06/93
305526	75483	61450	70093	75535	05/88-03/93
305527	75507	61474	70204	75559	04/88-06/93
305528	75512	61479	70210	75564	01/89-06/93

	BDTSO	*TSOL*	*MBSO*	*DTSO*		
305540	75501	70652	61468	75553	01/84-05/84	
305541	75502	70648	61469	75554	01/84-05/84	
305542	75503	70649	61470	75555	01/84-02/85	
305543	75504	70651	61471	75556	01/84-08/84	
305544	75505	70646	61472	75557	01/84-05/84	
305545	75506	70650	61473	75558	01/84-02/85	➲*305445*
305546	75507	70648	61474	75559	03/85-05/85	➲*305446*
305548	75509	70652	61476	75561	03/85-04/85	➲*305448*
305549	75510	70651	61477	75562	02/85-04/85	➲*305449*
305550	75511	70650	61478	75563	02/85-05/85	➲*305450*

	BDTCOL	*MBSO*	*TSOL*	*DTSO*		
305594	75199	61430	70085	75073	02/92-01/93	➲*302226*
305595	75193	61446	70079	75067	02/92-01/93	➲*302220*
305596	75356	61480	70224	75281	02/92-07/93	➲*302208*
305597	75195	61433	70081	75069	02/92-12/92	➲*302222*
305598	75190	61435	70076	75064	02/92-07/93	➲*302217*
305599	75090	61434	70065	75038	02/92-07/93	➲*302206*

Class 307 AM7

Southend Line
25kV ac overhead
307101-307132

	BDTBSO	*MSO*	*TSOL*	*DTCOL*			
307101	75001	61001	70001	75101		11/82-08/93	➲Dep
307102	75002	61002	70002	75102		01/80-08/93	
307103	75003	61003	70003	75103		10/82-08/93	
307104	75004	61004	70004	75104		01/82-08/93	
307105	75005	61005	70005	75105	90⇨**E**	09/82-08/93	
307106	75006	61006	70006	75106		02/80-08/93	➲Dep
307107	75007	61007	70007	75107		12/81-08/93	
307108	75008	61008	70008	75108		04/82-08/93	
307109	75009	61009	70009	75109		02/82-08/93	
307110	75010	61010	70010	75110		11/81-08/93	
307111	75011	61011	70011	75111	90⇨**E**	01/83-08/93	
307112	75012	61012	70012	75112		09/82-08/93	
307113	75013	61013	70013	75113		12/82-08/93	
307114	75014	61014	70014	75114		11/81-08/93	
307115	75015	61015	70015	75115		12/81-08/93	
307116	75016	61016	70016	75116		12/81-08/93	
307117	75017	61017	70017	75117	91⇨**SC**	07/82-08/93	
307118	75018	61018	70018	75118		02/82-08/93	➲*Dep 316998*
307119	75019	61019	70019	75119		06/82-08/93	
307120	75020	61020	70020	75120	90⇨**E**	09/81-08/93	
307121	75021	61021	70021	75121		04/82-08/93	➲Dep
307122	75022	61022	70022	75122	90⇨**E**	08/82-08/93	
307123	75023	61023	70023	75123		10/81-08/93	
307124	75024	61024	70024	75124		05/82-08/93	
307125	75025	61025	70025	75125		10/82-08/93	
307126	75026	61026	70026	75126		08/82-08/93	
307127	75027	61027	70027	75127		01/82-08/93	
307128	75028	61028	70028	75128		03/82-08/93	
307129	75029	61029	70029	75129		06/82-08/93	
307130	75030	61030	70030	75130	90⇨**E**	06/82-08/93	
307131	75031	61031	70031	75131		05/82-08/93	
307132	75032	61032	70032	75132		04/82-08/93	

Class 308/1 AM8

Clacton Line
25kV ac overhead
308133-308165

	BDTCOL	*MBSO*	*TSOL*	*DTSO*			
308133	75878	61883	70611	75887	04/81-05/93		
308134	75879	61884	70612	75888	08/81-09/93		
308135	75880	61885	70613	75889	08/81-07/92		
308135	*75910*	61885	*70634*	*75943*	07/92-12/93		⇦
308136	75881	61886	70614	75890	01/82-06/93		
308137	75882	61887	70615	75891	12/81-06/93		
308138	75883	61888	70367	75892	11/83-06/93		
308139	75884	61889	70617	75893	10/82-05/83		
308139	75884	61889	70617	*75223*	05/83-07/83		⇦
[illegible]	[illegible]	[illegible]	[illegible]	[illegible]	[illegible]		⇦
308140	75885	61890	70618	75894	05/81-06/93		
308141	75886	61891	70619	75895	08/81-09/93		
308142	75896	61892	70620	75929	01/82-05/93		
308143	75897	61893	70621	75930	01/82-06/93		
308144	75898	61894	70622	75931	12/81-09/90		
308144	*75435*	61894	70622	75931	09/90-06/93		⇦
308145	75899	61895	70623	75932	03/82-11/93		
308146	75900	61896	70624	75933	02/80-06/95		
308147	75901	61897	70625	75934	03/82-06/93		
308148	75902	61898	70626	75935	12/82-05/93		
308149	75903	61899	70627	75936	06/82-08/93		
308150	75904	61900	70628	75937	03/82-06/95	➲*Dep*	
308151	75905	61901	70629	75938	11/82-11/93	➲*937990*	
308152	75906	61902	70630	75939	05/83-02/89		
308152	*75913*	61902	70630	75939	02/89-06/93		⇦
308153	75907	61903	70631	75940	09/82-06/93		
308154	75908	61904	70632	75941	10/82-05/93		
308155	75909	61905	70633	75942	05/83-05/93		
308156	75910	61906	70634	75943	05/83-07/92		
308156	*75880*	61906	*70613*	*75889*	07/92-06/93	➲*308135*	⇦
308157	75911	61907	70635	75944	05/83-05/93		
308158	75912	61908	70636	75945	02/80-04/83	➲**308458**	
308158	75912	61908	70636	75945	05/83-06/93		⇦
308159	75913	61909	70637	75946	05/83-02/89		
308159	*75906*	61909	70637	75946	02/89-05/93		⇦
308160	75914	61910	70638	75947	05/83-06/93		
308161	75915	61911	70639	75948	01/80-04/83	➲**308461**	
308161	75915	61911	70639	75948	04/84-05/93		⇦
308162	75916	61912	70640	75949	07/83-06/93		
308163	75917	61913	70641	75950	07/83-05/93		
308164	75918	61914	70642	75951	02/80-05/93		
308165	75919	61915	70643	75952	02/81-06/93		

Three car units

	BDTCOL	*MBSO*	*DTSO*					
308133	75878	61883	75887			05/93-06/93		
308134	75879	61884	75888	93⇨**M**	95⇨**E**	09/93-09/99		
308134	75879	*61912*	75888			04/00-04/00		⇦
308136	75881	61886	75890			06/93-01/01		
308137	75882	61887	75891			06/93-03/01		
308138	75883	61888	75892			06/93-10/01		
308139	75884	61889	75893	93⇨**M**		11/93-09/95		
308140	75885	61890	75894	93⇨**M**		06/93-09/95		
308141	75886	61891	75895			09/93-04/01		
308142	75896	61892	75929			05/93-09/93		
308143	75897	61893	75930	93⇨**M**	95⇨**E**	06/93-06/01		
308144	75435	61894	75931			06/93-08/93		
308144	*75880*	61894	75931	93⇨**M**	95⇨**E**	08/93-02/01		⇦
308145	75899	61895	75932	93⇨**M**	95⇨**E**	11/93-06/01		
308146	75900	61896	75933			06/95-09/94	➲**937991**	
308147	75901	61897	75934	93⇨**M**	95⇨**E**	06/93-05/01		
308148	75902	61898	75935			05/93-09/93		
308149	75903	61899	75936			08/93-09/93		
308152	75913	61902	75939	93⇨**M**	95⇨**E**	06/93-05/01		
308153	75907	61903	75940	93⇨**M**	95⇨**E**	06/93-06/01		
308154	75908	61904	75941	93⇨**M**	95⇨**E**	05/93-01/01		
308155	75909	61905	75942	93⇨**M**	95⇨**E**	05/93-03/01		
308157	75911	61907	75944			05/93-10/94		
308157	*75915*	61907	75944	93⇨**M**	95⇨**E**	10/94-10/01		⇦
308158	75912	61908	75945	93⇨**M**	95⇨**E**	06/93-10/01		
308159	75906	61909	75946	93⇨**M**	95⇨**E**	05/93-01/01		
308160	75914	61910	75947	93⇨**M**		06/93-09/95		

308161	75915	61911	75948	93⇨**M**	05/93-10/94	
308161	*75911*	61911	75948	95⇨**E**	10/94-05/01	
308162	75916	61912	75949		06/93-04/00	
308162	75916	*61884*	75949		04/00-04/01	
308163	75917	61913	75950		05/93-01/01	
308164	75918	61914	75951	93⇨**M** 95⇨**E**	05/93-03/01	
308165	75919	61915	75952		06/93-04/01	

Class 308/2 AM8

Tilbury Line
25kV ac overhead
308313-308321

	BDTSOL	*MBSO*	*TSOL*	*DTSO*		
308313	75920	62431	70644	75953	01/82-06/85	
308314	75921	62434	70645	75954	06/81-01/85	
308315	75922	62433	70646	75955	02/82-01/84	
308316	75923	62432	70647	75956	06/81-01/85	

	BDTSOL	*MLV*	*TSOL*	*DTSO*		
308317	75924	68015	70648	75957	*82*-07/83	➲*308991*
308318	75925	68016	70649	75958	12/81-07/83	➲*308992*
308319	75926	68017	70650	75959	07/82-07/83	➲*308993*
308320	75927	68018	70651	75960	04/82-07/83	➲*308994*
308321	75928	68012	70652	75961	*82*-07/83	➲*308995*

Class 308/3 AM8

North East London Lines
25kV ac overhead
308453-308461

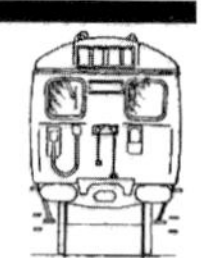

	BDTSO	*MBSO*	*DTSO*	
308453	75741	61689	75992	10/81-05/85
308453	*75743*	61689	75992	05/85-02/86
308454	75742	61690	75993	02/82-03/86
308455	75743	61691	75994	05/82-05/85
308455	*75741*	61691	75994	05/85-05/85

	BDTSOL	*MBS*	*TSOL*	*DTSO*	
308458	75912	61908	70636	75945	04/83-05/83
308461	75915	61911	70639	75948	04/83-04/84

Class 308/2 AM8

Parcels Units
25kV ac overhead
308991-308995

	BDTSOL	*MLV*	*DTLV*	
308991	75924	68015	75957	01/84-11/88
308992	75925	68016	75958	01/84-02/84
308993	75926	68017	75959	01/84-01/90
308994	75927	68018	75960	01/84-01/90
308995	75928	68012	75961	01/84-11/88
308995	*75347*	68012	75961	11/88-01/90

Class 309 AM9

Clacton & Walton Express Stock
25kV ac overhead
309601-309627

Units strengthened to 3-car units with the addition of converted Mark 1 coaches.

	DMBSOL	*TCsoL*	*BDTSOL*	
309601	61940	71573	75984	10/82-09/86
309602	61941	71574	75985	06/82-07/86
309603	61942	71575	75986	12/81-08/84
309604	61943	71576	75987	02/82-02/86

Units strengthened to 4-car units with the addition of converted Mark 1 coaches.

	DMBSO	*TSOL*	*TCsoL*	*BDTSOL*	
309601	61940	71569	71573	75984	09/86-05/93
309602	61941	71570	71574	75985	07/86-01/94
309603	61942	71571	71575	75986	08/84-05/93
309604	61943	71572	71576	75987	02/86-01/94

Units converted to 3-car units with the transfer of TSK to 309615-618 to allow withdrawal of Griddle cars.

	DMBSOL	*TCK*	*BDTSOL*	
309605	61944	71113	75988	12/81-03/85
309606	61945	71112	75989	12/81-07/85
309607	61946	71111	75990	11/82-07/85
309608	61947	71114	75991	09/82-10/85

Units reverting to 4-car units.

	DMBSO	*TSOL*	*TCsoL*	*BDTSOL*	
309605	61944	71108	71113	75988	03/85-03/98
309606	61945	71109	71112	75989	07/85-03/98
309607	61946	71107	71111	75990	07/85-02/94
309608	61947	71110	71114	75991	10/85-05/93

Units built as 4-car units with Griddle car.

	BDTC	*MBSK*	*TRB*	*DTC*	
309616	75642	61937	69108	75981	01/80- 81
309618	75644	61939	69107	75983	02/81-07/81

Griddle cars removed and replaced with converted Mark 1 coaches (some transferred from 309605-309608).

	BDTC	*MBSOL*	*TSOL*	*DTCOL*	
309611	75637	61932	71569	75976	03/81-09/86
309612	75638	61933	71570	75977	10/82-07/86
309613	75639	61934	71571	75978	06/82-08/84
309614	75640	61935	71572	75979	10/82-02/86
309615	75641	61936	71108	75980	09/82-03/85
309616	75642	61937	71109	75981	81-07/85
309617	75643	61938	71107	75982	10/82-07/85
309618	75644	61939	71110	75983	07/81-10/85

Units temporarily converted to 3-car units.

	BDTC	*MBSOL*	*DTSOL*	
309613	75639	61934	75978	08/84-04/86
309614	75640	61935	75979	02/86-07/86
309615	75641	61936	75980	03/85-09/86
309616	75642	61937	75981	07/85-04/86
309617	75643	61938	75982	07/85-04/86
309618	75644	61939	75983	10/85-01/86

Units strengthened to 4-car units with the addition of converted Mark 1 coaches.

	BDTC	*MBSO*	*TSO*	*DTSOL*			
309611	75637	61932	71754	75976		09/86-12/91	
309612	75638	61933	71755	75977		07/86-06/93	
309613	75639	61934	71756	75978	94⇨**M**	04/86-06/00	
309614	75640	61935	71757	75979		07/86-08/92	
309615	75641	61936	71758	75980		09/86-07/92	➲*309623*
309616	75642	61937	71759	75981	94⇨**M**	04/86-06/00	➲*Dep*
309617	75643	61938	71760	75982	94⇨**M**	04/86-06/00	➲*Dep*
309618	75644	61939	71761	75983		01/86-12/91	
309618	*75966*	61939	71761	75983	94⇨**M**	12/91-12/94	

Units built as 4-car units.

	BDTC	*MBSO*	*TSOL*	*DTSOL*			
309621	75962	61925	70253	75969		03/83-05/92	
309622	75963	61926	70254	75970		02/82-11/92	
309623	75964	61927	70255	75971		09/82-07/92	
309623	*75641*	61927	*71758*	*75980*	94⇨**M**	08/92-06/00	
309624	75965	61928	70256	75972	94⇨**M**	05/82-06/00	➲*Dep*
309625	75966	61929	70257	75973		04/82-12/91	
309626	75967	61930	70258	75974	94⇨**M**	03/82-12/94	
309627	75968	61931	70259	75975		10/82-02/92	
309627	*75644*	61931	70259	75975	94⇨**M**	02/92-11/99	

Class 310 AM10

London Midland Western Lines
25kV ac overhead
310046-310113

	BDTSOL	*MBSO*	*TSO*	*DTCOL*			
310046	76130	62071	70731	76180	88⇨**E**	*83*-05/01	
310047	76131	62072	70732	76181	88⇨**E**	03/82-06/01	
310048	76132	62073	70733	76182		04/81-09/89	➲**310108**
310049	76133	62074	70734	76183	88⇨**E**	08/81-06/01	
310050	76134	62075	70735	76184	88⇨**E**	09/82-10/01	
310051	76135	62076	70736	76185		06/81-10/01	
310052	76136	62077	70737	76186	88⇨**E**	02/80-06/01	
310053	76137	62078	70738	76187		11/82-10/89	➲**310109**
310054	76138	62079	70739	76188		07/81-11/89	➲**310110**
310055	76139	62080	70740	76189		12/81-10/88	➲**310102**
310056	76140	62081	70741	76190	88⇨**E**	02/80-04/93	
310056	*76158*	62081	70741	*76195*		04/93-04/94	

310057	76141	62082	70742	76191		03/82-08/00		
310058	76142	62083	70743	76192		12/81-06/01		
310059	76143	62084	70744	76205	88⇨**E**	12/79-07/01		
310060	76144	62085	70745	76194		04/81-06/01		
310061	76145	62086	70746	76195	88⇨**E**	03/82-04/93		
310061	*76140*	62086	70746	*76227*		04/93-09/94	**➲310112**	↩
310062	76146	62087	70747	76196		02/83-09/89	**➲310107**	
310063	76147	62088	70748	76197	88⇨**E**	06/81-03/90	**➲310111**	
310064	76148	62089	70749	76198	88⇨**E**	04/81-07/01		
310065	76149	62090	70750	76199	88⇨**E**	09/82-09/94		
310066	76228	62091	70751	76200	88⇨**E**	03/82-06/01		
310067	76151	62092	70752	76201	88⇨**E**	03/82-05/01		
310068	76152	62093	70753	76202	88⇨**E**	04/83-03/01		
310069	76153	62094	70754	76203	88⇨**E**	01/80-07/01		
310070	76154	62095	70755	76204	88⇨**E**	08/81-07/01		
310072	76156	62097	70757	76206	88⇨**E**	05/81-02/89	**➲310106**	
310073	76157	62098	70758	76207		12/81-09/88	**➲310101**	
310074	76158	62099	70759	76208	88⇨**E**	04/81-04/93		
310074	*76145*	62099	70759	76208		04/93-07/01		↩
310075	76159	62100	70760	76209	88⇨**E**	04/83-07/01		
310076	76160	62101	70761	76210		02/82-11/88	**➲310103**	
310077	76161	62102	70762	76211	88⇨**E**	12/81-06/01		
310078	76162	62103	70763	76212		03/82-01/89	**➲310104**	
310079	76163	62104	70764	76213	88⇨**E**	08/81-10/90		
310079	76163	62104	70764	*76222*		10/90-05/01		↩
310080	76164	62105	70765	76214	88⇨**E**	03/82-10/01		
310081	76165	62106	70766	76215	88⇨**E**	03/82-11/01		
310082	76166	62107	70767	76216	88⇨**E**	04/83-10/01		
310083	76167	62108	70768	76217	88⇨**E**	10/81-10/01		
310084	76168	62109	70769	76218	88⇨**E**	10/81-05/00		
310084	76168	62109	70769	*76206*		05/00-05/01		↩
310085	76169	62110	70770	76219	88⇨**E**	04/83-06/01		
310086	76170	62111	70771	76220		10/82-06/01		
310087	76171	62112	70772	76221	88⇨**E**	12/81-10/01		
310088	76172	62113	70773	76222	88⇨**E**	12/81-10/90		
310088	76172	62113	70773	*76213*		10/90-10/01		↩
310089	76173	62114	70774	76223	88⇨**E**	06/81-12/00		
310090	76174	62115	70775	76224		07/82-01/89	**➲310105**	
310091	76175	62116	70776	76225	88⇨**E**	04/83-05/01		
310092	76176	62117	70777	76226	88⇨**E**	02/83-10/01		
310093	76177	62118	70778	76227	88⇨**E**	07/82-04/93		
310093	76177	62118	70778	*76190*		04/93-11/01		↩
310094	76998	62119	70780	76193		01/83-06/01		
310095	76179	62120	70779	76229	88⇨**E**	04/81-05/01		

Refurbished units for Provincial Services

	BDTSOL	*MBSO*	*TSO*	*DTSOL*	
310101	76157	62098	70758	76207	09/88-02/96
310102	76139	62080	70740	76189	10/88-02/96
310103	76160	62101	70761	76210	11/88-02/96
310104	76162	62103	70763	76212	01/89-02/96
310105	76174	62115	70775	76224	01/89-02/96
310106	76156	62097	70757	76206	02/89-02/96
310107	76146	62087	70747	76196	09/89-02/96
310108	76132	62073	70733	76182	09/89-02/96
310109	76137	62078	70738	76187	10/89-02/96
310110	76138	62079	70739	76188	11/89-02/96
310111	76147	62088	70748	76197	03/90-02/96
310112	76140	62086	70746	76227	09/94-02/96

Units reduced to 3-car units

	BDTSOL	*MBSO*	*DTSOL*			
310101	76157	62098	76207	02/96-07/01		
310102	76139	62080	76189	02/96-09/01		
310103	76160	62101	76210	02/96-02/00		
310104	76162	62103	76212	02/96-07/01		
310105	76174	62115	76224	02/96-07/01		
310106	76156	62097	76206	02/96-05/00		
310106	76156	62097	*76218*	05/00-09/01		↩
310107	76146	62087	76196	02/96-07/01		
310108	76132	62073	76182	02/96-07/01		
310109	76137	62078	76187	02/96-07/01	➲Dep	
310110	76138	62079	76188	02/96-09/01		
310111	76147	62088	76197	02/96-05/01		
310112	76140	62086	76227	02/96-07/01		
310113	76158	62090	76195	09/94-07/01		

Class 311 AM11
Glasgow Suburban
25kV ac overhead
311092-311110

	DTSO	*MBSO*	*BDTSO*			
311092	76403	62163	76422	*05/79*-09/89		
311093	76404	62164	76423	*03/80*-12/87		
311094	76405	62165	76424	*03/80*-01/89		
311095	76406	62166	76425	*11/79*-01/89		
311096	76407	62167	76426	08/80-12/87		
311097	76408	62168	76427	07/80-09/89		
311098	76409	62169	76428	*08/79*-10/90		
311099	76410	62170	76429	06/80-10/90		
311100	76411	62171	76430	*05/79*-10/86		
311101	76412	62172	76431	*05/79*-12/87		
311102	76413	62173	76432	*03/80*-10/90		
311103	76414	62174	76433	*05/79-10/90*	**➲936103**	
311104	76415	62175	76434	*11/79-10/90*	**➲936104**	
311105	76416	62176	76435	*08/79*-09/90		
311106	76417	62177	76436	*03/80*-10/86		
311107	76418	62178	76437	06/80-07/90		
311107	*76421*	62178	76437	07/90-10/90		↩
311108	76419	62179	76438	*03/80*-10/90		
311109	76420	62180	76439	*08/79*-08/90		
311109	*75594*	62180	76439	08/90-10/90		↩
311110	76421	62181	76440	*80*-07/90		
311110	*76418*	62181	76440	07/90-10/90		↩

Class 312
GE/GN/Birmingham
25kV ac overhead
312001-312799

The Class 312 units were based on Class 310 and were built for several different services. Class 312/0 was built for Great Northern outer suburban services from Kings Cross to Royston. Class 312/1 was for Great Eastern outer suburban services out of Liverpool Street. Finally four units of Class 312/2 were built to work the Birmingham New Street to Birmingham International shuttle.

Eventually all the units were renumbered in the 3127xx units and the Birmingham area units moved to the GE section in 1988.

All the units were working on the GE section by the late 1980s, and then half the class moved to the Tilbury lines in 1991.

Class 312/0

	BDTSOL	*MBSO*	*TSO*	*DTCOL*		
312001	76949	62484	71168	78000	05/77-05/79	**➲312701**
312002	76950	62485	71169	78001	06/77-05/79	**➲312702**
312003	76951	62486	71170	78002	06/77-04/79	**➲312703**
312004	76952	62487	71171	78003	07/77-03/79	**➲312704**
312005	76953	62488	71172	78004	07/77-04/79	**➲312705**
312006	76954	62489	71173	78005	07/77-05/79	**➲312706**
312007	76955	62490	71174	78006	07/77-04/79	**➲312707**
312008	76956	62491	71175	78007	07/77-05/79	**➲312708**
312009	76957	62492	71176	78008	08/77-05/79	**➲312709**
312010	76958	62493	71177	78009	08/77-05/79	**➲312710**
312011	76959	62494	71178	78010	08/77-05/79	**➲312711**
312012	76960	62495	71179	78011	09/77-04/79	**➲312712**
312013	76961	62496	71180	78012	09/77-04/79	**➲312713**
312014	76962	62497	71181	78013	10/77-03/79	**➲312714**
312015	76963	62498	71182	78014	10/77-04/79	**➲312715**
312016	76964	62499	71183	78015	10/77-04/79	**➲312716**
312017	76965	62500	71184	78016	11/77-04/79	**➲312717**
312018	76966	62501	71185	78017	11/77-05/79	**➲312718**
312019	76967	62502	71186	78018	12/77-04/79	**➲312719**
312020	76968	62503	71187	78019	12/77-05/79	**➲312720**
312021	76969	62504	71188	78020	12/77-05/79	**➲312721**
312022	76970	62505	71189	78021	12/77-04/79	**➲312722**
312023	76971	62506	71190	78022	01/78-04/79	**➲312723**
312024	76972	62507	71191	78023	01/78-05/79	**➲312724**
312025	76973	62508	71192	78024	09/78-03/79	**➲312725**
312026	76974	62509	71193	78025	12/78-05/79	**➲312726**

Class 312/1

	BDTSOL	*MBSO*	*TSO*	*DTCOL*		
312101	76975	62510	71194	78026	03/75- 78	**➲312781**
312102	76976	62511	71195	78027	04/75- 78	**➲312782**
312103	76977	62512	71196	78028	04/75- 78	**➲312783**
312104	76978	62513	71197	78029	05/75- 78	**➲312784**
312105	76979	62514	71198	78030	06/75- 78	**➲312785**
312106	76980	62515	71199	78031	06/75- 78	**➲312786**
312107	76981	62516	71200	78032	06/75- 78	**➲312787**
312108	76982	62517	71201	78033	06/75- 78	**➲312788**
312109	76983	62518	71202	78034	07/75- 78	**➲312789**
312110	76984	62519	71203	78035	07/75- 78	**➲312790**
312111	76985	62520	71204	78036	07/75- 78	**➲312791**
312112	76986	62521	71205	78037	08/75- 78	**➲312792**
312113	76987	62522	71206	78038	08/75- 78	**➲312793**
312114	76988	62523	71207	78039	08/75- 78	**➲312794**
312115	76989	62524	71208	78040	09/75- 78	**➲312795**
312116	76990	62525	71209	78041	09/75- 78	**➲312796**
312117	76991	62526	71210	78042	09/75- 78	**➲312797**

312118	76992	62527	71211	78043	10/75- 78	➲**312798**
312119	76993	62528	71212	78044	10/75- 78	➲**312799**

Class 312/2

	BDTSOL	*MBSO*	*TSO*	*DTCOL*		
312201	76994	62657	71277	78045	02/76-04/88	➲**312727**
312202	76995	62658	71278	78046	01/76-04/88	➲**312728**
312203	76996	62659	71279	78047	02/76-05/88	➲**312729**
312204	76997	62660	71280	78048	12/75-05/88	➲**312730**

Class 312/0

	BDTSOL	*MBSO*	*TSO*	*DTCOL*	
312701	76949	62484	71168	78000	05/79-10/03
312702	76950	62485	71169	78001	05/79-09/03
312703	76951	62486	71170	78002	04/79-03/04
312704	76952	62487	71171	78003	03/79-09/03
312705	76953	62488	71172	78004	04/79-09/03
312706	76954	62489	71173	78005	05/79-09/03
312707	76955	62490	71174	78006	04/79-09/03
312708	76956	62491	71175	78007	05/79-09/03
312709	76957	62492	71176	78008	05/79-10/03
312710	76958	62493	71177	78009	05/79-09/03
312711	76959	62494	71178	78010	05/79-09/03
312712	76960	62495	71179	78011	04/79-09/04
312713	76961	62496	71180	78012	04/79-01/03
312714	76962	62497	71181	78013	03/79-03/04
312715	76963	62498	71182	78014	04/79-03/04
312716	76964	62499	71183	78015	04/79-09/03
312717	76965	62500	71184	78016	04/79-09/03
312718	76966	62501	71185	78017	05/79-05/04
312719	76967	62502	71186	78018	04/79-09/03
312720	76968	62503	71187	78019	05/79-09/03
312721	76969	62504	71188	78020	05/79-05/04
312722	76970	62505	71189	78021	04/79-05/04
312723	76971	62506	71190	78022	04/79-05/04
312724	76972	62507	71191	78023	05/79-09/03
312725	76973	62508	71192	78024	03/79-04/02
312726	76974	62509	71193	78025	05/79-11/01

Class 312/2

	BDTSOL	*MBSO*	*TSO*	*DTCOL*	
312727	76994	62657	71277	78045	04/88-11/01
312728	76995	62658	71278	78046	04/88-10/03
312729	76996	62659	71279	78047	05/88-12/01
312730	76997	62660	71280	78048	05/88-08/02

Class 312/1

	BDTSOL	*MBSO*	*TSO*	*DTCOL*	
312781	76975	62510	71194	78026	78-03/03
312782	76976	62511	71195	78027	78-11/01
312783	76977	62512	71196	78028	78-03/03
312784	76978	62513	71197	78029	78-03/03
312785	76979	62514	71198	78030	78-09/02
312786	76980	62515	71199	78031	78-02/02
312787	76981	62516	71200	78032	78-03/02
312788	76982	62517	71201	78033	78-03/02
312789	76983	62518	71202	78034	78-09/02
312790	76984	62519	71203	78035	78-02/02
312791	76985	62520	71204	78036	78-04/02
312792	76986	62521	71205	78037	78-03/03
312793	76987	62522	71206	78038	78-02/02
312794	76988	62523	71207	78039	78-12/01
312795	76989	62524	71208	78040	78-12/01
312796	76990	62525	71209	78041	78-12/01
312797	76991	62526	71210	78042	78-03/03
312798	76992	62527	71211	78043	78-02/02
312799	76993	62528	71212	78044	78-03/02

TOPS Numbered Southern Units

When BR started applying TOPs numbers to units, the Southern Region took a different route. The units were allocated six-digit unit numbers, but only the last four digits were applied to each unit. A few of the early Class 411 refurbished units displayed the full unit numbers for a short time.

Some class numbers were changed at this time so that the four-digit unit numbers series would be grouped together logically.

Class 421/4 4-CIG

Express Units
660-750V dc third rail
1100-1127

Units that were not facelifted.

	DTCsoL	*MBSO*	*TSO*	*DTCsoL*		
1100	76125	62066	71051	76071	06/87-10/92	➲**1751**
1105	76080	62021	70699	76026	06/87-12/87	
1105	76080	62021	70699	*76039*	12/87-09/92	➲**1750**
1110	76085	62026	70704	76031	06/87-03/92	➲**1745**
1111	76086	62027	70705	76032	06/87-12/91	➲**1742**
1114	76089	62030	70708	76035	06/87-11/91	➲**1741**
1116	76091	62032	70710	76037	06/87-04/92	➲**1746**
1118	76093	62034	70712	76039	06/87-12/87	
1118	76093	62034	70712	*76026*	12/87-04/92	➲**1747**
1121	76096	62037	70715	76042	05/87-01/88	➲**1732**
1123	76119	62060	70717	76065	07/86-11/92	➲**1752**
1127	76102	62043	70721	76048	06/87-01/93	➲**1753**

Class 411/9 3-CEP

Express Units
660-750V dc third rail
1101-1118

Three-car units for South Eastern Division services.

	DMSO(B)	*TBCK*	*DMSO(A)*	
1101	61330	70316	61331	10/98-04/03
1102	61232	70604	61231	10/98-04/03
1103	61751	70580	61750	09/98-04/03
1104	61761	70585	61760	11/98-12/02
1105	61953	70655	61952	11/98-04/03
1106	61364	70333	61365	05/99-06/02
1107	61380	70327	61343	05/99-03/03
1108	61399	70350	61398	05/99-02/03
1109	61409	70355	61408	05/99-06/02
1110	61322	70312	61323	05/99-08/02
1111	61338	70320	61339	05/99-01/03
1112	61368	70335	61369	07/99-03/03
1113	61370	70336	61371	05/99-04/03
1114	61376	70339	61377	05/99-04/03
1115	61719	70564	61718	05/99-08/02
1116	61757	70589	61756	05/99-03/03
1117	61705	70557	61704	07/99-03/03
1118	61709	70559	61708	05/99-03/03

Class 411/1 3-CEP

Express Units
660-750V dc third rail
1197-1199

Three-car units for the Lymington Branch.

	DMSO(B)	*TBCK*	*DMSO(A)*		
1197	61804	70539	61805	12/04-	Never formed
1198	61736	70573	61737	05/04-12/04	
1199	61328	70578	61329	01/03-05/04	

Class 421/2 4-CIG

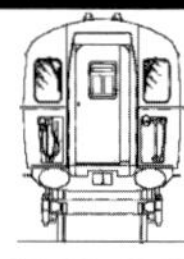

Express Units
660-750V dc third rail
1201-1300

	DTCsoL	*MBSO*	*TSO*	*DTCsoL*		
1201	76751	62389	71069	76822	06/87-02/92	➲**1868**
1202	76752	62390	71070	76823	05/87-06/91	➲**1860**

1203	76753	62391	71071	76824	08/87-11/89		
1203	76753	62391	71071	*76804*	11/89-02/92	⊃**1869**	☜
1204	76754	62392	71072	76825	06/87-07/92	⊃**1875**	
1205	76755	62393	71073	76826	07/87-07/92	⊃**1874**	
1206	76756	62394	71074	76827	08/87-03/92	⊃**1871**	
1208	76758	62396	71076	76829	07/87-11/90		
1208	*76771*	62396	71076	76829	11/90-05/92	⊃**1872**	☜
1209	76759	62397	71077	76830	07/87-06/92	⊃**1873**	
1210	76760	62398	71078	76831	05/87-09/92	⊃**1879**	
1211	76761	62399	71079	76832	08/87-07/92	⊃**1876**	
1212	76762	62400	71080	76833	09/87-10/92	⊃**1881**	
1213	76763	62401	71081	76834	09/87-07/92	⊃**1877**	
1214	76764	62402	71082	76835	09/87-11/92	⊃**1883**	
1215	76765	62403	71083	76836	08/87-10/92	⊃**1882**	
1216	76766	62404	71084	76837	09/87-12/92	⊃**1887**	
1217	76767	62405	71085	76838	09/87-11/92	⊃**1884**	
1218	76768	62406	71086	76839	09/87-08/92	⊃**1878**	
1219	76769	62407	71087	76840	09/87-12/92	⊃**1885**	
1220	76770	62408	71088	76841	06/87-09/92	⊃**1880**	
1221	76771	62409	71089	76842	08/87-11/90		
1221	*76758*	62409	71089	76842	11/90-03/91		☜
1221	*76108*	62409	71089	76842	03/91-04/92	⊃**1870**	☜
1222	76772	62410	71090	76843	08/87-12/92	⊃**1886**	
1223	76773	62411	71091	76844	08/87-01/93	⊃**1888**	
1224	76774	62412	71092	76845	09/87-01/93	⊃**1889**	
1225	76775	62413	71093	76846	08/87-02/93	⊃**1890**	
1226	76776	62414	71094	76847	08/87-03/93	⊃**1891**	
1237	76581	62287	70967	76611	08/87-05/88	⊃**1816**	
1238	76582	62288	70968	76612	06/87-06/90	⊃**1833**	
1239	76583	62289	70969	76613	08/87-05/88	⊃**1817**	
1240	76584	62290	70970	76614	09/87-04/88	⊃**1815**	
1241	76585	62291	70971	76615	08/87-04/90	⊃**1316**	
1242	76586	62292	70972	76616	09/87-07/88	⊃**1820**	
1243	76587	62293	70973	76617	09/87-08/90	⊃**1838**	
1244	76588	62294	70974	76618	06/87-04/90	⊃**1314**	
1245	76589	62295	70975	76619	06/87-10/90	⊃**1844**	
1246	76590	62296	70976	76620	06/87-11/90	⊃**1849**	
1247	76591	62297	70977	76621	06/87-12/90	⊃**1852**	
1248	76592	62298	70978	76622	06/87-07/88	⊃**1821**	
1249	76593	62299	70979	76623	09/87-07/90	⊃**1836**	
1250	76594	62300	70980	76624	08/87-07/88	⊃**1822**	
1251	76595	62301	70981	76625	08/87-04/88	⊃**1814**	
1252	76596	62302	70982	76626	09/87-04/90	⊃**1313**	
1253	76597	62303	70983	76627	09/87-11/90	⊃**1317**	
1254	76598	62304	70984	76628	11/87-05/90	⊃**1831**	
1255	76599	62305	70985	76629	02/88-10/90	⊃**1845**	
1256	76600	62306	70986	76630	06/87-11/90	⊃**1847**	
1257	76601	62307	70987	76631	07/87-06/90	⊃**1835**	
1258	76566	62282	70988	76576	09/87-06/90	⊃**1834**	
1259	76603	62309	70989	76633	06/87-09/90	⊃**1841**	
1260	76604	62310	70990	76634	06/87-05/91	⊃**1858**	
1261	76605	62311	70991	76635	08/87-11/90	⊃**1848**	
1262	76606	62312	70992	76636	05/87-01/91	⊃**1853**	
1263	76607	62313	70993	76637	07/87-08/90	⊃**1839**	
1264	76608	62314	70994	76638	07/87-04/90	⊃**1315**	
1266	76610	62316	70996	76640	05/87-04/91	⊃**1857**	
1267	76717	62355	71035	76788	08/87-06/88	⊃**1818**	
1268	76718	62356	71036	76789	06/87-12/90	⊃**1850**	
1269	76719	62357	71037	76790	05/87-05/90	⊃**1832**	
1270	76720	62358	71038	76791	08/87-01/91	⊃**1855**	
1271	76721	62359	71039	76792	08/87-12/90	⊃**1851**	
1272	76722	62360	71040	76793	06/87-07/90	⊃**1837**	
1273	76723	62361	71041	76794	06/87-06/88	⊃**1819**	
1274	76724	62362	71042	76795	06/87-08/90	⊃**1840**	
1275	76725	62363	71043	76796	06/87-09/90	⊃**1842**	
1276	76726	62364	71044	76797	08/87-10/89	⊃*2251*	
1277	76727	62365	71045	76798	08/87-06/91	⊃**1859**	
1278	76728	62366	71046	76799	06/87-10/89	⊃*2252*	
1279	76729	62367	71047	76800	06/87-09/89	⊃*2257*	
1280	76730	62368	71048	76801	06/87-04/89		
1281	76731	62369	71049	76802	06/87-10/90	⊃**1843**	
1282	76732	62370	71050	76803	06/87-10/89	⊃*2254*	
1284	76734	62372	71052	76805	06/87-10/89	⊃*2253*	
1285	76735	62373	71053	76806	06/87-07/91	⊃**1861**	
1286	76736	62374	71054	76807	06/87-08/91	⊃**1862**	
1287	76737	62375	71055	76808	06/87-11/90	⊃**1846**	
1288	76738	62376	71056	76809	06/87-01/91	⊃**1854**	
1289	76739	62377	71057	76810	07/87-02/91	⊃**1856**	
1290	76740	62378	71058	76811	09/87-10/89	⊃*2255*	
1291	76741	62379	71059	76812	06/87-09/91	⊃**1864**	
1292	76742	62380	71060	76813	06/87-09/91	⊃**1863**	
1293	76743	62381	71061	76814	06/87-12/91	⊃**1866**	
1294	76744	62382	71062	76815	05/87-01/92	⊃**1867**	
1295	76745	62383	71063	76816	08/87-11/89		
1295	76745	62383	71063	*76639*	11/89-11/91	⊃**1865**	☜
1296	76746	62384	71064	76817	06/87-11/89	⊃*2258*	
1297	76747	62385	71065	76818	06/87-11/89	⊃*2256*	
1298	76748	62386	71066	76819	08/87-11/89	⊃*2259*	
1299	76749	62387	71067	76820	05/87-11/89	⊃*2260*	
1300	76750	62388	71068	76821	06/87-10/89	⊃*2261*	

Class 421/5 4-CIG
Greyhound Units
660-750V dc third rail
1301-1322

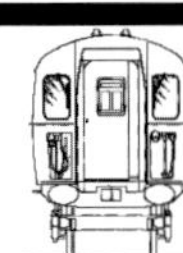

	DTCsoL	*MBSO*	*TSO*	*DTCsoL*		
1301	76595	62301	70981	76625	04/90-08/04	
1302	76584	62290	70970	76614	04/90-04/04	
1303	76581	62287	70967	76611	04/90-02/05	
1304	76583	62289	70969	76613	04/90-04/05	
1305	76717	62355	71035	76788	04/90-07/04	
1306	76723	62361	71041	76794	05/90-07/04	
1307	76586	62292	70972	76616	05/90-10/04	
1308	76592	62298	70978	76622	05/90-01/92	
1308	*76627*	62298	70978	76622	01/92-09/04	☜
1309	76594	62300	70980	76624	04/90-04/05	
1310	76567	62283	71926	76577	05/90-08/04	
1311	76561	62277	71927	76571	05/90-08/04	
1312	76562	62278	71928	76572	06/90-04/05	
1313	76596	62302	70982	76626	04/90-12/04	
1314	76588	62294	70974	76618	04/90-08/04	
1315	76608	62314	70994	76638	04/90-12/04	
1316	[illegible]	[illegible]	[illegible]	[illegible]	[illegible]	
1317	76597	62303	70983	76627	11/90-01/92	
1317	76597	62303	70983	*76592*	01/92-09/04	☜
1318	76590	62296	70976	76620	01/92-06/05	
1319	76591	62297	70977	76621	01/92-06/05	
1320	76593	62299	70979	76623	01/92-10/04	
1321	76589	62295	70975	76619	01/92-08/04	
1322	76587	62293	70973	76617	03/92-08/04	

Class 421/8 4-CIG
Express Units
660-750V dc third rail
1392-1399

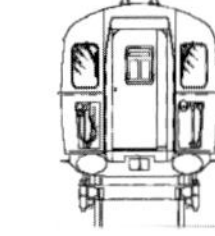

4-BIG units reformed to 4-CIG using a 4-CEP TSO.

	DTCsoL	*MBSO*	*TSO*	*DTCsoL*		
1392	76740	62378	70273	76811	07/99-05/05	
1393	76746	62384	70527	76817	07/99-04/05	
1394	76726	62364	70663	76797	08/99-12/04	⊃*1499*
1395	76779	62417	70662	76850	09/99-05/05	
1396	76732	62370	70531	76803	09/99-05/05	
1397	76749	62387	70515	76820	09/99-05/05	
1398	76748	62386	70292	76819	09/99-04/05	
1399	76747	62385	70508	76818	09/99-04/05	

Class 411/1 3-CEP
Express Units
660-750V dc third rail
1401-1406

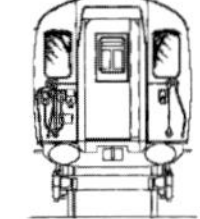

Three-car units for the Medway Valley, Tonbridge-Redhill and Sheerness services.

	DMSO(B)	*TBCK*	*DMSO(A)*		
1401	61352	70324	61353	05/93-06/94	
1402	61346	70341	61347	05/93-06/94	
1403	61236	70238	61235	07/93-06/94	
1404	61240	70240	61239	07/93-06/94	
1405	61378	70340	61379	07/93-06/94	
1406	61354	70328	61355	06/93-05/94	
1406	61354	70328	*61870*	05/94-06/94	☜

Class 421/4 4-BIG
Express Units
660-750V dc third rail
1401-1411

	DTCsoL	*MBSO*	*TSRB*	*DTCsoL*		
1401	76568	62284	69334	76578	06/97-07/97	⊃**1401**
1402	76564	62280	69336	76574	06/97-12/97	⊃**1402**
1403	76563	62279	69311	76573	06/97-12/97	⊃**1403**
1404	76602	62308	69338	76632	06/97-01/98	⊃**1404**
1405	76565	62281	69339	76575	06/97-08/97	⊃**1405**
1406	76728	62366	69312	76799	06/97-11/97	⊃**1406**

1407	76729	62367	69332	76800	09/97-11/97	**⊃1407**
1408	76750	62388	69301	76821	09/97-01/98	**⊃1408**
1409	76569	62285	69335	76579	09/97-12/97	**⊃1409**
1410	76734	62372	69313	76805	09/97-01/98	**⊃1410**
1411	76570	62286	69337	76580	09/97-02/98	**⊃1411**

Class 421/7 3-COP
Outer-Suburban Units (Coastway)
660-750V dc third rail
1401-1411

4-BIG units reformed to 3-COP for Coastway services.

	DTSsoL	MBSO	DTSsoL		
1401	76568	62284	76578	11/97-02/04	
1402	76564	62280	76574	12/97-04/02	
1403	76563	62279	76573	12/97-10/03	**⊃1403**
1404	76602	62308	76632	02/98-01/04	**⊃1404**
1405	76565	62281	76575	11/97-09/03	**⊃1405**
1406	76728	62366	76799	11/97-10/03	**⊃1406**
1407	76729	62367	76800	12/97-09/03	
1408	76750	62388	76821	01/98-11/03	
1409	76569	62285	76579	01/98-11/03	
1410	76734	62372	76805	02/98-10/03	**⊃1410**
1411	76570	62286	76580	02/98-11/03	**⊃1411**

Class 421/7 4-COP
Outer-Suburban Units (Coastway)
660-750V dc third rail
1403-1411

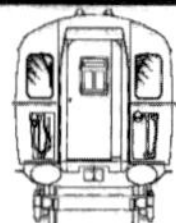

Coastway units augmented to four-car units with the addition of a TSO.

	DTSsoL	MBSO	TSO	DTSsoL	
1403	76563	62279	70703	76573	10/03-06/04
1404	76602	62308	70713	76632	01/04-03/05
1405	76565	62281	70716	76575	09/03-06/04
1406	76728	62366	70699	76799	10/03-12/04
1410	76734	62372	70720	76805	10/03-03/05
1411	76570	62286	70722	76580	11/03-04/05

Class 421/7 3-CIG
Express Units
660-750V dc third rail
1497-1499

Three-car units for the Lymington Branch.

	DTCsoL	MBSO	DTCsoL		
1497	76764	62402	76835	*Freshwater*	04/05-05/10
1498	76773	62411	76844	*Farringford*	04/05-05/10
1499	76726	62364	76797		12/04-05/05

Class 411/3 4-CEP
Express Units
660-750V dc third rail
1500

Prototype refurbished unit

	DMSO(B)	TSOL	TBCK	DMSO(A)	
1500	61388	70302	70345	61389	11/85-01/90

Class 411/4 4-CEP
Express Units
660-750V dc third rail
1501-1505

Refurbished units (original prototype units).

	DMSO(B)	TSOL	TBCK	DMSO(A)	
1501	61042	70034	70041	61041	05/80-03/93
1502	61039	70036	70040	61040	12/80-01/93
1503	61034	70033	70037	61033	10/82-03/93
1504	61037	71712	70042	61043	08/83-05/93
1505	61038	70035	70039	61044	01/84-03/93

Class 411/5 4-CEP
Express Units
660-750V dc third rail
1506-1621

Refurbished units.

	DMSO(B)	TSOL	TBCK	DMSO(A)			
1506	61348	70282	70325	61349	12/79-12/92		
1507	61362	70289	70332	61363	01/80-12/02		
1508	61304	70260	70303	61305	01/80-05/95		
1509	61334	70275	70318	61335	02/80-12/02		
1510	61364	70290	70333	61365	04/80-05/99	⊃*1106*	
1511	61366	70291	70334	61367	05/80-12/02		
1512	61320	70268	70311	61321	06/80-06/02		
1513	61340	70278	70321	61796	06/80-05/95		
1514	61326	70271	70314	61327	08/80-06/95		
1515	61344	70280	70323	61345	09/80-04/96		
1516	61318	70267	70310	61319	10/80-06/95		
1517	61316	70266	70309	61317	11/80-08/04		
1518	61332	70274	70317	61333	11/80-08/96		
1519	61402	70516	70352	61403	11/80-01/00		
1519	61402	*70536*	70352	61403	01/00-04/04		☞
1520	61380	70284	70327	61343	12/80-05/99	⊃*1107*	
1521	61352	70281	70324	61353	12/80-05/93	⊃*1401*	
1522	61346	70665	70341	61347	01/81-05/93	⊃*1402*	
1523	61382	70299	70342	61383	02/81-04/96		
1524	61308	70262	70305	61309	02/81-11/85		
1525	61236	70232	70238	61235	03/81-07/93	⊃*1403*	
1526	61240	70234	70240	61239	03/81-07/93	⊃*1404*	
1527	61238	70233	70239	61237	04/81-11/99		
1528	61378	70297	70340	61379	04/81-07/93	⊃*1405*	
1529	61354	70285	70328	61355	05/81-06/93	⊃*1406*	
1530	61330	70273	70316	61331	06/81-10/98	⊃*1101*	
1531	61234	70231	70237	61233	06/81-01/04		
1532	61390	71626	70346	61391	09/81-08/97		
1533	61385	71627	70347	61393	09/81-04/04		
1534	61404	71628	70353	61405	10/81-08/97		
1534	61404	*71626*	70353	61405	08/97-04/04		☞
1535	61396	71629	70349	61397	11/81-07/04		
1536	61398	71631	70350	61399	11/81-05/99	⊃*1108*	
1537	61230	70229	70235	61229	01/82-09/02	⊃*2325*	
1538	61306	70261	70304	61307	02/82-09/02	⊃*2327*	
1539	61400	71632	70351	61401	02/82-09/04		
1540	61384	70300	70343	61870	03/82-05/94		
1540	61384	70300	70343	*61355*	05/94-08/96	**⊃1698**	☞
1541	61409	71633	70355	61408	03/82-05/99	⊃*1109*	
1542	61394	71634	70348	61395	03/82-05/95		
1543	61322	70269	70312	61323	04/82-11/93		
1543	61322	*70297*	70312	61323	11/93-05/99	⊃*1110*	☞
1544	61314	70265	70308	61315	06/82-03/94		
1544	*61349*	70265	70308	61315	03/94-04/04		☞
1545	61358	70287	70330	61359	07/82-04/97	⊃*932545*	
1546	61356	70286	70329	61357	08/82-06/95		
1547	61328	70272	70315	61329	09/82-01/90		
1547	61328	70272	*70345*	61329	01/90-05/97		☞
1547	61328	70272	*70578*	61329	05/97-09/02	⊃*2326*	☞
1548	61374	70295	70338	61375	10/82-09/02	⊃*2322*	
1549	61338	70277	70320	61339	11/82-05/99	⊃*1111*	
1550	61312	70264	70307	61313	12/82-08/04		
1551	61324	70270	70313	61325	12/82-12/02		
1552	61372	70294	70337	61373	02/83-10/96	**⊃1697**	
1553	61350	70263	70306	61351	02/83-10/95		
1553	61350	70263	70306	*61728*	04/96-03/04		☞
1554	61368	70292	70335	61369	04/83-07/99	⊃*1112*	
1555	61310	70283	70326	61311	04/83-08/04		
1556	61370	70293	70336	61371	06/83-08/83	⊃*2701*	
1556	61370	70293	70336	61371	02/86-05/99	⊃*1113*	☞
1557	61360	70288	70331	61337	07/83-09/83	⊃*2702*	
1557	61360	70288	70331	61337	03/86-10/99		☞
1558	61336	70276	70319	61361	10/83-12/83	⊃*2704*	
1558	61336	70276	70319	61361	03/86-05/93		☞
1559	61376	70296	70339	61377	10/83-05/99	⊃*1114*	
1560	61386	70301	70344	61387	11/83-12/83	⊃*2703*	
1560	61386	70301	70344	61387	03/86-12/02		☞
1561	61232	70230	70604	61231	12/83-07/98		
1561	61232	*70663*	70604	61231	07/98-10/98	⊃*1102*	☞
1562	61406	70241	70236	61407	12/83-03/89	⊃*2308*	
1562	61406	70241	70236	61407	12/89-04/04		☞
1563	61741	70526	70575	61740	01/83-03/04		
1564	61789	70550	70599	61788	12/82-03/03		
1565	61763	71711	70586	61762	01/83-04/03		
1565	61763	71711	*70311*	61762	04/03-04/04		☞
1566	61723	70517	70566	61722	11/82-09/02	⊃*2324*	
1567	61787	70549	70598	61786	10/82-04/95		
1568	61767	70539	70588	61766	09/82-09/02	⊃*2321*	
1569	61783	70547	70596	61782	08/82-05/95		

1570	61739	70525	70574	61738	08/82-11/02	
1571	61807	71636	70608	61806	06/82-09/02	➲*2323*
1571	61807	*70289*	70608	61806	12/02-09/04	
1572	61735	70523	70572	61734	06/82-03/99	
1573	61727	70519	70568	61726	05/82-04/04	
1574	61793	71635	70601	61792	05/82-12/02	
1575	61769	70540	70583	61768	04/82-10/02	
1576	61771	70541	70590	61770	04/82-08/02	
1577	61719	70515	70564	61718	02/82-05/99	➲*1115*
1578	61701	70506	70555	61700	02/82-09/04	
1579	61773	70542	70591	61772	01/82-05/93	
1579	61773	*70281*	70591	61772	10/93-05/93	
1580	61757	70534	70589	61756	12/81-05/99	➲*1116*
1581	61785	70548	70597	61784	11/81-04/04	
1582	61797	71630	70603	61748	11/81-12/02	
1583	61747	70529	70578	61746	10/81-04/96	
1584	61753	70532	70581	61752	03/82-11/02	
1585	61711	70511	70560	61710	10/81-08/02	
1586	61715	70513	70562	61714	08/81-03/03	
1587	61765	71625	70587	61764	08/81-10/02	
1588	61721	70520	70044	61720	08/81-11/01	
1589	61743	70527	70576	61742	07/81-04/97	
1590	61697	70504	70553	61696	06/81-06/04	
1591	61791	70551	70600	61790	06/81-09/02	
1592	61779	70545	70594	61778	05/81-06/04	
1593	61731	70521	70570	61730	04/81-03/04	
1594	61755	70533	70582	61754	03/81-03/04	
1595	61705	70508	70557	61704	02/81-07/99	➲*1117*
[illegible]	[illegible]	[illegible]	[illegible]	[illegible]	01/81-04/96	
1597	61709	70510	70559	61708	01/81-05/99	➲*1118*
1598	61781	70546	70595	61780	11/80-09/95	
1599	61707	70509	70558	61706	10/80-01/03	
1600	61725	70518	70567	61724	09/80-03/96	
1601	61777	70544	70593	61776	09/80-05/95	
1602	61959	70279	70565	61720	08/80-08/81	
1602	61959	70279	70565	*61958*	08/81-04/04	
1603	61729	70298	70569	61728	07/80-10/95	
1604	61733	70522	70571	61732	07/80-08/85	
1605	61713	70512	70561	61712	04/80-06/96	➲**1699**
1606	61695	70503	70552	61694	03/80-08/95	
1607	61699	70505	70554	61698	03/80-06/03	
1608	61961	70666	70659	61960	02/80-06/95	
1609	61745	70528	70577	61744	02/83-12/02	
1610	61751	70531	70580	61750	02/83-09/98	➲*1103*
1611	61759	70537	70584	61758	03/83-12/02	
1612	61795	70535	70602	61794	03/83-04/04	
1613	61761	70536	70585	61760	04/83-11/98	➲*1104*
1614	61703	70507	70556	61702	04/83-03/03	
1615	61957	70664	70657	61956	05/83-04/04	
1616	61951	70543	70654	61950	06/83-09/02	
1616	61951	70543	70654	*61323*	09/02-03/03	
1617	61801	70661	70605	61800	07/83-10/99	
1618	61869	70663	70043	61868	09/83-04/94	
1619	61953	70662	70655	61952	10/83-11/98	➲*1105*
1620	61949	70660	70653	61948	11/83-01/93	➲**932620**
1621	61811	70524	70610	61810	03/84-05/93	

Class 411/6 4-CEP
Express Units
660-750V dc third rail
1697-1699

Units fitted with B6 power bogies.

	DMSO(B)	*TSOL*	*TBCK*	*DMSO(A)*	
1697	61372	70294	70337	61373	10/96-07/05
1698	61384	70300	70343	61355	08/96-09/05
1699	61713	70512	70561	61712	06/96-07/05

Class 421/3 4-CIG
Express Units
660-750V dc third rail
1701-1753

Facelifted units.

	DTCsoL	*MBSO*	*TSO*	*DTCsoL*		
1701	76087	62028	70706	76033	07/85-07/04	
1702	76101	62042	70720	76047	08/85-11/02	
1703	76097	62038	70716	76043	09/85-12/02	
1704	76092	62033	70711	76038	10/85-11/04	
1705	76076	62017	70695	76022	11/85-01/03	
1706	76094	62035	70713	76040	12/85-11/02	
1707	76084	62025	70703	76030	12/85-01/03	
1708	76110	62051	70729	76056	01/86-02/05	
1709	76103	62044	70722	76049	02/86-03/03	
1710	76078	62019	70697	76024	02/86-02/05	
1711	76114	62055	71766	76060	03/86-12/04	
1712	76079	62020	70698	76025	04/86-02/05	
1713	76128	62069	71767	76074	05/86-02/04	
1714	76077	62018	70696	76023	06/86-02/05	
1715	76082	62023	70701	76028	07/86-04/93	➲**1901**
1716	76100	62041	71768	76046	08/86-04/93	➲**1902**
1717	76083	62024	70702	76029	09/86-02/05	
1718	76081	62022	70700	76027	10/86-07/93	➲**1903**
1719	76116	62057	70719	76062	10/86-04/04	
1720	76098	62039	71769	76044	11/86-07/04	
1721	76090	62031	70709	76036	12/86-08/04	
1722	76106	62047	70725	76052	01/87-06/04	
1723	76107	62048	70726	76053	02/87-11/93	➲**1904**
1724	76120	62061	71770	76066	03/87-02/04	
1725	76088	62029	70707	76034	03/87-07/04	
1726	76109	62050	70728	76055	05/87-09/03	
1727	76111	62052	70730	76057	06/87-06/04	
1728	76099	62040	70718	76045	07/87-03/94	➲**1905**
1729	76104	62045	70723	76050	07/87-07/94	➲**1907**
1730	76105	62046	70724	76113	10/87-05/94	➲**1906**
1731	76095	62036	70714	76041	11/87-12/02	
1732	76096	62037	70715	76042	01/88-01/95	➲**1908**
1733	76122	62063	71047	76068	10/90-07/04	
1734	76063	62054	71044	76059	12/90-07/04	
[illegible]	[illegible]	[illegible]	[illegible]	[illegible]	[illegible]	
1736	76124	62065	71052	76070	02/91-03/03	
1737	76121	62062	71058	76067	03/91-09/03	
1738	76129	62064	71046	76069	05/91-03/03	
1739	76123	62070	71066	76075	01/92-06/04	
1740	76126	62067	71097	76072	11/91-04/04	
1741	76089	62030	70708	76035	11/91-02/05	
1742	76086	62027	70705	76032	12/91-07/04	
1743	76118	62059	71065	76064	01/92-02/05	
1744	76127	62068	71064	76073	02/92-02/04	
1745	76085	62026	70704	76031	03/92-06/03	
1746	76091	62032	70710	76037	04/92-07/04	
1747	76093	62034	70712	76026	04/92-09/03	
1748	76115	62056	71067	76061	05/92-05/04	
1749	76112	62053	71068	76058	05/92-09/95	
1750	76080	62021	70699	76039	09/92-01/03	
1751[2]	76125	62066	71051	76071	10/92-07/04	
1752[2]	76119	62060	70717	76065	11/92-07/04	
1753[2]	76102	62043	70721	76048	01/93-02/04	

Class 421/3 4-CIG
Express Units
660-750V dc third rail
1751-1762

4-BIG units reformed to 4-CIG.

	DTCsoL	*MBSO*	*TSO*	*DTCsoL*		
1751	76063	62054	71044	76059	10/89-12/90	➲**1734**
1752	76129	62064	71046	76069	10/89-05/91	➲**1738**
1753	76124	62065	71052	76070	10/89-02/91	➲**1736**
1754	76117	62058	71050	76051	10/89-02/91	➲**1735**
1755	76121	62062	71058	76067	10/89-03/91	➲**1737**
1756	76118	62059	71065	76064	11/89-01/92	➲**1743**
1757	76122	62063	71047	76068	09/89-10/90	➲**1733**
1758	76127	62068	71064	76073	11/89-02/92	➲**1744**
1759	76123	62070	71066	76075	11/89-01/92	➲**1739**
1760	76115	62056	71067	76061	11/89-05/92	➲**1748**
1761	76112	62053	71068	76058	10/89-05/92	➲**1749**
1762	76126	62067	71097	76072	12/89-11/91	➲**1740**

Class 421/4 4-CIG
Express Units
660-750V dc third rail
1800-1813

	DTCsoL	*MBSO*	*TSO*	*DTCsoL*		
1800	76599	62319	70958	76543	11/91-08/92	➲*3515*
1801	76777	62415	71095	76848	04/86-05/93	➲*2003*
1801	76777	62415	71095	76848	01/97-07/04	
1802	76779	62417	71097	76850	04/86-12/89	➲*2262*
1802	*76754*	*62392*	*71072*	*76825*	01/97-07/04	
1803	76780	62418	71098	76851	05/86-07/04	
1804	76778	62416	71096	76849	05/86-07/05	
1805	76782	62420	71100	76853	06/86-11/05	
1806	76783	62421	71101	76854	06/86-09/04	

1807	76784	62422	71102	76855	07/86-07/04	
1808	76785	62423	71103	76856	09/86-08/04	
1809	76786	62424	71104	76857	09/86-02/04	
1810	76787	62425	71105	76858	11/86-02/04	
1811	76781	62419	71099	76852	12/86-04/04	
1812	76757	62395	71075	76828	01/87-09/00	
1813	76859	62430	71106	76860	02/87-02/04	

Class 421/4 4-CIG
Express Units
660-750V dc third rail
1814-1891

Facelifted units.

	DTCsoL	*MBSO*	*TSO*	*DTCsoL*		
1814	76595	62301	70981	76625	04/88-04/90	➲**1301**
1815	76584	62290	70970	76614	04/88-04/90	➲**1302**
1816	76581	62287	70967	76611	05/88-04/90	➲**1303**
1817	76583	62289	70969	76613	05/88-04/90	➲**1304**
1818	76717	62355	71035	76788	06/88-04/90	➲**1305**
1819	76723	62361	71041	76794	06/88-05/90	➲**1306**
1820	76586	62292	70972	76616	07/88-05/90	➲**1307**
1821	76592	62298	70978	76622	07/88-05/90	➲**1308**
1822	76594	62300	70980	76624	07/88-04/90	➲**1309**
1823	76567	62283	71926	76577	10/88-05/90	➲**1310**
1824	76561	62277	71927	76571	11/88-05/90	➲**1311**
1825	76562	62278	71928	76572	12/88-06/90	➲**1312**
1830	76512	62332	70942	76729	12/91-01/92	➲*3501*
1831	76598	62304	70984	76628	05/90-05/05	
1832	76719	62357	71037	76790	05/90-07/05	
1833	76582	62288	70968	76612	06/90-07/04	
1834	76566	62282	70988	76576	06/90-02/05	
1835	76601	62307	70987	76631	06/90-10/04	
1836	76593	62299	70979	76623	07/90-01/92	➲**1320**
1837	76722	62360	71040	76793	07/90-02/05	
1838	76587	62293	70973	76617	08/90-03/92	➲**1322**
1839	76607	62313	70993	76637	08/90-05/04	
1840	76724	62362	71042	76795	08/90-05/04	
1841	76603	62309	70989	76633	09/90-07/04	
1842	76725	62363	71043	76796	09/90-04/04	
1843	76731	62369	71049	76802	10/90-10/04	
1844	76589	62295	70975	76619	10/90-01/92	➲**1321**
1845	76599	62305	70985	76629	10/90-11/91	
1845	*76544*	62305	70985	76629	11/91-08/92	
1845	*76599*	62305	70985	76629	08/92-10/99	
1845	76599	62305	70985	*76718*	10/99-12/04	
1846	76737	62375	71055	76808	11/90-02/05	
1847	76600	62306	70986	76630	11/90-02/05	
1848	76605	62311	70991	76635	11/90-02/05	
1849	76590	62296	70976	76620	11/90-01/92	➲**1318**
1850	76718	62356	71036	76789	12/90-10/99	
1850	*76629*	62356	71036	76789	10/99-06/03	
1851	76721	62359	71039	76792	12/90-02/05	
1852	76591	62297	70977	76621	12/90-01/92	➲**1319**
1853	76606	62312	70992	76636	01/91-05/05	
1854	76738	62376	71056	76809	01/91-04/05	
1855	76720	62358	71038	76791	01/91-12/04	
1856	76739	62377	71057	76810	02/91-04/05	
1857	76610	62316	70996	76640	04/91-12/05	
1858	76604	62310	70990	76634	05/91-07/05	
1859	76727	62365	71045	76798	06/91-06/05	
1860	76752	62390	71070	76823	06/91-07/05	
1861	76735	62373	71053	76806	07/91-06/05	
1862	76736	62374	71054	76807	08/91-06/05	
1863	76742	62380	71060	76813	09/91-06/05	
1864	76741	62379	71059	76812	09/91-08/05	
1865	76745	62383	71063	76639	11/91-05/05	
1866	76743	62381	71061	76814	12/91-11/05	
1867	76744	62382	71062	76815	01/92-06/05	
1868	76751	62389	71069	76822	02/92-05/05	
1869	76753	62391	71071	76804	02/92-06/05	
1870	76108	62409	71089	76842	04/92-07/04	
1871	76756	62394	71074	76827	04/92-08/04	
1872	76771	62396	71076	76829	05/92-09/04	
1873	76759	62397	71077	76830	06/92-08/04	
1874	76755	62393	71073	76826	07/92-02/05	
1875	76754	62392	71072	76825	07/92-05/93	➲*2001*
1876	76761	62399	71079	76832	07/92-08/04	
1877	76763	62401	71081	76834	07/92-08/04	
1878	76768	62406	71086	76839	08/92- 04	
1879	76760	62398	71078	76831	09/92-08/04	
1880	76770	62408	71088	76841	09/92-09/04	
1881	76762	62400	71080	76833	10/92-04/05	
1882	76765	62403	71083	76836	10/92-07/05	
1883	76764	62402	71082	76835	11/92-02/05	
1884	76767	62405	71085	76838	11/92-02/05	
1885	76769	62407	71087	76840	12/92-11/04	
1886	76772	62410	71090	76843	12/92-09/04	
1887	76766	62404	71084	76837	12/92-09/04	
1888	76773	62411	71091	76844	01/93-02/05	
1889	76774	62412	71092	76845	01/93-02/05	
1890	76775	62413	71093	76846	02/93-04/05	
1891	76776	62414	71094	76847	03/93-09/04	

Class 438/1 4-REP
Bournemouth Line Tractor Units
660-850V dc third rail
1901-1902

	DMSO	*TBSK*	*TFK*	*DMSO*	
1901	62141	70830	71163	62142	12/88-05/90
1902	62154	70824	70845	62153	02/89-04/90

	DMSO	*TBSK*	*TFK*	
1902	62153	70824	*70859*	04/90-06/90

Class 438/1 6-REP
Bournemouth Line Units
660-850V dc third rail
1903-1906

	DMSO	*TBSK*	*TFK*	*TFK*	*TBSK*	*DTSO*	
1903	62145	70834	70866	70853	70827	76324	04/90-09/90
1904	62154	70838	70870	70845	70839	76323	04/90-04/91
1905	62141	70829	70861	70847	70815	76321	05/90-04/91
1906	62142	70830	71163	70849	70817	76322	05/90-01/91

Class 438/1 6-REP
Bournemouth Line Units
660-850V dc third rail
1901-1905

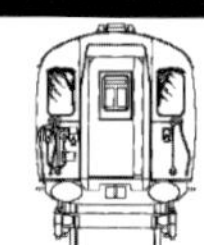

	DTSO	*TBSK*	*TFK*	*DMSO*	*TBSK*	*DTSO*	
1901^{2}	76324	70830	71163	62142	70824	76322	03/91-02/92
1902^{2}	76314	70834	70853	62153	70822	76303	09/90-12/90
1902^{2}	76314	70834	70853	62153	*70827*	76303	12/90-10/91
1903^{2}	76279	70817	70849	62145	70822	76280	01/91-06/91
1903^{2}	*76275*	*70829*	*70861*	62145	70822	76276	06/91-10/91
1904^{2}	76321	70838	70845	62141	70839	76323	07/91-10/91
1904^{2}	76321	70838	70845	62141	70839	*76275*	10/91-02/92

	DMSO	*TBSK*	*TFK*	*TFK*	*TBSK*	*DTSO*	
1905^{2}	62154	70829	70861	70847	70815	76323	04/91-06/91

Class 421/6 4-CIG
Express Units
660-750V dc third rail
1901-1908

Units fitted with B6 power bogies.

	DTCsoL	*MBSO*	*TSO*	*DTCsoL*		
1901^{3}	76082	62023	70701	76028	04/93-05/93	➲*2004*
1901^{3}	76082	62023	70701	76028	01/97-02/05	
1902^{3}	76100	62041	71768	76046	04/93-05/93	➲*2002*
1902^{3}	76100	62041	71768	76046	01/97-06/03	
1903^{3}	76081	62022	70700	76027	07/93-03/06	
1904^{3}	76107	62048	70726	76053	11/93-04/04	
1905^{3}	76099	62040	70718	76045	03/94-11/04	
1906^{2}	76105	62046	70724	76113	05/94-07/04	
1907	76104	62045	70723	76050	07/94-07/04	
1908	76096	62037	70715	76042	01/95-11/04	

Class 432 4-REP
Bournemouth Line Tractor Units
660-850V dc third rail
2001-2015

Previously Class 430
Later Class 438

	DMSO	TBFK	TRB	DMSO			
2001	62141	70801	69319	62142	06/86-09/86		
2001	62141	70801	*69326*	62142	09/86-12/87		☜
2002	62143	70802	69320	62144	05/86-01/88		
2003	62145	70803	69321	62146	09/86-12/87	⊃*2902*	
2004	62147	70804	69322	62148	06/86-12/87		
2005	62149	70805	69323	62150	08/86-01/88		
2006	62151	70806	69324	62152	06/86-12/86		
2007	62153	70807	69325	62154	06/86-03/88	⊃*2903*	
2009	62157	70809	69327	62158	06/86-06/87		
2010	62159	70810	69328	62160	09/86-06/87		
2011	62161	70811	69329	62162	09/86-01/87		
2012	62477	71156	69022	62476	05/86-06/87		
2013	62479	71157	69023	62478	05/86-12/87		
2014	62481	71158	69024	62480	04/86-03/88		
2015	62483	71159	69025	62482	04/86-11/86		

Class 438/1 4-REP
Bournemouth Line Tractor Units
660-850V dc third rail
2001-2007

	DMSO	TBFK	TRB	DMSO		
2001	62142	70810	69319	62141	05/88-06/88	
2001	62142	*70801*	69319	62141	06/88-06/88	☜
2003	62145	70803	69321	62146	04/88-04/90	
2007	62153	70807	69325	62154	05/88-02/89	

Class 422 8-DIG
Express Units
660-750V dc third rail
2001-2004

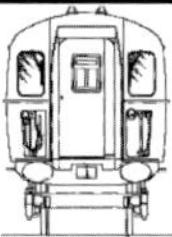

Eight-car units for working the London-Brighton "Capital Coast Express".

	DTCsoL	MBSO	TSO	DTCsoL	DTCsoL	TSRB	MBSO	DTCsoL	
2001[2]	76754	62392	71072	76825	76850	69333	62417	76779	05/93-01/97
2002[2]	76100	62041	71768	76046	76803	69306	62370	76732	05/93-01/97
2003[2]	76848	71095	62415	76777	76811	69310	62378	76740	05/93-01/97
2004[2]	76082	62023	70701	76028	76819	69318	62386	76748	05/93-01/97

Class 422/1 4-BIG
Express Buffet Units
660-750V dc third rail
2101-2112

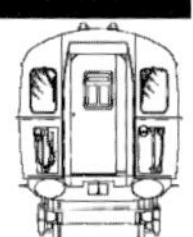

	DTCsoL	MBSO	TSRB	DTCsoL			
2101	76063	62054	69302	76059	04/85-10/89	⊃*1751*	
2102	76129	62064	69312	76069	04/85-10/89	⊃*1752*	
2103	76124	62065	69313	76070	04/85-10/89	⊃*1753*	
2104	76117	62058	69306	76051	05/85-10/89	⊃*1754*	
2105	76121	62062	69310	76067	05/85-10/89	⊃*1755*	
2106	76118	62059	69307	76064	04/85-11/89	⊃*1756*	
2107	76122	62063	69311	76068	04/85-09/89	⊃*1757*	
2108	76127	62068	69316	76073	09/85-11/89	⊃*1758*	
2109	76123	62070	69318	76075	10/85-11/89	⊃*1759*	
2110	76115	62056	69304	76061	11/85-11/89	⊃*1760*	
2111	76112	62053	69301	76058	09/85-10/89	⊃*1761*	
2112	76126	62067	69315	76072	04/86-07/88		
2112	76126	62067	*69333*	76072	07/88-12/89	⊃*1762*	☜

Class 422/2 4-BIG
Express Buffet Units
660-750V dc third rail
2201-2210

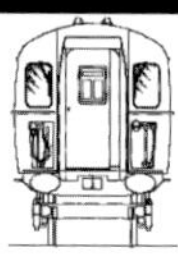

	DTCsoL	MBSO	TSRB	DTCsoL		
2201	76561	62277	69330	76571	06/85-11/88	⊃**1824**
2202	76562	62278	69331	76572	05/85-12/88	⊃**1825**
2203	76563	62279	69332	76573	04/85-06/97	⊃*1403*
2204	76564	62280	69336	76574	04/85-06/97	⊃**1402**
2205	76565	62281	69339	76575	04/85-06/97	⊃**1405**
2206	76602	62308	69338	76632	04/85-06/97	⊃**1404**
2207	76567	62283	69333	76577	04/85-07/88	⊃*1823*
2208	76568	62284	69334	76578	04/85-06/97	⊃**1401**
2209	76569	62285	69335	76579	04/85-09/97	⊃**1409**
2210	76570	62286	69337	76580	04/85-09/97	⊃**1411**

Class 422/3 4-BIG
Express Buffet Units
660-750V dc third rail
2251-2262

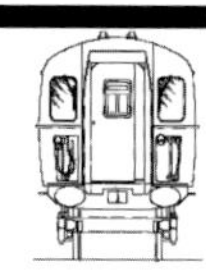

	DTCsoL	MBSO	TSRB	DTCsoL			
2251	76726	62364	69302	76797	10/89-05/99	⊃*1394*	
2252	76728	62366	69312	76799	10/89-06/97	⊃**1406**	
2253	76734	62372	69313	76805	10/89-09/97	⊃**1410**	
2254	76732	62370	69306	76803	10/89-05/93	⊃*2002*	
2254	76732	62370	69306	76803	01/97-07/99	⊃*1396*	☜
2255	76740	62378	69310	76811	10/89-05/93	⊃*2003*	
2255	76740	62378	69310	76811	01/97-04/99	⊃*1392*	☜
2256	76747	62385	69307	76818	11/89-09/99	⊃*1399*	
2257	76729	62367	69311	76800	09/89-12/91		
2257		62367	69311	*76511*	12/91-01/92		☜
2257	*76729*	62367	69311	*76800*	01/92-06/97		☜
2257	76729	62367	*69332*	76800	06/97-09/97	⊃**1407**	☜
2258	76746	62384	69316	76817	11/89-04/99	⊃*1393*	
2259	76748	62386	69318	76819	11/89-05/93	⊃*2004*	
2259	76748	62386	69318	76819	01/97-09/99	⊃*1398*	☜
2260	76749	62387	69304	76820	01/97-08/99	⊃*1397*	
2261	76750	62388	69301	76821	10/89-09/97	⊃**1408**	
2262	76779	62417	69333	76850	12/89-05/93	⊃*2001*	
2262	76779	62417	69333	76850	01/97-07/99	⊃*1395*	

Class 412 4-BEP
Express Buffet Units
660-750V dc third rail
2301-2308

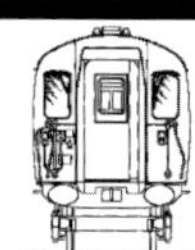

Refurbished units.

	DMSO(A)	TBCK	TSRB	DMSO(B)			
2301	61804	70607	69341	61805	02/82-09/02	⊃*2311*	
2302	61774	70592	69342	61775	06/83-04/91		
2302	61774	70592	69342	*61809*	04/91-09/02	⊃*2312*	☜
2303	61954	70656	69343	61955	09/83-09/02	⊃*2313*	
2304	61736	70573	69344	61737	11/83-09/02	⊃*2314*	
2305	61798	70354	69345	61799	12/83-09/02	⊃*2315*	
2306	61808	70609	69346	61809	02/84-03/89		
2306	61808	70609	69346	61809	04/89-04/91		☜
2306	61808	70609	69346	*61775*	04/91-09/02	⊃*2316*	☜
2307	61802	70606	69347	61803	03/84-09/02	⊃*2317*	
2308	61407	70236	69346	61406	03/89-04/89	⊃*1562*	

Class 411 4-CEP
'Greyhound' Units
660-750V dc third rail
2311-2317

South West Trains 4-BEP units renumbered after they were reformed to 4-CEP with the removal of the Buffet car.

	DMSO(A)	TBCK	TSOL	DMSO(B)		
2311	61804	70607	70539	61805	09/02-12/04	⊃*1197*
2312	61774	70592	70295	61809	09/02-10/04	
2313	61954	70656	71636	61955	09/02-10/04	
2314	61736	70573	70517	61737	09/02-05/04	⊃*1198*
2315	61798	70354	70229	61799	09/02-12/04	
2316	61808	70609	70272	61775	09/02-10/04	

2317	61802	70606	70261	61803	09/02-10/04	

Class 412 4-BEP
Express Buffet Units
660-750V dc third rail
2321-2327

South West Trains 4-CEP units renumbered after they were reformed to 4-BEP with the addition of a Buffet car.

	DMSO(B)	TSRB	TBCK	DMSO(A)		
2321	61767	69341	70588	61766	09/02-11/03	
2322	61374	69342	70338	61375	09/02-01/04	
2323	61806	69343	70608	61807	09/02-12/02	➲ *1571*
2324	61723	69344	70566	61722	09/02-11/03	
2325	61230	69345	70235	61229	09/02-12/03	
2326	61328	69346	70578	61329	09/02-01/03	➲ *1199*
2327	61306	69347	70304	61307	09/02-11/03	

Class 482 8-MIG
Express Buffet Units
660-750V dc third rail
2601-2602

Temporary eight-car buffet units for the London-Portsmouth line used during the CIG and BIG asbestos removal programme.

	DTCsoL	MBSO	TSO	DTCsoL	TSRB	MBSO	DTCsoL		
2601	76751	62389	71069	76822	1872	76752	62390	76823	05/83-10/83
2602	76753	62391	71071	76824	1873	76754	62392	76825	05/83-10/83

Class 422/7 4-TEP
Express Buffet Units
660-750V dc third rail
2701-2704

Temporary units for the Brighton Line used during the CIG and BIG asbestos removal programme.

	DMSO(B)	TRB	TBCK	DMSO(A)		
2701	61370	69010	70336	61371	08/83-02/86	➲ *1556*
2702	61360	69021	70331	61337	09/83-03/86	➲ *1557*
2703	61386	69020	70344	61387	12/83-03/86	➲ *1560*
2704	61336	69017	70319	61361	12/83-03/86	➲ *1558*

Class 492/8 4-TC
Bournemouth Line Trailer Units
660-850V dc third rail (unpowered)
2801-2807

	DTSO	TRB	TBSK	DTSO			
2801	76283	69319	70819	76284	12/86-12/87	➲ *8101*	
2802	76271	69324	70813	76272	12/86-09/87		
2802	76271	69324	*70814*	76272	09/87-01/88	➲ *8102*	↩
2803	76285	69025	70820	76286	12/86-12/87	➲ *8103*	
2804	76289	69329	70822	76290	02/87-12/87	➲ *8104*	
2805	76273	69327	70809	76274	06/87-06/87		
2805	76273	69327	*70814*	76274	06/87-09/87		↩
2805	76273	69327	*70813*	76274	09/87-12/87	➲ *8105*	↩
2806	76293	69328	70810	76294	06/87-12/87		
2807	76945	69022	71156	76946	06/87-04/88		
2807	76945	69022	*70854*	76946	04/88-05/89		↩

Class 492/0 5-TC
Bournemouth Line Trailer Units
660-850V dc third rail (unpowered)
2804-2809

	DTSO	TFK	TRB	TBSK	DTSO		
2804[2]	76286	70846	69020	70820	76285	05/88-04/89	
2805[2]	76273	70851	69023	70813	76274	04/88-10/88	
2806[2]	76294	70845	69025	70824	76293	05/88-09/88	➲ *8106*
2808	76275	70847	69025	70815	76276	09/88-01/89	➲ *8004*
2809	76329	71164	69025	70842	76330	01/89-05/89	➲ *8031*

Class 438/1 3-REP
Bournemouth Line Units
660-850V dc third rail
2901-2906

	DMSO	TRB	TBFK		
2901	62142	69025	70801	12/87-05/88	➲ *2001*
2902	62146	69321	70803	12/87-04/88	➲ *2003*
2903	62154	69325	70807	03/88-05/88	➲ *2007*
2904	62141	69319	70810	12/87-05/88	➲ *2001*
2905	62145	69023	71157	12/87-04/88	
2906	62153	69024	71158	03/88-05/88	

Class 423 4-VEP
Outer-Suburban Units
660-850V dc third rail
3000-3194

	DTCsoL	TSO	MBSO	DTCsoL			
3000	76804	70798	62200	76639	08/87-12/88	➲ *3454*	
3001	76230	70781	62121	76231	09/87-10/93	➲ *3401*	
3002	76232	70782	62122	76233	06/87-06/93	➲ *3402*	
3003	76234	70783	62123	76235	06/87-05/93	➲ *3403*	
3004	76236	70784	62124	76237	06/87-02/89		
3005	76238	70785	62125	76239	09/87-06/89	➲ *3405*	
3006	76240	70786	62126	76241	06/87-01/94	➲ *3406*	
3007	76242	70787	62127	76243	09/87-08/93	➲ *3407*	
3008	76244	70788	62128	76245	09/87-06/93	➲ *3408*	
3009	76246	70789	62129	76247	06/87-06/94	➲ *3409*	
3010	76369	70790	62130	76249	10/87-12/93	➲ *3410*	
3011	76250	70791	62131	76251	05/87-06/90	➲ *3411*	
3012	76252	70792	62132	76253	08/87-01/94	➲ *3412*	
3013	76254	70793	62133	76255	06/87-08/94	➲ *3413*	
3014	76248	70794	62134	76257	08/87-08/94	➲ *3414*	
3015	76258	70795	62135	76259	12/87-10/94	➲ *3415*	
3016	76260	70796	62136	76261	06/87-06/90		
3016	76260	70796	*62339*	76261	06/90-12/93	➲ *3416*	↩
3017	76262	70797	62137	76263	08/87-09/93	➲ *3417*	
3018	76264	70875	62138	76265	06/87-09/94	➲ *3418*	
3019	76266	70799	62139	76267	05/87-09/90		
3019	76266	70799	*62349*	76267	09/90-03/94	➲ *3419*	↩
3020	76268	70800	62140	76269	07/87-04/94	➲ *3420*	
3021	76333	70872	62182	76334	07/87-06/88	➲ *3429*	
3022	76335	70873	62183	76336	07/87-11/88	➲ *3449*	
3023	76337	70874	62184	76338	06/87-05/88	➲ *3425*	
3024	76339	71021	62185	76340	12/87-02/88		
3024	*76690*	71021	*62197*	76340	02/88-11/88	➲ *3452*	↩
3025	76341	70876	62186	76342	06/87-05/88	➲ *3435*	
3026	76343	70877	62187	76344	05/87-11/94	➲ *3569*	
3027	76345	70878	62188	76346	06/87-08/88	➲ *3437*	
3028	76347	70879	62189	76348	06/87-06/88	➲ **3430**	
3029	76349	70880	62190	76350	06/87-07/88	➲ **3436**	
3030	76351	70881	62191	76352	05/87-05/94	➲ *3558*	
3031	76353	70882	62192	76354	05/87-05/88	➲ *3424*	
3032	76355	70883	62193	76356	05/87-01/95	➲ **3578**	
3033	76357	70884	62194	76358	06/87-04/89		
3034	76359	70885	62195	76360	06/87-02/95	➲ **3580**	
3035	76361	70890	62196	76362	06/87-01/95	➲ **3576**	
3037	76365	70888	62198	76366	06/87-02/95	➲ **3581**	
3038	76367	70889	62199	76368	08/87-10/88	➲ *3444*	
3040	76371	70891	62201	76372	02/88-04/88	➲ **3422**	
3041	76373	70892	62202	76374	06/87-06/88	➲ *3427*	
3042	76375	70886	62203	76376	02/88-11/88	➲ *3448*	
3043	76377	70894	62204	76378	06/87-09/88	➲ *3441*	
3044	76379	70895	62205	76380	08/87-11/88	➲ *3447*	
3045	76381	70896	62206	76382	03/88-12/88	➲ *3453*	
3046	76383	70897	62207	76384	06/87-02/93	➲ **3536**	
3047	76385	70898	62208	76386	06/87-05/88	➲ **3426**	
3048	76387	70899	62209	76388	03/88-12/88	➲ *3455*	
3049	76389	70900	62210	76390	10/87-12/88		
3050	76391	70901	62211	76392	10/87-01/89	➲ *3457*	
3051	76393	70902	62212	76394	12/87-01/89	➲ *3458*	
3052	76395	70903	62213	76396	11/87-01/89	➲ *3459*	
3053	76397	70904	62214	76398	12/87-02/89	➲ *3463*	
3054	76399	70905	62215	76400	06/87-07/88	➲ *3432*	
3055	76401	70906	62216	76402	03/88-09/88	➲ *3439*	
3056	76441	70907	62217	76442	12/87-02/89	➲ *3464*	
3057	76443	70908	62218	76444	06/87-07/88	➲ *3433*	
3058	76445	70909	62219	76446	07/88-03/89	➲ *3467*	
3059	76447	70910	62220	76448	02/88-03/89	➲ *3468*	
3060	76449	70911	62221	76450	09/87-10/88	➲ *3445*	
3061	76451	70912	62222	76452	06/87-04/88	➲ **3423**	
3062	76453	70913	62223	76454	02/88-06/88	➲ **3428**	
3063	76455	70914	62224	76456	06/87-01/89	➲ *3456*	

Unit					Dates	To	
3064	76457	70915	62225	76458	06/87-06/88	➲ *3431*	
3065	76459	70916	62226	76460	03/88-11/88	➲ *3450*	
3066	76461	70917	62227	76462	08/87-07/88	➲ *3434*	
3067	76463	70918	62228	76464	08/87-07/88	➲ *3466*	
3068	76370	70919	62229	76466	09/87-07/91	➲ *3524*	
3069	76467	70920	62230	76468	06/87-02/92	➲ *3530*	
3070	76469	70921	62231	76470	08/87-01/90	➲ *3500*	
3071	76471	70922	62232	76472	06/87-02/90	➲ *3505*	
3072	76473	70923	62233	76474	10/87-07/89	➲ *3480*	
3073	76475	70924	62234	76476	10/87-08/89	➲ *3484*	
3074	76477	70925	62235	76478	10/87-09/89	➲ *3486*	
3075	76479	70926	62236	76480	08/87-09/93	➲ *3542*	
3076	76481	70927	62237	76482	06/87-10/89	➲ *3491*	
3077	76483	70928	62238	76484	06/87-08/90	➲ *3521*	
3078	76485	70929	62239	76486	06/87-06/94	➲ *3559*	
3079	76487	70930	62240	76488	08/87-11/88	➲ **3451**	
3080	76489	70931	62241	76490	06/87-02/94	➲ *3550*	
3081	76491	70932	62242	76492	07/87-10/88	➲ *3442*	
3082	76493	70933	62243	76494	05/87-09/88	➲ *3443*	
3083	76495	70934	62244	76496	07/87-04/89	➲ *3470*	
3084	76497	70935	62245	76498	05/87-04/89	➲ *3471*	
3085	76499	70936	62246	76500	05/87-05/89	➲ *3472*	
3086	76501	70937	62247	76502	05/87-05/89	➲ *3473*	
3087	76503	70938	62248	76504	05/87-05/89	➲ *3474*	
3088	76505	70939	62249	76506	05/87-10/92	➲ *3534*	
3089	76507	70940	62250	76508	05/87-08/89	➲ *3485*	
3090	76509	70941	62251	76510	06/87-09/89	➲ *3487*	
3091	76511	70942	62252	76512	06/87-12/89	➲ *3501*	
3092	76513	[illegible]	[illegible]	[illegible]	05/87-03/93	➲ *3537*	
3093	76515	70944	62254	76516	06/87-04/93	➲ *3538*	
3094	76517	70945	62255	76518	05/87-01/92	➲ *3528*	
3095	76519	70946	62256	76520	06/87-12/91	➲ *3527*	
3096	76521	70947	62257	76522	06/87-10/91	➲ *3525*	
3097	76523	70948	62258	76524	05/87-01/92	➲ *3526*	
3098	76525	70949	62259	76364	05/87-09/92	➲ *3533*	
3099	76527	70950	62260	76528	05/87-06/92	➲ *3532*	
3100	76529	70951	62261	76530	08/87-08/88	➲ *3438*	
3101	76531	70952	62262	76532	06/87-08/88	➲ *3446*	
3102	76533	70953	62263	76534	06/87-09/88	➲ *3440*	
3103	76535	70954	62264	76536	07/87-02/89	➲ *3462*	
3104	76537	70955	62265	76538	05/87-02/89	➲ *3461*	
3105	76539	70956	62266	76540	05/87-01/89	➲ *3460*	
3106	76542	70957	62267	76541	07/87-03/89	➲ *3465*	
3107	76544	70958	62268	76543	05/87-05/90	➲ *3515*	
3108	76546	70959	62269	76545	06/87-04/89	➲ *3469*	
3109	76548	70960	62270	76547	06/87-05/89	➲ *3476*	
3110	76550	70961	62271	76549	10/87-05/89	➲ *3477*	
3111	76552	70962	62272	76551	08/87-06/89	➲ *3475*	
3112	76554	70963	62273	76553	09/87-02/90	➲ *3506*	
3113	76556	70964	62274	76555	08/87-07/90	➲ **3519**	
3114	76558	70965	62275	76557	09/87-02/90	➲ *3507*	
3115	76560	70966	62276	76559	09/87-03/90	➲ *3509*	
3116	76642	70997	62317	76641	05/87-02/90	➲ *3510*	
3117	76644	70998	62318	76643	08/87-03/90	➲ *3508*	
3118	76646	70999	62319	76645	06/87-04/90	➲ *3511*	
3119	76648	71000	62320	76647	09/87-12/88		
3120	76650	71001	62321	76649	03/88-03/92	➲ *3531*	
3121	76652	71002	62322	76651	12/87-05/91	➲ *3523*	
3122	76654	71003	62323	76653	04/88-06/89	➲ *3478*	
3123	76656	71004	62324	76655	06/87-07/89	➲ *3479*	
3124	76658	71005	62325	76657	03/88 08/89	➲ *3482*	
3125	76660	71006	62326	76659	07/87-12/91	➲ *3529*	
3126	76662	71007	62327	76661	12/87-08/89	➲ *3483*	
3127	76664	71008	62328	76663	09/88-09/89	➲ *3488*	
3128	76666	71009	62329	76665	08/87-09/89	➲ *3489*	
3129	76668	71010	62330	76667	11/87-10/89	➲ *3492*	
3130	76670	71011	62331	76669	07/87-10/89	➲ *3493*	
3131	76672	71012	62332	76671	08/87-11/89	➲ *3497*	
3132	76674	71013	62333	76673	07/87-11/89	➲ *3496*	
3133	76676	71014	62334	76675	07/87-11/89	➲ *3494*	
3134	76678	71015	62335	76677	05/87-11/92	➲ **3535**	
3135	76680	71016	62336	76679	05/87-05/90	➲ *3512*	
3136	76682	71017	62337	76681	10/87-02/90	➲ *3503*	
3137	76684	71018	62338	76683	05/87-06/90	➲ *3514*	
3138	76686	71019	62339	76685	07/87-06/90	➲ *3517*	
3139	76688	71020	62340	76687	05/87-12/93	➲ *3546*	
3140	76363	70887	62341	76689	07/87-07/90	➲ *3518*	
3141	76692	71022	62342	76691	07/87-05/90	➲ *3513*	
3142	76694	71023	62343	76693	10/87-06/90	➲ *3516*	
3143	76696	71024	62344	76695	06/87-10/89	➲ *3490*	
3144	76698	71025	62345	76697	06/87-07/90	➲ *3520*	
3145	76700	71026	62346	76699	07/87-11/89	➲ *3495*	
3146	76702	71027	62347	76701	08/87-12/89	➲ *3498*	
3147	76704	71028	62348	76703	06/87-07/93	➲ *3541*	
3148	76706	71029	62349	76705	09/87-09/90	➲ *3522*	
3149	76708	71030	62350	76707	08/87-02/94	➲ *3549*	
3150	76710	71031	62351	76709	06/87-01/90	➲ *3502*	
3151	76712	71032	62352	76711	05/87-01/90	➲ *3504*	
3152	76714	71033	62353	76465	05/87-02/94	➲ *3551*	
3153	76716	71034	62354	76715	07/87-03/94	➲ *3552*	
3154	76862	71115	62435	76861	05/87-06/93	➲ *3539*	
3155	76864	71116	62436	76863	05/87-09/90		
3155	76864	71116	*62238*	76863	09/90-07/93	➲ *3540*	☜
3156	76866	71117	62437	76865	06/87-04/94	➲ *3555*	
3157	76868	71118	62438	76867	09/87-07/94	➲ *3561*	
3158	76870	71119	62439	76869	06/87-05/94	➲ *3557*	
3159	76872	71120	62440	76871	08/87-09/94	➲ *3567*	
3160	76874	71121	62441	76873	06/87-07/94	➲ *3563*	
3161	76876	71122	62442	76875	05/87-11/93	➲ *3545*	
3162	76878	71123	62443	76877	07/87-08/94	➲ *3565*	
3163	76880	71124	62444	76879	06/87-12/94	➲ *3572*	
3164	76882	71125	62445	76881	08/87-03/95	➲ *3584*	
3165	76884	71126	62446	76883	08/87-07/94	➲ *3564*	
3166	76886	71127	62447	76885	07/87-05/94	➲ *3556*	
3167	76888	71128	62448	76887	08/87-10/94	➲ *3568*	
3168	76890	71129	62449	76889	08/87-03/88	➲ **3421**	
3169	76892	71130	62450	76891	05/87-07/92		
3169	*76275*	71130	62450	76891	07/92-02/95	➲ *3582*	☜
3170	76894	71131	62451	76893	07/87-02/93		
3170	76894	71131	62451	*76892*	02/93-11/93	➲ *3544*	☜
3171	76896	71132	62452	76895	07/87-01/94	➲ *3547*	
3172	76898	71133	62453	76897	06/87-06/94	➲ *3560*	
3173	76900	71134	62454	76899	05/87-10/93	➲ *3543*	
3174	76902	71135	62455	76901	07/87-12/89	➲ *3499*	
3175	76904	71136	62456	76903	08/87-02/94	➲ *3548*	
3176	76906	71137	62457	76905	05/87-03/94	➲ *3554*	
3177	76908	71138	62458	76907	[illegible]	➲ *3562*	
3178	76910	71139	62463	76909	09/87-11/94	➲ *3570*	
3179	76912	71140	62460	76911	06/87-06/95	➲ *3589*	
3180	76914	71141	62461	76913	07/87-03/94	➲ *3553*	
3181	76916	71142	62462	76915	08/87-09/94	➲ *3566*	
3182	76918	71143	62459	76917	07/87-09/95	➲ *3591*	
3183	76920	71144	62464	76919	09/87-12/94	➲ *3573*	
3184	76922	71145	62465	76921	09/87-03/95	➲ *3586*	
3185	76924	71146	62466	76923	07/87-05/95	➲ *3588*	
3186	76926	71147	62467	76925	10/87-05/95	➲ *3587*	
3187	76928	71148	62468	76927	09/87-11/94	➲ *3571*	
3188	76930	71149	62469	76929	08/87-12/94	➲ *3574*	
3189	76932	71150	62470	76931	08/87-12/94	➲ *3575*	
3190	76934	71151	62471	76933	08/87-01/95	➲ *3577*	
3191	76936	71152	62472	76935	06/87-01/95	➲ *3579*	
3192	76938	71153	62473	76937	07/87-02/95	➲ *3583*	
3193	76940	71154	62474	76939	09/87-03/95	➲ *3585*	
3194	76942	71155	62475	76941	10/87-07/95	➲ *3590*	

Class 413/2 4-CAP
Outer-Suburban Units
660-750V dc third rail
3201-3213

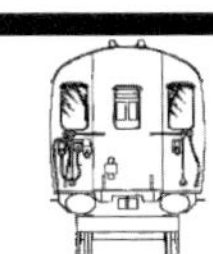

	DTSsoL	DMBSO	DMBSO	DTSsoL		
3201	77120	65398	65401	77123	05/82-11/94	
3201	*77117*	*65395*	65401	77123	11/94-02/95	☜
3202	77118	65396	65412	77134	05/82-09/93	
3203	77117	65395	65424	77146	05/82-11/94	
3204	77132	65410	65420	77142	04/82-02/95	
3205	77135	65413	65422	77144	05/82-03/95	
3206	77141	65419	65423	77145	04/82-08/91	
3207	77126	65404	65428	77150	05/82-09/94	
3208	77147	65425	65429	77151	05/82-09/91	
3208	77147	65425	65429	*77537*	09/91-01/94	☜
3209	77129	65407	65430	77152	04/82-05/91	
3210	77124	65402	65434	77156	05/82-05/91	
3211	77115	65393	65427	77149	06/82-05/93	
3212	77128	65406	65433	77155	04/82-05/91	
3213	77119	65397	65432	77154	05/82-09/91	

Class 413/3 4-CAP
Outer-Suburban Units
660-750V dc third rail
3301-3311

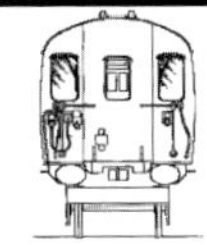

	DTSsoL	DMBSO	DMBSO	DTSsoL	
3301	75373	61253	61255	75375	05/82-01/95
3302	75361	61241	61244	75364	05/82-04/93
3303	75372	61252	61250	75370	04/82-01/94
3304	75402	61282	61283	75403	04/82-04/94
3305	75399	61279	61302	75422	05/82-05/94
3306	75374	61254	61256	75376	04/82-12/93
3307	75378	61258	61271	75391	05/82-12/93
3308	75366	61246	61264	75384	05/82-05/91
3309	75371	61251	61257	75377	05/82-05/91

3310	75363	61243	61266	75386	05/82-10/84	
3310	75363	61243	*61259*	75386	02/85-05/91	✍
3311	75411	61291	61297	75417	05/82-04/93	

Class 413/3 4-CAP
Outer-Suburban Units
660-750V dc third rail
3321-3325

	DMBSO	DTSsoL	DTSsoL	DMBSO		
3321	61268	75388	75398	61278	09/91-01/94	
3322	61300	75415	75420	61295	09/91-12/91	
3322	*61262*	*75382*	*75415*	61295	12/91-01/94	✍
3323	61273	75393	75382	61262	09/91-12/91	
3323	61273	75393	*75420*	*61300*	12/91-05/93	✍
3324	61270	75390	75423	61303	09/91-12/93	
3325	61261	75381	75418	61298	09/91-01/95	

Class 413/3 4-CAP
Outer-Suburban Units
660-750V dc third rail
3333

	DMBSO	DTCsoL	DTCsoL	DMBSO	
3333	65405	77127	75735	61683	09/91-01/92

Class 423/1 4-VEP
Outer-Suburban Units
660-850V dc third rail
3401-3591

	DTCsoL	TSO	MBSO	DTCsoL			
3401	76231	70781	62276	76230	10/93-06/02		
3401	*76872*	70781	62276	*76871*	07/02-04/05		✍
3402	76233	70782	62123	76232	06/93-04/05		
3403	76235	70783	62254	76234	05/93-02/05		
3404	76378	70894	62261	76236	02/90-08/04		
3405	76239	70785	62271	76238	06/89-04/05		
3406	76241	70786	62130	76240	01/94-06/04		
3407	76243	70787	62348	76242	08/93-04/05		
3408	76245	70788	62435	76244	06/93-03/05		
3409	76247	70789	62239	76246	06/94-07/04		
3410	76249	70790	62442	76369	12/93-05/04		
3411	76251	70791	62342	76250	06/90-04/05		
3412	76253	70792	62340	76252	01/94-08/05		
3413	76255	70793	62441	76254	08/94-08/04		
3414	76257	70794	62446	76248	09/94-08/04		
3415	76259	70795	62462	76258	10/94-02/05		
3416	76260	70796	62451	76261	12/93-08/05		
3417	76263	70797	62236	76262	09/93-		
3418	76264	70875	62133	76265	09/94-08/04		
3419	76266	70799	62354	76267	03/94-05/04		
3420	76268	70800	62349	76269	04/94-05/04		
3421	76890	71129	62449	76889	03/88-11/04		
3422	76371	70891	62201	76372	04/88-12/04		
3423	76451	70912	62222	76452	04/88-08/05		
3424	76353	70882	62185	76354	05/88-05/05		
3425	76337	70874	62192	76338	05/88-07/89		
3425	*76358*	70874	62192	76338	07/89-07/04		✍
3426	76385	70898	62208	76386	05/88-05/04		
3427	76373	70892	62184	76374	06/88-05/04		
3428	76453	70913	62223	76454	06/88-08/02		
3428	76453	70913	62223	*76360*	08/02-10/02		✍
3428	76453	70913	62223	*76231*	10/02-07/04		✍
3429	76333	70872	62202	76334	06/88-07/04		
3430	76347	70879	62189	76348	06/88-07/04		
3431	76457	70915	62182	76458	06/88-07/04		
3432	76399	70905	62225	76400	07/88-07/04		
3433	76443	70908	62215	76444	07/88-10/04		
3434	76461	70917	62218	76462	07/88-07/05		
3435	76341	70876	62228	76342	07/88-09/03	➲ *3814*	
3436	76349	70880	62190	76350	07/88-11/04		
3437	76345	70878	62186	76346	08/88-12/04		
3438	76529	70951	62262	76530	08/88-10/99	➲ **3910**	
3439	76401	70906	62227	76402	09/88-05/99	➲ **3901**	
3440	76533	70953	62188	76534	09/88-08/95	➲ **3802**	
3441	76377	70894	62261	76378	09/88-01/90	➲ *3404*	
3442	76491	70932	62216	76492	10/88-11/99	➲ **3912**	
3443	76493	70933	62263	76494	09/88-09/95	➲ **3803**	
3444	76367	70889	62204	76368	10/88-10/95	➲ **3804**	
3445	76449	70911	62242	76450	10/88-08/05		
3446	76531	70952	62243	76532	10/88-06/05		
3447	76379	70895	62199	76380	11/88-06/05		
3448	76375	70886	62221	76376	11/88-07/05		
3449	76335	70873	62205	76336	11/88-12/05		
3450	76459	70916	62203	76460	11/88-10/05		
3451	76487	70930	62240	76488	11/88-11/04		
3452	76690	71021	62183	76340	11/88-11/04		
3453	76381	70896	62226	76382	12/88-10/05		
3454	76389	70798	62200	76390	12/88-09/05		
3455	76387	70899	62206	76388	12/88-12/04		
3456	76455	70914	62210	76456	01/89-06/02		
3456	76455	70914	62210	*76230*	06/02-04/05		✍
3457	76391	70901	62197	76392	01/89-10/05		
3458	76393	70902	62209	76394	01/89-04/05		
3459	76395	70903	62224	76396	01/89-04/05		
3460	76539	70956	62211	76540	01/89-09/95	➲ **3805**	
3461	76537	70955	62212	76538	02/89-08/95	➲ **3806**	
3462	76535	70954	62213	76536	02/89-07/99	➲ **3903**	
3463	76397	70904	62266	76398	02/89-08/99	➲ **3905**	
3464	76441	70907	62265	76442	02/89-10/99	➲ **3908**	
3465	76541	70957	62264	76542	03/89-08/95	➲ **3807**	
3466	76463	70918	62214	76464	03/89-04/05		
3467	76445	70909	62217	76446	03/89-02/05		
3468	76447	70910	62267	76448	03/89-04/05		
3469	76545	70959	62219	76546	04/89-08/04		
3470	76495	70934	62220	76496	04/89-04/05		
3471	76497	70935	62269	76498	04/89-10/05		
3472	76499	70936	62244	76500	05/89-06/05		
3473	76501	70937	62245	76502	05/89-12/91		
3473	*76339*	70937	62245	76502	07/92-02/05		✍
3474	76503	70938	62246	76504	05/89-09/05		
3475	76551	70962	62270	76552	06/89-10/05		
3476	76547	70960	62247	76548	05/89-11/99	➲ **3911**	
3477	76549	70961	62248	76550	05/89-08/95	➲ **3808**	
3478	76654	71003	62125	76653	06/89-11/99	➲ **3913**	
3479	76656	71004	62272	76655	07/89-07/05		
3480	76473	70923	62323	76474	07/89-07/04		
3481	76648	70900	62324	76647	07/89-06/05		
3482	76658	71005	62320	76657	08/89-04/05		
3483	76662	71007	62233	76661	08/89-07/05		
3484	76475	70924	62325	76476	08/89-05/05		
3485	76507	70940	62327	76508	08/89-06/05		
3486	76477	70925	62234	76478	09/89-11/05		
3487	76509	70941	62250	76510	09/89-06/93		
3487	76509	70941	62250	*76645*	06/93-09/05		✍
3488	76664	71008	62235	76663	09/89-04/05		
3489	76666	71009	62251	76665	09/89-07/05		
3490	76696	71024	62328	76695	10/89-11/05		
3491	76481	70927	62329	76482	10/89-04/91		
3491	76481	70927	*62436*	*76337*	06/91-07/05		✍
3492	76668	71010	62344	76667	10/89- 05		
3493	76670	71011	62237	76669	10/89-11/04		
3494	76676	71014	62330	76675	11/89-05/05		
3495	76700	71026	62331	76699	11/89-08/05		
3496	76674	71013	62334	76673	11/89-08/05		
3497	76672	71012	62346	76671	11/89-08/05		
3498	76702	71027	62333	76701	12/89-08/05		
3499	76902	71135	62347	76901	12/89-06/05		
3500	76469	70921	62455	76470	01/90-07/04		
3500	76469	70921	62455	*76924*	07/04-10/05		✍
3501	76511	70942	62332	76512	12/89-12/91	➲ *1830*	
3501	76511	70942	62332	76512	01/92-02/05		✍
3502	76710	71031	62252	76709	01/90-06/96	➲ **3810**	
3503	76682	71017	62231	76681	02/90-09/03	➲ *3844*	
3504	76712	71032	62351	76711	01/90-09/03	➲ *3822*	
3505	76471	70922	62352	76472	02/90-11/05		
3506	76553	70963	62317	76554	02/90-01/00	➲ **3919**	
3507	76557	70965	62232	76558	02/90-12/99	➲ **3917**	
3508	76644	70998	62273	76643	03/90-03/05		
3509	76559	70966	62275	76560	03/90-07/04		
3510	76642	70997	62318	76641	03/90-05/04		
3511	76646	70999	62276	76645	04/90-06/93		
3511	76646	70999	*62135*	*76893*	11/94-05/05		✍
3512	76680	71016	62337	76679	05/90-05/04		
3513	76692	71022	62336	76691	05/90-07/99	➲ **3904**	
3514	76684	71018	62136	76683	06/90-11/05		
3515	76543	70958	62319	76544	05/90-11/91	➲ *1800*	
3515	76543	70958	62319	76544	08/92-10/04		✍
3516	76694	71023	62268	76693	06/90-04/05		
3517	76686	71019	62338	76685	06/90-06/04		
3518	76363	70887	62343	76689	07/90-09/03	➲ *3842*	
3519	76555	70964	62274	76556	07/90-05/04		
3520	76698	71025	62131	76697	07/90-08/02		
3520	*76359*	71025	62131	76697	08/02-10/02		✍
3520	*76698*	71025	62131	76697	10/02-04/05		✍
3521	76483	70928	62345	76484	08/90-09/05		
3522	76706	71029	62341	76705	09/90-09/99	➲ **3909**	
3523	76652	71002	62139	76651	05/91-07/05		
3524	76370	70919	62322	76466	07/91-04/05		

3525	76521	70947	62229	76522	10/91-08/95	➲ **3801**
3526	76523	70948	62255	76524	03/92-12/99	➲ **3915**
3527	76519	70946	62326	76520	12/91-11/99	➲ **3914**
3528	76517	70945	62258	76518	01/92-12/99	➲ **3916**
3529	76660	71006	62257	76659	12/91-06/04	
3530	76467	70920	62256	76468	02/92-11/05	
3531	76650	71001	62230	76649	03/92-05/05	
3532	76527	70950	62321	76528	06/92-01/00	➲ **3918**
3533	76525	70949	62260	76364	09/92-08/99	➲ **3902**
3534	76505	70939	62259	76506	10/92-09/99	➲ **3907**
3535	76678	71015	62335	76677	11/92-11/05	
3536	76383	70897	62207	76384	02/93-06/08	
3537	76513	70943	62249	76514	03/93-04/98	➲ **3811**
3538	76515	70944	62253	76516	04/93-06/96	➲ **3809**
3539	76862	71115	62122	76861	06/93-04/05	
3540	76864	71116	62128	76863	07/93-04/05	
3541	76704	71028	62238	76703	07/93-05/98	➲ **3812**
3542	76479	70926	62127	76480	09/93-04/05	
3543	76900	71134	62137	76899	10/93-11/04	
3544	76894	71131	62454	76892	11/93-09/05	
3545	76876	71122	62121	76875	11/93-10/05	
3546	76688	71020	62339	76687	12/93-05/04	
3547	76896	71132	62126	76895	01/94-10/05	
3548	76904	71136	62452	76903	02/94-08/05	
3549	76708	71030	62132	76707	02/94-10/04	
3550	76489	70931	62350	76490	02/94-09/99	➲ **3906**
3551	76714	71033	62456	76465	02/94-12/04	
3552	76716	71034	62353	76715	03/94-05/04	
3553	76914	71141	62241	76913	03/94-05/05	
3554	76906	71137	62461	76905	03/94-11/04	
3555	76866	71117	62140	76865	04/94-05/04	
3556	76886	71127	62457	76885	05/94-11/04	
3557	76870	71119	62437	76869	05/94-05/04	
3558	76351	70881	62447	76352	05/94-05/04	
3559	76485	70929	62439	76486	06/94-05/04	
3560	76898	71133	62191	76897	06/94-09/05	
3561	76868	71118	62453	76867	07/94-07/04	
3562	76908	71138	62129	76907	07/94-10/05	
3563	76874	71121	62438	76873	07/94-07/04	
3564	76884	71126	62458	76883	07/94-12/05	
3565	76878	71123	62134	76877	08/94-10/05	
3566	76916	71142	62443	76915	09/94-12/04	
3567	76872	71120	62138	76871	09/94-06/02	➲ *3401*
3568	76888	71128	62440	76887	10/94-10/05	
3569	76343	70877	62448	76344	11/94-04/05	
3570	76910	71139	62187	76909	11/94-11/04	
3571	76928	71148	62463	76927	11/94-12/04	
3572	76880	71124	62468	76879	12/94-06/05	
3573	76920	71144	62444	76919	12/94-07/05	
3574	76930	71149	62464	76929	12/94-08/05	
3575	76932	71150	62469	76931	12/94-11/04	
3576	76361	70890	62196	76362	01/95-04/05	
3577	76934	71151	62470	76933	01/95-04/96	
3577	76934	71151	*62459*	76933	04/96-06/05	
3578	76355	70883	62193	76356	01/95-08/04	
3579	76936	71152	62471	76935	01/95-08/05	
3580	76359	70885	62195	76360	02/95-08/02	
3580	76359	70885	62195	76360	04/03-08/04	
3581	76365	70888	62198	76366	02/95-03/05	
3582	76275	71130	62472	76891	02/95-05/04	
3583	76938	71153	62450	76937	02/95-07/05	
3584	76882	71125	62473	76881	03/95-08/05	
3585	76940	71154	62445	76939	03/95-07/05	
3586	76922	71145	62474	76921	03/95-08/05	
3587	76926	71147	62465	76925	05/95-10/05	
3588	76924	71146	62467	76923	05/95-05/04	
3589	76912	71140	62466	76911	06/95-07/05	
3590	76942	71155	62460	76941	07/95-10/05	
3591	76918	71143	62475	76917	09/95-06/05	

Class 423/1 4-VEP

Outer Suburban Units
660-850V dc third rail
3801-3812

Porterbrook units renumbered to differentiate them from Angel Trains units.

	DTCsoL	*TSO*	*MBSO*	*DTCsoL*		
3801	76521	70947	62229	76522	08/95-05/04	
3802	76533	70953	62188	76534	08/95-07/04	
3803	76493	70933	62263	76494	09/95-02/05	
3804	76367	70889	62204	76368	10/95-12/04	
3805	76539	70956	62211	76540	09/95-02/05	
3806	76537	70955	62212	76538	08/95-12/04	
3807	76541	70957	62264	76542	08/95-12/04	
3808	76549	70961	62248	76550	08/95-02/05	
3809	76515	70944	62253	76516	06/96-04/05	
3810	76710	71031	62252	76709	06/96-04/05	
3811	76513	70943	62249	76514	04/98-02/05	
3812	76704	71028	62238	76703	05/98-04/05	

Class 423/8 4-VIP

Outer-Suburban Units
660-750V dc third rail
3813-3844

Temporary units with first class at one end only.

	DTSsoL	*TSO*	*MBSO*	*DTCsoL*		
3813	76342	71003	62125	76653	09/03-11/04	
3814	76341	70876	62228	76654	09/03-10/04	
3821	76711	70951	62262	76530	09/03-08/05	
3822	76712	71032	62351	76529	09/03-08/05	
3841	76689	70946	62326	76520	09/03-07/04	
3842	76363	70887	62343	76519	09/03-07/05	
3843	76489	70931	62350	76681	09/03-04/05	
3844	76682	71017	62231	76490	09/03-07/05	

Class 423/2 4-VOP

Outer-Suburban Units
660-750V dc third rail
3901-3919

Downgraded to second class for the South London Metro services.

	DTSsoL	*TSO*	*MBSO*	*DTSsoL*		
3901	76401	70906	62227	76402	05/99-08/05	
3902	76525	70949	62260	76364	08/99-04/05	
3903	76535	70954	62213	76536	07/99-07/05	
3904	76692	71022	62336	76691	07/99-04/05	
3905	76397	70904	62266	76398	08/99-04/05	
3906	76489	70931	62350	76490	09/99-09/03	➲ *3843*
3907	76505	70939	62259	76506	09/99-03/05	
3908	76441	70907	62265	76442	10/99-06/05	
3909	76706	71029	62341	76705	09/99-11/04	
3910	76529	70951	62262	76530	10/99-09/03	➲ *3821*
3911	76547	70960	62247	76548	11/99-08/05	
3912	76491	70932	62216	76492	11/99-07/05	
3913	76654	71003	62125	76653	11/99-09/03	➲ *3813*
3914	76519	70946	62326	76520	11/99-09/03	➲ *3841*
3915	76523	70948	62255	76524	12/99-02/05	
3916	76517	70945	62258	76518	12/99-07/05	
3917	76557	70965	62232	76558	12/99-10/04	
3918	76527	70950	62321	76528	01/00-04/05	
3919	76553	70963	62317	76554	01/00-07/05	

Class 424 Classic

Adtranz Classic Prototype
660-750V dc third rail
4001

76112 was rebuilt by Adtranz in 1997 to evaluate a proposal to reuse the underframes from CEP, CIG and VEP vehicles with an aluminium 'Networker' body. This was in an attempt to find a cheaper way of replacing old stock. The vehicle was displayed at Victoria in 1998, but the project foundered after the strength of early underframes caused concern when involved in accidents.

	DTS	
4001	76112	97-

Class 414/2 2-HAP

Outer-Suburban Units
660-750V dc third rail
4201

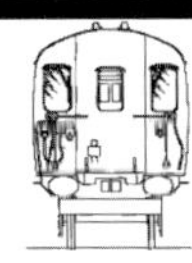

	DMBSO	*DTCsoL*		
4201	65405	77127	07/88-09/91	➲ *3333*

Class 414/3 2-HAP

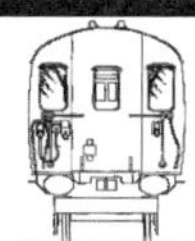

Outer-Suburban Units
660-750V dc third rail
4301-4322

	DMBSO	DTCsoL		
4301	61249	75369	07/88-07/91	
4302	61260	75380	06/88-07/91	
4303	61261	75381	05/88-09/91	➲ *3325*
4304	61262	75382	12/87-09/91	➲ *3323*
4305	61268	75388	04/88-09/91	➲ *3321*
4306	61270	75390	08/87-09/91	➲ *3324*
4307	61273	75393	10/87-09/91	➲ *3323*
4308	61275	75395	07/87-03/95	
4309	61276	75396	07/87-03/95	
4310	61278	75398	05/88-09/91	➲ *3321*
4311	61287	75407	07/87-03/95	
4312	61288	75408	07/88-07/91	
4313	61290	75410	07/87-03/95	
4314	61294	75414	07/87-11/94	
4315	61295	75415	11/87-09/91	➲ *3322*
4316	61296	75416	12/87-07/91	
4317	61298	75418	04/87-09/91	➲ *3325*
4318	61300	75420	05/87-09/91	➲ *3322*
4319	61303	75423	06/87-09/91	➲ *3324*
4320	61654	75706	11/87-07/91	
4321	61668	75720	05/88-05/92	
4322	61683	75735	06/88-09/91	➲ *3333*

5001-5281 Many units from the old series still ran in this period

Class 415/4 4-EPB

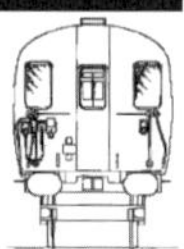

SR Suburban Units Facelifted
660-750V dc third rail
5401-5497

	DMBSO	TS	TS	DMBSO		
5401	14556	15449	15450	14521	03/77-03/94	
5402	14449	15020	15351	14407	03/80-01/85	
5402	14449	*15464*	*15465*	14407	01/85-04/93	
5403	14285	15221	15174	14286	09/80-11/94	
5404	14435	15036	15406	14436	10/80-04/94	
5405	14470	15053	15216	14469	03/81-01/94	
5406	14303	15230	15285	14356	01/81-05/92	➲Dep
5407	14428	15392	15060	14427	04/81-01/93	
5408	14297	15227	15313	14298	04/81-07/93	
5409	14206	15047	15065	14494	04/81-04/93	
5410	14528	15304	15386	14527	06/81-01/85	
5410	14528	15304	15386	*14540*	01/85-01/93	
5411	14475	15056	15192	14476	05/81-02/93	
5412	14415	15451	15452	14304	06/81-04/93	
5413	14396	15326	15191	14395	07/81-12/93	
5414	14441	15039	15182	14442	07/81-03/94	
5415	14466	15051	15040	14465	09/81-02/94	
5416	14421	15389	15324	14422	07/81-11/92	
5417	14478	15057	15041	14477	10/81-10/91	
5418	14282	15219	15063	14443	09/81-10/91	
5419	14473	15055	15058	14474	11/81-09/88	
5419	14473	15055	15058	14474	10/88-04/93	
5420	14240	15198	15202	14239	09/81-12/92	
5421	14500	15068	15073	14499	12/81-10/93	
5422	14467	15209	15050	14468	10/81-04/94	
5423	14511	15074	15212	14512	12/81-08/93	
5424	14447	15042	15052	14448	11/81-06/93	
5425	14538	15453	15454	14542	12/81-07/86	
5425	14538	15453	15454	*14570*	07/86-01/93	
5426	14517	15077	15066	14518	01/82-06/93	
5427	14453	15045	15046	14454	01/82-09/93	
5428	14430	15393	15061	14429	01/82-08/93	
5429	14410	15333	15383	14409	01/82-02/93	
5430	14509	15437	15438	14496	03/82-10/93	
5431	14423	15390	15400	14424	02/82-07/93	
5432	14486	15044	15447	14416	02/82-11/93	
5433	14472	15054	15424	14471	02/82-06/93	
5434	14497	15067	15455	14498	04/82-07/94	
5435	14491	15403	15431	14267	04/82-09/93	
5436	14534	15456	15457	14543	05/82-10/93	
5437	14411	15384	15394	14412	05/82-11/93	
5438	14530	15459	15458	14547	06/82-12/93	
5439	14487	15062	15432	14488	05/82-05/90	
5440	14514	15075	15445	14513	08/82-01/92	
5441	14397	15327	15377	14398	06/82-08/94	
5442	14537	15460	15461	14554	07/82-07/94	
5443	14504	15070	15440	14503	11/82-11/94	
5444	14535	15463	15462	14553	09/82-07/94	
5445	14540	15464	15465	14529	03/82-01/85	
5445	*14527*	*15020*	*15351*	14529	01/85-04/94	
5446	14531	15466	15467	14541	09/82-01/93	
5447	14532	15468	15469	14550	11/82-01/93	
5447	*14013*	15468	15469	14550	01/93-11/93	
5448	14539	15470	15471	14548	12/82-02/93	
5449	14438	15037	15407	14437	12/82-02/92	
5449	14438	*15291*	15407	14437	02/92-09/93	
5450	14533	15472	15473	14552	02/83-02/92	
5451	14526	15474	15475	14551	03/83-11/91	
5452	14546	15476	15477	14536	04/83-02/88	
5452	*14563*	15476	15477	14536	02/88-04/94	
5453	14525	15478	15479	14545	05/83-07/93	
5454	14524	15480	15481	14555	08/83-09/91	
5454	14524	15480	15481	*14264*	09/91-07/93	
5455	14062	15023	15027	14054	09/84-11/93	
5456	14482	15059	15001	14481	10/84-03/94	
5457	14502	15069	15439	14501	11/84-11/93	
5458	14431	15034	15404	14432	11/84-04/94	
5459	14505	15071	15441	14506	12/84-01/94	
5460	14515	15076	15446	14516	01/85-02/94	
5461	14519	15078	15448	14520	02/85-11/94	
5462	14021	15011	15111	14022	02/85-12/93	
5463	14037	15019	15119	14038	03/85-06/94	
5464	14081	15166	15159	14082	04/85-05/94	
5465	14350	15208	15196	14236	04/85-07/94	
5466	14004	15002	15220	14003	05/85-05/94	
5467	14006	15003	15177	14005	05/85-03/91	
5467	14006	*15062*	15177	14005	03/91-08/94	
5468	14212	15184	15332	14211	06/85-04/92	
5469	14007	15004	15201	14008	06/85-10/91	
5470	14315	15286	15215	14316	06/85-01/93	
5471	14255	15206	15231	14256	06/85-07/94	
5472	14508	15295	15169	14458	08/85-07/94	
5473	14058	15170	15029	14493	08/85-02/95	
5474	14065	15033	15224	14066	08/85-01/94	
5475	14019	15010	15048	14020	08/85-05/93	
5476	14016	15316	15319	14015	08/85-07/92	
5477	14057	15233	15180	14013	09/85-01/93	
5478	14059	15030	15167	14060	09/85-04/93	
5479	14322	15289	15317	14321	10/85-02/94	
5480	14264	15210	15291	14263	10/85-09/91	
5480	*14555*	15210	15291	14263	09/91-02/92	
5481	14330	15293	15226	14329	10/85-02/94	
5482	14017	15009	15297	14018	11/85-02/94	
5483	14052	15175	15329	14051	11/85-05/94	
5484	14061	15031	15308	14046	12/85-05/91	
5485	14105	15178	15185	14106	12/85-02/94	
5486	14071	15161	15125	14072	01/86-04/92	
5486	*14211*	15161	15125	14072	04/92-08/94	
5487	14361	15309	15359	14362	03/86-06/94	
5488	14386	15321	15371	14385	04/86-08/94	
5489	14024	15012	15112	14023	05/86-08/94	
5490	14205	15433	15128	14056	06/86-05/94	
5491	14029	15136	15115	14030	07/86-08/94	
5492	14223	15246	15240	14224	08/86-11/93	
5493	14028	15237	15114	14027	10/86-02/93	
5494	14073	15236	15137	14074	11/86-02/93	
5495	14095	15265	15148	14096	12/86-08/93	
5496	14400	15336	15378	14399	01/87-08/93	
5497	14246	15104	15251	14245	02/87-08/93	

Class 415/5 4-EPB

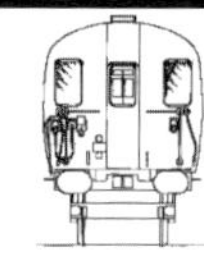

SR Suburban Units Facelifted
660-750V dc third rail
5501-5532

	DMBSO	TS	TS	DMBSO	
5501	14249	15294	15015	14250	05/88-05/91
5502	14366	15311	15318	14365	05/88-10/91
5503	14279	15288	15218	14359	05/88-10/91
5504	14076	15163	15302	14075	04/88-01/91
5505	14323	15290	15296	14324	05/88-05/90
5506	14302	15229	15232	14301	04/88-01/91
5507	14341	15299	15038	14342	04/88-05/90
5508	14036	15018	15164	14035	04/88-10/91
5509	14238	15197	15199	14237	04/88-05/90
5510	14344	15193	15084	14343	07/88-03/91
5511	14031	15016	15301	14032	05/88-05/90
5512	14210	15183	15223	14209	04/88-05/90
5513	14357	15307	15310	14358	05/88-05/91
5514	14367	15312	15330	14368	05/88-05/91
5515	14413	15385	15387	14414	04/88-08/91
5516	14063	15032	15211	14064	05/88-05/91
5517	14043	15022	15165	14044	05/88-01/91
5518	14293	15225	15322	14294	05/88-10/91

5519	14383	15217	15320	14274	05/88-10/91	
5520	14221	15189	15323	14222	05/88-10/91	
5521	14050	15213	15388	14270	05/88-07/91	
5522	14394	15325	15306	14393	05/88-10/91	
5523	14232	15194	15204	14231	04/88-01/91	➲ *5280*
5524	14287	15222	15284	14288	05/88-10/91	
5525	14272	15214	15049	14271	04/88-07/91	
5526	14374	15315	15391	14349	05/88-07/91	➲ *5281*
5527	14234	15195	15298	14233	04/88-05/91	
5528	14257	15207	15305	14258	05/88-10/90	➲ *5279*
5529	14085	15168	15176	14086	04/88-10/90	➲ *5278*
5530	14201	15179	15081	14202	04/88-01/91	
5531	14010	15005	15287	14009	04/88-05/91	
5532	14025	15013	15160	14026	05/88-06/91	➲ *Dep*

Class 415/6 4-EPB

Suburban Units

660-750V dc third rail

5601-5628

	DMBS	*TSso*	*TSso*	*DMBS*		
5601	61550	70409	70410	61551	07/87-05/93	
5602	61582	70441	70442	61583	07/87-09/93	
5602	*61550*	*70409*	70442	61583	09/93-02/95	
5603	61538	70397	70398	61539	06/87-11/94	
5604	61588	70447	70448	[illegible]	[illegible]	
5605	61540	70399	70400	61541	07/87-01/95	
5606	61536	70395	70396	61537	07/87-02/95	
5607	61590	70449	70450	61591	07/87-09/88	➲ **5626**
5608	61600	70459	70460	61601	06/87-09/88	➲ **5627**
5609	61604	70463	70464	61605	07/87-10/88	➲ **5628**
5610	61566	70425	70426	61567	07/87-11/94	
5611	61570	70429	70430	61571	07/87-10/94	
5612	61542	70401	70402	61543	06/87-03/95	
5613	61532	70391	70392	61533	07/87-03/95	
5614	61546	70405	70406	61547	06/87-05/93	
5614	61546	70405	70406	*61551*	05/93-03/95	
5615	61612	70471	70472	61613	07/87-02/95	
5616	61576	70435	70436	61577	07/87-02/95	
5617	61592	70451	70452	61593	07/87-03/95	
5618	61584	70443	70444	61585	07/87-05/91	
5619	61562	70421	70422	61563	07/87-01/95	
5620	61602	70461	70462	61603	07/87-01/95	
5621	61520	70379	70380	61521	07/87-02/95	
5622	61560	70419	70420	61561	07/87-01/95	
5623	61578	70437	70438	61579	07/87-02/92	
5623	61578	70437	70438	*61584*	02/92-02/95	
5624	61572	70431	70432	61573	07/87-03/95	
5625	61608	70455	70468	61609	07/87-03/95	
5626	61590	70449	70450	61591	09/88-10/94	
5627	61600	70459	70460	61601	09/88-03/95	
5628	61604	70463	70464	61605	10/88-10/94	

Class 416/2 2-EPB

Suburban Units

660-750V dc third rail

6202-6279

	DMBSO	*DTSso*		
6202	65301	77501	04/85-05/94	
6203	65302	77502	03/85-05/93	
6205	65304	77504	04/85-05/93	
6206	65305	77505	05/85-12/85	➲ **6406**
6207	65306	77506	01/85-05/91	
6210	65309	75636	04/85-01/86	
6212	65326	77511	03/85-09/91	
6213	65327	77512	04/85-01/95	
6214	65328	77513	09/84-12/86	➲ **6416**
6215	65329	77514	08/84-11/85	➲ **6404**
6216	65330	77515	03/85-01/86	➲ **6407**
6217	65331	77516	09/84- 94	➲ **931002**
6218	65332	77517	09/84-09/91	
6219	65333	77518	03/85-02/86	➲ **6411**
6220	65334	77519	05/85-03/86	➲ **6410**
6221	65335	77520	09/84-10/94	
6222	65336	77521	03/85-01/92	
6223	65337	77522	12/84-10/94	
6224	65338	77523	01/85-01/94	
6225	65339	77524	08/84-10/94	
6226	65340	77525	02/85-05/94	
6227	65341	77526	04/85-01/93	
6228	65342	77527	08/84-02/86	➲ **6408**
6229	65343	77528	08/84-05/91	
6230	65344	77529	12/84-05/94	
6231	65345	77530	03/85-05/93	
6232	65346	77531	07/85-09/85	➲ **6401**
6233	65347	77532	08/84-12/86	➲ **6405**
6234	65348	77533	09/84-09/86	➲ **6415**
6235	65349	77534	05/85-11/94	
6236	65350	77535	09/84-10/94	
6237	65351	77536	05/85-11/94	
6238	65352	77537	05/85-09/91	
6238	65352	*77151*	09/91-02/92	
6239	65353	77538	05/85-06/93	
6240	65354	77539	09/84-08/94	
6241	65355	77540	08/84-01/93	
6242	65356	77541	03/85-10/85	➲ **6403**
6243	65357	77542	03/85-01/92	
6244	65358	77543	08/84-09/91	
6245	65359	77544	04/85-11/94	
6246	65360	77545	01/85-02/87	➲ **6418**
6247	65361	77546	04/85-05/93	
6248	65362	77547	04/85-10/85	➲ **6402**
6249	65363	77548	05/85-05/94	
6250	65364	77549	03/85-03/86	➲ **6412**
6251	65365	77550	02/85-10/94	
6252	65366	77551	08/84-01/87	➲ **6417**
6253	65367	77552	07/84-05/93	
6254	65368	77553	07/84-06/86	➲ **6414**
6255	65369	77554	10/84-02/94	
6256	65370	77555	08/84-02/94	
6257	65371	77556	[illegible]-09/91	
6258	65372	77557	04/85-05/86	➲ **6413**
6259	65373	77558	10/84-01/95	
6260	65374	77559	12/84-01/94	
6261	65375	77560	09/84-02/94	
6262	65376	77561	07/84-01/94	
6263	65377	77562	12/84-01/95	
6264	65378	77563	03/85-12/94	
6265	65379	77564	07/84-01/94	
6267	65381	77566	09/84-04/94	
6268	65382	77567	09/84-01/94	
6269	65307	77568	04/85-12/91	
6270	65384	77569	08/84-03/94	
6271	65385	77570	09/84-05/94	
6272	65386	77571	09/84-05/93	
6273	65387	77572	08/84-01/95	
6274	65388	77573	08/84-04/94	
6275	65389	77574	08/84-04/94	
6276	65390	77575	08/84-05/91	
6277	65391	77576	08/84-11/94	
6278	65392	77577	09/84-01/94	
6279	65435	77578	08/84-05/87	

Class 416/2 2-EPB

Suburban Units

660-750V dc third rail

6281-6293

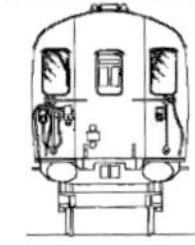

	DMBSO	*DTSso*		
6281	65311	77100	08/84-10/84	
6282	65312	77101	08/84-10/84	
6283	65313	77102	08/84-10/84	
6284	65314	77103	08/84-10/84	
6285	65315	77104	08/84-10/84	
6286	65316	77105	08/84-10/84	
6287	65317	77106	09/84-10/84	
6289	65319	77108	09/84-10/84	➲ **050**
6290	65320	77109	08/84-10/84	
6291	65321	77110	09/84-10/84	
6292	65322	77111	08/84-10/84	
6293	65323	77112	08/84-10/84	

Class 416/3 2-EPB

Suburban Units

660-750V dc third rail

6301-6335

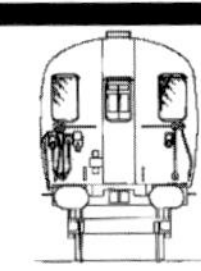

	DMBSO	*DTSso*	
6301	14577	16121	03/82-01/94
6302	14580	16124	03/82-03/94
6303	14576	16120	04/82-05/93
6304	14589	16133	04/82-05/93
6305	14587	16131	07/82-01/94
6306	14571	16115	10/82-08/94
6307	14573	16117	06/83-03/95
6308	14564	16108	06/83-03/95
6309	14562	16106	10/83-03/95

6310	14574	16118	01/84-11/94
6311	14565	16109	02/84-11/94
6312	14579	16123	02/84-05/94
6313	14558	16102	03/84-09/88
6313	14558	16102	10/88-07/93
6314	14586	16130	04/84-07/93
6315	14590	16134	04/84-10/94
6316	14559	16103	05/84-07/94
6317	14578	16122	05/84-07/93
6318	14566	16110	06/84-10/94
6319	14568	16112	07/84-09/94
6320	14561	16105	07/84-01/95
6321	14584	16128	07/84-12/86
6321	*14283*	16128	12/86-03/95
6322	14575	16119	08/84-12/89
6322	*14488*	16119	05/90-05/93
6323	14581	16125	08/84-01/94
6324	14560	16104	09/84-06/94
6325	14567	16111	10/84-06/94
6326	14585	16129	01/85-08/94
6327	14572	16116	02/85-05/93
6328	14582	16126	03/85-04/94
6329	14570	16114	03/85-07/86
6329	*14542*	16114	07/86-03/95
6330	14588	16132	05/85-03/95
6331	14583	16127	05/85-02/95
6332	14569	16113	06/85-03/95
6333	14557	16101	06/85-05/93
6334	14563	16107	06/85-02/88
6334	*14546*	16107	02/88-07/93
6335	14473	16102	09/88-10/88

Class 416/4 2-EPB
Suburban Units
660-750V dc third rail
6401-6418

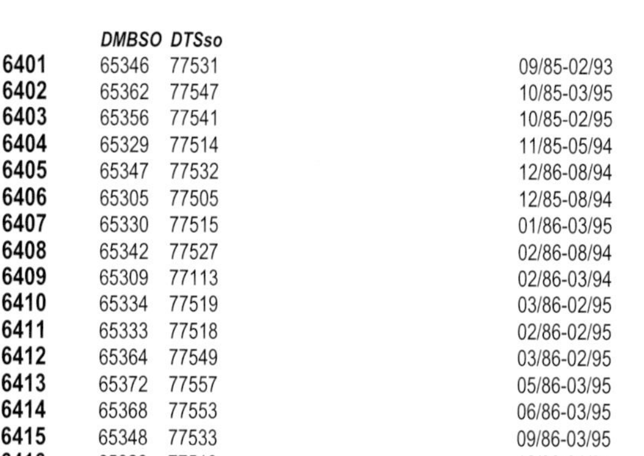

	DMBSO	*DTSso*	
6401	65346	77531	09/85-02/93
6402	65362	77547	10/85-03/95
6403	65356	77541	10/85-02/95
6404	65329	77514	11/85-05/94
6405	65347	77532	12/86-08/94
6406	65305	77505	12/85-08/94
6407	65330	77515	01/86-03/95
6408	65342	77527	02/86-08/94
6409	65309	77113	02/86-03/94
6410	65334	77519	03/86-02/95
6411	65333	77518	02/86-02/95
6412	65364	77549	03/86-02/95
6413	65372	77557	05/86-03/95
6414	65368	77553	06/86-03/95
6415	65348	77533	09/86-03/95
6416	65328	77513	12/86-01/94
6417	65366	77551	01/87-11/94
6418	65360	77545	02/87-01/94

Class 438 4-TC
Bournemouth Line Trailer Units
660-850V dc third rail (unpowered)
8001-8034

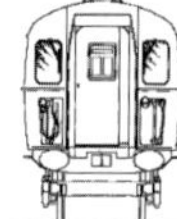

	DTSO	*TBSK*	*TFK*	*DTSO*		
8001	76332	70812	70844	76270	07/86-10/88	
8001	76332	*70821*	70844	76270	10/88-07/91	
8001	76332	70821	76270		07/91-09/92	
8002	76271	70813	70845	76272	06/86-12/86	➲ *2802*
8003	76274	70814	70846	76273	11/86-06/87	➲ *2805*
8004	76276	70815	70847	76275	10/86-09/88	➲ **2808**
8004	76276	70815	70847	76275	01/89-05/90	
8006	76279	70817	70849	76280	06/86-05/90	
8007	76282	70818	70850	76281	12/86-07/89	
8008	76283	70819	70851	76284	10/86-12/86	➲ *2801*
8010	76287	70821	70853	76288	08/86-10/88	
8010	76287	*70812*	70853	76288	10/88-04/90	➲ *8110*
8011	76289	70822	70854	76290	10/86-02/87	➲ *2804*
8012	76291	70823	70855	76292	06/86-08/88	
8012	76291	*70858*	70855	76292	08/88-09/88	
8012	76291	*70828*	70858	76292	09/88-05/91	
8013	76294	70824	70856	76293	05/86-06/87	➲ *2806*
8014	76296	70825	70857	76295	09/86-06/89	
8014	76296	70825	*70869*	76295	06/89-05/91	
8015	76298	70826	70858	76297	10/86-06/88	
8015	76298	*71158*	70858	76297	06/88-08/88	
8015	76298	71158	*70823*	76297	08/88-09/88	
8015	76298	*70823*	*70855*	76297	09/88-05/91	
8016	76300	70827	70859	76299	06/86-10/88	
8017	76301	70828	70860	76302	10/86-09/88	
8017	76301	*70826*	70860	76302	09/88-09/91	➲ **417**
8018	76304	70829	70861	76303	10/86-05/90	
8019	76305	70830	70862	76306	08/86-08/88	
8020	76308	70831	70863	76307	09/86-05/89	
8021	76310	70832	70864	76309	10/86-02/89	
8022	76311	70833	70865	76312	05/86-08/88	
8023	76314	70834	70866	76313	06/86-04/90	
8024	76315	70835	70867	76316	05/86-05/88	
8025	76318	70836	70868	76317	05/86-10/88	
8026	76320	70837	70869	76319	08/86-05/89	
8027	76322	70838	70870	76321	06/86-04/90	
8028	76323	70839	70871	76324	06/86-04/90	
8029	76325	70840	71162	76326	10/86-07/88	
8030	76327	70841	71163	76328	09/86-08/88	
8031	76329	70842	71164	76330	10/86-01/89	➲ **2809**
8031	76329	70842	71164	76330	05/89-08/89	
8032	76943	70843	71165	76944	06/86-07/88	
8033	76945	71160	71166	76946	09/86-06/87	
8034	76947	71161	71167	76948	09/86-09/88	

Class 438/1 4-TCT/5-TCT/3-TC
Bournemouth Line Trailer Units
660-850V dc third rail (unpowered)
8101-8106

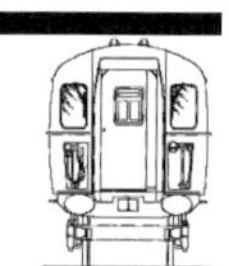

	DTSO	*TBSK*	*TFK*	*DTSO*			
8101	76283	70819	70852	76284		12/87-05/88	
8101	76283	70819	70852	*70856*	76284	05/88-08/88	
8102	76271	70814	70845	76272		01/88-04/88	
8102	76271	70814	76272			04/88-05/88	
8103	76285	70820	70846	76286		12/87-05/88	➲ *2804*
8104	76289	70822	70854	76290		12/87-04/88	
8104	76289	70822	76290			04/88-05/88	
8105	76274	70813	70851	76273		12/87-04/88	➲ *2805*
8106	76294	70824	70856	76293		12/87-05/88	➲ *2806*
8106	76294	70824	*70845*	76293		09/88-10/88	

Class 438/1 5-TC
Bournemouth Line Trailer Units
660-850V dc third rail (unpowered)
8110

	DTSO	*TBSK*	*TFK*	*TBSK*	*DTSO*	
8110	76287	70812	70859	70824	76288	06/90-03/91

Class 488
Gatwick Trailer Units
660-750V dc third rail (unpowered)
8201-8210, 8301-8319

In 1984 the Airport Express service from London Victoria to Gatwick airport was modernised. The service was powered by Class 73 electro-diesel locomotives, working in push-pull mode with converted Mark 2f loco hauled stock and a Gatwick luggage van at the other end of the formation.

The Mark 2f vehicles were formed into two and three car sets and were classified 488. Ten trains of up to eight coaches of these sets were formed.

Class 488/2

	TFOLH	*TSOLH*	
8201	72500	72638	01/84-01/01
8202	72501	72639	01/84-07/88
8202	72501	*72617*	07/88- 04
8203	72502	72640	03/84-01/01
8204	72503	72641	03/84-09/00
8205	72504	72628	04/84-02/01
8206	72505	72629	04/84- 04
8207	72506	72642	05/84-08/02
8208	72507	72643	05/84-07/00
8209	72508	72644	05/84- 04
8210	72509	72635	05/84-11/01

Class 488/3

	TSOLH	TOLS	TSOLH	
8301	72600	72700	72601	11/83-08/85
8302	72602	72701	72604	03/84-05/02
8303	72603	72702	72608	03/84-09/00
8304	72606	72703	72611	12/83-01/01
8305	72605	72704	72609	01/84-09/00
8306	72607	72705	72610	02/84-11/01
8307	72612	72706	72613	02/84-01/01
8308	72614	72707	72615	02/84-09/00
8309	72616	72708	72617	03/84-07/88
8309	72616	72708	*72639*	08/88-10/01
8310	72618	72709	72619	03/84-08/02
8311	72620	72710	72621	03/84- 05
8312	72622	72711	72623	04/84-07/00
8313	72624	72712	72625	04/84- 04
8314	72626	72713	72627	05/84-09/00
8315	72636	72714	72645	05/84-07/00
8316	72630	72715	72631	05/84-10/01
8317	72632	72716	72633	05/84-11/01
8318	72634	72717	72637	06/84-09/00
8319	72646	72718	72647	06/84-09/00

Class 489 1-GLV
Gatwick Trailer Units
660-750V dc third rail
9101-9110

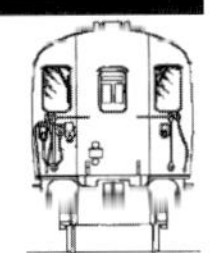

Ten Class 489 Gatwick Luggage Vans were formed to run with the Class 488 sets on the Airport Express service. They were converted from Class 414 HAP DMBS vehicles.

	DMLV	
9101	68500	01/84-11/01
9102	68501	01/84-07/00
9103	68502	02/84-02/01
9104	68503	02/84- 05
9105	68504	03/84-01/01
9106	68505	03/84-09/00
9107	68506	03/84-08/02
9108	68507	04/84- 04
9109	68508	04/84-10/01
9110	68509	05/84- 05

Departmental Stock

Instruction Unit

S10	DS40	DS41	DS42		04/56- 71	➲**053**

Mobile Test Unit

S15	DS70057	DS70058		61- 67

***Mobile Test Unit** (Conversion cancelled)*

S15[2]	DS70258	DS70260	DS70261	DS70259	-12/69
S90	DS347	DS348			-11/61
S91	DS349	DS350			-11/61

De-icing Units

S92	DS70044	DS70045	09/60-01/62	
S92	*DS70173*	DS70045	02/62- 68	➲**011**
S93	DS70090	DS70091	09/60- 68	➲**012**
S94	DS70092	DS70093	09/60- 68	➲**013**
S95	DS70094	DS70095	09/60- 68	➲**014**
S96	DS70096	DS70097	09/60- 68	➲**015**
S97	DS70098	DS70099	10/60- 68	➲**016**
S98	DS70100	DS70101	10/60- 68	➲**017**
S99	DS70102	DS70103	10/60- 68	➲**018**
S100	DS70104	DS70105	10/60- 68	➲**019**
S101	DS70106	DS70107	10/60- 68	➲**020**

Class 930 De-icing Units and Sandite Units

001	DS70268	S65364	07/68- 69	
001	DS70268	DS70273	69- 86	
001	ADB977365	ADB977366	86- 87	
001	ADB977365	*ADB977368*	87- 90	
002	DS70269	DS70271	69- 78	
002[3]	DS70270	DS70272	82- 87	
002[3]	*ADB977367*	ADB977366	87- 89	
003	DS70270	DS70272	69- 82	➲**002**[3]

De-icing Units

011	DS70173	DS70045	68- 79
012	DS70090	DS70091	68- 79
013	DS70092	DS70093	68- 79
014	DS70094	DS70095	68- 79
015	DS70096	DS70097	68- 79
016	DS70098	DS70099	68- 79
017	DS70100	DS70101	68- 79
018	DS70102	DS70103	68- 79
019	DS70104	DS70105	68- 79
020	DS70106	DS70107	68- 79

Class 930 De-icing Units and Sandite Units

002[2]	ADB975594	ADB975595	79- 82	➲**003**[2]
003[2]	ADB975594	ADB975595	82- *91*	➲**930003**
004	ADB975586	ADB975587	08/77-11/91	➲**930004**
005	ADB975588	ADB975589	77- *91*	➲**930005**
006	ADB975590	ADB975591	77- *91*	➲**930006**
007	ADB975592	ADB975593	77- *91*	➲**930007**
008	ADB975596	ADB975597	79- *91*	➲**930008**
009	ADB975598	ADB975599	79- *91*	➲**930009**
010	ADB975600	ADB975601	79- *91*	➲**930010**
011[2]	ADB975602	ADB975603	79- *91*	➲**930011**
012[2]	ADB975604	ADB975605	79- *91*	➲**930012**
013[2]	ADB975896	ADB975897	82- *91*	➲**930202**
015[2]	ADB977531	ADB977532	87- *91*	➲**930015**
016[2]	ADB977533	ADB977534	87- *91*	➲**930016**
017[2]	ADB977566	ADB977567	87- *91*	➲**930017**

Class 931 Stores Units

010	[illegible]	[illegible]	[illegible]
019[2]	ADB977068	ADB977069	02/87-06/91

Temporary Stores Unit

020[2]	ADB977213	ADB977214	02/84- 88

Class 931 Stores Units/Class 932 Tractor Unit

021	ADB977304	ADB977305	85- *91*	➲**932021**

Stores Units

022	DS70315	DS70318	04/70-12/83
023	DS70316	DS70317	05/70-02/84
024	ADB975250	ADB975251	73-12/84

Research Department Unit

024[2]	DS70321	DS70322	Unit **2037**	70- 75

Tractor Units

025	ADB977294	ADB977295	*05/85*-01/88

Class 930 Carriage Cleaning Fluid Unit

026	ADB977559	ADB977560	87- *90*	➲**062**

Research Units

051	ADB975027	ADB975028	ADB975029	69- 70
051	ADB975029	ADB975027	*ADB975030*	*70*-04/70
051	ADB975027	*ADB975030*		04/70-01/72
052	ADB975030	ADB975031	ADB975033	69- 70

Instruction Unit

053	DS40	DS41	DS42	71-05/74

Air Conditioning Test Unit

054	ADB975255	ADB975256	ADB975257	ADB975258	10/72- *75*

Instruction Unit

055	ADB975319	ADB975320	ADB975321	ADB975322	03/74-11/85

Service/Tractor Units

050	ADB977296	ADB977297	*91*-03/93	➲**932050**
051[2]	ADB977205	ADB977206	02/84-05/85	
052[2]	ADB977209	ADB977210	02/84- *89*	
053[2]	ADB977211	ADB977212	02/84- *90*	
054[2]	ADB977207	ADB977208	02/84- *90*	

Class 935 Prototype High Density Stock (PEP)

056	ADB975848	ADB975845	ADB975846	ADB975847	04/81- 85
057	ADB975844	ADB975849	ADB975850	ADB975851	80- 90

Class 931 Carriage Cleaning Fluid Unit

062	ADB977559	ADB977560	90- *91*

➲**931062**

Anglia Region Sandite Units

908	ADB977741	ADB977742	ADB977743	**305908**	05/92- 99	➲*937908*
996	ADB977598	ADB977599	ADB977600	**302996**	88- 96	➲*937996*
997	ADB977601	ADB977602	ADB977603	**302997**	88-11/92	➲*937997*
998	ADB977604	ADB977605	ADB977606	**302998**	88- 98	➲*937998*

SR Emergency Exercise Training Units

998	ADB977702	ADB977703	ADB977704	ADB977705	90- 91
999	ADB977688	ADB977689	ADB977690	ADB977691	90-03/92

Tractor Units

1053	ADB977505	ADB977507			02/87-03/93	⊃**930053**
1054	ADB977506	ADB977508			02/87- 96	⊃**930054**

Class 438 4-TC/6-TC Unit

8007	ADB977684	ADB977685	ADB977686	ADB977687	90- 92	
8007	ADB977684	ADB977685	*ADB977763* *ADB977764*	ADB977686 ADB977687 ☜	92- 94	

Special Duties Unit

303048	ADB977719	ADB977720	ADB977721	-

Demonstration/Test Unit

303999	TDB977711	TDB977712	TDB977713	03/91- *96*

InterCity Instruction Unit

305935	ADB977639	ADB977640	ADB977641	05/89-09/94

Crash Test Units

307101	ADB977668	ADB977669	ADB977670	ADB977671	11/91-03/93
307106	ADB977672	ADB977673	ADB977674	ADB977675	11/91-03/93
307121	ADB977676	ADB977677	ADB977678	ADB977679	11/91-03/93

Class 316 ex-Class 307 Test Unit (used for testing Class 323 equipment)
(Did not carry the departmental carriage numbers)

316999	ADB977708	ADB977709	ADB977710	03/93- 93	⊃**316997**
316997	ADB977708	ADB977709	ADB977710	93- 01	☜

Class 910 Brake Force Runner Sets

910001	72616	72708	72639	03- 06
910002	72612	72706	72613	03- 06
	72614	72707	72615	03- 04
	72630		72631	03- 06

Class 920 Prototype High Density Stock (PEP)

920001	ADB975430	ADB975431	ADB975432	05/75-04/86

Class 930 De-icing & Sandite Units

930001	ADB975604	ADB975605	08/97- *00*	
spare	ADB975598	ADB975605	*00- 04*	☜
930002	ADB975896	ADB975897	06/97- *04*	
930003	ADB975594	ADB975595	*91- 04*	
930004	ADB975586	ADB975587	11/91- *04*	
930005	ADB975588	ADB975589	*91- 03*	
930006	ADB975590	ADB975591	*91- 04*	
930007	ADB975592	ADB975593	*91- 03*	
930008	ADB975596	ADB975597	*91- 03*	
930009	ADB975598	ADB975599	*91- 00*	
930009	*ADB975604*	ADB975599	*00- 03*	☜
930010	ADB975600	ADB975601	*91- 04*	℗
930011	ADB975602	ADB975603	*91- 04*	
930012	ADB975604	ADB975605	*91*-08/97	⊃**930001**
930013	ADB975896	ADB975897	*91*-06/97	⊃**930002**
930014	ADB977207	ADB977609	90-06/97	⊃**930101**
930015	ADB977531	ADB977532	*91*-04/94	
930016	ADB977533	ADB977534	*91*-06/97	⊃**930102**
930017	ADB977566	ADB977567	*91*-10/97	⊃**930201**
930030	ADB977804	ADB977805	06/92-04/98	⊃**930202**
930031	ADB977864	ADB977865	08/93-10/97	⊃**930203**
930032	ADB977874	ADB977875	08/93-10/97	⊃**930204**
930033	ADB977871	ADB977872	08/93-06/97	⊃**930205**
930034	ADB977924	ADB977925	10/94-10/97	⊃**930206**
930053	ADB977505	ADB977507	*91*-03/93	
930054	ADB977506	ADB977508	*91*- 93	

Class 930 De-icing & Sandite Trailers

930078	ADB977578	89- *02*
930079	ADB977579	89- *02*

Class 930 Mobile Track Assessment Units

930080	DB977395	DB977396	07/91-04/94
930081	DB977397	DB977398	05/90-04/94

Class 930 Route LearningUnit/Training Unit

930082	ADB977861	ADB977862	ADB977863	05/93- *05*

Class 930/1 Tractor Unit

930101	ADB977207	ADB977609	06/97- *10*

Class 930/1 Sandite Unit

930102	ADB977533	ADB977534	06/97- *03*

Class 930/2 Sandite/De-icing/Tractor Units

930201	ADB977566	ADB977567	10/97- *05*
930202	ADB977804	ADB977805	04/98- *03*
930203	ADB977864	ADB977865	10/97- *04*
930204	ADB977874	ADB977875	10/97-06/09
930205	ADB977871	ADB977872	06/97- *05*
930206	ADB977924	ADB977925	10/97-09/09

Class 930 ATP Test Train Unit

930997	ADB977777	ADB977778	ADB977779	ADB977780	05/92-04/94

Class 931 Route Learning Units

931001	ADB977856	ADB977857	06/93- *04*
931002	ADB977917	ADB977918	94- *03*

Class 931 Carriage Cleaning Fluid Unit/Tractor Unit

931062	ADB977559	ADB977560	*The Sprinter*	*91- 04*

Class 931 ex-Class 419 Tractor Units

931090	68010	92- 99	
931091	68001	92- 98	
931092	68002	92- 03	
931093	68003	92- 98	⊃**9003**
931094	68004	92- 99	
931095	68005	92- 99	
931097	68007	92- 98	⊃**9007**
931098	68008	92- 99	
931099	68009	92- 98	⊃**9009**

Class 932 Tractor Units

932021	ADB977304	ADB977305	*91*-01/93
932050	ADB977296	ADB977297	*91*-03/93

Class 932 Test Units

932053	ADB977505	ADB977508	93- 96
932054	ADB977506	ADB977296	93- 96

Class 932 Tractor Units

932080	DB977395	DB977396	07/91-04/94
932081	DB977397	DB977398	05/90-04/94

Class 932 Test Units

932545	61358	70330	61359		04/97- 02
932620	61948	70653	70660	61949	01/93- 03

Class 936 Merseyrail Sandite Units

936001	ADB977345	ADB977346	86-09/97
936002	ADB977347	ADB977348	86-09/97
936003	ADB977349	ADB977350	*86- 02*

Class 936 Sandite Units

936103	ADB977844	ADB977845	ADB977846	10/93- *02*
936104	ADB977847	ADB977848	ADB977849	10/93-06/02

Class 936 Sandite Units

936501	ADB977385	ADB977386	04/87- 92

Class 937 Sandite & Tractor Units

937908	ADB977741	ADB977742	ADB977743	**305908**	05/92- 99
937990	DB977876	DB977877	DB977878	**308990**	09/94-05/02
937991	DB977926	DB977927	DB977928	**308991**	09/94- *02*
937996	ADB977598	ADB977599	ADB977600	**302996**	88- 96
937997	ADB977601	ADB977602	ADB977603	**302997**	88-11/92
937998	ADB977604	ADB977605	ADB977606	**302998**	88- 98

Class 960/1 Cab Signalling Test Unit

960101	977962	977963	977964	*West Coast Flyer*	*01*-02/09
960102	977965	977966	977967	*New Dalby*	*01*-02/09

Class 960 Hitachi 'V' Train

960201	977977	977978	977981	977980	12/02-03/07
spare	977979				12/02-

CMEE Test Units

ADB977307	ADB977309	ADB977308	(02/89)-

Mobile Track Assessment Unit

DB977543	DB977542	DB977545	DB977544	04/87- 92

Test Coaches

ADB977684	ADB977685	ADB977686	ADB977687	04/90- *96*
ADB977763	ADB977764			05/92-05/92

SR Radio Trials Units

ADB977729	ADB977730	-
ADB977731	ADB977732	92-05/92
ADB977733	ADB977734	-
ADB977735	ADB977736	-
ADB977737	ADB977738	92-11/92
ADB977739	ADB977740	-

Emergency Exercise Training Unit

ADB977797	ADB977798	ADB977799	ADB977800	-

Emergency Incident Unit

977919	977920	-

Conversion cancelled

977929	977930	977931	-

SR Towing Units

4202	8013	8014	03/54-01/55
4252	8738	8896	05/53-09/56
4302	8131	8132	02/61-11/61
4342	081269	081270	06/60-12/69
4402	8557	9810	02/53-06/53
4505	8736	8894	06/59-05/60
4543	081046	081047	09/56-05/59
4557	8741	8899	10/56-04/57
4559	8744	9802	03/55-10/57
4564	8746	9804	07/56-10/58

Shunting Unit

4623	11305	11306			82-	85

Thyristor Test Unit

4748	12789	10213	9028	8642	04/76-	76

Class 419 Tractor Units

9003	68003	98-	99
9007	68007	98-	99
9009	68009	98-	99

Above: One of the original 1903-built trains of clerestory roofed Mersey Railway stock is seen near the end of its life in June 1956 at Birkenhead Central. *J. W. Gahan*

Below: An amazing selection of enamel adverts overlooks a three-car overhead electric set at Victoria. *Ian Allan Library*

STAFFORD
Way out
1, 4 and 5
Waiting room

L. & N. W. AND L. E. R.
407J

WATFORD
B1
158
HELP YOUR BEANS GROW UP GIVE THEM A LADDER.

Above left: The AM10 (Class 310) units were built to work the longer distance services at the southern end of the LMR Western Lines electrified route. No 068 is seen at Nuneaton before working a service to Stafford on 14 August 1975. *Philip D. Hawkins*

Left: The LNWR and London Electric Railway joint tube stock was built in 1920 to allow through working from the Bakerloo Line through to the Watford line. Although built to tube dimensions the flooring was higher than usual as the trains served stations on the LNWR line with standard height platforms. No 407J was an LNWR-owned Driving Trailer vehicle, but it was not one of the vehicles retained by the LMS to work the Rickmansworth and Croxley Green services after the others were scrapped. *London Transport*

*Below left:*Class 501 units were normally formed in standard formations and they were known by the last three digits of the carriages. This number was not normally carried, but there were a few exceptions. When seen at Watford Junction on 1 May 1982, not only was this unit displaying the number 158 twice on the end, but the number on the jumper cable cover had the prefix 501, showing the full number 501158. *Michael J. Collins*

Above: In 1927 a joint order of GEC compartment stock was made for both the London area and the Southport line. DMBT M28310M was the last DMBT built for the Southport line and it is seen here at Aintree. *P. J. Sharpe*

Below: Motor M65446 and trailer M77165 of the BR Bury units are seen face to face at Bury on 1 March 1980. This was during the last month of operation at the original Bury station. *B. Watkins*

LIVERPOOL S
05
063

3
4
GIDEA PARK
98
081

GIDEA PARK
19
32s

Above left: Class 306 unit number 063 at Gidea Park on a service to Liverpool Street. This shows the units as converted to ac working. *P. J. Sharpe*

Left: Class 306 unit number 081 at Ilford on 15 September 1980. From this end of the unit the lower profile of the original cab roof can be seen. Before conversion from dc operation the pantograph was above the cab at this end. *John Fozard*

Below left: This interesting photo shows the two dc classes of unit working out of Liverpool Street before their conversion to ac working. On the left is Shenfield Line unit 19 (later Class 306 number 019) and on the right is Southend Line unit 32s (later Class 307 132). *G. M. Kichenside*

Above: Class 307 unit 122 is seen at Ilford on 25 June 1980 working an empty carriage stock train from Liverpool Street. After conversion to ac the front cab end carried a headcode box indicator between the cab windows. *M. L. Rogers*

Below: AM2 unit number 292 is seen heading a service to Chelmsford at Shenfield & Hutton Station. *P. J. Sharpe*

Left: Class 302 unit number 266 at Shoeburyness on 22 February 1981 working the 15.10 service to Fenchurch Street. *Brian Denton*

Below: On 10 September 1977 Class 305/1 unit number 424 is leaving Liverpool Street on the 12.40 service to Chingford. *Brian Morrison*

Bottom: Class 308/3 unit number 454 is seen at Thorrington on 12 June 1984 working the 10.25 Colchester to Clacton service. Note that this unit is incorrectly carrying the number 305454. The main difference between classes 305 and 308 was their electrical equipment. *Michael J. Collins*

Top: Class 305/2 unit number 512 heads Class 308/1 unit number 151 into Liverpool Street. They are working the 12.57 service from Bishop's Stortford on 10 September 1977. *Brian Morrison*

Above: Class 309 unit 608 heads No 611 at Colchester on the 09.50 Clacton to Liverpool Street service on 11 May 1977. No 608 retains its original wrap-around cab windows. *Brian Morrison*

Left: Class 309 unit number 626 is seen at Clacton on 12 January 1976. It carries the new revised cab windows. *Malcolm Pudduck*

MILNGAVIE
65
084

GOUROCK
105

302
302
91

Above left: Class 303 unit number 084 is at Bearsden on the 6 May 1974 working the 07.38 Springburn to Milngavie service. *D. G. Cameron*

Left: Class 311 unit number 105 is seen here at Port Glasgow working a service to Gourock. *G. M. Kichenside*

Below left: One of the short-lived 3-TC units, number 302 heads a train approaching Southampton on 8 February 1969. *John H. Bird*

Above: A typical Bournemouth line service formed of 4-TCs 423 and 426, powered by 4-REP unit 3013 at the rear. It is the 10.35 Waterloo to Weymouth service passing Vauxhall on 10 November 1984. The REP unit will be removed from the train at Bournemouth, with the TC units continuing to Weymouth hauled by a Class 33/1 diesel locomotive. *David Brown*

Below: The sole 7-TC set was disbanded in May 1969. Three surviving vehicles from the set are seen at Woking on 13 November 1969; S10573S, S10353S and S12107S, the others having been transferred into other sets. Out of these remaining three, only S10353S saw further service (in 4-SUB 4364). The other two vehicles, which had originally formed 2-BIL unit 2006, were scrapped. *John Scrace*

Above: Two South Eastern-bodied 3-SUB units headed by 1618 are seen passing Tadworth.
Ian Allan Library

Left: A 2-SL unit is seen here, easily identified by the low roof over both the cab ends where the collector bow had been located in the units' original incarnation as ac overhead South London sets.
Ian Allan Library

Below: A South London overhead train passes Clapham on 17 March 1928 on a Victoria to London Bridge service. It is formed of two 2-car units, each formed from a 1910 trailer and a 1909 motor car.
H. C. Casserley

Top: 2-BIL unit 2104 is seen here at Lancing heading the 15.15 Brighton to Portsmouth Harbour service on 30 April 1971. This view shows the corridor side of the unit. *John Scrace*

Above: Another 2-BIL unit, 2152 shows the smaller windows and larger number of doors on the compartment side of the unit. *P. J. Sharpe*

Left: 4-LAV unit 2925 is seen fresh out of works in sparkling green livery in this view. *Ian Allan Library*

Left: 4-LAV unit 2954 is seen passing Horsham on 10 October 1965. This was one of the final two 4-LAV units which externally resembled 2-HAL units. Compare this with the view of 2925. *John Scrace*

Centre left: 6-PUL unit 3001 is seen passing Haywards Heath. The Pullman vehicle can be clearly seen in full Pullman livery as the third vehicle in the set. *P. J. Sharpe*

Bottom left: 6-PAN unit 3035 is passing Hampden Park on a Victoria to Eastbourne service. *P Ransome-Wallis*

Opposite top left: 6-CIT set number 3042. These units had a larger percentage of first class seats for commuters to the City. *R. C. Riley*

Opposite top right: A number of condemned 6-COR units could be seen at Ford on 24 March 1969, including 3044 seen on the left. *John H. Bird*

Right centre: 5-BEL 'Brighton Belle' unit number 3051 is approaching Brighton. It is seen here in the Pullman Livery it carried until the late sixties. *P. J. Sharpe*

Right: An attempt was made to modernise the look of the 'Brighton Belle' units at the end of the sixties. They were repainted in a version of the BR blue and grey livery and the individual carriage names were removed. No 3052 is seen waiting to depart from Brighton with the 17.45 service to London Victoria on 20 August 1969. *John Scrace*

51

3044

3051

3052
BRIGHTON BELLE

Top: New 4-REP unit number 3003 is seen passing Micheldever on 18 March 1967. It is on a training run before entering service. *John H. Bird*

Above: 4-BUF unit number 3083 with S11191S leading is seen at Arundel on a Victoria Express service. *P. J. Sharpe*

Left: 4-COR unit number 3128 is seen approaching Portsmouth at the head of the 12.50 service from London Waterloo on 25 January 1969. *John H. Bird*

Top: 4-DD double-deck unit number 4001 is seen on a trial run on 14 September 1949. *BR*

Above: The new prototype 4-PEP unit 4001 is seen on a press trip at Waterloo on 4 June 1973. *C. Lang*

Right: 'A Very Great Train'. The first Sheba unit, 4101, is seen at the end of its life at Horsham on 3 August 1972. This was the first of the standard 4-SUB units, built in 1941, and due to the intervention of the war it was the only one of its type until more appeared in 1944. It's a shame it was not preserved. *John Scrace*

Top: 4-SUB 'Sheba' unit number 4105 passing Shortlands. *R. C. Riley*

Above: Standard 4-SUB unit 4114 at Mitcham Junction. *Ian Allan Library*

Left: 4-SUB 4298 passing Teddington on 22 December 1982 while working a Waterloo to Waterloo service via Richmond and Kingston. *David Brown*

Above right: 4-SUB unit number 4311 was a Southern-bodied unit which received an all-steel trailer when it was augmented from a 3-SUB unit. *Ian Allan Library*

Centre right: 4-SUB unit 4348 was unusual in that it contained two postwar all-steel trailers for a while in 1961. *P. J. Sharpe*

Right: LBSCR-bodied 4-SUB unit number 4506 at Wimbledon with S8717S leading. The carriages in this unit were all converted from ex-ac stock. *J .C. Beckett*

4348

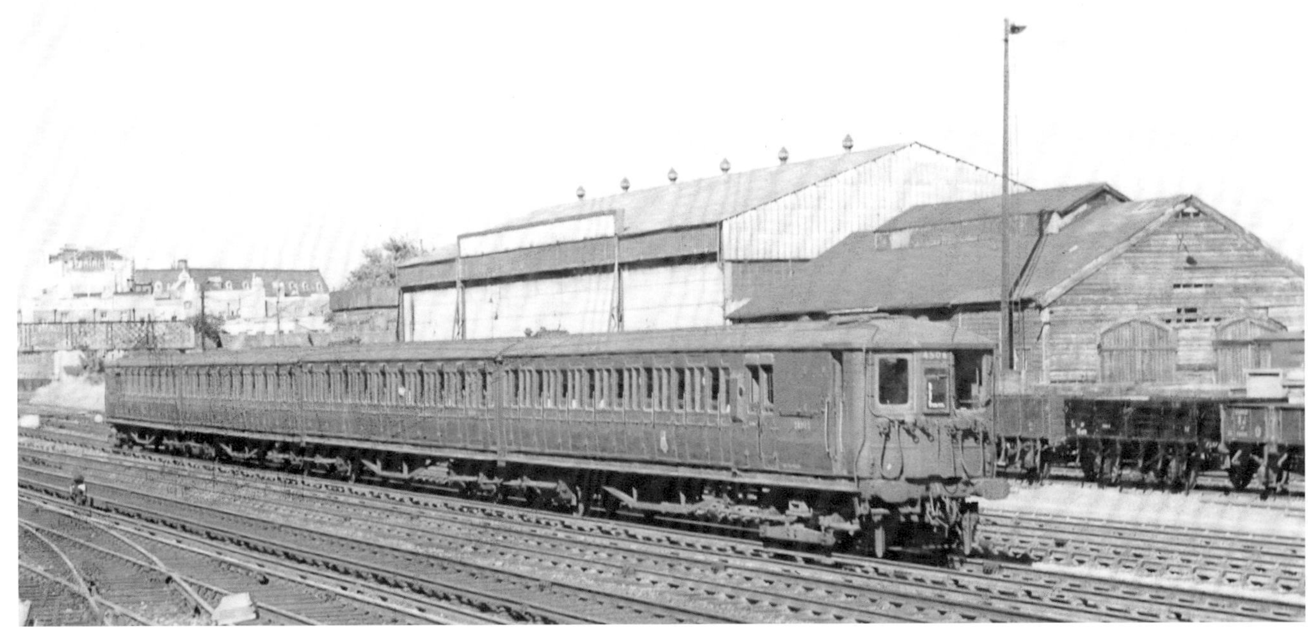

Above left: This is an interior view of a Motor Open Second in 4-SUB unit 4655 taken at Shepperton on 2 January 1980. This is a typical view of the open carriages used by many commuters in the London area for many years. Note the netted luggage racks above the seat backs. These worked well unless vandals had sliced through the netting! *J. G. Glover*

Above: 4-SUB unit 4629 stands next to Stores Unit 022 at Selhurst on 26 September 1983. 022 is formed from former 2-HAL vehicles. *John Scrace*

Left: More withdrawn units at Micheldever sidings. 4-SUB unit 4644 stands among others of the class in the sidings on 8 April 1980. *Luke Siemeszko*

Below left: 4-SUB unit 4649 is seen passing through Clapham Junction on 18 September 1974. *Brian Morrison*

Top: 4-SUB unit 4670 looks immaculate in its green livery. *P. J. Sharpe*

Above: Seen at Plumstead on 7 October 1971 and by now renumbered 4901, this is a close-up of the side of the double-deck unit. The upper compartments were interleaved with the lower compartment, and a narrow staircase was the means of access to the top level. This view also shows the inset doors on the guard's compartment and the lack of running boards and commode handles to the compartment doors. These features were all due to the units being built to the very extremes of the loading gauge. *John Scrace*

Right: 4-EPB units 5005 and 5049 are seen working the 11.41 Victoria to West Croydon service at Norwood Junction on 6 April 1978. This shows the style of the early units which did not have a rainstrip above the side windows. *Brian Morrison*

Left: 4-EPB unit 5227 at Waterloo shows the units which carried the rainstrip above the side windows. *Carl Symes*

Below: No 5317 is one of the BR version of the 4-EPB units and it is seen working the 09.35 Charing Cross to Gillingham service through Strood on 23 September 1978. *Les Bertram*

Bottom: SR 2-HAP unit 5604 at Ramsgate on 1 June 1959. *J. C. Haydon*

Top: In later blue livery, 2-HAP unit No 5601 is at Eastleigh on 18 July 1974. The corridor side of DTCL S16001S can be seen clearly. *John Scrace*

Above: SR-bodied 2-EPB number 5669 is at Waterloo on 22 April 1971. These units were built on the frames of former 2-NOL units. *D. L. Percival*

Right: BR 2-EPB unit 5727 is seen at Selsdon on 3 August 1981, after arriving on the 17.10 service from Elmers End. *John Scrace*

Left: Two downgraded 2-SAP units, 5947 and 5942, are ready to depart from Hampton Court with the 16.43 service to Waterloo on 11 March 1978. *Les Bertram*

Below: 2-HAP unit 6066 in green livery is seen here with DMBSO S61264 leading. *P. J. Sharpe*

Bottom: 4-BIG unit 7047 is leaving Gatwick Airport in the formation of the 15.23 Victoria to Littlehampton on 17 July 1983. *John Scrace*

Right: 4-BEP unit 7006 is seen here heading the 17.33 London Bridge to Ore & Seaford service at East Croydon on 7 September 1979. *John Scrace*

Below: 4-CIG unit 7350 at Fratton on 9 May 1980. *John Scrace*

Bottom: 4-VEP unit 7707 is seen here in early BR blue livery. *S. W. Stevens-Stratten*

Top: 4-VEG unit 7909 is displaying the name of the route it was designed for. Twelve of these units were converted in 1978 with extra luggage racks to work on this airport service. It is seen at Bognor Regis on 19 August 1979. *Les Bertram*

Above: The unique 8-VAB unit is seen at Romsey. In this photograph it is working a Waterloo to Bournemouth train, hauled by a Class 33 locomotive, which was diverted because of engineering work. *John H. Bird*

Left: A three-car set of Crystal Palace stock passes Wandsworth Common on 17 March 1928. This is the later formation with the motor car in the centre of the set. *H. C. Casserley*

Above: Two five-car sets of Coulsdon-Wallington stock are seen in the sidings at Coulsdon North on 28 May 1927. The Motor Luggage van can be clearly seen in the centre of the units. *H. C. Casserley*

Right: An LSWR three-car suburban unit carrying its original number E24. It later became SR 3-SUB unit 1224. *Ian Allan Library*

Below: On 30 March 1974 4-VEC unit 044 leaves Shanklin on the Isle of Wight with a train to Ryde. 3-TIS unit 034 is stored at the platform to the right. *R. E. Ruffell*

Top: This works photograph shows the Waterloo & City 1899 trailer car number 31. *English Electric*

Above: In 1940 the old stock on the Waterloo & City line was replaced with new stock. This photograph was taken at Waterloo and it shows the old stock on the left, awaiting removal for scrap, while the new stock on the right is waiting to be taken down the lift to the underground line. *Ian Allan Library*

Below: Four Class 302 units were converted to three-car parcels units with roller shutter doors in 1989. No 302990 is seen working the Norwich-Liverpool Street mails service at Ipswich on 24 February 1992. *Michael J. Collins*

Above: AM4 unit 029 is seen at Runcorn on a stopping service to Liverpool from Crewe. It is carrying the original green livery. It is one of the AM4/2 sub-class, as can be seen from the large windows between the seating bays on the leading driving trailer vehicle M75673. *P. J. Sharpe*

Right: The AM4 units were later classed 304. Class 304/1 unit 009 with M75053 leading is seen at Allerton depot. These early units (with smaller side windows) were originally ordered for the Manchester area, but they all ran as common-user sets throughout the electrified area. *D. L. Percival*

Right: No 303080 is working a Cathcart Circle service at Glasgow Central on 5 June 1982. It is carrying the revised front windows. *D. M. May*

Left: Unit 305508 is seen far from its original home at North Berwick on 6 August 1992. It is working the 12.20 service to Edinburgh Haymarket. *Ian S. Carr*

Below: Later in their lives the headcode indicator was again removed, as can be seen in this view of 307105. It is shown at Southend Victoria on 14 May 1983 coupled to unit 305511 working the 11.29 service from Liverpool Street. *Alex Dasi-Sutton*

Bottom: AM8/1 unit number 165 at Wickford. *P. J. Sharpe*

Right: Class 308/1 unit number 145 is seen working the summer Sunday 10.05 Colchester to Clacton and Walton via St Botolphs service at Great Bentley on 8 August 1971. *G. R. Mortimer*

Below: Class 308 unit number 314 is seen at Benfleet working the 12.45 Fenchurch Street to Shoeburyness service on 28 September 1980. *Les Bertram*

Bottom: Two class 310 units side by side at Bletchley on 20 March 1987 provide a comparison between the original and rebuilt front ends of these units. No 310064 has the original wrap-around front windows, while 310065 carries the newer flat windows which were designed to be safer and cheaper to replace if damaged. *Barry Smith*

Top: Class 312/0 unit 312008 is seen at Kings Cross on an evening train to Hitchin on 30 December 1977. *M. Hall*

Above: 312202 was one of the small batch of Class 312/2 units built for working in the Birmingham area. It is seen on arrival at Birmingham International working the 17.00 service from Birmingham New Street on 5 May 1976. *Philip D. Hawkins*

Left: Two Class 311 units stand side-by-side at the buffer stops at Glasgow Central on 20 May 1985. Nos 311102 and 310098 both carry the revised-style cab windows. *A. R. Johnston*

Right: Newly refurbished Class 411/5 4-CEP unit 411507 is seen on 25 January 1980. Only a few units were turned out with a full six-digit number, and this unit soon became 1507. *BR*

Below: Refurbished Class 411 4-CEP unit 1594 is at Waterloo East working the 10.05 Charing Cross to Ashford service on 28 March 1986. It is wearing the short-lived London & South East livery *David Brown*

Bottom: Facelifted Class 421/3 4-CIG units 1723 and 1721 in Network SouthEast livery are seen at Portsmouth Harbour forming the 12.30 to London Victoria on Saturday 11 April 1987. *Michael McGowan*

Left: Refurbished Class 412 4-BEP unit 2303 pauses at Guildford while working the 13.28 Waterloo to Portsmouth Harbour service on 21 August 1984. *David Brown*

Below: Class 482 8-MIG unit number 2602 is passing New Malden working the 07.28 Portsmouth Harbour to Waterloo semi-fast service on 18 June 1983. *David Brown*

Bottom: Class 413/3 4-CAP unit 3305 is seen at Worthing while working the 13.00 Littlehampton to Brighton service on 2 August 1982. This unit was formed from 2-HAP units 6081 and 6104. *John E. Oxley*

Left: Class 414/3 2-HAP unit 4304 leads Class 423 4-VEP unit 3119 at St Denys working the 13.42 Waterloo to Bournemouth service on 5 April 1988. *David Brown*

Below: Class 415/4 4-EPB unit 5404 leads Class 416/3 2-EPB units 6329, 6306, 6334 and 6310 out of Redhill while working the 4F58 Hastings to London Bridge service on 7 May 1988. *Alex Dasi-Sutton*

Left: Class 416/3 2-EPB unit number 6316 waits at West Croydon to work the 11.36 service to Wimbledon on 13 September 1991. This service was taken over by Class 456 units on 30 September that year. *Chris Wilson*

Above: Class 416/4 2-EPB unit 6402 is at Maidstone West on 11 April 1987, waiting to work the 12.44 service to Strood. *J. Critchley*

Left: The 11.15 Victoria to Gatwick Airport service passes Clapham Junction on 20 June 1984. It is formed of Class 488 Mark 2f Gatwick sets hauled by Class 73 73123 'Gatwick Express'. *David Brown*

Below: The Gatwick Express services were formed of Class 488 units with a Class 489 Driving Luggage Van at one end and a Class 73 locomotive at the other. GLV 9101 heads the 10.05 Gatwick Airport to Victoria service past Battersea Park on 12 October 1985. *Brian Morrison*

Above: North Tyneside 'B type' articulated unit E29121E and E29321E is seen at Monkseaton on 10 February 1967 on a Newcastle via Wallsend service. *Keith Pringle*

Below: The newly built Tyneside motor luggage van E68000 is seen out on test at Brighton on 24 November 1955. After the South Tyneside line was de-electrified, this van was transferred to the London Midland Southport line. *W. M. J. Jackson*

Bottom: BR standard South Tyneside unit E65314 and E77103 is seen on a stopping service to South Shields. These units were later transferred to the Southern Region, where this unit became 2-EPB 5784. *P. J. Sharpe*

Part 2. EMUs listed by Carriage numbers

British Railways

Class 307 Eastleigh

Motor Brake Second
MBS, later MS then MSO
E61001-E61032

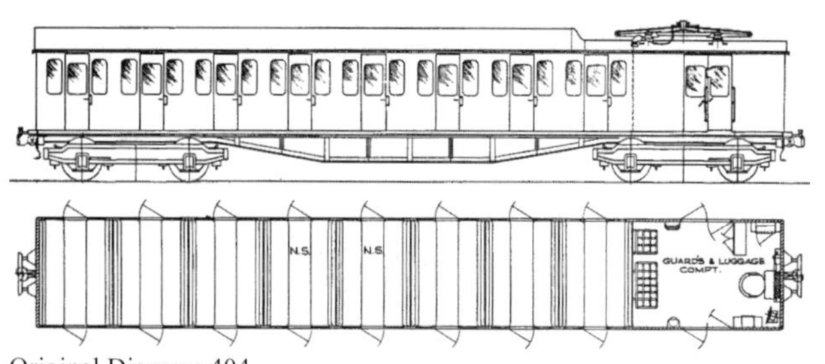

Original Diagram 404

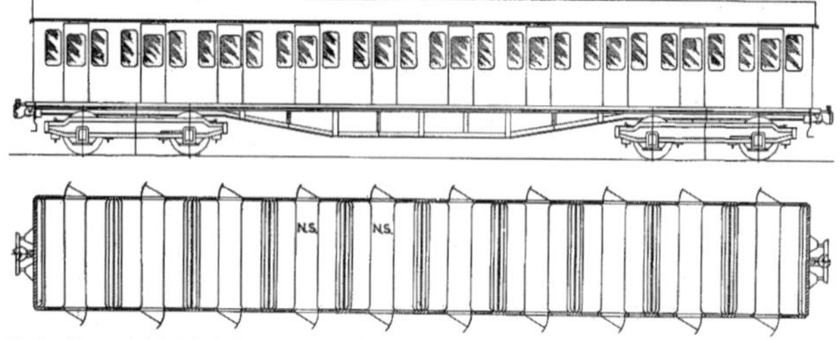

Rebuilt to MS 1960/61 at Stratford, Diagram 419

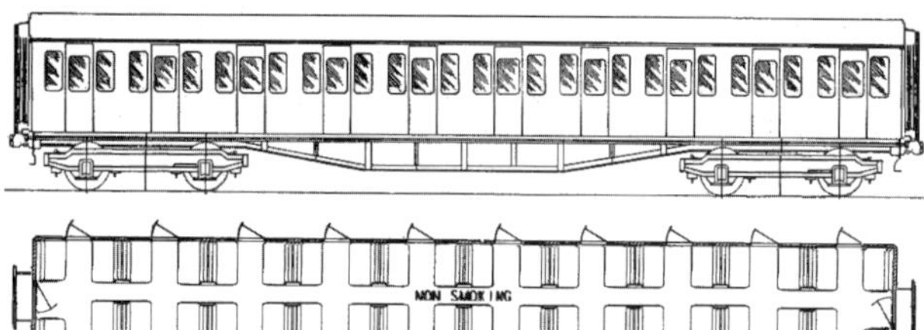

Refurbished 1983-84 Diagram EC204

Diagram:	404 419 EC204	Lot Number:	30203
Body:	63' 6" × 9' 3¼"	Weight:	46t 6cwt
Seats:	96 second, later 120 second then 98 second	Bogies:	Gresley
		Motors:	EE 2 × 174hp

E61001	02/56-08/93	➲**977669**	**01s**	02/56-*61*	**101**	*61*-11/82	**307101**	11/82-08/93
E61002	02/56-08/93	⊗08/93	**02s**	02/56-*61*	**102**	*61*-01/80	**307102**	01/80-08/93
E61003	02/56-09/93	⊗08/93	**03s**	02/56-02/60	**103**	02/60-10/82	**307103**	10/82-08/93
E61004	03/56-08/93	⊗08/93	**04s**	03/56-*61*	**104**	*61*-01/82	**307104**	01/82-08/93
E61005	03/56-09/93	⊗08/93	**05s**	03/56-*61*	**105**	*61*-09/82	**307105**	09/82-08/93
E61006	03/56-08/93	➲**977673**	**06s**	03/56-*61*	**106**	*61*-02/80	**307106**	02/80-08/93
E61007	04/56-08/93	⊗08/93	**07s**	04/56-*61*	**107**	*61*-12/81	**307107**	12/81-08/93
E61008	04/56-09/93	⊗08/93	**08s**	04/56-*61*	**108**	*61*-04/82	**307108**	04/82-08/93
E61009	04/56-08/93	⊗08/93	**09s**	04/56-*61*	**109**	*61*-02/82	**307109**	02/82-08/93
E61010	05/56-09/93	⊗08/93	**10s**	05/56-*61*	**110**	*61*-11/81	**307110**	11/81-08/93
E61011	05/56-09/93	⊗08/93	**11s**	05/56-*61*	**111**	*61*-01/83	**307111**	01/83-08/93
E61012	05/56-08/93	⊗08/93	**12s**	05/56-*61*	**112**	*61*-09/82	**307112**	09/82-08/93
E61013	05/56-09/93	⊗08/93	**13s**	05/56-*61*	**113**	*61*-12/82	**307113**	12/82-08/93
E61014	06/56-09/93	⊗08/93	**14s**	06/56-*61*	**114**	*61*-11/81	**307114**	11/81-08/93
E61015	06/56-08/93	⊗08/93	**15s**	06/56-*61*	**115**	*61*-12/81	**307115**	12/81-08/93
E61016	06/56-09/93	⊗08/93	**16s**	06/56-*61*	**116**	*61*-12/81	**307116**	12/81-08/93
E61017	06/56-08/93	⊗08/93	**17s**	06/56-*61*	**117**	*61*-07/82	**307117**	07/82-08/93
E61018	06/56-08/93	➲**977709**	**18s**	06/56-*61*	**118**	*61*-02/82	**307118**	02/82-08/93
E61019	07/56-08/93	⊗08/93	**19s**	07/56-*61*	**119**	*61*-06/82	**307119**	06/82-08/93
E61020	07/56-08/93	⊗08/93	**20s**	07/56-*61*	**120**	*61*-09/81	**307120**	09/81-08/93
E61021	07/56-08/93	➲**977677**	**21s**	07/56-*61*	**121**	*61*-04/82	**307121**	04/82-08/93
E61022	07/56-09/93	⊗08/93	**22s**	07/56-*61*	**122**	*61*-08/82	**307122**	08/82-08/93
E61023	08/56-09/93	⊗08/93	**23s**	08/56-*61*	**123**	*61*-10/81	**307123**	10/81-08/93
E61024	08/56-08/93	⊗08/93	**24s**	08/56-*61*	**124**	*61*-05/82	**307124**	05/82-08/93
E61025	09/56-09/93	⊗08/93	**25s**	09/56-*61*	**125**	*61*-10/82	**307125**	10/82-08/93
E61026	09/56-09/93	⊗08/93	**26s**	09/56-*61*	**126**	*61*-08/82	**307126**	08/82-08/93
E61027	09/56-09/93	⊗08/93	**27s**	09/56-*61*	**127**	*61*-01/82	**307127**	01/82-08/93
E61028	09/56-08/93	⊗08/93	**28s**	09/56-*61*	**128**	*61*-03/82	**307128**	03/82-08/93
E61029	09/56-10/93	⊗08/93	**29s**	09/56-*61*	**129**	*61*-06/82	**307129**	06/82-08/93
E61030	10/56-08/93	⊗08/93	**30s**	10/56-*61*	**130**	*61*-06/82	**307130**	06/82-08/93
E61031	10/56-09/93	⊗08/93	**31s**	10/56-*61*	**131**	*61*-05/82	**307131**	05/82-08/93
E61032	10/56-08/93	⊗08/93	**32s**	10/56-*61*	**132**	*61*-04/82	**307132**	04/82-08/93

Class 411 4-CEP Ashford/Eastleigh

Driving Motor Brake Second Open
DMBSO later DMSO(A) & DMSO(B)
S61033-S61040

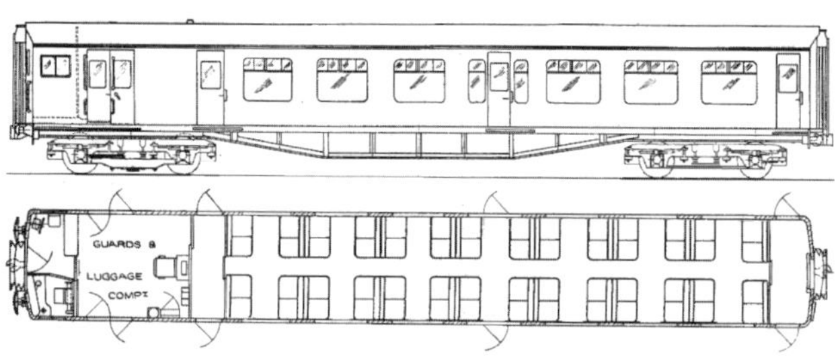

As built, Diagram 402

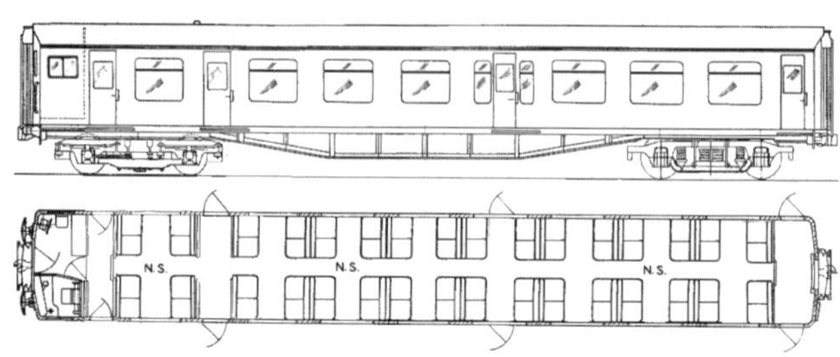

Refurbished, Diagram 884 DMSO(A) EA263, DMSO(B) EA264

Diagram:	402 884 EA263 EA264	Lot Number:	30108
Body:	64' 6" × 9' 3"	Weight:	40t 0cwt
Seats:	56 second, later 64 second	Bogies:	1 Mk 4 Motor 1 Mk 6, later Commonwealth
Motors:	EE507 2 × 250hp		

S61033	02/56-03/93	⊗06/93	**7101**	02/56-10/82	**1503**	10/82-03/93
S61034	02/56-03/93	⊗06/93	**7101**	02/56-10/82	**1503**	10/82-03/93
S61035	03/56-07/91	➲**977395**	**7102**	03/56-10/75		
S61036	03/56-10/75	⊗08/76	**7102**	03/56-10/75		
S61037	04/56-05/93	⊗08/96	**7103**	04/56-08/83	**1504**	08/83-05/93
S61038	04/56-05/93	➲**977863**	**7103**	04/56-08/83	**1505**	01/84-03/93
S61039	05/56-01/93	⊗04/93	**7104**	05/56-12/80	**1502**	12/80-01/93
S61040	05/56-01/93	⊗04/93	**7104**	05/56-12/80	**1502**	12/80-01/93

Class 410 4-BEP Ashford/Eastleigh

Driving Motor Brake Second Open
DMBSO later DMSO(A) & DMSO(B)
S61041-S61044

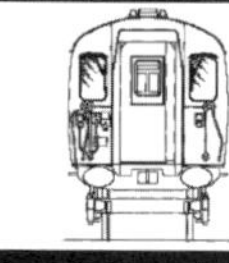

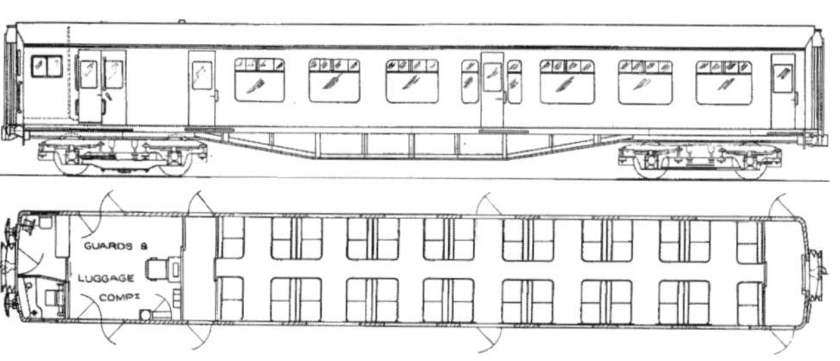

As built, Diagram 402

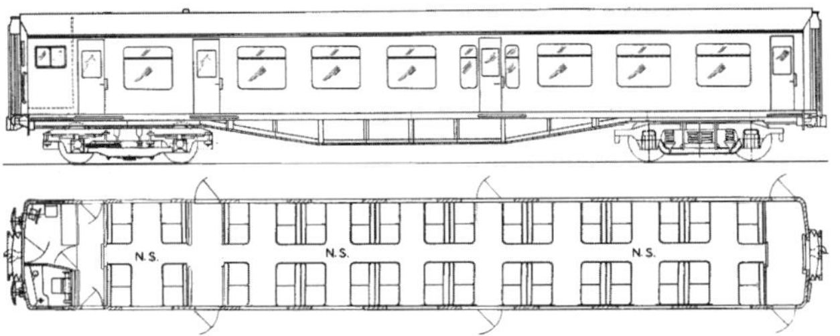

Refurbished, Diagram 884 DMSO(A) EA263, DMSO(B) EA264

Diagram:	402 884 EA263 EA264	Lot Number:	30111
Body:	64' 6" × 9' 3"	Weight:	40t 0cwt
Seats:	56 second, later 64 second	Bogies:	1 Mk 6 Motor 1 Mk 6 later Commonwealth
Motors:	EE507 2 × 250hp		

S61041	07/56-03/93	⊗04/93	**7001**	07/56-05/80	**1501**	05/80-03/93
S61042	07/56-03/93	⊗04/93	**7001**	07/56-05/80	**1501**	05/80-03/93
S61043	07/56-05/93	⊗08/96	**7002**	07/56-08/83	**1504**	08/83-05/93
301044	07/56-05/93	➲977881	**7002**	07/56-08/83	**1505**	01/84-03/93

Class 304/1 Wolverton
Motor Brake Second
MBS, later MBSO
M61045-M61059

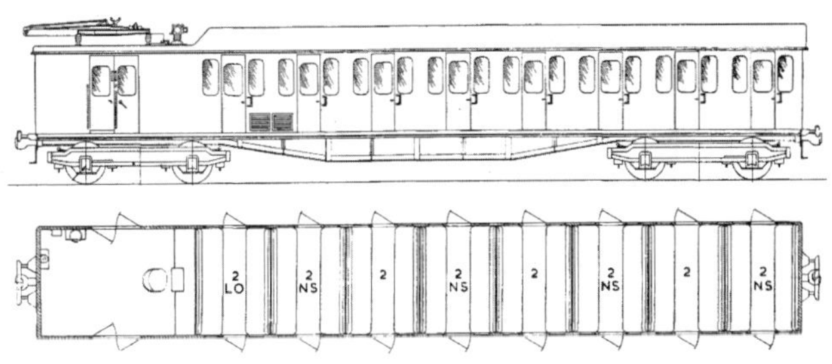

As built, Diagram 408

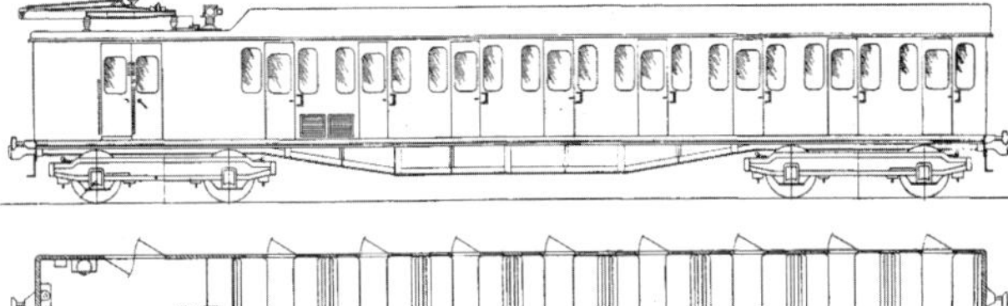

Rebuilt, Diagram ED215

Diagram:	408 ED215	Lot Number:	30428
Body:	63' 6⅛" × 9' 3"	Weight:	53t 12cwt
Seats:	96 second, later 82 second	Bogies:	Gresley
Motors:	BTH 2 × 207hp		

M61045	03/60-07/92	⊗07/92	**001**	03/60-10/82	**304001**	10/82-07/92
M61046	04/60-04/96	⊗05/96	**002**	04/60-04/82	**304002**	04/82-04/96
M61047	04/60-05/94	⊗10/00	**003**	04/60-07/81	**304003**	07/81-05/94
M61048	05/60-03/96	⊗01/97	**004**	05/60-09/83	**304004**	09/83-03/96
M61049	05/60-12/94	⊗05/96	**005**	05/60-10/81	**304005**	10/81-12/94
M61050	05/60-12/93	⊗11/97	**006**	05/60-12/82	**304006**	12/82-12/93
M61051	06/60-05/92	⊗05/92	**007**	06/60-04/82	**304007**	04/82-05/92
M61052	06/60-05/94	⊗10/00	**008**	06/60-08/81	**304008**	08/81-05/94
M61053	06/60-03/96	⊗01/97	**009**	06/60-04/81	**304009**	04/81-03/96
M61054	06/60-09/94	⊗06/96	**010**	06/60-12/81	**304010**	12/81-09/94
M61055	06/60-01/91	⊗*11/91*	**011**	06/60-01/80	**304011**	01/80-01/91
M61056	07/60-05/92	⊗04/92	**012**	07/60-04/82	**304012**	04/82-05/92
M61057	07/60-05/94	⊗11/97	**013**	07/60-07/81	**304013**	07/81-05/94
M61058	07/60-09/94	⊗05/96	**014**	07/60-06/81	**304014**	06/81-09/94
M61059	07/60-06/94	⊗06/96	**015**	07/60-08/82	**304015**	08/82-06/94

Class 302 York
Motor Brake Second
MBS, later MBSO
E61060-E61096

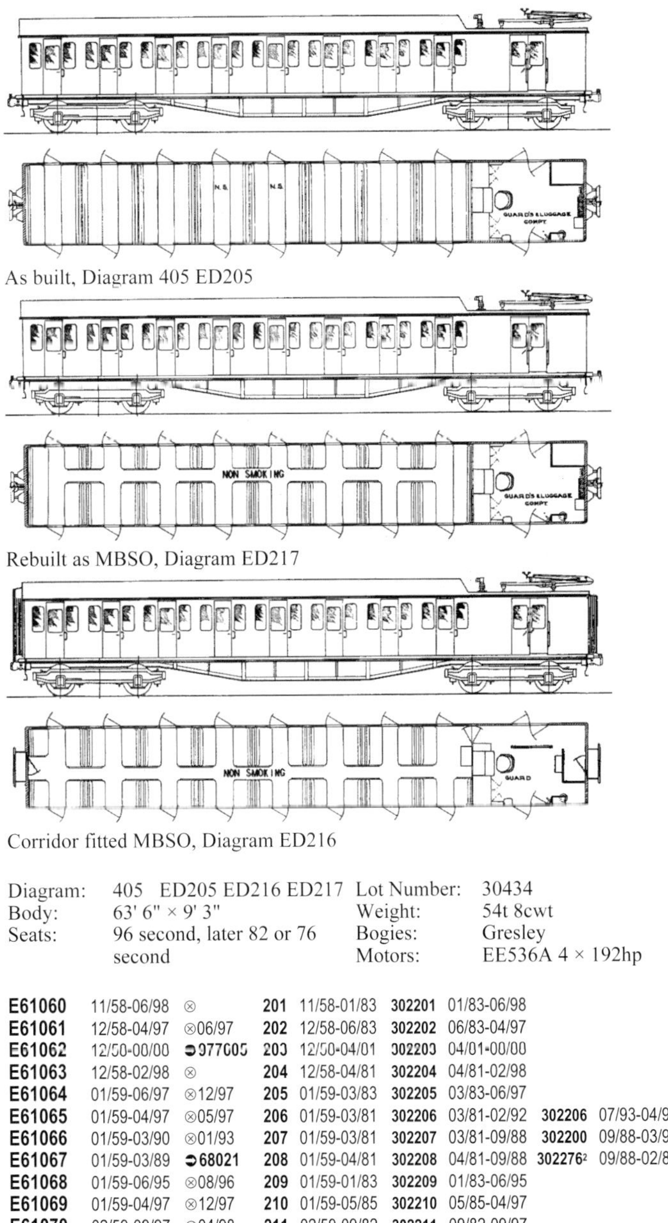

As built, Diagram 405 ED205

Rebuilt as MBSO, Diagram ED217

Corridor fitted MBSO, Diagram ED216

Diagram:	405 ED205 ED216 ED217	Lot Number:	30434
Body:	63' 6" × 9' 3"	Weight:	54t 8cwt
Seats:	96 second, later 82 or 76 second	Bogies:	Gresley
		Motors:	EE536A 4 × 192hp

E61060	11/58-06/98	⊗	**201**	11/58-01/83	**302201**	01/83-06/98		
E61061	12/58-04/97	⊗06/97	**202**	12/58-06/83	**302202**	06/83-04/97		
E61062	12/58-00/00	➲977605	**203**	12/58-04/01	**302203**	04/01-00/00		
E61063	12/58-02/98	⊗	**204**	12/58-04/81	**302204**	04/81-02/98		
E61064	01/59-06/97	⊗12/97	**205**	01/59-03/83	**302205**	03/83-06/97		
E61065	01/59-04/97	⊗05/97	**206**	01/59-03/81	**302206**	03/81-02/92	**302206**	07/93-04/97
E61066	01/59-03/90	⊗01/93	**207**	01/59-03/81	**302207**	03/81-09/88	**302200**	09/88-03/90
E61067	01/59-03/89	➲68021	**208**	01/59-04/81	**302208**	04/81-09/88	**302276**[2]	09/88-02/89
E61068	01/59-06/95	⊗08/96	**209**	01/59-01/83	**302209**	01/83-06/95		
E61069	01/59-04/97	⊗12/97	**210**	01/59-05/85	**302210**	05/85-04/97		
E61070	02/59-09/97	⊗04/98	**211**	02/59-09/82	**302211**	09/82-09/97		
E61071	02/59-02/97	⊗09/98	**212**	02/59-05/81	**302212**	05/81-02/97		
E61072	02/59-07/97	⊗	**213**	02/59-08/81	**302213**	08/81-07/97		
E61073	02/59-04/88	➲977599	**214**	02/59-04/81	**302214**	04/81-04/88		
E61074	02/59-04/97	⊗05/97	**215**	03/59-12/81	**302215**	12/81-04/97		
E61075	02/59-07/98	⊗	**216**	02/59-06/83	**302216**	06/83-07/98		
E61076	03/59-04/97	⊗06/97	**217**	03/59-07/84	**302217**	07/84-02/92	**302217**	07/93-04/97
E61077	04/59-07/97	⊗	**218**	04/59-06/81	**302218**	06/81-07/97		
E61078	04/59-04/97	⊗06/97	**219**	04/59-09/83	**302219**	09/83-04/97		
E61079	04/59-06/97	⊗09/98	**220**	04/59-09/83	**302220**	09/83-02/92	**302220**	01/93-06/97
E61080	04/59-06/97	⊗	**221**	04/59-09/83	**302221**	09/83-06/97		
E61081	04/59-06/96	⊗04/98	**222**	04/59-06/82	**302222**	06/82-02/92	**302222**	12/92-06/96
E61082	04/59-08/88	⊗08/90	**223**	06/59-05/81	**302223**	05/81-08/88		
E61083	04/59-08/97	⊗*08/00*	**224**	06/59-07/81	**302224**	07/81-08/97		
E61084	05/59-07/98	⊗	**225**	05/59-10/81	**302225**	10/81-07/98		
E61085	05/59-01/98	⊗	**226**	06/59-10/81	**302226**	10/81-02/92	**302226**	01/93-01/98
E61086	05/59-09/88	⊗07/90	**227**	06/59-*83*	**302227**	*83*-02/88	**302427**	02/88-06/88
			302227	06/88-07/88				
E61087	05/59-07/98	⊗	**228**	05/59-11/81	**302228**	11/81-07/98		
E61088	05/59-09/97	⊗09/98	**229**	05/59-08/82	**302229**	08/82-09/97		
E61089	05/59-08/88	⊗08/90	**230**	05/59-12/83	**302230**	12/83-08/88		
E61090	05/59-03/89	➲68020	**231**	05/59-07/84	**302231**	07/84-03/89		
E61091	05/59-07/98	⊗	**232**	05/59-03/85	**302232**	03/85-09/88	**302230**[2]	09/88-07/98
E61092	05/59-04/88	⊗04/88	**233**	06/59-07/84	**302233**	07/84-02/88	**302433**	02/88-04/88
			302233	04/88-04/88				
E61093	06/59-01/91	⊗03/91	**234**	06/59-12/83	**302234**	12/83-08/87	**302434**	08/87-01/88
			302234	01/88-01/91				

E61094	06/59-04/89	⊗07/90	**235**	06/59-04/81	**302235**	04/81-12/88	**302241**	12/88-03/89
E61095	06/59-02/86	⊗07/86	**236**	06/59-01/80	**302236**	01/80-02/86		
E61096	06/59-04/89	⊗03/89	**237**	06/59-11/84	**302237**	11/84-03/89		

Class 302 York

Motor Brake Second
MBS, later MBSO
E61097-E61132

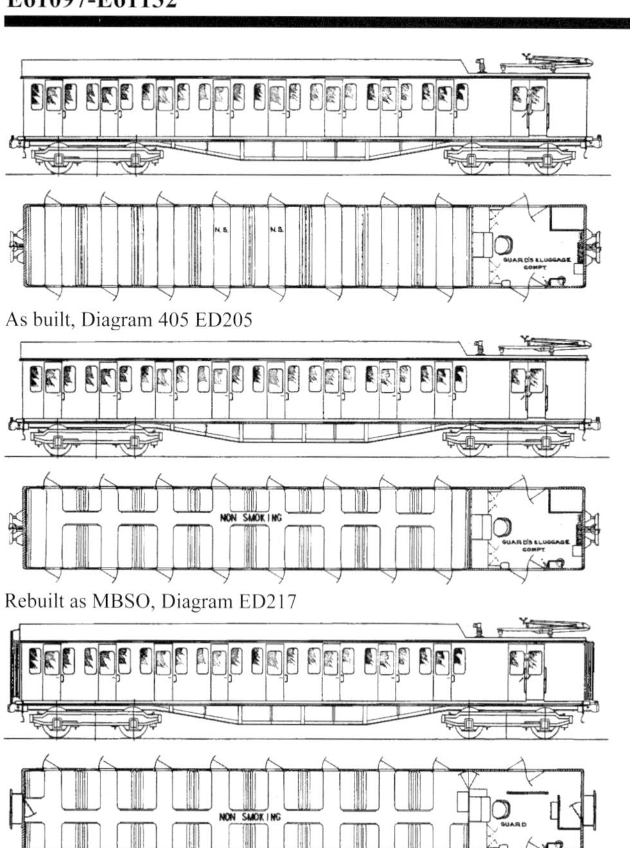

As built, Diagram 405 ED205

Rebuilt as MBSO, Diagram ED217

Corridor fitted MBSO, Diagram ED216

Diagram:	405 ED205 ED216 ED217	Lot Number:	30438
Body:	63' 6" × 9' 3"	Weight:	54t 8cwt
Seats:	96 second, later 82 or 76 second	Bogies:	Gresley
		Motors:	EE536A 4 × 192hp

E61097	06/59-09/89	⊗07/90	**238**	06/59-05/81	**302238**	05/81-09/89		
E61098	06/59-06/90	⊗07/90	**239**	06/59-01/83	**302239**	01/83-08/87	**302439**	08/87-01/88
			302239	01/88-06/90				
E61099	06/59-06/88	⊗03/89	**240**	06/59-11/82	**302240**	11/82-06/88		
E61100	06/59-04/89	⊗03/89	**241**	06/59-11/84	**302241**	11/84-12/88	**302235**	12/88-03/89
E61101	07/59-11/88	⊗11/88	**242**	07/59-01/82	**302242**	01/82-07/88		
E61102	07/59-09/89	⊗08/90	**243**	07/59-10/83	**302243**	10/83-09/89		
E61103	07/59-09/89	⊗08/90	**244**	07/59-10/70	**244**	06/72-06/82	**302244**	06/82-03/89
E61104	07/59-09/89	⊗07/90	**245**	07/59-08/81	**302245**	08/81-04/89		
E61105	07/59-09/89	⊗02/90	**246**	07/59- *83*	**302246**	*83*-09/89		
E61106	07/59-09/89	⊗04/90	**247**	07/59-01/82	**302247**	01/82-04/89		
E61107	07/59-09/89	⊗08/90	**248**	07/59-03/83	**302248**	03/83-03/83	**302399**	03/83-05/83
			302248	05/83-03/89				
E61108	08/59-09/89	⊗04/90	**249**	08/59-09/82	**302249**	09/82-09/89		
E61109	08/59-02/83	⊗02/84	**250**	08/59-04/82	**302250**	04/82-02/83		
E61110	08/59-10/90	⊗10/90	**251**	08/59-01/83	**302251**	01/83-10/90		
E61111	08/59-03/91	⊗03/91	**252**	08/59-08/82	**302252**	08/82-03/91		
E61112	08/59-05/85	⊗10/85	**253**	08/59-10/82	**302253**	10/82-05/85		
E61113	08/59-01/90	⊗03/90	**254**	08/59-03/83	**302254**	03/83-09/89		
E61114	08/59-07/83	⊗05/84	**255**	08/59-01/82	**302255**	01/82-07/83		
E61115	09/59-09/89	⊗04/90	**256**	09/59- *83*	**302256**	*83*-09/89		
E61116	09/59-03/90	⊗07/90	**257**	09/59-04/82	**302257**	04/82-03/89	**302296**	03/89-03/90
E61117	09/59-09/89	⊗05/90	**258**	09/59-05/81	**302258**	05/81-09/89		
E61118	09/59-03/90	⊗08/90	**259**	09/59-03/80	**302259**	03/80-11/87	**302459**	11/87-02/88
			302259	02/88-03/90				
E61119	09/59-05/85	⊗10/88	**260**	09/59-05/81	**302260**	05/81-05/85		
E61120	09/59-01/91	⊗03/91	**261**	09/59-03/83	**302261**	03/83-01/91		
E61121	09/59-01/91	⊗03/91	**262**	09/59-10/82	**302262**	10/82-11/87	**302462**	11/87-02/88
			302262	02/88-07/90				
E61122	09/59-06/96	⊗04/98	**263**	09/59-09/83	**302263**	09/83-09/88	**302203**[2]	09/88-06/96
E61123	09/59-09/89	⊗05/90	**264**	09/59-05/82	**302264**	05/82-09/89		
E61124	09/59-09/89	⊗04/90	**265**	09/59-09/82	**302265**	09/82-03/89		
E61125	09/59-01/88	⊗09/88	**266**	09/59-07/84	**302266**	07/84-01/88		
E61126	09/59-02/87	⊗10/87	**267**	09/59-02/80	**302267**	02/80-08/86		
E61127	10/59-09/89	⊗05/90	**268**	11/59-09/82	**302268**	09/82-09/89		
E61128	10/59-09/89	⊗04/90	**269**	11/59-01/82	**302269**	01/82-09/89		
E61129	10/59-09/89	⊗07/90	**270**	11/59- *83*	**302270**	*83*-09/89		
E61130	10/59-09/89	⊗08/90	**271**	11/59-04/82	**302271**	04/82-11/88		
E61131	10/59-06/90	⊗08/90	**272**	11/59-06/83	**302272**	06/83-06/90		
E61132	10/59-08/85	⊗10/85	**273**	11/59-03/82	**302273**	03/82-08/85	**302260**[2]	09/88-09/89

Class 501 Ashford/Eastleigh

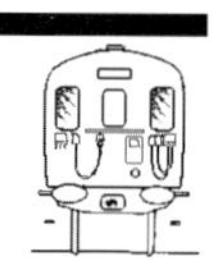

Driving Motor Brake Second Open
DMBSO
M61133-M61189

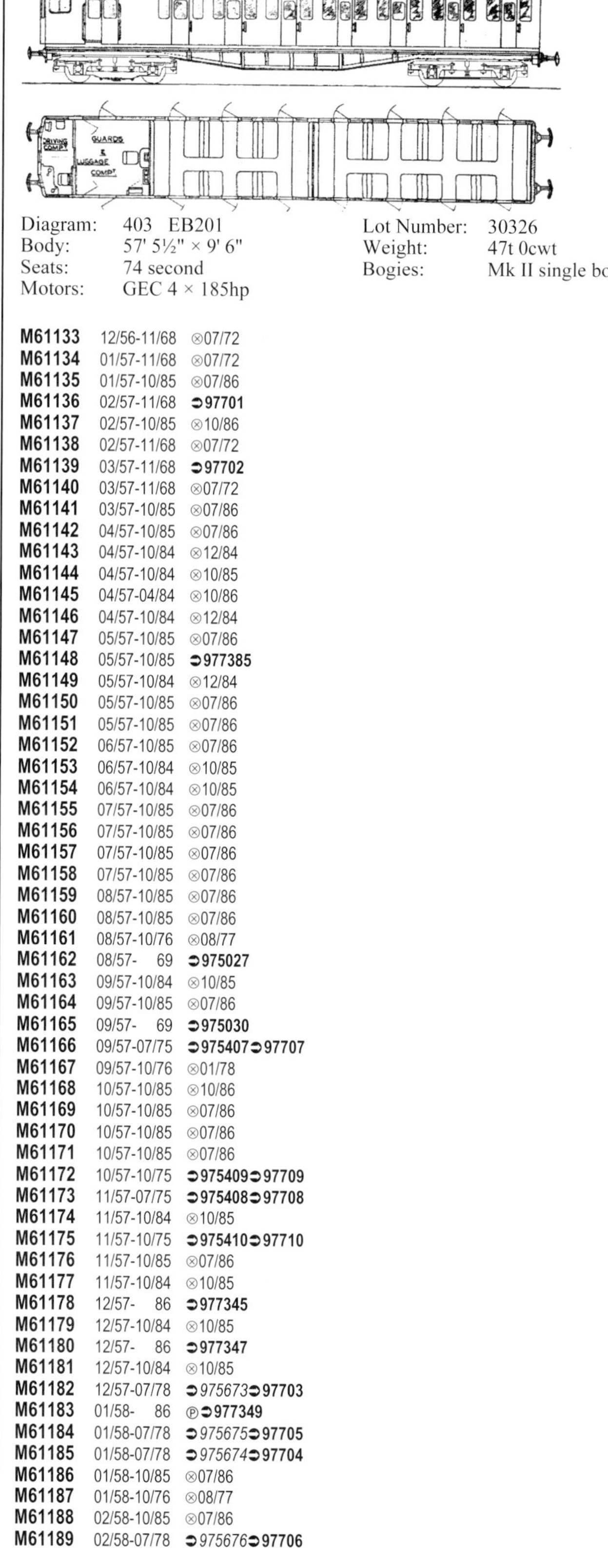

Diagram:	403 EB201	Lot Number:	30326
Body:	57' 5½" × 9' 6"	Weight:	47t 0cwt
Seats:	74 second	Bogies:	Mk II single bolster
Motors:	GEC 4 × 185hp		

M61133	12/56-11/68	⊗07/72
M61134	01/57-11/68	⊗07/72
M61135	01/57-10/85	⊗07/86
M61136	02/57-11/68	➲**97701**
M61137	02/57-10/85	⊗10/86
M61138	02/57-11/68	⊗07/72
M61139	03/57-11/68	➲**97702**
M61140	03/57-11/68	⊗07/72
M61141	03/57-10/85	⊗07/86
M61142	04/57-10/85	⊗07/86
M61143	04/57-10/84	⊗12/84
M61144	04/57-10/84	⊗10/85
M61145	04/57-04/84	⊗10/86
M61146	04/57-10/84	⊗12/84
M61147	05/57-10/85	⊗07/86
M61148	05/57-10/85	➲**977385**
M61149	05/57-10/84	⊗12/84
M61150	05/57-10/85	⊗07/86
M61151	05/57-10/85	⊗07/86
M61152	06/57-10/85	⊗07/86
M61153	06/57-10/84	⊗10/85
M61154	06/57-10/84	⊗10/85
M61155	07/57-10/85	⊗07/86
M61156	07/57-10/85	⊗07/86
M61157	07/57-10/85	⊗07/86
M61158	07/57-10/85	⊗07/86
M61159	08/57-10/85	⊗07/86
M61160	08/57-10/85	⊗07/86
M61161	08/57-10/76	⊗08/77
M61162	08/57- 69	➲**975027**
M61163	09/57-10/84	⊗10/85
M61164	09/57-10/85	⊗07/86
M61165	09/57- 69	➲**975030**
M61166	09/57-07/75	➲**975407**➲**97707**
M61167	09/57-10/76	⊗01/78
M61168	10/57-10/85	⊗10/86
M61169	10/57-10/85	⊗07/86
M61170	10/57-10/85	⊗07/86
M61171	10/57-10/85	⊗07/86
M61172	10/57-10/75	➲**975409**➲**97709**
M61173	11/57-07/75	➲**975408**➲**97708**
M61174	11/57-10/84	⊗10/85
M61175	11/57-10/75	➲**975410**➲**97710**
M61176	11/57-10/85	⊗07/86
M61177	11/57-10/84	⊗10/85
M61178	12/57- 86	➲**977345**
M61179	12/57-10/84	⊗10/85
M61180	12/57- 86	➲**977347**
M61181	12/57-10/84	⊗10/85
M61182	12/57-07/78	➲*975673*➲**97703**
M61183	01/58- 86	Ⓟ➲**977349**
M61184	01/58-07/78	➲*975675*➲**97705**
M61185	01/58-07/78	➲*975674*➲**97704**
M61186	01/58-10/85	⊗07/86
M61187	01/58-10/76	⊗08/77
M61188	02/58-10/85	⊗07/86
M61189	02/58-07/78	➲*975676*➲**97706**

Class 302 York

Motor Brake Second
MBS, later MBSO
E61190-E61228

As built, Diagram 405 ED205

Rebuilt as MBSO, Diagram ED217

Corridor fitted MBSO, Diagram ED216

Diagram:	405 ED205 ED216 ED217	Lot Number:	30438
Body:	63' 6" × 9' 3"	Weight:	54t 8cwt
Seats:	96 second, later 82 or 76 second	Bogies:	Gresley
		Motors:	EE536A 4 × 192hp

E61190	10/59-01/91	⊗03/91	**274**	11/59-05/82	**302274**	05/82-01/91		
E61191	10/59-07/83	⊗05/84	**275**	11/59-11/79	**302275**	11/79-07/83		
E61192	10/59-02/86	⊗04/86	**276**	11/59-01/80	**302276**	01/80-02/86		
E61193	10/59-01/98	⊗	**277**	11/59-01/83	**302277**	01/83-09/88	**302227**[2]	09/88-01/98
E61194	10/59-09/89	⊗05/90	**278**	01/60-11/84	**302278**	11/84-09/89		
E61195	10/59-02/88	⊗09/88	**279**	01/60-10/81	**302279**	10/81-02/88		
E61196	10/59-01/90	⊗03/90	**280**	01/60- *83*	**302280**	*83*-01/90		
E61197	11/59-02/87	⊗10/87	**281**	01/60-10/82	**302281**	10/82-10/86		
E61198	11/59-09/89	⊗05/90	**282**	11/59-02/82	**302282**	02/82-09/89		
E61199	12/59-03/91	⊗03/91	**283**	12/59-02/83	**302283**	02/83-07/90		
E61200	12/59-03/90	⊗05/91	**284**	12/59-10/81	**302284**	10/81-03/90		
E61201	12/59-06/90	⊗07/90	**285**	12/59-06/83	**302285**	06/83-05/90		
E61202	12/59-03/90	⊗08/90	**286**	12/59-05/82	**302286**	05/82-03/90		
E61203	11/59-10/85	⊗02/86	**287**	11/59-01/80	**302287**	01/80-10/85		
E61204	12/59-02/87	⊗04/88	**288**	12/59-12/82	**302288**	12/82-05/85		
E61205	01/60-09/89	⊗03/90	**289**	01/60-01/80	**302289**	01/80-09/89		
E61206	01/60-09/89	⊗04/90	**290**	01/60-10/82	**302290**	10/82-09/89		
E61207	01/60-09/89	⊗02/90	**291**	01/60- *83*	**302291**	*83*-09/89		
E61208	01/60-10/90	⊗10/90	**292**	01/60-03/83	**302292**	03/83-10/90		
E61209	01/60-07/97	⊗12/97	**293**	01/60-08/81	**302293**	08/81-09/88	**302223**[2]	09/88-07/97
E61210	01/60-06/88	⊗09/88	**294**	01/60-01/82	**302294**	01/82-11/87	**302494**	11/87-06/88
			302294	06/88-06/88				
E61211	01/60-09/89	⊗05/90	**295**	01/60-02/82	**302295**	02/82-09/89		
E61212	01/60-09/89	⊗05/90	**296**	01/60-04/84	**302296**	04/84-03/89	**302257**	03/89-09/89
E61213	02/60-09/89	⊗08/90	**297**	02/60-10/81	**302297**	10/81-11/87	**302497**	11/87-02/88
			302297	02/88-03/89	**302265**	03/89-09/89		
E61214	01/60-06/90	⊗09/90	**298**	01/60-03/83	**302298**	03/83-06/90		
E61215	01/60-09/89	⊗07/90	**299**	01/60-03/83	**302299**	03/83-11/88		
E61216	01/60-03/90	⊗08/90	**300**	01/60-07/83	**302300**	07/83-09/88	**302250**[2]	09/88-03/90
E61217	01/60-06/90	⊗07/90	**301**	01/60-01/83	**302301**	01/83-09/88	**302253**[2]	09/88-06/90
E61218	02/60-09/89	⊗02/90	**302**	02/60-02/80	**302302**	02/80-09/88		
E61219	06/60-01/90	⊗08/90	**303**	06/60-07/83	**302303**	07/83-09/88	**302255**[2]	09/88-01/90
E61220	02/60-09/97	⊗09/97	**304**	02/60-06/83	**302304**	06/83-09/88	**302214**[2]	09/88-09/96
E61221	01/60-01/90	⊗09/90	**305**	01/60- *83*	**302305**	*83*-01/90		
E61222	01/60-03/90	➲**68023**	**306**	01/60-03/83	**302306**	03/83-09/88	**302273**[2]	09/88-03/90
E61223	01/60-10/90	⊗10/90	**307**	01/60-10/83	**302307**	10/83-09/88	**302267**[2]	09/88-10/90
E61224	02/60-01/94	⊗12/97	**308**	02/60-02/83	**302308**	02/83-09/88	**302208**[2]	09/88-02/92
			302208	07/93-01/94				
E61225	01/60-12/85	⊗02/86	**309**	01/60-02/80	**302309**	02/80-12/85		
E61226	04/60-04/97	⊗05/97	**310**	04/60-09/83	**302310**	09/83-09/88	**302207**[2]	09/88-04/97
E61227	04/60-04/89	➲**68022**	**311**	04/60- *83*	**302311**	*83*-09/88	**302275**[2]	09/88-04/89
E61228	05/60-08/88	➲**977602**	**312**	05/60- *83*	**302312**	*83*-08/88		

Class 411 4-CEP Ashford/Eastleigh

Motor Brake Second Open
DMBSO later DMSO(A) & DMSO(B)
S61229-S61240

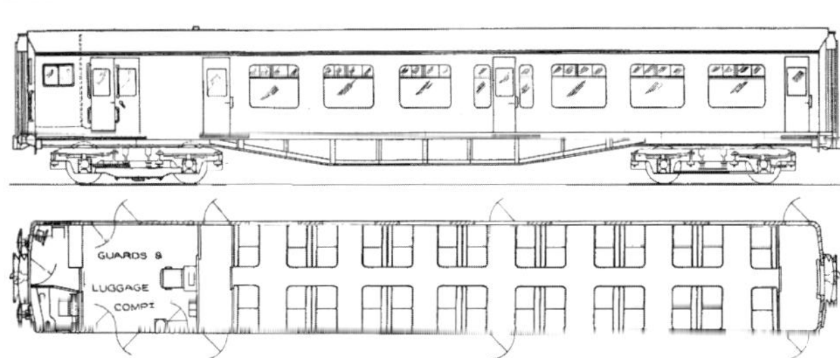

As built, Diagram 402

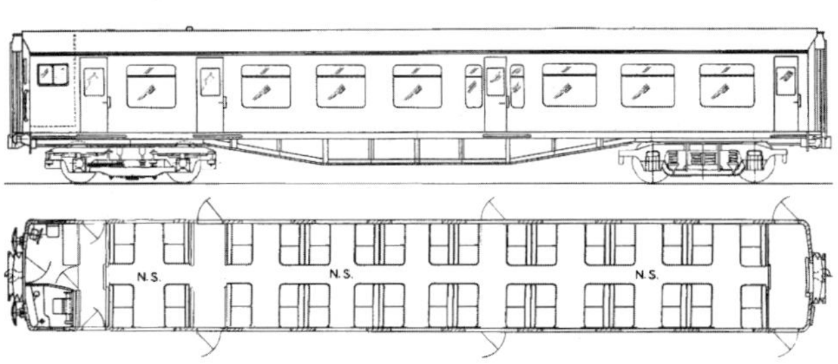

Refurbished, Diagram 884 DMSO(A) EA263, DMSO(B) EA264

Diagram:	402 884 EA263 EA264	Lot Number:	30116
Body:	64' 6" × 9' 3"	Weight:	40t 0cwt
Seats:	56 second, later 64 second	Bogies:	1 Mk 4 Motor
Motors:	EE507 2 × 250hp		1 Mk 3B or 4
			later Commonwealth

S61229	08/58-12/03	Ⓟ	**7105**	08/58-01/82	**1537**	01/82-09/02	**2325**	09/02-12/03
S61230	08/58-12/03	Ⓟ	**7105**	08/58-01/82	**1537**	01/82-09/02	**2325**	09/02-12/03
S61231	08/58-04/03	⊗04/03	**7106**	08/58-12/83	**1561**	12/83-10/98	**1102**	10/98-04/03
S61232	08/58-04/03	⊗04/03	**7106**	08/58-12/83	**1561**	12/83-10/98	**1102**	10/98-04/03
S61233	08/58-01/04	⊗02/04	**7107**	08/58-06/81	**1531**	06/81-01/04		
S61234	08/58-01/04	⊗02/04	**7107**	08/58-06/81	**1531**	06/81-01/04		
S61235	09/58-06/94	⊗07/95	**7108**	09/58-03/81	**1525**	03/81-07/93	**1403**	07/93-06/94
S61236	09/58-06/94	⊗07/95	**7108**	09/58-03/81	**1525**	03/81-07/93	**1403**	07/93-06/94
S61237	09/58-11/99	⊗05/04	**7109**	09/58-04/81	**1527**	04/81-11/99		
S61238	09/58-11/99	⊗	**7109**	09/58-04/81	**1527**	04/81-11/99		
S61239	09/58-06/94	⊗06/95	**7110**	09/58-03/81	**1526**	03/81-07/93	**1404**	07/93-06/94
S61240	09/58-06/94	⊗06/95	**7110**	09/58-03/81	**1526**	03/81-07/93	**1404**	07/93-06/94

Class 414 2-HAP Ashford/Eastleigh

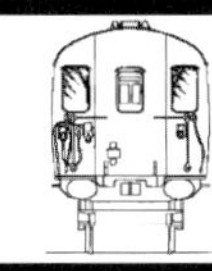

Driving Motor Brake Second Open
DMBSO
S61241-S61303

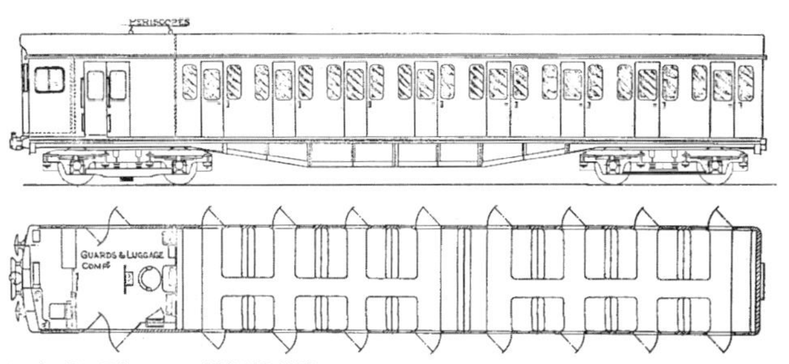

As built, Diagram 400 EB270

Diagram:	400 EB270	Lot Number:	30452
Body:	63' 11½" × 9' 3¼"	Weight:	41t 0cwt
Seats:	84 second, later 82 or 79	Bogies:	Mk 4
Motors:	EE507 2 × 250hp		

S61241	11/58-04/93	⊗08/93	**6043**	11/58-04/74	**5941**	04/74-03/80	**6043**	03/80-05/82
			3302	05/82-04/93				
S61242	12/58-10/83	⊗07/86	**6044**	12/58-04/74	**5942**	04/74-02/80	**6044**	02/80-10/83
S61243	12/58-05/91	⊗11/91	**6045**	12/58-05/77	**5943**	05/77-04/80	**6045**	04/80-05/82
			3310	05/82-10/84	**3310**	02/85-05/91		
S61244	12/58-04/93	⊗08/93	**6046**	12/58-05/77	**5944**	05/77-03/80	**6046**	03/80-05/82
			3302	05/82-04/93				
S61245	12/58-05/84	⊗02/85	**6047**	12/58-05/77	**5945**	05/77-04/80	**6047**	04/80-05/84
S61246	12/58-05/91	➲*977729*	**6048**	12/58-05/77	**5946**	05/77-03/80	**6048**	03/80-05/82
			3308	05/82-05/91				⊗08/91
S61247	01/59-05/84	⊗07/85	**6049**	01/59-05/77	**5947**	05/77-03/80	**6049**	03/80-05/84
S61248	01/59-10/82	⊗12/86	**6050**	01/59-05/77	**5948**	05/77-02/80	**6050**	02/80-10/82
S61249	01/59-07/91	⊗12/91	**6051**	01/59-05/77	**5949**	05/77-02/80	**6051**	05/80-07/88
			4301	07/88-07/91				
S61250	01/59-01/94	⊗05/94	**6052**	01/59-05/77	**5950**	05/77-05/80	**6052**	05/80-04/82
			3303	04/82-01/94				
S61251	01/59-05/91	⊗08/91	**6053**	01/59-05/77	**5951**	05/77-10/77	**6053**	10/77-05/82
			3309	05/82-05/91				
S61252	02/59-01/94	⊗05/94	**6054**	02/59-04/82	**3303**	04/82-01/94		
S61253	02/59-01/95	⊗11/94	**6055**	02/59-05/82	**3301**	05/82-01/95		
S61254	02/59-12/93	⊗01/94	**6056**	02/59-04/82	**3306**	04/82-12/93		
S61255	02/59-01/95	⊗11/94	**6057**	02/59-05/82	**3301**	05/82-01/95		
S61256	02/59-12/93	⊗01/94	**6058**	02/59-04/82	**3306**	04/82-12/93		
S61257	03/59-05/91	⊗08/91	**6059**	03/59-05/82	**3309**	05/82-05/91		
S61258	03/59-12/93	⊗01/94	**6060**	03/59-05/82	**3307**	05/82-12/93		
S61259	03/59-05/91	⊗11/91	**6061**	03/59-10/84	**3310**	02/85-05/91		
S61260	03/59-07/91	➲**977731**	**6062**	03/59-06/88	**4302**	06/88-07/91		
S61261	04/59-01/95	⊗02/95	**6063**	04/59-05/88	**4303**	05/88-09/91	**3325**	09/91-01/95
S61262	04/59-01/94	⊗02/94	**6064**	04/59-12/87	**4304**	12/87-09/91	**3323**	09/91-12/91
			3322	12/91-01/94				
S61263	04/59-10/83	⊗06/84	**6065**	04/59-10/83				
S61264	04/59-05/91	⊗08/91	**6066**	04/59-05/82	**3308**	05/82-05/91		
S61265	05/59-10/82	⊗12/86	**6067**	05/59-10/82				
S61266	05/59-10/84	⊗04/87	**6068**	05/59-05/82	**3310**	05/82-10/84		
S61267	05/59-05/82	℗➲**68507**	**6069**	05/59-05/82				
S61268	05/59-01/94	⊗02/94	**6070**	05/59-04/88	**4305**	04/88-09/91	**3321**	09/91-01/94
S61269	05/59-05/82	℗➲**68500**	**6071**	05/59-05/82				
S61270	06/59-12/93	⊗01/94	**6072**	06/59-08/87	**4306**	08/87-09/91	**3324**	09/91-12/93
S61271	06/59-12/93	⊗01/94	**6073**	06/59-05/82	**3307**	05/82-12/93		
S61272	06/59-05/82	➲**68508**	**6074**	06/59-05/82				
S61273	06/59-05/93	⊗08/93	**6075**	06/59-10/87	**4307**	10/87-09/91	**3323**	09/91-05/93
S61274	06/59-09/82	➲**68502**	**6076**	06/59-09/82				
S61275	06/59-03/95	℗	**6077**	06/59-07/87	**4308**	07/87-03/95		
S61276	07/59-03/95	⊗04/95	**6078**	07/59-07/87	**4309**	07/87-03/95		
S61277	07/59-09/82	℗➲**68503**	**6079**	07/59-09/82				
S61278	07/59-01/94	⊗02/94	**6080**	07/59-05/88	**4310**	05/88-09/91	**3321**	09/91-01/94
S61279	07/59-05/94	⊗06/94	**6081**	07/59-05/82	**3305**	05/82-05/94		
S61280	07/59-05/82	℗➲**68509**	**6082**	07/59-05/82				
S61281	07/59-05/82	➲**68501**	**6083**	07/59-05/82				
S61282	07/59-04/94	⊗06/94	**6084**	07/59-04/82	**3304**	04/82-04/94		
S61283	07/59-04/94	⊗06/94	**6085**	07/59-04/82	**3304**	04/82-04/94		
S61284	07/59-05/82	⊗09/87	**6086**	07/59-05/82				
S61285	08/59-10/84	⊗02/88	**6087**	08/59-10/84				
S61286	08/59-05/82	➲**68504**	**6088**	08/59-05/82				
S61287	08/59-03/95	℗	**6089**	08/59-07/87	**4311**	07/87-03/95		
S61288	08/59-07/91	➲*977733*	**6090**	08/59-07/88	**4312**	07/88-07/91		⊗12/91
S61289	08/59-10/83	⊗05/84	**6091**	08/59-10/83				
S61290	08/59-03/95	⊗04/95	**6092**	08/59-07/87	**4313**	07/87-03/95		
S61291	08/59-04/93	⊗08/93	**6093**	08/59-05/82	**3311**	05/82-04/93		
S61292	08/59-05/82	℗➲**68506**	**6094**	08/59-05/82				
S61293	08/59-10/82	⊗01/87	**6095**	08/59-10/82				
S61294	08/59-11/94	⊗11/94	**6096**	08/59-07/87	**4314**	07/87-11/94		
S61295	09/59-01/94	⊗02/94	**6097**	09/59-11/87	**4315**	11/87-09/91	**3322**	09/91-01/94
S61296	09/59-07/91	➲*977733*	**6098**	09/59-12/87	**4316**	12/87-07/91		⊗12/91
S61297	08/59-04/93	⊗08/93	**6099**	09/59-05/82	**3311**	05/82-04/93		
S61298	08/59-01/95	⊗02/95	**6100**	09/59-04/87	**4317**	04/87-09/91	**3325**	09/91-01/95
S61299	09/59-05/82	➲**68505**	**6101**	09/59-05/82				
S61300	09/59-05/93	⊗08/93	**6102**	09/59-05/87	**4318**	05/87-09/91	**3322**	09/91-12/91
			3323	12/91-05/93				
S61301	09/59-10/84	⊗02/88	**6103**	09/59-10/84				
S61302	09/59-05/94	⊗06/94	**6104**	09/59-05/82	**3305**	05/82-05/94		
S61303	09/59-12/93	⊗01/94	**6105**	09/59-06/87	**4319**	06/87-09/91	**3324**	09/91-12/93

Class 411 4-CEP Ashford/Eastleigh

Driving Motor Brake Second Open DMBSO later DMSO(A) & DMSO(B)

S61304-S61409 (61390 onwards Class 410 4-BEP)

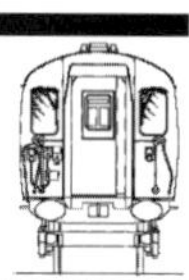

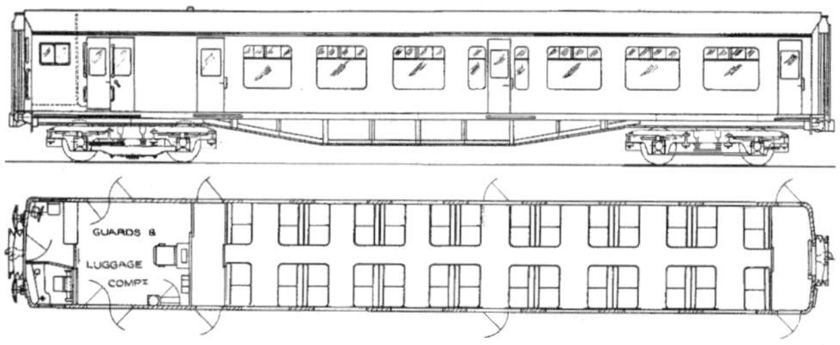

As built, Diagram 402

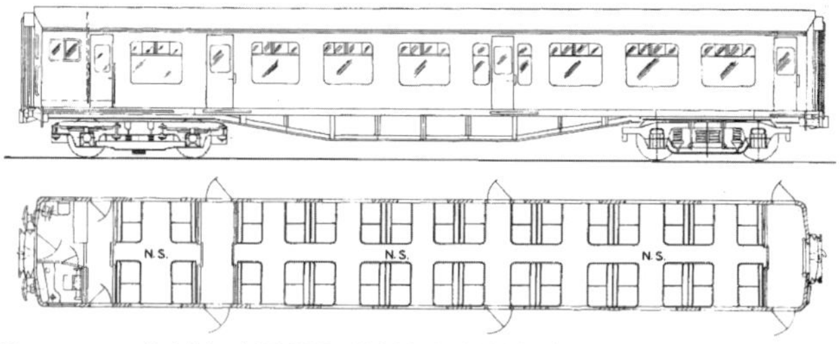

Prototype refurbished DMSO, 61388 & 61389 Diagram 882 EA262

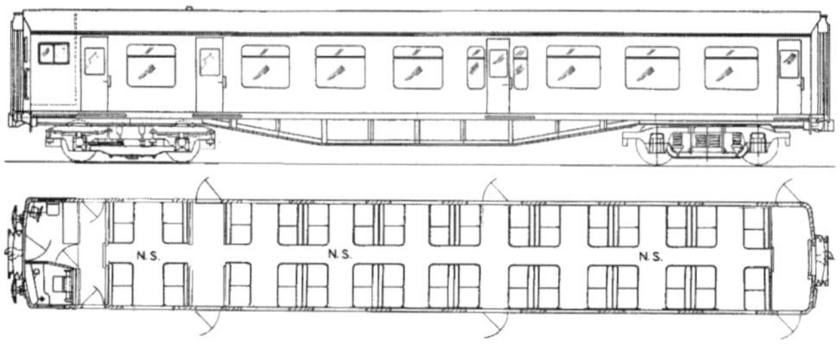

Refurbished as DMSO, Diagram 884 DMSO(A) EA263, DMSO(B) EA264

Diagram:	402 882 EA262 884 EA263 EA264	Lot Number:	30454
Body:	64' 6" × 9' 3"	Weight:	40t 0cwt
Seats:	56 second, later 64 second	Bogies:	1 Mk 4 Motor 1 Mk 6
Motors:	EE507 2 × 250hp		later Commonwealth

S61304	09/58-05/95	⊗06/95	**7111**	09/58-01/80	**1508**	01/80-05/95		
S61305	09/58-05/95	⊗06/95	**7111**	09/58-01/80	**1508**	01/80-05/95		
S61306	09/58-11/03	⊗02/04	**7112**	09/58-02/82	**1538**	02/82-09/02	**2327**	09/02-11/03
S61307	09/58-11/03	⊗02/04	**7112**	09/58-02/82	**1538**	02/82-09/02	**2327**	09/02-11/03
S61308	10/58-11/95	⊗04/96	**7113**	10/58-02/81	**1524**	02/81-11/85		
S61309	10/58-11/95	⊗04/96	**7113**	10/58-02/81	**1524**	02/81-11/85		
S61310	10/58-08/04	⊗08/04	**7114**	10/58-04/83	**1555**	04/83-08/04		
S61311	10/58-08/04	⊗08/04	**7114**	10/58-04/83	**1555**	04/83-08/04		
S61312	10/58-08/04	⊗08/04	**7115**	10/58-12/82	**1550**	12/82-08/04		
S61313	10/58-08/04	⊗08/04	**7115**	10/58-12/82	**1550**	12/82-08/04		
S61314	10/58-12/92	⊗03/94	**7116**	10/58-06/82	**1544**	06/82-03/94		
S61315	10/58-04/04	⊗05/04	**7116**	10/58-06/82	**1544**	06/82-04/04		
S61316	10/58-08/04	⊗08/04	**7117**	10/58-11/80	**1517**	11/80-08/04		
S61317	10/58-08/04	⊗08/04	**7117**	10/58-11/80	**1517**	11/80-08/04		
S61318	11/58-06/95	⊗07/95	**7118**	11/58-10/80	**1516**	10/80-06/95		
S61319	11/58-06/95	⊗07/95	**7118**	11/58-10/80	**1516**	10/80-06/95		
S61320	11/58-06/02	⊗	**7119**	11/58-06/80	**1512**	06/80-06/02		
S61321	11/58-06/02	⊗06/05	**7119**	11/58-06/80	**1512**	06/80-06/02		
S61322	11/58-08/02	⊗09/02	**7120**	11/58-04/82	**1543**	04/82-05/99	**1110**	05/99-08/02
S61323	11/58-03/03	⊗06/03	**7120**	11/58-04/82	**1543**	04/82-05/99	**1110**	05/99-08/02
			1616	09/02-03/03				
S61324	11/58-12/02	⊗01/03	**7121**	11/58-12/82	**1551**	12/82-12/02		
S61325	11/58-12/02	⊗01/03	**7121**	11/58-12/82	**1551**	12/82-12/02		
S61326	11/58-06/95	⊗06/95	**7122**	11/58-08/80	**1514**	08/80-06/95		
S61327	11/58-06/95	⊗06/95	**7122**	11/58-08/80	**1514**	08/80-06/95		
S61328	12/58-05/04	⊗08/04	**7123**	12/58-09/82	**1547**	09/82-09/02	**2326**	09/02-01/03
			1199	01/03-05/04				
S61329	12/58-05/04	⊗08/04	**7123**	12/58-09/82	**1547**	09/82-09/02	**2326**	09/02-01/03
			1199	01/03-05/04				
S61330	12/58-04/03	⊗04/03	**7124**	12/58-06/81	**1530**	06/81-10/98	**1101**	10/98-04/03
S61331	12/58-04/03	⊗04/03	**7124**	12/58-06/81	**1530**	06/81-10/98	**1101**	10/98-04/03
S61332	12/58-08/96	*⊗05/97*	**7125**	12/58-11/80	**1518**	11/80-08/96		
S61333	12/58-08/96	*⊗05/97*	**7125**	12/58-11/80	**1518**	11/80-08/96		
S61334	12/58-12/02	⊗12/02	**7126**	12/58-02/80	**1509**	02/80-12/02		
S61335	12/58-12/02	⊗12/02	**7126**	12/58-02/80	**1509**	02/80-12/02		

S61336	12/58-05/93	⊗11/93	**7127**	12/58-07/83	**1558**	10/83-12/83	**2704**	12/83-03/86
			1558	03/86-05/93				
S61337	12/58-10/99	⊗05/01	**7127**	12/58-07/83	**1557**	07/83-09/83	**2702**	09/83-03/86
			1557	03/86-10/99				
S61338	12/58-01/03	⊗01/03	**7128**	12/58-11/82	**1549**	11/82-05/99	**1111**	05/99-01/03
S61339	12/58-01/03	⊗01/03	**7128**	12/58-11/82	**1549**	11/82-05/99	**1111**	05/99-01/03
S61340	01/59-05/95	⊗06/95	**7129**	01/59-06/80	**1513**	06/80-05/95		
S61341	01/59-09/70	⊗02/79	**7129**	01/59-09/70				
S61342	01/59-07/91	⊃977396	**7130**	01/59-03/79				
S61343	01/59-03/03	⊗04/03	**7130**	01/59-03/79	**1520**	12/80-05/99	**1107**	05/99-03/03
S61344	01/59-04/96	⊗05/96	**7131**	01/59-09/80	**1515**	09/80-04/96		
S61345	01/59-04/96	⊗05/96	**7131**	01/59-09/80	**1515**	09/80-04/96		
S61346	01/59-06/94	⊗07/95	**7132**	01/59-12/80	**1522**	01/81-05/93	**1402**	05/93-06/94
S61347	01/59-06/94	⊗07/95	**7132**	01/59-12/80	**1522**	01/81-05/93	**1402**	05/93-06/94
S61348	01/59-01/93	⊗03/94	**7133**	01/59-12/79	**1506**	12/79-12/92		
S61349	01/59-04/04	⊗04/04	**7133**	01/59-12/79	**1506**	12/79-12/92	**1544**	03/94-04/04
S61350	01/59-03/04	⊗	**7134**	01/59-10/82	**1553**	02/83-10/95	**1553**	04/96-03/04
S61351	01/59-10/95	⊗04/96	**7134**	01/59-10/82	**1553**	02/83-10/95		
S61352	01/59-06/94	⊗06/95	**7135**	01/59-12/80	**1521**	12/80-05/93	**1401**	05/93-06/94
S61353	01/59-06/94	⊗06/95	**7135**	01/59-12/80	**1521**	12/80-05/93	**1401**	05/93-06/94
S61354	02/59-06/94	⊗07/95	**7136**	02/59-05/81	**1529**	05/81-06/93	**1406**	06/93-06/94
S61355	02/59-09/05	⊗12/05	**7136**	02/59-05/81	**1529**	05/81-06/93	**1406**	06/93-05/94
			1540	05/94-08/96	**1698**	08/96-09/05		
S61356	02/59-06/95	⊗06/95	**7137**	02/59-08/82	**1546**	08/82-06/95		
S61357	02/59-06/95	⊗06/95	**7137**	02/59-08/82	**1546**	08/82-06/95		
S61358	02/59-04/97	⊃Dep	**7138**	02/59-07/82	**1545**	07/82-04/97	**932545**	04/97- 02
S61359	02/59-04/97	⊃Dep	**7138**	02/59-07/82	**1545**	07/82-04/97	**932545**	04/97- 02
S61360	02/59-10/99	⊗05/01	**7139**	02/59-07/83	**1557**	07/83-09/83	**2702**	09/83-03/86
			1557	03/86-10/99				
S61361	02/59-05/93	⊗11/93	**7139**	02/59-07/83	**1558**	10/83-12/83	**2704**	12/83-03/86
			1558	03/86-05/93				
S61362	02/59-03/03	⊗03/03	**7140**	02/59-01/80	**1507**	01/80-12/02		
S61363	02/59-03/03	⊗03/03	**7140**	02/59-01/80	**1507**	01/80-12/02		
S61364	03/59-06/02	⊗09/02	**7141**	03/59-04/80	**1510**	04/80-05/99	**1106**	05/99-06/02
S61365	03/59-06/02	⊗09/02	**7141**	03/59-04/80	**1510**	04/80-05/99	**1106**	05/99-06/02
S61366	03/59-12/02	⊗01/03	**7142**	03/59-05/80	**1511**	05/80-12/02		
S61367	03/59-12/02	⊗01/03	**7142**	03/59-05/80	**1511**	05/80-12/02		
S61368	03/59-03/03	⊗04/03	**7143**	03/59-04/83	**1554**	04/83-07/99	**1112**	07/99-03/03
S61369	03/59-03/03	⊗04/03	**7143**	03/59-04/83	**1554**	04/83-07/99	**1112**	07/99-03/03
S61370	03/59-04/03	⊗04/03	**7144**	03/59-06/83	**1556**	06/83-08/83	**2701**	08/83-02/86
			1556	02/86-05/99	**1113**	05/99-04/03		
S61371	03/59-04/03	⊗04/03	**7144**	03/59-06/83	**1556**	06/83-08/83	**2701**	08/83-02/86
			1556	02/86-05/99	**1113**	05/99-04/03		
S61372	04/59-07/05	⊗12/05	**7145**	04/59-02/83	**1552**	02/83-10/96	**1697**	10/96-07/05
S61373	04/59-07/05	⊗12/05	**7145**	04/59-02/83	**1552**	02/83-10/96	**1697**	10/96-07/05
S61374	04/59-01/04	⊗02/04	**7146**	04/59-10/82	**1548**	10/82-09/02	**2322**	09/02-01/04
S61375	04/59-01/04	⊗02/04	**7146**	04/59-10/82	**1548**	10/82-09/02	**2322**	09/02-01/04
S61376	04/59-04/03	⊗04/03	**7147**	04/59-10/83	**1559**	10/83-05/99	**1114**	05/99-04/03
S61377	04/59-04/03	⊗04/03	**7147**	04/59-10/83	**1559**	10/83-05/99	**1114**	05/99-04/03
S61378	05/59-06/94	⊗07/95	**7148**	05/59-04/81	**1528**	04/81-07/93	**1405**	07/93-06/94
S61379	05/59-06/94	⊗07/95	**7148**	05/59-04/81	**1528**	04/81-07/93	**1405**	07/93-06/94
S61380	05/59-03/03	⊗04/03	**7149**	05/59-04/79	**1520**	12/80-05/99	**1107**	05/99-03/03
S61381	05/59-04/79	⊗02/81	**7149**	05/59-04/79				
S61382	06/59-04/96	⊗05/96	**7150**	06/59-02/81	**1523**	02/81-04/96		
S61383	06/59-04/96	℗	**7150**	06/59-02/81	**1523**	02/81-04/96		
S61384	06/59-09/05	⊗12/05	**7151**	06/59-03/82	**1540**	03/82-08/96	**1698**	08/96-09/05
S61385	06/59-04/04	⊗08/04	**7151**	06/59-04/71	**7004**	03/72-09/81	**1533**	09/81-04/04
S61386	06/59-12/02	⊗12/02	**7152**	06/59-11/83	**1560**	11/83-12/83	**2703**	12/83-03/86
			1560	03/86-12/02				
S61387	06/59-12/02	⊗12/02	**7152**	06/59-11/83	**1560**	11/83-12/83	**2703**	12/83-03/86
			1560	03/86-12/02				
S61388	06/59-05/90	⊃977397	**7153**	06/59-11/85	**1500**	11/85-01/90		
S61389	06/59-05/90	⊃977398	**7153**	06/59-11/85	**1500**	11/85-01/90		
S61390	03/59-08/97	⊗01/08	**7003**	03/59-09/81	**1532**	09/81-08/97		
S61391	03/59-08/97	⊗08/00	**7003**	03/59-09/81	**1532**	09/81-08/97		
S61392	04/59-01/72	⊗08/73	**7004**	04/59-01/72				
S61393	04/59-04/04	⊗08/04	**7004**	04/59-09/81	**1533**	09/81-04/04		
S61394	04/59-05/95	⊗06/95	**7005**	04/59-03/82	**1542**	03/82-05/95		
S61395	04/59-05/95	⊗06/95	**7005**	04/59-03/82	**1542**	03/82-05/95		
S61396	04/59-07/04	⊗	**7006**	04/59-11/81	**1535**	11/81-07/04		
S61397	04/59-07/04	⊗	**7006**	04/59-11/81	**1535**	11/81-07/04		
S61398	04/59-02/03	⊗03/03	**7007**	04/59-11/81	**1536**	11/81-05/99	**1108**	05/99-02/03
S61399	04/59-02/03	⊗03/03	**7007**	04/59-11/81	**1536**	11/81-05/99	**1108**	05/99-02/03
S61400	05/59-09/04	⊗09/04	**7008**	05/59-11/81	**1539**	02/82-09/04		
S61401	05/59-09/04	⊗09/04	**7008**	05/59-11/81	**1539**	02/82-09/04		
S61402	05/59-04/04	⊗05/04	**7009**	05/59-11/80	**1519**	11/80-04/04		
S61403	05/59-04/04	⊗05/04	**7009**	05/59-11/80	**1519**	11/80-04/04		
S61404	05/59-04/04	⊗08/04	**7010**	05/59-10/81	**1534**	10/81-04/04		
S61405	05/59-04/04	⊗08/04	**7010**	05/59-10/81	**1534**	10/81-04/04		
S61406	05/59-04/04	⊗06/04	**7011**	05/59-08/83	**1562**	12/83-03/89	**2308**	03/89-04/89
			1562	12/89-04/04				
S61407	05/59-04/04	⊗06/04	**7011**	05/59-08/83	**1562**	12/83-03/89	**2308**	03/89-04/89
			1562	12/89-04/04				
S61408	05/59-06/02	⊗09/02	**7012**	05/59-11/81	**1541**	03/82-05/99	**1109**	05/99-06/02
S61409	05/59-06/02	⊗09/02	**7012**	05/59-11/81	**1541**	03/82-05/99	**1109**	05/99-06/02

Class 305/2 York/Doncaster
Motor Brake Second
MBS, later MBSO
E61410-E61428

As built, Diagram 405 ED205

Rebuilt as MBSO, Diagram ED217

Corridor fitted MBSO, Diagram ED216

Diagram:	405 ED205 ED216 ED217	Lot Number:	30567
Body:	63' 6" × 9' 3"	Weight:	54t 8cwt
Seats:	96 second, later 82 or 76 second	Bogies:	Gresley
		Motors:	GEC WT380 4 × 200hp

E61410	10/59-12/01	⊗01/02	**501**	10/59-03/83	**305501**	03/83-12/01		
E61411	03/60-05/84	⊗07/86	**502**	03/60-04/83	**305502**	04/83-04/83		
E61412	04/60-11/97	⊗04/99	**503**	04/60-05/81	**305503**	05/81-11/97		
E61413	04/60-06/96	⊗07/96	**504**	04/60-11/81	**305504**	11/81-06/96		
E61414	04/60-09/90	⊗09/90	**505**	04/60-12/81	**305505**	05/83-09/90		
E61415	05/60-08/00	⊗04/03	**506**	05/60-07/81	**305506**	07/81-08/00		
E61416	05/60-11/97	⊗04/99	**507**	05/60-01/80	**305507**	01/80-11/97		
E61417	06/60-10/01	⊗11/01	**508**	06/60-03/83	**305508**	03/83-10/01		
E61418	07/60-05/98	⊗12/98	**509**	07/60- *83*	**305509**	*83*-10/95		
E61419	07/60-03/99	⊗04/99	**510**	07/60-03/83	**305510**	03/83-03/99		
E61420	07/60-07/00	⊗03/03	**511**	07/60-04/83	**305511**	04/83-07/00		
E61421	08/60-06/01	⊗11/01	**512**	08/60-09/81	**305499**	10/82-02/83	**305502**	04/83-06/01
E61422	08/60-06/96	⊗07/96	**513**	08/60-02/80	**305513**	02/80-06/96		
E61423	09/60-03/93	⊗09/93	**514**	09/60-02/81	**305514**	02/81-03/93		
E61424	10/60-11/97	⊗04/99	**515**	10/60-01/80	**305515**	01/80-11/97		
E61425	10/60-06/00	⊗03/03	**516**	10/60-02/83	**305516**	02/83-06/00		
E61426	10/60-12/01	⊗01/02	**517**	10/60-02/83	**305517**	02/83-12/01		
E61427	11/60-05/98	⊗12/98	**518**	11/60-08/81	**305518**	08/81-05/98		
E61428	11/60-12/01	⊗01/02	**519**	11/60-04/83	**305519**	04/83-12/01		

Class 305/1 York

Motor Brake Second Open
MBSO
E61429-E61480

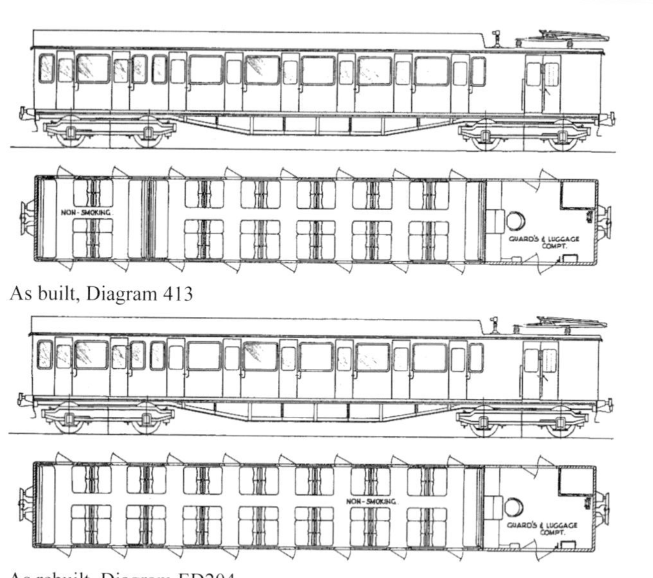

As built, Diagram 413

As rebuilt, Diagram ED204

Diagram:	413 ED204	Lot Number:	30571
Body:	63' 6⅛" × 9' 3"	Weight:	54t 6cwt
Seats:	84 second, later 76 second	Bogies:	Gresley
Motors:	GEC WT380 4 × 200hp		

E61429	03/60-06/96	⊗07/96	**401**	03/60-09/82	**305401**	09/82-06/96		
E61430	03/60-03/93	⊗02/95	**402**	03/60-08/83	**305402**	08/83-02/92	**305594**	02/92-01/93
E61431	03/60-03/93	⊗06/93	**403**	03/60-11/81	**305403**	11/81-07/87	**305521**	05/88-03/93
E61432	03/60-12/92	⊗11/94	**404**	03/60-08/81	**305404**	08/81-11/88	**305522**	11/88-12/92
E61433	04/60-12/92	⊗12/98	**405**	04/60-09/82	**305405**	09/82-10/82	**305405**	02/83-02/92
			305597	02/92-12/92				
E61434	04/60-07/95	⊗09/95	**406**	04/60-09/82	**305406**	09/82-01/92	**305599**	02/92-07/93
E61435	05/60-07/93	⊗03/94	**407**	05/60-11/81	**305407**	11/81-02/92	**305598**	02/92-07/93
E61436	03/60-09/91	➲**977742**	**408**	03/60-08/82	**305408**	08/82-09/91		
E61437	04/60-12/92	⊗02/94	**409**	04/60-06/83	**305409**	06/83-12/92		
E61438	06/60-06/96	⊗07/96	**410**	06/60-06/82	**305410**	06/82-06/96		
E61439	04/60-12/92	⊗08/93	**411**	04/60- *83*	**305411**	*83*-07/87	**305523**	04/88-12/92
E61440	04/60-08/93	⊗08/93	**412**	04/60-04/81	**305412**	04/81-08/93		
E61441	04/60-02/92	⊗03/94	**413**	04/60-05/81	**305413**	05/81-02/92		
E61442	06/60-12/92	⊗03/94	**414**	06/60-11/81	**305414**	11/81-07/87	**305524**	11/88-12/92
E61443	06/60-10/92	⊗03/94	**415**	06/60-11/81	**305415**	11/81-10/92		
E61444	05/60-06/96	⊗07/96	**416**	05/60-10/82	**305416**	10/82-06/96		
E61445	05/60-01/93	⊗02/94	**417**	05/60- *83*	**305417**	*83*-01/93		
E61446	06/60-03/93	⊗02/95	**418**	06/60-04/82	**305418**	04/82-02/92	**305595**	02/92-01/93
E61447	05/60-06/93	⊗09/94	**419**	05/60-05/82	**305419**	05/82-07/87	**305525**	02/92-06/93
E61448	06/60-06/96	⊗07/96	**420**	06/60-03/83	**305420**	03/83-06/96		
E61449	07/60-02/92	⊗03/94	**421**	07/60-07/83	**305421**	07/83-02/92		
E61450	07/60-03/93	⊗03/94	**422**	06/60-04/83	**305422**	04/83-06/87	**305526**	05/88-03/93
E61451	06/60-05/84	⊗08/85	**423**	06/60-01/82	**305423**	01/82-05/84		
E61452	06/60-05/84	⊗04/85	**424**	06/60-12/81	**305424**	12/81-05/84		
E61453	06/60-05/84	⊗03/85	**425**	06/60-08/82	**305425**	08/82-05/84		
E61454	07/60-05/84	⊗04/85	**426**	07/60- *83*	**305426**	*83*-05/84		
E61455	07/60-05/84	⊗10/85	**427**	07/60-02/80	**305427**	02/80-05/84		
E61456	07/60-05/84	⊗03/85	**428**	07/60-02/80	**305428**	02/80-05/84		
E61457	07/60-05/84	⊗04/85	**429**	07/60-08/81	**305429**	08/81-05/84		
E61458	07/60-05/84	⊗08/85	**430**	07/60-06/81	**305430**	06/81-05/84		
E61459	08/60-05/84	⊗07/85	**431**	08/60-03/83	**305431**	03/83-05/84		
E61460	08/60-05/84	⊗04/85	**432**	08/60- *83*	**305432**	*83*-05/84		
E61461	08/60-05/84	⊗04/85	**433**	08/60-04/82	**305433**	04/82-05/84		
E61462	08/60-05/84	⊗11/84	**434**	08/60-01/82	**305434**	01/82-05/84		
E61463	08/60-05/84	➲**977640**	**435**	08/60-10/82	**305435**	10/82-05/84		
E61464	08/60-05/84	⊗04/85	**436**	08/60-08/82	**305436**	08/82-05/84		
E61465	08/60-05/84	⊗02/86	**437**	08/60-07/81	**305437**	07/81-05/84		
E61466	08/60-05/84	⊗07/85	**438**	08/60-04/83	**305438**	04/83-05/84		
E61467	09/60-05/84	➲**977309**	**439**	09/60-11/82	**305439**	11/82-05/84		
E61468	09/60-05/84	⊗06/85	**440**	09/60-02/82	**305440**	02/82-01/84	**305540**	01/84-05/84
E61469	10/60-05/84	⊗06/85	**441**	11/60-06/81	**305441**	06/81-01/84	**305541**	01/84-05/84
E61470	10/60-02/85	⊗04/85	**442**	11/60-12/81	**305442**	12/81-01/84	**305542**	01/84-02/85
E61471	10/60-08/84	⊗03/85	**443**	11/60-01/82	**305443**	01/82-01/84	**305543**	01/84-08/84
E61472	10/60-05/84	⊗06/85	**444**	11/60-02/80	**305444**	02/80-01/84	**305544**	01/84-05/84
E61473	10/60-05/98	⊗12/98	**445**	11/60-06/82	**305445**	06/82-01/84	**305545**	01/84-02/85
			305445	02/85-07/87	**305403**[2]	07/87-05/98		
E61474	10/60-06/93	⊗08/93	**446**	11/60-05/82	**305446**	05/82-03/85	**305546**	03/85-05/85
			305446	05/85-04/88	**305527**	04/88-06/93		
E61475	10/60-12/92	⊗01/93	**447**	11/60-06/83	**305447**	06/83-07/87	**305404**	07/87-12/92
E61476	10/60-12/92	⊗12/93	**448**	11/60-01/82	**305448**	01/82-03/85	**305548**	03/85-04/85
			305448	04/85-07/87	**305411**[2]	07/87-12/92		
E61477	10/60-11/91	⊗11/91	**449**	11/60-12/82	**305449**	12/82-02/85	**305549**	02/85-04/85
			305449	04/85-07/87	**305414**[2]	07/87-11/91		
E61478	10/60-11/92	⊗03/94	**450**	11/60-12/83	**305450**	12/83-02/85	**305550**	02/85-05/85
			305450	05/85-07/87	**305419**[2]	07/87-11/92		
E61479	11/60-06/93	⊗08/93	**451**	11/60-03/81	**305451**	03/81-01/89	**305528**	01/89-06/93
E61480	11/60-07/93	⊗03/94	**452**	11/60-02/80	**305452**	02/80-06/87	**305422**[2]	06/87-02/92
			305596	02/92-07/93				

Class 303 Pressed Steel

Motor Brake Second Open
MBSO
SC61481-SC61515

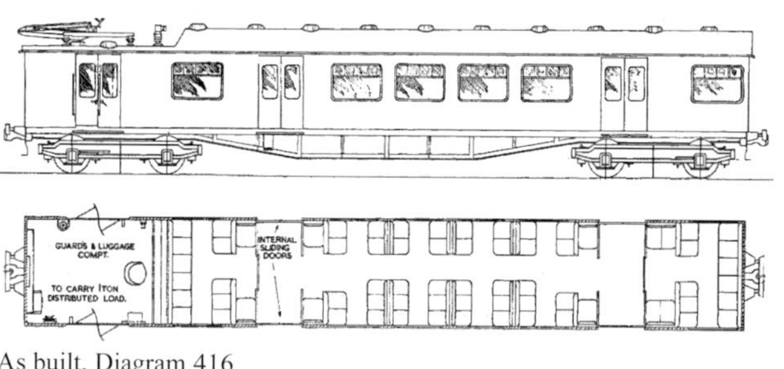

As built, Diagram 416

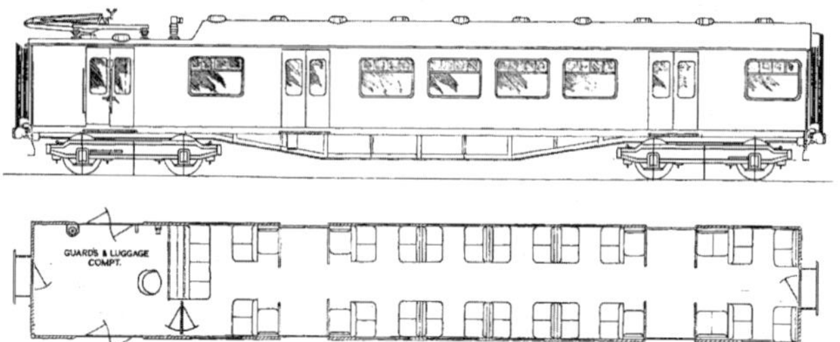

® Refurbished 2+2 seating

Diagram:	416 ED201	Lot Number:	30580
Body:	63' 6⅛" × 9' 3"	Weight:	55t 11cwt
Seats:	70 second, later 48 second	Bogies:	Gresley
Motors:	MV 4 × 207hp		

SC61481	07/59-12/02	⊗01/03	®	**001**	07/59-*11/79*	**303001**	*11/79*-12/02		
SC61482	09/59- 78	⊗12/82		**002**	09/59- 78				
SC61483	09/59-10/01	⊗01/03	®	**003**	09/59-*11/79*	**303003**	*11/79*-10/01		
SC61484	11/59-12/02	⊗01/03	®	**004**	11/59-*03/80*	**303004**	*03/80*-12/02		
SC61485	11/59-07/89	⊗11/91		**005**	11/59-*03/80*	**303005**	*03/80*-07/89		
SC61486	11/59-06/02	⊗09/02	®	**006**	11/59-*11/79*	**303006**	*11/79*-06/02		
SC61487	11/59- 78	⊗03/81		**007**	11/59- 78				
SC61488	12/59-01/02	⊗02/02	®	**008**	12/59-*11/79*	**303008**	*11/79*-01/02		
SC61489	12/59-08/00	⊗03/01	®	**009**	12/59-*03/80*	**303009**	*03/80*-08/00	**303024**	08/00-08/00
SC61490	12/59-01/01	⊗09/01	®	**010**	12/59-*11/79*	**303010**	*11/79*-01/01		
SC61491	12/59-12/02	⊗01/03	®	**011**	12/59-*05/79*	**303011**	*05/79*-12/02		
SC61492	01/60-02/02	⊗02/02	®	**012**	01/60- *80*	**303012**	*80*-02/02		
SC61493	01/60-10/01	⊗05/02	®	**013**	01/60- *80*	**303013**	*80*-10/01		
SC61494	01/60-07/01	⊗11/01	®	**014**	01/60-*03/80*	**303014**	*03/80*-07/01		
SC61495	01/60-12/87	⊗02/88		**015**	01/60-05/80	**303015**	05/80-12/87		
SC61496	02/60-01/02	⊗02/02	®	**016**	02/60- *80*	**303016**	*80*-01/02		
SC61497	02/60-12/82	⊗11/87		**017**	02/60-06/80	**303017**	06/80-12/82		
SC61498	02/60-12/87	⊗02/88		**018**	02/60-07/80	**303018**	07/80-12/87		
SC61499	02/60-03/02	⊗05/02	®	**019**	02/60-*03/80*	**303019**	*03/80*-03/02		
SC61500	02/60-06/02	⊗12/02	®	**020**	02/60- *80*	**303020**	*80*-06/02		
SC61501	03/60-06/02	⊗10/02	®	**021**	03/60-08/80	**303021**	08/80-06/02		
SC61502	03/60-12/82	⊗11/87		**022**	03/60-06/80	**303022**	06/80-12/82		
SC61503	03/60-07/02	℗	®	**023**	03/60-06/80	**303023**	06/80-07/02		
SC61504	03/60-09/02	⊗01/03	®	**024**	03/60-*11/79*	**303024**	*11/79*-05/98	**303009**	08/00-09/02
SC61505	03/60-07/00	⊗08/01	®	**025**	03/60-*08/79*	**303025**	*08/79*-09/00		
SC61506	04/60-12/87	⊗05/89		**026**	04/60- *80*	**303026**	*80*-12/87		
SC61507	04/60-09/02	⊗12/02	®	**027**	04/60-*03/80*	**303027**	*03/80*-09/02		
SC61508	04/60-04/02	⊗08/02	®	**028**	04/60-*11/79*	**303028**	*11/79*-07/99	**303037**	07/99-04/02
SC61509	04/60-09/90	⊗12/90		**029**	04/60-*03/80*	**303029**	*03/80*-09/90		
SC61510	04/60-12/87	⊗04/89		**030**	04/60-*11/79*	**303030**	*11/79*-12/87		
SC61511	05/60-02/88	⊗05/89		**031**	05/60- *80*	**303031**	*80*-12/87		
SC61512	05/60-06/02	⊗08/02	®	**032**	05/60-*05/79*	**303032**	*05/79*-06/02		
SC61513	05/60-05/77	⊗11/87		**033**	05/60-06/79				
SC61514	05/60-10/01	⊗05/02	®	**034**	05/60- *80*	**303034**	*80*-10/01		
SC61515	11/60-12/80	⊗12/82		**035**	11/60-06/80	**303035**	06/80-12/80		

Class 415 4-EPB Eastleigh

Driving Motor Brake Second
DMBS
S61516-S61627

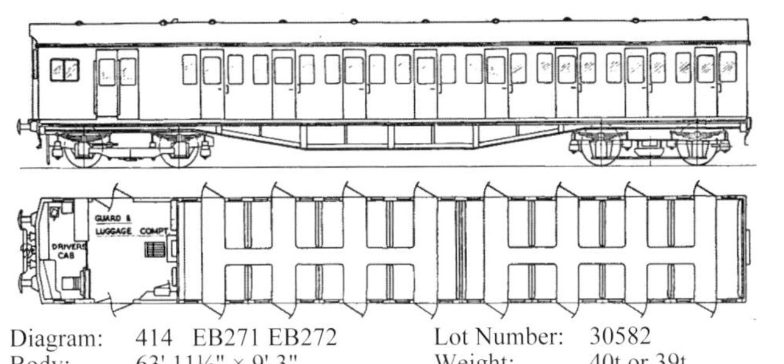

Diagram:	414 EB271 EB272		Lot Number:	30582
Body:	63' 11½" × 9' 3"		Weight:	40t or 39t
Seats:	84 second		Bogies:	Mk 3C or 3D
Motors:	EE507 2 × 250hp			

S61516	01/60-05/85	⊗01/86	**5303**	01/60-05/85				
S61517	01/60-05/85	⊗01/86	**5303**	01/60-05/85				
S61518	01/60-05/85	⊗05/86	**5304**	01/60-05/85				
S61519	01/60-05/85	⊗05/86	**5304**	01/60-05/85				
S61520	01/60-02/95	⊗05/95	**5305**	01/60-07/87	**5621**	07/87-02/95		
S61521	01/60-02/95	⊗05/95	**5305**	01/60-07/87	**5621**	07/87-02/95		
S61522	01/60-05/85	⊗06/86	**5306**	01/60-05/85				
S61523	01/60-05/85	⊗06/86	**5306**	01/60-05/85				
S61524	01/60-05/84	⊗10/85	**5307**	01/60-05/84				
S61525	01/60-05/84	⊗10/85	**5307**	01/60-05/84				
S61526	01/60-05/84	⊗06/86	**5308**	01/60-05/84				
S61527	01/60-05/84	⊗06/86	**5308**	01/60-05/84				
S61528	02/60-05/84	⊗08/85	**5309**	02/60-05/84				
S61529	02/60-05/84	⊗08/85	**5309**	02/60-05/84				
S61530	02/60-05/85	⊗02/86	**5310**	02/60-05/85				
S61531	02/60-05/85	⊗02/86	**5310**	02/60-05/85				
S61532	02/60-03/95	⊗03/95	**5311**	02/60-07/87	**5613**	07/87-03/95		
S61533	02/60-03/95	⊗03/95	**5311**	02/60-07/87	**5613**	07/87-03/95		
S61534	02/60-10/84	⊗10/85	**5312**	02/60-10/84				
S61535	02/60-10/84	⊗10/85	**5312**	02/60-10/84				
S61536	02/60-02/95	⊗03/95	**5313**	02/60-07/87	**5606**	07/87-02/95		
S61537	02/60-02/95	⊗03/95	**5313**	02/60-07/87	**5606**	07/87-02/95		
S61538	02/60-11/94	⊗02/95	**5314**	02/60-06/87	**5603**	06/87-11/94		
S61539	02/60-11/94	⊗02/95	**5314**	02/60-06/87	**5603**	06/87-11/94		
S61540	03/60-01/95	⊗01/95	**5315**	03/60-07/87	**5605**	07/87-01/95		
S61541	03/60-01/95	⊗01/95	**5315**	03/60-07/87	**5605**	07/87-01/95		
S61542	03/60-03/95	⊗04/95	**5316**	03/60-06/87	**5612**	06/87-03/95		
S61543	03/60-03/95	⊗04/95	**5316**	03/60-06/87	**5612**	06/87-03/95		
S61544	03/60-05/85	⊗04/86	**5317**	03/60-05/85				
S61545	03/60-05/85	⊗04/86	**5317**	03/60-05/85				
S61546	03/60-03/95	⊗04/95	**5318**	03/60-06/87	**5614**	06/87-03/95		
S61547	03/60-05/93	⊗11/93	**5318**	03/60-06/87	**5614**	06/87-05/93		
S61548	03/60-05/84	⊗02/85	**5319**	03/60-05/84				
S61549	03/60-05/84	⊗02/85	**5319**	03/60-05/84				
S61550	03/60-02/95	⊗03/95	**5320**	03/60-07/87	**5601**	07/87-05/93	**5602**	09/93-02/95
S61551	03/60-03/95	⊗04/95	**5320**	03/60-07/87	**5601**	07/87-05/93	**5614**	05/93-03/95
S61552	03/60-10/84	⊗11/85	**5321**	03/60-10/84				
S61553	03/60-10/84	⊗11/85	**5321**	03/60-10/84				
S61554	03/60-05/85	⊗07/87	**5322**	03/60-05/85				
S61555	03/60-05/85	⊗07/87	**5322**	03/60-05/85				
S61556	03/60-08/84	⊗10/86	**5323**	03/60-08/84				
S61557	03/60-08/84	⊗10/86	**5323**	03/60-08/84				
S61558	03/60-05/85	⊗05/86	**5324**	03/60-05/85				
S61559	03/60-05/85	⊗05/86	**5324**	03/60-05/85				
S61560	04/60-01/95	⊗02/95	**5325**	04/60-07/87	**5622**	07/87-01/95		
S61561	04/60-01/95	⊗02/95	**5325**	04/60-07/87	**5622**	07/87-01/95		
S61562	04/60-01/95	⊗02/95	**5326**	04/60-07/87	**5619**	07/87-01/95		
S61563	04/60-01/95	⊗02/95	**5326**	04/60-07/87	**5619**	07/87-01/95		
S61564	04/60-05/85	⊗08/86	**5327**	04/60-05/85				
S61565	04/60-05/85	⊗08/86	**5327**	04/60-05/85				
S61566	04/60-11/94	⊗12/94	**5328**	04/60-07/87	**5610**	07/87-11/94		
S61567	04/60-11/94	⊗12/94	**5328**	04/60-07/87	**5610**	07/87-11/94		
S61568	04/60-12/83	⊗12/86	**5329**	04/60-12/83				
S61569	04/60-12/83	⊗12/86	**5329**	04/60-12/83				
S61570	04/60-10/94	⊗11/94	**5330**	04/60-07/87	**5611**	07/87-10/94		
S61571	04/60-10/94	⊗11/94	**5330**	04/60-07/87	**5611**	07/87-10/94		
S61572	04/60-03/95	⊗03/95	**5331**	04/60-07/87	**5624**	07/87-03/95		
S61573	04/60-03/95	⊗03/95	**5331**	04/60-07/87	**5624**	07/87-03/95		
S61574	04/60-05/85	⊗04/86	**5332**	04/60-05/85				
S61575	04/60-05/85	⊗04/86	**5332**	04/60-05/85				
S61576	05/60-02/95	⊗03/95	**5333**	05/60-07/87	**5616**	07/87-02/95		
S61577	05/60-02/95	⊗03/95	**5333**	05/60-07/87	**5616**	07/87-02/95		
S61578	05/60-02/95	⊗03/95	**5334**	05/60-07/87	**5623**	07/87-02/95		
S61579	05/60-02/92	⊗12/92	**5334**	05/60-07/87	**5623**	07/87-02/92		
S61580	05/60-05/85	⊗05/86	**5335**	05/60-05/85				
S61581	05/60-05/85	⊗05/86	**5335**	05/60-05/85				
S61582	05/60-09/93	⊗11/93	**5336**	05/60-07/87	**5602**	07/87-09/93		
S61583	05/60-02/95	⊗03/95	**5336**	05/60-07/87	**5602**	07/87-02/95		
S61584	05/60-02/95	⊗03/95	**5337**	05/60-07/87	**5618**	07/87-05/91	**5623**	02/92-02/95
S61585	05/60-05/91	⊗04/92	**5337**	05/60-07/87	**5618**	07/87-05/91		
S61586	05/60-05/84	⊗07/85	**5338**	05/60-05/84				
S61587	05/60-05/84	⊗07/85	**5338**	05/60-05/84				
S61588	06/60-03/95	⊗04/95	**5339**	06/60-06/87	**5604**	06/87-03/95		
S61589	06/60-03/95	⊗04/95	**5339**	06/60-06/87	**5604**	06/87-03/95		
S61590	06/60-10/94	⊗11/94	**5340**	06/60-07/87	**5607**	07/87-09/88	**5626**	09/88-10/94
S61591	06/60-10/94	⊗11/94	**5340**	06/60-07/87	**5607**	07/87-09/88	**5626**	09/88-10/94
S61592	06/60-03/95	⊗04/95	**5341**	06/60-07/87	**5617**	07/87-03/95		
S61593	06/60-03/95	⊗04/95	**5341**	06/60-07/87	**5617**	07/87-03/95		
S61594	06/60-08/84	⊗11/85	**5342**	06/60-08/84				
S61595	06/60-08/84	⊗11/85	**5342**	06/60-08/84				
S61596	06/60-05/84	⊗10/85	**5343**	06/60-05/84				
S61597	06/60-05/84	⊗10/85	**5343**	06/60-05/84				
S61598	06/60-03/85	⊗10/86	**5344**	06/60-03/85				
S61599	06/60-03/85	⊗10/86	**5344**	06/60-03/85				
S61600	09/61-03/95	⊗05/95	**5345**	09/61-06/87	**5608**	06/87-09/88	**5627**	09/88-03/95
S61601	09/61-03/95	⊗05/95	**5345**	09/61-06/87	**5608**	06/87-09/88	**5627**	09/88-03/95
S61602	10/61-01/95	⊗02/95	**5346**	10/61-07/87	**5620**	07/87-01/95		
S61603	10/61-01/95	⊗02/95	**5346**	10/61-07/87	**5620**	07/87-01/95		
S61604	10/61-10/94	⊗11/94	**5347**	10/61-07/87	**5609**	07/87-10/88	**5628**	10/88-10/94
S61605	10/61-10/94	⊗11/94	**5347**	10/61-07/87	**5609**	07/87-10/88	**5628**	10/88-10/94
S61606	10/61-05/85	⊗05/86	**5348**	10/61-05/85				
S61607	10/61-05/85	⊗05/86	**5348**	10/61-05/85				
S61608	10/61-03/95	⊗04/95	**5349**	10/61-07/87	**5625**	07/87-03/95		
S61609	10/61-03/95	⊗04/95	**5349**	10/61-07/87	**5625**	07/87-03/95		
S61610	11/61-05/85	⊗12/85	**5350**	11/61-05/85				
S61611	11/61-05/85	⊗12/85	**5350**	11/61-05/85				
S61612	11/61-02/95	⊗03/95	**5351**	11/61-07/87	**5615**	07/87-02/95		
S61613	11/61-02/95	⊗03/95	**5351**	11/61-07/87	**5615**	07/87-02/95		
S61614	11/61-10/62	⊗*10/62*	**5352**	11/61-10/62				
S61615	11/61-02/85	⊗08/86	**5352**	11/61-10/62	**5352**	12/64-02/85		
S61616	11/61-05/85	⊗12/85	**5353**	11/61-05/85				
S61617	11/61-05/85	⊗12/85	**5353**	11/61-05/85				
S61618	12/61-05/85	⊗12/85	**5354**	12/61-05/85				
S61619	12/61-05/85	⊗12/85	**5354**	12/61-05/85				
S61620	12/61-05/85	⊗04/86	**5355**	12/61-05/85				
S61621	12/61-05/85	⊗04/86	**5355**	12/61-05/85				
S61622	01/62-05/85	⊗12/86	**5356**	01/62-05/85				
S61623	01/62-05/85	⊗12/86	**5356**	01/62-05/85				
S61624	01/60-02/85	⊗08/86	**5800**	01/60-12/64	**5352**	12/64-02/85		
S61625	01/60-08/87	⊗09/87	**5301**	01/60-08/87				
S61626	01/60-08/87	⊗09/87	**5301**	01/60-08/87				
S61627	02/60-12/83	⊃**977213**	**5302**	01/61-12/83				

Class 304/2 Wolverton

Motor Brake Second Open
MBSO
M61628-M61647

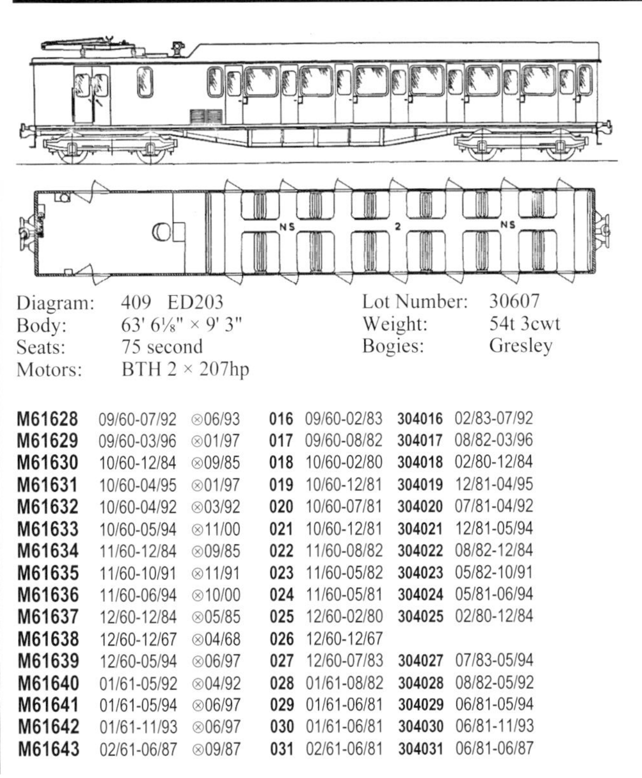

Diagram:	409 ED203		Lot Number:	30607
Body:	63' 6⅛" × 9' 3"		Weight:	54t 3cwt
Seats:	75 second		Bogies:	Gresley
Motors:	BTH 2 × 207hp			

M61628	09/60-07/92	⊗06/93	**016**	09/60-02/83	**304016**	02/83-07/92
M61629	09/60-03/96	⊗01/97	**017**	09/60-08/82	**304017**	08/82-03/96
M61630	10/60-12/84	⊗09/85	**018**	10/60-02/80	**304018**	02/80-12/84
M61631	10/60-04/95	⊗01/97	**019**	10/60-12/81	**304019**	12/81-04/95
M61632	10/60-04/92	⊗03/92	**020**	10/60-07/81	**304020**	07/81-04/92
M61633	10/60-05/94	⊗11/00	**021**	10/60-12/81	**304021**	12/81-05/94
M61634	11/60-12/84	⊗09/85	**022**	11/60-08/82	**304022**	08/82-12/84
M61635	11/60-10/91	⊗11/91	**023**	11/60-05/82	**304023**	05/82-10/91
M61636	11/60-06/94	⊗10/00	**024**	11/60-05/81	**304024**	05/81-06/94
M61637	12/60-12/84	⊗05/85	**025**	12/60-02/80	**304025**	02/80-12/84
M61638	12/60-12/67	⊗04/68	**026**	12/60-12/67		
M61639	12/60-05/94	⊗06/97	**027**	12/60-07/83	**304027**	07/83-05/94
M61640	01/61-05/92	⊗04/92	**028**	01/61-08/82	**304028**	08/82-05/92
M61641	01/61-05/94	⊗06/97	**029**	01/61-06/81	**304029**	06/81-05/94
M61642	01/61-11/93	⊗06/97	**030**	01/61-06/81	**304030**	06/81-11/93
M61643	02/61-06/87	⊗09/87	**031**	02/61-06/81	**304031**	06/81-06/87

M61644	02/61-05/96	⊗05/96	**032**	02/61-09/81	**304032**	09/81-05/96
M61645	02/61-04/96	⊗05/96	**033**	02/61-10/84	**304033**	10/84-04/96
M61646	03/61-01/94	⊗02/94	**034**	03/61-06/84	**304034**	06/84-01/94
M61647	06/61-11/91	⊗11/91	**035**	06/61-04/82	**304035**	04/82-11/91

Class 414 2-HAP Eastleigh

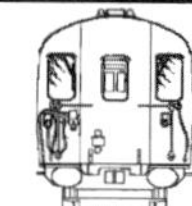

Driving Motor Brake Second Open
DMBSO
S61648-S61688

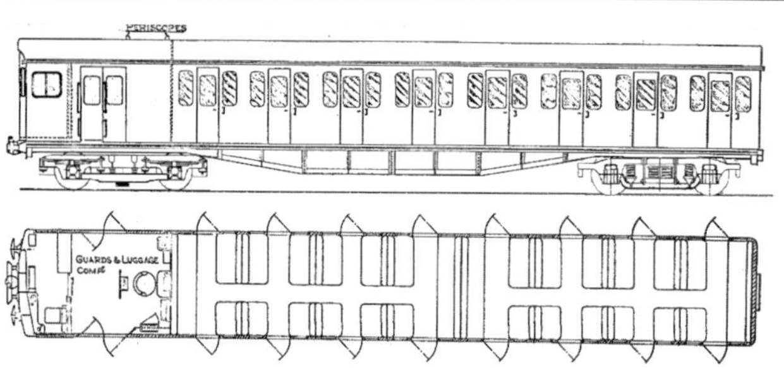

Diagram:	400 EB270	Lot Number:	30617
Body:	63' 11½" × 9' 3¼"	Weight:	41t 0cwt
Seats:	84 second	Bogies:	1 Mk 4
Motors:	EE507 2 × 250hp		1 Commonwealth

S61648	03/61-05/82	⊗05/84	**6106**	03/61-05/82				
S61649	04/61-05/82	⊗10/84	**6107**	04/61-05/82				
S61650	04/61-10/83	⊗10/84	**6108**	04/61-10/83				
S61651	04/61-10/83	⊗05/84	**6109**	04/61-10/83				
S61652	04/61-05/82	⊗10/84	**6110**	04/61-05/82				
S61653	04/61-10/83	⊗04/84	**6111**	04/61-10/83				
S61654	05/61-07/91	➲**977737**	**6112**	05/61-11/87	**4320**	11/87-07/91		
S61655	05/61-10/83	⊗05/84	**6113**	05/61-10/83				
S61656	05/61-05/83	⊗02/87	**6114**	05/61-05/83				
S61657	05/61-05/82	⊗04/84	**6115**	05/61-05/82				
S61658	05/61-10/83	➲**977207**	**6116**	05/61-10/83				
S61659	05/61-10/83	⊗09/84	**6117**	05/61-10/83				
S61660	05/61-10/83	⊗09/84	**6118**	05/61-10/83				
S61661	05/61-10/83	⊗03/90	**6119**	05/61-10/83				
S61662	05/61-05/82	⊗09/84	**6120**	05/61-05/82				
S61663	06/61-05/82	➲**977209**	**6121**	06/61-05/82				
S61664	06/61-05/82	⊗04/84	**6122**	06/61-05/82				
S61665	06/61-05/82	⊗04/84	**6123**	06/61-05/82				
S61666	06/61-05/83	⊗04/84	**6124**	06/61-05/83				
S61667	06/61-10/83	⊗06/84	**6125**	06/61-10/83				
S61668	07/61-05/92	➲*977739*	**6126**	07/61-05/88	**4321**	05/88-05/92		
S61669	07/61-01/82	⊗02/83	**6127**	07/61-01/82				
S61670	08/61-05/83	⊗08/86	**6128**	08/61-05/83				
S61671	08/61-05/82	⊗09/84	**6129**	08/61-05/82				
S61672	08/61-05/82	⊗05/84	**6130**	08/61-05/82				
S61673	09/61-05/83	⊗06/84	**6131**	09/61-05/83				
S61674	09/61-05/82	⊗05/82	**6132**	09/61-05/82				
S61675	09/61-10/83	⊗06/84	**6133**	09/61-10/83				
S61676	09/61-01/82	⊗02/82	**6134**	09/61-01/82				
S61677	09/61-05/82	⊗09/84	**6135**	09/61-05/82				
S61678	09/61-09/82	⊗04/84	**6136**	09/61-09/82				
S61679	10/61-09/82	⊗04/84	**6137**	10/61-09/82				
S61680	10/61-05/82	⊗09/84	**6138**	10/61-05/82				
S61681	11/61-10/83	⊗08/84	**6139**	11/61-10/83				
S61682	11/61-05/83	⊗06/84	**6140**	11/61-05/83				
S61683	11/61-01/92	⊗05/92	**6141**	11/61-06/88	**4322**	06/88-09/91	**3333**	09/91-01/92
S61684	11/61-05/82	➲**977211**	**6142**	11/61-05/82				
S61685	12/61-05/82	⊗10/84	**6143**	12/61-05/82				
S61686	12/61-04/83	⊗10/86	**6144**	12/61-04/83				
S61687	01/62-05/83	⊗03/90	**6145**	01/62-05/83				
S61688	01/62-10/83	⊗06/84	**6146**	01/62-10/83				

Class 308 York

Motor Brake Second Open
MBSO
E61689-E61691

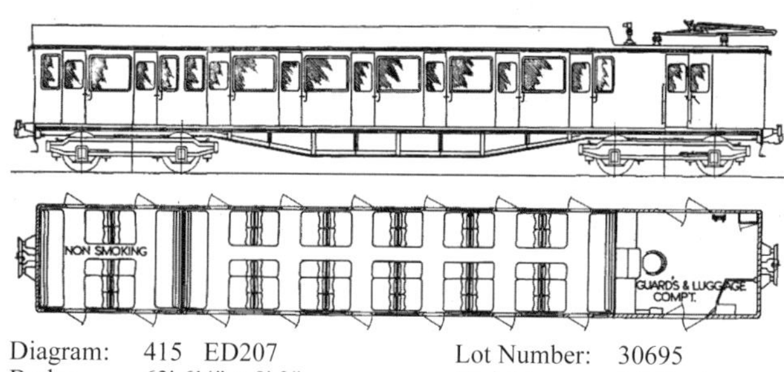

Diagram:	415 ED207	Lot Number:	30695
Body:	63' 6⅛" × 9' 3"	Weight:	54t 0cwt
Seats:	84 second	Bogies:	Gresley
Motors:	EE 4 × 200hp		

E61689	12/61-03/86	⊗02/86	**453**	12/61-10/81	**308453**	10/81-02/86
E61690	12/61-03/86	⊗07/86	**454**	12/61-02/82	**308454**	02/82-03/86
E61691	12/61-05/85	⊗06/85	**455**	12/61-05/82	**308455**	05/82-05/85

Class 411 4-CEP Ashford/Eastleigh

Driving Motor Brake Second Open
DMBSO later DMSO(A) & DMSO(B)
S61694-S61811 (61792 onwards Class 410 4-BEP)

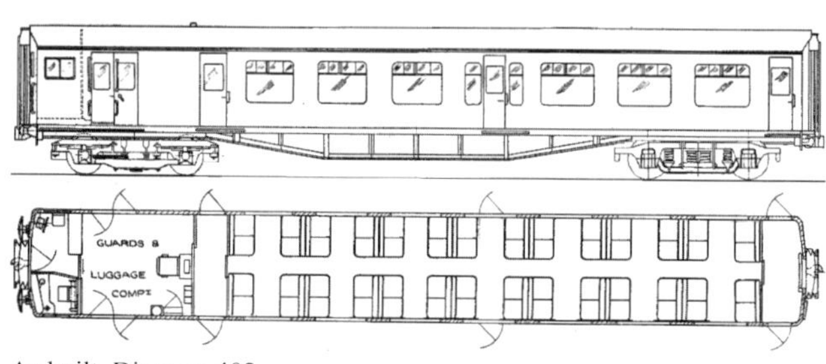

As built, Diagram 402

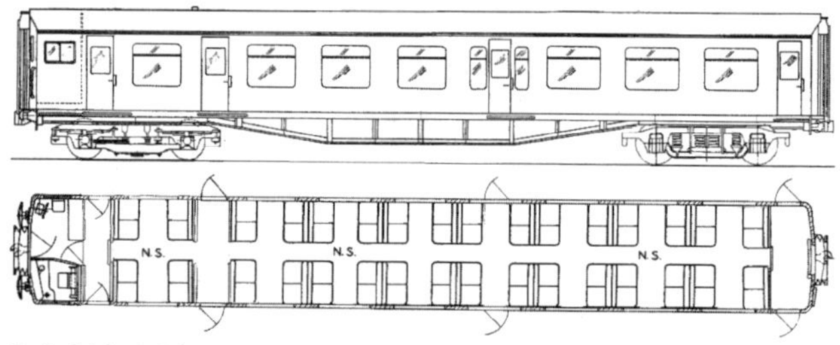

Refurbished, Diagram 884 DMSO(A) EA263, DMSO(B) EA264

Diagram:	402 884 EA263 EA264	Lot Number:	30619
Body:	64' 6" × 9' 3"	Weight:	40t 0cwt
Seats:	56 second, later 64 second	Bogies:	1 Mk 3B Motor
Motors:	EE507 2 × 250hp		1 Commonwealth

S61694	07/60-08/95	⊗*05/97*	**7154**	07/60-03/80	**1606**	03/80-08/95		
S61695	07/60-08/95	⊗*05/97*	**7154**	07/60-03/80	**1606**	03/80-08/95		
S61696	08/60-06/04	⊗06/04	**7155**	08/60-06/81	**1590**	06/81-06/04		
S61697	08/60-06/04	⊗06/04	**7155**	08/60-06/81	**1590**	06/81-06/04		
S61698	09/60-06/03	⊗06/03	**7156**	09/60-03/80	**1607**	03/80-06/03		
S61699	09/60-06/03	⊗06/03	**7156**	09/60-03/80	**1607**	03/80-06/03		
S61700	09/60-09/04	⊗09/04	**7157**	09/60-02/82	**1578**	02/82-09/04		
S61701	09/60-09/04	⊗09/04	**7157**	09/60-02/82	**1578**	02/82-09/04		
S61702	09/60-03/03	⊗06/03	**7158**	09/60-04/83	**1614**	04/83-03/03		
S61703	09/60-03/03	⊗06/03	**7158**	09/60-04/83	**1614**	04/83-03/03		
S61704	09/60-03/03	⊗04/03	**7159**	09/60-02/81	**1595**	02/81-07/99	**1117**	07/99-03/03
S61705	09/60-03/03	⊗04/03	**7159**	09/60-02/81	**1595**	02/81-07/99	**1117**	07/99-03/03
S61706	09/60-01/03	⊗01/03	**7160**	09/60-10/80	**1599**	10/80-01/03		
S61707	09/60-01/03	⊗01/03	**7160**	09/60-10/80	**1599**	10/80-01/03		
S61708	09/60-03/03	⊗04/03	**7161**	09/60-01/81	**1597**	01/81-05/99	**1118**	05/99-03/03
S61709	09/60-03/03	⊗04/03	**7161**	09/60-01/81	**1597**	01/81-05/99	**1118**	05/99-03/03
S61710	01/61-08/02	⊗09/02	**7162**	01/61-10/81	**1585**	10/81-08/02		
S61711	01/61-08/02	⊗09/02	**7162**	01/61-10/81	**1585**	10/81-08/02		
S61712	10/60-07/05	⊗12/05	**7163**	10/60-04/80	**1605**	04/80-06/96	**1699**	06/96-07/05
S61713	10/60-07/05	⊗12/05	**7163**	10/60-04/80	**1605**	04/80-06/96	**1699**	06/96-07/05

S61714	10/60-03/03	⊗03/03	**7164**	10/60-08/81	**1586**	08/81-03/03		
S61715	10/60-03/03	⊗03/03	**7164**	10/60-08/81	**1586**	08/81-03/03		
S61716	10/60-04/96	⊗05/96	**7165**	10/60-01/81	**1596**	01/81-04/96		
S61717	10/60-04/96	⊗05/96	**7165**	10/60-01/81	**1596**	01/81-04/96		
S61718	10/60-08/02	⊗09/02	**7166**	10/60-02/82	**1577**	02/82-05/99	**1115**	05/99-08/02
S61719	10/60-08/02	⊗09/02	**7166**	10/60-02/82	**1577**	02/82-05/99	**1115**	05/99-08/02
S61720	10/60-11/01	⊗09/02	**7167**	10/60-08/80	**1602**	08/80-08/81	**1588**	08/81-11/01
S61721	10/60-11/01	⊗09/02	**7167**	10/60-08/80	**1588**	08/81-11/01		
S61722	10/60-11/03	⊗02/04	**7168**	10/60-11/82	**1566**	11/82-09/02	**2324**	09/02-11/03
S61723	10/60-11/03	⊗02/04	**7168**	10/60-11/82	**1566**	11/82-09/02	**2324**	09/02-11/03
S61724	10/60-03/96	⊗06/96	**7169**	10/60-09/80	**1600**	09/80-03/96		
S61725	10/60-03/96	⊗06/96	**7169**	10/60-09/80	**1600**	09/80-03/96		
S61726	11/60-04/04	⊗05/04	**7170**	11/60-05/82	**1573**	05/82-04/04		
S61727	11/60-04/04	⊗05/04	**7170**	11/60-05/82	**1573**	05/82-04/04		
S61728	11/60-03/04	⊗	**7171**	11/60-07/80	**1603**	07/80-10/95	**1553**	04/96-03/04
S61729	11/60-10/95	⊗04/96	**7171**	11/60-07/80	**1603**	07/80-10/95		
S61730	11/60-03/04	⊗04/04	**7172**	11/60-04/81	**1593**	04/81-03/04		
S61731	11/60-03/04	⊗04/04	**7172**	11/60-04/81	**1593**	04/81-03/04		
S61732	11/60-08/95	⊗04/96	**7173**	11/60-07/80	**1604**	07/80-08/85		
S61733	11/60-08/95	⊗04/96	**7173**	11/60-07/80	**1604**	07/80-08/85		
S61734	11/60-03/99	⊗05/04	**7174**	11/60-06/82	**1572**	06/82-03/99		
S61735	11/60-03/99	⊗05/04	**7174**	11/60-06/82	**1572**	06/82-03/99		
S61736	11/60-12/04	℗	**7175**	11/60-11/83	**2304**	11/83-09/02	**2314**	09/02-05/04
			1198	05/04-12/04				
S61737	11/60-12/04	℗	**7175**	11/60-11/83	**2304**	11/83-09/02	**2314**	09/02-05/04
			1198	05/04-12/04				
S61738	11/60-11/02	⊗11/02	**7176**	11/60-08/82	**1570**	08/82-11/02		
S61739	11/60-11/02	⊗11/02	**7176**	11/60-08/82	**1570**	08/82-11/02		
S61740	12/60-03/04	⊗05/04	**7177**	12/60-01/83	**1563**	01/83-03/04		
S61741	12/60-03/04	⊗	**7177**	12/60-01/83	**1563**	01/83-03/04		
S61742	12/60-04/97	℗	**7178**	12/60-07/81	**1589**	07/81-04/97		
S61743	12/60-04/97	℗	**7178**	12/60-07/81	**1589**	07/81-04/97		
S61744	12/60-12/02	⊗01/03	**7179**	12/60-02/83	**1609**	02/83-12/02		
S61745	12/60-12/02	⊗01/03	**7179**	12/60-02/83	**1609**	02/83-12/02		
S61746	12/60-04/96	⊗04/96	**7180**	12/60-10/81	**1583**	10/81-04/96		
S61747	12/60-04/96	⊗04/96	**7180**	12/60-10/81	**1583**	10/81-04/96		
S61748	12/60-11/02	⊗12/02	**7181**	12/60-01/69	**7015**	07/70-11/81	**1582**	11/81-12/02
S61749	12/60-05/69	⊗01/69	**7181**	12/60-01/69				
S61750	01/61-04/03	⊗04/03	**7182**	01/61-02/83	**1610**	02/83-09/98	**1103**	09/98-04/03
S61751	01/61-04/03	⊗04/03	**7182**	01/61-02/83	**1610**	02/83-09/98	**1103**	09/98-04/03
S61752	01/61-11/02	⊗11/02	**7183**	01/61-03/82	**1584**	03/82-11/02		
S61753	01/61-11/02	⊗11/02	**7183**	01/61-03/82	**1584**	03/82-11/02		
S61754	01/61-03/04	⊗05/04	**7184**	01/61-03/81	**1594**	03/81-03/04		
S61755	01/61-03/04	⊗05/04	**7184**	01/61-03/81	**1594**	03/81-03/04		
S61756	01/61-03/03	⊗04/03	**7185**	01/61-12/81	**1580**	12/81-05/99	**1116**	05/99-03/03
S61757	01/61-03/03	⊗04/03	**7185**	01/61-12/81	**1580**	12/81-05/99	**1116**	05/99-03/03
S61758	02/61-12/02	⊗01/03	**7186**	02/61-03/83	**1611**	03/83-12/02		
S61759	02/61-12/02	⊗01/03	**7186**	02/61-03/83	**1611**	03/83-12/02		
S61760	02/61-12/02	⊗12/02	**7187**	02/61-04/83	**1613**	04/83-11/98	**1104**	11/98-12/02
S61761	02/61-12/02	⊗12/02	**7187**	02/61-04/83	**1613**	04/83-11/98	**1104**	11/98-12/02
S61762	02/61-04/04	⊗06/04	**7188**	02/61-01/83	**1565**	01/83-04/04		
S61763	02/61-04/04	⊗06/04	**7188**	02/61-01/83	**1565**	01/83-04/04		
S61764	02/61-10/02	⊗10/02	**7189**	02/61-08/81	**1587**	08/81-10/02		
S61765	02/61-10/02	⊗10/02	**7189**	02/61-08/81	**1587**	08/81-10/02		
S61766	03/61-11/03	⊗02/04	**7190**	03/61-09/82	**1568**	09/82-09/02	**2321**	09/02-11/03
S61767	03/61-11/03	⊗02/04	**7190**	03/61-09/82	**1568**	09/82-09/02	**2321**	09/02-11/03
S61768	03/61-10/02	⊗10/02	**7191**	03/61-12/81	**1575**	04/82-10/02		
S61769	03/61-10/02	⊗10/02	**7191**	03/61-12/81	**1575**	04/82-10/02		
S61770	03/61-08/02	⊗09/02	**7192**	03/61-04/82	**1576**	04/82-08/02		
S61771	03/61-08/02	⊗09/02	**7192**	03/61-04/82	**1576**	04/82-08/02		
S61772	03/61-06/95	⊗05/96	**7193**	03/61-01/82	**1579**	01/82-05/93	**1579**	10/93-05/93
S61773	03/61-06/95	⊗05/96	**7193**	03/61-01/82	**1579**	01/82-05/93	**1579**	10/93-05/93
S61774	04/61-10/04	⊗12/04	**7194**	04/61-06/83	**2302**	06/83-09/02	**2312**	09/02-10/04
S61775	04/61-10/04	⊗10/04	**7194**	04/61-06/83	**2302**	06/83-04/91	**2306**	04/91-09/02
			2316	09/02-10/04				
S61776	04/61-05/95	⊗04/96	**7195**	04/61-09/80	**1601**	09/80-05/95		
S61777	04/61-05/95	⊗04/96	**7195**	04/61-09/80	**1601**	09/80-05/95		
S61778	06/61-06/04	⊗06/04	**7196**	06/61-05/81	**1592**	05/81-06/04		
S61779	06/61-06/04	⊗06/04	**7196**	06/61-05/81	**1592**	05/81-06/04		
S61780	06/61-09/95	⊗04/96	**7197**	06/61-11/80	**1598**	11/80-09/95		
S61781	06/61-09/95	⊗04/96	**7197**	06/61-11/80	**1598**	11/80-09/95		
S61782	06/61-05/95	⊗06/95	**7198**	06/61-08/82	**1569**	08/82-05/95		
S61783	06/61-05/95	⊗06/95	**7198**	06/61-08/82	**1569**	08/82-05/95		
S61784	07/61-04/04	⊗05/04	**7199**	07/61-11/81	**1581**	11/81-04/04		
S61785	07/61-04/04	⊗05/04	**7199**	07/61-11/81	**1581**	11/81-04/04		
S61786	07/61-04/95	⊗06/95	**7200**	07/61-10/82	**1567**	10/82-04/95		
S61787	07/61-04/95	⊗06/95	**7200**	07/61-10/82	**1567**	10/82-04/95		
S61788	07/61-03/03	⊗03/03	**7201**	07/61-12/82	**1564**	12/82-03/03		
S61789	07/61-03/03	⊗03/03	**7201**	07/61-12/82	**1564**	12/82-03/03		
S61790	08/61-09/02	⊗09/02	**7202**	08/61-06/81	**1591**	06/81-09/02		
S61791	08/61-09/02	⊗09/02	**7202**	08/61-06/81	**1591**	06/81-09/02		
S61792	01/61-12/02	⊗12/02	**7013**	01/61-05/82	**1574**	05/82-12/02		
S61793	01/61-12/02	⊗12/02	**7013**	01/61-05/82	**1574**	05/82-12/02		
S61794	01/61-04/04	⊗05/04	**7014**	01/61-03/83	**1612**	03/83-04/04		
S61795	01/61-04/04	⊗04/04	**7014**	01/61-03/83	**1612**	03/83-04/04		
S61796	03/61-05/95	⊗06/95	**7015**	03/61-07/70	**7129**	09/70-06/80	**1513**	06/80-05/95
S61797	03/61-11/02	⊗12/02	**7015**	03/61-11/81	**1582**	11/81-12/02		
S61798	03/61-12/04	℗	**7016**	03/61-12/83	**2305**	12/83-09/02	**2315**	09/02-12/04
S61799	03/61-12/04	℗	**7016**	03/61-12/83	**2305**	12/83-09/02	**2315**	09/02-12/04
S61800	04/61-10/99	⊗05/01	**7017**	04/61-07/83	**1617**	07/83-10/99		
S61801	04/61-10/99	⊗05/01	**7017**	04/61-07/83	**1617**	07/83-10/99		
S61802	04/61-10/04	⊗10/04	**7018**	04/61-12/83	**2307**	03/84-09/02	**2317**	09/02-10/04
S61803	04/61-10/04	⊗10/04	**7018**	04/61-12/83	**2307**	03/84-09/02	**2317**	09/02-10/04
S61804	05/61-12/04	℗	**7019**	05/61-02/82	**2301**	02/82-09/02	**2311**	09/02-12/04
S61805	05/61-12/04	℗	**7019**	05/61-02/82	**2301**	02/82-09/02	**2311**	09/02-12/04
S61806	06/61-09/04	⊗09/04	**7020**	06/61-06/82	**1571**	06/82-09/02	**2323**	09/02-12/02
			1571	12/02-09/04				
S61807	06/61-09/04	⊗09/04	**7020**	06/61-06/82	**1571**	06/82-09/02	**2323**	09/02-12/02
			1571	12/02-09/04				
S61808	06/61-10/04	⊗10/04	**7021**	06/61-12/83	**2306**	02/84-09/02	**2316**	09/02-10/04
S61809	06/61-10/04	⊗12/04	**7021**	06/61-12/83	**2306**	02/84-04/91	**2302**	04/91-09/02
			2312	09/02-10/04				
S61810	09/61-05/93	⊗11/93	**7022**	09/61-09/83	**1621**	03/84-05/93		
S61811	09/61-05/93	⊗11/93	**7022**	09/61-09/83	**1621**	03/84-05/93		

Class 303 Pressed Steel

Motor Brake Second Open

MBSO

SC61812-SC61867

As built, Diagram 416

® Refurbished 2+2 seating

Diagram:	416 ED201	Lot Number:	30630
Body:	63' 6⅛" × 9' 3"	Weight:	55t 11cwt
Seats:	70 second, later 48 second	Bogies:	Gresley
Motors:	MV 4 × 207hp		

SC61812	05/60-10/89	⊗11/89		**036**	05/60- *80*	**303036**	*80*-10/89		
SC61813	06/60-07/99	⊗03/01	®	**037**	06/60-*03/80*	**303037**	*03/80*-07/91	**303037**	02/94-05/98
				303028	07/99-07/99				
SC61814	06/60-02/93	⊗ 93	®	**038**	06/60-*03/80*	**303038**	*03/80*-02/93		
SC61815	06/60-06/60	⊗10/90		**039**	06/60-*08/79*	**303039**	*08/79*-09/90		
SC61816	06/60-02/01	⊗04/04	®	**040**	06/60-*08/79*	**303040**	*08/79*-02/01		
SC61817	06/60-10/89	⊗11/89		**041**	06/60-*11/79*	**303041**	*11/79*-10/89		
SC61818	06/60-09/89	⊗08/90		**042**	06/60-*03/80*	**303042**	*03/80*-09/89		
SC61819	06/60-08/01	⊗01/03	®	**043**	06/60-06/80	**303043**	06/80-08/01		
SC61820	06/60-01/89	⊗08/90		**044**	06/60-06/80	**303044**	06/80-02/88		
SC61821	06/60-09/02	⊗12/02	®	**045**	06/60-*03/80*	**303045**	*03/80*-09/02		
SC61822	06/60-11/97	⊗11/97	®	**046**	06/60-06/80	**303046**	06/80-11/97		
SC61823	07/60-10/01	⊗05/02	®	**047**	07/60-*11/79*	**303047**	*11/79*-10/01		
SC61824	07/60-03/96	**➲977720**	℗⊗09/98			**048**	07/60- *80*	**303048**	*80*-03/96
SC61825	07/60-02/91	**➲977712**		**049**	07/60- *80*	**303049**	*80*-02/91		
SC61826	07/60-10/89	⊗11/89		**050**	07/60-*08/79*	**303050**	*08/79*-10/89		
SC61827	07/60-02/87	⊗12/89	®	**051**	07/60-*03/80*	**303051**	*03/80*-02/87		
SC61828	07/60-09/90	⊗11/90		**052**	07/60-*03/80*	**303052**	*03/80*-09/90		
SC61829	07/60-10/89	⊗11/89		**053**	07/60-*03/80*	**303053**	*03/80*-10/89		
SC61830	07/60-06/02	⊗08/02	®	**054**	07/60-*03/80*	**303054**	*03/80*-06/02		
SC61831	07/60-03/01	⊗03/01	®	**055**	07/60-*08/79*	**303055**	*08/79*-03/01		
SC61832	08/60-03/01	⊗09/01	®	**056**	08/60-*03/80*	**303056**	*03/80*-03/01		
SC61833	08/60-10/89	⊗11/89	®	**057**	08/60- *80*	**303057**	*80*-10/89		
SC61834	09/60-03/01	⊗08/01	®	**058**	09/60-*03/80*	**303058**	*03/80*-03/01		
SC61835	09/60-11/83	⊗11/83		**059**	09/60- *80*	**303059**	*80*-11/83		
SC61836	09/60-12/92	⊗02/94		**060**	09/60- *80*	**303060**	*80*-12/92		
SC61837	09/60-03/01	⊗03/01	®	**061**	09/60-*05/79*	**303061**	*05/79*-03/01		
SC61838	09/60-09/90	⊗11/91		**062**	09/60- *80*	**303062**	*80*-09/90		
SC61839	09/60-10/90	⊗08/92		**063**	09/60-*03/80*	**303063**	*03/80*-10/90		
SC61840	10/60-07/88	⊗03/90		**064**	10/60-*08/79*	**303064**	*08/79*-07/88		
SC61841	10/60-06/01	⊗08/01	®	**065**	10/60- *80*	**303065**	*80*-06/01		
SC61842	10/60-02/91	⊗04/91		**066**	10/60- *80*	**303066**	*80*-02/91		
SC61843	10/60-10/89	⊗02/91		**067**	10/60-*03/80*	**303067**	*03/80*-10/89		
SC61844	10/60-05/89	⊗05/90		**068**	10/60-05/80	**303068**	05/80-01/89		
SC61845	10/60-07/90	⊗01/91		**069**	10/60-*03/80*	**303069**	*03/80*-07/90		

SC61846	10/60-10/01	⊗08/02 ®	**070**	10/60-05/80	**303070**	05/80-10/01		
SC61847	11/60-07/89	⊗08/90 ®	**071**	11/60-08/79	**303071**	08/79-07/89		
SC61848	11/60-07/90	⊗12/90	**072**	11/60-05/79	**303072**	05/79-07/90		
SC61849	12/60-07/96	⊗07/96	**073**	12/60- 80	**303073**	80-07/96		
SC61850	12/60- 78	⊗12/82	**074**	12/60- 78				
SC61851	12/60-09/90	⊗08/90	**075**	12/60-06/80	**303075**	06/80-08/90		
SC61852	12/60-09/90	⊗01/91	**076**	12/60-03/80	**303076**	03/80-09/90		
SC61853	12/60-01/02	⊗02/02 ®	**077**	12/60-06/80	**303077**	06/80-01/02		
SC61854	01/61-10/89	⊗11/89	**078**	01/61-03/80	**303078**	03/80-10/89		
SC61855	01/61-06/02	⊗10/02 ®	**079**	01/61- 80	**303079**	80-06/02		
SC61856	01/61-10/01	⊗09/02 ®	**080**	01/61-08/79	**303080**	08/79-10/01		
SC61857	01/61-01/89	⊗01/90	**081**	01/61-08/79	**303081**	08/79-01/89		
SC61858	02/61-12/92	⊗08/94	**082**	02/61-03/80	**303082**	03/80-12/92		
SC61859	02/61-09/02	⊗03/03 ®	**083**	02/61-03/80	**303083**	03/80-09/02		
SC61860	02/61-06/02	⊗08/02 ®	**084**	02/61- 78	**033**	06/79-07/80	**303033**	07/80-06/02
SC61861	02/61-03/02	⊗08/02 ®	**085**	02/61-03/80	**303085**	03/80-03/02		
SC61862	02/61-05/89	⊗08/90	**086**	02/61-07/80	**303086**	07/80-05/98		
SC61863	02/61-04/02	⊗09/02 ®	**087**	02/61-05/79	**303087**	05/79-04/02		
SC61864	02/61-12/02	⊗07/03 ®	**088**	02/61- 80	**303088**	80-12/02		
SC61865	03/61-03/01	⊗04/01 ®	**089**	03/61-11/79	**303089**	11/79-03/01		
SC61866	04/61-04/02	⊗01/03 ®	**090**	04/61- 80	**303090**	80-04/02		
SC61867	07/61-06/02	⊗10/02 ®	**091**	07/61-08/79	**303091**	08/79-06/02		

Class 411 4-CEP Ashford/Eastleigh
Driving Motor Brake Second Open
DMBSO later DMSO(A) & DMSO(B)
S61868-S61871

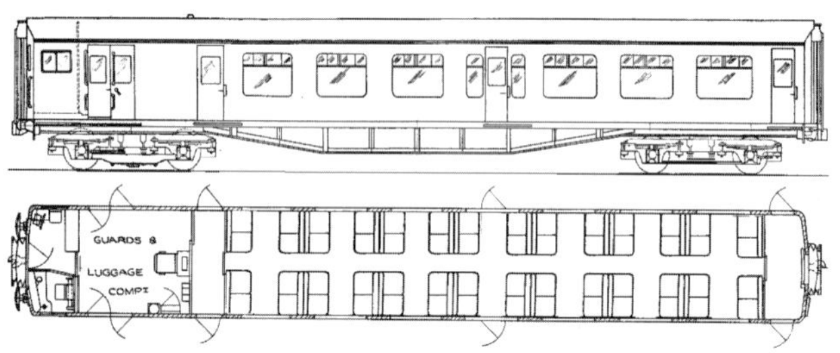

As built, Diagram 402

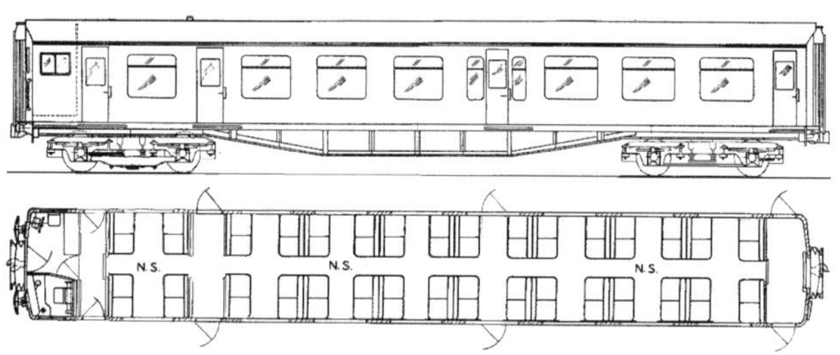

Refurbished, Diagram 884 DMSO(A) EA263, DMSO(B) EA264

Diagram:	402 884 EA263 EA264	Lot Number:	30638
Body:	64' 6" × 9' 3"	Weight:	41t 0cwt
Seats:	56 second, later 64 second	Bogies:	1 Mk 3B Motor
Motors:	EE507 2 × 250hp		1 Commonwealth

S61868	08/61-04/97	⊗05/01	**7203**	08/61-09/83	**1618**	09/83-04/94		
S61869	08/61-04/97	⊗05/01	**7203**	08/61-09/83	**1618**	09/83-04/94		
S61870	09/61-06/94	⊗07/95	**7204**	09/61-04/71	**7151**	04/71-03/82	**1540**	03/82-05/94
			1406	05/94-06/94				
S61871	09/61-06/71	⊗04/90	**7204**	09/61-04/71				

Class 415 Ashford/Eastleigh
Driving Motor Brake Second Open
DMBSO
S61872

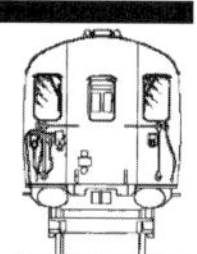

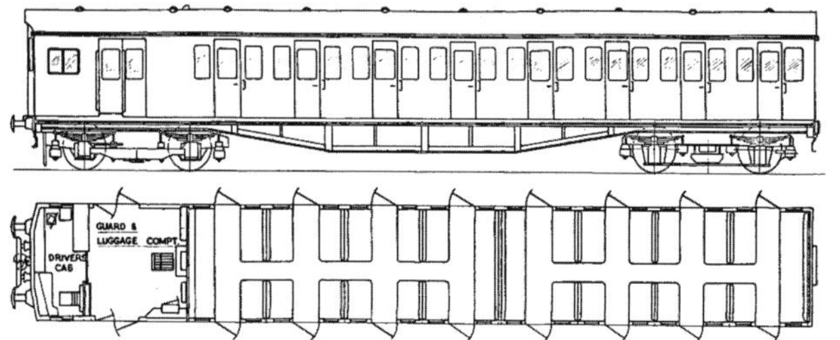

Diagram:	414 EB271 EB272	Lot Number:	30641
Body:	63' 11½" × 9' 3"	Weight:	40t or 39t
Seats:	84 second	Bogies:	Mk 4
Motors:	EE507 2 × 250hp		

S61872	03/61-10/83	⊗06/84	**5302**	01/61-01/72	**6151**	01/72-10/83

Class 304 Wolverton
Motor Brake Second Open
MBSO
M61873-M61882

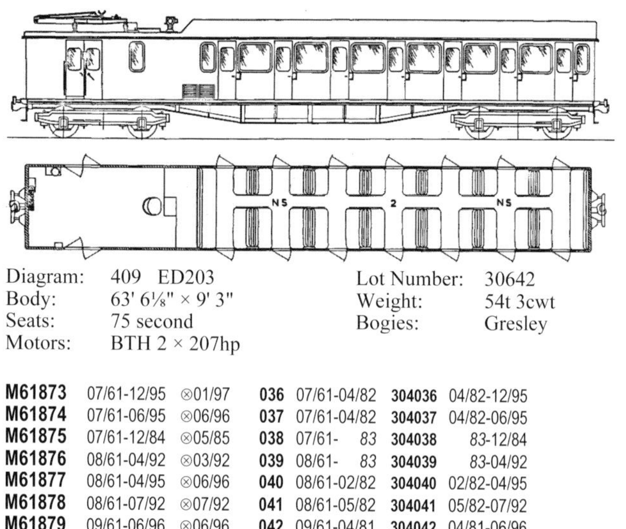

Diagram:	409 ED203	Lot Number:	30642
Body:	63' 6⅛" × 9' 3"	Weight:	54t 3cwt
Seats:	75 second	Bogies:	Gresley
Motors:	BTH 2 × 207hp		

M61873	07/61-12/95	⊗01/97	**036**	07/61-04/82	**304036**	04/82-12/95
M61874	07/61-06/95	⊗06/96	**037**	07/61-04/82	**304037**	04/82-06/95
M61875	07/61-12/84	⊗05/85	**038**	07/61- 83	**304038**	83-12/84
M61876	08/61-04/92	⊗03/92	**039**	08/61- 83	**304039**	83-04/92
M61877	08/61-04/95	⊗06/96	**040**	08/61-02/82	**304040**	02/82-04/95
M61878	08/61-07/92	⊗07/92	**041**	08/61-05/82	**304041**	05/82-07/92
M61879	09/61-06/96	⊗06/96	**042**	09/61-04/81	**304042**	04/81-06/96
M61880	09/61-05/94	⊗06/96	**043**	09/61-07/83	**304043**	07/83-05/94
M61881	09/61-12/84	⊗05/85	**044**	09/61-10/82	**304044**	10/82-12/84
M61882	10/61-07/92	⊗08/92	**045**	10/61-02/83	**304045**	02/83-07/92

Class 308/1 York
Motor Brake Second
MBS, later MBSO
E61883-E61891

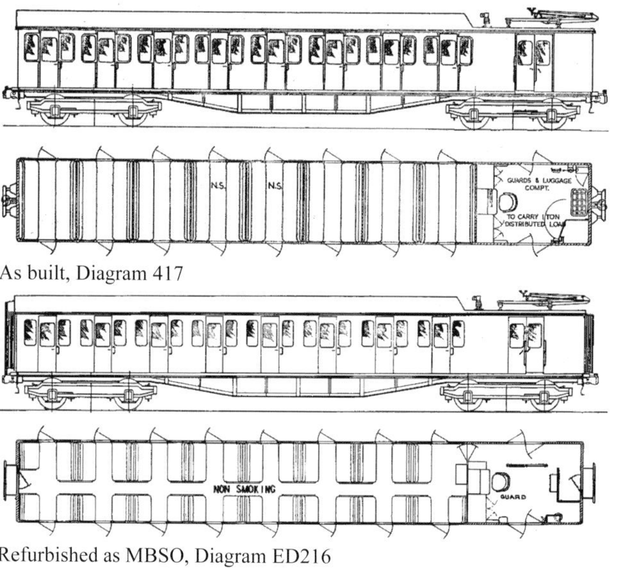

As built, Diagram 417

Refurbished as MBSO, Diagram ED216

Diagram:	417 ED216	Lot Number:	30653
Body:	63' 6" × 9' 3"	Weight:	54t 0cwt
Seats:	96 second, later 76 second	Bogies:	Gresley
Motors:	EE 4 × 200hp		

E61883	01/61-06/93	⊗06/94	**133**	01/61-04/81	**308133**	04/81-06/93		
E61884	01/61-04/01	⊗04/03	**134**	01/61-08/81	**308134**	08/81-09/99	**308162**	04/00-04/01
E61885	01/61-12/93	⊗03/94	**135**	01/61-08/81	**308135**	08/81-12/93		
E61886	01/61-01/01	⊗09/03	**136**	01/61-01/82	**308136**	01/82-01/01		
E61887	02/61-03/01	⊗06/03	**137**	02/61-12/81	**308137**	12/81-03/01		
E61888	02/61-10/01	⊗10/01	**138**	02/61-12/81	**308138**	11/83-10/01		
E61889	02/61-09/95	⊗09/95	**139**	02/61-10/82	**308139**	10/82-09/95		

E61890	02/61-09/95	⊗09/95	**140**	02/61-05/81	**308140**	05/81-09/95
E61891	03/61-04/01	⊗05/03	**141**	03/61-08/81	**308141**	08/81-04/01

Class 308/1 York

Motor Brake Second
MBS, later MBSO
E61892-E61915

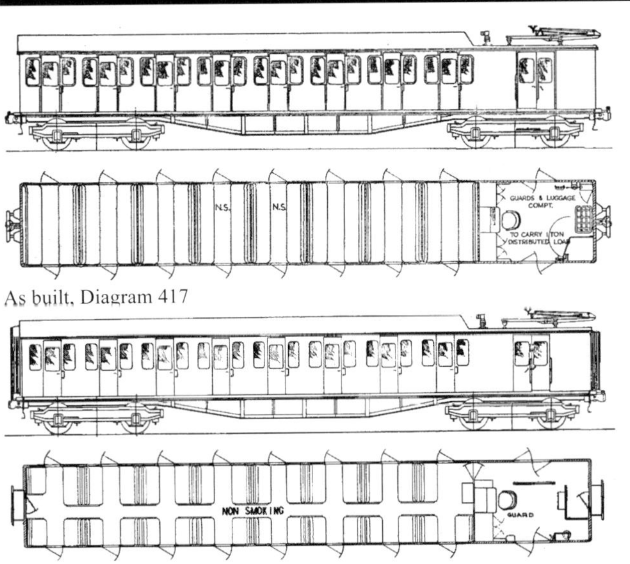

As built, Diagram 417

Refurbished as MBSO, Diagram ED216

Diagram:	417 ED216	Lot Number:	30657
Body:	63' 6" × 9' 3"	Weight:	54t 0cwt
Seats:	96 second, later 76 second	Bogies:	Gresley
Motors:	EE 4 × 200hp		

E61892	03/61-09/93	⊗04/97	**142**	03/61-01/82	**308142**	01/82-09/93		
E61893	03/61-06/01	℗10/01	**143**	03/61-01/82	**308143**	01/82-06/01		
E61894	03/61-02/01	○01/02	**144**	03/61-12/81	**308144**	12/81-02/01		
E61895	04/61-06/01	⊗10/01	**145**	04/61-03/82	**308145**	03/82-06/01		
E61896	04/61-09/94	➲977927	**146**	04/61-02/80	**308146**	02/80-09/94		
E61897	04/61-05/01	⊗06/03	**147**	04/61-03/82	**308147**	03/82-05/01		
E61898	04/61-09/93	⊗11/95	**148**	04/61-12/82	**308148**	12/82-09/93		
E61899	05/61-09/93	⊗02/95	**149**	05/61-06/82	**308149**	06/82-09/93		
E61900	05/61-*09/94*	➲977930	**150**	05/61-03/82	**308150**	03/82-06/95		
E61901	05/61-11/93	➲977877	**151**	05/61-11/82	**308151**	11/82-11/93		
E61902	06/61-05/01	⊗05/03	**152**	07/61-05/83	**308152**	05/83-05/01		
E61903	06/61-06/01	⊗11/01	**153**	07/61-09/82	**308153**	09/82-06/01		
E61904	06/61-01/01	⊗06/03	**154**	07/61-10/82	**308154**	10/82-01/01		
E61905	06/61-03/01	⊗05/03	**155**	07/61-05/83	**308155**	05/83-03/01		
E61906	07/61-09/93	⊗06/94	**156**	07/61-05/83	**308156**	05/83-06/93		
E61907	07/61-10/01	⊗10/01	**157**	07/61-05/83	**308157**	05/83-10/01		
E61908	07/61-10/01	⊗10/01	**158**	07/61-02/80	**308158**	02/80-04/83	**308458**	04/83-05/83
			308158	05/83-10/01				
E61909	07/61-01/01	⊗10/03	**159**	07/61-05/83	**308159**	05/83-01/01		
E61910	08/61-09/95	⊗09/95	**160**	08/61-05/83	**308160**	05/83-09/95		
E61911	08/61-05/01	⊗05/03	**161**	08/61-01/80	**308161**	01/80-04/83	**308461**	04/83-04/84
			308161	04/84-05/01				
E61912	09/61-04/00	⊗06/03	**162**	09/61-07/83	**308162**	07/83-04/00	**308134**	04/00-04/00
E61913	09/61-01/01	⊗09/03	**163**	09/61-07/83	**308163**	07/83-01/01		
E61914	09/61-03/01	⊗06/03	**164**	09/61-02/80	**308164**	02/80-03/01		
E61915	09/61-04/01	⊗05/03	**165**	09/61-02/81	**308165**	02/81-04/01		

Class 308 York

Motor Brake Second
MBS
E61916-E61924

Built as Motor Luggage Vans

E61916	➲**68011**
E61917	➲**68012**
E61918	➲**68013**
E61919	➲**68014**
E61920	➲**68015**
E61921	➲**68016**
E61922	➲**68017**
E61923	➲**68018**
E61924	➲**68019**

Class 309 York

Motor Brake Corridor Second
MBSK, later MBSO(T)
E61925-E61931

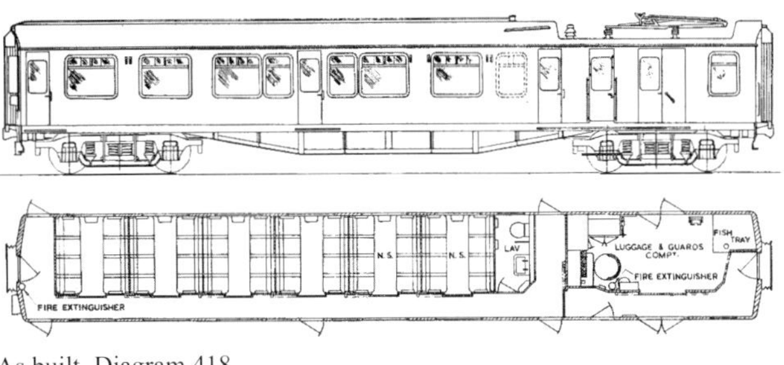

As built, Diagram 418

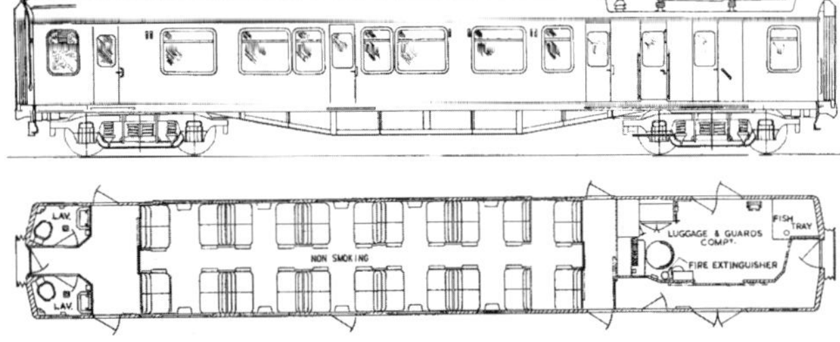

Later MBSOL ED209

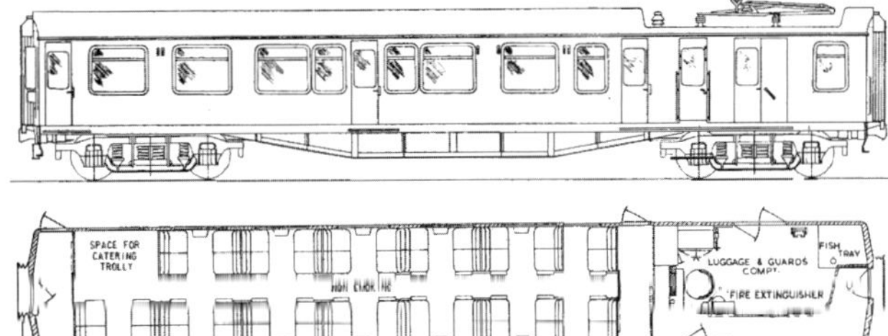

Later MBSO(T), Diagram ED218

Diagram:	418 ED209 ED218	Lot Number:	30676
Body:	64' 6" × 9' 3"	Weight:	56t 16cwt
Seats:	48 second 1 toilet, later 44 second 2 toilets, later 48 second no toilet	Bogies:	Commonwealth
		Motors:	GEC 4 × 282hp

E61925	07/62-05/92	⊗03/92	**621**	08/62-03/83	**309621**	03/83-05/92
E61926	09/62-11/92	⊗04/93	**622**	11/62-02/82	**309622**	02/82-11/92
E61927	11/62-06/00	⊗04/04	**623**	11/62-09/82	**309623**	09/82-06/00
E61928	11/62-06/00	℗➲977966	**624**	12/62-05/82	**309624**	05/82-06/00
E61929	12/62-12/91	⊗02/92	**625**	12/62-04/82	**309625**	04/82-12/91
E61930	10/62-12/94	⊗10/97	**626**	12/62-03/82	**309626**	03/82-12/94
E61931	10/62-11/99	⊗01/04	**627**	12/62-10/82	**309627**	10/82-11/99

Class 309 York

Motor Brake Corridor Second
MBSK, later MBSO(T)
E61932-E61939

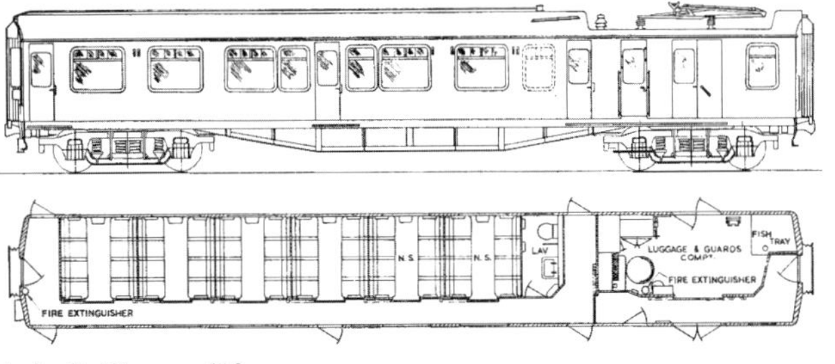

As built, Diagram 418

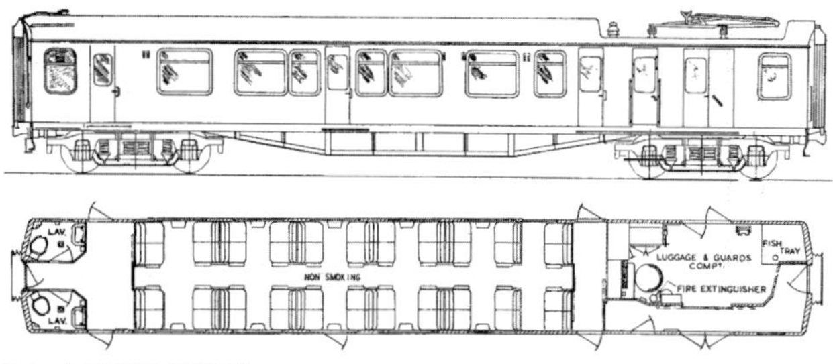

Later MBSOL ED209

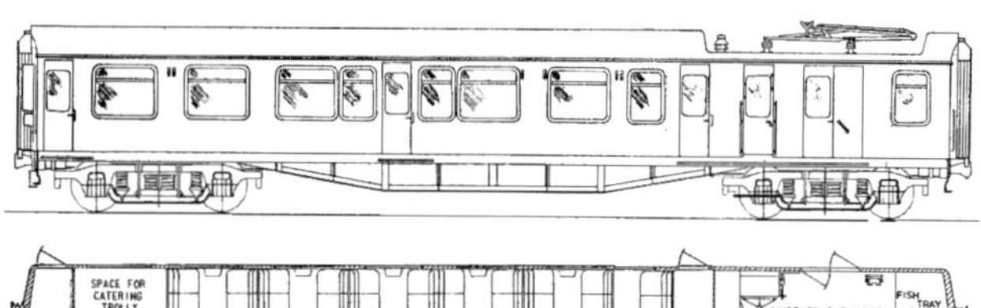

Later MBSO(T), Diagram ED218

Diagram:	418 ED209 ED218	Lot Number:	30680
Body:	64' 6" × 9' 3"	Weight:	56t 16cwt
Seats:	48 second 1 toilet, later 44 second 2 toilets, later 48 second no toilet	Bogies:	Commonwealth
		Motors:	GEC 4 × 282hp

E61932	09/62-12/91	⊗03/92	611	09/62-03/81	309611	03/81-12/91		
E61933	10/62-06/93	⊗04/93	612	10/62-10/82	309612	10/82-06/93		
E61934	10/62-06/00	⊗11/04	613	10/62-06/82	309613	06/82-06/00		
E61935	12/62-08/92	⊗07/92	614	12/62-10/82	309614	10/82-02/86	309614	07/86-08/92
E61936	12/62-08/92	⊗07/92	615	01/63-09/82	309615	09/82-03/85	309615	09/86-07/92
E61937	12/62-06/00	ⓟ➲977963	616	01/63-01/70	616	06/72-01/80	309616	01/80-07/85
			309616	04/86-06/00				
E61938	12/62-06/00	⊗08/04	617	02/63-10/82	309617	10/82-07/85	309617	04/86-06/00
E61939	12/62-12/94	⊗10/97	618	02/63-02/81	309618	02/81-12/94		

Class 309 York

Driving Motor Brake Corridor Second DMBSK, later DMBSO(T) E61940-E61947

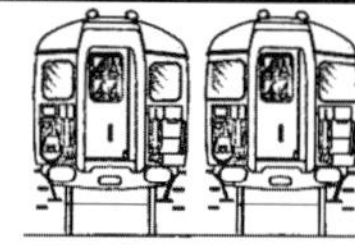

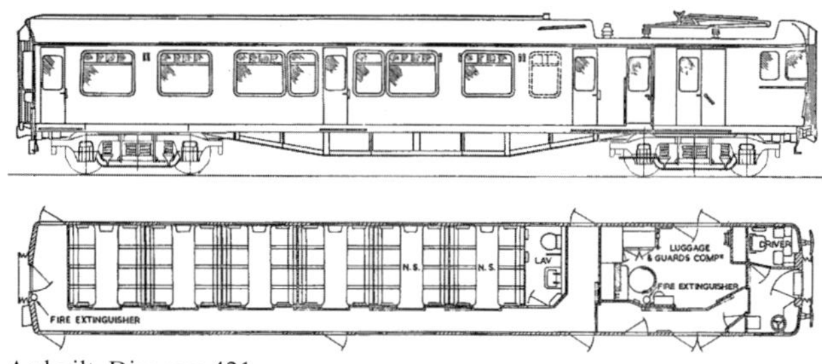

As built, Diagram 421

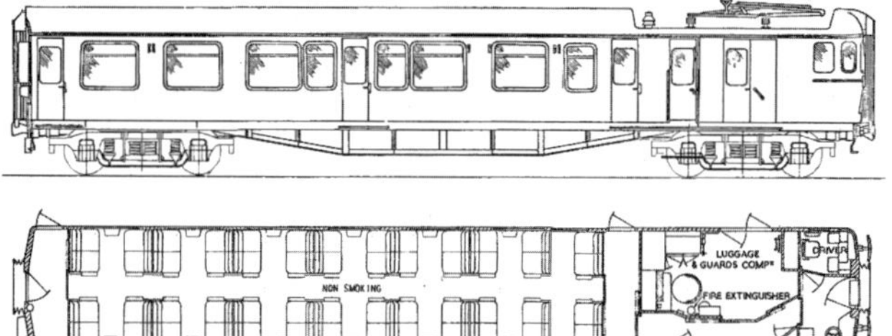

Later DMBSOL EB206

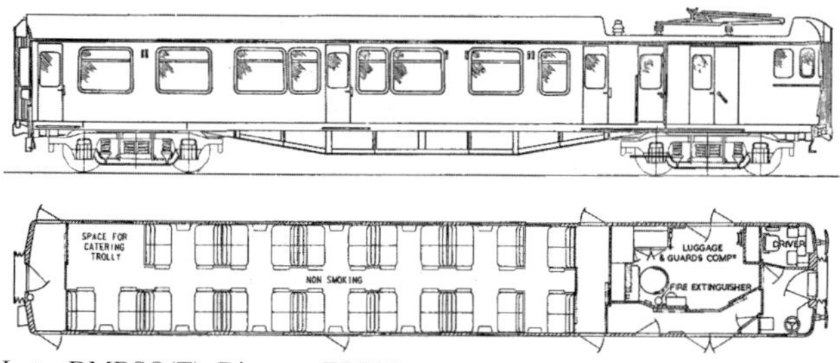

Later DMBSO(T), Diagram EB207

Diagram:	421 EB206 EB207	Lot Number:	30684
Body:	64' 9¾" × 9' 3"	Weight:	59t 6cwt
Seats:	48 second 1 toilet, later 52 second no toilet, later 48 second no toilet,	Bogies:	Commonwealth
		Motors:	GEC 4 × 282hp

E61940	09/62-05/93	⊗07/93	601	09/62-10/82	309601	10/82-05/93
E61941	12/62-01/94	⊗03/94	602	12/62-06/82	309602	06/82-01/94
E61942	01/63-05/93	⊗07/93	603	01/63-12/81	309603	12/81-05/93
E61943	02/63-01/94	⊗03/94	604	02/63-02/82	309604	02/82-01/94
E61944	02/63-03/98	⊗03/98	605	02/63-12/81	309605	12/81-03/98
E61945	03/63-03/98	⊗03/98	606	03/63-12/81	309606	12/81-03/98
E61946	03/63-02/94	⊗10/97	607	03/63-11/82	309607	11/82-02/94
E61947	03/63-05/93	⊗07/93	608	03/63-09/82	309608	09/82-05/93

Class 411 4-CEP Ashford/Eastleigh

Driving Motor Brake Second Open DMBSO later DMSO(A) & DMSO(B) S61948-S61961

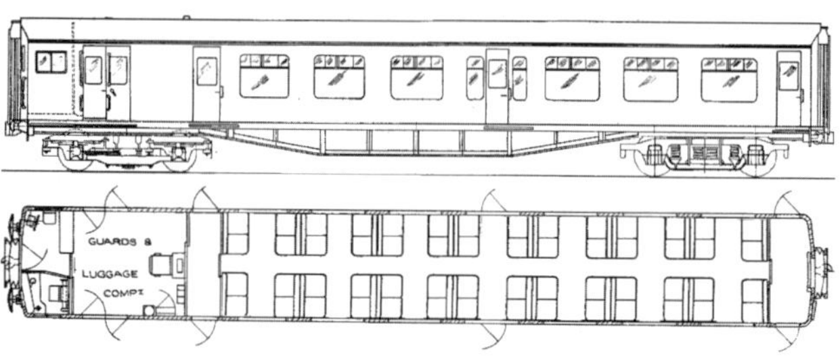

As built, Diagram 402

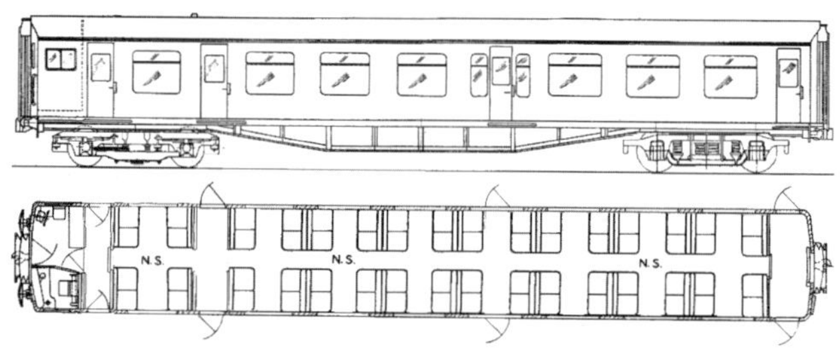

Refurbished, Diagram 884 DMSO(A) EA263, DMSO(B) EA264

Diagram:	402 884 EA263 EA264	Lot Number:	30708
Body:	64' 6" × 9' 3"	Weight:	41t 0cwt
Seats:	56 second, later 64 second	Bogies:	1 Mk 3B Motor
Motors:	EE507 2 × 250hp		1 Commonwealth

S61948	12/62-01/93	➲Dep	7205	12/62-11/83	1620	11/83-01/93	932620	01/93- 03
S61949	12/62-01/93	➲Dep	7205	12/62-11/83	1620	11/83-01/93	932620	01/93- 03
S61950	01/63-08/02	⊗09/02	7206	01/63-06/83	1616	06/83-09/02		
S61951	01/63-03/03	⊗06/03	7206	01/63-06/83	1616	06/83-03/03		
S61952	01/63-04/03	⊗04/03	7207	01/63-10/83	1619	10/83-11/98	1105	11/98-04/03
S61953	01/63-04/03	⊗04/03	7207	01/63-10/83	1619	10/83-11/98	1105	11/98-04/03
S61954	01/63-10/04	⊗10/04	7208	01/63-09/83	2303	09/83-09/02	2313	09/02-10/04
S61955	01/63-10/04	⊗12/04	7208	01/63-09/83	2303	09/83-09/02	2313	09/02-10/04
S61956	02/63-04/04	⊗06/04	7209	02/63-05/83	1615	05/83-04/04		
S61957	02/63-04/04	⊗06/04	7209	02/63-05/83	1615	05/83-04/04		
S61958	02/63-04/04	⊗08/04	7210	02/63-03/79	1602	08/81-04/04		
S61959	02/63-04/04	⊗06/04	7210	02/63-03/79	1602	08/80-04/04		
S61960	02/63-06/95	⊗06/95	7211	02/63-02/80	1608	02/80-06/95		
S61961	02/63-06/95	⊗06/95	7211	02/63-02/80	1608	02/80-06/95		

Class 414 2-HAP Ashford/Eastleigh

Driving Motor Brake Second Open
DMBSO
S61962-S61988

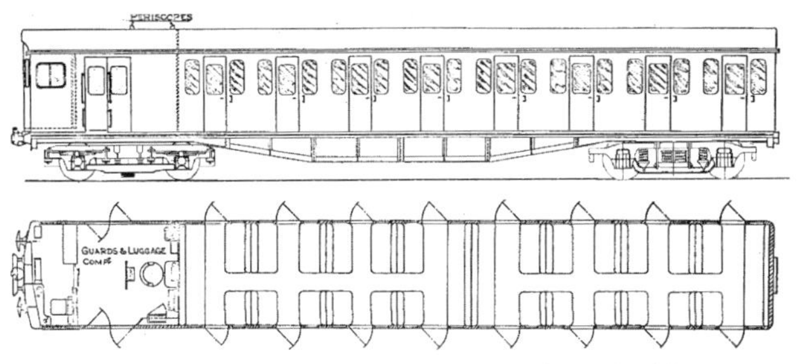

Diagram:	400 EB270	Lot Number:	30711
Body:	63' 11½" × 9' 3¼"	Weight:	41t 0cwt
Seats:	84 second	Bogies:	1 Mk 4
Motors:	EE507 2 × 250hp		1 Commonwealth

S61962	02/63-05/84	⊗10/84	**6147**	02/63-05/84
S61963	02/63-10/83	⊗08/84	**6148**	02/63-10/83
S61964	03/63-10/83	⊗04/84	**6149**	03/63-10/83
S61965	03/63-05/84	⊗10/84	**6150**	03/63-05/84
S61966	03/63-06/71	⊗01/72	**6151**	03/63-06/71
S61967	03/63-10/83	⊗06/84	**6152**	03/63-10/83
S61968	03/63-05/84	⊗11/84	**6153**	03/63-05/84
S61969	03/63-10/83	⊗06/84	**6154**	03/63-10/83
S61970	03/63-05/83	⊗08/86	**6155**	03/63-05/83
S61971	03/63-10/83	⊃**977205**	**6156**	03/63-10/83
S61972	04/63-10/83	⊗08/84	**6157**	04/63-10/83
S61973	04/63-10/83	⊗08/84	**6158**	04/63-10/83
S61974	04/63-05/84	⊗09/84	**6159**	04/63-05/84
S61975	04/63-10/83	⊗06/84	**6160**	04/63-10/83
S61976	04/63-05/84	⊗07/85	**6161**	04/63-05/84
S61977	04/63-05/84	⊗10/86	**6162**	04/63-05/84
S61978	04/63-05/84	⊗10/84	**6163**	04/63-05/84
S61979	04/63-06/82	⊗09/84	**6164**	04/63-06/82
S61980	05/63-10/83	⊗08/84	**6165**	05/63-10/83
S61981	05/63-05/84	⊗11/85	**6166**	05/63-05/84
S61982	05/63-05/84	⊗02/85	**6167**	05/63-05/84
S61983	05/63-10/83	⊗08/86	**6168**	05/63-10/83
S61984	05/63-05/84	⊗10/84	**6169**	05/63-05/84
S61985	05/63-10/84	⊗05/86	**6170**	05/63-10/84
S61986	05/63-05/84	⊗02/86	**6171**	05/63-05/84
S61987	05/63-05/84	⊗11/85	**6172**	05/63-05/84
S61988	05/63-10/84	⊗05/86	**6173**	05/63-10/84

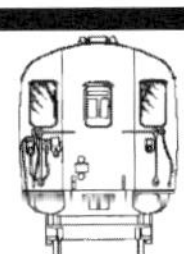

Class 415 4-EPB Ashford/Eastleigh

Driving Motor Brake Second Open
DMBSO
S61989-S62016

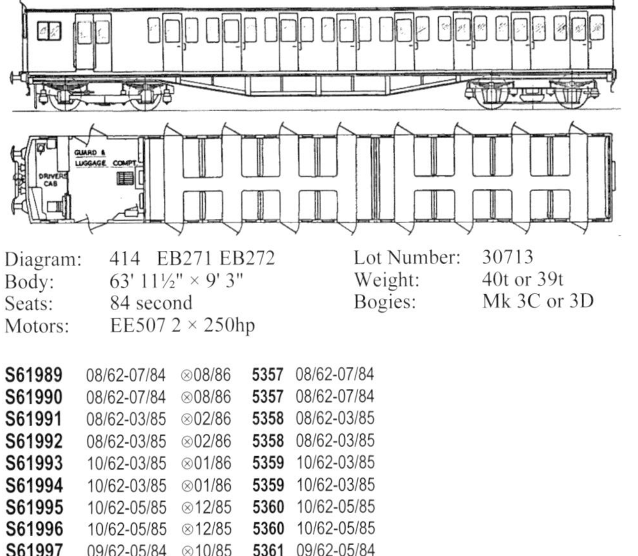

Diagram:	414 EB271 EB272	Lot Number:	30713
Body:	63' 11½" × 9' 3"	Weight:	40t or 39t
Seats:	84 second	Bogies:	Mk 3C or 3D
Motors:	EE507 2 × 250hp		

S61989	08/62-07/84	⊗08/86	**5357**	08/62-07/84
S61990	08/62-07/84	⊗08/86	**5357**	08/62-07/84
S61991	08/62-03/85	⊗02/86	**5358**	08/62-03/85
S61992	08/62-03/85	⊗02/86	**5358**	08/62-03/85
S61993	10/62-03/85	⊗01/86	**5359**	10/62-03/85
S61994	10/62-03/85	⊗01/86	**5359**	10/62-03/85
S61995	10/62-05/85	⊗12/85	**5360**	10/62-05/85
S61996	10/62-05/85	⊗12/85	**5360**	10/62-05/85
S61997	09/62-05/84	⊗10/85	**5361**	09/62-05/84
S61998	09/62-05/84	⊗10/85	**5361**	09/62-05/84
S61999	12/62-04/84	⊗11/86	**5362**	12/62-04/84
S62000	12/62-04/84	⊗11/86	**5362**	12/62-04/84
S62001	12/62-09/84	⊗07/86	**5363**	12/62-09/84
S62002	12/62-09/84	⊗07/86	**5363**	12/62-09/84
S62003	12/62-10/84	⊗04/86	**5364**	12/62-10/84
S62004	12/62-10/84	⊗04/86	**5364**	12/62-10/84
S62005	12/62-02/85	⊗04/86	**5365**	12/62-02/85
S62006	12/62-02/85	⊗04/86	**5365**	12/62-02/85
S62007	01/63-09/84	⊗11/85	**5366**	01/63-09/84
S62008	01/63-09/84	⊗11/85	**5366**	01/63-09/84
S62009	01/63-07/84	⊗11/85	**5367**	01/63-07/84
S62010	01/63-07/84	⊗11/85	**5367**	01/63-07/84
S62011	01/63-05/84	⊗11/85	**5368**	01/63-05/84
S62012	01/63-05/84	⊗11/85	**5368**	01/63-05/84
S62013	01/63-10/84	⊗04/86	**5369**	01/63-10/84
S62014	01/63-10/84	⊗04/86	**5369**	01/63-10/84
S62015	01/63-05/84	⊗11/85	**5370**	01/63-05/84
S62016	01/63-05/84	⊗11/85	**5370**	01/63-05/84

Class 421 4-CIG York

Motor Brake Second Open
MBSO
S62017-S62070 (62053 onwards Class 420 4-BIG)

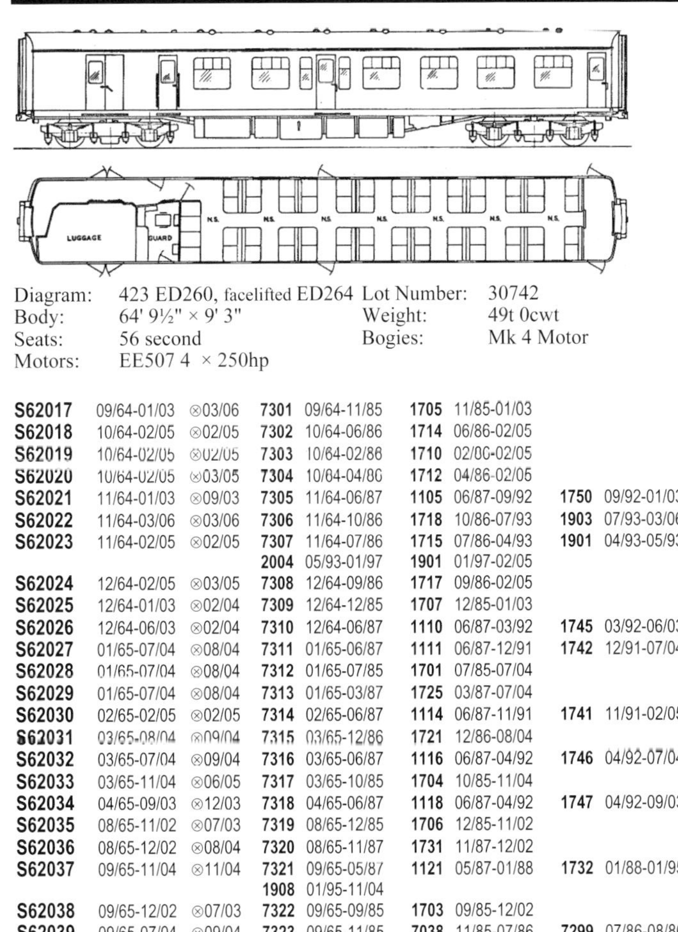

Diagram:	423 ED260, facelifted ED264	Lot Number:	30742
Body:	64' 9½" × 9' 3"	Weight:	49t 0cwt
Seats:	56 second	Bogies:	Mk 4 Motor
Motors:	EE507 4 × 250hp		

S62017	09/64-01/03	⊗03/06	**7301**	09/64-11/85	**1705**	11/85-01/03		
S62018	10/64-02/05	⊗02/05	**7302**	10/64-06/86	**1714**	06/86-02/05		
S62019	10/64-02/05	⊗02/05	**7303**	10/64-02/86	**1710**	02/86-02/05		
S62020	10/64-02/05	⊗03/05	**7304**	10/64-04/86	**1712**	04/86-02/05		
S62021	11/64-01/03	⊗09/03	**7305**	11/64-06/87	**1105**	06/87-09/92	**1750**	09/92-01/03
S62022	11/64-03/06	⊗03/06	**7306**	11/64-10/86	**1718**	10/86-07/93	**1903**	07/93-03/06
S62023	11/64-02/05	⊗02/05	**7307**	11/64-07/86	**1715**	07/86-04/93	**1901**	04/93-05/93
			2004	05/93-01/97	**1901**	01/97-02/05		
S62024	12/64-02/05	⊗03/05	**7308**	12/64-09/86	**1717**	09/86-02/05		
S62025	12/64-01/03	⊗02/04	**7309**	12/64-12/85	**1707**	12/85-01/03		
S62026	12/64-06/03	⊗02/04	**7310**	12/64-06/87	**1110**	06/87-03/92	**1745**	03/92-06/03
S62027	01/65-07/04	⊗08/04	**7311**	01/65-06/87	**1111**	06/87-12/91	**1742**	12/91-07/04
S62028	01/65-07/04	⊗08/04	**7312**	01/65-07/85	**1701**	07/85-07/04		
S62029	01/65-07/04	⊗08/04	**7313**	01/65-03/87	**1725**	03/87-07/04		
S62030	02/65-02/05	⊗02/05	**7314**	02/65-06/87	**1114**	06/87-11/91	**1741**	11/91-02/05
S62031	03/65-08/04	⊗09/04	**7315**	03/65-12/86	**1721**	12/86-08/04		
S62032	03/65-07/04	⊗09/04	**7316**	03/65-06/87	**1116**	06/87-04/92	**1746**	04/92-07/04
S62033	03/65-11/04	⊗06/05	**7317**	03/65-10/85	**1704**	10/85-11/04		
S62034	04/65-09/03	⊗12/03	**7318**	04/65-06/87	**1118**	06/87-04/92	**1747**	04/92-09/03
S62035	08/65-11/02	⊗07/03	**7319**	08/65-12/85	**1706**	12/85-11/02		
S62036	08/65-12/02	⊗08/04	**7320**	08/65-11/87	**1731**	11/87-12/02		
S62037	09/65-11/04	⊗11/04	**7321**	09/65-05/87	**1121**	05/87-01/88	**1732**	01/88-01/95
			1908	01/95-11/04				
S62038	09/65-12/02	⊗07/03	**7322**	09/65-09/85	**1703**	09/85-12/02		
S62039	09/65-07/04	⊗09/04	**7323**	09/65-11/85	**7038**	11/85-07/86	**7299**	07/86-08/86
			1720	11/86-07/04				
S62040	09/65-11/04	⊗11/04	**7324**	09/65-07/87	**1728**	07/87-03/94	**1905**	03/94-11/04
S62041	10/65-06/03	⊗11/03	**7325**	10/65-08/86	**1716**	08/86-04/93	**1902**	04/93-05/93
			2002	05/93-01/97	**1902**	01/97-06/03		
S62042	10/65-11/02	⊗08/03	**7326**	10/65-08/85	**1702**	08/85-11/02		
S62043	10/65-02/04	Ⓟ	**7327**	10/65-06/87	**1127**	06/87-01/93	**1753**	01/93-02/04
S62044	10/65-03/03	⊗02/04	**7328**	10/65-02/86	**1709**	02/86-03/03		
S62045	11/65-07/04	⊗09/04	**7329**	11/65-07/87	**1729**	07/87-07/94	**1907**	07/94-07/04
S62046	12/65-07/04	⊗07/04	**7330**	12/65-10/87	**1730**	10/87-05/94	**1906**	05/94-07/04
S62047	12/65-06/04	⊗06/04	**7331**	12/65-01/87	**1722**	01/87-06/04		
S62048	01/66-04/04	⊗03/06	**7332**	01/66-02/87	**1723**	02/87-11/93	**1904**	11/93-04/04
S62049	01/66-12/78	⊗04/79	**7333**	01/66-12/78				
S62050	01/66-09/03	⊗08/04	**7334**	01/66-05/87	**1726**	05/87-09/03		
S62051	01/66-02/05	⊗03/05	**7335**	01/66-01/86	**1708**	01/86-02/05		
S62052	02/66-06/04	⊗06/04	**7336**	02/66-06/87	**1727**	06/87-06/04		
S62053	04/65-09/95	⊗06/04	**7031**	04/65-09/85	**2111**	09/85-10/89	**1761**	10/89-05/92
			1749	05/92-09/95				
S62054	05/65-07/04	⊗07/04	**7032**	05/65-04/85	**2101**	04/85-10/89	**1751**	10/89-12/90
			1734	12/90-07/04				
S62055	05/65-12/04	⊗01/05	**7033**	05/65-03/86	**1711**	03/86-12/04		
S62056	06/65-05/04	⊗02/05	**7034**	06/65-11/85	**2110**	11/85-11/89	**1760**	11/89-05/92
			1748	05/92-05/04				
S62057	06/65-04/04	⊗08/04	**7035**	06/65-10/86	**1719**	10/86-04/04		

S62058	06/65-02/04	⊗08/04	**7036**	06/65-05/85	**2104**	05/85-10/89	**1754**	10/89-02/91
			1735	02/91-02/04				
S62059	08/65-02/05	⊗07/04	**7037**	08/65-04/85	**2106**	04/85-11/89	**1756**	11/89-01/92
			1743	01/92-02/05				
S62060	07/65-07/04	⊗01/05	**7038**	07/65-11/85	**7323**	11/85-07/86	**1123**	07/86-11/92
			1752	11/92-07/04				
S62061	08/65-02/04	⊗08/04	**7039**	08/65-10/86	**1724**	03/87-02/04		
S62062	11/65-09/03	⊗02/04	**7040**	11/65-08/79	**7300**	08/79-04/80	**7040**	04/80-05/85
			2105	05/85-10/89	**1755**	10/89-03/91	**1737**	03/91-09/03
S62063	11/65-07/04	⊗09/04	**7041**	11/65-04/85	**2107**	04/85-09/89	**1757**	09/89-10/90
			1733	10/90-07/04				
S62064	11/65-03/03	⊗02/04	**7042**	11/65-04/85	**2102**	04/85-10/89	**1752**	10/89-05/91
			1738	05/91-03/03				
S62065	12/65-03/03	⊗02/04	**7043**	12/65-04/85	**2103**	04/85-10/89	**1753**	10/89-02/91
			1736	02/91-03/03				
S62066	12/65-07/04	⊗03/05	**7044**	12/65-03/86	**7300**	03/86-06/87	**1100**	06/87-10/92
			1751	10/92-07/04				
S62067	12/65-04/04	⊗02/04	**7045**	12/65-04/86	**2112**	04/86-12/89	**1762**	12/89-11/91
			1740	11/91-04/04				
S62068	02/66-02/04	⊗08/04	**7046**	02/66-09/85	**2108**	09/85-11/89	**1758**	11/89-02/92
			1744	02/92-02/04				
S62069	02/66-02/04	⊗03/05	**7047**	02/66-05/86	**1713**	05/86-02/04		
S62070	02/66-06/04	⊗06/04	**7048**	02/66-10/85	**2109**	10/85-11/89	**1759**	11/89-01/92
			1739	01/92-06/04				

Class 310 Derby

Motor Brake Second Open
MBSO
M62071-M62120

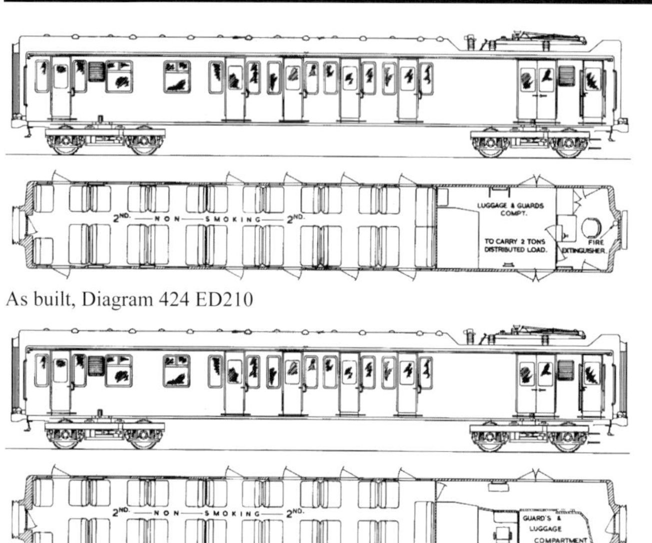

As built, Diagram 424 ED210

Rebuilt with through gangway, Diagram ED219

Diagram:	424 ED210 ED219	Lot Number:	30746
Body:	65' 4¼" × 9' 3"	Weight:	56t 6¾cwt
Seats:	70 second, later 68 second	Bogies:	B4
Motors:	EE546 4 × 270hp		

M62071	02/65-05/01	⊗10/07	**046**	02/65- *83*	**310046**	*83*-05/01		
M62072	03/65-06/01	⊗04/07	**047**	03/65-03/82	**310047**	03/82-06/01		
M62073	03/65-07/01	⊗07/08	**048**	03/65-04/81	**310048**	04/81-09/89	**310108**	09/89-07/01
M62074	03/65-06/01	⊗06/08	**049**	03/65-08/81	**310049**	08/81-06/01		
M62075	03/65-10/01	⊗02/09	**050**	03/65-09/82	**310050**	09/82-10/01		
M62076	08/65-10/01	⊗03/09	**051**	09/65-06/81	**310051**	06/81-10/01		
M62077	09/65-06/01	⊗02/07	**052**	09/65-02/80	**310052**	02/80-06/01		
M62078	09/65-07/01	➲977979	**053**	09/65-11/82	**310053**	11/82-10/89	**310109**	10/89-07/01
M62079	09/65-09/01	⊗09/08	**054**	09/65-07/81	**310054**	07/81-11/89	**310110**	11/89-09/01
M62080	08/65-09/01	⊗07/08	**055**	08/65-12/81	**310055**	12/81-10/88	**310102**	10/88-09/01
M62081	11/65-04/94	⊗11/95	**056**	11/65-02/80	**310056**	02/80-04/94		
M62082	10/65-08/00	⊗11/06	**057**	10/65-03/82	**310057**	03/82-08/00		
M62083	10/65-06/01	⊗03/07	**058**	10/65-12/81	**310058**	12/81-06/01		
M62084	10/65-07/01	⊗03/08	**059**	10/65-12/79	**310059**	12/79-07/01		
M62085	10/65-06/01	⊗07/07	**060**	10/65-04/81	**310060**	04/81-06/01		
M62086	08/65-07/01	⊗01/08	**061**	08/65-03/82	**310061**	03/82-09/94	**310112**	09/94-07/01
M62087	11/65-07/01	⊗02/07	**062**	11/65-02/83	**310062**	02/83-09/89	**310107**	09/89-07/01
M62088	08/65-05/01	⊗10/08	**063**	08/65-06/81	**310063**	06/81-03/90	**310111**	03/90-05/01
M62089	08/65-07/01	⊗01/08	**064**	08/65-04/81	**310064**	04/81-07/01		
M62090	08/65-07/01	➲977978	**065**	08/65-09/82	**310065**	09/82-09/94	**310113**	09/94-07/01
M62091	09/65-06/01	⊗09/07	**066**	09/65-03/82	**310066**	03/82-06/01		
M62092	09/65-05/01	⊗07/07	**067**	09/65-03/82	**310067**	03/82-05/01		
M62093	10/65-03/01	⊗08/06	**068**	10/65-04/83	**310068**	04/83-03/01		
M62094	10/65-07/01	⊗11/07	**069**	10/65-01/80	**310069**	01/80-07/01		
M62095	11/65-07/01	⊗04/08	**070**	11/65-08/81	**310070**	08/81-07/01		
M62096	12/65-01/70	⊗05/76	**071**	12/65-01/70				
M62097	12/65-09/01	⊗02/03	**072**	12/65-05/81	**310072**	05/81-02/89	**310106**	02/89-09/01
M62098	02/66-07/01	⊗06/07	**073**	02/66-12/81	**310073**	12/81-09/88	**310101**	09/88-07/01
M62099	06/66-07/01	⊗11/03	**074**	06/66-04/81	**310074**	04/81-07/01		
M62100	07/66-07/01	⊗11/03	**075**	07/66-04/83	**310075**	04/83-07/01		
M62101	07/66-02/00	⊗03/03	**076**	07/66-02/82	**310076**	02/82-11/88	**310103**	11/88-02/00
M62102	07/66-06/01	⊗03/03	**077**	07/66-12/81	**310077**	12/81-06/01		
M62103	08/66-07/01	⊗10/03	**078**	08/66-03/82	**310078**	03/82-01/89	**310104**	01/89-07/01
M62104	08/66-05/01	⊗10/03	**079**	08/66-08/81	**310079**	08/81-05/01		
M62105	08/66-10/01	⊗09/03	**080**	08/66-03/82	**310080**	03/82-10/01		
M62106	09/66-11/01	⊗09/03	**081**	09/66-03/82	**310081**	03/82-11/01		
M62107	09/66-10/01	⊗09/03	**082**	09/66-04/83	**310082**	04/83-10/01		
M62108	09/66-10/01	⊗09/03	**083**	09/66-10/81	**310083**	10/81-10/01		
M62109	10/66-05/01	⊗11/03	**084**	10/66-10/81	**310084**	10/81-05/01		
M62110	11/66-06/01	⊗11/03	**085**	11/66-04/83	**310085**	04/83-06/01		
M62111	10/66-06/01	⊗10/03	**086**	10/66-10/82	**310086**	10/82-06/01		
M62112	02/67-10/01	⊗11/03	**087**	02/67-12/81	**310087**	12/81-10/01		
M62113	12/66-10/01	⊗11/03	**088**	12/66-12/81	**310088**	12/81-10/01		
M62114	01/67-12/00	⊗03/03	**089**	01/67-06/81	**310089**	06/81-12/00		
M62115	11/66-07/01	⊗11/03	**090**	11/66-07/82	**310090**	07/82-01/89	**310105**	01/89-07/01
M62116	12/66-05/01	⊗11/03	**091**	12/66-04/83	**310091**	04/83-05/01		
M62117	12/66-10/01	⊗09/03	**092**	12/66-02/83	**310092**	02/83-10/01		
M62118	03/67-11/01	⊗11/03	**093**	03/67-07/82	**310093**	07/82-11/01		
M62119	02/67-06/01	⊗11/03	**094**	02/67-12/67	*stored*	12/67-04/75	**094**	04/75-01/83
			310094	01/83-06/01				
M62120	05/67-05/01	⊗11/03	**095**	05/67-04/81	**310095**	04/81-05/01		

Class 423 4-VEP Derby

Motor Brake Second Open
MBSO
S62121-S62140

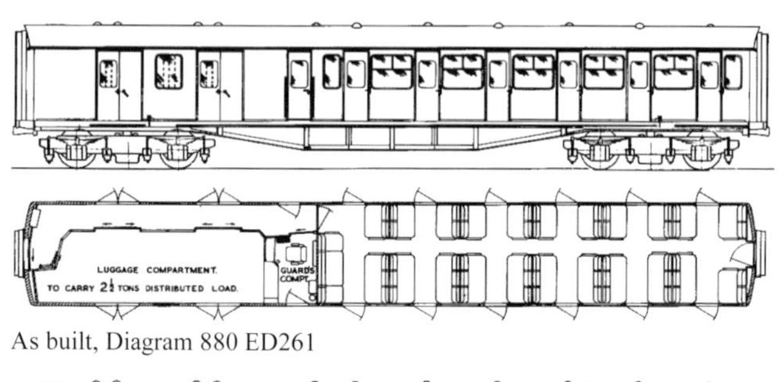

As built, Diagram 880 ED261

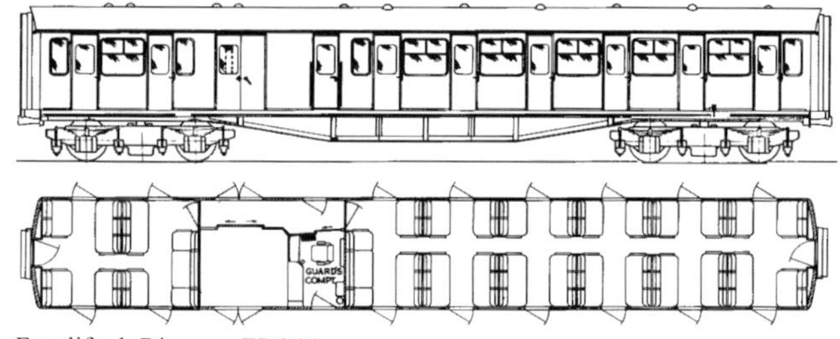

Facelifted, Diagram ED266

Diagram:	880 ED261 ED266	Lot Number:	30760
Body:	64' 9⅝" × 9' 3"	Weight:	47t 14cwt
Seats:	58 second, later 76 second	Bogies:	Mk 4 Motor
Motors:	EE507 4 × 250hp		

S62121	04/67-10/05	⊗12/05	**7701**	04/67-09/87	**3001**	09/87-10/93	**3545**	11/93-10/05
S62122	04/67-04/05	⊗04/05	**7702**	04/67-06/87	**3002**	06/87-06/93	**3539**	06/93-04/05
S62123	04/67-04/05	⊗04/05	**7703**	04/67-06/87	**3003**	06/87-05/93	**3402**	06/93-04/05
S62124	04/67-02/89	⊗06/89	**7704**	04/67-06/87	**3004**	06/87-02/89		
S62125	04/67-11/04	⊗03/05	**7705**	04/67-09/87	**3005**	09/87-06/89	**3478**	06/89-11/99
			3913	11/99-09/03	**3813**	09/03-11/04		
S62126	04/67-10/05	⊗12/05	**7706**	04/67-06/87	**3006**	06/87-01/94	**3547**	01/94-10/05
S62127	04/67-04/05	⊗04/05	**7707**	04/67-09/87	**3007**	09/87-08/93	**3542**	09/93-04/05
S62128	04/67-04/05	⊗04/05	**7708**	04/67-09/87	**3008**	09/87-06/93	**3540**	07/93-04/05
S62129	06/67-10/05	⊗10/05	**7709**	06/67-06/87	**3009**	06/87-06/94	**3562**	07/94-10/05
S62130	06/67-06/04	⊗07/04	**7710**	06/67-10/87	**3010**	10/87-12/93	**3406**	01/94-06/04
S62131	06/67-04/05	⊗08/05	**7711**	06/67-05/87	**3011**	05/87-06/90	**3520**	07/90-04/05
S62132	06/67-10/04	⊗10/04	**7712**	06/67-08/87	**3012**	08/87-01/94	**3549**	02/94-10/04
S62133	06/67-08/04	⊗	**7713**	06/67-06/87	**3013**	06/87-08/94	**3418**	09/94-08/04
S62134	06/67-10/05	⊗12/05	**7714**	06/67-04/71	**7714**	01/72-08/87	**3014**	08/87-08/94
			3565	08/94-10/05				
S62135	07/67-05/05	⊗05/05	**7715**	07/67-12/87	**3015**	12/87-10/94	**3511**	11/94-05/05
S62136	07/67-11/05	⊗12/05	**7716**	07/67-06/87	**3016**	06/87-06/90	**3514**	06/90-11/05
S62137	07/67-11/04	⊗02/05	**7717**	07/67-08/87	**3017**	08/87-09/93	**3543**	10/93-11/04
S62138	07/67-06/02	➲977981	**7718**	07/67-06/87	**3018**	06/87-09/94	**3567**	09/94-06/02
S62139	07/67-07/05	⊗07/05	**7719**	07/67-05/87	**3019**	05/87-09/90	**3523**	05/91-07/05
S62140	07/67-05/04	⊗06/04	**7720**	07/67-07/87	**3020**	07/87-04/94	**3555**	04/94-05/04

Class 430 4-REP York

Driving Motor Second Open
DMSO
S62141-S62162

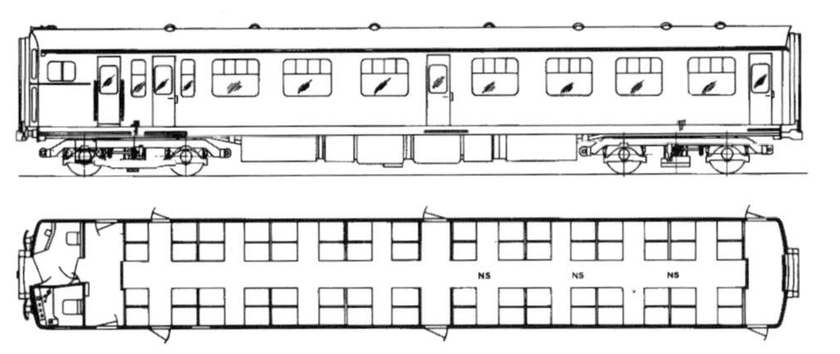

Diagram:	890A EA260	Lot Number:	30761
Body:	64' 9½" × 9' 3"	Weight:	51t 13cwt
Seats:	64 second	Bogies:	Mk 6 motor
Motors:	EE340B 4 × 400hp		

S62141	03/67-02/92	⊗05/92	**3001**	03/67-06/86	**2001**	06/86-12/87	**2904**	12/87-05/88
			2001	05/88-06/88	**1901**	12/88-05/90	**1905**	05/90-04/91
			1904	07/91-02/92				
S62142	03/67-02/92	⊗05/92	**3001**	03/67-06/86	**2001**	06/86-12/87	**2901**	12/87-05/88
			2001	05/88-06/88	**1901**	12/88-05/90	**1906**	05/90-01/91
			1901	03/91-02/92				
S62143	03/67-01/88	⊗12/89	**3002**	03/67-05/86	**2002**	05/86-01/88		
S62144	03/67-01/88	⊗12/89	**3002**	03/67-05/86	**2002**	05/86-01/88		
S62145	03/67-10/91	⊗11/91	**3003**	03/67-09/86	**2003**	09/86-12/87	**2905**	12/87-04/88
			2003	04/88-04/90	**1903**	04/90-09/90	**1903**	01/91-10/91
S62146	03/67-04/90	⊗	**3003**	03/67-09/86	**2003**	09/86-12/87	**2902**	12/87-04/88
			2003	04/88-04/90				
S62147	05/67-12/87	⊗04/90	**3004**	05/67-06/86	**2004**	06/86-12/87		
S62148	05/67-12/87	⊗04/90	**3004**	05/67-06/86	**2004**	06/86-12/87		
S62149	06/67-01/88	⊗04/89	**3005**	06/67-08/86	**2005**	08/86-01/88		
S62150	06/67-01/88	⊗04/89	**3005**	06/67-08/86	**2005**	08/86-01/88		
S62151	05/67-12/86	⊗06/90	**3006**	05/67-06/86	**2006**	06/86-12/86		
S62152	05/67-12/88	⊗06/90	**3006**	05/67-06/86	**2006**	06/86-12/86		
S62153	06/67-10/91	⊗11/91	**3007**	06/67-06/86	**2007**	06/86-03/88	**2906**	03/88-05/88
			2007	05/88-02/89	**1902**	02/89-10/91		
S62154	06/67-06/91	⊗03/92	**3007**	06/67-06/86	**2007**	[illegible]	[illegible]	[illegible]
			2007	05/88-02/89	**1902**	[illegible]	[illegible]	[illegible]
			1905	04/91-06/91				
S62155	05/67-10/88	⊗10/88	**3008**	05/67-09/86				
S62156	05/67-10/88	⊗10/88	**3008**	05/67-09/86				
S62157	06/67-06/87	⊗06/90	**3009**	06/67-06/86	**2009**	06/86-06/87		
S62158	06/67-06/87	⊗04/90	**3009**	06/67-06/86	**2009**	06/86-06/87		
S62159	07/67-06/87	⊗06/90	**3010**	07/67-09/86	**2010**	09/86-06/87		
S62160	07/67-06/87	⊗08/90	**3010**	07/67-09/86	**2010**	09/86-06/87		
S62161	07/67-01/87	⊗06/90	**3011**	07/67-09/86	**2011**	09/86-01/87		
S62162	07/67-01/87	⊗07/90	**3011**	07/67-09/86	**2011**	09/86-01/87		

Class 311 Cravens

Motor Brake Second Open
MBSO
SC62163-SC62181

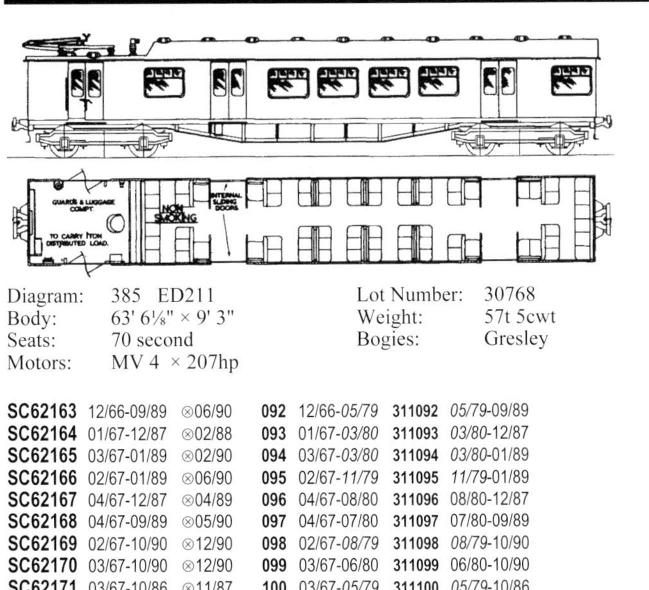

Diagram:	385 ED211	Lot Number:	30768
Body:	63' 6⅛" × 9' 3"	Weight:	57t 5cwt
Seats:	70 second	Bogies:	Gresley
Motors:	MV 4 × 207hp		

SC62163	12/66-09/89	⊗06/90	**092**	12/66-*05/79*	**311092**	*05/79*-09/89
SC62164	01/67-12/87	⊗02/88	**093**	01/67-*03/80*	**311093**	*03/80*-12/87
SC62165	03/67-01/89	⊗02/90	**094**	03/67-*03/80*	**311094**	*03/80*-01/89
SC62166	02/67-01/89	⊗06/90	**095**	02/67-*11/79*	**311095**	*11/79*-01/89
SC62167	04/67-12/87	⊗04/89	**096**	04/67-08/80	**311096**	08/80-12/87
SC62168	04/67-09/89	⊗05/90	**097**	04/67-07/80	**311097**	07/80-09/89
SC62169	02/67-10/90	⊗12/90	**098**	02/67-*08/79*	**311098**	*08/79*-10/90
SC62170	03/67-10/90	⊗12/90	**099**	03/67-06/80	**311099**	06/80-10/90
SC62171	03/67-10/86	⊗11/87	**100**	03/67-*05/79*	**311100**	*05/79*-10/86
SC62172	05/67-12/87	⊗04/90	**101**	05/67-*05/79*	**311101**	*05/79*-12/87
SC62173	04/67-10/90	⊗11/90	**102**	04/67-*03/80*	**311102**	*03/80*-10/90
SC62174	05/67-*10/90*	Ⓟ➲**977845**	**103**	05/67-*05/79*	**311103**	*05/79-10/90*
SC62175	05/67-*10/90*	➲**977848**	**104**	05/67-*11/79*	**311104**	*11/79-10/90*
SC62176	05/67-09/90	⊗01/91	**105**	05/67-*08/79*	**311105**	*08/79*-09/90
SC62177	05/67-10/86	⊗06/87	**106**	05/67-*03/80*	**311106**	*03/80*-10/86
SC62178	05/67-10/90	⊗11/90	**107**	05/67-06/80	**311107**	06/80-10/90
SC62179	06/67-10/90	⊗01/91	**108**	06/67-*03/80*	**311108**	*03/80*-10/90
SC62180	06/67-10/90	⊗01/91	**109**	06/67-*08/79*	**311109**	*08/79*-10/90
SC62181	07/67-10/90	⊗08/90	**110**	07/67- *80*	**311110**	*80*-10/90

Class 423 4-VEP York

Motor Brake Second Open
MBSO
S62182-S62216

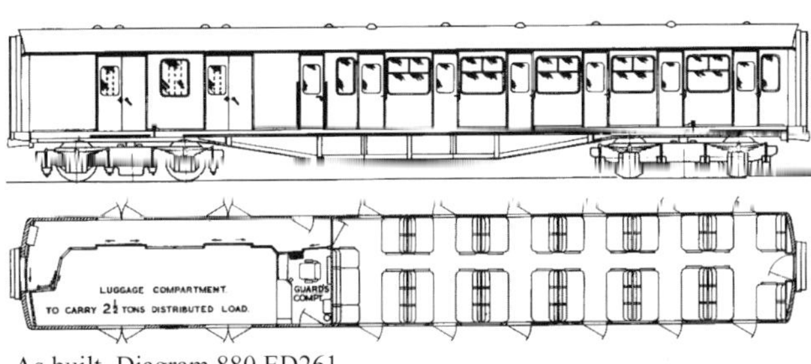

As built, Diagram 880 ED261

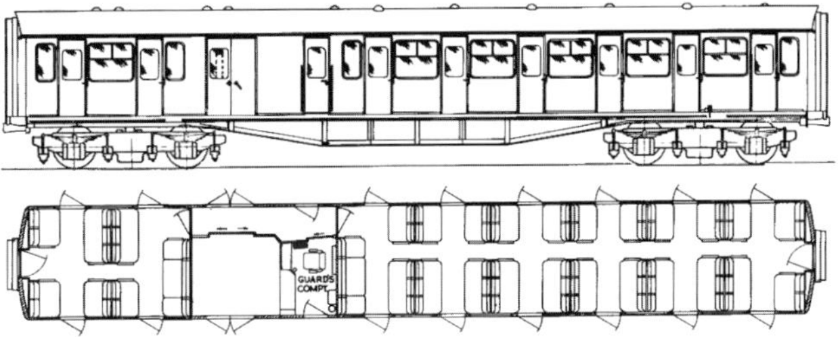

Facelifted, Diagram ED266

Diagram:	880 ED261 ED266	Lot Number:	30773
Body:	64' 9⅝" × 9' 3"	Weight:	47t 14cwt
Seats:	58 second, later 76 second	Bogies:	Mk 4 Motor
Motors:	EE507 4 × 250hp		

S62182	10/67-07/04	⊗08/04	**7721**	10/67-07/87	**3021**	07/87-06/88	**3431**	06/88-07/04
S62183	10/67-11/04	⊗10/04	**7722**	10/67-07/87	**3022**	07/87-11/88	**3452**	11/88-11/04
S62184	10/67-05/04	⊗06/04	**7723**	10/67-06/87	**3023**	06/87-05/88	**3427**	06/88-05/04
S62185	11/67-05/05	⊗05/05	**7724**	11/67-12/87	**3024**	12/87-02/88	**3424**	05/88-05/05
S62186	11/67-12/04	⊗03/05	**7725**	11/67-06/87	**3025**	06/87-07/88	**3437**	08/88-12/04
S62187	11/67-11/04	⊗02/05	**7726**	11/67-05/87	**3026**	05/87-11/94	**3570**	11/94-11/04
S62188	12/67-07/04	⊗08/04	**7727**	12/67-06/87	**3027**	06/87-08/88	**3440**	09/88-08/95
			3802	08/95-07/04				
S62189	12/67-07/04	⊗08/04	**7728**	12/67-06/87	**3028**	06/87-06/88	**3430**	06/88-07/04
S62190	12/67-11/04	⊗06/05	**7729**	12/67-06/87	**3029**	06/87-07/88	**3436**	07/88-11/04
S62191	12/67-09/05	⊗10/05	**7730**	12/67-05/87	**3030**	05/87-05/94	**3560**	06/94-09/05
S62192	12/67-07/04	⊗08/04	**7731**	12/67-05/87	**3031**	05/87-05/88	**3425**	05/88-07/04
S62193	12/67-08/04	⊗ 04	**7732**	12/67-05/87	**3032**	05/87-01/95	**3578**	01/95-08/04
S62194	12/67-05/90	⊗11/90	**7733**	12/67-06/87	**3033**	06/87-04/89		
S62195	01/68-08/04	⊗ 04	**7734**	01/68-06/87	**3034**	06/87-02/95	**3580**	02/95-08/02
			3580	04/03-08/04				
S62196	01/68-04/05	⊗06/05	**7735**	01/68-06/87	**3035**	06/87-01/95	**3576**	01/95-04/05
S62197	01/68-10/05	⊗10/05	**7736**	01/68-04/80	**3024**	02/88-11/88	**3457**	01/89-10/05
S62198	02/68-03/05	⊗07/05	**7737**	02/68-06/87	**3037**	06/87-02/95	**3581**	02/95-03/05
S62199	02/68-06/05	⊗06/05	**7738**	02/68-08/87	**3038**	08/87-10/88	**3447**	11/88-06/05
S62200	02/68-09/05	⊗09/05	**8001**	04/68-01/75	**7700**	10/84-08/87	**3000**	08/87-12/88
			3454	12/88-09/05				
S62201	02/68-12/04	⊗02/05	**7740**	02/68-02/88	**3040**	02/88-04/88	**3422**	04/88-12/04
S62202	03/68-07/04	⊗08/04	**8001**	04/68-01/75	**7741**	02/75-06/87	**3041**	06/87-06/88
			3429	06/88-07/04				
S62203	03/68-10/05	⊗12/05	**8001**	04/68-01/75	**7742**	02/75-02/88	**3042**	02/88-11/88
			3450	11/88-10/05				
S62204	04/68-12/04	⊗06/05	**7743**	04/68-06/87	**3043**	06/87-09/88	**3444**	10/88-10/95
			3804	10/95-12/04				
S62205	04/68-12/05	⊗12/05	**7744**	04/68-08/87	**3044**	08/87-11/88	**3449**	11/88-12/05
S62206	04/68-12/04	⊗01/05	**7745**	04/68-03/88	**3045**	03/88-12/88	**3455**	12/88-12/04
S62207	04/68-06/08	⊗09/09	**7746**	04/68-06/87	**3046**	06/87-02/93	**3536**	02/93-06/08
S62208	04/68-05/04	⊗06/04	**7747**	04/68-06/87	**3047**	06/87-05/88	**3426**	05/88-05/04
S62209	04/68-04/05	⊗04/05	**7748**	04/68-03/88	**3048**	03/88-12/88	**3458**	01/89-04/05
S62210	05/68-04/05	⊗04/05	**7749**	05/68-10/87	**3049**	10/87-12/88	**3456**	01/89-04/05
S62211	05/68-02/05	⊗02/05	**7750**	05/68-10/87	**3050**	10/87-01/89	**3460**	01/89-09/95
			3805	09/95-02/05				
S62212	05/68-12/04	⊗06/05	**7751**	05/68-12/87	**3051**	12/87-01/89	**3461**	02/89-08/95
			3806	08/95-12/04				

S62213	06/68-07/05	⊗06/05	**7752**	06/68-11/87	**3052**	11/87-01/89	**3462**	02/89-07/99
			3903	07/99-07/05				
S62214	06/68-04/05	⊗04/05	**7753**	06/68-12/87	**3053**	12/87-02/89	**3466**	03/89-04/05
S62215	07/68-10/04	⊗11/04	**7754**	07/68-06/87	**3054**	06/87-07/88	**3433**	07/88-10/04
S62216	07/68-07/05	⊗07/05	**7755**	07/68-03/88	**3055**	03/88-09/88	**3442**	10/88-11/99
			3912	11/99-07/05				

Class 423 4-VEP York

Motor Brake Second Open

MBSO

S62217-S62266

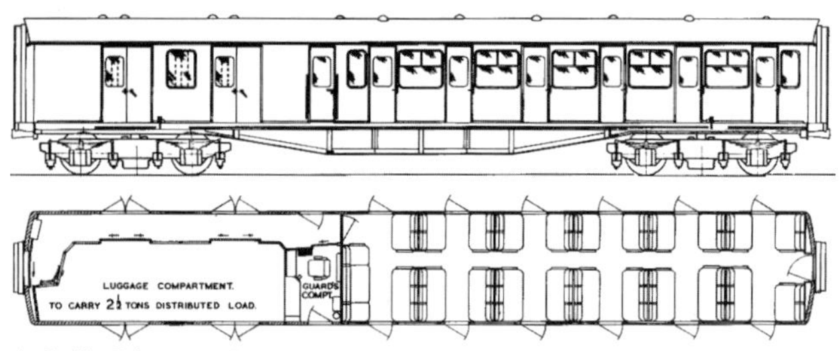

As built, Diagram 881 ED263

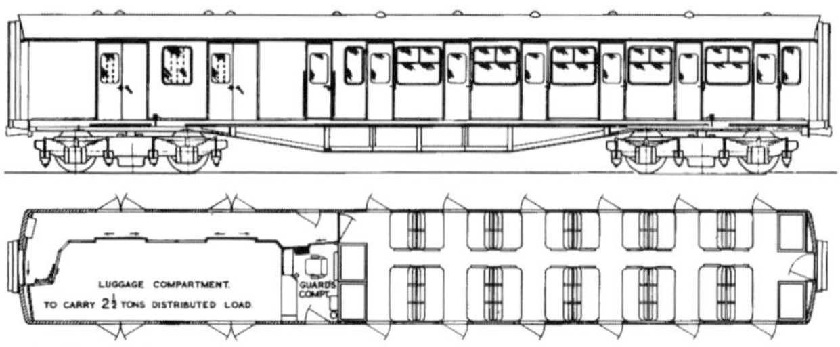

Rebuilt as Class 427 4-VEG for Gatwick services, Diagram 840 ED262

Facelifted, Diagram ED266

Diagram:	881 ED263 840 ED262 ED266	Lot Number:	30794
Body:	64' 9⅝" × 9' 3"	Weight:	49t 0cwt
Seats:	58 second, VEG 50 second later 76 second	Bogies:	Mk 4 Motor
		Motors:	EE507 4 × 250hp

S62217	01/69-02/05	⊗08/05	**7756**	01/69-12/87	**3056**	12/87-02/89	**3467**	03/89-02/05
S62218	01/69-07/05	⊗07/05	**7757**	01/69-06/87	**3057**	06/87-07/88	**3434**	07/88-07/05
S62219	01/69-08/04	⊗ 04	**7758**	01/69-07/88	**3058**	07/88-03/89	**3469**	04/89-08/04
S62220	02/69-04/05	⊗08/05	**7759**	02/69-02/88	**3059**	02/88-03/89	**3470**	04/89-04/05
S62221	02/69-07/05	⊗10/05	**7760**	02/69-09/87	**3060**	09/87-10/88	**3448**	11/88-07/05
S62222	02/69-08/05	⊗08/05	**7761**	02/69-06/87	**3061**	06/87-04/88	**3423**	04/88-08/05
S62223	02/69-07/04	⊗ 04	**7762**	02/69-02/88	**3062**	02/88-06/88	**3428**	06/88-07/04
S62224	02/69-04/05	⊗04/05	**7763**	02/69-06/87	**3063**	06/87-01/89	**3459**	01/89-04/05
S62225	02/69-07/04	⊗11/04	**7764**	02/69-06/87	**3064**	06/87-06/88	**3432**	07/88-07/04
S62226	03/69-10/05	⊗10/05	**7765**	03/69-03/88	**3065**	03/88-11/88	**3453**	12/88-10/05
S62227	03/69-08/05	⊗10/05	**7766**	03/69-08/87	**3066**	08/87-07/88	**3439**	09/88-05/99
			3901	05/99-08/05				
S62228	03/69-10/04	⊗10/04	**7767**	03/69-08/87	**3067**	08/87-07/88	**3435**	07/88-09/03
			3814	09/03-10/04				
S62229	03/69-05/04	⊗07/04	**7768**	03/69-03/74	**7768**	01/75-09/87	**3068**	09/87-07/91
			3525	10/91-08/95	**3801**	08/95-05/04		
S62230	03/69-05/05	⊗05/05	**7769**	03/69-06/87	**3069**	06/87-02/92	**3531**	03/92-05/05
S62231	04/69-07/05	⊗10/05	**7770**	04/69-08/87	**3070**	08/87-01/90	**3503**	02/90-09/03
			3844	09/03-07/05				
S62232	04/69-10/04	⊗10/04	**7771**	04/69-06/87	**3071**	06/87-02/90	**3507**	02/90-12/99
			3917	12/99-10/04				
S62233	04/69-07/05	⊗07/05	**7772**	04/69-10/87	**3072**	10/87-07/89	**3483**	08/89-07/05
S62234	04/69-11/05	⊗01/06	**7773**	04/69-10/87	**3073**	10/87-08/89	**3486**	09/89-11/05
S62235	05/69-04/05	⊗08/05	**7774**	05/69-10/87	**3074**	10/87-09/89	**3488**	09/89-04/05
S62236	05/69-	Ⓟ	**7775**	05/69-08/87	**3075**	08/87-09/93	**3417**	09/93-
				05/04 Named Gordon Pettitt				
S62237	05/69-11/04	⊗02/05	**7776**	05/69-06/87	**3076**	06/87-10/89	**3493**	10/89-11/04
S62238	05/69-04/05	⊗06/05	**7777**	05/69-06/87	**3077**	06/87-08/90	**3155**	09/90-07/93
			3541	07/93-05/98	**3812**	05/98-04/05		
S62239	05/69-07/04	⊗ 04	**7778**	05/69-06/87	**3078**	06/87-06/94	**3409**	06/94-07/04
S62240	05/69-11/04	⊗10/04	**7779**	05/69-08/87	**3079**	08/87-11/88	**3451**	11/88-11/04
S62241	06/69-05/05	⊗05/05	**7780**	06/69-06/87	**3080**	06/87-02/94	**3553**	03/94-05/05
S62242	06/69-08/05	⊗10/05	**7781**	06/69-07/87	**3081**	07/87-10/88	**3445**	10/88-08/05
S62243	06/69-06/05	⊗08/05	**7782**	06/69-05/87	**3082**	05/87-09/88	**3446**	10/88-06/05
S62244	07/69-06/05	⊗06/05	**7783**	07/69-07/87	**3083**	07/87-04/89	**3472**	05/89-06/05
S62245	07/69-02/05	⊗10/05	**7784**	07/69-05/87	**3084**	05/87-04/89	**3473**	05/89-12/91
			3473	07/92-02/05				
S62246	07/69-09/05	⊗12/05	**7785**	07/69-05/87	**3085**	05/87-05/89	**3474**	05/89-09/05
S62247	07/69-08/05	⊗10/05	**7786**	07/69-05/87	**3086**	05/87-05/89	**3476**	05/89-11/99
			3911	11/99-08/05				
S62248	07/69-02/05	⊗02/05	**7787**	07/69-05/87	**3087**	05/87-05/89	**3477**	05/89-08/95
			3808	08/95-02/05				
S62249	08/69-02/05	⊗02/05	**7788**	08/69-05/78	**7901**	05/78-05/84	**7788**	05/84-05/87
			3088	05/87-10/92	**3537**	03/93-04/98	**3811**	04/98-02/05
S62250	09/69-09/05	⊗09/05	**7789**	09/69-05/78	**7902**	05/78-05/84	**7789**	05/84-05/87
			3089	05/87-08/89	**3487**	09/89-09/05		
S62251	09/69-07/05	⊗10/05	**7790**	09/69-05/78	**7903**	05/78-05/84	**7790**	05/84-06/87
			3090	06/87-09/89	**3489**	09/89-07/05		
S62252	09/69-04/05	⊗06/05	**7791**	09/69-04/78	**7904**	04/78-05/84	**7791**	05/84-06/87
			3091	06/87-12/89	**3502**	01/90-06/96	**3810**	06/96-04/05
S62253	09/69-04/05	⊗06/05	**7792**	09/69-03/78	**7905**	03/78-05/84	**7792**	05/84-05/87
			3092	05/87-03/93	**3538**	04/93-06/96	**3809**	06/96-04/05
S62254	09/69-02/05	⊗06/05	**7793**	09/69-05/78	**7906**	05/78-05/84	**7793**	05/84-06/87
			3093	06/87-04/93	**3403**	05/93-02/05		
S62255	10/69-02/05	⊗02/05	**7794**	10/69-05/78	**7907**	05/78-05/84	**7794**	05/84-05/87
			3094	05/87-01/92	**3526**	03/92-12/99	**3915**	12/99-02/05
S62256	10/69-11/05	⊗01/06	**7795**	10/69-05/78	**7908**	05/78-05/84	**7795**	05/84-06/87
			3095	06/87-12/91	**3530**	02/92-11/05		
S62257	10/69-06/04	⊗06/04	**7796**	10/69-05/78	**7909**	05/78-05/84	**7796**	05/84-06/87
			3096	06/87-10/91	**3529**	12/91-06/04		
S62258	11/69-07/05	⊗12/05	**7797**	11/69-05/78	**7910**	05/78-05/84	**7797**	05/84-05/87
			3097	05/87-01/92	**3528**	01/92-12/99	**3916**	12/99-07/05
S62259	11/69-03/05	⊗06/05	**7798**	11/69-05/78	**7911**	05/78-06/80	**7911**	10/80-05/84
			7798	05/84-05/87	**3098**	05/87-09/92	**3534**	10/92-09/99
			3907	09/99-03/05				
S62260	11/69-04/05	⊗08/05	**7799**	11/69-05/78	**7912**	05/78-05/84	**7799**	05/84-05/87
			3099	05/87-06/92	**3533**	09/92-08/99	**3902**	08/99-04/05
S62261	11/69-08/04	⊗ 04	**7800**	11/69-08/87	**3100**	08/87-08/88	**3441**	09/88-01/90
			3404	02/90-08/04				
S62262	11/69-08/05	⊗08/05	**7801**	11/69-06/87	**3101**	06/87-08/88	**3438**	08/88-10/99
			3910	10/99-09/03	**3821**	09/03-08/05		
S62263	12/69-02/05	⊗02/05	**7802**	12/69-06/87	**3102**	06/87-09/88	**3443**	09/88-09/95
			3803	09/95-02/05				
S62264	12/69-12/04	⊗12/04	**7803**	12/69-07/87	**3103**	07/87-02/89	**3465**	03/89-08/95
			3807	08/95-12/04				
S62265	12/69-06/05	⊗06/05	**7804**	12/69-05/87	**3104**	05/87-02/89	**3464**	02/89-10/99
			3908	10/99-06/05				
S62266	12/69-04/05	Ⓟ	**7805**	12/69-05/87	**3105**	05/87-01/89	**3463**	02/89-08/99
			3905	08/99-04/05				

Class 423 4-VEP York

Motor Brake Second Open

MBSO

S62267-S62276

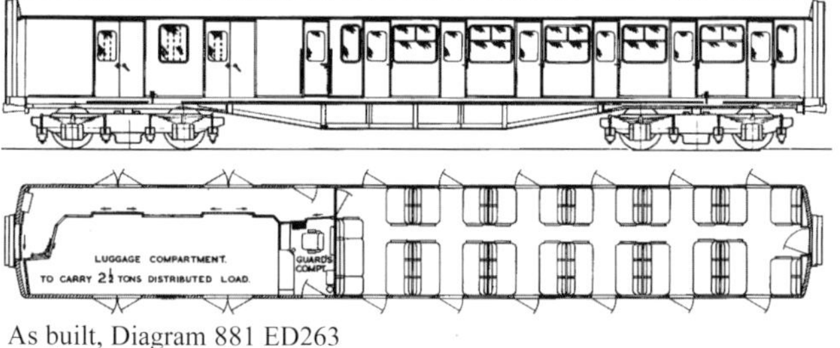

As built, Diagram 881 ED263

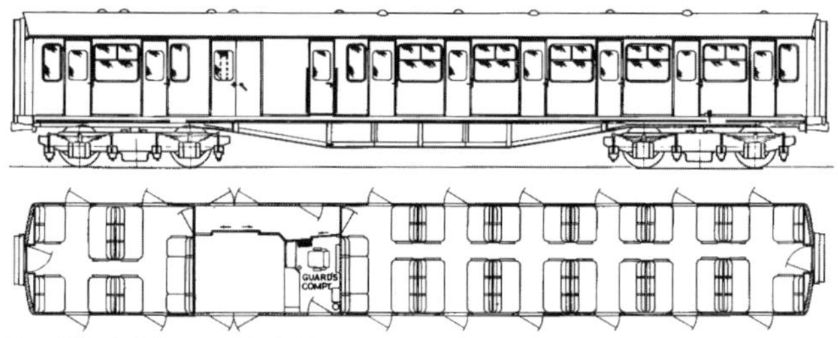

Facelifted, Diagram ED266

Diagram:	881 ED263 ED266	Lot Number:	30800
Body:	64' 9⅝" × 9' 3"	Weight:	49t 0cwt
Seats:	58 second, later 76 second	Bogies:	Mk 4 Motor
Motors:	EE507 4 × 250hp		

S62267	01/70-04/05	⊗04/05	**7806**	01/70-07/87	**3106**	07/87-03/89	**3468**	03/89-04/05
S62268	01/70-04/05	⊗06/05	**7807**	01/70-05/87	**3107**	05/87-05/90	**3516**	06/90-04/05
S62269	02/70-10/05	⊗12/05	**7808**	02/70-06/87	**3108**	06/87-04/89	**3471**	04/89-10/05

S62270	02/70-10/05	⊗10/05	**7809**	02/70-06/87	**3109**	06/87-05/89	**3475**	06/89-10/05
S62271	02/70-04/05	⊗04/05	**7810**	02/70-10/87	**3110**	10/87-05/89	**3405**	06/89-04/05
S62272	02/70-07/05	⊗07/05	**7811**	02/70-08/87	**3111**	08/87-06/89	**3479**	07/89-07/05
S62273	02/70-03/05	⊗07/05	**7812**	02/70-09/87	**3112**	09/87-02/90	**3508**	03/90-03/05
S62274	03/70-05/04	⊗07/04	**7813**	03/70-08/87	**3113**	08/87-07/90	**3519**	07/90-05/04
S62275	03/70-07/04	⊗08/04	**7814**	03/70-09/87	**3114**	09/87-02/90	**3509**	03/90-07/04
S62276	03/70-04/05	⊗06/05	**7815**	03/70-09/87	**3115**	09/87-03/90	**3511**	04/90-06/93
			3401	10/93-04/05				

Class 420 4-BIG York

Motor Brake Second Open

MBSO

S62277-S62286

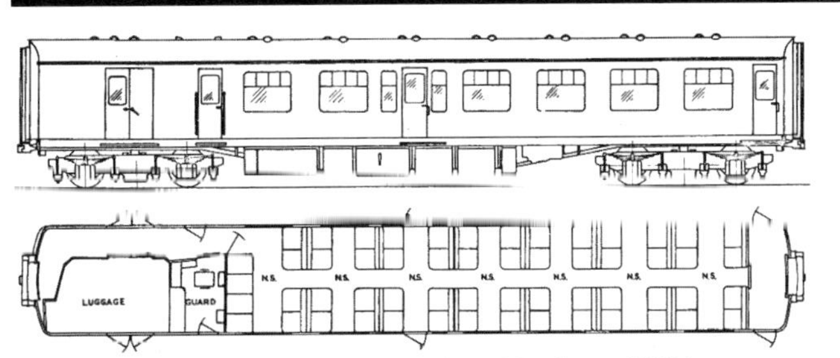

Diagram:	423 ED260, facelifted ED264	Lot Number:	30804
Body:	64' 9½" × 9' 3"	Weight:	49t 0cwt
Seats:	56 second	Bogies:	Mk 4 Motor
Motors:	EE507 4 × 250hp		

S62277	05/70-08/04	⊗09/04	**7049**	05/70-06/85	**2201**	06/85-11/88	**1824**	11/88-05/90
			1311	05/90-08/04				
S62278	06/70-04/05	⊗05/05	**7050**	06/70-05/85	**2202**	05/85-12/88	**1825**	12/88-06/90
			1312	06/90-04/05				
S62279	06/70-06/04	⊗07/04	**7051**	06/70-04/85	**2203**	04/85-06/97	**1403**	06/97-06/04
S62280	10/70-04/02	⊗11/03	**7052**	10/70-04/85	**2204**	04/85-06/97	**1402**	06/97-04/02
S62281	11/70-06/04	⊗07/04	**7053**	11/70-04/85	**2205**	04/85-06/97	**1405**	06/97-06/04
S62282	12/70-02/05	⊗10/05	**7358**	10/70-09/87	**1258**	09/87-06/90	**1834**	06/90-02/05
S62283	07/70-08/04	⊗ 04	**7055**	07/70-04/85	**2207**	04/85-07/88	**1823**	10/88-05/90
			1310	05/90-08/04				
S62284	08/70-02/04	⊗08/06	**7056**	08/70-04/85	**2208**	04/85-06/97	**1401**	06/97-07/97
			1401	11/97-02/04				
S62285	09/70-11/03	⊗11/03	**7057**	09/70-04/85	**2209**	04/85-09/97	**1409**	09/97-11/03
S62286	10/70-04/05	⊗06/05	**7058**	10/70-04/85	**2210**	04/85-09/97	**1411**	09/97-04/05

Class 421 4-CIG York

Motor Brake Second Open

MBSO

S62287-S62316

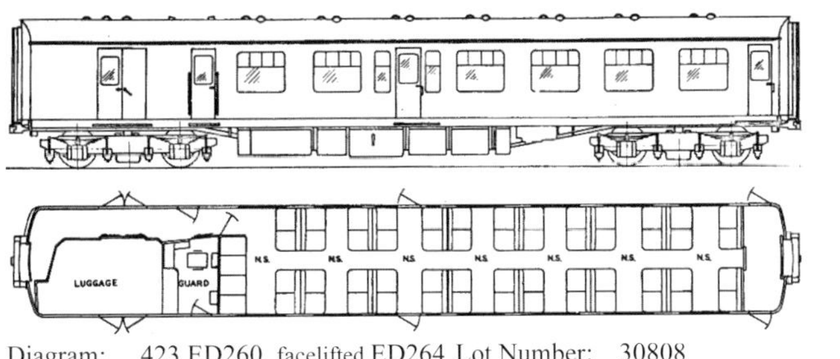

Diagram:	423 ED260, facelifted ED264	Lot Number:	30808
Body:	64' 9½" × 9' 3"	Weight:	49t 0cwt
Seats:	56 second	Bogies:	Mk 4 Motor
Motors:	EE507 4 × 250hp		

S62287	06/70-02/05	Ⓟ	**7337**	06/70-08/87	**1237**	08/87-05/88	**1816**	05/88-04/90
			1303	04/90-02/05				
S62288	05/70-07/04	⊗08/04	**7338**	05/70-06/87	**1238**	06/87-06/90	**1833**	06/90-07/04
S62289	05/70-04/05	⊗09/09	**7339**	05/70-08/87	**1239**	08/87-05/88	**1817**	05/88-04/90
			1304	04/90-04/05				
S62290	06/70-04/04	⊗04/05	**7340**	06/70-09/87	**1240**	09/87-04/88	**1815**	04/88-04/90
			1302	04/90-04/04				
S62291	06/70-05/05	⊗10/05	**7341**	06/70-08/87	**1241**	08/87-04/90	**1316**	04/90-05/05
S62292	08/70-10/04	⊗11/04	**7342**	08/70-09/87	**1242**	09/87-07/88	**1820**	07/88-05/90
			1307	05/90-10/04				
S62293	10/70-08/04	⊗09/04	**7343**	10/70-09/87	**1243**	09/87-08/90	**1838**	08/90-03/92
			1322	03/92-08/04				
S62294	10/70-08/04	⊗09/04	**7344**	10/70-06/87	**1244**	06/87-04/90	**1314**	04/90-08/04
S62295	11/70-08/04	⊗09/04	**7345**	11/70-06/87	**1245**	06/87-10/90	**1844**	10/90-01/92
			1321	01/92-08/04				
S62296	01/71-06/05	⊗06/05	**7346**	01/71-06/87	**1246**	06/87-11/90	**1849**	11/90-01/92
			1318	01/92-06/05				
S62297	01/71-06/05	⊗06/05	**7347**	01/71-06/87	**1247**	06/87-12/90	**1852**	12/90-01/92
			1319	01/92-06/05				
S62298	06/70-09/04	⊗10/04	**7348**	06/70-06/87	**1248**	06/87-07/88	**1821**	07/88-05/90
			1308	05/90-09/04				
S62299	07/70-10/04	⊗08/04	**7349**	07/70-09/87	**1249**	09/87-07/90	**1836**	07/90-01/92
			1320	01/92-10/04				
S62300	07/70-04/05	⊗05/05	**7350**	07/70-08/87	**1250**	08/87-07/88	**1822**	07/88-04/90
			1309	04/90-04/05				
S62301	08/70-08/04	⊗09/04	**7351**	08/70-08/87	**1251**	08/87-04/88	**1814**	04/88-04/90
			1301	04/90-08/04				
S62302	08/70-12/04	⊗01/05	**7352**	08/70-09/87	**1252**	09/87-04/90	**1313**	04/90-12/04
S62303	09/70-09/04	⊗10/04	**7353**	09/70-09/87	**1253**	09/87-11/90	**1317**	11/90-09/04
S62304	09/70-05/05	⊗07/05	**7354**	09/70-11/87	**1254**	11/87-05/90	**1831**	05/90-05/05
S62305	10/70-12/04	⊗02/05	**7355**	10/70-02/88	**1255**	02/88-10/90	**1845**	10/90-12/04
S62306	11/70-02/05	⊗02/05	**7356**	11/70-06/87	**1256**	06/87-11/90	**1847**	11/90-02/05
S62307	10/70-10/04	⊗10/04	**7357**	10/70-07/87	**1257**	07/87-06/90	**1835**	06/90-10/04
S62308	07/70-03/05	⊗06/05	**7054**	11/70-04/85	**2206**	04/85-06/97	**1404**	06/97-03/05
S62309	10/70-07/04	⊗08/04	**7359**	10/70-06/87	**1259**	06/87-09/90	**1841**	09/90-07/04
S62310	11/70-07/05	⊗07/05	**7360**	11/70-06/87	**1260**	06/87-05/91	**1858**	05/91-07/05
S62311	11/70-02/05	⊗02/05	**7361**	11/70-08/87	**1261**	08/87-11/90	**1848**	11/90-02/05
S62312	12/70-05/05	⊗05/05	**7362**	12/70-05/87	**1262**	05/87-01/91	**1853**	01/91-05/05
S62313	12/70-05/04	⊗06/04	**7363**	12/70-07/87	**1263**	07/87-08/90	**1839**	08/90-05/04
S62314	11/70-12/04	⊗06/05	**7364**	11/70-07/87	**1264**	07/87-04/90	**1315**	04/90-12/04
S62315	12/70-12/78	⊗04/79	**7365**	12/70-12/70				
S62316	01/71-12/05	⊗12/05	**7366**	01/71-05/87	**1266**	05/87-04/91	**1857**	04/91-12/05

Class 423 4-VEP York

Motor Brake Second Open

MBSO

S62317-S62354

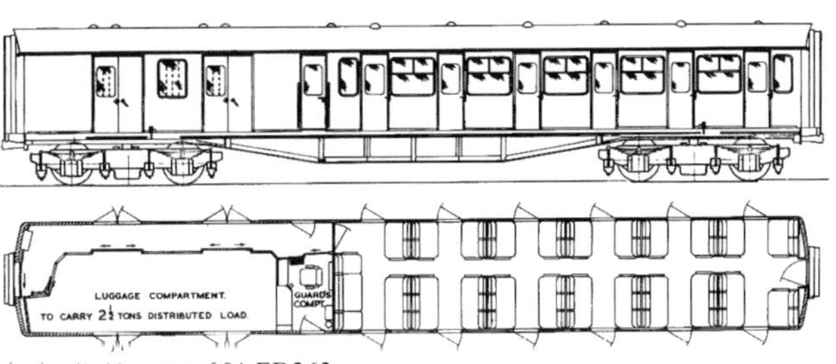

As built, Diagram 881 ED263

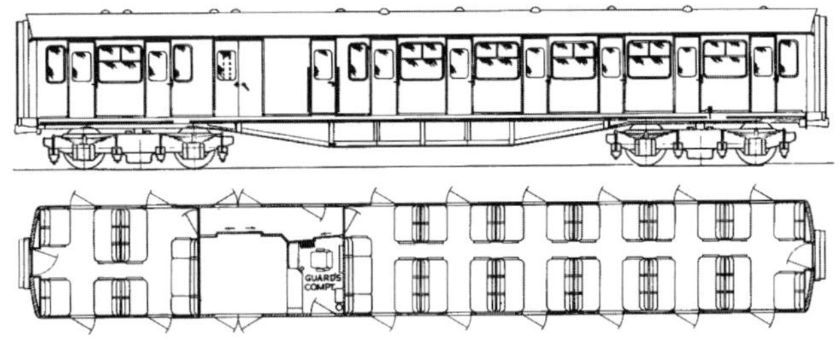

Facelifted, Diagram ED266

Diagram:	881 ED263 ED266	Lot Number:	30813
Body:	64' 9⅝" × 9' 3"	Weight:	49t 0cwt
Seats:	58 second, later 76 second	Bogies:	Mk 4 Motor
Motors:	EE507 4 × 250hp		

S62317	04/72-07/05	⊗08/05	**7816**	04/72-05/87	**3116**	05/87-02/90	**3506**	02/90-01/00
			3919	01/00-07/05				
S62318	04/72-05/04	⊗07/04	**7817**	04/72-08/87	**3117**	08/87-03/90	**3510**	03/90-05/04
S62319	04/72-10/04	⊗10/04	**7818**	04/72-06/87	**3118**	06/87-04/90	**3515**	05/90-11/91
			1800	11/91-08/92	**3515**	08/92-10/04		
S62320	04/72-04/05	⊗06/05	**7819**	04/72-09/87	**3119**	09/87-12/88	**3482**	08/89-04/05
S62321	05/72-04/05	Ⓟ	**7820**	05/72-03/88	**3120**	03/88-03/92	**3532**	06/92-01/00
			3918	01/00-04/05				
S62322	05/72-04/05	⊗05/05	**7821**	05/72-12/87	**3121**	12/87-05/91	**3524**	07/91-04/05
S62323	06/72-07/04	⊗08/04	**7822**	06/72-04/88	**3122**	04/88-06/89	**3480**	07/89-07/04
S62324	06/72-06/05	⊗06/05	**7823**	06/72-06/87	**3123**	06/87-07/89	**3481**	07/89-06/05
S62325	06/72-05/05	⊗05/05	**7824**	06/72-03/88	**3124**	03/88-08/89	**3484**	08/89-05/05
S62326	06/72-07/04	⊗07/04	**7825**	06/72-07/87	**3125**	07/87-12/91	**3527**	12/91-11/99
			3914	11/99-09/03	**3841**	09/03-07/04		
S62327	06/72-06/05	⊗10/05	**7826**	06/72-12/87	**3126**	12/87-08/89	**3485**	08/89-06/05
S62328	07/72-11/05	⊗01/06	**7827**	07/72-09/88	**3127**	09/88-09/89	**3490**	10/89-11/05
S62329	07/72-04/91	⊗10/91	**7828**	07/72-08/87	**3128**	08/87-09/89	**3491**	10/89-04/91
S62330	08/72-05/05	⊗05/05	**7829**	08/72-11/87	**3129**	11/87-10/89	**3494**	11/89-05/05
S62331	08/72-08/05	⊗10/05	**7830**	08/72-07/87	**3130**	07/87-10/89	**3495**	11/89-08/05
S62332	08/72-02/05	⊗ 05	**7831**	08/72-08/87	**3131**	08/87-11/89	**3501**	12/89-12/91
			1830	12/91-01/92	**3501**	01/92-02/05		
S62333	08/72-08/05	⊗10/05	**7832**	08/72-07/87	**3132**	07/87-11/89	**3498**	12/89-08/05
S62334	09/72-08/05	⊗10/05	**7833**	09/72-07/87	**3133**	07/87-11/89	**3496**	11/89-08/05
S62335	09/72-11/05	⊗12/05	**7834**	09/72-05/87	**3134**	05/87-11/92	**3535**	11/92-11/05

Vehicle	Dates	Fate	Unit	Dates	Unit	Dates	Unit	Dates
S62336	09/72-04/05	⊗07/05	**7835**	09/72-05/87	**3135**	05/87-05/90	**3513**	05/90-07/99
			3904	07/99-04/05				
S62337	09/72-05/04	⊗07/04	**7836**	09/72-10/87	**3136**	10/87-02/90	**3512**	05/90-05/04
S62338	09/72-06/04	⊗07/04	**7837**	09/72-05/87	**3137**	05/87-06/90	**3517**	06/90-06/04
S62339	10/72-05/04	⊗07/04	**7838**	10/72-07/87	**3138**	07/87-06/90	**3016**	06/90-12/93
			3546	12/93-05/04				
S62340	10/72-08/05	⊗10/05	**7839**	10/72-05/87	**3139**	05/87-12/93	**3412**	01/94-08/05
S62341	11/72-11/04	⊗11/04	**7840**	11/72-07/87	**3140**	07/87-07/90	**3522**	09/90-09/99
			3909	09/99-11/04				
S62342	11/72-04/05	⊗12/05	**7841**	11/72-07/87	**3141**	07/87-05/90	**3411**	06/90-04/05
S62343	12/72-07/05	⊗08/05	**7842**	12/72-10/87	**3142**	10/87-06/90	**3518**	07/90-09/03
			3842	09/03-07/05				
S62344	12/72- 05	⊗ 05	**7843**	12/72-06/87	**3143**	06/87-10/89	**3492**	10/89- 05
S62345	02/73-09/05	⊗12/05	**7844**	02/73-06/87	**3144**	06/87-07/90	**3521**	08/90-09/05
S62346	02/73-08/05	⊗10/05	**7845**	02/73-07/87	**3145**	07/87-11/89	**3497**	11/89-08/05
S62347	03/73-06/05	⊗08/05	**7846**	03/73-08/87	**3146**	08/87-12/89	**3499**	12/89-06/05
S62348	03/73-04/05	⊗04/05	**7847**	03/73-06/87	**3147**	06/87-07/93	**3407**	08/93-04/05
S62349	03/73-05/04	⊗07/04	**7848**	03/73-09/87	**3148**	09/87-09/90	**3019**	09/90-03/94
			3420	04/94-05/04				
S62350	04/73-04/05	⊗06/05	**7849**	04/73-08/87	**3149**	08/87-02/94	**3550**	02/94-09/99
			3906	09/99-09/03	**3843**	09/03-04/05		
S62351	04/73-08/05	⊗	**7850**	04/73-06/87	**3150**	06/87-01/90	**3504**	01/90-09/03
			3822	09/03-08/05				
S62352	05/73-11/05	⊗12/05	**7851**	05/73-05/87	**3151**	05/87-01/90	**3505**	02/90-11/05
S62353	05/73-05/04	⊗07/04	**7852**	05/73-05/87	**3152**	05/87-02/94	**3552**	03/94-05/04
S62354	05/73-05/04	⊗07/04	**7853**	05/73-07/87	**3153**	07/87-03/94	**3419**	03/94-05/04

Class 421 4-CIG York

Motor Brake Second Open
MBSO
S62355-S62425

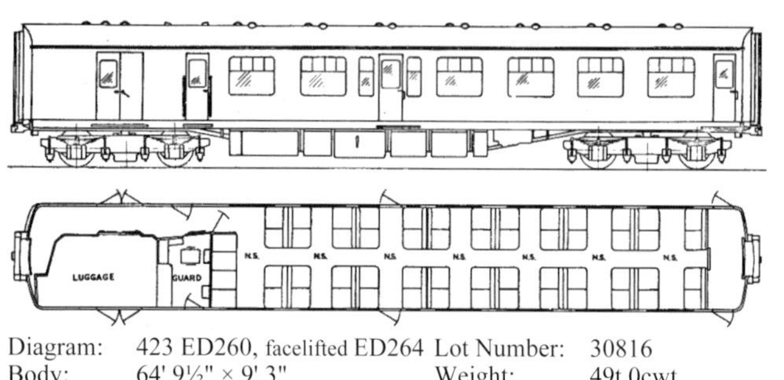

Diagram:	423 ED260, facelifted ED264	Lot Number:	30816
Body:	64' 9½" × 9' 3"	Weight:	49t 0cwt
Seats:	56 second	Bogies:	Mk 4 Motor
Motors:	EE507 4 × 250hp		

Vehicle	Dates	Fate	Unit	Dates	Unit	Dates	Unit	Dates
S62355	02/71-07/04	⊗09/04	**7367**	02/71-08/87	**1267**	08/87-06/88	**1818**	06/88-04/90
			1305	04/90-07/04				
S62356	02/71-06/03	➲999606	**7368**	02/71-06/87	**1268**	06/87-12/90	**1850**	12/90-06/03
S62357	02/71-07/05	⊗07/05	**7369**	02/71-05/87	**1269**	05/87-05/90	**1832**	05/90-07/05
S62358	03/71-12/04	⊗07/05	**7370**	03/71-08/87	**1270**	08/87-01/91	**1855**	01/91-12/04
S62359	02/71-02/05	⊗03/05	**7371**	02/71-08/87	**1271**	08/87-12/90	**1851**	12/90-02/05
S62360	02/71-02/05	⊗02/05	**7372**	02/71-06/87	**1272**	06/87-07/90	**1837**	07/90-02/05
S62361	02/71-07/04	⊗09/04	**7373**	02/71-06/87	**1273**	06/87-06/88	**1819**	06/88-05/90
			1306	05/90-07/04				
S62362	03/71-05/04	⊗06/04	**7374**	03/71-06/87	**1274**	06/87-08/90	**1840**	08/90-05/04
S62363	03/71-04/04	⊗06/04	**7375**	03/71-06/87	**1275**	06/87-09/90	**1842**	09/90-04/04
S62364	04/71-05/05	Ⓟ	**7376**	04/71-08/87	**1276**	08/87-10/89	**2251**	10/89-05/99
			1394	08/99-12/04	**1499**	12/04-05/05		
S62365	04/71-06/05	⊗10/05	**7377**	04/71-08/87	**1277**	08/87-06/91	**1859**	06/91-06/05
S62366	04/71-12/04	⊗01/05	**7378**	04/71-06/87	**1278**	06/87-10/89	**2252**	10/89-06/97
			1406	06/97-12/04				
S62367	04/71-09/03	⊗10/03	**7379**	04/71-06/87	**1279**	06/87-09/89	**2257**	09/89-09/97
			1407	09/97-09/03				
S62368	04/71-04/89	⊗02/90	**7380**	04/71-06/87	**1280**	06/87-04/89		
S62369	05/71-10/04	⊗01/05	**7381**	05/71-06/87	**1281**	06/87-10/90	**1843**	10/90-10/04
S62370	05/71-05/05	⊗06/05	**7382**	05/71-06/87	**1282**	06/87-10/89	**2254**	10/89-05/93
			2002	05/93-01/97	**2254**	01/97-07/99	**1396**	09/99-05/05
S62371	05/71-01/86	⊗07/86	**7383**	05/71-01/86				
S62372	05/71-03/05	⊗06/05	**7384**	05/71-06/87	**1284**	06/87-10/89	**2253**	10/89-09/97
			1410	09/97-03/05				
S62373	05/71-06/05	⊗10/05	**7385**	05/71-06/87	**1285**	06/87-07/91	**1861**	07/91-06/05
S62374	05/71-06/05	⊗10/05	**7386**	05/71-06/87	**1286**	06/87-08/91	**1862**	08/91-06/05
S62375	05/71-02/05	⊗02/05	**7387**	05/71-06/87	**1287**	06/87-11/90	**1846**	11/90-02/05
S62376	05/71-04/05	⊗05/05	**7388**	05/71-06/87	**1288**	06/87-01/91	**1854**	01/91-04/05
S62377	06/71-04/05	⊗05/05	**7389**	06/71-07/87	**1289**	07/87-02/91	**1856**	02/91-04/05
S62378	06/71-05/05	⊗	**7390**	06/71-09/87	**1290**	09/87-10/89	**2255**	10/89-05/93
			2003	05/93-01/97	**2255**	01/97-04/99	**1392**	07/99-05/05
S62379	06/71-08/05	⊗10/05	**7391**	06/71-06/87	**1291**	06/87-09/91	**1864**	09/91-08/05
S62380	06/71-06/05	⊗10/05	**7392**	06/71-06/87	**1292**	06/87-09/91	**1863**	09/91-06/05
S62381	06/71-11/05	⊗ 06	**7393**	06/71-06/87	**1293**	06/87-12/91	**1866**	12/91-11/05
S62382	06/71-06/05	⊗06/05	**7394**	06/71-05/87	**1294**	05/87-01/92	**1867**	01/92-06/05
S62383	07/71-05/05	⊗07/05	**7395**	07/71-08/87	**1295**	08/87-11/91	**1865**	11/91-05/05
S62384	07/71-04/05	Ⓟ	**7396**	07/71-06/87	**1296**	06/87-11/89	**2258**	11/89-04/99
			1393	07/99-04/05				
S62385	08/71-04/05	Ⓟ	**7397**	08/71-06/87	**1297**	06/87-11/89	**2256**	11/89-09/99
			1399	09/99-04/05				
S62386	08/71-04/05	⊗06/05	**7398**	08/71-08/87	**1298**	08/87-11/89	**2259**	11/89-05/93
			2004	05/93-01/97	**2259**	01/97-09/99	**1398**	09/99-04/05
S62387	08/71-05/05	⊗06/05	**7399**	08/71-05/87	**1299**	05/87-11/89	**2260**	01/97-08/99
			1397	09/99-05/05				
S62388	08/71-11/03	⊗11/03	**7400**	08/71-06/87	**1300**	06/87-10/89	**2261**	10/89-09/97
			1408	09/97-11/03				
S62389	09/71-05/05	⊗10/05	**7401**	09/71-05/83	**2601**	05/83-10/83	**7401**	10/83-06/87
			1201	06/87-02/92	**1868**	02/92-05/05		
S62390	09/71-07/05	⊗10/05	**7402**	09/71-05/83	**2601**	05/83-10/83	**7402**	10/83-05/87
			1202	05/87-06/91	**1860**	06/91-07/05		
S62391	09/71-06/05	⊗06/05	**7403**	09/71-05/83	**2602**	05/83-10/83	**7403**	10/83-08/87
			1203	08/87-02/92	**1869**	02/92-06/05		
S62392	09/71-07/04	⊗07/04	**7404**	09/71-05/83	**2602**	05/83-10/83	**7404**	10/83-06/87
			1204	06/87-07/92	**1875**	07/92-05/93	**2001**	05/93-01/97
			1802	01/97-07/04				
S62393	09/71-02/05	⊗03/05	**7405**	09/71-07/87	**1205**	07/87-07/92	**1874**	07/92-02/05
S62394	09/71-08/04	⊗08/04	**7406**	09/71-08/87	**1206**	08/87-03/92	**1871**	04/92-08/04
S62395	09/71-09/00	⊗11/05	**7407**	09/71-12/86	**1812**	01/87-09/00		
S62396	10/71-09/04	⊗09/04	**7408**	10/71-07/87	**1208**	07/87-05/92	**1872**	05/92-09/04
S62397	10/71-08/04	⊗09/04	**7409**	10/71-07/87	**1209**	07/87-06/92	**1873**	06/92-08/04
S62398	10/71-08/04	⊗08/04	**7410**	10/71-05/87	**1210**	05/87-09/92	**1879**	09/92-08/04
S62399	10/71-08/04	⊗09/04	**7411**	10/71-08/87	**1211**	08/87-07/92	**1876**	07/92-08/04
S62400	11/71-04/05	Ⓟ	**7412**	11/71-09/87	**1212**	09/87-10/92	**1881**	10/92-04/05
S62401	11/71-08/04	⊗09/04	**7413**	11/71-09/87	**1213**	09/87-07/92	**1877**	07/92-08/04
S62402	12/71-05/10	Ⓟ	**7414**	12/71-09/87	**1214**	09/87-11/92	**1883**	11/92-02/05
			1497	04/05-05/10				
S62403	12/71-07/05	⊗08/05	**7415**	12/71-08/87	**1215**	08/87-10/92	**1882**	10/92-07/05
S62404	12/71-09/04	⊗10/04	**7416**	12/71-09/87	**1216**	09/87-12/92	**1887**	12/92-09/04
S62405	12/71-02/05	⊗03/07	**7417**	12/71-09/87	**1217**	09/87-11/92	**1884**	11/92-02/05
S62406	12/71- 04	⊗ 04	**7418**	12/71-09/87	**1218**	09/87-08/92	**1878**	08/92- 04
S62407	12/71-11/04	⊗11/04	**7419**	12/71-09/87	**1219**	09/87-12/92	**1885**	12/92-11/04
S62408	01/72-09/04	⊗10/04	**7420**	01/72-06/87	**1220**	06/87-09/92	**1880**	09/92-09/04
S62409	01/72-07/04	⊗08/04	**7421**	01/72-08/87	**1221**	08/87-04/92	**1870**	04/92-07/04
S62410	01/72-09/04	⊗10/04	**7422**	01/72-08/87	**1222**	08/87-12/92	**1886**	12/92-09/04
S62411	01/72-05/10	Ⓟ	**7423**	01/72-08/87	**1223**	08/87-01/93	**1888**	01/93-02/05
			1498	04/05-05/10				
S62412	02/72-02/05	⊗08/05	**7424**	02/72-09/87	**1224**	09/87-01/93	**1889**	01/93-02/05
S62413	02/72-04/05	⊗08/05	**7425**	02/72-08/87	**1225**	08/87-02/93	**1890**	02/93-04/05
S62414	02/72-09/04	⊗10/04	**7426**	02/72-08/87	**1226**	08/87-03/93	**1891**	03/93-09/04
S62415	02/72-07/04	⊗07/04	**7427**	02/72-03/86	**1801**	04/86-05/93	**2003**	-01/97
			1801	01/97-07/04				
S62416	03/72-07/05	⊗07/05	**7428**	03/72-05/86	**1804**	05/86-07/05		
S62417	03/72-05/05	⊗05/05	**7429**	03/72-03/86	**1802**	04/86-12/89	**2262**	12/89-05/93
			2001	05/93-01/97	**2262**	01/97-07/99	**1395**	09/99-05/05
S62418	02/72-07/04	⊗09/04	**7430**	02/72-03/86	**1803**	05/86-07/04		
S62419	02/72-04/04	⊗04/04	**7431**	02/72-11/86	**1811**	12/86-04/04		
S62420	03/72-11/05	⊗01/05	**7432**	03/72-05/86	**1805**	06/86-11/05		
S62421	03/72-09/04	⊗09/04	**7433**	03/72-06/86	**1806**	06/86-09/04		
S62422	03/72-07/04	⊗08/04	**7434**	03/72-06/86	**1807**	07/86-07/04		
S62423	03/72-08/04	⊗08/04	**7435**	03/72-07/86	**1808**	09/86-08/04		
S62424	04/72-02/04	⊗03/04	**7436**	04/72-08/86	**1809**	09/86-02/04		
S62425	05/72-02/04	⊗03/04	**7437**	05/72-09/86	**1810**	11/86-02/04		

Class 445 4-PEP York

Motor Second Open
MSO
S62426-S62429 (Originally Class 462)

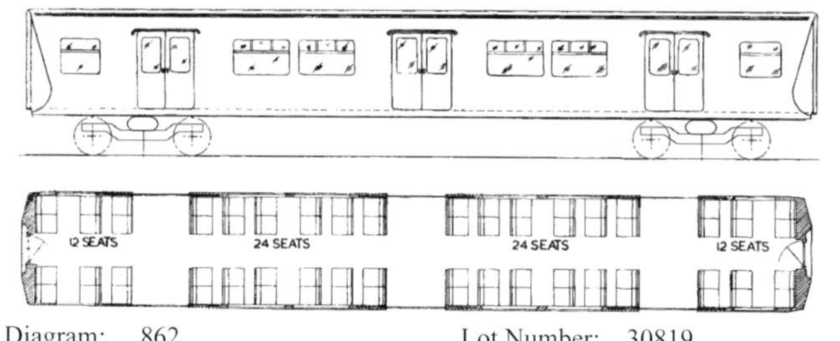

Diagram:	862	Lot Number:	30819
Body:	65' 4¼" × 9' 3"	Weight:	34t 6cwt
Seats:	72 second	Bogies:	4001 BT5, 4002 Mk 6
Motors:	GEC 4 × 100hp		

Vehicle	Dates	Fate	Unit	Dates
S62426	07/71-08/78	➲975849	**4002**	07/71-08/78
S62427	05/71-09/78	➲975845	**4001**	05/71-09/78
S62428	05/71-09/78	➲975846	**4001**	05/71-09/78
S62429	07/71-08/78	➲975850	**4002**	07/71-08/78

Class 421 4-CIG York

Motor Brake Second Open
MBSO
S62430

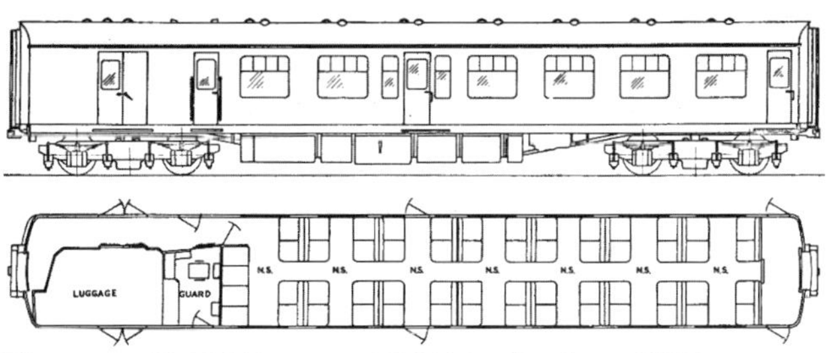

Diagram:	423 ED260, facelifted ED264	Lot Number:	30829
Body:	64' 9½" × 9' 3"	Weight:	49t 0cwt
Seats:	56 second	Bogies:	Mk 4 Motor
Motors:	EE507 4 × 250hp		

S62430	05/72-02/04	⊗12/04	7438	05/72-06/79	[illegible]	[illegible]	1810	[illegible]

Class 308 York (converted Wolverton)

Motor Brake Second Open
MBSO
E62431-E62434

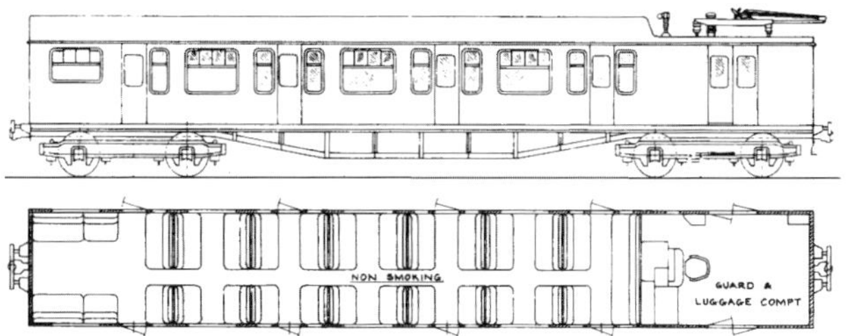

Diagram:	386 ED208	Lot Number:	c30701
Body:	63' 6" × 9' 3"	Weight:	
Seats:	76 second	Bogies:	Gresley
Motors:	EE 4 × 192hp		

Converted from MLV in 1971

E62431	06/71-06/85	⊗10/88	313	06/71-01/82	308313	01/82-06/85	⊂68011
E62432	07/71-01/85	⊗01/85	316	07/71-06/81	308316	06/81-01/85	⊂68014
E62433	08/71-06/85	⊗10/88	315	08/71-02/82	308315	02/82-01/84	⊂68013
E62434	10/71-01/85	⊗06/85	321	10/71-03/72	314	03/72-06/81	⊂68019
			308314	06/81-01/85			

Class 423 4-VEP York

Motor Brake Second Open
MBSO
S62435-S62475

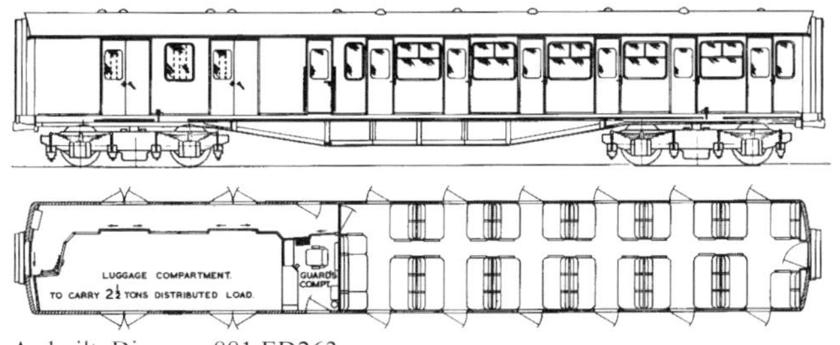

As built, Diagram 881 ED263

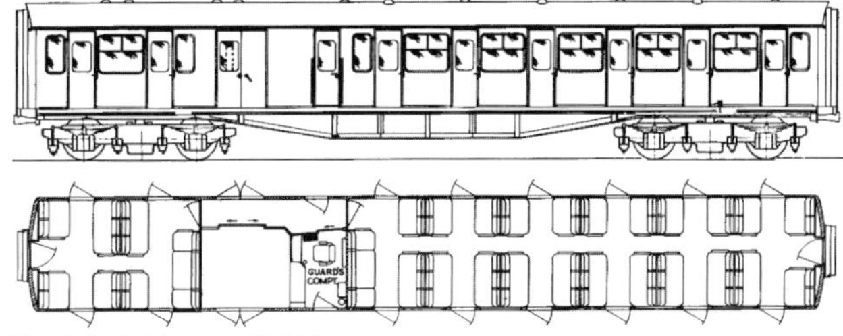

Facelifted, Diagram ED266

Diagram:	881 ED263 ED266	Lot Number:	30851
Body:	64' 9⅝" × 9' 3"	Weight:	49t 0cwt
Seats:	58 second, later 76 second	Bogies:	Mk 4 Motor
Motors:	EE507 4 × 250hp		

S62435	05/73-03/05	⊗10/05	7854	05/73-05/87	3154	05/87-06/93	3408	06/93-03/05
S62436	05/73-07/05	⊗10/05	7855	05/73-05/87	3155	05/87-09/90	3491	06/91-07/05
S62437	06/73-05/04	⊗06/04	7856	06/73-06/87	3156	06/87-04/94	3557	05/94-05/04
S62438	06/73-07/04	⊗08/04	7857	06/73-09/87	3157	09/87-07/94	3563	07/94-07/04
S62439	06/73-05/04	⊗06/04	7858	06/73-06/87	3158	06/87-05/94	3559	06/94-05/04
S62440	06/73-10/05	⊗	7859	06/73-08/87	3159	08/87-09/94	3568	10/94-10/05
S62441	07/73-[illegible]	⊗11/04	[illegible]	[illegible]	[illegible]	[illegible]	[illegible]	[illegible]
S62442	07/73-05/04	⊗07/04	7861	07/73-05/87	3161	05/87-11/93	3410	12/93-05/04
S62443	07/73-12/04	⊗02/05	7862	07/73-07/87	3162	07/87-08/94	3566	09/94-12/04
S62444	07/73-07/05	⊗07/05	7863	07/73-06/87	3163	06/87-12/94	3573	12/94-07/05
S62445	08/73-07/05	⊗07/05	7864	08/73-08/87	3164	08/87-03/95	3585	03/95-07/05
S62446	08/73-08/04	⊗	7865	08/73-08/87	3165	08/87-07/94	3414	09/94-08/04
S62447	08/73-05/04	⊗06/04	7866	08/73-07/87	3166	07/87-05/94	3558	05/94-05/04
S62448	08/73-04/05	⊗04/05	7867	08/73-08/87	3167	08/87-10/94	3569	11/94-04/05
S62449	09/73-11/04	⊗02/05	7868	09/73-08/87	3168	08/87-03/88	3421	03/88-11/04
S62450	09/73-07/05	⊗07/05	7869	09/73-05/87	3169	05/87-02/95	3583	02/95-07/05
S62451	09/73-08/05	⊗10/05	7870	09/73-07/87	3170	07/87-11/93	3416	12/93-08/05
S62452	09/73-08/05	⊗10/05	7871	09/73-07/87	3171	07/87-01/94	3548	02/94-08/05
S62453	10/73-07/04	⊗08/04	7872	10/73-06/87	3172	06/87-06/94	3561	07/94-07/04
S62454	10/73-09/05	⊗12/05	7873	10/73-05/87	3173	05/87-10/93	3544	11/93-09/05
S62455	10/73-10/05	⊗10/05	7874	10/73-07/87	3174	07/87-12/89	3500	01/90-10/05
S62456	10/73-12/04	⊗12/04	7875	10/73-08/87	3175	08/87-02/94	3551	02/94-12/04
S62457	11/73-11/04	⊗10/04	7876	11/73-05/87	3176	05/87-03/94	3556	05/94-11/04
S62458	12/73-12/05	⊗12/05	7877	12/73-08/87	3177	08/87-07/94	3564	07/94-12/05
S62459	01/74-06/05	⊗06/05	7878	01/74-07/87	3182	07/87-09/95	3577	04/96-06/05
S62460	01/74-10/05	⊗10/05	7879	01/74-06/87	3179	06/87-06/95	3590	07/95-10/05
S62461	02/74-11/04	⊗10/04	7880	02/74-07/87	3180	07/87-03/94	3554	03/94-11/04
S62462	02/74-02/05	⊗12/05	7881	02/74-08/87	3181	08/87-09/94	3415	10/94-02/05
S62463	12/73-12/04	⊗02/05	7882	12/73-07/87	3178	09/87-11/94	3571	11/94-12/04
S62464	02/74-08/05	⊗08/05	7883	02/74-09/87	3183	09/87-12/94	3574	12/94-08/05
S62465	02/74-10/05	⊗10/05	7884	02/74-09/87	3184	09/87-03/95	3587	05/95-10/05
S62466	02/74-07/05	⊗07/05	7885	02/74-07/87	3185	07/87-05/95	3589	06/95-07/05
S62467	03/74-05/04	⊗08/05	7886	03/74-10/87	3186	10/87-05/95	3588	05/95-05/04
S62468	03/74-06/05	⊗07/05	7887	03/74-09/87	3187	09/87-11/94	3572	12/94-06/05
S62469	03/74-11/04	⊗02/05	7888	03/74-08/87	3188	08/87-12/94	3575	12/94-11/04
S62470	03/74-12/04	⊗12/04	7889	03/74-08/87	3189	08/87-12/94	3577	01/95-04/96
S62471	04/74-08/05	⊗09/05	7890	04/74-08/87	3190	08/87-01/95	3579	01/95-08/05
S62472	04/74-05/04	⊗08/05	7891	04/74-06/87	3191	06/87-01/95	3582	02/95-05/04
S62473	04/74-08/05	⊗09/05	7892	04/74-07/87	3192	07/87-02/95	3584	03/95-08/05
S62474	05/74-08/05	⊗10/05	7893	05/74-09/87	3193	09/87-03/95	3586	03/95-08/05
S62475	05/74-06/05	⊗07/05	7894	05/74-10/87	3194	10/87-07/95	3591	09/95-06/05

Class 430 4-REP York

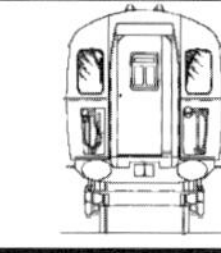

Driving Motor Second Open
DMSO
S62476-S62483

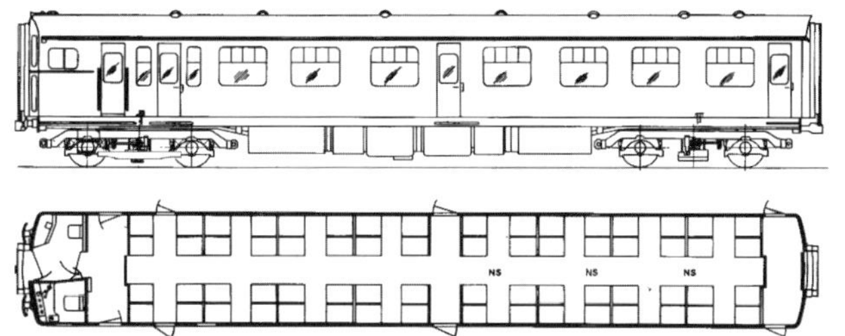

Diagram:	890A EA260	Lot Number:	30862
Body:	64' 9½" × 9' 3"	Weight:	51t 13cwt
Seats:	64 second	Bogies:	Mk 6 motor
Motors:	EE546B 4 × 400hp		

S62476	09/74-06/87	⊗06/90	3012	09/74-05/86	2012	05/86-06/87
S62477	09/74-06/87	⊗07/90	3012	09/74-05/86	2012	05/86-06/87
S62478	10/74-12/87	⊗03/90	3013	10/74-05/86	2013	05/86-12/87
S62479	10/74-02/88	⊗05/92	3013	10/74-05/86	2013	05/86-12/87

S62480	11/74-03/88	⊗04/90	**3014**	11/74-04/86	**2014**	04/86-03/88		
S62481	11/74-03/88	⊗04/90	**3014**	11/74-04/86	**2014**	04/86-03/88		
S62482	12/74-11/86	➲Dep	**3015**	12/74-04/86	**2015**	04/86-11/86	**999605**	01/07
S62483	12/74-11/86	➲999602	**3015**	12/74-04/86	**2015**	04/86-11/86		

Class 312/0 York
Motor Brake Second Open
MBSO
E62484-E62509

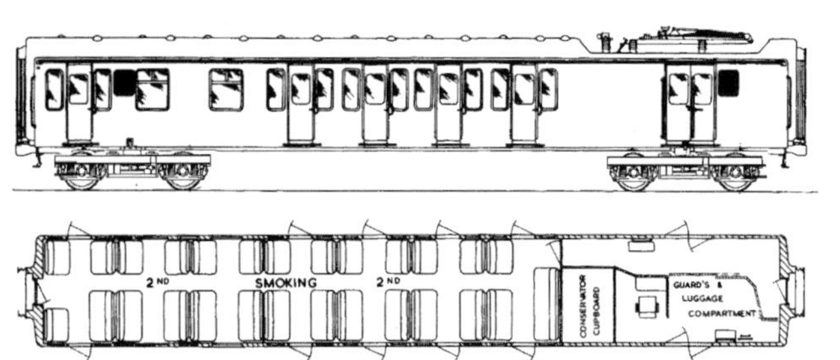

Diagram:	490 ED212	Lot Number:	30864
Body:	65' 4¼" × 9' 3"	Weight:	
Seats:	68 second	Bogies:	B4
Motors:	EE546 4 × 270hp		

E62484	05/77-10/03	⊗11/04	**312001**	05/77-05/79	**312701**	05/79-10/03
E62485	06/77-09/03	⊗10/04	**312002**	06/77-05/79	**312702**	05/79-09/03
E62486	06/77-03/04	⊗11/04	**312003**	06/77-04/79	**312703**	04/79-03/04
E62487	07/77-09/03	⊗10/03	**312004**	07/77-03/79	**312704**	03/79-09/03
E62488	07/77-09/03	⊗09/04	**312005**	07/77-04/79	**312705**	04/79-09/03
E62489	07/77-09/03	⊗12/04	**312006**	07/77-05/79	**312706**	05/79-09/03
E62490	07/77-09/03	⊗07/04	**312007**	07/77-04/79	**312707**	04/79-09/03
E62491	07/77-09/03	⊗10/03	**312008**	07/77-05/79	**312708**	05/79-09/03
E62492	08/77-10/03	⊗01/05	**312009**	08/77-05/79	**312709**	05/79-10/03
E62493	08/77-09/03	⊗10/03	**312010**	08/77-05/79	**312710**	05/79-09/03
E62494	08/77-09/03	⊗09/04	**312011**	08/77-05/79	**312711**	05/79-09/03
E62495	09/77-09/04	⊗11/04	**312012**	09/77-04/79	**312712**	04/79-09/04
E62496	09/77-01/03	⊗10/04	**312013**	09/77-04/79	**312713**	04/79-01/03
E62497	10/77-03/04	⊗12/04	**312014**	10/77-03/79	**312714**	03/79-03/04
E62498	10/77-03/04	⊗12/04	**312015**	10/77-04/79	**312715**	04/79-03/04
E62499	10/77-09/03	⊗10/03	**312016**	10/77-04/79	**312716**	04/79-09/03
E62500	11/77-09/03	⊗10/03	**312017**	11/77-04/79	**312717**	04/79-09/03
E62501	11/77-05/04	⊗07/04	**312018**	11/77-05/79	**312718**	05/79-05/04
E62502	12/77-09/03	⊗12/04	**312019**	12/77-04/79	**312719**	04/79-09/03
E62503	12/77-09/03	⊗10/03	**312020**	12/77-05/79	**312720**	05/79-09/03
E62504	12/77-05/04	⊗07/04	**312021**	12/77-05/79	**312721**	05/79-05/04
E62505	12/77-05/04	⊗12/04	**312022**	12/77-04/79	**312722**	04/79-05/04
E62506	01/78-05/04	⊗07/04	**312023**	01/78-04/79	**312723**	04/79-05/04
E62507	01/78-09/03	⊗09/04	**312024**	01/78-05/79	**312724**	05/79-09/03
E62508	09/78-04/02	⊗02/05	**312025**	09/78-03/79	**312725**	03/79-04/02
E62509	12/78-11/01	⊗02/05	**312026**	12/78-05/79	**312726**	05/79-11/01

Class 312/1 York
Motor Brake Second Open
MBSO
E62510-E62528

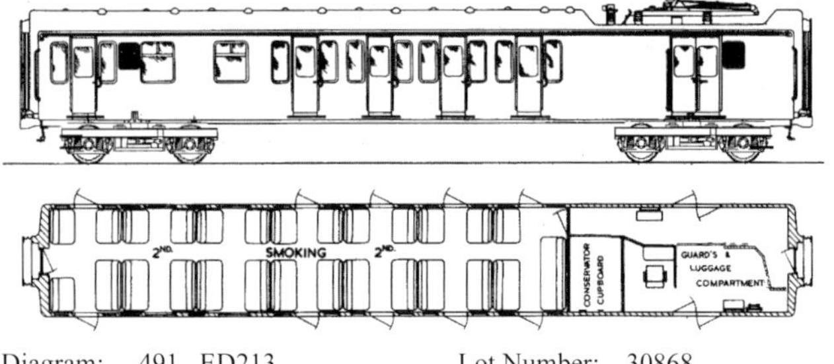

Diagram:	491 ED213	Lot Number:	30868
Body:	65' 4¼" × 9' 3"	Weight:	
Seats:	68 second	Bogies:	B4
Motors:	EE546 4 × 270hp		

E62510	03/75-03/03	⊗01/05	**312101**	03/75-	78	**312781**	78-03/03
E62511	04/75-11/01	⊗03/05	**312102**	04/75-	78	**312782**	78-11/01
E62512	04/75-03/03	⊗02/05	**312103**	04/75-	78	**312783**	78-03/03
E62513	05/75-03/03	⊗09/04	**312104**	05/75-	78	**312784**	78-03/03
E62514	06/75-09/02	⊗03/05	**312105**	06/75-	78	**312785**	78-09/02
E62515	06/75-02/02	⊗01/05	**312106**	06/75-	78	**312786**	78-02/02
E62516	06/75-03/02	⊗02/05	**312107**	06/75-	78	**312787**	78-03/02
E62517	06/75-03/02	⊗01/05	**312108**	06/75-	78	**312788**	78-03/02
E62518	07/75-09/02	⊗03/05	**312109**	07/75-	78	**312789**	78-09/02
E62519	07/75-02/02	⊗02/05	**312110**	07/75-	78	**312790**	78-02/02
E62520	07/75-04/02	⊗02/05	**312111**	07/75-	78	**312791**	78-04/02
E62521	08/75-03/03	⊗03/05	**312112**	08/75-	78	**312792**	78-03/03
E62522	08/75-02/02	⊗02/05	**312113**	08/75-	78	**312793**	78-02/02
E62523	08/75-12/01	⊗02/05	**312114**	08/75-	78	**312794**	78-12/01
E62524	09/75-12/01	⊗02/05	**312115**	09/75-	78	**312795**	78-12/01
E62525	09/75-12/01	⊗01/05	**312116**	09/75-	78	**312796**	78-12/01
E62526	09/75-03/03	⊗02/05	**312117**	09/75-	78	**312797**	78-03/03
E62527	10/75-02/02	⊗01/05	**312118**	10/75-	78	**312798**	78-02/02
E62528	10/75-03/02	⊗03/05	**312119**	10/75-	78	**312799**	78-03/02

E62529-62592	*Class 313*	*02/76*
E62593-62656	*Class 313*	*02/76*

Class 312/2 York
Motor Brake Second Open
MBSO
M62657-M62660

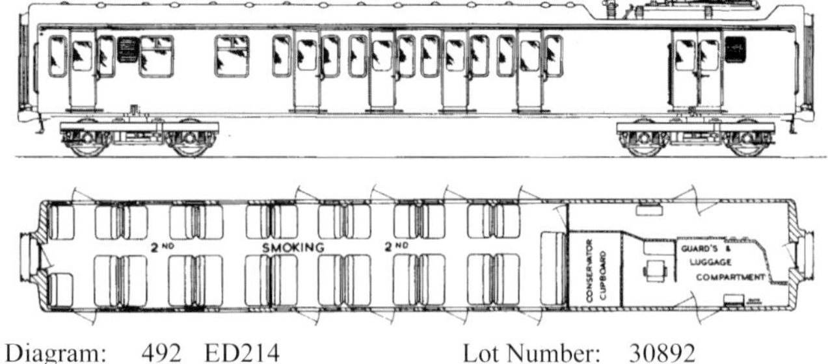

Diagram:	492 ED214	Lot Number:	30892
Body:	65' 4¼" × 9' 3"	Weight:	
Seats:	68 second	Bogies:	B4
Motors:	EE546 4 × 270hp		

M62657	02/76-11/01	⊗01/05	**312201**	02/76-04/88	**312727**	04/88-11/01
M62658	01/76-10/03	⊗01/05	**312202**	01/76-04/88	**312728**	04/88-10/03
M62659	02/76-12/01	⊗02/05	**312203**	02/76-05/88	**312729**	05/88-12/01
M62660	12/75-08/02	⊗03/05	**312204**	12/75-05/88	**312730**	05/88-08/02

62661-62708	*Class 317/1*	*09/81*
62709-62825	*Class 455*	*08/82*
62826-62845	*Class 455/9*	*02/85*
62846-62865	*Class 317/2*	*10/85*
62866-62885	*Class 318*	*06/86*
62886-62889	*Class 317/2*	*03/87*
62890	*Class 318*	*03/87*
62891-62936	*Class 319/0*	*09/87*
62937-62960	*Class 442*	*02/88*
62961-62974	*Class 319/0*	*06/88*
62975-63020	*Class 321/3*	*09/88*
63021-63042	*Class 320*	*04/90*
63043-63062	*Class 319/1*	*10/90*
63063-63092	*Class 321/4*	*07/89*
63093-63098	*Class 319/1*	*01/91*
63099-63104	*Class 321/4*	*12/89*
63105-63124	*Class 321/3*	*01/90*
63125-63136	*Class 321/4*	*11/89*
63137-63141	*Class 322*	*07/90*
63153-63155	*Class 321/9*	*07/91*
64001-64043	*Class 323*	*11/92*

Class 445 4-PEP 446 2-PEP York
Driving Motor Second Open
DMSO
S64300-S64305 (Originally Class 461)

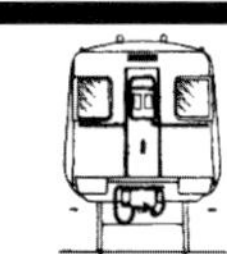

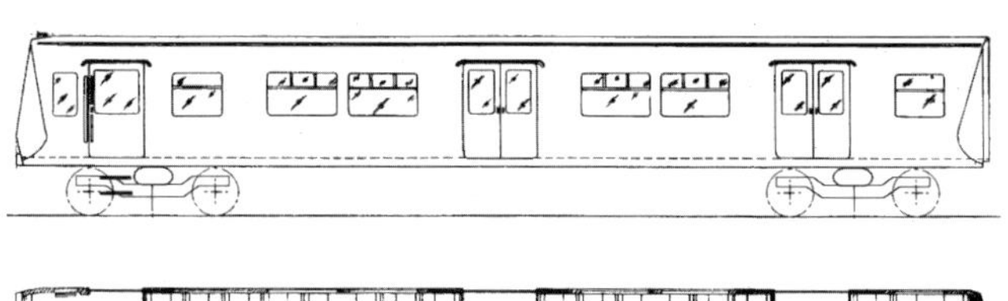

Diagram:	861	Lot Number:	30818

Body:	64' 11½" × 9' 3"	Weight:	35t 7cwt	
Seats:	68 second		64305 31t 6cwt (F type Bogies)	
Motors:	GEC 4 × 100hp	Bogies:	4001 BT5, 4002 Mk 6	

S64300	72-10/74	➲**975430**	**2001**	72-10/74		
S64301	05/71-10/74	➲**975432**	**4001**	05/71-08/73	**2001**	08/73-10/74
S64302	05/71-09/78	➲**975847**	**4001**	05/71-09/78		
S64303	07/71-08/78	➲**975848**	**4002**	07/71-08/78		
S64304	07/71-08/78	➲**975851**	**4002**	07/71-08/78		
S64305	72-09/78	➲**975844**	**2001**	72-08/73	**4001**	08/73-09/78

M64367-64399	***Class 507***	*78*
M64405-64437	***Class 507***	*78*
E64461-64582	***Class 315***	*05/80*
SC64583-64614	***Class 314***	*04/79*
S64649-64691	***Class 508***	*03/80*
S64692-64734	***Class 508***	*03/80*
64735-64758	***Class 456***	*04/91*
64759-64808	***Class 465/0***	*07/94*
64809-64858	***Class 465/0***	*07/94*
64860-64902	***Class 466***	*04/94*
65001-65043	***Class 323***	*11/92*

Class 416/2 2-EPB Ashford/Eastleigh
Driving Motor Brake Second Open
DMBSO
S65300-S65310

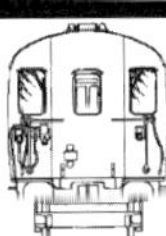

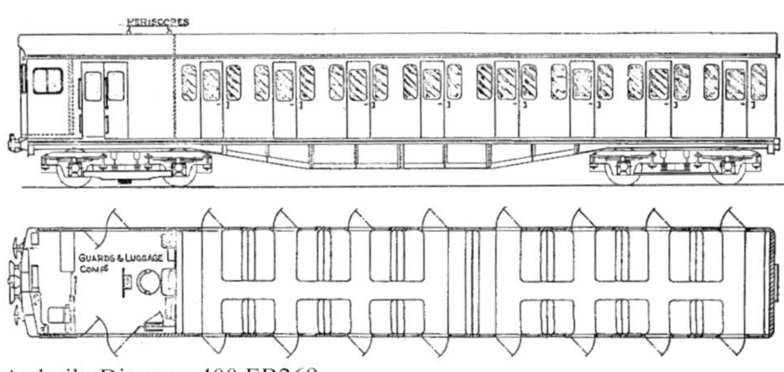

As built, Diagram 400 EB269

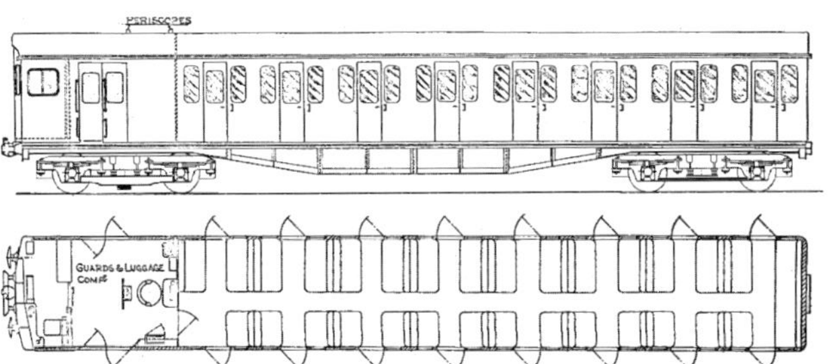

Class 416/4 6401-6409, rebuilt for revenue protection services, Diagram EB281

Diagram:	400 EB269 EB281	Lot Number:	30114
Body:	63' 11½" × 9' 3¼"	Weight:	41t 0cwt
Seats:	84 second, some later 79	Bogies:	Mk 3D
Motors:	EE507 2 × 250hp		

S65300	01/54-07/93	⊗08/93	**5701**	01/54-01/65	**5261**	08/65-07/93		
S65301	01/54-05/94	⊗06/94	**5702**	01/54-04/85	**6202**	04/85-05/94		
S65302	04/54-05/93	ⓟ➲**977874**	**5703**	04/54-03/85	**6203**	03/85-05/93		
S65303	04/54-02/92	⊗04/92	**5704**	04/54-01/65	**5262**	12/65-06/86	**5028**	06/86-07/87
			5169	07/87-02/92				
S65304	04/54-05/93	ⓟ➲**977875**	**5705**	04/54-04/85	**6205**	04/85-05/93		
S65305	04/54-08/94	⊗08/94	**5706**	04/54-05/85	**6206**	05/85-12/85	**6406**	12/85-08/94
S65306	04/54-05/91	⊗10/91	**5707**	04/54-01/85	**6207**	01/85-05/91		
S65307	05/54-12/91	⊗07/92	**5708**	05/54-01/65	**5247**	11/67-10/71	**5769**	10/71-04/85
			6269	04/85-12/91				
S65308	05/54-12/83	⊗06/86	**5709**	05/54-01/65	**5262**	12/65-01/72	**5302**	01/72-12/83
S65309	05/54-03/94	⊗04/94	**5710**	05/54-04/85	**6210**	04/85-01/86	**6409**	02/86-03/94
S65310	05/54-07/93	⊗08/93	**5711**	05/54-01/65	**5261**	08/65-07/93		

South Tyneside Eastleigh
Driving Motor Brake Second Open
DMBSO
E65311-E65325 Later Class 416/2 2-EPB

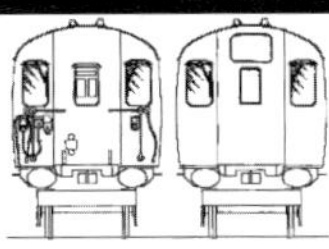

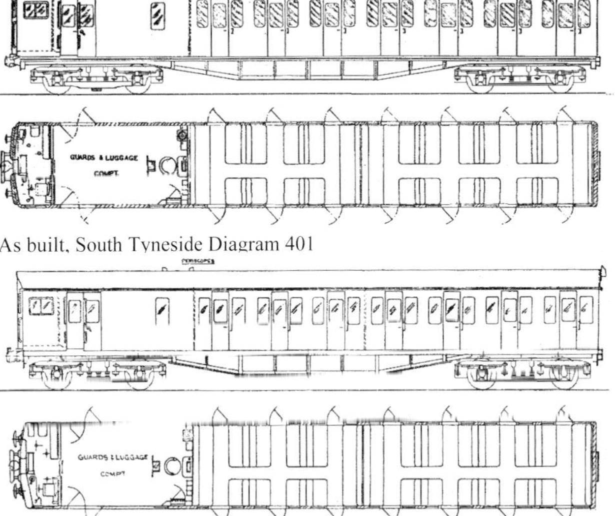

As built, South Tyneside Diagram 401

Converted to Southern Region 2-EPB, Diagram 422

Diagram:	401 422	Lot Number:	30116
Body:	63' 11½" × 9' 3¼"	Weight:	40t 0cwt
Seats:	74 second	Bogies:	Mk 3D
Motors:	EE507 2 × 250hp		

E65311	12/54-10/84	⊗11/91	08/63⇨**S**	**5781**	08/63-08/84	**6281**	08/84-10/84
E65312	12/54-10/84	➲**977566**	10/63⇨**S**	**5782**	10/63-08/84	**6282**	08/84-10/84
E65313	01/55-10/84	➲**977559**	07/63⇨**S**	**5783**	07/63-08/84	**6283**	08/84-10/84
E65314	01/55-10/84	➲**977567**	08/63⇨**S**	**5784**	08/63-08/84	**6284**	08/84-10/84
E65315	01/55-10/84	⊗01/93	09/63⇨**S**	**5785**	09/63-08/84	**6285**	08/84-10/84
E65316	02/55-10/84	➲*977394*	09/63⇨**S**	**5786**	09/63-08/84	**6286**	08/84-10/84
E65317	02/55-10/84	➲**977304**	08/63⇨**S**	**5787**	08/63-09/84	**6287**	09/84-10/84
E65318	02/55-05/84	➲**977290**	08/63⇨**S**	**5788**	08/63-05/84		
E65319	02/55-10/84	➲**977296**	07/63⇨**S**	**5789**	07/63-09/84	**6289**	09/84-10/84
E65320	02/55-10/84	➲**977560**	08/63⇨**S**	**5790**	08/63-08/84	**6290**	08/84-10/84
E65321	03/55-10/84	ⓟ➲**977505**	08/63⇨**S**	**5791**	08/63-09/84	**6291**	09/84-10/84
E65322	03/55-10/84	➲**977305**	09/63⇨**S**	**5792**	09/63-08/84	**6292**	08/84-10/84
E65323	03/55-10/84	➲**977506**	07/63⇨**S**	**5793**	07/63-08/84	**6293**	08/84-10/84
E65324	03/55-05/84	➲**977291**	08/63⇨**S**	**5794**	08/63-05/84		
E65325	04/55-05/84	⊗04/87	09/63⇨**S**	**5795**	09/63-05/84		

Class 416/2 2-EPB Ashford/Eastleigh
Driving Motor Brake Second Open
DMBSO
S65326-S65341

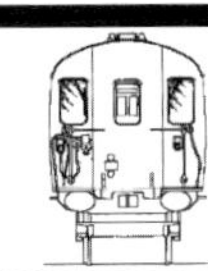

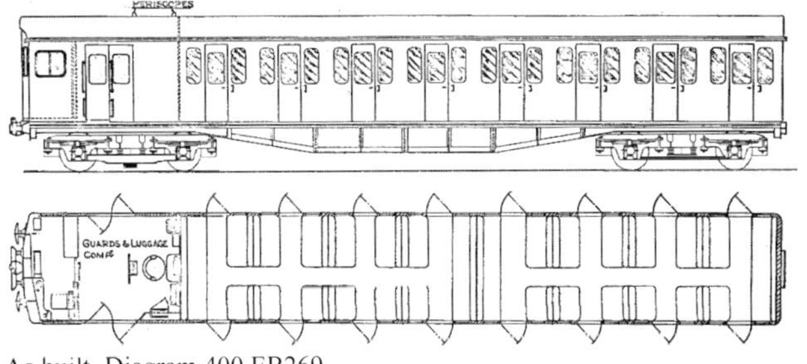

As built, Diagram 400 EB269

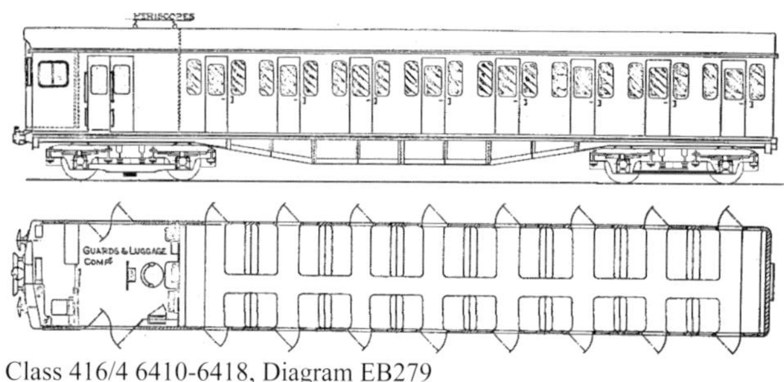

Class 416/4 6410-6418, Diagram EB279

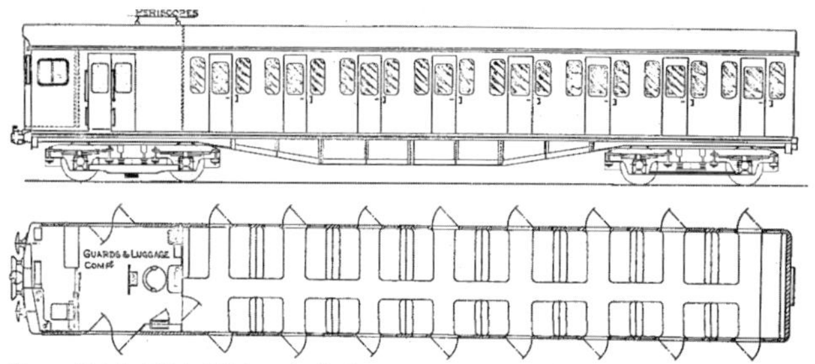

Class 416/4 6401-6409, rebuilt for revenue protection services, Diagram EB281

Diagram:	400 EB269 EB279 EB281	Lot Number:	30119
Body:	63' 11½" × 9' 3¼"	Weight:	41t 0cwt
Seats:	84 second, later 82 or 79	Bogies:	Mk 3D
Motors:	EE507 2 × 250hp		

S65326	08/54-09/91	⊗05/92	**5712**	08/54-03/85	**6212**	03/85-09/91		
S65327	08/54-01/95	⊗02/07	**5713**	08/54-04/85	**6213**	04/85-01/95		
S65328	08/54-01/94	⊗10/94	**5714**	08/54-09/84	**6214**	09/84-12/86	**6416**	12/86-01/94
S65329	08/54-05/94	⊗05/94	**5715**	08/54-08/84	**6215**	08/84-11/85	**6404**	11/85-05/94
S65330	09/54-03/95	⊗05/95	**5716**	09/54-03/85	**6216**	03/85-01/86	**6407**	01/86-03/95
S65331	09/54- 94	**➲977917**	**5717**	09/54-09/84	**6217**	09/84- 94		
S65332	09/54-09/91	⊗05/92	**5718**	09/54-09/84	**6218**	09/84-09/91		
S65333	09/54-02/95	⊗07/95	**5719**	09/54-03/85	**6219**	03/85-02/86	**6411**	02/86-02/95
S65334	10/54-02/95	⊗07/95	**5720**	10/54-05/85	**6220**	05/85-03/86	**6410**	03/86-02/95
S65335	10/54-10/94	⊗01/95	**5721**	10/54-09/84	**6221**	09/84-10/94		
S65336	10/54-01/92	**➲977804**	**5722**	10/54-03/85	**6222**	03/85-01/92		
S65337	10/54-10/94	⊗11/94	**5723**	10/54-12/84	**6223**	12/84-10/94		
S65338	10/54-01/94	⊗02/94	**5724**	10/54-01/85	**6224**	01/85-01/94		
S65339	11/54-10/94	⊗11/94	**5725**	11/54-08/84	**6225**	08/84-10/94		
S65340	11/54-05/94	⊗05/94	**5726**	11/54-02/85	**6226**	02/85-05/94		
S65341	11/54-01/93	**➲977864**	**5727**	11/54-04/85	**6227**	04/85-01/93		

Class 416/2 2-EPB Ashford/Eastleigh

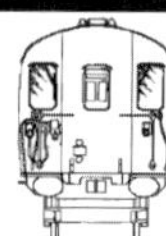

Driving Motor Brake Second Open
DMBSO
S65342-S65366

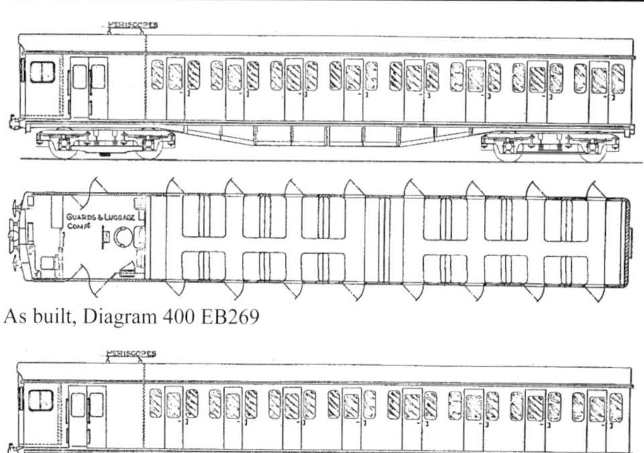

As built, Diagram 400 EB269

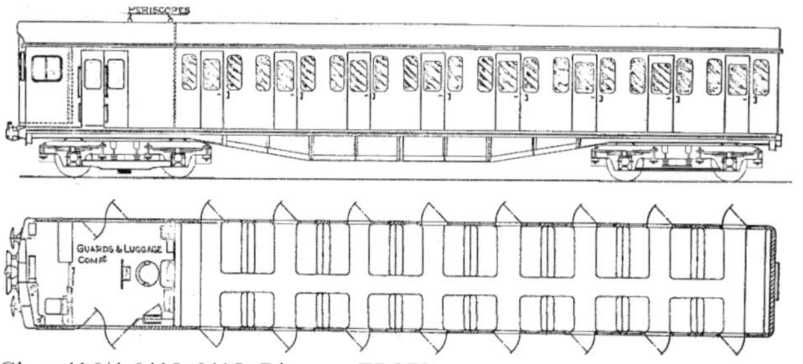

Class 416/4 6410-6418, Diagram EB279

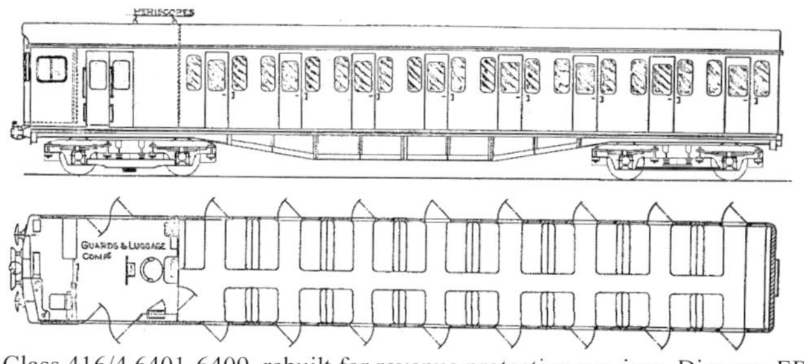

Class 416/4 6401-6409, rebuilt for revenue protection services, Diagram EB281

Diagram:	400 EB269 EB279 EB281	Lot Number:	30167
Body:	63' 11½" × 9' 3¼"	Weight:	41t 0cwt
Seats:	84 second, later 82 or 79	Bogies:	Mk 3D
Motors:	EE507 2 × 250hp		

S65342	04/55-08/94	⊗10/94	**5728**	04/55-08/84	**6228**	08/84-02/86	**6408**	02/86-08/94
S65343	05/55-05/91	⊗05/92	**5729**	05/55-06/77	**5800**	06/77-09/77	**5801**	09/77-12/77
			5800	12/77-11/80	**5729**	11/80-08/84	**6229**	08/84-05/91
S65344	05/55-05/94	⊗05/94	**5730**	05/55-12/84	**6230**	12/84-05/94		
S65345	05/55-05/93	⊗08/93	**5731**	05/55-03/85	**6231**	03/85-05/93		
S65346	05/55-02/93	**➲977857**	**5732**	05/55-07/85	**6232**	07/85-09/85	**6401**	09/85-02/93
S65347	06/55-08/94	⊗10/94	**5733**	06/55-08/84	**6233**	08/84-12/86	**6405**	12/86-08/94
S65348	06/55-03/95	⊗07/95	**5734**	06/55-09/84	**6234**	09/84-09/86	**6415**	09/86-03/95
S65349	06/55-11/94	⊗12/94	**5735**	06/55-05/85	**6235**	05/85-11/94		
S65350	06/55-10/94	⊗11/94	**5736**	06/55-09/84	**6236**	09/84-10/94		
S65351	07/55-11/94	⊗11/94	**5737**	07/55-05/85	**6237**	05/85-11/94		
S65352	07/55-02/92	⊗11/92	**5738**	07/55-05/85	**6238**	05/85-02/92		
S65353	07/55-06/93	**➲977871**	**5739**	07/55-05/85	**6239**	05/85-06/93		
S65354	07/55-08/94	⊗08/94	**5740**	07/55-09/84	**6240**	09/84-08/94		
S65355	07/55-01/93	**➲977865**	**5741**	07/55-08/84	**6241**	08/84-01/93		
S65356	08/55-02/95	⊗07/95	**5742**	08/55-03/85	**6242**	03/85-10/85	**6403**	10/85-02/95
S65357	08/55-01/92	**➲977805**	**5743**	08/55-03/85	**6243**	03/85-01/92		
S65358	08/55-09/91	⊗11/92	**5744**	08/55-08/84	**6244**	08/84-09/91		
S65359	09/55-11/94	⊗11/94	**5745**	09/55-04/85	**6245**	04/85-11/94		
S65360	09/55-01/94	⊗10/94	**5746**	09/55-01/85	**6246**	01/85-02/87	**6418**	02/87-01/94
S65361	09/55-05/93	⊗06/94	**5747**	09/55-04/85	**6247**	04/85-05/93		
S65362	09/55-03/95	⊗	**5748**	09/55-04/85	**6248**	04/85-10/85	**6402**	10/85-03/95
S65363	09/55-05/94	⊗06/94	**5749**	09/55-05/85	**6249**	05/85-05/94		
S65364	10/55-02/95	⊗07/95	**5750**	10/55-03/85	**6250**	03/85-03/86	**6412**	03/86-02/95
S65365	10/55-10/94	⊗01/95	**5751**	10/55-02/85	**6251**	02/85-10/94		
S65366	10/55-11/94	⊗*11/96*	**5752**	10/55-08/84	**6252**	08/84-01/87	**6417**	01/87-11/94

Class 416/2 2-EPB Ashford/Eastleigh
Driving Motor Brake Second Open
DMBSO
S65367-S65396 (65393 onwards Class 414 2-HAP)

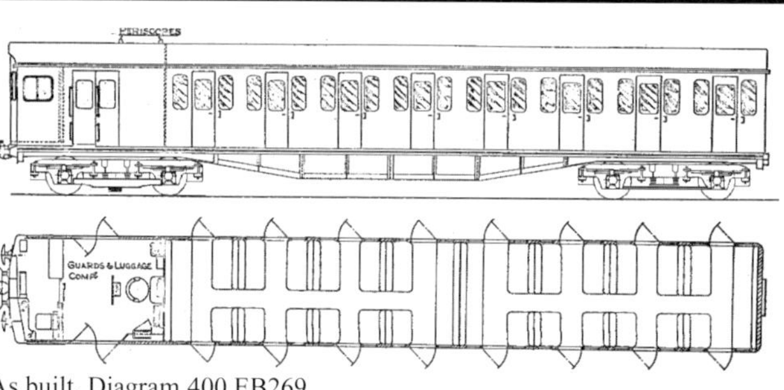

As built, Diagram 400 EB269

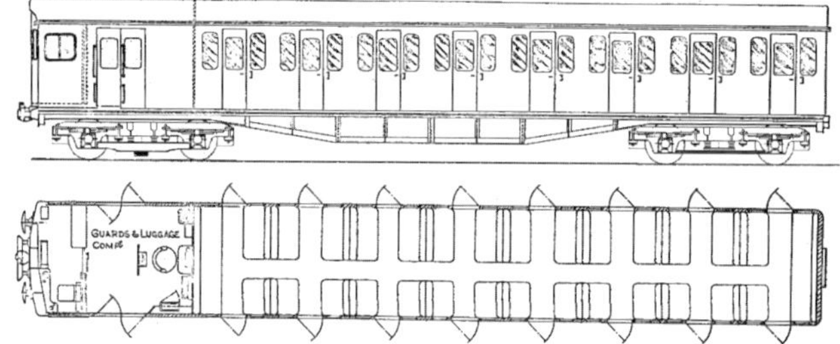

Class 416/4 6410-6418, Diagram EB279

Diagram:	400 EB269 EB279	Lot Number:	30314
Body:	63' 11½" × 9' 3¼"	Weight:	41t 0cwt
Seats:	84 second, some later 82	Bogies:	Mk 4
Motors:	EE507 2 × 250hp		

S65367	04/56-05/93	**➲977872**	**5753**	04/56-07/84	**6253**	07/84-05/93		
S65368	05/56-03/95	⊗07/95	**5754**	05/56-07/84	**6254**	07/84-06/86	**6414**	06/86-03/95

S65369	10/56-02/94	⊗03/94	**5755**	10/56-10/84	**6255**	10/84-02/94		
S65370	05/56-02/94	➲*977919*	**5756**	05/56-08/84	**6256**	08/84-02/94		
S65371	06/56-05/91	⊗11/91	**5757**	06/56-03/85	**6257**	03/85-05/91		
S65372	10/56-03/95	⊗07/95	**5758**	10/56-04/85	**6258**	04/85-05/86	**6413**	05/86-03/95
S65373	06/56-01/95	℗	**5759**	06/56-10/84	**6259**	10/84-01/95		
S65374	05/56-01/94	⊗02/94	**5760**	05/56-12/84	**6260**	12/84-01/94		
S65375	07/56-02/94	⊗03/94	**5761**	07/56-09/84	**6261**	09/84-02/94		
S65376	06/56-01/94	⊗02/94	**5762**	06/56-07/84	**6262**	07/84-01/94		
S65377	06/56-01/95	⊗01/95	**5763**	06/56-12/84	**6263**	12/84-01/95		
S65378	07/56-12/94	⊗03/95	**5764**	07/56-03/85	**6264**	03/85-12/94		
S65379	07/56-01/94	➲**977925**	**5765**	07/56-07/84	**6265**	07/84-01/94		
S65380	07/56-12/57	⊗12/57	**5766**	07/56-12/57				
S65381	08/56-04/94	⊗04/94	**5767**	08/56-09/84	**6267**	09/84-04/94		
S65382	08/56-01/94	➲**977924**	**5768**	08/56-09/84	**6268**	09/84-01/94		
S65383	09/56-09/92	⊗11/92	**5769**	09/56-09/71	**5246**	06/72-01/82	**5134**	03/82-09/92
S65384	09/56-03/94	⊗04/94	**5770**	09/56-08/84	**6270**	08/84-03/94		
S65385	09/56-05/94	⊗05/94	**5771**	09/56-09/84	**6271**	09/84-05/94		
S65386	09/56-05/93	⊗07/93	**5772**	09/56-09/84	**6272**	09/84-05/93		
S65387	09/56-01/95	⊗01/95	**5773**	09/56-08/84	**6273**	08/84-01/95		
S65388	10/56-04/94	⊗05/94	**5774**	10/56-06/77	**5800**	06/77-09/77	**5801**	09/77-12/77
			5800	12/77-11/80	**5774**	11/80-08/84	**6274**	08/84-04/94
S65389	10/56-04/94	⊗05/94	**5775**	10/56-08/84	**6275**	08/84-04/94		
S65390	10/56-05/91	⊗11/91	**5776**	10/56-08/84	**6276**	08/84-05/91		
S65391	11/56-11/94	⊗11/94	**5777**	11/56-08/84	**6277**	08/84-11/94		
S65392	11/56-01/94	⊗02/94	**5778**	11/56-09/84	**6278**	09/84-01/94		
S65393	06/57-05/93	⊗06/93	**6001**	06/57-05/74	**5901**	05/74-02/80	**6001**	02/80-06/82
			3211	06/82-05/93				
S65394	07/57-05/84	⊗01/85	**6002**	07/57-05/74	**5902**	05/74-05/80	**6002**	05/80-05/84
S65395	07/57-02/95	⊗05/95	**6003**	07/57-05/74	**5903**	05/74-04/80	**6003**	04/80-05/82
			3203	05/82-11/94	**3201**	11/94-02/95		
S65396	08/57-09/93	⊗11/93	**6004**	08/57-04/74	**5904**	04/74-07/80	**6004**	07/80-05/82
			3202	05/82-09/93				

Class 414 2-HAP Ashford/Eastleigh
Driving Motor Brake Second Open
DMBSO
S65397-S65403

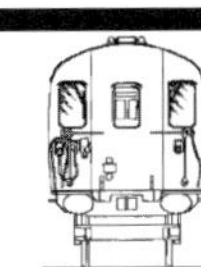

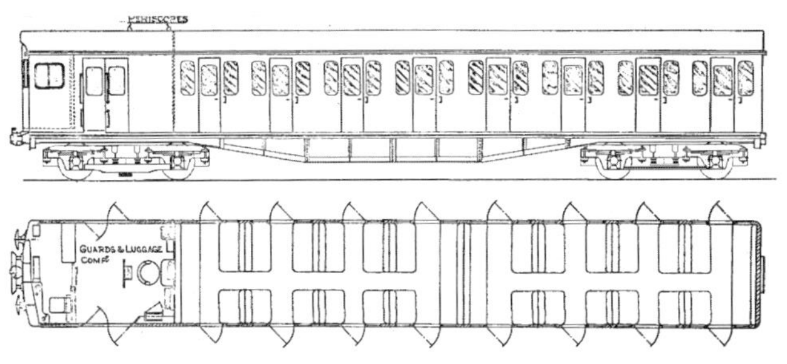

Diagram: 400 EB269
Body: 63' 11½" × 9' 3¼"
Seats: 84 second
Motors: EE507 2 × 250hp
Lot Number: 30319
Weight: 41t 0cwt
Bogies: Mk 4/3B

S65397	11/57-05/91	⊗09/91	**6005**	11/57-04/74	**5905**	04/74-04/80	**6005**	04/80-05/82
			3213	05/82-09/91				
S65398	11/57-11/94	⊗01/95	**6006**	11/57-04/74	**5906**	04/74-09/80	**6006**	09/80-05/82
			3201	05/82-11/94				
S65399	11/57-05/85	⊗09/87	**6007**	11/57-04/74	**5907**	04/74-04/80	**6007**	04/80-05/85
S65400	11/57-05/85	⊗09/87	**6008**	11/57-04/74	**5908**	04/74-05/80	**6008**	05/80-05/85
S65401	11/57-02/95	⊗05/95	**6009**	11/57-04/74	**5909**	04/74-09/80	**6009**	09/80-05/82
			3201	05/82-02/95				
S65402	11/57-05/91	⊗07/91	**6010**	11/57-05/74	**5910**	05/74-04/80	**6010**	04/80-05/82
			3210	05/82-05/91				
S65403	11/57-10/84	⊗02/88	**6011**	11/57-04/74	**5911**	04/74-04/80	**6011**	04/80-10/84

Class 414 2-HAP Ashford/Eastleigh
Driving Motor Brake Second Open
DMBSO
S65404-S65435 (65435 Class 416/2 2-EPB)

As built, Diagram 400 EB269

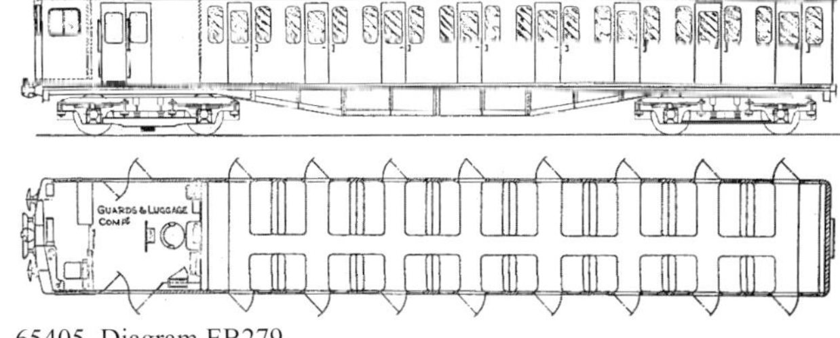

65405, Diagram EB279

Diagram: 400 EB269 EB279
Body: 63' 11½" × 9' 3¼"
Seats: 84 second, some later 82
Motors: EE507 2 × 250hp
Lot Number: 30388
Weight: 41t 0cwt
Bogies: Mk 4

S65404	02/58-09/94	⊗11/94	**6012**	02/58-04/74	**5912**	04/74-03/80	**6012**	03/80-05/82
			3207	05/82-09/94				
S65405	02/58-01/92	⊗05/92	**6013**	02/58-05/74	**5913**	05/74-05/80	**6013**	05/80-07/88
			4201	07/88-09/91	**3333**	09/91-01/92		
S65406	02/58-05/91	⊗11/91	**6014**	02/58-04/74	**5914**	04/74-04/80	**6014**	04/80-04/82
			3212	04/82-05/91				
S65407	02/58-05/91	⊗10/91	**6015**	02/58-05/74	**5915**	05/74-05/80	**6015**	05/80-04/82
			3209	04/82-05/91				
S65408	02/58-05/84	⊗10/85	**6016**	02/58-05/74	**5916**	05/74-02/80	**6016**	02/80-05/84
S65409	02/58-05/83	⊗10/86	**6017**	02/58-05/74	**5917**	05/74-03/79	**5624**	09/79-05/83
S65410	03/58-02/95	⊗03/95	**6018**	03/58-04/74	**5918**	04/74-04/80	**6018**	04/80-04/82
			3204	04/82-02/95				
S65411	03/58-05/84	⊗10/84	**6019**	03/58-04/74	**5919**	04/74-03/80	**6019**	03/80-05/84
S65412	03/58-09/93	⊗11/93	**6020**	03/58-05/74	**5920**	05/74-05/80	**6020**	05/80-05/82
			3202	05/82-09/93				
S65413	03/58-03/95	⊗03/95	**6021**	03/58-04/74	**5921**	04/74-03/80	**6021**	03/80-05/82
			3205	05/82-03/95				
S65414	03/58-05/86	➲977609	**6022**	03/58-05/86				
S65415	03/58-05/86	⊗11/87	**6023**	03/58-05/86				
S65416	03/58-05/84	⊗10/85	**6024**	03/58-04/74	**5922**	04/74-02/80	**6024**	02/80-05/84
S65417	03/58-05/84	⊗02/85	**6025**	03/58-04/74	**5923**	04/74-03/80	**6025**	03/80-05/84
S65418	03/58-05/84	⊗02/85	**6026**	03/58-04/74	**5924**	04/74-02/80	**6026**	02/80-05/84
S65419	03/58-08/91	⊗10/91	**6027**	03/58-04/74	**5925**	04/74-02/80	**6027**	02/80-04/82
			3206	04/82-08/91				
S65420	03/58-02/95	⊗03/95	**6028**	03/58-04/74	**5926**	04/74-03/80	**6028**	03/80-04/82
			3204	04/82-02/95				
S65421	04/58-05/84	⊗10/85	**6029**	04/58-04/74	**5927**	04/74-04/80	**6029**	04/80-05/84
S65422	04/58-03/95	⊗03/95	**6030**	04/58-05/74	**5928**	05/74-03/80	**6030**	03/80-05/82
			3205	05/82-03/95				
S65423	04/58-08/91	⊗10/91	**6031**	04/58-03/74	**5929**	03/74-04/80	**6031**	04/80-04/82
			3206	04/82-08/91				
S65424	04/58-11/94	⊗01/95	**6032**	04/58-04/74	**5930**	04/74-02/80	**6032**	02/80-05/82
			3203	05/82-11/94				
S65425	04/58-01/94	⊗02/94	**6033**	04/58-05/74	**5931**	05/74-02/80	**6033**	02/80-05/82
			3208	05/82-01/94				
S65426	04/58-05/84	⊗09/87	**6034**	04/58-04/74	**5932**	04/74-02/80	**6034**	02/80-05/84
S65427	05/58-05/93	⊗06/93	**6035**	05/58-04/74	**5933**	04/74-04/80	**6035**	04/80-06/82
			3211	06/82-05/93				
S65428	05/58-09/94	⊗11/94	**6036**	05/58-04/74	**5934**	04/74-06/80	**6036**	06/80-05/82
			3207	05/82-09/94				
S65429	05/58-01/94	⊗02/94	**6037**	05/58-04/74	**5935**	04/74-06/80	**6037**	06/80-05/82
			3208	05/82-01/94				
S65430	05/58-05/91	⊗10/91	**6038**	05/58-04/74	**5936**	04/74-02/80	**6038**	02/80-04/82
			3209	04/82-05/91				
S65431	05/58-06/84	⊗06/84	**6039**	05/58-04/74	**5937**	04/74-02/80	**6039**	02/80-06/84
S65432	05/58-05/91	⊗09/91	**6040**	05/58-04/74	**5938**	04/74-02/80	**6040**	02/80-05/82
			3213	05/82-09/91				
S65433	05/58-05/91	⊗11/91	**6041**	05/58-05/74	**5939**	05/74-05/80	**6041**	05/80-04/82
			3212	04/82-05/91				

S65434 05/58-05/91 ⊗07/91 **6042** 05/58-04/74 **5940** 04/74-02/80 **6042** 02/80-05/82 **3210** 05/82-05/91

S65435 06/58-05/87 ⊗09/87 **5779** 06/58-08/84 **6279** 08/84-05/87

Class 504 Manchester-Bury Wolverton

Driving Motor Brake Second Open

DMBSO

M65436-M65461

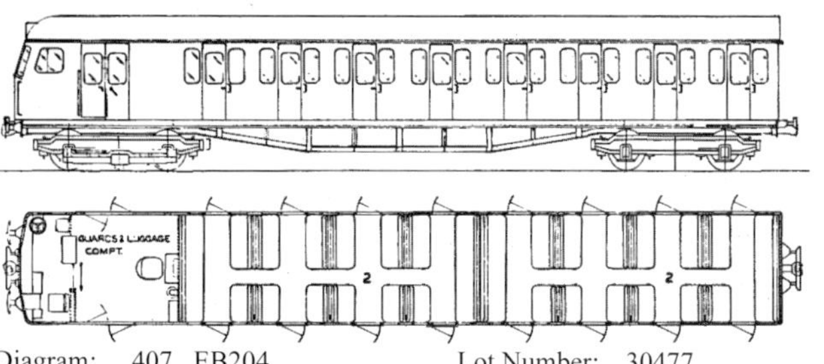

Diagram:	407 EB204	Lot Number:	30477
Body:	64' 0⅝" × 9' 3"	Weight:	49t 8cwt
Seats:	84 second	Bogies:	Gresley
Motors:	EE 4 × 141hp		

M65436 08/59-05/82 ⊗05/85

M65437 08/59-05/82 ⊗*06/82*

M65438 08/59-11/78 ⊗12/79

M65439 08/59-05/82 ⊗01/83

M65440 59-01/70 ⊗

M65441 59-05/82 ⊗01/83

M65442 59-05/82 ⊗01/83

M65443 59-05/82 ⊗05/85

M65444 59-08/91 ⊗09/91 **504444** 07/88-08/91

M65445 59-08/91 ⊗09/91 **504445** 07/88-08/91

M65446 59-08/91 ⊗08/91 **504446** 07/88-08/91

M65447 59-07/91 ⊗08/91 **504447** 07/88-07/91

M65448 59-07/86 ⊗*01/87*

M65449 59-07/91 ⊗08/91 **504449** 07/88-07/91

M65450 59-07/91 ⊗08/91 **504450** 07/88-07/91

M65451 59-08/91 ⓟ **504451** 07/88-08/91

M65452 59-08/91 ⊗08/91 **504452** 07/88-08/91

M65453 59-08/91 ⊗08/91 **504453** 07/88-08/91

M65454 59-07/91 ⊗08/91 **504454** 07/88-07/91

M65455 59-07/91 ⊗08/91 **504455** 07/88-07/91

M65456 59-09/91 ⊗09/91 **504456** 07/88-09/91

M65457 59-09/91 ⊗09/91 **504457** 07/88-09/91

M65458 59-07/91 ⊗08/91 **504458** 07/88-07/91

M65459 59-07/91 ⊗08/91 **504459** 07/88-07/91

M65460 59-08/91 ⊗08/91 **504460** 07/88-08/91

M65461 59-08/91 ⓟ⊗08/92**504461** 07/88-08/91

65501-65510 ***Class 482*** *03/93*

65700-65749 ***Class 465/2*** *12/93*

65750-65799 ***Class 465/2*** *12/93*

65800-65846 ***Class 465/1*** *12/93*

65847-65893 ***Class 465/1*** *12/93*

65894-65934 ***Class 365*** *08/96*

65935-65975 ***Class 365*** *08/96*

67300-67301 ***Class 457*** *06/88*

67400-67401 ***Class 457*** *06/88*

67501-67510 ***Class 482*** *03/93*

Tyneside Eastleigh

Driving Motor Luggage Van

DMLV

E68000 Later transferred to Southport Line

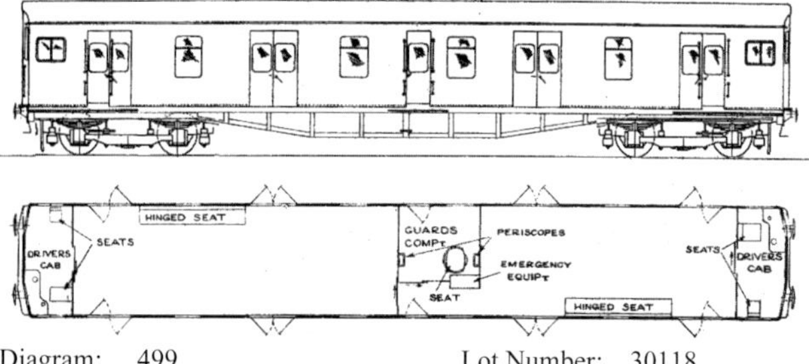

Diagram:	499	Lot Number:	30118
Body:	64' 5" × 9' 0¼"	Weight:	49t 0cwt
Bogies:	Mk 3B		
Motors:	EE507 2 × 250hp		

E68000 55- *64* ⊗ 08/63⇨**M**

Class 419 1-MLV Ashford/Eastleigh

Driving Motor Luggage Van

DMLV

S68001-S68002

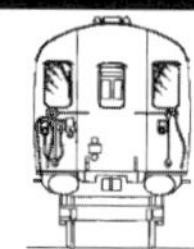

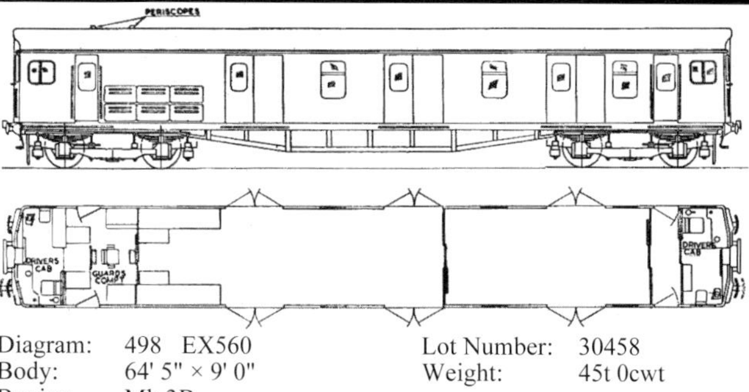

Diagram:	498 EX560	Lot Number:	30458
Body:	64' 5" × 9' 0"	Weight:	45t 0cwt
Bogies:	Mk 3B		
Motors:	EE507 2 × 250hp		

S68001 04/59- 92 ⓟ➲Dep **931091**

S68002 05/59- 92 ⓟ➲Dep **931092**

Class 419 1-MLV Ashford/Eastleigh

Driving Motor Luggage Van

DMLV

S68003-S68010

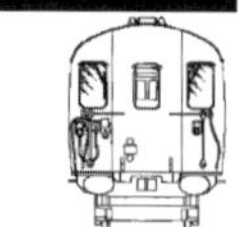

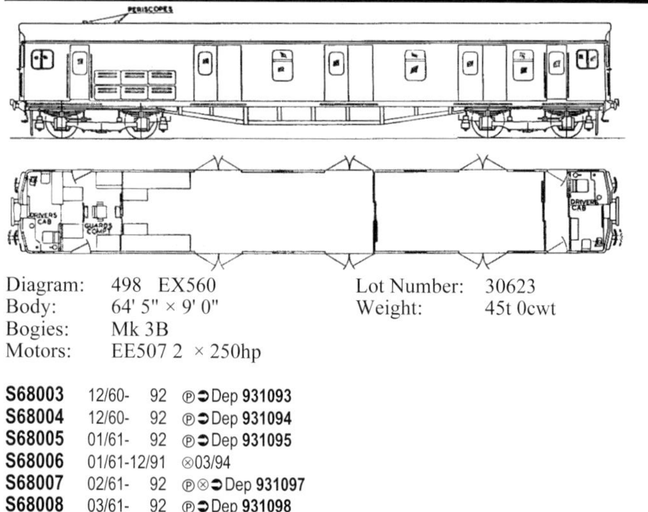

Diagram:	498 EX560	Lot Number:	30623
Body:	64' 5" × 9' 0"	Weight:	45t 0cwt
Bogies:	Mk 3B		
Motors:	EE507 2 × 250hp		

S68003 12/60- 92 ⓟ➲Dep **931093**

S68004 12/60- 92 ⓟ➲Dep **931094**

S68005 01/61- 92 ⓟ➲Dep **931095**

S68006 01/61-12/91 ⊗03/94

S68007 02/61- 92 ⓟ⊗➲Dep **931097**

S68008 03/61- 92 ⓟ➲Dep **931098**

S68009 03/61- 92 ⓟ➲Dep **931099**

S68010 03/61- 92 ⓟ➲Dep **931090**

Class 308 York

Motor Luggage Van

MLV

E68011-E68019

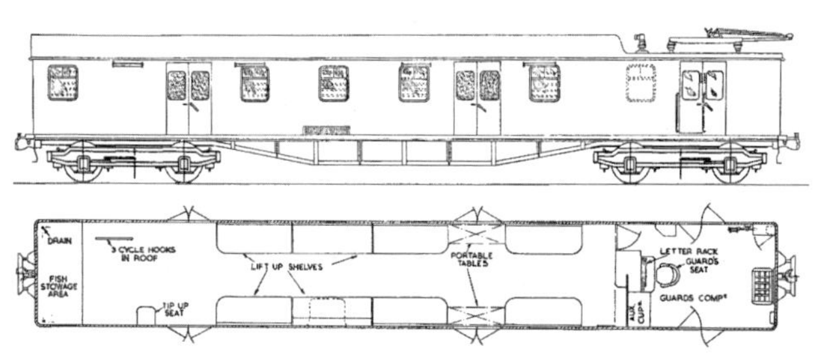

Diagram:	497 EY501	Lot Number:	30701
Body:	63' 6" × 9' 3"	Weight:	51t 12cwt
Bogies:	Gresley		
Motors:	EE 4 × 192hp		

E68011	05/61-06/71	⊃62431	313	05/61-06/71						⊂61916
E68012	09/61-01/90	⊗07/90	314	09/61-03/72	321	03/72- 82	308321	82-07/83		
			308995	01/84-01/90						⊂61917
E68013	09/61-08/71	⊃62433	315	09/61-08/71						⊂61918
E68014	10/61-07/71	⊃62432	316	10/61-07/71						⊂61919
E68015	10/61-11/88	⊗04/90	317	10/61- 82	308317	82-07/83	308991	01/84-11/88		⊂61920
E68016	11/61-02/84	⊗08/90	318	11/61-12/81	308318	12/81-07/83	308992	01/84-02/84		⊂61921
E68017	11/61-01/90	⊗04/90	319	11/61-07/82	308319	07/82-07/83	308993	01/84-01/90		⊂61922
E68018	11/61-01/90	⊗08/90	320	11/61-04/82	308320	04/82-07/83	308994	01/84-01/90		⊂61923
E68019	11/61-10/71	⊃62434	321	11/61-10/71						⊂61924

Class 302 York
Motor Luggage Van
MLV or MPMV
68020-68023

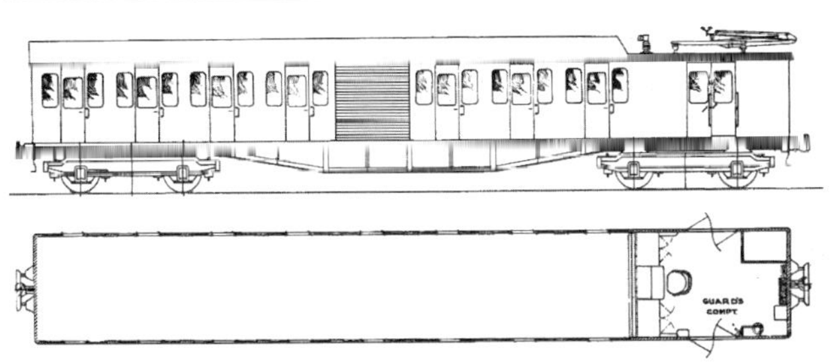

Diagram: ED501 Lot Number:
Body: 63' 6" × 9' 3" Weight:
Bogies: Gresley
Motors: EE536A 4 × 192hp

68020	03/89-10/95	⊗10/95	302990	03/89-10/95	⊂61090
68021	03/89-10/95	⊗11/95	302991	03/89-10/95	⊂61067
68022	04/89-11/93	⊗01/94	302992	04/89-11/93	⊂61227
68023	03/90-03/96	⊗11/95	302993	03/90-03/96	⊂61222

Class 302 York
Driving Trailer Luggage Van
DTLV or BDTPMV
68100-68103

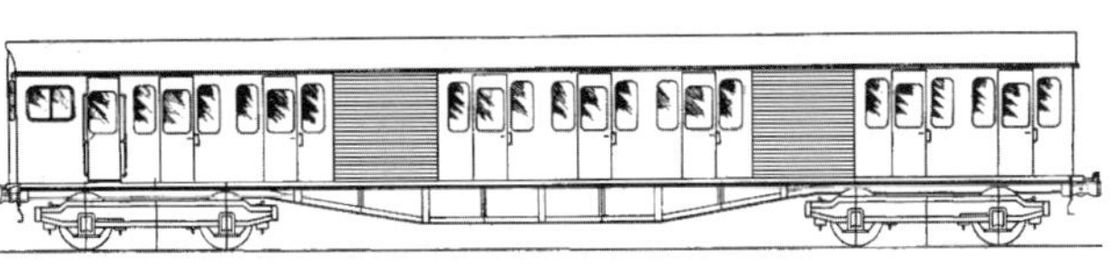

Diagram: EF501 Lot Number:
Body: 63' 11½" × 9' 3" Weight:
Bogies: Gresley

68100	03/89-10/95	⊗10/95	302990	03/89-10/95	⊂75084
68101	03/89-10/95	⊗11/95	302991	03/89-10/95	⊂75221
68102	04/89-11/93	⊗01/94	302992	04/89-11/93	⊂75220
68103	03/90-03/96	⊗11/95	302993	03/90-03/96	⊂75078

Class 419 1-TLV Pressed Steel
Trailer Luggage Van
TLV
S68201-S68206

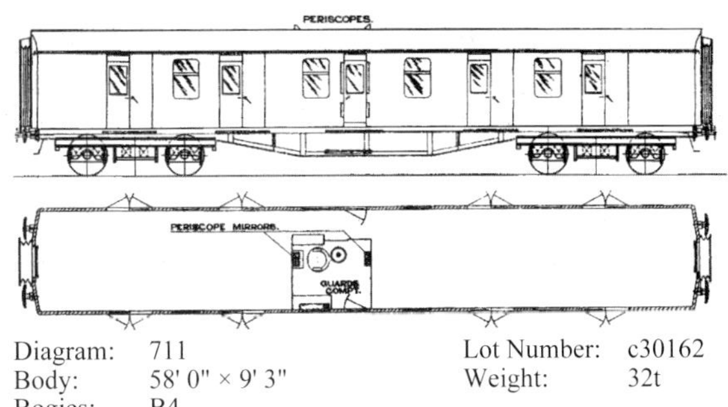

Diagram: 711 Lot Number: c30162
Body: 58' 0" × 9' 3" Weight: 32t
Bogies: B4

S68201	*01/68-09/74*	⊃975611	⊂80915
S68202	*01/68-09/74*	⊃975613	⊂80918
S68203	*01/68-09/74*	⊃975612	[illegible]
S68204	*01/68-09/74*	⊃975614	⊂80925
S68205	*01/68-09/74*	⊃975610	⊂80942
S68206	*01/68-09/74*	⊃975615	⊂80951

Class 302 York
Driving Trailer Luggage Van
DTLV or BDTPMV
68207-68210

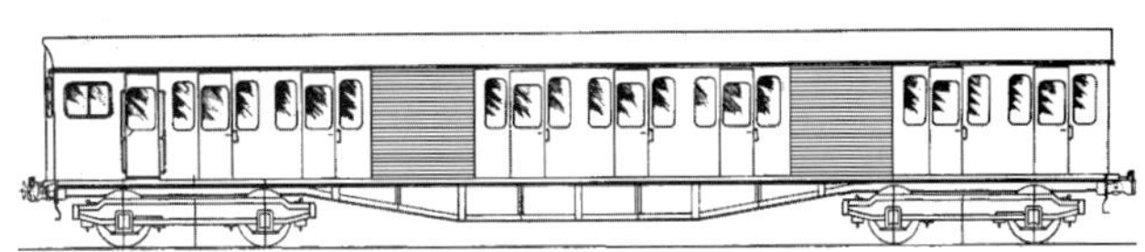

Diagram: EE501 Lot Number:
Body: 63' 11½" × 9' 3" Weight:
Bogies: Gresley

68207	03/89-10/95	⊗10/95	302990	03/89-10/95	⊂75082
68208	03/89-10/95	⊗11/95	302991	03/89-10/95	⊂75217
68209	04/89-11/93	⊗01/94	302992	04/89-11/93	⊂75218
68210	03/90-03/96	⊗11/95	302993	03/90-03/96	⊂75074

68300-68331	*Class 325*	*02/95*
68340-68355	*Class 325*	*02/95*
68360-68375	*Class 325*	*02/95*

Class 489 Gatwick Ashford/Eastleigh
Driving Motor Luggage Van
DMLV
S68500-S68509

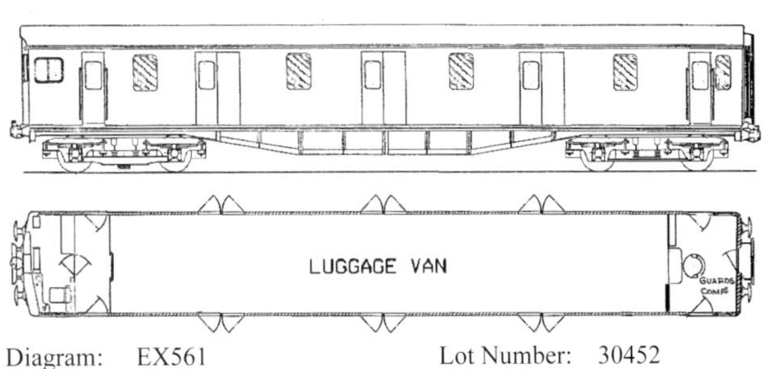

Diagram: EX561 Lot Number: 30452
Body: 63' 11½" × 9' 3¼" Weight: 44t 2cwt
Motors: EE507 2 × 250hp Bogies: Mk 4

S68500	01/84-11/01	Ⓟ	9101	01/84-11/01	⊂61269
S68501	01/84-07/00		9102	01/84-07/00	⊂61281

S68502	02/84-02/01	⊗06/03	**9103**	02/84-02/01	⊂61274
S68503	02/84- 05	ⓟ	**9104**	02/84- 05	⊂61277
S68504	03/84-01/01	⊗	**9105**	03/84-01/01	⊂61286
S68505	03/84-09/00	⊗	**9106**	03/84-09/00	⊂61299
S68506	03/84-08/02	ⓟ	**9107**	03/84-08/02	⊂61292
S68507	04/84- 04	ⓟ	**9108**	04/84- 04	⊂61267
S68508	04/84-10/01	⊗01/12	**9109**	04/84-10/01	⊂61272
S68509	05/84- 06	ⓟ	**9110**	05/84- 06	⊂61280

Class 410 4-BEP Ashford/Eastleigh
Trailer Buffet
TRB
S69000-S69001

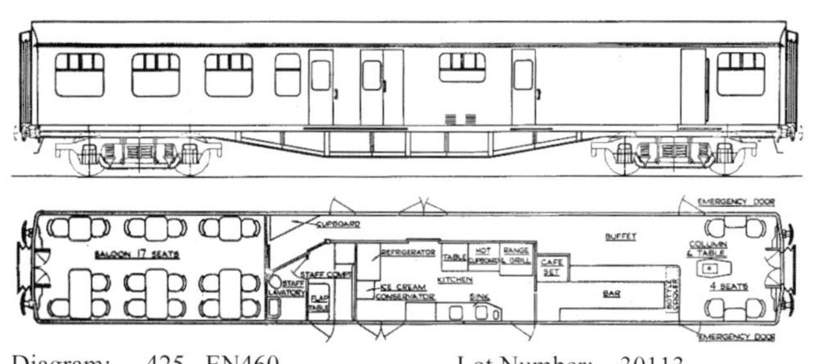

Diagram: 425 EN460 Lot Number: 30113
Body: 64' 6" × 9' 3" Weight: 35t 0cwt
Seats: 17 unclassified 4 buffet 1 staff toilet
Bogies: Commonwealth

S69000	07/57-04/81	⊗11/84	**7001**	07/56-05/80
S69001	07/57-08/83	⊗12/86	**7002**	07/56-08/83

Class 410 4-BEP Ashford/Eastleigh
Trailer Buffet
TRB
S69002-S69011

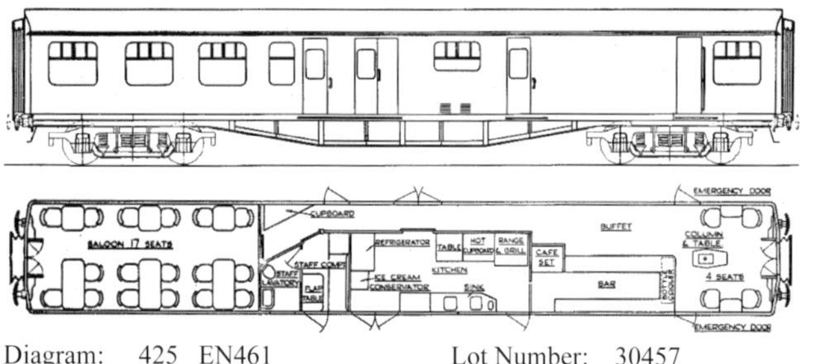

Diagram: 425 EN461 Lot Number: 30457
Body: 64' 6" × 9' 3" Weight: 35t 0cwt
Seats: 17 unclassified 4 buffet 1 staff toilet
Bogies: Commonwealth

S69002	03/59-11/81	⊗11/84	**7003**	03/59-09/81		
S69003	04/59-11/81	⊗11/84	**7004**	04/59-09/81		
S69004	04/59-11/81	⊗11/84	**7005**	04/59-03/82		
S69005	04/59-11/81	⊗11/84	**7006**	04/59-11/81		
S69006	04/59-11/81	⊗11/84	**7007**	04/59-11/81		
S69007	05/59-11/81	⊗11/84	**7008**	05/59-11/81		
S69008	05/59-11/81	⊗11/84	**7009**	05/59-11/80		
S69009	05/59-11/81	⊗11/84	**7010**	05/59-10/81		
S69010	05/59-05/86	⊗03/87	**7011**	05/59-08/83	**2701**	08/83-02/86
S69011	05/59-11/81	⊗03/85	**7012**	05/59-11/81		

Class 410 4-BEP Ashford/Eastleigh
Trailer Buffet
TRB
S69012-S69021

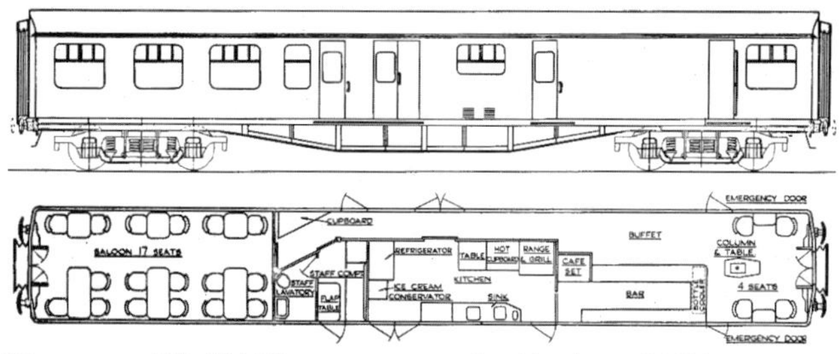

Diagram: 425 EN461 Lot Number: 30622
Body: 64' 6" × 9' 3" Weight: 35t 0cwt
Seats: 17 unclassified 4 buffet 1 staff toilet
Bogies: Commonwealth

S69012	01/61-11/83	➲69344	**7013**	01/61-05/82				
S69013	01/61-12/83	ⓟ➲69345	**7014**	01/61-03/83				
S69014	03/61-02/82	➲69341	**7015**	03/61-11/81				
S69015	03/61-03/84	➲69347	**7016**	03/61-12/83				
S69016	04/61-02/84	➲69346	**7017**	04/61-07/83				
S69017	04/61-05/86	⊗03/87	**7018**	04/61-12/83	**2704**	12/83-03/86		
S69018	05/61-09/83	➲69343	**7019**	05/61-02/82				
S69019	06/61-06/83	➲69342	**7020**	06/61-06/82				
S69020	06/61-05/86	⊗03/87	**7021**	06/61-12/83	**2703**	12/83-03/86	**2804**	05/88-04/89
S69021	09/61-05/86	⊗03/87	**7022**	09/61-09/83	**2702**	09/83-03/86		

Class 430 4-REP York
Trailer Buffet
TRB
S69022-S69025

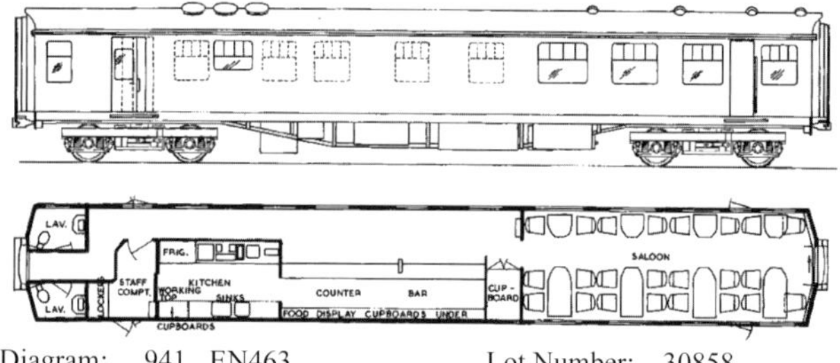

Diagram: 941 EN463 Lot Number: 30858
Body: 64' 6" × 9' 3" Weight: 38t 11cwt
Seats: 23 unclasssified 2 toilets Bogies: B5 (SR)

S69022	09/74-05/89	⊗12/89	**3012**	09/74-05/86	**2012**	05/86-06/87	**2807**	06/87-05/89
	The Brooklands							⊂1925
S69023	10/74-10/88	⊗03/89	**3013**	10/74-05/86	**2013**	05/86-12/87	**2905**	12/87-04/88
	The Avon		**2805**	04/88-10/88				⊂1932
S69024	11/74-04/89	⊗12/89	**3014**	11/74-04/86	**2014**	04/86-03/88	**2906**	03/88-05/88
	The New Forest							⊂1935
S69025	12/74-12/89	⊗12/89	**3015**	12/74-04/86	**2015**	04/86-11/86	**2803**	12/86-12/87
	The Stour		**2901**	12/87-05/88	**2806**	05/88-09/88	**2808**	09/88-01/89
			2809	01/89-05/89				⊂1939

Class 309 York
Trailer Griddle
TRB
E69100-E69107

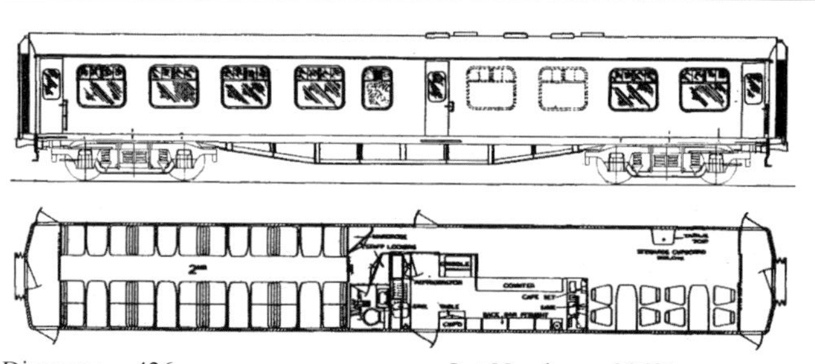

Diagram: 426 Lot Number: 30681
Body: 64' 6" × 9' 3" Weight: 35t 16cwt

Seats: 24 second 8 buffet 1 staff toilet
Bogies: Commonwealth

E69100	07/62-08/84	⊗08/84	**611**	09/62-12/80		
E69101	07/62-08/84	⊗08/84	**612**	10/62-05/81		
E69102	07/62-08/84	⊗08/84	**613**	10/62-12/80		
E69103	07/62-08/84	⊗08/84	**614**	12/62-02/81		
E69104	09/62-08/84	⊗08/84	**615**	01/63- 81		
E69105	10/62-01/70	⊗05/76	**616**	01/63-01/70		
E69106	12/62-08/84	⊗08/84	**617**	02/63- 81		
E69107	02/63-08/84	⊗08/84	**618**	02/63-02/81	**309618**	02/81-07/81

Class 309 Wolverton
Trailer Griddle
TRB
E69108

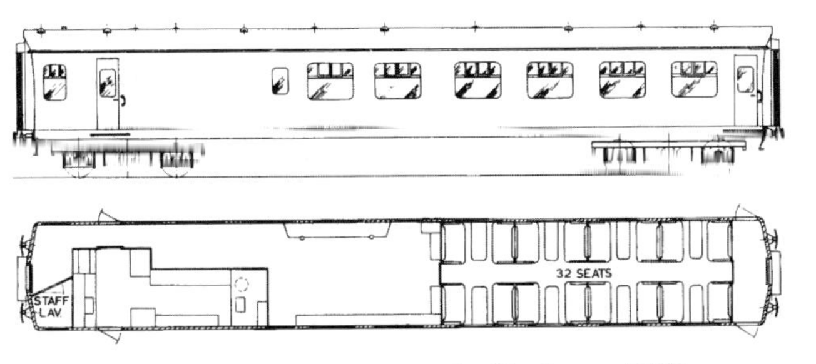

Diagram:	495	Lot Number:	c30707
Body:	64' 6⅛" × 9' 3"	Weight:	35t 16cwt
Seats:	32 second 1 staff toilet	Bogies:	B4

Rebuilt 06/72 from DMU 59831 (Diagram 569) to replace 69105.

E69108	06/63-08/84	⊗08/84	**616**	06/72-01/80	**309616**	01/80- 81	⊂59831

Class 420 4-BIG York
Trailer Buffet Unclassified
TSRB
S69301-S69318

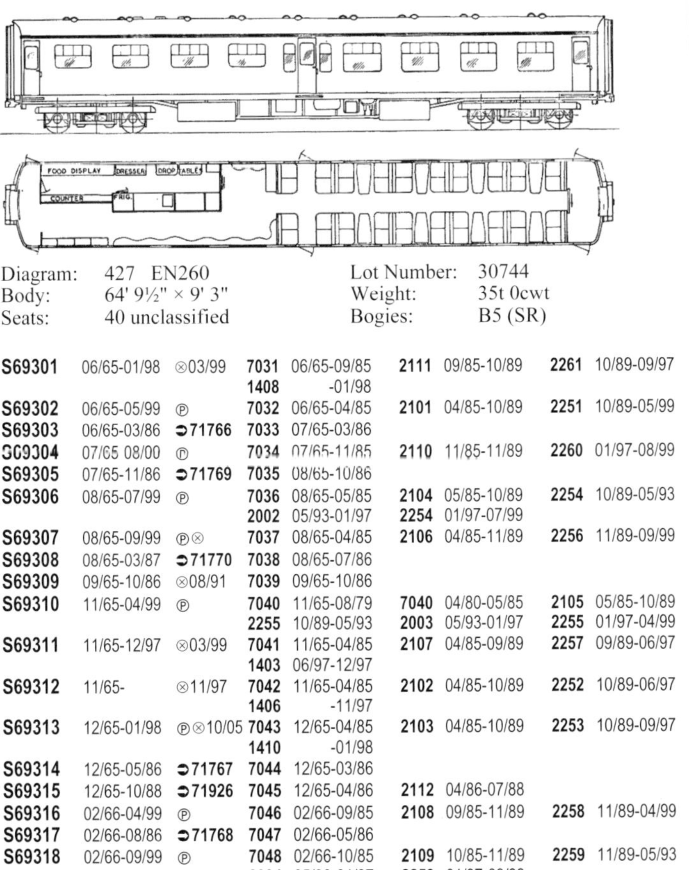

Diagram:	427 EN260	Lot Number:	30744
Body:	64' 9½" × 9' 3"	Weight:	35t 0cwt
Seats:	40 unclassified	Bogies:	B5 (SR)

S69301	06/65-01/98	⊗03/99	**7031**	06/65-09/85	**2111**	09/85-10/89	**2261**	10/89-09/97
			1408	-01/98				
S69302	06/65-05/99	Ⓟ	**7032**	06/65-04/85	**2101**	04/85-10/89	**2251**	10/89-05/99
S69303	06/65-03/86	⊃71766	**7033**	07/65-03/86				
S69304	07/65-08/00	Ⓟ	**7034**	07/65-11/85	**2110**	11/85-11/89	**2260**	01/97-08/99
S69305	07/65-11/86	⊃71769	**7035**	08/65-10/86				
S69306	08/65-07/99	Ⓟ	**7036**	08/65-05/85	**2104**	05/85-10/89	**2254**	10/89-05/93
			2002	05/93-01/97	**2254**	01/97-07/99		
S69307	08/65-09/99	Ⓟ⊗	**7037**	08/65-04/85	**2106**	04/85-11/89	**2256**	11/89-09/99
S69308	08/65-03/87	⊃71770	**7038**	08/65-07/86				
S69309	09/65-10/86	⊗08/91	**7039**	09/65-10/86				
S69310	11/65-04/99	Ⓟ	**7040**	11/65-08/79	**7040**	04/80-05/85	**2105**	05/85-10/89
			2255	10/89-05/93	**2003**	05/93-01/97	**2255**	01/97-04/99
S69311	11/65-12/97	⊗03/99	**7041**	11/65-04/85	**2107**	04/85-09/89	**2257**	09/89-06/97
			1403	06/97-12/97				
S69312	11/65-	⊗11/97	**7042**	11/65-04/85	**2102**	04/85-10/89	**2252**	10/89-06/97
			1406	-11/97				
S69313	12/65-01/98	Ⓟ⊗10/05	**7043**	12/65-04/85	**2103**	04/85-10/89	**2253**	10/89-09/97
			1410	-01/98				
S69314	12/65-05/86	⊃71767	**7044**	12/65-03/86				
S69315	12/65-10/88	⊃71926	**7045**	12/65-04/86	**2112**	04/86-07/88		
S69316	02/66-04/99	Ⓟ	**7046**	02/66-09/85	**2108**	09/85-11/89	**2258**	11/89-04/99
S69317	02/66-08/86	⊃71768	**7047**	02/66-05/86				
S69318	02/66-09/99	Ⓟ	**7048**	02/66-10/85	**2109**	10/85-11/89	**2259**	11/89-05/93
			2004	05/93-01/97	**2259**	01/97-09/99		

Class 430 4-REP York
Trailer Buffet
TRB
S69319-S69329

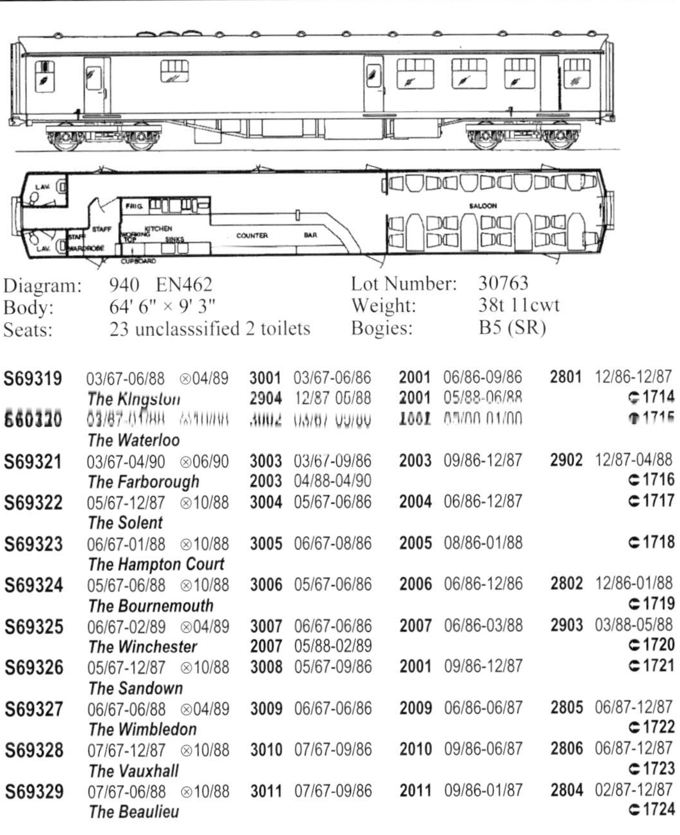

Diagram:	940 EN462	Lot Number:	30763
Body:	64' 6" × 9' 3"	Weight:	38t 11cwt
Seats:	23 unclasssified 2 toilets	Bogies:	B5 (SR)

S69319	03/67-06/88	⊗04/89	**3001**	03/67-06/86	**2001**	06/86-09/86	**2801**	12/86-12/87	
	The Kingston		**2904**	12/87-05/88	**2001**	05/88-06/88			⊂1714
S69320	03/67-01/88	⊗10/88	**3002**	03/67-09/86	**2002**	09/86-01/88			⊂1715
	The Waterloo								
S69321	03/67-04/90	⊗06/90	**3003**	03/67-09/86	**2003**	09/86-12/87	**2902**	12/87-04/88	
	The Farborough		**2003**	04/88-04/90					⊂1716
S69322	05/67-12/87	⊗10/88	**3004**	05/67-06/86	**2004**	06/86-12/87			⊂1717
	The Solent								
S69323	06/67-01/88	⊗10/88	**3005**	06/67-08/86	**2005**	08/86-01/88			⊂1718
	The Hampton Court								
S69324	05/67-06/88	⊗10/88	**3006**	05/67-06/86	**2006**	06/86-12/86	**2802**	12/86-01/88	
	The Bournemouth								⊂1719
S69325	06/67-02/89	⊗04/89	**3007**	06/67-06/86	**2007**	06/86-03/88	**2903**	03/88-05/88	
	The Winchester		**2007**	05/88-02/89					⊂1720
S69326	05/67-12/87	⊗10/88	**3008**	05/67-09/86	**2001**	09/86-12/87			⊂1721
	The Sandown								
S69327	06/67-06/88	⊗04/89	**3009**	06/67-06/86	**2009**	06/86-06/87	**2805**	06/87-12/87	
	The Wimbledon								⊂1722
S69328	07/67-12/87	⊗10/88	**3010**	07/67-09/86	**2010**	09/86-06/87	**2806**	06/87-12/87	
	The Vauxhall								⊂1723
S69329	07/67-06/88	⊗10/88	**3011**	07/67-09/86	**2011**	09/86-01/87	**2804**	02/87-12/87	
	The Beaulieu								⊂1724

Class 420 4-BIG York
Trailer Buffet Unclassified
TSRB
S69330-S69339

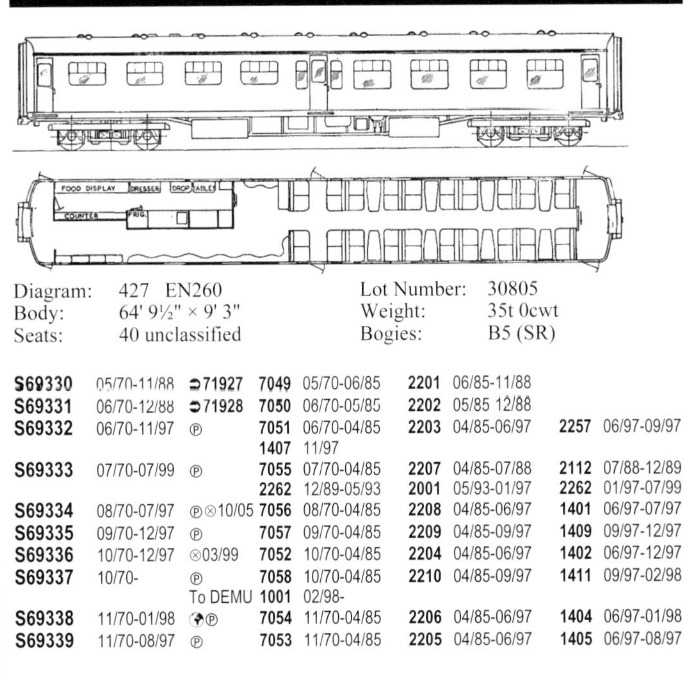

Diagram:	427 EN260	Lot Number:	30805
Body:	64' 9½" × 9' 3"	Weight:	35t 0cwt
Seats:	40 unclassified	Bogies:	B5 (SR)

S69330	05/70-11/88	⊃71927	**7049**	05/70-06/85	**2201**	06/85-11/88		
S69331	06/70-12/88	⊃71928	**7050**	06/70-05/85	**2202**	05/85-12/88		
S69332	06/70-11/97	Ⓟ	**7051**	06/70-04/85	**2203**	04/85-06/97	**2257**	06/97-09/97
			1407	11/97				
S69333	07/70-07/99	Ⓟ	**7055**	07/70-04/85	**2207**	04/85-07/88	**2112**	07/88-12/89
			2262	12/89-05/93	**2001**	05/93-01/97	**2262**	01/97-07/99
S69334	08/70-07/97	Ⓟ⊗10/05	**7056**	08/70-04/85	**2208**	04/85-06/97	**1401**	06/97-07/97
S69335	09/70-12/97	Ⓟ	**7057**	09/70-04/85	**2209**	04/85-09/97	**1409**	09/97-12/97
S69336	10/70-12/97	⊗03/99	**7052**	10/70-04/85	**2204**	04/85-06/97	**1402**	06/97-12/97
S69337	10/70-	Ⓟ	**7058**	10/70-04/85	**2210**	04/85-09/97	**1411**	09/97-02/98
		To DEMU	**1001**	02/98-				
S69338	11/70-01/98	✦Ⓟ	**7054**	11/70-04/85	**2206**	04/85-06/97	**1404**	06/97-01/98
S69339	11/70-08/97	Ⓟ	**7053**	11/70-04/85	**2205**	04/85-06/97	**1405**	06/97-08/97

Class 410 4-BEP Ashford/Eastleigh
Trailer Buffet Second
TRB
S69341-S69347

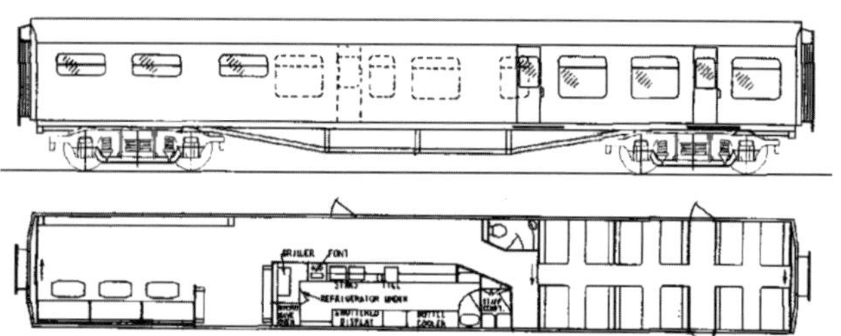

Diagram:	EN261	Lot Number:	30622
Body:	64' 6" × 9' 3"	Weight:	35t 0cwt
Seats:	24 second 9 buffet 1 toilet		
Bogies:	Commonwealth		

S69341	02/82-11/03	Ⓟ	**2301**	02/82-09/02	**2321**	09/02-11/03			⊂**69014**
S69342	06/83-01/04	⊗02/04	**2302**	06/83-09/02	**2322**	09/02-01/04			⊂**69019**
S69343	09/83-12/02	⊗11/05	**2303**	09/83-09/02	**2323**	09/02-12/02			⊂**69018**
S69344	11/83-11/03	⊗02/04	**2304**	11/83-09/02	**2324**	09/02-11/03			⊂**69012**
S69345	12/83-12/03	Ⓟ	**2305**	12/83-09/02	**2325**	09/02-12/03			⊂**69013**
S69346	02/84-01/03	⊗03/03	**2306**	02/84-03/89	**2308**	03/89-04/89	**2306**	04/89-09/02	
			2326	09/02-01/03					⊂**69016**
S69347	03/84-11/03	⊗02/04	**2307**	03/84-09/02	**2327**	09/02-11/03			⊂**69015**

Class 307 Ashford/Eastleigh
Trailer Composite (Semi-open) Lavatory
TCsoL, later TSOL
E70001-E70032

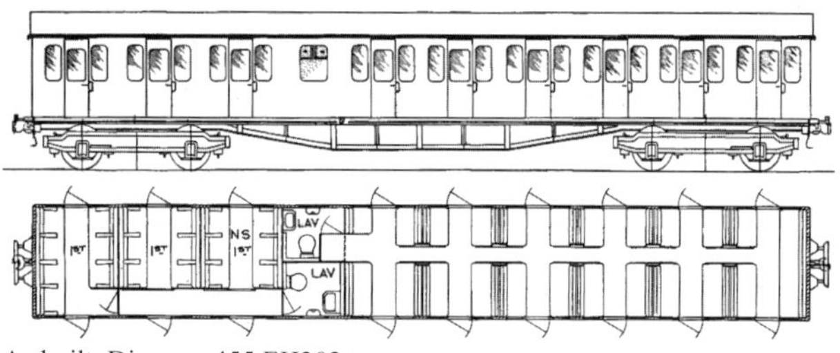

As built, Diagram 455 EH302

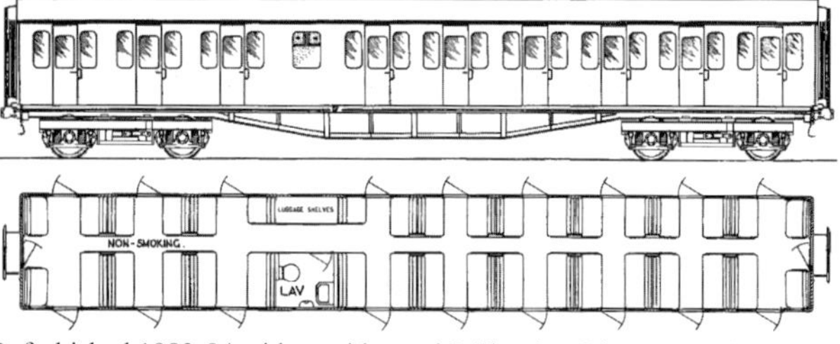

Refurbished 1983-84 with corridor and B4 bogies, Diagram EH222

Diagram:	455 EH302 EH222	Lot Number:	30204
Body:	63' 6" × 9' 3"	Weight:	30t 0cwt
Seats:	19 first 60 second 2 toilets later 86 second 1 toilet	Bogies:	Gresley later B4

E70001	02/56-08/93	⊃**977670**	**01s**	02/56-	*61*	**101**	*61*-11/82	**307101**	11/82-08/93
E70002	02/56-08/93	⊗03/95	**02s**	02/56-	*61*	**102**	*61*-01/80	**307102**	01/80-08/93
E70003	02/56-08/93	⊗11/98	**03s**	02/56-02/60		**103**	02/60-10/82	**307103**	10/82-08/93
E70004	03/56-09/93	⊗09/93	**04s**	03/56-	*61*	**104**	*61*-01/82	**307104**	01/82-08/93
E70005	03/56-09/93	⊗09/93	**05s**	03/56-	*61*	**105**	*61*-09/82	**307105**	09/82-08/93
E70006	03/56-08/93	⊃**977674**	**06s**	03/56-	*61*	**106**	*61*-02/80	**307106**	02/80-08/93
E70007	04/56-08/93	⊗03/95	**07s**	04/56-	*61*	**107**	*61*-12/81	**307107**	12/81-08/93
E70008	04/56-*09/93*	⊗11/98	**08s**	04/56-	*61*	**108**	*61*-04/82	**307108**	04/82-08/93
E70009	04/56-09/93	⊗09/93	**09s**	04/56-	*61*	**109**	*61*-02/82	**307109**	02/82-08/93
E70010	05/56-08/93	⊗12/98	**10s**	05/56-	*61*	**110**	*61*-11/81	**307110**	11/81-08/93
E70011	05/56-08/93	⊗12/98	**11s**	05/56-	*61*	**111**	*61*-01/83	**307111**	01/83-08/93
E70012	05/56-08/93	⊗ *96*	**12s**	05/56-	*61*	**112**	*61*-09/82	**307112**	09/82-08/93
E70013	05/56-08/93	⊗11/96	**13s**	05/56-	*61*	**113**	*61*-12/82	**307113**	12/82-08/93
E70014	06/56-09/93	⊗09/93	**14s**	06/56-	*61*	**114**	*61*-11/81	**307114**	11/81-08/93
E70015	06/56-08/93	⊗ *96*	**15s**	06/56-	*61*	**115**	*61*-12/81	**307115**	12/81-08/93
E70016	06/56-08/93	⊗03/93	**16s**	06/56-	*61*	**116**	*61*-12/81	**307116**	12/81-08/93
E70017	06/56-09/93	⊗09/93	**17s**	06/56-	*61*	**117**	*61*-07/82	**307117**	07/82-08/93
E70018	06/56-08/93	⊗03/95	**18s**	06/56-	*61*	**118**	*61*-02/82	**307118**	02/82-08/93
E70019	07/56-09/93	⊗09/93	**19s**	07/56-	*61*	**119**	*61*-06/82	**307119**	06/82-08/93
E70020	07/56-08/93	⊗03/95	**20s**	07/56-	*61*	**120**	*61*-09/81	**307120**	09/81-08/93
E70021	07/56-08/93	⊃**977678**	**21s**	07/56-	*61*	**121**	*61*-04/82	**307121**	04/82-08/93
E70022	07/56-08/93	⊗ *96*	**22s**	07/56-	*61*	**122**	*61*-08/82	**307122**	08/82-08/93
E70023	08/56-*09/93*	⊗03/96	**23s**	08/56-	*61*	**123**	*61*-10/81	**307123**	10/81-08/93
E70024	08/56-*08/93*	⊗03/95	**24s**	08/56-	*61*	**124**	*61*-05/82	**307124**	05/82-08/93
E70025	09/56-*08/93*	⊗03/95	**25s**	09/56-	*61*	**125**	*61*-10/82	**307125**	10/82-08/93
E70026	09/56-*09/93*	⊗ *96*	**26s**	09/56-	*61*	**126**	*61*-08/82	**307126**	08/82-08/93
E70027	09/56-09/93	⊗09/93	**27s**	09/56-	*61*	**127**	*61*-01/82	**307127**	01/82-08/93
E70028	09/56-*08/93*	⊗03/95	**28s**	09/56-	*61*	**128**	*61*-03/82	**307128**	03/82-08/93
E70029	09/56-*10/93*	⊗03/95	**29s**	09/56-	*61*	**129**	*61*-06/82	**307129**	06/82-08/93
E70030	10/56-*08/93*	⊗03/95	**30s**	10/56-	*61*	**130**	*61*-06/82	**307130**	06/82-08/93
E70031	10/56-*09/93*	⊗03/95	**31s**	10/56-	*61*	**131**	*61*-05/82	**307131**	05/82-08/93
E70032	10/56-*08/93*	⊗03/95	**32s**	10/56-	*61*	**132**	*61*-04/82	**307132**	04/82-08/93

Class 411 4-CEP Ashford/Eastleigh
Trailer Corridor Second
TSK, later TSOL
S70033-S70036

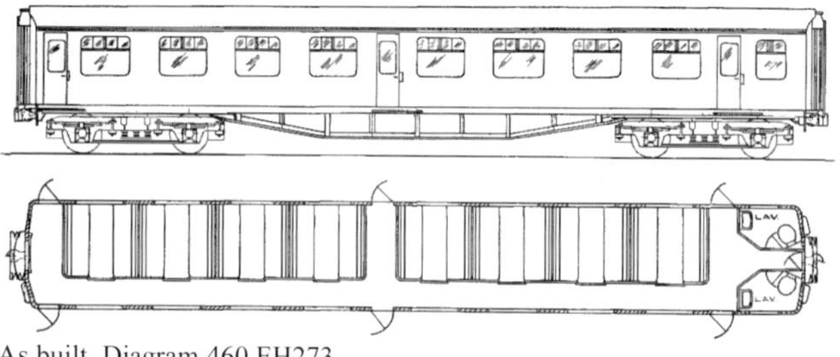

As built, Diagram 460 EH273

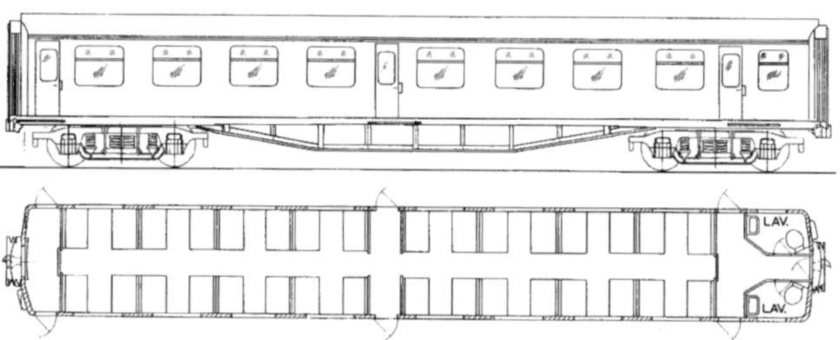

Refurbished as TSOL, Diagram 903 EH282

Diagram:	460 EH273 903 EH282	Lot Number:	30109
Body:	64' 6" × 9' 3"	Weight:	31t 0cwt
Seats:	64 second 2 toilets	Bogies:	Mk 6 later Commonwealth

S70033	02/56-03/93	⊗06/93	**7101**	02/56-10/82	**1503**	10/82-03/93
S70034	03/56-03/93	⊗04/93	**7102**	03/56-10/75	**1501**	05/80-03/93
S70035	04/56-05/93	⊗02/04	**7103**	04/56-08/83	**1505**	01/84-03/93
S70036	05/56-01/93	⊗04/93	**7104**	05/56-12/80	**1502**	12/80-01/93

Class 411 4-CEP Ashford/Eastleigh
Trailer Corridor Composite
TCK, later TBCK
S70037-S70040

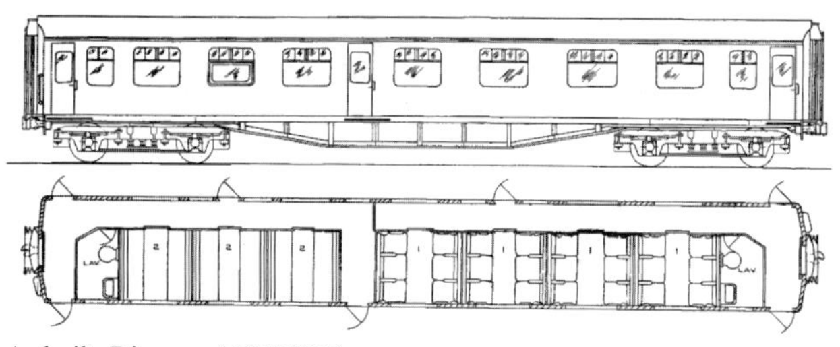

As built, Diagram 450 EH360

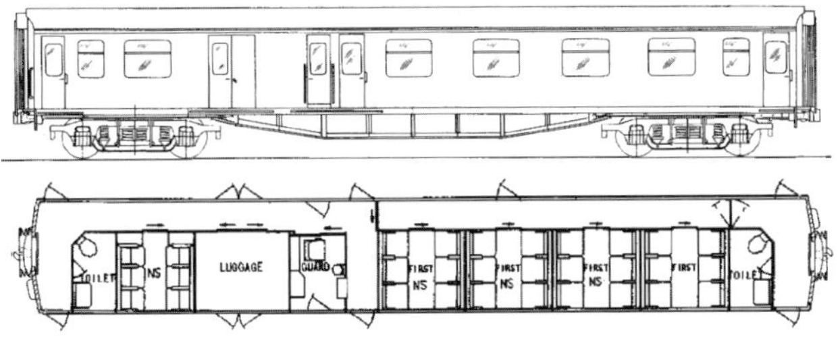

Refurbished as TBCK, Diagram 922 EJ361

Diagram:	450 EH360 922 EJ361	Lot Number:	30110
Body:	64' 6" × 9' 3"	Weight:	31t 0cwt
Seats:	24 first 24 second 2 toilets later 24 first 6 second 2 toilets	Bogies:	Mk 6 later Commonwealth

S70037	02/56-03/93	⊗06/93	**7101**	02/56-10/82	**1503**	10/82-03/93
S70038	03/56-10/75	⊗05/82	**7102**	03/56-10/75		
S70039	04/56-05/93	➲977862	**7103**	04/56-08/83	**1505**	01/84-03/93
S70040	05/56-01/93	⊗04/93	**7104**	05/56-12/80	**1502**	12/80-01/93

Class 410 4-BEP Ashford/Eastleigh

Trailer Corridor Composite
TCK, later TBCK
S70041-S70042

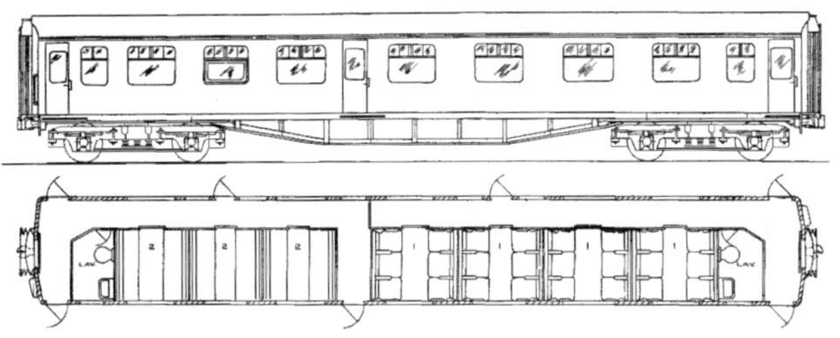

As built, Diagram 450 EH360

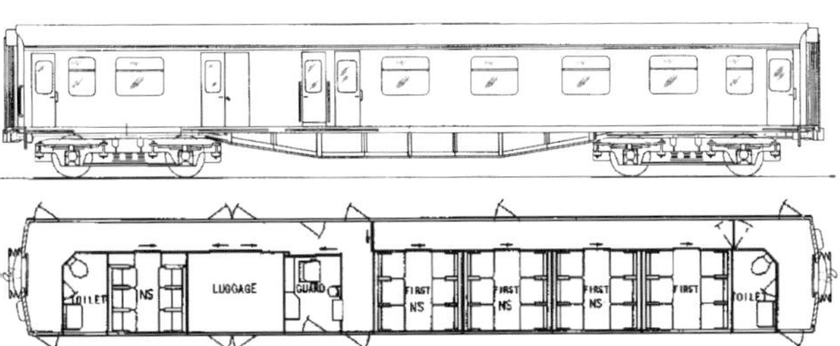

Refurbished as TBCK, Diagram 922 EJ361

Diagram:	450 EH360 922 EJ361	Lot Number:	30112
Body:	64' 6" × 9' 3"	Weight:	31t 0cwt
Seats:	24 first 24 second 2 toilets later 24 first 6 second 2 toilets	Bogies:	Mk 6 later Commonwealth

S70041	07/56-03/93	⊗04/93	**7001**	07/56-05/80	**1501**	05/80-03/93
S70042	07/56-05/93	⊗*05/97*	**7002**	07/56-08/83	**1504**	08/83-05/93

Class 411 4-CEP Ashford/Eastleigh

Trailer Corridor Composite
TCK, later TBCK
S70043-S70044

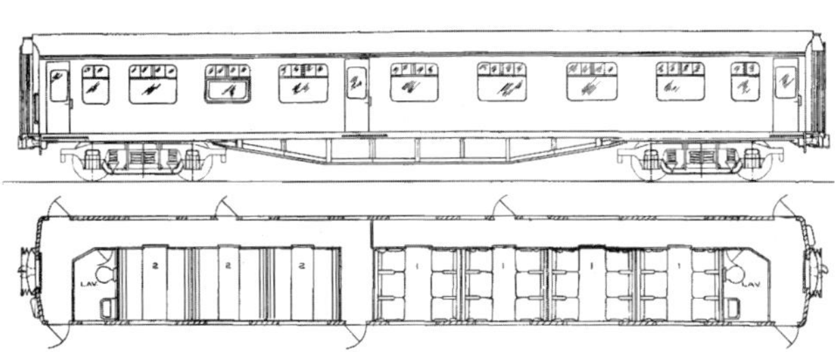

As built, Diagram 450 EH361

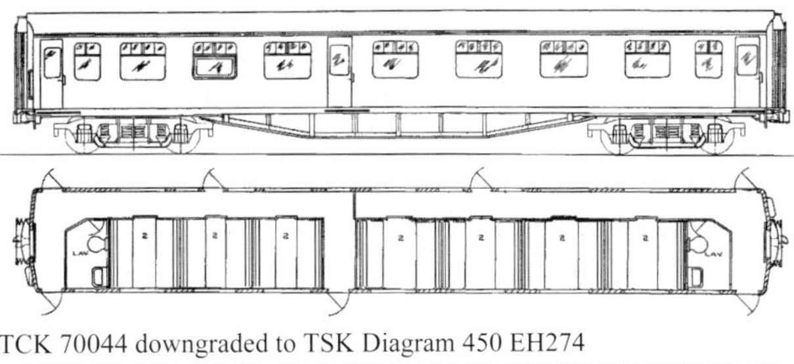

TCK 70044 downgraded to TSK Diagram 450 EH274

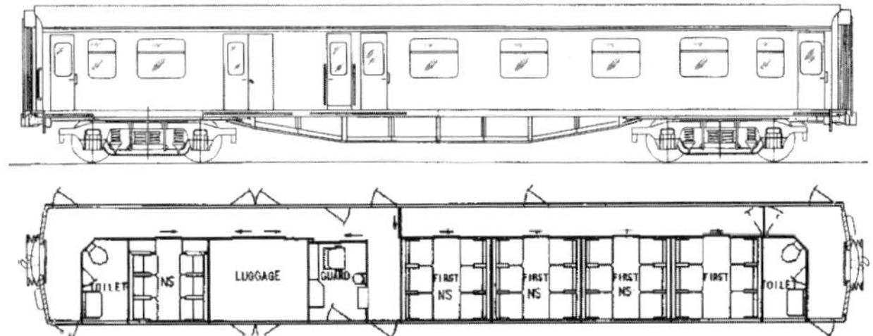

Refurbished as TBCK, Diagram 922 EJ361

Diagram:	450 EH361 922 EJ361	Lot Number:	30630
Body:	64' 6" × 9' 3"	Weight:	31t 0cwt
Seats:	24 first 24 second 2 toilets 70044 later 56 second 2 toilets later 24 first 6 second 2 toilets	Bogies:	Commonwealth

S70043	08/61-04/97	⊗05/01	**7203**	08/61-09/83	**1618**	09/83-04/94		
S70044	09/61-11/01	⊗09/02	**7204**	09/61-04/71	**7189**	11/71-08/81	**1588**	08/81-11/01

Class 304/1 Wolverton

Trailer Composite (Semi-open) Lavatory
TCsoL, later TSsoL
M70045-M70059

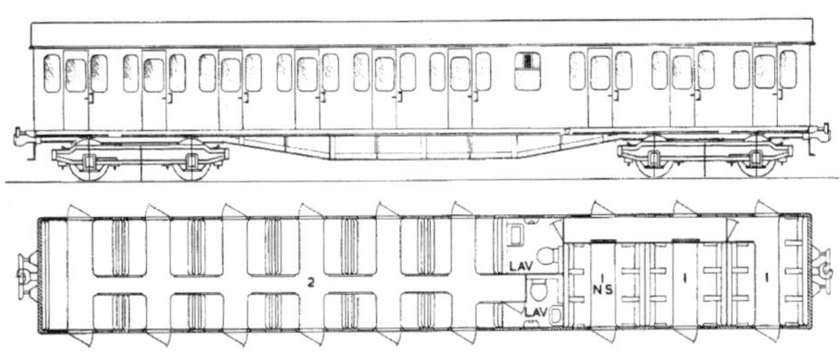

As built, Diagram 456 EH303

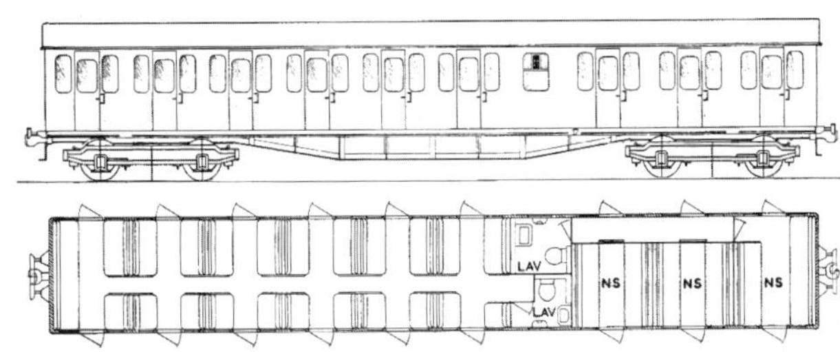

Downgraded 1979, Diagram EH225

Diagram:	456 EH303 EH225	Lot Number:	30431
Body:	63' 6⅛" × 9' 3"	Weight:	31t 5cwt
Seats:	19 first 60 second 2 toilets later 86 second 2 toilets	Bogies:	Gresley

M70045	03/60-05/86	⊗12/86	**001**	03/60-10/82	**304001**	10/82-12/86
M70046	04/60-05/86	⊗12/86	**002**	04/60-04/82	**304002**	04/82-12/86
M70047	04/60-05/86	⊗12/86	**003**	04/60-07/81	**304003**	07/81-12/86
M70048	05/60-05/86	⊗12/86	**004**	05/60-09/83	**304004**	09/83-12/86
M70049	05/60-05/86	⊗12/86	**005**	05/60-10/81	**304005**	10/81-12/86
M70050	05/60-05/86	⊗12/86	**006**	05/60-12/82	**304006**	12/82-12/86
M70051	06/60-05/86	⊗12/86	**007**	06/60-04/82	**304007**	04/82-12/86
M70052	06/60-05/86	⊗12/86	**008**	06/60-08/81	**304008**	08/81-07/84
M70053	06/60-05/86	⊗12/86	**009**	06/60-04/81	**304009**	04/81-12/86
M70054	06/60-05/86	⊗12/86	**010**	06/60-12/81	**304010**	12/81-12/86
M70055	06/60-05/86	⊗12/86	**011**	06/60-01/80	**304011**	01/80-12/86
M70056	07/60-05/86	⊗12/86	**012**	07/60-04/82	**304012**	04/82-12/86
M70057	07/60-05/86	⊗12/86	**013**	07/60-07/81	**304013**	07/81-12/86
M70058	07/60-05/86	⊗12/86	**014**	07/60-06/81	**304014**	06/81-12/86
M70059	07/60-05/86	⊗12/86	**015**	07/60-08/82	**304015**	08/82-12/86

Class 302 York/Doncaster

Trailer Composite (Semi-open) Lavatory
TCsoL, later TSOL
E70060-E70096

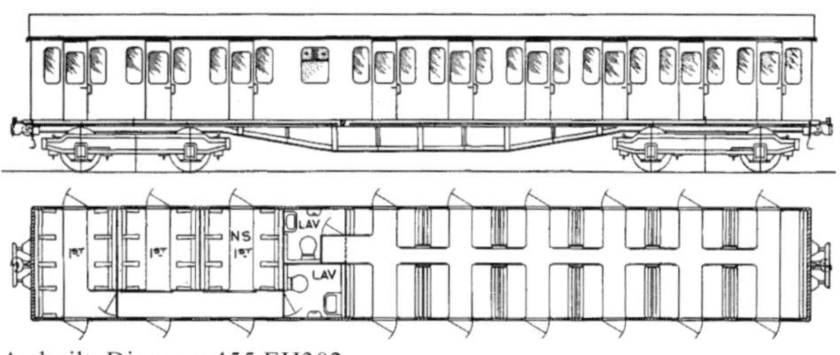

As built, Diagram 455 EH302

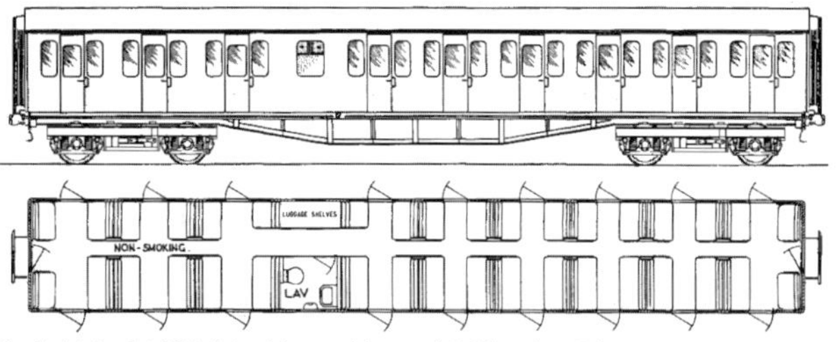

Refurbished 1983-84 with corridor and B4 bogies, Diagram EH223

Diagram:	455 EH302 EH223	Lot Number:	30437
Body:	63' 6" × 9' 3"	Weight:	30t 0cwt
Seats:	19 first 60 second 2 toilets later 86 second 1 toilet	Bogies:	Gresley later B4

E70060	10/58-06/98	⊗	**201**	11/58-01/83	**302201**	01/83-06/98		
E70061	12/58-04/97	⊗06/97	**202**	12/58-06/83	**302202**	06/83-04/97		
E70062	11/58-08/88	⊗06/90	**203**	12/58-04/81	**302203**	04/81-08/88		
E70063	11/58-02/98	⊗	**204**	12/58-04/81	**302204**	04/81-02/98		
E70064	11/58-06/97	⊗12/97	**205**	01/59-03/83	**302205**	03/83-06/97		
E70065	11/58-07/95	⊗09/95	**206**	01/59-03/81	**302206**	03/81-02/92	**305599**	02/92-07/93
			302206	07/93-03/94				
E70066	11/58-03/90	⊗08/90	**207**	01/59-03/81	**302207**	03/81-09/88	**302200**	09/88-03/90
E70067	12/58-09/89	⊗07/90	**208**	01/59-04/81	**302208**	04/81-09/88	**302276**[2]	09/88-02/89
E70068	12/58-06/95	⊗08/96	**209**	01/59-01/83	**302209**	01/83-06/95		
E70069	12/58-04/97	⊗12/97	**210**	01/59-05/85	**302210**	05/85-04/97		
E70070	12/58-09/97	⊗04/98	**211**	02/59-09/82	**302211**	09/82-09/97		
E70071	12/58-02/97	⊗09/98	**212**	02/59-05/81	**302212**	05/81-02/97		
E70072	12/58-07/97	⊗	**213**	02/59-08/81	**302213**	08/81-07/97		
E70073	01/59-01/91	⊗03/91	**214**	02/59-04/81	**302214**	04/81-04/88	**302261**	05/88-01/91
E70074	01/59-04/97	⊗05/97	**215**	03/59-12/81	**302215**	12/81-04/97		
E70075	01/59-07/98	⊗	**216**	02/59-06/83	**302216**	06/83-07/98		
E70076	01/59-04/97	⊗06/97	**217**	03/59-07/84	**302217**	07/84-02/92	**305598**	02/92-07/93
			302217	07/93-04/97				
E70077	01/59-07/97	⊗	**218**	04/59-06/81	**302218**	06/81-07/97		
E70078	01/59-04/97	⊗06/97	**219**	04/59-09/83	**302219**	09/83-04/97		
E70079	01/59-06/97	⊗09/98	**220**	04/59-09/83	**302220**	09/83-02/92	**305595**	02/92-01/93
			302220	01/93-06/97				
E70080	01/59-06/97	⊗	**221**	04/59-09/83	**302221**	09/83-06/97		
E70081	02/59-06/96	⊗04/98	**222**	04/59-06/82	**302222**	06/82-02/92	**305597**	02/92-12/92
			302222	12/92-06/96				
E70082	02/59-08/88	⊗06/90	**223**	06/59-05/81	**302223**	05/81-08/88		
E70083	02/59-08/97	⊗*09/00*	**224**	06/59-07/81	**302224**	07/81-08/97		
E70084	02/59-07/98	⊗	**225**	05/59-10/81	**302225**	10/81-07/98		
E70085	02/59-01/98	⊗	**226**	06/59-10/81	**302226**	10/81-02/92	**305594**	02/92-01/93
			302226	01/93-01/98				
E70086	02/59-10/90	⊗09/90	**227**	06/59- *83*	**302227**	*83*-02/88	**302272**	02/88-01/90
			302252	01/90-06/90				
E70087	03/59-07/98	⊗	**228**	05/59-11/81	**302228**	11/81-07/98		
E70088	03/59-09/97	⊗09/98	**229**	05/59-08/82	**302229**	08/82-09/97		
E70089	03/59-08/88	⊗06/90	**230**	05/59-12/83	**302230**	12/83-08/88		
E70090	03/59-09/89	⊗06/90	**231**	05/59-07/84	**302231**	07/84-03/89		
E70091	03/59-07/98	⊗	**232**	05/59-03/85	**302232**	03/85-09/88	**302230**[2]	09/88-07/98
E70092	03/59-09/89	⊗04/90	**233**	06/59-07/84	**302233**	07/84-02/88	**302297**	02/88-03/89
			302265	03/89-09/89				
E70093	04/59-03/93	⊗05/95	**234**	06/59-12/83	**302234**	12/83-08/87	**305526**	05/88-03/93
E70094	04/59-09/89	⊗07/90	**235**	06/59-04/81	**302235**	04/81-03/89		
E70095	04/59-02/86	⊗07/86	**236**	06/59-01/80	**302236**	01/80-02/86		
E70096	01/59-09/89	⊗06/90	**237**	06/59-11/84	**302237**	11/84-03/89		

Class 302 York

Trailer Composite (Semi-open) Lavatory
TCsoL, later TSOL
E70097-E70132

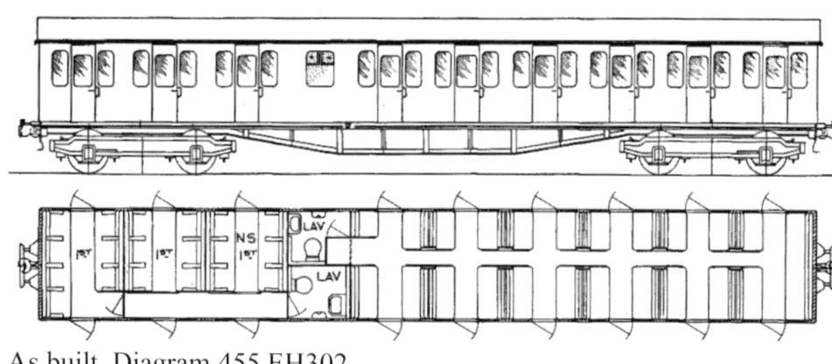

As built, Diagram 455 EH302

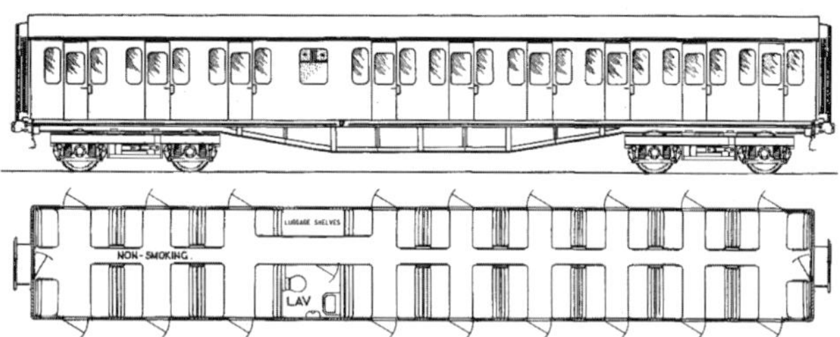

Refurbished 1983-84 with corridor and B4 bogies, Diagram EH223

Diagram:	455 EH302 EH223	Lot Number:	30441
Body:	63' 6" × 9' 3"	Weight:	30t 0cwt
Seats:	19 first 60 second 2 toilets later 86 second 1 toilet	Bogies:	Gresley later B4

E70097	02/59-09/88	⊗11/88	**238**	06/59-05/81	**302238**	05/81-08/88		
E70098	02/59-03/93	⊗05/95	**239**	06/59-01/83	**302239**	01/83-08/87	**302239**	01/88-02/88
			305521	05/88-03/93				
E70099	02/59-12/92	⊗05/95	**240**	06/59-11/82	**302240**	11/82-11/87	**305522**	11/88-12/92
E70100	02/59-09/89	⊗07/90	**241**	06/59-11/84	**302241**	11/84-03/89		
E70101	05/59-07/88	⊗06/90	**242**	07/59-01/82	**302242**	01/82-07/88		
E70102	02/59-09/89	⊗06/90	**243**	07/59-10/83	**302243**	10/83-09/89		
E70103	05/59-10/90	⊗10/90	**244**	07/59-10/70	**244**	06/72-06/82	**302244**	06/82-03/89
			302285	03/89-05/90	**302251**	05/90-10/90		
E70104	05/59-09/89	⊗06/90	**245**	07/59-08/81	**302245**	08/81-04/89		
E70105	05/59-09/89	⊗02/90	**246**	07/59- *83*	**302246**	*83*-09/89		
E70106	05/59-09/89	⊗06/90	**247**	07/59-01/82	**302247**	01/82-04/89		
E70107	03/59-09/89	⊗07/90	**248**	07/59-03/83	**302248**	03/83-03/83	**302399**	03/83-05/83
			302248	05/83-03/89				
E70108	06/59-03/90	⊗07/90	**249**	08/59-09/82	**302249**	09/82-09/89		
E70109	06/59-02/83	⊗01/85	**250**	08/59-04/82	**302250**	04/82-02/83		
E70110	05/59-07/90	⊗06/90	**251**	08/59-01/83	**302251**	01/83-05/90		
E70111	07/59-07/90	⊗08/90	**252**	08/59-08/82	**302252**	08/82-01/90	**302272**	01/90-06/90
E70112	02/59-09/89	⊗07/90	**253**	08/59-10/82	**302253**	10/82-05/85	**302312**	07/85-08/88
			302238	08/88-09/89				
E70113	03/59-09/89	⊗05/90	**254**	08/59-03/83	**302254**	03/83-03/89	**302264**	03/89-09/89
E70114	03/59-07/83	⊗*02/85*	**255**	08/59-01/82	**302255**	01/82-07/83		
E70115	03/59-09/89	⊗05/90	**256**	09/59- *83*	**302256**	*83*-09/89		
E70116	03/59-03/90	⊗08/90	**257**	09/59-04/82	**302257**	04/82-03/89	**302296**	03/89-03/90
E70117	03/59-03/90	⊗07/90	**258**	09/59-05/81	**302258**	05/81-09/89		
E70118	03/59-12/92	⊗05/95	**259**	09/59-03/80	**302259**	03/80-11/87	**305524**	11/88-12/92
E70119	03/59-05/85	⊗02/86	**260**	09/59-05/81	**302260**	05/81-05/85		
E70120	03/59-01/91	⊗03/91	**261**	09/59-03/83	**302261**	03/83-01/88	**302234**	01/88-01/91
E70121	04/59-11/88	⊗06/90	**262**	09/59-10/82	**302262**	10/82-11/87	**302240**	11/87-06/88
			302271	07/88-11/88				
E70122	04/59-06/96	⊗04/98	**263**	09/59-09/83	**302263**	09/83-09/88	**302203**[2]	09/88-06/96
E70123	04/59-09/89	⊗03/90	**264**	09/59-05/82	**302264**	05/82-03/89	**302254**	03/89-09/89
E70124	04/59-09/89	⊗06/90	**265**	09/59-09/82	**302265**	09/82-03/89	**302297**	03/89-03/89
E70125	04/59-06/90	⊗06/90	**266**	09/59-07/84	**302266**	07/84-01/88	**302239**	02/88-06/90
E70126	04/59-02/87	⊗10/87	**267**	09/59-02/80	**302267**	02/80-08/86		
E70127	11/59-09/89	⊗05/90	**268**	11/59-09/82	**302268**	09/82-09/89		
E70128	11/59-09/89	⊗04/90	**269**	11/59-01/82	**302269**	01/82-09/89		
E70129	11/59-09/89	⊗07/90	**270**	11/59- *83*	**302270**	*83*-09/89		
E70130	11/59-01/91	⊗03/91	**271**	11/59-04/82	**302271**	04/82-07/88	**302283**	08/88-07/90
E70131	11/59-01/91	⊗03/91	**272**	11/59-06/83	**302272**	06/83-02/88	**302262**	02/88-07/90
E70132	11/59-09/89	⊗02/90	**273**	11/59-03/82	**302273**	03/82-08/85	**302302**	09/85-09/88
			302260[2]	09/88-09/89				

Class 501 Ashford/Eastleigh
Trailer Second
TS later TSO
M70133-M70189

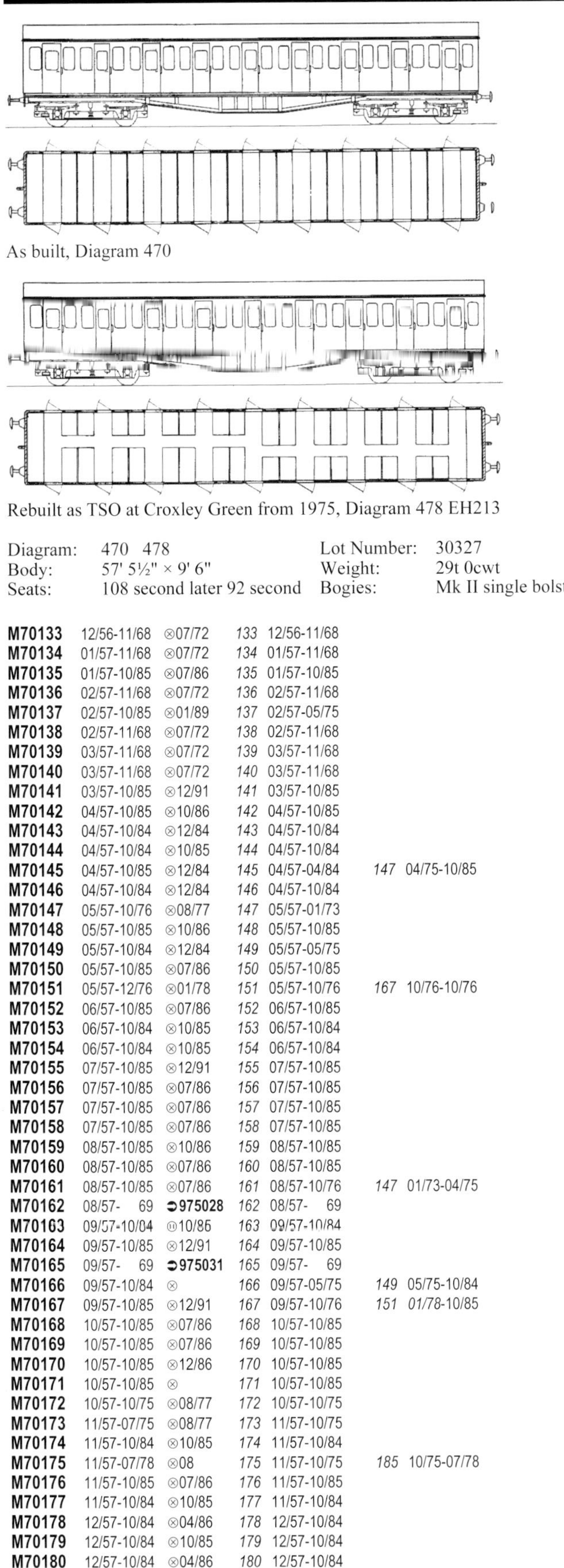

As built, Diagram 470

Rebuilt as TSO at Croxley Green from 1975, Diagram 478 EH213

Diagram:	470 478	Lot Number:	30327
Body:	57' 5½" × 9' 6"	Weight:	29t 0cwt
Seats:	108 second later 92 second	Bogies:	Mk II single bolster

M70133	12/56-11/68	⊗07/72	*133*	12/56-11/68		
M70134	01/57-11/68	⊗07/72	*134*	01/57-11/68		
M70135	01/57-10/85	⊗07/86	*135*	01/57-10/85		
M70136	02/57-11/68	⊗07/72	*136*	02/57-11/68		
M70137	02/57-10/85	⊗01/89	*137*	02/57-05/75		
M70138	02/57-11/68	⊗07/72	*138*	02/57-11/68		
M70139	03/57-11/68	⊗07/72	*139*	03/57-11/68		
M70140	03/57-11/68	⊗07/72	*140*	03/57-11/68		
M70141	03/57-10/85	⊗12/91	*141*	03/57-10/85		
M70142	04/57-10/85	⊗10/86	*142*	04/57-10/85		
M70143	04/57-10/84	⊗12/84	*143*	04/57-10/84		
M70144	04/57-10/84	⊗10/85	*144*	04/57-10/84		
M70145	04/57-10/85	⊗12/84	*145*	04/57-04/84	*147*	04/75-10/85
M70146	04/57-10/84	⊗12/84	*146*	04/57-10/84		
M70147	05/57-10/76	⊗08/77	*147*	05/57-01/73		
M70148	05/57-10/85	⊗10/86	*148*	05/57-10/85		
M70149	05/57-10/84	⊗12/84	*149*	05/57-05/75		
M70150	05/57-10/85	⊗07/86	*150*	05/57-10/85		
M70151	05/57-12/76	⊗01/78	*151*	05/57-10/76	*167*	10/76-10/76
M70152	06/57-10/85	⊗07/86	*152*	06/57-10/85		
M70153	06/57-10/84	⊗10/85	*153*	06/57-10/84		
M70154	06/57-10/84	⊗10/85	*154*	06/57-10/84		
M70155	07/57-10/85	⊗12/91	*155*	07/57-10/85		
M70156	07/57-10/85	⊗07/86	*156*	07/57-10/85		
M70157	07/57-10/85	⊗07/86	*157*	07/57-10/85		
M70158	07/57-10/85	⊗07/86	*158*	07/57-10/85		
M70159	08/57-10/85	⊗10/86	*159*	08/57-10/85		
M70160	08/57-10/85	⊗07/86	*160*	08/57-10/85		
M70161	08/57-10/85	⊗07/86	*161*	08/57-10/76	*147*	01/73-04/75
M70162	08/57- 69	➲975028	*162*	08/57- 69		
M70163	09/57-10/84	⊗10/86	*163*	09/57-10/84		
M70164	09/57-10/85	⊗12/91	*164*	09/57-10/85		
M70165	09/57- 69	➲975031	*165*	09/57- 69		
M70166	09/57-10/84	⊗	*166*	09/57-05/75	*149*	05/75-10/84
M70167	09/57-10/85	⊗12/91	*167*	09/57-10/76	*151*	*01/78*-10/85
M70168	10/57-10/85	⊗07/86	*168*	10/57-10/85		
M70169	10/57-10/85	⊗07/86	*169*	10/57-10/85		
M70170	10/57-10/85	⊗12/86	*170*	10/57-10/85		
M70171	10/57-10/85	⊗	*171*	10/57-10/85		
M70172	10/57-10/75	⊗08/77	*172*	10/57-10/75		
M70173	11/57-07/75	⊗08/77	*173*	11/57-10/75		
M70174	11/57-10/84	⊗10/85	*174*	11/57-10/84		
M70175	11/57-07/78	⊗08	*175*	11/57-10/75	*185*	10/75-07/78
M70176	11/57-10/85	⊗07/86	*176*	11/57-10/85		
M70177	11/57-10/84	⊗10/85	*177*	11/57-10/84		
M70178	12/57-10/84	⊗04/86	*178*	12/57-10/84		
M70179	12/57-10/84	⊗10/85	*179*	12/57-10/84		
M70180	12/57-10/84	⊗04/86	*180*	12/57-10/84		
M70181	12/57-10/84	⊗10/85	*181*	12/57-10/84		
M70182	12/57-10/84	⊗12/84	*182*	12/57-07/78		
M70183	01/58-10/84	⊗04/86	*183*	01/58-10/84		
M70184	01/58-10/84	⊗12/84	*184*	01/58-07/78		
M70185	01/58-10/85	⊗12/84	*185*	01/58-02/75	*137*	05/75-10/85
M70186	01/58-10/85	⊗07/86	*186*	01/58-10/85		
M70187	01/58-10/76	⊗08/77	*187*	01/58-10/76		
M70188	02/58-10/85	⊗07/86	*188*	02/58-10/85		
M70189	02/58-10/84	⊗12/84	*189*	02/58-07/78		

Class 302 York
Trailer Composite (Semi-open) Lavatory
TCsoL, later TSOL
E70190-E70228

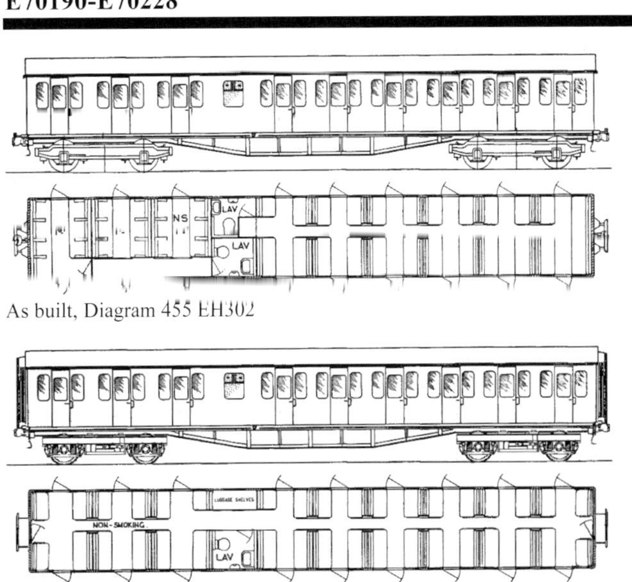

As built, Diagram 455 EH302

Refurbished 1983-84 with corridor and B4 bogies, Diagram EH223

Diagram:	455 EH302 EH223	Lot Number:	30441
Body:	63' 6" × 9' 3"	Weight:	30t 0cwt
Seats:	19 first 60 second 2 toilets later 86 second 1 toilet	Bogies:	Gresley later B4

E70190	11/59-03/90	⊗08/90	**274**	11/59-05/82	**302274**	05/82-04/89	**302286**	04/89-03/90
E70191	11/59-07/83	⊗05/84	**275**	11/59-11/79	**302275**	11/79-07/83		
E70192	11/59-02/86	⊗04/86	**276**	11/59-01/80	**302276**	01/80-02/86		
E70193	11/59-01/98	⊗	**277**	11/59-01/83	**302277**	01/83-09/88	**302227**[2]	09/88-01/98
E70194	01/60-09/89	⊗05/90	**278**	01/60-11/84	**302278**	11/84-09/89		
E70195	01/60-09/89	⊗05/90	**279**	01/60-10/81	**302279**	10/81-02/88	**302259**	02/88-03/89
			302282	03/89-09/89				
E70196	01/60-01/90	⊗03/90	**280**	01/60- *83*	**302280**	*83*-01/90		
E70197	01/60-01/90	⊗03/90	**281**	01/60-10/82	**302281**	10/82-10/86	**302305**	04/87-01/90
E70198	10/60-03/90	⊗08/90	**282**	10/60-02/82	**302282**	02/82-03/89	**302259**	03/89-03/90
E70199	11/60-09/88	⊗06/90	**283**	11/60-02/83	**302283**	02/83-08/88		
E70200	11/60-03/90	⊗05/91	**284**	11/60-10/81	**302284**	10/81-03/90		
E70201	11/60-09/89	⊗07/90	**285**	11/60-06/83	**302285**	06/83-03/89	**302244**	03/89-03/89
E70202	11/60-03/90	⊗06/90	**286**	12/60-05/82	**302286**	05/82-01/88	**302306**	01/88-09/88
			302273[2]	09/88-03/90				
E70203	12/60-10/85	⊗02/86	**287**	12/60-01/80	**302287**	01/80-10/85		
E70204	12/60-06/93	⊗05/95	**288**	12/60-12/82	**302288**	12/82-05/85	**305527**	04/88-06/93
E70205	12/60-09/89	⊗03/90	**289**	12/60-01/80	**302289**	01/80-09/89		
E70206	11/60-09/89	⊗04/90	**290**	11/60-10/82	**302290**	10/82-09/89		
E70207	11/60-09/89	⊗02/90	**291**	11/60- *83*	**302291**	*83*-09/89		
E70208	12/60-10/90	⊗10/90	**292**	12/60-03/83	**302292**	03/83-10/90		
E70209	12/60-07/97	⊗12/97	**293**	12/60-08/81	**302293**	08/81-09/88	**302223**[2]	09/88-07/97
E70210	12/60-06/93	⊗05/95	**294**	12/60-01/82	**302294**	01/82-11/87	**302294**	06/88-06/88
			305520	01/89 06/03				
E70211	12/60-09/89	⊗05/90	**295**	12/60-02/82	**302295**	02/82-09/89		
E70212	12/60-09/89	⊗05/90	**296**	12/60-04/84	**302296**	04/84-03/89	**302257**	03/89-09/89
E70213	12/60-06/93	⊗05/95	**297**	12/60-10/81	**302297**	10/81-11/87	**305525**	02/92-06/93
E70214	12/60-03/91	⊗03/91	**298**	12/60-03/83	**302298**	03/83-06/90	**302252**	06/90-03/91
E70215	12/60-11/88	⊗06/90	**299**	12/60-03/83	**302299**	03/83-11/88		
E70216	12/60-03/90	⊗08/90	**300**	12/60-07/83	**302300**	07/83-09/88	**302250**[2]	09/88-03/90
E70217	12/60-06/90	⊗06/90	**301**	12/60-01/83	**302301**	01/83-09/88	**302253**[2]	09/88-06/90
E70218	12/60-05/86	⊗10/86	**302**	12/60-02/80	**302302**	02/80-09/85		
E70219	12/60-03/90	⊗08/90	**303**	12/60-07/83	**302303**	07/83-09/88	**302255**[2]	09/88-01/90
E70220	12/60-09/97	⊗04/96	**304**	12/60-06/83	**302304**	06/83-09/88	**302214**[2]	09/88-09/96
E70221	12/60-12/92	⊗05/95	**305**	12/60- *83*	**302305**	*83*-04/87	**305523**	04/88-12/92
E70222	04/61-01/91	⊗03/91	**306**	04/61-03/83	**302306**	03/83-01/88	**302286**	01/88-04/89
			302274	04/89-01/91				
E70223	04/61-10/90	⊗10/90	**307**	04/61-10/83	**302307**	10/83-09/88	**302267**[2]	09/88-10/90
E70224	04/61-04/97	⊗	**308**	04/61-02/83	**302308**	02/83-09/88	**302208**[2]	09/88-02/92
			305596	02/92-07/93	**302208**	07/93-01/94	**302206**	03/94-04/97
E70225	01/60-12/85	⊗04/86	**309**	01/60-02/80	**302309**	02/80-12/85		
E70226	04/61-04/97	⊗05/97	**310**	04/61-09/83	**302310**	09/83-09/88	**302207**[2]	09/88-04/97
E70227	04/61-09/89	⊗06/90	**311**	04/61- *83*	**302311**	*83*-09/88	**302275**[2]	09/88-04/89
E70228	04/61-07/85	⊗08/85	**312**	04/61- *83*	**302312**	*83*-07/85		

Class 411 4-CEP Ashford/Eastleigh
Trailer Corridor Second
TSK, later TSOL
S70229-S70234

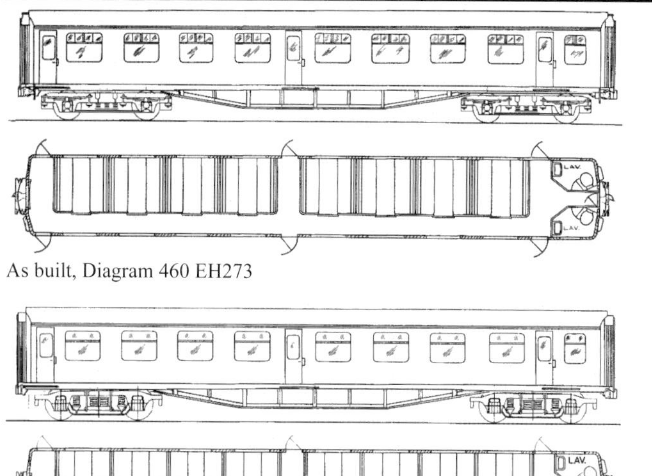

As built, Diagram 460 EH273

Refurbished as TSOL, Diagram 903 EH282

Diagram:	460 EH273 903 EH282	Lot Number:	30450
Body:	64' 6" × 9' 3"	Weight:	31t 0cwt
Seats:	64 second 2 toilets	Bogies:	Mk 6 later Commonwealth

S70229	08/58-12/04	Ⓟ	**7105**	08/58-01/82	**1537**	01/82-09/02	**2315**	09/02-12/04
S70230	08/58-07/98	⊗05/01	**7106**	08/58-12/83	**1561**	12/83-07/98		
S70231	08/58-01/04	⊗02/04	**7107**	08/58-06/81	**1531**	06/81-01/04		
S70232	09/58-07/93	⊗03/94	**7108**	09/58-03/81	**1525**	03/81-07/93		
S70233	09/58-11/99	⊗	**7109**	09/58-04/81	**1527**	04/81-11/99		
S70234	09/58-07/93	⊗11/93	**7110**	09/58-03/81	**1526**	03/81-07/93		

Class 411 4-CEP Ashford/Eastleigh
Trailer Corridor Composite
TCK, later TBCK
S70235-S70240

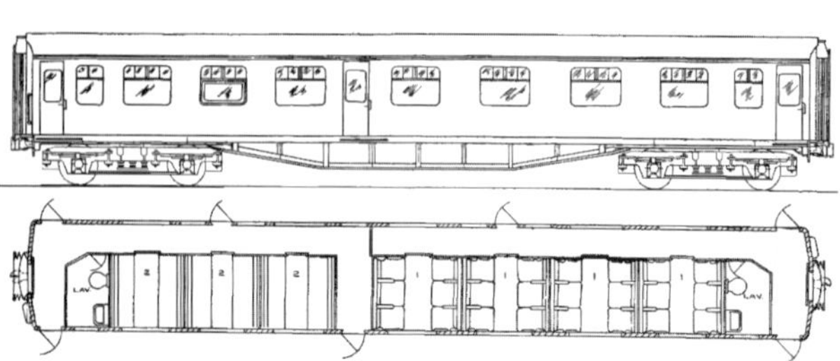

As built, Diagram 450 EH360

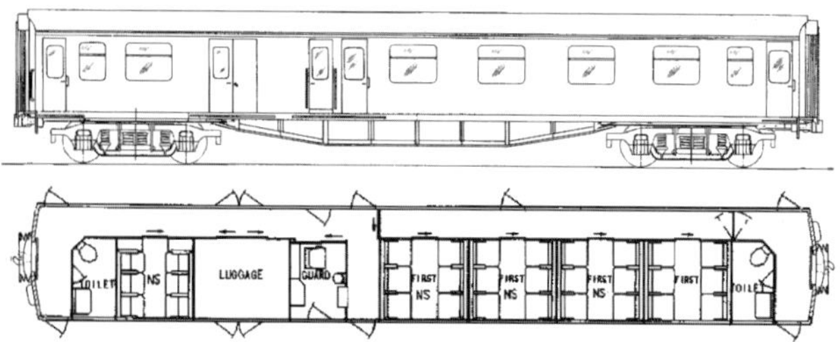

Refurbished as TBCK, Diagram 922 EJ361

Diagram:	450 EH360 922 EJ361	Lot Number:	30451
Body:	64' 6" × 9' 3"	Weight:	31t 0cwt
Seats:	24 first 24 second 2 toilets later 24 first 6 second 2 toilets	Bogies:	Mk 6 later Commonwealth

S70235	08/58-12/03	Ⓟ	**7105**	08/58-01/82	**1537**	01/82-09/02	**2325**	09/02-12/03
S70236	08/58-04/04	⊗06/04	**7106**	08/58-12/83	**1562**	12/83-03/89	**2308**	03/89-04/89
			1562	12/89-04/04				
S70237	08/58-01/04	⊗02/04	**7107**	08/58-06/81	**1531**	06/81-01/04		
S70238	09/58-06/94	⊗07/95	**7108**	09/58-03/81	**1525**	03/81-07/93	**1403**	07/93-06/94
S70239	09/58-11/99	⊗	**7109**	09/58-04/81	**1527**	04/81-11/99		
S70240	09/58-06/94	⊗06/95	**7110**	09/58-03/81	**1526**	03/81-07/93	**1404**	07/93-06/94

Class 411 4-CEP Ashford/Eastleigh
Trailer Corridor Second
TSK, later TSOL
S70241-S70242

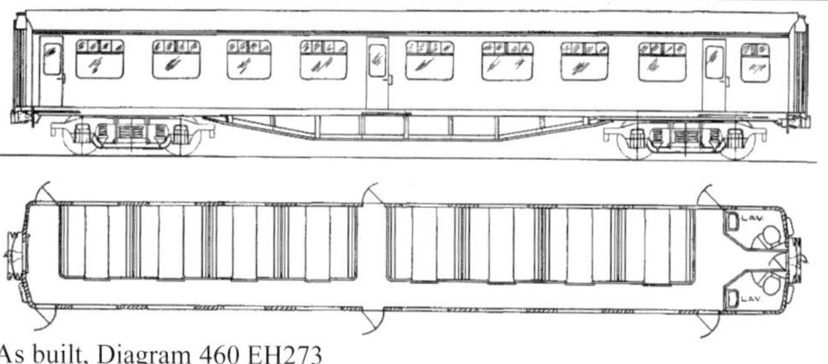

As built, Diagram 460 EH273

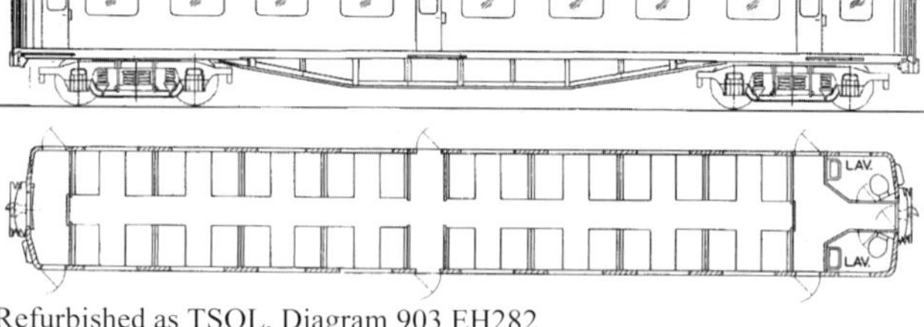

Refurbished as TSOL, Diagram 903 EH282

Diagram:	460 EH273 903 EH282	Lot Number:	30640
Body:	64' 6" × 9' 3"	Weight:	31t 0cwt
Seats:	64 second 2 toilets	Bogies:	Commonwealth

S70241	08/61-04/04	⊗06/04	**7203**	08/61-09/83	**1562**	12/83-03/89	**1562**	12/89-04/04
S70242	09/61-06/71	⊗*11/71*	**7204**	09/61-04/71				

Class 304/3 Wolverton
Trailer Composite (Semi-open) Lavatory
TCsoL, later TSsoL
M70243-M70252

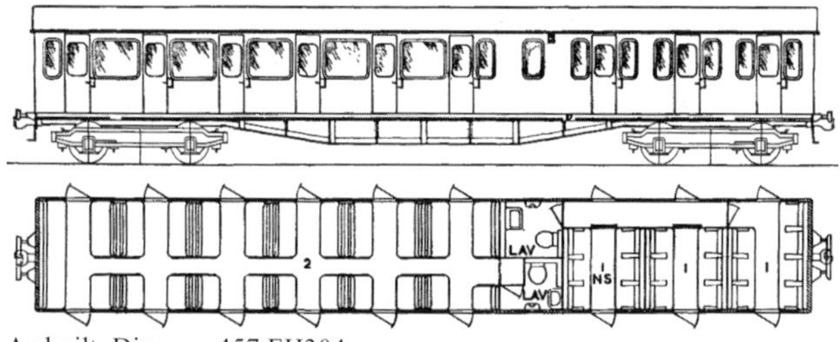

As built, Diagram 457 EH304

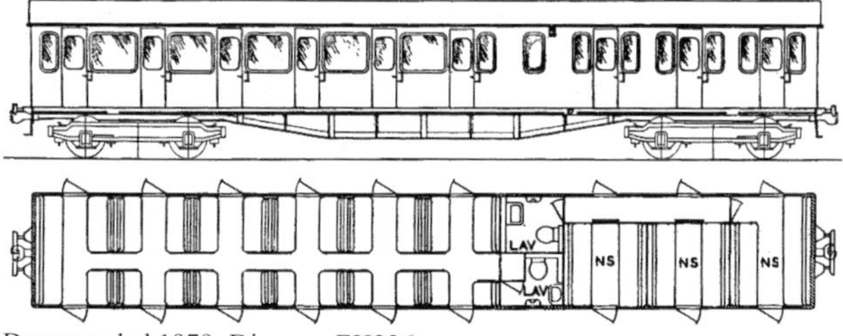

Downgraded 1979, Diagram EH226

Diagram:	457 EH304 EH226	Lot Number:	30644
Body:	63' 6⅛" × 9' 3"	Weight:	31t 15cwt
Seats:	19 first 60 second 2 toilets later 86 second 2 toilets	Bogies:	Gresley

M70243	07/61-10/84	⊗08/85	**036**	07/61-04/82	**304036**	04/82-10/84
M70244	07/61-10/84	⊗08/85	**037**	07/61-04/82	**304037**	04/82-10/84
M70245	07/61-12/84	⊗05/85	**038**	07/61- *83*	**304038**	*83*-12/84
M70246	08/61-10/84	⊗08/85	**039**	08/61- *83*	**304039**	*83*-10/84
M70247	08/61-10/84	⊗08/85	**040**	08/61-02/82	**304040**	02/82-10/84
M70248	08/61-10/84	⊗08/85	**041**	08/61-05/82	**304041**	05/82-10/84

M70249	09/61-01/85	⊗05/85	**042**	09/61-04/81	**304042**	04/81-07/84	**304008**	07/84-01/85
M70250	09/61-10/84	⊗08/85	**043**	09/61-07/83	**304043**	07/83-10/84		
M70251	09/61-12/84	⊗05/85	**044**	09/61-10/82	**304044**	10/82-12/84		
M70252	10/61-10/84	⊗08/85	**045**	10/61-02/83	**304045**	02/83-10/84		

Class 309 York

Trailer Second Open with Lavatory
TSOL
E70253-E70259

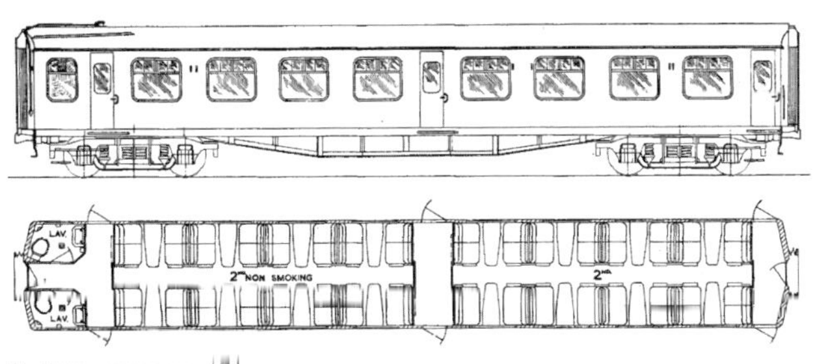

As built, Diagram 471

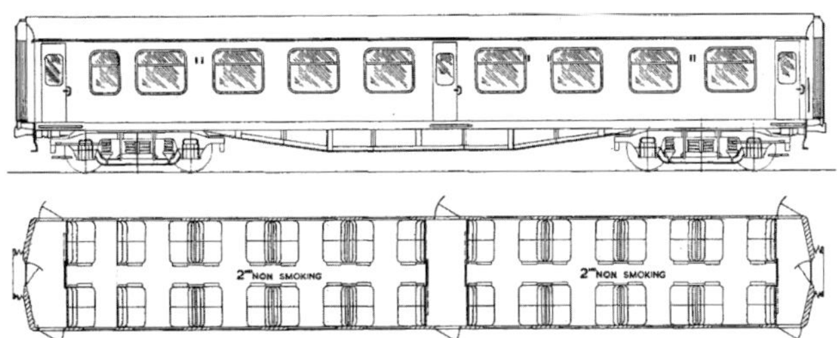

Refurbished Diagram EH206

Diagram:	471	Lot Number:	30677
Body:	64' 6" × 9' 3"	Weight:	34t 8cwt
Seats:	64 second 2 toilets	Bogies:	Commonwealth

E70253	07/62-05/92	⊗03/92	**621**	08/62-03/83	**309621**	03/83-05/92
E70254	07/62-11/92	⊗04/93	**622**	11/62-02/82	**309622**	02/82-11/92
E70255	07/62-08/92	⊗07/92	**623**	11/62-09/82	**309623**	09/82-07/92
E70256	07/62-06/00	⊗05/04	**624**	12/62-05/82	**309624**	05/82-06/00
E70257	07/62-12/91	⊗02/92	**625**	12/62-04/82	**309625**	04/82-12/91
E70258	07/62-12/94	⊗10/97	**626**	12/62-03/82	**309626**	03/82-12/94
E70259	07/62-11/99	⊗01/04	**627**	12/62-10/82	**309627**	10/82-11/99

Class 411 4-CEP Ashford/Eastleigh

Trailer Corridor Second
TSK later TSOL
S70260-S70302

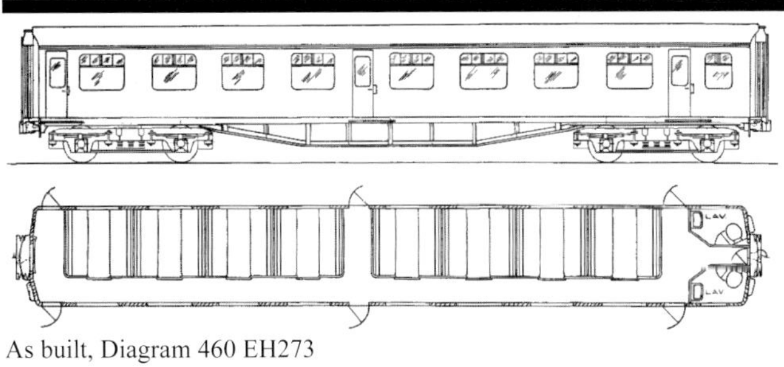

As built, Diagram 460 EH273

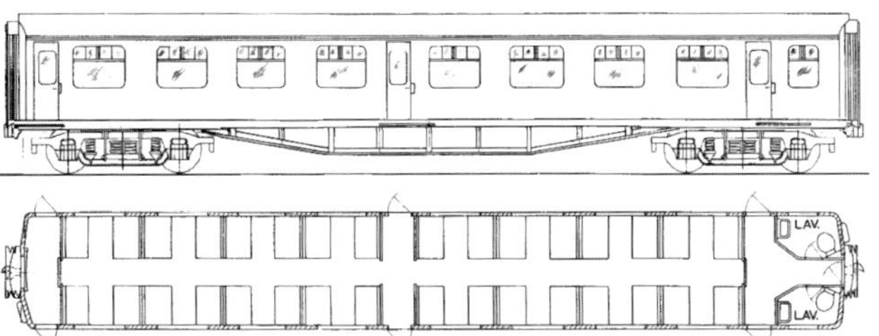

Prototype refurbished TSOL 70302, Diagram 901 EH277

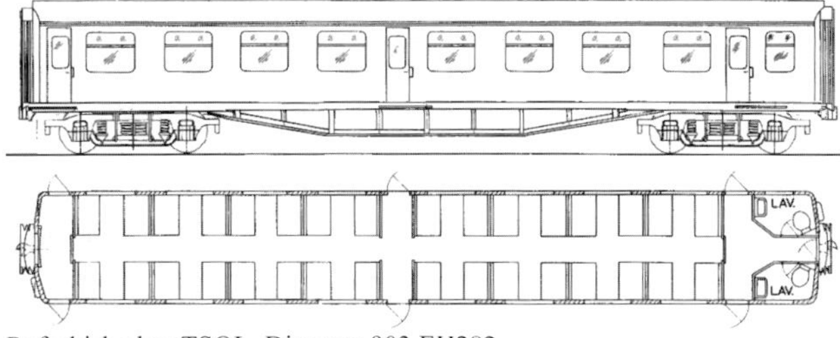

Refurbished as TSOL, Diagram 903 EH282

Diagram:	460 EH273 901 EH277 903 EH282	Lot Number:	30455
Body:	64' 6" × 9' 3"	Weight:	31t 0cwt
Seats:	64 second 2 toilets	Bogies:	Mk 6 later Commonwealth

S70260	09/58-05/95	⊗06/95	**7111**	09/58-01/80	**1508**	01/80-05/95		
S70261	09/58-10/04	⊗12/04	**7112**	09/58-02/82	**1538**	02/82-09/02	**2317**	09/02-10/04
S70262	10/58-	℗	**7113**	10/58-02/81	**1524**	02/81-11/85		
S70263	10/58-03/04	⊗	**7114**	10/58-10/82	**1553**	02/83-10/95	**1553**	04/96-03/04
S70264	10/58-08/04	⊗08/04	**7115**	10/58-12/82	**1550**	12/82-08/04		
S70265	10/58-04/04	⊗04/04	**7116**	10/58-06/82	**1544**	06/82-04/04		
S70266	10/58-08/04	⊗08/04	**7117**	10/58-11/80	**1517**	11/80-08/04		
S70267	11/58-06/95	⊗07/95	**7118**	11/58-10/80	[illegible]	[illegible]		
S70268	11/58-06/02	⊗	**7119**	11/58-06/80	**1512**	06/80-06/02		
S70269	11/58-07/93	⊗03/94	**7120**	11/58-04/82	**1543**	04/82-11/93		
S70270	11/58-12/02	⊗01/03	**7121**	11/58-12/82	**1551**	12/82-12/02		
S70271	11/58-06/95	⊗06/95	**7122**	11/58-08/80	**1514**	08/80-06/95		
S70272	12/58-10/04	⊗12/04	**7123**	12/58-09/82	**1547**	09/82-09/02	**2316**	09/02-10/04
S70273	12/58-05/05	℗	**7124**	12/58-06/81	**1530**	06/81-10/98	**1392**	07/99-05/05
S70274	12/58-08/96	⊗05/97	**7125**	12/58-11/80	**1518**	11/80-08/96		
S70275	12/58-12/02	⊗12/02	**7126**	12/58-02/80	**1509**	02/80-12/02		
S70276	12/58-05/93	⊗11/93	**7127**	12/58-07/83	**1558**	10/83-12/83	**1558**	03/86-05/93
S70277	12/58-05/99	⊗10/00	**7128**	12/58-11/82	**1549**	11/82-05/99		
S70278	01/59-05/95	⊗06/95	**7129**	01/59-06/80	**1513**	06/80-05/95		
S70279	01/59-04/04	⊗06/04	**7130**	01/59-03/79	**1602**	08/80-04/04		
S70280	01/59-04/96	⊗05/96	**7131**	01/59-09/80	**1515**	09/80-04/96		
S70281	01/59-06/95	⊗05/96	**7132**	01/59-12/80	**1521**	12/80-05/93	**1579**	10/93-05/93
S70282	01/59-01/93	⊗03/94	**7133**	01/59-12/79	**1506**	12/79-12/92		
S70283	01/59-08/04	⊗08/04	**7134**	01/59-10/82	**7114**	10/82-04/83	**1555**	04/83-08/04
S70284	01/59-05/99	℗	**7135**	01/59-12/80	**1520**	12/80-05/99		
S70285	02/59-11/93	⊗03/94	**7136**	02/59-05/81	**1529**	05/81-06/93		
S70286	02/59-06/95	⊗	**7137**	02/59-08/82	**1546**	08/82-06/95		
S70287	02/59-04/97	⊗04/99	**7138**	02/59-07/82	**1545**	07/82-04/97		
S70288	02/59-10/99	⊗05/01	**7139**	02/59-07/83	**1557**	07/83-09/83	**1557**	03/86-10/99
S70289	02/59-09/04	⊗09/04	**7140**	02/59-01/80	**1507**	01/80-12/02	**1571**	12/02-09/04
S70290	03/59-05/99	⊗03/01	**7141**	03/59-04/80	**1510**	04/80-05/99		
S70291	03/59-12/02	⊗01/03	**7142**	03/59-05/80	**1511**	05/80-12/02		
S70292	03/59-04/05	℗	**7143**	03/59-04/83	**1554**	04/83-07/99	**1398**	09/99-04/05
S70293	03/59-05/99	⊗08/11	**7144**	03/59-06/83	**1556**	06/83-08/83	**1556**	02/86-05/99
S70294	04/59-07/05	℗	**7145**	04/59-02/83	**1552**	02/83-10/96	**1697**	10/96-07/05
S70295	04/59-10/04	⊗12/04	**7146**	04/59-10/82	**1548**	10/82-09/02	**2312**	09/02-10/04
S70296	04/59-05/99	℗	**7147**	04/59-10/83	**1559**	10/83-05/99		
S70297	05/59-02/03	⊗02/03	**7148**	05/59-04/81	**1528**	04/81-07/93	**1543**	11/93-05/99
S70298	05/59-10/95	⊗04/96	**7149**	05/59-04/79	**1603**	07/80-10/95		
S70299	06/59-04/96	⊗05/96	**7150**	06/59-02/81	**1523**	02/81-04/96		
S70300	06/59-09/05	℗	**7151**	06/59-03/82	**1540**	03/82-08/96	**1698**	08/96-09/05
S70301	06/59-12/02	⊗12/02	**7152**	06/59-11/83	**1560**	11/83-12/83	**1560**	03/86-12/02
S70302	06/59-05/90	℗⊗	**7153**	06/59-11/85	**1500**	11/85-01/90		

Class 411 4-CEP Ashford/Eastleigh

Trailer Corridor Composite
TCK, later TBCK
S70303-S70355 (70346 onwards Class 410 4-BEP)

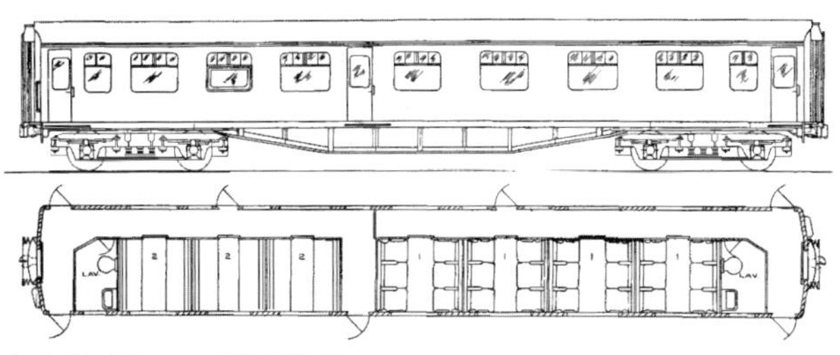

As built, Diagram 450 EH360

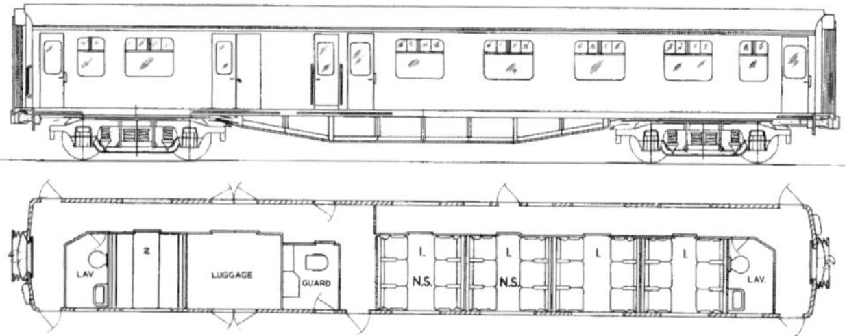

Prototype refurbished TBCK 70345, Diagram 921 EJ360

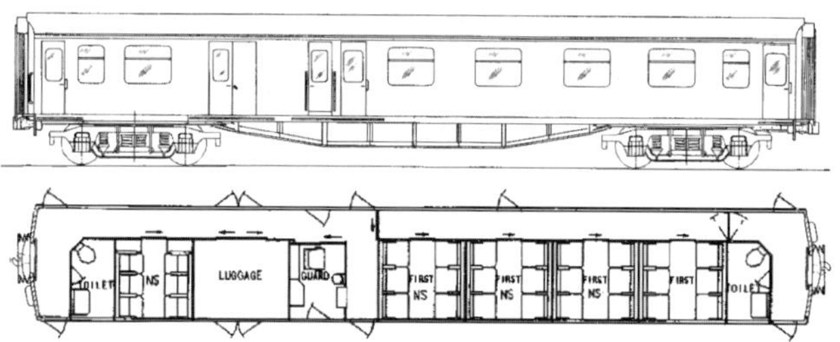

Refurbished as TBCK, Diagram 922 EJ361

Diagram:	450 EH360 922 EJ361	Lot Number:	30456
Body:	64' 6" × 9' 3"	Weight:	31t 0cwt
Seats:	24 first 24 second 2 toilets later 24 first 6 second 2 toilets	Bogies:	Mk 6 later Commonwealth

S70303	09/58-05/95	⊗06/95	**7111**	09/58-01/80	**1508**	01/80-05/95		
S70304	09/58-11/03	⊗02/04	**7112**	09/58-02/82	**1538**	02/82-09/02	**2327**	09/02-11/03
S70305	10/58-11/95	⊗04/96	**7113**	10/58-02/81	**1524**	02/81-11/85		
S70306	10/58-03/04	⊗	**7114**	10/58-10/82	**1553**	02/83-10/95	**1553**	04/96-03/04
S70307	10/58-08/04	⊗08/04	**7115**	10/58-12/82	**1550**	12/82-08/04		
S70308	10/58-04/04	⊗04/04	**7116**	10/58-06/82	**1544**	06/82-04/04		
S70309	10/58-08/04	⊗08/04	**7117**	10/58-11/80	**1517**	11/80-08/04		
S70310	11/58-06/95	⊗07/95	**7118**	11/58-10/80	**1516**	10/80-06/95		
S70311	11/58-04/04	⊗12/04	**7119**	11/58-06/80	**1512**	06/80-06/02	**1565**	04/03-04/04
S70312	11/58-08/02	⊗09/02	**7120**	11/58-04/82	**1543**	04/82-05/99	**1110**	05/99-08/02
S70313	11/58-12/02	⊗01/03	**7121**	11/58-12/82	**1551**	12/82-12/02		
S70314	11/58-06/95	⊗06/95	**7122**	11/58-08/80	**1514**	08/80-06/95		
S70315	12/58-01/90	⊗05/90	**7123**	12/58-09/82	**1547**	09/82-01/90		
S70316	12/58-04/03	⊗04/03	**7124**	12/58-06/81	**1530**	06/81-10/98	**1101**	10/98-04/03
S70317	12/58-08/96	⊗*05/97*	**7125**	12/58-11/80	**1518**	11/80-08/96		
S70318	12/58-12/02	⊗12/02	**7126**	12/58-02/80	**1509**	02/80-12/02		
S70319	12/58-05/93	⊗08/96	**7127**	12/58-07/83	**1558**	10/83-12/83	**2704**	12/83-03/86
			1558	03/86-05/93				
S70320	12/58-01/03	⊗01/03	**7128**	12/58-11/82	**1549**	11/82-05/99	**1111**	05/99-01/03
S70321	01/59-05/95	⊗06/95	**7129**	01/59-06/80	**1513**	06/80-05/95		
S70322	01/59-03/79	⊗02/80	**7130**	01/59-03/79				
S70323	01/59-04/96	⊗05/96	**7131**	01/59-09/80	**1515**	09/80-04/96		
S70324	01/59-06/94	⊗06/95	**7132**	01/59-12/80	**1521**	12/80-05/93	**1401**	05/93-06/94
S70325	01/59-01/93	⊗03/94	**7133**	01/59-12/79	**1506**	12/79-12/92		
S70326	01/59-08/04	⊗08/04	**7134**	01/59-10/82	**7114**	10/82-04/83	**1555**	04/83-08/04
S70327	01/59-03/03	⊗04/03	**7135**	01/59-12/80	**1520**	12/80-05/99	**1107**	05/99-03/03
S70328	02/59-06/94	⊗07/95	**7136**	02/59-05/81	**1529**	05/81-06/93	**1406**	06/93-06/94
S70329	02/59-06/95	⊗06/95	**7137**	02/59-08/82	**1546**	08/82-06/95		
S70330	02/59-04/97	➲Dep	**7138**	02/59-07/82	**1545**	07/82-04/97	**932545**	04/97- 02
S70331	02/59-10/99	⊗05/01	**7139**	02/59-07/83	**1557**	07/83-09/83	**2702**	09/83-03/86
			1557	03/86-10/99				
S70332	02/59-03/03	⊗03/03	**7140**	02/59-01/80	**1507**	01/80-12/02		
S70333	03/59-06/02	⊗09/02	**7141**	03/59-04/80	**1510**	04/80-05/99	**1106**	05/99-06/02
S70334	03/59-12/02	⊗01/03	**7142**	03/59-05/80	**1511**	05/80-12/02		
S70335	03/59-03/03	⊗04/03	**7143**	03/59-04/83	**1554**	04/83-07/99	**1112**	07/99-03/03
S70336	03/59-04/03	⊗04/03	**7144**	03/59-06/83	**1556**	06/83-08/83	**2701**	08/83-02/86
			1556	02/86-05/99	**1113**	05/99-04/03		
S70337	04/59-07/05	⊗12/05	**7145**	04/59-02/83	**1552**	02/83-10/96	**1697**	10/96-07/05
S70338	04/59-01/04	⊗02/04	**7146**	04/59-10/82	**1548**	10/82-09/02	**2322**	09/02-01/04
S70339	04/59-04/03	⊗04/03	**7147**	04/59-10/83	**1559**	10/83-05/99	**1114**	05/99-04/03
S70340	05/59-06/94	⊗07/95	**7148**	05/59-04/81	**1528**	04/81-07/93	**1405**	07/93-06/94
S70341	05/59-06/94	⊗07/95	**7149**	05/59-04/79	**1522**	01/81-05/93	**1402**	05/93-06/94
S70342	06/59-04/96	⊗05/96	**7150**	06/59-02/81	**1523**	02/81-04/96		
S70343	06/59-09/05	⊗12/05	**7151**	06/59-03/82	**1540**	03/82-08/96	**1698**	08/96-09/05
S70344	06/59-12/02	⊗12/02	**7152**	06/59-11/83	**1560**	11/83-12/83	**2703**	12/83-03/86
			1560	03/86-12/02				
S70345	06/59-06/97	Ⓟ	**7153**	06/59-11/85	**1500**	11/85-01/90	**1547**	01/90-05/97
S70346	03/59-08/97	Ⓟ⊗	**7003**	03/59-09/81	**1532**	09/81-08/97		
S70347	04/59-04/04	⊗08/04	**7004**	04/59-09/81	**1533**	09/81-04/04		
S70348	04/59-05/95	⊗06/95	**7005**	04/59-03/82	**1542**	03/82-05/95		
S70349	04/59-07/04	⊗	**7006**	04/59-11/81	**1535**	11/81-07/04		
S70350	04/59-02/03	⊗03/03	**7007**	04/59-11/81	**1536**	11/81-05/99	**1108**	05/99-02/03
S70351	05/59-09/04	⊗09/04	**7008**	05/59-11/81	**1539**	02/82-09/04		
S70352	05/59-04/04	⊗05/04	**7009**	05/59-11/80	**1519**	11/80-04/04		
S70353	05/59-04/04	⊗08/04	**7010**	05/59-10/81	**1534**	10/81-04/04		
S70354	05/59-12/04	Ⓟ	**7011**	05/59-08/83	**2305**	12/83-09/02	**2315**	09/02-12/04
S70355	05/59-06/02	⊗09/02	**7012**	05/59-11/81	**1541**	03/82-05/99	**1109**	05/99-06/02

Class 305/2 York/Doncaster

Trailer Composite (Semi-open) Lavatory

TCsoL, later TSOL

E70356-E70374

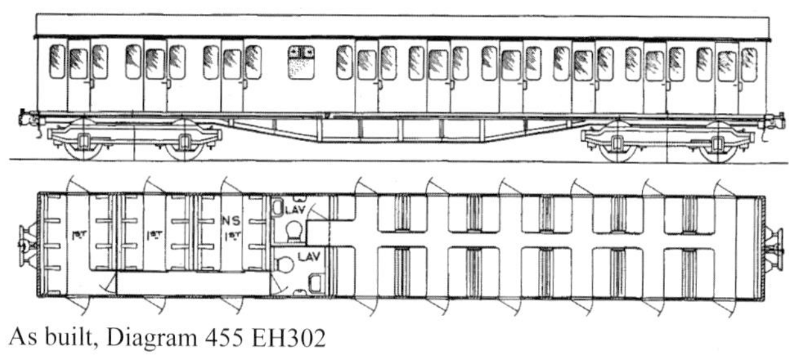

As built, Diagram 455 EH302

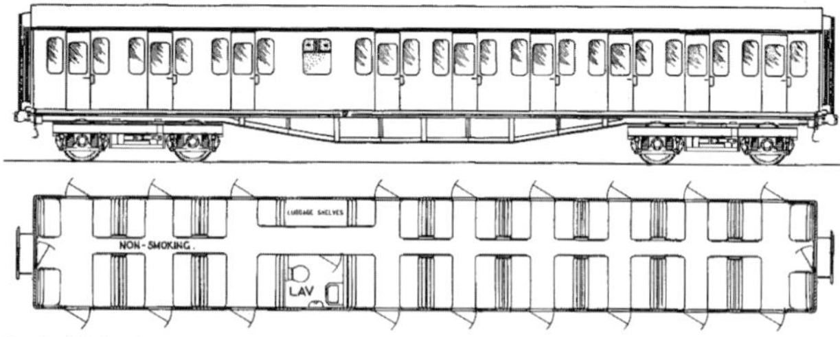

Refurbished 1983-84 with corridor and B4 bogies, Diagram EH223

Diagram:	455 EH302 EH223	Lot Number:	30568
Body:	63' 6" × 9' 3"	Weight:	30t 0cwt
Seats:	19 first 60 second 2 toilets later 86 second 1 toilet	Bogies:	Gresley later B4

E70356	10/59-12/01	⊗01/02	**501**	10/59-03/83	**305501**	03/83-12/01		
E70357	03/60-06/01	⊗11/01	**502**	03/60-04/83	**305502**	04/83-06/01		
E70358	04/60-03/93	⊗03/94	**503**	04/60-05/81	**305503**	05/81-03/93		
E70359	04/60-06/96	⊗07/96	**504**	04/60-11/81	**305504**	11/81-03/93	**305511**	03/93-06/96
E70360	04/60-03/93	⊗12/93	**505**	04/60-12/81	**305505**	05/83-09/90		
E70361	05/60-03/93	⊗09/93	**506**	05/60-07/81	**305506**	07/81-03/93		
E70362	05/60-11/97	⊗07/96	**507**	05/60-01/80	**305507**	01/80-03/93	**305515**	03/93-07/96
E70363	06/60-10/01	⊗11/01	**508**	06/60-03/83	**305508**	03/83-10/01		
E70364	07/60-03/93	⊗09/93	**509**	07/60- *83*	**305509**	*83*-03/93		
E70365	07/60-03/93	⊗09/93	**510**	07/60-03/83	**305510**	03/83-03/93		
E70366	07/60-03/93	⊗03/94	**511**	07/60-04/83	**305511**	04/83-03/93		
E70367	08/60-06/93	⊗02/94	**512**	08/60-09/81	**308138**	11/83-06/93		
E70368	08/60-10/95	⊗10/95	**513**	08/60-02/80	**305513**	02/80-03/93	**305503**	04/93-10/95
E70369	09/60-03/93	⊗09/93	**514**	09/60-02/81	**305514**	02/81-03/93		
E70370	10/60-03/93	⊗03/94	**515**	10/60-01/80	**305515**	01/80-03/93		
E70371	10/60-03/93	⊗03/94	**516**	10/60-02/83	**305516**	02/83-03/93		
E70372	10/60-12/01	⊗01/02	**517**	10/60-02/83	**305517**	02/83-12/01		
E70373	11/60-03/93	⊗10/95	**518**	11/60-08/81	**305518**	08/81-03/93	**305516**	03/93-03/93
E70374	11/60-12/01	⊗01/02	**519**	11/60-04/83	**305519**	04/83-12/01		

Class 415/2 4-EPB Eastleigh

Trailer Second (semi open)

TSso

S70375-S70482

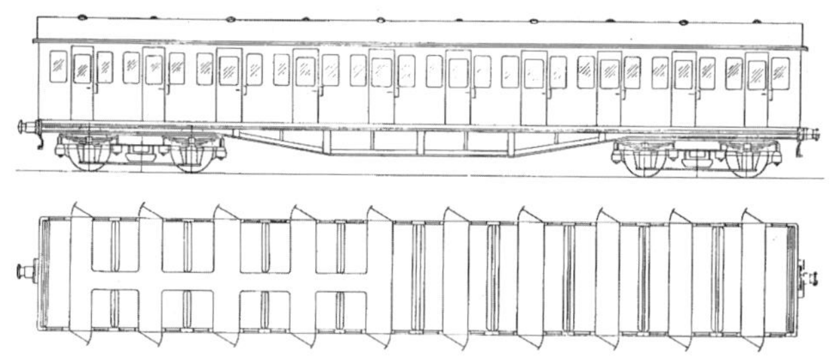

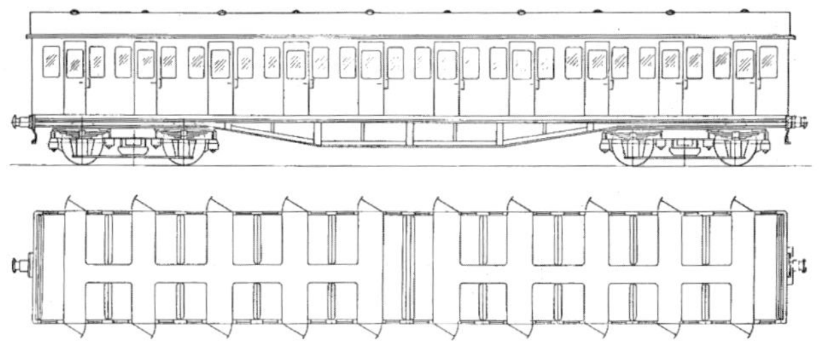

Facelifted and converted to open 1982-84 (units later renumbered in 56xx series)

Diagram:	480 EH271	Lot Number:	30583
Body:	63' 5⅛" × 9' 3"	Weight:	29t 0cwt
Seats:	112 second, facelifted 104 second	Bogies:	Mk 3D

Unit 5343 was damaged by an IRA bomb at Borough Market Junction in March 1976. S70455 was rebuilt and re-entered service as an open vehicle (prototype for the later facelifted units).

S70375	01/60-05/85	⊗01/86	**5303**	01/60-05/85				
[illegible]	[illegible]	[illegible]	[illegible]	[illegible]				
S70377	01/60-05/85	⊗05/86	**5304**	01/60-05/85				
S70378	01/60-05/85	⊗05/86	**5304**	01/60-05/85				
S70379	01/60-02/95	⊗05/95	**5305**	01/60-07/87	**5621**	07/87-02/95		
S70380	01/60-02/95	⊗05/95	**5305**	01/60-07/87	**5621**	07/87-02/95		
S70381	01/60-05/85	⊗06/86	**5306**	01/60-05/85				
S70382	01/60-05/85	⊗06/86	**5306**	01/60-05/85				
S70383	01/60-05/84	⊗10/85	**5307**	01/60-05/84				
S70384	01/60-05/84	⊗10/85	**5307**	01/60-05/84				
S70385	01/60-05/84	⊗06/86	**5308**	01/60-05/84				
S70386	01/60-05/84	⊗06/86	**5308**	01/60-05/84				
S70387	02/60-05/84	⊗08/85	**5309**	02/60-05/84				
S70388	02/60-05/84	⊗08/85	**5309**	02/60-05/84				
S70389	02/60-05/85	⊗02/86	**5310**	02/60-05/85				
S70390	02/60-05/85	⊗02/86	**5310**	02/60-05/85				
S70391	02/60-03/95	⊗03/95	**5311**	02/60-07/87	**5613**	07/87-03/95		
S70392	02/60-03/95	⊗03/95	**5311**	02/60-07/87	**5613**	07/87-03/95		
S70393	02/60-10/84	⊗10/85	**5312**	02/60-10/84				
S70394	02/60-10/84	⊗10/85	**5312**	02/60-10/84				
S70395	02/60-02/95	⊗03/95	**5313**	02/60-07/87	**5606**	07/87-02/95		
S70396	02/60-02/95	⊗03/95	**5313**	02/60-07/87	**5606**	07/87-02/95		
S70397	02/60-11/94	⊗02/95	**5314**	02/60-06/87	**5603**	06/87-11/94		
S70398	02/60-11/94	⊗02/95	**5314**	02/60-06/87	**5603**	06/87-11/94		
S70399	03/60-01/95	⊗01/95	**5315**	03/60-07/87	**5605**	07/87-01/95		
S70400	03/60-01/95	⊗01/95	**5315**	03/60-07/87	**5605**	07/87-01/95		
S70401	03/60-03/95	⊗04/95	**5316**	03/60-06/87	**5612**	06/87-03/95		
S70402	03/60-03/95	⊗04/95	**5316**	03/60-06/87	**5612**	06/87-03/95		
S70403	03/60-05/85	⊗04/86	**5317**	03/60-05/85				
S70404	03/60-05/85	⊗04/86	**5317**	03/60-05/85				
S70405	03/60-03/95	⊗04/95	**5318**	03/60-06/87	**5614**	06/87-03/95		
S70406	03/60-03/95	⊗04/95	**5318**	03/60-06/87	**5614**	06/87-03/95		
S70407	03/60-05/84	⊗02/85	**5319**	03/60-05/84				
S70408	03/60-05/84	⊗02/85	**5319**	03/60-05/84				
S70409	03/60-02/95	⊗03/95	**5320**	03/60-07/87	**5601**	07/87-05/93	**5602**	09/93-02/95
S70410	03/60-05/93	⊗11/93	**5320**	03/60-07/87	**5601**	07/87-05/93		
S70411	03/60-10/84	⊗11/85	**5321**	03/60-10/84				
S70412	03/60-10/84	⊗11/85	**5321**	03/60-10/84				
S70413	03/60-05/85	⊗07/87	**5322**	03/60-05/85				
S70414	03/60-05/85	⊗07/87	**5322**	03/60-05/85				
S70415	03/60-08/84	⊗10/86	**5323**	03/60-08/84				
S70416	03/60-08/84	⊗10/86	**5323**	03/60-08/84				
S70417	03/60-05/85	⊗05/86	**5324**	03/60-05/85				
S70418	03/60-05/85	⊗05/86	**5324**	03/60-05/85				
S70419	04/60-01/95	⊗02/95	**5325**	04/60-07/87	**5622**	07/87-01/95		
S70420	04/60-01/95	⊗02/95	**5325**	04/60-07/87	**5622**	07/87-01/95		
S70421	04/60-01/95	⊗02/95	**5326**	04/60-07/87	**5619**	07/87-01/95		
S70422	04/60-01/95	⊗02/95	**5326**	04/60-07/87	**5619**	07/87-01/95		
S70423	04/60-05/85	⊗08/86	**5327**	04/60-05/85				
S70424	04/60-05/85	⊗08/86	**5327**	04/60-05/85				
S70425	04/60-11/94	⊗12/94	**5328**	04/60-07/87	**5610**	07/87-11/94		
S70426	04/60-11/94	⊗12/94	**5328**	04/60-07/87	**5610**	07/87-11/94		
S70427	04/60-12/83	⊗12/86	**5329**	04/60-12/83				
S70428	04/60-12/83	⊗12/86	**5329**	04/60-12/83				
S70429	04/60-10/94	⊗11/94	**5330**	04/60-07/87	**5611**	07/87-10/94		
S70430	04/60-10/94	⊗11/94	**5330**	04/60-07/87	**5611**	07/87-10/94		
S70431	04/60-03/95	⊗03/95	**5331**	04/60-07/87	**5624**	07/87-03/95		
S70432	04/60-03/95	⊗03/95	**5331**	04/60-07/87	**5624**	07/87-03/95		
S70433	04/60-05/85	⊗04/86	**5332**	04/60-05/85				
S70434	04/60-05/85	⊗04/86	**5332**	04/60-05/85				
S70435	05/60-02/95	⊗03/95	**5333**	05/60-07/87	**5616**	07/87-02/95		
S70436	05/60-02/95	⊗03/95	**5333**	05/60-07/87	**5616**	07/87-02/95		
S70437	05/60-02/95	⊗03/95	**5334**	05/60-07/87	**5623**	07/87-02/95		
S70438	05/60-02/92	⊗03/95	**5334**	05/60-07/87	**5623**	07/87-02/95		
S70439	05/60-05/85	⊗05/86	**5335**	05/60-05/85				
S70440	05/60-05/85	⊗05/86	**5335**	05/60-05/85				
S70441	05/60-09/93	⊗11/93	**5336**	05/60-07/87	**5602**	07/87-09/93		
S70442	05/60-02/95	⊗03/95	**5336**	05/60-07/87	**5602**	07/87-02/95		
S70443	05/60-05/91	⊗11/92	**5337**	05/60-07/87	**5618**	07/87-05/91		
S70444	05/60-05/91	⊗01/92	**5337**	05/60-07/87	**5618**	07/87-05/91		
S70445	05/60-05/84	⊗07/85	**5338**	05/60-05/84				
S70446	05/60-05/84	⊗07/85	**5338**	05/60-05/84				
S70447	06/60-03/95	⊗04/95	**5339**	06/60-06/87	**5604**	06/87-03/95		
S70448	06/60-03/95	⊗04/95	**5339**	06/60-06/87	**5604**	06/87-03/95		
S70449	06/60-10/94	⊗11/94	**5340**	06/60-07/87	**5607**	07/87-09/88	**5626**	09/88-10/94
S70450	06/60-10/94	⊗11/94	**5340**	06/60-07/87	**5607**	07/87-09/88	**5626**	09/88-10/94
S70451	06/60-03/95	⊗04/95	**5341**	06/60-07/87	**5617**	07/87-03/95		
S70452	06/60-03/95	⊗04/95	**5341**	06/60-07/87	**5617**	07/87-03/95		
S70453	06/60-08/84	⊗11/85	**5342**	06/60-08/84				
S70454	06/60-08/84	⊗11/85	**5342**	06/60-08/84				
S70455	06/60-03/95	⊗04/95	**5343**	06/60-05/84	**5349**	05/84-07/87	**5625**	07/87-03/95
S70456	06/60-05/84	⊗10/85	**5343**	06/60-05/84				
S70457	06/60-03/85	⊗10/86	**5344**	06/60-03/85				
S70458	06/60-03/85	⊗10/86	**5344**	06/60-03/85				
S70459	09/61-03/95	⊗05/95	**5345**	09/61-06/87	**5608**	06/87-09/88	**5627**	09/88-03/95
S70460	09/61-03/95	⊗05/95	**5345**	09/61-06/87	**5608**	06/87-09/88	**5627**	09/88-03/95
S70461	10/61-01/95	⊗02/95	**5346**	10/61-07/87	**5620**	07/87-01/95		
S70462	10/61-01/95	⊗02/95	**5346**	10/61-07/87	**5620**	07/87-01/95		
S70463	10/61-10/94	⊗11/94	**5347**	10/61-07/87	**5609**	07/87-10/88	**5628**	10/88-10/94
S70464	10/61-10/94	⊗11/94	**5347**	10/61-07/87	**5609**	07/87-10/88	**5628**	10/88-10/94
S70465	10/61-05/85	⊗05/86	**5348**	10/61-05/85				
[illegible]	[illegible]	[illegible]	[illegible]	[illegible]				
S70467	10/61-05/84	⊗10/85	**5349**	10/61-05/84				
S70468	10/61-03/95	⊗04/95	**5349**	10/61-07/87	**5625**	07/87-03/95		
S70469	11/61-05/85	⊗12/85	**5350**	11/61-05/85				
S70470	11/61-05/85	⊗12/85	**5350**	11/61-05/85				
S70471	11/61-02/95	⊗03/95	**5351**	11/61-07/87	**5615**	07/87-02/95		
S70472	11/61-02/95	⊗03/95	**5351**	11/61-07/87	**5615**	07/87-02/95		
S70473	11/61-02/85	⊗08/86	**5352**	11/61-10/62	**5352**	12/64-02/85		
S70474	11/61-02/85	⊗08/86	**5352**	11/61-10/62	**5352**	12/64-02/85		
S70475	11/61-05/85	⊗12/85	**5353**	11/61-05/85				
S70476	11/61-05/85	⊗12/85	**5353**	11/61-05/85				
S70477	12/61-05/85	⊗12/85	**5354**	12/61-05/85				
S70478	12/61-05/85	⊗12/85	**5354**	12/61-05/85				
S70479	12/61-05/85	⊗04/86	**5355**	12/61-05/85				
S70480	12/61-05/85	⊗04/86	**5355**	12/61-05/85				
S70481	01/62-05/85	⊗12/86	**5356**	01/62-05/85				
S70482	01/62-05/85	⊗12/86	**5356**	01/62-05/85				

Class 304/2 Wolverton

Trailer Composite (Semi-open) Lavatory TCsoL, later TSsoL M70483-M70502

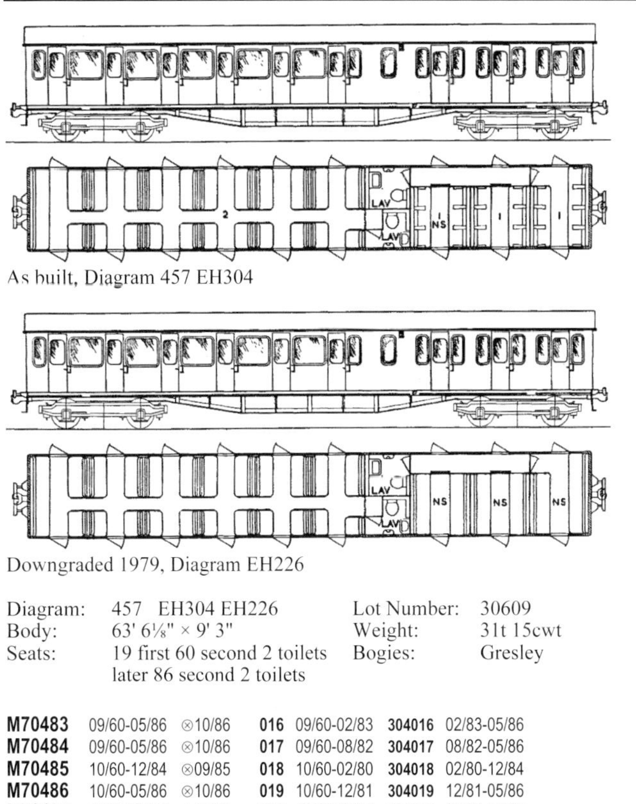

As built, Diagram 457 EH304

Downgraded 1979, Diagram EH226

Diagram:	457 EH304 EH226	Lot Number:	30609
Body:	63' 6⅛" × 9' 3"	Weight:	31t 15cwt
Seats:	19 first 60 second 2 toilets later 86 second 2 toilets	Bogies:	Gresley

M70483	09/60-05/86	⊗10/86	**016**	09/60-02/83	**304016**	02/83-05/86
M70484	09/60-05/86	⊗10/86	**017**	09/60-08/82	**304017**	08/82-05/86
M70485	10/60-12/84	⊗09/85	**018**	10/60-02/80	**304018**	02/80-12/84
M70486	10/60-05/86	⊗10/86	**019**	10/60-12/81	**304019**	12/81-05/86
M70487	10/60-05/86	⊗10/86	**020**	10/60-07/81	**304020**	07/81-05/86
M70488	10/60-05/86	⊗10/86	**021**	10/60-12/81	**304021**	12/81-05/86
M70489	11/60-12/84	⊗09/85	**022**	11/60-08/82	**304022**	08/82-12/84

M70490	11/60-09/85	⊗12/85	**023**	11/60-05/82	**304023**	05/82-09/85		
M70491	11/60-05/86	⊗10/86	**024**	11/60-05/81	**304024**	05/81-05/86		
M70492	12/60-12/84	⊗05/85	**025**	12/60-02/80	**304025**	02/80-12/84		
M70493	12/60-12/67	⊗*03/76*	**026**	12/60-12/67				
M70494	12/60-05/86	⊗10/86	**027**	12/60-07/83	**304027**	07/83-09/85	**304023**	09/85-05/86
M70495	01/61-09/85	⊗12/85	**028**	01/61-08/82	**304028**	08/82-09/85		
M70496	01/61-09/85	⊗12/85	**029**	01/61-06/81	**304029**	06/81-09/85		
M70497	01/61-05/85	⊗05/85	**030**	01/61-06/81	**304030**	06/81-05/85		
M70498	02/61-05/85	⊗08/85	**031**	02/61-06/81	**304031**	06/81-05/85		
M70499	02/61-10/84	⊗08/85	**032**	02/61-09/81	**304032**	09/81-10/84		
M70500	02/61-10/84	⊗08/85	**033**	02/61-10/84	**304033**	10/84-10/84		
M70501	03/61-10/84	⊗08/85	**034**	03/61-06/84	**304034**	06/84-10/84		
M70502	06/61-10/84	⊗08/85	**035**	06/61-04/82	**304035**	04/82-10/84		

Class 411 4-CEP Ashford/Eastleigh

Trailer Corridor Second
TSK, later TSOL
S70503-S70551

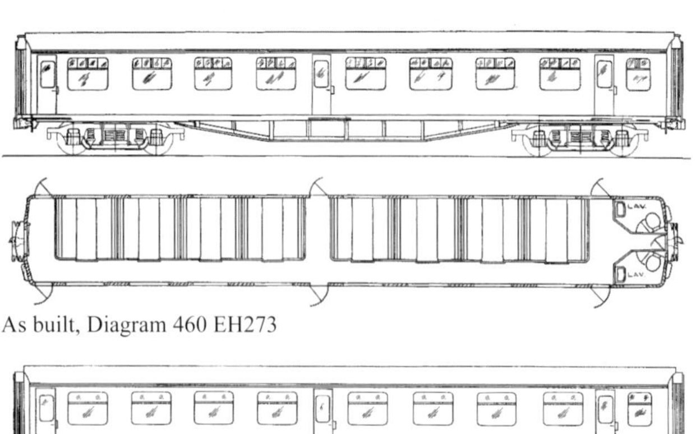

As built, Diagram 460 EH273

Refurbished as TSOL, Diagram 903 EH282

Diagram:	460 EH273 903 EH282	Lot Number:	30620
Body:	64' 6" × 9' 3"	Weight:	31t 0cwt
Seats:	64 second 2 toilets	Bogies:	Commonwealth

S70503	07/60-08/95	⊗*05/97*	**7154**	07/60-03/80	**1606**	03/80-08/95		
S70504	08/60-06/04	⊗06/04	**7155**	08/60-06/81	**1590**	06/81-06/04		
S70505	09/60-06/03	⊗06/03	**7156**	09/60-03/80	**1607**	03/80-06/03		
S70506	09/60-09/04	⊗09/04	**7157**	09/60-02/82	**1578**	02/82-09/04		
S70507	09/60-03/03	⊗06/03	**7158**	09/60-04/83	**1614**	04/83-03/03		
S70508	09/60-04/05	Ⓟ	**7159**	09/60-02/81	**1595**	02/81-07/99	**1399**	09/99-04/05
S70509	09/60-01/03	⊗01/03	**7160**	09/60-10/80	**1599**	10/80-01/03		
S70510	09/60-05/99	Ⓟ	**7161**	09/60-01/81	**1597**	01/81-05/99		
S70511	01/61-08/02	⊗09/02	**7162**	01/61-10/81	**1585**	10/81-08/02		
S70512	10/60-07/05	Ⓟ	**7163**	10/60-04/80	**1605**	04/80-06/96	**1699**	06/96-07/05
S70513	10/60-03/03	⊗03/03	**7164**	10/60-08/81	**1586**	08/81-03/03		
S70514	10/60-04/96	⊗05/96	**7165**	10/60-01/81	**1596**	01/81-04/96		
S70515	10/60-05/05	⊗06/05	**7166**	10/60-02/82	**1577**	02/82-05/99	**1397**	09/99-05/05
S70516	10/60-01/03	⊗05/05	**7167**	10/60-08/80	**1519**	11/80-01/00		
S70517	10/60-05/04	⊗	**7168**	10/60-11/82	**1566**	11/82-09/02	**2314**	09/02-05/04
S70518	10/60-03/96	⊗06/96	**7169**	10/60-09/80	**1600**	09/80-03/96		
S70519	11/60-04/04	⊗05/04	**7170**	11/60-05/82	**1573**	05/82-04/04		
S70520	11/60-11/01	⊗09/02	**7171**	11/60-07/80	**1588**	08/81-11/01		
S70521	11/60-03/04	⊗04/04	**7172**	11/60-04/81	**1593**	04/81-03/04		
S70522	11/60-08/95	⊗04/96	**7173**	11/60-07/80	**1604**	07/80-08/85		
S70523	11/60-03/99	⊗03/01	**7174**	11/60-06/82	**1572**	06/82-03/99		
S70524	11/60-05/93	⊗11/93	**7175**	11/60-11/83	**1621**	03/84-05/93		
S70525	11/60-11/02	⊗11/02	**7176**	11/60-08/82	**1570**	08/82-11/02		
S70526	12/60-03/04	⊗05/04	**7177**	12/60-01/83	**1563**	01/83-03/04		
S70527	12/60-04/05	Ⓟ	**7178**	12/60-07/81	**1589**	07/81-04/97	**1393**	07/99-04/05
S70528	12/60-12/02	⊗01/03	**7179**	12/60-02/83	**1609**	02/83-12/02		
S70529	12/60-04/96	⊗04/96	**7180**	12/60-10/81	**1583**	10/81-04/96		
S70530	12/60-05/69	⊗01/69	**7181**	12/60-01/69				
S70531	01/61-05/05	Ⓟ	**7182**	01/61-02/83	**1610**	02/83-09/98	**1396**	09/99-05/05
S70532	01/61-11/02	⊗11/02	**7183**	01/61-03/82	**1584**	03/82-11/02		
S70533	01/61-03/04	⊗05/04	**7184**	01/61-03/81	**1594**	03/81-03/04		
S70534	01/61-05/99	⊗01/03	**7185**	01/61-12/81	**1580**	12/81-05/99		
S70535	02/61-04/04	⊗05/04	**7186**	02/61-03/83	**1612**	03/83-04/04		
S70536	02/61-04/04	⊗05/04	**7187**	02/61-04/83	**1613**	04/83-11/98	**1519**	01/00-04/04
S70537	02/61-12/02	⊗01/03	**7188**	02/61-01/83	**1611**	03/83-12/02		
S70538	02/61-10/72	⊗12/73	**7189**	02/61-11/71				
S70539	03/61-12/04	Ⓟ	**7190**	03/61-09/82	**1568**	09/82-09/02	**2311**	09/02-12/04
S70540	03/61-10/02	⊗10/02	**7191**	03/61-12/81	**1575**	04/82-10/02		
S70541	03/61-08/02	⊗09/02	**7192**	03/61-04/82	**1576**	04/82-08/02		
S70542	03/61-05/93	⊗11/93	**7193**	03/61-01/82	**1579**	01/82-05/93		
S70543	04/61-03/03	⊗06/03	**7194**	04/61-06/83	**1616**	06/83-03/03		
S70544	04/61-05/95	⊗04/96	**7195**	04/61-09/80	**1601**	09/80-05/95		
S70545	06/61-06/04	⊗06/04	**7196**	06/61-05/81	**1592**	05/81-06/04		
S70546	06/61-09/95	⊗04/96	**7197**	06/61-11/80	**1598**	11/80-09/95		
S70547	06/61-05/95	Ⓟ	**7198**	06/61-08/82	**1569**	08/82-05/95		
S70548	07/61-04/04	⊗05/04	**7199**	07/61-11/81	**1581**	11/81-04/04		
S70549	07/61-04/95	Ⓟ	**7200**	07/61-10/82	**1567**	10/82-04/95		
S70550	07/61-03/03	⊗03/03	**7201**	07/61-12/82	**1564**	12/82-03/03		
S70551	08/61-09/02	⊗09/02	**7202**	08/61-06/81	**1591**	06/81-09/02		

Class 411 4-CEP Ashford/Eastleigh

Trailer Corridor Composite
TCK, later TBCK
S70552-S70610 **(70601 onwards Class 410 4-BEP)**

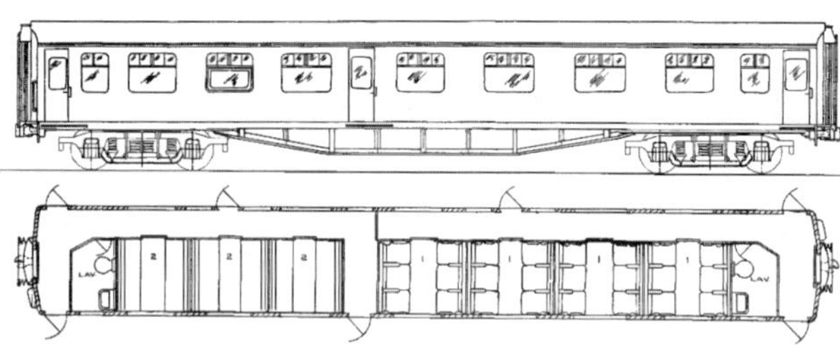

As built, Diagram 450 EH361

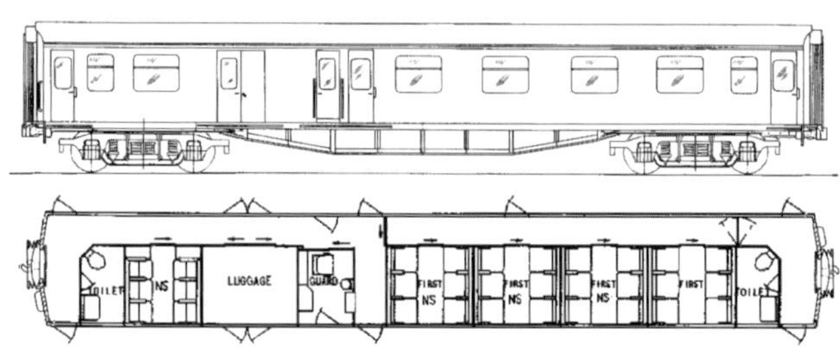

Refurbished as TBCK, Diagram 922 EJ361

Diagram:	450 EH361 922 EJ361	Lot Number:	30639
Body:	64' 6" × 9' 3"	Weight:	31t 0cwt
Seats:	24 first 24 second 2 toilets later 24 first 6 second 2 toilets	Bogies:	Commonwealth

S70552	07/60-08/95	⊗*05/97*	**7154**	07/60-03/80	**1606**	03/80-08/95		
S70553	08/60-06/04	⊗06/04	**7155**	08/60-06/81	**1590**	06/81-06/04		
S70554	09/60-06/03	⊗06/03	**7156**	09/60-03/80	**1607**	03/80-06/03		
S70555	09/60-09/04	⊗09/04	**7157**	09/60-02/82	**1578**	02/82-09/04		
S70556	09/60-03/03	⊗06/03	**7158**	09/60-04/83	**1614**	04/83-03/03		
S70557	09/60-03/03	⊗04/03	**7159**	09/60-02/81	**1595**	02/81-07/99	**1117**	07/99-03/03
S70558	09/60-01/03	⊗04/04	**7160**	09/60-10/80	**1599**	10/80-01/03		
S70559	09/60-03/03	⊗04/03	**7161**	09/60-01/81	**1597**	01/81-05/99	**1118**	05/99-03/03
S70560	01/61-08/02	⊗09/02	**7162**	01/61-10/81	**1585**	10/81-08/02		
S70561	10/60-07/05	⊗08/05	**7163**	10/60-04/80	**1605**	04/80-06/96	**1699**	06/96-07/05
S70562	10/60-03/03	⊗03/03	**7164**	10/60-08/81	**1586**	08/81-03/03		
S70563	10/60-04/96	⊗05/96	**7165**	10/60-01/81	**1596**	01/81-04/96		
S70564	10/60-08/02	⊗09/02	**7166**	10/60-02/82	**1577**	02/82-05/99	**1115**	05/99-08/02
S70565	10/60-04/04	⊗06/04	**7167**	10/60-08/80	**1602**	08/80-04/04		
S70566	10/60-04/04	⊗02/04	**7168**	10/60-11/82	**1566**	11/82-09/02	**2324**	09/02-11/03
S70567	10/60-03/96	⊗06/96	**7169**	10/60-09/80	**1600**	09/80-03/96		
S70568	11/60-04/04	⊗	**7170**	11/60-05/82	**1573**	05/82-04/04		
S70569	11/60-10/95	⊗04/96	**7171**	11/60-07/80	**1603**	07/80-10/95		
S70570	11/60-03/04	⊗04/04	**7172**	11/60-04/81	**1593**	04/81-03/04		
S70571	11/60-08/95	⊗04/96	**7173**	11/60-07/80	**1604**	07/80-08/85		
S70572	11/60-03/99	⊗03/01	**7174**	11/60-06/82	**1572**	06/82-03/99		
S70573	11/60-12/04	Ⓟ	**7175**	11/60-11/83	**2304**	11/83-09/02	**2314**	09/02-05/04
			1198	05/04-12/04				
S70574	11/60-11/02	⊗11/02	**7176**	11/60-08/82	**1570**	08/82-11/02		
S70575	12/60-03/04	⊗05/04	**7177**	12/60-01/83	**1563**	01/83-03/04		
S70576	12/60-04/97	Ⓟ	**7178**	12/60-07/81	**1589**	07/81-04/97		
S70577	12/60-12/02	⊗01/03	**7179**	12/60-02/83	**1609**	02/83-12/02		
S70578	12/60-05/04	⊗08/04	**7180**	12/60-10/81	**1583**	10/81-04/96	**1547**	05/97-09/02
			2326	09/02-01/03	**1199**	01/03-05/04		
S70579	12/60-05/69	⊗12/71	**7181**	12/60-01/69				
S70580	01/61-04/03	⊗04/03	**7182**	01/61-02/83	**1610**	02/83-09/98	**1103**	09/98-04/03
S70581	01/61-11/02	⊗11/02	**7183**	01/61-03/82	**1584**	03/82-11/02		
S70582	01/61-03/04	⊗05/04	**7184**	01/61-03/81	**1594**	03/81-03/04		
S70583	01/61-10/02	⊗10/02	**7185**	01/61-12/81	**1575**	04/82-10/02		
S70584	02/61-12/02	⊗01/03	**7186**	02/61-03/83	**1611**	03/83-12/02		
S70585	02/61-12/02	⊗12/02	**7187**	02/61-04/83	**1613**	04/83-11/98	**1104**	11/98-12/02
S70586	02/61-04/03	⊗05/03	**7188**	02/61-01/83	**1565**	01/83-04/03		

S70587	02/61-10/02	⊗10/02	**7189**	02/61-08/81	**1587**	08/81-10/02		
S70588	03/61-11/03	⊗02/04	**7190**	03/61-09/82	**1568**	09/82-09/02	**2321**	09/02-11/03
S70589	03/61-03/03	⊗04/03	**7191**	03/61-12/81	**1580**	12/81-05/99	**1116**	05/99-03/03
S70590	03/61-08/02	⊗09/02	**7192**	03/61-04/82	**1576**	04/82-08/02		
S70591	03/61-06/95	⊗05/96	**7193**	03/61-01/82	**1579**	01/82-05/93	**1579**	10/93-05/93
S70592	04/61-10/04	⊗12/04	**7194**	04/61-06/83	**2302**	06/83-09/02	**2312**	09/02-10/04
S70593	04/61-05/95	⊗04/96	**7195**	04/61-09/80	**1601**	09/80-05/95		
S70594	06/61-06/04	⊗06/04	**7196**	06/61-05/81	**1592**	05/81-06/04		
S70595	06/61-09/95	⊗04/96	**7197**	06/61-11/80	**1598**	11/80-09/95		
S70596	06/61-05/95	⊗06/95	**7198**	06/61-08/82	**1569**	08/82-05/95		
S70597	07/61-04/04	⊗05/04	**7199**	07/61-11/81	**1581**	11/81-04/04		
S70598	07/61-04/95	⊗06/95	**7200**	07/61-10/82	**1567**	10/82-04/95		
S70599	07/61-03/03	⊗03/03	**7201**	07/61-12/82	**1564**	12/82-03/03		
S70600	08/61-09/02	⊗09/02	**7202**	08/61-06/81	**1501**	06/81-09/02		
S70601	01/61-12/02	⊗12/02	**7013**	01/61-05/82	**1574**	05/82-12/02		
S70602	01/61-04/04	⊗04/04	**7014**	01/61-03/83	**1612**	03/83-04/04		
S70603	03/61-11/02	⊗12/02	**7015**	03/61-11/81	**1582**	11/81-12/02		
S70604	03/61-04/03	⊗04/03	**7016**	03/61-12/83	**1561**	12/83-10/98	**1102**	10/98-04/03
S70605	04/61-10/99	⊗05/01	**7017**	04/61-07/83	**1617**	07/83-10/99		
S70606	04/61-10/04	⊗12/04	**7018**	04/61-12/83	**2307**	03/84-09/02	**2317**	09/02-10/04
S70607	05/61-12/04	Ⓟ	**7019**	05/61-02/82	**2301**	02/82-09/02	**2311**	09/02-12/04
S70608	06/61-09/04	⊗09/04	**7020**	06/61-06/82	**1571**	06/82-09/02	**2323**	09/02-12/02
			1571	12/02-09/04				
S70609	06/61-10/04	⊗12/04	**7021**	06/61-12/83	**2306**	02/84-09/02	**2316**	09/02-10/04
S70610	03/61-05/03	⊗11/03	**7022**	03/61-09/83	**1621**	03/84-05/03		

Class 308/1 York

Trailer Composite (Semi-open) Lavatory
TCsoL, later TSOL
E70611-E70619

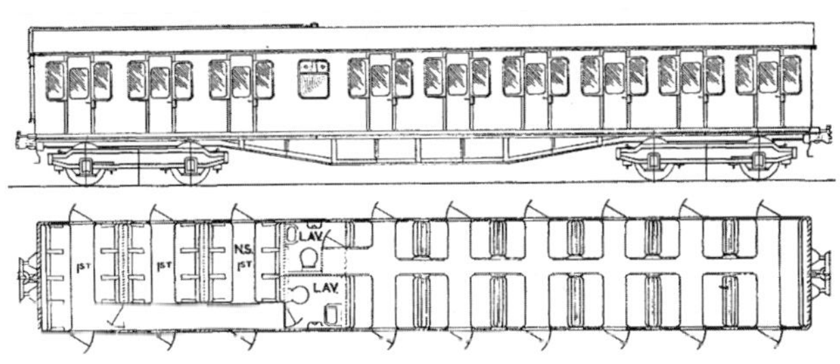

As built, Diagram 451 EH305

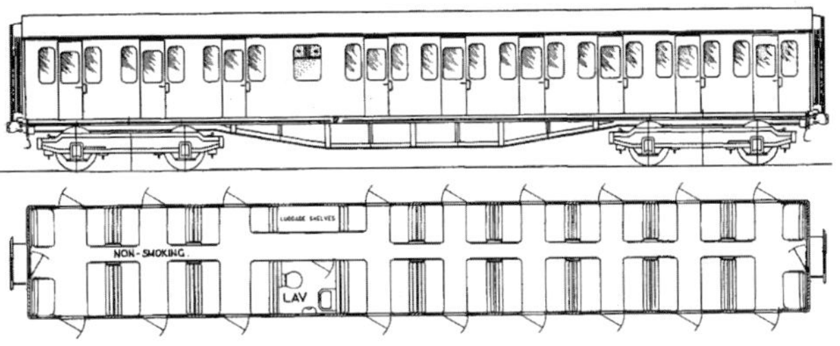

Refurbished as TSOL, Diagram EH223

Diagram:	451 EH305 EH223	Lot Number:	30654
Body:	63' 6⅛" × 9' 3"	Weight:	30t 18cwt
Seats:	19 first 60 second 2 toilets later 86 second 1 toilet	Bogies:	Gresley

E70611	01/61-05/93	⊗03/94	**133**	01/61-04/81	**308133**	04/81-05/93		
E70612	01/61-09/93	⊗01/05	**134**	01/61-08/81	**308134**	08/81-09/93		
E70613	01/61-06/93	⊗02/94	**135**	01/61-08/81	**308135**	08/81-07/92	**308156**	07/92-06/93
E70614	01/61-06/93	⊗02/94	**136**	01/61-01/82	**308136**	01/82-06/93		
E70615	02/61-06/93	⊗03/94	**137**	02/61-12/81	**308137**	12/81-06/93		
E70616	02/61-12/81	⊗06/82	**138**	02/61-12/81				
E70617	02/61-11/93	⊗06/94	**139**	02/61-10/82	**308139**	10/82-11/93		
E70618	02/61-06/93	⊗02/94	**140**	02/61-05/81	**308140**	05/81-06/93		
E70619	03/61-09/93	⊗02/94	**141**	03/61-08/81	**308141**	08/81-09/93		

Class 308/1 York

Trailer Composite (Semi-open) Lavatory
TCsoL, later TSOL
E70620-E70652 (70644 onwards Class 308/2)

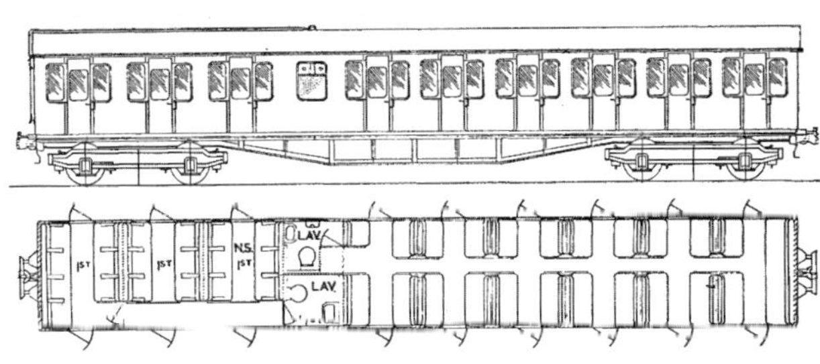

As built, Diagram 451 EH305

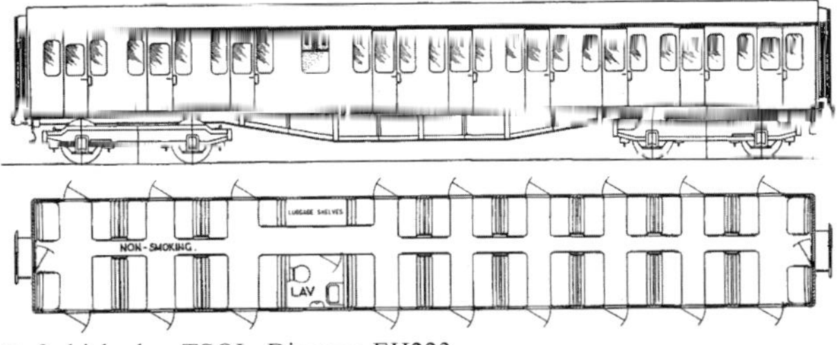

Refurbished as TSOL, Diagram EH223

Diagram:	451 EH305 EH223	Lot Number:	30658
Body:	63' 6⅛" × 9' 3"	Weight:	30t 18cwt
Seats:	19 first 60 second 2 toilets later 86 second 1 toilet	Bogies:	Gresley

E70620	03/61-05/93	⊗02/95	**142**	03/61-01/82	**308142**	01/82-05/93		
E70621	03/61-06/93	⊗05/04	**143**	03/61-01/82	**308143**	01/82-06/93		
E70622	03/61-06/93	⊗	**144**	03/61-12/81	**308144**	12/81-06/93		
E70623	04/61-11/93	⊗06/94	**145**	04/61-03/82	**308145**	03/82-11/93		
E70624	04/61-06/95	⊗06/95	**146**	04/61-02/80	**308146**	02/80-06/95		
E70625	04/61-06/93	⊗03/94	**147**	04/61-03/82	**308147**	03/02-06/93		
E70626	04/61-05/93	⊗03/94	**148**	04/61-12/82	**308148**	12/82-05/93		
E70627	05/61-08/93	⊗02/95	**149**	05/61-06/82	**308149**	06/82-08/93		
E70628	05/61-06/95	⊗06/95	**150**	05/61-03/82	**308150**	03/82-06/95		
E70629	05/61-11/93	⊗12/93	**151**	05/61-11/82	**308151**	11/82-11/93		
E70630	06/61-06/93	⊗02/94	**152**	07/61-05/83	**308152**	05/83-06/93		
E70631	06/61-06/93	⊗01/05	**153**	07/61-09/82	**308153**	09/82-06/93		
E70632	06/61-05/93	⊗02/94	**154**	07/61-10/82	**308154**	10/82-05/93		
E70633	06/61-05/93	⊗02/94	**155**	07/61-05/83	**308155**	05/83-05/93		
E70634	07/61-12/93	⊗12/93	**156**	07/61-05/83	**308156**	05/83-07/92	**308135**	07/92-12/93
E70635	07/61-05/93	⊗03/94	**157**	07/61-05/83	**308157**	05/83-05/93		
E70636	07/61-06/93	⊗02/94	**158**	07/61-02/80	**308158**	02/80-04/83	**308458**	04/83-05/83
			308158	05/83-06/93				
E70637	07/61-05/93	⊗02/94	**159**	07/61-05/83	**308159**	05/83-05/93		
E70638	08/61-06/93	⊗03/94	**160**	08/61-05/83	**308160**	05/83-06/93		
E70639	08/61-05/93	⊗03/94	**161**	08/61-01/80	**308161**	01/80-04/83	**308461**	04/83-04/84
			308161	04/84-05/93				
E70640	09/61-06/93	⊗01/05	**162**	09/61-07/83	**308162**	07/83-06/93		
E70641	09/61-05/93	⊗03/94	**163**	09/61-07/83	**308163**	07/83-05/93		
E70642	09/61-05/93	⊗03/94	**164**	09/61-02/80	**308164**	02/80-05/93		
E70643	09/61-06/93	⊗03/94	**165**	09/61-02/81	**308165**	02/81-06/93		
E70644	05/61-06/85	⊗01/88	**313**	05/61-01/82	**308313**	01/82-06/85		
E70645	09/61-01/85	⊗06/85	**314**	09/61-06/81	**308314**	06/81-01/85		
E70646	09/61-05/84	⊗04/86	**315**	09/61-02/82	**308315**	02/82-01/84	**305544**	01/84-05/84
E70647	10/61-01/85	⊗01/88	**316**	10/61-06/81	**308316**	06/81-01/85		
E70648	10/61-10/85	⊗10/85	**317**	10/61- *82*	**308317**	*82*-07/83	**305541**	01/84-05/84
			305546	03/85-05/85				
E70649	11/61-02/85	⊗01/88	**318**	11/61-12/81	**308318**	12/81-07/83	**305542**	01/84-02/85
E70650	11/61-10/85	⊗10/85	**319**	11/61-07/82	**308319**	07/82-07/83	**305545**	01/84-02/85
			305550	02/85-05/85				
E70651	11/61-05/86	⊗04/86	**320**	11/61-04/82	**308320**	04/82-07/83	**305543**	01/84-08/84
			305549	02/85-04/85				
E70652	11/61-05/86	⊗10/86	**321**	11/61- *82*	**308321**	*82*-07/83	**305540**	01/84-05/84
			305548	03/85-04/85				

Class 411 4-CEP Ashford/Eastleigh
Trailer Corridor Composite
TCK, later TBCK
S70653-S70659

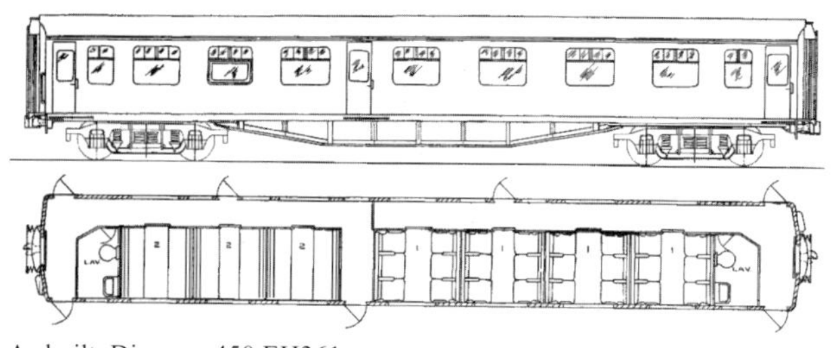

As built, Diagram 450 EH361

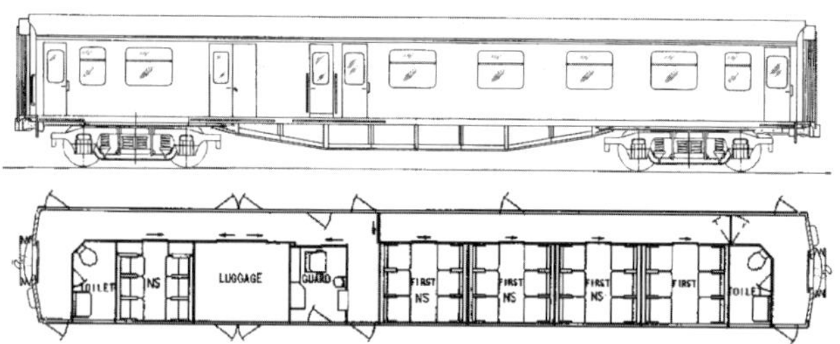

Refurbished as TBCK, Diagram 922 EJ361

Diagram:	450 EH361 922 EJ361	Lot Number:	30709
Body:	64' 6" × 9' 3"	Weight:	31t 0cwt
Seats:	24 first 24 second 2 toilets later 24 first 6 second 2 toilets	Bogies:	Commonwealth

S70653	12/62-01/93	➲Dep	**7205**	12/62-11/83	**1620**	11/83-01/93	**932620**	01/93- 03
S70654	01/63-03/03	⊗06/03	**7206**	01/63-06/83	**1616**	06/83-03/03		
S70655	01/63-04/03	⊗04/03	**7207**	01/63-10/83	**1619**	10/83-11/98	**1105**	11/98-04/03
S70656	01/63-10/04	⊗12/04	**7208**	01/63-09/83	**2303**	09/83-09/02	**2313**	09/02-10/04
S70657	02/63-04/04	⊗06/04	**7209**	02/63-05/83	**1615**	05/83-04/04		
S70658	02/63-03/79	⊗02/80	**7210**	02/63-03/79				
S70659	02/63-06/95	⊗06/95	**7211**	02/63-02/80	**1608**	02/80-06/95		

Class 411 4-CEP Ashford/Eastleigh
Trailer Corridor Second
TSK, later TSOL
S70660-S70666

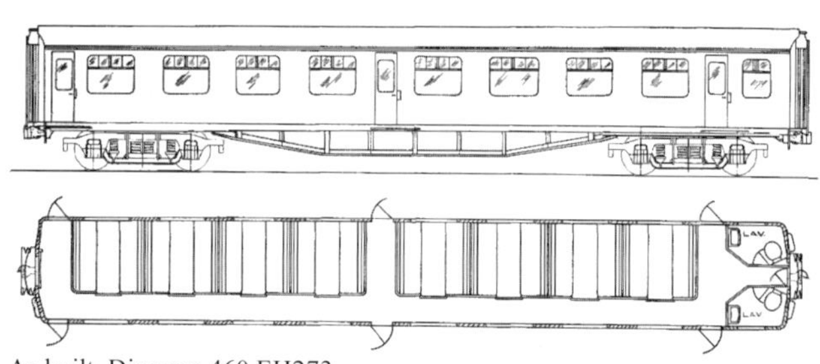

As built, Diagram 460 EH273

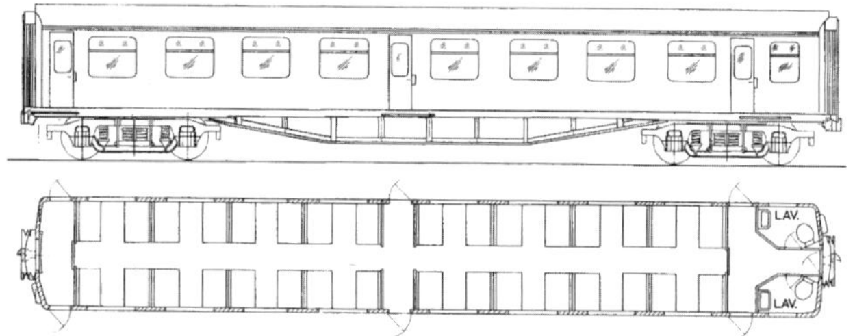

Refurbished as TSOL, Diagram 903 EH282

Diagram:	460 EH273 903 EH282	Lot Number:	30710
Body:	64' 6" × 9' 3"	Weight:	31t 0cwt
Seats:	64 second 2 toilets	Bogies:	Commonwealth

S70660	12/62-01/93	➲Dep	**7205**	12/62-11/83	**1620**	11/83-01/93	**932620**	01/93- 03
S70661	01/63-10/99	⊗05/01	**7206**	01/63-06/83	**1617**	07/83-10/99		
S70662	01/63-05/05	⊗05/05	**7207**	01/63-10/83	**1619**	10/83-11/98	**1395**	09/99-05/05
S70663	01/63-12/04	⊗02/05	**7208**	01/63-09/83	**1618**	09/83-04/94	**1561**	07/98-10/98
			1394	08/99-12/04				
S70664	02/63-04/04	⊗01/05	**7209**	02/63-05/83	**1615**	05/83-04/04		
S70665	02/63-05/93	⊗11/93	**7210**	02/63-03/79	**1522**	01/81-05/93		
S70666	02/63-06/95	⊗06/95	**7211**	02/63-02/80	**1608**	02/80-06/95		

Class 415/2 4-EPB Ashford/Eastleigh
Trailer Second (semi open)
TSso
S70667-S70694

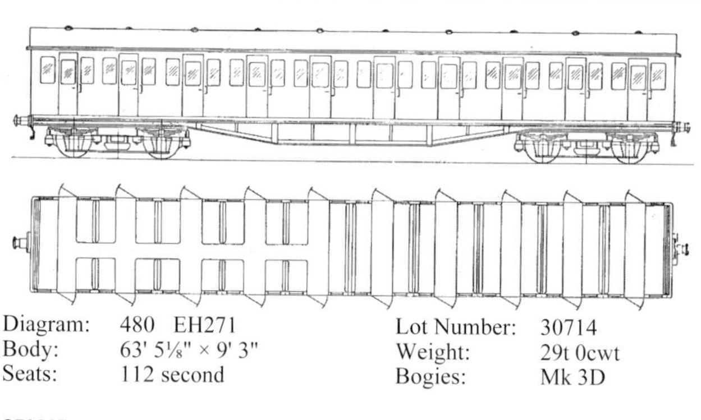

Diagram:	480 EH271	Lot Number:	30714
Body:	63' 5⅛" × 9' 3"	Weight:	29t 0cwt
Seats:	112 second	Bogies:	Mk 3D

S70667	08/62-07/84	⊗08/86	**5357**	08/62-07/84
S70668	08/62-07/84	⊗08/86	**5357**	08/62-07/84
S70669	08/62-03/85	⊗02/86	**5358**	08/62-03/85
S70670	08/62-03/85	⊗02/86	**5358**	08/62-03/85
S70671	10/62-03/85	⊗01/86	**5359**	10/62-03/85
S70672	10/62-03/85	⊗01/86	**5359**	10/62-03/85
S70673	10/62-05/85	⊗12/85	**5360**	10/62-05/85
S70674	10/62-05/85	⊗12/85	**5360**	10/62-05/85
S70675	09/62-05/84	⊗10/85	**5361**	09/62-05/84
S70676	09/62-05/84	⊗10/85	**5361**	09/62-05/84
S70677	12/62-04/84	⊗11/86	**5362**	12/62-04/84
S70678	12/62-04/84	⊗11/86	**5362**	12/62-04/84
S70679	12/62-09/84	⊗07/86	**5363**	12/62-09/84
S70680	12/62-09/84	⊗07/86	**5363**	12/62-09/84
S70681	12/62-10/84	⊗04/86	**5364**	12/62-10/84
S70682	12/62-10/84	⊗04/86	**5364**	12/62-10/84
S70683	12/62-02/85	⊗04/86	**5365**	12/62-02/85
S70684	12/62-02/85	⊗04/86	**5365**	12/62-02/85
S70685	01/63-09/84	⊗11/85	**5366**	01/63-09/84
S70686	01/63-09/84	⊗11/85	**5366**	01/63-09/84
S70687	01/63-07/84	⊗11/85	**5367**	01/63-07/84
S70688	01/63-07/84	⊗11/85	**5367**	01/63-07/84
S70689	01/63-05/84	⊗11/85	**5368**	01/63-05/84
S70690	01/63-05/84	⊗11/85	**5368**	01/63-05/84
S70691	01/63-10/84	⊗04/86	**5369**	01/63-10/84
S70692	01/63-10/84	⊗04/86	**5369**	01/63-10/84
S70693	01/63-05/84	⊗11/85	**5370**	01/63-05/84
S70694	01/63-05/84	⊗11/85	**5370**	01/63-05/84

Class 421 4-CIG York
Trailer Second Open
TSO
S70695-S70730

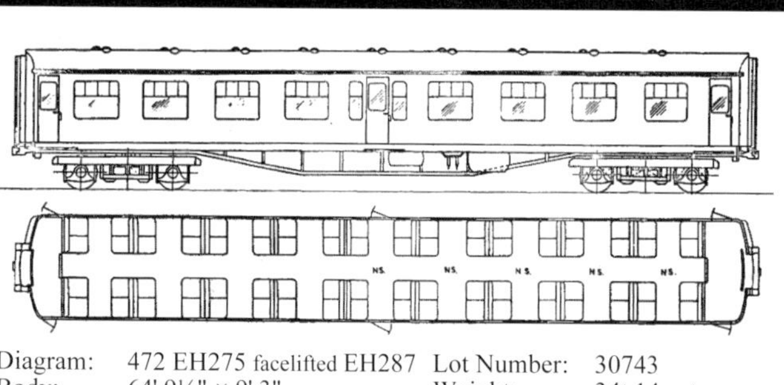

Diagram:	472 EH275 facelifted EH287	Lot Number:	30743
Body:	64' 9½" × 9' 3"	Weight:	34t 14cwt
Seats:	72 second	Bogies:	B5 (SR)

S70695	09/64-01/03	⊗03/06	**7301**	09/64-11/85	**1705**	11/85-01/03		
S70696	10/64-02/05	⊗02/05	**7302**	10/64-06/86	**1714**	06/86-02/05		
S70697	10/64-02/05	⊗02/05	**7303**	10/64-02/86	**1710**	02/86-02/05		
S70698	10/64-02/05	⊗03/05	**7304**	10/64-04/86	**1712**	04/86-02/05		
S70699	11/64-12/04	⊗01/05	**7305**	11/64-06/87	**1105**	06/87-09/92	**1750**	09/92-01/03
			1406	10/03-12/04				
S70700	11/64-03/06	⊗03/06	**7306**	11/64-10/86	**1718**	10/86-07/93	**1903**	07/93-03/06

S70701	11/64-02/05	⊗02/05	**7307**	11/64-07/86	**1715**	07/86-04/93	**1901**	04/93-05/93
			2004	05/93-01/97	**1901**	01/97-02/05		
S70702	12/64-02/05	⊗03/05	**7308**	12/64-09/86	**1717**	09/86-02/05		
S70703	12/64-06/04	⊗07/04	**7309**	12/64-12/85	**1707**	12/85-01/03	**1403**	10/03-06/04
S70704	12/64-06/03	⊗02/05	**7310**	12/64-06/87	**1110**	06/87-03/92	**1745**	03/92-06/03
S70705	01/65-07/04	⊗08/04	**7311**	01/65-06/87	**1111**	06/87-12/91	**1742**	12/91-07/04
S70706	01/65-07/04	⊗08/04	**7312**	01/65-07/85	**1701**	07/85-07/04		
S70707	01/65-07/04	⊗08/04	**7313**	01/65-03/87	**1725**	03/87-07/04		
S70708	02/65-02/05	⊗02/05	**7314**	02/65-06/87	**1114**	06/87-11/91	**1741**	11/91-02/05
S70709	03/65-08/04	⊗09/04	**7315**	03/65-12/86	**1721**	12/86-08/04		
S70710	03/65-07/04	⊗09/04	**7316**	03/65-06/87	**1116**	06/87-04/92	**1746**	04/92-07/04
S70711	03/65-11/04	⊗06/05	**7317**	03/65-10/85	**1704**	10/85-11/04		
S70712	04/65-09/03	⊗03/05	**7318**	04/65-06/87	**1118**	06/87-04/92	**1747**	04/92-09/03
S70713	08/65-11/02	⊗03/05	**7319**	08/65-12/85	**1706**	12/85-11/02	**1404**	01/04-03/05
S70714	08/65-12/02	⊗08/04	**7320**	08/65-11/87	**1731**	11/87-12/02		
S70715	09/65-11/04	⊗11/04	**7321**	09/65-05/87	**1121**	05/87-01/88	**1732**	01/88-01/95
			1908	01/95-11/04				
S70716	09/65-06/04	⊗12/04	**7322**	09/65-09/85	**1703**	09/85-12/02	**1405**	09/03-06/04
S70717	09/65-07/04	⊗08/04	**7323**	09/65-07/86	**1123**	07/86-11/02	**1752**	11/02-07/04
S70718	09/65-11/04	⊗11/04	**7324**	09/65-07/87	**1728**	07/87-03/94	**1905**	03/94-11/04
S70719	10/65-04/04	⊗12/04	**7325**	10/65-08/86	**1719**	10/86-04/04		
S70720	10/65-03/05	⊗03/05	**7326**	10/65-08/85	**1702**	08/85-11/02	**1410**	10/03-03/05
S70721	10/65-02/04	[illegible]	**7327**	[illegible]	**1127**	[illegible]	[illegible]	[illegible]
S70722	10/65-04/05	⊗05/05	**7328**	10/65-02/86	**1709**	02/86-03/03	**1411**	11/03-04/05
S70723	[illegible]	[illegible]	**7329**	11/65-07/87	**1729**	07/87-07/94	**1907**	07/94-07/04
S70724	12/65-07/04	⊗07/04	**7330**	12/65-10/87	**1730**	10/87-05/94	**1906**	05/94-07/04
S70725	12/65-06/04	⊗06/04	**7331**	12/65-01/87	**1722**	01/87-06/04		
S70726	01/66-04/04	⊗03/06	**7332**	01/66-02/87	**1723**	02/87-11/93	**1904**	11/93-04/04
S70727	01/66-12/78	⊗04/79	**7333**	01/66-12/78				
S70728	01/66-09/03	⊗08/04	**7334**	01/66-05/87	**1726**	05/87-09/03		
S70729	01/66-02/05	⊗03/05	**7335**	01/66-01/86	**1708**	01/86-02/05		
S70730	02/66-06/04	⊗06/04	**7336**	02/66-06/87	**1727**	06/87-06/04		

Class 310 Derby

Trailer Second Open

TSO

M70731-M70780

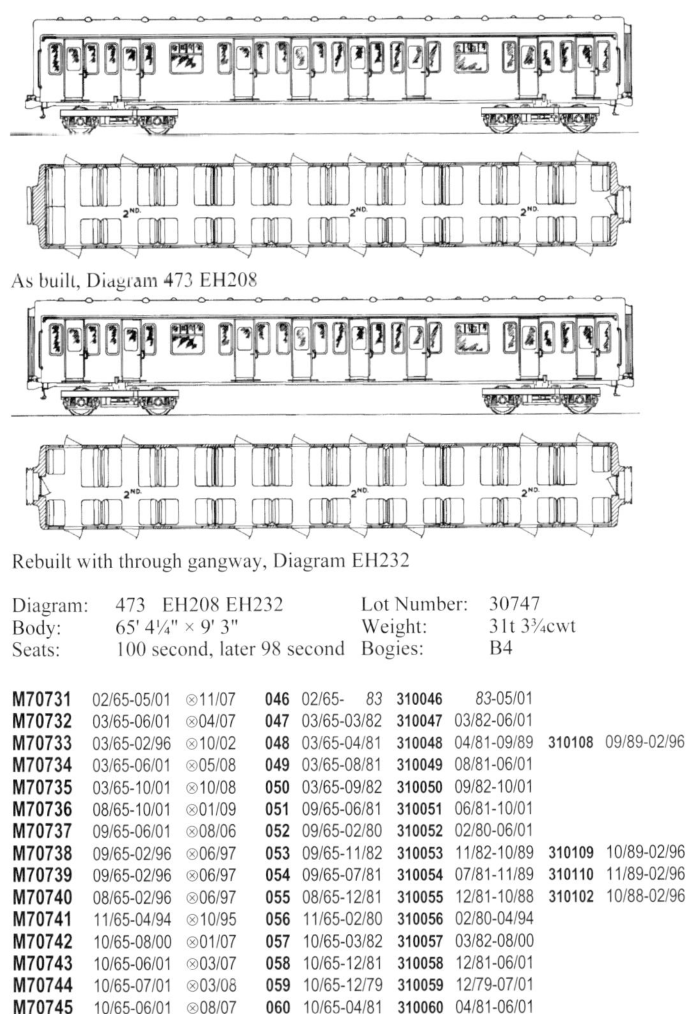

As built, Diagram 473 EH208

Rebuilt with through gangway, Diagram EH232

Diagram:	473 EH208 EH232	Lot Number:	30747
Body:	65' 4¼" × 9' 3"	Weight:	31t 3¾cwt
Seats:	100 second, later 98 second	Bogies:	B4

M70731	02/65-05/01	⊗11/07	**046**	02/65- *83*	**310046**	*83*-05/01		
M70732	03/65-06/01	⊗04/07	**047**	03/65-03/82	**310047**	03/82-06/01		
M70733	03/65-02/96	⊗10/02	**048**	03/65-04/81	**310048**	04/81-09/89	**310108**	09/89-02/96
M70734	03/65-06/01	⊗05/08	**049**	03/65-08/81	**310049**	08/81-06/01		
M70735	03/65-10/01	⊗10/08	**050**	03/65-09/82	**310050**	09/82-10/01		
M70736	08/65-10/01	⊗01/09	**051**	09/65-06/81	**310051**	06/81-10/01		
M70737	09/65-06/01	⊗08/06	**052**	09/65-02/80	**310052**	02/80-06/01		
M70738	09/65-02/96	⊗06/97	**053**	09/65-11/82	**310053**	11/82-10/89	**310109**	10/89-02/96
M70739	09/65-02/96	⊗06/97	**054**	09/65-07/81	**310054**	07/81-11/89	**310110**	11/89-02/96
M70740	08/65-02/96	⊗06/97	**055**	08/65-12/81	**310055**	12/81-10/88	**310102**	10/88-02/96
M70741	11/65-04/94	⊗10/95	**056**	11/65-02/80	**310056**	02/80-04/94		
M70742	10/65-08/00	⊗01/07	**057**	10/65-03/82	**310057**	03/82-08/00		
M70743	10/65-06/01	⊗03/07	**058**	10/65-12/81	**310058**	12/81-06/01		
M70744	10/65-07/01	⊗03/08	**059**	10/65-12/79	**310059**	12/79-07/01		
M70745	10/65-06/01	⊗08/07	**060**	10/65-04/81	**310060**	04/81-06/01		
M70746	08/65-02/96	⊗06/97	**061**	08/65-03/82	**310061**	03/82-09/94	**310112**	09/94-02/96
M70747	11/65-02/96	⊗11/02	**062**	11/65-02/83	**310062**	02/83-09/89	**310107**	09/89-02/96
M70748	08/65-02/96	⊗10/02	**063**	08/65-06/81	**310063**	06/81-03/90	**310111**	03/90-02/96
M70749	08/65-07/01	⊗08/06	**064**	08/65-04/81	**310064**	04/81-07/01		
M70750	08/65-01/96	⊗05/97	**065**	08/65-09/82	**310065**	09/82-09/94		
M70751	09/65-06/01	⊗09/07	**066**	09/65-03/82	**310066**	03/82-06/01		
M70752	09/65-05/01	⊗07/07	**067**	09/65-03/82	**310067**	03/82-05/01		
M70753	10/65-03/01	⊗11/06	**068**	10/65-04/83	**310068**	04/83-03/01		
M70754	10/65-07/01	⊗11/07	**069**	10/65-01/80	**310069**	01/80-07/01		
M70755	11/65-07/01	⊗04/08	**070**	11/65-08/81	**310070**	08/81-07/01		
M70756	12/65-04/75	⊃76998	**071**	12/65-01/70				
M70757	12/65-02/96	⊗10/02	**072**	12/65-05/81	**310072**	05/81-02/89	**310106**	02/89-02/96
M70758	02/66-02/96	⊗06/97	**073**	02/66-12/81	**310073**	12/81-09/88	**310101**	09/88-02/96
M70759	06/66-07/01	⊗11/03	**074**	06/66-04/81	**310074**	04/81-07/01		
M70760	07/66-07/01	⊗11/03	**075**	07/66-04/83	**310075**	04/83-07/01		
M70761	07/66-02/96	⊗02/98	**076**	07/66-02/82	**310076**	02/82-11/88	**310103**	11/88-02/96
M70762	07/66-06/01	⊗06/02	**077**	07/66-12/81	**310077**	12/81-06/01		
M70763	08/66-02/96	⊗10/02	**078**	08/66-03/82	**310078**	03/82-01/89	**310104**	01/89-02/96
M70764	08/66-05/01	⊗10/03	**079**	08/66-08/81	**310079**	08/81-05/01		
M70765	08/66-10/01	⊗09/03	**080**	08/66-03/82	**310080**	03/82-10/01		
M70766	09/66-11/01	⊗12/03	**081**	09/66-03/82	**310081**	03/82-11/01		
M70767	09/66-10/01	⊗09/03	**082**	09/66-04/83	**310082**	04/83-10/01		
M70768	09/66-10/01	⊗09/03	**083**	09/66-10/81	**310083**	10/81-10/01		
M70769	10/66-05/01	⊗11/03	**084**	10/66-10/81	**310084**	10/81-05/01		
M70770	11/66-06/01	⊗11/03	**085**	11/66-04/83	**310085**	04/83-06/01		
M70771	10/66-06/01	⊗10/03	**086**	10/66-10/82	**310086**	10/82-06/01		
M70772	02/67-10/01	⊗11/03	**087**	02/67-12/81	**310087**	12/81-10/01		
M70773	12/66-10/01	⊗11/03	**088**	12/66-12/81	**310088**	12/81-10/01		
M70774	01/67-12/00	⊗03/03	**089**	01/67-06/81	**310089**	06/81-12/00		
M70775	11/66-02/96	⊗02/98	**090**	11/66-07/82	**310090**	07/82-01/89	**310105**	01/89-02/96
M70776	12/66-05/01	⊗11/03	**091**	12/66-04/83	**310091**	04/83-05/01		
M70777	12/66-10/01	⊗09/03	**092**	12/66-02/83	**310092**	02/83-10/01		
M70778	03/67-11/01	⊗11/03	**093**	03/67-07/82	**310093**	07/82-11/01		
M70779	02/67-05/01	⊗11/03	**094**	02/67-12/67	**095**	12/67-04/81	**310095**	04/81-05/01
M70780	05/67-06/01	⊗10/03	**095**	05/67-12/67	**094**	04/75-01/83	**310094**	01/83-06/01

Class 423 4-VEP Derby

Trailer Second Open

TSO

S70781-S70800

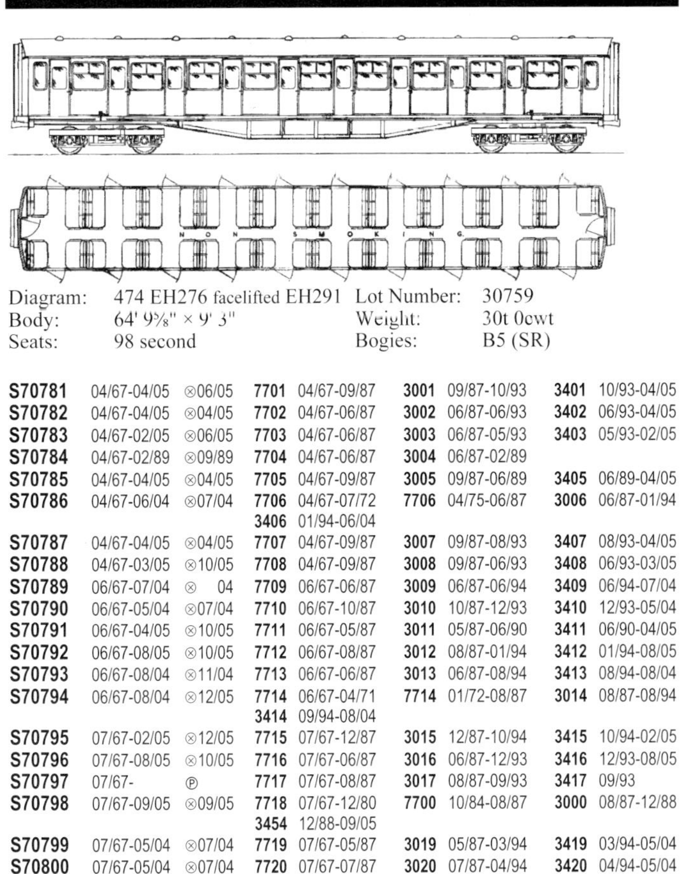

Diagram:	474 EH276 facelifted EH291	Lot Number:	30759
Body:	64' 9⅜" × 9' 3"	Weight:	30t 0cwt
Seats:	98 second	Bogies:	B5 (SR)

S70781	04/67-04/05	⊗06/05	**7701**	04/67-09/87	**3001**	09/87-10/93	**3401**	10/93-04/05
S70782	04/67-04/05	⊗04/05	**7702**	04/67-06/87	**3002**	06/87-06/93	**3402**	06/93-04/05
S70783	04/67-02/05	⊗06/05	**7703**	04/67-06/87	**3003**	06/87-05/93	**3403**	05/93-02/05
S70784	04/67-02/89	⊗09/89	**7704**	04/67-06/87	**3004**	06/87-02/89		
S70785	04/67-04/05	⊗04/05	**7705**	04/67-09/87	**3005**	09/87-06/89	**3405**	06/89-04/05
S70786	04/67-06/04	⊗07/04	**7706**	04/67-07/72	**7706**	04/75-06/87	**3006**	06/87-01/94
			3406	01/94-06/04				
S70787	04/67-04/05	⊗04/05	**7707**	04/67-09/87	**3007**	09/87-08/93	**3407**	08/93-04/05
S70788	04/67-03/05	⊗10/05	**7708**	04/67-09/87	**3008**	09/87-06/93	**3408**	06/93-03/05
S70789	06/67-07/04	⊗ 04	**7709**	06/67-06/87	**3009**	06/87-06/94	**3409**	06/94-07/04
S70790	06/67-05/04	⊗07/04	**7710**	06/67-10/87	**3010**	10/87-12/93	**3410**	12/93-05/04
S70791	06/67-04/05	⊗10/05	**7711**	06/67-05/87	**3011**	05/87-06/90	**3411**	06/90-04/05
S70792	06/67-08/05	⊗10/05	**7712**	06/67-08/87	**3012**	08/87-01/94	**3412**	01/94-08/05
S70793	06/67-08/04	⊗11/04	**7713**	06/67-06/87	**3013**	06/87-08/94	**3413**	08/94-08/04
S70794	06/67-08/04	⊗12/05	**7714**	06/67-04/71	**7714**	01/72-08/87	**3014**	08/87-08/94
			3414	09/94-08/04				
S70795	07/67-02/05	⊗12/05	**7715**	07/67-12/87	**3015**	12/87-10/94	**3415**	10/94-02/05
S70796	07/67-08/05	⊗10/05	**7716**	07/67-06/87	**3016**	06/87-12/93	**3416**	12/93-08/05
S70797	07/67-	Ⓟ	**7717**	07/67-08/87	**3017**	08/87-09/93	**3417**	09/93
S70798	07/67-09/05	⊗09/05	**7718**	07/67-12/80	**7700**	10/84-08/87	**3000**	08/87-12/88
			3454	12/88-09/05				
S70799	07/67-05/04	⊗07/04	**7719**	07/67-05/87	**3019**	05/87-03/94	**3419**	03/94-05/04
S70800	07/67-05/04	⊗07/04	**7720**	07/67-07/87	**3020**	07/87-04/94	**3420**	04/94-05/04

Class 430 4-REP York

Trailer Brake Corridor First

TBFK

S70801-S70811

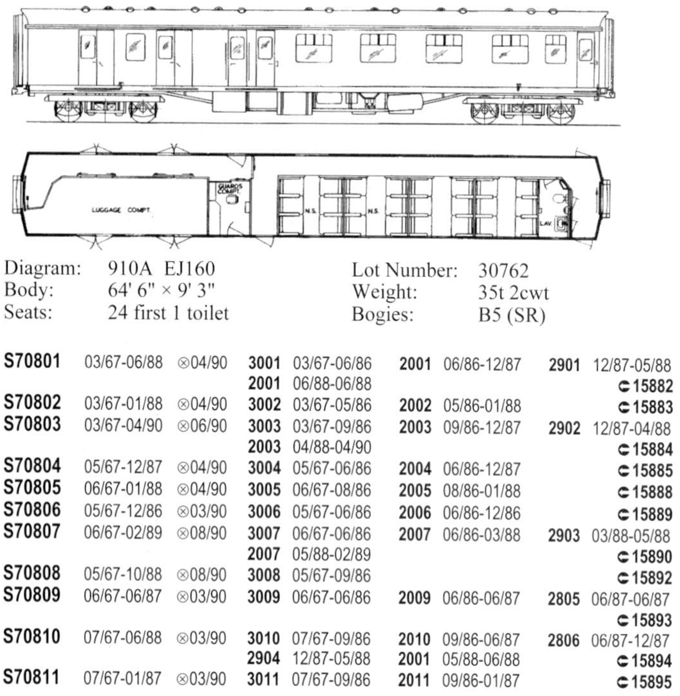

Diagram: 910A EJ160 | Lot Number: 30762
Body: 64' 6" × 9' 3" | Weight: 35t 2cwt
Seats: 24 first 1 toilet | Bogies: B5 (SR)

S70801	03/67-06/88	⊗04/90	3001	03/67-06/86	2001	06/86-12/87	2901	12/87-05/88	
			2001	06/88-06/88					⊂15882
S70802	03/67-01/88	⊗04/90	3002	03/67-05/86	2002	05/86-01/88			⊂15883
S70803	03/67-04/90	⊗06/90	3003	03/67-09/86	2003	09/86-12/87	2902	12/87-04/88	
			2003	04/88-04/90					⊂15884
S70804	05/67-12/87	⊗04/90	3004	05/67-06/86	2004	06/86-12/87			⊂15885
S70805	06/67-01/88	⊗04/90	3005	06/67-08/86	2005	08/86-01/88			⊂15888
S70806	05/67-12/86	⊗03/90	3006	05/67-06/86	2006	06/86-12/86			⊂15889
S70807	06/67-02/89	⊗08/90	3007	06/67-06/86	2007	06/86-03/88	2903	03/88-05/88	
			2007	05/88-02/89					⊂15890
S70808	05/67-10/88	⊗08/90	3008	05/67-09/86					⊂15892
S70809	06/67-06/87	⊗03/90	3009	06/67-06/86	2009	06/86-06/87	2805	06/87-06/87	
									⊂15893
S70810	07/67-06/88	⊗03/90	3010	07/67-09/86	2010	09/86-06/87	2806	06/87-12/87	
			2904	12/87-05/88	2001	05/88-06/88			⊂15894
S70811	07/67-01/87	⊗03/90	3011	07/67-09/86	2011	09/86-01/87			⊂15895

Class 491 4-TC York

Trailer Brake Corridor Second

TBSK

S70812-S70843 (70840 onwards Class 492 3-TC)

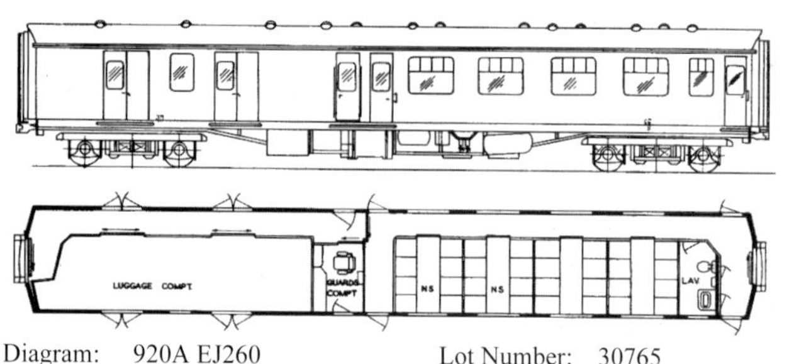

Diagram: 920A EJ260 | Lot Number: 30765
Body: 64' 6" × 9' 3" | Weight: 34t 16cwt
Seats: 32 second 1 toilet | Bogies: B5 (SR)

S70812	10/67-08/96	Ⓟ	401	10/67-07/86	8001	07/86-10/88	8010	10/88-04/90	
			8110	06/90-03/91	410	09/91-08/96			⊂34987
S70813	08/66-10/88	⊗04/90	402	08/66-06/86	8002	06/86-12/86	2802	12/86-09/87	
			2805	09/87-12/87	8105	12/87-04/88	2805	04/88-10/88	
									⊂34968
S70814	08/66-05/88	⊗08/90	403	08/66-11/86	8003	11/86-06/87	2805	06/87-09/87	
			2802	09/87-01/88	8102	01/88-05/88			⊂34969
S70815	08/66-06/91	⊗03/92	404	08/66-10/86	8004	10/86-09/88	2808	09/88-01/89	
			8004	01/89-05/90	1905	05/90-06/91			⊂34958
S70816	08/66-05/85	⊗ 87	405	08/66-05/85					⊂34959
S70817	08/66-06/91	⊗10/91	406	08/66-06/86	8006	06/86-05/90	1906	05/90-01/91	
			1903	01/91-06/91					⊂34960
S70818	09/66-07/89	➲977685	407	09/66-12/86	8007	12/86-07/89			⊂34961
S70819	08/66-08/88	⊗04/90	408	08/66-10/86	8008	10/86-12/86	2801	12/86-12/87	
			8101	12/87-08/88					⊂34962
S70820	09/66-04/89	⊗06/90	409	09/66-12/86	2803	12/86-12/87	8103	12/87-05/88	
			2804	05/88-04/89					⊂34963
S70821	09/66-09/92	⊗11/92	410	09/66-08/86	8010	08/86-10/88	8001	10/88-09/92	
									⊂34985
S70822	09/66-10/91	⊗11/91	411	09/66-10/86	8011	10/86-02/87	2804	02/87-12/87	
			8104	12/87-05/88	1902	09/90-12/90	1903	01/91-10/91	
									⊂34986
S70823	09/66-05/91	Ⓟ	412	09/66-06/86	8012	06/86-08/88	8015	08/88-05/91	
									⊂34970
S70824	10/66-02/92	Ⓟ	413	10/66-05/86	8013	05/86-06/87	8106	12/87-05/88	
			2806	05/88-09/88	8106	09/88-10/88	1902	02/89-06/90	
			8110	06/90-03/91	1901	03/91-02/92			⊂34984
S70825	10/66-05/91	➲977545	414	10/66-09/86	8014	09/86-05/91			⊂34996
S70826	11/66-08/99	Ⓟ	415	11/66-10/86	8015	10/86-06/88	8017	09/88-09/91	
			417	09/91-01/98					⊂34980
S70827	10/66-10/91	⊗11/91	416	10/66-06/86	8016	06/86-10/88	1903	04/90-09/90	
			1902	12/90-10/91					⊂34997
S70828	11/66-05/91	⊗03/92	417	11/66-10/86	8017	10/86-09/88	8012	09/88-05/91	
									⊂34998
S70829	11/66-10/91	⊗11/91	418	11/66-10/86	8018	10/86-05/90	1905	05/90-06/91	
			1903	06/91-10/91					⊂34981
S70830	11/66-02/92	⊗03/92	419	11/66-08/86	8019	08/86-08/88	1901	12/88-05/90	
			1906	05/90-01/91	1901	03/91-02/92			⊂34976
S70831	11/66-05/89	⊗07/90	420	11/66-09/86	8020	09/86-05/89			⊂34977
S70832	12/66-02/89	⊗03/92	421	12/66-10/86	8021	10/86-02/89			⊂34967
S70833	07/66-08/88	⊗03/90	422	07/67-05/86	8022	05/86-08/88			⊂34966
S70834	02/67-10/91	⊗11/91	423	02/67-06/86	8023	06/86-04/90	1903	04/90-09/90	
			1902	09/90-10/91					⊂34972
S70835	03/67-05/88	⊗04/90	424	03/67-05/86	8024	05/86-05/88			⊂34973
S70836	01/67-10/88	⊗01/90	425	01/67-05/86	8025	05/86-10/88			⊂34974
S70837	02/67-05/89	⊗03/92	426	02/67-08/86	8026	08/86-05/89			⊂34975
S70838	02/67-02/92	⊗05/92	427	02/67-06/86	8027	06/86-04/90	1904	04/90-02/92	
									⊂34979
S70839	03/67-02/92	⊗11/92	428	03/67-06/86	8028	06/86-04/90	1904	04/90-02/92	
									⊂34978
S70840	05/67-07/88	⊗03/90	301	05/67-06/74	429	06/74-10/86	8029	10/86-07/88	
									⊂34982
S70841	07/67-08/88	⊗03/90	302	07/67-07/74	430	07/74-09/86	8030	09/86-08/88	
									⊂34956
S70842	07/67-08/89	⊗07/90	303	08/67-06/74	431	06/74-10/86	8031	10/86-01/89	
			2809	01/89-05/89	8031	05/89-08/89			⊂34957
S70843	08/67-07/88	⊗05/90	304	08/67-02/75	432	02/75-06/86	8032	06/86-07/88	
									⊂34983

Class 491 4-TC York

Trailer Corridor First

TFK

S70844-S70871

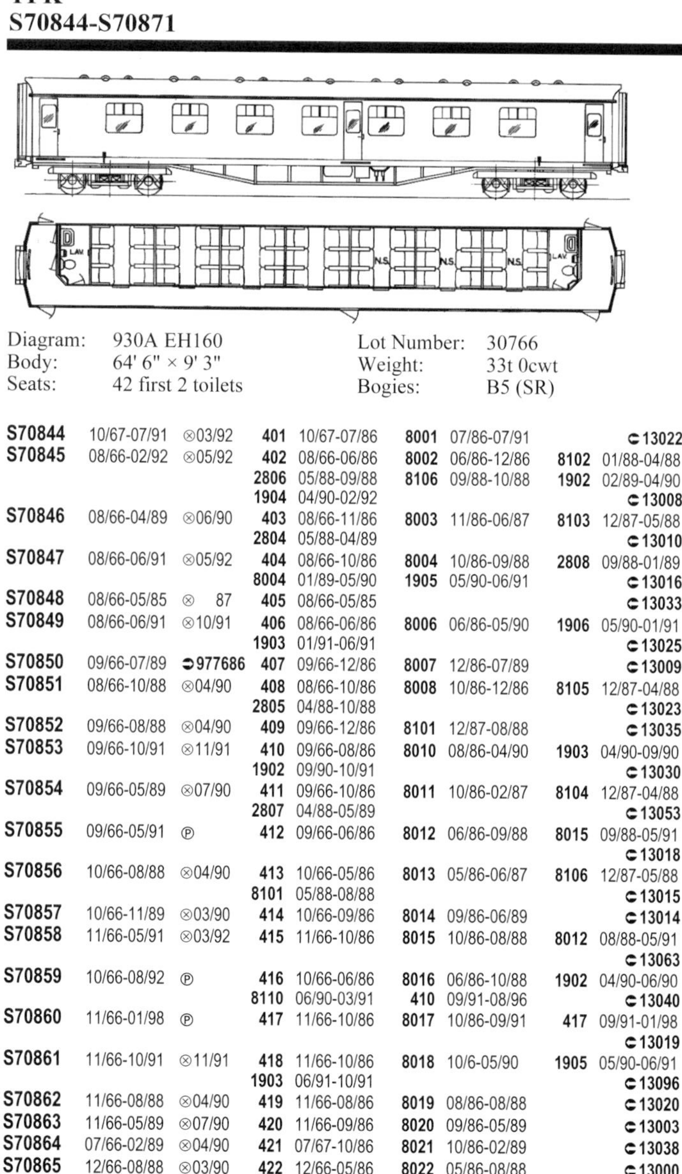

Diagram: 930A EH160 | Lot Number: 30766
Body: 64' 6" × 9' 3" | Weight: 33t 0cwt
Seats: 42 first 2 toilets | Bogies: B5 (SR)

S70844	10/67-07/91	⊗03/92	401	10/67-07/86	8001	07/86-07/91			⊂13022
S70845	08/66-02/92	⊗05/92	402	08/66-06/86	8002	06/86-12/86	8102	01/88-04/88	
			2806	05/88-09/88	8106	09/88-10/88	1902	02/89-04/90	
			1904	04/90-02/92					⊂13008
S70846	08/66-04/89	⊗06/90	403	08/66-11/86	8003	11/86-06/87	8103	12/87-05/88	
			2804	05/88-04/89					⊂13010
S70847	08/66-06/91	⊗05/92	404	08/66-10/86	8004	10/86-09/88	2808	09/88-01/89	
			8004	01/89-05/90	1905	05/90-06/91			⊂13016
S70848	08/66-05/85	⊗ 87	405	08/66-05/85					⊂13033
S70849	08/66-06/91	⊗10/91	406	08/66-06/86	8006	06/86-05/90	1906	05/90-01/91	
			1903	01/91-06/91					⊂13025
S70850	09/66-07/89	➲977686	407	09/66-12/86	8007	12/86-07/89			⊂13009
S70851	08/66-10/88	⊗04/90	408	08/66-10/86	8008	10/86-12/86	8105	12/87-04/88	
			2805	04/88-10/88					⊂13023
S70852	09/66-08/88	⊗04/90	409	09/66-12/86	8101	12/87-08/88			⊂13035
S70853	09/66-10/91	⊗11/91	410	09/66-08/86	8010	08/86-04/90	1903	04/90-09/90	
			1902	09/90-10/91					⊂13030
S70854	09/66-05/89	⊗07/90	411	09/66-10/86	8011	10/86-02/87	8104	12/87-04/88	
			2807	04/88-05/89					⊂13053
S70855	09/66-05/91	Ⓟ	412	09/66-06/86	8012	06/86-09/88	8015	09/88-05/91	
									⊂13018
S70856	10/66-08/88	⊗04/90	413	10/66-05/86	8013	05/86-06/87	8106	12/87-05/88	
			8101	05/88-08/88					⊂13015
S70857	10/66-11/89	⊗03/90	414	10/66-09/86	8014	09/86-06/89			⊂13014
S70858	11/66-05/91	⊗03/92	415	11/66-10/86	8015	10/86-08/88	8012	08/88-05/91	
									⊂13063
S70859	10/66-08/92	Ⓟ	416	10/66-06/86	8016	06/86-10/88	1902	04/90-06/90	
			8110	06/90-03/91	410	09/91-08/96			⊂13040
S70860	11/66-01/98	Ⓟ	417	11/66-10/86	8017	10/86-09/91	417	09/91-01/98	
									⊂13019
S70861	11/66-10/91	⊗11/91	418	11/66-10/86	8018	10/6-05/90	1905	05/90-06/91	
			1903	06/91-10/91					⊂13096
S70862	11/66-08/88	⊗04/90	419	11/66-08/86	8019	08/86-08/88			⊂13020
S70863	11/66-05/89	⊗07/90	420	11/66-09/86	8020	09/86-05/89			⊂13003
S70864	07/66-02/89	⊗04/90	421	07/67-10/86	8021	10/86-02/89			⊂13038
S70865	12/66-08/88	⊗03/90	422	12/66-05/86	8022	05/86-08/88			⊂13000

S70866	07/67-12/91	➲977764	**423**	07/67-06/86	**8023**	06/86-04/90	**1903**	04/90-09/90
								⊂**13037**
S70867	07/67-05/88	⊗04/90	**424**	07/67-05/86	**8024**	05/86-05/88		⊂**13021**
S70868	07/67-10/88	⊗01/90	**425**	07/67-05/86	**8025**	05/86-10/88		⊂**13001**
S70869	10/67-05/91	➲977542	**426**	10/67-08/86	**8026**	08/86-05/89	**8014**	06/89-05/91
								⊂**13002**
S70870	07/67-12/91	⊗03/92	**427**	07/67-06/86	**8027**	06/86-04/90	**1904**	04/90-04/91
								⊂**13032**
S70871	07/67-08/90	➲977763	**428**	07/67-06/86	**8028**	06/86-04/90		⊂**13017**

Class 423 4-VEP York

Trailer Second Open

TSO

S70872-S70906

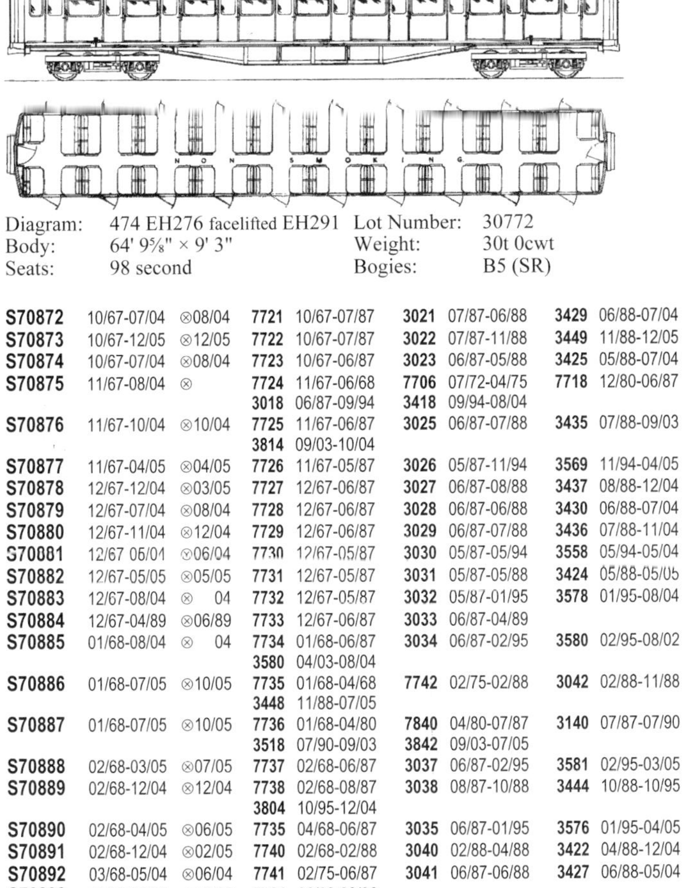

Diagram:	474 EH276 facelifted EH291	Lot Number:	30772
Body:	64' 9⅝" × 9' 3"	Weight:	30t 0cwt
Seats:	98 second	Bogies:	B5 (SR)

S70872	10/67-07/04	⊗08/04	**7721**	10/67-07/87	**3021**	07/87-06/88	**3429**	06/88-07/04
S70873	10/67-12/05	⊗12/05	**7722**	10/67-07/87	**3022**	07/87-11/88	**3449**	11/88-12/05
S70874	10/67-07/04	⊗08/04	**7723**	10/67-06/87	**3023**	06/87-05/88	**3425**	05/88-07/04
S70875	11/67-08/04	⊗	**7724**	11/67-06/68	**7706**	07/72-04/75	**7718**	12/80-06/87
			3018	06/87-09/94	**3418**	09/94-08/04		
S70876	11/67-10/04	⊗10/04	**7725**	11/67-06/87	**3025**	06/87-07/88	**3435**	07/88-09/03
			3814	09/03-10/04				
S70877	11/67-04/05	⊗04/05	**7726**	11/67-05/87	**3026**	05/87-11/94	**3569**	11/94-04/05
S70878	12/67-12/04	⊗03/05	**7727**	12/67-06/87	**3027**	06/87-08/88	**3437**	08/88-12/04
S70879	12/67-07/04	⊗08/04	**7728**	12/67-06/87	**3028**	06/87-06/88	**3430**	06/88-07/04
S70880	12/67-11/04	⊗12/04	**7729**	12/67-06/87	**3029**	06/87-07/88	**3436**	07/88-11/04
S70881	12/67-06/04	⊗06/04	**7730**	12/67-05/87	**3030**	05/87-05/94	**3558**	05/94-05/04
S70882	12/67-05/05	⊗05/05	**7731**	12/67-05/87	**3031**	05/87-05/88	**3424**	05/88-05/05
S70883	12/67-08/04	⊗ 04	**7732**	12/67-05/87	**3032**	05/87-01/95	**3578**	01/95-08/04
S70884	12/67-04/89	⊗06/89	**7733**	12/67-06/87	**3033**	06/87-04/89		
S70885	01/68-08/04	⊗ 04	**7734**	01/68-06/87	**3034**	06/87-02/95	**3580**	02/95-08/02
			3580	04/03-08/04				
S70886	01/68-07/05	⊗10/05	**7735**	01/68-04/68	**7742**	02/75-02/88	**3042**	02/88-11/88
			3448	11/88-07/05				
S70887	01/68-07/05	⊗10/05	**7736**	01/68-04/80	**7840**	04/80-07/87	**3140**	07/87-07/90
			3518	07/90-09/03	**3842**	09/03-07/05		
S70888	02/68-03/05	⊗07/05	**7737**	02/68-06/87	**3037**	06/87-02/95	**3581**	02/95-03/05
S70889	02/68-12/04	⊗12/04	**7738**	02/68-08/87	**3038**	08/87-10/88	**3444**	10/88-10/95
			3804	10/95-12/04				
S70890	02/68-04/05	⊗06/05	**7735**	04/68-06/87	**3035**	06/87-01/95	**3576**	01/95-04/05
S70891	02/68-12/04	⊗02/05	**7740**	02/68-02/88	**3040**	02/88-04/88	**3422**	04/88-12/04
S70892	03/68-05/04	⊗06/04	**7741**	02/75-06/87	**3041**	06/87-06/88	**3427**	06/88-05/04
S70893	03/68-05/86	⊗10/86	**7724**	06/68-08/86				
S70894	04/68-08/04	⊗ 04	**7743**	04/68-06/87	**3043**	06/87-09/88	**3441**	09/88-01/90
			3404	02/90-08/04				
S70895	04/68-06/05	⊗06/05	**7744**	04/68-08/87	**3044**	08/87-11/88	**3447**	11/88-06/05
S70896	04/68-10/05	⊗10/05	**7745**	04/68-03/88	**3045**	03/88-12/88	**3453**	12/88-10/05
S70897	04/68-06/08	⊗09/09	**7746**	04/68-06/87	**3046**	06/87-02/93	**3536**	02/93-06/08
S70898	04/68-05/04	⊗06/04	**7747**	04/68-06/87	**3047**	06/87-05/88	**3426**	05/88-05/04
S70899	04/68-12/04	⊗01/05	**7748**	04/68-03/88	**3048**	03/88-12/88	**3455**	12/88-12/04
S70900	05/68-06/05	⊗06/05	**7749**	05/68-10/87	**3049**	10/87-12/88	**3481**	07/89-06/05
S70901	05/68-10/05	⊗10/05	**7750**	05/68-10/87	**3050**	10/87-01/89	**3457**	01/89-10/05
S70902	05/68-04/05	⊗04/05	**7751**	05/68-12/87	**3051**	12/87-01/89	**3458**	01/89-04/05
S70903	06/68-04/05	⊗10/05	**7752**	06/68-11/87	**3052**	11/87-01/89	**3459**	01/89-04/05
S70904	06/68-04/05	Ⓟ	**7753**	06/68-12/87	**3053**	12/87-02/89	**3463**	02/89-08/99
			3905	08/99-04/05				
S70905	07/68-07/04	⊗11/04	**7754**	07/68-06/87	**3054**	06/87-07/88	**3432**	07/88-07/04
S70906	07/68-08/05	⊗10/05	**7755**	07/68-03/88	**3055**	03/88-09/88	**3439**	09/88-05/99
			3901	05/99-08/05				

Class 423 4-VEP York

Trailer Second Open

TSO

S70907-S70956

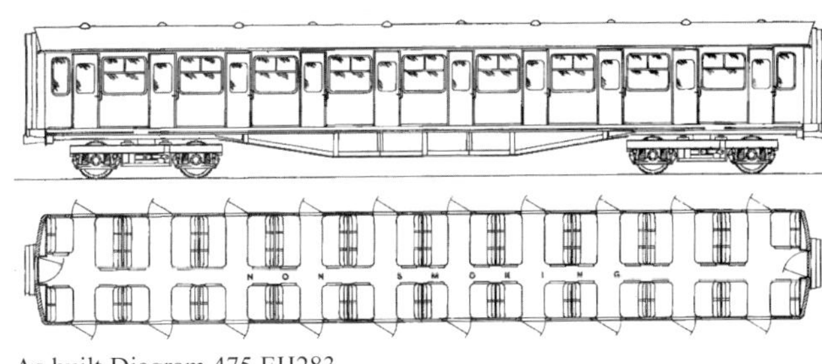

As built Diagram 475 EH283

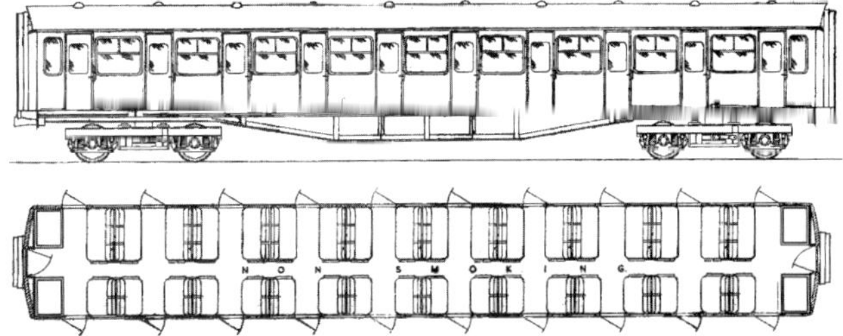

Rebuilt as Class 427 4-VEG for Gatwick services, Diagram 842 EH278

Diagram:	475 EH283 842 EH278 facelifted EH291	Lot Number:	30793
		Weight:	30t 0cwt
Body:	64' 9⅝" × 9' 3"	Bogies:	B5 (SR)
Seats:	98 second, VEG 90 second		

S70907	01/69-06/05	⊗06/05	**7756**	01/69-12/87	**3056**	12/87-02/89	**3464**	02/89-10/99
			3908	10/99-06/05				
S70908	01/69-10/04	⊗11/04	**7757**	01/69-06/87	**3057**	06/87-07/88	**3433**	07/88-10/04
S70909	01/69-02/05	⊗08/05	**7758**	01/69-07/88	**3058**	07/88-03/89	**3467**	03/89-02/05
S70910	02/69-04/05	⊗04/05	**7759**	02/69-02/88	**3059**	02/88-03/89	**3468**	03/89-04/05
S70911	02/69-08/05	⊗10/05	**7760**	02/69-09/87	**3060**	09/87-10/88	**3445**	10/88-08/05
S70912	02/69-08/05	⊗08/05	**7761**	02/69-06/87	**3061**	06/87-04/88	**3423**	04/88-08/05
S70913	02/69-07/04	⊗ 04	**7762**	02/69-02/88	**3062**	02/88-06/88	**3428**	06/88-07/04
S70914	02/69-04/05	⊗04/05	**7763**	02/69-06/87	**3063**	06/87-01/89	**3456**	01/89-04/05
S70915	02/69-07/04	⊗08/04	**7764**	02/69-06/87	**3064**	06/87-06/88	**3431**	06/88-07/04
S70916	03/69-10/05	⊗12/05	**7765**	03/69-03/88	**3065**	03/88-11/88	**3450**	11/88-10/05
S70917	03/69-07/05	⊗07/05	**7766**	03/69-08/87	**3066**	08/87-07/88	**3434**	07/88-07/05
S70918	03/69-04/05	⊗04/05	**7767**	03/69-08/87	**3067**	08/87-07/88	**3466**	03/89-04/05
S70919	03/69-04/05	⊗05/05	**7768**	03/69-03/74	**7768**	01/75-09/87	**3068**	09/87-07/91
			3524	07/91-04/05				
S70920	03/69-11/05	⊗01/06	**7769**	03/69-06/87	**3069**	06/87-02/92	**3530**	02/92-11/05
S70921	04/69-10/05	⊗10/05	**7770**	04/69-08/87	**3070**	08/87-01/90	**3500**	01/90-10/05
S70922	04/69-11/05	⊗12/05	**7771**	04/69-06/87	**3071**	06/87-02/90	**3505**	02/90-11/05
S70923	04/69-07/04	⊗08/04	**7772**	04/69-10/87	**3072**	10/87-07/89	**3480**	07/89-07/04
S70924	04/69-05/05	⊗05/05	**7773**	04/69-10/87	**3073**	10/87-08/89	**3484**	08/89-05/05
S70925	05/69-11/05	⊗01/06	**7774**	05/69-10/87	**3074**	10/87-09/89	**3486**	09/89-11/05
S70926	05/69-04/05	⊗04/05	**7775**	05/69-08/87	**3075**	08/87-09/93	**3542**	09/93-04/05
S70927	05/69-07/05	⊗10/05	**7776**	05/69-06/87	**3076**	06/87-10/89	**3491**	10/89-07/05
S70928	05/69-09/05	⊗12/05	**7777**	05/69-06/87	**3077**	06/87-08/90	**3521**	08/90-09/05
S70929	05/69-05/04	⊗06/04	**7778**	05/69-06/87	**3078**	06/87-06/94	**3559**	06/94-05/04
S70930	05/69-11/04	⊗02/05	**7779**	05/69-08/87	**3079**	08/87-11/88	**3451**	11/88-11/04
S70931	06/69-04/05	⊗06/05	**7780**	06/69-06/87	**3080**	06/87-02/94	**3550**	02/94-09/99
			3906	09/99-09/03	**3843**	09/03-04/05		
S70932	06/69-07/05	⊗07/05	**7781**	06/69-07/87	**3081**	07/87-10/88	**3442**	10/88-11/99
			3912	11/99-07/05				
S70933	06/69-02/05	⊗02/05	**7782**	06/69-05/87	**3082**	05/87-09/88	**3443**	09/88-09/95
			3803	09/95-02/05				
S70934	07/69-04/05	⊗08/05	**7783**	07/69-07/87	**3083**	07/87-04/89	**3470**	04/89-04/05
S70935	07/69-10/05	⊗12/05	**7784**	07/69-05/87	**3084**	05/87-04/89	**3471**	04/89-10/05
S70936	07/69-06/05	⊗06/05	**7785**	07/69-05/87	**3085**	05/87-05/89	**3472**	05/89-06/05
S70937	07/69-02/05	⊗08/05	**7786**	07/69-05/87	**3086**	05/87-05/89	**3473**	05/89-12/91
			3473	07/92-02/05				
S70938	07/69-09/05	⊗12/05	**7787**	07/69-05/87	**3087**	05/87-05/89	**3474**	05/89-09/05
S70939	08/69-03/05	⊗06/05	**7788**	08/69-05/78	**7901**	05/78-05/84	**7788**	05/84-05/87
			3088	05/87-10/92	**3534**	10/92-09/99	**3907**	09/99-03/05
S70940	09/69-06/05	⊗10/05	**7789**	09/69-05/78	**7902**	05/78-05/84	**7789**	05/84-05/87
			3089	05/87-08/89	**3485**	08/89-06/05		
S70941	09/69-09/05	⊗09/05	**7790**	09/69-05/78	**7903**	05/78-05/84	**7790**	05/84-06/87
			3090	06/87-09/89	**3487**	09/89-09/05		
S70942	09/69-02/05	⊗ 05	**7791**	09/69-04/78	**7904**	04/78-05/84	**7791**	05/84-06/87
			3091	06/87-12/89	**3501**	12/89-12/91	**1830**	12/91-01/92
			3501	01/92-02/05				
S70943	09/69-02/05	⊗05/05	**7792**	09/69-03/78	**7905**	03/78-05/84	**7792**	05/84-05/87
			3092	05/87-03/93	**3537**	03/93-04/98	**3811**	04/98-02/05
S70944	09/69-04/05	⊗06/05	**7793**	09/69-05/78	**7906**	05/78-05/84	**7793**	05/84-06/87
			3093	06/87-04/93	**3538**	04/93-06/96	**3809**	06/96-04/05

Vehicle	Dates	Fate	Unit	Period	Unit	Period	Unit	Period
S70945	10/69-07/05	⊗10/05	**7794**	10/69-05/78	**7907**	05/78-05/84	**7794**	05/84-05/87
			3094	05/87-01/92	**3528**	01/92-12/99	**3916**	12/99-07/05
S70946	10/69-07/04	⊗07/04	**7795**	10/69-05/78	**7908**	05/78-05/84	**7795**	05/84-06/87
			3095	06/87-12/91	**3527**	12/91-11/99	**3914**	11/99-09/03
			3841	09/03-07/04				
S70947	10/69-05/04	⊗07/04	**7796**	10/69-05/78	**7909**	05/78-05/84	**7796**	05/84-06/87
			3096	06/87-10/91	**3525**	10/91-08/95	**3801**	08/95-05/04
S70948	11/69-02/05	⊗02/05	**7797**	11/69-05/78	**7910**	05/78-05/84	**7797**	05/84-05/87
			3097	05/87-01/92	**3526**	03/92-12/99	**3915**	12/99-02/05
S70949	11/69-04/05	⊗08/05	**7798**	11/69-05/78	**7911**	05/78-06/80	**7911**	10/80-05/84
			7798	05/84-05/87	**3098**	05/87-09/92	**3533**	09/92-08/99
			3902	08/99-04/05				
S70950	11/69-04/05	Ⓟ	**7799**	11/69-05/78	**7912**	05/78-05/84	**7799**	05/84-05/87
			3099	05/87-06/92	**3532**	06/92-01/00	**3918**	01/00-04/05
S70951	11/69-08/05	⊗08/05	**7800**	11/69-08/87	**3100**	08/87-08/88	**3438**	08/88-10/99
			3910	10/99-09/03	**3821**	09/03-08/05		
S70952	11/69-06/05	⊗08/05	**7801**	11/69-06/87	**3101**	06/87-08/88	**3446**	10/88-06/05
S70953	12/69-07/04	⊗08/04	**7802**	12/69-06/87	**3102**	06/87-09/88	**3440**	09/88-08/95
			3802	08/95-07/04				
S70954	12/69-07/05	⊗06/05	**7803**	12/69-07/87	**3103**	07/87-02/89	**3462**	02/89-07/99
			3903	07/99-07/05				
S70955	12/69-12/04	⊗12/04	**7804**	12/69-05/87	**3104**	05/87-02/89	**3461**	02/89-08/95
			3806	08/95-12/04				
S70956	12/69-02/05	⊗02/05	**7805**	12/69-05/87	**3105**	05/87-01/89	**3460**	01/89-09/95
			3805	09/95-02/05				

Class 423 4-VEP York

Trailer Second Open
TSO
S70957-S70966

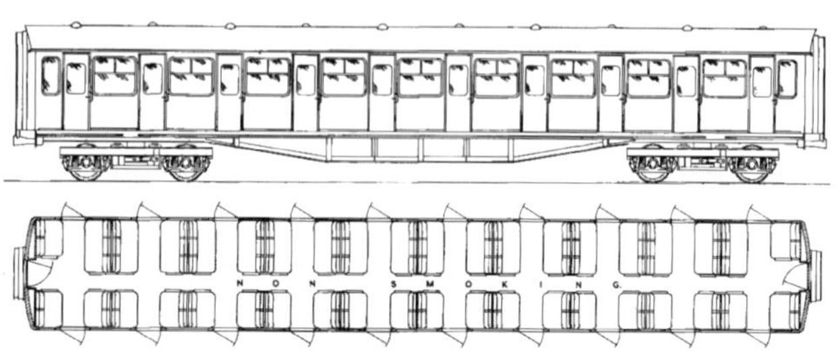

Diagram:	475 EH283 facelifted EH291	Lot Number:	30801
Body:	64' 9⅝" × 9' 3"	Weight:	30t 0cwt
Seats:	98 second	Bogies:	B5 (SR)

Vehicle	Dates	Fate	Unit	Period	Unit	Period	Unit	Period
S70957	01/70-12/04	⊗12/04	**7806**	01/70-07/87	**3106**	07/87-03/89	**3465**	03/89-08/95
			3807	08/95-12/04				
S70958	01/70-10/04	⊗10/04	**7807**	01/70-05/87	**3107**	05/87-05/90	**3515**	05/90-11/91
			1800	11/91-08/92	**3515**	08/92-10/04		
S70959	02/70-08/04	⊗10/05	**7808**	02/70-06/87	**3108**	06/87-04/89	**3469**	04/89-08/04
S70960	02/70-08/05	⊗02/05	**7809**	02/70-06/87	**3109**	06/87-05/89	**3476**	05/89-11/99
			3911	11/99-08/05				
S70961	02/70-02/05	⊗10/05	**7810**	02/70-10/87	**3110**	10/87-05/89	**3477**	05/89-08/95
			3808	08/95-02/05				
S70962	02/70-10/05	⊗10/05	**7811**	02/70-08/87	**3111**	08/87-06/89	**3475**	06/89-10/05
S70963	02/70-07/05	⊗08/05	**7812**	02/70-09/87	**3112**	09/87-02/90	**3506**	02/90-01/00
			3919	01/00-07/05				
S70964	03/70-05/04	⊗07/04	**7813**	03/70-08/87	**3113**	08/87-07/90	**3519**	07/90-05/04
S70965	03/70-10/04	⊗10/04	**7814**	03/70-09/87	**3114**	09/87-02/90	**3507**	02/90-12/99
			3917	12/99-10/04				
S70966	03/70-07/04	⊗08/04	**7815**	03/70-09/87	**3115**	09/87-03/90	**3509**	03/90-07/04

Class 421 4-CIG York

Trailer Second Open
TSO
S70967-S70996

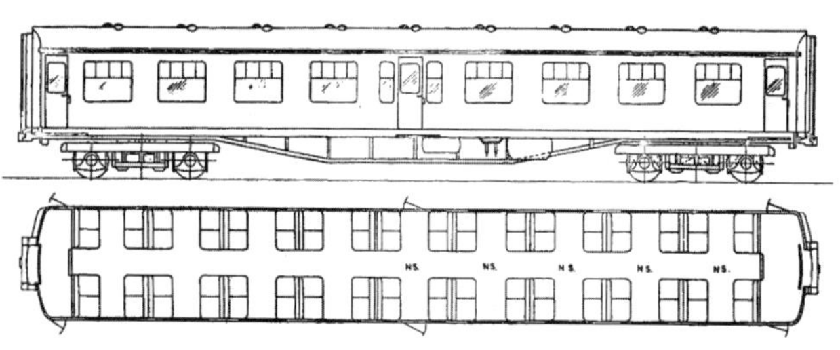

Diagram:	472 EH275 facelifted EH287	Lot Number:	30809
Body:	64' 9½" × 9' 3"	Weight:	34t 14cwt
Seats:	72 second	Bogies:	B5 (SR)

Vehicle	Dates	Fate	Unit	Period	Unit	Period	Unit	Period
S70967	06/70-02/05	⊗06/05	**7337**	06/70-08/87	**1237**	08/87-05/88	**1816**	05/88-04/90
			1303	04/90-02/05				
S70968	05/70-07/04	⊗08/04	**7338**	05/70-06/87	**1238**	06/87-06/90	**1833**	06/90-07/04
S70969	05/70-04/05	⊗09/09	**7339**	05/70-08/87	**1239**	08/87-05/88	**1817**	05/88-04/90
			1304	04/90-04/05				
S70970	06/70-04/04	⊗04/05	**7340**	06/70-09/87	**1240**	09/87-04/88	**1815**	04/88-04/90
			1302	04/90-04/04				
S70971	06/70-05/05	⊗05/05	**7341**	06/70-08/87	**1241**	08/87-04/90	**1316**	04/90-05/05
S70972	08/70-10/04	⊗11/04	**7342**	08/70-09/87	**1242**	09/87-07/88	**1820**	07/88-05/90
			1307	05/90-10/04				
S70973	10/70-08/04	⊗09/04	**7343**	10/70-09/87	**1243**	09/87-08/90	**1838**	08/90-03/92
			1322	03/92-08/04				
S70974	10/70-08/04	⊗09/04	**7344**	10/70-06/87	**1244**	06/87-04/90	**1314**	04/90-08/04
S70975	11/70-08/04	⊗09/04	**7345**	11/70-06/87	**1245**	06/87-10/90	**1844**	10/90-01/92
			1321	01/92-08/04				
S70976	01/71-06/05	⊗06/05	**7346**	01/71-06/87	**1246**	06/87-11/90	**1849**	11/90-01/92
			1318	01/92-06/05				
S70977	01/71-06/05	⊗06/05	**7347**	01/71-06/87	**1247**	06/87-12/90	**1852**	12/90-01/92
			1319	01/92-06/05				
S70978	06/70-09/04	⊗10/04	**7348**	06/70-06/87	**1248**	06/87-07/88	**1821**	07/88-05/90
			1308	05/90-09/04				
S70979	07/70-10/04	⊗06/05	**7349**	07/70-09/87	**1249**	09/87-07/90	**1836**	07/90-01/92
			1320	01/92-10/04				
S70980	07/70-04/05	⊗05/05	**7350**	07/70-08/87	**1250**	08/87-07/88	**1822**	07/88-04/90
			1309	04/90-04/05				
S70981	08/70-08/04	⊗09/04	**7351**	08/70-08/87	**1251**	08/87-04/88	**1814**	04/88-04/90
			1301	04/90-08/04				
S70982	08/70-12/04	⊗01/05	**7352**	08/70-09/87	**1252**	09/87-04/90	**1313**	04/90-12/04
S70983	09/70-09/04	⊗10/04	**7353**	09/70-09/87	**1253**	09/87-11/90	**1317**	11/90-09/04
S70984	09/70-05/05	⊗07/05	**7354**	09/70-11/87	**1254**	11/87-05/90	**1831**	05/90-05/05
S70985	10/70-12/04	⊗02/05	**7355**	10/70-02/88	**1255**	02/88-10/90	**1845**	10/90-12/04
S70986	11/70-02/05	⊗02/05	**7356**	11/70-06/87	**1256**	06/87-11/90	**1847**	11/90-02/05
S70987	10/70-10/04	⊗10/04	**7357**	10/70-07/87	**1257**	07/87-06/90	**1835**	06/90-10/04
S70988	10/70-02/05	⊗02/05	**7358**	10/70-09/87	**1258**	09/87-06/90	**1834**	06/90-02/05
S70989	10/70-07/04	⊗08/04	**7359**	10/70-06/87	**1259**	06/87-09/90	**1841**	09/90-07/04
S70990	11/70-07/05	⊗07/05	**7360**	11/70-06/87	**1260**	06/87-05/91	**1858**	05/91-07/05
S70991	11/70-02/05	⊗02/05	**7361**	11/70-08/87	**1261**	08/87-11/90	**1848**	11/90-02/05
S70992	12/70-05/05	⊗05/05	**7362**	12/70-05/87	**1262**	05/87-01/91	**1853**	01/91-05/05
S70993	12/70-05/04	⊗06/04	**7363**	12/70-07/87	**1263**	07/87-08/90	**1839**	08/90-05/04
S70994	11/70-12/04	⊗06/05	**7364**	11/70-07/87	**1264**	07/87-04/90	**1315**	04/90-12/04
S70995	12/70-05/80	⊗11/03	**7365**	12/70-12/78	**7300**	01/80-04/80		
S70996	01/71-12/05	⊗12/05	**7366**	01/71-05/87	**1266**	05/87-04/91	**1857**	04/91-12/05

Class 423 4-VEP York

Trailer Second Open
TSO
S70997-S71034

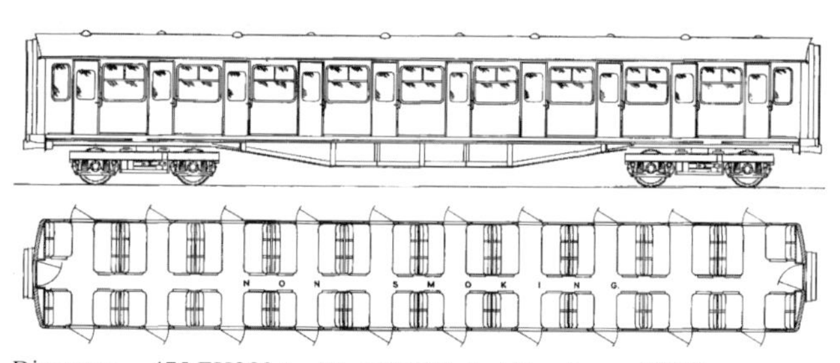

Diagram:	475 EH283 facelifted EH291	Lot Number:	30812
Body:	64' 9⅝" × 9' 3"	Weight:	30t 0cwt
Seats:	98 second	Bogies:	B5 (SR)

Vehicle	Dates	Fate	Unit	Period	Unit	Period	Unit	Period
S70997	04/72-05/04	⊗07/04	**7816**	04/72-05/87	**3116**	05/87-02/90	**3510**	03/90-05/04
S70998	04/72-03/05	⊗07/05	**7817**	04/72-08/87	**3117**	08/87-03/90	**3508**	03/90-03/05
S70999	04/72-05/05	⊗05/05	**7818**	04/72-06/87	**3118**	06/87-04/90	**3511**	04/90-06/93
			3511	11/94-05/05				
S71000	04/72-12/88	⊗10/90	**7819**	04/72-09/87	**3119**	09/87-12/88		
S71001	05/72-05/05	⊗05/05	**7820**	05/72-03/88	**3120**	03/88-03/92	**3531**	03/92-05/05
S71002	05/72-07/05	⊗07/05	**7821**	05/72-12/87	**3121**	12/87-05/91	**3523**	05/91-07/05
S71003	06/72-11/04	⊗03/05	**7822**	06/72-04/88	**3122**	04/88-06/89	**3478**	06/89-11/99
			3913	11/99-09/03	**3813**	09/03-11/04		
S71004	06/72-07/05	⊗07/05	**7823**	06/72-06/87	**3123**	06/87-07/89	**3479**	07/89-07/05
S71005	06/72-04/05	⊗06/05	**7824**	06/72-03/88	**3124**	03/88-08/89	**3482**	08/89-04/05
S71006	06/72-06/04	⊗06/04	**7825**	06/72-07/87	**3125**	07/87-12/91	**3529**	12/91-06/04
S71007	06/72-07/05	⊗07/05	**7826**	06/72-12/87	**3126**	12/87-08/89	**3483**	08/89-07/05
S71008	07/72-04/05	⊗08/05	**7827**	07/72-09/88	**3127**	09/88-09/89	**3488**	09/89-04/05
S71009	07/72-07/05	⊗10/05	**7828**	07/72-08/87	**3128**	08/87-09/89	**3489**	09/89-07/05
S71010	08/72- 05	⊗ 05	**7829**	08/72-11/87	**3129**	11/87-10/89	**3492**	10/89- 05
S71011	08/72-11/04	⊗02/05	**7830**	08/72-07/87	**3130**	07/87-10/89	**3493**	10/89-11/04
S71012	08/72-08/05	⊗10/05	**7831**	08/72-08/87	**3131**	08/87-11/89	**3497**	11/89-08/05
S71013	08/72-08/05	⊗10/05	**7832**	08/72-07/87	**3132**	07/87-11/89	**3496**	11/89-08/05
S71014	09/72-05/05	⊗05/05	**7833**	09/72-07/87	**3133**	07/87-11/89	**3494**	11/89-05/05
S71015	09/72-11/05	⊗12/05	**7834**	09/72-05/87	**3134**	05/87-11/92	**3535**	11/92-11/05
S71016	09/72-05/04	⊗07/04	**7835**	09/72-05/87	**3135**	05/87-05/90	**3512**	05/90-05/04
S71017	09/72-07/05	⊗10/05	**7836**	09/72-10/87	**3136**	10/87-02/90	**3503**	02/90-09/03
			3844	09/03-07/05				
S71018	09/72-11/05	⊗12/05	**7837**	09/72-05/87	**3137**	05/87-06/90	**3514**	06/90-11/05
S71019	10/72-06/04	⊗07/04	**7838**	10/72-07/87	**3138**	07/87-06/90	**3517**	06/90-06/04

S71020	10/72-05/04	⊗07/04	**7839**	10/72-05/87	**3139**	05/87-12/93	**3546**	12/93-05/04
S71021	11/72-11/04	⊗10/04	**7840**	11/72-04/80	**7299**	07/86-08/86	**7724**	08/86-12/87
			3024	12/87-11/88	**3452**	11/88-11/04		
S71022	11/72-04/05	⊗07/05	**7841**	11/72-07/87	**3141**	07/87-05/90	**3513**	05/90-07/99
			3904	07/99-04/05				
S71023	12/72-04/05	⊗06/05	**7842**	12/72-10/87	**3142**	10/87-06/90	**3516**	06/90-04/05
S71024	12/72-11/05	⊗01/06	**7843**	12/72-06/87	**3143**	06/87-10/89	**3490**	10/89-11/05
S71025	02/73-04/05	⊗08/05	**7844**	02/73-06/87	**3144**	06/87-07/90	**3520**	07/90-04/05
S71026	02/73-08/05	⊗10/05	**7845**	02/73-07/87	**3145**	07/87-11/89	**3495**	11/89-08/05
S71027	03/73-08/05	⊗10/05	**7846**	03/73-08/87	**3146**	08/87-12/89	**3498**	12/89-08/05
S71028	03/73-04/05	⊗06/05	**7847**	03/73-06/87	**3147**	06/87-07/93	**3541**	07/93-05/98
			3812	05/98-04/05				
S71029	03/73-11/04	⊗11/04	**7848**	03/73-09/87	**3148**	09/87-09/90	**3522**	09/90-09/99
			3909	09/99-11/04				
S71030	04/73-10/04	⊗10/04	**7849**	04/73-08/87	**3149**	08/87-02/94	**3549**	02/94-10/04
S71031	04/73-04/05	⊗06/05	**7850**	04/73-06/87	**3150**	06/87-01/90	**3502**	01/90-06/96
			3810	06/96-04/05				
S71032	05/73-08/05	Ⓟ⊗	**7851**	05/73-05/87	**3151**	05/87-01/90	**3504**	01/90-09/03
			3822	09/03-08/05				
S71033	05/73-12/04	⊗12/04	**7852**	05/73-05/87	**3152**	05/87-02/94	**3551**	02/94-12/04
S71034	05/73-05/04	⊗07/04	**7853**	05/73-07/87	**3153**	07/87-03/94	**3552**	03/94-05/04

Class 421 4-CIG York
Trailer Second Open
TSO
S71035-S71105

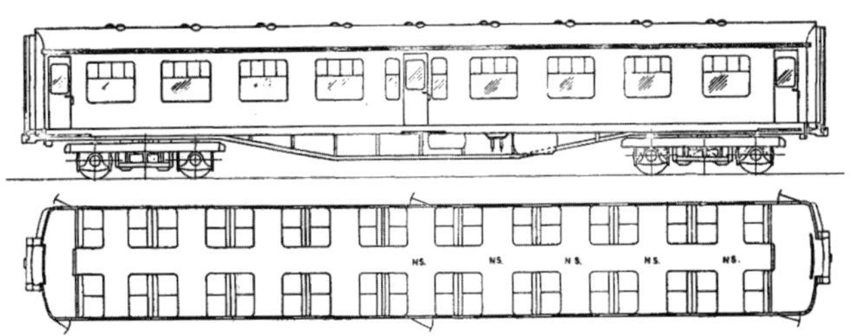

Diagram:	472 EH275 facelifted EH287	Lot Number:	30817
Body:	64' 9½" × 9' 3"	Weight:	34t 14cwt
Seats:	72 second	Bogies:	B5 (SR)

S71035	02/71-07/04	⊗09/04	**7367**	02/71-08/87	**1267**	08/87-06/88	**1818**	06/88-04/90
			1305	04/90-07/04				
S71036	02/71-06/03	⊗11/08	**7368**	02/71-06/87	**1268**	06/87-12/90	**1850**	12/90-06/03
S71037	02/71-07/05	⊗07/05	**7369**	02/71-05/87	**1269**	05/87-05/90	**1832**	05/90-07/05
S71038	03/71-12/04	⊗07/05	**7370**	03/71-08/87	**1270**	08/87-01/91	**1855**	01/91-12/04
S71039	02/71-02/05	⊗03/05	**7371**	02/71-08/87	**1271**	08/87-12/90	**1851**	12/90-02/05
S71040	02/71-02/05	⊗02/05	**7372**	02/71-06/87	**1272**	06/87-07/90	**1837**	07/90-02/05
S71041	02/71-07/04	Ⓟ	**7373**	02/71-06/87	**1273**	06/87-06/88	**1819**	06/88-05/90
			1306	05/90-07/04				
S71042	03/71-05/04	⊗06/04	**7374**	03/71-06/87	**1274**	06/87-08/90	**1840**	08/90-05/04
S71043	03/71-04/04	⊗06/04	**7375**	03/71-06/87	**1275**	06/87-09/90	**1842**	09/90-04/04
S71044	04/71-07/04	⊗07/04	**7376**	04/71-08/87	**1276**	08/87-10/89	**1751**	10/89-12/90
			1734	12/90-07/04				
S71045	04/71-06/05	⊗10/05	**7377**	04/71-08/87	**1277**	08/87-06/91	**1859**	06/91-06/05
S71046	04/71-03/03	⊗08/04	**7378**	04/71-06/87	**1278**	06/87-10/89	**1752**	10/89-05/91
			1738	05/91-03/03				
S71047	04/71-07/04	⊗09/04	**7379**	04/71-06/87	**1279**	06/87-09/89	**1757**	09/89-10/90
			1733	10/90-07/04				
S71048	04/71-04/89	⊗03/90	**7380**	04/71-06/87	**1280**	06/87-04/89		
S71049	05/71-10/04	⊗01/05	**7381**	05/71-06/87	**1281**	06/87-10/90	**1843**	10/90-10/04
S71050	05/71-02/04	⊗08/04	**7382**	05/71-06/87	**1282**	06/87-10/89	**1754**	10/89-02/91
			1735	02/91-02/04				
S71051	05/71-07/04	⊗03/05	**7383**	05/71-01/86	**7300**	03/86-06/87	**1100**	06/87-10/92
			1751	10/92-07/04				
S71052	05/71-03/03	⊗06/04	**7384**	05/71-06/87	**1284**	06/87-10/89	**1753**	10/89-02/91
			1736	02/91-03/03				
S71053	05/71-06/05	⊗10/05	**7385**	05/71-06/87	**1285**	06/87-07/91	**1861**	07/91-06/05
S71054	05/71-06/05	⊗10/05	**7386**	05/71-06/87	**1286**	06/87-08/91	**1862**	08/91-06/05
S71055	05/71-02/05	⊗02/05	**7387**	05/71-06/87	**1287**	06/87-11/90	**1846**	11/90-02/05
S71056	05/71-04/05	⊗05/05	**7388**	05/71-06/87	**1288**	06/87-01/91	**1854**	01/91-04/05
S71057	06/71-04/05	⊗05/05	**7389**	06/71-07/87	**1289**	07/87-02/91	**1856**	02/91-04/05
S71058	06/71-09/03	⊗08/04	**7390**	06/71-09/87	**1290**	09/87-10/89	**1755**	10/89-03/91
			1737	03/91-09/03				
S71059	06/71-08/05	⊗10/05	**7391**	06/71-06/87	**1291**	06/87-09/91	**1864**	09/91-08/05
S71060	06/71-06/05	⊗10/05	**7392**	06/71-06/87	**1292**	06/87-09/91	**1863**	09/91-06/05
S71061	06/71-11/05	⊗ 06	**7393**	06/71-06/87	**1293**	06/87-12/91	**1866**	12/91-11/05
S71062	06/71-06/05	⊗10/05	**7394**	06/71-05/87	**1294**	05/87-01/92	**1867**	01/92-06/05
S71063	07/71-05/05	⊗07/05	**7395**	07/71-08/87	**1295**	08/87-11/91	**1865**	11/91-05/05
S71064	07/71-02/04	⊗08/04	**7396**	07/71-06/87	**1296**	06/87-11/89	**1758**	11/89-02/92
			1744	02/92-02/04				
S71065	08/71-02/05	⊗03/05	**7397**	08/71-06/87	**1297**	06/87-11/89	**1756**	11/89-01/92
			1743	01/92-02/05				
S71066	08/71-06/04	⊗06/04	**7398**	08/71-08/87	**1298**	08/87-11/89	**1759**	11/89-01/92
			1739	01/92-06/04				
S71067	08/71-05/04	⊗08/04	**7399**	08/71-05/87	**1299**	05/87-11/89	**1760**	11/89-05/92
			1748	05/92-05/04				
S71068	08/71-09/95	⊗05/04	**7400**	08/71-06/87	**1300**	06/87-10/89	**1761**	10/89-05/92
			1749	05/92-09/95				
S71069	09/71-05/05	⊗10/05	**7401**	09/71-05/83	**2601**	05/83-10/83	**7401**	10/83-06/87
			1201	06/87-02/92	**1868**	02/92-05/05		
S71070	09/71-07/05	⊗10/05	**7402**	09/71-05/83	**7402**	10/83-05/87	**1202**	05/87-06/91
			1860	06/91-07/05				
S71071	09/71-06/05	⊗10/05	**7403**	09/71-05/83	**2602**	05/83-10/83	**7403**	10/83-08/87
			1203	08/87-02/92	**1869**	02/92-06/05		
S71072	09/71-07/04	⊗07/04	**7404**	09/71-05/83	**7404**	10/83-06/87	**1204**	06/87-07/92
			1875	07/92-05/93	**2001**	05/93-01/97	**1802**	01/97-07/04
S71073	09/71-02/05	⊗06/05	**7405**	09/71-07/87	**1205**	07/87-07/92	**1874**	07/92-02/05
S71074	09/71-08/04	⊗08/04	**7406**	09/71-08/87	**1206**	08/87-03/92	**1871**	04/92-08/04
S71075	09/71-09/00	⊗11/03	**7407**	09/71-12/86	**1812**	01/87-09/00		
S71076	10/71-09/04	⊗09/04	**7408**	10/71-07/87	**1208**	07/87-05/92	**1872**	05/92-09/04
S71077	10/71-08/04	⊗09/04	**7409**	10/71-07/87	**1209**	07/87-06/92	**1873**	06/92-08/04
S71078	10/71-08/04	⊗08/04	**7410**	10/71-05/87	**1210**	05/87-09/92	**1879**	09/92-08/04
S71079	10/71-08/04	⊗09/04	**7411**	10/71-08/87	**1211**	08/87-07/92	**1876**	07/92-08/04
S71080	11/71-04/05	Ⓟ	**7412**	11/71-09/87	**1212**	09/87-10/92	**1881**	10/92-04/05
S71081	11/71-08/04	⊗09/04	**7413**	11/71-09/87	**1213**	09/87-07/92	**1877**	07/92-08/04
S71082	12/71-02/05	⊗10/05	**7414**	12/71-09/87	**1214**	09/87-11/92	**1883**	11/92-02/05
S71083	12/71-07/05	⊗07/05	**7415**	12/71-08/87	**1215**	08/87-10/92	**1882**	10/92-07/05
S71084	12/71-09/04	⊗10/04	**7416**	12/71-09/87	**1216**	09/87-12/92	**1887**	12/92-09/04
S71085	12/71-02/05	Ⓟ	**7417**	12/71-09/87	**1217**	09/87-11/92	**1884**	11/92-02/05
S71086	12/71-[illegible]04	⊗[illegible]04	**7418**	12/71-09/87	**1218**	09/87-08/92	**1878**	08/92-[illegible]04
S71087	12/71-11/04	⊗11/04	**7419**	12/71-09/87	**1219**	09/87-12/92	**1885**	12/92-11/04
S71088	01/72-09/04	⊗10/04	**7420**	01/72-06/87	**1220**	06/87-09/92	**1880**	09/92-09/04
S71089	01/72-07/04	⊗08/04	**7421**	01/72-08/87	**1221**	08/87-04/92	**1870**	04/92-07/04
S71090	01/72-09/04	⊗10/04	**7422**	01/72-08/87	**1222**	08/87-12/92	**1886**	12/92-09/04
S71091	01/72-02/05	⊗10/05	**7423**	01/72-08/87	**1223**	08/87-01/93	**1888**	01/93-02/05
S71092	02/72-02/05	⊗08/05	**7424**	02/72-09/87	**1224**	09/87-01/93	**1889**	01/93-02/05
S71093	02/72-04/05	⊗08/05	**7425**	02/72-08/87	**1225**	08/87-02/93	**1890**	02/93-04/05
S71094	02/72-09/04	⊗10/04	**7426**	02/72-08/87	**1226**	08/87-03/93	**1891**	03/93-09/04
S71095	02/72-07/04	⊗07/04	**7427**	02/72-03/86	**1801**	04/86-05/93	**2003**	05/93-01/97
			1801	01/97-07/04				
S71096	03/72-07/05	⊗07/05	**7428**	03/72-05/86	**1804**	05/86-07/05		
S71097	03/72-04/04	⊗07/04	**7429**	03/72-03/86	**1802**	04/86-12/89	**1762**	12/89-11/91
			1740	11/91-04/04				
S71098	02/72-07/04	⊗09/04	**7430**	02/72-03/86	**1803**	05/86-07/04		
S71099	02/72-04/04	⊗04/04	**7431**	02/72-11/86	**1811**	12/86-04/04		
S71100	03/72-11/05	⊗01/05	**7432**	03/72-05/86	**1805**	06/86-11/05		
S71101	03/72-09/04	⊗09/04	**7433**	03/72-06/86	**1806**	06/86-09/04		
S71102	03/72-07/04	⊗08/04	**7434**	03/72-06/86	**1807**	07/86-07/04		
S71103	03/72-08/04	⊗08/04	**7435**	03/72-07/86	**1808**	09/86-08/04		
S71104	04/72-02/04	⊗03/04	**7436**	04/72-08/86	**1809**	09/86-02/04		
S71105	05/72-02/04	⊗03/04	**7437**	05/72-09/86	**1810**	11/86-02/04		

Class 421 4-CIG York
Trailer Second Open
TSO
S71106

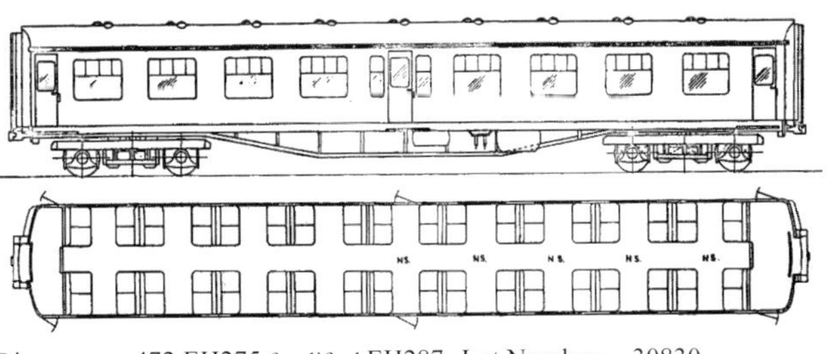

Diagram:	472 EH275 facelifted EH287	Lot Number:	30830
Body:	64' 9½" × 9' 3"	Weight:	34t 14cwt
Seats:	72 second	Bogies:	B5 (SR)

S71106	05/72-02/04	⊗12/04	**7438**	05/72-08/79	**7300**	08/79-01/80	**7438**	01/80-02/87
			1813	02/87-02/04				

Class 309 Wolverton

Trailer Corridor Second
TSK, TSO
E71107-E71110

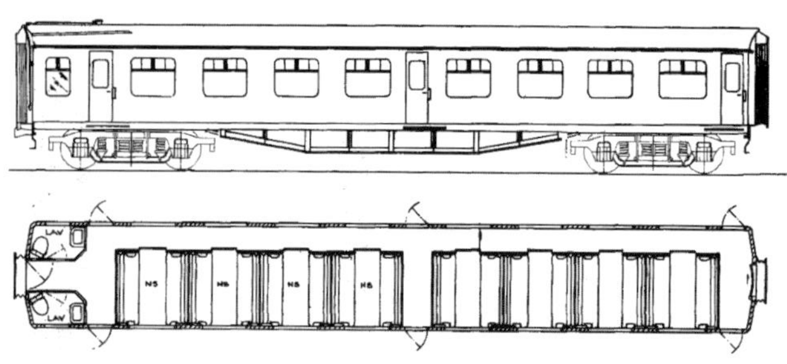

As converted, Diagram 469

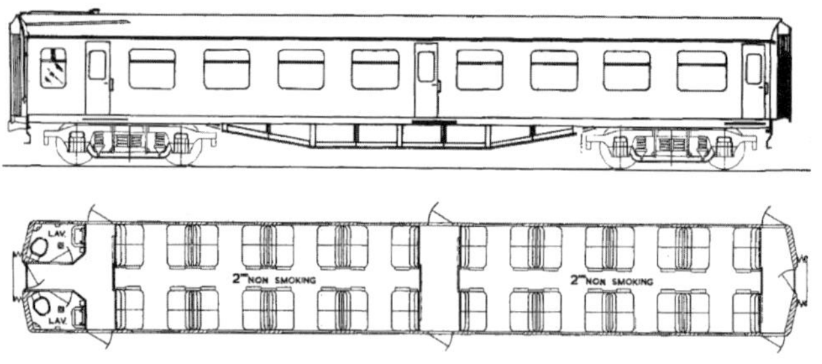

Later converted to TSOL, Diagram EH207

Diagram:	469 EH207	Lot Number:	30871
Body:	64' 6" × 9' 3"	Weight:	34t 0cwt
Seats:	64 second 2 toilets	Bogies:	Commonwealth

E71107	04/74-02/94	⊗10/97	**607**	04/74- 81	**617**	81-10/82	**309617**	10/82-07/85
			309607	07/85-02/94				⊂**26203**
E71108	05/74-03/98	⊗03/98	**605**	05/74- 81	**615**	81-09/82	**309615**	09/82-03/85
			309605	03/85-03/98				⊂**26189**
E71109	03/74-03/98	⊗03/98	**606**	03/74- 81	**309616**	81-07/85	**309606**	07/85-03/98
								⊂**26196**
E71110	04/74-05/93	⊗07/93	**608**	04/74-07/81	**309618**	07/81-10/85	**309608**	10/85-05/93
								⊂**26204**

Class 309 Wolverton

Trailer Corridor Composite
TCK, later TCsoL
E71111-E71114

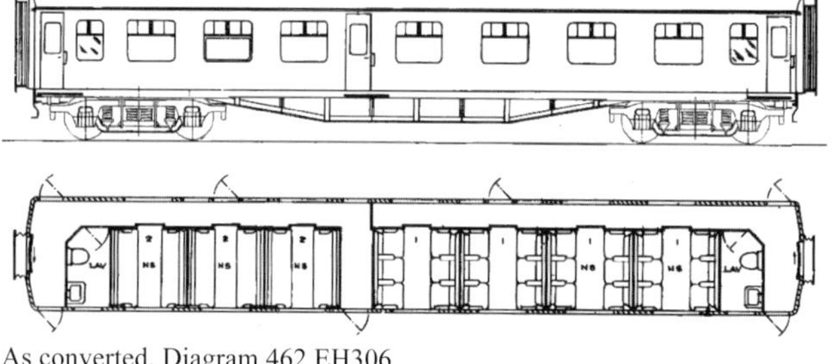

As converted, Diagram 462 EH306

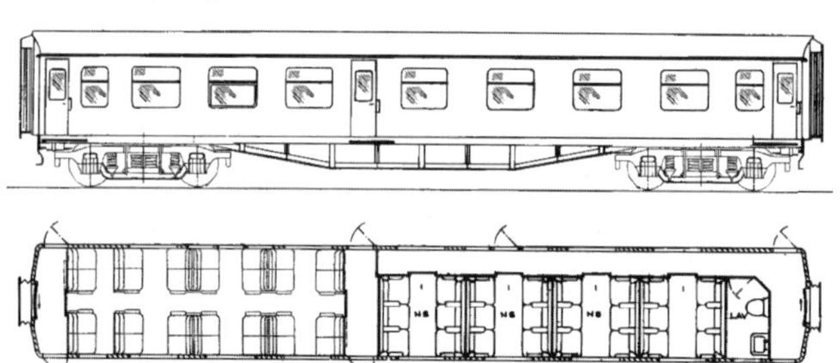

Later converted to TCsoL, Diagram EH309

Diagram:	462 EH306 EH309	Lot Number:	30872
Body:	64' 6" × 9' 3"	Weight:	35t 0cwt
Seats:	24 first 24 second 2 toilets later 24 first 28 second 1 toilet	Bogies:	Commonwealth

E71111	04/74-02/94	⊗10/97	**607**	04/74-11/82	**309607**	11/82-02/94	⊂**16246**
E71112	03/74-03/98	⊗03/98	**606**	03/74-12/81	**309606**	12/81-03/98	⊂**16249**
E71113	05/74-03/98	⊗03/98	**605**	05/74-12/81	**309605**	12/81-03/98	⊂**16244**
E71114	04/74-05/93	⊗07/93	**608**	04/74-09/82	**309608**	09/82-05/93	⊂**16252**

Class 423 4-VEP York

Trailer Second Open
TSO
S71115-S71155

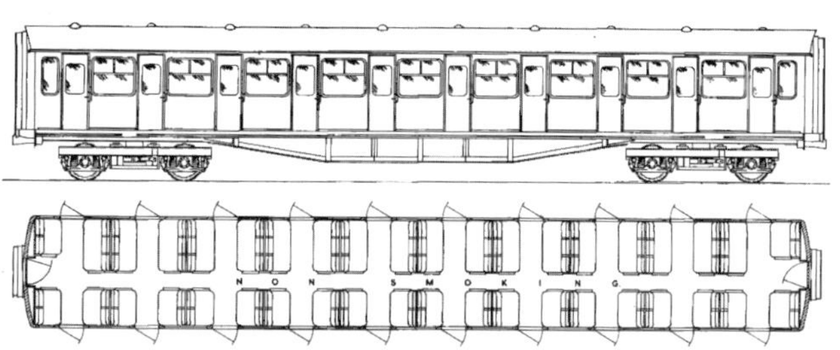

Diagram:	475 EH283 facelifted EH291	Lot Number:	30852
Body:	64' 9⅝" × 9' 3"	Weight:	30t 0cwt
Seats:	98 second	Bogies:	B5 (SR)

S71115	05/73-04/05	⊗04/05	**7854**	05/73-05/87	**3154**	05/87-06/93	**3539**	06/93-04/05
S71116	05/73-04/05	⊗04/05	**7855**	05/73-05/87	**3155**	05/87-07/93	**3540**	07/93-04/05
S71117	06/73-05/04	⊗06/04	**7856**	06/73-06/87	**3156**	06/87-04/94	**3555**	04/94-05/04
S71118	06/73-07/04	⊗08/04	**7857**	06/73-09/87	**3157**	09/87-07/94	**3561**	07/94-07/04
S71119	06/73-05/04	⊗06/04	**7858**	06/73-06/87	**3158**	06/87-05/94	**3557**	05/94-05/04
S71120	06/73-06/02	⊗10/03	**7859**	06/73-08/87	**3159**	08/87-09/94	**3567**	09/94-06/02
S71121	07/73-07/04	⊗08/04	**7860**	07/73-06/87	**3160**	06/87-07/94	**3563**	07/94-07/04
S71122	07/73-10/05	⊗12/05	**7861**	07/73-05/87	**3161**	05/87-11/93	**3545**	11/93-10/05
S71123	07/73-10/05	⊗12/05	**7862**	07/73-07/87	**3162**	07/87-08/94	**3565**	08/94-10/05
S71124	07/73-06/05	⊗07/05	**7863**	07/73-06/87	**3163**	06/87-12/94	**3572**	12/94-06/05
S71125	08/73-08/05	⊗09/05	**7864**	08/73-08/87	**3164**	08/87-03/95	**3584**	03/95-08/05
S71126	08/73-12/05	⊗12/05	**7865**	08/73-08/87	**3165**	08/87-07/94	**3564**	07/94-12/05
S71127	08/73-11/04	⊗10/04	**7866**	08/73-07/87	**3166**	07/87-05/94	**3556**	05/94-11/04
S71128	08/73-10/05	⊗	**7867**	08/73-08/87	**3167**	08/87-10/94	**3568**	10/94-10/05
S71129	09/73-11/04	⊗02/05	**7868**	09/73-08/87	**3168**	08/87-03/88	**3421**	03/88-11/04
S71130	09/73-05/04	⊗08/05	**7869**	09/73-05/87	**3169**	05/87-02/95	**3582**	02/95-05/04
S71131	09/73-09/05	⊗12/05	**7870**	09/73-07/87	**3170**	07/87-11/93	**3544**	11/93-09/05
S71132	09/73-10/05	⊗12/05	**7871**	09/73-07/87	**3171**	07/87-01/94	**3547**	01/94-10/05
S71133	10/73-09/05	⊗10/05	**7872**	10/73-06/87	**3172**	06/87-06/94	**3560**	06/94-09/05
S71134	10/73-11/04	⊗02/05	**7873**	10/73-05/87	**3173**	05/87-10/93	**3543**	10/93-11/04
S71135	10/73-06/05	⊗08/05	**7874**	10/73-07/87	**3174**	07/87-12/89	**3499**	12/89-06/05
S71136	10/73-08/05	⊗09/05	**7875**	10/73-08/87	**3175**	08/87-02/94	**3548**	02/94-08/05
S71137	11/73-11/04	⊗10/04	**7876**	11/73-05/87	**3176**	05/87-03/94	**3554**	03/94-11/04
S71138	12/73-10/05	⊗10/05	**7877**	12/73-08/87	**3177**	08/87-07/94	**3562**	07/94-10/05
S71139	01/74-11/04	⊗02/05	**7878**	01/74-07/87	**3178**	09/87-11/94	**3570**	11/94-11/04
S71140	01/74-07/05	⊗07/05	**7879**	01/74-06/87	**3179**	06/87-06/95	**3589**	06/95-07/05
S71141	02/74-05/05	⊗05/05	**7880**	02/74-07/87	**3180**	07/87-03/94	**3553**	03/94-05/05
S71142	02/74-12/04	⊗02/05	**7881**	02/74-08/87	**3181**	08/87-09/94	**3566**	09/94-12/04
S71143	12/73-06/05	⊗07/05	**7882**	12/73-07/87	**3182**	07/87-09/95	**3591**	09/95-06/05
S71144	02/74-07/05	⊗07/05	**7883**	02/74-09/87	**3183**	09/87-12/94	**3573**	12/94-07/05
S71145	02/74-08/05	⊗10/05	**7884**	02/74-09/87	**3184**	09/87-03/95	**3586**	03/95-08/05
S71146	02/74-05/04	⊗08/05	**7885**	02/74-07/87	**3185**	07/87-05/95	**3588**	05/95-05/04
S71147	03/74-10/05	⊗10/05	**7886**	03/74-10/87	**3186**	10/87-05/95	**3587**	05/95-10/05
S71148	03/74-12/04	⊗02/05	**7887**	03/74-09/87	**3187**	09/87-11/94	**3571**	11/94-12/04
S71149	03/74-08/05	⊗08/05	**7888**	03/74-08/87	**3188**	08/87-12/94	**3574**	12/94-08/05
S71150	03/74-11/04	⊗02/05	**7889**	03/74-08/87	**3189**	08/87-12/94	**3575**	12/94-11/04
S71151	04/74-06/05	⊗06/05	**7890**	04/74-08/87	**3190**	08/87-01/95	**3577**	01/95-06/05
S71152	04/74-08/05	⊗09/05	**7891**	04/74-06/87	**3191**	06/87-01/95	**3579**	01/95-08/05
S71153	04/74-07/05	⊗07/05	**7892**	04/74-07/87	**3192**	07/87-02/95	**3583**	02/95-07/05
S71154	05/74-07/05	⊗07/05	**7893**	05/74-09/87	**3193**	09/87-03/95	**3585**	03/95-07/05
S71155	05/74-10/05	⊗10/05	**7894**	05/74-10/87	**3194**	10/87-07/95	**3590**	07/95-10/05

Class 430 4-REP York

Trailer Brake Corridor First
TBFK
S71156-S71159

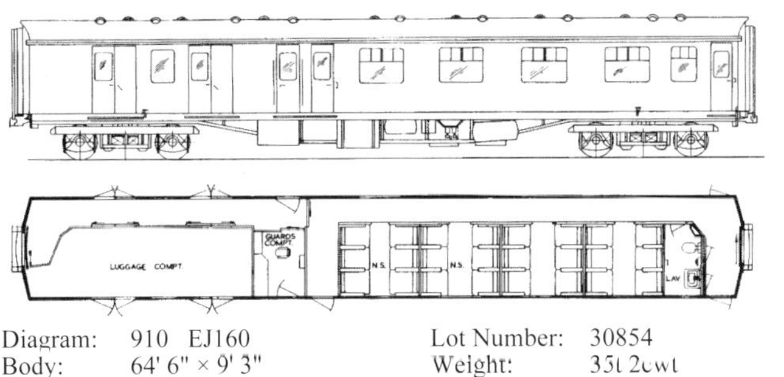

Diagram:	910 EJ160	Lot Number:	30854
Body:	64' 6" × 9' 3"	Weight:	35t 2cwt
Seats:	24 first 1 toilet	Bogies:	B5 (SR)

S71156	09/74-05/89	⊗06/90	**3012**	09/74-05/86	**2012**	05/86-06/87	**2807**	06/87-04/88	
									⊂15423
S71157	10/74-04/88	⊗08/90	**3013**	10/74-05/86	**2013**	05/86-12/87	**2905**	12/87-04/88	
									⊂15871
S71158	11/74-09/88	⊗04/90	**3014**	11/74-04/86	**2014**	04/86-03/88	**2906**	03/88-05/88	
			8015	06/88-09/88					⊂15876
S71159	12/74-11/86	⊗04/90	**3015**	12/74-04/86	**2015**	04/86-11/86			⊂15909

Class 491 4-TC York

Trailer Brake Corridor Second
TBSK
S71160-S71161

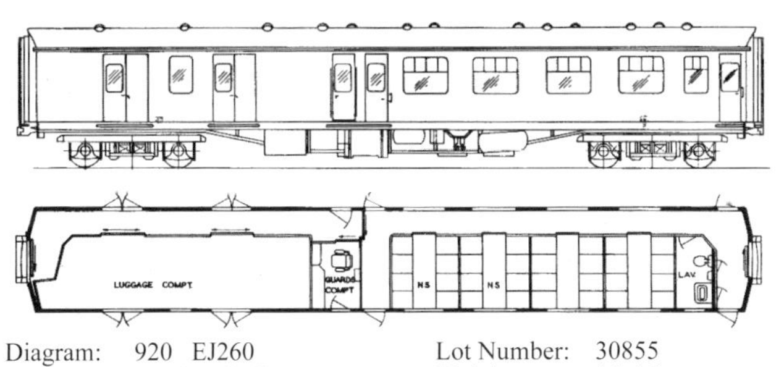

Diagram:	920 EJ260	Lot Number:	30855
Body:	64' 6" × 9' 3"	Weight:	34t 16cwt
Seats:	32 second 1 toilet	Bogies:	B5 (SR)

S71160	02/75-06/87	⊗04/90	**433**	02/75-09/86	**8033**	09/86-06/87	⊂34637
S71161	01/75-09/88	⊗08/90	**434**	01/75-09/86	**8034**	09/86-09/88	⊂34640

Class 491 4-TC York

Trailer Corridor First
TFK
S71162-S71167

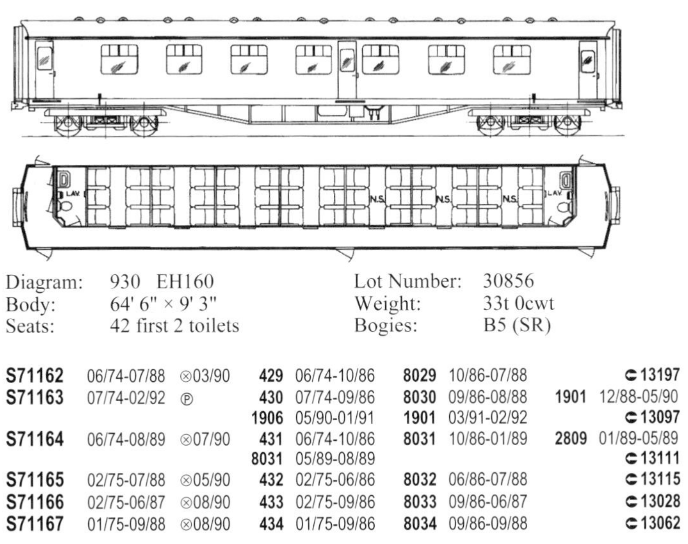

Diagram:	930 EH160	Lot Number:	30856
Body:	64' 6" × 9' 3"	Weight:	33t 0cwt
Seats:	42 first 2 toilets	Bogies:	B5 (SR)

S71162	06/74-07/88	⊗03/90	**429**	06/74-10/86	**8029**	10/86-07/88			⊂13197
S71163	07/74-02/92	Ⓟ	**430**	07/74-09/86	**8030**	09/86-08/88	**1901**	12/88-05/90	
			1906	05/90-01/91	**1901**	03/91-02/92			⊂13097
S71164	06/74-08/89	⊗07/90	**431**	06/74-10/86	**8031**	10/86-01/89	**2809**	01/89-05/89	
			8031	05/89-08/89					⊂13111
S71165	02/75-07/88	⊗05/90	**432**	02/75-06/86	**8032**	06/86-07/88			⊂13115
S71166	02/75-06/87	⊗08/90	**433**	02/75-09/86	**8033**	09/86-06/87			⊂13028
S71167	01/75-09/88	⊗08/90	**434**	01/75-09/86	**8034**	09/86-09/88			⊂13062

Class 312/0 York

Trailer Second Open
TSO
E71168-E71193

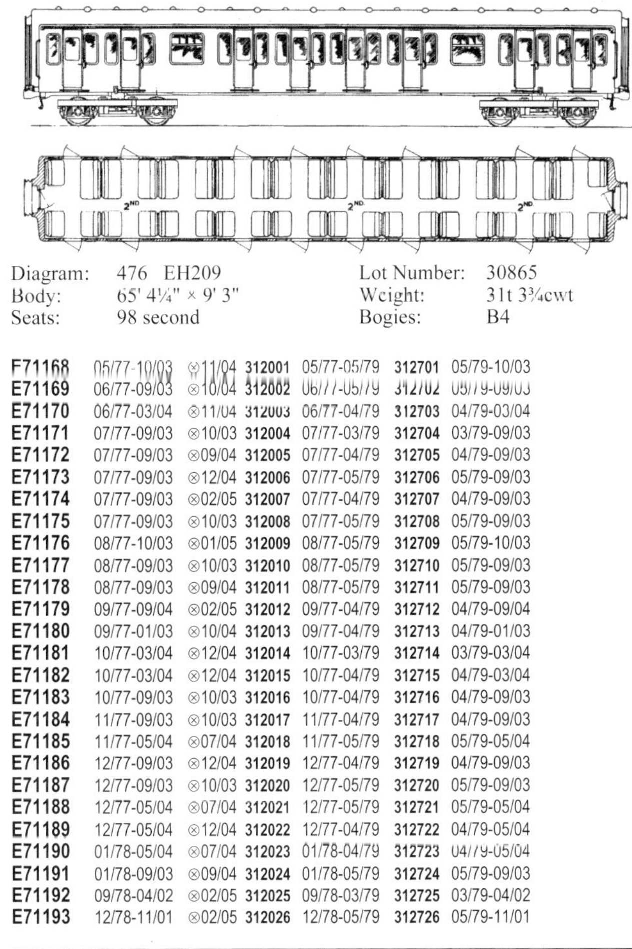

Diagram:	476 EH209	Lot Number:	30865
Body:	65' 4¼" × 9' 3"	Weight:	31t 3¾cwt
Seats:	98 second	Bogies:	B4

E71168	05/77-10/03	⊗11/04	**312001**	05/77-05/79	**312701**	05/79-10/03
E71169	06/77-09/03	⊗10/04	**312002**	06/77-05/79	**312702**	05/79-09/03
E71170	06/77-03/04	⊗11/04	**312003**	06/77-04/79	**312703**	04/79-03/04
E71171	07/77-09/03	⊗10/03	**312004**	07/77-03/79	**312704**	03/79-09/03
E71172	07/77-09/03	⊗09/04	**312005**	07/77-04/79	**312705**	04/79-09/03
E71173	07/77-09/03	⊗12/04	**312006**	07/77-05/79	**312706**	05/79-09/03
E71174	07/77-09/03	⊗02/05	**312007**	07/77-04/79	**312707**	04/79-09/03
E71175	07/77-09/03	⊗10/03	**312008**	07/77-05/79	**312708**	05/79-09/03
E71176	08/77-10/03	⊗01/05	**312009**	08/77-05/79	**312709**	05/79-10/03
E71177	08/77-09/03	⊗10/03	**312010**	08/77-05/79	**312710**	05/79-09/03
E71178	08/77-09/03	⊗09/04	**312011**	08/77-05/79	**312711**	05/79-09/03
E71179	09/77-09/04	⊗02/05	**312012**	09/77-04/79	**312712**	04/79-09/04
E71180	09/77-01/03	⊗10/04	**312013**	09/77-04/79	**312713**	04/79-01/03
E71181	10/77-03/04	⊗12/04	**312014**	10/77-03/79	**312714**	03/79-03/04
E71182	10/77-03/04	⊗12/04	**312015**	10/77-04/79	**312715**	04/79-03/04
E71183	10/77-09/03	⊗10/03	**312016**	10/77-04/79	**312716**	04/79-09/03
E71184	11/77-09/03	⊗10/03	**312017**	11/77-04/79	**312717**	04/79-09/03
E71185	11/77-05/04	⊗07/04	**312018**	11/77-05/79	**312718**	05/79-05/04
E71186	12/77-09/03	⊗12/04	**312019**	12/77-04/79	**312719**	04/79-09/03
E71187	12/77-09/03	⊗10/03	**312020**	12/77-05/79	**312720**	05/79-09/03
E71188	12/77-05/04	⊗07/04	**312021**	12/77-05/79	**312721**	05/79-05/04
E71189	12/77-05/04	⊗12/04	**312022**	12/77-04/79	**312722**	04/79-05/04
E71190	01/78-05/04	⊗07/04	**312023**	01/78-04/79	**312723**	04/79-05/04
E71191	01/78-09/03	⊗09/04	**312024**	01/78-05/79	**312724**	05/79-09/03
E71192	09/78-04/02	⊗02/05	**312025**	09/78-03/79	**312725**	03/79-04/02
E71193	12/78-11/01	⊗02/05	**312026**	12/78-05/79	**312726**	05/79-11/01

Class 312/1 York

Trailer Second Open
TSO
E71194-E71212

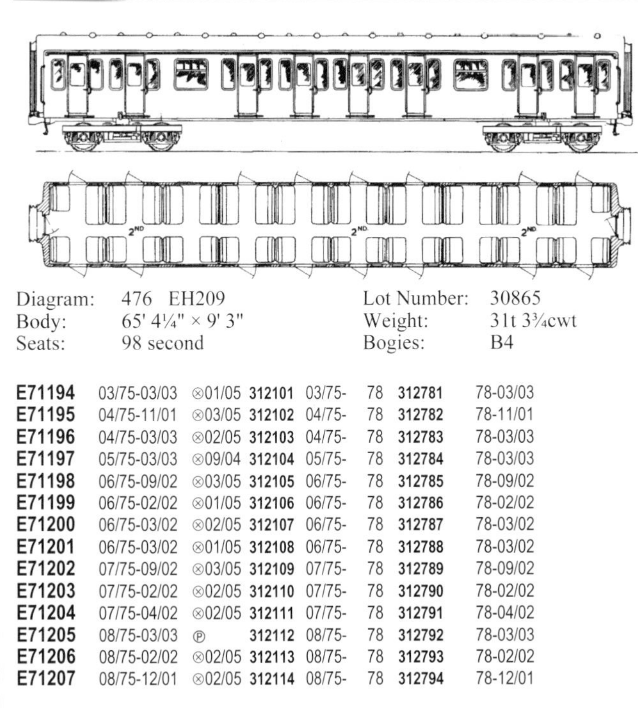

Diagram:	476 EH209	Lot Number:	30865
Body:	65' 4¼" × 9' 3"	Weight:	31t 3¾cwt
Seats:	98 second	Bogies:	B4

E71194	03/75-03/03	⊗01/05	**312101**	03/75-78	**312781**	78-03/03
E71195	04/75-11/01	⊗03/05	**312102**	04/75-78	**312782**	78-11/01
E71196	04/75-03/03	⊗02/05	**312103**	04/75-78	**312783**	78-03/03
E71197	05/75-03/03	⊗09/04	**312104**	05/75-78	**312784**	78-03/03
E71198	06/75-09/02	⊗03/05	**312105**	06/75-78	**312785**	78-09/02
E71199	06/75-02/02	⊗01/05	**312106**	06/75-78	**312786**	78-02/02
E71200	06/75-03/02	⊗02/05	**312107**	06/75-78	**312787**	78-03/02
E71201	06/75-03/02	⊗01/05	**312108**	06/75-78	**312788**	78-03/02
E71202	07/75-09/02	⊗03/05	**312109**	07/75-78	**312789**	78-09/02
E71203	07/75-02/02	⊗02/05	**312110**	07/75-78	**312790**	78-02/02
E71204	07/75-04/02	⊗02/05	**312111**	07/75-78	**312791**	78-04/02
E71205	08/75-03/03	Ⓟ	**312112**	08/75-78	**312792**	78-03/03
E71206	08/75-02/02	⊗02/05	**312113**	08/75-78	**312793**	78-02/02
E71207	08/75-12/01	⊗02/05	**312114**	08/75-78	**312794**	78-12/01

E71208 09/75-12/01 ⊗02/05 **312115** 09/75- 78 **312795** 78-12/01
E71209 09/75-12/01 ⊗01/05 **312116** 09/75- 78 **312796** 78-12/01
E71210 09/75-03/03 ⊗02/05 **312117** 09/75- 78 **312797** 78-03/03
E71211 10/75-02/02 ⊗01/05 **312118** 10/75- 78 **312798** 78-02/02
E71212 10/75-03/02 ⊗03/05 **312119** 10/75- 78 **312799** 78-03/02

E71213-71276 ***Class 313*** *02/76*

Class 312/2 York
Trailer Second Open
TSO
M71277-M71280

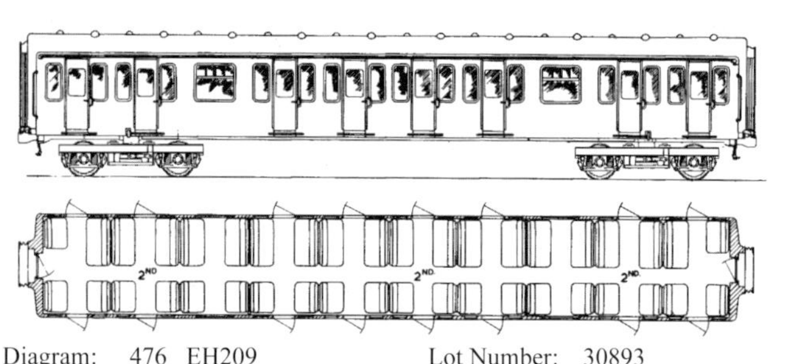

Diagram:	476 EH209	Lot Number:	30893
Body:	65' 4¼" × 9' 3"	Weight:	31t 3¾cwt
Seats:	98 second	Bogies:	B4

M71277 02/76-11/01 ⊗01/05 **312201** 02/76-04/88 **312727** 04/88-11/01
M71278 01/76-10/03 ⊗01/05 **312202** 01/76-04/88 **312728** 04/88-10/03
M71279 02/76-12/01 ⊗02/05 **312203** 02/76-05/88 **312729** 05/88-12/01
M71280 12/75-08/02 ⊗03/05 **312204** 12/75-05/88 **312730** 05/88-08/02

E71281-71341 ***Class 315*** *05/80*
M71342-71374 ***Class 507*** *78*
E71389-71449 ***Class 315*** *05/80*
SC71450-71465 ***Class 314*** *04/79*
S71483-71525 ***Class 508*** *03/80*
S71526-71568 ***Class 508*** *03/80*

Class 309 Wolverton
Trailer Second Open with Lavatory
TSOL
E71569-E71572

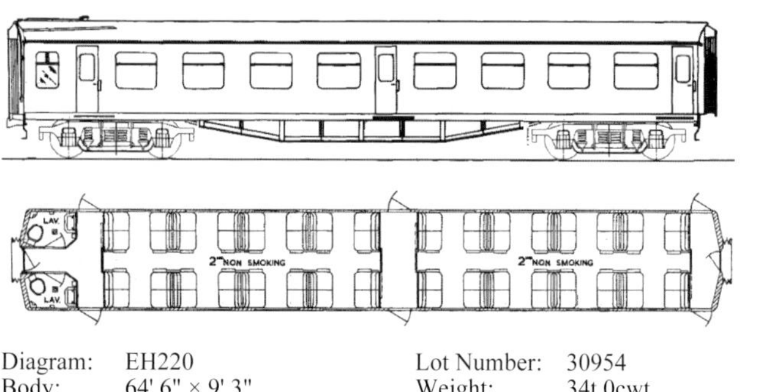

Diagram:	EH220	Lot Number:	30954
Body:	64' 6" × 9' 3"	Weight:	34t 0cwt
Seats:	64 second 2 toilets	Bogies:	Commonwealth

E71569 12/80-05/93 ⊗07/93 **309611** 12/80-09/86 **309601** 09/86-05/93 **⊂5047**
E71570 05/81-01/94 ⊗03/94 **309612** 05/81-07/86 **309602** 07/86-01/94 **⊂5050**
E71571 12/80-05/93 ⊗07/93 **309613** 12/80-08/84 **309603** 08/84-05/93 **⊂5059**
E71572 02/81-01/94 ⊗03/94 **309614** 02/81-02/86 **309604** 02/86-01/94 **⊂5061**

Class 309 Wolverton
Trailer Composite (Semi-open) Lavatory
TCsoL
E71573-E71576

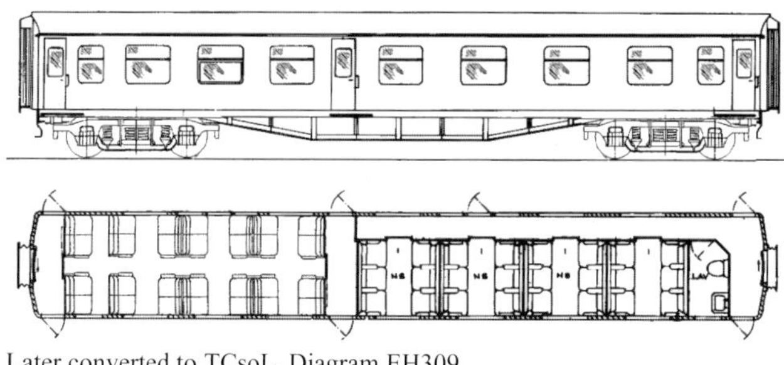

Later converted to TCsoL, Diagram EH309

Diagram:	EH309	Lot Number:	30954
Body:	64' 6" × 9' 3"	Weight:	35t 0cwt
Seats:	24 first 28 second 1 toilet	Bogies:	Commonwealth

E71573 08/81-05/93 ⊗07/93 **309601** 08/81-05/93 **⊂16264**
E71574 10/81-01/94 ⊗03/94 **309602** 10/81-01/94 **⊂16257**
E71575 09/81-05/93 ⊗07/93 **309603** 09/81-05/93 **⊂16242**
E71576 10/81-01/94 ⊗03/94 **309604** 10/81-01/94 **⊂16259**

71577-71624 ***Class 317/1*** *09/81*

Class 411/5 4-CEP
Trailer Second Open with Lavatory
TSOL
S71625-S71636

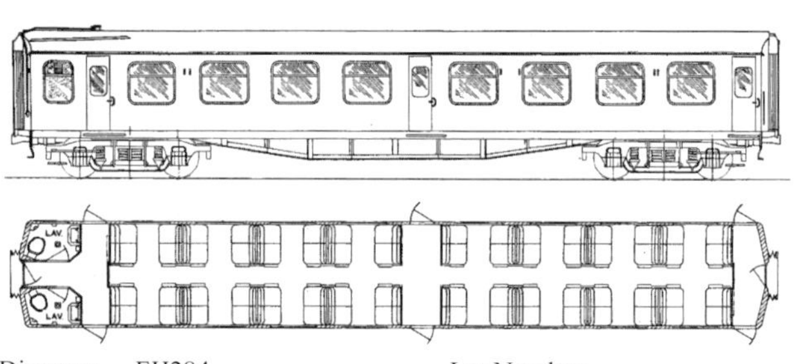

Diagram:	EH284	Lot Number:	
Body:	64' 6" × 9' 3"	Weight:	33t 10cwt
Seats:	64 second 2 toilets	Bogies:	Commonwealth

S71625 08/81-10/02 ⊗10/02 **1587** 08/81-10/02
S71626 09/81-04/04 ⊗08/04 **1532** 09/81-08/97 **1534** 08/97-04/04
S71627 09/81-04/04 ⊗08/04 **1533** 09/81-04/04
S71628 10/81-08/97 ⊗10/00 **1534** 10/81-08/97
S71629 11/81-07/04 ⊗ **1535** 11/81-07/04
S71630 11/81-11/02 ⊗12/02 **1582** 11/81-12/02
S71631 12/81-05/99 ⊗10/00 **1536** 11/81-05/99
S71632 02/82-09/04 ⊗09/04 **1539** 02/82-09/04
S71633 03/82-05/99 ⊗10/00 **1541** 03/82-05/99
S71634 03/82-05/95 ⊗ **1542** 03/82-05/95
S71635 04/82-12/02 ⊗12/02 **1574** 05/82-12/02
S71636 06/82-10/04 ⊗12/04 **1571** 06/82-09/02 **2313** 09/02-10/04

71637-71710 ***Class 455/8*** *08/82*

Class 411/5 4-CEP
Trailer Second Open with Lavatory
TSOL
S71711-S71712

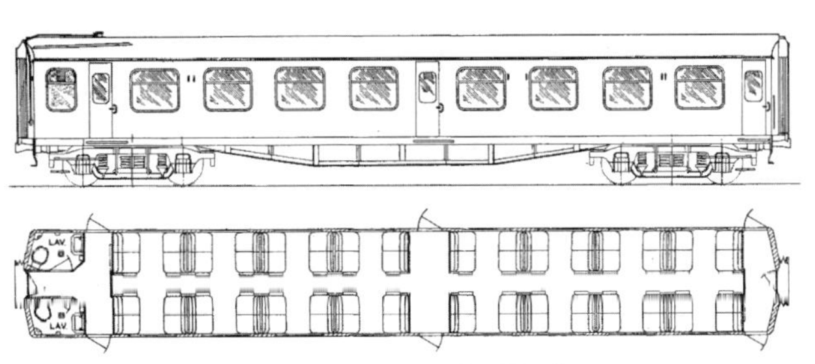

Diagram:	EH284	Lot Number:	
Body:	64' 6" × 9' 3"	Weight:	33t 10cwt
Seats:	64 second 2 toilets	Bogies:	Commonwealth

S71711	01/83-04/04	⊗12/04	**1565**	01/83-04/04	⊂3994
S71712	08/83-05/03	⊗07/03	**1504**	08/83-05/03	[illegible]

71714-71733	***Class 455/9***	*02/85*
71733	***Class 457***	*06/85*
71734-71753	***Class 317/2***	*10/85*

Class 309 Wolverton
Trailer Second Open
TSO
E71754-E71761

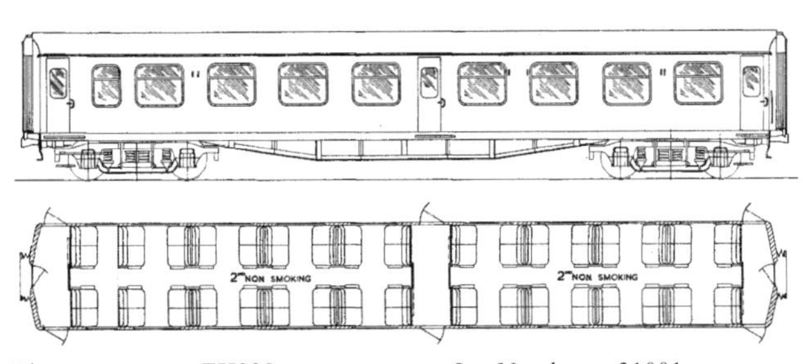

Diagram:	EH228	Lot Number:	31001
Body:	64' 6" × 9' 3"	Weight:	35t 0cwt
Seats:	68 second	Bogies:	Commonwealth

E71754	09/86-12/91	⊗03/92	**309611**	09/86-12/91			⊂5065
E71755	07/86-06/93	⊗04/93	**309612**	07/86-06/93			⊂5051
E71756	04/86-06/00	⊗01/04	**309613**	04/86-06/00			⊂5068
E71757	07/86-08/92	⊗07/92	**309614**	07/86-08/92			⊂5069
E71758	09/86-06/00	⊗	**309615**	09/86-07/92	**309623**	08/92-06/00	⊂5058
E71759	04/86-06/00	⊗02/05	**309616**	04/86-06/00			⊂5062
E71760	04/86-06/00	⊗04/04	**309617**	04/86-06/00			⊂5056
E71761	01/86-12/94	⊗10/97	**309618**	01/86-12/94			⊂5066

71762-71765	***Class 317/2***	*03/87*

Class 411/5 4-CEP
Trailer Second Open with Lavatory
TSOL
71766-71770

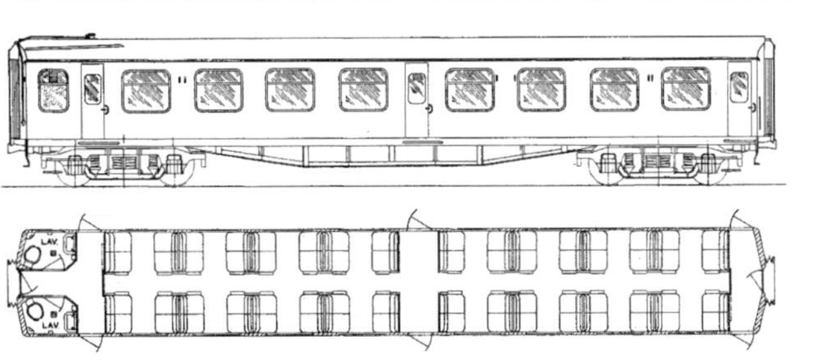

Diagram:	EH284	Lot Number:	
Body:	64' 6" × 9' 3"	Weight:	33t 10cwt
Seats:	64 second 2 toilets	Bogies:	Commonwealth

71766	03/86-12/04	⊗01/05	**1711**	03/86-12/04					⊂69303
71767	05/86-02/04	⊗08/04	**1713**	05/86-02/04					⊂69314
71768	08/86-06/03	⊗	**1716**	08/86-04/93	**1902**	04/93-05/93	**2002**	05/93-01/97	
			1902	01/97-06/03					⊂69317
71769	11/86-07/04	⊗09/04	**1720**	11/86-07/04					⊂69305
71770	03/87-02/04	⊗08/04	**1724**	03/87-02/04					⊂69308

71772-71817	***Class 319/0***	*09/87*
71818-71841	***Class 442***	*01/88*
71842-71865	***Class 442***	*01/88*
71866-71879	***Class 319/0***	*06/88*
71880-71925	***Class 321/3***	*09/88*

Class 411/5 4-CEP
Trailer Second Open with Lavatory
TSOL
71926-71928

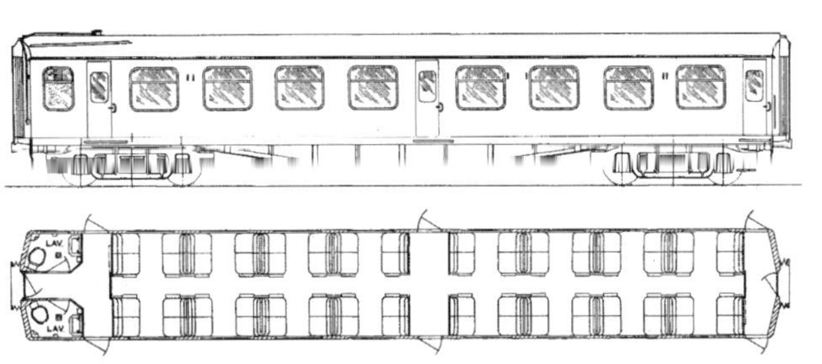

Diagram:	EH284	Lot Number:	
Body:	64' 6" × 9' 3"	Weight:	33t 10cwt
Seats:	64 second 2 toilets	Bogies:	Commonwealth

71926	10/88-08/04	⊗ 04	**1823**	10/88-05/90	**1310**	05/90-08/04	⊂69315
71927	11/88-08/04	⊗09/04	**1824**	11/88-05/90	**1311**	05/90-08/04	⊂69330
71928	11/88-04/05	⊗05/05	**1825**	12/88-06/90	**1312**	06/90-04/05	⊂69331

71929-71948	***Class 319/1***	*10/90*
71949-71978	***Class 321/4***	*07/89*
71979-71984	***Class 319/1***	*01/91*
71985-71990	***Class 321/4***	*12/89*
71991-72010	***Class 321/3***	*01/90*
72011-72022	***Class 321/4***	*11/89*
72023-72027	***Class 322***	*07/90*
72028-72127	***Class 465/0***	*07/94*
72128-72130	***Class 321/9***	*07/90*
72201-72239	***Class 323***	*11/92*
72240-72320 (evens)	***Class 365***	*08/96*
72241-72321 (odds)	***Class 365***	*08/96*
72340-72343	***Class 323***	*05/95*

Class 488 Gatwick Derby
Trailer First Lavatory (Handbrake)
TFOLH
S72500-S72509

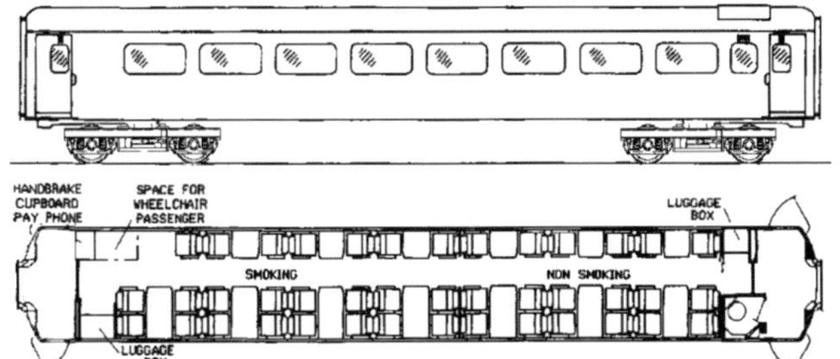

Diagram:	EP101	Lot Number:	30859
Body:	66' 0" × 9' 2⅜"	Weight:	33t
Seats:	41 first 1 toilet	Bogies:	B4

S72500	01/84-01/01	⊗	**8201**	01/84-01/01	⊂3413
S72501	01/84- 04	⊗	**8202**	01/84- 04	⊂3382
S72502	03/84-01/01	⊗	**8203**	03/84-01/01	⊂3321
S72503	03/84-09/00	⊃977983	**8204**	03/84-09/00	⊂3407
S72504	04/84-02/01	⊗11/03	**8205**	04/84-02/01	⊂3406
S72505	04/84- 04	⊗	**8206**	04/84- 04	⊂3415
S72506	05/84-08/02	⊗12/04	**8207**	05/84-08/02	⊂3335
S72507	05/84-07/00	⊗07/09	**8208**	05/84-07/00	⊂3412
S72508	05/84- 04	⊗05/08	**8209**	05/84- 04	⊂3409
S72509	05/84-11/01	⊗	**8210**	05/84-11/01	⊂3398

Class 488 Gatwick Derby
Trailer Second Lavatory (Handbrake)
TSOLH
S72600-S72647

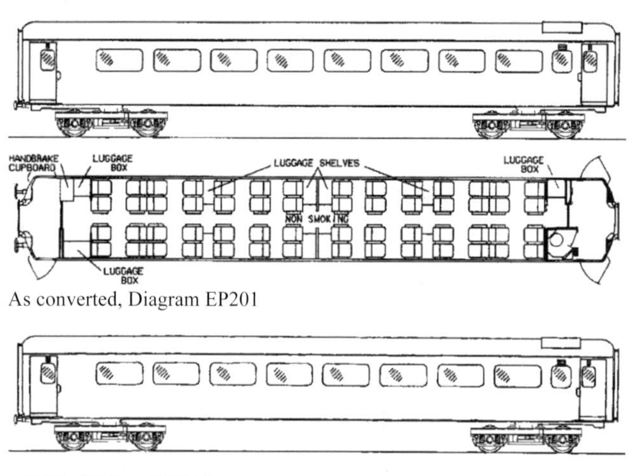

As converted, Diagram EP201

Converted with extra luggage space in1988, Diagram EP202

Diagram:	EP201 EP202	Lot Number:	30860
Body:	66' 0" × 9' 2⅜"	Weight:	33t
Seats:	56 second 1 toilet Later 48 second 1 toilet	Bogies:	B4

No.	Dates	Fate	Unit	Dates	Unit	Dates	Unit	Dates	Former
S72600	11/83-08/85	⊗02/92	**8301**	11/83-08/85					⊂6133
S72601	11/83-08/85	⊗02/92	**8301**	11/83-08/85					⊂6125
S72602	03/84-05/02	⊗09/03	**8302**	03/84-05/02					⊂6130
S72603	03/84-09/00	⊗03/07	**8303**	03/84-09/00					⊂6093
S72604	03/84-05/02	⊗09/03	**8302**	03/84-05/02					⊂6087
S72605	01/84-09/00	🌍	**8305**	01/84-09/00					⊂6082
S72606	12/83-01/01	⊗07/10	**8304**	12/83-01/01					⊂6084
S72607	02/84-11/01	⊗02/05	**8306**	02/84-11/01					⊂6020
S72608	03/84-09/00	⊗10/08	**8303**	03/84-09/00					⊂6077
S72609	01/84-09/00	🌍	**8305**	01/84-09/00					⊂6080
S72610	02/84-11/01	⊗	**8306**	02/84-11/01					⊂6074
S72611	12/83-01/01	⊗07/10	**8304**	12/83-01/01					⊂6083
S72612	02/84-01/01		**8307**	02/84-01/01	**910002**	03- 06			⊂6156
S72613	02/84-01/01	➲**977997**	**8307**	02/84-01/01	**910002**	03- 06			⊂6126
S72614	02/84-09/00		**8308**	02/84-09/00	➲Dep				⊂6090
S72615	02/84-09/00		**8308**	02/84-09/00	➲Dep				⊂5938
S72616	03/84-10/01		**8309**	03/84-10/01	**910001**	03- 06			⊂6007
S72617	03/84- 04	⊗	**8309**	03/84-07/88	**8202**	07/88- 04			⊂6086
S72618	03/84-08/02	⊗10/09	**8310**	03/84-08/02					⊂6044
S72619	03/84-08/02	⊗10/09	**8310**	03/84-08/02					⊂5909
S72620	03/84- 05	⊗	**8311**	03/84- 05					⊂6140
S72621	03/84- 05	⊗	**8311**	03/84- 05					⊂6108
S72622	04/84-07/00	⊗04/09	**8312**	04/84-07/00					⊂6004
S72623	04/84-07/00	⊗04/09	**8312**	04/84-07/00					⊂6118
S72624	04/84- 04	🌍05/08	**8313**	04/84- 04					⊂5972
S72625	04/84- 04	🌍05/08	**8313**	04/84- 04					⊂6085
S72626	05/84-09/00	🌍	**8314**	05/84-09/00					⊂6017
S72627	05/84-09/00	🌍	**8314**	05/84-09/00					⊂5974
S72628	04/84-02/01	⊗06/03	**8205**	04/84-02/01					⊂6058
S72629	04/84- 04	⊗	**8206**	04/84- 04					⊂6048
S72630	05/84-10/01		**8316**	05/84-10/01	➲Dep				⊂6094
S72631	05/84-10/01	⊗07/09	**8316**	05/84-10/01	➲Dep				⊂6096
S72632	05/84-11/01	⊗11/08	**8317**	05/84-11/01					⊂6072
S72633	05/84-11/01	⊗11/08	**8317**	05/84-11/01					⊂6129
S72634	06/84-09/00	🌍	**8318**	06/84-09/00					⊂6089
S72635	05/84-11/01	⊗	**8210**	05/84-11/01					⊂6128
S72636	05/84-07/00	⊗08/09	**8315**	05/84-07/00					⊂6071
S72637	06/84-09/00	🌍	**8318**	06/84-09/00					⊂6098
S72638	01/84-01/01	⊗02/05	**8201**	01/84-01/01					⊂6068
S72639	01/84-10/01		**8202**	01/84-07/88	**8309**	08/88-10/01	**910001**	03- 06	⊂6070
S72640	03/84-01/02	⊗06/07	**8203**	03/84-01/01					⊂6097
S72641	03/84-09/00	℗	**8204**	03/84-09/00					⊂6079
S72642	05/84-08/02	⊗12/04	**8207**	05/84-08/02					⊂6076
S72643	05/84-07/00	⊗08/09	**8208**	05/84-07/00					⊂6040
S72644	05/84- 04	🌍05/08	**8209**	05/84- 04					⊂6039
S72645	05/84-07/00	⊗08/09	**8315**	05/84-07/00					⊂5942
S72646	08/84-09/00	🌍	**8319**	06/84-09/00					⊂6078
S72647	08/84-09/00	🌍	**8319**	06/84-09/00					⊂6081

Class 488 Derby
Trailer Second Lavatory
TSOL
S72700-S72718

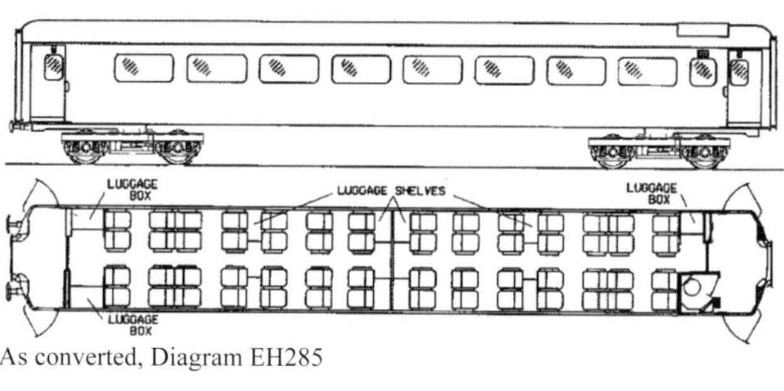

As converted, Diagram EH285

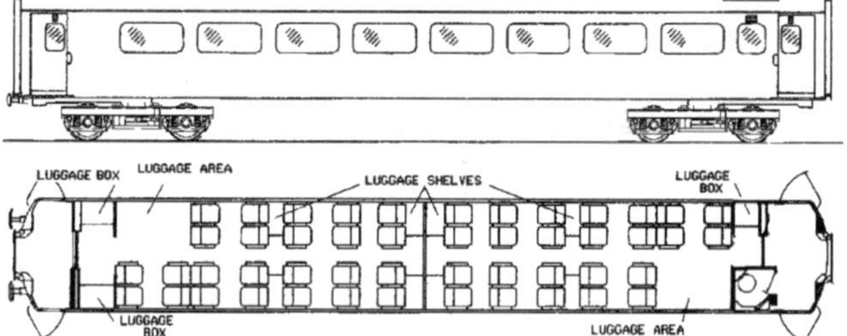

Converted with extra luggage space in1988, Diagram EH290

Diagram:	EH285 EH290	Lot Number:	30860
Body:	66' 0" × 9' 2⅜"	Weight:	33t
Seats:	56 second 1 toilet Later 48 second 1 toilet	Bogies:	B4

No.	Dates	Fate	Unit	Dates	Unit	Dates	Former
S72700	11/83-08/85	⊗03/87	**8301**	11/83-08/85			⊂6131
S72701	03/84-05/02	⊗09/03	**8302**	03/84-05/02			⊂6088
S72702	03/84-09/00	⊗01/09	**8303**	03/84-09/00			⊂6099
S72703	12/83-01/01	⊗09/09	**8304**	12/83-01/01			⊂6075
S72704	01/84-09/00	⊗07/03	**8305**	01/84-09/00			⊂6132
S72705	02/84-11/01	⊗	**8306**	02/84-11/01			⊂6032
S72706	02/84-01/01		**8307**	02/84-01/01	**910002**	03- 06	⊂6143
S72707	02/84-09/00		**8308**	02/84-09/00	➲Dep		⊂6127
S72708	03/84-10/01	⊗10/08	**8309**	03/84-10/01	**910001**	03- 06	⊂6095
S72709	03/84-08/02	⊗10/09	**8310**	03/84-08/02			⊂5982
S72710	03/84- 05	⊗	**8311**	03/84- 05			⊂6003
S72711	04/84-07/00	⊗04/09	**8312**	04/84-07/00			⊂6109
S72712	04/84- 04	🌍05/08	**8313**	04/84- 04			⊂6091
S72713	05/84-09/00	⊗	**8314**	05/84-09/00			⊂6023
S72714	05/84-07/00	⊗06/09	**8315**	05/84-07/00			⊂6092
S72715	05/84-10/01	➲**977985**	**8316**	05/84-10/01			⊂6019
S72716	05/84-11/01	⊗10/08	**8317**	05/84-11/01			⊂6114
S72717	06/84-09/01	⊗	**8318**	06/84-09/00			⊂6069
S72718	08/84-09/01	⊗07/03	**8319**	06/84-09/00			⊂5979

72719-72818 *Class 465/2* *12/93*
72900-72993 *Class 465/1* *12/93*

Class 307 Ashford/Eastleigh
Driving Trailer Second later Driving Trailer Brake Second
DTS later DTBS then BDTBSO
E75001-E75032

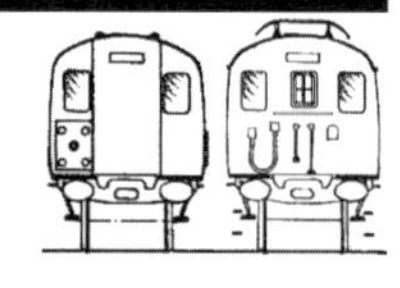

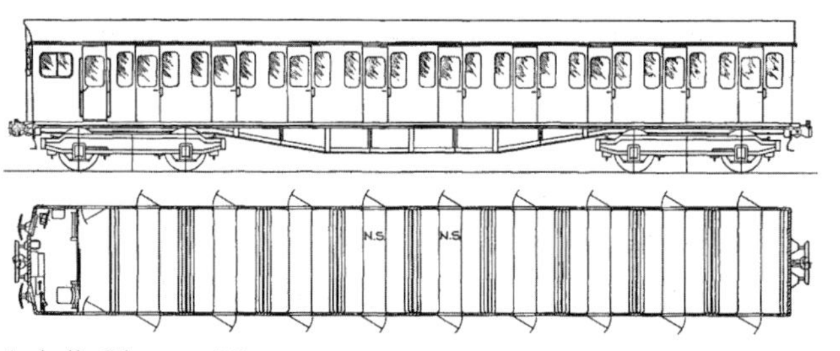

As built, Diagram 430

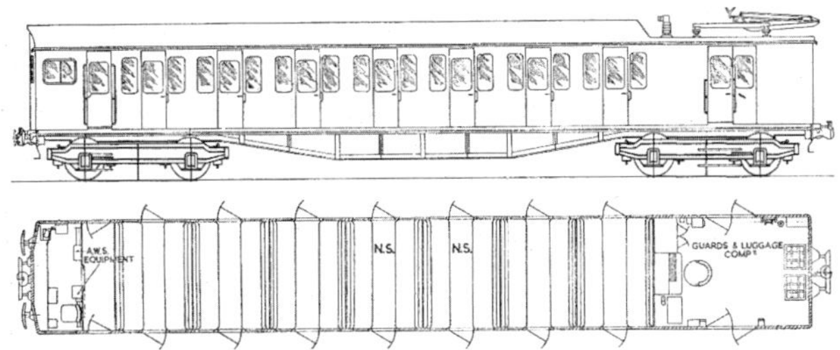
Rebuilt to DTBS 1960/61 at Stratford, Diagram 449

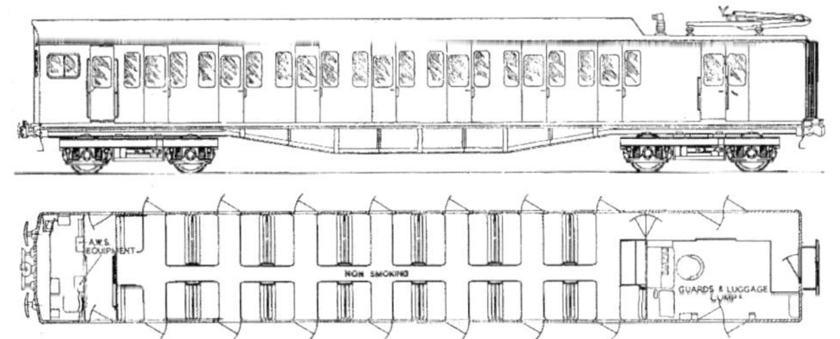
Refurbished 1983-84 with corridor and B5 bogies, Diagram EO202

Diagram:	430 449 EO202	Lot Number:	30205
Body:	63' 11½" × 9' 3¼"	Weight:	30t 5cwt
Seats:	108 second later 84 second later 66 second	Bogies:	Gresley later B5

E75001	02/56-08/93	⊃**977668**	**01s**	02/56- *61*	**101**	*61*-11/82	**307101**	11/82-08/93
E75002	02/56-08/93	⊗11/98	**02s**	02/56- *61*	**102**	*61*-01/80	**307102**	01/80-08/93
E75003	02/56-08/93	⊗*02/97*	**03s**	02/56-02/60	**103**	02/60-10/82	**307103**	10/82-08/93
E75004	03/56-08/93	⊃**94345**	**04s**	03/56- *61*	**104**	*61*-01/82	**307104**	01/82-08/93
E75005	03/56-08/93	⊃**94342**	**05s**	03/56- *61*	**105**	*61*-09/82	**307105**	09/82-08/93
E75006	03/56-08/93	⊃**977672**	**06s**	03/56- *61*	**106**	*61*-02/80	**307106**	02/80-08/93
E75007	04/56-08/93	⊃**94341**	**07s**	04/56- *61*	**107**	*61*-12/81	**307107**	12/81-08/93
E75008	04/56-08/93	⊃**94338**	**08s**	04/56- *61*	**108**	*61*-04/82	**307108**	04/82-08/93
E75009	04/56-10/93	⊗09/93	**09s**	04/56- *61*	**109**	*61*-02/82	**307109**	02/82-08/93
E75010	05/56-08/93	⊗11/96	**10s**	05/56- *61*	**110**	*61*-11/81	**307110**	11/81-08/93
E75011	05/56-08/93	⊃**94332**	**11s**	05/56- *61*	**111**	*61*-01/83	**307111**	01/83-08/93
E75012	05/56-08/93	⊃**94340**	**12s**	05/56- *61*	**112**	*61*-09/82	**307112**	09/82-08/93
E75013	05/56-10/93	⊗09/93	**13s**	05/56- *61*	**113**	*61*-12/82	**307113**	12/82-08/93
E75014	06/56-08/93	⊃**94344**	**14s**	06/56- *61*	**114**	*61*-11/81	**307114**	11/81-08/93
E75015	06/56-08/93	⊗*02/97*	**15s**	06/56- *61*	**115**	*61*-12/81	**307115**	12/81-08/93
E75016	06/56-08/93	⊃**94333**	**16s**	06/56- *61*	**116**	*61*-12/81	**307116**	12/81-08/93
E75017	06/56-08/93	⊃**94334**	**17s**	06/56- *61*	**117**	*61*-07/82	**307117**	07/82-08/93
E75018	06/56-08/93	⊃**977708**	**18s**	06/56- *61*	**118**	*61*-02/82	**307118**	02/82-08/93
E75019	07/56-08/93	⊗*02/97*	**19s**	07/56- *61*	**119**	*61*-06/82	**307119**	06/82-08/93
E75020	07/56-08/93	⊗11/98	**20s**	07/56- *61*	**120**	*61*-09/81	**307120**	09/81-08/93
E75021	07/56-08/93	⊃**977676**	**21s**	07/56- *61*	**121**	*61*-04/82	**307121**	04/82-08/93
E75022	07/56-08/93	⊃**94331**	**22s**	07/56- *61*	**122**	*61*-08/82	**307122**	08/82-08/93
E75023	08/56-08/93	Ⓟ	**23s**	08/56- *61*	**123**	*61*-10/81	**307123**	10/81-08/93
E75024	08/56-08/93	⊃**94339**	**24s**	08/56- *61*	**124**	*61*-05/82	**307124**	05/82-08/93
E75025	09/56-08/93	⊗11/98	**25s**	09/56- *61*	**125**	*61*-10/82	**307125**	10/82-08/93
E75026	09/56-08/93	⊗12/98	**26s**	09/56- *61*	**126**	*61*-08/82	**307126**	08/82-08/93
E75027	09/56-08/93	⊃**94343**	**27s**	09/56- *61*	**127**	*61*-01/82	**307127**	01/82-08/93
E75028	09/56-08/93	⊗ *96*	**28s**	09/56- *61*	**128**	*61*-03/82	**307128**	03/82-08/93
E75029	09/56-08/93	⊃**94337**	**29s**	09/56- *61*	**129**	*61*-06/82	**307129**	06/82-08/93
E75030	10/56-08/93	⊗12/98	**30s**	10/56- *61*	**130**	*61*-06/82	**307130**	06/82-08/93
E75031	10/56-08/93	⊃**94336**	**31s**	10/56- *61*	**131**	*61*-05/82	**307131**	05/82-08/93
E75032	10/56-08/93	⊃**94335**	**32s**	10/56- *61*	**132**	*61*-04/82	**307132**	04/82-08/93

Class 302 York

Driving Trailer Second
DTS, later DTSO
E75033-E75044

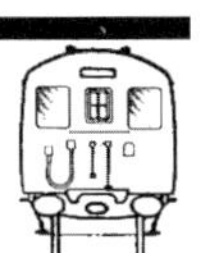

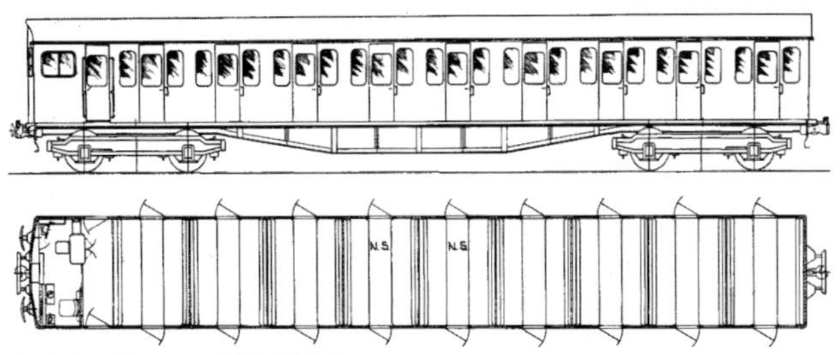
As built, Diagram 433 EE205

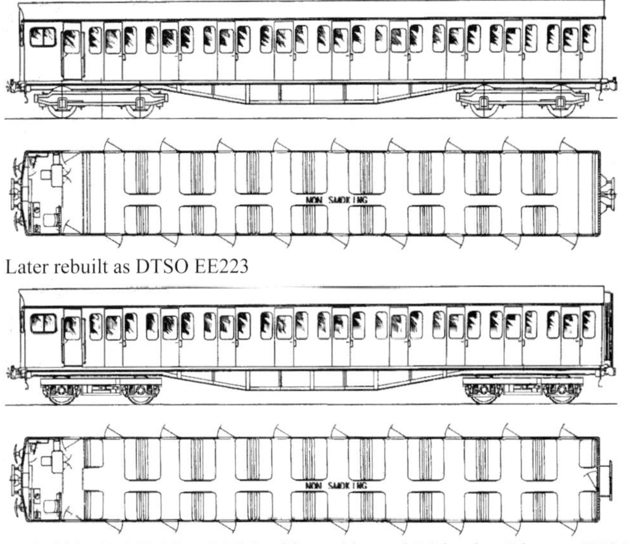
Later rebuilt as DTSO EE223

Refurbished 1983-84 as DTSO with corridor and B5 bogies, Diagram EE219

Diagram:	433 EE205 EE219 EE223	Lot Number:	30433
Body:	63' 11½" × 9' 3"	Weight:	32t 2cwt
Seats:	108 second, later 88 second or 92 second	Bogies:	Gresley later B5

E75033	11/58-06/98	Ⓟ	**201**	11/58-01/83	**302201**	01/83-06/98		
E75034	12/58-04/97	⊗06/97	**202**	12/58-06/83	**302202**	06/83-04/97		
E75035	12/58-08/88	⊃**977603**	**203**	12/58-04/81	**302203**	04/81-08/88		
E75036	12/58-02/98	⊗	**204**	12/58-04/81	**302204**	04/81-02/98		
E75037	01/59-06/97	⊗12/97	**205**	01/59-03/83	**302205**	03/83-06/97		
E75038	01/59-07/95	⊗09/95	**206**	01/59-03/81	**302206**	03/81-02/92	**305599**	02/92-07/93
			302206	07/93-03/94				
E75039	01/59-03/90	⊗08/90	**207**	01/59-03/81	**302207**	03/81-09/88	**302200**	09/88-03/90
E75040	01/59-03/90	⊗06/90	**208**	01/59-04/81	**302208**	04/81-09/88	**302276**[2]	09/88-02/89
E75041	01/59-06/95	⊗08/96	**209**	01/59-01/83	**302209**	01/83-06/95		
E75042	01/59-04/97	⊗12/97	**210**	01/59-05/85	**302210**	05/85-04/97		
E75043	01/59-09/97	⊗04/98	**211**	02/59-09/82	**302211**	09/82-09/97		
E75044	02/59-02/97	⊗09/98	**212**	02/59-05/81	**302212**	05/81-02/97		

Class 304/1 Wolverton

Battery Driving Trailer Second Open Lavatory
BDTSOL
M75045-M75059

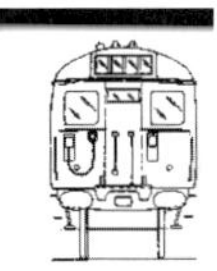

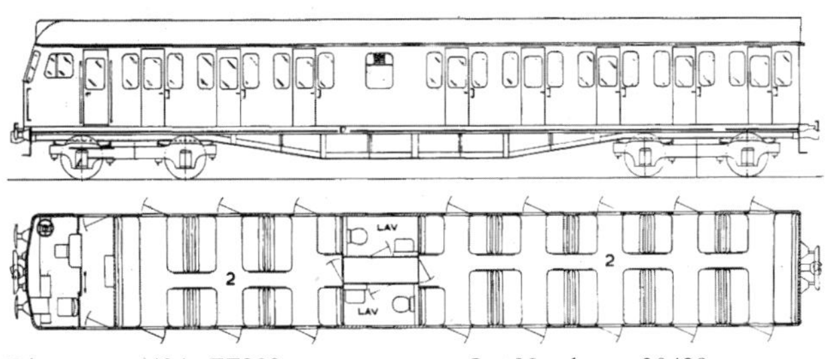

Diagram:	434 EF203	Lot Number:	30429
Body:	64' 0⅝" × 9' 3"	Weight:	35t 12cwt
Seats:	80 second 2 toilets	Bogies:	Gresley

M75045	03/60-07/92	⊗07/92	**001**	03/60-10/82	**304001**	10/82-07/92
M75046	04/60-04/90	⊗05/90	**002**	04/60-04/82	**304002**	04/82-04/90
M75047	04/60-05/94	⊗10/00	**003**	04/60-07/81	**304003**	07/81-05/94
M75048	05/60-03/96	⊗01/97	**004**	05/60-09/83	**304004**	09/83-03/96
M75049	05/60-12/94	⊗05/96	**005**	05/60-10/81	**304005**	10/81-12/94
M75050	05/60-12/93	⊗11/97	**006**	05/60-12/82	**304006**	12/82-12/93
M75051	06/60-05/92	⊗05/92	**007**	06/60-04/82	**304007**	04/82-05/92
M75052	06/60-05/94	⊗10/00	**008**	06/60-08/81	**304008**	08/81-05/94
M75053	06/60-03/96	⊗01/97	**009**	06/60-04/81	**304009**	04/81-03/96
M75054	06/60-09/94	⊗06/96	**010**	06/60-12/81	**304010**	12/81-09/94
M75055	06/60-01/91	⊗*11/91*	**011**	06/60-01/80	**304011**	01/80-01/91
M75056	07/60-05/92	⊗04/92	**012**	07/60-04/82	**304012**	04/82-05/92
M75057	07/60-05/94	⊗11/97	**013**	07/60-07/81	**304013**	07/81-05/94
M75058	07/60-09/94	⊗05/96	**014**	07/60-06/81	**304014**	06/81-09/94
M75059	07/60-06/94	⊗06/96	**015**	07/60-08/82	**304015**	08/82-06/94

Class 302 York

Driving Trailer Second
DTS, later DTSO
E75060-E75084

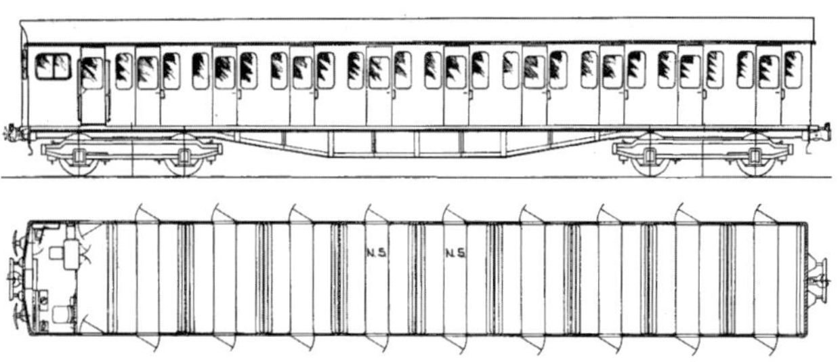

As built, Diagram 433 EE205

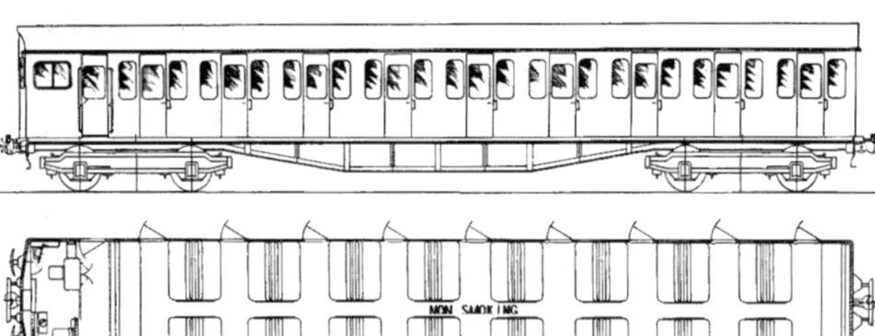

Later rebuilt as DTSO EE223

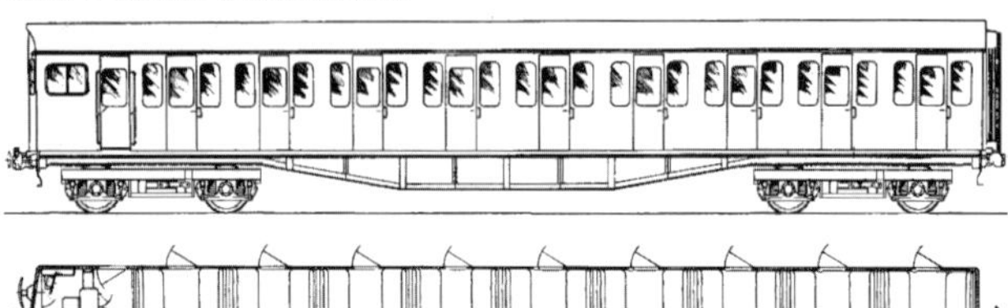

Refurbished 1983-84 as DTSO with corridor and B5 bogies, Diagram EE219

Diagram:	433 EE205 EE219 EE223	Lot Number:	30435
Body:	63' 11½" × 9' 3"	Weight:	32t 2cwt
Seats:	108 Second, later 88 second or 92 second	Bogies:	Gresley later B5

E75060	02/59-07/97	⊗	**213**	02/59-08/81	**302213**	08/81-07/97		
E75061	02/59-04/88	➲**977600**	**214**	02/59-04/81	**302214**	04/81-04/88		
E75062	03/59-04/97	⊗05/97	**215**	03/59-12/81	**302215**	12/81-04/97		
E75063	01/59-07/98	⊗	**216**	02/59-06/83	**302216**	06/83-07/98		
E75064	01/59-04/97	⊗06/97	**217**	03/59-07/84	**302217**	07/84-02/92	**305598**	02/92-07/93
			302217	07/93-04/97				
E75065	02/59-07/97	⊗	**218**	04/59-06/81	**302218**	06/81-07/97		
E75066	03/59-04/97	⊗06/97	**219**	04/59-09/83	**302219**	09/83-04/97		
E75067	03/59-06/97	⊗09/98	**220**	04/59-09/83	**302220**	09/83-02/92	**305595**	02/92-01/93
			302220	01/93-06/97				
E75068	03/59-06/97	⊗	**221**	04/59-09/83	**302221**	09/83-06/97		
E75069	04/59-06/96	⊗04/98	**222**	04/59-06/82	**302222**	06/82-02/92	**305597**	02/92-12/92
			302222	12/92-06/96				
E75070	06/59-08/88	➲**977606**	**223**	06/59-05/81	**302223**	05/81-08/88		
E75071	06/59-08/97	⊗	**224**	06/59-07/81	**302224**	07/81-08/97		
E75072	04/59-07/98	⊗	**225**	05/59-10/81	**302225**	10/81-07/98		
E75073	06/59-01/98	⊗	**226**	06/59-10/81	**302226**	10/81-02/92	**305594**	02/92-01/93
			302226	01/93-01/98				
E75074	06/59-03/90	➲**68210**	**227**	06/59- *83*	**302227**	*83*-02/88	**302427**	02/88-06/88
			302227	06/88-07/88	**302297**	07/88-03/89		
E75075	04/59-07/98	⊗	**228**	05/59-11/81	**302228**	11/81-07/98		
E75076	02/59-09/97	⊗09/98	**229**	05/59-08/82	**302229**	08/82-09/97		
E75077	03/59-08/88	➲**977604**	**230**	05/59-12/83	**302230**	12/83-08/88		
E75078	02/59-03/90	➲**68103**	**231**	05/59-07/84	**302231**	07/84-03/89		
E75079	02/59-07/98	⊗	**232**	05/59-03/85	**302232**	03/85-09/88	**302230**[2]	09/88-07/98
E75080	06/59-04/88	➲**977598**	**233**	06/59-07/84	**302233**	07/84-02/88	**302433**	02/88-04/88
			302233	04/88-04/88				
E75081	06/59-01/91	⊗03/91	**234**	06/59-12/83	**302234**	12/83-08/87	**302434**	08/87-01/88
			302234	01/88-01/91				
E75082	04/59-03/89	➲**68207**	**235**	06/59-04/81	**302235**	04/81-03/89		
E75083	04/59-02/86	⊗07/86	**236**	06/59-01/80	**302236**	01/80-02/86		
E75084	04/59-03/89	➲**68100**	**237**	06/59-11/84	**302237**	11/84-03/89		

Class 302 York/Doncaster

Battery Driving Trailer Second Open Lavatory
BDTSOL, later BDTCOL
E75085-E75100

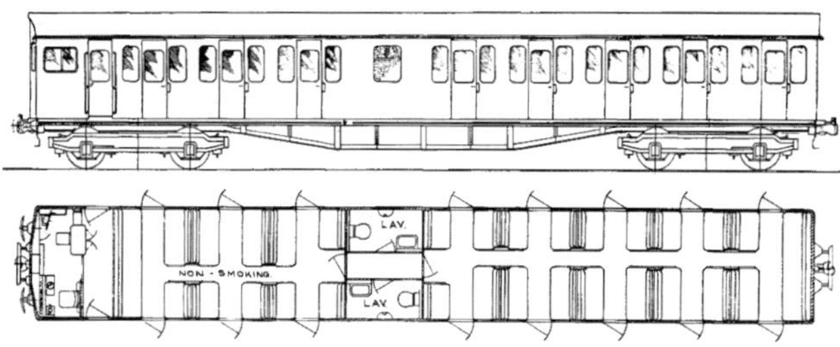

As built, Diagram 432 EF201

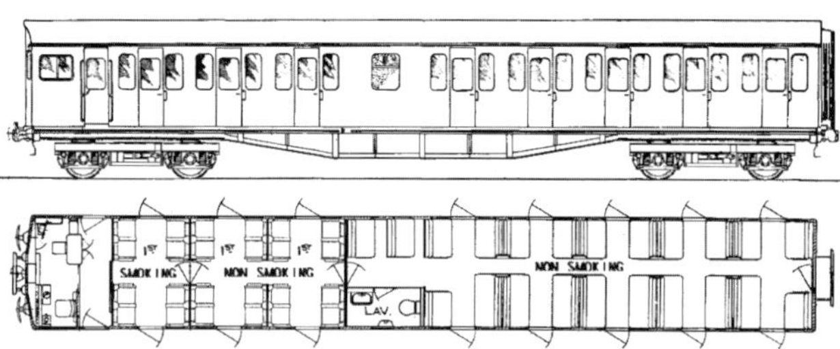

Refurbished 1983-84 with corridor and B5 bogies, Diagram EF303

Diagram:	432 EF201 EF303	Lot Number:	30436
Body:	63' 11½" × 9' 3"	Weight:	35t 15cwt
Seats:	80 second 2 toilets later 24 first 52 second 1 toilet	Bogies:	Gresley later B5

E75085	10/58-06/98	⊗	**201**	11/58-01/83	**302201**	01/83-06/98		
E75086	12/58-04/97	⊗06/97	**202**	12/58-06/83	**302202**	06/83-04/97		
E75087	11/58-08/88	⊗11/88	**203**	12/58-04/81	**302203**	04/81-08/88		
E75088	11/58-02/98	⊗	**204**	12/58-04/81	**302204**	04/81-02/98		
E75089	12/58-06/97	⊗	**205**	01/59-03/83	**302205**	03/83-06/97		
E75090	12/58-07/95	⊗10/95	**206**	01/59-03/81	**302206**	03/81-02/92	**305599**	02/92-07/93
			302206	07/93-03/94				
E75091	12/58-03/90	⊗07/90	**207**	01/59-03/81	**302207**	03/81-09/88	**302200**	09/88-03/90
E75092	12/58-01/90	⊗08/90	**208**	01/59-04/81	**302208**	04/81-09/88	**302276**[2]	09/88-02/89
			302255[2]	02/89-01/90				
E75093	01/59-06/95	⊗08/96	**209**	01/59-01/83	**302209**	01/83-06/95		
E75094	01/59-04/97	⊗12/97	**210**	01/59-05/85	**302210**	05/85-04/97		
E75095	01/59-09/97	⊗04/98	**211**	02/59-09/82	**302211**	09/82-09/97		
E75096	01/59-02/97	⊗09/98	**212**	02/59-05/81	**302212**	05/81-02/97		
E75097	01/59-07/97	⊗	**213**	02/59-08/81	**302213**	08/81-07/97		
E75098	02/59-04/88	⊗11/88	**214**	02/59-04/81	**302214**	04/81-04/88		
E75099	03/59-04/97	⊗05/97	**215**	03/59-12/81	**302215**	12/81-04/97		
E75100	02/59-07/98	⊗	**216**	02/59-06/83	**302216**	06/83-07/98		

Class 307 Ashford/Eastleigh

Driving Trailer Second Open Lavatory
DTSOL , later DTCOL
E75101-E75132

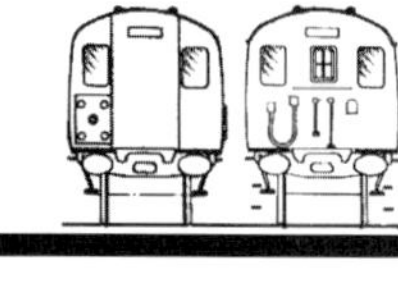

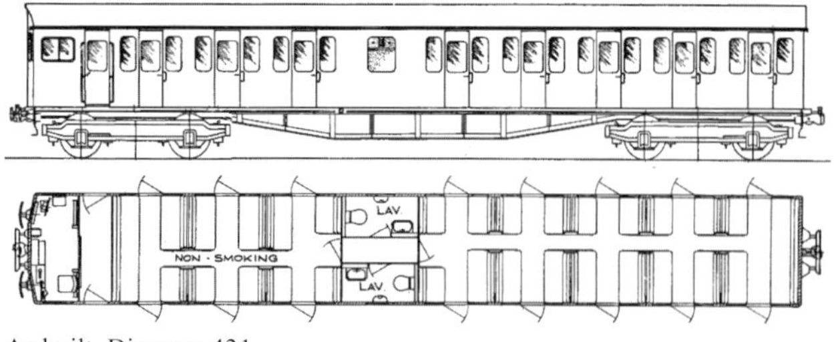

As built, Diagram 431

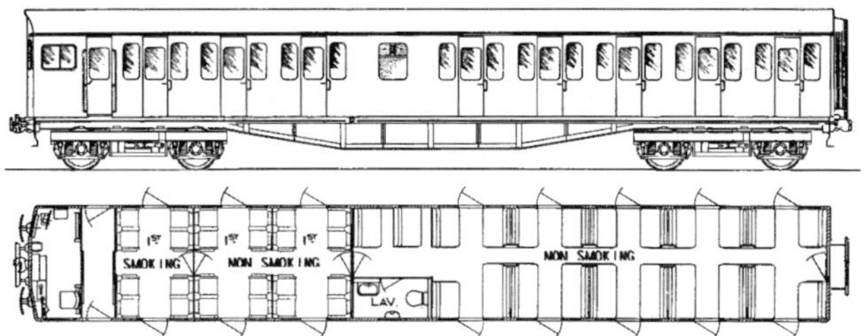

Refurbished 1983-84 as DTCOLwith corridor and B4 bogies, Diagram EE307

Diagram:	431 EE307	Lot Number:	30206
Body:	63' 11½" × 9' 3¼"	Weight:	30t 19cwt
Seats:	80 second 2 toilets later 24 first 52 second 1 toilet	Bogies:	Gresley later B4

E75101	02/56-08/93	**➲977671**	**01s**	02/56- *61*	**101**	*61*-11/82	**307101**	11/82-08/93
E75102	02/56-08/93	**➲94301**	**02s**	02/56- *61*	**102**	*61*-01/80	**307102**	01/80-08/93
E75103	02/56-08/93	**➲94324**	**03s**	02/56-02/60	**103**	02/60-10/82	**307103**	10/82-08/93
E75104	03/56-08/93	**➲94305**	**04s**	03/56- *61*	**104**	*61*-01/82	**307104**	01/82-08/93
E75105	03/56-08/93	**➲94311**	**05s**	03/56- *61*	**105**	*61*-09/82	**307105**	09/82-08/93
E75106	03/56-08/93	**➲977675**	**06s**	03/56- *61*	**106**	*61*-02/80	**307106**	02/80-08/93
E75107	04/56-08/93	**➲94304**	**07s**	04/56- *61*	**107**	*61*-12/81	**307107**	12/81-08/93
E75108	04/56-08/93	**➲94316**	**08s**	04/56- *61*	**108**	[illegible]	**307108**	04/82-08/93
E75109	04/56-08/93	**➲94314**	**09s**	04/56- *61*	**109**	*61*-02/82	**307109**	02/82-08/93
E75110	05/56-08/93	**➲94323**	**10s**	05/56- *61*	**110**	*61*-11/81	**307110**	11/81-08/93
E75111	05/56-08/93	**➲94322**	**11s**	05/56- *61*	**111**	*61*-01/83	**307111**	01/83-08/93
E75112	05/56-08/93	**➲94306**	**12s**	05/56- *61*	**112**	*61*-09/82	**307112**	09/82-08/93
E75113	05/56-08/93	**➲94325**	**13s**	05/56- *61*	**113**	*61*-12/82	**307113**	12/82-08/93
E75114	06/56-08/93	**➲94300**	**14s**	06/56- *61*	**114**	*61*-11/81	**307114**	11/81-08/93
E75115	06/56-08/93	**➲94318**	**15s**	06/56- *61*	**115**	*61*-12/81	**307115**	12/81-08/93
E75116	06/56-08/93	**➲94327**	**16s**	06/56- *61*	**116**	*61*-12/81	**307116**	12/81-08/93
E75117	06/56-08/93	**➲94317**	**17s**	06/56- *61*	**117**	*61*-07/82	**307117**	07/82-08/93
E75118	06/56-08/93	**➲977710**	**18s**	06/56- *61*	**118**	*61*-02/82	**307118**	02/82-08/93
E75119	07/56-08/93	**➲94310**	**19s**	07/56- *61*	**119**	*61*-06/82	**307119**	06/82-08/93
E75120	07/56-08/93	Ⓟ**➲94320**	**20s**	07/56- *61*	**120**	*61*-09/81	**307120**	09/81-08/93
E75121	07/56-08/93	**➲977679**	**21s**	07/56- *61*	**121**	*61*-04/82	**307121**	04/82-08/93
E75122	07/56-08/93	**➲94321**	**22s**	07/56- *61*	**122**	*61*-08/82	**307122**	08/82-08/93
E75123	08/56-08/93	**➲94326**	**23s**	08/56- *61*	**123**	*61*-10/81	**307123**	10/81-08/93
E75124	08/56-08/93	**➲94302**	**24s**	08/56- *61*	**124**	*61*-05/82	**307124**	05/82-08/93
E75125	09/56-08/93	**➲94308**	**25s**	09/56- *61*	**125**	*61*-10/82	**307125**	10/82-08/93
E75126	09/56-08/93	**➲94312**	**26s**	09/56- *61*	**126**	*61*-08/82	**307126**	08/82-08/93
E75127	09/56-08/93	**➲94307**	**27s**	09/56- *61*	**127**	*61*-01/82	**307127**	01/82-08/93
E75128	09/56-08/93	**➲94319**	**28s**	09/56- *61*	**128**	*61*-03/82	**307128**	03/82-08/93
E75129	09/56-08/93	**➲94313**	**29s**	09/56- *61*	**129**	*61*-06/82	**307129**	06/82-08/93
E75130	10/56-08/93	**➲94309**	**30s**	10/56- *61*	**130**	*61*-06/82	**307130**	06/82-08/93
E75131	10/56-08/93	**➲94303**	**31s**	10/56- *61*	**131**	*61*-05/82	**307131**	05/82-08/93
E75132	10/56-08/93	**➲94315**	**32s**	10/56- *61*	**132**	*61*-04/82	**307132**	04/82-08/93

Class 501 Ashford/Eastleigh

Driving Trailer Brake Second Open
DTBSO
M75133-M75189

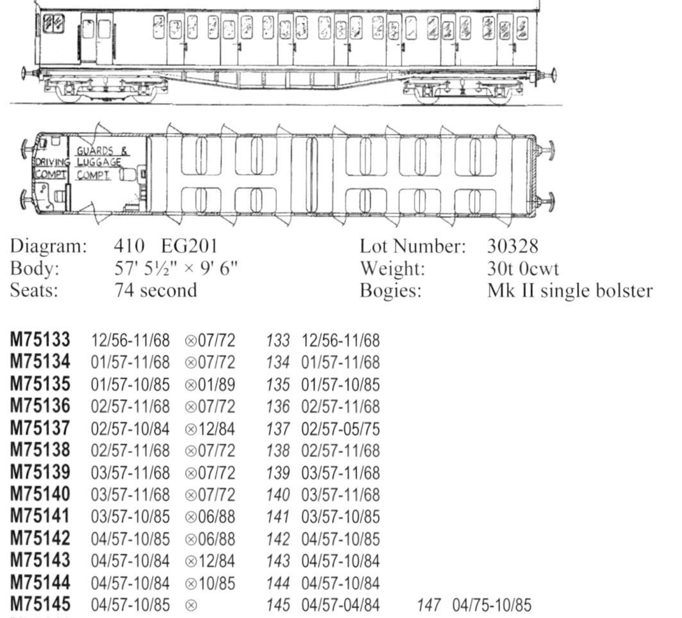

Diagram:	410 EG201	Lot Number:	30328
Body:	57' 5½" × 9' 6"	Weight:	30t 0cwt
Seats:	74 second	Bogies:	Mk II single bolster

M75133	12/56-11/68	⊗07/72	*133*	12/56-11/68		
M75134	01/57-11/68	⊗07/72	*134*	01/57-11/68		
M75135	01/57-10/85	⊗01/89	*135*	01/57-10/85		
M75136	02/57-11/68	⊗07/72	*136*	02/57-11/68		
M75137	02/57-10/84	⊗12/84	*137*	02/57-05/75		
M75138	02/57-11/68	⊗07/72	*138*	02/57-11/68		
M75139	03/57-11/68	⊗07/72	*139*	03/57-11/68		
M75140	03/57-11/68	⊗07/72	*140*	03/57-11/68		
M75141	03/57-10/85	⊗06/88	*141*	03/57-10/85		
M75142	04/57-10/85	⊗06/88	*142*	04/57-10/85		
M75143	04/57-10/84	⊗12/84	*143*	04/57-10/84		
M75144	04/57-10/84	⊗10/85	*144*	04/57-10/84		
M75145	04/57-10/85	⊗	*145*	04/57-04/84	*147*	04/75-10/85
M75146	04/57-10/84	⊗12/84	*146*	04/57-10/84		
M75147	05/57-10/76	⊗08/77	*147*	05/57-01/73		
M75148	05/57-10/85	⊗07/86	*148*	05/57-10/85		
M75149	05/57-10/84	⊗12/84	*149*	05/57-05/75		
M75150	05/57-10/85	⊗07/86	*150*	05/57-10/85		
M75151	05/57-10/85	⊗06/88	*151*	05/57-10/85		
M75152	06/57-10/85	⊗01/89	*152*	06/57-10/85		
M75153	06/57-10/84	⊗10/85	*153*	06/57-10/84		
M75154	06/57-10/84	⊗10/85	*154*	06/57-10/84		
M75155	07/57-10/85	⊗06/88	*155*	07/57-10/85		
M75156	07/57-10/85	⊗07/86	*156*	07/57-10/85		
M75157	07/57-10/85	⊗06/88	*157*	07/57-10/85		
M75158	07/57-10/85	⊗07/86	*158*	07/57-10/85		
M75159	08/57-10/85	⊗07/86	*159*	08/57-10/85		
M75160	08/57-10/85	⊗06/88	*160*	08/57-10/85		
M75161	08/57-10/85	⊗07/86	*161*	08/57-10/76	*147*	01/73-04/75
M75162	08/57- 69	**➲975029**	*162*	08/57- 69		
M75163	09/57-10/84	⊗10/85	*163*	09/57-10/84		
M75164	09/57-10/85	⊗01/89	*164*	09/57-10/85		
M75165	09/57- 69	**➲975032**	*165*	09/57- 69		
M75166	09/57-10/76	⊗08/77	*166*	09/57-05/75	*149*	05/75-10/84
M75167	09/57-10/85	⊗	*167*	09/57-10/76		
M75168	10/57-10/85	⊗01/89	*168*	10/57-10/85		
M75169	10/57-10/85	⊗01/89	*169*	10/57-10/85		
M75170	10/57-10/85	⊗01/89	*170*	10/57-10/85		
M75171	10/57-10/85	⊗01/89	*171*	10/57-10/85		
M75172	10/57-10/76	⊗08/77	*172*	10/57-10/76		
M75173	11/57-10/76	⊗08/77	*173*	11/57-07/75		
M75174	11/57-10/84	⊗10/85	*174*	11/57-10/84		
M75175	11/57-07/78	⊗	*175*	11/57-10/75	*185*	10/75-07/78
M75176	11/57-10/85	⊗01/89	*176*	11/57-10/85		
M75177	11/57-10/84	⊗10/85	*177*	11/57-10/84		
M75178	12/57-10/84	**➲977346**	*178*	12/57-10/84		
M75179	12/57-10/84	⊗10/85	*179*	12/57-10/84		
M75180	12/57-10/84	**➲977348**	*180*	12/57-10/84		
M75181	12/57-10/84	⊗10/85	*181*	12/57-10/84		
M75182	12/57-10/84	⊗12/84	*182*	12/57-07/78		
M75183	01/58-10/84	**➲977350**	*183*	01/58-10/84		
M75184	01/58-10/84	⊗12/84	*184*	01/58-07/78		
M75185	01/58-10/84	⊗12/84	*185*	01/58-02/75	*137*	05/75-10/85
M75186	01/58-10/85	Ⓟ	*186*	01/58-10/85		
M75187	01/58-10/76	⊗08/77	*187*	01/58-10/76		
M75188	02/58-10/85	⊗07/86	*188*	02/58-10/85		
M75189	02/58-(05/88)	**➲977386**	*189*	02/58-07/78		

Class 302 York/Doncaster

Battery Driving Trailer Second Open Lavatory
BDTSOL, later BDTCOL
E75190-E75210

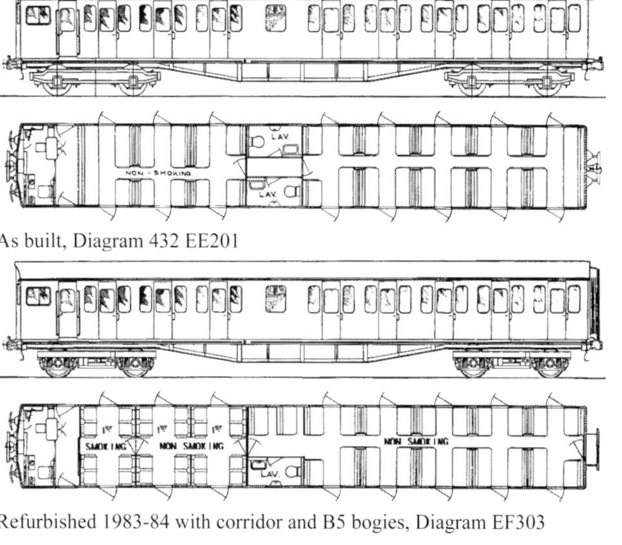

As built, Diagram 432 EE201

Refurbished 1983-84 with corridor and B5 bogies, Diagram EF303

Diagram:	432 EF201 EF303	Lot Number:	30436
Body:	63' 11½" × 9' 3"	Weight:	35t 15cwt
Seats:	80 second 2 toilets later 24 first 52 second 1 toilet	Bogies:	Gresley later B5

E75190	02/59-04/97	⊗06/97	**217**	03/59-07/84	**302217**	07/84-02/92	**305598**	02/92-07/93
					302217	07/93-04/97		
E75191	03/59-07/97	⊗	**218**	04/59-06/81	**302218**	06/81-07/97		
E75192	03/59-04/97	⊗06/97	**219**	04/59-09/83	**302219**	09/83-04/97		
E75193	03/59-06/97	⊗09/98	**220**	04/59-09/83	**302220**	09/83-02/92	**305595**	02/92-01/93
					302220	01/93-06/97		

E75194	03/59-06/97	⊗	**221**	04/59-09/83	**302221**	09/83-06/97		
E75195	04/59-06/96	⊗04/98	**222**	04/59-06/82	**302222**	06/82-02/92	**305597**	02/92-12/92
			302222	12/92-06/96				
E75196	04/59-08/88	⊗11/88	**223**	06/59-05/81	**302223**	05/81-08/88		
E75197	04/59-08/97	⊗	**224**	06/59-07/81	**302224**	07/81-08/97		
E75198	04/59-07/98	⊗	**225**	05/59-10/81	**302225**	10/81-07/98		
E75199	04/59-01/98	⊗	**226**	06/59-10/81	**302226**	10/81-02/92	**305594**	02/92-01/93
			302226	01/93-01/98				
E75200	04/59-02/86	⊗02/86	**227**	06/59- *83*	**302227**	*83*-10/85		
E75201	04/59-07/98	⊗	**228**	05/59-11/81	**302228**	11/81-07/98		
E75202	05/59-09/97	⊗09/98	**229**	05/59-08/82	**302229**	08/82-09/97		
E75203	05/59-08/88	⊗11/88	**230**	05/59-12/83	**302230**	12/83-08/88		
E75204	05/59-04/89	⊗03/89	**231**	05/59-07/84	**302231**	07/84-03/89		
E75205	05/59-07/98	⊗	**232**	05/59-03/85	**302232**	03/85-09/88	**302230**[2]	09/88-07/98
E75206	05/59-04/88	⊗04/88	**233**	06/59-07/84	**302233**	07/84-02/88	**302433**	02/88-04/88
			302233	04/88-04/88				
E75207	05/59-01/91	⊗03/91	**234**	06/59-12/83	**302234**	12/83-08/87	**302434**	08/87-01/88
			302234	01/88-01/91				
E75208	05/59-04/89	⊗03/89	**235**	06/59-04/81	**302235**	04/81-03/89		
E75209	05/59-02/86	⊗04/88	**236**	06/59-01/80	**302236**	01/80-02/86		
E75210	05/59-09/89	⊗06/90	**237**	06/59-11/84	**302237**	11/84-12/88	**302285**	12/88-03/89
			302244	03/89-03/89				

Class 302 York
Driving Trailer Second
DTS, later DTSO
E75211-E75285

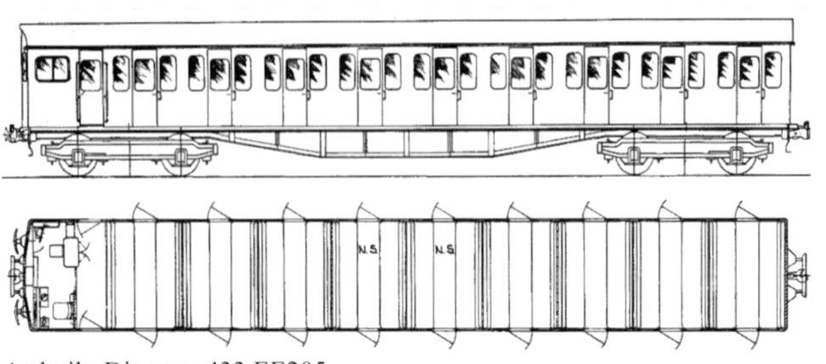

As built, Diagram 433 EE205

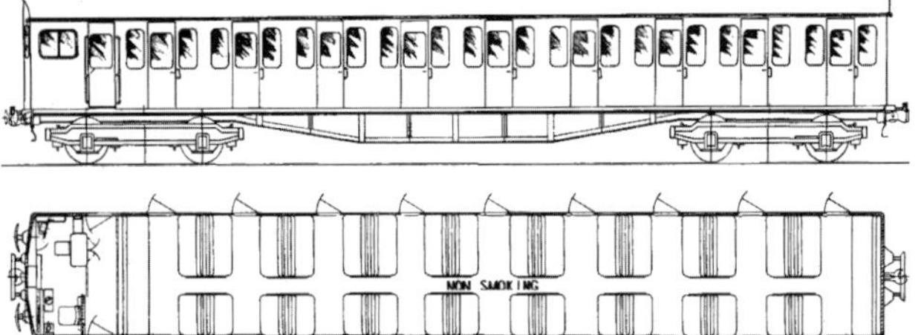

Later rebuilt as DTSO EE223

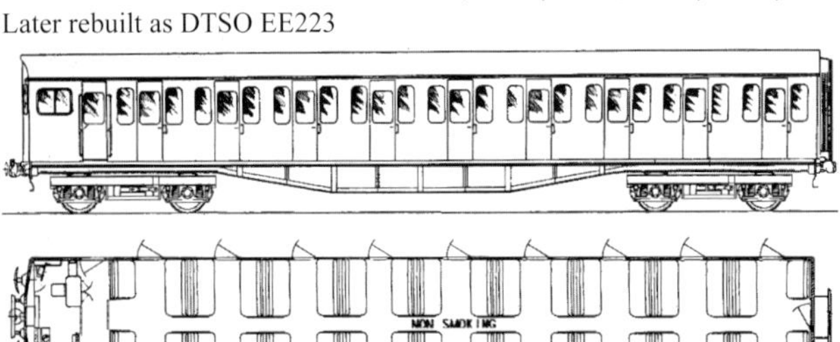

Refurbished 1983-84 as DTSO with corridor and B5 bogies, Diagram EE219

Diagram:	433 EE205 EE219 EE223	Lot Number:	30439
Body:	63' 11½" × 9' 3"	Weight:	32t 2cwt
Seats:	108 Second, later 88 second or 92 second	Bogies:	Gresley later B5

E75211	04/59-09/88	➲**977601**	**238**	06/59-05/81	**302238**	05/81-08/88		
E75212	04/59-01/90	⊗08/90	**239**	06/59-01/83	**302239**	01/83-08/87	**302439**	08/87-09/87
			302305	09/87-01/90				
E75213	05/59-06/88	⊗06/90	**240**	06/59-11/82	**302240**	11/82-06/88		
E75214	05/59-04/89	➲**977641**	**241**	06/59-11/84	**302241**	11/84-03/89		
E75215	05/59-07/88	⊗06/90	**242**	07/59-01/82	**302242**	01/82-07/88		
E75216	05/59-01/90	⊗06/90	**243**	07/59-10/83	**302243**	10/83-09/89		
E75217	05/59-03/89	➲**68208**	**244**	07/59-10/70	**244**	06/72-06/82	**302244**	06/82-03/89
E75218	05/59-04/89	➲**68209**	**245**	07/59-08/81	**302245**	08/81-04/89		
E75219	05/59-09/89	⊗02/90	**246**	07/59- *83*	**302246**	*83*-09/89		
E75220	05/59-04/89	➲**68102**	**247**	07/59-01/82	**302247**	01/82-04/89		
E75221	05/59-03/89	➲**68101**	**248**	07/59-03/83	**302248**	03/83-03/89		
E75222	05/59-03/90	⊗07/90	**249**	08/59-09/82	**302249**	09/82-09/89		
E75223	06/59-03/84	⊗01/85	**250**	08/59-04/82	**302250**	04/82-02/83	**302399**	03/83-05/83
			308139	05/83-07/83				
E75224	06/59-10/90	⊗10/90	**251**	08/59-01/83	**302251**	01/83-10/90		
E75225	06/59-10/90	⊗09/90	**252**	08/59-08/82	**302252**	08/82-06/90		
E75226	06/59-09/89	⊗04/90	**253**	08/59-10/82	**302253**	10/82-05/85	**302312**	07/85-08/88
			302238	08/88-09/89				
E75227	07/59-01/90	⊗03/90	**254**	08/59-03/83	**302254**	03/83-03/89	**302264**	03/89-09/89
E75228	06/59-07/83	⊗05/84	**255**	08/59-01/82	**302255**	01/82-07/83		
E75229	06/59-07/90	⊗07/90	**256**	09/59- *83*	**302256**	*83*-03/89	**302258**	03/89-09/89
E75230	06/59-09/89	⊗05/90	**257**	09/59-04/82	**302257**	04/82-09/89		
E75231	07/59-09/89	⊗05/90	**258**	09/59-05/81	**302258**	05/81-03/89	**302256**	03/89-09/89
E75232	07/59-07/90	⊗08/90	**259**	09/59-03/80	**302259**	03/80-11/87	**302459**	11/87-02/88
			302259	02/88-03/90				
E75233	07/59-05/85	⊗10/88	**260**	09/59-05/81	**302260**	05/81-05/85		
E75234	07/59-01/91	⊗03/91	**261**	09/59-03/83	**302261**	03/83-01/91		
E75235	07/59-01/91	⊗03/91	**262**	09/59-10/82	**302262**	10/82-11/87	**302462**	11/87-02/88
			302262	02/88-07/90				
E75236	07/59-06/96	⊗04/98	**263**	09/59-09/83	**302263**	09/83-09/88	**302203**[2]	09/88-06/96
E75237	07/59-02/87	⊗03/90	**264**	09/59-05/82	**302264**	05/82-02/87		
E75238	07/59-09/89	⊗04/90	**265**	09/59-09/82	**302265**	09/82-09/89		
E75239	08/59-01/88	⊗04/88	**266**	09/59-07/84	**302266**	07/84-01/88		
E75240	08/59-02/87	⊗10/87	**267**	09/59-02/80	**302267**	02/80-08/86		
E75241	08/59-09/89	⊗05/90	**268**	11/59-09/82	**302268**	09/82-09/89		
E75242	08/59-09/89	⊗04/90	**269**	11/59-01/82	**302269**	01/82-09/89		
E75243	08/59-09/89	⊗07/90	**270**	11/59- *83*	**302270**	*83*-09/89		
E75244	08/59-11/88	⊗11/88	**271**	11/59-04/82	**302271**	04/82-06/88		
E75245	08/59-06/90	⊗08/90	**272**	11/59-06/83	**302272**	06/83-06/90		
E75246	08/59-09/89	⊗02/90	**273**	11/59-03/82	**302273**	03/82-08/85	**302302**	09/85-09/88
			302260[2]	09/88-09/89				
E75247	08/59-01/91	⊗03/91	**274**	11/59-05/82	**302274**	05/82-01/91		
E75248	08/59-07/83	⊗05/84	**275**	11/59-11/79	**302275**	11/79-07/83		
E75249	08/59-02/86	⊗04/86	**276**	11/59-01/80	**302276**	01/80-02/86		
E75250	09/59-01/98	℗	**277**	11/59-01/83	**302277**	01/83-09/88	**302227**[2]	09/88-01/98
E75251	09/59-09/89	⊗05/90	**278**	01/60-11/84	**302278**	11/84-09/89		
E75252	09/59-02/88	⊗04/88	**279**	01/60-10/81	**302279**	10/81-02/88		
E75253	09/59-01/90	⊗03/90	**280**	01/60- *83*	**302280**	*83*-01/90		
E75254	09/59-09/89	⊗05/90	**281**	01/60-10/82	**302281**	10/82-10/86	**302264**	02/87-03/89
			302254	03/89-09/89				
E75255	09/59-09/89	⊗05/90	**282**	11/59-02/82	**302282**	02/82-09/89		
E75256	09/59-07/90	⊗03/91	**283**	12/59-02/83	**302283**	02/83-07/90		
E75257	09/59-03/90	⊗09/90	**284**	12/59-10/81	**302284**	10/81-03/90		
E75258	09/59-07/90	⊗06/90	**285**	12/59-06/83	**302285**	06/83-05/90		
E75259	09/59-03/90	⊗08/90	**286**	12/59-05/82	**302286**	05/82-03/90		
E75260	10/59-10/85	⊗02/86	**287**	11/59-01/80	**302287**	01/80-10/85		
E75261	10/59-02/87	⊗03/90	**288**	12/59-12/82	**302288**	12/82-05/85		
E75262	10/59-09/89	⊗03/90	**289**	01/60-01/80	**302289**	01/80-09/89		
E75263	10/59-09/89	⊗04/90	**290**	01/60-10/82	**302290**	10/82-09/89		
E75264	10/59-09/89	⊗02/90	**291**	01/60- *83*	**302291**	*83*-09/89		
E75265	10/59-06/90	⊗06/90	**292**	01/60-03/83	**302292**	03/83-06/90		
E75266	10/59-07/97	⊗12/97	**293**	01/60-08/81	**302293**	08/81-09/88	**302223**[2]	09/88-07/97
E75267	10/59-11/88	⊗11/88	**294**	01/60-01/82	**302294**	01/82-11/87	**302494**	11/87-06/88
			302294	06/88-06/88	**302271**	06/88-11/88		
E75268	10/59-09/89	⊗05/90	**295**	01/60-02/82	**302295**	02/82-09/89		
E75269	10/59-07/90	⊗08/90	**296**	01/60-04/84	**302296**	04/84-03/90		
E75270	10/59-12/85	⊗04/86	**297**	02/60-10/81	**302297**	10/81-12/85		
E75271	10/59-03/91	⊗03/91	**298**	01/60-03/83	**302298**	03/83-06/90	**302252**	06/90-03/91
E75272	11/59-10/90	⊗10/90	**299**	01/60-03/83	**302299**	03/83-11/88	**302239**	11/88-06/90
			302292	06/90-10/90				
E75273	11/59-03/90	⊗08/90	**300**	01/60-07/83	**302300**	07/83-09/88	**302250**[2]	09/88-03/90
E75274	10/59-06/90	⊗06/90	**301**	01/60-01/83	**302301**	01/83-09/88	**302253**[2]	09/88-06/90
E75275	12/59-10/85	⊗10/85	**302**	02/60-02/80	**302302**	02/80-09/85		
E75276	01/60-07/90	⊗08/90	**303**	06/60-07/83	**302303**	07/83-09/88	**302255**[2]	09/88-01/90
E75277	01/60-09/97	⊗04/96	**304**	02/60-06/83	**302304**	06/83-09/88	**302214**[2]	09/88-09/96
E75278	01/60-11/88	⊗03/89	**305**	01/60- *83*	**302305**	*83*-08/87	**302439**	09/87-01/88
			302239	01/88-11/88				
E75279	01/60-03/90	⊗06/90	**306**	01/60-03/83	**302306**	03/83-09/88	**302273**[2]	09/88-03/90
E75280	01/60-10/90	⊗10/90	**307**	01/60-10/83	**302307**	10/83-09/88	**302267**[2]	09/88-10/90
E75281	01/60-04/97	⊗05/97	**308**	02/60-02/83	**302308**	02/83-09/88	**302208**[2]	09/88-02/92
			305596	02/92-07/93	**302208**	07/93-01/94	**302206**	03/94-04/97
E75282	12/59-09/88	⊗03/89	**309**	01/60-02/80	**302309**	02/80-12/85	**302297**	12/85-11/87
			302497	11/87-02/88	**302297**	02/88-07/88		
E75283	01/60-04/97	⊗05/97	**310**	04/60-09/83	**302310**	09/83-09/88	**302207**[2]	09/88-04/97
E75284	01/60-09/89	⊗04/90	**311**	04/60- *83*	**302311**	*83*-09/88	**302275**[2]	09/88-04/89
E75285	03/60-07/85	⊗08/85	**312**	05/60- *83*	**302312**	*83*-07/85		

Class 302 York/Doncaster

Battery Driving Trailer Second Open Lavatory
BDTSOL, later BDTCOL
E75286-E75360

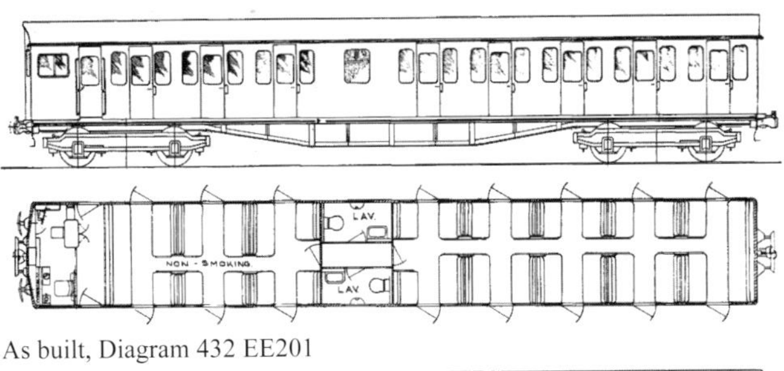

As built, Diagram 432 EE201

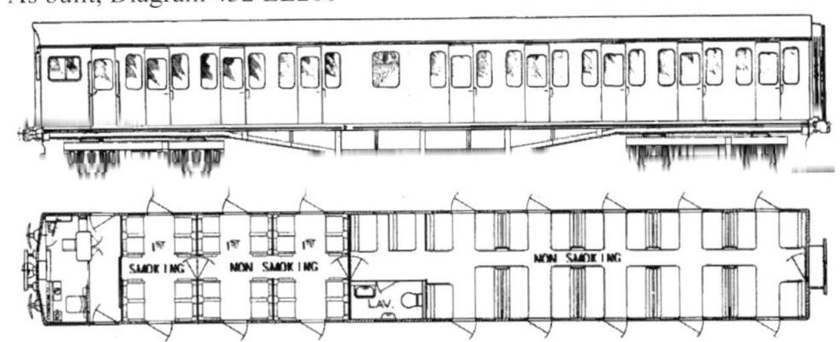

Refurbished 1983-84 with corridor and B5 bogies, Diagram EF303

Diagram:	432 EF201 EF303	Lot Number:	30440
Body:	63' 11½" × 9' 3"	Weight:	35t 15cwt
Seats:	80 second 2 toilets later 24 first 52 second 1 toilet	Bogies:	Gresley later B5

E75286	05/59-11/88	⊗11/88	**238**	06/59-05/81	**302238**	05/81-08/88		
E75287	05/59-06/90	⊗06/90	**239**	06/59-01/83	**302239**	01/83-08/87	**302439**	08/87-01/88
			302239	01/88-06/90				
E75288	05/59-06/88	⊗11/88	**240**	06/59-11/82	**302240**	11/82-06/88		
E75289	06/59-11/91	⊗11/91	**241**	06/59-11/84	**302241**	11/84-03/89	**305414**[2]	03/89-11/91
E75290	06/59-09/89	⊗06/90	**242**	07/59-01/82	**302242**	01/82-07/88	**302271**	08/88-11/88
E75291	06/59-09/89	⊗06/90	**243**	07/59-10/83	**302243**	10/83-09/89		
E75292	06/59-10/70	⊗*03/76*	**244**	07/59-10/70				
E75293	06/59-09/89	⊗06/90	**245**	07/59-08/81	**302245**	08/81-04/89		
E75294	06/59-09/89	⊗02/90	**246**	07/59- *83*	**302246**	*83*-09/89		
E75295	06/59-09/89	⊗04/90	**247**	07/59-01/82	**302247**	01/82-04/89		
E75296	06/59-09/89	⊗07/90	**248**	07/59-03/83	**302248**	03/83-03/83	**302399**	03/83-05/83
			302248	05/83-03/89				
E75297	06/59-07/90	⊗07/90	**249**	08/59-09/82	**302249**	09/82-09/89		
E75298	06/59-01/91	⊗03/91	**250**	08/59-04/82	**302250**	04/82-02/83	**302244**	09/83-03/89
			302285	03/89-05/90	**302261**	05/90-01/91		
E75299	07/59-10/90	⊗10/90	**251**	08/59-01/83	**302251**	01/83-10/90		
E75300	07/59-09/89	⊗05/90	**252**	08/59-08/82	**302252**	08/82-03/89	**302278**	03/89-09/89
E75301	07/59-05/85	⊗08/85	**253**	08/59-10/82	**302253**	10/82-05/85		
E75302	07/59-09/89	⊗05/90	**254**	08/59-03/83	**302254**	03/83-09/89		
E75303	07/59-07/83	⊗05/84	**255**	08/59-01/82	**302255**	01/82-07/83		
E75304	07/59-09/89	⊗05/90	**256**	09/59- *83*	**302256**	*83*-03/89	**302258**	03/89-09/89
E75305	07/59-09/89	⊗05/90	**257**	09/59-04/82	**302257**	04/82-09/89		
E75306	08/59-10/90	⊗09/90	**258**	09/59-05/81	**302258**	05/81-11/88	**302278**	11/88-03/89
			302252	03/89-06/90				
E75307	08/59-09/89	⊗05/90	**259**	09/59-03/80	**302259**	03/80-11/87	**302459**	11/87-02/88
			302259	02/88-03/89	**302282**	03/89-09/89		
E75308	08/59-05/85	⊗10/88	**260**	09/59-05/81	**302260**	05/81-05/85		
E75309	08/59-06/90	⊗06/90	**261**	09/59-03/83	**302261**	03/83-05/90		
E75310	08/59-07/90	⊗03/91	**262**	09/59-10/82	**302262**	10/82-11/87	**302462**	11/87-02/88
			302262	02/88-07/90				
E75311	08/59-06/96	⊗04/98	**263**	09/59-09/83	**302263**	09/83-09/88	**302203**[2]	09/88-06/96
E75312	08/59-01/90	⊗03/90	**264**	09/59-05/82	**302264**	05/82-09/89		
E75313	08/59-09/89	⊗06/90	**265**	09/59-09/82	**302265**	09/82-03/89	**302297**	03/89-03/89
E75314	08/59-01/88	⊗09/88	**266**	09/59-07/84	**302266**	07/84-01/88		
E75315	08/59-09/89	⊗05/90	**267**	09/59-02/80	**302267**	02/80-08/86	**302268**	08/86-09/89
E75316	08/59-02/87	⊗10/87	**268**	11/59-09/82	**302268**	09/82-08/86		
E75317	08/59-09/88	⊗09/88	**269**	11/59-01/82	**302269**	01/82-06/88		
E75318	08/59-09/89	⊗07/90	**270**	11/59- *83*	**302270**	*83*-09/89		
E75319	09/59-11/88	⊗11/88	**271**	11/59-04/82	**302271**	04/82-08/88		
E75320	09/59-09/89	⊗04/90	**272**	11/59-06/83	**302272**	06/83-04/89		
E75321	09/59-09/89	⊗02/90	**273**	11/59-03/82	**302273**	03/82-08/85	**302302**	09/85-09/88
			302260[2]	09/88-09/89				
E75322	09/59-03/90	⊗08/90	**274**	11/59-05/82	**302274**	05/82-04/89	**302286**	04/89-03/90
E75323	09/59-07/83	⊗05/84	**275**	11/59-11/79	**302275**	11/79-07/83		
E75324	09/59-02/86	⊗04/86	**276**	11/59-01/80	**302276**	01/80-02/86		
E75325	09/59-01/98	⊗	**277**	11/59-01/83	**302277**	01/83-09/88	**302227**[2]	09/88-01/98
E75326	10/59-03/90	⊗07/90	**278**	01/60-11/84	**302278**	11/84-11/88	**302258**	11/88-03/89
			302256	03/89-09/89				
E75327	10/59-02/88	⊗04/88	**279**	01/60-10/81	**302279**	10/81-02/88		
E75328	10/59-01/90	⊗03/90	**280**	01/60- *83*	**302280**	*83*-01/90		
E75329	10/59-03/90	⊗08/90	**281**	01/60-10/82	**302281**	10/82-10/86	**302282**	10/86-03/89
			302259	03/89-03/90				
E75330	10/59-08/86	⊗10/87	**282**	11/59-02/82	**302282**	02/82-08/86		
E75331	10/59-01/91	⊗03/91	**283**	12/59-02/83	**302283**	02/83-07/90		
E75332	10/59-03/90	⊗09/90	**284**	12/59-10/81	**302284**	10/81-03/90		
E75333	10/59-04/89	⊗03/89	**285**	12/59-06/83	**302285**	06/83-12/88	**302237**	12/88-03/89
E75334	10/59-01/91	⊗03/91	**286**	12/59-05/82	**302286**	05/82-04/89	**302274**	04/89-01/91
E75335	10/59-09/88	⊗09/88	**287**	11/59-01/80	**302287**	01/80-10/85	**302227**	10/85-02/88
			302427	02/88-06/88	**302227**	06/88-07/88		
E75336	10/59-05/85	⊗03/90	**288**	12/59-12/82	**302288**	12/82-05/85		
E75337	10/59-12/89	⊗03/90	**289**	01/60-01/80	**302289**	01/80-09/89		
E75338	11/59-09/89	⊗04/90	**290**	01/60-10/82	**302290**	10/82-09/89		
E75339	11/59-09/89	⊗02/90	**291**	01/60- *83*	**302291**	*83*-09/89		
E75340	11/59-10/90	⊗10/90	**292**	01/60-03/83	**302292**	03/83-10/90		
E75341	11/59-07/97	⊗12/97	**293**	01/60-08/81	**302293**	08/81-09/88	**302223**[2]	09/88-07/97
E75342	11/59-09/89	⊗04/90	**294**	01/60-01/82	**302294**	01/82-11/87	**302494**	11/87-06/88
			302294	06/88-06/88	**302269**	06/88-09/89		
E75343	11/59-09/89	⊗05/90	**295**	01/60-02/82	**302295**	02/82-09/89		
E75344	11/59-03/90	⊗08/90	**296**	01/60-04/84	**302296**	04/84-03/90		
E75345	11/59-09/89	⊗04/90	**297**	02/60-10/81	**302297**	10/81-11/87	**302497**	11/87-02/88
			302297	02/88-03/89	**302265**	03/89-09/89		
E75346	11/59-03/91	⊗03/91	**298**	01/60-03/83	**302298**	03/83-06/90	**302252**	06/90-03/91
E75347	11/59-01/90	⊗07/90	**299**	01/60-03/83	**302299**	03/83-11/88	**308995**	11/88-01/90
E75348	11/59-03/90	⊗08/90	**300**	01/60-07/83	**302300**	07/83-09/88	**302260**[2]	09/88-03/90
E75349	12/59-06/90	⊗06/90	**301**	01/60-01/83	**302301**	01/83-09/88	**302253**[2]	09/88-06/90
E75350	12/59-10/85	⊗10/85	**302**	02/60-02/80	**302302**	02/80-09/85		
[illegible]	[illegible]	[illegible]	[illegible]	[illegible]	[illegible]	[illegible]	[illegible]	[illegible]
E75352	12/59-09/97	⊗04/96	**304**	02/60-06/83	**302304**	06/83-09/88	**302214**[2]	09/88-09/96
E75353	12/59-01/90	⊗03/90	**305**	01/60- *83*	**302305**	*83*-01/90		
E75354	12/59-03/90	⊗06/90	**306**	01/60-03/83	**302306**	03/83-09/88	**302273**[2]	09/88-03/90
E75355	12/59-10/90	⊗10/90	**307**	01/60-10/83	**302307**	10/83-09/88	**302267**[2]	09/88-10/90
E75356	01/60-04/97	⊗05/97	**308**	02/60-02/83	**302308**	02/83-09/88	**302208**[2]	09/88-02/92
			305596	02/92-07/93	**302208**	07/93-01/94	**302206**	03/94-04/97
E75357	01/60-12/85	⊗02/86	**309**	01/60-02/80	**302309**	02/80-12/85		
E75358	01/60-04/97	⊗05/97	**310**	04/60-09/83	**302310**	09/83-09/88	**302207**[2]	09/88-04/97
E75359	01/60-06/90	⊗08/90	**311**	04/60- *83*	**302311**	*83*-09/88	**302275**[2]	09/88-04/89
			302272	04/89-06/90				
E75360	01/60-09/89	⊗06/90	**312**	05/60- *83*	**302312**	*83*-08/88	**302238**	08/88-09/89

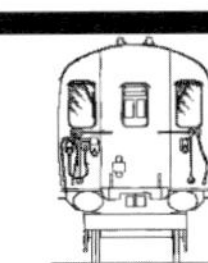

Class 414/3 2-HAP Ashford/Eastleigh

Driving Trailer Composite (Semi-open) Lavatory
DTCsoL, later DTSsoL
S75361-S75423

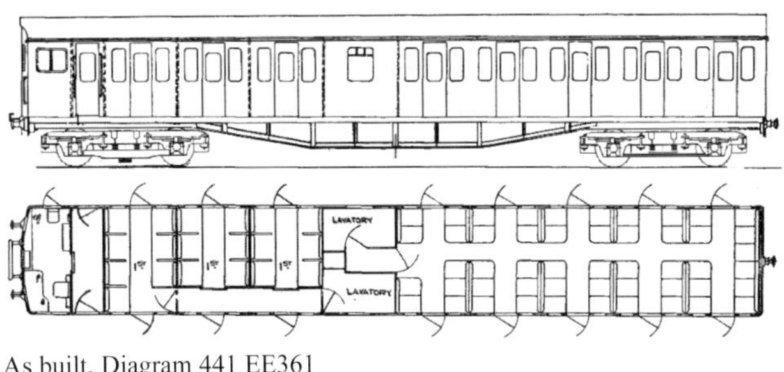

As built, Diagram 441 EE361

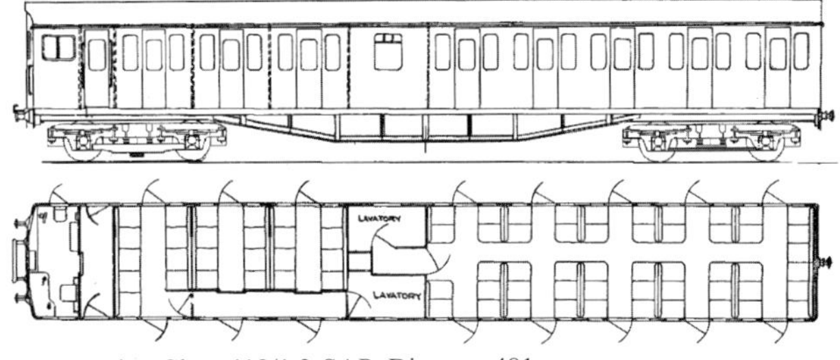

Converted to Class 418/1 2-SAP, Diagram 481

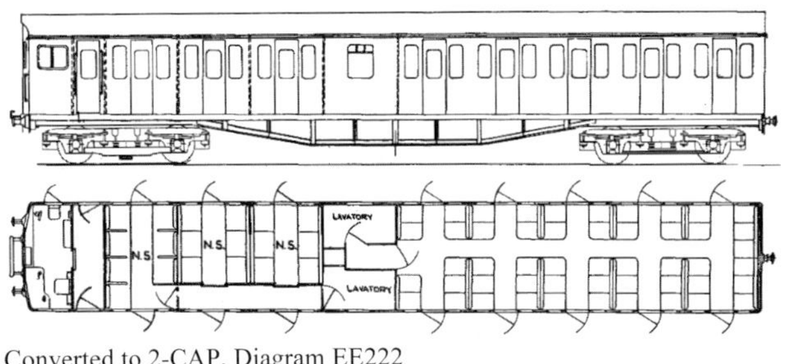

Converted to 2-CAP, Diagram EE222

Diagram:	441 481 EE361 EE222	Lot Number:	30453
Body:	63' 11½" × 9' 3"	Weight:	32t 0cwt

Seats: 19 first 50 second 2 toilets Bogies: Mk 4
later 76 second 2 toilets or 69 second 2 toilets

S75361	11/58-04/93	⊗08/93	**6043**	11/58-04/74	**5941**	04/74-03/80	**6043**	03/80-05/82
			3302	05/82-04/93				
S75362	12/58-10/83	➲**977214**	**6044**	12/58-04/74	**5942**	04/74-02/80	**6044**	02/80-10/83
S75363	12/58-05/91	⊗11/91	**6045**	12/58-05/77	**5943**	05/77-04/80	**6045**	04/80-05/82
			3310	05/82-10/84	**3310**	02/85-05/91		
S75364	12/58-04/93	⊗08/93	**6046**	12/58-05/77	**5944**	05/77-03/80	**6046**	03/80-05/82
			3302	05/82-04/93				
S75365	12/58-05/84	⊗02/85	**6047**	12/58-05/77	**5945**	05/77-04/80	**6047**	04/80-05/84
S75366	12/58-05/91	⊗08/91	**6048**	12/58-05/77	**5946**	05/77-03/80	**6048**	03/80-05/82
			3308	05/82-05/91				
S75367	01/59-05/84	⊗07/85	**6049**	01/59-05/77	**5947**	05/77-03/80	**6049**	03/80-05/84
S75368	01/59-10/82	⊗12/86	**6050**	01/59-05/77	**5948**	05/77-02/80	**6050**	02/80-10/82
S75369	01/59-07/91	➲*977730*	**6051**	01/59-05/77	**5949**	05/77-02/80	**6051**	05/80-07/88
			4301	07/88-07/91				
S75370	01/59-01/94	⊗05/94	**6052**	01/59-05/77	**5950**	05/77-05/80	**6052**	05/80-04/82
			3303	04/82-01/94				
S75371	01/59-05/91	⊗08/91	**6053**	01/59-05/77	**5951**	05/77-10/77	**6053**	10/77-05/82
			3309	05/82-05/91				
S75372	02/59-01/94	⊗05/94	**6054**	02/59-04/82	**3303**	04/82-01/94		
S75373	02/59-01/95	⊗11/94	**6055**	02/59-05/82	**3301**	05/82-01/95		
S75374	02/59-12/93	⊗01/94	**6056**	02/59-04/82	**3306**	04/82-12/93		
S75375	02/59-01/95	⊗11/94	**6057**	02/59-05/82	**3301**	05/82-01/95		
S75376	02/59-12/93	⊗01/94	**6058**	02/59-04/82	**3306**	04/82-12/93		
S75377	03/59-05/91	⊗08/91	**6059**	03/59-05/82	**3309**	05/82-05/91		
S75378	03/59-12/93	⊗01/94	**6060**	03/59-05/82	**3307**	05/82-12/93		
S75379	03/59-04/85	➲**977732**	**6061**	03/59-10/84				
S75380	03/59-07/91	⊗12/91	**6062**	03/59-06/88	**4302**	06/88-07/91		
S75381	04/59-01/95	⊗02/95	**6063**	04/59-05/88	**4303**	05/88-09/91	**3325**	09/91-01/95
S75382	04/59-01/94	⊗02/94	**6064**	04/59-12/87	**4304**	12/87-09/91	**3323**	09/91-12/91
			3322	12/91-01/94				
S75383	04/59-10/83	⊗06/84	**6065**	04/59-10/83				
S75384	04/59-05/91	⊗08/91	**6066**	04/59-05/82	**3308**	05/82-05/91		
S75385	05/59-10/82	⊗12/86	**6067**	05/59-10/82				
S75386	05/59-05/91	⊗11/91	**6068**	05/59-05/82	**3310**	05/82-10/84	**3310**	02/85-05/91
S75387	05/59-05/82	⊗04/84	**6069**	05/59-05/82				
S75388	05/59-01/94	⊗02/94	**6070**	05/59-04/88	**4305**	04/88-09/91	**3321**	09/91-01/94
S75389	05/59-05/82	⊗12/86	**6071**	05/59-05/82				
S75390	06/59-12/93	⊗01/94	**6072**	06/59-08/87	**4306**	08/87-09/91	**3324**	09/91-12/93
S75391	06/59-12/93	⊗01/94	**6073**	06/59-05/82	**3307**	05/82-12/93		
S75392	06/59-05/82	⊗01/87	**6074**	06/59-05/82				
S75393	06/59-05/93	⊗08/93	**6075**	06/59-10/87	**4307**	10/87-09/91	**3323**	09/91-05/93
S75394	06/59-09/82	⊗10/84	**6076**	06/59-09/82				
S75395	06/59-03/95	Ⓟ	**6077**	06/59-07/87	**4308**	07/87-03/95		
S75396	07/59-03/95	⊗04/95	**6078**	07/59-07/87	**4309**	07/87-03/95		
S75397	07/59-09/82	⊗06/84	**6079**	07/59-09/82				
S75398	07/59-01/94	⊗02/94	**6080**	07/59-05/88	**4310**	05/88-09/91	**3321**	09/91-01/94
S75399	07/59-05/94	⊗06/94	**6081**	07/59-05/82	**3305**	05/82-05/94		
S75400	07/59-05/82	⊗01/87	**6082**	07/59-05/82				
S75401	07/59-05/82	⊗12/86	**6083**	07/59-05/82				
S75402	07/59-04/94	⊗06/94	**6084**	07/59-04/82	**3304**	04/82-04/94		
S75403	07/59-04/94	⊗06/94	**6085**	07/59-04/82	**3304**	04/82-04/94		
S75404	07/59-05/82	⊗09/87	**6086**	07/59-05/82				
S75405	08/59-10/84	⊗02/88	**6087**	08/59-10/84				
S75406	08/59-05/82	⊗01/87	**6088**	08/59-05/82				
S75407	08/59-03/95	Ⓟ	**6089**	08/59-07/87	**4311**	07/87-03/95		
S75408	08/59-07/91	➲*977734*	**6090**	08/59-07/88	**4312**	07/88-07/91		
S75409	08/59-10/83	⊗05/84	**6091**	08/59-10/83				
S75410	08/59-03/95	⊗04/95	**6092**	08/59-07/87	**4313**	07/87-03/95		
S75411	08/59-04/93	⊗08/93	**6093**	08/59-05/82	**3311**	05/82-04/93		
S75412	08/59-05/82	⊗01/87	**6094**	08/59-05/82				
S75413	08/59-10/82	⊗01/87	**6095**	08/59-10/82				
S75414	08/59-11/94	⊗11/94	**6096**	08/59-07/87	**4314**	07/87-11/94		
S75415	09/59-01/94	⊗02/94	**6097**	09/59-11/87	**4315**	11/87-09/91	**3322**	09/91-01/94
S75416	09/59-07/91	➲*977736*	**6098**	09/59-12/87	**4316**	12/87-07/91		
S75417	08/59-04/93	⊗08/93	**6099**	09/59-05/82	**3311**	05/82-04/93		
S75418	08/59-01/95	⊗02/95	**6100**	09/59-04/87	**4317**	04/87-09/91	**3325**	09/91-01/95
S75419	09/59-05/82	⊗01/87	**6101**	09/59-05/82				
S75420	09/59-05/93	⊗08/93	**6102**	09/59-05/87	**4318**	05/87-09/91	**3322**	09/91-12/91
			3323	12/91-05/93				
S75421	09/59-10/84	⊗02/88	**6103**	09/59-10/84				
S75422	09/59-05/94	⊗06/94	**6104**	09/59-05/82	**3305**	05/82-05/94		
S75423	09/59-12/93	⊗01/94	**6105**	09/59-06/87	**4319**	06/87-09/91	**3324**	09/91-12/93

Class 305/2 York/Doncaster

Battery Driving Trailer Second Open Lavatory
BDTSOL, later BDTCOL
E75424-E75442

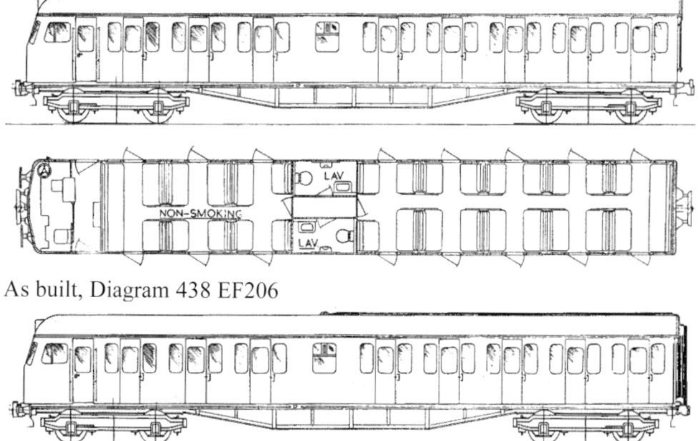

As built, Diagram 438 EF206

Refurbished as BDTCOL, Diagram EF304

Diagram: 438 EF206 EF304 Lot Number: 30566
Body: 64' 0⅝" × 9' 3" Weight: 35t 19cwt
Seats: 80 second 2 toilets Bogies: Gresley
later 24 first 52 second 1 toilet

E75424	10/59-12/01	⊗01/02	**501**	10/59-03/83	**305501**	03/83-12/01		
E75425	03/60-06/01	⊗11/01	**502**	03/60-04/83	**305502**	04/83-06/01		
E75426	04/60-11/97	⊗04/99	**503**	04/60-05/81	**305503**	05/81-11/97		
E75427	04/60-06/96	⊗07/96	**504**	04/60-11/81	**305504**	11/81-06/96		
E75428	04/60-12/81	⊗06/82	**505**	04/60-12/81				
E75429	05/60-08/00	⊗04/03	**506**	05/60-07/81	**305506**	07/81-08/00		
E75430	05/60-11/97	⊗04/99	**507**	05/60-01/80	**305507**	01/80-11/97		
E75431	06/60-10/01	⊗11/01	**508**	06/60-03/83	**305508**	03/83-10/01		
E75432	07/60-10/95	⊗10/95	**509**	07/60- *83*	**305509**	*83*-10/95		
E75433	07/60-03/99	⊗04/99	**510**	07/60-03/83	**305510**	03/83-03/99		
E75434	07/60-07/00	⊗04/03	**511**	07/60-04/83	**305511**	04/83-07/00		
E75435	08/60-03/94	⊗06/94	**512**	08/60-09/81	**305505**	05/83-09/90	**308144**	09/90-08/93
E75436	08/60-06/96	⊗07/96	**513**	08/60-02/80	**305513**	02/80-06/96		
E75437	09/60-03/93	⊗09/93	**514**	09/60-02/81	**305514**	02/81-03/93		
E75438	10/60-11/97	⊗04/99	**515**	10/60-01/80	**305515**	01/80-11/97		
E75439	10/60-06/00	⊗04/03	**516**	10/60-02/83	**305516**	02/83-06/00		
E75440	10/60-12/01	⊗01/02	**517**	10/60-02/83	**305517**	02/83-12/01		
E75441	11/60-05/98	⊗12/98	**518**	11/60-08/81	**305518**	08/81-05/98		
E75442	11/60-12/01	⊗01/02	**519**	11/60-04/83	**305519**	04/83-12/01		

Class 305/2 York/Doncaster

Driving Trailer Second
DTS, later DTSO
E75443-E75461

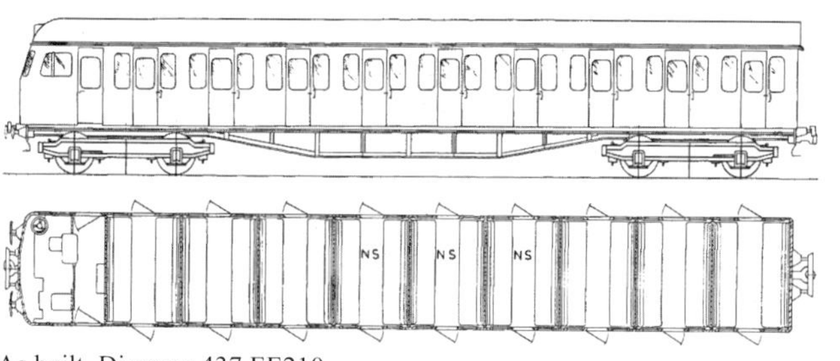

As built, Diagram 437 EE210

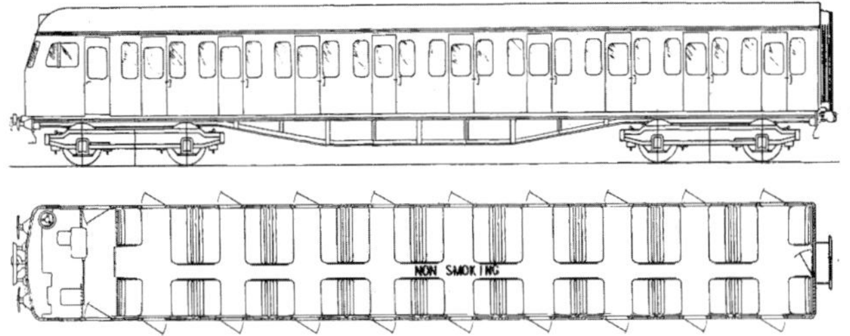

Refurbished as DTSO, Diagram EE220

Diagram: 437 EE210 — Lot Number: 30569
Body: 64' 0⅝" × 9' 3" — Weight: 32t 3cwt
Seats: 108 second later 88 second — Bogies: Gresley

E75443	10/59-12/01	⊗01/02	**501**	10/59-03/83	**305501**	03/83-12/01
E75444	03/60-06/01	⊗11/01	**502**	03/60-04/83	**305502**	04/83-06/01
E75445	04/60-11/97	⊗04/99	**503**	04/60-05/81	**305503**	05/81-11/97
E75446	04/60-06/96	⊗07/96	**504**	04/60-11/81	**305504**	11/81-06/96
E75447	04/60-03/93	⊗12/93	**505**	04/60-12/81	**305505**	[illegible]
[illegible]	[illegible]	[illegible]	**506**	[illegible]	[illegible]	[illegible]
E75449	[illegible]	⊗04/99	**507**	[illegible]	[illegible]	[illegible]
[illegible]	[illegible]	[illegible]	[illegible]	[illegible]	[illegible]	[illegible]
E75451	07/60-10/95	⊗10/95	**509**	07/60- *83*	**305509**	*83*-10/95
E75452	07/60-03/99	⊗04/99	**510**	07/60-03/83	**305510**	03/83-03/99
E75453	07/60-07/00	⊗03/03	**511**	07/60-04/83	**305511**	04/83-07/00
E75454	08/60-09/81	⊗06/82	**512**	08/60-09/81		
E75455	08/60-06/96	⊗07/96	**513**	08/60-02/80	**305513**	02/80-06/96
E75456	09/60-03/93	⊗09/93	**514**	09/60-02/81	**305514**	02/81-03/93
E75457	10/60-11/97	⊗04/99	**515**	10/60-01/80	**305515**	01/80-11/97
E75458	10/60-06/00	⊗04/03	**516**	10/60-02/83	**305516**	02/83-06/00
E75459	10/60-12/01	⊗01/02	**517**	10/60-02/83	**305517**	02/83-12/01
E75460	11/60-05/98	⊗12/98	**518**	11/60-08/81	**305518**	08/81-05/98
E75461	11/60-12/01	⊗01/02	**519**	11/60-04/83	**305519**	04/83-12/01

Class 305/1 York
Battery Driving Trailer Second Open
BDTSO
E75462-E75513

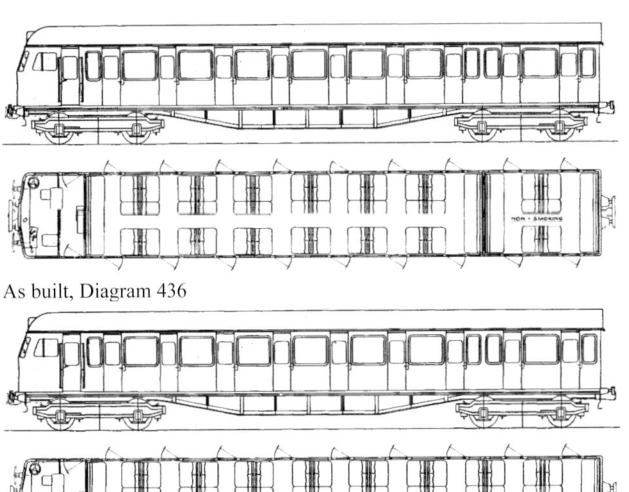

As built, Diagram 436

Facelifted, Diagram EF205

Diagram: 436 EF205 — Lot Number: 30570
Body: 64' 0⅝" × 9' 3" — Weight: 34t 6cwt
Seats: 94 second later 92 second — Bogies: Gresley

E75462	03/60-06/96	⊗07/96	**401**	03/60-09/82	**305401**	09/82-05/93	**305410**	05/93-06/96
E75463	03/60-02/92	⊗02/92	**402**	03/60-08/83	**305402**	08/83-02/92		
E75464	03/60-03/93	⊗06/93	**403**	03/60-11/81	**305403**	11/81-07/87	**305521**	05/88-03/93
E75465	03/60-12/92	⊗11/94	**404**	03/60-08/81	**305404**	08/81-11/88	**305522**	11/88-12/92
E75466	04/60-02/92	⊗02/92	**405**	04/60-09/82	**305405**	09/82-10/82	**305499**	10/82-02/83
			305405	02/83-02/92				
E75467	04/60-01/92	⊗02/92	**406**	04/60-09/82	**305406**	09/82-01/92		
E75468	05/60-03/92	⊗03/94	**407**	05/60-11/81	**305407**	11/81-02/92		
E75469	03/60-09/91	➲977741	**408**	03/60-08/82	**305408**	08/82-09/91		
E75470	04/60-12/92	⊗05/95	**409**	04/60-06/83	**305409**	06/83-12/92		
E75471	06/60-06/96	⊗07/96	**410**	06/60-06/82	**305410**	06/82-05/93	**305401**	05/93-06/96
E75472	04/60-12/92	⊗08/93	**411**	04/60- *83*	**305411**	*83*-07/87	**305523**	04/88-12/92
E75473	04/60-08/93	⊗08/93	**412**	04/60-04/81	**305412**	04/81-08/93		
E75474	04/60-02/92	⊗03/94	**413**	04/60-05/81	**305413**	05/81-02/92		
E75475	06/60-12/92	⊗03/94	**414**	06/60-11/81	**305414**	11/81-07/87	**305524**	11/88-12/92
E75476	06/60-01/93	⊗02/94	**415**	06/60-11/81	**305415**	11/81-01/92	**305417**	01/92-01/93
E75477	05/60-06/96	⊗07/96	**416**	05/60-10/82	**305416**	10/82-06/96		
E75478	05/60-10/92	⊗02/94	**417**	05/60- *83*	**305417**	*83*-01/92	**305415**	01/92-10/92
E75479	06/60-02/92	⊗02/92	**418**	06/60-04/82	**305418**	04/82-02/92		
E75480	05/60-06/93	⊗09/94	**419**	05/60-05/82	**305419**	05/82-07/87	**305525**	02/92-06/93
E75481	06/60-06/96	⊗07/96	**420**	06/60-03/83	**305420**	03/83-06/96		
E75482	07/60-02/92	⊗03/94	**421**	07/60-07/83	**305421**	07/83-02/92		
E75483	07/60-03/93	⊗03/94	**422**	06/60-04/83	**305422**	04/83-06/87	**305526**	05/88-03/93
E75484	06/60-05/84	⊗08/85	**423**	06/60-01/82	**305423**	01/82-05/84		
E75485	06/60-05/84	⊗04/85	**424**	06/60-12/81	**305424**	12/81-05/84		
E75486	06/60-05/84	⊗03/85	**425**	06/60-08/82	**305425**	08/82-05/84		
E75487	07/60-05/84	⊗04/85	**426**	07/60- *83*	**305426**	*83*-05/84		
E75488	07/60-05/84	⊗10/85	**427**	07/60-02/80	**305427**	02/80-05/84		
E75489	07/60-05/84	⊗04/85	**428**	07/60-02/80	**305428**	02/80-05/84		
E75490	07/60-05/84	⊗04/85	**429**	07/60-08/81	**305429**	08/81-05/84		
E75491	07/60-05/84	⊗08/85	**430**	07/60-06/81	**305430**	06/81-05/84		
E75492	08/60-05/84	⊗07/85	**431**	08/60-03/83	**305431**	03/83-05/84		
E75493	08/60-05/84	⊗04/85	**432**	08/60- *83*	**305432**	*83*-05/84		
E75494	08/60-05/84	⊗04/85	**433**	08/60-04/82	**305433**	04/82-05/84		
E75495	08/60-05/84	⊗11/84	**434**	08/60-01/82	**305434**	01/82-05/84		
[illegible]	[illegible]	[illegible]	[illegible]	[illegible]	[illegible]	[illegible]		
[illegible]	08/60-05/84	⊗04/85	**436**	08/60-08/82	**305436**	08/82-05/84		
[illegible]	[illegible]	[illegible]	**437**	08/60-07/81	[illegible]	07/81-05/84		
[illegible]	[illegible]	[illegible]	[illegible]	[illegible]	[illegible]	[illegible]		
E75500	09/60-05/84	➲977307	**439**	09/60-11/82	**305439**	11/82-05/84		
E75501	09/60-05/84	⊗06/85	**440**	09/60-02/82	**305440**	02/82-01/84	**305540**	01/84-05/84
E75502	10/60-05/84	⊗06/85	**441**	11/60-06/81	**305441**	06/81-01/84	**305541**	01/84-05/84
E75503	10/60-02/85	⊗09/85	**442**	11/60-12/81	**305442**	12/81-01/84	**305542**	01/84-02/85
E75504	10/60-08/84	⊗03/85	**443**	11/60-01/82	**305443**	01/82-01/84	**305543**	01/84-08/84
E75505	10/60-05/84	⊗06/85	**444**	11/60-02/80	**305444**	02/80-01/84	**305544**	01/84-05/84
E75506	10/60-05/98	⊗12/98	**445**	11/60-06/82	**305445**	06/82-01/84	**305545**	01/84-02/85
			305445	02/85-07/87	**305403**[2]	07/87-05/98		
E75507	10/60-06/93	⊗08/93	**446**	11/60-05/82	**305446**	05/82-03/85	**305546**	03/85-05/85
			305446	05/85-04/88	**305527**	04/88-06/93		
E75508	10/60-12/92	⊗01/93	**447**	11/60-06/83	**305447**	06/83-07/87	**305404**	07/87-12/92
E75509	10/60-12/92	⊗02/94	**448**	11/60-01/82	**305448**	01/82-03/85	**305548**	03/85-04/85
			305448	04/85-07/87	**305411**[2]	07/87-12/92		
E75510	10/60-02/92	⊗02/93	**449**	11/60-12/82	**305449**	12/82-02/85	**305549**	02/85-04/85
			305449	04/85-07/87	**305414**[2]	07/87-03/89		
E75511	10/60-11/92	⊗03/94	**450**	11/60-12/83	**305450**	12/83-02/85	**305550**	02/85-05/85
			305450	05/85-07/87	**305419**[2]	07/87-11/92		
E75512	11/60-06/93	⊗08/93	**451**	11/60-03/81	**305451**	03/81-01/89	**305528**	01/89-06/93
E75513	11/60-03/92	⊗12/93	**452**	11/60-02/80	**305452**	02/80-06/87	**305422**[2]	06/87-02/92

Class 305/1 York
Driving Trailer Second Open
DTSO
E75514-E75565

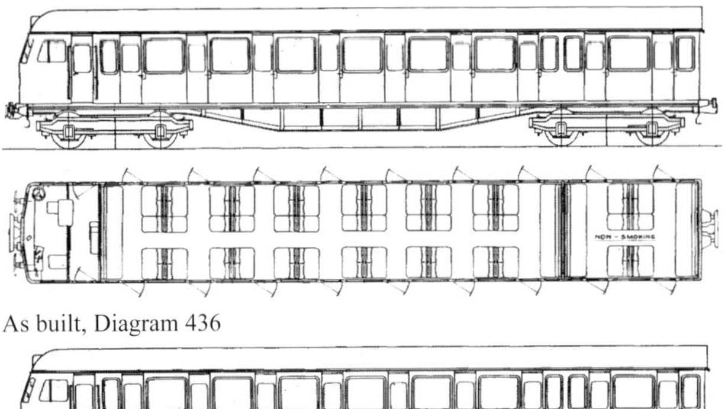

As built, Diagram 436

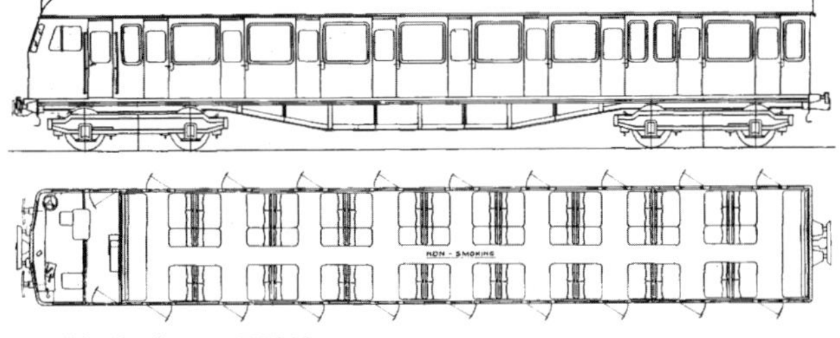

Facelifted, Diagram EE209

Diagram: 436 EE209 — Lot Number: 30572
Body: 64' 0⅝" × 9' 3" — Weight: 31t 0cwt
Seats: 94 second later 92 second — Bogies: Gresley

E75514	03/60-06/96	⊗07/96	**401**	03/60-09/82	**305401**	09/82-06/96		
E75515	03/60-02/92	⊗02/92	**402**	03/60-08/83	**305402**	08/83-02/92		
E75516	03/60-03/93	⊗06/93	**403**	03/60-11/81	**305403**	11/81-07/87	**305521**	05/88-03/93
E75517	03/60-12/92	⊗11/94	**404**	03/60-08/81	**305404**	08/81-11/88	**305522**	11/88-12/92
E75518	04/60-02/92	⊗02/92	**405**	04/60-09/82	**305405**	09/82-10/82	**305499**	10/82-02/83
			305405	02/83-02/92				

E75519	04/60-01/92	⊗02/92	**406**	04/60-09/82	**305406**	09/82-01/92		
E75520	05/60-03/92	⊗12/93	**407**	05/60-11/81	**305407**	11/81-02/92		
E75521	03/60-09/91	➲**977743**	**408**	03/60-08/82	**305408**	08/82-09/91		
E75522	04/60-12/92	⊗05/95	**409**	04/60-06/83	**305409**	06/83-12/92		
E75523	06/60-06/96	⊗07/96	**410**	06/60-06/82	**305410**	06/82-06/96		
E75524	04/60-12/92	⊗08/93	**411**	04/60- *83*	**305411**	*83*-07/87	**305523**	04/88-12/92
E75525	04/60-08/93	⊗08/93	**412**	04/60-04/81	**305412**	04/81-08/93		
E75526	04/60-02/92	⊗03/94	**413**	04/60-05/81	**305413**	05/81-02/92		
E75527	06/60-12/92	⊗03/94	**414**	06/60-11/81	**305414**	11/81-07/87	**305524**	11/88-12/92
E75528	06/60-10/92	⊗10/95	**415**	06/60-11/81	**305415**	11/81-10/92		
E75529	05/60-06/96	⊗07/96	**416**	05/60-10/82	**305416**	10/82-06/96		
E75530	05/60-01/93	⊗02/94	**417**	05/60- *83*	**305417**	*83*-01/93		
E75531	06/60-02/92	⊗02/92	**418**	06/60-04/82	**305418**	04/82-02/92		
E75532	05/60-06/93	⊗09/94	**419**	05/60-05/82	**305419**	05/82-07/87	**305525**	02/92-06/93
E75533	06/60-06/96	⊗07/96	**420**	06/60-03/83	**305420**	03/83-06/96		
E75534	07/60-02/92	⊗03/94	**421**	07/60-07/83	**305421**	07/83-02/92		
E75535	07/60-03/93	⊗03/94	**422**	06/60-04/83	**305422**	04/83-06/87	**305526**	05/88-03/93
E75536	06/60-05/84	⊗08/85	**423**	06/60-01/82	**305423**	01/82-05/84		
E75537	06/60-05/84	⊗04/85	**424**	06/60-12/81	**305424**	12/81-05/84		
E75538	06/60-05/84	⊗11/95	**425**	06/60-08/82	**305425**	08/82-05/84		
E75539	07/60-05/84	⊗04/85	**426**	07/60- *83*	**305426**	*83*-05/84		
E75540	07/60-05/84	⊗10/85	**427**	07/60-02/80	**305427**	02/80-05/84		
E75541	07/60-05/84	⊗03/85	**428**	07/60-02/80	**305428**	02/80-05/84		
E75542	07/60-05/84	⊗04/85	**429**	07/60-08/81	**305429**	08/81-05/84		
E75543	07/60-05/84	⊗08/85	**430**	07/60-06/81	**305430**	06/81-05/84		
E75544	08/60-05/84	⊗07/85	**431**	08/60-03/83	**305431**	03/83-05/84		
E75545	08/60-05/84	⊗04/85	**432**	08/60- *83*	**305432**	*83*-05/84		
E75546	08/60-05/84	⊗04/85	**433**	08/60-04/82	**305433**	04/82-05/84		
E75547	08/60-05/84	⊗11/84	**434**	08/60-01/82	**305434**	01/82-05/84		
E75548	08/60-05/84	➲**977639**	**435**	08/60-10/82	**305435**	10/82-05/84		
E75549	08/60-05/84	⊗04/85	**436**	08/60-08/82	**305436**	08/82-05/84		
E75550	08/60-05/84	⊗01/88	**437**	08/60-07/81	**305437**	07/81-05/84		
E75551	08/60-05/84	⊗07/85	**438**	08/60-04/83	**305438**	04/83-05/84		
E75552	09/60-05/84	➲**977308**	**439**	09/60-11/82	**305439**	11/82-05/84		
E75553	09/60-05/84	⊗06/85	**440**	09/60-02/82	**305440**	02/82-01/84	**305540**	01/84-05/84
E75554	10/60-05/84	⊗06/85	**441**	11/60-06/81	**305441**	06/81-01/84	**305541**	01/84-05/84
E75555	10/60-02/85	⊗09/85	**442**	11/60-12/81	**305442**	12/81-01/84	**305542**	01/84-02/85
E75556	10/60-08/84	⊗03/85	**443**	11/60-01/82	**305443**	01/82-01/84	**305543**	01/84-08/84
E75557	10/60-05/84	⊗06/85	**444**	11/60-02/80	**305444**	02/80-01/84	**305544**	01/84-05/84
E75558	10/60-05/98	⊗12/98	**445**	11/60-06/82	**305445**	06/82-01/84	**305545**	01/84-02/85
			305445	02/85-07/87	**305403**[2]	07/87-05/98		
E75559	10/60-06/93	⊗08/93	**446**	11/60-05/82	**305446**	05/82-03/85	**305546**	03/85-05/85
			305446	05/85-04/88	**305527**	04/88-06/93		
E75560	10/60-12/92	⊗01/93	**447**	11/60-06/83	**305447**	06/83-07/87	**305404**	07/87-12/92
E75561	10/60-12/92	⊗02/94	**448**	11/60-01/82	**305448**	01/82-03/85	**305548**	03/85-04/85
			305448	04/85-07/87	**305411**[2]	07/87-12/92		
E75562	10/60-11/91	⊗11/91	**449**	11/60-12/82	**305449**	12/82-02/85	**305549**	02/85-04/85
			305449	04/85-07/87	**305414**[2]	07/87-11/91		
E75563	10/60-11/92	⊗03/94	**450**	11/60-12/83	**305450**	12/83-02/85	**305550**	02/85-05/85
			305450	05/85-07/87	**305419**[2]	07/87-11/92		
E75564	11/60-06/93	⊗08/93	**451**	11/60-03/81	**305451**	03/81-01/89	**305528**	01/89-06/93
E75565	11/60-03/92	⊗12/93	**452**	11/60-02/80	**305452**	02/80-06/87	**305422**[2]	06/87-02/92

Class 303 Pressed Steel

Driving Trailer Second Open

DTSO

SC75566-SC75600

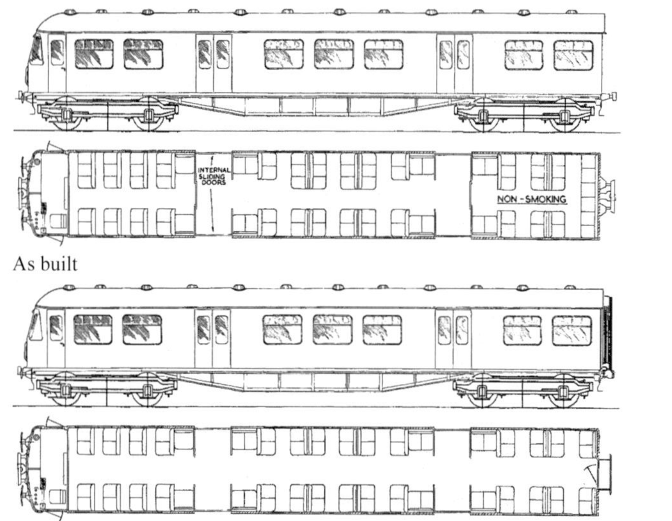

As built

® Refurbished with 2+2 seating and corridor. Shown with modified cab (see left hand cab view above).

Diagram:	439 EE206	Lot Number:	30579
Body:	63' 11⅝" × 9' 3"	Weight:	33t 17cwt
Seats:	83 second later 56 second	Bogies:	Gresley

SC75566	07/59-12/02	⊗01/03	®	**001**	07/59-*11/79*	**303001**	*11/79*-12/02		
SC75567	09/59- 78	⊗12/82		**002**	09/59- 78				
SC75568	09/59-10/01	⊗01/03	®	**003**	09/59-*11/79*	**303003**	*11/79*-10/01		
SC75569	11/59-12/02	⊗01/03	®	**004**	11/59-*03/80*	**303004**	*03/80*-12/02		
SC75570	11/59-07/89	⊗11/91		**005**	11/59-*03/80*	**303005**	*03/80*-07/89		
SC75571	11/59-06/02	⊗09/02	®	**006**	11/59-*11/79*	**303006**	*11/79*-06/02		
SC75572	11/59-07/00	⊗04/02		**007**	11/59- 78	**043**	06/79-06/80	**303043**	06/80-09/00
				303025	09/00				
SC75573	12/59-01/02	⊗02/02	®	**008**	12/59-*11/79*	**303008**	*11/79*-01/02		
SC75574	12/59-09/02	⊗01/03	®	**009**	12/59-*03/80*	**303009**	*03/80*-09/02		
SC75575	12/59-01/01	⊗09/01	®	**010**	12/59-*11/79*	**303010**	*11/79*-01/01		
SC75576	12/59-12/02	⊗01/03	®	**011**	12/59-*05/79*	**303011**	*05/79*-12/02		
SC75577	01/60-02/02	⊗02/02	®	**012**	01/60- *80*	**303012**	*80*-02/02		
SC75578	01/60-10/01	⊗05/02	®	**013**	01/60- *80*	**303013**	*80*-10/01		
SC75579	01/60-07/01	⊗11/01	®	**014**	01/60-*03/80*	**303014**	*03/80*-07/01		
SC75580	01/60-12/87	⊗02/88		**015**	01/60-05/80	**303015**	05/80-12/87		
SC75581	02/60-02/01	⊗01/03	®	**016**	02/60- *80*	**303016**	*80*-10/90	**303040**	10/90-02/01
SC75582	02/60-12/82	⊗11/87		**017**	02/60-06/80	**303017**	06/80-12/82		
SC75583	02/60-12/87	⊗02/88		**018**	02/60-07/80	**303018**	07/80-12/87		
SC75584	02/60-03/02	⊗05/02	®	**019**	02/60-*03/80*	**303019**	*03/80*-03/02		
SC75585	02/60-06/02	⊗12/02	®	**020**	02/60- *80*	**303020**	*80*-06/02		
SC75586	03/60-06/02	⊗10/02	®	**021**	03/60-08/80	**303021**	08/80-06/02		
SC75587	03/60-12/82	⊗06/87		**022**	03/60-06/80	**303022**	06/80-12/82		
SC75588	03/60-07/02	⊗08/02	®	**023**	03/60-06/80	**303023**	06/80-07/02		
SC75589	03/60-05/98	⊗03/01	®	**024**	03/60-*11/79*	**303024**	*11/79*-05/98	**303024**	08/00-08/00
SC75590	03/60-03/01	⊗06/02	®	**025**	03/60-*08/79*	**303025**	*08/79*-07/00	**303056**	09/00-03/01
SC75591	04/60-12/87	⊗05/89		**026**	04/60- *80*	**303026**	*80*-12/87		
SC75592	04/60-09/02	⊗12/02	®	**027**	04/60-*03/80*	**303027**	*03/80*-09/02		
SC75593	04/60-10/82	⊗03/83	®	**028**	04/60-*11/79*	**303028**	*11/79*-10/82		
SC75594	04/60-10/90	⊗01/91		**029**	04/60-*03/80*	**303029**	*03/80*-08/90	**311109**	08/90-10/90
SC75595	04/60-06/02	⊗08/02		**030**	04/60-*11/79*	**303030**	*11/79*-12/87	**303033**	07/88-06/02
SC75596	05/60-12/87	⊗04/90		**031**	05/60- *80*	**303031**	*80*-12/87		
SC75597	05/60-06/02	Ⓟ	®	**032**	05/60-*05/79*	**303032**	*05/79*-06/02		
SC75598	05/60-12/87	⊗08/92	®	**033**	05/60-07/80	**303033**	07/80-07/88		
SC75599	05/60-10/01	⊗05/02	®	**034**	05/60- *80*	**303034**	*80*-10/01		
SC75600	11/60-05/98	⊗03/01		**035**	11/60-06/80	**303035**	06/80-12/80	**303028**	10/82-07/99

Class 303 Pressed Steel

Battery Driving Trailer Second Open

BDTSO

SC75601-SC75635

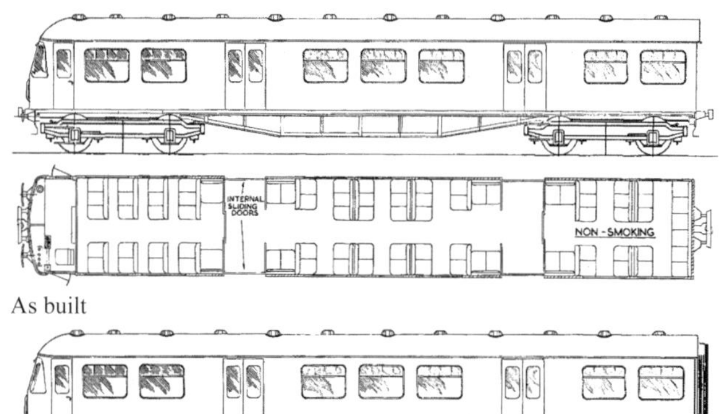

As built

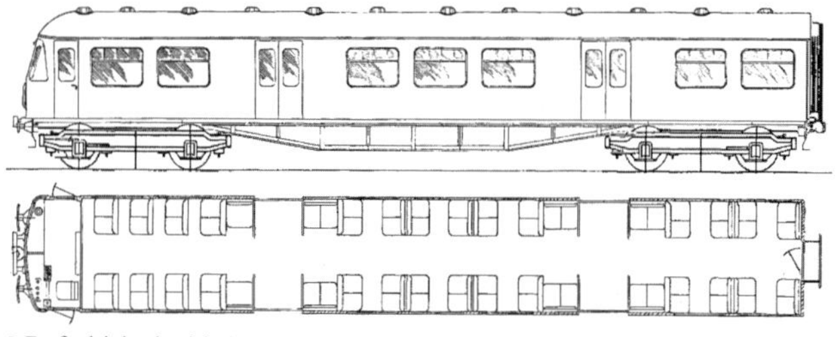

® Refurbished with 2+2 seating and corridor.

Diagram:	439 EF202	Lot Number:	30581
Body:	63' 11⅝" × 9' 3"	Weight:	37t 9cwt
Seats:	83 second later 56 second	Bogies:	Gresley

SC75601	07/59-12/02	⊗01/03	®	**001**	07/59-*11/79*	**303001**	*11/79*-12/02		
SC75602	09/59- 78	⊗10/81		**002**	09/59- 78				
SC75603	09/59-10/01	⊗01/03	®	**003**	09/59-*11/79*	**303003**	*11/79*-10/01		
SC75604	11/59-12/02	⊗01/03	®	**004**	11/59-*03/80*	**303004**	*03/80*-12/02		
SC75605	11/59-07/89	⊗04/90		**005**	11/59-*03/80*	**303005**	*03/80*-07/89		
SC75606	11/59-06/02	⊗09/02	®	**006**	11/59-*11/79*	**303006**	*11/79*-06/02		
SC75607	11/59-07/90	⊗01/91		**007**	11/59- 78	**069**	78-*03/80*	**303069**	*03/80*-07/90
SC75608	12/59-01/02	⊗02/02	®	**008**	12/59-*11/79*	**303008**	*11/79*-01/02		
SC75609	12/59-09/02	⊗01/03	®	**009**	12/59-*03/80*	**303009**	*03/80*-09/02		
SC75610	12/59-01/01	⊗09/01	®	**010**	12/59-*11/79*	**303010**	*11/79*-01/01		
SC75611	12/59-12/02	⊗01/03	®	**011**	12/59-*05/79*	**303011**	*05/79*-12/02		
SC75612	01/60-02/02	⊗02/02	®	**012**	01/60- *80*	**303012**	*80*-02/02		
SC75613	01/60-10/01	Ⓟ	®	**013**	01/60- *80*	**303013**	*80*-10/01		

SC75614	01/60-07/01	⊗11/01	®	**014**	01/60-*03/80*	**303014**	*03/80*-07/01		
SC75615	01/60-12/87	⊗09/90		**015**	01/60-05/80	**303015**	05/80-12/87		
SC75616	02/60-01/02	⊗02/03	®	**016**	02/60- *80*	**303016**	*80*-01/02		
SC75617	02/60-12/82	⊗11/87		**017**	02/60-06/80	**303017**	06/80-12/82		
SC75618	02/60-12/87	⊗02/88		**018**	02/60-07/80	**303018**	07/80-12/87		
SC75619	02/60-03/02	⊗05/02	®	**019**	02/60-*03/80*	**303019**	*03/80*-03/02		
SC75620	02/60-06/02	⊗12/02	®	**020**	02/60- *80*	**303020**	*80*-06/02		
SC75621	03/60-06/02	⊗10/02	®	**021**	03/60-08/80	**303021**	08/80-06/02		
SC75622	03/60-12/82	⊗11/87		**022**	03/60-06/80	**303022**	06/80-12/82		
SC75623	03/60-07/02	⊗08/02	®	**023**	03/60-06/80	**303023**	06/80-07/02		
SC75624	03/60-05/98	⊗03/04	®	**024**	03/60-*11/79*	**303024**	*11/79*-05/98	**303024**	08/00-08/00
SC75625	03/60-07/00	⊗09/01	®	**025**	03/60-*08/79*	**303025**	*08/79*-09/00		
SC75626	04/60-12/87	⊗05/89		**026**	04/60- *80*	**303026**	*80*-12/87		
SC75627	04/60-09/02	⊗12/02	®	**027**	04/60-*03/80*	**303027**	*03/80*-09/02		
SC75628	04/60-10/82	⊗05/83	®	**028**	04/60-*11/79*	**303028**	*11/79*-10/82		
SC75629	04/60-09/90	⊗12/90		**029**	04/60-*03/80*	**303029**	*03/80*-09/90		
SC75630	04/60-12/87	⊗04/89		**030**	04/60-*11/79*	**303030**	*11/79*-12/87		
SC75631	05/60-02/88	⊗05/89		**031**	05/60- *80*	**303031**	*80*-12/87		
SC75632	05/60-06/02	Ⓟ	®	**032**	05/60-*05/79*	**303032**	*05/79*-06/02		
SC75633	05/60-12/87	⊗08/92	®	**033**	05/60-07/80	**303033**	07/80-07/88		
SC75634	05/60-10/01	⊗05/02	®	**034**	05/60- *80*	**303034**	*80*-10/01		
SC75635	11/60-06/02	⊗10/02		**035**	11/60-06/80	**303035**	06/80-12/80	**303028**	10/82-07/99
				303079	07/99-06/02				

Class 416/2 2-EPB Eastleigh

Driving Trailer Second (Semi-open)

DTSso

S75636

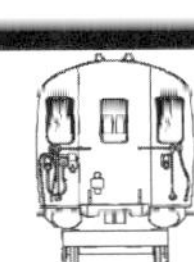

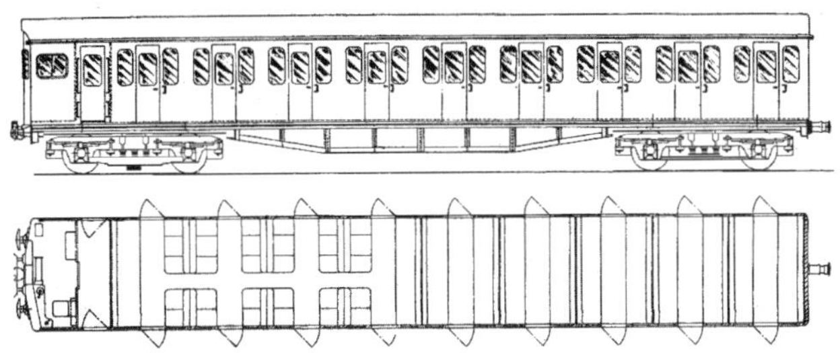

Diagram: 420 EE264
Body: 63' 11½" × 9' 3¼"
Seats: 102 second
Lot Number: 30584
Weight: 30t 0cwt
Bogies: Mk 3D

S75636	01/60-01/86	⊗03/90	**5800**	01/60-12/64	**5710**	12/64-04/85	**6210**	04/85-01/86

Class 309 York

Battery Driving Trailer Composite (Semi-open) Lavatory BDTCsoL

E75637-E75644

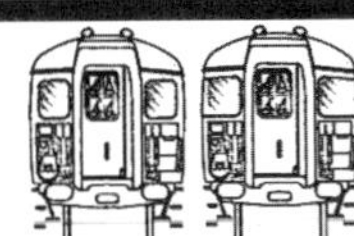

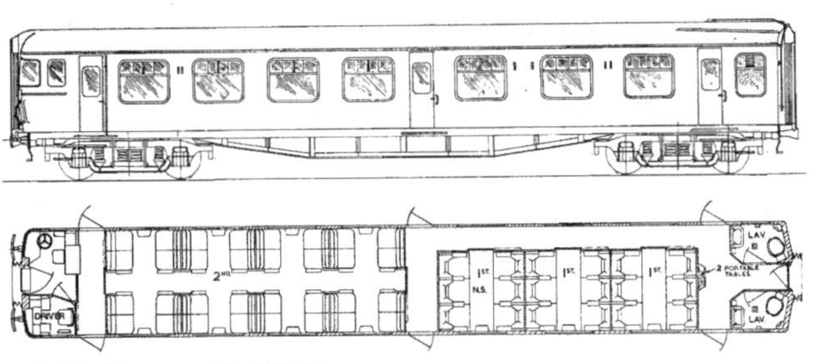

As built, Diagram 448 EF301

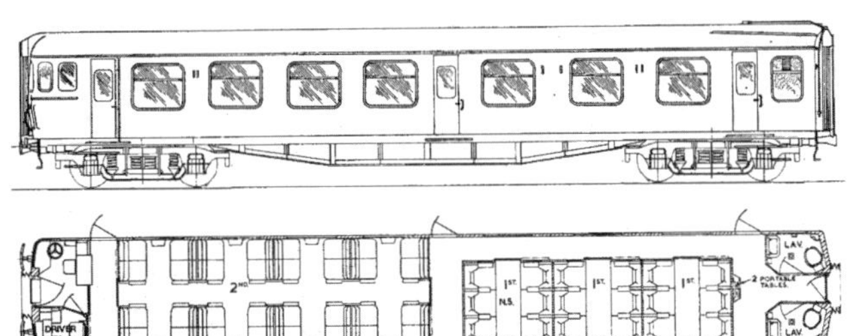

Refurbished, Diagram EF305. Shown with modified cab (see left hand cab view above).

Diagram: 448 EF301 EF305
Body: 64' 9¾" × 9' 3"
Seats: 18 first 32 second 2 toilets
Lot Number: 30679
Weight: 39t 7cwt
Bogies: Commonwealth

E75637	08/62-12/91	⊗03/92	**611**	09/62-03/81	**309611**	03/81-12/91		
E75638	09/62-06/93	⊗04/93	**612**	10/62-10/82	**309612**	10/82-06/93		
E75639	09/62-06/00	⊗04/04	**613**	10/62-06/82	**309613**	06/82-06/00		
E75640	09/62-08/92	⊗07/92	**614**	12/62-10/82	**309614**	10/82-02/86	**309614**	07/86-08/92
E75641	09/62-06/00	⊗04/04	**615**	01/63-09/82	**309615**	09/82-03/85	**309615**	09/86-07/92
			309623	08/92-06/00				
E75642	09/62-06/00	Ⓟ➲977962	**616**	01/63-01/70	**616**	06/72-01/80	**309616**	01/80-07/85
			309616	04/86-06/00				
E75643	09/62-06/00	⊗02/05	**617**	02/63-10/82	**309617**	10/82-07/85	**309617**	04/86-06/00
E75644	09/62-11/99	⊗02/04	**618**	02/63-02/81	**309618**	02/81-12/91	**309627**	02/92-11/99

Class 304/1 Wolverton

Driving Trailer Brake Second Open

DTBSO

M75645-M75659

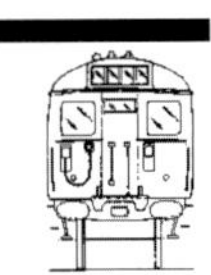

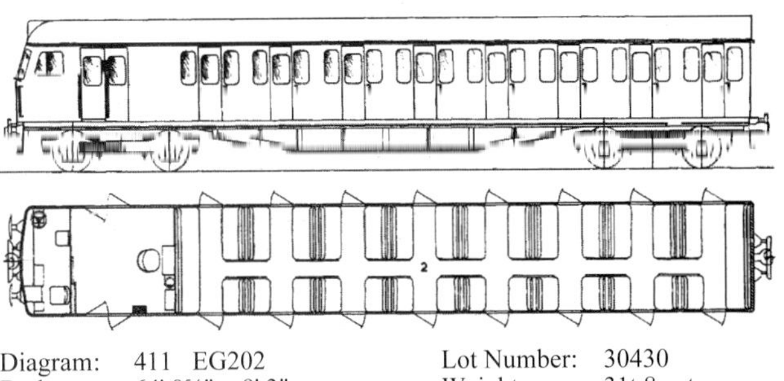

Diagram: 411 EG202
Body: 64' 0⅝" × 9' 3"
Seats: 82 second
Lot Number: 30430
Weight: 31t 8cwt
Bogies: Gresley

M75645	03/60-07/92	⊗07/92	**001**	03/60-10/82	**304001**	10/82-07/92
M75646	04/60-04/96	⊗05/96	**002**	04/60-04/82	**304002**	04/82-04/96
M75647	04/60-05/94	⊗10/00	**003**	04/60-07/81	**304003**	07/81-05/94
M75648	05/60-03/96	⊗01/97	**004**	05/60-09/83	**304004**	09/83-03/96
M75649	05/60-12/94	⊗05/96	**005**	05/60-10/81	**304005**	10/81-12/94
M75650	05/60-12/93	⊗11/97	**006**	05/60-12/82	**304006**	12/82-12/93
M75651	06/60-05/92	⊗05/92	**007**	06/60-04/82	**304007**	04/82-05/92
M75652	06/60-05/94	⊗10/00	**008**	06/60-08/81	**304008**	08/81-05/94
M75653	06/60-03/96	⊗01/97	**009**	06/60-04/81	**304009**	04/81-03/96
M75654	06/60-09/94	⊗06/96	**010**	06/60-12/81	**304010**	12/81-09/94
M75655	06/60-01/91	⊗*11/91*	**011**	06/60-01/80	**304011**	01/80-01/91
M75656	07/60-05/92	⊗04/92	**012**	07/60-04/82	**304012**	04/82-05/92
M75657	07/60-05/94	⊗11/97	**013**	07/60-07/81	**304013**	07/81-05/94
M75658	07/60-09/94	⊗05/96	**014**	07/60-06/81	**304014**	06/81-09/94
M75659	07/60-06/94	⊗06/96	**015**	07/60-08/82	**304015**	08/82-06/94

Class 304/2 Wolverton

Driving Trailer Brake Second Open

DTBSO

M75660-M75679

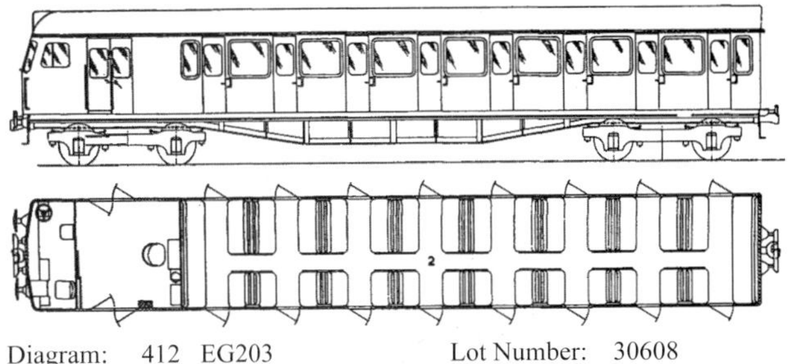

Diagram: 412 EG203
Body: 64' 0⅝" × 9' 3"
Seats: 82 second
Lot Number: 30608
Weight: 32t 0cwt
Bogies: Gresley

M75670 was cut up before it was officially withdrawn.

M75660	09/60-07/92	⊗06/93	**016**	09/60-02/83	**304016**	02/83-07/92
M75661	09/60-03/96	⊗01/97	**017**	09/60-08/82	**304017**	08/82-03/96
M75662	10/60-12/84	⊗09/85	**018**	10/60-02/80	**304018**	02/80-12/84
M75663	10/60-04/95	⊗01/97	**019**	10/60-12/81	**304019**	12/81-04/95
M75664	10/60-04/92	⊗03/92	**020**	10/60-07/81	**304020**	07/81-04/92
M75665	10/60-05/94	⊗11/00	**021**	10/60-12/81	**304021**	12/81-05/94
M75666	11/60-12/84	⊗09/85	**022**	11/60-08/82	**304022**	08/82-12/84
M75667	11/60-10/91	⊗11/91	**023**	11/60-05/82	**304023**	05/82-10/91
M75668	11/60-06/94	⊗10/00	**024**	11/60-05/81	**304024**	05/81-06/94
M75669	12/60-12/84	⊗05/85	**025**	12/60-02/80	**304025**	02/80-12/84

M75670	12/60-12/67	⊗03/67	**026**	12/60-12/67		
M75671	12/60-05/94	⊗06/97	**027**	12/60-07/83	**304027**	07/83-05/94
M75672	01/61-05/92	⊗04/92	**028**	01/61-08/82	**304028**	08/82-05/92
M75673	01/61-05/94	⊗06/97	**029**	01/61-06/81	**304029**	06/81-05/94
M75674	01/61-11/93	⊗06/97	**030**	01/61-06/81	**304030**	06/81-11/93
M75675	02/61-06/87	⊗09/87	**031**	02/61-06/81	**304031**	06/81-06/87
M75676	02/61-05/96	⊗05/96	**032**	02/61-09/81	**304032**	09/81-05/96
M75677	02/61-04/96	⊗05/96	**033**	02/61-10/84	**304033**	10/84-04/96
M75678	03/61-01/94	⊗02/94	**034**	03/61-06/84	**304034**	06/84-01/94
M75679	06/61-11/91	⊗11/91	**035**	06/61-04/82	**304035**	04/82-11/91

Class 304/2 Wolverton

Battery Driving Trailer Second Open Lavatory
BDTSOL
M75680-M75699

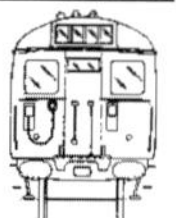

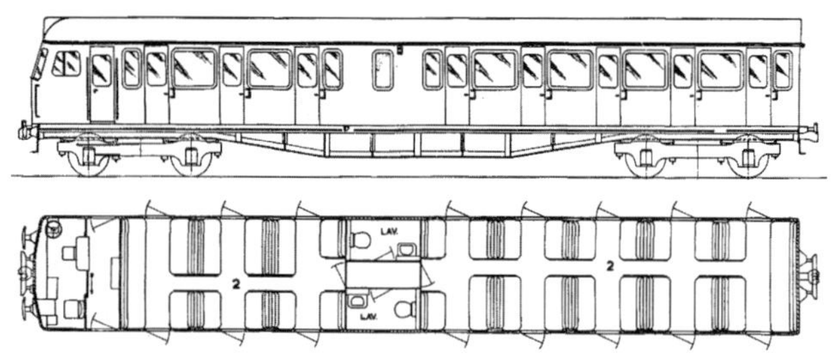

Diagram:	435 EF204	Lot Number:	30610
Body:	64' 0⅝" × 9' 3"	Weight:	36t 5cwt
Seats:	80 second 2 toilets	Bogies:	Gresley

M75680	09/60-07/92	⊗06/93	**016**	09/60-02/83	**304016**	02/83-07/92
M75681	09/60-03/96	⊗01/97	**017**	09/60-08/82	**304017**	08/82-03/96
M75682	10/60-12/84	⊗09/85	**018**	10/60-02/80	**304018**	02/80-12/84
M75683	10/60-04/95	⊗01/97	**019**	10/60-12/81	**304019**	12/81-04/95
M75684	10/60-04/92	⊗03/92	**020**	10/60-07/81	**304020**	07/81-04/92
M75685	10/60-05/94	⊗11/00	**021**	10/60-12/81	**304021**	12/81-05/94
M75686	11/60-12/84	⊗09/85	**022**	11/60-08/82	**304022**	08/82-12/84
M75687	11/60-10/91	⊗11/91	**023**	11/60-05/82	**304023**	05/82-10/91
M75688	11/60-06/94	⊗10/00	**024**	11/60-05/81	**304024**	05/81-06/94
M75689	12/60-12/84	⊗05/85	**025**	12/60-02/80	**304025**	02/80-12/84
M75690	12/60-12/67	⊗05/68	**026**	12/60-12/67		
M75691	12/60-05/94	⊗06/97	**027**	12/60-07/83	**304027**	07/83-05/94
M75692	01/61-05/92	⊗04/92	**028**	01/61-08/82	**304028**	08/82-05/92
M75693	01/61-05/94	⊗06/97	**029**	01/61-06/81	**304029**	06/81-05/94
M75694	01/61-11/93	⊗06/97	**030**	01/61-06/81	**304030**	06/81-11/93
M75695	02/61-06/87	⊗09/87	**031**	02/61-06/81	**304031**	06/81-06/87
M75696	02/61-05/96	⊗05/96	**032**	02/61-09/81	**304032**	09/81-05/96
M75697	02/61-04/96	⊗05/96	**033**	02/61-10/84	**304033**	10/84-04/96
M75698	03/61-01/94	⊗02/94	**034**	03/61-06/84	**304034**	06/84-01/94
M75699	06/61-11/91	⊗11/91	**035**	06/61-04/82	**304035**	04/82-11/91

Class 414/3 2-HAP Ashford/Eastleigh

Driving Trailer Composite (Semi-open) Lavatory
DTCsoL, later DTSsoL
S75700-S75740

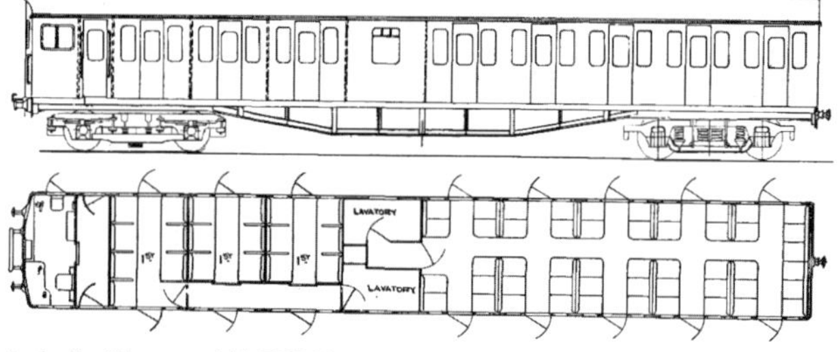

As built, Diagram 441 EE361

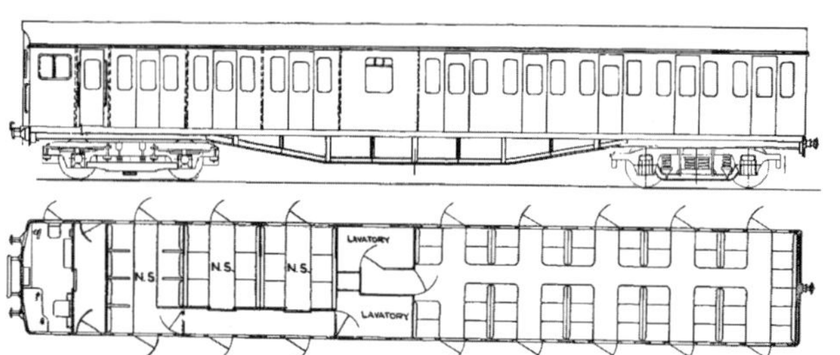

Converted to 2-CAP, Diagram EE222

Diagram:	441 EE361 EE222	Lot Number:	30618
Body:	63' 11½" × 9' 3"	Weight:	32t 0cwt
Seats:	19 first 50 second 2 toilets later 69 second 2 toilets	Bogies:	1 Mk 4 1 Commonwealth

S75700	03/61-05/82	⊗05/84	**6106**	03/61-05/82				
S75701	04/61-05/82	⊗10/84	**6107**	04/61-05/82				
S75702	04/61-10/83	⊗10/84	**6108**	04/61-10/83				
S75703	04/61-10/83	⊗05/84	**6109**	04/61-10/83				
S75704	04/61-05/82	⊗10/84	**6110**	04/61-05/82				
S75705	04/61-10/83	⊗04/84	**6111**	04/61-10/83				
S75706	05/61-07/91	➲**977738**	**6112**	05/61-11/87	**4320**	11/87-07/91		
S75707	05/61-10/83	⊗05/84	**6113**	05/61-10/83				
S75708	05/61-05/83	⊗05/84	**6114**	05/61-05/83				
S75709	05/61-05/82	⊗04/84	**6115**	05/61-05/82				
S75710	05/61-10/83	➲**977208**	**6116**	05/61-10/83				
S75711	05/61-10/83	⊗09/84	**6117**	05/61-10/83				
S75712	05/61-10/83	⊗09/84	**6118**	05/61-10/83				
S75713	05/61-10/83	⊗03/90	**6119**	05/61-10/83				
S75714	05/61-05/82	⊗09/84	**6120**	05/61-05/82				
S75715	06/61-05/82	➲**977210**	**6121**	06/61-05/82				
S75716	06/61-05/82	⊗04/84	**6122**	06/61-05/82				
S75717	06/61-05/82	⊗04/84	**6123**	06/61-05/82				
S75718	06/61-05/83	⊗04/84	**6124**	06/61-05/83				
S75719	06/61-10/83	⊗06/84	**6125**	06/61-10/83				
S75720	07/61-05/92	➲*977740*	**6126**	07/61-05/88	**4321**	05/88-05/92		
S75721	07/61-01/82	⊗02/83	**6127**	07/61-01/82				
S75722	08/61-05/83	⊗08/86	**6128**	08/61-05/83				
S75723	08/61-05/82	⊗09/84	**6129**	08/61-05/82				
S75724	08/61-05/82	⊗05/84	**6130**	08/61-05/82				
S75725	09/61-05/83	⊗06/84	**6131**	09/61-05/83				
S75726	09/61-05/82	⊗05/82	**6132**	09/61-05/82				
S75727	09/61-10/83	⊗06/84	**6133**	09/61-10/83				
S75728	09/61-01/82	⊗02/82	**6134**	09/61-01/82				
S75729	09/61-05/82	⊗09/84	**6135**	09/61-05/82				
S75730	09/61-09/82	⊗04/84	**6136**	09/61-09/82				
S75731	10/61-09/82	⊗04/84	**6137**	10/61-09/82				
S75732	10/61-05/82	⊗09/84	**6138**	10/61-05/82				
S75733	11/61-10/83	⊗08/84	**6139**	11/61-10/83				
S75734	11/61-05/83	⊗06/84	**6140**	11/61-05/83				
S75735	11/61-01/92	⊗05/92	**6141**	11/61-06/88	**4322**	06/88-09/91	**3333**	09/91-01/92
S75736	11/61-05/82	➲**977212**	**6142**	11/61-05/82				
S75737	12/61-05/82	⊗10/84	**6143**	12/61-05/82				
S75738	12/61-04/83	⊗10/86	**6144**	12/61-04/83				
S75739	01/62-05/83	⊗03/90	**6145**	01/62-05/83				
S75740	01/62-10/83	⊗06/84	**6146**	01/62-10/83				

Class 308/3 York

Battery Driving Trailer Second Open
BDTSO
E75741-E75743

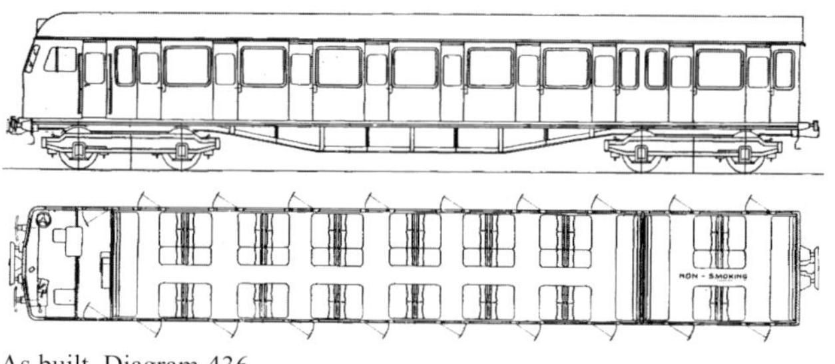

As built, Diagram 436

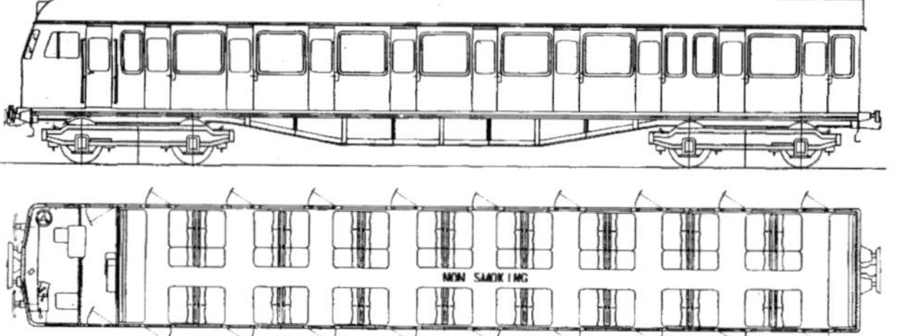

Facelifted, Diagram EF205

Diagram:	436 EF205	Lot Number:	30694
Body:	64' 0⅝" × 9' 3"	Weight:	34t 6cwt
Seats:	94 second, later 92 second	Bogies:	Gresley

E75741	12/61-05/85	⊗06/85	**453**	12/61-10/81	**308453**	10/81-05/85	**308455**	05/85-05/85

E75742	12/61-03/86	⊗07/86	**454** 12/61-02/82	**308454**	02/82-03/86		
E75743	12/61-05/85	⊗02/86	**455** 12/61-05/82	**308455**	05/82-05/85	**308453**	05/85-02/86

Class 303 Pressed Steel

Driving Trailer Second Open
DTSO
SC75746-SC75801

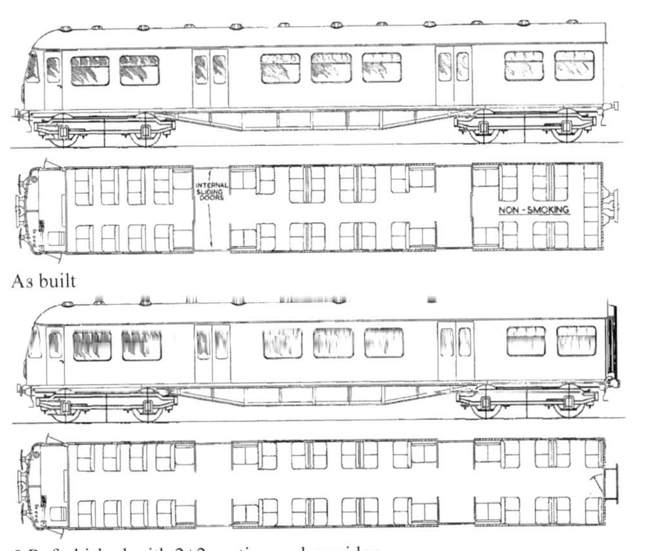

As built

® Refurbished with 2+2 seating and corridor

Diagram:	439 EE206	Lot Number:	30629
Body:	63' 11⅝" × 9' 3"	Weight:	33t 17cwt
Seats:	83 second later 56 second	Bogies:	Gresley

Number	Dates	Fate		Set	Dates	Unit	Dates	Unit	Dates
SC75746	05/60-10/89	⊗11/89		**036**	05/60- *80*	**303036**	*80*-10/89		
SC75747	06/60-08/91	⊗07/91	®	**037**	06/60-*03/80*	**303037**	*03/80*-07/91		
SC75748	06/60-02/93	⊗08/94	®	**038**	06/60-*03/80*	**303038**	*03/80*-02/93		
SC75749	06/60-09/90	⊗10/90		**039**	06/60-*08/79*	**303039**	*08/79*-09/90		
SC75750	06/60-01/02	⊗02/02		**040**	06/60-*08/79*	**303040**	*08/79*-10/90	**303016**	10/90-01/02
SC75751	06/60-10/89	⊗11/89		**041**	06/60-*11/79*	**303041**	*11/79*-10/89		
SC75752	06/60-10/89	Ⓟ➲**75758**		**042**	06/60-*03/80*	**303042**	*03/80*-09/89		
SC75753	06/60-05/77	⊗11/87		**043**	06/60-06/79				
SC75754	06/60-01/89	⊗05/89		**044**	06/60-06/80	**303044**	06/80-02/88		
SC75755	06/60-09/02	⊗12/02	®	**045**	06/60-*03/80*	**303045**	*03/80*-09/02		
SC75756	06/60-11/97	⊗01/98	®	**046**	06/60-06/80	**303046**	06/80-11/97		
SC75757	07/60-10/01	⊗05/02	®	**047**	07/60-*11/79*	**303047**	*11/79*-10/01		
SC75758	07/60-09/90	⊗11/90		**048**	07/60- *80*	**303048**	*80*-03/90	**303052**	03/90-09/90
				303048	10/90-03/96				
SC75758[2]	10/90-03/96	➲*977721*		Ⓟ⊗09/98					⊂**75752**
SC75759	07/60-02/91	➲**977711**		**049**	07/60- *80*	**303049**	*80*-02/91		
SC75760	07/60-10/89	⊗11/89		**050**	07/60-*08/79*	**303050**	*08/79*-10/89		
SC75761	07/60-02/87	⊗10/87	®	**051**	07/60-*03/80*	**303051**	*03/80*-02/87		
SC75762	07/60-03/90	⊗06/90		**052**	07/60-*03/80*	**303052**	*03/80*-03/90		
SC75763	07/60-10/89	⊗11/89		**053**	07/60-*03/80*	**303053**	*03/80*-10/89		
SC75764	07/60-06/02	⊗08/02	®	**054**	07/60-*03/80*	**303054**	*03/80*-06/02		
SC75765	07/60-03/01	⊗04/01	®	**055**	07/60-*08/79*	**303055**	*08/79*-03/01		
SC75766	08/60-08/01	⊗01/03	®	**056**	08/60-*03/80*	**303056**	*03/80*-09/00	**303043**	09/00-08/01
SC75767	08/60-10/89	⊗11/89	®	**057**	08/60- *80*	**303057**	*80*-10/89		
SC75768	09/60-03/01	⊗08/01	®	**058**	09/60-*03/80*	**303058**	*03/80*-03/01		
SC75769	09/60-11/83	⊗08/85		**059**	09/60- *80*	**303059**	*80*-11/83		
SC75770	09/60-12/92	⊗02/94		**060**	09/60- *80*	**303060**	*80*-12/92		
SC75771	09/60-03/01	⊗03/01	®	**061**	09/60-*05/79*	**303061**	*05/79*-03/01		
SC75772	09/60-09/90	⊗11/91		**062**	09/60- *80*	**303062**	*80*-09/90		
SC75773	09/60-10/90	⊗05/04		**063**	09/60-*03/80*	**303063**	*03/80*-10/90		
SC75774	10/60-07/88	⊗03/90		**064**	10/60-*08/79*	**303064**	*08/79*-07/88		
SC75775	10/60-06/01	⊗08/02	®	**065**	10/60- *80*	**303065**	*80*-06/01		
SC75776	10/60-02/91	⊗04/91		**066**	10/60- *80*	**303066**	*80*-02/91		
SC75777	10/60-10/89	⊗02/91		**067**	10/60-*03/80*	**303067**	*03/80*-10/89		
SC75778	10/60-01/89	⊗08/90		**068**	10/60-05/80	**303068**	05/80-01/89		
SC75779	10/60-07/90	⊗01/91		**069**	10/60-*03/80*	**303069**	*03/80*-07/90		
SC75780	10/60-10/01	⊗08/02	®	**070**	10/60-05/80	**303070**	05/80-10/01		
SC75781	11/60-04/02	⊗08/02	®	**071**	11/60-*08/79*	**303071**	*08/79*-07/89	**303037**	02/94-05/98
				303037	07/99-04/02				
SC75782	11/60-07/90	⊗12/90		**072**	11/60-*05/79*	**303072**	*05/79*-07/90		
SC75783	12/60-07/96	⊗07/96		**073**	12/60- *80*	**303073**	*80*-07/96		
SC75784	12/60- 78	⊗12/82		**074**	12/60- 78				
SC75785	12/60-12/92	⊗ 93		**075**	12/60-06/80	**303075**	06/80-08/90		
SC75786	12/60-09/90	⊗01/91		**076**	12/60-*03/80*	**303076**	*03/80*-09/90		
SC75787	12/60-01/02	⊗02/02	®	**077**	12/60-06/80	**303077**	06/80-01/02		
SC75788	01/61-10/89	⊗11/89		**078**	01/61-*03/80*	**303078**	*03/80*-10/89		
SC75789	01/61-06/02	⊗10/02	®	**079**	01/61- *80*	**303079**	*80*-06/02		
SC75790	01/61-10/01	⊗09/02	®	**080**	01/61-*08/79*	**303080**	*08/79*-10/01		
SC75791	01/61-01/89	⊗01/90		**081**	01/61-*08/79*	**303081**	*08/79*-01/89		
SC75792	02/61-12/92	⊗08/94		**082**	02/61-*03/80*	**303082**	*03/80*-12/92		
SC75793	02/61-09/02	⊗03/03	®	**083**	02/61-*03/80*	**303083**	*03/80*-09/02		
SC75794	02/61- 78	⊗11/87		**084**	02/61- 78				
SC75795	02/61-03/02	⊗08/02	®	**085**	02/61-*03/80*	**303085**	*03/80*-03/02		
SC75796	02/61-05/89	⊗09/90		**086**	02/61-07/80	**303086**	07/80-05/98		
SC75797	02/61-04/02	⊗09/02	®	**087**	02/61-*05/79*	**303087**	*05/79*-04/02		
SC75798	02/61-12/02	⊗01/03	®	**088**	02/61- *80*	**303088**	*80*-12/02		
SC75799	03/61-03/01	⊗04/01	®	**089**	03/61-*11/79*	**303089**	*11/79*-03/01		
SC75800	04/61-04/02	⊗01/03	®	**090**	04/61- *80*	**303090**	*80*-04/02		
SC75801	07/61-06/02	⊗10/02	®	**091**	07/61-*08/79*	**303091**	*08/79*-06/02		

Class 303 Pressed Steel

Battery Driving Trailer Second Open
BDTSO
SC75802-SC75857

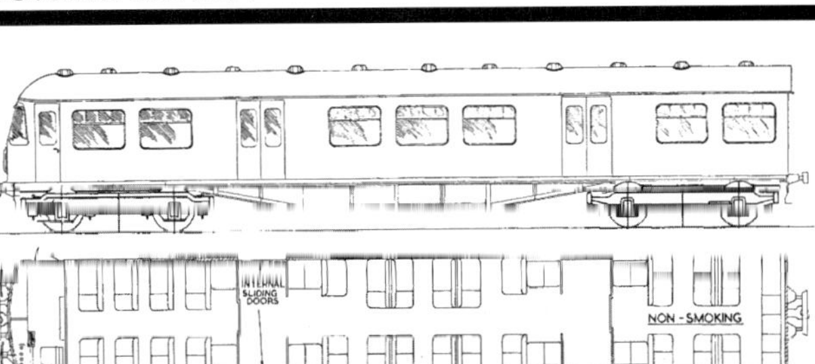

As built

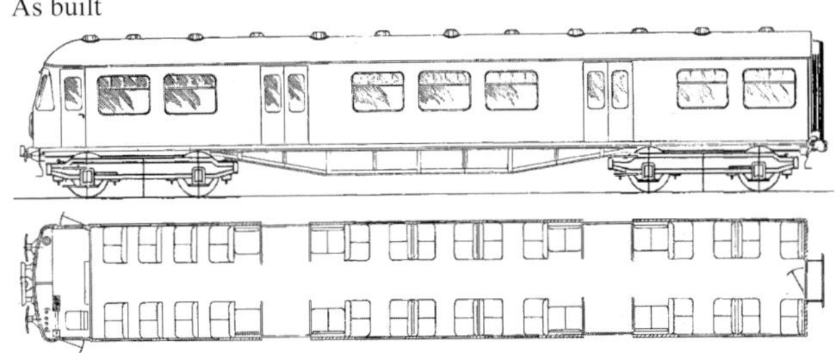

® Refurbished with 2+2 seating and corridor

Diagram:	439 EF202	Lot Number:	30631
Body:	63' 11⅝" × 9' 3"	Weight:	37t 9cwt
Seats:	83 second later 56 second	Bogies:	Gresley

Number	Dates	Fate		Set	Dates	Unit	Dates	Unit	Dates
SC75802	05/60-10/89	⊗11/89		**036**	05/60- *80*	**303036**	*80*-10/89		
SC75803	06/60-04/02	⊗08/02	®	**037**	06/60-*03/80*	**303037**	*03/80*-07/91	**303037**	02/94-05/98
				303037	07/99-04/02				
SC75804	06/60-02/93	⊗08/94	®	**038**	06/60-*03/80*	**303038**	*03/80*-02/93		
SC75805	06/60-09/90	⊗10/90		**039**	06/60-*08/79*	**303039**	*08/79*-09/90		
SC75806	06/60-02/01	⊗01/03	®	**040**	06/60-*08/79*	**303040**	*08/79*-02/01		
SC75807	06/60-10/89	⊗11/89		**041**	06/60-*11/79*	**303041**	*11/79*-10/89		
SC75808	06/60-10/89	Ⓟ➲**75814**		**042**	06/60-*03/80*	**303042**	*03/80*-09/89		
SC75809	06/60-08/01	⊗01/03	®	**043**	06/60-06/80	**303043**	06/80-08/01		
SC75810	06/60-01/88	⊗02/88		**044**	06/60-06/80	**303044**	06/80-02/88		
SC75811	06/60-09/02	⊗12/02	®	**045**	06/60-*03/80*	**303045**	*03/80*-09/02		
SC75812	06/60-11/97	⊗11/97	®	**046**	06/60-06/80	**303046**	06/80-11/97		
SC75813	07/60-10/01	⊗05/02	®	**047**	07/60-*11/79*	**303047**	*11/79*-10/01		
SC75814	07/60-09/90	⊗11/90		**048**	07/60- *80*	**303048**	*80*-03/90	**303052**	03/90-09/90
				303048	10/90-03/96				
SC75814[2]	10/90-03/96	➲*977719*		Ⓟ⊗09/98					⊂**75808**
SC75815	07/60-02/91	➲**977713**		**049**	07/60- *80*	**303049**	*80*-02/91		
SC75816	07/60-10/89	⊗11/89		**050**	07/60-*08/79*	**303050**	*08/79*-10/89		
SC75817	07/60-06/02	⊗08/02	®	**051**	07/60-*03/80*	**303051**	*03/80*-02/87	**303033**	07/88-06/02
SC75818	07/60-03/90	⊗06/90		**052**	07/60-*03/80*	**303052**	*03/80*-03/90		
SC75819	07/60-10/89	⊗11/89		**053**	07/60-*03/80*	**303053**	*03/80*-10/89		
SC75820	07/60-06/02	⊗08/02	®	**054**	07/60-*03/80*	**303054**	*03/80*-06/02		
SC75821	07/60-03/01	⊗03/01	®	**055**	07/60-*08/79*	**303055**	*08/79*-03/01		
SC75822	08/60-03/01	⊗09/01	®	**056**	08/60-*03/80*	**303056**	*03/80*-03/01		
SC75823	08/60-10/89	⊗11/89	®	**057**	08/60- *80*	**303057**	*80*-10/89		
SC75824	09/60-03/01	⊗04/04	®	**058**	09/60-*03/80*	**303058**	*03/80*-03/01		
SC75825	09/60-11/83	⊗08/85		**059**	09/60- *80*	**303059**	*80*-11/83		
SC75826	09/60-12/92	⊗02/94		**060**	09/60- *80*	**303060**	*80*-12/92		
SC75827	09/60-03/01	⊗03/01	®	**061**	09/60-*05/79*	**303061**	*05/79*-03/01		
SC75828	09/60-09/90	⊗11/91		**062**	09/60- *80*	**303062**	*80*-09/90		
SC75829	09/60-10/90	⊗08/92		**063**	09/60-*03/80*	**303063**	*03/80*-10/90		
SC75830	10/60-07/88	⊗03/90		**064**	10/60-*08/79*	**303064**	*08/79*-07/88		
SC75831	10/60-06/01	⊗09/01	®	**065**	10/60- *80*	**303065**	*80*-06/01		
SC75832	10/60-02/91	⊗04/91		**066**	10/60- *80*	**303066**	*80*-02/91		
SC75833	10/60-10/89	⊗02/91		**067**	10/60-*03/80*	**303067**	*03/80*-10/89		
SC75834	10/60-05/89	⊗04/90		**068**	10/60-05/80	**303068**	05/80-01/89		
SC75835	10/60- 78	⊗04/88		**069**	10/60- 78				
SC75836	10/60-10/01	⊗08/02	®	**070**	10/60-05/80	**303070**	05/80-10/01		
SC75837	11/60-07/89	⊗07/90	®	**071**	11/60-*08/79*	**303071**	*08/79*-07/89		
SC75838	11/60-07/90	⊗12/90		**072**	11/60-*05/79*	**303072**	*05/79*-07/90		
SC75839	12/60-07/96	⊗07/96		**073**	12/60- *80*	**303073**	*80*-07/96		

SC75840	12/60- 78	⊗10/81		**074**	12/60- 78				
SC75841	12/60-12/92	⊗ 93		**075**	12/60-06/80	**303075**	06/80-08/90		
SC75842	12/60-09/90	⊗01/91		**076**	12/60-*03/80*	**303076**	*03/80*-09/90		
SC75843	12/60-01/02	⊗02/02	®	**077**	12/60-06/80	**303077**	06/80-01/02		
SC75844	01/61-10/89	⊗11/89		**078**	01/61-*03/80*	**303078**	*03/80*-10/89		
SC75845	01/61-07/99	⊗03/01	®	**079**	01/61- *80*	**303079**	*80*-07/99	**303028**	07/99-07/99
SC75846	01/61-10/01	⊗09/02	®	**080**	01/61-*08/79*	**303080**	*08/79*-10/01		
SC75847	01/61-01/89	⊗01/90		**081**	01/61-*08/79*	**303081**	*08/79*-01/89		
SC75848	02/61-12/92	⊗08/94		**082**	02/61-*03/80*	**303082**	*03/80*-12/92		
SC75849	02/61-09/02	⊗03/03	®	**083**	02/61-*03/80*	**303083**	*03/80*-09/02		
SC75850	02/61- 78	⊗*06/86*		**084**	02/61- 78				
SC75851	02/61-03/02	⊗08/02	®	**085**	02/61-*03/80*	**303085**	*03/80*-03/02		
SC75852	02/61-05/89	⊗08/90		**086**	02/61-07/80	**303086**	07/80-05/98		
SC75853	02/61-04/02	⊗09/02	®	**087**	02/61-*05/79*	**303087**	*05/79*-04/02		
SC75854	02/61-12/02	⊗01/03	®	**088**	02/61- *80*	**303088**	*80*-12/02		
SC75855	03/61-03/01	⊗04/01	®	**089**	03/61-*11/79*	**303089**	*11/79*-03/01		
SC75856	04/61-04/02	⊗01/03	®	**090**	04/61- *80*	**303090**	*80*-04/02		
SC75857	07/61-06/02	⊗10/02	®	**091**	07/61-*08/79*	**303091**	*08/79*-06/02		

Class 304/3 Wolverton
Driving Trailer Brake Second Open
DTBSO
M75858-M75867

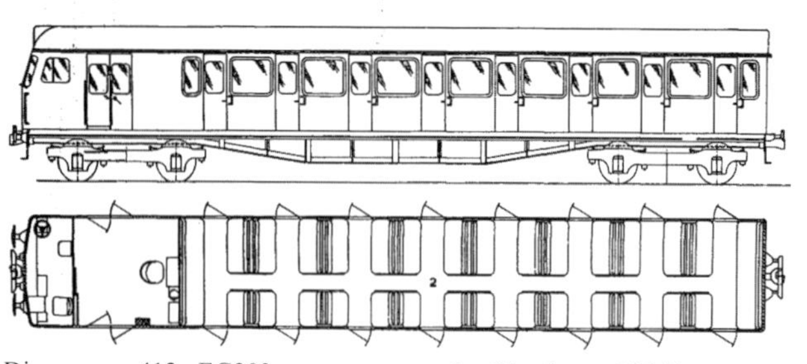

Diagram:	412 EG203	Lot Number:	30643
Body:	64' 0⅝" × 9' 3"	Weight:	32t 0cwt
Seats:	82 second	Bogies:	Gresley

M75858	07/61-12/95	⊗01/97	**036**	07/61-04/82	**304036**	04/82-12/95
M75859	07/61-06/95	⊗06/96	**037**	07/61-04/82	**304037**	04/82-06/95
M75860	07/61-12/84	⊗05/85	**038**	07/61- *83*	**304038**	*83*-12/84
M75861	08/61-04/92	⊗03/92	**039**	08/61- *83*	**304039**	*83*-04/92
M75862	08/61-04/95	⊗06/96	**040**	08/61-02/82	**304040**	02/82-04/95
M75863	08/61-07/92	⊗07/92	**041**	08/61-05/82	**304041**	05/82-07/92
M75864	09/61-06/96	⊗06/96	**042**	09/61-04/81	**304042**	04/81-06/96
M75865	09/61-05/94	⊗06/96	**043**	09/61-07/83	**304043**	07/83-05/94
M75866	09/61-12/84	⊗05/85	**044**	09/61-10/82	**304044**	10/82-12/84
M75867	10/61-07/92	⊗08/92	**045**	10/61-02/83	**304045**	02/83-07/92

Class 304/3 Wolverton
Battery Driving Trailer Second Open Lavatory
BDTSOL
M75868-M75877

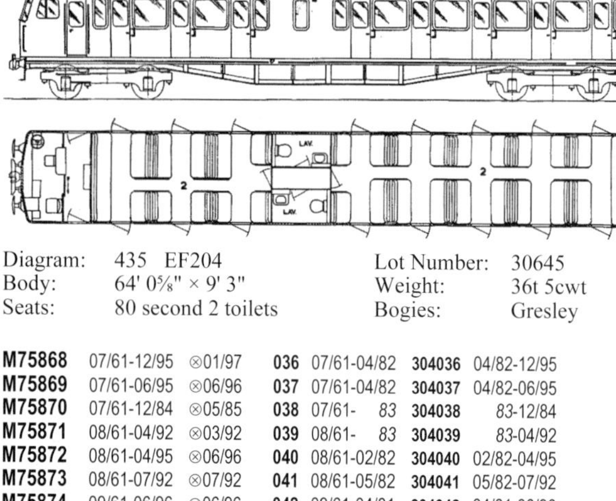

Diagram:	435 EF204	Lot Number:	30645
Body:	64' 0⅝" × 9' 3"	Weight:	36t 5cwt
Seats:	80 second 2 toilets	Bogies:	Gresley

M75868	07/61-12/95	⊗01/97	**036**	07/61-04/82	**304036**	04/82-12/95
M75869	07/61-06/95	⊗06/96	**037**	07/61-04/82	**304037**	04/82-06/95
M75870	07/61-12/84	⊗05/85	**038**	07/61- *83*	**304038**	*83*-12/84
M75871	08/61-04/92	⊗03/92	**039**	08/61- *83*	**304039**	*83*-04/92
M75872	08/61-04/95	⊗06/96	**040**	08/61-02/82	**304040**	02/82-04/95
M75873	08/61-07/92	⊗07/92	**041**	08/61-05/82	**304041**	05/82-07/92
M75874	09/61-06/96	⊗06/96	**042**	09/61-04/81	**304042**	04/81-06/96
M75875	09/61-05/94	⊗06/96	**043**	09/61-07/83	**304043**	07/83-05/94
M75876	09/61-12/84	⊗05/85	**044**	09/61-10/82	**304044**	10/82-12/84
M75877	10/61-07/92	⊗08/92	**045**	10/61-02/83	**304045**	02/83-07/92

Class 308/1 York
Battery Driving Trailer Second Open Lavatory
BDTSOL, later BDTCOL
E75878-E75886

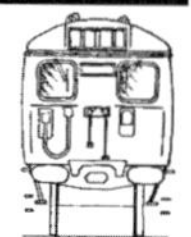

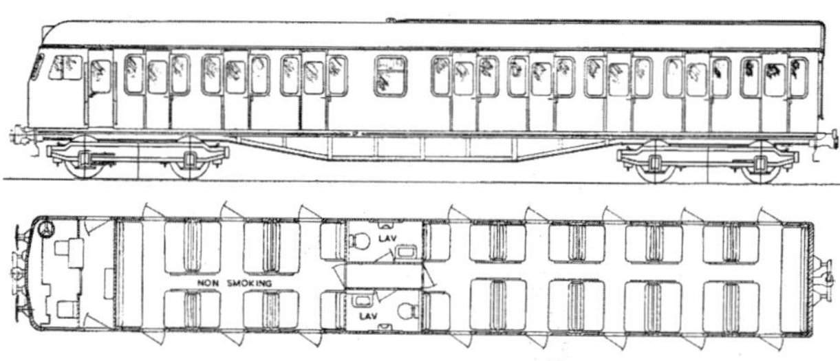

As built, Diagram 444 EF208

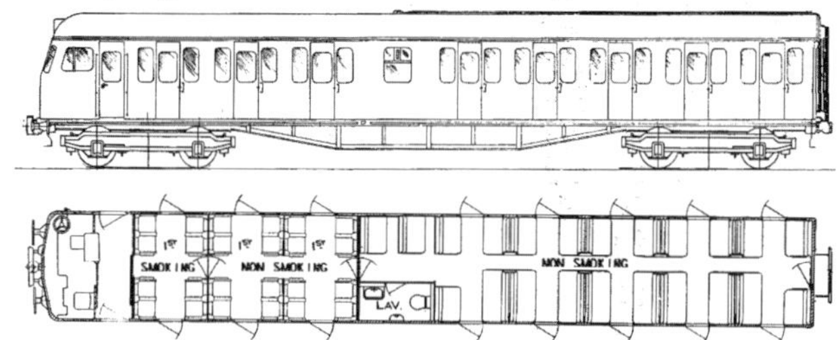

Refurbished as BDTCOL, Diagram EF304

Diagram:	444 EF208 EF304	Lot Number:	30652
Body:	64' 0⅝" × 9' 3"	Weight:	35t 15cwt
Seats:	80 second 2 toilets later 24 first 52 second 1 toilet	Bogies:	Gresley

E75878	01/61-06/93	⊗02/94	**133**	01/61-04/81	**308133**	04/81-06/93		
E75879	01/61-04/00	⊗06/03	**134**	01/61-08/81	**308134**	08/81-09/99	**308134**	04/00-04/00
E75880	01/61-02/01	⊗11/01	**135**	01/61-08/81	**308135**	08/81-07/92	**308156**	07/92-06/93
			308144	08/93-02/01				
E75881	01/61-01/01	Ⓟ	**136**	01/61-01/82	**308136**	01/82-01/01		
E75882	02/61-03/01	⊗05/03	**137**	02/61-12/81	**308137**	12/81-03/01		
E75883	02/61-10/01	⊗10/01	**138**	02/61-12/81	**308138**	11/83-10/01		
E75884	02/61-09/95	⊗09/95	**139**	02/61-10/82	**308139**	10/82-09/95		
E75885	02/61-09/95	⊗09/95	**140**	02/61-05/81	**308140**	05/81-09/95		
E75886	03/61-04/01	⊗05/03	**141**	03/61-08/81	**308141**	08/81-04/01		

Class 308/1 York
Driving Trailer Second
DTS, later DTSO
E75887-E75895

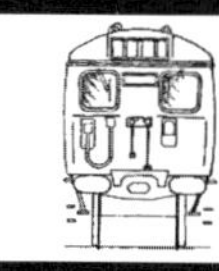

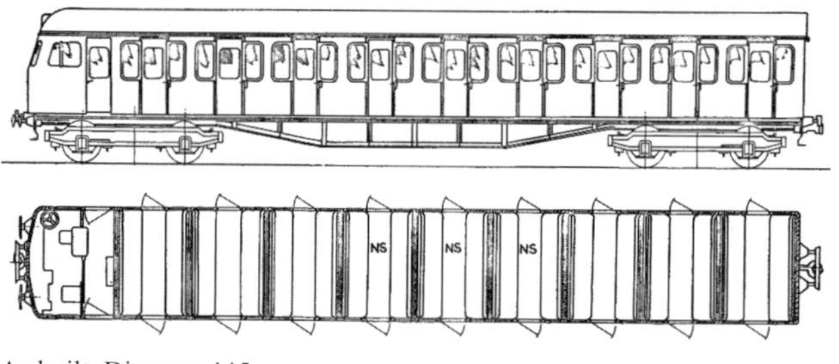

As built, Diagram 445

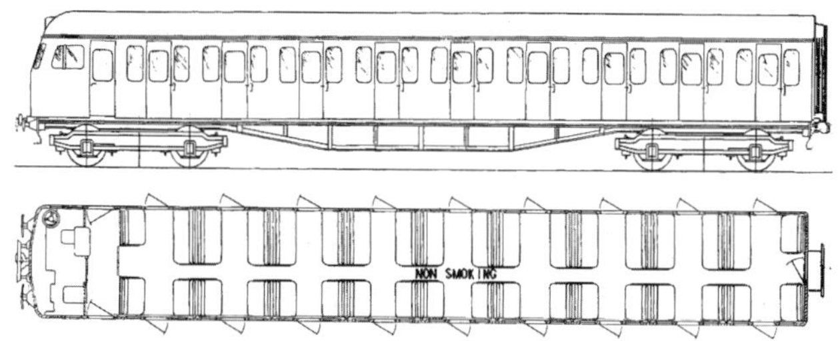

Refurbished as DTSO, Diagram EE220

Diagram:	445 EE220	Lot Number:	30655
Body:	64' 0⅝" × 9' 3"	Weight:	32t 8cwt
Seats:	90 second, later 88 second	Bogies:	Gresley

E75887	01/61-06/93	⊗02/94	**133**	01/61-04/81	**308133**	04/81-06/93		
E75888	01/61-04/00	⊗06/03	**134**	01/61-08/81	**308134**	08/81-09/99	**308134**	04/00-04/00
E75889	01/61-06/93	⊗06/94	**135**	01/61-08/81	**308135**	08/81-07/92	**308156**	07/92-06/93
E75890	01/61-01/00	⊗09/03	**136**	01/61-01/82	**308136**	01/82-01/01		
E75891	02/61-03/01	⊗05/03	**137**	02/61-12/81	**308137**	12/81-03/01		
E75892	02/61-10/01	⊗10/01	**138**	02/61-12/81	**308138**	11/83-10/01		
E75893	02/61-09/95	⊗09/95	**139**	02/61-10/82	**308139**	10/82-09/95		
E75894	02/61-09/95	⊗09/95	**140**	02/61-05/81	**308140**	05/81-09/95		
E75895	03/61-04/01	⊗04/03	**141**	03/61-08/81	**308141**	08/81-04/01		

Class 308/1 York

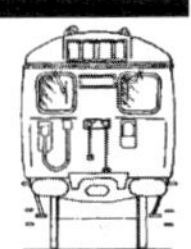

Battery Driving Trailer Second Open Lavatory
BDTSOL, later BDTCOL
E75896-E75928 (75920 onwards Class 308/2)

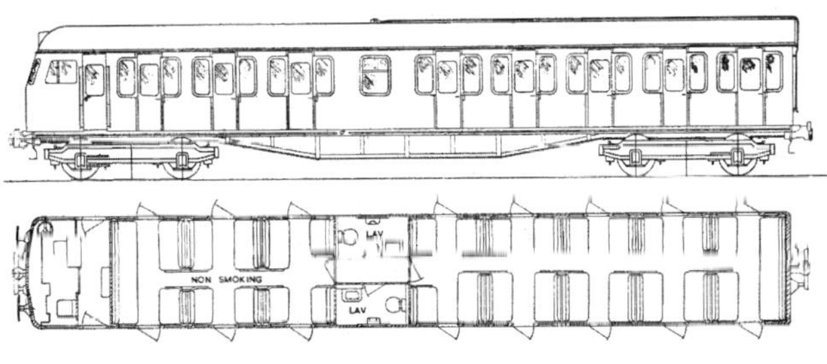

As built, Diagram 444 EF208

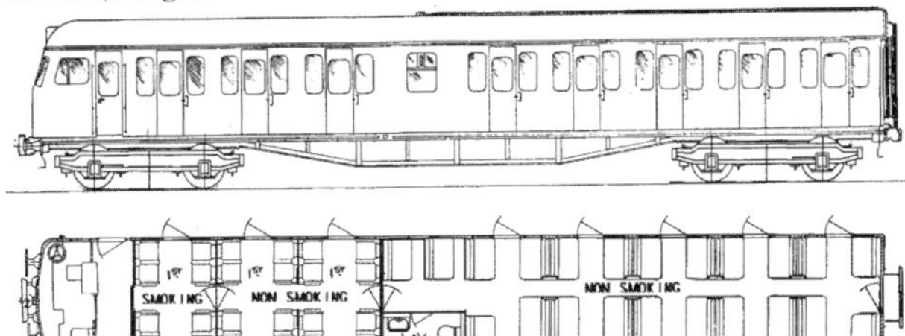

Refurbished as BDTCOL, Diagram EF304

Diagram:	444 EF208 EF304	Lot Number:	30656
Body:	64' 0⅝" × 9' 3"	Weight:	35t 15cwt
Seats:	80 second 2 toilets	Bogies:	Gresley
	later 24 first 52 second 1 toilet		

E75896	03/61-09/93	⊗04/97	**142**	03/61-01/82	**308142**	01/82-09/93		
E75897	03/61-06/01	⊗10/01	**143**	03/61-01/82	**308143**	01/82-06/01		
E75898	03/61-09/90	⊗02/93	**144**	03/61-12/81	**308144**	12/81-09/90		
E75899	04/61-06/01	⊗10/01	**145**	04/61-03/82	**308145**	03/82-06/01		
E75900	04/61-09/94	➲**977926**	**146**	04/61-02/80	**308146**	02/80-09/94		
E75901	04/61-05/01	⊗06/03	**147**	04/61-03/82	**308147**	03/82-05/01		
E75902	04/61-09/93	⊗11/95	**148**	04/61-12/82	**308148**	12/82-09/93		
E75903	05/61-09/93	⊗02/95	**149**	05/61-06/82	**308149**	06/82-09/93		
E75904	05/61-06/95	➲**977929**	**150**	05/61-03/82	**308150**	03/82-06/95		
E75905	05/61-11/93	➲**977876**	**151**	05/61-11/82	**308151**	11/82-11/93		
E75906	06/61-01/01	⊗09/03	**152**	07/61-05/83	**308152**	05/83-02/89	**308159**	02/89-01/01
E75907	06/61-06/01	⊗11/01	**153**	07/61-09/82	**308153**	09/82-06/01		
E75908	06/61-01/01	⊗06/03	**154**	07/61-10/82	**308154**	10/82-01/01		
E75909	06/61-03/01	⊗05/03	**155**	07/61-05/83	**308155**	05/83-03/01		
E75910	07/61-12/93	⊗12/93	**156**	07/61-05/83	**308156**	05/83-07/92	**308135**	07/92-12/93
E75911	07/61-05/01	⊗05/03	**157**	07/61-05/83	**308157**	05/83-10/94	**308161**	10/94-05/01
E75912	07/61-10/01	⊗10/01	**158**	07/61-02/80	**308158**	02/80-04/83	**308458**	04/83-05/83
			308158	05/83-10/01				
E75913	07/61-05/01	⊗05/03	**159**	07/61-05/83	**308159**	05/83-02/89	**308152**	02/89-05/01
E75914	08/61-09/95	⊗09/95	**160**	08/61-05/83	**308160**	05/83-09/95		
E75915	08/61-10/01	⊗10/01	**161**	08/61-01/80	**308161**	01/80-04/83	**308461**	04/83-04/84
			308161	04/84-10/94	**308157**	10/94-10/01		
E75916	09/61-04/01	⊗04/03	**162**	09/61-07/83	**308162**	07/83-04/01		
E75917	09/61-01/01	⊗09/03	**163**	09/61-07/83	**308163**	07/83-01/01		
E75918	09/61-03/01	⊗06/03	**164**	09/61-02/80	**308164**	02/80-03/01		
E75919	09/61-04/01	⊗05/03	**165**	09/61-02/81	**308165**	02/81-04/01		
E75920	05/61-06/85	⊗01/88	**313**	05/61-01/82	**308313**	01/82-06/85		
E75921	09/61-01/85	⊗06/85	**314**	09/61-06/81	**308314**	06/81-01/85		
E75922	09/61-06/85	⊗01/88	**315**	09/61-02/82	**308315**	02/82-01/84		
E75923	10/61-01/85	⊗01/85	**316**	10/61-06/81	**308316**	06/81-01/85		
E75924	10/61-11/88	⊗03/89	**317**	10/61- *82*	**308317**	*82*-07/83	**308991**	01/84-11/88
E75925	11/61-02/84	⊗07/85	**318**	11/61-12/81	**308318**	12/81-07/83	**308992**	01/84-02/84
E75926	11/61-01/90	⊗04/90	**319**	11/61-07/82	**308319**	07/82-07/83	**308993**	01/84-01/90
E75927	11/61-01/90	⊗07/90	**320**	11/61-04/82	**308320**	04/82-07/83	**308994**	01/84-01/90
E75928	11/61-11/88	⊗11/88	**321**	11/61- *82*	**308321**	*82*-07/83	**308995**	01/84-11/88

Class 308/1 York

Driving Trailer Second
DTS, later DTSO
E75929-E75961 (75953 onwards Class 308/2)

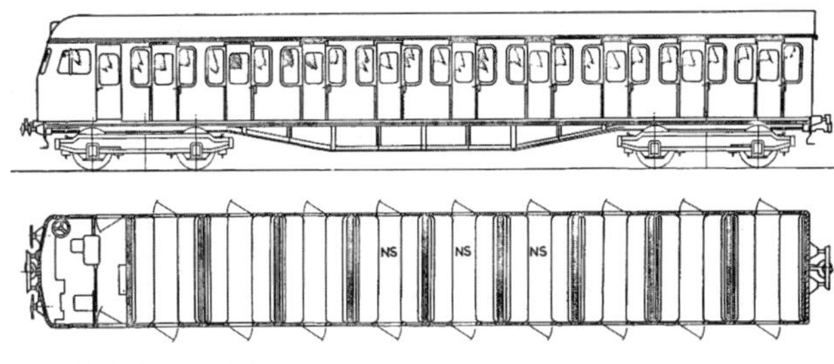

As built, Diagram 445

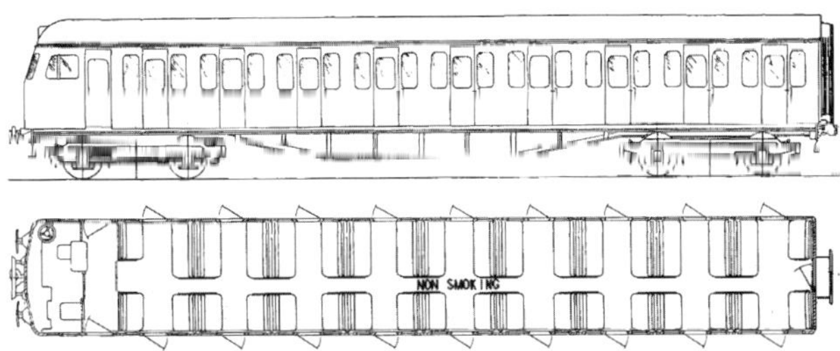

Refurbished as DTSO, Diagram EE220

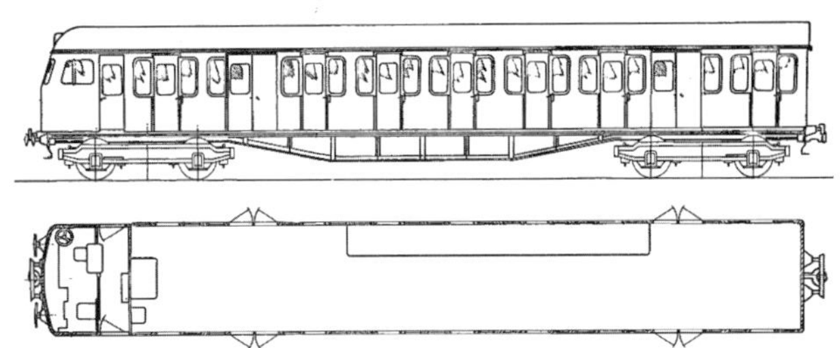

75957-75961. Converted to DTLV, EW501

Diagram:	445 EE220 EW501	Lot Number:	30659
Body:	64' 0⅝" × 9' 3"	Weight:	32t 8cwt
Seats:	90 second, later 88 second	Bogies:	Gresley

E75929	03/61-09/93	⊗04/97	**142**	03/61-01/82	**308142**	01/82-09/93		
E75930	03/61-06/01	⊗10/01	**143**	03/61-01/82	**308143**	01/82-06/01		
E75931	03/61-02/01	⊗11/01	**144**	03/61-12/81	**308144**	12/81-02/01		
E75932	04/61-06/01	⊗10/01	**145**	04/61-03/82	**308145**	03/82-06/01		
E75933	04/61-09/94	➲**977928**	**146**	04/61-02/80	**308146**	02/80-09/94		
E75934	04/61-05/01	⊗06/03	**147**	04/61-03/82	**308147**	03/82-05/01		
E75935	04/61-09/93	⊗11/95	**148**	04/61-12/82	**308148**	12/82-09/93		
E75936	05/61-09/93	⊗02/95	**149**	05/61-06/82	**308149**	06/82-09/93		
E75937	05/61-06/95	➲**977931**	**150**	05/61-03/82	**308150**	03/82-06/95		
E75938	05/61-11/93	➲**977878**	**151**	05/61-11/82	**308151**	11/82-11/93		
E75939	06/61-05/01	⊗05/03	**152**	07/61-05/83	**308152**	05/83-05/01		
E75940	06/61-06/01	⊗11/01	**153**	07/61-09/82	**308153**	09/82-06/01		
E75941	06/61-01/01	⊗06/03	**154**	07/61-10/82	**308154**	10/82-01/01		
E75942	06/61-03/01	⊗05/03	**155**	07/61-05/83	**308155**	05/83-03/01		
E75943	07/61-12/93	⊗12/93	**156**	07/61-05/83	**308156**	05/83-07/92	**308135**	07/92-12/93
E75944	07/61-10/01	⊗10/01	**157**	07/61-05/83	**308157**	05/83-10/01		
E75945	07/61-10/01	⊗10/01	**158**	07/61-02/80	**308158**	02/80-04/83	**308458**	04/83-05/83
			308158	05/83-10/01				
E75946	07/61-01/01	⊗10/03	**159**	07/61-05/83	**308159**	05/83-01/01		
E75947	08/61-09/95	⊗09/95	**160**	08/61-05/83	**308160**	05/83-09/95		
E75948	08/61-05/01	⊗05/03	**161**	08/61-01/80	**308161**	01/80-04/83	**308461**	04/83-04/84
			308161	04/84-05/01				
E75949	09/61-04/01	⊗04/03	**162**	09/61-07/83	**308162**	07/83-04/01		
E75950	09/61-01/01	⊗10/03	**163**	09/61-07/83	**308163**	07/83-01/01		
E75951	09/61-03/01	⊗05/03	**164**	09/61-02/80	**308164**	02/80-03/01		
E75952	09/61-04/01	⊗05/03	**165**	09/61-02/81	**308165**	02/81-04/01		
E75953	05/61-06/85	⊗01/88	**313**	05/61-01/82	**308313**	01/82-06/85		
E75954	09/61-01/85	⊗06/85	**314**	09/61-06/81	**308314**	06/81-01/85		
E75955	09/61-06/85	⊗01/88	**315**	09/61-02/82	**308315**	02/82-01/84		
E75956	10/61-01/85	⊗01/85	**316**	10/61-06/81	**308316**	06/81-01/85		
E75957	10/61-11/88	⊗03/89	**317**	10/61- *82*	**308317**	*82*-07/83	**308991**	01/84-11/88
E75958	11/61-02/84	⊗07/85	**318**	11/61-12/81	**308318**	12/81-07/83	**308992**	01/84-02/84
E75959	11/61-01/90	⊗04/90	**319**	11/61-07/82	**308319**	07/82-07/83	**308993**	01/84-01/90
E75960	11/61-01/90	⊗07/90	**320**	11/61-04/82	**308320**	04/82-07/83	**308994**	01/84-01/90
E75961	11/61-01/90	⊗07/90	**321**	11/61- *82*	**308321**	*82*-07/83	**308995**	01/84-01/90

Class 309 York

Battery Driving Trailer Composite (Semi-open) Lavatory BDTCsoL E75962-E75968

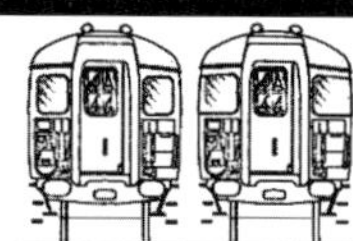

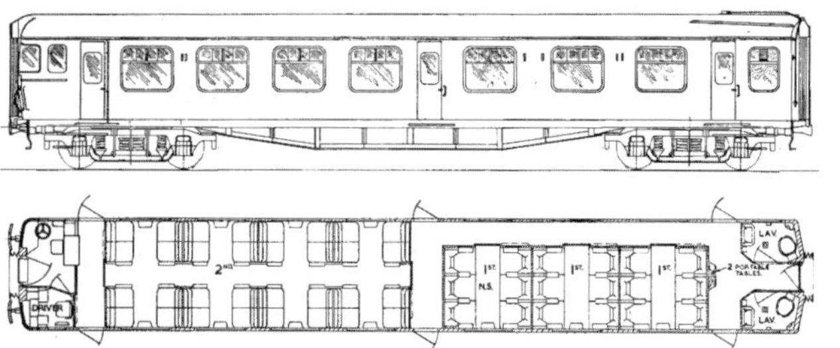

As built, Diagram 448 EF301

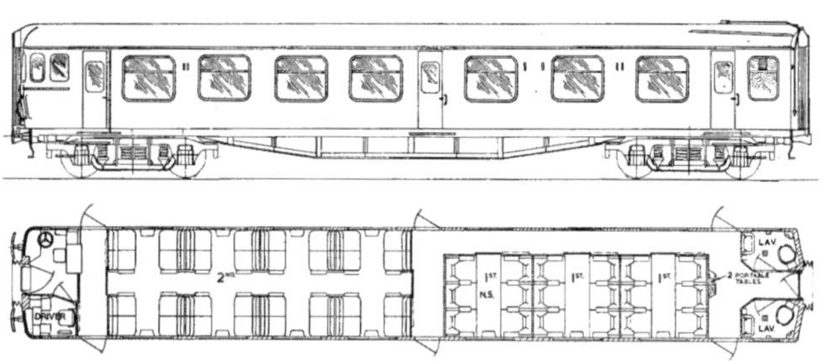

Refurbished, Diagram EF305

Diagram:	448 EF301 EF305	Lot Number:	30675
Body:	64' 9¾" × 9' 3"	Weight:	39t 7cwt
Seats:	18 first 32 second 2 toilets	Bogies:	Commonwealth

E75962	08/62-05/92	⊗03/92	**621**	08/62-03/83	**309621**	03/83-05/92		
E75963	11/62-11/92	⊗04/93	**622**	11/62-02/82	**309622**	02/82-11/92		
E75964	11/62-08/92	⊗07/92	**623**	11/62-09/82	**309623**	09/82-07/92		
E75965	12/62-06/00	Ⓟ➲**977965**	**624**	12/62-05/82	**309624**	05/82-06/00		
E75966	12/62-12/94	⊗10/97	**625**	12/62-04/82	**309625**	04/82-12/91	**309618**	12/91-12/94
E75967	12/62-12/94	⊗10/97	**626**	12/62-03/82	**309626**	03/82-12/94		
E75968	12/62-02/92	⊗02/92	**627**	12/62-10/82	**309627**	10/82-02/92		

Class 309 York

Driving Trailer Composite (Semi-open) Lavatory DTCsoL, later DTSOL E75969-E75975

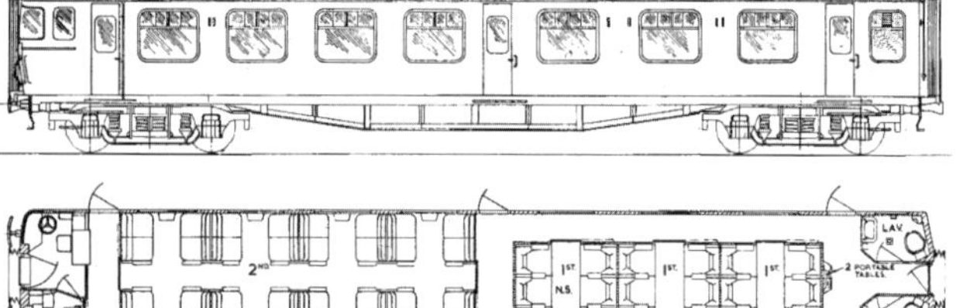

As built, Diagram 448

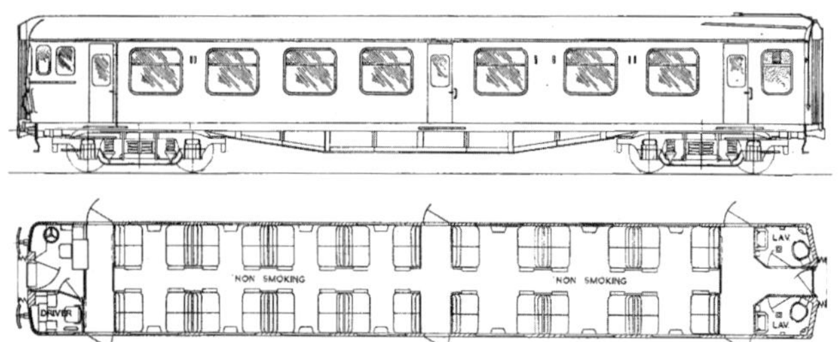

Rebuilt as DTSOL, Diagram EE229

Diagram:	448 EE229	Lot Number:	30678
Body:	64' 9¾" × 9' 3"	Weight:	36t 15cwt
Seats:	18 first 32 second 2 toilets later 56 second 2 toilets	Bogies:	Commonwealth

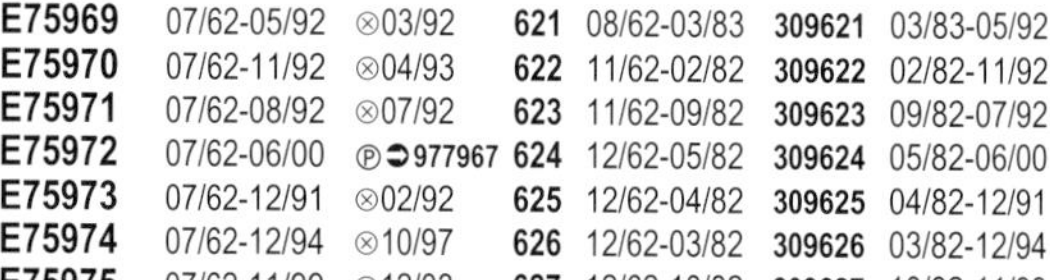

E75969	07/62-05/92	⊗03/92	**621**	08/62-03/83	**309621**	03/83-05/92
E75970	07/62-11/92	⊗04/93	**622**	11/62-02/82	**309622**	02/82-11/92
E75971	07/62-08/92	⊗07/92	**623**	11/62-09/82	**309623**	09/82-07/92
E75972	07/62-06/00	Ⓟ➲**977967**	**624**	12/62-05/82	**309624**	05/82-06/00
E75973	07/62-12/91	⊗02/92	**625**	12/62-04/82	**309625**	04/82-12/91
E75974	07/62-12/94	⊗10/97	**626**	12/62-03/82	**309626**	03/82-12/94
E75975	07/62-11/99	⊗12/03	**627**	12/62-10/82	**309627**	10/82-11/99

Class 309 York

Driving Trailer Composite Open Lavatory DTCOL, later DTSOL E75976-E75983

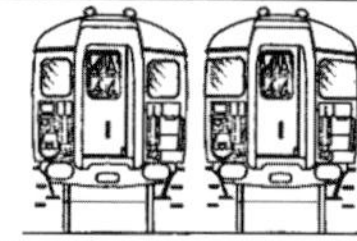

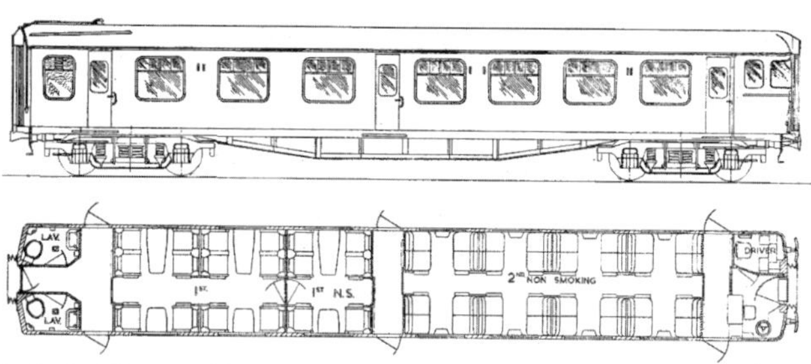

As built, Diagram 447

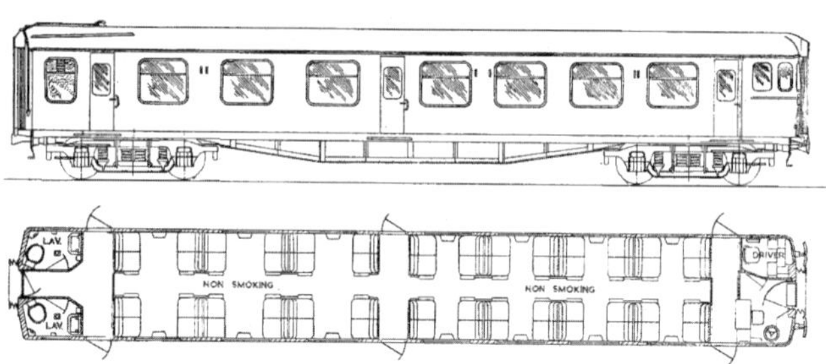

Rebuilt as DTSOL, Diagram EE229

Diagram:	447 EE229	Lot Number:	30682
Body:	64' 9¾" × 9' 3"	Weight:	36t 1cwt
Seats:	18 first 32 second 2 toilets later 56 second 2 toilets	Bogies:	Commonwealth

E75976	07/62-12/91	⊗03/92	**611**	09/62-03/81	**309611**	03/81-12/91		
E75977	09/62-06/93	⊗04/93	**612**	10/62-10/82	**309612**	10/82-06/93		
E75978	07/62-06/00	⊗04/04	**613**	10/62-06/82	**309613**	06/82-06/00		
E75979	12/62-08/92	⊗07/92	**614**	12/62-10/82	**309614**	10/82-02/86	**309614**	07/86-08/92
E75980	01/63-06/00	⊗04/04	**615**	01/63-09/82	**309615**	09/82-03/85	**309615**	09/86-07/92
			309623	08/92-06/00				
E75981	01/63-06/00	Ⓟ➲**977964**	**616**	01/63-01/70	**616**	06/72-01/80	**309616**	01/80-07/85
			309616	04/86-06/00				
E75982	02/63-06/00	⊗03/04	**617**	02/63-10/82	**309617**	10/82-07/85	**309617**	04/86-06/00
E75983	02/63-12/94	⊗10/97	**618**	02/63-02/81	**309618**	02/81-12/94		

Class 309 York

Battery Driving Trailer Second Open Lavatory BDTSOL E75984-E75991

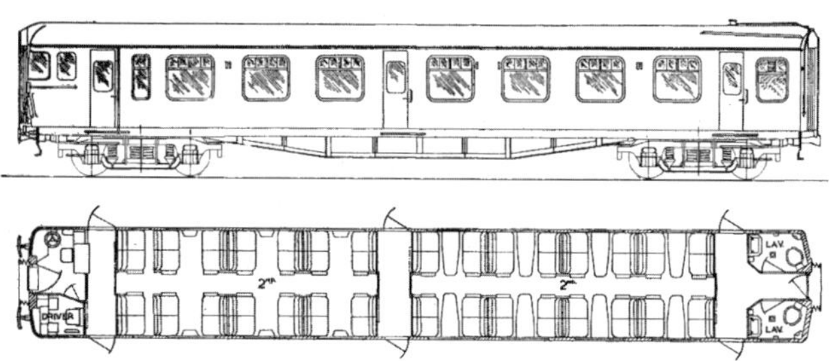

As built, Diagram 446 EF216

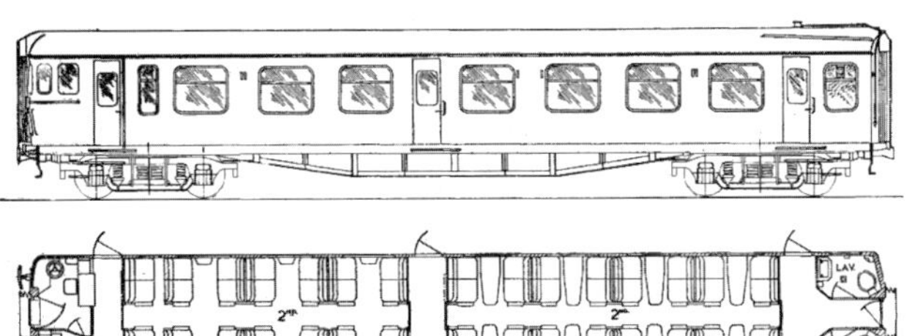

Refurbished, Diagram EF209

Diagram:	446 EF216 EF209	Lot Number:	30683
Body:	64' 9¾" × 9' 3"	Weight:	39t 11cwt
Seats:	60 second 2 toilets	Bogies:	Commonwealth

E75984	07/62-05/93	⊗07/93	**601**	09/62-10/82	**309601**	10/82-05/93
E75985	09/62-01/94	⊗03/94	**602**	12/62-06/82	**309602**	06/82-01/94
E75986	10/62-05/93	⊗07/93	**603**	01/63-12/81	**309603**	12/81-05/93
E75987	10/62-01/94	⊗03/94	**604**	02/63-02/82	**309604**	02/82-01/94
E75988	10/62-03/98	⊗03/98	**605**	02/63-12/81	**309605**	12/81-03/98
E75989	10/62-03/98	⊗03/98	**606**	03/63-12/81	**309606**	12/81-03/98
E75990	10/62-02/94	⊗10/97	**607**	03/63-11/82	**309607**	11/82-02/94
E75991	10/62-05/93	⊗07/93	**608**	03/63-09/82	**309608**	09/82-05/93

Class 308/3 York

Driving Trailer Second Open
DTSO
E75992-E75994

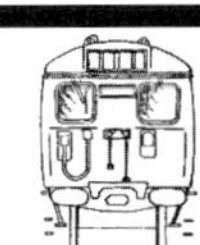

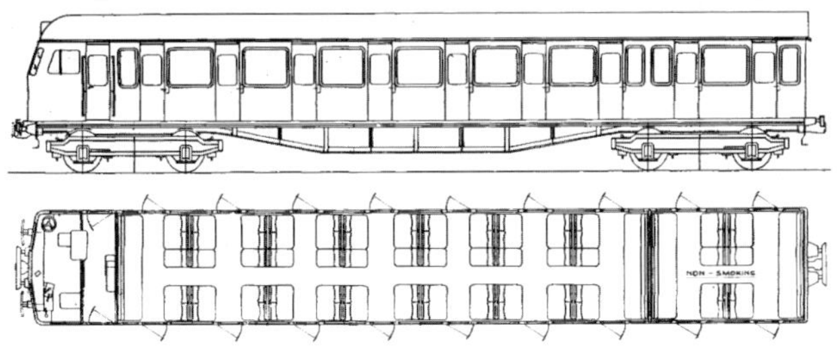

As built, Diagram 436

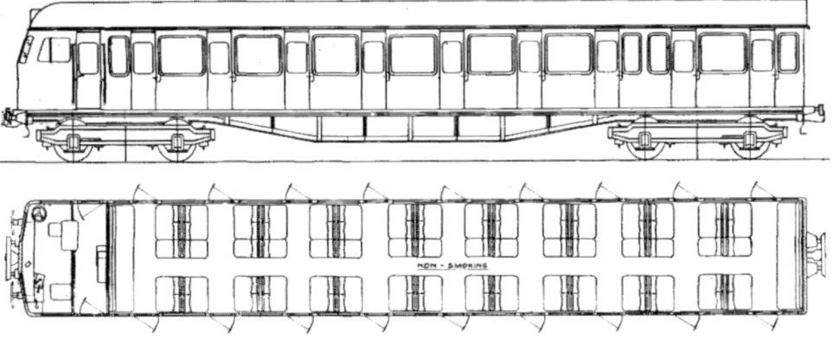

Facelifted, Diagram EE209

Diagram:	436 EE209	Lot Number:	30696
Body:	64' 0⅝" × 9' 3"	Weight:	31t 0cwt
Seats:	94 second, later 92 second	Bogies:	Gresley

E75992	12/61-03/86	⊗02/86	**453**	12/61-10/81	**308453**	10/81-02/86
E75993	12/61-03/86	⊗07/86	**454**	12/61-02/82	**308454**	02/82-03/86
E75994	12/61-05/85	⊗06/85	**455**	12/61-05/82	**308455**	05/82-05/85

Class 414/3 2-HAP Ashford/Eastleigh

Driving Trailer Composite (Semi-open) Lavatory
DTCsoL
S75995-S76021

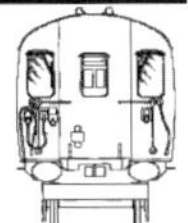

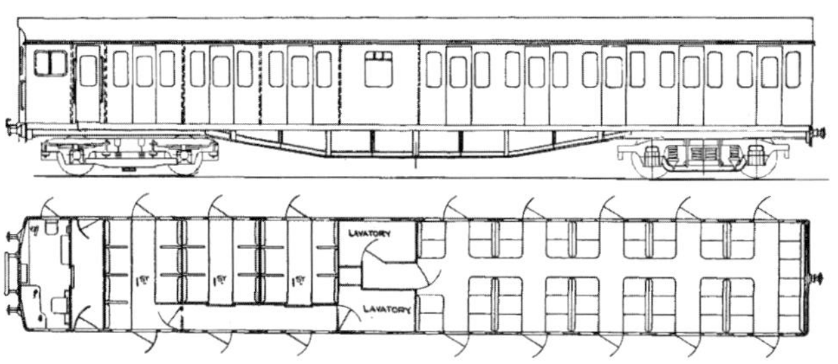

Diagram:	441 EE361	Lot Number:	30712
Body:	63' 11½" × 9' 3"	Weight:	32t 0cwt
Seats:	19 first 50 second 2 toilets	Bogies:	1 Mk 4 1 Commonwealth

S75995	02/63-05/84	⊗10/84	**6147**	02/63-05/84		
S75996	02/63-10/83	⊗08/84	**6148**	02/63-10/83		
S75997	03/63-10/83	⊗04/84	**6149**	03/63-10/83		
S75998	03/63-05/84	⊗10/84	**6150**	03/63-05/84		
S75999	03/63-10/83	⊗06/84	**6151**	03/63-06/71	**6151**	01/72-10/83
S76000	03/63-10/83	⊗06/84	**6152**	03/63-10/83		
S76001	03/63-05/84	⊗11/84	**6153**	03/63-05/84		
S76002	03/63-10/83	⊗06/84	**6154**	03/63-10/83		
S76003	03/63-05/83	⊗08/86	**6155**	03/63-05/83		
S76004	03/63-10/83	⊃977206	**6156**	03/63-10/83		
S76005	04/63-10/83	⊗08/84	**6157**	04/63-10/83		
S76006	04/63-10/83	⊗08/84	**6158**	04/63-10/83		
S76007	04/63-05/84	⊗09/84	**6159**	04/63-05/84		
S76008	04/63-10/83	⊗06/84	**6160**	04/63-10/83		
S76009	04/63-05/84	⊗07/85	**6161**	04/63-05/84		
S76010	04/63-05/84	⊗10/86	**6162**	04/63-05/84		
S76011	04/63-05/84	⊗10/84	**6163**	04/63-05/84		
S76012	04/63-06/82	⊗09/84	**6164**	04/63-06/82		
S76013	05/63-10/83	⊗08/84	**6165**	05/63-10/83		
S76014	05/63-05/84	⊗11/85	**6166**	05/63-05/84		
S76015	05/63-05/84	⊗02/85	**6167**	05/63-05/84		
S76016	05/63-10/83	⊗08/86	**6168**	05/63-10/83		
S76017	05/63-05/84	⊗10/84	**6169**	05/63-05/84		
S76018	05/63-10/84	⊗05/86	**6170**	05/63-10/84		
S76019	05/63-05/84	⊗02/86	**6171**	05/63-05/84		
S76020	05/63-05/84	⊗11/85	**6172**	05/63-05/84		
S76021	05/63-10/84	⊗05/86	**6173**	05/63-10/84		

Class 421 4-CIG York

Driving Trailer Composite (Semi-open) Lavatory
DTCsoL
S76022-S76075 (76058 onwards Class 420 4-BIG)

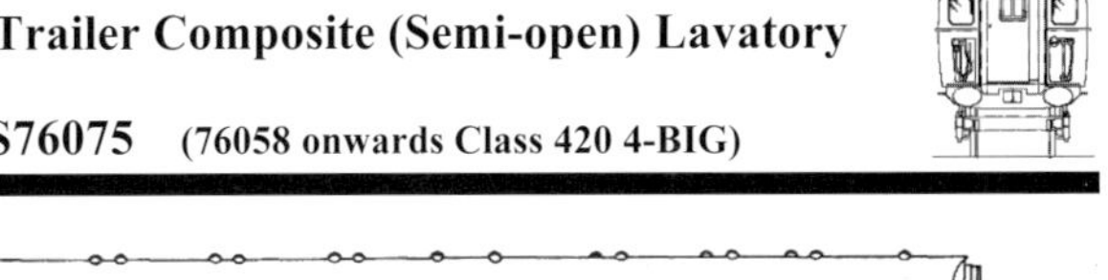

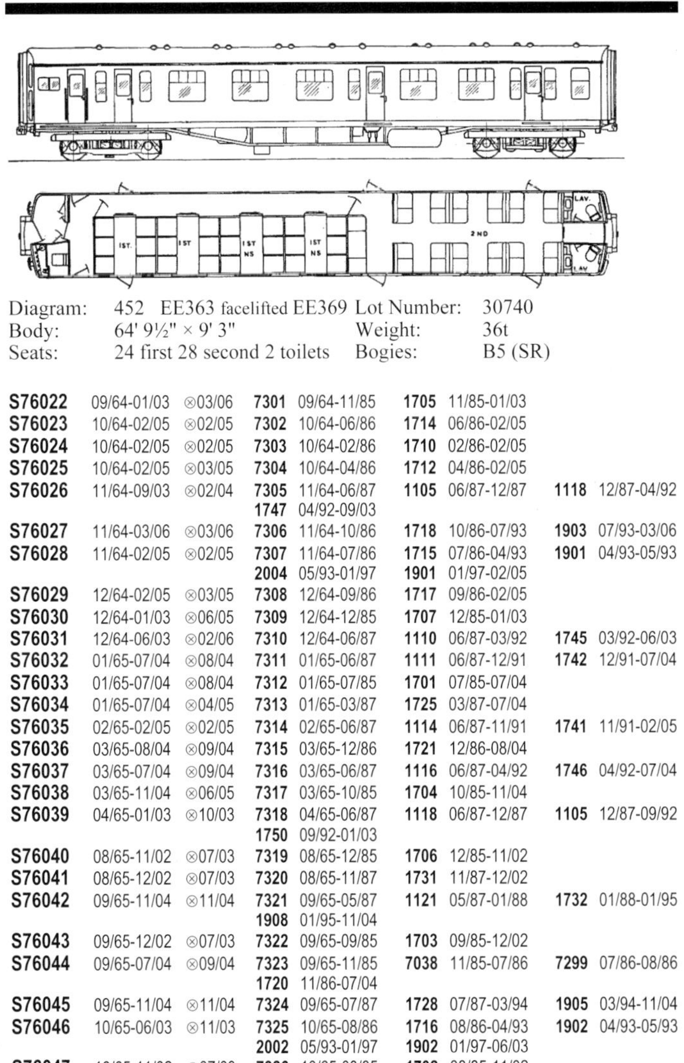

Diagram:	452 EE363 facelifted EE369	Lot Number:	30740
Body:	64' 9½" × 9' 3"	Weight:	36t
Seats:	24 first 28 second 2 toilets	Bogies:	B5 (SR)

S76022	09/64-01/03	⊗03/06	**7301**	09/64-11/85	**1705**	11/85-01/03		
S76023	10/64-02/05	⊗02/05	**7302**	10/64-06/86	**1714**	06/86-02/05		
S76024	10/64-02/05	⊗02/05	**7303**	10/64-02/86	**1710**	02/86-02/05		
S76025	10/64-02/05	⊗03/05	**7304**	10/64-04/86	**1712**	04/86-02/05		
S76026	11/64-09/03	⊗02/04	**7305**	11/64-06/87	**1105**	06/87-12/87	**1118**	12/87-04/92
			1747	04/92-09/03				
S76027	11/64-03/06	⊗03/06	**7306**	11/64-10/86	**1718**	10/86-07/93	**1903**	07/93-03/06
S76028	11/64-02/05	⊗02/05	**7307**	11/64-07/86	**1715**	07/86-04/93	**1901**	04/93-05/93
			2004	05/93-01/97	**1901**	01/97-02/05		
S76029	12/64-02/05	⊗03/05	**7308**	12/64-09/86	**1717**	09/86-02/05		
S76030	12/64-01/03	⊗06/05	**7309**	12/64-12/85	**1707**	12/85-01/03		
S76031	12/64-06/03	⊗02/06	**7310**	12/64-06/87	**1110**	06/87-03/92	**1745**	03/92-06/03
S76032	01/65-07/04	⊗08/04	**7311**	01/65-06/87	**1111**	06/87-12/91	**1742**	12/91-07/04
S76033	01/65-07/04	⊗08/04	**7312**	01/65-07/85	**1701**	07/85-07/04		
S76034	01/65-07/04	⊗04/05	**7313**	01/65-03/87	**1725**	03/87-07/04		
S76035	02/65-02/05	⊗02/05	**7314**	02/65-06/87	**1114**	06/87-11/91	**1741**	11/91-02/05
S76036	03/65-08/04	⊗09/04	**7315**	03/65-12/86	**1721**	12/86-08/04		
S76037	03/65-07/04	⊗09/04	**7316**	03/65-06/87	**1116**	06/87-04/92	**1746**	04/92-07/04
S76038	03/65-11/04	⊗06/05	**7317**	03/65-10/85	**1704**	10/85-11/04		
S76039	04/65-01/03	⊗10/03	**7318**	04/65-06/87	**1118**	06/87-12/87	**1105**	12/87-09/92
			1750	09/92-01/03				
S76040	08/65-11/02	⊗07/03	**7319**	08/65-12/85	**1706**	12/85-11/02		
S76041	08/65-12/02	⊗07/03	**7320**	08/65-11/87	**1731**	11/87-12/02		
S76042	09/65-11/04	⊗11/04	**7321**	09/65-05/87	**1121**	05/87-01/88	**1732**	01/88-01/95
			1908	01/95-11/04				
S76043	09/65-12/02	⊗07/03	**7322**	09/65-09/85	**1703**	09/85-12/02		
S76044	09/65-07/04	⊗09/04	**7323**	09/65-11/85	**7038**	11/85-07/86	**7299**	07/86-08/86
			1720	11/86-07/04				
S76045	09/65-11/04	⊗11/04	**7324**	09/65-07/87	**1728**	07/87-03/94	**1905**	03/94-11/04
S76046	10/65-06/03	⊗11/03	**7325**	10/65-08/86	**1716**	08/86-04/93	**1902**	04/93-05/93
			2002	05/93-01/97	**1902**	01/97-06/03		
S76047	10/65-11/02	⊗07/03	**7326**	10/65-08/85	**1702**	08/85-11/02		
S76048	10/65-02/04	Ⓟ	**7327**	10/65-06/87	**1127**	06/87-01/93	**1753**	01/93-02/04

S76049	10/65-03/03	⊗02/06	7328	10/65-02/86	1709	02/86-03/03		
S76050	11/65-07/04	⊗09/04	7329	11/65-07/87	1729	07/87-07/94	1907	07/94-07/04
S76051	12/65-02/04	⊗02/06	7330	12/65-06/83	7036	06/83-05/85	2104	05/85-10/89
			1754	10/89-02/91	1735	02/91-02/04		
S76052	12/65-06/04	⊗06/04	7331	12/65-01/87	1722	01/87-06/04		
S76053	01/66-04/04	⊗03/06	7332	01/66-02/87	1723	02/87-11/93	1904	11/93-04/04
S76054	01/66-12/78	⊗12/78	7333	01/66-12/78				
S76055	01/66-09/03	⊗08/04	7334	01/66-05/87	1726	05/87-09/03		
S76056	01/66-02/05	⊗02/06	7335	01/66-01/86	1708	01/86-02/05		
S76057	02/66-06/04	⊗06/04	7336	02/66-06/87	1727	06/87-06/04		
S76058	04/65-09/95	⊗	7031	04/65-09/85	2111	09/85-10/89	1761	10/89-05/92
			1749	05/92-09/95				
S76059	05/65-07/04	⊗07/04	7032	05/65-04/85	2101	04/85-10/89	1751	10/89-12/90
			1734	12/90-07/04				
S76060	05/65-12/04	⊗01/05	7033	05/65-03/86	1711	03/86-12/04		
S76061	06/65-05/04	⊗05/06	7034	06/65-11/85	2110	11/85-11/89	1760	11/89-05/92
			1748	05/92-05/04				
S76062	06/65-04/04	⊗06/05	7035	06/65-10/86	1719	10/86-04/04		
S76063	06/65-07/04	⊗07/04	7036	06/65-04/83	7032	04/83-04/85	2101	04/85-10/89
			1751	10/89-12/90	1734	12/90-07/04		
S76064	08/65-02/05	⊗03/05	7037	08/65-04/85	2106	04/85-11/89	1756	11/89-01/92
			1743	01/92-02/05				
S76065	07/65-07/04	⊗08/04	7038	07/65-11/85	7323	11/85-07/86	1123	07/86-11/92
			1752	11/92-07/04				
S76066	08/65-02/04	⊗ 06	7039	08/65-10/86	1724	03/87-02/04		
S76067	11/65-09/03	⊗03/06	7040	11/65-08/79	7300	08/79-04/80	7040	04/80-05/85
			2105	05/85-10/89	1755	10/89-03/91	1737	03/91-09/03
S76068	11/65-07/04	⊗09/04	7041	11/65-04/85	2107	04/85-09/89	1757	09/89-10/90
			1733	10/90-07/04				
S76069	11/65-03/03	⊗03/06	7042	11/65-04/85	2102	04/85-10/89	1752	10/89-05/91
			1738	05/91-03/03				
S76070	12/65-03/03	⊗08/04	7043	12/65-04/85	2103	04/85-10/89	1753	10/89-02/91
			1736	02/91-03/03				
S76071	12/65-07/04	⊗03/05	7044	12/65-03/86	7300	03/86-06/87	1100	06/87-10/92
			1751	10/92-07/04				
S76072	12/65-04/04	⊗02/06	7045	12/65-04/86	2112	04/86-12/89	1762	12/89-11/91
			1740	11/91-04/04				
S76073	02/66-02/04	⊗03/06	7046	02/66-09/85	2108	09/85-11/89	1758	11/89-02/92
			1744	02/92-02/04				
S76074	02/66-02/04	⊗03/05	7047	02/66-05/86	1713	05/86-02/04		
S76075	02/66-06/04	⊗06/04	7048	02/66-10/85	2109	10/85-11/89	1759	11/89-01/92
			1739	01/92-06/04				

Class 421 4-CIG York

Driving Trailer Composite (Semi-open) Lavatory

DTCsoL

S76076-S76129 (76113 onwards Class 420 4-BIG)

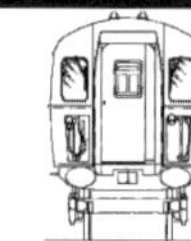

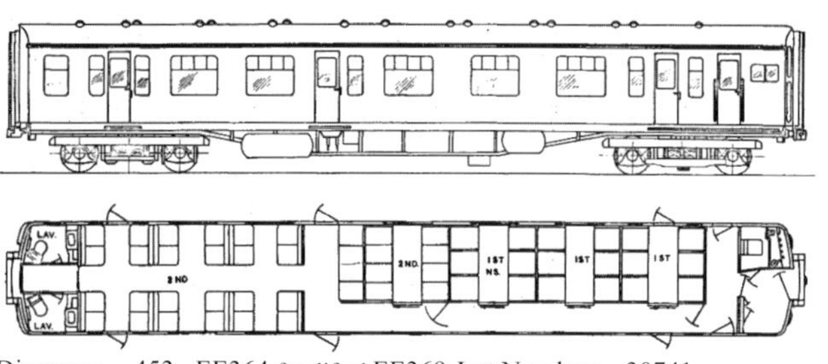

Diagram:	453 EE364 facelifted EE369	Lot Number:	30741
Body:	64' 9½" × 9' 3"	Weight:	35t 10 cwt
Seats:	18 first 36 second 2 toilets	Bogies:	B5 (SR)

76112 was rebuilt as Class 424 Networker Classic prototype in 1997 and carried the unit number 4001. It weighed 31t, was fitted with B4 bogies and seated 77 standard in 2+3 seating.

S76076	09/64-01/03	⊗03/06	7301	09/64-11/85	1705	11/85-01/03		
S76077	10/64-02/05	⊗02/05	7302	10/64-06/86	1714	06/86-02/05		
S76078	10/64-02/05	⊗02/05	7303	10/64-02/86	1710	02/86-02/05		
S76079	10/64-02/05	⊗03/05	7304	10/64-04/86	1712	04/86-02/05		
S76080	11/64-01/03	⊗09/03	7305	11/64-06/87	1105	06/87-09/92	1750	09/92-01/03
S76081	11/64-03/06	⊗03/06	7306	11/64-10/86	1718	10/86-07/93	1903	07/93-03/06
S76082	11/64-02/05	⊗02/05	7307	11/64-07/86	1715	07/86-04/93	1901	04/93-05/93
			2004	05/93-01/97	1901	01/97-02/05		
S76083	12/64-02/05	⊗03/05	7308	12/64-09/86	1717	09/86-02/05		
S76084	12/64-01/03	⊗06/05	7309	12/64-12/85	1707	12/85-01/03		
S76085	12/64-06/03	⊗02/06	7310	12/64-06/87	1110	06/87-03/92	1745	03/92-06/03
S76086	01/65-07/04	⊗08/04	7311	01/65-06/87	1111	06/87-12/91	1742	12/91-07/04
S76087	01/65-07/04	⊗08/04	7312	01/65-07/85	1701	07/85-07/04		
S76088	01/65-07/04	⊗08/04	7313	01/65-03/87	1725	03/87-07/04		
S76089	02/65-02/05	⊗02/05	7314	02/65-06/87	1114	06/87-11/91	1741	11/91-02/05
S76090	03/65-08/04	⊗09/04	7315	03/65-12/86	1721	12/86-08/04		
S76091	03/65-07/04	⊗09/04	7316	03/65-06/87	1116	06/87-04/92	1746	04/92-07/04
S76092	03/65-11/04	⊗06/05	7317	03/65-10/85	1704	10/85-11/04		
S76093	04/65-09/03	⊗03/05	7318	04/65-06/87	1118	06/87-04/92	1747	04/92-09/03
S76094	08/65-11/02	⊗07/03	7319	08/65-12/85	1706	12/85-11/02		
S76095	08/65-12/02	⊗07/03	7320	08/65-11/87	1731	11/87-12/02		
S76096	09/65-11/04	⊗11/04	7321	09/65-05/87	1121	05/87-01/88	1732	01/88-01/95
			1908	01/95-11/04				
S76097	09/65-12/02	⊗07/03	7322	09/65-09/85	1703	09/85-12/02		
S76098	09/65-07/04	⊗09/04	7323	09/65-11/85	7038	11/85-07/86	7299	07/86-08/86
			1720	11/86-07/04				
S76099	09/65-11/04	⊗11/04	7324	09/65-07/87	1728	07/87-03/94	1905	03/94-11/04
S76100	10/65-06/03	⊗11/03	7325	10/65-08/86	1716	08/86-04/93	1902	04/93-05/93
			2002	05/93-01/97	1902	01/97-06/03		
S76101	10/65-11/02	⊗08/03	7326	10/65-08/85	1702	08/85-11/02		
S76102	10/65-02/04	Ⓟ	7327	10/65-06/87	1127	06/87-01/93	1753	01/93-02/04
S76103	10/65-03/03	⊗02/06	7328	10/65-02/86	1709	02/86-03/03		
S76104	11/65-07/04	⊗09/04	7329	11/65-07/87	1729	07/87-07/94	1907	07/94-07/04
S76105	12/65-07/04	⊗07/04	7330	12/65-10/87	1730	10/87-05/94	1906	05/94-07/04
S76106	12/65-06/04	⊗08/04	7331	12/65-01/87	1722	01/87-06/04		
S76107	01/66-04/04	⊗03/06	7332	01/66-02/87	1723	02/87-11/93	1904	11/93-04/04
S76108	01/66-07/04	⊗08/04	7333	01/66-12/78	1221	03/91-04/92	1870	04/92-07/04
S76109	01/66-09/03	⊗06/04	7334	01/66-05/87	1726	05/87-09/03		
S76110	01/66-02/05	⊗03/05	7335	01/66-01/86	1708	01/86-02/05		
S76111	02/66-06/04	⊗06/04	7336	02/66-06/87	1727	06/87-06/04		
S76112	04/65-09/95	Rebuilt as class 424 classic 97			7031	04/65-09/85	2111	09/85-10/89
			1761	10/89-05/92	1749	05/92-09/95	4001	97-
S76113	05/65-07/04	⊗07/04	7032	05/65-04/83	7036	04/83-06/83	7330	06/83-10/87
			1730	10/87-05/94	1906	05/94-07/04		
S76114	05/65-12/04	⊗01/05	7033	05/65-03/86	1711	03/86-12/04		
S76115	06/65-05/04	⊗08/06	7034	06/65-11/85	2110	11/85-11/89	1760	11/89-05/92
			1748	05/92-05/04				
S76116	06/65-04/04	⊗06/05	7035	06/65-10/86	1719	10/86-04/04		
S76117	06/65-02/04	⊗03/06	7036	06/65-05/85	2104	05/85-10/89	1754	10/89-02/91
			1735	02/91-02/04				
S76118	08/65-02/05	⊗03/05	7037	08/65-04/85	2106	04/85-11/89	1756	11/89-01/92
			1743	01/92-02/05				
S76119	07/65-07/04	⊗08/04	7038	07/65-11/85	7323	11/85-07/86	1123	07/86-11/92
			1752	11/92-07/04				
S76120	08/65-02/04	⊗03/06	7039	08/65-10/86	1724	03/87-02/04		
S76121	11/65-09/03	⊗02/06	7040	11/65-08/79	7300	08/79-04/80	7040	04/80-05/85
			2105	05/85-10/89	1755	10/89-03/91	1737	03/91-09/03
S76122	11/65-07/04	⊗09/04	7041	11/65-04/85	2107	04/85-09/89	1757	09/89-10/90
			1733	10/90-07/04				
S76123	11/65-06/04	⊗06/04	7042	11/65-08/83	7048	08/83-10/85	2109	10/85-11/89
			1759	11/89-01/92	1739	01/92-06/04		
S76124	12/65-03/03	⊗08/04	7043	12/65-04/85	2103	04/85-10/89	1753	10/89-02/91
			1736	02/91-03/03				
S76125	12/65-07/04	⊗03/05	7044	12/65-03/86	7300	03/86-06/87	1100	06/87-10/92
			1751	10/92-07/04				
S76126	12/65-04/04	⊗06/05	7045	12/65-04/86	2112	04/86-12/89	1762	12/89-11/91
			1740	11/91-04/04				
S76127	02/66-02/04	⊗03/06	7046	02/66-09/85	2108	09/85-11/89	1758	11/89-02/92
			1744	02/92-02/04				
S76128	02/66-02/04	⊗03/05	7047	02/66-05/86	1713	05/86-02/04		
S76129	02/66-03/03	⊗ 06	7048	02/66-08/83	7042	08/83-04/85	2102	04/85-10/89
			1752	10/89-05/91	1738	05/91-03/03		

Class 310 Derby

Battery Driving Trailer Second Open Lavatory

BDTSOL

M76130-M76179

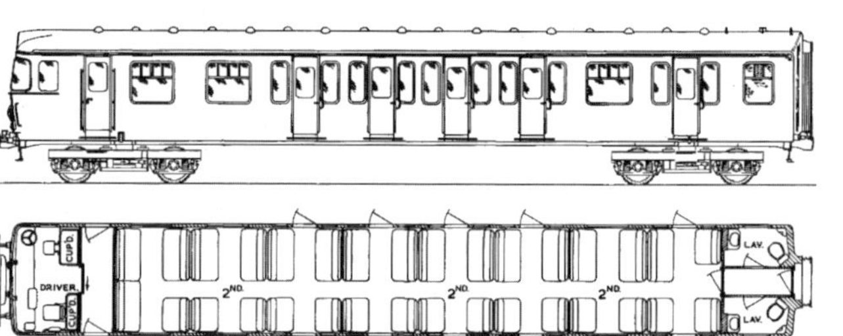

Diagram:	428 EF211	Lot Number:	30745
Body:	65' 1⅝" × 9' 3"	Weight:	36t 15¼cwt
Seats:	80 second 2 toilets	Bogies:	B4

M76130	02/65-05/01	⊗10/07	046	02/65- *83*	310046	*83*-05/01		
M76131	03/65-06/01	⊗04/07	047	03/65-03/82	310047	03/82-06/01		
M76132	03/65-07/01	⊗07/08	048	03/65-04/81	310048	04/81-09/89	310108	09/89-07/01
M76133	03/65-06/01	⊗06/08	049	03/65-08/81	310049	08/81-06/01		
M76134	03/65-10/01	⊗12/08	050	03/65-09/82	310050	09/82-10/01		
M76135	08/65-10/01	⊗02/09	051	09/65-06/81	310051	06/81-10/01		
M76136	09/65-06/01	⊗01/07	052	09/65-02/80	310052	02/80-06/01		
M76137	09/65-07/01	➲977977	053	09/65-11/82	310053	11/82-10/89	310109	10/89-07/01
M76138	09/65-09/01	⊗03/08	054	09/65-07/81	310054	07/81-11/89	310110	11/89-09/01
M76139	08/65-09/01	⊗06/08	055	08/65-12/81	310055	12/81-10/88	310102	10/88-09/01
M76140	11/65-07/01	⊗02/08	056	11/65-02/80	310056	02/80-04/93	310061	04/93-09/94
			310112	09/94-07/01				
M76141	10/65-08/00	⊗08/06	057	10/65-03/82	310057	03/82-08/00		
M76142	10/65-06/01	⊗04/07	058	10/65-12/81	310058	12/81-06/01		
M76143	10/65-07/01	⊗03/08	059	10/65-12/79	310059	12/79-07/01		
M76144	10/65-06/01	⊗07/07	060	10/65-04/81	310060	04/81-06/01		

M76145	08/65-07/01	⊗10/07	**061**	08/65-03/82	**310061**	03/82-04/93	**310074**	04/93-07/01
M76146	11/65-07/01	⊗12/06	**062**	11/65-02/83	**310062**	02/83-09/89	**310107**	09/89-07/01
M76147	08/65-05/01	⊗09/08	**063**	08/65-06/81	**310063**	06/81-03/90	**310111**	03/90-05/01
M76148	08/65-07/01	⊗01/08	**064**	08/65-04/81	**310064**	04/81-07/01		
M76149	08/65-01/96	⊗05/97	**065**	08/65-09/82	**310065**	09/82-09/94		
M76150	09/65-05/69	⊗07/69	**066**	09/65-04/69				
M76151	09/65-05/01	⊗06/07	**067**	09/65-03/82	**310067**	03/82-05/01		
M76152	10/65-03/01	⊗10/06	**068**	10/65-04/83	**310068**	04/83-03/01		
M76153	10/65-07/01	⊗12/07	**069**	10/65-01/80	**310069**	01/80-07/01		
M76154	11/65-07/01	⊗03/08	**070**	11/65-08/81	**310070**	08/81-07/01		
M76155	12/65-01/70	⊗05/76	**071**	12/65-01/70				
M76156	12/65-09/01	⊗01/08	**072**	12/65-05/81	**310072**	05/81-02/89	**310106**	02/89-09/01
M76157	02/66-07/01	⊗06/07	**073**	02/66-12/81	**310073**	12/81-09/88	**310101**	09/88-07/01
M76158	06/66-07/01	⊗04/04	**074**	06/66-04/81	**310074**	04/81-04/93	**310056**	04/93-04/94
			310113	09/94-07/01				
M76159	07/66-07/01	⊗11/03	**075**	07/66-04/83	**310075**	04/83-07/01		
M76160	07/66-02/00	⊗03/03	**076**	07/66-02/82	**310076**	02/82-11/88	**310103**	11/88-02/00
M76161	07/66-06/01	⊗08/04	**077**	07/66-12/81	**310077**	12/81-06/01		
M76162	08/66-07/01	⊗10/03	**078**	08/66-03/82	**310078**	03/82-01/89	**310104**	01/89-07/01
M76163	08/66-05/01	⊗10/03	**079**	08/66-08/81	**310079**	08/81-05/01		
M76164	08/66-10/01	⊗12/03	**080**	08/66-03/82	**310080**	03/82-10/01		
M76165	09/66-11/01	⊗09/03	**081**	09/66-03/82	**310081**	03/82-11/01		
M76166	09/66-10/01	⊗09/03	**082**	09/66-04/83	**310082**	04/83-10/01		
M76167	09/66-10/01	⊗[illegible]	**083**	09/66-10/81	**310083**	10/81-10/01		
M76168	10/66-05/01	⊗11/03	**084**	10/66-10/81	**310084**	10/81-05/01		
M76169	11/66-06/01	⊗11/03	**085**	11/66-04/83	**310085**	04/83-06/01		
M76170	10/66-06/01	⊗11/03	**086**	10/66-10/82	**310086**	10/82-08/01		
M76171	02/67-10/01	⊗11/03	**087**	02/67-12/81	**310087**	12/81-10/01		
M76172	12/66-10/01	⊗11/03	**088**	12/66-12/81	**310088**	12/81-10/01		
M76173	01/67-12/00	⊗03/03	**089**	01/67-06/81	**310089**	06/81-12/00		
M76174	11/66-07/01	⊗10/03	**090**	11/66-07/82	**310090**	07/82-01/89	**310105**	01/89-07/01
M76175	12/66-05/01	⊗11/03	**091**	12/66-04/83	**310091**	04/83-05/01		
M76176	12/66-10/01	⊗09/03	**092**	12/66-02/83	**310092**	02/83-10/01		
M76177	03/67-11/01	⊗11/03	**093**	03/67-07/82	**310093**	07/80-11/01		
M76178	02/67-12/68	⊗12/68	**094**	02/67-12/67				
M76179	05/67-05/01	⊗11/03	**095**	05/67-04/81	**310095**	04/81-05/01		

Class 310 Derby

Driving Trailer Composite Open Lavatory
DTCOL
M76180-M76229

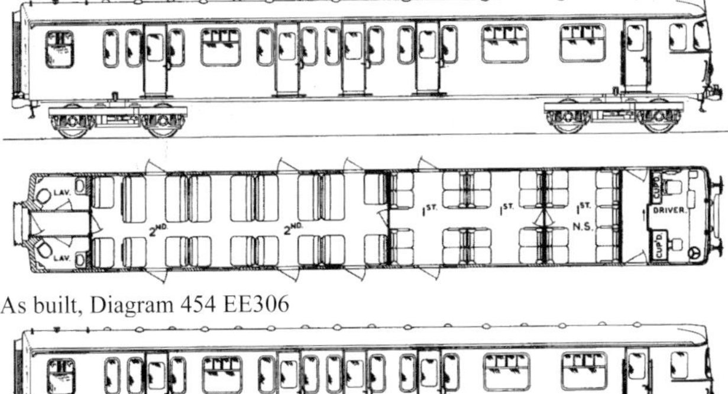

As built, Diagram 454 EE306

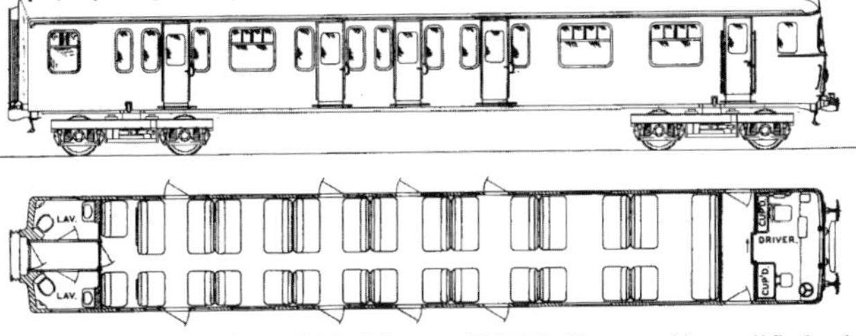

Rebuilt as Class 310/1 DTSOL, Diagram EE237. Shown with modified cab (see left hand cab view above).

76228 rebuilt as BDTSOL, Diagram EF210

Diagram:	454 EE306 EE237 EF210	Lot Number:	30748
Body:	65' 1⅝" × 9' 3"	Weight:	33t 16½cwt
Seats:	25 first 43 second 2 toilets	Bogies:	B4
	310/1: 75 second 2 toilets		
	76228: 68 second 2 toilets		

M76180	02/65-05/01	⊗10/07	**046**	02/65- *83*	**310046**	*83*-05/01		
M76181	03/65-06/01	⊗05/07	**047**	03/65-03/82	**310047**	03/82-06/01		
M76182	03/65-07/01	⊗07/08	**048**	03/65-04/81	**310048**	04/81-09/89	**310108**	09/89-07/01
M76183	03/65-06/01	⊗06/08	**049**	03/65-08/81	**310049**	08/81-06/01		
M76184	03/65-10/01	⊗11/08	**050**	03/65-09/82	**310050**	09/82-10/01		
M76185	08/65-10/01	⊗12/08	**051**	09/65-06/81	**310051**	06/81-10/01		
M76186	09/65-06/01	⊗01/07	**052**	09/65-02/80	**310052**	02/80-06/01		
M76187	09/65-07/01	⊃**977980**	**053**	09/65-11/82	**310053**	11/82-10/89	**310109**	10/89-07/01
M76188	09/65-09/01	⊗08/08	**054**	09/65-07/81	**310054**	07/81-11/89	**310110**	11/89-09/01
M76189	08/65-09/01	⊗08/08	**055**	08/65-12/81	**310055**	12/81-10/88	**310102**	10/88-09/01
M76190	11/65-11/01	⊗05/07	**056**	11/65-02/80	**310056**	02/80-04/93	**310093**	04/93-11/01
M76191	10/65-08/00	⊗01/07	**057**	10/65-03/82	**310057**	03/82-08/00		
M76192	10/65-06/01	⊗02/07	**058**	10/65-12/81	**310058**	12/81-06/01		
M76193	10/65-06/01	⊗02/08	**059**	10/65-09/71	**094**	04/75-01/83	**310094**	01/83-06/01
M76194	10/65-06/01	⊗09/07	**060**	10/65-04/81	**310060**	04/81-06/01		
M76195	08/65-07/01	⊗04/04	**061**	08/65-03/82	**310061**	03/82-04/93	**310056**	04/93-04/94
			310113	09/94-07/01				
M76196	11/65-07/01	⊗10/06	**062**	11/65-02/83	**310062**	02/83-09/89	**310107**	09/89-07/01
M76197	08/65-05/01	⊗09/08	**063**	08/65-06/81	**310063**	06/81-03/90	**310111**	03/90-05/01
M76198	08/65-07/01	⊗12/07	**064**	08/65-04/81	**310064**	04/81-07/01		
M76199	08/65-01/96	⊗07/97	**065**	08/65-09/82	**310065**	09/82-09/94		
M76200	09/65-06/01	⊗09/07	**066**	09/65-03/82	**310066**	03/82-06/01		
M76201	09/65-05/01	⊗07/07	**067**	09/65-03/82	**310067**	03/82-05/01		
M76202	10/65-03/01	⊗09/06	**068**	10/65-04/83	**310068**	04/83-03/01		
M76203	10/65-07/01	⊗11/07	**069**	10/65-01/80	**310069**	01/80-07/01		
M76204	11/65-07/01	⊗05/08	**070**	11/65-08/81	**310070**	08/81-07/01		
M76205	12/65-07/01	⊗[illegible]	**071**	12/65-11/70	**059**	09/71-12/79	**310059**	12/79-07/01
M76206	12/65-05/01	⊗05/07	**072**	12/65-05/81	**310072**	05/81-02/89	**310106**	02/89-05/00
			310084	05/00-05/01				
M76207	02/66-07/01	⊗05/07	**073**	02/66-12/81	**310073**	12/81-09/88	**310101**	09/88-07/01
M76208	06/66-07/01	⊗11/03	**074**	06/66-04/81	**310074**	04/81-07/01		
M76209	07/66-07/01	⊗11/03	**075**	07/66-04/83	**310075**	04/83-07/01		
M76210	07/66-02/00	⊗03/03	**076**	07/66-02/82	**310076**	02/82-11/88	**310103**	11/88-02/00
M76211	07/66-06/01	⊗08/04	**077**	07/66-12/81	**310077**	12/81-06/01		
M76212	08/66-07/01	⊗10/03	**078**	08/66-03/82	**310078**	03/82-01/89	**310104**	01/89-07/01
M76213	08/66-10/01	⊗11/03	**079**	08/66-08/81	**310079**	08/81-10/90	**310088**	10/90-10/01
M76214	08/66-10/01	⊗03/04	**080**	08/66-03/82	**310080**	03/82-10/01		
M76215	09/66-11/01	⊗09/03	**081**	09/66-03/82	**310081**	03/82-11/01		
M76216	09/66-10/01	⊗12/03	**082**	09/66-04/83	**310082**	04/83-10/01		
M76217	09/66-10/01	⊗09/03	**083**	09/66-10/81	**310083**	10/81-10/01		
M76218	10/66-09/01	⊗03/04	**084**	10/66-10/81	**310084**	10/81-05/00	**310106**	05/00-09/01
M76219	11/66-06/01	⊗11/03	**085**	11/66-04/83	**310085**	04/83-06/01		
M76220	10/66-06/01	⊗10/03	**086**	10/66-10/82	**310086**	10/82-06/01		
M76221	02/67-10/01	⊗10/03	**087**	02/67-12/81	**310087**	12/81-10/01		
M76222	12/66-05/01	⊗10/03	**088**	12/66-12/81	**310088**	12/81-10/90	**310079**	10/90-05/01
M76223	01/67-12/00	⊗03/03	**089**	01/67-06/81	**310089**	06/81-12/00		
M76224	11/66-07/01	⊗11/03	**090**	11/66-07/82	**310090**	07/82-01/89	**310105**	01/89-07/01
M76225	12/66-05/01	⊗11/03	**091**	12/66-04/83	**310091**	04/83-05/01		
M76226	12/66-10/01	⊗09/03	**092**	12/66-02/83	**310092**	02/83-10/01		
M76227	03/67-07/01	⊗10/03	**093**	03/67-07/82	**310093**	07/82-04/93	**310061**	04/93-09/94
			310112	09/94-07/01				
M76228	02/67-06/01	⊗11/03	**094**	02/67-12/67	**066**	04/69-03/82	**310066**	03/82-06/01
M76229	05/67-05/01	⊗11/03	**095**	05/67-04/81	**310095**	04/81-05/01		

Class 423 4-VEP York

Driving Trailer Composite (Semi-open) Lavatory
DTCsoL
S76230-S76269

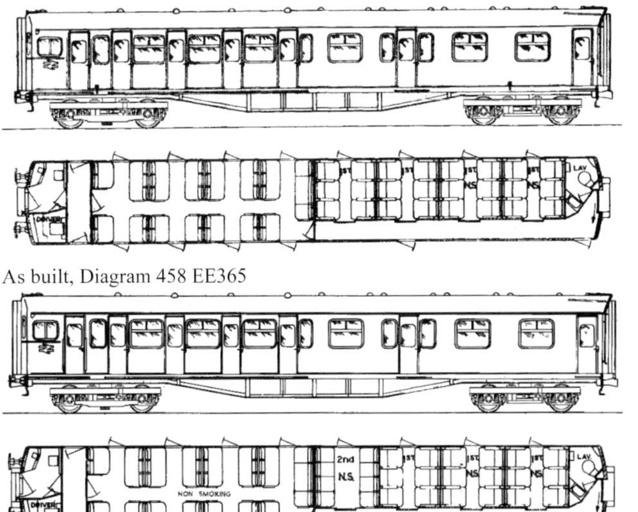

As built, Diagram 458 EE365

Facelifted EE373

Diagram:	458 EE365 EE373	Lot Number:	30758
Body:	64' 9⅝" × 9' 3"	Weight:	33t 17cwt

Seats:	24 first 38 second 1 toilet later 18 first 46 second 1 toilet	Bogies: B5 (SR)

Vehicle	Service	Fate	Unit	Dates	Unit	Dates	Unit	Dates
S76230	04/67-04/05	⊗04/05	**7701**	04/67-09/87	**3001**	09/87-10/93	**3401**	10/93-06/02
			3456	06/02-04/05				
S76231	04/67-07/04	⊗ 04	**7701**	04/67-09/87	**3001**	09/87-10/93	**3401**	10/93-06/02
			3428	10/02-07/04				
S76232	04/67-04/05	⊗04/05	**7702**	04/67-06/87	**3002**	06/87-06/93	**3402**	06/93-04/05
S76233	04/67-04/05	⊗04/05	**7702**	04/67-06/87	**3002**	06/87-06/93	**3402**	06/93-04/05
S76234	04/67-02/05	⊗06/05	**7703**	04/67-06/87	**3003**	06/87-05/93	**3403**	05/93-02/05
S76235	04/67-02/05	⊗06/05	**7703**	04/67-06/87	**3003**	06/87-05/93	**3403**	05/93-02/05
S76236	04/67-08/04	⊗ 04	**7704**	04/67-06/87	**3004**	06/87-02/89	**3404**	02/90-08/04
S76237	04/67-02/89	⊗06/89	**7704**	04/67-06/87	**3004**	06/87-02/89		
S76238	04/67-04/05	⊗04/05	**7705**	04/67-09/87	**3005**	09/87-06/89	**3405**	06/89-04/05
S76239	04/67-04/05	⊗04/05	**7705**	04/67-09/87	**3005**	09/87-06/89	**3405**	06/89-04/05
S76240	04/67-06/04	⊗07/04	**7706**	04/67-06/87	**3006**	06/87-01/94	**3406**	01/94-06/04
S76241	04/67-06/04	⊗07/04	**7706**	04/67-06/87	**3006**	06/87-01/94	**3406**	01/94-06/04
S76242	04/67-04/05	⊗04/05	**7707**	04/67-09/87	**3007**	09/87-08/93	**3407**	08/93-04/05
S76243	04/67-04/05	⊗04/05	**7707**	04/67-09/87	**3007**	09/87-08/93	**3407**	08/93-04/05
S76244	04/67-03/05	⊗10/05	**7708**	04/67-09/87	**3008**	09/87-06/93	**3408**	06/93-03/05
S76245	04/67-03/05	⊗10/05	**7708**	04/67-09/87	**3008**	09/87-06/93	**3408**	06/93-03/05
S76246	06/67-07/04	⊗ 04	**7709**	06/67-06/87	**3009**	06/87-06/94	**3409**	06/94-07/04
S76247	06/67-07/04	⊗ 04	**7709**	06/67-06/87	**3009**	06/87-06/94	**3409**	06/94-07/04
S76248	06/67-08/04	⊗ 04	**7710**	06/67-11/68	**7714**	01/72-08/87	**3014**	08/87-08/94
			3414	09/94-08/04				
S76249	06/67-05/04	⊗07/04	**7710**	06/67-10/87	**3010**	10/87-12/93	**3410**	12/93-05/04
S76250	06/67-04/05	⊗12/05	**7711**	06/67-05/87	**3011**	05/87-06/90	**3411**	06/90-04/05
S76251	06/67-04/05	⊗12/05	**7711**	06/67-05/87	**3011**	05/87-06/90	**3411**	06/90-04/05
S76252	06/67-08/05	⊗10/05	**7712**	06/67-08/87	**3012**	08/87-01/94	**3412**	01/94-08/05
S76253	06/67-08/05	⊗10/05	**7712**	06/67-08/87	**3012**	08/87-01/94	**3412**	01/94-08/05
S76254	06/67-08/04	⊗11/04	**7713**	06/67-06/87	**3013**	06/87-08/94	**3413**	08/94-08/04
S76255	06/67-08/04	⊗11/04	**7713**	06/67-06/87	**3013**	06/87-08/94	**3413**	08/94-08/04
S76256	06/67-04/71	⊗06/82	**7714**	06/67-04/71				
S76257	06/67-08/04	⊗ 04	**7714**	06/67-04/71	**7714**	01/72-08/87	**3014**	08/87-08/94
			3414	09/94-08/04				
S76258	07/67-02/05	⊗12/05	**7715**	07/67-12/87	**3015**	12/87-10/94	**3415**	10/94-02/05
S76259	07/67-02/05	⊗12/05	**7715**	07/67-12/87	**3015**	12/87-10/94	**3415**	10/94-02/05
S76260	07/67-08/05	⊗10/05	**7716**	07/67-06/87	**3016**	06/87-12/93	**3416**	12/93-08/05
S76261	07/67-08/05	⊗10/05	**7716**	07/67-06/87	**3016**	06/87-12/93	**3416**	12/93-08/05
S76262	07/67-	ⓟ	**7717**	07/67-08/87	**3017**	08/87-09/93	**3417**	09/93-
S76263	07/67-	ⓟ	**7717**	07/67-08/87	**3017**	08/87-09/93	**3417**	09/93-
S76264	07/67-08/04	⊗	**7718**	07/67-06/87	**3018**	06/87-09/94	**3418**	09/94-08/04
S76265	07/67-08/04	⊗	**7718**	07/67-06/87	**3018**	06/87-09/94	**3418**	09/94-08/04
S76266	07/67-05/04	⊗07/04	**7719**	07/67-05/87	**3019**	05/87-03/94	**3419**	03/94-05/04
S76267	07/67-05/04	⊗07/04	**7719**	07/67-05/87	**3019**	05/87-03/94	**3419**	03/94-05/04
S76268	07/67-05/04	⊗07/04	**7720**	07/67-07/87	**3020**	07/87-04/94	**3420**	04/94-05/04
S76269	07/67-05/04	⊗07/04	**7720**	07/67-07/87	**3020**	07/87-04/94	**3420**	04/94-05/04

Class 438 4-TC York
Driving Trailer Second Open
DTSO
S76270-S76332 (some 3-TC)

Diagram:	900A EE266	Lot Number:	30764
Body:	64' 7¾" × 9' 3"	Weight:	31t 19cwt
Seats:	64 second	Bogies:	B5 (SR)

Vehicle	Service	Fate	Unit	Dates	Unit	Dates	Unit	Dates	Reformed
S76270	08/67-09/92	⊗11/92	**304**	08/67-05/68	**401**	05/68-07/86	**8001**	07/86-09/92	
									⊂**4043**
S76271	08/66-05/88	⊗08/90	**402**	08/66-06/86	**8002**	06/86-12/86	**2802**	12/86-01/88	
			8102	01/88-05/88					⊂**4022**
S76272	08/66-05/88	⊗08/90	**402**	08/66-06/86	**8002**	06/86-12/86	**2802**	12/86-01/88	
			8102	01/88-05/88					⊂**4023**
S76273	08/66-10/88	⊗04/90	**403**	08/66-11/86	**8003**	11/86-06/87	**2805**	06/87-12/87	
			8105	12/87-04/88	**2805**	04/88-10/88			⊂**4021**
S76274	08/66-10/88	⊗04/90	**403**	08/66-11/86	**8003**	11/86-06/87	**2805**	06/87-12/87	
			8105	12/87-04/88	**2805**	04/88-10/88			⊂**4024**
S76275	08/66-05/04	ⓟ	**404**	08/66-10/86	**8004**	10/86-09/88	**2808**	09/88-01/89	
			8004	01/89-05/90	**1903**	06/91-10/91	**1904**	10/91-02/92	
			3169	07/92-02/95	**3582**	02/95-05/04			⊂**3929**
S76276	08/66-10/91	⊗11/91	**404**	08/66-10/86	**8004**	10/86-09/88	**2808**	09/88-01/89	
			8004	01/89-05/90	**1903**	06/91-10/91			⊂**4003**
S76277	08/66-05/85	➲977335	**405**	08/66-05/85					⊂**4005**
S76278	08/66-05/85	➲977336	**405**	08/66-05/85					⊂**4007**
S76279	08/66-06/91	⊗10/91	**406**	08/66-06/86	**8006**	06/86-05/90	**1903**	01/91-06/91	
									⊂**3926**
S76280	08/66-06/91	⊗10/91	**406**	08/66-06/86	**8006**	06/86-05/90	**1903**	01/91-06/91	
									⊂**4014**
S76281	09/66-07/89	➲977687	**407**	09/66-12/86	**8007**	12/86-07/89			⊂**4042**
S76282	09/66-07/89	➲977684	**407**	09/66-12/86	**8007**	12/86-07/89			⊂**4374**
S76283	09/66-08/88	⊗04/90	**408**	08/66-10/86	**8008**	10/86-12/86	**2801**	12/86-12/87	
			8101	12/87-08/88					⊂**3932**
S76284	09/66-01/90	⊗04/90	**408**	08/66-10/86	**8008**	10/86-12/86	**2801**	12/86-12/87	
			8101	12/87-08/88					⊂**4008**
S76285	09/66-04/89	⊗06/90	**409**	09/66-12/86	**2803**	12/86-12/87	**8103**	12/87-05/88	
			2804	05/88-04/89					⊂**4380**
S76286	09/66-04/89	⊗06/90	**409**	09/66-12/86	**2803**	12/86-12/87	**8103**	12/87-05/88	
			2804	05/88-04/89					⊂**4386**
S76287	09/66-08/96	⊗04/99	**410**	09/66-08/86	**8010**	08/86-04/90	**8110**	06/90-03/91	
			410	09/91-08/96					⊂**4379**
S76288	09/66-08/96	⊗03/03	**410**	09/66-08/86	**8010**	08/86-04/90	**8110**	06/90-03/91	
			410	09/91-08/96					⊂**4391**
S76289	09/66-05/88	⊗07/90	**411**	09/66-10/86	**8011**	10/86-02/87	**2804**	02/87-12/87	
			8104	12/87-05/88					⊂**4029**
S76290	09/66-05/88	⊗07/90	**411**	09/66-10/86	**8011**	10/86-02/87	**2804**	02/87-12/87	
			8104	12/87-05/88					⊂**4394**
S76291	09/66-05/91	⊗03/92	**412**	09/66-06/86	**8012**	06/86-05/91			⊂**3931**
S76292	09/66-05/91	⊗03/92	**412**	09/66-06/86	**8012**	06/86-05/91			⊂**3946**
S76293	10/66-10/88	⊗08/90	**413**	10/66-05/86	**8013**	05/86-06/87	**2806**	06/87-12/87	
			8106	12/87-05/88	**2806**	05/88-09/88	**8106**	09/88-10/88	
									⊂**3942**
S76294	10/66-10/88	⊗08/90	**413**	10/66-05/86	**8013**	05/86-06/87	**2806**	06/87-12/87	
			8106	12/87-05/88	**2806**	05/88-09/88	**8106**	09/88-10/88	
									⊂**3999**
S76295	10/66-05/91	➲977543	**414**	10/66-09/86	**8014**	09/86-05/91			⊂**3927**
S76296	10/66-10/91	➲977544	**414**	10/66-09/86	**8014**	09/86-05/91			⊂**3945**
S76297	11/66-05/91	ⓟ	**415**	11/66-10/86	**8015**	10/86-05/91			⊂**3938**
S76298	11/66-05/91	ⓟ	**415**	11/66-10/86	**8015**	10/86-05/91			⊂**4004**
S76299	10/66-10/88	⊗07/90	**416**	10/66-06/86	**8016**	06/86-10/88			⊂**3935**
S76300	10/66-10/88	⊗07/90	**416**	10/66-06/86	**8016**	06/86-10/88			⊂**3944**
S76301	11/66-08/99	ⓟ	**417**	11/66-10/86	**8017**	10/86-09/91	**417**	09/91-01/98	
									⊂**4375**
S76302	11/66-08/99	ⓟ	**417**	11/66-10/86	**8017**	10/86-09/91	**417**	09/91-01/98	
									⊂**4382**
S76303	11/66-10/91	⊗11/91	**418**	11/66-10/86	**8018**	10/86-05/90	**1902**	09/90-10/91	
									⊂**4017**
S76304	11/66-12/91	⊗05/92	**418**	11/66-10/86	**8018**	10/86-05/90			⊂**4384**
S76305	11/66-08/88	⊗04/90	**419**	11/66-08/86	**8019**	08/86-08/88			⊂**4016**
S76306	11/66-08/88	⊗04/90	**419**	11/66-08/86	**8019**	08/86-08/88			⊂**4383**
S76307	11/66-05/89	⊗07/90	**420**	11/66-09/86	**8020**	09/86-05/89			⊂**4041**
S76308	11/66-05/89	⊗07/90	**420**	11/66-09/86	**8020**	09/86-05/89			⊂**4390**
S76309	12/66-02/89	⊗04/90	**421**	12/66-10/86	**8021**	10/86-02/89			⊂**4006**
S76310	12/66-02/89	⊗04/90	**421**	12/66-10/86	**8021**	10/86-02/89			⊂**4027**
S76311	12/66-08/88	⊗03/90	**422**	12/66-05/86	**8022**	05/86-08/88			⊂**4001**
S76312	12/66-08/88	⊗03/90	**422**	12/66-05/86	**8022**	05/86-08/88			⊂**4015**
S76313	02/67-12/91	⊗05/92	**423**	02/67-06/86	**8023**	06/86-04/90			⊂**3941**
S76314	02/67-10/91	⊗11/91	**423**	02/67-06/86	**8023**	06/86-04/90	**1902**	09/90-10/91	
									⊂**3943**
S76315	03/67-05/88	⊗04/90	**424**	03/67-05/86	**8024**	05/86-05/88			⊂**4000**
S76316	03/67-05/88	⊗04/90	**424**	03/67-05/86	**8024**	05/86-05/88			⊂**4028**
S76317	01/67-10/88	⊗01/90	**425**	01/67-05/86	**8025**	05/86-10/88			⊂**3928**
S76318	01/67-10/88	⊗01/90	**425**	01/67-05/86	**8025**	05/86-10/88			⊂**4026**
S76319	02/67-05/89	⊗03/90	**426**	02/67-08/86	**8026**	08/86-05/89			⊂**3939**
S76320	02/67-05/89	⊗03/90	**426**	02/67-08/86	**8026**	08/86-05/89			⊂**3998**
S76321	02/67-02/92	⊗05/92	**427**	02/67-06/86	**8027**	06/86-04/90	**1905**	05/90-04/91	
			1904	07/91-02/92					⊂**3930**
S76322	02/67-02/92	ⓟ	**427**	02/67-06/86	**8027**	06/86-04/90	**1906**	05/90-01/91	
			1901	03/91-02/92					⊂**3936**
S76323	03/67-10/91	⊗12/91	**428**	03/67-06/86	**8028**	06/86-04/90	**1904**	04/90-04/91	
			1905	04/91-06/91	**1904**	07/91-10/91			⊂**3940**
S76324	03/67-02/92	⊗	**428**	03/67-06/86	**8028**	06/86-04/90	**1903**	04/90-09/90	
			1901	03/91-02/92					⊂**4009**
S76325	05/67-07/88	⊗03/90	**301**	05/67-06/74	**429**	06/74-10/86	**8029**	10/86-07/88	
									⊂**3933**
S76326	05/67-07/88	⊗03/90	**301**	05/67-06/74	**429**	06/74-10/86	**8029**	10/86-07/88	
									⊂**3934**
S76327	07/67-08/88	ⓟ⊗03/01	**302**	07/67-07/74	**430**	07/74-09/86	**8030**	09/86-08/88	
									⊂**4018**
S76328	07/67-08/88	⊗05/92	**302**	07/67-07/74	**430**	07/74-09/86	**8030**	09/86-08/88	
									⊂**4044**
S76329	07/67-08/89	⊗07/90	**303**	08/67-06/74	**431**	06/74-10/86	**8031**	10/86-01/89	
			2809	01/89-05/89	**8031**	05/89-08/89			⊂**4373**
S76330	07/67-08/89	⊗07/90	**303**	08/67-06/74	**431**	06/74-10/86	**8031**	10/86-01/89	
			2809	01/89-05/89	**8031**	05/89-08/89			⊂**4045**
S76331	10/67-07/90	⊗08/90	**401**	10/67-05/68	**304**	05/68-02/75			⊂**4388**
S76332	10/67-09/92	⊗11/92	**401**	10/67-07/86	**8001**	07/86-09/92			⊂**3937**

Class 423 4-VEP York

Driving Trailer Composite (Semi-open) Lavatory
DTCsoL
S76333-S76402

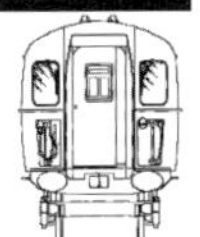

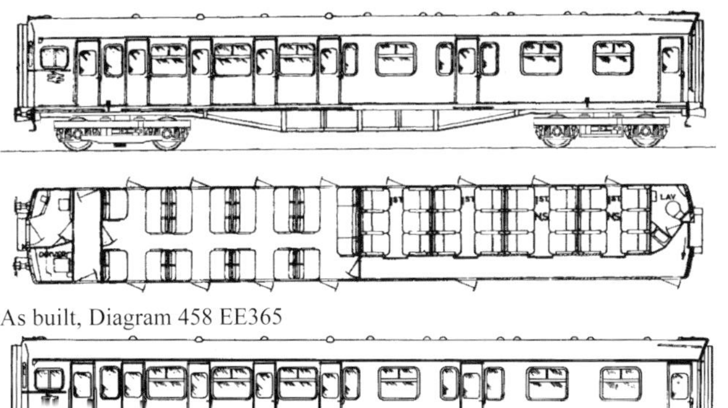

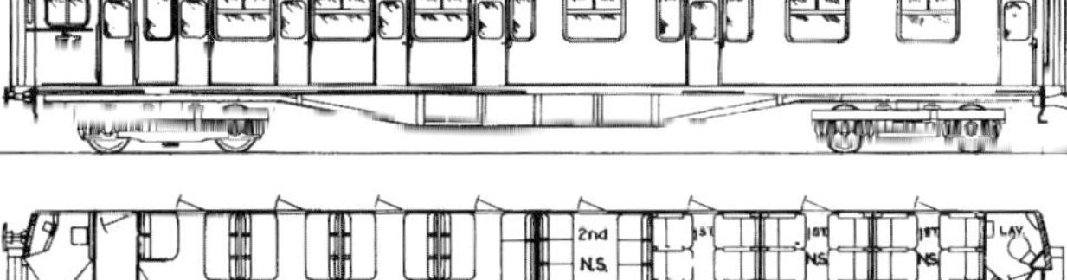

As built, Diagram 458 EE365

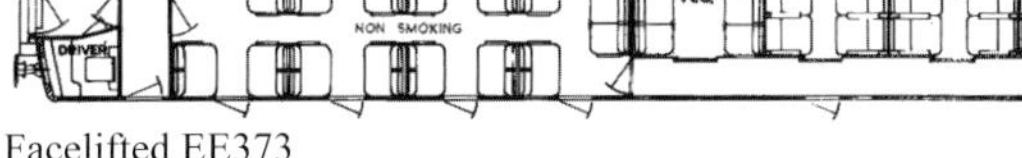

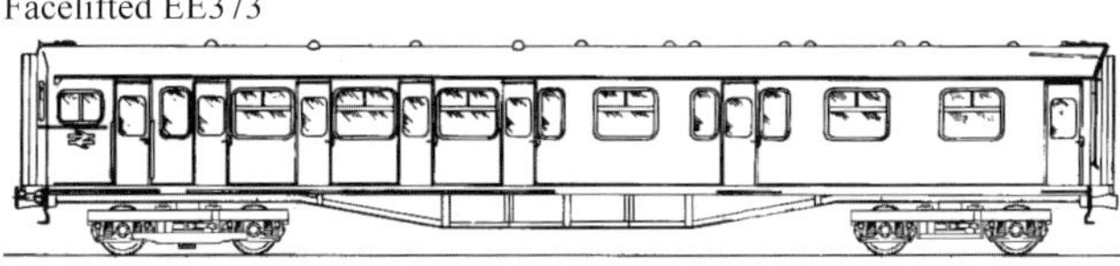

Facelifted EE373

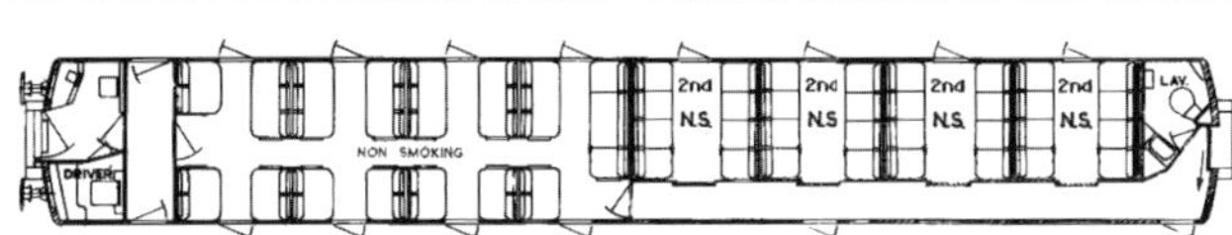

Modified as Class 423/2 4-VOP Metro units 3901-3919, Diagram EE281

Diagram:	458 EE365 EE373 EE281	Lot Number:	30771
Body:	64' 9⅝" × 9' 3"	Weight:	33t 17cwt
Seats:	24 first 38 second 1 toilet later 18 first 46 second 1 toilet VOP 70 second 1 toilet	Bogies:	B5 (SR)

S76333	10/67-07/04	⊗08/04	**7721**	10/67-07/87	**3021**	07/87-06/88	**3429**	06/88-07/04
S76334	10/67-07/04	⊗08/04	**7721**	10/67-07/87	**3021**	07/87-06/88	**3429**	06/88-07/04
S76335	10/67-12/05	⊗12/05	**7722**	10/67-07/87	**3022**	07/87-11/88	**3449**	11/88-12/05
S76336	10/67-12/05	⊗12/05	**7722**	10/67-07/87	**3022**	07/87-11/88	**3449**	11/88-12/05
S76337	10/67-07/05	⊗10/05	**7723**	10/67-06/87	**3023**	06/87-05/88	**3425**	05/88-07/89
			3491	06/91-07/05				
S76338	10/67-07/04	⊗08/04	**7723**	10/67-06/87	**3023**	06/87-05/88	**3425**	05/88-07/04
S76339	11/67-02/05	⊗10/05	**7724**	11/67-06/84	**7724**	10/84-12/87	**3024**	12/87-02/88
			3473	07/92-02/05				
S76340	11/67-11/04	⊗10/04	**7724**	11/67-12/87	**3024**	12/87-11/88	**3452**	11/88-11/04
S76341	11/67-10/04	⊗10/04	**7725**	11/67-06/87	**3025**	06/87-07/88	**3435**	07/88-09/03
			3814	09/03-10/04				
S76342	11/67-11/04	⊗03/05	**7725**	11/67-06/87	**3025**	06/87-07/88	**3435**	07/88-09/03
			3813	09/03-11/04				
S76343	11/67-04/05	⊗04/05	**7726**	11/67-05/87	**3026**	05/87-11/94	**3569**	11/94-04/05
S76344	11/67-04/05	⊗04/05	**7726**	11/67-05/87	**3026**	05/87-11/94	**3569**	11/94-04/05
S76345	12/67-12/04	⊗03/05	**7727**	12/67-06/87	**3027**	06/87-08/88	**3437**	08/88-12/04
S76346	12/67-12/04	⊗03/05	**7727**	12/67-06/87	**3027**	06/87-08/88	**3437**	08/88-12/04
S76347	12/67-07/04	⊗08/04	**7728**	12/67-06/87	**3028**	06/87-06/88	**3430**	06/88-07/04
S76348	12/67-07/04	⊗08/04	**7728**	12/67-06/87	**3028**	06/87-06/88	**3430**	06/88-07/04
S76349	12/67-11/04	⊗06/05	**7729**	12/67-06/87	**3029**	06/87-07/88	**3436**	07/88-11/04
S76350	12/67-11/04	Ⓟ	**7729**	12/67-06/87	**3029**	06/87-07/88	**3436**	07/88-11/04
S76351	12/67-05/04	⊗06/04	**7730**	12/67-05/87	**3030**	05/87-05/94	**3558**	05/94-05/04
S76352	12/67-05/04	⊗06/04	**7730**	12/67-05/87	**3030**	05/87-05/94	**3558**	05/94-05/04
S76353	12/67-05/05	⊗05/05	**7731**	12/67-05/87	**3031**	05/87-05/88	**3424**	05/88-05/05
S76354	12/67-05/05	⊗05/05	**7731**	12/67-05/87	**3031**	05/87-05/88	**3424**	05/88-05/05
S76355	12/67-08/04	⊗ 04	**7732**	12/67-05/87	**3032**	05/87-01/95	**3578**	01/95-08/04
S76356	12/67-08/04	⊗ 04	**7732**	12/67-05/87	**3032**	05/87-01/95	**3578**	01/95-08/04
S76357	12/67-04/89	⊗06/89	**7733**	12/67-06/87	**3033**	06/87-04/89		
S76358	12/67-07/04	⊗08/04	**7733**	12/67-06/87	**3033**	06/87-04/89	**3425**	07/89-07/04
S76359	01/68-08/04	⊗ 04	**7734**	01/68-06/87	**3034**	06/87-02/95	**3580**	02/95-08/02
			3520	08/02-10/02	**3580**	04/03-08/04		
S76360	01/68-08/04	⊗ 04	**7734**	01/68-06/87	**3034**	06/87-02/95	**3580**	02/95-08/02
			3428	08/02-10/02	**3580**	04/03-08/04		
S76361	01/68-04/05	⊗06/05	**7735**	01/68-06/87	**3035**	06/87-01/95	**3576**	01/95-04/05
S76362	01/68-04/05	⊗06/05	**7735**	01/68-06/87	**3035**	06/87-01/95	**3576**	01/95-04/05
S76363	01/68-07/05	⊗08/05	**7736**	01/68-04/80	**7840**	04/80-07/87	**3140**	07/87-07/90
			3518	07/90-09/03	**3842**	09/03-07/05		
S76364	01/68-04/05	⊗10/05	**7736**	01/68-04/80	**7911**	10/80-05/84	**7798**	05/84-05/87
			3098	05/87-09/92	**3533**	09/92-08/99	**3902**	08/99-04/05
S76365	02/68-03/05	⊗07/05	**7737**	02/68-06/87	**3037**	06/87-02/95	**3581**	02/95-03/05
S76366	02/68-03/05	⊗07/05	**7737**	02/68-06/87	**3037**	06/87-02/95	**3581**	02/95-03/05
S76367	02/68-12/04	⊗12/04	**7738**	02/68-08/87	**3038**	08/87-10/88	**3444**	10/88-10/95
			3804	10/95-12/04				
S76368	02/68-12/04	⊗12/04	**7738**	02/68-08/87	**3038**	08/87-10/88	**3444**	10/88-10/95
			3804	10/95-12/04				
S76369	02/68-05/04	⊗07/04	**7710**	11/68-10/87	**3010**	10/87-12/93	**3410**	12/93-05/04
S76370	02/68-04/05	⊗05/05	**7768**	01/75-09/87	**3068**	09/87-07/91	**3524**	07/91-04/05
S76371	02/68-12/04	⊗02/05	**7740**	02/68-02/88	**3040**	02/88-04/88	**3422**	04/88-12/04
S76372	02/68-12/04	⊗02/05	**7740**	02/68-02/88	**3040**	02/88-04/88	**3422**	04/88-12/04
S76373	03/68-05/04	⊗06/04	**8001**	04/68-01/75	**7741**	02/75-06/87	**3041**	06/87-06/88
			3427	06/88-05/04				
S76374	03/68-05/04	⊗06/04	**8001**	04/68-01/75	**7741**	02/75-06/87	**3041**	06/87-06/88
			3427	06/88-05/04				
S76375	03/68-07/05	⊗10/05	**8001**	04/68-01/75	**7742**	02/75-02/88	**3042**	02/88-11/88
			3448	11/88-07/05				
S76376	03/68-07/05	⊗10/05	**8001**	04/68-01/75	**7742**	02/75-02/88	**3042**	02/88-11/88
			3448	11/88-07/05				
S76377	04/68-01/90	⊗03/90	**7743**	04/68-06/87	**3043**	06/87-09/88	**3441**	09/88-01/90
S76378	04/68-08/04	⊗ 04	**7743**	04/68-06/87	**3043**	06/87-09/88	**3441**	09/88-01/90
			3404	02/90-08/04				
S76379	04/68-06/05	⊗06/05	**7744**	04/68-08/87	**3044**	08/87-11/88	**3447**	11/88-06/05
S76380	04/68-06/05	⊗06/05	**7744**	04/68-08/87	**3044**	08/87-11/88	**3447**	11/88-06/05
S76381	04/68-10/05	⊗10/05	**7745**	04/68-03/88	**3045**	03/88-12/88	**3453**	12/88-10/05
S76382	04/68-10/05	⊗09/05	**7745**	04/68-03/88	**3045**	03/88-12/88	**3453**	12/88-10/05
S76383	04/68-06/08	⊗06/08	**7746**	04/68-06/87	**3046**	06/87-02/93	**3536**	02/93-06/08
S76384	04/68-06/08	⊗06/08	**7746**	04/68-06/87	**3046**	06/87-02/93	**3536**	02/93-06/08
S76385	04/68-05/04	⊗06/04	**7747**	04/68-06/87	**3047**	06/87-05/88	**3426**	05/88-05/04
S76386	04/68-05/04	⊗06/04	**7747**	04/68-06/87	**3047**	06/87-05/88	**3426**	05/88-05/04
S76387	04/68-12/04	⊗01/05	**7748**	04/68-03/88	**3048**	03/88-12/88	**3455**	12/88-12/04
S76388	04/68-12/04	⊗01/05	**7748**	04/68-03/88	**3048**	03/88-12/88	**3455**	12/88-12/04
S76389	05/68-09/05	⊗09/05	**7749**	05/68-10/87	**3049**	10/87-12/88	**3454**	12/88-09/05
S76390	05/68-09/05	⊗09/05	**7749**	05/68-10/87	**3049**	10/87-12/88	**3454**	12/88-09/05
S76391	05/68-10/05	⊗10/05	**7750**	05/68-10/87	**3050**	10/87-01/89	**3457**	01/89-10/05
S76392	05/68-10/05	⊗10/05	**7750**	05/68-10/87	**3050**	10/87-01/89	**3457**	01/89-10/05
S76393	05/68-04/05	⊗04/05	**7751**	05/68-12/87	**3051**	12/87-01/89	**3458**	01/89-04/05
S76394	05/68-04/05	⊗04/05	**7751**	05/68-12/87	**3051**	12/87-01/89	**3458**	01/89-04/05
S76395	06/68-04/05	⊗04/05	**7752**	06/68-11/87	**3052**	11/87-01/89	**3459**	01/89-04/05
S76396	06/68-04/05	⊗04/05	**7752**	06/68-11/87	**3052**	11/87-01/89	**3459**	01/89-04/05
S76397	06/68-04/05	Ⓟ	**7753**	06/68-12/87	**3053**	12/87-02/89	**3463**	02/89-08/99
			3905	08/99-04/05				
S76398	06/68-04/05	Ⓟ	**7753**	06/68-12/87	**3053**	12/87-02/89	**3463**	02/89-08/99
			3905	08/99-04/05				
S76399	07/68-07/04	⊗11/04	**7754**	07/68-06/87	**3054**	06/87-07/88	**3432**	07/88-07/04
S76400	07/68-07/04	⊗11/04	**7754**	07/68-06/87	**3054**	06/87-07/88	**3432**	07/88-07/04
S76401	07/68-08/05	⊗10/05	**7755**	07/68-03/88	**3055**	03/88-09/88	**3439**	09/88-05/99
			3901	05/99-08/05				
S76402	07/68-08/05	⊗10/05	**7755**	07/68-03/88	**3055**	03/88-09/88	**3439**	09/88-05/99
			3901	05/99-08/05				

Class 311 Cravens

Driving Trailer Second Open
DTSO
SC76403-SC76421

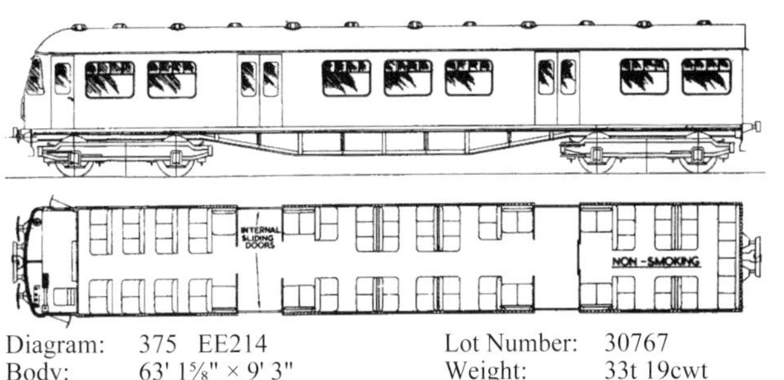

Diagram:	375 EE214	Lot Number:	30767
Body:	63' 1⅝" × 9' 3"	Weight:	33t 19cwt
Seats:	83 second	Bogies:	Gresley

Originally incorrectly allocated numbers 76130-76148. These numbers were already carried by Class 310 units. 092-095 & 098 ran in service carrying these numbers until 1968.

SC76403	12/66-09/89	⊗07/90	**092**	12/66-*05/79*	**311092**	*05/79*-09/89
SC76404	01/67-12/87	⊗02/88	**093**	01/67-*03/80*	**311093**	*03/80*-12/87
SC76405	03/67-01/89	⊗02/90	**094**	03/67-*03/80*	**311094**	*03/80*-01/89
SC76406	02/67-01/89	⊗07/90	**095**	02/67-*11/79*	**311095**	*11/79*-01/89
SC76407	04/67-12/87	⊗04/89	**096**	04/67-08/80	**311096**	08/80-12/87
SC76408	04/67-09/89	⊗04/90	**097**	04/67-07/80	**311097**	07/80-09/89
SC76409	02/67-10/90	⊗12/90	**098**	02/67-*08/79*	**311098**	*08/79*-10/90
SC76410	03/67-10/90	⊗12/90	**099**	03/67-06/80	**311099**	06/80-10/90
SC76411	03/67-10/86	⊗11/87	**100**	03/67-*05/79*	**311100**	*05/79*-10/86
SC76412	05/67-12/87	⊗04/90	**101**	05/67-*05/79*	**311101**	*05/79*-12/87

SC76413	04/67-10/90	⊗11/90	**102**	04/67-03/80	**311102**	03/80-10/90		
SC76414	05/67-10/90	Ⓟ➲977844	**103**	05/67-05/79	**311103**	05/79-10/90		
SC76415	05/67-10/90	➲977847	**104**	05/67-11/79	**311104**	11/79-10/90		
SC76416	05/67-09/90	⊗01/91	**105**	05/67-08/79	**311105**	08/79-09/90		
SC76417	05/67-10/86	⊗06/87	**106**	05/67-03/80	**311106**	03/80-10/86		
SC76418	05/67-10/90	⊗08/90	**107**	05/67-06/80	**311107**	06/80-07/90	**311110**	07/90-10/90
SC76419	06/67-10/90	⊗01/91	**108**	06/67-03/80	**311108**	03/80-10/90		
SC76420	06/67-09/90	⊗12/90	**109**	06/67-08/79	**311109**	08/79-08/90	**303029**	08/90-09/90
SC76421	07/67-10/90	⊗11/90	**110**	07/67- 80	**311110**	80-07/90	**311107**	07/90-10/90

Class 311 Cravens

Battery Driving Trailer Second Open

BDTSO

SC76422-SC76440

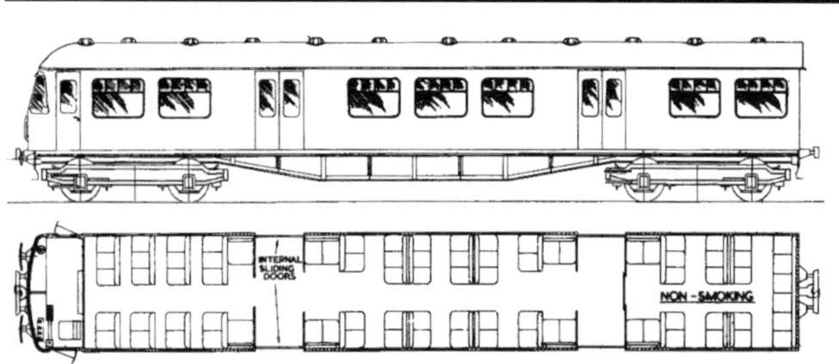

Diagram:	375 EF212	Lot Number:	30769
Body:	63' 1⅝" × 9' 3"	Weight:	36t 17cwt
Seats:	83 second	Bogies:	Gresley

Originally incorrectly allocated numbers 76149-76167. These numbers were already carried by Class 310 units. 092-095 & 098 ran in service carrying these numbers until 1968.

SC76422	12/66-09/89	⊗06/90	**092**	12/66-05/79	**311092**	05/79-09/89
SC76423	01/67-12/87	⊗02/88	**093**	01/67-03/80	**311093**	03/80-12/87
SC76424	03/67-01/89	⊗04/90	**094**	03/67-03/80	**311094**	03/80-01/89
SC76425	02/67-01/89	⊗06/90	**095**	02/67-11/79	**311095**	11/79-01/89
SC76426	04/67-12/87	⊗04/89	**096**	04/67-08/80	**311096**	08/80-12/87
SC76427	04/67-09/89	⊗05/90	**097**	04/67-07/80	**311097**	07/80-09/89
SC76428	02/67-10/90	⊗12/90	**098**	02/67-08/79	**311098**	08/79-10/90
SC76429	03/67-10/90	⊗11/90	**099**	03/67-06/80	**311099**	06/80-10/90
SC76430	03/67-10/86	⊗11/87	**100**	03/67-05/79	**311100**	05/79-10/86
SC76431	05/67-12/87	⊗02/90	**101**	05/67-05/79	**311101**	05/79-12/87
SC76432	04/67-10/90	⊗11/90	**102**	04/67-03/80	**311102**	03/80-10/90
SC76433	05/67-10/90	Ⓟ➲977846	**103**	05/67-05/79	**311103**	05/79-10/90
SC76434	05/67-10/90	➲977849	**104**	05/67-11/79	**311104**	11/79-10/90
SC76435	05/67-09/90	⊗01/91	**105**	05/67-08/79	**311105**	08/79-09/90
SC76436	05/67-10/86	⊗06/87	**106**	05/67-03/80	**311106**	03/80-10/86
SC76437	05/67-10/90	⊗11/90	**107**	05/67-06/80	**311107**	06/80-10/90
SC76438	06/67-10/90	⊗01/91	**108**	06/67-03/80	**311108**	03/80-10/90
SC76439	06/67-10/90	⊗01/91	**109**	06/67-08/79	**311109**	08/79-10/90
SC76440	07/67-10/90	⊗08/90	**110**	07/67- 80	**311110**	80-10/90

Class 423 4-VEP York

Driving Trailer Composite (Semi-open) Lavatory

DTCsoL

S76441-S76540

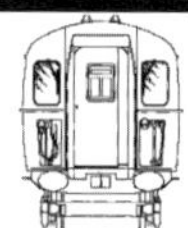

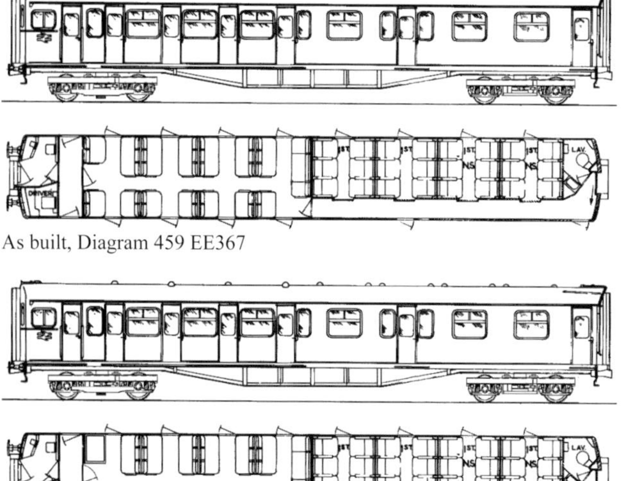

As built, Diagram 459 EE367

Rebuilt as Class 427 4-VEG for Gatwick services, Diagram 841 EE366

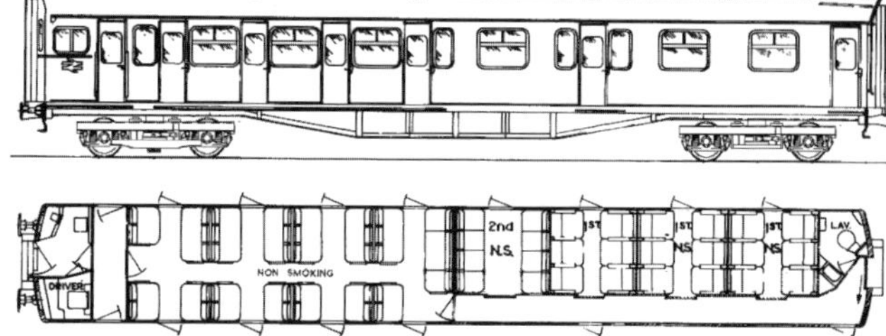

Facelifted EE373

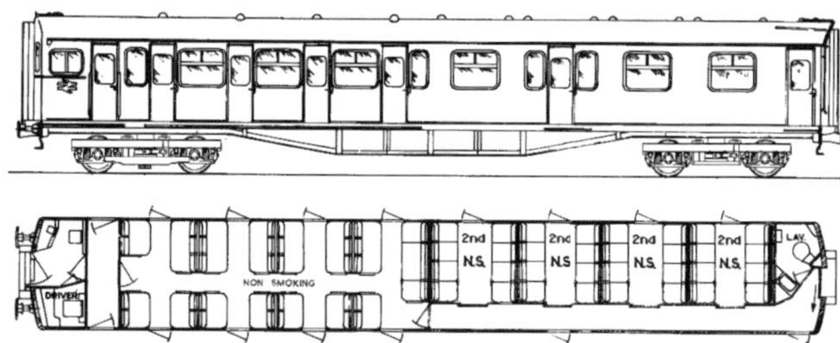

Modified as Class 423/2 4-VOP Metro units 3901-3919, Diagram EE281

Diagram:	459 EE367 841 EE366 EE373 EE281	Lot Number:	30792
Body:	64' 9⅝" × 9' 3"	Weight:	34t 5cwt
Seats:	24 first 38 second 1 toilet VEG 24 first 34 second 1 toilet later 18 first 46 second 1 toilet VOP 70 second 1 toilet	Bogies:	B5 (SR)

S76441	01/69-06/05	⊗06/05	**7756**	01/69-12/87	**3056**	12/87-02/89	**3464**	02/89-10/99
			3908	10/99-06/05				
S76442	01/69-06/05	⊗06/05	**7756**	01/69-12/87	**3056**	12/87-02/89	**3464**	02/89-10/99
			3908	10/99-06/05				
S76443	01/69-10/04	⊗11/04	**7757**	01/69-06/87	**3057**	06/87-07/88	**3433**	07/88-10/04
S76444	01/69-10/04	⊗11/04	**7757**	01/69-06/87	**3057**	06/87-07/88	**3433**	07/88-10/04
S76445	01/69-02/05	⊗08/05	**7758**	01/69-07/88	**3058**	07/88-03/89	**3467**	03/89-02/05
S76446	01/69-02/05	⊗08/05	**7758**	01/69-07/88	**3058**	07/88-03/89	**3467**	03/89-02/05
S76447	02/69-04/05	⊗04/05	**7759**	02/69-02/88	**3059**	02/88-03/89	**3468**	03/89-04/05
S76448	02/69-04/05	⊗04/05	**7759**	02/69-02/88	**3059**	02/88-03/89	**3468**	03/89-04/05
S76449	02/69-08/05	⊗10/05	**7760**	02/69-09/87	**3060**	09/87-10/88	**3445**	10/88-08/05
S76450	02/69-08/05	⊗10/05	**7760**	02/69-09/87	**3060**	09/87-10/88	**3445**	10/88-08/05
S76451	02/69-08/05	⊗08/05	**7761**	02/69-06/87	**3061**	06/87-04/88	**3423**	04/88-08/05
S76452	02/69-08/05	⊗08/05	**7761**	02/69-06/87	**3061**	06/87-04/88	**3423**	04/88-08/05
S76453	02/69-07/04	⊗ 04	**7762**	02/69-02/88	**3062**	02/88-06/88	**3428**	06/88-07/04
S76454	02/69-08/02	⊗11/03	**7762**	02/69-02/88	**3062**	02/88-06/88	**3428**	06/88-08/02
S76455	02/69-04/05	⊗04/05	**7763**	02/69-06/87	**3063**	06/87-01/89	**3456**	01/89-04/05
S76456	02/69-06/02	⊗11/03	**7763**	02/69-06/87	**3063**	06/87-01/89	**3456**	01/89-06/02
S76457	02/69-07/04	⊗08/04	**7764**	02/69-06/87	**3064**	06/87-06/88	**3431**	06/88-07/04
S76458	02/69-07/04	⊗08/04	**7764**	02/69-06/87	**3064**	06/87-06/88	**3431**	06/88-07/04
S76459	03/69-10/05	⊗12/05	**7765**	03/69-03/88	**3065**	03/88-11/88	**3450**	11/88-10/05
S76460	03/69-10/05	⊗12/05	**7765**	03/69-03/88	**3065**	03/88-11/88	**3450**	11/88-10/05
S76461	03/69-07/05	⊗07/05	**7766**	03/69-08/87	**3066**	08/87-07/88	**3434**	07/88-07/05
S76462	03/69-07/05	⊗07/05	**7766**	03/69-08/87	**3066**	08/87-07/88	**3434**	07/88-07/05
S76463	03/69-04/05	⊗04/05	**7767**	03/69-08/87	**3067**	08/87-07/88	**3466**	03/89-04/05
S76464	03/69-04/05	⊗04/05	**7767**	03/69-08/87	**3067**	08/87-07/88	**3466**	03/89-04/05
S76465	03/69-12/04	⊗12/04	**7768**	03/69-03/74	**7852**	03/74-05/87	**3152**	05/87-02/94
			3551	02/94-12/04				
S76466	03/69-04/05	⊗05/05	**7768**	03/69-03/74	**7768**	01/75-09/87	**3068**	09/87-07/91
			3524	07/91-04/05				
S76467	03/69-11/05	⊗01/06	**7769**	03/69-06/87	**3069**	06/87-02/92	**3530**	02/92-11/05
S76468	03/69-11/05	⊗01/06	**7769**	03/69-06/87	**3069**	06/87-02/92	**3530**	02/92-11/05
S76469	04/69-10/05	⊗10/05	**7770**	04/69-08/87	**3070**	08/87-01/90	**3500**	01/90-10/05
S76470	04/69-07/04	⊗08/05	**7770**	04/69-08/87	**3070**	08/87-01/90	**3500**	01/90-07/04
S76471	04/69-11/05	⊗12/05	**7771**	04/69-06/87	**3071**	06/87-02/90	**3505**	02/90-11/05
S76472	04/69-11/05	⊗12/05	**7771**	04/69-06/87	**3071**	06/87-02/90	**3505**	02/90-11/05
S76473	04/69-07/04	⊗08/04	**7772**	04/69-10/87	**3072**	10/87-07/89	**3480**	07/89-07/04
S76474	04/69-07/04	⊗08/04	**7772**	04/69-10/87	**3072**	10/87-07/89	**3480**	07/89-07/04
S76475	04/69-05/05	⊗05/05	**7773**	04/69-10/87	**3073**	10/87-08/89	**3484**	08/89-05/05
S76476	04/69-05/05	⊗05/05	**7773**	04/69-10/87	**3073**	10/87-08/89	**3484**	08/89-05/05
S76477	05/69-11/05	⊗01/06	**7774**	05/69-10/87	**3074**	10/87-09/89	**3486**	09/89-11/05
S76478	05/69-11/05	⊗01/06	**7774**	05/69-10/87	**3074**	10/87-09/89	**3486**	09/89-11/05
S76479	05/69-04/05	⊗04/05	**7775**	05/69-08/87	**3075**	08/87-09/93	**3542**	09/93-04/05
S76480	05/69-04/05	⊗04/05	**7775**	05/69-08/87	**3075**	08/87-09/93	**3542**	09/93-04/05
S76481	05/69-07/05	⊗10/05	**7776**	05/69-06/87	**3076**	06/87-10/89	**3491**	10/89-07/05
S76482	05/69-04/91	⊗10/91	**7776**	05/69-06/87	**3076**	06/87-10/89	**3491**	10/89-04/91
S76483	05/69-09/05	⊗12/05	**7777**	05/69-06/87	**3077**	06/87-08/90	**3521**	08/90-09/05
S76484	05/69-09/05	⊗12/05	**7777**	05/69-06/87	**3077**	06/87-08/90	**3521**	08/90-09/05
S76485	05/69-05/04	⊗06/04	**7778**	05/69-06/87	**3078**	06/87-06/94	**3559**	06/94-05/04
S76486	05/69-05/04	⊗06/04	**7778**	05/69-06/87	**3078**	06/87-06/94	**3559**	06/94-05/04
S76487	05/69-11/04	⊗10/04	**7779**	05/69-08/87	**3079**	08/87-11/88	**3451**	11/88-11/04
S76488	05/69-11/04	⊗10/04	**7779**	05/69-08/87	**3079**	08/87-11/88	**3451**	11/88-11/04

Vehicle	In service	Withdrawn	Unit	Dates	Unit	Dates	Unit	Dates
S76489	06/69-04/05	⊗06/05	**7780**	06/69-06/87	**3080**	06/87-02/94	**3550**	02/94-09/99
			3906	09/99-09/03	**3843**	09/03-04/05		
S76490	06/69-07/05	⊗10/05	**7780**	06/69-06/87	**3080**	06/87-02/94	**3550**	02/94-09/99
			3906	09/99-09/03	**3844**	09/03-07/05		
S76491	06/69-07/05	⊗07/05	**7781**	06/69-07/87	**3081**	07/87-10/88	**3442**	10/88-11/99
			3912	11/99-07/05				
S76492	06/69-07/05	⊗07/05	**7781**	06/69-07/87	**3081**	07/87-10/88	**3442**	10/88-11/99
			3912	11/99-07/05				
S76493	06/69-02/05	⊗02/05	**7782**	06/69-05/87	**3082**	05/87-09/88	**3443**	09/88-09/95
			3803	09/95-02/05				
S76494	06/69-02/05	⊗02/05	**7782**	06/69-05/87	**3082**	05/87-09/88	**3443**	09/88-09/95
			3803	09/95-02/05				
S76495	07/69-04/05	⊗08/05	**7783**	07/69-07/87	**3083**	07/87-04/89	**3470**	04/89-04/05
S76496	07/69-04/05	⊗08/05	**7783**	07/69-07/87	**3083**	07/87-04/89	**3470**	04/89-04/05
S76497	07/69-10/05	⊗12/05	**7784**	07/69-05/87	**3084**	05/87-04/89	**3471**	04/89-10/05
S76498	07/69-10/05	⊗12/05	**7784**	07/69-05/87	**3084**	05/87-04/89	**3471**	04/89-10/05
S76499	07/69-06/05	⊗06/05	**7785**	07/69-05/87	**3085**	05/87-05/89	**3472**	05/89-06/05
S76500	07/69-06/05	⊗06/05	**7785**	07/69-05/87	**3085**	05/87-05/89	**3472**	05/89-06/05
S76501	07/69-12/91	⊗08/96	**7786**	07/69-05/87	**3086**	05/87-05/89	**3473**	05/89-12/91
S76502	07/69-02/05	⊗10/05	**7786**	07/69-05/87	**3086**	05/87-05/89	**3473**	05/89-12/91
			3473	07/92-02/05				
S76503	07/69-09/05	⊗12/05	**7787**	07/69-05/87	**3087**	05/87-05/89	**3474**	05/89-09/05
S76504	07/69-09/05	⊗12/05	**7787**	07/69-05/87	**3087**	05/87-05/89	**3474**	05/89-09/05
S76505	08/69-03/05	⊗06/05	**7788**	08/69-05/78	**7901**	05/78-05/84	**7788**	05/84-05/87
			3088	05/87-10/92	**3534**	10/92-09/99	**3907**	09/99-03/05
S76506	08/69-03/05	⊗06/05	**7788**	08/69-05/78	**7901**	05/78-05/84	**7788**	05/84-05/87
			3088	06/87-10/92	**3534**	10/92-09/99	**3907**	09/99-03/05
S76507	09/69-06/05	⊗10/05	**7789**	09/69-05/78	**7902**	05/78-05/84	**7789**	05/84-05/87
			3089	05/87-08/89	**3485**	08/89-06/05		
S76508	09/69-06/05	⊗ 06	**7789**	09/69-05/78	**7902**	05/78-05/84	**7789**	05/84-05/87
			3089	05/87-08/89	**3485**	08/89-06/05		
S76509	09/69-09/05	⊗09/05	**7790**	09/69-05/78	**7903**	05/78-05/84	**7790**	05/84-06/87
			3090	06/87-09/89	**3487**	09/89-09/05		
S76510	09/69-06/93	⊗10/03	**7790**	09/69-05/78	**7903**	05/78-05/84	**7790**	05/84-06/87
			3090	06/87-09/89	**3487**	09/89-06/93		
S76511	09/69-02/05	⊗ 05	**7791**	09/69-04/78	**7904**	04/78-05/84	**7791**	05/84-06/87
			3091	06/87-12/89	**3501**	12/89-12/91	**2257**	12/91-01/92
			3501	01/92-02/05				
S76512	09/69-02/05	⊗ 05	**7791**	09/69-04/78	**7904**	04/78-05/84	**7791**	05/84-06/87
			3091	06/87-12/89	**3501**	12/89-12/91	**1830**	12/91-01/92
			3501	01/92-02/05				
S76513	09/69-02/05	⊗05/05	**7792**	09/69-03/78	**7905**	03/78-05/84	**7792**	05/84-05/87
			3092	05/87-03/93	**3537**	03/93-04/98	**3811**	04/98-02/05
S76514	09/69-02/05	⊗05/05	**7792**	09/69-03/78	**7905**	03/78-05/84	**7792**	05/84-05/87
			3092	05/87-03/93	**3537**	03/93-04/98	**3811**	04/98-02/05
S76515	09/69-04/05	⊗06/05	**7793**	09/69-05/78	**7906**	05/78-05/84	**7793**	05/84-06/87
			3093	06/87-04/93	**3538**	04/93-06/96	**3809**	06/96-04/05
S76516	09/69-04/05	⊗06/05	**7793**	09/69-05/78	**7906**	05/78-05/84	**7793**	05/84-06/87
			3093	06/87-04/93	**3538**	04/93-06/96	**3809**	06/96-04/05
S76517	10/69-07/05	⊗10/05	**7794**	10/69-05/78	**7907**	05/78-05/84	**7794**	05/84-05/87
			3094	05/87-01/92	**3528**	01/92-12/99	**3916**	12/99-07/05
S76518	10/69-07/05	⊗10/05	**7794**	10/69-05/78	**7907**	05/78-05/84	**7794**	05/84-05/87
			3094	05/87-01/92	**3528**	01/92-12/99	**3916**	12/99-07/05
S76519	10/69-07/05	⊗08/05	**7795**	10/69-05/78	**7908**	05/78-05/84	**7795**	05/84-06/87
			3095	06/87-12/91	**3527**	12/91-11/99	**3914**	11/99-09/03
			3842	09/03-07/05				
S76520	10/69-07/04	⊗07/04	**7795**	10/69-05/78	**7908**	05/78-05/84	**7795**	05/84-06/87
			3095	06/87-12/91	**3527**	12/91-11/99	**3914**	11/99-09/03
			3841	09/03-07/04				
S76521	10/69-05/04	⊗07/04	**7796**	10/69-05/78	**7909**	05/78-05/84	**7796**	05/84-06/87
			3096	06/87-10/91	**3525**	10/91-08/95	**3801**	08/95-05/04
S76522	10/69-05/04	⊗08/04	**7796**	10/69-05/78	**7909**	05/78-05/84	**7796**	05/04-06/87
			3096	06/87-10/91	**3525**	10/91-08/95	**3801**	08/95-05/04
S76523	11/69-02/05	⊗02/05	**7797**	11/69-05/78	**7910**	05/78-05/84	**7797**	05/84-05/87
			3097	05/87-01/92	**3526**	03/92-12/99	**3915**	12/99-02/05
S76524	11/69-02/05	⊗02/05	**7797**	11/69-05/78	**7910**	05/78-05/84	**7797**	05/84-05/87
			3097	05/87-01/92	**3526**	03/92-12/99	**3915**	12/99-02/05
S76525	11/69-04/05	⊗08/05	**7798**	11/69-05/78	**7911**	05/78-06/80	**7911**	10/80-05/84
			7798	05/84-05/87	**3098**	05/87-09/92	**3533**	09/92-08/99
			3902	08/99-04/05				
S76526	11/69-06/80	⊗05/82	**7798**	11/69-05/78	**7911**	05/78-06/80		
S76527	11/69-04/05	ⓟ	**7799**	11/69-05/78	**7912**	05/78-05/84	**7799**	05/84-05/87
			3099	05/87-06/92	**3532**	06/92-01/00	**3918**	01/00-04/05
S76528	11/69-04/05	ⓟ	**7799**	11/69-05/78	**7912**	05/78-05/84	**7799**	05/84-05/87
			3099	05/87-06/92	**3532**	06/92-01/00	**3918**	01/00-04/05
S76529	11/69-08/05	ⓟ⊗	**7800**	11/69-08/87	**3100**	08/87-08/88	**3438**	08/88-10/99
			3910	10/99-09/03	**3822**	09/03-08/05		
S76530	11/69-08/05	⊗08/05	**7800**	11/69-08/87	**3100**	08/87-08/88	**3438**	08/88-10/99
			3910	10/99-09/03	**3821**	09/03-08/05		
S76531	11/69-06/05	⊗08/05	**7801**	11/69-06/87	**3101**	06/87-08/88	**3446**	10/88-06/05
S76532	11/69-06/05	⊗08/05	**7801**	11/69-06/87	**3101**	06/87-08/88	**3446**	10/88-06/05
S76533	12/69-07/04	⊗08/04	**7802**	12/69-06/87	**3102**	06/87-09/88	**3440**	09/88-08/95
			3802	08/95-07/04				
S76534	12/69-07/04	⊗08/04	**7802**	12/69-06/87	**3102**	06/87-09/88	**3440**	09/88-08/95
			3802	08/95-07/04				
S76535	12/69-07/05	⊗06/05	**7803**	12/69-07/87	**3103**	07/87-02/89	**3462**	02/89-07/99
			3903	07/99-07/05				
S76536	12/69-07/05	⊗06/05	**7803**	12/69-07/87	**3103**	07/87-02/89	**3462**	02/89-07/99
			3903	07/99-07/05				
S76537	12/69-12/04	⊗06/05	**7804**	12/69-05/87	**3104**	05/87-02/89	**3461**	02/89-08/95
			3806	08/95-12/04				
S76538	12/69-12/04	⊗12/04	**7804**	12/69-05/87	**3104**	05/87-02/89	**3461**	02/89-08/95
			3806	08/95-12/04				
S76539	12/69-02/05	⊗02/05	**7805**	12/69-05/87	**3105**	05/87-01/89	**3460**	01/89-09/95
			3805	09/95-02/05				
S76540	12/69-02/05	⊗02/05	**7805**	12/69-05/87	**3105**	05/87-01/89	**3460**	01/89-09/95
			3805	09/95-02/05				

Class 423 4-VEP York

Driving Trailer Composite (Semi-open) Lavatory DTCsoL S76541-S76560

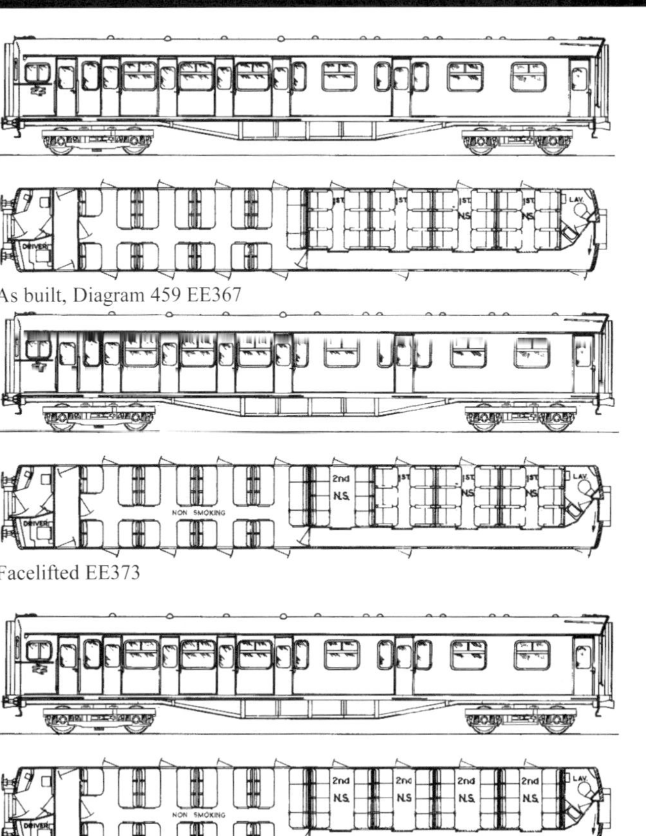

As built, Diagram 459 EE367

Facelifted EE373

Modified as Class 423/2 4-VOP Metro units 3901-3919, Diagram EE281

Diagram:	459 EE367 EE373 EE281	Lot Number:	30799
Body:	64' 9⅝" × 9' 3"	Weight:	34t 5cwt
Seats:	24 first 38 second 1 toilet later 18 first 46 second 1 toilet VOP 70 second 1 toilet	Bogies:	B5 (SR)

Vehicle	In service	Withdrawn	Unit	Dates	Unit	Dates	Unit	Dates
S76541	01/70-12/04	⊗12/04	**7806**	01/70-07/87	**3106**	07/87-03/89	**3465**	03/89-08/95
			3807	08/95-12/04				
S76542	01/70-12/04	⊗12/04	**7806**	01/70-07/87	**3106**	07/87-03/89	**3465**	03/89-08/95
			3807	08/95-12/04				
S76543	01/70-10/04	⊗10/04	**7807**	01/70-05/87	**3107**	05/87-05/90	**3515**	05/90-11/91
			1800	11/91-08/92	**3515**	08/92-10/04		
S76544	01/70-10/04	⊗10/04	**7807**	01/70-05/87	**3107**	05/87-05/90	**3515**	05/90-11/91
			1845	11/91-08/92	**3515**	08/92-10/04		
S76545	02/70-08/04	⊗ 04	**7808**	02/70-06/87	**3108**	06/87-04/89	**3469**	04/89-08/04
S76546	02/70-08/04	⊗ 04	**7808**	02/70-06/87	**3108**	06/87-04/89	**3469**	04/89-08/04
S76547	02/70-08/05	⊗10/05	**7809**	02/70-06/87	**3109**	06/87-05/89	**3476**	05/89-11/99
			3911	11/99-08/05				
S76548	02/70-08/05	⊗10/05	**7809**	02/70-06/87	**3109**	06/87-05/89	**3476**	05/89-11/99
			3911	11/99-08/05				
S76549	02/70-02/05	⊗02/05	**7810**	02/70-10/87	**3110**	10/87-05/89	**3477**	05/89-08/95
			3808	08/95-02/05				
S76550	02/70-02/05	⊗02/05	**7810**	02/70-10/87	**3110**	10/87-05/89	**3477**	05/89-08/95
			3808	08/95-02/05				
S76551	02/70-10/05	⊗10/05	**7811**	02/70-08/87	**3111**	08/87-06/89	**3475**	06/89-10/05
S76552	02/70-10/05	⊗10/05	**7811**	02/70-08/87	**3111**	08/87-06/89	**3475**	06/89-10/05
S76553	02/70-07/05	⊗08/05	**7812**	02/70-09/87	**3112**	09/87-02/90	**3506**	02/90-01/00
			3919	01/00-07/05				
S76554	02/70-07/05	⊗08/05	**7812**	02/70-09/87	**3112**	09/87-02/90	**3506**	02/90-01/00
			3919	01/00-07/05				
S76555	03/70-05/04	⊗07/04	**7813**	03/70-08/87	**3113**	08/87-07/90	**3519**	07/90-05/04
S76556	03/70-05/04	⊗07/04	**7813**	03/70-08/87	**3113**	08/87-07/90	**3519**	07/90-05/04
S76557	03/70-10/04	⊗10/04	**7814**	03/70-09/87	**3114**	09/87-02/90	**3507**	02/90-12/99
			3917	12/99-10/04				
S76558	03/70-10/04	⊗10/04	**7814**	03/70-09/87	**3114**	09/87-02/90	**3507**	02/90-12/99
			3917	12/99-10/04				
S76559	03/70-07/04	⊗08/04	**7815**	03/70-09/87	**3115**	09/87-03/90	**3509**	03/90-07/04
S76560	03/70-07/04	⊗08/04	**7815**	03/70-09/87	**3115**	09/87-03/90	**3509**	03/90-07/04

Class 420 4-BIG York

Driving Trailer Composite (Semi-open) Lavatory DTCsoL, some later DTSsoL S76561-S76570

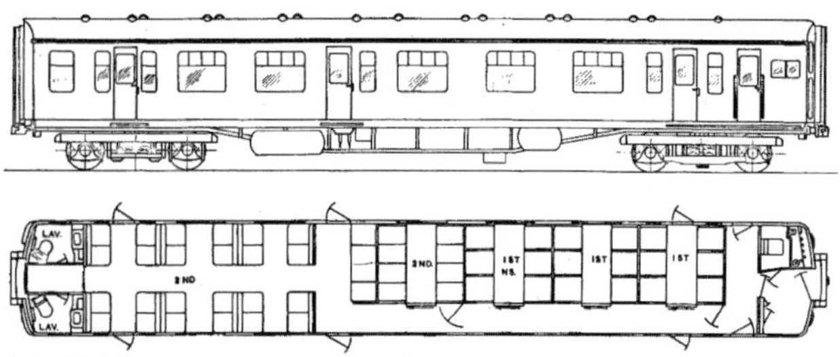

As built, Diagram 453 EE364, then facelifted EE369

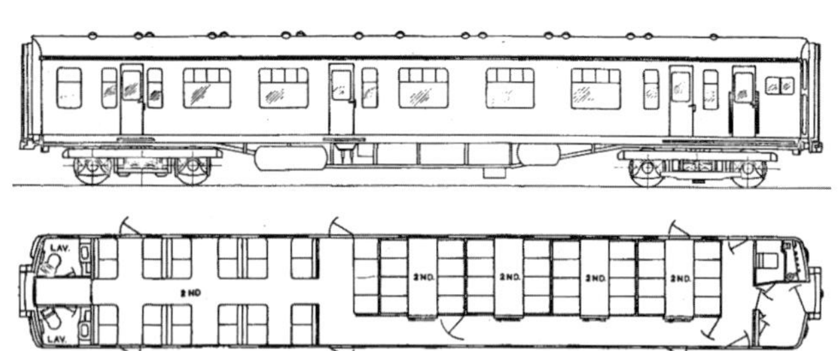

Converted to 3/4-COP units 1401-1411, Diagram EE245

Diagram:	453 EE364 EE369 EE245	Lot Number:	30802
Body:	64' 9½" × 9' 3"	Weight:	35t 10cwt
Seats:	18 first 36 second 2 toilets COP 60 second 2 toilets	Bogies:	B5 (SR)

S76561	05/70-08/04	⊗09/04	**7049**	05/70-06/85	**2201**	06/85-11/88	**1824**	11/88-05/90
			1311	05/90-08/04				
S76562	06/70-04/02	⊗04/05	**7050**	06/70-05/85	**2202**	05/85-12/88	**1825**	12/88-06/90
			1312	06/90-04/05				
S76563	06/70-06/04	⊗07/04	**7051**	06/70-04/85	**2203**	04/85-06/97	**1403**	06/97-06/04
S76564	10/70-04/02	⊗10/03	**7052**	10/70-04/85	**2204**	04/85-06/97	**1402**	06/97-04/02
S76565	11/70-06/04	⊗07/04	**7053**	11/70-04/85	**2205**	04/85-06/97	**1405**	06/97-06/04
S76566	12/70-02/05	⊗02/05	**7358**	10/70-09/87	**1258**	09/87-06/90	**1834**	06/90-02/05
S76567	07/70-08/04	⊗ 04	**7055**	07/70-04/85	**2207**	04/85-07/88	**1823**	10/88-05/90
			1310	05/90-08/04				
S76568	08/70-02/04	⊗08/05	**7056**	08/70-04/85	**2208**	04/85-06/97	**1401**	06/97-07/97
			1401	11/97-02/04				
S76569	09/70-11/03	⊗11/03	**7057**	09/70-04/85	**2209**	04/85-09/97	**1409**	09/97-11/03
S76570	10/70-04/05	⊗06/05	**7058**	10/70-04/85	**2210**	04/85-09/97	**1411**	09/97-04/05

Class 420 4-BIG York

Driving Trailer Composite (Semi-open) Lavatory DTCsoL, some later DTSsoL S76571-S76580

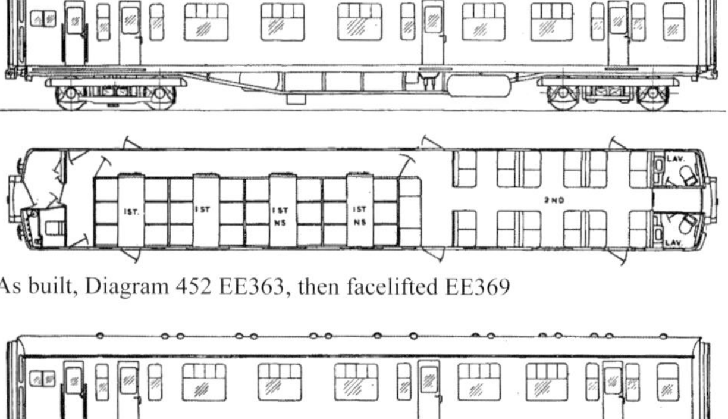

As built, Diagram 452 EE363, then facelifted EE369

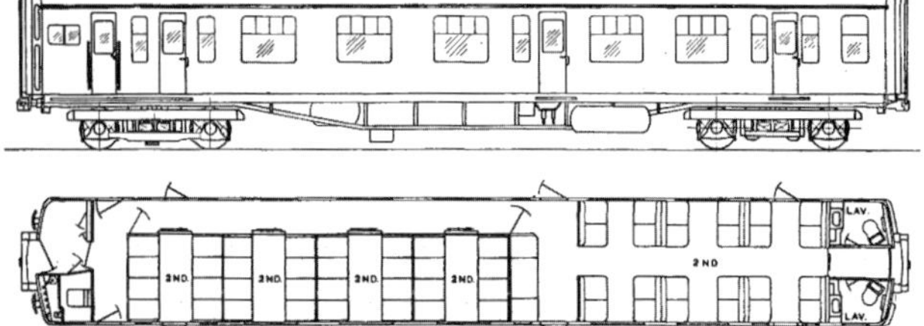

Converted to 3/4-COP units 1401-1411, Diagram EE246

Diagram:	452 EE363 EE369 EE246	Lot Number:	30803
Body:	64' 9½" × 9' 3"	Weight:	36t
Seats:	24 first 28 second 2 toilets COP 60 second 2 toilets	Bogies:	B5 (SR)

S76571	05/70-08/04	⊗09/04	**7049**	05/70-06/85	**2201**	06/85-11/88	**1824**	11/88-05/90
			1311	05/90-08/04				
S76572	06/70-04/05	⊗05/05	**7050**	06/70-05/85	**2202**	05/85-12/88	**1825**	12/88-06/90
			1312	06/90-04/05				
S76573	06/70-06/04	⊗07/04	**7051**	06/70-04/85	**2203**	04/85-06/97	**1403**	06/97-06/04
S76574	10/70-04/02	⊗11/03	**7052**	10/70-04/85	**2204**	04/85-06/97	**1402**	06/97-04/02
S76575	11/70-06/04	⊗07/04	**7053**	11/70-04/85	**2205**	04/85-06/97	**1405**	06/97-06/04
S76576	12/70-02/05	⊗02/05	**7358**	10/70-09/87	**1258**	09/87-06/90	**1834**	06/90-02/05
S76577	07/70-08/04	⊗ 04	**7055**	07/70-04/85	**2207**	04/85-07/88	**1823**	10/88-05/90
			1310	05/90-08/04				
S76578	08/70-02/04	⊗02/05	**7056**	08/70-04/85	**2208**	04/85-06/97	**1401**	06/97-07/97
			1401	11/97-02/04				
S76579	09/70-11/03	⊗11/03	**7057**	09/70-04/85	**2209**	04/85-09/97	**1409**	09/97-11/03
S76580	10/70-04/05	⊗06/05	**7058**	10/70-04/85	**2210**	04/85-09/97	**1411**	09/97-04/05

Class 421 4-CIG York

Driving Trailer Composite (Semi-open) Lavatory DTCsoL, some later DTSsoL S76581-S76610

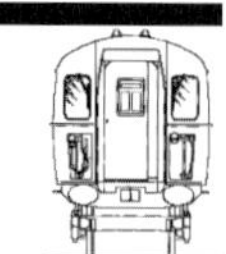

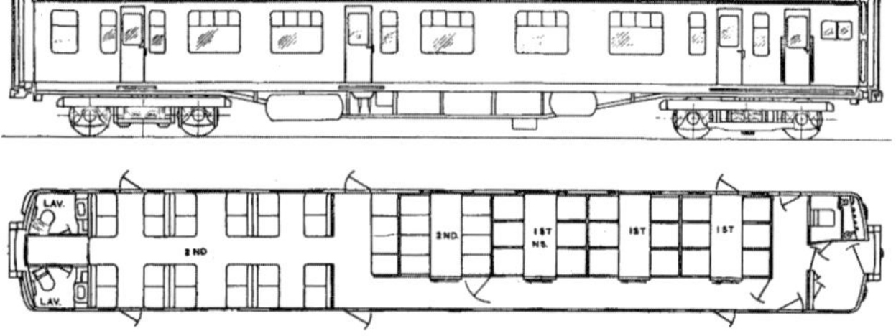

As built, Diagram 453 EE364, then facelifted EE369

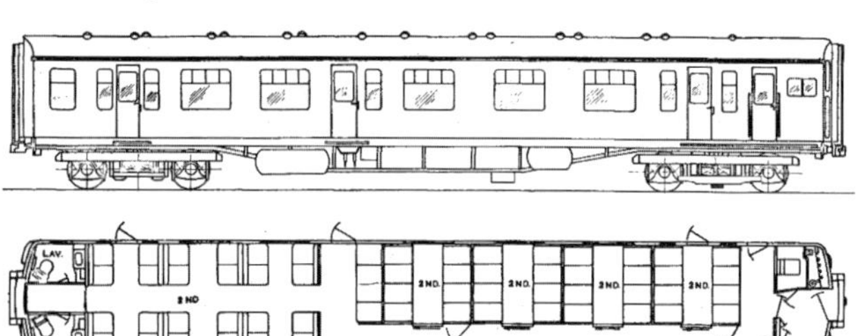

Converted to 3/4-COP units 1401-1411, Diagram EE245

Diagram:	453 EE364 EE369 EE245	Lot Number:	30806
Body:	64' 9½" × 9' 3"	Weight:	35t 10cwt
Seats:	18 first 36 second 2 toilets COP 60 second 2 toilets	Bogies:	B5 (SR)

S76581	06/70-02/05	⊗06/05	**7337**	06/70-08/87	**1237**	08/87-05/88	**1816**	05/88-04/90
			1303	04/90-02/05				
S76582	05/70-07/04	⊗08/04	**7338**	05/70-06/87	**1238**	06/87-06/90	**1833**	06/90-07/04
S76583	05/70-04/05	⊗06/09	**7339**	05/70-08/87	**1239**	08/87-05/88	**1817**	05/88-04/90
			1304	04/90-04/05				
S76584	06/70-04/04	⊗04/05	**7340**	06/70-09/87	**1240**	09/87-04/88	**1815**	04/88-04/90
			1302	04/90-04/04				
S76585	06/70-05/05	⊗05/05	**7341**	06/70-08/87	**1241**	08/87-04/90	**1316**	04/90-05/05
S76586	08/70-10/04	⊗11/04	**7342**	08/70-09/87	**1242**	09/87-07/88	**1820**	07/88-05/90
			1307	05/90-10/04				
S76587	10/70-08/04	⊗09/04	**7343**	10/70-09/87	**1243**	09/87-08/90	**1838**	08/90-03/92
			1322	03/92-08/04				
S76588	10/70-08/04	⊗09/04	**7344**	10/70-06/87	**1244**	06/87-04/90	**1314**	04/90-08/04
S76589	11/70-08/04	⊗09/04	**7345**	11/70-06/87	**1245**	06/87-10/90	**1844**	10/90-01/92
			1321	01/92-08/04				
S76590	01/71-06/05	⊗06/05	**7346**	01/71-06/87	**1246**	06/87-11/90	**1849**	11/90-01/92
			1318	01/92-06/05				
S76591	01/71-06/05	⊗06/05	**7347**	01/71-06/87	**1247**	06/87-12/90	**1852**	12/90-01/92
			1319	01/92-06/05				
S76592	06/70-09/04	⊗10/04	**7348**	06/70-06/87	**1248**	06/87-07/88	**1821**	07/88-05/90
			1308	05/90-01/92	**1317**	01/92-09/04		
S76593	07/70-10/04	⊗06/05	**7349**	07/70-09/87	**1249**	09/87-07/90	**1836**	07/90-01/92
			1320	01/92-10/04				
S76594	07/70-04/05	⊗05/05	**7350**	07/70-08/87	**1250**	08/87-07/88	**1822**	07/88-04/90
			1309	04/90-04/05				
S76595	08/70-08/04	⊗09/04	**7351**	08/70-08/87	**1251**	08/87-04/88	**1814**	04/88-04/90
			1301	04/90-08/04				
S76596	08/70-12/04	⊗01/05	**7352**	08/70-09/87	**1252**	09/87-04/90	**1313**	04/90-12/04
S76597	09/70-09/04	⊗10/04	**7353**	09/70-09/87	**1253**	09/87-11/90	**1317**	11/90-09/04
S76598	09/70-05/05	⊗07/05	**7354**	09/70-11/87	**1254**	11/87-05/90	**1831**	05/90-05/05

S76599	10/70-12/04	⊗02/05	**7355**	10/70-02/88	**1255**	02/88-10/90	**1845**	10/90-11/91
			1800	11/91-08/92	**1845**	08/92-12/04		
S76600	11/70-02/05	⊗02/05	**7356**	11/70-06/87	**1256**	06/87-11/90	**1847**	11/90-02/05
S76601	10/70-10/04	⊗10/04	**7357**	10/70-07/87	**1257**	07/87-06/90	**1835**	06/90-10/04
S76602	07/70-03/05	⊗06/05	**7054**	11/70-04/85	**2206**	04/85-06/97	**1404**	06/97-03/05
S76603	10/70-07/04	⊗08/04	**7359**	10/70-06/87	**1259**	06/87-09/90	**1841**	09/90-07/04
S76604	11/70-07/05	⊗07/05	**7360**	11/70-06/87	**1260**	06/87-05/91	**1858**	05/91-07/05
S76605	11/70-02/05	⊗02/05	**7361**	11/70-08/87	**1261**	08/87-11/90	**1848**	11/90-02/05
S76606	12/70-05/05	⊗05/05	**7362**	12/70-05/87	**1262**	05/87-01/91	**1853**	01/91-05/05
S76607	12/70-05/04	⊗06/04	**7363**	12/70-07/87	**1263**	07/87-08/90	**1839**	08/90-05/04
S76608	11/70-12/04	⊗06/05	**7364**	11/70-07/87	**1264**	07/87-04/90	**1315**	04/90-12/04
S76609	12/70-12/78	⊗12/78	**7365**	12/70-12/78				
S76610	01/71-12/05	⊗12/05	**7366**	01/71-05/87	**1266**	05/87-04/91	**1857**	04/91-12/05

Class 421 4-CIG York

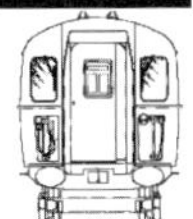

Driving Trailer Composite (Semi-open) Lavatory DTCsoL, some later DTSsoL S76611-S76640

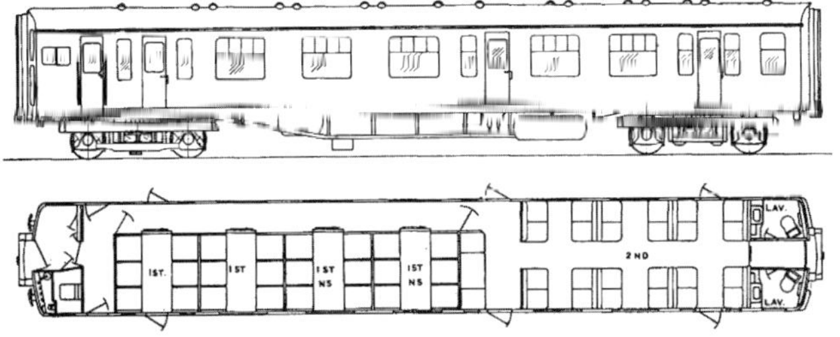

As built, Diagram 452 EE363, then facelifted EE369

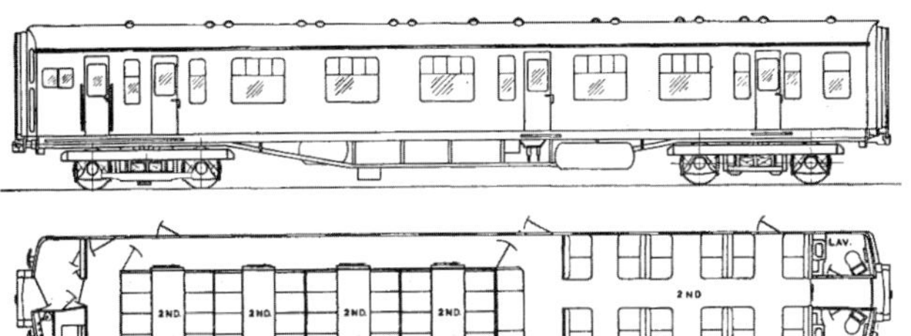

Converted to 3/4-COP units 1401-1411, Diagram EE246

Diagram:	452 EE363 EE369 EE246	Lot Number:	30807
Body:	64' 9½" × 9' 3"	Weight:	36t
Seats:	24 first 28 second 2 toilets COP 60 second 2 toilets	Bogies:	B5 (SR)

S76611	06/70-02/05	⊗06/05	**7337**	06/70-08/87	**1237**	08/87-05/88	**1816**	05/88-04/90
			1303	04/90-02/05				
S76612	05/70-07/04	⊗08/04	**7338**	05/70-06/87	**1238**	06/87-06/90	**1833**	06/90-07/04
S76613	05/70-04/05	⊗06/09	**7339**	05/70-08/87	**1239**	08/87-05/88	**1817**	05/88-04/90
			1304	04/90-04/05				
S76614	06/70-04/04	⊗04/05	**7340**	06/70-09/87	**1240**	09/87-04/88	**1815**	04/88-04/90
			1302	04/90-04/04				
S76615	06/70-05/05	⊗05/05	**7341**	06/70-08/87	**1241**	08/87-04/90	**1316**	04/90-05/05
S76616	08/70-10/04	⊗11/04	**7342**	08/70-09/87	**1242**	09/87-07/88	**1820**	07/88-05/90
			1307	05/90-10/04				
S76617	10/70-08/04	⊗09/04	**7343**	10/70-09/87	**1243**	09/87-08/90	**1838**	08/90-03/92
			1322	03/92-08/04				
S76618	10/70-08/04	⊗09/04	**7344**	10/70-06/87	**1244**	06/87-04/90	**1314**	04/90-08/04
S76619	11/70-08/04	⊗09/04	**7345**	11/70-06/87	**1245**	06/87-10/90	**1844**	10/90-01/92
			1321	01/92-08/04				
S76620	01/71-06/05	⊗06/05	Rebuilt with frame of 76713 08/74				**7346**	01/71-06/87
			1246	06/87-11/90	**1849**	11/90-01/92	**1318**	01/92-06/05
S76621	01/71-06/05	⊗06/05	**7347**	01/71-06/87	**1247**	06/87-12/90	**1852**	12/90-01/92
			1319	01/92-06/05				
S76622	06/70-09/04	⊗10/04	**7348**	06/70-06/87	**1248**	06/87-07/88	**1821**	07/88-05/90
			1308	05/90-09/04				
S76623	07/70-10/04	⊗06/05	**7349**	07/70-09/87	**1249**	09/87-07/90	**1836**	07/90-01/92
			1320	01/92-10/04				
S76624	07/70-04/05	⊗05/05	**7350**	07/70-08/87	**1250**	08/87-07/88	**1822**	07/88-04/90
			1309	04/90-04/05				
S76625	08/70-08/04	⊗09/04	**7351**	08/70-08/87	**1251**	08/87-04/88	**1814**	04/88-04/90
			1301	04/90-08/04				
S76626	08/70-12/04	⊗01/05	**7352**	08/70-09/87	**1252**	09/87-04/90	**1313**	04/90-12/04
S76627	09/70-09/04	⊗10/04	**7353**	09/70-09/87	**1253**	09/87-11/90	**1317**	11/90-01/92
			1308	01/92-09/04				
S76628	09/70-05/05	⊗07/05	**7354**	09/70-11/87	**1254**	11/87-05/90	**1831**	05/90-05/05
S76629	10/70-06/03	⊗02/07	**7355**	10/70-02/88	**1255**	02/88-10/90	**1845**	10/90-10/99
			1850	10/99-06/03				
S76630	11/70-02/05	⊗02/05	**7356**	11/70-06/87	**1256**	06/87-11/90	**1847**	11/90-02/05
S76631	10/70-10/04	⊗10/04	**7357**	10/70-07/87	**1257**	07/87-06/90	**1835**	06/90-10/04
S76632	07/70-03/05	⊗06/05	**7054**	11/70-04/85	**2206**	04/85-06/97	**1404**	06/97-03/05
S76633	10/70-07/04	⊗08/04	**7359**	10/70-06/87	**1259**	06/87-09/90	**1841**	09/90-07/04
S76634	11/70-07/05	⊗07/05	**7360**	11/70-06/87	**1260**	06/87-05/91	**1858**	05/91-07/05
S76635	11/70-02/05	⊗02/05	**7361**	11/70-08/87	**1261**	08/87-11/90	**1848**	11/90-02/05
S76636	12/70-05/05	⊗05/05	**7362**	12/70-05/87	**1262**	05/87-01/91	**1853**	01/91-05/05
S76637	12/70-05/04	⊗06/04	**7363**	12/70-07/87	**1263**	07/87-08/90	**1839**	08/90-05/04
S76638	11/70-12/04	⊗06/05	**7364**	11/70-07/87	**1264**	07/87-04/90	**1315**	04/90-12/04
S76639	12/70-05/05	⊗07/05	**7365**	12/70-12/78	**7724**	06/84-10/84	**7700**	10/84-08/87
			3000	08/87-12/88	**1295**	11/89-11/91	**1865**	11/91-05/05
S76640	01/71-12/05	⊗12/05	**7366**	01/71-05/87	**1266**	05/87-04/91	**1857**	04/91-12/05

Class 423 4-VEP York

Driving Trailer Composite (Semi-open) Lavatory DTCsoL S76641-S76716

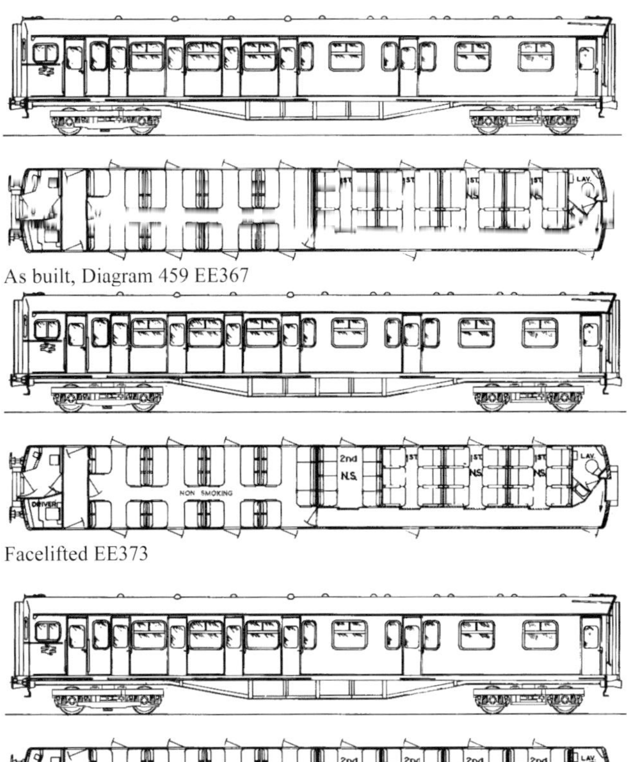

As built, Diagram 459 EE367

Facelifted EE373

Modified as Class 423/2 4-VOP Metro units 3901-3919, Diagram EE281

Diagram:	459 EE367 EE373 EE281	Lot Number:	30811
Body:	64' 9⅝" × 9' 3"	Weight:	34t 5cwt
Seats:	24 first 38 second 1 toilet later 18 first 46 second 1 toilet VOP 70 second 1 toilet	Bogies:	B5 (SR)

S76641	04/72-05/04	⊗07/04	**7816**	04/72-05/87	**3116**	05/87-02/90	**3510**	03/90-05/04
S76642	04/72-05/04	⊗07/04	**7816**	04/72-05/87	**3116**	05/87-02/90	**3510**	03/90-05/04
S76643	04/72-03/05	⊗07/05	**7817**	04/72-08/87	**3117**	08/87-03/90	**3508**	03/90-03/05
S76644	04/72-03/05	⊗07/05	**7817**	04/72-08/87	**3117**	08/87-03/90	**3508**	03/90-03/05
S76645	04/72-09/05	⊗09/05	**7818**	04/72-06/87	**3118**	06/87-04/90	**3511**	04/90-06/93
			3487	06/93-09/05				
S76646	04/72-05/05	⊗05/05	**7818**	04/72-06/87	**3118**	06/87-04/90	**3511**	04/90-06/93
			3511	11/94-05/05				
S76647	04/72-06/05	⊗06/05	**7819**	04/72-09/87	**3119**	09/87-12/88	**3481**	07/89-06/05
S76648	04/72-06/05	⊗06/05	**7819**	04/72-09/87	**3119**	09/87-12/88	**3481**	07/89-06/05
S76649	05/72-05/05	⊗05/05	**7820**	05/72-03/88	**3120**	03/88-03/92	**3531**	03/92-05/05
S76650	05/72-05/05	⊗05/05	**7820**	05/72-03/88	**3120**	03/88-03/92	**3531**	03/92-05/05
S76651	05/72-07/05	⊗07/05	**7821**	05/72-12/87	**3121**	12/87-05/91	**3523**	05/91-07/05
S76652	05/72-07/05	⊗07/05	**7821**	05/72-12/87	**3121**	12/87-05/91	**3523**	05/91-07/05
S76653	06/72-11/04	⊗03/05	**7822**	06/72-04/88	**3122**	04/88-06/89	**3478**	06/89-11/99
			3913	11/99-09/03	**3813**	09/03-11/04		
S76654	06/72-10/04	⊗10/04	**7822**	06/72-04/88	**3122**	04/88-06/89	**3478**	06/89-11/99
			3913	11/99-09/03	**3814**	09/03-10/04		
S76655	06/72-07/05	⊗07/05	**7823**	06/72-06/87	**3123**	06/87-07/89	**3479**	07/89-07/05
S76656	06/72-07/05	⊗07/05	**7823**	06/72-06/87	**3123**	06/87-07/89	**3479**	07/89-07/05
S76657	06/72-04/05	⊗06/05	**7824**	06/72-03/88	**3124**	03/88-08/89	**3482**	08/89-04/05
S76658	06/72-04/05	⊗06/05	**7824**	06/72-03/88	**3124**	03/88-08/89	**3482**	08/89-04/05
S76659	06/72-06/04	⊗06/04	**7825**	06/72-07/87	**3125**	07/87-12/91	**3529**	12/91-06/04
S76660	06/72-06/04	⊗06/04	**7825**	06/72-07/87	**3125**	07/87-12/91	**3529**	12/91-06/04
S76661	06/72-07/05	⊗07/05	**7826**	06/72-12/87	**3126**	12/87-08/89	**3483**	08/89-07/05
S76662	06/72-07/05	⊗07/05	**7826**	06/72-12/87	**3126**	12/87-08/89	**3483**	08/89-07/05
S76663	07/72-04/05	⊗08/05	**7827**	07/72-09/88	**3127**	09/88-09/89	**3488**	09/89-04/05

S76664	07/72-04/05	⊗08/05	**7827**	07/72-09/88	**3127**	09/88-09/89	**3488**	09/89-04/05
S76665	07/72-07/05	⊗10/05	**7828**	07/72-08/87	**3128**	08/87-09/89	**3489**	09/89-07/05
S76666	07/72-07/05	⊗ 06	**7828**	07/72-08/87	**3128**	08/87-09/89	**3489**	09/89-07/05
S76667	08/72- 05	⊗ 05	**7829**	08/72-11/87	**3129**	11/87-10/89	**3492**	10/89- 05
S76668	08/72- 05	⊗ 05	**7829**	08/72-11/87	**3129**	11/87-10/89	**3492**	10/89- 05
S76669	08/72-11/04	⊗02/05	**7830**	08/72-07/87	**3130**	07/87-10/89	**3493**	10/89-11/04
S76670	08/72-11/04	⊗02/05	**7830**	08/72-07/87	**3130**	07/87-10/89	**3493**	10/89-11/04
S76671	08/72-08/05	⊗10/05	**7831**	08/72-08/87	**3131**	08/87-11/89	**3497**	11/89-08/05
S76672	08/72-08/05	⊗10/05	**7831**	08/72-08/87	**3131**	08/87-11/89	**3497**	11/89-08/05
S76673	08/72-08/05	⊗10/05	**7832**	08/72-07/87	**3132**	07/87-11/89	**3496**	11/89-08/05
S76674	08/72-08/05	⊗10/05	**7832**	08/72-07/87	**3132**	07/87-11/89	**3496**	11/89-08/05
S76675	09/72-05/05	⊗05/05	**7833**	09/72-07/87	**3133**	07/87-11/89	**3494**	11/89-05/05
S76676	09/72-05/05	⊗05/05	**7833**	09/72-07/87	**3133**	07/87-11/89	**3494**	11/89-05/05
S76677	09/72-11/05	⊗12/05	**7834**	09/72-05/87	**3134**	05/87-11/92	**3535**	11/92-11/05
S76678	09/72-11/05	⊗12/05	**7834**	09/72-05/87	**3134**	05/87-11/92	**3535**	11/92-11/05
S76679	09/72-05/04	⊗07/04	**7835**	09/72-05/87	**3135**	05/87-05/90	**3512**	05/90-05/04
S76680	09/72-05/04	⊗07/04	**7835**	09/72-05/87	**3135**	05/87-05/90	**3512**	05/90-05/04
S76681	09/72-04/05	⊗06/05	**7836**	09/72-10/87	**3136**	10/87-02/90	**3503**	02/90-09/03
			3843	09/03-04/05				
S76682	09/72-07/05	⊗10/05	**7836**	09/72-10/87	**3136**	10/87-02/90	**3503**	02/90-09/03
			3844	09/03-07/05				
S76683	09/72-11/05	⊗12/05	**7837**	09/72-05/87	**3137**	05/87-06/90	**3514**	06/90-11/05
S76684	09/72-11/05	⊗12/05	**7837**	09/72-05/87	**3137**	05/87-06/90	**3514**	06/90-11/05
S76685	10/72-06/04	⊗07/04	**7838**	10/72-07/87	**3138**	07/87-06/90	**3517**	06/90-06/04
S76686	10/72-06/04	⊗02/05	**7838**	10/72-07/87	**3138**	07/87-06/90	**3517**	06/90-06/04
S76687	10/72-05/04	⊗06/04	**7839**	10/72-05/87	**3139**	05/87-12/93	**3546**	12/93-05/04
S76688	10/72-05/04	⊗07/04	**7839**	10/72-05/87	**3139**	05/87-12/93	**3546**	12/93-05/04
S76689	11/72-07/04	⊗02/05	**7840**	11/72-07/87	**3140**	07/87-07/90	**3518**	07/90-09/03
			3841	09/03-07/04				
S76690	11/72-11/04	⊗02/05	**7840**	11/72-04/80	**7700**	10/84-05/86	**3024**	02/88-11/88
			3452	11/88-11/04				
S76691	11/72-04/05	⊗07/05	**7841**	11/72-07/87	**3141**	07/87-05/90	**3513**	05/90-07/99
			3904	07/99-04/05				
S76692	11/72-04/05	⊗07/05	**7841**	11/72-07/87	**3141**	07/87-05/90	**3513**	05/90-07/99
			3904	07/99-04/05				
S76693	12/72-04/05	⊗06/05	**7842**	12/72-10/87	**3142**	10/87-06/90	**3516**	06/90-04/05
S76694	12/72-04/05	⊗06/05	**7842**	12/72-10/87	**3142**	10/87-06/90	**3516**	06/90-04/05
S76695	12/72-11/05	⊗01/06	**7843**	12/72-06/87	**3143**	06/87-10/89	**3490**	10/89-11/05
S76696	12/72-11/05	⊗01/06	**7843**	12/72-06/87	**3143**	06/87-10/89	**3490**	10/89-11/05
S76697	02/73-04/05	⊗08/05	**7844**	02/73-06/87	**3144**	06/87-07/90	**3520**	07/90-04/05
S76698	02/73-08/02	⊗04/05	**7844**	02/73-06/87	**3144**	06/87-07/90	**3520**	07/90-04/05
S76699	02/73-08/05	⊗10/05	**7845**	02/73-07/87	**3145**	07/87-11/89	**3495**	11/89-08/05
S76700	02/73-08/05	⊗10/05	**7845**	02/73-07/87	**3145**	07/87-11/89	**3495**	11/89-08/05
S76701	03/73-08/05	⊗10/05	**7846**	03/73-08/87	**3146**	08/87-12/89	**3498**	12/89-08/05
S76702	03/73-08/05	⊗10/05	**7846**	03/73-08/87	**3146**	08/87-12/89	**3498**	12/89-08/05
S76703	03/73-04/05	⊗06/05	**7847**	03/73-06/87	**3147**	06/87-07/93	**3541**	07/93-05/98
			3812	05/98-04/05				
S76704	03/73-04/05	⊗06/05	**7847**	03/73-06/87	**3147**	06/87-07/93	**3541**	07/93-05/98
			3812	05/98-04/05				
S76705	03/73-11/04	⊗11/04	**7848**	03/73-09/87	**3148**	09/87-09/90	**3522**	09/90-09/99
			3909	09/99-11/04				
S76706	03/73-11/04	⊗11/04	**7848**	03/73-09/87	**3148**	09/87-09/90	**3522**	09/90-09/99
			3909	09/99-11/04				
S76707	04/73-10/04	⊗10/04	**7849**	04/73-08/87	**3149**	08/87-02/94	**3549**	02/94-10/04
S76708	04/73-10/04	⊗10/04	**7849**	04/73-08/87	**3149**	08/87-02/94	**3549**	02/94-10/04
S76709	04/73-04/05	⊗06/05	**7850**	04/73-06/87	**3150**	06/87-01/90	**3502**	01/90-06/96
			3810	06/96-04/05				
S76710	04/73-04/05	⊗06/05	**7850**	04/73-06/87	**3150**	06/87-01/90	**3502**	01/90-06/96
			3810	06/96-04/05				
S76711	05/73-08/05	⊗08/05	**7851**	05/73-05/87	**3151**	05/87-01/90	**3504**	01/90-09/03
			3821	09/03-08/05				
S76712	05/73-08/05	Ⓟ⊗	**7851**	05/73-05/87	**3151**	05/87-01/90	**3504**	01/90-09/03
			3822	09/03-08/05				
S76713	05/73-09/74	➲**76620** (frame only)			**7852**	05/73-03/74		
S76714	05/73-12/04	⊗12/04	**7852**	05/73-05/87	**3152**	05/87-02/94	**3551**	02/94-12/04
S76715	05/73-05/04	⊗07/04	**7853**	05/73-07/87	**3153**	07/87-03/94	**3552**	03/94-05/04
S76716	05/73-05/04	⊗07/04	**7853**	05/73-07/87	**3153**	07/87-03/94	**3552**	03/94-05/04

Class 421 4-CIG York

Driving Trailer Composite (Semi-open) Lavatory DTCsoL, some later DTSsoL S76717-S76787

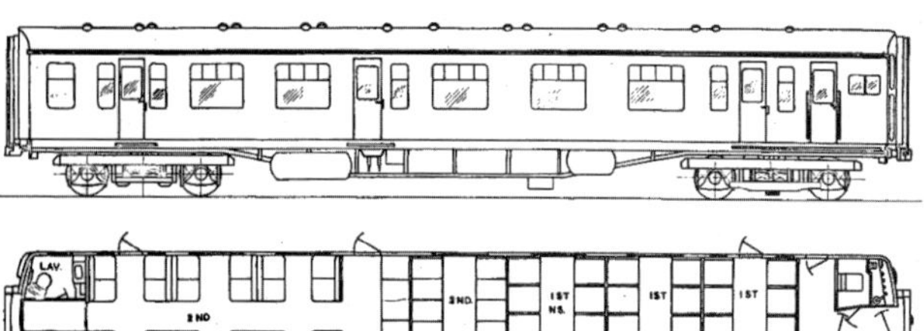

As built, Diagram 453 EE364, then facelifted EE369

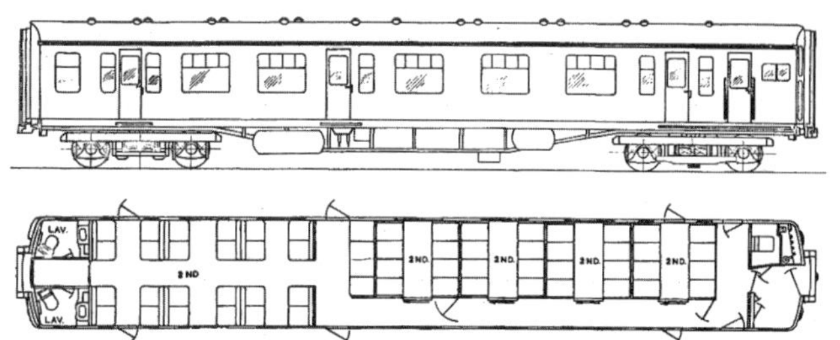

Converted to 3/4-COP units 1401-1411, Diagram EE245

Diagram:	453 EE364 EE369 EE245	Lot Number:	30814
Body:	64' 9½" × 9' 3"	Weight:	35t 10cwt
Seats:	18 first 36 second 2 toilets COP 60 second 2 toilets	Bogies:	B5 (SR)

S76717	02/71-07/04	⊗09/04	**7367**	02/71-08/87	**1267**	08/87-06/88	**1818**	06/88-04/90
			1305	04/90-07/04				
S76718	02/71-12/04	⊗02/05	**7368**	02/71-06/87	**1268**	06/87-12/90	**1850**	12/90-10/99
			1845	10/99-12/04				
S76719	02/71-07/05	⊗07/05	**7369**	02/71-05/87	**1269**	05/87-05/90	**1832**	05/90-07/05
S76720	03/71-12/04	⊗07/05	**7370**	03/71-08/87	**1270**	08/87-01/91	**1855**	01/91-12/04
S76721	02/71-02/05	⊗03/05	**7371**	02/71-08/87	**1271**	08/87-12/90	**1851**	12/90-02/05
S76722	02/71-02/05	⊗02/05	**7372**	02/71-06/87	**1272**	06/87-07/90	**1837**	07/90-02/05
S76723	02/71-07/04	⊗09/04	**7373**	02/71-06/87	**1273**	06/87-06/88	**1819**	06/88-05/90
			1306	05/90-07/04				
S76724	03/71-05/04	⊗06/04	**7374**	03/71-06/87	**1274**	06/87-08/90	**1840**	08/90-05/04
S76725	03/71-04/04	⊗06/04	**7375**	03/71-06/87	**1275**	06/87-09/90	**1842**	09/90-04/04
S76726	04/71-05/05	Ⓟ⊗	**7376**	04/71-08/87	**1276**	08/87-10/89	**2251**	10/89-05/99
			1394	08/99-12/04	**1499**	12/04-05/05		
S76727	04/71-06/05	⊗10/05	**7377**	04/71-08/87	**1277**	08/87-06/91	**1859**	06/91-06/05
S76728	04/71-12/04	⊗01/05	**7378**	04/71-06/87	**1278**	06/87-10/89	**2252**	10/89-06/97
			1406	06/97-12/04				
S76729	04/71-09/03	⊗10/03	**7379**	04/71-06/87	**1279**	06/87-09/89	**2257**	09/89-12/91
			1830	12/91-01/92	**2257**	01/92-09/97	**1407**	09/97-09/03
S76730	04/71-04/89	⊗02/90	**7380**	04/71-06/87	**1280**	06/87-04/89		
S76731	05/71-10/04	⊗01/05	**7381**	05/71-06/87	**1281**	06/87-10/90	**1843**	10/90-10/04
S76732	05/71-05/05	⊗06/05	**7382**	05/71-06/87	**1282**	06/87-10/89	**2254**	10/89-05/93
			2002	05/93-01/97	**2254**	01/97-07/99	**1396**	09/99-05/05
S76733	05/71-01/86	⊗07/86	**7383**	05/71-01/86				
S76734	05/71-03/05	⊗06/05	**7384**	05/71-06/87	**1284**	06/87-10/89	**2253**	10/89-09/97
			1410	09/97-03/05				
S76735	05/71-06/05	⊗10/05	**7385**	05/71-06/87	**1285**	06/87-07/91	**1861**	07/91-06/05
S76736	05/71-06/05	⊗10/05	**7386**	05/71-06/87	**1286**	06/87-08/91	**1862**	08/91-06/05
S76737	05/71-02/05	⊗02/05	**7387**	05/71-06/87	**1287**	06/87-11/90	**1846**	11/90-02/05
S76738	05/71-04/05	⊗05/05	**7388**	05/71-06/87	**1288**	06/87-01/91	**1854**	01/91-04/05
S76739	06/71-04/05	⊗05/05	**7389**	06/71-07/87	**1289**	07/87-02/91	**1856**	02/91-04/05
S76740	06/71-05/05	Ⓟ⊗	**7390**	06/71-09/87	**1290**	09/87-10/89	**2255**	10/89-05/93
			2003	05/93-01/97	**2255**	01/97-04/99	**1392**	07/99-05/05
S76741	06/71-08/05	⊗10/05	**7391**	06/71-06/87	**1291**	06/87-09/91	**1864**	09/91-08/05
S76742	06/71-06/05	⊗10/05	**7392**	06/71-06/87	**1292**	06/87-09/91	**1863**	09/91-06/05
S76743	06/71-11/05	⊗ 06	**7393**	06/71-06/87	**1293**	06/87-12/91	**1866**	12/91-11/05
S76744	06/71-06/05	⊗10/05	**7394**	06/71-05/87	**1294**	05/87-01/92	**1867**	01/92-06/05
S76745	07/71-05/05	⊗07/05	**7395**	07/71-08/87	**1295**	08/87-11/91	**1865**	11/91-05/05
S76746	07/71-04/05	Ⓟ⊗	**7396**	07/71-06/87	**1296**	06/87-11/89	**2258**	11/89-04/99
			1393	07/99-04/05				
S76747	08/71-04/05	Ⓟ	**7397**	08/71-06/87	**1297**	06/87-11/89	**2256**	11/89-09/99
			1399	09/99-04/05				
S76748	08/71-04/05	⊗06/05	**7398**	08/71-08/87	**1298**	08/87-11/89	**2259**	11/89-05/93
			2004	05/93-01/97	**2259**	01/97-09/99	**1398**	09/99-04/05
S76749	08/71-05/05	⊗06/05	**7399**	08/71-05/87	**1299**	05/87-11/89	**2260**	01/97-08/99
			1397	09/99-05/05				
S76750	08/71-11/03	⊗11/03	**7400**	08/71-06/87	**1300**	06/87-10/89	**2261**	10/89-09/97
			1408	09/97-11/03				
S76751	09/71-05/05	⊗10/05	**7401**	09/71-05/83	**2601**	05/83-10/83	**7401**	10/83-06/87
			1201	06/87-02/92	**1868**	02/92-05/05		
S76752	09/71-07/05	⊗10/05	**7402**	09/71-05/83	**2601**	05/83-10/83	**7402**	10/83-05/87
			1202	05/87-06/91	**1860**	06/91-07/05		
S76753	09/71-06/05	⊗10/05	**7403**	09/71-05/83	**2602**	05/83-10/83	**7403**	10/83-08/87
			1203	08/87-02/92	**1869**	02/92-06/05		
S76754	09/71-07/04	⊗07/04	**7404**	09/71-05/83	**2602**	05/83-10/83	**7404**	10/83-06/87
			1204	06/87-07/92	**1875**	07/92-05/93	**2001**	05/93-01/97
			1802	01/97-07/04				
S76755	09/71-02/05	⊗03/05	**7405**	09/71-07/87	**1205**	07/87-07/92	**1874**	07/92-02/05
S76756	09/71-08/04	⊗08/04	**7406**	09/71-08/87	**1206**	08/87-03/92	**1871**	04/92-08/04
S76757	09/71-09/00	⊗11/03	**7407**	09/71-12/86	**1812**	01/87-09/00		
S76758	10/71-04/91	⊗10/91	**7408**	10/71-07/87	**1208**	07/87-11/90	**1221**	11/90-03/91
S76759	10/71-08/04	⊗09/04	**7409**	10/71-07/87	**1209**	07/87-06/92	**1873**	06/92-08/04
S76760	10/71-08/04	⊗08/04	**7410**	10/71-05/87	**1210**	05/87-09/92	**1879**	09/92-08/04
S76761	10/71-08/04	⊗09/04	**7411**	10/71-08/87	**1211**	08/87-07/92	**1876**	07/92-08/04
S76762	11/71-04/05	Ⓟ	**7412**	11/71-09/87	**1212**	09/87-10/92	**1881**	10/92-04/05
S76763	11/71-08/04	⊗09/04	**7413**	11/71-09/87	**1213**	09/87-07/92	**1877**	07/92-08/04
S76764	12/71-05/10	Ⓟ	**7414**	12/71-09/87	**1214**	09/87-11/92	**1883**	11/92-02/05
			1497	04/05-05/10				
S76765	12/71-07/05	⊗06/08	**7415**	12/71-08/87	**1215**	08/87-10/92	**1882**	10/92-07/05
S76766	12/71-09/04	⊗10/04	**7416**	12/71-09/87	**1216**	09/87-12/92	**1887**	12/92-09/04
S76767	12/71-02/05	⊗ 10	**7417**	12/71-09/87	**1217**	09/87-11/92	**1884**	11/92-02/05
S76768	12/71- 04	⊗ 04	**7418**	12/71-09/87	**1218**	09/87-08/92	**1878**	08/92- 04
S76769	12/71-11/04	⊗11/04	**7419**	12/71-09/87	**1219**	09/87-12/92	**1885**	12/92-11/04

S76770	01/72-09/04	⊗10/04	**7420**	01/72-06/87	**1220**	06/87-09/92	**1880**	09/92-09/04
S76771	01/72-09/04	⊗09/04	**7421**	01/72-08/87	**1221**	08/87-11/90	**1208**	11/90-05/92
			1872	05/92-09/04				
S76772	01/72-09/04	⊗10/04	**7422**	01/72-08/87	**1222**	08/87-12/92	**1886**	12/92-09/04
S76773	01/72-05/10	℗	**7423**	01/72-08/87	**1223**	08/87-01/93	**1888**	01/93-02/05
			1498	04/05-05/10				
S76774	02/72-02/05	⊗01/07	**7424**	02/72-09/87	**1224**	09/87-01/93	**1889**	01/93-02/05
S76775	02/72-04/05	⊗10/07	**7425**	02/72-08/87	**1225**	08/87-02/93	**1890**	02/93-04/05
S76776	02/72-09/04	⊗10/04	**7426**	02/72-08/87	**1226**	08/87-03/93	**1891**	03/93-09/04
S76777	02/72-07/04	⊗07/04	**7427**	02/72-03/86	**1801**	04/86-05/93	**2003**	05/93-01/97
			1801	01/97-07/04				
S76778	03/72-07/05	⊗07/05	**7428**	03/72-05/86	**1804**	05/86-07/05		
S76779	03/72-05/05	⊗05/05	**7429**	03/72-03/86	**1802**	04/86-12/89	**2262**	12/89-05/93
			2001	05/93-01/97	**2262**	01/97-07/99	**1395**	09/99-05/05
S76780	02/72-07/04	⊗09/04	**7430**	02/72-03/86	**1803**	05/86-07/04		
S76781	02/72-04/04	⊗04/04	**7431**	02/72-11/86	**1811**	12/86-04/04		
S76782	03/72-11/05	⊗01/05	**7432**	03/72-05/86	**1805**	06/86-11/05		
S76783	03/72-09/04	⊗09/04	**7433**	03/72-06/86	**1806**	06/86-09/04		
S76784	03/72-07/04	⊗08/04	**7434**	03/72-06/86	**1807**	07/86-07/04		
S76785	03/72-08/04	⊗08/04	**7435**	03/72-07/86	**1808**	09/86-08/04		
S76786	04/72-02/04	⊗03/04	**7436**	04/72-08/86	**1809**	09/86-02/04		
S76787	05/72-02/04	⊗03/04	**7437**	05/72-09/86	**1810**	11/86-02/04		

Class 421 4-CIG York

Driving Trailer Composite (Semi open) Lavatory

DTCsoL, some later DTSsoL

S76788-S76858

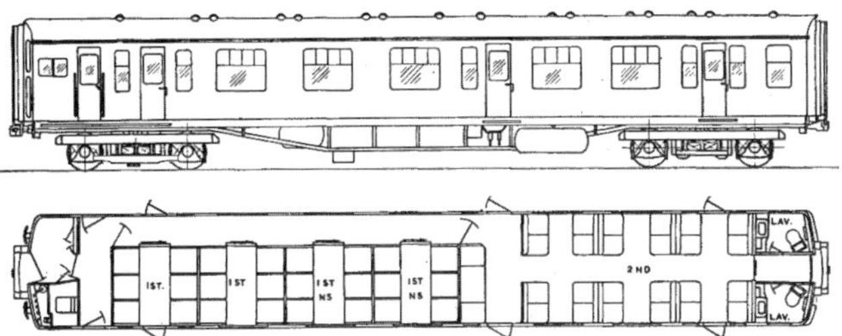

As built, Diagram 452 EE363, then facelifted EE369

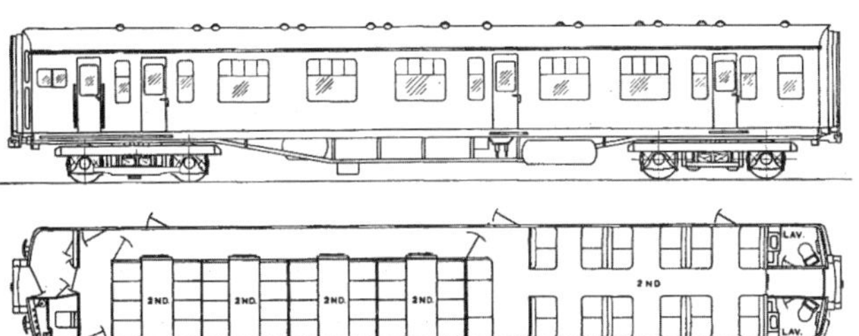

Converted to 3/4-COP units 1401-1411, Diagram EE246

Diagram:	452 EE363 EE369 EE246	Lot Number:	30815
Body:	64' 9½" × 9' 3"	Weight:	36t
Seats:	24 first 28 second 2 toilets COP 60 second 2 toilets	Bogies:	B5 (SR)

S76788	02/71-07/04	⊗09/04	**7367**	02/71-08/87	**1267**	08/87-06/88	**1818**	06/88-04/90
			1305	04/90-07/04				
S76789	02/71-06/03	⊗02/07	**7368**	02/71-06/87	**1268**	06/87-12/90	**1850**	12/90-06/03
S76790	02/71-07/05	⊗07/05	**7369**	02/71-05/87	**1269**	05/87-05/90	**1832**	05/90-07/05
S76791	03/71-12/04	⊗07/05	**7370**	03/71-08/87	**1270**	08/87-01/91	**1855**	01/91-12/04
S76792	02/71-02/05	⊗03/05	**7371**	02/71-08/87	**1271**	08/87-12/90	**1851**	12/90-02/05
S76793	02/71-02/05	⊗02/05	**7372**	02/71-06/87	**1272**	06/87-07/90	**1837**	07/90-02/05
S76794	02/71-07/04	⊗09/04	**7373**	02/71-06/87	**1273**	06/87-06/88	**1819**	06/88-05/90
			1306	05/90-07/04				
S76795	03/71-05/04	⊗06/04	**7374**	03/71-06/87	**1274**	06/87-08/90	**1840**	08/90-05/04
S76796	03/71-04/04	⊗06/04	**7375**	03/71-06/87	**1275**	06/87-09/90	**1842**	09/90-04/04
S76797	04/71-05/05	℗⊗	**7376**	04/71-08/87	**1276**	08/87-10/89	**2251**	10/89-05/99
			1394	08/99-12/04	**1499**	12/04-05/05		
S76798	04/71-06/05	⊗10/05	**7377**	04/71-08/87	**1277**	08/87-06/91	**1859**	06/91-06/05
S76799	04/71-12/04	⊗01/05	**7378**	04/71-06/87	**1278**	06/87-10/89	**2252**	10/89-06/97
			1406	06/97-12/04				
S76800	04/71-09/03	⊗10/03	**7379**	04/71-06/87	**1279**	06/87-09/89	**2257**	09/89-09/97
			1407	09/97-09/03				
S76801	04/71-04/89	⊗03/90	**7380**	04/71-06/87	**1280**	06/87-04/89		
S76802	05/71-10/04	⊗01/05	**7381**	05/71-06/87	**1281**	06/87-10/90	**1843**	10/90-10/04
S76803	05/71-05/05	⊗06/05	**7382**	05/71-06/87	**1282**	06/87-10/89	**2254**	10/89-05/93
			2002	05/93-01/97	**2254**	01/97-07/99	**1396**	09/99-05/05
S76804	05/71-06/05	⊗10/05	**7383**	05/71-01/86	**7700**	05/86-08/87	**3000**	08/87-12/88
			1203	11/89-02/92	**1869**	02/92-06/05		
S76805	05/71-03/05	⊗06/05	**7384**	05/71-06/87	**1284**	06/87-10/89	**2253**	10/89-09/97
			1410	09/97-03/05				
S76806	05/71-06/05	⊗10/05	**7385**	05/71-06/87	**1285**	06/87-07/91	**1861**	07/91-06/05
S76807	05/71-06/05	⊗10/05	**7386**	05/71-06/87	**1286**	06/87-08/91	**1862**	08/91-06/05
S76808	05/71-02/05	⊗02/05	**7387**	05/71-06/87	**1287**	06/87-11/90	**1846**	11/90-02/05
S76809	05/71-04/05	⊗05/05	**7388**	05/71-06/87	**1288**	06/87-01/91	**1854**	01/91-04/05
S76810	06/71-04/05	⊗05/05	**7389**	06/71-07/87	**1289**	07/87-02/91	**1856**	02/91-04/05
S76811	06/71-05/05	℗⊗	**7390**	06/71-09/87	**1290**	09/87-10/89	**2255**	10/89-05/93
			2003	05/93-01/97	**2255**	01/97-04/99	**1392**	07/99-05/05
S76812	06/71-08/05	⊗10/05	**7391**	06/71-06/87	**1291**	06/87-09/91	**1864**	09/91-08/05
S76813	06/71-06/05	⊗10/05	**7392**	06/71-06/87	**1292**	06/87-09/91	**1863**	09/91-06/05
S76814	06/71-11/05	⊗ 06	**7393**	06/71-06/87	**1293**	06/87-12/91	**1866**	12/91-11/05
S76815	06/71-06/05	⊗10/05	**7394**	06/71-05/87	**1294**	05/87-01/92	**1867**	01/92-06/05
S76816	07/71-11/89	⊗03/90	**7395**	07/71-08/87	**1295**	08/87-11/89		
S76817	07/71-04/05	℗⊗	**7396**	07/71-06/87	**1296**	06/87-11/89	**2258**	11/89-04/99
			1393	07/99-04/05				
S76818	08/71-04/05	℗	**7397**	08/71-06/87	**1297**	06/87-11/89	**2256**	11/89-09/99
			1399	09/99-04/05				
S76819	08/71-04/05	⊗06/05	**7398**	08/71-08/87	**1298**	08/87-11/89	**2259**	11/89-05/93
			2004	05/93-01/97	**2259**	01/97-09/99	**1398**	09/99-04/05
S76820	08/71-05/05	⊗06/05	**7399**	08/71-05/87	**1299**	05/87-11/89	**2260**	01/97-08/99
			1397	09/99-05/05				
S76821	08/71-11/03	⊗11/03	**7400**	08/71-06/87	**1300**	06/87-10/89	**2261**	10/89-09/97
			1408	09/97-11/03				
S76822	09/71-05/05	⊗10/05	**7401**	09/71-05/83	**2601**	05/83-10/83	**7401**	10/83-06/87
			1201	06/87-02/92	**1868**	02/92-05/05		
S76823	09/71-07/05	⊗10/05	**7402**	09/71-05/83	**2601**	05/83-10/83	**7402**	10/83-05/87
			1202	05/87-06/91	**1860**	06/91-07/05		
S76824	09/71-07/91	⊗03/99	**7403**	09/71-05/83	**2602**	05/83-10/83	**7403**	10/83-08/87
			1203	08/87-11/89				
S76825	09/71-07/04	⊗07/04	**7404**	09/71-05/83	**2602**	05/83-10/83	**7404**	10/83-06/87
			1204	06/87-07/92	**1875**	07/92-05/93	**2001**	05/93-01/97
			1802	01/97-07/04				
S76826	09/71-02/05	⊗06/05	**7405**	09/71-07/87	**1205**	07/87-07/92	**1874**	07/92-02/05
S76827	09/71-08/04	⊗08/04	**7406**	09/71-08/87	**1206**	08/87-03/92	**1871**	04/92-08/04
S76828	09/71-09/00	⊗11/03	**7407**	09/71-12/86	**1812**	01/87-09/00		
S76829	10/71-09/04	⊗09/04	**7408**	10/71-07/87	**1208**	07/87-05/92	**1872**	05/92-09/04
S76830	10/71-08/04	⊗09/04	**7409**	10/71-07/87	**1209**	07/87-06/92	**1873**	06/92-08/04
S76831	10/71-08/04	⊗08/04	**7410**	10/71-05/87	**1210**	05/87-09/92	**1879**	09/92-08/04
S76832	10/71-08/04	⊗09/04	**7411**	10/71-08/87	**1211**	08/87-07/92	**1876**	07/92-08/04
S76833	11/71-04/05	℗⊗10/11	**7412**	11/71-09/87	**1212**	09/87-10/92	**1881**	10/92-04/05
S76834	11/71-08/04	⊗09/04	**7413**	11/71-09/87	**1213**	09/87-07/92	**1877**	07/92-08/04
S76835	12/71-05/10	℗	**7414**	12/71-09/87	**1214**	09/87-11/92	**1883**	11/92-02/05
			1497	04/05-05/10				
S76836	12/71-07/05	⊗02/08	**7415**	12/71-08/87	**1215**	08/87-10/92	**1882**	10/92-07/05
S76837	12/71-09/04	⊗10/04	**7416**	12/71-09/87	**1216**	09/87-12/92	**1887**	12/92-09/04
S76838	12/71-02/05	℗⊗ 10	**7417**	12/71-09/87	**1217**	09/87-11/92	**1884**	11/92-02/05
S76839	12/71- 04	⊗ 04	**7418**	12/71-09/87	**1218**	09/87-08/92	**1878**	08/92- 04
S76840	12/71-11/04	⊗11/04	**7419**	12/71-09/87	**1219**	09/87-12/92	**1885**	12/92-11/04
S76841	01/72-09/04	⊗10/04	**7420**	01/72-06/87	**1220**	06/87-09/92	**1880**	09/92-09/04
S76842	01/72-07/04	⊗08/04	**7421**	01/72-08/87	**1221**	08/87-04/92	**1870**	04/92-07/04
S76843	01/72-09/04	⊗10/04	**7422**	01/72-08/87	**1222**	08/87-12/92	**1886**	12/92-09/04
S76844	01/72-05/10	℗	**7423**	01/72-08/87	**1223**	08/87-01/93	**1888**	01/93-02/05
			1498	04/05-05/10				
S76845	02/72-02/05	⊗01/07	**7424**	02/72-09/87	**1224**	09/87-01/93	**1889**	01/93-02/05
S76846	02/72-04/05	⊗02/09	**7425**	02/72-08/87	**1225**	08/87-02/93	**1890**	02/93-04/05
S76847	02/72-09/04	⊗10/04	**7426**	02/72-08/87	**1226**	08/87-03/93	**1891**	03/93-09/04
S76848	02/72-07/04	⊗07/04	**7427**	02/72-03/86	**1801**	04/86-05/93	**2003**	05/93-01/97
			1801	01/97-07/04				
S76849	03/72-07/05	⊗07/05	**7428**	03/72-05/86	**1804**	05/86-07/05		
S76850	03/72-05/05	⊗05/05	**7429**	03/72-03/86	**1802**	04/86-12/89	**2262**	12/89-05/93
			2001	05/93-01/97	**2262**	01/97-07/99	**1395**	09/99-05/05
S76851	02/72-07/04	⊗09/04	**7430**	02/72-03/86	**1803**	05/86-07/04		
S76852	02/72-04/04	⊗04/04	**7431**	02/72-11/86	**1811**	12/86-04/04		
S76853	03/72-11/05	⊗01/05	**7432**	03/72-05/86	**1805**	06/86-11/05		
S76854	03/72-09/04	⊗09/04	**7433**	03/72-06/86	**1806**	06/86-09/04		
S76855	03/72-07/04	⊗08/04	**7434**	03/72-06/86	**1807**	07/86-07/04		
S76856	03/72-08/04	⊗08/04	**7435**	03/72-07/86	**1808**	09/86-08/04		
S76857	04/72-02/04	⊗03/04	**7436**	04/72-08/86	**1809**	09/86-02/04		
S76858	05/72-02/04	⊗03/04	**7437**	05/72-09/86	**1810**	11/86-02/04		

Class 421 4-CIG York

Driving Trailer Composite (Semi-open) Lavatory

DTCsoL

S76859

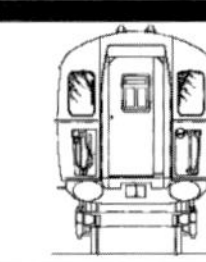

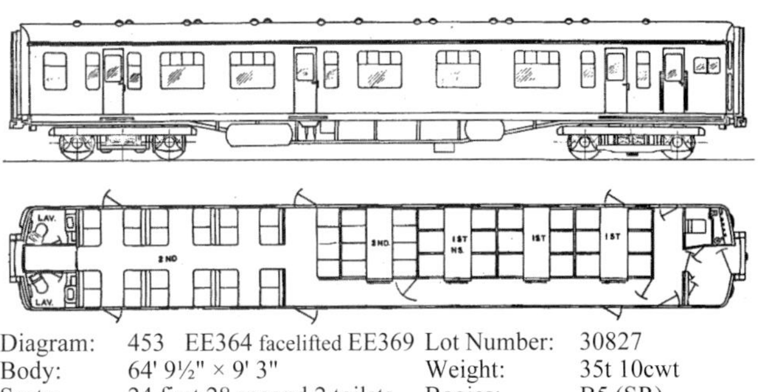

Diagram:	453 EE364 facelifted EE369	Lot Number:	30827
Body:	64' 9½" × 9' 3"	Weight:	35t 10cwt
Seats:	24 first 28 second 2 toilets	Bogies:	B5 (SR)

S76859	05/72-02/04	⊗12/04	**7438**	05/72-08/79	**7438**	01/80-02/87	**1813**	02/87-02/04

Class 421 4-CIG York

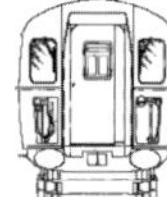

Driving Trailer Composite (Semi-open) Lavatory
DTCsoL
S76860

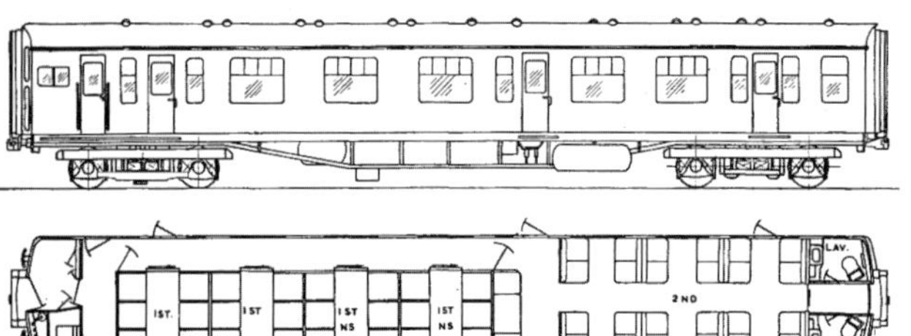

Diagram:	452 EE363 facelifted EE369	Lot Number:	30828
Body:	64' 9½" × 9' 3"	Weight:	36t
Seats:	24 first 28 second 2 toilets	Bogies:	B5 (SR)

S76860	05/72-02/04	⊗12/04	**7438**	05/72-08/79	**7438**	01/80-02/87	**1813**	02/87-02/04

Class 423 4-VEP York

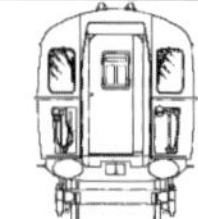

Driving Trailer Composite (Semi-open) Lavatory
DTCsoL
S76861-S76942

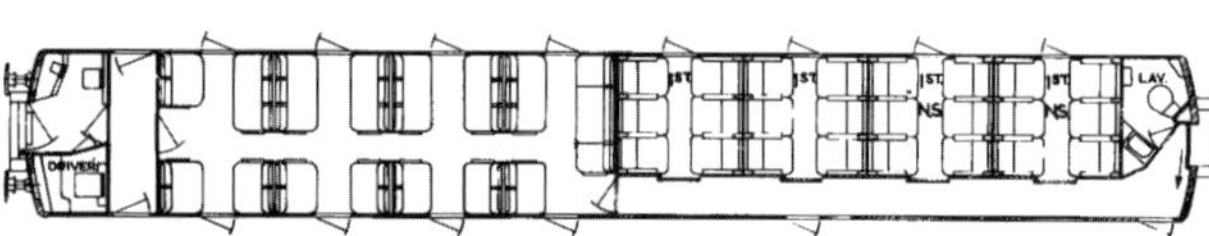

As built, Diagram 459 EE368

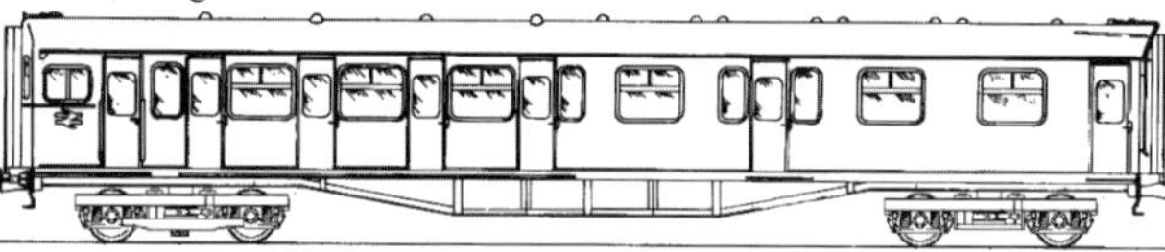

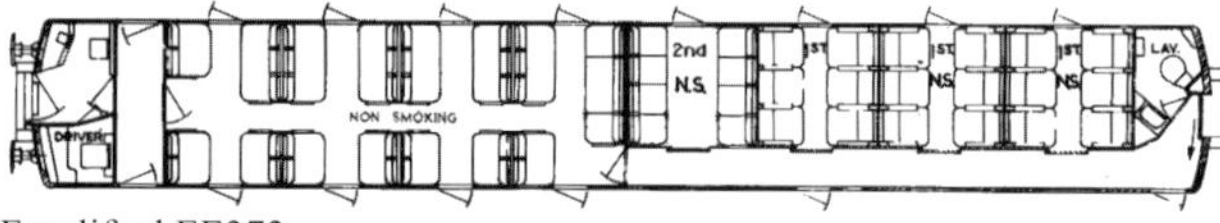

Facelifted EE373

Diagram:	459 EE368 EE373	Lot Number:	30853
Body:	64' 9⅝" × 9' 3"	Weight:	34t 5cwt
Seats:	24 first 38 second 1 toilet later 18 first 46 second 1 toilet	Bogies:	B5 (SR)

S76861	05/73-04/05	⊗04/05	**7854**	05/73-05/87	**3154**	05/87-06/93	**3539**	06/93-04/05
S76862	05/73-04/05	⊗04/05	**7854**	05/73-05/87	**3154**	05/87-06/93	**3539**	06/93-04/05
S76863	05/73-04/05	⊗04/05	**7855**	05/73-05/87	**3155**	05/87-07/93	**3540**	07/93-04/05
S76864	05/73-04/05	⊗04/05	**7855**	05/73-05/87	**3155**	05/87-07/93	**3540**	07/93-04/05
S76865	06/73-05/04	⊗06/04	**7856**	06/73-06/87	**3156**	06/87-04/94	**3555**	04/94-05/04
S76866	06/73-05/04	⊗06/04	**7856**	06/73-06/87	**3156**	06/87-04/94	**3555**	04/94-05/04
S76867	06/73-07/04	⊗08/04	**7857**	06/73-09/87	**3157**	09/87-07/94	**3561**	07/94-07/04
S76868	06/73-07/04	⊗08/04	**7857**	06/73-09/87	**3157**	09/87-07/94	**3561**	07/94-07/04
S76869	06/73-05/04	⊗06/04	**7858**	06/73-06/87	**3158**	06/87-05/94	**3557**	05/94-05/04
S76870	06/73-05/04	⊗06/04	**7858**	06/73-06/87	**3158**	06/87-05/94	**3557**	05/94-05/04
S76871	06/73-04/05	⊗06/05	**7859**	06/73-08/87	**3159**	08/87-09/94	**3567**	09/94-06/02
			3401	07/02-04/05				
S76872	06/73-04/05	⊗06/05	**7859**	06/73-08/87	**3159**	08/87-09/94	**3567**	09/94-06/02
			3401	07/02-04/05				
S76873	07/73-07/04	⊗08/04	**7860**	07/73-06/87	**3160**	06/87-07/94	**3563**	07/94-07/04
S76874	07/73-07/04	⊗08/04	**7860**	07/73-06/87	**3160**	06/87-07/94	**3563**	07/94-07/04
S76875	07/73-10/05	Ⓟ	**7861**	07/73-05/87	**3161**	05/87-11/93	**3545**	11/93-10/05
S76876	07/73-10/05	⊗12/05	**7861**	07/73-05/87	**3161**	05/87-11/93	**3545**	11/93-10/05
S76877	07/73-10/05	⊗02/06	**7862**	07/73-07/87	**3162**	07/87-08/94	**3565**	08/94-10/05
S76878	07/73-10/05	⊗02/06	**7862**	07/73-07/87	**3162**	07/87-08/94	**3565**	08/94-10/05
S76879	07/73-06/05	⊗07/05	**7863**	07/73-06/87	**3163**	06/87-12/94	**3572**	12/94-06/05
S76880	07/73-06/05	⊗07/05	**7863**	07/73-06/87	**3163**	06/87-12/94	**3572**	12/94-06/05
S76881	08/73-08/05	⊗09/05	**7864**	08/73-08/87	**3164**	08/87-03/95	**3584**	03/95-08/05
S76882	08/73-08/05	⊗09/05	**7864**	08/73-08/87	**3164**	08/87-03/95	**3584**	03/95-08/05
S76883	08/73-12/05	⊗12/05	**7865**	08/73-08/87	**3165**	08/87-07/94	**3564**	07/94-12/05
S76884	08/73-12/05	⊗12/05	**7865**	08/73-08/87	**3165**	08/87-07/94	**3564**	07/94-12/05
S76885	08/73-11/04	⊗10/04	**7866**	08/73-07/87	**3166**	07/87-05/94	**3556**	05/94-11/04
S76886	08/73-11/04	⊗10/04	**7866**	08/73-07/87	**3166**	07/87-05/94	**3556**	05/94-11/04
S76887	08/73-10/05	Ⓟ	**7867**	08/73-08/87	**3167**	08/87-10/94	**3568**	10/94-10/05
S76888	08/73-10/05	⊗02/06	**7867**	08/73-08/87	**3167**	08/87-10/94	**3568**	10/94-10/05
S76889	09/73-11/04	⊗02/05	**7868**	09/73-08/87	**3168**	08/87-03/88	**3421**	03/88-11/04
S76890	09/73-11/04	⊗02/05	**7868**	09/73-08/87	**3168**	08/87-03/88	**3421**	03/88-11/04
S76891	09/73-05/04	⊗10/05	**7869**	09/73-05/87	**3169**	05/87-02/95	**3582**	02/95-05/04
S76892	09/73-09/05	⊗12/05	**7869**	09/73-05/87	**3169**	05/87-07/92	**3170**	02/93-11/93
			3544	11/93-09/05				
S76893	09/73-05/05	⊗05/05	**7870**	09/73-07/87	**3170**	07/87-02/93	**3511**	11/94-05/05
S76894	09/73-09/05	⊗12/05	**7870**	09/73-07/87	**3170**	07/87-11/93	**3544**	11/93-09/05
S76895	09/73-10/05	⊗12/05	**7871**	09/73-07/87	**3171**	07/87-01/94	**3547**	01/94-10/05
S76896	09/73-10/05	⊗12/05	**7871**	09/73-07/87	**3171**	07/87-01/94	**3547**	01/94-10/05
S76897	10/73-09/05	⊗10/05	**7872**	10/73-06/87	**3172**	06/87-06/94	**3560**	06/94-09/05
S76898	10/73-09/05	⊗10/05	**7872**	10/73-06/87	**3172**	06/87-06/94	**3560**	06/94-09/05
S76899	10/73-11/04	⊗02/05	**7873**	10/73-05/87	**3173**	05/87-10/93	**3543**	10/93-11/04
S76900	10/73-11/04	⊗02/05	**7873**	10/73-05/87	**3173**	05/87-10/93	**3543**	10/93-11/04
S76901	10/73-06/05	⊗08/05	**7874**	10/73-07/87	**3174**	07/87-12/89	**3499**	12/89-06/05
S76902	10/73-06/05	⊗08/05	**7874**	10/73-07/87	**3174**	07/87-12/89	**3499**	12/89-06/05
S76903	10/73-08/05	⊗10/05	**7875**	10/73-08/87	**3175**	08/87-02/94	**3548**	02/94-08/05
S76904	10/73-08/05	⊗10/05	**7875**	10/73-08/87	**3175**	08/87-02/94	**3548**	02/94-08/05
S76905	11/73-11/04	⊗10/04	**7876**	11/73-05/87	**3176**	05/87-03/94	**3554**	03/94-11/04
S76906	11/73-11/04	⊗10/04	**7876**	11/73-05/87	**3176**	05/87-03/94	**3554**	03/94-11/04
S76907	12/73-10/05	⊗10/05	**7877**	12/73-08/87	**3177**	08/87-07/94	**3562**	07/94-10/05
S76908	12/73-10/05	⊗10/05	**7877**	12/73-08/87	**3177**	08/87-07/94	**3562**	07/94-10/05
S76909	01/74-11/04	⊗02/05	**7878**	01/74-07/87	**3178**	09/87-11/94	**3570**	11/94-11/04
S76910	01/74-11/04	⊗02/05	**7878**	01/74-07/87	**3178**	09/87-11/94	**3570**	11/94-11/04
S76911	01/74-07/05	⊗07/05	**7879**	01/74-06/87	**3179**	06/87-06/95	**3589**	06/95-07/05
S76912	01/74-07/05	⊗07/05	**7879**	01/74-06/87	**3179**	06/87-06/95	**3589**	06/95-07/05
S76913	02/74-05/05	⊗05/05	**7880**	02/74-07/87	**3180**	07/87-03/94	**3553**	03/94-05/05
S76914	02/74-05/05	⊗05/05	**7880**	02/74-07/87	**3180**	07/87-03/94	**3553**	03/94-05/05
S76915	02/74-12/04	⊗02/05	**7881**	02/74-08/87	**3181**	08/87-09/94	**3566**	09/94-12/04
S76916	02/74-12/04	⊗02/05	**7881**	02/74-08/87	**3181**	08/87-09/94	**3566**	09/94-12/04
S76917	12/73-06/05	⊗07/05	**7882**	12/73-07/87	**3182**	07/87-09/95	**3591**	09/95-06/05
S76918	12/73-06/05	⊗07/05	**7882**	12/73-07/87	**3182**	07/87-09/95	**3591**	09/95-06/05
S76919	02/74-07/05	⊗07/05	**7883**	02/74-09/87	**3183**	09/87-12/94	**3573**	12/94-07/05
S76920	02/74-07/05	⊗07/05	**7883**	02/74-09/87	**3183**	09/87-12/94	**3573**	12/94-07/05
S76921	02/74-08/05	⊗10/05	**7884**	02/74-09/87	**3184**	09/87-03/95	**3586**	03/95-08/05
S76922	02/74-08/05	⊗10/05	**7884**	02/74-09/87	**3184**	09/87-03/95	**3586**	03/95-08/05
S76923	02/74-05/04	⊗08/05	**7885**	02/74-07/87	**3185**	07/87-05/95	**3588**	05/95-05/04
S76924	02/74-05/04	⊗10/05	**7885**	02/74-07/87	**3185**	07/87-05/95	**3588**	05/95-05/04
			3500	07/04-10/05				
S76925	03/74-10/05	⊗10/05	**7886**	03/74-10/87	**3186**	10/87-05/95	**3587**	05/95-10/05
S76926	03/74-10/05	⊗10/05	**7886**	03/74-10/87	**3186**	10/87-05/95	**3587**	05/95-10/05
S76927	03/74-12/04	⊗02/05	**7887**	03/74-09/87	**3187**	09/87-11/94	**3571**	11/94-12/04
S76928	03/74-12/04	⊗02/05	**7887**	03/74-09/87	**3187**	09/87-11/94	**3571**	11/94-12/04
S76929	03/74-08/05	⊗08/05	**7888**	03/74-08/87	**3188**	08/87-12/94	**3574**	12/94-08/05
S76930	03/74-08/05	⊗08/05	**7888**	03/74-08/87	**3188**	08/87-12/94	**3574**	12/94-08/05
S76931	03/74-11/04	⊗02/05	**7889**	03/74-08/87	**3189**	08/87-12/94	**3575**	12/94-11/04
S76932	03/74-11/04	⊗02/05	**7889**	03/74-08/87	**3189**	08/87-12/94	**3575**	12/94-11/04
S76933	04/74-06/05	⊗06/05	**7890**	04/74-08/87	**3190**	08/87-01/95	**3577**	01/95-06/05
S76934	04/74-06/05	⊗06/05	**7890**	04/74-08/87	**3190**	08/87-01/95	**3577**	01/95-06/05
S76935	04/74-08/05	⊗10/05	**7891**	04/74-06/87	**3191**	06/87-01/95	**3579**	01/95-08/05
S76936	04/74-08/05	⊗10/05	**7891**	04/74-06/87	**3191**	06/87-01/95	**3579**	01/95-08/05
S76937	04/74-07/05	⊗07/05	**7892**	04/74-07/87	**3192**	07/87-02/95	**3583**	02/95-07/05
S76938	04/74-07/05	⊗07/05	**7892**	04/74-07/87	**3192**	07/87-02/95	**3583**	02/95-07/05
S76939	05/74-07/05	⊗07/05	**7893**	05/74-09/87	**3193**	09/87-03/95	**3585**	03/95-07/05
S76940	05/74-07/05	⊗07/05	**7893**	05/74-09/87	**3193**	09/87-03/95	**3585**	03/95-07/05
S76941	05/74-10/05	⊗10/05	**7894**	05/74-10/87	**3194**	10/87-07/95	**3590**	07/95-10/05
S76942	05/74-10/05	⊗10/05	**7894**	05/74-10/87	**3194**	10/87-07/95	**3590**	07/95-10/05

Class 438 4-TC York

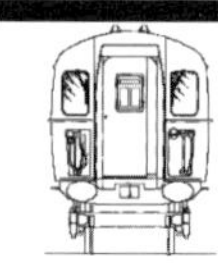

Driving Trailer Second Open
DTSO
S76943-S76948

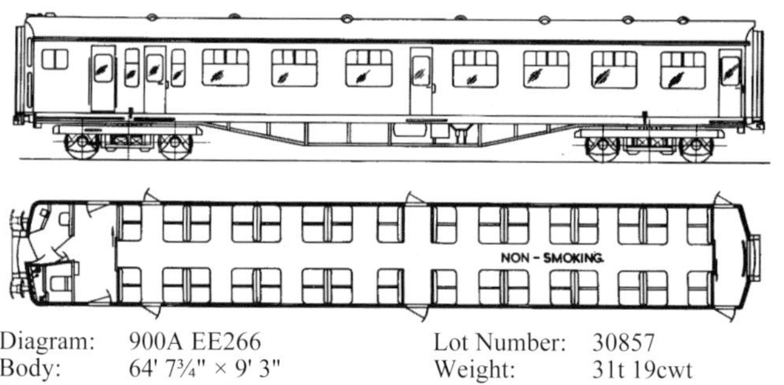

Diagram:	900A EE266	Lot Number:	30857
Body:	64' 7¾" × 9' 3"	Weight:	31t 19cwt
Seats:	64 second	Bogies:	B5 (SR)

S76943	02/75-07/88	⊗05/90	**432**	02/75-06/86	**8032**	06/86-07/88	⊂**3913**
S76944	02/75-07/88	⊗05/90	**432**	02/75-06/86	**8032**	06/86-07/88	⊂**3987**

S76945	02/75-05/89	⊗06/90	**433**	02/75-09/86	**8033**	09/86-06/87	**2807**	06/87-05/89 ⊂**4030**
S76946	02/75-05/89	⊗06/90	**433**	02/75-09/86	**8033**	09/86-06/87	**2807**	06/87-05/89 ⊂**4032**
S76947	01/75-09/88	⊗08/90	**434**	01/75-09/86	**8034**	09/86-09/88		⊂**4034**
S76948	01/75-09/88	⊗08/90	**434**	01/75-09/86	**8034**	09/86-09/88		⊂**4073**

Class 312/0 York

Battery Driving Trailer Second Open Lavatory
BDTSOL
E76949-E76974

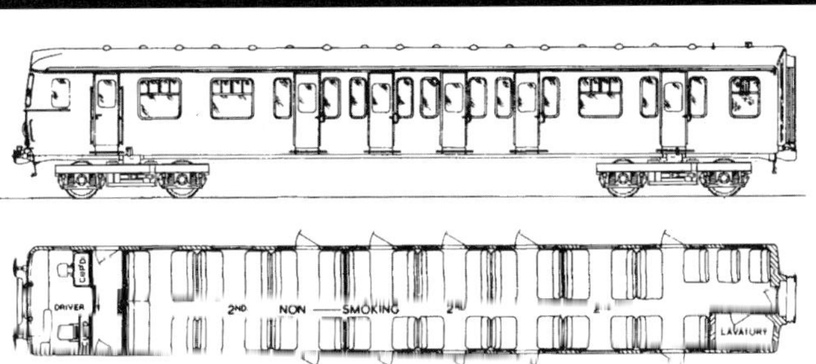

Diagram:	465 EF213	Lot Number:	30863
Body:	65' 1⅝" × 9' 3"	Weight:	34t 5cwt
Seats:	84 second 1 toilet	Bogies:	B4

E76949	05/77-10/03	⊗11/04	**312001**	05/77-05/79	**312701**	05/79-10/03
E76950	06/77-09/03	⊗10/04	**312002**	06/77-05/79	**312702**	05/79-09/03
E76951	06/77-03/04	⊗11/04	**312003**	06/77-04/79	**312703**	04/79-03/04
E76952	07/77-09/03	⊗10/03	**312004**	07/77-03/79	**312704**	03/79-09/03
E76953	07/77-09/03	⊗09/04	**312005**	07/77-04/79	**312705**	04/79-09/03
E76954	07/77-09/03	⊗12/04	**312006**	07/77-05/79	**312706**	05/79-09/03
E76955	07/77-09/03	⊗07/04	**312007**	07/77-04/79	**312707**	04/79-09/03
E76956	07/77-09/03	⊗10/03	**312008**	07/77-05/79	**312708**	05/79-09/03
E76957	08/77-10/03	⊗01/05	**312009**	08/77-05/79	**312709**	05/79-10/03
E76958	08/77-09/03	⊗10/03	**312010**	08/77-05/79	**312710**	05/79-09/03
E76959	08/77-09/03	⊗09/04	**312011**	08/77-05/79	**312711**	05/79-09/03
E76960	09/77-09/04	⊗11/04	**312012**	09/77-04/79	**312712**	04/79-09/04
E76961	09/77-01/03	⊗10/04	**312013**	09/77-04/79	**312713**	04/79-01/03
E76962	10/77-03/04	⊗12/04	**312014**	10/77-03/79	**312714**	03/79-03/04
E76963	10/77-03/04	⊗12/04	**312015**	10/77-04/79	**312715**	04/79-03/04
E76964	10/77-09/03	⊗10/03	**312016**	10/77-04/79	**312716**	04/79-09/03
E76965	11/77-09/03	⊗10/03	**312017**	11/77-04/79	**312717**	04/79-09/03
E76966	11/77-05/04	⊗07/04	**312018**	11/77-05/79	**312718**	05/79-05/04
E76967	12/77-09/03	⊗12/04	**312019**	12/77-04/79	**312719**	04/79-09/03
E76968	12/77-09/03	⊗10/03	**312020**	12/77-05/79	**312720**	05/79-09/03
E76969	12/77-05/04	⊗07/04	**312021**	12/77-05/79	**312721**	05/79-05/04
E76970	12/77-05/04	⊗12/04	**312022**	12/77-04/79	**312722**	04/79-05/04
E76971	01/78-05/04	⊗07/04	**312023**	01/78-04/79	**312723**	04/79-05/04
E76972	01/78-09/03	⊗09/04	**312024**	01/78-05/79	**312724**	05/79-09/03
E76973	09/78-04/02	⊗02/05	**312025**	09/78-03/79	**312725**	03/79-04/02
E76974	12/78-11/01	⊗02/05	**312026**	12/78-05/79	**312726**	05/79-11/01

Class 312/1 York

Battery Driving Trailer Second Open Lavatory
BDTSOL
E76975-E76993

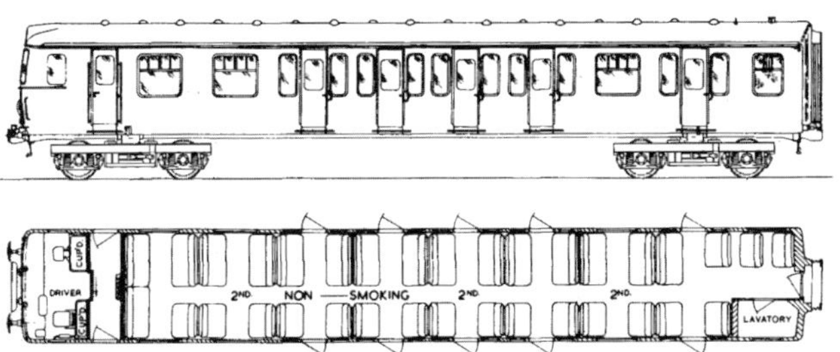

Diagram:	465 EF213	Lot Number:	30867
Body:	65' 1⅝" × 9' 3"	Weight:	34t 5cwt
Seats:	84 second 1 toilet	Bogies:	B4

E76975	03/75-03/03	⊗01/05	**312101**	03/75-78	**312781**	78-03/03
E76976	04/75-11/01	⊗03/05	**312102**	04/75-78	**312782**	78-11/01
E76977	04/75-03/03	⊗02/05	**312103**	04/75-78	**312783**	78-03/03
E76978	05/75-03/03	⊗09/04	**312104**	05/75-78	**312784**	78-03/03
E76979	06/75-09/02	⊗03/05	**312105**	06/75-78	**312785**	78-09/02
E76980	06/75-02/02	⊗01/05	**312106**	06/75-78	**312786**	78-02/02
E76981	06/75-03/02	⊗02/05	**312107**	06/75-78	**312787**	78-03/02
E76982	06/75-03/02	⊗01/05	**312108**	06/75-78	**312788**	78-03/02
E76983	07/75-09/02	⊗03/05	**312109**	07/75-78	**312789**	78-09/02
E76984	07/75-02/02	⊗02/05	**312110**	07/75-78	**312790**	78-02/02
E76985	07/75-04/02	⊗02/05	**312111**	07/75-78	**312791**	78-04/02
E76986	08/75-03/03	⊗03/05	**312112**	08/75-78	**312792**	78-03/03
E76987	08/75-02/02	⊗02/05	**312113**	08/75-78	**312793**	78-02/02
E76988	08/75-12/01	⊗02/05	**312114**	08/75-78	**312794**	78-12/01
E76989	09/75-12/01	⊗02/05	**312115**	09/75-78	**312795**	78-12/01
E76990	09/75-12/01	⊗01/05	**312116**	09/75-78	**312796**	78-12/01
E76991	09/75-03/03	⊗02/05	**312117**	09/75-78	**312797**	78-03/03
E76992	10/75-02/02	⊗01/05	**312118**	10/75-78	**312798**	78-02/02
E76993	10/75-03/02	⊗03/05	**312119**	10/75-78	**312799**	78-03/02

Class 312/2 York

Battery Driving Trailer Second Open Lavatory
BDTSOL
M76994-M76997

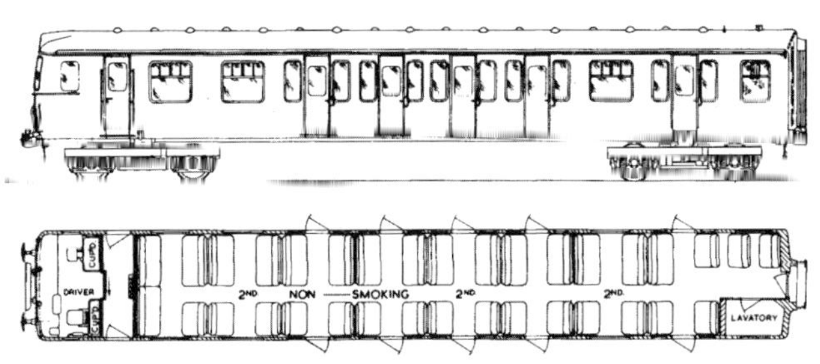

Diagram:	465 EF213	Lot Number:	30891
Body:	65' 1⅝" × 9' 3"	Weight:	34t 5cwt
Seats:	84 second 1 toilet	Bogies:	B4

M76994	02/76-11/01	⊗01/05	**312201**	02/76-04/88	**312727**	04/88-11/01
M76995	01/76-10/03	⊗01/05	**312202**	01/76-04/88	**312728**	04/88-10/03
M76996	02/76-12/01	⊗02/05	**312203**	02/76-05/88	**312729**	05/88-12/01
M76997	12/75-08/02	⊗03/05	**312204**	12/75-05/88	**312730**	05/88-08/02

Class 310 Wolverton

Battery Driving Trailer Second Open
BDTSO
M76998

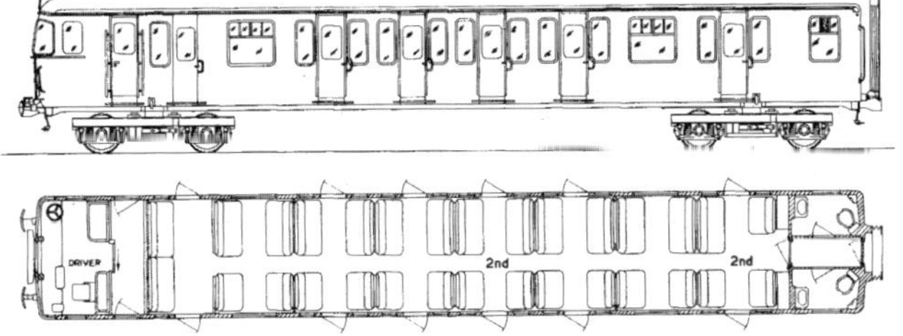

Diagram:	482 EF214	Lot Number:	c30747
Body:	65' 1⅝" × 9' 3"	Weight:	34t 5cwt
Seats:	75 second 2 toilets	Bogies:	B4

M76998	04/75-06/01	⊗	**094**	04/75-01/83	**310094**	01/83-06/01	⊂**70756**

77000-77095 *Class 317/1* *09/81*

South Tyneside Eastleigh
Driving Trailer Second (Semi-open)
DTCso later DTSso
E77100-E77114 Later Class 416/2 2-EPB

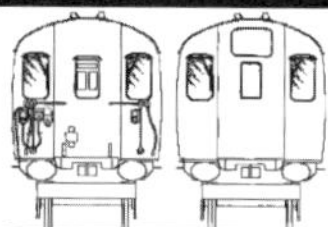

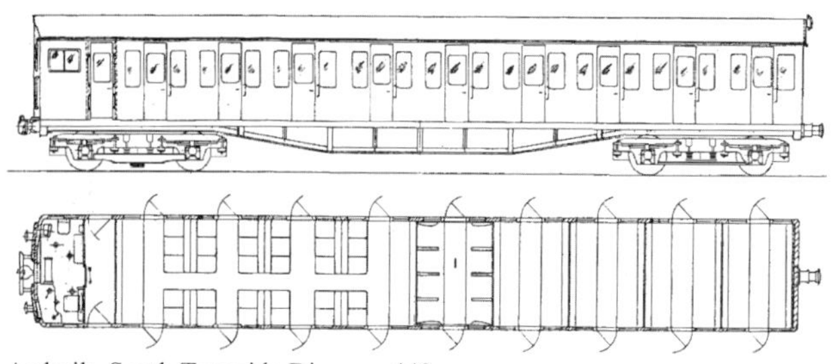

As built, South Tyneside Diagram 440

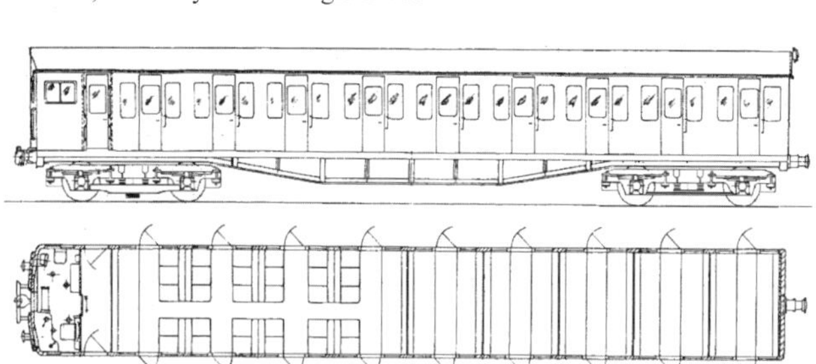

Converted to Southern Region 2-EPB, Diagram 429

Diagram:	440 later 429	Lot Number:	30117
Body:	63' 11½" × 9' 3¼"	Weight:	30t 0cwt
Seats:	90 second 8 first later 102 second		
Bogies:	Mk 3D		

E77100	12/54-10/84	⊗11/91	08/63⇨**S**	**5781**	08/63-08/84	**6281**	08/84-10/84
E77101	12/54-10/84	**➲977578**	10/63⇨**S**	**5782**	10/63-08/84	**6282**	08/84-10/84
E77102	01/55-10/84	**➲977690**	07/63⇨**S**	**5783**	07/63-08/84	**6283**	08/84-10/84
E77103	01/55-10/84	**➲977691**	08/63⇨**S**	**5784**	08/63-08/84	**6284**	08/84-10/84
E77104	01/55-10/84	⊗01/93	09/63⇨**S**	**5785**	09/63-08/84	**6285**	08/84-10/84
E77105	02/55-10/84	⊗11/91	09/63⇨**S**	**5786**	09/63-08/84	**6286**	08/84-10/84
E77106	02/55-10/84	**➲977689**	08/63⇨**S**	**5787**	08/63-09/84	**6287**	09/84-10/84
E77107	02/55-05/84	⊗03/90	08/63⇨**S**	**5788**	08/63-05/84		
E77108	02/55-10/84	**➲977297**	07/63⇨**S**	**5789**	07/63-09/84	**6289**	09/84-10/84
E77109	02/55-10/84	**➲977579**	08/63⇨**S**	**5790**	08/63-08/84	**6290**	08/84-10/84
E77110	03/55-10/84	**➲977507**	08/63⇨**S**	**5791**	08/63-09/84	**6291**	09/84-10/84
E77111	03/55-10/84	**➲977688**	09/63⇨**S**	**5792**	09/63-08/84	**6292**	08/84-10/84
E77112	03/55-10/84	**➲977508**	07/63⇨**S**	**5793**	07/63-08/84	**6293**	08/84-10/84
E77113	03/55-03/94	⊗04/94	08/63⇨**S**	**5794**	08/63-05/84	**6409**	02/86-03/94
E77114	04/55-05/84	⊗04/87	09/63⇨**S**	**5795**	09/63-05/84		

Class 414/2 2-HAP Ashford/Eastleigh
Driving Trailer Composite (Semi-open) Lavatory
DTCsoL, later DTSsoL
S77115-S77118

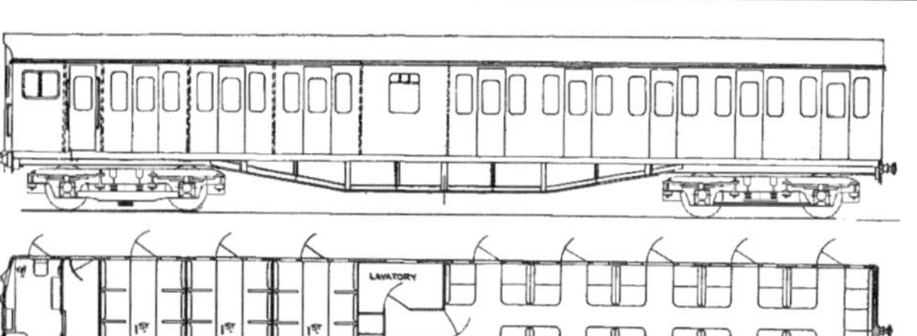

As built, Diagram 441 EE361

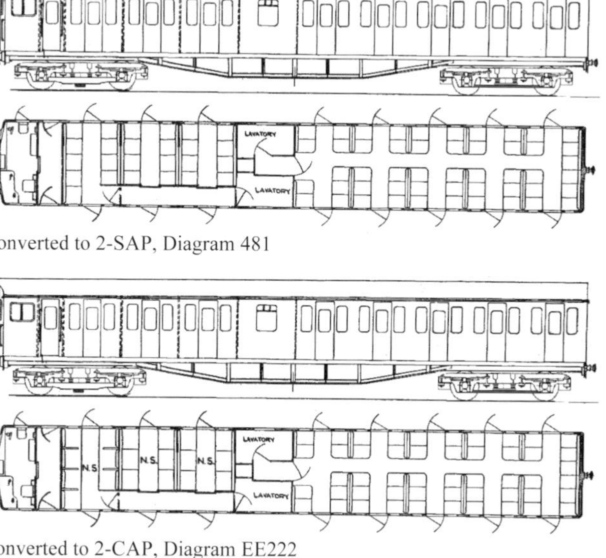

Converted to 2-SAP, Diagram 481

Converted to 2-CAP, Diagram EE222

Diagram:	441 481 EE361 EE222	Lot Number:	30316
Body:	63' 11½" × 9' 3"	Weight:	32t 0cwt
Seats:	19 first 50 second 2 toilets	Bogies:	Mk 4
	later 76 second 2 toilets or 69 second 2 toilets		

S77115	06/57-05/93	⊗06/93	**6001**	06/57-05/74	**5901**	05/74-02/80	**6001**	02/80-06/82
			3211	06/82-05/93				
S77116	07/57-05/84	⊗01/85	**6002**	07/57-05/74	**5902**	05/74-05/80	**6002**	05/80-05/84
S77117	07/57-02/95	⊗05/95	**6003**	07/57-05/74	**5903**	05/74-04/80	**6003**	04/80-05/82
			3203	05/82-11/94	**3201**	11/94-02/95		
S77118	08/57-09/93	⊗11/93	**6004**	08/57-04/74	**5904**	04/74-07/80	**6004**	07/80-05/82
			3202	05/82-09/93				

Class 414/2 2-HAP Ashford/Eastleigh
Driving Trailer Composite (Semi-open) Lavatory
DTCsoL, later DTSsoL
S77119-S77125

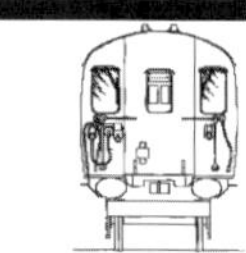

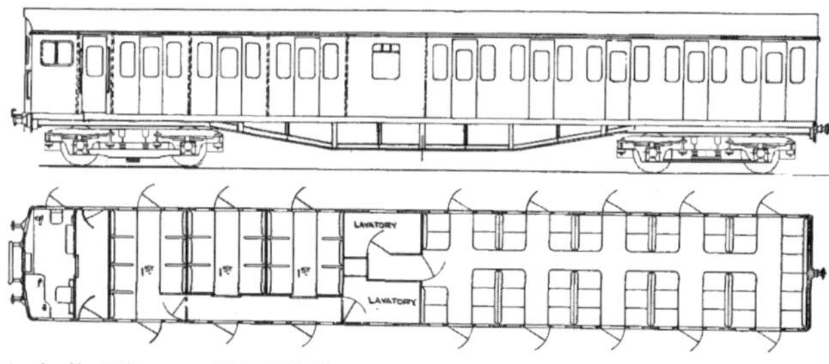

As built, Diagram 441 EE361

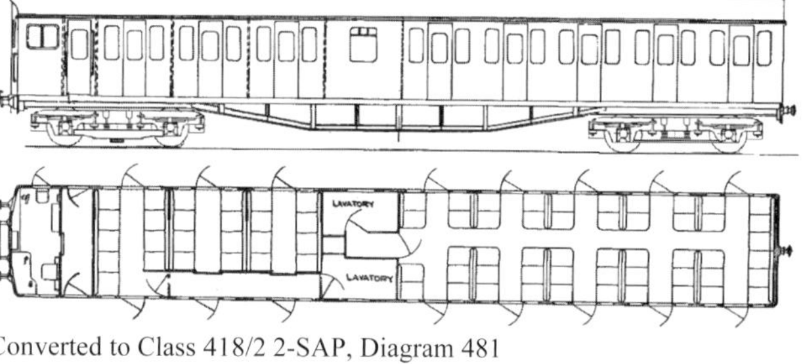

Converted to Class 418/2 2-SAP, Diagram 481

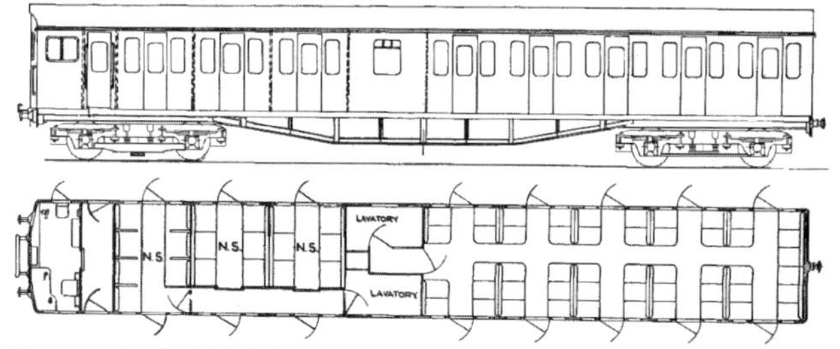

Converted to 2-CAP, Diagram EE222

Diagram:	441 481 EE361 EE222	Lot Number:	30320
Body:	63' 11½" × 9' 3"	Weight:	32t 0cwt
Seats:	19 first 50 second 2 toilets	Bogies:	Mk 4
	later 76 second 2 toilets or 69 second 2 toilets		

S77119	11/57-05/91	⊗09/91	**6005**	11/57-04/74	**5905**	04/74-04/80	**6005**	04/80-05/82
			3213	05/82-09/91				
S77120	11/57-11/94	⊗01/95	**6006**	11/57-04/74	**5906**	04/74-09/80	**6006**	09/80-05/82
			3201	05/82-11/94				
S77121	11/57-05/85	⊗09/87	**6007**	11/57-04/74	**5907**	04/74-04/80	**6007**	04/80-05/85
S77122	11/57-05/85	⊗09/87	**6008**	11/57-04/74	**5908**	04/74-05/80	**6008**	05/80-05/85
S77123	11/57-02/95	⊗05/95	**6009**	11/57-04/74	**5909**	04/74-09/80	**6009**	09/80-05/82
			3201	05/82-02/95				
S77124	11/57-05/91	⊗07/91	**6010**	11/57-05/74	**5910**	05/74-04/80	**6010**	04/80-05/82
			3210	05/82-05/91				
S77125	11/57-10/84	⊗02/88	**6011**	11/57-04/74	**5911**	04/74-04/80	**6011**	04/80-10/84

Class 414/2 2-HAP Ashford/Eastleigh

Driving Trailer Composite (Semi-open) Lavatory
DTCsoL, later DTSsoL
S77126-S77156

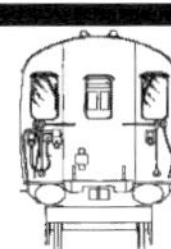

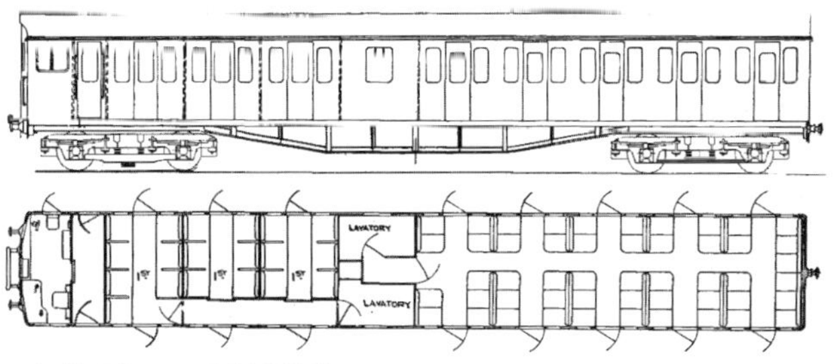

As built, Diagram 441 EE361

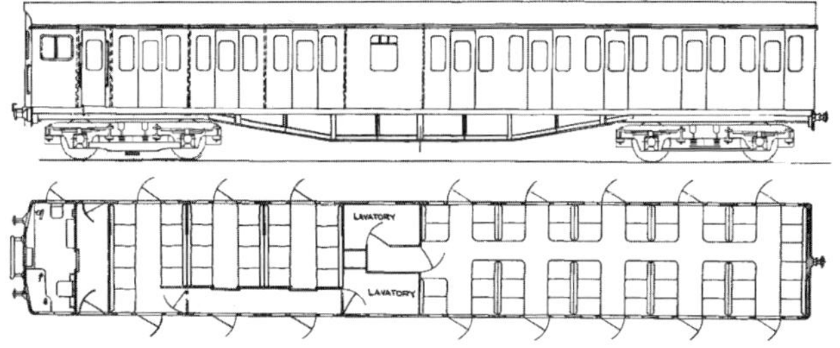

Converted to Class 418/2 2-SAP, Diagram 481

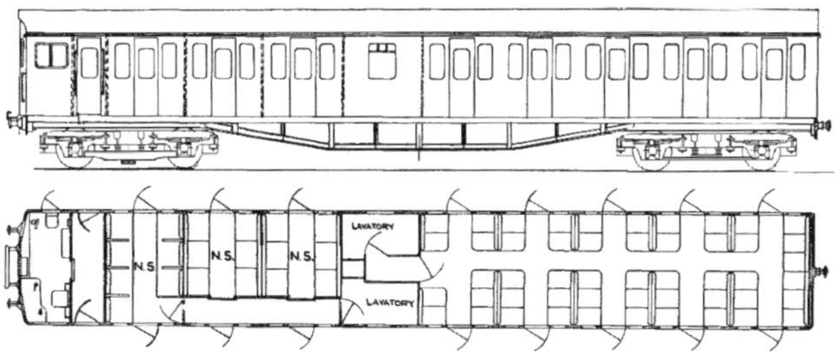

Converted to 2-CAP, Diagram EE222

Diagram:	441 481 EE361 EE222	Lot Number:	30389
Body:	63' 11½" × 9' 3"	Weight:	32t 0cwt
Seats:	19 first 50 second 2 toilets	Bogies:	Mk 4
	later 76 second 2 toilets or 69 second 2 toilets		

S77126	02/58-09/94	⊗11/94	**6012**	02/58-04/74	**5912**	04/74-03/80	**6012**	03/80-05/82
			3207	05/82-09/94				
S77127	02/58-01/92	⊗05/92	**6013**	02/58-05/74	**5913**	05/74-05/80	**6013**	05/80-07/88
			4201	07/88-09/91	**3333**	09/91-01/92		
S77128	02/58-05/91	⊗11/91	**6014**	02/58-04/74	**5914**	04/74-04/80	**6014**	04/80-04/82
			3212	04/82-05/91				
S77129	02/58-05/91	⊗10/91	**6015**	02/58-05/74	**5915**	05/74-05/80	**6015**	05/80-04/82
			3209	04/82-05/91				
S77130	02/58-05/84	⊗10/85	**6016**	02/58-05/74	**5916**	05/74-02/80	**6016**	02/80-05/84
S77131	02/58-03/79	⊗03/84	**6017**	02/58-05/74	**5917**	05/74-03/79		
S77132	03/58-02/95	⊗03/95	**6018**	03/58-04/74	**5918**	04/74-04/80	**6018**	04/80-04/82
			3204	04/82-02/95				
S77133	03/58-05/84	⊗10/84	**6019**	03/58-04/74	**5919**	04/74-03/80	**6019**	03/80-05/84
S77134	03/58-09/93	⊗11/93	**6020**	03/58-05/74	**5920**	05/74-05/80	**6020**	05/80-05/82
			3202	05/82-09/93				
S77135	03/58-03/95	⊗03/95	**6021**	03/58-04/74	**5921**	04/74-03/80	**6021**	03/80-05/82
			3205	05/82-03/95				
S77136	03/58-05/86	➲*977610*	**6022**	03/58-05/86				
S77137	03/58-05/86	⊗11/87	**6023**	03/58-05/86				
S77138	03/58-05/84	⊗10/85	**6024**	03/58-04/74	**5922**	04/74-02/80	**6024**	02/80-05/84
S77139	03/58-05/84	⊗02/85	**6025**	03/58-04/74	**5923**	04/74-03/80	**6025**	03/80-05/84
S77140	03/58-05/84	⊗02/85	**6026**	03/58-04/74	**5924**	04/74-02/80	**6026**	02/80-05/84
S77141	03/58-08/91	⊗10/91	**6027**	03/58-04/74	**5925**	04/74-02/80	**6027**	02/80-04/82
			3206	04/82-08/91				
S77142	03/58-02/95	⊗03/95	**6028**	03/58-04/74	**5926**	04/74-03/80	**6028**	03/80-04/82
			3204	04/82-02/95				
S77143	04/58-05/84	⊗10/85	**6029**	04/58-04/74	**5927**	04/74-04/80	**6029**	04/80-05/84
S77144	04/58-03/95	⊗03/95	**6030**	04/58-05/74	**5928**	05/74-03/80	**6030**	03/80-05/82
			3205	05/82-03/95				
S77145	04/58-08/91	⊗10/91	**6031**	04/58-03/74	**5929**	03/74-04/80	**6031**	04/80-04/82
			3206	04/82-08/91				
S77146	04/58-11/94	⊗01/95	**6032**	04/58-04/74	**5930**	04/74-02/80	**6032**	02/80-05/82
			3203	05/82-11/94				
S77147	04/58-01/94	⊗02/94	**6033**	04/58-05/74	**5931**	05/74-02/80	**6033**	02/80-05/82
			3208	05/82-01/94				
S77148	04/58-05/84	⊗09/87	**6034**	04/58-04/74	**5932**	04/74-02/80	**6034**	02/80-05/84
S77149	05/58-05/93	⊗06/93	**6035**	05/58-04/74	**5933**	04/74-04/80	**6035**	04/80-06/82
			3211	06/82-05/93				
S77150	05/58-09/94	⊗11/94	**6036**	05/58-04/74	**5934**	04/74-06/80	**6036**	06/80-05/82
			3207	05/82-09/94				
S77151	05/58-02/92	⊗11/92	**6037**	05/58-04/74	**5935**	04/74-06/80	**6037**	06/80-05/82
			3208	05/82-09/91	**6238**	09/91-02/92		
S77152	05/58-05/91	⊗10/91	**6038**	05/58-04/74	**5936**	04/74-02/80	**6038**	02/80-04/82
			3209	04/82-05/91				
S77153	05/58-08/84	⊗06/84	**6039**	06/58-04/74	**5937**	04/74-02/80	**6039**	02/80-06/84
S77154	05/58-05/91	⊗09/91	**6040**	05/58-04/74	**5938**	04/74-02/80	**6040**	02/80-05/82
			3213	05/82-09/91				
S77155	05/58-05/91	⊗11/91	**6041**	05/58-05/74	**5939**	05/74-05/80	**6041**	05/80-04/82
			3212	04/82-05/91				
S77156	05/58-05/91	⊗07/91	**6042**	05/58-04/74	**5940**	04/74-02/80	**6042**	02/80-05/82
			3210	05/82-05/91				

Class 504 Manchester-Bury Wolverton

Driving Trailer Composite Open
DTCso, later DTSso
M77157-M77182

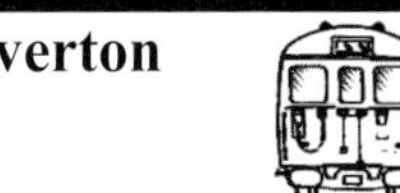

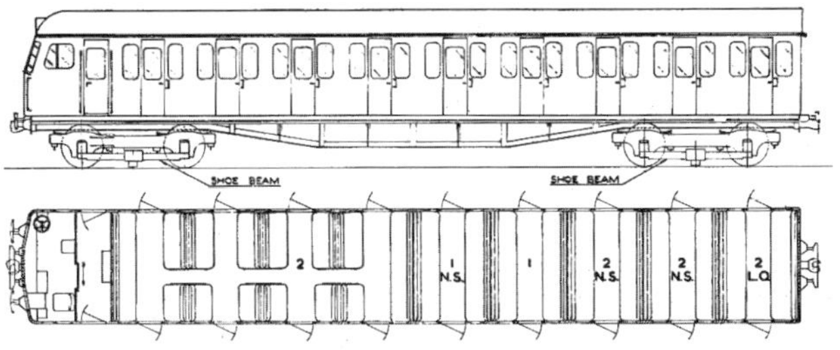

As built, Diagram 443

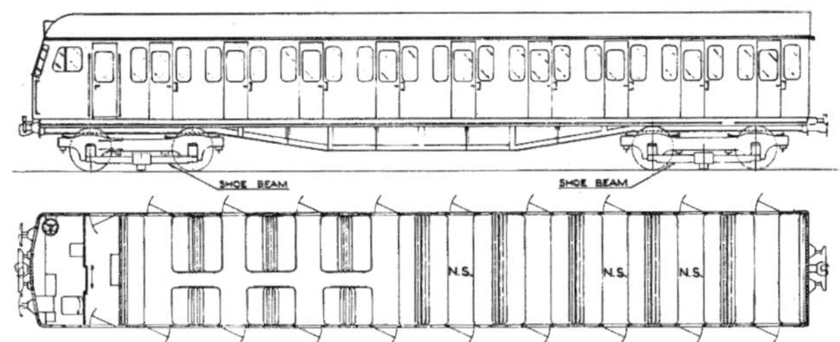

Downgraded to second class EE215

Diagram:	443 EE215	Lot Number:	30478
Body:	64' 0⅝" × 9' 3"	Weight:	32t 9cwt
Seats:	16 first 78 second	Bogies:	Gresley
	then 102 second, then 94 second		

M77157	08/59-05/82	⊗*06/82*						
M77158	08/59-05/82	⊗05/85						
M77159	08/59-11/78	⊗*06/82*						
M77160	08/59-05/82	⊗01/83						
M77161	59-11/69	⊗04/71						
M77162	59-05/82	⊗01/83						
M77163	59-05/82	⊗ *83*						
M77164	59-09/83	⊗05/85		09/70⇨**E**	**244**	06/72-06/82	**302244**	06/82-09/83
M77165	59-08/91	⊗09/91	**504444**	07/88-08/91				
M77166	59-08/91	⊗09/91	**504445**	07/88-08/91				
M77167	59-08/91	⊗08/91	**504446**	07/88-08/91				
M77168	59-07/91	⊗08/91	**504447**	07/88-07/91				
M77169	59-12/84	⊗03/91						
M77170	59-07/91	⊗08/91	**504449**	07/88-07/91				
M77171	59-07/91	⊗08/91	**504450**	07/88-07/91				
M77172	59-08/91	Ⓟ	**504451**	07/88-08/91				
M77173	59-08/91	⊗08/91	**504452**	07/88-08/91				
M77174	59-07/91	⊗08/91	**504453**	07/88-08/91				

M77175	59-08/91	⊗08/91	**504454**	07/88-07/91
M77176	59-07/91	⊗08/91	**504455**	07/88-07/91
M77177	59-09/91	⊗09/91	**504456**	07/88-09/91
M77178	59-09/91	⊗09/91	**504457**	07/88-09/91
M77179	59-07/91	⊗08/91	**504458**	07/88-07/91
M77180	59-07/91	⊗08/91	**504459**	07/88-07/91
M77181	59-08/91	⊗08/91	**504460**	07/88-08/91
M77182	59-08/91	Ⓟ⊗08/92	**504461**	07/88-08/91

77200-77219	***Class 317/2***	*10/85*
77220-77239	***Class 317/2***	*10/85*
77240-77259	***Class 318***	*06/86*
77260-77279	***Class 318***	*06/86*
77280-77283	***Class 317/2***	*03/87*
77284-77287	***Class 317/2***	*03/87*
77288	***Class 318***	*03/87*
77289	***Class 318***	*03/87*
***77290-77380** (evens)*	***Class 319/0***	*09/87*
***77291-77381** (odds)*	***Class 319/0***	*09/87*
77382-77405	***Class 442***	*01/88*
77406-77429	***Class 442***	*01/88*
***77430-77456** (evens)*	***Class 319/0***	*06/88*
***77431-77457** (odds)*	***Class 319/0***	*06/88*
***77458-77496** (evens)*	***Class 319/1***	*10/90*
***77459-77497** (odds)*	***Class 319/1***	*10/90*

Class 416 Ashford/Eastleigh
Driving Trailer Second (Semi-open)
DTSso, later DTSO
S77500-S77510

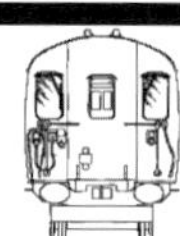

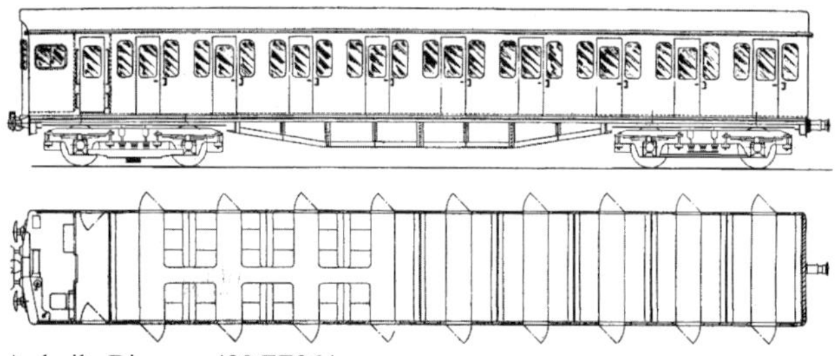

As built, Diagram 420 EE264

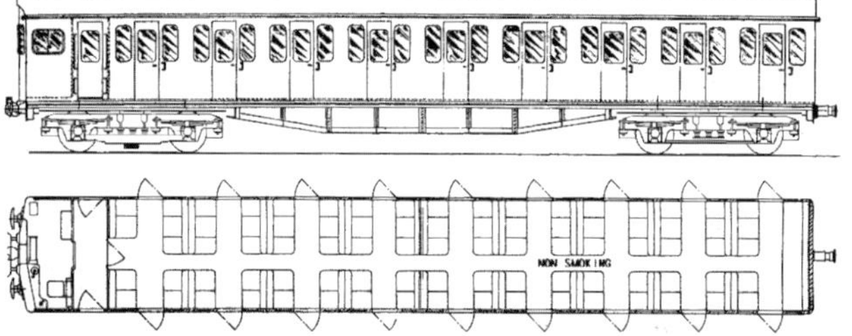

Class 416/4 6401-6409, rebuilt for revenue protection services, Diagram EE274

Diagram:	420 EE264 EE274	Lot Number:	30115
Body:	63' 11½" × 9' 3¼"	Weight:	30t 0cwt
Seats:	102 second later 92 second	Bogies:	Mk 3D

S77500	01/54-10/87	⊗01/89	**5701**	01/54-01/65	DEMU **1201**	01/65-		
S77501	01/54-05/94	⊗06/94	**5702**	01/54-04/85	**6202**	04/85-05/94		
S77502	04/54-05/93	⊗07/93	**5703**	04/54-03/85	**6203**	03/85-05/93		
S77503	04/54-08/87	⊗02/88	**5704**	04/54-01/65	DEMU **1202**	01/65-		
S77504	04/54-05/93	⊗07/93	**5705**	04/54-04/85	**6205**	04/85-05/93		
S77505	04/54-08/94	⊗08/94	**5706**	04/54-05/85	**6206**	05/85-12/85	**6406**	12/85-08/94
S77506	04/54-05/91	⊗10/91	**5707**	04/54-01/85	**6207**	01/85-05/91		
S77507	05/54-09/87	⊗12/88	**5708**	05/54-01/65	DEMU **1203**	01/65-		
S77508	05/54-11/87	⊗10/88	**5709**	05/54-01/65	DEMU **1204**	01/65-		
S77509	05/54-08/87	⊗01/89	**5710**	05/54-12/64	DEMU **1205**	01/65-		
S77510	05/54-08/87	⊗11/85	**5711**	05/54-01/65	DEMU **1206**	01/65-		

Class 416 Ashford/Eastleigh
Driving Trailer Second (Semi-open)
DTSso, later DTSO
S77511-S77526

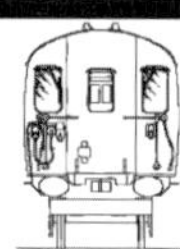

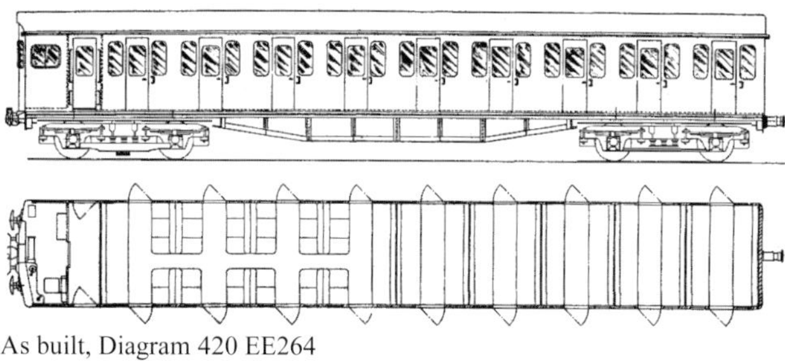

As built, Diagram 420 EE264

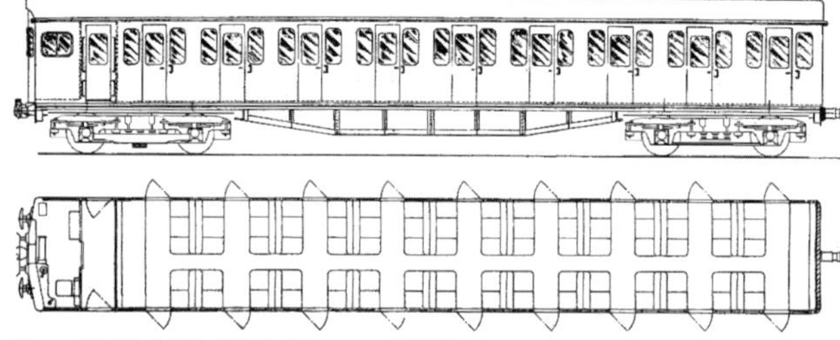

Class 416/4 6410-6418, Diagram EE271

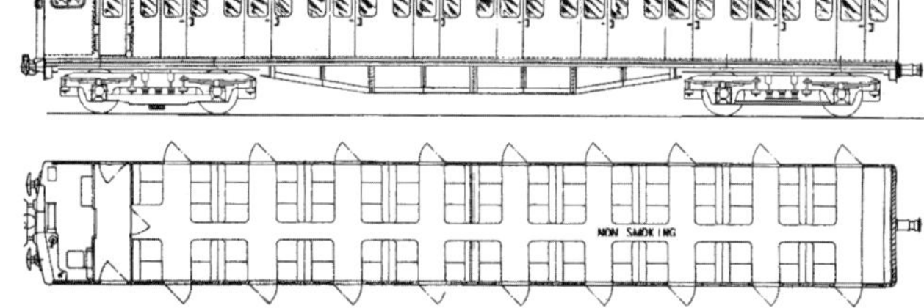

Class 416/4 6401-6409, rebuilt for revenue protection services, Diagram EE274

Diagram:	420 EE264 EE271 EE274	Lot Number:	30120
Body:	63' 11½" × 9' 3¼"	Weight:	30t 0cwt
Seats:	102 second, later 92 second or 90 second	Bogies:	Mk 3D

S77511	08/54-09/91	⊗05/92	**5712**	08/54-03/85	**6212**	03/85-09/91		
S77512	08/54-01/95	⊗	**5713**	08/54-04/85	**6213**	04/85-01/95		
S77513	08/54-01/94	⊗10/94	**5714**	08/54-09/84	**6214**	09/84-12/86	**6416**	12/86-01/94
S77514	08/54-05/94	⊗05/94	**5715**	08/54-08/84	**6215**	08/84-11/85	**6404**	11/85-05/94
S77515	09/54-03/95	⊗05/95	**5716**	09/54-03/85	**6216**	03/85-01/86	**6407**	01/86-03/95
S77516	09/54- 94	➲**977918**	**5717**	09/54-09/84	**6217**	09/84- 94		
S77517	09/54-09/91	⊗05/92	**5718**	09/54-09/84	**6218**	09/84-09/91		
S77518	09/54-02/95	⊗07/95	**5719**	09/54-03/85	**6219**	03/85-02/86	**6411**	02/86-02/95
S77519	10/54-02/95	⊗07/95	**5720**	10/54-05/85	**6220**	05/85-03/86	**6410**	03/86-02/95
S77520	10/54-10/94	⊗01/95	**5721**	10/54-09/84	**6221**	09/84-10/94		
S77521	10/54-01/92	⊗11/92	**5722**	10/54-03/85	**6222**	03/85-01/92		
S77522	10/54-10/94	⊗11/94	**5723**	10/54-12/84	**6223**	12/84-10/94		
S77523	10/54-01/94	⊗02/94	**5724**	10/54-01/85	**6224**	01/85-01/94		
S77524	11/54-10/94	⊗11/94	**5725**	11/54-08/84	**6225**	08/84-10/94		
S77525	11/54-05/94	⊗05/94	**5726**	11/54-02/85	**6226**	02/85-05/94		
S77526	11/54-01/93	⊗04/93	**5727**	11/54-04/85	**6227**	04/85-01/93		

Class 416 Ashford/Eastleigh
Driving Trailer Second (Semi-open)
DTSso, later DTSO
S77527-S77551

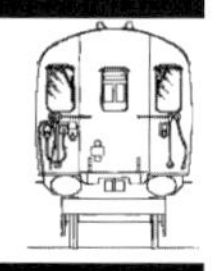

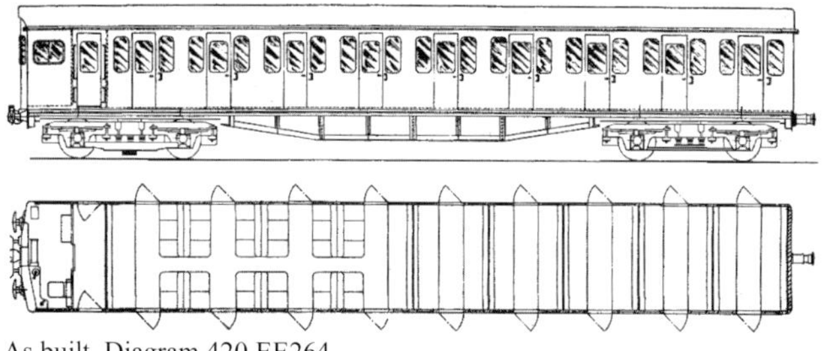

As built, Diagram 420 EE264

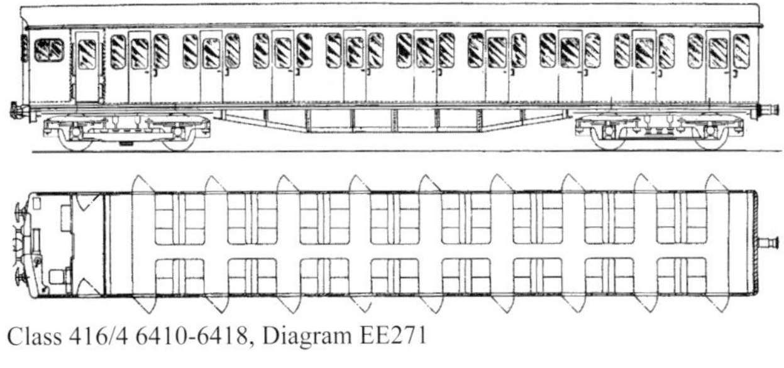

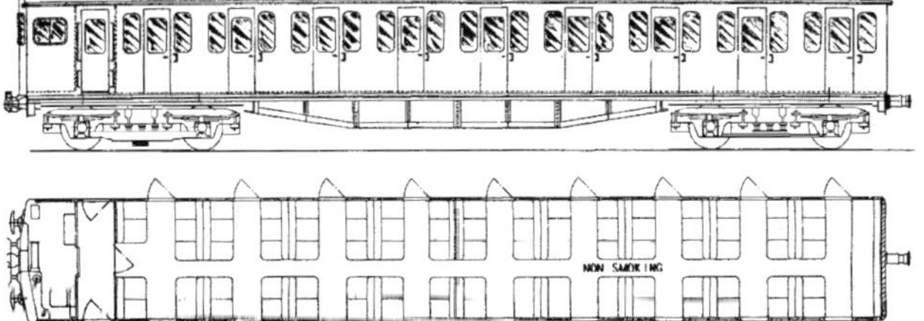

Class 416/4 6410-6418, Diagram EE271

Class 416/4 6401-6409, rebuilt for revenue protection services, Diagram EE274

Diagram:	420 EE264 EE271 EE274	Lot Number:	30168
Body:	63' 11½" × 9' 3¼"	Weight:	30t 0cwt
Seats:	102 second, later 92 second or 90 second	Bogies:	Mk 3D

S77527	04/55-08/94	⊗10/94	**5728**	04/55-08/84	**6228**	08/84-02/86	**6408**	02/86-08/94
S77528	05/55-05/91	⊗05/92	**5729**	05/55-06/77	**5729**	11/80-08/84	**6229**	08/84-05/91
S77529	05/55-05/94	⊗05/94	**5730**	05/55-12/84	**6230**	12/84-05/94		
S77530	05/55-05/93	⊗08/93	**5731**	05/55-03/85	**6231**	03/85-05/93		
S77531	05/55-02/93	➲**977856**	**5732**	05/55-07/85	**6232**	07/85-09/85	**6401**	09/85-02/93
S77532	06/55-08/94	⊗10/94	**5733**	06/55-08/84	**6233**	08/84-12/86	**6405**	12/86-08/94
S77533	06/55-03/95	⊗07/95	**5734**	06/55-09/84	**6234**	09/84-09/86	**6415**	09/86-03/95
S77534	06/55-11/94	⊗12/94	**5735**	06/55-05/85	**6235**	05/85-11/94		
S77535	06/55-10/94	⊗11/94	**5736**	06/55-09/84	**6236**	09/84-10/94		
S77536	07/55-11/94	⊗11/94	**5737**	07/55-05/85	**6237**	05/85-11/94		
S77537	07/55-01/94	⊗02/94	**5738**	07/55-05/85	**6238**	05/85-09/91	**3208**	09/91-01/94
S77538	07/55-06/93	⊗07/93	**5739**	07/55-05/85	**6239**	05/85-06/93		
S77539	07/55-08/94	⊗08/94	**5740**	07/55-09/84	**6240**	09/84-08/94		
S77540	07/55-01/93	⊗04/93	**5741**	07/55-08/84	**6241**	08/84-01/93		
S77541	08/55-02/95	⊗07/95	**5742**	08/55-03/85	**6242**	03/85-10/85	**6403**	10/85-02/95
S77542	08/55-01/92	⊗11/92	**5743**	08/55-03/85	**6243**	03/85-01/92		
S77543	08/55-09/91	⊗11/92	**5744**	08/55-08/84	**6244**	08/84-09/91		
S77544	09/55-11/94	⊗11/94	**5745**	09/55-04/85	**6245**	04/85-11/94		
S77545	09/55-01/94	⊗10/94	**5746**	09/55-01/85	**6246**	01/85-02/87	**6418**	02/87-01/94
S77546	09/55-05/93	⊗06/94	**5747**	09/55-04/85	**6247**	04/85-05/93		
S77547	09/55-03/95	⊗	**5748**	09/55-04/85	**6248**	04/85-10/85	**6402**	10/85-03/95
S77548	09/55-05/94	⊗06/94	**5749**	09/55-05/85	**6249**	05/85-05/94		
S77549	10/55-02/95	⊗07/95	**5750**	10/55-03/85	**6250**	03/85-03/86	**6412**	03/86-02/95
S77550	10/55-10/94	⊗01/95	**5751**	10/55-02/85	**6251**	02/85-10/94		
S77551	10/55-11/94	⊗*11/96*	**5752**	10/55-08/84	**6252**	08/84-01/87	**6417**	01/87-11/94

Class 416 Ashford/Eastleigh
Driving Trailer Second (Semi-open)
DTSso, later DTSO
S77552-S77577

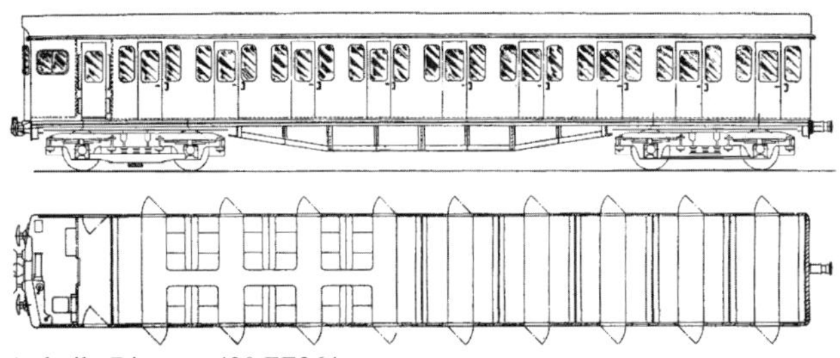

As built, Diagram 420 EE264

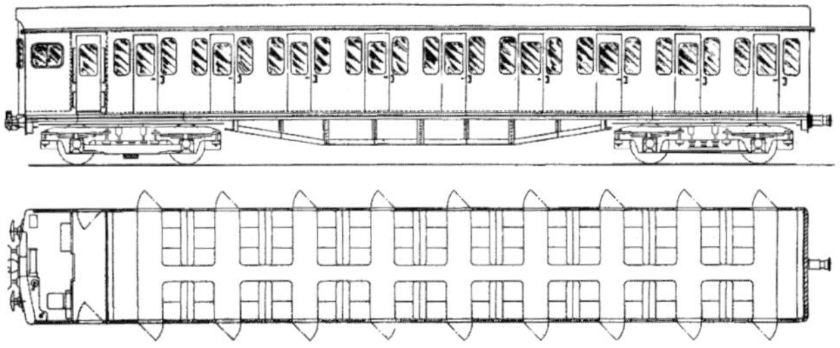

Class 416/4 6410-6418, Diagram EE271

Diagram:	420 EE264 EE271	Lot Number:	30315
Body:	63' 11½" × 9' 3¼"	Weight:	30t 0cwt
Seats:	102 second, later 92 second	Bogies:	Mk 3D

S77552	04/56-05/93	⊗07/93	**5753**	04/56-07/84	**6253**	07/84-05/93		
S77553	05/56-03/95	⊗07/95	**5754**	05/56-07/84	**6254**	07/84-06/86	**6414**	06/86-03/95
S77554	10/56-02/94	⊗03/94	**5755**	10/56-10/84	**6255**	10/84-02/94		
S77555	05/56-02/94	➲*977920*	**5756**	05/56-08/84	**6256**	08/84-02/94		
S77556	06/56-05/91	⊗11/91	**5757**	06/56-03/85	**6257**	03/85-05/91		
S77557	10/56-03/95	⊗07/95	**5758**	10/56-04/85	**6258**	04/85-05/86	**6413**	05/86-03/95
S77558	06/56-01/95	Ⓡ	**5759**	06/56-10/84	**6259**	10/84-01/95		
S77559	05/56-01/94	⊗02/94	**5760**	05/56-12/84	**6260**	12/84-01/94		
S77560	07/56-02/94	⊗03/94	**5761**	07/56-09/84	**6261**	09/84-02/94		
S77561	06/56-01/94	⊗02/94	**5762**	06/56-07/84	**6262**	07/84-01/94		
S77562	06/56-01/95	⊗01/95	**5763**	06/56-12/84	**6263**	12/84-01/95		
S77563	07/56-12/94	⊗03/95	**5764**	07/56-03/85	**6264**	03/85-12/94		
S77564	07/56-01/94	⊗09/94	**5765**	07/56-07/84	**6265**	07/84-01/94		
S77565	07/56-12/57	⊗12/57	**5766**	07/56-12/57				
S77566	08/56-04/94	⊗04/94	**5767**	08/56-09/84	**6267**	09/84-04/94		
S77567	08/56-01/94	⊗09/94	**5768**	08/56-09/84	**6268**	09/84-01/94		
S77568	09/56-12/91	⊗07/92	**5769**	09/56-04/85	**6269**	04/85-12/91		
S77569	09/56-03/94	⊗04/94	**5770**	09/56-08/84	**6270**	08/84-03/94		
S77570	09/56-05/94	⊗05/94	**5771**	09/56-09/84	**6271**	09/84-05/94		
S77571	09/56-05/93	⊗07/93	**5772**	09/56-09/84	**6272**	09/84-05/93		
S77572	09/56-01/95	⊗01/95	**5773**	09/56-08/84	**6273**	08/84-01/95		
S77573	10/56-04/94	⊗05/94	**5774**	10/56-06/77	**5774**	11/80-08/84	**6274**	08/84-04/94
S77574	10/56-04/94	⊗05/94	**5775**	10/56-08/84	**6275**	08/84-04/94		
S77575	10/56-05/91	⊗11/91	**5776**	10/56-08/84	**6276**	08/84-05/91		
S77576	11/56-11/94	⊗11/94	**5777**	11/56-08/84	**6277**	08/84-11/94		
S77577	11/56-01/94	⊗02/94	**5778**	11/56-09/84	**6278**	09/84-01/94		

Class 416 Ashford/Eastleigh
Driving Trailer Second (Semi-open)
DTSso
S77578

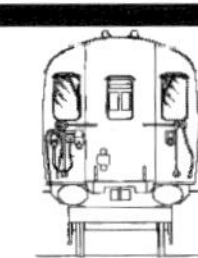

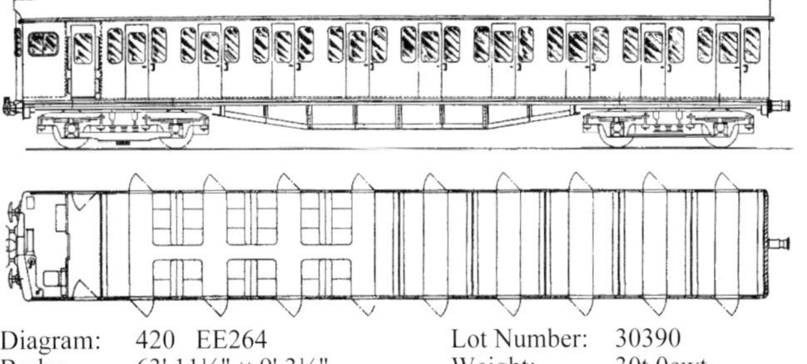

Diagram:	420 EE264	Lot Number:	30390
Body:	63' 11½" × 9' 3¼"	Weight:	30t 0cwt
Seats:	102 second	Bogies:	Mk 3D

S77578	06/58-05/87	⊗09/87	**5779**	06/58-08/84	**6279**	08/84-05/87

77579-77812	***Class 455***	*08/82*
77813-77852	***Class 455/9***	*02/85*
77853-77898	***Class 321/3***	*09/88*
77899-77920	***Class 320***	*04/90*
77921-77942	***Class 320***	*04/90*
77943-77972	***Class 321/4***	*07/89*
77973-77983 (odds)	***Class 319/1***	*01/91*
77974-77984 (evens)	***Class 319/1***	*01/91*
77985-77989	***Class 322***	*07/90*
77990-77992	***Class 321/9***	*07/91*
77993-77995	***Class 321/9***	*07/91*

Class 312/0 York

Driving Trailer Composite Open Lavatory
DTCOL
E78000-E78025

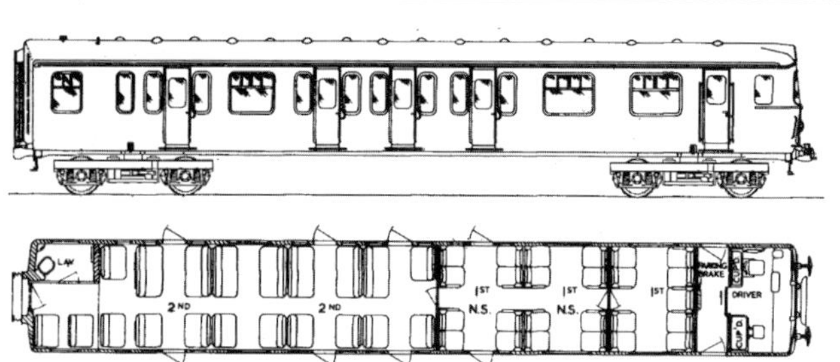

Diagram:	461 EE305		Lot Number:	30866
Body:	65' 1⅝" × 9' 3"		Weight:	33t 16½cwt
Seats:	25 first 47 second 1 toilet		Bogies:	B4

E78000	05/77-10/03	⊗11/04	**312001**	05/77-05/79	**312701**	05/79-10/03
E78001	06/77-09/03	⊗10/04	**312002**	06/77-05/79	**312702**	05/79-09/03
E78002	06/77-03/04	⊗11/04	**312003**	06/77-04/79	**312703**	04/79-03/04
E78003	07/77-09/03	⊗10/03	**312004**	07/77-03/79	**312704**	03/79-09/03
E78004	07/77-09/03	⊗09/04	**312005**	07/77-04/79	**312705**	04/79-09/03
E78005	07/77-09/03	⊗12/04	**312006**	07/77-05/79	**312706**	05/79-09/03
E78006	07/77-09/03	⊗12/04	**312007**	07/77-04/79	**312707**	04/79-09/03
E78007	07/77-09/03	⊗10/03	**312008**	07/77-05/79	**312708**	05/79-09/03
E78008	08/77-10/03	⊗01/05	**312009**	08/77-05/79	**312709**	05/79-10/03
E78009	08/77-09/03	⊗10/03	**312010**	08/77-05/79	**312710**	05/79-09/03
E78010	08/77-09/03	⊗09/04	**312011**	08/77-05/79	**312711**	05/79-09/03
E78011	09/77-09/04	⊗11/04	**312012**	09/77-04/79	**312712**	04/79-09/04
E78012	09/77-01/03	⊗10/04	**312013**	09/77-04/79	**312713**	04/79-01/03
E78013	10/77-03/04	⊗12/04	**312014**	10/77-03/79	**312714**	03/79-03/04
E78014	10/77-03/04	⊗12/04	**312015**	10/77-04/79	**312715**	04/79-03/04
E78015	10/77-09/03	⊗10/03	**312016**	10/77-04/79	**312716**	04/79-09/03
E78016	11/77-09/03	⊗10/03	**312017**	11/77-04/79	**312717**	04/79-09/03
E78017	11/77-05/04	⊗07/04	**312018**	11/77-05/79	**312718**	05/79-05/04
E78018	12/77-09/03	⊗12/04	**312019**	12/77-04/79	**312719**	04/79-09/03
E78019	12/77-09/03	⊗10/03	**312020**	12/77-05/79	**312720**	05/79-09/03
E78020	12/77-05/04	⊗07/04	**312021**	12/77-05/79	**312721**	05/79-05/04
E78021	12/77-05/04	⊗12/04	**312022**	12/77-04/79	**312722**	04/79-05/04
E78022	01/78-05/04	⊗07/04	**312023**	01/78-04/79	**312723**	04/79-05/04
E78023	01/78-09/03	⊗09/04	**312024**	01/78-05/79	**312724**	05/79-09/03
E78024	09/78-04/02	⊗02/05	**312025**	09/78-03/79	**312725**	03/79-04/02
E78025	12/78-11/01	⊗02/05	**312026**	12/78-05/79	**312726**	05/79-11/01

Class 312/1 York

Driving Trailer Composite Open Lavatory
DTCOL
E78026-E78044

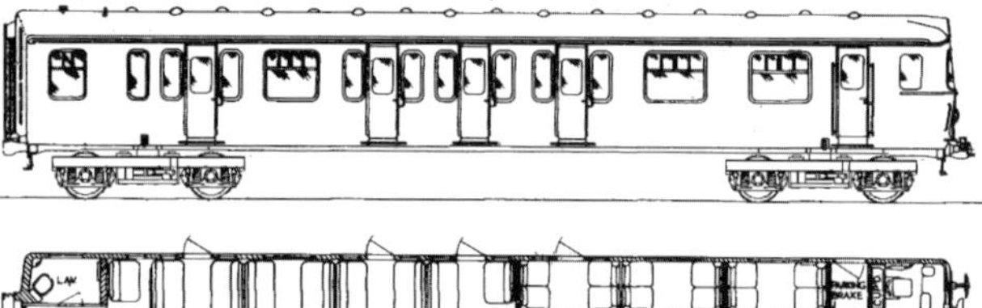

Diagram:	461 EE305		Lot Number:	30870
Body:	65' 1⅝" × 9' 3"		Weight:	33t 16½cwt
Seats:	25 first 47 second 1 toilet		Bogies:	B4

E78026	03/75-03/03	⊗01/05	**312101**	03/75-	78	**312781**	78-03/03
E78027	04/75-11/01	⊗03/05	**312102**	04/75-	78	**312782**	78-11/01
E78028	04/75-03/03	⊗02/05	**312103**	04/75-	78	**312783**	78-03/03
E78029	05/75-03/03	⊗09/04	**312104**	05/75-	78	**312784**	78-03/03
E78030	06/75-09/02	⊗03/05	**312105**	06/75-	78	**312785**	78-09/02
E78031	06/75-02/02	⊗01/05	**312106**	06/75-	78	**312786**	78-02/02
E78032	06/75-03/02	⊗02/05	**312107**	06/75-	78	**312787**	78-03/02
E78033	06/75-03/02	⊗01/05	**312108**	06/75-	78	**312788**	78-03/02
E78034	07/75-09/02	⊗03/05	**312109**	07/75-	78	**312789**	78-09/02
E78035	07/75-02/02	⊗02/05	**312110**	07/75-	78	**312790**	78-02/02
E78036	07/75-04/02	⊗02/05	**312111**	07/75-	78	**312791**	78-04/02
E78037	08/75-03/03	℗	**312112**	08/75-	78	**312792**	78-03/03
E78038	08/75-02/02	⊗02/05	**312113**	08/75-	78	**312793**	78-02/02
E78039	08/75-12/01	⊗02/05	**312114**	08/75-	78	**312794**	78-12/01
E78040	09/75-12/01	⊗02/05	**312115**	09/75-	78	**312795**	78-12/01
E78041	09/75-12/01	⊗01/05	**312116**	09/75-	78	**312796**	78-12/01
E78042	09/75-03/03	⊗02/05	**312117**	09/75-	78	**312797**	78-03/03
E78043	10/75-02/02	⊗01/05	**312118**	10/75-	78	**312798**	78-02/02
E78044	10/75-03/02	⊗03/05	**312119**	10/75-	78	**312799**	78-03/02

Class 312/2 York

Driving Trailer Composite Open Lavatory
DTCOL
M78045-M78048

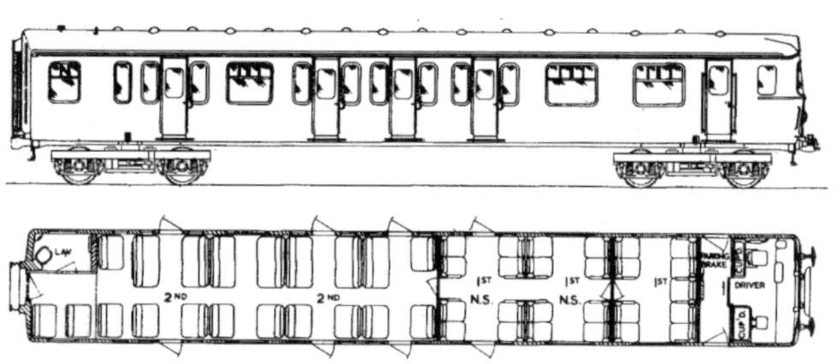

Diagram:	461 EE305		Lot Number:	30894
Body:	65' 1⅝" × 9' 3"		Weight:	33t 16½cwt
Seats:	25 first 47 second 1 toilet		Bogies:	B4

M78045	02/76-11/01	⊗01/05	**312201**	02/76-04/88	**312727**	04/88-11/01
M78046	01/76-10/03	⊗01/05	**312202**	01/76-04/88	**312728**	04/88-10/03
M78047	02/76-12/01	⊗02/05	**312203**	02/76-05/88	**312729**	05/88-12/01
M78048	12/75-08/02	⊗03/05	**312204**	12/75-05/88	**312730**	05/88-08/02

78049-78162	***Class 321***	*09/88*
78163-78167	***Class 322***	*07/90*
78250-78273	***Class 456***	*04/91*
78274-78311	***Class 321***	*12/89*
78312-78354	***Class 466***	*04/94*

Hauled Stock used in EMUs

Mark I Pressed Steel

Buffet/Restaurant
RB
S1758-S1759

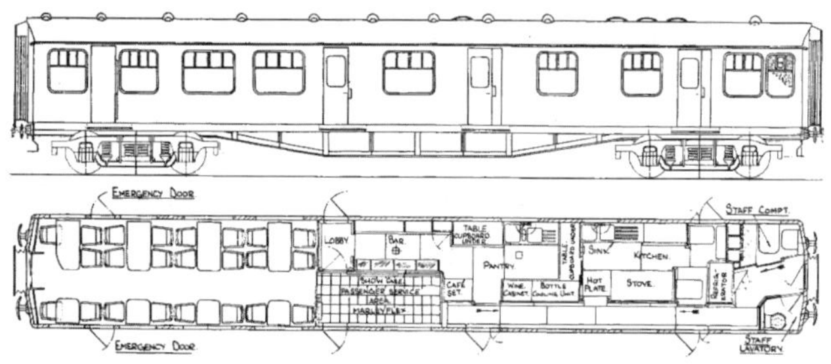

Diagram:	24 AJ402		Lot Number:	30636
Body:	64' 6" × 9' 3"		Weight:	38t
Seats:	23 unclassified		Bogies:	Commonwealth

S1758	⊗10/88	04/68- *74*	**spare**	04/68- *74*
S1759	⊗06/77	04/68-01/75	**8001**	04/68-01/75

Mark I Wolverton
Open Second with Miniature Buffet
RMB
S1872-S1873

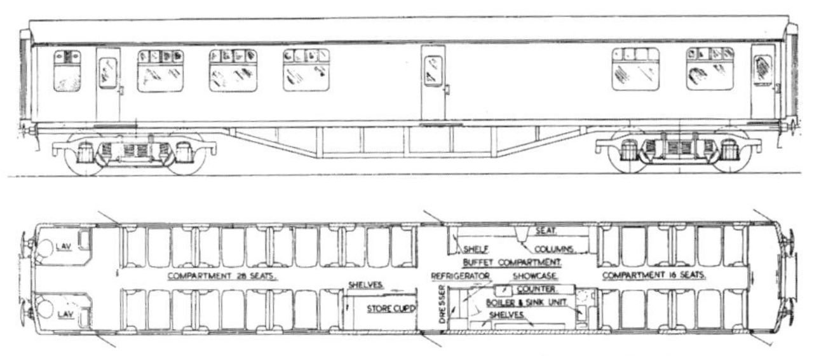

Diagram:	99 AN203	Lot Number:	30702
Body:	64' 6" × 9' 3"	Weight:	38t
Seats:	44 second, 2 toilets	Bogies:	Commonwealth

S1872	⊗	05/83-10/83	2601	05/83-10/83
S1873	⊗	05/83-10/83	2602	05/83-10/83

Southern Railway

Class 405 4-SUB Eastleigh
Driving Motor Brake Third Open
DMBTO
S8616S-S8655S

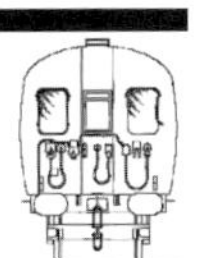

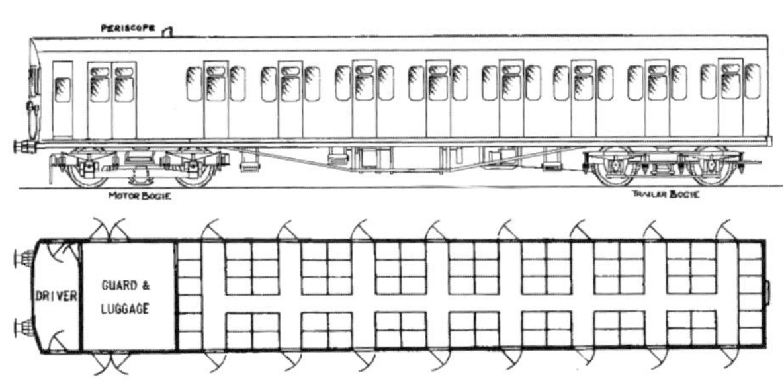

Diagram:	2126 EB265	HO Number:	3638
Body:	62' 6" × 9' 0"	Weight:	39-43t
Seats:	82 third	Bogies:	SR
Motor:	EE507C 2 × 250hp		

S8616S	07/51-06/81	⊗08/82	4735	07/51-06/81			↵8332
S8617S	07/51-06/81	⊗08/82	4735	07/51-06/81			↵8329
S8618S	07/51-04/76	⊗	4736	07/51-12/70	4736	05/71-04/76	↵8288
S8619S	07/51-04/76	⊗	4736	07/51-04/76			↵8408
S8620S	08/51-01/83	⊗06/84	4737	08/51-10/71	4722	10/71-01/83	↵8344
S8621S	08/51-10/71	⊗03/72	4737	08/51-10/71			↵8331
S8622S	08/51-08/83	⊗07/85	4738	08/51-08/83			↵8311
S8623S	08/51-03/76	⊗10/76	4738	08/51-03/76			↵8272
S8624S	08/51-06/81	⊗12/81	4739	08/51-06/81			↵8235
S8625S	08/51-06/81	⊗12/81	4739	08/51-06/81			↵8273
S8626S	08/51-04/76	⊗08/76	4740	08/51-04/76			↵8492
S8627S	08/51-04/76	⊗08/76	4740	08/51-04/76			↵8312
S8628S	08/51-04/76	⊗11/76	4741	08/51-04/76			↵8236
S8629S	08/51-04/76	⊗11/76	4741	08/51-04/76			↵8259
S8630S	08/51-06/83	⊗04/86	4742	08/51-06/83			↵8317
S8631S	08/51-06/83	⊗04/86	4742	08/51-06/83			
S8632S	09/51-05/83	⊗04/86	4743	09/51-05/83			↵8318
S8633S	09/51-05/83	⊗04/86	4743	09/51-05/83			↵8300
S8634S	09/51-01/76	⊗06/76	4744	09/51-01/76			↵8407
S8635S	09/51-01/76	⊗06/76	4744	09/51-01/76			
S8636S	09/51-10/73	⊗03/74	4745	09/51-10/73			↵8293
S8637S	09/51-10/73	⊗03/74	4745	09/51-10/73			↵8287
S8638S	09/51-04/76	⊗	4746	09/51-04/76			↵8231
S8639S	09/51-04/76	⊗	4746	09/51-04/76			↵8271
S8640S	10/51-05/83	⊗02/84	4747	10/51-05/83			↵8243
S8641S	10/51-05/83	⊗02/84	4747	10/51-05/83			↵8489
S8642S	10/51-04/76	⊗05/80	4748	10/51-04/76			↵8232
S8643S	10/51-03/74	⊗01/77	4748	10/51-03/74			↵8244
S8644S	10/51-05/83	⊗04/84	4749	10/51-09/82	4692	12/82-05/83	↵8386
S8645S	10/51-09/82	⊗06/84	4749	10/51-09/82			↵8349
S8646S	10/51-10/82	⊗10/85	4750	10/51-10/82	4687	01/83-05/83	↵8393
S8647S	10/51-10/82	⊗06/84	4750	10/51-10/82			↵8248
S8648S	10/51-07/83	⊗07/85	4751	10/51-07/83			↵8385
S8649S	10/51-06/81	⊗04/82	4751	10/51-11/65	4701	11/65-06/81	↵8247
S8650S	11/51-04/76	⊗08/76	4752	11/51-04/76			↵8339
S8651S	11/51-04/76	⊗08/76	4752	11/51-04/76			↵8483
S8652S	12/51-09/78	⊗10/79	4753	12/51-09/78			↵8485
S8653S	12/51-09/78	⊗10/79	4753	12/51-09/78			↵8484
S8654S	12/51-07/83	⊗12/87	4754	12/51-10/59	4680	10/59-07/83	
S8655S	12/51-07/83	⊗12/87	4754	12/51-10/59	4680	10/59-07/83	

4-EPB Eastleigh
Driving Motor Brake Second Open
DMBSO
S8656S-S8673S

Numbers not used. Renumbered before entering service.

S8656S	⊃14001
S8657S	⊃14002
S8658S	⊃14003
S8659S	⊃14004
S8660S	⊃14005
S8661S	⊃14006
S8662S	⊃14007
S8663S	⊃14008
S8664S	⊃14009
S8665S	⊃14010
S8666S	⊃14011
S8667S	⊃14012
S8668S	⊃14013
S8669S	⊃14014
S8670S	⊃14015
S8671S	⊃14016
S8672S	⊃14017
S8673S	⊃14018

Class 405 4-SUB Eastleigh
Trailer Third
TT
S8901S-S8935S

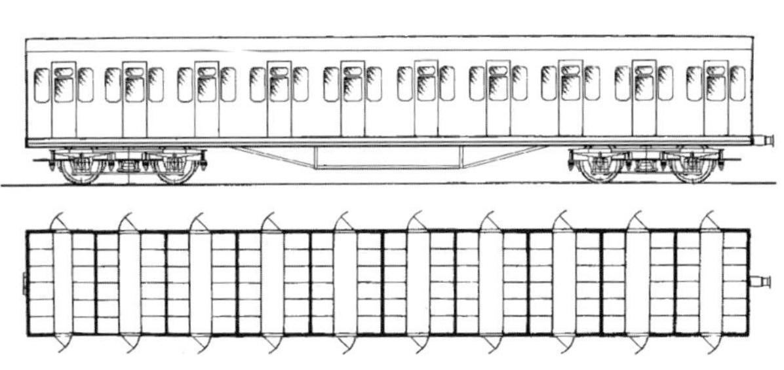

Diagram:	2013 EH263	HO Number:	3504
Body:	62' 0" × 9' 0"	Weight:	26-29t
Seats:	120 third	Bogies:	SR

S8901S	05/49-06/76	⊗08/76	4621	05/49-06/76			↵9690
S8902S	05/49-05/74	⊗03/76	4622	05/49-05/74			↵9685
S8903S	05/49-07/81	⊗10/85	4623	05/49-07/81			↵9676
S8904S	05/49-04/76	⊗07/81	4624	05/49-04/76			
S8905S	06/49-05/74	⊗03/76	4625	06/49-05/74			↵9669
S8906S	06/49-05/76	⊗	4626	06/49-05/76			↵9708
S8907S	06/49-05/76	⊗07/76	4627	06/49-05/76			
S8908S	06/49-06/81	⊗06/82	4628	06/49-06/81			↵9702
S8909S	07/49-06/81	⊗06/82	4629	07/49-06/81			
S8910S	07/49-06/81	⊗08/82	4630	07/49-06/81			↵9711
S8911S	07/49-06/76	⊗07/76	4631	07/49- *51*	4718	05/52-06/76	↵9700
S8912S	07/49-06/81	⊗08/82	4632	07/49-09/78	4632	06/79-06/81	↵9699
S8913S	07/49-06/76	⊗05/80	4633	07/49-06/76			
S8914S	07/49-05/74	⊗04/76	4634	07/49-05/74			↵9666
S8915S	08/49-06/81	⊗06/82	4635	08/49-06/81			↵9680
S8916S	09/49-06/81	⊗07/85	4636	09/49-06/81			
S8917S	09/49-05/76	⊗10/76	4637	09/49-05/76			
S8918S	09/49-06/81	⊗04/82	4638	09/49-06/81			
S8919S	09/49-03/75	⊗03/76	4639	09/49-03/75			
S8920S	10/49-11/73	⊗01/76	4640	10/49-11/73			↵9556
S8921S	10/49-06/81	⊗06/82	4641	10/49-06/81			
S8922S	10/49-05/73	⊗07/82	4642	10/49-05/73			↵9714
S8923S	10/49-04/81	⊗	4643	10/49-04/81			
S8924S	10/49-04/76	⊗05/80	4644	10/49-04/76			
S8925S	11/49-12/75	⊗01/77	4645	11/49-12/75			
S8926S	11/49-04/76	⊗07/76	4646	11/49-04/76			
S8927S	11/49-04/76	⊗08/82	4647	11/49-04/76			
S8928S	11/49-06/81	⊗	4648	11/49-05/81			

S8929S	11/49-03/75	⊗03/76	**4649**	11/49-03/75					
S8930S	12/49-04/76	⊗08/76	**4650**	12/49-04/58	**4752**	06/58-04/76			
S8931S	12/49-07/76	⊗08/76	**4651**	12/49-07/76					
S8932S	12/49-04/61	⊗ *61*	**4652**	12/49-04/61					
S8933S	12/49-06/81	⊗06/82	**4653**	12/49-06/81					
S8934S	01/50-07/76	⊗	**4654**	01/50-07/76					
S8935S	01/50-06/81	⊗03/83	**4655**	01/50-06/81					↩**9688**

Class 405 4-SUB Eastleigh

Trailer Third
TT
S8936S-S8939S

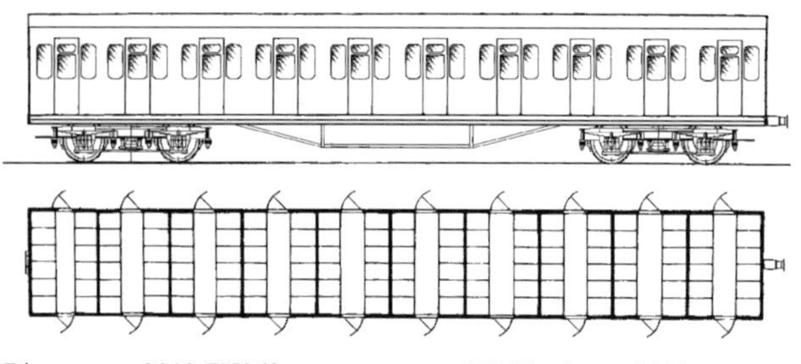

Diagram: 2013 EH263 HO Number: 3505
Body: 62' 0" × 9' 0" Weight: 26-29t
Seats: 120 third Bogies: SR

S8936S	01/50-06/76	⊗08/76	**4656**	01/50-06/76
S8937S	01/50-05/76	⊗08/76	**4657**	01/50-05/76
S8938S	02/50-05/76	⊗08/76	**4658**	02/50-05/76
S8939S	02/50-06/76	⊗	**4659**	02/50-06/76

Class 405 4-SUB Eastleigh

Trailer Third
TT
S8940S-S8946S

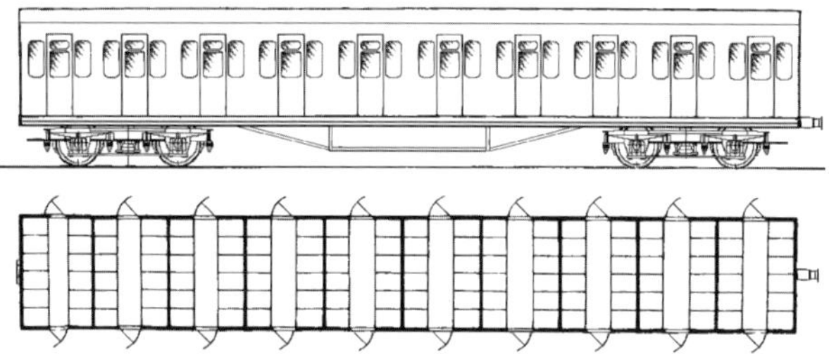

Diagram: 2013 EH263 HO Number: 3506
Body: 62' 0" × 9' 0" Weight: 26-29t
Seats: 120 third Bogies: SR

S8940S	02/50-07/81	⊗06/82	**4660**	02/50-07/81				
S8941S	02/50-04/76	⊗09/81	**4661**	02/50-05/66	**4368**	05/66-08/67	**4661**	08/67-03/74
			4607	03/74-04/76				
S8942S	02/50-07/76	⊗10/76	**4662**	02/50-07/76				
S8943S	02/50-05/72	⊗05/74	**4663**	02/50-05/72				
S8944S	03/50-11/80	⊗	**4664**	03/50-11/80				
S8945S	03/50-04/76	⊗05/80	**4665**	03/50-04/76				
S8946S	03/50-05/83	⊗07/76	**4666**	03/50-05/76				

Class 405 4-SUB Eastleigh

Trailer Third Open
TTO
S8947S-S8989S

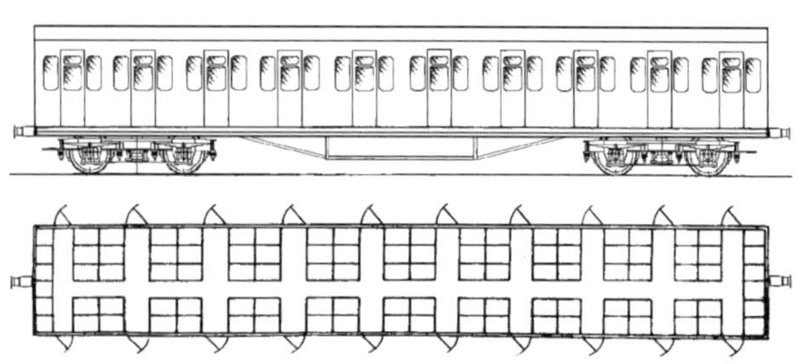

Diagram: 2018 EH266 HO Number: 3617
Body: 62' 0" × 9' 0" Weight: 27-29t
Seats: 102 third Bogies: SR

S8947S	05/50-09/83	⊗08/85	**4667**	05/50-11/70	**4623**	10/72-05/82	**4279**	07/82-09/83	
									↩**9624**
S8948S	05/50-05/83	⊗	**4668**	05/50-05/83					↩**9696**
S8949S	05/50-05/82	⊗02/84	**4669**	05/50-05/82					↩**9645**
S8950S	05/50-05/83	⊗	**4670**	05/50-05/83					↩**9625**
S8951S	05/50-10/82	⊗02/84	**4671**	05/50-10/82					↩**9693**
S8952S	05/50-10/82	⊗06/84	**4672**	05/50-10/82					↩**9670**
S8953S	06/50-10/82	⊗02/84	**4673**	06/50-10/82					↩**9704**
S8954S	06/50-10/82	⊗02/84	**4674**	06/50-10/82					↩**9632**
S8955S	06/50-06/81	⊗06/82	**4675**	06/50-10/58	**4675**	04/59-06/81			↩**9713**
S8956S	06/50-10/82	⊗11/83	**4676**	06/50-04/76	**4637**	05/76-10/82			↩**9575**
S8957S	06/50-10/82	⊗06/84	**4677**	06/50-08/67	**4677**	01/68-06/81	**4683**	07/81-10/82	
S8958S	07/50-05/83	⊗06/84	**4678**	07/50-05/83					↩**9637**
S8959S	07/50-10/82	⊗02/84	**4679**	07/50-10/82					↩**9511**
S8960S	07/50-07/83	⊗12/87	**4680**	07/50-07/83					↩**9505**
S8961S	07/50-10/82	⊗02/84	**4681**	07/50-05/81	**4673**	05/81-10/82			↩**9640**
S8962S	07/50-04/83	⊗02/84	**4682**	07/50-04/83					↩**9531**
S8963S	08/50-10/82	⊗06/84	**4683**	08/50-10/82					↩**9715**
S8964S	08/50-05/82	⊗06/84	**4684**	08/50-05/82					↩**9533**
S8965S	08/50-02/79	⊗06/80	**4685**	08/50-04/76	**4662**	07/76-02/79			↩**9543**
S8966S	08/50-10/82	⊗06/84	**4686**	08/50-04/76	**4750**	06/76-10/82			↩**9549**
S8967S	09/50-05/83	⊗10/85	**4687**	09/50-05/56	**4687**	*08/57*-05/83			
S8968S	09/50-04/83	⊗02/84	**4688**	09/50-04/76	**4682**	06/76-04/83			↩**9572**
S8969S	09/50-06/81	⊗01/82	**4689**	09/50-06/81					↩**9510**
S8970S	09/50-05/83	⊗12/87	**4690**	09/50-04/76	**4620**	05/76-05/83			↩**9694**
S8971S	09/50-07/83	⊗02/85	**4691**	09/50-04/76	**4726**	06/76-07/83			↩**9525**
S8972S	09/50-05/83	⊗04/84	**4692**	09/50-05/83					↩**9567**
S8973S	09/50-06/81	⊗06/82	**4693**	09/50-06/81					↩**9695**
S8974S	09/50-10/82	⊗02/84	**4694**	09/50-04/76	**4674**	06/76-10/82			↩**9564**
S8975S	09/50-05/82	⊗06/84	**4695**	09/50-06/81	**4684**	07/81-05/82			↩**9634**
S8976S	10/50-07/83	⊗11/84	**4696**	10/50-05/81	**4714**	05/81-07/83			
S8977S	10/50-07/81	⊗04/86	**4697**	10/50-06/81	**4742**	07/81-06/83			↩**9576**
S8978S	10/50-10/82	⊗11/83	**4698**	10/50-04/76	**4659**	06/76-10/82			↩**9545**
S8979S	10/50-10/82	⊗	**4699**	10/50-04/76	**4293**	05/76-10/82			↩**9519**
S8980S	10/50-02/81	⊃**15451**	**4700**	10/50-04/76	**4621**	06/76-12/80			↩**9542**
S8981S	11/50-06/81	⊗04/82	**4701**	11/50-06/81					↩**9577**
S8982S	11/50-05/83	⊗06/84	**4702**	11/50-04/76	**4678**	06/76-05/83			↩**9536**
S8983S	11/50-05/83	⊗	**4703**	11/50-04/76	**4668**	06/76-05/83			↩**9488**
S8984S	11/50-10/82	⊗05/85	**4704**	11/50-09/75	**4645**	12/75-10/82			
S8985S	11/50-06/81	⊗	**4705**	11/50-06/81					↩**9562**
S8986S	11/50-07/83	⊗10/85	**4706**	11/50-04/76	**4710**	06/76-07/83			↩**9716**
S8987S	12/50-01/78	⊗02/81	**4707**	12/50-04/76	**4718**	06/76-01/78			↩**9520**
S8988S	12/50- 73	⊗03/75	**4708**	12/50-09/72					↩**9535**
S8989S	12/50-05/83	⊗04/84	**4709**	12/50-05/81	**4692**	05/81-05/83			↩**9534**

Class 405 4-SUB Eastleigh

Trailer Third Open
TTO
S8990S-S9034S

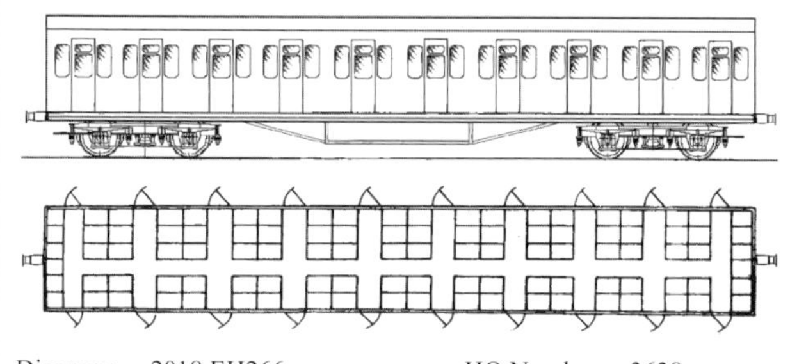

Diagram: 2018 EH266 HO Number: 3638
Body: 62' 0" × 9' 0" Weight: 27-29t
Seats: 102 third Bogies: SR

S8990S	12/50-07/83	⊗10/85	**4710**	12/50-07/83					↩**9578**
S8991S	12/50-10/82	⊗02/84	**4711**	12/50-10/56	**4711**	07/58-12/70	**4711**	05/71-04/76	
			4671	06/76-10/82					↩**9566**
S8992S	01/51-07/83	⊗07/85	**4712**	01/51-04/76	**4657**	05/76-07/83			↩**9524**
S8993S	01/51-05/83	⊗02/85	**4713**	01/51-04/76	**4666**	05/76-05/83			↩**9516**
S8994S	01/51-07/83	⊗11/84	**4714**	01/51-07/83					↩**9689**
S8995S	01/51-10/82	⊗10/82	**4715**	01/51-11/74	**4730**	11/74-10/82			↩**9485**
S8996S	02/51-07/83	⊗06/84	**4716**	02/51-07/83					↩**9560**
S8997S	02/51-09/82	⊗06/84	**4717**	02/51-04/76	**4749**	05/76-09/82			↩**9612**
S8998S	02/51-01/78	⊗02/81	**4718**	02/51-06/51	**4718**	05/52-01/78			↩**9512**
S8999S	03/51-06/83	⊗10/85	**4719**	03/51-06/83					↩**9528**
S9000S	03/51-05/83	⊗10/85	**4720**	03/51-04/76	**4687**	06/76-05/83			↩**9491**
S9001S	03/51-09/83	⊗11/84	**4721**	03/51-09/83					↩**9537**
S9002S	04/51-05/83	⊗02/85	**4722**	04/51-03/71	**4722**	10/71-05/83			↩**9611**
S9003S	04/51-07/83	⊗12/87	**4723**	04/51-04/76	**4680**	05/76-07/83			↩**9538**
S9004S	04/51-08/83	⊗07/85	**4724**	07/51-04/76	**4291**	06/76-08/83			↩**9667**

S9005S	04/51-01/82	⊗08/82	**4725**	04/51-10/81			
S9006S	05/51-07/83	⊗02/85	**4726**	05/51-07/83			
S9007S	05/51-05/83	⊗10/85	**4727**	05/51-04/76	**4294**	05/76-05/83	↩**9613**
S9008S	06/51-05/83	⊗04/86	**4728**	06/51-04/76	**4743**	06/76-05/83	↩**9530**
S9009S	06/51-03/74	⊗01/77	**4729**	06/51-03/74			↩**9616**
S9010S	06/51-10/82	⊗10/82	**4730**	06/51-10/82			↩**9522**
S9011S	06/51-08/83	⊗07/85	**4731**	06/51-04/76	**4738**	04/76-08/83	↩**9550**
S9012S	06/51-11/74	⊗01/76	**4732**	06/51-11/74			↩**9487**
S9013S	06/51-05/82	⊗10/85	**4733**	06/51-05/82			↩**9532**
S9014S	07/51-10/82	⊗	**4734**	07/51-04/76	**4658**	05/76-10/82	↩**9559**
S9015S	07/51-06/81	⊗08/82	**4735**	07/51-06/81			↩**9574**
S9016S	07/51-10/82	⊗06/84	**4736**	07/51-04/76	**4672**	05/76-10/82	↩**9502**
S9017S	08/51-10/71	⊗03/72	**4737**	08/51-10/71			↩**9557**
S9018S	08/51-08/83	⊗07/85	**4738**	08/51-08/83			↩**9499**
S9019S	08/51-06/81	⊗12/81	**4739**	08/51-06/81			↩**9544**
S9020S	08/51-10/79	⊗06/80	**4740**	08/51-04/76	**4651**	07/76-10/79	↩**9504**
S9021S	08/51-05/83	⊗02/85	**4741**	08/51-04/76	**4722**	05/76-05/83	↩**9529**
S9022S	08/51-06/83	⊗04/86	**4742**	08/51-06/83			↩**9514**
S9023S	09/51-05/83	⊗04/86	**4743**	09/51-05/83			↩**9573**
S9024S	09/51-01/76	⊗06/76	**4744**	09/51-01/76			↩**9498**
S9025S	09/51-10/73	⊗03/74	**4745**	09/51-10/73			↩**9539**
S9026S	09/51-10/82	⊗05/84	**4746**	09/51-04/76	**4626**	05/76-10/82	↩**9683**
S9027S	10/51-05/83	⊗02/84	**4747**	10/51-05/83			↩**9565**
S9028S	10/51-01/82	⊗08/82	**4748**	10/51-04/76	**4725**	06/76-10/81	↩**9614**
S9029S	10/51-09/82	⊗06/84	**4749**	10/51-09/82			↩**9513**
S9030S	10/51-10/82	⊗06/84	**4750**	10/51-10/82			↩**9515**
S9031S	10/51-07/83	⊗07/85	**4751**	10/51-07/83			↩**9551**
S9032S	11/51-10/82	⊗06/84	**4752**	11/51-04/76	**4656**	06/76-10/82	↩**9554**
S9033S	12/51-09/78	⊗10/79	**4753**	12/51-09/78			↩**9617**
S9034S	12/51-09/83	⊗10/84	**4754**	12/51-09/83			↩**9523**

4-EPB Eastleigh

Trailer Third

TT

S9035S-S9043S

Numbers not used. Renumbered before entering service.

S9035S	➲**15101**
S9036S	➲**15102**
S9037S	➲**15103**
S9038S	➲**15104**
S9039S	➲**15105**
S9040S	➲**15106**
S9041S	➲**15107**
S9042S	➲**15108**
S9043S	➲**15109**

6-PUL Lancing/Eastleigh

Trailer Corridor Third Lavatory

TTK

S10001S-S10020S

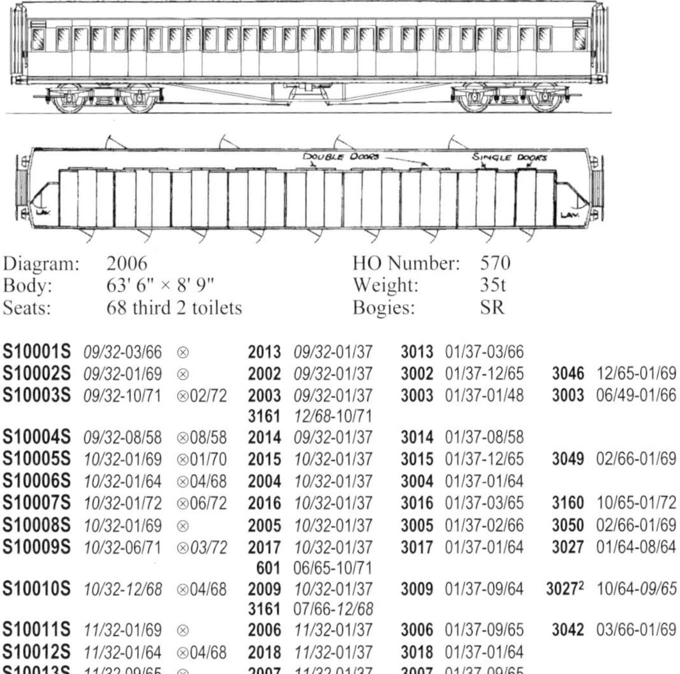

Diagram:	2006	HO Number:	570
Body:	63' 6" × 8' 9"	Weight:	35t
Seats:	68 third 2 toilets	Bogies:	SR

S10001S	*09/32*-03/66	⊗	**2013**	*09/32*-01/37	**3013**	01/37-03/66		
S10002S	*09/32*-01/69	⊗	**2002**	*09/32*-01/37	**3002**	01/37-12/65	**3046**	12/65-01/69
S10003S	*09/32*-10/71	⊗02/72	**2003**	*09/32*-01/37	**3003**	01/37-01/48	**3003**	06/49-01/66
			3161	*12/68*-10/71				
S10004S	*09/32*-08/58	⊗08/58	**2014**	*09/32*-01/37	**3014**	01/37-08/58		
S10005S	*10/32*-01/69	⊗01/70	**2015**	*10/32*-01/37	**3015**	01/37-12/65	**3049**	02/66-01/69
S10006S	*10/32*-01/64	⊗04/68	**2004**	*10/32*-01/37	**3004**	01/37-01/64		
S10007S	*10/32*-01/72	⊗06/72	**2016**	*10/32*-01/37	**3016**	01/37-03/65	**3160**	10/65-01/72
S10008S	*10/32*-01/69	⊗	**2005**	*10/32*-01/37	**3005**	01/37-02/66	**3050**	02/66-01/69
S10009S	*10/32*-06/71	⊗03/72	**2017**	*10/32*-01/37	**3017**	01/37-01/64	**3027**	01/64-08/64
			601	06/65-10/71				
S10010S	*10/32*-*12/68*	⊗04/68	**2009**	*10/32*-01/37	**3009**	01/37-09/64	**3027**[2]	10/64-*09/65*
			3161	07/66-*12/68*				
S10011S	*11/32*-01/69	⊗	**2006**	*11/32*-01/37	**3006**	01/37-09/65	**3042**	03/66-01/69
S10012S	*11/32*-01/64	⊗04/68	**2018**	*11/32*-01/37	**3018**	01/37-01/64		
S10013S	*11/32*-09/65	⊗	**2007**	*11/32*-01/37	**3007**	01/37-09/65		
S10014S	*11/32*-06/71	⊗*03/72*	**2020**	*11/32*-01/37	**3020**	01/37-01/64	**3027**	01/64-08/64
			601	06/65-10/71				
S10015S	*11/32*-01/64	⊗	**2019**	*11/32*-01/37	**3019**	01/37-01/64		
S10016S	*11/32*-01/69	⊗	**2010**	*11/32*-01/37	**3010**	01/37-11/65	**3044**	11/65-01/69
S10017S	*12/32*-10/68	⊗	**2001**	*12/32*-01/37	**3001**	01/37-04/66	**3043**	04/66-10/68
S10018S	*12/32*-12/65	⊗	**2011**	*12/32*-01/37	**3011**	01/37-12/65	**3048**	01/66- 66
S10019S	*12/32*-02/66	⊗	**2008**	*12/32*-01/37	**3008**	01/37-02/66		
S10020S	*12/32*-09/65	⊗	**2012**	*12/32*-01/37	**3012**	01/37-09/65		

6-PAN Lancing/Eastleigh

Trailer Corridor Third Lavatory

TTK

S10021S-S10054S

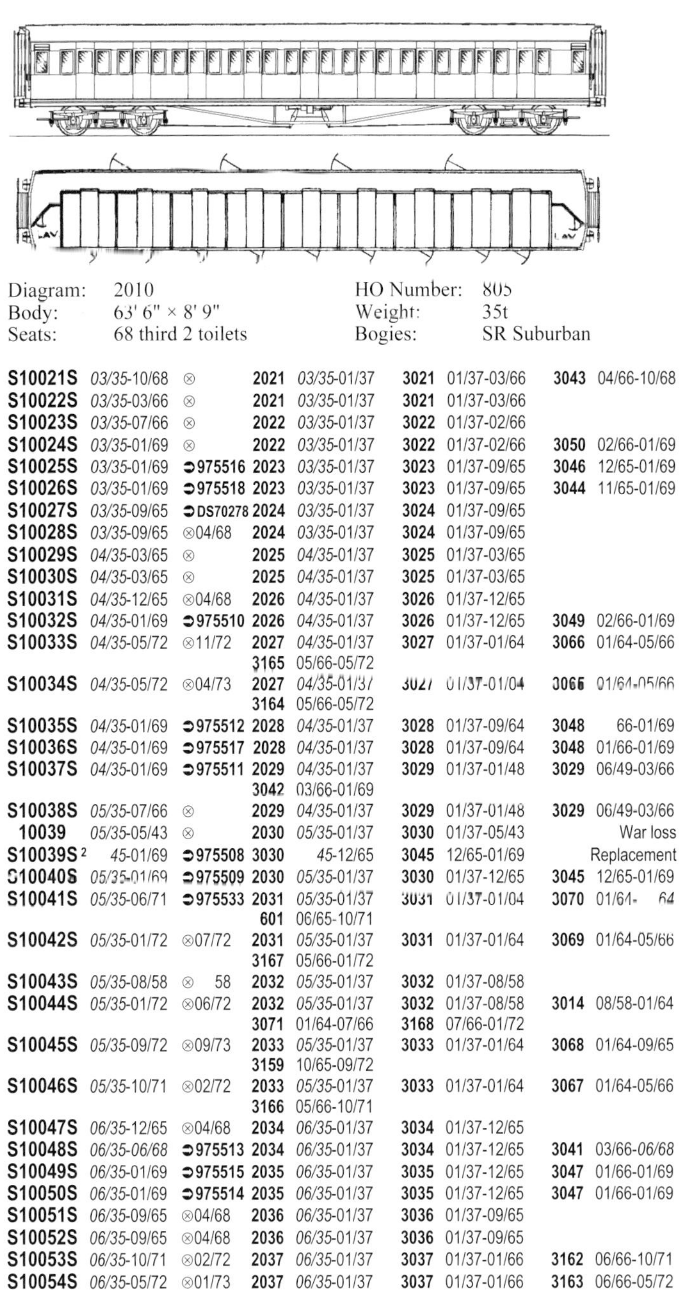

Diagram:	2010	HO Number:	805
Body:	63' 6" × 8' 9"	Weight:	35t
Seats:	68 third 2 toilets	Bogies:	SR Suburban

S10021S	*03/35*-10/68	⊗	**2021**	*03/35*-01/37	**3021**	01/37-03/66	**3043**	04/66-10/68
S10022S	*03/35*-03/66	⊗	**2021**	*03/35*-01/37	**3021**	01/37-03/66		
S10023S	*03/35*-07/66	⊗	**2022**	*03/35*-01/37	**3022**	01/37-02/66		
S10024S	*03/35*-01/69	⊗	**2022**	*03/35*-01/37	**3022**	01/37-02/66	**3050**	02/66-01/69
S10025S	*03/35*-01/69	➲**975516**	**2023**	*03/35*-01/37	**3023**	01/37-09/65	**3046**	12/65-01/69
S10026S	*03/35*-01/69	➲**975518**	**2023**	*03/35*-01/37	**3023**	01/37-09/65	**3044**	11/65-01/69
S10027S	*03/35*-09/65	➲**DS70278**	**2024**	*03/35*-01/37	**3024**	01/37-09/65		
S10028S	*03/35*-09/65	⊗04/68	**2024**	*03/35*-01/37	**3024**	01/37-09/65		
S10029S	*04/35*-03/65	⊗	**2025**	*04/35*-01/37	**3025**	01/37-03/65		
S10030S	*04/35*-03/65	⊗	**2025**	*04/35*-01/37	**3025**	01/37-03/65		
S10031S	*04/35*-12/65	⊗04/68	**2026**	*04/35*-01/37	**3026**	01/37-12/65		
S10032S	*04/35*-01/69	➲**975510**	**2026**	*04/35*-01/37	**3026**	01/37-12/65	**3049**	02/66-01/69
S10033S	*04/35*-05/72	⊗11/72	**2027**	*04/35*-01/37	**3027**	01/37-01/64	**3066**	01/64-05/66
			3165	05/66-05/72				
S10034S	*04/35*-05/72	⊗04/73	**2027**	*04/35*-01/37	**3027**	01/37-01/64	**3066**	01/64-05/66
			3164	05/66-05/72				
S10035S	*04/35*-01/69	➲**975512**	**2028**	*04/35*-01/37	**3028**	01/37-09/64	**3048**	66-01/69
S10036S	*04/35*-01/69	➲**975517**	**2028**	*04/35*-01/37	**3028**	01/37-09/64	**3048**	01/66-01/69
S10037S	*04/35*-01/69	➲**975511**	**2029**	*04/35*-01/37	**3029**	01/37-01/48	**3029**	06/49-03/66
			3042	03/66-01/69				
S10038S	*05/35*-07/66	⊗	**2029**	*04/35*-01/37	**3029**	01/37-01/48	**3029**	06/49-03/66
10039	*05/35*-05/43	⊗	**2030**	*05/35*-01/37	**3030**	01/37-05/43		War loss
S10039S[2]	*45*-01/69	➲**975508**	**3030**	*45*-12/65	**3045**	12/65-01/69		Replacement
S10040S	*05/35*-01/69	➲**975509**	**2030**	*05/35*-01/37	**3030**	01/37-12/65	**3045**	12/65-01/69
S10041S	*05/35*-06/71	➲**975533**	**2031**	*05/35*-01/37	**3031**	01/37-01/64	**3070**	01/64- *64*
			601	06/65-10/71				
S10042S	*05/35*-01/72	⊗07/72	**2031**	*05/35*-01/37	**3031**	01/37-01/64	**3069**	01/64-05/66
			3167	05/66-01/72				
S10043S	*05/35*-08/58	⊗ 58	**2032**	*05/35*-01/37	**3032**	01/37-08/58		
S10044S	*05/35*-01/72	⊗06/72	**2032**	*05/35*-01/37	**3032**	01/37-08/58	**3014**	08/58-01/64
			3071	01/64-07/66	**3168**	07/66-01/72		
S10045S	*05/35*-09/72	⊗09/73	**2033**	*05/35*-01/37	**3033**	01/37-01/64	**3068**	01/64-09/65
			3159	10/65-09/72				
S10046S	*05/35*-10/71	⊗02/72	**2033**	*05/35*-01/37	**3033**	01/37-01/64	**3067**	01/64-05/66
			3166	05/66-10/71				
S10047S	*06/35*-12/65	⊗04/68	**2034**	*06/35*-01/37	**3034**	01/37-12/65		
S10048S	*06/35*-06/68	➲**975513**	**2034**	*06/35*-01/37	**3034**	01/37-12/65	**3041**	03/66-*06/68*
S10049S	*06/35*-01/69	➲**975515**	**2035**	*06/35*-01/37	**3035**	01/37-12/65	**3047**	01/66-01/69
S10050S	*06/35*-01/69	➲**975514**	**2035**	*06/35*-01/37	**3035**	01/37-12/65	**3047**	01/66-01/69
S10051S	*06/35*-09/65	⊗04/68	**2036**	*06/35*-01/37	**3036**	01/37-09/65		
S10052S	*06/35*-09/65	⊗04/68	**2036**	*06/35*-01/37	**3036**	01/37-09/65		
S10053S	*06/35*-10/71	⊗02/72	**2037**	*06/35*-01/37	**3037**	01/37-01/66	**3162**	06/66-10/71
S10054S	*06/35*-05/72	⊗01/73	**2037**	*06/35*-01/37	**3037**	01/37-01/66	**3163**	06/66-05/72

Class 404 4-COR Lancing/Eastleigh
Trailer Corridor Third Lavatory
TTK
S10055S-S10083S

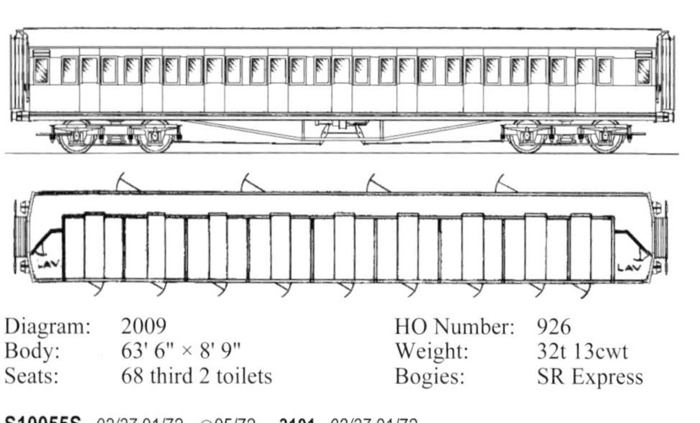

Diagram:	2009	HO Number:	926
Body:	63' 6" × 8' 9"	Weight:	32t 13cwt
Seats:	68 third 2 toilets	Bogies:	SR Express

S10055S	*02/37-01/72*	⊗05/72	**3101**	*02/37-01/72*			
S10056S	*02/37-10/72*	⊗02/73	**3102**	*02/37-10/72*			
S10057S	*02/37-05/72*	⊗02/73	**3103**	*02/37-05/72*			
S10058S	*02/37-05/72*	⊗11/72	**3104**	*02/37-05/72*			
S10059S	*02/37-05/72*	⊗11/72	**3105**	*02/37-05/72*			
S10060S	*02/37-05/72*	⊗11/72	**3106**	*02/37-05/72*			
S10061S	*02/37-01/72*	⊗05/72	**3107**	*02/37-01/72*			
S10062S	*02/37-09/72*	⊗05/73	**3108**	*02/37-09/72*			
S10063S	*02/37-09/72*	⊗05/73	**3109**	*02/37-09/72*			
S10064S	*03/37-10/71*	➲**975526**	**3110**	*03/37-10/71*			
S10065S	*03/37-05/72*	⊗11/72	**3111**	*03/37-05/72*			
S10066S	*03/37-01/72*	⊗07/72	**3112**	*03/37-01/72*			
S10067S	*03/37-01/72*	⊗06/72	**3113**	*03/37-01/72*			
S10068S	*03/37-05/72*	⊗11/72	**3114**	*03/37-05/72*			
S10069S	*03/37-01/72*	⊗06/72	**3115**	*03/37-01/72*			
S10070S	*03/37-12/72*	⊗02/73	**3116**	*03/37-12/72*			
10071	*03/37-01/41*	⊗03/41	**3117**	*03/37-01/41*			War loss
S10071S[2]	*10/46-05/72*	⊗11/72	**3117**	*09/46-05/72*			Replacement
S10072S	*03/37-08/72*	⊗02/73	**3118**	*03/37-08/72*			
10073	*03/37-01/41*	⊗03/41	**3119**	*03/37-01/41*			War loss
S10073S[2]	*10/46-05/72*	⊗04/73	**3041**	07/46-02/47	**3119**	*02/47-05/72*	Replacement
S10074S	*04/37-05/72*	⊗11/72	**3120**	*04/37-05/72*			
S10075S	*04/37-10/71*	⊗03/72	**3121**	*04/37-10/71*			
S10076S	*04/37-08/72*	⊗05/73	**3122**	*04/37-08/72*			
S10077S	*04/37-12/72*	⊗02/73	**3123**	*04/37-12/72*			
S10078S	*04/37-10/71*	⊗02/72	**3124**	*04/37-10/71*			
S10079S	*04/37-01/72*	➲**975529**	**3125**	*04/37-01/72*			
S10080S	*04/37-01/72*	⊗05/72	**3126**	*04/37-01/72*			
S10081S	*04/37-01/70*	➲**975519**	**3127**	*04/37-01/70*			
S10082S	*04/37-09/72*	⊗05/73	**3128**	*04/37-09/72*			
S10083S	*04/37-05/72*	⊗11/72	**3129**	*04/37-05/72*			

Class 404 4-COR Lancing/Eastleigh
Trailer Corridor Third Lavatory
TTK
S10084S-S10109S

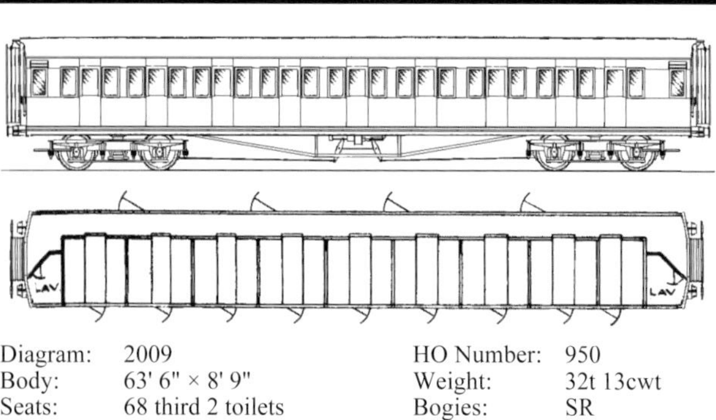

Diagram:	2009	HO Number:	950
Body:	63' 6" × 8' 9"	Weight:	32t 13cwt
Seats:	68 third 2 toilets	Bogies:	SR

S10084S	*01/38-05/72*	⊗02/74	**3130**	*05/38-05/72*			
S10085S	*01/38-09/72*	⊗07/73	**3131**	*05/38-09/72*			
S10086S	*01/38-09/72*	⊗02/73	**3132**	*05/38-09/72*			
S10087S	*01/38-05/72*	⊗01/73	**3133**	*05/38-05/72*			
S10088S	*01/38-01/72*	➲**083145**	**3134**	*05/38-02/63*	**3134**	*04/64-01/72*	
S10089S	*01/38-09/72*	⊗07/73	**3135**	*05/38-09/72*			
S10090S	*02/38-09/72*	⊗02/73	**3136**	*05/38-09/72*			
10091	*02/38-08/40*	⊗	**3137**	*05/38-08/40*			War loss
S10091S[2]	*10/46-08/72*	⊗	**3137**	*47-08/72*			Replacement
S10092S	*02/38-01/72*	⊗06/72	**3138**	*06/38-01/72*			
S10093S	*02/38-01/72*	⊗06/72	**3139**	*06/38-01/72*			
S10094S	*02/38-05/72*	⊗01/73	**3140**	*06/38-05/72*			
S10095S	*02/38-09/72*	⊗02/73	**3141**	*06/38-09/72*			
S10096S	*02/38-12/72*	Ⓟ	**3142**	*06/38-12/72*			
S10097S	*03/38-10/72*	⊗02/73	**3143**	*06/38-10/72*			
10098	*03/38-08/40*	⊗	**3144**	*06/38-06/40*			War loss
S10098S[2]	*10/46-01/72*	⊗07/72	**3156**	*10/46-01/72*			Replacement
S10099S	*03/38- 72*	⊗02/73	**3145**	*06/38- 72*			
S10100S	*03/38-01/72*	⊗02/72	**3146**	*06/38-01/72*			
S10101S	*03/38-01/72*	⊗06/72	**3147**	*07/38-01/72*			
S10102S	*03/38-12/71*	⊗06/72	**3148**	*07/38-12/71*			
S10103S	*03/38-01/72*	➲**975532**	**3149**	*07/38-01/72*			
S10104S	*04/38-12/71*	⊗07/72	**3150**	*07/38-12/71*			
S10105S	*04/38-08/72*	⊗05/73	**3151**	*07/38-08/72*			
S10106S	*04/38-01/72*	⊗05/72	**3152**	*07/38-01/72*			
S10107S	*04/38-01/72*	⊗07/72	**3153**	*07/38-01/72*			
S10108S	*04/38-09/72*	⊗07/72	**3154**	*07/38-09/72*			
S10109S	*04/38-01/72*	⊗06/72	**3155**	*07/38-01/72*			

Class 404 4-COR Lancing/Eastleigh
Trailer Corridor Third Lavatory
TTK
S10110S-S10112S

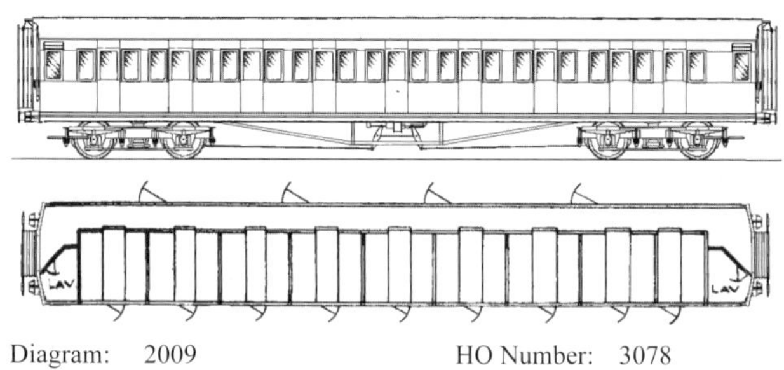

Diagram:	2009	HO Number:	3078
Body:	63' 6" × 8' 9"	Weight:	32t 13cwt
Seats:	68 third 2 toilets	Bogies:	SR

War loss replacements for 12606/15/17

S10110S	10/46-05/72	⊗02/74	**3158**	10/46-05/72
S10111S	10/46-10/71	⊗02/72	**3144**	10/46-10/71
S10112S	10/46-01/72	⊗06/72	**3157**	10/46-01/72

6-CIT Lancing/Eastleigh
Trailer Corridor Third Lavatory
TTK
S10113S-S10115S

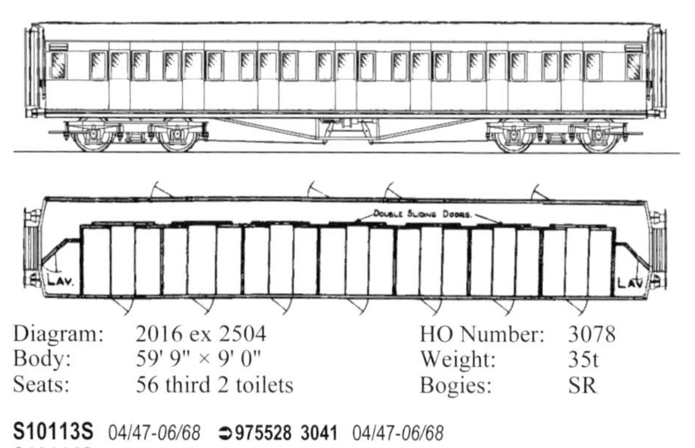

Diagram:	2016 ex 2504	HO Number:	3078
Body:	59' 9" × 9' 0"	Weight:	35t
Seats:	56 third 2 toilets	Bogies:	SR

S10113S	04/47-*06/68*	➲**975528**	**3041**	04/47-*06/68*	⊂**12254**
S10114S	12/47-09/65	⊗	**3042**	12/47-09/65	⊂**12259**
S10115S	12/47-03/66	⊗	**3043**	12/47-03/66	⊂**12253**

Class 405 4-SUB Eastleigh

Trailer Third Open
TTO
S10121S-S10143S

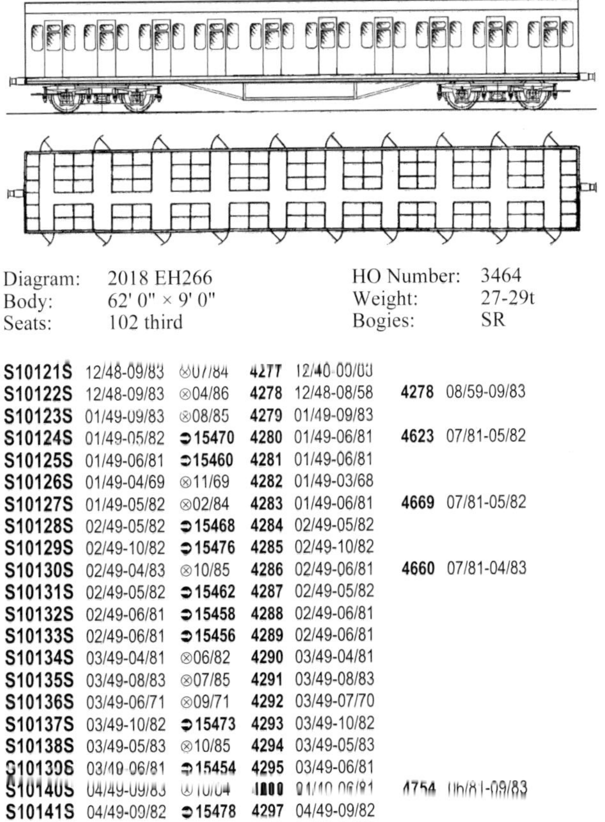

Diagram:	2018 EH266		HO Number:	3464
Body:	62' 0" × 9' 0"		Weight:	27-29t
Seats:	102 third		Bogies:	SR

S10121S	12/48-09/83	⊗07/84	**4277**	12/48-09/83		
S10122S	12/48-09/83	⊗04/86	**4278**	12/48-08/58	**4278**	08/59-09/83
S10123S	01/49-09/83	⊗08/85	**4279**	01/49-09/83		
S10124S	01/49-05/82	**⊃15470**	**4280**	01/49-06/81	**4623**	07/81-05/82
S10125S	01/49-06/81	**⊃15460**	**4281**	01/49-06/81		
S10126S	01/49-04/69	⊗11/69	**4282**	01/49-03/68		
S10127S	01/49-05/82	⊗02/84	**4283**	01/49-06/81	**4669**	07/81-05/82
S10128S	02/49-05/82	**⊃15468**	**4284**	02/49-05/82		
S10129S	02/49-10/82	**⊃15476**	**4285**	02/49-10/82		
S10130S	02/49-04/83	⊗10/85	**4286**	02/49-06/81	**4660**	07/81-04/83
S10131S	02/49-05/82	**⊃15462**	**4287**	02/49-05/82		
S10132S	02/49-06/81	**⊃15458**	**4288**	02/49-06/81		
S10133S	02/49-06/81	**⊃15456**	**4289**	02/49-06/81		
S10134S	03/49-04/81	⊗06/82	**4290**	03/49-04/81		
S10135S	03/49-08/83	⊗07/85	**4291**	03/49-08/83		
S10136S	03/49-06/71	⊗09/71	**4292**	03/49-07/70		
S10137S	03/49-10/82	**⊃15473**	**4293**	03/49-10/82		
S10138S	03/49-05/83	⊗10/85	**4294**	03/49-05/83		
S10139S	03/49-06/81	**⊃15454**	**4295**	03/49-06/81		
S10140S	04/49-09/83	⊗10/84	[illegible]	04/49-06/81	**4754**	06/81-09/83
S10141S	04/49-09/82	**⊃15478**	**4297**	04/49-09/82		
S10142S	04/49-09/83	⊗04/86	**4298**	04/49-09/83		
S10143S	04/49-06/81	**⊃15457**	**4299**	04/49-11/73	**4299**	06/74-06/81

Class 405 4-SUB Eastleigh

Trailer Third
TT
S10144S-S10166S

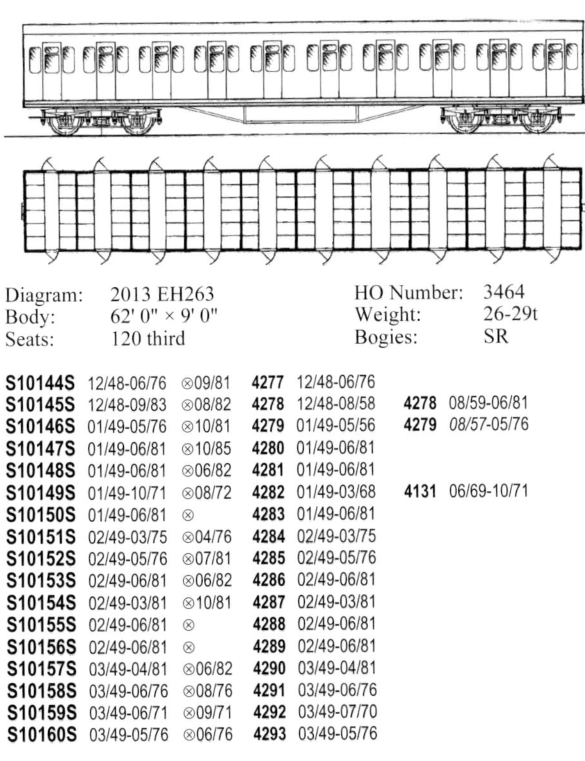

Diagram:	2013 EH263		HO Number:	3464
Body:	62' 0" × 9' 0"		Weight:	26-29t
Seats:	120 third		Bogies:	SR

S10144S	12/48-06/76	⊗09/81	**4277**	12/48-06/76		
S10145S	12/48-09/83	⊗08/82	**4278**	12/48-08/58	**4278**	08/59-06/81
S10146S	01/49-05/76	⊗10/81	**4279**	01/49-05/56	**4279**	*08/57*-05/76
S10147S	01/49-06/81	⊗10/85	**4280**	01/49-06/81		
S10148S	01/49-06/81	⊗06/82	**4281**	01/49-06/81		
S10149S	01/49-10/71	⊗08/72	**4282**	01/49-03/68	**4131**	06/69-10/71
S10150S	01/49-06/81	⊗	**4283**	01/49-06/81		
S10151S	02/49-03/75	⊗04/76	**4284**	02/49-03/75		
S10152S	02/49-05/76	⊗07/81	**4285**	02/49-05/76		
S10153S	02/49-06/81	⊗06/82	**4286**	02/49-06/81		
S10154S	02/49-03/81	⊗10/81	**4287**	02/49-03/81		
S10155S	02/49-06/81	⊗	**4288**	02/49-06/81		
S10156S	02/49-06/81	⊗	**4289**	02/49-06/81		
S10157S	03/49-04/81	⊗06/82	**4290**	03/49-04/81		
S10158S	03/49-06/76	⊗08/76	**4291**	03/49-06/76		
S10159S	03/49-06/71	⊗09/71	**4292**	03/49-07/70		
S10160S	03/49-05/76	⊗06/76	**4293**	03/49-05/76		
S10161S	03/49-05/76	⊗06/76	**4294**	03/49-05/76		
S10162S	03/49-06/81	⊗	**4295**	03/49-06/81		
S10163S	04/49-06/81	⊗	**4296**	04/49-06/81		
S10164S	04/49-07/76	⊗09/81	**4297**	04/49-07/76		
S10165S	04/49-07/76	⊗08/82	**4298**	04/49-07/76		
S10166S	04/49-11/73	⊗01/76	**4299**	04/49-11/73		

Class 405 4-SUB Eastleigh

Trailer Third
TT
S10167S-S10169S

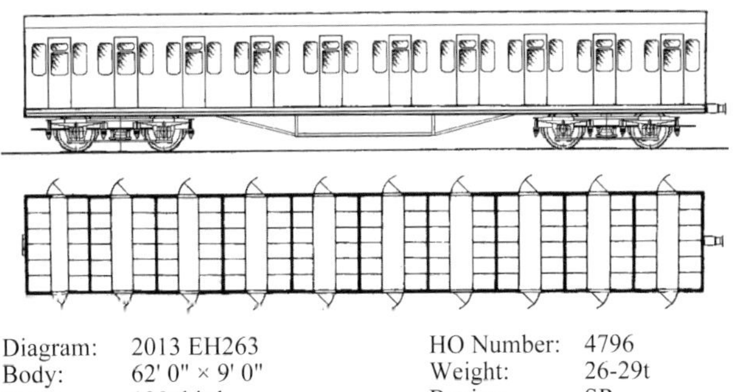

Diagram:	2013 EH263		HO Number:	4796
Body:	62' 0" × 9' 0"		Weight:	26-29t
Seats:	120 third		Bogies:	SR

S10167S	*01/48*-07/56	**⊃15054**	**4534**	*01/48*-07/56
S10168S	*01/48*-12/56	**⊃15074**	**4550**	*01/48*-12/56
S10169S	*01/48*-06/52	**⊃15012**	**4568**	*01/48*-06/52

Class 405 4-SUB Eastleigh

Trailer Third
TT
S10170S-S10229S

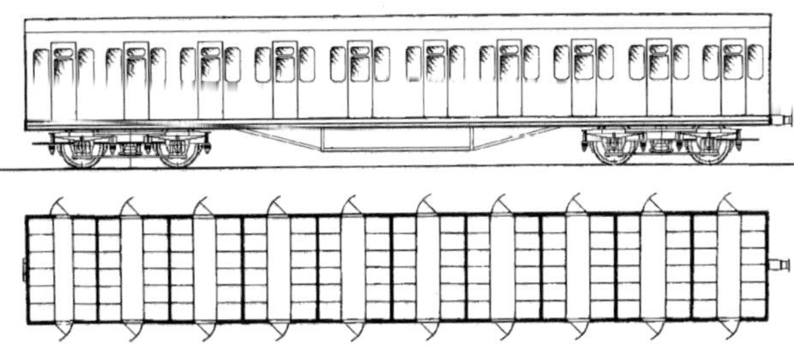

Diagram:	2013 EH263		HO Number:	3463
Body:	62' 0" × 9' 0"		Weight:	26-29t
Seats:	120 third		Bogies:	SR

S10170S	01/48-05/72	⊗02/73	**4368**	01/48-08/67	**4368**	03/68-05/72		
S10171S	02/48-10/73	**⊃975320**	**4367**	02/48-10/73				
S10172S	03/48-01/74	⊗10/76	**4366**	03/48-01/74				
S10173S	03/48-05/74	⊗03/76	**4365**	03/48-02/68	**4379**	04/69-05/74		
S10174S	*01/48*-06/52	**⊃15011**	**4571**	*01/48*-06/52				
S10175	*01/48*-12/51	**⊃15022**	**4517**	*01/48*-04/53				
S10176S	*02/48*-06/56	**⊃15049**	**4553**	*02/48*-06/56				
S10177S	*02/48*-05/53	**⊃15020**	**4519**	*02/48-05/53*				
S10178S	*02/48*-09/56	**⊃15062**	**4543**	*02/48*-09/56				
S10179S	*02/48*-12/56	**⊃15072**	**4558**	*02/48*-12/56				
S10180S	*02/48*-11/56	**⊃15070**	**4523**	*02/48-01/49*	**4531**	*01/49*-11/56		
S10181S	*02/48*-04/76	⊗	**4584**	*02/48*-05/49	**4570**	05/49-04/51	**4724**	04/51-07/51
			4736	07/51-04/76				
S10182S	*02/48*-08/56	**⊃15078**	**4524**	*02/48*-05/49	**4529**	05/49-08/56		
S10183S	*02/48*-11/56	**⊃15068**	**4528**	*02/48*-11/56				
S10184S	*02/48-06/52*	**⊃15014**	**4586**	*02/48-06/52*				
S10185S	*03/48*-12/56	**⊃15073**	**4563**	*03/48*-03/49	**4533**	03/49-12/56		
S10186S	*03/48*-10/56	**⊃15066**	**4581**	*03/48*-08/49	**4544**	08/49-10/56		
S10187S	*03/48*-01/57	**⊃15075**	**4555**	*03/48*-01/57				
S10188S	*03/48*-09/56	**⊃15058**	**4582**	*03/48*-05/49	**4548**	05/49-*04/50*	**4532**	*05/50*-09/56
S10189S	*03/48*-06/52	**⊃15013**	**4583**	*03/48-02/49*	**4566**	*02/49*-06/52		
S10190S	*03/48*-08/56	**⊃15056**	**4575**	*03/48-02/49*	**4545**	*02/49*-08/56		
S10191S	*03/48*-12/56	**⊃15071**	**4562**	*03/48-01/49*	**4539**	*01/49*-12/56		
S10192S	*03/48*-08/53	**⊃15031**	**4580**	*03/48*-08/53				
S10193S	*03/48*-08/56	**⊃15057**	**4576**	*03/48*-08/49	**4530**	08/49-08/56		
S10194S	*04/48*-10/56	**⊃15063**	**4538**	*04/48*-10/56				
S10195S	*04/48*-07/60	**⊃15079**	**4578**	*04/48-10/49*	**4588**	*10/49-10/51*	**4331**	*10/51*-07/60
S10196S	03/48-02/74	⊗10/76	**4364**	03/48-02/74				
S10197S	04/48-02/74	⊗03/75	**4363**	04/48-02/74				
S10198S	04/48-02/74	⊗03/75	**4363**	04/48-02/74				
S10199S	04/48-10/73	⊗10/76	**4362**	04/48-10/73				

S10200S	04/48-10/73	⊗10/76	4362	04/48-10/73		
S10201S	04/48-02/52	➲15009	4585	04/48-01/49	4567	01/49-02/52
S10202S	04/48-05/53	➲15029	4525	04/48-01/49	4536	01/49-05/53
S10203S	04/48-01/52	➲15004	4522	05/48-01/49	4518	01/49-01/52
S10204S	04/48-08/56	➲15077	4577	05/48-01/49	4547	01/49-08/56
S10205S	04/48-05/74	⊗10/76	4361	04/48-05/74		
S10206S	04/48-05/74	⊗10/76	4361	04/48-05/74		
S10207S	04/48-09/64	➲15082	4360	04/48-09/64		
S10208S	04/48-09/64	➲15081	4360	04/48-09/64		
S10209S	05/48-01/74	⊗07/76	4359	05/48-01/74		
S10210S	05/48-01/74	⊗07/76	4359	05/48-01/74		
S10211S	05/48-06/56	➲15051	4540	05/48-06/56		
S10212S	05/48-10/56	➲15065	4557	06/48-10/56		
S10213S	05/48-04/76	⊗05/80	4574	06/48-09/51	4748	10/51-04/76
S10214S	05/48-01/74	⊗	4358	05/48-01/74		
S10215S	05/48-01/74	⊗	4358	05/48-01/74		
S10216S	05/48-07/73	⊗02/74	4357	05/48-07/73		
S10217S	05/48-07/73	⊗02/74	4357	05/48-07/73		
S10218S	06/48-01/74	⊗10/76	4356	06/48-01/74		
S10219S	06/48-01/74	⊗10/76	4356	06/48-01/74		
S10220S	06/48-05/72	⊗06/73	4355	06/48-05/72		
S10221S	06/48-05/72	⊗06/73	4355	06/48-05/72		
S10222S	07/48-03/56	➲15037	4542	07/48-03/56		
S10223S	07/48-06/56	➲15052	4546	07/48-06/56		
S10224S	07/48-05/56	➲15044	4565	07/48-04/55	4215	05/55-05/56
S10225S	07/48-11/56	➲15069	4541	07/48-11/56		
S10226S	07/48-09/56	➲15061	4535	07/48-09/56		
S10227S	07/48-01/57	➲15076	4554	07/48-01/57		
S10228	07/48-11/51	➲15007	4526	07/48-11/51		
S10229S	07/48-02/56	➲15035	4559	07/48-10/54	4520	10/54-02/56

Class 405 4-SUB   Eastleigh

Trailer Third
TT
S10230S-S10345

Diagram: 2013 EH263   HO Number: 3351
Body: 62' 0" × 9' 0"   Weight: 26-29t
Seats: 120 third   Bogies: SR

S10230S	10/46-04/76	⊗10/76	4488	01/47-07/47	4436	08/47-06/50	4676	06/50-04/76
S10231S	10/46-04/76	⊗08/76	4491	10/46-11/50	4706	11/50-04/76		
S10232S	10/46-05/81	⊗	4473	10/46-09/50	4692	09/50-05/81		
S10233S	10/46-06/81	⊗	4452	02/47-12/50	4709	12/50-05/81		
S10234S	10/46-06/81	⊗08/82	4407	10/46-07/51	4735	07/51-06/81		
S10235S	10/46-06/76	⊗08/76	4476	10/46-04/51	4725	04/51-06/76		
S10236S	10/46-04/76	⊗06/76	4459	10/46-10/50	4699	10/50-04/76		
S10237S	10/46-04/76	⊗07/81	4465	10/46-04/50	4606	04/50-04/76		
S10238S	10/46-02/53	➲15018	4409	10/46-02/53				
S10239S	10/46-10/83	℗	4413	10/46-06/51	4732	06/51-10/83		
S10240S	10/46-06/76	⊗07/81	4448	10/46-03/50	4601	04/50-10/58	4601	06/59-06/76
S10241S	11/46-10/73	⊗03/74	4514	11/46-08/51	4745	09/51-10/73		
S10242S	11/46-05/76	⊗09/76	4442[1]	11/46-02/48	4442[2]	02/48-04/50	4602	04/50-06/72
			4620	06/72-05/76				
S10243S	11/46-07/81	⊗07/85	4437	11/46-02/51	4719	03/51-07/81		
S10244S	11/46-06/81	⊗	4506	11/46-09/51	4752	11/51-06/58	4650	06/58-06/81
S10245S	11/46-06/76	⊗07/81	4492	11/46-04/50	4601	04/50-10/58	4601	06/59-06/76
S10246S	11/46-04/56	➲15039	4425	11/46-04/56				
S10247S	11/46-06/81	⊗08/82	4472	11/46-06/50	4677	06/50-08/67	4677	01/68-06/81
S10248S	11/46-04/76	⊗07/81	4463	11/46-04/50	4606	04/50-04/76		
S10249S	11/46-06/76	⊗04/81	4435	11/46-05/50	4670	05/50-06/76		
S10250S	11/46-04/76	⊗08/76	4455	11/46-10/50	4700	10/50-04/76		
S10251S	11/46-03/53	➲15016	4411	11/46-03/53				
S10252S	11/46-05/76	⊗10/76	4511	11/46-01/51	4718	02/51-06/51	4731	06/51-04/76
S10253	11/46-07/51	➲15006	4422	11/46-07/51				
S10254S	12/46-03/53	➲15021	4405	12/46-03/53				
S10255S	12/46-04/76	⊗08/76	4439[1]	12/46-02/49	4439[2]	02/49-07/51	4740	08/51-04/76
S10256S	12/46-04/76	⊗07/76	4481	12/46-01/51	4713	01/51-04/76		
S10257S	12/46-06/81	⊗	4502	12/46-09/51	4754	12/51-06/81		
S10258S	12/46-06/81	⊗06/82	4433	12/46-06/50	4675	06/50-10/58	4675	04/59-06/81
S10259S	12/46-02/81	⊗10/81	4478	12/46-04/50	4605	04/50-05/77	4619	05/77-02/81
S10260S	12/46-04/56	➲15050	4424	12/46-04/56				
S10261S	12/46-07/81	⊗	4487	12/46-04/50	4669	05/50-07/81		
S10262S	12/46-11/74	⊗11/74	4508	12/46-02/51	4730	06/51-11/74		
S10263S	12/46-04/76	⊗06/76	4446	12/46-09/50	4694	09/50-04/76		
S10264S	12/46-06/76	⊗05/76	4490	12/46-04/50	4668	05/50-06/76		
S10265S	12/46-04/76	⊗04/80	4445	12/46-04/50	4604	04/50-04/76		
S10266S	12/46-03/53	➲15024	4418	12/46-03/53				
S10267S	01/47-06/76	⊗08/76	4498	01/47-08/50	4687	09/50-05/56	4279	05/56-08/57
			4687	08/57-06/76				
S10268S	01/47-05/76	⊗07/76	4431	01/47-09/51	4749	10/51-05/76		
S10269S	01/47-05/81	⊗	4430	01/47-08/51	4747	10/51-05/81		
S10270S	01/47-07/81	⊗10/85	4406[1]	01/47-11/47	4406[2]	11/47-07/50	4684	08/50-07/81
S10271S	01/47-06/81	⊗06/82	4453	01/47-11/50	4705	11/50-06/81		
S10272S	01/47-04/53	➲15028	4515	01/47-04/53				
S10273S	01/47-06/76	⊗08/76	4512	01/47-09/51	4743	09/51-06/76		
S10274S	01/47-04/76	⊗08/76	4467	01/47-07/50	4686	08/50-04/76		
S10275S	01/47-04/56	➲15043	4427	01/47-04/56				
S10276S	01/47-06/72	⊗05/74	4441	01/47-04/50	4602	04/50-06/72		
S10277S	01/47-07/52	➲15015	4503	01/47-07/52				
S10278S	01/47-07/53	➲15030	4510	01/47-07/53				
S10279S	01/47-06/76	⊗08/76	4454	01/47-04/50	4671	05/50-06/76		
S10280S	02/47-07/53	➲15032	4412	02/47-07/53				
S10281S	02/47-02/53	➲15027	4408	02/47-02/53				
S10282S	02/47-04/76	⊗08/76	4444	02/47-06/50	4690	09/50-04/76		
S10283S	02/47-04/56	➲15042	4429	02/47-04/56				
S10284S	02/47-04/76	⊗08/76	4451	02/47-04/51	4724	04/51-04/76		
S10285S	02/47-03/56	➲15040	4426	02/47-03/56				
S10286S	02/47-06/81	⊗04/82	4460	02/47-10/50	4697	10/50-06/81		
S10287S	02/47-06/76	⊗09/82	4462	02/47-03/50	4603	04/50-06/76		
S10288S	02/47-04/76	⊗11/76	4404	02/47-08/51	4741	08/51-04/76		
S10289S	02/47-06/76	⊗08/76	4421	02/47-10/50	4591	10/50-08/51	4750	10/51-06/76
S10290S	02/47-07/81	⊗08/82	4440	03/47-07/50	4683	08/50-07/81		
S10291S	02/47-06/71	⊗07/72	4488	07/47-04/50	4667	05/50-11/70		
S10292S	02/47-02/53	➲15017	4402	02/47-02/53				
S10293S	03/47-06/76	⊗08/76	4464	03/47-06/50	4682	07/50-06/76		
S10294S	03/47-04/76	⊗08/76	4450	03/47-01/51	4712	01/51-04/76		
S10295S	03/47-09/75	⊗01/77	4479	03/47-11/50	4704	11/50-09/75		
S10296S	03/47-06/75	⊗06/76	4438	03/47-06/50	4674	06/50-06/76		
S10297S	03/47-06/76	⊗09/82	4456	03/47-04/50	4603	04/50-06/76		
S10298S	03/47-05/53	➲15026	4420	03/47-05/53				
S10299S	03/47-04/56	➲15048	4428	03/47-04/56				
S10300S	03/47-07/81	⊗04/82	4434	03/47-02/51	4716	02/51-07/81		
S10301S	03/47-06/81	⊗01/82	4485	03/47-09/50	4689	09/50-06/81		
S10302S	03/47-07/81	⊗06/82	4410	03/47-07/51	4751	10/51-07/81		
S10303S	03/47-04/76	⊗08/76	4496	04/47-09/50	4691	09/50-04/76		
S10304S	03/47-05/76	⊗08/76	4499	03/47-07/50	4680	07/50-05/76		
S10305S	03/47-06/81	⊗04/82	4466	03/47-11/50	4701	11/50-06/81		
S10306S	04/47-04/76	⊗07/76	4432	04/47-02/51	4717	02/51-04/76		
S10307S	04/47-11/74	⊗	4449	04/47-01/51	4715	01/51-11/74		
S10308S	04/47-10/71	⊗03/72	4415	04/47-07/51	4737	08/51-10/71		
S10309S	04/47-04/53	➲15023	4505	04/47-04/53				
S10310S	04/47-03/76	⊗10/76	4483[1]	04/47-02/49	4483[2]	02/49-06/51	4738	08/51-03/76
S10311S	04/47-04/76	⊗06/76	4500	04/47-11/50	4703	11/50-04/76		
S10312S	04/47-12/73	⊗03/75	4416	04/47-05/50	4607	05/50-12/73		
S10313S	04/47-01/76	⊗06/76	4509	04/47-08/51	4744	09/51-01/76		
S10314S	04/47-04/76	⊗10/76	4458	04/47-08/50	4685	08/50-04/76		
S10315S	04/47-04/76	⊗06/76	4513	04/47-02/51	4727	05/51-04/76		
S10316S	04/47-04/76	⊗	4423	04/47-07/51	4746	09/51-04/76		
S10317S	04/47- 73	⊗03/75	4469	04/47-12/50	4708	12/50-09/72		
S10318S	04/47-05/76	⊗05/80	4474	04/47-06/50	4679	07/50-05/76		
S10319S	05/47-06/83	⊗04/82	4414	05/47-08/51	4742	08/51-07/81		
S10320S	05/47-05/76	⊗	4495	05/47-04/50	4672	05/50-05/76		
S10321S	05/47-06/81	⊗	4497	05/47-07/50	4681	07/50-05/81		
S10322S	05/47-03/56	➲15041	4477	05/47- 50	4560	50-03/56		
S10323S	05/47-06/76	⊗07/76	4494	05/47-07/50	4678	07/50-06/76		
S10324S	05/47-05/81	⊗08/82	4489	05/47-01/51	4714	01/51-05/81		
S10325S	05/47-04/76	⊗04/80	4484	05/47-04/50	4604	04/50-04/76		
S10326S	05/47-09/78	⊗10/79	4504	05/47-09/51	4753	12/51-09/78		
S10327S	05/47-06/81	⊗06/82	4486	05/47-09/50	4693	09/50-06/81		
S10328S	05/47-07/81	⊗	4507	05/47-12/51	4631	05/52-07/81		
S10329S	05/47-04/76	⊗08/76	4482	05/47-10/50	4698	10/50-04/76		
S10330S	05/47-04/76	⊗08/76	4443	05/47-12/50	4711	12/50-10/56	4711	07/58-12/70
			4711	05/71-04/76				
S10331S	05/47-04/76	⊗07/76	4475	05/47-11/50	4702	11/50-04/76		
S10332S	05/47-03/53	➲15019	4401	05/47-03/53				
S10333	06/47-12/51	➲15003	4516	06/47-12/51				
S10334S	06/47-06/81	⊗10/85	4468	12/47-09/50	4695	09/50-06/81		
S10335S	06/47-01/52	➲15008	4419	06/47-01/52				
S10336S	06/47-06/76	⊗08/76	4471	06/47-03/51	4726	05/51-06/76		
S10337S	06/47-07/75	➲15450	4480	06/47-03/50	4605	04/50-07/75		
S10338S	06/47-04/76	⊗08/76	4403	06/47-07/51	4734	07/51-04/76		
S10339S	06/47-06/76	⊗10/81	4447	06/47-03/51	4721	03/51-06/76		
S10340S	06/47-04/76	⊗08/76	4470	06/47-03/51	4720	03/51-04/76		
S10341S	06/47-05/76	⊗11/76	4501	06/47-03/51	4722	04/51-03/71	4722	10/71-05/76
S10342S	06/47-06/76	⊗08/76	4493	06/47-12/50	4710	12/50-06/76		
S10343S	06/47-04/76	⊗07/76	4461	06/47-12/50	4707	12/50-04/76		
S10344S	06/47-05/81	⊗	4457	06/47-06/50	4673	06/50-05/81		
S10345	06/47-07/51	➲15002	4417	06/47-07/51				

Class 405 4-SUB Lancing/Eastleigh
Trailer Third
TT
S10346S-S10400S

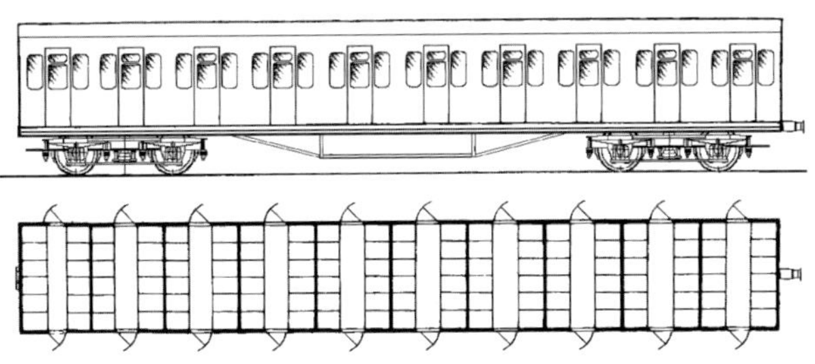

Diagram:	2013 EH263	HO Number:	1094
Body:	62' 0" × 9' 0"	Weight:	26-29t
Seats:	120 third	Bogies:	SR

10391-10400 were the first all steel trailers.

S10346S	*06/45*-10/71	⊗08/72	**4329**	*06/45*-01/62	**900**	09/63-06/66	**701**	06/66-05/69
			4131	06/69-10/71				
S10347S	*06/45*-04/61	⊗07/63	**4343**	*06/45*-04/61				
S10348S	*06/45*-09/60	⊗12/63	**4332**	*06/45*-11/48	**4332**	05/50-09/60		
S10349S	*06/45*-10/71	⊗08/72	**4346**	*06/45*-12/61	**900**	09/63-06/66	**701**	06/66-05/69
			4132	09/69-10/71				
S10350S	*06/45*-11/59	⊗01/64	**4354**	*06/45*-11/59				
S10351S	*07/45*-10/71	⊗08/72	**4328**	*07/45*-08/60	**900**	09/63-06/66	**701**	06/66-05/69
			4132	09/69-10/71				
S10352S	*07/45*-11/60	⊗08/63	**4339**	*07/45*-11/60	**4348**	03/61-01/62		
S10353S	*07/45*-02/74	⊗10/76	**4352**	*07/45*-11/61	**900**	09/63-06/66	**701**	06/66-05/69
			4364	*07/70*-02/74				
S10354S	*07/45*-05/60	⊗01/64	**4341**	*07/45*-05/60				
S10355S	*07/45*-07/60	⊗01/64	**4319**	*07/45*-07/60				
S10356S	*08/45*-05/72	⊗10/72	**4334**	*08/45*-08/60	**4108**	01/61-05/72		
S10357S	*08/45*-11/60	⊗*07/63*	**4315**	*08/45*-11/60	**4308**	11/60-11/60		
S10358S	*08/45*-06/60	⊗07/60	**4342**	*08/45*-06/60				
S10359S	*08/45*-10/73	⊗04/69	**4338**	*08/45*-11/61	**2926**	01/62-05/68	**4369**	04/69-10/73
S10360S	*08/45*-05/61	⊗07/63	**4347**	*08/45*-05/61				
S10361S	*09/45*-01/62	⊗08/63	**4331**	*09/45*-*10/51*	**4348**	*10/51*-01/62		
S10362S	*09/45*-04/61	⊗07/63	**4326**	*09/45*-04/61				
S10363S	*09/45*-08/60	⊗09/63	**4353**	*09/45*-08/60				
S10364S	*09/45*-01/62	⊗08/63	**4337**	*09/45*-01/62				
S10365S	*09/45*-*01/60*	⊗11/63	**4336**	*09/45*-*01/60*				
S10366S	*10/45*-03/60	⊗01/64	**4316**	*10/45*-03/60				
S10367S	*10/45*-02/60	⊗*10/63*	**4318**	*10/45*-02/60				
S10368S	*10/45*-01/62	⊗11/63	**4330**	*10/45*-01/62				
S10369S	*10/45*-09/60	⊗12/63	**4309**	*10/45*-09/60				
S10370S	*10/45*-05/60	⊗12/63	**4325**	*10/45*-05/60				
S10371S	*11/45*-02/60	⊗12/63	**4303**	*11/45*-02/60				
S10372S	*11/45*-09/60	⊗12/63	**4310**	*11/45*-03/58	**4309**	*04/58*-09/60		
S10373S	*11/45*-11/61	⊗09/63	**4350**	*11/45*-05/50	**4607**	05/50-05/60	**4333**	05/60-11/61
S10374S	*11/45*-04/60	⊗01/64	**4307**	*11/45*-04/60				
S10375S	*11/45*-10/61	⊗10/63	**4322**	*11/45*-10/61				
S10376S	*12/45*-01/62	⊗09/63	**4313**	*12/45*-12/49	**4594**	12/49-10/52	**4335**	10/52-01/62
S10377S	*12/45*-04/61	⊗07/63	**4323**	*12/45*-04/61				
S10378S	*12/45*-06/60	⊗11/63	**4312**	*12/45*-06/60				
S10379S	*12/45*-04/61	⊗07/63	**4311**	*12/45*-04/61				
S10380S	*12/45*-11/60	⊗	**4308**	*12/45*-11/60				
S10381S	*01/46*-01/62	⊗	**4302**	*01/46*-11/60	**4335**	11/60-01/62		
S10382S	*01/46*-05/61	⊗07/63	**4305**	*01/46*-05/61				
S10383S	*01/46*-10/61	⊗10/63	**4301**	*01/46*-10/60	**4322**	12/60-10/61		
S10384S	*01/46*-*03/58*	⊗05/58	**4300**	*01/46*-*03/58*				
S10385S	*01/46*-10/61	⊗09/63	**4321**	*01/46*-12/59	**4324**	02/61-10/61		
S10386S	*02/46*-10/61	⊗12/63	**4324**	*02/46*-10/61				
S10387S	*02/46*-04/60	⊗01/64	**4320**	*02/46*-04/60				
S10388S	*02/46*-04/60	⊗06/64	**4306**	*02/46*-04/60				
S10389S	*02/46*-04/61	⊗10/63	**4314**	*02/46*-04/61				
S10390S	*02/46*-03/60	⊗01/64	**4317**	*02/46*-03/60				
S10391S	*03/46*-*06/52*	⊃**15010**	**4335**	*03/46*-*06/52*				
S10392S	*03/46*-04/59	⊃**DS70050**	**4345**	*03/46*-04/59				
S10393S	*03/46*-03/74	⊗01/77	**4348**	*03/46*-06/51	**4729**	06/51-03/74		
S10394S	*03/46*-01/60	⊃**15228**[2]	**4327**	*03/46*-01/60				
S10395S	*03/46*-07/60	⊃**15083**	**4344**	*03/46*-07/60				
S10396S	*04/46*-01/72	⊗06/72	**4340**	*04/46*-07/60	**4115**	09/63-01/72		
S10397S	*04/46*-06/60	⊃**DS70086**	**4304**	*04/46*-06/60				
S10398	*04/46*-01/51	⊃**15001**	**4333**	*04/46*- 51				
S10399S	*04/46*-04/59	⊃**DS70051**	**4351**	*04/46*-08/60				
S10400S	*04/46*-07/60	⊃**DS70087**	**4349**	*04/46*-07/60			later **977364** ⊗02/10	

2-T Eastleigh
Trailer Third
TT
S10401S-S10418S

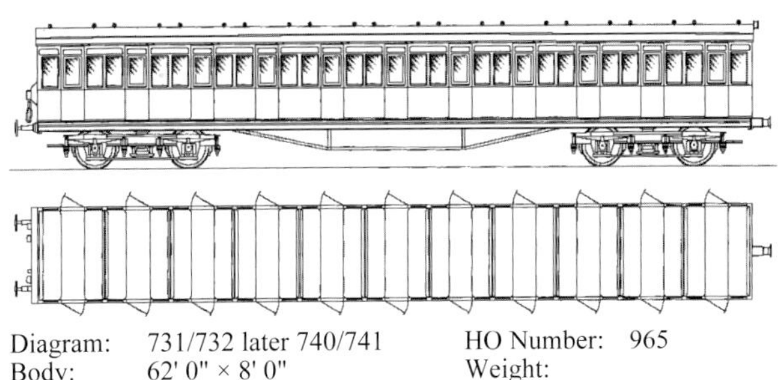

Diagram:	731/732 later 740/741	HO Number:	965
Body:	62' 0" × 8' 0"	Weight:	
Seats:	110 third	Bogies:	SR

Steel panelled on lower bodyside.

S10401S	*01/38-11/55*	↳**15429**	**1093**	38-09/43	**4149**	09/43-11/55		
S10402S	*01/38-06/55*	↳**15316**	**994**	*03/38-* 44	**4166**	44-06/55		
S10403S	*02/38-04/53*	↳**15167**	**993**	*03/38*-10/44	**4141**	[illegible]		
S10404S	*02/38-03/54*	↳**15204**	**1090**	38-01/48	**4188**	48-*03/54*		
S10405S	*02/38*-04/54	↳**15226**	**1108**	38-03/42	**4134**	03/42-03/53	**4411**	03/53-04/54
S10406S	*02/38-06/55*	↳**15362**	**997**	*05/38*-08/46	**4171**	08/46-06/55		
S10407S	*03/38-09/54*	↳**15320**	**1099**	38-02/43	**4143**	02/43-*09/54*		
S10408S	*03/38-05/53*	↳**15170**	**1051**	38-08/48	**4192**	08/48-05/53		
S10409S	*03/38-08/53*	↳**15174**	**995**	*04/38*-07/47	**4179**	07/47-08/53		
S10410S	*03/38-09/54*	↳**15331**	**991**	*02/38*-01/42	**4144**	01/42-*09/54*		
S10411S	*04/38-12/55*	↳**15421**	**989**	*01/38*-09/39	**4131**	04/41-12/55		
S10412S	*04/38-09/55*	↳**15333**	**1082**	38-06/45	**4158**	06/45-09/55		
S10413S	*04/38-10/55*	↳**15402**	**992**	*02/38-* 43	**4150**	43-10/55		
S10414S	*04/38-05/54*	↳**15216**	**1086**	38-11/42	**4146**	*11/42-05/54*		
S10415S	*05/38-09/54*	↳**15227**	**996**	*04/38-* 45	**4163**	45-09/54		
S10416S	*05/38-08/55*	↳**15323**	**1104**	38-06/44	**4152**	06/44-08/55		
S10417S	*05/38-11/55*	↳**15403**	**990**	*01/38-* 45	**4162**	45-11/55		
S10418S	*05/38-08/53*	↳**15198**	**1061**	*01/38*-02/44	**4154**	09/44-08/53		

Class 405 4-SUB Lancing/Eastleigh
Trailer Third
TT
S10419S-S10428S

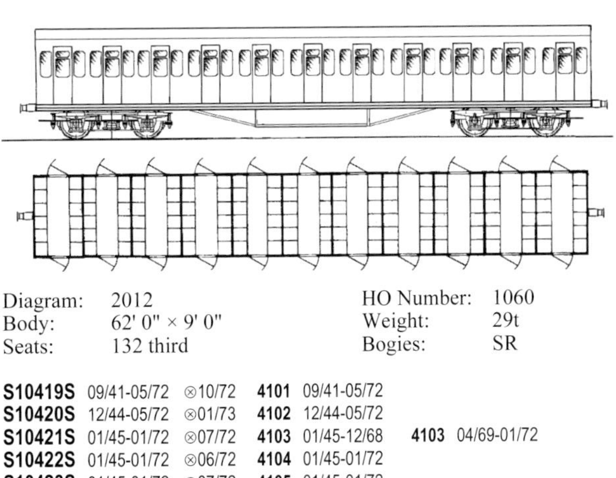

Diagram:	2012	HO Number:	1060
Body:	62' 0" × 9' 0"	Weight:	29t
Seats:	132 third	Bogies:	SR

S10419S	09/41-05/72	⊗10/72	**4101**	09/41-05/72		
S10420S	12/44-05/72	⊗01/73	**4102**	12/44-05/72		
S10421S	01/45-01/72	⊗07/72	**4103**	01/45-12/68	**4103**	04/69-01/72
S10422S	01/45-01/72	⊗06/72	**4104**	01/45-01/72		
S10423S	01/45-01/72	⊗07/72	**4105**	01/45-01/72		
S10424S	02/45-04/72	⊗02/73	**4106**	02/45-04/72		
S10425S	02/45-05/72	⊗10/72	**4107**	02/45-05/72		
S10426S	03/45-05/72	⊗10/72	**4108**	03/45-05/72		
S10427S	03/45-01/72	⊗06/72	**4109**	03/45-01/72		
S10428S	03/45-05/72	⊗04/73	**4110**	03/45-05/72		

Class 405 4-SUB Eastleigh
Trailer Third
TT
S10429S-S10438S

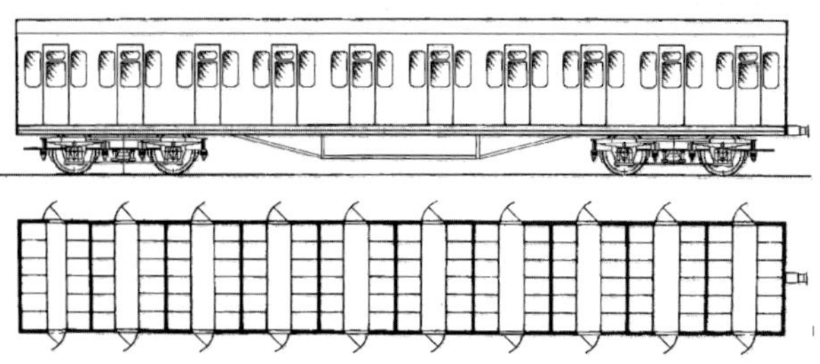

Diagram: 2014 HO Number: 1060
Body: 62' 0" × 9' 0" Weight: 26-29t
Seats: 120 third Bogies: SR

S10429S	04/46-05/72	⊗10/72	**4111**	04/46-05/72		
S10430S	04/46-05/74	⊗10/76	**4112**	04/46-05/74		
S10431S	05/46-10/73	⊗06/76	**4113**	05/46-10/73		
S10432S	05/46-05/72	⊗01/73	**4114**	05/46-05/72		
S10433S	06/46-01/72	⊗06/72	**4115**	06/46-01/72		
S10434S	06/46-05/72	⊗08/73	**4116**	06/46-05/72		
S10435S	06/46-10/73	⊗10/76	**4117**	06/46-10/73		
S10436S	07/46-01/72	⊗07/72	**4118**	07/46-01/72		
S10437S	07/46-10/73	⊗09/74	**4119**	07/46-10/73		
S10438S	07/46-05/72	⊗10/72	**4120**	07/46- *61*	**4120**	02/62-05/72

Class 405 4-SUB Eastleigh
Trailer Third Open
TTO
S10439S-S10448S

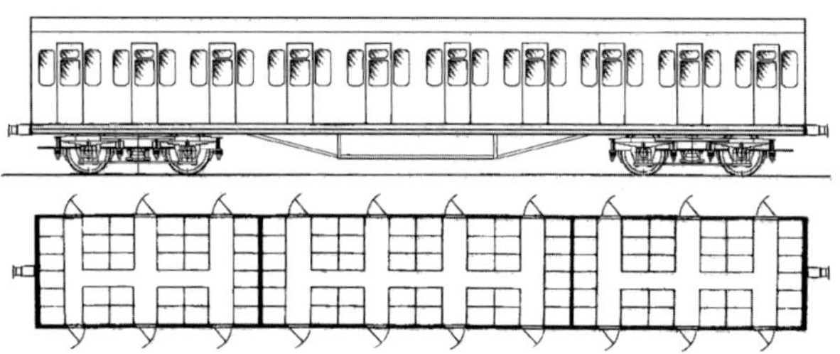

Diagram: 2015 EH265 HO Number: 1060
Body: 62' 0" × 9' 0" Weight: 27-29t
Seats: 106 third Bogies: SR

S10439S	08/46-07/82	**➲15471**	**4121**	08/46-04/76	**4279**	05/76-07/82		
S10440S	08/46-03/72	**➲15449**	**4122**	08/46-03/72				
S10441S	08/46-10/71	⊗07/72	**4123**	08/46-10/71				
S10442S	08/46-09/83	⊗04/86	**4124**	08/46-04/76	**4298**	07/76-09/83		
S10443S	09/46-09/83	⊗11/84	**4125**	09/46-04/76	**4721**	06/76-09/83		
S10444S	09/46-06/82	**➲15466**	**4126**	09/46-04/76	**4601**	06/76-05/77	**4617**	05/77-06/82
S10445S	09/46-10/82	**➲15475**	**4127**	09/46-04/76	**4603**	06/76-05/77	**4618**	05/77-10/82
S10446S	09/46-10/82	**➲15474**	**4128**	09/46-05/74	**4127**	03/75-04/76	**4603**	06/76-05/77
			4618	05/77-10/82				
S10447S	09/46-06/72	⊗04/73	**4129**	09/46-06/72				
S10448S	10/46-06/82	**➲15467**	**4130**	10/46-05/74	**4126**	01/75-04/76	**4601**	06/76-05/77
			4617	05/77-06/82				

Eastleigh
Trailer Third
TT
S10449S-S10471S

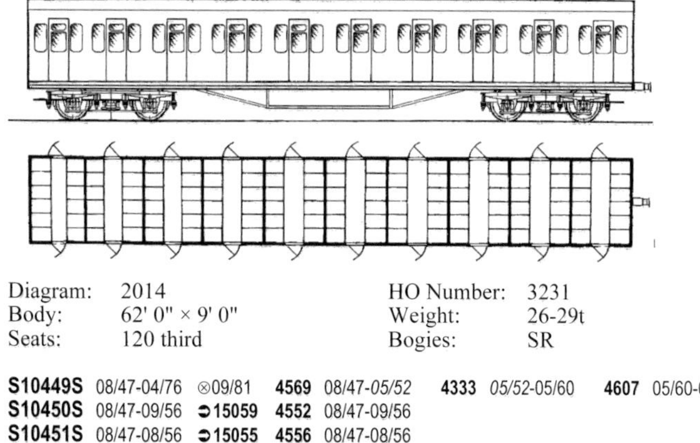

Diagram: 2014 HO Number: 3231
Body: 62' 0" × 9' 0" Weight: 26-29t
Seats: 120 third Bogies: SR

S10449S	08/47-04/76	⊗09/81	**4569**	08/47-*05/52*	**4333**	*05/52*-05/60	**4607**	05/60-04/76
S10450S	08/47-09/56	**➲15059**	**4552**	08/47-09/56				
S10451S	08/47-08/56	**➲15055**	**4556**	08/47-08/56				
S10452S	08/47-05/56	**➲15045**	**4572**	08/47-05/56				
S10453S	08/47-10/56	**➲15067**	**4551**	08/47-10/56				
S10454S	08/47-05/74	⊗10/76	**4374**	11/47-05/74				
S10455S	08/47-01/74	⊗	**4373**	12/47-01/74				
S10456S	08/47-*03/53*	**➲15025**	**4521**	08/47-*03/53*				
S10457S	08/47-02/74	⊗10/76	**4375**	11/47-02/74				
S10458S	08/47-10/73	⊗	**4376**	10/47-10/73				
S10459S	08/47-02/56	**➲15036**	**4564**	08/47-02/56				
S10460S	08/47-07/53	**➲15033**	**4579**	08/47-07/53				
S10461S	08/47-05/73	⊗09/73	**4370**	01/48-05/73				
S10462S	08/47-10/73	⊗09/74	**4371**	12/47-10/73				
S10463S	08/47-09/83	⊗07/84	**4377**	06/48-06/67	**4377**	02/68-04/76	**4277**	06/76-09/83
S10464S	08/47-03/68	⊗11/69	**4369**	01/48-03/68				
S10465S	08/47-05/72	⊗10/72	**4372**	12/47-05/72				
S10466S	08/47-08/55	**➲15046**	**4537**	08/47-05/56				
S10467S	08/47-05/56	**➲15060**	**4561**	08/47-07/56				
S10468S	08/47-07/56	**➲15047**	**4549**	08/47-05/56				
S10469S	08/47-05/56	**➲15064**	**4532**	08/47-*04/50*	**4548**	*04/50*-10/56		
S10470S	08/47-07/53	**➲15034**	**4520**	08/47-07/53	**4520**	10/54-02/56		
S10471S	08/47-02/56	**➲15053**	**4527**	08/47-07/56				

Class 405 4-SUB Eastleigh
Trailer Third
TT
S10472S-S10481S

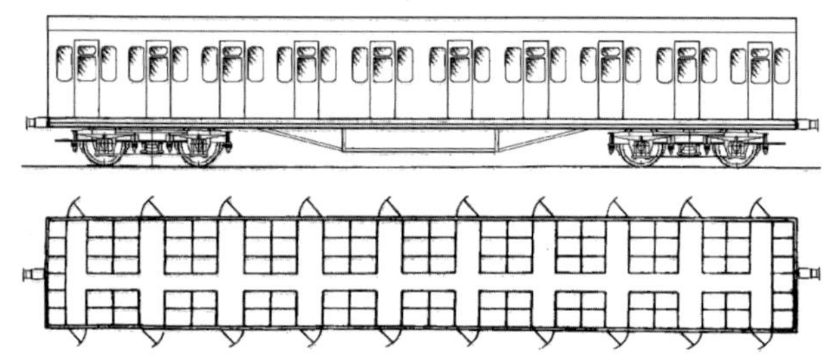

Diagram: 2018 EH266 HO Number: 3384
Body: 62' 0" × 9' 0" Weight: 26-29t
Seats: 102 third Bogies: SR

S10472S	09/48-05/72	⊗06/73	**4378**	09/48-05/72
S10473S	10/48-08/67	⊗11/69	**4379**	10/48-08/67
S10474S	10/48-04/76	⊗	**4380**	10/48-04/76
S10475S	10/48-11/73	⊗01/76	**4381**	10/48-11/73
S10476S	11/48-05/74	⊗03/76	**4382**	11/48-05/74
S10477S	09/48-04/72	⊗02/73	**4383**	09/48-04/72
S10478S	10/48-04/76	⊗10/81	**4384**	10/48-04/76
S10479S	10/48-04/76	⊗	**4385**	10/48-04/76
S10480S	10/48-05/74	⊗01/77	**4386**	10/48-05/74
S10481S	11/48-04/76	⊗09/82	**4387**	11/48-04/76

4-LAV Eastleigh

Driving Motor Brake Third
DMBT
S10497S-S10500S

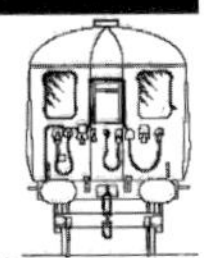

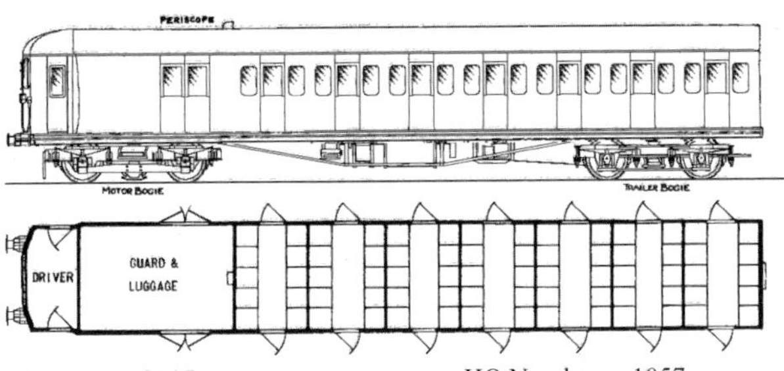

Diagram:	2117	HO Number:	1057
Body:	62' 6" × 9' 0"	Weight:	44t
Seats:	70 third	Bogies:	SR Suburban
Motor:	MV339 2 × 275hp later EE507C 2 × 250hp in 1950s		

S10497S	02/40-05/68	➲DS70270	2954	02/40-05/68
S10498S	02/40-05/68	➲DS70271	2954	02/40-05/68
S10499S	05/40-07/68	➲DS70272	2955	05/40-07/68
S10500S	05/40-07/68	➲DS70273	2955	05/40-07/68

4-LAV Lancing/Eastleigh

Driving Motor Brake Third
DMBT
S10501S-S10566S

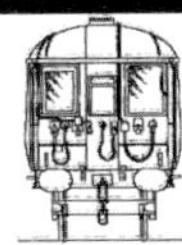

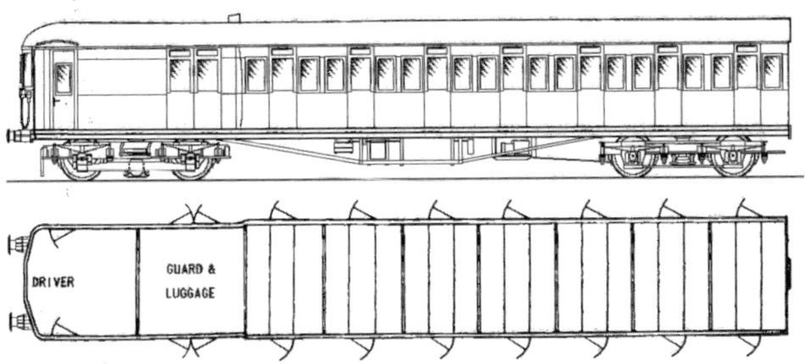

Diagram:	2106	HO Number:	569
Body:	62' 6" × 9' 0"	Weight:	41t
Seats:	70 third	Bogies:	SR Suburban
Motor:	MV339 2 × 275hp, later EE507C 2 × 250hp in 1950s		

S10501S	07/31-01/68	⊗03/68	1921	07/31-01/37	2921	01/37-01/68		
S10502S	07/31-01/68	⊗03/68	1921	07/31-01/37	2921	01/37-01/68		
S10503S	07/31-04/68	⊗12/68	1922	07/31-01/37	2922	01/37-04/68		
S10504S	07/31-04/68	⊗12/68	1922	07/31-01/37	2922	01/37-04/68		
S10505S	07/31-10/68	⊗	1923	07/31-01/37	2923	01/37-10/68		
S10506S	07/31-10/68	⊗	1923	07/31-01/37	2923	01/37-10/68		
S10507S	07/31-05/69	⊗ 69	1924	07/31-01/37	2924	01/37-05/69		
S10508S	07/31-05/69	⊗ 69	1924	07/31-01/37	2924	01/37-05/69		
S10509S	07/31-02/68	⊗10/68	1925	07/31-01/37	2925	01/37-02/68		
S10510S	07/31-02/68	⊗10/68	1925	07/31-01/37	2925	01/37-02/68		
10511	08/31-10/47	⊗10/47	1926	08/31-01/37	2926	01/37-10/47		
S10512S	08/31-10/67	⊗	1926	08/31-01/37	2926	01/37-10/47	2926	02/48-09/61
			2926	01/62-10/67				
S10513S	08/31-02/68	⊗05/68	1927	08/31-01/37	2927	01/37-02/68		
S10514S	08/31-02/68	⊗05/68	1927	08/31-01/37	2927	01/37-02/68		
S10515S	08/31-02/69	⊗07/69	1928	08/31-01/37	2928	01/37-02/69		
S10516S	08/31-02/69	⊗07/69	1928	08/31-01/37	2928	01/37-02/69		
S10517S	08/31-01/68	⊗08/68	1929	08/31-01/37	2929	01/37-01/68		
S10518S	08/31-01/68	⊗08/68	1929	08/31-01/37	2929	01/37-01/68		
S10519S	08/31-03/68	⊗04/68	1930	08/31-01/37	2930	01/37-03/68		
S10520S	08/31-03/68	⊗04/68	1930	08/31-01/37	2930	01/37-03/68		
S10521S	09/31-03/68	⊗05/68	1931	09/31-01/37	2931	01/37-03/68		
S10522S	09/31-03/68	⊗05/68	1931	09/31-01/37	2931	01/37-03/68		
S10523S	09/31-05/67	⊗03/68	1932	09/31-01/37	2932	01/37-05/67		
S10524S	09/31-05/67	⊗03/68	1932	09/31-01/37	2932	01/37-05/67		
S10525S	09/31-07/68	⊗11/68	1933	09/31-01/37	2933	01/37-07/68		
S10526S	09/31-07/68	⊗11/68	1933	09/31-01/37	2933	01/37-07/68		
S10527S	09/31-01/68	⊗03/68	1934	09/31-01/37	2934	01/37-01/68		
S10528S	09/31-01/68	⊗03/68	1934	09/31-01/37	2934	01/37-01/68		
S10529S	09/31-01/68	⊗10/68	1935	09/31-01/37	2935	01/37-01/68		
S10530S	09/31-01/68	⊗10/68	1935	09/31-01/37	2935	01/37-01/68		
S10531S	10/31-03/68	⊗10/68	1936	10/31-01/37	2936	01/37-03/68		
S10532S	10/31-03/68	⊗10/68	1936	10/31-01/37	2936	01/37-03/68		
S10533S	10/31-07/68	⊗12/68	1937	10/31-01/37	2937	01/37-07/68		
S10534S	10/31-07/68	⊗12/68	1937	10/31-01/37	2937	01/37-07/68		
S10535S	10/31-01/68	⊗03/68	1938	10/31-01/37	2938	01/37-01/68		
S10536S	10/31-01/68	⊗03/68	1938	10/31-01/37	2938	01/37-01/68		
S10537S	10/31-02/69	⊗07/69	1939	10/31-01/37	2939	01/37-02/69		
S10538S	10/31-02/69	⊗07/69	1939	10/31-01/37	2939	01/37-02/69		
S10539S	10/31-02/68	⊗03/68	1940	10/31-01/37	2940	01/37-02/68		
S10540S	10/31-02/68	⊗03/68	1940	10/31-01/37	2940	01/37-02/68		
S10541S	10/31-12/67	⊗03/68	1941	10/31-01/37	2941	01/37-12/67		
S10542S	10/31-05/68	⊗04/69	1941	10/31-01/37	2941	01/37-12/67	2926	12/67-05/68
S10543S	11/31-05/68	⊗	1942	11/31-01/37	2942	01/37-05/68		
S10544S	11/31-05/68	⊗	1942	11/31-01/37	2942	01/37-05/68		
S10545S	12/31-11/66	⊗	1943	12/31-01/37	2943	01/37-11/66		
S10546S	12/31-05/68	⊗10/68	1943	12/31-01/37	2943	01/37-05/68		
S10547S	01/32-02/68	⊗10/68	1944	01/32-01/37	2944	01/37-02/68		
S10548S	01/32-02/68	⊗10/68	1944	01/32-01/37	2944	01/37-02/68		
S10549S	01/32-01/68	⊗10/68	1945	01/32-01/37	2945	01/37-01/68		
S10550S	01/32-01/68	⊗10/68	1945	01/32-01/37	2945	01/37-01/68		
S10551S	02/32-03/68	⊗10/68	1946	02/32-01/37	2946	01/37-03/68		
S10552S	02/32-03/68	⊗10/68	1946	02/32-01/37	2946	01/37-03/68		
S10553S	03/32-05/68	⊗10/68	1947	03/32-01/37	2947	01/37-05/68		
S10554S	03/32-05/68	⊗10/68	1947	03/32-01/37	2947	01/37-05/68		
S10555S	04/32-05/68	⊗03/68	1948	04/32-01/37	2948	01/37-05/68		
S10556S	04/32-05/68	⊗03/68	1948	04/32-01/37	2948	01/37-05/68		
S10557S	05/32-02/69	⊗08/69	1949	05/32-01/37	2949	01/37-02/69		
S10558S	05/32-02/69	⊗08/69	1949	05/32-01/37	2949	01/37-02/69		
S10559S	06/32-02/69	⊗08/69	1950	06/32-01/37	2950	01/37-02/69		
S10560S	06/32-02/69	⊗08/69	1950	06/32-01/37	2950	01/37-02/69		
S10561S	07/32-05/68	⊗03/68	1951	07/32-01/37	2951	01/37-05/68		
S10562S	07/32-05/68	⊗03/68	1951	07/32-01/37	2951	01/37-05/68		
S10563S	08/32-03/68	⊗08/68	1952	08/32-01/37	2952	01/37-03/68		
S10564S	08/32-03/68	⊗08/68	1952	08/32-01/37	2952	01/37-03/68		
S10565S	09/32-01/68	⊗03/68	1953	09/32-01/37	2953	01/37-01/68		
S10566S	09/32-01/68	⊗03/68	1953	09/32-01/37	2953	01/37-01/68		

Class 401 2-BIL Lancing/Eastleigh

Driving Motor Brake Third Lavatory
DMBTL
S10567S

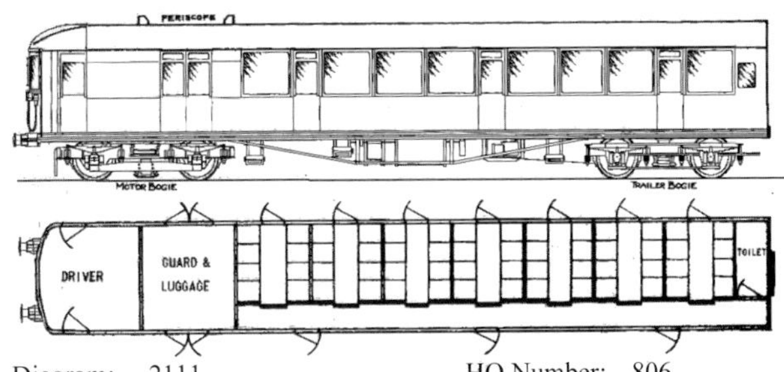

Diagram:	2111	HO Number:	806
Body:	62' 6" × 9' 0"	Weight:	43t 10cwt
Seats:	56 third 1 toilet	Bogies:	SR Suburban
Motor:	MV339 2 × 275hp, later EE507C 2 × 250hp in 1950s		

S10567S	02/35-07/68	⊗11/69	1900	02/35-01/36	1890	01/36-01/37	2010	01/37-07/68

Class 401 2-BIL Lancing/Eastleigh

Driving Motor Brake Third Lavatory
DMBTL
S10568S-S10576S

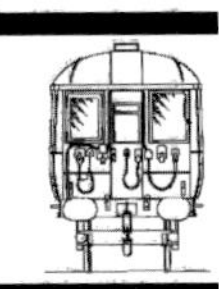

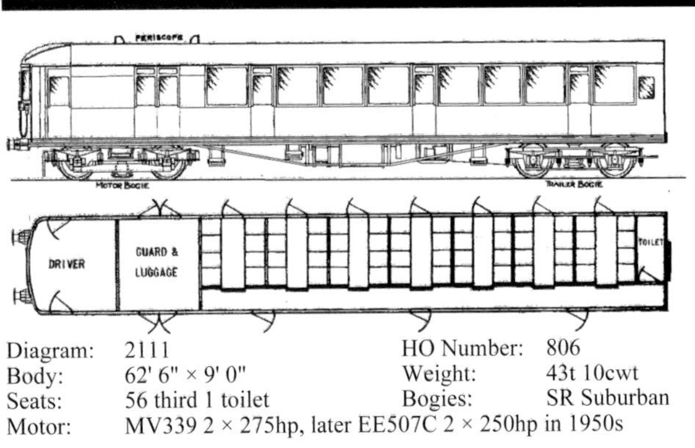

Diagram:	2111	HO Number:	806
Body:	62' 6" × 9' 0"	Weight:	43t 10cwt
Seats:	56 third 1 toilet	Bogies:	SR Suburban
Motor:	MV339 2 × 275hp, later EE507C 2 × 250hp in 1950s		

S10568S	03/35-04/69	⊗09/69	1891	03/35-01/37	2001	01/37-04/69
S10569S	03/35-05/69	⊗09/69	1892	03/35-01/37	2002	01/37-05/69
S10570S	03/35-04/69	⊗09/69	1893	03/35-01/37	2003	01/37-04/69
S10571S	03/35-03/69	⊗05/69	1894	03/35-01/37	2004	01/37-03/69

S10572S	*03/35*-04/69	⊗	**1895**	*03/35*-01/37	**2005**	01/37-04/69		
S10573S	*03/35*-05/69	⊗11/69	**1896**	*03/35*-01/37	**2006**	01/37-09/63	**900**	09/63-06/66
			701	06/66-05/69				
S10574S	*03/35*-07/68	⊗	**1897**	*03/35*-01/37	**2007**	01/37-07/68		
S10575S	*03/35*-04/69	⊗*09/69*	**1898**	*03/35*-01/37	**2008**	01/37-04/69		
S10576S	*03/35*-04/69	⊗09/69	**1899**	*03/35*-01/37	**2009**	01/37-04/69		

Class 401 2-BIL Lancing/Eastleigh
Driving Motor Brake Third Lavatory
DMBTL
S10577S-S10612S

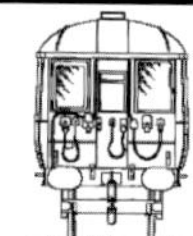

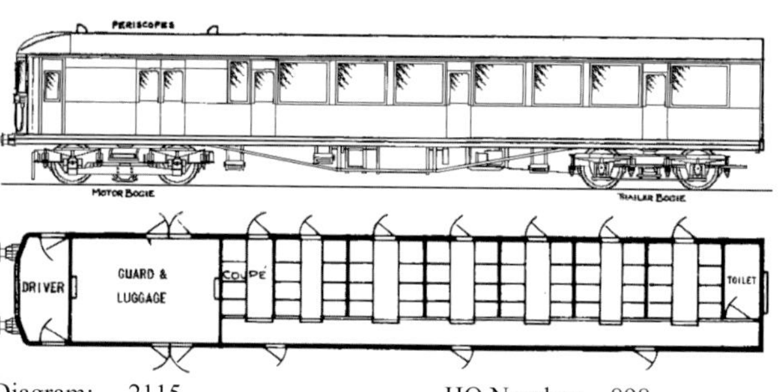

Diagram: 2115 HO Number: 898
Body: 62' 6" × 9' 0" Weight: 43t 10cwt
Seats: 52 third 1 toilet Bogies: SR Suburban
Motor: EE339 2 × 275hp

S10577S	*08/36*-11/70	⊗09/71	**1901**	*08/36*-01/37	**2011**	01/37-11/70		
S10578S	*08/36*-09/69	⊗10/70	**1902**	*08/36*-01/37	**2012**	01/37-09/69		
S10579S	*08/36*-09/69	⊗11/69	**1903**	*08/36*-01/37	**2013**	01/37-09/69		
10580	*08/36*-05/43	⊗05/43	**1904**	*08/36*-01/37	**2014**	01/37-05/43		
S10581S	*08/36*-05/69	⊗09/69	**1905**	*08/36*-01/37	**2015**	01/37-05/69		
S10582S	*08/36*-07/71	⊗03/72	**1906**	*08/36*-01/37	**2016**	01/37-07/71		
S10583S	*08/36*-10/70	⊗05/71	**1907**	*08/36*-01/37	**2017**	01/37-10/70		
S10584S	*08/36*-04/69	⊗02/70	**1908**	*08/36*-01/37	**2018**	01/37-04/69		
S10585S	*09/36*-01/70	⊗04/70	**1909**	*09/36*-01/37	**2019**	01/37-01/70		
S10586S	*09/36*-05/69	⊗09/69	**1910**	*09/36*-01/37	**2020**	01/37-05/69		
S10587S	*09/36*-06/70	⊗01/71	**1911**	*09/36*-01/37	**2021**	01/37-06/70		
S10588S	*09/36*-11/70	⊗07/71	**1912**	*09/36*-01/37	**2022**	01/37-11/70		
S10589S	*09/36*-09/69	⊗12/69	**1913**	*09/36*-01/37	**2023**	01/37-09/69		
S10590S	*09/36*-04/71	⊗09/71	**1914**	*09/36*-01/37	**2024**	01/37-04/71		
S10591S	*09/36*-11/70	⊗09/71	**1915**	*09/36*-01/37	**2025**	01/37-11/70		
S10592S	*10/36*-02/70	⊗09/70	**1916**	*10/36*-01/37	**2026**	01/37-02/70		
S10593S	*10/36*-11/70	⊗05/71	**1917**	*10/36*-01/37	**2027**	01/37-11/70		
S10594S	*10/36*-04/71	⊗09/71	**1918**	*10/36*-01/37	**2028**	01/37-10/66	**2028**	03/69-04/71
S10595S	*10/36*-10/70	⊗07/71	**1919**	*10/36*-01/37	**2029**	01/37-10/70		
S10596S	*10/36*-09/69	⊗10/70	**1920**	*10/36*-01/37	**2030**	01/37-09/69		
S10597S	*10/36*-01/70	⊗05/70	**1954**	*10/36*-01/37	**2031**	01/37-01/70		
S10598S	*10/36*-04/71	⊗09/71	**1955**	*10/36*-01/37	**2032**	01/37-04/71		
S10599S	*11/36*-04/71	⊗09/71	**1956**	*11/36*-01/37	**2033**	01/37-04/71		
S10600S	*11/36*-07/71	⊗04/72	**1957**	*11/36*-01/37	**2034**	01/37-07/71		
S10601S	*11/36*-01/70	⊗06/70	**1958**	*11/36*-01/37	**2035**	01/37-01/70		
S10602S	*11/36*-06/71	⊗01/72	**1959**	*11/36*-01/37	**2036**	01/37-06/71		
S10603S	*11/36*-02/70	➲**DS70321**	**1960**	*11/36*-01/37	**2037**	01/37-02/70		
S10604S	*11/36*-11/70	⊗09/71	**1961**	*11/36*-01/37	**2038**	01/37-11/70		
S10605S	*11/36*-12/69	⊗05/70	**1962**	*11/36*-01/37	**2039**	01/37-12/69		
S10606S	*12/36*-09/69	⊗03/70	**1963**	*12/36*-01/37	**2040**	01/37-09/69		
S10607S	*12/36*-04/69	⊗05/69	**1964**	*12/36*-01/37	**2041**	01/37-04/69		
S10608S	*12/36*-06/69	⊗11/69	**1965**	*12/36*-01/37	**2042**	01/37-06/69		
S10609S	*12/36*-10/70	⊗04/71	**1966**	*12/36*-01/37	**2043**	01/37-10/70		
S10610S	*12/36*-02/69	⊗05/69	**1967**	*12/36*-01/37	**2044**	01/37-02/69		
S10611S	*12/36*-10/70	⊗05/71	**1968**	*12/36*-01/37	**2045**	01/37-10/70		
S10612S	*12/36*-01/70	⊗04/70	**1969**	*12/36*-01/37	**2046**	01/37-01/70		

Class 401 2-BIL Lancing/Eastleigh
Driving Motor Brake Third Lavatory
DMBTL
S10613S-S10614S

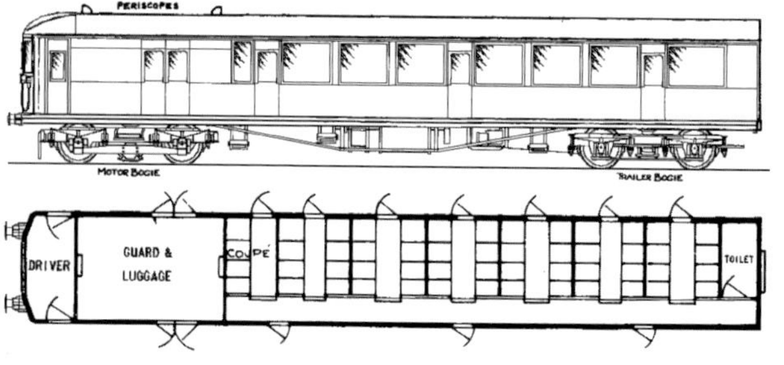

Diagram: 2115 HO Number: 903
Body: 62' 6" × 9' 0" Weight: 43t 10cwt
Seats: 52 third 1 toilet Bogies: SR Suburban
Motor: EE339 2 × 275hp

S10613S	*12/36*-01/70	⊗04/70	**1970**	*12/36*-01/37	**2047**	01/37-01/70
S10614S	01/37-01/70	⊗06/70	**1971**	01/37-01/37	**2048**	01/37-01/70

Class 401 2-BIL Lancing/Eastleigh
Driving Motor Brake Third Lavatory
DMBTL
S10615S-S10682S

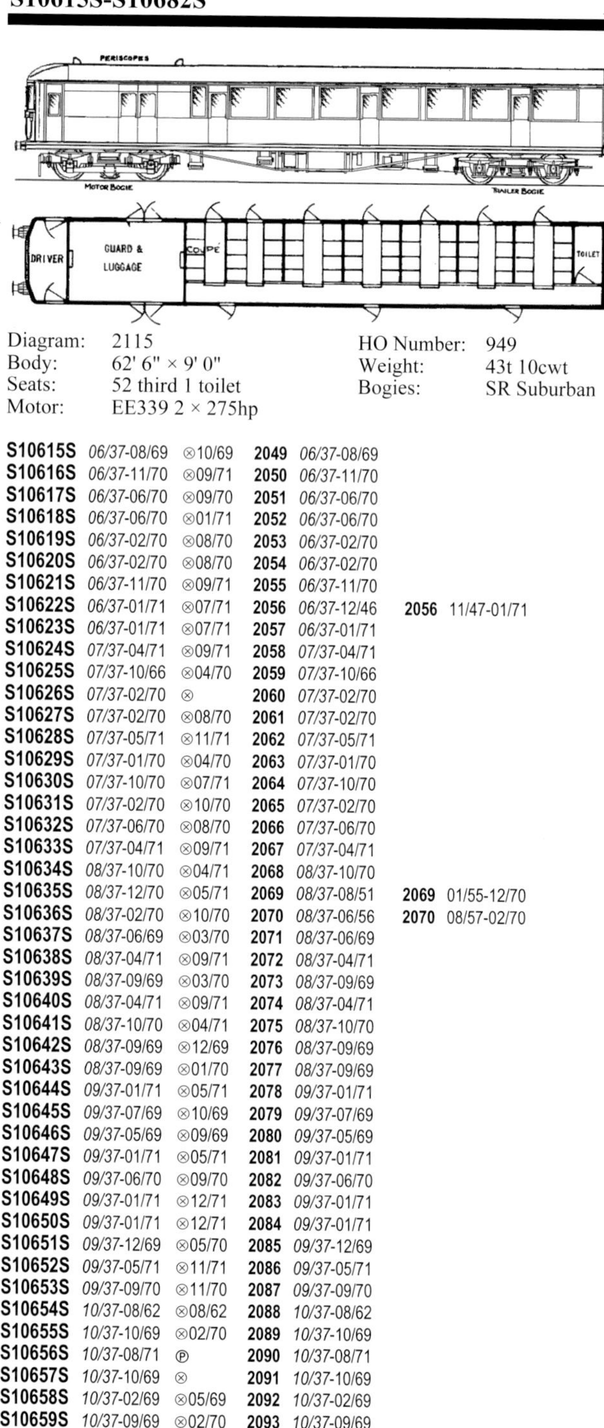

Diagram: 2115 HO Number: 949
Body: 62' 6" × 9' 0" Weight: 43t 10cwt
Seats: 52 third 1 toilet Bogies: SR Suburban
Motor: EE339 2 × 275hp

S10615S	*06/37*-08/69	⊗10/69	**2049**	*06/37-08/69*		
S10616S	*06/37*-11/70	⊗09/71	**2050**	*06/37-11/70*		
S10617S	*06/37*-06/70	⊗09/70	**2051**	*06/37-06/70*		
S10618S	*06/37*-06/70	⊗01/71	**2052**	*06/37-06/70*		
S10619S	*06/37*-02/70	⊗08/70	**2053**	*06/37-02/70*		
S10620S	*06/37*-02/70	⊗08/70	**2054**	*06/37-02/70*		
S10621S	*06/37*-11/70	⊗09/71	**2055**	*06/37-11/70*		
S10622S	*06/37*-01/71	⊗07/71	**2056**	*06/37-12/46*	**2056**	11/47-01/71
S10623S	*06/37*-01/71	⊗07/71	**2057**	*06/37-01/71*		
S10624S	*07/37*-04/71	⊗09/71	**2058**	*07/37-04/71*		
S10625S	*07/37*-10/66	⊗04/70	**2059**	*07/37-10/66*		
S10626S	*07/37*-02/70	⊗	**2060**	*07/37-02/70*		
S10627S	*07/37*-02/70	⊗08/70	**2061**	*07/37-02/70*		
S10628S	*07/37*-05/71	⊗11/71	**2062**	*07/37-05/71*		
S10629S	*07/37*-01/70	⊗04/70	**2063**	*07/37-01/70*		
S10630S	*07/37*-10/70	⊗07/71	**2064**	*07/37-10/70*		
S10631S	*07/37*-02/70	⊗10/70	**2065**	*07/37-02/70*		
S10632S	*07/37*-06/70	⊗08/70	**2066**	*07/37-06/70*		
S10633S	*07/37*-04/71	⊗09/71	**2067**	*07/37-04/71*		
S10634S	*08/37*-10/70	⊗04/71	**2068**	*08/37-10/70*		
S10635S	*08/37*-12/70	⊗05/71	**2069**	*08/37-08/51*	**2069**	01/55-12/70
S10636S	*08/37*-02/70	⊗10/70	**2070**	*08/37-06/56*	**2070**	08/57-02/70
S10637S	*08/37*-06/69	⊗03/70	**2071**	*08/37-06/69*		
S10638S	*08/37*-04/71	⊗09/71	**2072**	*08/37-04/71*		
S10639S	*08/37*-09/69	⊗03/70	**2073**	*08/37-09/69*		
S10640S	*08/37*-04/71	⊗09/71	**2074**	*08/37-04/71*		
S10641S	*08/37*-10/70	⊗04/71	**2075**	*08/37-10/70*		
S10642S	*08/37*-09/69	⊗12/69	**2076**	*08/37-09/69*		
S10643S	*08/37*-09/69	⊗01/70	**2077**	*08/37-09/69*		
S10644S	*09/37*-01/71	⊗05/71	**2078**	*09/37-01/71*		
S10645S	*09/37*-07/69	⊗10/69	**2079**	*09/37-07/69*		
S10646S	*09/37*-05/69	⊗09/69	**2080**	*09/37-05/69*		
S10647S	*09/37*-01/71	⊗05/71	**2081**	*09/37-01/71*		
S10648S	*09/37*-06/70	⊗09/70	**2082**	*09/37-06/70*		
S10649S	*09/37*-01/71	⊗12/71	**2083**	*09/37-01/71*		
S10650S	*09/37*-01/71	⊗12/71	**2084**	*09/37-01/71*		
S10651S	*09/37*-12/69	⊗05/70	**2085**	*09/37-12/69*		
S10652S	*09/37*-05/71	⊗11/71	**2086**	*09/37-05/71*		
S10653S	*09/37*-09/70	⊗11/70	**2087**	*09/37-09/70*		
S10654S	*10/37*-08/62	⊗08/62	**2088**	*10/37-08/62*		
S10655S	*10/37*-10/69	⊗02/70	**2089**	*10/37-10/69*		
S10656S	*10/37*-08/71	ⓟ	**2090**	*10/37-08/71*		
S10657S	*10/37*-10/69	⊗	**2091**	*10/37-10/69*		
S10658S	*10/37*-02/69	⊗05/69	**2092**	*10/37-02/69*		
S10659S	*10/37*-09/69	⊗02/70	**2093**	*10/37-09/69*		
S10660S	*10/37*-09/69	⊗11/69	**2094**	*10/37-09/69*		
S10661S	*10/37*-02/70	⊗06/70	**2095**	*10/37-02/70*		
S10662S	*10/37*-12/69	⊗05/70	**2096**	*10/37-12/69*		
S10663S	*10/37*-09/69	⊗11/69	**2097**	*10/37-09/69*		
S10664S	*11/37*-06/71	⊗04/72	**2098**	*11/37-06/71*		
S10665S	*11/37*-04/71	⊗09/71	**2099**	*11/37-04/71*		
S10666S	*11/37*-06/70	⊗12/70	**2100**	*11/37-08/51*	**2100**	01/55-06/70
S10667S	*11/37*-05/71	⊗11/71	**2101**	*11/37-05/71*		
10668	*11/37*-08/40	⊗08/40	**2102**	*11/37-08/40*		
S10669S	*11/37*-11/70	⊗05/71	**2103**	*11/37-11/70*		
S10670S	*11/37*-05/71	⊗06/72	**2104**	*11/37-05/71*		

S10671S	*11/37-05/68*	⊗10/68	**2105**	*11/37-09/65*	**2943**	11/66-05/68
S10672S	*11/37-02/69*	⊗05/69	**2106**	*11/37-02/69*		
S10673S	*11/37-09/69*	⊗11/69	**2107**	*11/37-09/69*		
S10674S	*12/37-08/69*	⊗10/69	**2108**	*12/37-08/69*		
S10675S	*12/37-06/69*	⊗10/69	**2109**	*12/37-06/69*		
S10676S	*12/37-03/70*	⊗06/70	**2110**	*12/37-03/70*		
S10677S	*12/37-01/71*	⊗01/72	**2111**	*12/37-01/71*		
S10678S	*12/37-01/71*	⊗12/71	**2112**	*12/37-01/71*		
S10679S	*12/37-02/71*	⊗04/71	**2113**	*12/37-09/59*	**2113**	03/62-02/71
S10680S	*12/37-11/70*	⊗07/71	**2114**	*12/37-11/70*		
S10681S	*12/37-10/69*	⊗02/70	**2115**	*12/37-10/69*		
S10682S	*12/37-09/70*	⊗11/70	**2116**	*12/37-09/70*		

Class 401 2-BIL Lancing/Eastleigh

Driving Motor Brake Third Lavatory
DMBTL
S10683S-S10718S

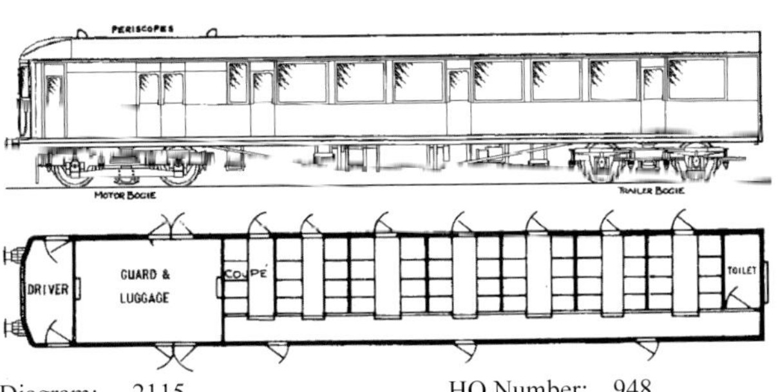

Diagram:	2115	HO Number:	948
Body:	62' 6" × 9' 0"	Weight:	43t 10cwt
Seats:	52 third 1 toilet	Bogies:	SR Suburban
Motor:	EE339 2 × 275hp		

S10683S	*08/38-09/70*	⊗11/70	**2117**	*08/38-09/70*		
S10684S	*08/38-12/69*	⊗05/70	**2118**	*08/38-12/69*		
10685	*08/38-12/44*	⊗12/44	**2119**	*08/38-12/44*		
S10686S	*08/38-04/69*	⊗02/70	**2120**	*08/38-04/69*		
S10687S	*08/38-08/69*	⊗02/70	**2121**	*08/38-08/69*		
S10688S	*08/38-02/69*	⊗	**2122**	*08/38-02/69*		
S10689S	*08/38-12/70*	⊗03/72	**2123**	*08/38-12/70*		
S10690S	*08/38-09/70*	⊗11/70	**2124**	*08/38-09/70*		
S10691S	*08/38-08/69*	⊗10/69	**2125**	*08/38-08/69*		
S10692S	*08/38-09/69*	⊗11/69	**2126**	*08/38-09/69*		
S10693S	*09/38-09/69*	⊗11/69	**2127**	*09/38-09/69*		
S10694S	*09/38-10/69*	⊗01/70	**2128**	*09/38-10/69*		
S10695S	*09/38-07/69*	⊗10/69	**2129**	*09/38-07/69*		
S10696S	*09/38-01/71*	⊗07/71	**2130**	*09/38-01/71*		
10697	*09/38-08/40*	⊗08/40	**2131**	*09/38-08/40*		
S10698S	*09/38-04/71*	⊗09/71	**2132**	*09/38-04/71*		
S10699S	*09/38-01/71*	⊗12/71	**2133**	*09/38-11/52*	**2133**	02/55-*01/71*
S10700S	*09/38-06/70*	⊗12/70	**2134**	*09/38-06/70*		
S10701S	*09/38-06/71*	⊗02/72	**2135**	*09/38-06/71*		
S10702S	*10/38-06/70*	⊗09/70	**2136**	*10/38-06/70*		
S10703S	*10/38-03/71*	⊗12/71	**2137**	*10/38-03/71*		
S10704S	*10/38-10/69*	⊗	**2138**	*10/38-10/69*		
S10705S	*10/38-01/71*	⊗12/71	**2139**	*10/38-01/71*		
S10706S	*10/38-08/71*	⊗02/72	**2140**	*10/38-08/71*		
S10707S	*10/38-01/71*	⊗12/71	**2141**	*10/38-01/71*		
S10708S	*10/38-05/69*	⊗09/69	**2142**	*10/38-05/69*		
S10709S	*10/38-07/69*	⊗10/69	**2143**	*10/38-07/69*		
S10710S	*10/38-10/69*	⊗02/70	**2144**	*10/38-10/69*		
S10711S	*11/38-01/70*	⊗05/70	**2145**	*11/38-01/70*		
S10712S	*11/38-01/71*	⊗07/71	**2146**	*11/38-01/71*		
S10713S	*11/38-03/71*	⊗11/71	**2147**	*11/38-03/71*		
S10714S	*11/38-05/69*	⊗	**2148**	*11/38-05/69*		
S10715S	*11/38-10/69*	⊗	**2149**	*11/38-10/69*		
S10716S	*11/38-09/70*	⊗07/71	**2150**	*11/38-09/70*		
S10717S	*11/38-02/70*	⊗10/70	**2151**	*11/38-02/70*		
S10718S	*11/38-02/70*	⊗10/70	**2152**	*11/38-02/70*		

Class 402 2-HAL Lancing/Eastleigh

Driving Motor Brake Third
DMBT
S10719S-S10794S

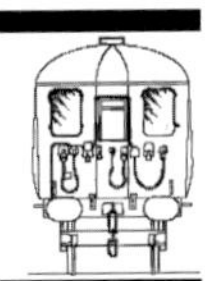

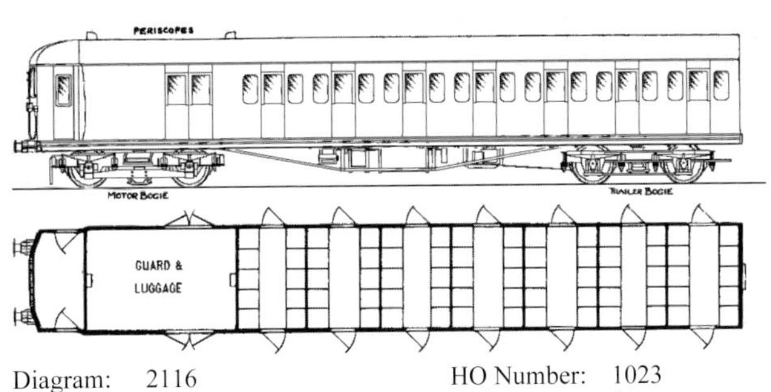

Diagram:	2116	HO Number:	1023
Body:	62' 6" × 9' 0"	Weight:	44t
Seats:	70 third	Bogies:	SR Suburban
Motor:	EE339 2 × 275hp		

S10719S	*01/39-02/70*	⊗00/70	**2601**	*01/39-02/70*				
S10720S	*01/39-01/71*	⊗12/71	**2602**	*01/39-01/71*				
S10721S	*01/39-01/71*	⊗12/71	**2603**	*01/39-01/71*				
S10722S	*01/39-11/70*	⊗06/72	**2604**	*01/39-11/70*	**061**	11/70-06/72		
S10723S	*01/39-11/70*	⊗02/73	**2605**	*01/39-11/70*	**062**	11/70-02/73		
S10724S	*01/39-12/69*	⊗05/70	**2606**	*01/39-12/69*				
S10725S	*01/39-11/70*	⊗04/71	**2607**	*01/39-11/70*				
S10726S	*01/39-07/67*	➲**DS70268**	**2608**	*01/39-07/67*				
S10727S	*01/39-09/69*	⊗10/70	**2609**	*01/39-09/69*				
S10728S	*01/39-08/71*	⊗06/72	**2610**	*01/39-08/71*				
S10729S	*01/39-06/70*	⊗11/70	**2611**	*01/39-06/70*				
S10730S	*01/39-10/70*	⊗04/71	**2612**	*01/39-10/70*				
S10731S	*01/39-12/69*	➲**DS70315**	**2613**	*01/39-12/69*				
S10732S	*01/39-01/70*	⊗04/70	**2614**	*01/39-01/70*				
S10733S	*02/39-01/71*	⊗05/73	**2615**	*02/39-01/71*				
S10734S	*02/39-01/71*	⊗07/71	**2616**	*02/39-01/71*				
S10735S	*02/39-09/69*	⊗01/70	**2617**	*02/39-09/69*				
S10736S	*02/39-06/70*	⊗01/71	**2618**	*02/39-06/70*				
S10737S	*02/39-06/71*	⊗04/72	**2619**	*02/39-06/71*				
S10738S	*02/39-12/70*	⊗09/71	**2620**	*02/39-12/70*				
S10739S	*02/39-10/70*	⊗07/71	**2621**	*02/39-10/70*				
S10740S	*02/39-10/71*	⊗08/72	**2622**	*02/39-04/69*	**4131**	06/69-10/71		
S10741S	*02/39-08/71*	⊗05/72	**2623**	*02/39-08/71*				
S10742S	*02/39-12/69*	➲**DS70317**	**2624**	*02/39-12/69*				
S10743S	*02/39-01/70*	⊗05/70	**2625**	*02/39-01/70*				
S10744S	*02/39-10/69*	⊗10/70	**2626**	*02/39-09/66*	**2626**	01/67-10/69		
S10745S	*02/39-07/71*	⊗06/72	**2627**	*02/39-07/71*				
S10746S	*02/39-07/71*	⊗03/72	**2628**	*02/39-07/71*				
S10747S	*02/39-07/71*	⊗	**2629**	*02/39-07/71*				
S10748S	*03/39-02/70*	⊗09/70	**2630**	*03/39-02/70*				
S10749S	*03/39-01/70*	⊗05/70	**2631**	*03/39-01/70*				
S10750S	*03/39-01/71*	⊗12/71	**2632**	*03/39-01/71*				
S10751S	*03/39-01/71*	⊗12/71	**2633**	*03/39-01/71*				
S10752S	*03/39-01/70*	⊗04/70	**2634**	*03/39-01/70*				
S10753S	*03/39-12/69*	⊗05/70	**2635**	*03/39-12/69*				
S10754S	*03/39-10/70*	⊗07/71	**2636**	*03/39-10/70*				
S10755S	*03/39-10/71*	⊗08/72	**2637**	*03/39-05/69*	**4132**	09/69-10/71		
S10756S	*03/39-06/70*	⊗06/72	**2638**	*03/39-06/70*	**063**	06/70-06/72		
S10757S	*03/39-07/69*	⊗11/69	**2639**	*03/39-07/69*				
S10758S	*03/39-10/70*	⊗05/71	**2640**	*03/39-10/70*				
S10759S	*03/39-07/71*	⊗01/72	**2641**	*03/39-07/71*				
S10760S	*03/39-12/69*	➲**DS70318**	**2642**	*03/39-12/69*				
S10761S	*03/39-02/70*	⊗05/70	**2643**	*03/39-02/70*				
S10762S	*03/39-01/72*	⊗07/72	**2644**	*03/39-04/69*	**4103**	04/69-01/72		
S10763S	*03/39-11/70*	⊗07/72	**2645**	*03/39-11/70*	**064**	11/70-07/72		
S10764S	*04/39-05/68*	➲**DS70269**	**2646**	*04/39-11/47*	**2926**	*02/48-09/61*	**2926**	01/62-05/68
S10765S	*04/39-02/70*	⊗10/70	**2647**	*04/39-02/70*				
S10766S	*04/39-01/71*	⊗07/71	**2648**	*04/39-01/71*				
S10767S	*04/39-01/71*	⊗05/71	**2649**	*04/39-01/71*				
S10768S	*04/39-02/70*	⊗10/70	**2650**	*04/39-02/70*				
S10769S	*04/39-10/69*	⊗	**2651**	*04/39-10/69*				
S10770S	*04/39-12/69*	⊗05/70	**2652**	*04/39-12/69*				
S10771S	*04/39-04/69*	⊗02/69	**2653**	*04/39- 50*	**2653**	01/51-02/69		
S10772S	*04/39-12/70*	⊗09/71	**2654**	*04/39-12/70*				
S10773S	*04/39-06/70*	⊗08/70	**2655**	*04/39-06/70*				
S10774S	*04/39-05/71*	⊗11/71	**2656**	*04/39-05/71*				
S10775S	*04/39-01/70*	⊗04/70	**2657**	*04/39-01/70*				
S10776S	*04/39-05/69*	⊗09/69	**2658**	*04/39-05/69*				
S10777S	*04/39-10/71*	⊗08/72	**2659**	*04/39-04/69*	**4131**	06/69-10/71		
S10778S	*04/39-11/70*	⊗05/71	**2660**	*04/39-11/70*				
S10779S	*04/39-08/71*	⊗04/72	**2661**	*04/39-08/71*				
S10780S	*05/39-09/69*	⊗06/70	**2662**	*05/39-09/69*				
S10781S	*05/39-01/70*	⊗05/70	**2663**	*05/39-01/70*				
S10782S	*05/39-01/70*	⊗05/70	**2664**	*05/39-01/70*				

S10783S	*05/39-04/71*	⊗09/71	**2665**	*05/39-04/71*
S10784S	*05/39-10/70*	⊗05/71	**2666**	*05/39-10/70*
S10785S	*05/39-01/71*	⊗07/71	**2667**	*05/39-01/71*
S10786S	*05/39-01/71*	⊗07/71	**2668**	*05/39-01/71*
S10787S	*05/39-12/69*	⊃**DS70316**	**2669**	*05/39-12/69*
S10788S	*05/39-09/69*	⊗10/70	**2670**	*05/39-09/69*
S10789S	*05/39-01/70*	⊗05/70	**2671**	*05/39-01/70*
S10790S	*05/39-03/71*	⊗05/73	**2672**	*05/39-03/71*
S10791S	*05/39-12/69*	⊗05/70	**2673**	*05/39-12/69*
S10792S	*05/39-08/71*	⊗01/72	**2674**	*05/39-08/71*
S10793S	*05/39-11/70*	⊗05/71	**2675**	*05/39-11/70*
S10794S	*05/39-04/71*	⊗09/71	**2676**	*05/39-04/71*

Class 402 2-HAL Lancing/Eastleigh

Driving Motor Brake Third
DMBT
S10795S-S10810S

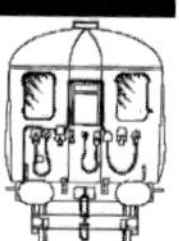

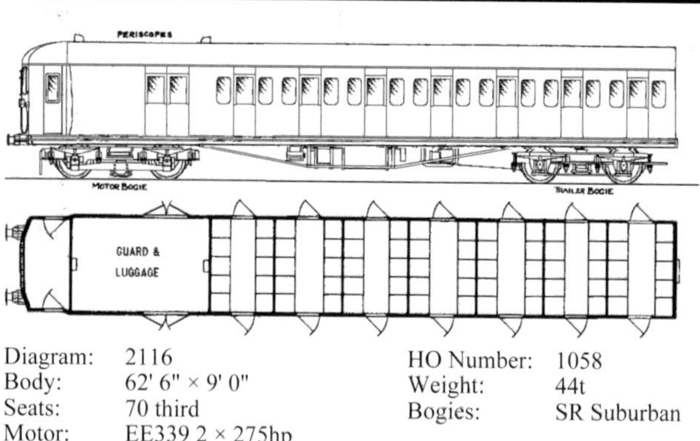

Diagram:	2116	HO Number:	1058
Body:	62' 6" × 9' 0"	Weight:	44t
Seats:	70 third	Bogies:	SR Suburban
Motor:	EE339 2 × 275hp		

S10795S	*11/39-05/71*	⊗11/71	**2677**	*11/39-05/71*			
S10796S	*11/39-08/69*	⊗10/69	**2678**	*11/39-08/69*			
S10797S	*11/39-07/71*	⊗05/72	**2679**	*11/39-07/71*			
S10798S	*11/39-04/56*	⊗08/60	**2680**	*11/39-04/56*			Part of underframe to **10895**
S10799S	*11/39-06/70*	⊗08/70	**2681**	*11/39-06/70*			
S10800S	*11/39-06/69*	⊗10/69	**2682**	*11/39-06/69*			
S10801S	*12/39-12/70*	⊗09/71	**2683**	*12/39-12/70*			
S10802S	*12/39-04/71*	⊗09/71	**2684**	*12/39-04/71*			
S10803S	*12/39-05/71*	⊗12/71	**2685**	*12/39-05/71*			
S10804S	*12/39-06/70*	⊗12/70	**2686**	*12/39-06/70*			
S10805S	*12/39-12/70*	⊗09/71	**2687**	*12/39-12/70*			
S10806S	*12/39-10/71*	⊗08/72	**2688**	*12/39-06/69*	**4132**	09/69-10/71	
S10807S	*12/39-10/70*	⊗07/72	**2689**	*12/39-10/70*	**065**	10/70-07/72	
S10808S	*12/39-10/70*	⊗07/71	**2690**	*12/39-10/70*			
S10809S	*12/39-01/70*	⊗05/70	**2691**	*12/39-01/70*			
S10810S	*12/39-12/70*	⊗07/72	**2692**	*12/39-12/70*	**066**	12/70-07/72	

Class 402 2-HAL Lancing/Eastleigh

Driving Motor Brake Third
DMBT
S10811S-S10817S

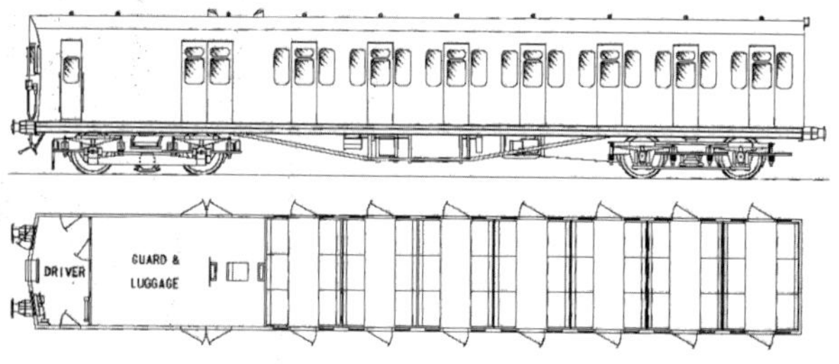

Diagram:	2121	HO Number:	3230
Body:	62' 6" × 9' 0"	Weight:	42t
Seats:	84 third	Bogies:	SR Suburban
Motor:	EE339 2 × 275hp		

S10811S	11/48-02/74	⊗10/76	**2693**	*11/48-07/70*	**4364**	*07/70-02/74*
S10812S	11/48-08/71	⊗05/72	**2694**	11/48-08/71		
S10813S	11/48-08/71	⊗01/72	**2695**	11/48-08/71		
S10814S	12/48-04/71	⊗11/71	**2696**	12/48-04/71		
S10815S	12/48-05/74	⊗03/76	**2697**	12/48-04/71	**4625**	04/71-05/74
S10816S	12/48-07/71	⊗05/72	**2698**	12/48-07/71		
S10817S	12/48-07/71	⊗03/72	**2699**	12/48-07/71		

Class 405 4-SUB Eastleigh

Driving Motor Brake Third Open
DMBTO
S10829S-S10848S

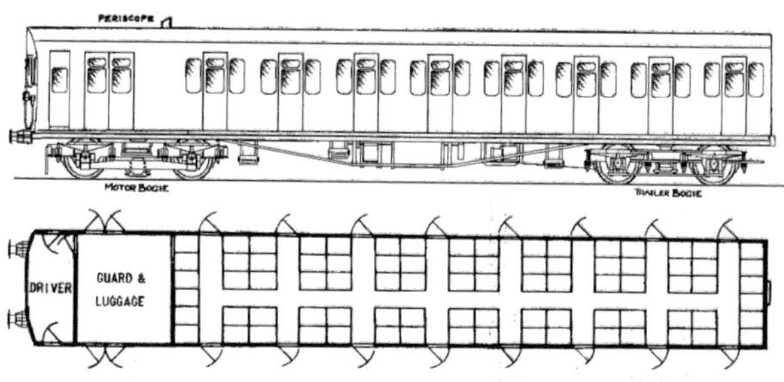

Diagram:	2126 EB265	HO Number:	3384
Body:	62' 6" × 9' 0"	Weight:	43t
Seats:	82 third	Bogies:	SR
Motor:	EE339 2 × 275hp		

S10829S	09/48-05/72	⊃**975250**	**4378**	09/48-05/72		
S10830S	09/48-05/72	⊃**975251**	**4378**	09/48-05/72		
S10831S	10/48-05/74	⊗03/76	**4379**	10/48-08/67	**4379**	04/69-05/74
S10832S	10/48-05/74	⊗03/76	**4379**	10/48-08/67	**4379**	04/69-05/74
S10833S	10/48-04/76	⊃**975590**	**4380**	10/48-04/76		
S10834S	10/48-04/76	⊃**975591**	**4380**	10/48-04/76		
S10835S	10/48-11/73	⊗01/76	**4381**	10/48-11/73		
S10836S	10/48-11/73	⊗01/76	**4381**	10/48-11/73		
S10837S	11/48-05/74	⊗03/76	**4382**	11/48-05/74		
S10838S	11/48-05/74	⊗03/76	**4382**	11/48-05/74		
S10839S	09/48-04/72	⊗02/73	**4383**	09/48-04/72		
S10840S	09/48-05/76	⊗07/76	**4383**	09/48-04/72	**4627**	04/72-05/76
S10841S	10/48-04/76	⊗10/81	**4384**	10/48-04/76		
S10842S	10/48-04/76	⊗10/81	**4384**	10/48-04/76		
S10843S	10/48-04/76	⊃**975601**	**4385**	10/48-04/76		
S10844S	10/48-04/76	⊃**975596**	**4385**	10/48-04/76		
S10845S	10/48-05/74	⊗01/77	**4386**	10/48-05/74		
S10846S	10/48-05/74	⊗01/77	**4386**	10/48-05/74		
S10847S	11/48-06/81	⊗08/82	**4387**	11/48-04/76	**4696**	06/77-05/81
S10848S	11/48-04/76	⊗09/82	**4387**	11/48-04/76		⊠05/74-10/74

Class 405 4-SUB Eastleigh

Driving Motor Brake Third Open
DMBTO
S10849S-S10894S

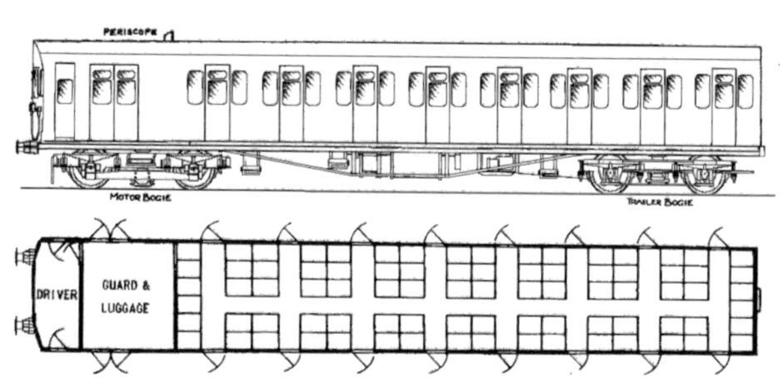

Diagram:	2126 EB265	HO Number:	3464
Body:	62' 6" × 9' 0"	Weight:	39t
Seats:	82 third	Bogies:	SR
Motor:	EE507C 2 × 250hp		

S10849S	12/48-09/83	⊗07/84	**4277**	12/48-09/83				
S10850S	12/48-09/83	⊗07/84	**4277**	12/48-09/83				
S10851S	12/48-09/83	⊗04/86	**4278**	12/48-08/58	**4278**	08/59-09/83		
S10852S	12/48-09/83	⊗04/86	**4278**	12/48-08/58	**4686**	08/58-04/59	**4278**	08/59-09/83
S10853S	01/49-09/83	⊗08/85	**4279**	01/49-09/83				
S10854S	01/49-09/83	⊗08/85	**4279**	01/49-09/83				
S10855S	01/49-06/81	⊗10/85	**4280**	01/49-06/81				
S10856S	01/49-06/81	⊗10/85	**4280**	01/49-06/81				
S10857S	01/49-06/81	⊗06/82	**4281**	01/49-06/81				
S10858S	01/49-06/81	⊗06/82	**4281**	01/49-06/81				
S10859S	01/49-04/69	⊗11/69	**4282**	01/49-03/68				
S10860S	01/49-05/72	⊗02/73	**4282**	01/49-03/68	**4368**	03/68-05/72		
S10861S	01/49-06/81	⊗	**4283**	01/49-06/81				
S10862S	01/49-10/82	⊗02/84	**4283**	01/49-06/81	**4679**	08/81-10/82		
S10863S	02/49-05/82	⊗	**4284**	02/49-05/82				
S10864S	02/49-05/82	⊗	**4284**	02/49-05/82				
S10865S	02/49-10/82	⊗ *84*	**4285**	02/49-10/82				

S10866S	02/49-10/82	⊗ *84*	**4285**	02/49-10/82				
S10867S	02/49-06/81	⊗06/82	**4286**	02/49-06/81				
S10868S	02/49-08/70	⊗09/71	**4286**	02/49-08/70				
S10869S	02/49-05/82	⊗ *84*	**4287**	02/49-05/82				
S10870S	02/49-05/82	⊗	**4287**	02/49-05/82				
S10871S	02/49-06/81	⊗	**4288**	02/49-06/81				
S10872S	02/49-06/81	⊗	**4288**	02/49-06/81				
S10873S	02/49-06/81	⊗08/82	**4289**	02/49-02/63	**4632**	02/63-09/78	**4655**	09/78-06/79
			4632	06/79-06/81				
S10874S	02/49-06/81	⊗	**4289**	02/49-06/81				
S10875S	03/49-12/76	⊗09/81	**4290**	03/49-12/76				
S10876S	03/49-04/81	⊗06/82	**4290**	03/49-04/81				
S10877S	03/49-08/83	⊗07/85	**4291**	03/49-08/83				
S10878S	03/49-08/83	⊗07/85	**4291**	03/49-08/83				
S10879S	03/49-06/71	⊗09/71	**4292**	03/49-07/70				
S10880S	03/49-06/81	⊗06/82	**4292**	03/49-07/70	**4286**	08/70-06/81		
S10881S	03/49-10/82	⊗ *84*	**4293**	03/49-10/82				
S10882S	03/49-10/82	⊗ *84*	**4293**	03/49-10/82				
S10883S	03/49-05/83	⊗10/85	**4294**	03/49-05/83				
S10884S	03/49-05/83	⊗10/85	**4294**	03/49-05/83				
S10885S	03/49-06/81	⊗	**4295**	03/49-06/81				
S10886S	03/49-06/81	⊗	**4295**	03/49-06/81				
S10887S	04/49-06/81	⊗	**4296**	04/49-06/81				
S10888S	04/49-06/81	⊗	**4296**	04/49-06/81				
S10889S	04/49-09/82	⊗ *84*	**4297**	04/49-09/82				
S10890S	04/49-09/82	⊗ *84*	**4297**	04/49-09/82				
S10891S	04/49-09/83	⊗04/86	**4298**	04/49-09/83				
S10892S	04/49-09/83	⊗04/86	**4298**	04/49-09/83				
S10893S	04/49-06/81	⊗	**4299**	04/49-11/73	**4299**	06/74-06/81		
S10894S	04/49-11/73	⊗01/76	**4299**	04/49-11/73				

Class 405 4-SUB Eastleigh

Driving Motor Brake Third
DMBT
S10895S-S10940S

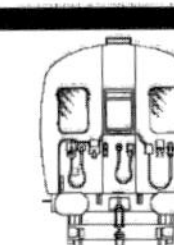

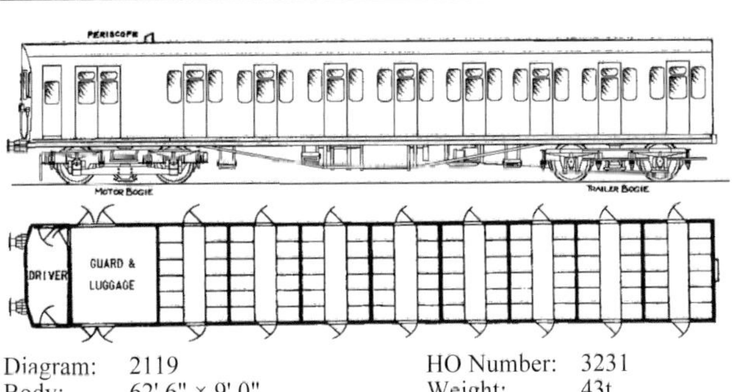

Diagram:	2119	HO Number:	3231
Body:	62' 6" × 9' 0"	Weight:	43t
Seats:	96 third	Bogies:	SR
Motor:	MV339 2 × 275hp		

S10895S	06/48-05/72	⊗06/73	**4355**	06/48-05/72 rebuilt with part of underframe of **10798** 07/60				
S10896S	06/48-03/72	⊗02/73	**4355**	06/48-03/72				
S10897S	06/48-01/74	⊗10/76	**4356**	06/48-01/74				
S10898S	06/48-01/74	⊗10/76	**4356**	06/48-01/74				
S10899S	05/48-07/73	⊗02/74	**4357**	05/48-07/73				
S10900S	05/48-07/73	⊗02/74	**4357**	05/48-07/73				
S10901S	05/48-01/74	⊗	**4358**	05/48-01/74				
S10902S	05/48-01/74	⊗	**4358**	05/48-01/74				
S10903S	05/48-04/70	⊗*04/70*	**4359**	05/48-06/58	**4364**	06/58-04/70		
S10904S	05/48-01/74	⊗07/76	**4359**	05/48-01/74				
S10905S	04/48-09/64	⊗ *64*	**4360**	04/48-09/64				
S10906S	04/48-04/76	⊗08/76	**4360**	04/48-09/64	**4720**	*01/65*-04/76		
S10907S	04/48-05/74	➲**975586**	**4361**	04/48-05/74				
S10908S	04/48-05/74	➲**975587**	**4361**	04/48-05/74				
S10909S	04/48-10/73	⊗10/76	**4362**	04/48-10/73				
S10910S	04/48-10/73	⊗10/76	**4362**	04/48-10/73				
S10911S	04/48-02/74	⊗03/75	**4363**	04/48-02/74				
S10912S	04/48-02/74	⊗03/75	**4363**	04/48-02/74				
S10913S	03/48-02/74	⊗10/76	**4364**	03/48-02/74				
S10914S	03/48-01/74	⊗07/76	**4364**	03/48-06/58	**4359**	06/58-01/74		
S10915S	03/48-01/72	⊗	**4365**	03/48-02/68	**4627**	02/68-01/72		
S10916S	03/48-02/69	⊗11/69	**4365**	03/48-02/68				
S10917S	03/48-01/74	⊗10/76	**4366**	03/48-01/74				
S10918S	03/48-01/74	⊗10/76	**4366**	03/48-01/74				
S10919S	02/48-10/73	➲**975319**	**4367**	02/48-10/73				
S10920S	02/48-10/73	➲**975322**	**4367**	02/48-10/73				
S10921S	01/48-08/67	⊗*03/68*	**4368**	01/48-08/67				
S10922S	01/48-05/72	⊗02/73	**4368**	01/48-08/67	**4368**	03/68-05/72		
S10923S	01/48-03/68	⊗11/69	**4369**	01/48-03/68				
S10924S	01/48-10/73	⊗	**4369**	01/48-03/68	**4369**	04/69-10/73		
S10925S	01/48-05/73	⊗09/73	**4370**	01/48-05/73				
S10926S	01/48-05/73	⊗09/73	**4370**	01/48-05/73				
S10927S	12/47-10/73	⊗09/74	**4371**	12/47-10/73				
S10928S	12/47-10/73	⊗09/74	**4371**	12/47-10/73				
S10929S	12/47-05/72	⊗10/72	**4372**	12/47-05/72				
S10930S	12/47-05/72	⊗10/72	**4372**	12/47-05/72				
S10931S	12/47-01/74	⊗01/74	**4373**	12/47-01/74	⊠10/73-12/73			
S10932S	12/47-01/74	⊗01/74	**4373**	12/47-01/74	⊠10/73-12/73			
S10933S	11/47-05/74	⊗10/76	**4374**	11/47-05/74				
S10934S	11/47-05/74	⊗10/76	**4374**	11/47-05/74				
S10935S	11/47-02/74	⊗10/76	**4375**	11/47-02/74				
S10936S	11/47-02/74	⊗10/76	**4375**	11/47-02/74				
S10937S	10/47-10/73	⊗	**4376**	10/47-10/73				
S10938S	10/47-10/73	⊗	**4376**	10/47-10/73				
S10939S	06/48-04/76	➲**975604**	**4377**	06/48-06/67	**2932**	06/67-02/68	**4377**	02/68-04/76
S10940S	06/48-04/76	➲**975605**	**4377**	06/48-06/67	**2932**	06/67-02/68	**4377**	02/68-04/76

Class 405 4-SUB Lancing/Eastleigh

Driving Motor Brake Third
DMBT
S10941S-S10960S

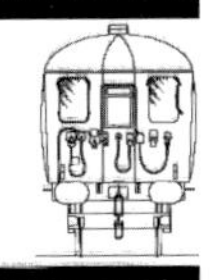

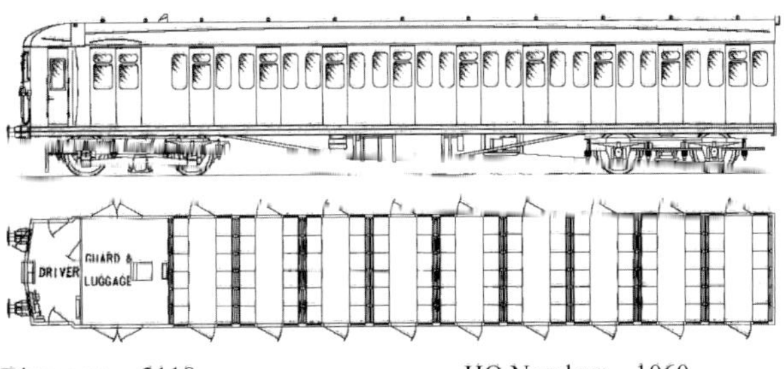

Diagram:	2118	HO Number:	1060
Body:	62' 6" × 9' 0"	Weight:	43t
Seats:	108 third	Bogies:	SR
Motor:	MV339 2 × 275hp		

S10941S	09/41-05/72	⊗10/72	**4101**	09/41-05/72		
S10942S	09/41-05/72	⊗10/72	**4101**	09/41-05/72		
S10943S	12/44-05/72	⊗01/73	**4102**	12/44-05/72		
S10944S	12/44-05/72	⊗01/73	**4102**	12/44-05/72		
S10945S	01/45-01/72	⊗07/72	**4103**	01/45-12/68	**4103**	04/69-01/72
S10946S	01/45-12/68	⊗12/68	**4103**	01/45-12/68		
S10947S	01/45-01/72	⊗06/72	**4104**	01/45-01/72		
S10948S	01/45-01/72	⊗06/72	**4104**	01/45-01/72		
S10949S	01/45-01/72	⊗07/72	**4105**	01/45-01/72		
S10950S	01/45-01/72	⊗07/72	**4105**	01/45-01/72		
S10951S	02/45-04/72	⊗02/73	**4106**	02/45-04/72		
S10952S	02/45-05/72	⊗06/73	**4106**	02/45-04/72	**4355**	04/72-05/72
S10953S	02/45-05/72	⊗10/72	**4107**	02/45-05/72		
S10954S	02/45-05/72	⊗10/72	**4107**	02/45-05/72		
S10955S	03/45-05/72	⊗10/72	**4108**	03/45-05/72		
S10956S	03/45-05/72	⊗10/72	**4108**	03/45-05/72		
S10957S	03/45-01/72	⊗06/72	**4109**	03/45-01/72		
S10958S	03/45-01/72	⊗06/72	**4109**	03/45-01/72		
S10959S	03/45-05/72	⊗04/73	**4110**	03/45-05/72		
S10960S	03/45-05/72	⊗04/73	**4110**	03/45-05/72		

Class 405 4-SUB Eastleigh

Driving Motor Brake Third
DMBT
S10961S-S10980S

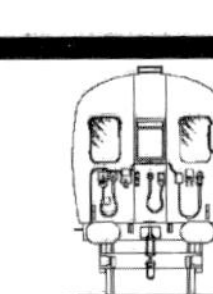

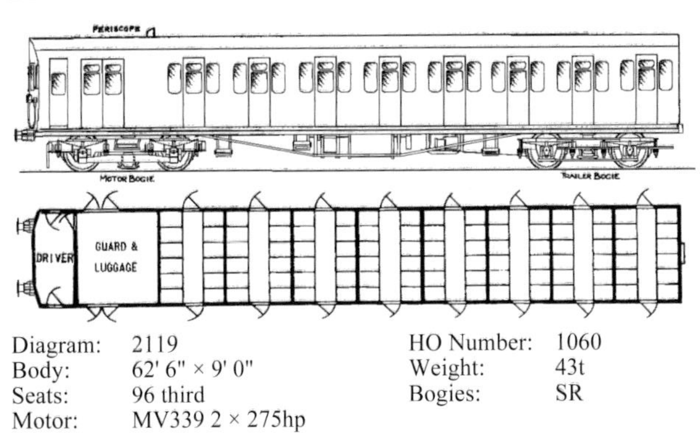

Diagram:	2119	HO Number:	1060
Body:	62' 6" × 9' 0"	Weight:	43t
Seats:	96 third	Bogies:	SR
Motor:	MV339 2 × 275hp		

S10961S	04/46-05/72	⊗10/72	**4111**	04/46-05/72
S10962S	04/46-05/72	⊗10/72	**4111**	04/46-05/72
S10963S	04/46-05/74	⊗10/76	**4112**	04/46-05/74
S10964S	04/46-05/74	⊗10/76	**4112**	04/46-05/74
S10965S	05/46-10/73	⊗06/76	**4113**	05/46-10/73
S10966S	05/46-10/73	⊗06/76	**4113**	05/46-10/73

S10967S	05/46-05/72	⊗01/73	**4114**	05/46-05/72		
S10968S	05/46-05/72	⊗01/73	**4114**	05/46-05/72		
S10969S	06/46-01/72	⊗06/72	**4115**	06/46-01/72		
S10970S	06/46-01/72	⊗06/72	**4115**	06/46-01/72		
S10971S	06/46-05/72	⊗08/73	**4116**	06/46-05/72		
S10972S	06/46-05/72	⊗08/73	**4116**	06/46-05/72		
S10973S	06/46-10/73	⊗10/76	**4117**	06/46-10/73		
S10974S	06/46-10/73	⊗10/76	**4117**	06/46-10/73		
S10975S	07/46-01/72	⊗07/72	**4118**	07/46-01/72		
S10976S	07/46-01/72	⊗07/72	**4118**	07/46-01/72		
S10977S	07/46-10/73	⊗09/74	**4119**	07/46-10/73		
S10978S	07/46-10/73	⊗09/74	**4119**	07/46-10/73		
S10979S	07/46-05/72	⊗10/72	**4120**	07/46- *61*	**4120**	02/62-05/72
S10980S	07/46- *61*	⊗ *62*	**4120**	07/46- *61*		

Class 405 4-SUB Eastleigh

Driving Motor Brake Third Open

DMBTO

S10981S-S11000S

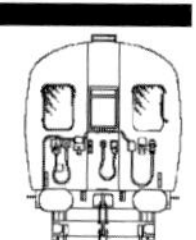

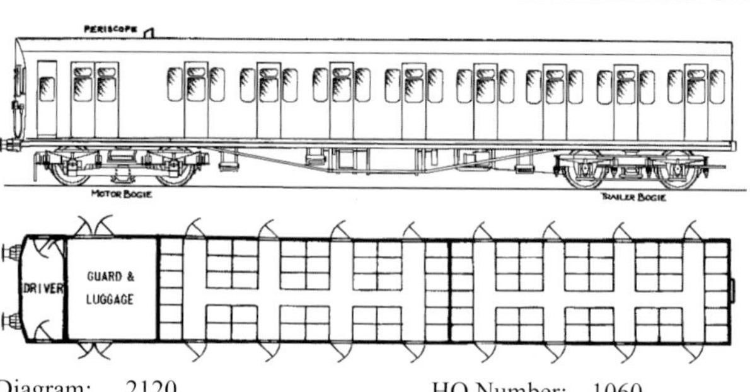

Diagram:	2120	HO Number:	1060
Body:	62' 6" × 9' 0"	Weight:	39t
Seats:	84 third	Bogies:	SR
Motor:	EE507C 2 × 250hp		

S10981S	08/46-04/76	**➲975588**	**4121**	08/46-04/76
S10982S	08/46-04/76	**➲975589**	**4121**	08/46-04/76
S10983S	08/46-03/72	⊗04/73	**4122**	08/46-03/72
S10984S	08/46-03/72	⊗04/73	**4122**	08/46-03/72
S10985S	08/46-10/71	⊗07/72	**4123**	08/46-10/71
S10986S	08/46-10/71	⊗07/72	**4123**	08/46-10/71
S10987S	08/46-04/76	**➲975597**	**4124**	08/46-04/76
S10988S	08/46-04/76	**➲975600**	**4124**	08/46-04/76
S10989S	09/46-04/76	**➲975598**	**4125**	09/46-04/76
S10990S	09/46-04/76	**➲975599**	**4125**	09/46-04/76
S10991S	09/46-04/76	**➲975602**	**4126**	09/46-04/76
S10992S	09/46-04/76	**➲975603**	**4126**	09/46-04/76
S10993S	09/46-04/76	**➲975592**	**4127**	09/46-04/76
S10994S	09/46-04/76	**➲975595**	**4127**	09/46-04/76
S10995S	09/46-05/74	⊗03/76	**4128**	09/46-05/74
S10996S	09/46-05/74	⊗03/76	**4128**	09/46-05/74
S10997S	09/46-06/72	⊗04/73	**4129**	09/46-06/72
S10998S	09/46-06/72	⊗04/73	**4129**	09/46-06/72
S10999S	10/46-05/74	⊗03/76	**4130**	10/46-05/74
S11000S	10/46-05/74	⊗03/76	**4130**	10/46-05/74

Prototype main-line unit, later 6-CIT

Birmingham RC&W

Driving Motor Brake Third Open

DMBTO

S11001S

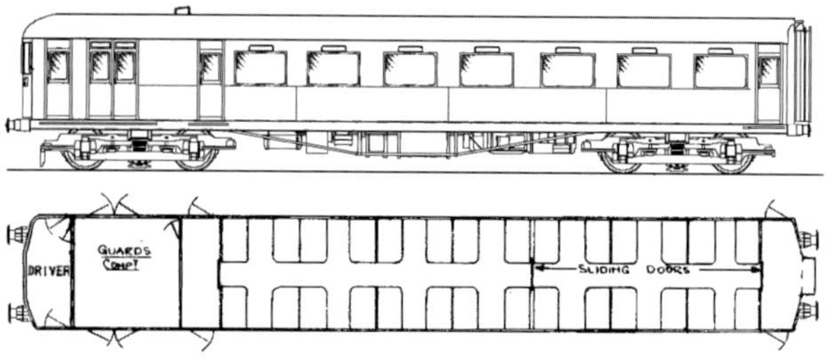

Diagram:	2108	HO Number:	external contract
Body:	63' 3" × 9' 5"	Weight:	57t
Seats:	56 third	Bogies:	SR
Motor:	MV163 4 × 225hp		

S11001S	11/31-*06/68*	⊗06/69	**2001**	11/31-11/32	**2041**	11/32-01/37	**3041**	01/37-*06/68*

Prototype main-line unit, later 6-CIT

Metropolitan CW&F

Driving Motor Brake Third Open

DMBTO

S11002S

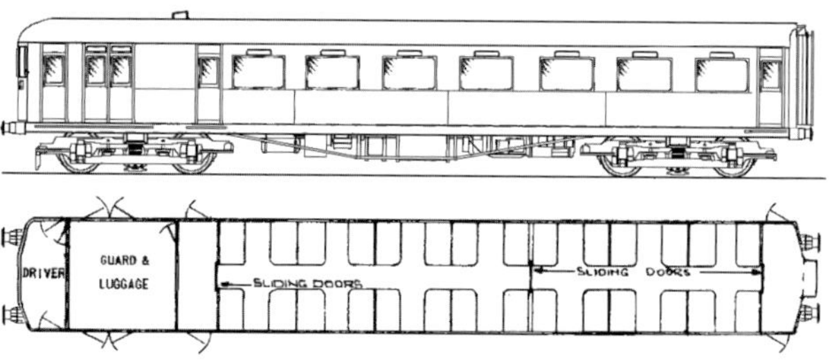

Diagram:	2109	HO Number:	external contract
Body:	63' 3" × 9' 5"	Weight:	58t
Seats:	56 third	Bogies:	SR
Motor:	MV163 4 × 225hp		

S11002S	11/31-09/65	⊗04/66	**2001**	11/31-11/32	**2042**	*11/32*-01/37	**3042**	01/37-02/47
			3042	12/47-09/65				

6-PUL Birmingham RC&W (11003-24)

Metropolitan Cammell (11025-42)

Driving Motor Brake Third Open

DMBTO

S11003S-S11042S (11041-11042 6-CIT)

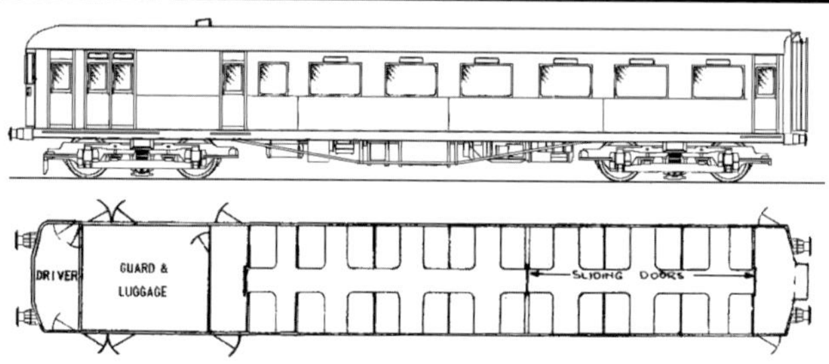

Diagram:	2107	HO Number:	external contract
Body:	63' 6" × 9' 0⅝"	Weight:	59t
Seats:	52 third	Bogies:	SR
Motor:	MV163 4 × 225hp		

S11003S	*09/32*-01/69	⊗	**2002**	*09/32*-01/37	**3002**	01/37-12/65	**3046**	12/65-01/69
S11004S	*09/32*-01/69	⊗	**2002**	*09/32*-01/37	**3002**	01/37-12/65	**3046**	12/65-01/69
S11005S	*09/32*-01/66	⊗	**2003**	*09/32*-01/37	**3003**	01/37-01/48	**3003**	06/49-01/66
S11006S	*09/32*-12/65	⊗	**2003**	*09/32*-01/37	**3003**	01/37-01/48	**3026**	06/49-12/65
S11007S	*10/32*-01/64	⊗	**2004**	*10/32*-01/37	**3004**	01/37-01/64		
S11008S	*10/32*-01/64	⊗07/65	**2004**	*10/32*-01/37	**3004**	01/37-01/64		
S11009S	*10/32*-01/69	⊗	**2005**	*10/32*-01/37	**3005**	01/37-02/66	**3050**	02/66-01/69
S11010S	*10/32*-01/69	⊗	**2005**	*10/32*-01/37	**3005**	01/37-02/66	**3050**	02/66-01/69
S11011S	*11/32*-01/69	⊗06/69	**2006**	*11/32*-01/37	**3006**	01/37-09/65	**3042**	03/66-01/69
S11012S	*11/32*-01/69	⊗06/69	**2006**	*11/32*-01/37	**3006**	01/37-09/65	**3042**	03/66-01/69
S11013S	*11/32*-09/65	⊗04/66	**2007**	*11/32*-01/37	**3007**	01/37-09/65		
S11014S	*11/32*-09/65	⊗04/66	**2007**	*11/32*-01/37	**3007**	01/37-09/65		
S11015S	12/32-03/66	⊗07/66	**2043**	12/32-01/37	**3043**	01/37-03/66		
S11016S	12/32-03/66	⊗07/66	**2043**	12/32-01/37	**3043**	01/37-03/66		
S11017S	*10/32*-09/64	⊗05/65	**2009**	*10/32*-01/37	**3009**	01/37-09/64		
S11018S	*10/32-09/65*	⊗	**2009**	*10/32*-01/37	**3009**	01/37-09/64	**3027**[2]	10/64-*09/65*
S11019S	*11/32*-12/65	⊗	**2010**	*11/32*-01/37	**3010**	01/37-11/65	**3044**	11/65-01/69
S11020S	*11/32*-01/69	⊗	**2010**	*11/32*-01/37	**3010**	01/37-11/65	**3044**	11/65-01/69
S11021S	*12/32*-01/69	⊗06/69	**2011**	*12/32*-01/37	**3011**	01/37-12/65	**3048**	01/66-01/69
S11022S	*12/32*-01/69	⊗06/69	**2011**	*12/32*-01/37	**3011**	01/37-12/65	**3048**	01/66-01/69
S11023S	*12/32*-09/65	⊗04/66	**2012**	*12/32*-01/37	**3012**	01/37-09/65		
S11024S	*12/32*-09/65	⊗04/66	**2012**	*12/32*-01/37	**3012**	01/37-09/65		
S11025S	*09/32*-03/66	⊗	**2013**	*09/32*-01/37	**3013**	01/37-03/66		
S11026S	*09/32*-03/66	⊗	**2013**	*09/32*-01/37	**3013**	01/37-03/66		
S11027S	*09/32*-08/58	⊗08/58	**2014**	*09/32*-01/37	**3014**	01/37-08/58		
S11028S	*09/32*-01/64	⊗07/65	**2014**	*09/32*-01/37	**3014**	01/37-01/64		
S11029S	*10/32*-01/69	⊗01/70	**2015**	*10/32*-01/37	**3015**	01/37-12/65	**3049**	02/66-01/69
S11030S	*10/32*-01/69	⊗06/69	**2015**	*10/32*-01/37	**3015**	01/37-12/65	**3049**	02/66-01/69
S11031S	*10/32*-03/65	⊗07/65	**2016**	*10/32*-01/37	**3016**	01/37-03/65		
S11032S	*10/32*-03/65	⊗07/65	**2016**	*10/32*-01/37	**3016**	01/37-03/65		
S11033S	*10/32*-01/64	⊗	**2017**	*10/32*-01/37	**3017**	01/37-01/64		
S11034S	*10/32*-07/65	⊗	**2017**	*10/32*-01/37	**3017**	01/37-01/64	**3124**	06/64-07/65
S11035S	*11/32-09/65*	⊗04/66	**2018**	*11/32*-01/37	**3018**	01/37-01/64	**3027**[2]	10/64-*09/65*
S11036S	*11/32*-07/65	⊗	**2018**	*11/32*-01/37	**3018**	01/37-01/64	**3148**	06/64-07/65

S11037S	11/32-01/64	⊗04/66	**2019**	11/32-01/37	**3019**	01/37-01/64		
S11038S	11/32-01/64	⊗	**2019**	11/32-01/37	**3019**	01/37-01/64		
S11039S	11/32-01/64	⊗08/65	**2020**	11/32-01/37	**3020**	01/37-01/64		
S11040S	11/32-01/64	⊗	**2020**	11/32-01/37	**3020**	01/37-01/64		
S11041S	11/32-06/68	⊗06/69	**2041**	11/32-01/37	**3041**	01/37-06/68		
S11042S	11/32-09/65	⊗04/66	**2042**	11/32-01/37	**3042**	01/37-02/47	**3042**	12/47-09/65

6-PUL Metropolitan Cammell

Driving Motor Brake Third Open
DMBTO
S11043S-S11044S

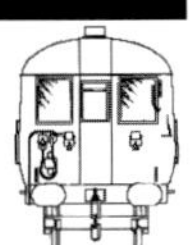

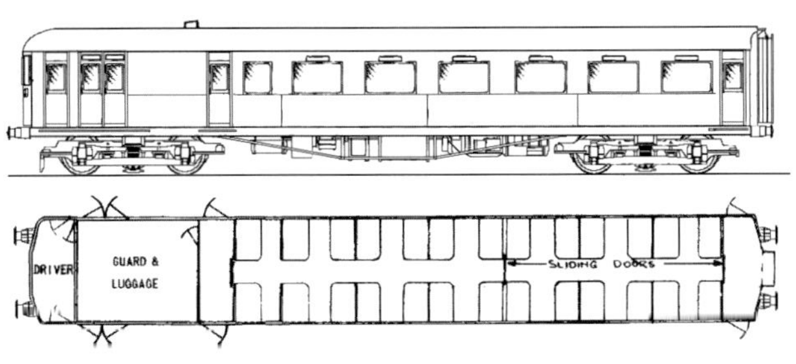

Diagram: 2107 HO Number: external contract
Body: 63' 6" × 9' 0⅝" Weight: 52t-59t
Seats: 52 third Bogies: SR
Motor: MV163 4 × 225hp

S11043S	12/32-10/68	⊗	**2001**	12/32-01/37	**3001**	01/37-04/66	**3043**	04/66-10/68
S11044S	12/32-10/68	⊗	**2001**	12/32-01/37	**3001**	01/37-04/66	**3043**	04/66-10/68

6-PUL Metropolitan Cammell

Driving Motor Brake Third Open
DMBTO
S11045S-S11046S

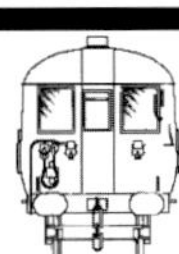

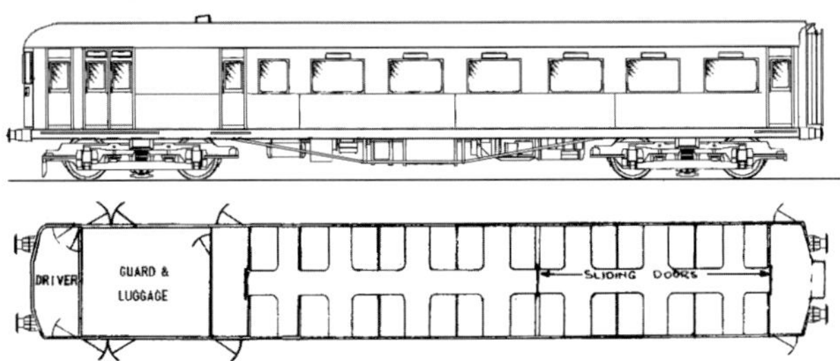

Diagram: 2107 HO Number: external contract
Body: 63' 6" × 9' 0⅝" Weight: 52t-59t
Seats: 52 third Bogies: SR
Motor: MV163 4 × 225hp

S11045S	12/32-02/66	⊗	**2008**	12/32-01/37	**3008**	01/37-02/66
S11046S	12/32-02/66	⊗	**2008**	12/32-01/37	**3008**	01/37-02/66

6-PAN Metropolitan Cammell (11047-63) Birmingham RC&W (11064-80)

Driving Motor Brake Third Open
DMBTO
S11047S-S11080S

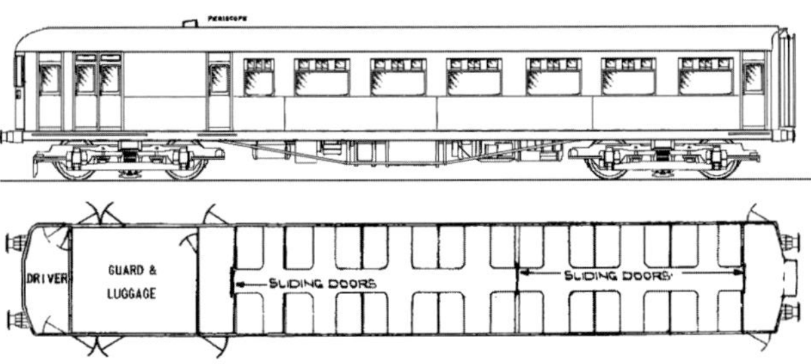

Diagram: 2112 HO Number: external contract
Body: 63' 6" × 9' 0⅝" Weight: 52t
Seats: 52 third Bogies: SR Suburban
Motor: EE163 4 × 225hp

S11047S	03/35-03/66	⊗07/66	**2021**	03/35-01/37	**3021**	01/37-03/66		
S11048S	03/35-03/66	⊗07/66	**2021**	03/35-01/37	**3021**	01/37-03/66		
S11049S	03/35-07/66	⊗07/66	**2022**	03/35-01/37	**3022**	01/37-02/66		
S11050S	03/35-07/66	⊗	**2022**	03/35-01/37	**3022**	01/37-02/66		
S11051S	03/35-09/65	⊗	**2023**	03/35-01/37	**3023**	01/37-09/65		
S11052S	03/35-09/65	⊗07/66	**2023**	03/35-01/37	**3023**	01/37-09/65		
S11053S	04/35-12/65	⊗	**2026**	04/35-01/37	**3026**	01/37-12/65		
S11054S	04/35-03/65	⊗07/65	**2026**	04/35-01/37	**3026**	01/37-06/49	**3025**	06/49-03/65
S11055S	04/35-07/66	⊗07/66	**2029**	04/35-01/37	**3029**	01/37-01/48	**3029**	06/49-03/66
S11056S	04/35-01/66	⊗	**2029**	04/35-01/37	**3029**	01/37-01/48	**3003**	06/49-01/66
S11057S	05/35-01/64	➲**DS70258**	**2031**	05/35-01/37	**3031**	01/37-01/64		
S11058S	05/35-01/64	➲**DS70259**	**2031**	05/35-01/37	**3031**	01/37-01/64		
S11059S	05/35-01/64	⊗07/65	**2033**	05/35-01/37	**3033**	01/37-01/64		
S11060S	05/35-01/64	⊗07/65	**2033**	05/35-01/37	**3033**	01/37-01/64		
S11061S	06/35-01/69	⊗01/70	**2035**	06/35-01/37	**3035**	01/37-12/65	**3047**	01/66-01/69
S11062S	06/35-01/69	⊗01/70	**2035**	06/35-01/37	**3035**	01/37-12/65	**3047**	01/66-01/69
S11063S	06/35-01/66	⊗07/66	**2037**	06/35-01/37	**3037**	01/37-01/66		
S11064S	03/35-09/65	⊗	**2024**	03/35-01/37	**3024**	01/37-09/65		
S11065S	03/35-09/65	⊗	**2024**	03/35-01/37	**3024**	01/37-09/65		
S11066S	04/35-07/66	⊗07/66	**2025**	04/35-01/37	**3025**	01/37-06/49	**3029**	06/49-03/66
S11067S	04/35-03/65	⊗08/65	**2025**	04/35-01/37	**3025**	01/37-03/65		
S11068S	04/35-08/64	⊗	**2027**	04/35-01/37	**3027**	01/37-08/64		
S11069S	04/35-08/64	⊗10/65	**2027**	04/35-01/37	**3027**	01/37-08/64		
S11070S	04/35-09/64	⊗	**2028**	04/35-01/37	**3028**	01/37-09/64		
S11071S	04/35-09/64	⊗	**2028**	04/35-01/37	**3028**	01/37-09/64		
S11072S	05/35-01/69	⊗06/69	**2030**	05/35-01/37	**3030**	01/37-12/65	**3045**	12/65-01/69
S11073S	06/35-12/65	⊗	**2034**	06/35-01/37	**3034**	01/37-12/65		
S11074S	05/35-01/59	⊗	**2032**	05/35-01/37	**3032**	01/37-08/58	**3014**	08/58-01/59
S11075S	05/35-01/64	⊗	**2032**	05/35-01/37	**3032**	01/37-08/58	**3014**	01/59-01/64
S11076S	06/35-12/65	⊗	**2034**	06/35-01/37	**3034**	01/37-12/65		
S11077S	05/35-01/69	⊗06/69	**2030**	05/35-01/37	**3030**	01/37-12/65	**3045**	12/65-01/69
S11078S	06/35-09/65	⊗	**2036**	06/35-01/37	**3036**	01/37-09/65		
S11079S	06/35-09/65	⊗	**2036**	06/35-01/37	**3036**	01/37-09/65		
S11080S	06/35-01/66	⊗07/66	**2037**	06/35-01/37	**3037**	01/37-01/66		

Class 404 4-COR Lancing/Eastleigh

Driving Motor Brake Third Open
DMBTO
S11081S-S11138S

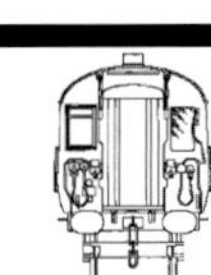

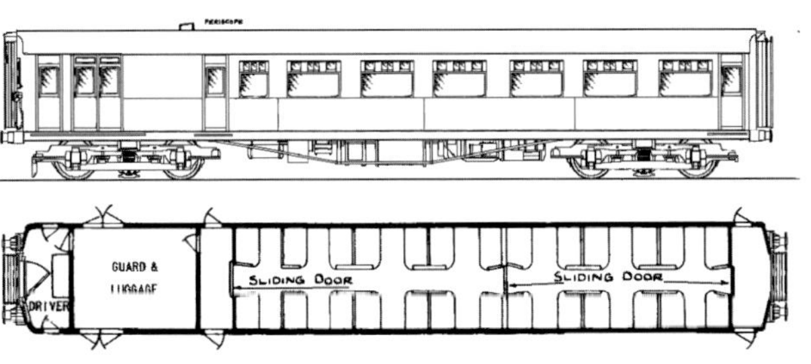

Diagram: 2114 HO Number: 924
Body: 63' 6" × 9' 0" Weight: 46t 10cwt
Seats: 52 third Bogies: SR Express
Motor: EE163 4 × 250hp

War Loss replacements built to HO 3075

S11081S	02/37-01/72	⊗05/72	**3101**	02/37-01/72	
11082	02/37-06/44	↪**11212**	**3101**	02/37-06/44	War loss
S11082S[2]	07/46-08/72	⊗	**3137**	47-08/72	Replacement
S11083S	02/37-10/72	⊗02/73	**3102**	02/37-10/72	
S11084S	02/37-10/72	⊗02/73	**3102**	02/37-10/72	
S11085S	02/37-05/72	⊗02/73	**3103**	02/37-05/72	
S11086S	02/37-05/72	⊗02/73	**3103**	02/37-05/72	
S11087S	02/37-05/72	⊗11/72	**3104**	02/37-05/72	
S11088S	02/37-05/72	⊗11/72	**3104**	02/37-05/72	
S11089S	02/37-05/72	⊗11/72	**3105**	02/37-05/72	
S11090S	02/37-05/72	⊗11/72	**3105**	02/37-05/72	
S11091S	02/37-05/72	⊗11/72	**3106**	02/37-05/72	
S11092S	02/37-05/72	⊗11/72	**3106**	02/37-05/72	
S11093S	02/37-01/72	⊗05/72	**3107**	02/37-01/72	
S11094S	02/37-01/72	⊗05/72	**3107**	02/37-01/72	
S11095S	02/37-09/72	⊗05/73	**3108**	02/37-09/72	
S11096S	02/37-09/72	⊗05/73	**3108**	02/37-09/72	
S11097S	02/37-09/72	⊗05/73	**3109**	02/37-09/72	
S11098S	02/37-09/72	⊗05/73	**3109**	02/37-09/72	
S11099S	03/37-10/71	⊗01/72	**3110**	03/37-10/71	
S11100S	03/37-10/71	⊗01/72	**3110**	03/37-10/71	
S11101S	03/37-05/72	⊗11/72	**3111**	03/37-05/72	
S11102S	03/37-05/72	⊗11/72	**3111**	03/37-05/72	

S11103S	03/37-01/72	⊗07/72	**3112**	03/37-01/72					
S11104S	03/37-01/72	⊗03/72	**3112**	03/37- 45	**3149**	45-01/72			
S11105S	03/37-01/72	⊗06/72	**3113**	03/37-01/72					
S11106S	03/37-01/72	⊗06/72	**3113**	03/37-01/72					
S11107S	03/37-05/72	⊗11/72	**3114**	03/37-05/72					
S11108S	03/37-05/72	⊗11/72	**3114**	03/37-05/72					
S11109S	03/37-01/72	⊗06/72	**3115**	03/37-01/72					
S11110S	03/37-01/72	⊗06/72	**3115**	03/37-01/72					
S11111S	03/37- 72	⊗02/73	**3116**	03/37- 64	**3145**	64- 72			
S11112S	03/37-10/70	⊗	**3116**	03/37- 45	**3083**	45-10/70			
11113	03/37-01/41	⊗03/41	**3117**	03/37-01/41					War loss
S11113S[2]	07/46-08/72	⊗	**3137**	47-08/72					Replacement
11114	03/37-01/41	⊗03/41	**3117**	03/37-01/41					War loss
S11114S[2]	08/46-05/72	⊗11/72	**3117**	09/46-05/72					Replacement
S11115S	03/37-01/72	⊗06/72	**3118**	03/37-01/70	**3138**	01/70-01/72			
S11116S	03/37-08/72	⊗02/73	**3118**	03/37-08/72					
11117	03/37-01/41	⊗03/41	**3119**	03/37-01/41					War loss
S11117S[2]	08/46-05/72	⊗04/73	**3119**	02/47-05/72					Replacement
11118	03/37-01/41	⊗03/41	**3119**	03/37-01/41					War loss
S11118S[2]	08/46-05/72	⊗11/72	**3117**	09/46-05/72					Replacement
S11119S	04/37-05/72	⊗11/72	**3120**	04/37-05/72					
S11120S	04/37-05/72	⊗11/72	**3120**	04/37-05/72					
S11121S	04/37-05/71	⊗05/71	**3121**	04/37-05/71					
S11122S	04/37-05/71	⊗05/71	**3121**	04/37-05/71					
S11123S	04/37-08/72	⊗05/73	**3122**	04/37-08/72					
S11124S	04/37-08/72	⊗05/73	**3122**	04/37-08/72					
S11125S	04/37-12/72	⊗02/73	**3123**	04/37-12/72					
S11126S	04/37-12/72	⊗02/73	**3123**	04/37-12/72					
S11127S	04/37-10/71	⊗02/72	**3124**	04/37-10/71					
S11128S	04/37-10/71	⊗02/72	**3124**	04/37-06/64	**3059**	09/64-07/65	**3124**	07/65-10/71	
S11129S	04/37-01/72	⊗	**3125**	04/37-01/72					
S11130S	04/37-01/72	⊗	**3125**	04/37-01/72					
S11131S	04/37-01/72	⊗05/72	**3126**	04/37-01/72					
S11132S	04/37-01/72	⊗05/72	**3126**	04/37-01/72					
S11133S	04/37-08/72	⊗02/73	**3127**	04/37-01/70	**3118**	01/70-08/72			
S11134S	04/37-01/70	⊗01/70	**3127**	04/37-01/70					
S11135S	04/37-09/72	⊗05/73	**3128**	04/37-09/72					
S11136S	04/37-09/72	⊗05/73	**3128**	04/37-09/72					
S11137S	04/37-05/72	⊗11/72	**3129**	04/37-05/72					
S11138S	04/37-05/72	⊗11/72	**3129**	04/37-05/72					

Class 404 4-RES Lancing/Eastleigh

Driving Motor Brake Third Open
DMBTO
S11139S-S11176S

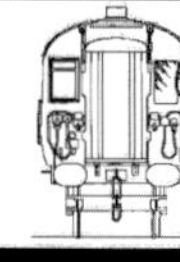

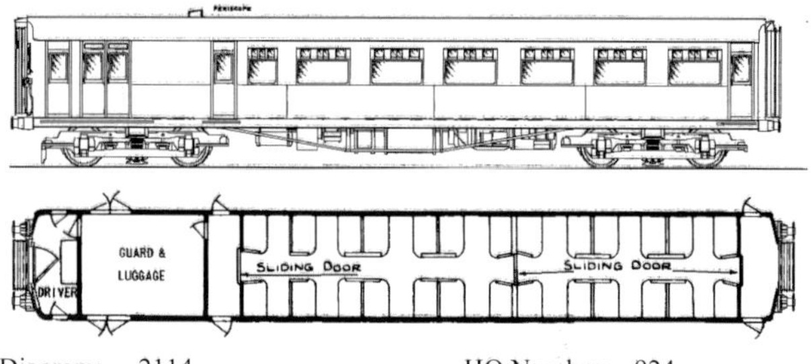

Diagram:	2114	HO Number:	924
Body:	63' 6" × 9' 0"	Weight:	46t 10cwt
Seats:	52 third	Bogies:	SR Express
Motor:	EE163 4 × 250hp		

War Loss replacements built to HO 3075

S11139S	04/37-05/72	⊗	**3054**	04/37- 45	**3130**	45-05/72			
S11140S	04/37-10/71	⊗02/72	**3054**	04/37-06/66	**3161**	07/66-10/71			
S11141S	04/37-10/71	⊗02/72	**3055**	04/37-06/66	**3162**	06/66-10/71			
S11142S	04/37-10/71	⊗02/72	**3055**	04/37-06/66	**3162**	06/66-10/71			
S11143S	04/37-05/71	⊗06/72	**3056**	04/37-12/63	**3086**	12/63-05/71			
S11144S	04/37-05/71	⊗06/72	**3056**	04/37-12/63	**3086**	12/63-05/71			
S11145S	04/37-07/70	⊗05/71	**3057**	04/37-03/66	**3163**	06/66-07/70			
S11146S	04/37-05/72	⊗01/73	**3057**	04/37-03/66	**3163**	06/66-05/72			
S11147S	04/37-01/72	⊗06/72	**3058**	04/37-12/40	**3148**	45-06/64	**3147**	07/65-01/72	
S11148S	04/37-10/71	⊗03/72	**3058**	04/37-12/40	**3073**	12/40-10/70	**3121**	05/71-10/71	
S11149S	04/37-01/72	⊗06/72	**3059**	04/37-07/65	**3160**	10/65-01/72			
S11150S	04/37-12/72	⊗02/73	**3059**	04/37- 45	**3116**	45-12/72			
11151	04/37-01/41	⊗	**3060**	04/37-01/41					War loss
S11151S[2]	10/46-01/72	⊗06/72	**3157**	10/46-01/72					Replacement
11152	04/37-01/41	⊗	**3060**	04/37-01/41					War loss
S11152S[2]	10/46-01/72	⊗06/72	**3157**	10/46-01/72					Replacement
S11153S	04/37-01/72	⊗06/72	**3061**	04/37-01/64	**3056**	01/64-07/65	**3160**	10/65-01/72	
S11154S	04/37-06/71	⊗03/72	**3061**	04/37-01/64	**3056**	01/64-09/64	**601**	06/65-10/71	
S11155S	04/37-05/72	⊗02/73	**3062**	04/37-01/64	**3065**	01/64-05/66	**3164**	05/66-05/72	
S11156S	04/37-05/72	⊗02/73	**3062**	04/37-01/64	**3065**	01/64-05/66	**3164**	05/66-05/72	
11157	04/37-06/44	⊗	**3063**	04/37-06/44					War loss
S11157S[2]	10/46-10/71	⊗02/72	**3144**	10/46-10/71					Replacement
S11158S	04/37-05/72	⊗06/72	**3063**	04/37-06/44	**3158**	10/46-05/72			
S11159S	05/37-09/72	⊗09/73	**3064**	05/37-01/64	**3068**	01/64-09/65	**3159**	10/65-09/72	
S11160S	05/37-09/72	⊗09/73	**3064**	05/37-01/64	**3068**	01/64-09/65	**3159**	10/65-09/72	
S11161S	05/37-12/72	Ⓟ	**3065**	05/37- 45	**3142**	45-12/72			
S11162S	05/37-05/71	➲975255	**3065**	05/37-12/63	**3087**	12/63-05/71			
S11163S	05/37-05/72	⊗11/72	**3066**	05/37-05/66	**3165**	05/66-05/72			
S11164S	05/37-05/72	⊗11/72	**3066**	05/37-05/66	**3165**	05/66-05/72			
S11165S	05/37-10/71	⊗02/72	**3067**	05/37-05/66	**3166**	05/66-10/71			
S11166S	05/37-10/71	⊗02/72	**3067**	05/37-05/66	**3166**	05/66-10/71			
S11167S	05/37-05/71	⊗06/72	**3068**	05/37-12/63	**3088**	12/63-05/71			
S11168S	05/37-05/71	⊗06/72	**3068**	05/37-12/63	**3088**	12/63-05/71			
S11169S	05/37-01/72	⊗07/72	**3069**	05/37-05/66	**3167**	05/66-01/72			
S11170S	05/37-01/72	⊗07/72	**3069**	05/37-05/66	**3167**	05/66-01/72			
S11171S	05/37-01/72	⊗06/72	**3070**	05/37- 64	**3147**	64-01/72			
S11172S	05/37-10/70	⊗05/71	**3070**	05/37- 45	**3059**	45-09/64	**3074**	09/64-10/70	
S11173S	05/37-01/72	⊗06/72	**3071**	05/37-07/66	**3168**	07/66-01/72			
S11174S	05/37-01/72	⊗06/72	**3071**	05/37-07/66	**3168**	07/66-01/72			
S11175S	05/37-05/71	⊗	**3072**	05/37-05/71					
S11176S	05/37-05/71	⊗	**3072**	05/37-05/71					

Class 404 4-COR Lancing/Eastleigh

Driving Motor Brake Third Open
DMBTO
S11177S-S11228S

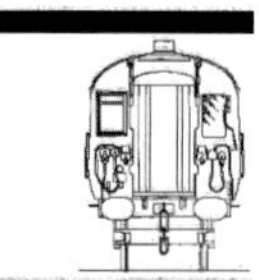

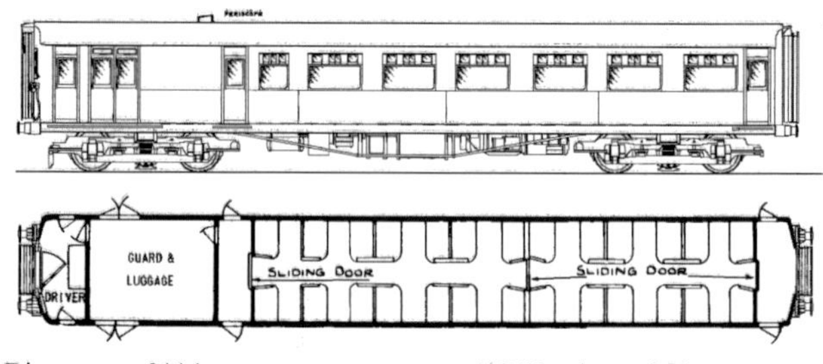

Diagram:	2114	HO Number:	950
Body:	63' 6" × 9' 0"	Weight:	46t 10cwt
Seats:	52 third	Bogies:	SR Express
Motor:	EE163 4 × 250hp		

War Loss replacements built to HO 3075

S11177S	05/38-05/72	⊗02/74	**3130**	05/38- 45	**3054**	45-06/66	**3161**	07/66-12/68	
S11178S	05/38-05/72	⊗02/74	**3130**	05/38-05/72					
S11179S	05/38-09/72	Ⓟ	**3131**	05/38-09/72					
S11180S	05/38-09/72	⊗07/73	**3131**	05/38-09/72					
11181	05/38-01/41	⊗	**3132**	05/38-01/41					War loss
S11181S[2]	10/46-09/72	⊗02/73	**3132**	10/46-09/72					Replacement
S11182S	05/38-09/72	⊗02/73	**3132**	05/38-09/72					
S11183S	05/38-05/72	⊗01/73	**3133**	05/38-05/72					
S11184S	05/38-05/72	⊗01/73	**3133**	05/38-05/72					
S11185S	05/38-01/72	⊗06/72	**3134**	05/38- 45	**3139**	45-01/72			
S11186S	05/38-02/63	⊗02/63	**3134**	05/38-02/63					
S11187S	05/38-09/72	Ⓟ	**3135**	05/38-09/72					
S11188S	05/38-09/72	⊗07/73	**3135**	05/38-09/72					
S11189S	05/38-09/72	⊗02/73	**3136**	05/38-09/72					
S11190S	05/38-09/72	⊗02/73	**3136**	05/38-09/72					
S11191S	05/38-10/70	⊗09/71	**3137**	05/38-08/40	**3083**	45-10/70			
11192	05/38-08/40	⊗	**3137**	05/38-08/40					War loss
S11192S[2]	11/46-05/72	⊗04/73	**3119**	02/47-05/72					Replacement
S11193S	06/38-01/72	⊗06/72	**3138**	06/38-01/72					
S11194S	06/38-01/70	⊗01/70	**3138**	06/38-01/70					
S11195S	06/38-01/72	⊗12/71	**3139**	06/38- 45	**3134**	45-01/72			
S11196S	06/38-01/72	⊗06/72	**3139**	06/38-01/72					
S11197S	06/38-05/72	⊗01/73	**3140**	06/38-05/72					
S11198S	06/38-05/72	⊗01/73	**3140**	06/38-05/72					
S11199S	06/38-09/72	⊗02/73	**3141**	06/38-09/72					
S11200S	06/38-09/72	⊗02/73	**3141**	06/38-09/72					
S11201S	06/38-12/72	Ⓟ	**3142**	06/38-12/72					
S11202S	06/38-05/71	➲975258	**3142**	06/38- 45	**3065**	45-12/63	**3087**	12/63-05/71	
S11203S	06/38-10/72	⊗02/73	**3143**	06/38-10/72					
S11204S	06/38-10/72	⊗02/73	**3143**	06/38-10/72					
11205	06/38-04/41	⊗	**3144**	06/38-08/40					War loss
S11205S[2]	11/46-10/71	⊗02/72	**3144**	10/46-10/71					Replacement
S11206S	06/38-10/70	⊗	**3144**	06/38-08/40	**3082**	06/44-10/70			
S11207S	06/38- 72	⊗02/73	**3145**	06/38- 72					
S11208S	06/38-12/71	⊗06/72	**3145**	06/38- 64	**3148**	06/64-12/71			
S11209S	06/38-01/72	⊗02/72	**3146**	06/38-01/72					
S11210S	06/38-01/72	⊗02/72	**3146**	06/38-01/72					
S11211S	07/38-12/72	⊗02/73	**3147**	07/38- 64	**3116**	64-12/72			
S11212S	07/38-07/65	⊗07/65	**3147**	07/38-07/65					
					12/55 damaged, then rebuilt on frame from **11082**				
S11213S	07/38-09/64	⊗09/64	**3148**	07/38- 45	**3074**	10/48-09/64			

S11214S	*07/38-12/71*	⊗06/72	**3148**	*07/38-06/64*	**3056**	09/64-07/65	**3148**	07/65-12/71
S11215S	*07/38-01/72*	⊗03/72	**3149**	*07/38-01/72*				
S11216S	*07/38-01/72*	⊗07/72	**3149**	*07/38- 45*	**3112**	*45*-01/72		
S11217S	*07/38-12/71*	⊗07/72	**3150**	*07/38-12/71*				
S11218S	*07/38-01/72*	⊗07/72	**3150**	*07/38- 45*	**3156**	*10/46*-01/72		
S11219S	*07/38-08/72*	⊗05/73	**3151**	*07/38-08/72*				
S11220S	*07/38-08/72*	⊗05/73	**3151**	*07/38-08/72*				
S11221S	*07/38-01/72*	⊗05/72	**3152**	*07/38-01/72*				
S11222S	*07/38-01/72*	⊗05/72	**3152**	*07/38-01/72*				
S11223S	*07/38-01/72*	⊗07/72	**3153**	*07/38-01/72*				
S11224S	*07/38-01/72*	⊗07/72	**3153**	*07/38-01/72*				
S11225S	*07/38-09/72*	⊗07/72	**3154**	*07/38-09/72*				
S11226S	*07/38-09/72*	⊗07/72	**3154**	*07/38-09/72*				
S11227S	*07/38-01/72*	⊗06/72	**3155**	*07/38-01/72*				
S11228S	*07/38-01/72*	⊗06/72	**3155**	*07/38-01/72*				

Class 404 4-BUF Lancing/Eastleigh

Driving Motor Brake Third Open
DMBTO
S11229S-S11254S

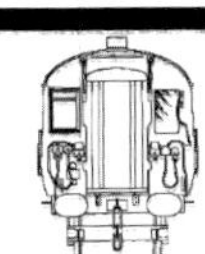

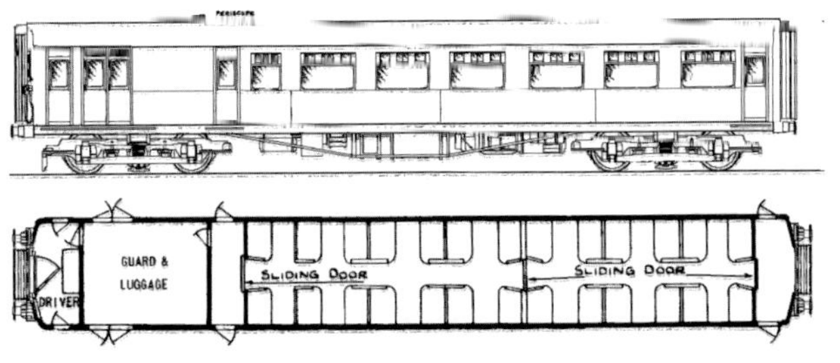

Diagram:	2114	HO Number:	951
Body:	63' 6" × 9' 0"	Weight:	46t 10cwt
Seats:	52 third	Bogies:	SR Express
Motor:	EE163 4 × 250hp		

S11229S	*05/38-06/71*	*⊗03/72*	**3073**	*05/38-09/40*	**3070**	*45- 64*	**601**	06/65-10/71
S11230S	*05/38-10/71*	⊗03/72	**3073**	*05/38-10/70*	**3121**	05/71-10/71		
S11231S	*05/38-10/70*	⊗05/71	**3074**	*05/38-09/40*	**3074**	10/48-10/70		
S11232S	*05/38-01/72*	⊗07/72	**3074**	*05/38-09/40*	**3156**	*10/46*-01/72		
S11233S	*05/38-01/71*	⊗09/71	**3075**	*05/38-01/71*				
S11234S	*05/38-01/71*	⊗09/71	**3075**	*05/38-01/71*				
S11235S	*05/38-10/70*	⊗05/71	**3076**	*05/38-10/70*				
S11236S	*05/38-10/70*	⊗05/71	**3076**	*05/38-10/70*				
S11237S	*06/38-02/71*	⊗12/71	**3077**	*06/38-02/71*				
S11238S	*06/38-02/71*	⊗12/71	**3077**	*06/38-02/71*				
S11239S	*06/38-12/71*	⊗07/72	**3078**	*06/38- 45*	**3150**	*45*-12/71		
S11240S	*06/38-10/70*	⊗05/71	**3078**	*06/38-10/70*				
S11241S	*06/38-01/72*	⊗12/71	**3079**	*06/38-09/62*	**3134**	*04/64*-01/72		
S11242S	*06/38-09/62*	*⊗06/63*	**3079**	*06/38-09/62*				
S11243S	*06/38-01/71*	⊗09/71	**3080**	*06/38-01/71*				
S11244S	*06/38-01/72*	⊗05/72	**3080**	*06/38- 45*	**3101**	*45*-01/72		
S11245S	*06/38-12/68*	⊗05/71	**3081**	*06/38-12/68*				
S11246S	*06/38-10/71*	⊗02/72	**3081**	*06/38-12/68*	**3161**	*12/68*-10/71		
S11247S	*07/38-05/72*	⊗06/72	**3082**	*07/38- 45*	**3158**	10/46-05/72		
S11248S	*07/38-10/70*	⊗02/72	**3082**	*07/38-10/70*				
S11249S	*07/38-05/72*	⊗01/73	**3083**	*07/38- 45*	**3078**	*45*-10/70	**3163**	10/70-05/72
S11250S	*07/38-01/71*	⊗09/71	**3083**	*07/38- 45*	**3080**	*45*-01/71		
S11251S	*07/38-10/70*	⊗02/72	**3084**	*07/38-10/70*				
S11252S	*07/38-10/70*	⊗02/72	**3084**	*07/38-10/70*				
S11253S	*07/38-02/71*	⊗09/71	**3085**	*07/38-02/71*				
S11254S	*07/38-02/71*	⊗09/71	**3085**	*07/38-02/71*				

Class 405 4-SUB Eastleigh

Driving Motor Brake Third Open
DMBTO
S11301S-S11370S

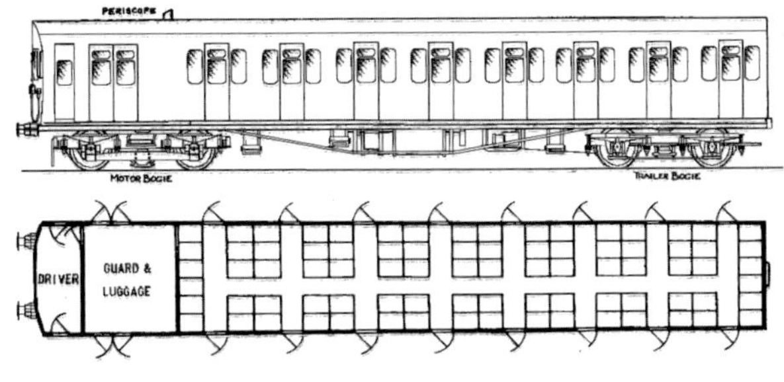

Diagram:	2126 EB265	HO Number:	3504
Body:	62' 6" × 9' 0"	Weight:	39t
Seats:	82 third	Bogies:	SR
Motor:	EE507C 2 × 250hp		

11302-11358 MV163 motors until 1960

S11301S	05/49-10/82	⊗11/83	**4621**	05/49-12/80	**4659**	12/80-10/82			
S11302S	05/49-09/72	⊗03/75	**4621**	05/49-09/72					
S11303S	05/49-05/74	⊗03/76	**4622**	05/49-05/74					↩8847
S11304S	05/49-05/74	⊗03/76	**4622**	05/49-05/74					
S11305S	05/49-05/82	➲977294	**4623**	05/49-07/72	**4624**	07/72-10/72	**4623**	10/72-05/82	↩8662
S11306S	05/49-05/82	➲977295	**4623**	05/49-05/82					↩8846
S11307S	05/49-04/76	⊗07/81	**4624**	05/49-04/76					
S11308S	05/49-04/76	⊗07/81	**4624**	05/49-04/76					↩8669
S11309S	06/49-*03/71*	⊗09/71	**4625**	06/49-*03/71*					↩8843
S11310S	06/49-05/74	⊗03/76	**4625**	06/49-05/74					↩8618
S11311S	06/49-10/82	⊗05/84	**4626**	06/49-10/82					↩8619
S11312S	06/49-02/79	⊗06/80	**4626**	06/49-02/79					↩8677
S11313S	06/49-06/81	⊗	**4627**	06/49-06/81					↩8620
S11314S	06/49-02/68	⊗11/69	**4627**	06/49-02/68					↩8661
S11315S	06/49-06/81	⊗06/82	**4628**	06/49-06/81					↩8671
S11316S	06/49-06/81	⊗06/82	**4628**	06/49-06/81					↩8665
S11317S	07/49-09/83	⊗07/84	**4629**	07/49-09/83					↩8617
S11318S	07/49-09/83	⊗07/84	**4629**	07/49-09/83					↩8837
S11319S	07/49-05/83	⊗06/85	**4630**	07/49-05/83					↩8679
S11320S	07/49-05/83	⊗06/85	**4630**	07/49-05/83					↩8666
S11321S	07/49-05/82	⊗ *84*	**4631**	07/49- *51*	**4631**	05/52-05/82			↩8841
S11322S	07/49-05/82	⊗	**4631**	07/49- *51*	**4631**	05/52-05/82			↩8638
S11323S	07/49-06/81	⊗	**4632**	07/49-02/63	**4289**	03/63-06/81			↩8670
S11324S	07/49-06/81	⊗08/82	**4632**	07/49-09/78	**4632**	06/79-06/81			↩8637
S11325S	07/49-10/82	⊗07/85	**4633**	07/49-10/82					↩8675
S11326S	07/49-10/82	⊗07/85	**4633**	07/49-10/82					↩8629
S11327S	07/49-05/74	⊗04/76	**4634**	07/49-05/74					↩8647
S11328S	07/49-05/74	⊗04/76	**4634**	07/49-05/74					↩8648
S11329S	08/49-06/81	⊗	**4635**	08/49-06/81					↩8630
S11330S	08/49-07/73	⊗01/77	**4635**	08/49-07/73					↩8627
S11331S	09/49-06/81	⊗07/85	**4636**	09/49-06/81					↩8626
S11332S	09/49-06/81	⊗07/85	**4636**	09/49-06/81					↩8668
S11333S	09/49-10/82	⊗11/83	**4637**	09/49-10/82					↩8674
S11334S	09/49-10/82	⊗11/83	**4637**	09/49-10/82					↩8845
S11335S	09/49-06/81	⊗04/82	**4638**	09/49-06/81					
S11336S	09/49-06/81	⊗04/82	**4638**	09/49-06/81					↩8840
S11337S	09/49-05/82	⊗	**4639**	09/49-05/82					↩8643
S11338S	09/49-05/82	⊗	**4639**	09/49-05/82					↩8628
S11339S	10/49-06/81	⊗	**4640**	10/49-11/73	**4299**	06/74-06/81			↩8649
S11340S	10/49-11/73	⊗01/76	**4640**	10/49-11/73					
S11341S	10/49-06/81	⊗06/82	**4641**	10/49-06/81					↩8650
S11342S	10/49-06/81	⊗06/82	**4641**	10/49-06/81					↩8663
S11343S	10/49-06/81	⊗06/82	**4642**	10/49-05/73	**4635**	07/73-06/81			
S11344S	10/49-05/73	⊗07/82	**4642**	10/49-05/73					
S11345S	10/49-04/81	⊗	**4643**	10/49-04/81					↩8664
S11346S	10/49-04/81	⊗	**4643**	10/49-04/81					↩8842
S11347S	10/49-04/76	⊗05/80	**4644**	10/49-04/76					↩8593
S11348S	10/49-04/76	⊗05/80	**4644**	10/49-04/76					↩8683
S11349S	11/49-05/83	⊗02/85	**4645**	11/49-10/82	**4722**	01/83-05/83			↩8644
S11350S	11/49-10/82	⊗05/85	**4645**	11/49-10/82					↩8635
S11351S	11/49-06/81	⊗	**4646**	11/49-04/76	**4627**	05/76-06/81			↩8623
S11352S	11/49-04/76	⊗	**4646**	11/49-04/76					↩8586
S11353S	11/49-04/76	⊗08/82	**4647**	11/49-04/76					↩8633
S11354S	11/49-06/76	⊗08/82	**4647**	11/49-04/76	**4674**	06/76-12/77			↩8676
S11355S	11/49-06/81	⊗	**4648**	11/49-05/81					↩8634
S11356S	11/49-06/81	⊗	**4648**	11/49-05/81					↩8651
S11357S	11/49-06/82	⊗03/83	**4649**	11/49-06/82					↩8588
S11358S	11/49-06/82	⊗03/83	**4649**	11/49-06/82					↩8592
S11359S	12/49-06/81	⊗	**4650**	12/49-06/81					↩8639
S11360S	12/49-06/81	⊗	**4650**	12/49-06/81					↩8642
S11361S	12/49-10/82	⊗ *84*	**4651**	12/49-10/82					↩8631 or 8632?
S11362S	12/49-10/82	⊗ *84*	**4651**	12/49-10/82					↩8589
S11363S	12/49-05/72	⊗10/72	**4652**	12/49-04/61	**4120**	02/62-05/72			↩8656
S11364S	12/49-04/61	⊗04/61	**4652**	12/49-04/61					↩8636
S11365S	12/49-06/81	⊗06/82	**4653**	12/49-06/81					
S11366S	12/49-06/81	⊗06/82	**4653**	12/49-06/81					↩8657
S11367S	01/50-10/82	⊗11/83	**4654**	01/50-10/82					↩8646
S11368S	01/50-10/82	⊗11/83	**4654**	01/50-10/82					
S11369S	01/50-06/81	⊗03/83	**4655**	01/50-09/78	**4655**	06/79-06/81			↩8587
S11370S	01/50-06/81	⊗03/83	**4655**	01/50-06/81					↩8624

Class 405 4-SUB Eastleigh

Driving Motor Brake Third Open
DMBTO
S11371S-S11378S

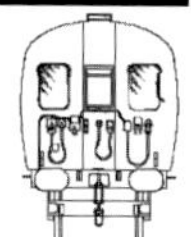

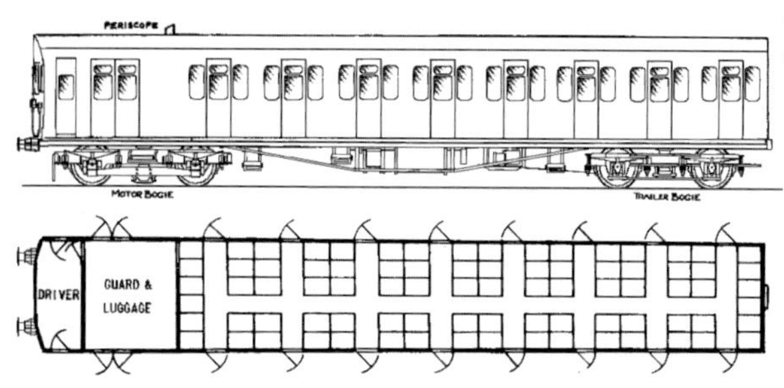

Diagram:	2126 EB265	HO Number:	3505
Body:	62' 6" × 9' 0"	Weight:	39t
Seats:	82 third	Bogies:	SR
Motor:	EE507C 2 × 250hp		

S11371S	01/50-10/82	⊗06/84	**4656**	01/50-10/82	↩8645
S11372S	01/50-10/82	⊗06/84	**4656**	01/50-10/82	↩8685
S11373S	01/50-07/83	⊗07/85	**4657**	01/50-07/83	↩8641
S11374S	01/50-07/83	⊗07/85	**4657**	01/50-07/83	↩8684
S11375S	02/50-10/82	⊗ *84*	**4658**	02/50-10/82	↩8594
S11376S	02/50-10/82	⊗ *84*	**4658**	02/50-10/82	↩8655
S11377S	02/50-10/82	⊗11/83	**4659**	02/50-10/82	↩8640
S11378S	02/50-12/80	⊗	**4659**	02/50-12/80	↩8652

Class 405 4-SUB Eastleigh

Driving Motor Brake Third Open
DMBTO
S11379S-S11392S

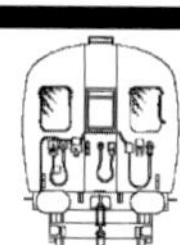

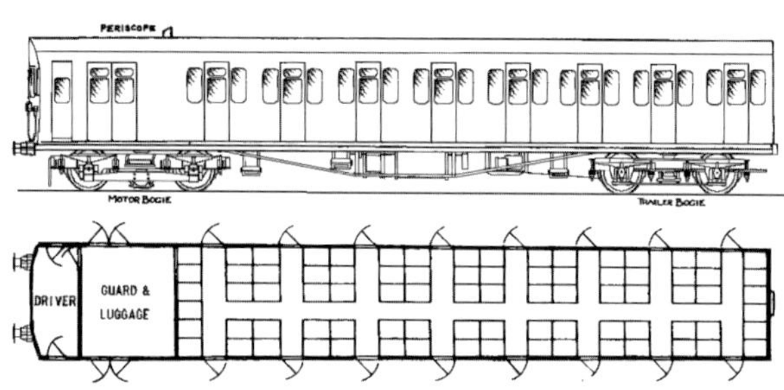

Diagram:	2126 EB265	HO Number:	3506
Body:	62' 6" × 9' 0"	Weight:	39t
Seats:	82 third	Bogies:	SR
Motor:	EE507C 2 × 250hp		

S11379S	02/50-04/83	⊗10/85	**4660**	02/50-04/83					↩8850
S11380S	02/50-04/83	⊗10/85	**4660**	02/50-04/83					↩8590
S11381S	02/50-03/74	⊗03/75	**4661**	02/50-06/51	**4718**	05/52-02/59	**4661**	02/59-05/66	
			4661	11/66-03/74					↩8858
S11382S	02/50-04/76	⊗09/81	**4661**	02/50-05/66	**4661**	11/66-03/74	**4607**	03/74-04/76	
									↩8644
S11383S	02/50-10/82	⊗05/84	**4662**	02/50-02/79	**4626**	02/79-10/82			↩8667
S11384S	02/50-02/79	⊗06/80	**4662**	02/50-02/79					
S11385S	02/50-05/72	⊗05/74	**4663**	02/50-05/72					↩8565
S11386S	02/50-05/72	⊗05/74	**4663**	02/50-05/72					
S11387S	03/50-11/80	➲975896	**4664**	03/50-11/80					
S11388S	03/50-11/80	➲975897	**4664**	03/50-08/67	**4664**	01/68-11/80			
S11389S	03/50-04/76	⊗05/80	**4665**	03/50-04/76					
S11390S	03/50-04/76	⊗05/80	**4665**	03/50-04/76					
S11391S	03/50-05/83	⊗02/85	**4666**	03/50-05/83					
S11392S	03/50-05/83	⊗02/85	**4666**	03/50-05/83					

Class 405 4-SUB Eastleigh

Trailer Third
TT
S11448S-S11470S

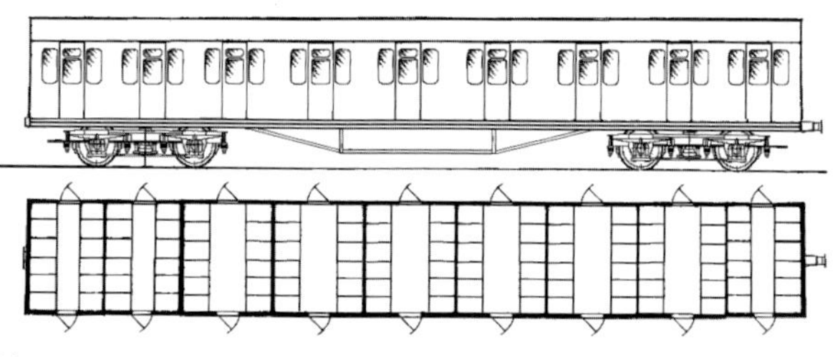

Diagram:	2314 EH262	HO Number:	3231
Body:	62' 0" × 9' 0"	Weight:	26-29t
Seats:	108 third	Bogies:	SR

Built as TC, used as TT

S11448S	*08/47*-06/76	⊗10/81	**4602**	*08/47*-06/48	**4610**	06/48-*02/49*	**4591**	*02/49-10/50*
			4696	10/50-06/76				
S11449S	*08/47*-04/76	⊗08/76	**4614**	*08/47-01/49*	**4589**	*01/49-01/51*	**4728**	06/51-04/76
S11450S	*08/47*-04/76	⊗08/76	**4613**	*08/47*-08/49	**4560**	08/49- *50*	**4477**	*50*-09/50
			4688	09/50-04/76				
S11451S	*08/47*-03/56	➲15038	**4605**	*08/47-02/49*	**4590**	02/49-03/56		
S11452S	*08/47*-06/76	⊗	**4603**	*08/47-02/49*	**4592**	*02/49-06/51*	**4739**	08/51-06/76
S11453S	*08/47*-10/75	⊗03/76	**4601**	*08/47*-05/49	**4587**	05/49-*05/51*	**4733**	06/51-10/75
S11454S	*08/47-11/51*	➲15005	**4606**	*08/47-01/49*	**4573**	*01/49-11/51*		
S11455S	*08/47*-04/76	⊗08/76	**4604**	*08/47*-05/49	**4593**	05/49-*03/51*	**4723**	04/51-04/76
S11456S	*08/47*-05/60	➲15080	**4607**	*08/47-02/48*	**4608**	*02/48-03/49*	**4594**	*03/49*-12/49
			4313	12/49-05/60				
S11457S	06/48-04/76	⊗	**4377**	06/48-06/67	**4377**	02/68-04/76		
S11458S	10/47-10/73	⊗	**4376**	10/47-10/73				
S11459S	11/47-02/74	⊗10/76	**4375**	11/47-02/74				
S11460S	11/47-05/74	⊗10/76	**4374**	11/47-05/74				
S11461S	03/48-04/70	⊗*04/70*	**4364**	03/48-04/70				
S11462S	03/48-05/74	⊗03/76	**4365**	03/48-02/68	**4379**	04/69-05/74		
S11463S	12/47-10/73	⊗09/74	**4371**	12/47-10/73				
S11464S	12/47-05/72	⊗10/72	**4372**	12/47-05/72				
S11465S	12/47-01/74	⊗	**4373**	12/47-01/74				
S11466S	01/48-10/73	⊗	**4369**	01/48-03/68	**4369**	04/69-10/73		
S11467S	01/48-05/73	⊗09/73	**4370**	01/48-05/73				
S11468S	01/48-05/72	⊗02/73	**4368**	01/48-05/66	**4661**	11/66-08/67	**4368**	03/68-05/72
S11469S	03/48-01/74	⊗10/76	**4366**	03/48-01/74				
S11470S	02/48-10/73	➲975321	**4367**	02/48-10/73				

Class 405 4-SUB Lancing/Eastleigh

Trailer Third
TT
S11471S-S11480S

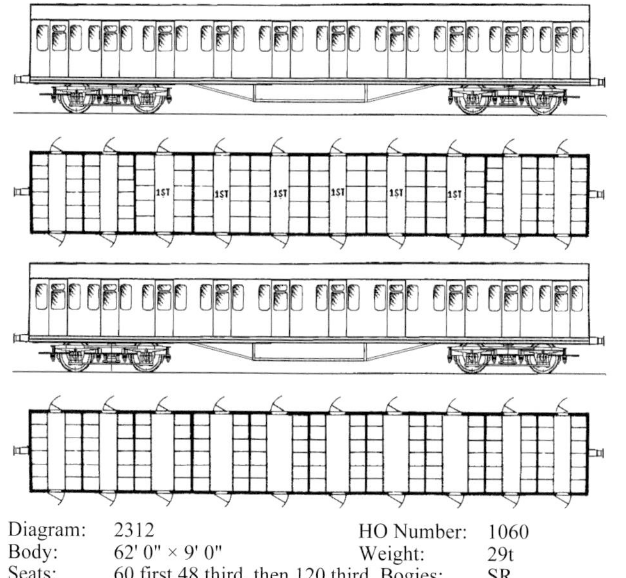

Diagram:	2312	HO Number:	1060
Body:	62' 0" × 9' 0"	Weight:	29t
Seats:	60 first 48 third, then 120 third	Bogies:	SR

Built as TC, used as TT. 11471 used as TC when first built.

S11471S	09/41-05/72	⊗10/72	**4101**	09/41-05/72		
S11472S	12/44-05/72	⊗01/73	**4102**	12/44-05/72		
S11473S	01/45-01/72	⊗07/72	**4103**	01/45-12/68	**4103**	04/69-01/72
S11474S	01/45-01/72	⊗06/72	**4104**	01/45-01/72		
S11475S	01/45-01/72	⊗07/72	**4105**	01/45-01/72		
S11476S	02/45-04/72	⊗02/73	**4106**	02/45-04/72		
S11477S	02/45-05/72	⊗10/72	**4107**	02/45-05/72		
S11478S	03/45-01/61	⊗03/61	**4108**	03/45-01/61		
S11479S	03/45-01/72	⊗06/72	**4109**	03/45-01/72		
S11480S	03/45-05/72	⊗04/73	**4110**	03/45-05/72		

Class 405 4-SUB Eastleigh

Trailer Third

TT

S11481S-S11490S

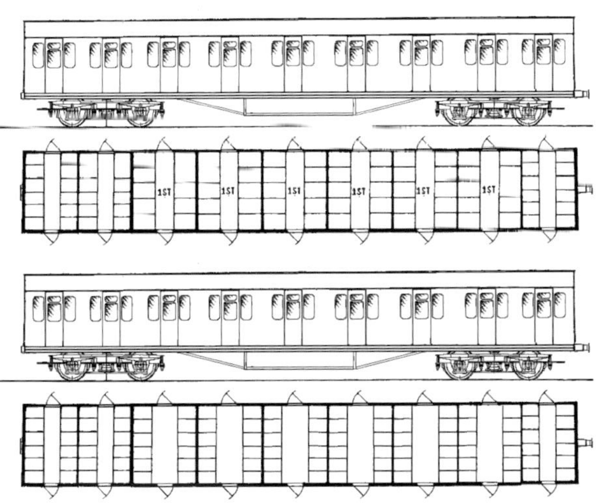

Diagram:	2314 EH262	HO Number:	1060
Body:	62' 0" × 9' 0"	Weight:	26-29t
Seats:	60 first 36 third, then 108 third	Bogies:	SR

Built as TC, used as TT. 11485 used as TC while in 7-TC unit 900/701.

S11481S	04/46-05/72	⊗10/72	**4111**	04/46-05/72				
S11482S	04/46-05/74	⊗10/76	**4112**	04/46-05/74				
S11483S	05/46-10/73	⊗06/76	**4113**	05/46-10/73				
S11484S	05/46-05/72	⊗01/73	**4114**	05/46-05/72				
S11485S	06/46-05/69	⊃15084	**4115**	06/46-09/63	**900**	09/63-06/66	**701**	06/66-05/69
S11486S	06/46-05/72	⊗08/73	**4116**	06/46-05/72				
S11487S	06/46-10/73	⊗10/76	**4117**	06/46-10/73				
S11488S	07/46-01/72	⊗07/72	**4118**	07/46-01/72				
S11489S	07/46-10/73	⊗09/74	**4119**	07/46-10/73				
S11490S	07/46-05/72	⊗10/72	**4120**	07/46- 61	**4120**	02/62-05/72		

Class 405 4-SUB Eastleigh

Trailer Third

TT

S11491S-S11500S

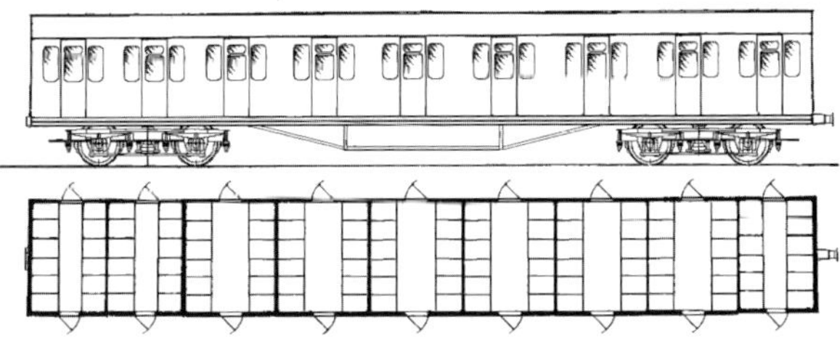

Diagram:	2314 EH262	HO Number:	1060
Body:	62' 0" × 9' 0"	Weight:	26-29t
Seats:	108 third	Bogies:	SR

Built as TC, used as TT

S11491S	08/46-04/76	⊗	**4121**	08/46-04/76
S11492S	08/46-03/72	⊗04/73	**4122**	08/46-03/72
S11493S	08/46-10/71	⊗07/72	**4123**	08/46-10/71
S11494S	08/46-04/76	⊗	**4124**	08/46-04/76
S11495S	09/46-04/76	⊗	**4125**	09/46-04/76
S11496S	09/46-01/75	⊗03/76	**4126**	09/46-01/75
S11497S	09/46-03/75	⊗03/76	**4127**	09/46-03/75
S11498S	09/46-05/74	⊗03/76	**4128**	09/46-05/74
S11499S	09/46-06/72	⊗04/73	**4129**	09/46-06/72
S11500S	10/46-05/74	⊗03/76	**4130**	10/46-05/74

4-LAV Lancing/Eastleigh

Trailer Composite

TC

S11501S-S11533S

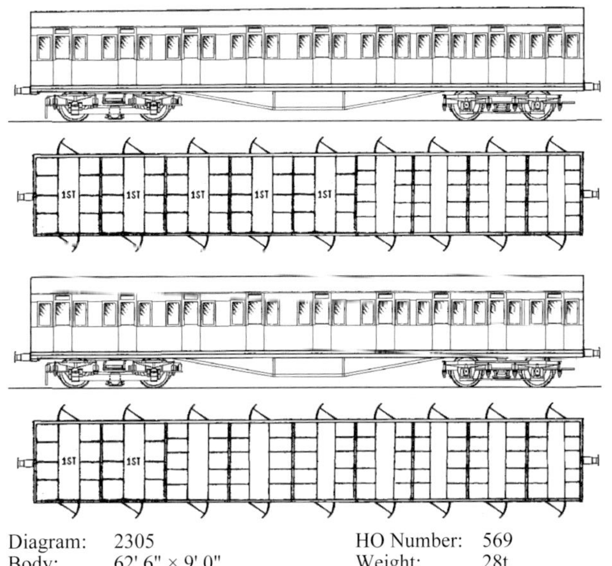

Diagram:	2305	HO Number:	569
Body:	62' 6" × 9' 0"	Weight:	28t
Seats:	40 first 40 third, later 16 first 70 third	Bogies:	SR Suburban

S11501S	07/31-01/68	⊗03/68	**1921**	07/31-01/37	**2921**	01/37-01/68		
S11502S	07/31-04/68	⊗12/68	**1922**	07/31-01/37	**2922**	01/37-04/68		
S11503S	08/31-01/68	⊗08/68	**1929**	08/31-01/37	**2929**	01/37-01/68		
S11504S	08/31-02/68	⊗05/68	**1927**	08/31-01/37	**2927**	01/37-02/68		
S11505S	10/31-02/69	⊗07/69	**1939**	10/31-01/37	**2939**	01/37-02/69		
S11506S	07/31-05/69	⊗ 69	**1924**	07/31-01/37	**2924**	01/37-05/69		
S11507S	09/31-02/68	⊗03/68	**1932**	09/31-01/37	**2932**	01/37-02/68		
S11508S	08/31-02/69	⊗07/69	**1928**	08/31-01/37	**2928**	01/37-02/69		
S11509S	08/31-05/68	⊗04/69	**1926**	08/31-01/37	**2926**	01/37-10/47	**2926**	02/48-09/61
			2926	01/62-05/68				
S11510S	07/31-02/68	⊗10/68	**1925**	07/31-01/37	**2925**	01/37-02/68		
S11511S	10/31-01/68	⊗03/68	**1938**	10/31-01/37	**2938**	01/37-01/68		
S11512S	10/31-02/68	⊗03/68	**1940**	10/31-01/37	**2940**	01/37-02/68		
S11513S	09/31-01/68	⊗10/68	**1935**	09/31-01/37	**2935**	01/37-01/68		
S11514S	09/31-01/68	⊗03/68	**1934**	09/31-01/37	**2934**	01/37-01/68		
S11515S	10/31-03/68	⊗10/68	**1936**	10/31-01/37	**2936**	01/37-03/68		
S11516S	09/31-07/68	⊗11/68	**1933**	09/31-01/37	**2933**	01/37-07/68		
S11517S	07/31-10/68	⊗	**1923**	07/31-01/37	**2923**	01/37-10/68		
S11518S	08/31-03/68	⊗04/68	**1930**	08/31-01/37	**2930**	01/37-03/68		
S11519S	10/31-07/68	⊗12/68	**1937**	10/31-01/37	**2937**	01/37-07/68		
S11520S	09/31-03/68	⊗05/68	**1931**	09/31-01/37	**2931**	01/37-03/68		
S11521S	10/31-12/67	⊗03/68	**1941**	10/31-01/37	**2941**	01/37-12/67		
S11522S	11/31-05/68	⊗	**1942**	11/31-01/37	**2942**	01/37-05/68		
S11523S	12/31-05/68	⊗10/68	**1943**	12/31-01/37	**2943**	01/37-05/68		
S11524S	01/32-02/68	⊗10/68	**1944**	01/32-01/37	**2944**	01/37-02/68		
S11525S	01/32-01/68	⊗10/68	**1945**	01/32-01/37	**2945**	01/37-01/68		
S11526S	02/32-03/68	⊗10/68	**1946**	02/32-01/37	**2946**	01/37-03/68		
S11527S	03/32-05/68	⊗10/68	**1947**	03/32-01/37	**2947**	01/37-05/68		
S11528S	04/32-05/68	⊗03/68	**1948**	04/32-01/37	**2948**	01/37-05/68		
S11529S	05/32-02/69	⊗08/69	**1949**	05/32-01/37	**2949**	01/37-02/69		
S11530S	06/32-02/69	⊗08/69	**1950**	06/32-01/37	**2950**	01/37-02/69		
S11531S	07/32-05/68	⊗03/68	**1951**	07/32-01/37	**2951**	01/37-05/68		
S11532S	08/32-03/68	⊗08/68	**1952**	08/32-01/37	**2952**	01/37-03/68		
S11533S	09/32-01/68	⊗03/68	**1953**	09/32-01/37	**2953**	01/37-01/68		

4-LAV Eastleigh

Trailer Composite
TC
S11534S-S11535S

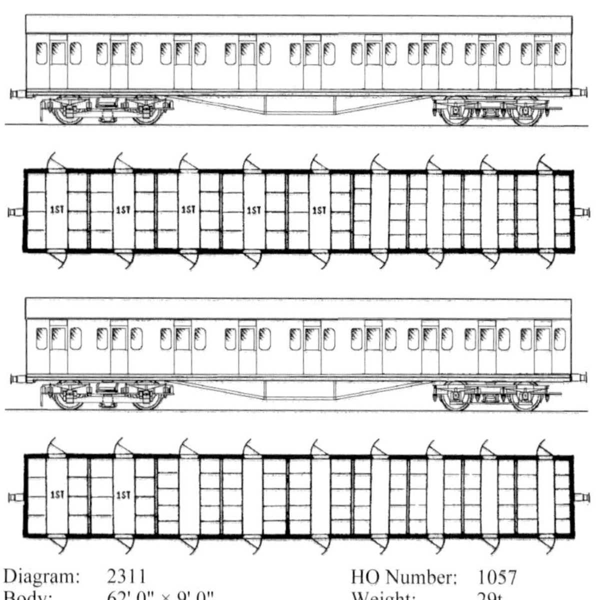

Diagram:	2311	HO Number:	1057
Body:	62' 0" × 9' 0"	Weight:	29t
Seats:	40 first 40 third, later 16 first 70 third	Bogies:	SR Suburban

S11534S	*02/40*-05/68	⊗03/75	**2954**	02/40-05/68
S11535S	*05/40*-*07/68*	⊗07/72	**2955**	05/40-*07/68*

4-PUL Lancing/Eastleigh

Trailer Composite Corridor Lavatory
TCK
S11751S-S11790S

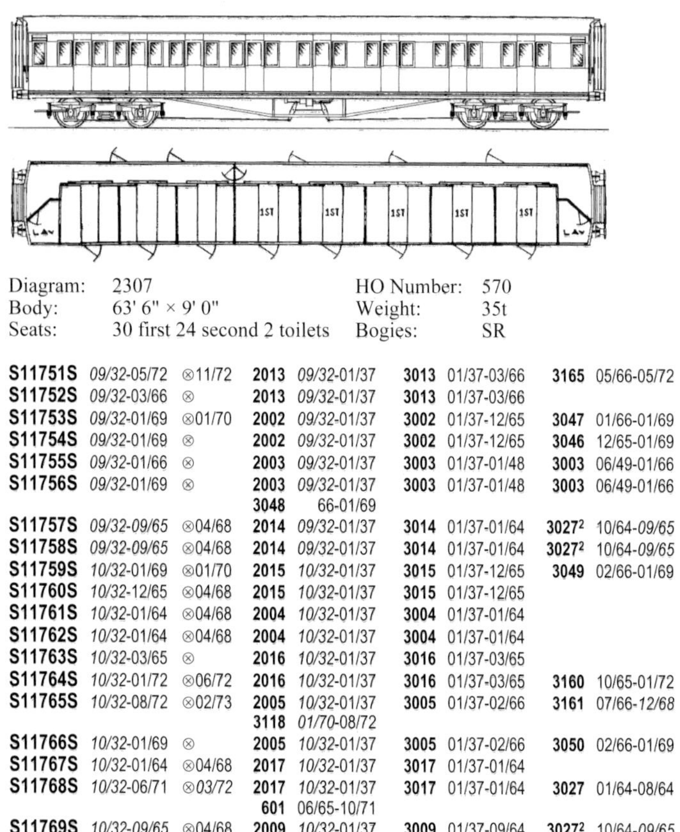

Diagram:	2307	HO Number:	570
Body:	63' 6" × 9' 0"	Weight:	35t
Seats:	30 first 24 second 2 toilets	Bogies:	SR

S11751S	*09/32*-05/72	⊗11/72	**2013**	*09/32*-01/37	**3013**	01/37-03/66	**3165**	05/66-05/72
S11752S	*09/32*-03/66	⊗	**2013**	*09/32*-01/37	**3013**	01/37-03/66		
S11753S	*09/32*-01/69	⊗01/70	**2002**	*09/32*-01/37	**3002**	01/37-12/65	**3047**	01/66-01/69
S11754S	*09/32*-01/69	⊗	**2002**	*09/32*-01/37	**3002**	01/37-12/65	**3046**	12/65-01/69
S11755S	*09/32*-01/66	⊗	**2003**	*09/32*-01/37	**3003**	01/37-01/48	**3003**	06/49-01/66
S11756S	*09/32*-01/69	⊗	**2003**	*09/32*-01/37	**3003**	01/37-01/48	**3003**	06/49-01/66
			3048	66-01/69				
S11757S	*09/32*-*09/65*	⊗04/68	**2014**	*09/32*-01/37	**3014**	01/37-01/64	**3027**[2]	10/64-*09/65*
S11758S	*09/32*-*09/65*	⊗04/68	**2014**	*09/32*-01/37	**3014**	01/37-01/64	**3027**[2]	10/64-*09/65*
S11759S	*10/32*-01/69	⊗01/70	**2015**	*10/32*-01/37	**3015**	01/37-12/65	**3049**	02/66-01/69
S11760S	*10/32*-12/65	⊗04/68	**2015**	*10/32*-01/37	**3015**	01/37-12/65		
S11761S	*10/32*-01/64	⊗04/68	**2004**	*10/32*-01/37	**3004**	01/37-01/64		
S11762S	*10/32*-01/64	⊗04/68	**2004**	*10/32*-01/37	**3004**	01/37-01/64		
S11763S	*10/32*-03/65	⊗	**2016**	*10/32*-01/37	**3016**	01/37-03/65		
S11764S	*10/32*-01/72	⊗06/72	**2016**	*10/32*-01/37	**3016**	01/37-03/65	**3160**	10/65-01/72
S11765S	*10/32*-08/72	⊗02/73	**2005**	*10/32*-01/37	**3005**	01/37-02/66	**3161**	07/66-*12/68*
			3118	*01/70*-08/72				
S11766S	*10/32*-01/69	⊗	**2005**	*10/32*-01/37	**3005**	01/37-02/66	**3050**	02/66-01/69
S11767S	*10/32*-01/64	⊗04/68	**2017**	*10/32*-01/37	**3017**	01/37-01/64		
S11768S	*10/32*-06/71	⊗*03/72*	**2017**	*10/32*-01/37	**3017**	01/37-01/64	**3027**	01/64-08/64
			601	06/65-10/71				
S11769S	*10/32*-*09/65*	⊗04/68	**2009**	*10/32*-01/37	**3009**	01/37-09/64	**3027**[2]	10/64-*09/65*
S11770S	*10/32*-09/64	⊗04/68	**2009**	*10/32*-01/37	**3009**	01/37-09/64		
S11771S	*11/32*-09/65	⊗	**2006**	*11/32*-01/37	**3006**	01/37-09/65		
S11772S	*11/32*-01/69	⊗	**2006**	*11/32*-01/37	**3006**	01/37-09/65	**3042**	03/66-01/69
S11773S	*11/32*-09/72	Ⓟ	**2018**	*11/32*-01/37	**3018**	01/37-01/64	**3159**	10/65-09/72
S11774S	*11/32*-01/64	⊗04/68	**2018**	*11/32*-01/37	**3018**	01/37-01/64		
S11775S	*11/32*-10/71	⊗02/72	**2007**	*11/32*-01/37	**3007**	01/37-09/65	**3166**	05/66-10/71
S11776S	*11/32*-01/72	⊗06/72	**2007**	*11/32*-01/37	**3007**	01/37-09/65	**3168**	07/66-01/72
S11777S	*11/32*-01/64	⊗04/68	**2020**	*11/32*-01/37	**3020**	01/37-01/64		
S11778S	*11/32*-01/64	⊗07/64	**2020**	*11/32*-01/37	**3020**	01/37-01/64		
S11779S	*11/32*-01/64	⊗	**2019**	*11/32*-01/37	**3019**	01/37-01/64		
S11780S	*11/32*-01/64	⊗	**2019**	*11/32*-01/37	**3019**	01/37-01/64		
S11781S	*11/32*-01/69	⊗	**2010**	*11/32*-01/37	**3010**	01/37-11/65	**3044**	11/65-01/69
S11782S	*11/32*-01/69	⊗	**2010**	*11/32*-01/37	**3010**	01/37-11/65	**3045**	12/65-01/69
S11783S	*12/32*-10/68	⊗	**2001**	*12/32*-01/37	**3001**	01/37-04/66	**3043**	04/66-10/68
S11784S	*12/32*-01/72	⊗07/72	**2001**	*12/32*-01/37	**3001**	01/37-04/66	**3167**	05/66-01/72
S11785S	*12/32*-12/65	⊗04/68	**2011**	*12/32*-01/37	**3011**	01/37-12/65	**3048**	01/66- 66
S11786S	*12/32*-12/65	⊗04/68	**2011**	*12/32*-01/37	**3011**	01/37-12/65		
S11787S	*12/32*-05/72	⊗04/73	**2008**	*12/32*-01/37	**3008**	01/37-02/66	**3164**	05/66-05/72
S11788S	*12/32*-05/72	⊗01/73	**2008**	*12/32*-01/37	**3008**	01/37-02/66	**3163**	06/66-05/72
S11789S	*12/32*-10/71	⊗02/72	**2012**	*12/32*-01/37	**3012**	01/37-09/65	**3162**	06/66-10/71
S11790S	*12/32*-09/65	⊗	**2012**	*12/32*-01/37	**3012**	01/37-09/65		

Class 404 4-COR Lancing/Eastleigh

Trailer Composite Corridor Lavatory
TCK
S11791S-S11819S

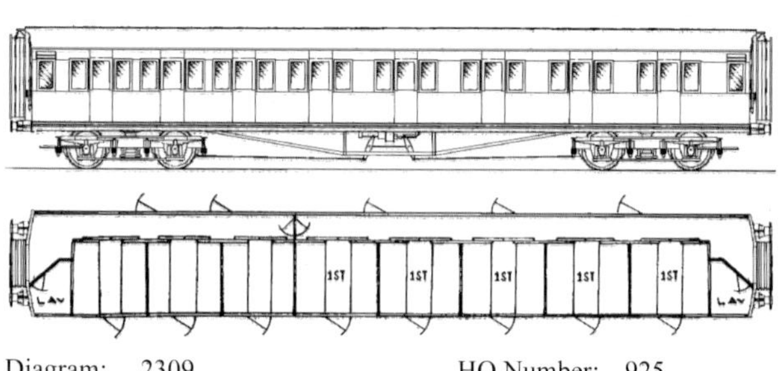

Diagram:	2309	HO Number:	925
Body:	62' 0" × 9' 0"	Weight:	32t 12cwt
Seats:	30 first 24 second 2 toilets	Bogies:	SR Express

War Loss replacements built to HO 3079

S11791S	*02/37*-01/72	⊗05/72	**3101**	*02/37*-01/72			
S11792S	*02/37*-10/72	⊗02/73	**3102**	*02/37*-10/72			
S11793S	*02/37*-05/72	⊗02/73	**3103**	*02/37*-05/72			
S11794S	*02/37*-05/72	⊗11/72	**3104**	*02/37*-05/72			
S11795S	*02/37*-05/72	⊗11/72	**3105**	*02/37*-05/72			
S11796S	*02/37*-05/72	⊗11/72	**3106**	*02/37*-05/72			
S11797S	*02/37*-01/72	⊗05/72	**3107**	*02/37*-01/72			
S11798S	*02/37*-09/72	⊗05/73	**3108**	*02/37*-09/72			
S11799S	*02/37*-09/72	⊗05/73	**3109**	*02/37*-09/72			
S11800S	*03/37*-10/71	**➲975527**	**3110**	*03/37*-10/71			
S11801S	*03/37*-05/72	⊗11/72	**3111**	*03/37*-05/72			
S11802S	*03/37*-01/72	**➲975531**	**3112**	*03/37- 45*	**3149**	*45*-01/72	
S11803S	*03/37*-01/72	⊗06/72	**3113**	*03/37*-01/72			
S11804S	*03/37*-05/72	⊗11/72	**3114**	*03/37*-05/72			
S11805S	*03/37*-01/72	⊗06/72	**3115**	*03/37*-01/72			
S11806S	*03/37*-12/72	⊗02/73	**3116**	*03/37*-12/72			
11807	*03/37*-01/41	⊗03/41	**3117**	*03/37*-01/41			War loss
S11807S[2]	46-01/72	⊗07/72	**3156**	*10/46*-01/72			Replacement
S11808S	*03/37*-01/72	⊗06/72	**3118**	*03/37*-*01/70*	**3138**	*01/70*-01/72	
11809	*03/37*-01/41	⊗03/41	**3119**	*03/37*-01/41			War loss
S11809S[2]	46-05/72	⊗11/72	**3117**	*09/46*-05/72			Replacement
S11810S	*04/37*-05/72	⊗11/72	**3120**	*04/37*-05/72			
S11811S	*04/37*-10/71	⊗03/72	**3121**	*04/37*-10/71			
S11812S	*04/37*-08/72	⊗05/73	**3122**	*04/37*-08/72			
S11813S	*04/37*-12/72	⊗02/73	**3123**	*04/37*-12/72			
S11814S	*04/37*-10/71	⊗02/72	**3124**	*04/37*-10/71			
S11815S	*04/37*-01/72	**➲975530**	**3125**	*04/37*-01/72			
S11816S	*04/37*-01/72	⊗05/72	**3126**	*04/37*-01/72			
S11817S	*04/37*-01/70	**➲975524**	**3127**	*04/37*-01/70			
S11818S	*04/37*-09/72	⊗05/73	**3128**	*04/37*-09/72			
S11819S	*04/37*-05/72	⊗11/72	**3129**	*04/37*-05/72			

Class 404 4-COR   Lancing/Eastleigh

Trailer Composite Corridor Lavatory

TCK

S11820S-S11845S

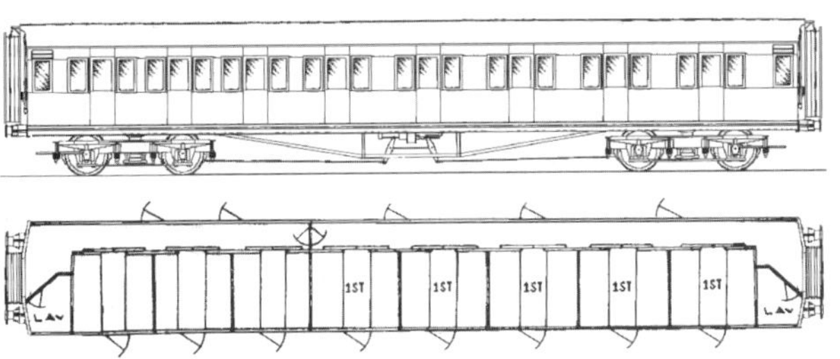

Diagram:	2309	HO Number:	951
Body:	62' 0" × 9' 0"	Weight:	32t 12cwt
Seats:	30 first 24 second 2 toilets	Bogies:	SR

War Loss replacements built to HO 3079

S11820S	*05/38*-05/72	⊗02/74	**3130**	*05/38*-05/72			
S11821S	*05/38*-09/72	⊗07/73	**3131**	*05/38*-09/72			
S11822S	*05/38*-09/72	⊗02/73	**3132**	*05/38*-09/72			
S11823S	*05/38*-05/72	⊗01/73	**3133**	*05/38*-05/72			
S11824S	*05/38*-05/72	⊗06/72	**3134**	*05/38*-02/63	**3158**	*02/64*-05/72	
S11825S	*05/38*-09/72	℗	**3135**	*05/38*-09/72			
S11826S	*05/38*-09/72	⊗02/73	**3136**	*05/38*-09/72			
11827	*05/38*-08/40	⊗	**3137**	*05/38*-08/40			War loss
S11827S[2]	46-08/72	⊗	**3137**	*47*-08/72			Replacement
S11828S	*06/38*-10/71	⊗02/72	**3138**	*06/38*-*11/68*	**3161**	*11/68*-10/71	
S11829S	*06/38*-01/72	⊗06/72	**3139**	*06/38*-01/72			
S11830S	*06/38*-05/72	⊗01/73	**3140**	*06/38*-05/72			
S11831S	*06/38*-09/72	⊗02/73	**3141**	*06/38*-09/72			
S11832S	*06/38*-12/72	⊗07/73	**3142**	*06/38*-12/72			
S11833S	*06/38*-10/72	⊗02/73	**3143**	*06/38*-10/72			
11834	*06/38*-04/41	⊗	**3144**	*06/38*-08/40			War loss
S11834S[2]	46-10/71	⊗02/72	**3144**	10/46-10/71			Replacement
S11835S	*06/38*- 72	⊗02/73	**3145**	*06/38*- 72			
S11836S	*06/38*-01/72	⊗[illegible]	**3146**	*06/38*-01/72			
S11837S	*07/38*-01/72	⊗06/72	**3147**	*07/38*-01/72			
S11838S	*07/38*-12/71	⊗06/72	**3148**	*07/38*-12/71			
S11839S	*07/38*-01/72	⊗07/72	**3149**	*07/38*- *45*	**3112**	*45*-01/72	
S11840S	*07/38*-12/71	⊗07/72	**3150**	*07/38*-12/71			
S11841S	*07/38*-08/72	⊗05/73	**3151**	*07/38*-08/72			
S11842S	*07/38*-01/72	⊗05/72	**3152**	*07/38*-01/72			
S11843S	*07/38*-01/72	⊗07/72	**3153**	*07/38*-01/72			
S11844S	*07/38*-09/72	⊗07/72	**3154**	*07/38*-09/72			
S11845S	*07/38*-01/72	➲975525	**3155**	*07/38*-01/72			

Class 404 4-BUF   Lancing/Eastleigh

Trailer Composite Corridor Lavatory

TCK

S11846S-S11858S

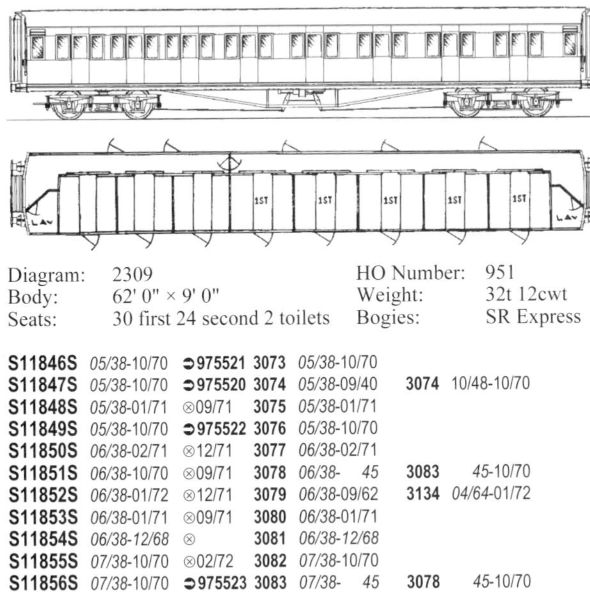

Diagram:	2309	HO Number:	951
Body:	62' 0" × 9' 0"	Weight:	32t 12cwt
Seats:	30 first 24 second 2 toilets	Bogies:	SR Express

S11846S	*05/38*-10/70	➲975521	**3073**	*05/38*-10/70		
S11847S	*05/38*-10/70	➲975520	**3074**	*05/38*-09/40	**3074**	10/48-10/70
S11848S	*05/38*-01/71	⊗09/71	**3075**	*05/38*-01/71		
S11849S	*05/38*-10/70	➲975522	**3076**	*05/38*-10/70		
S11850S	*06/38*-02/71	⊗12/71	**3077**	*06/38*-02/71		
S11851S	*06/38*-10/70	⊗09/71	**3078**	*06/38*- *45*	**3083**	*45*-10/70
S11852S	*06/38*-01/72	⊗12/71	**3079**	*06/38*-09/62	**3134**	*04/64*-01/72
S11853S	*06/38*-01/71	⊗09/71	**3080**	*06/38*-01/71		
S11854S	*06/38*-*12/68*	⊗	**3081**	*06/38*-*12/68*		
S11855S	*07/38*-10/70	⊗02/72	**3082**	*07/38*-10/70		
S11856S	*07/38*-10/70	➲975523	**3083**	*07/38*- *45*	**3078**	*45*-10/70
S11857S	*07/38*-10/70	℗	**3084**	*07/38*-10/70		
S11858S	*07/38*-02/71	⊗09/71	**3085**	*07/38*-02/71		

6-CIT then 4-COR   Lancing/Eastleigh

Trailer Composite Corridor Lavatory

TCK

S11859S

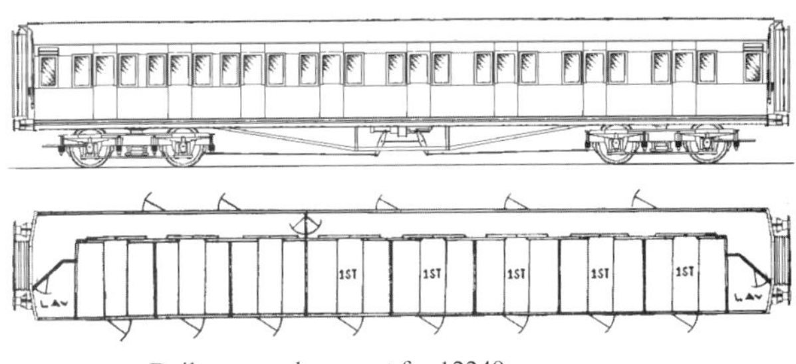

Built as a replacement for 12249.

Diagram:	2309	HO Number:	3079
Body:	62' 0" × 9' 0"	Weight:	32t 12cwt
Seats:	30 first 24 second 2 toilets	Bogies:	SR

S11859S	07/46-05/72	⊗04/73	**3042**	07/46-02/47	**3119**	*02/47*-05/72

Class 404 4-COR   Lancing/Eastleigh

Trailer Composite Corridor Lavatory

TCK

S11860S

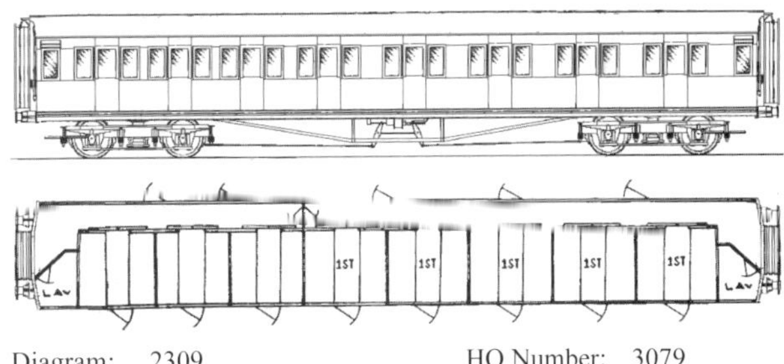

Diagram:	2309	HO Number:	3079
Body:	62' 0" × 9' 0"	Weight:	32t 12cwt
Seats:	30 first 24 second 2 toilets	Bogies:	SR Express

Built as a replacement for 12234 rebuilt as TCK by 1957.

S11860S	10/46-01/72	⊗06/72	**3157**	10/46-01/72

Class 404 4-COR   Lancing/Eastleigh

Trailer Composite Corridor Lavatory

TCK

S11861S

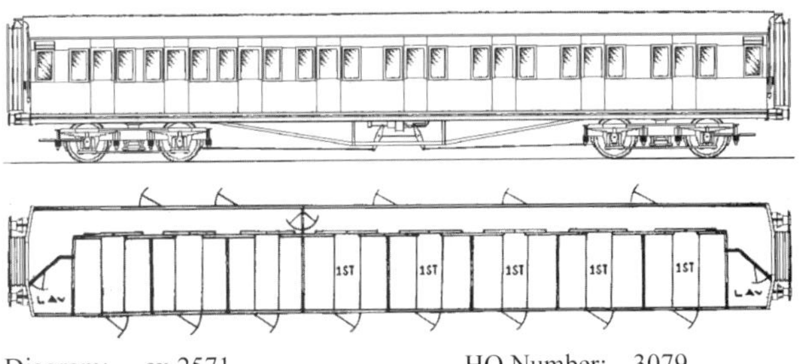

Diagram:	ex 2571	HO Number:	3079
Body:	63' 6" × 9' 0"	Weight:	32t 12cwt
Seats:	30 first 24 second 2 toilets	Bogies:	SR Express

S11861S	10/46-*02/64*	➲**DS70280**	**3158**	10/46-*02/64*	⊗05/68 after use as an office	⊂**12232**

Left: No 305935 was used as an InterCity Instruction unit. It is seen here at York on Sunday 26 April 1987 next to Class 101 DMU 53128. *Adrian White*

Above: DMBSO S61777 is seen heading 4-CEP unit 7195 at Canterbury East. *P. J. Sharpe*

Left: Two Class 309 units cab-to-cab, showing the two different cab window styles. E61946 was built to work in a two-car unit, and as such has the pantograph just behind the front cab, rather than in the centre of the unit for the four-car sets. *Ian Allan Library*

Left: Motor Luggage Van 68001 is seen next to 4-CEP 7124 at Dover Western Docks on 24 August 1979. No 68001 has arrived at the head of a boat train from London, 7124 is waiting to leave on a local service to Faversham. *J. G. Glover*

Below: Class 501 Driving Trailer M75148 is seen at the head of a Richmond service at Broad Street on 24 July 1980. Note the bars on the windows which were a feature of trains on this line, due to some restricted width tunnels. *M. L. Rogers*

Bottom: Driving Trailer E75483 is seen heading AM5 unit number 422 on a Chingford to Liverpool Street service. *P. J. Sharpe*

Top: AM3 DTSO SC75749 in North Clydeside set 039 is seen in its original Caledonian Blue livery. It does not seem to be carrying a unit number this early in its life. *P. J. Sharpe*

Above: S11157S in 4-COR unit 3144 is at Eastleigh on 28 February 1968. *John Scrace*

Left: Many southern units spent time after withdrawal in the yard at Micheldever. Two such units are seen here on 18 May 1963. On the left with the condemned sign attached is S8442S of unit 4338. This had been withdrawn from service in November 1961 and was finally scrapped in January 1964. The other vehicle seen here was luckier. S8143S was part of unit 4308 and was withdrawn in November 1960, but it survived to be preserved as part of the National Collection. *T. F. Williams*

Top: Southern-bodied trailer number S9458S in 4-SUB unit 4323. *G. M. Kichenside*

Above: Trailer third S9475S of 4-SUB unit 4557 is seen at Hampton Court in May 1956. This started its life as LBSCR Crystal Palace trailer 4072, later renumbered 9888. It was converted for dc use in 1930, becoming 9475. *G. M. Kichenside*

Right: This photograph shows a four-car LYR set for the Southport line. The driving vehicles are both 1904 clerestory roofed stock, while the two trailers are from the 1910 curved roof batch. No 3021 (later 28453) is at the head of the unit. *Ian Allan Library*

Top: Southern-bodied trailer number S9595S in 4-SUB unit 4327. *G. M. Kichenside*

Above: Motor vehicle S9815S in unit 4501 (second series) was an LSWR-bodied vehicle, built on the frame of an LBSCR ac electric coach. *G. M. Kichenside*

Left: Class 487 Waterloo & City motor car S52S is seen at Waterloo with a train for Bank on 8 December 1979. *Brian Morrison*

Above: Motor Luggage van 10114 at Coulsdon North. *H. C. Casserley*

Right: A beautiful period photo showing a three-car North Tyneside set, heading towards New Bridge Street. The leading vehicle is clerestory roofed DMT number 3229, one of the original 1904-built vehicles. *Ian Allan Library*

Below: Crystal Palace Driving Motor Brake Third number 3260. This did not carry its allocated SR number 8596, before being converted to dc working as 9281 in 2-T unit 1180 in 1930. *O. J. Morris*

EUSTON
M 28247 M

Above left: M28003 was one of the London area GEC compartment stock motor coaches. It is seen here at Watford on 23 July 1949. *H. C. Casserley*

Left: The London area Oerlikon sets were admired for their comfort and smooth ride. They were open sets, not fitted with the compartments that were usual for commuter stock in those days. M28247M is pictured on a London Euston service. Nos 28247 and 28282 were badly damaged at Euston in 1941 and were rebuilt with flush panelled sides and the later style of guard's doors and four grilles to the equipment compartment. *Ian Allan Library*

Below left: When the Lancaster to Morecambe and Heysham line was rebuilt as a test bed for high voltage ac working, the original LNWR Siemens units from the London area were converted to run on the service. They were known as AM1 units. M28222M is seen with its new pantograph above the cab. *P. J. Sharpe*

Above: M28219M is at Heysham on 6 November 1965. Compare this photograph with that of M28222M. The power compartment has a completely different set of radiator grilles on the side, reflecting that this was very much an experimental conversion. *John Marshall*

Below: The new stock built in 1939-41 to replace older stock on the Southport line was completely different to the earlier stock. In some ways it resembled the new open stock on the Wirral line, with air-operated sliding doors. Motor vehicle M28343M is seen here at Blundellsands & Crosby. *P. J. Sharpe*

Left: When the underground loop line was built in Liverpool city centre in 1977, the stock for the line was rebuilt with through doors to allow passengers to exit from the train in the tube section of the line in an emergency. M28376M is seen at Rock Ferry on 30 October 1984 with a train for Liverpool, showing the end doors. *K. I. Bond*

Above: Lancashire & Yorkshire Railway Driving Motor Brake Third No 3037 was one of the 1906-built carriages built to work the Liverpool-Southport line. It became No 14538 then 28464 in LMS days. This view clearly shows the unique inset doors used on the LYR units. The doors were set in at an angle so that when they opened outwards, they did not extend past the side of the carriage. *BR*

Left: What later became known as the Class 503 stock for the Wirral and Mersey lines, consisted of two identical batches of units built in 1938 and 1956. M28690M of the 1938 batch is seen at Birkenhead North on a Liverpool-bound service. *G. M. Kichenside*

Right: One of the original Bury line units led by motor vehicle M28514 is seen at Bury on 24 April 1951. The Bury line was unique in using a side-contact third rail system, with the power rail protected by wooden planking. *H. C. Casserley*

Below right: The original Bury station was replaced with the new Bury Interchange, where M77165 is seen working on 24 May 1986. *Colin Boocock*

Below: This photograph shows the original Lancaster, Morecambe and Heysham power car number 2236. It later became M28610M It is partnered with one of the 54ft-long trailer vehicles, working as a two-car set. *Ian Allan Library*

24

MORECAMBE (PROM)
M 29023 M
M 29023 M

M 29212 M

Left: Another of the Dingle sets is seen here on the Lancashire & Yorkshire section led by car No 1008 (later 28697). *Ian Allan Library*

Centre left: AM1 trailer M29023M is seen here at Morecambe. *P. J. Sharpe*

Below left: On 1 February 1964 withdrawn Bury line trailer M29212M was to be seen at Horwich works in use as a workman's hut. *John R. Hillier*

Right: This view, taken at the Liverpool Overhead Railway's Pier Head station, shows one of the Dingle units built by the Lancashire & Yorkshire Railway for through working to the Southport line. *J. B. Horne*

Right: The Southport stock later became known as Class 502. Driving trailer M29888M is seen here at Hall Road working the 15.50 Liverpool Central to Southport train on 8 June 1977. *D. A. Idle*

Below: A three-car Lancaster, Morecambe and Heysham unit is shown here with the power car flanked by two trailers. The leading vehicle is Midland Railway trailer number 01174, which was used on the line for a while before the Grouping. *Ian Allan Library*

Above: Metropolitan-Cammell-built North Tyneside 'A type' articulated unit with E29101E leading. *P. J. Sharpe*

Left: The pantograph end of a Class 506 unit is seen in this view of M59401M at Broadbottom on 26 April 1980. These units always carried an M suffix to the numbers where an E suffix would have been more appropriate. *Keith Smith*

Bolow: As part of the 1937 order for articulated units from Metropolitan-Cammell, four single vehicles were ordered, including this Motor Luggage Van. E29468E is seen at Manors on 28 May 1962 heading from Newcastle towards Jesmond. *M. Mensing*

Right: A Class 506 unit headed by driving trailer M59607M is seen ready to depart from Manchester Piccadilly on a service to Hadfield on 23 August 1980. These LNER-designed units were almost identical to the unrebuilt Shenfield units (later Class 306) working the lines out of Liverpool Street. *Peter Harris*

Below: When the Class 306 units were rebuilt the pantograph was relocated on the intermediate trailer vehicle. GE65401 carries the short-lived GE prefix used on the Great Eastern line in the early sixties. These vehicles never carried the E suffix which would have been appropriate for vehicles numbered in the LNER series. *P. J. Sharpe*

Right: The Tyneside 1920-22 stock was built to replace the units destroyed in the Heaton car-shed fire in 1918. They took the numbers of the earlier stock, but were clearly distinguishable by the elliptical roofs rather than the clerestory roofs of the earlier stock. No 23785 is seen at the head of a train formed of the new stock. It finished its life numbered E29386E. *LNER*

6-CIT Lancing/Eastleigh

Trailer Composite Corridor Lavatory
TCK
S11862S-S11867S

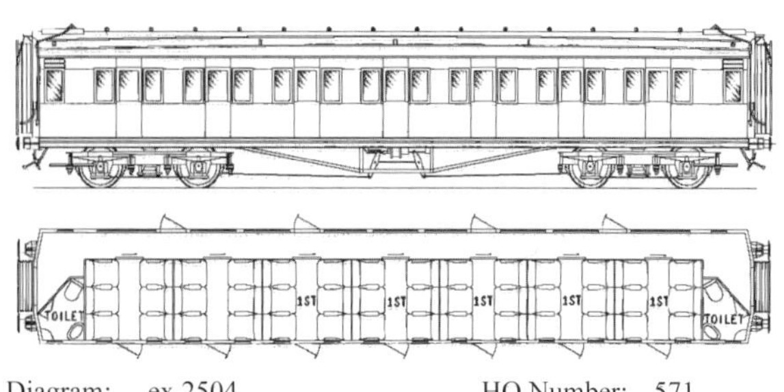

Diagram:	ex 2504	HO Number:	571
Body:	59' 0" × 9' 0"	Weight:	34t
Seats:	30 first 12 third 2 toilets	Bogies:	SR

Two compartments derated from first.

S11862S	04/47-06/68	⊗	**3041**	04/47-06/68	⊂12255
S11863S	04/47-06/66	⊗	**3041**	04/47-03/66	⊂12256
S11864S	12/47-09/65	⊗	**3042**	12/47-09/65	⊂12258
S11865S	12/47-09/65	⊗	**3042**	12/47-09/65	⊂12257
S11866S	12/47-03/66	⊗	**3043**	12/47-03/66	⊂12251
S11867S	12/47-03/66	⊗	**3043**	12/47-03/66	⊂12252

4-LAV Eastleigh

Trailer Composite Lavatory
TCL
S11999S-S12000S

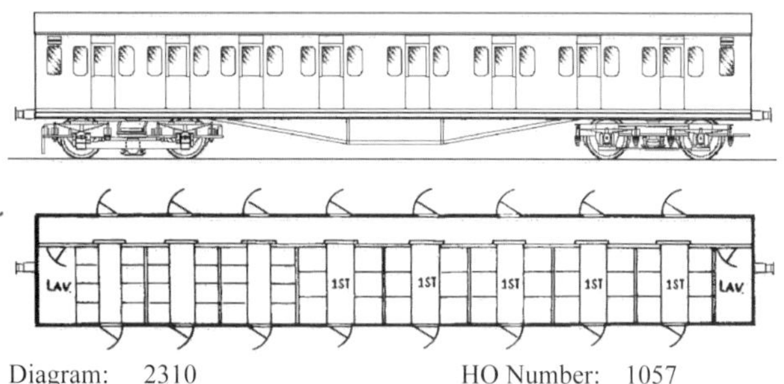

Diagram:	2310	HO Number:	1057
Body:	62' 0" × 9' 0"	Weight:	30t
Seats:	30 first 24 second 2 toilets	Bogies:	SR Suburban

S11999S	02/40-05/68	⊗03/75	**2954**	02/40-05/68
S12000S	05/40-07/68	⊗07/72	**2955**	05/40-07/68

4-LAV Lancing/Eastleigh

Trailer Composite Lavatory
TCL
S12001S-S12033S

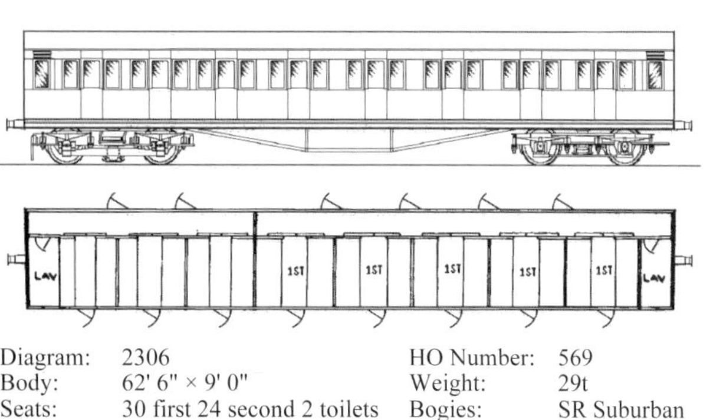

Diagram:	2306	HO Number:	569
Body:	62' 6" × 9' 0"	Weight:	29t
Seats:	30 first 24 second 2 toilets	Bogies:	SR Suburban

S12001S	08/31-09/61	⊗	**1926**	08/31-01/37	**2926**	01/37-10/47	**2926**	02/48-09/61
S12002S	07/31-01/68	⊗03/68	**1921**	07/31-01/37	**2921**	01/37-01/68		
S12003S	07/31-02/68	⊗10/68	**1925**	07/31-01/37	**2925**	01/37-02/68		
S12004S	07/31-04/68	⊗12/68	**1922**	07/31-01/37	**2922**	01/37-04/68		
S12005S	07/31-05/69	⊗ 69	**1924**	07/31-01/37	**2924**	01/37-05/69		
S12006S	08/31-02/68	⊗05/68	**1927**	08/31-01/37	**2927**	01/37-02/68		
S12007S	08/31-01/68	⊗08/68	**1929**	08/31-01/37	**2929**	01/37-01/68		
S12008S	08/31-03/68	⊗04/68	**1930**	08/31-01/37	**2930**	01/37-03/68		
S12009S	10/31-07/68	⊗12/68	**1937**	10/31-01/37	**2937**	01/37-07/68		
S12010S	09/31-02/68	⊗03/68	**1932**	09/31-01/37	**2932**	01/37-02/68		
S12011S	09/31-01/68	⊗03/68	**1934**	09/31-01/37	**2934**	01/37-01/68		
S12012S	08/31-02/69	⊗07/69	**1928**	08/31-01/37	**2928**	01/37-02/69		
S12013S	07/31-10/68	⊗	**1923**	07/31-01/37	**2923**	01/37-10/68		
S12014S	09/31-01/68	⊗10/68	**1935**	09/31-01/37	**2935**	01/37-01/68		
S12015S	10/31-02/69	⊗07/69	**1939**	10/31-01/37	**2939**	01/37-02/69		
S12016S	09/31-07/68	⊗11/68	**1933**	09/31-01/37	**2933**	01/37-07/68		
S12017S	10/31-01/68	⊗03/68	**1938**	10/31-01/37	**2938**	01/37-01/68		
S12018S	10/31-02/68	⊗03/68	**1940**	10/31-01/37	**2940**	01/37-02/68		
S12019S	10/31-03/68	⊗10/68	**1936**	10/31-01/37	**2936**	01/37-03/68		
S12020S	09/31-03/68	⊗05/68	**1931**	09/31-01/37	**2931**	01/37-03/68		
S12021S	10/31-12/67	⊗03/68	**1941**	10/31-01/37	**2941**	01/37-12/67		
S12022S	11/31-05/68	⊗	**1942**	11/31-01/37	**2942**	01/37-05/68		
S12023S	12/31-05/68	⊗10/68	**1943**	12/31-01/37	**2943**	01/37-05/68		
S12024S	01/32-02/68	⊗10/68	**1944**	01/32-01/37	**2944**	01/37-02/68		
S12025S	01/32-01/68	⊗10/68	**1945**	01/32-01/37	**2945**	01/37-01/68		
S12026S	02/32-03/68	⊗10/68	**1946**	02/32-01/37	**2946**	01/37-03/68		
S12027S	03/32-05/68	⊗10/68	**1947**	03/32-01/37	**2947**	01/37-05/68		
S12028S	04/32-05/68	⊗03/68	**1948**	04/32-01/37	**2948**	01/37-05/68		
S12029S	05/32-02/69	⊗08/69	**1949**	05/32-01/37	**2949**	01/37-02/69		
S12030S	06/32-02/69	⊗08/69	**1950**	06/32-01/37	**2950**	01/37-02/69		
S12031S	07/32-05/68	⊗03/68	**1951**	07/32-01/37	**2951**	01/37-05/68		
S12032S	08/32-03/68	⊗08/68	**1952**	08/32-01/37	**2952**	01/37-03/68		
S12033S	09/32-01/68	⊗03/68	**1953**	09/32-01/37	**2953**	01/37-01/68		

Class 401 2-BIL Lancing/Eastleigh

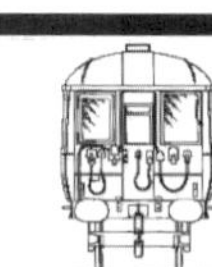

Driving Trailer Composite Lavatory
DTCL
S12034S-S12069S

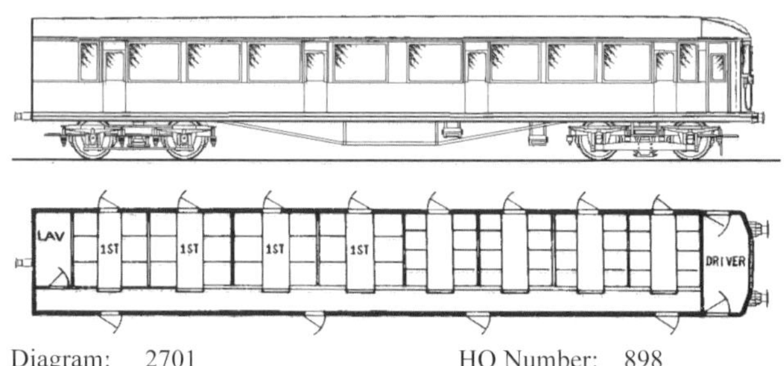

Diagram:	2701	HO Number:	898
Body:	62' 6" × 9' 0"	Weight:	31t 5cwt
Seats:	24 first 32 second 1 toilet	Bogies:	SR Suburban

S12034S	08/36-11/70	⊗09/71	**1901**	08/36-01/37	**2011**	01/37-11/70		
S12035S	08/36-09/69	⊗10/70	**1902**	08/36-01/37	**2012**	01/37-09/69		
S12036S	08/36-09/69	⊗11/69	**1903**	08/36-01/37	**2013**	01/37-09/69		
12037	08/36-05/43	↪**12855**	**1904**	08/36-01/37	**2014**	01/37-05/43		
S12038S	08/36-05/69	⊗09/69	**1905**	08/36-01/37	**2015**	01/37-05/69		
S12039S	08/36-07/71	⊗03/72	**1906**	08/36-01/37	**2016**	01/37-07/71		
S12040S	08/36-10/70	⊗05/71	**1907**	08/36-01/37	**2017**	01/37-10/70		
S12041S	08/36-04/69	⊗02/70	**1908**	08/36-01/37	**2018**	01/37-04/69		
S12042S	09/36-01/70	⊗04/70	**1909**	09/36-01/37	**2019**	01/37-01/70		
S12043S	09/36-05/69	⊗09/69	**1910**	09/36-01/37	**2020**	01/37-05/69		
S12044S	09/36-06/70	⊗01/71	**1911**	09/36-01/37	**2021**	01/37-06/70		
S12045S	09/36-11/70	⊗07/71	**1912**	09/36-01/37	**2022**	01/37-11/70		
S12046S	09/36-09/69	⊗12/69	**1913**	09/36-01/37	**2023**	01/37-09/69		
S12047S	09/36-04/71	⊗09/71	**1914**	09/36-01/37	**2024**	01/37-04/71		
S12048S	09/36-11/70	⊗09/71	**1915**	09/36-01/37	**2025**	01/37-11/70		
S12049S	10/36-02/70	⊗09/70	**1916**	10/36-01/37	**2026**	01/37-02/70		
S12050S	10/36-11/70	⊗05/71	**1917**	10/36-01/37	**2027**	01/37-11/70		
S12051S	10/36-10/69	⊗10/70	**1918**	10/36-01/37	**2028**	01/37-10/66	**2626**	01/67-10/69
S12052S	10/36-04/69	⊗09/69	**1919**	10/36-01/37	**2029**	01/37-08/51	**2008**	08/51-04/69
S12053S	10/36-09/69	⊗10/70	**1920**	10/36-01/37	**2030**	01/37-09/69		
S12054S	10/36-01/70	⊗05/70	**1954**	10/36-01/37	**2031**	01/37-01/70		
S12055S	10/36-04/71	⊗09/71	**1955**	10/36-01/37	**2032**	01/37-04/71		
S12056S	11/36-04/71	⊗09/71	**1956**	11/36-01/37	**2033**	01/37-04/71		
S12057S	11/36-07/71	⊗04/72	**1957**	11/36-01/37	**2034**	01/37-07/71		
S12058S	11/36-01/70	⊗06/70	**1958**	11/36-01/37	**2035**	01/37-01/70		
S12059S	11/36-06/71	⊗01/72	**1959**	11/36-01/37	**2036**	01/37-06/71		
S12060S	11/36-02/70	⊃DS70322	**1960**	11/36-01/37	**2037**	01/37-02/70		
S12061S	11/36-11/70	⊗09/71	**1961**	11/36-01/37	**2038**	01/37-11/70		
S12062S	11/36-12/69	⊗05/70	**1962**	11/36-01/37	**2039**	01/37-12/69		
S12063S	12/36-09/69	⊗03/70	**1963**	12/36-01/37	**2040**	01/37-09/69		
S12064S	12/36-04/69	⊗05/69	**1964**	12/36-01/37	**2041**	01/37-04/69		
S12065S	12/36-06/69	⊗11/69	**1965**	12/36-01/37	**2042**	01/37-06/69		
S12066S	12/36-10/70	⊗04/71	**1966**	12/36-01/37	**2043**	01/37-10/70		
S12067S	12/36-02/69	⊗05/69	**1967**	12/36-01/37	**2044**	01/37-02/69		
S12068S	12/36-10/70	⊗05/71	**1968**	12/36-01/37	**2045**	01/37-10/70		
S12069S	12/36-01/70	⊗04/70	**1969**	12/36-01/37	**2046**	01/37-01/70		

Class 401 2-BIL Lancing/Eastleigh
Driving Trailer Composite Lavatory
DTCL
S12070S-S12071S

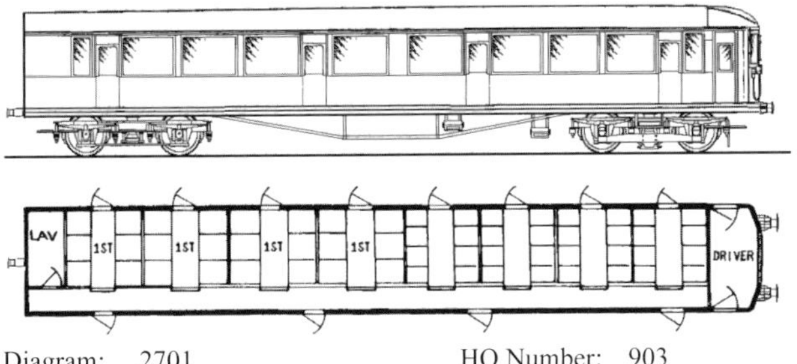

Diagram:	2701	HO Number:	903
Body:	62' 6" × 9' 0"	Weight:	31t 5cwt
Seats:	24 first 32 second 1 toilet	Bogies:	SR Suburban

S12070S	12/36-01/70	⊗04/70	**1070**	12/36-01/37	**2047**	01/37-01/70
S12071S	01/37-01/70	⊗06/70	**1971**	01/37-01/37	**2048**	01/37-01/70

Class 401 2-BIL Lancing/Eastleigh
Driving Trailer Composite Lavatory
DTCL
S12072S-S12100S

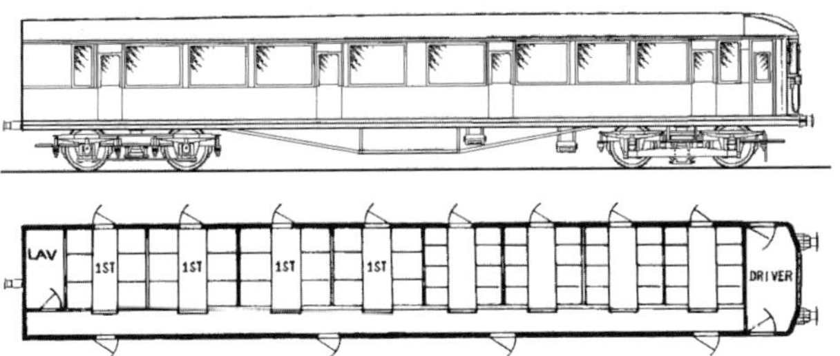

Diagram:	2701	HO Number:	949
Body:	62' 6" × 9' 0"	Weight:	31t 5cwt
Seats:	24 first 32 second 1 toilet	Bogies:	SR Suburban

S12072S	*06/37-08/69*	⊗10/69	**2049**	*06/37-08/69*				
S12073S	*06/37-11/70*	⊗09/71	**2050**	*06/37-11/70*				
S12074S	*06/37-06/70*	⊗09/70	**2051**	*06/37-06/70*				
S12075S	*06/37-06/70*	⊗01/71	**2052**	*06/37-06/70*				
S12076S	*06/37-02/70*	⊗08/70	**2053**	*06/37-02/70*				
S12077S	*06/37-02/70*	⊗08/70	**2054**	*06/37-02/70*				
S12078S	*06/37-07/68*	⊗ 69	**2055**	*06/37-07/68*				
12079	*06/37-12/46*	⊗12/46	**2056**	*06/37-12/46*				
S12080S	*06/37-01/71*	⊗07/71	**2057**	*06/37-01/71*				
S12081S	*07/37-04/71*	⊗09/71	**2058**	*07/37-04/71*				
S12082S	*07/37-10/66*	⊗04/70	**2059**	*07/37-10/66*				
S12083S	*07/37-02/70*	⊗	**2060**	*07/37-02/70*				
S12084S	*07/37-02/70*	⊗08/70	**2061**	*07/37-02/70*				
S12085S	*07/37-05/71*	⊗11/71	**2062**	*07/37-05/71*				
S12086S	*07/37-01/70*	⊗04/70	**2063**	*07/37-01/70*				
S12087S	*07/37-10/70*	⊗07/71	**2064**	*07/37-10/70*				
S12088S	*07/37-02/70*	⊗10/70	**2065**	*07/37-02/70*				
S12089S	*07/37-06/70*	⊗08/70	**2066**	*07/37-06/70*				
S12090S	*07/37-04/71*	⊗09/71	**2067**	*07/37-04/71*				
S12091S	*08/37-10/70*	⊗04/71	**2068**	*08/37-10/70*				
S12092	*08/37-08/51*	⊗08/51	**2069**	*08/37-08/51*				
S12093S	*08/37-02/70*	⊗10/70	**2070**	*08/37-06/56*	**2601**	06/56-08/57	**2070**	08/57-02/70
S12094S	*08/37-06/69*	⊗03/70	**2071**	*08/37-06/69*				
S12095S	*08/37-04/71*	⊗09/71	**2072**	*08/37-04/71*				
S12096S	*08/37-09/69*	⊗03/70	**2073**	*08/37-09/69*				
S12097S	*08/37-04/71*	⊗09/71	**2074**	*08/37-04/71*				
S12098S	*08/37-10/70*	⊗04/71	**2075**	*08/37-10/70*				
S12099S	*08/37-09/69*	⊗12/69	**2076**	*08/37-09/69*				
S12100S	*08/37-09/69*	⊗01/70	**2077**	*08/37-09/69*				

Class 401 2-BIL Lancing/Eastleigh
Driving Trailer Composite Lavatory
DTCL
S12101S

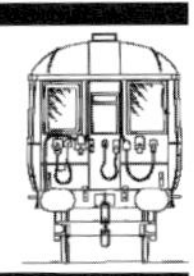

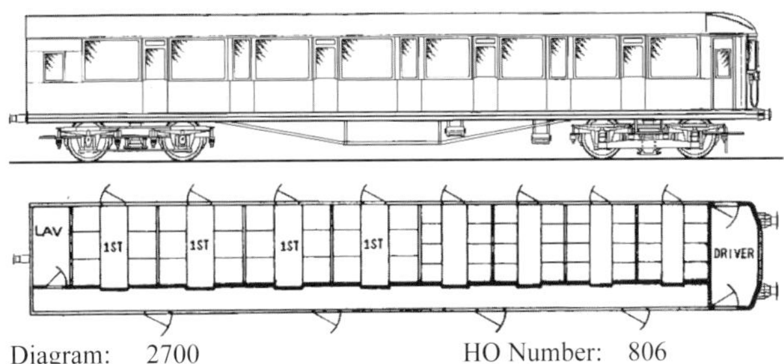

Diagram:	2700	HO Number:	806
Body:	62' 6" × 9' 0"	Weight:	31t 5cwt
Seats:	24 first 32 second 1 toilet	Bogies:	SR Suburban

S12101S	02/35-12/69	⊗05/70	**1900**	02/35-01/36	**1890**	01/36-01/37	**2010**	01/37-07/68
			2096	07/69-12/69				

Class 401 2-BIL Lancing/Eastleigh
Driving Trailer Composite Lavatory
DTCL
S12102S-S12110S

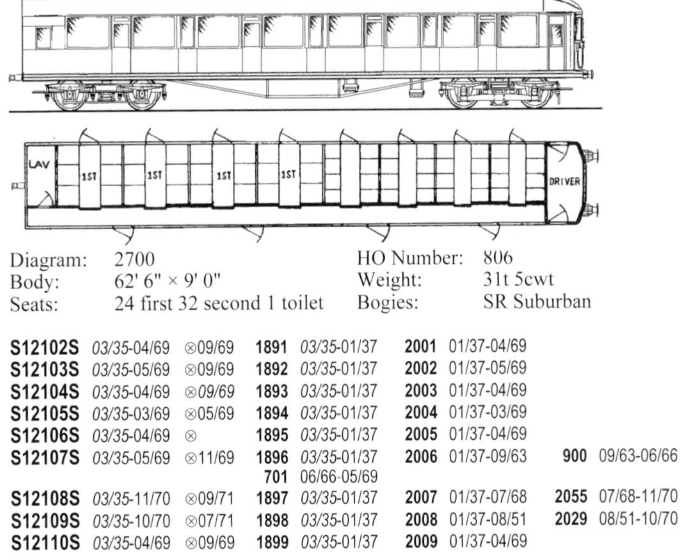

Diagram:	2700	HO Number:	806
Body:	62' 6" × 9' 0"	Weight:	31t 5cwt
Seats:	24 first 32 second 1 toilet	Bogies:	SR Suburban

S12102S	*03/35-04/69*	⊗09/69	**1891**	*03/35-01/37*	**2001**	01/37-04/69		
S12103S	*03/35-05/69*	⊗09/69	**1892**	*03/35-01/37*	**2002**	01/37-05/69		
S12104S	*03/35-04/69*	*⊗09/69*	**1893**	*03/35-01/37*	**2003**	01/37-04/69		
S12105S	*03/35-03/69*	⊗05/69	**1894**	*03/35-01/37*	**2004**	01/37-03/69		
S12106S	*03/35-04/69*	⊗	**1895**	*03/35-01/37*	**2005**	01/37-04/69		
S12107S	*03/35-05/69*	⊗11/69	**1896**	*03/35-01/37*	**2006**	01/37-09/63	**900**	09/63-06/66
			701	06/66-05/69				
S12108S	*03/35-11/70*	⊗09/71	**1897**	*03/35-01/37*	**2007**	01/37-07/68	**2055**	07/68-11/70
S12109S	*03/35-10/70*	⊗07/71	**1898**	*03/35-01/37*	**2008**	01/37-08/51	**2029**	08/51-10/70
S12110S	*03/35-04/69*	⊗09/69	**1899**	*03/35-01/37*	**2009**	01/37-04/69		

Class 401 2-BIL Lancing/Eastleigh
Driving Trailer Composite Lavatory
DTCL
S12111S-S12149S

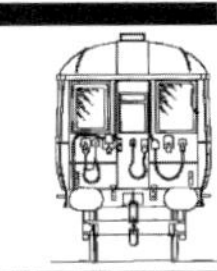

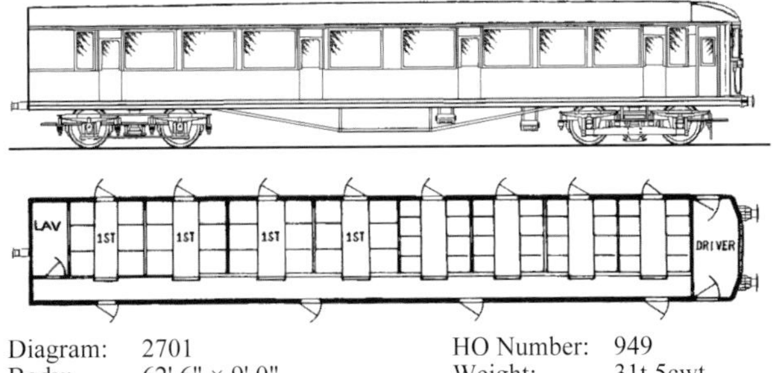

Diagram:	2701	HO Number:	949
Body:	62' 6" × 9' 0"	Weight:	31t 5cwt
Seats:	24 first 32 second 1 toilet	Bogies:	SR

S12111S	*09/37-01/71*	⊗05/71	**2078**	*09/37-01/71*
S12112S	*09/37-07/69*	⊗10/69	**2079**	*09/37-07/69*
S12113S	*09/37-05/69*	⊗09/69	**2080**	*09/37-05/69*
S12114S	*09/37-01/71*	⊗05/71	**2081**	*09/37-01/71*
S12115S	*09/37-06/70*	⊗09/70	**2082**	*09/37-06/70*

S12116S	09/37-01/71	⊗12/71	**2083**	09/37-01/71				
S12117S	09/37-01/71	⊗12/71	**2084**	09/37-01/71				
S12118S	09/37-12/69	⊗05/70	**2085**	09/37-12/69				
S12119S	09/37-05/71	⊗11/71	**2086**	09/37-05/71				
S12120S	09/37-09/70	⊗11/70	**2087**	09/37-09/70				
S12121	10/37- 50	↳**12854**	**2088**	10/37- 50				
S12122S	10/37-10/69	⊗02/70	**2089**	10/37-10/69				
S12123S	10/37-08/71	Ⓟ	**2090**	10/37-08/71				
S12124S	10/37-10/69	⊗	**2091**	10/37-10/69				
S12125S	10/37-02/69	⊗05/69	**2092**	10/37-02/69				
S12126S	10/37-09/69	⊗02/70	**2093**	10/37-09/69				
S12127S	10/37-09/69	⊗11/69	**2094**	10/37-09/69				
S12128S	10/37-02/70	⊗06/70	**2095**	10/37-02/70				
S12129S	10/37-07/69	⊗11/69	**2096**	10/37-07/69				
S12130S	10/37-09/69	⊗11/69	**2097**	10/37-09/69				
S12131S	11/37-06/71	⊗04/72	**2098**	11/37-06/71				
S12132S	11/37-04/71	⊗09/71	**2099**	11/37-04/71				
S12133	11/37-08/51	↳**12856**	**2100**	11/37-08/51				
S12134S	11/37-05/71	⊗11/71	**2101**	11/37-05/71				
12135	11/37-08/40	⊗08/40	**2102**	11/37-08/40				
S12136S	11/37-11/70	⊗05/71	**2103**	11/37-11/70				
S12137S	11/37-05/71	⊗06/72	**2104**	11/37-05/71				
S12138S	11/37-09/65	⊗09/65	**2105**	11/37-09/65				
S12139S	11/37-02/69	⊗05/69	**2106**	11/37-02/69				
S12140S	11/37-09/69	⊗11/69	**2107**	11/37-09/69				
S12141S	12/37-08/69	⊗10/69	**2108**	12/37-08/69				
S12142S	12/37-06/69	⊗10/69	**2109**	12/37-06/69				
S12143S	12/37-03/70	⊗06/70	**2110**	12/37-03/70				
S12144S	12/37-01/71	⊗01/72	**2111**	12/37-01/71				
S12145S	12/37-01/71	⊗12/71	**2112**	12/37-01/71				
S12146S	12/37-02/71	⊗04/71	**2113**	12/37-09/59	**2611**	09/59-03/62	**2113**	03/62-02/71
S12147S	12/37-11/70	⊗07/71	**2114**	12/37-11/70				
S12148S	12/37-10/69	⊗02/70	**2115**	12/37-10/69				
S12149S	12/37-09/70	⊗11/70	**2116**	12/37-09/70				

Class 401 2-BIL Lancing/Eastleigh

Driving Trailer Composite Lavatory
DTCL
S12150S-S12185S

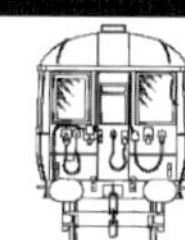

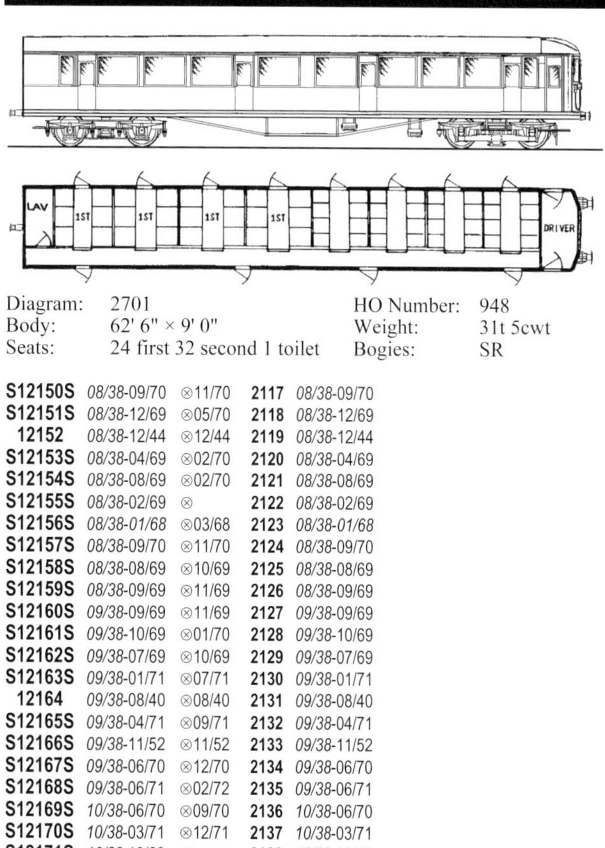

Diagram:	2701	HO Number:	948
Body:	62' 6" × 9' 0"	Weight:	31t 5cwt
Seats:	24 first 32 second 1 toilet	Bogies:	SR

S12150S	08/38-09/70	⊗11/70	**2117**	08/38-09/70
S12151S	08/38-12/69	⊗05/70	**2118**	08/38-12/69
12152	08/38-12/44	⊗12/44	**2119**	08/38-12/44
S12153S	08/38-04/69	⊗02/70	**2120**	08/38-04/69
S12154S	08/38-08/69	⊗02/70	**2121**	08/38-08/69
S12155S	08/38-02/69	⊗	**2122**	08/38-02/69
S12156S	08/38-01/68	⊗03/68	**2123**	08/38-01/68
S12157S	08/38-09/70	⊗11/70	**2124**	08/38-09/70
S12158S	08/38-08/69	⊗10/69	**2125**	08/38-08/69
S12159S	08/38-09/69	⊗11/69	**2126**	08/38-09/69
S12160S	09/38-09/69	⊗11/69	**2127**	09/38-09/69
S12161S	09/38-10/69	⊗01/70	**2128**	09/38-10/69
S12162S	09/38-07/69	⊗10/69	**2129**	09/38-07/69
S12163S	09/38-01/71	⊗07/71	**2130**	09/38-01/71
12164	09/38-08/40	⊗08/40	**2131**	09/38-08/40
S12165S	09/38-04/71	⊗09/71	**2132**	09/38-04/71
S12166S	09/38-11/52	⊗11/52	**2133**	09/38-11/52
S12167S	09/38-06/70	⊗12/70	**2134**	09/38-06/70
S12168S	09/38-06/71	⊗02/72	**2135**	09/38-06/71
S12169S	10/38-06/70	⊗09/70	**2136**	10/38-06/70
S12170S	10/38-03/71	⊗12/71	**2137**	10/38-03/71
S12171S	10/38-10/69	⊗	**2138**	10/38-10/69
S12172S	10/38-01/71	⊗12/71	**2139**	10/38-01/71
S12173S	10/38-08/71	⊗02/72	**2140**	10/38-08/71
S12174S	10/38-01/71	⊗12/71	**2141**	10/38-01/71
S12175S	10/38-05/69	⊗09/69	**2142**	10/38-05/69
S12176S	10/38-07/69	⊗10/69	**2143**	10/38-07/69
S12177S	10/38-10/69	⊗02/70	**2144**	10/38-10/69
S12178S	11/38-01/70	⊗05/70	**2145**	11/38-01/70
S12179S	11/38-01/71	⊗07/71	**2146**	11/38-01/71
S12180S	11/38-03/71	⊗11/71	**2147**	11/38-03/71
S12181S	11/38-05/69	⊗	**2148**	11/38-05/69
S12182S	11/38-10/69	⊗	**2149**	11/38-10/69
S12183S	11/38-09/70	⊗07/71	**2150**	11/38-09/70
S12184S	11/38-02/70	⊗10/70	**2151**	11/38-02/70
S12185S	11/38-02/70	⊗10/70	**2152**	11/38-02/70

Class 402 2-HAL Lancing/Eastleigh

Driving Trailer Composite Lavatory
DTCL
S12186S-S12231S

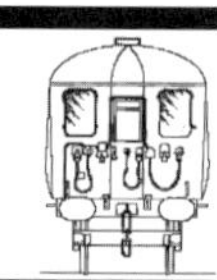

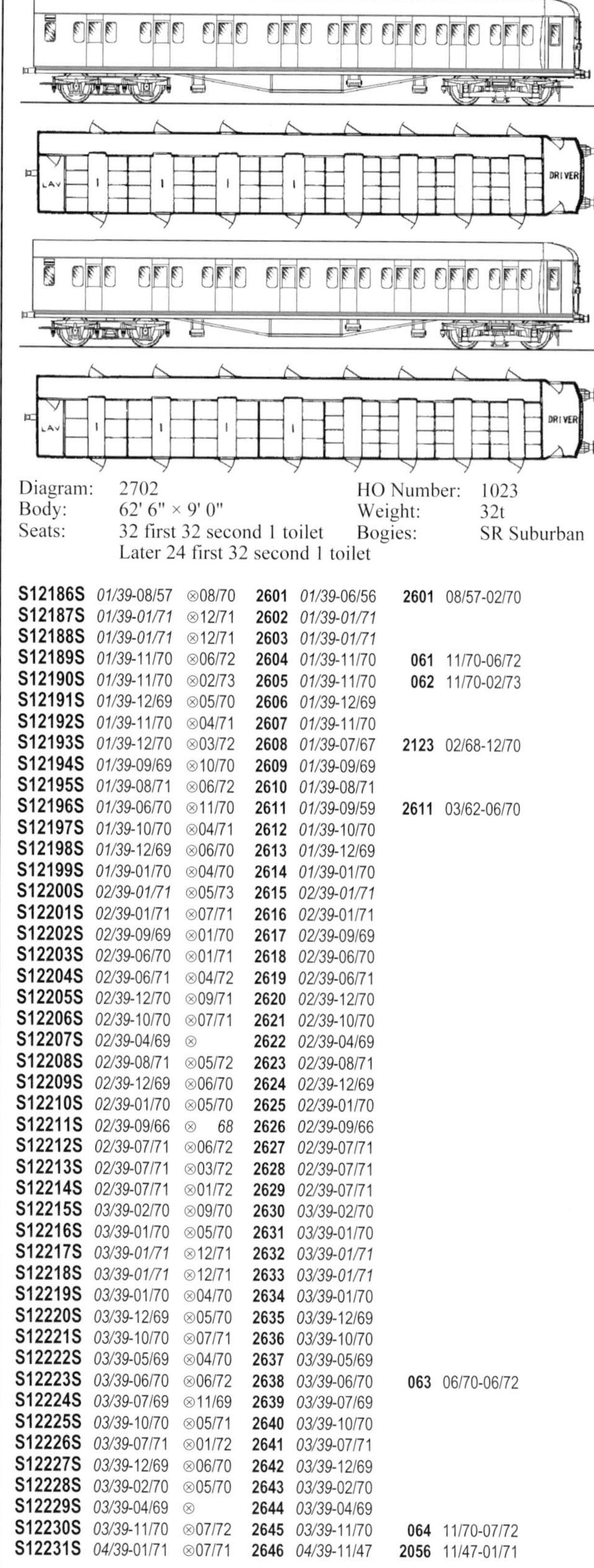

Diagram:	2702	HO Number:	1023
Body:	62' 6" × 9' 0"	Weight:	32t
Seats:	32 first 32 second 1 toilet	Bogies:	SR Suburban
	Later 24 first 32 second 1 toilet		

S12186S	01/39-08/57	⊗08/70	**2601**	01/39-06/56	**2601**	08/57-02/70
S12187S	01/39-01/71	⊗12/71	**2602**	01/39-01/71		
S12188S	01/39-01/71	⊗12/71	**2603**	01/39-01/71		
S12189S	01/39-11/70	⊗06/72	**2604**	01/39-11/70	**061**	11/70-06/72
S12190S	01/39-11/70	⊗02/73	**2605**	01/39-11/70	**062**	11/70-02/73
S12191S	01/39-12/69	⊗05/70	**2606**	01/39-12/69		
S12192S	01/39-11/70	⊗04/71	**2607**	01/39-11/70		
S12193S	01/39-12/70	⊗03/72	**2608**	01/39-07/67	**2123**	02/68-12/70
S12194S	01/39-09/69	⊗10/70	**2609**	01/39-09/69		
S12195S	01/39-08/71	⊗06/72	**2610**	01/39-08/71		
S12196S	01/39-06/70	⊗11/70	**2611**	01/39-09/59	**2611**	03/62-06/70
S12197S	01/39-10/70	⊗04/71	**2612**	01/39-10/70		
S12198S	01/39-12/69	⊗06/70	**2613**	01/39-12/69		
S12199S	01/39-01/70	⊗04/70	**2614**	01/39-01/70		
S12200S	02/39-01/71	⊗05/73	**2615**	02/39-01/71		
S12201S	02/39-01/71	⊗07/71	**2616**	02/39-01/71		
S12202S	02/39-09/69	⊗01/70	**2617**	02/39-09/69		
S12203S	02/39-06/70	⊗01/71	**2618**	02/39-06/70		
S12204S	02/39-06/71	⊗04/72	**2619**	02/39-06/71		
S12205S	02/39-12/70	⊗09/71	**2620**	02/39-12/70		
S12206S	02/39-10/70	⊗07/71	**2621**	02/39-10/70		
S12207S	02/39-04/69	⊗	**2622**	02/39-04/69		
S12208S	02/39-08/71	⊗05/72	**2623**	02/39-08/71		
S12209S	02/39-12/69	⊗06/70	**2624**	02/39-12/69		
S12210S	02/39-01/70	⊗05/70	**2625**	02/39-01/70		
S12211S	02/39-09/66	⊗ 68	**2626**	02/39-09/66		
S12212S	02/39-07/71	⊗06/72	**2627**	02/39-07/71		
S12213S	02/39-07/71	⊗03/72	**2628**	02/39-07/71		
S12214S	02/39-07/71	⊗01/72	**2629**	02/39-07/71		
S12215S	03/39-02/70	⊗09/70	**2630**	03/39-02/70		
S12216S	03/39-01/70	⊗05/70	**2631**	03/39-01/70		
S12217S	03/39-01/71	⊗12/71	**2632**	03/39-01/71		
S12218S	03/39-01/71	⊗12/71	**2633**	03/39-01/71		
S12219S	03/39-01/70	⊗04/70	**2634**	03/39-01/70		
S12220S	03/39-12/69	⊗05/70	**2635**	03/39-12/69		
S12221S	03/39-10/70	⊗07/71	**2636**	03/39-10/70		
S12222S	03/39-05/69	⊗04/70	**2637**	03/39-05/69		
S12223S	03/39-06/70	⊗06/72	**2638**	03/39-06/70	**063**	06/70-06/72
S12224S	03/39-07/69	⊗11/69	**2639**	03/39-07/69		
S12225S	03/39-10/70	⊗05/71	**2640**	03/39-10/70		
S12226S	03/39-07/71	⊗01/72	**2641**	03/39-07/71		
S12227S	03/39-12/69	⊗06/70	**2642**	03/39-12/69		
S12228S	03/39-02/70	⊗05/70	**2643**	03/39-02/70		
S12229S	03/39-04/69	⊗	**2644**	03/39-04/69		
S12230S	03/39-11/70	⊗07/72	**2645**	03/39-11/70	**064**	11/70-07/72
S12231S	04/39-01/71	⊗07/71	**2646**	04/39-11/47	**2056**	11/47-01/71

Class 404 4-RES Metropolitan-Cammell

Trailer Restaurant First
TFRK
12232-S12250S

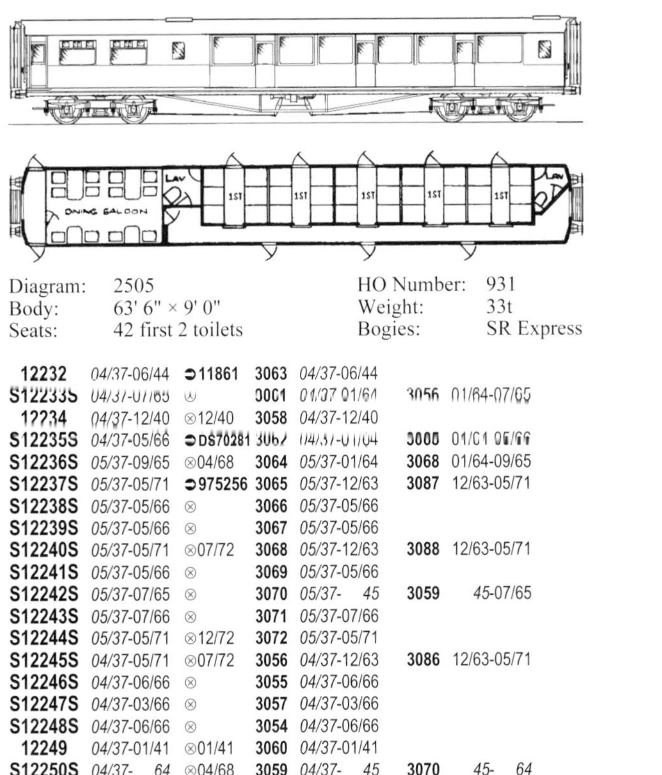

Diagram:	2505	HO Number:	931
Body:	63' 6" × 9' 0"	Weight:	33t
Seats:	42 first 2 toilets	Bogies:	SR Express

12232	04/37-06/44	➲11861	**3063**	04/37-06/44		
S12233S	04/37-07/65	⊗	**3061**	04/37-01/64	**3056**	01/64-07/65
12234	04/37-12/40	⊗12/40	**3058**	04/37-12/40		
S12235S	04/37-05/66	➲DS70281	**3062**	04/37-01/64	**3066**	01/64-05/66
S12236S	05/37-09/65	⊗04/68	**3064**	05/37-01/64	**3068**	01/64-09/65
S12237S	05/37-05/71	➲975256	**3065**	05/37-12/63	**3087**	12/63-05/71
S12238S	05/37-05/66	⊗	**3066**	05/37-05/66		
S12239S	05/37-05/66	⊗	**3067**	05/37-05/66		
S12240S	05/37-05/71	⊗07/72	**3068**	05/37-12/63	**3088**	12/63-05/71
S12241S	05/37-05/66	⊗	**3069**	05/37-05/66		
S12242S	05/37-07/65	⊗	**3070**	05/37- 45	**3059**	45-07/65
S12243S	05/37-07/66	⊗	**3071**	05/37-07/66		
S12244S	05/37-05/71	⊗12/72	**3072**	05/37-05/71		
S12245S	04/37-05/71	⊗07/72	**3056**	04/37-12/63	**3086**	12/63-05/71
S12246S	04/37-06/66	⊗	**3055**	04/37-06/66		
S12247S	04/37-03/66	⊗	**3057**	04/37-03/66		
S12248S	04/37-06/66	⊗	**3054**	04/37-06/66		
12249	04/37-01/41	⊗01/41	**3060**	04/37-01/41		
S12250S	04/37- 64	⊗04/68	**3059**	04/37- 45	**3070**	45- 64

6-CIT Lancing/Eastleigh

Trailer First Corridor
TFK
12251-12259

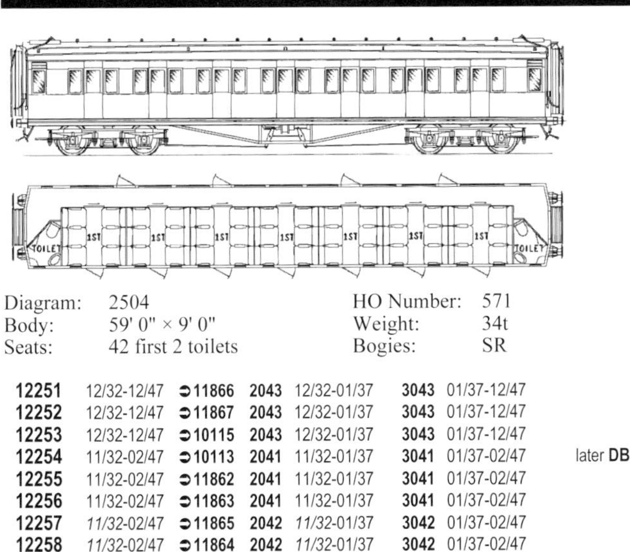

Diagram:	2504	HO Number:	571
Body:	59' 0" × 9' 0"	Weight:	34t
Seats:	42 first 2 toilets	Bogies:	SR

12251	12/32-12/47	➲11866	**2043**	12/32-01/37	**3043**	01/37-12/47	
12252	12/32-12/47	➲11867	**2043**	12/32-01/37	**3043**	01/37-12/47	
12253	12/32-12/47	➲10115	**2043**	12/32-01/37	**3043**	01/37-12/47	
12254	11/32-02/47	➲10113	**2041**	11/32-01/37	**3041**	01/37-02/47	later **DB975528**
12255	11/32-02/47	➲11862	**2041**	11/32-01/37	**3041**	01/37-02/47	
12256	11/32-02/47	➲11863	**2041**	11/32-01/37	**3041**	01/37-02/47	
12257	11/32-02/47	➲11865	**2042**	11/32-01/37	**3042**	01/37-02/47	
12258	11/32-02/47	➲11864	**2042**	11/32-01/37	**3042**	01/37-02/47	
12259	11/32-02/47	➲10114	**2042**	11/32-01/37	**3042**	01/37-02/47	

6-PAN Lancing/Eastleigh

Trailer First Corridor
TFK
S12260S-S12276S

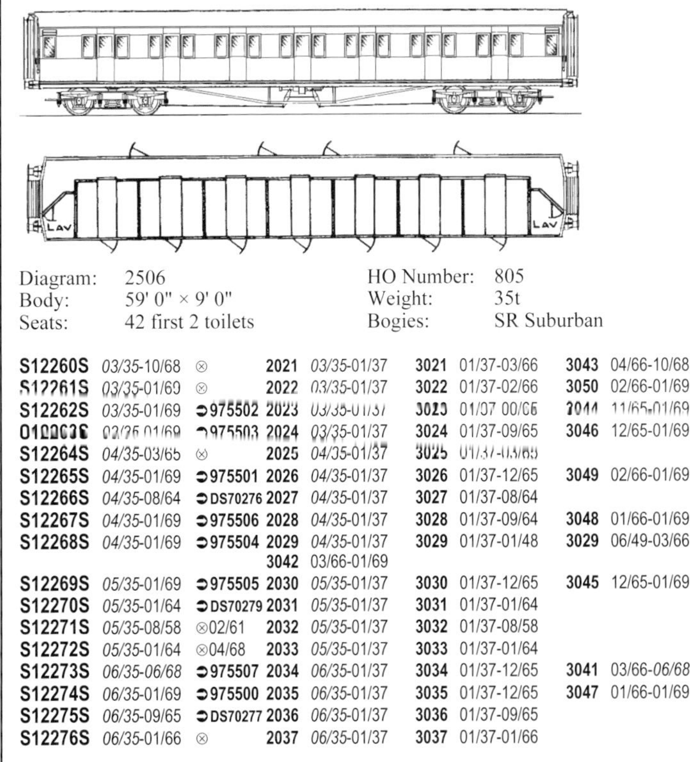

Diagram:	2506	HO Number:	805
Body:	59' 0" × 9' 0"	Weight:	35t
Seats:	42 first 2 toilets	Bogies:	SR Suburban

S12260S	03/35-10/68	⊗	**2021**	03/35-01/37	**3021**	01/37-03/66	**3043**	04/66-10/68
S12261S	03/35-01/69	⊗	**2022**	03/35-01/37	**3022**	01/37-02/66	**3050**	02/66-01/69
S12262S	03/35-01/69	➲975502	**2023**	03/35-01/37	**3023**	01/37-09/65	**3044**	11/65-01/69
S12263S	03/35-01/69	➲975503	**2024**	03/35-01/37	**3024**	01/37-09/65	**3046**	12/65-01/69
S12264S	04/35-03/65	⊗	**2025**	04/35-01/37	**3025**	01/37-03/65		
S12265S	04/35-01/69	➲975501	**2026**	04/35-01/37	**3026**	01/37-12/65	**3049**	02/66-01/69
S12266S	04/35-08/64	➲DS70276	**2027**	04/35-01/37	**3027**	01/37-08/64		
S12267S	04/35-01/69	➲975506	**2028**	04/35-01/37	**3028**	01/37-09/64	**3048**	01/66-01/69
S12268S	04/35-01/69	➲975504	**2029**	04/35-01/37	**3029**	01/37-01/48	**3029**	06/49-03/66
			3042	03/66-01/69				
S12269S	05/35-01/69	➲975505	**2030**	05/35-01/37	**3030**	01/37-12/65	**3045**	12/65-01/69
S12270S	05/35-01/64	➲DS70279	**2031**	05/35-01/37	**3031**	01/37-01/64		
S12271S	05/35-08/58	⊗02/61	**2032**	05/35-01/37	**3032**	01/37-08/58		
S12272S	05/35-01/64	⊗04/68	**2033**	05/35-01/37	**3033**	01/37-01/64		
S12273S	06/35-06/68	➲975507	**2034**	06/35-01/37	**3034**	01/37-12/65	**3041**	03/66-06/68
S12274S	06/35-01/69	➲975500	**2035**	06/35-01/37	**3035**	01/37-12/65	**3047**	01/66-01/69
S12275S	06/35-09/65	➲DS70277	**2036**	06/35-01/37	**3036**	01/37-09/65		
S12276S	06/35-01/66	⊗	**2037**	06/35-01/37	**3037**	01/37-01/66		

Class 405 4-SUB Eastleigh

Trailer Third Open
TTO
S12351S-S12360S

Diagram:	2018 EH266	HO Number:	3384/3385
Body:	62' 0" × 9' 0"	Weight:	27-29t
Seats:	102 third	Bogies:	SR

S12351S	09/48-05/72	⊗06/73	**4378**	09/48-05/72				
S12352S	10/48-08/67	⊗11/69	**4379**	10/48-08/67				
S12353S	10/48-10/82	➲15479	**4380**	10/48-04/76	**4285**	05/76-10/82		
S12354S	10/48-10/83	℗	**4381**	10/48-11/73	**4732**	11/74-10/83		
S12355S	11/48-06/82	➲15465	**4382**	11/48-05/74	**4649**	03/75-06/82		
S12356S	09/48-04/72	⊗02/73	**4383**	09/48-04/72				
S12357S	10/48-05/83	⊗06/85	**4384**	10/48-04/76	**4696**	06/76-05/81	**4630**	06/81-05/83
S12358S	10/48-09/82	➲15481	**4385**	10/48-04/76	**4297**	07/76-09/82		
S12359S	10/48-05/82	➲15463	**4386**	10/48-05/74	**4605**	07/75-05/77	**4619**	05/77-02/81
			4287	03/81-05/82				
S12360S	11/48-06/81	➲15453	**4387**	11/48-04/76	**4739**	06/76-06/81		

Class 405 4-SUB Eastleigh
Trailer Third Open
TTO
S12361S-S12395S

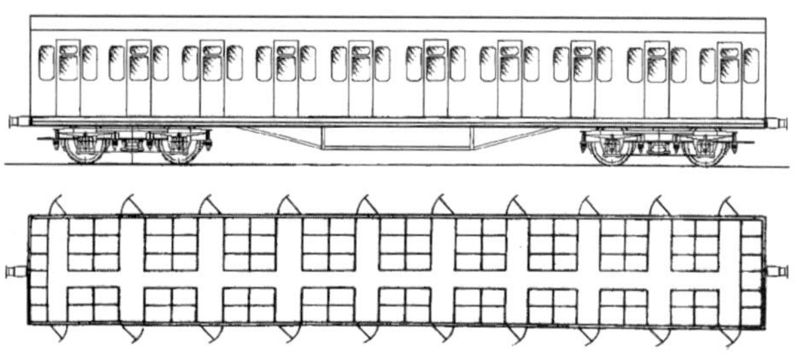

Diagram:	2018 EH266	HO Number:	3504
Body:	62' 0" × 9' 0"	Weight:	27-29t
Seats:	102 third	Bogies:	SR

S12361S	05/49-02/81	⊃**15452**	**4621**	05/49-12/80					↩**9707**
S12362S	05/49-05/82	⊗	**4622**	05/49-05/74	**4639**	03/75-05/82			↩**9698**
S12363S	05/49-07/72	⊗01/77	**4623**	05/49-07/72					↩**9709**
S12364S	05/49-10/82	⊗11/83	**4624**	05/49-04/76	**4654**	07/76-10/82			↩**9712**
S12365S	06/49-05/82	⊗10/85	**4625**	06/49-05/74	**4733**	10/75-05/82			↩**9684**
S12366S	06/49-10/82	⊗05/84	**4626**	06/49-10/82					↩**9705?**
S12367S	06/49-06/81	⊗	**4627**	06/49-06/81					↩**9710?**
S12368S	06/49-09/83	⊗07/84	**4628**	06/49-06/81	**4629**	06/81-09/83			↩**9679**
S12369S	07/49-09/83	⊗07/84	**4629**	07/49-09/83					↩**9697**
S12370S	07/49-05/83	⊗06/85	**4630**	07/49-05/83					
S12371S	07/49-10/82	⊗11/83	**4631**	07/49- *51*	**4631**	05/52-05/82	**4637**	05/82-10/82	↩**9701**
S12372S	07/49-09/83	⊗04/86	**4632**	07/49-09/78	**4632**	06/79-06/81	**4278**	06/81-09/83	↩**9682**
S12373S	07/49-10/82	⊗07/85	**4633**	07/49-10/82					↩**9668**
S12374S	07/49-05/82	⊗ *84*	**4634**	07/49-05/74	**4284**	03/75-05/82			↩**9681**
S12375S	08/49-07/83	⊗07/85	**4635**	08/49-06/81	**4751**	07/81-07/83			
S12376S	09/49-06/83	⊗10/85	**4636**	09/49-06/81	**4719**	07/81-06/83			
S12377S	09/49-05/82	⊗ *84*	**4637**	09/49-05/82					↩**9675**
S12378S	09/49-07/83	⊗06/84	**4638**	09/49-06/81	**4716**	07/81-07/83			
S12379S	09/49-05/82	⊗	**4639**	09/49-05/82					
S12380S	10/49-06/81	⊗	**4640**	10/49-11/73	**4299**	06/74-06/81			↩**9517**
S12381S	10/49-06/81	⊃**15459**	**4641**	10/49-06/81					
S12382S	10/49-05/73	⊗07/82	**4642**	10/49-05/73					↩**9509**
S12383S	10/49-04/81	⊗	**4643**	10/49-04/81					
S12384S	10/49-10/82	⊗07/85	**4644**	10/49-04/76	**4633**	06/76-10/82			↩**9678**
S12385S	11/49-10/82	⊗05/85	**4645**	11/49-10/82					
S12386S	11/49-06/81	⊗	**4646**	11/49-04/76	**4627**	05/76-06/81			
S12387S	11/49-05/83	⊗	**4647**	11/49-04/76	**4670**	06/76-05/83			
S12388S	11/49-05/83	⊗02/84	**4648**	11/49-05/81	**4747**	05/81-05/83			
S12389S	11/49-06/82	⊃**15464**	**4649**	11/49-06/82					
S12390S	12/49-05/82	⊃**15469**	**4650**	12/49-06/81	**4631**	07/81-05/82			
S12391S	12/49-10/82	⊃**15472**	**4651**	12/49-10/82					
S12392S	12/49-04/61	⊃**15278**[2]	**4652**	12/49-04/61					↩**9691**
S12393S	12/49-06/81	⊃**15461**	**4653**	12/49-06/81					
S12394S	01/50-10/82	⊗11/83	**4654**	01/50-10/82					
S12395S	01/50-06/81	⊗03/83	**4655**	01/50-06/81					

Class 405 4-SUB Eastleigh
Trailer Third Open
TTO
S12396S-S12399S

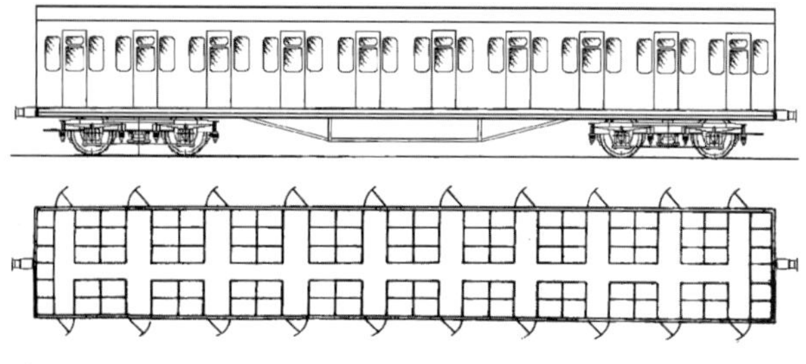

Diagram:	2018 EH266	HO Number:	3505
Body:	62' 0" × 9' 0"	Weight:	27-29t
Seats:	102 third	Bogies:	SR

S12396S	01/50-10/82	⊗06/84	**4656**	01/50-10/82
S12397S	01/50-07/83	⊗07/85	**4657**	01/50-07/83
S12398S	02/50-10/82	⊃**15480**	**4658**	02/50-10/82
S12399S	02/50-10/82	⊗11/83	**4659**	02/50-10/82

Class 405 4-SUB Eastleigh
Trailer Third Open
TTO
S12400S-S12406S

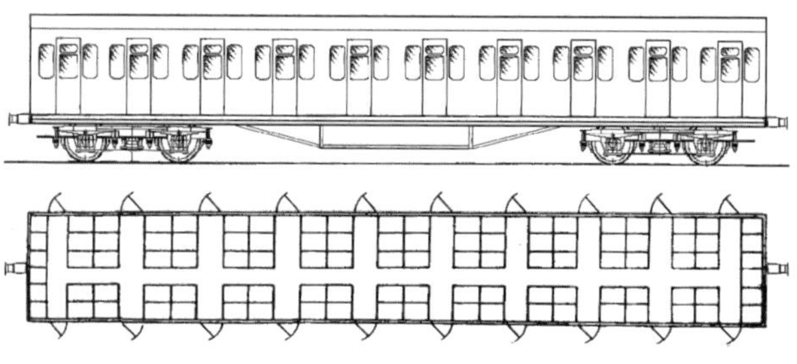

Diagram:	2018 EH266	HO Number:	3506
Body:	62' 0" × 9' 0"	Weight:	27-29t
Seats:	102 third	Bogies:	SR

S12400S	02/50-04/83	⊗10/85	**4660**	02/50-04/83		
S12401S	02/50-03/74	⊗03/75	**4661**	02/50-05/66	**4661**	11/66-03/74
S12402S	02/50-10/82	⊃**15477**	**4662**	02/50-02/79	**4651**	10/79-10/82
S12403S	02/50-05/83	⊗12/87	**4663**	02/50-05/72	**4620**	06/72-05/83
S12404S	03/50-11/80	⊃**15455**	**4664**	03/50-11/80		
S12405S	03/50-10/82	⊗02/84	**4665**	03/50-04/76	**4679**	05/76-10/82
S12406S	03/50-05/83	⊗02/85	**4666**	03/50-05/83		

6-PAN Lancing/Eastleigh
Trailer Pantry First
TFRBK
S12501S-S12517S

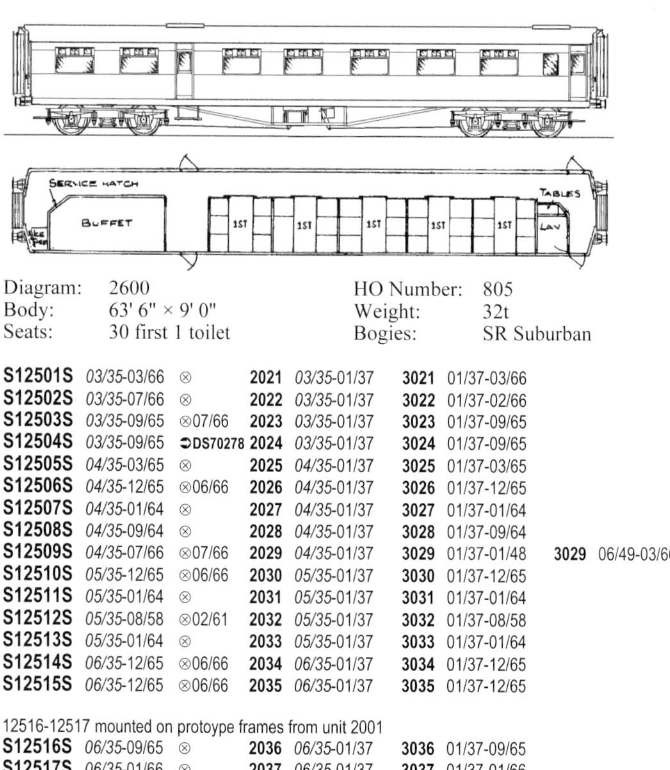

Diagram:	2600	HO Number:	805
Body:	63' 6" × 9' 0"	Weight:	32t
Seats:	30 first 1 toilet	Bogies:	SR Suburban

S12501S	*03/35*-03/66	⊗	**2021**	*03/35*-01/37	**3021**	01/37-03/66		
S12502S	*03/35*-07/66	⊗	**2022**	*03/35*-01/37	**3022**	01/37-02/66		
S12503S	*03/35*-09/65	⊗07/66	**2023**	*03/35*-01/37	**3023**	01/37-09/65		
S12504S	*03/35*-09/65	⊃**DS70278**	**2024**	*03/35*-01/37	**3024**	01/37-09/65		
S12505S	*04/35*-03/65	⊗	**2025**	*04/35*-01/37	**3025**	01/37-03/65		
S12506S	*04/35*-12/65	⊗06/66	**2026**	*04/35*-01/37	**3026**	01/37-12/65		
S12507S	*04/35*-01/64	⊗	**2027**	*04/35*-01/37	**3027**	01/37-01/64		
S12508S	*04/35*-09/64	⊗	**2028**	*04/35*-01/37	**3028**	01/37-09/64		
S12509S	*04/35*-07/66	⊗07/66	**2029**	*04/35*-01/37	**3029**	01/37-01/48	**3029**	06/49-03/66
S12510S	*05/35*-12/65	⊗06/66	**2030**	*05/35*-01/37	**3030**	01/37-12/65		
S12511S	*05/35*-01/64	⊗	**2031**	*05/35*-01/37	**3031**	01/37-01/64		
S12512S	*05/35*-08/58	⊗02/61	**2032**	*05/35*-01/37	**3032**	01/37-08/58		
S12513S	*05/35*-01/64	⊗	**2033**	*05/35*-01/37	**3033**	01/37-01/64		
S12514S	*06/35*-12/65	⊗06/66	**2034**	*06/35*-01/37	**3034**	01/37-12/65		
S12515S	*06/35*-12/65	⊗06/66	**2035**	*06/35*-01/37	**3035**	01/37-12/65		

12516-12517 mounted on protoype frames from unit 2001

S12516S	*06/35*-09/65	⊗	**2036**	*06/35*-01/37	**3036**	01/37-09/65
S12517S	*06/35*-01/66	⊗	**2037**	*06/35*-01/37	**3037**	01/37-01/66

Class 404 4-BUF Lancing/Eastleigh

Trailer Buffet
TRB
12518-S12530S

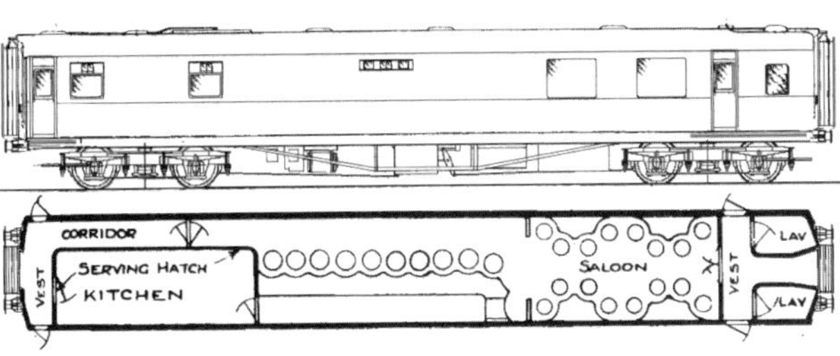

Diagram:	2601	HO Number:	951
Body:	63' 6" × 9' 0"	Weight:	37t
Seats:	16 seats 10 stools 2 toilets	Bogies:	SR Express

All stored from May 1942 to January 1946.

12518	*05/38-09/40*	⊗	3073	*05/38-09/40*				War loss
S12518S²	10/48-10/70	➲080336	3074	10/48-10/70				Replacement
S12519	*05/38-10/48*	⊗City of Portsmouth			3074	*05/38-09/40*	3073	*12/40*-10/70
S12520S	*05/38-01/71*	⊗09/71	3075	*05/38-01/71*				
S12521S	*05/38-10/70*	⊗	3076	*05/38-10/70*				
S12522S	*06/38-02/71*	⊗12/71	3077	*06/38-02/71*				
S12523S	*06/38-10/70*	⊗	3078	*06/38-10/70*				
S12524S	*06/38-09/62*	⊗	3079	*06/38-09/62*				
S12525S	*06/38-01/71*	⊗09/71	3080	*06/38-01/71*				
S12526S	*06/38-12/68*	⊗	3081	*06/38-12/68*				
S12527S	*07/38-10/70*	⊗02/72	3082	*07/38-10/70*				
S12528S	*07/38-10/70*	⊗09/71	3083	*07/38-10/70*				
S12529S	*07/38-10/70*	⊗02/72	3084	*07/38-10/70*				Reserved for National Collection, but then destroyed by fire
S12530S	*07/38-02/71*	⊗09/71	3085	*07/38-02/71*				

Class 404 4-RES Birmingham RC&W

Trailer Restaurant Kitchen
TRKB, some later TKRG
S12601S-S12619S

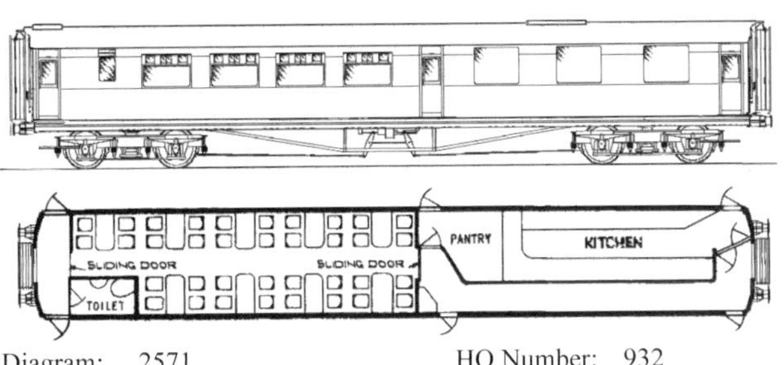

Diagram:	2571	HO Number:	932
Body:	62' 0" × 9' 0"	Weight:	35t
Seats:	36 third 1 toilet	Bogies:	SR Express

S12601S	*05/37-01/64*	⊗08/64	3064	*05/37-01/64*			
S12602S	*05/37-05/71*	➲975257	3068	*05/37-12/63*	3087	12/63-05/71	to griddle 61/62
S12603S	*05/37-01/64*	⊗07/66	3069	*05/37-01/64*			
S12604S	*05/37-01/64*	⊗08/64	3066	*05/37-01/64*			
S12605S	*05/37-05/71*	⊗07/72	3065	*05/37-12/63*	3086	12/63-05/71	to griddle 61/62
12606	*04/37-12/40*	⊗12/40	3058	*04/37-12/40*			
S12607S	*04/37-01/64*	⊗ *66*	3061	*04/37-01/64*			
S12608S	*05/37-01/64*	⊗08/64	3067	*05/37-01/64*			
S12609S	*04/37-05/71*	⊗07/72	3056	*04/37-12/63*	3088	12/63-05/71	to griddle 61/62
S12610S	*04/37-01/64*	⊗08/64	3055	*04/37-01/64*			
S12611S	*04/37-01/64*	⊗ *66*	3057	*04/37-01/64*			
S12612S	*04/37-01/64*	⊗ *66*	3059	*04/37-01/64*			
S12613S	*05/37-05/71*	⊗07/72	3072	*05/37-05/71*			Fire damage 02/54. Rebuilt as buffet 55. Later became transport café
S12614S	*05/37-01/64*	⊗ *66*	3070	*05/37-01/64*			
12615	*04/37-01/41*	⊗01/41	3060	*04/37-01/41*			
S12616S	*04/37-01/64*	⊗08/64	3062	*04/37-01/64*			
12617	*04/37-06/44*	⊗06/44	3063	*04/37-06/44*			
S12618S	*05/37-01/64*	➲IU	3071	*05/37-01/64*			
S12619S	*04/37-01/64*	⊗08/64	3054	*04/37-01/64*			

Class 405 4-SUB Eastleigh

Driving Motor Brake Third Open
DMBTO
S12650S-S12664S

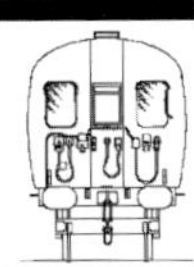

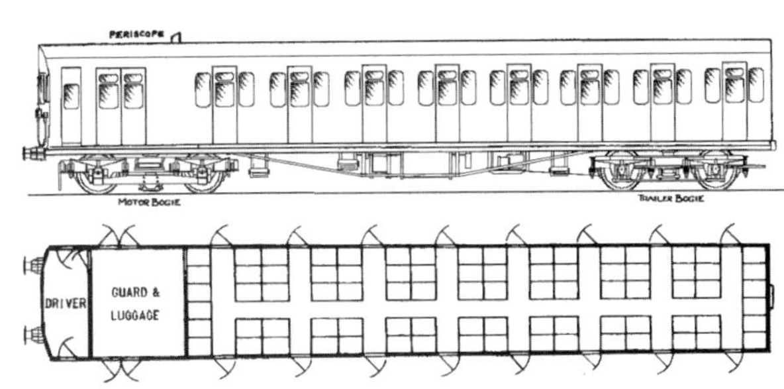

Diagram:	2126 EB265	HO Number:	3618
Body:	62' 6" × 9' 0"	Weight:	39t
Seats:	82 third	Bogies:	SR
Motor:	EE507C 2 × 250hp		

S12650S	04/50-06/82	⊗03/83	4601	04/50-10/58	4601	06/59-05/77	4617	05/77-06/82
S12651S	04/50-06/81	⊗06/82	4601	04/50-10/58	4675	04/59-06/81		
S12652S	04/50-05/83	⊗12/87	4602	04/50-06/72	4620	06/72-05/83		
S12653S	04/50-05/83	⊗12/87	4602	04/50-06/72	4620	06/72-05/83		
S12654S	04/50-10/82	⊗ *84*	4603	04/50-05/77	4618	05/77-10/82		
S12655S	04/50-02/81	⊗10/81	4605	04/50-05/77	4619	05/77-02/81		
S12656S	04/50-02/81	⊗10/81	4605	04/50-05/77	4619	05/77-02/81		
S12657S	04/50-10/82	⊗ *84*	4603	04/50-05/77	4618	05/77-10/82		
S12658S	04/50-04/76	➲975594	4604	04/50-04/76				
S12659S	04/50-04/76	➲975593	4604	04/50-04/76				
S12660S	04/50-04/81	⊗06/82	4606	04/50-04/76	4290	12/76-04/81		
S12661S	04/50-04/76	⊗07/81	4606	04/50-04/76				
S12662S	05/50-04/76	⊗09/81	4607	05/50-04/76				
S12663S	05/50-12/73	⊗03/75	4607	05/50-12/73				
S12664S	05/50-10/73	⊗	4590	*05/50*-07/54	2700	02/55-03/68	4369	04/69-10/73

Class 405 4-SUB Eastleigh

Driving Motor Brake Third Open
DMBTO
S12665S-S12750S

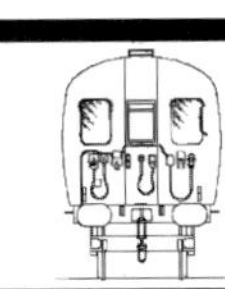

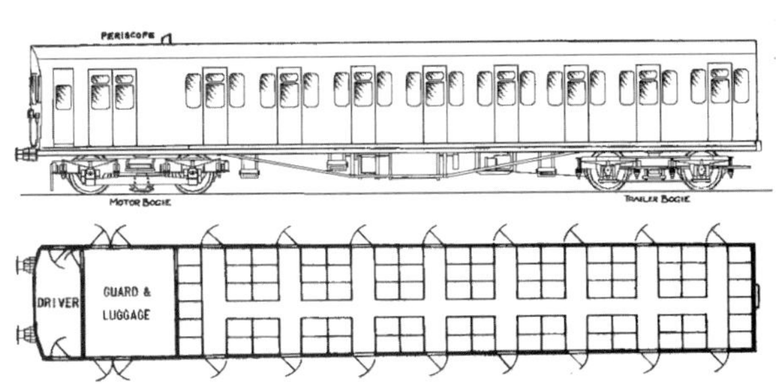

Diagram:	2126 EB265	HO Number:	3617
Body:	62' 6" × 9' 0"	Weight:	39-43t
Seats:	82 third	Bogies:	SR
Motor:	EE507C 2 × 250hp		

S12665S	05/50-02/81	⊗	4667	05/50-11/70	4703	11/70-06/73	4621	06/73-12/80
S12666S	05/50-06/71	⊗07/72	4667	05/50-11/70				
S12667S	05/50-05/83	⊗	4668	05/50-05/83				
S12668S	05/50-05/83	⊗	4668	05/50-05/83				↩8839
S12669S	05/50-05/82	⊗02/84	4669	05/50-05/82				↩8873
S12670S	05/50-05/82	⊗02/84	4669	05/50-05/82				↩8506
S12671S	05/50-05/83	⊗	4670	05/50-05/83				↩8507
S12672S	05/50-05/83	⊗	4670	05/50-05/83				↩8653
S12673S	05/50-10/82	⊗02/84	4671	05/50-10/82				↩8508
S12674S	05/50-10/82	⊗02/84	4671	05/50-10/82				↩8654
S12675S	05/50-10/82	⊗06/84	4672	05/50-10/82				↩8526
S12676S	05/50-10/82	⊗06/84	4672	05/50-10/82				↩8548
S12677S	06/50-10/82	⊗02/84	4673	06/50-10/82				↩8547
S12678S	06/50-10/82	⊗02/84	4673	06/50-10/82				↩8505
S12679S	06/50-10/82	⊗02/84	4674	06/50-10/82				↩8525
S12680S	06/50-10/82	⊗02/84	4674	06/50-06/76	4674	12/77-10/82		↩8682
S12681S	06/50-06/82	⊗03/83	4675	06/50-10/58	4601	06/59-05/77	4617	05/77-06/82
S12682S	06/50-06/81	⊗06/82	4675	06/50-10/58	4675	04/59-06/81		↩8848
S12683S	06/50-04/76	⊗10/76	4676	06/50-04/76				↩8672
S12684S	06/50-04/76	⊗10/76	4676	06/50-04/76				↩8522
S12685S	06/50-06/81	⊗08/82	4677	06/50-08/67	4677	01/68-06/81		↩8532

S12686S	06/50-06/81	⊗08/82	**4677**	06/50-08/67	**4664**	08/67-01/68	**4677**	01/68-06/81	↵8531
S12687S	07/50-05/83	⊗06/84	**4678**	07/50-05/83					↵8415
S12688S	07/50-05/83	⊗06/84	**4678**	07/50-05/83					↵8537
S12689S	07/50-05/82	⊗06/84	**4679**	07/50-07/59	**4684**	07/59-05/82			↵8345
S12690S	07/50-05/82	⊗06/84	**4679**	07/50-07/59	**4684**	07/59-05/82			↵8249
S12691S	07/50-09/83	⊗10/84	**4680**	07/50-10/59	**4754**	10/59-09/83			
S12692S	07/50-09/83	⊗10/84	**4680**	07/50-10/59	**4754**	10/59-09/83			
S12693S	07/50-06/81	⊗	**4681**	07/50-05/81					↵8410
S12694S	07/50-06/81	⊗	**4681**	07/50-05/81					↵8348
S12695S	07/50-04/83	⊗02/84	**4682**	07/50-04/83					
S12696S	07/50-04/83	⊗02/84	**4682**	07/50-04/83					↵8250
S12697S	08/50-10/82	⊗06/84	**4683**	08/50-10/82					↵8416
S12698S	08/50-10/82	⊗06/84	**4683**	08/50-10/82					↵8409
S12699S	08/50-08/81	⊗	**4684**	08/50-07/59	**4679**	07/59-08/81			↵8521
S12700S	08/50-10/82	⊗02/84	**4684**	08/50-07/59	**4679**	07/59-10/82			↵8538
S12701S	08/50-04/76	⊗10/76	**4685**	08/50-04/76					↵8388
S12702S	08/50-04/76	⊗10/76	**4685**	08/50-04/76					↵8333
S12703S	08/50-04/76	⊗08/76	**4686**	08/50-04/76					↵8384
S12704S	08/50-04/76	⊗08/76	**4686**	08/50-08/58	**4686**	04/59-04/76			↵8383
S12705S	09/50-12/82	⊗06/84	**4687**	09/50-05/56	**4687**	*08/57*-12/82			↵8227
S12706S	09/50-05/83	⊗10/85	**4687**	09/50-05/56	**4687**	*08/57*-05/83			↵8347
S12707S	09/50-04/76	⊗08/76	**4688**	09/50-04/76					
S12708S	09/50-04/76	⊗08/76	**4688**	09/50-04/76					↵8413
S12709S	09/50-06/81	⊗01/82	**4689**	09/50-06/81					↵8387
S12710S	09/50-06/81	⊗01/82	**4689**	09/50-06/81					
S12711S	09/50-04/76	⊗08/76	**4690**	09/50-04/76					
S12712S	09/50-04/76	⊗08/76	**4690**	09/50-04/76					↵8591
S12713S	09/50-04/76	⊗08/76	**4691**	09/50-04/76					↵8414
S12714S	09/50-04/76	⊗08/76	**4691**	09/50-04/76					↵8267
S12715S	09/50-05/83	⊗04/84	**4692**	09/50-05/83					
S12716S	09/50-12/82	⊗06/84	**4692**	09/50-12/82					↵8400
S12717S	09/50-06/81	⊗06/82	**4693**	09/50-06/81					
S12718S	09/50-06/81	⊗06/82	**4693**	09/50-06/81					↵8322
S12719S	09/50-04/76	⊗06/76	**4694**	09/50-04/76					↵8256
S12720S	09/50-04/76	⊗06/76	**4694**	09/50-04/76					
S12721S	09/50-06/81	⊗10/85	**4695**	09/50-06/81					
S12722S	09/50-06/81	⊗10/85	**4695**	09/50-06/81					↵8285
S12723S	10/50-04/76	⊗08/76	**4696**	10/50-01/65	**4720**	*01/65*-04/76			
S12724S	10/50-06/81	⊗08/82	**4696**	10/50-05/81					↵8374
S12725S	10/50-06/81	⊗04/82	**4697**	10/50-06/81					↵8341
S12726S	10/50-06/81	⊗04/82	**4697**	10/50-06/81					↵8268
S12727S	10/50-04/76	⊗08/76	**4698**	10/50-04/76					↵8342
S12728S	10/50-04/76	⊗08/76	**4698**	10/50-04/76					
S12729S	10/50-04/76	⊗06/76	**4699**	10/50-04/76					↵8286
S12730S	10/50-04/76	⊗06/76	**4699**	10/50-04/76					↵8389
S12731S	10/50-04/76	⊗08/76	**4700**	10/50-04/76					↵8390
S12732S	10/50-04/76	⊗08/76	**4700**	10/50-04/76					↵8399?
S12733S	11/50-06/81	⊗04/82	**4701**	11/50-06/81					↵8323?
S12734S	11/50-07/83	⊗07/85	**4701**	11/50-11/65	**4751**	*01/66*-07/83			↵8228
S12735S	11/50-04/76	⊗07/76	**4702**	11/50-04/76					↵8281
S12736S	11/50-04/76	⊗07/76	**4702**	11/50-04/76					↵8289
S12737S	11/50-11/70	⊗07/72	**4703**	11/50-11/70					↵8306
S12738S	11/50-04/76	⊗06/76	**4703**	11/50-04/76					↵8324
S12739S	11/50-05/82	⊗10/85	**4704**	11/50-09/75	**4733**	10/75-05/82			↵8276
S12740S	11/50-04/76	⊗08/76	**4704**	11/50-*07/58*	**4711**	07/58-12/70	**4736**	12/70-05/71	
			4711	05/71-04/76					↵8275
S12741S	11/50-06/81	⊗06/82	**4705**	11/50-06/81					↵8320
S12742S	11/50-06/81	⊗06/82	**4705**	11/50-06/81					↵8319
S12743S	11/50-04/76	⊗08/76	**4706**	11/50-04/76					↵8305
S12744S	11/50-04/76	⊗08/76	**4706**	11/50-04/76					↵8316
S12745S	12/50-04/76	⊗07/76	**4707**	12/50-04/76					↵8351
S12746S	12/50-04/76	⊗07/76	**4707**	12/50-04/76					↵8352
S12747S	12/50-04/76	⊗06/76	**4708**	12/50-09/72	**4621**	09/72-06/73	**4703**	06/73-04/76	↵8315
S12748S	12/50- 73	⊗03/75	**4708**	12/50-09/72					↵8475
S12749S	12/50-06/81	⊗	**4709**	12/50-05/81					↵8411
S12750S	12/50-06/81	⊗	**4709**	12/50-05/81					↵8328

Class 405 4-SUB Eastleigh

Driving Motor Brake Third Open

DMBTO

S12751S-S12800S

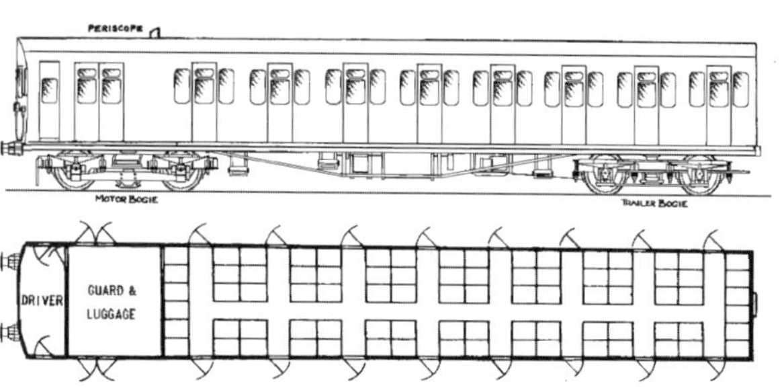

Diagram:	2126 EB265	HO Number:	3638
Body:	62' 6" × 9' 0"	Weight:	39-43t
Seats:	82 third	Bogies:	SR
Motor:	EE507C 2 × 250hp		

S12751S	12/50-03/78	⊗02/81	**4710**	12/50-03/78					↵8327
S12752S	12/50-07/83	⊗10/85	**4710**	12/50-07/83					↵8412
S12753S	12/50-04/76	⊗08/76	**4711**	12/50-10/56	**4711**	07/58-12/70	**4711**	05/71-04/76	↵8396
S12754S	12/50-09/75	⊗ 75	**4711**	12/50-10/56	**4704**	07/58-09/75			↵8251
S12755S	01/51-04/76	⊗08/76	**4712**	01/51-04/76					↵8252
S12756S	01/51-04/76	⊗08/76	**4712**	01/51-04/76					↵8395
S12757S	01/51-04/76	⊗07/76	**4713**	01/51-04/76					↵8476
S12758S	01/51-04/76	⊗07/76	**4713**	01/51-04/76					
S12759S	01/51-07/83	⊗11/84	**4714**	01/51-07/83					↵8233
S12760S	01/51-07/83	⊗11/84	**4714**	01/51-07/83					↵8301
S12761S	01/51-11/74	⊗10/74	**4715**	01/51-11/74					↵8302
S12762S	01/51-12/81	⊗08/82	**4715**	01/51-11/74	**4730**	11/74-12/81			↵8239
S12763S	02/51-07/83	⊗06/84	**4716**	02/51-07/83					↵8240
S12764S	02/51-07/83	⊗06/84	**4716**	02/51-07/83					↵8297
S12765S	02/51-04/76	⊗07/76	**4717**	02/51-04/76					↵8381
S12766S	02/51-04/76	⊗07/76	**4717**	02/51-04/76					↵8359
S12767S	02/51-07/83	⊗10/85	**4718**	02/51-06/51	**4661**	06/51-02/59	**4718**	02/59-01/78	
			4710	03/78-07/83					↵8394
S12768S	02/51-01/78	⊗02/81	**4718**	02/51-06/51	**4718**	05/52-01/78			↵8298
S12769S	03/51-06/83	⊗10/85	**4719**	03/51-06/83					↵8292
S12770S	03/51-06/83	⊗10/85	**4719**	03/51-06/83					↵8291
S12771S	03/51-03/77	⊗06/81	**4720**	03/51-12/64	**4696**	01/65-03/77			↵8478
S12772S	03/51-12/64	⊗	**4720**	03/51-12/64					↵8477
S12773S	03/51-09/83	⊗11/84	**4721**	03/51-09/83					↵8401
S12774S	03/51-09/83	⊗11/84	**4721**	03/51-09/83					↵8303
S12775S	04/51-03/71	⊗*03/71*	**4722**	04/51-03/71					↵8402
S12776S	04/51-05/83	⊗02/85	**4722**	04/51-03/71	**4722**	10/71-05/83			↵8360
S12777S	04/51-04/76	⊗08/76	**4723**	04/51-04/76					↵8480
S12778S	04/51-04/76	⊗08/76	**4723**	04/51-04/76					↵8346
S12779S	04/51-04/76	⊗08/76	**4724**	04/51-04/76					
S12780S	04/51-04/76	⊗08/76	**4724**	04/51-04/76					↵8299
S12781S	04/51-10/82	⊗10/82	**4725**	04/51-10/81	**4730**	12/81-10/82			↵8260
S12782S	04/51-01/82	⊗08/82	**4725**	04/51-10/81					↵8326
S12783S	05/51-07/83	⊗02/85	**4726**	05/51-07/83					
S12784S	05/51-07/83	⊗02/85	**4726**	05/51-07/83					↵8343
S12785S	05/51-04/76	⊗06/76	**4727**	05/51-04/76					↵8363
S12786S	05/51-04/76	⊗06/76	**4727**	05/51-04/76					↵8364
S12787S	06/51-04/76	⊗08/76	**4728**	06/51-04/76					↵8304
S12788S	06/51-04/76	⊗08/76	**4728**	06/51-04/76					↵8479
S12789S	06/51-04/76	⊗05/80	**4729**	06/51-03/74	**4748**	03/74-04/76			↵8487
S12790S	06/51-03/74	⊗01/77	**4729**	06/51-03/74					↵8258
S12791S	06/51-11/74	⊗11/74	**4730**	06/51-11/74					↵8488
S12792S	06/51-10/82	⊗10/82	**4730**	06/51-10/82					↵8257
S12793S	06/51-08/83	⊗07/85	**4731**	06/51-04/76	**4738**	04/76-08/83			↵8490
S12794S	06/51-05/76	⊗10/76	**4731**	06/51-04/76					↵8365
S12795S	06/51-10/83	Ⓟ	**4732**	06/51-10/83					↵8309
S12796S	06/51-10/83	Ⓟ	**4732**	06/51-10/83					↵8310
S12797S	06/51-05/82	⊗10/85	**4733**	06/51-05/82					↵8370
S12798S	06/51-10/75	⊗03/76	**4733**	06/51-10/75					↵8274
S12799S	07/51-04/76	⊗08/76	**4734**	07/51-04/76					↵8237
S12800S	07/51-04/76	⊗08/76	**4734**	07/51-04/76					↵8325

Class 402 2-HAL Lancing/Eastleigh

Driving Trailer Composite Lavatory

DTCL

S12801S-S12846S

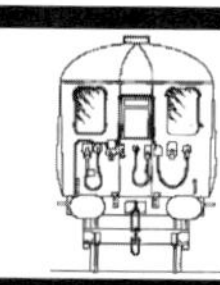

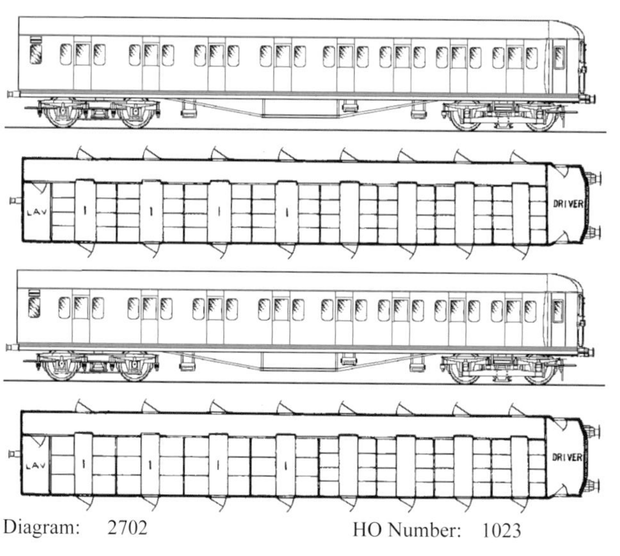

Diagram: 2702 HO Number: 1023

Body: 62' 6" × 9' 0" Weight: 32t
Seats: 32 first 32 second 1 toilet Bogies: SR Suburban
Later 24 first 32 second 1 toilet

S12801S *04/39*-02/70 ⊗10/70 **2647** *04/39*-02/70
S12802S *04/39*-01/71 ⊗07/71 **2648** *04/39*-01/71
S12803S *04/39*-01/71 ⊗05/71 **2649** *04/39*-01/71
S12804S *04/39*-02/70 ⊗10/70 **2650** *04/39*-02/70
S12805S *04/39*-10/69 ⊗ **2651** *04/39*-10/69
S12806S *04/39*-12/69 ⊗05/70 **2652** *04/39*-12/69
S12807S *04/39*-08/62 ⊗08/62 **2653** *04/39*- 50 **2088** 50-08/62
S12808S *04/39*-12/70 ⊗09/71 **2654** *04/39*-12/70
S12809S *04/39*-06/70 ⊗08/70 **2655** *04/39*-06/70
S12810S *04/39*-05/71 ⊗11/71 **2656** *04/39*-05/71
S12811S *04/39*-01/70 ⊗04/70 **2657** *04/39*-01/70
S12812S *04/39*-05/69 ⊗09/69 **2658** *04/39*-05/69
S12813S *04/39*-04/69 ⊗02/70 **2659** *04/39*-04/69
S12814S *04/39*-11/70 ⊗05/71 **2660** *04/39*-11/70
S12815S *04/39*-08/71 ⊗04/72 **2661** *04/39*-08/71
S12816S *05/39*-09/69 ⊗06/70 **2662** *05/39*-09/69
S12817S *05/39*-01/70 ⊗05/70 **2663** *05/39*-01/70
S12818S *05/39*-01/70 ⊗05/70 **2664** *05/39*-01/70
S12819S *05/39*-04/71 ⊗09/71 **2665** *05/39*-04/71
S12820S *05/39*-10/70 ⊗05/71 **2666** *05/39*-10/70
S12821S *05/39*-01/71 ⊗07/71 **2667** *05/39*-01/71
S12822S *05/39*-01/71 ⊗07/71 **[illegible]** [illegible] 01/71
S12823S *05/39*-12/69 ⊗06/70 **[illegible]** [illegible] 12/69
S12824S *05/39*-09/69 ⊗10/70 **2670** *05/39*-09/69
S12825S *05/39*-01/70 ⊗05/70 **2671** *05/39*-01/70
S12826S *05/39*-03/71 ⊗05/73 **2672** *05/39*-03/71
S12827S *05/39*-12/69 ⊗05/70 **2673** *05/39*-12/69
S12828S *05/39*-08/71 ⊗01/72 **2674** *05/39*-08/71
S12829S *05/39*-11/70 ⊗05/71 **2675** *05/39*-11/70
S12830S *05/39*-04/71 ⊗09/71 **2676** *05/39*-04/71
S12831S *11/39*-05/71 ⊗11/71 **2677** *11/39*-05/71
S12832S *11/39*-08/69 ⊗10/69 **2678** *11/39*-08/69
S12833S *11/39*-07/71 ⊗05/72 **2679** *11/39*-07/71
S12834S *11/39*-04/56 ⊗04/56 **2680** *11/39*-04/56
S12835S *11/39*-06/70 ⊗08/70 **2681** *11/39*-06/70
S12836S *11/39*-06/69 ⊗10/69 **2682** *11/39*-06/69
S12837S *12/39*-12/70 ⊗09/71 **2683** *12/39*-12/70
S12838S *12/39*-04/71 ⊗09/71 **2684** *12/39*-04/71
S12839S *12/39*-05/71 ⊗12/71 **2685** *12/39*-05/71
S12840S *12/39*-06/70 ⊗12/70 **2686** *12/39*-06/70
S12841S *12/39*-12/70 ⊗09/71 **2687** *12/39*-12/70
S12842S *12/39*-03/68 ⊗04/68 **2688** *12/39*-03/68
S12843S *12/39*-10/70 ⊗07/72 **2689** *12/39*-10/70 **065** 10/70-07/72
S12844S *12/39*-10/70 ⊗07/71 **2690** *12/39*-10/70
S12845S *12/39*-01/70 ⊗05/70 **2691** *12/39*-01/70
S12846S *12/39*-12/70 ⊗07/72 **2692** *12/39*-12/70 **066** 12/70-07/72

Class 402 2-HAL Lancing/Eastleigh

Driving Trailer Composite Lavatory
DTCL
S12847S-S12853S

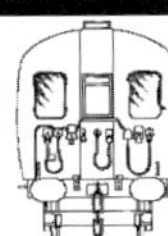

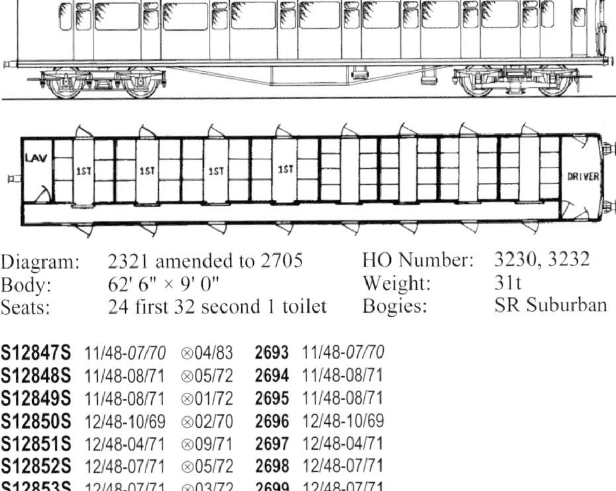

Diagram: 2321 amended to 2705 HO Number: 3230, 3232
Body: 62' 6" × 9' 0" Weight: 31t
Seats: 24 first 32 second 1 toilet Bogies: SR Suburban

S12847S 11/48-*07/70* ⊗04/83 **2693** 11/48-*07/70*
S12848S 11/48-08/71 ⊗05/72 **2694** 11/48-08/71
S12849S 11/48-08/71 ⊗01/72 **2695** 11/48-08/71
S12850S 12/48-10/69 ⊗02/70 **2696** 12/48-10/69
S12851S 12/48-04/71 ⊗09/71 **2697** 12/48-04/71
S12852S 12/48-07/71 ⊗05/72 **2698** 12/48-07/71
S12853S 12/48-07/71 ⊗03/72 **2699** 12/48-07/71

Class 402 2-HAL Lancing/Eastleigh

Driving Trailer Composite Lavatory
DTCL
S12854S

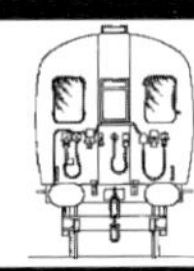

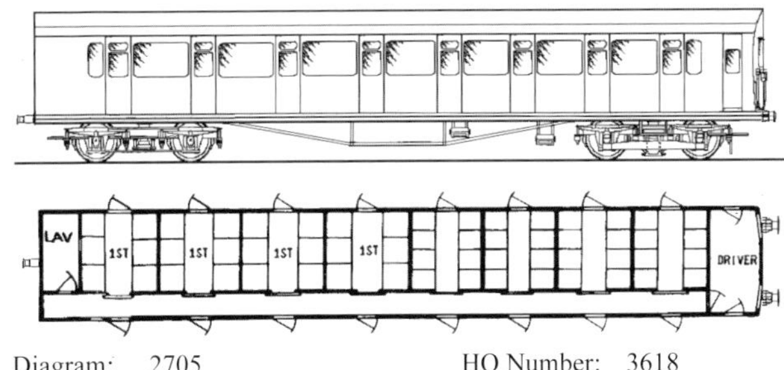

Diagram: 2705 HO Number: 3618
Body: 62' 6" × 9' 0" Weight: 31t
Seats: 24 first 32 second 1 toilet Bogies: SR

S12854S 01/55-04/71 ⊗09/71 **2653** 01/51-02/69 **2028** 03/69-04/71
Built on frame of **12121** fire loss replacement

Class 401 2-BIL Eastleigh

Driving Trailer Composite Lavatory
DTCL
S12855S-S12858S (12855 Class 402 2-HAL)

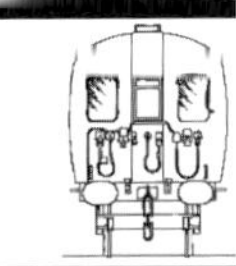

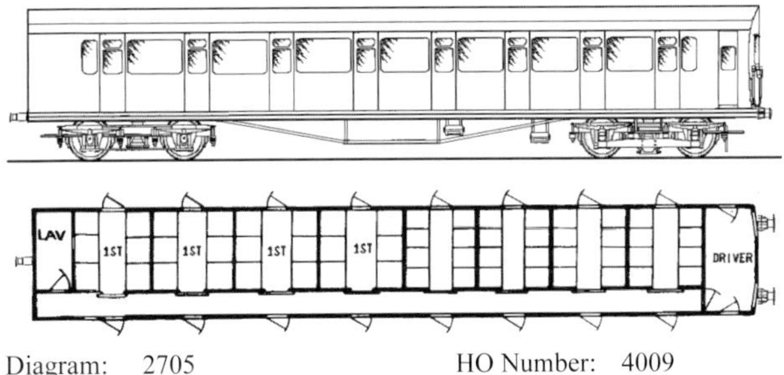

Diagram: 2705 HO Number: 4009
Body: 62' 6" × 9' 0" Weight: 31t
Seats: 24 first 32 second 1 toilet Bogies: SR

S12855S 01/55-04/71 ⊗11/71 **2700** 02/55-03/68 **2688** 03/68-06/69 **2696** 10/69-04/71
Built on frame of **12037** war loss replacement
S12856S 01/55-*01/71* ⊗12/71 **2133** 02/55-*01/71*
Built on frame of **12133** accident loss replacement
S12857S 01/55-06/70 ⊗12/70 **2100** 01/55-06/70 replacement
S12858S 01/55-12/70 ⊗05/71 **2069** 01/55-12/70 replacement

4-DD Lancing/Eastleigh

Driving Motor Brake Third (Double Deck)
DMBT
S13001S-S13004S

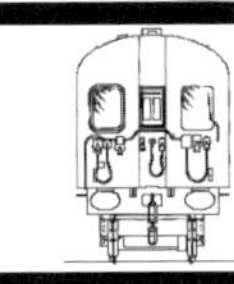

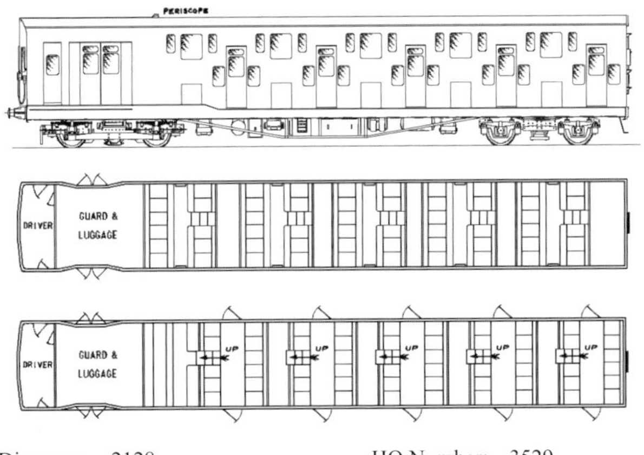

Diagram: 2128 HO Number: 3529
Body: 62' 6" × 9' 0" Weight: 39t
Seats: 120 third Bogies: SR
Motor: EE507C 2 × 250hp

S13001S	10/49-10/71	⊗11/71	**4001**	10/49-10/70	**4901**	10/70-10/71
S13002S	10/49-10/71	⊗11/71	**4001**	10/49-10/70	**4901**	10/70-10/71
S13003S	10/49-10/71	Ⓟ	**4002**	10/49-10/70	**4902**	10/70-10/71
S13004S	10/49-10/71	Ⓟ	**4002**	10/49-10/70	**4902**	10/70-10/71

4-DD Lancing/Eastleigh
Trailer Third (Double Deck)
TT
S13501S-S13504S

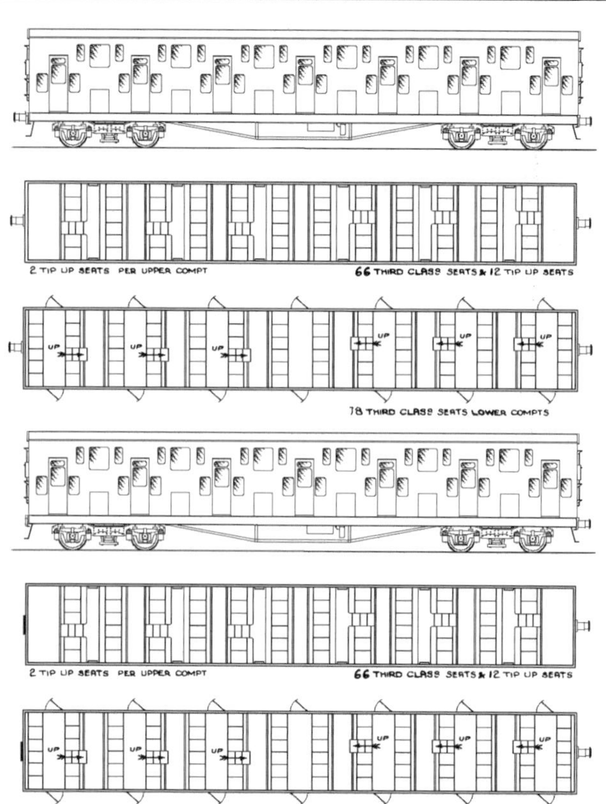

Diagram:	2100 2101	HO Number:	3529
Body:	62' 6" × 9' 0"	Weight:	28t
Seats:	156 third	Bogies:	SR

S13501S	10/49-10/71	⊗11/71	**4001**	10/49-10/70	**4901**	10/70-10/71
S13502S	10/49-10/71	⊗11/71	**4001**	10/49-10/70	**4901**	10/70-10/71
S13503S	10/49-10/71	Ⓟ⊗08/84	**4002**	10/49-10/70	**4902**	10/70-10/71
S13504S	10/49-10/71	⊗11/71	**4002**	10/49-10/70	**4902**	10/70-10/71

Class 415/1 4-EPB Eastleigh
Driving Motor Brake Third Open
DMBTO
S14001S-S14030S

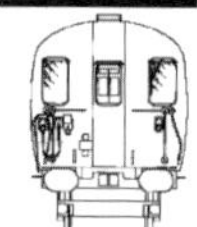

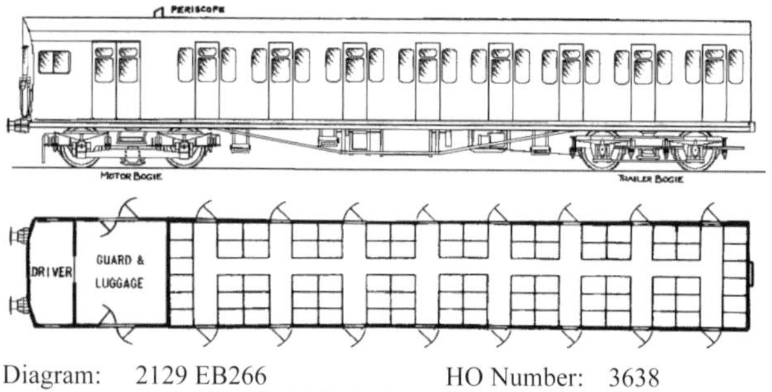

Diagram:	2129 EB266 Refurbished EB277 EB279	HO Number:	3638
		Weight:	40t
Body:	62' 6" × 9' 0"	Bogies:	SR 40ft type
Seats:	82 third	Motor:	EE507C 2 × 250hp

14001-14018 originally to be numbered 8656-8673

S14001S	12/51-03/95	⊗04/04	**5001**	12/51-11/88	**5265**	11/88-11/90	**5001**	11/90-03/95	↩**8391**
S14002S	12/51-03/95	⊗04/04	**5001**	12/51-11/88	**5265**	11/88-11/90	**5001**	11/90-03/95	↩**8335**
S14003S	02/52-05/94	⊗06/94	**5002**	02/52-04/85	**5466**	05/85-05/94			↩**8254**
S14004S	02/52-05/94	⊗06/94	**5002**	02/52-04/85	**5466**	05/85-05/94			↩**8406**
S14005S	03/52-08/94	⊗09/94	**5003**	03/52-03/85	**5467**	05/85-08/94			↩**8397**
S14006S	03/52-08/94	⊗09/94	**5003**	03/52-03/85	**5467**	05/85-08/94			↩**8392**
S14007S	03/52-10/91	⊗11/91	**5004**	03/52-06/85	**5469**	06/85-10/91			↩**8279**
S14008S	03/52-10/91	⊗11/91	**5004**	03/52-06/85	**5469**	06/85-10/91			↩**8367**
S14009S	04/52-05/91	⊗09/91	**5005**	04/52-04/88	**5531**	04/88-05/91			↩**8368**
S14010S	04/52-05/91	⊗09/91	**5005**	04/52-04/88	**5531**	04/88-05/91			↩**8296**
S14011S	04/52-07/87	⊗12/88	**5006**	04/52-07/87					↩**8307**
S14012S	04/52-01/86	⊗10/87	**5006**	04/52-08/85					↩**8377**
S14013S	04/52-11/93	⊗12/93	**5007**	04/52-07/85	**5477**	09/85-01/93	**5447**	01/93-11/93	↩**8405**
S14014S	04/52-11/81	⊗04/83	**5007**	04/52-11/81					↩**8353**
S14015S	05/52-07/92	⊗09/92	**5008**	05/52-08/59	**5008**	08/60-06/85	**5476**	08/85-07/92	↩**8362**
S14016S	05/52-07/92	⊗09/92	**5008**	05/52-08/59	**5008**	08/60-06/85	**5476**	08/85-07/92	↩**8372**
S14017S	05/52-02/94	⊗06/94	**5009**	05/52-08/85	**5482**	11/85-02/94			↩**8486**
S14018S	05/52-02/94	⊗06/94	**5009**	05/52-08/85	**5482**	11/85-02/94			↩**8265**
S14019S	06/52-05/93	⊗05/93	**5010**	06/52-06/85	**5475**	08/85-05/93			↩**8246**
S14020S	06/52-05/93	⊗05/93	**5010**	06/52-06/85	**5475**	08/85-05/93			↩**8241**
S14021S	06/52-12/93	⊗12/93	**5011**	06/52-02/85	**5462**	02/85-12/93			↩**8295**
S14022S	06/52-12/93	⊗12/93	**5011**	06/52-02/85	**5462**	02/85-12/93			↩**8494**
S14023S	07/52-08/94	⊗08/94	**5012**	07/52-05/86	**5489**	05/86-08/94			↩**8361**
S14024S	07/52-08/94	⊗08/94	**5012**	07/52-05/86	**5489**	05/86-08/94			↩**8284**
S14025S	08/52-06/91	⊗10/91	**5013**	08/52-05/88	**5532**	05/88-06/91			↩**8313**
S14026S	08/52-06/91	⊗10/91	**5013**	08/52-05/88	**5532**	05/88-06/91			↩**8338**
S14027S	08/52-02/93	⊗02/93	**5014**	08/52-10/86	**5493**	10/86-02/93			↩**8398**
S14028S	08/52-02/93	⊗02/93	**5014**	08/52-10/86	**5493**	10/86-02/93			↩**8266**
S14029S	08/52-08/94	⊗09/94	**5015**	08/52-01/86	**5491**	07/86-08/94			↩**8277**
S14030S	08/52-08/94	⊗09/94	**5015**	08/52-01/86	**5491**	07/86-08/94			↩**8366**

Class 415/1 4-EPB Eastleigh
Driving Motor Brake Third Open
DMBTO
S14031S-S14066S

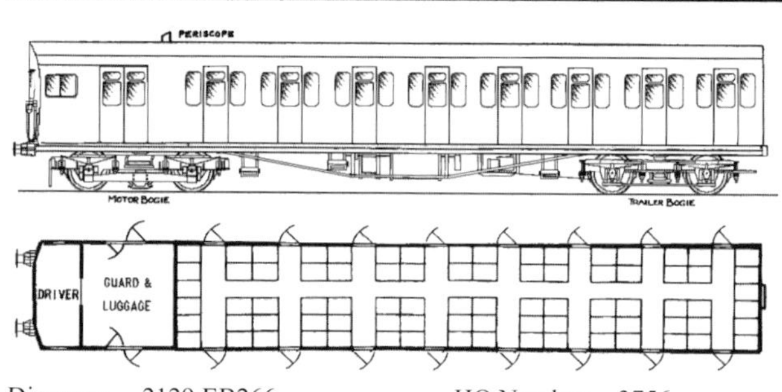

Diagram:	2129 EB266 Refurbished EB277 EB279	HO Number:	3756
		Weight:	40t
Body:	62' 6" × 9' 0"	Bogies:	SR 40ft type
Seats:	82 third	Motor:	EE507C 2 × 250hp

S14031S	04/53-05/90	⊗11/90	**5016**	04/53-05/88	**5511**	05/88-05/90					↩**8375**
S14032S	04/53-05/90	⊗11/90	**5016**	04/53-05/88	**5511**	05/88-05/90					↩**8493**
S14033S	05/53-07/87	⊗12/89	**5017**	05/53-07/87							↩**8262**
S14034S	05/53-07/87	⊗12/89	**5017**	05/53-07/87							↩**8245**
S14035S	05/53-10/91	⊗11/91	**5018**	05/53-04/88	**5508**	04/88-10/91					↩**8337**
S14036S	05/53-10/91	⊗11/91	**5018**	05/53-04/88	**5508**	04/88-10/91					↩**8357**
S14037S	05/53-06/94	⊗06/94	**5019**	05/53-03/85	**5463**	03/85-06/94					↩**8403**
S14038S	05/53-06/94	⊗06/94	**5019**	05/53-03/85	**5463**	03/85-06/94					↩**8354**
S14039S	05/53-01/93	⊗12/92	**5020**	05/53-06/58	**5020**	11/58-11/88	**5266**	11/88-02/91	**5209**	02/91-01/93	↩**8264**
S14040S	05/53-01/93	⊗01/93	**5020**	05/53-06/58	**5020**	11/58-11/88	**5266**	11/88-01/93			↩**9853**
S14041S	05/53-02/59	⊗04/59	**5021**	05/53-02/59							↩**8229**
S14042S	05/53-09/92	⊗11/92	**5021**	05/53-02/59	**5021**	10/59-02/84	**5027**	02/84-11/88	**5267**	11/88-09/92	↩**8261**
S14043S	06/53-01/91	⊗03/91	**5022**	06/53-05/88	**5517**	05/88-01/91					↩**8404**
S14044S	06/53-01/91	⊗03/91	**5022**	06/53-05/88	**5517**	05/88-01/91					↩**8552**
S14045S	06/53-07/58	⊗07/58	**5023**	06/53-07/58							↩**8263**
S14046S	06/53-05/91	⊗03/92	**5023**	06/53-07/58	**5031**	09/58-12/85	**5484**	12/85-05/91			↩**9854**
S14047S	06/53-07/87	➲**977531**	**5024**	06/53-07/87							↩**8358**
S14048S	06/53-07/87	➲**977532**	**5024**	06/53-07/87							↩**8542**
S14049S	06/53-12/85	⊗02/90	**5025**	06/53-12/85							↩**8314**
S14050S	06/53-07/91	⊗09/91	**5025**	06/53-12/85	**5135**	12/85-05/88	**5521**	05/88-07/91			↩**8541**
S14051S	07/53-05/94	⊗05/94	**5026**	07/53-11/85	**5483**	11/85-05/94					↩**8504**
S14052S	07/53-05/94	⊗05/94	**5026**	07/53-11/85	**5483**	11/85-05/94					↩**8551**
S14053S	07/53-09/92	⊗11/92	**5027**	07/53-11/88	**5267**	11/88-09/92					↩**8503**
S14054S	07/53-11/93	⊗11/93	**5027**	07/53-02/84	**5021**	02/84-09/84	**5455**	09/84-11/93			↩**9844**
S14055S	08/53-07/87	⊗12/87	**5028**	08/53-07/87							↩**9813**

S14056S	08/53-05/94	⊗05/94	**5028**	08/53-06/86	**5490**	06/86-05/94			↵**8269**
S14057S	08/53-04/93	⊗01/93	**5029**	08/53-09/79	**5203**	09/79-05/80	**5007**	01/82-07/85	
			5477	09/85-01/93					↵**8270**
S14058S	08/53-02/95	⊗02/95	**5029**	08/53-08/85	**5473**	08/85-02/95			↵**8308**
S14059S	08/53-04/93	⊗05/93	**5030**	08/53-09/85	**5478**	09/85-04/93			↵**8230**
S14060S	08/53-04/93	⊗05/93	**5030**	08/53-09/85	**5478**	09/85-04/93			↵**8282**
S14061S	08/53-05/91	⊗12/92	**5031**	08/53-12/85	**5484**	12/85-05/91			↵**8501**
S14062S	08/53-11/93	⊗11/93	**5031**	08/53-09/58	**5021**	10/59-09/84	**5455**	09/84-11/93	
									↵**9843**
S14063S	08/53-05/91	⊗10/91	**5032**	08/53-05/88	**5516**	05/88-05/91			↵**8502**
S14064S	08/53-05/91	⊗10/91	**5032**	08/53-05/88	**5516**	05/88-05/91			↵**9836**
S14065S	09/53-01/94	⊗01/94	**5033**	09/53-08/85	**5474**	08/85-01/94			↵**9835**
S14066S	09/53-01/94	⊗01/94	**5033**	09/53-08/85	**5474**	08/85-01/94			↵**8560**

Class 415/1 4-EPB Eastleigh

Driving Motor Brake Third Open

DMBTO

S14067S-S14106S

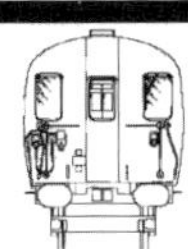

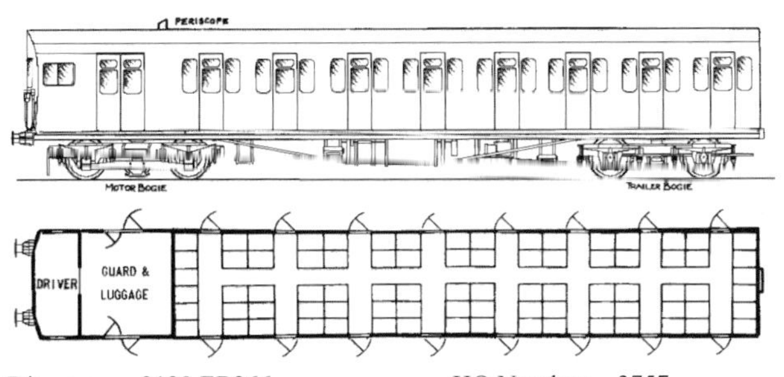

Diagram:	2129 EB266 Refurbished EB277 EB279	HO Number: Weight:	3757 40t
Body:	62' 6" × 9' 0"	Bogies:	SR 40ft type
Seats:	82 third	Motor:	EE507C 2 × 250hp

S14067S	09/53-12/85	⊗01/88	**5034**	09/53-12/85					↵**8574**
S14068S	09/53-12/85	⊗01/88	**5034**	09/53-12/85					↵**8530**
S14069S	09/53-08/93	⊗08/93	**5035**	09/53-11/88	**5268**	11/88-08/93			↵**8529**
S14070S	09/53-08/93	⊗08/93	**5035**	09/53-11/88	**5268**	11/88-08/93			↵**8545**
S14071S	09/53-04/92	⊗07/92	**5036**	09/53-01/86	**5486**	01/86-04/92			↵**9851**
S14072S	09/53-08/94	⊗09/94	**5036**	09/53-01/86	**5486**	01/86-08/94			↵**8519**
S14073S	10/53-02/93	⊗09/93	**5037**	10/53-11/86	**5494**	11/86-02/93			↵**8527**
S14074S	10/53-02/93	⊗09/93	**5037**	10/53-11/86	**5494**	11/86-02/93			↵**8580**
S14075S	10/53-01/91	⊗02/92	**5038**	10/53-04/88	**5504**	04/88-01/91			↵**8581**
S14076S	10/53-01/91	⊗02/92	**5038**	10/53-04/88	**5504**	04/88-01/91			↵**8511**
S14077S	10/53-06/77	⊗06/77	**5039**	10/53-06/77					↵**8546**
S14078S	10/53-01/93	⊗01/93	**5039**	10/53-11/88	**5269**	11/88-01/93			↵**8575**
S14079S	10/53-05/93	⊗07/93	**5040**	10/53-11/88	**5270**	11/88-05/93			↵**8820**
S14080S	10/53-05/93	⊗07/93	**5040**	10/53-11/88	**5270**	11/88-05/93			↵**8206**
S14081S	10/53-05/94	⊗06/94	**5041**	10/53-04/85	**5464**	04/85-05/94			↵**8690**
S14082S	10/53-05/94	⊗06/94	**5041**	10/53-04/85	**5464**	04/85-05/94			↵**8528**
S14083S	11/53-01/91	⊗09/91	**5042**	11/53-11/88	**5271**	11/88-01/91			↵**8520**
S14084S	11/53-01/91	⊗09/91	**5042**	11/53-11/88	**5271**	11/88-01/91			↵**9852**
S14085S	11/53-05/91	⊗10/91	**5043**	11/53-04/88	**5529**	04/88-10/90	**5278**	10/90-05/91	
									↵**8578**
S14086S	11/53-05/91	⊗10/91	**5043**	11/53-04/88	**5529**	04/88-10/90	**5278**	10/90-05/91	
									↵**8495**
S14087S	11/53-01/91	⊗09/91	**5044**	11/53-11/88	**5272**	11/88-01/91			↵**8515**
S14088S	11/53-01/91	⊗09/91	**5044**	11/53-11/88	**5272**	11/88-01/91			↵**8496**
S14089S	11/53-10/90	⊗10/91	**5045**	11/53-11/88	**5273**	11/88-10/90			↵**8856**
S14090S	11/53-10/90	⊗10/91	**5045**	11/53-11/88	**5273**	11/88-10/90			↵**8516**
S14091S	11/53-10/90	⊗04/92	**5046**	11/53-11/88	**5274**	11/88-10/90			↵**8512**
S14092S	11/53-10/90	⊗04/92	**5046**	11/53-11/88	**5274**	11/88-10/90			↵**8828**
S14093S	11/53-08/77	⊗06/77	**5047**	11/53-06/77					↵**8556**
S14094S	11/53-01/93	⊗01/93	**5047**	11/53-06/77	**5039**	08/77-11/88	**5269**	11/88-01/93	
									↵**8544**
S14095S	11/53-08/93	⊗09/93	**5048**	11/53-12/86	**5495**	12/86-08/93			↵**8543**
S14096S	11/53-08/93	⊗09/93	**5048**	11/53-12/86	**5495**	12/86-08/93			↵**8196**
S14097S	12/53-04/93	⊗05/93	**5049**	12/53-09/88	**5275**	11/88-04/93			↵**8183**
S14098S	12/53-04/93	⊗05/93	**5049**	12/53-09/88	**5275**	11/88-04/93			↵**8812**
S14099S	01/54-05/91	⊗02/92	**5050**	01/54-01/85	**5150**	01/85-11/85	**5150**	09/87-05/91	
									↵**8509**
S14100S	01/54-07/87	⊗12/88	**5050**	01/54-01/85	**5006**	08/85-07/87			↵**8510**
S14101S	01/54-05/92	⊗07/92	**5051**	01/54-11/88	**5276**	11/88-05/92			↵**8810**
S14102S	01/54-05/92	⊗07/92	**5051**	01/54-11/88	**5276**	11/88-05/92			↵**8524**
S14103S	01/54-05/93	⊗05/93	**5052**	01/54-06/72	**5240**	06/72-05/93			↵**8498**
S14104S	01/54-05/93	⊗06/93	**5052**	01/54-11/88	**5277**	11/88-05/93			↵**8497**
S14105S	02/54-02/94	⊗03/94	**5053**	02/54-12/85	**5485**	12/85-02/94			↵**8826**
S14106S	02/54-02/94	⊗03/94	**5053**	02/54-12/85	**5485**	12/85-02/94			↵**8212**

Class 415/1 4-EPB Eastleigh

Driving Motor Brake Third Open

DMBTO

S14201S-S14210S

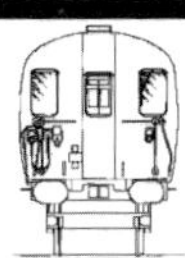

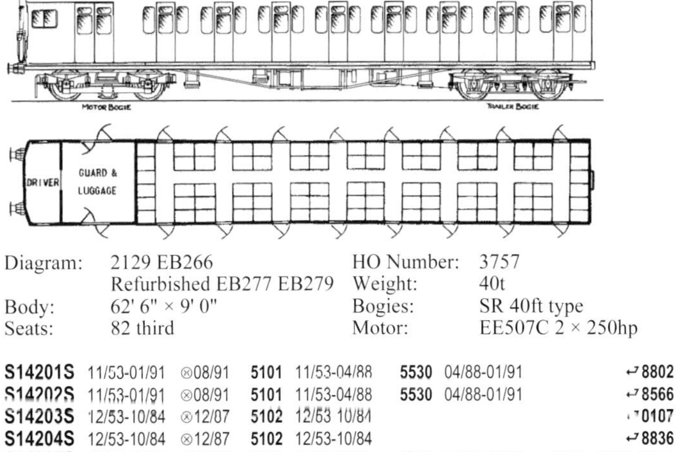

Diagram:	2129 EB266 Refurbished EB277 EB279	HO Number: Weight:	3757 40t
Body:	62' 6" × 9' 0"	Bogies:	SR 40ft type
Seats:	82 third	Motor:	EE507C 2 × 250hp

S14201S	11/53-01/91	⊗08/91	**5101**	11/53-04/88	**5530**	04/88-01/91			↵**8802**
S14202S	11/53-01/91	⊗08/91	**5101**	11/53-04/88	**5530**	04/88-01/91			↵**8566**
S14203S	12/53-10/84	⊗12/07	**5102**	12/53-10/84					↵**0107**
S14204S	12/53-10/84	⊗12/87	**5102**	12/53-10/84					↵**8836**
S14205S	12/53-05/94	⊗05/94	**5103**	12/53-09/71	**5262**	01/72-06/86	**5490**	06/86-05/94	
									↵**8194**
S14206S	12/53-04/93	⊗05/94	**5103**	12/53-09/71	**5769**	09/71-10/71	**5247**	10/71-04/81	
			5409	04/81-04/93					↵**8567**
S14207S	01/54-11/92	⊗01/93	**5104**	01/54-11/92					↵**8795**
S14208S	01/54-11/92	⊗01/93	**5104**	01/54-11/92					↵**8523**
S14209S	01/54-05/90	⊗*12/90*	**5105**	01/54-04/88	**5512**	04/88-05/90			↵**8181**
S14210S	01/54-05/90	⊗*12/90*	**5105**	01/54-04/88	**5512**	04/88-05/90			↵**8190**

Class 415/1 4-EPB Eastleigh

Driving Motor Brake Third Open

DMBTO

S14211S-S14310S

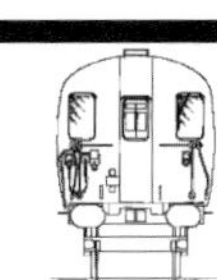

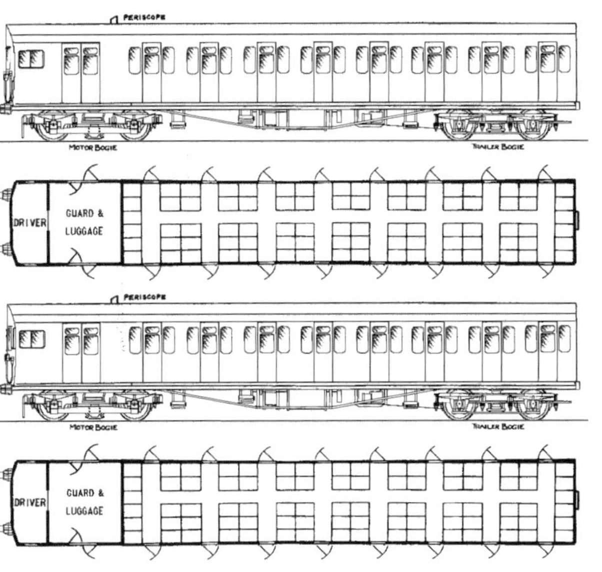

14275 onwards fitted with rainstrips

Diagram:	2129 EB266 Refurbished EB277 EB279	HO Number: Weight:	4016 40t
Body:	62' 6" × 9' 0"	Bogies:	SR 40ft type
Seats:	82 third	Motor:	EE507C 2 × 250hp

S14211S	02/54-08/94	⊗09/94	**5106**	02/54-03/85	**5468**	06/85-04/92	**5486**	04/92-08/94	
									↵**8797**
S14212S	02/54-04/92	⊗07/92	**5106**	02/54-03/85	**5468**	06/85-04/92			↵**8804**
S14213S	02/54-10/90	⊗11/91	**5107**	02/54-10/90					↵**8833**
S14214S	02/54-10/90	⊗11/91	**5107**	02/54-10/90					↵**8830**
S14215S	03/54-07/87	⊗12/89	**5108**	03/54-07/87					↵**8204**
S14216S	03/54-07/87	⊗12/89	**5108**	03/54-07/87					↵**8817**
S14217S	03/54-07/87	⊗04/89	**5109**	03/54-07/87					↵**8825**
S14218S	03/54-07/87	⊗04/89	**5109**	03/54-07/87					↵**8818**
S14219S	03/54-07/87	⊗01/88	**5110**	03/54-07/87					↵**8211**
S14220S	03/54-11/83	⊗10/87	**5110**	03/54-11/83					↵**8806**

S14221S	03/54-01/92	⊗02/92	**5111**	03/54-05/88	**5520**	05/88-10/91			↵8192
S14222S	03/54-01/92	⊗02/92	**5111**	03/54-05/88	**5520**	05/88-10/91			↵8216
S14223S	03/54-11/93	⊗11/93	**5112**	03/54-08/86	**5492**	08/86-11/93			↵8793
S14224S	03/54-11/93	⊗11/93	**5112**	03/54-08/86	**5492**	08/86-11/93			↵8179
S14225S	04/54-05/91	⊗09/91	**5113**	04/54-05/91					↵8514
S14226S	04/54-05/91	⊗09/91	**5113**	04/54-05/91					↵8184
S14227S	04/54-02/92	⊃977797	**5114**	04/54-02/92					↵8796
S14228S	04/54-02/92	⊃977800	**5114**	04/54-02/92					↵8219
S14229S	04/54-10/92	⊗11/92	**5115**	04/54-01/69	**5115**	08/69-10/92			↵8794
S14230S	04/54-10/92	⊗11/92	**5115**	04/54-01/69	**5115**	08/69-10/92			↵8182
S14231S	04/54-02/93	⊗03/93	**5116**	04/54-04/88	**5523**	04/88-01/91	**5280**	01/91-02/93	↵8203
S14232S	04/54-02/93	⊗03/93	**5116**	04/54-04/88	**5523**	04/88-01/91	**5280**	01/91-02/93	↵8180
S14233S	05/54-05/91	⊗02/92	**5117**	05/54-04/88	**5527**	04/88-05/91			↵8185
S14234S	05/54-05/91	⊗02/92	**5117**	05/54-04/88	**5527**	04/88-05/91			↵8799
S14235S	05/54-07/87	⊗10/87	**5118**	05/54-11/83					↵8579
S14236S	05/54-07/94	⊗08/94	**5118**	05/54-04/85	**5465**	04/85-07/94			↵8202
S14237S	05/54-05/90	⊗10/90	**5119**	05/54-04/88	**5509**	04/88-05/90			↵8214
S14238S	05/54-05/90	⊗10/90	**5119**	05/54-04/88	**5509**	04/88-05/90			↵8218
S14239S	05/54-12/92	⊗01/93	**5120**	05/54-09/81	**5420**	09/81-12/92			↵9823
S14240S	05/54-12/92	⊗01/93	**5120**	05/54-09/81	**5420**	09/81-12/92			↵8224
S14241S	06/54-10/92	⊗12/92	**5121**	06/54-10/92					↵8835
S14242S	06/54-10/91	⊗05/92	**5121**	06/54-09/91					↵8808
S14243S	06/54-07/87	⊗05/89	**5122**	06/54-04/71	**5122**	09/71-07/87			↵8816
S14244S	06/54-07/87	⊗05/89	**5122**	06/54-04/71	**5122**	09/71-07/87			↵8210
S14245S	06/54-08/93	⊗09/93	**5123**	06/54-02/87	**5497**	02/87-08/93			↵8200
S14246S	06/54-08/93	⊗09/93	**5123**	06/54-02/87	**5497**	02/87-08/93			↵8824
S14247S	06/54-01/93	⊗02/93	**5124**	06/54-01/93					↵8513
S14248S	06/54-01/93	⊗02/93	**5124**	06/54-01/93					↵8535
S14249S	06/54-05/91	⊗11/91	**5125**	06/54-05/88	**5501**	05/88-05/91			↵8577
S14250S	06/54-05/91	⊗11/91	**5125**	06/54-05/88	**5501**	05/88-05/91			↵8559
S14251S	07/54-10/85	⊗	**5126**	07/54-01/85					↵8809
S14252S	07/54-07/92	⊗09/92	**5126**	07/54-07/92					↵8207
S14253S	07/54-06/85	⊗10/87	**5127**	07/54-06/85					↵9822
S14254S	07/54-06/85	⊗10/87	**5127**	07/54-06/85					↵8555
S14255S	08/54-07/94	⊗08/94	**5128**	08/54-05/85	**5471**	06/85-07/94			↵8821
S14256S	08/54-07/94	⊗08/94	**5128**	08/54-05/85	**5471**	06/85-07/94			↵8540
S14257S	08/54-02/94	⊗03/94	**5129**	08/54-05/88	**5528**	05/88-10/90	**5279**	11/90-02/94	↵8803
S14258S	08/54-02/94	⊗03/94	**5129**	08/54-05/88	**5528**	05/88-10/90	**5279**	11/90-02/94	↵8534
S14259S	08/54-12/73	⊗12/87	**5130**	08/54-12/73					↵8539
S14260S	08/54-09/93	⊗09/93	**5130**	08/54-12/73	**5220**	12/73-09/93			↵8189
S14261S	09/54-05/93	⊗05/93	**5131**	09/54-05/93					↵8822
S14262S	09/54-05/93	⊗05/93	**5131**	09/54-05/93					↵8557
S14263S	09/54-02/92	⊗02/92	**5132**	09/54-08/85	**5480**	10/85-02/92			↵8223
S14264S	09/54-07/93	⊗07/93	**5132**	09/54-08/85	**5480**	10/85-09/91	**5454**	09/91-07/93	↵9810
S14265S	09/54-12/91	⊗02/92	**5133**	09/54-12/91					↵8063
S14266S	09/54-12/91	⊗02/92	**5133**	09/54-12/91					↵8558
S14267S	09/54-09/93	⊗09/93	**5134**	09/54-03/82	**5435**	04/82-09/93			↵8123
S14268S	09/54-09/92	⊗11/92	**5134**	09/54-09/92					↵8208
S14269S	09/54-07/87	⊗02/90	**5135**	09/54-12/85	**5025**	01/86-07/87			↵9811
S14270S	09/54-07/91	⊗09/91	**5135**	09/54-05/88	**5521**	05/88-07/91			↵8576
S14271S	10/54-07/91	⊗02/92	**5136**	10/54-04/88	**5525**	04/88-07/91			↵8570
S14272S	10/54-07/91	⊗02/92	**5136**	10/54-04/88	**5525**	04/88-07/91			↵8105
S14273S	10/54-09/87	⊃977533	**5137**	10/54-01/76	**5192**	01/76-07/87			↵8571
S14274S	10/54-01/92	⊗02/92	**5137**	10/54-05/88	**5519**	05/88-10/91			↵8533
S14275S	10/54-09/93	⊗09/93	**5138**	10/54-09/93					↵8779
S14276S	10/54-09/93	⊗09/93	**5138**	10/54-09/93					↵8031
S14277S	10/54-02/92	⊗04/92	**5139**	10/54-02/92					↵9845
S14278S	10/54-02/92	⊗04/92	**5139**	10/54-02/92					↵8815
S14279S	11/54-10/91	⊗01/92	**5140**	11/54-05/88	**5503**	05/88-10/91			↵8201
S14280S	11/54-06/88	⊗02/90	**5140**	11/54-05/87					↵8018
S14281S	11/54-07/61	⊗07/61	**5141**	11/54-07/61					↵8032
S14282S	11/54-10/91	⊗01/92	**5141**	11/54-07/61	**5245**	09/61-05/81	**5418**	09/81-10/91	↵8790
S14283S	11/54-03/95	⊗05/95	**5142**	11/54-12/86	**6321**	12/86-03/95			↵8047
S14284S	11/54-07/87	⊗12/87	**5142**	11/54-12/86					↵8765
S14285S	11/54-11/94	⊗11/94	**5143**	11/54-09/80	**5403**	09/80-11/94			↵8008
S14286S	11/54-11/94	⊗11/94	**5143**	11/54-09/80	**5403**	09/80-11/94			↵8007
S14287S	11/54-10/91	⊗05/92	**5144**	11/54-05/88	**5524**	05/88-10/91			↵9850
S14288S	11/54-10/91	⊗05/92	**5144**	11/54-05/88	**5524**	05/88-10/91			↵9849
S14289S	11/54-04/93	⊗05/93	**5145**	11/54-04/93					↵8051
S14290S	11/54-04/93	⊗05/93	**5145**	11/54-04/93					↵8052
S14291S	12/54-01/91	⊗08/91	**5146**	12/54-01/91					↵8756
S14292S	12/54-01/91	⊗08/91	**5146**	12/54-01/91					↵9831
S14293S	12/54-10/91	⊗07/92	**5147**	12/54-05/88	**5518**	05/88-10/91			↵8010
S14294S	12/54-10/91	⊗07/92	**5147**	12/54-05/88	**5518**	05/88-10/91			↵8778
S14295S	12/54-11/90	⊗10/91	**5148**	12/54-11/90					↵8009
S14296S	12/54-11/90	⊗10/91	**5148**	12/54-11/90					↵8120
S14297S	01/55-07/93	⊗07/93	**5149**	01/55-10/80	**5408**	04/81-07/93			↵8056
S14298S	01/55-07/93	⊗07/93	**5149**	01/55-10/80	**5408**	04/81-07/93			↵9832
S14299S	01/55-05/91	⊗02/92	**5150**	01/55-11/85	**5150**	09/87-05/91			↵8095
S14300S	01/55-05/85	⊗12/87	**5150**	01/55-01/85	**5050**	01/85-01/85			↵8834
S14301S	01/55-01/91	⊗03/92	**5151**	01/55-04/88	**5506**	04/88-01/91			↵8781
S14302S	01/55-01/91	⊗03/92	**5151**	01/55-04/88	**5506**	04/88-01/91			↵8220
S14303S	01/55-05/92	⊃977777	**5152**	01/55-01/81	**5406**	01/81-05/92			↵8055
S14304S	01/55-04/93	⊗04/93	**5152**	01/55-01/81	**5412**	06/81-04/93			↵8066
S14305S	01/55-05/93	⊗07/93	**5153**	01/55-05/93					↵8099
S14306S	01/55-05/93	⊗07/93	**5153**	01/55-05/93					↵8772
S14307S	02/55-04/93	⊗05/93	**5154**	02/55-04/93					↵8757
S14308S	02/55-04/93	⊗05/93	**5154**	02/55-04/93					↵8058
S14309S	02/55-11/92	⊗12/92	**5155**	02/55-11/92					↵8084
S14310S	02/55-11/92	⊗12/92	**5155**	02/55-11/92					↵8057

Class 415/1 4-EPB Eastleigh

Driving Motor Brake Third Open
DMBTO
S14311S-S14410S

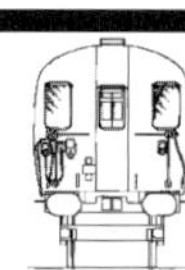

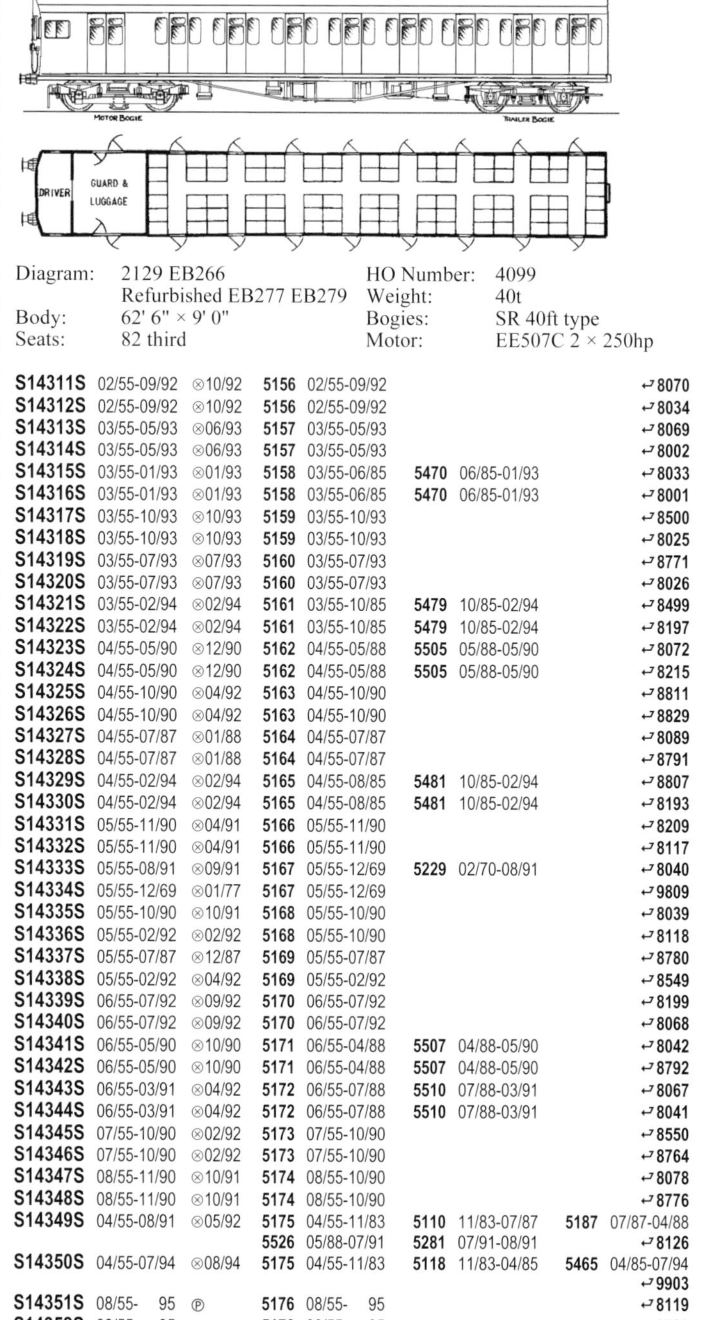

Diagram:	2129 EB266	HO Number:	4099
	Refurbished EB277 EB279	Weight:	40t
Body:	62' 6" × 9' 0"	Bogies:	SR 40ft type
Seats:	82 third	Motor:	EE507C 2 × 250hp

S14311S	02/55-09/92	⊗10/92	**5156**	02/55-09/92					↵8070
S14312S	02/55-09/92	⊗10/92	**5156**	02/55-09/92					↵8034
S14313S	03/55-05/93	⊗06/93	**5157**	03/55-05/93					↵8069
S14314S	03/55-05/93	⊗06/93	**5157**	03/55-05/93					↵8002
S14315S	03/55-01/93	⊗01/93	**5158**	03/55-06/85	**5470**	06/85-01/93			↵8033
S14316S	03/55-01/93	⊗01/93	**5158**	03/55-06/85	**5470**	06/85-01/93			↵8001
S14317S	03/55-10/93	⊗10/93	**5159**	03/55-10/93					↵8500
S14318S	03/55-10/93	⊗10/93	**5159**	03/55-10/93					↵8025
S14319S	03/55-07/93	⊗07/93	**5160**	03/55-07/93					↵8771
S14320S	03/55-07/93	⊗07/93	**5160**	03/55-07/93					↵8026
S14321S	03/55-02/94	⊗02/94	**5161**	03/55-10/85	**5479**	10/85-02/94			↵8499
S14322S	03/55-02/94	⊗02/94	**5161**	03/55-10/85	**5479**	10/85-02/94			↵8197
S14323S	04/55-05/90	⊗12/90	**5162**	04/55-05/88	**5505**	05/88-05/90			↵8072
S14324S	04/55-05/90	⊗12/90	**5162**	04/55-05/88	**5505**	05/88-05/90			↵8215
S14325S	04/55-10/90	⊗04/92	**5163**	04/55-10/90					↵8811
S14326S	04/55-10/90	⊗04/92	**5163**	04/55-10/90					↵8829
S14327S	04/55-07/87	⊗01/88	**5164**	04/55-07/87					↵8089
S14328S	04/55-07/87	⊗01/88	**5164**	04/55-07/87					↵8791
S14329S	04/55-02/94	⊗02/94	**5165**	04/55-08/85	**5481**	10/85-02/94			↵8807
S14330S	04/55-02/94	⊗02/94	**5165**	04/55-08/85	**5481**	10/85-02/94			↵8193
S14331S	05/55-11/90	⊗04/91	**5166**	05/55-11/90					↵8209
S14332S	05/55-11/90	⊗04/91	**5166**	05/55-11/90					↵8117
S14333S	05/55-08/91	⊗09/91	**5167**	05/55-12/69	**5229**	02/70-08/91			↵8040
S14334S	05/55-12/69	⊗01/77	**5167**	05/55-12/69					↵9809
S14335S	05/55-10/90	⊗10/91	**5168**	05/55-10/90					↵8039
S14336S	05/55-02/92	⊗02/92	**5168**	05/55-10/90					↵8118
S14337S	05/55-07/87	⊗12/87	**5169**	05/55-07/87					↵8780
S14338S	05/55-02/92	⊗04/92	**5169**	05/55-02/92					↵8549
S14339S	06/55-07/92	⊗09/92	**5170**	06/55-07/92					↵8199
S14340S	06/55-07/92	⊗09/92	**5170**	06/55-07/92					↵8068
S14341S	06/55-05/90	⊗10/90	**5171**	06/55-04/88	**5507**	04/88-05/90			↵8042
S14342S	06/55-05/90	⊗10/90	**5171**	06/55-04/88	**5507**	04/88-05/90			↵8792
S14343S	06/55-03/91	⊗04/92	**5172**	06/55-07/88	**5510**	07/88-03/91			↵8067
S14344S	06/55-03/91	⊗04/92	**5172**	06/55-07/88	**5510**	07/88-03/91			↵8041
S14345S	07/55-10/90	⊗02/92	**5173**	07/55-10/90					↵8550
S14346S	07/55-10/90	⊗02/92	**5173**	07/55-10/90					↵8764
S14347S	08/55-11/90	⊗10/91	**5174**	08/55-10/90					↵8078
S14348S	08/55-11/90	⊗10/91	**5174**	08/55-10/90					↵8776
S14349S	04/55-08/91	⊗05/92	**5175**	04/55-11/83	**5110**	11/83-07/87	**5187**	07/87-04/88	
			5526	05/88-07/91	**5281**	07/91-08/91			↵8126
S14350S	04/55-07/94	⊗08/94	**5175**	04/55-11/83	**5118**	11/83-04/85	**5465**	04/85-07/94	↵9903
S14351S	08/55- 95	℗	**5176**	08/55- 95					↵8119
S14352S	08/55- 95	℗	**5176**	08/55- 95					↵8789
S14353S	08/55-05/93	⊗05/93	**5177**	08/55-05/93					↵8090
S14354S	08/55-05/93	⊗05/93	**5177**	08/55-05/93					↵8116
S14355S	08/55-04/81	⊗04/81	**5178**	08/55-10/80					↵8115
S14356S	08/55-05/92	⊃977780	**5178**	08/55-10/80	**5406**	01/81-05/92			↵8098
S14357S	09/55-05/91	⊗07/91	**5179**	09/55-05/88	**5513**	05/88-05/91			↵8813
S14358S	09/55-05/91	⊗07/91	**5179**	09/55-05/88	**5513**	05/88-05/91			↵8097
S14359S	09/55-10/91	⊗01/92	**5180**	09/55-05/87	**5140**	05/87-05/88	**5503**	05/88-10/91	↵8112
S14360S	09/55-09/87	⊗02/90	**5180**	09/55-05/87					↵8569
S14361S	09/55-06/94	⊗06/94	**5181**	09/55-03/86	**5487**	03/86-06/94			↵8111
S14362S	09/55-06/94	⊗06/94	**5181**	09/55-03/86	**5487**	03/86-06/94			↵8767
S14363S	09/55-10/91	⊗01/92	**5182**	09/55-10/91					↵8053
S14364S	09/55-10/91	⊗01/92	**5182**	09/55-10/91					↵8568

S14365S	10/55-10/91	⊗11/91	**5183**	10/55-05/88	**5502**	05/88-10/91			↵8784
S14366S	10/55-10/91	⊗11/91	**5183**	10/55-05/88	**5502**	05/88-10/91			↵8102
S14367S	10/55-05/91	⊗11/91	**5184**	10/55-05/88	**5514**	05/88-05/91			↵8022
S14368S	10/55-05/91	⊗11/91	**5184**	10/55-05/88	**5514**	05/88-05/91			↵8583
S14369S	10/55-01/93	⊗12/92	**5185**	10/55-01/93					↵8019
S14370S	10/55-01/93	⊗12/92	**5185**	10/55-01/93					↵8020
S14371S	10/55-07/87	⊗01/88	**5186**	10/55-07/87					↵8122
S14372S	10/55-07/87	⊗01/88	**5186**	10/55-07/87					↵8030
S14373S	10/55-07/87	⊗01/88	**5187**	10/55-07/87					↵8121
S14374S	10/55-09/92	⊗10/92	**5187**	10/55-04/88	**5526**	05/88-07/91	**5281**	07/91-09/92	↵8852
S14375S	11/55-06/85	⊗12/87	**5188**	11/55-01/85					↵8043
S14376S	11/55-07/92	⊗09/92	**5188**	11/55-01/85	**5126**	01/85-07/92			↵8760
S14377S	11/55-11/90	⊗07/91	**5189**	11/55-11/90					↵8044
S14378S	11/55-11/90	⊗07/91	**5189**	11/55-11/90					↵8686
S14379S	11/55-04/93	⊗05/93	**5190**	11/55-04/93					↵8777
S14380S	11/55-04/93	⊗05/93	**5190**	11/55-04/93					↵8093
S14381S	11/55-10/90	⊗04/92	**5191**	11/55-10/90					↵8749
S14382S	11/55-10/90	⊗04/92	**5191**	11/55-10/90					↵8083
S14383S	11/55-01/92	⊗02/92	**5192**	11/55-01/76	**5137**	01/76-05/88	**5519**	05/88-10/91	↵8094
S14384S	11/55-07/87	➲**977534**	**5192**	11/55-07/87					↵9807
S14385S	11/55-08/94	⊗09/94	**5193**	11/55-04/86	**5488**	04/86-08/94			↵8011
S14386S	11/55-08/94	⊗09/94	**5193**	11/55-04/86	**5488**	04/86-08/94			↵8012
S14387S	11/55-10/93	⊗10/93	**5194**	11/55-10/93					↵8754
S14388S	11/55-10/93	⊗10/93	**5194**	11/55-10/93					↵8753
S14389S	12/55-09/93	⊗10/93	**5195**	12/55-09/93					↵8811
S14390S	12/55-09/93	⊗10/93	**5195**	12/55-09/93					↵8561
S14391S	12/55-07/94	⊗08/94	**5196**	12/55-07/94					↵8751
S14392S	12/55-07/94	⊗08/94	**5196**	12/55-07/94					↵9859
S14393S	12/55-10/91	⊗10/91	**5197**	12/55-05/88	**5522**	05/88-10/91			↵9860
S14394S	12/55-10/91	⊗02/92	**5197**	12/55-05/88	**5522**	05/88-10/91			↵8046
S14395S	12/55-12/93	⊗01/94	**5198**	12/55-04/81	**5413**	07/81-12/93			↵8049
S14396S	12/55-12/93	⊗01/94	**5198**	12/55-04/81	**5413**	07/81-12/93			↵8103
S14397S	12/55-08/94	⊗08/94	**5199**	12/55-06/82	**5441**	06/82-08/94			↵8050
S14398S	12/55-08/94	⊗08/94	**5199**	12/55-06/82	**5441**	06/82-08/94			↵8782
S14399S	12/55-08/93	⊗08/93	**5200**	12/55-11/86	**5496**	01/87-08/93			↵8104
S14400S	12/55-08/93	⊗08/93	**5200**	12/55-11/86	**5496**	01/87-08/93			↵8038
S14401S	12/55-01/91	⊗12/91	**5201**	12/55-01/91					↵8096
S14402S	12/55-01/91	⊗12/91	**5201**	12/55-01/91					↵8037
S14403S	01/56-10/90	⊗05/92	**5202**	01/56-10/90					↵8024
S14404S	01/56-10/90	⊗05/92	**5202**	01/56-10/90					↵8758
S14405S	01/56-10/93	⊗10/93	**5203**	01/56-05/80	**5243**	02/81-10/93			↵8027
S14406S	01/56-06/80	⊗06/80	**5203**	01/56-09/79					↵8080
S14407S	01/56-04/93	⊗04/93	**5204**	01/56-12/57	**5225**	06/58-03/80	**5402**	03/80-04/93	↵8079
S14408S	01/56-12/57	⊗12/57	**5204**	01/56-12/57					↵8045
S14409S	01/56-02/93	⊗03/93	**5205**	01/56-01/82	**5429**	01/82-02/93			↵8005
S14410S	01/56-02/93	⊗03/93	**5205**	01/56-01/82	**5429**	01/82-02/93			↵8028

Class 415/1 4-EPB Eastleigh

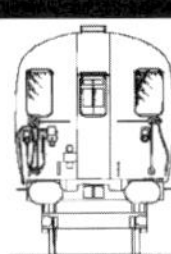

Driving Motor Brake Second Open
DMBSO
S14411S-S14430S

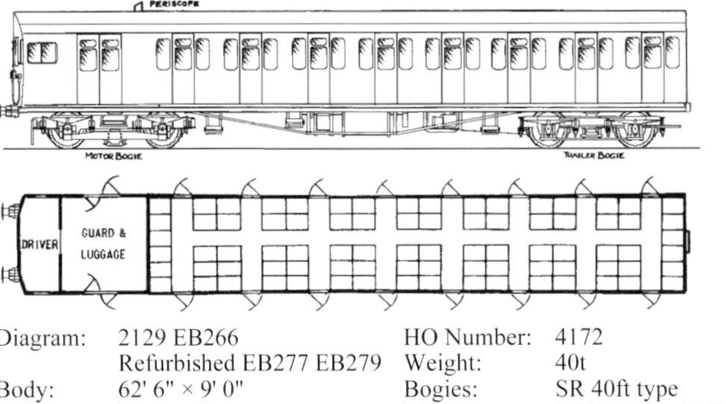

Diagram:	2129 EB266 Refurbished EB277 EB279	HO Number:	4172
		Weight:	40t
Body:	62' 6" × 9' 0"	Bogies:	SR 40ft type
Seats:	82 second	Motor:	EE507C 2 × 250hp

S14411S	02/56-11/93	⊗10/93	**5206**	02/56-05/82	**5437**	05/82-11/93			↵8065
S14412S	02/56-11/93	⊗10/93	**5206**	02/56-05/82	**5437**	05/82-11/93			↵8774
S14413S	02/56-10/92	⊗12/92	**5207**	02/56-04/88	**5515**	04/88-08/91	**5121**	09/91-10/92	↵8584
S14414S	02/56-09/92	⊗10/92	**5207**	02/56-04/88	**5515**	04/88-08/91	**5281**	08/91-09/92	↵8585
S14415S	02/56-04/93	⊗04/93	**5208**	02/56-01/81	**5412**	06/81-04/93			↵9833
S14416S	02/56-11/93	⊗11/93	**5208**	02/56-01/81	**5432**	02/82-11/93			↵8759
S14417S	02/56-01/93	⊗12/92	**5209**	02/56-01/93					↵8195
S14418S	02/56-01/93	⊗01/93	**5209**	02/56-02/91	**5266**	02/91-01/93			↵8221
S14419S	03/56-09/92	⊗10/92	**5210**	03/56-09/92					↵8562
S14420S	03/56-09/92	⊗10/92	**5210**	03/56-09/92					↵8029
S14421S	03/56-11/92	⊗01/93	**5211**	03/56-07/81	**5416**	07/81-11/92			↵8785
S14422S	03/56-11/92	⊗01/93	**5211**	03/56-07/81	**5416**	07/81-11/92			↵8061
S14423S	03/56-07/93	⊗08/93	**5212**	03/56-02/82	**5431**	02/82-07/93			↵8107
S14424S	03/56-07/93	⊗08/93	**5212**	03/56-02/82	**5431**	02/82-07/93			↵9837
S14425S	03/56-11/92	⊗01/93	**5213**	03/56-11/92					↵8062
S14426S	03/56-11/92	⊗01/93	**5213**	03/56-11/92					↵9838
S14427S	03/56-01/93	⊗01/93	**5214**	03/56-04/81	**5407**	04/81-01/93			↵8087
S14428S	03/56-01/93	⊗01/93	**5214**	03/56-04/81	**5407**	04/81-01/93			↵8088
S14429S	04/56-08/93	⊗08/93	**5215**	04/56-01/82	**5428**	01/82-08/93			↵8768
S14430S	04/56-08/93	⊗08/93	**5215**	04/56-01/82	**5428**	01/82-08/93			↵9848

Class 415/1 4-EPB Eastleigh

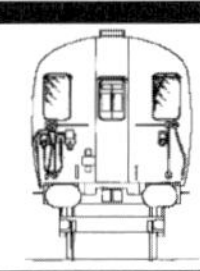

Driving Motor Brake Second Open
DMBSO
S14431S-S14520S

Diagram:	2129 EB266 Refurbished EB277 EB279	HO Number:	4173
		Weight:	40t
Body:	62' 6" × 9' 0"	Bogies:	SR 40ft type
Seats:	82 second	Motor:	EE507C 2 × 250hp

S14431S	04/56-04/94	⊗04/94	**5216**	04/56-11/84	**5458**	11/84-04/94			↵9847
S14432S	04/56-04/94	⊗04/94	**5216**	04/56-11/84	**5458**	11/84-04/94			↵8770
S14433S	04/56-11/92	⊗12/92	**5217**	04/56-11/92					↵8060
S14434S	04/56-11/92	⊗12/92	**5217**	04/56-11/92					↵8054
S14435S	04/56-04/94	⊗04/94	**5218**	04/56-10/80	**5404**	10/80-04/94			↵8114
S14436S	04/56-04/94	⊗04/94	**5218**	04/56-10/80	**5404**	10/80-04/94			↵9808
S14437S	05/56-09/93	⊗12/93	**5219**	05/56-12/82	**5449**	12/82-09/93			↵8077
S14438S	05/56-09/93	⊗12/93	**5219**	05/56-12/82	**5449**	12/82-09/93			↵8082
S14439S	05/56-09/93	⊗09/93	**5220**	05/56-01/73	**5220**	12/73-09/93			↵8775
S14440S	05/56-01/73	⊗03/73	**5220**	05/56-01/73					↵8081
S14441S	05/56-03/94	⊗04/94	**5221**	05/56-05/81	**5414**	07/81-03/94			↵8092
S14442S	05/56-03/94	⊗04/94	**5221**	05/56-05/81	**5414**	07/81-03/94			↵8761
S14443S	06/56-10/91	⊗01/92	**5222**	06/56-05/81	**5418**	09/81-10/91			↵8035
S14444S	06/56-01/91	⊗04/91	**5222**	06/56-01/91					↵8205
S14445S	06/56-07/91	⊗01/92	**5223**	06/56-07/91					↵8074
S14446S	06/56-07/91	⊗01/92	**5223**	06/56-07/91					↵8819
S14447S	06/56-06/93	⊗06/93	**5224**	06/56-07/81	**5424**	11/81-06/93			↵8021
S14448S	06/56-06/93	⊗06/93	**5224**	06/56-07/81	**5424**	11/81-06/93			↵8091
S14449S	06/56-04/93	⊗04/93	**5225**	06/56-08/57	**5225**	06/58-03/80	**5402**	03/80-04/93	↵8572
S14450S	06/56-08/57	⊗08/57	**5225**	06/56-08/57					↵8073
S14451S	07/56-11/92	⊗12/92	**5226**	07/56-11/92					↵8075
S14452S	07/56-11/92	⊗12/92	**5226**	07/56-11/92					↵8853
S14453S	07/56-09/93	⊗10/93	**5227**	07/56-01/82	**5427**	01/82-09/93			↵8076
S14454S	07/56-09/93	⊗10/93	**5227**	07/56-01/82	**5427**	01/82-09/93			↵8573
S14455S	07/56-10/90	⊗11/91	**5228**	07/56-10/90					↵8858
S14456S	07/56-10/90	⊗11/91	**5228**	07/56-10/90					↵8692
S14457S	07/56-08/91	⊗09/91	**5229**	07/56-08/91					↵8687
S14458S	07/56-07/94	⊗07/94	**5229**	07/56-02/70	**5254**	05/70-07/85	**5472**	08/85-07/94	↵9793
S14459S	08/56-10/90	⊗05/92	**5230**	08/56-10/90					↵8225
S14460S	08/56-10/90	⊗05/92	**5230**	08/56-10/90					↵9794
S14461S	08/56-05/91	⊗10/91	**5231**	08/56-05/91					↵8689
S14462S	08/56-05/91	⊗10/91	**5231**	08/56-05/91					↵9791
S14463S	08/56-04/93	⊗07/93	**5232**	08/56-04/93					↵9792
S14464S	08/56-04/93	⊗07/93	**5232**	08/56-04/93					↵9806
S14465S	09/56-02/94	⊗02/94	**5233**	09/56-09/81	**5415**	09/81-02/94			↵8023
S14466S	09/56-02/94	⊗02/94	**5233**	09/56-09/81	**5415**	09/81-02/94			↵8006
S14467S	09/56-04/94	⊗04/94	**5234**	09/56-10/81	**5422**	10/81-04/94			↵8085
S14468S	09/56-04/94	⊗04/94	**5234**	09/56-10/81	**5422**	10/81-04/94			↵8769
S14469S	09/56-01/94	⊗01/94	**5235**	09/56-03/81	**5405**	03/81-01/94			↵8752
S14470S	09/56-01/94	⊗01/94	**5235**	09/56-03/81	**5405**	03/81-01/94			↵9796
S14471S	09/56-06/93	⊗06/93	**5236**	09/56-02/82	**5433**	02/82-06/93			↵9795
S14472S	09/56-06/93	⊗06/93	**5236**	09/56-02/82	**5433**	02/82-06/93			↵8110
S14473S	10/56-04/93	⊗04/93	**5237** **5419**	10/56-11/81 10/88-04/93	**5419**	11/81-09/88	**6335**	09/88-10/88	↵8109
S14474S	10/56-04/93	⊗04/93	**5237**	10/56-11/81	**5419**	11/81-04/93			↵9800
S14475S	10/56-02/93	⊗02/93	**5238**	10/56-05/81	**5411**	05/81-02/93			↵9799
S14476S	10/56-02/93	⊗02/93	**5238**	10/56-05/81	**5411**	05/81-02/93			↵8106
S14477S	10/56-10/91	⊗01/92	**5239**	10/56-10/81	**5417**	10/81-10/91			↵8773
S14478S	10/56-10/91	⊗01/92	**5239**	10/56-10/81	**5417**	10/81-10/91			↵8071
S14479S	10/56-06/72	⊗01/77	**5240**	10/56-06/72					↵8766
S14480S	10/56-05/93	⊗05/93	**5240**	10/56-05/93					↵8762
S14481S	10/56-03/94	⊗05/94	**5241**	10/56-10/84	**5456**	10/84-03/94			↵8036
S14482S	10/56-03/94	⊗05/94	**5241**	10/56-10/84	**5456**	10/84-03/94			↵8787

S14483S	11/56-05/91	⊗01/92	**5242**	11/56-05/91							↩8798
S14484S	11/56-05/91	⊗01/92	**5242**	11/56-05/91							↩8048
S14485S	11/56-10/93	⊗10/93	**5243**	11/56-10/93							↩9789
S14486S	11/56-11/93	⊗11/93	**5243**	11/56-02/81	**5432**	02/82-11/93					↩9790
S14487S	11/56-05/90	➲977702	**5244**	11/56-05/82	**5439**	05/82-05/90					↩8783
S14488S	11/56-05/93	⊗06/93	**5244**	11/56-05/82	**5439**	05/82-05/90	**6322**	05/90-05/93			↩9876
S14489S	11/56-07/61	⊗07/61	**5245**	11/56-07/61							↩8554
S14490S	11/56-01/91	⊗04/91	**5245**	11/56-05/81	**5222**	05/81-01/91					↩8186
S14491S	11/56-09/93	⊗09/93	**5246**	11/56-01/82	**5435**	04/82-09/93					↩9855
S14492S	11/56-08/93	⊗08/93	**5246**	11/56-06/72	**5248**	06/72-08/93					↩8800
S14493S	12/56-02/95	⊗02/95	**5247**	12/56-11/67	**5624**	11/67-09/79	**5029**	09/79-08/85	**5473**	08/85-02/95	↩8755
S14494S	12/56-04/93	⊗05/94	**5247**	12/56-04/81	**5409**	04/81-04/93					↩9812
S14495S	12/56-05/93	⊗06/93	**5248**	12/56-06/72	**5052**	06/72-11/88	**5277**	11/88-05/93			↩9834
S14496S	12/56-10/93	⊗10/93	**5248**	12/56-01/82	**5430**	03/82-10/93					↩9856
S14497S	01/57-07/94	⊗08/94	**5249**	01/57-03/82	**5434**	04/82-07/94					↩8603
S14498S	01/57-07/94	⊗08/94	**5249**	01/57-03/82	**5434**	04/82-07/94					↩8582
S14499S	01/57-10/93	⊗10/93	**5250**	01/57-09/81	**5421**	12/81-10/93					↩9840
S14500S	01/57-10/93	⊗10/93	**5250**	01/57-09/81	**5421**	12/81-10/93					↩9839
S14501S	01/57-11/93	⊗12/93	**5251**	01/57-11/84	**5457**	11/84-11/93					↩8611
S14502S	01/57-11/93	⊗12/93	**5251**	01/57-11/84	**5457**	11/84-11/93					↩8610
S14503S	01/57-11/94	⊗11/94	**5252**	01/57-11/82	**5443**	11/82-11/94					↩8014
S14504S	01/57-11/94	⊗11/94	**5252**	01/57-11/82	**5443**	11/82-11/94					↩9842
S14505S	01/57-01/94	⊗06/94	**5253**	01/57-12/84	**5459**	12/84-01/94					↩8113
S14506S	01/57-01/94	⊗06/94	**5253**	01/57-12/84	**5459**	12/84-01/94					↩8059
S14507S	02/57-02/70	⊗02/70	**5254**	02/57-02/70							↩9841
S14508S	02/57-07/94	⊗07/94	**5254**	02/57-07/85	**5472**	08/85-07/94					↩8553
S14509S	02/57-10/93	⊗10/93	**5255**	02/57-03/82	**5430**	03/82-10/93					↩8017
S14510S	02/57-08/93	⊗08/93	**5255**	02/57-03/82	**5248**	03/82-08/93					↩8191
S14511S	02/57-08/93	⊗09/93	**5256**	02/57-12/81	**5423**	12/81-08/93					↩8763
S14512S	02/57-08/93	⊗09/93	**5256**	02/57-12/81	**5423**	12/81-08/93					↩8086
S14513S	02/57-01/92	⊗01/92	**5257**	02/57-08/82	**5440**	08/82-01/92					↩9798
S14514S	02/57-01/92	⊗01/92	**5257**	02/57-08/82	**5440**	08/82-01/92					↩8786
S14515S	03/57-02/94	⊗03/94	**5258**	03/57-01/85	**5460**	01/85-02/94					↩8831
S14516S	03/57-02/94	⊗03/94	**5258**	03/57-01/85	**5460**	01/85-02/94					↩9797
S14517S	03/57-06/93	⊗06/93	**5259**	03/57-01/82	**5426**	01/82-06/93					↩8108
S14518S	03/57-06/93	⊗06/93	**5259**	03/57-01/82	**5426**	01/82-06/93					↩9846
S14519S	03/57-11/94	⊗02/95	**5260**	03/57-02/85	**5461**	02/85-11/94					↩8217
S14520S	03/57-11/94	⊗02/95	**5260**	03/57-02/85	**5461**	02/85-11/94					↩9886

Class 414/1 2-HAP Eastleigh

Driving Motor Brake Second Open
DMBSO
S14521S-S14556S

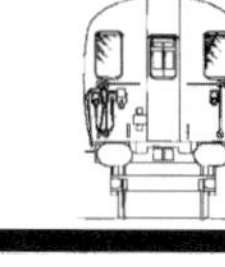

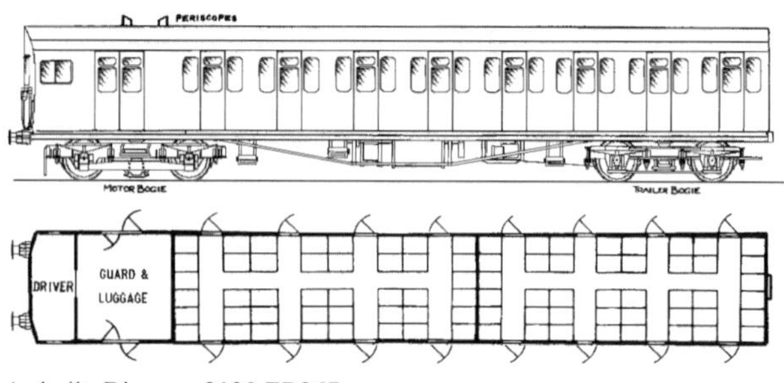

As built, Diagram 2130 EB267

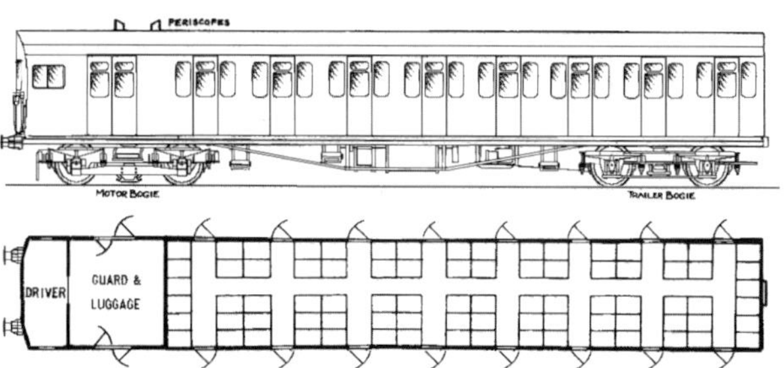

Refurbished, Diagram EB278 EB280

Diagram:	2130 EB267 EB278 EB280	HO Number:	4281
Body:	62' 6" × 9' 0"	Weight:	40t
Seats:	84 second, later 82 second	Bogies:	SR 40ft type
Motor:	EE507C 2 × 250hp		

S14521S	02/58-04/76	⊗04/94	**5601**	02/58-04/76	**5263**	06/76-03/77	**5401**	03/77-03/94	↩9906
S14522S	02/58-11/92	⊗01/93	**5602**	02/58-09/77	**5264**	09/77-11/92			↩9782
S14523S	02/58-11/92	⊗01/93	**5603**	02/58-09/77	**5264**	09/77-11/92			↩9907
S14524S	02/58-07/93	⊗07/93	**5604**	02/58-05/83	**5454**	08/83-07/93			↩8602
S14525S	02/58-07/93	⊗07/93	**5605**	02/58-05/83	**5453**	05/83-07/93			↩8608
S14526S	06/58-11/91	⊗01/92	**5606**	06/58-02/83	**5451**	03/83-11/91			↩8607
S14527S	06/58-04/94	⊗05/94	**5607**	06/58-01/81	**5410**	06/81-01/85	**5445**	01/85-04/94	↩9910
S14528S	07/58-01/93	⊗11/93	**5608**	07/58-01/81	**5410**	06/81-01/93			↩8606
S14529S	07/58-04/94	⊗05/94	**5609**	07/58-03/82	**5445**	03/82-04/94			↩9787
S14530S	07/58-12/93	⊗01/94	**5610**	07/58-06/82	**5438**	06/82-12/93			↩8600
S14531S	06/58-01/93	⊗04/93	**5611**	06/58-07/82	**5446**	09/82-01/93			↩9784
S14532S	06/58-01/93	⊗04/93	**5612**	08/58-08/82	**5447**	11/82-01/93			↩9788
S14533S	06/58-02/92	⊗11/92	**5613**	08/58-10/82	**5450**	02/83-02/92			↩9781
S14534S	06/58-02/82	⊗10/93	**5614**	08/58-02/82	**5436**	05/82-10/93			↩8613
S14535S	06/58-07/94	⊗09/94	**5615**	08/58-05/82	**5444**	09/82-07/94			↩9883
S14536S	06/58-04/94	⊗05/94	**5616**	08/58-04/83	**5452**	04/83-04/94			↩9786
S14537S	06/58-07/94	⊗08/94	**5617**	08/58-04/82	**5442**	07/82-07/94			↩8601
S14538S	06/58-01/93	⊗02/93	**5618**	08/58-10/80	**5425**	12/81-01/93			↩9891
S14539S	09/58-02/93	⊗03/93	**5619**	09/58-09/82	**5448**	12/82-02/93			↩9785
S14540S	09/58-01/85	⊗11/93	**5620**	09/58-03/82	**5445**	03/82-01/85	**5410**	01/85-01/93	↩8609
S14541S	09/58-01/93	⊗01/93	**5621**	09/58-07/82	**5446**	09/82-01/93			↩8615
S14542S	09/58-03/95	⊗05/95	**5622**	09/58-10/80	**5425**	12/81-07/86	**6329**	07/86-03/95	↩8596
S14543S	09/58-10/93	⊗10/93	**5623**	09/58-02/82	**5436**	05/82-10/93			↩9902
S14544S	09/58-11/67	⊗*11/67*	**5624**	09/58-11/67					↩9863
S14545S	09/58-07/93	⊗07/93	**5625**	09/58-05/83	**5453**	05/83-07/93			↩8612
S14546S	09/58-07/93	⊗07/93	**5626**	09/58-04/83	**5452**	04/83-02/88	**6334**	02/88-07/93	↩9783
S14547S	09/58-12/93	⊗01/94	**5627**	09/58-03/82	**5438**	06/82-12/93			↩9899
S14548S	09/58-02/93	⊗03/93	**5628**	09/58-09/82	**5448**	12/82-02/93			↩9908
S14549S	10/58-09/82	➲977068	**5629**	10/58-09/82					↩9904
S14550S	10/58-11/93	⊗12/93	**5630**	10/58-08/82	**5447**	11/82-11/93			↩9909
S14551S	10/58-11/91	⊗01/92	**5631**	10/58-02/83	**5451**	03/83-11/91			↩9900
S14552S	10/58-02/92	⊗11/92	**5632**	10/58-10/82	**5450**	02/83-02/92			↩9905
S14553S	10/58-07/94	⊗09/94	**5633**	10/58-05/82	**5444**	09/82-07/94			↩8614
S14554S	10/58-07/94	⊗08/94	**5634**	10/58-04/82	**5442**	07/82-07/94			↩8598
S14555S	10/58-02/92	⊗02/92	**5635**	10/58-05/83	**5454**	08/83-09/91	**5480**	09/91-02/92	↩8597
S14556S	10/58-03/94	⊗04/94	**5636**	10/58-04/76	**5263**	06/76-03/77	**5401**	03/77-03/94	↩8599

Class 416/1 2-EPB Eastleigh

Driving Motor Brake Second Open
DMBSO
S14557S-S14590S

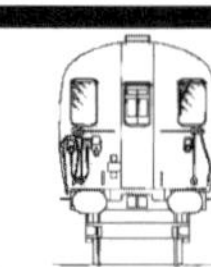

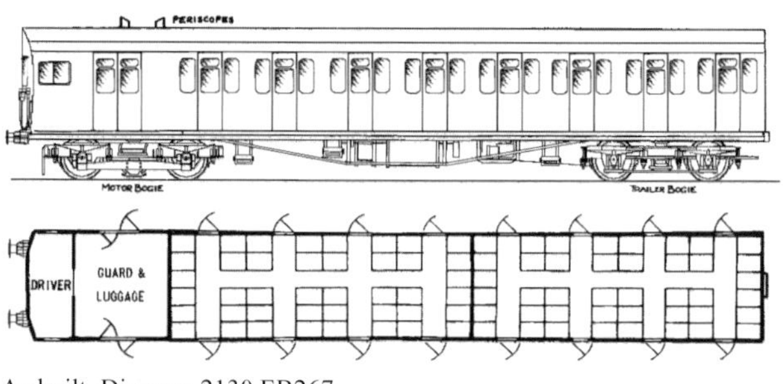

As built, Diagram 2130 EB267

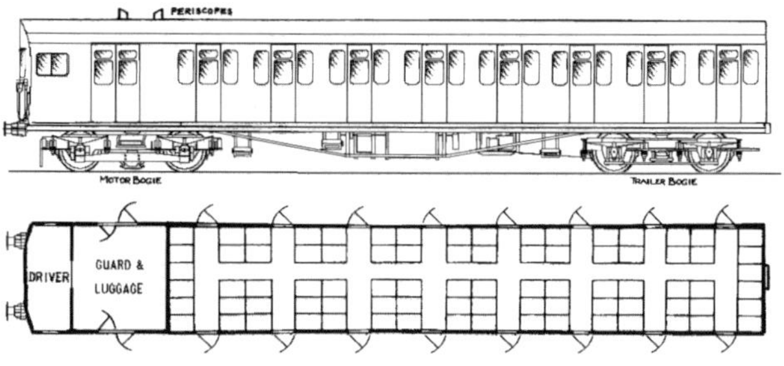

Refurbished, Diagram EB278 EB280

Diagram:	2130 EB267 EB278 EB280	HO Number:	4281
Body:	62' 6" × 9' 0"	Weight:	40t
Seats:	84 second, later 82 second	Bogies:	SR 40ft type
Motor:	EE507C 2 × 250hp		

S14557S	09/59-05/93	⊗05/93	**5651**	09/59-06/85	**6333**	06/85-05/93			↩9872
S14558S	10/59-07/93	⊗07/93	**5652**	10/59-03/84	**6313**	03/84-07/93			↩9893
S14559S	10/59-07/94	⊗08/94	**5653**	10/59-05/84	**6316**	05/84-07/94			↩9867
S14560S	10/59-06/94	⊗06/94	**5654**	10/59-09/84	**6324**	09/84-06/94			↩9898
S14561S	10/59-01/95	⊗03/95	**5655**	10/59-07/84	**6320**	07/84-01/95			↩9869
S14562S	10/59-03/95	⊗	**5656**	10/59-10/83	**6309**	10/83-03/95			↩9889
S14563S	10/59-04/94	⊗05/94	**5657**	10/59-06/85	**6334**	06/85-02/88	**5452**	02/88-04/94	↩9897
S14564S	10/59-03/95	⊗09/06	**5658**	10/59-06/83	**6308**	06/83-03/95			↩9895
S14565S	10/59-11/94	⊗11/94	**5659**	10/59-02/84	**6311**	02/84-11/94			↩9873

S14566S	10/59-10/94	⊗11/94	**5660**	10/59-06/84	**6318**	06/84-10/94			↩**9894**
S14567S	10/59-06/94	⊗06/94	**5661**	10/59-10/84	**6325**	10/84-06/94			↩**9871**
S14568S	10/59-09/94	⊗09/94	**5662**	10/59-07/84	**6319**	07/84-09/94			↩**9896**
S14569S	10/59-03/95	⊗07/95	**5663**	10/59-06/85	**6332**	06/85-03/95			↩**9862**
S14570S	10/59-01/93	⊗02/93	**5664**	10/59-03/85	**6329**	03/85-07/86	**5425**	07/86-01/93	↩**9882**
S14571S	10/59-08/94	⊗10/94	**5665**	10/59-10/82	**6306**	10/82-08/94			↩**9870**
S14572S	11/59-05/93	⊗06/93	**5666**	11/59-02/85	**6327**	02/85-05/93			↩**9877**
S14573S	11/59-03/95	Ⓟ	**5667**	11/59-06/83	**6307**	06/83-03/95			↩**9892**
S14574S	11/59-11/94	⊗12/94	**5668**	11/59-01/84	**6310**	01/84-11/94			↩**9864**
S14575S	11/59-12/89	⊃**977702**	**5669**	11/59-08/84	**6322**	08/84-12/89			↩**9885**
S14576S	11/59-05/93	⊗06/93	**5670**	11/59-04/82	**6303**	04/82-05/93			↩**9881**
S14577S	12/59-01/94	⊗02/94	**5671**	12/59-03/82	**6301**	03/82-01/94			↩**9868**
S14578S	12/59-07/93	⊗08/93	**5672**	12/59-05/84	**6317**	05/84-07/93			↩**9875**
S14579S	12/59-05/94	⊗05/94	**5673**	12/59-02/84	**6312**	02/84-05/94			↩**9865**
S14580S	12/59-03/94	⊗04/94	**5674**	12/59-03/82	**6302**	03/82-03/94			↩**9888**
S14581S	12/59-01/94	⊗02/94	**5675**	12/59-08/84	**6323**	08/84-01/94			↩**8605**
S14582S	12/59-04/94	⊗05/94	**5676**	12/59-03/85	**6328**	03/85-04/94			↩**9890**
S14583S	12/59-02/95	⊗07/95	**5677**	12/59-05/85	**6331**	05/85-02/95			↩**9884**
S14584S	12/59-07/87	⊗12/87	**5678**	12/59-07/84	**6321**	07/84-12/86			↩**9887**
S14585S	12/59-08/94	⊗08/94	**5679**	12/59-01/85	**6326**	01/85-08/94			↩**9861**
S14586S	12/59-07/93	⊗07/93	**5680**	12/59-04/84	**6314**	04/84-07/93			↩**9878**
S14587S	12/59-01/94	⊗02/94	**5681**	12/59-07/82	**6305**	07/82-01/94			↩**9874**
S14588S	12/59-03/95	⊗05/95	**5682**	12/59-05/85	**6330**	05/85-03/95			↩**9880**
S14589S	12/59-05/93	⊗05/93	**5683**	12/59-04/82	**6304**	04/82-05/93			↩**9800**
S14590S	12/59-10/94	⊗11/94	**5684**	12/59-04/84	**6315**	04/84-10/94			↩**9879**

Class 415/1 4-EPB Eastleigh

Trailer Third
TT
S15001S-S15033S

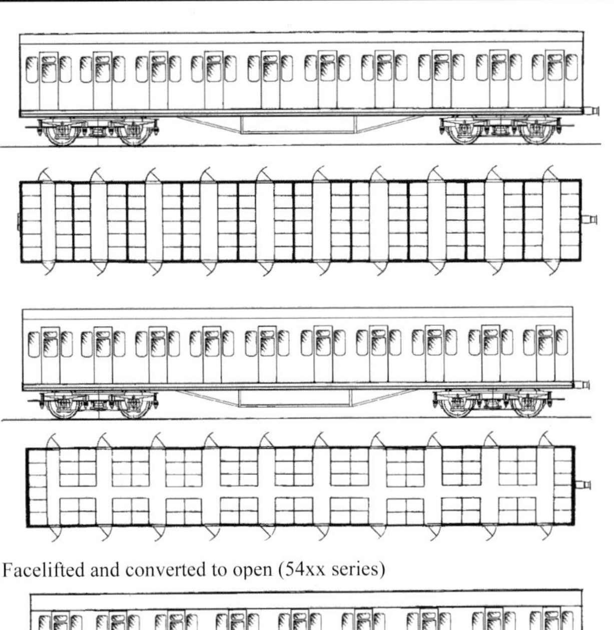

Facelifted and converted to open (54xx series)

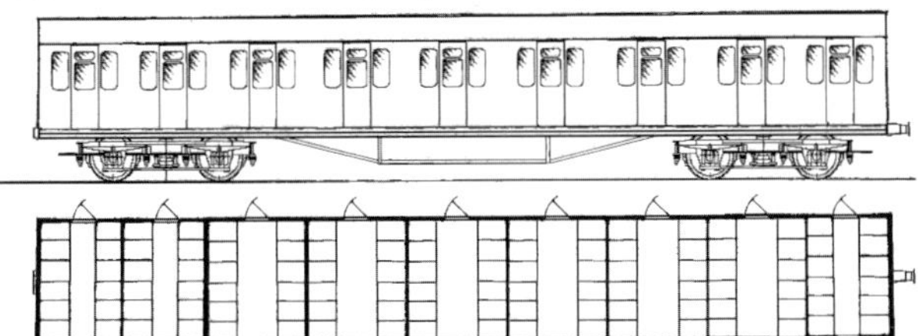

15005, Diagram 2314 EH267

Diagram:	2013 EH268	HO Number:	3798/99
Body:	62' 6" × 9' 0"	Weight:	28t
Seats:	120 or 108 third Facelifted 102 second	Bogies:	SR 40ft type

Rewired and renumbered from 4-SUB stock.

S15001S	12/51-03/94	⊗05/94	**5001**	12/51-01/84	**5241**	01/84-10/84	**5456**	10/84-03/94	⊂**10398**
S15002S	02/52-05/94	⊗06/94	**5002**	02/52-04/85	**5466**	05/85-05/94			⊂**10345**
S15003S	03/52-03/91	⊗10/91	**5003**	03/52-03/85	**5467**	05/85-03/91			⊂**10333**
S15004S	03/52-10/91	⊗11/91	**5004**	03/52-06/85	**5469**	06/85-10/91			⊂**10203**
S15005S	04/52-05/91	⊗09/91	**5005**	04/52-04/88	**5531**	04/88-05/91			⊂**11454**
S15006S	04/52-07/87	⊗12/88	**5006**	04/52-07/87					⊂**10253**
S15007S	04/52-03/86	⊗05/86	**5007**	04/52-07/85					⊂**10228**
S15008S	05/52-08/59	⊗09/59	**5008**	05/52-08/59					⊂**10335**
S15009S	05/52-02/94	⊗06/94	**5009**	05/52-08/85	**5482**	11/85-02/94			⊂**10201**
S15010S	06/52-05/93	⊗05/93	**5010**	06/52-06/85	**5475**	08/85-05/93			⊂**10391**
S15011S	06/52-12/93	⊗12/93	**5011**	06/52-02/85	**5462**	02/85-12/93			⊂**10174**
S15012S	07/52-08/94	⊗08/94	**5012**	07/52-05/86	**5489**	05/86-08/94			⊂**10169**
S15013S	08/52-06/91	⊃**977703**	**5013**	08/52-05/88	**5532**	05/88-06/91			⊂**10189**
S15014S	08/52-07/87	⊗04/89	**5014**	08/52-10/86	**5109**	10/86-07/87			⊂**10184**
S15015S	08/52-05/91	⊗11/91	**5015**	08/52-01/86	**5125**	01/86-05/88	**5501**	05/88-05/91	⊂**10277**
S15016S	04/53-05/90	⊗11/90	**5016**	04/53-05/88	**5511**	05/88-05/90			⊂**10251**
S15017S	05/53-07/87	⊗12/89	**5017**	05/53-07/87					⊂**10292**
S15018S	05/53-10/91	⊗11/91	**5018**	05/53-04/88	**5508**	04/88-10/91			⊂**10238**
S15019S	05/53-06/94	⊗06/94	**5019**	05/53-03/85	**5463**	03/85-06/94			⊂**10332**
S15020S	05/53-04/94	⊗05/94	**5020**	05/53-06/58	**5225**	06/58-03/80	**5402**	03/80-01/85	
			5445	01/85-04/94					⊂**10177**
S15021S	05/53-02/59	⊗ *61*	**5021**	05/53-02/59					⊂**10254**
S15022S	06/53-01/91	⊗03/91	**5022**	06/53-05/88	**5517**	05/88-01/91			⊂**10175**
S15023S	06/53-11/93	⊗11/93	**5023**	06/53-07/58	**5021**	10/59-09/84	**5455**	09/84-11/93	⊂**10309**
S15024S	06/53-07/87	⊗01/88	**5024**	06/53-07/87					⊂**10266**
S15025S	06/53-07/87	⊗02/90	**5025**	06/53-07/87					⊂**10456**
S15026S	07/53-06/88	⊗12/87	**5026**	07/53-11/85					⊂**10298**
S15027S	07/53-11/93	⊗11/93	**5027**	07/53-02/84	**5021**	02/84-09/84	**5455**	09/84-11/93	⊂**10281**
S15028S	08/53-07/87	⊗12/87	**5028**	08/53-07/87					⊂**10272**
S15029S	08/53-02/95	⊗02/95	**5029**	08/53-08/85	**5473**	08/85-02/95			⊂**10202**
S15030S	08/53-04/93	⊗05/93	**5030**	08/53-09/85	**5478**	09/85-04/93			⊂**10278**
S15031S	08/53-05/91	⊗12/92	**5031**	08/53-12/85	**5484**	12/85-05/91			⊂**10192**
S15032S	08/53-05/91	⊗10/91	**5032**	08/53-05/88	**5516**	05/88-05/91			⊂**10280**
S15033S	09/53-01/94	⊗01/94	**5033**	09/53-08/85	**5474**	08/85-01/94			⊂**10460**

Class 415/1 4-EPB Eastleigh

Trailer Second
TS
S15034S-S15078S

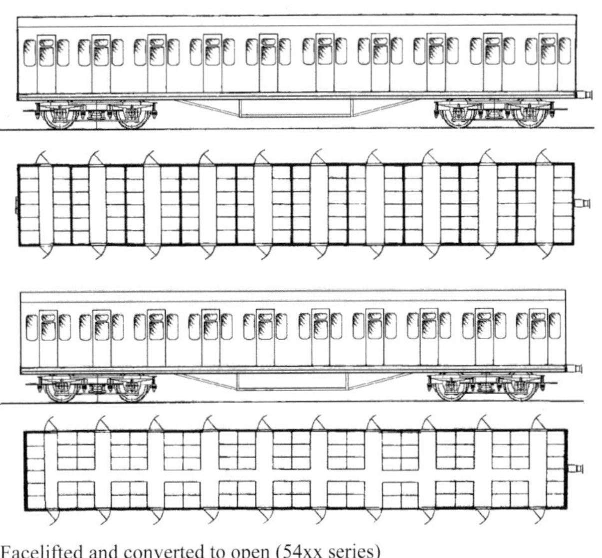

Facelifted and converted to open (54xx series)

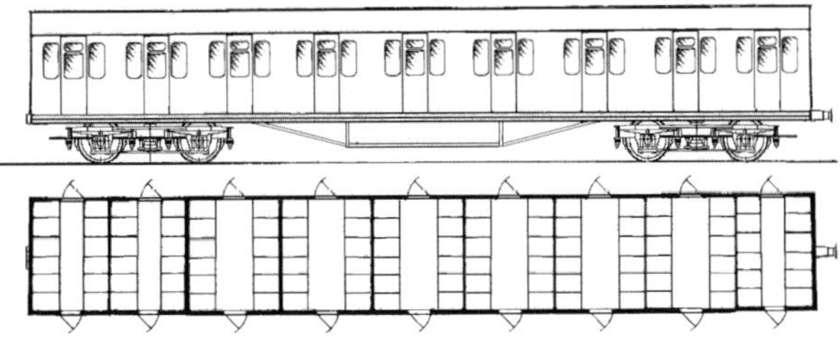

15038, Diagram 2314 EH267

Diagram:	2013 EH268	HO Number:	4174
Body:	62' 6" × 9' 0"	Weight:	28t
Seats:	120 or 108 second Facelifted 102 second	Bogies:	SR 40ft type

Rewired and renumbered from 4-SUB stock.

S15034S	04/56-04/94	⊗04/94	**5216**	04/56-11/84	**5458**	11/84-04/94			⊂**10470**
S15035S	04/56-06/85	⊗	**5217**	04/56-06/85					⊂**10229**
S15036S	04/56-04/94	⊗04/94	**5218**	04/56-10/80	**5404**	10/80-04/94			⊂**10459**
S15037S	05/56-02/92	⊗02/92	**5219**	05/56-12/82	**5449**	12/82-02/92			⊂**10222**
S15038S	05/56-05/90	⊗10/90	**5220**	05/56-01/73	**5220**	12/73-04/88	**5507**	04/88-05/90	⊂**11451**

S15039S	05/56-03/94	⊗04/94	**5221**	05/56-05/81	**5414**	07/81-03/94			⊂**10246**
S15040S	06/56-02/94	⊗02/94	**5222**	06/56-09/81	**5415**	09/81-02/94			⊂**10285**
S15041S	06/56-10/91	⊗01/92	**5223**	06/56-10/81	**5417**	10/81-10/91			⊂**10322**
S15042S	06/56-06/93	⊗06/93	**5224**	06/56-07/81	**5424**	11/81-06/93			⊂**10283**
S15043S	06/56-08/87	⊗09/87	**5225**	06/56-08/57	**5301**	01/60-08/87			⊂**10275**
S15044S	07/56-11/93	⊗11/93	**5226**	07/56-02/82	**5432**	02/82-11/93			⊂**10224**
S15045S	07/56-09/93	⊗10/93	**5227**	07/56-01/82	**5427**	01/82-09/93			⊂**10452**
S15046S	07/56-09/93	⊗10/93	**5228**	07/56-01/82	**5427**	01/82-09/93			⊂**10466**
S15047S	07/56-04/93	⊗05/94	**5229**	07/56-04/81	**5409**	04/81-04/93			⊂**10468**
S15048S	08/56-05/93	⊗05/93	**5230**	08/56-06/85	**5475**	08/85-05/93			⊂**10299**
S15049S	08/56-07/91	⊗02/92	**5231**	08/56-04/88	**5525**	04/88-07/91			⊂**10176**
S15050S	08/56-04/94	⊗04/94	**5232**	08/56-10/81	**5422**	10/81-04/94			⊂**10260**
S15051S	09/56-02/94	⊗02/94	**5233**	09/56-09/81	**5415**	09/81-02/94			⊂**10211**
S15052S	09/56-06/93	⊗06/93	**5234**	09/56-10/81	**5424**	11/81-06/93			⊂**10223**
S15053S	09/56-01/94	⊗01/94	**5235**	09/56-03/81	**5405**	03/81-01/94			⊂**10471**
S15054S	09/56-06/93	⊗06/93	**5236**	09/56-02/82	**5433**	02/82-06/93			⊂**10167**
S15055S	10/56-04/93	⊗04/93	**5237**	10/56-11/81	**5419**	11/81-04/93			⊂**10451**
S15056S	10/56-02/93	⊗02/93	**5238**	10/56-05/81	**5411**	05/81-02/93			⊂**10190**
S15057S	10/56-10/91	⊗01/92	**5239**	10/56-10/81	**5417**	10/81-10/91			⊂**10193**
S15058S	10/56-04/93	⊗04/93	**5240**	10/56-11/81	**5419**	11/81-04/93			⊂**10188**
S15059S	10/56-03/94	⊗05/94	**5241**	10/56-10/84	**5456**	10/84-03/94			⊂**10450**
S15060S	11/56-01/93	⊗01/93	**5242**	11/56-04/81	**5407**	04/81-01/93			⊂**10467**
S15061S	11/56-08/93	⊗08/93	**5243**	11/56-10/80	**5246**	10/80-01/82	**5428**	01/82-08/93	⊂**10226**
S15062S	11/56-08/94	⊗09/94	**5244**	11/56-05/82	**5439**	05/82-05/90	**5467**	03/91-08/94	⊂**10178**
S15063S	11/56-10/91	⊗01/92	**5245**	11/56-05/81	**5418**	09/81-10/91			⊂**10194**
S15064S	11/56-06/72	⊗	**5246**	11/56-03/75					⊂**10469**
S15065S	12/56-04/93	⊗05/94	**5247**	12/56-04/81	**5409**	04/81-04/93			⊂**10212**
S15066S	12/56-06/93	⊗06/93	**5248**	12/56-01/82	**5426**	01/82-06/93			⊂**10186**
S15067S	01/57-07/94	⊗08/94	**5249**	01/57-03/82	**5434**	04/82-07/94			⊂**10453**
S15068S	01/57-10/93	⊗10/93	**5250**	01/57-09/81	**5421**	12/81-10/93			⊂**10183**
S15069S	01/57-11/93	⊗12/93	**5251**	01/57-11/84	**5457**	11/84-11/93			⊂**10225**
S15070S	01/57-11/94	⊗11/94	**5252**	01/57-11/82	**5443**	11/82-11/94			⊂**10180**
S15071S	01/57-01/94	⊗06/94	**5253**	01/57-12/84	**5459**	12/84-01/94			⊂**10191**
S15072S	10/54-02/81	⊗02/81	**5254**	02/57-02/70	**5137**	03/70-01/76	**5203**	03/79-03/80	⊂**10179**
S15073S	02/57-10/93	⊗10/93	**5255**	02/57-09/81	**5421**	12/81-10/93			⊂**10185**
S15074S	02/57-08/93	⊗09/93	**5256**	02/57-12/81	**5423**	12/81-08/93			⊂**10168**
S15075S	02/57-01/92	⊗01/92	**5257**	02/57-08/82	**5440**	08/82-01/92			⊂**10187**
S15076S	03/57-02/94	⊗03/94	**5258**	03/57-01/85	**5460**	01/85-02/94			⊂**10227**
S15077S	03/57-06/93	⊗06/93	**5259**	03/57-01/82	**5426**	01/82-06/93			⊂**10204**
S15078S	03/57-11/94	⊗02/95	**5260**	03/57-02/85	**5461**	02/85-11/94			⊂**10182**

Class 415/1 4-EPB Eastleigh

Trailer Second
TS
S15079S-S15084S

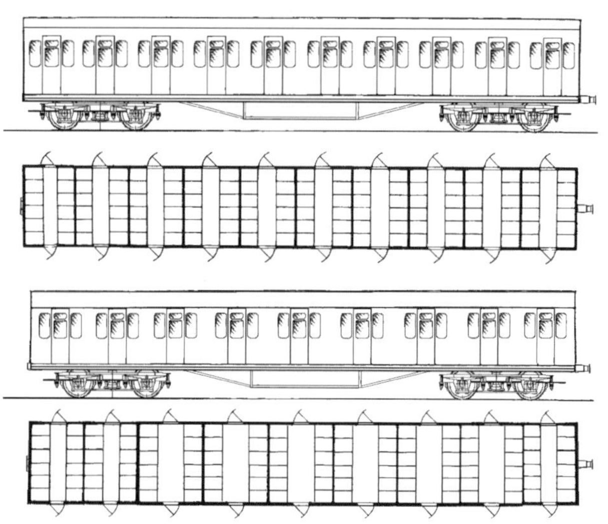

15080 & 15084, Diagram 2314 EH267

Diagram:	2013 EH268	HO Number:	
Body:	62' 6" × 9' 0"	Weight:	28t
Seats:	120 or 108 second	Bogies:	SR 40ft type

Rewired and renumbered from 4-SUB stock.

S15079S	01/61-12/83	⊗06/86	**5302**	01/61-12/83			⊂**10195**
S15080S	08/60-06/85	⊗12/87	**5008**	08/60-06/85			⊂**11456**
S15081S	08/65-01/91	⊗08/91	**5261**	08/65-04/88	**5530**	04/88-01/91	⊂**10208**
S15082S	08/65-06/88	⊗	**5261**	08/65-08/87			⊂**10207**
S15083S	12/65-07/87	⊗12/87	**5262**	12/65-06/86	**5028**	06/86-07/87	⊂**10395**
S15084S	01/69-03/91	⊗04/92	**5115**	08/69-07/88	**5510**	07/88-03/91	⊂**11485**

Class 415/1 4-EPB Eastleigh

Trailer Third Open
TTO
S15101S-S15115S

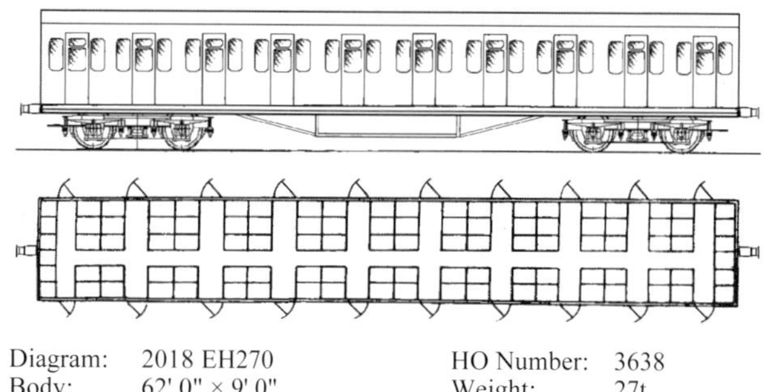

Diagram:	2018 EH270	HO Number:	3638
Body:	62' 0" × 9' 0"	Weight:	27t
Seats:	102 third	Bogies:	SR 40ft type

15101-15109 originally to be numbered 9035-9043

S15101S	12/51-03/95	⊗04/04	**5001**	12/51-11/88	**5265**	11/88-11/90	**5001**	11/90-03/95	↩**9526**
S15102S	02/52-07/87	⊗12/87	**5002**	02/52-04/85	**5142**	04/85-12/86			↩**9569**
S15103S	03/52-05/93	⊗06/93	**5003**	03/52-03/85	**5052**	03/85-11/88	**5277**	11/88-05/93	↩**9493**
S15104S	03/52-08/93	⊗09/93	**5004**	03/52-06/85	**5123**	06/85-02/87	**5497**	02/87-08/93	↩**9506**
S15105S	04/52-10/93	⊗10/93	**5005**	04/52-04/88	**5159**	04/88-10/93			↩**9508**
S15106S	04/52-07/87	⊗12/88	**5006**	04/52-07/87					↩**9552**
S15107S	04/52-11/92	⊗12/92	**5007**	04/52-07/85	**5155**	07/85-11/92			↩**9563**
S15108S	05/52-10/90	⊗04/92	**5008**	05/52-08/59	**5008**	08/60-06/85	**5191**	08/85-10/90	↩**9507**
S15109S	05/52-02/92	⊗04/92	**5009**	05/52-08/85	**5169**	08/85-02/92			↩**9561**
S15110S	06/52-10/90	⊗05/92	**5010**	06/52-06/85	**5230**	06/85-10/90			↩**9615**
S15111S	06/52-12/93	⊗12/93	**5011**	06/52-02/85	**5462**	02/85-12/93			↩**9609**
S15112S	07/52-08/94	⊗08/94	**5012**	07/52-05/86	**5489**	05/86-08/94			↩**9555**
S15113S	08/52-08/93	⊗08/93	**5013**	08/52-05/88	**5035**	05/88-11/88	**5268**	11/88-08/93	↩**9541**
S15114S	08/52-02/93	⊗02/93	**5014**	08/52-10/86	**5493**	10/86-02/93			↩**9558**
S15115S	08/52-08/94	⊗09/94	**5015**	08/52-01/86	**5491**	07/86-08/94			↩**9548**

Class 415/1 4-EPB Eastleigh

Trailer Third Open
TTO
S15116S-S15133S

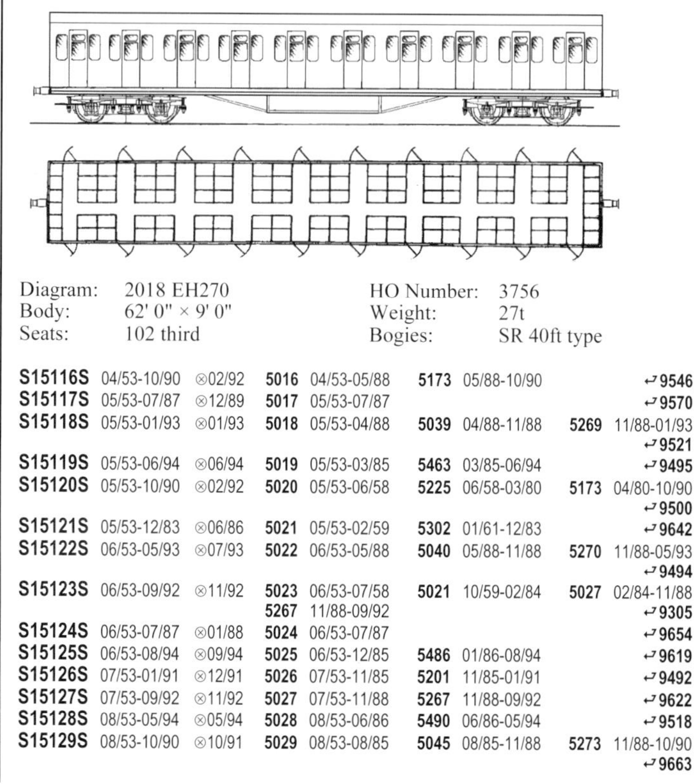

Diagram:	2018 EH270	HO Number:	3756
Body:	62' 0" × 9' 0"	Weight:	27t
Seats:	102 third	Bogies:	SR 40ft type

S15116S	04/53-10/90	⊗02/92	**5016**	04/53-05/88	**5173**	05/88-10/90			↩**9546**
S15117S	05/53-07/87	⊗12/89	**5017**	05/53-07/87					↩**9570**
S15118S	05/53-01/93	⊗01/93	**5018**	05/53-04/88	**5039**	04/88-11/88	**5269**	11/88-01/93	↩**9521**
S15119S	05/53-06/94	⊗06/94	**5019**	05/53-03/85	**5463**	03/85-06/94			↩**9495**
S15120S	05/53-10/90	⊗02/92	**5020**	05/53-06/58	**5225**	06/58-03/80	**5173**	04/80-10/90	↩**9500**
S15121S	05/53-12/83	⊗06/86	**5021**	05/53-02/59	**5302**	01/61-12/83			↩**9642**
S15122S	06/53-05/93	⊗07/93	**5022**	06/53-05/88	**5040**	05/88-11/88	**5270**	11/88-05/93	↩**9494**
S15123S	06/53-09/92	⊗11/92	**5023** **5267**	06/53-07/58 11/88-09/92	**5021**	10/59-02/84	**5027**	02/84-11/88	↩**9305**
S15124S	06/53-07/87	⊗01/88	**5024**	06/53-07/87					↩**9654**
S15125S	06/53-08/94	⊗09/94	**5025**	06/53-12/85	**5486**	01/86-08/94			↩**9619**
S15126S	07/53-01/91	⊗12/91	**5026**	07/53-11/85	**5201**	11/85-01/91			↩**9492**
S15127S	07/53-09/92	⊗11/92	**5027**	07/53-11/88	**5267**	11/88-09/92			↩**9622**
S15128S	08/53-05/94	⊗05/94	**5028**	08/53-06/86	**5490**	06/86-05/94			↩**9518**
S15129S	08/53-10/90	⊗10/91	**5029**	08/53-08/85	**5045**	08/85-11/88	**5273**	11/88-10/90	↩**9663**

S15130S	08/53-01/91	⊗09/91	**5030**	08/53-09/85	**5042**	09/85-11/88	**5271**	11/88-01/91	↩**9571**
S15131S	08/53-09/87	⊗02/90	**5031**	08/53-12/85	**5180**	12/85-05/87			↩**9768**
S15132S	08/53-12/91	⊗02/92	**5032**	08/53-05/88	**5133**	05/88-12/91			↩**9547**
S15133S	09/53-01/91	⊗08/91	**5033**	09/53-08/85	**5146**	08/85-01/91			↩**9623**

Class 415/1 4-EPB Eastleigh

Trailer Third Open
TTO
S15134S-S15153S

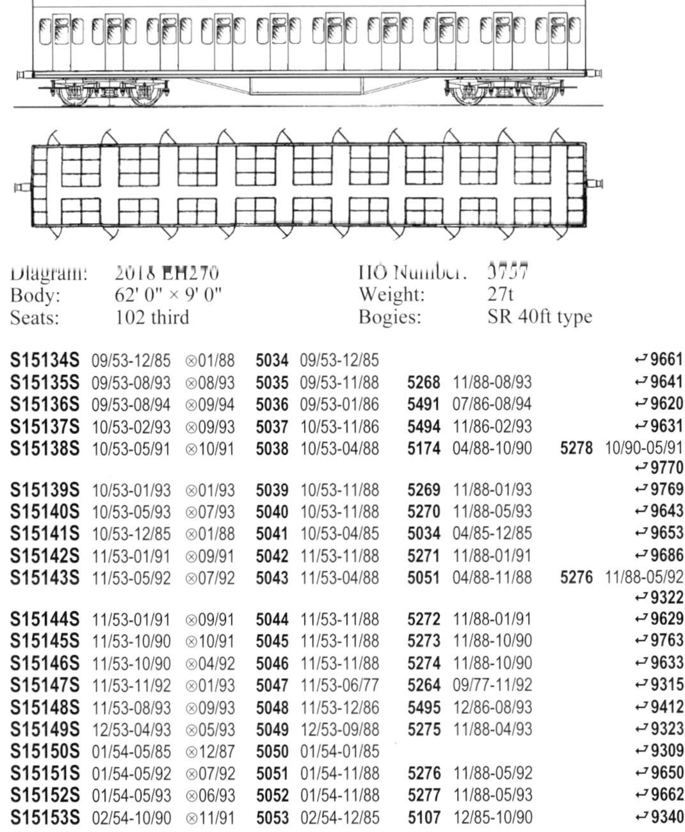

Diagram: 2018 EH270 HO Number: 3757
Body: 62' 0" × 9' 0" Weight: 27t
Seats: 102 third Bogies: SR 40ft type

S15134S	09/53-12/85	⊗01/88	**5034**	09/53-12/85					↩**9661**
S15135S	09/53-08/93	⊗08/93	**5035**	09/53-11/88	**5268**	11/88-08/93			↩**9641**
S15136S	09/53-08/94	⊗09/94	**5036**	09/53-01/86	**5491**	07/86-08/94			↩**9620**
S15137S	10/53-02/93	⊗09/93	**5037**	10/53-11/86	**5494**	11/86-02/93			↩**9631**
S15138S	10/53-05/91	⊗10/91	**5038**	10/53-04/88	**5174**	04/88-10/90	**5278**	10/90-05/91	↩**9770**
S15139S	10/53-01/93	⊗01/93	**5039**	10/53-11/88	**5269**	11/88-01/93			↩**9769**
S15140S	10/53-05/93	⊗07/93	**5040**	10/53-11/88	**5270**	11/88-05/93			↩**9643**
S15141S	10/53-12/85	⊗01/88	**5041**	10/53-04/85	**5034**	04/85-12/85			↩**9653**
S15142S	11/53-01/91	⊗09/91	**5042**	11/53-11/88	**5271**	11/88-01/91			↩**9686**
S15143S	11/53-05/92	⊗07/92	**5043**	11/53-04/88	**5051**	04/88-11/88	**5276**	11/88-05/92	↩**9322**
S15144S	11/53-01/91	⊗09/91	**5044**	11/53-11/88	**5272**	11/88-01/91			↩**9629**
S15145S	11/53-10/90	⊗10/91	**5045**	11/53-11/88	**5273**	11/88-10/90			↩**9763**
S15146S	11/53-10/90	⊗04/92	**5046**	11/53-11/88	**5274**	11/88-10/90			↩**9633**
S15147S	11/53-11/92	⊗01/93	**5047**	11/53-06/77	**5264**	09/77-11/92			↩**9315**
S15148S	11/53-08/93	⊗09/93	**5048**	11/53-12/86	**5495**	12/86-08/93			↩**9412**
S15149S	12/53-04/93	⊗05/93	**5049**	12/53-09/88	**5275**	11/88-04/93			↩**9323**
S15150S	01/54-05/85	⊗12/87	**5050**	01/54-01/85					↩**9309**
S15151S	01/54-05/92	⊗07/92	**5051**	01/54-11/88	**5276**	11/88-05/92			↩**9650**
S15152S	01/54-05/93	⊗06/93	**5052**	01/54-11/88	**5277**	11/88-05/93			↩**9662**
S15153S	02/54-10/90	⊗11/91	**5053**	02/54-12/85	**5107**	12/85-10/90			↩**9340**

Class 415/1 4-EPB Eastleigh

Trailer Third Open
TTO
S15154S-S15158S

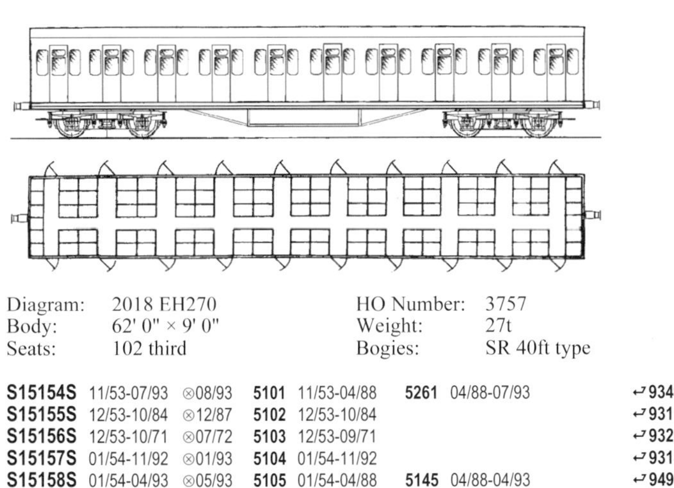

Diagram: 2018 EH270 HO Number: 3757
Body: 62' 0" × 9' 0" Weight: 27t
Seats: 102 third Bogies: SR 40ft type

S15154S	11/53-07/93	⊗08/93	**5101**	11/53-04/88	**5261**	04/88-07/93	↩**9349**
S15155S	12/53-10/84	⊗12/87	**5102**	12/53-10/84			↩**9311**
S15156S	12/53-10/71	⊗07/72	**5103**	12/53-09/71			↩**9326**
S15157S	01/54-11/92	⊗01/93	**5104**	01/54-11/92			↩**9318**
S15158S	01/54-04/93	⊗05/93	**5105**	01/54-04/88	**5145**	04/88-04/93	↩**9490**

Class 415/1 4-EPB Eastleigh

Trailer Third Open
TTO
S15159S-S15178S

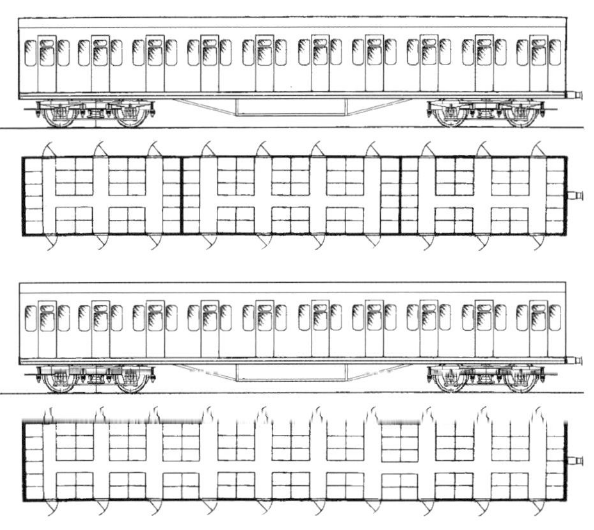

Facelifted, Diagram EH280

Diagram: 2015 EH265 EH280 HO Number: 3757
Body: 62' 0" × 9' 0" Weight: 28t
Seats: 106 third, later 102 second Bogies: SR 40ft type

S15159S	09/53-05/94	⊗06/94	**5034**	09/53-04/85	**5464**	04/85-05/94			↩**9761**
S15160S	09/53-06/91	➲**977704**	**5035**	09/53-05/88	**5532**	05/88-06/91			↩**9635**
S15161S	09/53-08/94	⊗09/94	**5036**	09/53-01/86	**5486**	01/86-08/94			↩**9334**
S15162S	10/53-07/87	⊗12/89	**5037**	10/53-11/86	**5108**	11/86-07/87			↩**9664**
S15163S	10/53-01/91	⊗02/92	**5038**	10/53-04/88	**5504**	04/88-01/91			↩**9627**
S15164S	10/53-10/91	⊗11/91	**5039**	10/53-04/88	**5508**	04/88-10/91			↩**9665**
S15165S	10/53-01/91	⊗03/91	**5040**	10/53-05/88	**5517**	05/88-01/91			↩**9644**
S15166S	10/53-05/94	⊗06/94	**5041**	10/53-04/85	**5464**	04/85-05/94			↩**9660**
S15167S	11/53-04/93	⊗05/93	**5042**	11/53-09/85	**5478**	09/85-04/93			↩**10403**
S15168S	11/53-10/90	⊗10/91	**5043**	11/53-04/88	**5529**	04/88-10/90			↩**9350**
S15169S	11/53-07/94	⊗07/94	**5044**	11/53-07/85	**5472**	08/85-07/94			↩**9692**
S15170S	11/53-02/95	⊗02/95	**5045**	11/53-08/85	**5473**	08/85-02/95			↩**10408**
S15171S	11/53-07/87	⊗	**5046**	11/53-07/87					↩**9636**
S15172S	11/53-08/77	⊗06/77	**5047**	11/53-06/77					↩**9771**
S15173S	11/53-06/88	⊗05/89	**5048**	11/53-12/86	**5122**	12/86-07/87			↩**9175**
S15174S	12/53-11/94	⊗11/94	**5049**	12/53-09/80	**5403**	09/80-11/94			↩**10409**
S15175S	01/54-05/94	⊗05/94	**5050**	01/54-01/85	**5150**	01/85-11/85	**5483**	11/85-05/94	↩**9338**
S15176S	01/54-10/90	⊗10/91	**5051**	01/54-04/88	**5529**	04/88-10/90			↩**9177**
S15177S	01/54-08/94	⊗09/94	**5052**	01/54-03/85	**5467**	05/85-08/94			↩**9316**
S15178S	02/54-02/94	⊗03/94	**5053**	02/54-12/85	**5485**	12/85-02/94			↩**9167**

Class 415/1 4-EPB Eastleigh

Trailer Third Open
TTO
S15179S-S15183S

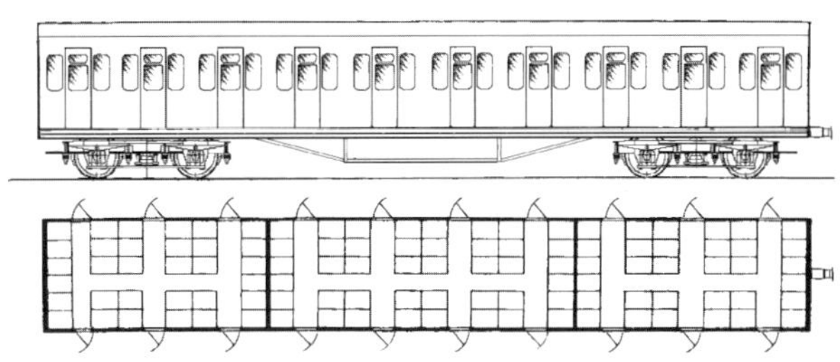

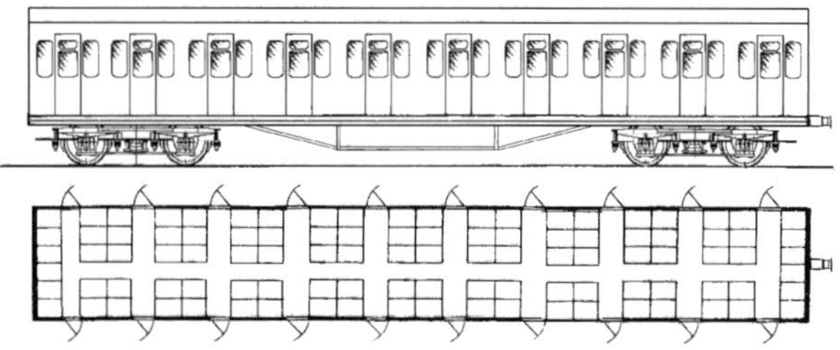

Facelifted, Diagram EH280

Diagram:	2015 EH265 EH280	HO Number:	3757
Body:	62' 0" × 9' 0"	Weight:	28t
Seats:	106 third, later 102 second	Bogies:	SR 40ft type

Number	Dates	Fate	Unit	Dates	Unit	Dates	Unit	Dates	To
S15179S	11/53-01/91	⊗08/91	**5101**	11/53-04/88	**5530**	04/88-01/91			↩**9687**
S15180S	12/53-04/93	⊗04/93	**5102**	12/53-10/84	**5477**	09/85-01/93			↩**9184**
S15181S	12/53-10/80	⊗04/81	**5103**	12/53-09/71	**5246**	03/75-10/80			↩**9230**
S15182S	01/54-03/94	⊗04/94	**5104**	01/54-05/81	**5414**	07/81-03/94			↩**9197**
S15183S	01/54-05/90	⊗*12/90*	**5105**	01/54-04/88	**5512**	04/88-05/90			↩**9206**

Class 415/1 4-EPB Eastleigh

Trailer Third Open
TTO
S15184S-S15233S

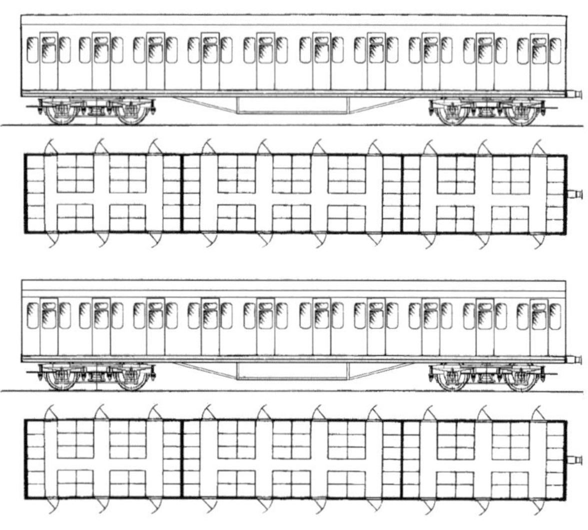

15216 onwards fitted with rainstrips

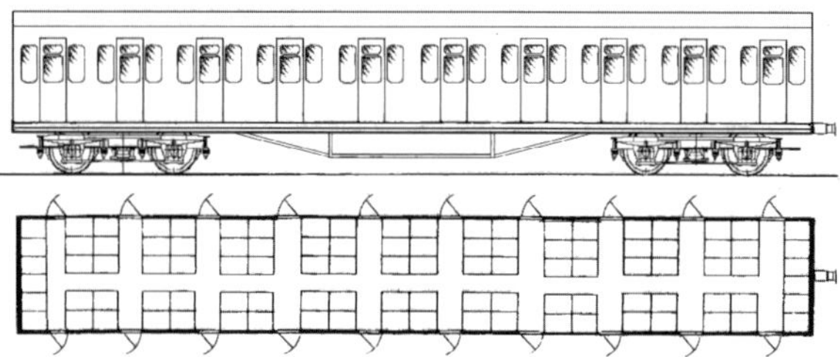

Facelifted, Diagram EH280

Diagram:	2015 EH265	HO Number:	4016
Body:	62' 0" × 9' 0"	Weight:	28t
Seats:	106 third, later 102 second	Bogies:	SR 40ft type

Number	Dates	Fate	Unit	Dates	Unit	Dates	Unit	Dates	To
S15184S	02/54-04/92	⊗07/92	**5106**	02/54-03/85	**5468**	06/85-04/92			↩**9628**
S15185S	02/54-02/94	⊗03/94	**5107**	02/54-12/85	**5485**	12/85-02/94			↩**9209**
S15186S	03/54-07/87	⊗12/89	**5108**	03/54-07/87					↩**9218**
S15187S	03/54-07/87	⊗04/89	**5109**	03/54-07/87					↩**9240**
S15188S	03/54-11/83	⊗10/87	**5110**	03/54-11/83					↩**9196**
S15189S	03/54-01/92	⊗02/92	**5111**	03/54-05/88	**5520**	05/88-10/91			↩**9320**
S15190S	03/54-07/87	⊗01/88	**5112**	03/54-08/86	**5192**	08/86-07/87			↩**9202**
S15191S	04/54-12/93	⊗01/94	**5113**	04/54-04/81	**5413**	07/81-12/93			↩**9203**
S15192S	04/54-02/93	⊗02/93	**5114**	04/54-05/81	**5411**	05/81-02/93			↩**9171**
S15193S	04/54-03/91	⊗04/92	**5115**	04/54-01/69	**5172**	01/69-07/88	**5510**	07/88-03/91	↩**9189**
S15194S	04/54-01/91	⊗04/91	**5116**	04/54-04/88	**5523**	04/88-01/91			↩**9244**
S15195S	05/54-05/91	⊗02/92	**5117**	05/54-04/88	**5527**	04/88-05/91			↩**9192**
S15196S	05/54-07/94	⊗08/94	**5118**	05/54-04/85	**5465**	04/85-07/94			↩**9250**
S15197S	05/54-05/90	⊗10/90	**5119**	05/54-04/88	**5509**	04/88-05/90			↩**9328**
S15198S	05/54-12/92	⊗01/93	**5120**	05/54-09/81	**5420**	09/81-12/92			↩**10418**
S15199S	06/54-10/92	⊗10/90	**5121**	06/54-04/88	**5509**	04/88-05/90			↩**9647**
S15200S	06/54-04/71	⊗11/71	**5122**	06/54-04/71					↩**9208**
S15201S	06/54-10/91	⊗11/91	**5123**	06/54-06/85	**5469**	06/85-10/91			↩**9367**
S15202S	06/54-12/92	⊗01/93	**5124**	06/54-09/81	**5420**	09/81-12/92			↩**9301**
S15203S	06/54-07/87	⊗02/90	**5125**	06/54-01/86	**5025**	01/86-07/87			↩**9212**
S15204S	07/54-01/91	⊗04/91	**5126**	07/54-04/88	**5523**	04/88-01/91			↩**10404**
S15205S	07/54-06/85	⊗10/87	**5127**	07/54-06/85					↩**9638**
S15206S	08/54-07/94	⊗08/94	**5128**	08/54-05/85	**5471**	06/85-07/94			↩**9216**
S15207S	08/54-03/95	⊗04/04	**5129**	08/54-05/88	**5528**	05/88-10/90	**5001**	11/90-03/95	↩**9649**
S15208S	08/54-07/94	⊗08/94	**5130**	08/54-12/73	**5192**	01/76-04/85	**5465**	04/85-07/94	↩**9249**
S15209S	09/54-04/94	⊗04/94	**5131**	09/54-07/81	**5422**	10/81-04/94			↩**9767**
S15210S	09/54-02/92	⊗02/92	**5132**	09/54-08/85	**5480**	10/85-02/92			↩**9201**
S15211S	09/54-05/91	⊗10/91	**5133**	09/54-05/88	**5516**	05/88-05/91			↩**9220**
S15212S	09/54-08/93	⊗09/93	**5134**	09/54-12/81	**5423**	12/81-08/93			↩**9161**
S15213S	09/54-07/91	⊗09/91	**5135**	09/54-05/88	**5521**	05/88-07/91			↩**9651**
S15214S	10/54-07/91	⊗02/92	**5136**	10/54-04/88	**5525**	04/88-07/91			↩**9337**
S15215S	10/54-01/93	⊗01/93	**5137**	10/54-03/70	**5122**	09/71-06/85	**5470**	06/85-01/93	↩**9178**
S15216S	10/54-01/94	⊗01/94	**5138**	10/54-03/81	**5405**	03/81-01/94			↩**10414**
S15217S	10/54-10/91	⊗02/92	**5139**	10/54-05/88	**5519**	05/88-10/91			↩**9236**
S15218S	11/54-10/91	⊗01/92	**5140**	11/54-05/88	**5503**	05/88-10/91			↩**9187**
S15219S	11/54-10/91	⊗01/92	**5141**	11/54-07/61	**5245**	09/61-05/81	**5418**	09/81-10/91	↩**9773**
S15220S	11/54-05/94	⊗06/94	**5142**	11/54-04/85	**5466**	05/85-05/94			↩**9235**
S15221S	11/54-11/94	⊗11/94	**5143**	11/54-09/80	**5403**	09/80-11/94			↩**9297**
S15222S	11/54-10/91	⊗05/92	**5144**	11/54-05/88	**5524**	05/88-10/91			↩**9234**
S15223S	11/54-05/90	⊗*12/90*	**5145**	11/54-04/88	**5512**	04/88-05/90			↩**9231**
S15224S	12/54-01/94	⊗01/94	**5146**	12/54-08/85	**5474**	08/85-01/94			↩**9168**
S15225S	12/54-10/91	⊗07/92	**5147**	12/54-05/88	**5518**	05/88-10/91			↩**9214**
S15226S	12/54-02/94	⊗02/94	**5148**	12/54-08/85	**5481**	10/85-02/94			↩**10405**
S15227S	01/55-07/93	⊗07/93	**5149**	01/55-10/80	**5408**	04/81-07/93			↩**10415**
S15228S	01/55-05/63	⊗05/63	**5150**	01/55-05/63					↩**9223**
S15228S[2]	05/63-06/88	⊗01/88	**5150**	05/63-01/85					↩**10394**
S15229S	01/55-01/91	⊗03/92	**5151**	01/55-04/88	**5506**	04/88-01/91			↩**9205**
S15230S	01/55-05/92	➲977778	**5152**	01/55-01/81	**5406**	01/81-05/92			↩**9332**
S15231S	01/55-07/94	⊗08/94	**5153**	01/55-05/85	**5471**	06/85-07/94			↩**9827**
S15232S	02/55-01/91	⊗03/92	**5154**	02/55-04/88	**5506**	04/88-01/91			↩**9159**
S15233S	02/55-04/93	⊗04/93	**5155**	02/55-07/85	**5477**	09/85-01/93			↩**9248**

Class 415/1 4-EPB Eastleigh

Trailer Third Open
TTO
S15234S-S15283S

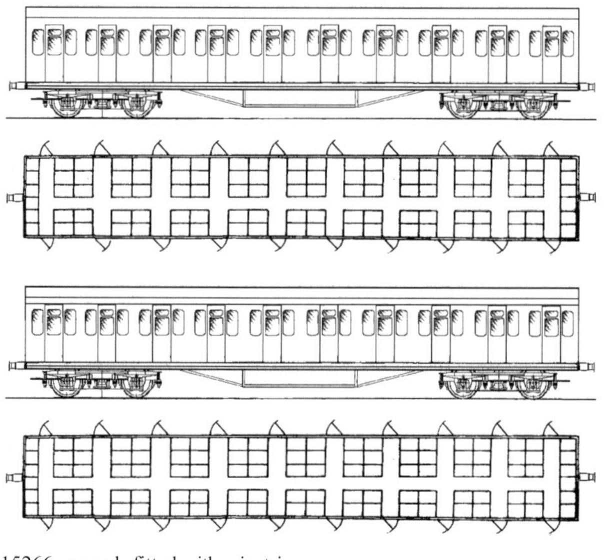

15266 onwards fitted with rainstrips

Diagram:	2018 EH270	HO Number:	4099
Body:	62' 0" × 9' 0"	Weight:	27t
Seats:	102 third	Bogies:	SR 40ft type

Number	Dates	Fate	Unit	Dates	Unit	Dates	Unit	Dates	To
S15234S	02/54-01/93	⊗01/93	**5106**	02/54-03/85	**5020**	03/85-11/88	**5266**	11/88-01/93	↩**9324**
S15235S	02/54-10/90	⊗11/91	**5107**	02/54-10/90					↩**9347**
S15236S	03/54-02/93	⊗09/93	**5108**	03/54-11/86	**5494**	11/86-02/93			↩**9376**
S15237S	03/54-02/93	⊗02/93	**5109**	03/54-10/86	**5493**	10/86-02/93			↩**9339**
S15238S	03/54-07/87	⊗01/88	**5110**	03/54-07/87					↩**9331**
S15239S	03/54-09/93	⊗10/93	**5111**	03/54-05/88	**5195**	05/88-09/93			↩**9191**
S15240S	03/54-11/93	⊗11/93	**5112**	03/54-08/86	**5492**	08/86-11/93			↩**9312**
S15241S	04/54-05/91	⊗09/91	**5113**	04/54-05/91					↩**9307**

S15242S	04/54-02/92	➲977798	**5114**	04/54-02/92					↩**9310**
S15243S	04/54-10/92	⊗11/92	**5115**	04/54-01/69	**5115**	08/69-10/92			↩**9308**
S15244S	04/54-07/92	⊗09/92	**5116**	04/54-04/88	**5126**	04/88-07/92			↩**9313**
S15245S	05/54-07/92	⊗09/92	**5117**	05/54-04/88	**5170**	04/88-07/92			↩**9342**
S15246S	05/54-11/93	⊗11/93	**5118**	05/54-04/85	**5192**	04/85-08/86	**5492**	08/86-11/93	↩**9346**
S15247S	05/54-10/92	⊗12/92	**5119**	05/54-04/88	**5121**	04/88-10/92			↩**9302**
S15248S	05/54-01/93	⊗02/93	**5120**	05/54-09/81	**5124**	09/81-01/93			↩**9409**
S15249S	06/54-10/92	⊗12/92	**5121**	06/54-10/92					↩**9344**
S15250S	06/54-04/71	⊗04/71	**5122**	06/54-04/71					↩**9765**
S15251S	06/54-08/93	⊗09/93	**5123**	06/54-02/87	**5497**	02/87-08/93			↩**9404**
S15252S	06/54-01/93	⊗02/93	**5124**	06/54-01/93					↩**9179**
S15253S	06/54-11/90	⊗04/91	**5125**	06/54-05/88	**5166**	05/88-11/90			↩**9406**
S15254S	07/54-07/92	⊗09/92	**5126**	07/54-07/92					↩**9317**
S15255S	07/54-06/85	⊗10/87	**5127**	07/54-06/85					↩**9335**
S15256S	08/54-05/93	⊗07/93	**5128**	08/54-05/85	**5153**	05/85-05/93			↩**9639**
S15257S	08/54-05/93	⊗05/93	**5129**	08/54-05/88	**5177**	05/88-05/93			↩**9652**
S15258S	08/54-11/92	⊗01/93	**5130**	08/54-12/73	**5264**	09/77-11/92			↩**9336**
S15259S	09/54-05/93	⊗05/93	**5131**	09/54-05/93					↩**9361**
S15260S	09/54-10/90	⊗04/92	**5132**	09/54-08/85	**5163**	08/85-10/90			↩**9484**
S15261S	09/54-12/91	⊗02/92	**5133**	09/54-12/91					↩**9655**
S15262S	09/54-09/92	⊗11/92	**5134**	09/54-09/92					↩**9330**
S15263S	09/54-09/92	⊗10/92	**5135**	09/54-05/88	**5210**	05/88-09/92			↩**9368**
S15264S	10/54-05/91	⊗10/91	**5136**	10/54-04/88	**5231**	04/88-05/91			↩**9329**
S15265S	10/54-08/93	⊗09/93	**5137**	10/54-03/70	**5122**	09/71-12/86	**5495**	12/86-08/93	↩**9306**
S15266S	10/54-09/93	⊗09/93	**5138**	10/54-09/93					↩**9173**
S15267S	10/54-02/92	⊗04/92	**5139**	10/54-02/92					↩**9775**
S15268S	11/54-07/93	⊗07/93	**5140**	11/54-05/88	**5160**	05/88-07/93			↩**9411**
S15269S	11/54-07/61	⊗07/61	**5141**	11/54-07/61					↩**9415**
S15270S	11/54-07/87	⊗12/87	**5142**	11/54-12/86					↩**9359**
S15271S	11/54-04/93	⊗05/93	**5143**	11/54-09/80	**5049**	09/80-09/88	**5275**	11/88-04/93	↩**9386**
S15272S	11/54-09/92	⊗10/92	**5144**	11/54-05/88	**5156**	05/88-09/92			↩**9366**
S15273S	11/54-04/93	⊗05/93	**5145**	11/54-04/93					↩**9345**
S15274S	12/54-01/91	⊗08/91	**5146**	12/54-01/91					↩**9399**
S15275S	12/54-10/93	⊗10/93	**5147**	12/54-05/88	**5194**	05/88-10/93			↩**9188**
S15276S	12/54-11/90	⊗10/91	**5148**	12/54-11/90					↩**9402**
S15277S	01/55-01/93	⊗12/92	**5149**	01/55-10/80	**5185**	10/80-01/93			↩**9766**
S15278S	01/55-05/63	⊗05/63	**5150**	01/55-05/63					↩**9423**
S15278S[2]	05/63-05/91	⊗02/92	**5150**	05/63-11/85	**5150**	09/87-05/91			↩**12392**
S15279S	01/55-04/93	⊗05/93	**5151**	01/55-04/88	**5154**	04/88-04/93			↩**9393**
S15280S	01/55-11/92	⊗12/92	**5152**	01/55-01/81	**5226**	04/82-11/92			↩**9378**
S15281S	01/55-05/93	⊗07/93	**5153**	01/55-05/93					↩**9348**
S15282S	02/55-04/93	⊗05/93	**5154**	02/55-04/93					↩**9360**
S15283S	02/55-11/92	⊗12/92	**5155**	02/55-11/92					↩**9356**

Class 415/1 4-EPB Eastleigh

Trailer Third Open
TTO
S15284S-S15333S

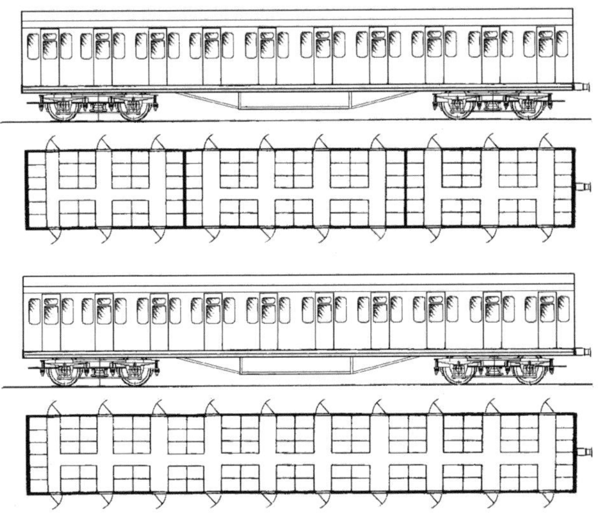

Facelifted, Diagram EH280

Diagram:	2015 EH265 EH280	HO Number:	4099
Body:	62' 0" × 9' 0"	Weight:	28t
Seats:	106 third, later 102 second	Bogies:	SR 40ft type

S15284S	02/55-10/91	⊗05/92	**5156**	02/55-05/88	**5524**	05/88-10/91			↩**9242**
S15285S	03/55-05/92	➲977779	**5157**	03/55-03/80	**5203**	03/80-05/80	**5406**	01/81-05/92	↩**9232**
S15286S	03/55-01/93	⊗01/93	**5158**	03/55-06/85	**5470**	06/85-01/93			↩**9185**
S15287S	03/55-05/91	⊗09/91	**5159**	03/55-04/88	**5531**	04/88-05/91			↩**9180**
S15288S	03/55-10/91	⊗01/92	**5160**	03/55-05/88	**5503**	05/88-10/91			↩**9251**
S15289S	03/55-02/94	⊗02/94	**5161**	03/55-10/85	**5479**	10/85-02/94			↩**9176**
S15290S	04/55-05/90	⊗12/90	**5162**	04/55-05/88	**5505**	05/88-05/90			↩**9243**
S15291S	04/55-09/93	⊗12/93	**5163**	04/55-08/85	**5480**	10/85-02/92	**5449**	02/92-09/93	↩**9825**
S15292S	04/55-07/87	⊗01/88	**5164**	04/55-07/87					↩**9182**
S15293S	04/55-02/94	⊗02/94	**5165**	04/55-08/85	**5481**	10/85-02/94			↩**9253**
S15294S	05/55-05/91	⊗11/91	**5166**	05/55-05/88	**5501**	05/88-05/91			↩**9226**
S15295S	05/55-07/94	⊗07/94	**5167**	05/55-12/69	**5254**	05/70-07/85	**5472**	08/85-07/94	↩**9219**
S15296S	05/55-05/90	⊗12/90	**5168**	05/55-05/88	**5505**	05/88-05/90			↩**9626**
S15297S	05/55-02/94	⊗06/94	**5169**	05/55-08/85	**5482**	11/85-02/94			↩**9183**
S15298S	06/55-05/91	⊗02/92	**5170**	06/55-04/88	**5527**	04/88-05/91			↩**9299**
S15299S	06/55-05/90	⊗10/90	**5171**	06/55-04/88	**5507**	04/88-05/90			↩**9826**
S15300S	06/55-01/69	⊗11/69	**5172**	06/55-01/69					↩**9228**
S15301S	07/55-05/90	⊗11/90	**5173**	07/55-05/88	**5511**	05/88-05/90			↩**9170**
S15302S	08/55-01/91	⊗02/92	**5174**	08/55-04/88	**5504**	04/88-01/91			↩**9194**
S15303S	04/55-08/84	⊗10/87	**5175**	04/55-11/83					↩**9829**
S15304S	08/55-01/93	⊗11/93	**5176**	08/55-01/81	**5410**	06/81-01/93			↩**9199**
S15305S	08/55-10/90	⊗05/92	**5177**	08/55-05/88	**5528**	05/88-10/90			↩**8691**
S15306S	08/55-10/91	⊗02/92	**5178**	08/55-10/80	**5243**	10/80-05/88	**5522**	05/88-10/91	↩**9233**
S15307S	09/55-05/91	⊗07/91	**5179**	09/55-05/88	**5513**	05/88-05/91			↩**9314**
S15308S	09/55-05/91	⊗03/92	**5180**	09/55-12/85	**5484**	12/85-05/91			↩**9215**
S15309S	09/55-06/94	⊗06/94	**5181**	09/55-03/86	**5487**	03/86-06/94			↩**9224**
S15310S	09/55-05/91	⊗07/91	**5182**	09/55-05/88	**5513**	05/88-05/91			↩**10648**
S15311S	10/55-10/91	⊗11/91	**5183**	10/55-05/88	**5502**	05/88-10/91			↩**9181**
S15312S	10/55-05/91	⊗11/91	**5184**	10/55-05/88	**5514**	05/88-05/91			↩**9428**
S15313S	10/55-07/93	⊗07/93	**5185**	10/55-10/80	**5408**	04/81-07/93			↩**9157**
S15314S	10/55-07/87	⊗01/88	**5186**	10/55-07/87					↩**9213**
S15315S	10/55-08/91	⊗01/92	**5187**	10/55-07/87	**5526**	05/88-07/91			↩**9217**
S15316S	11/55-07/92	⊗09/92	**5188**	11/55-01/85	**5476**	08/85-07/92			↩**10402**
S15317S	11/55-02/94	⊗02/94	**5189**	11/55-10/85	**5479**	10/85-02/94			↩**9174**
S15318S	11/55-10/91	⊗11/91	**5190**	11/55-05/88	**5502**	05/88-10/91			↩**9229**
S15319S	11/55-07/92	⊗09/92	**5191**	11/55-08/85	**5476**	08/85-07/92			↩**9254**
S15320S	11/55-10/91	⊗02/92	**5192**	11/55-01/76	**5137**	01/76-05/88	**5519**	05/88-10/91	↩**10407**
S15321S	11/55-08/94	⊗09/94	**5193**	11/55-04/86	**5488**	04/86-08/94			↩**9255**
S15322S	11/55-10/91	⊗07/92	**5194**	11/55-05/88	**5518**	05/88-10/91			↩**9211**
S15323S	12/55-10/91	⊗02/92	**5195**	12/55-05/88	**5520**	05/88-10/91			↩**10416**
S15324S	12/55-11/92	⊗01/93	**5196**	12/55-07/81	**5416**	07/81-11/92			↩**9195**
S15325S	12/55-10/91	⊗02/92	**5197**	12/55-05/88	**5522**	05/88-10/91			↩**9207**
S15326S	12/55-12/93	⊗01/94	**5198**	12/55-04/81	**5413**	07/81-12/93			↩**9300**
S15327S	12/55-08/94	⊗08/94	**5199**	12/55-06/82	**5441**	06/82-08/94			↩**9172**
S15328S	12/55-06/88	⊗05/89	**5200**	12/55-11/86	**5122**	12/86-07/87			↩**8563**
S15329S	12/55-05/94	⊗05/94	**5201**	12/55-11/85	**5483**	11/85-05/94			↩**9238**
S15330S	01/56-05/91	⊗11/91	**5202**	01/56-05/88	**5514**	05/88-05/91			↩**8854**
S15331S	01/56-05/80	⊗06/80	**5203**	01/56-03/79					↩**10410**
S15332S	01/56-04/92	⊗07/92	**5204**	01/56-12/57	**5020**	11/58-03/85	**5468**	06/85-04/92	↩**9241**
S15333S	01/56-02/93	⊗03/93	**5205**	01/56-01/82	**5429**	01/82-02/93			↩**10412**

Class 415/1 4-EPB Eastleigh

Trailer Third Open
TTO
S15334S-S15383S

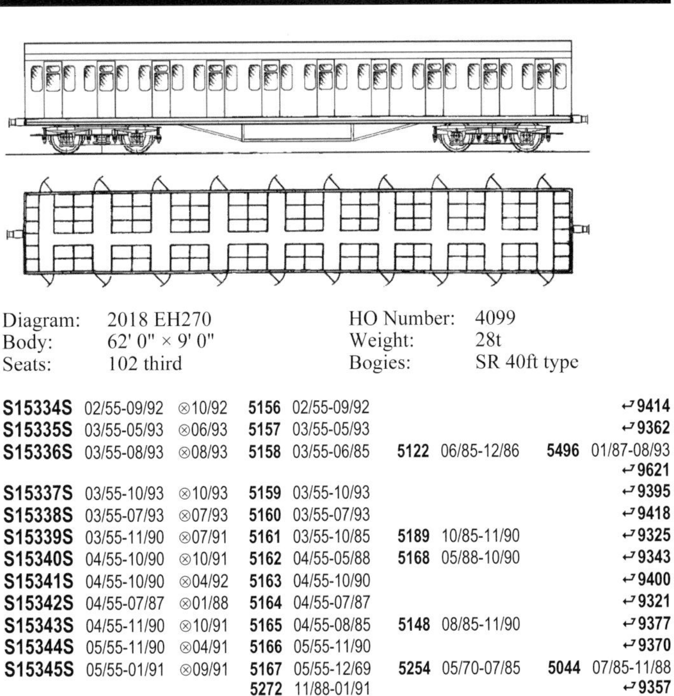

Diagram:	2018 EH270	HO Number:	4099
Body:	62' 0" × 9' 0"	Weight:	28t
Seats:	102 third	Bogies:	SR 40ft type

S15334S	02/55-09/92	⊗10/92	**5156**	02/55-09/92					↩**9414**
S15335S	03/55-05/93	⊗06/93	**5157**	03/55-05/93					↩**9362**
S15336S	03/55-08/93	⊗08/93	**5158**	03/55-06/85	**5122**	06/85-12/86	**5496**	01/87-08/93	↩**9621**
S15337S	03/55-10/93	⊗10/93	**5159**	03/55-10/93					↩**9395**
S15338S	03/55-07/93	⊗07/93	**5160**	03/55-07/93					↩**9418**
S15339S	03/55-11/90	⊗07/91	**5161**	03/55-10/85	**5189**	10/85-11/90			↩**9325**
S15340S	04/55-10/90	⊗10/91	**5162**	04/55-05/88	**5168**	05/88-10/90			↩**9343**
S15341S	04/55-10/90	⊗04/92	**5163**	04/55-10/90					↩**9400**
S15342S	04/55-07/87	⊗01/88	**5164**	04/55-07/87					↩**9321**
S15343S	04/55-11/90	⊗10/91	**5165**	04/55-08/85	**5148**	08/85-11/90			↩**9377**
S15344S	05/55-11/90	⊗04/91	**5166**	05/55-11/90					↩**9370**
S15345S	05/55-01/91	⊗09/91	**5167**	05/55-12/69	**5254**	05/70-07/85	**5044**	07/85-11/88	
			5272	11/88-01/91					↩**9357**

S15346S	05/55-10/90	⊗10/91	**5168**	05/55-10/90					↵**9646**
S15347S	05/55-02/92	⊗04/92	**5169**	05/55-02/92					↵**9401**
S15348S	06/55-07/92	⊗09/92	**5170**	06/55-07/92					↵**9327**
S15349S	06/55-09/93	⊗09/93	**5171**	06/55-04/88	**5220**	04/88-09/93			↵**9385**
S15350S	06/55-10/92	⊗11/92	**5172**	06/55-07/88	**5115**	07/88-10/92			↵**9394**
S15351S	07/55-04/94	⊗05/94	**5173**	07/55-03/80	**5225**	03/80-03/80	**5402**	03/80-01/85	
			5445	01/85-04/94					↵**9419**
S15352S	08/55-10/90	⊗10/91	**5174**	08/55-10/90	**5278**	10/90-05/91			↵**9397**
S15353S	04/55-11/92	⊗01/93	**5175**	04/55-11/83	**5110**	11/83-07/87	**5187**	07/87-04/88	
			5213	04/88-11/92					↵**9413**
S15354S	08/55- 95	Ⓟ	**5176**	08/55- 95					↵**9410**
S15355S	08/55-05/93	⊗05/93	**5177**	08/55-05/93					↵**9433**
S15356S	08/55-10/93	⊗10/93	**5178**	08/55-10/80	**5243**	10/80-10/93			↵**9252**
S15357S	09/55-10/91	⊗01/92	**5179**	09/55-05/88	**5182**	05/88-10/91			↵**9430**
S15358S	09/55-09/87	⊗02/90	**5180**	09/55-05/87					↵**9416**
S15359S	09/55-06/94	⊗06/94	**5181**	09/55-03/86	**5487**	03/86-06/94			↵**9369**
S15360S	09/55-10/91	⊗01/92	**5182**	09/55-10/91					↵**9384**
S15361S	10/55-04/93	⊗05/93	**5183**	10/55-05/88	**5190**	05/88-04/93			↵**9388**
S15362S	10/55-11/90	⊗05/92	**5184**	10/55-05/88	**5202**	05/88-10/90			↵**10406**
S15363S	10/55-01/93	⊗12/92	**5185**	10/55-01/93					↵**9354**
S15364S	10/55-10/90	⊗04/92	**5186**	10/55-07/87	**5046**	07/87-11/88	**5274**	11/88-10/90	
									↵**9405**
S15365S	10/55-03/88	⊗01/88	**5187**	10/55-04/88					↵**9417**
S15366S	11/55-11/92	⊗12/92	**5188**	11/55-01/85	**5217**	06/85-11/92			↵**9434**
S15367S	11/55-11/90	⊗07/91	**5189**	11/55-11/90					↵**9381**
S15368S	11/55-04/93	⊗05/93	**5190**	11/55-04/93					↵**9387**
S15369S	11/55-10/90	⊗04/92	**5191**	11/55-10/90					↵**9421**
S15370S	11/55-05/91	⊗02/92	**5192**	11/55-07/87	**5150**	09/87-05/91			↵**9319**
S15371S	11/55-08/94	⊗09/94	**5193**	11/55-04/86	**5488**	04/86-08/94			↵**9193**
S15372S	11/55-10/93	⊗10/93	**5194**	11/55-10/93					↵**9483**
S15373S	12/55-09/93	⊗10/93	**5195**	12/55-09/93					↵**9352**
S15374S	12/55-07/94	⊗08/94	**5196**	12/55-07/94					↵**9398**
S15375S	12/55-10/93	⊗10/93	**5197**	12/55-05/88	**5243**	05/88-10/93			↵**9374**
S15376S	12/55-05/91	⊗09/91	**5198**	12/55-04/81	**5113**	04/81-05/91			↵**9372**
S15377S	12/55-08/94	⊗08/94	**5199**	12/55-06/82	**5441**	06/82-08/94			↵**9383**
S15378S	12/55-08/93	⊗08/93	**5200**	12/55-11/86	**5496**	01/87-08/93			↵**9375**
S15379S	12/55-01/91	⊗12/91	**5201**	12/55-01/91					↵**9425**
S15380S	01/56-02/94	⊗03/94	**5202**	01/56-10/90	**5279**	11/90-02/94			↵**9422**
S15381S	01/56-05/93	⊗06/93	**5203**	01/56-05/80	**5157**	05/80-05/93			↵**9431**
S15382S	01/56-01/93	⊗01/93	**5204**	01/56-12/57	**5020**	11/58-11/88	**5266**	11/88-01/93	
									↵**9403**
S15383S	01/56-02/93	⊗03/93	**5205**	01/56-01/82	**5429**	01/82-02/93			↵**9420**

Class 415/1 4-EPB Eastleigh

Trailer Second Open
TSO
S15384S-S15393S

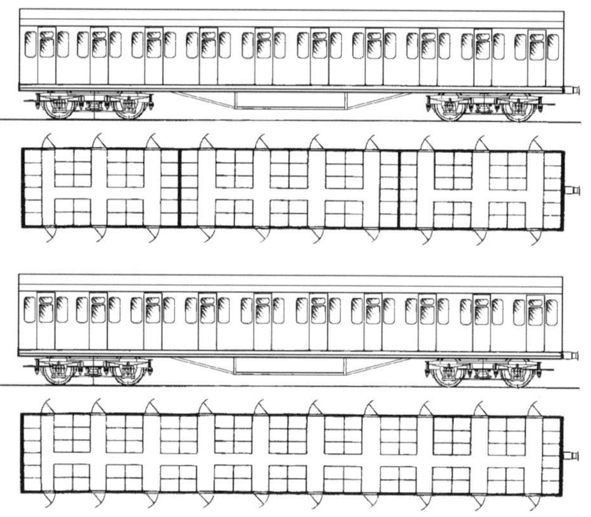

Facelifted, Diagram EH280

Diagram:	2015 EH265 EH280	HO Number:	4172
Body:	62' 0" × 9' 0"	Weight:	28t
Seats:	106 second, later 102 second	Bogies:	SR 40ft type

S15384S	02/56-11/93	⊗10/93	**5206**	02/56-05/82	**5437**	05/82-11/93	↵**9246**
S15385S	02/56-08/91	⊗10/91	**5207**	02/56-04/88	**5515**	04/88-08/91	↵**9210**
S15386S	02/56-01/93	⊗11/93	**5208**	02/56-01/81	**5410**	06/81-01/93	↵**9390**
S15387S	02/56-08/91	⊗10/91	**5209**	02/56-04/88	**5515**	04/88-08/91	↵**9221**
S15388S	03/56-07/91	⊗09/91	**5210**	03/56-05/88	**5521**	05/88-07/91	↵**9358**
S15389S	03/56-11/92	⊗01/93	**5211**	03/56-07/81	**5416**	07/81-11/92	↵**9392**
S15390S	03/56-07/93	⊗08/93	**5212**	03/56-02/82	**5431**	02/82-07/93	↵**9424**
S15391S	03/56-08/91	⊗01/92	**5213**	03/56-04/88	**5526**	05/88-07/91	↵**9247**
S15392S	03/56-01/93	⊗01/93	**5214**	03/56-04/81	**5407**	04/81-01/93	↵**9363**

S15393S	04/56-08/93	⊗08/93	**5215**	04/56-01/82	**5428**	01/82-08/93	↵**9389**

Class 415/1 4-EPB Eastleigh

Trailer Second Open
TSO
S15394S-S15403S

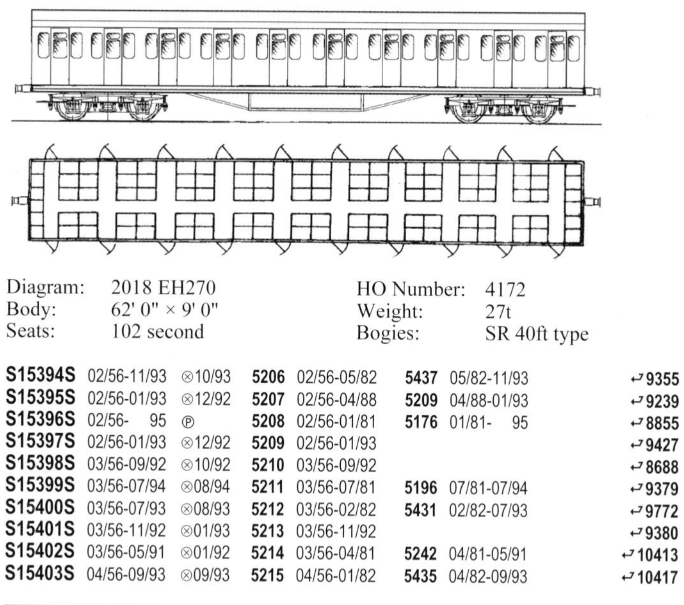

Diagram:	2018 EH270	HO Number:	4172
Body:	62' 0" × 9' 0"	Weight:	27t
Seats:	102 second	Bogies:	SR 40ft type

S15394S	02/56-11/93	⊗10/93	**5206**	02/56-05/82	**5437**	05/82-11/93	↵**9355**
S15395S	02/56-01/93	⊗12/92	**5207**	02/56-04/88	**5209**	04/88-01/93	↵**9239**
S15396S	02/56- 95	Ⓟ	**5208**	02/56-01/81	**5176**	01/81- 95	↵**8855**
S15397S	02/56-01/93	⊗12/92	**5209**	02/56-01/93			↵**9427**
S15398S	03/56-09/92	⊗10/92	**5210**	03/56-09/92			↵**8688**
S15399S	03/56-07/94	⊗08/94	**5211**	03/56-07/81	**5196**	07/81-07/94	↵**9379**
S15400S	03/56-07/93	⊗08/93	**5212**	03/56-02/82	**5431**	02/82-07/93	↵**9772**
S15401S	03/56-11/92	⊗01/93	**5213**	03/56-11/92			↵**9380**
S15402S	03/56-05/91	⊗01/92	**5214**	03/56-04/81	**5242**	04/81-05/91	↵**10413**
S15403S	04/56-09/93	⊗09/93	**5215**	04/56-01/82	**5435**	04/82-09/93	↵**10417**

Class 415/1 4-EPB Eastleigh

Trailer Second Open
TSO
S15404S-S15448S

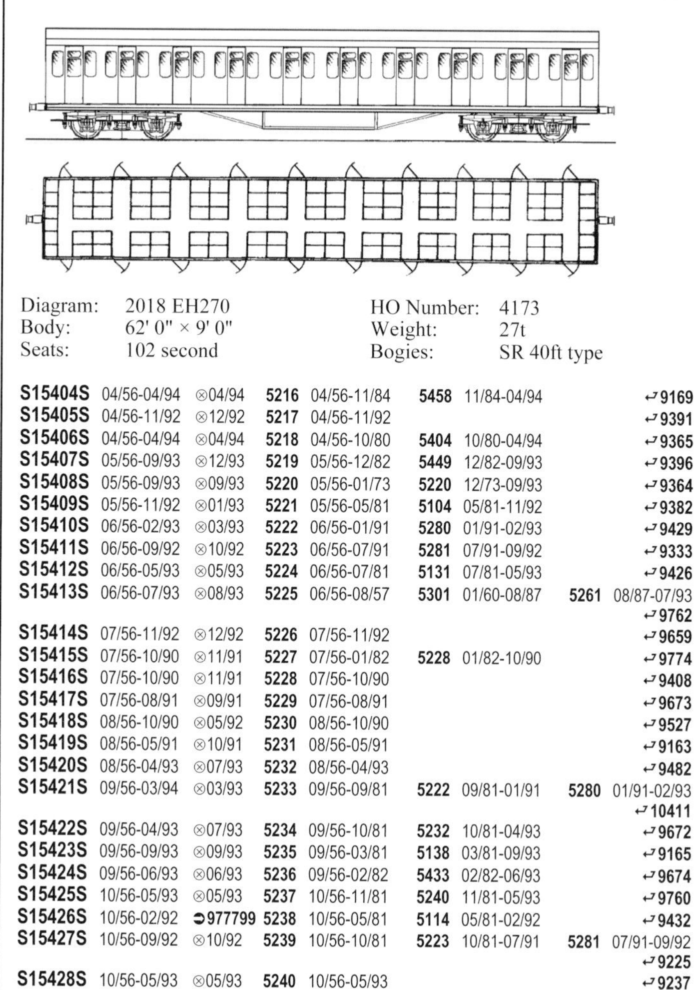

Diagram:	2018 EH270	HO Number:	4173
Body:	62' 0" × 9' 0"	Weight:	27t
Seats:	102 second	Bogies:	SR 40ft type

S15404S	04/56-04/94	⊗04/94	**5216**	04/56-11/84	**5458**	11/84-04/94			↵**9169**
S15405S	04/56-11/92	⊗12/92	**5217**	04/56-11/92					↵**9391**
S15406S	04/56-04/94	⊗04/94	**5218**	04/56-10/80	**5404**	10/80-04/94			↵**9365**
S15407S	05/56-09/93	⊗12/93	**5219**	05/56-12/82	**5449**	12/82-09/93			↵**9396**
S15408S	05/56-09/93	⊗09/93	**5220**	05/56-01/73	**5220**	12/73-09/93			↵**9364**
S15409S	05/56-11/92	⊗01/93	**5221**	05/56-05/81	**5104**	05/81-11/92			↵**9382**
S15410S	06/56-02/93	⊗03/93	**5222**	06/56-01/91	**5280**	01/91-02/93			↵**9429**
S15411S	06/56-09/92	⊗10/92	**5223**	06/56-07/91	**5281**	07/91-09/92			↵**9333**
S15412S	06/56-05/93	⊗05/93	**5224**	06/56-07/81	**5131**	07/81-05/93			↵**9426**
S15413S	06/56-07/93	⊗08/93	**5225**	06/56-08/57	**5301**	01/60-08/87	**5261**	08/87-07/93	
									↵**9762**
S15414S	07/56-11/92	⊗12/92	**5226**	07/56-11/92					↵**9659**
S15415S	07/56-10/90	⊗11/91	**5227**	07/56-01/82	**5228**	01/82-10/90			↵**9774**
S15416S	07/56-10/90	⊗11/91	**5228**	07/56-10/90					↵**9408**
S15417S	07/56-08/91	⊗09/91	**5229**	07/56-08/91					↵**9673**
S15418S	08/56-10/90	⊗05/92	**5230**	08/56-10/90					↵**9527**
S15419S	08/56-05/91	⊗10/91	**5231**	08/56-05/91					↵**9163**
S15420S	08/56-04/93	⊗07/93	**5232**	08/56-04/93					↵**9482**
S15421S	09/56-03/94	⊗03/93	**5233**	09/56-09/81	**5222**	09/81-01/91	**5280**	01/91-02/93	
									↵**10411**
S15422S	09/56-04/93	⊗07/93	**5234**	09/56-10/81	**5232**	10/81-04/93			↵**9672**
S15423S	09/56-09/93	⊗09/93	**5235**	09/56-03/81	**5138**	03/81-09/93			↵**9165**
S15424S	09/56-06/93	⊗06/93	**5236**	09/56-02/82	**5433**	02/82-06/93			↵**9674**
S15425S	10/56-05/93	⊗05/93	**5237**	10/56-11/81	**5240**	11/81-05/93			↵**9760**
S15426S	10/56-02/92	➲**977799**	**5238**	10/56-05/81	**5114**	05/81-02/92			↵**9432**
S15427S	10/56-09/92	⊗10/92	**5239**	10/56-10/81	**5223**	10/81-07/91	**5281**	07/91-09/92	
									↵**9225**
S15428S	10/56-05/93	⊗05/93	**5240**	10/56-05/93					↵**9237**

S15429S 10/56-02/94 ⊗03/94 **5241** 10/56-01/84 **5001** 01/84-11/88 **5265** 11/88-11/90
5279 11/90-02/94 ↵**10401**
S15430S 11/56-05/91 ⊗01/92 **5242** 11/56-05/91 ↵**8604**
S15431S 11/56-09/93 ⊗09/93 **5243** 11/56-10/80 **5246** 10/80-01/82 **5435** 04/82-09/93 ↵**9303**
S15432S 11/56-06/91 ⊗10/91 **5244** 11/56-05/82 **5439** 05/82-05/90 ↵**9373**
S15433S 11/56-05/94 ⊗05/94 **5245** 11/56-07/61 **5262** 12/65-06/86 **5490** 06/86-05/94 ↵**9222**
S15434S 11/56-10/93 ⊗04/81 **5246** 11/56-10/80 ↵**9928**
S15435S 12/56-08/91 ⊗09/91 **5247** 12/56-04/81 **5229** 04/81-08/91 ↵**9927**
S15436S 12/56-08/93 ⊗08/93 **5248** 12/56-08/93 ↵**8198**
S15437S 01/57-10/93 ⊗10/93 **5249** 01/57-03/82 **5430** 03/82-10/93 ↵**9935**
S15438S 01/57-10/93 ⊗10/93 **5250** 01/57-09/81 **5255** 09/81-03/82 **5430** 03/82-10/93 ↵**9671**
S15439S 01/57-11/93 ⊗12/93 **5251** 01/57-11/84 **5457** 11/84-11/93 ↵**9204**
S15440S 01/57-11/94 ⊗11/94 **5252** 01/57-11/82 **5443** 11/82-11/94 ↵**8013**
S15441S 01/57-01/94 ⊗06/94 **5253** 01/57-12/84 **5459** 12/84-01/94 ↵**9190**
S15442S 02/57-02/92 ⊗04/92 **5254** 02/57-02/70 **5137** 03/70-05/88 **5139** 05/88-02/92 ↵**8213**
S15443S 02/57-08/93 ⊗08/93 **5255** 02/57-03/82 **5248** 03/82-08/93 ↵**9245**
S15444S 02/57-09/92 ⊗11/92 **5256** 02/57-12/81 **5134** 12/81-09/92 ↵**9407**
S15445S 02/57-01/92 ⊗01/92 **5257** 02/57-08/82 **5440** 08/82-01/92 ↵**9759**
S15446S 03/57-02/94 ⊗03/94 **5258** 03/57-01/85 **5460** 01/85-02/94 ↵**9828**
S15447S 03/57-11/93 ⊗11/93 **5259** 03/57-01/82 **5432** 02/82-11/93 ↵**9934**
S15448S 03/57-11/94 ⊗02/95 **5260** 03/57-02/85 **5461** 02/85-11/94 ↵**9186**

Class 415/1 4-EPB Eastleigh

Trailer Second Open
TSO
S15449S-S15450S

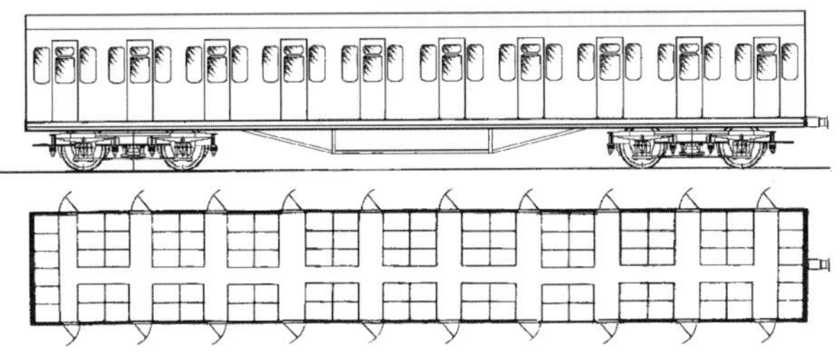

Diagram: 2013 EH263 EH279 HO Number:
Body: 62' 0" × 9' 0" Weight: 27t
Seats: 102 second Bogies: SR 40ft type

Prototype facelifted vehicles.

S15449S 06/76-03/94 ⊗04/94 **5263** 06/76-03/77 **5401** 03/77-03/94 ⊂**10440**
S15450S 06/76-03/94 ⊗04/94 **5263** 06/76-03/77 **5401** 03/77-03/94 ⊂**10337**

Class 415/1 4-EPB Eastleigh

Trailer Second Open
TSO
S15451S-S15481S

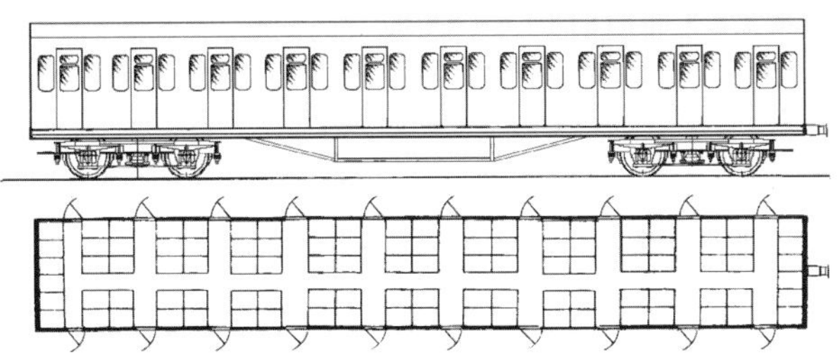

Diagram: 2013 EH263 EH279 HO Number:
Body: 62' 0" × 9' 0" Weight: 27t
Seats: 102 second Bogies: SR 40ft type

Spare 4-SUB trailers built to EPB standards.

S15451S 06/81-04/93 ⊗04/93 **5412** 06/81-04/93 ⊂**8980**
S15452S 06/81-04/93 ⊗04/93 **5412** 06/81-04/93 ⊂**12361**
S15453S 12/81-01/93 ⊗02/93 **5425** 12/81-01/93 ⊂**12360**
S15454S 12/81-01/93 ⊗02/93 **5425** 12/81-01/93 ⊂**10139**
S15455S 04/82-07/94 ⊗08/94 **5434** 04/82-07/94 ⊂**12404**
S15456S 05/82-10/93 ⊗10/93 **5436** 05/82-10/93 ⊂**10133**
S15457S 05/82-10/93 ⊗10/93 **5436** 05/82-10/93 ⊂**10143**
S15458S 06/82-12/93 ⊗01/94 **5438** 06/82-12/93 ⊂**10132**
S15459S 06/82-12/93 ⊗01/94 **5438** 06/82-12/93 ⊂**12381**
S15460S 07/82-07/94 ⊗08/94 **5442** 07/82-07/94 ⊂**10125**
S15461S 07/82-07/94 ⊗08/94 **5442** 07/82-07/94 ⊂**12393**
S15462S 09/82-07/94 ⊗09/94 **5444** 09/82-07/94 ⊂**10131**
S15463S 09/82-07/94 ⊗09/94 **5444** 09/82-07/94 ⊂**12359**
S15464S 03/82-04/93 ⊗04/93 **5445** 03/82-01/85 **5402** 01/85-04/93 ⊂**12389**
S15465S 03/82-04/93 ⊗04/93 **5445** 03/82-01/85 **5402** 01/85-04/93 ⊂**12355**
S15466S 09/82-01/93 ⊗01/93 **5446** 09/82-01/93 ⊂**10444**
S15467S 09/82-01/93 ⊗01/93 **5446** 09/82-01/93 ⊂**10448**
S15468S 11/82-11/93 ⊗12/93 **5447** 11/82-11/93 ⊂**10128**
S15469S 11/82-11/93 ⊗12/93 **5447** 11/82-11/93 ⊂**12390**
S15470S 12/82-02/93 ⊗03/93 **5448** 12/82-02/93 ⊂**10124**
S15471S 12/82-02/93 ⊗03/93 **5448** 12/82-02/93 ⊂**10439**
S15472S 02/83-02/92 ⊗11/92 **5450** 02/83-02/92 ⊂**12391**
S15473S 02/83-02/92 ⊗11/92 **5450** 02/83-02/92 ⊂**10137**
S15474S 03/83-11/91 ⊗01/92 **5451** 03/83-11/91 ⊂**10446**
S15475S 03/83-11/91 ⊗01/92 **5451** 03/83-11/91 ⊂**10445**
S15476S 04/83-04/94 ⊗05/94 **5452** 04/83-04/94 ⊂**10129**
S15477S 04/83-04/94 ⊗05/94 **5452** 04/83-04/94 ⊂**12402**
S15478S 05/83-07/93 ⊗07/93 **5453** 05/83-07/93 ⊂**10141**
S15479S 05/83-07/93 ⊗07/93 **5453** 05/83-07/93 ⊂**12353**
S15480S 08/83-07/93 ⊗07/93 **5454** 08/83-07/93 ⊂**12398**
S15481S 08/83-07/93 ⊗07/93 **5454** 08/83-07/93 ⊂**12358**

Class 414/1 2-HAP Eastleigh

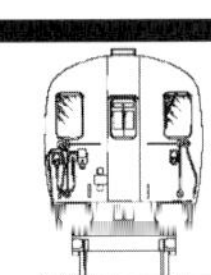

Driving Trailer Composite Lavatory
DTCL, later DTSL
S16001S-S16036S

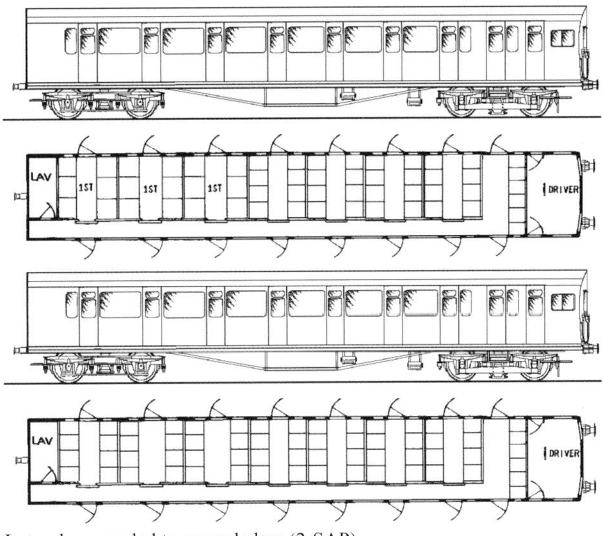

Later downgraded to second class (2-SAP)

Diagram: 2703 HO Number: 4281
Body: 62' 6" × 9' 0" Weight: 32t
Seats: 18 first 38 second 1 toilet Bogies: SR 40ft type
later 62 second

S16001S 02/58-04/76 ⊗01/77 **5601** 02/58-04/76 ↵**9924**
S16002S 02/58-09/77 ⊗04/81 **5602** 02/58-09/77 ↵**9931**
S16003S 02/58-09/77 ⊗07/83 **5603** 02/58-09/77 ↵**9914**
S16004S 02/58-05/83 ⊗05/83 **5604** 02/58-05/83 ↵**9932**
S16005S 02/58-05/83 ⊗05/83 **5605** 02/58-05/83 ↵**9996**
S16006S 06/58-02/83 ⊗02/83 **5606** 06/58-02/83 ↵**9930**
S16007S 06/58-01/81 ⊗04/81 **5607** 06/58-01/81 ↵**9926**
S16008S 07/58-01/81 ⊗04/81 **5608** 07/58-01/81 ↵**9991**
S16009S 07/58-03/82 ⊗12/82 **5609** 07/58-03/82 ↵**9980**
S16010S 07/58-06/82 ⊗*12/82* **5610** 07/58-06/82 ↵**9913**
S16011S 06/58-07/82 ⊗*12/82* **5611** 06/58-07/82 ↵**9916**
S16012S 06/58-08/82 ⊗*12/82* **5612** 08/58-08/82 ↵**9919**
S16013S 06/58-10/82 ⊗10/82 **5613** 08/58-10/82 ↵**9937**
S16014S 06/58-02/82 ⊗*12/82* **5614** 08/58-02/82 ↵**9995**
S16015S 06/58-05/82 ⊗*12/82* **5615** 08/58-05/82 ↵**9922**
S16016S 06/58-05/83 ⊗05/83 **5616** 08/58-04/83 ↵**9912**
S16017S 06/58-04/82 ⊗*12/82* **5617** 08/58-04/82 ↵**9988**
S16018S 06/58-10/80 ⊗ **5618** 08/58-10/80 ↵**9933**
S16019S 09/58-09/82 ⊗*12/82* **5619** 09/58-09/82 ↵**9972**
S16020S 09/58-06/82 ⊗*12/82* **5620** 09/58-03/82 ↵**9918**
S16021S 09/58-07/82 ⊗*12/82* **5621** 09/58-07/82 ↵**9925**
S16022S 09/58-10/80 ⊗ **5622** 09/58-10/80 ↵**9936**
S16023S 09/58-02/82 ⊗*12/82* **5623** 09/58-02/82 ↵**9939**
S16024S 09/58-05/83 ⊗10/86 **5624** 09/58-05/83 ↵**9997**
S16025S 09/58-05/83 ⊗05/83 **5625** 09/58-05/83 ↵**9920**
S16026S 09/58-05/83 ⊗05/83 **5626** 09/58-04/83 ↵**9929**
S16027S 09/58-03/82 ⊗*12/82* **5627** 09/58-03/82 ↵**9917**
S16028S 09/58-09/82 ⊗01/83 **5628** 09/58-09/82 ↵**9993**
S16029S 10/58-09/82 ➲**977069** **5629** 10/58-09/82 ↵**9998**

S16030S	10/58-08/82	⊗*12/82*	**5630**	10/58-08/82		↩**9994**
S16031S	10/58-02/83	⊗02/83	**5631**	10/58-02/83		↩**9921**
S16032S	10/58-10/82	⊗10/82	**5632**	10/58-10/82		↩**9989**
S16033S	10/58-05/82	⊗*12/82*	**5633**	10/58-05/82		↩**9938**
S16034S	10/58-04/82	⊗*12/82*	**5634**	10/58-04/82		↩**9915**
S16035S	10/58-05/83	⊗05/83	**5635**	10/58-05/83		↩**9923**
S16036S	10/58-04/76	⊗01/77	**5636**	10/58-04/76		↩**9999**

Class 416/1 2-EPB Eastleigh

Driving Trailer Second Open

DTS

S16101S-S16134S

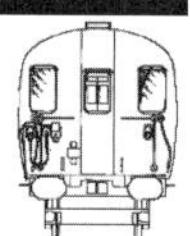

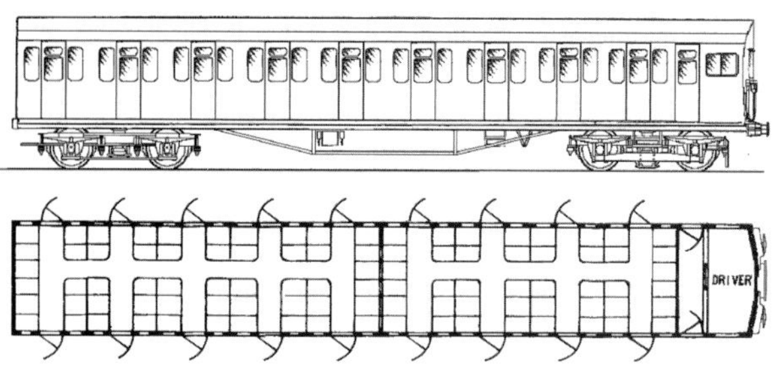

Diagram: 2704 EE262
Body: 62' 6" × 9' 0"
Seats: 94 second

HO Number: 4281
Weight: 30t
Bogies: SR 40ft type

S16101S	09/59-05/93	⊗05/93	**5651**	09/59-06/85	**6333**	06/85-05/93			↩**9950**
S16102S	10/59-07/93	⊗07/93	**5652**	10/59-03/84	**6313**	03/84-09/88	**6335**	09/88-10/88	
			6313	10/88-07/93					↩**9982**
S16103S	10/59-07/94	⊗08/94	**5653**	10/59-05/84	**6316**	05/84-07/94			↩**9964**
S16104S	10/59-06/94	⊗06/94	**5654**	10/59-09/84	**6324**	09/84-06/94			↩**9978**
S16105S	10/59-01/95	⊗03/95	**5655**	10/59-07/84	**6320**	07/84-01/95			↩**9983**
S16106S	10/59-03/95	⊗	**5656**	10/59-10/83	**6309**	10/83-03/95			↩**9986**
S16107S	10/59-07/93	⊗07/93	**5657**	10/59-06/85	**6334**	06/85-07/93			↩**9975**
S16108S	10/59-03/95	⊗09/06	**5658**	10/59-06/83	**6308**	06/83-03/95			↩**9965**
S16109S	10/59-11/94	⊗11/94	**5659**	10/59-02/84	**6311**	02/84-11/94			↩**9974**
S16110S	10/59-10/94	⊗11/94	**5660**	10/59-06/84	**6318**	06/84-10/94			↩**9948**
S16111S	10/59-06/94	⊗06/94	**5661**	10/59-10/84	**6325**	10/84-06/94			↩**9940**
S16112S	10/59-09/94	⊗09/94	**5662**	10/59-07/84	**6319**	07/84-09/94			↩**9962**
S16113S	10/59-03/95	⊗07/95	**5663**	10/59-06/85	**6332**	06/85-03/95			↩**9987**
S16114S	10/59-03/95	⊗05/95	**5664**	10/59-03/85	**6329**	03/85-03/95			↩**9984**
S16115S	10/59-08/94	⊗10/94	**5665**	10/59-10/82	**6306**	10/82-08/94			↩**9969**
S16116S	11/59-05/93	⊗06/93	**5666**	11/59-02/85	**6327**	02/85-05/93			↩**9973**
S16117S	11/59-03/95	Ⓟ	**5667**	11/59-06/83	**6307**	06/83-03/95			↩**9985**
S16118S	11/59-11/94	⊗12/94	**5668**	11/59-01/84	**6310**	01/84-11/94			↩**9949**
S16119S	11/59-05/93	⊗06/93	**5669**	11/59-08/84	**6322**	08/84-12/89	**6322**	05/90-05/93	↩**9971**
S16120S	11/59-05/93	⊗06/93	**5670**	11/59-04/82	**6303**	04/82-05/93			↩**9970**
S16121S	12/59-01/94	⊗02/94	**5671**	12/59-03/82	**6301**	03/82-01/94			↩**9977**
S16122S	12/59-07/93	⊗08/93	**5672**	12/59-05/84	**6317**	05/84-07/93			↩**9943**
S16123S	12/59-05/94	⊗05/94	**5673**	12/59-02/84	**6312**	02/84-05/94			↩**9944**
S16124S	12/59-03/94	⊗04/94	**5674**	12/59-03/82	**6302**	03/82-03/94			↩**9947**
S16125S	12/59-01/94	⊗02/94	**5675**	12/59-08/84	**6323**	08/84-01/94			↩**9942**
S16126S	12/59-04/94	⊗05/94	**5676**	12/59-03/85	**6328**	03/85-04/94			↩**9966**
S16127S	12/59-02/95	⊗07/95	**5677**	12/59-05/85	**6331**	05/85-02/95			↩**9968**
S16128S	12/59-03/95	⊗05/95	**5678**	12/59-07/84	**6321**	07/84-03/95			↩**9981**
S16129S	12/59-08/94	⊗08/94	**5679**	12/59-01/85	**6326**	01/85-08/94			↩**9941**
S16130S	12/59-07/93	⊗07/93	**5680**	12/59-04/84	**6314**	04/84-07/93			↩**9967**
S16131S	12/59-01/94	⊗02/94	**5681**	12/59-07/82	**6305**	07/82-01/94			↩**9976**
S16132S	12/59-03/95	⊗05/95	**5682**	12/59-05/85	**6330**	05/85-03/95			↩**9979**
S16133S	12/59-05/93	⊗05/93	**5683**	12/59-04/82	**6304**	04/82-05/93			↩**9963**
S16134S	12/59-10/94	⊗11/94	**5684**	12/59-04/84	**6315**	04/84-10/94			↩**9945**

Southern Railway (Older stock)

3-SUB Eastleigh

Driving Motor Brake Third

DMBT

S8001S-S8126S

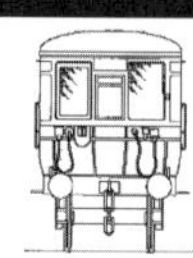

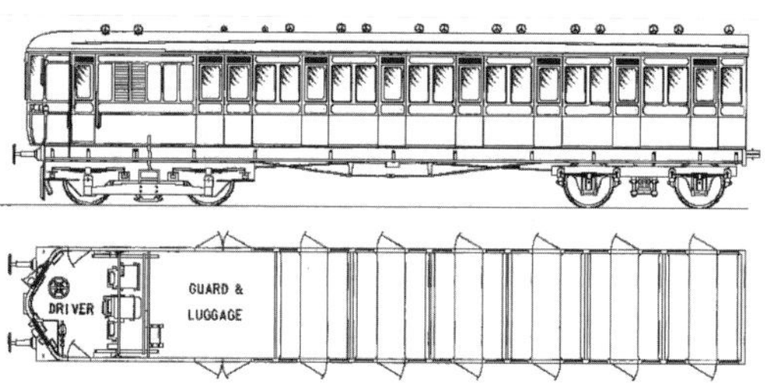

As built

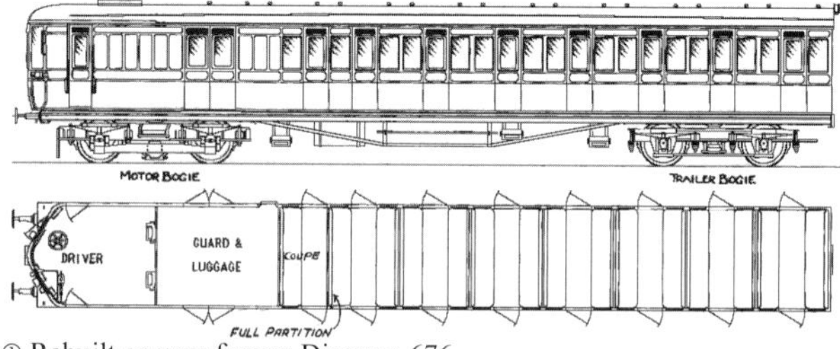

① Rebuilt on new frames Diagram 676

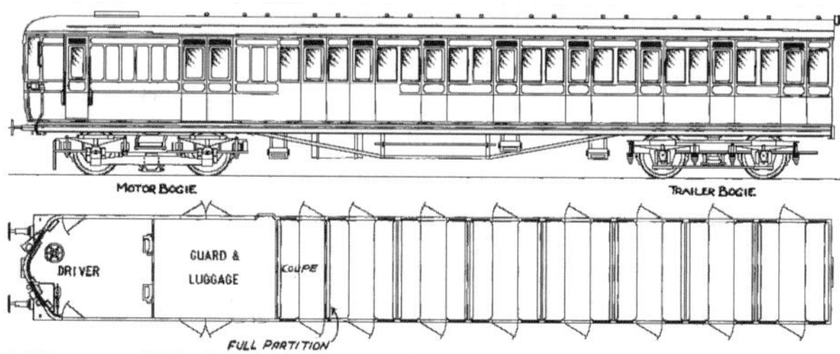

② Diagram 676. Steel lower panelling on added compartments.

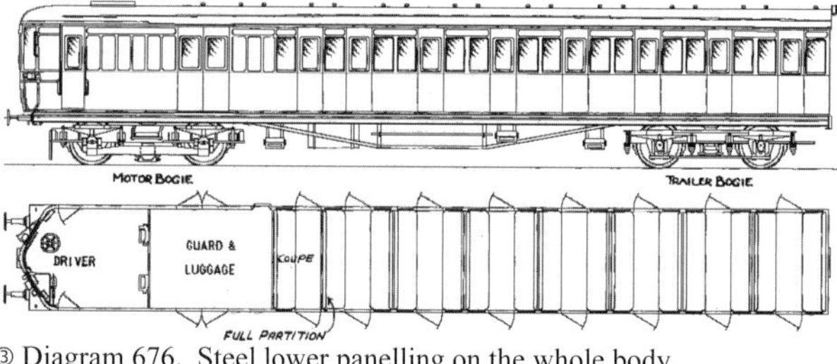

③ Diagram 676. Steel lower panelling on the whole body.

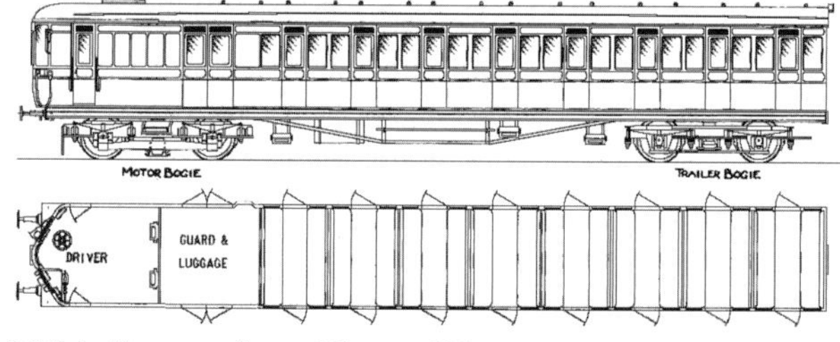

①**C** Rebuilt on new frames Diagram 685

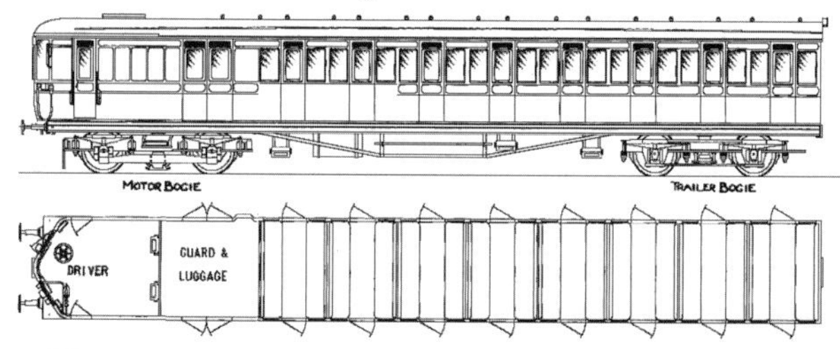

②**C** Diagram 685. Steel lower panelling on added compartments.

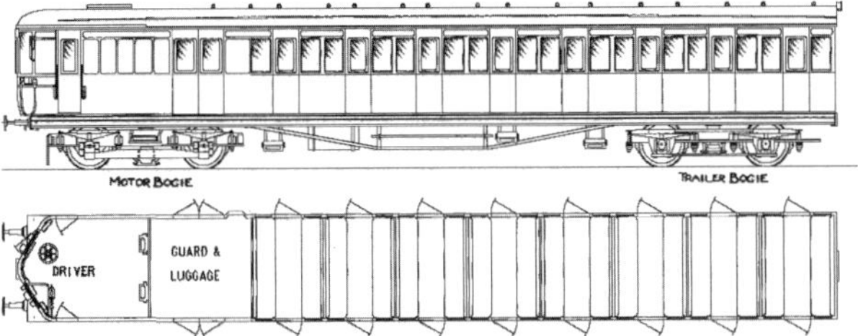

③C Diagram 685. Steel lower panelling on the whole body.

Diagram:	660 later 676 or c 685	Order Number:	LSWR
Body:	52' 0" × 8' 0" later 62' 6" × 8' 0"	Weight:	33t later 42t
Seats:	60 third later 75 or 80 third	Bogies:	LSWR later SR
Motors:	BTH 2 × 250hp, later MV339 or EE339 2 × 275hp		

For rebuilding dates, see the unit listings.

S8001S	③	23-*06/54*	↪14316	1201	23-03/43	4200	03/43-*06/54*			⊂6701
S8002S	③	23-*06/54*	↪14314	1201	23-03/43	4200	03/43-*06/54*			⊂6702
8003		23-12/39	⊗10/40	1202	23-12/39		Body to 8581			⊂6703
8004		23-12/39	⊗03/40	1202	23-12/39					⊂6704
S8005S	①c	23-04/55	↪14409	1203	23-08/46	4228	08/46-04/55			⊂6705
S8006S	③c	23-12/55	↪14466	1204	23-04/41	4131	04/41-12/55			⊂6706
S8007S	②	23-*06/54*	↪14286	1205	23-07/47	4211	07/47-*06/54*			⊂6707
S8008S	②	23-*06/54*	↪14285	1205	23-07/47	4211	07/47-*06/54*			⊂6708
S8009S	②	23-*07/56*	↪14295	1206	23-08/43	4218	08/43-*07/56*			⊂6709
S8010S	②	23-*07/56*	↪14293	1206	23-08/43	4218	08/43-*07/56*			⊂6710
S8011S	①c	23-08/55	↪14385	1207	23-10/45	4160	10/45-08/55			⊂6711
S8012S	①c	23-08/55	↪14386	1208	23-06/44	4152	06/44-08/55			⊂6712
S8013S	③	23-03/54	↪15440	1209	23-08/43	4202	09/43-03/54			⊂6713
S8014S	③	23-03/54	↪14503	1209	23-08/43	4202	09/43-03/54			⊂6714
8015		23-12/39	⊗03/40	1210	23-12/39					⊂6715
8016		23-12/39	⊗03/40	1210	23-12/39					⊂6716
S8017S	①c	23-08/53	↪14509	1211	23- *44*	4154	09/44-08/53			⊂6717
S8018S	③c	23-*05/54*	↪14280	1212	23-*11/42*	4146	*11/42-05/54*			⊂6718
S8019S	③	23-04/55	↪14369	1213	23-09/42	4199	09/42-04/55			⊂6719
S8020S	③	23-04/55	↪14370	1213	23-09/42	4199	09/42-04/55			⊂6720
S8021S	③	23-05/55	↪14447	1214	23-02/44	4226	02/44-05/55			⊂6721
S8022S	③	23-05/55	↪14367	1214	23-02/44	4226	02/44-05/55			⊂6722
S8023S	①c	23-03/56	↪14465	1215	23-09/44	4153	09/44-09/54	4590	09/54-03/56	
										⊂6723
S8024S	③c	23-09/55	↪14403	1216	23-06/45	4158	06/45-09/55			⊂6724
S8025S	③	23-*10/54*	↪14318	1217	23-09/43	4203	09/43-*10/54*			⊂6725
S8026S	③	23-*10/54*	↪14320	1217	23-09/43	4203	09/43-*10/54*			⊂6726
S8027S	③	23-10/55	↪14405	1218	23-11/47	4232	11/47-10/55			⊂6727
S8028S	③	23-10/55	↪14410	1218	23-11/47	4232	11/47-10/55			⊂6728
S8029S	①c	23-11/55	↪14420	1219	23- 45	4162	45-11/55			⊂6729
S8030S	③c	23-06/55	↪14372	1220	23- 44	4156	44-06/55			⊂6730
S8031S	③	23-*04/54*	↪14276	1221	23-01/46	4207	01/46-*04/54*			⊂6731
S8032S	③	23-*04/54*	↪14281	1221	23-01/46	4207	01/46-*04/54*			⊂6732
8033		23-11/37	⊗11/37	1222	23-11/37					⊂6733
S8033S[2]	①	38-*10/54*	↪14315	1222	38-08/46	4229	08/46-*10/54*			
							Newly converted body on new frame			
S8034S	①	23-*10/54*	↪14312	1222	23-08/46	4229	08/46-*10/54*			⊂6734
S8035S	②c	23-01/56	↪14443	1223	23-08/46	4170	08/46-01/56			⊂6735
S8036S	②c	23-05/56	↪14481	1224	23-12/45	4164	12/45-08/55	4537	08/55-05/56	
										⊂6736
S8037S	③	23-09/55	↪14402	1225	23-08/46	4208	08/46-09/55			⊂6737
S8038S	③	23-09/55	↪14400	1225	23-08/46	4208	08/46-09/55			⊂6738
S8039S	③	23-*12/54*	↪14335	1226	23-02/43	4223	02/43-*12/54*			⊂6739
S8040S	③	23-*12/54*	↪14333	1226	23-02/43	4223	02/43-*12/54*			⊂6740
S8041S	①c	23-02/55	↪14344	1227	23-01/43	4141	01/43-02/55			⊂6741
S8042S	①c	23-12/54	↪14341	1228	23- 46	4165	46-12/54			⊂6742
S8043S	③	23-06/55	↪14375	1229	23-06/43	4201	06/43-06/55			⊂6743
S8044S	③	23-06/55	↪14377	1229	23-06/43	4201	06/43-06/55			⊂6744
S8045S	③	23-04/55	↪14408	1230	23-08/46	4228	08/46-04/55			⊂6745
S8046S	③	23-08/55	↪14394	1230	23-08/46	4169	08/46-08/55			⊂6746
S8047S	①c	23-*06/54*	↪14283	1231	23-09/42	4140	09/42-*06/54*			⊂6747
S8048S	①c	23-05/56	↪14484	1232	23-09/42	4133	09/42-05/56			⊂6748
S8049S	③	23-09/55	↪14395	1233	23-04/44	4205	04/44-09/55			⊂6749
S8050S	③	23-09/55	↪14397	1233	23-04/44	4205	04/44-09/55			⊂6750
S8051S	②	23-*07/54*	↪14289	1234	23-11/42	4216	11/42-*07/54*			⊂6751
S8052S	②	23-*07/54*	↪14290	1234	23-11/42	4216	11/42-*07/54*			⊂6752
S8053S	③c	23-04/55	↪14363	1235	23-09/42	4138	09/42-04/55			⊂6753
S8054S	③c	23-12/55	↪14434	1236	23-10/45	4159	10/45-12/55			⊂6754
S8055S	②	23-04/55	↪14303	1237	23-04/42	4198	04/42-04/55			⊂6755
S8056S	②	23-04/55	↪14297	1237	23-04/42	4198	04/42-04/55			⊂6756
S8057S	③	23-10/54	↪14310	1238	23-09/46	4230	09/46-10/54			⊂6757
S8058S	③	23-10/54	↪14308	1238	23-09/46	4230	09/46-10/54			⊂6758
S8059S	①c	23-02/55	↪14506	1239	23-02/42	4132	02/42-02/55			⊂6759
S8060S	①c	23-12/55	↪14433	1240	23- *42*	4135	*42*-12/55			⊂6760
S8061S	②	23-11/55	↪14422	1241	23-02/44	4204	02/44-11/55			⊂6761
S8062S	②	23-11/55	↪14425	1241	23-02/44	4204	02/44-11/55			⊂6762
S8063S	③	23-*04/54*	↪14265	1242	23-01/44	4224	01/44-*04/54*			⊂6763
S8064	③	23-04/48	⊗ *51*	1242	23-01/44	4224	01/44-04/48			⊂6764
S8065S	①c	23-10/55	↪14411	1243	23-11/42	4150	43-10/55			⊂6765
S8066S	①c	23-*08/54*	↪14304	1244	23- 46	4167	46-*08/54*			⊂6766
S8067S	③	23-02/55	↪14343	1245	23-01/46	4209	01/46-02/55			⊂6767
S8068S	③	23-02/55	↪14340	1245	23-01/46	4209	01/46-02/55			⊂6768
S8069S	①	23-*10/54*	↪14313	1246	23-09/43	4220	09/43-*10/54*			⊂6769
S8070S	①	23-*10/54*	↪14311	1246	23-09/43	4220	09/43-*10/54*			⊂6770
S8071S	③c	23-05/56	↪14478	1247	23-03/42	4134	03/42-05/56			⊂6771
S8072S	①c	23-*11/54*	↪14323	1248	23-10/42	4147	11/42-*11/54*			⊂6772
S8073S	③	23-10/55	↪14450	1249	23-08/47	4213	08/47-10/55			⊂6773
S8074S	③	23-10/55	↪14445	1249	23-08/47	4213	08/47-10/55			⊂6774
S8075S	③	23-11/55	↪14451	1250	23-10/47	4231	10/47-11/55			⊂6775
S8076S	③	23-11/55	↪14453	1250	23-10/47	4231	10/47-11/55			⊂6776
S8077S	①c	23-12/55	↪14437	1251	23- 46	4166	46-12/55			⊂6777
S8078S	①c	23-03/55	↪14347	1252	23- 44	4151	44-03/55			⊂6778
S8079S	③	23-10/55	↪14407	1253	23-08/46	4210	08/46-10/55			⊂6779
S8080S	③	23-10/55	↪14406	1253	23-08/46	4210	08/46-10/55			⊂6780
S8081S	③	23-12/55	↪14440	1254	23-09/43	4221	09/43-12/55			⊂6781
S8082S	③	23-12/55	↪14438	1254	23-09/43	4221	09/43-12/55			⊂6782
S8083S	①c	23-*09/54*	↪14382	1255	23-02/43	4143	02/43-*09/54*			⊂6783
S8084S	①c	23-*07/54*	↪14309	1256	23-05/45	4157	05/45-*07/54*			⊂6784
S8085S	③	23-05/55	↪14467	1257	23-01/42	4195	01/42-05/55			⊂6785
S8086S	③	23-05/55	↪14512	1257	23-01/42	4195	01/42-05/55			⊂6786
S8087S	②	23-11/55	↪14427	1258	23-08/43	4219	08/43-11/55			⊂6787
S8088S	②	23-11/55	↪14428	1258	23-08/43	4219	08/43-11/55			⊂6788
S8089S	①c	23-*12/54*	↪14327	1259	23-11/42	4145	11/42-*12/54*			⊂6789
S8090S	①c	23-*11/54*	↪14353	1260	23-07/42	4137	07/42-*11/54*			⊂6790
S8091S	①	23-01/56	↪[illegible]	1261	23- 45	4206	45-01/56			⊂6791
S8092S	①	23-01/56	↪14441	1261	23- 45	4206	45-01/56			⊂6792
S8093S	②	23-07/55	↪14380	1262	23-03/43	4217	03/43-07/55			⊂6793
S8094S	②	23-07/55	↪14383	1262	23-03/43	4217	03/43-07/55			⊂6794
S8095S	①c	23-09/54	↪14299	1263	23- 45	4163	45-09/54			⊂6795
S8096S	①c	23-*09/54*	↪14401	1264	23-01/42	4144	01/42-*09/54*			⊂6796
S8097S	②	23-03/55	↪14358	1265	23-12/47	4214	12/47-03/55			⊂6797
S8098S	②	23-03/55	↪14356	1265	23-12/47	4214	12/47-03/55			⊂6798
S8099S	②	23-*04/52*	↪14305	1266	23-11/47	4233	11/47-*04/52*			⊂6799
S8100S	②	23-*04/52*	⊗*08/52*	1266	23-11/47	4233	11/47-*04/52*			⊂6800
8101	①c	23-10/44	⊗10/44	1267	23-08/44					⊂6801
S8102S	①c	23-06/55	↪14366	1268	23-08/46	4171	08/46-06/55			⊂6802
S8103S	②	23-06/55	↪14396	1269	23-10/42	4196	10/42-06/55			⊂6803
S8104S	②	23-06/55	↪14399	1269	23-10/42	4196	10/42-06/55			⊂6804
S8105S	③	23-05/54	↪14272	1270	23-12/43	4225	12/43-05/54			⊂6805
S8106S	③	23-02/56	↪14476	1270	23-12/43	4225	12/43-05/54	4520	10/54-02/56	
										⊂6806
S8107S	①c	23-*01/54*	↪14423	1271	23-09/42	4139	09/42-*01/54*			⊂6807
S8108S	①c	23-06/56	↪14517	1272	23-11/42	4142	11/42-06/56			⊂6808
S8109S	③	23-05/56	↪14473	1273	23-03/48	4215	03/48-05/56			⊂6809
S8110S	③	23-05/56	↪14472	1273	23-03/48	4215	03/48-05/56			⊂6810
S8111S	③	23-05/55	↪14361	1274	23-11/47	4234	11/47-05/55			⊂6811
S8112S	③	23-05/55	↪14359	1274	23-11/47	4234	11/47-05/55			⊂6812
S8113S	③c	23-11/55	↪14505	1275	23-09/43	4149	09/43-11/55			⊂6813
S8114S	②c	23-*11/53*	↪14435	1276	23- 45	4161	45-*11/53*			⊂6814
S8115S	③	23-03/55	↪14355	1277	23-07/47	4212	07/47-03/55			⊂6815
S8116S	③	23-03/55	↪14354	1277	23-07/47	4212	07/47-03/55			⊂6816
S8117S	③	23-*06/54*	↪14332	1278	23-12/44	4227	12/44-*06/54*			⊂6817
S8118S	③	23-*06/54*	↪14336	1278	23-12/44	4227	12/44-*06/54*			⊂6818
S8119S	①c	23-03/55	↪14351	1279	23-09/43	4148	09/43-03/55			⊂6819
S8120S	①c	23-*05/54*	↪14296	1280	23-09/42	4136	09/42-*05/54*			⊂6820
S8121S	③	23-*08/54*	↪14373	1281	23- 42	4197	42-*08/54*			⊂6821
S8122S	③	23-*08/54*	↪14371	1281	23- 42	4197	42-*08/54*			⊂6822
S8123S	②	23-*04/54*	↪14267	1282	23-02/43	4222	02/43-11/47	4224	06/48-*04/54*	
										⊂6823
8124	②	23-11/47	⊗11/47	1282	23-02/43	4222	02/43-11/47			⊂6824
8125	①c	23-10/40	⊗12/40	1283	23-10/40					⊂6825
S8126S	①c	23-01/55	↪14349	1284	23-01/46	4168	01/46-01/55			⊂6826

3-SUB Metropolitan CW&F

Driving Motor Brake Third
DMBT
S8127S-S8178S

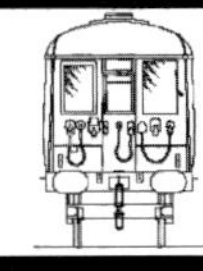

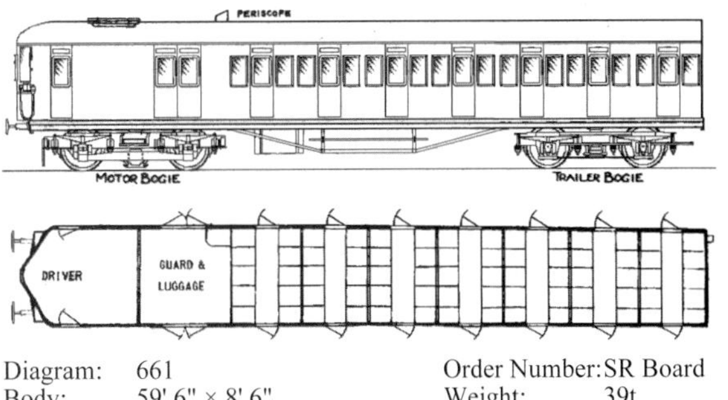

Diagram:	661	Order Number:	SR Board
Body:	59' 6" × 8' 6"	Weight:	39t
Seats:	70 third	Bogies:	SR
Motors:	MV339 2 × 275hp		

S8127S	05/25-03/58	⊗05/58	**1285**	05/25-01/46	**4300**	01/46-03/58		
S8128S	05/25-05/60	⊗05/60	**1285**	05/25-01/46	**4300**	01/46-03/58	**4310**	04/58-05/60
S8129S	05/25-10/60	⊗01/61	**1286**	05/25-01/46	**4301**	01/46-10/60		
S8130S	05/25-10/60	⊗01/61	**1286**	05/25-01/46	**4301**	01/46-10/60		
S8131S	05/25-11/60	⊗11/61	**1287**	05/25-01/46	**4302**	01/46-11/60		
S8132S	05/25-11/60	⊗11/61	**1287**	05/25-01/46	**4302**	01/46-11/60		
S8133S	05/25-02/60	⊗02/60	**1288**	05/25-11/45	**4303**	11/45-02/60		
S8134S	05/25-02/60	⊗02/60	**1288**	05/25-11/45	**4303**	11/45-02/60		
S8135S	06/25-06/60	⊗07/60	**1289**	06/25-04/46	**4304**	04/46-06/60		
S8136S	06/25-06/60	⊗07/60	**1289**	06/25-04/46	**4304**	04/46-06/60		
S8137S	06/25-05/61	⊗06/61	**1290**	06/25-01/46	**4305**	01/46-05/61		
S8138S	06/25-05/61	⊗06/61	**1290**	06/25-01/46	**4305**	01/46-05/61		
S8139S	06/25-04/60	⊗05/60	**1291**	06/25-02/46	**4306**	02/46-04/60		
S8140S	06/25-04/60	⊗05/60	**1291**	06/25-02/46	**4306**	02/46-04/60		
S8141S	06/25-04/60	⊗05/60	**1292**	06/25-11/45	**4307**	11/45-04/60		
S8142S	06/25-04/61	⊗11/61	**1292**	06/25-	**1299**	-02/46	**4314**	02/46-04/61
S8143S	06/25-11/60	Ⓟ	**1293**	06/25-12/45	**4308**	12/45-11/60		
S8144S	06/25-11/60	⊗02/61	**1293**	06/25-12/45	**4308**	12/45-11/60		
S8145S	06/25-09/60	⊗09/60	**1294**	06/25-10/45	**4309**	10/45-09/60		
S8146S	06/25-09/60	⊗09/60	**1294**	06/25-10/45	**4309**	10/45-09/60		
S8147S	06/25-05/60	⊗05/60	**1295**	06/25-11/45	**4310**	11/45-05/60		
S8148S	06/25-11/60	⊗01/61	**1295**	06/25-11/45	**4310**	11/45-03/58	**4339**	04/58-11/60
S8149S	06/25-04/61	⊗06/61	**1296**	06/25-12/45	**4311**	12/45-04/61		
S8150S	06/25-04/61	⊗06/61	**1296**	06/25-12/45	**4311**	12/45-04/61		
S8151S	07/25-06/60	⊗07/60	**1297**	07/25-12/45	**4312**	12/45-06/60		
S8152S	07/25-06/60	⊗07/60	**1297**	07/25-12/45	**4312**	12/45-06/60		
S8153S	07/25-05/60	⊗06/60	**1298**	07/25-12/45	**4313**	12/45-05/60		
S8154S	07/25-05/60	⊗06/60	**1298**	07/25-12/45	**4313**	12/45-05/60		
S8155S	07/25-05/60	⊗05/60	**1299**	07/25-	**1292**	-11/45	**4307**	11/45-04/60
S8156S	07/25-04/61	⊗11/61	**1299**	07/25-02/46	**4314**	02/46-04/61		
S8157S	07/25-11/60	⊗02/61	**1300**	07/25-08/45	**4315**	08/45-11/60		
S8158S	07/25-11/60	⊗02/61	**1300**	07/25-08/45	**4315**	08/45-11/60		
S8159S	07/25-03/60	⊗05/60	**1301**	07/25-10/45	**4316**	10/45-03/60		
S8160S	07/25-03/60	⊗05/60	**1301**	07/25-10/45	**4316**	10/45-03/60		
S8161S	07/25-03/60	⊗04/60	**1302**	07/25-02/46	**4317**	02/46-03/60		
S8162S	07/25-03/60	⊗04/60	**1302**	07/25-02/46	**4317**	02/46-03/60		
S8163S	07/25-02/60	⊗02/60	**1303**	07/25-10/45	**4318**	10/45-02/60		
S8164S	07/25-02/60	⊗02/60	**1303**	07/25-10/45	**4318**	10/45-02/60		
S8165S	07/25-07/60	⊗08/60	**1304**	07/25-07/45	**4319**	07/45-07/60		
S8166S	07/25-07/60	⊗08/60	**1304**	07/25-07/45	**4319**	07/45-07/60		
S8167S	07/25-04/60	⊗04/60	**1305**	07/25-02/46	**4320**	02/46-04/60		
S8168S	07/25-04/60	⊗04/60	**1305**	07/25-02/46	**4320**	02/46-04/60		
S8169S	07/25-12/59	⊗02/60	**1306**	07/25-01/46	**4321**	01/46-12/59		
S8170S	07/25-12/59	⊗02/60	**1306**	07/25-01/46	**4321**	01/46-12/59		
S8171S	08/25-10/61	⊗06/62	**1307**	08/25-11/45	**4322**	11/45-10/61		
S8172S	08/25-10/61	⊗06/62	**1307**	08/25-11/45	**4322**	11/45-10/61		
S8173S	08/25-04/61	⊗05/61	**1308**	08/25-12/45	**4323**	12/45-04/61		
S8174S	08/25-04/61	⊗05/61	**1308**	08/25-12/45	**4323**	12/45-04/61		
S8175S	08/25-10/61	⊗06/62	**1309**	08/25-02/46	**4324**	02/46-10/61		
S8176S	08/25-10/61	⊗06/62	**1309**	08/25-02/46	**4324**	02/46-10/61		
S8177S	08/25-05/60	⊗05/60	**1310**	08/25-10/45	**4325**	10/45-05/60		
S8178S	08/25-05/60	⊗05/60	**1310**	08/25-10/45	**4325**	10/45-05/60		

3-SUB Lancing/Ashford (LSWR bodies)

Driving Motor Brake Third

DMBT

S8179S-8222

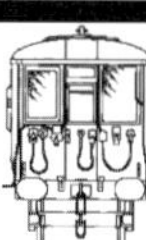

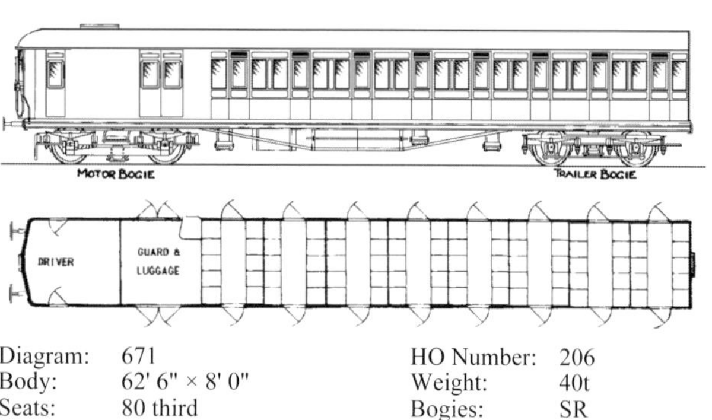

Diagram:	671	HO Number:	206
Body:	62' 6" × 8' 0"	Weight:	40t
Seats:	80 third	Bogies:	SR
Motors:	MV339 2 × 275hp		

S8179S	09/27-10/53	↳**14224**	**1658**	09/27-08/46	**4172**	08/46-10/53
S8180S	01/28-09/54	↳**14232**	**1659**	01/28-08/48	**4194**	08/48-09/54
S8181	01/28-06/49	↳**14209**	**1660**	01/28-08/48	**4193**	08/48-06/49
S8182S	01/28-10/53	↳**14230**	**1661**	01/28-05/47	**4174**	05/47-10/53
S8183S	01/28-07/53	↳**14097**	**1662**	01/28-02/47	**4177**	02/47-07/53
S8184S	01/28-09/53	↳**14226**	**1663**	01/28-12/47	**4185**	12/47-09/53
S8185S	01/28-12/53	↳**14233**	**1664**	01/28-07/47	**4180**	07/47-12/53
S8186S	01/28-04/55	↳**14490**	**1665**	01/28-08/47	**4181**	08/47-04/55
S8187S	01/28-05/53	↳**14203**	**1666**	01/28-08/48	**4192**	08/48-05/53
8188	01/28-06/45	⊗06/45	**1667**	01/28-06/45		
S8189S	01/28-03/54	↳**14260**	**1668**	01/28- 48	**4188**	48-03/54
S8190S	01/28-08/53	↳**14210**	**1669**	01/28-12/47	**4249**	12/47-08/53
S8191S	02/28-08/52	↳**14510**	**1670**	02/28-10/47	**4184**	10/47-08/52
S8192S	02/28-10/53	↳**14221**	**1671**	02/28-02/47	**4173**	02/47-10/53
S8193S	02/28-12/54	↳**14330**	**1672**	02/28- 48	**4187**	48-12/54
S8194S	02/28-05/53	↳**14205**	**1673**	02/28-10/47	**4255**	12/47-05/53
S8195S	02/28-07/53	↳**14417**	**1674**	02/28-09/48	**4189**	09/48-07/53
S8196S	02/28-07/53	↳**14096**	**1675**	02/28-08/47	**4183**	08/47-07/53
S8197S	02/28-11/54	↳**14322**	**1676**	02/28-05/47	**4178**	05/47-11/54
S8198S	02/28-08/53	↳**15436**	**1677**	02/28-07/47	**4179**	07/47-08/53
S8199S	02/28-01/55	↳**14339**	**1678**	02/28-09/48	**4250**[2]	09/48-01/55
S8200S	02/28-03/53	↳**14245**	**1679**	02/28-08/47	**4521**	08/47-03/53
S8201S	02/28-05/54	↳**14279**	**1680**	02/28-08/47	**4182**	08/47-05/54
S8202S	03/28-12/53	↳**14236**	**1681**	03/28-09/48	**4242**	09/48-12/53
S8203S	03/28-09/53	↳**14231**	**1682**	03/28-02/47	**4175**	02/47-09/53
S8204S	03/28-09/53	↳**14215**	**1683**	03/28-05/48	**4186**	05/48-09/53
S8205S	03/28-01/56	↳**14444**	**1684**	03/28-05/47	**4176**	05/47-01/56
S8206S	03/28-04/53	↳**14080**	**1685**	03/28-07/48	**4191**	07/48-04/53
S8207S	03/28-02/54	↳**14252**	**1686**	03/28-01/43	**4236**	01/43-02/54
S8208S	03/28-03/54	↳**14268**	**1687**	03/28-11/42	**4245**	08/48-03/54
S8209S	03/28-05/54	↳**14331**	**1688**	03/28-12/47	**4239**	12/47-05/54
S8210S	03/28-08/53	↳**14244**	**1689**	03/28-11/47	**4237**	11/47-08/53
S8211S	03/28-11/53	↳**14219**	**1690**	03/28-08/48	**4248**	08/48-11/53
S8212S	03/28-08/53	↳**14106**	**1691**	03/28-07/48	**4243**	07/48-08/53
S8213S	04/28-01/54	↳**15442**	**1692**	04/28-09/44	**4155**	09/44-01/54
S8214S	04/28-12/53	↳**14237**	**1693**	04/28-04/48	**4244**	04/48-12/53
S8215S	04/28-12/54	↳**14324**	**1694**	04/28-07/48	**4247**	07/48-12/54
S8216S	04/28-07/53	↳**14222**	**1695**	04/28-05/47	**4235**	05/47-07/53
S8217S	04/28-05/56	↳**14519**	**1696**	04/28-08/47	**4572**	08/47-05/56
S8218S	04/28-09/53	↳**14238**	**1697**	04/28-03/48	**4246**	03/48-09/53
S8219S	04/28-09/53	↳**14228**	**1698**	04/28-10/47	**4240**	10/47-09/53
S8220S	04/28-09/54	↳**14302**	**1699**	04/28-10/47	**4238**	10/47-09/54
S8221S	04/28-07/53	↳**14418**	**1700**	04/28-02/48	**4241**	02/48-07/53
8222	04/28-03/47	⊗03/47	**1701**	04/28-03/47		

3-SUB Lancing/Ashford (LSWR bodies)

Driving Motor Brake Third

DMBT

S8223S-S8225S

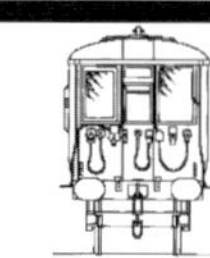

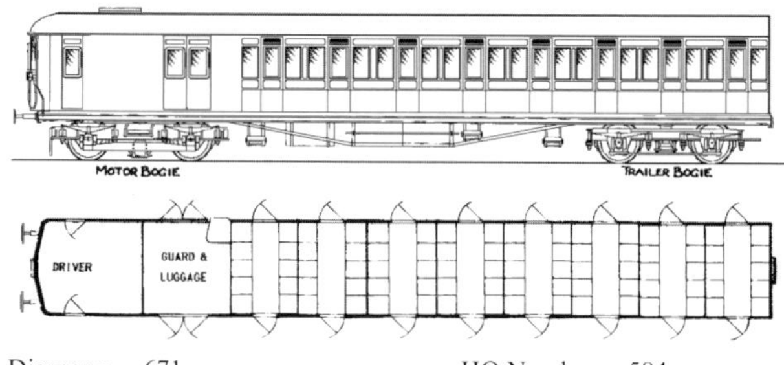

Diagram:	671	HO Number:	584
Body:	62' 6" × 8' 0"	Weight:	
Seats:	80 third	Bogies:	SR
Motors:	MV339 2 × 275hp		

S8223S	11/30-12/53	↳**14263**	**1783**	11/30-02/48	**4594**	03/49-12/53
S8224S	11/30-04/53	↳**14240**	**1784**	11/30-01/48	**4517**	01/48-04/53
S8225S	11/30-02/56	↳**14459**	**1785**	11/30-07/48	**4526**	07/48-02/56

3-SUB Lancing/Ashford (LSWR bodies)

Driving Motor Brake Third

DMBT

8226

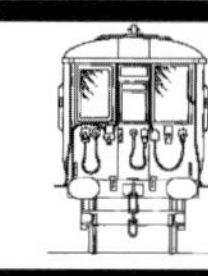

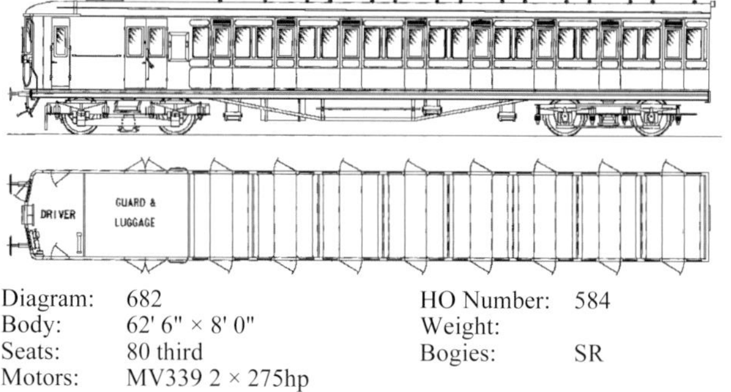

Diagram:	682	HO Number:	584
Body:	62' 6" × 8' 0"	Weight:	
Seats:	80 third	Bogies:	SR
Motors:	MV339 2 × 275hp		

8226	01/31-11/47	⊗11/47	**1786**	01/31-01/47	**4406**[1]	01/47-11/47

3-SUB Ashford (SER bodies)

Driving Motor Brake Third
DMBT
S8227-S8246

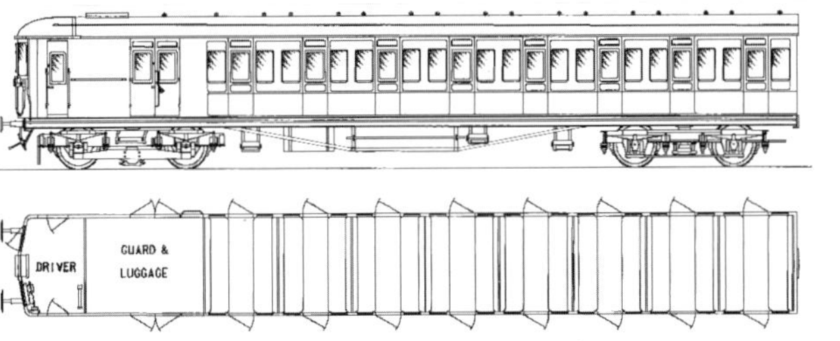

Diagram:	662	HO Number:	Pre SR (Joint committee)
Body:	62' 6" × 8' 0"	Weight:	
Seats:	80 third	Bogies:	SR
Motors:	EE DK77 2 × 300hp, later MV339 2 × 275hp		

S8227	*02/25-11/49*	↪**12705**	**1401**	*02/25-11/49*		
S8228	*02/25-11/49*	↪**12734**	**1401**	*02/25-11/49*		
S8229	*02/25-02/51*	↪**14041**	**1402**	*02/25-04/47*	**4432**	*04/47-02/51*
S8230	*02/25-02/51*	↪**14059**	**1402**	*02/25-04/47*	**4432**	*04/47-02/51*
S8231	*02/25-06/50*	↪**8638**	**1403**	*02/25-12/46*	**4433**	*12/46-06/50*
S8232	*02/25-06/50*	↪**8642**	**1403**	*02/25-12/46*	**4433**	*12/46-06/50*
S8233	*02/25-01/49*	↪**12759**	**1404**	*02/25-01/49*		
8234	*02/25-06/45*	⊗06/45	**1404**	*02/25-06/45*		
S8235	*02/25-02/51*	↪**8624**	**1405**	*02/25-03/47*	**4434**	*03/47-02/51*
S8236	*02/25-02/51*	↪**8628**	**1405**	*02/25-03/47*	**4434**	*03/47-02/51*
S8237	*02/25-07/50*	↪**12799**	**1406**	*02/25-11/47*	**4406**²	*11/47-07/50*
S8238	*02/25-07/50*	⊗	**1406**	*02/25-11/47*	**4406**²	*11/47-07/50*
S8239	*02/25-05/50*	↪**12762**	**1407**	*02/25-11/46*	**4435**	*11/46-06/50*
S8240	*02/25-05/50*	↪**12763**	**1407**	*02/25-11/46*	**4435**	*11/46-06/50*
S8241	*02/25-11/49*	↪**14020**	**1408**	*02/25-11/49*		
S8242	*02/25-11/49*	⊗	**1408**	*02/25-11/49*		
S8243	*02/25-06/50*	↪**8640**	**1409**	*02/25-08/47*	**4436**	*08/47-06/50*
S8244	*02/25-06/50*	↪**8643**	**1409**	*02/25-08/47*	**4436**	*08/47-06/50*
S8245	*03/25-02/51*	↪**14034**	**1410**	*03/25-11/46*	**4437**	*11/46-02/51*
S8246	*03/25-02/51*	↪**14019**	**1410**	*03/25-11/46*	**4437**	*11/46-02/51*

3-SUB Ashford (SER bodies)

Driving Motor Brake Third
DMBT
S8247-S8258

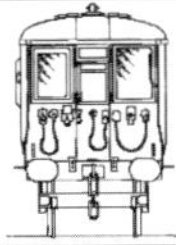

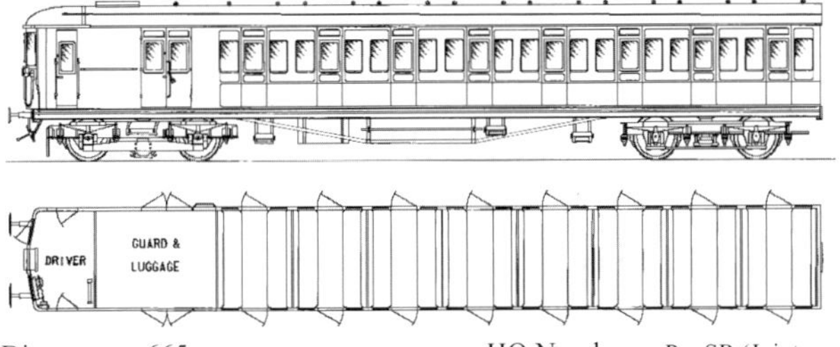

Diagram:	665	HO Number:	Pre SR (Joint committee)
Body:	62' 6" × 8' 0"	Weight:	
Seats:	80 third	Bogies:	SR
Motors:	EE DK77 2 × 300hp, later MV339 2 × 275hp		

S8247	*03/25-06/50*	↪**8649**	**1411**	*03/25-03/47*	**4438**	*03/47-06/50*
S8248	*03/25-06/50*	↪**8647**	**1411**	*03/25-03/47*	**4438**	*03/47-06/50*
S8249	*03/25-02/49*	↪**12690**	**1412**	*03/25-12/46*	**4439**¹	*12/46-02/49*
S8250	*03/25-02/49*	↪**12696**	**1412**	*03/25-12/46*	**4439**¹	*12/46-02/49*
S8251	*03/25-07/50*	↪**12754**	**1413**	*03/25-03/47*	**4440**	*03/47-07/50*
S8252	*03/25-07/50*	↪**12755**	**1413**	*03/25-03/47*	**4440**	*03/47-07/50*
8253	*03/25-10/40*	⊗11/40	**1414**	*03/25-10/40*		
S8254	*03/25-04/51*	↪**14003**	**1414**	*03/25-01/47*	**4441**	*01/47-04/51*
S8255	*03/25-02/48*	⊗02/48	**1415**	*03/25-11/46*	**4442**¹	*11/46-02/48*
S8256	*03/25-02/48*	↪**12719**	**1415**	*03/25-11/46*	**4442**¹	*11/46-02/48*
S8257	*03/25-12/50*	↪**12792**	**1416**	*03/25-05/47*	**4443**	*05/47-12/50*
S8258	*03/25-12/50*	↪**12790**	**1416**	*03/25-05/47*	**4443**	*05/47-12/50*

3-SUB Ashford (SER bodies)

Driving Motor Brake Third
DMBT
S8259-S8297

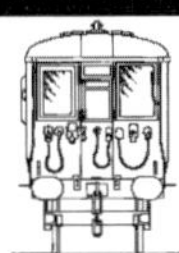

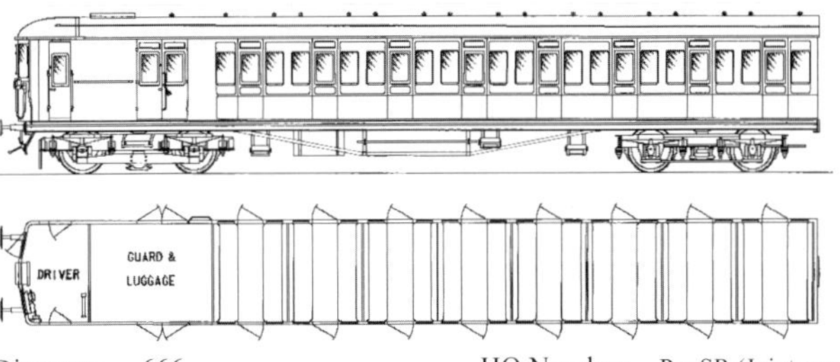

Diagram:	666	HO Number:	Pre SR (Joint committee)
Body:	62' 6" × 8' 0"	Weight:	
Seats:	80 third	Bogies:	SR
Motors:	EE DK77 2 × 300hp, later MV339 2 × 275hp		

S8259	*03/25-08/50*	↪**8629**	**1417**	*03/25-*	**1437**	*-04/47*	**4458**	*04/47-08/50*
S8260	*03/25-09/50*	↪**12781**	**1417**	*03/25-02/47*	**4444**	*02/47-09/50*		
S8261	*04/25-05/51*	↪**14042**	**1418**	*04/25-12/46*	**4445**	*12/46-05/51*		
S8262	*04/25-05/51*	↪**14033**	**1418**	*04/25-12/46*	**4445**	*12/46-05/51*		
S8263	*04/25-09/50*	↪**14045**	**1419**	*04/25-12/46*	**4446**	*12/46-10/50*		
S8264	*04/25-09/50*	↪**14039**	**1419**	*04/25-12/46*	**4446**	*12/46-10/50*		
S8265	*04/25-03/51*	↪**14018**	**1420**	*04/25-06/47*	**4447**	*06/47-03/51*		
S8266	*04/25-03/51*	↪**14028**	**1420**	*04/25-06/47*	**4447**	*06/47-03/51*		
S8267	*04/25-11/49*	↪**12714**	**1421**	*04/25-11/49*				
S8268	*04/25-11/49*	↪**12726**	**1421**	*04/25-11/49*				
S8269	*04/25-03/50*	↪**14056**	**1422**	*04/25-10/46*	**4448**	*10/46-03/50*		
S8270	*04/25-03/50*	↪**14057**	**1422**	*04/25-10/46*	**4448**	*10/46-03/50*		
S8271	*04/25-01/51*	↪**8639**	**1423**	*04/25-04/47*	**4449**	*04/47-01/51*		
S8272	*04/25-01/51*	↪**8623**	**1423**	*04/25-04/47*	**4449**	*04/47-01/51*		
S8273	*04/25-01/51*	↪**8625**	**1424**	*04/25-03/47*	**4450**	*03/47-01/51*		
S8274	*04/25-01/51*	↪**12798**	**1424**	*04/25-03/47*	**4450**	*03/47-01/51*		
S8275	*04/25-11/49*	↪**12740**	**1425**	*04/25-11/49*				
S8276	*04/25-11/49*	↪**12739**	**1425**	*04/25-11/49*				
S8277	*04/25-04/51*	↪**14029**	**1426**	*04/25-02/47*	**4451**	*02/47-04/51*		
8278	*04/25-10/40*	⊗11/40	**1426**	*04/25-10/40*				
S8279	*05/25-09/50*	↪**14007**	**1427**	*05/25-01/45*	**1483**	*03/46-05/47*	**4486**	*05/47-09/50*
8280	*05/25-01/45*	⊗01/45	**1427**	*05/25-01/45*				
8281	*05/25-11/40*	↪**12735**	**1428**	*05/25-01/45*				
S8282	*05/25-10/50*	↪**14060**	**1428**	*05/25-04/41*	**1475**	*42-05/47*	**4482**	*05/47-10/50*
8283	*05/25-01/47*	⊗ 47	**1429**	*05/25-01/47*				
8284	*05/25-01/42*	↪**14024**	**1429**	*05/25-02/47*	**4452**	*02/47-12/50*		
S8285	*05/25-11/49*	↪**12722**	**1430**	*05/25-11/49*				
S8286	*05/25-11/49*	↪**12729**	**1430**	*05/25-11/49*				
S8287	*05/25-11/50*	↪**8637**	**1431**	*05/25-01/47*	**4453**	*01/47-12/50*		
S8288	*05/25-11/50*	↪**8618**	**1431**	*05/25-01/47*	**4453**	*01/47-12/50*		
8289	*05/25-11/40*	↪**12736**	**1432**	*05/25-11/40*				
8290	*05/25- 42*	⊗	**1432**	*05/25-11/40*	**1428**	*04/41-01/45*		
S8291	*05/25-04/50*	↪**12770**	**1433**	*05/25-01/47*	**4454**	*01/47-04/50*		
S8292	*05/25-04/50*	↪**12769**	**1433**	*05/25-01/47*	**4454**	*01/47-04/50*		
S8293	*05/25-10/50*	↪**8636**	**1434**	*05/25-11/46*	**4455**	*11/46-11/50*		
8294	*05/25-11/40*	⊗11/40	**1434**	*05/25-11/40*				
S8295	*05/25-05/51*	↪**14021**	**1435**	*05/25-03/47*	**4456**	*03/47-05/51*		
S8296	*05/25-05/51*	↪**14010**	**1435**	*05/25-03/47*	**4456**	*03/47-05/51*		
S8297	*06/25-06/50*	↪**12764**	**1436**	*06/25-06/47*	**4457**	*06/47-06/50*		

3-SUB Ashford (SER bodies)

Driving Motor Brake Third
DMBT
S8298-S8326

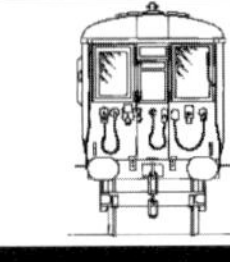

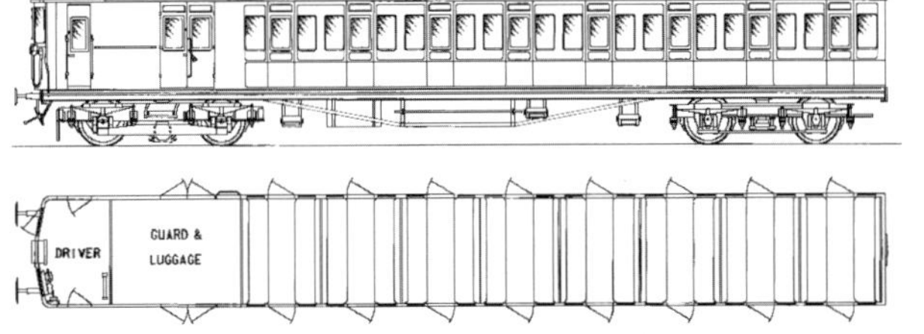

Diagram:	665	HO Number:	Pre SR (Joint committee)
Body:	62' 6" × 8' 0"	Weight:	
Seats:	80 third	Bogies:	SR
Motors:	EE DK77 2 × 300hp, later MV339 2 × 275hp		

S8298	*06/25-06/50*	↪**12768**	**1436**	*06/25-06/47*	**4457**	*06/47-06/50*		
S8299	*06/25-09/50*	↪**12780**	**1437**	*06/25-*	**1417**	*-02/47*	**4444**	*02/47-09/50*

S8300	*06/25-08/50*	↳**8633**	**1437**	*06/25-04/47*	**4458**	*04/47-08/50*		
S8301	*06/25-11/49*	↳**12760**	**1438**	*06/25-11/49*				
S8302	*06/25-11/49*	↳**12761**	**1438**	*06/25-11/49*				
S8303	*06/25-10/50*	↳**12774**	**1439**	*06/25-10/46*	**4459**	*10/46-10/50*		
S8304	*06/25-10/50*	↳**12787**	**1439**	*06/25-10/46*	**4459**	*10/46-10/50*		
S8305	*06/25-11/49*	↳**12743**	**1440**	*06/25-11/49*				
S8306	*06/25-11/49*	↳**12737**	**1440**	*06/25-11/49*				
S8307	*06/25-10/50*	↳**14011**	**1441**	*06/25-02/47*	**4460**	*02/47-10/50*		
S8308	*06/25-10/50*	↳**14058**	**1441**	*06/25-02/47*	**4460**	*02/47-10/50*		
S8309	*06/25-12/50*	↳**12795**	**1442**	*06/25-06/47*	**4461**	*06/47-12/50*		
S8310	*06/25-12/50*	↳**12796**	**1442**	*06/25-06/47*	**4461**	*06/47-12/50*		
S8311	*06/25-03/50*	↳**8622**	**1443**	*06/25-02/47*	**4462**	*02/47-03/50*		
S8312	*06/25-03/50*	↳**8627**	**1443**	*06/25-02/47*	**4462**	*02/47-03/50*		
S8313	*06/25-05/51*	↳**14025**	**1444**	*06/25-11/46*	**4463**	*11/46-05/51*		
S8314	*06/25-05/51*	↳**14049**	**1444**	*06/25-11/46*	**4463**	*11/46-05/51*		
S8315	*07/25-11/49*	↳**12747**	**1445**	*07/25-11/49*				
S8316	*07/25-11/49*	↳**12744**	**1445**	*07/25-11/49*				
S8317	*07/25-06/50*	↳**8630**	**1446**	*07/25-03/47*	**4464**	*03/47-06/50*		
S8318	*07/25-06/50*	↳**8632**	**1446**	*07/25-03/47*	**4464**	*03/47-06/50*		
S8319	*07/25-04/50*	↳**12742**	**1447**	*07/25-10/46*	**4465**	*10/46-04/50*		
S8320	*07/25-04/50*	↳**12741**	**1447**	*07/25-10/46*	**4465**	*10/46-04/50*		
S8321	*07/25-09/40*	⊗09/40	**1448**	*07/25-09/40*				
S8322	*07/25-11/49*	↳**12718**	**1448**	*07/25-11/49*				
S8323	*07/25-11/49*	↳**12733**	**1449**	*07/25-11/49*				
S8324	*07/25-11/49*	↳**12738**	**1449**	*07/25-11/49*				
S8325	*07/25-11/50*	↳**12800**	**1450**	*07/25-03/47*	**4466**	*03/47-11/50*		
S8326	*07/25-11/50*	↳**12782**	**1450**	*07/25-03/47*	**4466**	*03/47-11/50*		

3-SUB Ashford (SER bodies)

Driving Motor Brake Third

DMBT

S8327-S8416

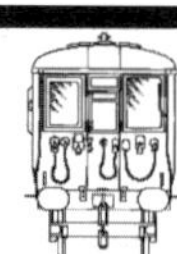

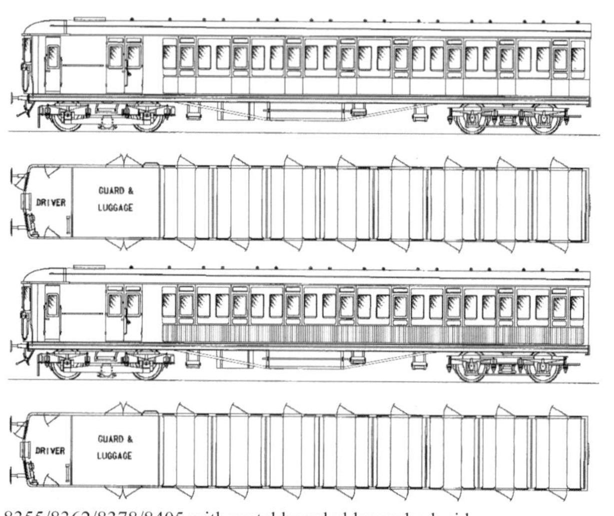

8355/8362/8378/8405 with matchboarded lower bodysides.

Diagram:	662	HO Number:	Pre SR (Joint committee)
Body:	62' 6" × 8' 0"	Weight:	
Seats:	80 third	Bogies:	SR
Motors:	EE DK77 2 × 300hp, later MV339 2 × 275hp		

S8327	*07/25-07/50*	↳**12751**	**1451**	*07/25-01/47*	**4467**	*01/47-07/50*		
S8328	*07/25-07/50*	↳**12750**	**1451**	*07/25-01/47*	**4467**	*01/47-07/50*		
S8329	*07/25-09/50*	↳**8617**	**1452**	*07/25- 47*	**4468**	*12/47-09/50*		
8330	*07/25-11/47*	⊗	**1452**	*07/25-11/47*				
S8331	*07/25-12/50*	↳**8621**	**1453**	*07/25-04/47*	**4469**	*04/47-12/50*		
S8332	*07/25-12/50*	↳**8616**	**1453**	*07/25-04/47*	**4469**	*04/47-12/50*		
S8333	*08/25-11/49*	↳**12702**	**1454**	*08/25-09/40*	**1448**	09/40-11/49		
8334	*08/25-09/40*	⊗09/40	**1454**	*08/25-09/40*				
S8335	*08/25-03/51*	↳**14002**	**1455**	*08/25-06/47*	**4470**	*06/47-03/51*		
8336	*08/25-03/46*	⊗ *42*	**1455**	*08/25-03/46*				
S8337	*08/25-03/51*	↳**14035**	**1456**	*08/25-06/47*	**4471**	*06/47-03/51*		
S8338	*08/25-03/51*	↳**14026**	**1456**	*08/25-06/47*	**4471**	*06/47-03/51*		
S8339	*08/25-06/50*	↳**8650**	**1457**	*08/25-11/46*	**4472**	*11/46-06/50*		
8340	*08/25-12/41*	⊗12/41	**1457**	*08/25-12/41*				
S8341	*08/25-11/49*	↳**12725**	**1458**	*08/25-11/49*				
S8342	*08/25-11/49*	↳**12727**	**1458**	*08/25-11/49*				
S8343	*08/25-09/50*	↳**12784**	**1459**	*08/25-10/46*	**4473**	*10/46-09/50*		
S8344	*08/25-09/50*	↳**8620**	**1459**	*08/25-10/46*	**4473**	*10/46-09/50*		
S8345	*08/25- 49*	↳**12689**	**1460**	*08/25-04/47*	**4474**	*04/47- 49*		
S8346	*08/25-06/50*	↳**12778**	**1460**	*08/25-04/47*	**4474**	*04/47-06/50*		
S8347	*08/25-11/49*	↳**12706**	**1461**	*08/25-11/49*				
S8348	*08/25-11/49*	↳**12694**	**1461**	*08/25-11/49*				
S8349	*09/25-06/50*	↳**8645**	**1462**	*09/25-12/41*	**1457**	12/41-11/46	**4472**	*11/46-06/50*
8350	*09/25-12/41*	⊗12/41	**1462**	*09/25-12/41*				
S8351	*09/25-11/49*	↳**12745**	**1463**	*09/25-11/49*				
S8352	*09/25-11/49*	↳**12746**	**1463**	*09/25-11/49*				
S8353	*09/25-11/50*	↳**14014**	**1464**	*09/25-05/47*	**4475**	*05/47-11/50*		
S8354	*09/25-11/50*	↳**14038**	**1464**	*09/25-05/47*	**4475**	*05/47-11/50*		
S8355	*09/25-11/49*	⊗	**1465**	*09/25-11/49*				
S8356	*09/25-11/49*	⊗	**1465**	*09/25-11/49*				
S8357	*09/25-04/51*	↳**14036**	**1466**	*09/25-10/46*	**4476**	*10/46-04/51*		
S8358	*09/25-04/51*	↳**14047**	**1466**	*09/25-10/46*	**4476**	*10/46-04/51*		
S8359	*09/25-09/50*	↳**12766**	**1467**	*09/25-05/47*	**4477**	*05/47-09/50*		
S8360	*09/25-09/50*	↳**12776**	**1467**	*09/25-05/47*	**4477**	*05/47-09/50*		
S8361	*09/25-05/51*	↳**14023**	**1468**	*09/25-12/46*	**4478**	*12/46-05/51*		
S8362	*09/25-05/51*	↳**14015**	**1468**	*09/25-12/46*	**4478**	*12/46-05/51*		
S8363	*09/25-11/50*	↳**12785**	**1469**	*09/25-03/47*	**4479**	*03/47-11/50*		
S8364	*09/25-11/50*	↳**12786**	**1469**	*09/25-03/47*	**4479**	*03/47-11/50*		
S8365	*09/25-01/51*	↳**12794**	**1470**	*09/25-* 40	**4481**	48-01/51		
S8366	*09/25-12/50*	↳**14030**	**1470**	*09/25-* 40	**1429**	01/47-*02/47*	**4452**	*02/47-12/50*
S8367	*10/25-03/50*	↳**14008**	**1471**	*10/25-06/47*	**4480**	*06/47-03/50*		
S8368	*10/25-03/50*	↳**14009**	**1471**	*10/25-06/47*	**4480**	*06/47-03/50*		
S8369	*10/25- 50*	⊗ 50	**1472**	*10/25-12/46*	**4481**	*12/46- 50*		
S8370	*10/25-01/51*	↳**12797**	**1472**	*10/25-12/46*	**4481**	*12/46-01/51*		
8371	*10/25-11/40*	⊗11/40	**1473**	*10/25-10/40*		original body accident loss 04/37		
S8372	*10/25-04/51*	↳**14016**	**1473**	*10/25-10/40*	**1414**	11/40-*01/47*	**4441**	*01/47-04/51*
S8373	*10/25- 51*	⊗	**1474**	*10/25-10/46*				
S8374	*10/25-09/50*	↳**12724**	**1474**	*10/25-10/46*	**1452**	11/47- *47*	**4468**	*12/47-09/50*
S8375	*10/25-10/50*	↳**14031**	**1475**	*10/25-05/47*	**4482**	*05/47-10/50*		
S8376	*10/25-01/49*	⊗	**1475**	*10/25- 42*	**1404**	06/45-*01/49*		
S8377	*10/25-04/51*	↳**14012**	**1476**	*10/25-08/40*	**1426**	11/40-*02/47*	**4451**	*02/47-04/51*
8378	*10/25-08/40*	⊗08/40	**1476**	*10/25-08/40*				
S8379	*10/25-02/49*	⊗02/49	**1477**	*10/25-04/47*	**4483**[1]	*04/47-02/49*		
S8380	*10/25-06/50*	⊗	**1477**	*10/25-04/47*	**4483**[1]	*04/47-02/49*	**4474**	*49-06/50*
S8381	*10/25-04/50*	↳**12765**	**1478**	*10/25-05/47*	**4484**	*05/47-04/50*		
S8382	*10/25-04/50*	⊗ *56*	**1478**	*10/25-05/47*	**4484**	*05/47-04/50*		
S8383	*10/25-11/49*	↳**12704**	**1479**	*10/25-11/49*				
S8384	*10/25-11/49*	↳**12703**	**1479**	*10/25-11/49*				
S8385	*11/25-09/50*	↳**8648**	**1480**	*11/25-03/47*	**4485**	*03/47-09/50*		
S8386	*11/25-09/50*	↳**8644**	**1480**	*11/25-03/47*	**4485**	*03/47-09/50*		
S8387	*11/25-11/49*	↳**12709**	**1481**	*11/25-11/49*				
S8388	*11/25-11/49*	↳**12701**	**1481**	*11/25-11/49*				
S8389	*11/25-11/49*	↳**12730**	**1482**	*11/25-11/49*				
S8390	*11/25-11/49*	↳**12731**	**1482**	*11/25-11/49*				
S8391	*11/25-03/51*	↳**14001**	**1483**	*11/25-03/46*	**1455**	03/46-*06/47*	**4470**	*06/47-03/51*
S8392	*11/25-09/50*	↳**14006**	**1483**	*11/25-05/47*	**4486**	*05/47-09/50*		
S8393	*11/25-04/50*	↳**8646**	**1484**	*11/25-12/46*	**4487**	*12/46-04/50*		
S8394	*11/25-04/50*	↳**12767**	**1484**	*11/25-12/46*	**4487**	*12/46-04/50*		
S8395	*11/25-04/50*	↳**12756**	**1485**	*11/25-01/47*	**4488**	01/47-*04/50*		
S8396	*11/25-04/50*	↳**12753**	**1485**	*11/25-01/47*	**4488**	01/47-*04/50*		
S8397	*11/25-01/51*	↳**14005**	**1486**	*11/25-05/47*	**4489**	*05/47-02/51*		
S8398	*11/25-01/51*	↳**14027**	**1486**	*11/25-05/47*	**4489**	*05/47-02/51*		
S8399	*11/25-11/49*	↳**12733**	**1487**	*11/25-11/49*				
S8400	*11/25-11/49*	↳**12716**	**1487**	*11/25-11/49*				
S8401	*11/25-04/50*	↳**12773**	**1488**	*11/25-12/46*	**4490**	*12/46-04/50*		
S8402	*11/25-04/50*	↳**12775**	**1488**	*11/25-12/46*	**4490**	*12/46-04/50*		
S8403	*12/25-11/50*	↳**14037**	**1489**	*12/25-10/46*	**4491**	*10/46-11/50*		
S8404	*12/25-11/50*	↳**14043**	**1489**	*12/25-10/46*	**4491**	*10/46-11/50*		
S8405	*12/25-06/51*	↳**14013**	**1490**	*12/25-11/46*	**4492**	*11/46-06/51*		
S8406	*12/25-06/51*	↳**14004**	**1490**	*12/25-11/46*	**4492**	*11/46-06/51*		
S8407	*12/25-12/50*	↳**8634**	**1491**	*12/25-06/47*	**4493**	*06/47-12/50*		
S8408	*12/25-12/50*	↳**8619**	**1491**	*12/25-06/47*	**4493**	*06/47-12/50*		
S8409	*12/25-11/49*	↳**12698**	**1492**	*12/25-11/49*				
S8410	*12/25-11/49*	↳**12693**	**1492**	*12/25-11/49*				
S8411	*12/25-07/50*	↳**12749**	**1493**	*12/25-05/47*	**4494**	*05/47-07/50*		
S8412	*12/25-07/50*	↳**12752**	**1493**	*12/25-05/47*	**4494**	*05/47-07/50*		
S8413	*12/25-11/49*	↳**12708**	**1494**	*12/25-11/49*				
S8414	*12/25-11/49*	↳**12713**	**1494**	*12/25-11/49*				
S8415	*12/25-11/49*	↳**12687**	**1495**	*12/25-11/49*				
S8416	*12/25-11/49*	↳**12697**	**1495**	*12/25-11/49*				

3-SUB Metropolitan CW&F

Driving Motor Brake Third

DMBT

S8417S-S8474S

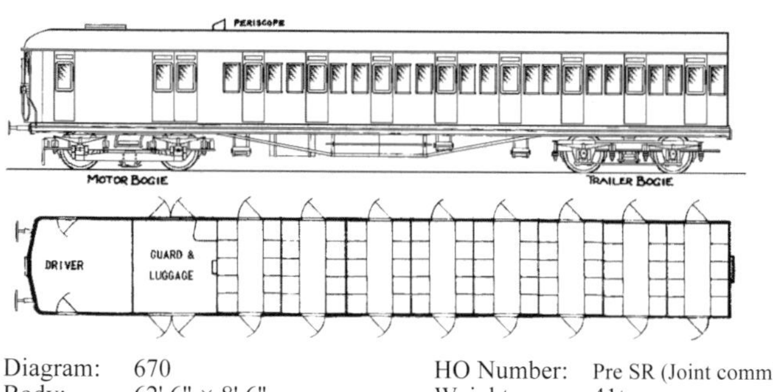

Diagram:	670	HO Number:	Pre SR (Joint committee)
Body:	62' 6" × 8' 6"	Weight:	41t

Seats: 80 third Bogies: SR
Motors: EE DK77 2 × 300hp, later MV339 2 × 275hp

S8417S	09/25-04/61	⊗05/61	1496	09/25-09/45	4326	09/45-04/61		
S8418S	09/25-04/61	⊗05/61	1496	09/25-09/45	4326	09/45-04/61		
S8419S	09/25-01/60	⊗07/60	1497	09/25-03/46	4327	03/46-01/60		
S8420S	09/25-01/60	⊃DS70057	1497	09/25-03/46	4327	03/46-01/60		
S8421S	09/25-08/60	⊃DS70103	1498	09/25-07/45	4328	07/45-08/60		
S8422S	09/25-08/60	⊃DS70102	1498	09/25-07/45	4328	07/45-08/60		
S8423S	09/25-07/60	⊃DS70107	1499	09/25-	1501	-09/45	4331	09/45-07/60
S8424S	09/25-01/62	⊗01/64	1499	09/25-06/45	4329	06/45-01/62		
S8425S	09/25-01/62	⊗11/63	1500	09/25-10/45	4330	10/45-01/62		
S8426S	09/25-01/62	⊗11/63	1500	09/25-10/45	4330	10/45-01/62		
S8427S	09/25-07/60	⊃DS70106	1501	09/25-09/45	4331	09/45-07/60		
S8428S	09/25-01/62	⊗01/64	1501	09/25-	1499	-06/45	4329	06/45-01/62
S8429	09/25-11/48	⊗	1502	09/25-06/45	4332	06/45-11/48		
S8430S	09/25-09/60	⊃DS70104	1502	09/25-06/45	4332	06/45-11/48	4332	05/50-09/60
S8431S	09/25-05/61	⊗06/61	1503	09/25-	1517	-08/45	4347	08/45-05/61
S8432S	09/25-11/61	⊗	1503	09/25-04/46	4333	04/46- 51	4333	05/52-11/61
S8433S	09/25-08/60	⊃DS70096	1504	09/25-08/45	4334	08/45-08/60		
S8434S	09/25-08/60	⊃DS70097	1504	09/25-08/45	4334	08/45-08/60		
S8435S	09/25-01/62	⊗09/63	1505	09/25-03/46	4335	03/46-06/52	4335	10/52-01/62
S8436S	09/25-01/62	⊗09/63	1505	09/25-03/46	4335	03/46-06/52	4335	10/52-01/62
S8437S	09/25-01/60	⊗12/60	1506	09/25-09/45	4336	09/45-01/60		
S8438S	09/25-01/60	⊗12/60	1506	09/25-09/45	4336	09/45-01/60		
S8439S	09/25-01/62	⊗	1507	09/25-09/45	4337	09/45-01/62		
S8440S	09/25-01/62	⊗	1507	09/25-09/45	4337	09/45-01/62		
S8441S	07/25-11/61	⊗01/64	1508	07/25-08/45	4338	08/45-11/61		
S8442S	07/25-11/61	⊗01/64	1508	07/25-08/45	4338	08/45-11/61		
S8443S	07/25-11/60	⊗01/61	1509	07/25-07/45	4339	07/45-11/60		
S8444S	07/25-04/58	⊗	1509	07/25-07/45	4339	07/45-04/58		
S8445S	07/25-07/60	⊃DS70091	1510	07/25-04/46	4340	04/46-07/60		
S8446S	07/25-07/60	⊃DS70090	1510	07/25-04/46	4340	04/46-07/60		
S8447S	07/25-05/60	⊗06/60	1511	07/25-07/45	4341	07/45-05/60		
S8448S	07/25-05/60	⊗06/60	1511	07/25-07/45	4341	07/45-05/60		
S8449S	08/25-06/60	⊃081269	1512	08/25-08/45	4342	08/45-06/60		
S8450S	08/25-06/60	⊃081270	1512	08/25-08/45	4342	08/45-06/60		
S8451S	08/25-04/61	⊗05/61	1513	08/25-06/45	4343	06/45-04/61		
S8452S	08/25-04/61	⊗05/61	1513	08/25-06/45	4343	06/45-04/61		
S8453S	08/25-07/60	⊃DS70094	1514	08/25-03/46	4344	03/46-07/60		
S8454S	08/25-07/60	⊃DS70095	1514	08/25-03/46	4344	03/46-07/60		
S8455S	08/25-04/59	⊃DS70045	1515	08/25-03/46	4345	03/46-04/59		
S8456S	08/25-04/59	⊃DS70044	1515	08/25-03/46	4345	03/46-04/59		
S8457S	08/25-12/61	⊃DS70173	1516	08/25-06/45	4346	06/45-12/61		
S8458S	08/25-12/61	⊗03/62	1516	08/25-06/45	4346	06/45-12/61		
S8459S	09/25-05/61	⊗06/61	1517	09/25-08/45	4347	08/45-05/61		
S8460S	09/25-11/61	⊗	1517	09/25-	1503	-04/46	4333	04/46- 51
			4333	05/52-11/61				
S8461S	09/25-01/62	⊗08/63	1518	09/25-03/46	4348	03/46-01/62		
S8462S	09/25-01/62	⊗08/63	1518	09/25-03/46	4348	03/46-01/62		
S8463S	09/25-07/60	⊃DS70092	1519	09/25-04/46	4349	04/46-07/60		
S8464S	09/25-07/60	⊃DS70093	1519	09/25-04/46	4349	04/46-07/60		
S8465S	09/25-09/60	⊃DS70105	1520	09/25-11/45	4350	11/45-05/50	4332	05/50-09/60
8466	09/25-11/40	⊗11/40	1520	09/25-11/40				
S8467S	10/25-08/60	⊃DS70100	1521	10/25-09/45	4351	04/46-08/60		
S8468S	10/25-08/60	⊃DS70101	1521	10/25-09/45	4351	04/46-08/60		
S8469S	10/25-11/61	⊗01/62	1522	10/25-07/45	4352	07/45-11/61		
S8470S	10/25-11/61	⊗01/62	1522	10/25-07/45	4352	07/45-11/61		
S8471S	10/25-08/60	⊃DS70098	1523	10/25-09/45	4353	09/45-08/60		
S8472S	10/25-08/60	⊃DS70099	1523	10/25-09/45	4353	09/45-08/60		
S8473S	10/25-11/59	⊃DS70058	1524	10/25-06/45	4354	06/45-11/59		
S8474S	10/25-11/59	⊗11/59	1524	10/25-06/45	4354	06/45-11/59		

3-SUB Birmingham RC&W/ Ashford (SER bodies)

Driving Motor Brake Third
DMBT
S8475-S8494

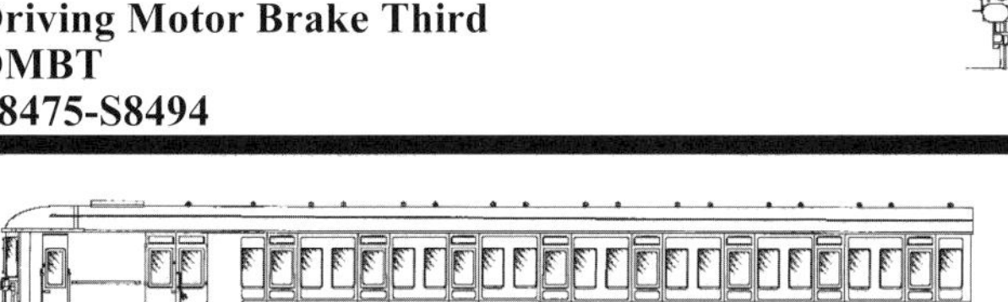

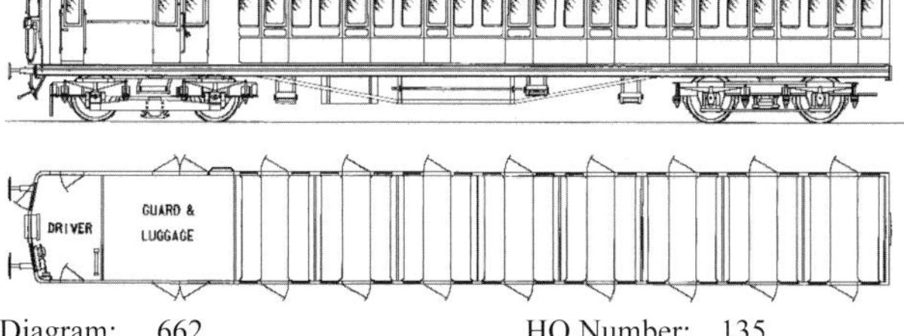

Diagram: 662 HO Number: 135
Body: 62' 6" × 8' 0" Weight:
Seats: 80 third Bogies: SR
Motors: EE DK77 2 × 300hp, later MV339 2 × 275hp

S8475	06/26-04/50	↪12748	1525	06/26-02/48	4442[2]	02/48-04/50		
S8476	06/26-04/50	↪12757	1525	06/26-02/48	4442[2]	02/48-04/50		
S8477	06/26-04/50	↪12772	1526	06/26-05/47	4495	05/47-04/50		
S8478	06/26-04/50	↪12771	1526	06/26-05/47	4495	05/47-04/50		
S8479	06/26-09/50	↪12788	1527	06/26-04/47	4496	04/47-09/50		
S8480	06/26-09/50	↪12777	1527	06/26-04/47	4496	04/47-09/50		
S8481	06/26-08/49	⊗	1528	06/26-08/49				
S8482	06/26-08/49	⊗	1528	06/26-08/49				
S8483	06/26-07/50	↪8651	1529	06/26-05/47	4497	05/47-07/50		
S8484	06/26-07/50	↪8653	1529	06/26-05/47	4497	05/47-07/50		
S8485	06/26-10/50	↪8652	1530	06/26-11/40	1434	11/40-11/46	4455	11/46-11/50
S8486	06/26-05/50	↪14017	1530	06/26-11/40	1520	11/40-11/45	4350	11/45-05/50
S8487	06/26-08/50	↪12789	1531	06/26-01/47	4498	01/47-08/50		
S8488	06/26-08/50	↪12791	1531	06/26-01/47	4498	01/47-08/50		
S8489	06/26-07/50	↪8641	1532	06/26-03/47	4499	03/47-07/50		
S8490	06/26-07/50	↪12793	1532	06/26-03/47	4499	03/47-07/50		
S8491	06/26-11/50	⊗	1533	06/26-04/47	4500	04/47-11/50		
S8492	06/26-11/50	↪8626	1533	06/26-04/47	4500	04/47-11/50		
S8493	06/26-03/51	↪14032	1534	06/26-06/47	4501	06/47-03/51		
S8494	06/26-03/51	↪14022	1534	06/26-06/47	4501	06/47-03/51		

3-SUB Ashford (SER bodies)

Driving Motor Brake Third
DMBT
S8495-S8524

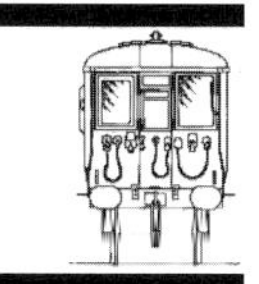

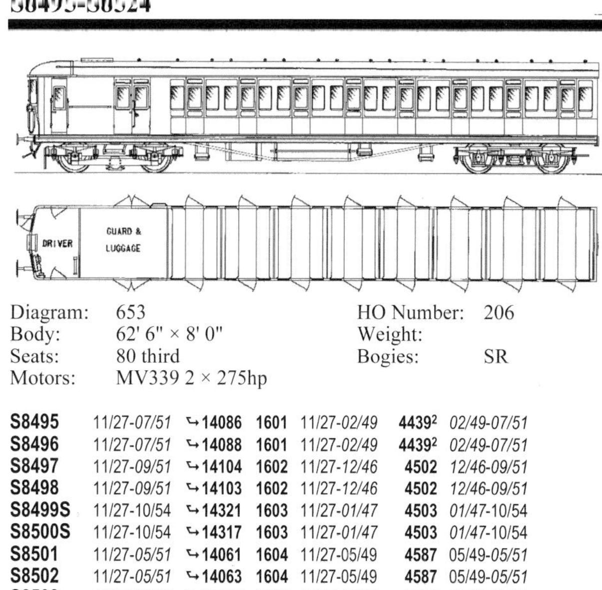

Diagram: 653 HO Number: 206
Body: 62' 6" × 8' 0" Weight:
Seats: 80 third Bogies: SR
Motors: MV339 2 × 275hp

S8495	11/27-07/51	↪14086	1601	11/27-02/49	4439[2]	02/49-07/51		
S8496	11/27-07/51	↪14088	1601	11/27-02/49	4439[2]	02/49-07/51		
S8497	11/27-09/51	↪14104	1602	11/27-12/46	4502	12/46-09/51		
S8498	11/27-09/51	↪14103	1602	11/27-12/46	4502	12/46-09/51		
S8499S	11/27-10/54	↪14321	1603	11/27-01/47	4503	01/47-10/54		
S8500S	11/27-10/54	↪14317	1603	11/27-01/47	4503	01/47-10/54		
S8501	11/27-05/51	↪14061	1604	11/27-05/49	4587	05/49-05/51		
S8502	11/27-05/51	↪14063	1604	11/27-05/49	4587	05/49-05/51		
S8503	11/27-09/51	↪14053	1605	11/27-05/47	4504	05/47-09/51		
S8504	11/27-09/51	↪14051	1605	11/27-05/47	4504	05/47-09/51		
S8505	11/27-11/49	↪12678	1606	11/27-11/49				
S8506	11/27-11/49	↪12670	1606	11/27-11/49				
S8507	12/27-11/49	↪12671	1607	12/27-11/49				
S8508	12/27-11/49	↪12673	1607	12/27-11/49				
S8509S	12/27-04/53	↪14099	1608	12/27-04/47	4505	04/47-04/53		
S8510S	12/27-04/53	↪14100	1608	12/27-04/47	4505	04/47-04/53		
S8511	12/27-10/51	↪14076	1609	12/27-04/48	4588	10/49-10/51		
S8512	12/27-10/51	↪14091	1609	12/27-04/48	4588	10/49-10/51		
S8513S	12/27-07/53	↪14247	1610	12/27-02/44	1621	06/44-01/47	4510	01/47-07/53
S8514	12/27-06/51	↪14225	1610	12/27-02/49	4483[2]	02/49-06/51		
S8515	12/27-09/51	↪14087	1611	12/27-11/46	4506	11/46-09/51		
S8516	12/27-09/51	↪14090	1611	12/27-11/46	4506	11/46-09/51		
8517	12/27-05/41	⊗	1612	12/27-05/41				Grounded Lancing 05/41
8518	12/27-05/41	⊗05/41	1612	12/27-05/41				
S8519	01/28-12/51	↪14072	1613	01/28-05/47	4507	05/47-12/51		
S8520	01/28-12/51	↪14083	1613	01/28-05/47	4507	05/47-12/51		
S8521	01/28-11/49	↪12699	1614	01/28-11/49				
S8522	01/28-11/49	↪12684	1614	01/28-11/49				
8523	01/28-04/37	⊗04/37	1615	01/28-04/37				
S8523[2]	04/37-02/51	↪14208	1615	04/37-12/46	4508	12/46-02/51		
				Replacement with LSWR body on new underframe				
S8524	01/28-02/51	↪14102	1615	01/28-12/46	4508	12/46-02/51		

3-SUB Ashford (SER bodies)

Driving Motor Brake Third
DMBT
S8525-S8538

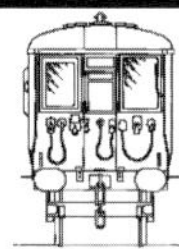

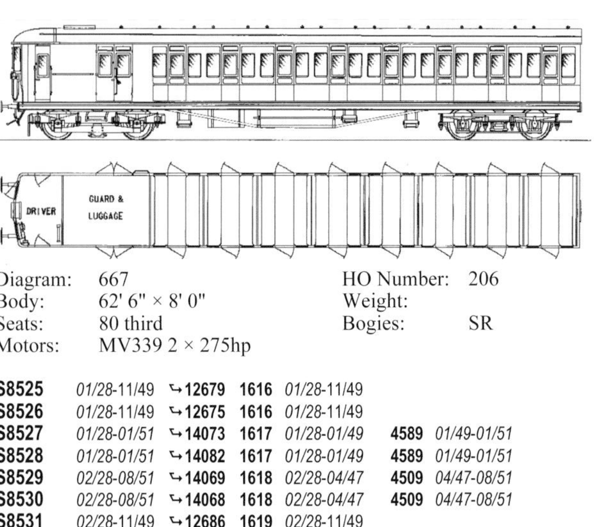

Diagram: 667 | HO Number: 206
Body: 62' 6" × 8' 0" | Weight:
Seats: 80 third | Bogies: SR
Motors: MV339 2 × 275hp

S8525	*01/28-11/49*	↳**12679**	**1616**	*01/28-11/49*		
S8526	*01/28-11/49*	↳**12675**	**1616**	*01/28-11/49*		
S8527	*01/28-01/51*	↳**14073**	**1617**	*01/28-01/49*	**4589**	*01/49-01/51*
S8528	*01/28-01/51*	↳**14082**	**1617**	*01/28-01/49*	**4589**	*01/49-01/51*
S8529	*02/28-08/51*	↳**14069**	**1618**	*02/28-04/47*	**4509**	*04/47-08/51*
S8530	*02/28-08/51*	↳**14068**	**1618**	*02/28-04/47*	**4509**	*04/47-08/51*
S8531	*02/28-11/49*	↳**12686**	**1619**	*02/28-11/49*		
S8532	*02/28-11/49*	↳**12685**	**1619**	*02/28-11/49*		
S8533S	*02/28-03/54*	↳**14274**	**1620**	*02/28-03/48*	**4580**	*03/48-03/54*
S8534S	*02/28-03/54*	↳**14258**	**1620**	*02/28-03/48*	**4580**	*03/48-03/54*
S8535S	*02/28-07/53*	↳**14248**	**1621**	*02/28-01/47*	**4510**	*01/47-07/53*
8536	*02/28-06/44*	⊗06/44	**1621**	*02/28-06/44*		
S8537	*02/28-11/49*	↳**12688**	**1622**	*02/28-11/49*		
S8538	*02/28-11/49*	↳**12700**	**1622**	*02/28-11/49*		

3-SUB Ashford (SER bodies)

Driving Motor Brake Third
DMBT
S8539-S8548

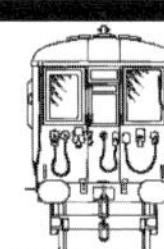

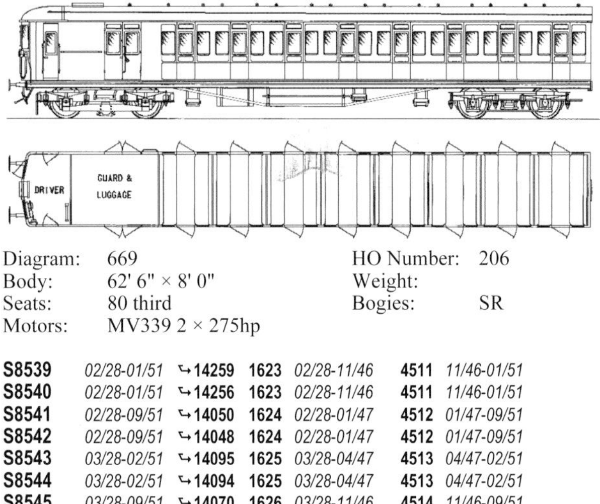

Diagram: 669 | HO Number: 206
Body: 62' 6" × 8' 0" | Weight:
Seats: 80 third | Bogies: SR
Motors: MV339 2 × 275hp

S8539	*02/28-01/51*	↳**14259**	**1623**	*02/28-11/46*	**4511**	*11/46-01/51*
S8540	*02/28-01/51*	↳**14256**	**1623**	*02/28-11/46*	**4511**	*11/46-01/51*
S8541	*02/28-09/51*	↳**14050**	**1624**	*02/28-01/47*	**4512**	*01/47-09/51*
S8542	*02/28-09/51*	↳**14048**	**1624**	*02/28-01/47*	**4512**	*01/47-09/51*
S8543	*03/28-02/51*	↳**14095**	**1625**	*03/28-04/47*	**4513**	*04/47-02/51*
S8544	*03/28-02/51*	↳**14094**	**1625**	*03/28-04/47*	**4513**	*04/47-02/51*
S8545	*03/28-09/51*	↳**14070**	**1626**	*03/28-11/46*	**4514**	*11/46-09/51*
S8546	*03/28-09/51*	↳**14077**	**1626**	*03/28-11/46*	**4514**	*11/46-09/51*
S8547	*03/28-11/49*	↳**12677**	**1627**	*03/28-11/49*		
S8548	*03/28-11/49*	↳**12676**	**1627**	*03/28-11/49*		

3-SUB Ashford (SER bodies)

Driving Motor Brake Third
DMBT
S8549S-S8553S

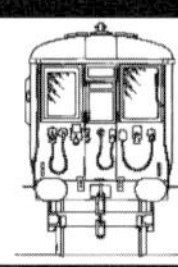

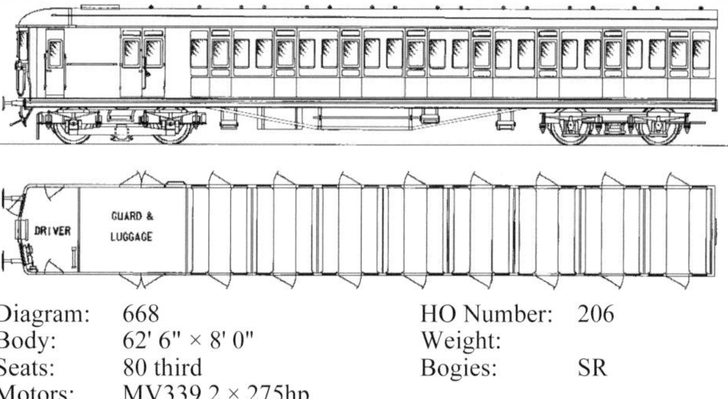

Diagram: 668 | HO Number: 206
Body: 62' 6" × 8' 0" | Weight:
Seats: 80 third | Bogies: SR
Motors: MV339 2 × 275hp

S8549S	*03/28-01/55*	↳**14338**	**1628**	*03/28-01/47*	**4515**	*01/47-01/55*
S8550S	*03/28-01/55*	↳**14345**	**1628**	*03/28-01/47*	**4515**	*01/47-01/55*
S8551S	*03/28-04/53*	↳**14052**	**1629**	*03/28-06/47*	**4516**	*06/47-12/51*
S8552S	*03/28-04/53*	↳**14044**	**1629**	*03/28-06/47*	**4516**	*06/47-12/51*
S8553S	*03/28-01/55*	↳**14508**	**1630**	*03/28-02/48*	**4586**	*02/48-01/55*

3-SUB Ashford (SER bodies)

Driving Motor Brake Third
DMBT
S8554S

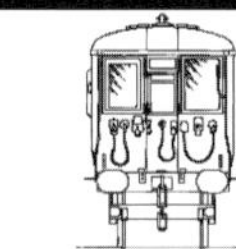

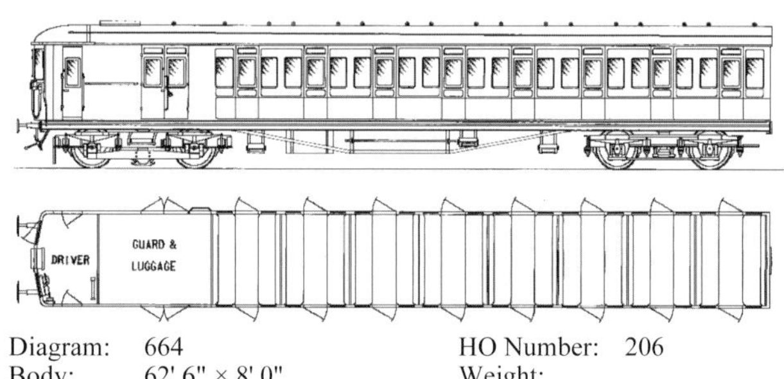

Diagram: 664 | HO Number: 206
Body: 62' 6" × 8' 0" | Weight:
Seats: 80 third | Bogies: SR
Motors: MV339 2 × 275hp

S8554S	*03/28-01/55*	↳**14489**	**1630**	*03/28-02/48*	**4586**	*02/48-01/55*

3-SUB Lancing/Ashford (LSWR bodies)

Driving Motor Brake Third
DMBT
S8555S-S8563

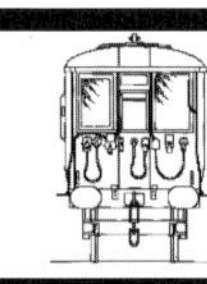

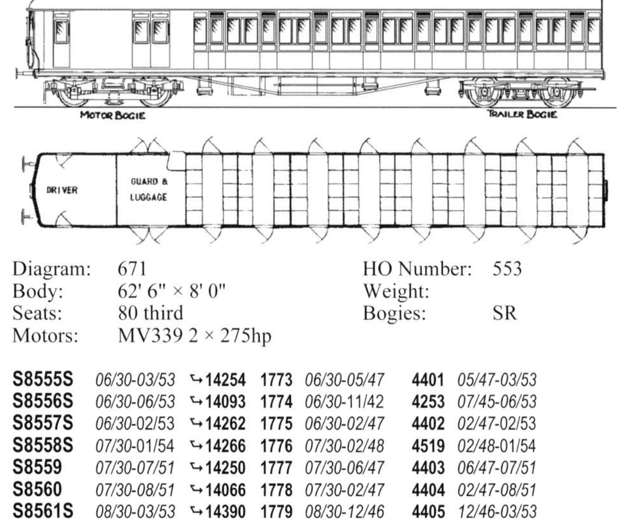

Diagram: 671 | HO Number: 553
Body: 62' 6" × 8' 0" | Weight:
Seats: 80 third | Bogies: SR
Motors: MV339 2 × 275hp

S8555S	*06/30-03/53*	↳**14254**	**1773**	*06/30-05/47*	**4401**	*05/47-03/53*
S8556S	*06/30-06/53*	↳**14093**	**1774**	*06/30-11/42*	**4253**	*07/45-06/53*
S8557S	*06/30-02/53*	↳**14262**	**1775**	*06/30-02/47*	**4402**	*02/47-02/53*
S8558S	*07/30-01/54*	↳**14266**	**1776**	*07/30-02/48*	**4519**	*02/48-01/54*
S8559	*07/30-07/51*	↳**14250**	**1777**	*07/30-06/47*	**4403**	*06/47-07/51*
S8560	*07/30-08/51*	↳**14066**	**1778**	*07/30-02/47*	**4404**	*02/47-08/51*
S8561S	*08/30-03/53*	↳**14390**	**1779**	*08/30-12/46*	**4405**	*12/46-03/53*

S8562S	08/30-03/54	↪**14419**	**1780**	08/30-01/49	**4573**	01/49-06/52	**4418**	06/52-03/54
S8563	08/30-09/51	↪**15328**	**1781**	08/30-06/48	**4574**	06/48-09/51		

3-SUB Lancing (AC frame) /Ashford (LSWR bodies)

Driving Motor Brake Third
DMBT
S8564S

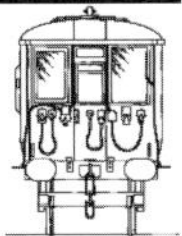

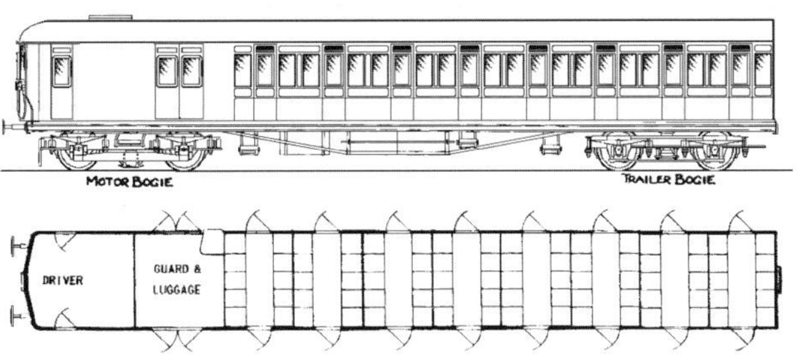

Diagram:	671	HO Number:	553
Body:	62' 6" × 8' 0"	Weight:	
Seats:	80 third	Bogies:	SR
Motors:	MV339 2 × 275hp		

S8564S	08/30-07/53	⊃**DS40**	**1782**	08/30-08/47	**4579**	08/47-07/53

3-SUB Lancing/Ashford (LSWR bodies)

Driving Motor Brake Third
DMBT
8565-S8571S

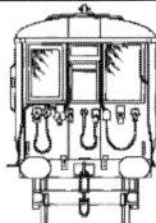

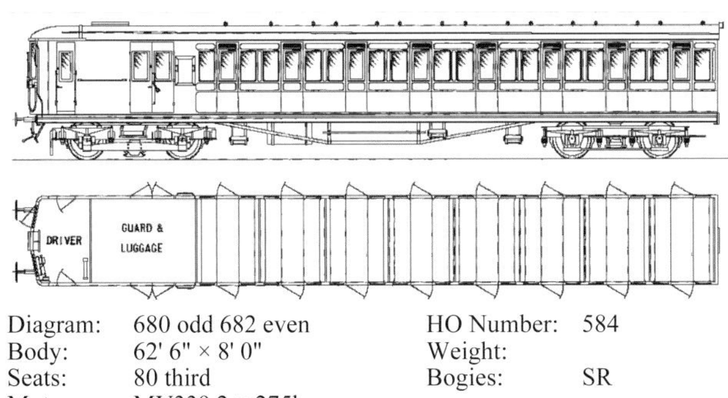

Diagram:	680 odd 682 even	HO Number:	584
Body:	62' 6" × 8' 0"	Weight:	
Seats:	80 third	Bogies:	SR
Motors:	MV339 2 × 275hp		

8565	01/31-11/47	↪**11385**	**1786**	01/31-01/47	**4406**[1]	01/47-11/47
S8566	01/31-07/51	↪**14202**	**1787**	01/31-10/46	**4407**	10/46-07/51
S8567	01/31-07/51	↪**14206**	**1787**	01/31-10/46	**4407**	10/46-07/51
S8568S	01/31-02/53	↪**14364**	**1788**	01/31-02/47	**4408**	02/47-02/53
S8569S	01/31-02/53	↪**14360**	**1788**	01/31-02/47	**4408**	02/47-02/53
S8570S	01/31-04/54	↪**14271**	**1789**	01/31-10/46	**4409**	10/46-04/54
S8571S	01/31-04/54	↪**14273**	**1789**	01/31-10/46	**4409**	10/46-04/54

3-SUB Lancing/Ashford (LSWR bodies)

Driving Motor Brake Third
DMBT
S8572S

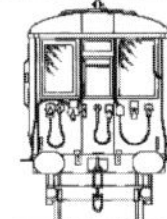

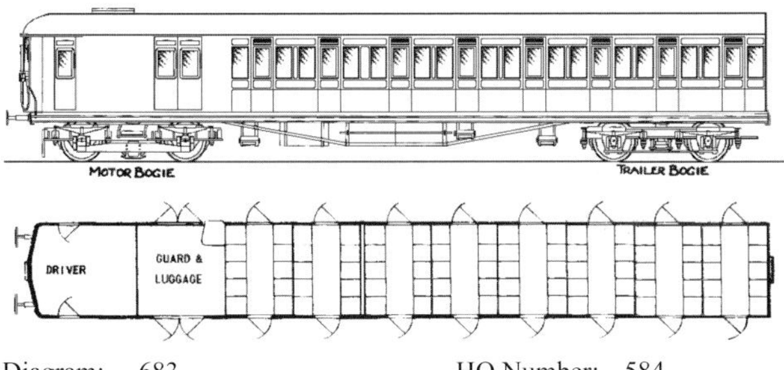

Diagram:	683	HO Number:	584
Body:	62' 6" × 8' 0"	Weight:	
Seats:	80 third	Bogies:	SR
Motors:	MV339 2 × 275hp		

8572	01/31-04/34	⊗04/34	**1790**	01/31-04/34		
S8572S[2]	04/34-01/56	↪**14449**	**1790**	04/34-08/48	**4190**	08/48-01/56

Replacement with LSWR body on new underframe

3-SUB Lancing/Ashford (LSWR bodies)

Driving Motor Brake Third
DMBT
S8573S-S8580

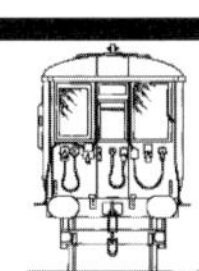

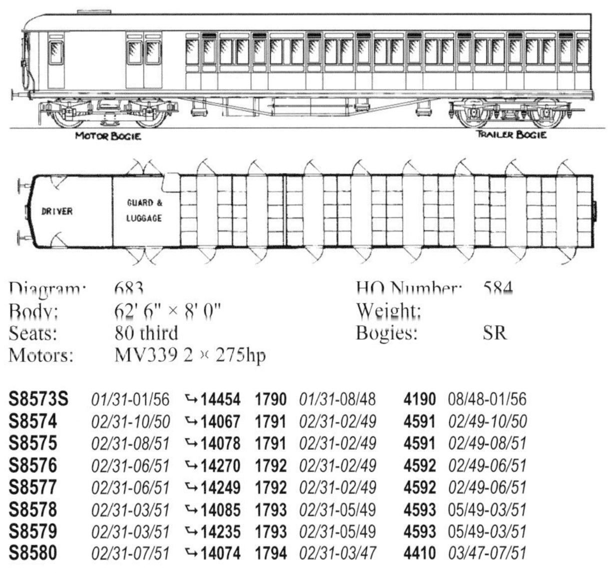

Diagram:	683	HO Number:	584
Body:	62' 6" × 8' 0"	Weight:	
Seats:	80 third	Bogies:	SR
Motors:	MV339 2 × 275hp		

S8573S	01/31-01/56	↪**14454**	**1790**	01/31-08/48	**4190**	08/48-01/56
S8574	02/31-10/50	↪**14067**	**1791**	02/31-02/49	**4591**	02/49-10/50
S8575	02/31-08/51	↪**14078**	**1791**	02/31-02/49	**4591**	02/49-08/51
S8576	02/31-06/51	↪**14270**	**1792**	02/31-02/49	**4592**	02/49-06/51
S8577	02/31-06/51	↪**14249**	**1792**	02/31-02/49	**4592**	02/49-06/51
S8578	02/31-03/51	↪**14085**	**1793**	02/31-05/49	**4593**	05/49-03/51
S8579	02/31-03/51	↪**14235**	**1793**	02/31-05/49	**4593**	05/49-03/51
S8580	02/31-07/51	↪**14074**	**1794**	02/31-03/47	**4410**	03/47-07/51

3-SUB Lancing/Ashford (LSWR bodies)

Driving Motor Brake Third
DMBT
S8581

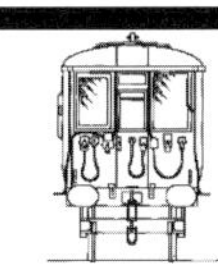

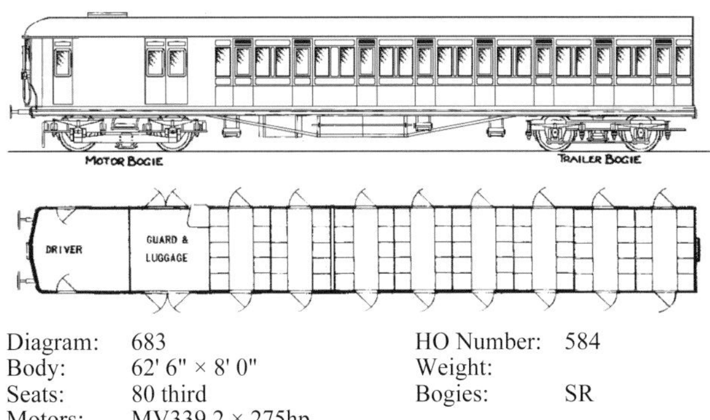

Diagram:	683	HO Number:	584
Body:	62' 6" × 8' 0"	Weight:	
Seats:	80 third	Bogies:	SR
Motors:	MV339 2 × 275hp		

8581	02/31-09/39	⊗09/39	**1794**	02/31-09/39		
S8581[2]	40-07/51	↪**14075**	**1794**	40-03/47	**4410**	03/47-07/51

Replaced in 1940 with rebuilt body from **8003**

3-SUB Lancing/Ashford (LSWR bodies)

Driving Motor Brake Third
DMBT
S8582-S8585

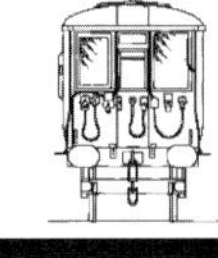

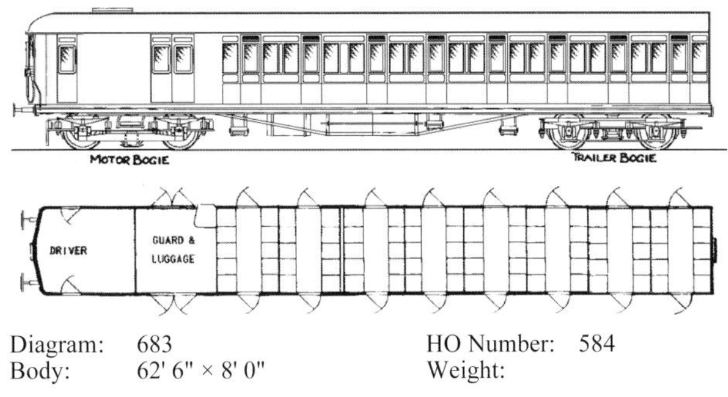

Diagram:	683	HO Number:	584
Body:	62' 6" × 8' 0"	Weight:	

Seats:	80 third	Bogies:	SR
Motors:	MV339 2 × 275hp		

S8582	11/31-*08/51*	↳**14498**	**1795**	11/31-*01/47*	**4430**	*01/47-08/51*
S8583	11/31-*08/51*	↳**14368**	**1795**	11/31-*01/47*	**4430**	*01/47-08/51*
S8584	11/31-*09/51*	↳**14413**	**1796**	11/31-*01/47*	**4431**	*01/47-09/51*
S8585	11/31-*09/51*	↳**14414**	**1796**	11/31-*01/47*	**4431**	*01/47-09/51*

3-SUB Lancing/Ashford (LBSCR bodies)

Driving Motor Brake Third
DMBT
S8586-S8589

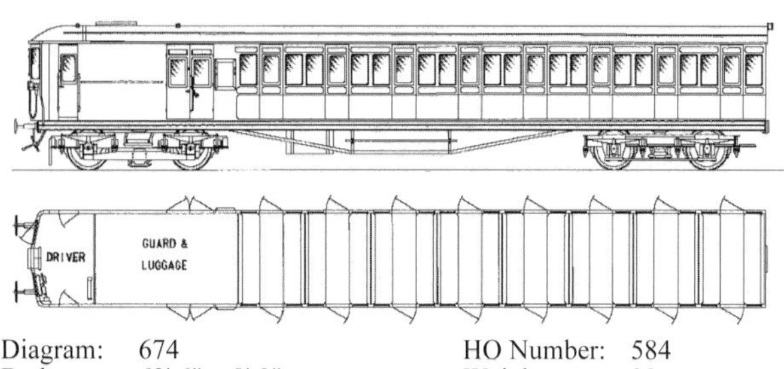

Diagram:	674	HO Number:	584
Body:	62' 6" × 8' 0"	Weight:	39t
Seats:	80 third	Bogies:	SR
Motors:	MV339 2 × 275hp		

S8586	01/32-02/49	↳**11352**	**1797**	01/32-*03/48*	**4583**	*03/48*-02/49	⊂**1752/2168**
S8587	01/32-02/49	↳**11369**	**1797**	01/32-*03/48*	**4583**	*03/48*-02/49	⊂**1687/2157**
S8588	01/32-05/49	↳**11357**	**1798**	01/32-*02/48*	**4584**	*02/48*-05/49	⊂**1734/2166**
S8589	01/32-05/49	↳**11362**	**1798**	01/32-*02/48*	**4584**	*02/48*-05/49	⊂**1592/2144**

3-SUB Lancing/Ashford (LBSCR bodies)

Driving Motor Brake Third
DMBT
8590-S8595

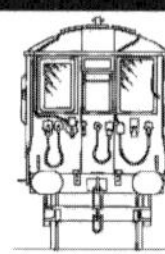

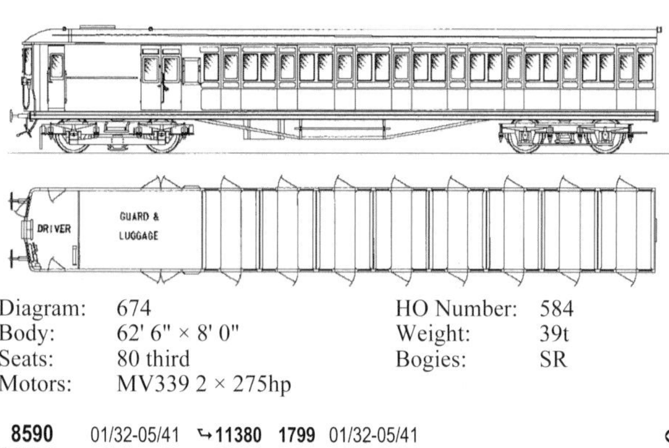

Diagram:	674	HO Number:	584
Body:	62' 6" × 8' 0"	Weight:	39t
Seats:	80 third	Bogies:	SR
Motors:	MV339 2 × 275hp		

8590	01/32-05/41	↳**11380**	**1799**	01/32-05/41					⊂**1286/3777**
S8591	01/32- 48	↳**12712**	**1799**	01/32-10/46					⊂**1275/3767**
S8592	01/32-05/48	↳**11358**	**1800**	01/32-05/48					⊂**1311/3800**
S8593	01/32-05/48	↳**11347**	**1800**	01/32-05/48					⊂**1304/3793**
S8594	01/32-02/48	↳**11375**	**1801**	01/32- 34	**1600**	34-*08/47*	**4607**	*08/47*-02/48	⊂**1287/3778**
S8595	01/32-02/48	⊗02/48	**1801**	01/32- 34	**1600**	34-*08/47*	**4607**	*08/47*-02/48	⊂**1305/3794**

2-NOL Lancing or Lancing/Eastleigh (LSWR bodies)

Driving Motor Brake Third
DMBT
S8596S-S8615S

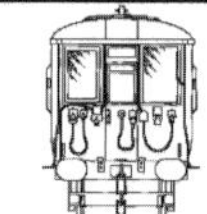

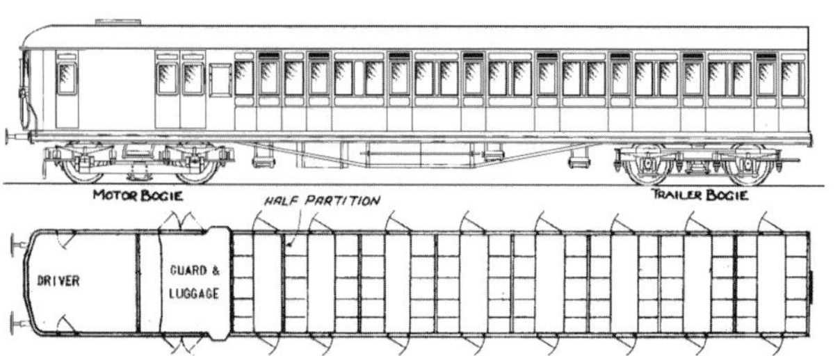

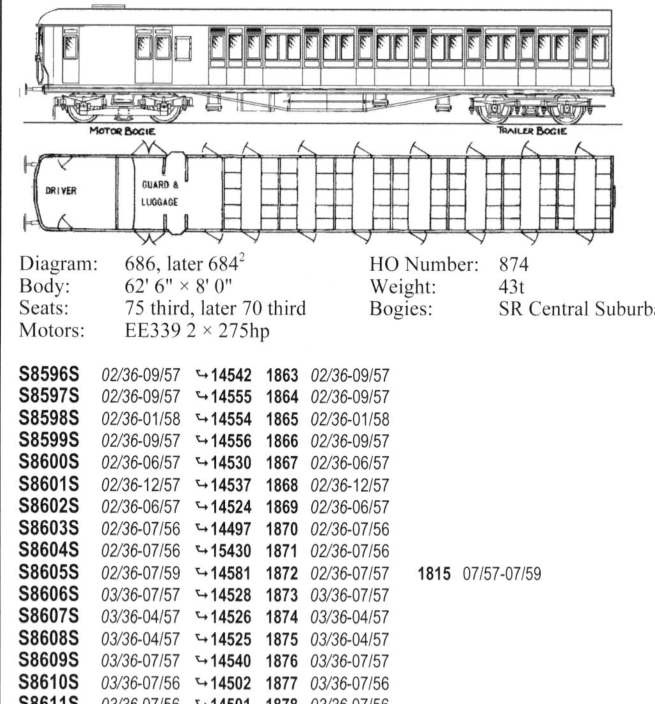

Diagram:	686, later 684[2]	HO Number:	874
Body:	62' 6" × 8' 0"	Weight:	43t
Seats:	75 third, later 70 third	Bogies:	SR Central Suburban
Motors:	EE339 2 × 275hp		

S8596S	*02/36*-09/57	↳**14542**	**1863**	*02/36*-09/57		
S8597S	*02/36*-09/57	↳**14555**	**1864**	*02/36*-09/57		
S8598S	*02/36*-01/58	↳**14554**	**1865**	*02/36*-01/58		
S8599S	*02/36*-09/57	↳**14556**	**1866**	*02/36*-09/57		
S8600S	*02/36*-06/57	↳**14530**	**1867**	*02/36*-06/57		
S8601S	*02/36*-12/57	↳**14537**	**1868**	*02/36*-12/57		
S8602S	*02/36*-06/57	↳**14524**	**1869**	*02/36*-06/57		
S8603S	*02/36*-07/56	↳**14497**	**1870**	*02/36*-07/56		
S8604S	*02/36*-07/56	↳**15430**	**1871**	*02/36*-07/56		
S8605S	*02/36*-07/59	↳**14581**	**1872**	*02/36*-07/57	**1815**	07/57-07/59
S8606S	*03/36*-07/57	↳**14528**	**1873**	*03/36*-07/57		
S8607S	*03/36*-04/57	↳**14526**	**1874**	*03/36*-04/57		
S8608S	*03/36*-04/57	↳**14525**	**1875**	*03/36*-04/57		
S8609S	*03/36*-07/57	↳**14540**	**1876**	*03/36*-07/57		
S8610S	*03/36*-07/56	↳**14502**	**1877**	*03/36*-07/56		
S8611S	*03/36*-07/56	↳**14501**	**1878**	*03/36*-07/56		
S8612S	*03/36*-08/57	↳**14545**	**1879**	*03/36*-08/57		
S8613S	*03/36*-10/57	↳**14534**	**1880**	*03/36*-10/57		
S8614S	*03/36*-05/57	↳**14553**	**1881**	*03/36*-05/57		
S8615S	*03/36*-09/57	↳**14541**	**1882**	*03/36*-09/57		

3-SUB Lancing/Ashford (LBSCR bodies)

Driving Motor Brake Third
DMBT
S8617-S8639

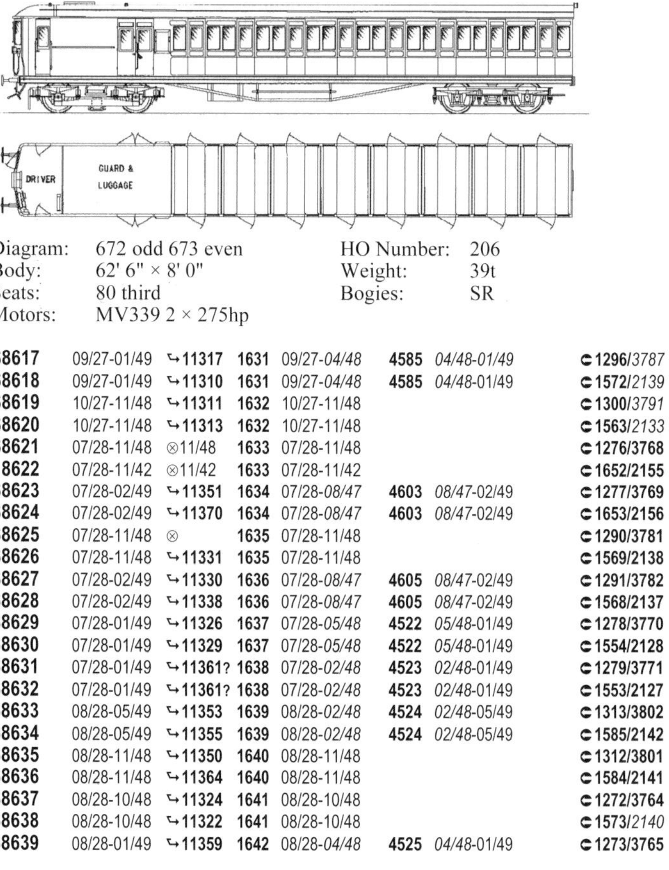

Diagram:	672 odd 673 even	HO Number:	206
Body:	62' 6" × 8' 0"	Weight:	39t
Seats:	80 third	Bogies:	SR
Motors:	MV339 2 × 275hp		

S8617	09/27-01/49	↳**11317**	**1631**	09/27-*04/48*	**4585**	*04/48-01/49*	⊂**1296**/*3787*
S8618	09/27-01/49	↳**11310**	**1631**	09/27-*04/48*	**4585**	*04/48*-01/49	⊂**1572**/*2139*
S8619	10/27-11/48	↳**11311**	**1632**	10/27-11/48			⊂**1300**/*3791*
S8620	10/27-11/48	↳**11313**	**1632**	10/27-11/48			⊂**1563**/*2133*
S8621	07/28-11/48	⊗11/48	**1633**	07/28-11/48			⊂**1276/3768**
8622	07/28-11/42	⊗11/42	**1633**	07/28-11/42			⊂**1652/2155**
S8623	07/28-02/49	↳**11351**	**1634**	07/28-*08/47*	**4603**	*08/47*-02/49	⊂**1277/3769**
S8624	07/28-02/49	↳**11370**	**1634**	07/28-*08/47*	**4603**	*08/47*-02/49	⊂**1653/2156**
S8625	07/28-11/48	⊗	**1635**	07/28-11/48			⊂**1290/3781**
S8626	07/28-11/48	↳**11331**	**1635**	07/28-11/48			⊂**1569/2138**
S8627	07/28-02/49	↳**11330**	**1636**	07/28-*08/47*	**4605**	*08/47*-02/49	⊂**1291/3782**
S8628	07/28-02/49	↳**11338**	**1636**	07/28-*08/47*	**4605**	*08/47*-02/49	⊂**1568/2137**
S8629	07/28-01/49	↳**11326**	**1637**	07/28-*05/48*	**4522**	*05/48*-01/49	⊂**1278/3770**
S8630	07/28-01/49	↳**11329**	**1637**	07/28-*05/48*	**4522**	*05/48*-01/49	⊂**1554/2128**
S8631	07/28-01/49	↳**11361**?	**1638**	07/28-*02/48*	**4523**	*02/48*-01/49	⊂**1279/3771**
S8632	07/28-01/49	↳**11361**?	**1638**	07/28-*02/48*	**4523**	*02/48*-01/49	⊂**1553/2127**
S8633	08/28-05/49	↳**11353**	**1639**	08/28-*02/48*	**4524**	*02/48*-05/49	⊂**1313/3802**
S8634	08/28-05/49	↳**11355**	**1639**	08/28-*02/48*	**4524**	*02/48*-05/49	⊂**1585/2142**
S8635	08/28-11/48	↳**11350**	**1640**	08/28-11/48			⊂**1312/3801**
S8636	08/28-11/48	↳**11364**	**1640**	08/28-11/48			⊂**1584/2141**
S8637	08/28-10/48	↳**11324**	**1641**	08/28-10/48			⊂**1272/3764**
S8638	08/28-10/48	↳**11322**	**1641**	08/28-10/48			⊂**1573**/*2140*
S8639	08/28-01/49	↳**11359**	**1642**	08/28-*04/48*	**4525**	*04/48*-01/49	⊂**1273/3765**

3-SUB Lancing/Ashford (LBSCR bodies)

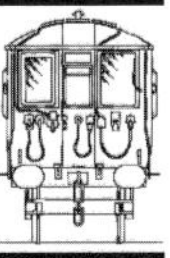

Driving Motor Brake Third
DMBT
S8640-S8644

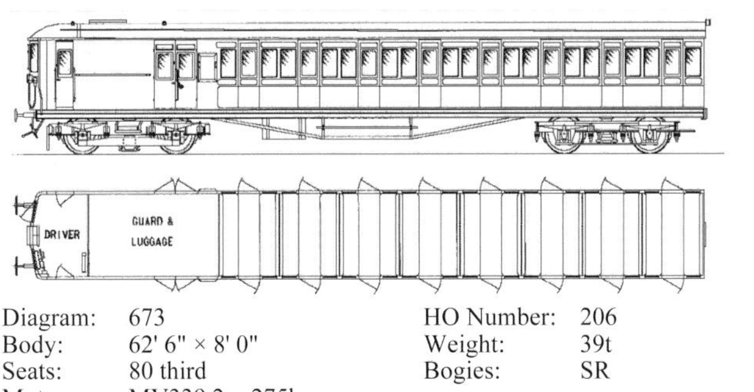

Diagram:	673	HO Number:	206
Body:	62' 6" × 8' 0"	Weight:	39t
Seats:	80 third	Bogies:	SR
Motors:	MV339 2 × 275hp		

S8640	08/28-01/49	↳11377	1642	08/28-04/48	4525	04/48-01/49	⊂1564/2134
S8641	09/28-05/49	↳11373	1643	09/28-08/47	4601	08/47-05/49	⊂1565/2135
S8642	[illegible]	[illegible]	[illegible]	[illegible]	4601	[illegible]	[illegible]
S8643	09/28-01/49	↳11337	1644	09/28-03/48	4562	03/48-01/49	⊂1605/2148
S8644	09/28-01/49	↳11349	1644	09/28-03/48	4562	03/48-01/49	⊂1603/2147

3-SUB Lancing/Ashford (LBSCR bodies)

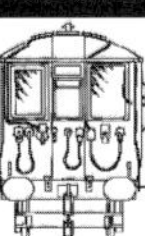

Driving Motor Brake Third
DMBT
S8645-S8651

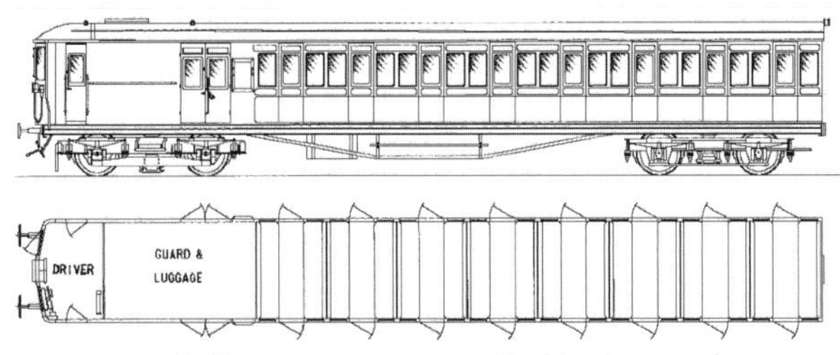

Diagram:	672/673	HO Number:	206
Body:	62' 6" × 8' 0"	Weight:	39t
Seats:	80 third	Bogies:	SR
Motors:	MV339 2 × 275hp		

S8645	09/28-06/49	↳11371	1645	09/28-08/47	4604	08/47-05/49	⊂1261/3762
S8646	09/28-05/49	↳11367	1645	09/28-08/47	4604	08/47-05/49	⊂1555/2129
S8647	09/28-11/48	↳11327	1646	09/28-11/48			⊂1262/3763
S8648	09/28-11/48	↳11328	1646	09/28-11/48			⊂1556/2130
S8649	10/28-02/49	↳11339	1647	10/28-08/47	4610	06/48-02/49	⊂1274/3766
S8650	10/28-02/49	↳11341	1647	10/28-08/47	4610	06/48-02/49	⊂1529/2119
S8651	10/28-01/49	↳11356	1648	10/28-08/47	4606	08/47-01/49	⊂1295/3786

3-SUB Lancing/Ashford (LBSCR bodies)

Driving Motor Brake Third
DMBT
S8652-S8656

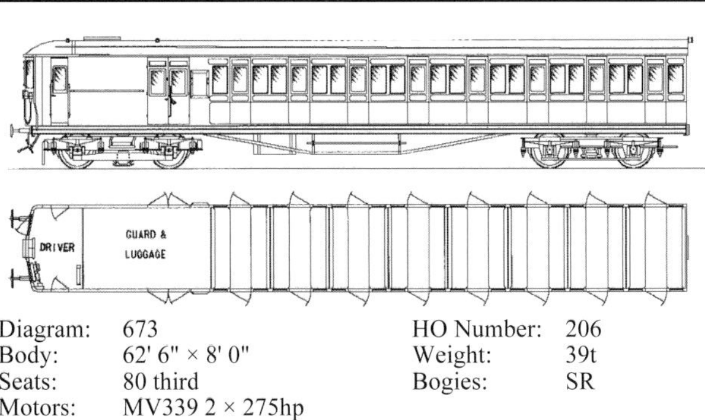

Diagram:	673	HO Number:	206
Body:	62' 6" × 8' 0"	Weight:	39t
Seats:	80 third	Bogies:	SR
Motors:	MV339 2 × 275hp		

S8652	10/28-01/49	↳11378	1648	10/28-08/47	4606	08/47-01/49	⊂1530/2120
S8653	10/28-10/49	↳12672	1649	10/28-02/48	4257	02/48-10/49	⊂1525/2118
S8654	10/28-10/49	↳12674	1649	10/28-02/48	4257	02/48-10/49	⊂1524/2117
S8655	10/28-02/49	↳11376	1650	10/28-03/48	4575	03/48-02/49	⊂1561/2131
S8656	10/28-02/49	↳11363	1650	10/28-03/48	4575	03/48-02/49	⊂1562/2132

3-SUB Lancing/Ashford (LBSCR bodies)

Driving Motor Brake Third
DMBT
S8657-S8670

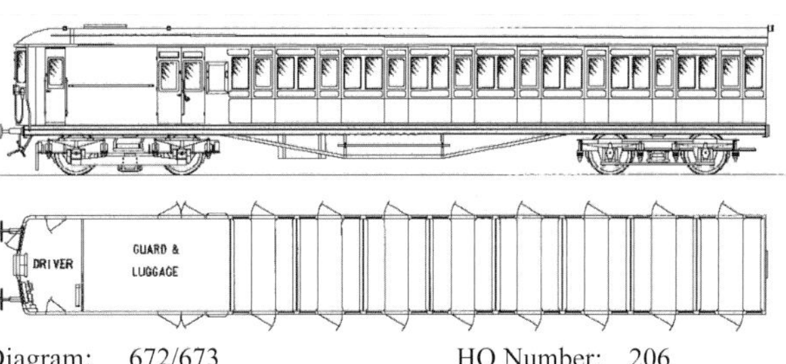

Diagram:	672/673	HO Number:	206
Body:	62' 6" × 8' 0"	Weight:	39t
Seats:	80 third	Bogies:	SR
Motors:	MV339 2 × 275hp		

S8657	11/28-02/49	↳11366	1651	11/28-02/48	4608	02/48-02/49	⊂1309/3798
S8658	11/28-02/49	↳11381	1651	11/28-02/48	4608	02/48-02/49	⊂1631/2153
S8659	11/28-08/49	⊗	1652	11/28-08/47	4613	08/47-08/49	⊂584/3760
S8660	11/28-08/49	↳12660?	1652	11/28-08/47	4613	08/47-08/49	⊂1709/2162
S8661	11/28-01/49	↳11314	1653	11/28-08/47	4614	08/47-01/49	⊂585/3761
S8662	11/28-01/49	↳11305	1653	11/28-08/47	4614	08/47-01/49	⊂1708/2161
S8663	12/28-11/48	↳11342	1654	12/28-11/48			⊂1632/2154
S8664	12/28-11/48	↳11345	1654	12/28-11/48			⊂1620/2149
S8665	12/28-11/48	↳11316	1655	12/28-11/48			⊂1621/2150
S8666	12/28-11/48	↳11320	1655	12/28-11/48			⊂1719/2163
S8667	05/28-11/48	↳11383	1656	05/28-11/48			⊂1597/2145
S8668	05/28-11/48	↳11332	1656	05/28-11/48			⊂1598/2146
S8669	04/28-01/49	↳11308	1657	04/28-01/49			⊂1627/2152
S8670	04/28-01/49	↳11323	1657	04/28-01/49			⊂1626/2151

3-SUB Lancing/Ashford (LBSCR bodies)

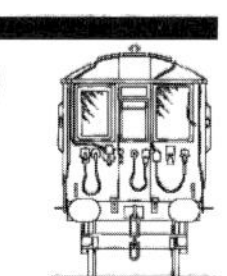

Driving Motor Brake Third
DMBT
S8671-S8685

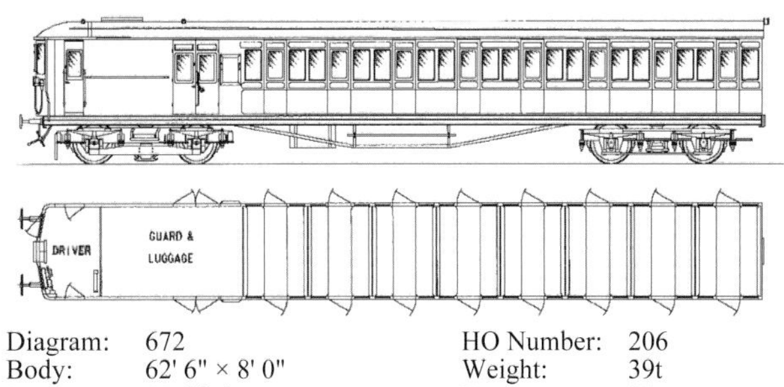

Diagram:	672	HO Number:	206
Body:	62' 6" × 8' 0"	Weight:	39t
Seats:	80 third	Bogies:	SR
Motors:	MV339 2 × 275hp		

S8671	10/27-09/48	↳11315	1702	10/27-09/48			⊂1297/3788
S8672	10/27-10/49	↳12683	1703	10/27-02/48	4256	02/48-10/49	⊂1301/3792
S8673	10/27-08/49	↳12669	1704	10/27-03/48	4576	03/48-08/49	⊂1306/3795
S8674	10/27-11/48	↳11333	1705	10/27-11/48			⊂1298/3789
S8675	07/28-01/49	↳11325	1706	07/28-05/48	4577	05/48-01/49	⊂1299/3790
S8676	07/28-06/48	↳11354	1707	07/28-08/47	4602	08/47-06/48	⊂1307/3796
S8677	08/28-01/49	↳11312	1708	08/28-01/49			⊂1288/3779
8678	08/28-11/47	⊗11/47	1709	08/28-08/43	4250[1]	08/43-11/47	⊂1289/3780
S8679	09/28-07/48	↳11319	1710	09/28-07/48			⊂1292/3783
S8680	09/28-11/48	⊗	1711	09/28-11/48			⊂1293/3784
S8681	10/28-08/48	⊗	1712	10/28-08/48			⊂1282/3774
S8682	10/28-10/49	↳12680	1713	10/28-04/48	4578	04/48-10/49	⊂1283/3775
S8683	11/28-03/49	↳11348	1714	11/28-03/48	4563	03/48-03/49	⊂1308/3797
S8684	12/28-08/49	↳11374	1715	12/28-03/48	4581	03/48-08/49	⊂1281/3773
S8685	12/28-05/49	↳11372	1716	12/28-03/48	4582	03/48-05/49	⊂1280/3772

3-SUB Ashford (ex AC stock)

Driving Motor Brake Third
DMBT
S8686S-S8692S

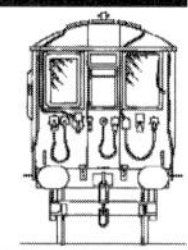

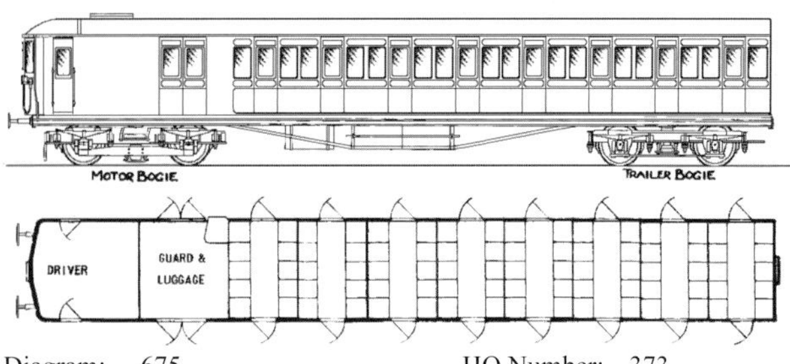

Diagram: 675 HO Number: 373
Body: 62' 6" × 8' 0" Weight: 39t
Seats: 80 third Bogies: LBSCR
Motors: MV339 2 × 275hp

S8686S	01/29-*07/55*	↳**14378**	**1717**	01/29-*03/48*	**4566**	*02/49-07/55*			⊂**9811**
S8687S	01/29-02/56	↳**14457**	**1718**	01/29-*04/48*	**4567**	*01/49*-02/56			⊂**9824**
S8688S	02/29-06/52	↳**15398**	**1719**	02/29-*01/48*	**4568**	*01/48*-06/52			⊂**9816**
S8689S	02/29-02/56	↳**14461**	**1720**	02/29-08/47	**4569**	08/47-*05/52*	**4573**	06/52-02/56	
									⊂**9820**
S8690	02/29-04/51	↳**14081**	**1721**	02/29-*02/48*	**4570**	05/49-*05/51*			⊂**9821**
S8691S	02/29-05/54	↳**15305**	**1722**	02/29-04/41	**1728**	45-08/47	**4520**	08/47-07/53	
									⊂**9814**
S8692S	02/29-03/56	↳**14456**	**1723**	02/29-*01/48*	**4571**	*01/48*-03/56			⊂**9822**

3-SUB Ashford (ex AC stock)

Driving Motor Brake Third
DMBT
S8693S-S8696S

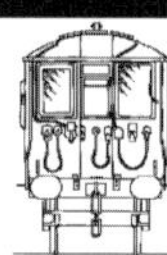

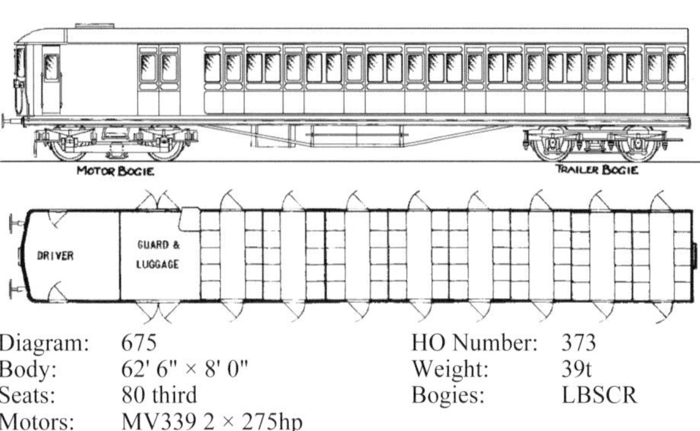

Diagram: 675 HO Number: 373
Body: 62' 6" × 8' 0" Weight: 39t
Seats: 80 third Bogies: LBSCR
Motors: MV339 2 × 275hp

S8693S	05/29-07/56	⊗*07/56*	**1724**	05/29-08/47	**4527**	08/47-07/56			⊂**9823**
S8694S	05/29-11/59	⊗*11/59*	**1725**	05/29-*02/48*	**4528**	*02/48*-06/55	**4555**	06/55-01/57	
			4515	01/57-11/59					⊂**9815**
S8695S	06/29-08/56	⊗*08/56*	**1726**	06/29-*02/48*	**4529**	05/49-08/56			⊂**9813**
S8696S	06/29-08/56	⊗*08/56*	**1727**	06/29-*04/48*	**4530**	08/49-08/56			⊂**9812**

3-SUB Ashford (ex AC stock)

Driving Motor Brake Third
DMBT
S8697S-S8705S

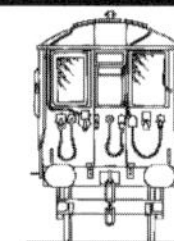

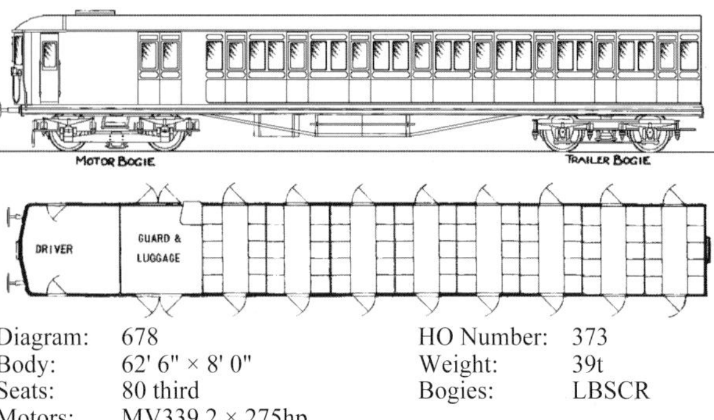

Diagram: 678 HO Number: 373
Body: 62' 6" × 8' 0" Weight: 39t
Seats: 80 third Bogies: LBSCR
Motors: MV339 2 × 275hp

S8697S	06/29-09/56	⊗	**1728**	06/29-06/44	**1728**	*12/44*-08/47	**4520**	08/47-07/53	
			4520	10/54-02/56					⊂*9203*
S8698S	06/29-12/56	➲**DS349**	**1729**	06/29-08/47	**4531**	*01/49*-11/56			⊂*9199*
8699	09/29-*10/46*	⊗	**1730**	09/29-*10/46*					⊂**9180**
S8700S	09/29-10/56	⊗*10/56*	**1731**	09/29-08/47	**4532**	08/47-*04/50*	**4548**	*04/50*-10/56	
									⊂**9171**
S8701S	07/29-10/59	⊗*11/59*	**1732**	07/29-03/49	**4533**	03/49-12/56	**4514**	12/56-10/59	
									⊂*9208*
S8702S	07/29-07/56	⊗*07/56*	**1733**	07/29-*01/48*	**4534**	*01/48*-07/56			⊂*9191*
S8703S	08/29-10/59	⊗*10/59*	**1734**	08/29-*07/48*	**4535**	*07/48*-09/56	**4507**	09/56-10/59	
									⊂**9174**
S8704S	08/29-05/53	⊗	**1735**	08/29-*01/49*	**4536**	*01/49*-05/53			⊂**9179**
S8705S	08/29-11/58	⊗*11/59*	**1736**	08/29-03/44	**4251**	03/44-11/56	**4518**	01/57-11/58	
									⊂**9178**

3-SUB Eastleigh (ex AC stock)

Driving Motor Brake Third
DMBT
S8706S-S8707S

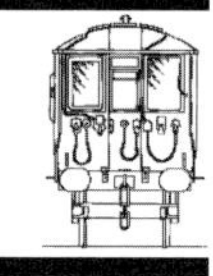

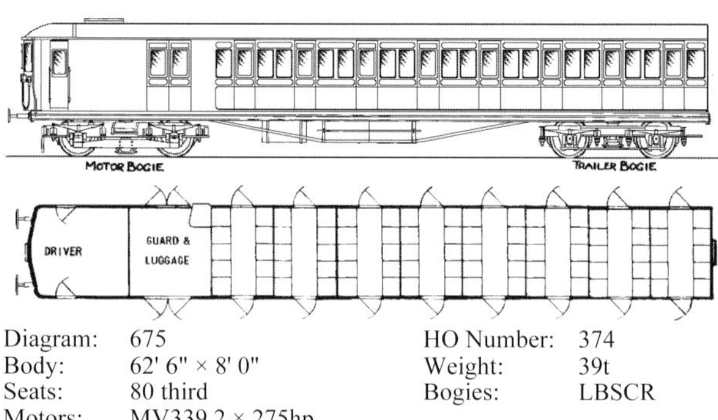

Diagram: 675 HO Number: 374
Body: 62' 6" × 8' 0" Weight: 39t
Seats: 80 third Bogies: LBSCR
Motors: MV339 2 × 275hp

S8706S	06/29-08/55	⊗*08/55*	**1737**	06/29-08/47	**4537**	08/47-08/55			⊂**9817**
S8707S	06/29-01/60	⊗01/60	**1738**	06/29-*04/48*	**4538**	*04/48*-10/56	**4508**	10/56-01/60	
									⊂**9818**

3-SUB Eastleigh (ex AC stock)

Driving Motor Brake Third
DMBT
S8708S

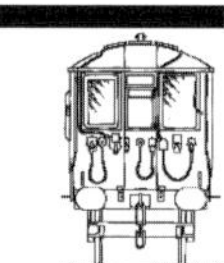

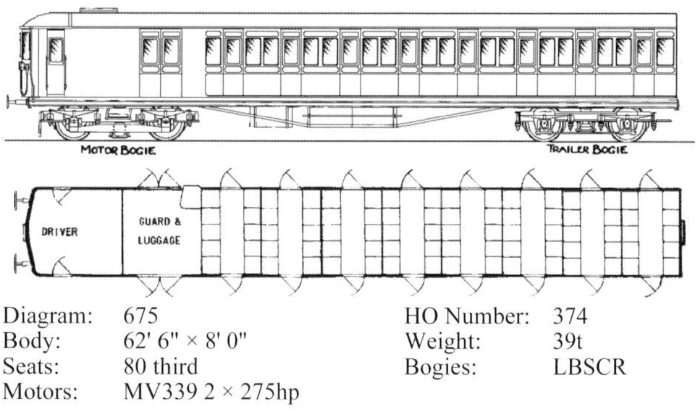

Diagram: 675 HO Number: 374
Body: 62' 6" × 8' 0" Weight: 39t
Seats: 80 third Bogies: LBSCR
Motors: MV339 2 × 275hp

S8708S	06/29-12/59	⊗01/60	**1739**	06/29-*01/49*	**4539**	*01/49*-12/56	**4512**	12/56-12/59	
									⊂**9819**

3-SUB Eastleigh (ex AC stock)

Driving Motor Brake Third
DMBT
S8709S-S8722S

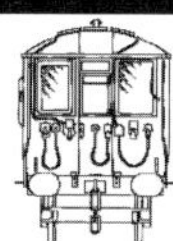
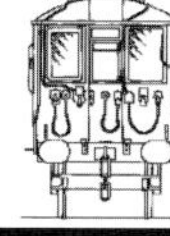

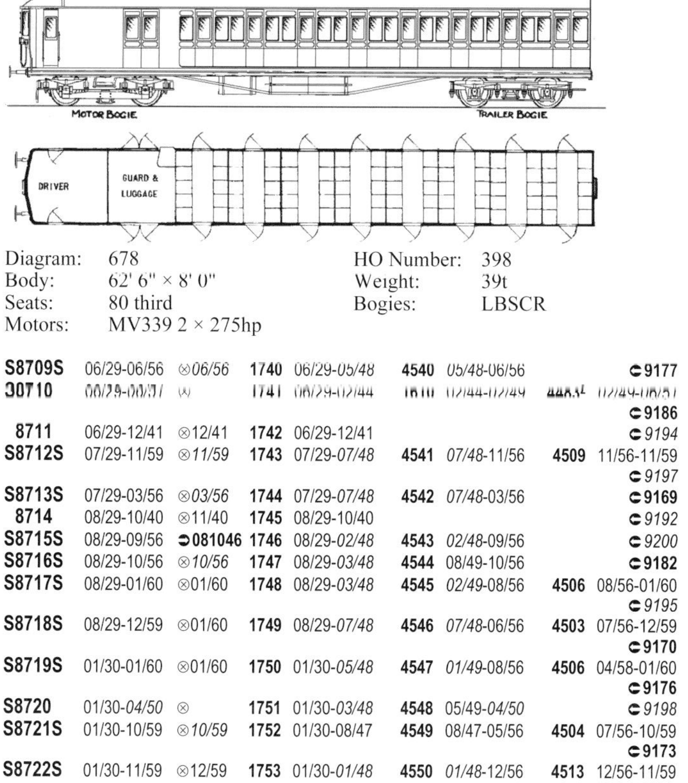

Diagram:	678	HO Number:	398
Body:	62' 6" × 8' 0"	Weight:	39t
Seats:	80 third	Bogies:	LBSCR
Motors:	MV339 2 × 275hp		

S8709S	06/29-06/56	⊗*06/56*	**1740**	06/29-*05/48*	**4540**	*05/48*-06/56			⊂**9177**
[illegible]8710	*06/29-06/51*	⊗	**1741**	*06/29-02/44*	**1810**	*02/44-02/49*	**4483**	*02/49-06/51*	⊂**9186**
8711	06/29-12/41	⊗12/41	**1742**	06/29-12/41					⊂*9194*
S8712S	07/29-11/59	⊗*11/59*	**1743**	07/29-*07/48*	**4541**	*07/48*-11/56	**4509**	11/56-11/59	⊂*9197*
S8713S	07/29-03/56	⊗*03/56*	**1744**	07/29-*07/48*	**4542**	*07/48*-03/56			⊂**9169**
8714	08/29-10/40	⊗11/40	**1745**	08/29-10/40					⊂*9192*
S8715S	08/29-09/56	⊃**081046**	**1746**	08/29-*02/48*	**4543**	*02/48*-09/56			⊂*9200*
S8716S	08/29-10/56	⊗*10/56*	**1747**	08/29-*03/48*	**4544**	08/49-10/56			⊂**9182**
S8717S	08/29-01/60	⊗01/60	**1748**	08/29-*03/48*	**4545**	*02/49*-08/56	**4506**	08/56-01/60	⊂*9195*
S8718S	08/29-12/59	⊗01/60	**1749**	08/29-*07/48*	**4546**	*07/48*-06/56	**4503**	07/56-12/59	⊂**9170**
S8719S	01/30-01/60	⊗01/60	**1750**	01/30-*05/48*	**4547**	*01/49*-08/56	**4506**	04/58-01/60	⊂**9176**
S8720	01/30-*04/50*	⊗	**1751**	01/30-*03/48*	**4548**	05/49-*04/50*			⊂*9198*
S8721S	01/30-10/59	⊗*10/59*	**1752**	01/30-08/47	**4549**	08/47-05/56	**4504**	07/56-10/59	⊂**9173**
S8722S	01/30-11/59	⊗12/59	**1753**	01/30-*01/48*	**4550**	*01/48*-12/56	**4513**	12/56-11/59	⊂*9206*

2-SL Lancing (ex AC stock)

Driving Motor Brake Third
DMBT
S8723S-S8730S

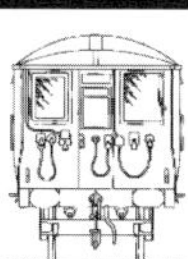

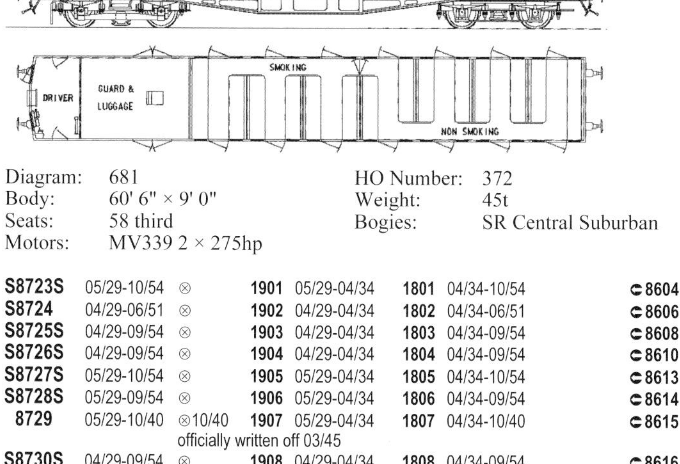

Diagram:	681	HO Number:	372
Body:	60' 6" × 9' 0"	Weight:	45t
Seats:	58 third	Bogies:	SR Central Suburban
Motors:	MV339 2 × 275hp		

S8723S	05/29-10/54	⊗	**1901**	05/29-04/34	**1801**	04/34-10/54	⊂**8604**
S8724	04/29-06/51	⊗	**1902**	04/29-04/34	**1802**	04/34-06/51	⊂**8606**
S8725S	04/29-09/54	⊗	**1903**	04/29-04/34	**1803**	04/34-09/54	⊂**8608**
S8726S	04/29-09/54	⊗	**1904**	04/29-04/34	**1804**	04/34-09/54	⊂**8610**
S8727S	05/29-10/54	⊗	**1905**	05/29-04/34	**1805**	04/34-10/54	⊂**8613**
S8728S	05/29-09/54	⊗	**1906**	05/29-04/34	**1806**	04/34-09/54	⊂**8614**
8729	05/29-10/40	⊗10/40 officially written off 03/45	**1907**	05/29-04/34	**1807**	04/34-10/40	⊂**8615**
S8730S	04/29-09/54	⊗	**1908**	04/29-04/34	**1808**	04/34-09/54	⊂**8616**

3-SUB Ashford (ex AC stock)

Driving Motor Brake Third
DMBT
S8731S-S8733S

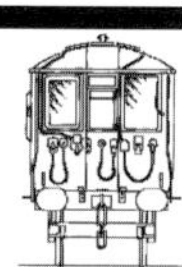

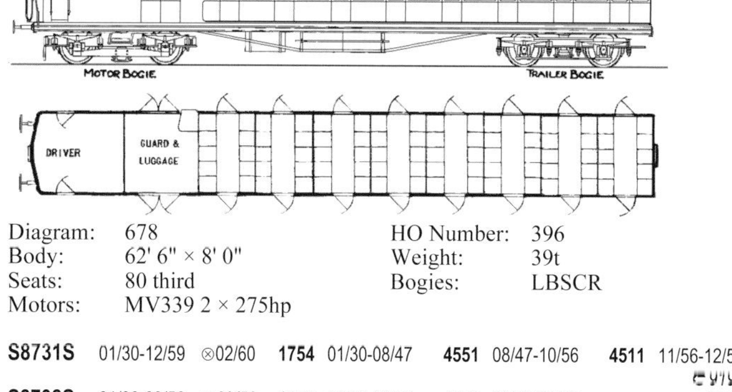

Diagram:	678	HO Number:	396
Body:	62' 6" × 8' 0"	Weight:	39t
Seats:	80 third	Bogies:	LBSCR
Motors:	MV339 2 × 275hp		

S8731S	01/30-12/59	⊗02/60	**1754**	01/30-08/47	**4551**	08/47-10/56	**4511**	11/56-12/59	⊂*9190*
S8732S	01/30-09/56	⊗*09/56*	**1755**	01/30-08/47	**4552**	08/47-09/56			⊂**9188**
S8733S	01/30-12/59	⊗01/60	**1756**	01/30-*02/48*	**4553**	*02/48*-06/56	**4502**	06/56-12/59	⊂*9202*

3-SUB Ashford (ex AC stock)

Driving Motor Brake Third
DMBT
S8734S-S8745S

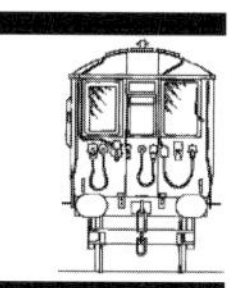

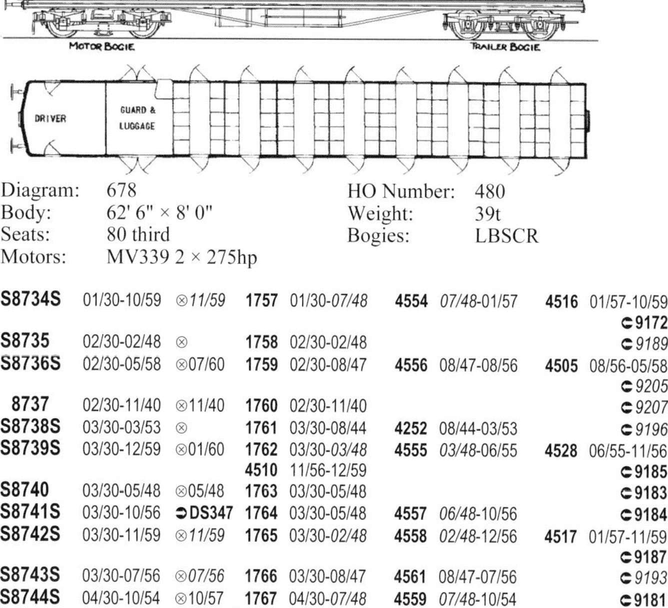

Diagram:	678	HO Number:	480
Body:	62' 6" × 8' 0"	Weight:	39t
Seats:	80 third	Bogies:	LBSCR
Motors:	MV339 2 × 275hp		

S8734S	01/30-10/59	⊗*11/59*	**1757**	01/30-*07/48*	**4554**	*07/48*-01/57	**4516**	01/57-10/59	⊂**9172**
S8735	02/30-02/48	⊗	**1758**	02/30-02/48					⊂*9189*
S8736S	02/30-05/58	⊗07/60	**1759**	02/30-08/47	**4556**	08/47-08/56	**4505**	08/56-05/58	⊂*9205*
8737	02/30-11/40	⊗11/40	**1760**	02/30-11/40					⊂*9207*
S8738S	03/30-03/53	⊗	**1761**	03/30-08/44	**4252**	08/44-03/53			⊂*9196*
S8739S	03/30-12/59	⊗01/60	**1762**	03/30-*03/48*	**4555**	*03/48*-06/55	**4528**	06/55-11/56	
			4510	11/56-12/59					⊂**9185**
S8740	03/30-05/48	⊗05/48	**1763**	03/30-05/48					⊂**9183**
S8741S	03/30-10/56	⊃**DS347**	**1764**	03/30-05/48	**4557**	*06/48*-10/56			⊂**9184**
S8742S	03/30-11/59	⊗*11/59*	**1765**	03/30-*02/48*	**4558**	*02/48*-12/56	**4517**	01/57-11/59	⊂**9187**
S8743S	03/30-07/56	⊗*07/56*	**1766**	03/30-08/47	**4561**	08/47-07/56			⊂*9193*
S8744S	04/30-10/54	⊗10/57 towing unit 03/55-09/55 and 57	**1767**	04/30-*07/48*	**4559**	*07/48*-10/54			⊂**9181**
S8745S	04/30-03/56	⊗*03/56*	**1768**	04/30-*05/47*	**4560**	08/49-03/56			⊂**9175**

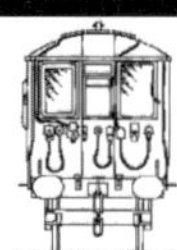

3-SUB Ashford (ex AC stock)

Driving Motor Brake Third

DMBT

S8746S

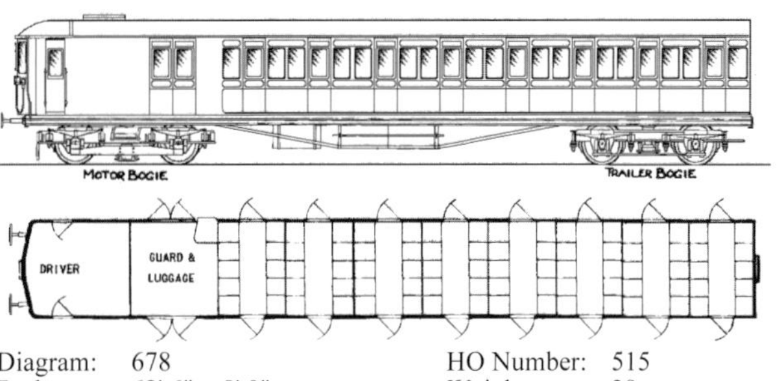

Diagram:	678	HO Number:	515
Body:	62' 6" × 8' 0"	Weight:	39t
Seats:	80 third	Bogies:	LBSCR
Motors:	MV339 2 × 275hp		

S8746S	06/30-02/56	⊗*02/56*	**1769**	06/30-08/47	**4564**	08/47-02/56	**⊂9204**

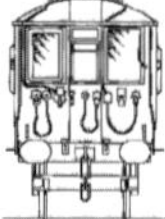

3-SUB Ashford (ex AC stock)

Driving Motor Brake Third

DMBT

8747-S8748

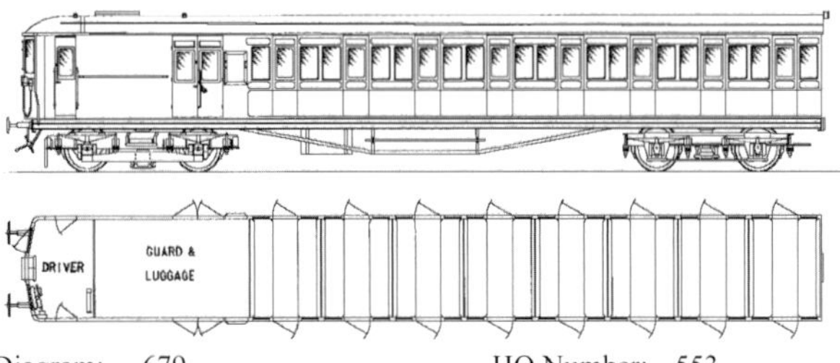

Diagram:	679	HO Number:	553
Body:	62' 6" × 8' 0"	Weight:	39t
Seats:	80 third	Bogies:	LBSCR
Motors:	MV339 2 × 275hp		

8747	06/30-10/47	⊗10/47	**1770**	06/30-10/47	**⊂1731/2165**
S8748	06/30-11/48	⊗	**1771**	06/30-11/48	**⊂1691/2160**

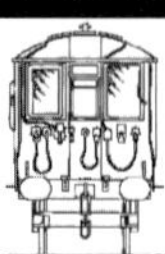

3-SUB Ashford (ex AC stock)

Driving Motor Brake Third

DMBT

S8749S

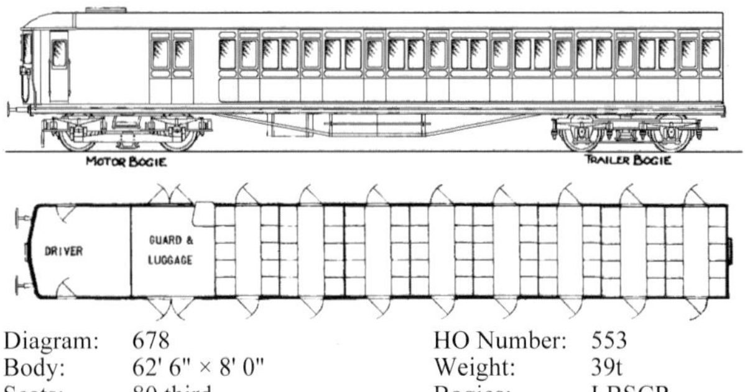

Diagram:	678	HO Number:	553
Body:	62' 6" × 8' 0"	Weight:	39t
Seats:	80 third	Bogies:	LBSCR
Motors:	MV339 2 × 275hp		

S8749S	06/30-04/55	↳**14381**	**1772**	06/30-*07/48*	**4565**	*07/48*-04/55	*⊂9201*

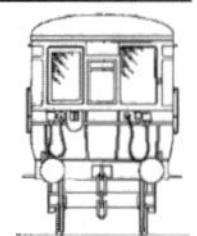
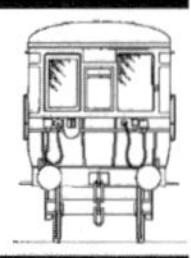

3-SUB Eastleigh

Driving Motor Brake Composite

DMBC

S8751S-S8792S

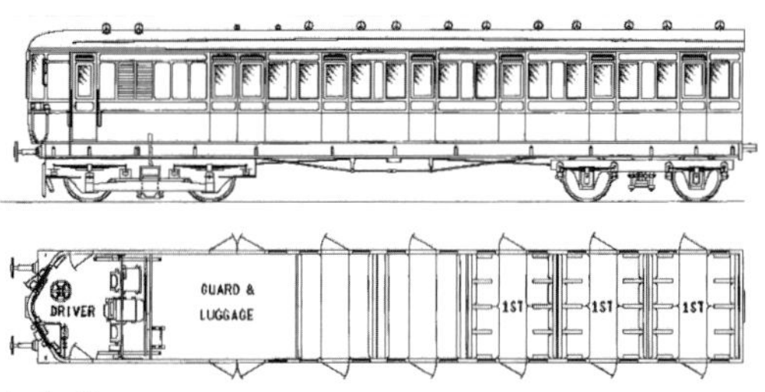

As built

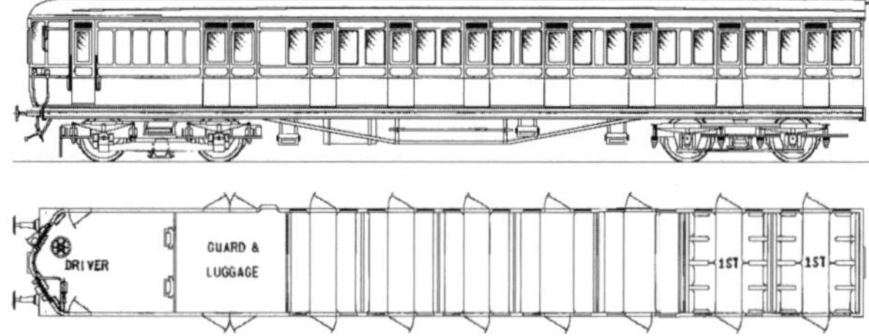

① Rebuilt on new frames Diagram 698

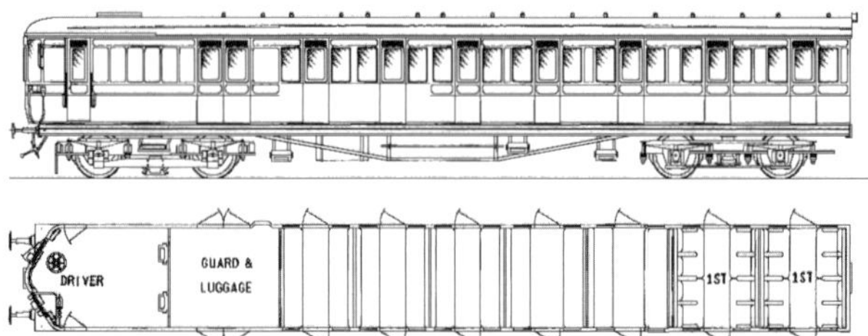

② Diagram 698. Steel lower panelling on added compartments.

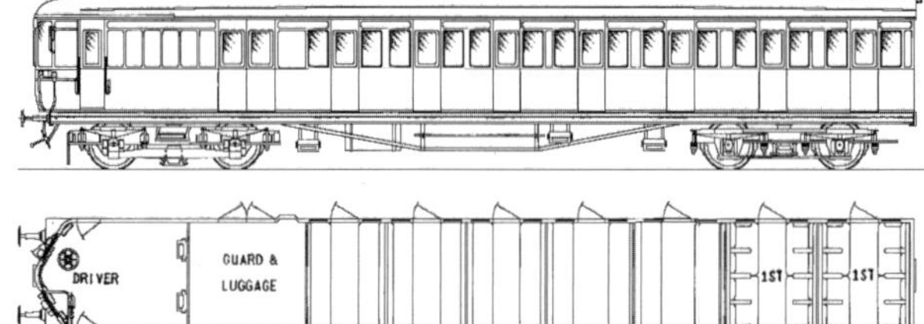

③ Diagram 698. Steel lower panelling on the whole body.

Diagram:	690 later 698	HO Number:	LSWR
Body:	52' 0" × 8' 0" later 62' 6" × 8' 0"	Weight:	39t later 42t 10cwt
Seats:	24 first 20 third later 16 first 50 third	Bogies:	LSWR later SR
Motors:	BTH 2 × 250hp, later MV339 or EE339 2 × 275hp		

S8751S	①	23-08/55	↳**14391**	**1203**	23-08/46	**4169**	08/46-08/55			**⊂7201**
S8752S	③	23-12/55	↳**14469**	**1204**	23-04/41	**4131**	04/41-12/55			**⊂7202**
S8753S	①	23-08/55	↳**14388**	**1207**	23-10/45	**4160**	10/45-08/55			**⊂7203**
S8754S	①	23-08/55	↳**14387**	**1208**	23-06/44	**4152**	06/44-08/55			**⊂7204**
S8755S	①	23-08/53	↳**14493**	**1211**	23- *44*	**4154**	09/44-08/53			**⊂7205**
S8756S	③	23-*05/54*	↳**14291**	**1212**	23-*11/42*	**4146**	*11/42-05/54*			**⊂7206**
S8757S	①	23-09/54	↳**14307**	**1215**	23-09/44	**4153**	09/44-09/54			**⊂7207**
S8758S	③	23-09/55	↳**14404**	**1216**	23-06/45	**4158**	06/45-09/55			**⊂7208**
S8759S	①	23-11/55	↳**14416**	**1219**	23- 45	**4162**	45-11/55			**⊂7209**
S8760S	③	23-06/55	↳**14376**	**1220**	23- 44	**4156**	44-06/55			**⊂7210**
S8761S	②	23-01/56	↳**14442**	**1223**	23-08/46	**4170**	08/46-01/56			**⊂7211**
S8762S	②	23-05/56	↳**14480**	**1224**	23-12/45	**4164**	12/45-08/55	**4537**	08/55-05/56	**⊂7212**
S8763S	①	23-02/55	↳**14511**	**1227**	23-01/43	**4141**	01/43-02/55			**⊂7213**
S8764S	①	23-12/54	↳**14346**	**1228**	23- 46	**4165**	46-12/54			**⊂7214**
S8765S	①	23-*06/54*	↳**14284**	**1231**	23-09/42	**4140**	09/42-*06/54*			**⊂7215**
S8766S	①	23-05/56	↳**14479**	**1232**	23-09/42	**4133**	09/42-05/56			**⊂7216**
S8767S	③	23-04/55	↳**14362**	**1235**	23-09/42	**4138**	09/42-04/55			**⊂7217**
S8768S	③	23-12/55	↳**14429**	**1236**	23-10/45	**4159**	10/45-12/55			**⊂7218**
S8769S	①	23-02/55	↳**14468**	**1239**	23-02/42	**4132**	02/42-02/55			**⊂7219**
S8770S	①	23-12/55	↳**14432**	**1240**	23- *42*	**4135**	*42*-12/55			**⊂7220**
S8771S	①	23-*11/54*	↳**14319**	**1243**	23-11/42	**4147**	11/42-*11/54*			**⊂7221**
S8772S	①	23-*08/54*	↳**14306**	**1244**	23- 46	**4167**	46-*08/54*			**⊂7222**
S8773S	③	23-05/56	↳**14477**	**1247**	23-03/42	**4134**	03/42-05/56			**⊂7223**

S8774S	①	23-10/55	↳**14412**	**1248**	23-10/42	**4150**	43-10/55			⊂**7224**
S8775S	①	23-12/55	↳**14439**	**1251**	23- 46	**4166**	46-12/55			⊂**7225**
S8776S	①	23-03/55	↳**14348**	**1252**	23- 44	**4151**	44-03/55			⊂**7226**
S8777S	①	23-09/54	↳**14379**	**1255**	23-02/43	**4143**	02/43-09/54			⊂**7227**
S8778S	①	23-07/54	↳**14294**	**1256**	23-05/45	**4157**	05/45-07/54			⊂**7228**
S8779S	①	23-09/53	↳**14275**	**1259**	23-12/40	**1697**	12/40-03/48	**4246**	03/48-09/53	⊂**7229**
S8780S	①	23-11/54	↳**14337**	**1260**	23-07/42	**4137**	07/42-11/54			⊂**7230**
S8781S	①	23-09/54	↳**14301**	**1263**	23- 45	**4163**	45-09/54			⊂**7231**
S8782S	①	23-09/54	↳**14398**	**1264**	23-01/42	**4144**	01/42-09/54			⊂**7232**
S8783S	①	23-01/54	↳**14487**	**1267**	23-08/44	**1692**	08/44-09/44	**4155**	09/44-01/54	⊂**7233**
S8784S	①	23-06/55	↳**14365**	**1268**	23-08/46	**4171**	08/46-06/55			⊂**7234**
S8785S	①	23-01/54	↳**14421**	**1271**	23-09/42	**4139**	09/42-01/54			⊂**7235**
S8786S	②	23-06/56	↳**14514**	**1272**	23-11/42	**4142**	11/42-06/56			⊂**7236**
S8787S	③	23-11/55	↳**14482**	**1275**	23-09/43	**4149**	09/43-11/55			⊂**7237**
8788	②	23-10/47	⊗10/47	**1276**	23- 45	**4161**	45-10/47			⊂**7238**
S8789S	①	23-03/55	↳**14352**	**1279**	23-09/43	**4148**	09/43-03/55			⊂**7239**
S8790S	①	23-05/54	↳**14282**	**1280**	23-09/42	**4136**	09/42-05/54			⊂**7240**
S8791S	①	23-12/54	↳**14328**	**1283**	23-10/40	**1259**	12/40-11/42	**4145**	11/42-12/54	⊂**7241**
S8792S	①	23-01/55	↳**14342**	**1284**	23-01/46	**4168**	01/46-01/55			⊂**7242**

3-SUB Lancing/Ashford (LSWR bodies)

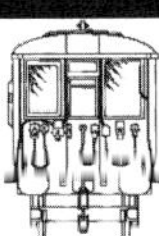

Driving Motor Brake Composite
DMBC
S8793S-S8836S

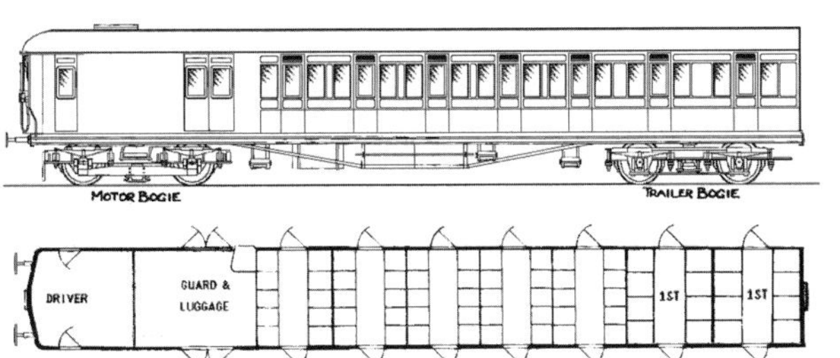

Diagram:	691	HO Number:	206
Body:	62' 6" × 8' 0"	Weight:	
Seats:	24 first 40 third	Bogies:	SR
Motors:	MV339 2 × 275hp		

S8793S	09/27-10/53	↳**14223**	**1658**	09/27-08/46	**4172**	08/46-10/53		
S8794S	01/28-09/54	↳**14229**	**1659**	01/28-08/48	**4194**	08/48-09/54		
S8795	01/28-06/49	↳**14207**	**1660**	01/28-08/48	**4193**	08/48-06/49		
S8796S	01/28-10/53	↳**14227**	**1661**	01/28-05/47	**4174**	05/47-10/53		
S8797S	01/28-05/52	↳**14211**	**1662**	01/28-02/47	**4177**	02/47-05/52		
S8798S	01/28-06/56	↳**14483**	**1663**	01/28-12/47	**4185**	12/47-09/53	**4546**	09/53-06/56
S8799S	01/28-12/53	↳**14234**	**1664**	01/28-07/47	**4180**	07/47-12/53		
S8800S	01/28-04/55	↳**14492**	**1665**	01/28-08/47	**4181**	08/47-04/55		
S8801S	01/28-05/53	⊗05/53	**1666**	01/28-08/48	**4192**	08/48-05/53		
S8802S	01/28-06/53	↳**14201**	**1667**	01/28-06/45	**4253**	07/45-06/53		
S8803S	01/28-03/54	↳**14257**	**1668**	01/28- 48	**4188**	48-03/54		
S8804S	01/28-08/53	↳**14212**	**1669**	01/28-12/47	**4249**	12/47-08/53		
S8805S	02/28-08/52	⊗08/52	**1670**	02/28-10/47	**4184**	10/47-08/52		
S8806S	02/28-10/53	↳**14220**	**1671**	02/28-02/47	**4173**	02/47-10/53		
S8807S	02/28-12/54	↳**14329**	**1672**	02/28- 48	**4187**	48-12/54		
S8808S	02/28-11/53	↳**14242**	**1673**	02/28-10/47	**4161**	10/47-11/53		
S8809S	02/28-07/53	↳**14251**	**1674**	02/28-09/48	**4189**	09/48-07/53		
S8810S	02/28-07/53	↳**14101**	**1675**	02/28-08/47	**4183**	08/47-07/53		
S8811S	02/28-11/54	↳**14325**	**1676**	02/28-05/47	**4178**	05/47-11/54		
S8812S	02/28-08/53	↳**14098**	**1677**	02/28-07/47	**4179**	07/47-08/53		
S8813S	02/28-01/55	↳**14357**	**1678**	02/28-09/48	**4250**[2]	09/48-01/55		
8814	02/28-12/41	⊗12/41	**1679**	02/28-12/41				
S8815S	02/28-05/54	↳**14278**	**1680**	02/28-08/47	**4182**	08/47-05/54		
S8816S	03/28-12/53	↳**14243**	**1681**	03/28-09/48	**4242**	09/48-12/53		
S8817S	03/28-09/53	↳**14216**	**1682**	03/28-02/47	**4175**	02/47-09/53		
S8818S	03/28-09/53	↳**14218**	**1683**	03/28-05/48	**4186**	05/48-09/53		
S8819S	03/28-01/56	↳**14446**	**1684**	03/28-05/47	**4176**	05/47-01/56		
S8820S	03/28-04/53	↳**14079**	**1685**	03/28-07/48	**4191**	07/48-04/53		
S8821S	03/28-02/54	↳**14255**	**1686**	03/28-01/43	**4236**	01/43-02/54		
S8822S	03/28-03/54	↳**14261**	**1687**	03/28-11/42	**4245**	08/48-03/54		
8823	03/28-11/42	⊗11/42	**1688**	03/28-11/42				
S8824S	03/28-08/53	↳**14246**	**1689**	03/28-11/47	**4237**	11/47-08/53		
S8825S	03/28-11/53	↳**14217**	**1690**	03/28-08/48	**4248**	08/48-11/53		
S8826S	03/28-08/53	↳**14105**	**1691**	03/28-07/48	**4243**	07/48-08/53		
8827	04/28-06/44	⊗08/44	**1692**	04/28-06/44				
S8828S	04/28-12/53	↳**14092**	**1693**	04/28-04/48	**4244**	04/48-12/53		
S8829S	04/28-12/54	↳**14326**	**1694**	04/28-07/48	**4247**	07/48-12/54		
S8830S	04/28-07/53	↳**14214**	**1695**	04/28-05/47	**4235**	05/47-07/53		
S8831S	04/28-05/56	↳**14515**	**1696**	04/28-08/47	**4572**	08/47-05/56		
8832	04/28-10/40	⊗11/40	**1697**	04/28-10/40				
S8833S	04/28-09/53	↳**14213**	**1698**	04/28-10/47	**4240**	10/47-09/53		
S8834S	04/28-09/54	↳**14300**	**1699**	04/28-10/47	**4238**	10/47-09/54		
S8835S	04/28-07/53	↳**14241**	**1700**	04/28-02/48	**4241**	02/48-07/53		
S8836S	04/28-05/53	↳**14204**	**1701**	04/28-03/47	**4255**	12/47-05/53		

3-SUB Lancing/Ashford (LBSCR bodies)

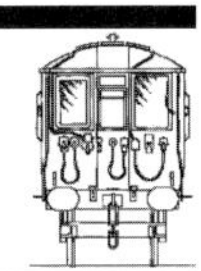

Driving Motor Brake Composite
DMBC
S8837-S8851

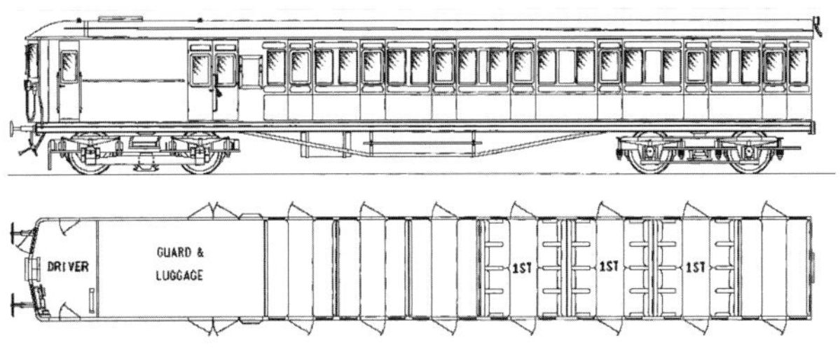

Diagram:	692	HO Number:	206
Body:	62' 6" × 8' 0"	Weight:	39t
Seats:	24 first 40 third	Bogies:	SR
Motors:	MV339 2 × 275hp		

S8837	10/27-09/48	↳**11318**	**1702**	10/27-09/48			⊂**571**/6079
S8838	10/27-10/49	⊗	**1703**	10/27-02/48	**4256**	02/48-10/49	⊂**575**/6083
S8839	10/27-08/49	↳**12668**	**1704**	10/27-03/48	**4576**	03/48-08/49	⊂**580/6088**
S8840	10/27-11/48	↳**11336**	**1705**	10/27-01/49			⊂**572**/6080
S8841	07/28-01/49	↳**11321**	**1706**	07/28-05/48	**4577**	05/48-01/49	⊂**564/6072**
S8842	07/28-06/48	↳**11346**	**1707**	07/28-08/47	**4602**	08/47-06/48	⊂**551/6059**
S8843	08/28-01/49	↳**11309**	**1708**	08/28-01/49			⊂**562/6070**
8844	08/28-11/47	↳**11382**	**1709**	08/28-08/43	**4250**[1]	08/43-11/47	⊂**552/6060**
S8845	09/28-07/48	↳**11334**	**1710**	09/28-07/48			⊂**586/6094**
S8846	09/28-11/48	↳**11306**	**1711**	09/28-11/48			⊂**566**/6074
S8847	10/28-08/48	↳**11303**	**1712**	10/28-08/48			⊂**576/6084**
S8848	10/28-10/49	↳**12682**	**1713**	10/28-04/48	**4578**	04/48-10/49	⊂**557/6065**
S8849	11/28-03/49	⊗	**1714**	11/28-03/48	**4563**	03/48-03/49	⊂**583/6091**
S8850	12/28-08/49	↳**11379**	**1715**	12/28-03/48	**4581**	03/48-08/49	⊂**554/6062**
S8851	12/28-05/49	⊗	**1716**	12/28-03/48	**4582**	03/48-05/49	⊂**68/6051**

3-SUB Ashford (ex AC stock)

Driving Motor Brake Composite
DMBC
S8852S-S8858S

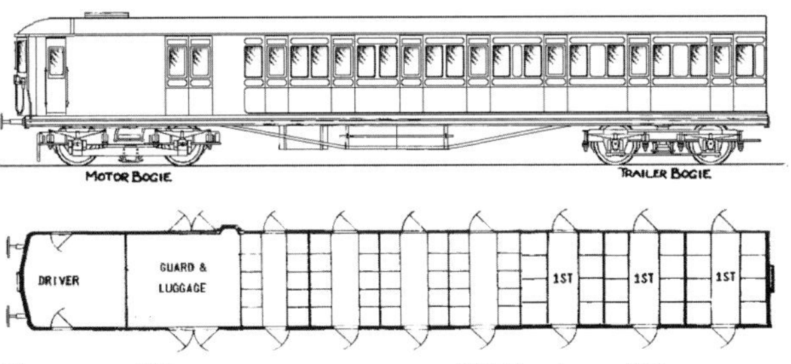

Diagram:	693	HO Number:	373
Body:	62' 6" × 8' 0"	Weight:	
Seats:	24 first 40 third	Bogies:	LBSCR
Motors:	MV339 2 × 275hp		

S8852S	01/29-07/55	↳**14374**	**1717**	01/29-03/48	**4566**	02/49-07/55	⊂**9892**
S8853S	01/29-02/56	↳**14452**	**1718**	01/29-04/48	**4567**	01/49-02/56	⊂**9860**
S8854S	02/29-06/52	↳**15330**	**1719**	02/29-01/48	**4568**	01/48-06/52	⊂**9854**
S8855S	02/29-05/52	↳**15396**	**1720**	02/29-08/47	**4569**	08/47-05/52	⊂**9874**
S8856	02/29-04/51	↳**14089**	**1721**	02/29-02/48	**4570**	05/49-05/51	⊂9846
8857	02/29-04/41	⊗04/41	**1722**	02/29-04/41			⊂**9883**
S8858S	02/29-03/56	↳**14455**	**1723**	02/29-01/48	**4571**	01/48-03/56	⊂9880

3-SUB Ashford (ex AC stock)

Driving Motor Brake Composite
DMBC
S8859S-S8862S

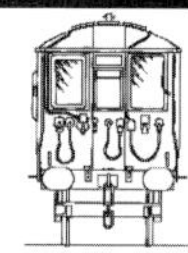

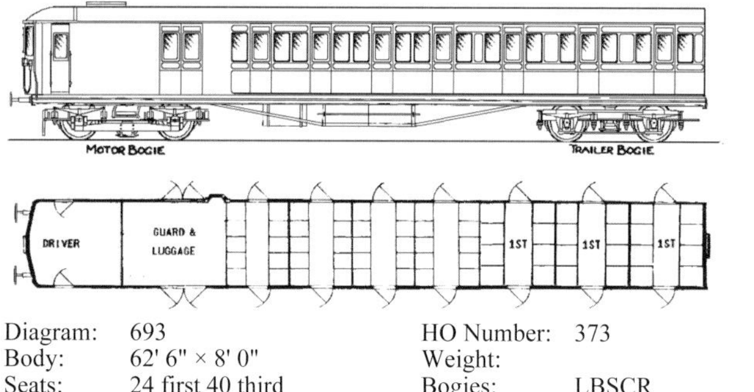

Diagram:	693	HO Number:	373
Body:	62' 6" × 8' 0"	Weight:	
Seats:	24 first 40 third	Bogies:	LBSCR
Motors:	MV339 2 × 275hp		

Vehicle	Dates	Fate	Unit	Dates	Unit	Dates	Unit	Dates
S8859S	05/29-10/59	⊗*10/59*	**1724**	05/29-08/47	**4527**	08/47-07/56	**4504**	07/56-10/59 **⊂9837**
S8860S	05/29-12/59	⊗01/60	**1725**	05/29-*02/48*	**4528**	*02/48*-11/56	**4510**	11/56-12/59 **⊂9857**
S8861S	06/29-08/56	⊗*08/56*	**1726**	06/29-*02/48*	**4529**	05/49-08/56		**⊂9849**
S8862S	06/29-08/56	⊗*08/56*	**1727**	06/29-*04/48*	**4530**	08/49-08/56		**⊂9847**

3-SUB Ashford (ex AC stock)

Driving Motor Brake Composite
DMBC
8863-S8871S

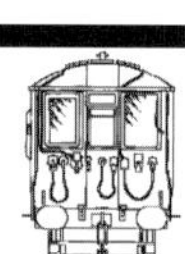

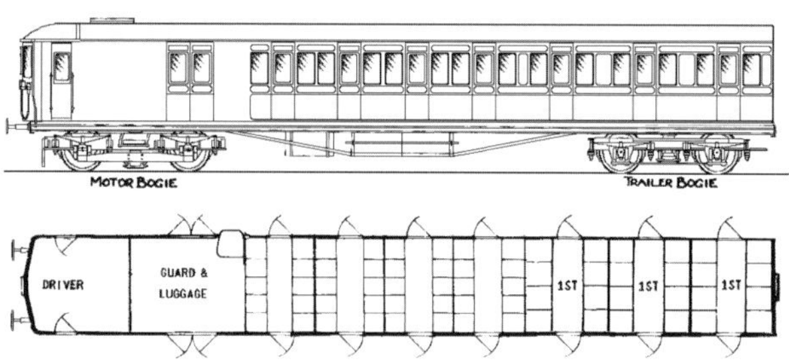

Diagram:	694	HO Number:	373
Body:	62' 6" × 8' 0"	Weight:	
Seats:	24 first 40 third	Bogies:	LBSCR
Motors:	MV339 2 × 275hp		

Vehicle	Dates	Fate	Unit	Dates	Unit	Dates	Unit	Dates
8863	06/29-06/44	⊗06/44	**1728**	06/29-06/44				⊂*9664*
S8864S	06/29-11/56	**⊃DS350**	**1729**	06/29-08/47	**4531**	*01/49*-11/56		**⊂9658**
S8865S	09/29-09/56	⊗*09/56*	**1730**	09/29-*10/46*	**4254**	10/46-03/56		**⊂9656**
S8866S	09/29-10/59	⊗*10/59*	**1731**	09/29-08/47	**4532**	08/47-09/56	**4507**	09/56-10/59 ⊂9667
S8867S	07/29-10/59	⊗*11/59*	**1732**	07/29-03/49	**4533**	03/49-12/56	**4514**	12/56-10/59 ⊂*9668*
S8868S	07/29-12/59	⊗01/60	**1733**	07/29-*01/48*	**4534**	*01/48*-07/56	**4503**	07/56-12/59 ⊂*9659*
S8869S	08/29-09/56	⊗*09/56*	**1734**	08/29-*07/48*	**4535**	*07/48*-09/56		**⊂9672**
S8870S	08/29-05/53	⊗	**1735**	08/29-*01/49*	**4536**	*01/49*-05/53		⊂*9669*
S8871S	08/29-11/58	⊗*11/59*	**1736**	08/29-03/44	**4251**	03/44-11/56	**4518**	01/57-11/58 **⊂9661**

3-SUB Eastleigh (ex AC stock)

Driving Motor Brake Composite
DMBC
S8872S-S8874S

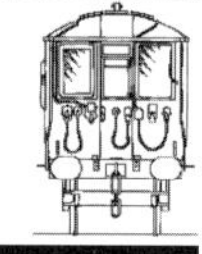

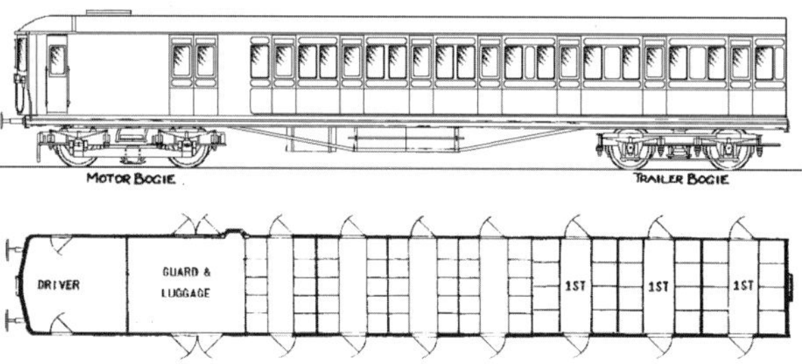

Diagram:	693	HO Number:	374
Body:	62' 6" × 8' 0"	Weight:	
Seats:	24 first 40 third	Bogies:	LBSCR
Motors:	MV339 2 × 275hp		

Vehicle	Dates	Fate	Unit	Dates	Unit	Dates	Unit	Dates
S8872S	06/29-08/55	⊗*08/55*	**1737**	06/29-08/47	**4537**	08/47-08/55		**⊂9881**
S8873S	06/29-01/60	⊗01/60	**1738**	06/29-*04/48*	**4538**	*04/48*-10/56	**4508**	10/56-01/60 **⊂9836**
S8874S	06/29-12/59	⊗01/60	**1739**	06/29-*01/49*	**4539**	*01/49*-12/56	**4512**	12/56-12/59 **⊂9829**

3-SUB Eastleigh (ex AC stock)

Driving Motor Brake Composite
DMBC
S8875S-S8884S

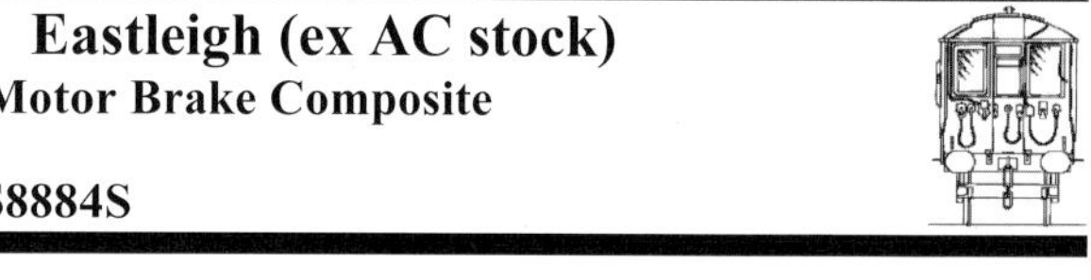

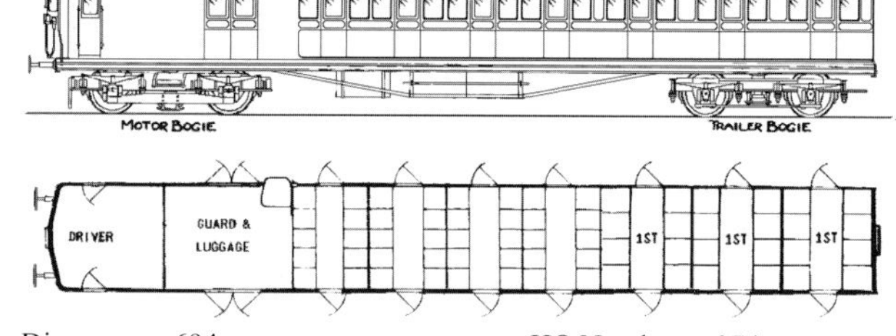

Diagram:	694	HO Number:	374
Body:	62' 6" × 8' 0"	Weight:	
Seats:	24 first 40 third	Bogies:	LBSCR
Motors:	MV339 2 × 275hp		

Vehicle	Dates	Fate	Unit	Dates	Unit	Dates	Unit	Dates
S8875S	06/29-06/56	⊗*06/56*	**1740**	06/29-*05/48*	**4540**	*05/48*-06/56		⊂*9665*
8876	06/29-02/44	⊗02/44	**1741**	06/29-02/44				**⊂9674**
S8877S	06/29-09/56	⊗*09/56*	**1742**	06/29-12/41	**1633**	11/42-11/48	**1771**	11/48-02/49
			4590	02/49-*05/50*	**4532**	*05/50*-09/56		**⊂9662**
S8878S	07/29-*11/59*	⊗*11/59*	**1743**	07/29-*07/48*	**4541**	*07/48*-11/56	**4509**	11/56-*11/59* **⊂9657**
S8879S	07/29-03/56	⊗*03/56*	**1744**	07/29-*07/48*	**4542**	*07/48*-03/56		⊂*9666*
8880	08/29-11/40	⊗11/40	**1745**	08/29-10/40				**⊂9655**
S8881S	08/29-09/56	**⊃081047**	**1746**	08/29-*02/48*	**4543**	*02/48*-09/56		⊂*9671*
S8882S	08/29-10/56	⊗*10/56*	**1747**	08/29-*03/48*	**4544**	08/49-10/56		⊂*9670*
S8883S	08/29-04/58	⊗	**1748**	08/29-*03/48*	**4545**	*02/49*-08/56	**4506**	08/56-04/58 **⊂9673**
S8884S	08/29-09/53	⊗*09/53*	**1749**	08/29-*07/48*	**4546**	*07/48*-09/53		⊂*9660*

3-SUB Ashford (ex AC stock)

Driving Motor Brake Composite
DMBC
S8885S-S8888S

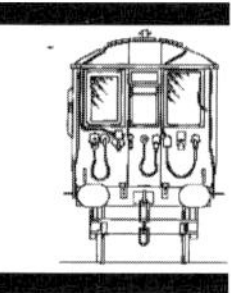

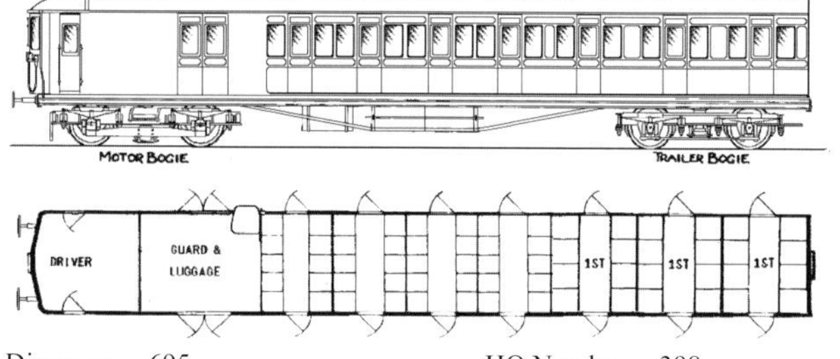

Diagram:	695	HO Number:	398
Body:	62' 6" × 8' 0"	Weight:	
Seats:	24 first 40 third	Bogies:	LBSCR
Motors:	MV339 2 × 275hp		

Vehicle	Dates	Fate	Unit	Dates	Unit	Dates	Unit	Dates
S8885S	*01/30*-08/56	⊗*08/56*	**1750**	*01/30-05/48*	**4547**	*01/49*-08/56		⊂*9911*
S8886S	*01/30*-10/56	⊗*10/56*	**1751**	*01/30-03/48*	**4548**	05/49-10/56		**⊂9896**
S8887S	*01/30*-05/56	⊗*05/56*	**1752**	*01/30*-08/47	**4549**	08/47-05/56		**⊂9902**
S8888S	*01/30*-11/59	⊗12/59	**1753**	*01/30-01/48*	**4550**	*01/48*-12/56	**4513**	12/56-11/59 ⊂*9905*

3-SUB Ashford (ex AC stock)

Driving Motor Brake Composite
DMBC
S8889S

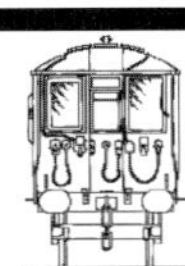

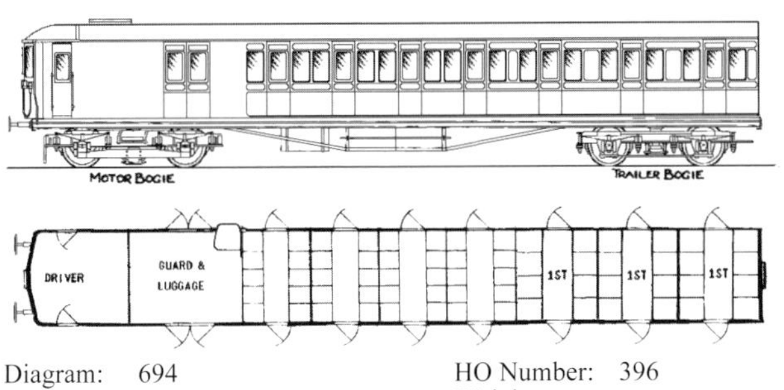

Diagram:	694	HO Number:	396
Body:	62' 6" × 8' 0"	Weight:	
Seats:	24 first 40 third	Bogies:	LBSCR
Motors:	MV339 2 × 275hp		

S8889S	11/29-12/59	⊗02/60	**1754**	11/29-08/47	**4551**	08/47-10/56	**4511**	11/56-12/59 ⊂**9663**

3-SUB Ashford (ex AC stock)

Driving Motor Brake Composite
DMBC
S8890S-S8891S

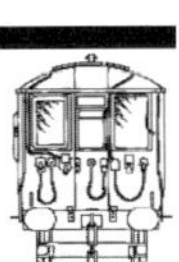

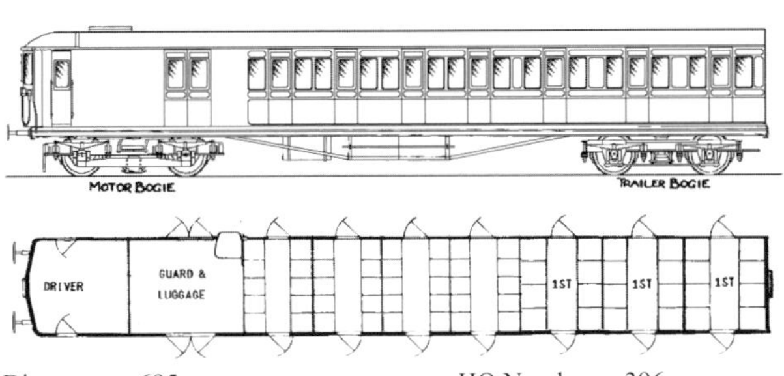

Diagram:	695	HO Number:	396
Body:	62' 6" × 8' 0"	Weight:	
Seats:	24 first 40 third	Bogies:	LBSCR
Motors:	MV339 2 × 275hp		

S8890S	12/29-09/56	⊗09/56	**1755**	12/29-08/47	**4552**	08/47-09/56		⊂**9913**
S8891S	12/29-12/59	⊗01/60	**1756**	12/29-02/48	**4553**	02/48-06/56	**4502**	06/56-12/59 ⊂**9900**

3-SUB Ashford (ex AC stock)

Driving Motor Brake Composite
DMBC
S8892S-S8900S

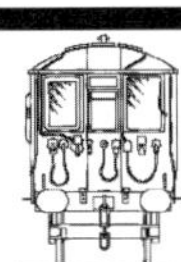

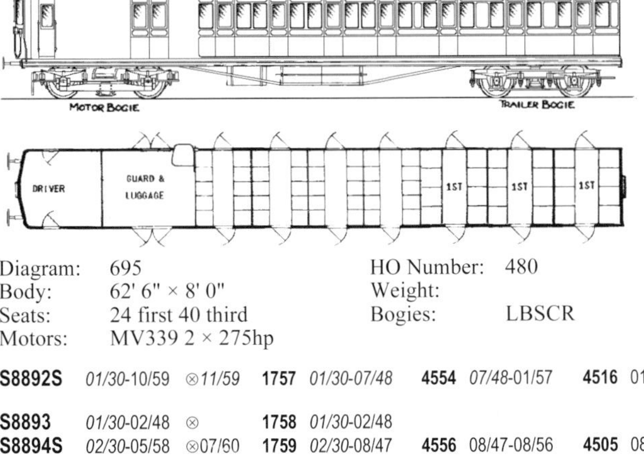

Diagram:	695	HO Number:	480
Body:	62' 6" × 8' 0"	Weight:	
Seats:	24 first 40 third	Bogies:	LBSCR
Motors:	MV339 2 × 275hp		

S8892S	01/30-10/59	⊗11/59	**1757**	01/30-07/48	**4554**	07/48-01/57	**4516**	01/57-10/59 ⊂**9914**
S8893	01/30-02/48	⊗	**1758**	01/30-02/48				⊂9910
S8894S	02/30-05/58	⊗07/60	**1759**	02/30-08/47	**4556**	08/47-08/56	**4505**	08/56-05/58 ⊂**9912**
S8895S	02/30-01/60	⊗01/60	**1760**	02/30-11/40	**1785**	11/40-07/48	**4526**	07/48-02/56
			4501	06/56-01/60				⊂9907
S8896S	03/30-03/53	⊗	**1761**	03/30-08/44	**4252**	08/44-03/53		⊂9906
S8897S	03/30-11/59	⊗11/59	**1762**	03/30-03/48	**4555**	03/48-01/57	**4515**	01/57-11/59 ⊂**9909**
S8898	04/30-05/48	⊗05/48	**1763**	04/30-05/48				⊂9899
S8899S	04/30-10/56	⊃**DS348**	**1764**	04/30-05/48	**4557**	06/48-10/56		⊂9901
S8900S	05/30-11/59	⊗11/59	**1765**	05/30-02/48	**4558**	02/48-12/56	**4517**	01/57-11/59 ⊂9904

2-T Eastleigh (ex LSWR hauled stock)

Trailer Third
TT
S8901-8912

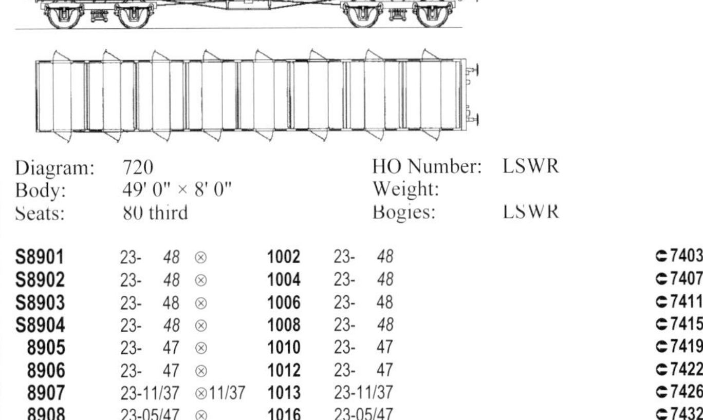

Diagram:	720	HO Number:	LSWR
Body:	49' 0" × 8' 0"	Weight:	
Seats:	80 third	Bogies:	LSWR

S8901	23- 48	⊗	**1002**	23- 48		⊂**7403**
S8902	23- 48	⊗	**1004**	23- 48		⊂**7407**
S8903	23- 48	⊗	**1006**	23- 48		⊂**7411**
S8904	23- 48	⊗	**1008**	23- 48		⊂**7415**
8905	23- 47	⊗	**1010**	23- 47		⊂**7419**
8906	23- 47	⊗	**1012**	23- 47		⊂**7422**
8907	23-11/37	⊗11/37	**1013**	23-11/37		⊂**7426**
8908	23-05/47	⊗	**1016**	23-05/47		⊂**7432**
S8909	23-01/48	⊗	**1017**	23-01/48		⊂**7434**
8910	23-05/43	⊗	**1021**	23- 43	Grounded at Eardley 43	⊂**7442**
8911	23-12/47	⊗	**1022**	23-12/47		⊂**7444**
8912	23-05/47	⊗	**1024**	23-05/47		⊂**7448**

2-T Eastleigh (ex LSWR hauled stock)

Trailer Third
TT
8913-8924

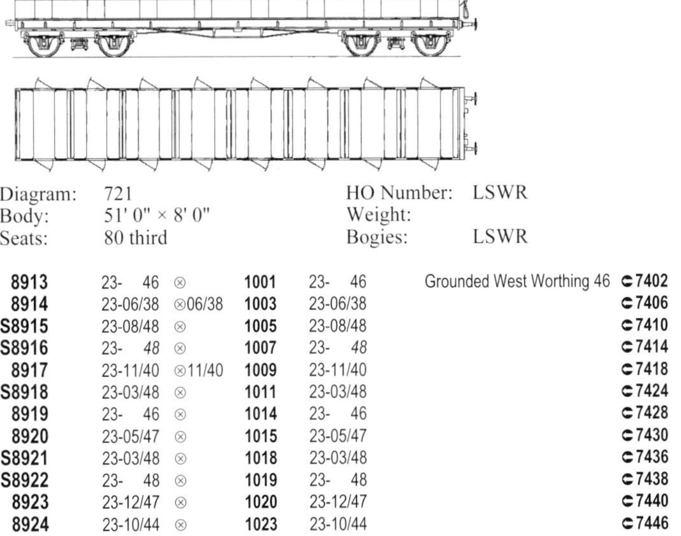

Diagram:	721	HO Number:	LSWR
Body:	51' 0" × 8' 0"	Weight:	
Seats:	80 third	Bogies:	LSWR

8913	23- 46	⊗	**1001**	23- 46	Grounded West Worthing 46	⊂**7402**
8914	23-06/38	⊗06/38	**1003**	23-06/38		⊂**7406**
S8915	23-08/48	⊗	**1005**	23-08/48		⊂**7410**
S8916	23- 48	⊗	**1007**	23- 48		⊂**7414**
8917	23-11/40	⊗11/40	**1009**	23-11/40		⊂**7418**
S8918	23-03/48	⊗	**1011**	23-03/48		⊂**7424**
8919	23- 46	⊗	**1014**	23- 46		⊂**7428**
8920	23-05/47	⊗	**1015**	23-05/47		⊂**7430**
S8921	23-03/48	⊗	**1018**	23-03/48		⊂**7436**
S8922	23- 48	⊗	**1019**	23- 48		⊂**7438**
8923	23-12/47	⊗	**1020**	23-12/47		⊂**7440**
8924	23-10/44	⊗	**1023**	23-10/44		⊂**7446**

2-T Eastleigh (ex LSWR hauled stock)

Trailer Third
TT
8925-8948

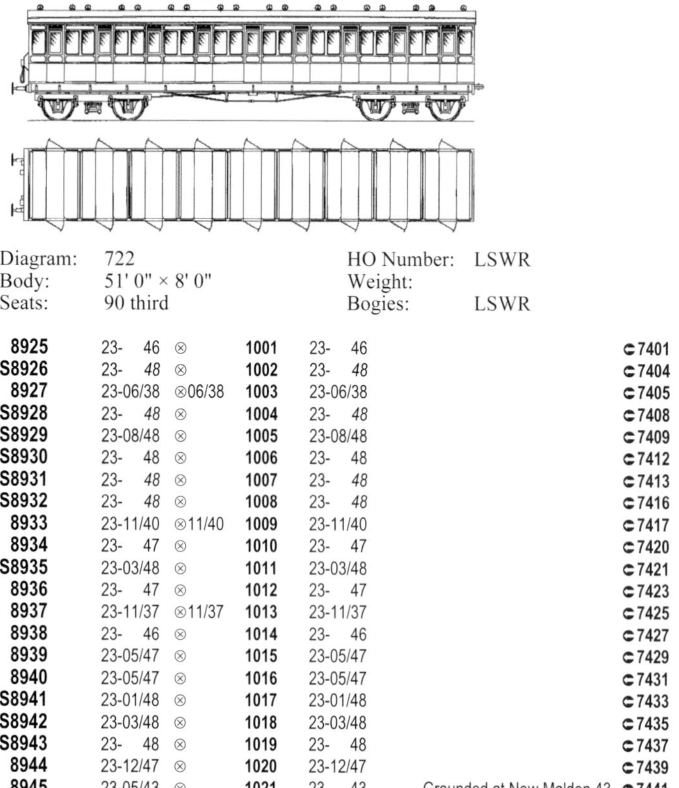

Diagram:	722	HO Number:	LSWR
Body:	51' 0" × 8' 0"	Weight:	
Seats:	90 third	Bogies:	LSWR

8925	23- 46	⊗	**1001**	23- 46		**⊂7401**
S8926	23- *48*	⊗	**1002**	23- *48*		**⊂7404**
8927	23-06/38	⊗06/38	**1003**	23-06/38		**⊂7405**
S8928	23- *48*	⊗	**1004**	23- *48*		**⊂7408**
S8929	23-08/48	⊗	**1005**	23-08/48		**⊂7409**
S8930	23- 48	⊗	**1006**	23- 48		**⊂7412**
S8931	23- *48*	⊗	**1007**	23- *48*		**⊂7413**
S8932	23- *48*	⊗	**1008**	23- *48*		**⊂7416**
8933	23-11/40	⊗11/40	**1009**	23-11/40		**⊂7417**
8934	23- 47	⊗	**1010**	23- 47		**⊂7420**
S8935	23-03/48	⊗	**1011**	23-03/48		**⊂7421**
8936	23- 47	⊗	**1012**	23- 47		**⊂7423**
8937	23-11/37	⊗11/37	**1013**	23-11/37		**⊂7425**
8938	23- 46	⊗	**1014**	23- 46		**⊂7427**
8939	23-05/47	⊗	**1015**	23-05/47		**⊂7429**
8940	23-05/47	⊗	**1016**	23-05/47		**⊂7431**
S8941	23-01/48	⊗	**1017**	23-01/48		**⊂7433**
S8942	23-03/48	⊗	**1018**	23-03/48		**⊂7435**
S8943	23- 48	⊗	**1019**	23- 48		**⊂7437**
8944	23-12/47	⊗	**1020**	23-12/47		**⊂7439**
8945	23-05/43	⊗	**1021**	23- 43	Grounded at New Malden 43	**⊂7441**
8946	23-12/47	⊗	**1022**	23-12/47		**⊂7443**
8947	23-10/44	⊗	**1023**	23-10/44		**⊂7445**
8948	23-05/47	⊗	**1024**	23-05/47		**⊂7447**

2-T Lancing (ex LBSCR hauled stock)

Trailer Third
TT
8949-S8974

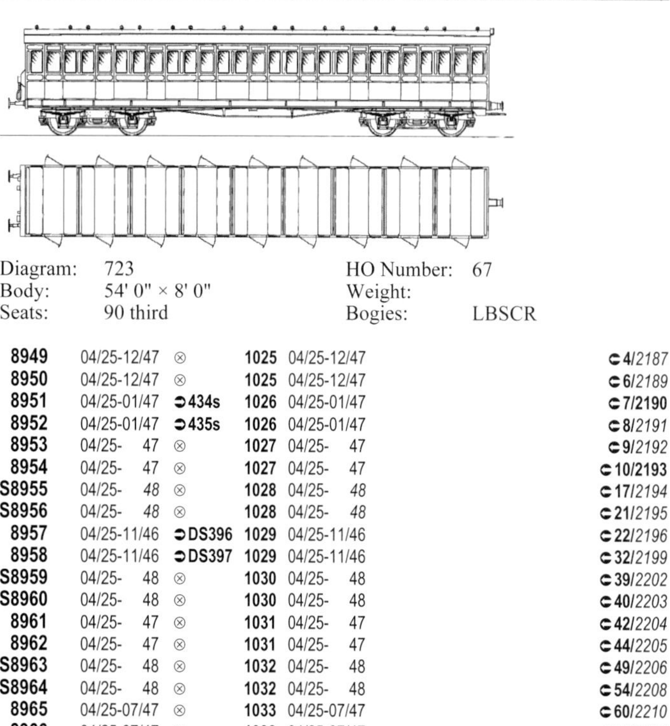

Diagram:	723	HO Number:	67
Body:	54' 0" × 8' 0"	Weight:	
Seats:	90 third	Bogies:	LBSCR

8949	04/25-12/47	⊗	**1025**	04/25-12/47	**⊂4/***2187*
8950	04/25-12/47	⊗	**1025**	04/25-12/47	**⊂6/***2189*
8951	04/25-01/47	**⊃434s**	**1026**	04/25-01/47	**⊂7/2190**
8952	04/25-01/47	**⊃435s**	**1026**	04/25-01/47	**⊂8/***2191*
8953	04/25- 47	⊗	**1027**	04/25- 47	**⊂9/***2192*
8954	04/25- 47	⊗	**1027**	04/25- 47	**⊂10/2193**
S8955	04/25- *48*	⊗	**1028**	04/25- *48*	**⊂17/***2194*
S8956	04/25- *48*	⊗	**1028**	04/25- *48*	**⊂21/***2195*
8957	04/25-11/46	**⊃DS396**	**1029**	04/25-11/46	**⊂22/***2196*
8958	04/25-11/46	**⊃DS397**	**1029**	04/25-11/46	**⊂32/***2199*
S8959	04/25- 48	⊗	**1030**	04/25- 48	**⊂39/***2202*
S8960	04/25- 48	⊗	**1030**	04/25- 48	**⊂40/***2203*
8961	04/25- 47	⊗	**1031**	04/25- 47	**⊂42/***2204*
8962	04/25- 47	⊗	**1031**	04/25- 47	**⊂44/***2205*
S8963	04/25- 48	⊗	**1032**	04/25- 48	**⊂49/***2206*
S8964	04/25- 48	⊗	**1032**	04/25- 48	**⊂54/***2208*
8965	04/25-07/47	⊗	**1033**	04/25-07/47	**⊂60/***2210*
8966	04/25-07/47	⊗	**1033**	04/25-07/47	**⊂64/***2211*
S8967	05/25- 48	⊗	**1034**	05/25- 48	**⊂66/***2212*
S8968	05/25- 48	⊗	**1034**	05/25- 48	**⊂67/2213**
8969	04/25-10/47	⊗	**1035**	04/25-10/47	**⊂71/***2215*
8970	04/25-10/47	⊗	**1035**	04/25-10/47	**⊂73/***2216*
8971	04/25-06/47	⊗	**1036**	04/25-06/47	**⊂74/***2217*
8972	04/25-06/47	⊗	**1036**	04/25-06/47	**⊂77/***2218*
S8973	04/25- 48	⊗	**1037**	04/25- 48	**⊂78/***2219*
S8974	04/25- 48	⊗	**1037**	04/25- 48	**⊂81/***2220*

2-T Lancing (ex SECR hauled stock)

Trailer Third
TT
8975-8998

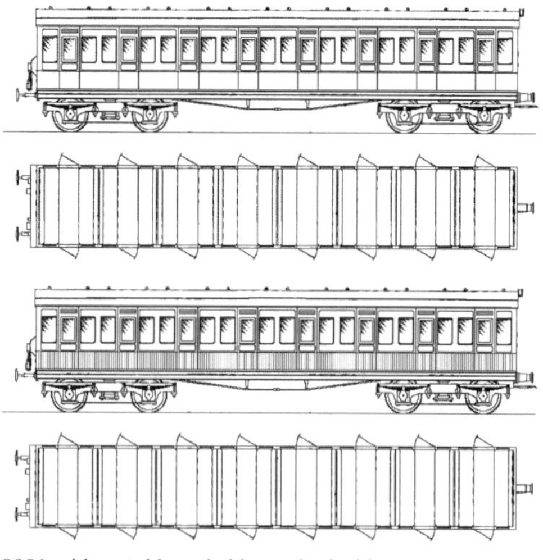

8981 with matchboarded lower bodysides.

Diagram:	725	HO Number:	214
Body:	48' 0" × 8' 0"	Weight:	
Seats:	80 third	Bogies:	SECR

8975	03/28-10/47	⊗	**1121**	03/28-10/47	**⊂3462/***1029*
8976	03/28-03/46	⊗	**1122**	03/28-03/46	**⊂2307/1013**
8977	03/28-03/43	⊗	**1123**	03/28-03/43	**⊂708/1003** Grounded Yeovil Junction 03/43
8978	03/28-11/47	⊗	**1124**	03/28-01/43	**⊂713/9012/***1008*
8979	03/28-09/42	⊗	**1125**	03/28-09/42	**⊂3454/1021** Grounded Staines 09/42
8980	04/28-04/42	⊗	**1126**	04/28-04/42	**⊂3461/1028** Grounded Lancing Works 04/42
8981	04/28-09/43	⊗	**1127**	04/28-09/43	**⊂2308/1014** Grounded Bevois Park 09/43
S8982	04/28-08/48	⊗	**1128**	04/28-08/48	**⊂3485/1051**
8983	04/28-09/40	⊗09/40	**1129**	04/28-09/40	**⊂698/996**
8984	05/28-05/47	⊗	**1130**	05/28-05/47	**⊂712/1007**
8985	05/28-02/43	⊗	**1131**	05/28-02/43	**⊂3457/1024** Grounded Redhill 02/43
8986	05/28-02/43	⊗	**1132**	05/28-02/43	**⊂2314/9023/***1019* Grounded Eastleigh 02/43
8987	05/28-11/47	⊗	**1133**	05/28-11/47	**⊂3465/***1032*
8988	05/28-09/43	⊗	**1134**	05/28-09/43	**⊂3459/1026**
8989	05/28-10/47	⊗	**1135**	05/28-10/47	**⊂3456/1023**
8990	05/28-11/47	⊗	**1136**	05/28-11/47	**⊂3472/1039**
8991	04/28-10/47	⊗	**1137**	04/28-10/47	**⊂3463/***1030*
8992	04/28-11/44	⊗	**1138**	04/28-11/44	**⊂2310/1015**
8993	04/28-02/44	⊗	**1139**	04/28-02/44	**⊂2312/1017** Grounded Southampton Old Docks 02/44
8994	05/28-01/46	⊗	**1140**	05/28-01/46	**⊂700/***997*
8995	05/28-02/44	⊗	**1141**	05/28-02/44	**⊂709/***1004* Grounded St Denys 02/44
S8996	05/28-02/48	⊗	**1142**	05/28-02/48	**⊂3464/***1031*
8997	05/28-08/43	⊗	**1143**	05/28-08/43	**⊂2313/1018** Grounded Eastleigh Works 08/43
8998	04/28-03/43	⊗	**1144**	04/28-03/43	**⊂706/***1002* Grounded Yeovil 03/43

2-T Lancing (ex LBSCR hauled stock)

Trailer Third

TT

S8999-9116 (some Metropolitan Amalgamated RC&W)

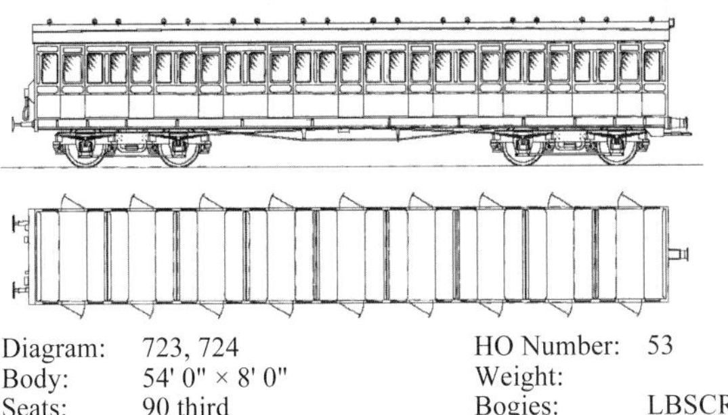

Diagram:	723, 724	HO Number:	53
Body:	54' 0" × 8' 0"	Weight:	
Seats:	90 third	Bogies:	LBSCR

Converted from LBSCR nine-compartment steam hauled third vehicles. These had been rebuilt at Lancing in 1910-1911 from six-wheeled five-compartment thirds with new underframes.

New built:
1-886 (2189-2240) Lancing 1912/1921
1351-1400 (2241-2290) Metropolitan Amalgamated RC&W 1910-1911

No.	Dates	Fate	Unit	Dates	Unit	Dates	Origin / Notes
S8999	06/25-08/48	⊗	1051	06/25-08/48			⊂1/2186
9000	06/25-10/40	⊗10/40	1059	06/25- 36	1039	37-10/40	⊂515/2316
9001	06/25-03/43	⊗	1052	06/25-03/43			⊂5/2188
							Grounded Wokingham 03/43
9002	06/25-03/43	⊗	1052	06/25-03/43			⊂522/2317
							Grounded Eastleigh 03/43
9003	06/25-11/45	➲DS356	1060	07/25-11/45			⊂546/2318
							Grounded Halwill Junc 07/43
9004	06/25-07/43	⊗	1066	06/25-07/43			⊂551/2319
S9005	06/25- 48	⊗	1058	06/25- 48			⊂555/2320
S9006	06/25- 48	⊗	1057	06/25- 48			⊂557/2321
9007	06/25-07/43	⊗	1066	06/25-07/43			⊂561/2322
							Grounded Southampton Old Docks 07/43
S9008	06/25- 48	⊗	1057	06/25- 48			⊂562/2323
9009	06/25-12/43	⊗	1069	07/25-12/43			⊂571/2324
							Grounded Folkestone 12/43
9010	06/25-12/45	➲DS351	1065	06/25-12/45			⊂26/2197
S9011	07/25- 48	⊗	1056	07/25- 48			⊂31/2198
9012	07/25- 44	⊗	1059	07/25- 44			⊂1156/2325
							Grounded Eastleigh C&W 44
9013	06/25-11/45	➲DS353	1053	06/25-11/45			⊂36/2200
S9014	06/25- 48	⊗	1056	06/25- 48			⊂38/2201
9015	07/25-09/40	⊗09/40	1063	07/25-09/40			⊂1166/2326
9016	07/25-09/40	⊗09/40	1063	07/25-09/40			⊂1167/2327
9017	07/25-07/47	⊗	1092	07/25- 36	1092	36-07/47	⊂1168/2328
9018	07/25- 45	⊗	1072	07/25- 45			⊂1169/2329
9019	08/25-09/40	⊗09/40	1067	08/25- 37	1120	02/37-09/40	⊂1174/2330
9020	07/25-09/40	⊗	1072	07/25- 37	1038	37-09/40	⊂51/2207
9021	08/25-02/47	⊗	1070	08/25-02/47			⊂1247/2331
9022	07/25-05/47	⊗	1068	08/25- 37	1098	37-05/47	⊂56/2209
9023	09/25- 47	⊗	1079	09/25-07/44			⊂1251/2332
							Grounded Lancing 47
9024	10/25-11/42	⊗	1084	10/25- 37	1000	07/37-11/42	⊂1253/2333
							Grounded Effingham Junction 11/42
9025	01/26-03/42	⊗	1107	01/26-03/42			⊂1380/2270
							Grounded Redhill MPD 03/42
9026	01/26-03/42	⊗	1107	01/26-03/42			⊂1381/2271
							Grounded Southampton 03/42
9027	10/25-09/42	⊗	1087	10/25- 35	1198	35-09/42	⊂70/2214
							Grounded Tunbridge Wells West 09/42
9028	12/25-08/47	⊗	1097	12/25- 36	1044	36-08/47	⊂1382/2272
							Grounded Gravesend West 03/43
9029	12/25-03/43	⊗	1100	12/25-03/43			⊂1383/2273
9030	12/25-08/46	⊗	1103	12/25-03/37	1067	37-08/46	⊂1384/2274
S9031	12/25- 48	⊗	1102	12/25- 48			⊂1385/2275
9032	01/26-12/45	⊗12/45	1109	01/26-12/45			⊂1386/2276
9033	01/26-06/44	⊗	1104	01/26-06/44			⊂1387/2277
9034	07/25-08/47	⊗	1073	07/25- 36	1041	36-08/47	⊂86/2221
9035	10/25-12/45	⊗	1085	10/25-07/37	999	09/37-12/45	⊂330/2291
9036	08/25-11/42	⊗11/42	1071	07/25- 36	1048	36-11/42	⊂357/2292
9037	10/25-10/40	⊗10/40	1081	10/25-10/40			⊂360/2293
9038	10/25-11/42	⊗	1086	10/25-11/42			⊂377/2294
							Grounded Wimbledon 43
9039	10/25-11/43	⊗	1086	10/25-02/38	992	02/38-11/43	⊂388/2295
9040	12/25-11/42	⊗	1089	12/25-11/42			⊂410/2296
							Grounded Orpington 11/42
9041	10/25-11/42	⊗	1089	12/25-11/42			⊂413/2297
							Grounded Bricklayers Arms 11/42
S9042	10/25- 48	⊗	1091	10/25-12/47			⊂416/2298
9043	10/25-04/42	⊗09/42	1080	10/25-04/42			⊂418/2299
							Frame used for Brake 3rd 3861
9044	10/25-02/47	⊗	1087	10/25-02/47			⊂423/2300
9045	12/25-05/47	⊗	1097	12/25- 36	1043	36-05/47	⊂424/2301
9046	12/25-09/44	⊗	1098	11/25-03/37	1103	03/37-09/44	⊂431/2302
S9047	12/25-08/48	⊗	1096	12/25- 36	1042	36-08/48	⊂436/2303
9048	05/25-10/40	⊗	1054	05/25-10/40			⊂437/2304
9049	12/25-02/43	⊗	1099	12/25-02/43			⊂438/2305
							Grounded Wimbledon Park 02/43
9050	12/25-03/42	⊗	1108	12/25-03/42			⊂459/2306
S9051	12/25-07/48	⊗	1101	12/25-07/48			⊂460/2307
9052	05/25-10/45	⊗	1055	05/25- 36	1040	36-10/45	⊂461/2308
9053	09/25- 47	⊗12/47	1079	09/25-07/44			⊂465/2309
9054	12/25-08/46	⊗	1108	12/25- 38	997	05/38-08/46	⊂484/2310
S9055	12/25- 48	⊗	1102	12/25- 48			⊂488/2311
9056	05/25-10/41	⊗	1054	05/25-10/41			⊂495/2312
							Grounded Fratton 41
9057	12/25-03/43	⊗	1100	12/25-03/43			⊂501/2313
							Grounded Micheldever 03/43
9058	12/25- 45	⊗	1104	12/25- 38	996	04/38- 45	⊂502/2314
9059	09/25-05/43	⊗	1077	09/25-05/43			⊂503/2315
							Grounded Brighton C&W 05/43
9060	07/25-11/45	➲DS355	1060	07/25-11/45			⊂855/2222
9061	07/25-01/45	⊗	1065	07/25-12/45			⊂856/2223
9062	07/25-03/43	⊗	1062	07/25-03/43			⊂857/2224
							Grounded Wareham 03/43
9063	07/25-02/44	⊗02/44	1051	07/25-02/44			⊂858/2225
9064	07/25-03/43	⊗	1062	07/25-03/43			⊂859/2226
							Grounded Tooting Junc 03/43
9065	07/25-12/45	⊗	1061	07/25- 38	990	01/38- 45	⊂860/2227
9066	07/25- 46	⊗	1070	07/25- 36	1071	36- 46	⊂861/2228
9067	07/25-09/42	⊗	1071	07/25- 36	1047	36-09/42	⊂862/2229
							Grounded Raynes Park 09/42
9068	07/25-12/43	⊗	1069	07/25-12/43			⊂863/2230
							Grounded Bricklayers Arms 12/43
9069	05/25-11/45	➲DS354	1053	05/25-11/45			⊂864/2231
9070	07/25- 46	⊗	1098	12/25-03/37	1199	03/37- 46	⊂872/2232
S9071	07/25-05/48	⊗	1064	07/25-05/48			⊂873/2233
9072	07/25-09/43	⊗	1073	07/25-09/43			⊂874/2234
							Grounded Sutton 09/43
S9073	07/25- 48	⊗	1074	07/25- 48			⊂879/2235
9074	10/25-06/45	⊗	1082	10/25-06/45			⊂880/2236
S9075	10/25-01/48	⊗01/48	1090	10/25-01/48			⊂883/2237
S9076	08/25- 48	⊗	1074	08/25- 48			⊂884/2238
9077	08/25-08/46	⊗	1068	08/25- 37	1119	02/37-08/46	⊂885/2239
9078	09/25-08/35	⊗07/36	1078	09/25-08/35			⊂886/2240
S9078S[2]	37-01/56	⊗01/56	1078	37-08/48	4190	08/48-01/56	Replacement
9079	10/25-11/46	➲DS398	1083	10/25-11/46			⊂1351/2241
S9080	09/25- 48	⊗	1076	09/25- 48			⊂1352/2242
9081	09/25-07/43	⊗	1075	09/25-07/43			⊂1353/2243
9082	09/25-05/43	⊗	1077	09/25-05/43			⊂1354/2244
							Grounded Brighton C&W 05/43
9083	10/25- 47	⊗	1088	10/25- 47			⊂1355/2245
9084	09/25-12/42	⊗	1082	10/25- 38	991	02/38-01/42	⊂1356/2246
							Grounded Wimbledon 01/42
9085	09/25-04/42	⊗	1080	09/25-04/42			⊂1357/2247
9086	10/25-10/44	⊗	1090	10/25- 38	993	03/38-10/44	⊂1358/2248
9087	10/25-12/47	⊗	1091	10/25-12/47			⊂1359/2249
9088	11/25-09/43	⊗	1094	11/25-09/43			⊂1360/2250
							Grounded Fratton 09/43
9089	10/25-11/46	➲DS399	1083	10/25-11/46			⊂1361/2251
9090	09/25-07/43	⊗	1075	09/25-07/43			⊂1362/2252
							Grounded Worthing Central 07/43
S9091	10/25-09/48	⊗	1085	10/25-07/37	998	09/37-09/48	⊂1363/2253
S9092	09/25-08/48	⊗	1078	09/25-08/48			⊂1364/2254
9093	10/25-09/42	⊗	1092	10/25- 36	1046	36-09/42	⊂1365/2255
							Grounded Farnham 09/42
9094	10/25-01/46	⊗	1081	10/25- 37	1095	37-01/46	⊂1366/2256
9095	10/25- 46	⊗	1084	10/25- 37	1200	07/37- 46	⊂1367/2257
9096	10/25- 47	⊗	1088	10/25- 47			⊂1368/2258
9097	10/25-08/47	⊗	1092	10/25- 36	1045	36-08/47	⊂1369/2259
9098	11/25-08/46	⊗	1095	10/25-09/37	1084	37-08/46	⊂1370/2260
9099	11/25-09/44	⊗	1095	11/25-09/37	1085	09/37-11/40	⊂1371/2261
			1081	11/40-09/44			
9100	05/25-09/39	⊗09/39	1093	11/25- 38	989	01/38-09/39	⊂1372/2262
9101	12/25-07/47	⊗	1099	12/25-02/38	995	04/38-07/47	⊂1373/2263
9102	11/25-09/43	⊗	1093	11/25-09/43			⊂1374/2264
							Grounded Eastleigh Works 09/43
S9103	07/25- 48	⊗	1058	07/25- 48			⊂1375/2265
9104	11/25-02/47	⊗	1096	11/25-02/47			⊂1376/2266
9105	11/25-09/43	⊗	1094	11/25-09/43			⊂1377/2267
9106	11/25- 44	⊗	1093	11/25- 38	994	03/38- 44	⊂1378/2268
S9107	11/25-08/48	⊗	1098	11/25-03/37	1039	37-10/40	⊂1379/2269
S9108	09/25- 48	⊗	1076	09/25- 48			⊂1392/2282
S9109	12/25-08/48	⊗	1103	12/25-03/37	1068	37-08/48	⊂1393/2283
S9110	12/25-07/48	⊗	1101	12/25-07/48			⊂1394/2284
S9111	01/26-08/48	⊗	1106	01/26-08/48			⊂1395/2285
S9112	01/26- 48	⊗	1105	01/26- 48			⊂1396/2286
S9113	01/26- 48	⊗	1105	01/26- 48			⊂1397/2287
S9114	01/26-08/48	⊗	1106	01/26-08/48			⊂1398/2288

9115	05/25-12/40	⊗12/40	**1055**	05/25-12/40	**⊂1399/***2289*
9116	01/26-12/45	**⊃DS352**	**1109**	01/26-12/45	**⊂1400/2290**

2-T Lancing (ex LBSCR hauled stock)

Trailer Third
TT
9117-9120

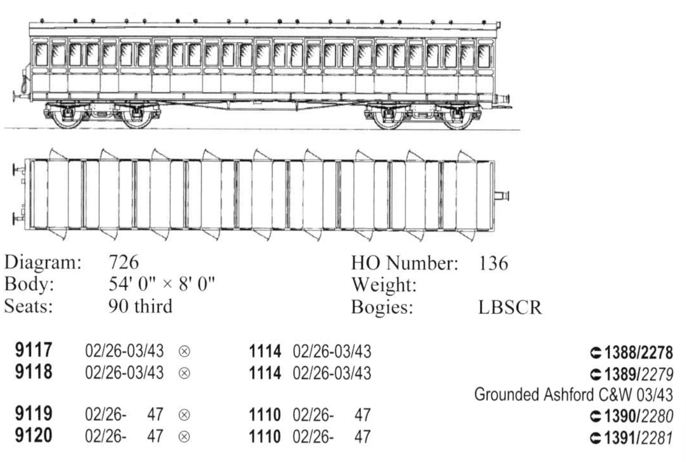

Diagram: 726 HO Number: 136
Body: 54' 0" × 8' 0" Weight:
Seats: 90 third Bogies: LBSCR

9117	02/26-03/43	⊗	**1114**	02/26-03/43	**⊂1388/2278**
9118	02/26-03/43	⊗	**1114**	02/26-03/43	**⊂1389/***2279*
					Grounded Ashford C&W 03/43
9119	02/26- 47	⊗	**1110**	02/26- 47	**⊂1390/***2280*
9120	02/26- 47	⊗	**1110**	02/26- 47	**⊂1391/***2281*

2-T Lancing (ex LBSCR hauled stock)

Trailer Third
TT
9121-9132

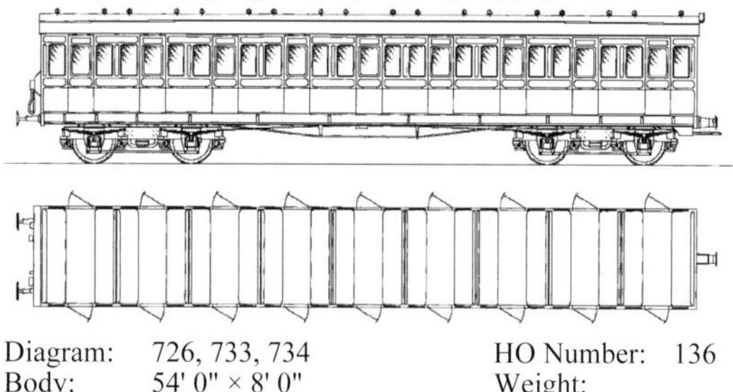

Diagram: 726, 733, 734 HO Number: 136
Body: 54' 0" × 8' 0" Weight:
Seats: 90 third Bogies: LBSCR

9121	02/26-07/42	⊗	**1111** 02/26- 36	**1050**	36-07/42	**⊂1531/***2121*
9122	02/26-09/42	⊗	**1113** 02/26- 36	**1097**	36-09/42	**⊂1532/***2122*
						Grounded Wimbledon CMEE 09/42
S9123	02/26- 48	⊗	**1070** *08/25*- 36	**1049**	36- 48	**⊂1533/***2123*
9124	03/26-10/47	⊗	**1112** 03/26-10/47			**⊂1534/***2124*
9125	03/26-11/42	⊗	**1113** 03/26-11/42			**⊂1535/***2125*
						Grounded Tonbridge 11/42
S9126	03/26-09/48	⊗	**1112** 03/26- 36	**1111**	36-09/48	**⊂1537/***2126*
9127	04/26-05/45	⊗	**1117** 04/26-05/45			**⊂1590/***2143*
9128	04/26-09/42	⊗	**1116** 04/26-09/42			**⊂1688/***2158*
						Grounded Lancing 09/42
9129	02/26-01/43	⊗	**1115** 02/26-01/43			**⊂1727/***2164*
						Grounded Ashford 01/43
9130	04/26-10/45	⊗	**1117** 04/26- 35	**1195**	35-10/45	**⊂1768/***2169*
9131	04/26-09/39	⊗09/39	**1116** 04/26- 35	**1197**	35-09/39	**⊂1778/2171**
9132	03/26-05/47	⊗	**1115** 03/26- 35	**1196**	35-05/47	**⊂1781/2172**

2-T Lancing (ex SECR hauled stock)

Trailer Third
TT
9133-9155

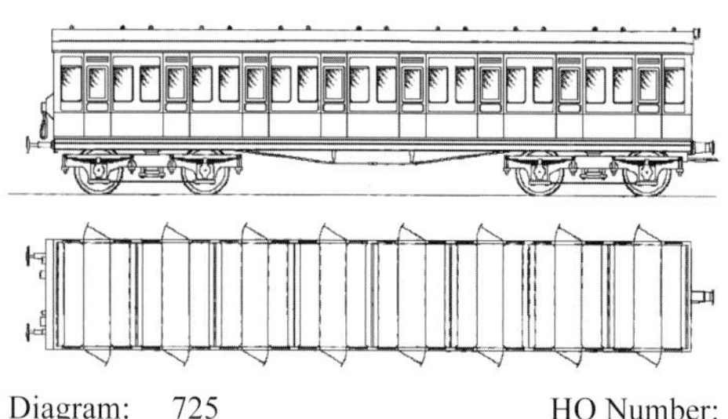

Diagram: 725 HO Number: 214
Body: 48' 0" × 8' 0" Weight:
Seats: 80 third Bogies: SECR

9133	04/28-07/47	⊗	**1145**	04/28-07/47	**⊂3476/1042**
9134	11/28-11/47	⊗	**1146**	11/28-11/47	**⊂3482/***1048*
9135	11/28-11/42	⊗	**1147**	11/28-11/42	**⊂3471/1038**
					Grounded Selhurst CMEE 11/42
9136	01/29-01/46	⊗	**1148**	01/29-01/46	**⊂699/***997*
9137	10/28-08/47	⊗	**1149**	10/28-08/47	**⊂704/***1000*
9138	01/29-04/44	⊗	**1150**	01/29-04/44	**⊂3466/***1033*
					Grounded Mitcham 04/44
9139	01/29-08/46	⊗	**1151**	01/29-08/46	**⊂3467/1034**
9140	01/29-08/37	⊗08/37	**1152**	01/29-08/37	**⊂3468/1035**
					Accident loss
S9140[2]	38-08/48	⊗	**1152**	38-08/48	Replacement
9141	12/28-08/46	⊗	**1153**	10/28-08/46	**⊂2311/***1016*
9142	12/28-09/43	⊗	**1154**	12/28-09/43	**⊂3480/***1046*
					Grounded Brighton Top Yard 09/43
S9143	12/28-07/48	⊗	**1155**	12/28-07/48	**⊂3481/***1047*
S9144	02/29-04/48	⊗	**1156**	02/29-04/48	**⊂714/1009**
9145	02/29-08/43	⊗	**1157**	02/29-08/43	**⊂3479/1045**
					Grounded Bevois Park 08/43
9146	02/29-11/47	⊗	**1158**	02/29-11/47	**⊂3475/1041**
9147	02/29-11/40	⊗11/40	**1159**	02/29-11/40	**⊂705/1001**
9148	02/29-08/46	⊗	**1160**	02/29-08/46	**⊂3460/1027**
9149	01/29-01/44	⊗	**1161**	01/29-01/44	**⊂3470/1037**
S9150	02/29-03/48	⊗	**1162**	02/29-03/48	**⊂702/999**
					Grounded Three Bridges 03/48
9151	02/29-09/43	⊗	**1163**	02/29-09/43	**⊂711/1006**
9152	02/29-12/47	⊗	**1164**	02/29-12/47	**⊂3469/***1036*
9153	02/29-12/47	⊗	**1165**	02/29-12/47	**⊂710/1005**
9154	02/29-06/43	⊗	**1166**	02/29-06/43	**⊂3484/1050**
					Grounded Twickenham 06/43
9155	02/29-08/47	⊗	**1167**	02/29-08/47	**⊂3487/1053**

2-T Lancing

Trailer Third
TT
9156-S9167S

Odd Numbers (ex LBSCR CP stock):

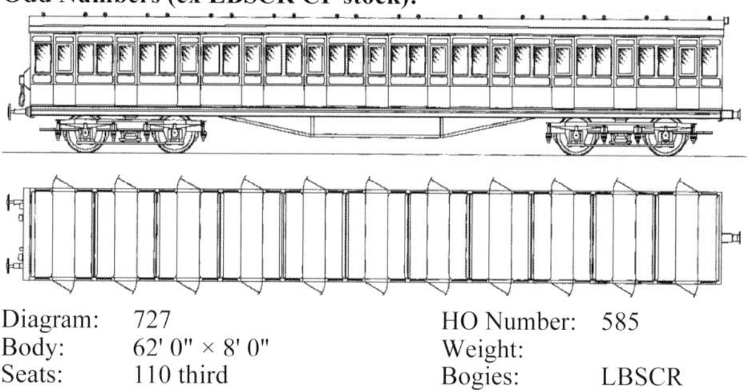

Diagram: 727 HO Number: 585
Body: 62' 0" × 8' 0" Weight:
Seats: 110 third Bogies: LBSCR

Even Numbers (ex-SECR hauled stock):

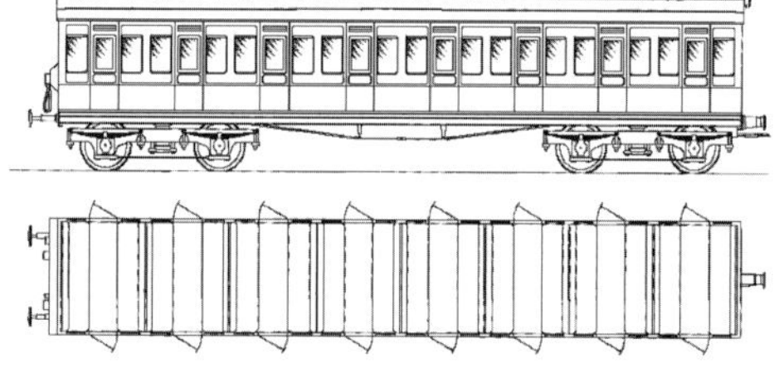

Diagram: 725 HO Number: 585
Body: 48' 0" × 8' 0" Weight:
Seats: 80 third Bogies: SR

9156	02/31-01/42	⊗01/42	**1189**	02/31-01/42			**⊂3453/1020**
S9157S	02/31-05/55	↳**15313**	**1189**	02/31-01/42	**4195**	01/42-05/55	
9158	02/31-09/46	⊗	**1190**	02/31-09/46			**⊂3455/1022**
S9159S	02/31-10/54	↳**15232**	**1190**	02/31-09/46	**4230**	09/46-10/54	
9160	02/31-12/43	⊗	**1191**	02/31-12/43			**⊂715/1010**
S9161S	02/31-05/54	↳**15212**	**1191**	02/31-12/43	**4225**	12/43-05/54	
9162	02/31-10/42	⊗	**1192**	03/31-10/42			**⊂2306/1012**
S9163S	03/31-06/55	↳**15419**	**1192**	03/31-10/42	**4196**	10/42-06/55	
9164	03/31-11/44	⊗11/44	**1193**	03/31-11/44			**⊂3458/9029/1025**
9165	03/31-11/44	↳**15423**	**1193**	03/31-11/44			
S9166	03/31-07/48	⊗	**1194**	03/31-07/48			**⊂3475/1040**
S9167S	03/31-08/53	↳**15178**	**1194**	03/31-07/48	**4243**	07/48-*08/53*	

2-T Lancing (LSWR bodies)

Trailer Third

TT

S9168S-S9175S

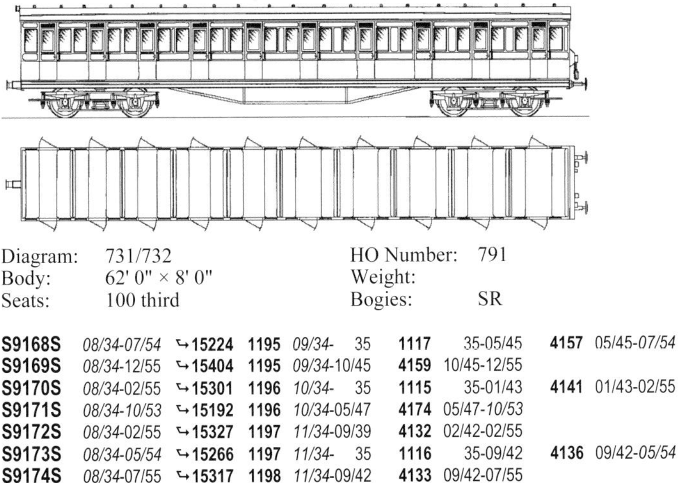

Diagram: 731/732 HO Number: 791
Body: 62' 0" × 8' 0" Weight:
Seats: 100 third Bogies: SR

S9168S	*08/34-07/54*	↳**15224**	**1195**	*09/34-* 35	**1117**	35-05/45	**4157**	05/45-*07/54*
S9169S	*08/34*-12/55	↳**15404**	**1195**	*09/34*-10/45	**4159**	10/45-12/55		
S9170S	*08/34*-02/55	↳**15301**	**1196**	*10/34-* 35	**1115**	35-01/43	**4141**	01/43-02/55
S9171S	*08/34-10/53*	↳**15192**	**1196**	*10/34*-05/47	**4174**	05/47-*10/53*		
S9172S	*08/34*-02/55	↳**15327**	**1197**	*11/34*-09/39	**4132**	02/42-02/55		
S9173S	*08/34-05/54*	↳**15266**	**1197**	*11/34-* 35	**1116**	35-09/42	**4136**	09/42-*05/54*
S9174S	*08/34*-07/55	↳**15317**	**1198**	*11/34*-09/42	**4133**	09/42-07/55		
S9175S	*08/34*-07/53	↳**15173**	**1198**	*11/34-* 35	**1087**	35-02/47	**4177**	02/47-07/53

2-T Lancing (LSWR bodies)

Trailer Third

TT

S9176S-S9191S

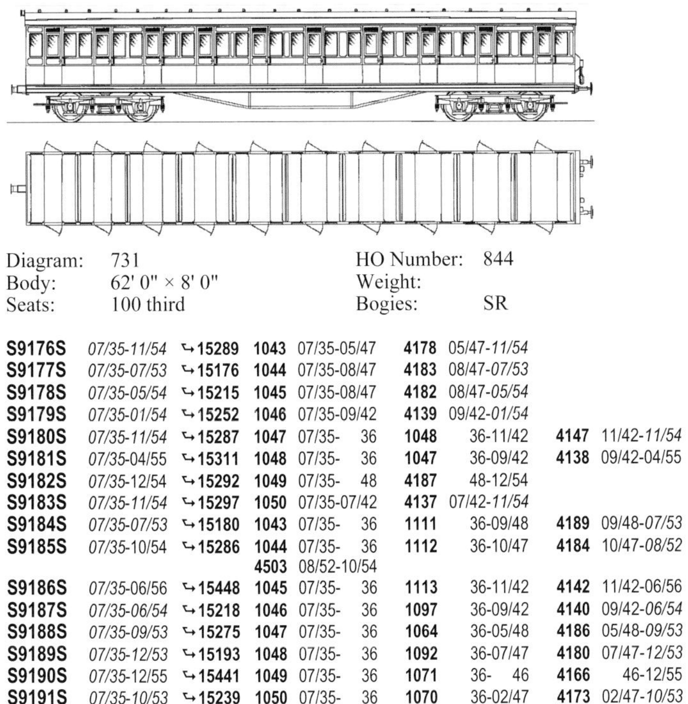

Diagram: 731 HO Number: 844
Body: 62' 0" × 8' 0" Weight:
Seats: 100 third Bogies: SR

S9176S	*07/35-11/54*	↳**15289**	**1043**	07/35-05/47	**4178**	05/47-*11/54*		
S9177S	*07/35-07/53*	↳**15176**	**1044**	07/35-08/47	**4183**	08/47-*07/53*		
S9178S	*07/35-05/54*	↳**15215**	**1045**	07/35-08/47	**4182**	08/47-*05/54*		
S9179S	*07/35-01/54*	↳**15252**	**1046**	07/35-09/42	**4139**	09/42-*01/54*		
S9180S	*07/35-11/54*	↳**15287**	**1047**	07/35- 36	**1048**	36-11/42	**4147**	11/42-*11/54*
S9181S	*07/35*-04/55	↳**15311**	**1048**	07/35- 36	**1047**	36-09/42	**4138**	09/42-04/55
S9182S	*07/35*-12/54	↳**15292**	**1049**	07/35- 48	**4187**	48-12/54		
S9183S	*07/35-11/54*	↳**15297**	**1050**	07/35-07/42	**4137**	07/42-*11/54*		
S9184S	*07/35-07/53*	↳**15180**	**1043**	07/35- 36	**1111**	36-09/48	**4189**	09/48-*07/53*
S9185S	*07/35*-10/54	↳**15286**	**1044**	07/35- 36	**1112**	36-10/47	**4184**	10/47-*08/52*
			4503	08/52-10/54				
S9186S	*07/35*-06/56	↳**15448**	**1045**	07/35- 36	**1113**	36-11/42	**4142**	11/42-06/56
S9187S	*07/35-06/54*	↳**15218**	**1046**	07/35- 36	**1097**	36-09/42	**4140**	09/42-*06/54*
S9188S	*07/35-09/53*	↳**15275**	**1047**	07/35- 36	**1064**	36-05/48	**4186**	05/48-*09/53*
S9189S	*07/35-12/53*	↳**15193**	**1048**	07/35- 36	**1092**	36-07/47	**4180**	07/47-*12/53*
S9190S	*07/35*-12/55	↳**15441**	**1049**	07/35- 36	**1071**	36- 46	**4166**	46-12/55
S9191S	*07/35-10/53*	↳**15239**	**1050**	07/35- 36	**1070**	36-02/47	**4173**	02/47-*10/53*

2-T Lancing (LSWR bodies)

Trailer Third

TT

S9192S-S9199S

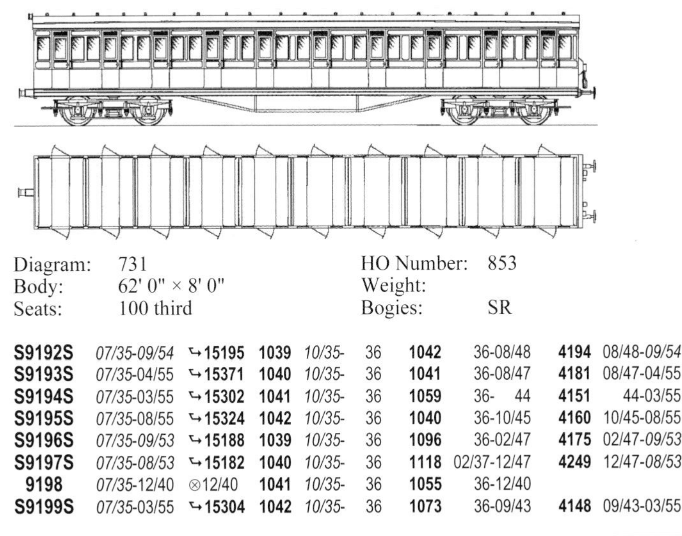

Diagram: 731 HO Number: 853
Body: 62' 0" × 8' 0" Weight:
Seats: 100 third Bogies: SR

S9192S	*07/35-09/54*	↳**15195**	**1039**	*10/35-* 36	**1042**	36-08/48	**4194**	08/48-*09/54*
S9193S	*07/35*-04/55	↳**15371**	**1040**	*10/35-* 36	**1041**	36-08/47	**4181**	08/47-04/55
S9194S	*07/35*-03/55	↳**15302**	**1041**	*10/35-* 36	**1059**	36- 44	**4151**	44-03/55
S9195S	*07/35*-08/55	↳**15324**	**1042**	*10/35-* 36	**1040**	36-10/45	**4160**	10/45-08/55
S9196S	*07/35-09/53*	↳**15188**	**1039**	*10/35-* 36	**1096**	36-02/47	**4175**	02/47-*09/53*
S9197S	*07/35-08/53*	↳**15182**	**1040**	*10/35-* 36	**1118**	02/37-12/47	**4249**	12/47-*08/53*
9198	*07/35*-12/40	⊗12/40	**1041**	*10/35-* 36	**1055**	36-12/40		
S9199S	*07/35*-03/55	↳**15304**	**1042**	*10/35-* 36	**1073**	36-09/43	**4148**	09/43-03/55

2-T Eastleigh (LSWR bodies)

Trailer Third

TT

9200-S9208S

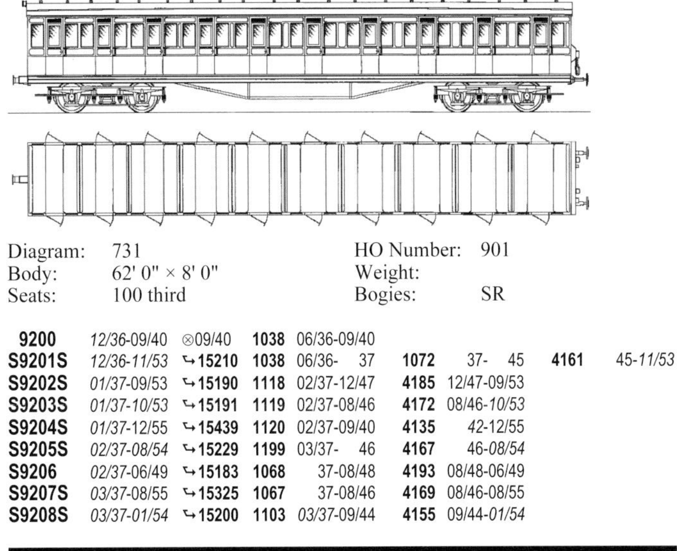

Diagram: 731 HO Number: 901
Body: 62' 0" × 8' 0" Weight:
Seats: 100 third Bogies: SR

9200	*12/36*-09/40	⊗09/40	**1038**	06/36-09/40				
S9201S	*12/36-11/53*	↳**15210**	**1038**	06/36- 37	**1072**	37- 45	**4161**	45-*11/53*
S9202S	*01/37*-09/53	↳**15190**	**1118**	02/37-12/47	**4185**	12/47-09/53		
S9203S	*01/37-10/53*	↳**15191**	**1119**	02/37-08/46	**4172**	08/46-*10/53*		
S9204S	*01/37*-12/55	↳**15439**	**1120**	02/37-09/40	**4135**	*42*-12/55		
S9205S	*02/37-08/54*	↳**15229**	**1199**	03/37- 46	**4167**	46-*08/54*		
S9206	*02/37*-06/49	↳**15183**	**1068**	37-08/48	**4193**	08/48-06/49		
S9207S	*03/37*-08/55	↳**15325**	**1067**	37-08/46	**4169**	08/46-08/55		
S9208S	*03/37-01/54*	↳**15200**	**1103**	*03/37*-09/44	**4155**	09/44-*01/54*		

2-T Lancing (LSWR bodies)

Trailer Third

TT

S9209S-S9255S

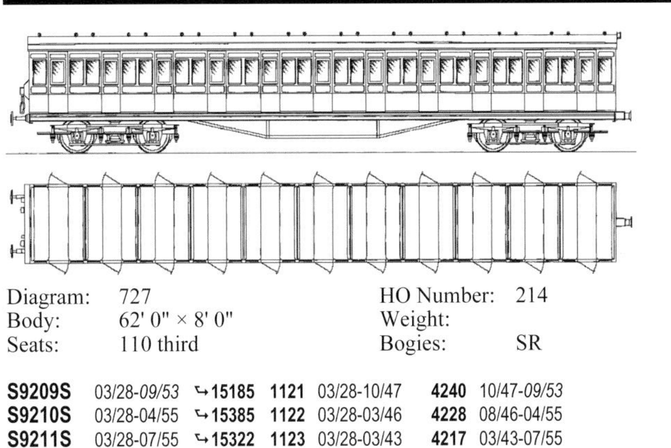

Diagram: 727 HO Number: 214
Body: 62' 0" × 8' 0" Weight:
Seats: 110 third Bogies: SR

S9209S	03/28-*09/53*	↳**15185**	**1121**	03/28-10/47	**4240**	10/47-*09/53*
S9210S	03/28-04/55	↳**15385**	**1122**	03/28-03/46	**4228**	08/46-04/55
S9211S	03/28-07/55	↳**15322**	**1123**	03/28-03/43	**4217**	03/43-07/55

S9212S	03/28-*02/54*	↳**15203**	**1124**	03/28-01/43	**4236**	01/43-*02/54*		
S9213S	03/28-04/55	↳**15314**	**1125**	03/28-09/42	**4199**	09/42-04/55		
S9214S	04/28-04/55	↳**15225**	**1126**	04/28-04/42	**4198**	04/42-04/55		
S9215S	04/28-03/54	↳**15308**	**1127**	04/28-09/43	**4202**	09/43-03/54		
S9216S	04/28-*03/54*	↳**15206**	**1128**	04/28-08/48	**4245**	08/48-*03/54*		
S9217S	04/28-*08/54*	↳**15315**	**1129**	04/28-09/40	**4197**	42-*08/54*		
S9218S	05/28-*07/53*	↳**15186**	**1130**	05/28-05/47	**4235**	05/47-*07/53*		
S9219S	05/28-*12/54*	↳**15295**	**1131**	05/28-02/43	**4223**	02/43-*12/54*		
S9220S	05/28-*12/53*	↳**15211**	**1132**	05/28-02/43	**4222**	02/43-11/47	**4242**	09/48-*12/53*
S9221S	05/28-*04/52*	↳**15387**	**1133**	05/28-11/47	**4233**	11/47-*04/52*		
S9222S	05/28-12/55	↳**15433**	**1134**	05/28-09/43	**4221**	09/43-12/55		
S9223S	05/28-*09/54*	↳**15228**	**1135**	05/28-10/47	**4238**	10/47-*09/54*		
S9224S	05/28-05/55	↳**15309**	**1136**	05/28-11/47	**4234**	11/47-05/55		
S9225S	04/28-11/55	↳**15427**	**1137**	04/28-10/47	**4231**	10/47-11/55		
S9226S	04/28-*06/54*	↳**15294**	**1138**	04/28-11/44	**4227**	12/44-*06/54*		
9227	04/28-10/40	⊗10/40	**1139**	04/28-10/40				
S9228S	05/28-02/55	↳**15300**	**1140**	05/28-01/46	**4209**	01/46-02/55		
S9229S	05/28-05/55	↳**15318**	**1141**	05/28-02/44	**4226**	02/44-05/55		
S9230S	05/28-*07/53*	↳**15181**	**1142**	05/28-02/48	**4241**	02/48-*07/53*		
S9231S	05/28-*07/56*	↳**15223**	**1143**	05/28-08/43	**4218**	08/43-*07/56*		
S9232S	04/28-*06/54*	↳**15285**	**1144**	04/28-03/43	**4200**	03/43-*06/54*		
S9233S	04/28-03/55	↳**15306**	**1145**	04/28-07/47	**4212**	07/47-03/55		
S9234S	11/28-08/53	↳**15222**	**1146**	11/28-11/47	**4237**	11/47-08/53		
S9235S	11/28-*07/54*	↳**15220**	**1147**	11/28-11/42	**4216**	11/42-*07/54*		
S9236S	01/29-*04/54*	↳**15217**	**1148**	01/29-01/46	**4207**	01/46-*04/54*		
S9237S	10/28-10/55	↳**15428**	**1149**	10/28-08/47	**4213**	08/47-10/55		
S9238S	01/29-09/55	↳**15329**	**1150**	01/29-04/44	**4205**	04/44-09/55		
S9239S	01/29-10/55	↳**15395**	**1151**	01/29-08/46	**4210**	08/46-10/55		
S9240S	01/29-*11/53*	↳**15187**	**1152**	01/29-08/48	**4248**	08/48-*11/53*		
S9241S	12/28-09/55	↳**15332**	**1153**	12/28-08/46	**4208**	08/46-09/55		
S9242S	12/28-*10/54*	↳**15284**	**1154**	12/28-09/43	**4220**	09/43-*10/54*		
S9243S	12/28-12/54	↳**15290**	**1155**	12/28-07/48	**4247**	07/48-12/54		
S9244S	02/29-*12/53*	↳**15194**	**1156**	02/29-04/48	**4244**	04/48-*12/53*		
S9245S	02/29-11/55	↳**15443**	**1157**	02/29-08/43	**4219**	08/43-11/55		
S9246S	02/29-10/55	↳**15384**	**1158**	02/29-11/47	**4232**	11/47-10/55		
S9247S	02/29-11/55	↳**15391**	**1159**	02/2911/40	**1139**	12/40-02/44	**4204**	02/44-11/55
S9248S	02/29-*10/54*	↳**15233**	**1160**	02/29-08/46	**4229**	08/46-*10/54*		
S9249S	01/29-*04/54*	↳**15208**	**1161**	01/29-01/44	**4224**	01/44-*04/54*		
S9250S	02/29-*09/53*	↳**15196**	**1162**	02/29-03/48	**4246**	03/48-*09/53*		
S9251S	02/29-*10/54*	↳**15288**	**1163**	02/29-09/43	**4203**	09/43-*10/54*		
S9252S	02/29-03/55	↳**15356**	**1164**	02/29-12/47	**4214**	12/47-03/55		
S9253S	02/29-*05/54*	↳**15293**	**1165**	02/29-12/47	**4239**	12/47-*05/54*		
S9254S	02/29-06/55	↳**15319**	**1166**	02/29-06/43	**4201**	06/43-06/55		
S9255S	02/29-*05/55*	↳**15321**	**1167**	02/29-08/47	**4215**	03/48-*05/55*		

2-T Lancing (ex LBSCR CP stock)

Trailer Third
TT
9256-S9277

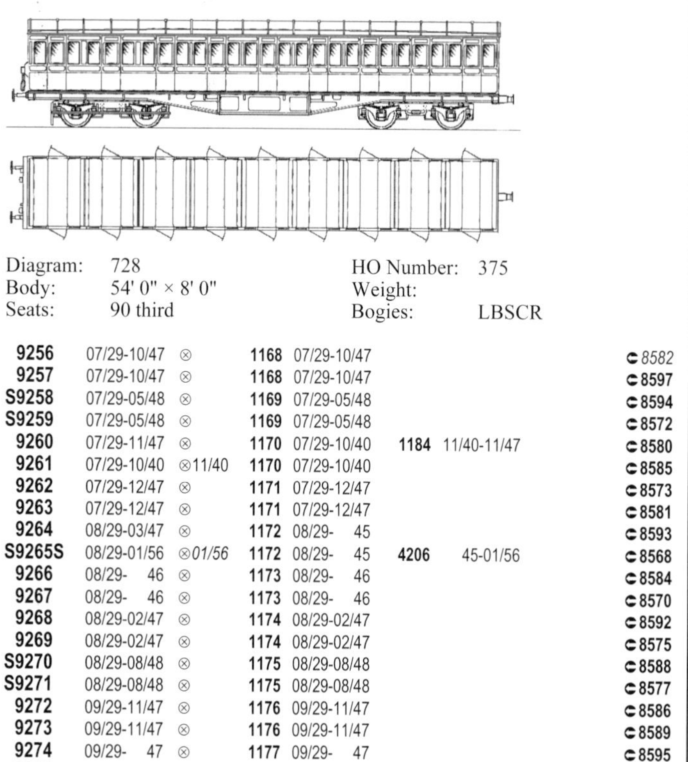

Diagram: 728 | HO Number: 375
Body: 54' 0" × 8' 0" | Weight:
Seats: 90 third | Bogies: LBSCR

9256	07/29-10/47	⊗	**1168**	07/29-10/47			⊂*8582*
9257	07/29-10/47	⊗	**1168**	07/29-10/47			⊂8597
S9258	07/29-05/48	⊗	**1169**	07/29-05/48			⊂8594
S9259	07/29-05/48	⊗	**1169**	07/29-05/48			⊂8572
9260	07/29-11/47	⊗	**1170**	07/29-10/40	**1184**	11/40-11/47	⊂8580
9261	07/29-10/40	⊗11/40	**1170**	07/29-10/40			⊂8585
9262	07/29-12/47	⊗	**1171**	07/29-12/47			⊂8573
9263	07/29-12/47	⊗	**1171**	07/29-12/47			⊂8581
9264	08/29-03/47	⊗	**1172**	08/29- 45			⊂8593
S9265S	08/29-01/56	⊗*01/56*	**1172**	08/29- 45	**4206**	45-01/56	⊂8568
9266	08/29- 46	⊗	**1173**	08/29- 46			⊂8584
9267	08/29- 46	⊗	**1173**	08/29- 46			⊂8570
9268	08/29-02/47	⊗	**1174**	08/29-02/47			⊂8592
9269	08/29-02/47	⊗	**1174**	08/29-02/47			⊂8575
S9270	08/29-08/48	⊗	**1175**	08/29-08/48			⊂8588
S9271	08/29-08/48	⊗	**1175**	08/29-08/48			⊂8577
9272	09/29-11/47	⊗	**1176**	09/29-11/47			⊂8586
9273	09/29-11/47	⊗	**1176**	09/29-11/47			⊂8589
9274	09/29- 47	⊗	**1177**	09/29- 47			⊂8595
9275	09/29- 47	⊗	**1177**	09/29- 47			⊂8576
S9276	09/29-08/48	⊗	**1178**	09/29-08/48	Grounded Eastleigh Works 08/48		⊂8590
S9277	09/29-08/48	⊗	**1178**	09/29-08/48			⊂8591

2-T Lancing (ex LBSCR CP stock)

Trailer Third
TT
S9278-9281

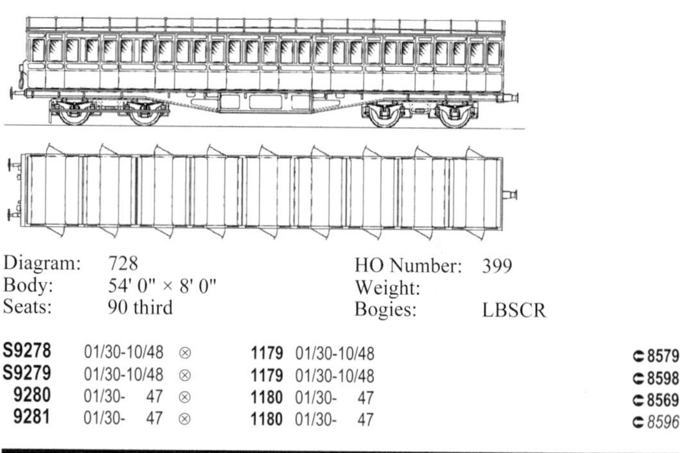

Diagram: 728 | HO Number: 399
Body: 54' 0" × 8' 0" | Weight:
Seats: 90 third | Bogies: LBSCR

S9278	01/30-10/48	⊗	**1179**	01/30-10/48	⊂8579
S9279	01/30-10/48	⊗	**1179**	01/30-10/48	⊂8598
9280	01/30- 47	⊗	**1180**	01/30- 47	⊂8569
9281	01/30- 47	⊗	**1180**	01/30- 47	⊂*8596*

2-T Lancing (ex LBSCR CP/CW stock)

Trailer Third
TT
S9282-9293

Odd Numbers:

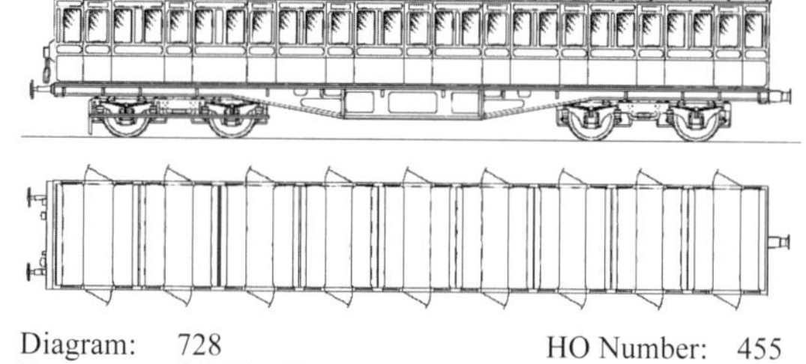

Diagram: 728 | HO Number: 455
Body: 54' 0" × 8' 0" | Weight:
Seats: 90 third | Bogies: LBSCR

Even Numbers (9282/88/90):

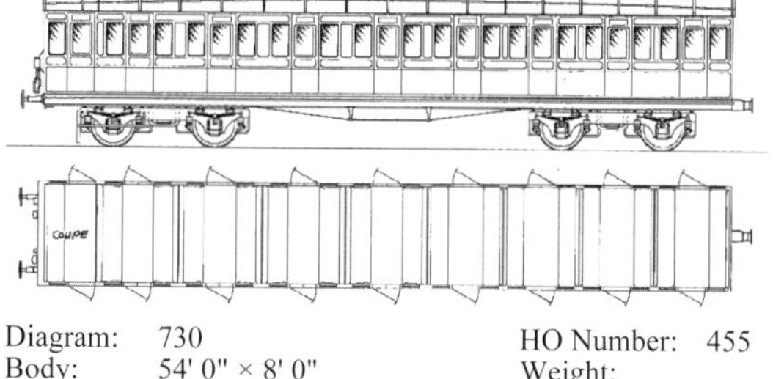

Diagram: 730 | HO Number: 455
Body: 54' 0" × 8' 0" | Weight:
Seats: 85 third | Bogies: LBSCR

Even Numbers (9284/86/92):

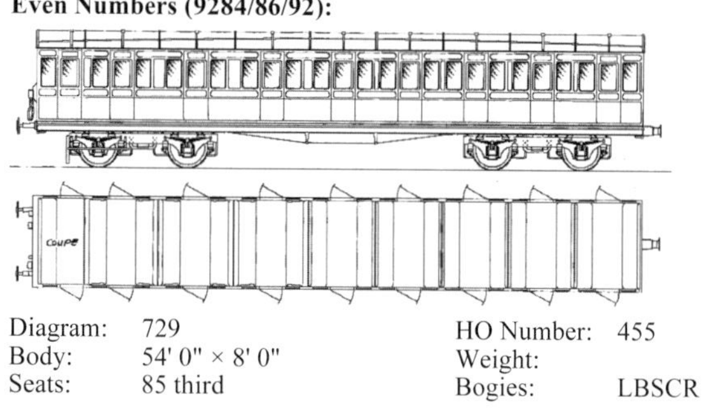

Diagram: 729 | HO Number: 455
Body: 54' 0" × 8' 0" | Weight:
Seats: 85 third | Bogies: LBSCR

S9282	02/30-05/48	⊗	**1181**	02/30-05/48	⊂9908
S9283	02/30-05/48	⊗	**1181**	02/30-05/48	⊂8599
9284	02/30-04/47	⊗	**1182**	02/30-04/47	⊂9841

9285	02/30-04/47 ⊗	**1182**	02/30-04/47			⊂**8583**
9286	02/30- 45 ⊗	**1183**	02/30- 45			⊂**9856**
9287	02/30- 45 ⊗	**1183**	02/30- 45			⊂**8578**
9288	02/30-11/47 ⊗	**1184**	02/30-11/47			⊂**9893**
9289	02/30-11/40 ⊗11/40	**1184**	02/30-11/40			⊂**8587**
9290	02/30-10/40 ⊗10/40	**1185**	03/30-10/40			⊂**9894**
9291	03/30-10/41 ⊗	**1185**	03/30-10/40	**1054**	10/40-10/41	⊂**8571**
9292	03/30-06/47 ⊗	**1186**	03/30-06/47			⊂*9895*
9293	03/30-06/47 ⊗	**1186**	03/30-06/47			⊂**8600**

2-T Lancing (ex LBSCR CP stock)
Trailer Third
TT
S9294-S9295

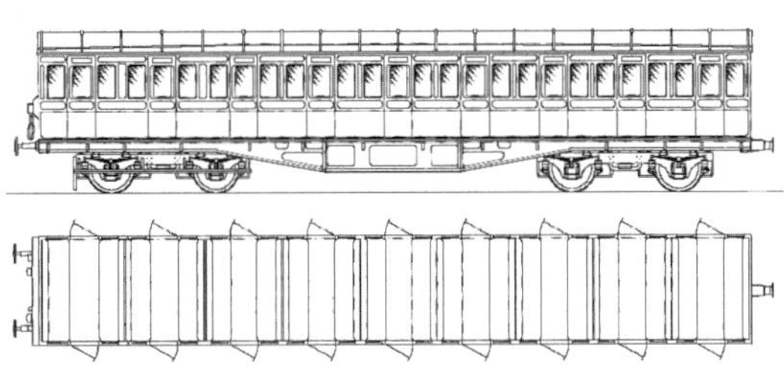

Diagram: 728 HO Number: 516
Body: 54' 0" × 8' 0" Weight:
Seats: 90 third Bogies: LBSCR

S9294	07/30-04/48 ⊗	**1187**	07/30-04/48	⊂**8567**
S9295	07/30-04/48 ⊗	**1187**	07/30-04/48	⊂**8574**

2-T Lancing (ex SECR hauled stock)
Trailer Third
TT
9296

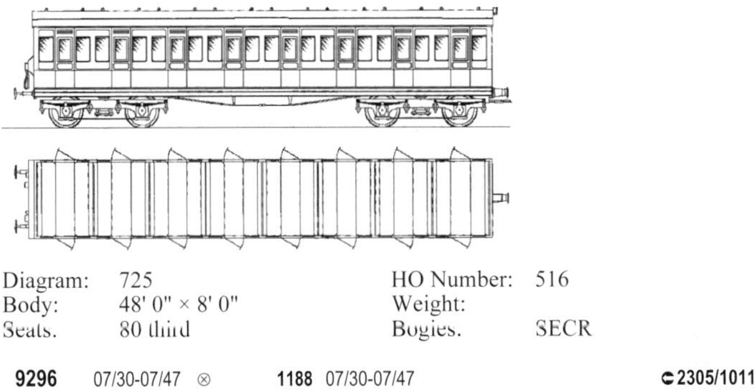

Diagram: 725 HO Number: 516
Body: 48' 0" × 8' 0" Weight:
Seats: 80 third Bogies: SECR

9296 07/30-07/47 ⊗ **1188** 07/30-07/47 ⊂**2305/1011**

2-T Lancing (ex LSWR body)
Trailer Third
TT
S9297S

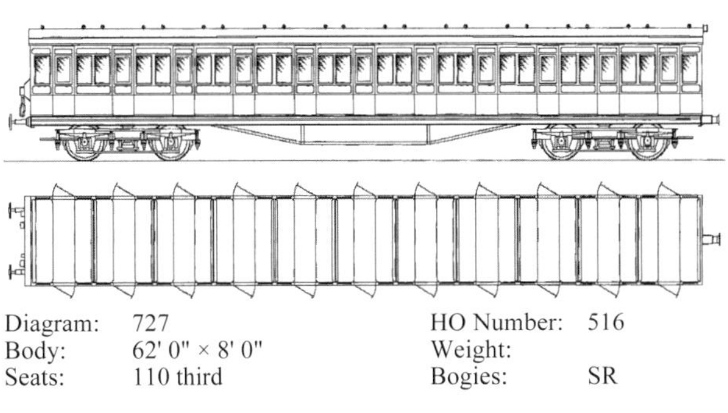

Diagram: 727 HO Number: 516
Body: 62' 0" × 8' 0" Weight:
Seats: 110 third Bogies: SR

S9297S 07/30-*06/54* ↪**15221** **1188** 07/30-07/47 **4211** 07/47-*06/54*

2-T Eastleigh (LSWR body)
Trailer Third
TT
S9298S

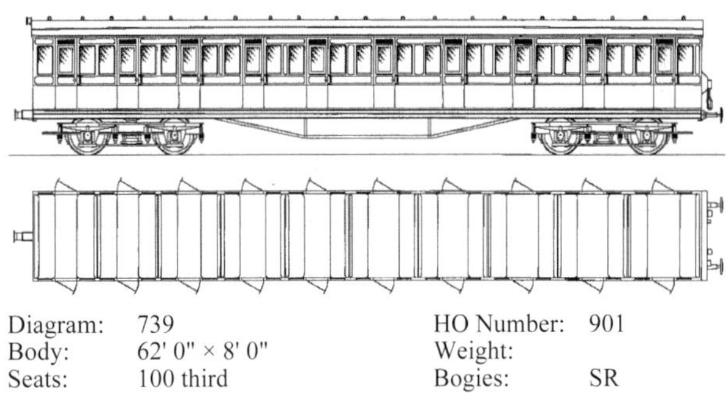

Diagram: 739 HO Number: 901
Body: 62' 0" × 8' 0" Weight:
Seats: 100 third Bogies: SR

S9298S 01/37-01/56 ⊗*01/56* **1098** 03/37-05/47 **4176** 05/47-01/56

2-T Eastleigh (LSWR body)
Trailer Third
TT
S9299S

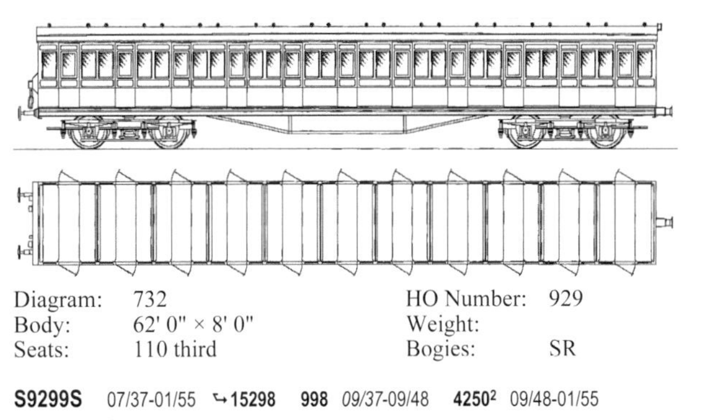

Diagram: 732 HO Number: 929
Body: 62' 0" × 8' 0" Weight:
Seats: 110 third Bogies: SR

S9299S 07/37-01/55 ↪**15298** **998** *09/37*-09/48 **4250**[2] 09/48-01/55

2-T Eastleigh (LSWR body)
Trailer Third
TT
S9300S

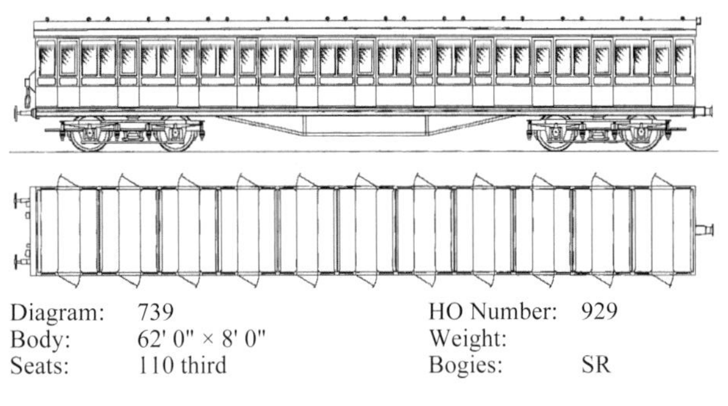

Diagram: 739 HO Number: 929
Body: 62' 0" × 8' 0" Weight:
Seats: 110 third Bogies: SR

S9300S 07/37-08/55 ↪**15326** **999** *09/37*-12/45 **4164** 12/45-08/55

3-SUB Lancing/Ashford (LSWR body)

Trailer Composite
TC
S9301S

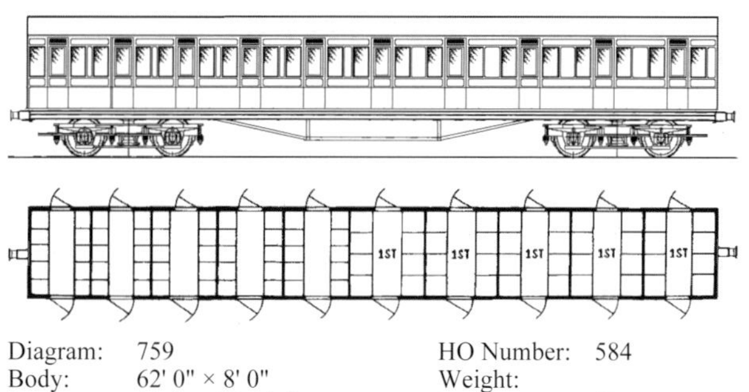

Diagram:	759	HO Number:	584
Body:	62' 0" × 8' 0"	Weight:	
Seats:	40 first 50 third	Bogies:	SR

S9301S	11/30-*12/53*	↳**15202**	**1783**	*11/30-02/48*	**4594**	*03/49-12/53*

3-SUB Lancing/Ashford (LSWR bodies)

Trailer Composite
TC
S9302S-S9303S

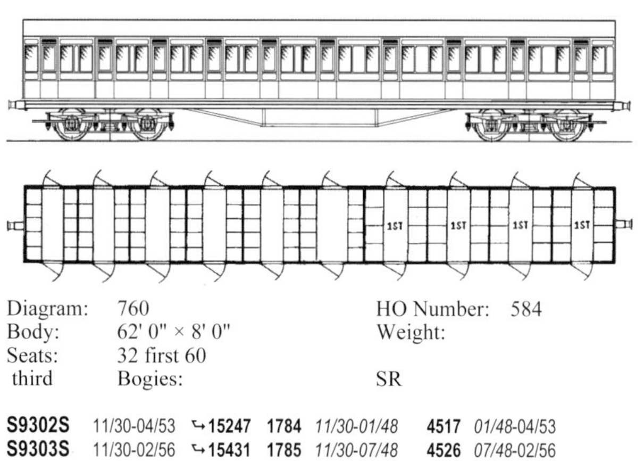

Diagram:	760	HO Number:	584
Body:	62' 0" × 8' 0"	Weight:	
Seats:	32 first 60		
third	Bogies:		SR

S9302S	11/30-04/53	↳**15247**	**1784**	*11/30-01/48*	**4517**	*01/48*-04/53
S9303S	11/30-02/56	↳**15431**	**1785**	*11/30-07/48*	**4526**	*07/48*-02/56

3-SUB Lancing/Ashford (LSWR bodies)

Trailer Composite
TC
9304-S9306S

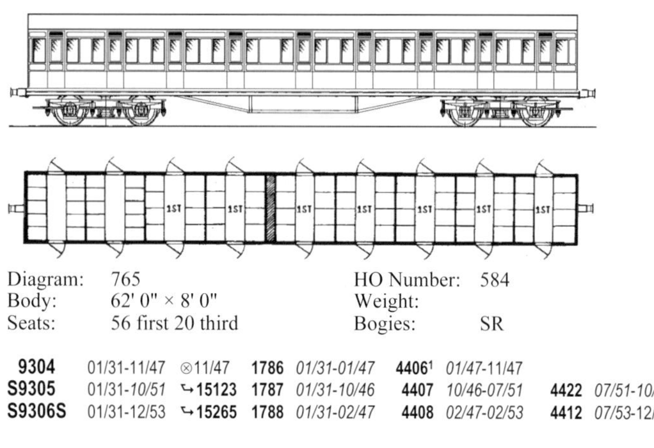

Diagram:	765	HO Number:	584
Body:	62' 0" × 8' 0"	Weight:	
Seats:	56 first 20 third	Bogies:	SR

9304	01/31-11/47	⊗11/47	**1786**	*01/31-01/47*	**4406**[1]	*01/47*-11/47		
S9305	01/31-*10/51*	↳**15123**	**1787**	*01/31-10/46*	**4407**	*10/46-07/51*	**4422**	*07/51-10/51*
S9306S	01/31-12/53	↳**15265**	**1788**	*01/31-02/47*	**4408**	*02/47-02/53*	**4412**	*07/53*-12/53

3-SUB Lancing/Ashford (LSWR bodies)

Trailer Composite
TC
S9307S-S9343S

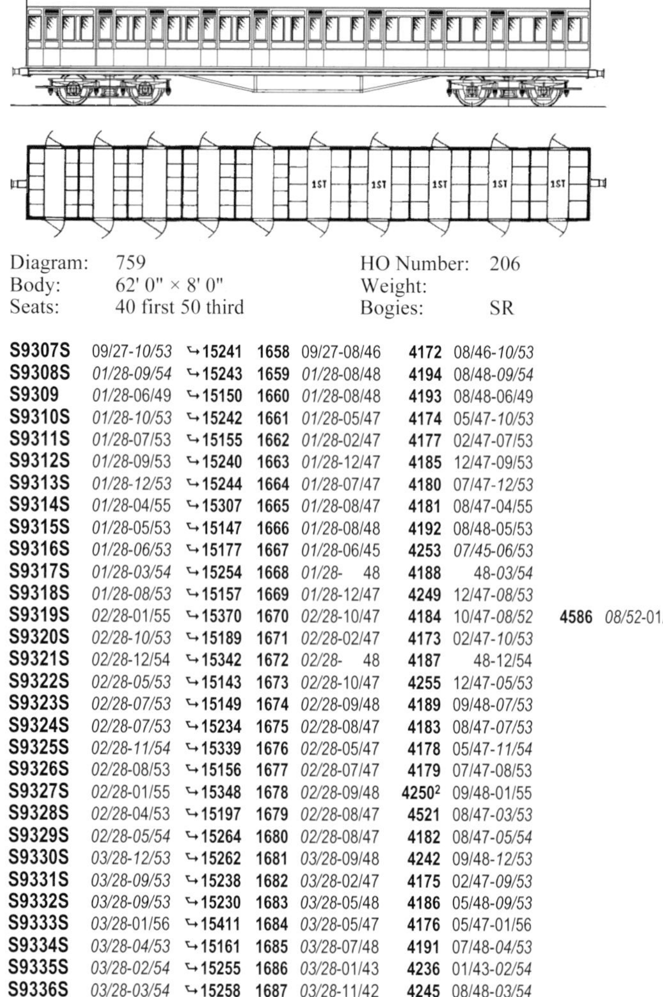

Diagram:	759	HO Number:	206
Body:	62' 0" × 8' 0"	Weight:	
Seats:	40 first 50 third	Bogies:	SR

S9307S	09/27-*10/53*	↳**15241**	**1658**	09/27-08/46	**4172**	08/46-*10/53*		
S9308S	*01/28-09/54*	↳**15243**	**1659**	*01/28*-08/48	**4194**	08/48-*09/54*		
S9309	*01/28*-06/49	↳**15150**	**1660**	*01/28*-08/48	**4193**	08/48-06/49		
S9310S	*01/28-10/53*	↳**15242**	**1661**	*01/28*-05/47	**4174**	05/47-*10/53*		
S9311S	*01/28*-07/53	↳**15155**	**1662**	*01/28*-02/47	**4177**	02/47-07/53		
S9312S	*01/28*-09/53	↳**15240**	**1663**	*01/28*-12/47	**4185**	12/47-09/53		
S9313S	*01/28-12/53*	↳**15244**	**1664**	*01/28*-07/47	**4180**	07/47-*12/53*		
S9314S	*01/28*-04/55	↳**15307**	**1665**	*01/28*-08/47	**4181**	08/47-04/55		
S9315S	*01/28*-05/53	↳**15147**	**1666**	*01/28*-08/48	**4192**	08/48-05/53		
S9316S	*01/28-06/53*	↳**15177**	**1667**	*01/28*-06/45	**4253**	*07/45-06/53*		
S9317S	*01/28-03/54*	↳**15254**	**1668**	*01/28-* 48	**4188**	48-*03/54*		
S9318S	*01/28-08/53*	↳**15157**	**1669**	*01/28*-12/47	**4249**	12/47-*08/53*		
S9319S	*02/28*-01/55	↳**15370**	**1670**	*02/28*-10/47	**4184**	10/47-*08/52*	**4586**	*08/52*-01/55
S9320S	*02/28-10/53*	↳**15189**	**1671**	*02/28*-02/47	**4173**	02/47-*10/53*		
S9321S	*02/28*-12/54	↳**15342**	**1672**	*02/28-* 48	**4187**	48-12/54		
S9322S	*02/28-05/53*	↳**15143**	**1673**	*02/28*-10/47	**4255**	12/47-*05/53*		
S9323S	*02/28-07/53*	↳**15149**	**1674**	*02/28*-09/48	**4189**	09/48-*07/53*		
S9324S	*02/28-07/53*	↳**15234**	**1675**	*02/28*-08/47	**4183**	08/47-*07/53*		
S9325S	*02/28-11/54*	↳**15339**	**1676**	*02/28*-05/47	**4178**	05/47-*11/54*		
S9326S	*02/28*-08/53	↳**15156**	**1677**	*02/28*-07/47	**4179**	07/47-08/53		
S9327S	*02/28*-01/55	↳**15348**	**1678**	*02/28*-09/48	**4250**[2]	09/48-01/55		
S9328S	*02/28*-04/53	↳**15197**	**1679**	*02/28*-08/47	**4521**	08/47-*03/53*		
S9329S	*02/28-05/54*	↳**15264**	**1680**	*02/28*-08/47	**4182**	08/47-*05/54*		
S9330S	*03/28-12/53*	↳**15262**	**1681**	*03/28*-09/48	**4242**	09/48-*12/53*		
S9331S	*03/28-09/53*	↳**15238**	**1682**	*03/28*-02/47	**4175**	02/47-*09/53*		
S9332S	*03/28-09/53*	↳**15230**	**1683**	*03/28*-05/48	**4186**	05/48-*09/53*		
S9333S	*03/28*-01/56	↳**15411**	**1684**	*03/28*-05/47	**4176**	05/47-01/56		
S9334S	*03/28-04/53*	↳**15161**	**1685**	*03/28*-07/48	**4191**	07/48-*04/53*		
S9335S	*03/28-02/54*	↳**15255**	**1686**	*03/28*-01/43	**4236**	01/43-*02/54*		
S9336S	*03/28-03/54*	↳**15258**	**1687**	*03/28*-11/42	**4245**	08/48-*03/54*		
S9337S	*03/28-05/54*	↳**15214**	**1688**	*03/28*-12/47	**4239**	12/47-*05/54*		
S9338S	*03/28*-08/53	↳**15175**	**1689**	*03/28*-11/47	**4237**	11/47-08/53		
S9339S	*03/28-11/53*	↳**15237**	**1690**	*03/28*-08/48	**4248**	08/48-*11/53*		
S9340S	*03/28-08/53*	↳**15153**	**1691**	*03/28*-07/48	**4243**	07/48-*08/53*		
9341	*04/28*-06/44	⊗08/44	**1692**	*04/28*-06/44				
S9342S	*04/28-12/53*	↳**15245**	**1693**	*04/28*-04/48	**4244**	04/48-*12/53*		
S9343S	*04/28*-12/54	↳**15340**	**1694**	*04/28*-07/48	**4247**	07/48-12/54		

3-SUB Lancing/Ashford (LSWR bodies)

Trailer Composite
TC
S9344S

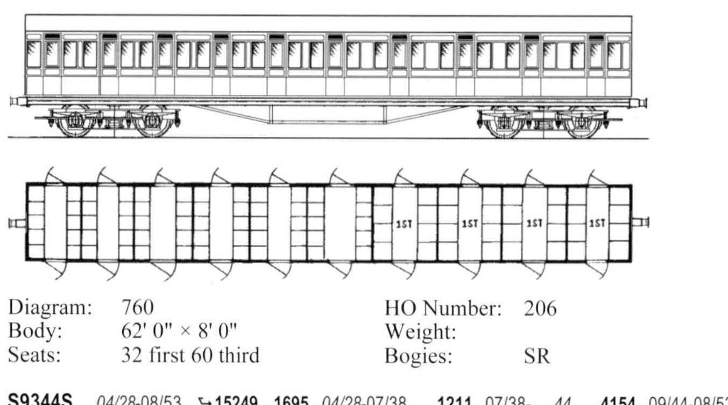

Diagram:	760	HO Number:	206
Body:	62' 0" × 8' 0"	Weight:	
Seats:	32 first 60 third	Bogies:	SR

S9344S	*04/28*-08/53	↳**15249**	**1695**	*04/28*-07/38	**1211**	07/38- *44*	**4154**	09/44-08/53

3-SUB Lancing/Ashford (LSWR bodies)

Trailer Composite
TC
S9345S-S9350S

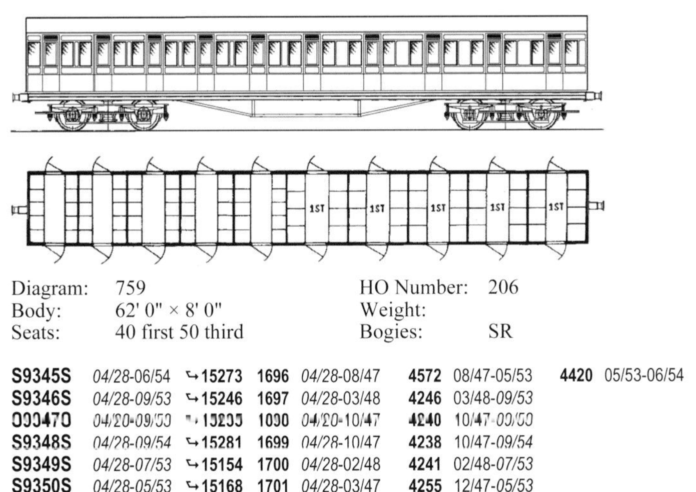

Diagram:	759			HO Number:	206			
Body:	62' 0" × 8' 0"			Weight:				
Seats:	40 first 50 third			Bogies:	SR			

No.	Dates		Unit	Dates	Unit	Dates	Unit	Dates
S9345S	*04/28-06/54*	↳**15273**	**1696**	*04/28-08/47*	**4572**	08/47-05/53	**4420**	05/53-06/54
S9346S	*04/28-09/53*	↳**15246**	**1697**	*04/28-03/48*	**4246**	03/48-*09/53*		
S9347S	*04/28-09/53*	↳**15235**	**1698**	*04/28-10/47*	**4240**	10/47-*09/53*		
S9348S	*04/28-09/54*	↳**15281**	**1699**	*04/28-10/47*	**4238**	10/47-*09/54*		
S9349S	*04/28-07/53*	↳**15154**	**1700**	*04/28-02/48*	**4241**	02/48-*07/53*		
S9350S	*04/28-05/53*	↳**15168**	**1701**	*04/28-03/47*	**4255**	12/47-*05/53*		

3-SUB Eastleigh

Trailer Composite
TC
9351-9371

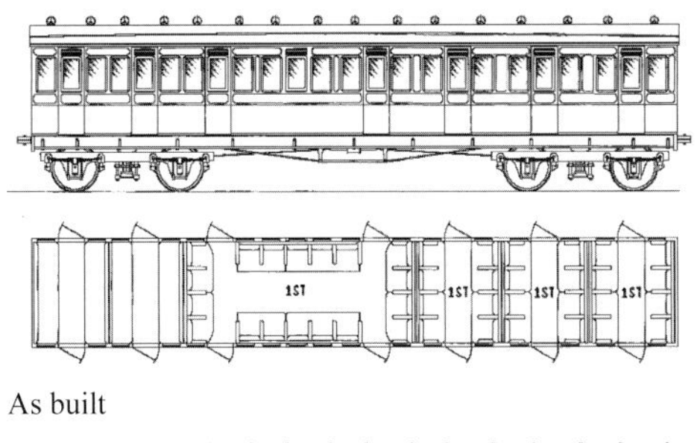

As built

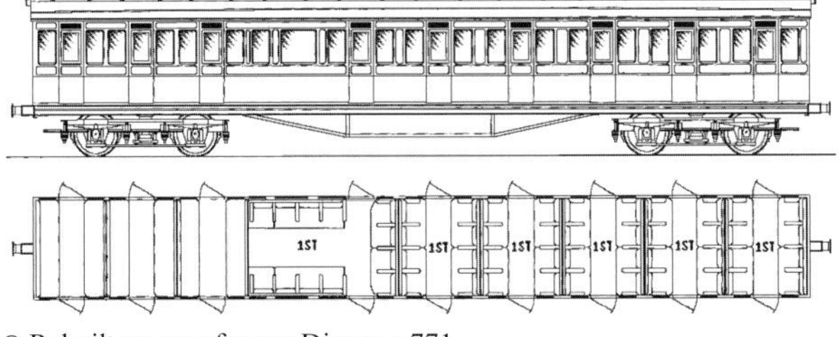

① Rebuilt on new frames Diagram 771

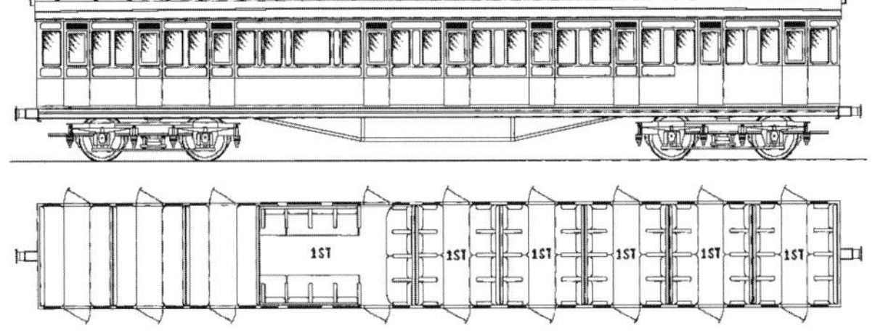

② Diagram 771. Steel lower panelling on added compartments.

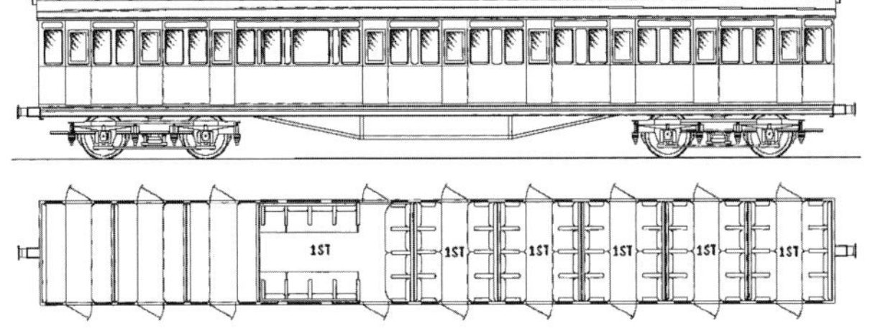

③ Diagram 771. Steel lower panelling on the whole body.

Diagram:	750 later 771	HO Number:	LSWR
Body:	49' 0" × 8' 0" later 62' 0" × 8' 0"	Weight:	29t
Seats:	42 first 20 third later 52 first 30 third	Bogies:	LSWR later SR

No.		Dates		Unit	Dates	Unit	Dates	Unit	Dates	
9351		23-12/39	⊗*12/39*	**1202**	23-12/39					⊂**7552**
S9352S	②	23-07/55	↳**15373**	**1206**	23- *38*	**1262**	*38*-03/43	**4217**	03/43-07/55	⊂**7556**
9353		23-12/39	⊗*12/39*	**1210**	23-12/39					⊂**7560**
S9354S	③	23-05/55	↳**15363**	**1214**	23-02/44	**4226**	02/44-05/55			⊂**7564**
S9355S	③	23-10/55	↳**15394**	**1218**	23-11/47	**4232**	11/47-10/55			⊂**7568**
S9356S	①	23-*10/54*	↳**15283**	**1222**	23-08/46	**4229**	08/46-*10/54*			⊂**7572**
S9357S	③	23-*12/54*	↳**15345**	**1226**	23-02/43	**4223**	02/43-*12/54*			⊂**7576**
S9358S	③	23-04/55	↳**15388**	**1230**	23-08/46	**4228**	08/46-04/55			⊂**7580**
S9359S	②	23-*07/54*	↳**15270**	**1234**	23-11/42	**4216**	11/42-*07/54*			⊂**7584**
S9360S	③	23-10/54	↳**15282**	**1238**	23-09/46	**4230**	09/46-10/54			⊂**7588**
S9361S	③	23-*04/54*	↳**15259**	**1242**	23-01/44	**4224**	01/44-*04/54*			⊂**7592**
S9362S	①	23-*10/54*	↳**15335**	**1246**	23-09/43	**4220**	09/43-*10/54*			⊂**7596**
S9363S	③	23-11/55	↳**15392**	**1250**	23-10/47	**4231**	10/47-11/55			⊂**7600**
S9364S	③	23-12/55	↳**15408**	**1254**	23-09/43	**4221**	09/43-12/55			⊂**7604**
S9365S	②	23-11/55	↳**15406**	**1258**	23-08/43	**4219**	08/43-11/55			⊂**7608**
S9366S	②	23-*07/56*	↳**15272**	**1262**	23- *38*	**1206**	*38*-08/43	**4218**	08/43-*07/56*	⊂**7612**
S9367S	②	23-*12/53*	↳**15201**	**1266**	23-11/47	**4233**	11/47-*04/52*	**4594**	10/52-*12/53*	⊂**7616**
S9368S	③	23-05/54	↳**15263**	**1270**	23-12/43	**4225**	12/43-05/54			⊂**7620**
S9369S	③	23-05/55	↳**15359**	**1274**	23-11/47	**4234**	11/47-05/55			⊂**7624**
S9370S	①	23-*08/54*	↳**15344**	**1278**	23-12/41	**4227**	12/41-*08/54*			●**7628**
9371	②	23-11/47	⊗11/47	**1282**	23-02/43	**4222**	02/43-11/47			⊂**7632**

3-SUB Eastleigh

Trailer Composite
TC
S9372S-S9413S

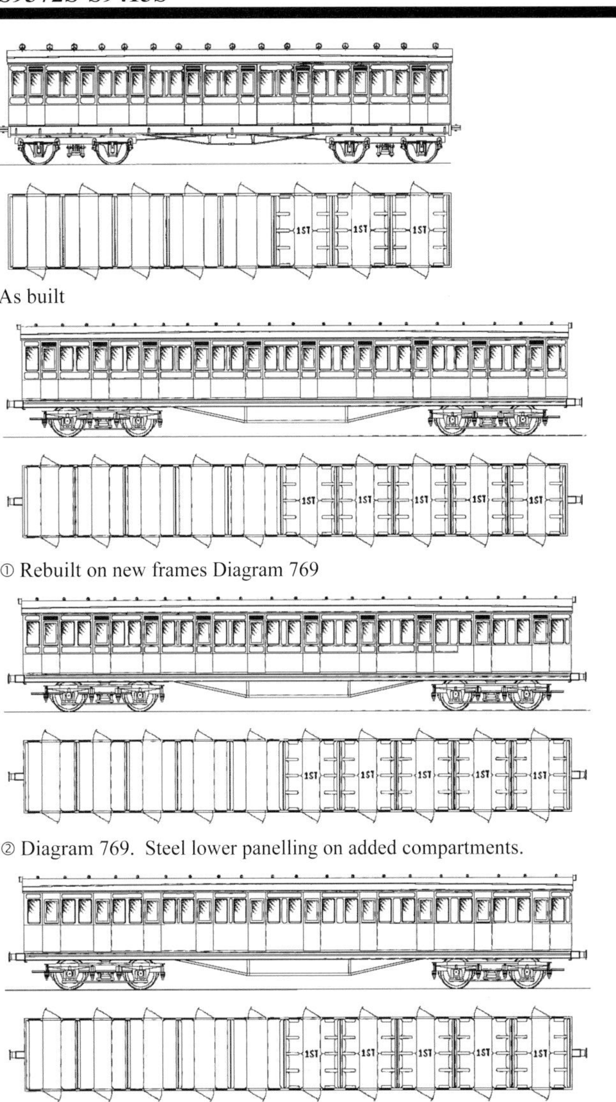

As built

① Rebuilt on new frames Diagram 769

② Diagram 769. Steel lower panelling on added compartments.

③ Diagram 769. Steel lower panelling on the whole body.

Diagram:	751 later 769	HO Number:	LSWR
Body:	49' 0" × 8' 0" later 62' 0" × 8' 0"	Weight:	29t

Seats: 24 first 50 third later 40 first 50 third Bogies: LSWR later SR

S9372S	①	23-08/55	↪**15376**	**1203**	23-08/46	**4169**	08/46-08/55			**⊂7553**
S9373S	③	23-12/55	↪**15432**	**1204**	23-04/41	**4131**	04/41-12/55			**⊂7554**
S9374S	①	23-08/55	↪**15375**	**1207**	23-10/45	**4160**	10/45-08/55			**⊂7557**
S9375S	①	23-08/55	↪**15378**	**1208**	23-06/44	**4152**	06/44-08/55			**⊂7558**
S9376S	①	23-*07/53*	↪**15236**	**1211**	23-07/38	**1695**	07/38-05/47	**4235**	05/47-*07/53*	**⊂7561**
S9377S	③	23-*05/54*	↪**15343**	**1212**	23-*11/42*	**4146**	*11/42-05/54*			**⊂7562**
S9378S	①	23-09/54	↪**15280**	**1215**	23-09/44	**4153**	09/44-09/54			**⊂7565**
S9379S	③	23-09/55	↪**15399**	**1216**	23-06/45	**4158**	06/45-09/55			**⊂7566**
S9380S	①	23-11/55	↪**15401**	**1219**	23- 45	**4162**	45-11/55			**⊂7569**
S9381S	③	23-06/55	↪**15367**	**1220**	23- 44	**4156**	44-06/55			**⊂7570**
S9382S	②	23-01/56	↪**15409**	**1223**	23-08/46	**4170**	08/46-01/56			**⊂7573**
S9383S	②	23-08/55	↪**15377**	**1224**	23-12/45	**4164**	12/45-08/55			**⊂7574**
S9384S	①	23-02/55	↪**15360**	**1227**	23-01/43	**4141**	01/43-02/55			**⊂7577**
S9385S	①	23-12/54	↪**15349**	**1228**	23- 46	**4165**	46-12/54			**⊂7578**
S9386S	①	23-*06/54*	↪**15271**	**1231**	23-09/42	**4140**	09/42-*06/54*			**⊂7581**
S9387S	①	23-07/55	↪**15368**	**1232**	23-09/42	**4133**	09/42-07/55			**⊂7582**
S9388S	③	23-04/55	↪**15361**	**1235**	23-09/42	**4138**	09/42-04/55			**⊂7585**
S9389S	③	23-12/55	↪**15393**	**1236**	23-10/45	**4159**	10/45-12/55			**⊂7586**
S9390S	①	23-02/55	↪**15386**	**1239**	23-02/42	**4132**	02/42-02/55			**⊂7589**
S9391S	①	23-12/55	↪**15405**	**1240**	23- *42*	**4135**	*42*-12/55			**⊂7590**
S9392S	①	23-10/55	↪**15389**	**1243**	23-11/42	**4150**	43-10/55			**⊂7593**
S9393S	①	23-*08/54*	↪**15279**	**1244**	23- 46	**4167**	46-*08/54*			**⊂7594**
S9394S	③	23-03/53	↪**15350**	**1247**	23-03/42	**4134**	03/42-03/53			**⊂7597**
S9395S	①	23-*11/54*	↪**15337**	**1248**	23-10/42	**4147**	11/42-*11/54*			**⊂7598**
S9396S	①	23-12/55	↪**15407**	**1251**	23- 46	**4166**	46-12/55			**⊂7601**
S9397S	①	23-03/55	↪**15352**	**1252**	23- 44	**4151**	44-03/55			**⊂7602**
S9398S	①	23-*09/54*	↪**15374**	**1255**	23-02/43	**4143**	02/43-*09/54*			**⊂7605**
S9399S	①	23-*07/54*	↪**15274**	**1256**	23-05/45	**4157**	05/45-*07/54*			**⊂7606**
S9400S	①	23-*12/54*	↪**15341**	**1259**	23-11/42	**4145**	11/42-*12/54*			**⊂7609**
S9401S	①	23-*11/54*	↪**15347**	**1260**	23-07/42	**4137**	07/42-*11/54*			**⊂7610**
S9402S	①	23-09/54	↪**15276**	**1263**	23- 45	**4163**	45-09/54			**⊂7613**
S9403S	①	23-*09/54*	↪**15382**	**1264**	23-01/42	**4144**	01/42-*09/54*			**⊂7614**
S9404S	①	23-*01/54*	↪**15251**	**1267**	23-08/44	**1692**	08/44-09/44	**4155**	09/44-*01/54*	**⊂7617**
S9405S	①	23-06/55	↪**15364**	**1268**	23-08/46	**4171**	08/46-06/55			**⊂7618**
S9406S	①	23-*01/54*	↪**15253**	**1271**	23-09/42	**4139**	09/42-*01/54*			**⊂7621**
S9407S	②	23-06/56	↪**15444**	**1272**	23-11/42	**4142**	11/42-06/56			**⊂7622**
S9408S	③	23-11/55	↪**15416**	**1275**	23-09/43	**4149**	09/43-11/55			**⊂7625**
S9409S	②	23-*11/53*	↪**15248**	**1276**	23- 45	**4161**	45-*11/53*			**⊂7626**
S9410S	①	23-03/55	↪**15354**	**1279**	23-09/43	**4148**	09/43-03/55			**⊂7629**
S9411S	①	23-*05/54*	↪**15268**	**1280**	23-09/42	**4136**	09/42-*05/54*			**⊂7630**
S9412S	①	23-07/53	↪**15148**	**1283**	23-10/40	**1305**	04/41-*02/46*	**4320**	*02/46*-05/50	
				4416	*05/50*-07/53					**⊂7633**
S9413S	①	23-01/55	↪**15353**	**1284**	23-01/46	**4168**	01/46-01/55			**⊂7634**

3-SUB Eastleigh

Trailer Composite

TC

S9414S-S9434S

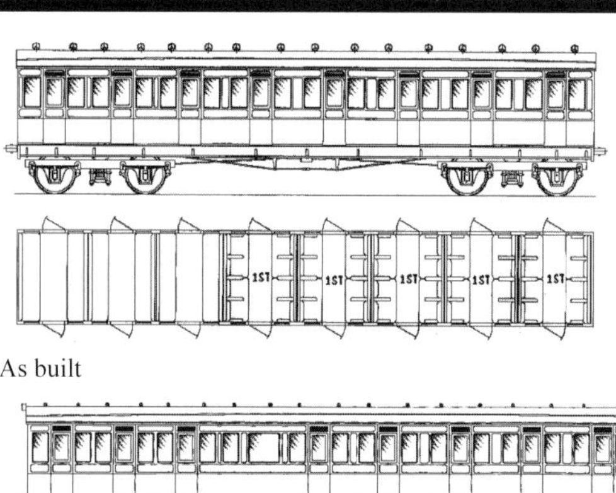

As built

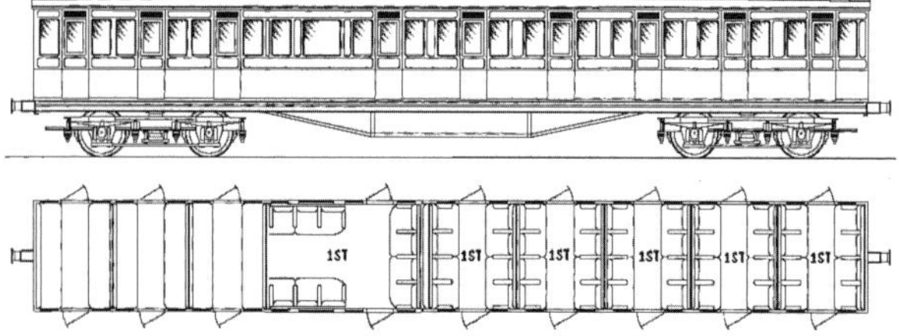

① Rebuilt on new frames Diagram 772

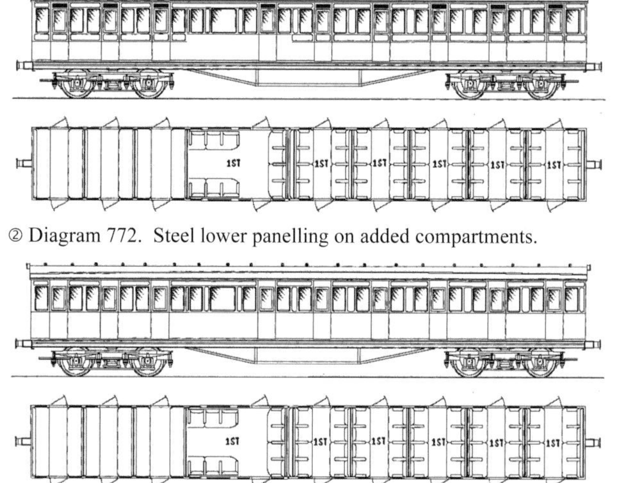

② Diagram 772. Steel lower panelling on added compartments.

③ Diagram 772. Steel lower panelling on the whole body.

Diagram:	752 later 772	HO Number:	LSWR
Body:	51' 0" × 8' 0" later 62' 0" × 8' 0"	Weight:	29t
Seats:	40 first 30 third later 50 first 30 third	Bogies:	LSWR later SR

S9414S	③	23-*06/54*	↪**15334**	**1201**	23-03/43	**4200**	03/43-*06/54*	**⊂7551**
S9415S	②	23-*06/54*	↪**15269**	**1205**	23-07/47	**4211**	07/47-*06/54*	**⊂7555**
S9416S	③	23-03/54	↪**15358**	**1209**	23-08/43	**4202**	09/43-03/54	**⊂7559**
S9417S	③	23-04/55	↪**15365**	**1213**	23-09/42	**4199**	09/42-04/55	**⊂7563**
S9418S	③	23-*10/54*	↪**15338**	**1217**	23-09/43	**4203**	09/43-*10/54*	**⊂7567**
S9419S	③	23-*04/54*	↪**15351**	**1221**	23-01/46	**4207**	01/46-*04/54*	**⊂7571**
S9420S	③	23-09/55	↪**15383**	**1225**	23-08/46	**4208**	08/46-09/55	**⊂7575**
S9421S	③	23-06/55	↪**15369**	**1229**	23-06/43	**4201**	06/43-06/55	**⊂7579**
S9422S	③	23-09/55	↪**15380**	**1233**	23-04/44	**4205**	04/44-09/55	**⊂7583**
S9423S	②	23-04/55	↪**15278**	**1237**	23-04/42	**4198**	04/42-04/55	**⊂7587**
S9424S	②	23-11/55	↪**15390**	**1241**	23-02/44	**4204**	02/44-11/55	**⊂7591**
S9425S	③	23-02/55	↪**15379**	**1245**	23-01/46	**4209**	01/46-02/55	**⊂7595**
S9426S	③	23-10/55	↪**15412**	**1249**	23-08/47	**4213**	08/47-10/55	**⊂7599**
S9427S	③	23-10/55	↪**15397**	**1253**	23-08/46	**4210**	08/46-10/55	**⊂7603**
S9428S	③	23-05/55	↪**15312**	**1257**	23-01/42	**4195**	01/42-05/55	**⊂7607**
S9429S	①	23-01/56	↪**15410**	**1261**	23- 45	**4206**	45-01/56	**⊂7611**
S9430S	②	23-03/55	↪**15357**	**1265**	23-12/47	**4214**	12/47-03/55	**⊂7615**
S9431S	②	23-06/55	↪**15381**	**1269**	23-10/42	**4196**	10/42-06/55	**⊂7619**
S9432S	③	23-05/56	↪**15426**	**1273**	23-03/48	**4215**	03/48-05/56	**⊂7623**
S9433S	③	23-03/55	↪**15355**	**1277**	23-07/47	**4212**	07/47-03/55	**⊂7627**
S9434S	③	23-*08/54*	↪**15366**	**1281**	23- 42	**4197**	42-*08/54*	**⊂7631**

3-SUB Cammell Laird/ Midland RC&W

Trailer Composite

TC

S9435S-S9460S

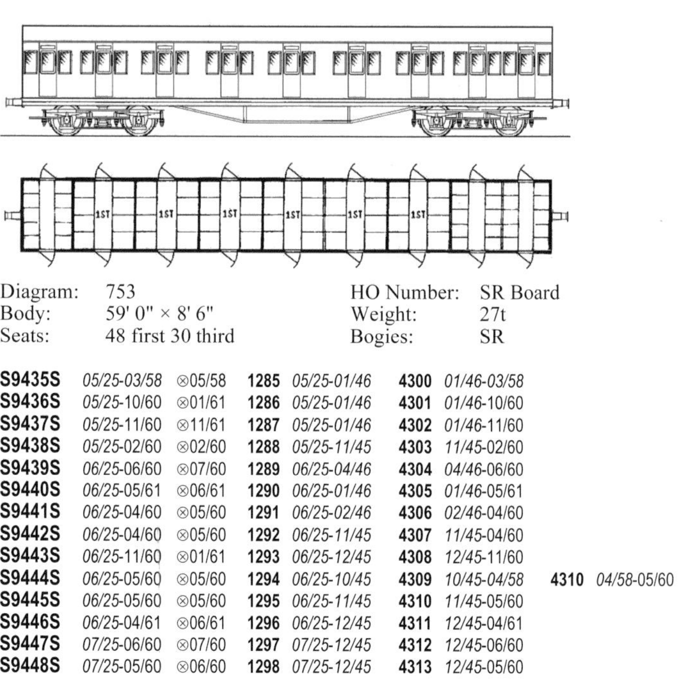

Diagram:	753	HO Number:	SR Board
Body:	59' 0" × 8' 6"	Weight:	27t
Seats:	48 first 30 third	Bogies:	SR

S9435S	*05/25-03/58*	⊗05/58	**1285**	*05/25-01/46*	**4300**	*01/46-03/58*		
S9436S	*05/25*-10/60	⊗01/61	**1286**	*05/25-01/46*	**4301**	*01/46*-10/60		
S9437S	*05/25*-11/60	⊗11/61	**1287**	*05/25-01/46*	**4302**	*01/46*-11/60		
S9438S	*05/25*-02/60	⊗02/60	**1288**	*05/25-11/45*	**4303**	*11/45*-02/60		
S9439S	*06/25*-06/60	⊗07/60	**1289**	*06/25-04/46*	**4304**	*04/46*-06/60		
S9440S	*06/25*-05/61	⊗06/61	**1290**	*06/25-01/46*	**4305**	*01/46*-05/61		
S9441S	*06/25*-04/60	⊗05/60	**1291**	*06/25-02/46*	**4306**	*02/46*-04/60		
S9442S	*06/25*-04/60	⊗05/60	**1292**	*06/25-11/45*	**4307**	*11/45*-04/60		
S9443S	*06/25*-11/60	⊗01/61	**1293**	*06/25-12/45*	**4308**	*12/45*-11/60		
S9444S	*06/25*-05/60	⊗05/60	**1294**	*06/25-10/45*	**4309**	*10/45-04/58*	**4310**	*04/58*-05/60
S9445S	*06/25*-05/60	⊗05/60	**1295**	*06/25-11/45*	**4310**	*11/45*-05/60		
S9446S	*06/25*-04/61	⊗06/61	**1296**	*06/25-12/45*	**4311**	*12/45*-04/61		
S9447S	*07/25*-06/60	⊗07/60	**1297**	*07/25-12/45*	**4312**	*12/45*-06/60		
S9448S	*07/25*-05/60	⊗06/60	**1298**	*07/25-12/45*	**4313**	*12/45*-05/60		

S9449S	07/25-04/61	⊗11/61	**1299**	07/25-02/46	**4314**	02/46-04/61
S9450S	07/25-11/60	⊗02/61	**1300**	07/25-08/45	**4315**	08/45-11/60
S9451S	07/25-03/60	⊗05/60	**1301**	07/25-10/45	**4316**	10/45-03/60
S9452S	07/25-03/60	⊗04/60	**1302**	07/25-02/46	**4317**	02/46-03/60
S9453S	07/25-02/60	⊗02/60	**1303**	07/25-10/45	**4318**	10/45-02/60
S9454S	07/25-07/60	⊗08/60	**1304**	07/25-07/45	**4319**	07/45-07/60
9455	07/25-04/41	⊗	**1305**	07/25-04/41		
S9456S	07/25-12/59	⊗02/60	**1306**	07/25-01/46	**4321**	01/46-12/59
S9457S	08/25-12/60	⊗02/61	**1307**	08/25-11/45	**4322**	11/45-12/60
S9458S	08/25-04/61	⊗05/61	**1308**	08/25-12/45	**4323**	12/45-04/61
S9459S	08/25-02/61	⊗03/61	**1309**	08/25-02/46	**4324**	02/46-02/61
S9460S	08/25-05/60	⊗05/60	**1310**	08/25-10/45	**4325**	10/45-05/60

3-SUB Ashford (ex AC stock)

Trailer Composite
TC
S9461S-S9464S

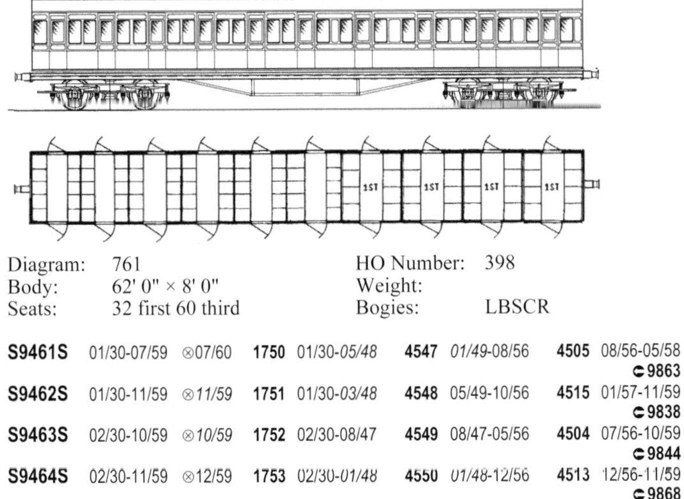

Diagram: 761 HO Number: 398
Body: 62' 0" × 8' 0" Weight:
Seats: 32 first 60 third Bogies: LBSCR

S9461S	01/30-07/59	⊗07/60	**1750**	01/30-*05/48*	**4547**	*01/49*-08/56	**4505**	08/56-05/58	**⊂9863**
S9462S	01/30-11/59	⊗*11/59*	**1751**	01/30-*03/48*	**4548**	05/49-10/56	**4515**	01/57-11/59	**⊂9838**
S9463S	02/30-10/59	⊗*10/59*	**1752**	02/30-08/47	**4549**	08/47-05/56	**4504**	07/56-10/59	**⊂9844**
S9464S	02/30-11/59	⊗12/59	**1753**	02/30-*01/48*	**4550**	*01/48*-12/56	**4513**	12/56-11/59	**⊂9868**

3-SUB Ashford (ex AC stock)

Trailer Composite
TC
S9465-S9467S

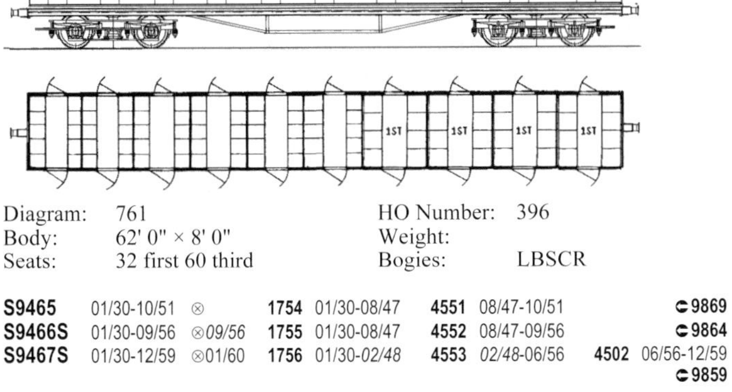

Diagram: 761 HO Number: 396
Body: 62' 0" × 8' 0" Weight:
Seats: 32 first 60 third Bogies: LBSCR

S9465	01/30-10/51	⊗	**1754**	01/30-08/47	**4551**	08/47-10/51			**⊂9869**
S9466S	01/30-09/56	⊗*09/56*	**1755**	01/30-08/47	**4552**	08/47-09/56			**⊂9864**
S9467S	01/30-12/59	⊗01/60	**1756**	01/30-*02/48*	**4553**	*02/48*-06/56	**4502**	06/56-12/59	**⊂9859**

3-SUB Ashford (ex AC stock)

Trailer Composite
TC
S9468S-S9479S

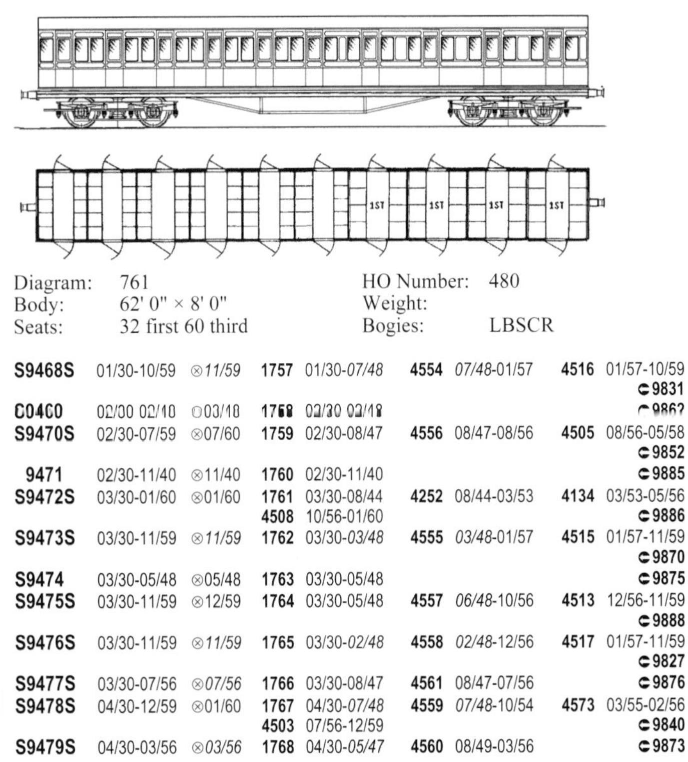

Diagram: 761 HO Number: 480
Body: 62' 0" × 8' 0" Weight:
Seats: 32 first 60 third Bogies: LBSCR

S9468S	01/30-10/59	⊗*11/59*	**1757**	01/30-*07/48*	**4554**	*07/48*-01/57	**4516**	01/57-10/59	**⊂9831**
C04C0	02/00 02/10	⊗03/18	**1758**	02/30 02/18					**⊂9862**
S9470S	02/30-07/59	⊗07/60	**1759**	02/30-08/47	**4556**	08/47-08/56	**4505**	08/56-05/58	**⊂9852**
9471	02/30-11/40	⊗11/40	**1760**	02/30-11/40					**⊂9885**
S9472S	03/30-01/60	⊗01/60	**1761**	03/30-08/44	**4252**	08/44-03/53	**4134**	03/53-05/56	
			4508	10/56-01/60					**⊂9886**
S9473S	03/30-11/59	⊗*11/59*	**1762**	03/30-*03/48*	**4555**	*03/48*-01/57	**4515**	01/57-11/59	**⊂9870**
S9474	03/30-05/48	⊗05/48	**1763**	03/30-05/48					**⊂9875**
S9475S	03/30-11/59	⊗12/59	**1764**	03/30-05/48	**4557**	*06/48*-10/56	**4513**	12/56-11/59	**⊂9888**
S9476S	03/30-11/59	⊗*11/59*	**1765**	03/30-*02/48*	**4558**	*02/48*-12/56	**4517**	01/57-11/59	**⊂9827**
S9477S	03/30-07/56	⊗*07/56*	**1766**	03/30-08/47	**4561**	08/47-07/56			**⊂9876**
S9478S	04/30-12/59	⊗01/60	**1767**	04/30-*07/48*	**4559**	*07/48*-10/54	**4573**	03/55-02/56	
			4503	07/56-12/59					**⊂9840**
S9479S	04/30-03/56	⊗*03/56*	**1768**	04/30-*05/47*	**4560**	08/49-03/56			**⊂9873**

3-SUB Ashford (ex AC stock)

Trailer Composite
TC
S9480S

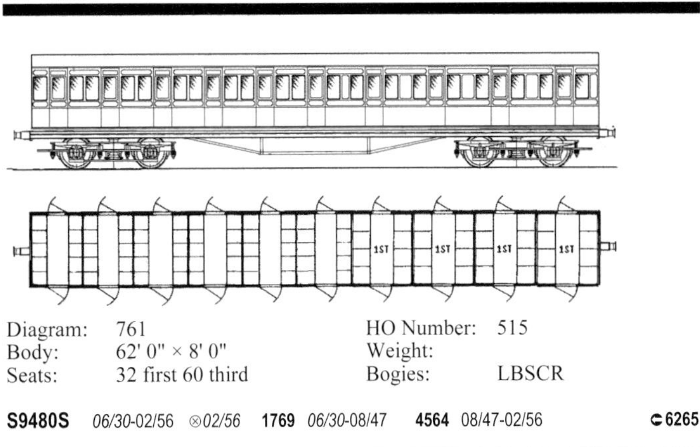

Diagram: 761 HO Number: 515
Body: 62' 0" × 8' 0" Weight:
Seats: 32 first 60 third Bogies: LBSCR

S9480S	*06/30*-02/56	⊗*02/56*	**1769**	*06/30*-08/47	**4564**	08/47-02/56	**⊂6265**

3-SUB Ashford (ex AC stock)

Trailer Composite
TC
9481-S9483S

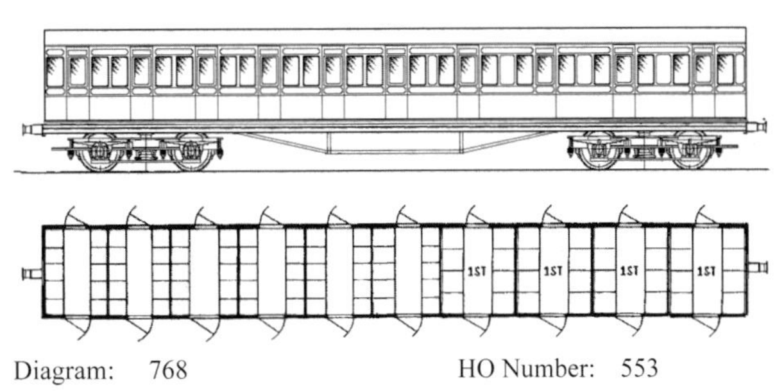

Diagram: 768 HO Number: 553

Body: 62' 0" × 8' 0" Weight:
Seats: 32 first 60 third Bogies: LBSCR

9481	06/30-10/47	⊗10/47	**1770**	06/30-10/47			⊂**6266**
S9482S	07/30-03/56	↳**15420**	**1771**	07/30-02/49	**4590**	02/49-03/56	⊂**6270**
S9483S	08/30-04/55	↳**15372**	**1772**	08/30-*07/48*	**4565**	*07/48*-04/55	⊂**6267**

3-SUB Lancing/Ashford (LSWR bodies)

Trailer Composite

TC

S9484S

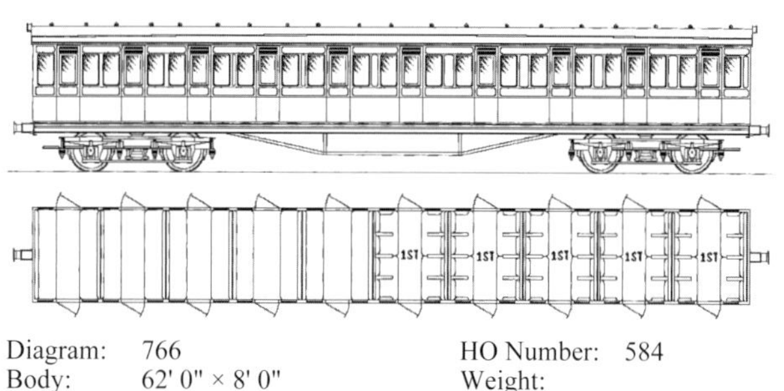

Diagram: 766 HO Number: 584
Body: 62' 0" × 8' 0" Weight:
Seats: 40 first 50 third Bogies: SR

S9484S	01/31-04/54	↳**15260**	**1789**	*01/31-10/46*	**4409**	*10/46*-04/54

3-SUB Ashford (SER bodies)

Trailer Composite

TC

S9485-9579

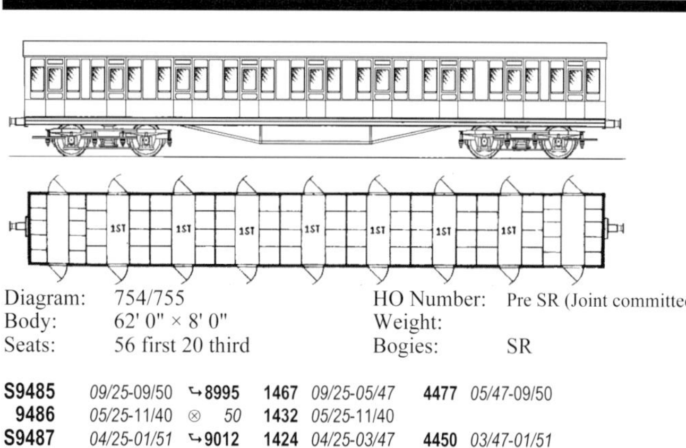

Diagram: 754/755 HO Number: Pre SR (Joint committee)
Body: 62' 0" × 8' 0" Weight:
Seats: 56 first 20 third Bogies: SR

S9485	*09/25-09/50*	↳**8995**	**1467**	*09/25-05/47*	**4477**	*05/47-09/50*		
9486	*05/25*-11/40	⊗ *50*	**1432**	*05/25*-11/40				
S9487	*04/25-01/51*	↳**9012**	**1424**	*04/25-03/47*	**4450**	*03/47-01/51*		
S9488	*04/25*-11/49	↳**8983**	**1425**	*04/25*-11/49				
9489	*10/25*-10/40	⊗11/40	**1473**	*10/25*-10/40				
S9490S	*05/25*-07/53	↳**15158**	**1427**	*05/25*-01/45	**1728**	45-08/47	**4520**	08/47-07/53
S9491	*11/25-04/50*	↳**9000**	**1488**	*11/25-12/46*	**4490**	*12/46-04/50*		
S9492	*09/25-11/50*	↳**15126**	**1464**	*09/25-05/47*	**4475**	*05/47-11/50*		
S9493	*04/25*-06/51	↳**15103**	**1422**	*04/25-10/46*	**4448**	*10/46*-03/50	**4492**	04/50-06/51
S9494	*12/25-11/50*	↳**15122**	**1489**	*12/25-10/46*	**4491**	*10/46-11/50*		
S9495	*06/25-05/51*	↳**15119**	**1443**	*06/25-02/47*	**4462**	*02/47*-03/50	**4456**	04/50-*05/51*
S9496	*02/25-11/49*	⊗	**1408**	*02/25-11/49*				
9497	*08/25*-09/40	⊗09/40	**1454**	*08/25*-09/40				
S9498	*02/25-07/50*	↳**9024**	**1406**	*02/25-11/47*	**4406**[2]	*11/47-07/50*		
S9499	*08/25-03/51*	↳**9018**	**1455**	*08/25-06/47*	**4470**	*06/47-03/51*		
S9500	*10/25-05/51*	↳**15120**	**1478**	*10/25-05/47*	**4484**	*05/47-04/50*	**4445**	*05/50-05/51*
S9501	*02/25-09/50*	⊗	**1403**	*02/25-12/46*	**4433**	*12/46-06/50*	**4444**	*06/50-09/50*
S9502	*02/25-02/51*	↳**9016**	**1405**	*02/25-03/47*	**4434**	*03/47-02/51*		
S9503	*07/25-09/50*	⊗	**1452**	*07/25- 47*	**4468**	*12/47-09/50*		
S9504	*09/25-11/50*	↳**9020**	**1469**	*09/25-03/47*	**4479**	*03/47-11/50*		
S9505	*03/25*-10/49	↳**8960**	**1415**	*03/25-11/46*	**4442**[1]	*11/46-02/48*	**4256**	*02/48*-10/49
S9506	*03/25-04/51*	↳**15104**	**1414**	*03/25-01/47*	**4441**	*01/47-04/51*		
S9507	*09/25-04/51*	↳**15108**	**1466**	*09/25-10/46*	**4476**	*10/46-04/51*		
S9508	*11/25-09/50*	↳**15105**	**1483**	*11/25-05/47*	**4486**	*05/47-09/50*		
S9509	*03/25-02/49*	↳**12382**	**1412**	*03/25-12/46*	**4439**[1]	*12/46-02/49*		
S9510	*12/25*-11/49	↳**8969**	**1492**	*12/25*-11/49				
S9511	*08/25*-11/49	↳**8959**	**1461**	*08/25*-11/49				
S9512	*05/25-04/50*	↳**8998**	**1433**	*05/25-01/47*	**4454**	*01/47-04/50*		
S9513	*02/25-06/50*	↳**9029**	**1409**	*02/25*-08/47	**4436**	08/47-*06/50*		
S9514	*04/25-01/51*	↳**9022**	**1423**	*04/25-04/47*	**4449**	*04/47-01/51*		
S9515	*11/25-09/50*	↳**9030**	**1480**	*11/25-03/47*	**4485**	*03/47-09/50*		
S9516	*11/25-04/50*	↳**8993**	**1485**	*11/25-01/47*	**4488**	01/47-*04/50*		
S9517	*02/25-01/49*	↳**12380**	**1404**	*02/25-01/49*				
S9518	*02/25-02/51*	↳**15128**	**1402**	*02/25-04/47*	**4432**	*04/47-02/51*		
S9519	*09/25*-11/49	↳**8979**	**1465**	*09/25*-11/49				
S9520	*11/25-04/50*	↳**8987**	**1484**	*11/25-12/46*	**4487**	*12/46-04/50*		
S9521	*12/25*-06/51	↳**15118**	**1490**	*12/25-11/46*	**4492**	*11/46*-06/51		
S9522	*06/25-12/50*	↳**9010**	**1442**	*06/25-06/47*	**4461**	*06/47-12/50*		
S9523	*04/25-09/50*	↳**9034**	**1419**	*04/25-12/46*	**4446**	*12/46-10/50*		
S9524	*02/25*-05/50	↳**8992**	**1407**	*02/25-11/46*	**4435**	*11/46-06/50*		
S9525	*11/25*-11/49	↳**8971**	**1487**	*11/25*-11/49				
S9526	*04/25-03/51*	↳**15101**	**1420**	*04/25-06/47*	**4447**	*06/47-03/51*		
S9527S	*10/25-06/56*	↳**15418**	**1474**	*10/25-10/46*	**4254**	10/46-03/56		
S9528	*03/25-09/50*	↳**8999**	**1417**	*03/25-02/47*	**4444**	*02/47-09/50*		
S9529	*10/25-10/50*	↳**9021**	**1475**	*10/25-05/47*	**4482**	*05/47-10/50*		
S9530	*12/25-12/50*	↳**9008**	**1491**	*12/25-06/47*	**4493**	*06/47-12/50*		
S9531	*02/25*-11/49	↳**8962**	**1401**	*02/25*-11/49				
S9532	*03/25-12/50*	↳**9013**	**1416**	*03/25-05/47*	**4443**	*05/47-12/50*		
S9533	*11/25-11/49*	↳**8964**	**1481**	*11/25-11/49*				
S9534	*03/25-07/50*	↳**8989**	**1413**	*03/25-03/47*	**4440**	*03/47-07/50*		
S9535	*07/25-07/50*	↳**8988**	**1451**	*07/25-01/47*	**4467**	*01/47-07/50*		
S9536	*07/25*-11/49	↳**8982**	**1449**	*07/25*-11/49				
S9537	*08/25-06/50*	↳**9001**	**1460**	*08/25-04/47*	**4474**	*04/47-06/50*		
S9538	*06/25-10/50*	↳**9003**	**1439**	*06/25-10/46*	**4459**	*10/46-10/50*		
S9539	*07/25-11/50*	↳**9025**	**1450**	*07/25-03/47*	**4466**	*03/47-11/50*		
9540	*09/25-* 40	⊗ 40	**1470**	*09/25-* 45				
S9541	*07/25-05/51*	↳**15113**	**1447**	*07/25-10/46*	**4465**	*10/46*-04/50	**4463**	04/50-*05/51*
S9542	*06/25*-11/49	↳**8980**	**1440**	*06/25*-11/49				
S9543	*07/25*-11/49	↳**8965**	**1448**	*07/25*-11/49				
S9544	*07/25-06/50*	↳**9019**	**1446**	*07/25-03/47*	**4464**	*03/47-06/50*		
S9545	*05/25*-11/49	↳**8978**	**1430**	*05/25*-11/49				
S9546	*03/25-02/51*	↳**15116**	**1410**	*03/25-11/46*	**4437**	*11/46-02/51*		
S9547	*08/25-03/51*	↳**15132**	**1456**	*08/25-06/47*	**4471**	*06/47-03/51*		
S9548	*05/25-12/50*	↳**15115**	**1429**	*05/25-02/47*	**4452**	*02/47-12/50*		
S9549	*10/25*-11/49	↳**8966**	**1479**	*10/25*-11/49				
S9550	*06/25-08/50*	↳**9011**	**1437**	*06/25-04/47*	**4458**	*04/47-08/50*		
S9551	*08/25-06/50*	↳**9031**	**1457**	*08/25-11/46*	**4472**	*11/46-06/50*		
S9552	*04/25-05/51*	↳**15106**	**1418**	*04/25-12/46*	**4445**	*12/46-05/51*		
9553	*05/25*-01/45	⊗01/45	**1428**	*05/25*-01/45				
S9554	*03/25-06/50*	↳**9032**	**1411**	*03/25-03/47*	**4438**	*03/47-06/50*		
S9555	*06/25-05/51*	↳**15112**	**1444**	*06/25-11/46*	**4463**	*11/46-05/51*		
S9556	*10/25-02/49*	↳**8920**	**1477**	*10/25-04/47*	**4483**[1]	*04/47-02/49*		
S9557	*10/25*-01/51	↳**9017**	**1472**	*10/25-12/46*	**4481**	*12/46*-01/51		
S9558	*10/25-05/51*	↳**15114**	**1471**	*10/25-06/47*	**4480**	*06/47*-03/50	**4478**	04/50-*05/51*
S9559	*08/25-09/50*	↳**9014**	**1459**	*08/25-10/46*	**4473**	*10/46-09/50*		
S9560	*06/25-06/50*	↳**8996**	**1436**	*06/25-06/47*	**4457**	*06/47-06/50*		
S9561	*09/25-05/51*	↳**15109**	**1468**	*09/25-12/46*	**4478**	*12/46-05/51*		
S9562	*07/25*-11/49	↳**8985**	**1445**	*07/25*-11/49				
S9563	*05/25-05/51*	↳**15107**	**1435**	*05/25-03/47*	**4456**	*03/47-05/51*		
S9564	*04/25*-11/49	↳**8974**	**1421**	*04/25*-11/49				
S9565	*05/25*-11/50	↳**9027**	**1431**	*05/25-01/47*	**4453**	*01/47-12/50*		
S9566	*06/25*-11/49	↳**8991**	**1438**	*06/25*-11/49				
S9567	*11/25*-11/49	↳**8972**	**1482**	*11/25*-11/49				
S9568	*10/25*-08/40	⊗08/40	**1476**	*10/25*-08/40				
S9569	*11/25*-01/51	↳**15102**	**1486**	*11/25-05/47*	**4489**	*05/47-02/51*		
S9570	*06/25-10/50*	↳**15117**	**1441**	*06/25-02/47*	**4460**	*02/47-10/50*		
S9571	*05/25-10/50*	↳**15130**	**1434**	*05/25-11/46*	**4455**	*11/46-11/50*		
S9572	*08/25*-11/49	↳**8968**	**1458**	*08/25*-11/49				
S9573	*04/25-04/51*	↳**9023**	**1426**	*04/25-02/47*	**4451**	*02/47-04/51*		
S9574	*07/25-12/50*	↳**9015**	**1453**	*07/25-04/47*	**4469**	*04/47-12/50*		
S9575	*12/25*-11/49	↳**8956**	**1495**	*12/25*-11/49				
S9576	*12/25*-11/49	↳**8977**	**1494**	*12/25*-11/49				
S9577	*09/25*-11/49	↳**8981**	**1463**	*09/25*-11/49				
S9578	*12/25-07/50*	↳**8990**	**1493**	*12/25-05/47*	**4494**	*05/47-07/50*		
9579	*09/25*-12/41	⊗12/41	**1462**	*09/25*-12/41				

3-SUB Birmingham RC&W

Trailer Composite

TC

S9580S-S9608S

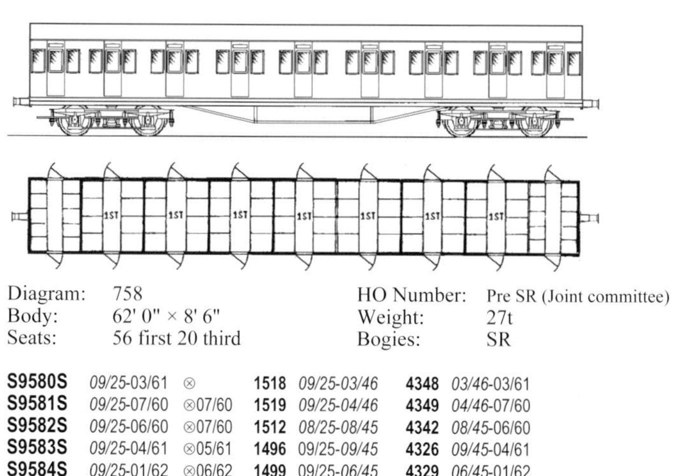

Diagram: 758 HO Number: Pre SR (Joint committee)
Body: 62' 0" × 8' 6" Weight: 27t
Seats: 56 first 20 third Bogies: SR

S9580S	*09/25*-03/61	⊗	**1518**	*09/25-03/46*	**4348**	*03/46*-03/61
S9581S	*09/25*-07/60	⊗07/60	**1519**	*09/25-04/46*	**4349**	*04/46*-07/60
S9582S	*09/25*-06/60	⊗07/60	**1512**	*08/25-08/45*	**4342**	*08/45*-06/60
S9583S	*09/25*-04/61	⊗05/61	**1496**	*09/25-09/45*	**4326**	*09/45*-04/61
S9584S	*09/25*-01/62	⊗06/62	**1499**	*09/25-06/45*	**4329**	*06/45*-01/62

S9585S	09/25-08/60	⊗	**1523**	10/25-09/45	**4353**	09/45-08/60		
S9586S	09/25-12/61	⊗06/62	**1516**	08/25-06/45	**4346**	06/45-12/61		
S9587S	09/25-01/62	⊗	**1507**	09/25-09/45	**4337**	09/45-01/62		
S9588S	09/25-01/60	⊗12/60	**1506**	09/25-09/45	**4336**	09/45-01/60		
S9589S	09/25-07/60	⊗09/60	**1510**	07/25-04/46	**4340**	04/46-07/60		
S9590S	09/25-05/61	⊗06/61	**1517**	09/25-08/45	**4347**	08/45-05/61		
S9591S	09/25-08/60	⊗09/61	**1498**	09/25-07/45	**4328**	07/45-08/60		
S9592S	09/25-07/60	⊗08/60	**1514**	08/25-03/46	**4344**	03/46-07/60		
S9593S	09/25-04/60	⊗04/60	**1520**	09/25-11/45	**4350**	11/45-05/50	**4320**	05/50-04/60
S9594S	09/25-04/61	⊗05/61	**1513**	08/25-06/45	**4343**	06/45-04/61		
S9595S	09/25-01/60	⊗02/60	**1497**	09/25-03/46	**4327**	03/46-01/60		
S9596S	09/25-11/61	⊗06/62	**1508**	07/25-08/45	**4338**	08/45-11/61		
S9597S	09/25-11/60	⊗02/61	**1505**	09/25-03/46	**4335**	03/46-06/52	**4335**	10/52-11/60
S9598S	09/25-09/60	⊗09/61	**1502**	09/25-06/45	**4332**	06/45-11/48	**4332**	05/50-09/60
S9599S	09/25-05/60	⊗06/60	**1511**	07/25-07/45	**4341**	07/45-05/60		
S9600S	09/25-11/60	⊗01/61	**1509**	07/25-07/45	**4339**	07/45-11/60		
S9601S	09/25-04/59	⊗09/61	**1521**	10/25-09/45	**4351**	04/46-04/59		
S9602S	09/25-11/61	⊗01/62	**1522**	10/25-07/45	**4352**	07/45-11/61		
S9603S	09/25-01/62	⊗11/63	**1500**	09/25-10/45	**4330**	10/45-01/62		
S9604S	09/25-07/60	⊗11/60	**1501**	09/25-09/45	**4331**	09/45-07/60		
S9605S	09/25-11/59	⊗02/60	**1524**	10/25-06/45	**4354**	06/45-11/59		
S9606S	09/25-11/61	⊗	**1503**	09/25-04/46	**4333**	04/46- 51	**4333**	05/52-11/61
S9607S	09/25-08/60	⊗09/61	**1504**	09/25-08/45	**4334**	08/45-08/60		
S9608S	09/25-08/60	⊗09/61	**1515**	08/25-03/46	**4345**	03/46-04/59	**4351**	04/59-08/60

3 SUB Birmingham RC&W/Ashford (SER bodies)
Trailer Composite
TC
S9609-9618

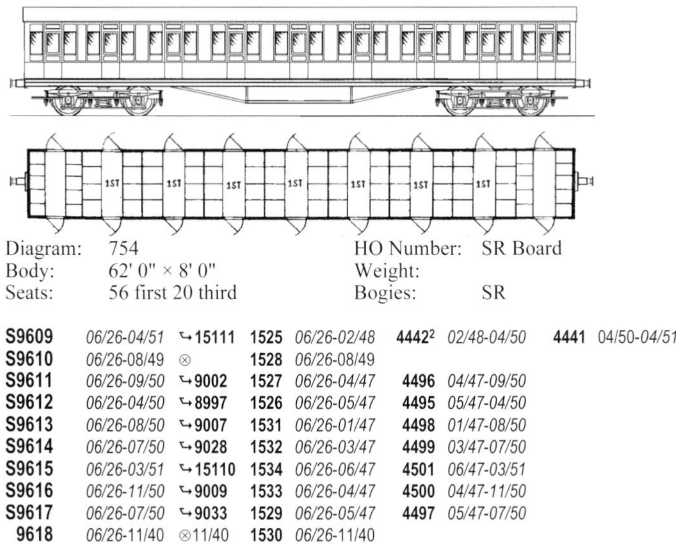

Diagram: 754 HO Number: SR Board
Body: 62' 0" × 8' 0" Weight:
Seats: 56 first 20 third Bogies: SR

S9609	06/26-04/51	↪**15111**	**1525**	06/26-02/48	**4442**[2]	02/48-04/50	**4441**	04/50-04/51
S9610	06/26-08/49	⊗	**1528**	06/26-08/49				
S9611	06/26-09/50	↪**9002**	**1527**	06/26-04/47	**4496**	04/47-09/50		
S9612	06/26-04/50	↪**8997**	**1526**	06/26-05/47	**4495**	05/47-04/50		
S9613	06/26-08/50	↪**9007**	**1531**	06/26-01/47	**4498**	01/47-08/50		
S9614	06/26-07/50	↪**9028**	**1532**	06/26-03/47	**4499**	03/47-07/50		
S9615	06/26-03/51	↪**15110**	**1534**	06/26-06/47	**4501**	06/47-03/51		
S9616	06/26-11/50	↪**9009**	**1533**	06/26-04/47	**4500**	04/47-11/50		
S9617	06/26-07/50	↪**9033**	**1529**	06/26-05/47	**4497**	05/47-07/50		
9618	06/26-11/40	⊗11/40	**1530**	06/26-11/40				

3-SUB Ashford (SER bodies)
Trailer Composite
TC
S9619-S9624

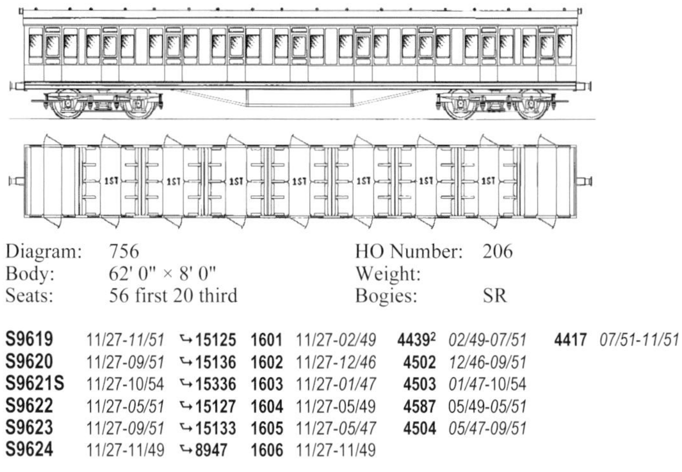

Diagram: 756 HO Number: 206
Body: 62' 0" × 8' 0" Weight:
Seats: 56 first 20 third Bogies: SR

S9619	11/27-11/51	↪**15125**	**1601**	11/27-02/49	**4439**[2]	02/49-07/51	**4417**	07/51-11/51
S9620	11/27-09/51	↪**15136**	**1602**	11/27-12/46	**4502**	12/46-09/51		
S9621S	11/27-10/54	↪**15336**	**1603**	11/27-01/47	**4503**	01/47-10/54		
S9622	11/27-05/51	↪**15127**	**1604**	11/27-05/49	**4587**	05/49-05/51		
S9623	11/27-09/51	↪**15133**	**1605**	11/27-05/47	**4504**	05/47-09/51		
S9624	11/27-11/49	↪**8947**	**1606**	11/27-11/49				

3-SUB Ashford (SER bodies)
Trailer Composite
TC
S9625-S9628

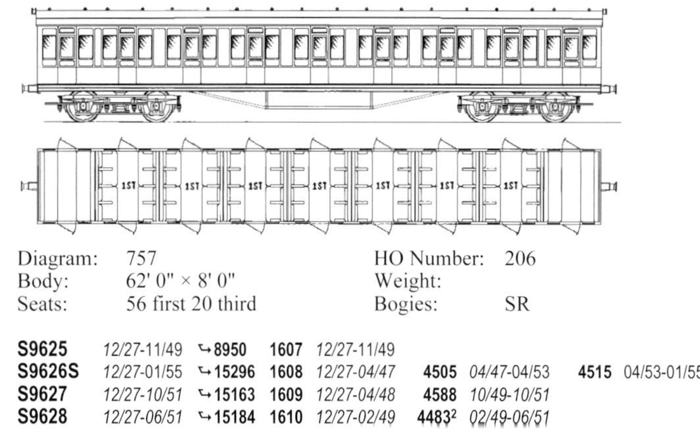

Diagram: 757 HO Number: 206
Body: 62' 0" × 8' 0" Weight:
Seats: 56 first 20 third Bogies: SR

S9625	12/27-11/49	↪**8950**	**1607**	12/27-11/49				
S9626S	12/27-01/55	↪**15296**	**1608**	12/27-04/47	**4505**	04/47-04/53	**4515**	04/53-01/55
S9627	12/27-10/51	↪**15163**	**1609**	12/27-04/48	**4588**	10/49-10/51		
S9628	12/27-06/51	↪**15184**	**1610**	12/27-02/49	**4483**[2]	02/49-06/51		

3-SUB Ashford (SER bodies)
Trailer Composite
TC
S9629-S9631

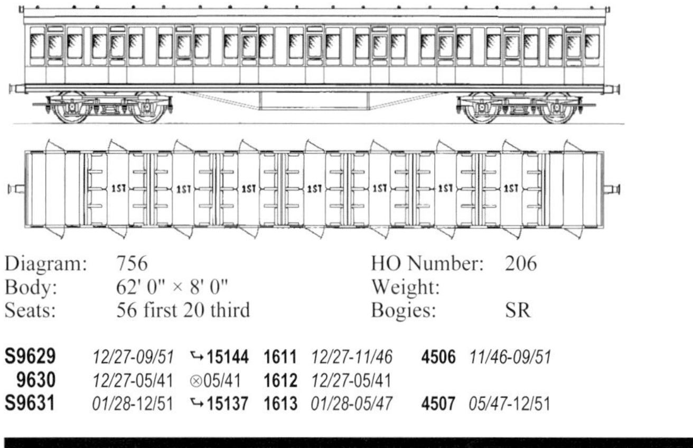

Diagram: 756 HO Number: 206
Body: 62' 0" × 8' 0" Weight:
Seats: 56 first 20 third Bogies: SR

S9629	12/27-09/51	↪**15144**	**1611**	12/27-11/46	**4506**	11/46-09/51
9630	12/27-05/41	⊗05/41	**1612**	12/27-05/41		
S9631	01/28-12/51	↪**15137**	**1613**	01/28-05/47	**4507**	05/47-12/51

3-SUB Ashford (SER bodies)
Trailer Composite
TC
S9632

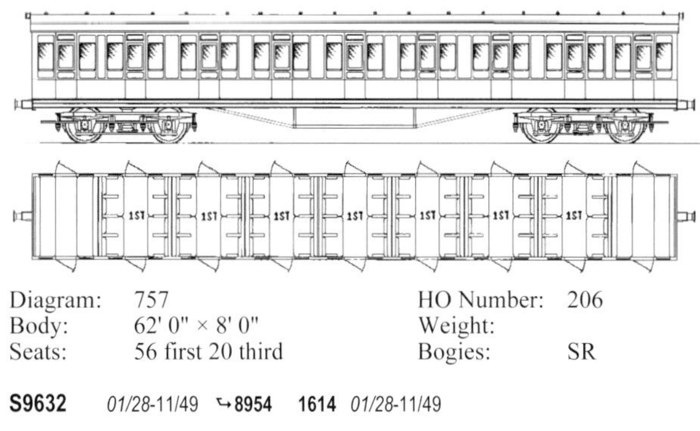

Diagram: 757 HO Number: 206
Body: 62' 0" × 8' 0" Weight:
Seats: 56 first 20 third Bogies: SR

S9632	01/28-11/49	↪**8954**	**1614**	01/28-11/49

3-SUB Ashford (SER bodies)
Trailer Composite
TC
S9633-S9648S

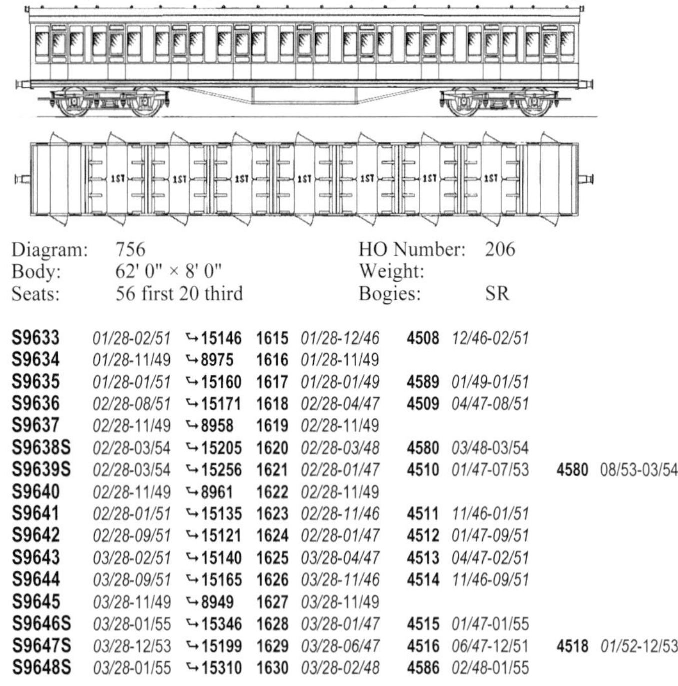

Diagram:	756	HO Number:	206
Body:	62' 0" × 8' 0"	Weight:	
Seats:	56 first 20 third	Bogies:	SR

S9633	01/28-02/51	↳**15146**	**1615**	01/28-12/46	**4508**	12/46-02/51		
S9634	01/28-11/49	↳**8975**	**1616**	01/28-11/49				
S9635	01/28-01/51	↳**15160**	**1617**	01/28-01/49	**4589**	01/49-01/51		
S9636	02/28-08/51	↳**15171**	**1618**	02/28-04/47	**4509**	04/47-08/51		
S9637	02/28-11/49	↳**8958**	**1619**	02/28-11/49				
S9638S	02/28-03/54	↳**15205**	**1620**	02/28-03/48	**4580**	03/48-03/54		
S9639S	02/28-03/54	↳**15256**	**1621**	02/28-01/47	**4510**	01/47-07/53	**4580**	08/53-03/54
S9640	02/28-11/49	↳**8961**	**1622**	02/28-11/49				
S9641	02/28-01/51	↳**15135**	**1623**	02/28-11/46	**4511**	11/46-01/51		
S9642	02/28-09/51	↳**15121**	**1624**	02/28-01/47	**4512**	01/47-09/51		
S9643	03/28-02/51	↳**15140**	**1625**	03/28-04/47	**4513**	04/47-02/51		
S9644	03/28-09/51	↳**15165**	**1626**	03/28-11/46	**4514**	11/46-09/51		
S9645	03/28-11/49	↳**8949**	**1627**	03/28-11/49				
S9646S	03/28-01/55	↳**15346**	**1628**	03/28-01/47	**4515**	01/47-01/55		
S9647S	03/28-12/53	↳**15199**	**1629**	03/28-06/47	**4516**	06/47-12/51	**4518**	01/52-12/53
S9648S	03/28-01/55	↳**15310**	**1630**	03/28-02/48	**4586**	02/48-01/55		

3-SUB Lancing/Ashford (LSWR bodies)
Trailer Composite
TC
S9649S-S9655S

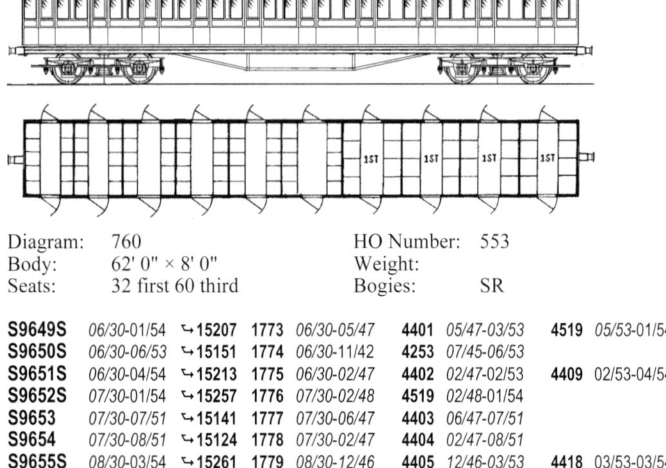

Diagram:	760	HO Number:	553
Body:	62' 0" × 8' 0"	Weight:	
Seats:	32 first 60 third	Bogies:	SR

S9649S	06/30-01/54	↳**15207**	**1773**	06/30-05/47	**4401**	05/47-03/53	**4519**	05/53-01/54
S9650S	06/30-06/53	↳**15151**	**1774**	06/30-11/42	**4253**	07/45-06/53		
S9651S	06/30-04/54	↳**15213**	**1775**	06/30-02/47	**4402**	02/47-02/53	**4409**	02/53-04/54
S9652S	07/30-01/54	↳**15257**	**1776**	07/30-02/48	**4519**	02/48-01/54		
S9653	07/30-07/51	↳**15141**	**1777**	07/30-06/47	**4403**	06/47-07/51		
S9654	07/30-08/51	↳**15124**	**1778**	07/30-02/47	**4404**	02/47-08/51		
S9655S	08/30-03/54	↳**15261**	**1779**	08/30-12/46	**4405**	12/46-03/53	**4418**	03/53-03/54

3-SUB Lancing (AC frame) /Ashford (LSWR bodies)
Trailer Composite
TC
S9656S-S9658S

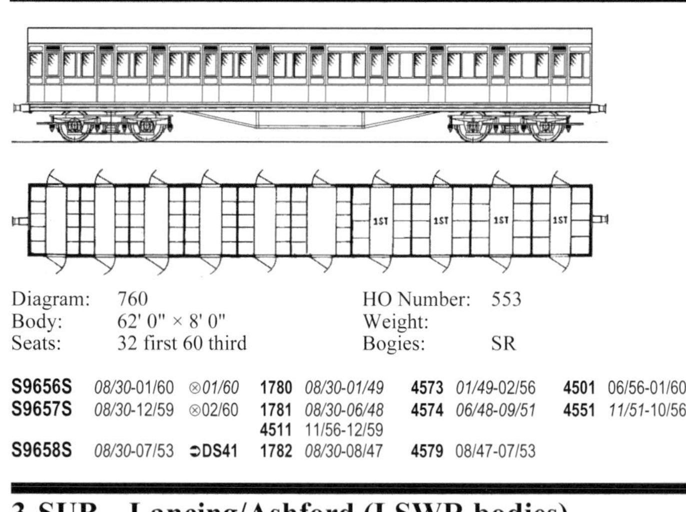

Diagram:	760	HO Number:	553
Body:	62' 0" × 8' 0"	Weight:	
Seats:	32 first 60 third	Bogies:	SR

S9656S	08/30-01/60	⊗01/60	**1780**	08/30-01/49	**4573**	01/49-02/56	**4501**	06/56-01/60
S9657S	08/30-12/59	⊗02/60	**1781**	08/30-06/48	**4574**	06/48-09/51	**4551**	11/51-10/56
			4511	11/56-12/59				
S9658S	08/30-07/53	⊃**DS41**	**1782**	08/30-08/47	**4579**	08/47-07/53		

3-SUB Lancing/Ashford (LSWR bodies)
Trailer Composite
TC
S9659S-S9661

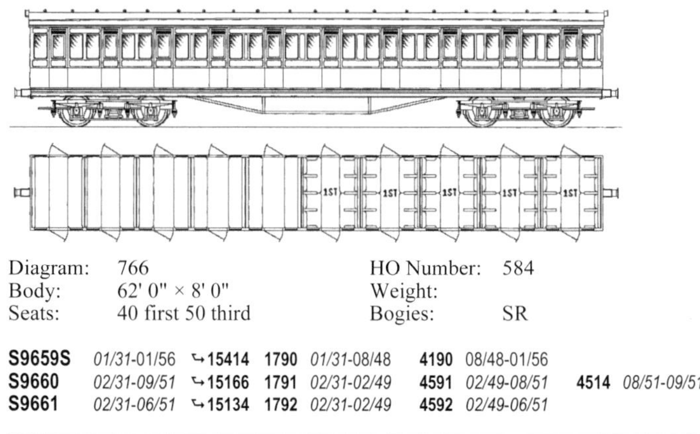

Diagram:	766	HO Number:	584
Body:	62' 0" × 8' 0"	Weight:	
Seats:	40 first 50 third	Bogies:	SR

S9659S	01/31-01/56	↳**15414**	**1790**	01/31-08/48	**4190**	08/48-01/56		
S9660	02/31-09/51	↳**15166**	**1791**	02/31-02/49	**4591**	02/49-08/51	**4514**	08/51-09/51
S9661	02/31-06/51	↳**15134**	**1792**	02/31-02/49	**4592**	02/49-06/51		

3-SUB Lancing/Ashford (LSWR bodies)
Trailer Composite
TC
S9662-S9663

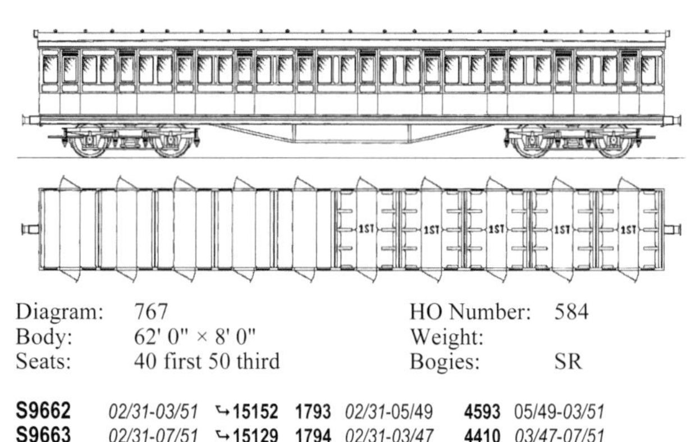

Diagram:	767	HO Number:	584
Body:	62' 0" × 8' 0"	Weight:	
Seats:	40 first 50 third	Bogies:	SR

S9662	02/31-03/51	↳**15152**	**1793**	02/31-05/49	**4593**	05/49-03/51
S9663	02/31-07/51	↳**15129**	**1794**	02/31-03/47	**4410**	03/47-07/51

3-SUB Lancing/Ashford (LSWR bodies)

Trailer Composite

TC

S9664-S9665

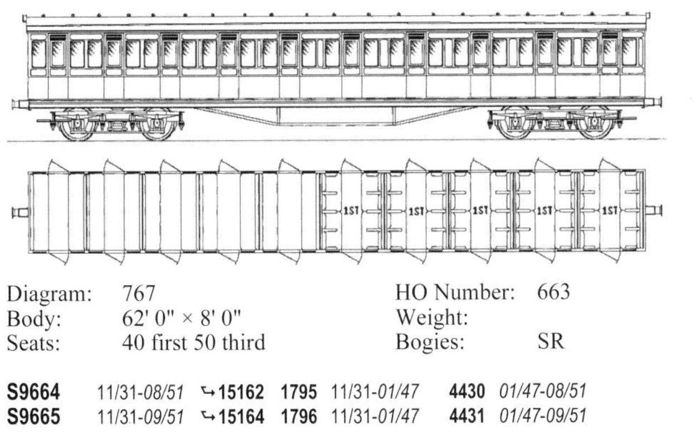

Diagram:	767	HO Number:	663
Body:	62' 0" × 8' 0"	Weight:	
Seats:	40 first 50 third	Bogies:	SR

S9664	11/31-08/51	↳15162	1795	11/31-01/47	4430	01/47-08/51
S9665	11/31-09/51	↳15164	1796	11/31-01/47	4431	01/47-09/51

3-SUB Lancing/Ashford (LBSCR bodies)

Trailer Composite

TC

S9666-S9670

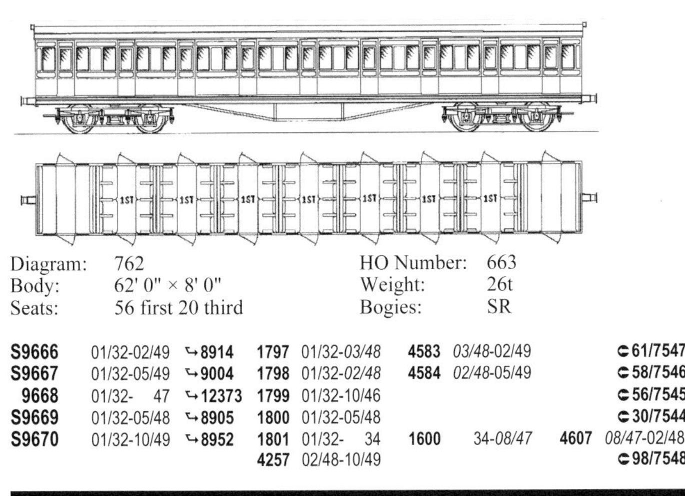

Diagram:	762	HO Number:	663
Body:	62' 0" × 8' 0"	Weight:	26t
Seats:	56 first 20 third	Bogies:	SR

S9666	01/32-02/49	↳8914	1797	01/32-03/48	4583	03/48-02/49			⊂61/7547
S9667	01/32-05/49	↳9004	1798	01/32-02/48	4584	02/48-05/49			⊂58/7546
9668	01/32- 47	↳12373	1799	01/32-10/46					⊂56/7545
S9669	01/32-05/48	↳8905	1800	01/32-05/48					⊂30/7544
S9670	01/32-10/49	↳8952	1801	01/32- 34	1600	34-08/47	4607	08/47-02/48	
			4257	02/48-10/49					⊂98/7548

3-SUB Eastleigh (LSWR bodies)

Trailer Composite

TC

S9671S-S9674S

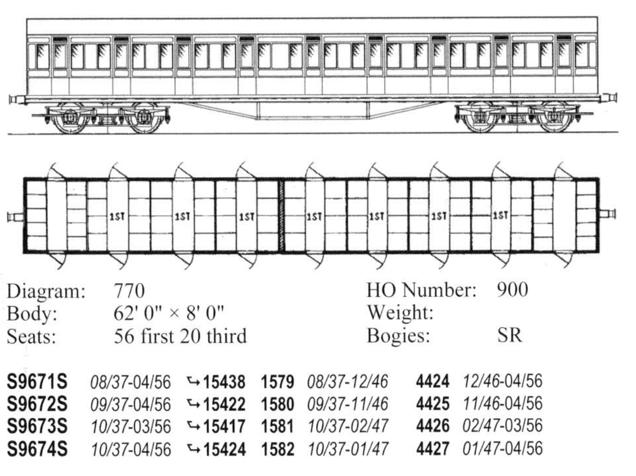

Diagram:	770	HO Number:	900
Body:	62' 0" × 8' 0"	Weight:	
Seats:	56 first 20 third	Bogies:	SR

S9671S	08/37-04/56	↳15438	1579	08/37-12/46	4424	12/46-04/56
S9672S	09/37-04/56	↳15422	1580	09/37-11/46	4425	11/46-04/56
S9673S	10/37-03/56	↳15417	1581	10/37-02/47	4426	02/47-03/56
S9674S	10/37-04/56	↳15424	1582	10/37-01/47	4427	01/47-04/56

3-SUB Lancing/Ashford (LBSCR bodies)

Trailer Composite

TC

S9675-S9701

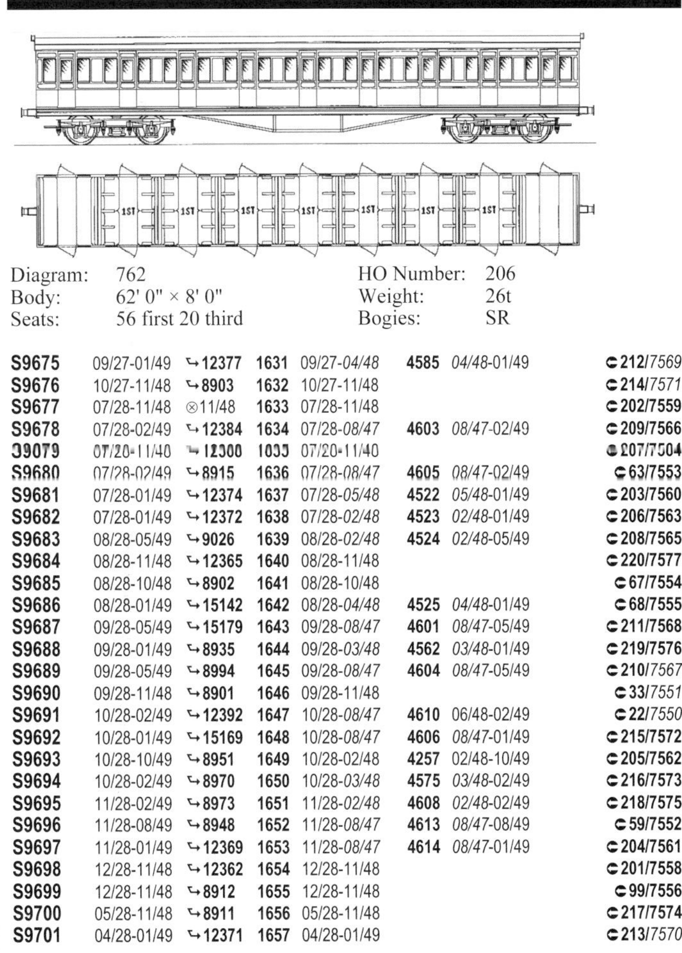

Diagram:	762	HO Number:	206
Body:	62' 0" × 8' 0"	Weight:	26t
Seats:	56 first 20 third	Bogies:	SR

S9675	09/27-01/49	↳12377	1631	09/27-04/48	4585	04/48-01/49	⊂212/7569
S9676	10/27-11/48	↳8903	1632	10/27-11/48			⊂214/7571
S9677	07/28-11/48	⊗11/48	1633	07/28-11/48			⊂202/7559
S9678	07/28-02/49	↳12384	1634	07/28-08/47	4603	08/47-02/49	⊂209/7566
S9679	07/28-11/48	↳12[illegible]	1635	07/28-11/48			⊂207/7564
S9680	07/28-02/49	↳8915	1636	07/28-08/47	4605	08/47-02/49	⊂63/7553
S9681	07/28-01/49	↳12374	1637	07/28-05/48	4522	05/48-01/49	⊂203/7560
S9682	07/28-01/49	↳12372	1638	07/28-02/48	4523	02/48-01/49	⊂206/7563
S9683	08/28-05/49	↳9026	1639	08/28-02/48	4524	02/48-05/49	⊂208/7565
S9684	08/28-11/48	↳12365	1640	08/28-11/48			⊂220/7577
S9685	08/28-10/48	↳8902	1641	08/28-10/48			⊂67/7554
S9686	08/28-01/49	↳15142	1642	08/28-04/48	4525	04/48-01/49	⊂68/7555
S9687	09/28-05/49	↳15179	1643	09/28-08/47	4601	08/47-05/49	⊂211/7568
S9688	09/28-01/49	↳8935	1644	09/28-03/48	4562	03/48-01/49	⊂219/7576
S9689	09/28-05/49	↳8994	1645	09/28-08/47	4604	08/47-05/49	⊂210/7567
S9690	09/28-11/48	↳8901	1646	09/28-11/48			⊂33/7551
S9691	10/28-02/49	↳12392	1647	10/28-08/47	4610	06/48-02/49	⊂22/7550
S9692	10/28-01/49	↳15169	1648	10/28-08/47	4606	08/47-01/49	⊂215/7572
S9693	10/28-10/49	↳8951	1649	10/28-02/48	4257	02/48-10/49	⊂205/7562
S9694	10/28-02/49	↳8970	1650	10/28-03/48	4575	03/48-02/49	⊂216/7573
S9695	11/28-02/49	↳8973	1651	11/28-02/48	4608	02/48-02/49	⊂218/7575
S9696	11/28-08/49	↳8948	1652	11/28-08/47	4613	08/47-08/49	⊂59/7552
S9697	11/28-01/49	↳12369	1653	11/28-08/47	4614	08/47-01/49	⊂204/7561
S9698	12/28-11/48	↳12362	1654	12/28-11/48			⊂201/7558
S9699	12/28-11/48	↳8912	1655	12/28-11/48			⊂99/7556
S9700	05/28-11/48	↳8911	1656	05/28-11/48			⊂217/7574
S9701	04/28-01/49	↳12371	1657	04/28-01/49			⊂213/7570

3-SUB Lancing/Ashford (LBSCR bodies)

Trailer Composite

TC

9702-S9716

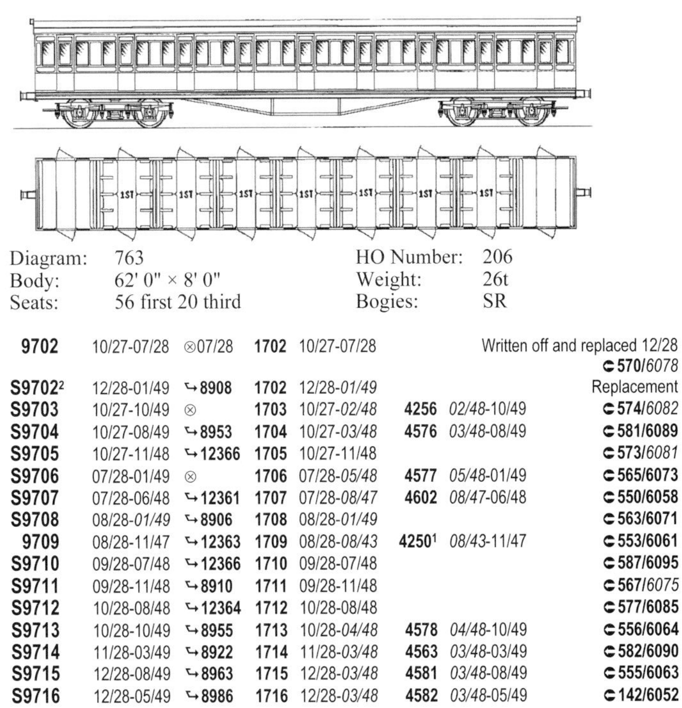

Diagram:	763	HO Number:	206
Body:	62' 0" × 8' 0"	Weight:	26t
Seats:	56 first 20 third	Bogies:	SR

9702	10/27-07/28	⊗07/28	1702	10/27-07/28			Written off and replaced 12/28 ⊂570/6078
S9702[2]	12/28-01/49	↳8908	1702	12/28-01/49			Replacement
S9703	10/27-10/49	⊗	1703	10/27-02/48	4256	02/48-10/49	⊂574/6082
S9704	10/27-08/49	↳8953	1704	10/27-03/48	4576	03/48-08/49	⊂581/6089
S9705	10/27-11/48	↳12366	1705	10/27-11/48			⊂573/6081
S9706	07/28-01/49	⊗	1706	07/28-05/48	4577	05/48-01/49	⊂565/6073
S9707	07/28-06/48	↳12361	1707	07/28-08/47	4602	08/47-06/48	⊂550/6058
S9708	08/28-01/49	↳8906	1708	08/28-01/49			⊂563/6071
9709	08/28-11/47	↳12363	1709	08/28-08/43	4250[1]	08/43-11/47	⊂553/6061
S9710	09/28-07/48	↳12366	1710	09/28-07/48			⊂587/6095
S9711	09/28-11/48	↳8910	1711	09/28-11/48			⊂567/6075
S9712	10/28-08/48	↳12364	1712	10/28-08/48			⊂577/6085
S9713	10/28-10/49	↳8955	1713	10/28-04/48	4578	04/48-10/49	⊂556/6064
S9714	11/28-03/49	↳8922	1714	11/28-03/48	4563	03/48-03/49	⊂582/6090
S9715	12/28-08/49	↳8963	1715	12/28-03/48	4581	03/48-08/49	⊂555/6063
S9716	12/28-05/49	↳8986	1716	12/28-03/48	4582	03/48-05/49	⊂142/6052

3-SUB Ashford (ex AC stock)
Trailer Composite
TC
S9717S-S9736S

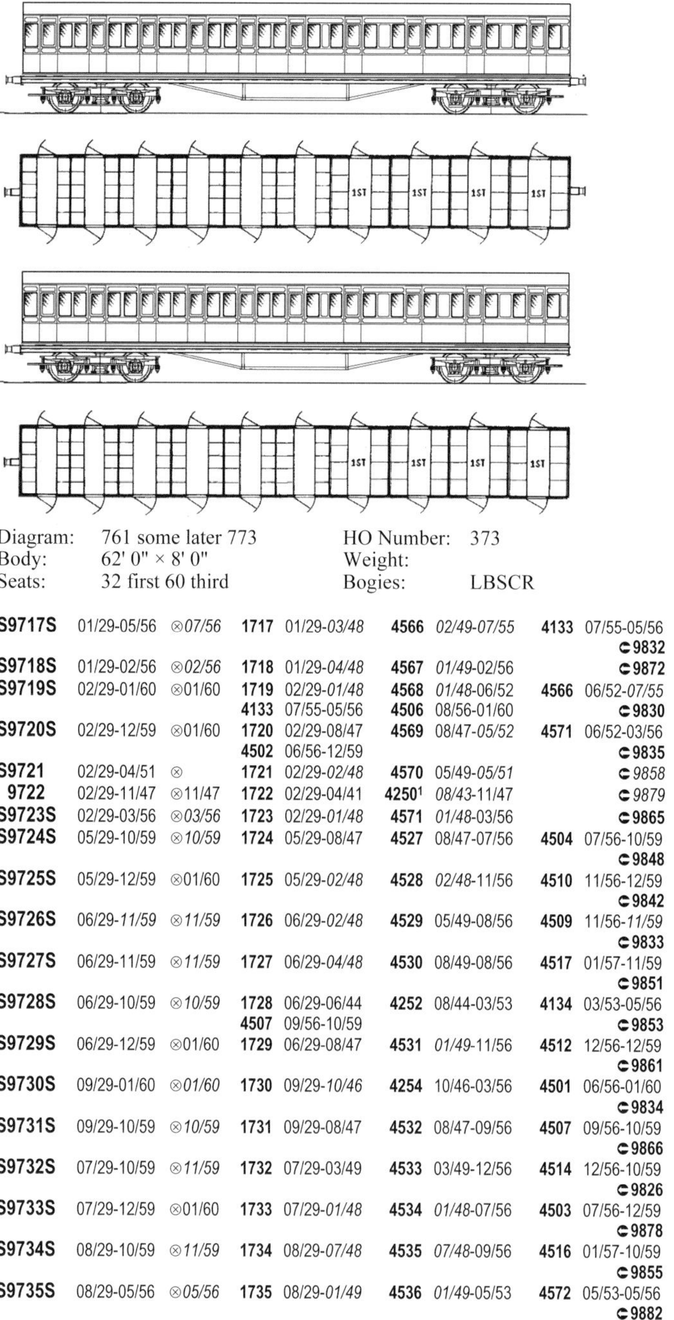

Diagram:	761 some later 773	HO Number:	373
Body:	62' 0" × 8' 0"	Weight:	
Seats:	32 first 60 third	Bogies:	LBSCR

No.	Dates	Withdrawn	Unit	Dates	Unit	Dates	Unit	Dates	
S9717S	01/29-05/56	⊗*07/56*	**1717**	01/29-*03/48*	**4566**	*02/49-07/55*	**4133**	07/55-05/56	**⊂9832**
S9718S	01/29-02/56	⊗*02/56*	**1718**	01/29-*04/48*	**4567**	*01/49*-02/56			**⊂9872**
S9719S	02/29-01/60	⊗01/60	**1719**	02/29-*01/48*	**4568**	*01/48*-06/52	**4566**	06/52-*07/55*	
			4133	07/55-05/56	**4506**	08/56-01/60			**⊂9830**
S9720S	02/29-12/59	⊗01/60	**1720**	02/29-08/47	**4569**	08/47-*05/52*	**4571**	06/52-03/56	
			4502	06/56-12/59					**⊂9835**
S9721	02/29-04/51	⊗	**1721**	02/29-*02/48*	**4570**	05/49-*05/51*			**⊂***9858*
9722	02/29-11/47	⊗11/47	**1722**	02/29-04/41	**4250**[1]	*08/43*-11/47			**⊂***9879*
S9723S	02/29-03/56	⊗*03/56*	**1723**	02/29-*01/48*	**4571**	*01/48*-03/56			**⊂9865**
S9724S	05/29-10/59	⊗*10/59*	**1724**	05/29-08/47	**4527**	08/47-07/56	**4504**	07/56-10/59	**⊂9848**
S9725S	05/29-12/59	⊗01/60	**1725**	05/29-*02/48*	**4528**	*02/48*-11/56	**4510**	11/56-12/59	**⊂9842**
S9726S	06/29-*11/59*	⊗*11/59*	**1726**	06/29-*02/48*	**4529**	05/49-08/56	**4509**	11/56-*11/59*	**⊂9833**
S9727S	06/29-11/59	⊗*11/59*	**1727**	06/29-*04/48*	**4530**	08/49-08/56	**4517**	01/57-11/59	**⊂9851**
S9728S	06/29-10/59	⊗*10/59*	**1728**	06/29-06/44	**4252**	08/44-03/53	**4134**	03/53-05/56	
			4507	09/56-10/59					**⊂9853**
S9729S	06/29-12/59	⊗01/60	**1729**	06/29-08/47	**4531**	*01/49*-11/56	**4512**	12/56-12/59	**⊂9861**
S9730S	09/29-01/60	⊗*01/60*	**1730**	09/29-*10/46*	**4254**	10/46-03/56	**4501**	06/56-01/60	**⊂9834**
S9731S	09/29-10/59	⊗*10/59*	**1731**	09/29-08/47	**4532**	08/47-09/56	**4507**	09/56-10/59	**⊂9866**
S9732S	07/29-10/59	⊗*11/59*	**1732**	07/29-03/49	**4533**	03/49-12/56	**4514**	12/56-10/59	**⊂9826**
S9733S	07/29-12/59	⊗01/60	**1733**	07/29-*01/48*	**4534**	*01/48*-07/56	**4503**	07/56-12/59	**⊂9878**
S9734S	08/29-10/59	⊗*11/59*	**1734**	08/29-*07/48*	**4535**	*07/48*-09/56	**4516**	01/57-10/59	**⊂9855**
S9735S	08/29-05/56	⊗*05/56*	**1735**	08/29-*01/49*	**4536**	*01/49*-05/53	**4572**	05/53-05/56	**⊂9882**
S9736S	08/29-11/58	⊗*11/59*	**1736**	08/29-03/44	**4251**	03/44-11/56	**4518**	01/57-11/58	**⊂9843**

3-SUB Eastleigh (ex AC stock)
Trailer Composite
TC
S9737S-S9749S

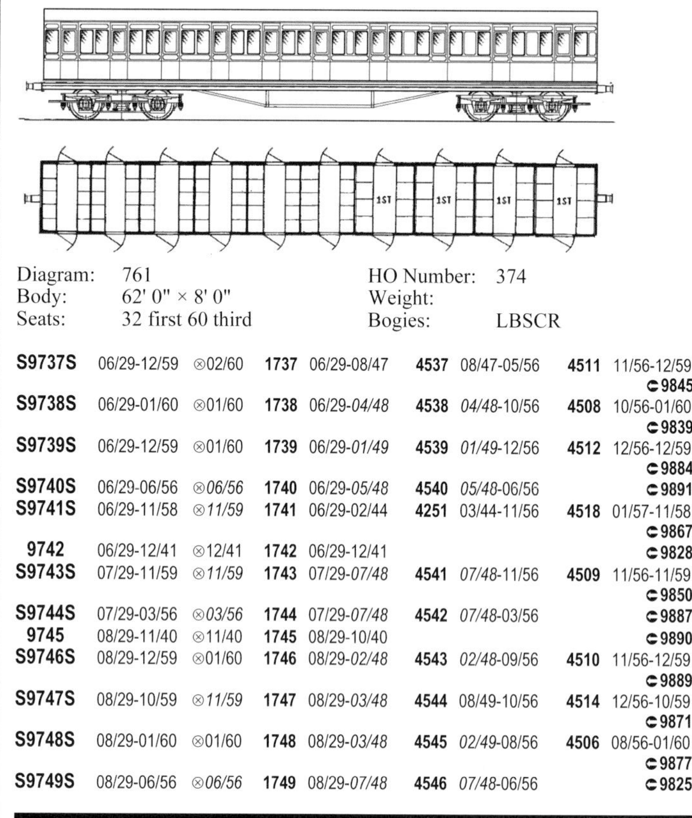

Diagram:	761	HO Number:	374
Body:	62' 0" × 8' 0"	Weight:	
Seats:	32 first 60 third	Bogies:	LBSCR

No.	Dates	Withdrawn	Unit	Dates	Unit	Dates	Unit	Dates	
S9737S	06/29-12/59	⊗02/60	**1737**	06/29-08/47	**4537**	08/47-05/56	**4511**	11/56-12/59	**⊂9845**
S9738S	06/29-01/60	⊗01/60	**1738**	06/29-*04/48*	**4538**	*04/48*-10/56	**4508**	10/56-01/60	**⊂9839**
S9739S	06/29-12/59	⊗01/60	**1739**	06/29-*01/49*	**4539**	*01/49*-12/56	**4512**	12/56-12/59	**⊂9884**
S9740S	06/29-06/56	⊗*06/56*	**1740**	06/29-*05/48*	**4540**	*05/48*-06/56			**⊂9891**
S9741S	06/29-11/58	⊗*11/59*	**1741**	06/29-02/44	**4251**	03/44-11/56	**4518**	01/57-11/58	**⊂9867**
9742	06/29-12/41	⊗12/41	**1742**	06/29-12/41					**⊂9828**
S9743S	07/29-11/59	⊗*11/59*	**1743**	07/29-*07/48*	**4541**	*07/48*-11/56	**4509**	11/56-11/59	**⊂9850**
S9744S	07/29-03/56	⊗*03/56*	**1744**	07/29-*07/48*	**4542**	*07/48*-03/56			**⊂9887**
9745	08/29-11/40	⊗11/40	**1745**	08/29-10/40					**⊂9890**
S9746S	08/29-12/59	⊗01/60	**1746**	08/29-*02/48*	**4543**	*02/48*-09/56	**4510**	11/56-12/59	**⊂9889**
S9747S	08/29-10/59	⊗*11/59*	**1747**	08/29-*03/48*	**4544**	08/49-10/56	**4514**	12/56-10/59	**⊂9871**
S9748S	08/29-01/60	⊗01/60	**1748**	08/29-*03/48*	**4545**	*02/49*-08/56	**4506**	08/56-01/60	**⊂9877**
S9749S	08/29-06/56	⊗*06/56*	**1749**	08/29-*07/48*	**4546**	*07/48*-06/56			**⊂9825**

2-SL Lancing (ex AC stock)
Driving Trailer Composite
DTC
S9751S-S9758S

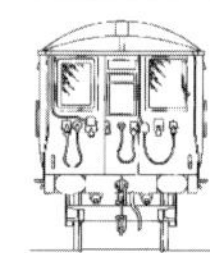

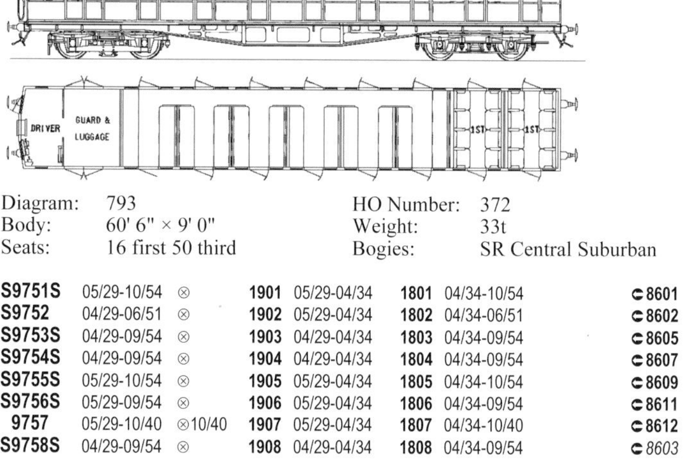

Diagram:	793	HO Number:	372
Body:	60' 6" × 9' 0"	Weight:	33t
Seats:	16 first 50 third	Bogies:	SR Central Suburban

No.	Dates	Withdrawn	Unit	Dates	Unit	Dates	
S9751S	05/29-10/54	⊗	**1901**	05/29-04/34	**1801**	04/34-10/54	**⊂8601**
S9752	04/29-06/51	⊗	**1902**	05/29-04/34	**1802**	04/34-06/51	**⊂8602**
S9753S	04/29-09/54	⊗	**1903**	04/29-04/34	**1803**	04/34-09/54	**⊂8605**
S9754S	04/29-09/54	⊗	**1904**	04/29-04/34	**1804**	04/34-09/54	**⊂8607**
S9755S	05/29-10/54	⊗	**1905**	05/29-04/34	**1805**	04/34-10/54	**⊂8609**
S9756S	05/29-09/54	⊗	**1906**	05/29-04/34	**1806**	04/34-09/54	**⊂8611**
9757	05/29-10/40	⊗10/40	**1907**	05/29-04/34	**1807**	04/34-10/40	**⊂8612**
S9758S	04/29-09/54	⊗	**1908**	04/29-04/34	**1808**	04/34-09/54	**⊂***8603*

3-SUB Eastleigh (LSWR bodies)

Trailer Composite
TC
S9759S-S9760

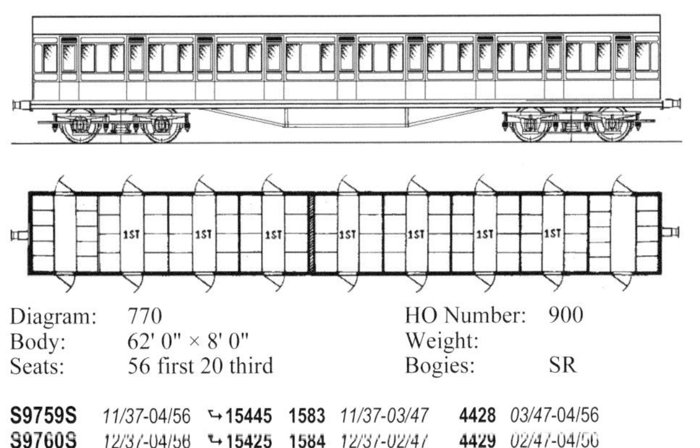

Diagram:	770	HO Number:	900
Body:	62' 0" × 8' 0"	Weight:	
Seats:	56 first 20 third	Bogies:	SR

S9759S	*11/37-04/56*	↳**15445**	**1583**	*11/37-03/47*	**4428**	*03/47-04/56*
S9760S	*12/37-04/56*	↳**15425**	**1584**	*12/37-02/47*	**4429**	*02/47-04/56*

3-SUB Eastleigh (LSWR bodies)

Trailer Composite
TC
S9761-S9765S

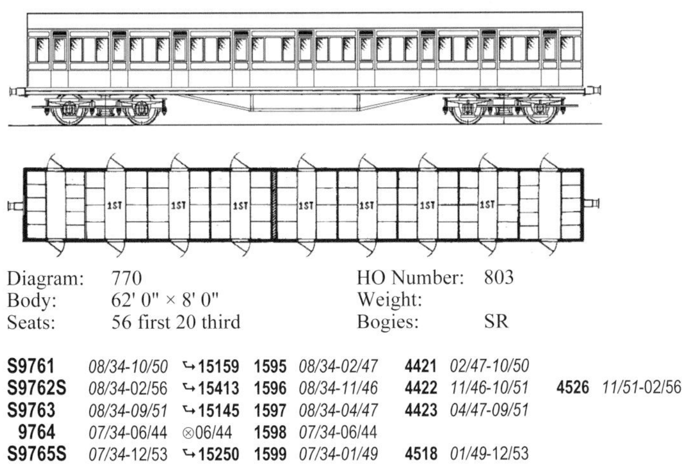

Diagram:	770	HO Number:	803
Body:	62' 0" × 8' 0"	Weight:	
Seats:	56 first 20 third	Bogies:	SR

S9761	*08/34-10/50*	↳**15159**	**1595**	*08/34-02/47*	**4421**	*02/47-10/50*		
S9762S	*08/34-02/56*	↳**15413**	**1596**	*08/34-11/46*	**4422**	*11/46-10/51*	**4526**	*11/51-02/56*
S9763	*08/34-09/51*	↳**15145**	**1597**	*08/34-04/47*	**4423**	*04/47-09/51*		
9764	*07/34-06/44*	⊗06/44	**1598**	*07/34-06/44*				
S9765S	*07/34-12/53*	↳**15250**	**1599**	*07/34-01/49*	**4518**	*01/49-12/53*		

3-SUB Eastleigh (LSWR bodies)

Trailer Composite
TC
S9766S-S9775S

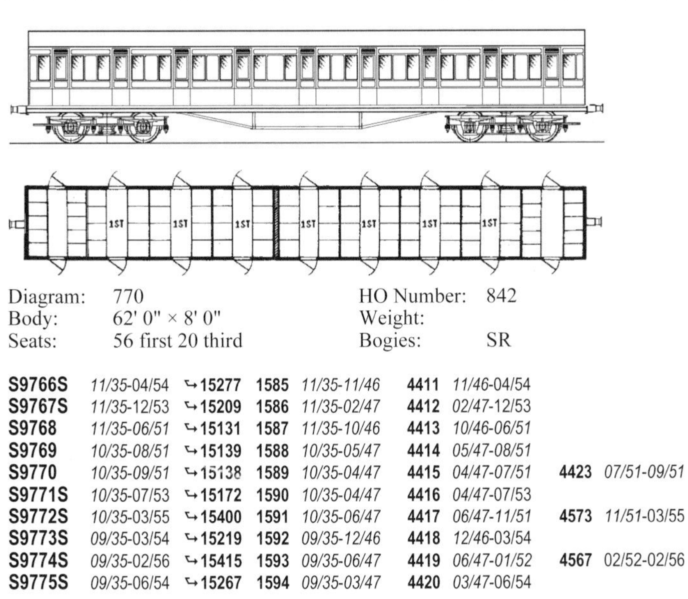

Diagram:	770	HO Number:	842
Body:	62' 0" × 8' 0"	Weight:	
Seats:	56 first 20 third	Bogies:	SR

S9766S	*11/35-04/54*	↳**15277**	**1585**	*11/35-11/46*	**4411**	*11/46-04/54*		
S9767S	*11/35-12/53*	↳**15209**	**1586**	*11/35-02/47*	**4412**	*02/47-12/53*		
S9768	*11/35-06/51*	↳**15131**	**1587**	*11/35-10/46*	**4413**	*10/46-06/51*		
S9769	*10/35-08/51*	↳**15139**	**1588**	*10/35-05/47*	**4414**	*05/47-08/51*		
S9770	*10/35-09/51*	↳**15138**	**1589**	*10/35-04/47*	**4415**	*04/47-07/51*	**4423**	*07/51-09/51*
S9771S	*10/35-07/53*	↳**15172**	**1590**	*10/35-04/47*	**4416**	*04/47-07/53*		
S9772S	*10/35-03/55*	↳**15400**	**1591**	*10/35-06/47*	**4417**	*06/47-11/51*	**4573**	*11/51-03/55*
S9773S	*09/35-03/54*	↳**15219**	**1592**	*09/35-12/46*	**4418**	*12/46-03/54*		
S9774S	*09/35-02/56*	↳**15415**	**1593**	*09/35-06/47*	**4419**	*06/47-01/52*	**4567**	02/52-02/56
S9775S	*09/35-06/54*	↳**15267**	**1594**	*09/35-03/47*	**4420**	*03/47-06/54*		

2-NOL Lancing or Lancing /Eastleigh (LSWR bodies)

Driving Motor Brake Third
DMBT
S9781S-S9788S

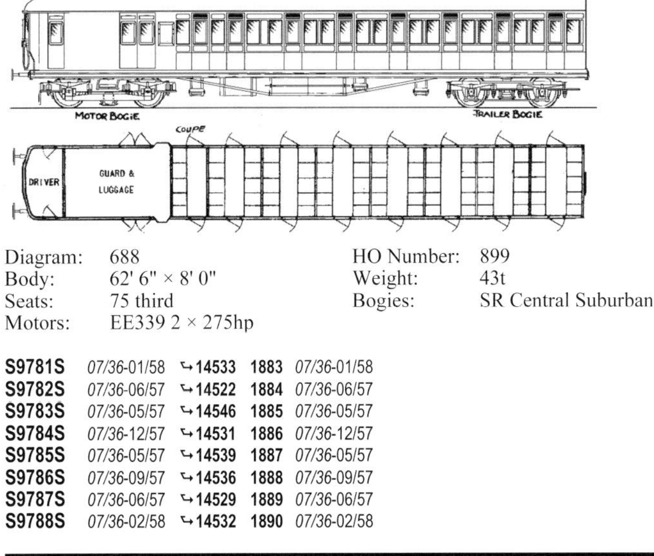

Diagram:	688	HO Number:	899
Body:	62' 6" × 8' 0"	Weight:	43t
Seats:	75 third	Bogies:	SR Central Suburban
Motors:	EE339 2 × 275hp		

S9781S	*07/36-01/58*	↳**14533**	**1883**	*07/36-01/58*
S9782S	*07/36-06/57*	↳**14522**	**1884**	*07/36-06/57*
S9783S	*07/36-05/57*	↳**14546**	**1885**	*07/36-05/57*
S9784S	*07/36-12/57*	↳**14531**	**1886**	*07/36-12/57*
S9785S	*07/36-05/57*	↳**14539**	**1887**	*07/36-05/57*
S9786S	*07/36-09/57*	↳**14536**	**1888**	*07/36-09/57*
S9787S	*07/36-06/57*	↳**14529**	**1889**	*07/36-06/57*
S9788S	*07/36-02/58*	↳**14532**	**1890**	*07/36-02/58*

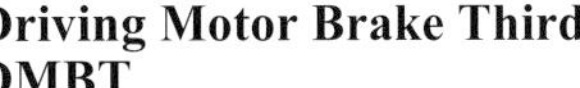

3-SUB Eastleigh (LSWR bodies)

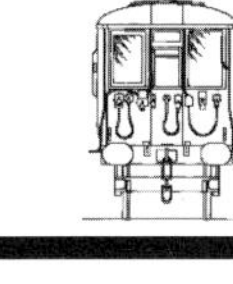

Driving Motor Brake Third
DMBT
S9789S-S9800S

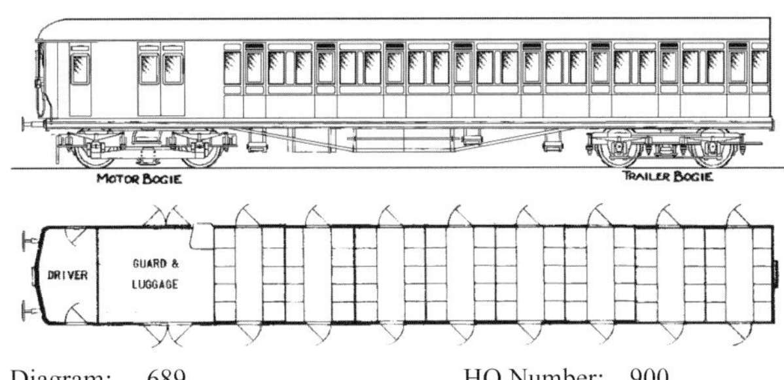

Diagram:	689	HO Number:	900
Body:	62' 0" × 8' 0"	Weight:	
Seats:	80 third	Bogies:	SR
Motors:	EE339 2 × 275hp		

S9789S	*08/37-04/56*	↳**14485**	**1579**	*08/37-12/46*	**4424**	*12/46-04/56*
S9790S	*08/37-04/56*	↳**14486**	**1579**	*08/37-12/46*	**4424**	*12/46-04/56*
S9791S	*09/37-04/56*	↳**14462**	**1580**	*09/37-11/46*	**4425**	*11/46-04/56*
S9792S	*09/37-04/56*	↳**14463**	**1580**	*09/37-11/46*	**4425**	*11/46-04/56*
S9793S	*10/37-03/56*	↳**14458**	**1581**	*10/37-02/47*	**4426**	*02/47-03/56*
S9794S	*10/37-03/56*	↳**14460**	**1581**	*10/37-02/47*	**4426**	*02/47-03/56*
S9795S	*10/37-04/56*	↳**14471**	**1582**	*10/37-01/47*	**4427**	*01/47-04/56*
S9796S	*10/37-04/56*	↳**14470**	**1582**	*10/37-01/47*	**4427**	*01/47-04/56*
S9797S	*11/37-04/56*	↳**14516**	**1583**	*11/37-03/47*	**4428**	*03/47-04/56*
S9798S	*11/37-04/56*	↳**14513**	**1583**	*11/37-03/47*	**4428**	*03/47-04/56*
S9799S	*12/37-04/56*	↳**14475**	**1584**	*12/37-02/47*	**4429**	*02/47-04/56*
S9800S	*12/37-04/56*	↳**14474**	**1584**	*12/37-02/47*	**4429**	*02/47-04/56*

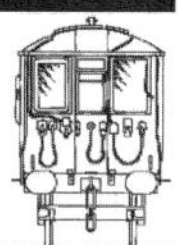

3-SUB Ashford (ex AC stock)

Driving Motor Brake Composite
DMBC
S9801S-S9803

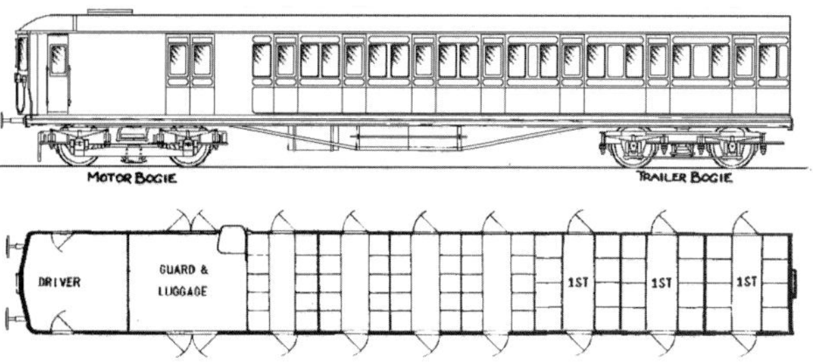

Diagram:	695	HO Number:	480
Body:	62' 6" × 8' 0"	Weight:	
Seats:	24 first 40 third	Bogies:	LBSCR
Motors:	EE339 2 × 275hp		

S9801S	05/30-07/56	⊗07/56	**1766**	05/30-08/47	**4561**	08/47-07/56	⊂9898
S9802S	06/30-10/54	⊗	**1767**	06/30-07/48	**4559**	07/48-10/54	⊂9903
S9803S	06/30-03/56	⊗03/56	**1768**	06/30-05/47	**4560**	08/49-03/56	⊂9897

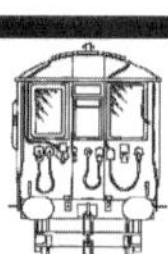

3-SUB Ashford (ex AC stock)

Driving Motor Brake Composite
DMBC
S9804S

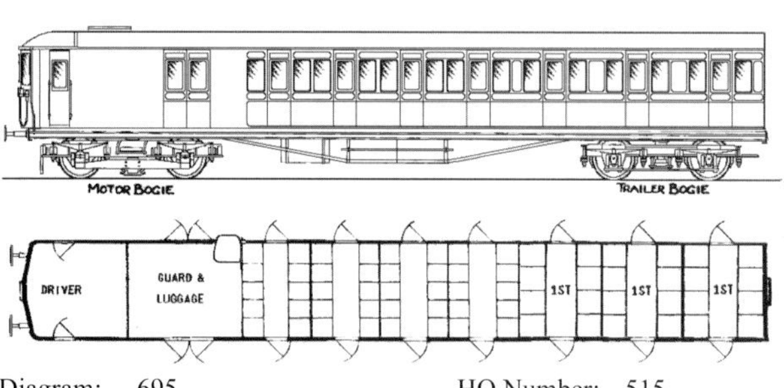

Diagram:	695	HO Number:	515
Body:	62' 6" × 8' 0"	Weight:	
Seats:	24 first 40 third	Bogies:	LBSCR
Motors:	EE339 2 × 275hp		

S9804S	06/30-02/56	⊗02/56	**1769**	06/30-08/47	**4564**	08/47-02/56	⊂6260

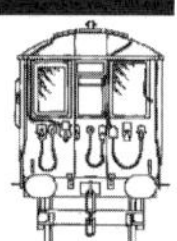

3-SUB Ashford (ex AC stock)

Driving Motor Brake Composite
DMBC
9805-S9807S

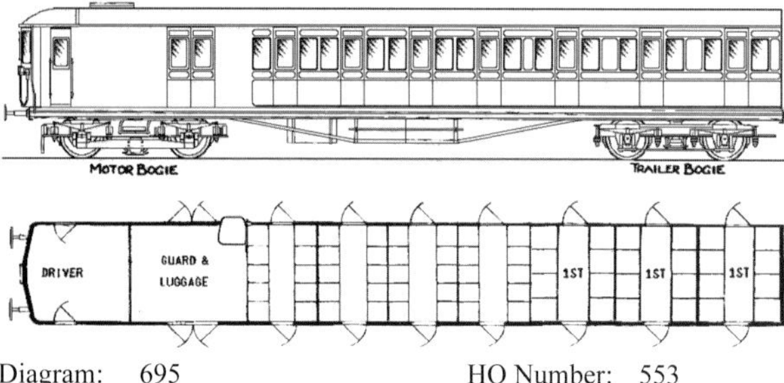

Diagram:	695	HO Number:	553
Body:	62' 6" × 8' 0"	Weight:	
Seats:	24 first 40 third	Bogies:	LBSCR
Motors:	EE339 2 × 275hp		

9805	06/30-10/47	⊗10/47	**1770**	06/30-10/47			⊂6256
S9806S	07/30-03/56	↳**14464**	**1771**	07/30-02/49	**4590**	02/49-03/56	⊂6251
S9807S	08/30-04/55	↳**14384**	**1772**	08/30-07/48	**4565**	07/48-04/55	⊂6259

3-SUB Lancing/Ashford (LSWR bodies)

Driving Motor Brake Composite
DMBC
S9808S-S9814S

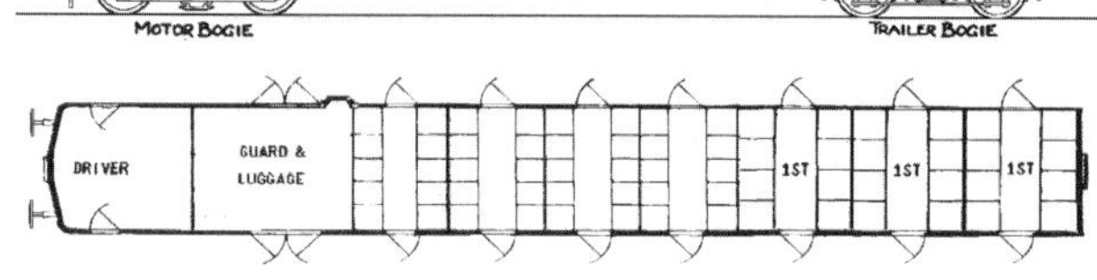

Diagram:	697	HO Number:	553
Body:	62' 6" × 8' 0"	Weight:	
Seats:	24 first 40 third	Bogies:	SR
Motors:	EE339 2 × 275hp		

S9808S	06/30-03/53	↳**14436**	**1773**	06/30-05/47	**4401**	05/47-03/53		
S9809S	06/30-05/54	↳**14334**	**1774**	06/30-11/42	**1688**	11/42-12/47	**4239**	12/47-05/54
S9810S	06/30-02/53	↳**14264**	**1775**	06/30-02/47	**4402**	02/47-02/53		
S9811S	07/30-01/54	↳**14269**	**1776**	07/30-02/48	**4519**	02/48-01/54		
S9812	07/30-07/51	↳**14494**	**1777**	07/30-06/47	**4403**	06/47-07/51		
S9813	07/30-08/51	↳**14055**	**1778**	07/30-02/47	**4404**	02/47-08/51		
S9814S	08/30-03/53	↳**14389**	**1779**	08/30-12/46	**4405**	12/46-03/53		

3-SUB Lancing (AC frame)/ Ashford (LSWR bodies)

Driving Motor Brake Composite
DMBC
S9815S-S9817S

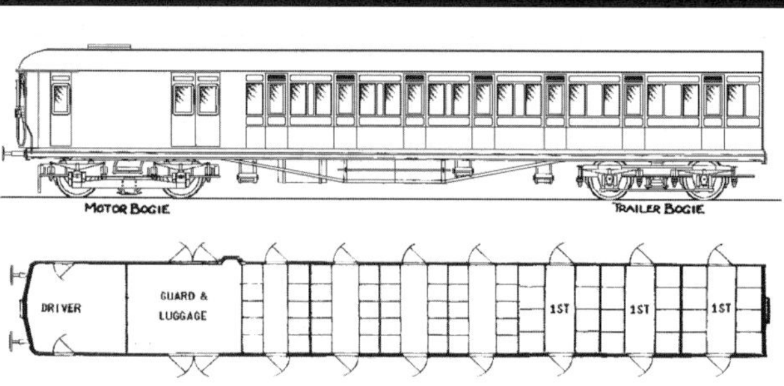

Diagram:	697	HO Number:	553
Body:	62' 6" × 8' 0"	Weight:	
Seats:	24 first 40 third	Bogies:	LBSCR
Motors:	EE339 2 × 275hp		

S9815S	08/30-01/60	⊗01/60	**1780**	08/30-01/49	**4573**	01/49-02/56	**4501**	06/56-01/60
S9816	08/30-09/51	⊗04/53	**1781**	08/30-06/48	**4574**	06/48-09/51		
S9817S	08/30-07/53	⊃**DS42**	**1782**	08/30-08/47	**4579**	08/47-07/53		

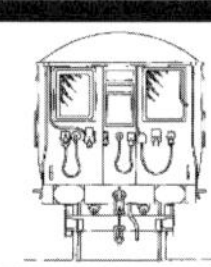

2-WIM Lancing (ex AC stock)

Driving Motor Brake Composite
DMBC
S9818S-S9821S

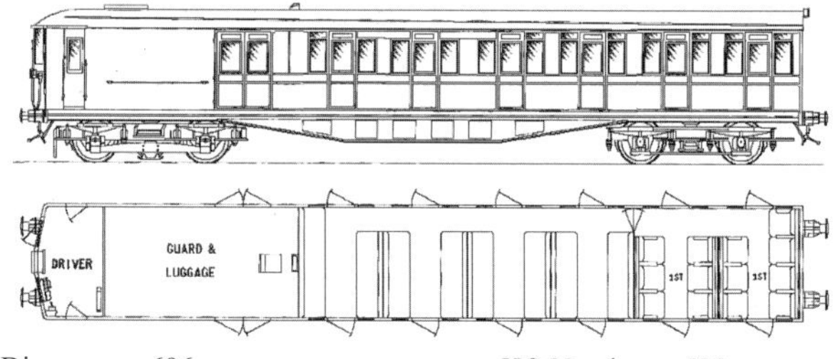

Diagram:	696	HO Number:	530
Body:	60' 6" × 9' 0"	Weight:	44t
Seats:	13 first 33 third	Bogies:	SR Central Suburban
Motors:	MV339 2 × 275hp		

S9818S	06/30-01/54	⊗	**1909**	06/30-04/34	**1809**	04/34-01/54	⊂7651
S9819S	06/30-10/54	⊗	**1910**	06/30-04/34	**1810**	04/34-10/54	⊂7644

S9820S	06/30-10/54 ⊗	**1911**	06/30-04/34	**1811**	04/34-10/54		⊂**7649**
S9821S	06/30-08/54 ⊗	**1912**	06/30-04/34	**1812**	04/34-08/54		⊂**7647**

3-SUB Lancing/Ashford (LSWR bodies)

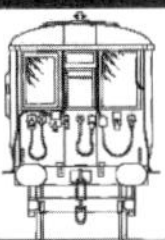

Driving Motor Brake Composite
DMBC
S9822S-9824

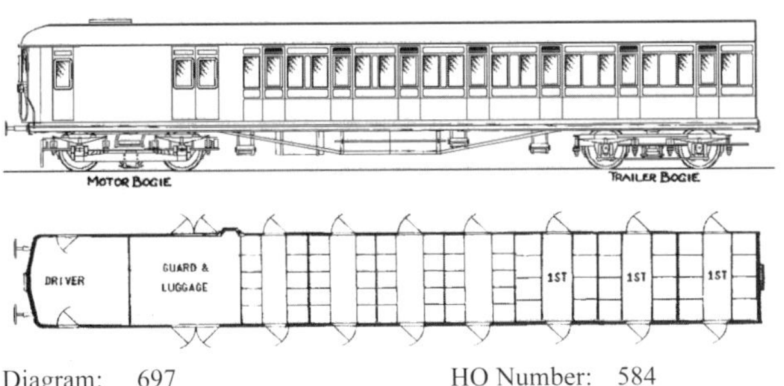

Diagram:	697	HO Number:	584
Body:	62' 6" × 8' 0"	Weight:	
Seats:	24 first 40 third	Bogies:	SR
Motors:	EE339 2 × 275hp		

S9822S	11/30-12/53	↳**14253**	**1783**	11/30-02/48	**4594**	03/49-12/53
S9823S	11/30-04/53	↳**14239**	**1784**	11/30-01/48	**4517**	01/48-04/53
9824	11/30-11/40	⊗11/40	**1785**	11/30-11/40		

2-T Eastleigh (LSWR bodies)
Trailer Third
TT
S9825S-9830

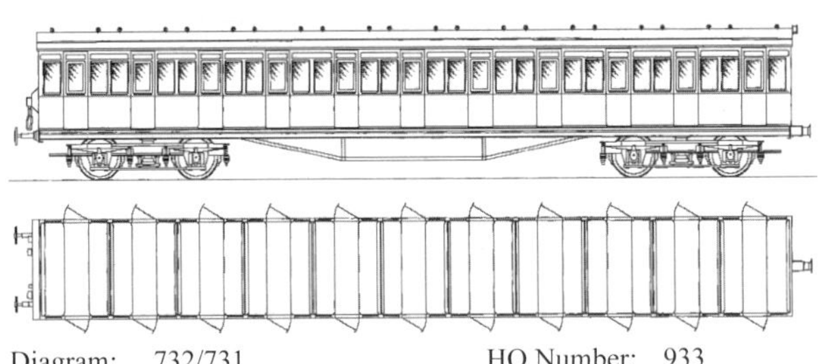

Diagram:	732/731	HO Number:	933
Body:	62' 0" × 8' 0"	Weight:	
Seats:	110 third	Bogies:	SR

Steel panelled on lower bodyside.

S9825S	07/37-12/54	↳**15291**	**1000**	07/37-11/42	**4145**	11/42-12/54
S9826S	07/37-12/54	↳**15299**	**1200**	07/37- 46	**4165**	46-12/54
S9827S	09/37-09/54	↳**15231**	**1081**	37-09/44	**4153**	09/44-09/54
S9828S	09/37-01/56	↳**15446**	**1084**	37-08/46	**4170**	08/46-01/56
S9829S	09/37-01/55	↳**15303**	**1095**	37-01/46	**4168**	01/46-01/55
9830	09/37-11/40	⊗11/40	**1085**	09/37-11/40		

3-SUB Eastleigh (LSWR bodies)

Driving Motor Brake Third
DMBT
S9831S-S9860S

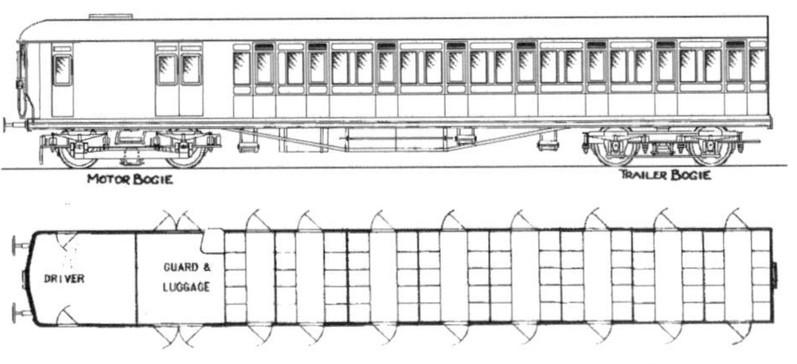

Diagram:	687	HO Number:	933
Body:	62' 6" × 8' 0"	Weight:	
Seats:	75 third	Bogies:	SR
Motors:	MV339 2 × 275hp		

S9831S	11/35-04/54	↳**14292**	**1585**	11/35-11/46	**4411**	11/46-04/54		
S9832S	11/35-04/54	↳**14298**	**1585**	11/35-11/46	**4411**	11/46-04/54		
S9833S	11/35-12/53	↳**14415**	**1586**	11/35-02/47	**4412**	02/47-12/53		
S9834S	11/35-12/53	↳**14495**	**1586**	11/35-02/47	**4412**	02/47-12/53		
S9835	11/35-06/51	↳**14065**	**1587**	11/35-10/46	**4413**	10/46-06/51		
S9836	11/35-06/51	↳**14064**	**1587**	11/35-10/46	**4413**	10/46-06/51		
S9837	10/35-08/51	↳**14424**	**1588**	10/35-05/47	**4414**	05/47-08/51		
S9838	10/35-08/51	↳**14426**	**1588**	10/35-05/47	**4414**	05/47-08/51		
S9839	10/35-07/51	↳**14500**	**1589**	10/35-04/47	**4415**	04/47-07/51		
S9840	10/35-07/51	↳**14499**	**1589**	10/35-04/47	**4415**	04/47-07/51		
S9841S	10/35-07/53	↳**14507**	**1590**	10/35-04/47	**4416**	04/47-07/53		
S9842S	10/35-07/53	↳**14504**	**1590**	10/35-04/47	**4416**	04/47-07/53		
S9843	10/35-11/51	↳**14062**	**1591**	10/35-06/47	**4417**	06/47-11/51		
S9844	10/35-11/51	↳**14054**	**1591**	10/35-06/47	**4417**	06/47-11/51		
S9845S	09/35-07/53	↳**14277**	**1592**	09/35-12/46	**4418**	12/46-05/52	**4177**	05/52-07/53
S9846S	09/35-03/54	↳**14518**	**1592**	09/35-12/46	**4418**	12/46-03/54		
S9847S	09/35-01/52	↳**14431**	**1593**	09/35-06/47	**4419**	06/47-01/52		
S9848S	09/35-01/52	↳**14430**	**1593**	09/35-06/47	**4419**	06/47-01/52		
S9849S	09/35-06/54	↳**14288**	**1594**	09/35-03/47	**4420**	03/47-06/54		
S9850S	09/35-06/54	↳**14287**	**1594**	09/35-03/47	**4420**	03/47-06/54		
S9851	08/34-10/50	↳**14071**	**1595**	08/34-02/47	**4421**	02/47-10/50		
S9852	08/34-08/51	↳**14084**	**1595**	08/34-02/47	**4421**	02/47-10/50	**4591**	10/50-08/51
S9853	08/34-10/51	↳**14040**	**1596**	08/34-11/46	**4422**	11/46-10/51		
S9854	08/34-10/51	↳**14046**	**1596**	08/34-11/46	**4422**	11/46-10/51		
S9855	08/34-09/51	↳**14491**	**1597**	08/34-04/47	**4423**	04/47-09/51		
S9856	08/34-09/51	↳**14496**	**1597**	08/34-04/47	**4423**	04/47-09/51		
9857	07/34-06/44	⊗06/44	**1598**	07/34-06/44				
9858	07/34-06/44	⊗06/44	**1598**	07/34-06/44				
S9859S	07/34-12/53	↳**14392**	**1599**	07/34-01/49	**4518**	01/49-12/53		
S9860S	07/34-12/53	↳**14393**	**1599**	07/34-01/49	**4518**	01/49-12/53		

2-NOL Lancing or Lancing/Eastleigh (LSWR bodies)
Driving Motor Brake Third
DMBT
S9861S-S9871S

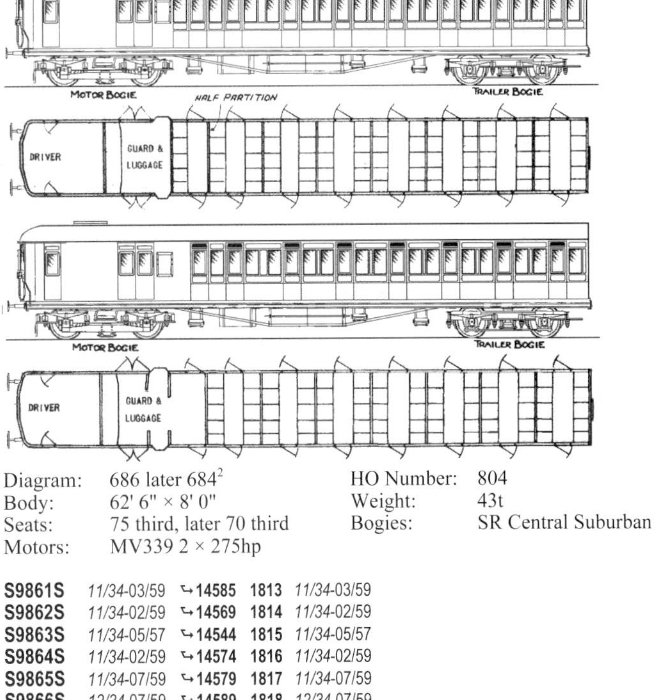

Diagram:	686 later 684[2]	HO Number:	804
Body:	62' 6" × 8' 0"	Weight:	43t
Seats:	75 third, later 70 third	Bogies:	SR Central Suburban
Motors:	MV339 2 × 275hp		

S9861S	11/34-03/59	↳**14585**	**1813**	11/34-03/59		
S9862S	11/34-02/59	↳**14569**	**1814**	11/34-02/59		
S9863S	11/34-05/57	↳**14544**	**1815**	11/34-05/57		
S9864S	11/34-02/59	↳**14574**	**1816**	11/34-02/59		
S9865S	11/34-07/59	↳**14579**	**1817**	11/34-07/59		
S9866S	12/34-07/59	↳**14589**	**1818**	12/34-07/59		
S9867S	12/34-05/58	↳**14559**	**1819**	12/34-01/51	**1819**	05/51-05/58
S9868S	12/34-07/59	↳**14577**	**1820**	12/34-07/59		
S9869S	12/34-02/59	↳**14561**	**1821**	12/34-02/59		
S9870S	12/34-07/59	↳**14571**	**1822**	12/34-07/59		
S9871S	12/34-10/58	↳**14567**	**1823**	12/34-10/58		

2-NOL Lancing or Lancing/Eastleigh (LSWR bodies)

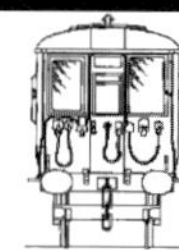

Driving Motor Brake Third
DMBT
S9872S-S9910S

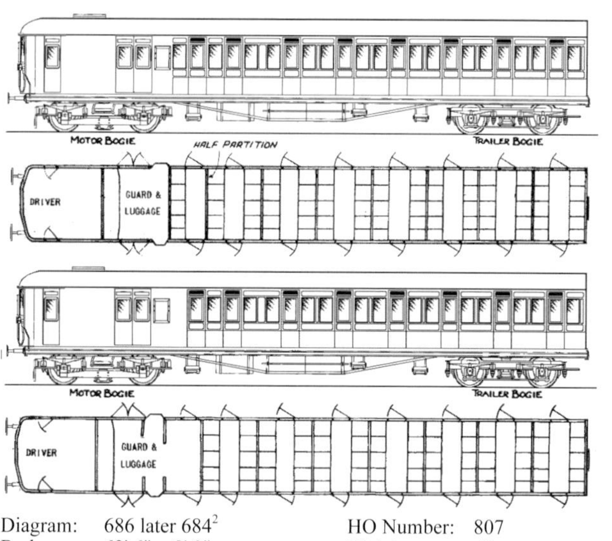

Diagram:	686 later 684[2]	HO Number:	807
Body:	62' 6" × 8' 0"	Weight:	43t
Seats:	75 third, later 70 third	Bogies:	SR Central Suburban
Motors:	MV339 2 × 275hp		

S9872S	*01/35-02/59*	↳**14557**	**1824**	*01/35-02/59*				
S9873S	*01/35-03/59*	↳**14565**	**1825**	*01/35-03/59*				
S9874S	*01/35-08/59*	↳**14587**	**1826**	*01/35-08/59*				
S9875S	*01/35-06/59*	↳**14578**	**1827**	*01/35-06/59*				
S9876S	*01/35-03/56*	↳**14488**	**1828**	*01/35-05/41*	**1799**	06/41-10/46	**4254**	10/46-03/56
S9877S	*01/35-07/59*	↳**14572**	**1829**	*01/35-07/59*				
S9878S	*01/35-08/59*	↳**14586**	**1830**	*01/35-08/59*				
S9879S	*01/35-02/59*	↳**14590**	**1831**	*01/35-02/59*				
S9880S	*02/35-07/59*	↳**14588**	**1832**	*02/35-07/59*				
S9881S	*02/35-06/58*	↳**14576**	**1833**	*02/35-06/58*				
S9882S	*02/35-06/59*	↳**14570**	**1834**	*02/35-06/59*				
S9883S	*02/35-02/58*	↳**14535**	**1835**	*02/35-02/58*				
S9884S	*02/35-06/59*	↳**14583**	**1836**	*02/35-06/59*				
S9885S	*02/35-03/59*	↳**14575**	**1837**	*02/35-03/59*				
S9886	*02/35-05/51*	↳**14520**	**1838**	*02/35-05/51*				
S9887S	*02/35-07/59*	↳**14584**	**1839**	*02/35-07/59*				
S9888S	*03/35-07/59*	↳**14580**	**1840**	*03/35-07/59*				
S9889S	*03/35-02/59*	↳**14562**	**1841**	*03/35-02/59*				
S9890S	*03/35-07/59*	↳**14582**	**1842**	*03/35-07/59*				
S9891S	*03/35-02/58*	↳**14538**	**1843**	*03/35-02/58*				
S9892S	*03/35-06/59*	↳**14573**	**1844**	*03/35-06/59*				
S9893S	*03/35-03/59*	↳**14558**	**1845**	*03/35-03/59*				
S9894S	*03/35-03/59*	↳**14566**	**1846**	*03/35-03/59*				
S9895S	*03/35-02/59*	↳**14564**	**1847**	*03/35-02/59*				
S9896S	*04/35-06/59*	↳**14568**	**1848**	*04/35-06/59*				
S9897S	*04/35-03/59*	↳**14563**	**1849**	*04/35-03/59*				
S9898S	*04/35-03/59*	↳**14560**	**1850**	*04/35-03/59*				
S9899S	*04/35-04/57*	↳**14547**	**1851**	*04/35-04/57*				
S9900S	*04/35-12/57*	↳**14551**	**1852**	*04/35-12/57*				
S9901S	*04/35-12/55*	⊗12/55	**1853**	*04/35-12/55*				
S9902S	*04/35-11/57*	↳**14543**	**1854**	*04/35-11/57*				
S9903S	*04/35-03/53*	↳**14350**	**1855**	*04/35-11/41*	**1679**	12/41-08/47	**4521**	08/47-*03/53*
S9904S	*04/35-07/57*	↳**14549**	**1856**	*04/35-07/57*				
S9905S	*05/35-05/57*	↳**14552**	**1857**	*05/35-05/57*				
S9906S	*05/35-04/57*	↳**14521**	**1858**	*05/35-04/57*				
S9907S	*05/35-04/57*	↳**14523**	**1859**	*05/35-04/57*				
S9908S	*05/35-09/57*	↳**14548**	**1860**	*05/35-09/57*				
S9909S	*05/35-06/57*	↳**14550**	**1861**	*05/35-06/57*				
S9910S	*05/35-06/57*	↳**14527**	**1862**	*05/35-06/57*				

2-NOL Lancing or Lancing/Eastleigh (LSWR bodies)

Driving Trailer Composite
DTC
S9912S-S9919S

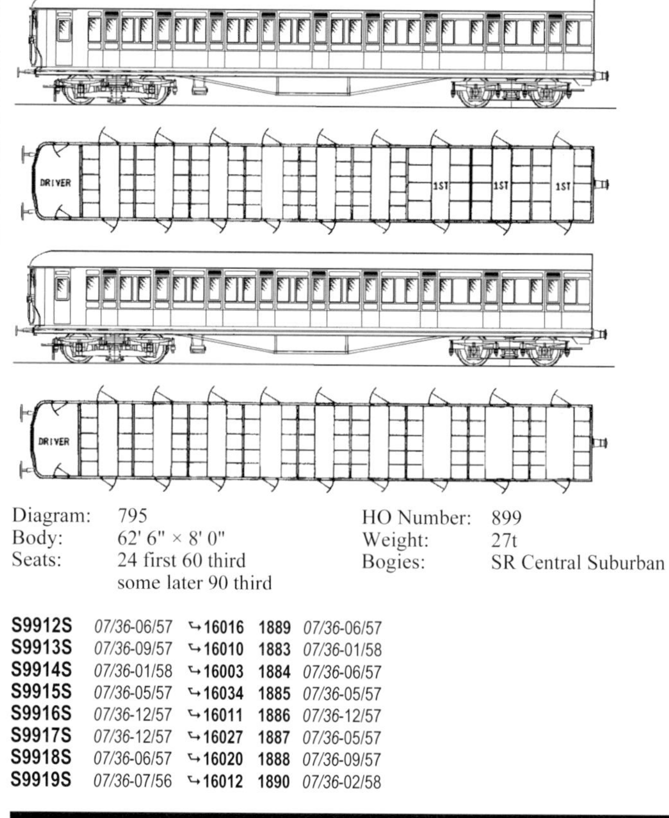

Diagram:	795	HO Number:	899
Body:	62' 6" × 8' 0"	Weight:	27t
Seats:	24 first 60 third some later 90 third	Bogies:	SR Central Suburban

S9912S	*07/36-06/57*	↳**16016**	**1889**	*07/36-06/57*
S9913S	*07/36-09/57*	↳**16010**	**1883**	*07/36-01/58*
S9914S	*07/36-01/58*	↳**16003**	**1884**	*07/36-06/57*
S9915S	*07/36-05/57*	↳**16034**	**1885**	*07/36-05/57*
S9916S	*07/36-12/57*	↳**16011**	**1886**	*07/36-12/57*
S9917S	*07/36-12/57*	↳**16027**	**1887**	*07/36-05/57*
S9918S	*07/36-06/57*	↳**16020**	**1888**	*07/36-09/57*
S9919S	*07/36-07/56*	↳**16012**	**1890**	*07/36-02/58*

2-NOL Lancing or Lancing/Eastleigh (LSWR bodies)

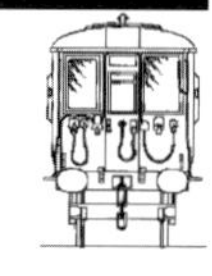

Driving Trailer Composite
DTC
S9920S-S9939S

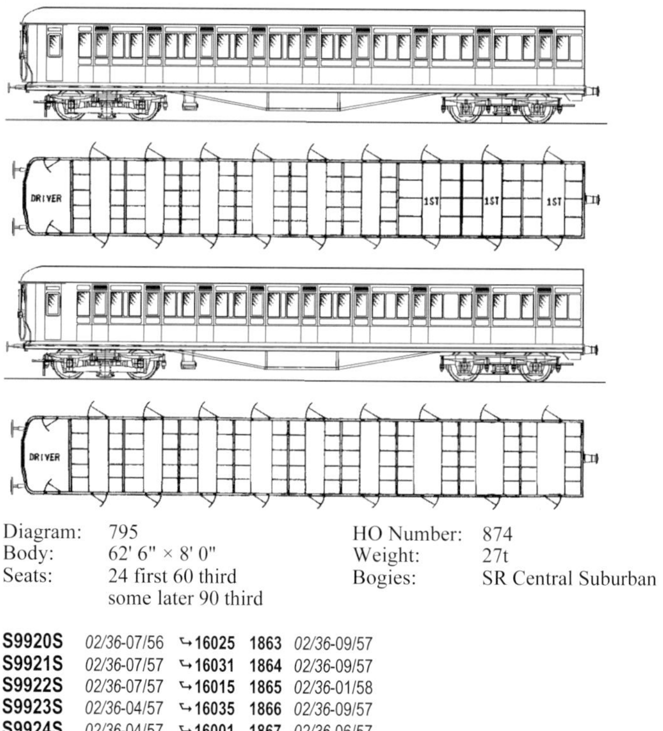

Diagram:	795	HO Number:	874
Body:	62' 6" × 8' 0"	Weight:	27t
Seats:	24 first 60 third some later 90 third	Bogies:	SR Central Suburban

S9920S	*02/36-07/56*	↳**16025**	**1863**	*02/36-09/57*
S9921S	*02/36-07/57*	↳**16031**	**1864**	*02/36-09/57*
S9922S	*02/36-07/57*	↳**16015**	**1865**	*02/36-01/58*
S9923S	*02/36-04/57*	↳**16035**	**1866**	*02/36-09/57*
S9924S	*02/36-04/57*	↳**16001**	**1867**	*02/36-06/57*

S9925S	*02/36*-07/57	↳**16021**	**1868**	*02/36*-12/57
S9926S	*02/36*-07/56	↳**16007**	**1869**	*02/36*-06/57
S9927S	*02/36*-07/56	↳**15435**	**1870**	*02/36*-07/56
S9928S	*02/36*-08/57	↳**15434**	**1871**	*02/36*-07/56
S9929S	*02/36*-10/57	↳**16026**	**1872**	*02/36*-07/57
S9930S	*03/36*-05/57	↳**16006**	**1873**	*03/36*-07/57
S9931S	*03/36*-09/57	↳**16002**	**1874**	*03/36*-04/57
S9932S	*03/36*-01/58	↳**16004**	**1875**	*03/36*-04/57
S9933S	*03/36*-06/57	↳**16018**	**1876**	*03/36*-07/57
S9934S	*03/36*-06/57	↳**15447**	**1877**	*03/36*-07/56
S9935S	*03/36*-01/58	↳**15437**	**1878**	*03/36*-07/56
S9936S	*03/36*-05/57	↳**16022**	**1879**	*03/36*-08/57
S9937S	*03/36*-09/57	↳**16013**	**1880**	*03/36*-10/57
S9938S	*03/36*-07/57	↳**16033**	**1881**	*03/36*-05/57
S9939S	*03/36*-02/58	↳**16023**	**1882**	*03/36*-09/57

2-NOL Lancing or Lancing/Eastleigh (LSWR bodies)

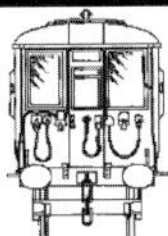

Driving Trailer Composite
DTC
S9940S-S9950S

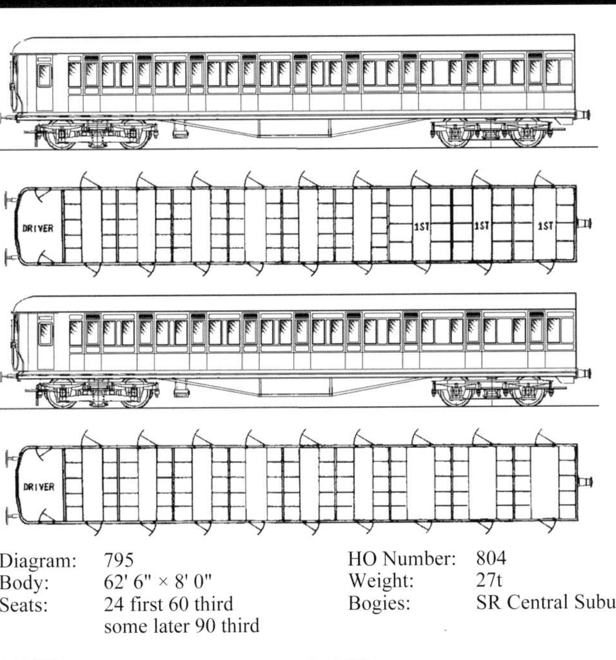

Diagram:	795	HO Number:	804
Body:	62' 6" × 8' 0"	Weight:	27t
Seats:	24 first 60 third some later 90 third	Bogies:	SR Central Suburban

S9940S	*11/34*-03/59	↳**16111**	**1813**	*11/34*-03/59
S9941S	*11/34*-02/59	↳**16130**	**1814**	*11/34*-02/59
S9942S	*11/34*-07/59	↳**16125**	**1815**	*11/34*-07/59
S9943S	*11/34*-02/59	↳**16122**	**1816**	*11/34*-02/59
S9944S	*11/34*-07/59	↳**16123**	**1817**	*11/34*-07/59
S9945S	*12/34*-07/59	↳**16134**	**1818**	*12/34*-07/59
S9946	*12/34*-01/51	⊗01/51	**1819**	*12/34*-01/51
S9947S	*12/34*-07/59	↳**16124**	**1820**	*12/34*-07/59
S9948S	*12/34*-02/59	↳**16110**	**1821**	*12/34*-02/59
S9949S	*12/34*-07/59	↳**16118**	**1822**	*12/34*-07/59
S9950S	*12/34*-10/58	↳**16101**	**1823**	*12/34*-10/58

2-WIM Brighton (ex AC stock)

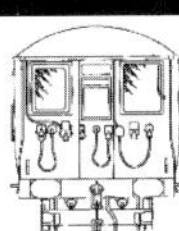

Driving Trailer Third
DTT
S9951S-S9954S

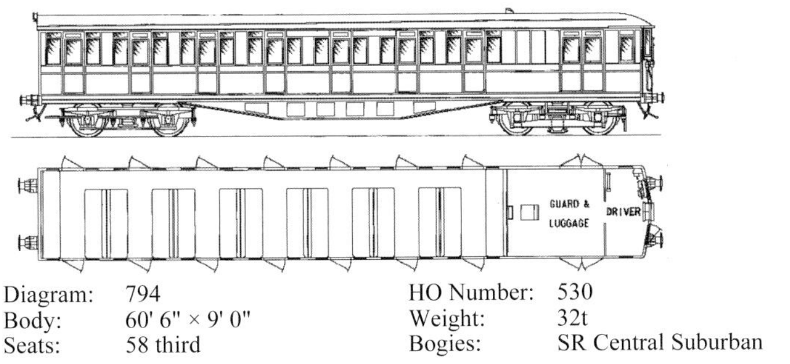

Diagram:	794	HO Number:	530
Body:	60' 6" × 9' 0"	Weight:	32t
Seats:	58 third	Bogies:	SR Central Suburban

S9951S	06/30-*01/54*	⊗	**1909**	06/30-04/34	**1809**	04/34-*01/54*	⊂**7645**
S9952S	06/30-10/54	⊗	**1910**	06/30-04/34	**1810**	04/34-10/54	⊂**7646**
S9953S	06/30-10/54	⊗	**1911**	06/30-04/34	**1811**	04/34-10/54	⊂**7648**
S9954S	06/30-08/54	⊗	**1912**	06/30-04/34	**1812**	04/34-08/54	⊂**7650**

2-NOL Lancing or Lancing/Eastleigh (LSWR bodies)

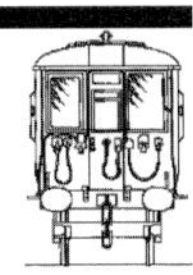

Driving Trailer Composite
DTC
9961-S9999S

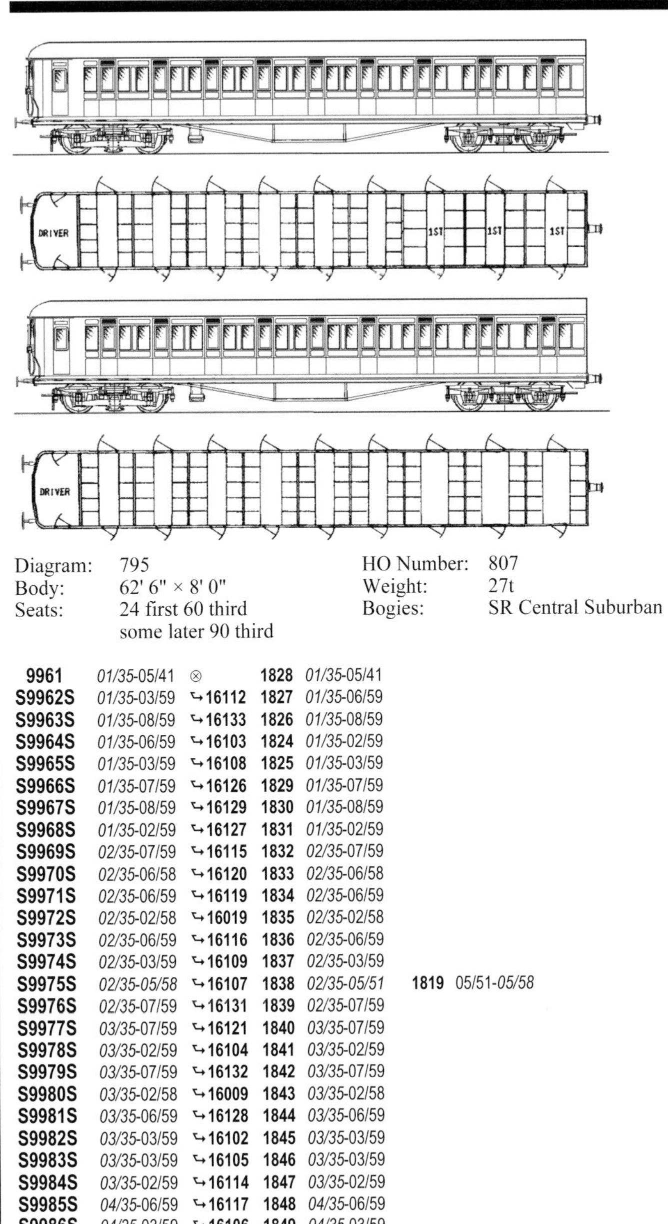

Diagram:	795	HO Number:	807
Body:	62' 6" × 8' 0"	Weight:	27t
Seats:	24 first 60 third some later 90 third	Bogies:	SR Central Suburban

9961	*01/35*-05/41	⊗	**1828**	*01/35*-05/41		
S9962S	*01/35*-03/59	↳**16112**	**1827**	*01/35*-06/59		
S9963S	*01/35*-08/59	↳**16133**	**1826**	*01/35*-08/59		
S9964S	*01/35*-06/59	↳**16103**	**1824**	*01/35*-02/59		
S9965S	*01/35*-03/59	↳**16108**	**1825**	*01/35*-03/59		
S9966S	*01/35*-07/59	↳**16126**	**1829**	*01/35*-07/59		
S9967S	*01/35*-08/59	↳**16129**	**1830**	*01/35*-08/59		
S9968S	*01/35*-02/59	↳**16127**	**1831**	*01/35*-02/59		
S9969S	*02/35*-07/59	↳**16115**	**1832**	*02/35*-07/59		
S9970S	*02/35*-06/58	↳**16120**	**1833**	*02/35*-06/58		
S9971S	*02/35*-06/59	↳**16119**	**1834**	*02/35*-06/59		
S9972S	*02/35*-02/58	↳**16019**	**1835**	*02/35*-02/58		
S9973S	*02/35*-06/59	↳**16116**	**1836**	*02/35*-06/59		
S9974S	*02/35*-03/59	↳**16109**	**1837**	*02/35*-03/59		
S9975S	*02/35*-05/58	↳**16107**	**1838**	*02/35*-05/51	**1819**	05/51-*05/58*
S9976S	*02/35*-07/59	↳**16131**	**1839**	*02/35*-07/59		
S9977S	*03/35*-07/59	↳**16121**	**1840**	*03/35*-07/59		
S9978S	*03/35*-02/59	↳**16104**	**1841**	*03/35*-02/59		
S9979S	*03/35*-07/59	↳**16132**	**1842**	*03/35*-07/59		
S9980S	*03/35*-02/58	↳**16009**	**1843**	*03/35*-02/58		
S9981S	*03/35*-06/59	↳**16128**	**1844**	*03/35*-06/59		
S9982S	*03/35*-03/59	↳**16102**	**1845**	*03/35*-03/59		
S9983S	*03/35*-03/59	↳**16105**	**1846**	*03/35*-03/59		
S9984S	*03/35*-02/59	↳**16114**	**1847**	*03/35*-02/59		
S9985S	*04/35*-06/59	↳**16117**	**1848**	*04/35*-06/59		
S9986S	*04/35*-03/59	↳**16106**	**1849**	*04/35*-03/59		
S9987S	*04/35*-03/59	↳**16113**	**1850**	*04/35*-03/59		
S9988S	*04/35*-04/57	↳**16017**	**1851**	*04/35*-04/57		
S9989S	*04/35*-12/57	↳**16032**	**1852**	*04/35*-12/57		
S9990S	*04/35*-12/55	⊗12/55	**1853**	*04/35*-12/55		
S9991S	*04/35*-11/57	↳**16008**	**1854**	*04/35*-11/57		
9992	*04/35*-11/41	⊗11/41	**1855**	*04/35*-11/41		
S9993S	*04/35*-07/57	↳**16028**	**1856**	*04/35*-07/57		
S9994S	*05/35*-05/57	↳**16030**	**1857**	*05/35*-05/57		
S9995S	*05/35*-04/57	↳**16014**	**1858**	*05/35*-04/57		
S9996S	*05/35*-04/57	↳**16005**	**1859**	*05/35*-04/57		
S9997S	*05/35*-09/57	↳**16024**	**1860**	*05/35*-09/57		
S9998S	*05/35*-06/57	↳**16029**	**1861**	*05/35*-06/57		
S9999S	*05/35*-06/57	↳**16036**	**1862**	*05/35*-06/57		

Pullman Cars

All Pullman cars were stored from May 1942 to January 1946.

6-PUL Metropolitan-Cammell

Pullman Trailer Kitchen Composite
TPCK
S256S-S278S (Some 6-CIT)

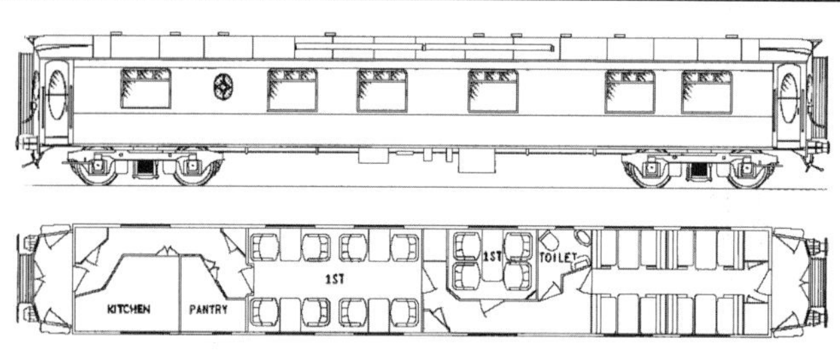

Body: 65' 0" × 9' 0" Weight: 43t
Seats: 12 first 16 third 1 toilet Bogies: SR Express

S256S	*09/32*-03/66	62➲**300**	**2002**	*09/32*-01/37	**3002**	01/37-05/42	**3043**	12/47-03/66
	Rita							
S257S	*09/32*-01/66	62➲**297**	**2003**	*09/32*-01/37	**3003**	01/37-05/42	**3003**	46-01/48
	Grace		**3003**	06/49-01/66				
S258S	*09/32*-03/66	62➲**294**	**2013**	*09/32*-01/37	**3013**	01/37-05/42	**3013**	46-03/66
	Brenda							
S259S	*09/32*-09/64	62➲**296**	**2014**	*09/32*-01/37	**3014**	01/37-05/42	**3014**	46-01/64
	Enid		**3059**	01/64-09/64				
S260S	*10/32*-02/66	62➲**295**	**2004**	*10/32*-01/37	**3004**	01/37-05/42	**3004**	46-01/64
	Elinor		**3057**	01/64-02/66				
S261S	*10/32*-12/65	62➲**299**	**2015**	*10/32*-01/37	**3015**	01/37-05/42	**3015**	46-12/65
	Joyce							
S262S	*10/32*-09/65	62➲**298**	**2016**	*10/32*-01/37	**3016**	01/37-05/42	**3016**	46-03/65
	Iris		**3006**	04/65-09/65				
S263S	*10/32*-06/66	⊗06/66	**2005**	*10/32*-01/37	**3005**	01/37-05/42	**3005**	46-02/66
	Ida							
S264S	*10/32*-09/65	Ⓟ➲DS70260	**2017**	*10/32*-01/37	**3017**	01/37-05/42	**3042**	12/47-09/65
	Ruth							
S265S	*11/32*-04/65	⊗	**2006**	*11/32*-01/37	**3006**	01/37-05/42	**3006**	46-04/65
	Rose							
S266S	*11/32*-09/65	⊗04/66	**2007**	*11/32*-01/37	**3007**	01/37-05/42	**3007**	46-09/65
	Violet							
S267S	*11/32*-09/65	⊗06/66	**2018**	*11/32*-01/37	**3018**	01/37-05/42	**3041**	04/47-09/65
	May							
S268S	*11/32*-01/64	⊗	**2019**	*11/32*-01/37	**3019**	01/37-05/42	**3019**	46-01/64
	Peggy							
S269S	*11/32*-06/66	⊗	**2020**	*11/32*-01/37	**3020**	01/37-05/42	**3020**	46-01/64
	Clara		**3054**	01/64-06/66				
S270S	12/32-07/65	⊗06/66	**2043**	12/32-01/37	**3043**	01/37-05/42	**3018**	05/46-01/64
	Ethel		**3056**	01/64-07/65				
S271S	*10/32*-06/66	⊗	**2009**	*10/32*-01/37	**3009**	01/37-05/42	**3009**	46-09/64
	Alice		**3059**	09/64-07/65	**3041**	09/65-03/66		
S272S	11/32-06/66	⊗	**2041**	11/32-01/37	**3041**	01/37-05/42	**3017**	05/46-01/64
	Gwladys		**3055**	01/64-06/66				
S273S	*11/32*-12/65	⊗	**2042**	*11/32*-01/37	**3042**	01/37-05/42	**3002**	05/46-12/65
	Olive							
S274S	*11/32*-12/65	⊗	**2010**	*11/32*-01/37	**3010**	01/37-05/42	**3010**	46-11/65
	Daisy							
S275S	*12/32*-09/65	⊗04/66	**2001**	*12/32*-01/37	**3001**	01/37-05/42	**3001**	46- 48
	Anne		**3012**	48-09/65				
S276S	*12/32*-12/65	⊗06/66	**2011**	*12/32*-01/37	**3011**	01/37-05/42	**3011**	46-12/65
	Naomi							
S277S	*12/32*-03/66	⊗	**2008**	*12/32*-01/37	**3008**	01/37-05/42	**3008**	46-02/66
	Lorna		**3057**	02/66-03/66				
S278S	*12/32*-06/66	Ⓟ➲DS70261	**2012**	*12/32*-01/37	**3012**	01/37-05/42	**3012**	46- 48
	Bertha		**3001**	48-04/66				

Class 405 5-BEL Metropolitan-Cammell

Brighton Belle Trailer Kitchen First
TKRK
S279S-S284S

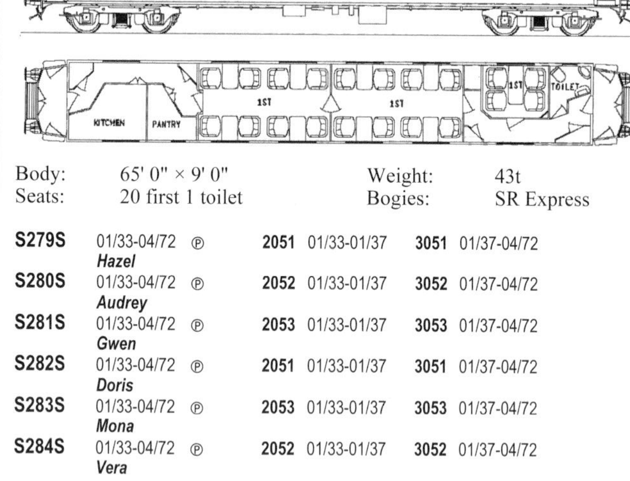

Body: 65' 0" × 9' 0" Weight: 43t
Seats: 20 first 1 toilet Bogies: SR Express

S279S	01/33-04/72	Ⓟ	**2051**	01/33-01/37	**3051**	01/37-04/72
	Hazel					
S280S	01/33-04/72	Ⓟ	**2052**	01/33-01/37	**3052**	01/37-04/72
	Audrey					
S281S	01/33-04/72	Ⓟ	**2053**	01/33-01/37	**3053**	01/37-04/72
	Gwen					
S282S	01/33-04/72	Ⓟ	**2051**	01/33-01/37	**3051**	01/37-04/72
	Doris					
S283S	01/33-04/72	Ⓟ	**2053**	01/33-01/37	**3053**	01/37-04/72
	Mona					
S284S	01/33-04/72	Ⓟ	**2052**	01/33-01/37	**3052**	01/37-04/72
	Vera					

Class 405 5-BEL Metropolitan-Cammell

Brighton Belle Trailer Parlour Second
TPS
S285S-S287S

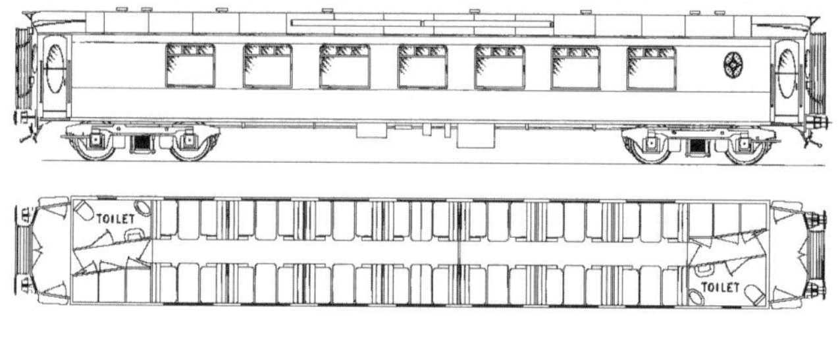

Body: 65' 0" × 9' 0" Weight: 39t
Seats: 56 third 1 toilet sBogies: SR Express

S285S	01/33-04/72	Ⓟ	**2053**	01/33-01/37	**3053**	01/37-04/72
	Car Number 85					
S286S	01/33-04/72	Ⓟ	**2051**	01/33-01/37	**3051**	01/37-04/72
	Car Number 86					
S287S	01/33-04/72	Ⓟ	**2052**	01/33-01/37	**3052**	01/37-04/72
	Car Number 87					

Class 405 5-BEL Metropolitan-Cammell

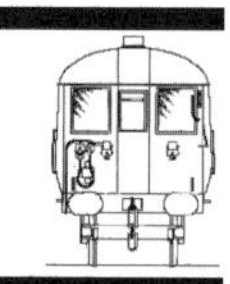

Brighton Belle Motor Brake Parlour Second
DMPBS
S288S-S293S

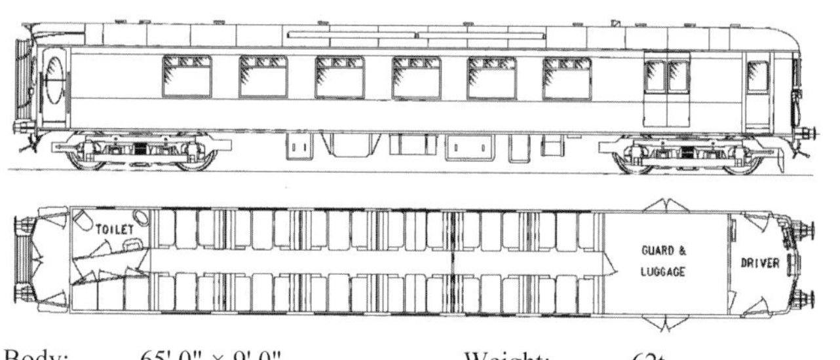

Body: 65' 0" × 9' 0" Weight: 62t
Seats: 48 third 1 toilet Bogies: SR Express
Motor: BTH 4 × 225hp

S288S	01/33-04/72	Ⓟ	**2051**	01/33-01/37	**3051**	01/37-04/72
	Car Number 88					

S289S 01/33-04/72 Ⓟ
2051 01/33-01/37**3051** 01/37-04/72
Car Number 89

S290S 01/33-04/72 Ⓟ⊗ **2052** 01/33-01/37 **3052** 01/37-04/72
Car Number 90

S291S 01/33-04/72 Ⓟ **2052** 01/33-01/37 **3052** 01/37-04/72
Car Number 91

S292S 01/33-04/72 Ⓟ **2053** 01/33-01/37 **3053** 01/37-04/72
Car Number 92

S293S 01/33-04/72 Ⓟ **2053** 01/33-01/37 **3053** 01/37-04/72
Car Number 93

Waterloo & City

1899 stock Jackson Sharp

Single-ended Motor Third
DMT
1-12

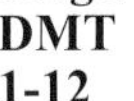

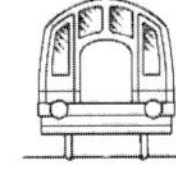

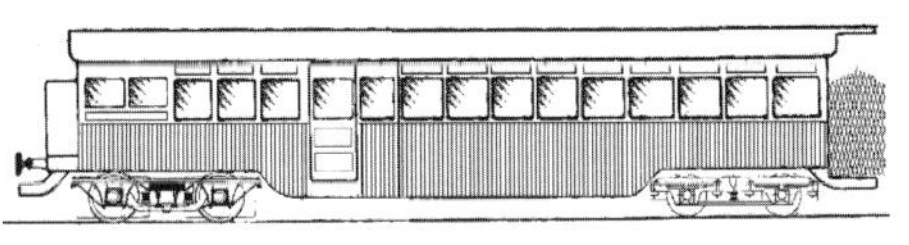

Diagram:
Body: 51' 3" × 8' 6" Weight:
Seats: 46 third Bogies:
Motors: Siemens 120hp

1	98-11/40	⊗	*43*
2	98-11/40	⊗	*43*
3	98-11/40	⊗	*43*
4	98-11/40	⊗	*43*
5	98-11/40	⊗	*43*
6	98-11/40	⊗	*43*
7	98-11/40	⊗	*43*
8	98-11/40	⊗	*43*
9	98-11/40	⊗	*43*
10	98-11/40	⊗	*43*
11	98-11/40	⊗	*43*
12	98-11/40	⊗	*43*

1899 Stock Dick Kerr

Double-ended Motor Third
DMT
13-17

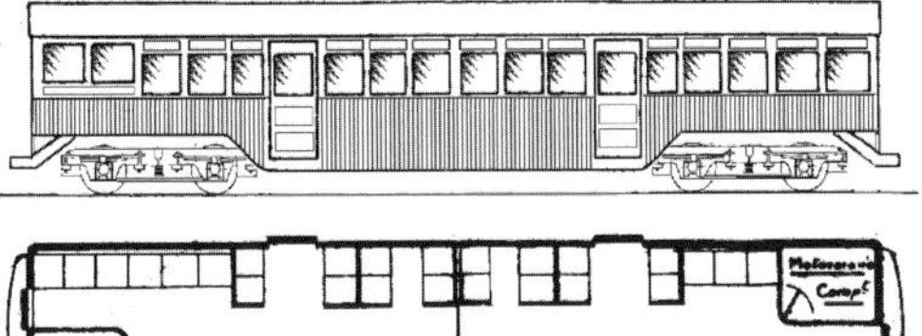

Diagram:
Body: 50' 9" × 8' 6" Weight:
Seats: 50 third Bogies:
Motors: Siemens 120hp

13	99-11/40	⊗	*43*
14	99-11/40	⊗	*48*
15	99-11/40	⊗	*43*
16	00-11/40	⊗	*43*
17	00-11/40	⊗	*43*

1898 stock Jackson Sharp

Trailer Third
TT
21-30

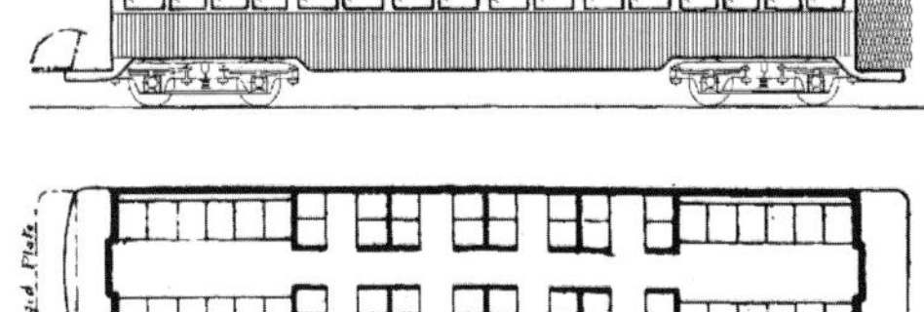

Diagram:
Body: 49' 9" × 8' 6" Weight:
Seats: 56 third Bogies:
Motors:

21	98-11/40	⊗	*43*
22	98-11/40	⊗	*43*
23	98-11/40	⊗	*43*
24	98-11/40	⊗	*43*
25	98-11/40	⊗	*43*
26	98-11/40	⊗	*43*
27	98-11/40	⊗	*43*
28	98-11/40	⊗	*43*
29	98-11/40	⊗	*43*
30	98-11/40	⊗	*43*

1904 stock Electric TW

Trailer Third
TT
31-31

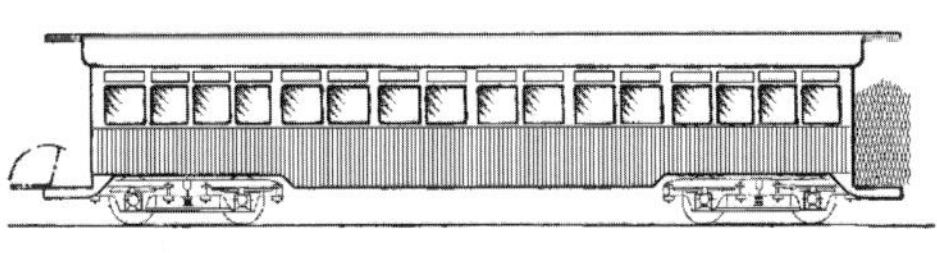

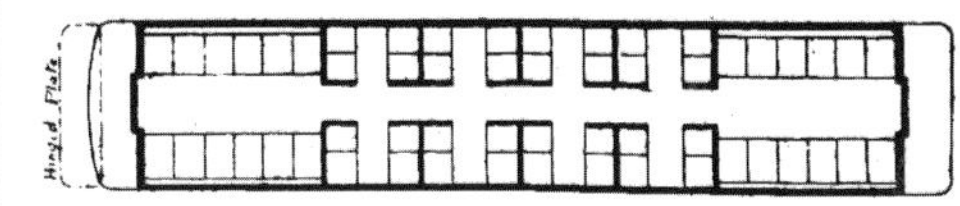

Diagram:
Body: 49' 9" × 8' 6" Weight:
Seats: 56 third Bogies:

31	04-11/40	⊗	*43*
32	04-11/40	⊗	*43*

1904 stock Eastleigh

Trailer Third
TT
33-36

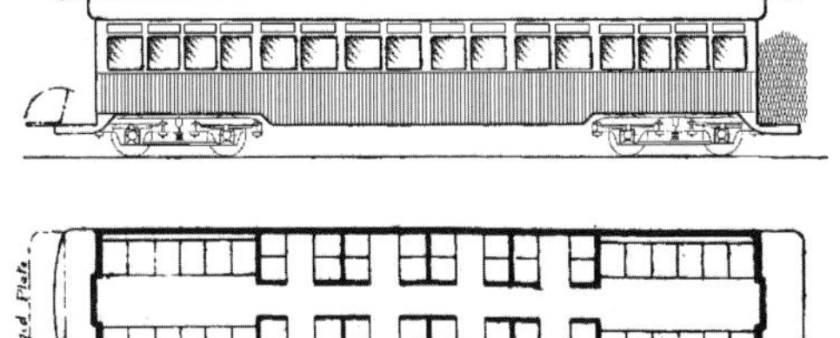

Diagram:
Body: 49' 2" × 8' 6" Weight:
Seats: 56 third Bogies:

33	22-11/40	⊗	*43*
34	22-11/40	⊗	*43*
35	22-11/40	⊗	*43*
36	22-11/40	⊗	*48*

Class 487 Dick Kerr

Driving Motor Second Open
DMSO
S51S-S62S

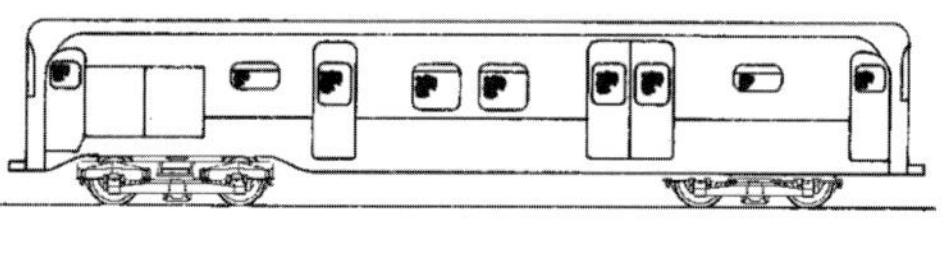

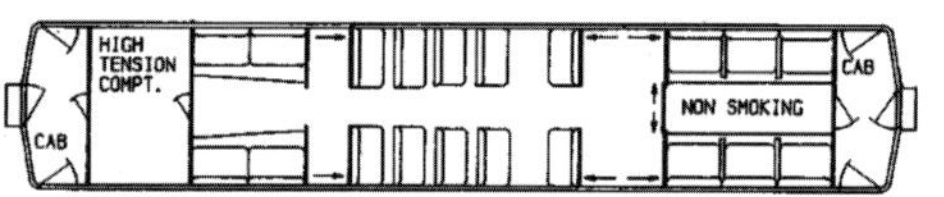

Diagram:	842 EB260	HO Number:	
Body:	49' 1¾" × 8' 7¾"	Weight:	23t
Seats:	40 second	Bogies:	
Motors:	EE500 2 × 190hp		

S51S	03/40-05/93	⊗06/93
S52S	03/40-09/82	⊗08/88
S53S	03/40-05/93	⊗06/93
S54S	03/40-05/93	⊗07/93
S55S	03/40-10/86	⊗02/90
S56S	03/40-05/93	⊗07/93
S57S	05/40-05/93	⊗06/93
S58S	05/40-04/91	⊗05/93
S59S	06/40-05/93	⊗06/93
S60S	06/40-05/93	⊗06/93
S61S	07/40-05/93	Ⓟ
S62S	07/40-04/93	⊗05/93

Class 487 Dick Kerr

Trailer Second Open
TSO
S71S-S86S

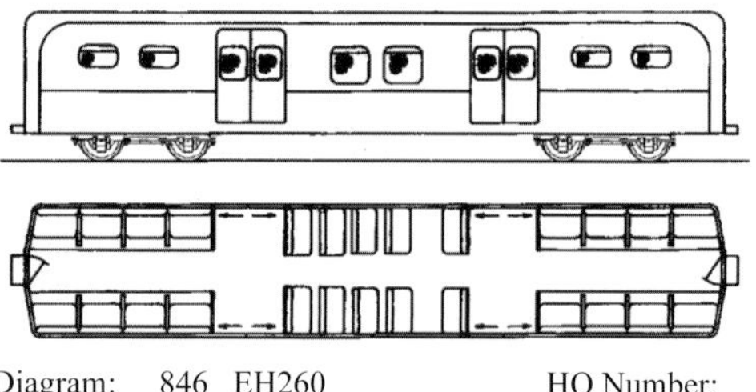

Diagram:	846 EH260	HO Number:	
Body:	49' 1¾" × 8' 7¾"	Weight:	19t
Seats:	52 second	Bogies:	

S71S	05/40-08/87	⊗08/90
S72S	03/40-05/93	⊗06/93
S73S	03/40-05/93	⊗06/93
S74S	03/40-05/93	⊗06/93
S75S	06/40-05/93	⊗06/93
S76S	06/40-05/93	⊗06/93
S77S	06/40-05/93	⊗06/93
S78S	07/40-05/93	⊗06/93
S79S	03/40-06/87	⊗08/90
S80S	03/40-05/93	⊗06/93
S81S	03/40-02/83	⊗05/93
S82S	03/40-09/82	⊗08/88
S83S	03/40-05/93	⊗06/93
S84S	03/40-05/93	⊗06/93
S85S	05/40-05/93	⊗06/93
S86S	05/40-05/93	⊗06/93

Isle of Wight

Class 485/486 Metropolitan C&W

Driving Motor Brake Second
MBSO
S1S-S25S (some built by UCC (Feltham))

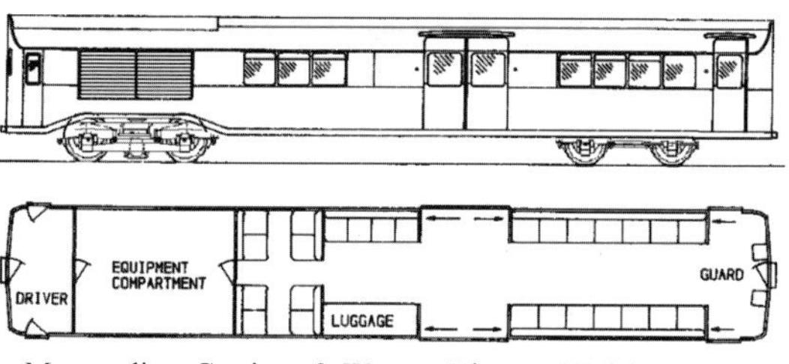

M Metropolitan Carriage & Wagon, Diagram EB261

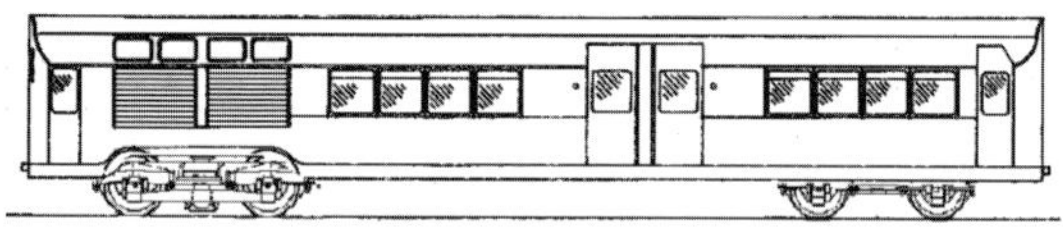

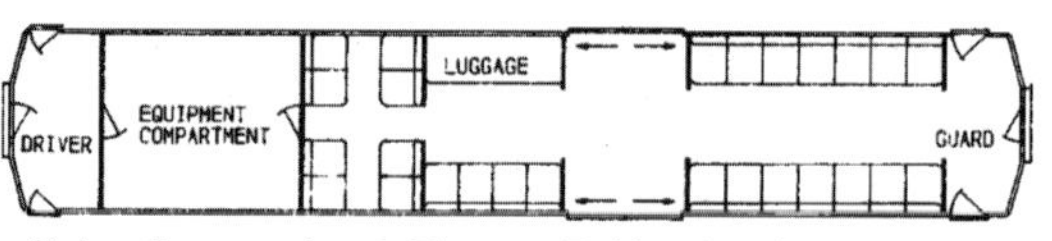

U Union Construction & Finance (Feltham) , Diagram EB262

Diagram:	848 EB261 EB262	Lot Number:	
Body:	54' 8½" × 8' 8"	Weight:	29t
Seats:	26 second	Bogies:	LT
Motors:	EE 4 × 240hp		

S1S	03/67-06/90	⊗01/93	**031**	03/67- 83	**041**	83- 84			⊂**3703** (**M** 11/34)
			485041	84- 89					
S2S	03/67-09/90	Ⓟ	**043**	03/67- 84	**485043**	84- 89			⊂**3706** (**M** 02/35)
S3S	03/67- 89	⊗10/90	**032**	03/67- 68	**042**	68-09/71			⊂**3251** (**M** 06/32)
			032	09/71- 84	**486032**	84- 85	**485042**	85- 89	
S4S	03/67-09/89	⊗10/90	**044**	03/67- 84	**485044**	84- 85			⊂**3702** (**M** 01/35)
			485042	85- 89					
S5S	03/67-05/91	⊗04/94	**033**	03/67-12/82	**043**	82- 84			⊂**3185** (**M** 04/32)
			485043	85- 89					
S6S	03/67-02/90	⊗08/91	**045**	03/67- 84	**485045**	84- 85			⊂**3084** (**M** 12/31)
			485043	85- 89					
S7S	03/67-09/90	Ⓟ	**034**	03/67- 84	**486034**	84- 85			⊂**3209** (**M** 05/32)
			485044	85- 89					
S8S	03/67-06/90	⊗01/93	**046**	03/67-10/80	**036**	10/80- 84			⊂**3074** (**M** 12/31)
			486036	84- 85	**485044**	85- 89			
S9S	03/67-10/89	⊗08/91	**035**	03/67-09/73	**045**	74- 83			⊂**3223** (**M** 06/32)
			035	83- 84	**486035**	84- 85	**485045**	85- 89	
S10S	03/67-06/90	⊗01/93	**037**	*spare*	**042**	68-09/71			⊂**3696** (**M** 11/34)
			034	76- 82	**485045**	85- 89			
S11S	03/67-02/90	⊗01/93	**036**	03/67- 74	**035**	74- 83			⊂**3705** (**M** 12/34)
			045	83- 84	**485045**	84- 85	**486031**	85- 89	
S13S	03/67-03/85	⊗06/87	**041**	03/67- 83	**031**	83- 84			⊂**3141** (**M** 03/32)
			486031	84- 85					
S15S[1]	03/67-10/67	⊗05/69	**042**	03/67- 68					⊂**3253** (**M** 06/32)
S15S[2]	03/71-04/88	⊗05/89	**042**	09/71- 84	**485042**	84- 85			⊂**3073** (**M** 12/31)
			486032	85-08/88					
S19S	03/67-12/82	⊃**083569**	**043**	03/67- 82	**485043**	84- 85			⊂**3045** (**U** 03/29)
S20S	03/67-04/88	⊗05/89	**041**	83- 84	**485041**	84- 85			⊂**3308** (**U** 10/29)
			486031	85-08/87	**486032**	08/87- 88			
S21S	03/67-03/85	⊗06/87	**044**	03/67- 84	**485044**	84- 85			⊂**3041** (03/29)
									Carried **S17S** (**036**) before entering service
S22S	03/67-11/86	⊗05/89	**042**	03/67- 68	**032**	68-09/71			⊂**3010** (06/30)
			042	09/71- 84	**485042**	84- 85	**486032**	85-08/87	
									Carried **S12S** (**043**) before entering service
S23S	03/67-09/73	⊗11/75	**045**	03/67-09/73					⊂**3315** (**M** 06/29)
S25S	03/67-09/75	⊗02/82	**046**	03/67-09/75					⊂**3313** (**M** 06/29)

Class 485/486 Metropolitan C&W

Driving Trailer Second
DTSO
S26S-S36S

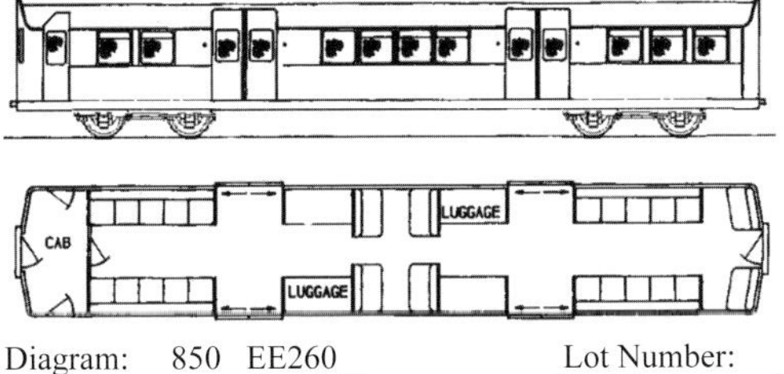

Diagram:	850 EE260	Lot Number:	
Body:	50' 2¼" × 8' 8"	Weight:	27t
Seats:	38 second	Bogies:	LT

No.	Dates	Disposal	Unit	Period	Unit	Period	Unit	Period	Former
S26S	03/67-09/90	⊗04/94	**031**	03/67- 84	**486031**	84- 85			⊂**5294** (08/26)
			485041	85- 89	Carried **S38S** (**037**) before entering service				
S27S	03/67-01/90	Ⓟ	**041**	03/67- 84	**485041**	84- 89			⊂**5279** (08/26)
S28S	03/67-05/91	⊗04/94	**032**	03/67- 68	**042**	68-09/71			⊂**5304** (09/26)
			032	09/71- 84	**486032**	84- 85	**485042**	85- 87	
			486031	08/87- 89					
S29S	03/67 09/89	⊗10/90	**042**	03/67- 68	**032**	68-09/71			⊂**5293** (09/26)
			042	09/71- 84	**485042**	84- 89			
S30S	03/67-12/82	⊃**083570**	**033**	03/67-12/82					⊂**5312** (10/26)
S31S	03/67-05/91	⊗04/94	**043**	03/67- 84	**485043**	84- 89			⊂**5283** (08/26)
S32S	03/67-09/89	⊗10/90	**034**	03/67- 84	**486034**	84- 85			⊂**5290** (09/26)
			485043	85- 89					
S33S	03/67-09/89	⊗10/90	**044**	03/67- 84	**485044**	84- 89			⊂**5291** (09/26)
S34S	03/67-06/90	⊗10/90	**035**	03/67-09/73	**045**	74- 84			⊂**5302** (09/26)
			485045	84- 89					
S36S	03/67-03/85	⊗06/87	**036**	03/67- 74	**035**	74- 84			⊂**5350** (05/29)
			486035	84- 85					

Class 485/486 Cammell Laird

Trailer Second
TSO
S41S-S49S, S92S-S96S

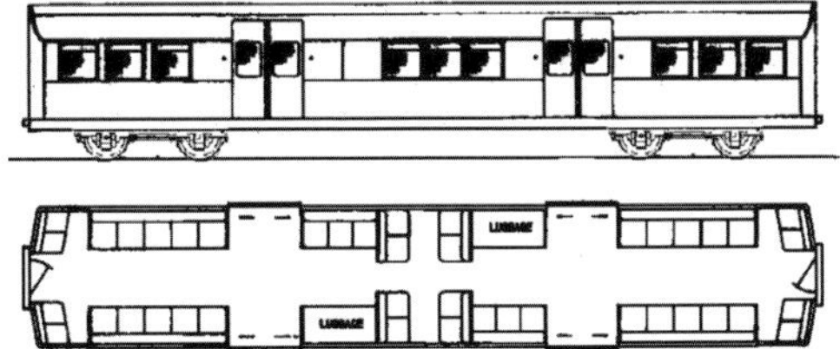

Diagram:	849 EH261	Lot Number:	
Body:	49' 9¼" × 8' 8"	Weight:	19t
Seats:	42 second	Bogies:	LT

No.	Dates	Disposal	Unit	Period	Unit	Period	Unit	Period	Former
S41S	03/67-09/86	⊗05/89	**041**	03/67- 84	**485041**	84- 85			⊂**7286** (02/24)
S42S	03/67-11/86	⊗05/89	**042**	03/67- 68	**032**	68-09/71			⊂**7280** (01/24)
			042	09/71- 84	**485042**	84- 87			
S43S	03/67-09/88	⊗10/90	**043**	03/67- 84	**485043**	84- 89			⊂**7275** (01/24)
S44S	03/67-02/90	Ⓟ	**044**	03/67- 84	**485044**	84- 89			⊂**7281** (01/24)
S45S	03/67-09/73	⊗11/75	**045**	03/67-09/73					⊂**7293** (02/24)
S46S	03/67-02/86	⊗05/89	**046**	03/67-10/80	**036**	10/80- 84			⊂**7283** (02/24)
			486036	84- 85					
S47S	03/67-11/87	⊗10/90	**031**	03/67- 84	**486031**	84- 85			⊂**7279** (01/24)
			485042	87- 89					
S48S	03/67-09/73	⊗11/75	**045**	03/67-09/73					⊂**7298** (02/24)
S49S	03/67-09/90	Ⓟ	**046**	03/67-10/80	**036**	10/80- 84			⊂**7296** (02/24)
			486036	84- 85	**485044**	85- 89			
S92S	03/67-10/88	⊗10/90	**032**	03/67- 68	**042**	68-09/71			⊂**7285** (01/24)
			032	09/71- 84	**486032**	84- 85	**485041**	85- 89	
S93S	03/67-01/90	⊗10/90	**033**	03/67-12/82	**485045**	85- 89			⊂**7282** (01/24)
S94S	03/67-10/89	⊗10/90	**034**	03/67- 84	**486034**	84- 85			⊂**7287** (02/24)
			485045	85- 89					
S95S	03/67-03/90	⊗10/90	**035**	03/67-09/73	**045**	74- 84			⊂**7292** (02/24)
			485045	84- 85	**485042**	87- 89			
S96S	03/67-03/85	⊗06/87	**036**	03/67- 74	**035**	74- 84			⊂**7290** (02/24)
			486035	84- 85					

121-129	***Class 483***	*89*
221-229	***Class 483***	*89*

Southern Railway (AC Units)

CP Crystal Palace Metropolitan Amalgamated RC&W

Driving Motor Brake Third
DMTB
8567-8600

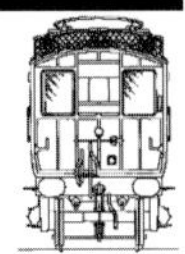

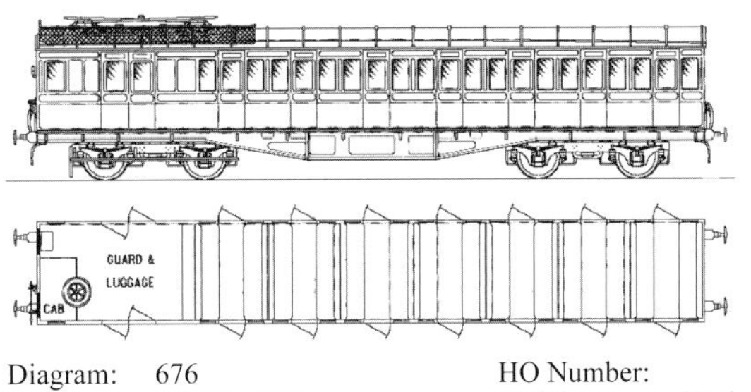

Diagram:	676	HO Number:	
Body:	54' 0" × 8' 0"	Weight:	51t 6cwt
Seats:	70 third	Bogies:	LBSCR
Motors:	Winter Eichberg 4 × 150hp		

No.	Dates	Renumbered	Former
8567	07/24-07/30	⊃**9294**	⊂3231
8568	09/26-08/29	⊃**9265**	⊂3232
8569	12/25-01/30	⊃**9280**	⊂3233
8570	05/26-08/29	⊃**9267**	⊂3234
8571	01/28-03/30	⊃**9291**	⊂3235
8572	01/27-07/29	⊃**9259**	⊂3236
8573	12/24-07/29	⊃**9262**	⊂3237
8574	03/25-07/30	⊃**9295**	⊂3238
8575	03/27-08/29	⊃**9269**	⊂3239
8576	09/26-09/29	⊃**9275**	⊂3240
8577	12/24-08/29	⊃**9271**	⊂3241
8578	05/24-02/30	⊃**9287**	⊂3242
8579	12/25-01/30	⊃**9278**	⊂3243
8580	05/26-07/29	⊃**9260**	⊂3244
8581	06/27-07/29	⊃**9263**	⊂3245
8582	-07/29	⊃**9256**	⊂3246
8583	09/25-02/30	⊃**9285**	⊂3247
8584	06/27-08/29	⊃**9266**	⊂3248
8585	09/27-07/29	⊃**9261**	⊂3249
8586	10/24-10/29	⊃**9272**	⊂3250
8587	09/27-02/30	⊃**9289**	⊂3251
8588	05/24-08/29	⊃**9270**	⊂3252
8589	10/24-09/29	⊃**9273**	⊂3253
8590	01/27-09/29	⊃**9276**	⊂3254
8591	06/25-09/29	⊃**9277**	⊂3255
8592	01/24-08/29	⊃**9268**	⊂3256
8593	06/25-08/29	⊃**9264**	⊂3257
8594	10/25-07/29	⊃**9258**	⊂3258
8595	07/24-09/29	⊃**9274**	⊂3259
8596	-01/30	⊃**9281**	⊂3260
8597	04/27-07/29	⊃**9257**	⊂3261
8598	01/24-01/30	⊃**9279**	⊂3262
8599	01/28-02/30	⊃**9283**	⊂3263
8600	03/25-03/30	⊃**9293**	⊂3264

SL South London Metropolitan Amalgamated RC&W

Driving Motor Brake Third
DMBT
8601-8616

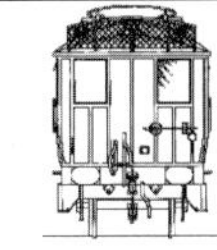

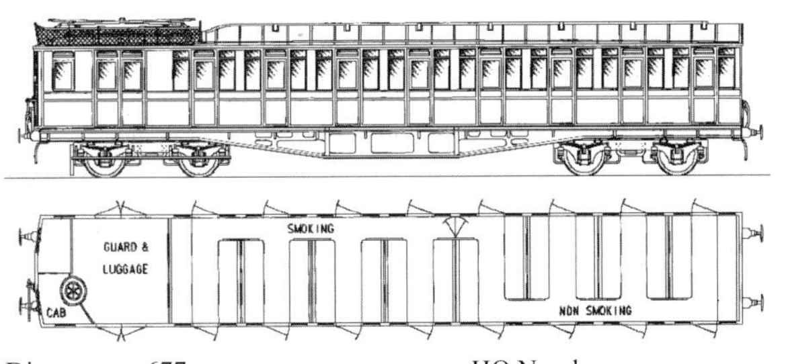

Diagram:	677	HO Number:	
Body:	60' 0" × 9' 0"	Weight:	54t
Seats:	66 third (82 crush)	Bogies:	LBSCR
Motors:	Winter Eichberg 4 × 115hp		

8601	02/25-05/29	⊃**9751**	⊂**3201**
8602	09/24-04/29	⊃**9752**	⊂**3203**
8603	-04/29	⊃**9758**	⊂**3204**
8604	04/24-05/29	⊃**8723**	⊂**3206**
8605	12/25-04/29	⊃**9753**	⊂**3207**
8606	08/27-04/29	⊃**8724**	⊂**3209**
8607	10/25-04/29	⊃**9754**	⊂**3210**
8608	06/25-04/29	⊃**8725**	⊂**3212**
8609	03/26-05/29	⊃**9755**	⊂**3213**
8610	06/26-04/29	⊃**8726**	⊂**3215**
8611	01/27-05/29	⊃**9756**	⊂**3216**
8612	11/24-05/29	⊃**9757**	⊂**3218**
8613	01/24-05/29	⊃**8727**	⊂**3219**
8614	05/27-05/29	⊃**8728**	⊂**3221**
8615	04/25-05/29	⊃**8729**	⊂**3222**
8616	07/24-04/29	⊃**8730**	⊂**3224**

CW Coulsdon-Wallington Metro/Eastleigh/Lancing

Driving Trailer Third
DTT
9169-9208

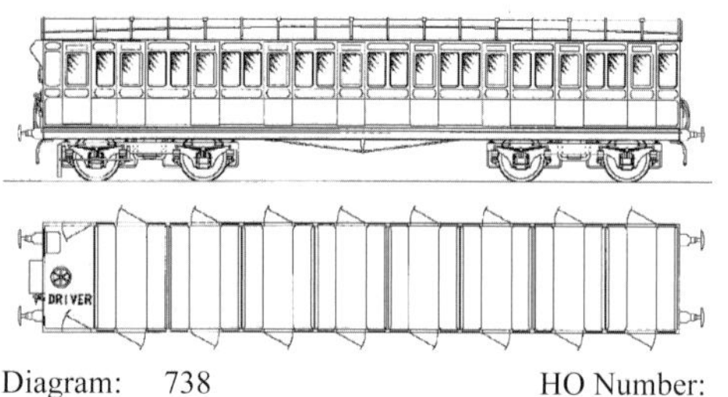

Diagram:	738	HO Number:	
Body:	48' 0" × 8' 0"	Weight:	24t
Seats:	80 third	Bogies:	LBSCR

9169-9171 were built by Metropolitan Amalgamated
9172-9188 were built by Eastleigh on Lancing frames
3268-3287, which did not carry their Southern numbers, were built at Lancing

9169	12/23-07/29	⊃**8713**	⊂*3265*
9170	12/23-08/29	⊃**8718**	⊂*3266*
9171	12/23-09/29	⊃**8700**	⊂*3267*
9172	11/23-01/30	⊃**8734**	⊂*3288*
9173	11/23-01/30	⊃**8721**	⊂*3289*
9174	11/23-08/29	⊃**8703**	⊂*3290*
9175	11/23-04/30	⊃**8745**	⊂*3291*
9176	12/23-01/30	⊃**8719**	⊂*3292*
9177	12/23-06/29	⊃**8709**	⊂*3293*
9178	12/23-08/29	⊃**8705**	⊂*3294*
9179	12/23-08/29	⊃**8704**	⊂*3295*
9180	02/24-09/29	⊃**8699**	⊂*3296*
9181	02/24-04/30	⊃**8744**	⊂*3297*
9182	02/24-08/29	⊃**8716**	⊂*3298*
9183	02/24-03/30	⊃**8740**	⊂*3299*
9184	02/24-03/30	⊃**8741**	⊂*3300*
9185	02/24-03/30	⊃**8739**	⊂*3301*
9186	02/24-06/29	⊃**8710**	⊂*3302*
9187	02/24-03/30	⊃**8742**	⊂*3303*
9188	02/24-01/30	⊃**8732**	⊂*3304*
9189	-02/30	⊃**8735**	⊂**3268**
9190	-01/30	⊃**8731**	⊂**3269**
9191	-07/29	⊃**8702**	⊂**3270**
9192	-08/29	⊃**8714**	⊂**3271**
9193	-03/30	⊃**8743**	⊂**3272**
9194	-06/29	⊃**8711**	⊂**3273**
9195	-08/29	⊃**8717**	⊂**3274**
9196	-03/30	⊃**8738**	⊂**3275**
9197	-07/29	⊃**8712**	⊂**3276**
9198	-01/30	⊃**8720**	⊂**3277**
9199	-06/29	⊃**8698**	⊂**3278**
9200	-08/29	⊃**8715**	⊂**3279**
9201	-06/30	⊃**8749**	⊂**3280**
9202	-01/30	⊃**8733**	⊂**3281**
9203	-06/29	⊃**8697**	⊂**3282**
9204	-06/30	⊃**8746**	⊂**3283**
9205	-02/30	⊃**8736**	⊂**3284**
9206	-01/30	⊃**8722**	⊂**3285**
9207	-02/30	⊃**8737**	⊂**3286**
9208	-07/29	⊃**8701**	⊂**3287**

CW Coulsdon-Wallington Lancing/Eastleigh/Metro

Driving Trailer Composite
DTC
9655-9674

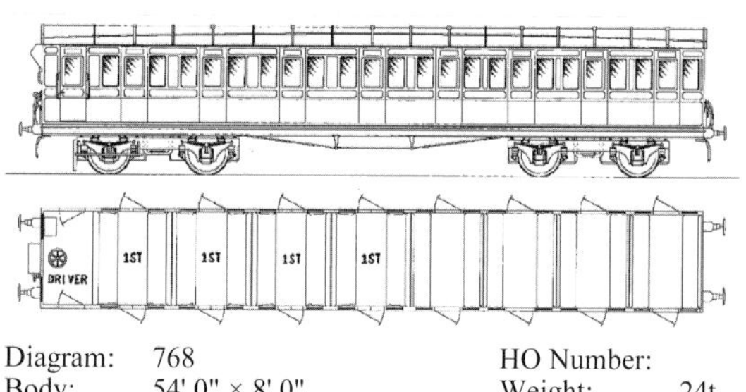

Diagram:	768	HO Number:	
Body:	54' 0" × 8' 0"	Weight:	24t
Seats:	32 first 40 third	Bogies:	LBSCR

9672-9674 were built by Metropolitan Amalgamated
9655-9658 & 9661-9663 were built by Eastleigh on Lancing frames
4119-4128, which did not carry their Southern numbers, were built at Lancing

9655	11/23-08/29	⊃**8880**	⊂*4129*
9656	11/23-09/29	⊃**8865**	⊂*4130*
9657	12/23-07/29	⊃**8878**	⊂*4131*
9658	12/23-06/29	⊃**8864**	⊂*4132*
9659	-07/29	⊃**8868**	⊂**4127**
9660	-08/29	⊃**8884**	⊂**4128**
9661	02/24-08/29	⊃**8871**	⊂*4133*
9662	02/24-06/29	⊃**8877**	⊂*4134*
9663	02/24-01/30	⊃**8889**	⊂*4135*
9664	-06/29	⊃**8863**	⊂**4119**
9665	-06/29	⊃**8875**	⊂**4120**
9666	-07/29	⊃**8879**	⊂**4121**
9667	-09/29	⊃**8866**	⊂**4122**
9668	-07/29	⊃**8867**	⊂**4123**
9669	-08/29	⊃**8870**	⊂**4124**
9670	-08/29	⊃**8882**	⊂**4125**
9671	-08/29	⊃**8881**	⊂**4126**
9672	12/23-08/29	⊃**8869**	⊂*4136*
9673	12/23-08/29	⊃**8883**	⊂*4137*
9674	12/23-06/29	⊃**8876**	⊂*4138*

SL South London Lancing

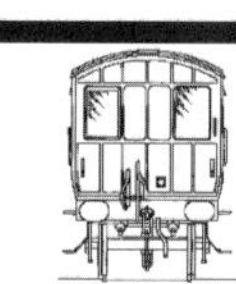

Driving Trailer Composite
DTC
9811-9824

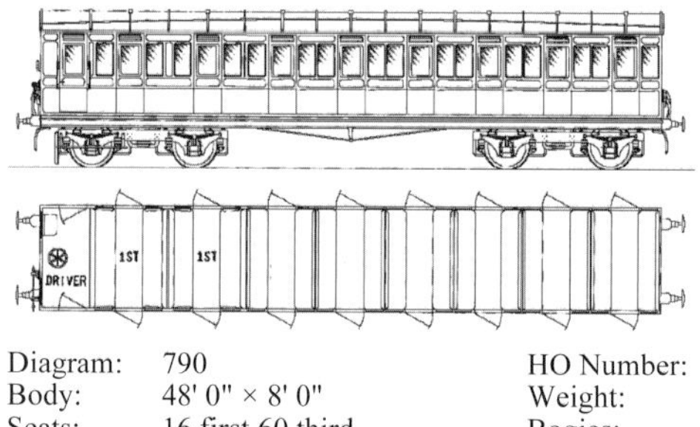

Diagram:	790	HO Number:	
Body:	48' 0" × 8' 0"	Weight:	20t 8cwt
Seats:	16 first 60 third	Bogies:	LBSCR

9811	12/25-01/29	⊃**8686**	⊂**3225**
9812	05/24-06/29	⊃**8696**	⊂**3226**
9813	10/25-06/29	⊃**8695**	⊂**3227**
9814	05/27-02/29	⊃**8691**	⊂**3228**
9815	01/27-05/29	⊃**8694**	⊂**3229**
9816	07/24-02/29	⊃**8688**	⊂**3230**
9817	08/27-06/29	⊃**8706**	⊂**4057**
9818	10/24-06/29	⊃**8707**	⊂**4058**
9819	01/24-06/29	⊃**8708**	⊂**4059**
9820	03/25-02/29	⊃**8689**	⊂**4060**
9821	*12/12-* 23	⊃**8690**	⊂**4065**
9822	*12/12-* 23	⊃**8692**	⊂**4066**
9823	*12/12-* 23	⊃**8693**	⊂**4067**
9824	*12/12-* 23	⊃**8687**	⊂**4068**

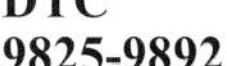

CP Crystal Palace
Metropolitan Amalgamated 9825-54/81-84, Lancing 9855-78/85-92
Driving Trailer Composite
DTC
9825-9892

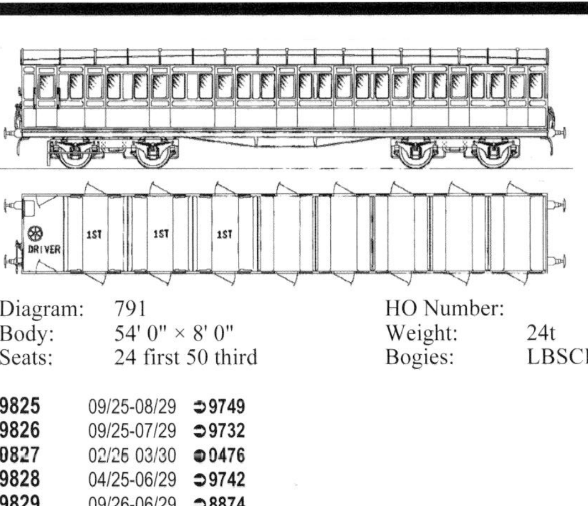

Diagram:	791	HO Number:	
Body:	54' 0" × 8' 0"	Weight:	24t
Seats:	24 first 50 third	Bogies:	LBSCR

No.	Dates	To	
9825	09/25-08/29	➲**9749**	⊂**4001**
9826	09/25-07/29	➲**9732**	⊂**4002**
9827	02/25 03/30	●**0476**	⊂**4003**
9828	04/25-06/29	➲**9742**	⊂**4004**
9829	09/26-06/29	➲**8874**	⊂**4005**
9830	05/24-02/29	➲**9719**	⊂**4006**
9831	07/24-02/30	➲**9468**	⊂**4007**
9832	01/24-01/29	➲**9717**	⊂**4008**
9833	10/25-06/29	➲**9726**	⊂**4009**
9834	06/27-09/29	➲**9730**	⊂**4010**
9835	01/24-02/29	➲**9720**	⊂**4011**
9836	09/26-06/29	➲**8873**	⊂**4012**
9837	09/26-05/29	➲**8859**	⊂**4013**
9838	12/24-01/30	➲**9462**	⊂**4014**
9839	09/26-06/29	➲**9738**	⊂**4015**
9840	06/27-04/30	➲**9478**	⊂**4016**
9841	04/27-02/30	➲**9284**	⊂**4017**
9842	03/25-05/29	➲**9725**	⊂**4018**
9843	09/24-08/29	➲**9736**	⊂**4019**
9844	12/24-02/30	➲**9463**	⊂**4020**
9845	09/27-06/29	➲**9737**	⊂**4021**
9846	-02/29	➲**8856**	⊂**4022**
9847	04/27-06/29	➲**8862**	⊂**4023**
9848	06/27-05/29	➲**9724**	⊂**4024**
9849	10/27-06/29	➲**8861**	⊂**4025**
9850	09/27-07/29	➲**9743**	⊂**4026**
9851	10/27-06/29	➲**9727**	⊂**4027**
9852	01/28-02/30	➲**9470**	⊂**4028**
9853	04/26-06/29	➲**9728**	⊂**4029**
9854	01/24-02/29	➲**8854**	⊂**4030**
9855	12/25-08/29	➲**9734**	⊂**4031**
9856	01/28-02/30	➲**9286**	⊂**4032**
9857	01/27-05/29	➲**8860**	⊂**4033**
9858	-02/29	➲**9721**	⊂**4034**
9859	01/28-01/30	➲**9467**	⊂**4035**
9860	01/24-01/29	➲**8853**	⊂**4036**
9861	02/25-06/29	➲**9729**	⊂**4037**
9862	07/24-02/30	➲**9469**	⊂**4038**
9863	01/27 01/30	➲**9461**	⊂**4039**
9864	12/24-01/30	➲**9466**	⊂**4040**
9865	01/24-02/29	➲**9723**	⊂**4041**
9866	02/25-09/29	➲**9731**	⊂**4042**
9867	07/24-06/29	➲**9741**	⊂**4043**
9868	12/24-02/30	➲**9464**	⊂**4044**
9869	09/25-01/30	➲**9465**	⊂**4045**
9870	06/27-03/30	➲**9473**	⊂**4046**
9871	06/25-08/29	➲**9747**	⊂**4047**
9872	05/24-01/29	➲**9718**	⊂**4048**
9873	06/25-04/30	➲**9479**	⊂**4049**
9874	01/24-02/29	➲**8855**	⊂**4050**
9875	01/27-03/30	➲**9474**	⊂**4051**
9876	06/25-03/30	➲**9477**	⊂**4052**
9877	04/26-08/29	➲**9748**	⊂**4053**
9878	01/27-07/29	➲**9733**	⊂**4054**
9879	-02/29	➲**9722**	⊂**4055**
9880	-02/29	➲**8858**	⊂**4056**
9881	10/24-06/29	➲**8872**	⊂**4061**
9882	07/24-08/29	➲**9735**	⊂**4062**
9883	05/24-02/29	➲**8857**	⊂**4063**
9884	10/24-06/29	➲**9739**	⊂**4064**
9885	01/26-02/30	➲**9471**	⊂**4069**
9886	12/25-02/30	➲**9472**	⊂**4070**
9887	05/26-07/29	➲**9744**	⊂**4071**
9888	10/25-03/30	➲**9475**	⊂**4072**
9889	12/25-08/29	➲**9746**	⊂**4073**
9890	01/28-08/29	➲**9745**	⊂**4074**
9891	04/26-06/29	➲**9740**	⊂**4075**
9892	05/24-01/29	➲**8852**	⊂**4076**

CW Coulsdon-Wallington Lancing
Driving Trailer Composite
DTC
9893-9914

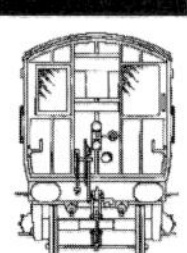

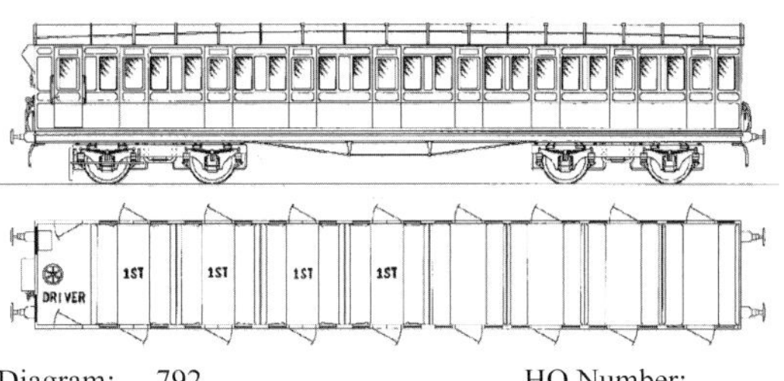

Diagram:	792	HO Number:	
Body:	54' 0" × 8' 0"	Weight:	24t
Seats:	32 first 40 third	Bogies:	LBSCR

9893 & 9894 worked as CP stock.

No.	Dates	To	
9893	04/27-02/30	➲**9288**	⊂**4084**
9894	03/27-03/30	➲**9290**	⊂**4085**
9895	-03/30	➲**9292**	⊂**4077**
9896	05/24-01/30	➲**8886**	⊂**4078**
9897	-04/30	➲**9803**	⊂**4079**
9898	-03/30	➲**9801**	⊂**4080**
9899	-03/30	➲**8898**	⊂**4081**
9900	05/24-01/30	➲**8891**	⊂**4082**
9901	-03/30	➲**8899**	⊂**4083**
9902	05/24-01/30	➲**8887**	⊂**4086**
9903	05/24-04/30	➲**9802**	⊂**4087**
9904	-03/30	➲**8900**	⊂**4088**
9905	-02/30	➲**8888**	⊂**4089**
9906	-02/30	➲**8896**	⊂**4090**
9907	-02/30	➲**8895**	⊂**4091**
9908	05/24-02/30	➲**9282**	⊂**4092**
9909	05/24-02/30	➲**8897**	⊂**4093**
9910	-02/30	➲**8893**	⊂**4094**
9911	-01/30	➲**8885**	⊂**4095**
9912	05/24-02/30	➲**8894**	⊂**4096**
9913	05/24-01/30	➲**8890**	⊂**4097**
9914	05/24-02/30	➲**8892**	⊂**4098**

CW Coulsdon-Wallington
Metropolitan Amalgamated RC&W
Motor Brake Van
MBV
10101-10121

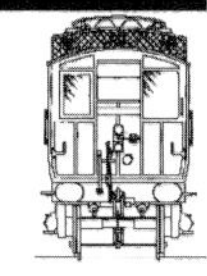

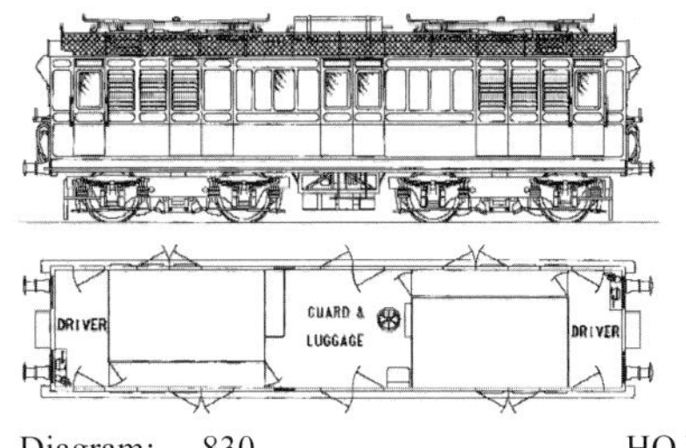

Diagram:	830	HO Number:	
Body:	38' 5" × 8' 0"	Weight:	62t
Motors:	GEC 4 × 250hp	Bogies:	LBSCR

No.	Dates	To
10101	12/23-09/29	08/34➲**56272**
10102	12/23-09/29	07/34➲**56273**
10103	12/23-09/29	12/34➲**56274**
10104	12/23-09/29	07/34➲**56275**
10105	12/23-09/29	10/34➲**56276**
10106	12/23-09/29	03/34➲**56261**
10107	12/23-09/29	05/34➲**56262**
10108	12/23-09/29	09/33➲**56263**
10109	01/24-09/29	06/34➲**56264**
10110	01/24-09/29	08/34➲**56277**
10111	01/24-09/29	01/35➲**56278**
10112	01/24-09/29	03/34➲**56265**
10113	01/24-09/29	04/34➲**56266**

10114	01/24-09/29	03/34⊃**56267**
10115	01/24-09/29	04/34⊃**56268**
10116	01/24-09/29	07/34⊃**56279**
10117	03/24-09/29	05/34⊃**56269**
10118	03/24-09/29	09/34⊃**56270**
10119	04/24-09/29	10/34⊃**56280**
10120	04/24-09/29	03/34⊃**56271**
10121	04/24-09/29	08/34⊃**56281**

Hauled Stock (ex EMU)

ex-CW Coulsdon-Wallington Lancing

Trailer Composite
DTC
6251-6270

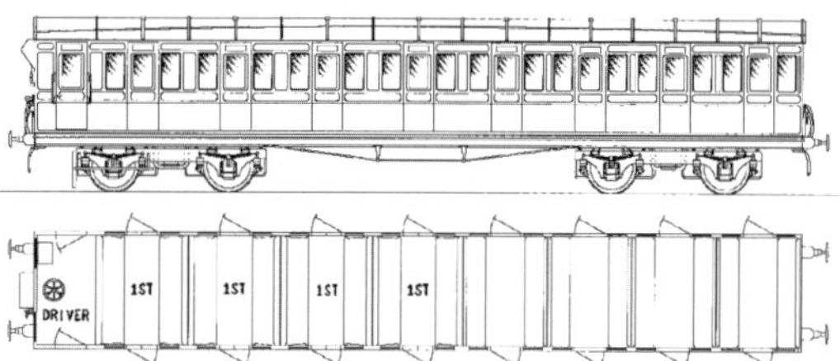

6251-6269 Diagram 792 later 284 (driving cab converted to luggage compartment)

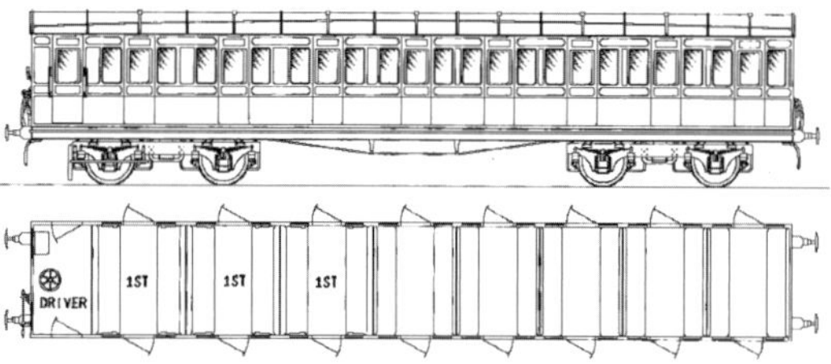

6265-6270 Diagram 285 (driving cab converted to luggage compartment)

Diagram:	352	HO Number:	
Body:	54' 0" × 8' 0"	Weight:	24t
Seats:	24 first 50 third	Bogies:	LBSCR

These were built before and during the First World War for Coulsdon-Wallington services. They were put into store then entered service as hauled stock.

6251	10/24-06/30	⊃**9806**	⊂**4099**
6252	11/24-04/32	⊃**2186**⊗07/44	⊂**4100**
6253	06/25-05/32	⊃**2187**⊗08/58	⊂**4101**
6254	11/26-03/32	⊃**2188**⊗12/58	⊂**4102**
6255	04/27-10/31	⊃**2189**⊗01/38	⊂**4103**
6256	09/24-06/30	⊃**9805**	⊂**4104**
6257	10/27-03/31	⊃**6939**⊗08/37	⊂**4105**
6258	10/26-04/32	⊃**2190**⊗08/59	⊂**4106**
6259	12/24-06/30	⊃**9807**	⊂**4113**
6260	05/25-06/30	⊃**9804**	⊂**4114**
6261	07/27-03/31	⊃**6940**⊗10/59	⊂**4115**
6262	08/25-04/32	⊃**2191**⊗04/59	⊂**4116**
6263	08/26-03/31	⊃**6941**⊗10/58	⊂**4117**
6264	06/27-01/32	⊃**2192**⊗12/39	⊂**4118**
6265	11/25-04/30	⊃**9480**	⊂**4107**
6266	04/25-06/30	⊃**9481**	⊂**4108**
6267	10/27-06/30	⊃**9483**	⊂**4109**
6268	07/27-01/32	⊃**2193**⊗08/61	⊂**4110**
6269	10/26-01/32	⊃**2194**⊗12/39	⊂**4111**
6270	10/26-06/30	⊃**9482**	⊂**4112**

ex-SL South London
Metropolitan Amalgamated RC&W

Trailer First
TF
7644-7651

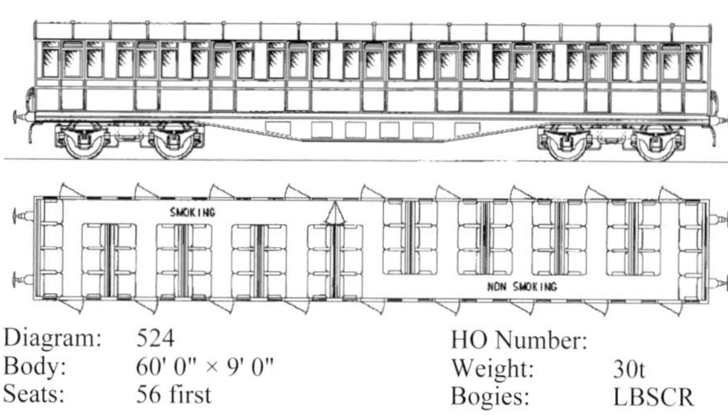

Diagram:	524	HO Number:	
Body:	60' 0" × 9' 0"	Weight:	30t
Seats:	56 first	Bogies:	LBSCR

The original South London first class trailers were taken out of use in about 1910. They later became steam-hauled first class carriages, before being rebuilt again for dc use.

7644	11/27-06/30	⊃**9819**	⊂**3202**
7645	03/28-06/30	⊃**9951**	⊂**3205**
7646	06/27-06/30	⊃**9952**	⊂**3208**
7647	02/28-06/30	⊃**9821**	⊂**3211**
7648	07/27-06/30	⊃**9953**	⊂**3214**
7649	11/27-06/30	⊃**9820**	⊂**3217**
7650	02/28-06/30	⊃**9954**	⊂**3220**
7651	08/27-06/30	⊃**9818**	⊂**3223**

London Brighton & South Coast Railway

SL South London
Metropolitan Amalgamated RC&W

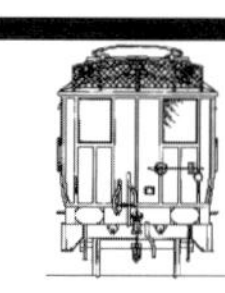

Driving Motor Brake Third and Trailer First
DMBT and TF
3201-3224

For details see SR 8601-8616 and 7644-7651

3201	12/08-02/25	⊃**8601**
3202	12/08-11/27	⊃**7644**
3203	12/08-09/24	⊃**8602**
3204	04/09-04/29	⊃*8603*
3205	04/09-03/28	⊃**7645**
3206	04/09-04/24	⊃**8604**
3207	*05/09*-12/25	⊃**8605**
3208	*05/09*-06/27	⊃**7646**
3209	*05/09*-08/27	⊃**8606**
3210	*06/09*-10/25	⊃**8607**
3211	*06/09*-02/28	⊃**7647**
3212	*06/09*-06/25	⊃**8608**
3213	*06/09*-03/26	⊃**8609**
3214	*06/09*-07/27	⊃**7648**
3215	*06/09*-06/26	⊃**8610**
3216	*07/09*-01/27	⊃**8611**
3217	*07/09*-11/27	⊃**7649**
3218	*07/09*-11/24	⊃**8612**
3219	*07/09*-01/24	⊃**8613**
3220	*07/09*-02/28	⊃**7650**
3221	*07/09*-05/27	⊃**8614**
3222	*08/09*-04/25	⊃**8615**
3223	*08/09*-08/27	⊃**7651**
3224	*08/09*-07/24	⊃**8616**

SL South London Lancing
Driving Trailer Composite
DTC
3225-3230

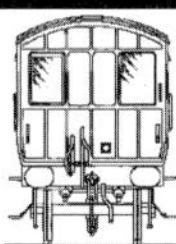

For details see SR 9811-9816

3225	06/10-12/25	⊃**9811**	Built *12/00*	⊂**594**
3226	06/10-05/24	⊃**9812**	Built 96	⊂**1236**
3227	06/10-10/25	⊃**9813**	Built *06/97*	⊂**1240**
3228	06/10-05/27	⊃**9814**	Built *06/99*	⊂**1270**
3229	06/10-01/27	⊃**9815**	Built *06/99*	⊂**1271**
3230	06/10-07/24	⊃**9816**	Built *12/00*	⊂**1284**

CP Crystal Palace
Metropolitan Amalgamated RC&W
Driving Motor Brake Third
DMTB
3231-3264

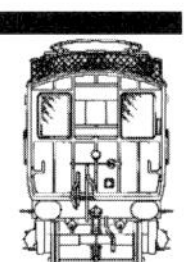

For details see SR 8567-8600

3231	11-07/24	⊃**8567**
3232	11-09/26	⊃**8568**
3233	11-12/25	⊃**8569**
3234	11-05/26	⊃**8570**
3235	11-01/28	⊃**8571**
3236	11-01/27	⊃**8572**
3237	11-12/24	⊃**8573**
3238	11-03/25	⊃**8574**
3239	11-03/27	⊃**8575**
3240	11-09/26	⊃**8576**
3241	11-12/24	⊃**8577**
3242	11-05/24	⊃**8578**
3243	11-12/25	⊃**8579**
3244	11-05/26	⊃**8580**
3245	11-06/27	⊃**8581**
3246	11-07/29	⊃*8582*
3247	11-09/25	⊃**8583**
3248	11-06/27	⊃**8584**
3249	11-09/27	⊃**8585**
3250	11-10/24	⊃**8586**
3251	11-09/27	⊃**8587**
3252	11-05/24	⊃**8588**
3253	11-10/24	⊃**8589**
3254	11-01/27	⊃**8590**
3255	11-06/25	⊃**8591**
3256	11-01/24	⊃**8592**
3257	11-06/25	⊃**8593**
3258	11-10/25	⊃**8594**
3259	11-07/24	⊃**8595**
3260	11-01/30	⊃*8596*
3261	12-04/27	⊃**8597**
3262	12-01/24	⊃**8598**
3263	12-01/28	⊃**8599**
3264	12-03/25	⊃**8600**

CW Coulsdon-Wallington
Metro/Eastleigh/Lancing
Driving Trailer Third
DTT
3268-3287

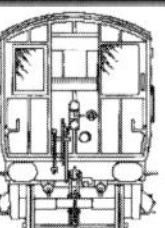

For details see SR 9189-9208

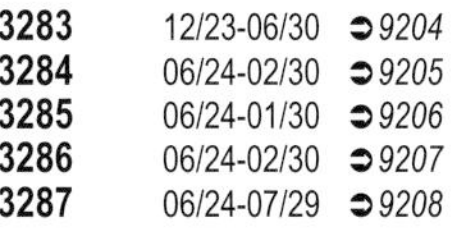

3268	12/23-02/30	⊃*9189*
3269	12/23-01/30	⊃*9190*
3270	12/23-07/29	⊃*9191*
3271	12/23-08/29	⊃*9192*
3272	12/23-03/30	⊃*9193*
3273	12/23-06/29	⊃*9194*
3274	12/23-08/29	⊃*9195*
3275	12/23-03/30	⊃*9196*
3276	12/23-07/29	⊃*9197*
3277	12/23-01/30	⊃*9198*
3278	12/23-06/29	⊃*9199*
3279	12/23-08/29	⊃*9200*
3280	12/23-06/30	⊃*9201*
3281	12/23-01/30	⊃*9202*
3282	12/23-06/29	⊃*9203*
3283	12/23-06/30	⊃*9204*
3284	06/24-02/30	⊃*9205*
3285	06/24-01/30	⊃*9206*
3286	06/24-02/30	⊃*9207*
3287	06/24-07/29	⊃*9208*

CP Crystal Palace
Metro 4001-30, 4055/56,
Lancing 4031-54
Driving Trailer Composite
DTC
4001-4056

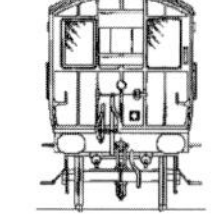

For details see SR 9825-9880

4001	11-09/25	⊃**9825**
4002	11-09/25	⊃**9826**
4003	11-02/25	⊃**9827**
4004	11-04/25	⊃**9828**
4005	11-09/26	⊃**9829**
4006	11-05/24	⊃**9830**
4007	11-07/24	⊃**9831**
4008	11-01/24	⊃**9832**
4009	11-10/25	⊃**9833**
4010	11-06/27	⊃**9834**
4011	11-01/24	⊃**9835**
4012	11-09/26	⊃**9836**
4013	11-09/26	⊃**9837**
4014	11-12/24	⊃**9838**
4015	11-09/26	⊃**9839**
4016	11-06/27	⊃**9840**
4017	11-04/27	⊃**9841**
4018	11-03/25	⊃**9842**
4019	11-09/24	⊃**9843**
4020	11-12/24	⊃**9844**
4021	11-09/27	⊃**9845**
4022	11-02/29	⊃*9846*
4023	11-04/27	⊃**9847**
4024	11-06/27	⊃**9848**
4025	11-10/27	⊃**9849**
4026	11-09/27	⊃**9850**
4027	11-10/27	⊃**9851**
4028	11-01/28	⊃**9852**
4029	11-04/26	⊃**9853**
4030	11-01/24	⊃**9854**
4031	11-12/25	⊃**9855**
4032	11-01/28	⊃**9856**
4033	11-01/27	⊃**9857**
4034	11-02/29	⊃*9858*
4035	11-01/28	⊃**9859**
4036	11-01/24	⊃**9860**
4037	11-02/25	⊃**9861**
4038	11-07/24	⊃**9862**
4039	11-01/27	⊃**9863**
4040	11-12/24	⊃**9864**
4041	11-01/24	⊃**9865**
4042	11-02/25	⊃**9866**
4043	11-07/24	⊃**9867**
4044	11-12/24	⊃**9868**
4045	11-09/25	⊃**9869**
4046	11-06/27	⊃**9870**
4047	11-06/25	⊃**9871**
4048	11-05/24	⊃**9872**
4049	11-06/25	⊃**9873**
4050	11-01/24	⊃**9874**
4051	11-01/27	⊃**9875**
4052	11-06/25	⊃**9876**
4053	11-04/26	⊃**9877**
4054	11-01/27	⊃**9878**
4055	11-02/29	⊃*9879*
4056	11-02/29	⊃*9880*

SL South London Lancing
Driving Trailer Composite
DTC
4057-4060

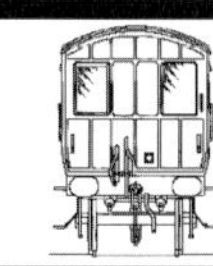

For details see SR 9817-9820

4057	06/11-08/27	⊃**9817**	Built *12/98*	⊂**1268**
4058	06/11-10/24	⊃**9818**	Built *06/00*	⊂**1320**
4059	06/11-01/24	⊃**9819**	Built *06/01*	⊂**710**
4060	06/11-03/25	⊃**9820**	Built *06/01*	⊂**718**

CP Crystal Palace Metro
Driving Trailer Composite
DTC
4061-4064

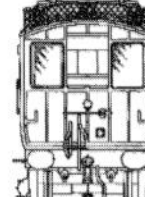

For details see SR 9881-9884

4061	12-10/24	➲**9881**
4062	12-07/24	➲**9882**
4063	12-05/24	➲**9883**
4064	12-10/24	➲**9884**

SL South London Lancing
Driving Trailer Composite
DTC

4065-4068

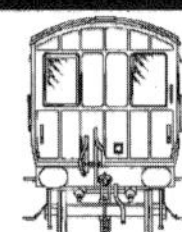

For details see SR 9821-9824

4065	12/12-12/24	➲**9821**	Built *12/00*	⊂**708**
4066	12/12-05/25	➲**9822**	Built *06/00*	⊂**1321**
4067	12/12-03/26	➲**9823**	Built *06/01*	⊂**1302**
4068	12/12-07/26	➲**9824**	Built *06/01*	⊂**1303**

CP Crystal Palace Lancing
Driving Trailer Composite
DTC
4069-4076

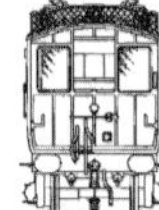

For details see SR 9885-9892

4069	13-01/26	➲**9885**
4070	13-12/25	➲**9886**
4071	13-05/26	➲**9887**
4072	13-10/25	➲**9888**
4073	13-12/25	➲**9889**
4074	13-01/28	➲**9890**
4075	13-04/26	➲**9891**
4076	13-05/24	➲**9892**

CW Coulsdon-Wallington Lancing
Driving Trailer Composite

DTC
4077-4098

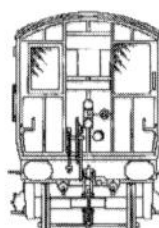

For details see SR 9893-9914

4077	14-03/30	➲*9895*
4078	14-05/24	➲**9896**
4079	14-04/30	➲*9897*
4080	14-03/30	➲*9898*
4081	14-03/30	➲*9899*
4082	14-05/24	➲**9900**
4083	14-03/30	➲*9901*
4084	14-04/27	➲**9893**
4085	14-03/27	➲**9894**
4086	14-05/24	➲**9902**
4087	14-05/24	➲**9903**
4088	14-03/30	➲*9904*
4089	15-02/30	➲*9905*
4090	15-02/30	➲*9906*
4091	15-02/30	➲*9907*
4092	15-05/24	➲**9908**
4093	15-05/24	➲**9909**
4094	15-02/30	➲*9910*
4095	15-01/30	➲*9911*
4096	15-05/24	➲**9912**
4097	15-05/24	➲**9913**
4098	15-05/24	➲**9914**

CW Coulsdon-Wallington Lancing
Driving Trailer Composite
DTC
4099-4118

For details see SR 6251-6270

4099	15-10/24	➲**6251**
4100	15-11/24	➲**6252**
4101	15-06/25	➲**6253**
4102	15-11/26	➲**6254**
4103	15-04/27	➲**6255**
4104	12/19-09/24	➲**6256**
4105	12/19-10/27	➲**6257**
4106	12/19-*10/26*	➲**6258**
4107	12/19-11/25	➲**6265**
4108	12/19-04/25	➲**6266**
4109	12/19-10/27	➲**6267**
4110	12/19-07/27	➲**6268**
4111	12/19-10/26	➲**6269**
4112	12/19-10/26	➲**6270**
4113	06/21-12/24	➲**6259**
4114	06/21-05/25	➲**6260**
4115	06/21-07/27	➲**6261**
4116	06/21-08/25	➲**6262**
4117	06/21-08/26	➲**6263**
4118	06/21-06/27	➲**6264**

CW Coulsdon-Wallington Lancing
Trailer Composite
TC
4119-4128

For details see 9659-9660 & 9664-9671

4119	12/23-06/29	➲*9664*
4120	12/23-06/29	➲*9665*
4121	12/23-07/29	➲*9666*
4122	12/23-09/29	➲*9667*
4123	12/23-07/29	➲*9668*
4124	12/23-08/29	➲*9669*
4125	12/23-08/29	➲*9670*
4126	12/23-08/29	➲*9671*
4127	01/24-07/29	➲*9659*
4128	06/24-08/29	➲*9660*

CW Coulsdon-Wallington
Metropolitan Amalgamated RC&W
Motor Brake Van
MBV
10101-10121

For details see SR 10101-10121. These retained the same LBSC numbers in SR days.

London & South Western Railway

3-SUB Eastleigh
Driving Motor Brake Third
DMBT
6701-6826

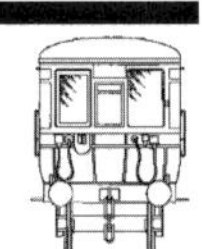

For details see SR 8001-8126

6701	11/14-	23	➲**8001**	**E1**	11/14-	23
6702	11/14-	23	➲**8002**	**E1**	11/14-	23
6703	11/14-	23	➲**8003**	**E2**	11/14-	23
6704	11/14-	23	➲**8004**	**E2**	11/14-	23
6705	11/14-	23	➲**8005**	**E3**	11/14-	23
6706	06/14-	23	➲**8006**	**E4**	06/14-	23
6707	11/14-	23	➲**8007**	**E5**	11/14-	23
6708	11/14-	23	➲**8008**	**E5**	11/14-	23
6709	11/14-	23	➲**8009**	**E6**	11/14-	23
6710	11/14-	23	➲**8010**	**E6**	11/14-	23
6711	*12/14-*	23	➲**8011**	**E7**	*12/14-*	23

6712	12/14-	23	➲**8012**	**E8**	12/14-	23
6713	12/14-	23	➲**8013**	**E9**	12/14-	23
6714	12/14-	23	➲**8014**	**E9**	12/14-	23
6715	12/14-	23	➲**8015**	**E10**	12/14-	23
6716	12/14-	23	➲**8016**	**E10**	12/14-	23
6717	01/15-	23	➲**8017**	**E11**	01/15-	23
6718	01/15-	23	➲**8018**	**E12**	01/15-	23
6719	01/15-	23	➲**8019**	**E13**	01/15-	23
6720	01/15-	23	➲**8020**	**E13**	01/15-	23
6721	01/15-	23	➲**8021**	**E14**	01/15-	23
6722	01/15-	23	➲**8022**	**E14**	01/15-	23
6723	01/15-	23	➲**8023**	**E15**	01/15-	23
6724	02/15-	23	➲**8024**	**E16**	02/15-	23
6725	02/15-	23	➲**8025**	**E17**	02/15-	23
6726	02/15-	23	➲**8026**	**E17**	02/15-	23
6727	02/15-	23	➲**8027**	**E18**	02/15-	23
6728	02/15-	23	➲**8028**	**E18**	02/15-	23
6729	02/15-	23	➲**8029**	**E19**	02/15-	23
6730	03/15-	23	➲**8030**	**E20**	03/15-	23
6731	03/15-	23	➲**8031**	**E21**	03/15-	23
6732	03/15-	23	➲**8032**	**E21**	03/15-	23
6733	03/15-	23	➲**8033**	**E22**	03/15-	23
6734	03/15-	23	➲**8034**	**E22**	03/15-	23
6735	03/15-	23	➲**8035**	**E23**	03/15-	23
6736	03/15-	23	➲**8036**	**E24**	03/15-	23
6737	04/15-	23	➲**8037**	**E25**	04/15-	23
6738	04/15-	23	➲**8038**	**E25**	04/15-	23
6739	04/15-	23	➲**8039**	**E26**	04/15-	23
6740	04/15-	23	➲**8040**	**E26**	04/15-	23
6741	04/15-	23	➲**8041**	**E27**	04/15-	23
6742	04/15-	23	➲**8042**	**E28**	04/15-	23
6743	05/15-	23	➲**8043**	**E29**	05/15-	23
6744	05/15-	23	➲**8044**	**E29**	05/15-	23
6745	05/15-	23	➲**8045**	**E30**	05/15-	23
6746	05/15-	23	➲**8046**	**E30**	05/15-	23
6747	05/15-	23	➲**8047**	**E31**	05/15-	23
6748	05/15-	23	➲**8048**	**E32**	05/15-	23
6749	06/15-	23	➲**8049**	**E33**	06/15-	23
6750	06/15-	23	➲**8050**	**E33**	06/15-	23
6751	06/15-	23	➲**8051**	**E34**	06/15-	23
6752	06/15-	23	➲**8052**	**E34**	06/15-	23
6753	06/15-	23	➲**8053**	**E35**	06/15-	23
6754	06/15-	23	➲**8054**	**E36**	06/15-	23
6755	07/15-	23	➲**8055**	**E37**	07/15-	23
6756	07/15-	23	➲**8056**	**E37**	07/15-	23
6757	07/15-	23	➲**8057**	**E38**	07/15-	23
6758	07/15-	23	➲**8058**	**E38**	07/15-	23
6759	07/15-	23	➲**8059**	**E39**	07/15-	23
6760	08/15-	23	➲**8060**	**E40**	08/15-	23
6761	08/15-	23	➲**8061**	**E41**	08/15-	23
6762	08/15-	23	➲**8062**	**E41**	08/15-	23
6763	08/15-	23	➲**8063**	**E42**	08/15-	23
6764	08/15-	23	➲**8064**	**E42**	08/15-	23
6765	09/15-	23	➲**8065**	**E43**	09/15-	23
6766	09/15-	23	➲**8066**	**E44**	09/15-	23
6767	09/15-	23	➲**8067**	**E45**	09/15-	23
6768	09/15-	23	➲**8068**	**E45**	09/15-	23
6769	12/15-	23	➲**8069**	**E46**	12/15-	23
6770	12/15-	23	➲**8070**	**E46**	12/15-	23
6771	12/15-	23	➲**8071**	**E47**	12/15-	23
6772	12/15-	23	➲**8072**	**E48**	12/15-	23
6773	02/16-	23	➲**8073**	**E49**	02/16-	23
6774	02/16-	23	➲**8074**	**E49**	02/16-	23
6775	02/16-	23	➲**8075**	**E50**	02/16-	23
6776	02/16-	23	➲**8076**	**E50**	02/16-	23
6777	02/16-	23	➲**8077**	**E51**	02/16-	23
6778	03/16-	23	➲**8078**	**E52**	03/16-	23
6779	03/16-	23	➲**8079**	**E53**	03/16-	23
6780	03/16-	23	➲**8080**	**E53**	03/16-	23
6781	03/16-	23	➲**8081**	**E54**	03/16-	23
6782	03/16-	23	➲**8082**	**E54**	03/16-	23
6783	06/16-	23	➲**8083**	**E55**	06/16-	23
6784	06/16-	23	➲**8084**	**E56**	06/16-	23
6785	07/16-	23	➲**8085**	**E57**	07/16-	23
6786	07/16-	23	➲**8086**	**E57**	07/16-	23
6787	07/16-	23	➲**8087**	**E58**	07/16-	23
6788	07/16-	23	➲**8088**	**E58**	07/16-	23
6789	08/16-	23	➲**8089**	**E59**	08/16-	23
6790	08/16-	23	➲**8090**	**E60**	08/16-	23
6791	09/16-	23	➲**8091**	**E61**	09/16-	23
6792	09/16-	23	➲**8092**	**E61**	09/16-	23
6793	09/16-	23	➲**8093**	**E62**	09/16-	23
6794	09/16-	23	➲**8094**	**E62**	09/16-	23
6795	10/16-	23	➲**8095**	**E63**	10/16-	23
6796	10/16-	23	➲**8096**	**E64**	10/16-	23
6797	10/16-	23	➲**8097**	**E65**	10/16-	23
6798	10/16-	23	➲**8098**	**E65**	10/16-	23
6799	11/16-	23	➲**8099**	**E66**	11/16-	23
6800	11/16-	23	➲**8100**	**E66**	11/16-	23
6801	11/16-	23	➲**8101**	**E67**	11/16-	23
6802	11/16-	23	➲**8102**	**E68**	11/16-	23
6803	12/16-	23	➲**8103**	**E69**	12/16-	23
6804	12/16-	23	➲**8104**	**E69**	12/16-	23
6805	12/16-	23	➲**8105**	**E70**	12/16-	23
6806	12/16-	23	➲**8106**	**E70**	12/16-	23
6807	12/16-	23	➲**8107**	**E71**	12/16-	23
6808	01/17-	23	➲**8108**	**E72**	01/17-	23
6809	01/17-	23	➲**8109**	**E73**	01/17-	23
6810	01/17-	23	➲**8110**	**E73**	01/17-	23
6811	01/17-	23	➲**8111**	**E74**	01/17-	23
6812	01/17-	23	➲**8112**	**E74**	01/17-	23
6813	02/17-	23	➲**8113**	**E75**	02/17-	23
6814	02/17-	23	➲**8114**	**E76**	02/17-	23
6815	02/17-	23	➲**8115**	**E77**	02/17-	23
6816	02/17-	23	➲**8116**	**E77**	02/17-	23
6817	03/17-	23	➲**8117**	**E78**	03/17-	23
6818	03/17-	23	➲**8118**	**E78**	03/17-	23
6819	03/17-	23	➲**8119**	**E79**	03/17-	23
6820	03/17-	23	➲**8120**	**E80**	03/17-	23
6821	08/17-	23	➲**8121**	**E81**	08/17-	23
6822	08/17-	23	➲**8122**	**E81**	08/17-	23
6823	08/17-	23	➲**8123**	**E82**	08/17-	23
6824	08/17-	23	➲**8124**	**E82**	08/17-	23
6825	04/17-	23	➲**8125**	**E83**	04/17-	23
6826	08/17-	23	➲**8126**	**E84**	08/17-	23

3-SUB Eastleigh

Driving Motor Brake Composite
DMBC
7201-7242

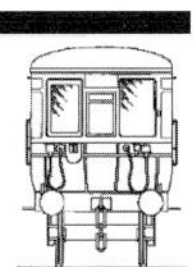

For details see SR 8751-8792

7201	11/14-	23	➲**8751**	**E3**	11/14-	23
7202	06/14-	23	➲**8752**	**E4**	06/14-	23
7203	12/14-	23	➲**8753**	**E7**	12/14-	23
7204	12/14-	23	➲**8754**	**E8**	12/14-	23
7205	01/15-	23	➲**8755**	**E11**	01/15-	23
7206	01/15-	23	➲**8756**	**E12**	01/15-	23
7207	01/15-	23	➲**8757**	**E15**	01/15-	23
7208	02/15-	23	➲**8758**	**E16**	02/15-	23
7209	02/15-	23	➲**8759**	**E19**	02/15-	23
7210	03/15-	23	➲**8760**	**E20**	03/15-	23
7211	03/15-	23	➲**8761**	**E23**	03/15-	23
7212	03/15-	23	➲**8762**	**E24**	03/15-	23
7213	04/15-	23	➲**8763**	**E27**	04/15-	23
7214	04/15-	23	➲**8764**	**E28**	04/15-	23
7215	05/15-	23	➲**8765**	**E31**	05/15-	23
7216	05/15-	23	➲**8766**	**E32**	05/15-	23
7217	06/15-	23	➲**8767**	**E35**	06/15-	23
7218	06/15-	23	➲**8768**	**E36**	06/15-	23
7219	07/15-	23	➲**8769**	**E39**	07/15-	23
7220	08/15-	23	➲**8770**	**E40**	08/15-	23
7221	09/15-	23	➲**8771**	**E43**	09/15-	23
7222	09/15-	23	➲**8772**	**E44**	09/15-	23
7223	12/15-	23	➲**8773**	**E47**	12/15-	23
7224	12/15-	23	➲**8774**	**E48**	12/15-	23
7225	02/16-	23	➲**8775**	**E51**	02/16-	23
7226	03/16-	23	➲**8776**	**E52**	03/16-	23
7227	06/16-	23	➲**8777**	**E55**	06/16-	23
7228	06/16-	23	➲**8778**	**E56**	06/16-	23
7229	08/16-	23	➲**8779**	**E59**	08/16-	23
7230	08/16-	23	➲**8780**	**E60**	08/16-	23
7231	10/16-	23	➲**8781**	**E63**	10/16-	23
7232	10/16-	23	➲**8782**	**E64**	10/16-	23
7233	11/16-	23	➲**8783**	**E67**	11/16-	23
7234	11/16-	23	➲**8784**	**E68**	11/16-	23
7235	12/16-	23	➲**8785**	**E71**	12/16-	23
7236	01/17-	23	➲**8786**	**E72**	01/17-	23
7237	02/17-	23	➲**8787**	**E75**	02/17-	23
7238	02/17-	23	➲**8788**	**E76**	02/17-	23
7239	03/17-	23	➲**8789**	**E79**	03/17-	23
7240	03/17-	23	➲**8790**	**E80**	03/17-	23
7241	04/17-	23	➲**8791**	**E83**	04/17-	23
7242	08/17-	23	➲**8792**	**E84**	08/17-	23

2-T Eastleigh (ex LSWR hauled stock)

Trailer Third

TT

7401-7448

For details see SR 8901-8948

7401	01/20-	23	➲**8925**	**T1**	01/20-	23
7402	01/20-	23	➲**8913**	**T1**	01/20-	23
7403	01/20-	23	➲**8901**	**T2**	01/20-	23
7404	01/20-	23	➲**8926**	**T2**	01/20-	23
7405	04/20-	23	➲**8927**	**T3**	04/20-	23
7406	04/20-	23	➲**8914**	**T3**	04/20-	23
7407	04/20-	23	➲**8902**	**T4**	04/20-	23
7408	04/20-	23	➲**8928**	**T4**	04/20-	23
7409	04/20-	23	➲**8929**	**T5**	04/20-	23
7410	04/20-	23	➲**8915**	**T5**	04/20-	23
7411	01/20-	23	➲**8903**	**T6**	01/20-	23
7412	01/20-	23	➲**8930**	**T6**	01/20-	23
7413	04/20-	23	➲**8931**	**T7**	04/20-	23
7414	04/20-	23	➲**8916**	**T7**	04/20-	23
7415	05/20-	23	➲**8904**	**T8**	05/20-	23
7416	05/20-	23	➲**8932**	**T8**	05/20-	23
7417	05/20-	23	➲**8933**	**T9**	05/20-	23
7418	05/20-	23	➲**8917**	**T9**	05/20-	23
7419	05/20-	23	➲**8905**	**T10**	05/20-	23
7420	05/20-	23	➲**8934**	**T10**	05/20-	23
7421	10/20-	23	➲**8935**	**T11**	10/20-	23
7422	10/20-	23	➲**8906**	**T12**	10/20-	23
7423	10/20-	23	➲**8936**	**T12**	10/20-	23
7424	10/20-	23	➲**8918**	**T11**	10/20-	23
7425	12/21-	23	➲**8937**	**T13**	12/21-	23
7426	12/21-	23	➲**8907**	**T13**	12/21-	23
7427	12/21-	23	➲**8938**	**T14**	12/21-	23
7428	12/21-	23	➲**8919**	**T14**	12/21-	23
7429	12/21-	23	➲**8939**	**T15**	12/21-	23
7430	12/21-	23	➲**8920**	**T15**	12/21-	23
7431	12/21-	23	➲**8940**	**T16**	12/21-	23
7432	12/21-	23	➲**8908**	**T16**	12/21-	23
7433	12/21-	23	➲**8941**	**T17**	12/21-	23
7434	12/21-	23	➲**8909**	**T17**	12/21-	23
7435	12/21-	23	➲**8942**	**T18**	12/21-	23
7436	12/21-	23	➲**8921**	**T18**	12/21-	23
7437	11/22-	23	➲**8943**	**T19**	11/22-	23
7438	11/22-	23	➲**8922**	**T19**	11/22-	23
7439	12/22-	23	➲**8944**	**T20**	12/22-	23
7440	12/22-	23	➲**8923**	**T20**	12/22-	23
7441	12/22-	23	➲**8945**	**T21**	12/22-	23
7442	12/22-	23	➲**8910**	**T21**	12/22-	23
7443	12/22-	23	➲**8946**	**T22**	12/22-	23
7444	12/22-	23	➲**8911**	**T22**	12/22-	23
7445	12/22-	23	➲**8947**	**T23**	12/22-	23
7446	12/22-	23	➲**8924**	**T23**	12/22-	23
7447	12/22-	23	➲**8948**	**T24**	12/22-	23
7448	12/22-	23	➲**8912**	**T24**	12/22-	23

3-SUB Eastleigh

Trailer Composite

TC

7551-7634

For details see SR 9351-9434

7551	11/14-	23	➲**9414**	**E1**	11/14-	23
7552	11/14-	23	➲**9351**	**E2**	11/14-	23
7553	11/14-	23	➲**9372**	**E3**	11/14-	23
7554	06/14-	23	➲**9373**	**E4**	06/14-	23
7555	11/14-	23	➲**9415**	**E5**	11/14-	23
7556	11/14-	23	➲**9352**	**E6**	11/14-	23
7557	*12/14-*	23	➲**9374**	**E7**	*12/14-*	23
7558	*12/14-*	23	➲**9375**	**E8**	*12/14-*	23
7559	*12/14-*	23	➲**9416**	**E9**	*12/14-*	23
7560	*12/14-*	23	➲**9353**	**E10**	*12/14-*	23
7561	*01/15-*	23	➲**9376**	**E11**	*01/15-*	23
7562	*01/15-*	23	➲**9377**	**E12**	*01/15-*	23
7563	*01/15-*	23	➲**9417**	**E13**	*01/15-*	23
7564	*01/15-*	23	➲**9354**	**E14**	*01/15-*	23
7565	*01/15-*	23	➲**9378**	**E15**	*01/15-*	23
7566	*02/15-*	23	➲**9379**	**E16**	*02/15-*	23
7567	*02/15-*	23	➲**9418**	**E17**	*02/15-*	23
7568	*02/15-*	23	➲**9355**	**E18**	*02/15-*	23
7569	*02/15-*	23	➲**9380**	**E19**	*02/15-*	23
7570	*03/15-*	23	➲**9381**	**E20**	*03/15-*	23
7571	*03/15-*	23	➲**9419**	**E21**	*03/15-*	23
7572	*03/15-*	23	➲**9356**	**E22**	*03/15-*	23
7573	*03/15-*	23	➲**9382**	**E23**	*03/15-*	23
7574	*03/15-*	23	➲**9383**	**E24**	*03/15-*	23
7575	*04/15-*	23	➲**9420**	**E25**	*04/15-*	23
7576	*04/15-*	23	➲**9357**	**E26**	*04/15-*	23
7577	*04/15-*	23	➲**9384**	**E27**	*04/15-*	23
7578	*04/15-*	23	➲**9385**	**E28**	*04/15-*	23
7579	*05/15-*	23	➲**9421**	**E29**	*05/15-*	23
7580	*05/15-*	23	➲**9358**	**E30**	*05/15-*	23
7581	*05/15-*	23	➲**9386**	**E31**	*05/15-*	23
7582	*05/15-*	23	➲**9387**	**E32**	*05/15-*	23
7583	*06/15-*	23	➲**9422**	**E33**	*06/15-*	23
7584	*06/15-*	23	➲**9359**	**E34**	*06/15-*	23
7585	*06/15-*	23	➲**9388**	**E35**	*06/15-*	23
7586	*06/15-*	23	➲**9389**	**E36**	*06/15-*	23
7587	*07/15-*	23	➲**9423**	**E37**	*07/15-*	23
7588	*07/15-*	23	➲**9360**	**E38**	*07/15-*	23
7589	*07/15-*	23	➲**9390**	**E39**	*07/15-*	23
7590	*08/15-*	23	➲**9391**	**E40**	*08/15-*	23
7591	*08/15-*	23	➲**9424**	**E41**	*08/15-*	23
7592	*08/15-*	23	➲**9361**	**E42**	*08/15-*	23
7593	*09/15-*	23	➲**9392**	**E43**	*09/15-*	23
7594	*09/15-*	23	➲**9393**	**E44**	*09/15-*	23
7595	*09/15-*	23	➲**9425**	**E45**	*09/15-*	23
7596	12/15-	23	➲**9362**	**E46**	12/15-	23
7597	12/15-	23	➲**9394**	**E47**	12/15-	23
7598	12/15-	23	➲**9395**	**E48**	12/15-	23
7599	02/16-	23	➲**9426**	**E49**	02/16-	23
7600	02/16-	23	➲**9363**	**E50**	02/16-	23
7601	02/16-	23	➲**9396**	**E51**	02/16-	23
7602	03/16-	23	➲**9397**	**E52**	03/16-	23
7603	03/16-	23	➲**9427**	**E53**	03/16-	23
7604	03/16-	23	➲**9364**	**E54**	03/16-	23
7605	*06/16-*	23	➲**9398**	**E55**	*06/16-*	23
7606	*06/16-*	23	➲**9399**	**E56**	*06/16-*	23
7607	*07/16-*	23	➲**9428**	**E57**	*07/16-*	23
7608	*07/16-*	23	➲**9365**	**E58**	*07/16-*	23
7609	*08/16-*	23	➲**9400**	**E59**	*08/16-*	23
7610	*08/16-*	23	➲**9401**	**E60**	*08/16-*	23
7611	*09/16-*	23	➲**9429**	**E61**	*09/16-*	23
7612	*09/16-*	23	➲**9366**	**E62**	*09/16-*	23
7613	*10/16-*	23	➲**9402**	**E63**	*10/16-*	23
7614	*10/16-*	23	➲**9403**	**E64**	*10/16-*	23
7615	*10/16-*	23	➲**9430**	**E65**	*10/16-*	23
7616	*11/16-*	23	➲**9367**	**E66**	*11/16-*	23
7617	*11/16-*	23	➲**9404**	**E67**	*11/16-*	23
7618	*11/16-*	23	➲**9405**	**E68**	*11/16-*	23
7619	*12/16-*	23	➲**9431**	**E69**	*12/16-*	23
7620	*12/16-*	23	➲**9368**	**E70**	*12/16-*	23
7621	*12/16-*	23	➲**9406**	**E71**	*12/16-*	23
7622	*01/17-*	23	➲**9407**	**E72**	*01/17-*	23
7623	*01/17-*	23	➲**9432**	**E73**	*01/17-*	23
7624	*01/17-*	23	➲**9369**	**E74**	*01/17-*	23
7625	*02/17-*	23	➲**9408**	**E75**	*02/17-*	23
7626	*02/17-*	23	➲**9409**	**E76**	*02/17-*	23
7627	*02/17-*	23	➲**9433**	**E77**	*02/17-*	23
7628	*03/17-*	23	➲**9370**	**E78**	*03/17-*	23
7629	*03/17-*	23	➲**9410**	**E79**	*03/17-*	23
7630	*03/17-*	23	➲**9411**	**E80**	*03/17-*	23
7631	08/17-	23	➲**9434**	**E81**	08/17-	23
7632	08/17-	23	➲**9371**	**E82**	08/17-	23
7633	04/17-	23	➲**9412**	**E83**	04/17-	23
7634	08/17-	23	➲**9413**	**E84**	08/17-	23

London Midland & Scottish Railway 1933 Numbering

LNWR Oerlikon Metropolitan CW&F

Driving Motor Brake Third
DMBT
M28000M London Area

As built

Corridor connection later removed

Diagram:		Weight:	55t 0cwt
Body:	57' 6" × 9' 6"	Bogies:	LNWR
Seats:	48 third	Motors:	Oerlikon 4 × 260hp

M28000M	33-12/60	⊗11/60	⊂5796

LNWR GEC Metropolitan CW&F

Driving Motor Brake Third
DMBT
M28001M-M28017M London Area

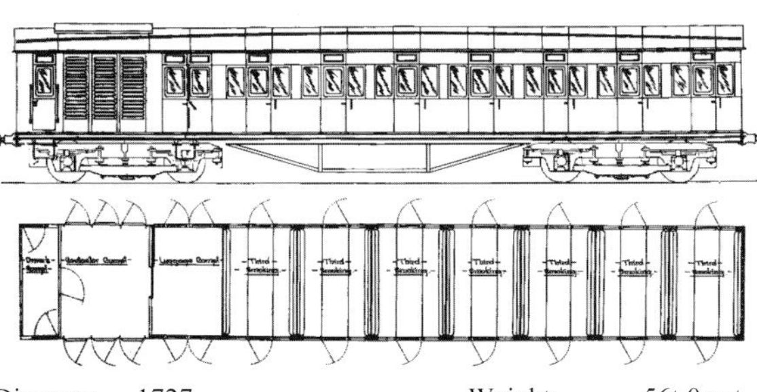

Diagram:	1727	Weight:	56t 0cwt
Body:	59' 0" × 9' 2¼"	Bogies:	LNWR
Seats:	84 third	Motors:	GEC 4 × 280hp

M28001M	33-11/63	⊗	⊂4605
M28002M	33-11/63	⊗	⊂4606
M28003M	33-11/63	⊗	⊂4607
M28004M	33-11/63	⊗	⊂4608
M28005M	33-11/63	⊗	⊂4609
M28006M	33-11/63	⊗	⊂4610
M28007M	33-11/63	⊗	⊂5801
M28008M	33-06/62	⊗	⊂8800
M28009M	33-11/63	⊗	⊂8880
M28010M	33-11/63	⊗	⊂8881
M28011M	33-11/63	⊗	⊂8882
M28012M	33-11/63	⊗	⊂8883
M28013M	33-11/63	⊗	⊂8884
M28014M	33-11/63	⊗	⊂8885
M28015M	33-11/63	⊗	⊂8886
M28016M	33-11/63	⊗	⊂8887
M28017M	33-11/63	⊗	⊂8888

LNWR GEC Wolverton

Driving Motor Brake Third
DMBT
M28018M-M28025M London Area

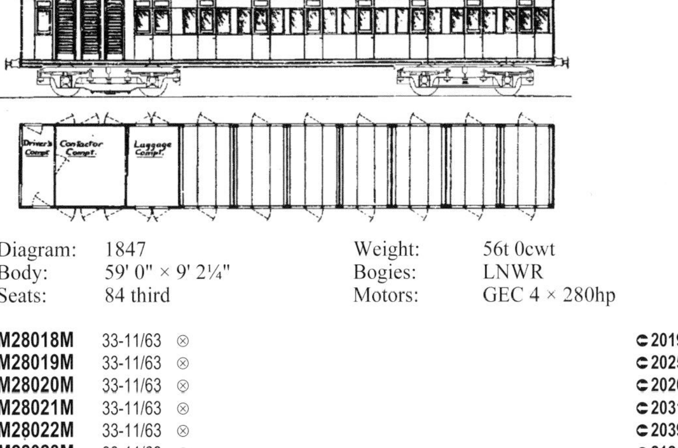

Diagram:	1847	Weight:	56t 0cwt
Body:	59' 0" × 9' 2¼"	Bogies:	LNWR
Seats:	84 third	Motors:	GEC 4 × 280hp

M28018M	33-11/63	⊗	⊂2019
M28019M	33-11/63	⊗	⊂2025
M28020M	33-11/63	⊗	⊂2026
M28021M	33-11/63	⊗	⊂2031
M28022M	33-11/63	⊗	⊂2039
M28023M	33-11/63	⊗	⊂2121
M28024M	33-11/63	⊗	⊂2234
M28025M	33-11/63	⊗	⊂2253

Tube Joint Metropolitan CW&F

Driving Motor Brake Third
DMBT
M28213-M28218 London Area

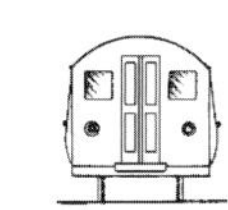

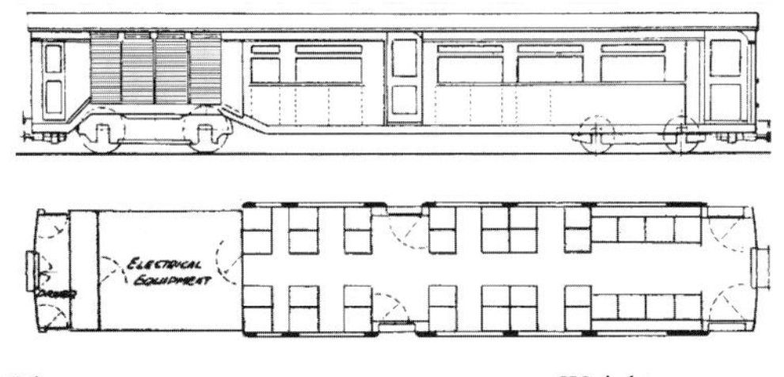

Diagram:		Weight:	
Body:	50' 10" ×	Bogies:	
Seats:	36 third	Motors:	BTH 2 × 240hp

M28213	33-07/48	⊗	49	⊂2394
M28214	33-07/48	⊗	49	⊂2415
M28215	33-07/48	⊗	49	⊂2416
M28216	33-07/48	⊗	49	⊂904
M28217	33-07/48	⊗	49	⊂770
M28218	33-07/48	⊗	49	⊂825

LNWR Siemens Metropolitan CW&F

Driving Motor Brake Third
DMBT
M28219M-M28222M London Area (later AM1)

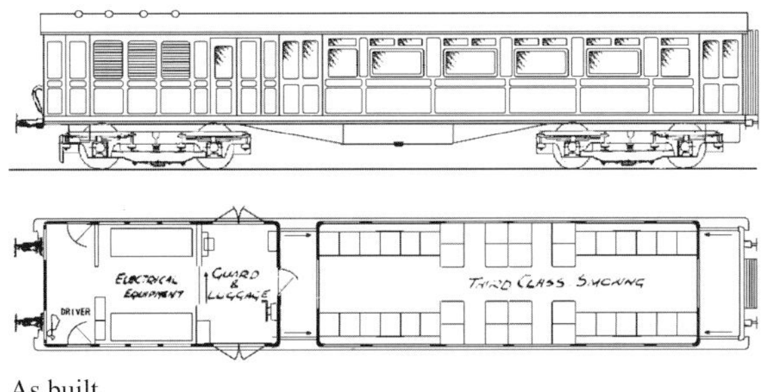

As built

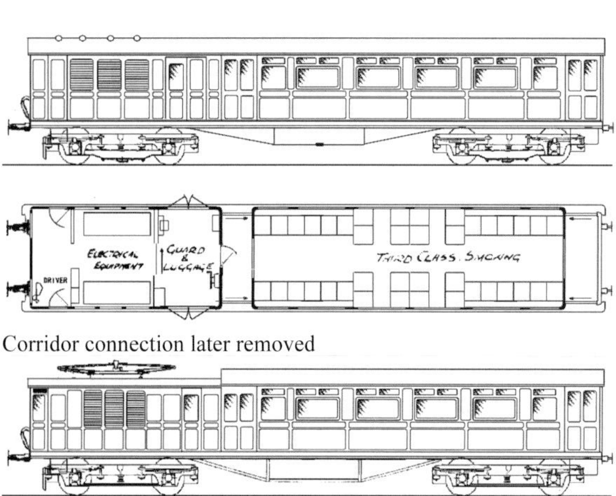

Corridor connection later removed

Converted for ac working

Diagram:		Weight:	53t 0cwt
Body:	57' 6" × 9' 6"	Bogies:	LNWR
Seats:	40 third	Motors:	Siemens 4 × 250hp later EE 4 × 125hp

M28219M	33-02/67	⊗	⊂5721
M28220M	33-02/67	⊗	⊂5722
M28221M	33-02/67	⊗	⊂5723
M28222M	33-02/67	⊗	⊂5724

LNWR Oerlikon Metropolitan CW&F
Driving Motor Brake Third
DMBT
M28223M-M28260M London Area

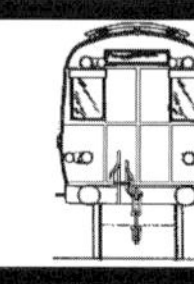

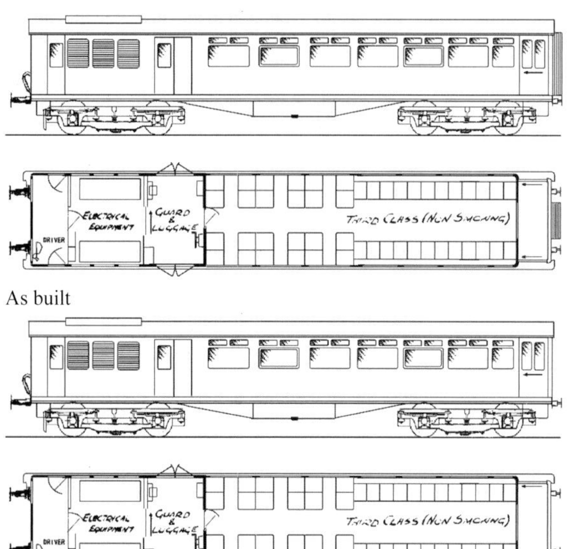

As built

Corridor connection later removed

Diagram:		Weight:	55t 0cwt
Body:	57' 6" × 9' 6"	Bogies:	LNWR
Seats:	48 third	Motors:	Oerlikon 4 × 260hp

M28223M	33-10/57	⊗11/57	⊂5725
M28224M	33-12/60	⊗12/60	⊂5726
M28225M	33-12/60	⊗12/60	⊂5727
M28226M	33-12/60	⊗	⊂5728
M28227M	33-03/55	⊗	⊂5729
M28228M	33-12/60	⊗12/60	⊂5730
M28229M	33-12/60	⊗11/60	⊂5731
M28230M	33-12/60	⊗11/60	⊂5732
M28231M	33-06/56	⊗	⊂5733
M28232	33-02/51	⊗	⊂5734
M28233M	33-07/57	⊗08/57	⊂5735
M28234M	33-12/55	⊗	⊂5736
M28235M	33-06/57	⊗07/57	⊂5737
28236	33-02/42	⊗10/40	⊂5738
M28237M	33-12/60	⊗12/60	⊂5739
M28238M	33-08/56	⊗	⊂5740
M28239M	33-10/55	⊗	⊂5741
M28240M	33-03/53	⊗	⊂5742
M28241M	33-02/54	⊗	⊂5743
M28242M	33-12/60	⊗12/60	⊂5744
M28243M	33-09/57	⊗10/57	⊂5745
M28244M	33-07/57	⊗09/57	⊂5746
M28245M	33-03/54	⊗	⊂5747
M28246M	33-12/60	⊗11/60	⊂5748
M28247M	33-08/57	⊗10/57	⊂5749
M28248M	33-12/60	⊗12/60	⊂5750
M28249M	33-05/62	℗	⊂5751
M28250M	33-12/54	⊗	⊂5752
M28251M	33-12/53	⊗	⊂5753
M28252M	33-12/60	⊗12/60	⊂5754
M28253M	33-06/59	⊗08/59	⊂5755
M28254M	33-06/59	⊗08/59	⊂5756
M28255M	33-12/60	⊗12/60	⊂5757
M28256M	33-12/60	⊗12/60	⊂5758
M28257M	33-12/60	⊗	⊂5759
M28258M	33-09/57	⊗10/57	⊂5760
M28259M	33-12/60	⊗03/69	⊂5761
M28260M	33-11/57	⊗12/57	⊂5762

LNWR Oerlikon Metropolitan CW&F
Driving Motor Brake Third
DMBT
M28261M-M28264M London Area

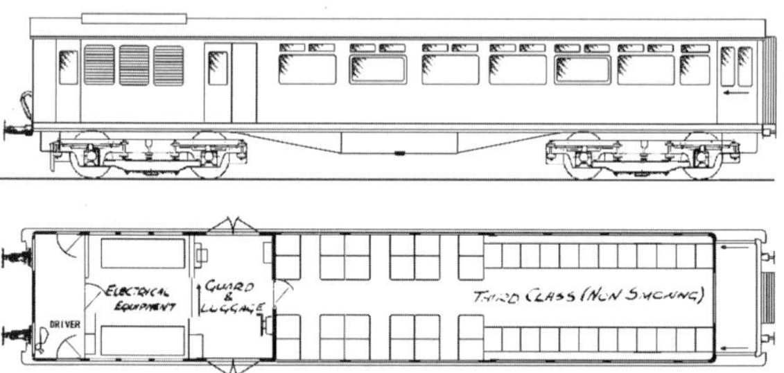

As built

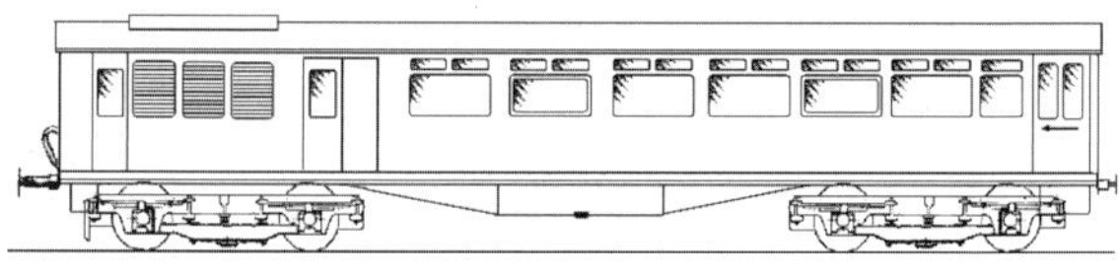

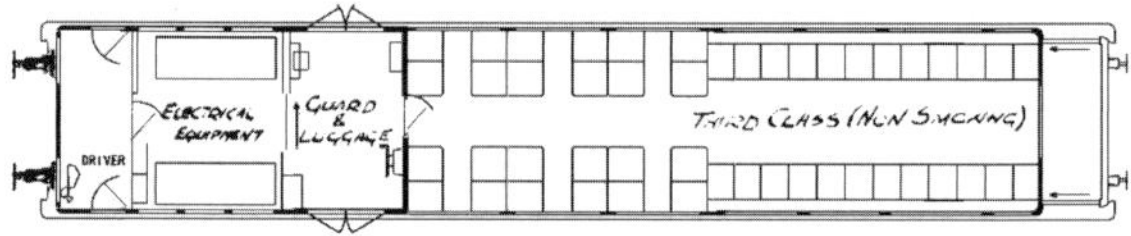

Corridor connection later removed

Diagram:		Weight:	55t 0cwt
Body:	57' 6" × 9' 6"	Bogies:	LNWR
Seats:	48 third	Motors:	Oerlikon 4 × 260hp

M28261M	33-11/60	⊗11/60	⊂5793
M28262M	33-12/61	⊗03/69	⊂5794
M28263M	33-11/60	⊗11/60	⊂5795
M28264M	33-12/60	⊗11/60	⊂5798

LNWR Oerlikon Metropolitan CW&F

Driving Motor Brake Third
DMBT
M28265M-M28294M London Area

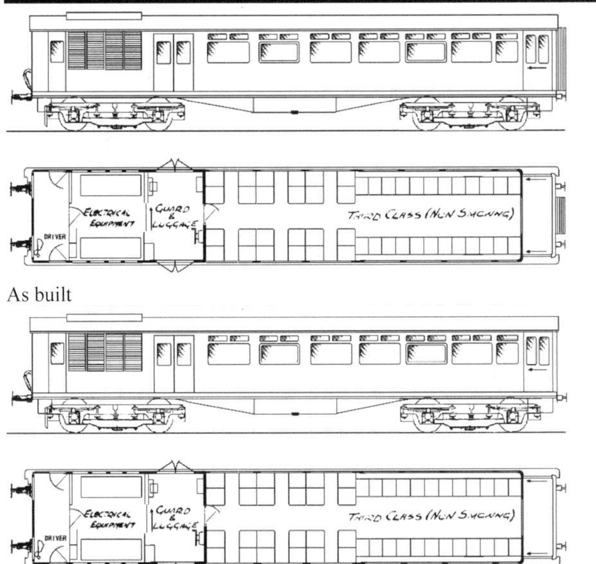

As built

Corridor connection later removed

Diagram:		Weight:	55t 0cwt
Body:	57' 6" × 9' 6"	Bogies:	LNWR
Seats:	48 third	Motors:	Oerlikon 4 × 260hp

M28265M	33-12/60	⊗12/60	⊂5763
M28266M	33-06/59	⊗08/59	⊂5764
M28267M	33-04/59	⊗06/59	⊂5765
M28268M	33-03/55	⊗	⊂5766
M28269M	33-12/60	⊗	⊂5767
M28270M	33-06/59	⊗06/59	⊂5768
M28271M	33-07/56	⊗	⊂5769
M28272M	33-10/57	⊗12/57	⊂5770
M28273M	33-12/57	⊗03/58	⊂5771
M28274M	33-11/60	⊗11/60	⊂5772
M28275M	33-12/59	⊗04/60	⊂5773
M28276M	33-08/56	⊗	⊂5774
M28277M	33-12/60	⊗12/60	⊂5775
M28278M	33-09/56	⊗	⊂5776
M28279M	33-12/60	⊗12/60	⊂5777
M28280M	33-10/59	⊗10/59	⊂5778
M28281M	33-03/59	⊗05/59	⊂5779
M28282M	33-12/60	⊗11/60	⊂5780
M28283M	33-12/60	⊗11/60	⊂5781
M28284M	33-12/60	⊗12/60	⊂5782
M28285M	33-12/60	⊗11/60	⊂5783
M28286M	33-10/57	⊗12/57	⊂5784
M28287M	33-12/60	⊗11/60	⊂5785
M28288M	33-12/60	⊗12/60	⊂5786
M28289M	33-12/60	⊗12/60	⊂5787
M28290M	33-11/60	⊗11/60	⊂5788
M28291M	33-01/55	⊗	⊂5789
M28292M	33-12/60	⊗12/60	⊂5790
M28293M	33-08/57	⊗10/57	⊂5791
M28294M	33-12/60	⊗11/60	⊂5792

LNWR Oerlikon Metropolitan CW&F

Driving Motor Brake Third
DMBT
M28295M-M28297M London Area

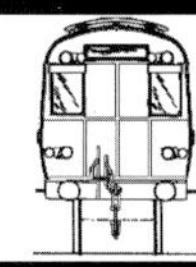

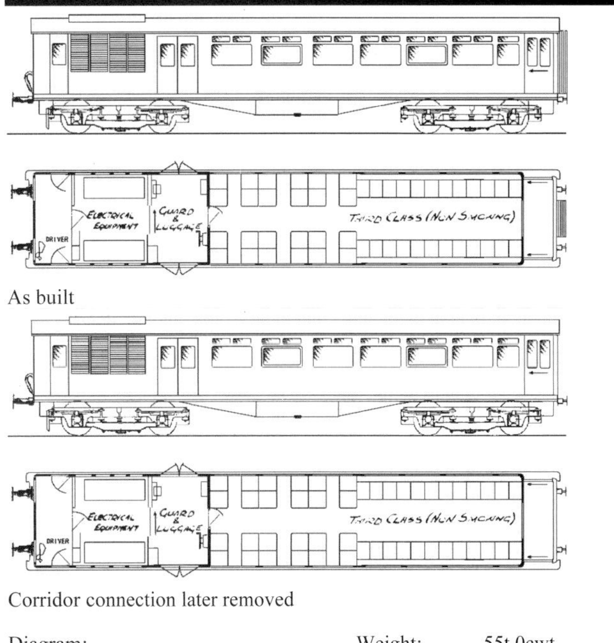

As built

Corridor connection later removed

Diagram:		Weight:	55t 0cwt
Body:	57' 6" × 9' 6"	Bogies:	LNWR
Seats:	48 third	Motors:	Oerlikon 4 × 260hp

M28295M	33-12/60	⊗12/60	⊂5797
M28296M	33-12/57	⊗03/58	⊂5799
M28297M	33-12/60	⊗	⊂5800

LNWR Oerlikon Metropolitan CW&F

Driving Motor Brake Third
DMBT
M28298M-M28299M London Area

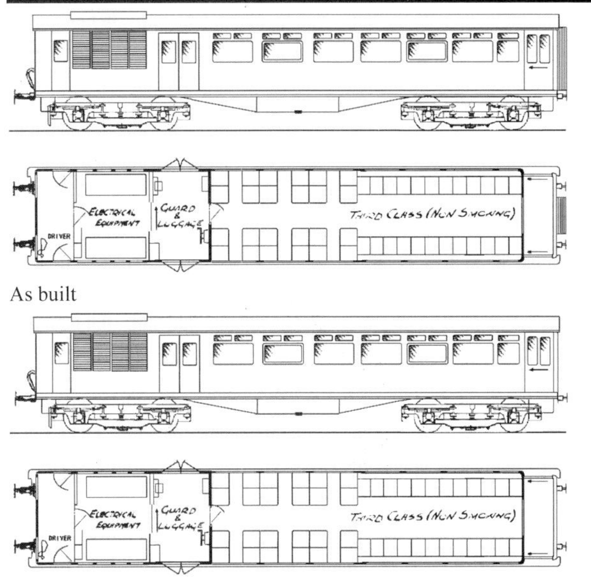

As built

Corridor connection later removed

Diagram:		Weight:	55t 0cwt
Body:	57' 6" × 9' 6"	Bogies:	LNWR
Seats:	48 third	Motors:	Oerlikon 4 × 260hp

M28298M	33-07/59	⊗08/59	⊂5719
M28299M	33-03/59	⊗08/59	⊂5720

LNWR Liverpool
Driving Motor Brake Third
DMBT
M28300M-M28310M Liverpool Area

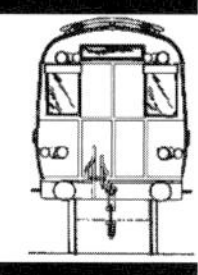

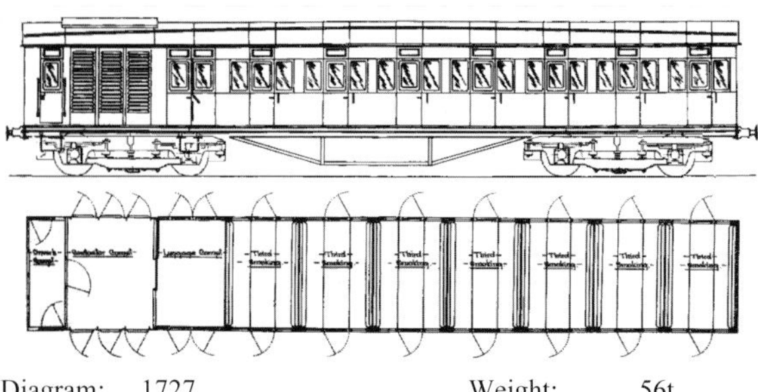

Diagram:	1727	Weight:	56t
Body:	59' 0" × 9' 2¼"	Bogies:	LNWR
Seats:	84 third	Motors:	Metro Vic 4 × 265hp

M28300M	33-04/53	⊃**28496**	⊂**8889**
M28301M	33-02/63	⊗01/63	⊂**8890**
M28302M	33-02/63	⊗01/63	⊂**8891**
M28303M	33-02/63	⊗01/63	⊂**8892**
M28304M	33-02/63	⊗01/63	⊂**8893**
M28305M	33-07/63	⊗01/63	⊂**8894**
M28306M	33-02/63	⊗01/63	⊂**8895**
M28307M	33-02/63	⊗01/63	⊂**8896**
M28308M	33-07/63	⊗07/63	⊂**8897**
M28309M	33-02/63	⊗02/63	⊂**8898**
M28310M	33-02/63	⊗02/63	⊂**8899**

Class 502 Derby
Driving Motor Brake Second
DMBS
M28311M-M28369M Liverpool-Southport

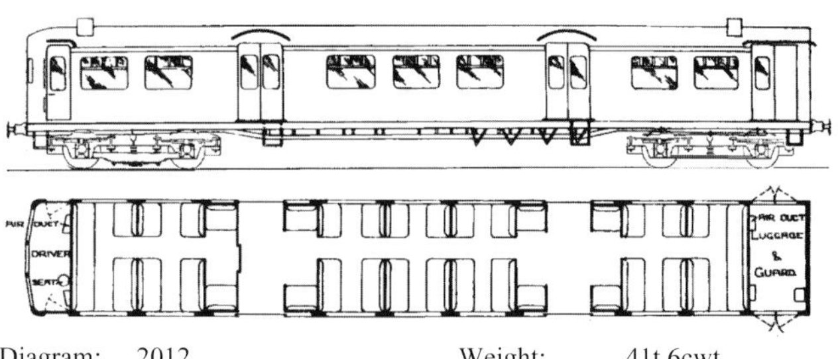

Diagram:	2012	Weight:	41t 6cwt
Body:	66' 5¼" × 9' 7"	Bogies:	
Seats:	88 second	Motors:	EE 4 × 235hp

M28311M	39-12/78	⊗02/80
M28312M	39-11/80	⊗03/81
M28313M	39-12/77	⊗
M28314M	39-12/78	⊗09/81
M28315M	39-12/77	⊗*06/83*
M28316M	39-06/74	⊗
M28317M	39-10/68	⊗03/69
M28318M	39-11/80	⊗03/81
M28319M	39-11/80	⊃**977017**
M28320M	39-12/50	⊗
M28321M	39-06/62	⊗06/62
M28322M	39-05/79	⊗02/80
M28323M	39-11/80	⊗09/81
M28324M	39-10/68	⊗03/69
M28325M	39-01/63	⊗
M28326M	39-09/79	⊗03/80
M28327M	39-06/74	⊗
M28328M	39-09/79	⊗05/81
M28329M	39-06/62	⊗
M28330M	39-05/79	⊗05/80
M28331M	39-09/79	⊗08/80
M28332M	39-11/80	⊗03/82
M28333M	39-03/80	⊗08/80
M28334M	39-11/80	⊃**977018**
M28335M	39-11/80	⊗03/81
M28336M	39-10/68	⊗03/69
M28337M	39-11/80	⊗09/81
M28338M	39-11/80	⊗03/82
M28339M	39-05/79	⊗09/81
M28340M	39-12/77	⊗*06/83*
M28341M	39-05/79	⊗02/80
M28342M	39-10/68	⊗03/69
M28343M	39-08/79	⊗02/80
M28344M	39-06/74	⊗
M28345M	39-10/68	⊗03/69
M28346M	39-01/50	⊗
M28347M	39-11/80	⊗03/81
M28348M	39-10/68	⊗03/69
M28349M	39-09/79	⊗03/81
M28350M	39-10/68	⊗03/69
M28351M	39-11/80	⊗08/81
M28352M	39-09/79	⊗03/80
M28353M	39-05/79	⊗02/80
M28354M	39-11/80	⊗
M28355M	39-09/79	⊗03/80
M28356M	39-08/79	⊗02/80
M28357M	39-11/80	⊗
M28358M	39-09/79	⊗04/81
M28359M	39-09/79	⊗07/80
M28360M	39-04/80	⊗08/80
M28361M	39-08/80	Ⓟ
M28362M	39-12/78	⊗02/80
M28363M	39-10/68	⊗03/69
M28364M	39-11/80	⊗09/81
M28365M	39-10/68	⊗03/69
M28366M	39-11/80	⊗03/81
M28367M	39-10/68	⊗03/69
M28368M	39-10/68	⊗03/69
M28369M	39-12/77	⊗*06/83*

Class 503 Metropolitan-Cammell
Driving Motor Brake Second
DMBS
M28371M-M28394M Wirral & Mersey

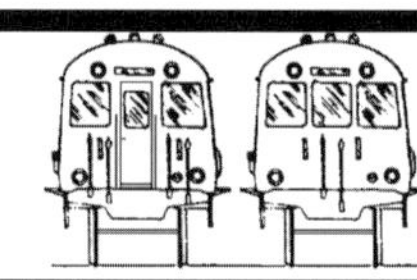

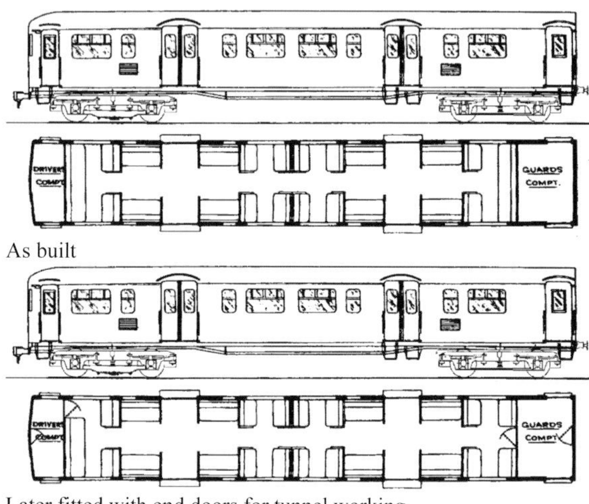

As built

Later fitted with end doors for tunnel working

Diagram:	2004 EB203	Weight:	37t
Body:	58' 0" × 9' 1"	Bogies:	Single Bolster
Seats:	58 second, later 56 second	Motors:	BTH 540hp

M28371M	56-05/85	⊗12/85
M28372M	56-03/85	⊗10/85
M28373M	56-03/85	⊗10/85
M28374M	56-10/84	⊗12/84
M28375M	56-11/84	⊗10/85
M28376M	56-12/84	⊗04/86
M28377M	56-02/85	⊗04/86
M28378M	56-12/84	⊗06/85
M28379M	56-02/85	⊗05/86
M28380M	56-10/84	⊗12/84
M28381M	56-12/84	⊗11/85
M28382M	56-10/84	⊗07/85
M28383M	56-11/84	⊗12/85
M28384M	56-11/84	⊗11/85
M28385M	56-12/84	⊗05/86
M28386M	56-10/84	⊗12/84
M28387M	56-02/85	⊗03/87
M28388M	56-11/84	⊗02/86
M28389M	56-10/84	⊗12/84
M28390M	56-10/84	⊗12/84
M28391M	56-02/85	⊗04/86
M28392M	56-03/85	⊗09/85
M28393M	56-02/85	⊗07/85
M28394M	56-05/85	⊗11/85

Mersey Milnes, Hadley
Driving Motor First
DMF
M28405M-M28416M

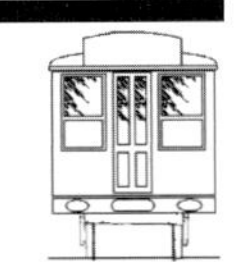

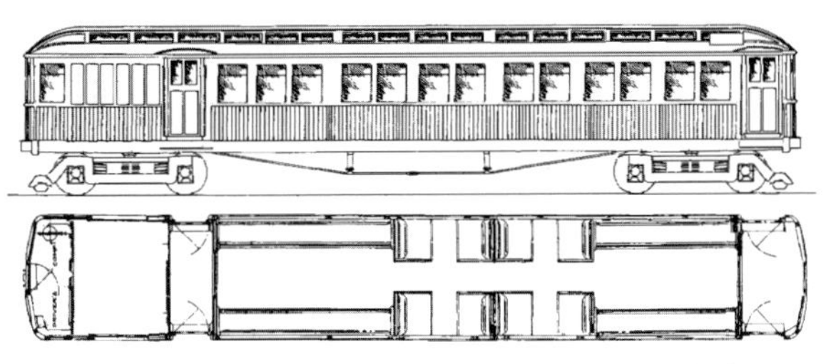

Diagram:		Weight:	36t 10cwt
Body:	59' 0" × 8' 7"	Bogies:	Baldwin Equalised
Seats:	46 first	Motors:	Westinghouse 4 × 115hp

M28405M	48-12/57	⊗09/58	⊂1
M28406M	48-10/56	⊗10/56	⊂2
M28407M	48-02/57	⊗02/57	⊂3
M28408M	48-05/57	⊗05/57	⊂4
M28409M	48-03/57	⊗03/57	⊂5
M28410M	48-10/56	⊗10/56	⊂6
M28411M	48-08/57	⊗09/57	⊂7
M28412M	48-03/57	⊗03/57	⊂8
M28413M	48-11/56	⊗11/56	⊂9
M28414M	48-08/57	⊗08/57	⊂10
M28415M	48-11/56	⊗11/56	⊂11
M28416M	48-12/56	⊗12/56	⊂12

Mersey Cravens
Driving Motor First
DMF
M28417M-M28418M

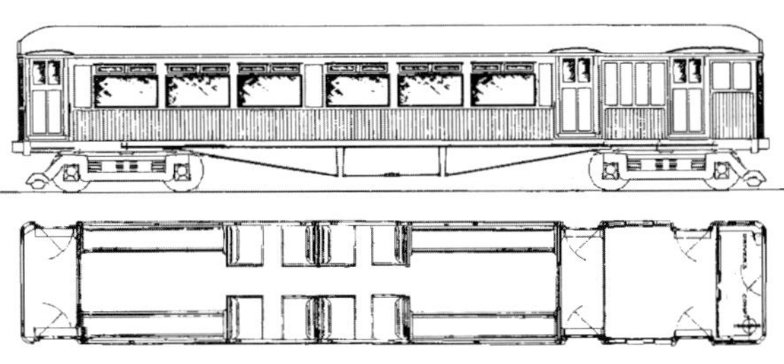

Diagram:		Weight:	36t 10cwt
Body:	59' 0" × 8' 7"	Bogies:	Baldwin Equalised
Seats:	40 first	Motors:	Westinghouse 4 × 125hp

M28417M	48-06/57	⊗06/57	⊂13
M28418M	48-10/56	⊗10/56	⊂14

Mersey Milnes, Hadley
Driving Motor Third
DMT
M28419M-M28430M

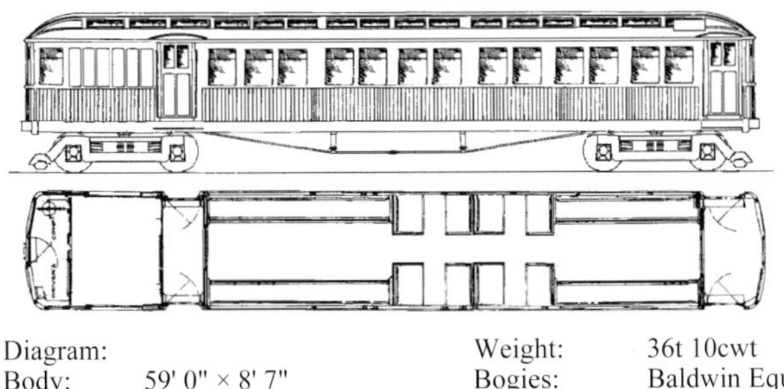

Diagram:		Weight:	36t 10cwt
Body:	59' 0" × 8' 7"	Bogies:	Baldwin Equalised
Seats:	50 third	Motors:	MV 4 × 125hp

M28419M	48-03/57	⊗03/57	⊂26
M28420M	48-05/57	⊗05/57	⊂27
M28421M	48-08/57	⊗09/57	⊂28
M28422M	48-03/57	⊗09/57	⊂29
M28423M	48-02/57	⊗02/57	⊂30
M28424M	48-12/56	⊗12/56	⊂31
M28425M	48-10/56	⊗10/56	⊂32
M28426M	48-01/56	⊗01/56	⊂33
M28427M	48-08/57	⊗08/57	⊂34
M28428M	48-08/57	⊗09/57	⊂35
M28429M	48-11/56	⊗11/56	⊂36
M28430M	48-10/56	⊗10/56	⊂37

Mersey Cravens
Driving Motor Third
DMT
M28431M-M28432M

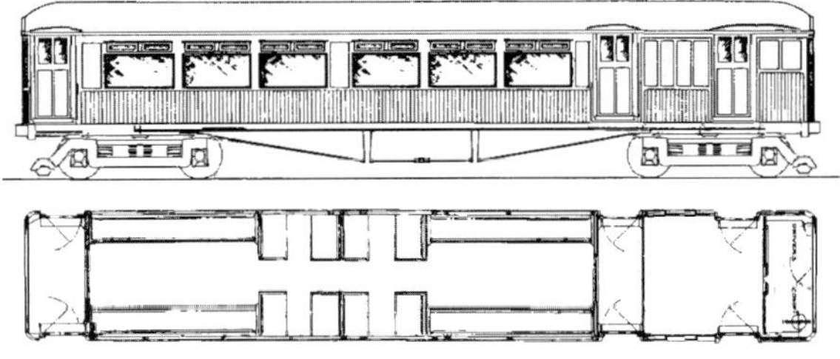

Diagram:		Weight:	36t 10cwt
Body:	59' 0" × 8' 7"	Bogies:	Baldwin Equalised
Seats:	48 third	Motors:	MV 4 × 125hp

M28431M	48-10/56	⊗10/56	⊂38
M28432M	48-06/57	⊗06/57	⊂39

LYR Liverpool Newton Heath
Driving Motor Brake Third
DMBT
28433-28459 Liverpool-Southport

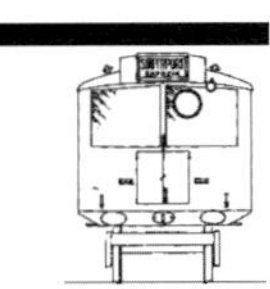

Diagram:	56	Weight:	46t
Body:	60' 5" × 10' 0"	Bogies:	LYR
Seats:	80 third	Motors:	Dick Kerr 4 × 150hp, later 4 × 250hp

28433	33-02/41	⊗02/41	⊂14527
28434	33-03/41	⊗03/41	⊂14501
28435	33-06/40	⊗05/40	⊂14502
28436	33-09/40	⊗08/40	⊂14503
28437	33-10/40	⊗09/40	⊂14504
28438	33-06/46	⊗06/46	⊂14505
28439	33-10/40	⊗10/40	⊂14506
28440	33-04/45	⊗04/45	⊂14507
28441	33-01/40	⊗01/40	⊂14508
28442	33-06/40	⊗04/40	⊂14509
28443	33-03/41	⊗03/41	⊂14511
28444	33-02/41	⊗12/40	⊂14512
28445	33-10/40	⊗11/40	⊂14513
28446	33-06/40	⊗04/40	⊂14514
28447	33-12/45	⊗12/45	⊂14515
28448	33-06/46	⊗06/46	⊂14517
28449	33-10/40	⊗10/40	⊂14518
28450	33-07/40	⊗06/40	⊂14519
28451	33-06/41	⊗05/41	⊂14520
28452	33-09/40	⊗09/40	⊂14521
28453	33-09/40	⊗09/40	⊂14522
28454	33-11/38	⊗04/39	⊂14523
28455	33-06/41	⊗05/41	⊂14525
28456	33-04/45	⊗04/45	⊂14526
28457	33-12/45	⊗10/45	⊂14528
28458	33-04/43	⊗10/45	⊂14531
28459	33-07/39	⊗12/39	⊂14532

LYR Liverpool Newton Heath

Driving Motor Brake Third
DMBT
28460-28469 Liverpool-Southport

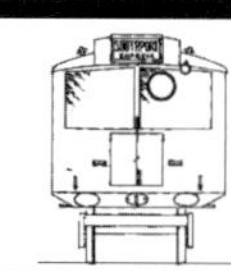

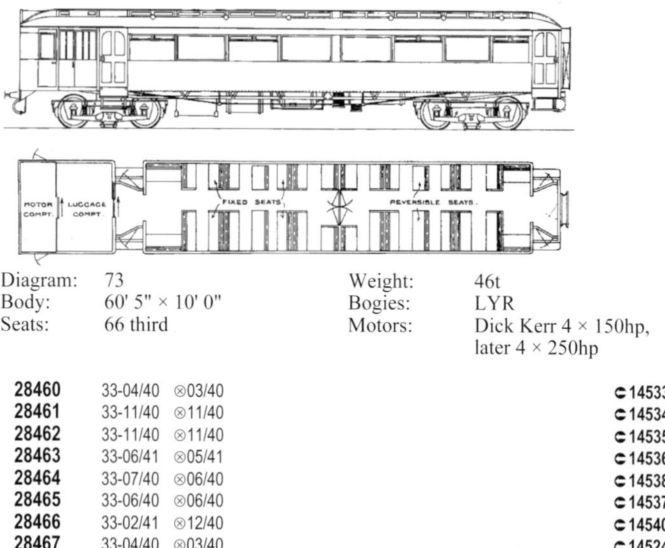

Diagram:	73	Weight:	46t
Body:	60' 5" × 10' 0"	Bogies:	LYR
Seats:	66 third	Motors:	Dick Kerr 4 × 150hp, later 4 × 250hp

28460	33-04/40	⊗03/40	⊂14533
28461	33-11/40	⊗11/40	⊂14534
28462	33-11/40	⊗11/40	⊂14535
28463	33-06/41	⊗05/41	⊂14536
28464	33-07/40	⊗06/40	⊂14538
28465	33-06/40	⊗06/40	⊂14537
28466	33-02/41	⊗12/40	⊂14540
28467	33-04/40	⊗03/40	⊂14524
28468	33-08/40	⊗07/40	⊂14516
28469	33-09/40	⊗08/40	⊂14539

LYR Liverpool Newton Heath

Driving Motor Brake Third
DMBT
28470-28471 Liverpool-Southport

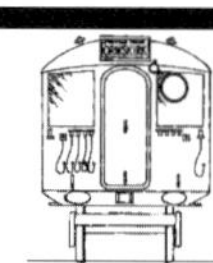

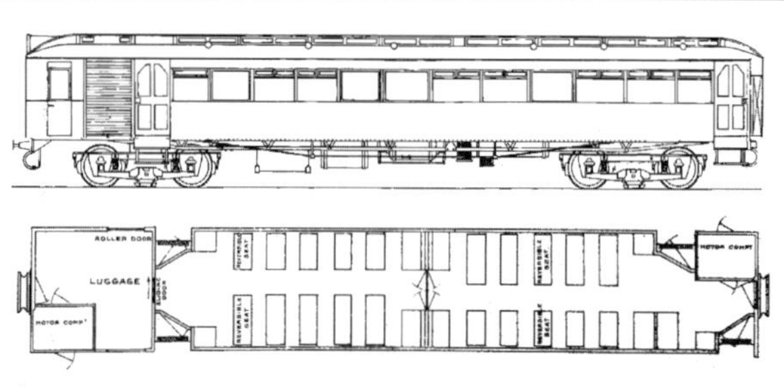

Diagram:	89	Weight:	46t
Body:	60' 0" × 10' 0"	Bogies:	LYR
Seats:	66 third	Motors:	Dick Kerr 4 × 150hp, later 4 × 250hp

28470	33-07/39	⊗09/39	⊂14548
28471	33-05/40	⊗05/40	⊂14549

LYR Liverpool Newton Heath

Driving Motor Third
DMT
28472-28476 Liverpool-Southport

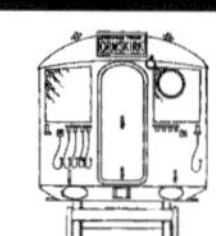

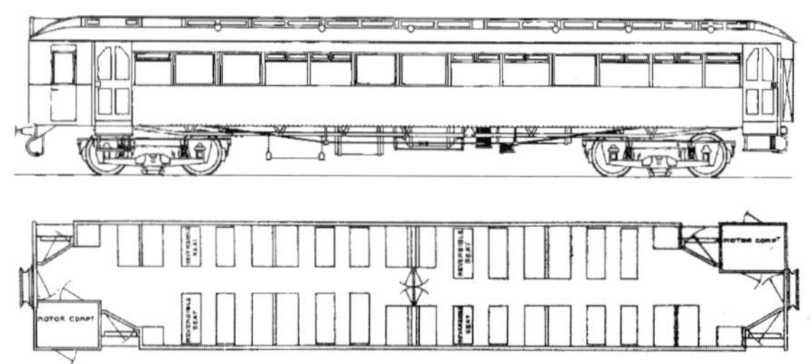

Diagram:	88	Weight:	46t
Body:	60' 0" × 10' 0"	Bogies:	LYR
Seats:	80 third	Motors:	Dick Kerr 4 × 150hp, later 4 × 250hp

28472	33-07/39	⊗12/39	⊂14541
28473	33-10/37	⊗06/39	⊂14542
28474	33-06/36	⊗06/39	⊂14543
28475	33-02/40	⊗01/40	⊂14544
28476	33-02/40	⊗01/40	⊂14545

LYR Liverpool Newton Heath

Driving Motor Brake Third
DMBT
28477-28478 Liverpool-Southport

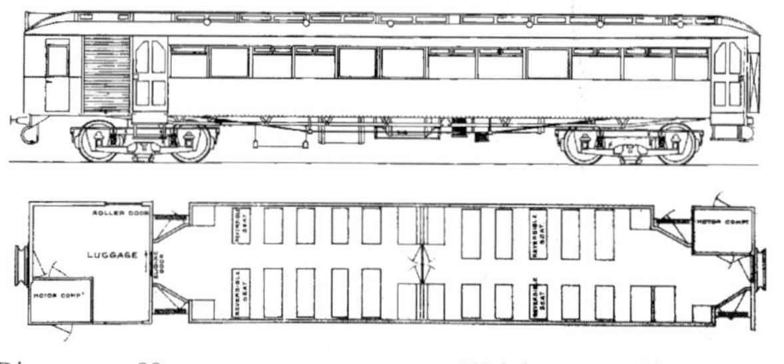

Diagram:	89	Weight:	46t
Body:	60' 0" × 10' 0"	Bogies:	LYR
Seats:	66 third	Motors:	Dick Kerr 4 × 150hp, later 4 × 250hp

28477	33-04/40	⊗04/40	⊂14547
28478	33-04/40	⊗04/40	⊂14550

LYR Liverpool Newton Heath

Driving Motor Third
DMT
28479 Liverpool-Southport

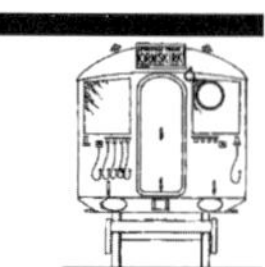

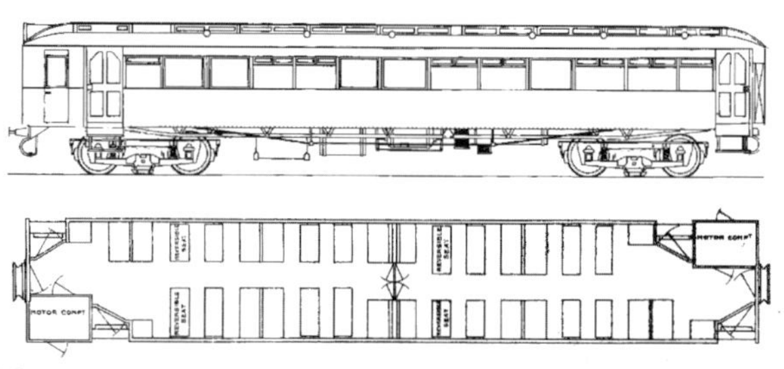

Diagram:	88	Weight:	46t
Body:	60' 0" × 10' 0"	Bogies:	LYR
Seats:	80 third	Motors:	Dick Kerr 4 × 150hp, later 4 × 250hp

28479	33-05/40	⊗05/40	⊂14552

LYR Liverpool Newton Heath

Driving Motor Brake Third
DMBT
28480-28481 Liverpool-Southport

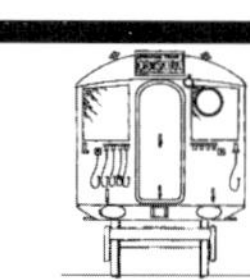

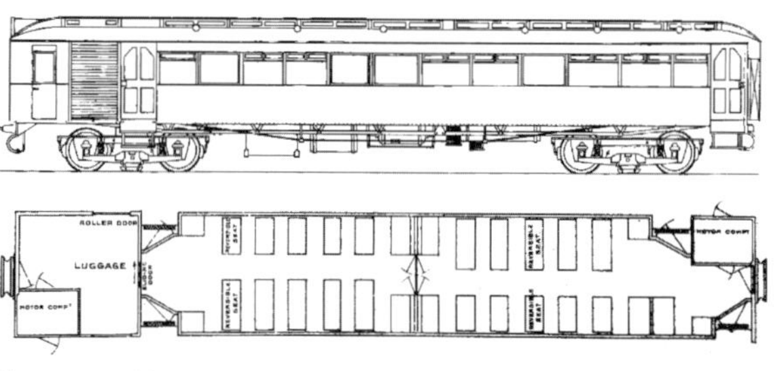

Diagram:	89	Weight:	46t
Body:	60' 0" × 10' 0"	Bogies:	LYR
Seats:	66 third	Motors:	Dick Kerr 4 × 150hp, later 4 × 250hp

28480	33-10/40	⊗09/40	⊂14546
28481	33-07/39	⊗10/39	⊂14551

LYR Liverpool Newton Heath
Driving Motor Brake Third
DMBT
28482 Liverpool-Southport

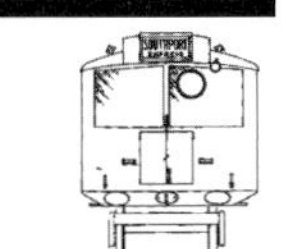

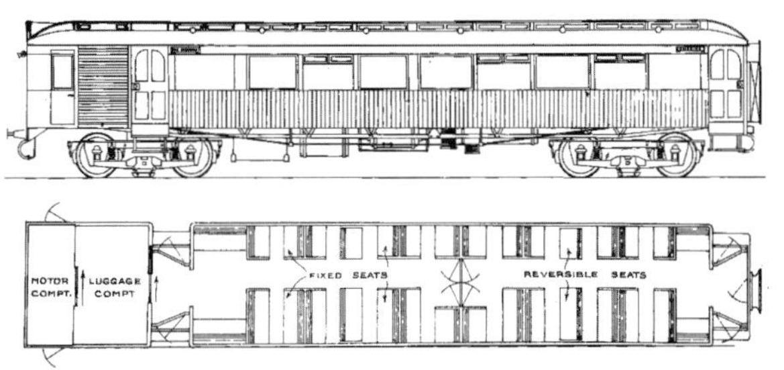

Diagram:	56B	Weight:	46t
Body:	60' 5" × 10' 0"	Bogies:	LYR
Seats:	78 third	Motors:	Dick Kerr 4 × 150hp, later 4 × 250hp

28482	33-01/40	⊗06/40	⊂14510

LYR Liverpool Newton Heath
Driving Motor Brake Third
DMBT
28483-28490 Liverpool-Southport

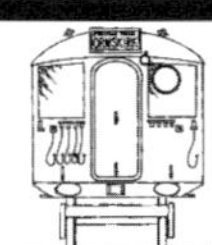

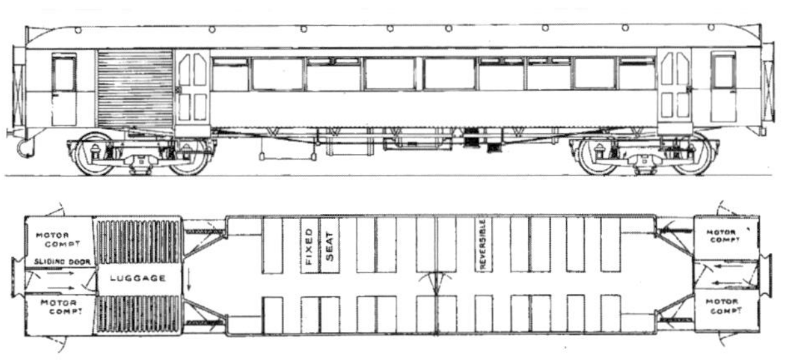

Diagram:	128	Weight:	46t
Body:	63' 7" × 10' 0"	Bogies:	LYR
Seats:	66 third	Motors:	Dick Kerr 4 × 150hp, later 4 × 250hp

28483	33-07/39	⊗07/39	⊂14553
28484	33-06/40	⊗06/40	⊂14554
28485	33-08/40	⊗08/40	⊂14555
28486	33-07/40	⊗07/40	⊂14556
28487	33-08/39	⊗08/39	⊂14557
28488	33-06/40	⊗06/40	⊂14558
28489	33-08/40	⊗08/40	⊂14559
28490	33-04/40	⊗04/40	⊂14560

LYR Liverpool Newton Heath
Driving Motor Brake Third
DMBT
28491-28496 Liverpool-Southport

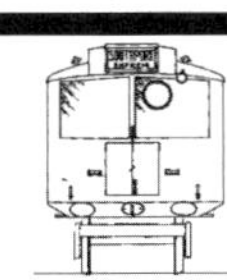

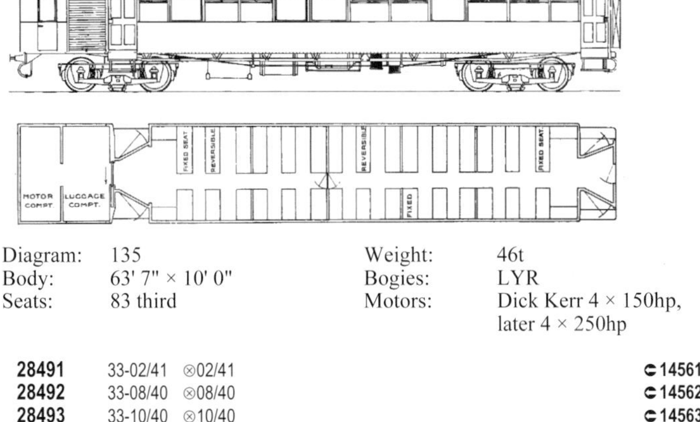

Diagram:	135	Weight:	46t
Body:	63' 7" × 10' 0"	Bogies:	LYR
Seats:	83 third	Motors:	Dick Kerr 4 × 150hp, later 4 × 250hp

28491	33-02/41	⊗02/41	⊂14561
28492	33-08/40	⊗08/40	⊂14562
28493	33-10/40	⊗10/40	⊂14563
28494	33-04/40	⊗04/40	⊂14564
28495	33-07/40	⊗07/40	⊂14565
28496	33-10/40	⊗10/40	⊂14566

LNWR Liverpool
Baggage Car

M28496M Liverpool-Southport

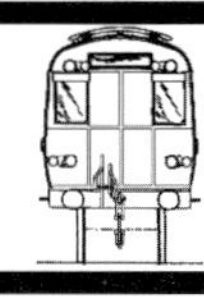

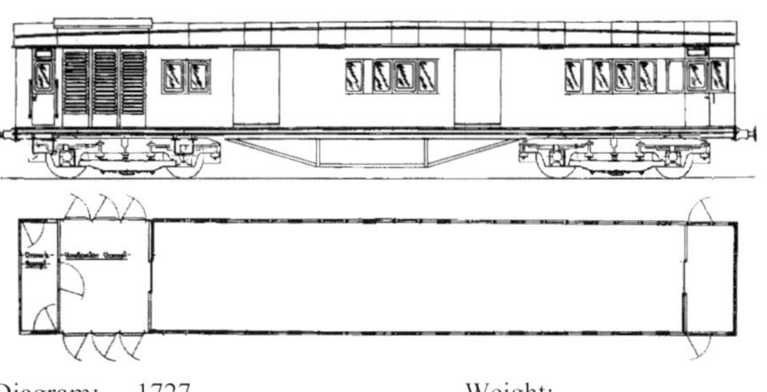

Diagram:	1727	Weight:	
Body:	59' 0" × 9' 2¼"	Bogies:	LNWR
Motors:	Metro Vic 2 × 265hp		

M28496M	204/53-02/66	⊗	⊂28300

LYR Liverpool Newton Heath
Baggage Car

28497-M28499M Liverpool-Southport

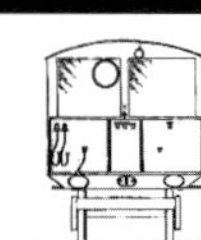

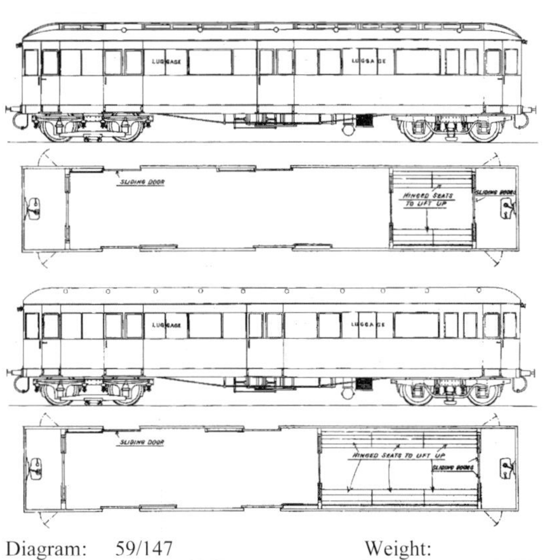

Diagram:	59/147	Weight:	
Body:	54' 0" × 9' 6"	Bogies:	LYR
Motors:	Dick Kerr 4 × 150hp, later 4 × 250hp		

28497	33-05/41	⊗09/41	⊂14529
M28498M	33-04/52	⊗03/52	⊂14530
M28499M	33-04/52	⊗03/52	⊂14567

LNWR Liverpool
Baggage Car

M28497M Liverpool-Southport

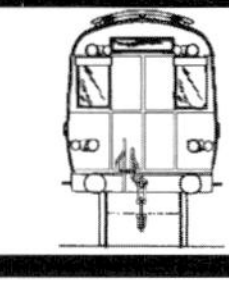

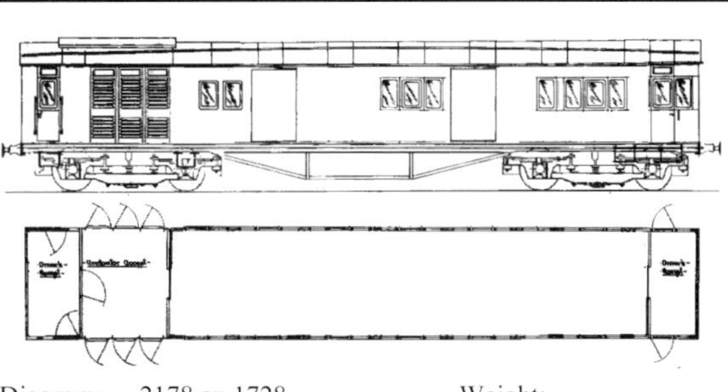

Diagram:	2178 ex 1728	Weight:	

Body:	57' 0" × 9' 2¼"	Bogies:	LNWR
Motors:	Metro Vic 2 × 265hp		

M28497M	²04/53-02/66	⊗	⊂29106

LYR Bury Newton Heath

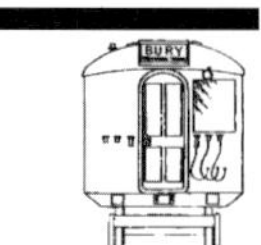

Driving Motor Brake Third
DMBT
M28500M-M28537M Manchester-Bury

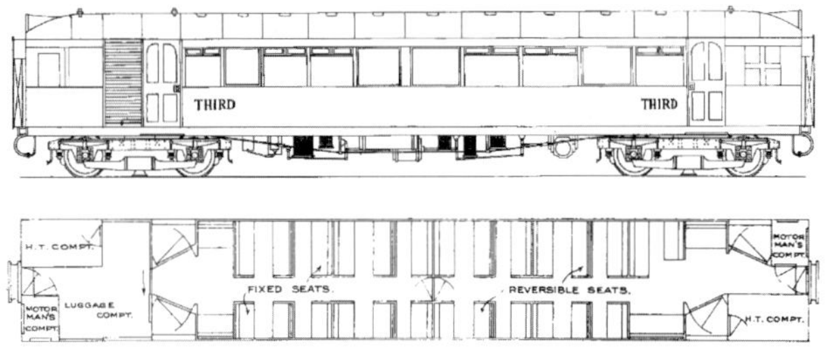

Diagram:	136	Weight:	55t 0cwt
Body:	63' 7" × 9' 6"	Bogies:	LYR
Seats:	74 third	Motors:	Dick Kerr 4 × 200hp

M28500M	33-11/59	⊗11/59	⊂14572
M28501M	33-06/59	⊗06/59	⊂14573
M28502M	33-05/59	⊗06/59	⊂14574
M28503M	33-12/59	⊗12/59	⊂14575
M28504M	33-10/59	⊗11/59	⊂14576
M28505M	33-05/60	⊗06/60	⊂14577
M28506M	33-01/60	⊗04/60	⊂14578
M28507M	33-05/59	⊗06/59	⊂14579
M28508M	33-07/60	⊗08/60	⊂14580
M28509M	33-09/60	⊗09/60	⊂14581
M28510M	33-09/60	⊗09/60	⊂14582
M28511M	33-04/60	⊗05/60	⊂14583
M28512M	33-09/60	⊗09/60	⊂14584
M28513M	33-09/60	⊗09/60	⊂14585
M28514M	33-09/60	⊗01/61	⊂14586
M28515M	33-06/60	⊗06/60	⊂14587
M28516M	33-04/60	⊗04/60	⊂14588
M28517M	33-03/60	⊗04/60	⊂14589
M28518M	33-12/59	⊗12/59	⊂14590
M28519M	33-09/60	⊗09/60	⊂14591
M28520M	33-08/53	⊗11/53	⊂14592
M28521M	33-10/59	⊗11/59	⊂14593
M28522M	33-09/60	⊗12/60	⊂14594
M28523M	33-09/59	⊗11/59	⊂14595
M28524M	33-09/60	⊗10/60	⊂14596
M28525M	33-06/59	⊗06/59	⊂14597
M28526M	33-05/60	⊗06/60	⊂14598
M28527M	33-06/60	⊗06/60	⊂14599
M28528M	33-09/59	⊗11/59	⊂14600
M28529M	33-11/59	⊗12/59	⊂14601
M28530M	33-09/60	⊗10/60	⊂14602
M28531M	33-09/60	⊗10/60	⊂14603
M28532M	33-09/60	⊗10/60	⊂14604
M28533M	33-09/60	⊗10/60	⊂14605
M28534M	33-08/59	⊗10/59	⊂14606
M28535M	33-02/60	⊗05/60	⊂14607
28536	33-12/47	⊗	⊂14608
M28537M	33-06/60	⊗06/60	⊂14609

MSJA Metropolitan-Cammell

Driving Motor Brake Third
DMBT
M28571M-M28594M Manchester-Altrincham

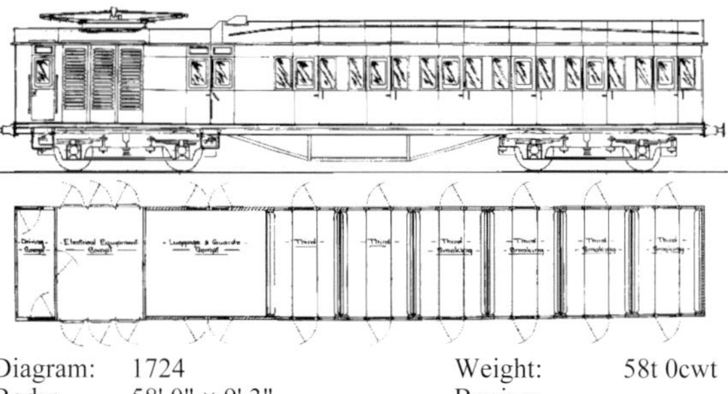

Diagram:	1724	Weight:	58t 0cwt
Body:	58' 0" × 9' 3"	Bogies:	
Seats:	72 third	Motors:	GEC 4 × 328hp

M28571M	48-05/71	⊗05/71	⊂1
M28572M	48-05/71	⊗05/71	⊂2
M28573M	48-05/71	*⊗05/71*	⊂3
M28574M	48-05/71	*⊗05/71*	⊂4
M28575M	48-11/63	⊗	⊂5
M28576M	48-05/71	*⊗05/71*	⊂6
M28577M	48-07/66	⊗10/66	⊂7
M28578M	48-05/71	⊗05/71	⊂8
M28579M	48-05/71	*⊗05/71*	⊂9
M28580M	48-05/71	*⊗05/71*	⊂10
M28581M	48-05/71	⊗05/71	⊂11
M28582M	48-10/66	⊗12/66	⊂12
M28583M	48-08/70	*⊗05/71*	⊂13
M28584M	48-10/66	⊗12/66	⊂14
M28585M	48-05/71	*⊗05/71*	⊂15
M28586M	48-07/66	⊗10/66	⊂16
M28587M	48-05/71	*⊗05/71*	⊂17
M28588M	48-05/71	*⊗05/71*	⊂18
M28589M	48-05/71	⊗05/71	⊂19
M28590M	48-05/71	*⊗05/71*	⊂20
M28591M	48-07/66	⊗10/66	⊂21
M28592M	48-05/71	*⊗05/71*	⊂22
M28593M	48-05/71	*⊗05/71*	⊂23
M28594M	48-12/66	⊗	⊂24

LYR Liverpool Newton Heath

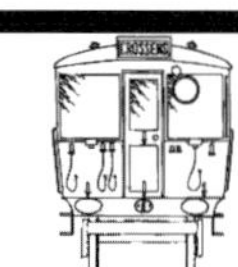

Driving Motor Third
DMT
28600-28602 Liverpool Overhead Railway through trains

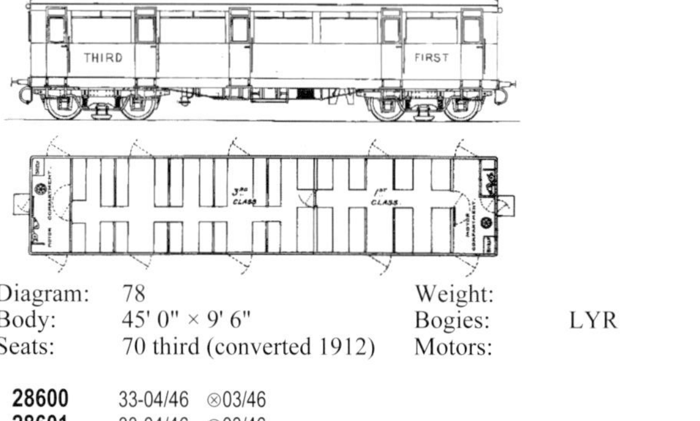

Diagram:	78	Weight:	
Body:	45' 0" × 9' 6"	Bogies:	LYR
Seats:	70 third (converted 1912)	Motors:	

28600	33-04/46	⊗03/46	⊂14610
28601	33-04/46	⊗03/46	⊂14611
28602	33-10/42	⊗03/46	⊂14612

Midland Lancaster-Morecambe/Heysham

Driving Motor Third
DMT
M28610M-M28612M

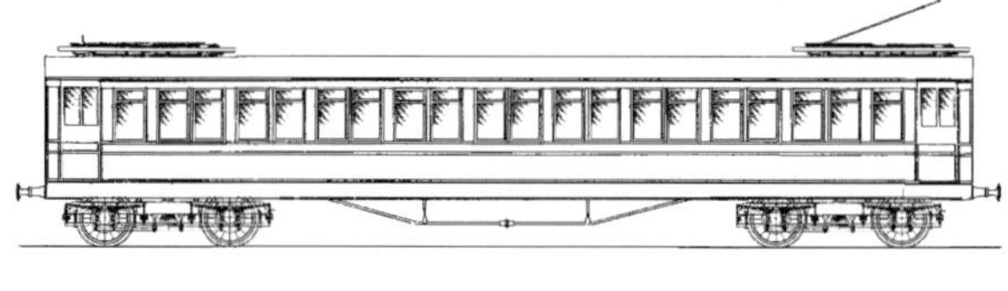

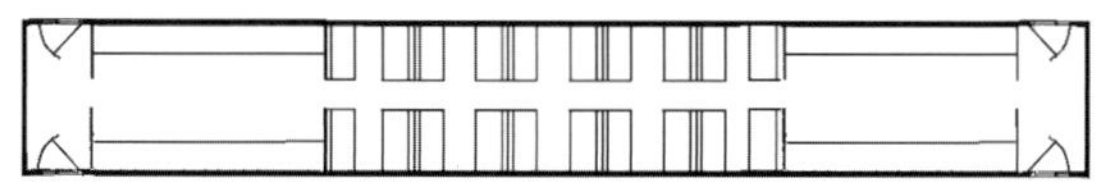

Diagram:	537	Weight:	36t 5cwt
Body:	60' 0" ×	Bogies:	Midland
Seats:	56 third	Motors:	Siemens 2 × 110hp later Westinghouse

M28610M	33-09/52	⊗	⊂2236
M28611M	33-01/52	⊗	⊂2237
M28612M	33-07/53	⊗	⊂2238

Class 503 Metropolitan-Cammell

Driving Motor Brake Second
DMBS
M28672M-M28690M Wirral & Mersey

As built

Later fitted with end doors for tunnel working

Diagram:	2004 EB203	Weight:	36t
Body:	58' 0" × 9' 1"	Bogies:	Single Bolster
Seats:	58 second, later 56 second	Motors:	BTH 540hp

M28672M	38-03/85	⊗10/85
M28673M	38-10/84	⊗12/84
M28674M	38-10/84	⊗12/84
M28675M	38-10/84	⊗12/84
M28676M	38-10/84	⊗12/84
M28677M	38-10/84	⊗12/84
M28678M	38-10/84	⊗07/85
M28679M	38-10/84	⊗12/84
M28680M	38-05/85	⊗11/85
M28681M	38-10/84	⊗12/84
M28682M	38-10/84	⊗12/84
M28683M	38-*06/82*	⊗01/84
M28684M	38-10/84	⊗12/84
M28685M	38-10/84	⊗12/84
M28686M	38-02/83	⊗09/83
M28687M	38-10/84	⊗12/84
M28688M	38-10/84	⊗07/85
M28689M	38-10/84	⊗12/84
M28690M	38-05/85	℗

LYR Liverpool Dick Kerr, Preston

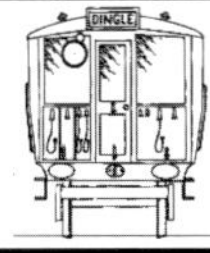

Driving Motor Composite
DMC
28691 Liverpool Overhead Railway through trains

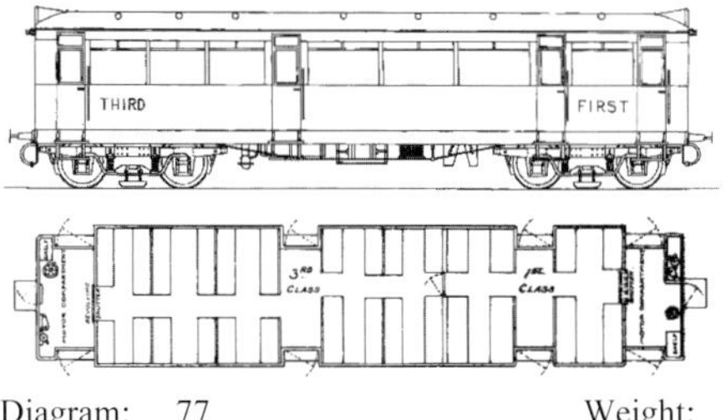

Diagram:	77	Weight:	
Body:	45' 0" × 9' 6"	Bogies:	LYR
Seats:	20 first 50 third	Motors:	

Prototype vehicle with recessed side doors.

28691	33-05/36	⊗ *40*	⊂11702

LYR Liverpool Newton Heath

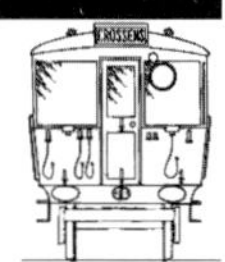

Driving Motor Composite
DMC
28692-28699 Liverpool Overhead Railway through trains

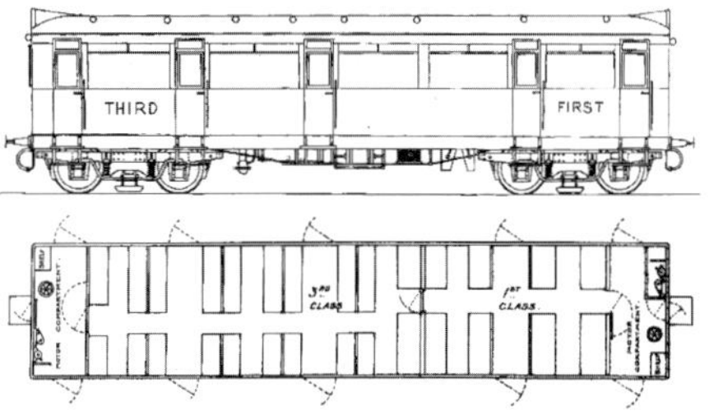

Diagram:	78	Weight:	
Body:	45' 0" × 9' 6"	Bogies:	LYR
Seats:	20 first 50 third	Motors:	

28692	33-11/33	⊗ *40*	⊂11703
28693	33-04/46	⊗02/46	⊂11704
28694	33-04/46	⊗03/46	⊂11705
28695	33-04/46	⊗03/46	⊂11706
28696	33-05/42	⊗02/46	⊂11707
28697	33-05/42	⊗04/46	⊂11708
28698	33-04/46	⊗02/46	⊂11709
28699	33-05/42	⊗04/46	⊂11710

LYR Bury Newton Heath

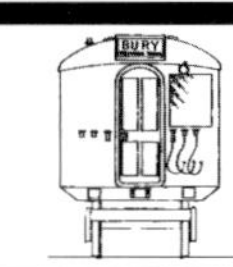

Driving Trailer First
DTF
M28700M-M28713M Manchester-Bury

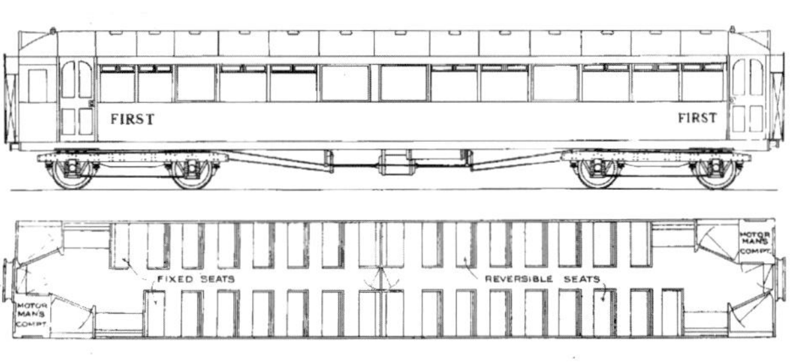

Diagram:	138	Weight:	39t 0cwt
Body:	63' 7" × 9' 6"	Bogies:	LYR
Seats:	72 first		

M28700M	33-05/60	⊗06/60	⊂10933
M28701M	33-09/60	⊗10/60	⊂10934
M28702M	33-09/60	⊗10/60	⊂10935
M28703M	33-07/60	⊗09/60	⊂10936
M28704M	33-11/59	⊗11/59	⊂10937
M28705M	33-01/60	⊗04/60	⊂10938
M28706M	33-09/59	⊗10/59	⊂10939
M28707M	33-05/59	⊗06/59	⊂10940
M28708M	33-09/60	⊗10/60	⊂10941
M28709M	33-03/60	⊗05/60	⊂10942
M28710M	33-09/60	⊗09/60	⊂10943
M28711M	33-03/60	⊗05/60	⊂10944
M28712M	33-12/59	⊗12/59	⊂10945
M28713M	33-05/59	⊗06/59	⊂10946

Mersey Milnes, Hadley
Trailer First
TF
M28787M-M28798M

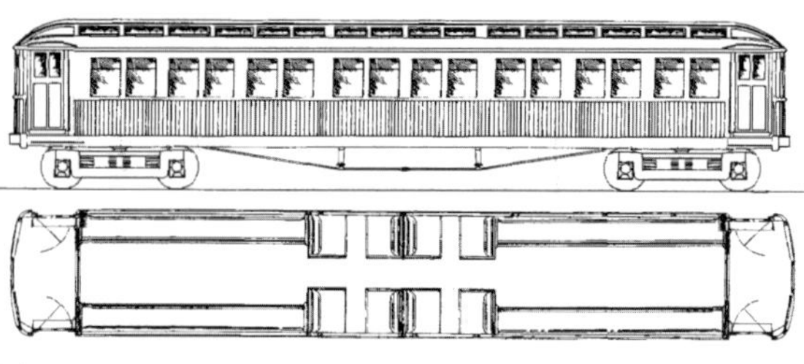

Diagram: | Weight: 20t
Body: 58' 0" × 8' 7" | Bogies: Baldwin Equalised
Seats: 56 first

M28787M	48-08/57	⊗08/57	⊂51
M28788M	48-03/57	⊗03/57	⊂52
M28789M	48-12/56	⊗12/56	⊂53
M28790M	48-03/57	⊗03/57	⊂54
M28791M	48-10/56	⊗10/56	⊂55
M28792M	48-05/57	⊗05/57	⊂56
M28793M	48-02/57	⊗02/57	⊂57
M28794M	48-10/56	⊗10/56	⊂58
M28795M	48-05/57	⊗06/57	⊂59
M28796M	48-11/56	⊗11/56	⊂60
M28797M	48-11/56	⊗11/56	⊂61
M28798M	48-03/57	⊗03/57	⊂62

Mersey Cravens
Trailer First
TF
M28799M

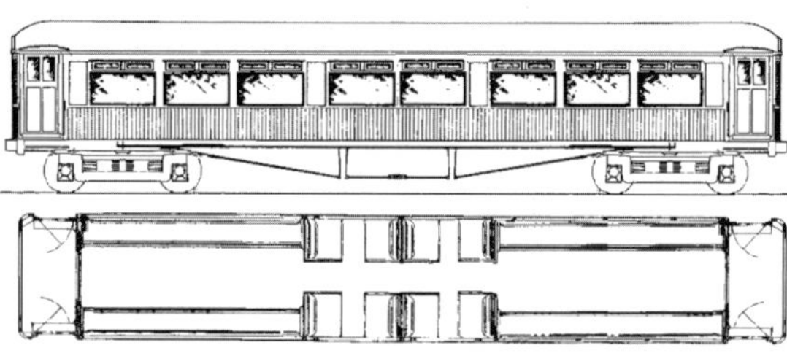

Diagram: | Weight: 20t
Body: 58' 0" × 8' 7" | Bogies: Baldwin Equalised
Seats: 56 first

M28799M	48-10/56	⊗10/56	⊂64

LNWR GEC Midland RC&W
Driving Trailer Third
DTT
M28800M-M28811M London Area

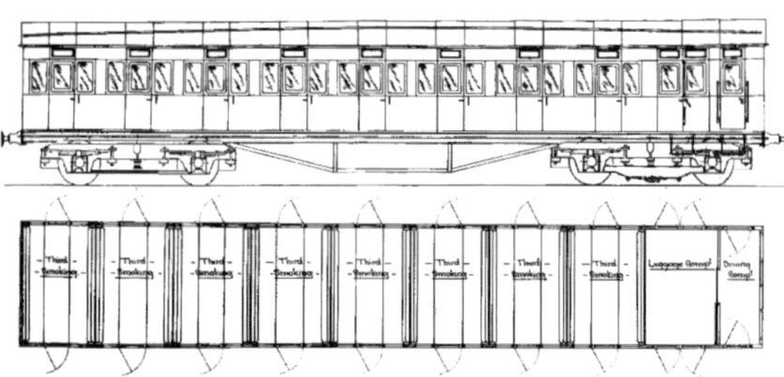

Diagram: 1728 | Weight: 30t
Body: 57' 0" × 9' 2¼" | Bogies: LNWR
Seats: 96 third

M28800M	33-11/63	⊗03/64	⊂4611
M28801M	33-11/63	⊗06/64	⊂4612
M28802M	33-11/63	⊗02/64	⊂4613
M28803M	33-11/63	⊗03/64	⊂4614
M28804M	33-11/63	⊗06/64	⊂5236
M28805M	33-11/63	⊗06/64	⊂5237
M28806M	33-11/63	⊗06/64	⊂5238
M28807M	33-11/63	⊗06/64	⊂5239
M28808M	33-11/63	⊗06/64	⊂5240
M28809M	33-11/63	⊗01/64	⊂5241
M28810M	33-11/63	⊗01/64	⊂5242
M28811M	33-11/63	⊗01/64	⊂5243

LNWR GEC Wolverton
Driving Trailer Third
DTT
M28812M-M28824M London Area

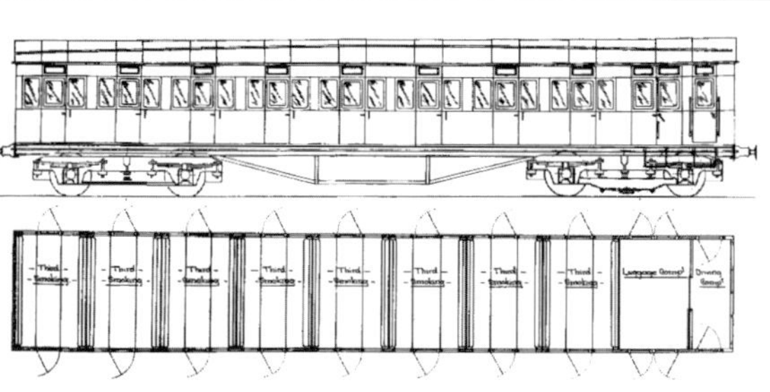

Diagram: 1728 | Weight: 30t
Body: 57' 0" × 9' 2¼" | Bogies: LNWR
Seats: 96 third

M28812M	33-11/63	⊗02/64		⊂1931
M28813M	33-11/63	⊗01/64		⊂1934
M28814M	33-11/63	⊗06/64		⊂1939
M28815M	33-11/63	⊗02/64		⊂1952
M28816M	33-11/63	⊗06/64		⊂1956
M28817M	33-11/63	⊗06/64		⊂1959
M28818M	33-11/63	⊗06/64		⊂1964
M28819M	33-11/63	⊗06/64		⊂1965
M28820M	33-11/63	⊗06/64		⊂1968
M28821M	33-11/63	⊗02/64		⊂1971
M28822M	33-11/63	⊗06/64		⊂1976
M28823M	33-11/63	⊗02/64		⊂1984
M28824M	33-11/63	⊗10/65	Stonebridge Park Shunter 11/63-10/65	⊂1993

LNWR Siemens Metropolitan CW&F
Driving Trailer Third
DTT/DTSO
M29021M-M29024M London Area (later AM1)

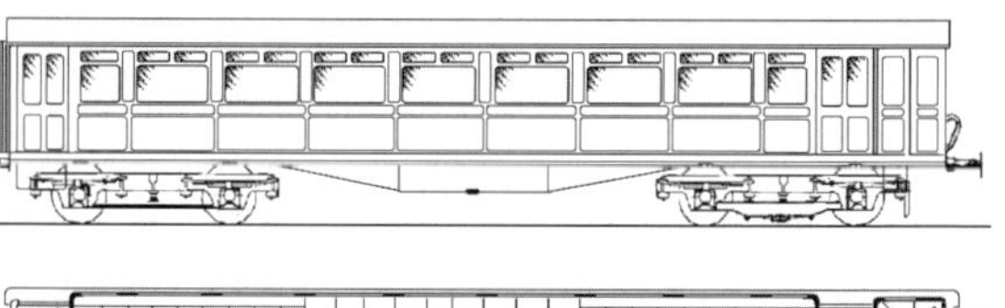

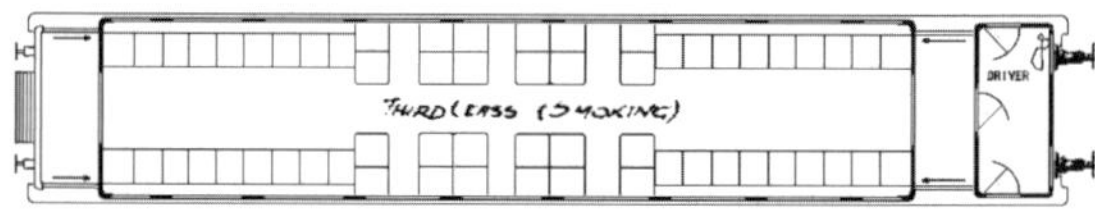

As built

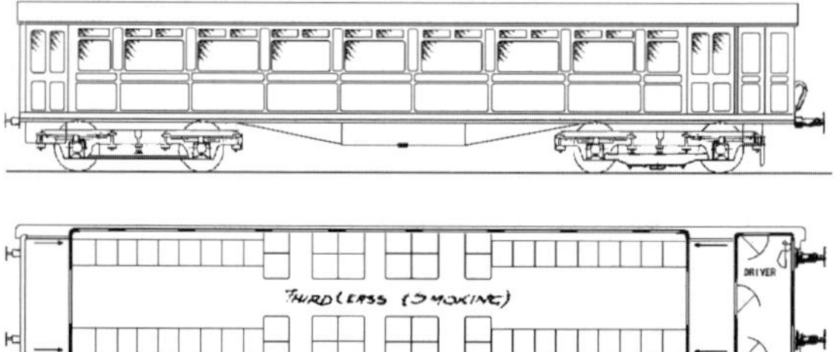

Corridor connection later removed

Diagram: | Weight: 28t 0cwt
Body: 57' 6" × 9' 6" | Bogies: LNWR
Seats: 60 third

M29021M	33-02/67	⊗	⊂9941
M29022M	33-02/67	⊗	⊂9942
M29023M	33-02/67	⊗	⊂9943
M29024M	33-02/67	⊗	⊂9944

LNWR Oerlikon Wolverton

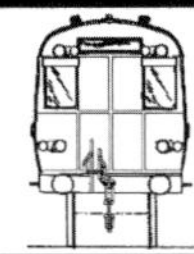

Driving Trailer Third
DTT
M29025M-M29062M London Area

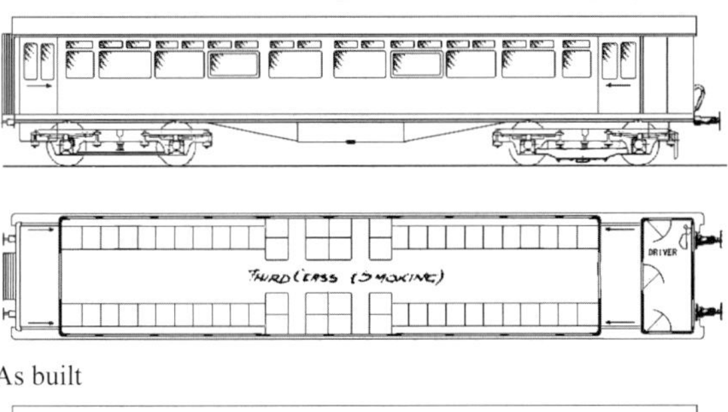

As built

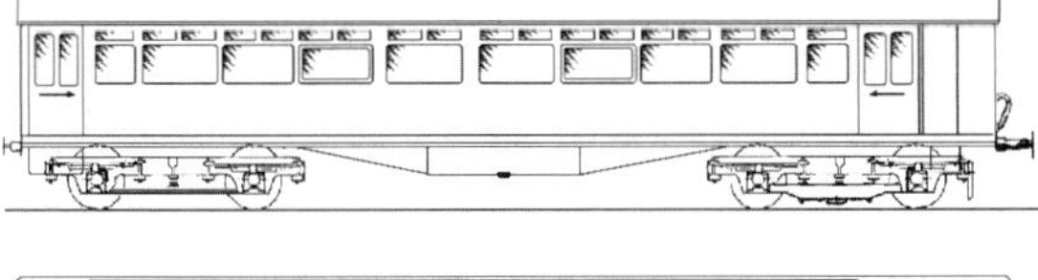

Corridor connection later removed

Diagram:		Weight:	29t 0cwt
Body:	57' 6" × 9' 6"	Bogies:	LNWR
Seats:	60 third		

M29025M	33-02/57	⊗09/59		⊂9945
M29026M	33-11/55	⊗		⊂9946
M29027M	33-12/61	⊗03/69		⊂9947
M29029M	33-09/56	⊗		⊂9949
M29030M	33-03/56	⊗		⊂9950
M29031M	33-06/60	⊗		⊂9951
M29032M	33-03/59	⊗06/59		⊂9952
M29033M	33-05/62	⊗	Later used as Shunting set Stonebridge Park	⊂9953
M29034M	33-04/59	⊗06/59		⊂9954
M29035M	33-11/55	⊗		⊂9955
M29036M	33-12/60	⊗12/60		⊂9956
M29037M	33-11/55	⊗		⊂9957
M29038M	33-05/59	⊗07/59		⊂9958
M29039M	33-05/60	⊗		⊂9959
M29040M	33-11/55	⊗		⊂9960
M29041M	33-10/57	⊗11/57		⊂9961
M29042M	33-11/60	⊗11/60		⊂9962
M29043M	33-03/57	⊗06/61		⊂9973
M29044M	33-05/60	⊗		⊂9974
M29045M	33-06/59	⊗08/59		⊂9975
M29046M	33-06/59	⊗06/59		⊂9976
M29047M	33-11/55	⊗		⊂9977
M29048M	33-02/57	⊗03/57		⊂9978
M29049M	33-07/59	⊗09/57		⊂9979
M29050M	33-07/60	⊗		⊂9980
M29051M	33-11/60	⊗11/60		⊂9981
M29052M	33-11/60	⊗11/60		⊂9963
M29053M	33-08/60	⊗		⊂9964
M29054M	33-11/60	⊗11/60		⊂9965
M29055M	33-07/60	⊗		⊂9966
M29056M	33-07/57	⊗09/57		⊂9967
M29057M	33-06/57	⊗08/57		⊂9968
M29058M	33-06/57	⊗03/63		⊂9969
M29059M	33-06/60	⊗		⊂9970
M29060M	33-08/57	⊗09/57		⊂9971
M29061M	33-11/60	⊗11/60		⊂9972
M29062M	33-08/57	⊗10/57		⊂9982

LNWR Oerlikon Wolverton

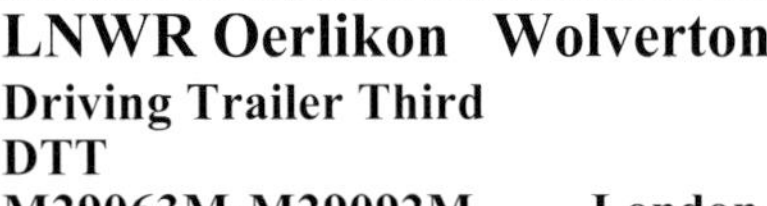

Driving Trailer Third
DTT
M29063M-M29092M London Area

As built

Corridor connection later removed

Diagram:		Weight:	29t 0cwt
Body:	57' 6" × 9' 6"	Bogies:	LNWR
Seats:	60 third		

M29063M	33-07/57	⊗09/57	⊂9983
M29064M	33-06/60	⊗	⊂9984
M29065M	33-11/56	⊗	⊂9985
M29066M	33-11/60	⊗11/60	⊂9986
M29067M	33-10/59	⊗11/66	⊂9987
M29068M	33-11/57	⊗12/57	⊂9988
M29069M	33-10/59	⊗11/66	⊂9989
M29070M	33-11/60	⊗11/60	⊂9990
M29071M	33-03/59	⊗10/59	⊂9991
M29072M	33-11/60	⊗11/60	⊂9992
M29073M	33-12/60	⊗11/60	⊂9993
M29074M	33-11/60	⊗11/60	⊂9994
M29075M	33-08/60	⊗	⊂9995
M29076M	33-01/61	⊗05/64	⊂9996
M29077M	33-11/57	⊗12/57	⊂9997
M29078M	33-11/60	⊗11/60	⊂9998
M29079M	33-06/60	⊗	⊂9999
M29080M	33-11/60	⊗11/60	⊂10000
M29081M	33-11/60	⊗11/60	⊂10001
M29082M	33-11/60	⊗11/60	⊂10002
M29083M	33-11/60	⊗11/60	⊂10003
M29084M	33-12/59	⊗12/59	⊂10004
M29085M	33-07/60	⊗	⊂10005
M29086M	33-11/60	⊗11/60	⊂10006
M29087M	33-07/59	⊗08/57	⊂10007
M29088M	33-06/60	⊗06/60	⊂10008
M29089M	33-05/60	⊗	⊂10009
M29090M	33-01/61	⊃040851	⊂10010
M29091M	33-11/60	⊗11/60	⊂10011
M29092M	33-08/60	⊗	⊂10012

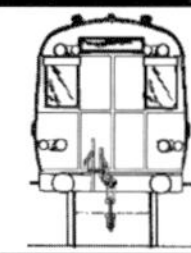
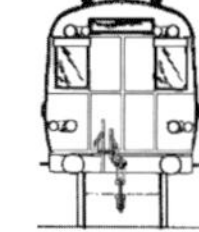

LNWR Oerlikon Wolverton

Driving Trailer Third
DTT
M29093M-M29099M London Area

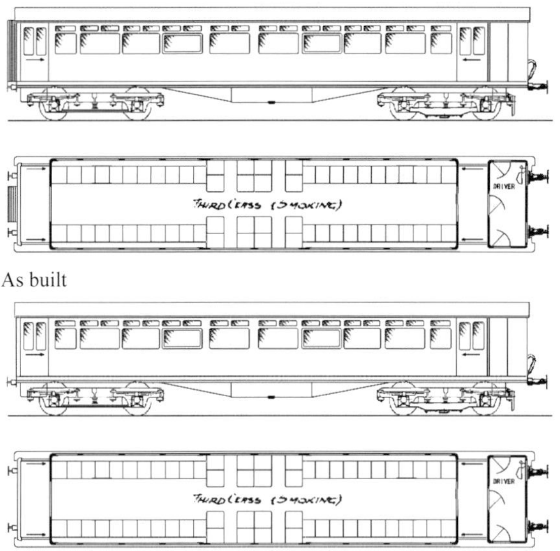

As built

Corridor connection later removed

Diagram:			
Body:	57' 6" × 9' 6"	Weight:	29t 0cwt
Seats:	60 third	Bogies:	LNWR

M29093M	33-12/57	⊗04/58	⊂10013
M29094M	33-08/60	⊗	⊂10014
M29095M	33-11/60	⊗11/60	⊂10015
M29096M	33-11/60	⊗11/60	⊂10016
29097	33-02/41	⊗10/40	⊂10017
M29098M	33-05/60	⊗	⊂10018
M29099M	33-06/60	⊗	⊂10019

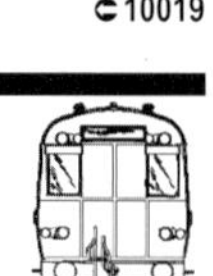

LNWR Liverpool

Driving Trailer Third
DTT
M29100M-M29110M Liverpool Area

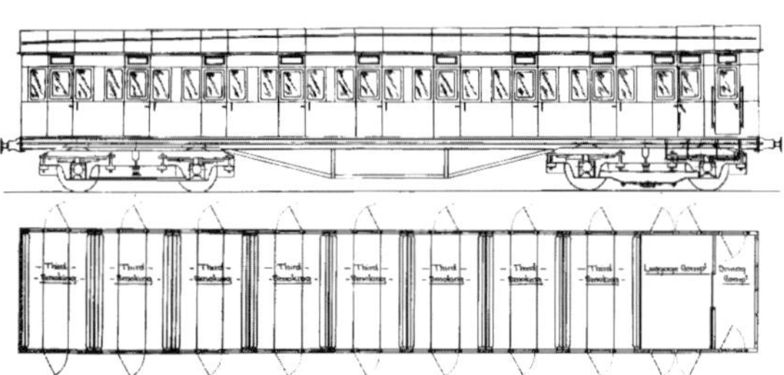

Diagram:	1728	Weight:	30t
Body:	57' 0" × 9' 2¼"	Bogies:	LNWR
Seats:	96 third		

M29100M	33-02/63	⊗02/63	⊂5244
M29101M	33-07/63	⊗07/63	⊂5245
M29102M	33-07/63	⊗07/63	⊂5246
M29103M	33-02/63	⊗02/63	⊂5247
M29104M	33-02/63	⊗01/63	⊂5248
M29105M	33-02/63	⊗01/63	⊂5249
M29106M	33-04/53	➲28497	⊂5250
M29107M	33-02/63	⊗01/63	⊂5358
M29108M	33-02/63	⊗02/63	⊂5359
M29109M	33-02/63	⊗02/63	⊂5360
M29110M	33-02/63	⊗02/63	⊂10020

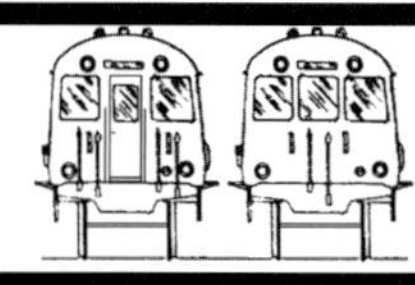

Class 503 Birmingham RC&W

Driving Trailer Second
DTS
M29131M-M29156M Wirral & Mersey

As built

Later fitted with end doors for tunnel working

Diagram:	2006 EE202	Weight:	22t
Body:	58' 0" × 9' 1"	Bogies:	Single Bolster
Seats:	68 second, later 65 second		

M29131M	56-03/85	⊗10/85	28371	56-	57	28373	57-03/85
M29132M	56-03/85	⊗12/85	28372	56-03/85			
M29133M	56-11/84	⊗02/86	28389	56-	57	28388	57-11/84
M29134M	56-12/84	⊗06/85	28378	56-12/84			
M29135M	56-10/84	⊗12/85	28380	56-10/84			
M29136M	56-10/84	⊗12/84	28387	56-	57	28389	57-10/84
M29137M	56-10/84	⊗12/84	28374	56-10/84			
M29138M	56-11/84	⊗10/85	28375	56-11/84			
M29139M	56-02/85	⊗02/86	28377	56-02/85			
M29140M	56-05/85	⊗12/85	28373	56-	57	28371	57-05/85
M29141M	56-05/85	⊗11/85	28394	56-05/85			
M29142M	56-12/84	⊗11/85	28381	56-12/84			
M29143M	56-03/85	⊗09/85	28392	56-03/85			
M29144M	56-02/85	⊗07/85	28393	56-02/85			
M29145M	56-02/85	⊗05/86	28379	56-02/85			
M29146M	56-12/84	⊗04/86	28376	56-12/84			
M29147M	56-10/84	⊗07/85	28382	56-10/84			
M29148M	56-02/85	⊗06/86	28391	56-02/85			
M29149M	56-10/84	⊗12/84	28386	56-10/84			
M29150M	56-11/84	⊗12/85	28383	56-11/84			
M29151M	56-11/84	⊗11/85	28384	56-11/84			
M29152M	56-12/84	⊗05/86	28385	56-12/84			
M29153M	56-02/85	⊗02/86	28388	56-	57	28387	57-02/85
M29154M	56-10/84	⊗12/84	28390	56-10/84			
M29155M	56-10/84	⊗07/85	28678	56-10/84			
M29156M	56-10/84	⊗12/84	28687	56-10/84			

Mersey Milnes, Hadley

Trailer Third
TT
M29157M-M29180M

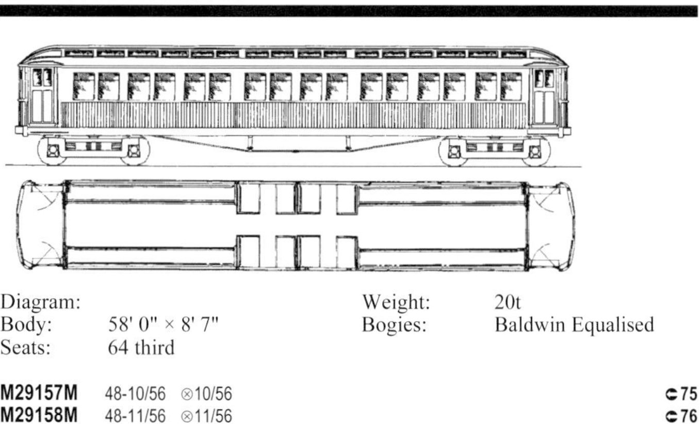

Diagram:		Weight:	20t
Body:	58' 0" × 8' 7"	Bogies:	Baldwin Equalised
Seats:	64 third		

M29157M	48-10/56	⊗10/56	⊂75
M29158M	48-11/56	⊗11/56	⊂76
M29159M	48-10/56	⊗10/56	⊂77
M29160M	48-12/56	⊗12/56	⊂78

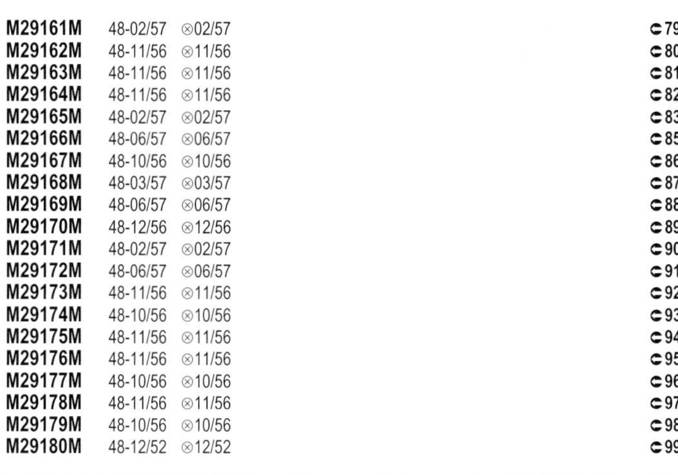

M29161M 48-02/57 ⊗02/57 ⊂79
M29162M 48-11/56 ⊗11/56 ⊂80
M29163M 48-11/56 ⊗11/56 ⊂81
M29164M 48-11/56 ⊗11/56 ⊂82
M29165M 48-02/57 ⊗02/57 ⊂83
M29166M 48-06/57 ⊗06/57 ⊂85
M29167M 48-10/56 ⊗10/56 ⊂86
M29168M 48-03/57 ⊗03/57 ⊂87
M29169M 48-06/57 ⊗06/57 ⊂88
M29170M 48-12/56 ⊗12/56 ⊂89
M29171M 48-02/57 ⊗02/57 ⊂90
M29172M 48-06/57 ⊗06/57 ⊂91
M29173M 48-11/56 ⊗11/56 ⊂92
M29174M 48-10/56 ⊗10/56 ⊂93
M29175M 48-11/56 ⊗11/56 ⊂94
M29176M 48-11/56 ⊗11/56 ⊂95
M29177M 48-10/56 ⊗10/56 ⊂96
M29178M 48-11/56 ⊗11/56 ⊂97
M29179M 48-10/56 ⊗10/56 ⊂98
M29180M 48-12/52 ⊗12/52 ⊂99

Mersey Craven
Trailer Third
TT
M29181M-M29182M

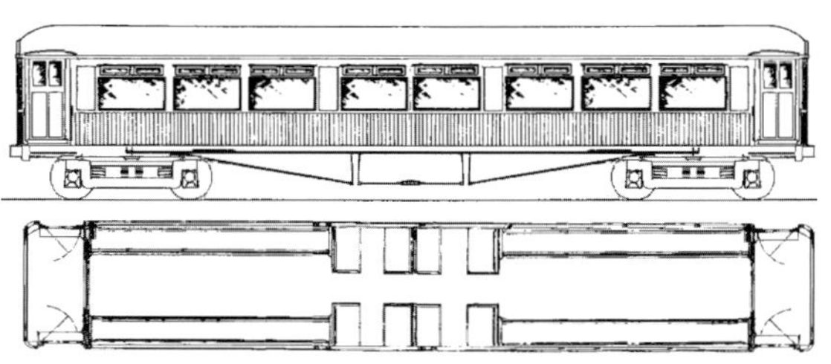

Diagram: Weight: 20t
Body: 58' 0" × 8' 7" Bogies: Baldwin Equalised
Seats: 64 third

M29181M 48-10/56 ⊗10/56 ⊂100
M29182M 48-10/56 ⊗10/56 ⊂101

Mersey Gloucester C&W
Trailer Third
TT
M29183M-M29192M

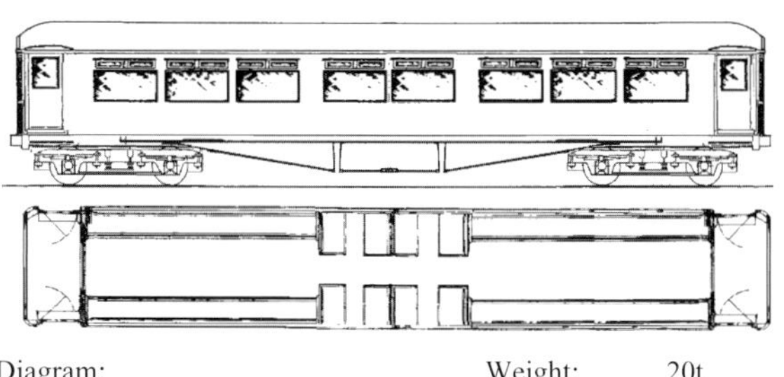

Diagram: Weight: 20t
Body: 58' 0" × 8' 7" Bogies:
Seats: 68 third

M29183M 48-03/57 ⊗03/57 ⊂102
M29184M 48-03/57 ⊗03/57 ⊂103
M29185M 48-03/57 ⊗03/57 ⊂104
M29186M 48-08/57 ⊗08/57 ⊂105
M29187M 48-05/57 ⊗05/57 ⊂106
M29188M 48-05/57 ⊗05/57 ⊂107
M29189M 48-08/57 ⊗08/57 ⊂108
M29190M 48-03/57 ⊗03/57 ⊂109
M29191M 48-08/57 ⊗09/57 ⊂110
M29192M 48-05/57 ⊗05/57 ⊂111

Mersey Wolverton
Trailer Third
TT
M29193M

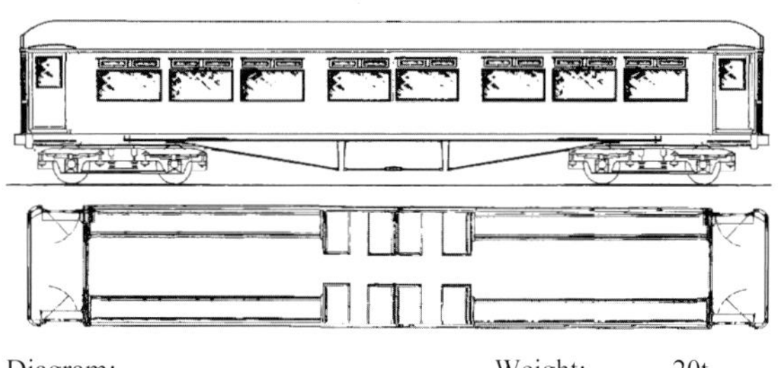

Diagram: Weight: 20t
Body: 58' 0" × 8' 7" Bogies:
Seats: 64 third

M29193M 48-08/57 ⊗08/57 ⊂112

LYR Liverpool Newton Heath
Trailer Third
TT, later DTT, later TT
29194 Liverpool-Southport

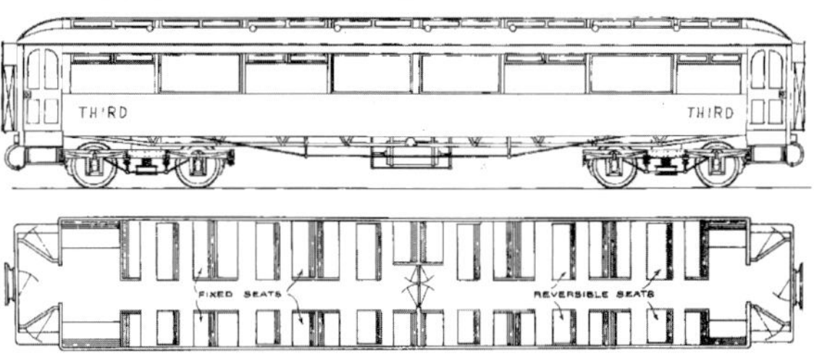

Diagram: 68 Weight: 20t
Body: 60' 0" × 10' 0" Bogies: LYR
Seats: 98 third, later 76 third, later 89 third

29194 33- *39* ⊗10/39 ⊂14616

LYR Liverpool Newton Heath
Trailer Third
TT, later DTT, later TT
29195 Liverpool-Southport

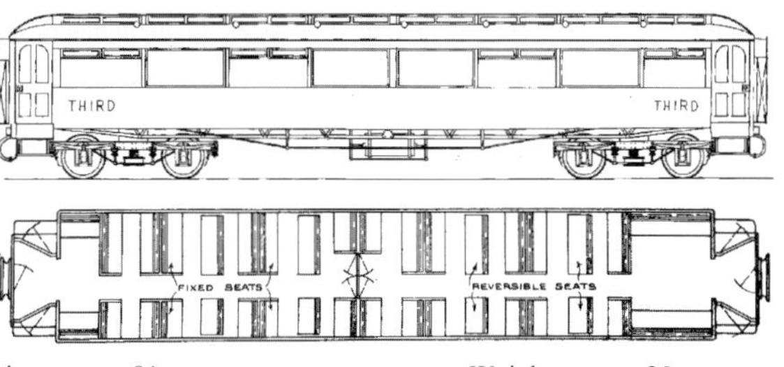

Diagram: 81 Weight: 20t
Body: 60' 0" × 10' 0" Bogies: LYR
Seats: 80 third, later 76 third, later 86 third

29195 33- *39* ⊗10/39 ⊂14633

LYR Liverpool Newton Heath
Driving Trailer Third
DTT
29196-29199 Manchester-Bury

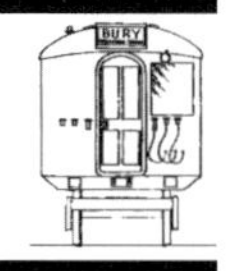

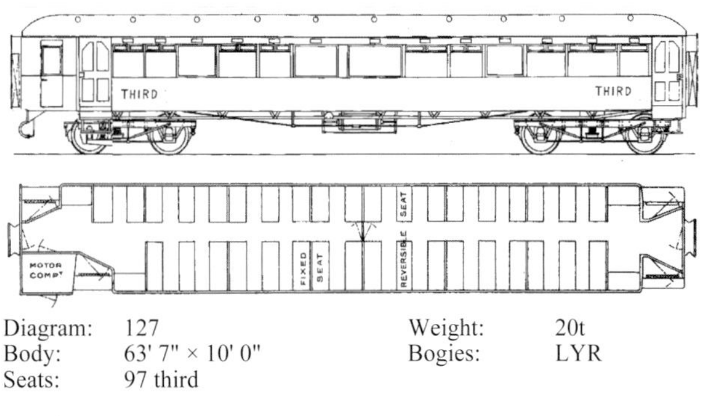

Diagram:	127	Weight:	20t
Body:	63' 7" × 10' 0"	Bogies:	LYR
Seats:	97 third		

29196	33-07/40	⊗04/40		⊂14643
29197	33- *39*	⊗09/39		⊂14644
29198	33- *39*	⊗06/39		⊂14645
29199	33-08/40	⊗03/40		⊂14646

LYR Bury Newton Heath
Driving Trailer Third
DTT
M29200M-M29213M Manchester-Bury

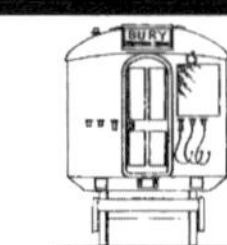

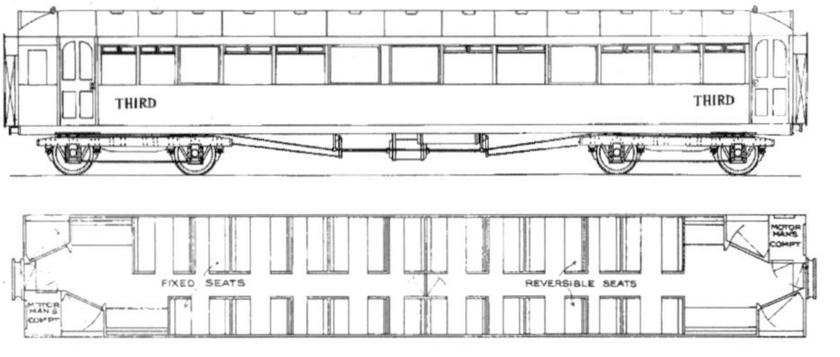

Diagram:	137	Weight:	
Body:	63' 7" × 9' 6"	Bogies:	LYR
Seats:	95 third		

M29200M	33-01/60	⊗04/60	Grounded Cheetwood	⊂14669
M29201M	33-12/59	⊗12/59		⊂14670
M29202M	33-10/59	⊗11/59		⊂14671
M29203M	33-01/60	⊗04/60	Grounded Cheetwood	⊂14672
M29204M	33-08/53	⊗11/53		⊂14673
M29205M	33-09/60	⊗10/60		⊂14674
M29206M	33-01/60	⊗04/60		⊂14675
M29207M	33-09/60	⊗10/60		⊂14676
M29208M	33-09/60	⊗10/60		⊂14677
M29209M	33-07/57	⊗07/57		⊂14678
M29210M	33-06/60	⊗06/60		⊂14679
M29211M	33-10/59	⊗11/59		⊂14680
M29212M	33-11/59	⊗ *64*		⊂14681
M29213M	33-09/60	⊗10/60		⊂14682

MSJA Metropolitan-Cammell
Driving Trailer Third
DTT
M29231M-M29252M Manchester-Altrincham

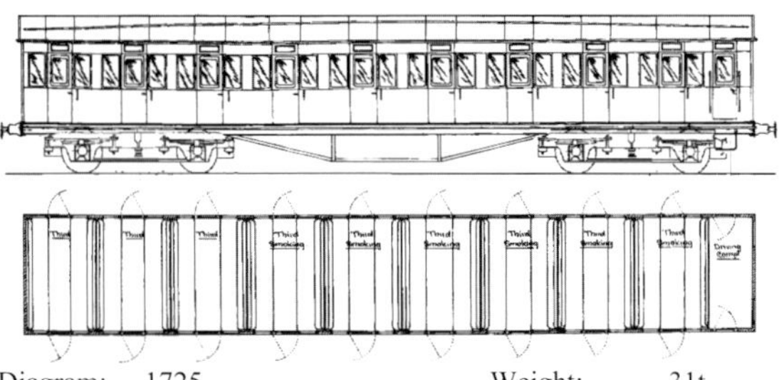

Diagram:	1725	Weight:	31t
Body:	58' 0" × 9' 3"	Bogies:	
Seats:	108 third		

M29231M	48-05/71	⊗10/71	⊂51
M29232M	48-05/71	⊗10/71	⊂52
M29233M	48-05/71	⊗10/71	⊂53
M29234M	48-07/66	⊗10/66	⊂54
M29235M	48-05/71	⊗05/71	⊂55
M29236M	48-08/70	⊗10/71	⊂56
M29237M	48-10/66	⊗01/67	⊂58
M29238M	48-05/71	⊗05/71	⊂74
M29239M	48-05/71	⊗10/71	⊂59
M29240M	48-05/71	⊗10/71	⊂60
M29241M	48-05/71	⊗10/71	⊂61
M29242M	48-05/71	⊗05/71	⊂62
M29243M	48-05/71	⊗10/71	⊂63
M29244M	48-05/71	⊗10/71	⊂64
M29245M	48-10/66	⊗01/67	⊂65
M29246M	48-05/71	⊗10/71	⊂66
M29247M	48-05/71	⊗05/71	⊂67
M29248M	48-05/71	⊗10/71	⊂68
M29249M	48-07/66	⊗10/66	⊂69
M29250M	48-05/71	⊗05/71	⊂70
M29251M	48-05/71	⊗10/71	⊂71
M29252M	48-07/66	⊗10/66	⊂72

Class 503 Birmingham RC&W
Driving Trailer Second
DTS
M29271M-M29289M Wirral & Mersey

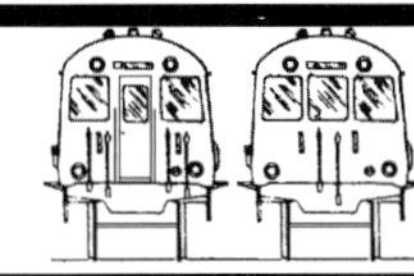

As built

Later fitted with end doors for tunnel working

Diagram:	2006 EE202	Weight:	21t
Body:	58' 0" × 9' 1"	Bogies:	Single Bolster
Seats:	68 second, later 66 second		

M29271M	38-03/85	⊗10/85	**28672**	38-03/85
M29272M	38-10/84	⊗12/84	**28673**	38-10/84
M29273M	38-10/84	⊗12/84	**28674**	38-10/84
M29274M	38-10/84	⊗12/84	**28675**	38-10/84
M29275M	38-10/84	⊗12/84	**28676**	38-10/84
M29276M	38-10/84	⊗12/84	**28677**	38-10/84
29277	38-03/41	⊗09/41	**28678**	38-03/41
M29278M	38-10/84	⊗12/84	**28679**	38-10/84
M29279M	38-05/85	⊗11/85	**28680**	38-05/85
M29280M	38-10/84	⊗12/84	**28681**	38-10/84
M29281M	38-10/84	⊗12/84	**28682**	38-10/84
M29282M	38-*06/82*	⊗01/84	**28683**	38-*06/82*
M29283M	38-10/84	⊗12/84	**28684**	38-10/84
M29284M	38-10/84	⊗12/84	**28685**	38-10/84
M29285M	38-02/83	⊗09/83	**28686**	38-02/83
29286	38-03/41	⊗09/41	**28687**	38-03/41
M29287M	38-10/84	⊗07/85	**28688**	38-10/84
M29288M	38-10/84	⊗12/84	**28689**	38-10/84
M29289M	38-05/85	Ⓟ	**28690**	38-05/85

Midland Lancaster Morecambe & Heysham
Driving Trailer Third
DTT
29290-29293

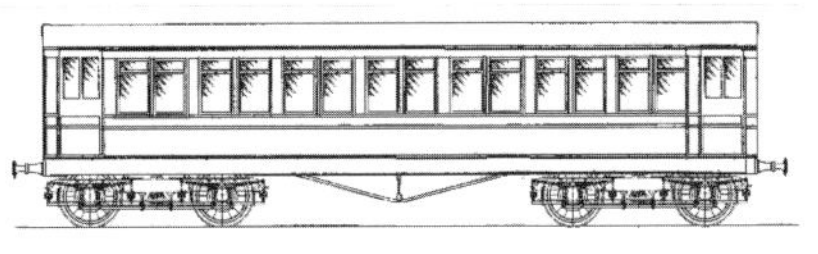

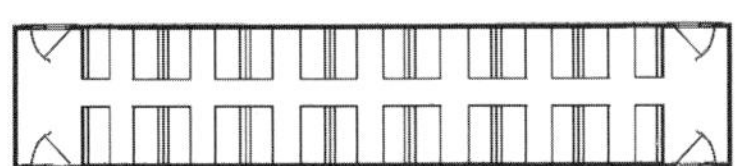

Diagram:	538	Weight:	26t 3cwt
Body:	43' 0" ×	Bogies:	Midland
Seats:	70 third		

29290	33- 38 ⊗	⊂**2239**
M29291M	33-09/52 ⊗	⊂**2240**
M29292M	33-09/52 ⊗	⊂**2241**
29293	33- 38 ⊗	⊂**2242**

Midland Lancaster Morecambe &Heysham
Driving Trailer Third
DTT
29298-29299

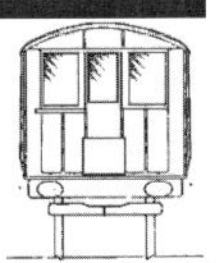

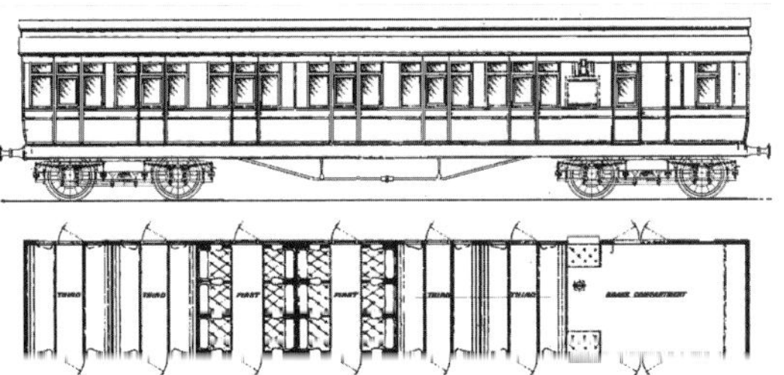

Diagram:	519A	Weight:	
Body:	54' 0" ×	Bogies:	Midland
Seats:	12 first 32 third		

Some sources show these numbered as 29294 & 29295

29298	- *44* ⊗	⊂**3439**
29299	- *44* ⊗	⊂**3441**

LYR Liverpool Newton Heath
Trailer First
TF
29300-29327 Liverpool-Southport

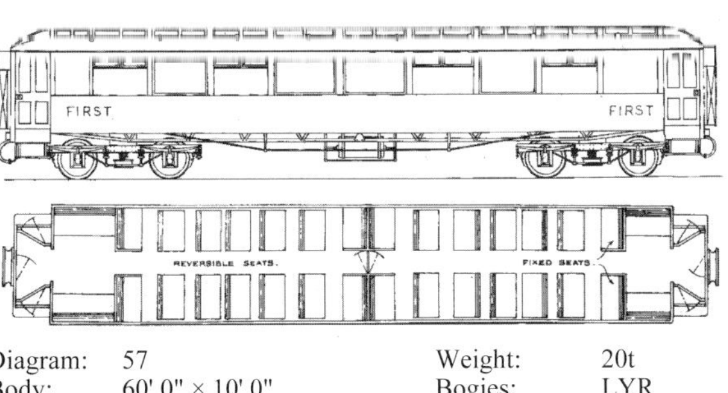

Diagram:	57	Weight:	20t
Body:	60' 0" × 10' 0"	Bogies:	LYR
Seats:	66 first		

29300	33-06/40	⊗05/40	⊂**10891**
29301	33-07/40	⊗06/40	⊂**10892**
29302	33-01/40	⊗01/40	⊂**10893**
29303	33-06/37	⊗06/37	⊂**10894**
29304	33-02/40	⊗01/40	⊂**10895**
29305	33-04/40	⊗03/40	⊂**10896**
29306	33-04/40	⊗04/40	⊂**10897**
29307	33- *39*	⊗06/39	⊂**10898**
29308	33- *39*	⊗12/39	⊂**10899**
29309	33- *39*	⊗04/39	⊂**10900**
29310	33- *39*	⊗10/39	⊂**10901**
29311	33-06/40	⊗06/40	⊂**10902**
29312	33-06/40	⊗06/40	⊂**10903**
29313	33-08/40	⊗08/40	⊂**10904**
29314	33-05/40	⊗05/40	⊂**10905**
29315	33-08/40	⊗08/40	⊂**10906**
29316	33-04/40	⊗03/40	⊂**10907**
29317	33-07/40	⊗06/40	⊂**10908**
29318	33-06/40	⊗04/40	⊂**10909**
29319	33-03/41	⊗03/41	⊂**10910**
29320	33-09/40	⊗08/40	⊂**10911**
29321	33-02/41	⊗10/45	⊂**10912**
29322	33-10/40	⊗11/40	⊂**10913**
29323	33-12/40	⊗06/46	⊂**10914**
29324	33-04/45	⊗04/45	⊂**10915**
29325	33-06/40	⊗04/40	⊂**10916**
29326	33-07/40	⊗06/40	⊂**10917**
29327	33-10/40	⊗10/40	⊂**10918**

LYR Liverpool Newton Heath
Trailer First
TF
29328-29333 Liverpool-Southport

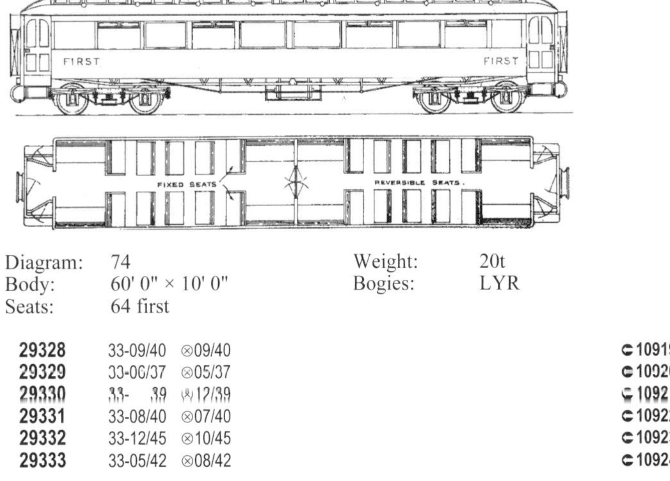

Diagram:	74	Weight:	20t
Body:	60' 0" × 10' 0"	Bogies:	LYR
Seats:	64 first		

29328	33-09/40	⊗09/40	⊂**10919**
29329	33-06/37	⊗05/37	⊂**10920**
29330	33- *39*	⊗12/39	⊂**10921**
29331	33-08/40	⊗07/40	⊂**10922**
29332	33-12/45	⊗10/45	⊂**10923**
29333	33-05/42	⊗08/42	⊂**10924**

LYR Liverpool Newton Heath
Trailer First
TF
29334-29340 Liverpool-Southport

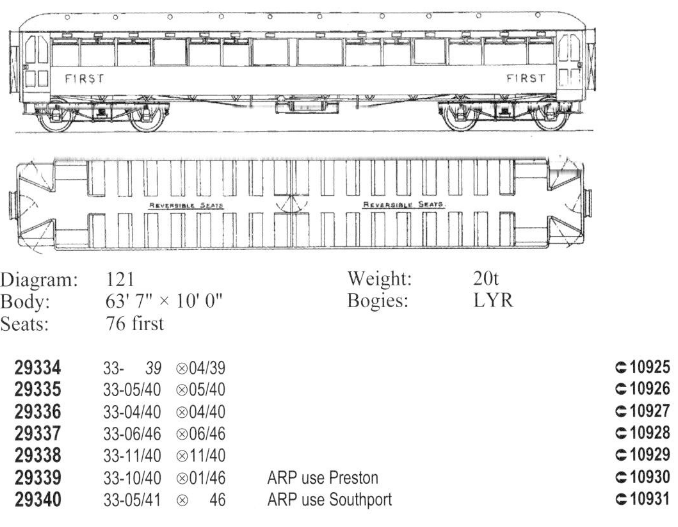

Diagram:	121	Weight:	20t
Body:	63' 7" × 10' 0"	Bogies:	LYR
Seats:	76 first		

29334	33- *39*	⊗04/39		⊂**10925**
29335	33-05/40	⊗05/40		⊂**10926**
29336	33-04/40	⊗04/40		⊂**10927**
29337	33-06/46	⊗06/46		⊂**10928**
29338	33-11/40	⊗11/40		⊂**10929**
29339	33-10/40	⊗01/46	ARP use Preston	⊂**10930**
29340	33-05/41	⊗ 46	ARP use Southport	⊂**10931**

MSJA Metropolitan-Cammell
Trailer Third
TT
M29390M-M29396M Manchester-Altrincham

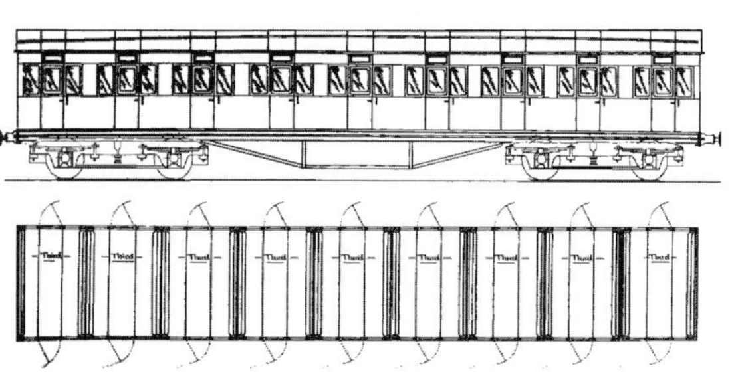

Diagram:	1684	Weight:	28t
Body:	57' 0" × 9' 2¼"	Bogies:	
Seats:	108 third		

M29390M	48-04/54	**➲12278**	54 to Loco Hauled Stock	**⊂151**
M29391M	48-04/54	**➲12279**	54 to Loco Hauled Stock	**⊂152**
M29392M	48-04/54	**➲12280**	54 to Loco Hauled Stock	**⊂154**
M29393M	48-10/54	**➲12281**	54 to Loco Hauled Stock	**⊂155**
M29394M	48-10/54	**➲12282**	54 to Loco Hauled Stock	**⊂156**
M29395M	48-10/54	**➲12283**	54 to Loco Hauled Stock	**⊂157**
M29396M	48-07/66			**⊂158**

LNWR GEC Wolverton
Trailer Third
TT
29400-M29409M London Area

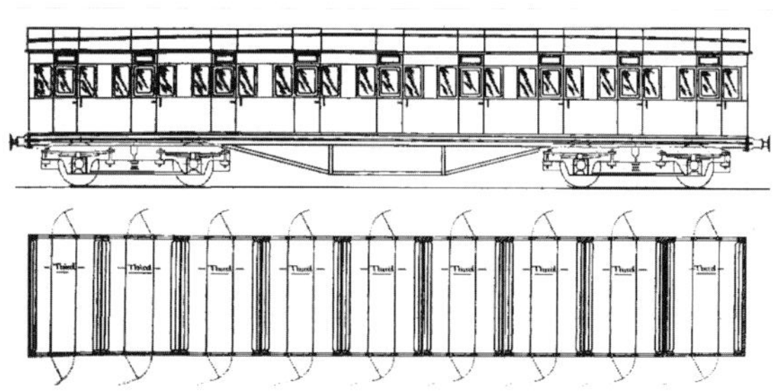

Diagram:	1684	Weight:	28t
Body:	57' 0" × 9' 2¼"	Bogies:	LNWR
Seats:	108 third		

29400	- 29	**➲29622**	**⊂14403**
29401	33- 39	**➲29237**	**⊂14404**
M29402M	33-02/57	⊗05/57	**⊂14405**
M29403M	33-11/63	⊗01/64	**⊂14406**
M29404M	33-02/57	⊗06/57	**⊂14407**
M29405M	33-06/57	⊗	**⊂14408**
M29406M	33-03/57	⊗07/57	**⊂14409**
29407	- 29	**➲29623**	**⊂14410**
29408	- 29	**➲29624**	**⊂14411**
M29409M	33-11/63	⊗03/64	**⊂14412**

Tube Joint Metropolitan CW&F
Trailer Third
TT
M29497-M29498 London Area

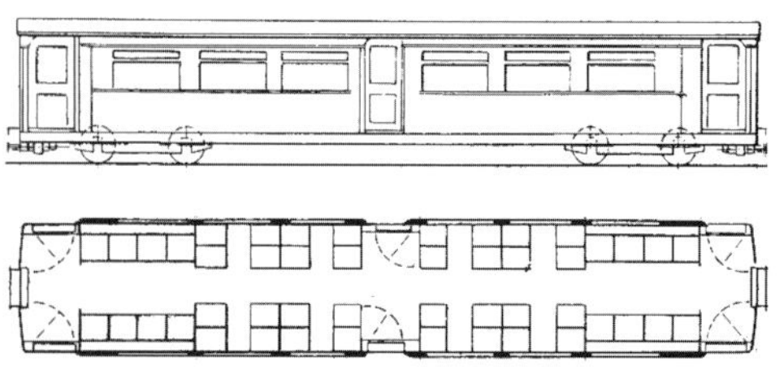

Diagram:		Weight:	
Body:	50' 10" ×	Bogies:	
Seats:	48 third		

M29497	33-07/48	⊗	49	**⊂337**
M29498	33-07/48	⊗	49	**⊂593**

Tube Joint Metropolitan CW&F
Trailer Third
TT ex DTT
M29499 London Area

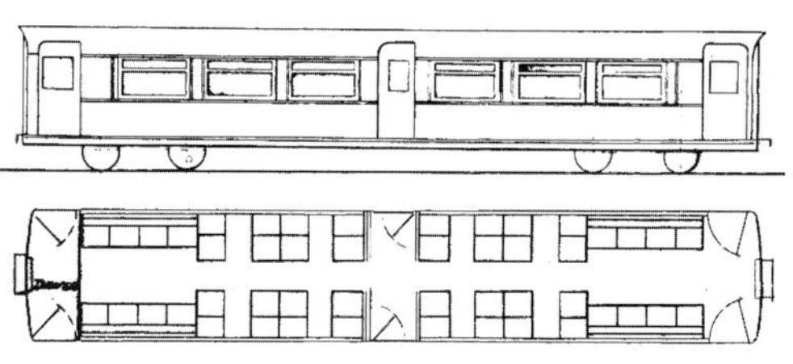

Diagram:		Weight:	
Body:	50' 10" ×	Bogies:	
Seats:	48 third		

M29499	33-07/48	⊗	49	**⊂640**

LYR Liverpool Newton Heath
Trailer Third
TT
29500-29510 Liverpool-Southport

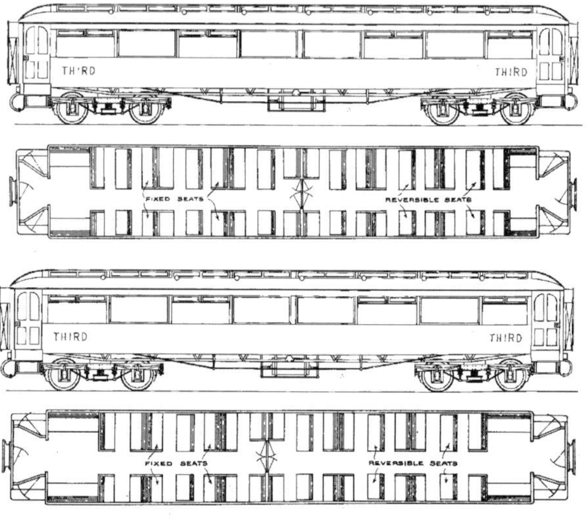

Diagram:	68/69	Weight:	20t
Body:	60' 0" × 10' 0"	Bogies:	LYR
Seats:	98 third (29500 92 third)		

29500	33- *39*	⊗09/39	**⊂14617**
29501	33-05/40	⊗04/40	**⊂14618**
29502	33- *39*	⊗09/39	**⊂14619**
29503	33-12/40	⊗06/46	**⊂14620**
29504	33-04/40	⊗03/40	**⊂14621**
29505	33-12/45	⊗10/45	**⊂14622**
29506	33-10/40	⊗10/45	**⊂14623**
29507	33- *39*	⊗01/40	**⊂14624**
29508	33-01/40	⊗01/40	**⊂14625**
29509	33-08/40	⊗08/40	**⊂14626**
29510	33-03/41	⊗03/41	**⊂14627**

LYR Liverpool Newton Heath
Trailer Third
TT
29511-29515 Liverpool-Southport

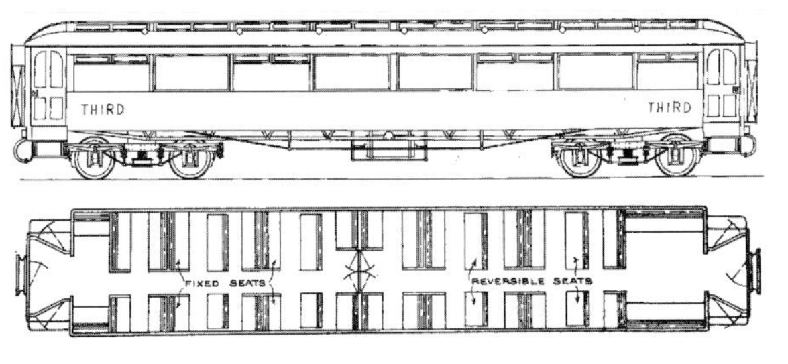

Diagram: 81 Weight: 20t
Body: 60' 0" × 10' 0" Bogies: LYR
Seats: 80 third

29511	33-03/41	⊗03/41	⊂14628
29512	33-08/40	⊗08/40	⊂14629
29513	33-06/40	⊗05/40	⊂14630
29514	33-05/41	⊗01/46	⊂14631
29515	33-09/40	⊗09/40	⊂14632

LYR Liverpool Newton Heath
Trailer Third
TT
29516-29521 Liverpool-Southport

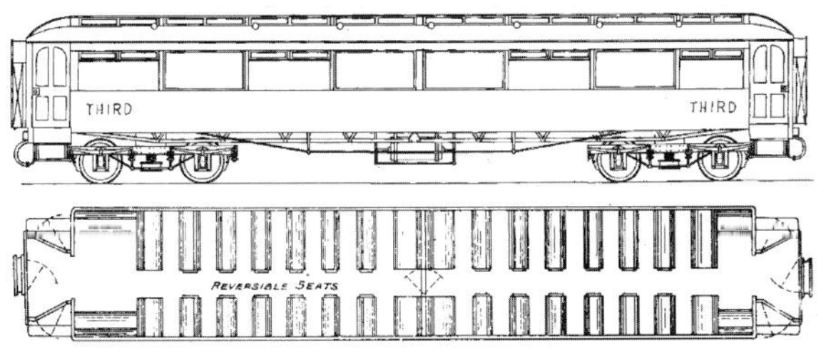

Diagram: 96 Weight: 20t
Body: 60' 0" × 10' 0" Bogies: LYR
Seats: 90 third

29516	33-06/45	⊗06/46	⊂14634
29517	33-04/45	⊗04/45	⊂14635
29518	33-01/40	⊗01/40	⊂14636
29519	33-04/40	⊗03/40	⊂14637
29520	33-02/41	⊗12/40	⊂14638
29521	33-10/40	⊗09/40	⊂14639

LYR Liverpool Newton Heath
Trailer Third
TT
29522-29544 Liverpool-Southport

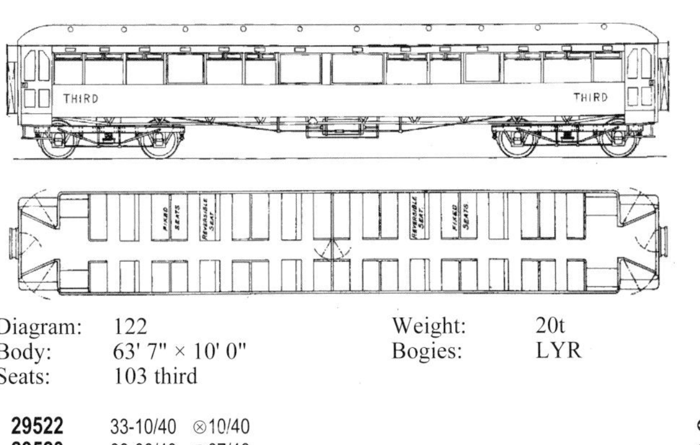

Diagram: 122 Weight: 20t
Body: 63' 7" × 10' 0" Bogies: LYR
Seats: 103 third

29522	33-10/40	⊗10/40	⊂14640
29523	33-08/40	⊗07/40	⊂14641
29524	33- *39*	⊗06/39	⊂14642
29525	33-07/40	⊗06/40	⊂14647
29526	33-06/40	⊗06/40	⊂14648
29527	33-09/40	⊗08/40	⊂14649
29528	33-10/40	⊗11/40	⊂14650
29529	33-06/40	⊗06/40	⊂14651
29530	33-06/37	⊗04/37	⊂14652
29531	33- *39*	⊗12/39	⊂14653
29532	33-09/40	⊗08/40	⊂14654
29533	33-10/40	⊗11/40	⊂14655
29534	33-02/41	⊗12/40	⊂14656
29535	33-12/45	⊗10/45	⊂14657
29536	33-06/40	⊗06/40	⊂14658
29537	33-11/40	⊗11/40	⊂14659
29538	33-04/40	⊗04/40	⊂14660
29539	33-10/42	⊗05/41	⊂14661
29540	33-07/40	⊗06/40	⊂14662
29541	33-06/40	⊗04/40	⊂14663
29542	33-04/40	⊗03/40	⊂14664
29543	33-04/45	⊗04/45	⊂14665
29544	33-02/40	⊗01/40	⊂14666

Class 502 Derby
Trailer Second
TS
M29544M-M29599M Liverpool-Southport

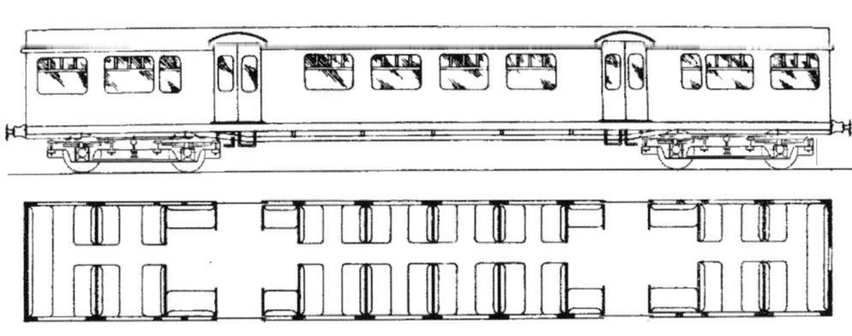

Diagram: 2011 Weight: 23t 10cwt
Body: 66' 5¼" × 9' 7" Bogies:
Seats: 102 second

M29544M[2]	*50*-01/63	⊗	**28332**	*50*-01/63					⊂29817
M29545M	39-09/79	⊗10/81	**28311**	39-05/73	**28355**	10/76-09/79			
M29546M	39-11/80	⊗11/81	**28312**	39-11/80					
M29547M	39-12/78	⊗02/80	**28313**	39-03/73	**28314**	01/77-12/78			
M29548M	39-11/80	⊗10/82	**28314**	39-05/73	**28333**	12/77-03/80			
M29549M	39-12/77	⊗06/78	**28315**	39-05/73	**28340**	01/77-12/77			
M29550M	39-06/75	⊗06/75	**28316**	39-03/73					
M29551M	39-10/68	⊗03/69	**28317**	39-10/68					
M29552M	39-05/79	⊗02/80	**28318**	39-11/79					
M29553M	39-10/68	⊗03/69	**28319**	39-10/68					
M29554M	39-09/79	⊗03/80	**28320**	39-02/50	**28349**	50-06/71	**28328**	10/76-09/79	
M29555M	39-11/80	⊗11/81	**28321**	39-06/62	**28350**	*63*-10/68	**28319**	68-11/79	
M29556M	39-11/80	⊗01/82	**28323**	39-11/80					
M29557M	39-11/80	⊗06/86	**28325**	39-07/62	**28369**	07/62-12/77	**28351**	12/77-11/80	
M29558M	39-06/75	⊗06/75	**28327**	39-09/70					
M29559M	39-11/80	⊗11/81	**28329**	39-06/62	**28334**	06/62-11/80			
M29560M	39-12/78	⊗09/79	**28331**	39-05/73					
M29561M	39-11/80	⊗11/81	**28333**	39-05/73	**28351**	10/76-12/77	**28335**	04/78-11/80	
			28338	06/80-11/80					
M29562M	39-11/80	⊗11/81	**28335**	39-04/78	**28354**	04/78-11/80			
M29563M	39-10/68	⊗03/69	**28336**	39-10/68					
M29564M	39-11/80	⊗11/81	**28337**	39-06/80	**28332**	06/80-11/80			
M29565M	39-11/80	⊗11/81	**28338**	39- *76*	**28341**	10/76-05/79	**28318**	11/79-11/80	
M29566M	39-11/80	⊗06/80	**28339**	39-05/73	**28332**	10/76-06/80			
M29567M	39-11/80	⊗11/81	**28340**	39-03/73	**28364**	01/77-11/80			
M29568M	39-09/79	⊗10/82	**28341**	39-*02/76*	**28331**	*02/76*-09/79			
M29569M	39-10/68	⊗03/69	**28342**	39-10/68					
M29570M	39-05/79	⊗02/80	**28343**	39-04/79					
M29571M	39-06/75	⊗06/75	**28344**	39-12/71					
M29572M	39-10/68	⊗03/69	**28345**	39-10/68					
M29573M	39-08/79	⊗02/80	**28346**	39-01/50	**28326**	12/58-01/79	**28343**	04/79-08/79	
M29574M	39-11/80	⊗11/81	**28347**	39-11/80					
M29575M	39-10/68	⊗09/14	**28348**	39-10/68					
29576	39-01/42	⊗05/41	**28349**	39-01/42					
M29577M	39-09/79	⊗11/81	**28350**	39- *63*	**28332**	01/63-03/73	**28315**	01/77-12/77	
M29578M	39-09/79	⊗10/82	**28351**	39-12/58	**28359**	12/58-04/79			
M29579M	39-09/79	⊗10/81	**28352**	39-09/79					
M29580M	39-05/79	⊗02/80	**28353**	39-05/79					
M29581M	39-09/79	⊗03/80	**28354**	39-04/78	**28311**	04/78-11/78	**28358**	11/78-09/79	
M29582M	39-11/80	⊗03/81	**28355**	39-03/73	**28338**	10/76-06/80			
M29583M	39-08/79	⊗02/80	**28356**	39-08/79					
M29584M	39-11/80	⊗11/81	**28357**	39-11/80					
M29585M	39-05/79	⊗02/80	**28358**	39-03/73	**28330**	10/76-05/79			
M29586M	39-12/77	⊗*06/83*	**28359**	39-12/58	**28351**	12/58-05/73	**28313**	10/76-12/77	
M29587M	39-11/80	⊗10/82	**28360**	39-04/80	**28357**	06/80-11/80			
M29588M	39-11/80	⊗11/81	**28361**	39-08/80					
M29589M	39-12/78	⊗10/79	**28362**	39-03/76	**28362**	12/77-12/78			
M29590M	39-10/68	⊗03/69	**28363**	39-10/68					

M29591M	39-12/78	⊗09/79	**28364**	39-05/73			
M29592M	39-10/68	⊗03/69	**28365**	39-10/68			
M29593M	39-11/80	⊗11/81	**28366**	39-11/80		incorrectly numbered **29543** 02/77	
M29594M	39-10/68	⊗03/69	**28367**	39-10/68			
M29595M	*50*-09/79	⊗07/83	**28322**	*50*-01/79	**28326**	01/79-09/79	**⊂29812**
M29596M	*50*-10/68	⊗03/69	**28324**	*50*-10/68			**⊂29813**
M29597M	*50*-12/58	**⊃29862**	**28326**	*50*-12/58			**⊂29814**
M29598M	*50*-05/79	⊗02/80	**28328**	*50*-05/73	**28339**	01/77-05/79	**⊂29815**
M29599M	*50*-12/78	⊗10/79	**28330**	*50*-03/73	**28311**	10/76-04/78	**⊂29816**
			28358	12/77-11/78	**28311**	11/78-12/78	

LNWR GEC Clayton

Trailer Composite later Third
TC later TT
M29600M-M29611M London Area

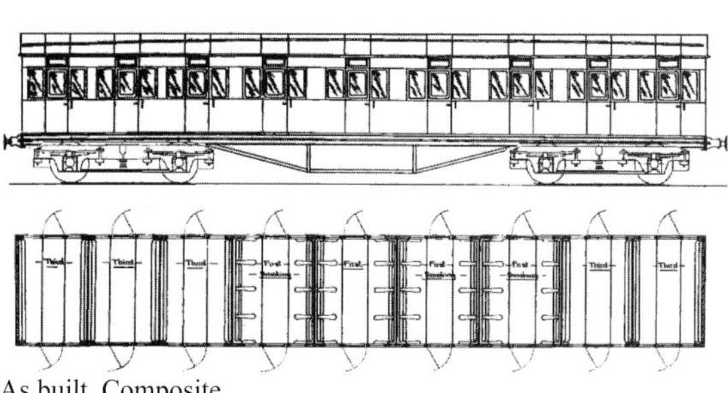

As built, Composite

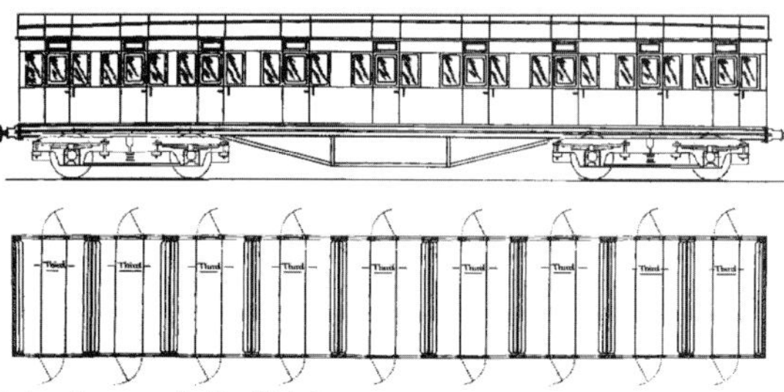

Later downgraded to Third

Diagram: 1691 Weight: 28t
Body: 57' 0" × 9' 2¼" Bogies: LNWR
Seats: 32 first 60 third, later 108 third

M29600M	33-02/57	⊗06/57	**⊂4615**
M29601M	33-11/63	⊗02/64	**⊂4616**
M29602M	33-11/63	⊗02/64	**⊂4617**
M29603M	33-11/63	⊗01/64	**⊂4618**
M29604M	33-11/63	⊗01/64	**⊂5713**
M29605M	33-11/63	⊗03/64	**⊂5714**
M29606M	33-11/63	⊗01/64	**⊂5715**
M29607M	33-11/63	⊗01/64	**⊂5716**
M29608M	33-11/63	⊗01/64	**⊂5717**
M29609M	33-11/63	⊗02/64	**⊂5718**
M29610M	33-11/63	⊗01/64	**⊂10679**
M29611M	33-11/63	⊗01/64	**⊂10680**

LNWR GEC Wolverton

Trailer Composite later Third
TC later TT
M29612M-M29621M London Area

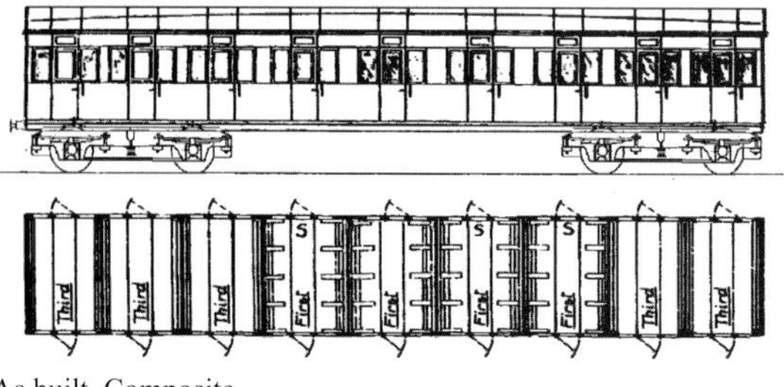

As built, Composite

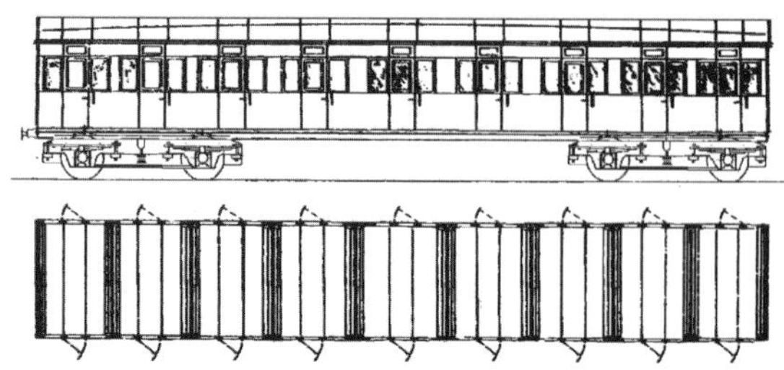

Later downgraded to Third

Diagram: 1846 Weight: 28t
Body: 57' 0" × 9' 2¼" Bogies: LNWR
Seats: 32 first 60 third, later 108 third

M29612M	33-11/63	⊗02/64	**⊂1886**
M29613M	33-11/63	⊗01/64	**⊂1892**
M29614M	33-11/63	⊗02/64	**⊂1895**
M29615M	33-11/63	⊗01/64	**⊂1898**
M29616M	33-11/63	⊗02/64	**⊂1901**
M29617M	33-11/63	⊗02/64	**⊂1905**
M29618M	33-11/63	⊗02/64	**⊂1912**
M29619M	33-11/63	⊗01/64	**⊂1917**
M29620M	33-11/63	⊗02/64	**⊂1922**
M29621M	33-11/63	⊗01/64	**⊂1923**

LNWR GEC Wolverton

Trailer Composite
TC
M29622M-M29624M London Area

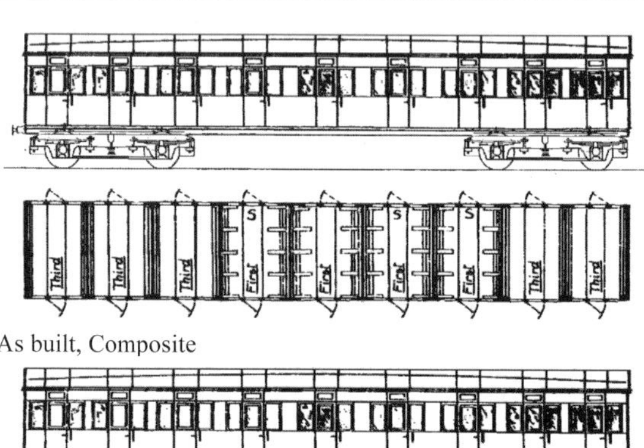

As built, Composite

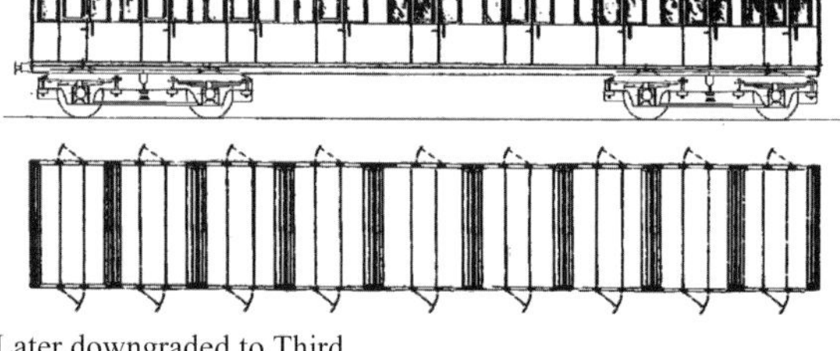

Later downgraded to Third

Diagram: 1846 Weight: 28t
Body: 57' 0" × 9' 2¼" Bogies: LNWR
Seats: 32 first 60 third, later 108 third

M29622M	33-11/63	⊗10/65	Stonebridge Park Shunter 11/63-10/65	**⊂*29400***
M29623M	33-11/63	⊗02/64		**⊂*29407***
M29624M	33-11/63	⊗02/64		**⊂*29408***

MSJA Metropolitan-Cammell

Trailer Composite
TC
M29650M-M29671M Manchester-Altrincham

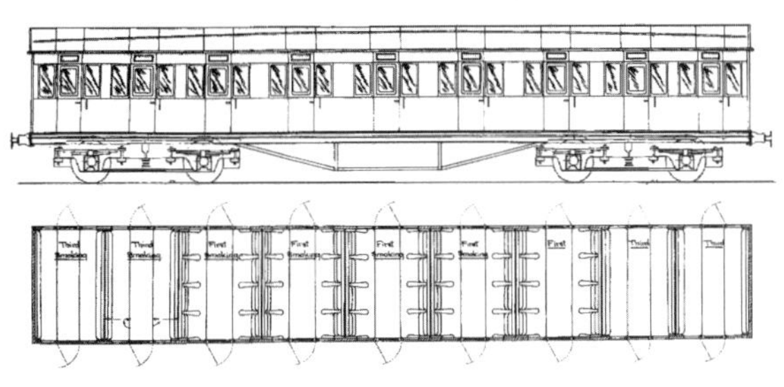

Diagram: 1726 Weight: 30t
Body: 58' 0" × 9' 3" Bogies:
Seats: 40 first 48 third, later 24 first 72 third

M29650M	48-05/71	⊗10/71	⊂101
M29651M	48-10/66	⊗12/66	⊂102
M29652M	48-10/66	⊗12/66	⊂103
M29653M	48-05/71	⊗10/71	⊂104
M29654M	48-05/71	⊗10/71	⊂105
M29655M	48-05/71	⊗10/71	⊂106
M29656M	48-05/71	⊗10/71	⊂107
M29657M	48-05/71	⊗05/71	⊂108
M29658M	48-05/71	⊗10/71	⊂109
M29659M	48-07/66	⊗10/66	⊂110
M29660M	48-05/71	⊗10/71	⊂111
M29661M	48-08/70	⊗10/71	⊂112
M29662M	48-05/71	⊗05/71	⊂113
M29663M	48-05/71	Ⓟ⊗08/06	⊂114
M29664M	48-11/63	⊗	⊂115
M29665M	48-07/66	⊗05/71	⊂116
M29666M	48-05/71	Ⓟ	⊂117
M29667M	48-05/71	⊗10/71	⊂118
M29668M	48-05/71	⊗10/71	⊂119
M29669M	48-05/71	⊗10/71	⊂120
M29670M	48-05/71	Ⓟ	⊂121
M29671M	48-05/71	⊗10/71	⊂122

Class 503 Birmingham RC&W Metropolitan-Cammell (29713 onwards)

Trailer Composite later Second
TC later TS
M29702M-M29720M Wirral & Mersey

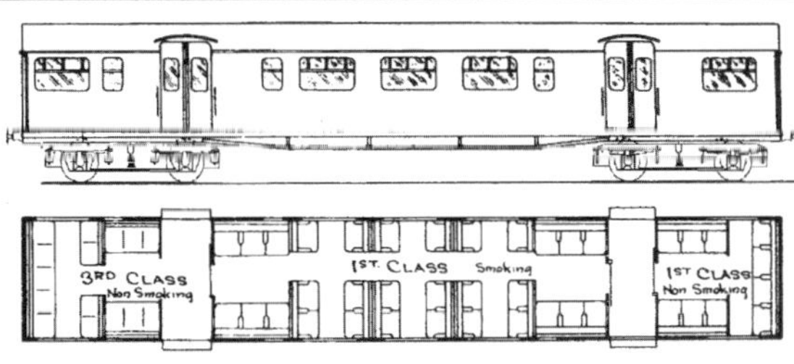

As built

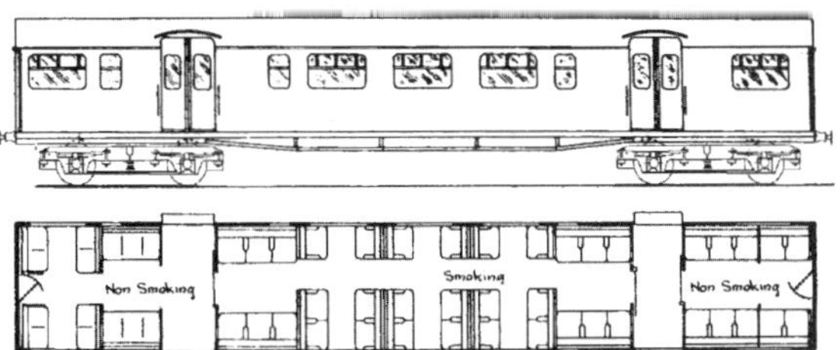

Later downgraded and fitted with end doors for tunnel working

Diagram: 2005 EH214 Weight: 20t
Body: 58' 0" × 9' 1" Bogies: Single Bolster
Seats: 40 first 15 second, later 54 second

M29702M	38-03/85	⊃977115	**28672**	38-03/85
M29703M	38-10/84	⊗12/84	**28673**	38-10/84
M29704M	38-10/84	⊗12/84	**28674**	38-10/84
M29705M	38-10/84	⊗12/84	**28675**	38-10/84
M29706M	38-10/84	⊗12/84	**28676**	38-10/84
M29707M	38-10/84	⊗12/84	**28677**	38-10/84
29708	38-03/41	⊗09/41	**28678**	38-03/41
M29709M	38-10/84	⊗12/84	**28679**	38-10/84
M29710M	38-05/85	⊗11/85	**28680**	38-05/85
M29711M	38-10/84	⊗12/84	**28681**	38-10/84
M29712M	38-10/84	⊗12/84	**28682**	38-10/84
M29713M	38-*06/82*	⊗01/84	**28683**	38-*06/82*
M29714M	38-10/84	⊗12/84	**28684**	38-10/84
M29715M	38-10/84	⊗12/84	**28685**	38-10/84
M29716M	38-02/83	⊗09/83	**28686**	38-02/83
29717	38-03/41	⊗09/41	**28687**	38-03/41
M29718M	38-10/84	⊗07/85	**28688**	38-10/84
M29719M	38-10/84	⊗12/84	**28689**	38-10/84
M29720M	38-05/85	Ⓟ	**28690**	38-05/85

LNWR Siemens Metropolitan CW&F

Trailer Composite
TC
M29721M-M29724M London Area (later AM1)

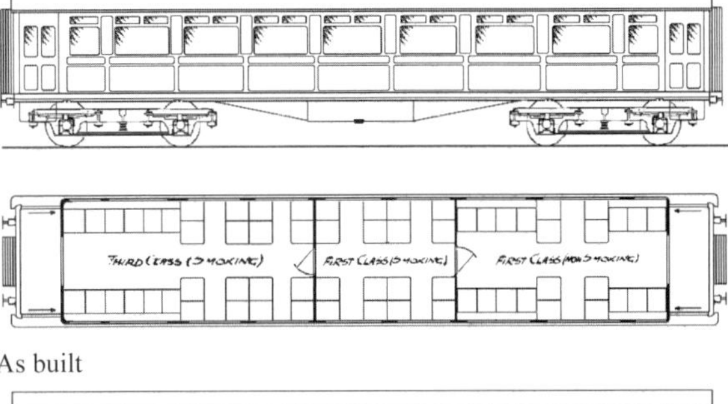

As built

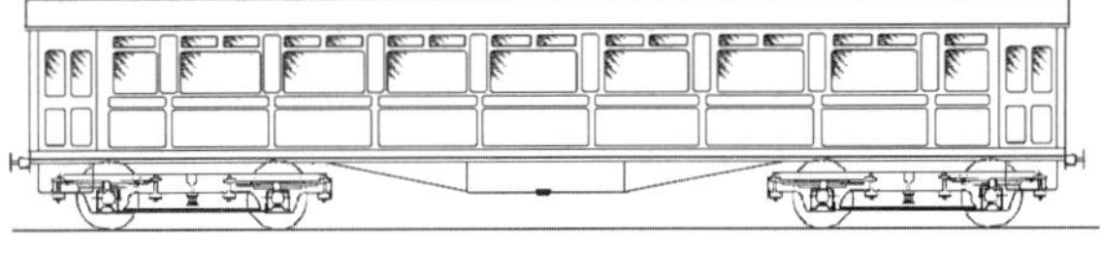

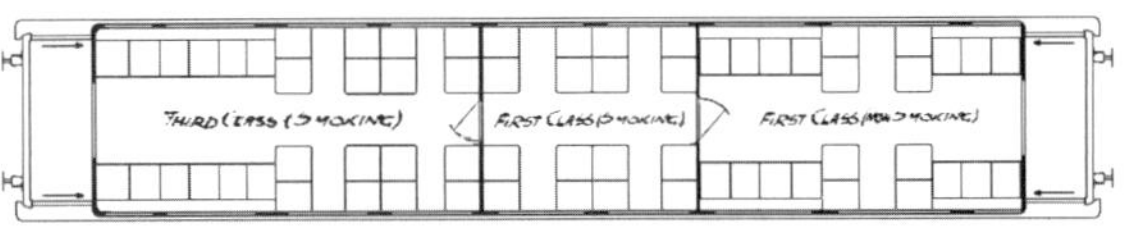

Corridor connection later removed

Diagram: Weight: 28t 0cwt
Body: 57' 6" × 9' 6" Bogies: LNWR
Seats: 38 first 28 second, later 63 second

M29721M	33-02/67	⊗	⊂8801
M29722M	33-02/67	⊗	⊂8802
M29723M	33-02/67	⊗	⊂8803
M29724M	33-02/67	⊗	⊂8804

LNWR Oerlikon Wolverton

Trailer Composite
TC, later TS
M29725M-M29762M London Area

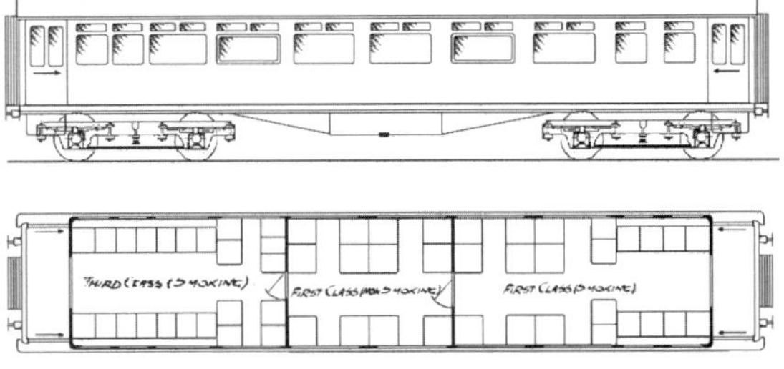

As built

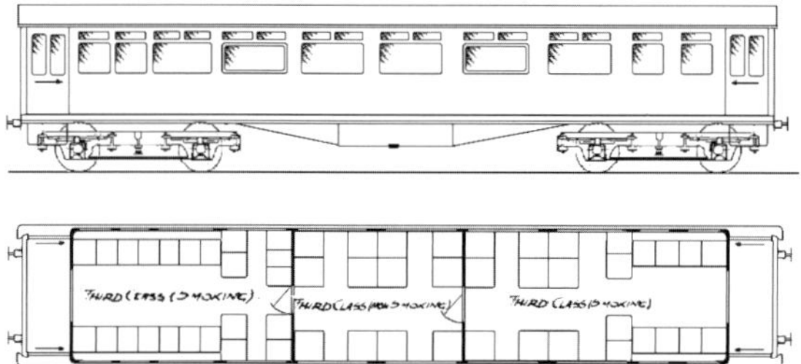

Corridor connection later removed and downgraded

Diagram:		Weight:	28t 0cwt
Body:	57' 6" × 9' 6"	Bogies:	LNWR
Seats:	33 first 22 second, later 60 third		

M29725M	33-02/57	⊗02/59	⊂8805
M29726M	33-12/55	⊗	⊂8806
M29727M	33-07/60	⊗	⊂8807
M29729M	33-09/56	⊗	⊂8809
M29730M	33-05/56	⊗	⊂8810
M29731M	33-06/60	⊗	⊂8811
M29732M	33-03/59	⊗05/59	⊂8812
M29733M	33-05/62	⊗	⊂8813
M29734M	33-04/59	⊗05/59	⊂8814
M29735M	33-11/55	⊗	⊂8815
M29736M	33-12/60	⊗12/60	⊂8816
M29737M	33-11/55	⊗	⊂8817
M29738M	33-06/59	⊗08/59	⊂8818
M29739M	33-05/60	⊗	⊂8819
M29740M	33-12/55	⊗	⊂8820
M29741M	33-10/57	⊗12/57	⊂8821
M29742M	33-05/60	⊗	⊂8822
M29743M	33-03/57	⊗05/61	⊂8823
M29744M	33-08/60	⊗	⊂8824
M29745M	33-06/59	⊗08/59	⊂8825
M29746M	33-06/60	⊗	⊂8826
M29747M	33-11/55	⊗	⊂8827
M29748M	33-02/57	⊗03/57	⊂8828
M29749M	33-07/60	⊗	⊂8829
M29750M	33-05/60	⊗	⊂8830
M29751M	33-06/59	⊗06/59	⊂8831
M29752M	33-05/60	⊗	⊂8832
M29753M	33-05/60	⊗	⊂8833
M29754M	33-06/60	⊗	⊂8834
M29755M	33-08/60	⊗	⊂8835
M29756M	33-07/57	⊗08/57	⊂8836
M29757M	33-06/57	⊗07/57	⊂8837
M29758M	33-06/57	⊗03/63	⊂8838
M29759M	33-05/60	⊗	⊂8839
M29760M	33-08/57	⊗10/57	⊂8840
M29761M	33-07/60	⊗	⊂8841
M29762M	33-08/57	⊗01/58 Grounded Watford Goods	⊂8842

LNWR Oerlikon Wolverton
Trailer Composite
TC, Later TS
M29763M-M29792M London Area

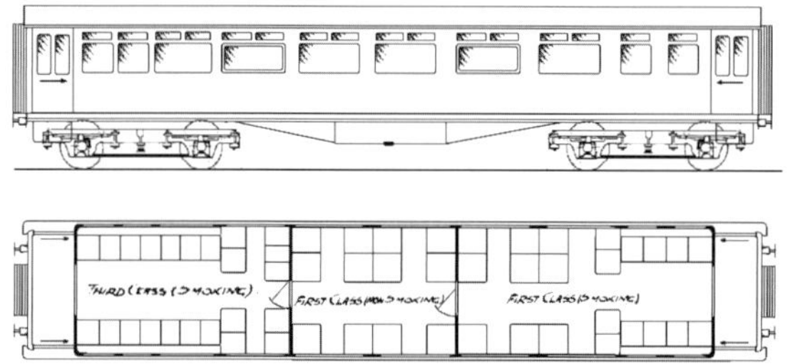

As built

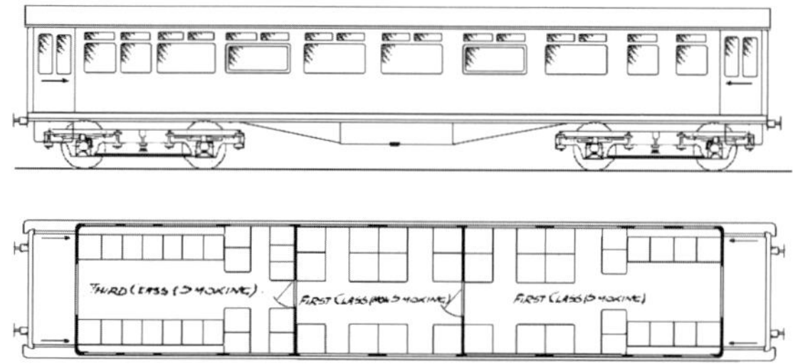

Corridor connection later removed and downgraded

Diagram:		Weight:	28t 0cwt
Body:	57' 6" × 9' 6"	Bogies:	LNWR
Seats:	33 first 22 second, later 60 third		

M29763M	33-07/57	⊗08/57	⊂8843
M29764M	33-06/60	⊗	⊂8844
M29765M	33-11/56	⊗	⊂8845
M29766M	33-07/60	⊗	⊂8846
M29767M	33-06/60	⊗06/60	⊂8847
M29768M	33-11/57	⊗03/58	⊂8848
M29769M	33-10/59	➲**040927**	⊂8849
M29770M	33-07/58	➲**040926**	⊂8850
M29771M	33-03/59	⊗09/59	⊂8851
M29772M	33-07/58	➲Internal User	⊂8852
M29773M	33-08/60	⊗	⊂8853
M29774M	33-06/60	⊗	⊂8854
M29775M	33-07/60	⊗	⊂8855
M29776M	33-09/57	➲**023450**	⊂8856
M29777M	33-11/57	⊗	⊂8857
M29778M	33-09/60	⊗	⊂8858
M29779M	3-05/60	⊗	⊂8859
M29780M	33-12/60	⊗12/60	⊂8860
M29781M	33-05/60	⊗	⊂8861
M29782M	33-09/60	⊗	⊂8862
M29783M	33-12/59	⊗	⊂8863
M29784M	33-05/60	⊗05/60	⊂8864
M29785M	33-06/60	⊗06/60	⊂8865
M29786M	33-05/60	⊗	⊂8866
M29787M	33-07/60	⊗	⊂8867
M29788M	33-05/60	⊗06/60	⊂8868
M29789M	33-05/60	⊗	⊂8869
M29790M	33-01/61	⊗05/64	⊂8870
M29791M	33-06/60	⊗06/60	⊂8871
M29792M	33-07/60	⊗	⊂8872

LNWR Oerlikon Wolverton
Trailer Composite
TC
M29793M-M29799M London Area

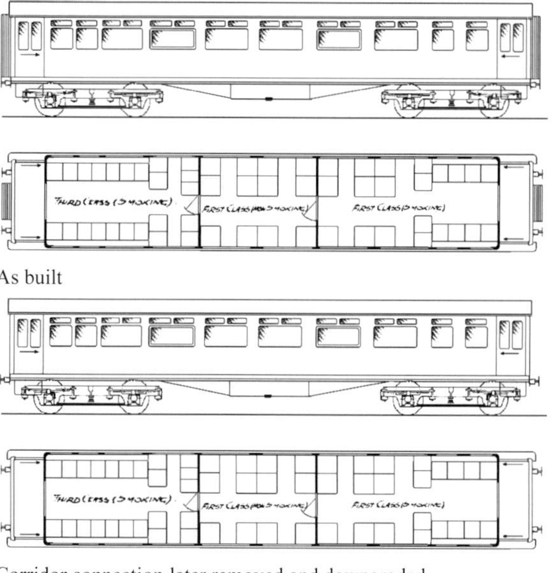

As built

Corridor connection later removed and downgraded

Diagram:		Weight:	28t 0cwt
Body:	57' 6" × 9' 6"	Bogies:	LNWR

Seats: 33 first 22 second, later 60 third

M29793M	33-12/57	⊗03/58	⊂**8873**
M29794M	33-08/60	⊗	⊂**8874**
M29795M	33-07/60	⊗	⊂**8875**
M29796M	33-08/60	⊗	⊂**8876**
M29797M	33-02/57	⊗10/57	⊂**8877**
M29798M	33-05/60	⊗	⊂**8878**
M29799M	33-06/60	⊗	⊂**8879**

LNWR Liverpool

Trailer Composite
TC
29800-29811 Liverpool Area

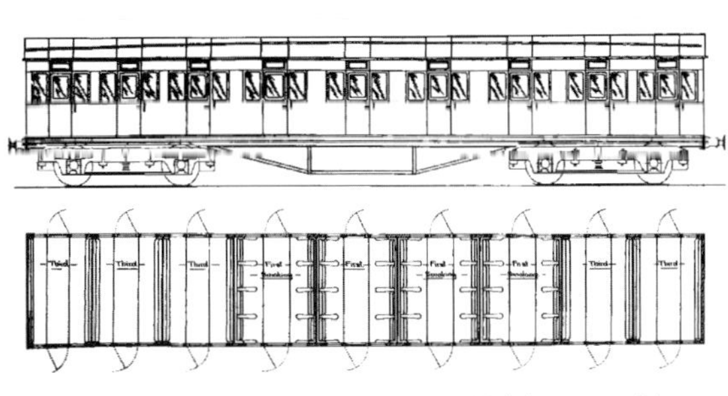

Diagram: 1691 Weight: 28t
Body: 57' 0" × 9' 2¼" Bogies: LNWR
Seats: 32 first 60 third

29800	33- 39	⊃ MSJA **154**	⊂**10682**
M29801M	33-02/63	⊗02/63	⊂**10683**
29802	33- 39	⊃ MSJA **155**	⊂**10684**
29803	33- 39	⊃ MSJA **156**	⊂**10685**
M29804M	33-02/63	⊗02/63	⊂**10686**
M29805M	33-02/63	⊗01/63	⊂**10687**
M29806M	33-02/63	⊗02/63	⊂**10688**
M29807M	33-02/63	⊗02/63	⊂**10689**
29808	33- 39	⊃ MSJA **157**	⊂**10690**
M29809M	33-02/63	⊗07/63	⊂**10691**
M29810M	33-02/63	⊗01/63	⊂**10692**
29811	33- 39	⊃ MSJA **158**	⊂**10693**

Class 502 Derby

Trailer Composite
TC
M29812-M29820M Liverpool-Southport

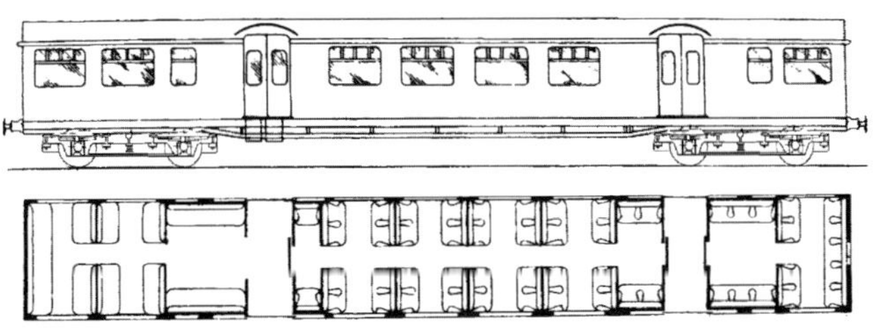

Diagram: 2009 Weight:
Body: 66' 5¼" × 9' 7" Bogies:
Seats: 53 first 29 second

M29812	39- *50*	⊃**29595**	**28322**	39- *50*
M29813	39- *50*	⊃**29596**	**28324**	39- *50*
M29814	39- *50*	⊃**29597**	**28326**	39- *50*
M29815	39- *50*	⊃**29598**	**28328**	39- *50*
M29816	39- *50*	⊃**29599**	**28330**	39- *50*
M29817	39- *50*	⊃**29544**	**28332**	39- *50*
M29818M	39-09/60	⊃**29863**	**28334**	39-09/60
M29819M	39-11/59	⊃**29864**	**28368**	39-*11/59*
M29820M	39-*04/59*	⊃**29865**	**28369**	39-*04/59*

Class 503 Birmingham RC&W
Metropolitan-Cammell (29833 onwards)

Trailer Composite later Second
TC later TS
M29821M-M29846M Wirral & Mersey

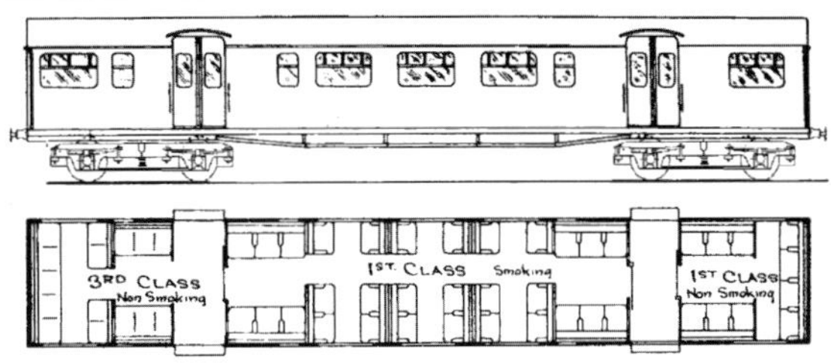

As built

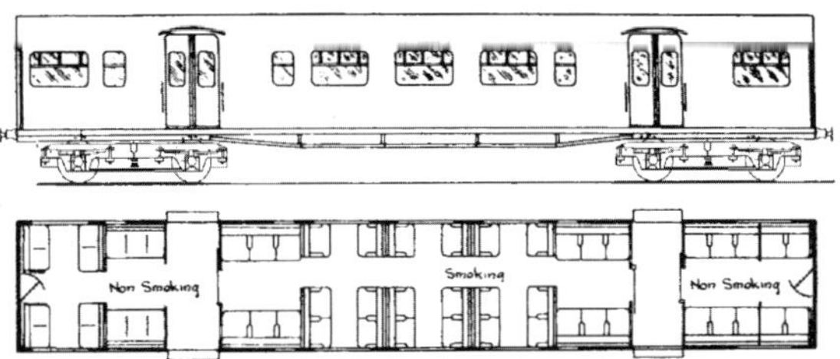

Later downgraded and fitted with end doors for tunnel working

Diagram: 2005 EH214 Weight: 20t
Body: 58' 0" × 9' 1" Bogies: Single Bolster
Seats: 40 first 15 second, later 53 second

M29821M	56-11/84	⊗10/85	**28375**	56-11/84			
M29822M	56-12/84	⊗05/86	**28376**	56-12/84			
M29823M	56-02/85	⊗03/86	**28377**	56-02/85			
M29824M	56-02/85	⊗05/86	**28379**	56-02/85			
M29825M	56-10/84	⊗12/84	**28380**	56-10/84			
M29826M	56-10/84	⊗07/85	**28382**	56-10/84			
M29827M	56-02/85	⊗06/86	**28391**	56-02/85			
M29828M	56-11/84	⊗11/85	**28384**	56-11/84			
M29829M	56-11/84	⊗02/86	**28387**	56-	57	**28388**	57-11/84
M29830M	56-10/84	⊗12/84	**28390**	56-10/84			
M29831M	56-10/84	⊗07/85	**28678**	56-10/84			
M29832M	56-10/84	⊗12/84	**28687**	56-10/84			
M29833M	56-10/84	⊗12/84	**28389**	56-10/84			
M29834M	56-03/85	⊗09/85	**28392**	56-03/85			
M29835M	56-02/85	⊗07/85	**28393**	56-02/85			
M29836M	56-05/85	⊗11/85	**28394**	56-05/85			
M29837M	56-12/84	⊗11/85	**28381**	56-12/84			
M29838M	56-03/85	⊗10/85	**28371**	56-	57	**28373**	57-03/85
M29839M	56-12/84	⊗05/86	**28385**	56-12/84			
M29840M	56-11/84	⊗12/85	**28383**	56-11/84			
M29841M	56-03/85	⊗10/85	**28372**	56-03/85			
M29842M	56-10/84	⊗12/84	**28386**	56-10/84			
M29843M	56-05/85	⊗12/85	**28373**	56-	57	**28371**	57-05/85
M29844M	56-12/84	⊗06/85	**28378**	56-12/84			
M29845M	56-10/84	⊗12/84	**28374**	56-10/84			
M29846M	56-10/84	⊗03/86	**28388**	56-	57	**28387**	57-02/85

Class 502 Derby

Driving Trailer Composite
DTC
M29862M-M29899M Liverpool-Southport

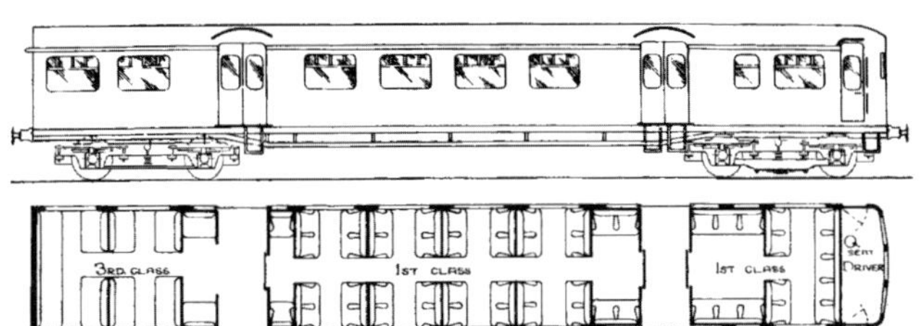

Diagram: 2013 393 EE207 Weight: 25t 1cwt
Body: 66' 5¼" × 9' 7" Bogies:
Seats: 53 first 25 second

M29862M	12/58-05/79	⊗02/80	**28351**	12/58-12/77	**28330**	12/77-05/79			⊂**29597**
M29863M	09/60-09/79	⊗03/80	**28354**	09/60-04/78	**28311**	04/78-11/78	**28358**	11/78-09/79	⊂**29818**
M29864M	11/59-09/79	⊗03/80	**28328**	11/59-09/79					⊂**29819**
M29865M	*04/59*-07/80	⊗08/80	**28360**	*04/59*-04/80					⊂**29820**
M29866M	39-09/79	⊗03/80	**28311**	39-12/77	**28358**	12/77-11/78	**28322**	11/78-01/79	
			28326	01/79-09/79					
M29867M	39-11/80	⊗03/81	**28312**	39-11/80					
M29868M	39-12/78	⊗02/80	**28313**	39-12/77	**28362**	12/77-12/78			
M29869M	39-12/78	⊗02/80	**28314**	39-*02/74*	**28356**	*02/74*-03/76	**28362**	03/76-01/77	
			28314	01/77-12/78					
M29870M	39-11/80	⊗03/81	**28315**	39- 68	**28344**	68-12/71	**28338**	72-06/80	
M29871M	39-05/79	⊗09/81	**28316**	39-03/73	**28358**	03/73-01/77	**28359**	01/77-04/79	
			28318	04/79-11/79					
M29872M	39-11/80	⊗02/82	**28317**	39-10/68	**28332**	68-11/80			
M29873M	39-09/79	⊗08/80	**28318**	39-04/79	**28359**	04/79-09/79			
M29874M	39-11/80	⊗03/81	**28319**	39- 68	**28315**	68-12/77	**28366**	06/79-11/80	
M29875M	39-11/80	⊗09/81	**28320**	39-02/50	**28349**	50-06/71	**28364**	05/73-11/80	
M29876M	39-08/79	⊗02/80	**28321**	39-06/62	**28326**	*63*-01/79	**28343**	04/79-08/79	
M29877M	39-11/80	⊗09/81	**28323**	39-11/80					
M29878M	39-09/79	⊗08/80	**28325**	39-07/62	**28369**	07/62-12/77	**28351**	12/77-11/79	
M29879M	39-08/79	⊗09/81	**28327**	39-09/70	**28330**	*06/71*-12/77	**28356**	12/77-08/79	
M29880M	39-11/80	⊗02/82	**28329**	39-06/62	**28334**	06/62-11/80			
M29881M	39-09/79	⊗08/80	**28331**	39-09/79					
M29882M	39-03/80	⊗08/80	**28333**	39-03/80					
M29883M	39-11/80	⊗03/81	**28335**	39-04/78	**28354**	04/78-11/80			
M29884M	39-07/80	⊗07/80	**28337**	39-11/80					
M29885M	39-05/79	⊗10/80	**28339**	39-03/76	**28359**	03/76- 76	**28339**	01/77-05/79	
M29886M	39-11/80	⊗03/81	**28341**	39-*02/76*	**28341**	10/76-05/79	**28318**	11/79-11/80	
M29887M	39-05/79	⊗09/81	**28343**	39-04/79					
M29888M	39-09/79	⊗03/80	**28345**	39-10/68	**28352**	68-09/79			
M29889M	39-11/80	⊗03/81	**28347**	39-11/80					
M29890M	39-11/80	⊗02/82	**28349**	39-01/42	**28350**	50-10/68	**28319**	68-11/79	
M29891M	39-12/77	⊗06/78	**28351**	39-12/58	**28359**	12/58-03/73	**28340**	03/73-12/77	
M29892M	39-05/79	⊗02/80	**28353**	39-05/79					
M29893M	39-09/79	⊗03/80	**28355**	39-09/79					
M29894M	39-11/80	⊗02/82	**28357**	39-01/80	**28335**	01/80-06/80	**28338**	06/80-11/80	
M29895M	39-11/80	⊗02/82	**28359**	39-12/58	**28342**	12/58-10/68	**28366**	68-06/79	
			28351	11/79-11/80					
M29896M	39-08/80	Ⓟ	**28361**	39-08/80					
M29897M	39-11/80	⊗03/81	**28363**	39-10/68	**28322**	68-02/74	**28360**	*02/74*-11/79	
			28335	11/79-01/80					
M29898M	39-10/68	⊗03/69	**28365**	39-10/68					
M29899M	39-10/68	⊗03/69	**28367**	39-10/68					

London Midland & Scottish Railway 1923 Numbering

Tube Joint Metropolitan CW&F
Trailer Third
TT
337, 593

For details see LMS 29497-29498

337	23-	33	⊃**29497**	⊂**214J**
593	23-	33	⊃**29498**	⊂**213J**

Tube Joint Metropolitan CW&F
Driving Trailer Third
DTT
640

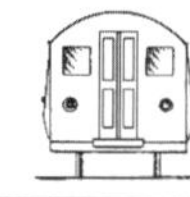

For details see LMS 29499

640	23-	33	⊃**29499**	⊂**401J**

Tube Joint Metropolitan CW&F
Driving Motor Brake Third
DMBT
770, 825, 904

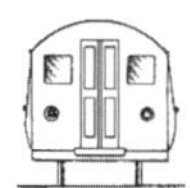

For details see LMS 28216-28218

770	23-	33	⊃**28217**	⊂**31J**
825	23-	33	⊃**28218**	⊂**32J**
904	23-	33	⊃**28216**	⊂**35J**

LNWR London Wolverton
Trailer Composite later Third
TC later TT
Between 1886 and 1923

For details see LMS 29612-29621

1886	33-	33	⊃**29612**
1892	33-	33	⊃**29613**
1895	33-	33	⊃**29614**
1898	33-	33	⊃**29615**
1901	33-	33	⊃**29616**
1905	33-	33	⊃**29617**
1912	33-	33	⊃**29618**
1917	33-	33	⊃**29619**
1922	33-	33	⊃**29620**
1923	33-	33	⊃**29621**

LNWR London Wolverton
Driving Trailer Third
DTT
Between 1931 and 1993

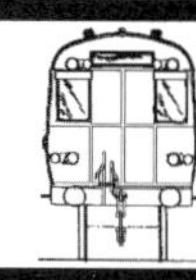

For details see LMS 28812-28824

1931	33-	33	⊃**28812**
1934	33-	33	⊃**28813**
1939	33-	33	⊃**28814**
1952	33-	33	⊃**28815**
1956	33-	33	⊃**28816**
1959	33-	33	⊃**28817**
1964	33-	33	⊃**28818**
1965	33-	33	⊃**28819**
1968	33-	33	⊃**28820**
1971	33-	33	⊃**28821**
1976	33-	33	⊃**28822**
1984	33-	33	⊃**28823**
1993	33-	33	⊃**28824**

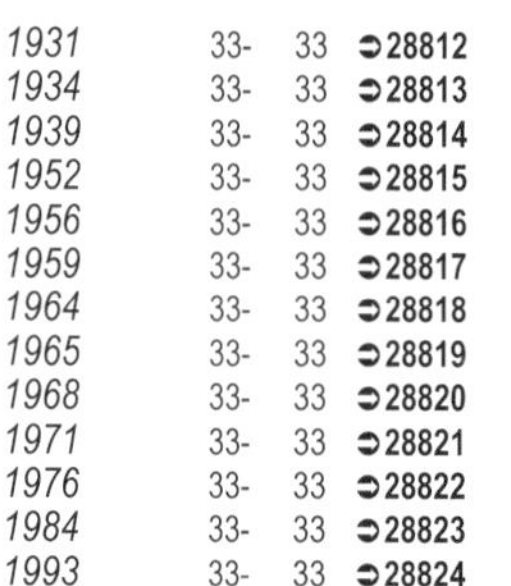

LNWR London Wolverton
Driving Motor Brake Third
DMBT
Between 2019 and 2253

For details see LMS 28018-28025

2019	33-	33	⊃**28018**
2025	33-	33	⊃**28019**
2026	33-	33	⊃**28020**
2031	33-	33	⊃**28021**
2039	33-	33	⊃**28022**
2121	33-	33	⊃**28023**
2234	33-	33	⊃**28024**
2253	33-	33	⊃**28025**

Tube Joint Metropolitan CW&F
Driving Motor Brake Third
DMBT
2394, 2415, 2416

For details see LMS 28213-28215

2394	23-	33	⊃**28213**	⊂**5J**
2415	23-	33	⊃**28214**	⊂**12J**
2416	23-	33	⊃**28215**	⊂**16J**

LNWR London Metropolitan CW&F
Driving Motor Brake Third
DMBT
4605-4610

For details see LMS 28001-28006

4605	27-	33	⊃**28001**
4606	27-	33	⊃**28002**
4607	27-	33	⊃**28003**

4608 27- 33 ⊃28004
4609 27- 33 ⊃28005
4610 27- 33 ⊃28006

LNWR London Midland RC&W
Driving Trailer Third
DTT
4611-4614

For details see LMS 28800-28803

4611 27- 33 ⊃28800
4612 27- 33 ⊃28801
4613 27- 33 ⊃28802
4614 27- 33 ⊃28803

LNWR London Clayton
Trailer Composite later Third
TC later TT
4615-4618

For details see LMS 29600-29603

4615 27- 33 ⊃29600
4616 27- 33 ⊃29601
4617 27- 33 ⊃29602
4618 27- 33 ⊃29603

LNWR London Midland RC&W
Driving Trailer Third
DTT
5236-5243

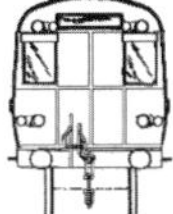

For details see LMS 28804-28811

5236 27- 33 ⊃28804
5237 27- 33 ⊃28805
5238 27- 33 ⊃28806
5239 27- 33 ⊃28807
5240 27- 33 ⊃28808
5241 27- 33 ⊃28809
5242 27- 33 ⊃28810
5243 27- 33 ⊃28811

LNWR Liverpool Wolverton
Driving Trailer Third
DTT
5244-5250, 5358-5360

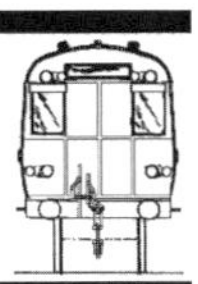

For details see LMS 29100-29109

5244 27- 33 ⊃29100
5245 27- 33 ⊃29101
5246 27- 33 ⊃29102
5247 27- 33 ⊃29103
5248 27- 33 ⊃29104
5249 27- 33 ⊃29105
5250 27- 33 ⊃29106
5358 27- 33 ⊃29107
5359 27- 33 ⊃29108
5360 27- 33 ⊃29109

LNWR London Clayton
Trailer Composite later Third
TC later TT
5713-5718

For details see LMS 29604-29609

5713 27- 33 ⊃29604
5714 27- 33 ⊃29605
5715 27- 33 ⊃29606
5716 27- 33 ⊃29607
5717 27- 33 ⊃29608
5718 27- 33 ⊃29609

LNWR London Metropolitan CW&F
Driving Motor Brake Third
DMBT
5719-5720

For details see LMS 28298-28299

5719 23- 33 ⊃28298
5720 23- 33 ⊃28299

LNWR London Metropolitan CW&F
Driving Motor Brake Third
DMBT
5721-5724

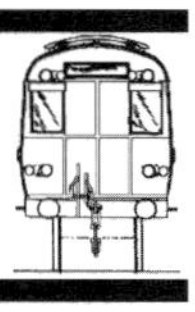

For details see LMS 28219-28222

5721 23- 33 ⊃28219 ⊂1E
5722 23- 33 ⊃28220 ⊂2E
5723 23- 33 ⊃28221 ⊂3E
5724 23- 33 ⊃28222 ⊂4E

LNWR London Metropolitan CW&F
Driving Motor Brake Third
DMBT
5725-5762

For details see LMS 28223-28260

5725 23- 33 ⊃28223 ⊂5E
5726 23- 33 ⊃28224 ⊂6E
5727 23- 33 ⊃28225 ⊂7E
5728 23- 33 ⊃28226 ⊂8E
5729 23- 33 ⊃28227 ⊂9E
5730 23- 33 ⊃28228 ⊂10E
5731 23- 33 ⊃28229 ⊂11E
5732 23- 33 ⊃28230 ⊂12E
5733 23- 33 ⊃28231 ⊂13E
5734 23- 33 ⊃28232 ⊂14E
5735 23- 33 ⊃28233 ⊂15E
5736 23- 33 ⊃28234 ⊂16E
5737 23- 33 ⊃28235 ⊂17E
5738 23- 33 ⊃28236 ⊂18E
5739 23- 33 ⊃28237 ⊂19E
5740 23- 33 ⊃28238 ⊂20E
5741 23- 33 ⊃28239 ⊂21E
5742 23- 33 ⊃28240 ⊂22E
5743 23- 33 ⊃28241 ⊂23E
5744 23- 33 ⊃28242 ⊂24E
5745 23- 33 ⊃28243 ⊂25E
5746 23- 33 ⊃28244 ⊂26E
5747 23- 33 ⊃28245 ⊂27E
5748 23- 33 ⊃28246 ⊂28E
5749 23- 33 ⊃28247 ⊂29E
5750 23- 33 ⊃28248 ⊂30E
5751 23- 33 ⊃28249 Ⓟ ⊂31E
5752 23- 33 ⊃28250 ⊂32E
5753 23- 33 ⊃28251 ⊂33E
5754 23- 33 ⊃28252 ⊂34E
5755 23- 33 ⊃20253 ⊂35E
5756 23- 33 ⊃28254 ⊂36E
5757 23- 33 ⊃28255 ⊂37E
5758 23- 33 ⊃28256 ⊂38E
5759 23- 33 ⊃28257 ⊂39E
5760 23- 33 ⊃28258 ⊂40E
5761 23- 33 ⊃28259 ⊂41E
5762 23- 33 ⊃28260 ⊂42E

LNWR London Metropolitan CW&F
Driving Motor Brake Third
DMBT
5763-5792

For details see LMS 28265-28294

5763 23- 33 ⊃28265 ⊂43E
5764 23- 33 ⊃28266 ⊂44E
5765 23- 33 ⊃28267 ⊂45E
5766 23- 33 ⊃28268 ⊂46E

5767	23-	33	⊃28269	⊂47E
5768	23-	33	⊃28270	⊂48E
5769	23-	33	⊃28271	⊂49E
5770	23-	33	⊃28272	⊂50E
5771	23-	33	⊃28273	⊂51E
5772	23-	33	⊃28274	⊂52E
5773	23-	33	⊃28275	⊂53E
5774	23-	33	⊃28276	⊂54E
5775	23-	33	⊃28277	⊂55E
5776	23-	33	⊃28278	⊂56E
5777	23-	33	⊃28279	⊂57E
5778	23-	33	⊃28280	⊂58E
5779	23-	33	⊃28281	⊂59E
5780	23-	33	⊃28282	⊂60E
5781	23-	33	⊃28283	⊂61E
5782	23-	33	⊃28284	⊂62E
5783	23-	33	⊃28285	⊂63E
5784	23-	33	⊃28286	⊂64E
5785	23-	33	⊃28287	⊂65E
5786	23-	33	⊃28288	⊂66E
5787	23-	33	⊃28289	⊂67E
5788	23-	33	⊃28290	⊂68E
5789	23-	33	⊃28291	⊂69E
5790	23-	33	⊃28292	⊂70E
5791	23-	33	⊃28293	⊂71E
5792	23-	33	⊃28294	⊂72E

LNWR London Metropolitan CW&F
Driving Motor Brake Third
DMBT
5793-5796

For details see LMS 28261-28263 & 28000

5793	23-	33	⊃28261	⊂250E
5794	23-	33	⊃28262	⊂251E
5795	23-	33	⊃28263	⊂252E
5796	23-	33	⊃28000 rebuilt 1926	⊂253E

LNWR London Metropolitan CW&F
Driving Motor Brake Third
DMBT
5797

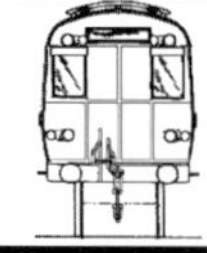

For details see LMS 28295

5797	23-	33	⊃28295	⊂254E

LNWR London Metropolitan CW&F
Driving Motor Brake Third
DMBT
5798

For details see LMS 28264

5798	23-	33	⊃28264	⊂255E

LNWR London Metropolitan CW&F
Driving Motor Brake Third
DMBT
5799-5800

For details see LMS 28296-28297

5799	23-	33	⊃28296	⊂256E
5800	23-	33	⊃28297	⊂257E

LNWR London Metropolitan CW&F
Driving Motor Brake Third
DMBT
5801, 8800

For details see LMS 28007-28008

5801	27-	33	⊃28007
8800	27-	33	⊃28008

LNWR London Metropolitan CW&F
Trailer Composite
TC
8801-8804

For details see LMS 29721-29724

8801	23-	33	⊃29721	⊂301E
8802	23-	33	⊃29722	⊂302E
8803	23-	33	⊃29723	⊂303E
8804	23-	33	⊃29724	⊂304E

LNWR London Wolverton
Trailer Composite
TC
8805-8842

For details see LMS 29725-29762

8805	23-	33	⊃29725	⊂305E
8806	23-	33	⊃29726	⊂306E
8807	23-	33	⊃29727	⊂307E
8808	23-	33	⊗01/34	⊂308E
8809	23-	33	⊃29729	⊂309E
8810	23-	33	⊃29730	⊂310E
8811	23-	33	⊃29731	⊂311E
8812	23-	33	⊃29732	⊂312E
8813	23-	33	⊃29733	⊂313E
8814	23-	33	⊃29734	⊂314E
8815	23-	33	⊃29735	⊂315E
8816	23-	33	⊃29736	⊂316E
8817	23-	33	⊃29737	⊂317E
8818	23-	33	⊃29738	⊂318E
8819	23-	33	⊃29739	⊂319E
8820	23-	33	⊃29740	⊂320E
8821	23-	33	⊃29741	⊂321E
8822	23-	33	⊃29742	⊂322E
8823	23-	33	⊃29743	⊂323E
8824	23-	33	⊃29744	⊂324E
8825	23-	33	⊃29745	⊂325E
8826	23-	33	⊃29746	⊂326E
8827	23-	33	⊃29747	⊂327E
8828	23-	33	⊃29748	⊂328E
8829	23-	33	⊃29749	⊂329E
8830	23-	33	⊃29750	⊂330E
8831	23-	33	⊃29751	⊂331E
8832	23-	33	⊃29752	⊂332E
8833	23-	33	⊃29753	⊂333E
8834	23-	33	⊃29754	⊂334E
8835	23-	33	⊃29755	⊂335E
8836	23-	33	⊃29756	⊂336E
8837	23-	33	⊃29757	⊂337E
8838	23-	33	⊃29758	⊂338E
8839	23-	33	⊃29759	⊂339E
8840	23-	33	⊃29760	⊂340E
8841	23-	33	⊃29761	⊂341E
8842	23-	33	⊃29762	⊂342E

LNWR London Wolverton
Trailer Composite
TC
8843-8872

For details see LMS 29763-29792

8843	23-	33	⊃29763	⊂343E
8844	23-	33	⊃29764	⊂344E
8845	23-	33	⊃29765	⊂345E
8846	23-	33	⊃29766	⊂346E
8847	23-	33	⊃29767	⊂347E
8848	23-	33	⊃29768	⊂348E
8849	23-	33	⊃29769	⊂349E
8850	23-	33	⊃29770	⊂350E
8851	23-	33	⊃29771	⊂351E
8852	23-	33	⊃29772	⊂352E
8853	23-	33	⊃29773	⊂353E
8854	23-	33	⊃29774	⊂354E
8855	23-	33	⊃29775	⊂355E
8856	23-	33	⊃29776	⊂356E
8857	23-	33	⊃29777	⊂357E
8858	23-	33	⊃29778	⊂358E
8859	23-	33	⊃29779	⊂359E

8860	23-	33	⊃29780	⊂360E
8861	23-	33	⊃29781	⊂361E
8862	23-	33	⊃29782	⊂362E
8863	23-	33	⊃29783	⊂363E
8864	23-	33	⊃29784	⊂364E
8865	23-	33	⊃29785	⊂365E
8866	23-	33	⊃29786	⊂366E
8867	23-	33	⊃29787	⊂367E
8868	23-	33	⊃29788	⊂368E
8869	23-	33	⊃29789	⊂369E
8870	23-	33	⊃29790	⊂370E
8871	23-	33	⊃29791	⊂371E
8872	23-	33	⊃29792	⊂372E

LNWR London Wolverton
Trailer Composite
TC
8873-8879

For details see LMS 29793-29799

8873	23-	33	⊃29793
8874	23-	33	⊃29794
8875	23-	33	⊃29795
8876	23-	33	⊃29796
8877	23-	33	⊃29797
8878	23-	33	⊃29798
8879	23-	33	⊃29799

LNWR London Metropolitan CW&F
Driving Motor Brake Third
DMBT
8880-8888

For details see LMS 28009-28017

8880	27-	33	⊃28009
8881	27-	33	⊃28010
8882	27-	33	⊃28011
8883	27-	33	⊃28012
8884	27-	33	⊃28013
8885	27-	33	⊃28014
8886	27-	33	⊃28015
8887	27-	33	⊃28016
8888	27-	33	⊃28017

LNWR Liverpool Wolverton
Driving Motor Brake Third
DMBT
8889-8899

For details see LMS 28300-28310

8889	27-	33	⊃28300
8890	27-	33	⊃28301
8891	27-	33	⊃28302
8892	27-	33	⊃28303
8893	27-	33	⊃28304
8894	27-	33	⊃28305
8895	27-	33	⊃28306
8896	27-	33	⊃28307
8897	27-	33	⊃28308
8898	27-	33	⊃28309
8899	27-	33	⊃28310

LNWR London Metropolitan CW&F
Driving Trailer Third
DTT/DTSO
9941-9944

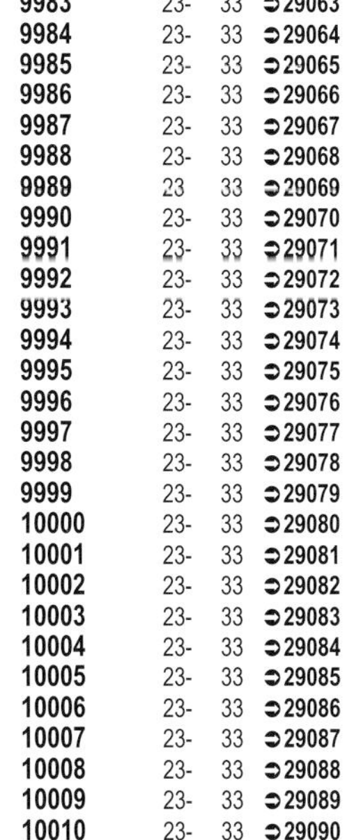

For details see LMS 29021-29024

9941	23-	33	⊃29021	⊂601E
9942	23-	33	⊃29022	⊂602E
9943	23-	33	⊃29023	⊂603E
9944	23-	33	⊃29024	⊂604E

LNWR London Wolverton
Driving Trailer Third
DTT
9945-9982

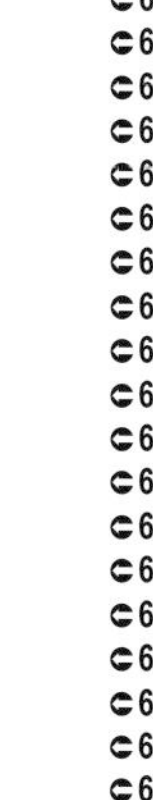

For details see LMS 29025-29062

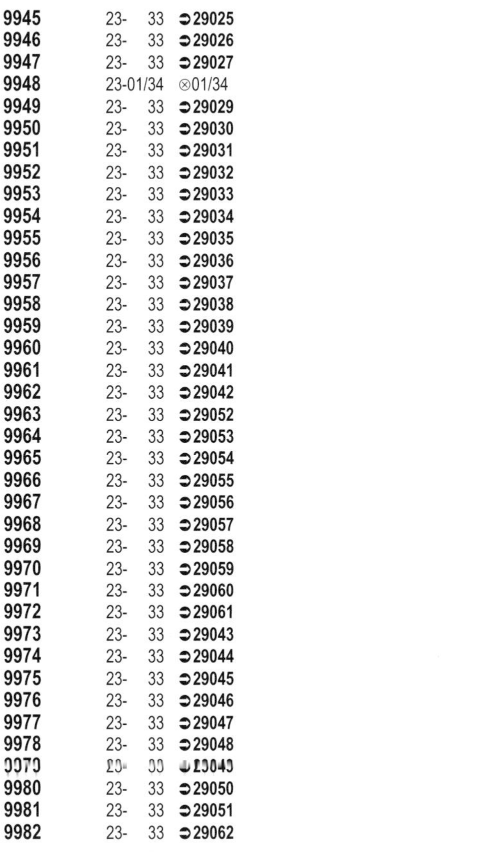

9945	23-	33	⊃29025	⊂605E
9946	23-	33	⊃29026	⊂606E
9947	23-	33	⊃29027	⊂607E
9948	23-01/34		⊗01/34	⊂608E
9949	23-	33	⊃29029	⊂609E
9950	23-	33	⊃29030	⊂610E
9951	23-	33	⊃29031	⊂611E
9952	23-	33	⊃29032	⊂612E
9953	23-	33	⊃29033	⊂613E
9954	23-	33	⊃29034	⊂614E
9955	23-	33	⊃29035	⊂615E
9956	23-	33	⊃29036	⊂616E
9957	23-	33	⊃29037	⊂617E
9958	23-	33	⊃29038	⊂618E
9959	23-	33	⊃29039	⊂619E
9960	23-	33	⊃29040	⊂620E
9961	23-	33	⊃29041	⊂621E
9962	23-	33	⊃29042	⊂622E
9963	23-	33	⊃29052	⊂623E
9964	23-	33	⊃29053	⊂624E
9965	23-	33	⊃29054	⊂625E
9966	23-	33	⊃29055	⊂626E
9967	23-	33	⊃29056	⊂627E
9968	23-	33	⊃29057	⊂628E
9969	23-	33	⊃29058	⊂629E
9970	23-	33	⊃29059	⊂630E
9971	23-	33	⊃29060	⊂631E
9972	23-	33	⊃29061	⊂632E
9973	23-	33	⊃29043	⊂633E
9974	23-	33	⊃29044	⊂634E
9975	23-	33	⊃29045	⊂635E
9976	23-	33	⊃29046	⊂636E
9977	23-	33	⊃29047	⊂637E
9978	23-	33	⊃29048	⊂638E
9979	23-	33	⊃29049	⊂639E
9980	23-	33	⊃29050	⊂640E
9981	23-	33	⊃29051	⊂641E
9982	23-	33	⊃29062	⊂642E

LNWR London Wolverton
Driving Trailer Third
DTT
9983-10012

For details see LMS 29063-29092

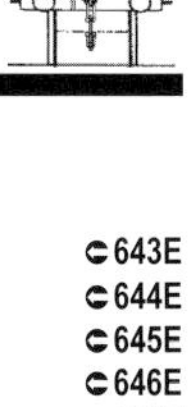

9983	23-	33	⊃29063	⊂643E
9984	23-	33	⊃29064	⊂644E
9985	23-	33	⊃29065	⊂645E
9986	23-	33	⊃29066	⊂646E
9987	23-	33	⊃29067	⊂647E
9988	23-	33	⊃29068	⊂648E
9989	23	33	⊃29069	⊂649E
9990	23-	33	⊃29070	⊂650E
9991	23-	33	⊃29071	⊂651E
9992	23-	33	⊃29072	⊂652E
9993	23-	33	⊃29073	⊂653E
9994	23-	33	⊃29074	⊂654E
9995	23-	33	⊃29075	⊂655E
9996	23-	33	⊃29076	⊂656E
9997	23-	33	⊃29077	⊂657E
9998	23-	33	⊃29078	⊂658E
9999	23-	33	⊃29079	⊂659E
10000	23-	33	⊃29080	⊂660E
10001	23-	33	⊃29081	⊂661E
10002	23-	33	⊃29082	⊂662E
10003	23-	33	⊃29083	⊂663E
10004	23-	33	⊃29084	⊂664E
10005	23-	33	⊃29085	⊂665E
10006	23-	33	⊃29086	⊂666E
10007	23-	33	⊃29087	⊂667E
10008	23-	33	⊃29088	⊂668E
10009	23-	33	⊃29089	⊂669E
10010	23-	33	⊃29090	⊂670E
10011	23-	33	⊃29091	⊂671E
10012	23-	33	⊃29092	⊂672E

LNWR London Wolverton
Driving Trailer Third
DTT
10013-10019

For details see LMS 29093-29099

10013	23-	33	➲**29093**
10014	23-	33	➲**29094**
10015	23-	33	➲**29095**
10016	23-	33	➲**29096**
10017	23-	33	➲**29097**
10018	23-	33	➲**29098**
10019	23-	33	➲**29099**

LNWR Liverpool Wolverton
Driving Trailer Third
DTT
10020

For details see LMS 29110

10020	27-	33	➲**29110**

LNWR London Clayton
Trailer Composite later Third
TC later TT
10679-10680

For details see LMS 29610-29611

10679	27-	33	➲**29610**
10680	27-	33	➲**29611**

LNWR Liverpool Wolverton
Trailer Composite
TC
10682-10693

For details see LMS 29800-29811

10682	27-	33	➲**29800**
10683	27-	33	➲**29801**
10684	27-	33	➲**29802**
10685	27-	33	➲**29803**
10686	27-	33	➲**29804**
10687	27-	33	➲**29805**
10688	27-	33	➲**29806**
10689	27-	33	➲**29807**
10690	27-	33	➲**29808**
10691	27-	33	➲**29809**
10692	27-	33	➲**29810**
10693	27-	33	➲**29811**

LYR Liverpool Newton Heath
Trailer First
TF
10891-10918

For details see LMS 29300-29327

10891	23-	33	➲**29300**	⊂**400**
10892	23-	33	➲**29301**	⊂**401**
10893	23-	33	➲**29302**	⊂**402**
10894	23-	33	➲**29303**	⊂**403**
10895	23-	33	➲**29304**	⊂**404**
10896	23-	33	➲**29305**	⊂**405**
10897	23-	33	➲**29306**	⊂**406**
10898	23-	33	➲**29307**	⊂**407**
10899	23-	33	➲**29308**	⊂**408**
10900	23-	33	➲**29309**	⊂**409**
10901	23-	33	➲**29310**	⊂**410**
10902	23-	33	➲**29311**	⊂**411**
10903	23-	33	➲**29312**	⊂**412**
10904	23-	33	➲**29313**	⊂**413**
10905	23-	33	➲**29314**	⊂**414**
10906	23-	33	➲**29315**	⊂**415**
10907	23-	33	➲**29316**	⊂**416**
10908	23-	33	➲**29317**	⊂**417**
10909	23-	33	➲**29318**	⊂**418**
10910	23-	33	➲**29319**	⊂**419**
10911	23-	33	➲**29320**	⊂**420**
10912	23-	33	➲**29321**	⊂**421**
10913	23-	33	➲**29322**	⊂**422**
10914	23-	33	➲**29323**	⊂**423**
10915	23-	33	➲**29324**	⊂**424**
10916	23-	33	➲**29325**	⊂**425**
10917	23-	33	➲**29326**	⊂**426**
10918	23-	33	➲**29327**	⊂**427**

LYR Liverpool Newton Heath
Trailer First
TF
10919-10924

For details see LMS 29328-29333

10919	23-	33	➲**29328**	⊂**428**
10920	23-	33	➲**29329**	⊂**429**
10921	23-	33	➲**29330**	⊂**430**
10922	23-	33	➲**29331**	⊂**431**
10923	23-	33	➲**29332**	⊂**432**
10924	23-	33	➲**29333**	⊂**433**

LYR Liverpool Newton Heath
Trailer First
TF
10925-10931

For details see LMS 29334-29340

10925	23-	33	➲**29334**	⊂**434**
10926	23-	33	➲**29335**	⊂**435**
10927	23-	33	➲**29336**	⊂**436**
10928	23-	33	➲**29337**	⊂**437**
10929	23-	33	➲**29338**	⊂**438**
10930	23-	33	➲**29339**	⊂**439**
10931	23-	33	➲**29340**	⊂**440**

LYR Bury Newton Heath
Driving Trailer First
DTF
10933-10946

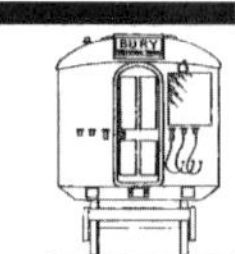

For details see LMS 28700-28713

10933	23-	33	➲**28700**	⊂**500**
10934	23-	33	➲**28701**	⊂**501**
10935	23-	33	➲**28702**	⊂**502**
10936	23-	33	➲**28703**	⊂**503**
10937	23-	33	➲**28704**	⊂**504**
10938	23-	33	➲**28705**	⊂**505**
10939	23-	33	➲**28706**	⊂**506**
10940	23-	33	➲**28707**	⊂**507**
10941	23-	33	➲**28708**	⊂**508**
10942	23-	33	➲**28709**	⊂**509**
10943	23-	33	➲**28710**	⊂**510**
10944	23-	33	➲**28711**	⊂**511**
10945	23-	33	➲**28712**	⊂**512**
10946	23-	33	➲**28713**	⊂**513**

LYR Liverpool Dick Kerr, Preston
Driving Motor Composite
DMC
11702 **(Liverpool Overhead Railway through trains)**

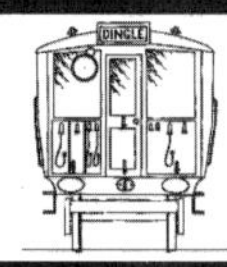

For details see LMS 28691

11702	23-	33	➲*28691*	⊂**1000**

LYR Liverpool Newton Heath

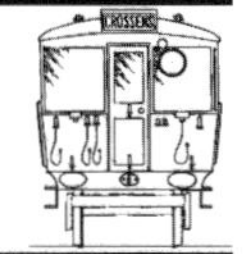

Driving Motor Composite
DMC
11703-11710 **(Liverpool Overhead Railway through trains)**

For details see LMS 28692-28699

11703	23-	33	⊃*28692*	⊂**1001**
11704	23-	33	⊃**28693**	⊂**1002**
11705	23-	33	⊃**28694**	⊂**1004**
11706	23-	33	⊃**28695**	⊂**1005**
11707	23-	33	⊃**28696**	⊂**1007**
11708	23-	33	⊃**28697**	⊂**1008**
11709	23-	33	⊃**28698**	⊂**1010**
11710	23-	33	⊃**28699**	⊂**1011**

LNWR London Wolverton

Trailer Third
TT
14403-14412

For details see LMS 29400-29409

14403	29-	33	⊃*29400*
14404	29-	33	⊃**29401**
14405	29-	33	⊃**29402**
14406	29-	33	⊃**29403**
14407	29-	33	⊃**29404**
14408	29-	33	⊃**29405**
14409	29-	33	⊃**29406**
14410	29-	33	⊃*29407*
14411	29-	33	⊃*29408*
14412	29-	33	⊃**29409**

LYR Liverpool Newton Heath

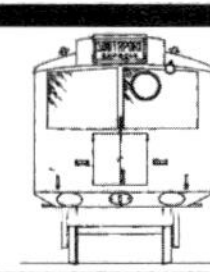

Driving Motor Brake Third
DMBT
14501-14528

For details see LMS 28433-28459, 28467, 28468, 28482

14501	23-	33	⊃**28434**	⊂**3000**
14502	23-	33	⊃**28435**	⊂**3001**
14503	23-	33	⊃**28436**	⊂**3002**
14504	23-	33	⊃**28437**	⊂**3003**
14505	23-	33	⊃**28438**	⊂**3004**
14506	23-	33	⊃**28439**	⊂**3005**
14507	23-	33	⊃**28440**	⊂**3006**
14508	23-	33	⊃**28441**	⊂**3007**
14509	23-	33	⊃**28442**	⊂**3008**
14510	23-	33	⊃**28482**	⊂**3009**
14511	23-	33	⊃**28443**	⊂**3010**
14512	23-	33	⊃**28444**	⊂**3011**
14513	23-	33	⊃**28445**	⊂**3012**
14514	23-	33	⊃**28446**	⊂**3013**
14515	23-	33	⊃**28447**	⊂**3014**
14516	23-	33	⊃**28468**	⊂**3015**
14517	23-	33	⊃**28448**	⊂**3016**
14518	23-	33	⊃**28449**	⊂**3017**
14519	23-	33	⊃**28450**	⊂**3018**
14520	23-	33	⊃**28451**	⊂**3019**
14521	23-	33	⊃**28452**	⊂**3020**
14522	23-	33	⊃**28453**	⊂**3021**
14523	23-	33	⊃**28454**	⊂**3022**
14524	23-	33	⊃**28467**	⊂**3023**
14525	23-	33	⊃**28455**	⊂**3024**
14526	23-	33	⊃**28456**	⊂**3025**
14527	23-	33	⊃**28433**	⊂**3026**
14528	23-	33	⊃**28457**	⊂**3027**

LYR Liverpool Newton Heath

Baggage Car

14529-14530

For details see LMS 28497-28498

14529	23-	33	⊃**28497**	⊂**3028**
14530	23-	33	⊃**28498**	⊂**3029**

LYR Liverpool Newton Heath

Driving Motor Brake Third
DMBT
14531-14532

For details see LMS 28458-28459

14531	23-	33	⊃**28458**	⊂**3030**
14532	23-	33	⊃**28459**	⊂**3031**

LYR Liverpool Newton Heath

Driving Motor Brake Third
DMBT
14533-14540

For details see LMS 28460-28469

14533	23-	33	⊃**28460**	⊂**3032**
14534	23-	33	⊃**28461**	⊂**3033**
14535	23-	33	⊃**28462**	⊂**3034**
14536	23-	33	⊃**28463**	⊂**3035**
14537	23-	33	⊃**28465**	⊂**3036**
14538	23-	33	⊃**28464**	⊂**3037**
14539	23-	33	⊃**28469**	⊂**3038**
14540	23-	33	⊃**28466**	⊂**3039**

LYR Liverpool Newton Heath

Driving Motor Third
DMT
14541-14545

For details see LMS 28472-28476

14541	23-	33	⊃**28472**	⊂**3040**
14542	23-	33	⊃**28473**	⊂**3041**
14543	23-	33	⊃**28474**	⊂**3042**
14544	23-	33	⊃**28475**	⊂**3043**
14545	23-	33	⊃**28476**	⊂**3044**

LYR Liverpool Newton Heath

Driving Motor Brake Third
DMBT
14546-14551

For details see LMS 28470-28471, 28477-28478, 28480-28481

14546	23-	33	⊃**28480**	⊂**3045**
14547	23-	33	⊃**28477**	⊂**3046**
14548	23-	33	⊃**28470**	⊂**3047**
14549	23-	33	⊃**28471**	⊂**3048**
14550	23-	33	⊃**28478**	⊂**3049**
14551	23-	33	⊃**28481**	⊂**3050**

LYR Liverpool Newton Heath

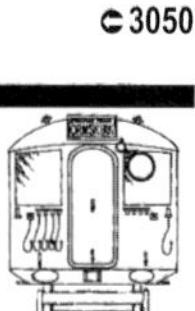

Driving Motor Third
DMT
14552

For details see LMS 28479

14552	23-	33	⊃**28479**	⊂**3051**

LYR Liverpool Newton Heath
Driving Motor Brake Third
DMBT
14553-14560

For details see LMS 28483-28490

14553	23-	33	⊃28483	⊂3052
14554	23-	33	⊃28484	⊂3053
14555	23-	33	⊃28485	⊂3054
14556	23-	33	⊃28486	⊂3055
14557	23-	33	⊃28487	⊂3056
14558	23-	33	⊃28488	⊂3057
14559	23-	33	⊃28489	⊂3058
14560	23-	33	⊃28490	⊂3059

LYR Liverpool Newton Heath
Driving Motor Brake Third
DMBT
14561-14566

For details see LMS 28491-28496

14561	23-	33	⊃28491	⊂3060
14562	23-	33	⊃28492	⊂3061
14563	23-	33	⊃28493	⊂3062
14564	23-	33	⊃28494	⊂3063
14565	23-	33	⊃28495	⊂3064
14566	23-	33	⊃28496	⊂3065

LYR Liverpool Newton Heath
Baggage Car

14567

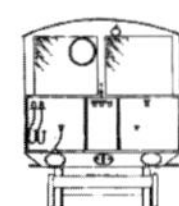

For details see LMS 28499

14567	23-	33	⊃28499	⊂3066

LYR Holcombe Brook Newton Heath
Driving Motor Brake Third
DMBT
14570-14571

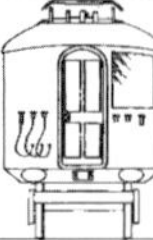

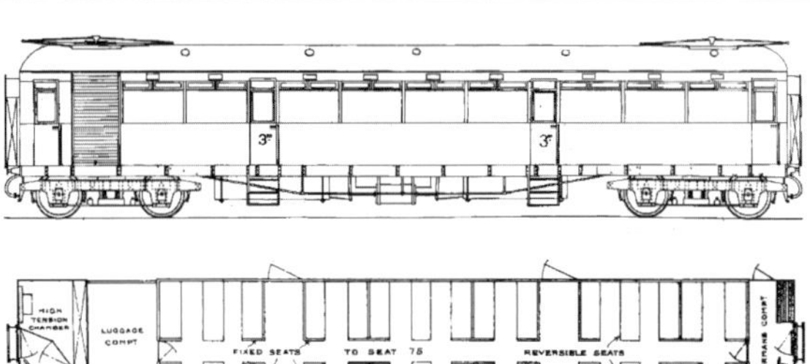

Diagram:	133	Weight:	
Body:	60' 0" × 9' 6"	Bogies:	LYR
Seats:	75 third	Motors:	Dick Kerr 4 × 150hp , 14571 4 × 250hp

After withdrawal these were converted into an experimental DMU

14570	23-	19	⊗ 33	⊂3500
14571	23-	19	⊗ 33	⊂3501

LYR Bury Newton Heath
Driving Motor Brake Third
DMBT
14572-14609

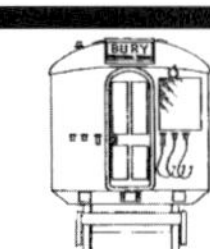

For details see LMS 28500-28537

14572	23-	33	⊃28500	⊂3502
14573	23-	33	⊃28501	⊂3503
14574	23-	33	⊃28502	⊂3504
14575	23-	33	⊃28503	⊂3505
14576	23-	33	⊃28504	⊂3506
14577	23-	33	⊃28505	⊂3507
14578	23-	33	⊃28506	⊂3508
14579	23-	33	⊃28507	⊂3509
14580	23-	33	⊃28508	⊂3510
14581	23-	33	⊃28509	⊂3511
14582	23-	33	⊃28510	⊂3512
14583	23-	33	⊃28511	⊂3513
14584	23-	33	⊃28512	⊂3514
14585	23-	33	⊃28513	⊂3515
14586	23-	33	⊃28514	⊂3516
14587	23-	33	⊃28515	⊂3517
14588	23-	33	⊃28516	⊂3518
14589	23-	33	⊃28517	⊂3519
14590	23-	33	⊃28518	⊂3520
14591	23-	33	⊃28519	⊂3521
14592	23-	33	⊃28520	⊂3522
14593	23-	33	⊃28521	⊂3523
14594	23-	33	⊃28522	⊂3524
14595	23-	33	⊃28523	⊂3525
14596	23-	33	⊃28524	⊂3526
14597	23-	33	⊃28525	⊂3527
14598	23-	33	⊃28526	⊂3528
14599	23-	33	⊃28527	⊂3529
14600	23-	33	⊃28528	⊂3530
14601	23-	33	⊃28529	⊂3531
14602	23-	33	⊃28530	⊂3532
14603	23-	33	⊃28531	⊂3533
14604	23-	33	⊃28532	⊂3534
14605	23-	33	⊃28533	⊂3535
14606	23-	33	⊃28534	⊂3536
14607	23-	33	⊃28535	⊂3537
14608	23-	33	⊃28536	⊂3538
14609	23-	33	⊃28537	⊂3539

LYR Liverpool Newton Heath
Driving Motor Third
DMT
14610-14612 **(Liverpool Overhead Railway through trains)**

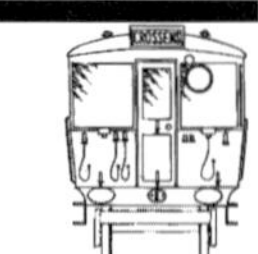

For details see LMS 28600-28602

14610	23-	33	⊃28600	⊂1003
14611	23-	33	⊃28601	⊂1006
14612	23-	33	⊃28602	⊂1009

LYR Liverpool Newton Heath
Trailer Third
TT, later DTT, later TT
14616

For details see LMS 29194

14616	23-	33	⊃29194	⊂3100

LYR Liverpool Newton Heath
Trailer Third
TT
14617-14627

For details see LMS 29500-29510

14617	23-	33	⊃29500	⊂3101
14618	23-	33	⊃29501	⊂3102
14619	23-	33	⊃29502	⊂3103
14620	23-	33	⊃29503	⊂3104
14621	23-	33	⊃29504	⊂3105
14622	23-	33	⊃29505	⊂3106
14623	23-	33	⊃29506	⊂3107
14624	23-	33	⊃29507	⊂3108
14625	23-	33	⊃29508	⊂3109
14626	23-	33	⊃29509	⊂3110
14627	23-	33	⊃29510	⊂3111

LYR Liverpool Newton Heath
Trailer Third
TT
14628-14632

For details see LMS 29511-29515

14628	23-	33	➲29511	⊂3112
14629	23-	33	➲29512	⊂3113
14630	23-	33	➲29513	⊂3114
14631	23-	33	➲29514	⊂3115
14632	23-	33	➲29515	⊂3116

LYR Liverpool Newton Heath
Trailer Third
TT, later DTT, later TT
14633

For details see LMS 29195

14633	23-	33	➲29195	⊂3117

LYR Liverpool Newton Heath
Trailer Third
TT
14634-14639

For details see LMS 29516-29521

14634	23-	33	➲29516	⊂3118
14635	23-	33	➲29517	⊂3119
14636	23-	33	➲29518	⊂3120
14637	23-	33	➲29519	⊂3121
14638	23-	33	➲29520	⊂3122
14639	23-	33	➲29521	⊂3123

LYR Liverpool Newton Heath
Trailer Third
TT
14640-14642

For details see LMS 29522-29524

14640	23-	33	➲29522	⊂3124
14641	23-	33	➲29523	⊂3125
14642	23-	33	➲29524	⊂3126

LYR Liverpool Newton Heath
Trailer Third
TT
14643-14646

For details see LMS 29196-29199

14643	23-	33	➲29196	⊂3127
14644	23-	33	➲29197	⊂3128
14645	23-	33	➲29198	⊂3129
14646	23-	33	➲29199	⊂3130

LYR Liverpool Newton Heath
Trailer Third
TT
14647-14666

For details see LMS 29525-29544

14647	23-	33	➲29525	⊂3131
14648	23-	33	➲29526	⊂3132
14649	23-	33	➲29527	⊂3133
14650	23-	33	➲29528	⊂3134
14651	23-	33	➲29529	⊂3135
14652	23-	33	➲29530	⊂3136
14653	23-	33	➲29531	⊂3137
14654	23-	33	➲29532	⊂3138
14655	23-	33	➲29533	⊂3139
14656	23-	33	➲29534	⊂3140
14657	23-	33	➲29535	⊂3141
14658	23-	33	➲29536	⊂3142
14659	23-	33	➲29537	⊂3143
14660	23-	33	➲29538	⊂3144
14661	23-	33	➲29539	⊂3145
14662	23-	33	➲29540	⊂3146
14663	23-	33	➲29541	⊂3147
14664	23-	33	➲29542	⊂3148
14665	23-	33	➲29543	⊂3149
14666	23-	33	➲29544	⊂3150

LYR Holcombe Brook Newton Heath
Driving Trailer Third
DTT
14667-14668

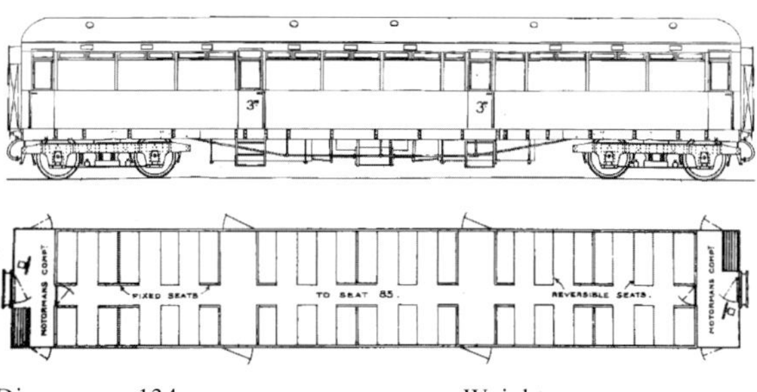

Diagram:	134	Weight:	
Body:	60' 0" × 9' 6"	Bogies:	LYR
Seats:	85 third		

After withdrawal these were converted into an experimental DMU

14667	23-	19 ⊗	33	⊂3600
14668	23-	19 ⊗	33	⊂3601

LYR Bury Newton Heath
Driving Trailer Third
DTT
14669-14682

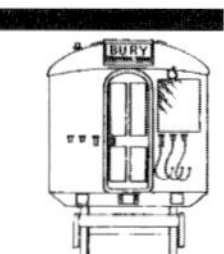

For details see LMS 29200-29213

14669	23-	33	➲29200	⊂3602
14670	23-	33	➲29201	⊂3603
14671	23-	33	➲29202	⊂3604
14672	23-	33	➲29203	⊂3605
14673	23-	33	➲29204	⊂3606
14674	23-	33	➲29205	⊂3607
14675	23-	33	➲29206	⊂3608
14676	23-	33	➲29207	⊂3609
14677	23-	33	➲29208	⊂3610
14678	23-	33	➲29209	⊂3611
14679	23-	33	➲29210	⊂3612
14680	23-	33	➲29211	⊂3613
14681	23-	33	➲29212	⊂3614
14682	23-	33	➲29213	⊂3615

Midland Railway

Midland Lancaster Morecambe & Heysham
Driving Motor Third
DMT
2236-2238

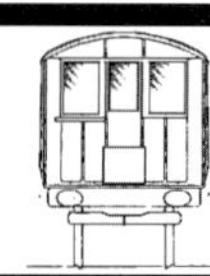

For details see LMS 28610-28612

2236	08-	33	➲28610
2237	08-	33	➲28611
2238	08-	33	➲28612

Midland Lancaster Morecambe/Heysham
Driving Trailer Third
DTT
2239-2242

For details see LMS 29290-29293

2239	08-	33	➲**29290**
2240	08-	33	➲**29291**
2241	08-	33	➲**29292**
2242	08-	33	➲**29293**

One Midland Railway diagram 490 bogie third vehicle was used as a trailer on this line before 1923. No other details are available.

01174 ⊗

Mersey Railway

Mersey Milnes, Hadley
Driving Motor First
DMF
1-12

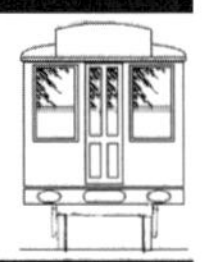

For details see LMS 28405-28416

1	03-	48	➲**28405**
2	03-	48	➲**28406**
3	03-	48	➲**28407**
4	03-	48	➲**28408**
5	03-	48	➲**28409**
6	03-	48	➲**28410**
7	03-	48	➲**28411**
8	03-	48	➲**28412**
9	03-	48	➲**28413**
10	03-	48	➲**28414**
11	03-	48	➲**28415**
12	03-	48	➲**28416**

Mersey Craven
Driving Motor First
DMF
13-14

For details see LMS 28417-28418

13	23-	48	➲**28417**
14	25-	48	➲**28418**

Mersey Milnes, Hadley
Driving Motor Third
DMT
26-37

For details see LMS 28419-28430

26	03-	48	➲**28419**
27	03-	48	➲**28420**
28	03-	48	➲**28421**
29	03-	48	➲**28422**
30	03-	48	➲**28423**
31	03-	48	➲**28424**
32	03-	48	➲**28425**
33	03-	48	➲**28426**
34	03-	48	➲**28427**
35	03-	48	➲**28428**
36	03-	48	➲**28429**
37	03-	48	➲**28430**

Mersey Craven
Driving Motor Third
DMT
38-39

For details see LMS 28431-28432

38	23-	48	➲**28431**
39	25-	48	➲**28432**

Mersey Milnes, Hadley
Trailer First
TF
51-63

For details see LMS 28787-28798

51	03-	48	➲**28787**	
52	03-	48	➲**28788**	
53	03-	48	➲**28789**	
54	03-	48	➲**28790**	
55	03-	48	➲**28791**	
56	03-	48	➲**28792**	
57	03-	48	➲**28793**	
58	03-	48	➲**28794**	
59	03-	48	➲**28795**	
60	03-	48	➲**28796**	
61	03-	48	➲**28797**	
62	08-	48	➲**28798**	⊂**119**
63	08-	37	➲**75**	⊂**110**

Mersey Craven
Trailer First
TF
64

For details see LMS 28799

64	25-	48	➲**28799**

Mersey Milnes, Hadley
Trailer Third
TT
75-99

For details see LMS 29157-29180

75	08-	48	➲**29157**	⊂**110** and **63**
76	03-	48	➲**29158**	
77	03-	48	➲**29159**	
78	03-	48	➲**29160**	
79	03-	48	➲**29161**	
80	03-	48	➲**29162**	
81	03-	48	➲**29163**	
82	03-	48	➲**29164**	
83	03-	48	➲**29165**	
84	03-	40	⊗	
85	03-	48	➲**29166**	
86	03-	48	➲**29167**	
87	03-	48	➲**29168**	
88	03-	48	➲**29169**	
89	03-	48	➲**29170**	
90	03-	48	➲**29171**	
91	03-	48	➲**29172**	
92	03-	48	➲**29173**	
93	08-	48	➲**29174**	⊂**116**
94	08-	48	➲**29175**	⊂**117**
95	08-	48	➲**29176**	⊂**118**
96	03-	48	➲**29177**	
97	03-	48	➲**29178**	
98	03-	48	➲**29179**	
99	03-	48	➲**29180**	

Mersey Craven
Trailer Third
TT
100-101

For details see LMS 29181-29182

100	25-	48	➲**29181**
101	25-	48	➲**29182**

Mersey Gloucester C&W
Trailer Third
TT
102-111

For details see LMS 29183-29192

102	36-	48	➲**29183**
103	36-	48	➲**29184**
104	36-	48	➲**29185**
105	36-	48	➲**29186**
106	36-	48	➲**29187**
107	36-	48	➲**29188**
108	36-	48	➲**29189**
109	36-	48	➲**29190**
110[2]	36-	48	➲**29191**
111	36-	48	➲**29192**

Mersey Wolverton
Trailer Third
TT
112

For details see LMS 29193. Replacement for 84.

112	44-	48	➲**29193**

Mersey Milnes, Hadley
Trailer Composite
TT
110 & 116-119

110	03-	08	➲**63** then **75**
116	03-	08	➲**93**
117	03-	08	➲**94**
118	03-	08	➲**95**
119	03-	08	➲**62**

Lancashire & Yorshire Railway

LYR Liverpool Newton Heath
Trailer First
TF
400-427

For details see LMS 29300-29327

400	04-	23	➲**10091**	29300
401	04-	23	➲**10892**	29301
402	04-	23	➲**10893**	29302
403	04-	23	➲**10894**	29303
404	04-	23	➲**10895**	29304
405	04-	23	➲**10896**	29305
406	04-	23	➲**10897**	29306
407	04-	23	➲**10898**	29307
408	04-	23	➲**10899**	29308
409	04-	23	➲**10900**	29309
410	04-	23	➲**10901**	29310
411	04-	23	➲**10902**	29311
412	04-	23	➲**10903**	29312
413	04-	23	➲**10904**	29313
414	04-	23	➲**10905**	29314
415	04-	23	➲**10906**	29315
416	04-	23	➲**10907**	29316
417	04-	23	➲**10908**	29317
418	04-	23	➲**10909**	29318
419	04-	23	➲**10910**	29319
420	04-	23	➲**10911**	29320
421	05-	23	➲**10912**	29321
422	05-	23	➲**10913**	29322
423	05-	23	➲**10914**	29323
424	05-	23	➲**10915**	29324
425	05-	23	➲**10916**	29325
426	05-	23	➲**10917**	29326
427	05-	23	➲**10918**	29327

LYR Liverpool Newton Heath
Trailer First
TF
428-433

For details see LMS 29328-29333

428	05-	23	➲**10919**	29328
429	05-	23	➲**10920**	29329
430	05-	23	➲**10921**	29330
431	05-	23	➲**10922**	29331
432	05-	23	➲**10923**	29332
433	05-	23	➲**10924**	29333

LYR Liverpool Newton Heath
Trailer First
TF
434-440

For details see LMS 29334-29340

434	11-	23	➲**10925**	29334
435	11-	23	➲**10926**	29335
436	12-	23	➲**10927**	29336
437	12-	23	➲**10928**	29337
438	14-	23	➲**10929**	29338
439	14-	23	➲**10930**	29339
440	14-	23	➲**10931**	29340

LYR Bury Newton Heath
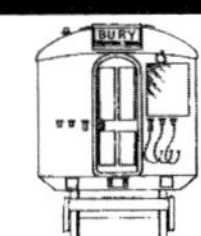

Driving Trailer First
DTF
500-513

For details see LMS 28700-28713

500	15-	23	➲**10933**	28700
501	15-	23	➲**10934**	28701
502	15-	23	➲**10935**	28702
503	15-	23	➲**10936**	28703
504	15-	23	➲**10937**	28704
505	15-	23	➲**10938**	28705
506	15-	23	➲**10939**	28706
507	16-	23	➲**10940**	28707
508	16-	23	➲**10941**	28708
509	20-	23	➲**10942**	28709
510	20-	23	➲**10943**	28710
511	20-	23	➲**10944**	28711
512	20-	23	➲**10945**	28712
513	20-	23	➲**10946**	28713

LYR Liverpool Dick Kerr, Preston
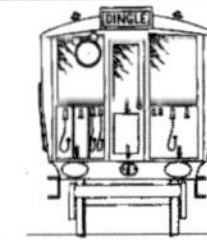

Driving Motor Composite
DMC
1000 **(Liverpool Overhead Railway through trains)**

For details see LMS 28691

1000	05-	23	➲**11702**	*28691*

LYR Liverpool Newton Heath
Driving Motor Composite
DMC
1001-1011 (Liverpool Overhead Railway through trains)

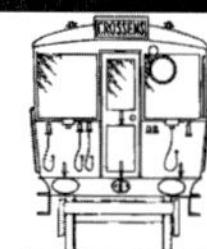

For details see LMS 28600-28602, 28692-28699

1001	05-	23	⊃**11703**	*28692*
1002	05-	23	⊃**11704**	28693
1003	05-	23	⊃**14610**	28600
1004	05-	23	⊃**11705**	28694
1005	05-	23	⊃**11706**	28695
1006	05-	23	⊃**14611**	28601
1007	05-	23	⊃**11707**	28696
1008	05-	23	⊃**11708**	28697
1009	05-	23	⊃**14612**	28602
1010	05-	23	⊃**11709**	28698
1011	05-	23	⊃**11710**	28699

LYR Liverpool Newton Heath
Driving Motor Brake Third
DMBT
3000-3027

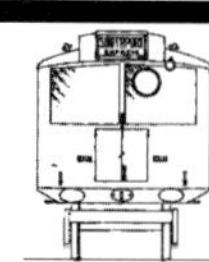

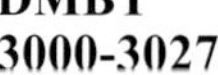

For details see LMS 28433-28459, 28467, 28468, 28482

3000	04-	23	⊃**14501**	28434
3001	04-	23	⊃**14502**	28435
3002	04-	23	⊃**14503**	28436
3003	04-	23	⊃**14504**	28437
3004	04-	23	⊃**14505**	28438
3005	04-	23	⊃**14506**	28439
3006	04-	23	⊃**14507**	28440
3007	04-	23	⊃**14508**	28441
3008	04-	23	⊃**14509**	28442
3009	04-	23	⊃**14510**	28482
3010	04-	23	⊃**14511**	28443
3011	04-	23	⊃**14512**	28444
3012	04-	23	⊃**14513**	28445
3013	04-	23	⊃**14514**	28446
3014	04-	23	⊃**14515**	28447
3015	04-07/05	⊗07/05		Original 3015 destroyed in crash 07/05
3015²	06-	23	⊃**14516**	28468
3016	04-	23	⊃**14517**	28448
3017	04-	23	⊃**14518**	28449
3018	04-	23	⊃**14519**	28450
3019	04-	23	⊃**14520**	28451
3020	04-	23	⊃**14521**	28452
3021	04-	23	⊃**14522**	28453
3022	04-	23	⊃**14523**	28454
3023	04-07/05	⊗07/05		Original 3023 destroyed in crash 07/05
3023²	06-	23	⊃**14524**	28467
3024	04-	23	⊃**14525**	28455
3025	04-	23	⊃**14526**	28456
3026	04-	23	⊃**14527**	28433
3027	05-	23	⊃**14528**	28457

LYR Liverpool Newton Heath
Baggage Car
3028-3029

For details see LMS 28497-28498

3028	03-	23	⊃**14529**	28497
3029	04-	23	⊃**14530**	28498

LYR Liverpool Newton Heath
Driving Motor Brake Third
DMBT
3030-3031

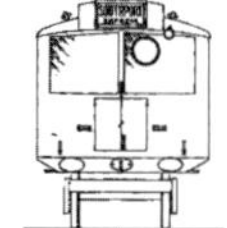

For details see LMS 28458-28459

3030	06-	23	⊃**14531**	28458
3031	06-	23	⊃**14532**	28459

LYR Liverpool Newton Heath
Driving Motor Brake Third
DMBT
3032-3039

For details see LMS 28460-28469

3032	05-	23	⊃**14533**	28460
3033	05-	23	⊃**14534**	28461
3034	06-	23	⊃**14535**	28462
3035	06-	23	⊃**14536**	28463
3036	06-	23	⊃**14537**	28465
3037	06-	23	⊃**14538**	28464
3038	06-	23	⊃**14539**	28469
3039	06-	23	⊃**14540**	28466

LYR Liverpool Newton Heath
Driving Motor Third
DMT
3040-3044

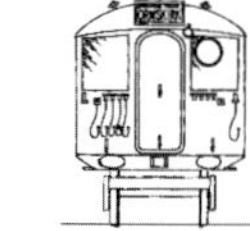

For details see LMS 28472-28476

3040	07-	23	⊃**14541**	28472
3041	07-	23	⊃**14542**	28473
3042	07-	23	⊃**14543**	28474
3043	07-	23	⊃**14544**	28475
3044	07-	23	⊃**14545**	28476

LYR Liverpool Newton Heath
Driving Motor Brake Third
DMBT
3045-3050

For details see LMS 28470-28471, 28477-28478, 28480-28481

3045	08-	23	⊃**14546**	28480
3046	08-	23	⊃**14547**	28477
3047	07-	23	⊃**14548**	28470
3048	07-	23	⊃**14549**	28471
3049	10-	23	⊃**14550**	28478
3050	10-	23	⊃**14551**	28481

LYR Liverpool Newton Heath
Driving Motor Third
DMT
3051

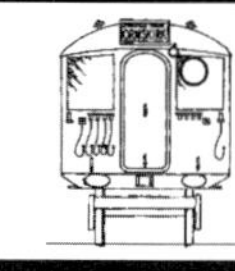

For details see LMS 28479

3051	08-	23	⊃**14552**	28479

LYR Liverpool Newton Heath
Driving Motor Brake Third
DMBT
3052-3059

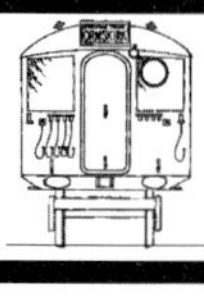

For details see LMS 28483-28490

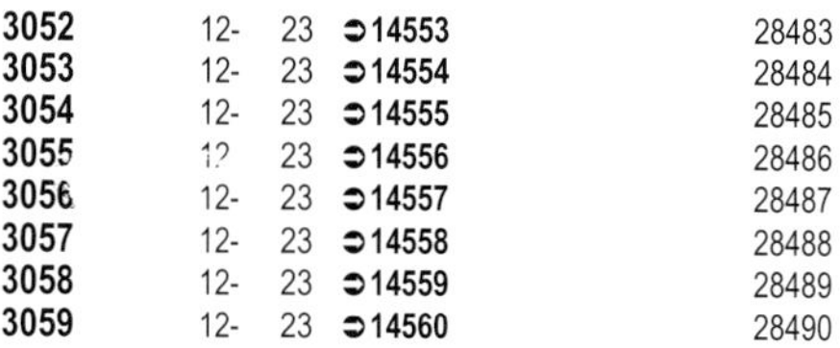

3052	12-	23	⊃**14553**	28483
3053	12-	23	⊃**14554**	28484
3054	12-	23	⊃**14555**	28485
3055	12-	23	⊃**14556**	28486
3056	12-	23	⊃**14557**	28487
3057	12-	23	⊃**14558**	28488
3058	12-	23	⊃**14559**	28489
3059	12-	23	⊃**14560**	28490

LYR Liverpool Newton Heath
Driving Motor Brake Third
DMBT
3060-3065

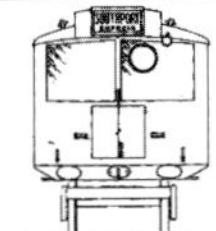

For details see LMS 28491-28496

3060	14-	23	**➲14561**	28491
3061	14-	23	**➲14562**	28492
3062	14-	23	**➲14563**	28493
3063	14-	23	**➲14564**	28494
3064	14-	23	**➲14565**	28495
3065	14-	23	**➲14566**	28496

LYR Liverpool Newton Heath
Baggage Car

3066

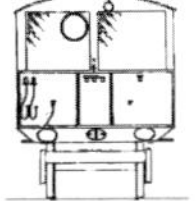

For details see LMS 28499

3066	21-	23	**➲14567**	28499

LYR Liverpool Newton Heath
Trailer Third
TT, later DTT, later TT
3100

For details see LMS 29194

3100	05-	23	**➲14616**	29194

LYR Liverpool Newton Heath
Trailer Third
TT
3101-3111

For details see LMS 29500-29510

3101	05-	23	**➲14617**	29500
3102	05-	23	**➲14618**	29501
3103	05-	23	**➲14619**	29502
3104	05-	23	**➲14620**	29503
3105	05-	23	**➲14621**	29504
3106	05-	23	**➲14622**	29505
3107	05-	23	**➲14623**	29506
3108	05-	23	**➲14624**	29507
3109	05-	23	**➲14625**	29508
3110	05-	23	**➲14626**	29509
3111	05-	23	**➲14627**	29510

LYR Liverpool Newton Heath
Trailer Third
TT
3112-3116

For details see LMS 29511-29515

3112	06-	23	**➲14628**	29511
3113	06-	23	**➲14629**	29512
3114	06-	23	**➲14630**	29513
3115	06-	23	**➲14631**	29514
3116	06-	23	**➲14632**	29515

LYR Liverpool Newton Heath
Trailer Third
TT, later DTT, later TT
3117

For details see LMS 29195

3117	06-	23	**➲14633**	29195

LYR Liverpool Newton Heath
Trailer Third
TT
3118-3123

For details see LMS 29516-29521

3118	08-	23	**➲14634**	29516
3119	08-	23	**➲14635**	29517
3120	08-	23	**➲14636**	29518
3121	08-	23	**➲14637**	29519
3122	08-	23	**➲14638**	29520
3123	08-	23	**➲14639**	29521

LYR Liverpool Newton Heath
Trailer Third
TT
3124-3126

For details see LMS 29522-29524

3124	10-	23	**➲14640**	29522
3125	10-	23	**➲14641**	29523
3126	10-	23	**➲14642**	29524

LYR Liverpool Newton Heath
Trailer Third
TT
3127-3130

For details see LMS 29196-29199

3127	12-	23	**➲14643**	29196
3128	12-	23	**➲14644**	29197
3129	12-	23	**➲14645**	29198
3130	12-	23	**➲14646**	29199

LYR Liverpool Newton Heath
Trailer Third
TT
3131-3150

For details see LMS 29525-29544

3131	13-	23	**➲14647**	29525
3132	13-	23	**➲14648**	29526
3133	13-	23	**➲14649**	29527
3134	13-	23	**➲14650**	29528
3135	13-	23	**➲14651**	29529
3136	13-	23	**➲14652**	29530
3137	13-	23	**➲14653**	29531
3138	13-	23	**➲14654**	29532
3139	13-	23	**➲14655**	29533
3140	13-	23	**➲14656**	29534
3141	13-	23	**➲14657**	29535
3142	13-	23	**➲14658**	29536
3143	13-	23	**➲14659**	29537
3144	13-	23	**➲14660**	29538
3145	14-	23	**➲14661**	29539
3146	14-	23	**➲14662**	29540
3147	14-	23	**➲14663**	29541
3148	14-	23	**➲14664**	29542
3149	14-	23	**➲14665**	29543
3150	14-	23	**➲14666**	29544

LYR Holcombe Brook Newton Heath
Driving Motor Brake Third
DMBT
3500-3501

For details see LMS 14570-14571

3500	13-	19	**➲14570**
3501	13-	19	**➲14571**

LYR Bury Newton Heath
Driving Motor Brake Third
DMBT
3502-3539

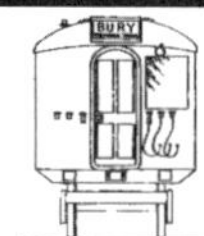

For details see LMS 28500-28537

3502	15-	23	**⊃14572**	28500
3503	15-	23	**⊃14573**	28501
3504	15-	23	**⊃14574**	28502
3505	15-	23	**⊃14575**	28503
3506	15-	23	**⊃14576**	28504
3507	15-	23	**⊃14577**	28505
3508	15-	23	**⊃14578**	28506
3509	15-	23	**⊃14579**	28507
3510	15-	23	**⊃14580**	28508
3511	15-	23	**⊃14581**	28509
3512	16-	23	**⊃14582**	28510
3513	16-	23	**⊃14583**	28511
3514	16-	23	**⊃14584**	28512
3515	16-	23	**⊃14585**	28513
3516	16-	23	**⊃14586**	28514
3517	16-	23	**⊃14587**	28515
3518	16-	23	**⊃14588**	28516
3519	16-	23	**⊃14589**	28517
3520	16-	23	**⊃14590**	28518
3521	16-	23	**⊃14591**	28519
3522	16-	23	**⊃14592**	28520
3523	16-	23	**⊃14593**	28521
3524	16-	23	**⊃14594**	28522
3525	16-	23	**⊃14595**	28523
3526	16-	23	**⊃14596**	28524
3527	16-	23	**⊃14597**	28525
3528	16-	23	**⊃14598**	28526
3529	16-	23	**⊃14599**	28527
3530	20-	23	**⊃14600**	28528
3531	20-	23	**⊃14601**	28529
3532	20-	23	**⊃14602**	28530
3533	20-	23	**⊃14603**	28531
3534	20-	23	**⊃14604**	28532
3535	20-	23	**⊃14605**	28533
3536	20-	23	**⊃14606**	28534
3537	21-	23	**⊃14607**	28535
3538	21-	23	**⊃14608**	28536
3539	21-	23	**⊃14609**	28537

LYR Holcombe Brook Newton Heath
Driving Trailer Third
DTT
3600-3601

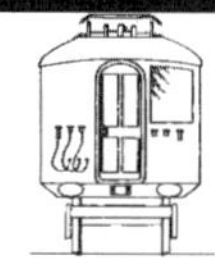

For details see LMS 14667-14668

3600	13-	19	**⊃14667**
3601	13-	19	**⊃14668**

LYR Bury Newton Heath
Driving Trailer Third
DTT
3602-3615

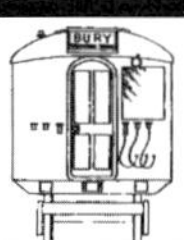

For details see LMS 29200-29213

3602	15-	23	**⊃14669**	29200
3603	15-	23	**⊃14670**	29201
3604	15-	23	**⊃14671**	29202
3605	15-	23	**⊃14672**	29203
3606	15-	23	**⊃14673**	29204
3607	15-	23	**⊃14674**	29205
3608	15-	23	**⊃14675**	29206
3609	16-	23	**⊃14676**	29207
3610	16-	23	**⊃14677**	29208
3611	20-	23	**⊃14678**	29209
3612	20-	23	**⊃14679**	29210
3613	20-	23	**⊃14680**	29211
3614	20-	23	**⊃14681**	29212
3615	20-	23	**⊃14682**	29213

Manchester South Junction and Altrincham Railway

MSJA Metropolitan-Cammell
Driving Motor Brake Third
DMBT
1-24

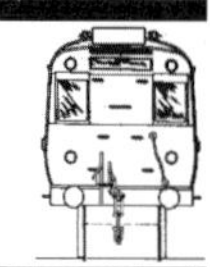

For details see LMS 28571-28594

1	31-	48	**⊃28571**
2	31-	48	**⊃28572**
3	31-	48	**⊃28573**
4	31-	48	**⊃28574**
5	31-	48	**⊃28575**
6	31-	48	**⊃28576**
7	31-	48	**⊃28577**
8	31-	48	**⊃28578**
9	31-	48	**⊃28579**
10	31-	48	**⊃28580**
11	31-	48	**⊃28581**
12	31-	48	**⊃28582**
13	31-	48	**⊃28583**
14	31-	48	**⊃28584**
15	31-	48	**⊃28585**
16	31-	48	**⊃28586**
17	31-	48	**⊃28587**
18	31-	48	**⊃28588**
19	31-	48	**⊃28589**
20	31-	48	**⊃28590**
21	31-	48	**⊃28591**
22	31-	48	**⊃28592**
23	31-	48	**⊃28593**
24	31-	48	**⊃28594**

MSJA Metropolitan-Cammell
Driving Trailer Third
DTT
51-74

For details see LMS 29231-29252

51	31-	48	**⊃29231**
52	31-	48	**⊃29232**
53	31-	48	**⊃29233**
54	31-	48	**⊃29234**
55	31-	48	**⊃29235**
56	31-	48	**⊃29236**
57	31-	48	⊗
58	31-	48	**⊃29237**
59	31-	48	**⊃29239**
60	31-	48	**⊃29240**
61	31-	48	**⊃29241**
62	31-	48	**⊃29242**
63	31-	48	**⊃29243**
64	31-	48	**⊃29244**
65	31-	48	**⊃29245**
66	31-	48	**⊃29246**
67	31-	48	**⊃29247**
68	31-	48	**⊃29248**
69	31-	48	**⊃29249**
70	31-	48	**⊃29250**
71	31-	48	**⊃29251**
72	31-	48	**⊃29252**
74	48-	48	**⊃29238 ⊂153**

MSJA Metropolitan-Cammell
Trailer Composite
TC
101-122

For details see LMS 29650-29671

101	31-	48	**⊃29650**
102	31-	48	**⊃29651**
103	31-	48	**⊃29652**
104	31-	48	**⊃29653**
105	31-	48	**⊃29654**

106	31-	48	⊃29655		
107	31-	48	⊃29656		
108	31-	48	⊃29657		
109	31-	48	⊃29658		
110	31-	48	⊃29659		
111	31-	48	⊃29660		
112	31-	48	⊃29661		
113	31-	48	⊃29662		
114	31-	48	⊃29663	Ⓟ⊗	
115	31-	48	⊃29664		
116	31-	48	⊃29665		
117	31-	48	⊃29666	Ⓟ	
118	31-	48	⊃29667		
119	31-	48	⊃29668		
120	31-	48	⊃29669		
121	31-	48	⊃29670	Ⓟ	
122	31-	48	⊃29671		

MSJA Metropolitan-Cammell
Trailer Composite
TC
151-158

For details see LMS 29390-29396

151	39-	48	⊃29390	
152	39-	48	⊃29391	
153	39-	48	⊃74	⊂29401
154	39-	48	⊃29392	⊂29800
155	39-	48	⊃29393	⊂29802
156	39-	48	⊃29394	⊂29803
157	39-	48	⊃29395	⊂29808
158	39-	48	⊃29396	⊂29811

London & North Western Railway

LNWR London Metropolitan CW&F

Driving Motor Brake Third
DMBT
1E-4E

For details see LMS 28219-28222

1E	14-	23	⊃5721	28219
2E	14-	23	⊃5722	28220
3E	14-	23	⊃5723	28221
4E	14-	23	⊃5724	28222

LNWR London Metropolitan CW&F

Driving Motor Brake Third
DMBT
5E-42E

For details see LMS 28223-28260

5E	15-	23	⊃5725	28223	
6E	15-	23	⊃5726	28224	
7E	15-	23	⊃5727	28225	
8E	15-	23	⊃5728	28226	
9E	15-	23	⊃5729	28227	
10E	15-	23	⊃5730	28228	
11E	15-	23	⊃5731	28229	
12E	15-	23	⊃5732	28230	
13E	15-	23	⊃5733	28231	
14E	15-	23	⊃5734	28232	
15E	15-	23	⊃5735	28233	
16E	15-	23	⊃5736	28234	
17E	15-	23	⊃5737	28235	
18E	15-	23	⊃5738	28236	
19E	15-	23	⊃5739	28237	
20E	15-	23	⊃5740	28238	
21E	15-	23	⊃5741	28239	
22E	15-	23	⊃5742	28240	
23E	15-	23	⊃5743	28241	
24E	15-	23	⊃5744	28242	
25E	15-	23	⊃5745	28243	
26E	15-	23	⊃5746	28244	
27E	15-	23	⊃5747	28245	
28E	15-	23	⊃5748	28246	
29E	15-	23	⊃5749	28247	
30E	15-	23	⊃5750	28248	
31E	15-	23	⊃5751	28249	Ⓟ
32E	15-	23	⊃5752	28250	
33E	15-	23	⊃5753	28251	
34E	15-	23	⊃5754	28252	
35E	15-	23	⊃5755	28253	
36E	15-	23	⊃5756	28254	
37E	15-	23	⊃5757	28255	
38E	15-	23	⊃5758	28256	
39E	15-	23	⊃5759	28257	
40E	15-	23	⊃5760	28258	
41E	15-	23	⊃5761	28259	
42E	15-	23	⊃5762	28260	

LNWR London Metropolitan CW&F
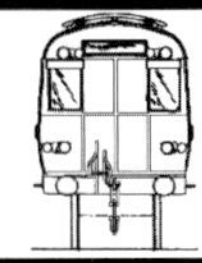
Driving Motor Brake Third
DMBT
43E-47E

For details see LMS 28261-28264 & 28000

43E	15-	23	⊃251E	28262
44E	15-	23	⊃250E	28261
45E	15-	23	⊃253E	28000
46E	15-	23	⊃252E	28263
47E	15-	23	⊃255E	28264

LNWR London Metropolitan CW&F
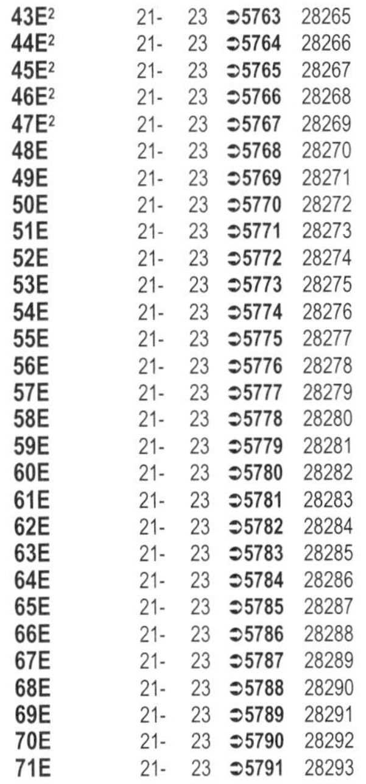
Driving Motor Brake Third
DMBT
43E-72E

For details see LMS 28265-28294

43E[2]	21-	23	⊃5763	28265
44E[2]	21-	23	⊃5764	28266
45E[2]	21-	23	⊃5765	28267
46E[2]	21-	23	⊃5766	28268
47E[2]	21-	23	⊃5767	28269
48E	21-	23	⊃5768	28270
49E	21-	23	⊃5769	28271
50E	21-	23	⊃5770	28272
51E	21-	23	⊃5771	28273
52E	21-	23	⊃5772	28274
53E	21-	23	⊃5773	28275
54E	21-	23	⊃5774	28276
55E	21-	23	⊃5775	28277
56E	21-	23	⊃5776	28278
57E	21-	23	⊃5777	28279
58E	21-	23	⊃5778	28280
59E	21-	23	⊃5779	28281
60E	21-	23	⊃5780	28282
61E	21-	23	⊃5781	28283
62E	21-	23	⊃5782	28284
63E	21-	23	⊃5783	28285
64E	21-	23	⊃5784	28286
65E	21-	23	⊃5785	28287
66E	21-	23	⊃5786	28288
67E	21-	23	⊃5787	28289
68E	21-	23	⊃5788	28290
69E	21-	23	⊃5789	28291
70E	21-	23	⊃5790	28292
71E	21-	23	⊃5791	28293
72E	21-	23	⊃5792	28294

LNWR London Metropolitan CW&F
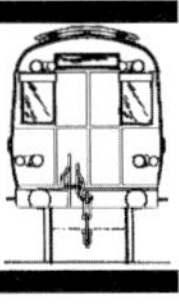
Driving Motor Brake Third
DMBT
250E-253E

For details see LMS 28261-28263 & 28000

250E	15-	23	⊃5793	28261	⊂44E
251E	15-	23	⊃5794	28262	⊂43E
252E	15-	23	⊃5795	28263	⊂46E
253E	15-	23	⊃5796	28000	⊂45E

LNWR London Metropolitan CW&F
Driving Motor Brake Third
DMBT
254E

For details see LMS 28295

254E 21- 23 ⊃5797 28295

LNWR London Metropolitan CW&F
Driving Motor Brake Third
DMBT
255E

For details see LMS 28264

255E 15- 23 ⊃5798 28264 ⊂47E

LNWR London Metropolitan CW&F
Driving Motor Brake Third
DMBT
256E-257E

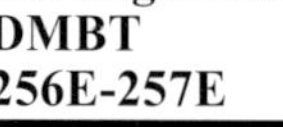

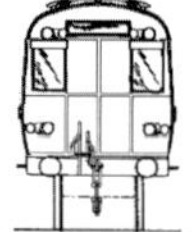

For details see LMS 28296-28297

256E 21- 23 ⊃5799 28296
257E 21- 23 ⊃5800 28297

LNWR London Metropolitan CW&F
TC
301E-304E

For details see LMS 29721-29724

301E 14- 23 ⊃8801 29721
302E 14- 23 ⊃8802 29722
303E 14- 23 ⊃8803 29723
304E 14- 23 ⊃8804 29724

LNWR London Wolverton
Trailer Composite
TC
305E-342E

For details see LMS 29725-29762

305E 15- 23 ⊃8805 29725
306E 15- 23 ⊃8806 29726
307E 15- 23 ⊃8807 29727
308E 15- 23 ⊃8808
309E 15- 23 ⊃8809 29729
310E 15- 23 ⊃8810 29730
311E 15- 23 ⊃8811 29731
312E 15- 23 ⊃8812 29732
313E 15- 23 ⊃8813 29733
314E 15- 23 ⊃8814 29734
315E 15- 23 ⊃8815 29735
316E 15- 23 ⊃8816 29736
317E 15- 23 ⊃8817 29737
318E 15- 23 ⊃8818 29738
319E 15- 23 ⊃8819 29739
320E 15- 23 ⊃8820 29740
321E 15- 23 ⊃8821 29741
322E 15- 23 ⊃8822 29742
323E 15- 23 ⊃8823 29743
324E 15- 23 ⊃8824 29744
325E 15- 23 ⊃8825 29745
326E 15- 23 ⊃8826 29746
327E 15- 23 ⊃8827 29747
328E 15- 23 ⊃8828 29748
329E 15- 23 ⊃8829 29749
330E 15- 23 ⊃8830 29750
331E 15- 23 ⊃8831 29751
332E 15- 23 ⊃8832 29752
333E 15- 23 ⊃8833 29753
334E 15- 23 ⊃8834 29754
335E 15- 23 ⊃8835 29755
336E 15- 23 ⊃8836 29756
337E 15- 23 ⊃8837 29757
338E 15- 23 ⊃8838 29758
339E 15- 23 ⊃8839 29759
340E 15- 23 ⊃8840 29760
341E 15- 23 ⊃8841 29761
342E 15- 23 ⊃8842 29762

LNWR London Wolverton
Trailer Composite
TC
343E-372E

For details see LMS 29763-29792

343E 21- 23 ⊃8843 29763
344E 21- 23 ⊃8844 29764
345E 21- 23 ⊃8845 29765
346E 21- 23 ⊃8846 29766
347E 21- 23 ⊃8847 29767
348E 21- 23 ⊃8848 29768
349E 21- 23 ⊃8849 29769
350E 21- 23 ⊃8850 29770
351E 21- 23 ⊃8851 29771
352E 21- 23 ⊃8852 29772
353E 21- 23 ⊃8853 29773
354E 21- 23 ⊃8854 29774
355E 21- 23 ⊃8855 29775
356E 21- 23 ⊃8856 29776
357E 21- 23 ⊃8857 29777
358E 21- 23 ⊃8858 29778
359E 21- 23 ⊃8859 29779
360E 21- 23 ⊃8860 29780
361E 21- 23 ⊃8861 29781
362E 21- 23 ⊃8862 29782
363E 21- 23 ⊃8863 29783
364E 21- 23 ⊃8864 29784
365E 21- 23 ⊃8865 29785
366E 21- 23 ⊃8866 29786
367E 21- 23 ⊃8867 29787
368E 21- 23 ⊃8868 29788
369E 21- 23 ⊃8869 29789
370E 21- 23 ⊃8870 29790
371E 21- 23 ⊃8871 29791
372E 21- 23 ⊃8872 29792

LNWR London Metropolitan CW&F
Driving Trailer Third
DTT/DTSO
601E-604E

For details see LMS 29021-29024

601E 14- 23 ⊃9941 29021
602E 14- 23 ⊃9942 29022
603E 14- 23 ⊃9943 29023
604E 14- 23 ⊃9944 29024

LNWR London Wolverton
Driving Trailer Third
DTT
605E-642E

For details see LMS 29025-29062

605E 15- 23 ⊃9945 29025
606E 15- 23 ⊃9946 29026
607E 15- 23 ⊃9947 29027
608E 15- 23 ⊃9948
609E 15- 23 ⊃9949 29029
610E 15- 23 ⊃9950 29030
611E 15- 23 ⊃9951 29031
612E 15- 23 ⊃9952 29032
613E 15- 23 ⊃9953 29033
614E 15- 23 ⊃9954 29034
615E 15- 23 ⊃9955 29035
616E 15- 23 ⊃9956 29036
617E 15- 23 ⊃9957 29037
618E 15- 23 ⊃9958 29038
619E 15- 23 ⊃9959 29039
620E 15- 23 ⊃9960 29040
621E 15- 23 ⊃9961 29041

622E	15-	23	**⊃9962**	29042
623E	15-	23	**⊃9963**	29052
624E	15-	23	**⊃9964**	29053
625E	15-	23	**⊃9965**	29054
626E	15-	23	**⊃9966**	29055
627E	15-	23	**⊃9967**	29056
628E	15-	23	**⊃9968**	29057
629E	15-	23	**⊃9969**	29058
630E	15-	23	**⊃9970**	29059
631E	15-	23	**⊃9971**	29060
632E	15-	23	**⊃9972**	29061
633E	15-	23	**⊃9973**	29043
634E	15-	23	**⊃9974**	29044
635E	15-	23	**⊃9975**	29045
636E	15-	23	**⊃9976**	29046
637E	15-	23	**⊃9977**	29047
638E	15-	23	**⊃9978**	29048
639E	15-	23	**⊃9979**	29049
640E	15-	23	**⊃9980**	29050
641E	15-	23	**⊃9981**	29051
642E	15-	23	**⊃9982**	29062

LNWR London Wolverton
Driving Trailer Third
DTT
643E-672E

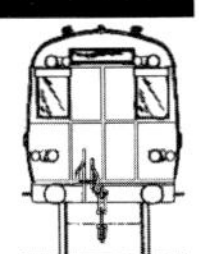

For details see LMS 29063-29092

643E	21-	23	**⊃9983**	29063
644E	21-	23	**⊃9984**	29064
645E	21-	23	**⊃9985**	29065
646E	21-	23	**⊃9986**	29066
647E	21-	23	**⊃9987**	29067
648E	21-	23	**⊃9988**	29068
649E	21-	23	**⊃9989**	29069
650E	21-	23	**⊃9990**	29070
651E	21-	23	**⊃9991**	29071
652E	21-	23	**⊃9992**	29072
653E	21-	23	**⊃9993**	29073
654E	21-	23	**⊃9994**	29074
655E	21-	23	**⊃9995**	29075
656E	21-	23	**⊃9996**	29076
657E	21-	23	**⊃9997**	29077
658E	21-	23	**⊃9998**	29078
659E	21-	23	**⊃9999**	29079
660E	21-	23	**⊃10000**	29080
661E	21-	23	**⊃10001**	29081
662E	21-	23	**⊃10002**	29082
663E	21-	23	**⊃10003**	29083
664E	21-	23	**⊃10004**	29084
665E	21-	23	**⊃10005**	29085
666E	21-	23	**⊃10006**	29086
667E	21-	23	**⊃10007**	29087
668E	21-	23	**⊃10008**	29088
669E	21-	23	**⊃10009**	29089
670E	21-	23	**⊃10010**	29090
671E	21-	23	**⊃10011**	29091
672E	21-	23	**⊃10012**	29092

Tube Joint Metropolitan CW&F
Driving Motor Brake Third
DMBT
Between 1J & 36J

For details see LMS 28213-28218

1J	20-			
2J	20-			
3J	20-			
4J	20-			
5J	20-	23	**⊃2394**	28213
6J	20-			
7J	20-			
8J	20-			
9J	20-			
10J	20-			
11J	20-			
12J	20-	23	**⊃2415**	28214
13J	20-			
14J	20-			
15J	20-			
16J	20-	23	**⊃2416**	28215
17J	20-			
18J	20-			
19J	20-			
20J	20-			
21J	20-			
22J	20-			
23J	20-			
24J	20-			
25J	20-			
26J	20-			
27J	20-			
28J	20-			
29J	20-			
30J	20-			
31J	20-	23	**⊃770**	28217
32J	20-	23	**⊃825**	28218
33J	20-			
34J	20-			
35J	20-	23	**⊃904**	28216
36J	20-			

Tube Joint Metropolitan CW&F
Trailer Third
TT
201J-224J

For details see LMS 29497-29498

201J	20-			
202J	20-			
203J	20-			
204J	20-			
205J	20-			
206J	20-			
207J	20-			
208J	20-			
209J	20-			
210J	20-			
211J	20-			
212J	20-			
213J	20-	23	**⊃593**	29498
214J	20-	23	**⊃337**	29497
215J	20-			
216J	20-			
217J	20-			
218J	20-			
219J	20-			
220J	20-			
221J	20-			
222J	20-			
223J	20-			
224J	20-			

Tube Joint Metropolitan CW&F
Driving Trailer Third
DTT
401J-412J

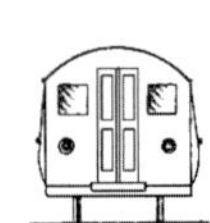

For details see LMS 29499

401J	20-	23	**⊃640**	29499
402J	20-			
403J	20-			
404J	20-			
405J	20-			
406J	20-			
407J	20-			
408J	20-			
409J	20-			
410J	20-			
411J	20-			
412J	20-			

LNER Railway 1943 Numbering

From 1965 onwards all the Tyneside units carried the **NE** prefix.

Tyneside Metropolitan-Cammell
Driving Motor Third
DMT
E29101E-E29112

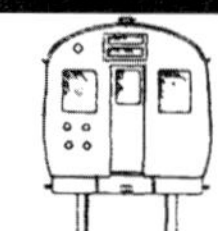

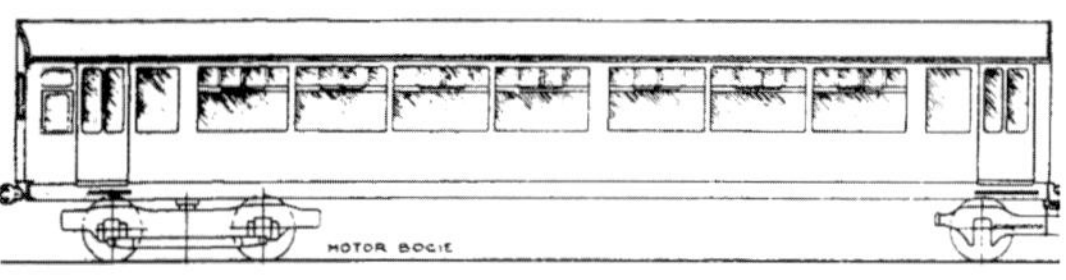

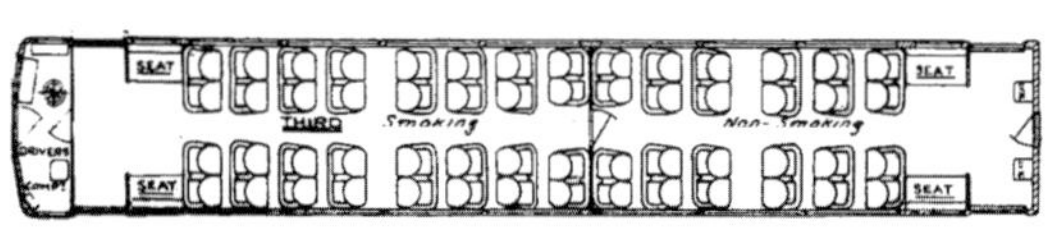

Diagram:	234	LNER Class:	MS3
Body:	55' 9" × 9' 0¾"	Weight:	54t 19cwt unit
Seats:	64 third	Bogies:	LNER Articulated
Motors:	Crompton Parkinson 2 × 154hp		

E29101E	43-04/67 ⊗		⊂24145
E29102E	43-06/67 ⊗		⊂24147
E29103E	43-04/67 ⊗		⊂24149
E29104E	43-04/67 ⊗		⊂24151
E29105E	43-06/67 ⊗		⊂24153
E29106E	43-06/67 ⊗		⊂24155
E29107E	43-06/67 ⊗		⊂24157
E29108E	43-04/67 ⊗		⊂24159
E29109E	43-04/67 ⊗		⊂24161
E29110E	43-04/67 ⊗		⊂24163
E29111E	43-06/67 ⊗		⊂24165
E29112	43-08/51	⊃29131	⊂24167

Tyneside Metropolitan-Cammell
Driving Motor Brake Third
DMBT
E29113E-E29128E

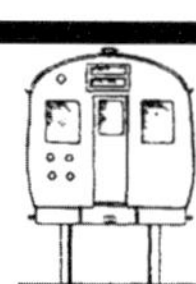

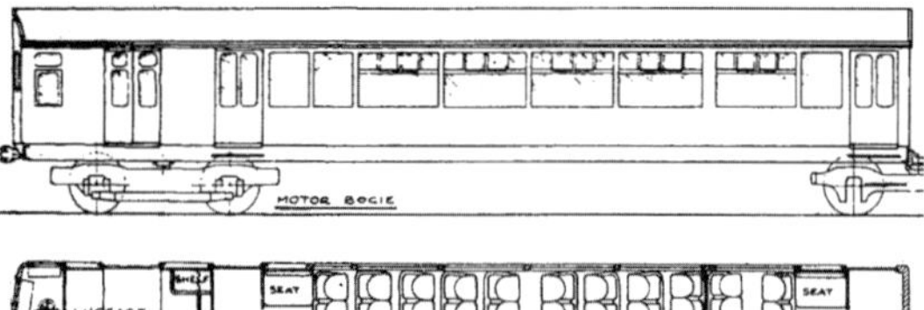

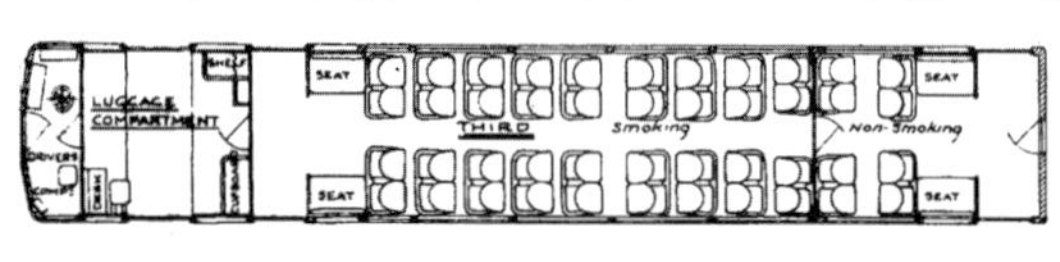

Diagram:	233	LNER Class:	LMS3
Body:	55' 9" × 9' 0¾"	Weight:	55t 7cwt unit
Seats:	52 third	Bogies:	LNER Articulated
Motors:	Crompton Parkinson 2 × 154hp		

E29113E	43-06/67 ⊗	⊂24169
E29114E	43-06/67 ⊗	⊂24171
E29115E	43-06/67 ⊗	⊂24173
E29116E	43-06/67 ⊗	⊂24175
E29117E	43-06/67 ⊗	⊂24177
E29118E	43-06/67 ⊗	⊂24179
E29119E	43-06/67 ⊗	⊂24181
E29120E	43-06/67 ⊗	⊂24183
E29121E	43-06/67 ⊗	⊂24185
E29122E	43-06/67 ⊗	⊂24187
E29123E	43-06/67 ⊗	⊂24189
E29124E	43-06/67 ⊗	⊂24191
E29125E	43-06/67 ⊗	⊂24193
E29126E	43-04/67 ⊗	⊂24195
E29127E	43-06/67 ⊗	⊂24197
E29128E	43-06/67 ⊗	⊂24199

Tyneside Metropolitan-Cammell
Driving Motor Third
DMT
E29129E-E29146E

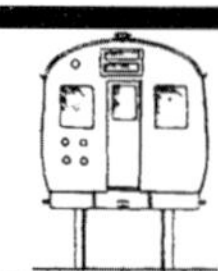

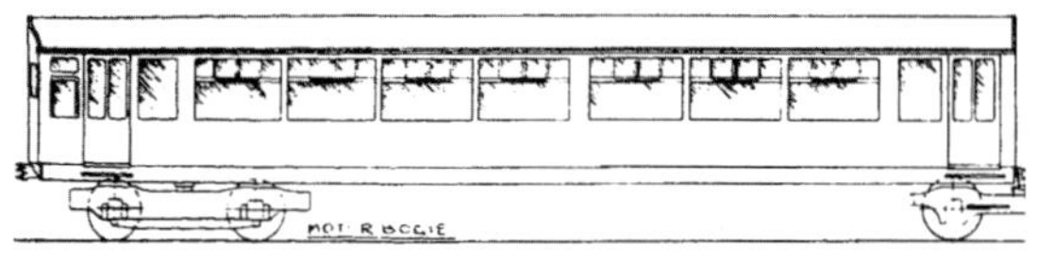

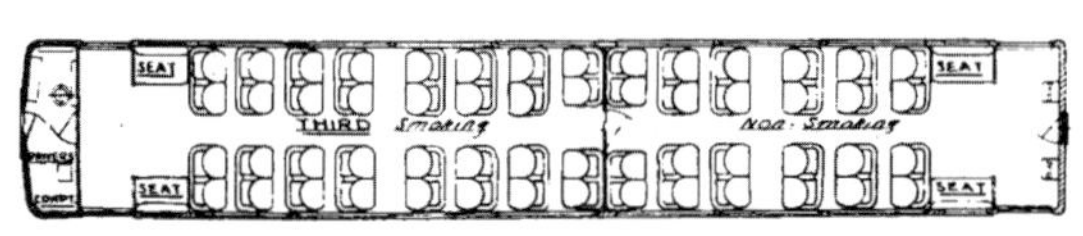

Diagram:	235	LNER Class:	MS3
Body:	55' 9" × 9' 0¾"	Weight:	53t 12cwt unit
Seats:	64 third	Bogies:	LNER Articulated
Motors:	Crompton Parkinson 2 × 154hp		

E29129E	43-06/64 ⊗	⊂24201
E29130E	43-04/67 ⊗	⊂24203
E29131	43-08/51 ⊗	⊂24205
E29131E[2]	08/51-06/64 ⊗	⊂29112
E29132E	43-06/67 ⊗	⊂24207
E29133E	43-06/64 ⊗	⊂24209
E29134E	43-04/67 ⊗	⊂24211
E29135E	43-06/64 ⊗	⊂24213
E29136E	43-04/67 ⊗	⊂24215
E29137E	43-06/64 ⊗	⊂24217
E29138E	43-04/67 ⊗	⊂24219
E29139E	43-06/64 ⊗	⊂24221
E29140E	43-06/64 ⊗	⊂24223
E29141E	43-06/64 ⊗	⊂24225
E29142E	43-06/64 ⊗	⊂24227
29143	- 40 ⊗	⊂24229
E29144E	43-06/67 ⊗	⊂24231
E29145E	43-06/64 ⊗	⊂24233
E29146E	43-06/64 ⊗	⊂24235

Tyneside Metropolitan-Cammell
Trailer Composite
TC
E29147E-E29164E

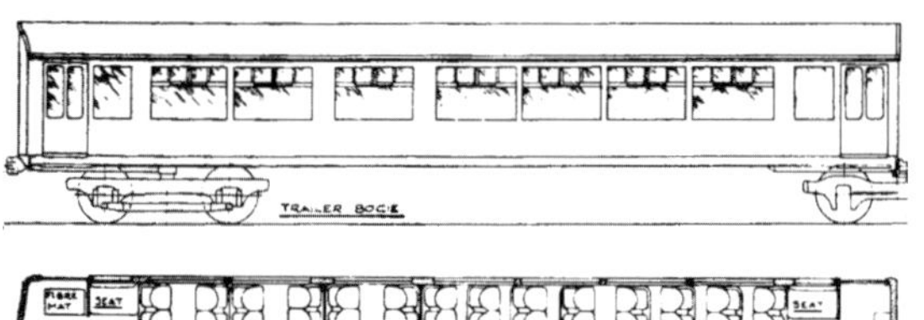

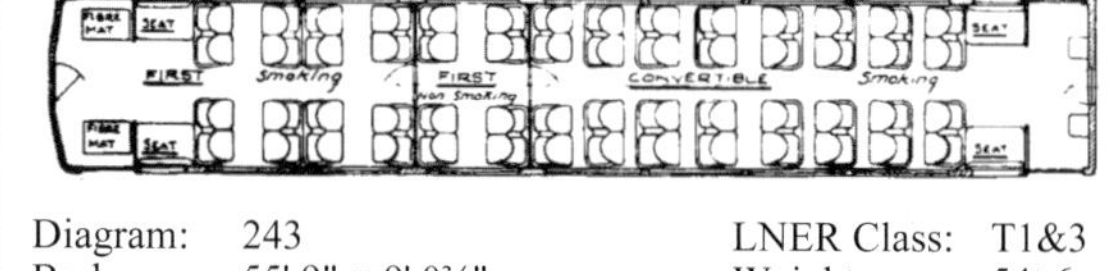

Diagram:	243	LNER Class:	T1&3
Body:	55' 9" × 9' 0¾"	Weight:	54t 6cwt unit
Seats:	28 first 36 convertible	Bogies:	LNER Articulated

E29147E	43-06/67 ⊗	⊂24237
E29148E	43-04/67 ⊗	⊂24239
E29149E	43-06/67 ⊗	⊂24241
E29150E	43-06/64 ⊗	⊂24243
E29151E	43-04/67 ⊗	⊂24245
E29152E	43-06/67 ⊗	⊂24247
E29153E	43-04/67 ⊗	⊂24249
E29154E	43-06/64 ⊗	⊂24251
E29155E	43-06/64 ⊗	⊂24253
E29156E	43-06/67 ⊗	⊂24255
E29157E	43-04/67 ⊗	⊂24257
E29158E	43-04/67 ⊗	⊂24259
E29159E	43-06/67 ⊗	⊂24261
E29160E	43-06/67 ⊗	⊂24263
E29161E	43-06/67 ⊗	⊂24265
E29162E	43-06/64 ⊗	⊂24267
E29163E	43-06/67 ⊗	⊂24269
E29164E	43-06/67 ⊗	⊂24271

Tyneside Metropolitan-Cammell
Driving Motor Brake Third
DMBT
E29165E-E29166E

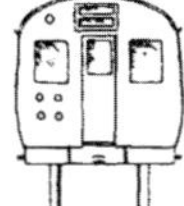

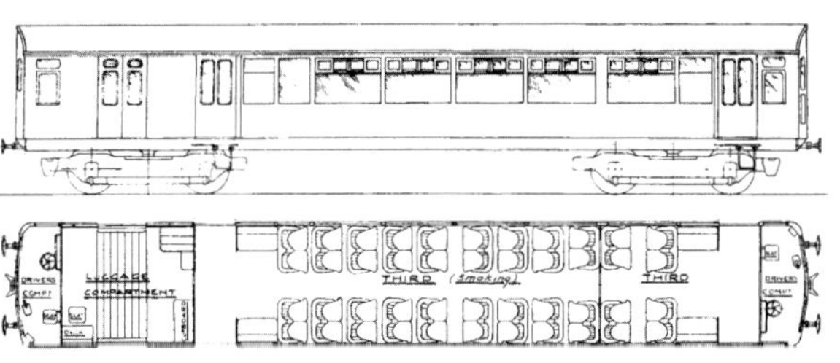

Diagram:	280	LNER Class:	LMD3
Body:	59' 0" × 9' 0¾"	Weight:	47t 4cwt (29165)
Seats:	52 third		47t 5cwt (29166)
Motors:	Crompton Parkinson 2 × 154hp	Bogies:	LNER 2 axle

E29165E	43-05/67 ⊗	⊂24273
E29166E	43-05/67 ⊗	⊂24274

Tyneside York
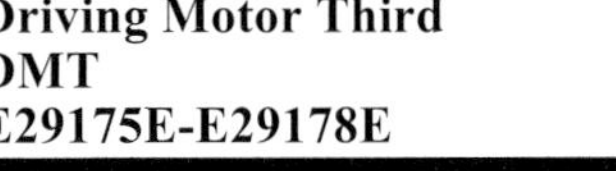

Driving Motor Third
DMT
E29175E-E29178E

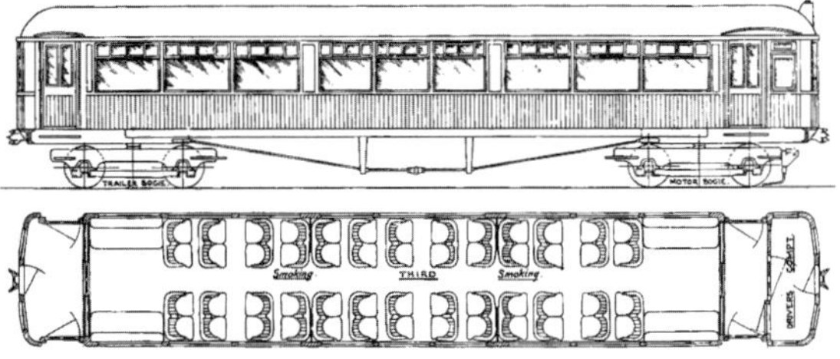

Diagram:	221	LNER Class:	MS3
Body:	56' 6" × 9' 2½"	Weight:	variable (33t)
Seats:	64 third	Bogies:	NER
Motors:	Crompton Parkinson 2 × 154hp		

Renovated in 1938.

E29175E	43- 55 ⊗	⊂23212
E29176E	43- 55 ⊗	⊂23219
E29177E	43- 55 ⊗	⊂23221
E29178E	43- 55 ⊗	⊂23225

Tyneside York
Driving Motor Third
DMT
E29179E-E29183E

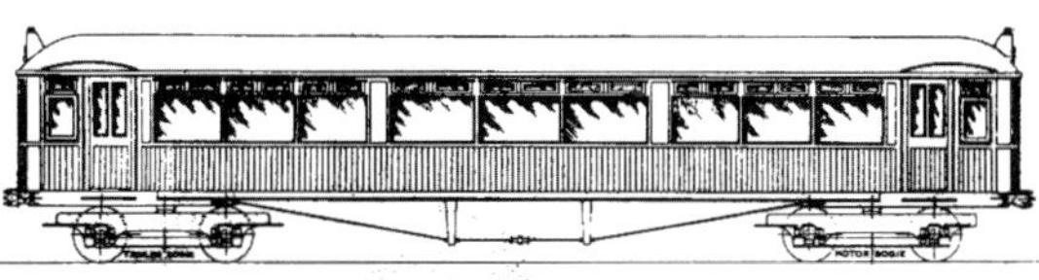

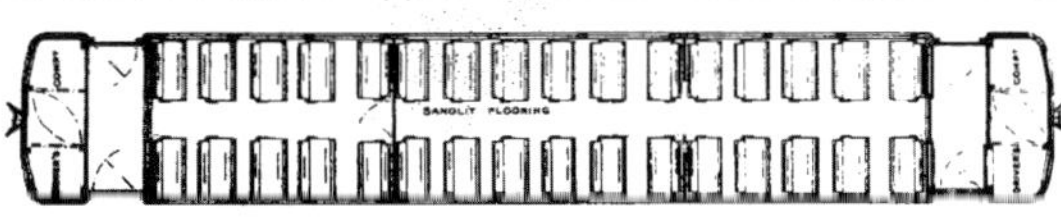

Diagram:	223 (mod)	LNER Class:	MS3
Body:	56' 6" × 9' 2½"	Weight:	
Seats:	60 third	Bogies:	NER
Motors:	Crompton Parkinson 2 × 154hp		

E29179E	43- 55 ⊗	⊂23226
E29180E	43- 55 ⊗	⊂23227
E29181E	43- 55 ⊗	⊂23228
E29182E	43- 55 ⊗	⊂23520
E29183E	43- 55 ⊗	⊂23521

Tyneside York
Driving Motor Brake Composite
DMBC
E29184E-E29185E

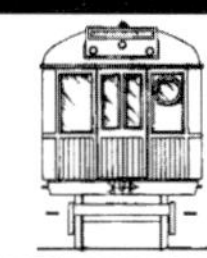

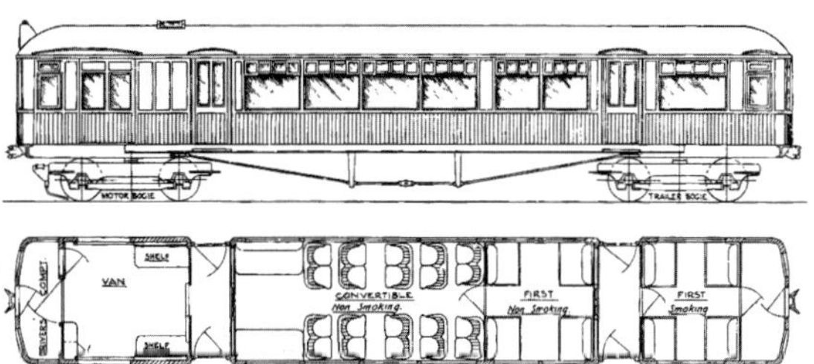

Diagram:	219	LNER Class:	LMD1
Body:	56' 6" × 9' 2½"	Weight:	34t 17cwt
Seats:	20 first 28 convertible	Bogies:	NER
Motors:	Crompton Parkinson 2 × 154hp		

Converted in1938 to LMS1. 16 first 26 convertible 34t 3cwt.

E29184E	43-03/55 ⊗	⊂23238
E29185E	43-05/55 ⊗	⊂23241

Tyneside York
Driving Motor Brake Composite
DMBC
E29186E-E29191E

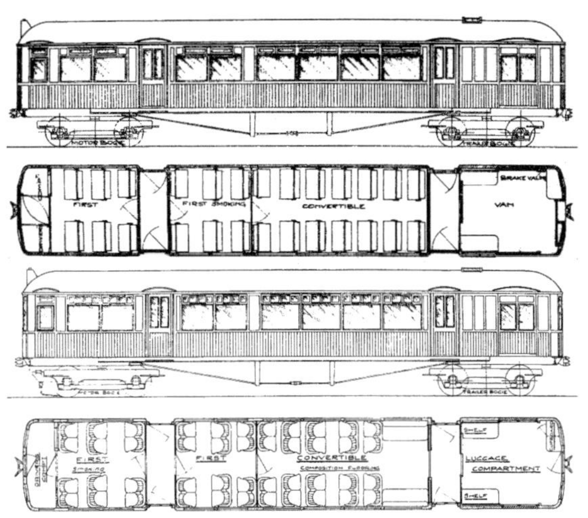

Diagram:	132 then 281	LNER Class:	LMS1
Body:	56' 6" × 9' 2½"	Weight:	33t 17cwt
Seats:	24 first 28 convertible,		then 34t 3cwt
	then 24 first 26 convertible	Bogies:	NER
Motors:	Crompton Parkinson 2 × 154hp		

Converted in 1938

E29186E	43- 55 ⊗	⊂23243
E29187E	43- 55 ⊗	⊂23246
E29189E	43- 55 ⊗	⊂23250
E29190E	43- 55 ⊗	⊂23251
E29191E	43- 55 ⊗	⊂23253

Tyneside York
Driving Motor Brake Composite
DMBC
E29192E

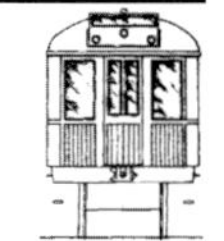

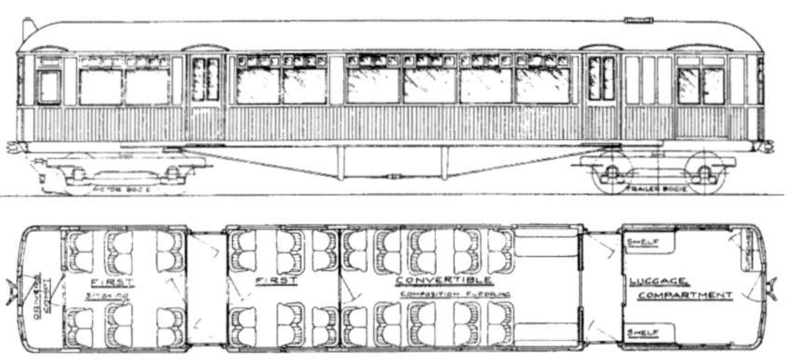

Diagram: 281 LNER Class: LMS1
Body: 56' 6" × 9' 2½" Weight: 34t 3cwt
Seats: 24 first 26 convertible Bogies: NER
Motors: Crompton Parkinson 2 × 154hp

E29192E 43- 55 ⊗ ⊂**24465**

Tyneside Metropolitan-Cammell
Trailer Third
TT
E29229E-E29246E

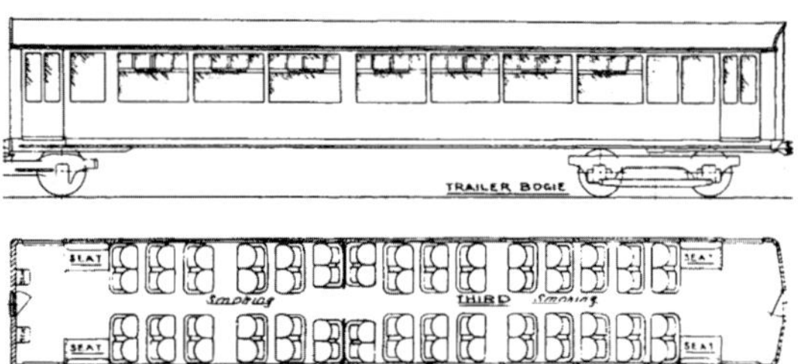

Diagram: 235 LNER Class: T3
Body: 55' 9" × 9' 0¾" Weight: 53t 12cwt unit
Seats: 68 third Bogies: LNER Articulated

E29229E 43-06/64 ⊗ ⊂**24202**
E29230E 43-04/67 ⊗ ⊂**24204**
E29231E 43-06/64 ⊗ ⊂**24206**
E29232E 43-06/67 ⊗ ⊂**24208**
E29233E 43-06/64 ⊗ ⊂**24210**
E29234E 43-04/67 ⊗ ⊂**24212**
E29235E 43-06/64 ⊗ ⊂**24214**
E29236E 43-04/67 ⊗ ⊂**24216**
E29237E 43-06/64 ⊗ ⊂**24218**
E29238E 43-04/67 ⊗ ⊂**24220**
E29239E 43-06/64 ⊗ ⊂**24222**
E29240E 43-06/64 ⊗ ⊂**24224**
E29241E 43-06/64 ⊗ ⊂**24226**
E29242E 43-06/64 ⊗ ⊂**24228**
29243 - 40 ⊗ ⊂**24230**
E29244E 43-06/67 ⊗ ⊂**24232**
E29245E 43-06/64 ⊗ ⊂**24234**
E29246E 43-06/64 ⊗ ⊂**24236**

Tyneside Metropolitan-Cammell
Driving Motor Brake Third
DMBT
E29247E-E29264E

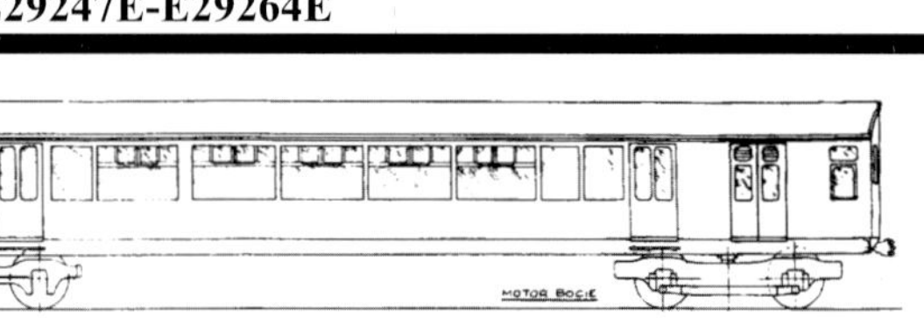

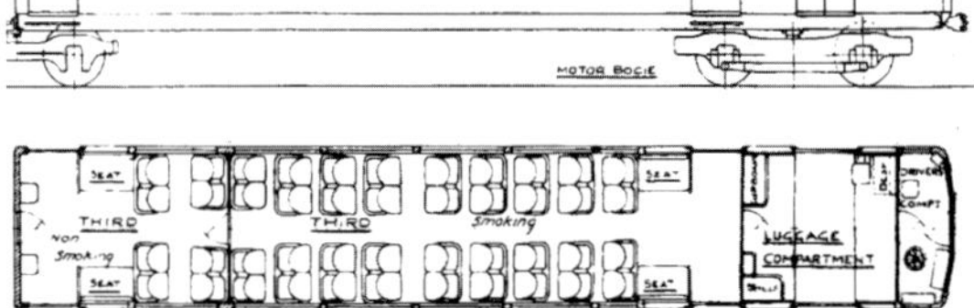

Diagram: 243 LNER Class: LMS3
Body: 55' 9" × 9' 0¾" Weight: 54t 6cwt unit
Seats: 52 third Bogies: LNER Articulated
Motors: Crompton Parkinson 2 × 154hp

E29247E 43-06/67 ⊗ ⊂**24238**
E29248E 43-04/67 ⊗ ⊂**24240**
E29249E 43-06/67 ⊗ ⊂**24242**
E29250E 43-06/64 ⊗ ⊂**24244**
E29251E 43-04/67 ⊗ ⊂**24246**
E29252E 43-06/67 ⊗ ⊂**24248**
E29253E 43-04/67 ⊗ ⊂**24250**
E29254E 43-06/64 ⊗ ⊂**24252**
E29255E 43-06/64 ⊗ ⊂**24254**
E29256E 43-06/67 ⊗ ⊂**24256**
E29257E 43-04/67 ⊗ ⊂**24258**
E29258E 43-04/67 ⊗ ⊂**24260**
E29259E 43-06/67 ⊗ ⊂**24262**
E29260E 43-06/67 ⊗ ⊂**24264**
E29261E 43-06/67 ⊗ ⊂**24266**
E29262E 43-06/64 ⊗ ⊂**24268**
E29263E 43-06/67 ⊗ ⊂**24270**
E29264E 43-06/67 ⊗ ⊂**24272**

Tyneside York
Controlled set Trailer Composite
E29269E

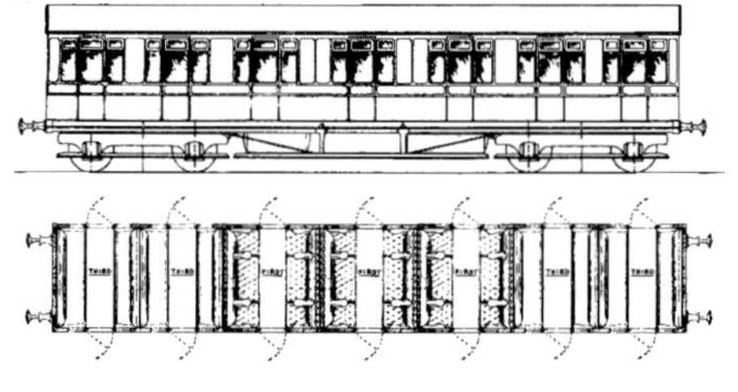

Diagram: 146 Weight:
Body: Bogies: NER
Seats: 24 first 40 third

E29269E 43-02/61 ⊗06/64 ⊂**23694**

Tyneside York
Controlled set Trailer Third
E29270E-E29274E

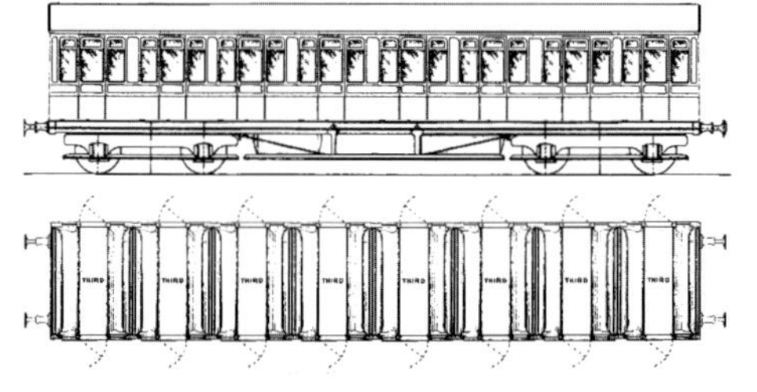

Diagram: 149 Weight:
Body: 49' Bogies: NER
Seats: 80 third

E29270E 43-02/61 ⊗05/62 ⊂**23731**
E29271E 43-02/61 ⊗12/61 ⊂**23733**
E29272E 43-02/61 ⊗08/61 ⊂**23744**
E29273E 43-02/61 ⊗05/62 ⊂**23745**
E29274E 43-02/61 ⊗12/61 ⊂**23747**

Tyneside Metropolitan-Cammell
Driving Trailer Third
DTT
E29301E-E29312E

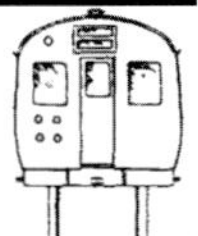

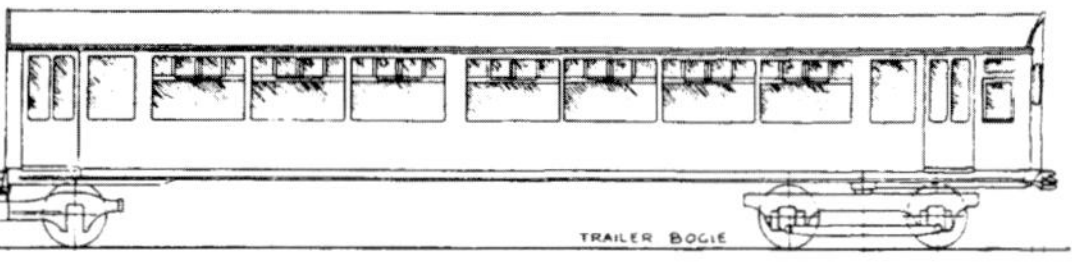

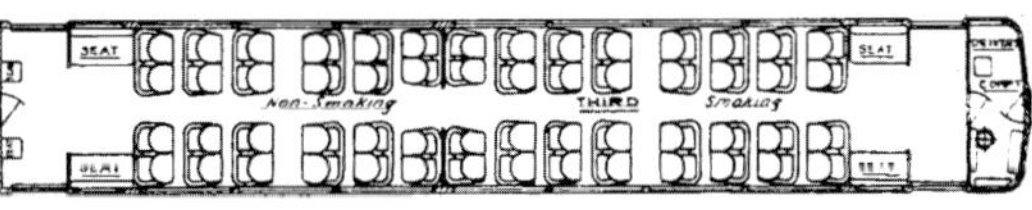

Diagram:	234	LNER Class:	TS3
Body:	55' 9" × 9' 0¾"	Weight:	54t 19cwt unit
Seats:	64 third	Bogies:	LNER Articulated

E29301E	43-04/67	⊗	⊂24146
E29302E	43-06/67	⊗	⊂24148
E29303E	43-04/67	⊗	⊂24150
E29304E	43-04/67	⊗	⊂24152
E29305E	43-06/67	⊗	⊂24154
E29306E	43-06/67	⊗	⊂24156
E29307E	43-06/67	⊗	⊂24158
E29308E	43-04/67	⊗	⊂24160
E29309E	43-04/67	⊗	⊂24162
E29310E	43-04/67	⊗	⊂24164
E29311E	43-06/67	⊗	⊂24166
E29312E	43-08/51	⊗	⊂24168

Tyneside Metropolitan-Cammell
Driving Trailer Composite
DTC
E29313E-E29328E

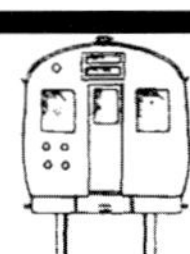

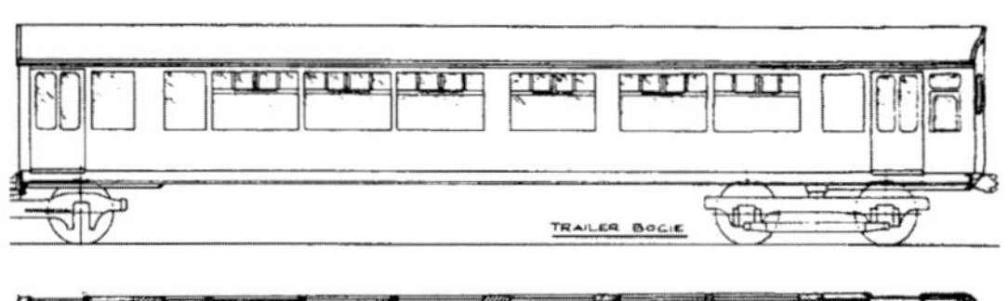

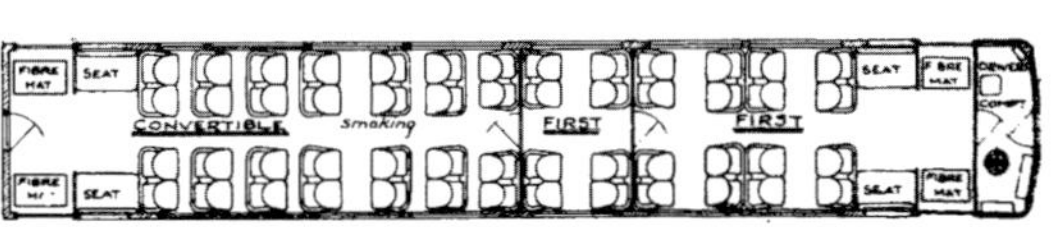

Diagram:	233	LNER Class:	TS1&3
Body:	55' 9" × 9' 0¾"	Weight:	55t 7cwt unit
Seats:	28 first 32 convertible	Bogies:	LNER Articulated

E29313E	43-06/67	⊗	⊂24170
E29314E	43-06/67	⊗	⊂24172
E29315E	43-06/67	⊗	⊂24174
E29316E	43-06/67	⊗	⊂24176
E29317E	43-06/67	⊗	⊂24178
E29318E	43-06/67	⊗	⊂24180
E29319E	43-06/67	⊗	⊂24182
E29320E	43-06/67	⊗	⊂24184
E29321E	43-06/67	⊗	⊂24186
E29322E	43-06/67	⊗	⊂24188
E29323E	43-06/67	⊗	⊂24190
E29324E	43-06/67	⊗	⊂24192
E29325E	43-06/67	⊗	⊂24194
E29326E	43-04/67	⊗	⊂24196
E29327E	43-06/67	⊗	⊂24198
E29328E	43-06/67	⊗	⊂24200

Tyneside York
Driving Trailer Third
DTT
E29375E-E29389E

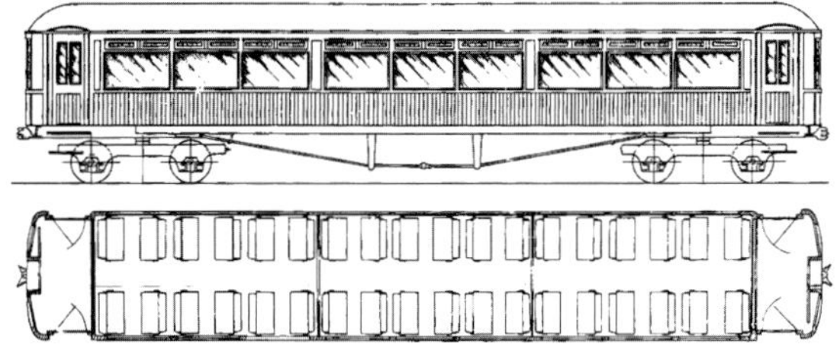

Diagram:	218	LNER Class:	TS3
Body:	56' 6" × 9' 2½"	Weight:	25t 8cwt
Seats:	72 third later 68 third	Bogies:	NER

E29375E	43-03/55	⊗	⊂23180
E29376E	43-07/62	⊗08/64	⊂23195
E29377E	43-03/55	⊗	⊂23197
E29378E	43-10/54	⊗	⊂23198
E29379E	43-03/55	⊗	⊂23204
E29380E	43-03/55	⊗	⊂23211
E29381E	43-03/55	⊗	⊂23507
E29382E	43-03/55	⊗	⊂23508
E29383E	43-03/55	⊗	⊂23512
E29384E	43-03/55	⊗	⊂23513
E29385E	43-03/55	⊗	⊂23518
E29386E	43-03/55	⊗	⊂23785
E29387E	43-07/62	⊗06/64	⊂23788
E29388E	43-05/60	⊗07/66 Grounded Shildon	⊂23790
E29389E	43-03/55	⊗	⊂23791

Tyneside York
Driving Trailer Third
DTT
E29390E

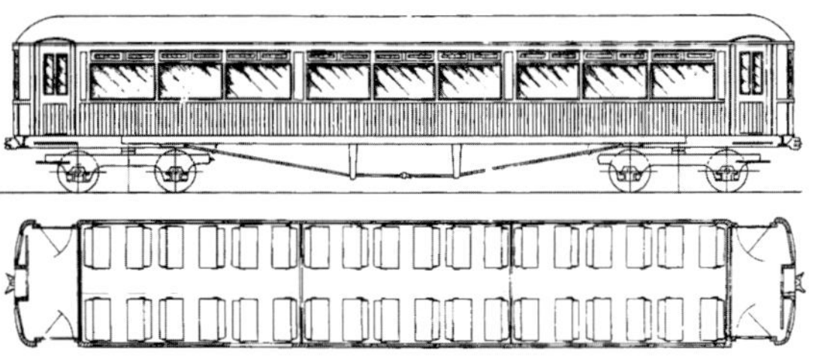

Diagram:	218 ex 221 Motor Third	LNER Class:	TS3
Body:	56' 6" × 9' 2½"	Weight:	26t 14cwt
Seats:	64 third	Bogies:	NER

E29390E	43-05/60	⊗11/60	⊂23217

Tyneside York
Driving Trailer Third
DTT
E29391E-E29392E

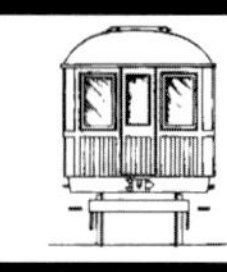

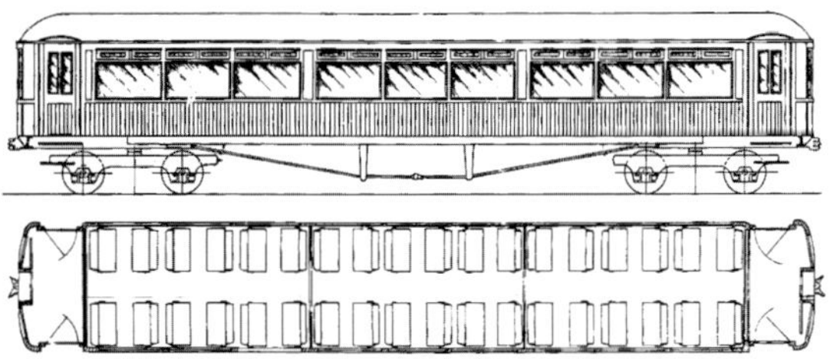

Diagram:	218 ex 97 or 175 Motor Third	LNER Class:	TS3
Body:	56' 6" × 9' 2½"	Weight:	
Seats:	60 third	Bogies:	NER

E29391E	43-03/55	⊗	⊂23268
E29392E	43-03/55	⊗	⊂23524

Tyneside Metropolitan-Cammell

Motor Luggage Van
MLV
E29467E-E29468E

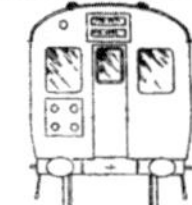

Diagram:	277		
Body:	59' 0" × 9' 0¾"	Weight:	38t 15cwt (29467)
Bogies:	LNER 2 axle		38t 18cwt (29468)
Motors:	Crompton Parkinson 4 × 154hp		

E29467E 43-06/67 ⊗ ⊂2424
E29468E 43-06/67 ⊗ ⊂2425

Tyneside York

Motor Luggage Van
MLV
E29493E

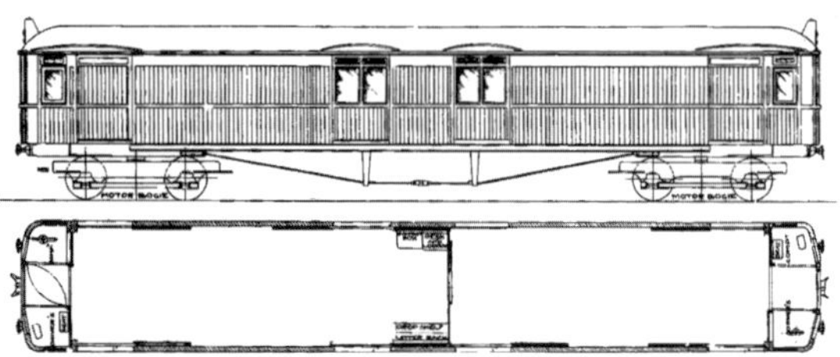

Diagram:	222	Weight:	39t 6cwt
Body:	56' 6" × 9' 2½"	Bogies:	NER
Motors:	Crompton Parkinson 2 × 154hp		

E29493E 43- 56 ⊗ ⊂23795

Class 506 Metropolitan-Cammell

Driving Motor Brake Second
DMBS
M59401-M59408 Manchester-Glossop-Hadfield

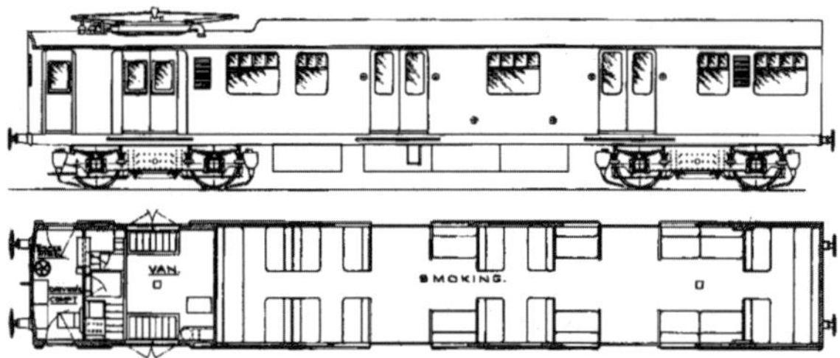

Diagram:	363 EB205	Weight:	50t 12cwt
Body:	60' 4¼" × 9' 3"	Bogies:	Thompson
Seats:	52 second	Motors:	GEC 4 × 185hp

The Manchester-Glossop-Hadfield units correctly carried the **E** prefix after nationalisation, but then later carried an **M** prefix without the correct **E** suffix, and later the incorrect **M** suffix.

59406 was renumbered 59408 for a while from April 1984 until withdrawal when it ran in that unit. Similarly 59401 carried the number 59402 on the cab end in October 1984.

M59401M 06/54-12/84 ⊗05/85
M59402M 06/54-12/84 ⊗05/85
M59403M 06/54-12/84 ⊗05/85
M59404M 06/54-12/84 ⓟ
M59405M 06/54-12/84 ⊗05/85

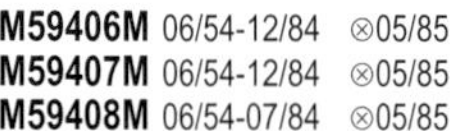

M59406M 06/54-12/84 ⊗05/85
M59407M 06/54-12/84 ⊗05/85
M59408M 06/54-07/84 ⊗05/85

Class 506 Metropolitan-Cammell

Trailer Composite later Trailer Second
TC later TS
M59501-M59508 Manchester-Glossop-Hadfield

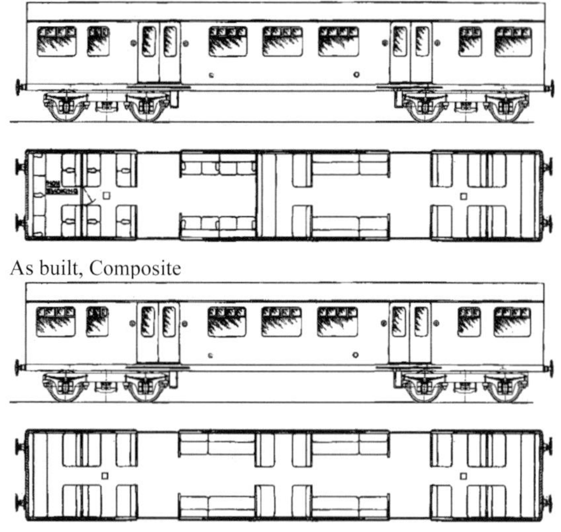

As built, Composite

Later downgraded

Diagram:	366 EH204	Weight:	26t 8cwt
Body:	55' 0½" × 9' 3"	Bogies:	Thompson
Seats:	24 first 38 second, later 62 second		

M59501M 06/54-12/84 ⊗05/85
M59502M 06/54-12/84 ⊗05/85
M59503M 06/54-12/84 ⊗05/85
M59504M 06/54-12/84 ⓟ
M59505M 06/54-12/84 ⊗05/85
M59506M 06/54-11/83 ⊗05/85
M59507M 06/54-12/84 ⊗05/85
M59508M 06/54-12/84 ⊗05/85

Class 506 Birmingham RC&W

Driving Trailer Second
DTS
M59601-M59608 Manchester-Glossop-Hadfield

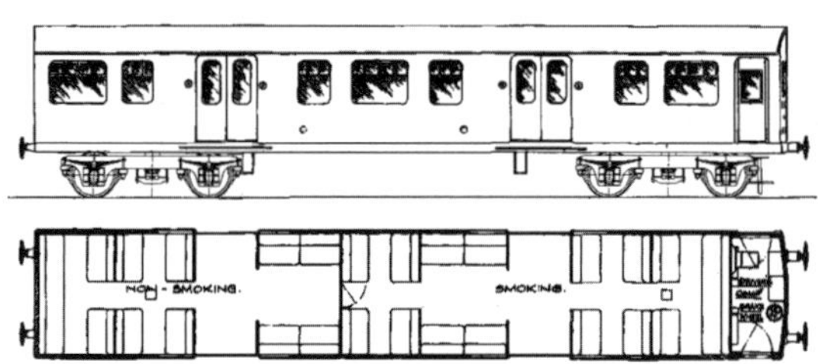

Diagram:	365 EE204	Weight:	27t 9cwt
Body:	55' 4¼" × 9' 3"	Bogies:	Thompson
Seats:	60 second		

M59601M 06/54-12/84 ⊗05/85
M59602M 06/54-12/84 ⊗05/85
M59603M 06/54-12/84 ⊗05/85
M59604M 06/54-12/84 ⓟ
M59605M 06/54-12/84 ⊗05/85
M59606M 06/54-11/83 ⊗05/85
M59607M 06/54-12/84 ⊗05/85
M59608M 06/54-12/84 ⊗05/85

Class 306 Metropolitan-Cammell

Driving Motor Brake Second
DMBTO later DMBSO
E65201-E65292 Shenfield

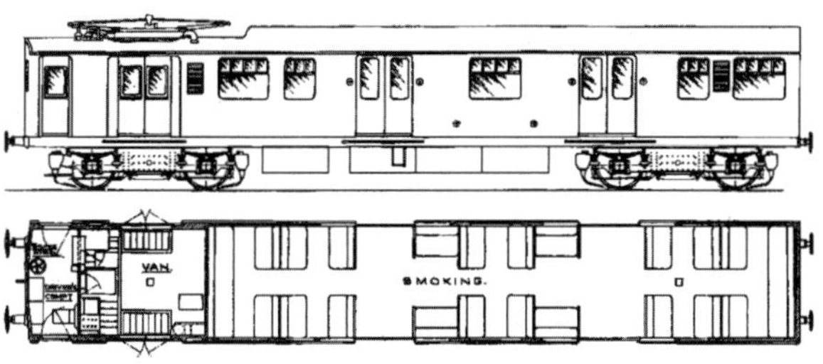

As built

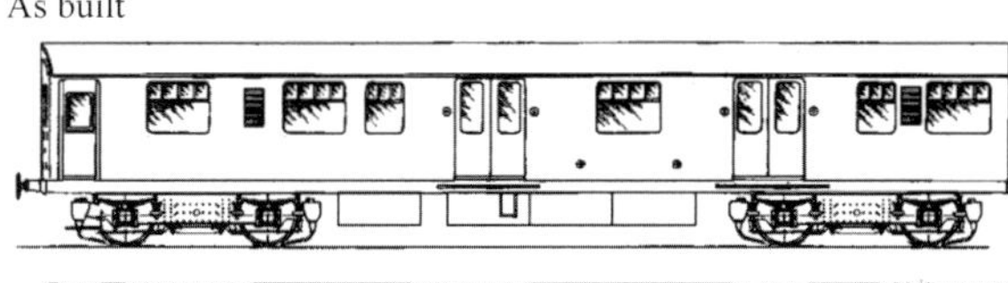

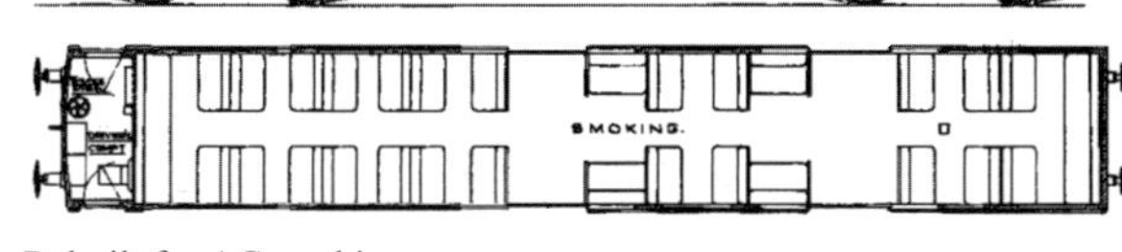

Rebuilt for AC working

Diagram:		Weight:	50t 12cwt
Body:	60' 4¼" × 9' 3"	Bogies:	Thompson
Seats:	48 third, later 62 second	Motors:	EE 504 4 × 210hp

The Shenfield units never carried the **E** suffix, but they carried a **GE** prefix in the early sixties.

E65201	11/49-04/81	⊗02/82	**01**	11/49-	*60*	**001**	*60*-04/81	
E65202	11/49-03/81	⊗09/81	**02**	11/49-	*60*	**002**	*60*-03/81	
E65203	11/49-03/81	⊗10/81	**03**	11/49-	*60*	**003**	*60*-08/80	
E65204	11/49-05/80	⊗07/82	**04**	11/49-	*60*	**004**	*60*-05/80	
E65205	11/49-11/81	⊗07/84	**05**	11/49-	*60*	**005**	*60*-11/81	
E65206	11/49-03/81	⊗10/81	**06**	11/49-	*60*	**006**	*60*-03/81	
E65207	11/49-09/81	⊗03/82	**07**	11/49-	*60*	**007**	*60*-09/81	
E65208	11/49-03/81	⊗10/81	**08**	11/49-	*60*	**008**	*60*-03/81	
E65209	11/49-04/81	⊗09/81	**09**	11/49-	*60*	**009**	*60*-04/81	
E65210	11/49-11/81	⊗07/84	**10**	11/49-	*60*	**010**	*60*-11/81	
E65211	11/49-03/81	⊗10/81	**11**	11/49-	*60*	**011**	*60*-03/81	
E65212	11/49-03/81	⊗09/81	**12**	11/49-	*60*	**012**	*60*-03/81	
E65213	11/49-03/81	⊗10/81	**13**	11/49-	*60*	**013**	*60*-03/81	
E65214	11/49-11/81	⊗07/84	**14**	11/49-	*60*	**014**	*60*-11/81	
E65215	11/49-11/81	⊗07/84	**15**	11/49-	*60*	**015**	*60*-11/81	
E65216	11/49-06/81	⊗09/82	**16**	11/49-	*60*	**016**	*60*-06/81	
E65217	11/49-11/81	Ⓟ	**17**	11/49-	*60*	**017**	*60*-11/81	
E65218	11/49-03/81	⊗10/81	**18**	11/49-	*60*	**018**	*60*-03/81	
E65219	11/49-08/81	⊗06/82	**19**	11/49-	*60*	**019**	*60*-08/81	
E65220	11/49-03/81	⊗10/81	**20**	11/49-	*60*	**020**	*60*-03/81	
E65221	11/49-08/81	⊗04/82	**21**	11/49-	*60*	**021**	*60*-08/81	
E65222	11/49-06/81	⊗04/82	**22**	11/49-	*60*	**022**	*60*-06/81	
E65223	11/49-05/81	⊗03/82	**23**	11/49-	*60*	**023**	*60*-05/81	
E65224	11/49-03/81	⊗10/81	**24**	11/49-	*60*	**024**	*60*-03/81	
E65225	11/49-03/81	⊗09/81	**25**	11/49-	*60*	**025**	*60*-03/81	
E65226	11/49-06/81	⊗03/82	**26**	11/49-	*60*	**026**	*60*-06/81	
E65227	11/49-03/81	⊗10/81	**27**	11/49-	*60*	**027**	*60*-03/81	
E65228	11/49-08/81	⊗08/82	**28**	11/49-	*60*	**028**	*60*-08/81	
E65229	11/49-08/81	⊗03/82	**29**	11/49-	*60*	**029**	*60*-08/81	
E65230	11/49-04/68	⊗ 70	**30**	11/49-	*60*	**030**	*60*-04/68	
E65231	11/49-09/81	⊗04/82	**31**	11/49-	*60*	**031**	*60*-09/81	
E65232	11/49-06/81	⊗03/85	**32**	11/49-	*60*	**032**	*60*-06/81	
E65233	11/49-08/81	⊗09/82	**33**	11/49-	*60*	**033**	*60*-08/81	
E65234	11/49-11/81	⊗09/84	**34**	11/49-	*60*	**034**	*60*-11/81	
E65235	11/49-03/81	⊗10/81	**35**	11/49-	*60*	**035**	*60*-03/81	
E65236	11/49-08/81	⊗01/82	**36**	11/49-	*60*	**036**	*60*-03/81	
E65237	11/49-11/81	⊗10/82	**37**	11/49-	*60*	**037**	*60*-11/81	
E65238	11/49-06/81	⊗07/84	**38**	11/49-	*60*	**038**	*60*-06/81	
E65239	11/49-03/81	⊗09/81	**39**	11/49-	*60*	**039**	*60*-03/81	
E65240	11/49-08/81	⊗02/82	**40**	11/49-	*60*	**040**	*60*-08/81	
E65241	11/49-09/81	⊗08/82	**41**	11/49-	*60*	**041**	*60*-09/81	
E65242	11/49-03/81	⊗10/81	**42**	11/49-	*60*	**042**	*60*-03/81	
E65243	11/49-08/81	⊗02/82	**43**	11/49-	*60*	**043**	*60*-08/81	
E65244	11/49-05/80	⊗07/82	**44**	11/49-	*60*	**044**	*60*-05/80	
E65245	11/49-03/81	⊗10/81	**45**	11/49-	*60*	**045**	*60*-03/81	
E65246	11/49-03/81	⊗11/83	**46**	11/49-	*60*	**046**	*60*-03/81	
E65247	11/49-09/81	⊗04/82	**47**	11/49-	*60*	**047**	*60*-09/81	
E65248	11/49-03/81	⊃IU	**48**	11/49-	*60*	**048**	*60*-03/81	
E65249	11/49-09/81	⊗04/82	**49**	11/49-	*60*	**049**	*60*-09/81	
E65250	11/49-06/81	⊗09/82	**50**	11/49-	*60*	**050**	*60*-06/81	
E65251	11/49-03/81	⊗10/81	**51**	11/49-	*60*	**051**	*60*-03/81	
E65252	11/49-09/81	⊗08/82	**52**	11/49-	*60*	**052**	*60*-09/81	
E65253	11/49-03/81	⊗11/83	**53**	11/49-	*60*	**053**	*60*-03/81	
E65254	11/49-06/81	⊗09/84	**54**	11/49-	*60*	**054**	*60*-04/81	
E65255	11/49-08/81	⊗08/82	**55**	11/49-	*60*	**055**	*60*-08/81	
E65256	11/49-03/81	⊗10/81	**56**	11/49-	*60*	**056**	*60*-03/81	
E65257	11/49-03/81	⊗11/83	**57**	11/49-	*60*	**057**	*60*-03/81	
E65258	11/49-11/81	⊗03/85	**58**	11/49-	*60*	**058**	*60*-11/81	
E65259	11/49-03/81	⊗	**59**	11/49-	*60*	**059**	*60*-03/81	
E65260	11/49-03/81	⊗10/81	**60**	11/49-	*60*	**060**	*60*-03/81	
E65261	11/49-11/81	⊗09/84	**61**	11/49-	*60*	**061**	*60*-11/81	
E65262	11/49-11/81	⊗07/84	**62**	11/49-	*60*	**062**	*60*-11/81	
E65263	11/49-11/81	⊗07/84	**63**	11/49-	*60*	**063**	*60*-11/81	
E65264	11/49-08/81	⊗04/82	**64**	11/49-	*60*	**064**	*60*-08/81	
E65265	11/49-03/81	⊗05/82	**65**	11/49-	*60*	**065**	*60*-03/81	
E65266	11/49-03/81	⊗07/84	**66**	11/49-	*60*	**066**	*60*-03/81	
E65267	11/49-06/81	⊗04/82	**67**	11/49-	*60*	**067**	*60*-06/81	
E65268	11/49-11/81	⊗03/85	**68**	11/49-	*60*	**068**	*60*-11/81	
E65269	11/49-09/81	⊗04/82	**69**	11/49-	*60*	**069**	*60*-09/81	
E65270	11/49-06/81	⊗03/82	**70**	11/49-	*60*	**070**	*60*-05/81	
E65271	11/49-06/81	⊗08/82	**71**	11/49-	*60*	**071**	*60*-06/81	
E65272	11/49-11/81	⊗*02/83*	**72**	11/49-	*60*	**072**	*60*-04/80	**072** 08/80-11/81
E65273	11/49-09/81	⊗09/82	**73**	11/49-	*60*	**073**	*60*-09/81	
E65274	11/49-06/81	⊗09/81	**74**	11/49-	*60*	**074**	*60*-06/81	
E65275	11/49-09/81	⊗08/82	**75**	11/49-	*60*	**075**	*60*-09/81	
E65276	11/49-09/81	⊗04/82	**76**	11/49-	*60*	**076**	*60*-09/81	
E65277	11/49-09/81	⊗09/82	**77**	11/49-	*60*	**077**	*60*-09/81	
E65278	11/49-08/81	⊗02/82	**78**	11/49-	*60*	**078**	*60*-08/81	
E65279	11/49-08/81	⊗04/82	**79**	11/49-	*60*	**079**	*60*-08/81	
E65280	11/49-09/81	⊗06/82	**80**	11/49-	*60*	**080**	*60*-09/81	
E65281	11/49-03/81	⊗04/82	**81**	11/49-	*60*	**081**	*60*-03/81	
E65282	11/49-11/81	⊗07/84	**82**	11/49-	*60*	**082**	*60*-11/81	
E65283	11/49-09/81	⊗05/82	**83**	11/49-	*60*	**083**	*60*-09/81	
E65284	11/49-11/81	⊗09/84	**84**	11/49-	*60*	**084**	*60*-11/81	
E65285	11/49-09/81	⊗05/82	**85**	11/49-	*60*	**085**	*60*-09/81	
E65286	11/49-08/81	⊗01/82	**86**	11/49-	*60*	**086**	*60*-08/81	
E65287	11/49-03/81	⊗09/81	**87**	11/49-	*60*	**087**	*60*-03/81	
E65288	11/49-09/81	⊗04/82	**88**	11/49-	*60*	**088**	*60*-09/81	
E65289	11/49-03/81	⊗09/81	**89**	11/49-	*60*	**089**	*60*-03/81	
E65290	11/49-09/81	⊗09/82	**90**	11/49-	*60*	**090**	*60*-09/81	
E65291	11/49-06/81	⊗04/82	**91**	11/49-	*60*	**091**	*60*-06/81	
E65292	11/49-03/81	⊗10/81	**92**	11/49-	*60*	**092**	*60*-03/81	

Class 306 Metropolitan-Cammell

Trailer Third Open later Pantograph Trailer Second Open
TTO later PTSB
E65401-E65492 Shenfield

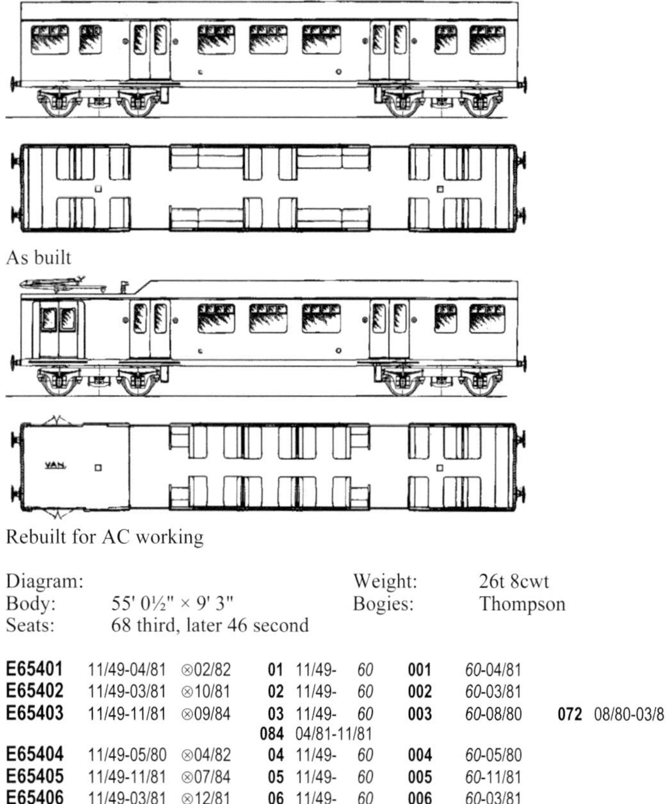

As built

Rebuilt for AC working

Diagram:		Weight:	26t 8cwt
Body:	55' 0½" × 9' 3"	Bogies:	Thompson
Seats:	68 third, later 46 second		

E65401	11/49-04/81	⊗02/82	**01**	11/49-	*60*	**001**	*60*-04/81	
E65402	11/49-03/81	⊗10/81	**02**	11/49-	*60*	**002**	*60*-03/81	
E65403	11/49-11/81	⊗09/84	**03**	11/49-	*60*	**003**	*60*-08/80	**072** 08/80-03/81
			084	04/81-11/81				
E65404	11/49-05/80	⊗04/82	**04**	11/49-	*60*	**004**	*60*-05/80	
E65405	11/49-11/81	⊗07/84	**05**	11/49-	*60*	**005**	*60*-11/81	
E65406	11/49-03/81	⊗12/81	**06**	11/49-	*60*	**006**	*60*-03/81	
E65407	11/49-09/81	⊗03/82	**07**	11/49-	*60*	**007**	*60*-09/81	

E65408	11/49-03/81	⊗09/81	**08**	11/49-	*60*	**008**	*60*-03/81		
E65409	11/49-04/81	⊗12/81	**09**	11/49-	*60*	**009**	*60*-04/81		
E65410	11/49-11/81	⊗07/84	**10**	11/49-	*60*	**010**	*60*-11/81		
E65411	11/49-05/80	⊗07/82	**11**	11/49-	*60*	**011**	*60*-04/80		
E65412	11/49-03/81	⊗12/81	**12**	11/49-	*60*	**012**	*60*-03/81		
E65413	11/49-03/81	⊗11/81	**13**	11/49-	*60*	**013**	*60*-03/81		
E65414	11/49-11/81	⊗07/84	**14**	11/49-	*60*	**014**	*60*-11/81		
E65415	11/49-11/81	⊗07/84	**15**	11/49-	*60*	**015**	*60*-11/81		
E65416	11/49-03/81	⊗09/81	**16**	11/49-	*60*	**016**	*60*-03/81		
E65417	11/49-11/81	Ⓟ	**17**	11/49-	*60*	**017**	*60*-11/81		
E65418	11/49-06/81	⊗07/84	**18**	11/49-	*60*	**018**	*60*-03/81		
E65419	11/49-08/81	⊗06/82	**19**	11/49-	*60*	**019**	*60*-08/81		
E65420	11/49-03/81	⊗12/81	**20**	11/49-	*60*	**020**	*60*-03/81		
E65421	11/49-08/81	⊗04/82	**21**	11/49-	*60*	**021**	*60*-08/81		
E65422	11/49-06/81	⊗03/82	**22**	11/49-	*60*	**022**	*60*-06/81		
E65423	11/49-05/81	⊗07/84	**23**	11/49-	*60*	**023**	*60*-05/81		
E65424	11/49-03/81	⊗09/81	**24**	11/49-	*60*	**024**	*60*-03/81		
E65425	11/49-03/81	⊗09/81	**25**	11/49-	*60*	**025**	*60*-03/81		
E65426	11/49-06/81	⊗03/82	**26**	11/49-	*60*	**026**	*60*-06/81		
E65427	11/49-06/81	⊗12/81	**27**	11/49-	*60*	**027**	*60*-11/80	**074**	11/80-06/81
E65428	11/49-08/81	⊗08/82	**28**	11/49-	*60*	**028**	*60*-08/81		
E65429	11/49-08/81	⊗03/82	**29**	11/49-	*60*	**029**	*60*-08/81		
E65430	11/49-04/68	⊗11/69	**30**	11/49-	*60*	**030**	*60*-04/68		
E65431	11/49-09/81	⊗04/82	**31**	11/49-	*60*	**031**	*60*-09/81		
E65432	11/49-06/81	⊗03/85	**32**	11/49-	*60*	**032**	*60*-06/81		
E65433	11/49-08/81	⊗09/82	**33**	11/49-	*60*	**033**	*60*-08/81		
E65434	11/49-11/81	⊗09/84	**34**	11/49-	*60*	**034**	*60*-11/81		
E65435	11/49-06/81	⊗03/82	**35**	11/49-	*60*	**035**	*60*-03/81	**016**	03/81-06/81
E65436	11/49-08/81	⊗01/82	**36**	11/49-	*60*	**036**	*60*-03/81		
E65437	11/49-11/81	⊗10/82	**37**	11/49-	*60*	**037**	*60*-11/81		
E65438	11/49-09/81	⊗05/82	**38**	11/49-	*60*	**038**	*60*-06/81	**083**	06/81-09/81
E65439	11/49-03/81	⊗09/81	**39**	11/49-	*60*	**039**	*60*-03/81		
E65440	11/49-08/81	⊗02/82	**40**	11/49-	*60*	**040**	*60*-08/81		
E65441	11/49-09/81	⊗08/82	**41**	11/49-	*60*	**041**	*60*-09/81		
E65442	11/49-03/81	⊗09/81	**42**	11/49-	*60*	**042**	*60*-03/81		
E65443	11/49-08/81	⊗02/82	**43**	11/49-	*60*	**043**	*60*-08/81		
E65444	11/49-03/81	⊗11/81	**44**	11/49-	*60*	**044**	*60*-05/80	**011**	05/80-03/81
E65445	11/49-03/81	⊗03/82	**45**	11/49-	*60*	**045**	*60*-03/81		
E65446	11/49-03/81	⊗03/82	**46**	11/49-	*60*	**046**	*60*-10/80	**027**	11/80-03/81
E65447	11/49-09/81	⊗04/82	**47**	11/49-	*60*	**047**	*60*-09/81		
E65448	11/49-03/81	⊗11/83	**48**	11/49-	*60*	**048**	*60*-03/81		
E65449	11/49-06/81	⊗02/82	**49**	11/49-	*60*	**049**	*60*-01/81		
E65450	11/49-06/81	⊗09/82	**50**	11/49-	*60*	**050**	*60*-06/81		
E65451	11/49-03/81	⊗03/82	**51**	11/49-	*60*	**051**	*60*-03/81		
E65452	11/49-09/81	⊗08/82	**52**	11/49-	*60*	**052**	*60*-09/81		
E65453	11/49-03/81	⊗11/83	**53**	11/49-	*60*	**053**	*60*-03/81		
E65454	11/49-09/81	⊗04/82	**54**	11/49-	*60*	**054**	*60*-04/81	**049**	04/81-09/81
E65455	11/49-08/81	⊗08/82	**55**	11/49-	*60*	**055**	*60*-08/81		
E65456	11/49-03/81	⊗11/81	**56**	11/49-	*60*	**056**	*60*-03/81		
E65457	11/49-03/81	⊗11/83	**57**	11/49-	*60*	**057**	*60*-03/81		
E65458	11/49-11/81	⊗03/85	**58**	11/49-	*60*	**058**	*60*-11/81		
E65459	11/49-03/81	➲**041368**	**59**	11/49-	*60*	**059**	*60*-03/81		
E65460	11/49-03/81	⊗11/81	**60**	11/49-	*60*	**060**	*60*-03/81		
E65461	11/49-11/81	⊗09/84	**61**	11/49-	*60*	**061**	*60*-11/81		
E65462	11/49-11/81	⊗07/84	**62**	11/49-	*60*	**062**	*60*-11/81		
E65463	11/49-11/81	⊗07/84	**63**	11/49-	*60*	**063**	*60*-11/81		
E65464	11/49-08/81	⊗03/82	**64**	11/49-	*60*	**064**	*60*-08/81		
E65465	11/49-03/81	⊗05/82	**65**	11/49-	*60*	**065**	*60*-03/81		
E65466	11/49-09/81	⊗09/82	**66**	11/49-	*60*	**066**	*60*-03/81	**090**	03/81-09/81
E65467	11/49-06/81	⊗04/82	**67**	11/49-	*60*	**067**	*60*-06/81		
E65468	11/49-11/81	⊗03/85	**68**	11/49-	*60*	**068**	*60*-11/81		
E65469	11/49-09/81	⊗04/82	**69**	11/49-	*60*	**069**	*60*-09/81		
E65470	11/49-11/81	⊗07/84	**70**	11/49-	*60*	**070**	*60*-05/81	**082**	06/81-11/81
E65471	11/49-06/81	⊗08/82	**71**	11/49-	*60*	**071**	*60*-06/81		
E65472	11/49-03/81	⊗12/81	**72**	11/49-	*60*	**072**	*60*-04/80	**011**	04/80-05/80
E65473	11/49-09/81	⊗09/82	**73**	11/49-	*60*	**073**	*60*-09/81		
E65474	11/49-03/81	⊗03/82	**74**	11/49-	*60*	**074**	*60*-10/80	**046**	10/80-03/81
E65475	11/49-09/81	⊗08/82	**75**	11/49-	*60*	**075**	*60*-09/81		
E65476	11/49-09/81	⊗04/82	**76**	11/49-	*60*	**076**	*60*-09/81		
E65477	11/49-09/81	⊗09/82	**77**	11/49-	*60*	**077**	*60*-09/81		
E65478	11/49-03/81	⊗04/82	**78**	11/49-	*60*	**078**	*60*-03/81		
E65479	11/49-08/81	⊗04/82	**79**	11/49-	*60*	**079**	*60*-08/81		
E65480	11/49-11/81	⊗*02/83*	**80**	11/49-	*60*	**080**	*60*-03/81	**072**	03/81-11/81
E65481	11/49-03/81	⊗04/82	**81**	11/49-	*60*	**081**	*60*-03/81		
E65482	11/49-05/81	⊗04/82	**82**	11/49-	*60*	**082**	*60*-06/81		
E65483	11/49-06/81	⊗07/84	**83**	11/49-	*60*	**083**	*60*-06/81		
E65484	11/49-08/81	⊗02/82	**84**	11/49-	*60*	**084**	*60*-03/81	**078**	03/81-08/81
E65485	11/49-09/81	⊗05/82	**85**	11/49-	*60*	**085**	*60*-09/81		
E65486	11/49-08/81	⊗01/82	**86**	11/49-	*60*	**086**	*60*-08/81		
E65487	11/49-03/81	⊗10/81	**87**	11/49-	*60*	**087**	*60*-03/81		
E65488	11/49-09/81	⊗04/82	**88**	11/49-	*60*	**088**	*60*-09/81		
E65489	11/49-03/81	⊗12/81	**89**	11/49-	*60*	**089**	*60*-03/81		
E65490	11/49-06/81	⊗09/84	**90**	11/49-	*60*	**090**	*60*-03/81		
E65491	11/49-06/81	⊗04/82	**91**	11/49-	*60*	**091**	*60*-06/81		
E65492	11/49-09/81	⊗06/82	**92**	11/49-	*60*	**092**	*60*-03/81	**080**	03/81-09/81

Class 306 Birmingham RC&W

Driving Trailer Second Open
DTTO later DTSO
E65601-E65692 Shenfield

Diagram:
Body: 55' 4¼" × 9' 3"
Seats: 60 third
Weight: 27t 9cwt
Bogies: Thompson

E65601	11/49-04/81	⊗07/84	**01**	11/49-	*60*	**001**	*60*-04/81		
E65602	11/49-03/81	⊗10/81	**02**	11/49-	*60*	**002**	*60*-03/81		
E65603	11/49-11/81	⊗09/84	**03**	11/49-	*60*	**003**	*60*-08/80	**072**	08/80-03/81
			084	04/81-11/81					
E65604	11/49-05/80	➲IU	**04**	11/49-	*60*	**004**	*60*-05/80		
E65605	11/49-11/81	⊗07/84	**05**	11/49-	*60*	**005**	*60*-11/81		
E65606	11/49-03/81	⊗12/81	**06**	11/49-	*60*	**006**	*60*-03/81		
E65607	11/49-09/81	⊗03/82	**07**	11/49-	*60*	**007**	*60*-09/81		
E65608	11/49-03/81	⊗11/81	**08**	11/49-	*60*	**008**	*60*-03/81		
E65609	11/49-04/81	⊗12/81	**09**	11/49-	*60*	**009**	*60*-04/81		
E65610	11/49-11/81	⊗07/84	**10**	11/49-	*60*	**010**	*60*-11/81		
E65611	11/49-05/80	⊗07/82	**11**	11/49-	*60*	**011**	*60*-04/80		
E65612	11/49-03/81	⊗12/81	**12**	11/49-	*60*	**012**	*60*-03/81		
E65613	11/49-03/81	⊗11/81	**13**	11/49-	*60*	**013**	*60*-03/81		
E65614	11/49-11/81	⊗07/84	**14**	11/49-	*60*	**014**	*60*-11/81		
E65615	11/49-11/81	⊗07/84	**15**	11/49-	*60*	**015**	*60*-11/81		
E65616	11/49-06/81	⊗03/82	**16**	11/49-	*60*	**016**	*60*-03/81	**026**	03/81-06/81
E65617	11/49-11/81	Ⓟ	**17**	11/49-	*60*	**017**	*60*-11/81		
E65618	11/49-06/81	⊗12/81	**18**	11/49-	*60*	**018**	*60*-03/81		
E65619	11/49-08/81	⊗06/82	**19**	11/49-	*60*	**019**	*60*-08/81		
E65620	11/49-03/81	⊗12/81	**20**	11/49-	*60*	**020**	*60*-03/81		
E65621	11/49-08/81	⊗04/82	**21**	11/49-	*60*	**021**	*60*-08/81		
E65622	11/49-09/81	➲IU	**22**	11/49-	*60*	**022**	*60*-06/81		
E65623	11/49-05/81	⊗01/82	**23**	11/49-	*60*	**023**	*60*-05/81		
E65624	11/49-03/81	⊗09/81	**24**	11/49-	*60*	**024**	*60*-03/81		
E65625	11/49-03/81	⊗09/81	**25**	11/49-	*60*	**025**	*60*-03/81		
E65626	11/49-03/81	⊗03/82	**26**	11/49-	*60*	**026**	*60*-03/81		
E65627	11/49-06/81	⊗12/81	**27**	11/49-	*60*	**027**	*60*-11/80	**074**	11/80-06/81
E65628	11/49-08/81	⊗08/82	**28**	11/49-	*60*	**028**	*60*-08/81		
E65629	11/49-08/81	⊗03/82	**29**	11/49-	*60*	**029**	*60*-08/81		
E65630	11/49-04/68	⊗ 70	**30**	11/49-	*60*	**030**	*60*-04/68		
E65631	11/49-09/81	⊗04/82	**31**	11/49-	*60*	**031**	*60*-09/81		
E65632	11/49-06/81	⊗03/85	**32**	11/49-	*60*	**032**	*60*-06/81		
E65633	11/49-08/81	⊗09/82	**33**	11/49-	*60*	**033**	*60*-08/81		
E65634	11/49-11/81	⊗09/84	**34**	11/49-	*60*	**034**	*60*-11/81		
E65635	11/49-06/81	⊗04/82	**35**	11/49-	*60*	**035**	*60*-03/81	**016**	03/81-06/81
E65636	11/49-03/81	⊗01/82	**36**	11/49-	*60*	**036**	*60*-03/81		
E65637	11/49-11/81	⊗10/82	**37**	11/49-	*60*	**037**	*60*-11/81		
E65638	11/49-09/81	⊗05/82	**38**	11/49-	*60*	**038**	*60*-06/81	**083**	06/81-09/81
E65639	11/49-03/81	⊗09/81	**39**	11/49-	*60*	**039**	*60*-03/81		
E65640	11/49-08/81	⊗02/82	**40**	11/49-	*60*	**040**	*60*-08/81		
E65641	11/49-09/81	⊗08/82	**41**	11/49-	*60*	**041**	*60*-09/81		
E65642	11/49-03/81	⊗09/81	**42**	11/49-	*60*	**042**	*60*-03/81		
E65643	11/49-08/81	⊗02/82	**43**	11/49-	*60*	**043**	*60*-08/81		
E65644	11/49-03/81	⊗11/81	**44**	11/49-	*60*	**044**	*60*-05/80	**011**	05/80-03/81
E65645	11/49-03/81	⊗03/82	**45**	11/49-	*60*	**045**	*60*-03/81		
E65646	11/49-03/81	⊗03/82	**46**	11/49-	*60*	**046**	*60*-10/80	**027**	11/80-03/81
E65647	11/49-09/81	⊗04/82	**47**	11/49-	*60*	**047**	*60*-09/81		
E65648	11/49-03/81	⊗11/83	**48**	11/49-	*60*	**048**	*60*-03/81		
E65649	11/49-06/81	⊗04/82	**49**	11/49-	*60*	**049**	*60*-01/81	**067**	01/81-06/81
E65650	11/49-06/81	⊗09/82	**50**	11/49-	*60*	**050**	*60*-06/81		
E65651	11/49-03/81	⊗03/82	**51**	11/49-	*60*	**051**	*60*-03/81		
E65652	11/49-09/81	⊗08/82	**52**	11/49-	*60*	**052**	*60*-09/81		
E65653	11/49-03/81	⊗11/83	**53**	11/49-	*60*	**053**	*60*-03/81		
E65654	11/49-04/81	⊗04/82	**54**	11/49-	*60*	**054**	*60*-04/81		
E65655	11/49-08/81	⊗08/82	**55**	11/49-	*60*	**055**	*60*-08/81		
E65656	11/49-03/81	⊗11/81	**56**	11/49-	*60*	**056**	*60*-03/81		
E65657	11/49-03/81	⊗11/83	**57**	11/49-	*60*	**057**	*60*-03/81		
E65658	11/49-11/81	⊗03/85	**58**	11/49-	*60*	**058**	*60*-11/81		
E65659	11/49-03/81	⊗	**59**	11/49-	*60*	**059**	*60*-03/81		
E65660	11/49-03/81	⊗11/81	**60**	11/49-	*60*	**060**	*60*-03/81		
E65661	11/49-11/81	⊗09/84	**61**	11/49-	*60*	**061**	*60*-11/81		
E65662	11/49-11/81	⊗07/84	**62**	11/49-	*60*	**062**	*60*-11/81		
E65663	11/49-11/81	⊗07/84	**63**	11/49-	*60*	**063**	*60*-11/81		
E65664	11/49-03/81	⊗11/81	**64**	11/49-	*60*	**064**	*60*-03/81		
E65665	11/49-03/81	⊗05/82	**65**	11/49-	*60*	**065**	*60*-03/81		

E65666	11/49-09/81	⊗09/82	**66**	11/49- *60*	**066**	*60*-03/81	**090**	03/81-09/81
E65667	11/49-09/81	⊗05/81	**67**	11/49- *60*	**067**	*60*-01/81	**049**	04/81-09/81
E65668	11/49-11/81	⊗03/85	**68**	11/49- *60*	**068**	*60*-11/81		
E65669	11/49-09/81	⊗04/82	**69**	11/49- *60*	**069**	*60*-09/81		
E65670	11/49-11/81	⊗07/84	**70**	11/49- *60*	**070**	*60*-05/81	**082**	06/81-11/81
E65671	11/49-06/81	⊗08/82	**71**	11/49- *60*	**071**	*60*-06/81		
E65672	11/49-03/81	⊗12/81	**72**	11/49- *60*	**072**	*60*-04/80	**011**	04/80-05/80
E65673	11/49-09/81	⊗09/82	**73**	11/49- *60*	**073**	*60*-09/81		
E65674	11/49-08/81	⊗03/82	**74**	11/49- *60*	**074**	*60*-10/80	**046**	10/80-03/81
			064	03/81-08/81				
E65675	11/49-06/81	⊗03/82	**75**	11/49- *60*	**075**	*60*-06/81		
E65676	11/49-09/81	⊗04/82	**76**	11/49- *60*	**076**	*60*-09/81		
E65677	11/49-09/81	⊗09/82	**77**	11/49- *60*	**077**	*60*-09/81		
E65678	11/49-09/81	⊗08/82	**78**	11/49- *60*	**078**	*60*-03/81	**075**	06/81-09/81
E65679	11/49-08/81	⊗04/82	**79**	11/49- *60*	**079**	*60*-08/81		
E65680	11/49-11/81	⊗*02/83*	**80**	11/49- *60*	**080**	*60*-03/81	**072**	03/81-11/81
E65681	11/49-03/81	⊗04/82	**81**	11/49- *60*	**081**	*60*-03/81		
E65682	11/49-05/81	⊗04/82	**82**	11/49- *60*	**082**	*60*-06/81		
E65683	11/49-06/81	⊗07/84	**83**	11/49- *60*	**083**	*60*-06/81		
E65684	11/49-08/81	⊗02/82	**84**	11/49- *60*	**084**	*60*-03/81	**078**	03/81-08/81
E65685	11/49-09/81	⊗05/82	**85**	11/49- *60*	**085**	*60*-09/81		
E65686	11/49-08/81	⊗01/82	**86**	11/49- *60*	**086**	*60*-08/81		
E65687	11/49-03/81	⊗10/81	**87**	11/49- *60*	**087**	*60*-03/81		
E65688	11/49-09/81	⊗04/82	**88**	11/49- *60*	**088**	*60*-09/81		
E65689	11/49-03/81	⊗12/81	**89**	11/49- *60*	**089**	*60*-03/81		
E65690	11/49-06/81	⊗09/84	**90**	11/49- *60*	**090**	*60*-03/81		
E65691	11/49-06/81	⊗04/82	**91**	11/49- *60*	**091**	*60*-06/81		
E65692	11/49-09/81	⊗06/82	**92**	11/49- *60*	**092**	*60*-03/81	**080**	03/81-09/81

LNER Railway 1923 Numbering

Tyneside Metropolitan-Cammell
Motor Luggage Van
MLV
2424-2425

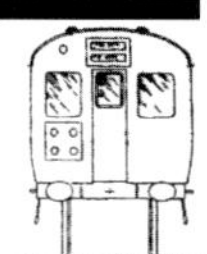

For details see LNER 29467-29468

2424	23-	43	➲**29467**
2425	23-	43	➲**29468**

Tyneside York
1904-1915 stock & 1920-1922 stock
Between 23130 & 23795

The 1920-1922 stock was built carrying the numbers of withdrawn 1904-1915 stock which had been destroyed in the Heaton Shed fire of 11th August 1918.

For details of the 1904-1915 stock see NER 3181-3794.
For details of the 1920-1922 stock see LNER 29xxx numbers as shown.

23180	23-	43	➲**29375**	1920-1922 stock	⊂**3180**
23181	23-	38	⊗		⊂**3181**
23182	23-	38	⊗		⊂**3182**
23183	23-	38	⊗		⊂**3183**
23184	23-	38	⊗		⊂**3184**
23185	23-	38	⊗		⊂**3185**
23186	23-	38	⊗		⊂**3186**
23187	23-	38	⊗		⊂**3187**
23188	23-	38	⊗		⊂**3188**
23189	23-	38	⊗		⊂**3189**
23190	23-	38	⊗		⊂**3190**
23191	23-	38	⊗		⊂**3191**
23192	23-	38	⊗		⊂**3192**
23193	23-	38	⊗		⊂**3193**
23194	23-	38	⊗		⊂**3194**
23195	23-	43	➲**29376**	1920-1922 stock	⊂**3195**
23196	23-	38	⊗		⊂**3196**
23197	23-	43	➲**29377**	1920-1922 stock	⊂**3197**
23198	23-	43	➲**29378**	1920-1922 stock	⊂**3198**
23199	23-	38	⊗		⊂**3199**
23200	23-	38	⊗		⊂**3200**
23201	23-	38	⊗		⊂**3201**
23202	23-	38	⊗		⊂**3202**
23203	23-	38	⊗		⊂**3203**
23204	23-	43	➲**29379**	1920-1922 stock	⊂**3204**
23205	23-	38	⊗		⊂**3205**
23206	23-	38	⊗		⊂**3206**
23207	23-	38	⊗		⊂**3207**
23208	23-	38	⊗		⊂**3208**
23209	23-	38	⊗		⊂**3209**
23210	23-	38	⊗		⊂**3210**
23211	23-	43	➲**29380**	1920-1922 stock	⊂**3211**
23212	23-	43	➲**29175**	1920-1922 stock	⊂**3212**
23213	23-	38	⊗		⊂**3213**
23214	23-	38	⊗		⊂**3214**
23215	23-	38	⊗		⊂**3215**
23216	23-	38	⊗		⊂**3216**
23217	23-	43	➲**29390**	1920-1922 stock	⊂**3217**
23218	23-	38	⊗		⊂**3218**
23219	23-	43	➲**29176**	1920-1922 stock	⊂**3219**
23220	23-	38	⊗		⊂**3220**
23221	23-	43	➲**29177**	1920-1922 stock	⊂**3221**
23222	23-	38	⊗		⊂**3222**
23223	23-	38	⊗		⊂**3223**
23224	23-	38	⊗		⊂**3224**
23225	23-	43	➲**29178**	1920-1922 stock	⊂**3225**
23226	23-	43	➲**29179**	1920-1922 stock	⊂**3226**
23227	23-	43	➲**29180**	1920-1922 stock	⊂**3227**
23228	23-	43	➲**29181**	1920-1922 stock	⊂**3228**
23229	23-	38	⊗		⊂**3229**
23230	23-	38	⊗		⊂**3230**
23231	23-	38	⊗		⊂**3231**
23232	23-	38	⊗		⊂**3232**
23233	23-	38	⊗		⊂**3233**
23234	23-	38	⊗		⊂**3234**
23235	23-	38	⊗		⊂**3235**
23236	23-	38	⊗		⊂**3236**
23237	23-	38	⊗		⊂**3237**
23238	23-	43	➲**29184**	1920-1922 stock	⊂**3238**
23239	23-	38	⊗		⊂**3239**
23240	23-	38	⊗		⊂**3240**
23241	23-	43	➲**29185**	1920-1922 stock	⊂**3241**
23242	23-	38	⊗		⊂**3242**
23243	23-	43	➲**29186**	1920-1922 stock	⊂**3243**
23244	23-	38	⊗		⊂**3244**
23245	23-	38	⊗		⊂**3245**
23246	23-	43	➲**29187**	1920-1922 stock	⊂**3246**
23247	23-	38	⊗		⊂**3247**
23248	23-	38	⊗		⊂**3248**
23249	*23-05/41*		⊗05/41	1920-1922 stock	⊂**3249**
23250	23-	43	➲**29189**	1920-1922 stock	⊂**3250**
23251	23-	43	➲**29190**	1920-1922 stock	⊂**3251**
23252	*23-11/33*		⊗ *33*		⊂**3252**
23253	*23-08/26*		⊗ *26*		⊂**3253**
23253[2]	28-	55	➲**29191**	1920-1922 stock	⊂**3253**
23254	23-	38	⊗		⊂**3254**
23255	23-	38	⊗		⊂**3255**
23256	23-	38	⊗		⊂**3256**
23257	23-	38	⊗		⊂**3257**
23258	23-	38	⊗		⊂**3258**
23259	23-	38	⊗		⊂**3259**
23260	23-	38	⊗		⊂**3260**
23261	23-	38	⊗		⊂**3261**
23262	23-	38	⊗		⊂**3262**
23263	23-	38	⊗		⊂**3263**
23264	23-	38	⊗		⊂**3264**
23265	23-	38	⊗		⊂**3265**
23266	23-	38	➲**900729**		⊂**3266**
23267	23-	38	➲**900730**	℗	⊂**3267**
23268	23-	43	➲**29391**	1920-1922 stock	⊂**3268**
23269	23-	38	⊗		⊂**3269**
23507	23-	43	➲**29381**	1920-1922 stock	⊂**3507**
23508	23-	43	➲**29382**	1920-1922 stock	⊂**3508**
23509	23-	38	⊗		⊂**3509**
23510	23-	38	⊗		⊂**3510**
23511	23-	38	⊗		⊂**3511**
23512	23-	43	➲**29383**	1920-1922 stock	⊂**3512**
23513	23-	43	➲**29384**	1920-1922 stock	⊂**3513**
23514	23-	38	⊗		⊂**3514**
23515	23-	38	⊗		⊂**3515**
23516	23-	38	⊗		⊂**3516**
23517	23-	38	⊗		⊂**3517**
23518	23-	43	➲**29385**	1920-1922 stock	⊂**3518**
23519	23-	40	⊗ *45*		⊂**3519**
23520	23-	43	➲**29182**	1920-1922 stock	⊂**3520**
23521	23-	43	➲**29183**	1920-1922 stock	⊂**3521**
23522	23-	40	⊗ *45*		⊂**3522**
23523	23-	40	⊗ *45*		⊂**3523**
23524	23-	43	➲**29392**	1920-1922 stock	⊂**3524**
23525	23-	38	⊗		⊂**3525**
23694	23-	43	➲**29269**	Controlled set	⊂**3694**
23731	23-	43	➲**29270**	Controlled set	⊂**3731**
23733	23-	43	➲**29271**	Controlled set	⊂**3733**
23744	23-	43	➲**29272**	Controlled set	⊂**3744**
23745	23-	43	➲**29273**	Controlled set	⊂**3745**
23747	23-	43	➲**29274**	Controlled set	⊂**3747**
23770	23-	40	⊗ *45*		⊂**3770**
23771	23-	40	⊗ *45*		⊂**3771**
23781	23-	40	⊗ *45*		⊂**3781**
23782	23-	40	⊗ *45*		⊂**3782**

23783	23-	40	⊗ *45*		⊂3783
23784	23-	40	⊗ *45*		⊂3784
23785	23-	43	➲**29386**	1920-1922 stock	⊂3785
23786	23-	40	⊗ *45*		⊂3786
23787	23-	40	⊗ *45*		⊂3787
23788	23-	43	➲**29387**	1920-1922 stock	⊂3788
23789	23-	40	⊗ *45*		⊂3789
23790	23-	43	➲**29388**	1920-1922 stock	⊂3790
23791	23-	43	➲**29389**	1920-1922 stock	⊂3791
23792	23-	40	⊗ *45*		⊂3792
23793	23-	40	⊗ *45*		⊂3793
23794	23-	40	⊗ *45*		⊂3794
23795	23-	43	➲**29493**	1920-1922 stock	⊂3795

Tyneside Metropolitan-Cammell
Driving Motor Third + Driving Trailer Third
Articulated DMT+DTT
24145-24168

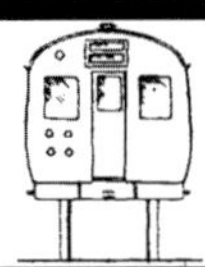

For details see LNER 29101-29112 and 29301-29312

24145	37-	43	➲**29101**
24146	37-	43	➲**29301**
24147	37-	43	➲**29102**
24148	37-	43	➲**29302**
24149	37-	43	➲**29103**
24150	37-	43	➲**29303**
24151	37-	43	➲**29104**
24152	37-	43	➲**29304**
24153	37-	43	➲**29105**
24154	37-	43	➲**29305**
24155	37-	43	➲**29106**
24156	37-	43	➲**29306**
24157	37-	43	➲**29107**
24158	37-	43	➲**29307**
24159	37-	43	➲**29108**
24160	37-	43	➲**29308**
24161	37-	43	➲**29109**
24162	37-	43	➲**29309**
24163	37-	43	➲**29110**
24164	37-	43	➲**29310**
24165	37-	43	➲**29111**
24166	37-	43	➲**29311**
24167	37-	43	➲**29112**
24168	37-	43	➲**29312**

Tyneside Metropolitan-Cammell
Driving Motor Brake Third + Driving Trailer Composite
Articulated DMBT+DTT
24169-24200

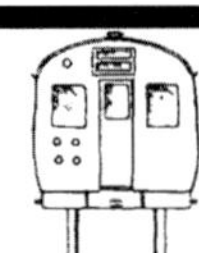

For details see LNER 29113-29128 and 29313-29328

24169	37-	43	➲**29113**
24170	37-	43	➲**29313**
24171	37-	43	➲**29114**
24172	37-	43	➲**29314**
24173	37-	43	➲**29115**
24174	37-	43	➲**29315**
24175	37-	43	➲**29116**
24176	37-	43	➲**29316**
24177	37-	43	➲**29117**
24178	37-	43	➲**29317**
24179	37-	43	➲**29118**
24180	37-	43	➲**29318**
24181	37-	43	➲**29119**
24182	37-	43	➲**29319**
24183	37-	43	➲**29120**
24184	37-	43	➲**29320**
24185	37-	43	➲**29121**
24186	37-	43	➲**29321**
24187	37-	43	➲**29122**
24188	37-	43	➲**29322**
24189	37-	43	➲**29123**
24190	37-	43	➲**29323**
24191	37-	43	➲**29124**
24192	37-	43	➲**29324**
24193	37-	43	➲**29125**
24194	37-	43	➲**29325**
24195	37-	43	➲**29126**
24196	37-	43	➲**29326**
24197	37-	43	➲**29127**
24198	37-	43	➲**29327**
24199	37-	43	➲**29128**
24200	37-	43	➲**29328**

Tyneside Metropolitan-Cammell
Driving Motor Third + Trailer Third
Articulated DMT+TT
24201-24236

For details see LNER 29129-29146 and 29229-29246

24201	37-	43	➲**29129**
24202	37-	43	➲**29229**
24203	37-	43	➲**29130**
24204	37-	43	➲**29230**
24205	37-	43	➲**29131**
24206	37-	43	➲**29231**
24207	37-	43	➲**29132**
24208	37-	43	➲**29232**
24209	37-	43	➲**29133**
24210	37-	43	➲**29233**
24211	37-	43	➲**29134**
24212	37-	43	➲**29234**
24213	37-	43	➲**29135**
24214	37-	43	➲**29235**
24215	37-	43	➲**29136**
24216	37-	43	➲**29236**
24217	37-	43	➲**29137**
24218	37-	43	➲**29237**
24219	37-	43	➲**29138**
24220	37-	43	➲**29238**
24221	37-	43	➲**29139**
24222	37-	43	➲**29239**
24223	37-	43	➲**29140**
24224	37-	43	➲**29240**
24225	37-	43	➲**29141**
24226	37-	43	➲**29241**
24227	37-	43	➲**29142**
24228	37-	43	➲**29242**
24229	37-	*40*	➲*29143*
24230	37-	*40*	➲*29243*
24231	37-	43	➲**29144**
24232	37-	43	➲**29244**
24233	37-	43	➲**29145**
24234	37-	43	➲**29245**
24235	37-	43	➲**29146**
24236	37-	43	➲**29246**

Tyneside Metropolitan-Cammell
Trailer Composite + Driving Motor Brake Third
Articulated TC+DMBT
24237-24272

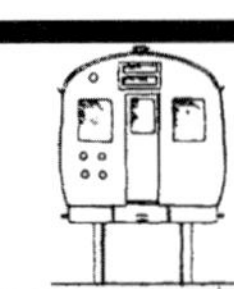

For details see LNER 29147-29164 and 29247-29264

24237	38-	43	➲**29147**
24238	38-	43	➲**29247**
24239	38-	43	➲**29148**
24240	38-	43	➲**29248**
24241	38-	43	➲**29149**
24242	38-	43	➲**29249**
24243	38-	43	➲**29150**
24244	38-	43	➲**29250**
24245	38-	43	➲**29151**
24246	38-	43	➲**29251**
24247	38-	43	➲**29152**
24248	38-	43	➲**29252**
24249	38-	43	➲**29153**
24250	38-	43	➲**29253**
24251	38-	43	➲**29154**
24252	38-	43	➲**29254**
24253	38-	43	➲**29155**
24254	38-	43	➲**29255**
24255	38-	43	➲**29156**
24256	38-	43	➲**29256**
24257	38-	43	➲**29157**
24258	38-	43	➲**29257**
24259	38-	43	➲**29158**
24260	38-	43	➲**29258**
24261	38-	43	➲**29159**
24262	38-	43	➲**29259**
24263	38-	43	➲**29160**
24264	38-	43	➲**29260**
24265	38-	43	➲**29161**
24266	38-	43	➲**29261**
24267	38-	43	➲**29162**

24268	38-	43	➲**29262**
24269	38-	43	➲**29163**
24270	38-	43	➲**29263**
24271	38-	43	➲**29164**
24272	38-	43	➲**29264**

Tyneside Metropolitan-Cammell
Driving Motor Brake Third
DMBT
24273-24274

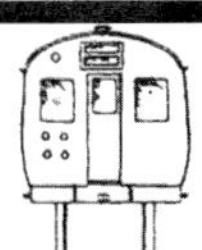

For details see LNER 29273-29274

24273	38-	43	➲**29165**
24274	38-	43	➲**29166**

Tyneside York
Driving Motor Brake Composite
DMBC
24465

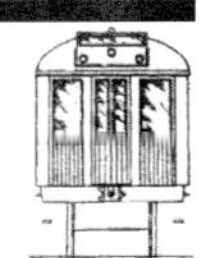

For details see LNER 29192

24465	38-	43	➲**29192**

North Eastern Railway

Tyneside York
Trailer Third
TT
3180-3206

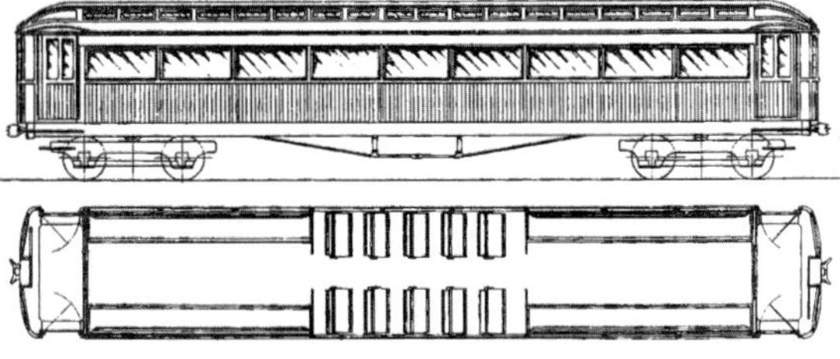

As built, Diagram 92

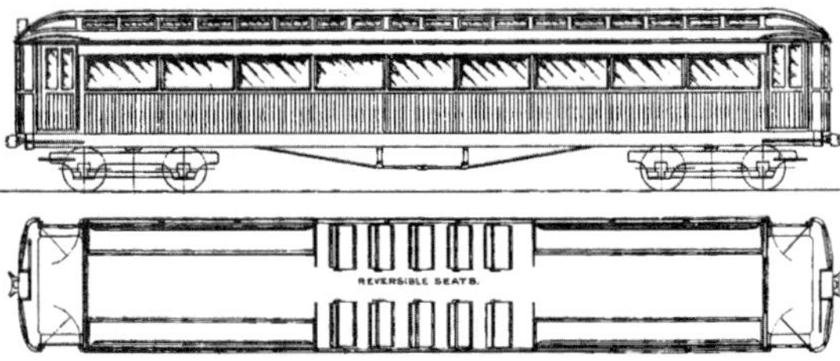

Modified, Diagram 92A

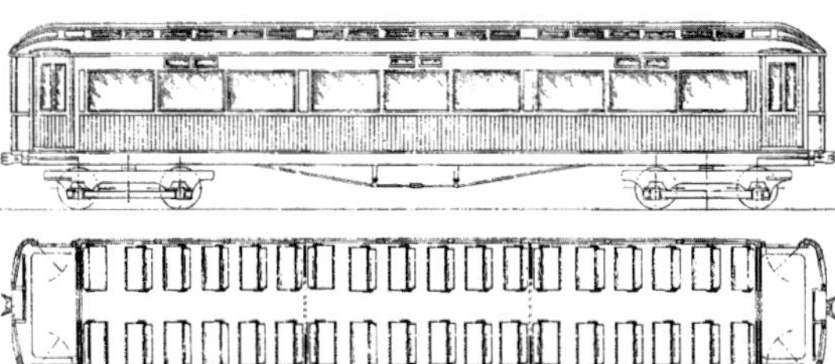

3204 Diagram 202

Diagram:	92 92A 202	LNER Class:	T3 or TS3
Body:	56' 6" × 9' 2½"	Weight:	21t 15cwt
Seats:	68 third	Bogies:	NER

3204 to Diagram 202 after accident, 72 third 22t 16cwt
3185/8-93/5-9, 3200/6 to Diagram 92A

3180	04-08/18		⊗08/18
3181	04-	23	➲**23181**
3182	04-	23	➲**23182**
3183	04-	23	➲**23183**
3184	04-	23	➲**23184**
3185	04-	23	➲**23185**
3186	04-	23	➲**23186**
3187	04-	23	➲**23187**
3188	04-	23	➲**23188**
3189	04-	23	➲**23189**
3190	04-	23	➲**23190**
3191	04-	23	➲**23191**
3192	04-	23	➲**23192**
3193	04-	23	➲**23193**
3194	04-	23	➲**23194**
3195	04-08/18		⊗08/18
3196	04-	23	➲**23196**
3197	04-08/18		⊗08/18
3198	04-08/18		⊗08/18
3199	04-	23	➲**23199**
3200	04-	23	➲**23200**
3201	04-	23	➲**23201**
3202	04-	23	➲**23202**
3203	04-	23	➲**23203**
3204	04-08/18		⊗08/18
3205	04-	23	➲**23205**
3206	04-	23	➲**23206**

Tyneside York
Driving Trailer Third
DTT
3207-3211

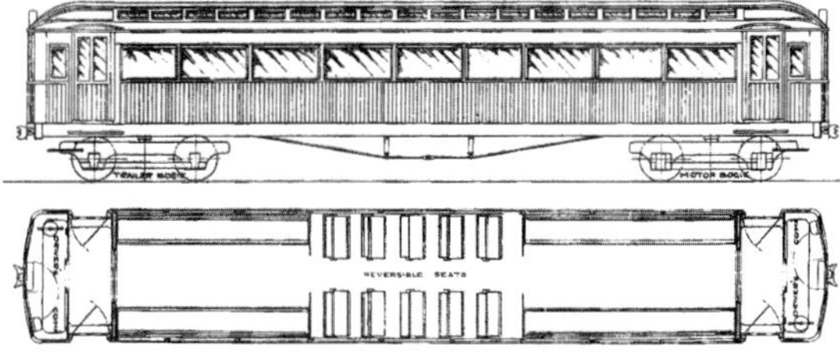

Diagram:	99	LNER Class:	TD3
Body:	56' 6" × 9' 2½"	Weight:	
Seats:	64 third	Bogies:	NER

3207	04-	23	➲**23207**
3208	04-	23	➲**23208**
3209	04-	23	➲**23209**
3210	04-	23	➲**23210**
3211	04-08/18		⊗08/18

Tyneside York
Driving Motor Third
DMT
3212-3235

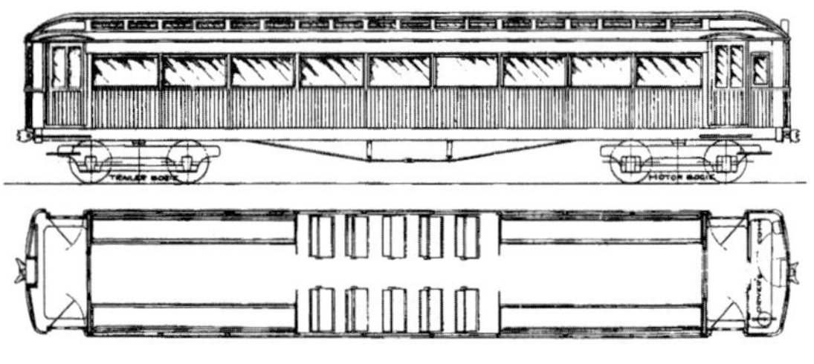

Diagram 91

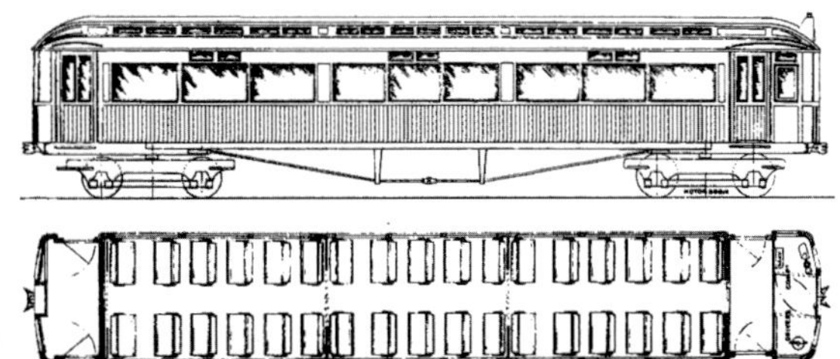

3213 Diagram 203

Diagram:	91	LNER Class:	MS3
Body:	56' 6" × 9' 2½"	Weight:	29t 15cwt
Seats:	64 third	Bogies:	NER
Motors:	BTH 2 × 125hp		

3212 To Diagram 203, 68 third

3212	04-08/18	⊗08/18
3213	04- 23	**➲23213**
3214	04- 23	**➲23214**
3215	04- 23	**➲23215**
3216	04- 23	**➲23216**
3217	04-08/18	⊗08/18
3218	04- 23	**➲23218**
3219	04-08/18	⊗08/18
3220	04- 23	**➲23220**
3221	04-08/18	⊗08/18
3222	04- 23	**➲23222**
3223	04- 23	**➲23223**
3224	04- 23	**➲23224**
3225	04-08/18	⊗08/18
3226	04-08/18	⊗08/18
3227	04-08/18	⊗08/18
3228	04-08/18	⊗08/18
3229	04- 23	**➲23229**
3230	04- 23	**➲23230**
3231	04- 23	**➲23231**
3232	04- 23	**➲23232**
3233	04- 23	**➲23233**
3234	04- 23	**➲23234**
3235	04- 23	**➲23235**

Tyneside York
Driving Motor Third
DMT
3236

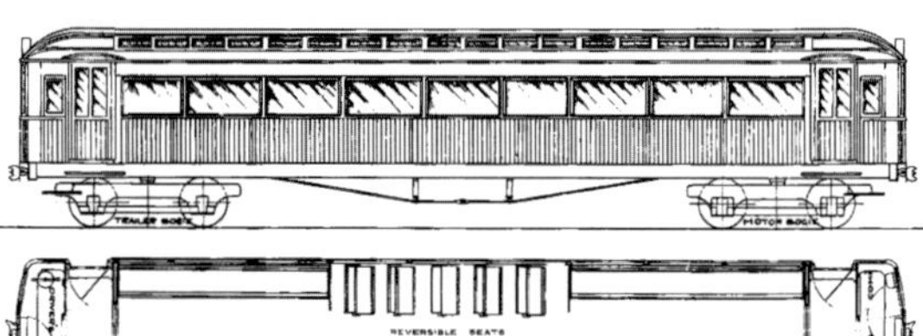

Diagram:	96	LNER Class:	MD3
Body:	56' 6" × 9' 2½"	Weight:	
Seats:	64 third	Bogies:	NER
Motors:	BTH 2 × 125hp		

3236	04- 23	**➲23236**

Tyneside York
Driving Motor Brake Third later Composite
DMBT
3237-3238

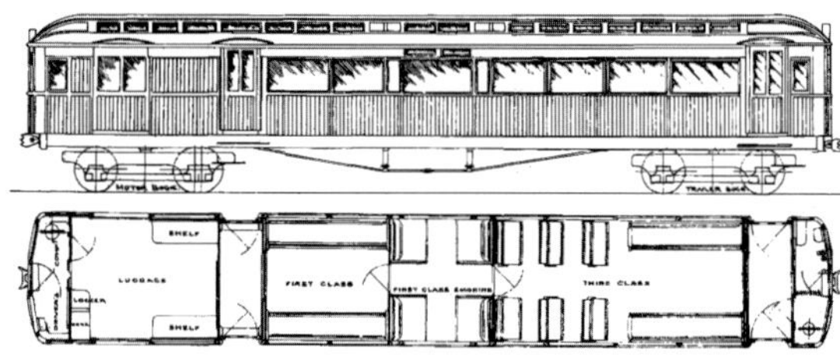

Diagram:	98	LNER Class:	LMD3 later LMD1
Body:	56' 6" × 9' 2½"	Weight:	
Seats:	42 third, later 18 first 24 third	Bogies:	NER
Motors:	BTH 2 × 125hp		

3237	04- 23	**➲23237**
3238	04-08/18	⊗08/18

Tyneside York
Driving Motor Brake Composite
DMBC
3239-3262

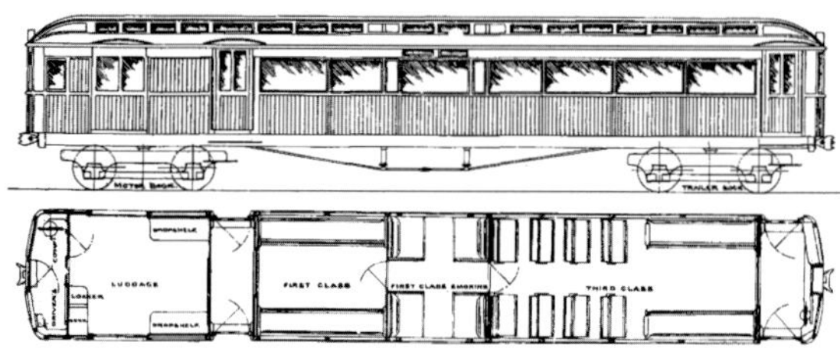

Diagram 90

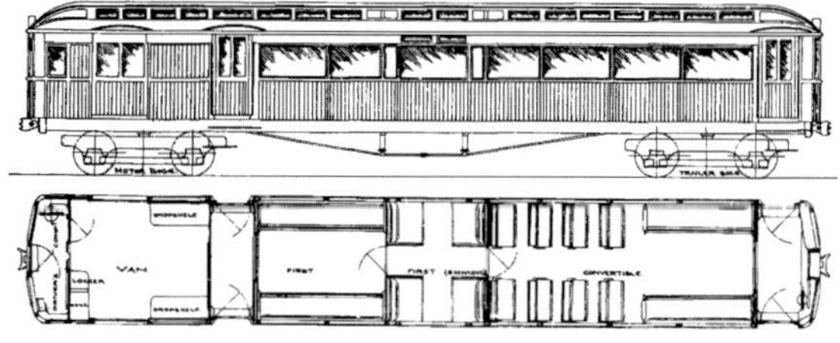

Diagram 90A

Diagram:	90 90A	LNER Class:	LMS1 or LMD1
Body:	56' 6" × 9' 2½"	Weight:	30t 15cwt
Seats:	44 first, later 18 first 26 third	Bogies:	NER
Motors:	BTH 2 × 125hp		

3240/41/60/61 to Diagram 90A LMD1, 18 first 26 convertible

3239	04- 23	**➲23239**
3240	04- 23	**➲23240**
3241	04-08/18	⊗08/18
3242	04- 23	**➲23242**
3243	04-08/18	⊗08/18
3244	04- 23	**➲23244**
3245	04- 23	**➲23245**
3246	04-08/18	⊗08/18
3247	04- 23	**➲23247**
3248	04- 23	**➲23248**
3249	04-08/18	⊗08/18
3250	04-08/18	⊗08/18
3251	04-08/18	⊗08/18
3252	04- 23	**➲23252**
3253	04- 23	**➲23253**
3254	04- 23	**➲23254**
3255	04- 23	**➲23255**
3256	04- 23	**➲23256**
3257	04- 23	**➲23257**
3258	04- 23	**➲23258**
3259	04- 23	**➲23259**
3260	04- 23	**➲23260**
3261	04- 23	**➲23261**
3262	04- 23	**➲23262**

Tyneside York
Driving Motor Brake Third later Composite
DMBT
3263-3265

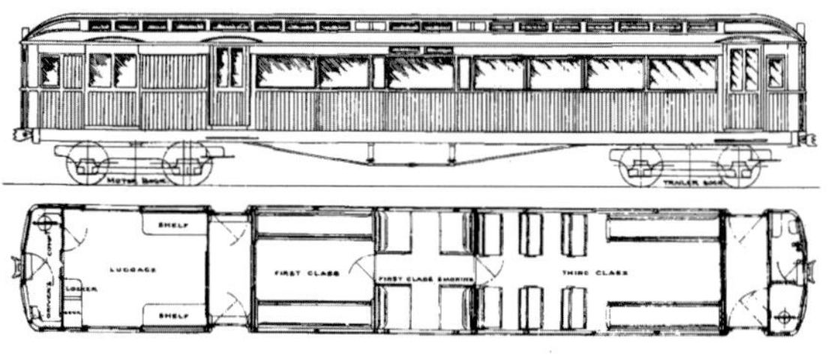

Diagram:	98	LNER Class:	LMD3 later LMD1
Body:	56' 6" × 9' 2½"	Weight:	
Seats:	42 third, later 18 first 24 third	Bogies:	NER
Motors:	BTH 2 × 125hp		

3263 04- 23 ➲**23263**
3264 04- 23 ➲**23264**
3265 04- 23 ➲**23265**

Tyneside York
Motor Parcels Van
MLV
3266-3267

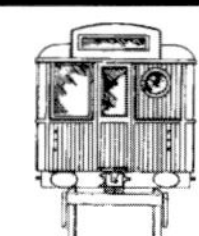

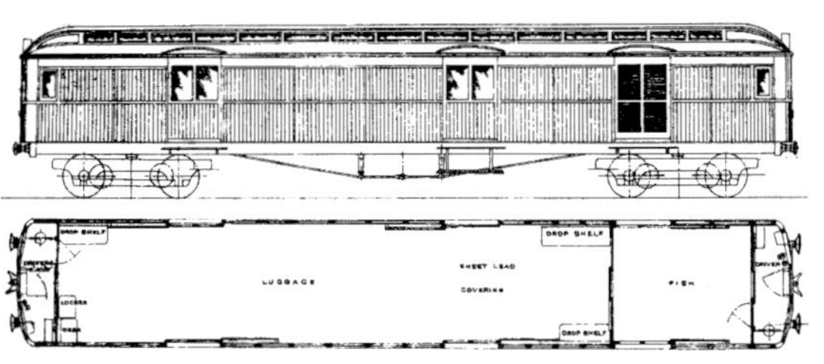

Diagram:	100		
Body:	56' 6" × 9' 2½"	Weight:	
Motors:	BTH 2 × 125hp	Bogies:	NER

3266 04- 23 ➲**23266**
3267 04- 23 ➲**23267** Ⓟ

Tyneside York
Driving Motor Third
DMT
3268-3269

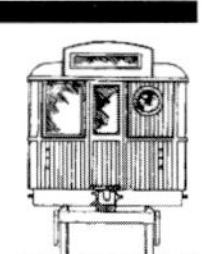

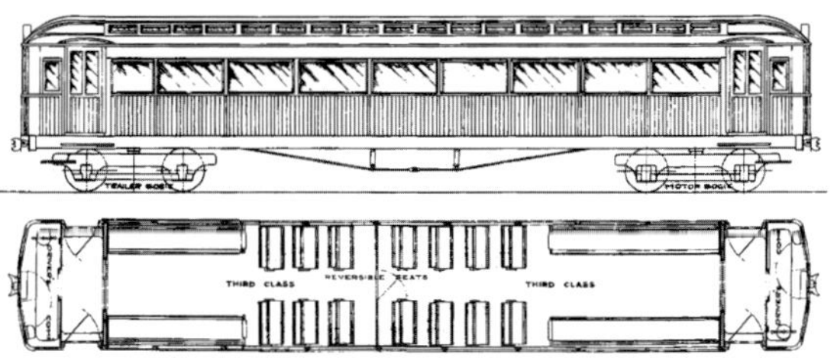

Diagram:	97	LNER Class:	MD3
Body:	56' 6" × 9' 2½"	Weight:	
Seats:	60 third	Bogies:	NER
Motors:	BTH 2 × 125hp		

3268 04-08/18 ⊗08/18
3269 04- 23 ➲**23269**

Tyneside York
Driving Trailer Third
DTT
3507-3518

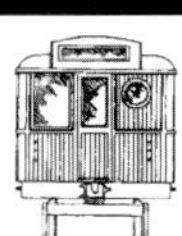

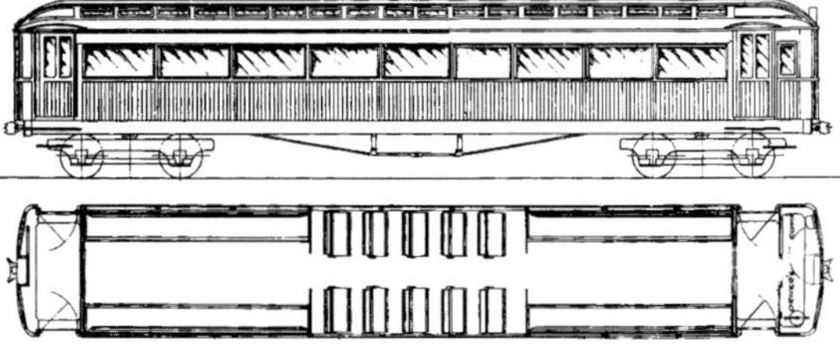

Diagram:	106	LNER Class:	TS3
Body:	56' 6" × 9' 2½"	Weight:	
Seats:	64 third	Bogies:	NER

3507 05-08/18 ⊗08/18
3508 05-08/18 ⊗08/18
3509 05- 23 ➲**23509**
3510 05- 23 ➲**23510**
3511 05- 23 ➲**23511**
3512 05-08/18 ⊗08/18
3513 05-08/18 ⊗08/18
3514 05- 23 ➲**23514**
3515 05- 23 ➲**23515**
3516 05- 23 ➲**23516**
3517 05- 23 ➲**23517**
3518 05-08/18 ⊗08/18

Tyneside York
Driving Motor Third
DMT
3519-3524

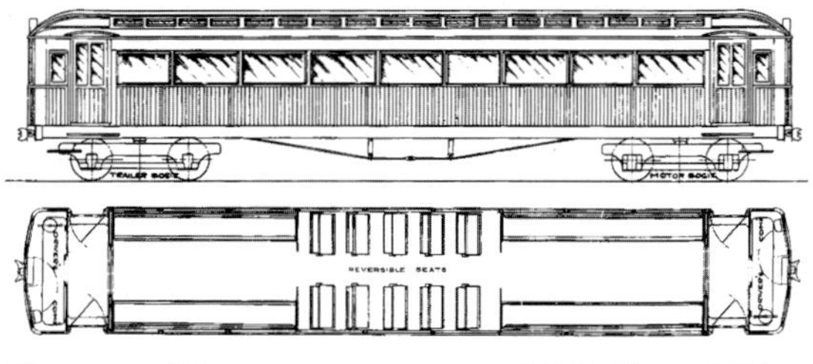

Diagram:	175	LNER Class:	MD3
Body:	56' 6" × 9' 2½"	Weight:	
Seats:	64 third	Bogies:	NER
Motors:	BTH 2 × 125hp		

3519 09- 23 ➲**23519**
3520 09-08/18 ⊗08/18
3521 09-08/18 ⊗08/18
3522 09- 23 ➲**23522**
3523 09- 23 ➲**23523**
3524 09-08/18 ⊗08/18

Tyneside York
Motor Luggage Van
MLV
3525

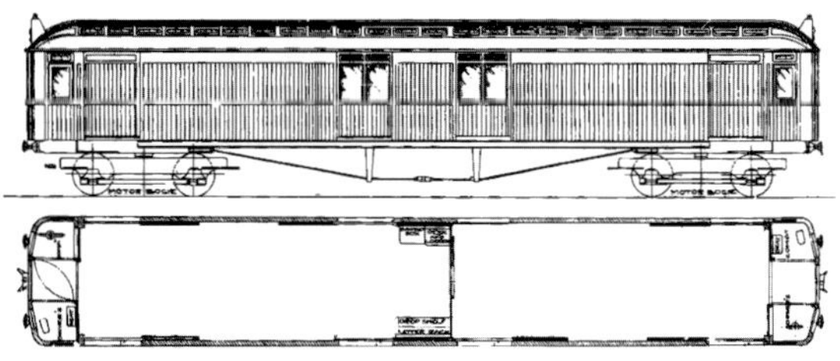

Diagram:	172		
Body:	56' 6" × 9' 2½"	Weight:	39t 6cwt
Motors:	BTH 2 × 125hp	Bogies:	NER

3525 08- 23 ➲**23525**

Tyneside York
Controlled set Trailer Composite
TC
3694

For details see LNER 29269

3694 07- 23 ➲**23694** 29269

Tyneside York
Controlled set Trailer Third
TT
3731-3747

For details see LNER 29270-29274

3731 08- 23 ➲**23731** 29270
3733 08- 23 ➲**23733** 29271
3744 08- 23 ➲**23744** 29272
3745 08- 23 ➲**23745** 29273
3747 08- 23 ➲**23747** 29274

Tyneside York
Driving Motor Brake Composite
DMBC
3770-3771

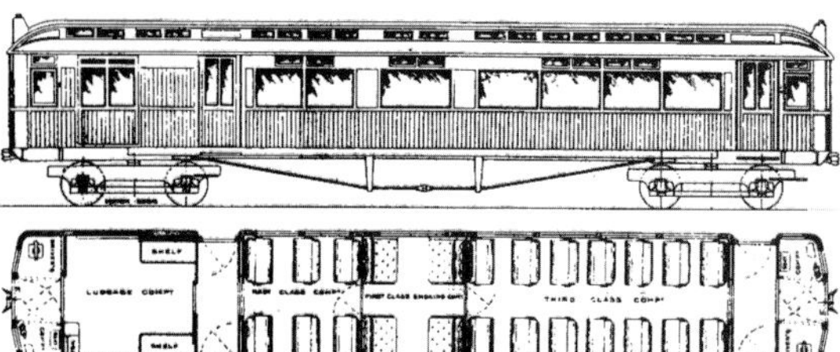

Diagram:	192	LNER Class:	LMD1
Body:	56' 6" × 9' 2½"	Weight:	
Seats:	20 first 28 third	Bogies:	NER
Motors:	BTH 2 × 125hp		

3770	12- 23	**➲23770**
3771	12- 23	**➲23771**

Tyneside York
Trailer Third
TT
3781-3791

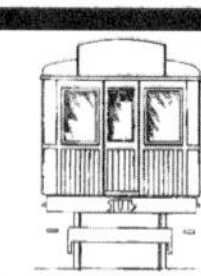

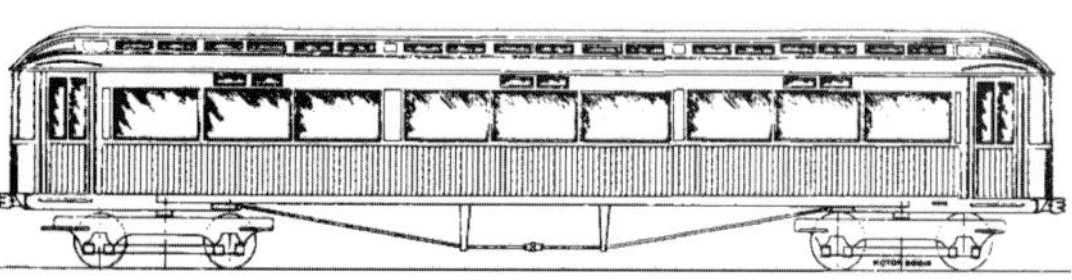

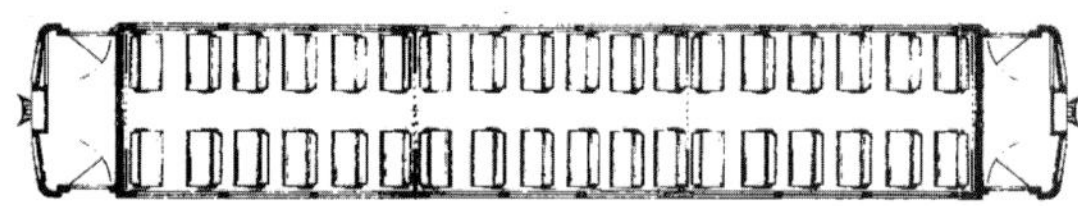

Diagram:	206	LNER Class:	T3
Body:	56' 6" × 9' 2½"	Weight:	22t 16cwt
Seats:	72 third	Bogies:	NER

3781	15- 23	**➲23781**
3782	15- 23	**➲23782**
3783	15- 23	**➲23783**
3784	15- 23	**➲23784**
3785	15-08/18	⊗08/18
3786	15- 23	**➲23786**
3787	15- 23	**➲23787**
3788	15-08/18	⊗08/18
3789	15- 23	**➲23789**
3790	15-08/18	⊗08/18
3791	15-08/18	⊗08/18

Tyneside York
Driving Motor Third
DMT
3792-3793

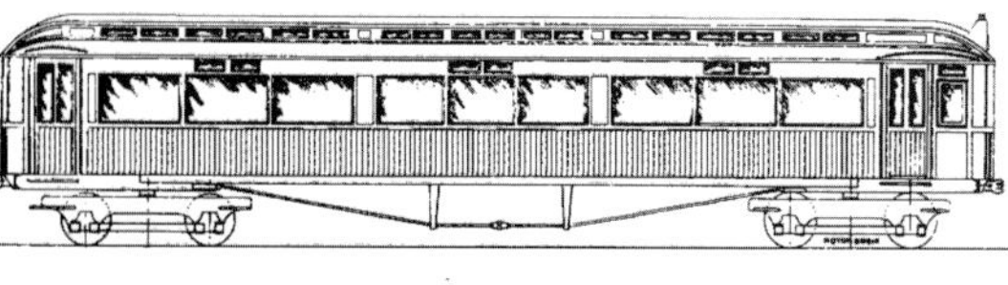

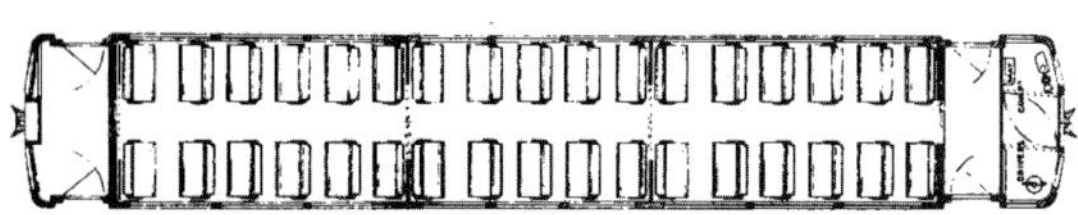

Diagram:	203	LNER Class:	MS3
Body:	56' 6" × 9' 2½"	Weight:	
Seats:	68 third	Bogies:	NER
Motors:	BTH 2 × 125hp		

3792	15- 23	**➲23792**
3793	15- 23	**➲23793**

Tyneside York
Driving Motor Brake Composite
DMBC
3794

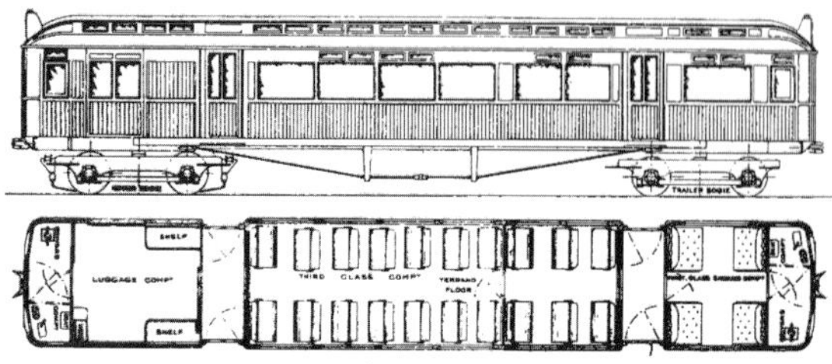

Diagram:	208	LNER Class:	LMD1
Body:	56' 6" × 9' 2½"	Weight:	
Seats:	20 first 28 third	Bogies:	NER
Motors:	BTH 2 × 125hp		

3794	15- 23	**➲23794**

NER 1920-22 stock

The 1920-1922 stock was built carrying the numbers of withdrawn 1904-1915 stock which had been destroyed in the Heaton Shed fire of 11th August 1918.

Tyneside York
Driving Trailer Third
DTT
Between 3180 & 3211

For details see LNER 29375-29380

3180[2]	*20-* 23	**➲23180**	29375
3195[2]	*20-* 23	**➲23195**	29376
3197[2]	*20-* 23	**➲23197**	29377
3198[2]	*20-* 23	**➲23198**	29378
3204[2]	*20-* 23	**➲23204**	29379
3211[2]	*20-* 23	**➲23211**	29380

Tyneside York
Driving Motor Third
DMT
Between 3212 & 3225

For details see LNER 29175-29178 & 29390

3212[2]	*20-* 23	**➲23212**	29175
3217[2]	*20-* 23	**➲23217**	29390
3219[2]	*20-* 23	**➲23219**	29176
3221[2]	*20-* 23	**➲23221**	29177
3225[2]	*20-* 23	**➲23225**	29178

Tyneside York
Driving Motor Third
DMT
3226-3228

For details see LNER 29179-29183

3226[2]	*21-* 23	**➲23226**	29179
3227[2]	*21-* 23	**➲23227**	29180
3228[2]	*21-* 23	**➲23228**	29181

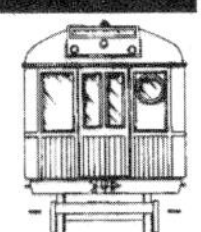

Tyneside York
Driving Motor Brake Composite
DMBC
3238 & 3241

For details see LNER 29184-29185

3238[2]	20-	23	➲**23238**	29184
3241[2]	20-	23	➲**23241**	29185

Tyneside York
Driving Motor Brake Composite
DMBC
Between 3243 & 3253

For details see LNER 29186-29191

3243[2]	20-	23	➲**23243**	29186
3246[2]	20-	23	➲**23246**	29187
3249[2]	20-	23	➲**23249**	
3250[2]	20-	23	➲**23250**	29189
3251[2]	20-	23	➲**23251**	29190

Tyneside York
Driving Trailer Third
DTT
3268

For details see LNER 29391

3268[2]	20-	23	➲**23268**	29391

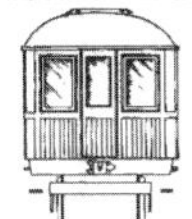

Tyneside York
Driving Trailer Third
DTT
Between 3507-3518

For details see LNER 29381-29385

3507[2]	20-	23	➲**23507**	29381
3508[2]	20-	23	➲**23508**	29382
3512[2]	20-	23	➲**23512**	29383
3513[2]	20-	23	➲**23513**	29384
3518[2]	20-	23	➲**23518**	29385

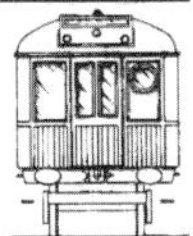

Tyneside York
Driving Motor Third
DMT
3520-3521

For details see LNER 29182-29183

3520[2]	21-	23	➲**23520**	29182
3521[2]	21-	23	➲**23521**	29183

Tyneside York
Driving Trailer Third
DTT
3524

For details see LNER 29392

3524[2]	20-	23	➲**23524**	29392

Tyneside York
Driving Trailer Third
DTT
Between 3785 & 3791

For details see LNER 29386-29389

3785[2]	20-	23	➲**23785**	29386
3788[2]	20-	23	➲**23788**	29387
3790[2]	20-	23	➲**23790**	29388
3791[2]	20-	23	➲**23791**	29389

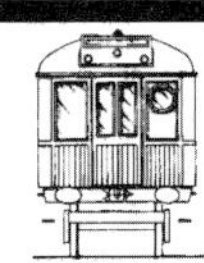

Tyneside York
Motor Luggage Van
MLV
3795

For details see LNER 29493

3795	21-	23	➲**23795**	29493

Departmental Stock

ADB975027	**M61162**	69- 86	⊗12/87	CM&EE Test Coach	
ADB975028	**M70162**	69- *79*	⊗11/79	CM&EE Test Coach	
ADB975029	**M75162**	69- *81*	⊗03/81	CM&EE Test Coach	
ADB975030	**M61165**	69- *81*	⊗03/81	CM&EE Test Coach	
ADB975031	**M70165**	69- *79*	⊗11/79	CM&EE Test Coach	
ADB975032	**M75165**	69- *97*	⊗08/97	CM&EE Test Coach, DT Test Car *Mars*	
*L*DB975178	**M61136**	01/73-07/83	⊗06/94	Battery Locomotive	07/83➲**97701**
*L*DB975179	**M61139**	01/73-07/83	⊗06/94	Battery Locomotive	07/83➲**97702**
ADB975250	**S10829S**	73-12/84	⊗03/90	SR Stores Unit **024**	
ADB975251	**S10830S**	73-12/84	⊗03/90	SR Stores Unit **024**	
ADB975255	**S11162S**	10/72- *75*	⊗06/75	SR Air-Conditioning Test Unit **054**	
ADB975256	**S12237S**	10/72- *75*	⊗06/75	SR Air-Conditioning Test Unit **054**	
ADB975257	**S12602S**	10/72- *75*	⊗06/75	SR Air-Conditioning Test Unit **054**	
ADB975258	**S11202S**	10/72- *75*	⊗06/75	SR Air-Conditioning Test Unit **054**	
ADB975319	**S10919S**	03/74-11/85	⊗07/87	SR Instruction Unit **055**	
ADB975320	**S10171S**	03/74-11/85	⊗07/87	SR Instruction Unit **055**	
ADB975321	**S11470S**	03/74-11/85	⊗07/87	SR Instruction Unit **055**	
ADB975322	**S10920S**	03/74-11/85	⊗07/87	SR Instruction Unit **055**	
ADB975407	**M61166**	07/75- *80*	⊗10/95	Battery Locomotive	*80*➲**97707** **LDB** when built
ADB975408	**M61173**	07/75- *80*	⊗10/95	Battery Locomotive	*80*➲**97708** **LDB** when built
ADB975409	**M61172**	10/75- *80*	⊗09/95	Battery Locomotive	*80*➲**97709** **LDB** when built
ADB975410	**M61175**	10/75- *80*	⊗09/95	Battery Locomotive	*80*➲**97710** **LDB** when built
ADB975430	**S64300**	05/75-12/86	⊗02/87	Electrification Test Unit **920001**	
ADB975431	*new*	04/75- 86	⊗11/87	Electrification Test Unit **920001**	
ADB975432	**S64301**	05/75-04/86	⊗04/86	Electrification Test Unit **920001**	
DB975500	**S12274S**	06/71-03/93	⊗02/94	Manta Long-Welded Rail Wagon	06/89⇨**KDB** S&T General Materials Wagon
DB975501	**S12265S**	06/71-08/93	⊗09/93	Manta Long-Welded Rail Wagon	06/89⇨**KDB** S&T General Materials Wagon
DB975502	**S12262S**	06/71-03/93	⊗02/94	Manta Long-Welded Rail Wagon	06/89⇨**KDB** S&T General Materials Wagon
DB975503	**S12263S**	06/71-03/93	⊗02/94	Manta Long-Welded Rail Wagon	06/89⇨**KDB** S&T General Materials Wagon
DB975504	**S12268S**	06/71-08/93	⊗09/93	Manta Long-Welded Rail Wagon	06/89⇨**KDB** S&T General Materials Wagon
DB975505	**S12269S**	06/71-11/92	⊗10/93	Manta Long-Welded Rail Wagon	06/89⇨**KDB** S&T General Materials Wagon
DB975506	**S12267S**	06/71-11/92	⊗10/93	Manta Long-Welded Rail Wagon	06/89⇨**KDB** S&T General Materials Wagon
DB975507	**S12273S**	06/71-11/92	⊗10/93	Manta Long-Welded Rail Wagon	06/89⇨**KDB** S&T General Materials Wagon
DB975508	**S10039S**	06/71-03/92	⊗06/92	Marlin Long-Welded Rail Wagon	06/89⇨**KDB** S&T Hoist Auxiliary Wagon
DB975509	**S10040S**	06/71-03/92	⊗06/92	Marlin Long-Welded Rail Wagon	06/89⇨**KDB** S&T Hoist Auxiliary Wagon
DB975510	**S10032S**	06/71- 04	Ⓟ	Marlin Long-Welded Rail Wagon	
DB975511	**S10037S**	06/71-07/92	⊗09/92	Marlin Long-Welded Rail Wagon	06/89⇨**KDB** S&T General Materials Wagon 10/92⇨**DB**
DB975512	**S10035S**	06/71- 99	⊗11/04	Marlin Long-Welded Rail Wagon	
DB975513	**S10048S**	71-11/93	⊗08/94	Marlin Long-Welded Rail Wagon	*90*⇨**KDB** Marlin Bogie Carrier
DB975514	**S10050S**	71-05/93	⊗01/05	Marlin Long-Welded Rail Wagon	➲**083656**
DB975515	**S10049S**	71-11/92	⊗10/93	Marlin Long-Welded Rail Wagon	06/89⇨**KDB** S&T General Materials Wagon
DB975516	**S10025S**	71-11/92	⊗10/93	Marlin Long-Welded Rail Wagon	06/89⇨**KDB** S&T General Materials Wagon
DB975517	**S10036S**	71-11/92	⊗10/93	Marlin Long-Welded Rail Wagon	06/89⇨**KDB** S&T General Materials Wagon
DB975518	**S10026S**	71-03/93	⊗07/99	Marlin Long-Welded Rail Wagon	

DB975519 **S10081S** 71-07/92 ⊗09/92 Marlin Long-Welded Rail Wagon
06/89⇨**KDB** S&T General Materials Wagon 10/92⇨**DB**
DB975520 **S11847S** 71-07/92 ⊗09/92 Marlin Long-Welded Rail Wagon
06/89⇨**KDB** S&T General Materials Wagon 10/92⇨**DB**
DB975521 **S11846S** 71-05/92 ⊗07/99 Marlin Long-Welded Rail Wagon
DB975522 **S11849S** 71- 02 ⊗09/04 Marlin Long-Welded Rail Wagon
DB975523 **S11856S** 71-11/92 ⊗10/93 Marlin Long-Welded Rail Wagon
06/89⇨**KDB** S&T General Materials Wagon
DB975524 **S11817S** 71-12/93 ⊗07/99 Marlin Long-Welded Rail Wagon
DB975525 **S11854S** 71-11/92 ⊗10/93 Marlin Long-Welded Rail Wagon
06/89⇨**KDB** S&T General Materials Wagon
DB975526 **S10064S** 71-11/93 ⊗08/94 Marlin Long-Welded Rail Wagon
90⇨**KDB** Marlin Bogie Carrier
DB975527 **S11800S** 71-11/92 ⊗10/93 Marlin Long-Welded Rail Wagonr
06/89⇨**KDB** S&T General Materials Wagon
DB975528 **S10113S** 71-11/93 ⊗08/94 Marlin Long-Welded Rail Wagon
(ex **S12254S**)
DB975529 **S10079S** 71- 99 ⊗03/03 Marlin Long-Welded Rail Wagon
90⇨**KDB** Marlin Bogie Carrier
DB975530 **S11815S** 71-07/92 ⊗08/94 Marlin Long-Welded Rail Wagon
06/89⇨**KDB** S&T General Materials Wagon 10/92⇨**DB**
DB975531 **S11802S** 71-03/93 ⊗07/99 Marlin Long-Welded Rail Wagon
DB975532 **S10103S** 71-11/92 ⊗10/93 Marlin Long-Welded Rail Wagon
06/89⇨**KDB** S&T General Materials Wagon
DB975533 **S10041S** 71-07/93 ⊗02/94 Marlin Long-Welded Rail Wagon
90⇨**KDB** Marlin Bogie Carrier
ADB975586 **S10907S** 05/77- *04* ⊗10/04 SR De-icing Unit **004** 11/91➲**930004**
ADB975587 **S10908S** 05/77- *04* ⊗09/04 SR De-icing Unit **004** 11/91➲**930004**
ADB975588 **S10981S** 12/77- *03* ⊗12/03 SR De-icing Unit **005** ➲**930005**
ADB975589 **S10982S** 12/77- *03* ⊗12/03 SR De-icinq Unit **005** ➲**930005**
ADB975590 **S10833S** 04/78- *04* ⊗09/04 SR De-icing Unit **006** ➲**930006**
ADB975591 **S10834S** 04/78- *04* ⊗09/04 SR De-icing Unit **006** ➲**930006**
ADB975592 **S10993S** 07/78- ⊗06/03 SR De-icing Unit **007** ➲**930007**
ADB975593 **S12659S** 07/78- ⊗06/03 SR De-icing Unit **007** ➲**930007**
ADB975594 **S12658S** 07/78- *04* ⊗11/04 SR De-icing Unit **003** ➲**930003**
ADB975595 **S10994S** 07/78- *04* ⊗11/04 SR De-icing Unit **003** ➲**930003**
ADB975596 **S10844S** 77- *03* ⊗06/03 SR De-icing Unit **008** ➲**930008**
ADB975597 **S10987S** 77- *03* ⊗05/03 SR De-icing Unit **008** ➲**930008**
ADB975598 **S10989S** 77- *04* ⊗02/10 SR De-icing Unit **009** ➲**930009**
ADB975599 **S10990S** 77- ⊗ SR De-icing Unit **009** ➲**930009**
ADB975600 **S10988S** 77- *04* SR De-icing Unit **010** ➲**930010**
ADB975601 **S10843S** 77- *04* SR De-icing Unit **010** ➲**930010**
ADB975602 **S10991S** 77- *04* ⊗11/04 SR De-icing Unit **011** ➲**930011**
ADB975603 **S10992S** 77- *04* ⊗11/04 SR De-icing Unit **011** ➲**930011**
ADB975604 **S10939S** 77- *03* ⊗06/03 SR De-icing Unit **012** ➲**930012**
08/97➲**930001**
ADB975605 **S10940S** 77- *04* ⊗02/10 SR De-icing Unit **012** ➲**930012**
08/97➲**930001**
ADB975610 **S68205** 09/74-03/96 ⊗03/96 Enparts Van (ex **M80942**)
76⇨Stores Van 84⇨ BTU Tool Van
ADB975611 **S68201** 09/74-09/11 ⊗09/11 Enparts Van (ex **M80915**)
76⇨Stores Van 84⇨ BTU Tool Van
ADB975612 **S68203** 09/74-09/11 ⊗09/11 Enparts Van (ex **M80922**)
76⇨Stores Van 84⇨ BTU Tool Van
ADB975613 **S68202** 08/78-09/11 ⊗09/11 HST Enparts Van (ex **M80918**)
76⇨Stores Van 84⇨ BTU Tool Van
ADB975614 **S68204** 78- ⊗03/96 HST Enparts Van (ex **M80925**)
76⇨Stores Van 84⇨ BTU Tool Van
ADB975615 **S68206** 78-11/05 ⊗01/08 HST Enparts Van (ex **M80951**)
76⇨Stores Van 84⇨ BTU Tool Van
LDB975673 **M61182** Cancelled ⊗09/95 Battery Locomotive **97703**
LDB975674 **M61185** Cancelled ⊗09/95 Battery Locomotive **97704**
LDB975675 **M61184** Cancelled ⊗10/95 Battery Locomotive **97705**
LDB975676 **M61189** Cancelled ⊗10/95 Battery Locomotive **97706**
ADB975844 **S64305** 80- 85 ⊗11/90 SR Experimental Unit **057**
ADB975845 **S62427** 04/81- 84 ⊗07/86 SR Experimental Unit **056**
ADB975846 **S62428** 04/81- 84 ⊗07/86 SR Experimental Unit **056**
ADB975847 **S64302** 04/81- 84 ⊗07/86 SR Experimental Unit **056**
ADB975848 **S64303** 04/81- 84 ⊗07/86 SR Experimental Unit **056**
ADB975849 **S62426** 80- 85 ⊗11/90 SR Experimental Unit **057**
ADB975850 **S62429** 80- 85 ⊗11/90 SR Experimental Unit **057**
ADB975851 **S64304** 80- 85 ⊗11/90 SR Experimental Unit **057**
ADB975896 **S11387S** 79- *04* ⊗09/04 SR De-icing Unit **930013** 06/97➲**930202**
ADB975897 **S11388S** 79- *04* ⊗09/04 SR De-icing Unit **930013** 06/97➲**930202**
ADB977017 **M28319M** 81-04/83 ⊗12/85 De-icing and Sandite Unit
ADB977018 **M28334M** 81-04/83 ⊗12/85 De-icing and Sandite Unit
ADB977068 **S14549S** 02/87-06/91 ⊗09/93 CM&EE Stores Van Unit **019**
ADB977069 **S16029S** 02/87-06/91 ⊗09/93 CM&EE Stores Van Unit **019**
ADB977115 **M29702M** 82-04/83 ⊗10/85 Sandite Coach
ADB977205 **S61971** 02/84-05/85 ⊗11/85 RM&EE Tractor Unit **051**
ADB977206 **S76004** 02/84-05/85 ⊗11/85 RM&EE Tractor Unit **051**
ADB977207 **S61658** 02/84- *10* ⊗02/10 RM&EE Tractor Unit **054, 930014**
06/97➲**930101**
ADB977208 **S75710** 02/84- *90* ⊗07/90 RM&EE Tractor Unit **054**
ADB977209 **S61663** 02/84- *89* ⊗06/89 RM&EE Tractor Unit **052**
ADB977210 **S75715** 02/84- *89* ⊗06/89 RM&EE Tractor Unit **052**
ADB977211 **S61684** 02/84- *90* ⊗07/90 RM&EE Tractor Unit **053**
ADB977212 **S75736** 02/84- *90* ⊗07/90 RM&EE Tractor Unit **053**
ADB977213 **S61627** 02/84- 88 ⊗04/88 RM&EE Temporary Stores Unit **020**
ADB977214 **S75362** 02/84- 88 ⊗04/88 RM&EE Temporary Stores Unit **020**
ADB977290 **S65318** 03/85-06/91 ⊗09/93 RM&EE Stores Unit **018**
ADB977291 **S65324** 03/85-06/91 ⊗09/93 RM&EE Stores Unit **018**
ADB977294 **S11305S** *05/85*-01/88 ⊗11/90 RM&EE Tractor Unit **025**
ADB977295 **S11306S** *05/85*-01/88 ⊗11/90 RM&EE Tractor Unit **025**
ADB977296 **S65319** 12/85-09/97 ⊗09/97 RM&EE Tractor Unit **050, 932054**
ADB977297 **S77108** 12/85-03/93 ⊗10/93 RM&EE Tractor Unit **050**
ADB977304 **S65317** 85-01/93 ⊗03/95 RM&EE Lathe Shunter Unit **021**
ADB977305 **S65322** 85-01/93 ⊗03/95 RM&EE Lathe Shunter Unit **021**
ADB977307 **E75500** (02/89)- ⊗10/88 CM&EE Test Coach
ADB977308 **E75552** (02/89)- ⊗10/88 CM&EE Test Coach
ADB977309 **E61467** (02/89)- ⊗10/88 CM&EE Test Coach
DB977335 **S76277** 12/87-04/04 Ⓟ Support Coach 04/03⇨□ (ex **S4005**)
DB977336 **S76278** 12/87-08/92 ⊗06/93 Support Coach (ex **S4007**)
ADB977345 **M61178** 86-09/97 ⊗12/97 De-Icing & Sandite Unit **936001**
ADB977346 **M75178** 86- ⊗07/02 De-Icing & Sandite Unit **936001**
ADB977347 **M61180** 86-09/97 ⊗12/97 De-Icing & Sandite Unit **936002**
ADB977348 **M75180** 86- ⊗07/02 De-Icing & Sandite Unit **936002**
ADB977349 **M61183** 86-11/06 Ⓟ De-Icing & Sandite Unit **936003**
ADB977350 **M75183** 86- ⊗07/02 De-Icing & Sandite Unit **936003**
ADB977362 **ADS70050** 86-*08/93* ⊗02/94 RM&EE De-Icing Coach (ex **S10392S**)
(09/91 **DB977362** carried by **97701** in error)
ADB977363 **ADS70051** 86- 90 ⊗09/93 RM&EE De-Icing Coach (ex **S10399S**)
(09/91 **DB977363** carried by **97702** in error)
ADB977364 **ADS70087** 86-02/10 Ⓟ RM&EE De-Icing Coach (ex **S10400S**)
ADB977365 **ADS70268** 86- 90 ⊗08/93 RM&EE De-Icing Unit **001** (ex **S10726S**)
ADB977366 **ADS70273** 86- 89 ⊗08/93 RM&EE De-Icing Unit **001/002**(ex **S10500S**)
ADB977367 **ADS70270** 86- 89 ⊗08/93 RM&EE De-Icing Unit **002** (ex **S10497S**)
ADB977368 **ADS70272** 86- 90 ⊗08/93 RM&EE De-Icing Unit **002/001**(ex **S10499S**)
ADB977385 **M61148** 04/87- 92 ⊗09/97 RM&EE De-Icing & Sandite Unit
"The Beastie"
ADB977386 **M75189** 04/87- 92 ⊗10/93 RM&EE De-Icing & Sandite Unit
DB977394 **65316** Cancelled ⊗11/91 Mobile Track Assessment Coach
DB977395 **61035** 07/91-04/94 ⊗01/96 Mobile Track Assessment Coach
Tractor Unit **930080** (**65312** originally allocated)
DB977396 **61342** 07/91-04/94 ⊗01/96 Mobile Track Assessment Coach
Tractor Unit **930080** (**65313** originally allocated)
DB977397 **61388** 05/90-04/94 ⊗01/96 Mobile Track Assessment Coach
Tractor Unit **930081**
DB977398 **61389** 05/90-04/94 ⊗01/96 Mobile Track Assessment Coach
Tractor Unit **930081**
ADB977505 **65321** 02/87- 96 Ⓟ M&EE Tractor Unit **1053 930053**
ADB977506 **65323** 02/87- 96 ⊗10/96 M&EE Tractor Unit **1054 930054**
ADB977507 **77110** 02/87-03/93 ⊗10/93 M&EE Tractor Unit **1053 930053**
ADB977508 **77112** 02/87- 96 Ⓟ M&EE Tractor Unit **1054 930054**
ADB977531 **S14047S** 87-04/94 ⊗03/95 M&EE Sandite & Tractor Unit **930015**
ADB977532 **S14048S** 87-04/94 ⊗03/95 M&EE Sandite & Tractor Unit **930015**
ADB977533 **S14273S** 87- *03* ⊗07/03 M&EE Sandite & Tractor Unit **930016**
06/97➲**930102**
ADB977534 **S14384S** 87- *03* ⊗07/03 M&EE Sandite & Tractor Unit **930016**
06/97➲**930102**
DB977542 **70869** 10/91-12/91 ⊗12/91 Mobile Track Assessment Coach
(ex **S13002**)
DB977543 **76295** 10/91-09/93 ⊗09/93 Mobile Track Assessment Coach
(ex **S3927**)
DB977544 **76296** 10/91-09/93 ⊗09/93 Mobile Track Assessment Coach
(ex **S3945**)
DB977545 **70825** 10/91-12/91 ⊗12/91 Mobile Track Assessment Coach
(ex **S34996**)
ADB977559 **65313** 87- *04* ⊗08/04 M&EE Carriage Cleaning Fluid & Tractor Unit **062**
ADB977560 **65320** 87- *04* ⊗08/04 M&EE Carriage Cleaning Fluid & Tractor Unit **062**
ADB977566 **65312** 87- *05* ⊗02/05 M&EE Sandite Unit **930017** 10/97➲**930201**
ADB977567 **65314** 87- *05* ⊗11/05 M&EE Sandite Unit **930017** 10/97➲**930201**
ADB977578 **77101** 89- *02* ⊗06/02 Sandite Coach **930078** used with Cl 317/319
ADB977579 **77109** 89- *02* ⊗06/02 Sandite Coach **930079** used with Cl 317/319
ADB977598 **75080** 88-04/94 ⊗03/97 M&EE Sandite & Tractor Unit **937996**
ADB977599 **61073** 88-04/94 ⊗03/97 M&EE Sandite & Tractor Unit **937996**
ADB977600 **75061** 88-04/94 ⊗03/97 M&EE Sandite & Tractor Unit **937996**
ADB977601 **75211** 88-04/94 ⊗04/94 M&EE Sandite & Tractor Unit **937997**
ADB977602 **61228** 88-03/94 ⊗04/94 M&EE Sandite & Tractor Unit **937997**
ADB977603 **75035** 88-11/92 ⊗04/94 M&EE Sandite & Tractor Unit **937997**
ADB977604 **75077** 88-04/94 ⊗04/99 M&EE Sandite & Tractor Unit **937998**
ADB977605 **61062** 88-04/94 ⊗05/99 M&EE Sandite & Tractor Unit **937998**
ADB977606 **75070** 88-04/94 ⊗04/99 M&EE Sandite & Tractor Unit **937998**
ADB977609 **65414** 88- *10* ⊗02/10 Tractor Unit
90⇨M&EE De-Icing & Sandite Unit **930014** 06/97➲**930101**
ADB977610 **77136** 88- *90* ⊗07/90 Tractor Unit
90⇨M&EE De-Icing & Sandite Unit
ADB977639 **75548** 05/89-09/94 Ⓟ M&EE Electrification Instruction Unit **305935**
ADB977640 **61463** 05/89-09/94 Ⓟ M&EE Electrification Instruction Unit **305935**
ADB977641 **75214** 05/89-09/94 Ⓟ M&EE Electrification Instruction Unit **305935**
ADB977668 **75001** 11/91-03/93 ⊗08/94 Crash Test Coach
ADB977669 **61001** 11/91-03/93 ⊗04/93 Crash Test Coach
ADB977670 **70001** 11/91-03/93 ⊗03/93 Crash Test Coach
ADB977671 **75101** 11/91-03/93 ⊗04/93 Crash Test Coach
ADB977672 **75006** 11/91-03/93 ⊗08/94 Crash Test Coach
ADB977673 **61006** 11/91-03/93 ⊗04/93 Crash Test Coach
ADB977674 **70006** 11/91-03/93 ⊗08/94 Crash Test Coach
ADB977675 **75106** 11/91-03/93 ⊗03/93 Crash Test Coach
ADB977676 **75021** 11/91-03/93 ⊗08/94 Crash Test Coach
ADB977677 **61021** 11/91-03/93 ⊗04/93 Crash Test Coach
ADB977678 **70021** 11/91-03/93 ⊗08/94 Crash Test Coach
ADB977679 **75121** 11/91-03/93 ⊗03/93 Crash Test Coach
ADB977684 **76282** 04/90- *96* ⊗10/96 Test Coach (ex **S4374**)
ADB977685 **70818** 04/90- *96* ⊗10/96 Test Coach (ex **S34961**)
ADB977686 **70850** 04/90- *96* ⊗10/96 Test Coach (ex **S13009**)
ADB977687 **76281** 04/90-10/94 ⊗10/96 Test Coach (ex **S4042**)
ADB977688 **77111** 90-03/92 ⊗07/92 Emergency Exercise Training Unit **999**
ADB977689 **77106** 90-03/92 ⊗07/92 Emergency Exercise Training Unit **999**
ADB977690 **77102** 90-03/92 ⊗07/92 Emergency Exercise Training Unit **999**
ADB977691 **77103** 90-03/92 ⊗07/92 Emergency Exercise Training Unit **999**
ADB977702 **S14575S** - ⊗10/91 Mobile Instruction Coach
ADB977703 **S15013S** - ⊗10/91 Mobile Instruction Coach
ADB977704 **S15160S** - ⊗10/91 Mobile Instruction Coach
ADB977705 **S14487S** - ⊗10/91 Mobile Instruction Coach

Number	Original	Dates	Withdrawn	Use	Notes
ADB977708	75018	03/93-08/94	⊗ 94	Power Collection Test Coach **316998** then **316997**	
ADB977709	61018	03/93-08/94	⊗06/01	Power Collection Test Coach **316998** then **316997**	
ADB977710	75118	03/93-08/94	⊗07/01	Power Collection Test Coach **316998** then **316997**	
TDB977711	75759	03/91- *96*	⊗07/96	Test Train **303999**	
TDB977712	61825	03/91- *96*	⊗05/97	Test Train **303999**	
TDB977713	75815	03/91- *96*	⊗05/97	Test Train **303999**	
ADB977719	75814	Cancelled		Special Duties Unit **303048**	(ex **SC75808**)
ADB977720	61824	Cancelled		Special Duties Unit **303048**	
ADB977721	75758	Cancelled		Special Duties Unit **303048**	(ex **SC75752**)
ADB977729	61249	Cancelled	⊗12/92		
ADB977730	75369	Cancelled	⊗12/92		
ADB977731	61260	92-05/92	⊗05/92	Radio Trials Coach	
ADB977732	75379	92-05/92	⊗05/92	Radio Trials Coach	
ADB977733	61288	Cancelled	⊗12/92		
ADB977734	75408	Cancelled	⊗12/92		
ADB977735	61296	Cancelled	⊗12/92		
ADB977736	75416	Cancelled	⊗12/92		
ADB977737	61651	92-11/92	⊗12/92	Cancelled	
ADB977738	75706	92-11/92	⊗12/92	Cancelled	
ADB977739	61668	Cancelled	⊗05/92		
ADB977740	75720	Cancelled	⊗05/92		
ADB977741	75469	-	⊗04/99	Sandite Coach **937908**	
ADB977742	61436	-	⊗04/99	Sandite Coach **937908**	
ADB977743	75521	-	⊗04/99	Sandite Coach **937908**	
ADB977763	70871	05/92-05/92	⊗10/96	Test Coach	Conversion Cancelled (ex **S13017**)
ADB977764	70866	05/92-05/92	⊗10/05	Test Coach	Conversion Cancelled (ex **S13037**)
ADB977777	S14303S	05/92-04/94	⊗04/94	ATP Test Train Unit **930997**	
ADB977778	S15230S	05/92-04/94	⊗04/94	ATP Test Train Unit **930997**	
ADB977779	S15285S	05/92-04/94	⊗04/94	ATP Test Train Unit **930997**	
ADB977780	S14356S	05/92-04/94	⊗04/94	ATP Test Train Unit **930997**	
ADB977797	S14227S	-	⊗10/92	Emergency Exercise Training Coach	
ADB977798	S15242S	-	⊗10/92	Emergency Exercise Training Coach	
ADB977799	S15426S	-	⊗10/92	Emergency Exercise Training Coach	
ADB977800	S14228S	-	⊗10/92	Emergency Exercise Training Coach	
ADB977804	65336	06/92- *04*	⊗02/04	De-icing Unit **930030**	04/98➲**930202**
ADB977805	65357	06/92- *04*	⊗02/04	De-icing Unit **930030**	04/98➲**930202**
ADB977844	76414	10/93-09/93	⊗08/06	Sandite Coach **936103**	
ADB977845	62174	10/93-06/02	℗	Sandite Coach **936103**	
ADB977846	76433	10/93-09/93	℗	Sandite Coach **936103**	
ADB977847	76415	10/93-06/02	⊗07/02	Sandite Coach **936104**	
ADB977848	62175	10/93-09/93	⊗06/02	Sandite Coach **936104**	
ADB977849	76434	10/93-06/02	⊗09/02	Sandite Coach **936104**	
ADB977856	77531	06/93- *04*	⊗02/04	Route Learning Unit **931001**	
ADB977857	65346	06/93- *04*	⊗03/04	Route Learning Unit **931001**	
ADB977861	61044	05/93- *05*	⊗12/05	Route Learning Unit **930082**	
ADB977862	70039	05/93- *05*	⊗12/05	Route Learning Unit **930082**	
ADB977863	61038	05/93- *05*	⊗11/05	Route Learning Unit **930082**	
ADB977864	65341	08/93- *04*	⊗11/04	De-Icing Unit **930031**	10/97➲**930203**
ADB977865	65355	08/93- *04*	⊗11/05	De-Icing Unit **930031**	10/97➲**930203**
ADB977871	65353	08/93- *05*	⊗11/05	De-Icing Unit **930033**	06/97➲**930205**
ADB977872	65367	08/93- *05*	⊗12/05	De-Icing Unit **930033**	06/97➲**930205**
ADB977874	65302	08/93-06/09	℗	De-Icing Unit **930032**	10/97➲**930204**
ADB977875	65304	08/93-06/09	℗	De-Icing Unit **930032**	10/97➲**930204**
DB977876	75905	09/94-	⊗08/02	Sandite Unit **937990**	
DB977877	61901	09/94-	⊗07/02	Sandite Unit **937990**	
DB977878	75938	09/94-05/02	⊗05/02	Sandite Unit **937990**	
DB977917	65331	94- *03*	⊗12/03	Route Learning Unit **931002**	
DB977918	77516	94- *03*	⊗12/03	Route Learning Unit **931002**	
977919	65370	Cancelled	⊗ 95	Emergency Incident Unit	
977920	77555	Cancelled	⊗ 95	Emergency Incident Unit	
ADB977924	65382	10/94-09/09	℗	Sandite Coach **930034**	10/97➲**930206**
ADB977925	65379	10/94-09/09	℗	Sandite Coach **930034**	10/97➲**930206**
DB977926	75900	09/94- *02*	⊗07/02	Sandite Coach **937991**	
DB977927	61896	09/94- *02*	⊗07/02	Sandite Coach **937991**	
DB977928	75933	09/94- *02*	⊗06/02	Sandite Coach **937991**	
977929	75904	Cancelled	⊗06/95		
977930	61900	Cancelled	⊗06/95		
977931	75937	Cancelled	⊗06/95		
977962	75642	-02/09	℗	Cab Signalling Test Unit	West Coast Flyer
977963	61937	-02/09	℗	Cab Signalling Test Unit	West Coast Flyer
977964	75981	-02/09	℗	Cab Signalling Test Unit	West Coast Flyer
977965	75965	-02/09	℗	Cab Signalling Test Unit	New Dalby
977966	61928	-02/09	℗	Cab Signalling Test Unit	New Dalby
977967	75972	-02/09	℗	Cab Signalling Test Unit	New Dalby
977977	76137	12/02-03/07	⊗03/07	Hitachi V-Train	
977978	62090	12/02-03/07	⊗03/07	Hitachi V-Train	
977979	62078	12/02-03/07	⊗03/07	Hitachi V-Train	
977980	76187	12/02-03/07	⊗06/07	Hitachi V-Train	
977981	62138	12/02-06/05	⊗06/05	Hitachi V-Train	
977983	72503	06/10-		Network Rail Hot Box Detection Coach	(ex **3407**)
DB977985	72715	05/03-11/05		Structure Gauging Support Coach (ex **6019**) Later Brake Force Runner	
977997	72613	09/09-		Radio Survey Coach	(ex **W6126**)
DB999602	S62483	88- 93	⊗	Ultrasonic Test Train Instrumentation Coach	
DB999603	S62482	88-01/07	⊗	Ultrasonic Test Train Coach	
999606	S62356	05-	⊗	Ultrasonic Test Train Coach	
97701	M61136	07/83-07/93	⊗06/94	Battery Locomotive	(ex **DB975178**)
97702	M61139	07/83-07/93	⊗06/94	Battery Locomotive	(ex **DB975179**)
97703	M61182	01/80-04/95	⊗09/95	Battery Locomotive	(ex *DB975673*)
97704	M61185	01/80-04/95	⊗09/95	Battery Locomotive	(ex *DB975674*)
97705	M61184	04/80-04/95	⊗10/95	Battery Locomotive	(ex *DB975675*)
97706	M61189	04/80-04/95	⊗10/95	Battery Locomotive	(ex *DB975676*)
97707	M61166	*80*-04/95	⊗10/95	Battery Locomotive	(ex **ADB975407**)
97708	M61173	*80*-04/95	⊗10/95	Battery Locomotive	(ex **ADB975408**)
97709	M61172	*80-07/87*	⊗09/95	Battery Locomotive	(ex **ADB975409**)
97710	M61175	*80-07/87*	⊗09/95	Battery Locomotive	(ex **ADB975410**)
61358		04/97- 02	⊗ 02	Class 932 Test Unit **932545**	
61359		04/97- 02	⊗ 02	Class 932 Test Unit **932545**	
61948		01/93- 03		Class 932 Test Class 932 Test Unit **932620**	
61949		01/93- 03		Class 932 Test Unit **932620**	
68001		92- 99		Tractor Unit **931091**	
68002		92- 03		Tractor Unit **931092**	
68003		92- 99		Tractor Unit **931093**	
68004		92- 99		Tractor Unit **931094**	
68005		92- 99		Tractor Unit **931095**	
68007		92- 99		Tractor Unit **931097**	
68008		92- 99		Tractor Unit **931098**	
68009		92- 99		Tractor Unit **931099**	
68010		92- 99		Tractor Unit **931090**	
70330		04/97- 02		Class 932 Test Unit **932545**	
70653		01/93- 03		Class 932 Test Unit **932620**	
70660		01/93- 03		Class 932 Test Unit **932620**	
72613		07/09-			(ex **6126**)
72631		07/09-			(ex **6096**)
S8642S		04/76- 76		Thyristor Test Unit **4748**	
S9028S		04/76- 76		Thyristor Test Unit **4748**	
S10213S		04/76- 76		Thyristor Test Unit **4748**	
S12789S		04/76- 76		Thyristor Test Unit **4748**	
DS40	S8564S	04/56-05/74	⊗05/76	Instruction Unit **S10**, later unit **053**	
DS41	S9658S	04/56-05/74	⊗05/76	Instruction Unit **S10**, later unit **053**	
DS42	S9817S	04/56-05/74	⊗05/76	Instruction Unit **S10**, later unit **053**	
DS347	8741	-11/61	⊗*02/62*	Unit **S90**	
DS348	8899	-11/61	⊗*02/62*	Unit **S90**	
DS349	8698	-11/61	⊗*02/62*	Unit **S91**	
DS350	8864	-11/61	⊗*02/62*	Unit **S91**	
DS351	9010	12/45-12/56	⊗ 58	De-icing Van	
DS352	9116	12/45-05/61	⊗05/61	De-icing Van	
DS353	9013	11/45-06/61	⊗06/61	De-icing Van	
DS354	9069	11/45-02/61	⊗04/61	De-icing Van	
DS355	9060	11/45-12/56	⊗	De-icing Van	
DS356	9003	11/45- *61*	⊗	De-icing Van	
DS396	8957	11/46-02/61	⊗04/61	De-icing Van	
DS397	8958	11/46-02/61	⊗04/61	De-icing Van	
DS398	9079	11/46-05/61	⊗04/61	De-icing Van	
DS399	9089	11/46- *62*	⊗	De-icing Van	
DS434	8951	01/47-	⊗	Departmental Trailer	
DS435	8952	01/47-	⊗	Departmental Trailer	
DS590	8961	09/47-	⊗	CMEE Stores Van	
DS70044	S8456S	09/60-01/62	⊗	De-icing Unit **S92**	
DS70045	S8455S	09/60- 79	⊗	De-icing Unit **S92**, later unit **011**	
DS70050	S10392S	05/59- 86	⊗02/94	De-icing Trailer 70➲**ADS** 86➲**ADB977362**	
DS70051	S10399S	05/59- 86	⊗09/93	De-icing Trailer 70➲**ADS** 86➲**ADB977363**	
DS70057	S8420S	61- 67	⊗01/70	Mobile Test Unit **S15**	
DS70058	S8473S	61- 67	⊗01/70	Mobile Test Unit **S15**	
DS70086	S10397S	06/60-		De-icing Trailer 70➲**ADS**	
DS70087	S10400S	06/60- 86	℗	De-icing Trailer 70➲**ADS** 86➲**ADB977364**	
DS70090	S8446S	09/60- 79	⊗05/80	De-icing Unit **S93**, later unit **012**	
DS70091	S8445S	09/60- 79	⊗05/80	De-icing Unit **S93**, later unit **012**	
DS70092	S8463S	09/60- 79	⊗09/80	De-icing Unit **S94**, later unit **013**	
DS70093	S8464S	09/60- 79	⊗09/80	De-icing Unit **S94**, later unit **013**	
DS70094	S8453S	09/60- 79	⊗	De-icing Unit **S95**, later unit **014**	
DS70095	S8454S	09/60- 79	⊗	De-icing Unit **S95**, later unit **014**	
DS70096	S8433S	09/60- 79	⊗04/80	De-icing Unit **S96**, later unit **015**	
DS70097	S8434S	09/60- 79	⊗04/80	De-icing Unit **S96**, later unit **015**	
DS70098	S8471S	10/60- 79	⊗	De-icing Unit **S97**, later unit **016**	
DS70099	S8472S	10/60- 79	⊗	De-icing Unit **S97**, later unit **016**	
DS70100	S8467S	10/60- 79	⊗	De-icing Unit **S98**, later unit **017**	
DS70101	S8468S	10/60- 79	⊗	De-icing Unit **S98**, later unit **017**	
DS70102	S8422S	10/60- 79	⊗	De-icing Unit **S99**, later unit **018**	
DS70103	S8421S	10/60- 79	⊗	De-icing Unit **S99**, later unit **018**	
DS70104	S8430S	10/60- 79	⊗05/80	De-icing Unit **S100**, later unit **019**	
DS70105	S8465S	10/60- 79	⊗05/80	De-icing Unit **S100**, later unit **019**	
DS70106	S8427S	10/60- 79	⊗	De-icing Unit **S101**, later unit **020**	
DS70107	S8423S	10/60- 79	⊗	De-icing Unit **S101**, later unit **020**	
DS70173	S8457S	10/60- 79	⊗	De-icing Unit **S92**, later unit **011**	
DS70258	S11057S	-12/69	⊗03/72	Mobile Test Unit **S15**[2]	*Conversion Cancelled*
DS70259	S11058S	-12/69	⊗03/72	Mobile Test Unit **S15**[2]	*Conversion Cancelled*
DS70260	264 *Ruth*	-12/69	℗	Mobile Test Unit **S15**[2]	*Conversion Cancelled*
DS70261	278 *Bertha*	-12/69	℗	Mobile Test Unit **S15**[2]	*Conversion Cancelled*
DS70268	S10726S	69- 86	⊗ 93	De-icing Unit **001**	86➲**ADB977365**
DS70269	S10764S	69- 78	⊗05/80	De-icing Unit **002**	
DS70270	S10497S	69- 86	⊗ 93	De-icing Unit **003**, later unit **002**	86➲**ADB977367**
DS70271	S10498S	69- 78	⊗05/80	De-icing Unit **002**	
DS70272	S10499S	69- 86	⊗ 93	De-icing Unit **003**, later unit **002**	86➲**ADB977368**
DS70273	S10500S	69- 86	⊗ 93	De-icing Unit **001**	86➲**ADB977366**
DS70276	S12266S	-		Crane Runner (Underframe Only)	
DS70277	S12275S	- 01	℗	Crane Runner (Underframe Only)	

DS70278	**S10027S**	- 02	℗	Crane Runner (Underframe Only)	
DS70279	**S12270S**	-	℗	Crane Runner (Underframe Only)	
DS70280	**S11861S**	-	℗	Crane Runner (Underframe Only)	(ex **S12232S**)
DS70281	**S12235S**	- 01	℗	Crane Runner (Underframe Only)	
DS70315	**S10731S**	04/70-12/83	⊗12/85	Stores Unit **022**	
DS70316	**S10787S**	04/70-12/83	⊗12/85	Stores Unit **023**	
DS70317	**S10742S**	05/70-02/84	⊗05/86	Stores Unit **023**	
DS70318	**S10760S**	05/70-02/84	⊗05/86	Stores Unit **022**	
DS70321	**S10603S**	70- 75	⊗ 75	Research Department Unit **024** (**2037**)	
DS70322	**S12060S**	70- 75	⊗ 75	Research Department Unit **024** (**2037**)	
DE900729	**NE23266E**		⊗	De-icing Vehicle	
DE900730	**NE23267E**		℗	De-icing Vehicle	

Internal User Vehicles

023450	**M29776M**		⊗	
040851	**M29090M**		⊗	
040926	**M29770M**		⊗	
040927	**M29769M**		⊗	
041368	**E65459**		⊗	
080336	**S12518S**		⊗	
081046	**S8715S**	09/56-05/59	⊗05/59	Towing Unit **4543**
081047	**S8881S**	09/56-05/59	⊗05/59	Towing Unit **4543**
081269	**S8449S**	07/60-12/69	⊗12/70	Towing Unit **4342**
081270	**S8450S**	07/60-12/69	⊗12/70	Towing Unit **4342**
083145	**S10088S**			

E65248	⊗
E65604	⊗
E65622	⊗
M29772M	⊗
S12618S	⊗

EMU vehicles re-used as PCVs

PCV Ashford/Eastleigh
Propelling Control Vehicle
PCV
94300-94345

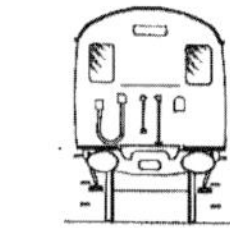

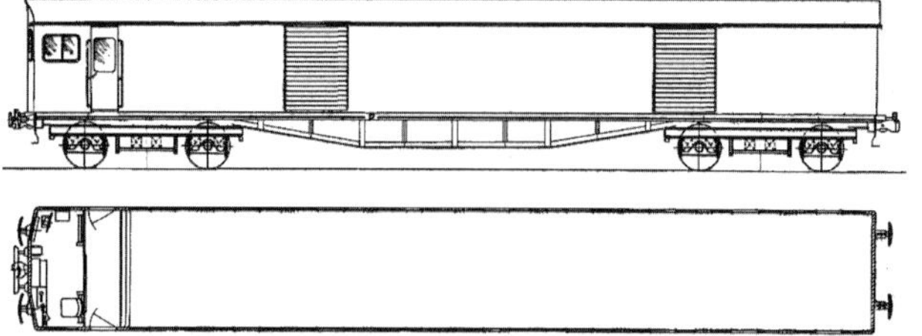

Diagram: NA508
Lot Number: 30565
Builder: Ashford/Eastleigh Rebuilt Hunslet/Barclay
94300-94301 Rebuilt Derby EDU 1993
Built: 1954-1956 Rebuilt 1994-1996
Bogies: B5

94300	09/93-12/98	⊃**95300**	⊂**75114**
94301	09/93-12/98	⊃**95301**	⊂**75102**
94302	04/96-03/04		⊂**75124**
94303	11/95-01/04		⊂**75131**
94304	05/96-04/02		⊂**75107**
94305	04/96-01/04	⊗04/07	⊂**75104**
94306	02/96-03/04		⊂**75112**
94307	11/95-01/04	⊗ 13	⊂**75127**
94308	03/96-02/04		⊂**75125**
94309	12/95-03/04	⊗02/07	⊂**75130**
94310	01/96-02/04		⊂**75119**
94311	01/96-02/04		⊂**75105**
94312	11/95-01/04	⊗09/07	⊂**75126**
94313	01/96-02/04		⊂**75129**
94314	11/95-08/03	⊗09/07	⊂**75109**
94315	12/95-01/04	⊗08/06	⊂**75132**
94316	02/96-02/04		⊂**75108**
94317	12/95-01/04		⊂**75117**
94318	01/96-04/02	⊗ 13	⊂**75115**
94319	11/95-01/04	⊗ 4/07	⊂**75128**
94320	02/96-06/04	℗	⊂**75120**
94321	01/96-01/04	⊗04/07	⊂**75122**
94322	02/96-09/03		⊂**75111**
94323	02/96-03/04		⊂**75110**
94324	02/96-01/04	⊗09/07	⊂**75103**
94325	12/95-03/04	⊗02/07	⊂**75113**
94326	02/96-02/04		⊂**75123**
94327	06/96-01/04	⊗05/07	⊂**75116**
94331	10/96-02/04	⊗ 13	⊂**75022**
94332	11/96-02/04		⊂**75011**
94333	10/96 02/04		⊂**75016**
94334	08/96-06/04		⊂**75017**
94335	09/96-02/04		⊂**75032**
94336	06/96-03/04		⊂**75031**
94337	08/96-02/04		⊂**75029**
94338	09/96-02/04		⊂**75008**
94339	11/96-01/04	⊗02/07	⊂**75024**
94340	07/96-02/04		⊂**75012**
94341	05/96-03/04	⊗02/07	⊂**75007**
94342	09/96-01/04	⊗04/07	⊂**75005**
94343	03/96-02/03		⊂**75027**
94344	05/96-03/04		⊂**75014**
94345	02/96-01/04	⊗04/07	⊂**75004**

PCV Ashford/Eastleigh
Propelling Control Vehicle
PCV
95300-95301

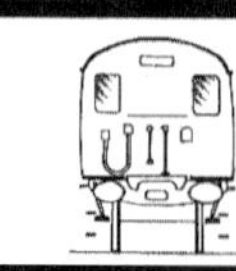

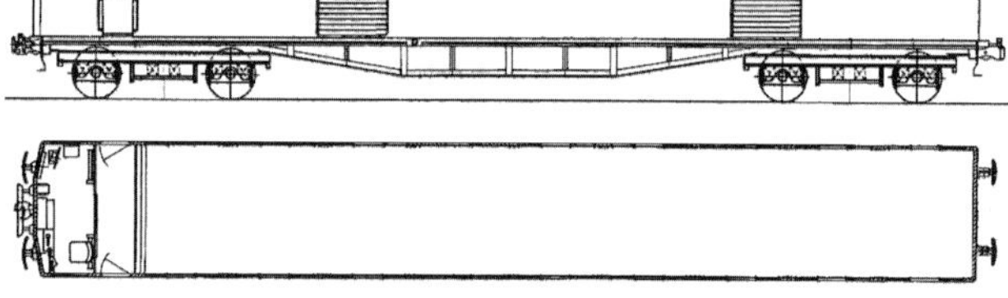

Diagram: NA508
Lot Number: 30565
Builder: Ashford/Eastleigh Rebuilt Derby EDU
Built: 1954-1956 Rebuilt 1994-1996
Bogies: B5

95300	12/98-08/03	**94300**
95301	12/98-08/03	⊂**94301**

Above: De-icing trailer ADS70086 was converted from 4-SUB trailer S10397S in 1960. It is pictured at Eastleigh on 7 May 1976. *John Scrace*

Below: Instruction unit S10 was formed in 1956 from the three original carriages from LSWR bodied 3-SUB unit 1782. It is seen here at Fratton on 30 July 1970. *John Scrace*

Above: Departmental de-icing unit number 93 at Pulborough on 4 March 1967. This later became unit number 012. The unit was formed from the power cars of 4-SUB unit 4340 in 1960. *John Scrace*

Left: De-icing unit 003 was formed in 1969 from two HAL-styled vehicles which had been used in 4-LAV sets. It was renumbered 002 in 1982. ADS70270, leading, was originally 10497 in unit 2954, while ADS70272 started life as 10499 in 2955. The unit is seen at Selhurst on 4 October 1983. *John Scrace*

Below: The second de-icing unit numbered 003 was converted in 1979 from 4-SUB motor cars and was originally numbered 002. It is seen at Selhurst on 6 October 1983. *John Scrace*

Above: De-icing unit 013 was originally numbered S94 and was converted from the power cars of 4-SUB unit 4349 in 1960. It is pictured at Wimbledon on 3 December 1979, shortly after withdrawal. *John Scrace*

Left: No 017 was a similar unit converted from the power cars of 4-SUB 4351, and it is seen at Eastleigh on 2 November 1968. *John H. Bird*

Below: No 018 was a stores unit formed from ex-South Tyneside MBSOs. These stores units worked to all the major depots on a weekly cycle. It is seen at East Wimbledon on 4 July 1985. *Colin J. Marsden*

Above: No 022 was a stores unit formed from ex 2-HAL motor vehicles in 1970. It was at Selhurst on 4 October 1983. *John Scrace*

Right: Nos 052 and 053 were Service/Tractor units formed from 2-HAP sets 6121 and 6142. They are seen here at Ashford in Kent displaying their new unit numbers on 16 December 1982. It was not until 1984 that they received carriage numbers in the departmental series. *T. J. Saunders*

Below: DB975179 was a battery locomotive converted from Class 501 motor vehicle M61139 in 1973. It was later numbered 97702 in the departmental locomotive number series. *Ian Allan Library*

Appendix : BR Lot Numbers

Lot	Type	Numbers	Builder	Year
30001	CK	15000	Eastleigh	1952
30002	SK	24000-24179	Derby	1951
30003	BSK	34000-34094	Derby	1951-52
30004	CK	15001-15020	Derby	1952
30005	CK	15065-15270	Metro-Cammell	1952-53
30006	BCK	21000-21019	Metro-Cammell	1954
30007	SK	24332-24396	BRCW	1953
30008	FO	3003-3019	BRCW	1954
30009	BG	80500-80529	Derby	1952-53
30010	FO	3000-3002	York	1951
30011	TSO	3700-3705	York	1951
30012	RFO	1-11	York	1951
30013	RF	301-305	Doncaster	1952
30014	RSO	1000-1013	York	1951
30015	SK	24180-24219	Doncaster	1951-52
30016	CK	15271-15310	Cravens	1952-53
30017	TSO	3706-3720	Cravens	1952
30018	RK	80000-80009	Doncaster	1951
30019	FK	13000-13032	Swindon	1951-52
	FK	13036-13059	Swindon	1951-52
30020	SK	24302-24331	Ashford/Eastleigh	1951-52
30021	BCK	[illegible]	Ashford/Eastleigh	1952
30022	CK	15021-15064	Ashford/Eastleigh	1952
30023	BG	80530-80535	Eastleigh	1951
30024				
30025	BSK	34096-34224	Wolverton	1951-52
30026	SK	24220-24301	York	1951-52
30027	FK	13060-13064	Swindon	1953
30028	S	46000-46018	Swindon	1954
30029				
30030	SK	24397-24436	Derby	1953
30031	SO	3721-3735	Derby	1954
30032	BSK	34285-34289	Wolverton	1952
	BSK	34372-34388	Wolverton	1952
	BSK	34410-34412	Wolverton	1952
30033	CK	15311-15349	Derby	1953
30034	BCK	21020-21024	Derby	1954
30035	SLF	2000-2009	Wolverton	1957-58
30036	SLSTP	2500-2521	Doncaster	1957
30037	S	46019-46062	Swindon	1955
30038	S	46109-46198	Wolverton	1954
30039	BG	80536-80566	Derby	1954
30040	BG	80567-80596	Wolverton	1954-55
30041				
30042	FO	3020-3039	Doncaster	1953-53
30043	TSO	3736-3753	Doncaster	1953
	TSO	3773-3788	Doncaster	1953
30044	SK	24557-24568	York	1952
30045	BS	43100-43161	York	1954-55
30046	BG	80597-80671	York	1954
30047	BS	43162-43170	Swindon	1955
		ex-53036-53051		
	BS	43260-43266	Swindon	1955
30048				
30049				
30050				
30051	S	46063-46108	Derby	1954
30052	FK	13033-13035	Eastleigh	1951
30053	SO	3500-3514	Eastleigh	1953
30054	TSO	3824-3849	Ashford/Eastleigh	1953-54
	TSO	3886-3903	Eastleigh	1954
30055				
30056				
30057	SK	24576-24675	BRCW	1953-54
30058	SK	24676-24700	Cravens	1953
30059	SK	24701-24720	Cravens	1953
30060	BSK	34451-34500	Gloucester	1953-54
30061	BSK	34501-34520	Charles Roberts	1954
30062	CK	15443-15532	Metro-Cammell	1953-54
30063	CK	15533-15542	Metro-Cammell	1954
30064	BSK	34413-34450	Wolverton	1953
30065	BSK	34290-34301	Wolverton	1953
30066	FK	13065-13076	Swindon	1953
30067	TSO	4358-4362	Eastleigh	1955
30068	SK	24539-24548	York	1952
30069				
30070	SK	24469-24538	York	1954
	SK	24549-24556	York	1954
	SK	24569-24575	York	1954
30071	C	41000-41022	Wolverton	1954
30072	SK	24437-24446	Wolverton	1953
30073	SK	24721-24745	Wolverton	1953
30074	BSK	34316-34371	Wolverton	1953
	BSK	34389-34409	Wolverton	1954
30075	CK	15350-15424	Derby	1954
30076	CK	15425-15435	Derby	1953
30077	SK	24746-24753	Swindon	1953-54
30078	SK	24754-24795	Swindon	1954
30079	TSO	3754-3772	York	1953
	TSO	3789-3823	York	1953
30080	TSO	3850-3885	York	1953-54
30081	CK	15436-15442	Derby	1954
30082	BSK	34302-34315	Wolverton	1954
30083	FK	13077-13084	Swindon	1953
30084	DMBS	79000-79007	Derby	1954
30085	DMCL	79500-79507	Derby	1954
30086	TSO	3904-3969	Eastleigh	1954-55
30087	BS	43267-43359	York	1955
		ex-53078-53170		
30088	SK	24447-24468	Swindon	1954
30089	FK	13085-13107	Swindon	1954
30090	TSO	3970-3997	York	1954
30091	FO	3040-3057	Doncaster	1954
30092	SLO	48000-48027	Doncaster	1955
30093	BS	43171-43259	Doncaster	1954
		ex-53171-53259		
30094	CL	43000-43049	Doncaster	1954-55
30095	BSK	34521-34584	Wolverton	1955
30096	SLC	2400-2401	Wolverton	1957
30097				
30098	S	46199-46266	Derby	1955
30099	SO[NG]	48035-48042	Derby	1955
30100	BS	43360-43367	Derby	1955
30101	S	46299-46306	Derby	1955
30102	C	41023-41042	Wolverton	1955
	C	41049-41059	Wolverton	1955
30103	C	41043-41048	Swindon	1955
30104	S	46267-46279	Swindon	1954-55
30105	SO[NG]	48043-48053	Swindon	1955
30106	BS	43368-43373	Swindon	1955
		ex-53268-53273		
30107	FK	13108-13125	Swindon	1954
30108	**DMBSO**	**61033-61040**	**Ashford/Eastleigh**	**1956**
30109	**TSK**	**70033-70036**	**Ashford/Eastleigh**	**1956**
30110	**TCK**	**70037-70040**	**Ashford/Eastleigh**	**1956**
30111	**DMBSO**	**61041-61044**	**Ashford/Eastleigh**	**1956**
30112	**TCK**	**70041-70042**	**Ashford/Eastleigh**	**1956**
30113	**TRB**	**69000-69001**	**Ashford/Eastleigh**	**1957**
30114	**DMBSO**	**65300-65310**	**Ashford/Eastleigh**	**1954**
30115	**DTSso**	**77500-77510**	**Ashford/Eastleigh**	**1954**
30116	**DMBSO**	**65311-65325**	**Eastleigh**	**1954-55**
30117	**DTSso**	**77100-77114**	**Eastleigh**	**1955**
30118	**DMLV**	**68000**	**Eastleigh**	**1955**
30119	**DMBSO**	**65326-65341**	**Ashford/Eastleigh**	**1954**
30120	**DTSso**	**77511-77526**	**Ashford/Eastleigh**	**1954**
30121	SO	4363-4372	Eastleigh	1955
30122				
30123	DMBS	79008-79020	Derby	1955
30124	DTCL	79600-79612	Derby	1955
30125	Fish	87000-87499	Faverdale	1954-55
30126	DMBS	79021-79033	Derby	1955
30127	DTCL	79613-79625	Derby	1955
30128	DMS	79740	BUT	1953
	TS	79741	BUT	1953
	DMBS	79742	BUT	1953
30129	ROY	499	Wolverton	1956
30130	ROY	2900	Wolverton	1955
30131	ROY	2901	Wolverton	1957
30132	BCK	21025-21059	Metro-Cammell	1954-55
30133	BCK	21060-21091	Metro-Cammell	1955
30134	CK	15543-15562	Metro-Cammell	1955
30135	CK	15563-15584	Metro-Cammell	1955
30136	BG	80672-80724	Metro-Cammell	1955
30137	SK	24796-24818	BRCW	1955
30138	CK	15585-15596	BRCW	1955
30139	CK	15597-15624	BRCW	1955
30140	BG	80725-80802	BRCW	1955-56
30141	BSK	34585-34612	Gloucester	1955
30142	BSK	34613-34630	Gloucester	1955
30143	BSK	34631-34654	Charles Roberts	1954-55
30144	BG	80803-80854	Cravens	1955
30145	SO[NG]	48028-48034	Doncaster	1955
30146	HB	96300-96414	Earlestown	1958
30147	FK	13126-13184	Swindon	1955
30148	BFK	14000-14001	Ashford/Swindon	1959
30149	TSO	3998-4097	Ashford/Swindon	1956-57
30150	S	46280-46298	Swindon	1955
30151	BS	43374-43383	Swindon	1956
30152	C	41060-41064	Swindon	1956
30153	SK	24819-24944	Derby	1955-56
30154	SK	24945-24974	Derby	1956
30155	SK	25045-25164	Wolverton	1955-56
30156	BSK	34655-34748	Wolverton	1955
30157	BSK	34749-34808	Wolverton	1955
30158	CK	15625-15694	Wolverton	1956
30159	SLF	2010-2019	Wolverton	1958
30160	SLSTP	2522-2526	York/Doncaster	1957
30161	SLC	2402-2403	Wolverton	1957
30162	BG	80855-80964	Pressed Steel	1956-57
30163	BG	81205-81265	Pressed Steel	1957
30164				
30165				
30166				
30167	**DMBSO**	**65342-65366**	**Ashford/Eastleigh**	**1955**
30168	**DTSso**	**77527-77551**	**Ashford/Eastleigh**	**1955**
30169	FO	3058-3070	Doncaster	1955
30170	BSO	9200-9276	Doncaster	1955-56
30171	TSO	4098-4197	York	1955-56
30172	TSO	4198-4257	York	1956
30173	BG	80965-81014	York	1956
30174	DMBS	79743-79744	BUT	1955
30175	DMS	79745	BUT	1955
30176	TS	79746-79747	BUT	1955
30177	DMBS	79034-79046	Derby	1955
30178	DTCL	79250-79262	Derby	1955
30179	CK	15695-15770	Metro-Cammell	1955-56
30180	CK	15771-15820	Metro-Cammell	1955-56
30181				
30182				
30183				
30184				
30185	BCK	21092-21118	Metro-Cammell	1956
30186	BCK	21119-21133	Metro-Cammell	1956
30187	BCK	21134-21168	Charles Roberts	1955-56
30188	GUV	86500	York	1956
30189	CCT	94100	Doncaster	1955
30190	DMBS	79047-79075	Metro-Cammell	1956
	DMBS	79076-79082	Metro-Cammell	1955
30191	DTSL	79263-79291	Metro-Cammell	1956
	DTCL	79626-79632	Metro-Cammell	1955
30192	DMC	79508-79512	Derby	1955
30193	DMS	79150-79154	Derby	1955
30194	TBSL	79325-79329	Derby	1955
30195	TSL	79400-79404	Derby	1955
30196	DMBSL	79083-79090	Swindon	1956
	DMBSL	79095	Swindon	1956
30197	TFKRB	79440-79447	Swindon	1957
30198	TFK	79470-79482	Swindon	1957
30199	DMSL	79155-79168	Swindon	1957
30200	DMBSL	79091-79094	Swindon	1957
	DMBSL	79096-79111	Swindon	1957
30201	DMBSL	79143-79149	Derby	1956
30202	DTCL	79663-79669	Derby	1956
30203	**MS**	**61001-61032**	**Ashford/Eastleigh**	**1956**
30204	**TCsoL**	**70001-70032**	**Ashford/Eastleigh**	**1956**
30205	**DTBS**	**75001-75032**	**Ashford/Eastleigh**	**1956**
30206	**DTCOL**	**75101-75132**	**Ashford/Eastleigh**	**1956**
30207	TSO	4258-4357	BRCW	1956
30208	SK	24975-25044	Derby	1956
30209	DMBS	50001-50048	Derby	1958
30210	DTCL	56001-56049	Derby	1958
30211	DMBS	50050-50091	Derby	1957
30212	TC	59000-59031	Derby	1957
30213	DMS	50092-50133	Derby	1957
30214	DMS	79748	BUT	1957
30215	TS	79749	BUT	1957
30216	DMBS	79750	BUT	1957
30217	FK	13185-13219	Ashford/Swindon	1957-59
30218	BFK	14002-14006	Ashford/Swindon	1959-60
30219	TSO	4373-4412	Ashford/Swindon	1957
30220	BSK	34809-34868	Gloucester	1956
30221	CK	15821-15860	Metro-Cammell	1956
30222	CK	15861-15915	Metro-Cammell	1956
30223	BSK	34869-34880	Charles Roberts	1956
30224	BG	81015-81054	Cravens	1956
30225	BSK	34881-34930	Charles Roberts	1957
30226	TSO	4413-4472	BRCW	1956-57
30227	SO	4473-4487	BRCW	1957
30228	BG	81055-81179	Metro-Cammell	1957-58
30229	BSK	34931-35023	Metro-Cammell	1957
30230	SK	25165-25247	Metro-Cammell	1957
30231	SK	25248-25279	Metro-Cammell	1957-58
30232	BSK	35024-35038	Gloucester	1956
30233	BSK	35039-35113	Gloucester	1957
30234	BG	81180-81204	Cravens	1956-57
30235	DMBSL	79118-79126	Derby	1956
30236	DTCL	79639-79647	Derby	1956
30237				
30238				
30239				
30240	DMBSL	79127-79136	Derby	1956
	DMBSL	79137-79140	Derby	1956
30241	DTCL	79648-79657	Derby	1956
	DTCL	79658-79661	Derby	1956
30242	FO	3071-3080	York/Doncaster	1956
30243	TSO	4488-4636	York	1956-57
30244	BSO	9277-9321	Doncaster	1956
30245	SLSTP	2527-2536	York/Doncaster	1957
30246	DMBSL	79141-79142	Derby	1956
30247	DTCL	79662	Derby	1956
30248	DMBS	50134-50137	Metro-Cammell	1957
30249	DMCL	50138-50151	Metro-Cammell	1956
30250	TSL	59042-59048	Metro-Cammell	1956
30251	TBSL	59049-59055	Metro-Cammell	1956
30252	DMBS	50152-50157	Metro-Cammell	1956
30253	DMCL	50158-50163	Metro-Cammell	1956
30254	DMBS	50164-50167	Metro-Cammell	1957
30255	DMCL	50168-50171	Metro-Cammell	1957
30256	DMCL	50172-50197	Metro-Cammell	1957
30257	TSL	59060-59072	Metro-Cammell	1957
30258	TBSL	59073-59085	Metro-Cammell	1957
30259	DMBS	50198-50209	Metro-Cammell	1957
30260	DTCL	56050-56061	Metro-Cammell	1957
30261	DMBS	50210-50233	Metro-Cammell	1957
30262	DTCL	56062-56085	Metro-Cammell	1957
30263	DMCL	50234-50245	Metro-Cammell	1957
30264	TSL	59086-59091	Metro-Cammell	1957
30265	TBSL	59092-59097	Metro-Cammell	1957
30266	DMBS	50250-50259	Metro-Cammell	1957
30267	DMCL	50260-50269	Metro-Cammell	1957
30268	DMCL	50270-50279	Metro-Cammell	1957-58
30269	TSL	59100-59109	Metro-Cammell	1957-58
30270	DMBS	50290-50296	Metro-Cammell	1957
30271	DMCL	50745-50751	Metro-Cammell	1957
30272	DTCL	56086-56089	Metro-Cammell	1957
30273	TSL	59302-59306	Metro-Cammell	1957
30274	TBSL	59112-59113	Metro-Cammell	1957
30275	DMBS	50303-50320	Metro-Cammell	1958
30276	DMCL	50321-50338	Metro-Cammell	1958
30277	TCL	59114-59131	Metro-Cammell	1958
30278	DMBS	50339-50358	Gloucester	1957
30279	DTCL	56094-56113	Gloucester	1957
30280	DMBS	50359-50372	Cravens	1956-58
30281	DTCL	56114-56127	Cravens	1956-57
30282	DMBS	50373-50389	Cravens	1957
30283	DTCL	56128-56144	Cravens	1957
30284	DMBS	50390-50394	Cravens	1957
30285	DTCL	56145-56149	Cravens	1957
30286	DMBS	50395-50414	Park Royal	1957-58
30287	DTCL	56150-56169	Park Royal	1957-58
30288	DMBS	50415-50419	Wickham	1958
30289	DTCL	56170-56174	Wickham	1958
30290	DMBS	50420-50423	BRCW	1957
30291	DMCL	50424-50427	BRCW	1957
30292	TCL	59132-59135	BRCW	1957
30293	DMBS	50428-50479	BRCW	1957-58
30294	DMCL	50480-50531	BRCW	1957-58
30295	TCL	59136-59187	BRCW	1957-58
30296	DMBS	50532-50541	BRCW	1958
30297	DTCL	56175-56184	BRCW	1958
30298	DMCL	50542-50583	BRCW	1958
30299	TSL	59188-59208	BRCW	1958
30300	TBSL	59209-59229	BRCW	1958
30301	DMCL	50584-50593	BRCW	1959
30302	TSL	59230-59234	BRCW	1959
30303	TBSL	59240-59244	BRCW	1959
30304				
30305				
30306				
30307				
30308				
30309				
30310				
30311				
30312				
30313				
30314	**DMBSO**	**65367-65396**	**Ashford/Eastleigh**	**1956-57**
30315	**DTSso**	**77552-77577**	**Ashford/Eastleigh**	**1956**
30316	**DTCsoL**	**77115-77118**	**Ashford/Eastleigh**	**1957**
30317	CK	15916-15985	Wolverton	1956-57
30318	SLF	2020-2029	York	1958
30319	**DMBSO**	**65397-65403**	**Ashford/Eastleigh**	**1957**
30320	**DTCsoL**	**77119-77125**	**Ashford/Eastleigh**	**1957**
30321	DMBSL	79169-79181	Derby	1956
30322	DTCL	79670-79684	Derby	1956
30323	BG	81266-81312	Pressed Steel	1957
30324	DMBS	79184-79188	Derby	1956
30325	DMCL	79189-79193	Derby	1956
30326	**DMBSO**	**61133-61189**	**Ashford/Eastleigh**	**1957-58**
30327	**TS**	**70133-70189**	**Ashford/Eastleigh**	**1957-58**
30328	**DTBSO**	**75133-75189**	**Ashford/Eastleigh**	**1957-58**
30329	DMBS	60000-60013	Ashford/Eastleigh	1957
30330	TFK	60700-60706	Ashford/Eastleigh	1957
30331	TSOL	60500-60520	Ashford/Eastleigh	1957

30332	DMBSO	60100-60117	Ashford/Eastleigh	1957
30333	DTCsoL	60800-60817	Ashford/Eastleigh	1957
30334	DMSL	50647-50695	Swindon	1958-59
30335	DMBC	50696-50744	Swindon	1958-59
30336	TSLRB	59255-59301	Swindon	1958-59
30337	DTCL	56090-56093	Metro-Cammell	1957
30338	DMBS	50280-50289	Metro-Cammell	1957-58
30339	DMBS	50246-50248	Metro-Cammell	1957
30340	DTCL	56218-56220	Metro-Cammell	1957
30341	DMBS	50000	Derby	1956
30342	DTCL	56000	Derby	1956
30343	GUV	86501-86520	Doncaster	1957
30344	Fish	87500-87692	Faverdale	1960
30345	FRUIT D	92000-92064	Swindon	1957-58
30346	RKB	1546	Ashford/Eastleigh	1956
30347	RB	1700	Eastleigh	1956
30348	RU	1900	Eastleigh	1956
30349	SK	25283-25402	Wolverton	1957
30350	SK	25403-25454	Wolverton	1957
30351	CK	15986-16057	Wolverton	1956-57
30352	DMBS	50752-50784	Cravens	1957-58
30353	DMCL	50785-50817	Cravens	1957-58
30354	TCL	59307-59325	Cravens	1957-58
30355	FK	13220	Metro-Cammell	1957
30356	SK	25455	Metro-Cammell	1957
30357	FK	13221	Gloucester	1957
30358	SK	25456	Gloucester	1957
30359	FO	3081	BRCW	1957
30360	SO	4637	BRCW	1957
30361	FO	3082	Cravens	1957
30362	TSO	4638	Cravens	1957
30363	DMBS	50818-50870	Derby	1957-58
30364	DMS	50871-50923	Derby	1957-58
30365	TC	59326-59376	Derby	1957-58
30366				
30367				
30368	BDMBS	79998	Derby/Cowlairs	1958
30368	BDTCL	79999	Derby/Cowlairs	1958
30369				
30370	FK	13222	Doncaster	1957
30371	SK	25457	Doncaster	1957
30372	FO	3083	Doncaster	1957
30373	FO	3084	Doncaster	1957
30374	SK	25458-25507	York	1958
30375	TSO	4639-4726	York	1957
	TSO	4739-4778	York	1957
30376	SO	4779-4809	York	1957
30377	SLF	2030-2063	York	1959
30378				
30379	SLSTP	2537-2573	York/Doncaster	1957-58
30380	DMBS	79900	Derby	1956
30381	FK	13223-13238	Ashford/Swindon	1959
30382	BFK	14007-14012	Ashford/Swindon	1960
30383	FRUIT D	92065-92114	Swindon	1958-59
30384	Fish	87693-87957	Faverdale	1960-61
30385	TS	59032-59041	Derby	1957
30386	BSK	35114-35175	Charles Roberts	1958
30387	DMBS	79901	Derby	1956
30388	**DMBSO**	**65404-65435**	**Ashford/Eastleigh**	**1958**
30389	**DTCsoL**	**77126-77156**	**Ashford/Eastleigh**	**1958**
30390	**DTSso**	**77578**	**Ashford/Eastleigh**	**1958**
30391	DMBSO	60020-60045	Ashford/Eastleigh	1957-58
30392	TFK	60710-60722	Ashford/Eastleigh	1957-58
30393	TRB	60750-60756	Ashford/Eastleigh	1958
30394	TSOL	60530-60561	Ashford/Eastleigh	1957-58
30395	DMBSO	60014-60019	Ashford/Eastleigh	1957
30396	TFK	60707-60709	Ashford/Eastleigh	1957
30397	TSOL	60521-60529	Ashford/Eastleigh	1957
30398	DMBSO	60118-60121	Ashford/Eastleigh	1958
30399	DTCsoL	60818-60821	Ashford/Eastleigh	1958
30400	BG	81313-81497	Pressed Steel	1957-58
30401	RU	1901-1912	Ashford/Swindon	1957
30402	GUV	86521-86654	York/Glasgow	1958-60
30403				
30404	DMBS	50594-50598	BRCW	1958
30405	DTCL	56185-56189	BRCW	1958
30406	DMBS	50599-50624	Derby	1958
30407	DMBS	50625-50629	Derby	1958
30408	DMCL	50630-50646	Derby	1958
30409	DTCL	56190-56210	Derby	1958
30410	DTCL	56211-56215	Derby	1959
30411	TSL	59380-59385	Derby	1958
30412	TBSL	59245-59250	Derby	1958
30413	DMSL	50936	Swindon	1959
	DMSL	51008-51029	Swindon	1959
30414	DMBSL	51030-51051	Swindon	1959
30415	TFK	59391-59400	Swindon	1959
30416	TCL	59402-59412	Swindon	1959
30417	GUV	86078-86499	Pressed Steel	1958-59
30418	DMPMV	55997-55999	Cravens	1958
30419	DMBS	55000-55019	Gloucester	1958
30420	DTS	56291-56299	Gloucester	1958
30421	DMBC	51052-51079	Gloucester	1958-59
30422	DMSL	51080-51107	Gloucester	1958-59
30423	TSLRB	59413-59437	Gloucester	1958-59
30424	BCK	21169-21194	Charles Roberts	1958-59
30425	BCK	21195-21224	Metro-Cammell	1958
30426	SK	25558-25703	Wolverton	1957-58
30427	BSK	35176-35273	Wolverton	1959
30428	**MBS**	**61045-61059**	**Wolverton**	**1960**
30429	**DTSOL**	**75045-75059**	**Wolverton**	**1960**
30430	**DTBSO**	**75645-75659**	**Wolverton**	**1960**
30431	**TCsoL**	**70045-70059**	**Wolverton**	**1960**
30432	FK	13239-13251	Ashford/Swindon	1959
30433				
30434	**MBS**	**61060-61096**	**York**	**1958-59**
30435	**DTS**	**75033-75044**	**York**	**1958-59**
	DTS	**75060-75084**	**York**	**1959**
30436	**DTSOL**	**75085-75100**	**York/Doncaster**	**1958-59**
	DTSOL	**75190-75210**	**York/Doncaster**	**1959**
30437	**TCsoL**	**70060-70096**	**York/Doncaster**	**1958-59**
30438	**MBS**	**61097-61132**	**York**	**1959**
	MBS	**61190-61228**	**York**	**1959-60**
30439	**DTS**	**75211-75285**	**York**	**1959-60**
30440	**DTSOL**	**75286-75360**	**York/Doncaster**	**1959**
30441	**TCsoL**	**70097-70132**	**York**	**1959**
	TCsoL	**70190-70228**	**York**	**1959-61**
30442	Fish	87958-88057	Faverdale	1961
30443	BSO	9322-9362	Gloucester	1959-60
30444	DMBS	51108-51127	Gloucester	1957-58
30445	DTCL	56300-56319	Gloucester	1957-58
30446	DMBS	51128-51140	Derby	1958
30447	DMS	51141-51153	Derby	1958
30448	TC	59438-59448	Derby	1958

30449	**DMBSO**	**61229-61240**	**Ashford/Eastleigh**	**1958**
30450	**TSK**	**70229-70234**	**Ashford/Eastleigh**	**1958**
30451	**TCK**	**70235-70240**	**Ashford/Eastleigh**	**1958**
30452	**DMBSO**	**61241-61303**	**Ashford/Eastleigh**	**1958-59**
30453	**DTCsoL**	**75361-75423**	**Ashford/Eastleigh**	**1958-59**
30454	**DMBSO**	**61304-61409**	**Ashford/Eastleigh**	**1958-59**
30455	**TSK**	**70260-70302**	**Ashford/Eastleigh**	**1958-59**
30456	**TCK**	**70303-70355**	**Ashford/Eastleigh**	**1958-59**
30457	**TRB**	**69002-69011**	**Ashford/Eastleigh**	**1959**
30458	**DMLV**	**68001-68002**	**Ashford/Eastleigh**	**1959**
30459	DMBS	50049	Derby	1957
30460	DMBS	50924-50935	Derby	1959-60
30461	DMCL	51561-51572	Derby	1959-60
30462	DMS	50988-51007	Derby	1958-59
30463	TS	59449-59468	Derby	1958-59
30464	DMBS	51154-51173	Derby	1958-59
30465	DMBS	50938-50987	Derby	1959
30466	DTCL	56221-56270	Derby	1959
30467	DMBS	51174-51253	Metro-Cammell	1958-59
30468	DTCL	56332-56411	Metro-Cammell	1958-59
30469	DMBS	51254-51301	Cravens	1958-59
30470	DTCL	56412-56459	Cravens	1958-59
30471	CK	16058-16092	Metro-Cammell	1958-59
30472	FO	3085-3094	BRCW	1959
30473	SO	4810-4829	BRCW	1959
30474	BCK	21225-21230	Charles Roberts	1959
30475	CK	16093-16107	Charles Roberts	1959
30476	RU	1913-1924	Ashford/Swindon	1958
30477	**DMBSO**	**65436-65461**	**Wolverton**	**1959**
30478	**DTSO**	**77157-77182**	**Wolverton**	**1959**
30479	DMBS	79975-79979	AC Cars	1958
30480	DMBS	79970-79974	Park Royal	1958
30481	DMBS	79965-79969	Wickham	1959
30482	DMBS	79960-79964	Waggon & Masch.	1958
30483	DMBS	79958-79959	BRCW	1958
30484	BG	81498-81572	Pressed Steel	1958
30485	RMB	1801-1812	York	1957-58
30486	POS	80300-80305	Wolverton	1959
30487	POS	80306-80308	Wolverton	1959
30488	POT	80400-80402	Wolverton	1959
30489	BPOT	80450-80455	Wolverton	1959
30490	SLF	2064-2104	Metro-Cammell	1959
30491	SLSTP	2574-2578	Metro-Cammell	1959
30492	SLC	2404-2426	Metro-Cammell	1959-60
30493	TSL	59386-59390	Derby	1958
30494	SK	25280-25282	Metro-Cammell	1958
30495				
30496				
30497				
30498	DMBS	51416-51424	Derby	1960
30499	DTCL	56271-56279	Derby	1960
30500	DMBS	51425-51470	Metro-Cammell	1959
30501	DMCL	51495-51540	Metro-Cammell	1959
30502	TCL	59523-59568	Metro-Cammell	1959
30503	DMBS	51471-51494	Cravens	1959
30504	DTCL	56460-56483	Cravens	1959
30505	DMBS	50249	Cravens	1959
30506	TSO	4830-4839	Wolverton	1959
30507	RMB	1838-1852	Wolverton	1960
30508	DMBS	51541-51550	Metro-Cammell	1959-60
30509	DMCL	51551-51560	Metro-Cammell	1959-60
30510	TSL	59569-59572	Metro-Cammell	1959
30511	RF	306-309	BRCW	1961
30512	RB	1701-1738	BRCW	1960
30513	RU	1925-1943	BRCW	1959-60
30514	RKB	1500-1526	Cravens	1959-60
30515	DMBCL	51573-51581	Swindon	1961
30516	DMSL	51582-51590	Swindon	1961
30517	TSL	59579-59588	Swindon	1961
30518	DMBS	55020-55035	Pressed Steel	1960-61
30519	DTS	56280-56289	Pressed Steel	1960-61
30520	RMB	1813-1837	Wolverton	1960
30521	DMBS	51591-51650	Derby	1959
30522	TSL	59589-59618	Derby	1959
30523	TS	59619-59648	Derby	1959
30524	RK	80010-80021	Charles Roberts	1962
30525	TSO	4840-4899	Wolverton	1959-60
30526	RSO	1014-1017	Wolverton	1960
30527	RB	1739-1754	BRCW	1961
30528	SLF	2105-2106	Wolverton	1959
30529	SLSTP	2579-2606	Wolverton	1959-60
30530	DMBS	51651-51680	Derby	1960
30531	TS	59649-59663	Derby	1960
30532	TCL	59664-59678	Derby	1960
30533	DMBS	51681-51705	Cravens	1959
30534	DMCOL	51706-51730	Cravens	1959
30535	DMBS	51731-51755	Cravens	1960
30536	DMCOL	51756-51780	Cravens	1960
30537	TFKRB	59098-59099	Swindon	1961
30538	SLC	2427	Metro-Cammell	1960
30539	RK	80022-80027	Charles Roberts	1962
30540	DMBSO	60122-60125	Ashford/Eastleigh	1959
30541	DTCsoL	60822-60825	Ashford/Eastleigh	1959
30542	TSO	60650-60671	Ashford/Eastleigh	1959
30543	DMBS	51302-51316	BRCW	1960
30544	TCL	59469-59483	BRCW	1960
30545	DMS	51317-51331	BRCW	1960
30546	DMBS	51332-51373	Pressed Steel	1959-60
30547	TCL	59484-59522	Pressed Steel	1959-60
30548	DMS	51374-51415	Pressed Steel	1959-60
30549	CCT	94101-94300	Earlestown	1959-60
30550	FK	13252	Swindon	1963
30551	DMPMV	55991-55996	Gloucester	1960
30552	DMPMV	55987-55990	Gloucester	1959
30553	DMBFL	60090-60093	Metro-Cammell	1960
30554	DMBS	60094-60099	Metro-Cammell	1960
30555	MPSL	60644-60649	Metro-Cammell	1960
30556	MFLRK	60730-60733	Metro-Cammell	1960
30557	TFLRK	60734-60739	Metro-Cammell	1960
30558	TPFL	60740-60749	Metro-Cammell	1960
30559	DMBC	51781-51787	Swindon	1959-60
30560	DMSL	51788-51794	Swindon	1959-60
30561	TSLRB	59679-59685	Swindon	1959-60
30562	CCT	94301-94454	Earlestown	1960
30563	CCT	94455-94595	Earlestown	1960
30564	CCT	94596-94692	Earlestown	1960-61
30565	GUV	86655-86834	Pressed Steel	1959
30566	**DTSOL**	**75424-75442**	**York/Doncaster**	**1960**
30567	**MBS**	**61410-61428**	**York/Doncaster**	**1959-60**
30568	**TCsoL**	**70356-70374**	**York/Doncaster**	**1960**
30569	**DTS**	**75443-75461**	**York/Doncaster**	**1960**
30570	**DTSO**	**75462-75513**	**York**	**1960**
30571	**MBSO**	**61429-61480**	**York**	**1960**
30572	**DTSO**	**75514-75565**	**York**	**1960**

30573	BSK	35274-35293	Gloucester	1960
30574	BCK	21231-21235	Gloucester	1960
30575	RU	1944-1958	Ashford/Swindon	1960
30576	FO	3095-3100	BRCW	1959
30577	CK	16108-16152	Metro-Cammell	1959-60
30578	FK	13253-13302	Metro-Cammell	1960
30579	**DTSO**	**75566-75600**	**Pressed Steel**	**1959-61**
30580	**MBSO**	**61481-61515**	**Pressed Steel**	**1959-61**
30581	**DTBSO**	**75601-75635**	**Pressed Steel**	**1959-61**
30582	**DMBS**	**61516-61627**	**Eastleigh**	**1960-61**
30583	**TSso**	**70375-70482**	**Eastleigh**	**1960-61**
30584	**DTSso**	**75636**	**Eastleigh**	**1960**
30585	RK	80028-80039	Charles Roberts	1962-63
30586	SLSTP	2607-2658	Wolverton	1960-61
30587	DMBS	51795-51801	Metro-Cammell	1959
30588	DMCL	51802-51808	Metro-Cammell	1959
30589	TCL	59686-59692	Metro-Cammell	1959
30590	SLF	2107-2120	Metro-Cammell	1960
30591	SLC	2428-2437	Metro-Cammell	1960
30592	DMBC	51809-51828	BRCW	1961
30593	DMCL	51829-51848	BRCW	1961
30594	TSL	59693-59712	BRCW	1961
30595	DMBS	51849-51860	Derby	1960
30596	TS	59713-59718	Derby	1960
30597	TCL	59719-59724	Derby	1960
30598	DMBS	51861-51900	Derby	1960
30599	TS	59725-59744	Derby	1960
30600	TCL	59745-59764	Derby	1960
30601	DMBS	51901-51950	Derby	1960-61
30602	DTCL	56484-56504	Derby	1960
30603	DMC	51951-51967	Swindon	1960
30604	MBSK	51968-51984	Swindon	1960
30605	TSL	59765-59773	Swindon	1960
30606	TFLRB	59774-59781	Swindon	1960
30607	**MBSO**	**61628-61647**	**Wolverton**	**1960-61**
30608	**DTBSO**	**75660-75679**	**Wolverton**	**1960-61**
30609	**TCsoL**	**70483-70502**	**Wolverton**	**1960-61**
30610	**DTSOL**	**75680-75699**	**Wolverton**	**1960-61**
30611	DMBS	51985-52010	Derby	1960-61
30612	DMCL	52011-52036	Derby	1960-61
30613	TSL	59782-59807	Derby	1960-61
30614	CCT	94693-94892	Earlestown	1960-61
30615	TSLRB	59573-59578	Metro-Cammell	1960
30616	GUV	86835-86984	Pressed Steel	1959-60
30617	**DMBSO**	**61648-61688**	**Eastleigh**	**1961**
30618	**DTCsoL**	**75700-75740**	**Ashford/Eastleigh**	**1961**
30619	**DMBSO**	**61694-61811**	**Ashford/Eastleigh**	**1960-61**
30620	**TSK**	**70503-70551**	**Ashford/Eastleigh**	**1960-61**
30621	**TCK**	**70552-70610**	**Ashford/Eastleigh**	**1960-61**
30622	**TRB**	**69012-69021**	**Ashford/Eastleigh**	**1961**
30623	**DMLV**	**68003-68010**	**Ashford/Eastleigh**	**1960-61**
30624	RKB	1547-1569	Cravens	1961
30625	DMBSO	60126-60144	Ashford/Eastleigh	1962
30626	TCsoL	60600-60618	Ashford/Eastleigh	1961
30627	DTSO	60900-60918	Ashford/Eastleigh	1962
30628	RB	1644-1699	Pressed Steel	1960-61
30629	**DTSO**	**75746-75801**	**Pressed Steel**	**1960-61**
30630	**MBSO**	**61812-61867**	**Pressed Steel**	**1960-61**
30631	**DTBSO**	**75802-75857**	**Pressed Steel**	**1960-61**
30632	RU	1959-1991	Ashford/Swindon	1960-61
30633	RF	310-342	Ashford/Swindon	1962
30634	RK	80040	Charles Roberts	1963
30635	RKB	1527-1529	Cravens	1961
30636	RB	1755-1772	Pressed Steel	1961-62
30637	RG	1100-1102	Ashford/Eastleigh	1960
30638	**DMBSO**	**61868-61871**	**Ashford/Eastleigh**	**1961**
30639	**TCK**	**70043-70044**	**Ashford/Eastleigh**	**1961**
30640	**TSK**	**70241-70242**	**Ashford/Eastleigh**	**1961**
30641	**DMBSO**	**61872**	**Ashford/Eastleigh**	**1961**
30642	**MBSO**	**61873-61882**	**Wolverton**	**1961**
30643	**DTBSO**	**75858-75867**	**Wolverton**	**1961**
30644	**TCsoL**	**70243-70252**	**Wolverton**	**1961**
30645	**DTSOL**	**75868-75877**	**Wolverton**	**1961**
30646	TSO	4900-4917	Wolverton	1961
30647	RUO	1018-1057	Wolverton	1961
30648	FO	3101-3103	Wolverton	1961
30649	SLC	2438	Wolverton	1961
30650	SLF	2121-2125	Wolverton	1961
30651	CCT	94893-94922	Earlestown	1961
30652	**DTSOL**	**75878-75886**	**York**	**1961**
30653	**MBS**	**61883-61891**	**York**	**1961**
30654	**TCsoL**	**70611-70619**	**York**	**1961**
30655	**DTS**	**75887-75895**	**York**	**1961**
30656	**DTSOL**	**75896-75928**	**York**	**1961**
30657	**MBS**	**61892-61915**	**York**	**1961**
30658	**TCsoL**	**70620-70652**	**York**	**1961**
30659	**DTS**	**75929-75961**	**York**	**1961**
30660	DMCL	52037-52065	Derby	1961
30661	POS	80309-80314	Wolverton	1961
30662	POS	80315-80317	Wolverton	1961
30663	POS	80318	Wolverton	1961
30664	TCV	96286-96299	Newton Chambers	1961-62
30665	CK	16153-16197	Derby	1961
30666	CK	16198-16225	Derby	1961
30667	FK	13303-13360	Swindon	1962
30668	BFK	14013-14022	Swindon	1961
30669	BCK	21236-21251	Swindon	1961-62
30670	RMB	1853-1864	Wolverton	1961-62
30671	DMBSO	60145-60151	Ashford/Eastleigh	1962
30672	TSO	60672-60678	Ashford/Eastleigh	1962
30673	DTCsoL	60826-60832	Ashford/Eastleigh	1962
30674	CCT	96200-96203	Doncaster	1960
30675	**DTCsoL**	**75962-75968**	**York**	**1962**
30676	**MBSK**	**61925-61931**	**York**	**1962**
30677	**TSOL**	**70253-70259**	**York**	**1962**
30678	**DTCsoL**	**75969-75975**	**York**	**1962**
30679	**DTCsoL**	**75637-75644**	**York**	**1962**
30680	**MBSK**	**61932-61939**	**York**	**1962**
30681	**TRB**	**69100-69107**	**York**	**1962-63**
30682	**DTCOL**	**75976-75983**	**York**	**1962-63**
30683	**DTSOL**	**75984-75991**	**York**	**1962**
30684	**DMBSK**	**61940-61947**	**York**	**1962-63**
30685	SK	25704-25905	Derby	1961-62
30686	SK	25906-25972	Derby	1962
30687	SLF	2126-2130	Wolverton	1961
30688	SLC	2439-2442	Wolverton	1961
30689	SLSTP	2659-2666	Wolverton	1961
30690	TSO	4918-5044	Wolverton	1961-62
30691	DMBC	52066-52075	BRCW	1961-62
30692	DMCL	52076-52085	BRCW	1961-62
30693	TSL	59808-59817	BRCW	1961-62
30694	**DTSO**	**75741-75743**	**York**	**1961**
30695	**MBSO**	**61689-61691**	**York**	**1961**
30696	**DTSO**	**75992-75994**	**York**	**1961**

Lot	Type	Numbers	Builder	Year
30697	FO	3104-3129	Swindon	1962-63
30698	BSO	9363-9380	Wolverton	1963
30699	BSK	35294-35400	Wolverton	1963
30700	BSK	35401-35406	Wolverton	1963
30701	MLV	68011-68019	York	1961
30702	RMB	1865-1882	Wolverton	1962
30703	DMBSL	52086-52095	Swindon	1963
30704	DMSK	52096-52105	Swindon	1963
30705	TCK	59818-59827	Swindon	1963
30706	TSL	59235-59239	Swindon	1963
30707	TSLRB	59828-59832	Swindon	1963
30708	DMBSO	61948-61961	Ashford/Eastleigh	1963
30709	TCK	70653-70659	Ashford/Eastleigh	1963
30710	TSK	70660-70666	Ashford/Eastleigh	1963
30711	DMBSO	61962-61988	Ashford/Eastleigh	1963
30712	DTCsoL	75995-76021	Ashford/Eastleigh	1963
30713	DMBSO	61989-62016	Ashford/Eastleigh	1962-63
30714	TSso	70667-70694	Ashford/Eastleigh	1962-63
30715	BG	81573-81592	Gloucester	1962
30716	BG	81593-81612	Gloucester	1962
30717	FO	3130-3151	Swindon	1963
30718	BFK	14023-14027	Swindon	1963
30719	SK	25973-26059	Derby	1962
30720	SK	26060-26137	Derby	1962-63
30721	BSK	35407-35446	Wolverton	1963
	BSK	35450-35499	Wolverton	1963
30722	SLF	2131-2132	Wolverton	1962
30723	SLSTP	2667-2681	Wolverton	1962
30724	TSO	5045-5069	York	1963
30725	BG	81613-81628	Gloucester	1963
30726	SK	26138-26217	York	1962-63
30727	SLC	2443-2445	Wolverton	1962-63
30728	BSK	35447-35449	Wolverton	1963
30729	CK	16226-16240	Derby	1963
30730	CK	16241-16267	Derby	1963
30731	BCK	21252-21262	Derby	1963
30732	BCK	21263-21275	Derby	1964
30733	FK	13361-13378	Derby	1964
30734	FK	13379-13406	Derby	1964
30735	SLSTP	2682-2691	Wolverton	1963
30736	SLC	2446-2454	Wolverton	1963-64
30737	SK	25508-25509	Derby	1964
30738	FK	13407-13409	Derby	1964
30739	TSO	4727-4729	Derby	1964
30740	DTCsoL	76022-76075	York	1964-66
30741	DTCsoL	76076-76129	York	1964-66
30742	MBSO	62017-62070	York	1964-66
30743	TSO	70695-70730	York	1964-66
30744	TSORB	69301-69318	York	1965-66
30745	DTSOL	76130-76179	Derby	1965-67
30746	MBSO	62071-62120	Derby	1965-67
30747	TSO	70731-70780	Derby	1965-67
30748	DTCOL	76180-76229	Derby	1965-67
30749	FK	13410-13431	Derby	1964
30750	FK	13432-13433	Derby	1964
30751	TSO	5070-5228	Derby	1965-67
30752	SO	5229-5256	Derby	1966
30753	PB	580-586	Derby	1966
30754	PC	540-553	Derby	1966
30755	PK	500-507	Derby	1966
30756	BFK	14028-14055	Derby	1966
30757	BSO	9381-9416	Derby	1966
30758	DTCsoL	76230-76269	York	1967
30759	TSO	70781-70800	Derby	1967
30760	MBSO	62121-62140	Derby	1967
30761	DMSO	62141-62162	York	1967
30762	TBFK	70801-70811	York	1967
30763	TRB	69319-69329	York	1967
30764	DTSO	76270-76332	York	1966-67
30765	TBSK	70812-70843	York	1966-67
30766	TFK	70844-70871	York	1966-67
30767	DTSO	76403-76421	Cravens	1967
30768	MBSO	62163-62181	Cravens	1967
30769	DTSO	76422-76440	Cravens	1967
30770	CARTIC-4	95001-95016	Rootes/Pressed Steel	1966-67
	CARTIC-4	95051-95066	Rootes/Pressed Steel	1966-67
30771	DTCsoL	76333-76402	York	1967-68
30772	TSO	70872-70906	York	1967-68
30773	MBSO	62182-62216	York	1967-68
30774	FK	13434-13463	Derby	1968
30775	BFK	14056-14077	Derby	1967-68
30776	TSO	5257-5345	Derby	1967-68
30777	BSO	9417-9425	Derby	1967
30778	POS	80319-80327	York	1968-69
30779	POS	80328-80338	York	1968-69
30780	POS	80339-80355	York	1968-69
30781	POT	80415-80424	York	1968
30782	BPOT	80456-80458	York	1968
30783	RG	1106	Derby	1968
30784	Bar	1883	Derby	1968
30785	FK	13464-13475	Derby	1968
30786	BFK	14078-14103	Derby	1968
30787	TSO	5346-5433	Derby	1968
30788	BSO	9426-9438	Derby	1968
30789	FK	13476-13513	Derby	1969
30790	BFK	14104-14112	Derby	1969
30791	TSO	5434-5497	Derby	1969
30792	DTCsoL	76441-76540	York	1968-69
30793	TSO	70907-70956	York	1968-69
30794	MBSO	62217-62266	York	1968-69
30795	TSO	5498-5615	Derby	1969-70
30796	BFK	14113-14138	Derby	1969-70
30797	FK	13514-13561	Derby	1969-70
30798	BSO	9439-9448	Derby	1970
30799	DTCsoL	76541-76560	York	1970
30800	MBSO	62267-62276	York	1970
30801	TSO	70957-70966	York	1970
30802	TCK	76561-76570	York	1970
30803	TCK	76571-76580	York	1970
30804	MBSO	62277-62286	York	1970-71
30805	TSORB	69330-69339	York	1970
30806	DTCsoL	76581-76610	York	1970-71
30807	DTCsoL	76611-76640	York	1970-71
30808	MBSO	62287-62316	York	1970-71
30809	TSO	70967-70996	York	1971
30810	FO	3152-3169	Derby	1970
30811	DTCsoL	76641-76716	York	1973
30812	TSO	70997-71034	York	1972-73
30813	MBSO	62317-62354	York	1972-73
30814	DTCsoL	76717-76787	York	1970-72
30815	DTCsoL	76788-76858	York	1970-72
30816	MBSO	62355-62425	York	1970-72
30817	TSO	71035-71105	York	1970-72
30818	DMBSO	64300-64305	York	1971
30819	MSO	62426-62429	York	1971-72
30820	BSO	9449-9478	Derby	1970
30821	FO	3170-3216	Derby	1971-72
30822	TSO	5616-5743	Derby	1971-72
30823	BFK	14139-14172	Derby	1971-72
30824	BSO	9479-9495	Derby	1971
30825	FK	13562-13610	Derby	1971-72
30826	BCV	85000	Derby	1970
30827	DTCsoL	76859	York	1972
30828	DTCsoL	76860	York	1972
30829	MBSO	62430	York	1972
30830	TSO	71106	York	1972
30831	BFB	99500-99503	Derby	1971
30832	TSO	12003	Derby	1972
30833	FO	11003	Derby	1972
30834				
30835				
30836				
30837	TSO	5744-5804	Derby	1972
30838	BSO	9496-9509	Derby	1972
30839	POS	80356-80380	York	1973
30840	POT	80425-80430	York	1973
30841	ExhibVan	99602-99613	Swindon (conversion)	1973
30842	ExhibVan	99614	Swindon (conversion)	1976
	ExhibVan	99620-99625	Swindon (conversion)	1976
30843	FO	3221-3275	Derby	1973
30844	TSO	5809-5907	Derby	1973
30845	FO	3276-3320	Derby	1973
30846	TSO	5908-5958	Derby	1973
30847	TSO	12000-12002	Derby	1972
30848	FO	11000-11002	Derby	1972
30849	RUB	10000	Derby	1973
30850	RUK	10100	Derby	1973
30851	MBSO	62435-62475	York	1974
30852	TSO	71115-71155	York	1974
30853	DTCsoL	76861-76942	York	1974
30854	TBFK	71156-71159	York	1974
30855	TBSK	71160-71161	York	1974
30856	TFK	71162-71167	York	1974
30857	DTSO	76943-76948	York	1974
30858	TRB	69022-69025	York	1974
30859	FO	3321-3428	Derby	1974
30860	TSO	5959-6170	Derby	1974
30861	BSO	9510-9539	Derby	1974
30862	DMSO	62476-62483	York	1974
30863	DTSOL	76949-76974	York	1977-78
30864	MBSO	62484-62509	York	1977-78
30865	TSO	71168-71193	York	1977-78
30866	DTCOL	78000-78025	York	1977-78
30867	DTSOL	76975-76993	York	1975-76
30868	MBSO	62510-62528	York	1975-76
30869	TSO	71194-71212	York	1975-76
30870	DTCOL	78026-78044	York	1975-76
30871	TSK	71107-71110	Wolverton	1974
30872	TCK	71111-71114	Wolverton	1974
30873	FO	3429-3439	Derby	1975
30874	TSO	6171-6184	Derby	1975
30875	DMB	43000-43001	Crewe	1974
30876	DMB	43002-43055	Crewe	1977
30877	TSO	12004-12168	Derby	1977
30878	FO	11004-11063	Derby	1976
30879	DMSO	62529-62592	York	1976-77
30880	TSO	71213-71276	York	1976-77
30881	TF	41003-41056	Derby	1977
30882	TS	42003-42090	Derby	1977
30883	TRSB	40001-40027	Derby	1977
30884	TRUK	40501-40520	Derby	1977
30885	BDMSO	62593-62656	York	1976-77
30886	ROY	2903	Wolverton	1977
30887	ROY	2904	Wolverton	1977
30888	ROY	2905	Wolverton	1977
30889	ROY	2906	Wolverton	1977
30890	RFB	10001-10028	Derby	1980
30891	DTSOL	76994-76997	York	1976
30892	MBSO	62657-62660	York	1976
30893	TSO	71277-71280	York	1976
30894	DTCOL	78045-78048	York	1976
30895	DMB	43056-43123	Crewe	1979
30896	TF	41057-41120	Derby	1978
30897	TS	42091-42250	Derby	1979
30898				
30899	TRSB	40028-40037	Derby	1977
30900	POS	80381-80395	York	1977
30901	POT	80431-80439	York	1976
30902	DMSO	64461-64582	York	1980-81
30903	PTSO	71389-71449	York	1980-81
30904	TSO	71281-71341	York	1980-81
30905				
30906	BDMSO	64367-64399	York	1978-80
30907	TSO	71342-71374	York	1978-80
30908	DMSO	64405-64437	York	1978-80
30909				
30910				
30911				
30912	DMSO	64583-64614	York	1979
30913	TSO	71450-71465	York	1979
30914				
30915				
30916				
30917				
30918				
30919				
30920				
30921	TRUB	40300-40321	Derby	1979
30922	PVG	85500-85507	Wolverton	1978
	PVG	85508-85534	Doncaster	1978
30923	DTS	48101-48107	Derby	1980
30924	TS	48201-48206	Derby	1980
30925	TRSB	48401-48406	Derby	1980
30926	TF	48501-48506	Derby	1980
30927	TBF	48601-48607	Derby	1980
30928	M	49001-49006	Derby	1980
30929				
30930	DMBSO	53001	Derby	1980
30931	DMSO	53000	Derby	1980
30932	TSO	57000-57001	Derby	1980
30933	TCOL	58000	Derby	1980
30934	DTSO	54000-54001	Derby	1980
30935				
30936				
30937				
30938	TF	41121-41148	Derby	1980
30939	TS	42251-42305	Derby	1980
30940	TRUB	40322-40335	Derby	1980
30941	DMB	43124-43152	Crewe	1981
30942	DMSO	64649-64687	York	1979-80
30943	TSO	71483-71520	York	1979-80
30944	TSO	71526-71568	York	1977-80
30945	BDMSO	64692-64729	York	1980
30946	DM	43153-43190	Crewe	1981
30947	TF	41149-41166	Derby	1980
30948	TRUB	40336-40353	Derby	1981
30949	TGS	44001-44090	Derby	1982
30950	ExhibVan	99629	Stewarts Lane (conv.)	1979
30951	ExhibVan	99630	Stewarts Lane (conv.)	1979
30952	ExhibVan	99631	Stewarts Lane (conv.)	1979
30953	TGS	44000	Derby	1980
30954	TSOL	71569-71572	Wolverton	1981
	TCsoL	71573-71576	Wolverton	1981
30955	DTSO	77000-77047	York	1981-82
30956	DTSO	77048-77095	York	1981-82
30957	TCOL	71577-71624	Derby	1981-82
30958	MSO	62661-62708	York	1981-82
30959	TU	48301-48306	Derby	1980
30960	SLEP	10500-10619	Derby	1983
30961	SLE	10646-10733	Derby	1984
30962	DMS	55500	Derby/Leyland Bus	1980
	DMSL	55501	Derby/Leyland Bus	1980
30963	TF	41167-41169	Derby	1982
30964	TGS	44091-44094	Derby	1982
30965				
30966	TRUB	40354-40357	Derby	1982
30967	TF	41170-41174	Derby	1982
30968	DM	43191-43198	Crewe	1982
30969	TS	42306-42322	Derby	1982
30970	TGS	44095-44101	Derby	1982
30971	ExhibVan	99641-99642	Stewarts Lane (conv.)	1981
30972	DTSO	77579-77726	York	1982-84
30973	MSO	62709-62782	York	1984-85
30974	TSO	71637-71710	York	1982-84
30975	MSO	62783-62825	York	1985
30976	DTSO	77727-77812	York	1984-85
30977	DMS	55502-55521	Derby/Leyland Bus	1984
30978	DMSL	55522-55541	Derby/Leyland Bus	1984
30979	DMSO	64688-64691	York	1979-80
30980	TSO	71521-71525	York	1980
30981	BDMSO	64730-64734	York	1980
30982	FO	11064-11101	Derby	1985
30983	TS	42323-42341	Derby	1985
30984	DMSL	55200-55201	York	1984
30985	DMS	55300-55301	York	1984
30986	MS	55400	York	1984
	MS	55401	York	1984
30987	DMSL	55202-55203	Metro-Cammell	1985
30988	DMS	55302-55303	Metro-Cammell	1985
30989	MS	55402-55403	Metro-Cammell	1985
30990	BFO	17173-17175	Derby	1986
30991	DTSO	77813-77852	York	1985
30992	MSO	62826-62845	York	1985
30993	TSO	71714-71733	York	1985
30994	DTSO	77200-77219	York	1985-86
30995	DTSO	77220-77239	York	1985-86
30996	MSO	62846-62865	York	1985-86
30997	TCOL	71734-71753	York	1985-86
30998	MSOL	62866-62885	York	1985-86
30999	DTSOL	77240-77259	York	1985-86
31000	DTSO	77260-77279	York	1985-86
31001	TSO	71754-71761	Wolverton	1981
31002	ROY	2914-2915	Derby/Wolverton	1985
31003	DMS	55542-55591	Derby/Leyland Bus	1985-86
31004	DMSL	55592-55641	Derby/Leyland Bus	1985-86
31005	DMS	55642-55666	Alexander/Barclay	1985-86
31006	DMSL	55667-55691	Alexander/Barclay	1985-86
31007	DTSO	77280-77283	York	1987
31008	DTSO	77284-77287	York	1987
31009	MSO	62886-62889	York	1987
31010	TCOL	71762-71765	York	1981
31011	DMSL	52101-52150	York	1985-86
31012	DMS	57101-57150	York	1985-86
31013	DMS	55701-55746	Derby/Leyland Bus	1987
31014	DMSL	55747-55792	Derby/Leyland Bus	1987
31015	DMS	55801-55823	Derby/Alexander	1986-87
31016	DMSL	55824-55846	Derby/Alexander	1986-87
31017	DMSL	52201-52285	York	1986-87
31018	DMS	57201-57285	York	1986-87
31019	MSO	62890	York	1987
31020	DTSL	77288	York	1987
31021	DTS	77289	York	1987
31022	DTS(A)	77291-77381 odds	York	1987-88
31023	MSO	62891-62936	York	1987-88
31024	TSOL	71772-71817	York	1987-88
31025	DTSL	77290-77380 evens	York	1987-88
31026	DMSL	52301-52335	Leyland Bus	1987-88
31027	DMS	57301-57335	Leyland Bus	1987-88
31028	DMSL	52401-52514	Metro-Cammell	1988-89
31029	DMS	57401-57514	Metro-Cammell	1988-89
31030	DTCsoL	77382-77405	Derby	1988-89
31031	DTSOL	77406-77429	Derby	1988-89
31032	TSOL(A)	71818-71841	Derby	1988-89
31033	TSOL(B)	71842-71865	Derby	1988-89
31034	MBRSM	62937-62960	Derby	1988-89
31035	ROY	2922	Derby/Wolverton	1989
31036	ROY	2923	Derby/Wolverton	1989
31037	MS	55850-55859	Derby/Alexander	1987
31038	DTSO	77431-77457 odds	York	1988
31039	MSO	62961-62974	York	1988
31040	TSOL	71866-71879	York	1988
31041	DTSOL	77430-77456 evens	York	1988
31042	DVT	82101-82152	Derby	1988
31043	DVT	82200-82231	Metro-Cammell	1988
31044	ROY	2920	Derby/Wolverton	1988
31045	RFB	10300-10333	Metro-Cammell	1989
31046	FO	11200-11271	Metro-Cammell	1989-92
31047	TSOEnd	12200-12231	Metro-Cammell	1989-91
31048	TSOD	12300-12330	Metro-Cammell	1989-91
31049	TSO	12400-12512	Metro-Cammell	1989-92
31050	MS	58701-58739	Derby	1991-92
31051	DMSO(A)	52701-52894	Derby	1989-93
	DMSO(A)	52901-52910	Derby	1990-92
31052	DMSO(B)	57701-57894	Derby	1989-92
	DMSO(B)	57901-57910	Derby	1990-92
31053	DTCO	78049-78094	York	1988-90
	DTCO	78131-78150	York	1988-90

31054	MSO	62975-63020	York	1988-90
	MSO	63105-63124	York	1988-90
31055	TSOL	71880-71925	York	1988-90
	TSOL	71991-72010	York	1988-90
31056	DTSO	77853-77898	York	1988-90
	DTSO	78280-78299	York	1988-90
31057	DMS(A)	52341-52347	Leyland Bus	1988
31058	DMS(B)	57341-57347	Leyland Bus	1988
31059	ROY	2916	Derby/Wolverton	1988
31060	DTSO(A)	77899-77920	York	1990
31061	DTSO(B)	77921-77942	York	1990
31062	MSO	63021-63042	York	1990
31063	DTCO	77459-77497 odds	York	1990
	DTCO	77973-77983 odds	York	1990
31064	MSO	63043-63062	York	1990
	MSO	63093-63098	York	1990
31065	TSOL	71929-71948	York	1990
	TSOL	71979-71984	York	1990
31066	DTSO	77458-77496 evens	York	1990
	DTSO	77974-77984 evens	York	1990
31067	DTCO	78095-78130	York	1989-90
	DTCO	78151-78162	York	1989-90
31068	MSO	63063-63092	York	1989-90
	MSO	63099-63104	York	1989-90
	MSO	63125-63136	York	1989-90
31069	TSOL	71949-71978	York	1989-90
	TSOL	71985-71990	York	1989-90
	TSOL	72011-72022	York	1989-90
31070	DTSO	77943-77972	York	1989-90
	DTSO	78274-78279	York	1989-90
	DTSO	78300-78311	York	1989-90
31071	DMSO(A)	121-129	Metro-Cammell (conv.)	1989-90
31072	DMSO(B)	221-229	Metro-Cammell (conv.)	1989-90
31073	DMSO	64735-64758	York	1990-91
31074	DTSO	78250-78273	York	1990-91
31075				
31076				
31077				
31078				
31079				
31080				
31081				
31082				
31083	ROY	2918	Wolverton	1990
31084	ROY	2917	Wolverton	1990
31085	ROY	2919	Wolverton	1990
31086	ROY	2920	Wolverton	1990
31087	DMCL	58801-58822	York	1991-92
	DMCL	58873-58878	York	1991-92
31088	DMS	58834-58872	York	1991-92
31089	DMCL	58823-58833	York	1991-92
31090	MS	55404-55414	York	1991-92
31091	DTSO	77985-77989	York	1990
31092	TSOL	72023-72027	York	1990
31093	MSO	63137-63141	York	1990
31094	DTCO	78163-78167	York	1990
31095	Cl 33	83301		1990
31096	DMCL	58879-58898	York	1992
31097	DMS	58916-58952	York	1992
31098	DMCL	58953-58969	York	1992
31099	MS	55415-55431	York	1992
31100	DMSO(A)	64759-64808	York	1991-93
	DMSO(B)	64809-64858	York	1991-93
31101	TSOL	72029-72127 odds	York	1991-93
	TSOL	72901-72993 odds	York	1993-94
31102	TSO	72028-72126 evens	York	1991-93
	TSO	72900-72992 evens	York	1993-94
31103	DMSO(A)	65700-65749	Metro-Cammell	1991-93
	DMSO(B)	65750-65799	Metro-Cammell	1991-93
31104	TSOL	72719-72817 odds	Metro-Cammell	1991-92
31105	TSO	72720-72818 evens	Metro-Cammell	1991-92
31106				
31107				
31108	DTSO(A)	77990-77992	York	1991
31109	MSO	63153-63155	York	1991
	TSOL	72128-72130	York	1991
31110				
31111	DTSO(B)	77993-77995	York	1991
31112	DMSO(A)	64001-64043	Hunslet	1992-93
31113	TSOL	72201-72239	Hunslet	1992-93
	TSOL	72340-72343	Hunslet	1992-93
31114	DMSO(B)	65001-65043	Hunslet	1992-93
31115	DMSL	52301-52335	Rebuilt	1991-92
	DMSL	57351-57385	Rebuilt	1991-92
31116	DMCL(A)	58101-58121	York	1992-93
	DMCL(B)	58122-58142	York	1992-93
31117	MS	58601-58621	York	1992-93
31118	DM	3730010-3730220	every 10th	1992-95
	DM	3731010-3731080	every 10th	1992-95
	DM	3732010-3732320	every 10th	1992-95
	DM	3733010-3733140	every 10th	1992-95
	DM	3739990		1992-95
31119	MS	3730011-3730221	every 10th	1992-95
	MS	3731011-3731081	every 10th	1992-95
	MS	3732011-3732321	every 10th	1992-95
	MS	3733011-3733141	every 10th	1992-95
31120	TS	3730012-3730222	every 10th	1992-95
	TS	3731012-3731082	every 10th	1992-95
	TS	3732012-3732322	every 10th	1992-95
	TS	3733012-3733142	every 10th	1992-95
31121	TS	3730013-3730223	every 10th	1992-95
	TS	3731013-3731083	every 10th	1992-95
	TS	3732013-3732323	every 10th	1992-95
	TS	3733013-3733143	every 10th	1992-95
31122	TS	3730014-3730224	every 10th	1992-95
	TS	3731014-3731084	every 10th	1992-95
	TS	3732014-3732324	every 10th	1992-95
31123	TS	3730015-3730225	every 10th	1992-95
	TS	3731015-3731085	every 10th	1992-95
	TS	3732015-3732325	every 10th	1992-95
	TS	3733015-3733145	every 10th	1992-95
31124	RB	3730016-3730226	every 10th	1992-95
	RB	3731016-3731086	every 10th	1992-95
	RB	3732016-3732326	every 10th	1992-95
	RB	3733016-3733146	every 10th	1992-95
31125	TFOH	3730017-3730227	every 10th	1992-95
	TFOH	3731017-3731087	every 10th	1992-95
	TFOH	3732017-3732327	every 10th	1992-95
	TFOH	3733017-3733147	every 10th	1992-95
31126	TFOH	3730018-3730228	every 10th	1992-95
	TFOH	3731018-3731088	every 10th	1992-95
	TFOH	3732018-3732328	every 10th	1992-95
31127	TBF	3730019-3730229	every 10th	1992-95
	TBF	3731019-3731089	every 10th	1992-95
	TBF	3732019-3732329	every 10th	1992-95
	TBF	3733019-3733149	every 10th	1992-95
31128	DMSO	64860-64902	GEC/Alsthom	1993-94
31129	DTSO	78312-78354	GEC/Alsthom	1993-94
31130	DMSO(A)	65800-65846	York	1993-94
	DMSO(B)	65847-65893	York	1993-94
31131				
31132				
31133	DMCO(A)	65894-65934	York	1994-95
31134	TSOL	72241-72321 odds	York	1994-95
31135	PTSOL	72240-72320 evens	York	1994-95
31136	DMCO(B)	65935-65975	York	1994-95
31137				
31138				
31139				
31140				
31141				
31142				
31143				
31144	DTPMV	68300-68331	Derby	1995
31145	MPMV	68340-68355	Derby	1995
31146	TPMV	68360-68375	Derby	1995

Three generations of EMUs stand side-by-side at Wimbledon Park on 7 September 1977. De-icing unit 015 is formed from two vehicles which were built in 1925 as part of 3-SUB unit 1504. The vehicle in the centre is ADB975027 which was converted from a 1957-built LMR London area dc unit, number M61162. It was converted in 1969 to work in research unit number 051, and survived as a test coach until 1986. The final unit seen here is 4-PEP number 4002, one of the 1971-built prototypes for new suburban stock. Between them these three units represent the main types of suburban trains to run in the UK for the last 100 years. *John Scrace*